PREFACE

The Longman Anthology of Modern and Contemporary Drama: A Global Perspective offers students of dramatic literature and theater a global collection of plays from the late nineteenth century to the beginning of the twenty-first. While we acknowledge the presence of other fine drama anthologies, few focus solely on modern (c. 1879–1960) and contemporary (1960–present) works. We are pleased to offer a richly varied selection from Europe and the United States, Asia, Africa, and especially Latin America and the Caribbean, regions noticeably underrepresented in current texts.

Breadth of Selections

By including 31 plays we offer teachers and students maximum flexibility, whether they are pursuing a traditional course of study devoted to European and American drama or exploring the diversity of voices in the world's theater, or a combination of the two. Given the contemporary student's predisposition for film and video, we include works for which there are—in our estimation—quality videos. For instance, students may supplement their study of Bernard Shaw, Tennessee Williams, and Sam Shepard by watching *Heartbreak House*, *Cat on a Hot Tin Roof*, and *True West*, respectively. We have specifically selected some plays that complement one another: Tom Stoppard's *Rosencrantz and Guildernstern Are Dead* and Derek Walcott's *Pantomime* share thematic similarities that encourage discussion and understanding. Students can explore two versions of *Hamlet*, first by Stoppard and then a postmodern treatment by Germany's Heiner Müller.

In addition to 20 essential plays from the West's modern canon, we present a broad range of drama from around the globe, including works from:

China: *The Bus Stop*, by Chinese dissident and Nobel Laureate Gao Xingjian, offers a glimpse inside contemporary China heretofore unseen by Western audiences.

Africa: Athol Fugard's *"MASTER HAROLD"* . . . *and the boys* and Wole Soyinka's *Death and the King's Horseman* allow students to examine important works by Africa's foremost playwrights.

Latin America: *Personal Effects* by Argentina's Griselda Gambaro, the premiere Latin American female playwright, presents a dark comedy in the absurdist tradition, while *Paper Flowers* by Egon Wolff is a surrealistic drama from Chile that is equal parts political tract and a mythic battle of the sexes.

The Caribbean: *Pantomime* by Nobel Laureate Derek Walcott (Trinidad-Tobago) explores the problems of the contemporary Caribbean in light of its Colonial past.

We have purposefully chosen a number of Western plays that are indebted to other cultures for both their thematic material and their performance style, including:

- Bertolt Brecht's *The Good Woman of Setzuan* and David Henry Hwang's *The Dance and the Railroad* employ techniques from the Chinese theater.

- Federico García Lorca's *Blood Wedding* fuses Spanish folk drama with symbolist drama to create a modern tragedy.
- Luis Valdez's *Zoot Suit* celebrates the Aztec heritage of contemporary Chicanos.
- August Wilson's *Fences* and Suzan-Lori Parks's *Topdog/Underdog* address the African Diaspora within the context of contemporary American social drama.
- Diane Glancy's *The Woman Who Was a Red Deer Dressed for the Deer Dance* uses a centuries-old storytelling tradition drawn from her Native American heritage.

The finest contemporary dramatists from the West are well represented:

- The founders of Social Realism (Ibsen, Chekhov, Shaw, O'Neill)
- The pioneers of nonrealistic forms such as Expressionism (Strindberg, Treadwell)
- The most critically acclaimed contemporary playwrights (Williams, Albee, Beckett, Shepard, Pinter, Fugard, and Wilson)
- Five Nobel Prize Laureates (O'Neill, Beckett, Soyinka, Walcott, and Gao Xingjian), and seven Pulitzer Prize playwrights (O'Neill, Williams, Albee, Shepard, Wilson, Kushner, Parks)

Important voices, heretofore underrepresented, are also heard:

- Acclaimed women playwrights (Sophie Treadwell, Caryl Churchill, Maria Irene Fornes, Griselda Gambaro, Diane Glancey, Suzan-Lori Parks)
- Minority playwrights (Luis Valdez, David Henry Hwang, August Wilson, Diane Glancey, Suzan-Lori Parks)
- Innovative new dramatists (e.g., Tony Kushner) who address current issues in a world that is redefining itself

Rituals, Ceremonies, and Folk Customs

In addition to an unequaled offering of international plays, we describe many examples of rituals, ceremonies, and folk customs that enhance our understanding of the human need to create theater as well as specific plays. For example, we explain how the Yoruban Obatala festival relates to Soyinka's *Death and the King's Horseman* and how the Italian *tarantella* and other healing dances shaped a significant moment in Ibsen's *A Doll's House*. In addition, the discussion of ritual theater in Mesoamerica provides an important cultural context for Valdez's *Zoot Suit*.

Flexible Organization

We offer *The Longman Anthology of Modern and Contemporary Drama: A Global Perspective* as another necessary step in the evolution of drama anthologies, and we do so with a sense of awe at the rich variety of plays and performance styles produced by artists throughout the world. The anthology provides the most comprehensive coverage of the evolution of theater over the past 150 years available in comparable texts. We have organized it to allow a broad variety of teaching and learning approaches for such courses as Theater History, Comparative and/or Dramatic Literature, and World Theater. The individual plays can be taught by themselves or with as much of the supporting historical and cultural material as time and inclination allow.

After an initial survey of those theatrical and dramatic forms that immediately preceded Ibsen and his contemporaries, we have divided this survey of plays into three parts, each corresponding to the generally accepted eras of early Modernism, mature and declining Modernism, and Postmodernism. Because the history of the theater presents many complex issues, as well as an overlapping of themes and styles, it is difficult to categorize events with such apparent precision, and there is legitimate debate among academics about such divisions.

Prologue: The Precursors of Modern Drama
Summarizes the drama of the mid-nineteenth century; several influential styles are discussed with summaries of representative plays (e.g., the romantic melodrama and Hugo's *Hernani*, the problem play and Dumas *fils's Camille*). Buchner's *Woyzeck* is included in its entirety as a touchstone for discussions of the drama that followed it.

Part I: Early Modern Drama: 1870–1918
Traces the rise of Realism under Ibsen, Chekhov, and Shaw, and then discusses early alternatives such as Strindberg's Expressionism.

Part II: Late Modern Drama: 1920–63
Illustrates how the work of the pioneers has been fused to create even more innovative dramas that incorporate Realism and Expressionism, Pirandello's Relativism, Brecht's Epic Theatre, and the Theater of the Absurd.

Part III: Contemporary and Postmodern Drama: 1964–The Present
Surveys a variety of approaches to contemporary and postmodern drama, including the theater of menace, the theater of the fabulous, the theater of images, docudramas, multicultural theater, and feminist drama.

We believe this framework provides a useful starting point for an exploration of modern and contemporary drama, whether chronologically (the primary design of the text), by themes, or by styles selected by the individual instructor. While we recognize that it is difficult to cover in a semester all plays herein, we believe instructors can select a representative number of plays to meet their goals and the ability level of their students.

Pedagogical Support

Headnotes
We introduce each play with a thorough headnote that provides a biography of its playwright (often with commentary by the playwright and those who have interpreted his work on stage) and a short introduction to the historical and/or stylistic context of the play.

Commentaries
To encourage students to read the play without a preconceived interpretation, we have placed a commentary *after* each play, with the proviso that our essays represent only a single interpretation of that play. We suggest additional essays that may be consulted for other points of view. Because we acknowledge that the contemporary student is the product of a media age, we also include the titles of relevant videos and films related to the play and its author as an added feature. Students are directed to videos of the actual play, other plays by the playwright, and videos about the playwright. Many feature films are readily available at video rental stores, and many university and college libraries now possess the suggested educational videos.

Because we are all practicing theater artists who have acted in, directed, or reviewed many of these plays, we enthusiastically explore the performance dimensions of the plays so that students may better appreciate their theatrical, as well as their literary, appeal.

Showcases
Throughout the text, students may read over 40 Showcases, or "mini-lessons," on a rich variety of theater topics. Showcases are concise (rarely more than two pages of text) and enable students to examine a topic quickly. Showcases are used in a variety of ways. They:

- Provide a **brief history lesson** on a theater company (e.g., the Group Theatre), a significant theater (e.g., the Moscow Art Theatre), or influential movements in the development of the theater (e.g., performance art).

- Summarize **historically important plays** that influenced the development of drama but cannot be included in the text because of space limitations (e.g., *Camille*, *A Raisin in the Sun*) or because publishing rights are not available or cost prohibitive (e.g., *Waiting for Godot* and *Death of a Salesman*).
- Highlight **cultural phenomena** that are relevant to a particular play (e.g., "The Trinidad Carnival" accompanies Walcott's *Pantomime*). These Showcases allow students to learn about the very impulses that contributed to the development of theater.
- Acquaint students with **the process of creating theater** as the ideas of playwrights, directors, actors, and designers are featured (e.g., Harold Clurman discusses *Heartbreak House* from a director's perspective, and Haibo Yu describes his designs for *Blood Wedding*).

Collectively, the Showcases expose students to a variety of approaches for writing about theater and drama. Instructors may assign as many Showcases as inclination and time allow. In our own teaching we have found that short essays appeal to students because they are focused and more easily comprehended.

Timelines
In lieu of a lengthy timeline at the opening of each part of the text, we have opted for shorter, more focused timelines that accompany each play. Timeline entries consider both global events and those that are particular to the play. We have also included entries that help students see the cultural—including "pop culture"—contexts of a given play.

Photos and Illustrations
Because "theater" derives from a Greek word meaning "the *seeing* place," we have also included illustrations to help students visualize the possibilities for theatrical production, especially those involving nonrealistic styles.

Appendix
To supplement the text, we offer a **glossary** that defines principal terms.

Because some students may not have had an introduction to theater course, three additional appendices and a lengthy bibliography are available on a Website. Regrettably, the economics of publishing a text of this size necessitated the use of a Website rather than including this material with the text.

These are designed to familiarize novice theater students with some key terms and concepts; more experienced students may find the material useful as review material. The following material may be downloaded and/or printed at no charge:

- **The Elements of Drama**: An introduction to the six primary elements of drama and theater as defined by Aristotle in *The Poetics*. The discussion notes both the classical and contemporary use of the elements, with reference to specific works in this anthology. For students new to the study of drama, this appendix provides a useful vocabulary for the discussion of plays.
- **The Genres of Drama**: A brief overview of the three principal genres of drama: Tragedy, Comedy, and Tragicomedy. Although the latter is the primary genre found in modern and contemporary drama, students may better comprehend Tragicomedy with an elementary knowledge of the two major genres that preceded it.
- **Styles and Conventions**: A brief summary of styles of theatrical production and the conventions that help define those styles; specific examples from this collection are used as referents.

Supplements
Either of the following supplements can be shrinkwrapped for FREE with *The Longman Anthology of Modern and Contemporary Drama*:

- *Evaluating a Performance: A Student's Guide to Writing the Play Review*, an innovative workbook that guides students through the process of writing about a play in performance. Not only does this 60-page booklet show students how to write an informed play review, it also advises them how to find a play, purchase tickets, respond to the theater experience from the moment they enter the theater, and so on. Worksheets also help students evaluate the play and the various artists who bring it to life on the stage.

- *Evaluating a Film: A Student's Guide to Watching a Play on Film*, another short text that introduces students to a basic vocabulary of film. Much like *Evaluating a Performance*, this workbook leads students through the process of talking about plays from a cinematic perspective.

Please contact your local Longman representative if you would like to take advantage of this opportunity.

Permission to reprint some scripts either was unavailable or prohibitively expensive. However, as Penguin is Longman's sister company, works such as Arthur Miller's *Death of a Salesman* and David Henry Hwang's *M. Butterfly* can be shrinkwrapped at a substantial discount with *The Longman Anthology of Modern and Contemporary Drama*. Please contact your Longman representative if you would like to order a value-pack. Also note that this text includes critical commentary on *Death of a Salesman*, as well as Jo Mielziner's account of his designs for the play in 1949.

Acknowledgments

We are indebted to many people who have contributed their expertise to the completion of this volume. To them we offer Shakespeare's words from *Twelfth Night*:

> [We] can no other answer make but thanks,
> And thanks; and ever oft good turns
> Are shuffled off with such uncurrent pay.

We begin with Erika Berg, Longman's Acquisitions Editor, who first suggested and then guided this project; our production editors at Longman Publishers, Barbara Santoro and Dianne Hall, for patiently steering the final manuscript to press; and Chrysta Meadowbrooke, for her superb copyediting on this enormous project.

Our colleagues across the nation who served as external reviewers offered comments and suggestions that helped make this a better and more accurate text. As is often the case, we learned and benefited most from our severest critics, and we trust they will see their input in the completed project: Kate Basham, University of Minnesota-Deluth; Robert Bender, University of Missouri-Columbia; Henry Bial, University of New Mexico; Franz G. Blaha, University of Nebraska-Lincoln; Meiling Cheng, University of Southern California; Bill Dynes, University of Indianapolis; Adam J. Frisch, Briar Cliff University; Janet V. Haedicke, University of Louisiana at Monroe; Lincoln Konkle, The College of New Jersey; John M. McInerney, University of Scranton; Ed Menta, Kalamazoo College; Georgeann Murphy, University of New Hampshire; Matthew Roudané, Georgia State University; Katy Ryan, West Virginia University; John Shout, State University of New York at Plattsburgh; Roger Stanley, Union University; and Julia Walker, University of Illinois at Urbarna-Champaign.

Others contributed to the completion of this project, and to them we offer our deepest gratitude: Dr. Allen Alford of Temple (TX) Community College, Pat Nies, Margaret Moser, Jody Flippen, Matthew Parker, and John Charron.

And finally, though most importantly, we thank our families for their patience and support. We dedicate this book with our love.

MICHAEL GREENWALD

ROBERTO DARIO POMO

ROGER SCHULTZ

ANNE MARIE WELSH

PROLOGUE

The Precursors of
Modern Drama

Woyzeck, the superfluous little man about whom no one cares, considers his death as two women look on without feeling. The postmodern production of Woyzeck *pictured here was produced at Brooklyn Academy of Music Harvey Theater in October 2002 and directed by Robert Wilson.*

PROLOGUE: THE PRECURSORS OF MODERN DRAMA

Premodern Theater and Drama

The Norwegian playwright Henrik Ibsen is generally recognized as the progenitor of the modern theater in the West, and his play *A Doll's House* (1879) is often referred to as "the first modern play." While some respected theater scholars may contest this assertion, most would allow that Ibsen's social dramas prompted a revolution in the development of the theater and its drama. Just as painter Vincent van Gogh and composer Claude Debussy revolutionized their arts in the last quarter of the nineteenth century, Ibsen and other dramatists contributed to the growth of *Modernism*, a cultural movement that largely rejected the classical Greco-Roman and Judeo-Christian traditions in favor of a secular, nonelitist worldview. Modernism was the dominant mode of cultural expression in Europe and the United States for about one hundred years. It may be divided into three phases:

1. *Early Modernism*, from c. 1870 through World War I (1914–18), in which artists (and, of course, those in other segments of society) defined the principles of Modernism.
2. *High Modernism*, from c. 1920 through World War II (1939–45)
3. *Declining Modernism*, from c. 1945 through the mid-1960s.

The first phase is discussed in Part I of this anthology. The second and third phases saw the triumph of Modernism and, as is the case with all artistic movements, its decline and gradual replacement by a subsequent generation of artistic rebels. Part II considers both High Modernism and its decline. Modernism itself was supplanted by the so-called postmodern era (c. 1965–present), a much debated term that is addressed in Part III.

A cursory examination of most general (as opposed to specific-interest) anthologies of Western drama suggests that there was very little theatrical activity from the time of Molière and the English Restoration (1660–1700) to the emergence of Ibsen in the late nineteenth century. While relatively few plays from this nearly two-hundred-year span are performed today (save the English comedies of Oliver Goldsmith and Richard Brindsley Sheridan), there were nonetheless major cultural changes taking place that laid the foundation for the work of the early social Realists. In Asia, a similar upheaval was taking place as the Japanese Kabuki and the Peking Opera emerged in the eighteenth and nineteenth centuries, partly in response to middle class calls for new entertainment. In the mid-to-late twentieth century, the theaters of Africa and Latin America also turned toward the social drama, sometimes portraying life in the style of Euro-American Realism, at others employing the more overtly theatrical traditions that have served them well for centuries as they confront modern problems. Many of these, notably the works of South Africa's Athol Fugard, show a pronounced influence of the early European Realists, who were themselves inspired by the Romantics.

Emile Zola (1840–1902), a French novelist, playwright, and social critic, acknowledged this debt when he wrote, "Romanticism is the first step toward realism." In addition to Realism (and its extension, Naturalism), such theatrical movements as Expressionism, the Epic Theatre, and the Theater of the Absurd also evolved in the modern era. These various styles shared a common impulse: the desire to examine humans as social beings trapped in outmoded political, economic, and philosophical systems. While the spirit of Romanticism may be found in modern plays, its idealism has generally been supplanted by a cynicism or—more accurately—a more "realistic" assessment of the human dilemma in a rapidly changing world.

Romanticism

Romanticism was both an outgrowth of and a reaction to the Enlightenment, the eighteenth-century philosophical movement that extolled free thought, rationality, and scientific inquiry. While the Enlightenment actually began in northwest Europe in the mid-seventeenth century and spread to England, its sanction came from France, then the beacon of European culture and thought. Three Frenchmen in particular exerted enormous influence on the new intellectualism; significantly, all involved themselves in the media best suited to reach mass audiences: the theater. They were Denis Diderot, Voltaire, and Jean-Jacques Rousseau, who collectively bore the title of the *Philosophes*. They compiled one of the world's first encyclopedias on such diverse topics as science, politics, and the arts.

Diderot (1713–84) wanted scientific empiricism applied to drama to teach moral lessons. The theater, he argued, ought to be "a spectacle destined for bourgeois [i.e., middle-class] audiences, representing a striking moral picture of one's own social milieu." Diderot's call championed both the middle class as a subject for drama and Realism as its artistic style. His essays prepared the way for Victor Hugo, Ibsen, and other nineteenth-century playwrights.

Voltaire (*née* François-Marie Arouet, 1694–1778) was an outspoken critic of the French monarchy whose candor got him imprisoned in the infamous Bastille. In 1726 he was exiled to England where he saw the plays of Shakespeare, which were unlike anything he had experienced in France. When he returned to France in 1729, he argued for political and artistic freedom of expression and even wrote tragedies whose style was neoclassic but whose spirit was romantic.

Rousseau (1712–78) was the most influential of the *Philosophes*. Although he wrote several treatises on dramatic theory and a play (*Pygmalion*, 1775), it was Rosseau's political writings that, in part, inspired both the American and French Revolutions and the subsequent artistic movement that we call Romanticism. (The term does not refer to "love stories"; it originally meant "in the Roman manner" and was applied to literary works that imitated popular Italian novellas set in natural, as opposed to urban, environments.) Rousseau wrote that humans were born free but found themselves shackled by tyrannical governments, science, and the new urbanization spreading across Europe. He called for a return to a natural state in which people were in harmony with nature. Rousseau admired the indigenous peoples of the Americas, whom Romantics called "Noble Savages," a term of respect for those uncorrupted by urban civilization.

Such thinking inspired a number of "antique plays," such as *Spartacus* (about a slave uprising in ancient Rome) and medieval plays that praised the glories of a country's historical past. Friedrich Schiller's *William Tell* (1804), a Robin Hood–like drama in which commoners fight tyranny from the shelter of the forest, is among the best of these. This fascination with history manifested itself in scenic design and, very importantly, costuming. Setting became central to the drama, while the move to historically accurate dress was intended to evoke the beauty of the past. Romantic dramas invariably portrayed common people as the saviors of their nations. Rousseau's countryman Caron de Beaumarchais (1732–99), a fine playwright himself, argued that "the nearer the suffering [of the protagonist] is to my station, the greater his claim upon my sympathy. We identify with people, not kings."

Although there are many facets of Romantic thought, three in particular help define the impulse behind the Romantic Revolution.

1. "Freedom" became the battle cry of the new thinkers of the mid-eighteenth century—freedom from political oppression, freedom to think for oneself, freedom to create art independent of stultifying rules and traditions.
2. The heroes of the Romantic Revolution were the common man and woman. This was after all the age when Thomas Jefferson wrote that "All men are created equal" and French workers stormed the Bastille with the cry of "Liberty, Equality, and Fraternity."
3. Passion and feeling supplanted what the Romantics perceived to be the cold, analytical thought of the Enlightenment. William Wordsworth, a leading romantic poet, scolded scientists and the new empiricism when he argued that "we murder to dissect."

The Romantic Melodrama That Changed Western Theater

On February 25, 1830, Victor Hugo's *Hernani* premiered at Paris's Comedie Francaise in one of the most famous opening nights in the history of the theater. It was a defining moment for Western drama as it incorporated true romantic drama into the popular theater. The story, however, began several years earlier. In 1827 actors from London's Covent Garden Theatre performed Shakespeare's plays in Paris, the bastion of Neoclassicism. Playgoers at the Odeon Theatre were enthralled by the romantic drama of Shakespeare, who freely mixed comedy with tragedy while defying the classical unities in his sprawling epics. The English actors sparked the imaginations of young intellectuals, most notably the 25-year-old Victor Hugo (1802–85), who hurriedly wrote a play, *Cromwell*, in the manner of Shakespearean drama. Though a flawed work, Hugo's preface to the play became the manifesto for a new generation of playwrights, and his next play, *Hernani*, became the most celebrated and controversial French drama since Corneille's *Le Cid* (1636). The avant-garde clashed openly with traditionalists, brawls ensued, and the papers were filled with essays about the merits of Hugo's bold experiment. Audiences voted at the box office, and the phenomenal success of *Hernani* finally released the neoclassical stranglehold on European drama and promoted experimentation with form and content. Furthermore, it represented the triumph of populism in the French theater, thus making the common voice a respectable, as well as economically powerful, influence on subsequent drama. Note that Hugo remains "good box office" even today: *Les Miserables* (1989), adapted from his 1862 novel, is among the most successful musical dramas in the world.

The plot of *Hernani* typifies romantic melodrama. Hernani, an aristocratic Spaniard, seeks to revenge his father's death at the hands of King Carlos, who has also forbidden a marriage between Hernani and the beautiful noblewoman, Doña Sol, whom Carlos loves. The King's tyranny reminds us that antimonarchist sentiments frequently dominated romantic dramas. To complicate matters, Doña Sol's guardian, Don Ruy Gomez, also loves the woman. Acts II and III are comprised of a series of encounters between the King and Hernani, who each bow to the demands of honor and refuse to kill one another. In Act IV the King undergoes an astonishing transformation: inspired by the tomb of the Emperor Charlemagne (in a scene in which the environment is the controlling factor of the action), Carlos vows to become a noble monarch. Hernani is given permission to marry Doña Sol, and the play seems headed for a joyful ending with the lovers united and the King reformed. However, the vengeful Don Ruy appears at the wedding, disguised in a red mask, to demand that Hernani honor an earlier promise to give his life to the old nobleman upon demand. Rather than violate his oath, Hernani and Doña Sol choose death together. They commit suicide, as does Don Ruy, who is shamed by his vindictive act. Though Hugo was attempting high tragedy in the best Shakespearean manner, the play is unquestionably a melodrama. Though Hernani and his lover die, and however much we regret their passing, they are nonetheless victims of external forces—Don Ruy's treachery, a code of honor they have inherited, even the playwright's contrivances. Hernani does not contain the seeds of his own destruction, and nowhere is there the discovery of his own contribution to his death. Though the ending of *Hernani* may be engrossing theater (it received thunderous ovations at the Comedie Français), it fails to achieve true tragic dignity.

Nonetheless, the play transformed the French theater and broke the stranglehold of Neoclassicism that had dominated dramaturgy for two hundred years. The unities of time, place, and a single action were replaced by sprawling plots that covered years, numerous locales, and subplots. In *Hernani*, we see five distinct locales housing a story line that covers many days in the telling. The comic and tragic impulses were frequently mixed in a single play, and characters were no longer bound by the strict rules of decorum. For instance, Doña Sol—a noblewoman who in an earlier play might be limited to only the most dignified of speeches—tells her oppressor that he "would do better to tear their young from the tigers than the one I love from me." While the comparison with a jungle creature was judged undignified to the old guard, it was audacious and thrilling to the new. Don Carlos, the Spanish King, involves himself in mundane conversations about the time of day and hides in a closet; such behavior provoked laughter from conservatives in the audience and drew cheers from Hugo's youthful admirers.

In another supreme act of defiance against Neoclassicism, Hugo appropriated that most distinctive convention of Shakespeare's theater—the soliloquy. Though lengthy, passionate speeches (*tirades*) were common in classical French drama, characters alone on stage could not speak their thoughts aloud because it violated verisimilitude ("likeness to life"), which gave plays their moral authority. Hugo not only concluded his first act with a soliloquy by Hernani expressing antimonarchist sentiments, he also made Don Carlos's soliloquy in Act IV the moral centerpiece of the play. Set in the crypt of Charlemagne, who symbolizes the mythic past the Romantics revered, the scene depicts the reformation of the truant King Carlos, who is inspired by the emperor's nobility of purpose. His lengthy soliloquy at the tomb rings with the spirit of nineteenth-century Romanticism:

. . . who will make me great? Who will give me counsel? Charlemagne—you will! Since God, before whom all obstacles fall back, has taken our two majesties and set them face to face, then from the depths of this your grave, imbue my heart with the sublime!

Albert Bremel, an authority on French literature, considers Carlos's soliloquy "apart from one or two passages in *The Song of Roland*, the finest monologue in the French language."

The settings throughout the play also represent a major departure for European drama, especially those of Charlemagne's tomb and a magnificent portrait gallery in the castle. With *Hernani* locale becomes an indispensable character within the drama. The portrait scene in Act III—in which Don Ruy hides Hernani to protect him from the King (and thereby secures the pledge of death)—cannot be performed without the scenic effects Hugo scripted. Charlemagne's tomb is also indispensable, although one might argue the power of Don Carlos's words evokes the memory of the great emperor and the soliloquy could be played on a bare stage. But the dramatic point is that Carlos is dwarfed by the monument and vows to reform so that he might achieve Charlemagne's greatness. The expansive setting, which stunned the audience in its magnificence, created the right ambience to make Carlos's words necessary. In terms of Western theater history, such scenes created not only the possibility but also the necessity of humans performing *in* an environment instead of *in front of* one; even more importantly, characters are influenced by their environment. These are necessary steps on the road to Realism. Because *Hernani* succeeded on so many levels as literature and as theater, it remains among the most important plays of the premodern era.

The Melodrama

Consequently, melodrama and its ringing passions became the theatrical embodiment of romantic idealism. Melodrama is as old as Euripides; Shakespeare wrote romantic melodramas (e.g., *Cymbeline*), as did Lope de Vega in Spain. However, melodrama as a full-fledged genre evolved in Europe in the late eighteenth century, and by 1830 it was the dominant theatrical form in Europe and America. Though it is associated with the French theater during the years immediately after the Revolution of 1789, there was a significant German movement, the *Sturm und Drang* ("storm and stress"). In 1776 Friedrich Klinger (1752–1831) wrote a drama expressing many of the same political sentiments that sparked the political revolutions in the American colonies and in France. Klinger first called his play *Der Wirrwarr* ("The Hurly-Burly") but retitled it *Sturm und Drang* because it reflected the "storm and stress" Germany was experiencing.

The play's title was soon applied to a brigade of young intellectuals who wrote tumultuous dramas that rebelled against political, economic, and artistic tyranny. Their plays celebrated ordinary people in natural—even primitive—settings; they depicted heroic peasants overthrowing villainous land barons and tyrannical princes. Using the language of the common man and woman, the plays contained sensational action and elemental conflicts between the forces of good and evil. Schiller's *The Robbers* (1781) established the plot and character prototypes for the melodrama: the damsel in distress, the falsely accused hero, and the ruthless villain whose castle is filled with dungeons, secret passageways, and trap doors. Note that many of our finest composers (e.g., Beethoven) wrote music to accompany such melodramas. Rossini's overture to *William Tell* is among the best known of these compositions, largely because it became the theme music for the television show, *The Lone Ranger*, which itself was a thoroughly romantic view of the American West.

Historically true melodrama was born on the boulevards of Paris after the Revolution. At this time, Parisian theaters were of two kinds:

1. The "restricted theaters" that were licensed to perform classical drama
2. Playhouses located on the boulevards of working-class neighborhoods where laborers gathered to watch popular entertainments such as animal acts, prizefighting, and variety shows

Among the favorite diversions at these "boulevard theaters" were *pantomimes*, which appealed to a largely nonliterate audience. Pantomimes evolved into *tableau vivants* ("living pictures") depicting spectacular scenes of violence and suspense (e.g., a hero dangling from a cliff) as well as historical events such as the storming of the Bastille.

A young writer named Guilbert de Pixerecourt (1773–1844) frequented such theaters and began writing full-length plays that incorporated spectacles and violence—or at least dangerous situations. In 1796 he wrote *Victor, The Child of the Forest*, the play that defines "melodrama" as an art form. Pixerecourt's melodramas gained international popularity as they championed justice and liberty. In Germany, August Iffland (1759–1814) wrote *familienstucke*, middle-class dramas dealing with families in crisis (e.g., foreclosure on the old homestead by a heartless banker). August Kotzebue (1761–1819), the most popular playwright in the Western world by 1810, wrote melodramas that appealed to middle-class morality. William Dunlap, the "Father of the American Theater," imported many of Kotzebue's dramas and thus began America's long-standing fascination with the melodrama, the most popular of which was *Uncle Tom's Cabin* (1852). However, it was Victor Hugo's romantic melodrama, *Hernani* (1830), that most transformed Western theater by loosening the grip of neoclassic dogma that demanded that plays be written according to the principles of the classic dramas of ancient Greece and Rome. (See Showcase, "*Hernani*: The Romantic Melodrama That Changed Western Theater.")

Melodrama often carries a negative connotation and suggests tawdry dramas in which moustache-twirling villains tie damsels in distress to the railroad tracks while square-jawed heroes ride to the rescue. This is "meller-dramer," a nineteenth-century variant on the much older, more respected melodrama. In truth many plays, including some of our most esteemed tragedies, have melodramatic elements. Stripped of its cosmic implications, *Hamlet* is a lurid melodrama filled with ghosts skulking about castles, cloak-and-dagger espionage, and violent deaths; Tom Stoppard's *Rosencrantz and Guildenstern Are Dead* (Part III) derives much of its humor by exposing the melodramatic elements in Shakespeare's tragedy.

Originally, a "*melo drame*" was a serious play accompanied by music to heighten its emotional impact. In 1775 Rousseau coined the term to describe his short play, *Pygmalion* (a monologue set to music). Eventually, "melodrama" was applied to a sensational play in which:

- Ingenious plots produce moments of danger for the protagonists.
- Characters are thinly drawn symbols of singular virtues and vices pitted against one another.
- Morality is reduced to its most simple elements.
- The emotional appeal surpasses any intellectual pretensions.
- Poetic justice triumphs by the final curtain.

Like tragedy, the melodrama asks us to feel for the protagonists, to experience pity and fear, and to come away from the experience cleansed. But in melodrama the conflicts are almost always external, and the protagonists are frequently victims of villains. Tragedy demands that the hero's own personality contains the seeds of his or her downfall and that the hero ultimately recognizes this truth. While melodrama may flirt with tragic import by putting its heroes in life-threatening situations, its reliance on purely external circumstances diminishes the possibility of tragedy.

Many social dramas, especially those with an undercurrent of propaganda, are steeped in melodramatic techniques because they rely on oppressive villains (bankers, landowners, and bosses) to stir their audiences to action. Arthur Miller's first successful play, *All My Sons*, an outstanding play by any criterion, is at heart a melodrama, despite its attempt to reach tragic proportions. The term need not be pejorative, as there are numerous respected plays that are properly classified as melodramas.

Because melodramas emphasized plotting over character development, the sensational over the profound, simple morality over complex issues, the quality of the playwriting diminished. "I write for those who cannot read," Pixerecourt once said. As a result, the scene designer, the technical wizard, and the costume designer became forces as powerful as the actor and the playwright. Scenery drew people into the theater because middle-class audiences were eager to escape into the magical illusions created by designers. The death-defying situations melodramatists imposed upon their heroes and heroines necessitated the invention of new stage machinery—and vice versa. Dioramas, panoramas, treadmills, trap doors, elevators for moving scenery on and off stage, and flying devices were developed to stage train wrecks, horse races, apparitions, and disappearances. Playwrights and theater managers often incorporated special effects into the plays simply because the machinery existed. *Uncle Tom's Cabin*—which depicts a shipwreck, Eliza trapped on the ice floes of the Ohio River, and a concluding *tableau*—illustrates the kinds of effects audiences clamored to see in 1852, just as modern movie audiences thrill to the sinking of the *Titanic*. Of more importance to the evolution of drama, however, this fascination with scenery placed a primary value on the environment in which a play's characters found themselves; and environment, as you will see, became a major concern of the early Modernists.

The Well-Made Play

Although the romantic spirit swept Europe and America, there was also a continuation of the scientific revolution fostered by the Enlightenment. It was spurred by empiricism, which placed a primary value on observation and experience. Consequently, this phenomenon inspired a new approach to playwriting that created a central component in the fully developed social drama: the well-made play.

Despite the success of *Hernani*, Hugo was soon replaced as Paris's most popular playwright by Eugene Scribe (1791–1861), whom Eric Bentley has called the greatest nongenius of drama. Scribe perfected the well-made play (*pièce bien fait*), a formula for playwriting that virtually guaranteed the box office appeal of intricate, believable plots in which suspense, action, and brilliantly theatrical moments take precedence over characterization and theme. Scribe, who composed over 400 stage works, disdained melodrama's penchant for improbable events and applied the scientific principles of "causality" to make them plausible or—as he said—to make "the accidental seem necessary." Instead of romantic settings, Scribe favored domestic scenes in his gently satiric dramas of the Parisian bourgeois. (See Showcase, "Eugene Scribe's Well-Made Play: *The Glass of Water*.")

The well-made play depicts essentially two-dimensional characters that are lively enough to engage audiences. Its plots are based upon a withheld secret (thereby creating suspense), which is hinted at in the well-crafted exposition of Act I. A series of reversals advance the action as the protagonist undergoes a battle of wits with an archrival. These reversals are credibly explained by letters, mistaken identities, carefully timed entrances and exits, and a *quid pro quo*, that is, a moment in which two or more characters misinterpret a situation that further enmeshes them in the action. Late in the play there is a climactic reversal—"the obligatory scene" (or *scène à faire*). This moment usually represents the hero's low point until the secret is revealed to vindicate him and vanquish the villain. All is explained logically and credibly in the play's final moments. This pattern is repeated in subtler ways in each scene and act, and each act ends on a moment of reversal to ensure suspense and to provide an ominous "curtain line."

Scribe did not, of course, invent the well-made play. That honor goes to Sophocles, whose *Oedipus the King* remains its prototype because it relies on a withheld secret. But Scribe did perfect the formula, which was codified in 1863 by the German theorist, Gustav Freitag (1816–95), whose short work "The Technique of the Drama" is the standard treatment of the topic. Thus the well-made play became the model for other European and American playwrights at mid-century. Ibsen oversaw the production of numerous Scribean plays at the state theater he managed in Norway. He drew upon Scribe's formula as he fashioned his first thesis dramas to attack contemporary social problems. *A Doll's House* turns on a secret (Nora's forgery of the bank note) and the letter from Krogstad which reverses the fortunes of the Helmer household forever.

The well-made play is still very much with us, most notably in film and television scriptwriting. Bound by well-defined time blocks and the need to stop the action for commercial messages (the equivalent of the nineteenth-century "curtain line"), TV writers necessarily adhere to the Scribean formula as they, too, write for mass audiences.

SHOWCASE ■ EUGENE SCRIBE'S WELL-MADE PLAY

The Glass of Water

Although the prolific Scribe wrote almost four hundred plays, few are performed today. Nonetheless, because he was among the most influential playwrights of the mid-nineteenth century, it is useful to familiarize yourself with at least one of his works. A careful reading of *The Glass of Water* (1840), perhaps Scribe's best-known work, reveals his mastery of the technique of the "well-made play."

While much has been written about Scribe's rather mechanical style, among the best analyses of the standard structural features of his work is one rendered by Stephen S. Stanton, who includes this comedy in his short anthology of nineteenth-century French drama, *Camille and Other Plays*. According to Stanton, the Scribean well-made play:

- Is based on a secret which is known to the audience but withheld from certain antagonists until the secret or its consequences are revealed in the climactic or obligatory scene, which unmasks the villain and restores the good fortune of the hero, with whom the audience sympathizes
- Displays a pattern of increasingly intense action and intrigue which has been preceded by meticulous exposition, facilitated by contrived entrances and exits, letters, and other devices
- Features a series of ups and downs in the hero's fortunes caused by his antagonist
- Reaches its climax in the *scène à faire*—obligatory scene—in which the withheld secret is revealed or disclosed to the opposing forces
- Includes a central misunderstanding (or *quid pro quo*) made obvious to the spectator but withheld from the participants
- Follows through to a probable and necessary denouement
- Reproduces this pattern in the action of each act

Let us apply these devices to a summary of *The Glass of Water*, which was written at the height of Scribe's popularity among Parisian audiences.

Set early in eighteenth-century London during the reign of Queen Anne, *The Glass of Water* presents the parallel plights of two young men: that of the likable soldier, Arthur Masham, and his quest for the love of Abigail Churchill; and that of the dashing young political operative, the soon-to-be Viscount Bolingbroke (Henry St. Johns), and his quest for "the good of England" in his battle with the powerful Duchess of Marlborough [*exposition*]. While Masham seeks a position for Abigail in Queen Anne's court, Bolingbroke seeks an audience with Queen Anne for Louis XIV's ambassador, M. de Torcy, to facilitate an end to the war [*more exposition*]. Standing between both is the ever-present Duchess of Marlborough, the Queen's favorite, who jealously and tyrannically controls the palace [*complication*]. Bolingbroke, having ascertained that the poor shopgirl, Abigail, is the obscure relative of Marlborough [*exposition*], threatens to expose Marlborough if the Duchess refuses to admit Abigail into Anne's service [*complication*]. In response, the Duchess, having purchased a creditor's claim against him, threatens to have Bolingbroke imprisoned [*minor crisis*]. In the meantime, Masham, having been insulted, challenges the elder Viscount to a duel, kills him, and is threatened with execution [*crisis/reversal*]. Now, however, an anonymous protector intervenes, securing a captaincy for Masham, and Bolingbroke, discovering that it is the Duchess of Marlborough herself [*exposition*], forces the Duchess to find a place for Abigail in Anne's service [*reversal*]. The charming Abigail wins over the Queen, who confesses that she is in love with Masham, thus presenting Abigail with two rivals—the Queen and the Duchess—both of whom arrange meetings with Masham [*complication/crisis*]. Although these meetings are ostensibly mere audiences,

poor Abigail considers them as amorous rendezvous, and she is not mistaken. She imparts this sad news and confesses her grief to Bolingbroke, who promises to protect her and save Masham for her. Bolingbroke meets the Duchess and informs her of the Queen's secret love; although he does not name Masham, he tells her she will soon recognize him by a prearranged signal—the Queen's asking him for a glass of water [*exposition/complication*]. When this takes place and the Duchess learns that it is, in fact, the Queen who is her rival for Masham, she intervenes and haughtily invokes court custom and privilege and her "rights as a lady of honor" to serve the Queen a glass of water, which the Duchess proceeds to spill all over the Queen [*crisis/reversal*]. Disgraced and seeking vengeance, the Duchess, now aware of the Queen's love for Masham, denounces him as a murderer, and the Queen is obliged to have him arrested [*reversal*]. Happily, however, it is Bolingbroke who has custody, and Masham's captivity is not long, for he soon has permission for a secret rendezvous with Abigail in, of all places, the Queen's boudoir. In a final attempt to defeat Bolingbroke and Masham, the Duchess, who knows everything and who has kept the keys to the Queen's boudoir, appears and interrupts what she has told all the court is a royal assignation [*quid pro quo*]. But Abigail's presence in the room saves the Queen's honor, and the Duchess is confronted by Bolingbroke [*obligatory scene*], who intervenes and orders the new favorite, Abigail, to marry Masham [*reversal*]. The Duchess is now hopelessly ruined [*climax*], Abigail succeeds her in Anne's favor, Bolingbroke is made minister, the Duke of Marlborough is recalled, and the peace treaty is signed [*denouement*]—"And all, thanks to a glass of water!"

The final line—"thanks to a glass of water"—humorously illustrates a central point in Scribe's dramaturgy that he articulates earlier in a speech by Bolingbroke: "Great effects are produced by small causes. That is my system. . . . I have confidence in it." This is, of course, the principle of causality upon which drama has been based since Sophocles in ancient Greece, and it was very much a philosophy of the Naturalists who maintained that heredity and environment were the "cause" of human behavior.

The principle of reversal that propelled the well-made play can be appreciated by looking at a story Masham tells Bolingbroke in the first act. Scribe wrote the sequence as a dialogue between the two gentlemen, but it is abridged here as a monologue. Note how Masham's fortunes reverse up and down throughout the speech:

. . . for many years, as you know, I had hoped for a place in the palace of the Queen. The difficulty came, of course, in presenting my petition to her Majesty. However, on the day that Parliament opened, I forced my way through the crowd which surrounded her carriage. . . . indeed I was almost touching it [*up*] when suddenly a large gentleman knocked against me, turned around and . . . snapped a finger in my face [*down*]. . . . in that moment the crowd came between us and practically threw me against the carriage, to whom I tossed my petition [*up*]. For a fortnight there was no answer [*down*]. Then I received a letter for an audience with her Majesty! [*up*] You can imagine how I hastened to present myself at the palace. . . . I was practically within two steps of St. James Palace [*still up*], when a carriage driving pell-mell down the street, splattered me from head to foot with mud [*down*]. . . .

The speech continues with alternating moments of success and failure for an-other half-page (yes, Masham gets his appointment to the Palace as an ensign in the Queen's Guards). Even this short passage indicates the mechanistic structure of the well-made play, the move from positive to negative reversals of fortune that creates suspense and keeps the audience engaged in the action. It is a formula that served playwrights well then—and now.

For further study:

Arvin, Neil Cole. *Eugene Scribe and the French Theatre: 1815–1860.* Cambridge: Harvard U Press, 1924.

Stanton, Stephen S. (ed.). *Camille and Other Plays.* New York: Mermaid Books, 1957. Contains the complete text of and commentary on *The Glass of Water.*

———. "Shaw's Debt to Scribe." *PMLA* LXXVI (December 1961), 388–402.

The Problem Play

In the next section you will learn that sociologists, evolutionists, philosophers, socialists, and psychologists created an atmosphere that precipitated radical changes in drama in the late nineteenth century. But, as is often the case, an earlier dramatist anticipated such changes. In 1849 Alexandre Dumas *fils* (1824–95) wrote *La Dame aux Camélias* in which he attempted to defend the dignity of the "fallen woman" as he portrayed a love affair between a well-bred young man and a courtesan. Though this much imitated play, known as *Camille*, is a melodrama, Dumas *fils* broke new ground that Ibsen and his successors would harvest a quarter-century later. (See Showcase, "The Original Problem Play: *La Dame aux Camélias*.")

Camille is often regarded as the first "thesis" (*pièce à thèse*), "problem," or "discussion" play because it provoked the characters on stage, as well as audiences, into discussing a topical problem; in truth, however, plays have provoked discussion of contemporary problems since Greek playwrights confronted audiences with issues that challenged Athens and other city states. Specifically, the late-nineteenth-century "problem play" was the product of then-liberal artists who questioned the validity of traditional thinking, especially in matters related to the emancipation of women, sexual behavior, and business ethics. Such dramas made open appeals to the social conscience of the audience, much like the phenomenally popular novels of social reformers like Charles Dickens.

Although Ibsen's social dramas are generally regarded as the epitome of the problem play, other pre-Ibsen playwrights merit attention. Dumas *fils*'s more conservative countryman, Emile Augier (1820–89), wrote similar plays, including *Olympe's Marriage* (1855), which portrayed the disastrous results of a marriage between a courtesan and an aristocrat. Augier's play was, in essence, a rebuttal to *Camille*. In England T. W. Robertson (1829–71) wrote a series of plays in the 1860s, of which *Caste* (1867) is the best known. Robertson's plays are often collectively referred to as "cup and saucer dramas" because characters discussed the problems of the day (such as inequities in England's caste system) while sipping tea. Robertson's "cup and saucer realism" would eventually give way to "kitchen sink realism," named for the squalid conditions portrayed in social realist dramas.

SHOWCASE — **THE ORIGINAL PROBLEM PLAY**

La Dame aux Camélias [Camille]

You may have seen one of the most popular and critically acclaimed films of 2002, Baz Lurhmann's *Moulin Rouge*, the story of an ill-fated love affair between an aristocratic young man and a dancer at Paris's fabled night club, the Moulin Rouge. The plot, with which Luhrmann and his cowriters have taken liberties, is derived (in part) from one of the most important and controversial plays of the mid-nineteenth century: *La Dame aux Camélias* (*The Lady of the Camellias*), or more simply, *Camille*. It was written by Alexandre Dumas *fils* (1824–95), the son of one of France's major romantic authors (who wrote the novel *The Count of Monte Cristo*, which also became one of the most popular of the nineteenth-century melodramatic plays; there have been 17 films of the play, the most recent in 2002).

Camille, a five-act play, tells the somewhat autobiographical story of the unhappy love affair between Armand Duval, a wealthy young man, and Marguerite Gauthier, the most beautiful and sought-after courtesan in Paris. (Do not think of the courtesan as a common prostitute; Marguerite was a "high-class" woman who wore spectacular clothing that was adorned with a bouquet of camellias.) When Armand meets Marguerite, she is "kept" by Count de Varville, who has agreed to pay her debts if she becomes his mistress. Marguerite is desperate for money, partly because she grew up in poverty, mostly because she has "consumption," a dreaded disease of the lungs. She justifies her dissolute lifestyle to Armand, whom she initially rejects as a lover:

> If I had to care for myself, my dear man, I would die. Don't you understand that the way I live keeps me alive? It is easy for women who have family and friends to care for themselves; but for a woman like me, the moment I am no longer attractive to others, I am left alone. . . . I know. I was alone in bed for two months and no one came to see me.

Here we see the playwright's attempt to build sympathy for the so-called "fallen woman," and it is speeches like this that make *Camille* a major point of departure for nineteenth-century social drama, for it "discusses" a "problem" of concern to mid-nineteenth-century French society.

Armand eventually wins Marguerite's love, and at the conclusion of Act II the courtesan rejects all suitors in favor of Armand. Act III, however, brings about a dramatic reversal when Armand's father, who has heard about his son's affair, appears at Marguerite's salon and begs the woman to reject his son because:

> . . . society makes its demands on us. Your love for Armand may be pure in your heart, but the world does not see a pure heart. It sees your wicked past and all doors will be closed to you and Armand. . . . I beg you, Marguerite, in the name of your love for Armand, give me the happiness of my child.

Marguerite responds to Duval's plea in a moving speech that defines the problem of the play:

> Whatever she may do, the fallen woman may not rise again. God may forgive her—but the world will never forgive her. What man wants her for a wife, what child a mother? One day you may tell Armand's daughter, should he have one, of a beautiful woman who sacrificed her happiness for one thing, your son's happiness, and she died for it. Because, you see, I shall die, and then perhaps I will be forgiven for my past.

Marguerite, after much anguish, does "the noble thing" and tells Armand she cannot see him anymore. Assuming that she loves another, he angrily showers her with bank notes in a public setting, treating her like the whore he assumes her to be. He exits, screaming, *"I call upon you to witness that I owe this woman nothing!"* The curtain falls on Act IV as Marguerite gives "a cry and falls to the ground." (This, by the way, is known as a "curtain line," a throwback to the melodrama that invariably brought down the curtain at a moment of high drama.)

Act V, among the most famous in all nineteenth-century theater and a favorite of actresses, takes place a half-year later in Marguerite's bedroom, where she is dying. Armand, who has since married a "respectable" woman, tearfully returns. He begs his former lover to live, but she replies that although she is dying, "I am happy, too . . . and it is only my happiness that you see." She dies quietly, and her maid speaks her epitaph: "Rest in peace, Marguerite. You will be forgiven many things, for you have loved much."

Sentimental? Melodramatic? Contrived for effect? Yes on all counts, but *Camille* (and its numerous imitations) remained a staple of European and American theater well into the twentieth century. It even spawned a phrase in our vocabulary: to do "a Camille" meant to use teary effects to get one's way. Predictably, the play was made into a film in the 1930s with Bette Davis in the title role. By contrast, in 1984 the British playwright Pam Gems adapted the play into a cold, unsentimental treatise about the exploitation of women.

But *Camille* is important for reasons other than its extraordinary popularity. It is the prototype of the "discussion drama," "problem play," or "thesis play" (*pièce à thèse*)—it goes by many names—that Ibsen and his successors would make the cornerstone of the New Drama a quarter-century later. Dumas *fils* himself defined the genre in a letter to a friend. It is worth noting that he actually wrote the play in 1849, but it was not performed until 1852 because of its controversial subject matter. Dumas's letter was a defense of his intentions; the italicized portions here most directly reflect the spirit of the drama that followed.

I realize the prime requisites of a play are laughter, tears, passion, emotion, interest, curiosity: to leave life at the cloak room. But I maintain that if, by means of all these ingredients, and without minimizing one of them, I can exercise some influence over society; if, instead of treating effects, I can treat causes; if, for example, while I satirize and dramatize adultery, *I can find means to force people to discuss the problems* and the law makers to revise the law, I shall have done more than my part as a poet, I shall have done my duty as a man. . . . We need invent nothing, we have only to observe, remember, feel, coordinate, restore. *As for the basis, the real*; as for the facts, what is possible; as for means, what is ingenious: that is all that can be asked of us. [Emphasis ours]

Despite his best intentions—i.e., to give dignity to the fallen woman—Dumas *fils*, it may be argued, dispatched poor, dying Marguerite for other than dramatic reasons (and there is no denying that her death is outstanding theater and drama). A mid-nineteenth-century audience may well have accepted the argument that a woman with a past merited sympathy and understanding. But the prevailing morality of the time also demanded that the wanton woman (however golden her heart) be punished. Men, of course, were judged by an entirely different standard; hence Armand returns to his wife to live "happily" ever after. Ironically, Marguerite's death allowed Parisian audiences—and those who flocked to see the play elsewhere—to have their theatrical cake and eat it, too. They left the theater with a new perspective on women, but satisfied that they did not have to confront the reality of Marguerite being a respectable woman within their society.

Other plays followed, each dutifully discussing the need for understanding of lifestyles considered deviant, and each dutifully dispatching these "fallen angels." Bernard Shaw, a critic as well as a playwright, noted that such women "died of the fifth act" because playwrights—like his contemporary Arthur Wing Pinero—did not always show the courage of their convictions when discussing the "problem" of women in their thesis plays. It was Shaw himself who took a giant step forward in *Mrs. Warren's Profession* (1892) when his protagonist, a madam in the world's oldest profession, not only lives but becomes a wealthy, respectable member of Victorian society. Her daughter Vivie, an exemplar of the New Woman, ultimately rejects Mrs. Warren, not because she is involved in prostitution but because she has become too conventional.

For further reading:

Stanton, Stephen S. (ed.). *Camille and Other Plays*. New York: Mermaid Books, 1957. This useful anthology contains the text of *Camille* as well as the most thorough commentary on Scribe's well-made play.

Given their lack of opportunities in a male-dominated society, we might expect that women would have written problem plays and other social dramas in the nineteenth century. There is little available evidence that this was the case, partly because women were largely discouraged from active participation in theater, and mostly because the novel was their literary weapon of choice. (Tellingly, a woman often had to adopt a male pseudonym when writing novels and, only later, plays.) The social dramas of Ibsen and his successors emboldened women, who used the stage as a soapbox to further their cause, especially suffrage. By the turn of the century, women were indeed writing "problem plays," such as Elizabeth Robins's *Votes for Women* (1907), which featured a spectacular rally by Suffragettes in London's Trafalgar Square (which Robins wrote from transcripts of actual rallies she had attended). In Scandinavia, Charlotte Leffler (1849–92) and Victoria Benedictsson (1849–88) addressed women's issues; the latter, it should be noted, was first known as "Ernest Ahlgren" to her Swedish audiences!

The "Other" First Modern Play?

Ironically, for all the popularity of romantic melodramas, well-made plays, and problem plays, an obscure play—which was not even produced until 1913—perhaps most thoroughly anticipates the extraordinary changes that the theater would experience in the late nineteenth and early twentieth centuries. *Woyzeck* (1836), written by Georg Buchner, contains elements of Romanticism, Social Realism, Naturalism, Expressionism, Surrealism, Symbolism, and even the Theater of the Absurd and Postmodernism—all of which will be explored in greater depth elsewhere in this text. We shall use *Woyzeck* as a touchstone for our exploration of modern and contemporary drama and refer to it often as we discuss the elements of style and theme. Buchner's biography, the text of this visionary play, and the interpretive essay that follows it should provide you with an important first step in your introduction to modern and even postmodern drama.

WOYZECK
Georg Buchner

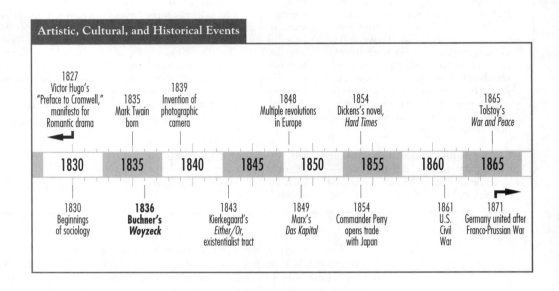

Artistic, Cultural, and Historical Events

1827
Victor Hugo's
"Preface to Cromwell,"
manifesto for
Romantic drama

1835
Mark Twain
born

1839
Invention of
photographic
camera

1848
Multiple revolutions
in Europe

1854
Dickens's novel,
Hard Times

1865
Tolstoy's
War and Peace

| 1830 | 1835 | 1840 | 1845 | 1850 | 1855 | 1860 | 1865 |

1830
Beginnings
of sociology

**1836
Buchner's
Woyzeck**

1843
Kierkegaard's
Either/Or,
existentialist tract

1849
Marx's
Das Kapital

1854
Commander Perry
opens trade
with Japan

1861
U.S.
Civil
War

1871
Germany united after
Franco-Prussian War

GEORG BUCHNER (1813–37)

Ironically, when Buchner died at 23 of typhoid fever without ever having seen his plays produced, it marked the end of the tempestuous life of an artist whose few plays manifested the deterministic philosophy that humans are doomed to a destiny over which they have no control. Although he technically did not write for the modern (i.e., post-Ibsen) theater, Buchner's small body of work anticipates the major strains of modern and contemporary drama: Social Realism, Naturalism, Expressionism, Surrealism, the Absurd, Existentialism, and even the Postmodern. Indeed, his dramaturgy was so far ahead of its time that he was largely ignored until Gerhart Hauptmann, a pioneer of German Naturalism, rediscovered his genius in the late nineteenth century.

The son of a German physician, Buchner studied medicine at the University of Strasbourg where he became involved in the *Junges Deutschland* (Young Germany) movement, a revolutionary cadre committed to the social and political changes sweeping Europe after the French Revolution. His peers believed change was best effected by the educated, but Buchner argued that the lower classes must be at the vanguard of the new order. In 1834 Buchner founded the Secret Society for the Rights of Man and wrote its manifesto ("The Hessian Courier"), which called for a rebellion by the peasant class. The government retaliated, and Buchner was forced to flee to his home near Darmstadt, where he began his first play, *Danton's Death* (1835), a darkly romantic drama that paralleled events of the French Revolution with the plight of contemporary young Germans. The play contains a speech by its titular hero that epitomizes the playwright's pessimistic worldview: "What are we but puppets, manipulated on wires by unknown powers? We are nothing, nothing in ourselves: we are the swords that spirits fight with—except no one sees the hands."

Buchner, a declared enemy of the state, was forbidden to travel and received his doctoral degree from the University of Zurich *in absentia*, although in 1836 he was finally permitted to move to Switzerland, where he taught anatomy. Free from German censorship, Buchner continued to write in Zurich, first *Leonce and Lena*, an absurd fairy tale that satirized repressive governments, and finally *Woyzeck*, his acknowledged masterpiece. Discovered only after the playwright's untimely death, *Woyzeck* appeared to be a work-in-progress whose 29 scenes were in no discernable order (see below). Thus the play was not published until 1879 (the year *A Doll's House* premiered), and it was not performed until 1913 (the age of German Expressionism). It is with justification considered by some scholars to be truly "the first modern play."

In 1835 Buchner wrote a letter to his parents in which he defined his mission as a playwright; the letter also serves as a manifesto for much of the new drama that emerged in Europe during the latter half of the nineteenth century and beyond. We offer it here as a preface to the dramas that follow Buchner's visionary work.

> . . . if someone were to say to me that the poet ought not to show the world as it is, but as it ought to be, then I would answer him that I will not make it better than the Good Lord, who must certainly have made it as it ought to be. As regards to the so-called Idealist poets [e.g., Schiller and the Romantics], I find that they have given us nothing more than marionettes with sky-blue noses and affected pathos, but not human beings of flesh and blood, who make us feel their joy with them, and whose deeds and actions fill me with revulsion or admiration.

As You Read *Woyzeck*

If the structure of this play—a series of seemingly unrelated scenes that form only a shadow of a plot—seems strange to you, imagine how those who discovered the play among Buchner's papers in 1837 must have felt. Or the editors who tried to organize the 29 unnumbered scenes into a cogent whole as they prepared the play for publication in 1879. That, however, is precisely the point: the scene order matters little because the action (or inaction) is seen solely through the eyes of the protagonist, the barber-soldier Johan Christian Woyzeck (an actual person who killed his mistress in Leipzig in 1824). Notably, a theater company in New York once performed the play by drawing the scene numbers randomly each night and found that the play invariably "worked" in whatever sequence fate decreed. Each scene is calculated to illustrate but one point: the world treats the hapless soldier cruelly and thus forces him to a single violent act that defines him forever. Consider the play as a great circle with the 29 scenes surrounding its hub—the lonely, isolated figure of Woyzeck. Cumulatively the scenes explain why the passive barber suddenly explodes into violence. Even if the killing is performed early in the play, the other scenes become flashbacks that illuminate the mounting injustices that prompted the murder. Woyzeck and his lover, Marie, are the only multidimensional characters in the play; the others are little more than caricatures, but not because of any inadequacies on the playwright's part. Rather, Buchner wished us to see the world precisely as Woyzeck sees it: hostile, cruel, and reduced to its most elemental horrors. In scenes 4 and 5 Woyzeck finds himself in a carnival. In fact, throughout the play he is trapped in a grotesque world of fun-house mirrors, hence the nightmare distortions in the structure, grotesque characterizations, shifting performance styles, and ultimately the message of this horrific drama.

WOYZECK

GEORG BUCHNER

Translated by Carl R. Mueller

CHARACTERS
WOYZECK
MARIE
CAPTAIN
DOCTOR
DRUM MAJOR
SERGEANT
ANDRES
MARGRET
PROPRIETOR OF THE BOOTH
CHARLATAN
OLD MAN WITH BARREL-ORGAN
JEW
INNKEEPER
APPRENTICES
KATHY
KARL THE TOWN IDIOT
GRANDMOTHER
POLICEMAN
SOLDIERS, STUDENTS, YOUNG MEN *and* GIRLS, CHILDREN, JUDGE, COURT CLERK, PEOPLE

SCENE 1—AT THE CAPTAIN'S

The Captain in a chair. Woyzeck shaving him.

CAPTAIN. Not so fast, Woyzeck, not so fast! One thing at a time! You're making me dizzy. What am I to do with the ten extra minutes that you'll finish early today? Just think, Woyzeck: you still have thirty beautiful years to live! Thirty years! That makes three hundred and sixty months! And days! Hours! Minutes! What do you think you'll do with all that horrible stretch of time? Have you ever thought about it, Woyzeck?

WOYZECK. Yes, sir, Captain.

CAPTAIN. It frightens me when I think about the world . . . when I think about eternity. Busyness, Woyzeck, busyness! There's the eternal: that's eternal, that is eternal. That you can understand. But then again it's not eternal. It's only a moment. A mere moment. Woyzeck, it makes me shudder when I think that the earth turns itself about in a single day! What a waste of time! Where will it all end? Woyzeck, I can't even look at a mill wheel any more without becoming melancholy.

WOYZECK. Yes, sir, Captain.

CAPTAIN. Woyzeck, you always seem so exasperated! A good man isn't like that. A good man with a good conscience, that is. Well, say something, Woyzeck! What's the weather like today?

WOYZECK. Bad, Captain, sir, bad: wind!

CAPTAIN. I feel it already. Sounds like a real storm out there. A wind like that has the same effect on me as a mouse. [*Cunningly.*] I think it must be something out of the north-south.

WOYZECK. Yes, sir, Captain.

CAPTAIN. Ha! Ha! Ha! North-south! Ha! Ha! Ha! Oh, he's a stupid one! Horribly stupid! [*Moved.*] Woyzeck, you're a good man, but [*With dignity.*] Woyzeck, you have no morality! Morality, that's when you have morals, you understand. It's a good word. You have a child without the blessings of the Church, just like our Right Reverend Garrison Chaplain says: "Without the blessings of the Church." It's not *my* phrase.

WOYZECK. Captain, sir, the good Lord's not going to look at a poor worm just because they said Amen over it before they went at it. The Lord said: "Suffer little children to come unto me."

CAPTAIN. What's that you said? What kind of strange answer's that? You're confusing me with your answers!

WOYZECK. It's us poor people that . . . You see, Captain, sir . . . Money, money! Whoever hasn't got money . . . Well, who's got morals when he's bringing something like me into the world? We're flesh and blood, too. Our kind is miserable only once: in this world and in the next. I think if we ever got to Heaven we'd have to help with the thunder.

CAPTAIN. Woyzeck, you have no virtue! You're not a virtuous human being! Flesh and blood? Whenever I rest at the window, when it's finished raining, and my eyes follow the white stockings along as they hurry across the street . . . Damnation, Woyzeck, I know what love is, too, then! I'm made of flesh and blood, too. But, Woyzeck: Virtue! Virtue! How was I to get rid of the time? I always say to myself: "You're a virtuous man [*Moved*], a good man, a good man."

WOYZECK. Yes, Captain, sir: Virtue. I haven't got much of that. You see, us common people, we haven't got virtue. That's the way it's got to be. But if I could be a gentleman, and if I could have a hat and a watch and a cane, and if I could talk refined, I'd want to be virtuous, all right. There must be something beautiful in virtue, Captain, sir. But I'm just a poor good-for-nothing!

CAPTAIN. Good, Woyzeck. You're a good man, a good man. But you think too much. It eats at you. You always seem so exasperated. Our discussion has affected me deeply. You can go now. And don't run so! Slowly! Nice and slowly down the street!

SCENE 2—AN OPEN FIELD. THE TOWN IN THE DISTANCE

*Woyzeck and Andres cut twigs from the bushes.
Andres whistles.*

WOYZECK. Andres? You know this place is cursed? Look at that light streak over there on the grass. There where the toadstools grow up. That's where the head rolls every night. One time somebody picked it up. He thought it was a hedgehog. Three days and three nights and he was in a box. [*Low.*] Andres, it was the Freemasons, don't you see, it was the Freemasons!

ANDRES [*sings*].

Two little rabbits sat on a lawn
Eating, oh, eating the green green grass . . .

WOYZECK. Quiet! Can you hear it, Andres? Can you hear it? Something moving!

ANDRES [*sings*].

Eating, oh, eating the green green grass
Till all the grass was gone.

WOYZECK. It's moving behind me! Under me! [*Stamps on the ground.*] Listen! Hollow! It's all hollow down there! It's the Freemasons!

ANDRES. I'm afraid.

WOYZECK. Strange how still it is. You almost want to hold your breath. Andres!

ANDRES. What?

WOYZECK. Say something! [*Looks about fixedly.*] Andres! How bright it is! It's all glowing over the town! A fire's sailing around the sky and a noise coming down like trumpets. It's coming closer! Let's get out of here! Don't look back! [*Drags him into the bushes.*]

ANDRES [*after a pause*]. Woyzeck? Do you still hear it?

WOYZECK. It's quiet now. So quiet. Like the world's dead.

ANDRES. Listen! I can hear the drums inside. We've got to go!

SCENE 3—THE TOWN

*Marie with her Child at the window. Margret. The
Retreat passes, The Drum Major at its head.*

MARIE [*rocking The Child in her arms*]. Ho, boy! Da-da-da-da! Can you hear! They're coming! There!

MARGRET. What a man! Built like a tree!

MARIE. He walks like a lion. [*The Drum Major salutes Marie.*]

MARGRET. Oh, what a look he threw you, neighbor! We're not used to such things from you.

MARIE [*sings*].

Soldiers, oh, you pretty lads . . .

MARGRET. Your eyes are still shining.

MARIE. And if they are? Take *your* eyes to the Jew's and let him clean them for you. Maybe he can shine them so you can sell them for a pair of buttons!

MARGRET. Look who's talking! Just look who's talking! If it isn't the Virgin herself! I'm a respectable person. But you! Everyone knows you could stare your way through seven layers of leather pants!

MARIE. Slut! [*Slams the window shut.*] Come, boy! What's it to them, anyway! Even if you are just a poor whore's baby, your dishonorable little face still makes your mother happy! [*Sings.*]

I have my trouble and bother
But, baby dear, where is your father?
Why should I worry and fight
I'll hold you and sing through the night:
Heio popeio, my baby, my dove
What do I want now with love?

[*A knock at the window.*] Who's there? Is it you, Franz? Come in!

WOYZECK. Can't. There's roll call.

MARIE. Did you cut wood for the Captain?

WOYZECK. Yes, Marie.

MARIE. What is it, Franz? You look so troubled.

WOYZECK. Marie, it happened again, only there was more. Isn't it written: "And there arose a smoke out of the pit, as the smoke of a great furnace"?

MARIE. Oh, Franz!

WOYZECK. Shh! Quiet! I've got it! The Freemasons! There was a terrible noise in the sky and everything was on fire! I'm on the trail of something, something big. It followed me all the way to the town. Something that I can't put my hands on, or understand. Something that drives us mad. What'll come of it all?

MARIE. Franz!

WOYZECK. Don't you see? Look around you! Everything hard and fixed, so gloomy. What's moving back there? When God goes, everything goes. I've got to get back.

MARIE. And the child?

WOYZECK. My God, the boy!—Tonight at the fair! I've saved something again.

[He leaves.]

MARIE. That man! Seeing things like that! He'll go mad if he keeps thinking that way! He frightened me! It's so gloomy here. Why are you so quiet, boy? Are you afraid? It's growing so dark. As if we were going blind. Only that street lamp shining in from outside. [Sings.]
    And what if your cradle is bad
    Sleep tight, my lovey, my lad.
I can't stand it! It makes me shiver!

[She goes out.]

SCENE 4—FAIR BOOTHS. LIGHTS, PEOPLE

Old Man with a Child, Woyzeck, Marie, Charlatan, Wife, Drum Major, and Sergeant

OLD MAN [sings while The Child dances to the barrel-organ].
    There's nothing on this earth will last,
    Our lives are as the fields of grass,
    Soon all is past, is past.

WOYZECK. Ho! Hip-hop there, boy! Hip-hop! Poor man, old man! Poor child, young child! Trouble and happiness!

MARIE. My God, when fools still have their senses, then we're all fools. Oh, what a mad world! What a beautiful world!

[They go over to The Charlatan who stands in front of a booth, his Wife in trousers, and a monkey in costume.]

CHARLATAN. Gentlemen, gentlemen! You see here before you a creature as God created it! But it is nothing this way! Absolutely nothing! But now look at what Art can do. It walks upright. Wears coat and pants. And even carries a saber. This monkey here is a regular soldier. So what if he *isn't* much different! So what if he *is* still on the bottom rung of the human ladder! Hey there, take a bow! That's the way! Now you're a baron, at least. Give us a kiss! [The monkey trumpets.] This little customer's musical, too. And, gentlemen, in here you will see the astronomical horse and the little lovebirds. Favorites of all the crowned heads of Europe. They'll tell you anything: how old you are, how many children you have, what your ailments are. The performance is about to begin. And at the beginning. The beginning of the beginning!

WOYZECK. You know, I had a little dog once who kept sniffing around the rim of a big hat, and I thought I'd be good to him and make it easier for him and sat him on top of it. And all the people stood around and clapped.

GENTLEMEN. Oh, grotesque! How really grotesque!

WOYZECK. Don't you believe in God either? It's an honest fact I don't believe in God.—You call that grotesque? I like what's grotesque. See that? That grotesque enough for you?—[To Marie.] You want to go in?

MARIE. Sure. That must be nice in there. Look at the tassels on him! And his wife's got pants on!

[They go inside.]

DRUM MAJOR. Wait a minute! Did you see her? What a piece!

SERGEANT. Hell, she could whelp a couple regiments of cavalry!

DRUM MAJOR. *And* breed drum majors!

SERGEANT. Look at the way she carries that head! You'd think all that black hair would pull her down like a weight. And those eyes!

DRUM MAJOR. Like looking down a well . . . or up a chimney. Come on, let's go after her!

SCENE 5—INTERIOR OF THE BRIGHTLY LIGHTED BOOTH

Marie, Woyzeck, Proprietor of the Booth, Sergeant, and Drum Major

MARIE. All these lights!

WOYZECK. Sure, Marie. Black cats with fiery eyes.

PROPRIETOR OF THE BOOTH [*bringing forward a horse*]. Show your talent! Show your brute reason! Put human society to shame! Gentlemen, this animal you see here, with a tail on its torso, and standing on its four hoofs, is a member of all the learnèd societies—as well as a professor at our university where he teaches students how to ride and fight. But that requires simple intelligence. Now think with your double reason! What do you do when you think with your double reason? Is there a jackass in this learnèd assembly? [*The nag shakes its head.*] How's that for double reasoning? That's physiognomy for you. This is no dumb animal. This is a person! A human being! But still an animal. A beast. [*The nag conducts itself indecently.*] That's right, put society to shame. As you can see, this animal is still in a state of Nature. Not ideal Nature, of course! Take a lesson from him! But ask your doctor first, it may prove highly dangerous! What we have been told by this is: Man must be natural! You are created of dust, sand, and dung. Why must you be more than dust, sand, and dung? Look there at his reason. He can figure even if he can't count it off on his fingers. And why? Because he cannot express himself, can't explain. A metamorphosed human being. Tell the gentlemen what time it is! Which of you ladies and gentlemen has a watch? A watch?

SERGEANT. A watch? [*He pulls a watch imposingly and measuredly from his pocket.*] There you are, my good man!

MARIE. I want to see this. [*She clambers down to the first row of seats; The Sergeant helps her.*]

DRUM MAJOR. What a piece!

SCENE 6—MARIE'S ROOM

Marie with her Child

MARIE [*sitting her Child on her lap, a piece of mirror in her hand*]. He told Franz to get the hell out, so what could he do! [*Looks at herself in the mirror.*] Look how the stones shine! What kind are they, I wonder? What kind did he say they were? Sleep, boy! Close your eyes! Tight! Stay that way now. Don't move or he'll get you! [*Sings.*]

> Hurry, lady, close up tight
> A gypsy lad is out tonight
> And he will take you by the hand
> And lead you into gypsyland.

[*Continues to look at herself in the mirror.*] They must be gold! I wonder how they'll look on me at the dance? Our kind's got only a little corner in the world

and a piece of broken mirror. But my mouth is just as red as any of the fine ladies with their mirrors from top to bottom, and their handsome gentlemen that kiss their hands for them! I'm just a poor common piece! [*The Child sits up.*] Quiet, boy! Close your eyes! There's the sandman! Look at him run across the wall! [*She flashes with the mirror.*] Eyes tight! Or he'll look into them and make you blind!

[*Woyzeck enters behind her. She jumps up, her hands at her ears.*]

WOYZECK. What's that?

MARIE. Nothing.

WOYZECK. There's something shiny in your hands.

MARIE. An earring. I found it.

WOYZECK. I never have luck like that! Two at a time!

MARIE. Am I human or not?

WOYZECK. I'm sorry, Marie.—Look at the boy asleep. Lift his arm, the chair's hurting him. Look at the shiny drops on his forehead. Everything under the sun works! We even sweat in our sleep. Us poor people! Here's some money again, Marie. My pay and something from the Captain.

MARIE. God bless you, Franz.

WOYZECK. I've got to get back. Tonight, Marie! I'll see you tonight!

[*He goes off.*]

MARIE [*alone, after a pause*]. I am bad, I am! I could run myself through with a knife! Oh, what a life, what a life! We'll all end up in hell, anyway, in the end: man, woman, and child!

SCENE 7—AT THE DOCTOR'S

The Doctor and Woyzeck

DOCTOR. I don't believe it, Woyzeck! And a man of your word!

WOYZECK. What's that, Doctor, sir?

DOCTOR. I saw it all, Woyzeck. You pissed on the street! You were pissing on the wall like a dog! And here I'm giving you three groschen a day plus board! That's terrible, Woyzeck! The world's becoming a terrible place, a terrible place!

WOYZECK. But, Doctor, sir, when Nature . . .

DOCTOR. When Nature? When Nature? What has Nature to do with it? Did I or did I not prove to you that the *musculus constrictor vesicae* is controlled by your will? Nature! Woyzeck, man is free! In Mankind alone we see glorified the individual's will to freedom! And you couldn't hold your water! [*Shakes his head, places his hands behind the small of his back, and walks back and forth.*] Have you eaten your peas today, Woyzeck? Nothing but peas! *Cruciferae!* Remember that! There's going to be a revolution in science! I'm going to blow it sky-high! *Urea Oxygen.* Ammonium hydrochloratem hyperoxidic. Woyzeck, couldn't you just *try* to piss again? Go in the other room there and make another try.

WOYZECK. Doctor, sir, I can't.

DOCTOR [*disturbed*]. But you could piss on the wall. I have it here in black and white. Our contract is right here! I saw it. I saw it with these very eyes. I had just stuck my head out the window, opening it to let in the rays of the sun, so as to execute the process of sneezing. [*Going toward him.*] No, Woyzeck, I'm not going to vex myself. Vexation is unhealthy. Unscientific. I'm calm now, completely calm. My pulse is beating at its accustomed sixty, and I am speaking to you in utmost cold-bloodedness. Why should I vex myself over a man, God forbid! A man! Now if he were a Proteus, it would be worth the vexation! But, Woyzeck, you really shouldn't have pissed on the wall.

WOYZECK. You see, Doctor, sir, sometimes a person's got a certain kind of character, like when he's made a certain way. But with Nature it's not the same, you see. With Nature [*He snaps his fingers.*], it's like *that!* How should I explain, it's like——

DOCTOR. Woyzeck, you're philosophizing again.

WOYZECK [*confidingly*]. Doctor, sir, did you ever see anything with double nature? Like when the sun stops at noon, and it's like the world was going up in fire? That's when I hear a terrible voice saying things to me!

DOCTOR. Woyzeck, you have an *aberratio!*

WOYZECK [*places his finger at his nose*]. It's in the toadstools, Doctor, sir, that's where it is. Did you ever see the shapes the toadstools make when they grow up out of the earth? If only somebody could read what they say!

DOCTOR. Woyzeck, you have a most beautiful *aberratio mentalis partialis* of a secondary order! And so wonderfully developed! Woyzeck, your salary is increased! *Idée fixe* of a secondary order, and with a generally rational state. You go about your business normally? Still shaving the Captain?

WOYZECK. Yes, sir.

DOCTOR. You eat your peas?

WOYZECK. Just as always, Doctor, sir. My wife gets the money for the household.

DOCTOR. Still in the army?

WOYZECK. Yes, sir, Doctor.

DOCTOR. You're an interesting case. Patient Woyzeck, you're to have an increase in salary. So behave yourself! Let's feel the pulse. Ah yes.

SCENE 8—MARIE'S ROOM

Drum Major and Marie

DRUM MAJOR. Marie!

MARIE [*looking at him, with expression*]. Go on, show me how you march!—Chest broad as a bull's and a beard like a lion! There's not another man in the world like that! And there's not a prouder woman than me!

DRUM MAJOR. Wait till Sunday when I wear my helmet with the plume and my white gloves! Damn, that'll be a sight for you! The Prince always says: "My God, there goes a real man!"

MARIE [*scoffing*]. Ha! [*Goes toward him.*] A man?

DRUM MAJOR. You're not such a bad piece yourself! Hell, we'll plot a whole brood of drum majors! Right? [*He puts his arm around her.*]

MARIE [*annoyed*]. Let go!

DRUM MAJOR. Bitch!

MARIE [*fiercely*]. You just touch me!

DRUM MAJOR. There's devils in your eyes.

MARIE. Let there be, for all I care! What's the difference!

SCENE 9—STREET

Captain and Doctor. The Captain comes panting along the street, stops; pants, looks about.

CAPTAIN. Ho, Doctor, don't run so fast! Don't paddle the air so with your stick! You're only courting death that way! A good man with a good conscience never walks as fast as that. A good man . . . [*He catches him by the coat.*] Doctor, permit me to save a human life!

DOCTOR. I'm in a hurry, Captain, I'm in a hurry!

CAPTAIN. Doctor, I'm so melancholy. I have such fantasies. I start to cry every time I see my coat hanging on the wall.

DOCTOR. Hm! Bloated, fat, thick neck: apoplectic constitution. Yes, Captain, you'll be having *apoplexia cerebri* any time now. Of course you could have it on only one side. In which case you'll be paralyzed down that one side. Or if things go really well you'll be mentally disabled so that you can vegetate away for the rest of your days. You may look forward to something approximately like that within the next four weeks! And, furthermore, I can assure you that you give promise of being a most interesting case. And if it is God's will that only one half of your tongue become paralyzed, then we will conduct the most immortal of experiments.

CAPTAIN. Doctor, you mustn't scare me that way! People are said to have died of fright. Of pure, sheer fright. I can see them now with lemons in their hands. But they'll say: "He was a good man, a good man." You devil's coffinnail-maker!

DOCTOR [*extending his hat toward him*]. Do you know who this is, Captain? This is Sir Hollowhead, my most honorable Captain Drilltheirassesoff!

CAPTAIN [*makes a series of folds in his sleeve*]. And so you know who this is, Doctor? This is Sir Manifold, my dear devil's coffinnail-maker! Ha! Ha! Ha! But no harm meant! I'm a good man, but I can play, too, when I want to, Doctor, when I want to . . .

[*Woyzeck comes toward them and tries to pass in a hurry.*]

CAPTAIN. Ho! Woyzeck! Where are you off to in such a hurry? Stay awhile, Woyzeck! Running through the world like an open razor, you're liable to cut someone. He runs as if he had to shave a castrated regiment and would be hung before he discovered and cut the longest hair that wasn't there. But on the subject of long beards . . . What was it I wanted to say? Woyzeck, why was I thinking about beards?

DOCTOR. The wearing of long beards on the chin, remarks Pliny, is a habit of which soldiers must be broken—

CAPTAIN [*continues*]. Ah, yes, this thing about beards! Tell me, Woyzeck, have you found any long hairs from beards in your soup bowl lately? Ho, I don't think he understands! A hair from a human face, from the beard of an engineer, a sergeant, a . . . a drum major? Well, Woyzeck? But then he's got a good wife. It's not the same as with the others.

WOYZECK. Yes, sir, Captain! What was it you wanted to say to me, Captain, sir?

CAPTAIN. What a face he's making! Well, maybe not in his soup, but if he hurries home around the corner I'll wager he might still find one on a certain pair of lips. A pair of lips, Woyzeck. I know what love is, too, Woyzeck. Look at him, he's white as chalk!

WOYZECK. Captain, sir, I'm just a poor devil. And there's nothing else I've got in the world but her. Captain, sir, if you're just making a fool of me . . .

CAPTAIN. A fool? Me? Making a fool of you, Woyzeck?

DOCTOR. Your pulse, Woyzeck, your pulse! Short, hard, skipping, irregular.

WOYZECK. Captain, sir, the earth's hot as coals in hell. But I'm cold as ice, cold as ice. Hell is cold. I'll bet you. I don't believe it! God! God! I don't believe it!

CAPTAIN. Look here, you, how would you . . . how'd you like a pair of bullets in your skull? You keep stabbing at me with those eyes of yours, and I'm only trying to help. Because you're a good man, Woyzeck, a good man.

DOCTOR. Facial muscles rigid, taut, occasionally twitches. Condition strained, excitable.

WOYZECK. I'm going. Anything's possible. The bitch! Anything's possible.—The weather's nice, Captain, sir. Look, a beautiful, hard, gray sky. You'd almost like to pound a nail in up there and hang yourself on it. And only because of that little dash between Yes and Yes again . . . and No. Captain, sir: Yes and No: did No make Yes or Yes make No? I must think about that.

[*He goes off with long strides, slowly at first, then faster and faster.*]

DOCTOR [*shouting after him*]. Phenomenon! Woyzeck, you get a raise!

CAPTAIN. I get so dizzy around such people. Look at him go! Long-legged rascals like him step out like a shadow running away from its own spider. But short ones only dawdle along. The long-legged ones are the lightning, the short ones the thunder. Haha . . . Grotesque! Grotesque!

SCENE 10—MARIE'S ROOM

Woyzeck and Marie

WOYZECK [*looks fixedly at her and shakes his head*]. Hm! I don't see it! I don't see it! My God, why can't I see it, why can't I take it in my fists!

MARIE [*frightened*]. Franz, what is it?—You're raving, Franz.

WOYZECK. A sin so swollen and big—it stinks to smoke the angels out of Heaven! You have a red mouth, Marie! No blisters on it? Marie, you're beautiful as sin. How can mortal sin be so beautiful?

MARIE. Franz, it's your fever making you talk this way!

WOYZECK. Damn you! Is this where he stood? Like this? Like this?

MARIE. While the day's long and the world's old a lot of people can stand in one spot, one right after the other.—Why are you looking at me so strange, Franz! I'm afraid!

WOYZECK. It's a nice street for walking, uh? You could walk corns on your feet! It's nice walking on the street, going around in society.

MARIE. Society?

WOYZECK. A lot of people pass through this street here, don't they! And you talk to them—to whoever you want—but that's not my business!—Why wasn't it me!

MARIE. You expect me to tell people to keep off the street—and take their mouths with them when they leave?

WOYZECK. And don't you ever leave your lips at home, they're too beautiful, it would be a sin! But then I guess the wasps like to light on them, uh?

MARIE. And what wasp stung you! You're like a cow chased by hornets!

WOYZECK. I saw him!

MARIE. You can see a lot with two eyes while the sun shines!

WOYZECK. Whore! [*He goes after her.*]

MARIE. Don't you touch me, Franz! I'd rather have a knife in my body than your hands touch me. When I looked at him, my father didn't dare lay a hand on me from the time I was ten.

WOYZECK. Whore! No, it should show on you! Something! Every man's a chasm. It makes you dizzy when you look down in. It's got to show! And she looks like innocence itself. So, innocence, there's a spot on you. But I can't prove it—can't prove it! Who can prove it?

[*He goes off.*]

SCENE 11—THE GUARDHOUSE

Woyzeck and Andres

ANDRES [*sings*].
        Our hostess she has a pretty maid
        She sits in her garden night and day
        She sits within her garden . . .

WOYZECK. Andres!

ANDRES. Hm?

WOYZECK. Nice weather.

ANDRES. Sunday weather.—They're playing music tonight ouside the town. All the whores are already there. The men stinking and sweating. Wonderful, uh?

WOYZECK [*restlessly*]. They're dancing, Andres, they're dancing!

ANDRES. Sure. So what? [*Sings.*]
        She sits within her garden
        But when the bells have tollèd
        Then she waits at her garden gate
        Or so the soldiers say.

WOYZECK. Andres, I can't keep quiet.

ANDRES. You're a fool!

WOYZECK. I've got to go out there. It keeps turning and turning in my head. They're dancing, dancing! Will she have hot hands, Andres? God damn her, Andres! God damn her!

ANDRES. What do you want?

WOYZECK. I've got to go out there. I've got to see them.

ANDRES. Aren't you ever satisfied? What's all this for a whore?

WOYZECK. I've got to get out of here! I can't stand the heat!

SCENE 12—THE INN

Apprentices

[*The windows are open. Dancing. Benches in front of the inn.*]

FIRST APPRENTICE [*sings*].
        This shirt I've got on, it is not mine
        And my soul it stinketh of brandywine . . .

SECOND APPRENTICE. Brother, let me be a real friend and knock a hole in your nature! Forward! I'll knock a hole in his nature! Hell, I'm as good a man as he is; I'll kill every flea on his body!

FIRST APPRENTICE. My soul, my soul stinketh of brandywine!—And even money passeth into decay! Forget me not, but the world's a beautiful place! Brother, my sadness could fill a barrel with tears! I wish our noses were two bottles so we could pour them down one another's throats.

THE OTHERS [*in chorus*].
        A hunter from the Rhine
        Once rode through a forest so fine
        Hallei-hallo, he called to me
        From high on a meadow, open and free
        A hunter's life for me.

[*Woyzeck stands at the window. Marie and The Drum Major dance past without noticing him.*]

WOYZECK. Both of them! God damn her!

MARIE [*dancing past*]. Don't stop! Don't stop!

WOYZECK [*seats himself on the bench, trembling, as he looks from there through the window*]. Listen! Listen! Ha, roll on each other, roll and turn! Don't stop, don't stop, she says!

IDIOT. Pah! It stinks!

WOYZECK. Yes, it stinks! Her cheeks are red, red, why should she stink already? Karl, what is it you smell?

IDIOT. I smell, I smell blood.

WOYZECK. Blood? Why are all things red that I look at now? Why are they all rolling in a sea of blood, one on top of the other, tumbling, tumbling! Ha, the sea is red!—Don't stop! Don't stop! [*He starts up passionately, then sinks down again onto the bench.*] Don't stop! Don't stop! [*Beating his hands together.*] Turn and roll and roll and turn! God, blow out the sun and let them roll on each other in their lechery! Man and woman and man and beast! They'll do it in the light of the sun! They'll do it in the palm of your hand like flies! Whore! That whore's red as coals, red as coals! Don't stop! Don't stop! [*Jumps up.*] Watch how the bastard takes hold of her! Touching her body! He's holding her now, holding her . . . the way I held her once. [*He slumps down in a stupor.*]

FIRST APPRENTICE [*preaching from a table*]. I say unto you, forget not the wanderer who standeth leaning against the stream of time, and who giveth himself answer with the wisdom of God, and saith: What is Man? What is Man? Yea, verily I say unto you: How should the farmer, the cooper, the shoemaker, the doctor, live, had not God created Man for their use? How should the tailor live had not God endowed Man with the need to slaughter himself? And therefore doubt ye not, for all things are lovely and sweet! Yet the world with all its things is evil place, and even money passeth into decay. In conclusion, my belovèd brethren, let us piss once more upon the Cross so that somewhere a Jew will die!

[*Amid the general shouting and laughing Woyzeck wakens. People are leaving the inn.*]

ANDRES. What are you doing there?
WOYZECK. What time is it?
ANDRES. Ten.
WOYZECK. Is that all it is? I think it should go faster—I want to think about it before night.
ANDRES. Why?
WOYZECK. So it'd be over.
ANDRES. What?
WOYZECK. The fun.
ANDRES. What are you sitting here by the door for?
WOYZECK. Because it feels good, and because I know—a lot of people sit by doors, but they don't know—they don't know till they're dragged out of the door feet first.
ANDRES. Come with me!
WOYZECK. It feels good here like this—and even better if I laid myself down . . .
ANDRES. There's blood on your head.
WOYZECK. *In* my head, maybe.—If they all knew what time it was they'd strip themselves naked and put on a silk shirt and let the carpenter make their bed of wood shavings.

ANDRES. He's drunk.

[*Goes off with the others.*]

WOYZECK. The world is out of order! Why did the streetlamp cleaner forget to wipe my eyes—everything's dark. Devil damn you, God! I lay in my own way: jump over myself. Where's my shadow gone? There's no safety in the kennels any more. Shine the moon through my legs again to see if my shadow's here. [*Sings.*]

Eating, oh, eating the green green grass
Eating, oh, eating the green green grass
Till all the grass was go-o-one.

What's that lying over there? Shining like that? It's making me look. How it sparkles. I've got to have it.

[*He rushes off.*]

SCENE 13—AN OPEN FIELD

Woyzeck

WOYZECK. Don't stop! Don't stop! Hishh! Hashh! That's how the fiddles and pipes go.—Don't stop! Don't stop!—Stop your playing! What's that talking down there? [*He stretches out on the ground.*] What? What are you saying? What? Louder! Louder! Stab? Stab the goat-bitch dead? Stab? Stab her? The goat-bitch dead? Should I? Must I? Do I hear it there, too? Does the wind say so, too? Won't it ever stop, ever stop? Stab her! Stab her! Dead! Dead!

SCENE 14—A ROOM IN THE BARRACKS. NIGHT

Andres and Woyzeck in a bed.

WOYZECK [*softly.*] Andres! [*Andres murmurs in his sleep. Shakes Andres.*] Andres! Hey, Andres!
ANDRES. Mmmmm! What do you want?
WOYZECK. I can't sleep! When I close my eyes everything turns and turns. I hear voices in the fiddles: Don't stop! Don't stop! And then the walls start to talk. Can't you hear it?
ANDRES. Sure. Let them dance! I'm tired. God bless us all, Amen.
WOYZECK. It's always saying: Stab! Stab! And then when I close my eyes it keeps shining there, a big, broad knife, on a table by a window in a narrow, dark street, and an old man sitting behind it. And the knife is always in front of my eyes.
ANDRES. Go to sleep, you fool!

WOYZECK. Andres! There's something outside. In the ground. They're always pointing to it. Don't you hear them now, listen, now, knocking on the walls? Somebody must have seen me out the window. Don't you hear? I hear it all day long. Don't stop. Stab! Stab the——

ANDRES. Lay down. You ought to go to the hospital. They'll give you a schnapps with a powder in it. It'll cut your fever.

WOYZECK. Don't stop! Don't stop!

ANDRES. Go to sleep!

[He goes back to sleep.]

SCENE 15—THE DOCTOR'S COURTYARD

Students and Woyzeck below, The Doctor in the attic window.

DOCTOR. Gentlemen, I find myself on the roof like David when he beheld Bathsheba. But all I see are the Parisian panties of the girls' boarding school drying in the garden. Gentlemen, we are concerned with the weighty question of the relationship of the subject to the object. If, for example, we were to take one of those innumerable things in which we see the highest manifestation of the self-affirmation of the Godhead, and examine its relationship to space, to the earth, and to the planetary constellations . . . Gentlemen, if we were to take this cat and toss it out the window: how would this object conduct itself in conformity with its own instincts towards its *centrum gravitationis*? Well, Woyzeck! *[Roars.]* Woyzeck!

WOYZECK *[picks up the cat]*. Doctor, sir, she's biting me!

DOCTOR. Damn, why do you handle the beast so tenderly! It's not your grandmother! *[He descends.]*

WOYZECK. Doctor, I'm shaking.

DOCTOR *[utterly delighted]*. Excellent, Woyzeck, excellent! *[Rubs his hands, takes the cat.]* What's this, gentlemen? The new species of rabbit louse! A beautiful species . . . *[He pulls out a magnifying glass; the cat runs off.]* Animals, gentlemen, simply have no scientific instincts. But in its place you may see something else. Now, observe: for three months this man has eaten nothing but peas. Notice the effect. Feel how irregularly his pulse beats! And look at his eyes!

WOYZECK. Doctor, sir, everything's going dark! *[He sits down.]*

DOCTOR. Courage, Woyzeck! A few more days and then it will all be over with. Feel, gentlemen, feel! *[They fumble over his temples, pulse, and chest.]*

DOCTOR. Apropos, Woyzeck, wiggle your ears for the gentlemen! I've meant to show you this before. He uses only two muscles. Let's go, let's go! You stupid animal, shall I wiggle them for you? Trying to run out on us like the cat? There you are, gentlemen! Here you see an example of the transition into a donkey: frequently the result of being raised by women and of a persistent usage of the Germanic language. How much hair has your mother pulled out recently for sentimental remembrances of you? It's become so thin these last few days. It's the peas, gentlemen, the peas!

SCENE 16—THE INN

Woyzeck. The Sergeant

WOYZECK *[sings]*.
　　Oh, daughter, my daughter
　　And didn't you know
　　That sleeping with coachmen
　　Would bring you low?

What is it that our Good Lord God cannot do? What? He cannot make what is done undone. Ha! Ha! Ha!—But that's the way it is, and that's the way it should be. But to make things better is to make things better. And a respectable man loves his life, and a man who loves his life has no courage, and a virtuous man has no courage. A man with courage is a dirty dog.

SERGEANT *[with dignity]*. You're forgetting yourself in the presence of a brave man.

WOYZECK. I wasn't talking about anybody, I wasn't talking about anything, not like the Frenchmen do when they talk, but it was good of you.—But a man with courage is a dirty dog.

SERGEANT. Damn you! You broken mustache cup! You watch or I'll see you drink a pot of your own piss and swallow your own razor!

WOYZECK. Sir, you do yourself an injustice! Was it *you* I talked about? Did I say *you* had courage? Don't torment me, sir! My name is science. Every week for my scientific career I get half a guilder. You mustn't cut me in two or I'll go hungry. I'm a *Spinosa pericyclia*; I have a Latin behind. I am a living skeleton. All Mankind studies me.—What is Man? Bones! Dust, sand, dung. What is Nature? Dust, sand, dung. But poor, stupid Man, stupid Man! We must be friends. If only you had no courage, there would be no science. Only Nature, no amputation, no articulation. What is this? Woyzeck's arm, flesh, bones, veins. What is this? Dung. Why is it rooted in dung? Must I cut off my arm? No, Man is selfish, he beats, shoots, stabs his own kind. [*He sobs.*] We must be friends. I wish our noses were two bottles that we could pour down each other's throats. What a beautiful place the world is! Friend! My friend! The world! [*Moved.*] Look! The sun coming through the clouds—like God emptying His bedpan on the world. [*He cries.*]

SCENE 17—THE BARRACKS YARD

Woyzeck. Andres

WOYZECK. What have you heard?

ANDRES. He's still inside with a friend.

WOYZECK. He said something.

ANDRES. How do you know? Why do I have to be the one to tell you? Well, he laughed and then he said she was some piece. And then something or other about her thighs—and that she was hot as a red poker.

WOYZECK [*quite coldly*]. So, he said that? What was that I dreamed about last night? About a knife? What stupid dreams we get!

ANDRES. Hey, friend! Where you off to?

WOYZECK. Get some wine for the Captain. Andres, you know something? There aren't many girls like she was.

ANDRES. Like who was?

WOYZECK. Nothing. I'll see you.

[*Goes off.*]

SCENE 18—THE INN

Drum Major, Woyzeck, and People

DRUM MAJOR. I'm a man! [*He pounds his chest.*] A man, you hear? Anybody say different? Anybody who's not as crocked as the Lord God Himself better keep off. I'll screw his nose up his own ass! I'll . . . [*To Woyzeck.*] You there, get drunk! I wish the world was schnapps, schnapps! You better start drinking! [*Woyzeck whistles.*] Son-of-a-bitch, you want me to pull your tongue out and wrap it around your middle? [*They wrestle; Woyzeck loses.*] You want I should leave enough wind in you for a good old lady's fart? Uh! [*Exhausted and trembling, Woyzeck seats himself on the bench.*] The son-of-a-bitch can whistle himself blue in the face for all I care. [*Sings.*]

Brandy's all my life, my life
Brandy gives me courage!

A MAN. He sure got more than he asked for.

ANOTHER. He's bleeding.

WOYZECK. One thing after another.

SCENE 19—PAWNBROKER'S SHOP

Woyzeck and The Jew

WOYZECK. The pistol costs too much.

JEW. So you want it or not? Make up your mind.

WOYZECK. How much was the knife?

JEW. It's straight and sharp. What do you want it for? To cut your throat? So what's the matter? You get it as cheap here as anywhere else. You'll die cheap enough, but not for nothing. What's the matter? It'll be a cheap death.

WOYZECK. This'll cut more than bread.

JEW. Two groschen.

WOYZECK. There!

[*He goes out.*]

JEW. There, he says! Like it was nothing! And it's real money!—Dog!

SCENE 20—MARIE'S ROOM

The Idiot. The Child. Marie

IDIOT [*lying down, telling fairy tales on his fingers*]. This one has the golden crown. He's the Lord King. Tomorrow I'll bring the Lady Queen her child. Bloodsausage says: Come, Liversausage . . .

MARIE [*paging through her Bible*]. "And no guile is found in his mouth." Lord God, Lord God! Don't look at me! [*Paging further.*] "And the Scribes and Pharisees brought unto him a woman taken in adultery, and set her in the midst . . . And Jesus said unto her: Neither do I condemn thee; go, and sin no more." [*Striking her hands together.*] Lord God! Lord God! I can't. Lord God, give me only so much strength that I may pray. [*The Child presses himself close to her.*] The child is a sword in my heart. [*To The Idiot.*] Karl!—I've strutted it in the light of the sun, like the whore I am—my sin, my sin! [*The Idiot takes The Child and grows quiet.*] Franz hasn't come. Not yesterday. Not today. It's getting hot in here! [*She opens the window and reads further.*] "And stood at his feet weeping, and began to wash his feet with tears, and did wipe them with the hairs of her head, and anointed them with ointment." [*Striking her breast.*] Everything dead! Saviour! Saviour! If only I might anoint Your feet!

SCENE 21—AN OPEN FIELD

WOYZECK [*buries the knife in a hole*]. Thou shalt not kill. Lay here! I can't stay here!

[*He rushes off.*]

SCENE 22—THE BARRACKS

*Andres. Woyzeck rummages through
his belongings.*

WOYZECK. Andres, this jacket's not part of the uniform, but you can use it, Andres.

ANDRES [*replies numbly to almost everything with*]. Sure.

WOYZECK. The cross is my sister's. And the ring.

ANDRES. Sure.

WOYZECK. I've got a Holy Picture, too: two hearts—they're real gold. I found it in my mother's Bible, and it said:

O Lord with wounded head so sore
So may my heart be evermore.

My mother only feels now when the sun shines on her hands . . . that doesn't matter.

ANDRES. Sure.

WOYZECK [*pulls out a paper*]. Friedrich Johann Franz Woyzeck. Soldier. Rifleman, Second Regiment, Second Battalion, Fourth Company. Born: the Feast of the Annunciation, twentieth of July. Today I'm thirty years old, seven months and twelve days.

ANDRES. Go to the hospital, Franz. Poor guy, you've got to drink some schnapps with a powder in it. It'll kill the fever.

WOYZECK. You know, Andres—when the carpenter puts those boards together, nobody knows who it's made for.

SCENE 23—THE STREET

*Marie with little Girls in front of the house door.
Grandmother. Later Woyzeck*

GIRLS [*singing*].

The sun shone bright on Candlemas Day
And the corn was all in bloom
And they marched along the meadow way
They marched by two and two.
The pipers marched ahead
The fiddlers followed through
And their socks were scarlet red . . .

FIRST CHILD. I don't like that one.

SECOND CHILD. Why do you always want to be different?

FIRST CHILD. *You* sing for us, Marie!

MARIE. I can't.

SECOND CHILD. Why?

MARIE. Because.

SECOND CHILD. But *why* because?

THIRD CHILD. Grandmother, *you* tell us a story!

GRANDMOTHER. All right, you little crab apples!—Once upon a time there was a poor little girl who had no father and no mother. Everyone was dead, and there was no one left in the whole wide world. Everyone was dead. And the little girl went out and looked for someone night and day. And because there was no one left on the earth, she wanted to go to Heaven. And the moon looked down so friendly at her. And when she finally got to the moon, it was a piece of rotten wood. And so she went to the sun, and it was a faded sunflower. And when she got to the stars, they were little golden flies, stuck up there as if they were caught in a spider's web. And when she wanted to go back to earth, the earth was an upside-down pot. And she was all alone. And she sat down there and she cried. And she sits there to this day, all, all alone.

WOYZECK [*appears*]. Marie!

MARIE [*startled*]. What!

WOYZECK. Let's go. It's getting time.

MARIE. Where to?

WOYZECK. How should I know?

SCENE 24—A POND BY THE EDGE OF THE WOODS

Marie and Woyzeck

MARIE. Then the town must be out that way. It's so dark.

WOYZECK. You can't go yet. Come, sit down.

MARIE. But I've got to get back.

WOYZECK. You don't want to run your feet sore.

MARIE. What's happened to you?

WOYZECK. You know how long it's been, Marie?

MARIE. Two years from Pentecost.

WOYZECK. You know how much longer it'll last?

MARIE. I've got to get back. Supper's not made yet.

WOYZECK. Are you freezing, Marie? And still you're so warm. Your lips are hot as coals! Hot as coals, the hot breath of a whore! And still I'd give up Heaven just to kiss them again. Are you freezing? When you're cold through, you won't freeze any more. The morning dew won't freeze you.

MARIE. What are you talking about?

WOYZECK. Nothing. [*Silence.*]

MARIE. Look how red the moon is! It's rising.

WOYZECK. Like a knife washed in blood.

MARIE. What are you going to do? Franz, you're so pale. [*He raises the knife.*]

MARIE. Franz! Stop! For Heaven's sake! Help me! Help me!

WOYZECK [*stabbing madly*]. There! There! Why can't you die? There! There! Ha, she's still shivering! Still not dead? Still not dead? Still shivering? [*Stabbing at her again.*] Are you dead? Dead! Dead!

[*He drops the knife and runs away.*]

[*Two men approach.*]

FIRST MAN. Wait!

SECOND MAN. You hear something? Shh! Over there!

FIRST MAN. Whhh! There! What a sound!

SECOND MAN. It's the water, it's calling. It's a long time since anyone drowned here. Let's go! I don't like hearing such sounds!

FIRST MAN. Whhh! There it is again! Like a person, dying!

SECOND MAN. It's uncanny! So foggy, nothing but gray mist as far as you can see—and the hum of beetles like broken bells. Let's get out of here!

FIRST MAN. No, it's too clear, it's too loud! Let's go up this way! Come on!

[*They hurry on.*]

SCENE 25—THE INN

Woyzeck, Kathy, Innkeeper, Idiot, and People

WOYZECK. Dance! Everybody! Don't stop! Sweat and stink! He'll get you all in the end! [*Sings.*]
>   Oh, daughter, my daughter
>   And didn't you know
>   That sleeping with coachmen
>   Would bring you low?

[*He dances.*] Ho, Kathy! Sit down! I'm so hot, so hot! [*Takes off his coat.*] That's the way it is: the devil takes one and lets the other get away. Kathy, you're hot as coals! Why, tell me why? Kathy, you'll be cold one day, too. Be reasonable.—Can't you sing something?

KATHY [*sings*].
>   That Swabian land I cannot bear
>   And dresses long I will not wear
>   For dresses long and pointed shoes
>   Are clothes a chambermaid never should choose.

WOYZECK. No shoes, no shoes! We can get to hell without shoes.

KATHY [*sings*].
>   To such and like I'll not be prone
>   Take back your gold and sleep alone.

WOYZECK. Sure, sure! What do I want to get all bloody for?

KATHY. Then what's that on your hand?

WOYZECK. Me? Me?

KATHY. Red! It's blood! [*People gather round him.*]

WOYZECK. Blood? Blood?

INNKEEPER. Blood!

WOYZECK. I think I cut myself. Here, on my right hand.

INNKEEPER. Then why is there blood on your elbow?

WOYZECK. I wiped it off.

INNKEEPER. Your right hand and you wiped it on your right elbow? You're a smart one!

IDIOT. And then the Giant said: "I smell, I smell the flesh of Man." Pew, it stinks already!

WOYZECK. What do you want from me? Is it your business? Out of my way or the first one who . . . Damn you! Do I look like I murdered somebody? Do I look like a murderer? What are you looking at? Look at yourselves! Look! Out of my way!

[*He runs off.*]

SCENE 26—AT THE POND

Woyzeck, alone.

WOYZECK. The knife! Where's the knife? I left it here. It'll give me away! Closer! And closer! What is this place? What's that noise? Something's moving! It's quiet now.—It's got to be here, close to her. Marie? Ha, Marie! Quiet. Everything's quiet! Why are you so pale, Marie? Why are you wearing those red beads around your neck? Who was it gave you that necklace for sinning with him? Your sins made you black, Marie, they made you black! Did I make you so pale? Why is your hair uncombed? Did you forget to twist your braids today? The knife, the knife! I've got it! There! [*He runs toward the water.*] There, into the water! [*He throws the knife into the water.*] It dives like a stone into the black water. No, it's not out far enough for when they swim! [*He wades into the pond and throws it out farther.*] There! Now! But in the summer when they dive for mussels? Ha, it'll get rusty, who'll ever notice it! Why didn't I break it first! Am I still bloody? I've got to wash myself. There, there's a spot, and there's another . . . [*He goes farther out into the water.*]

SCENE 27—THE STREET

Children

FIRST CHILD. Let's go find Marie!

SECOND CHILD. What happened?

FIRST CHILD. Don't you know? Everybody's out there. They found a body!

SECOND CHILD. Where?

FIRST CHILD. By the pond, out in the woods.

SECOND CHILD. Hurry, so we can still see something. Before they bring it back.

[*They rush off.*]

SCENE 28—IN FRONT OF MARIE'S HOUSE

Idiot. Child. Woyzeck.

IDIOT [*holding The Child on his knee, points to Woyzeck as he enters*]. Looky there, he fell in the water, he fell in the water, he fell in the water!

WOYZECK. Boy! Christian!

IDIOT [*looks at him fixedly*]. He fell in the water.

WOYZECK [*wanting to embrace The Child tenderly, but it turns from him and screams*]. My God! My God!

IDIOT. He fell in the water.

WOYZECK. I'll buy you a horsey, Christian. There, there. [*The Child pulls away. To the Idiot*]. Here, buy the boy a horsey! [*The Idiot stares at him.*] Hop! Hop! Hip-hop, horsey!

IDIOT [*shouting joyously*]. Hop! Hop! Hip-hop, horsey! Hip-hop, horsey!

[*He runs off with The Child. Woyzeck is alone.*]

SCENE 29—THE MORGUE

Judge, Court Clerk, Policeman, Captain, Doctor, Drum Major, Sergeant, Idiot, and others. Woyzeck

POLICEMAN. What a murder! A good, genuine, beautiful murder! Beautiful a murder as you could hope for! It's been a long time since we had one like this!

[*Woyzeck stands in their midst, dumbly looking at the body of Marie; he is bound, the dogmatic atheist, tall, haggard, timid, good-natured, scientific.*]

COMMENTARY

Note: The following essay represents a single interpretation of the play. For other perspectives on Woyzeck, *consult the essays listed below.*

In scene 18 Woyzeck wrestles with the pompous Drum Major (who later steals his lover) and is humiliated before a crowd of onlookers. Bleeding and broken, the barber stumbles to his feet while muttering "One thing after another." Woyzeck's entire life, as well as the play's thematic concerns, are crystallized in that simple line. And metaphorically the line represents the "last straw" for the hapless Woyzeck, who—as we have seen in the many scenes that precede scene 18—has been taunted and humiliated by virtually everyone with whom he has come in contact. He has been made a human guinea pig for his doctor's experiment, called a monkey by a carnival charlatan, and had his mind poisoned by a jealous captain who accuses Marie of infidelities, which the arrogant Drum Major makes a painful reality. Even in those scenes in which he is not present (e.g., scene 23, in which the Grandmother tells an odd story that defines human loneliness and isolation) we get a sense of the petty cruelties that defeat Woyzeck.

Thus the play becomes the first "modern tragedy" as it examines the catastrophe of the alienated, even superfluous, "little man" (whom Arthur Miller would rechristen "Loman" over a century later). Woyzeck is the prototype of Chekhov's befuddled characters who cannot cope with a radically changing world, of the isolated men and women who chase unattainable "pipe dreams" in the dramas of O'Neill and Williams, of the enigmatic souls of Pinter and Shepard who are terrified by a menacing world they don't understand, and mostly of the damned who inhabit Beckett's barren landscapes. The recent docudrama, *The Laramie Project,* is arguably a twenty-first-century variant on the themes raised by Buchner, although Matthew Shepherd does not kill—but is killed by louts even more cruel than the Drum Major or the Captain. His death becomes "one more thing" in a world as senseless as that of Buchner's. (See Showcase: "Docudrama.")

As you progress through the plays in this anthology, you will encounter the varied styles that comprise modern and contemporary drama. Most of these have their roots in Buchner's imaginative experiment of 1836.

- *Naturalism:* Woyzeck is unquestionably a product—better yet, a victim—of both his heredity and his environment. Born into poverty and trapped in the uncompromising environment of a hierarchical military and a middle class that cares little for the plight of the poor, Woyzeck articulates the creed of the Naturalists and Social Realists who would follow him 50 years later: ". . . who's got morals when he's bringing me into the world? We're flesh and blood, too. Our kind is miserable only once: in this world and in the next" (Sc. 1). Note, too, that Woyzeck is the subject of a coldly objective scientific analysis by the Doctor; it was the mode used by such early Naturalists as Emile Zola who sought to depict a "slice of life" in the theater, which they deemed as a bell jar for their dramatic experiments.
- *Expressionism and Surrealism:* We view the world solely through Woyzeck's eyes, hence the grotesque renderings of all characters save the poor soldier and Marie. Again, the image of the carnival fun house, as defined in scenes 4 and 5, defines the nightmarish quality of Woyzeck's world. Some scenes—e.g., scene 13, in which Woyzeck is reduced to a clod of dirt who hears the earth speaking—transcend Expressionism and approach the Surreal.
- *The Absurd:* Like Sisyphus (the Greek martyr whom Albert Camus cited as the exemplar of the absurdist hero in his work, *The Myth of Sisyphus*), our lonely protagonist is trapped in an unfathomable world over which he has no control. Each new encounter brings him another humiliation, yet he continues to push "the rock" of his humanity up the steep hill.
- *Tragicomedy:* The play's tone swings wildly between the pathetic and the grotesquely comic: we laugh ironically at Woyzeck's plight even as we pity his situation.

- *Psychological Realism:* Like Arthur Miller's *Death of a Salesman*, the play takes place "inside his head" (Miller's original title for the Willy Loman story). Few plays in this collection surpass Buchner's exploration of the deteriorating mind of its protagonist. Here you will find the antecedent to the tormented characters of Strindberg, O'Neill, and Tennessee Williams.
- *The Epic Theatre:* Like his countryman Bertolt Brecht a hundred years later, Buchner uses an epic structure, that is, a series of scenes that are linked thematically (as opposed to causally) to explore a social problem. And like Brecht, Buchner uses various alienation devices (songs, storytelling, caricatures) to distance the audience from the play's action so that it might better judge the events that precipitate Woyzeck's catastrophe. Indeed, one might legitimately mistake Buchner's script for one by Brecht.

Do not be concerned if many of the preceding references are unfamiliar to you at this time. As you progress through this anthology, you are likely to think often of the alienated soldier who committed "a murder as beautiful as you could hope for."

Other perspectives on *Woyzeck*:

Otten, Terry. "*Woyzeck* and *Othello*: The Dimension of Melodrama." *Comparative Drama* 12 (1978): 23–36.

Patterson, Michael. "Contradictions Concerning Time in Buchner's *Woyzeck*." *German Life and Letters* 32 (1989): 115–21.

See *Woyzeck* on film/video:

Georg Buchner: Woyzeck. Films for the Humanities, 49 min., 1975.

Woyzeck. Dir. Werner Herzog. Perf. Klaus Kinski and Eva Mattes. New Yorker Films, 82 min., 1978.

PART I

Early Modern Drama: 1870–1918

Nora frantically dances the tarantella to distract her husband so that he does not read Krogstad's incriminating letter in the original production of A Doll's House in 1879. You may read about the tarantella and other healing dances in the Showcase that follows Ibsen's groundbreaking drama.

PART I: EARLY MODERN DRAMA: 1870–1918

Realism

The Modern Theater—that is, the New Drama begun by Ibsen and his immediate contemporaries in Europe—is most associated with the style we call "Realism," although that term is difficult to define with precision. In accounts of acting in earlier centuries, such terms as "real," "lifelike," and "natural" are common. Audiences attending a Restoration comedy at London's Dorset Garden Theater in 1675 no doubt remarked how the action was so much like the life they lived in their homes. Hugo's *Hernani* (1830), discussed previously, attempted to replicate everyday speech and movement, as did Scribe's well-made plays on the boulevards of Paris in the mid-nineteenth century.

Yet were we to see these plays performed as they were in earlier times, few of us would call the performances "realistic" or "lifelike." Rather, we use the films of Al Pacino or a TV show such as *NYPD Blue* as our referents, or perhaps the plays of David Mamet or Marsha Norman. Yet, one suspects that 150 years from now audiences may not consider such works as "realistic" as we do; each generation defines the term from its perspective and value systems.

Still, the works of Ibsen, Chekhov, and their late-nineteenth- and early-twentieth-century contemporaries are identifiably realistic, and when compared to the works that preceded them, their plays indeed seem to have led the theater in new directions. With few exceptions the new drama was "realistic" in its attempt to recreate actual life on stage in a manner that employed the details and routines of daily dress, speech, environment, and situations. Much of the impetus for this artistic revolution in the theater can be traced to the Enlightenment and its emphasis on rational inquiry and science. To appreciate the changes in drama (and indeed most of the arts), it is necessary to examine life beyond the theater.

Influences on Realism

The Enlightenment championed empiricism, which transformed society into a laboratory for sciences unknown to Galileo: sociology, economics, and especially psychology. Out of these would grow prescriptions for reordering human behavior as the nineteenth century's most provocative thinkers attempted to redress injustices spawned by outmoded beliefs about class, gender, and workers' rights. During the Industrial Revolution, which began in the late eighteenth century and peaked by the mid-nineteenth, cities expanded to house factories and provide jobs for people who had previously tilled the soil. Some people prospered, largely by exploiting workers, especially women and children, but many people were condemned to lives of poverty in teeming slums that bred disease and crime. Just as serfs rebelled against feudal lords (as the Russians did in 1861, an issue that Chekhov raised in *The Cherry Orchard*) and plebeians toppled monarchs, so too would workers eventually rise against industry's leaders and political systems. There were numerous political revolutions throughout Europe in 1848; these often led to more tyrannical measures by the ruling class and thus provided citizens—and the artists who spoke for them—with further reason to address social problems.

Predictably, there was a cultural revolution in which the arts addressed social problems. The theater became a meeting place in which audiences observed contemporary ills, live and close-up, considered arguments for their solution, and (in theory) returned to their communities to improve the world for all. Theater became a "here and now" enterprise that no longer looked at the human situation through the romantic past. A concern for social problems is hardly a new phenomenon emanating from Western stages. Because it is a communal activity, the theater has an innate social dimension. What made the late nineteenth century's social voice so distinctive was its insistence upon being heard in uncompromising and realistic terms.

While Romantic philosophers and literary artists laid much of the foundation for the socially conscious dramas, there were other important contributors who changed the theater, though they were not themselves artists. Six are noteworthy because they represent significant new disciplines that changed Western drama.

- *Auguste Comte* (1798–1857), often called "The Father of Sociology," was a mathematician and philosopher who defined "the science of society." Comte and his disciples applied the empirical methodology of the hard sciences to social problems. Appropriating Comte's methods for the stage, artists saw the theater as a "bell jar" in which the precise conditions of a social problem (e.g., poverty, the subjugation of women) were recreated. The audience observed such issues with the detachment and rationality of a lab scientist as the problem was dissected and a cure was suggested.
- *Charles Darwin* (1809–92) wrote *The Origin of Species* in 1859 and radically altered human thought, especially concerning the evolution of our species. His studies of plant and animal life in the South Seas caused Darwin to conclude that:

1. Beings (including humans) are products of their heredity and environment.
2. Life involves a perpetual battle in which only the "fittest" survive.

Darwin's controversial theories, articulated by Herbert Spencer in his writings about "social Darwinism," had a number of implications for the theater. Darwin's emphasis on environment provoked theater artists to create as faithfully as possible the environment that created social problems. Whether it be the stultifying propriety of the Helmer household in Ibsen's *A Doll's House* (1879) or the dismal squalor of Maxim Gorky's Russian flophouse in *The Lower Depths* (1902), playwrights, directors, and scene designers labored to create absolute worlds in which characters acted as their heredity and environments dictated.

- *Friedrich Nietzsche* (1844–1900), a German philosopher and theater critic, proclaimed "God is dead" in 1885. Nietzsche was not espousing an atheistic worldview as much as he was observing that the new sciences discussed here had replaced the older Judeo-Christian tradition as the measure of human endeavor; this is a primary characteristic of Modernism. Because heredity and environment were viewed as determinants of human behavior, the role of Divine Providence was significantly reduced in dramatic literature. Miraculous endings disappeared, and tragic resolutions, which implied a kind of cosmic justice, gave way to the unhappy (or often unresolved) ending. Villainy diminished as moral absolutism was replaced by situational ethics and playwrights argued that miscreants were victims of forces beyond their control.
- *Karl Marx* (1818–83) advanced socialism, a term that had existed long before he wrote his famous manifesto, *Das Kapital*, in 1867. Like Darwin, Marx argued that change was inevitable and that workers could change their social and economic institutions by banding together to overthrow their oppressors. For Marx, art was the property of the bourgeois (who had usurped the monarchy), and it needed to reflect the plight of the proletariat, whom he esteemed as rulers in a classless society. Many early realistic plays, such as Gerhart Hauptman's *The Weavers* (1892), reflected Marx's attitudes in their focus on the economic conditions that repressed workers. Dramatists, such as Bernard Shaw in England and Eugene O'Neill in the United States, reflected many of the concerns espoused by Europe's socialist reformers. Today the Marxist school of literary criticism considers art in terms of its class and economic issues.
- *Sigmund Freud* (1856–1939) and *Karl Jung* (1875–1961) studied the workings of the mind and popularized psychology. Though their approaches differed, both were concerned with motivations for human behavior. For Freud, actions were the result of an interior battle among one's id (the agent of pleasure in the psyche), the ego (choosing self), and the superego (the "punishing" or "parent" agent). For Jung, the struggle was between one's conscious and a shared unconscious between male and female elements of the psyche. While the ideas of these early psychologists are too complex to summarize here, their influence on drama and performance was enormous. Playwrights often dealt with abnormal states of mind, as in August Strindberg's *The Ghost Sonata*. Formerly taboo subjects, such as sexual frustration, became commonplace. Unconventional, even deviant, behavior was no longer condemned, for behavior was now considered a product of a mental state over which one had little control. Most importantly, the classical Aristotelian element of character usurped the primacy of

The Rise of the Director and Germany's Meiningen Players

While we generally think of playwrights as the harbingers of change in the theater, those who produce new plays—and often old ones—also contribute to the evolution of theatrical styles. Even as Zola and Ibsen were writing their groundbreaking works in the 1870s, another equally important contribution to the modern theater was underway in Germany. In the small duchy of Saxe-Meiningen, Duke Georg II (1826–1914) indulged his passion for theater by mounting extraordinary productions in which all of the elements of acting, scenery, costume, music, and stage pictures were coordinated by a single vision: the Duke's. In 1874 Berlin hosted the Meiningen Players, who arrived in the capital for a four-week engagement. However, they extended their run by six weeks to satisfy audiences clamoring for the new "realism" they brought to the stage. This obscure company soon became world renowned and, it may be argued, influenced the evolution of the modern theater as much as the plays of Ibsen, Zola, Strindberg, Chekov, and others. In fact, Stanislavsky's contact with the Meiningen Players inspired his work with the Moscow Art Theatre.

Before examining the particulars of the Meiningen Players' phenomenal story, it is worth considering why it became necessary that the stage director—or *regissuer* as the title was known in late-nineteenth-century Europe—emerged as a central figure in Western theater. In ancient Greece playwrights such as Aeschylus and Sophocles worked directly with the actors who performed their plays; Aeschylus was in fact a very good actor and a respected choreographer. In Rome Plautus was also an actor who coached his actors as they performed his comedies. In the Middle Ages a professional *maître des jeux* ("master of the plays") was often hired to coordinate the efforts of the guildsmen who performed the epic cycle plays that portrayed the history of

humanity from the Creation to the Last Judgment; the *maître des jeux* was likely more of a logistics expert than a stage director who helped the actors interpret the play. Shakespeare and Molière, as well as their contemporaries, not only wrote plays but also performed in them; hence, they were *de facto* directors of their works. One can imagine Shakespeare himself saying much the same thing to his actors at the Globe as Hamlet does in his famous advice to the players in Act III of the tragedy. Molière actually wrote a short play (*The Versailles Impromptu*) that allows us to see how a play was rehearsed in seventeenth-century France.

With the emergence of the scene designer in the sixteenth century and later the costume designer (especially in the early nineteenth century, when historically accurate costuming became popular), with the advent of lighting in the theater (which evolved in stages throughout the nineteenth century), and especially with the popularity of revivals of plays by long-dead playwrights, it became necessary for someone with a controlling vision to coordinate the various artistic elements of a production. Throughout the eighteenth century and well into the nineteenth, this task was handled mostly by the "actor-manager," usually a leading actor such as David Garrick (1717–79) in England, who conducted rehearsals (rarely more than a half-dozen of a new play and perhaps a single rehearsal for a revival). Garrick was a bold innovator who supervised careful readings of the plays with his casts to ensure a uniform interpretation. Women, by the way, contributed to this process, most notably Caroline Neuber (1697–1760) in Germany and Madame Elizabeth Vestris (1797–1856) in England. Neuber raised production and acting standards in the German theater, while Vestris demanded close textual study from her actors. She also restored Shakespeare's original texts and is cred-

ited with bringing the "box set" to England. In Germany Johann Wolfgang von Goethe (1749–1832) ran the state theater at Weimar and conducted arduous rehearsals for a new production; to produce more lifelike and interesting stage pictures, he moved actors about the stage according to a carefully planned grid on the floor. He often pounded out the tempo of a scene with his cane. In the 1860s Edwin Booth (1833–93), the finest actor-manager in America, planned meticulous productions of *Hamlet* and *Richard III* that were noted for the unity of their look and interpretation.

However, it is Georg II, the Duke of Saxe-Meiningen, who is generally acknowledged as the progenitor of modern stage direction. Working with Ludwig Chronegk, his stage manager and stern taskmaster, the Duke meticulously created realistic worlds for such plays as Shakespeare's *Julius Caesar* and Schiller's *William Tell*. To prepare for the former, the Duke went to Rome, sketchpad in hand, and carefully drew pictures of authentic Roman clothing, weaponry, and architecture. He meticulously researched the period of a play and demanded that his artists render historically accurate details in weaponry and furniture on his stages. Even the stage floor, which had largely been ignored as a decorative element in the theater, was carefully painted to enhance the overall visual effects.

More importantly, the Duke and Chronegk were determined to create a more holistic approach to acting. The star system, which dominated Western theater in the nineteenth century, was replaced by an ensemble approach to performance. The Duke invented appropriate stage business for even the most faceless "extra" and grouped his crowds in aesthetically appealing compositions that often made them look much larger than they actually were. Typical rehearsals lasted about six hours, during which each moment in a scene was dissected and tried, retried, and discussed until it was deemed stage worthy. The Duke wrote copious notes about movement and interpretation in a *Regiebuch* (or what we now call a "prompt book," a standard tool in stage production); 28 of these still exist and provide excellent insights into the Duke's methods. A Meiningen production was noted for its exceptional attention to detail and the lifelike quality of its performances. Little wonder the Berlin engagement was a phenomenal success that created the demand for a European tour.

By 1880 the Meiningen Players were the most admired theatrical troupe in the Western world. They toured throughout Europe, Scandinavia, and eventually Russia—where the young Stanislavsky saw them and was inspired to liberate the Russian theater from its ponderous acting techniques. Andre Antoine in France and Henry Irving in England also acknowledged their indebtedness to the Meiningen troupe. By the early twentieth century the stage director had become a fixture in the theater, and names such as Jacques Copeau (France), Augustin Daly and David Belasco (America), and Herbert Beerbohm-Tree (England) could attract theater patrons as readily as those of the most renowned playwrights and actors.

Today the stage director is often a more powerful figure than playwrights or actors; some have even referred to the contemporary era as the age of "directors' theater." For example, we often refer to a production as "Brook's Dream," when we actually mean "William Shakespeare's *A Midsummer Night's Dream* as directed by Sir Peter Brook." Trevor Nunn, who directed *Cats* and *Les Miserables* as well as numerous Shakespeare plays, is among the wealthiest artists in today's theater solely from the royalties on the productions he has directed.

Once a mostly male-dominated profession, directing is now open to women. Julie Taymor, who directed *The Lion King* on Broadway, has as much "star power" as any playwright or actor in the contemporary theater. Among the most admired and innovative directors in the theater are such women as Arianne Mnouchkine, Anne Bogart, Joanne Akolitis, and Mary Zimmerman, whose production of *Metamorphoses* (which Zimmerman adapted from the fourteen-volume epic by the Roman poet, Ovid) is a current phenomenon.

plot in dramatic structure. Modern playwrights were—and mostly still are—more concerned with revealing the complexities of the human mind than telling intricate stories. For actors, the psychologist's concern for the reasons behind human behavior was translated into a new acting style in which words like "subtext," "intentions," and "motivations" were paramount.

The decade of the 1870s was especially important in the Western theater's march toward Realism. Although Ibsen wrote *The Pillars of Society* in 1877 and *A Doll's House* two years later (the works most often cited as among the first "problem plays") events in Germany and France helped create the cultural atmosphere for Ibsen's daring new works. The success of the Meiningen Players, under the direction of their Duke, Georg II of Saxe-Meiningen, in 1874 transformed the manner in which plays were produced. It was there that the theater gave birth to its newest artist: the stage director. The evolution of the stage director and the importance of the Meiningen Players are discussed in the accompanying Showcase.

Naturalism

Meanwhile in France, Emile Zola (1840–1902), who had applied Comte's theories to the novel, turned the theater into a social laboratory where audiences could observe humans in the environments that shaped their behaviors. Zola declared that he was "anti-art" because art—especially in the French theater, now dominated by tawdry melodramas and farces—was too contrived to be effective. He wanted a theater that depicted random, mundane events: "One simply takes from life the history of a being, or a group of beings, whose acts one faithfully records." Zola referred to such actions, and the all-important environment in which they take place, as *"la tranche a vie"* ("slice of life"), a key term in the evolution of realistic drama.

Actually, Zola, like his countryman Henri Becque (1837–99) and the Swedish playwright August Strindberg (1849–1912), was advancing an extreme form of Realism: *Naturalism*. The term defines two things, a philosophy and a theatrical style.

1. Naturalism is a philosophy of determinism (derived from Darwin and Spencer) contending that humans are products of their heredity and their environments. Natural-

istic plays are often characterized by gloominess and pessimism because their characters are trapped in a world from which there is no escape.

2. Naturalism, as a theatrical style, places a premium on actualistic details in scenery, costumes, and lighting, and it demands an acting style that is thoroughly lifelike. Naturalism is familiar, largely in the form of modern films about the "mean streets." Actors such as Robert Duval, Denzel Washington, Meryl Streep, and Edward James Olmos specialize in naturalistic films. Film accommodates Naturalism especially well because the camera takes us to actual locations and captures their details with photographic precision; the very psychology of film is that the camera photographs life in all its detail.

At the risk of oversimplifying complex issues, one might say that Naturalism places Realism under a microscope in its quest to portray life on stage. Or as one wit put it, "Realism shows life as it is, while Naturalism shows life as it is—only worse."

Concerns with heredity and environment have lasted well into our own era. The 1957 Broadway musical, *West Side Story*, illustrates these points in one of the play's most humorous and provocative songs, "Gee, Officer Krupke." The Jets, a street gang, satirize their frequent encounters with police officers, social workers, psychologists, and penologists. At one point they defend their delinquency with the lines:

> *Our mothers all are junkies,*
> *Our fathers all are drunks,*
> *Golly Moses, naturally we're punks.*

We might refer to this as "the hereditary principle." Later in the song, one of the Jets asserts that "I'm depraved on accounta I'm deprived." This is the other half of the equation, which we might call "the environmental principle." Although lyricist Stephen Sondheim and composer Leonard Bernstein were satirizing social problems in the 1950s, they echoed the concerns of the early Realists in the previous century.

While Zola was a visionary, he was more successful as a novelist than as a playwright because he found it difficult to reduce the random details of his novels for the stage. Despite his calls for reform, his plays, such as *Therese Raquin* (1873), retained an essentially melodramatic quality in which sensationalism supersedes logic. Zola's Preface to *Therese Raquin*, a manifesto for the Naturalists, is perhaps more important than the play itself. Zola's call for a "history of a group of beings" was realized by Anton Chekhov and his successors. Zola's call for a theater language that replicates "spoken conversation . . . free from declamation, big words, and grand sentiments" manifests itself in the writings of Sophie Treadwell (see *Machinal* in Part II) and such contemporary dramatists as David Mamet, whose early play *American Buffalo* (1976) features dialogue that is indeed "free from declamation, big words, and grand sentiments." That play ends with an exchange between Don, the owner of a seedy pawnshop, and Bob, his some-time employee who has attempted to steal a valuable coin:

DON: Bob.
BOB: What?
DON: Get up. (*Pause*) Bob, I'm sorry.
BOB: What?
DON: I'm sorry.
BOB: I fucked up.
DON: No. You did real good.
BOB: No.
DON: Yeah. You did real good. (*Pause*)
BOB: Thank you.
DON: That's all right. (*Pause*)
BOB: I'm sorry, Donny.
DON: That's all right. (*Lights dim*)

The triumph of Zola's ideal may be found in Marsha Norman's Pulitzer Prize–winning play, 'Night Mother (1983), which probes a woman's suicide in one lengthy act; the play's action takes place in a lower-class kitchen and consists largely of a conversation between the woman and her aging mother.

Artists in other media also reflected Europe's fascination with Realism and Naturalism. The novels of Charles Dickens (e.g., Hard Times, 1854) depicted the squalor of the new industrialism, as did those of the French writers Zola and Gustav Flaubert (1821–80); the latter wrote Madame Bovary (1857), which treated adultery in uncompromising terms. In Russia Count Leo Tolstoy (1828–1910) and Fyodor Dostoevsky (1821–81) exposed the problems of industrialism and the newly liberated serfs in their novels. In his most admired novel, The Brothers Karamazov (1879), Dostoevsky asks how a benevolent God could allow suffering in a seemingly indifferent world. The paintings of the Frenchmen Gustave Courbet (1819–77) and François Millet (1814–75) refused to portray the world according to the "pretty" values of the old aesthetics; rather, they rendered a grim reality in such works as Courbet's A Burial at Orleans (1849), in which a funeral is depicted as an egalitarian social rite, not a religious ceremony based on old-order hierarchies. In music we find the new realism projected in the operas of Giuseppe Verdi (1813–1901); in fact, one of his best-known operas, La Traviata (1853), was based on Dumas fils's drama, Camille (see Showcase in the Prologue). Similarly, the successful Broadway rock-opera, Rent, which depicts social outcasts in Greenwich Village, is based on the opera La Boheme by Giacomo Puccini, who drew his subject matter from a collection of short stories written in Paris even as Dumas fils was writing Camille. And we must not forget that the invention of the camera in 1839—by the Frenchman Louis Daguerre (1787–1851) and the Englishman William Talbot (1800–77)—encouraged artists of all stripes to turn a "realistic eye" toward the world. Photographic pictures soon became artworks unto themselves (e.g., United States Civil War photographs of Matthew Brady, which deromanticized war). The Swedish playwright August Strindberg was among the first to use photographs as art.

The First Generation of Realists: Ibsen, Strindberg, Chekhov, and Stanislavsky

Ironically, true realism in the modern theater sprang from the least likely places: Scandinavia and Russia. The geographical and cultural remoteness of Norway, Sweden, and czarist Russia allowed the Scandinavians Henrik Ibsen and August Strindberg and the Russians Anton Chekhov and Constantin Stanislavsky the freedom to experiment with new forms, unfettered by the weight of long-standing dramatic traditions.

Ibsen's most famous works were shaped in no small part by popular continental dramas, particularly Scribe's well-made plays. From Scribe he learned how to engage an audience through a well-structured play that builds to a satisfying climax. Ibsen's genius, as Bernard Shaw pointed out in his perceptive essay "The Quintessence of Ibsenism" (1913), was revealed in the way he inserted pointed discussions about social issues between the crisis and climax of the old Scribean formula. Shaw's analysis remains among the best explications of Ibsen's method:

> Formerly you had what was called a well-made play: an exposition in the first act, a situation in the second, an unraveling in the third. Now you have exposition, situation, and discussion; and the discussion is the test of the playwright. The critics protest in vain. They declare that discussions are not dramatic, and that art should not be didactic. Neither the playwrights nor the public take the smallest notice of them. The discussion conquered Europe in Ibsen's A Doll's House and now the serious playwright recognizes in the discussion not only the main test of his highest powers, but also the real center of the play's interest.

Ibsen's provocative dramas struck a chord as he outraged the old establishment that considered him dangerous; he left Norway and wrote the majority of his works in Germany and

---

The Birthplace (and the Mother) of the Modern American Theater

If Eugene O'Neill is regarded as "The Father of the Modern American Theater," it is no less fitting to remember Susan Glaspell (1882–1948) as its "Mother." Though not as well known as O'Neill, Glaspell was an integral part of the movement that brought American drama to maturity in the early years of the twentieth century. In 1931 she became the first woman to win a Pulitzer Prize for drama (*Alison's House*, a drama based loosely on the life of poet Emily Dickinson), an award that helped mark the acceptance of women in the American theater.

The Iowa-born Glaspell attended Drake University in Des Moines, where she studied literature and journalism. While working as a journalist in 1908, she met George Cram Cook, a professor at Iowa University, whom she married in 1913 (after his first marriage ended in divorce and after she had experienced the *avant-garde* artistic movements of Paris). The couple gravitated to Provincetown, a resort town on Cape Cod, where they joined other artists, including O'Neill, to produce short plays modeled upon the new European drama. They also discussed the formation of a theater—much like the new independent theaters they had heard about in Europe (e.g., Antoine's Théâtre Libre in Paris, Grein's Indepen-

dent Theatre in London)—where they could produce their then-experimental works. They returned to New York in the autumn of 1915, where they founded the Provincetown Playhouse on Macdougal Street in Greenwich Village; it was here that the modern American theater was born. (See Showcase, "Independent and Intimate Theaters," later in Part I for an account of this important theater.)

The first play produced at Provincetown was *Suppressed Desires*—coauthored by Glaspell and Cook—a still amusing satire on Freudian psychology. This was followed by other plays by Glaspell (most notably *Trifles*), O'Neill, e. e. cummings, Sherwood Anderson, and Edna Ferber. These bold experiments caught the attention of New York theater patrons who were intrigued by the Realism, Expressionism, and other experimental styles performed in this noncommercial setting. In 1925 Glaspell and Cook distanced themselves from the Provincetown Players when O'Neill assumed the leadership of the theater while the couple was in Greece (where Cook died).

Throughout her literary career Glaspell maintained the spirit of innovation and the contemporary thrust that marked the Provincetown enterprise. In her full-length play, *The Inheri-*

tors (1921), she challenged jingoistic Americanism in World War I while calling for greater individual freedom (especially for women) and tolerance of unpopular viewpoints. Her Pulitzer Prize was tainted by controversy, largely because she held such liberal ideas. Also in 1921 she wrote her most experimental work, *The Verge*, an expressionistic drama that portrayed the inner workings of the mind of the so-called "new woman." In both her short and longer pieces, Glaspell presented strong central female characters who sought autonomy in a male-dominated society. *Trifles* (1916) remains the best known, most produced of these plays. A one-act play written in the style of the new realism, *Trifles* tells the story of a murder in a remote farmhouse. As the town sheriff and other men search for clues, two women discuss oddities (or "trifles") about the house; to their horror, they discover their friend, Minnie, has killed her abusive husband.

From 1936 to 1938 Glaspell was chief administrator of the government-sponsored Federal Theater Project's Midwest Bureau, a position that acknowledged her importance as a founder of the community and regional theater movement in America and as a prominent standard-bearer for women's issues in art.

Italy. The new generation saw in Ibsen's works a defiant voice that spoke for them: Hauptmann in Germany, Shaw in England, and James A. Herne in America. Women also emerged as important voices, both as characters in plays and, gradually, as writers. The Scandanavian playwright Helen Wuolijoki, like Ibsen, wrote problem plays in defense of the emancipation of women. Susan Glaspell, instrumental in the emergence of a new American drama, also wrote Ibsen-like plays as early as 1915. (See Showcase, "The Provincetown Playhouse and Susan Glaspell: The Birthplace (and the Mother) of the Modern American Theater.") Sophie Treadwell also explored the subjugation of women and the tyranny of authoritarian marriages in her masterpiece, *Machinal*. Furthermore, American actresses, such as Minnie Maddern Fiske, built their reputations, in part, by playing Ibsen's well-etched heroines.

In Sweden Strindberg was also writing the new drama, though his plays are less concerned with the social implications of their protagonists' dilemmas. Strindberg, who suffered periods of mental illness, was drawn more to the inner workings of his characters' minds. If Ibsen was the most influential in portraying social dilemmas, Strindberg inspired Modernists with his intense psychological portraits in naturalistic plays (*Miss Julie*, 1888) and expressionistic dramas (*The Ghost Sonata*, 1907). In particular, the Swedish playwright had a profound effect on the style and thematic concerns of Eugene O'Neill, whose autobiographical plays *A Long Day's Journey into Night* and *A Moon for the Misbegotten* are more aligned with Strindberg's dramaturgy than that of Ibsen.

With the benefit of a hundred years of hindsight, we can now say that it was the Russian Anton Chekhov (1860–1904) who most fully portrayed realism on stage. Although Ibsen claimed that he wished "to produce the illusion of reality," his plays retain elements associated with nineteenth-century melodrama. Chekhov, however, devised a drama of what has been called "the action of inaction." In a letter to a friend, Chekhov defined his theatrical purpose: "Let the things that happen on stage be just as complex and yet as simple as they are in real life. For instance, people are having a meal at a table, just having a meal, but at the same time their happiness is being created or their lives are being smashed up." Here Chekhov suggests a primary characteristic of his dramaturgy: the action most often occurs off stage, and his protagonists are most often unaware of the changes in their lives. Hence, Chekhovian plays are frequently considered "anticlimactic" because they do not build to a traditional climax and a resolution of the conflict. As so often happens in life, characters continue in their ignorance, trapped by their own inertia. Sadly, they are unable to change in a world that is changing rapidly.

The typical Chekhov play consists primarily of a series of seemingly inconsequential conversations among a variety of characters. Rather than place an audience's emotional investment in a single character, Chekhov diffuses the sympathetic response to distance audiences from the dramatic action so they can see the folly (a comic response) of the frustrated, nearly tragic lives of his characters. For this reason, Chekhov's plays are customarily designated as tragicomedies. With their lack of discernable action, the absence of theatrical climaxes, their focus on the mundane, and their refusal to resolve conflicts in either the traditional comedic or tragic ways, Chekhov's dramas are, in Francis Ferguson's estimation, "the closest to the reality of the human situation." Both realists (e.g., Tennessee Williams) and nonrealists (e.g., Samuel Beckett) have acknowledged their indebtedness to Chekhov's style.

Alternatives to Realism and Naturalism

Relativism

Realism, once intended as an antidote to the drama that preceded it, was itself challenged by subsequent theater artists. Even as Ibsen was writing his realistic social dramas, Expressionism was being cultivated in Sweden and Germany, and soon there would come other "Isms" that usurped Realism's hold on the modern theater. Whereas the Realists had been influenced by the cultural air they breathed, as conditioned by Compte, Darwin, and other new thinkers, the antirealists were similarly influenced by advances in the physical (as opposed to social) sciences, most notably physics. In 1905 Albert Einstein (1879–1955) challenged the principles of Newtonian physics, which for 200 years stated that the physical laws of nature are determined by fixed points of reference (e.g., objects fall because of the earth's gravitational pull). But Einstein's famous Theory of Relativity ($E = mc^2$) challenged Newton's laws by arguing that space and time are not bound by fixed points but are only "relative" from one's point in space or time (e.g., the laws of gravity are suspended 12 miles above the earth, and the light we see today from a star was transmitted thousands of light-years ago). Artists formulated their version of the theory of relativity by showing that the world could be portrayed from multiple perspectives and by means other than realistic. For instance, the Cubists (e.g., Picasso) painted pictures that did not attempt to portray objects realistically: rather, they fragmented an object, such as the human face, into various geometrical shapes and showed that the parts of the whole could exist simultaneously by allowing the viewer to witness the parts from a single perspective. Hence, a mouth, an ear, and a nose could be placed on the same plane. "Relativity," "relativism," "multiple vantage points," "simultaneous action," and "contiguity" are all significant terms in the vocabulary of modern dramatists who are concerned (even obsessed?) with showing human experience from a variety of perspectives. Luigi Pirandello's *Six Characters in Search of an Author* is the prototype of relativist drama; better yet, the title of one of his plays—*It Is So if You Think It Is So* (or *Right You Are if You Think You Are*)—may well be the battle cry of the new drama of multiple perspectives. (Because it was written in 1921, we have included a synopsis of Pirandello's *Six Characters in Search of an Author* in Part II; see Showcase: "The Prototype of the Relativist Drama.") The postmodern theater, as we shall see in Part III, carries these early-twentieth-century beliefs to even greater lengths.

Expressionism

Actually, it was not theater artists who led the assault on Realism; rather, painters in the late nineteenth century began portraying the world they saw in other than realistic terms. First, the impressionists (e.g., Cezanne, Renoir, van Gogh, and Monet) painted pictures of water lilies and starry nights that emphasized color and shape—that is, their "impression" of an object caught at a particular moment in time and under certain lighting conditions. "Reality" was thus filtered through the eye of the beholder.

With the Expressionists reality was filtered through the mind of the beholder, and it was often distorted by the artist's personal perceptions of the world. Knowingly or otherwise, the Expressionists used art to illustrate the theories of Freud, Jung, and other practitioners of the then-new science of psychology who probed the workings of the mind. Ironically, the Expressionists were reacting, in part, to the advancements of science, which they claimed dehumanized people. Kasimir Edschmid defined the impulses that motivated him and his fellow Expressionists: "We do not work as photographers [i.e., the Realists] but we are overcome by visions. We are not concerned with descriptions but lived experience. We do not reproduce but create." Among the most important of the new expressionistic painters was Ibsen's countryman, Edvard Munch (1863–1944), whose well-known work, *The Scream* (1893), epitomizes the nightmarish view of life posited by the antirealists. The fiction of Franz Kafka (1883–1924), such as *The Trial* (1914), represents an important literary attempt to portray Expressionism in the novel. Harold Pinter's *The Birthday Party* (1957; see Part II) shows indebtedness to Kafka's parable about the modern police state. Expressionism can be found in the radical new music of the era, most notably in the atonal compositions of Arnold Schoenberg (1874–1914) and Igor Stravinsky (1882–1971). The latter's *The Rite of Spring* (1913) helped inaugurate the era of Modernism in dance.

Expressionism also became a fixture in the theater, first in Sweden in the work of August Strindberg, and later in Germany. As effective as he was in his naturalistic works, perhaps Strindberg's greatest achievement can be found in his experimental works, notably a series of expressionistic dramas such as *The Dream Play* (1902) and *The Ghost Sonata* (1907). The titles of these works suggest an "unreal," "dreamlike," or, more accurately, "nightmarish" depiction of human existence. Strindberg and the subsequent Expressionists sought to portray subjective states of the human mind realistically. This is, of course, a contradiction of terms: have you ever tried to explain a dream to someone? Nonetheless, the Expressionists attempted to construct authentic dream worlds on stage through the use of distorted scenic pictures, bizarre lighting effects, dialogue that defied logic, and nonrealistic acting. Strindberg defines some of the characteristics of expressionistic drama in the notes accompanying *A Dream Play*, which he wrote to:

> . . . imitate the incoherent but ostensibly logical form of our dreams. Anything can happen; everything is possible and probable. Time and space do not exist. Working with some insignificant real events as a background, the imagination spins out its threads of thoughts and weaves them into new patterns—a mixture of memories, experiences, spontaneous ideas, impossibilities and improbabilities.

The characters split, double, multiply, dissolve, condense, float apart, coalesce. But one mind stands over and above them all, the mind of the dreamer. . . .

Expressionism thrived in Germany during the early years of the twentieth century (1910–1924), partly as a means by which young writers, disillusioned by World War I, could attack the old order. Unlike Strindberg, who sought to project "dream states" on stage, the German Expressionists resorted to an intense subjectivism—i.e., externalization of their most private inner feelings—to illustrate their outrage at a society that had betrayed them. German Expressionism used characters to symbolize abstractions of social vices rather than psychological realities, lyrical dialogue that superseded the logic of plot, and scenery that reflected purely subjective realities in concrete terms. Writers such as Frank Wedekind, Georg Kaiser, Paul Kornfeld, and Karl Sternheim represent the best of German expressionistic drama. Bertolt Brecht inherited their tradition when he entered the theater in the 1920s, and it would become the basis for his Epic Theatre (see Part II).

Expressionism had an impact in early films, such as the historically important German films *The Cabinet of Doctor Caligari* (1917) and *Metropolis* (1927). The tricks of the moviemaker—crosscutting, dissolves, superimpositions, and bizarre camera angles—lent themselves to expressionistic storytelling. Expressionism could also be found in other European dramas; Luigi Pirandello's *Six Characters in Search of an Author* has expressionistic elements, although it is not, strictly speaking, an expressionistic play. Some of the most admired American playwrights (O'Neill, Elmer Rice, Sophie Treadwell, Tennessee Williams, Adrienne Kennedy, and Arthur Miller), all freely used expressionistic elements in their dramas. Most importantly, Expressionism did much to restore theatricality and poetry to the drama that was becoming increasingly obsessed with putting real life on stage.

The devastation created by World War I (1914–18) radically altered the way humans saw themselves and their world, a phenomenon that will be addressed in Part II. Among other things, the disillusionment that sprang from "the war to end all wars" prompted artists, theatrical and otherwise, to experiment with other forms such as Surrealism, Futurism, and Constructivism, also discussed in Part II. Suffice it to say, however, that the groundwork laid by the early Realists and Naturalists, as well as the thoroughly *avant-garde* works of the Expressionists, provided the subsequent generation of Modernists with both the philosophy and the methodology to continue the transformation of drama.

By the outbreak of World War I in 1914, the theater—indeed, the Western world—had changed in extraordinary ways. Thus the stage was set for "modern drama" in the post–World War I era. Realism and Naturalism, as well as an imaginative variety of nonrealistic (or even antirealistic) styles, competed for an audience's favor. Ironically, some of the most compelling plays produced between 1925 and 1960 were in fact a fusion of these seemingly disparate styles. Arthur Miller's *Death of a Salesman* (1949) is equal parts Realism and Expressionism. The many experiments with style and content that began at the end of the nineteenth century grew in the first two decades of the twentieth century, rapidly expanding the boundaries of Western theater more than at any time since its inception 2,300 years ago.

A DOLL'S HOUSE

HENRIK IBSEN

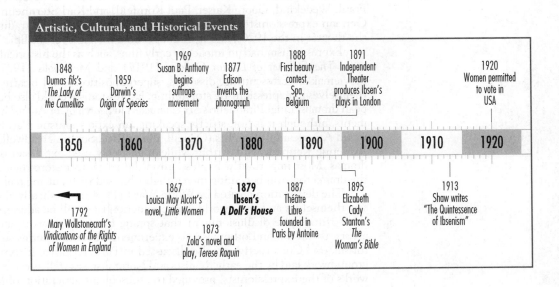

Artistic, Cultural, and Historical Events

1848
Dumas *fils's*
*The Lady of
the Camellias*

1859
Darwin's
Origin of Species

1969
Susan B. Anthony
begins
suffrage
movement

1877
Edison
invents the
phonograph

1888
First beauty
contest,
Spa,
Belgium

1891
Independent
Theater
produces Ibsen's
plays in London

1920
Women permitted
to vote in
USA

| 1850 | 1860 | 1870 | 1880 | 1890 | 1900 | 1910 | 1920 |

1792
Mary Wollstonecraft's
*Vindications of the Rights
of Women* in England

1867
Louisa May Alcott's
novel, *Little Women*

1873
Zola's novel and
play, *Terese Raquin*

1879
**Ibsen's
A Doll's House**

1887
Théâtre
Libre
founded in
Paris by Antoine

1895
Elizabeth
Cady
Stanton's
*The
Woman's Bible*

1913
Shaw writes
"The Quintessence
of Ibsenism"

HENRIK IBSEN (1828–1906)

Ibsen, often called "The Father of Modern Drama," was born in the small village of Skien in southeastern Norway. The son of a prosperous merchant, he was raised in the relative comfort of a large mansion until 1836, when his father declared bankruptcy. The move to less plush environs and ostracism from the local community left a permanent mark on Ibsen. His bitterness is reflected in many of his early poems, his 1881 unfinished biography, and particularly in the thematic concerns of his great social dramas.

Working as an apprentice to an apothecary, the young Ibsen dreamed of becoming a doctor. When the qualifying exams proved too much for him, he immersed himself in the theater as both a scholar and manager. While he was a successful scholar, theater management was not his forte. At the age of 23 he accepted the position of stage manager at the new theater in Bergen, and six years later he was named artistic director of the Christiana (Oslo) Norwegian Theatre. Neither venue proved successful, and when the Christiana Theatre closed in 1862, Ibsen began a self-imposed exile. He spent almost thirty years in Italy and Germany sharpening his critical vision of late-nineteenth-century Europe and honing his craft as a playwright. He returned to his homeland in 1891 where, incapacitated by paralyzing strokes in 1900, he died in 1906.

His dramatic works may be divided into five distinct literary styles. His earliest works, completed between 1850 and 1865, consisted of verse dramas such as *Cataline* (1850). Out of this period grew a series of dramatic poems, *Peer Gynt* (1867), based on his native history, that were epic tales of individual struggles. His next plays, usually called "social protest plays," included *The Pillars of Society* (1877), *A Doll's House* (1879), *Ghosts* (1881), and *An Enemy of the People* (1882). They dealt with the social and economic inequities he observed throughout Europe. As he continued to mature he moved to psychological dramas about interpersonal relationships; *The Wild Duck* (1885) and *Hedda Gabler* (1890) typify these plays. He concluded his career deeply immersed in plays that were "visionary"—*The Master Builder* (1892) and *When We Dead Awaken* (1900).

Bernard Shaw, his chief defender in England, saw Ibsen as an innovator who placed discussion at the heart of modern drama and as a courageous leader who tackled social injustice no matter how unpopular the subject matter. Indeed, it was not uncommon for critics to declare Ibsen vulgar and coarse, as suggested by a variety of critical commentaries that greeted *Ghosts* in 1881:

> "Ibsen's positively abominable play entitled *Ghosts* [is a] disgusting representation. . . . An open drain; a loathsome sore unbandaged; a dirty act done publicly. . . . Absolutely loathsome and fetid . . . a mass of vulgarity, egotism, coarseness, and absurdity."

> "As foul and filthy a concoction as has ever been allowed to disgrace the boards of an English theatre. . . . Dull and disgusting. . . . Nastiness and malodorousness laid on thickly as with a trowel."

In spite of this reception, Ibsen's work still survives.

While his poetic dramas are marked by episodic plots, his important social and psychological plays are essentially realistic. They use climactic plots growing from a gradual illumination of past transgressions, the discovery of which leads to the major reversal in the play. In *A Doll's House* the revelation of Nora's loan precipitates the climax of the play. In these works, Ibsen employs the components of the well-made play: the withheld secret and the obligatory scene. Rather than using them as a springboard to move the action swiftly to its resolution, he suspends the action as the play nears its climax for an in-depth discussion of the play's social issues. Thus, his plays move from the realm of entertainment, sentimentality, and melodrama into genuine social commentary.

The conflicts between one's duty to self and one's duty to society, between social and moral restrictions and one's quest for personal sovereignty, are Ibsen's primary thematic concerns. His leading characters, whether in pursuit of personal or political goals, invariably end up unfulfilled because they either sacrifice their own integrity or achieve success at the expense of others upon whom they trample. *Peer Gynt* illustrates this concept: the youthful Peer follows a life of hedonism and compromise, only to find himself facing death with no sense of integrity, purpose, or accomplishment.

AS YOU READ *A DOLL'S HOUSE*

Pay particular attention to the stage directions of Ibsen's play since they are filled with actualistic details that help create a specific world. With few exceptions, the theater had not seen this kind of detail prior to Ibsen. However, do not think of the detailed stage directions as the playwright's attempt to infuse a novelistic style with drama. Rather, the objects in this play tell us much about the characters and their relationships because, in the New Drama, the things of this world often tell us who and what we are. Note especially objects like the Christmas tree (and how it changes during the course of the action), the macaroons, the letter-box, and the parlor itself. Such items not only represent a "real" world in which people live but also are symbols of the conflicts and issues of the play.

In Act III Nora tells her husband, Torvald, to "sit down here" because "you and I have a lot to talk about." Although the play has been comprised of a series of discussions among the various characters (and note the small cast, a major innovation in 1879), this moment epitomizes the discussion drama that revolutionized Western theater, and its historical significance cannot be underestimated.

A DOLL'S HOUSE

HENRIK IBSEN

Translated by Michael Meyer

Scene: The action takes place in the Helmers' apartment.

ACT I

A comfortably and tastefully, but not expensively furnished room. Backstage right a door leads out to the hall; backstage left, another door to Helmer's study. Between these two doors stands a piano. In the middle of the left-hand wall is a door, with a window downstage of it. Near the window, a round table with armchairs and a small sofa. In the right-hand wall, slightly upstage, is a door, downstage of this, against the same wall, a stove lined with porcelain tiles, with a couple of armchairs and a rocking-chair in front of it. Between the stove and the side door is a small table. Engravings on the wall. A what-not with china and other bric-a-brac; a small bookcase with leather-bound books. A carpet on the floor; a fire in the stove. A winter day.

A bell rings in the hall outside. After a moment, we hear the front door being opened. Nora enters the room, humming contentedly to herself. She is wearing outdoor clothes and carrying a lot of parcels, which she puts down on the table right. She leaves the door to the hall open; through it, we can see a Porter carrying a Christmas tree and a bas-ket. He gives these to the Maid, who has opened the door for them.

NORA. Hide that Christmas tree away, Helen. The children mustn't see it before I've decorated it this evening. (*To the porter, taking out her purse.*) How much—?

PORTER. A shilling.

NORA. Here's half a crown. No, keep it.

The Porter touches his cap and goes. Nora closes the door. She continues to laugh happily to herself as she removes her coat, etc. She takes from her pocket a bag containing macaroons and eats a couple. Then, she tiptoes across and listens at her husband's door.

NORA. Yes, he's here. (*Starts humming again as she goes over to the table, right.*)

HELMER (*from his room*). Is that my skylark twittering out there?

NORA (*opening some of the parcels*). It is!

HELMER. Is that my squirrel rustling?

NORA. Yes!

HELMER. When did my squirrel come home?

NORA. Just now. (*Pops the bag of macaroons in her pocket and wipes her mouth.*) Come out here, Torvald, and see what I've bought.

HELMER. You mustn't disturb me! (*Short pause; then he opens the door and looks in, his pen in his hand.*) Bought, did you say? All that? Has my little squanderbird been overspending again?

NORA. Oh, Torvald, surely we can let ourselves go a little this year! It's the first Christmas we don't have to scrape.

HELMER. Well, you know, we can't afford to be extravagant.

NORA. Oh yes, Torvald, we can be a little extravagant now. Can't we? Just a tiny bit? You've got a big salary now, and you're going to make lots and lots of money.

HELMER. Next year, yes. But my new salary doesn't start till April.

NORA. Pooh; we can borrow till then.

HELMER. Nora! (*Goes over to her and takes her playfully by the ear.*) What a little spendthrift you are! Suppose I were to borrow fifty pounds today, and you spent it all over Christmas, and then on New Year's Eve a tile fell off a roof onto my head—

NORA (*puts her hand over his mouth*). Oh, Torvald! Don't say such dreadful things!

HELMER. Yes, but suppose something like that did happen? What then?

NORA. If any thing as frightful as that happened, it wouldn't make much difference whether I was in debt or not.

HELMER. But what about the people I'd borrowed from?

NORA. Them? Who cares about them? They're strangers.

HELMER. Oh, Nora, Nora, how like a woman! No, but seriously, Nora, you know how I feel about this. No debts! Never borrow! A home that is founded on debts can never be a place of freedom and beauty. We two have stuck it out bravely up to now; and we shall continue to do so for the short time we still have to.

NORA (*goes over towards the stove*). Very well, Torvald. As you say.

HELMER (*follows her*). Now, now! My little songbird mustn't droop her wings. What's this? Is little squirrel sulking? (*Takes out his purse.*) Nora; guess what I've got here!

NORA (*turns quickly*). Money!

HELMER. Look. (*Hands her some banknotes.*) I know how these small expenses crop up at Christmas.

NORA (*counts them*). One—two—three—four. Oh, thank you, Torvald, thank you! I should be able to manage with this.

HELMER. You'll have to.

NORA. Yes, yes, of course I will. But come over here, I want to show you everything I've bought. And so cheaply! Look, here are new clothes for Ivar—and a sword. And a horse and a trumpet for Bob. And a doll and a cradle for Emmy—they're nothing much, but she'll pull them apart in a few days. And some bits of material and handkerchiefs for the maids. Old Anne-Marie ought to have had something better, really.

HELMER. And what's in that parcel?

NORA (*cries*). No, Torvald, you mustn't see that before this evening!

HELMER. Very well. But now, tell me, you little spendthrift, what do you want for Christmas?

NORA. Me? Oh, pooh, I don't want anything.

HELMER. Oh, yes, you do. Now tell me, what, within reason, would you most like?

NORA. No, I really don't know. Oh, yes—Torvald—!

HELMER. Well?

NORA (*plays with his coat-buttons; not looking at him*). If you really want to give me something, you could—you could—

HELMER. Come on, out with it.

NORA (*quickly*). You could give me money, Torvald. Only as much as you feel you can afford; then later I'll buy something with it.

HELMER. But, Nora—

NORA. Oh yes, Torvald dear, please! Please! Then I'll wrap up the notes in pretty gold paper and hang them on the Christmas tree. Wouldn't that be fun?

HELMER. What's the name of that little bird that can never keep any money?

NORA. Yes, yes, squanderbird; I know. But let's do as I say, Torvald; then I'll have time to think about what I need most. Isn't that the best way? Mm?

HELMER (*smiles*). To be sure it would be, if you could keep what I give you and really buy yourself something with it. But you'll spend it on all sorts of useless things for the house, and then I'll have to put my hand in my pocket again.

NORA. Oh, but Torvald—

HELMER. You can't deny it, Nora dear. (*Puts his arm round her waist.*) The squanderbird's a pretty little creature, but she gets through an awful lot of money. It's incredible what an expensive pet she is for a man to keep.

NORA. For shame! How can you say such a thing? I save every penny I can.

HELMER (*laughs*). That's quite true. Every penny you can. But you can't.

NORA (*hums and smiles, quietly gleeful*). Hm. If you only knew how many expenses we larks and squirrels have, Torvald.

HELMER. You're a funny little creature. Just like your father used to be. Always on the look-out for some way to get money, but as soon as you have any it just runs through your fingers, and you never know where it's gone. Well, I suppose I must take you as you are. It's in your blood. Yes, yes, yes, these things are hereditary, Nora.

NORA. Oh, I wish I'd inherited more of Papa's qualities.

HELMER. And I wouldn't wish my darling little songbird to be any different from what she is. By the way, that reminds me. You look awfully—how shall I put it?—awfully guilty today.

NORA. Do I?

HELMER. Yes, you do. Look me in the eyes.

NORA (*looks at him*). Well?

HELMER (*wags his finger*). Has my little sweet-tooth been indulging herself in town today, by any chance?

NORA. No, how can you think such a thing?

HELMER. Not a tiny little digression into a pastry shop?

NORA. No, Torvald, I promise—

HELMER. Not just a wee jam tart?

NORA. Certainly not.

HELMER. Not a little nibble at a macaroon?

NORA. No, Torvald—I promise you, honestly—

HELMER. There, there. I was only joking.

NORA (*goes over to the table, right*). You know I could never act against your wishes.

HELMER. Of course not. And you've given me your word—(*Goes over to her.*) Well, my beloved Nora, you keep your little Christmas secrets to yourself. They'll be revealed this evening, I've no doubt, once the Christmas tree has been lit.

NORA. Have you remembered to invite Dr. Rank?

HELMER. No. But there's no need; he knows he'll be dining with us. Anyway, I'll ask him when he comes this morning. I've ordered some good wine. Oh Nora, you can't imagine how I'm looking forward to this evening.

NORA. So am I. And, Torvald, how the children will love it!

HELMER. Yes, it's a wonderful thing to know that one's position is assured and that one has an ample income. Don't you agree? It's good to know that, isn't it?

NORA. Yes, it's almost like a miracle.

HELMER. Do you remember last Christmas? For three whole weeks you shut yourself away every evening to make flowers for the Christmas tree, and all those other things you were going to surprise us with. Ugh, it was the most boring time I've ever had in my life.

NORA. I didn't find it boring.

HELMER (*smiles*). But it all came to nothing in the end, didn't it?

NORA. Oh, are you going to bring that up again? How could I help the cat getting in and tearing everything to bits?

HELMER. No, my poor little Nora, of course you couldn't. You simply wanted to make us happy, and that's all that matters. But it's good that those hard times are past.

NORA. Yes, it's wonderful.

HELMER. I don't have to sit by myself and be bored. And you don't have to tire your pretty eyes and your delicate little hands—

NORA (*claps her hands*). No, Torvald, that's true, isn't it—I don't have to any longer? Oh, it's really all just like a miracle. (*Takes his arm.*) Now, I'm going to tell you what I thought we might do, Torvald. As soon as Christmas is over—(*A bell rings in the hall.*) Oh, there's the doorbell. (*Tidies up one or two things in the room.*) Someone's coming. What a bore.

HELMER. I'm not at home to any visitors. Remember!

MAID (*in the doorway*). A lady's called, madam. A stranger.

NORA. Well, ask her to come in.

MAID. And the doctor's here too, sir.

HELMER. Has he gone to my room?

MAID. Yes, sir.

Helmer goes into his room. The Maid shows in Mrs. Linde, who is dressed in traveling clothes, and closes the door.

MRS. LINDE (*shyly and a little hesitantly*). Good evening, Nora.

NORA (*uncertainly*). Good evening—

MRS. LINDE. I don't suppose you recognize me.

NORA. No, I'm afraid I—Yes, wait a minute—surely—(*Exclaims.*) Why, Christine! Is it really you?

MRS. LINDE. Yes, it's me.

NORA. Christine! And I didn't recognize you! But how could I—? (*More quietly.*) How you've changed, Christine!

MRS. LINDE. Yes, I know. It's been nine years—nearly ten—

NORA. Is it so long? Yes, it must be. Oh, these last eight years have been such a happy time for me! So you've come to town? All that way in winter! How brave of you!

MRS. LINDE. I arrived by the steamer this morning.

NORA. Yes, of course—to enjoy yourself over Christmas. Oh, how splendid! We'll have to celebrate! But take off your coat. You're not cold, are you? (*Helps her off with it.*) There! Now let's sit down here by the stove and be comfortable. No, you take the armchair. I'll sit here in the rocking-chair. (*Clasps Mrs. Linde's hands.*) Yes, now you look like your old self. It was just at first that—you've got a little paler, though, Christine. And perhaps a bit thinner.

MRS. LINDE. And older, Nora. Much, much older.

NORA. Yes, perhaps a little older. Just a tiny bit. Not much. (*Checks herself suddenly and says earnestly.*) Oh, but how thoughtless of me to sit here and chatter away like this! Dear, sweet Christine, can you forgive me?

MRS. LINDE. What do you mean, Nora?

NORA (*quietly*). Poor Christine, you've become a widow.

MRS. LINDE. Yes. Three years ago.

NORA. I know, I know—I read it in the papers. Oh, Christine, I meant to write to you so often, honestly. But I always put it off, and something else always cropped up.

MRS. LINDE. I understand, Nora dear.

NORA. No, Christine, it was beastly of me. Oh, my poor darling, what you've gone through! And he didn't leave you anything?

MRS. LINDE. No.

NORA. No children, either?

MRS. LINDE. No.

NORA. Nothing at all, then?

MRS. LINDE. Not even a feeling of loss or sorrow.

NORA (*looks incredulously at her*). But, Christine, how is that possible?

MRS. LINDE (*smiles sadly and strokes Nora's hair*). Oh, these things happen, Nora.

NORA. All alone. How dreadful that must be for you. I've three lovely children. I'm afraid you can't see them now, because they're out with nanny. But you must tell me everything—

MRS. LINDE. No, no, no. I want to hear about you.

NORA. No, you start. I'm not going to be selfish today, I'm just going to think about you. Oh, but there's one thing I *must* tell you. Have you heard of the wonderful luck we've just had?

MRS. LINDE. No. What?

NORA. Would you believe it—my husband's just been made manager of the bank!

MRS. LINDE. Your husband? Oh, how lucky—!

NORA. Yes, isn't it? Being a lawyer is so uncertain, you know, especially if one isn't prepared to touch any case that isn't—well—quite nice. And of course Torvald's been very firm about that—and I'm absolutely with him. Oh, you can imagine how happy we are! He's joining the bank in the New Year, and he'll be getting a big salary, and lots of percentages too. From now on we'll be able to live quite differently—we'll be able to do whatever we want. Oh, Christine, it's such a relief! I feel so happy! Well, I mean, it's lovely to have heaps of money and not to have to worry about anything. Don't you think?

MRS. LINDE. It must be lovely to have enough to cover one's needs, anyway.

NORA. Not just our needs! We're going to have heaps and heaps of money!

MRS. LINDE (*smiles*). Nora, Nora, haven't you grown up yet? When we were at school you were a terrible little spendthrift.

NORA (*laughs quietly*). Yes, Torvald still says that. (*Wags her finger.*) But "Nora, Nora" isn't as silly as you think. Oh, we've been in no position for me to waste money. We've both had to work.

MRS. LINDE. You too?

NORA. Yes, little things—fancy work, crocheting, embroidery and so forth. (*Casually.*) And other things too. I suppose you know Torvald left the Ministry when we got married? There were no prospects of promotion in his department, and of course he needed more money. But the first year he overworked himself quite dreadfully. He had to take on all sorts of extra jobs, and worked day and night. But it was too much for him, and he became frightfully ill. The doctors said he'd have to go to a warmer climate.

MRS. LINDE. Yes, you spent a whole year in Italy, didn't you?

NORA. Yes. It wasn't easy for me to get away, you know. I'd just had Ivar. But of course we had to do it. Oh, it was a marvelous trip! And it saved Torvald's life. But it cost an awful lot of money, Christine.

MRS. LINDE. I can imagine.

NORA. Two hundred and fifty pounds. That's a lot of money, you know.

MRS. LINDE. How lucky you had it.

NORA. Well, actually, we got it from my father.

MRS. LINDE. Oh, I see. Didn't he die just about that time?

NORA. Yes, Christine, just about then. Wasn't it dreadful, I couldn't go and look after him. I was expecting little Ivar any day. And then I had my poor Torvald to care for—we really didn't think he'd live. Dear, kind Papa! I never saw him again, Christine. Oh, it's the saddest thing that's happened to me since I got married.

MRS. LINDE. I know you were very fond of him. But you went to Italy—?

NORA. Yes. Well, we had the money, you see, and the doctors said we mustn't delay. So we went the month after Papa died.

MRS. LINDE. And your husband came back completely cured?

NORA. Fit as a fiddle!

MRS. LINDE. But—the doctor?

NORA. How do you mean?

MRS. LINDE. I thought the maid said that the gentleman who arrived with me was the doctor.

NORA. Oh yes, that's Doctor Rank, but he doesn't come because anyone's ill. He's our best friend, and he looks us up at least once every day. No, Torvald hasn't had a moment's illness since we went away. And the children are fit and healthy and so am I. (*Jumps up and claps her hands.*) Oh God, oh God, Christine, isn't it a wonderful thing to be alive and happy! Oh, but how beastly of me! I'm only talking about myself. (*Sits on a footstool and rests her arms on Mrs. Linde's knee.*) Oh, please don't be angry with me! Tell me, is it really true you didn't love your husband? Why did you marry him, then?

MRS. LINDE. Well, my mother was still alive; and she was helpless and bedridden. And I had my two little brothers to take care of. I didn't feel I could say no.

NORA. Yes, well, perhaps you're right. He was rich then, was he?

MRS. LINDE. Quite comfortably off, I believe. But his business was unsound, you see, Nora. When he died it went bankrupt, and there was nothing left.

NORA. What did you do?

MRS. LINDE. Well, I had to try to make ends meet somehow, so I started a little shop, and a little school, and anything else I could turn my hand to. These last three years have been just one endless slog for me, without a moment's rest. But now it's over, Nora. My poor dear mother doesn't need me any more; she's passed away. And the boys don't need me either; they've got jobs now and can look after themselves.

NORA. How relieved you must feel—

MRS. LINDE. No, Nora. Just unspeakably empty. No one to live for any more. (*Gets up restlessly.*) That's why I couldn't bear to stay out there any longer, cut off from the world. I thought it'd be easier to find some work here that will exercise and occupy my mind. If only I could get a regular job—office work of some kind—

NORA. Oh, but Christine, that's dreadfully exhausting; and you look practically finished already. It'd be much better for you if you could go away somewhere.

MRS. LINDE (*goes over to the window*). I have no Papa to pay for my holidays, Nora.

NORA (*gets up*). Oh, please don't be angry with me.

MRS. LINDE. My dear Nora, it's I who should ask you not to be angry. That's the worst thing about this kind of situation—it makes one so bitter. One has no one to work for; and yet one has to be continually sponging for jobs. One has to live; and so one becomes completely egocentric. When you told me about this luck you've just had with Torvald's new job—can you imagine?—I was happy not so much on your account, as on my own.

NORA. How do you mean? Oh, I understand. You mean Torvald might be able to do something for you?

MRS. LINDE. Yes, I was thinking that.

NORA. He will too, Christine. Just you leave it to me. I'll lead up to it so delicately, so delicately; I'll get him in the right mood. Oh, Christine, I do so want to help you.

MRS. LINDE. It's sweet of you to bother so much about me, Nora. Especially since you know so little of the worries and hardships of life.

NORA. I? You say I know little of—?

MRS. LINDE (*smiles*). Well, good heavens—those bits of fancy work of yours—well, really—! You're a child, Nora.

NORA (*tosses her head and walks across the room*). You shouldn't say that so patronizingly.

MRS. LINDE. Oh?

NORA. You're like the rest. You all think I'm incapable of getting down to anything serious—

MRS. LINDE. My dear—

NORA. You think I've never had any worries like the rest of you.

MRS. LINDE. Nora dear, you've just told me about all your difficulties—

NORA. Pooh—that! (*Quietly.*) I haven't told you about the big thing.

MRS. LINDE. What big thing? What do you mean?

NORA. You patronize me, Christine; but you shouldn't. You're proud that you've worked so long and so hard for your mother.

MRS. LINDE. I don't patronize anyone, Nora. But you're right—I am both proud and happy that I was able to make my mother's last months on earth comparatively easy.

NORA. And you're also proud of what you've done for your brothers.

MRS. LINDE. I think I have a right to be.

NORA. I think so too. But let me tell you something, Christine. I too have done something to be proud and happy about.

MRS. LINDE. I don't doubt it. But—how do you mean?

NORA. Speak quietly! Suppose Torvald should hear! He mustn't, at any price—no one must know, Christine—no one but you.

MRS. LINDE. But what is this?

NORA. Come over here. (*Pulls her down on to the sofa beside her.*) Yes, Christine—I too have done something to be happy and proud about. It was I who saved Torvald's life.

MRS. LINDE. Saved his—? How did you save it?

NORA. I told you about our trip to Italy. Torvald couldn't have lived if he hadn't managed to get down there—

MRS. LINDE. Yes, well—your father provided the money—

NORA (*smiles*). So Torvald and everyone else thinks. But—

MRS. LINDE. Yes?

NORA. Papa didn't give us a penny. It was I who found the money.

MRS. LINDE. You? All of it?

NORA. Two hundred and fifty pounds. What do you say to that?

MRS. LINDE. But Nora, how could you? Did you win a lottery or something?

NORA (*scornfully*). Lottery? (*Sniffs.*) What would there be to be proud of in that?

MRS. LINDE. But where did you get it from, then?

NORA (*hums and smiles secretively*). Hm; tra-la-la-la.

MRS. LINDE. You couldn't have borrowed it.

NORA. Oh? Why not?

MRS. LINDE. Well, a wife can't borrow money without her husband's consent.

NORA (*tosses her head*). Ah, but when a wife has a little business sense, and knows how to be clever—

MRS. LINDE. But Nora, I simply don't understand—

NORA. You don't have to. No one has said I borrowed the money. I could have got it in some other way. (*Throws herself back on the sofa.*) I could have got it from an admirer. When a girl's as pretty as I am—

MRS. LINDE. Nora, you're crazy!

NORA. You're dying of curiosity now, aren't you, Christine?

MRS. LINDE. Nora dear, you haven't done anything foolish?

NORA (*sits up again*). Is it foolish to save one's husband's life?

MRS. LINDE. I think it's foolish if without his knowledge, you—

NORA. But the whole point was that he mustn't know! Great heavens, don't you see? He hadn't to know how dangerously ill he was. I was the one they told that his life was in danger and that only going to a warm climate could save him. Do you suppose I didn't try to think of other ways of getting him down there? I told him how wonderful it would be for me to go abroad like other young wives; I cried and prayed; I asked him to remember my condition, and said he ought to be nice and tender to me; and then I suggested he might quite easily borrow the money. But then he got almost angry with me, Christine. He said I was frivolous, and that it was his duty as a husband not to pander to my moods and caprices—I think that's what he called them. Well, well, I thought, you've got to be saved somehow. And then I thought of a way—

MRS. LINDE. But didn't your husband find out from your father that the money hadn't come from him?

NORA. No, never. Papa died just then. I'd thought of letting him into the plot and asking him not to tell. But since he was so ill—! And as things turned out, it didn't become necessary.

MRS. LINDE. And you've never told your husband about this?

NORA. For heaven's sake, no! What an idea! He's frightfully strict about such matters. And besides—he's so proud of being a *man*—it'd be so painful and humiliating for him to know that he owed anything to me. It'd completely wreck our relationship. This life we have built together would no longer exist.

MRS. LINDE. Will you never tell him?

NORA (*thoughtfully, half-smiling*). Yes—some time, perhaps. Years from now, when I'm no longer pretty. You mustn't laugh! I mean of course, when Torvald no longer loves me as he does now; when it no longer amuses him to see me dance and dress up and play the fool for him. Then it might be useful to have something up my sleeve. (*Breaks off.*) Stupid, stupid, stupid! That time will never come. Well, what do you think of my big secret, Christine? I'm not completely useless, am I? Mind you, all this has caused me a frightful lot of worry. It hasn't been easy for me to meet my obligations punctually. In case you don't know, in the world of business there are things called quarterly installments and interest, and they're a terrible problem to cope with. So I've had to scrape a little here and save a little there as best I can. I haven't been able to save much on the housekeeping money, because Torvald likes to live well; and I couldn't let the children go short of clothes—I couldn't take anything out of what he gives me for them. The poor little angels!

MRS. LINDE. So you've had to stint yourself, my poor Nora?

NORA. Of course. Well, after all, it was my problem. Whenever Torvald gave me money to buy myself new clothes, I never used more than half of it; and I always bought what was cheapest and plainest. Thank heaven anything suits me, so that Torvald's never noticed. But it made me a bit sad sometimes, because it's lovely to wear pretty clothes. Don't you think?

MRS. LINDE. Indeed it is.

NORA. And then I've found one or two other sources of income. Last winter I managed to get a lot of copying to do. So I shut myself away and wrote every evening, late into the night. Oh, I often got so tired, so tired. But it was great fun, though, sitting there working and earning money. It was almost like being a man.

MRS. LINDE. But how much have you managed to pay off like this?

NORA. Well, I can't say exactly. It's awfully difficult to keep an exact check on these kind of transactions. I only know I've paid everything I've managed to scrape together. Sometimes I really didn't know where to turn. (*Smiles.*) Then I'd sit here and imagine some rich old gentleman had fallen in love with me—

MRS. LINDE. What! What gentleman?

NORA. Silly! And that now he'd died and when they opened his will it said in big letters: "Everything I possess is to be paid forthwith to my beloved Mrs. Nora Helmer in cash."

MRS. LINDE. But, Nora dear, who was this gentleman?

NORA. Great heavens, don't you understand? There wasn't any old gentleman, he was just something I used to dream up as I sat here evening after evening wondering how on earth I could raise some money. But what does it matter? The old bore can stay imaginary as far as I'm concerned, because now I don't have to worry any longer! (*Jumps up.*) Oh, Christine, isn't it wonderful? I don't have to worry any more! No more troubles! I can play all day with the children, I can fill the house with pretty things, just the way Torvald likes. And, Christine, it will soon be spring, and the air will be fresh and the skies blue—and then perhaps we'll be able to take a little trip somewhere. I shall be able to see the sea again. Oh, yes, yes, it's a wonderful thing to be alive and happy!

The bell rings in the hall.

MRS. LINDE (*gets up*). You've a visitor. Perhaps I'd better go.

NORA. No, stay. It won't be for me. It's someone for Torvald—

MAID (*in the doorway*). Excuse me, madam, a gentleman's called who says he wants to speak to the master. But I didn't know—seeing as the doctor's with him—

NORA. Who is this gentleman?

KROGSTAD (*in the doorway*). It's me, Mrs. Helmer.

Mrs. Linde starts, composes herself; and turns away to the window.

NORA (*takes a step toward him and whispers tensely*). You? What is it? What do you want to talk to my husband about?

KROGSTAD. Business—you might call it. I hold a minor post in the bank, and I hear your husband is to become our new chief—

NORA. Oh—then it isn't—?

KROGSTAD. Pure business, Mrs. Helmer. Nothing more.

NORA. Well, you'll find him in his study.

Nods indifferently as she closes the hall door behind him. Then she walks across the room and sees to the stove.

MRS. LINDE. Nora, who was that man?

NORA. A lawyer called Krogstad.

MRS. LINDE. It was him, then.

NORA. Do you know that man?

MRS. LINDE. I used to know him—some years ago. He was a solicitor's clerk in our town, for a while.

NORA. Yes, of course, so he was.

MRS. LINDE. How he's changed!

NORA. He was very unhappily married, I believe.

MRS. LINDE. Is he a widower now?

NORA. Yes, with a lot of children. Ah, now it's alight.

She closes the door of the stove and moves the rocking-chair a little to one side.

MRS. LINDE. He does—various things now, I hear?

NORA. Does he? It's quite possible—I really don't know. But don't let's talk about business. It's so boring.

Dr. Rank enters from Helmer's study.

RANK (*still in the doorway*). No, no, my dear chap, don't see me out. I'll go and have a word with your wife. (*Closes the door and notices Mrs. Linde.*) Oh, I beg your pardon. I seem to be *de trop* here too.

NORA. Not in the least. (*Introduces them.*) Dr. Rank. Mrs. Linde.

RANK. Ah! A name I have often heard in this house. I believe I passed you on the stairs as I came up.

MRS. LINDE. Yes. Stairs tire me; I have to take them slowly.

RANK. Oh, have you hurt yourself?

MRS. LINDE. No, I'm just a little run down.

RANK. Ah, is that all? Then I take it you've come to town to cure yourself by a round of parties?

MRS. LINDE. I have come here to find work.

RANK. Is that an approved remedy for being run down?

MRS. LINDE. One has to live, Doctor.

RANK. Yes, people do seem to regard it as a necessity.

NORA. Oh, really, Dr. Rank. I bet you want to stay alive.

RANK. You bet I do. However miserable I sometimes feel, I still want to go on being tortured for as long as possible. It's the same with all my patients; and with people who are morally sick, too. There's a moral cripple in with Helmer at this very moment—

MRS. LINDE (*softly*). Oh!

NORA. Whom do you mean?

RANK. Oh, a lawyer fellow called Krogstad—you wouldn't know him. He's crippled all right; morally twisted. But even he started off by announcing, as though it were a matter of enormous importance, that he had to live.

NORA. Oh? What did he want to talk to Torvald about?

RANK. I haven't the faintest idea. All I heard was something about the bank.

NORA. I didn't know that Krog—that this man Krogstad had any connection with the bank.

RANK. Yes, he's got some kind of job down there. (*To Mrs. Linde.*) I wonder if in your part of the world you too have a species of human being that spends its time fussing around trying to smell out moral corruption? And when they find a case they give him some nice, comfortable position so that they can keep a good watch on him. The healthy ones just have to lump it.

MRS. LINDE. But surely it's the sick who need care most?

RANK (*shrugs his shoulders*). Well, there we have it. It's that attitude that's turning human society into a hospital.

Nora, lost in her own thoughts, laughs half to herself and claps her hands.

RANK. Why are you laughing? Do you really know what society is?

NORA. What do I care about society? I think it's a bore. I was laughing at something else—something frightfully funny. Tell me, Dr. Rank—will everyone who works at the bank come under Torvald now?

RANK. Do you find that particularly funny?

NORA (*smiles and hums*). Never you mind! Never you mind! (*Walks around the room.*) Yes, I find it very amusing to think that we—I mean, Torvald—has obtained so much influence over so many people. (*Takes the paper bag from her pocket.*) Dr. Rank, would you like a small macaroon?

RANK. Macaroons! I say! I thought they were forbidden here.

NORA. Yes, well, these are some Christine gave me.

MRS. LINDE. What? I—?

NORA. All right, all right, don't get frightened. You weren't to know Torvald had forbidden them. He's afraid they'll ruin my teeth. But, dash it—for once—! Don't you agree, Dr. Rank? Here! (*Pops a macaroon into his mouth.*) You too, Christine. And I'll have one too. Just a little one. Two at the most. (*Begins to walk round again.*) Yes, now I feel really, really happy. Now there's just one thing in the world I'd really love to do.

RANK. Oh? And what is that?

NORA. Just something I'd love to say to Torvald.

RANK. Well, why don't you say it?

NORA. No, I daren't. It's too dreadful.

MRS. LINDE. Dreadful?

RANK. Well, then, you'd better not. But you can say it to us. What is it you'd so love to say to Torvald?

NORA. I've the most extraordinary longing to say: "Bloody hell!"

RANK. Are you mad?

MRS. LINDE. My dear Nora—!

RANK. Say it. Here he is.

NORA (*hiding the bag of macaroons*). Ssh! Ssh!

Helmer, with his overcoat on his arm and his hat in his hand, enters from his study.

NORA (*goes to meet him*). Well, Torvald dear, did you get rid of him?

HELMER. Yes, he's just gone.

NORA. May I introduce you—? This is Christine. She's just arrived in town.

HELMER. Christine—? Forgive me, but I don't think—

NORA. Mrs. Linde, Torvald dear. Christine Linde.

HELMER. Ah. A childhood friend of my wife's, I presume?

MRS. LINDE. Yes, we knew each other in earlier days.

NORA. And imagine, now she's traveled all this way to talk to you.

HELMER. Oh?

MRS. LINDE. Well, I didn't really—

NORA. You see, Christine's frightfully good at office work, and she's mad to come under some really clever man who can teach her even more than she knows already—

HELMER. Very sensible, madam.

NORA. So when she heard you'd become head of the bank—it was in her local paper—she came here as quickly as she could and—Torvald, you will, won't you? Do a little something to help Christine? For my sake?

HELMER. Well, that shouldn't be impossible. You are a widow, I take it, Mrs. Linde?

MRS. LINDE. Yes.

HELMER. And you have experience of office work?

MRS. LINDE. Yes, quite a bit.

HELMER. Well then, it's quite likely I may be able to find some job for you—

NORA (*claps her hands*). You see, you see!

HELMER. You've come at a lucky moment, Mrs. Linde.

MRS. LINDE. Oh, how can I ever thank you—?

HELMER. There's absolutely no need. (*Puts on his overcoat.*) But now I'm afraid I must ask you to excuse me—

RANK. Wait. I'll come with you.

He gets his fur coat from the hall and warms it at the stove.

NORA. Don't be long, Torvald dear.

HELMER. I'll only be an hour.

NORA. Are you going too, Christine?

MRS. LINDE (*puts on her outdoor clothes*). Yes, I must start to look round for a room.

HELMER. Then perhaps we can walk part of the way together.

NORA (*helps her*). It's such a nuisance we're so cramped here—I'm afraid we can't offer to—

MRS. LINDE. Oh, I wouldn't dream of it. Goodbye, Nora dear, and thanks for everything.

NORA. *Au revoir.* You'll be coming back this evening, of course. And, you too, Dr. Rank. What? If you're well enough? Of course you'll be well enough. Wrap up warmly, though.

They go out, talking, into the hall. Children's voices are heard from the stairs.

NORA. Here they are! Here they are!

She runs out and opens the door. Anne-Marie, the nurse, enters with the children.

NORA. Come in, come in! (*Stoops down and kisses them.*) Oh, my sweet darlings—! Look at them, Christine! Aren't they beautiful?

RANK. Don't stand here chattering in this draught!

HELMER. Come, Mrs. Linde. This is for mothers only.

Dr. Rank, Helmer, and Mrs. Linde go down the stairs. The Nurse brings the children into the room. Nora follows, and closes the door to the hall.

NORA. How well you look! What red cheeks you've got! Like apples and roses! (*The children answer her inaudibly as she talks to them.*) Have you had fun? That's splendid. You gave Emmy and Bob a ride on the sledge? What, both together? I say! What a clever boy you are, Ivar! Oh, let me hold her for a moment, Anne-Marie! My sweet little baby doll! (*Takes the smallest child from the nurse and dances with her.*) Yes, yes, Mummy will dance with Bob too. What? Have you been throwing snowballs? Oh, I wish I'd been there! No, don't—I'll undress them myself, Anne-Marie. No, please let me; it's such fun. Go inside and warm yourself; you look frozen. There's some hot coffee on the stove. (*The nurse goes into the room on the left. Nora takes off the children's outdoor clothes and throws them anywhere while they all chatter simultaneously.*) What? A big dog ran after you? But he didn't bite you? No, dogs don't bite lovely little baby dolls. Leave those parcels alone, Ivar. What's in them? Ah, wouldn't you like to know! No, no; it's nothing nice. Come on, let's play a game. What shall we play? Hide and seek. Yes, let's play hide and seek. Bob shall hide first. You want me to? All right, let me hide first.

Nora and the children play around the room, and in the adjacent room to the left, laughing and shouting. At length Nora hides under the table. The children rush in, look, but cannot find her. Then they hear her half-stifled laughter, run to the table, lift up the cloth, and see her. Great excitement. She crawls out as though to frighten them. Further excitement. Meanwhile, there has been a knock on the door leading from the hall, but no one has noticed it. Now the door is half-opened and Krogstad enters. He waits for a moment; the game continues.

KROGSTAD. Excuse me, Mrs. Helmer—

NORA (*turns with a stifled cry and half jumps up*). Oh! What do you want?

KROGSTAD. I beg your pardon; the front door was ajar. Someone must have forgotten to close it.

NORA (*gets up*). My husband is not at home, Mr. Krogstad.

KROGSTAD. I know.

NORA. Well, what do want here, then?

KROGSTAD. A word with you.

NORA. With—? (*To the children, quietly.*) Go inside to Anne-Marie. What? No, the strange gentleman won't do anything to hurt Mummy. When he's gone we'll start playing again.

She takes the children into the room on the left and closes the door behind them.

NORA (*uneasy, tense*). You want to speak to me?

KROGSTAD. Yes.

NORA. Today? But it's not the first of the month yet.

KROGSTAD. No, it is Christmas Eve. Whether or not you have a merry Christmas depends on you.

NORA. What do you want? I can't give you anything today—

KROGSTAD. We won't talk about that for the present. There's something else. You have a moment to spare?

NORA. Oh, yes. Yes, I suppose so; though—

KROGSTAD. Good. I was sitting in the café down below and I saw your husband cross the street—

NORA. Yes.

KROGSTAD. With a lady.

NORA. Well?

KROGSTAD. Might I be so bold as to ask: was not that lady a Mrs. Linde?

NORA. Yes.

KROGSTAD. Recently arrived in town?

NORA. Yes, today.

KROGSTAD. She is a good friend of yours, is she not?

NORA. Yes, she is. But I don't see—

KROGSTAD. I used to know her too once.

NORA. I know.

KROGSTAD. Oh? You've discovered that. Yes, I thought you would. Well then, may I ask you a straight question: is Mrs. Linde to be employed at the bank?

NORA. How dare you presume to cross-examine me, Mr. Krogstad? You, one of my husband's employees? But since you ask, you shall have an answer. Yes, Mrs. Linde is to be employed by the bank. And I arranged it, Mr. Krogstad. Now you know.

KROGSTAD. I guessed right, then.

NORA (*walks up and down the room*). Oh, one has a little influence, you know. Just because one's a woman it doesn't necessarily mean that—When one is in a humble position, Mr. Krogstad, one should think twice before offending someone who—hm—

KROGSTAD. —who has influence?

NORA. Precisely.

KROGSTAD (*changes his tone*). Mrs. Helmer, will you have the kindness to use your influence on my behalf?

NORA. What? What do you mean?

KROGSTAD. Will you be so good as to see that I keep my humble position at the bank?

NORA. What do you mean? Who is thinking of removing you from your position?

KROGSTAD. Oh, you don't need to play innocent with me. I realize it can't be very pleasant for your friend to risk bumping into me; and now I also realize whom I have to thank for being hounded out like this.

NORA. But I assure you—

KROGSTAD. Look, let's not beat about the bush. There's still time, and I'd advise you to use your influence to stop it.

NORA. But, Mr. Krogstad, I have no influence—

KROGSTAD. Oh? I thought you just said—

NORA. But I didn't mean it like that! I? How on earth could you imagine that I would have any influence over my husband?

KROGSTAD. Oh, I've known your husband since we were students together. I imagine he has his weaknesses like other married men.

NORA. If you speak impertinently of my husband, I shall show you the door.

KROGSTAD. You're a bold woman, Mrs. Helmer.

NORA. I'm not afraid of you any longer. Once the New Year is in, I'll soon be rid of you.

KROGSTAD (*more controlled*). Now listen to me, Mrs. Helmer. If I'm forced to, I shall fight for my little job at the bank as I would fight for my life.

NORA. So it sounds.

KROGSTAD. It isn't just the money; that's the last thing I care about. There's something else—well, you might as well know. It's like this, you see. You know of course, as every one else does, that some years ago I committed an indiscretion.

NORA. I think I did hear something—

KROGSTAD. It never came into court; but from that day, every opening was barred to me. So I turned my hand to the kind of business you know about. I had to do something; and I don't think I was one of the worst. But now I want to give up all that. My sons are growing up; for their sake, I must try to regain what respectability I can. This job in the bank was the first step on the ladder. And now your husband wants to kick me off that ladder back into the dirt.

NORA. But my dear Mr. Krogstad, it simply isn't in my power to help you.

KROGSTAD. You say that because you don't want to help me. But I have the means to make you.

NORA. You don't mean you'd tell my husband that I owe you money?

KROGSTAD. And if I did?

NORA. That'd be a filthy trick! (*Almost in tears.*) This secret that is my pride and my joy—that he should hear about it in such a filthy, beastly way—hear about it from you! It'd involve me in the most dreadful unpleasantness—

KROGSTAD. Only—unpleasantness?

NORA (*vehemently*). All right, do it! You'll be the one who'll suffer. It'll show my husband the kind of man you are, and then you'll never keep your job.

KROGSTAD. I asked you whether it was merely domestic unpleasantness you were afraid of.

NORA. If my husband hears about it, he will of course immediately pay you whatever is owing. And then we shall have nothing more to do with you.

KROGSTAD (*takes a step closer*). Listen, Mrs. Helmer. Either you've a bad memory or else you know very little about financial transactions. I had better enlighten you.

NORA. What do you mean?

KROGSTAD. When your husband was ill, you came to me to borrow two hundred and fifty pounds.

NORA. I didn't know anyone else.

KROGSTAD. I promised to find that sum for you—

NORA. And you did find it.

KROGSTAD. I promised to find that sum for you on certain conditions. You were so worried about your husband's illness and so keen to get the money to take him abroad that I don't think you bothered much about the details. So it won't be out of place if I refresh your memory. Well—I promised to get you the money in exchange for an I.O.U., which I drew up.

NORA. Yes, and which I signed.

KROGSTAD. Exactly. But then I added a few lines naming your father as security for the debt. This paragraph was to be signed by your father.

NORA. Was to be? He did sign it.

KROGSTAD. I left the date blank for your father to fill in when he signed this paper. You remember, Mrs. Helmer?

NORA. Yes, I think so—

KROGSTAD. Then I gave you back this I.O.U. for you to post to your father. Is that not correct?

NORA. Yes.

KROGSTAD. And of course you posted it at once; for within five or six days you brought it along to me with your father's signature on it. Whereupon I handed you the money.

NORA. Yes, well. Haven't I repaid the installments as agreed?

KROGSTAD. Mm—yes, more or less. But to return to what we were speaking about—that was a difficult time for you just then, wasn't it, Mrs. Helmer?

NORA. Yes, it was.

KROGSTAD. And your father was very ill, if I am not mistaken.

NORA. He was dying.

KROGSTAD. He did in fact die shortly afterwards?

NORA. Yes.

KROGSTAD. Tell me, Mrs. Helmer, do you by any chance remember the date of your father's death? The day of the month, I mean.

NORA. Papa died on the twenty-ninth of September.

KROGSTAD. Quite correct; I took the trouble to confirm it. And that leaves me with a curious little problem—(*Takes out a paper.*)—which I simply cannot solve.

NORA. Problem? I don't see—

KROGSTAD. The problem, Mrs. Helmer, is that your father signed this paper three days after his death.

NORA. What? I don't understand—

KROGSTAD. Your father died on the twenty-ninth of September. But look at this. Here your father has dated his signature the second of October. Isn't that a curious little problem, Mrs. Helmer? (*Nora is silent.*) Can you suggest any explanation? (*She remains silent.*) And there's another curious thing. The words "second of October" and the year are written in a hand

which is not your father's, but which I seem to know. Well, there's a simple explanation to that. Your father could have forgotten to write in the date when he signed, and someone else could have added it before the news came of his death. There's nothing criminal about that. It's the signature itself I'm wondering about. It is genuine, I suppose, Mrs. Helmer? It was your father who wrote his name here?

NORA (*after a short silence, throws back her head and looks defiantly at him*). No, it was not. It was I who wrote Papa's name there.

KROGSTAD. Look, Mrs. Helmer, do you realize this is a dangerous admission?

NORA. Why? You'll get your money.

KROGSTAD. May I ask you a question? Why didn't you send this paper to your father?

NORA. I couldn't. Papa was very ill. If I'd asked him to sign this, I'd have had to tell him what the money was for. But I couldn't have told him in his condition that my husband's life was in danger. I couldn't have done that!

KROGSTAD. Then you would have been wiser to have given up your idea of a holiday.

NORA. But I couldn't! It was to save my husband's life. I couldn't put it off.

KROGSTAD. But didn't it occur to you that you were being dishonest towards me?

NORA. I couldn't bother about that. I didn't care about you. I hated you because of all the beastly difficulties you'd put in my way when you knew how dangerously ill my husband was.

KROGSTAD. Mrs. Helmer, you evidently don't appreciate exactly what you have done. But I can assure you that it is no bigger nor worse a crime than the one I once committed, and thereby ruined my whole social position.

NORA. You? Do you expect me to believe that you would have taken a risk like that to save your wife's life?

KROGSTAD. The law does not concern itself with motives.

NORA. Then the law must be very stupid.

KROGSTAD. Stupid or not, if I show this paper to the police, you will be judged according to it.

NORA. I don't believe that. Hasn't a daughter the right to shield her father from worry and anxiety when he's old and dying? Hasn't a wife the right to save her husband's life? I don't know much about the law but there must be something somewhere that says that such things are allowed. You ought to know about that, you're meant to be a lawyer, aren't you? You can't be a very good lawyer, Mr. Krogstad.

KROGSTAD. Possibly not. But business, the kind of business we two have been transacting—I think you'll admit I understand something about that? Good. Do as you please. But I tell you this. If I get thrown into the gutter for a second time, I shall take you with me.

He bows and goes out through the hall.

NORA (*stands for a moment in thought, then tosses her head*). What nonsense! He's trying to frighten me! I'm not that stupid. (*Busies herself gathering together the children's clothes; then she suddenly stops.*) But—? No, it's impossible. I did it for love, didn't I?

CHILDREN (*in the doorway, left*). Mummy, the strange gentleman's gone out into the street.

NORA. Yes, yes, I know. But don't talk to anyone about the strange gentleman. You hear? Not even to Daddy.

CHILDREN. No, Mummy. Will you play with us again now?

NORA. No, no. Not now.

CHILDREN. Oh but, Mummy, you promised!

NORA. I know, but I can't just now. Go back to the nursery. I've a lot to do. Go away, my darlings, go away. (*She pushes them gently into the other room and closes the door behind them. She sits on the sofa, takes up her embroidery, stitches for a few moments, but soon stops.*) No! (*Throws the embroidery aside, gets up, goes to the door leading to the hall, and calls.*) Helen! Bring in the Christmas tree! (*She goes to the table on the left and opens the drawer in it; then pauses again.*) No, but it's utterly impossible!

MAID (*enters with the tree*). Where shall I put it, madam?

NORA. There, in the middle of the room.

MAID. Will you be wanting anything else?

NORA. No, thank you, I have everything I need.

The Maid puts down the tree and goes out.

NORA (*busy decorating the tree*). Now—candles here—and flowers here. That loathsome man! Nonsense, nonsense, there's nothing to be frightened about. The Christmas tree must be beautiful. I'll do everything that you like, Torvald. I'll sing for you, dance for you—

Helmer, with a bundle of papers under his arm, enters.

NORA. Oh—are you back already?

HELMER. Yes. Has anyone been here?

NORA. Here? No.

HELMER. That's strange. I saw Krogstad come out of the front door.

NORA. Did you? Oh yes, that's quite right—Krogstad was here for a few minutes.

HELMER. Nora, I can tell from your face, he's been here and asked you to put in a good word for him.

NORA. Yes.

HELMER. And you were to pretend you were doing it of your own accord? You weren't going to tell me he'd been here? He asked you to do that too, didn't he?

NORA. Yes, Torvald. But—

HELMER. Nora, Nora! And you were ready to enter into such a conspiracy? Talking to a man like that, and making him promises—and then, on top of it all, to tell me an untruth!

NORA. An untruth?

HELMER. Didn't you say no one had been here? (*Wags his finger.*) My little songbird must never do that again. A songbird must have a clean beak to sing with; otherwise she'll start twittering out of tune. (*Puts his arm round her waist.*) Isn't that the way we want things? Yes, of course it is. (*Lets go of her.*) So let's hear no more about that. (*Sits down in front of the stove.*) Ah, how cozy and peaceful it is here. (*Glances for a few moments at his papers.*)

NORA (*busy with the tree; after a short silence*). Torvald.

HELMER. Yes.

NORA. I'm terribly looking forward to that fancy dress ball at the Stenborgs on Boxing Day.

HELMER. And I'm terribly curious to see what you're going to surprise me with.

NORA. Oh, it's so maddening.

HELMER. What is?

NORA. I can't think of anything to wear. It all seems so stupid and meaningless.

HELMER. So my little Nora's come to that conclusion, has she?

NORA (*behind his chair, resting her arms on its back*). Are you very busy, Torvald?

HELMER. Oh—

NORA. What are those papers?

HELMER. Just something to do with the bank.

NORA. Already?

HELMER. I persuaded the trustees to give me authority to make certain immediate changes in the staff and organization. I want to have everything straight by the New Year.

NORA. Then that's why this poor man Krogstad—

HELMER. Hm.

NORA (*still leaning over his chair, slowly strokes the back of his head*). If you hadn't been so busy, I was going to ask you an enormous favor, Torvald.

HELMER. Well, tell me. What was it to be?

NORA. You know I trust your taste more than anyone's. I'm so anxious to look really beautiful at the fancy dress ball. Torvald, couldn't you help me to decide what I shall go as, and what kind of costume I ought to wear?

HELMER. Aha! So little Miss Independent's in trouble and needs a man to rescue her, does she?

NORA. Yes, Torvald. I can't get anywhere without your help.

HELMER. Well, well, I'll give the matter thought. We'll find something.

NORA. Oh, how kind of you! (*Goes back to the tree. Pause.*) How pretty these red flowers look! But, tell me, is it so dreadful, this thing that Krogstad's done?

HELMER. He forged someone else's name. Have you any idea what that means?

NORA. Mightn't he have been forced to do it by some emergency?

HELMER. He probably just didn't think—that's what usually happens. I'm not so heartless as to condemn a man for an isolated action.

NORA. No, Torvald, of course not!

HELMER. Men often succeed in re-establishing themselves if they admit their crime and take their punishment.

NORA. Punishment?

HELMER. But Krogstad didn't do that. He chose to try and trick his way out of it; and that's what has morally destroyed him.

NORA. You think that would—?

HELMER. Just think how a man with that load on his conscience must always be lying and cheating and dissembling; how he must wear a mask even in the presence of those who are dearest to him, even his own wife and children! Yes, the children. That's the worst danger, Nora.

NORA. Why?

HELMER. Because an atmosphere of lies contaminates and poisons every corner of the home. Every breath that the children draw in such a house contains the germs of evil.

NORA (*comes closer behind him*). Do you really believe that?

HELMER. Oh, my dear, I've come across it so often in my work at the bar. Nearly all young criminals are the children of mothers who are constitutional liars.

NORA. Why do you say mothers?

HELMER. It's usually the mother; though of course the father can have the same influence. Every lawyer knows that only too well. And yet this fellow Krogstad has been sitting at home all these years poisoning his children with his lies and pretenses. That's why I say that, morally speaking, he is dead.

(*Stretches out his hands towards her.*) So my pretty little Nora must promise me not to plead his case. Your hand on it. Come, come, what's this? Give me your hand. There. That's settled, now. I assure you it'd be quite impossible for me to work in the same building as him. I literally feel physically ill in the presence of a man like that.

NORA (*draws her hand from his and goes over to the other side of the Christmas tree*). How hot it is in here! And I've so much to do.

HELMER (*gets up and gathers his papers*). Yes, and I must try to get some of this read before dinner. I'll think about your costume too. And I may even have something up my sleeve to hang in gold paper on the Christmas tree. (*Lays his hand on her head.*) My precious little songbird!

He goes into his study and closes the door.

NORA (*softly, after a pause*). It's nonsense. It must be. It's impossible. It *must* be impossible!

NURSE (*in the doorway, left*). The children are asking if they can come in to Mummy.

NORA. No, no, no; don't let them in! You stay with them, Anne-Marie.

NURSE. Very good, madam. (*Closes the door.*)

NORA (*pale with fear*). Corrupt my little children—! Poison my home! (*Short pause. She throws back her head.*) It isn't true! It *couldn't* be true!

ACT II

The same room. In the corner by the piano the Christmas tree stands, stripped and disheveled, its candles burned to their sockets. Nora's outdoor clothes lie on the sofa. She is alone in the room, walking restlessly to and fro. At length she stops by the sofa and picks up her coat.

NORA (*drops the coat again*). There's someone coming! (*Goes to the door and listens.*) No, it's no one. Of course—no one'll come today, it's Christmas Day. Nor tomorrow. But perhaps—! (*Opens the door and looks out.*) No. Nothing in the letter-box. Quite empty. (*Walks across the room.*) Silly, silly. Of course he won't do anything. It couldn't happen. It isn't possible. Why, I've three small children.

The Nurse, carrying a large cardboard box, enters from the room on the left.

NURSE. I found those fancy dress clothes at last, madam.

NORA. Thank you. Put them on the table.

NURSE (*does so*). They're all rumpled up.

NORA. Oh, I wish I could tear them into a million pieces!

NURSE. Why, madam! They'll be all right. Just a little patience.

NORA. Yes, of course. I'll go and get Mrs. Linde to help me.

NURSE. What, out again? In this dreadful weather? You'll catch a chill, madam.

NORA. Well, that wouldn't be the worst. How are the children?

NURSE. Playing with their Christmas presents, poor little dears. But—

NORA. Are they still asking to see me?

NURSE. They're so used to having their Mummy with them.

NORA. Yes, but, Anne-Marie, from now on I shan't be able to spend so much time with them.

NURSE. Well, children get used to anything in time.

NORA. Do you think so? Do you think they'd forget their mother if she went away from them—for ever?

NURSE. Mercy's sake, madam! For ever!

NORA. Tell me, Anne-Marie—I've so often wondered. How could you bear to give your child away—to strangers?

NURSE. But I had to when I came to nurse my little Miss Nora.

NORA. Do you mean you wanted to?

NURSE. When I had the chance of such a good job? A poor girl what's got into trouble can't afford to pick and choose. That good-for-nothing didn't lift a finger.

NORA. But your daughter must have completely forgotten you.

NURSE. Oh no, indeed she hasn't. She's written to me twice, once when she got confirmed and then again when she got married.

NORA (*hugs her*). Dear old Anne-Marie, you were a good mother to me.

NURSE. Poor little Miss Nora, you never had any mother but me.

NORA. And if my little ones had no one else, I know you would—no, silly, silly, silly! (*Opens the cardboard box.*) Go back to them, Anne-Marie. Now I must— Tomorrow you'll see how pretty I shall look.

NURSE. Why, there'll be no one at the ball as beautiful as my Miss Nora.

She goes into the room, left.

NORA (*begins to unpack the clothes from the box, but soon throws them down again*). Oh, if only I dared to go

out! If I could be sure no one would come, and nothing would happen while I was away! Stupid, stupid! No one will come. I just mustn't think about it. Brush this muff. Pretty gloves, pretty gloves! Don't think about it, don't think about it! One, two, three, four, five, six—(*Cries.*) Ah—they're coming—!

She begins to run toward the door, but stops uncertainly. Mrs. Linde enters from the hall, where she has been taking off her outdoor clothes.

NORA. Oh, it's you, Christine. There's no one else out there, is there? Oh, I'm so glad you've come.

MRS. LINDE. I hear you were at my room asking for me.

NORA. Yes, I just happened to be passing. I want to ask you to help me with something. Let's sit down here on the sofa. Look at this. There's going to be a fancy dress ball tomorrow night upstairs at Consul Stenborg's, and Torvald wants me to go as a Neapolitan fisher-girl and dance the tarantella. I learned it on Capri.

MRS. LINDE. I say, are you going to give a performance?

NORA. Yes, Torvald says I should. Look, here's the dress. Torvald had it made for me in Italy; but now it's all so torn, I don't know—

MRS. LINDE. Oh, we'll soon put that right; the stitching's just come away. Needle and thread? Ah, here we are.

NORA. You're being awfully sweet.

MRS. LINDE (*sews*). So you're going to dress up tomorrow, Nora? I must pop over for a moment to see how you look. Oh, but I've completely forgotten to thank you for that nice evening yesterday.

NORA (*gets up and walks across the room*). Oh, I didn't think it was as nice as usual. You ought to have come to town a little earlier, Christine. . . . Yes, Torvald understands how to make a home look attractive.

MRS. LINDE. I'm sure you do, too. You're not your father's daughter for nothing. But, tell me. Is Dr. Rank always in such low spirits as he was yesterday?

NORA. No, last night it was very noticeable. But he's got a terrible disease; he's got spinal tuberculosis, poor man. His father was a frightful creature who kept mistresses and so on. As a result Dr. Rank has been sickly ever since he was a child—you understand—

MRS. LINDE (*puts down her sewing*). But, my dear Nora, how on earth did you get to know about such things?

NORA (*walks about the room*). Oh, don't be silly, Christine—when one has three children, one comes into contact with women who—well, who know about medical matters, and they tell one a thing or two.

MRS. LINDE (*sews again; a short silence*). Does Dr. Rank visit you every day?

NORA. Yes, every day. He's Torvald's oldest friend, and a good friend to me too. Dr. Rank's almost one of the family.

MRS. LINDE. But, tell me—is he quite sincere? I mean, doesn't he rather say the sort of thing he thinks people want to hear?

NORA. No, quite the contrary. What gave you that idea?

MRS. LINDE. When you introduced me to him yesterday, he said he'd often heard my name mentioned here. But later I noticed your husband had no idea who I was. So how could Dr. Rank—?

NORA. Yes, that's quite right, Christine. You see, Torvald's so hopelessly in love with me that he wants to have me all to himself—those were his very words. When we were first married, he got quite jealous if I as much as mentioned any of my old friends back home. So naturally, I stopped talking about them. But I often chat with Dr. Rank about that kind of thing. He enjoys it, you see.

MRS. LINDE. Now listen, Nora. In many ways you're still a child; I'm a bit older than you and have a little more experience of the world. There's something I want to say to you. You ought to give up this business with Dr. Rank.

NORA. What business?

MRS. LINDE. Well, everything. Last night you were speaking about this rich admirer of yours who was going to give you money—

NORA. Yes, and who doesn't exist—unfortunately. But what's that got to do with—?

MRS. LINDE. Is Dr. Rank rich?

NORA. Yes.

MRS. LINDE. And he has no dependents?

NORA. No, no one. But—

MRS. LINDE. And he comes here to see you every day?

NORA. Yes, I've told you.

MRS. LINDE. But how dare a man of his education be so forward?

NORA. What on earth are you talking about?

MRS. LINDE. Oh, stop pretending, Nora. Do you think I haven't guessed who it was who lent you that two hundred pounds?

NORA. Are you out of your mind? How could you imagine such a thing? A friend, someone who comes here every day! Why, that'd be an impossible situation!

MRS. LINDE. Then it really wasn't him?

NORA. No, of course not. I've never for a moment dreamed of—anyway, he hadn't any money to lend then. He didn't come into that till later.

MRS. LINDE. Well, I think that was a lucky thing for you, Nora dear.

NORA. No, I could never have dreamed of asking Dr. Rank—Though I'm sure that if I ever did ask him—

MRS. LINDE. But of course you won't.

NORA. Of course not. I can't imagine that it should ever become necessary. But I'm perfectly sure that if I did speak to Dr. Rank—

MRS. LINDE. Behind your husband's back?

NORA. I've got to get out of this other business; and *that's* been going on behind his back. I've *got* to get out of it.

MRS. LINDE. Yes, well, that's what I told you yesterday. But—

NORA (*walking up and down*). It's much easier for a man to arrange these things than a woman—

MRS. LINDE. One's own husband, yes.

NORA. Oh, bosh. (*Stops walking.*) When you've completely repaid a debt, you get your I.O.U. back, don't you?

MRS. LINDE. Yes, of course.

NORA. And you can tear it into a thousand pieces and burn the filthy, beastly thing!

MRS. LINDE (*looks hard at her, puts down her sewing, and gets up slowly*). Nora, you're hiding something from me.

NORA. Can you see that?

MRS. LINDE. Something has happened since yesterday morning. Nora, what is it?

NORA (*goes toward her*). Christine! (*Listens.*) Ssh! There's Torvald. Would you mind going into the nursery for a few minutes? Torvald can't bear to see sewing around. Anne-Marie'll help you.

MRS. LINDE (*gathers some of her things together*). Very well. But I shan't leave this house until we've talked this matter out.

She goes into the nursery, left. As she does so, Helmer enters from the hall.

NORA (*runs to meet him*). Oh, Torvald dear, I've been so longing for you to come back!

HELMER. Was that the dressmaker?

NORA. No, it was Christine. She's helping me mend my costume. I'm going to look rather splendid in that.

HELMER. Yes, that was quite a bright idea of mine, wasn't it?

NORA. Wonderful! But wasn't it nice of me to give in to you?

HELMER (*takes her chin in his hand*). Nice—to give in to your husband? All right, little silly, I know you didn't mean it like that. But I won't disturb you. I expect you'll be wanting to try it on.

NORA. Are you going to work now?

HELMER. Yes. (*Shows her a bundle of papers.*) Look at these. I've been down to the bank—(*Turns to go into his study.*)

NORA. Torvald.

HELMER (*stops*). Yes.

NORA. If little squirrel asked you really prettily to grant her a wish—

HELMER. Well?

NORA. Would you grant it to her?

HELMER. First I should naturally have to know what it was.

NORA. Squirrel would do lots of pretty tricks for you if you granted her wish.

HELMER. Out with it, then.

NORA. Your little skylark would sing in every room—

HELMER. My little skylark does that already.

NORA. I'd turn myself into a little fairy and dance for you in the moonlight, Torvald.

HELMER. Nora, it isn't that business you were talking about this morning?

NORA (*comes closer*). Yes, Torvald—oh, please! I beg of you!

HELMER. Have you really the nerve to bring that up again?

NORA. Yes, Torvald, yes, you must do as I ask! You must let Krogstad keep his place at the bank!

HELMER. My dear Nora, his is the job I'm giving to Mrs. Linde.

NORA. Yes, that's terribly sweet of you. But you can get rid of one of the other clerks instead of Krogstad.

HELMER. Really, you're being incredibly obstinate. Just because you thoughtlessly promised to put in a word for him, you expect me to—

NORA. No, it isn't that, Helmer. It's for your own sake. That man writes for the most beastly newspapers— you said so yourself. He could do you tremendous harm. I'm so dreadfully frightened of him—

HELMER. Oh, I understand. Memories of the past. That's what's frightening you.

NORA. What do you mean?

HELMER. You're thinking of your father, aren't you?

NORA. Yes, yes. Of course. Just think what those dreadful men wrote in the papers about Papa! The most frightful slanders. I really believe it would have lost him his job if the Ministry hadn't sent you down to investigate, and you hadn't been so kind and helpful to him.

HELMER. But my dear little Nora, there's a considerable difference between your father and me. Your father was not a man of unassailable reputation. But I am; and I hope to remain so all my life.

NORA. But no one knows what spiteful people may not dig up. We could be so peaceful and happy now, Torvald—we could be free from every worry—you and I and the children. Oh, please, Torvald, please—!

HELMER. The very fact of your pleading his cause makes it impossible for me to keep him. Everyone at the bank already knows that I intend to dismiss Krogstad. If the rumor got about that the new manager had allowed his wife to persuade him to change his mind—

NORA. Well, what then?

HELMER. Oh, nothing, nothing. As long as my little Miss Obstinate gets her way—Do you expect me to make a laughing-stock of myself before my entire staff—give people the idea that I am open to outside influence? Believe me, I'd soon feel the consequences! Besides— there's something else that makes it impossible for Krogstad to remain in the bank while I am its manager.

NORA. What is that?

HELMER. I might conceivably have allowed myself to ignore his moral obloquies—

NORA. Yes, Torvald, surely?

HELMER. And I hear he's quite efficient at his job. But we—well, we were school friends. It was one of those friendships that one enters into over hastily and so often comes to regret later in life. I might as well confess the truth. We—well, we're on Christian name terms. And the tactless idiot makes no attempt to conceal it when other people are present. On the contrary, he thinks it gives him the right to be familiar with me. He shows off the whole time, with "Torvald this," and "Torvald that." I can tell you, I find it damned annoying. If he stayed, he'd make my position intolerable.

NORA. Torvald, you can't mean this seriously.

HELMER. Oh? And why not?

NORA. But it's so petty.

HELMER. What did you say? Petty? You think *I* am petty?

NORA. No, Torvald dear, of course you're not. That's just why—

HELMER. Don't quibble! You call my motives petty. Then I must be petty too. Petty! I see. Well, I've had enough of this. (*Goes to the door and calls into the hall.*) Helen!

NORA. What are you going to do?

HELMER (*searching among his papers*). I'm going to settle this matter once and for all. (*The Maid enters.*) Take this letter downstairs at once. Find a messenger and see that he delivers it. Immediately! The address is on the envelope. Here's the money.

MAID. Very good, sir. (*Goes out with the letter.*)

HELMER (*putting his papers in order*). There now, little Miss Obstinate.

NORA (*tensely*). Torvald—what was in that letter?

HELMER. Krogstad's dismissal.

NORA. Call her back, Torvald! There's still time. Oh, Torvald, call her back! Do it for my sake—for your own sake—for the children! Do you hear me, Torvald? Please do it! You don't realize what this may do to us all!

HELMER. Too late.

NORA. Yes. Too late.

HELMER. My dear Nora, I forgive you this anxiety. Though it is a bit of an insult to me. Oh, but it is! Isn't it an insult to imply that I should be frightened by the vindictiveness of a depraved hack journalist? But I forgive you, because it so charmingly testifies to the love you bear me. (*Takes her in his arms.*) Which is as it should be, my own dearest Nora. Let what will happen, happen. When the real crisis comes, you will not find me lacking in strength or courage. I am man enough to bear the burden for us both.

NORA (*fearfully*). What do you mean?

HELMER. The whole burden, I say—

NORA (*calmly*). I shall never let you do that.

HELMER. Very well. We shall share it, Nora—as man and wife. And that is as it should be. (*Caresses her.*) Are you happy now? There, there, there; don't look at me with those frightened little eyes. You're simply imagining things. You go ahead now and do your tarantella, and get some practice on that tambourine. I'll sit in my study and close the door. Then I won't hear anything, and you can make all the noise you want. (*Turns in the doorway.*) When Dr. Rank comes, tell him where to find me. (*He nods to her, goes into his room with his papers, and closes the door.*)

NORA (*desperate with anxiety, stands as though transfixed, and whispers*). He said he'd do it. He will do it. He will do it, and nothing'll stop him. No, never that. I'd rather anything. There must be some escape—Some way out—! (*The bell rings in the hall.*) Dr. Rank—! Anything but that! Anything, I don't care—!

She passes her hand across her face, composes herself, walks across, and opens the door to the hall. Dr. Rank is standing there, hanging up his fur coat. During the following scene, it begins to grow dark.

NORA. Good evening, Dr. Rank. I recognized your ring. But you mustn't go to Torvald yet. I think he's busy.

RANK. And—you?

NORA (*as he enters the room and she closes the door behind him*). Oh, you know very well I've always time to talk to you.

RANK. Thank you. I shall avail myself of that privilege as long as I can.

NORA. What do you mean by that? As long as you *can*?

RANK. Yes. Does that frighten you?

NORA. Well, it's rather a curious expression. Is something going to happen?

RANK. Something I've been expecting to happen for a long time. But I didn't think it would happen quite so soon.

NORA (*seizes his arm*). What is it? Dr. Rank, you must tell me!

RANK (*sits down by the stove*). I'm on the way out. And there's nothing to be done about it.

NORA (*sighs with relief*). Oh, it's you—?

RANK. Who else? No, it's no good lying to oneself. I am the most wretched of all my patients, Mrs. Helmer. These last few days I've been going through the books of this poor body of mine, and I find I am bankrupt. Within a month I may be rotting up there in the churchyard.

NORA. Ugh, what a nasty way to talk!

RANK. The facts aren't exactly nice. But the worst is that there's so much else that's nasty to come first. I've only one more test to make. When that's done I'll have a pretty accurate idea of when the final disintegration is likely to begin. I want to ask you a favour. Helmer's a sensitive chap, and I know how he hates anything ugly. I don't want him to visit me when I'm in hospital—

NORA. Oh but, Dr. Rank—

RANK. I don't want him there. On any pretext. I shan't have him allowed in. As soon as I know the worst, I'll send you my visiting card with a black cross on it, and then you'll know that the final filthy process has begun.

NORA. Really, you're being quite impossible this evening. And I did hope you'd be in a good mood.

RANK. With death on my hands? And all this to atone for someone else's sin? Is there justice in that? And in every single family, in one way or another, the same merciless law of retribution is at work—

NORA (*holds her hands to her ears*). Nonsense! Cheer up! Laugh!

RANK. Yes, you're right. Laughter's all the damned thing's fit for. My poor innocent spine must pay for the fun my father had as a gay young lieutenant.

NORA (*at the table, left*). You mean he was too fond of asparagus and *foie gras*?

RANK. Yes, and truffles too.

NORA. Yes, of course, truffles, yes. And oysters too, I suppose?

RANK. Yes, oysters, oysters. Of course.

NORA. And all that port and champagne to wash them down. It's too sad that all those lovely things should affect one's spine.

RANK. Especially a poor spine that never got any pleasure out of them.

NORA. Oh yes, that's the saddest thing of all.

RANK (*looks searchingly at her*). Hm—

NORA (*after a moment*). Why did you smile?

RANK. No, it was you who laughed.

NORA. No, it was you who smiled, Dr. Rank!

RANK (*gets up*). You're a worse little rogue than I thought.

NORA. Oh, I'm full of stupid tricks today.

RANK. So it seems.

NORA (*puts both her hands on his shoulders*). Dear, dear Dr. Rank, you mustn't die and leave Torvald and me.

RANK. Oh, you'll soon get over it. Once one is gone, one is soon forgotten.

NORA (*looks at him anxiously*). Do you believe that?

RANK. One finds replacements, and then—

NORA. Who will find a replacement?

RANK. You and Helmer both will, when I am gone. You seem to have made a start already, haven't you? What was this Mrs. Linde doing here yesterday evening?

NORA. Aha! But surely you can't be jealous of poor Christine?

RANK. Indeed I am. She will be my successor in this house. When I have moved on, this lady will—

NORA. Ssh—don't speak so loud! She's in there!

RANK. Today again? You see!

NORA. She's only come to mend my dress. Good heavens, how unreasonable you are! (*Sits on the sofa.*) Be nice now, Dr. Rank. Tomorrow you'll see how beautifully I shall dance; and you must imagine that I'm doing it just for you. And for Torvald of course; obviously. (*Takes some things out of the box.*) Dr. Rank, sit down here and I'll show you something.

RANK (*sits*). What's this?

NORA. Look here! Look!

RANK. Silk stockings!

NORA. Flesh-colored. Aren't they beautiful? It's very dark in here now, of course, but tomorrow—No, no, no; only the soles. Oh well, I suppose you can look a bit higher if you want to.

RANK. Hm—

NORA. Why are you looking so critical? Don't you think they'll fit me?

RANK. I can't really give you a qualified opinion on that.

NORA (*looks at him for a moment*). Shame on you! (*Flicks him on the ear with the stockings.*) Take that. (*Puts them back in the box.*)

RANK. What other wonders are to be revealed to me?

NORA. I shan't show you anything else. You're being naughty.

She hums a little and looks among the things in the box.

RANK (*after a short silence*). When I sit here like this being so intimate with you, I can't think—I cannot imagine what would have become of me if I had never entered this house.

NORA (*smiles*). Yes, I think you enjoy being with us, don't you?

RANK (*more quietly, looking into the middle distance*). And now to have to leave it all—

NORA. Nonsense. You're not leaving us.

RANK (*as before*). And not to be able to leave even the most wretched token of gratitude behind; hardly even a passing sense of loss; only an empty place, to be filled by the next comer.

NORA. Suppose I were to ask you to—? No—

RANK. To do what?

NORA. To give me proof of your friendship—

RANK. Yes, yes?

NORA. No, I mean—to do me a very great service—

RANK. Would you really for once grant me that happiness?

NORA. But you've no idea what it is.

RANK. Very well, tell me, then.

NORA. No, but, Dr. Rank, I can't. It's far too much—I want your help and advice, and I want you to do something for me.

RANK. The more the better. I've no idea what it can be. But tell me. You do trust me, don't you?

NORA. Oh, yes, more than anyone. You're my best and truest friend. Otherwise I couldn't tell you. Well then, Dr. Rank—there's something you must help me to prevent. You know how much Torvald loves me—he'd never hesitate for an instant to lay down his life for me—

RANK (*leans over towards her*). Nora—do you think he is the only one—?

NORA (*with a slight start*). What do you mean?

RANK. Who would gladly lay down his life for you?

NORA (*sadly*). Oh, I see.

RANK. I swore to myself I would let you know that before I go. I shall never have a better opportunity. . . . Well, Nora, now you know that. And now you also know that you can trust me as you can trust nobody else.

NORA (*rises; calmly and quietly*). Let me pass, please.

RANK (*makes room for her but remains seated*). Nora—

NORA (*in the doorway to the hall*). Helen, bring the lamp. (*Goes over to the stove.*) Oh, dear Dr. Rank, this was really horrid of you.

RANK (*gets up*). That I have loved you as deeply as anyone else has? Was that horrid of me?

NORA. No—but that you should go and tell me. That was quite unnecessary—

RANK. What do you mean? Did you know, then—?

The Maid enters with the lamp, puts it on the table, and goes out.

RANK. Nora—Mrs. Helmer—I am asking you, did you know this?

NORA. Oh, what do I know, what did I know, what didn't I know—I really can't say. How could you be so stupid, Dr. Rank? Everything was so nice.

RANK. Well, at any rate now you know that I am ready to serve you, body and soul. So—please continue.

NORA (*looks at him*). After this?

RANK. Please tell me what it is.

NORA. I can't possibly tell you now.

RANK. Yes, yes! You mustn't punish me like this. Let me be allowed to do what I can for you.

NORA. You can't do anything for me now. Anyway; I don't need any help. It was only my imagination— you'll see. Yes, really. Honestly. (*Sits in the rocking-chair, looks at him, and smiles.*) Well, upon my word you *are* a fine gentleman, Dr. Rank. Aren't you ashamed of yourself, now that the lamp's been lit?

RANK. Frankly, no. But perhaps I ought to say—*adieu*?

NORA. Of course not. You will naturally continue to visit us as before. You know quite well how Torvald depends on your company.

RANK. Yes, but you?

NORA. Oh, I always think it's enormous fun having you here.

RANK. That was what misled me. You're a riddle to me, you know. I'd often felt you'd just as soon be with me as with Helmer.

NORA. Well, you see, there are some people whom one loves, and others whom it's almost more fun to be with.

RANK. Oh yes, there's some truth in that.

NORA. When I was at home, of course I loved Papa best. But I always used to think it was terribly amusing to go down and talk to the servants; because they never told me what I ought to do; and they were such fun to listen to.

RANK. I see. So I've taken their place?

NORA (*jumps up and runs over to him*). Oh, dear, sweet Dr. Rank, I didn't mean that at all. But I'm sure you understand—I feel the same about Torvald as I did about Papa.

MAID (*enters from the hall*). Excuse me, madam. (*Whispers to her and hands her a visiting card.*)

NORA (*glances at the card*). Oh! (*Puts it quickly in her pocket.*)

RANK. Anything wrong?

NORA. No, no, nothing at all. It's just something that— it's my new dress.

RANK. What? But your costume is lying over there.

NORA. Oh—that, yes—but there's another—I ordered it specially—Torvald mustn't know—

RANK. Ah, so that's your big secret?

NORA. Yes, yes. Go in and talk to him—he's in his study—keep him talking for a bit—

RANK. Don't worry. He won't get away from me. (*Goes into Helmer's study.*)

NORA (*to the Maid*). Is he waiting in the kitchen?

MAID. Yes, madam, he came up the back way—

NORA. But didn't you tell him I had a visitor?

MAID. Yes, but he wouldn't go.

NORA. Wouldn't go?

MAID. No, madam, not until he'd spoken with you.

NORA. Very well, show him in; but quietly. Helen, you mustn't tell anyone about this. It's a surprise for my husband.

MAID. Very good, madam. I understand. (*Goes.*)

NORA. It's happening. It's happening after all. No, no, no, it can't happen, it mustn't happen.

She walks across and bolts the door of Helmer's study. The Maid opens the door from the hall to admit Krogstad, and closes it behind him. He is wearing an overcoat, heavy boots, and a fur cap.

NORA (*goes towards him*). Speak quietly. My husband's at home.

KROGSTAD. Let him hear.

NORA. What do you want from me?

KROGSTAD. Information.

NORA. Hurry up, then. What is it?

KROGSTAD. I suppose you know I've been given the sack.

NORA. I couldn't stop it, Mr. Krogstad. I did my best for you, but it didn't help.

KROGSTAD. Does your husband love you so little? He knows what I can do to you, and yet he dares to—

NORA. Surely you don't imagine I told him?

KROGSTAD. No. I didn't really think you had. It wouldn't have been like my old friend Torvald Helmer to show that much courage—

NORA. Mr. Krogstad, I'll trouble you to speak respectfully of my husband.

KROGSTAD. Don't worry, I'll show him all the respect he deserves. But since you're so anxious to keep this matter hushed up, I presume you're better informed than you were yesterday of the gravity of what you've done?

NORA. I've learned more than you could ever teach me.

KROGSTAD. Yes, a bad lawyer like me—

NORA. What do you want from me?

KROGSTAD. I just wanted to see how things were with you, Mrs. Helmer. I've been thinking about you all day. Even duns and hack journalists have hearts, you know.

NORA. Show some heart, then. Think of my little children.

KROGSTAD. Have you and your husband thought of mine? Well, let's forget that. I just wanted to tell you, you don't need to take this business too seriously. I'm not going to take any action, for the present.

NORA. Oh, no—you won't, will you? I knew it.

KROGSTAD. It can all be settled quite amicably. There's no need for it to become public. We'll keep it among the three of us.

NORA. My husband must never know about this.

KROGSTAD. How can you stop him? Can you pay the balance of what you owe me?

NORA. Not immediately.

KROGSTAD. Have you any means of raising the money during the next few days?

NORA. None that I would care to use.

KROGSTAD. Well, it wouldn't have helped anyway. However much money you offered me now I wouldn't give you back that paper.

NORA. What are you going to do with it?

KROGSTAD. Just keep it. No one else need ever hear about it. So in case you were thinking of doing anything desperate—

NORA. I am.

KROGSTAD. Such as running away—

NORA. I am.

KROGSTAD. Or anything more desperate—

NORA. How did you know?

KROGSTAD. —just give up the idea.

NORA. How did you know?

KROGSTAD. Most of us think of that at first. I did. But I hadn't the courage—

NORA (dully). Neither have I.

KROGSTAD (relieved). It's true, isn't it? You haven't the courage either?

NORA. No. I haven't. I haven't.

KROGSTAD. It'd be a stupid thing to do anyway. Once the first little domestic explosion is over. . . . I've got a letter in my pocket here addressed to your husband—

NORA. Telling him everything?

KROGSTAD. As delicately as possible.

NORA (quickly). He must never see that letter. Tear it up. I'll find the money somehow—

KROGSTAD. I'm sorry, Mrs. Helmer, I thought I'd explained—

NORA. Oh, I don't mean the money I owe you. Let me know how much you want from my husband, and I'll find it for you.

KROGSTAD. I'm not asking your husband for money.

NORA. What do you want, then?

KROGSTAD. I'll tell you. I want to get on my feet again, Mrs. Helmer. I want to get to the top. And your husband's going to help me. For eighteen months now my record's been clean. I've been in hard straits all that time; I was content to fight my way back inch by inch. Now I've been chucked back into the mud, and I'm not going to be satisfied with just getting back my job. I'm going to get to the top, I tell you. I'm going to get back into the bank, and it's going to be higher up. Your husband's going to create a new job for me—

NORA. He'll never do that!

KROGSTAD. Oh, yes he will. I know him. He won't dare to risk a scandal. And once I'm in there with him, you'll see! Within a year I'll be his right-hand man. It'll be Nils Krogstad who'll be running that bank, not Torvald Helmer!

NORA. That will never happen.

KROGSTAD. Are you thinking of—?

NORA. Now I *have* the courage.

KROGSTAD. Oh, you can't frighten me. A pampered little pretty like you—

NORA. You'll see! You'll see!

KROGSTAD. Under the ice? Down in the cold, black water? And then, in the spring, to float up again, ugly, unrecognizable, hairless—?

NORA. You can't frighten me.

KROGSTAD. And you can't frighten me. People don't do such things, Mrs. Helmer. And anyway, what'd be the use? I've got him in my pocket.

NORA. But afterwards? When I'm no longer—?

KROGSTAD. Have you forgotten that then your reputation will be in my hands? (*She looks at him speechlessly.*) Well, I've warned you. Don't do anything silly. When Helmer's read my letter, he'll get in touch with me. And remember, it's your husband who's forced me to act like this. And for that I'll never forgive him. Goodbye, Mrs. Helmer. (*He goes out through the hall.*)

NORA (*runs to the hall door, opens it a few inches, and listens*). He's going. He's not going to give him the letter. Oh, no, no, it couldn't possibly happen. (*Opens the door a little wider.*) What's he doing? Standing outside the front door. He's not going downstairs. Is he changing his mind? Yes, he—!

A letter falls into the letter-box. Krogstad's footsteps die away down the stairs.

NORA (*with a stifled cry runs across the room towards the table by the sofa. A pause*). In the letter-box. (*Steals timidly over towards the hall door.*) There it is! Oh, Torvald, Torvald! Now we're lost!

MRS. LINDE (*enters from the nursery with Nora's costume*). Well, I've done the best I can. Shall we see how it looks—?

NORA (*whispers hoarsely*). Christine, come here.

MRS. LINDE (*throws the dress on the sofa*). What's wrong with you? You look as though you'd seen a ghost!

NORA. Come here. Do you see that letter? There—look—through the glass of the letter-box.

MRS. LINDE. Yes, yes, I see it.

NORA. That letter's from Krogstad—

MRS. LINDE. Nora! It was Krogstad who lent you the money!

NORA. Yes. And now Torvald's going to discover everything.

MRS. LINDE. Oh, believe me, Nora, it'll be best for you both.

NORA. You don't know what's happened. I've committed a forgery—

MRS. LINDE. But, for heaven's sake—!

NORA. Christine, all I want is for you to be my witness.

MRS. LINDE. What do you mean? Witness what?

NORA. If I should go out of my mind—and it might easily happen—

MRS. LINDE. Nora!

NORA. Or if anything else should happen to me—so that I wasn't here any longer—

MRS. LINDE. Nora, Nora, you don't know what you're saying!

NORA. If anyone should try to take the blame, and say it was all his fault—you understand—?

MRS. LINDE. Yes, yes—but how can you think?

NORA. Then you must testify that it isn't true, Christine. I'm not mad—I know exactly what I'm saying—and I'm telling you, no one else knows anything about this. I did it entirely on my own. Remember that.

MRS. LINDE. All right. But I simply don't understand—

NORA. Oh, how could you understand? A—miracle—is about to happen.

MRS. LINDE. Miracle?

NORA. Yes. A miracle. But it's so frightening, Christine. It *mustn't* happen, not for anything in the world.

MRS. LINDE. I'll go over and talk to Krogstad.

NORA. Don't go near him. He'll only do something to hurt you.

MRS. LINDE. Once upon a time he'd have done anything for my sake.

NORA. He?

MRS. LINDE. Where does he live?

NORA. Oh, how should I know—? Oh, yes, wait a moment—! (*Feels in her pocket.*) Here's his card. But the letter, the letter—!

HELMER (*from his study, knocks on the door*). Nora!

NORA (*cries in alarm*). What is it?

HELMER. Now, now, don't get alarmed. We're not coming in; you've closed the door. Are you trying on your costume?

NORA. Yes, yes—I'm trying on my costume. I'm going to look so pretty for you, Torvald.

MRS. LINDE (*who has been reading the card*). Why, he lives just around the corner.

NORA. Yes; but it's no use. There's nothing to be done now. The letter's lying there in the box.

MRS. LINDE. And your husband has the key?

NORA. Yes, he always keeps it.

MRS. LINDE. Krogstad must ask him to send the letter back unread. He must find some excuse—

NORA. But Torvald always opens the box at just about this time—

MRS. LINDE. You must stop him. Go in and keep him talking. I'll be back as quickly as I can.

She hurries out through the hall.

NORA (*goes over to Helmer's door, opens it and peeps in*). Torvald!

HELMER (*offstage*). Well, may a man enter his own drawing-room again? Come on, Rank, now we'll see what—(*In the doorway.*) But what's this?

NORA. What, Torvald dear?

HELMER. Rank's been preparing me for some great transformation scene.

RANK (*in the doorway*). So I understood. But I seem to have been mistaken.

NORA. Yes, no one's to be allowed to see me before tomorrow night.

HELMER. But, my dear Nora, you look quite worn out. Have you been practicing too hard?

NORA. No, I haven't practiced at all yet.

HELMER. Well, you must.

NORA. Yes, Torvald, I must, I know. But I can't get anywhere without your help. I've completely forgotten everything.

HELMER. Oh, we'll soon put that to rights.

NORA. Yes, help me, Torvald. Promise me you will? Oh, I'm so nervous. All those people—! You must forget everything except me this evening. You mustn't think of business—I won't even let you touch a pen. Promise me, Torvald?

HELMER. I promise. This evening I shall think of nothing but you—my poor, helpless little darling. Oh, there's just one thing I must see to—(*Goes towards the hall door.*)

NORA. What do you want out there?

HELMER. I'm only going to see if any letters have come.

NORA. No, Torvald, no!

HELMER. Why, what's the matter?

NORA. Torvald, I beg you. There's nothing there.

HELMER. Well, I'll just make sure.

He moves towards the door. Nora runs to the piano and plays the first bars of the tarantella.

HELMER (*at the door, turns*). Aha!

NORA. I can't dance tomorrow if I don't practice with you now.

HELMER (*goes over to her*). Are you really so frightened, Nora dear?

NORA. Yes, terribly frightened. Let me start practicing now, at once—we've still time before dinner. Oh, do sit down and play for me, Torvald dear. Correct me, lead me, the way you always do.

HELMER. Very well, my dear, if you wish it.

He sits down at the piano. Nora seizes the tambourine and a long multi-colored shawl from the cardboard box, wraps the latter hastily around her, then takes a quick leap into the center of the room.

NORA. Play for me! I want to dance!

Helmer plays and Nora dances. Dr. Rank stands behind Helmer at the piano and watches her.

HELMER (*as he plays*). Slower, slower!

NORA. I can't!

HELMER. Not so violently, Nora.

NORA. I must!

HELMER (*stops playing*). No, no, this won't do at all.

NORA (*laughs and swings her tambourine*). Isn't that what I told you?

RANK. Let me play for her.

HELMER (*gets up*). Yes, would you? Then it'll be easier for me to show her.

Rank sits down at the piano and plays. Nora dances more and more wildly. Helmer has stationed himself by the stove and tries repeatedly to correct her, but she seems not to hear him. Her hair works loose and falls over her shoulders; she ignores it and continues to dance. Mrs. Linde enters.

MRS. LINDE (*stands in the doorway as though tongue-tied*). Ah—!

NORA (*as she dances*). Oh, Christine, we're having such fun!

HELMER. But, Nora darling, you're dancing as if your life depended on it.

NORA. It does.

HELMER. Rank, stop it! This is sheer lunacy. Stop it, I say!

Rank ceases playing. Nora suddenly stops dancing.

HELMER (*goes over to her*). I'd never have believed it. You've forgotten everything I taught you.

NORA (*throws away the tambourine*). You see!

HELMER. I'll have to show you every step.

NORA. You see how much I need you! You must show me every step of the way. Right to the end of the dance. Promise me you will, Torvald?

HELMER. Never fear. I will.

NORA. You mustn't think about anything but me—today or tomorrow. Don't open any letters—don't even open the letter-box—

HELMER. Aha, you're still worried about that fellow—

NORA. Oh, yes, yes, him too.

HELMER. Nora, I can tell from the way you're behaving, there's a letter from him already lying there.

NORA. I don't know. I think so. But you mustn't read it now. I don't want anything ugly to come between us till it's all over.

RANK (*quietly, to Helmer*). Better give her her way.

HELMER (*puts his arm round her*). My child shall have her way. But tomorrow night, when your dance is over—

NORA. Then you will be free.

MAID (*appears in the doorway, right*). Dinner is served, madam.

NORA. Put out some champagne, Helen.

MAID. Very good, madam. (*Goes.*)

HELMER. I say! What's this, a banquet?

NORA. We'll drink champagne until dawn! (*Calls.*) And, Helen! Put out some macaroons! Lots of macaroons—for once!

HELMER (*takes her hands in his*). Now, now, now. Don't get so excited. Where's my little songbird, the one I know?

NORA. All right. Go and sit down—and you too, Dr. Rank. I'll be with you in a minute. Christine, you must help me put my hair up.

RANK (*quietly, as they go*). There's nothing wrong, is there? I mean, she isn't—er—expecting—?

HELMER. Good heavens no, my dear chap. She just gets scared like a child sometimes—I told you before—

They go out right.

NORA. Well?

MRS. LINDE. He's left town.

NORA. I saw it from your face.

MRS. LINDE. He'll be back tomorrow evening. I left a note for him.

NORA. You needn't have bothered. You can't stop anything now. Anyway, it's wonderful really, in a way—sitting here and waiting for the miracle to happen.

MRS. LINDE. Waiting for what?

NORA. Oh, you wouldn't understand. Go in and join them. I'll be with you in a moment.

Mrs. Linde goes into the dining-room.

NORA (*stands for a moment as though collecting herself. Then she looks at her watch*). Five o'clock. Seven hours till midnight. Then another twenty-four hours till midnight tomorrow. And then the tarantella will be finished. Twenty-four and seven? Thirty-one hours to live.

HELMER (*appears in the doorway, right*). What's happened to my little songbird?

NORA (*runs to him with her arms wide*). Your songbird is here!

ACT III

The same room. The table which was formerly by the sofa has been moved into the center of the room; the chairs surround it as before. The door to the hall stands open. Dance music can be heard from the floor above. Mrs. Linde is seated at the table, absent-mindedly glancing through a book. She is trying to read, but seems unable to keep her mind on it. More than once she turns and listens anxiously towards the front door.

MRS. LINDE (*looks at her watch*). Not here yet. There's not much time left. Please God he hasn't—! (Listens again.) Ah, here he is. (*Goes out into the hall and cautiously opens the front door. Footsteps can be heard softly ascending the stairs. She whispers.*) Come in. There's no one here.

KROGSTAD (*in the doorway*). I found a note from you at my lodgings. What does this mean?

MRS. LINDE. I must speak with you.

KROGSTAD. Oh? And must our conversation take place in this house?

MRS. LINDE. We couldn't meet at my place; my room has no separate entrance. Come in. We're quite alone. The maid's asleep, and the Helmers are at the dance upstairs.

KROGSTAD (*comes into the room*). Well, well! So the Helmers are dancing this evening? Are they indeed?

MRS. LINDE. Yes, why not?

KROGSTAD. True enough. Why not?

MRS. LINDE. Well, Krogstad. You and I must have a talk together.

KROGSTAD. Have we two anything further to discuss?

MRS. LINDE. We have a great deal to discuss.

KROGSTAD. I wasn't aware of it.

MRS. LINDE. That's because you've never really understood me.

KROGSTAD. Was there anything to understand? It's the old story, isn't it—a woman chucking a man because something better turns up?

MRS. LINDE. Do you really think I'm so utterly heartless? You think it was easy for me to give you up?

KROGSTAD. Wasn't it?

MRS. LINDE. Oh, Nils, did you really believe that?

KROGSTAD. Then why did you write to me the way you did?

MRS. LINDE. I had to. Since I had to break with you, I thought it my duty to destroy all the feelings you had for me.

KROGSTAD (*clenches his fists*). So that was it. And you did this for money!

MRS. LINDE. You mustn't forget I had a helpless mother to take care of, and two little brothers. We couldn't wait for you, Nils. It would have been so long before you'd had enough to support us.

KROGSTAD. Maybe. But you had no right to cast me off for someone else.

MRS. LINDE. Perhaps not. I've often asked myself that.

KROGSTAD (*more quietly*). When I lost you, it was just as though all solid ground had been swept from under my feet. Look at me. Now I am a shipwrecked man, clinging to a spar.

MRS. LINDE. Help may be near at hand.

KROGSTAD. It was near. But then you came, and stood between it and me.

MRS. LINDE. I didn't know, Nils. No one told me till today that this job I'd found was yours.

KROGSTAD. I believe you, since you say so. But now you know, won't you give it up?

MRS. LINDE. No—because it wouldn't help you even if I did.

KROGSTAD. Wouldn't it? I'd do it all the same.

MRS. LINDE. I've learned to look at things practically. Life and poverty have taught me that.

KROGSTAD. And life has taught me to distrust fine words.

MRS. LINDE. Then it's taught you a useful lesson. But surely you still believe in actions?

KROGSTAD. What do you mean?

MRS. LINDE. You said you were like a shipwrecked man clinging to a spar.

KROGSTAD. I have good reason to say it.

MRS. LINDE. I'm in the same position as you. No one to care about, no one to care for.

KROGSTAD. You made your own choice.

MRS. LINDE. I had no choice—then.

KROGSTAD. Well?

MRS. LINDE. Nils, suppose we two shipwrecked souls could join hands?

KROGSTAD. What are you saying?

MRS. LINDE. Castaways have a better chance of survival together than on their own.

KROGSTAD. Christine!

MRS. LINDE. Why do you suppose I came to this town?

KROGSTAD. You mean—you came because of me?

MRS. LINDE. I must work if I'm to find life worth living. I've always worked, for as long as I can remember; it's been the greatest joy of my life—my only joy. But now I'm alone in the world, and I feel so dreadfully lost and empty. There's no joy in working just for oneself. Oh, Nils, give me something—someone—to work for.

KROGSTAD. I don't believe all that. You're just being hysterical and romantic. You want to find an excuse for self-sacrifice.

MRS. LINDE. Have you ever known me to be hysterical?

KROGSTAD. You mean you really—? Is it possible? Tell me—you know all about my past?

MRS. LINDE. Yes.

KROGSTAD. And you know what people think of me here?

MRS. LINDE. You said just now that with me you might have become a different person.

KROGSTAD. I know I could have.

MRS. LINDE. Couldn't it still happen?

KROGSTAD. Christine—do you really mean this? Yes—you do—I see it in your face. Have you really the courage—?

MRS. LINDE. I need someone to be a mother to; and your children need a mother. And you and I need each other. I believe in you, Nils. I am afraid of nothing—with you.

KROGSTAD (clasps her hands). Thank you, Christine—thank you! Now I shall make the world believe in me as you do! Oh—but I'd forgotten—

MRS. LINDE (listens). Ssh! The tarantella! Go quickly, go!

KROGSTAD. Why? What is it?

MRS. LINDE. You hear that dance? As soon as it's finished, they'll be coming down.

KROGSTAD. All right, I'll go. It's no good, Christine. I'd forgotten—you don't know what I've just done to the Helmers.

MRS. LINDE. Yes, Nils. I know.

KROGSTAD. And yet you'd still have the courage to—?

MRS. LINDE. I know what despair can drive a man like you to.

KROGSTAD. Oh, if only I could undo this!

MRS. LINDE. You can. Your letter is still lying in the box.

KROGSTAD. Are you sure?

MRS. LINDE. Quite sure. But—

KROGSTAD (looks searchingly at her). Is that why you're doing this? You want to save your friend at any price? Tell me the truth. Is that the reason?

MRS. LINDE. Nils, a woman who has sold herself once for the sake of others doesn't make the same mistake again.

KROGSTAD. I shall demand my letter back.

MRS. LINDE. No, no.

KROGSTAD. Of course I shall. I shall stay here till Helmer comes down. I'll tell him he must give me back my letter—I'll say it was only to do with my dismissal, and that I don't want him to read it—

MRS. LINDE. No, Nils, you mustn't ask for that letter back.

KROGSTAD. But—tell me—wasn't that the real reason you asked me to come here?

MRS. LINDE. Yes—at first, when I was frightened. But a day has passed since then, and in that time I've seen incredible things happen in this house. Helmer must know the truth. This unhappy secret of Nora's must be revealed. They must come to a full understanding; there must be an end of all these shiftings and evasions.

KROGSTAD. Very well. If you're prepared to risk it. But one thing I can do—and at once—

MRS. LINDE (listens). Hurry! Go, go! The dance is over. We aren't safe here another moment.

KROGSTAD. I'll wait for you downstairs.

MRS. LINDE. Yes, do. You can see me home.

KROGSTAD. I've never been so happy in my life before!

He goes out through the front door. The door leading from the room into the hall remains open.

MRS. LINDE (*tidies the room a little and gets her hat and coat*). What a change! Oh, what a change! Someone to work for—to live for! A home to bring joy into! I won't let this chance of happiness slip through my fingers. Oh, why don't they come? (*Listens.*) Ah, here they are. I must get my coat on.

She takes her hat and coat. Helmer's and Nora's voices become audible outside. A key is turned in the lock and Helmer leads Nora almost forcibly into the hall. She is

*dressed in an Italian costume with a large black shawl.
He is in evening dress, with a black cloak.*

NORA (*still in the doorway, resisting him*). No, no, no—not
in here! I want to go back upstairs. I don't want to
leave so early.

HELMER. But my dearest Nora—

NORA. Oh, please, Torvald, please! Just another hour!

HELMER. Not another minute, Nora, my sweet. You
know what we agreed. Come along, now. Into the
drawing-room. You'll catch cold if you stay out here.

*He leads her, despite her efforts to resist him, gently
into the room.*

MRS. LINDE. Good evening.

NORA. Christine!

HELMER. Oh, hullo, Mrs. Linde. You still here?

MRS. LINDE. Please forgive me. I did so want to see Nora
in her costume.

NORA. Have you been sitting here waiting for me?

MRS. LINDE. Yes. I got here too late, I'm afraid. You'd already gone up. And I felt I really couldn't go back
home without seeing you.

HELMER (*takes off Nora's shawl*). Well, take a good look at
her. She's worth looking at, don't you think? Isn't she
beautiful, Mrs. Linde?

MRS. LINDE. Oh, yes, indeed—

HELMER. Isn't she unbelievably beautiful? Everyone at
the party said so. But dreadfully stubborn she is, bless
her pretty little heart. What's to be done about that?
Would you believe it, I practically had to use force to
get her away!

NORA. Oh, Torvald, you're going to regret not letting me
stay—just half an hour longer.

HELMER. Hear that, Mrs. Linde? She dances her tarantella—makes a roaring success—and very well deserved—though possibly a trifle too realistic—more
so than was aesthetically necessary, strictly speaking.
But never mind that. Main thing is—she had a success—roaring success. Was I going to let her stay on
after that and spoil the impression? No, thank you. I
took my beautiful little Capri signorina—my capricious little Capricienne, what?—under my arm—a
swift round of the ballroom, a curtsey to the company, and, as they say in novels, the beautiful apparition disappeared! An exit should always be dramatic,
Mrs. Linde. But unfortunately that's just what I can't
get Nora to realize. I say, it's hot in here. (*Throws his
cloak on a chair and opens the door to his study.*) What's
this? It's dark in here. Ah, yes, of course—excuse me.
(*Goes in and lights a couple of candles.*)

NORA (*whispers swiftly, breathlessly*). Well?

MRS. LINDE (*quietly*). I've spoken to him.

NORA. Yes?

MRS. LINDE. Nora—you must tell your husband everything.

NORA (*dully*). I knew it.

MRS. LINDE. You've nothing to fear from Krogstad. But
you must tell him.

NORA. I shan't tell him anything.

MRS. LINDE. Then the letter will.

NORA. Thank you, Christine. Now I know what I must
do. Ssh!

HELMER (*returns*). Well, Mrs. Linde, finished admiring
her?

MRS. LINDE. Yes. Now I must say good night.

HELMER. Oh, already? Does this knitting belong to you?

MRS. LINDE (*takes it*). Thank you, yes. I nearly forgot it.

HELMER. You knit, then?

MRS. LINDE. Why, yes.

HELMER. Know what? You ought to take up embroidery.

MRS. LINDE. Oh? Why?

HELMER. It's much prettier. Watch me, now. You hold the
embroidery in your left hand, like this, and then you
take the needle in your right hand and go in and out
in a slow, easy movement—like this. I am right,
aren't I?

MRS. LINDE. Yes, I'm sure—

HELMER. But knitting, now—that's an ugly business—
can't help it. Look—arms all huddled up—great
clumsy needles going up and down—makes you look
like a damned Chinaman. I say, that really was a
magnificent champagne they served us.

MRS. LINDE. Well, good night, Nora. And stop being
stubborn. Remember!

HELMER. Quite right, Mrs. Linde!

MRS. LINDE. Good night, Mr. Helmer.

HELMER (*accompanies her to the door*). Good night, good
night! I hope you'll manage to get home all right? I'd
gladly—but you haven't far to go, have you? Good
night, good night. (*She goes. He closes the door behind
her and returns.*) Well, we've got rid of her at last.
Dreadful bore that woman is!

NORA. Aren't you very tired, Torvald?

HELMER. No, not in the least.

NORA. Aren't you sleepy?

HELMER. Not a bit. On the contrary, I feel extraordinarily
exhilarated. But what about you? Yes, you look very
sleepy and tired.

NORA. Yes, I am very tired. Soon I shall sleep.

HELMER. You see, you see! How right I was not to let you
stay longer!

NORA. Oh, you're always right, whatever you do.

HELMER (*kisses her on the forehead*). Now my little song-bird's talking just like a real big human being. I say, did you notice how cheerful Rank was this evening?

NORA. Oh? Was he? I didn't have a chance to speak with him.

HELMER. I hardly did. But I haven't seen him in such a jolly mood for ages. (*Looks at her for a moment, then comes closer.*) I say, it's nice to get back to one's home again, and be all alone with you. Upon my word, you're a distractingly beautiful young woman.

NORA. Don't look at me like that, Torvald!

HELMER. What, not look at my most treasured possession? At all this wonderful beauty that's mine, mine alone, all mine.

NORA (*goes round to the other side of the table*). You mustn't talk to me like that tonight.

HELMER (*follows her*). You've still the tarantella in your blood, I see. And that makes you even more desirable. Listen! Now the other guests are beginning to go. (*More quietly.*) Nora—soon the whole house will be absolutely quiet.

NORA. Yes, I hope so.

HELMER. Yes, my beloved Nora, of course you do! Do you know—when I'm out with you among other people like we were tonight, do you know why I say so little to you, why I keep so aloof from you, and just throw you an occasional glance? Do you know why I do that? It's because I pretend to myself that you're my secret mistress, my clandestine little sweetheart, and that nobody knows there's anything at all between us.

NORA. Oh, yes, yes, yes—I know you never think of anything but me.

HELMER. And then when we're about to go, and I wrap the shawl round your lovely young shoulders, over this wonderful curve of your neck—then I pretend to myself that you are my young bride, that we've just come from the wedding, that I'm taking you to my house for the first time—that, for the first time, I am alone with you—quite alone with you, as you stand there young and trembling and beautiful. All evening I've had no eyes for anyone but you. When I saw you dance the tarantella, like a huntress, a temptress, my blood grew hot, I couldn't stand it any longer! That was why I seized you and dragged you down here with me—

NORA. Leave me, Torvald! Get away from me! I don't want all this.

HELMER. What? Now, Nora, you're joking with me. Don't want, don't want—? Aren't I your husband—?

There is a knock on the front door.

NORA (*starts*). What was that?

HELMER (*goes towards the hall*). Who is it?

RANK (*outside*). It's me. May I come in for a moment?

HELMER (*quietly, annoyed*). Oh, what does he want now? (*Calls.*) Wait a moment. (*Walks over and opens the door.*) Well! Nice of you not to go by without looking in.

RANK. I thought I heard your voice, so I felt I had to say goodbye. (*His eyes travel swiftly around the room.*) Ah, yes—these dear rooms, how well I know them. What a happy, peaceful home you two have.

HELMER. You seemed to be having a pretty happy time yourself upstairs.

RANK. Indeed I did. Why not? Why shouldn't one make the most of this world? As much as one can, and for as long as one can. The wine was excellent—

HELMER. Especially the champagne.

RANK. You noticed that too? It's almost incredible how much I managed to get down.

NORA. Torvald drank a lot of champagne too, this evening.

RANK. Oh?

NORA. Yes. It always makes him merry afterwards.

RANK. Well, why shouldn't a man have a merry evening after a well-spent day?

HELMER. Well-spent? Oh, I don't know that I can claim that.

RANK (*slaps him across the back*). I can though, my dear fellow!

NORA. Yes, of course, Dr. Rank—you've been carrying out a scientific experiment today, haven't you?

RANK. Exactly.

HELMER. Scientific experiment! Those are big words for my little Nora to use!

NORA. And may I congratulate you on the finding?

RANK. You may indeed.

NORA. It was good, then?

RANK. The best possible finding—both for the doctor and the patient. Certainty.

NORA (*quickly*). Certainty?

RANK. Absolute certainty. So aren't I entitled to have a merry evening after that?

NORA. Yes, Dr. Rank. You were quite right to.

HELMER. I agree. Provided you don't have to regret it tomorrow.

RANK. Well, you never get anything in this life without paying for it.

NORA. Dr. Rank—you like masquerades, don't you?

RANK. Yes, if the disguises are sufficiently amusing.

NORA. Tell me. What shall we two wear at the next masquerade?

HELMER. You little gadabout! Are you thinking about the next one already?

RANK. We two? Yes, I'll tell you. You must go as the Spirit of Happiness—

HELMER. You try to think of a costume that'll convey that.

RANK. Your wife need only appear as her normal, everyday self—

HELMER. Quite right! Well said! But what are you going to be? Have you decided that?

RANK. Yes, my dear friend. I have decided that.

HELMER. Well?

RANK. At the next masquerade, I shall be invisible.

HELMER. Well, that's a funny idea.

RANK. There's a big, black hat—haven't you heard of the invisible hat? Once it's over your head, no one can see you any more.

HELMER (*represses a smile*). Ah yes, of course.

RANK. But I'm forgetting what I came for. Helmer, give me a cigar. One of your black Havanas.

HELMER. With the greatest pleasure. (*Offers him the box.*)

RANK (*takes one and cuts off the tip*). Thank you.

NORA (*strikes a match*). Let me give you a light.

RANK. Thank you. (*She holds out the match for him. He lights his cigar.*) And now—goodbye.

HELMER. Goodbye, my dear chap, goodbye.

NORA. Sleep well, Dr. Rank.

RANK. Thank you for that kind wish.

NORA. Wish me the same.

RANK. You? Very well—since you ask. Sleep well. And thank you for the light. (*He nods to them both and goes.*)

HELMER (*quietly*). He's been drinking too much.

NORA (*abstractedly*). Perhaps.

Helmer takes his bunch of keys from his pocket and goes out into the hall.

NORA. Torvald, what do you want out there?

HELMER. I must empty the letter-box. It's absolutely full. There'll be no room for the newspapers in the morning.

NORA. Are you going to work tonight?

HELMER. You know very well I'm not. Hullo, what's this? Someone's been at the lock.

NORA. At the lock—?

HELMER. Yes, I'm sure of it. Who on earth—? Surely not one of the maids? Here's a broken hairpin. Nora, it's yours—

NORA (*quickly*). Then it must have been the children.

HELMER. Well, you'll have to break them of that habit. Hm, hm. Ah, that's done it. (*Takes out the contents of the box and calls into the kitchen.*) Helen! Put out the light on the staircase. (*Comes back into the drawing-room with the letters in his hand and closes the door to the hall.*) Look at this! You see how they've piled up? (*Glances through them.*) What on earth's this?

NORA (*at the window*). The letter! Oh, no, Torvald, no!

HELMER. Two visiting cards—from Rank.

NORA. From Dr. Rank?

HELMER (*looks at them*). Peter Rank, M.D. They were on top. He must have dropped them in as he left.

NORA. Has he written anything on them?

HELMER. There's a black cross above his name. Look. Rather gruesome, isn't it? It looks just as though he was announcing his death.

NORA. He is.

HELMER. What? Do you know something? Has he told you anything?

NORA. Yes. When these cards come, it means he's said goodbye to us. He wants to shut himself up in his house and die.

HELMER. Ah, poor fellow. I knew I wouldn't be seeing him for much longer. But so soon—! And now he's going to slink away and hide like a wounded beast.

NORA. When the time comes, it's best to go silently. Don't you think so, Torvald?

HELMER (*walks up and down*). He was so much a part of our life. I can't realize that he's gone. His suffering and loneliness seemed to provide a kind of dark background to the happy sunlight of our marriage. Well, perhaps it's best this way. For him, anyway. (*Stops walking.*) And perhaps for us too, Nora. Now we have only each other. (*Embraces her.*) Oh, my beloved wife—I feel as though I could never hold you close enough. Do you know, Nora, often I wish some terrible danger might threaten you, so that I could offer my life and my blood, everything, for your sake.

NORA (*tears herself loose and says in a clear, firm voice*). Read your letters now, Torvald.

HELMER. No, no. Not tonight. Tonight I want to be with you, my darling wife—

NORA. When your friend is about to die—?

HELMER. You're right. This news has upset us both. An ugliness has come between us; thoughts of death and dissolution. We must try to forget them. Until then—you go to your room; I shall go to mine.

NORA (*throws her arms around his neck*). Good night, Torvald! Good night!

HELMER (*kisses her on the forehead*). Good night, my darling little songbird. Sleep well, Nora. I'll go and read my letters.

He goes into the study with the letters in his hand, and closes the door.

NORA (*wild-eyed, fumbles around, seizes Helmer's cloak, throws it round herself and whispers quickly, hoarsely*). Never see him again. Never. Never. Never. (*Throws the shawl over her head.*) Never see the children again. Them too. Never. Never. Oh—the icy black water! Oh—that bottomless—that—! Oh, if only it were all over! Now he's got it—he's reading it. Oh, no, no! Not yet! Goodbye, Torvald! Goodbye, my darlings!

She turns to run into the hall. As she does so, Helmer throws open his door and stands there with an open letter in his hand.

HELMER. Nora!

NORA (*shrieks*). Ah—!

HELMER. What is this? Do you know what is in this letter?

NORA. Yes, I know. Let me go! Let me go!

HELMER (*holds her back*). Go? Where?

NORA (*tries to tear herself loose*). You mustn't try to save me, Torvald!

HELMER (*staggers back*). Is it true? Is it true, what he writes? Oh, my God! No, no—it's impossible, it can't be true!

NORA. It *is* true. I've loved you more than anything else in the world.

HELMER. Oh, don't try to make silly excuses.

NORA (*takes a step towards him*). Torvald—

HELMER. Wretched woman! What have you done?

NORA. Let me go! You're not going to suffer for my sake. I won't let you!

HELMER. Stop being theatrical. (*Locks the front door.*) You're going to stay here and explain yourself. Do you understand what you've done? Answer me! Do you understand?

NORA (*looks unflinchingly at him and, her expression growing colder, says*). Yes. Now I am beginning to understand.

HELMER (*walking around the room*). Oh, what a dreadful awakening! For eight whole years—she who was my joy and my pride—a hypocrite, a liar—worse, worse—a criminal! Oh, the hideousness of it! Shame on you, shame!

Nora is silent and stares unblinkingly at him.

HELMER (*stops in front of her*). I ought to have guessed that something of this sort would happen. I should have foreseen it. All your father's recklessness and instability—be quiet!—I repeat, all your father's recklessness and instability he has handed on to you. No religion, no morals, no sense of duty! Oh, how I have been punished for closing my eyes to his faults! I did it for your sake. And now you reward me like this.

NORA. Yes. Like this.

HELMER. Now you have destroyed all my happiness. You have ruined my whole future. Oh, it's too dreadful to contemplate! I am in the power of a man who is completely without scruples. He can do what he likes with me, demand what he pleases, order me to do anything—I dare not disobey him. I am condemned to humiliation and ruin simply for the weakness of a woman.

NORA. When I am gone from this world, you will be free.

HELMER. Oh, don't be melodramatic. Your father was always ready with that kind of remark. How would it help me if you were "gone from this world," as you put it? It wouldn't assist me in the slightest. He can still make all the facts public; and if he does, I may quite easily be suspected of having been an accomplice in your crime. People may think that I was behind it—that it was I who encouraged you! And for all this I have to thank you, you whom I have carried on my hands through all the years of our marriage! Now do you realize what you've done to me?

NORA (*coldly calm*). Yes.

HELMER. It's so unbelievable I can hardly credit it. But we must try to find some way out. Take off that shawl. Take it off, I say! I must try to buy him off somehow. This thing must be hushed up at any price. As regards our relationship—we must appear to be living together just as before. Only *appear*, of course. You will therefore continue to reside here. That is understood. But the children shall be taken out of your hands. I dare no longer entrust them to you. Oh, to have to say this to the woman I once loved so dearly—and whom I still—! Well, all that must be finished. Henceforth there can be no question of happiness; we must merely strive to save what shreds and tatters—(*The front door bell rings. Helmer starts.*) What can that be? At this hour? Surely not—? He wouldn't—? Hide yourself, Nora. Say you're ill.

Nora does not move. Helmer goes to the door of the room and opens it. The Maid is standing half-dressed in the hall.

MAID. A letter for madam.

HELMER. Give it to me. (*Seizes the letter and shuts the door.*) Yes, it's from him. You're not having it. I'll read this myself.

NORA. Read it.

HELMER (*by the lamp*). I hardly dare to. This may mean the end for us both. No, I must know. (*Tears open the letter hastily; reads a few lines; looks at a piece of paper which is enclosed with it; utters a cry of joy.*) Nora! (*She looks at him questioningly.*) Nora! No—I must read it once more. Yes, yes, it's true! I am saved! Nora, I am saved!

NORA. What about me?

HELMER. You too, of course. We're both saved, you and I. Look! He's returning your I.O.U. He writes that he is sorry for what has happened—a happy accident has changed his life—oh, what does it matter what he writes? We are saved, Nora! No one can harm you now. Oh, Nora, Nora—no, first let me destroy this filthy thing. Let me see—! (*Glances at the I.O.U.*) No, I don't want to look at it. I shall merely regard the whole business as a dream. (*He tears the I.O.U. and both letters into pieces, throws them into the stove, and watches them burn.*) There. Now they're destroyed. He wrote that ever since Christmas Eve you've been—oh, these must have been three dreadful days for you, Nora.

NORA. Yes. It's been a hard fight.

HELMER. It must have been terrible—seeing no way out except—no, we'll forget the whole sordid business. We'll just be happy and go on telling ourselves over and over again: "It's over! It's over!" Listen to me. Nora. You don't seem to realize. It's over! Why are you looking so pale? Ah, my poor little Nora, I understand. You can't believe that I have forgiven you. But I have, Nora. I swear it to you. I have forgiven you everything. I know that what you did you did for your love of me.

NORA. That is true.

HELMER. You have loved me as a wife should love her husband. It was simply that in your inexperience you chose the wrong means. But do you think I love you any the less because you don't know how to act on your own initiative? No, no. Just lean on me. I shall counsel you. I shall guide you. I would not be a true man if your feminine helplessness did not make you doubly attractive in my eyes. You mustn't mind the hard words I said to you in those first dreadful moments when my whole world seemed to be tumbling about my ears. I have forgiven you, Nora. I swear it to you; I have forgiven you.

NORA. Thank you for your forgiveness.

She goes out through the door, right.

HELMER. No, don't go—(*Looks in.*) What are you doing there?

NORA (*offstage*). Taking off my fancy dress.

HELMER (*by the open door*). Yes, do that. Try to calm yourself and get your balance again, my frightened little songbird. Don't be afraid. I have broad wings to shield you. (*Begins to walk around near the door.*) How lovely and peaceful this little home of ours is, Nora. You are safe here; I shall watch over you like a hunted dove which I have snatched unharmed from the claws of the falcon. Your wildly beating little heart shall find peace with me. It will happen, Nora; it will take time, but it will happen, believe me. Tomorrow all this will seem quite different. Soon everything will be as it was before. I shall no longer need to remind you that I have forgiven you; your own heart will tell you that it is true. Do you really think I could ever bring myself to disown you, or even to reproach you? Ah, Nora, you don't understand what goes on in a husband's heart. There is something indescribably wonderful and satisfying for a husband in knowing that he has forgiven his wife—forgiven her unreservedly, from the bottom of his heart. It means that she has become his property in a double sense; he has, as it were, brought her into the world anew; she is now not only his wife but also his child. From now on that is what you shall be to me, my poor, helpless, bewildered little creature. Never be frightened of anything again, Nora. Just open your heart to me. I shall be both your will and your conscience. What's this? Not in bed? Have you changed?

NORA (*in her everyday dress*). Yes, Torvald. I've changed.

HELMER. But why now—so late—?

NORA. I shall not sleep tonight.

HELMER. But, my dear Nora—

NORA (*looks at her watch*). It isn't that late. Sit down here, Torvald. You and I have a lot to talk about.

She sits down on one side of the table.

HELMER. Nora, what does this mean? You look quite drawn—

NORA. Sit down. It's going to take a long time. I've a lot to say to you.

HELMER (*sits down on the other side of the table*). You alarm me, Nora. I don't understand you.

NORA. No, that's just it. You don't understand me. And I've never understood you—until this evening. No, don't interrupt me. Just listen to what I have to say. You and I have got to face facts, Torvald.

HELMER. What do you mean by that?

NORA (*after a short silence*). Doesn't anything strike you about the way we're sitting here?

HELMER. What?

NORA. We've been married for eight years. Does it occur to you that this is the first time that we two, you and I, man and wife, have ever had a serious talk together?

HELMER. Serious? What do you mean, serious?

NORA. In eight whole years—no, longer—ever since we first met—we have never exchanged a serious word on a serious subject.

HELMER. Did you expect me to drag you into all my worries—worries you couldn't possibly have helped me with?

NORA. I'm not talking about worries. I'm simply saying that we have never sat down seriously to try to get to the bottom of anything.

HELMER. But, my dear Nora, what on earth has that got to do with you?

NORA. That's just the point. You have never understood me. A great wrong has been done to me, Torvald. First by Papa, and then by you.

HELMER. What? But we two have loved you more than anyone in the world!

NORA (shakes her head). You have never loved me. You just thought it was fun to be in love with me.

HELMER. Nora, what kind of a way is this to talk?

NORA. It's the truth, Torvald. When I lived with Papa, he used to tell me what he thought about everything, so that I never had any opinions but his. And if I did have any of my own, I kept them quiet, because he wouldn't have liked them. He called me his little doll, and he played with me just the way I played with my dolls. Then I came here to live in your house—

HELMER. What kind of a way is that to describe our marriage?

NORA (undisturbed). I mean, then I passed from Papa's hands into yours. You arranged everything the way you wanted it, so that I simply took over your taste in everything—or pretended I did—I don't really know—I think it was a little of both—first one and then the other. Now I look back on it, it's as if I've been living here like a pauper, from hand to mouth. I performed tricks for you, and you gave me food and drink. But that was how you wanted it. You and Papa have done me a great wrong. It's your fault that I have done nothing with my life.

HELMER. Nora, how can you be so unreasonable and ungrateful? Haven't you been happy here?

NORA. No; never. I used to think I was; but I haven't ever been happy.

HELMER. Not—not happy?

NORA. No. I've just had fun. You've always been very kind to me. But our home has never been anything but a playroom. I've been your doll-wife, just as I used to be Papa's doll-child. And the children have been my dolls. I used to think it was fun when you came in and played with me, just as they think it's fun when I

go in and play games with them. That's all our marriage has been, Torvald.

HELMER. There may be a little truth in what you say, though you exaggerate and romanticize. But from now on it'll be different. Playtime is over. Now the time has come for education.

NORA. Whose education? Mine or the children's?

HELMER. Both yours and the children's, my dearest Nora.

NORA. Oh, Torvald, you're not the man to educate me into being the right wife for you.

HELMER. How can you say that?

NORA. And what about me? Am I fit to educate the children?

HELMER. Nora!

NORA. Didn't you say yourself a few minutes ago that you dare not leave them in my charge?

HELMER. In a moment of excitement. Surely you don't think I meant it seriously?

NORA. Yes. You were perfectly right. I'm not fitted to educate them. There's something else I must do first. I must educate myself. And you can't help me with that. It's something I must do by myself. That's why I'm leaving you.

HELMER (jumps up). What did you say?

NORA. I must stand on my own feet if I am to find out the truth about myself and about life. So I can't go on living here with you any longer.

HELMER. Nora, Nora!

NORA. I'm leaving you now, at once. Christine will put me up for tonight—

HELMER. You're out of your mind! You can't do this! I forbid you!

NORA. It's no use your trying to forbid me any more. I shall take with me nothing but what is mine. I don't want anything from you, now or ever.

HELMER. What kind of madness is this?

NORA. Tomorrow I shall go home—I mean, to where I was born. It'll be easiest for me to find some kind of a job there.

HELMER. But you're blind! You've no experience of the world—

NORA. I must try to get some, Torvald.

HELMER. But to leave your home, your husband, your children! Have you thought what people will say?

NORA. I can't help that. I only know that I must do this.

HELMER. But this is monstrous! Can you neglect your most sacred duties?

NORA. What do you call my most sacred duties?

HELMER. Do I have to tell you? Your duties towards your husband, and your children.

NORA. I have another duty which is equally sacred.

HELMER. You have not. What on earth could that be?

NORA. My duty towards myself.

HELMER. First and foremost you are a wife and a mother.

NORA. I don't believe that any longer. I believe that I am first and foremost a human being, like you—or anyway, that I must try to become one. I know most people think as you do, Torvald, and I know there's something of the sort to be found in books. But I'm no longer prepared to accept what people say and what's written in books. I must think things out for myself, and try to find my own answer.

HELMER. Do you need to ask where your duty lies in your own home? Haven't you an infallible guide in such matters—your religion?

NORA. Oh, Torvald, I don't really know what religion means.

HELMER. What are you saying?

NORA. I only know what Pastor Hansen told me when I went to confirmation. He explained that religion meant this and that. When I get away from all this and can think things out on my own, that's one of the questions I want to look into. I want to find out whether what Pastor Hansen said was right—or anyway, whether it is right for me.

HELMER. But it's unheard of for so young a woman to behave like this! If religion cannot guide you, let me at least appeal to your conscience. I presume you have some moral feelings left? Or—perhaps you haven't? Well, answer me.

NORA. Oh, Torvald, that isn't an easy question to answer. I simply don't know. I don't know where I am in these matters. I only know that these things mean something quite different to me from what they do to you. I've learned now that certain laws are different from what I'd imagined them to be; but I can't accept that such laws can be right. Has a woman really not the right to spare her dying father pain, or save her husband's life? I can't believe that.

HELMER. You're talking like a child. You don't understand how society works.

NORA. No, I don't. But now I intend to learn. I must try to satisfy myself which is right, society or I.

HELMER. Nora, you're ill; you're feverish. I almost believe you're out of your mind.

NORA. I've never felt so sane and sure in my life.

HELMER. You feel sure that it is right to leave your husband and your children?

NORA. Yes. I do.

HELMER. Then there is only one possible explanation.

NORA. What?

HELMER. That you don't love me any longer.

NORA. No, that's exactly it.

HELMER. Nora! How can you say this to me?

NORA. Oh, Torvald, it hurts me terribly to have to say it, because you've always been so kind to me. But I can't help it. I don't love you any longer.

HELMER (*controlling his emotions with difficulty*). And you feel quite sure about this too?

NORA. Yes, absolutely sure. That's why I can't go on living here any longer.

HELMER. Can you also explain why I have lost your love?

NORA. Yes, I can. It happened this evening, when the miracle failed to happen. It was then that I realized you weren't the man I'd thought you to be.

HELMER. Explain more clearly. I don't understand you.

NORA. I've waited so patiently, for eight whole years—well, good heavens, I'm not such a fool as to suppose that miracles occur every day. Then this dreadful thing happened to me, and then I *knew*: "Now the miracle will take place!" When Krogstad's letter was lying out there, it never occurred to me for a moment that you would let that man trample over you. I *knew* that you would say to him: "Publish the facts to the world." And when he had done this—

HELMER. Yes, what then? When I'd exposed my wife's name to shame and scandal—

NORA. Then I was certain that you would step forward and take all the blame on yourself, and say: "I am the one who is guilty!"

HELMER. Nora!

NORA. You're thinking I wouldn't have accepted such a sacrifice from you? No, of course I wouldn't! But what would my word have counted for against yours? That was the miracle I was hoping for, and dreading. And it was to prevent it happening that I wanted to end my life.

HELMER. Nora, I would gladly work for you night and day, and endure sorrow and hardship for your sake. But no man can be expected to sacrifice his honor, even for the person he loves.

NORA. Millions of women have done it.

HELMER. Oh, you think and talk like a stupid child.

NORA. That may be. But you neither think nor talk like the man I could share my life with. Once you'd got over your fright—and you weren't frightened of what might threaten me, but only of what threatened you—once the danger was past, then as far as you were concerned it was exactly as though nothing had happened. I was your little songbird just as before—your doll whom henceforth you would take particular care to protect from the world because she was so weak and fragile. (*Gets up*.) Torvald, in that moment

I realized that for eight years I had been living here with a complete stranger, and had borne him three children—! Oh, I can't bear to think of it! I could tear myself to pieces!

HELMER (*sadly*). I see it, I see it. A gulf has indeed opened between us. Oh, but Nora—couldn't it be bridged?

NORA. As I am now, I am no wife for you.

HELMER. I have the strength to change.

NORA. Perhaps—if your doll is taken from you.

HELMER. But to be parted—to be parted from you! No, no, Nora, I can't conceive of it happening!

NORA (*goes into the room, right*). All the more necessary that it should happen.

She comes back with her outdoor things and a small traveling-bag, which she puts down on a chair by the table.

HELMER. Nora, Nora, not now! Wait till tomorrow!

NORA (*puts on her coat*). I can't spend the night in a strange man's house.

HELMER. But can't we live here as brother and sister, then—?

NORA (*fastens her hat*). You know quite well it wouldn't last. (*Puts on her shawl.*) Goodbye, Torvald. I don't want to see the children. I know they're in better hands than mine. As I am now, I can be nothing to them.

HELMER. But some time, Nora—some time—?

NORA. How can I tell? I've no idea what will happen to me.

HELMER. But you are my wife, both as you are and as you will be.

NORA. Listen, Torvald. When a wife leaves her husband's house, as I'm doing now, I'm told that according to the law he is freed of any obligations towards her. In any case, I release you from any such obligations. You mustn't feel bound to me in any way, however small, just as I shall not feel bound to you. We must both be quite free. Here is your ring back. Give me mine.

HELMER. That too?

NORA. That too.

HELMER. Here it is.

NORA. Good. Well, now it's over. I'll leave the keys here. The servants know about everything to do with the house—much better than I do. Tomorrow, when I have left town, Christine will come to pack the things I brought here from home. I'll have them sent on after me.

HELMER. This is the end then! Nora, will you never think of me any more?

NORA. Yes, of course. I shall often think of you and the children and this house.

HELMER. May I write to you, Nora?

NORA. No, never. You mustn't do that.

HELMER. But at least you must let me send you—

NORA. Nothing. Nothing.

HELMER. But if you should need help?—

NORA. I tell you, no. I don't accept things from strangers.

HELMER. Nora—can I never be anything but a stranger to you?

NORA (*picks up her bag*). Oh, Torvald! Then the miracle of miracles would have to happen.

HELMER. The miracle of miracles?

NORA. You and I would both have to change so much that—oh, Torvald, I don't believe in miracles any longer.

HELMER. But I want to believe in them. Tell me. We should have to change so much that—?

NORA. That life together between us two could become a marriage. Goodbye.

She goes out through the hall.

HELMER (*sinks down on a chair by the door and buries his face in his hands*). Nora! Nora! (*Looks round and gets up.*) Empty! She's gone! (*A hope strikes him.*) The miracle of miracles—?

The street door is slammed shut downstairs.

COMMENTARY

Note: The following essay represents a single interpretation of the play. For other perspectives on A Doll's House, *consult the essays listed below.*

Like many realistic plays, *A Doll's House* is based on an actual occurrence. A young mother named Laura Kieler illegally signed a large bank note to finance treatment for her tubercular husband. Trying to cash a forged check, she was apprehended, charged as an unfit mother by her husband, and committed to an asylum. Similarly, *A Doll's House* tells the simple story of a young wife, Nora Helmer, who appears to be the ideal model of a nineteenth-century homemaker. She is totally devoted to her husband and children, but she unknowingly creates a potentially explosive situation. To borrow money to finance a life-saving trip for her sick husband, Torvald, Nora forged her father's name, thus violating both social customs and public statutes. After her husband's recovery, the Helmers are "one happy little family" until the loan's originator, Nils Krogstad, attempts to blackmail Nora. She assumes that Torvald will appreciate her life-saving initiative when her secret is revealed, but Nora's life is shattered when her husband castigates her as "a hypocrite, a liar—worse than that—a criminal!" with "no religion, no moral code, no sense of duty." Horrified, Nora refuses to continue playing the "doll's role" and tells Torvald that she is leaving. When he reminds her that should she leave she would "be betraying [her] most sacred duty . . . towards [her] husband and [her] children," she reveals that she must follow "another duty just as sacred. . . . My duty to myself." Then, as Nora exited and "the street door is slammed shut," the reverberation was heard throughout the Western theatrical world.

The ending of the play was so shocking that many producers refused to stage the play and demanded that the ending be changed. (A leading actress of the day turned down the role of Nora for fear that her admirers might see her as one who supported Nora's "unwomanly" action.) To secure venues for his work, Ibsen wrote an alternate ending to the play in which Nora remained with Torvald, an outcome much more palatable to his conservative, Victorian audience. Defiantly, Ibsen wrote *Ghosts* to depict the disastrous consequences when a wife does not leave her oppressive husband.

Both the content and form of the play were shocking for nineteenth-century audiences. Accustomed to seeing sentimental comedies, well-made plays, and melodramas wherein traditional values always triumphed, the original audiences of *A Doll's House* were taken aback by the effrontery of a woman who asserts her individuality at the expense of her family. As the climax of the play approached, they no doubt anticipated a contrite Nora who would be forgiven by a benevolent Torvald, thereby ensuring a happy ending.

The dramatic form in which Ibsen's ideas were expressed was equally foreign to audiences in 1879. While they were accustomed to plays in which the emotional intensity grew gradually from the exposition to the climax, Ibsen halted the action in mid-crisis to discuss the reasons behind Nora's forgery and for her leaving. The audience was thus forced to hold its emotions in check to consider the social implications of her actions.

Because of its revolutionary style, two additional problems arise when analyzing the play. First, Ibsen's basic premise was misunderstood. Original audiences mistakenly assumed, "much to Ibsen's chagrin," as theater historian Oscar Brockett has noted, that he was promoting a "feminist" point of view. True, the play served as a rallying point for early advocates of feminism who demanded more legal rights and suffrage. While considering this interpretation, we must remember that fundamentally the play advocates the sovereignty of the individual, and it is not a piece of feminist propaganda. Michael Meyer, among Ibsen's most respected biographers, argues that the play stresses "that the primary duty of anyone was to find out who he or she really was and to become that person." Indeed, Ibsen himself, in an address to the Norwegian Women's Rights League, stated that he "must disclaim the honor of having consciously worked for the women's rights movement. I am not even quite clear what this women's rights movement really is. To me it has seemed a problem of humanity in general."

Second, what we regard as a glaring error in Ibsen's craftsmanship went essentially unnoticed during early productions of the play. While those who debated the appropriateness of Nora's departure focused on her action, the most disconcerting aspect from the point of view of the play's construction is that in the discussion scene Nora, heretofore a rather sheltered "plaything" or "doll," suddenly metamorphoses into an articulate social advocate. She launches into an exquisite discourse on the new morality, which champions the rights of the individual over the expectations of society. Her sudden transformation seems an abrupt departure from the logic of the action that governed the play to that point.

Furthermore, the 1879 audience may have overlooked another innovative aspect of Ibsen's style: his use of the setting as an analogy for theme. Even contemporary audiences, predisposed to adopt a feminist reading of the play, might also overlook the significance of the setting so carefully described by Ibsen. While neoclassic writers confined the action to a single location and romantic writers, who disdained the unity of place, presented their action as sprawling across a continent, Ibsen confined the action to a single setting to enhance his theme rather than to observe or oppose any "rules." In *A Doll's House*, Ibsen gives us the literal and figurative creation of Torvald's "doll's house."

It is no accident that the play transpires in what Victorians called the "parlor" (literally, a room for talk or discussion). Today we might call it a "living room." The first words of the text describe it as "A comfortably and tastefully, but not expensively furnished room." Complete with all the amenities of the day—"a piano . . . a small sofa . . . a [porcelain lined] stove . . . a couple of armchairs and a rocking chair . . ."—it is a cozy home for a "twittering little lark," a safe habitat for a "bustling little squirrel." In the opening scenes it is an ideal "doll's house." But before we are twenty minutes into the play, it is clear that this comfortable "living room" becomes an uncomfortable "dying room" where Nora is incarcerated. She has been sentenced by Torvald and society to spend her life shuffling between the other important rooms—the bedroom, the kitchen, and the children's room—to carry out the traditional roles of the Victorian woman. Nora is confronted with the choice of accepting this fate or exerting her individuality.

Should she remain confined in this room where there is security without liberty? Or, should she liberate herself at the expense of security? While she initially accepts her imprisonment because she believes there is the possibility of what Torvald calls "the wonderful" happening in their marriage, her optimism is destroyed by Torvald's reaction to her secret. His selfishness, his preoccupation with his public reputation, and his attacks on her fitness as wife and mother expose him as a self-centered manipulator, not as a loving husband. Ironically, the living room eventually becomes not only a "liberating room" for Nora but also a prison for Torvald, its former warden.

Other perspectives on *A Doll's House*:

McDonald, Jan. "New Women in the New Drama." *New Theatre Quarterly* 6 (February 1990): 31–42.

Templeton, Joan. "The *Doll's House* Backlash: Criticism, Feminism, and Ibsen." *PMLA* 104 (January 1989) 1: 28–40.

See *A Doll's House* on video:

A Doll's House. Dir. Patrick Garland. Perf. Claire Bloom, Anthony Hopkins, and Ralph Richardson. 95 min., 1973.

A Doll's House. Dir. Joseph Losey. Perf. Jane Fonda, Edward Fox, and Trevor Howard. 105 min., 1973.

Other Ibsen plays on video/film:

An Enemy of the People. Dir. Jack O'Brien. Perf. John Glover and George Grizzard. 118 min., 1990.

Ghosts. Perf. Dorothy Tutin and Richard Pasco. 90 min., 1983.

Hedda Gabler. Adapted by John Osborne. Perf. Diana Rigg, Denis Lil, and Philip Bond. 78 min., 1976.

About Ibsen:

Henrik Ibsen: The Master Playwright. Films for the Humanities, 58 min., 1987.

Henrik Ibsen: Sphinx—Who Are You? Films for the Humanities, 52 min., 1999.

Immortal Ibsen. Films for the Humanities, 50 min., N.D.

SHOWCASE | THE *TARANTELLA* AND OTHER HEALING DANCES

Nora's frenzied *tarantella* in the second act of *A Doll's House* derives from a centuries-old Italian "healing dance" in which the dancer performs convulsive movements in frenetic 6/8 time. In the late Middle Ages Italy was afflicted with *tarantism*, an epidemic illness associated with the venomous bite of a tarantula (hence the name, *tarantella*). The poison caused the bite victim to lapse into a hysterical fury, often foaming at the mouth, and the cure—or so it was believed—was to perform a violent, swirling dance that distributed the poison throughout the body and forced the dancer to "sweat out" the venom. The town of Taranto, in Italy's southern Puglia region, became most associated with the *tarantella* (also the title of an Italian folk song). Incidentally, such acclaimed European composers as Chopin, Liszt, and Carl Maria von Weber wrote *tarantellas* for the piano. Ibsen, of course, lived in Italy while in self-imposed exile from Norway and likely saw the *tarantella* performed there. Thus, he wisely scripted the *tarantella* into his most famous play, for Nora is indeed trying to exorcise the "poison" that has infected the Helmer household. The dance not only enhances the play's central theme, it is also a remarkably theatrical moment in an otherwise realistic play.

Healing dances are virtually as old as humanity itself, and considerable evidence suggests that the theater grew from various forms of ecstatic dancing, many in worship of gods (e.g., rites in honor of Dionysus in ancient Greece), others specifically intended to "cast out" evil spirits. Often, of course, the two functions were combined.

The early Middle Ages in Europe were a particularly fertile time for ecstatic dances that grew out of the Catholic mass. Some dealt with death, a very real presence to people in the plague-ridden Middle Ages. The Dance of Death, also known as the *danse macabre* or *totentanz*, was especially popular. A dancer playing Death seized onlookers, regardless of their age or social status, and led them in a frenzied dance that reminded all that Death was indiscriminate. The renowned Swedish filmmaker Ingmar Bergman uses this dance to great effect in his allegorical movie, *The Seventh Seal*. Ibsen, also a Scandinavian, surely knew the dance.

The St. Vitus Dance, which dates from the 11th and 12th centuries in Northern Europe, may be the forerunner of the *tarantella* (versions of the St. Vitus Dance could be found in Italy in the 14th century). It was performed by masses of people, all dancing and screaming hysterically, often in response to the epileptic-like seizures associated with the Black Death that periodically ravaged Europe. Like the *tarantella*, the St. Vitus Dance was intended to purge illness from the dancers by forcing them to sweat out impurities. Such healing dances purge the body, and the Greek word for "purgation" was *catharsis*, the cornerstone of Aristotle's theory of the restorative powers of drama and theater. Once again a folk rite invests the theater with its power to heal the illnesses of both the individual and society.

THE CHERRY ORCHARD

ANTON CHEKHOV

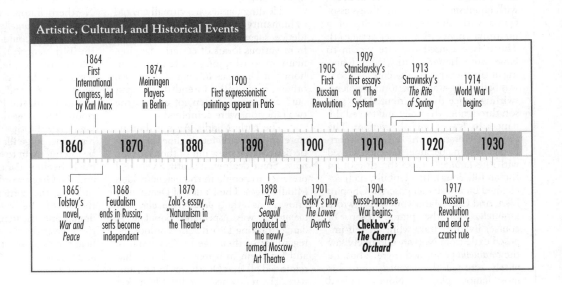

Artistic, Cultural, and Historical Events

1864
First
International
Congress, led
by Karl Marx

1874
Meiningen
Players
in Berlin

1900
First expressionistic
paintings appear in Paris

1905
First
Russian
Revolution

1909
Stanislavsky's
first essays
on "The
System"

1913
Stravinsky's
The Rite
of Spring

1914
World War I
begins

1860 1870 1880 1890 1900 1910 1920 1930

1865
Tolstoy's
novel,
War and
Peace

1868
Feudalism
ends in Russia;
serfs become
independent

1879
Zola's essay,
"Naturalism in
the Theater"

1898
The
Seagull
produced at
the newly
formed Moscow
Art Theatre

1901
Gorky's play
The Lower
Depths

1904
Russo-Japanese
War begins;
Chekhov's
The Cherry
Orchard

1917
Russian
Revolution
and end of
czarist rule

ANTON CHEKHOV (1860–1904)

Few playwrights have achieved such an exalted reputation on the basis of so few plays. Other than a number of short plays and farces (e.g., *The Marriage Proposal* and *The Boor*), Chekhov's place in the Pantheon of great dramatists rests upon four principal works: *The Sea Gull* (1895), *Uncle Vanya* (1899), *The Three Sisters* (1901), and *The Cherry Orchard* (1903). Perhaps more than any other of his contemporaries in Realism, Chekhov has inspired subsequent generations of writers to attempt his facile portrayal of the day-to-day drama of life in all its simplicity. Tennessee Williams, William Inge, Samuel Beckett, and Wendy Wasserstein, to name but a few, are among the many playwrights who have acknowledged Chekhov as their mentor. Even Bernard Shaw attempted to write "a fantasia in the Russian manner" (his subtitle for *Heartbreak House*) and produced the kind of play Chekhov might have written were he Ibsen. (You may read this play later in Part I.)

The son of a despotic storekeeper from the seaport village of Taganrog, Chekhov wrote to support himself while studying medicine at the University of Moscow. He wrote superb short stories and "vaudevilles," many based on his observations as a doctor. His daily rounds permitted him to see firsthand the rhythms of life: births, deaths, recoveries, lingering illnesses, despair, joy, uncertainty, and faith. These became the subjects of his stories and particularly his dramatic masterpieces. His own life was marked by many of these same difficulties. His first attempts at serious drama were rejected, largely because they were misunderstood. He was chronically ill and spent his last years in the warm-weather city of Yalta struggling against the tuberculosis that eventually killed him in 1904. He did not see his plays performed successfully until Stanislavsky and the Moscow Art Theatre (MAT) toured the Crimea in 1900. And like many of his characters, he was victimized by unrequited love. In 1890 he trekked to the Sakhalin *gulag* to study penal conditions, motivated in part by his immense humanitarianism, and in part to forget the woman who spurned him. In 1901 he married a leading actress of the MAT, Olga Knipper, only to die three years later. Amidst the disappointments that plagued him, he remained a lover of humanity despite its shortcomings. In *The Sea Gull*, Nina perhaps comes closer than any of his characters to articulating Chekhov's credo: ". . . what matters most for us, whether we're writers or actors, isn't fame or glamour, or any of the things I used to dream of. What matters most is knowing how to endure, knowing how to bear your cross and still have faith. I have faith now and I can stand my suffering. . . . I am not afraid of life."

In the introductory material to Part I, Chekhov's distinctive techniques were discussed in conjunction with the rise of realistic drama. His use of the anticlimax, his focus on a number of individuals rather than a central protagonist, and his depiction of trivial actions and seemingly inconsequential exchanges among his characters are trademarks of his dramaturgy. Perhaps the most innovative aspect of Chekhov's dramas, however, is the use of the parallel monologue. His subtle plots are structured around a series of shared monologues in which characters voice their innermost desires, fears, and delusions. In this sense he is among the foremost psychological Realists. But in these ongoing monologues—which are interspersed with those of the other characters—there is a failure to communicate. Chekhov's depiction of individuals trapped in an isolated universe anticipates the work of the Absurdists in the mid-twentieth century.

Unfortunately, Chekhov's plays are often misinterpreted (and are even a source of embarrassment among the Russian people) when they are presented as exercises in gloomy melancholy, largely because the monologues are rendered as angst-ridden laments by actors who take Chekhov's description of his plays as showing "all the grayness of everyday life" too literally. Chekhov and Stanislavsky clashed over the MAT's overly somber treatment of Chekhov's plays, which the writer believed turned his characters into pathetic whiners. For Chekhov, the plays were comedies, albeit serious ones, in which his characters—among whom there are no villains—are like so many people in life: destined to fail, partly because of the inexorable march of time, mostly because of the folly of their misguided aspirations.

Prior to Chekhov, the theater had not faced such characters nor the unflinching realism in which their predicaments were handled. Fortunately, his friend and literary colleague, Count Leo Tolstoy, accurately predicted Chekhov's legacy: ". . . it is possible that in the future, perhaps a hundred years hence, people will be amazed at what they find in Chekhov about the inner workings of the human soul."

AS YOU READ *THE CHERRY ORCHARD*

To the uninitiated Chekhov can be challenging because both readers and audiences in the theater, accustomed to rapidly paced plays and dialogue that usually creates tension, find the Russian's plays deliberately paced and lacking obvious conflict. Though there is a well-defined story that creates suspense in *The Cherry Orchard*—what will happen to Madame Ranevskaya's estate?—most of the play consists of a series of conversations in which the characters express their feelings and fears, yet no one seems to listen. That is because other characters are expressing their feelings and fears (often indirectly) at precisely the same time. Initially, the dialogue seems to lack the conflict we normally expect in a drama. As you read this play, it may be helpful to think of the dialogue not as exchanges between two or more characters but as a series of parallel monologues or even soliloquies. Here we get the pathos that permeates Chekhov's plays as we listen (even if the other characters do not) to lives "being smashed up"—Chekhov's words—while they are simply having dinner.

But the plays are also as comic as they are pathetic, and at precisely the same time. When a character becomes especially morose or filled with self-pity, Chekhov invariably adds a comic moment to undercut the pathos. For instance, at the beginning of Act II Charlotta delivers a long, melancholic tale about her troubled life as she eats a cucumber! It is impossible to do this speech seriously while eating a cucumber. So as you read, listen to the many sad tales told by the various characters, but always watch for the cucumber.

THE CHERRY ORCHARD

—A N T O N C H E K H O V—

Translated by Ann Dunnigan

C H A R A C T E R S

RANEVSKAYA, LYUBOV ANDREYEVNA, *a landowner*
ANYA, *her daughter, seventeen years old*
VARYA, *her adopted daughter, twenty-four years old*
GAYEV, LEONID ANDREYEVICH, *Madame Ranevskaya's brother*
LOPAKHIN, YERMOLAI ALEKSEYEVICH, *a merchant*
TROFIMOV, PYOTR SERGEYEVICH, *a student*
SEMYONOV-PISHCHIK, BORIS BORISOVICH, *a landowner*
CHARLOTTA IVANOVNA, *a governess*
YEPIKHODOV, SEMYON PANTELEYEVICH, *a clerk*
DUNYASHA, *a maid*
FIRS, *an old valet, eighty-seven years old*
YASHA, *a young footman*
A STRANGER
THE STATIONMASTER
A POST-OFFICE CLERK
GUESTS, SERVANTS

The action takes place on Madame Ranevskaya's estate.

ACT I

(*A room that is still called the nursery. One of the doors leads into Anya's room. Dawn; the sun will soon rise. It is May, the cherry trees are in bloom, but it is cold in the orchard; there is a morning frost. The windows in the room are closed. Enter Dunyasha with a candle, and Lopakhin with a book in his hand.*)

LOPAKHIN. The train is in, thank God. What time is it?

DUNYASHA. Nearly two. (*Blows out the candle.*) It's already light.

LOPAKHIN. How late is the train, anyway? A couple of hours at least. (*Yawns and stretches.*) I'm a fine one!

What a fool I've made of myself! Came here on purpose to meet them at the station, and then overslept.... Fell asleep in the chair. It's annoying.... You might have waked me.

DUNYASHA. I thought you had gone. (*Listens.*) They're coming now, I think!

LOPAKHIN (*listens*). No ... they've got to get the luggage and one thing and another. (*Pause.*) Lyubov Andreyevna has lived abroad for five years, I don't know what she's like now.... She's a fine person. Sweet-tempered, simple. I remember when I was a boy of fifteen, my late father—he had a shop in the village then—gave me a punch in the face and made my nose bleed.... We had come into the yard here for some reason or other, and he'd had a drop too much. Lyubov Andreyevna—I remember as if it were yesterday—still young, and so slender, led me to the washstand in this very room, the nursery. "Don't cry, little peasant," she said, "it will heal in time for your wedding...." (*Pause.*) Little peasant ... my father was a peasant, it's true, and here I am in a white waistcoat and tan shoes. Like a pig in a pastry shop.... I may be rich, I've made a lot of money, but if you think about it, analyze it, I'm a peasant through and through. (*Turning pages of the book.*) Here I've been reading this book, and I didn't understand a thing. Fell asleep over it. (*Pause.*)

DUNYASHA. The dogs didn't sleep all night: They can tell that their masters are coming.

LOPAKHIN. What's the matter with you, Dunyasha, you're so ...

DUNYASHA. My hands are trembling. I'm going to faint.

LOPAKHIN. You're much too delicate, Dunyasha. You dress like a lady, and do your hair like one, too. It's not right. You should know your place.

(Enter Yepikhodov with a bouquet; he wears a jacket and highly polished boots that squeak loudly. He drops the flowers as he comes in.)

YEPIKHODOV *(picking up the flowers)*. Here, the gardener sent these. He says you're to put them in the dining room. *(Hands the bouquet to Dunyasha.)*

LOPAKHIN. And bring me some kvas.[1]

DUNYASHA. Yes, sir. *(Goes out.)*

YEPIKHODOV. There's a frost this morning—three degrees—and the cherry trees are in bloom. I cannot approve of our climate. *(Sighs.)* I cannot. Our climate is not exactly conducive. And now, Yermolai Alekseyevich, permit me to append: The day before yesterday I bought myself a pair of boots, which, I venture to assure you, squeak so that it's quite infeasible. What should I grease them with?

LOPAKHIN. Leave me alone. You make me tired.

YEPIKHODOV. Every day some misfortune happens to me. But I don't complain, I'm used to it, I even smile.

(Dunyasha enters, serves Lopakhin the kvas.)

YEPIKHODOV. I'm going. *(Stumbles over a chair and upsets it.)* There! *(As if in triumph.)* Now you see, excuse the expression . . . the sort of circumstances, incidentally. . . . It's really quite remarkable! *(Goes out.)*

DUNYASHA. You know, Yermolai Alekseyich, I have to confess that Yepikhodov has proposed to me.

LOPAKHIN. Ah!

DUNYASHA. And I simply don't know. . . . He's a quiet man, but sometimes, when he starts talking, you can't understand a thing he says. It's nice, and full of feeling, only it doesn't make sense. I sort of like him. He's madly in love with me. But he's an unlucky fellow: Every day something happens to him. They tease him about it around here; they call him Two-and-twenty Troubles.

LOPAKHIN *(listening)*. I think I hear them coming . . .

DUNYASHA. They're coming! What's the matter with me? I'm cold all over.

LOPAKHIN. They're really coming. Let's go and meet them. Will she recognize me? It's five years since we've seen each other.

DUNYASHA *(agitated)*. I'll faint this very minute . . . oh, I'm going to faint!

(Two carriages are heard driving up to the house. Lopakhin and Dunyasha go out quickly. The stage is empty. There is a hubbub in the adjoining rooms. Firs hurriedly crosses the stage leaning on a stick. He

has been to meet Lyubov Andreyevna and wears old-fashioned livery and a high hat. He mutters something to himself, not a word of which can be understood. The noise offstage grows louder and louder. A voice: "Let's go through here. . . ." Enter Lyubov Andreyevna, Anya, Charlotta Ivanovna with a little dog on a chain, all in traveling dress; Varya wearing a coat and kerchief; Gayev, Semyonov-Pishchik, Lopakhin, Dunyasha with a bundle and parasol; servants with luggage—all walk through the room.)*

ANYA. Let's go this way. Do you remember, Mama, what room this is?

LYUBOV ANDREYEVNA *(joyfully, through tears)*. The nursery!

VARYA. How cold it is! My hands are numb. *(To Lyubov Andreyevna.)* Your rooms, both the white one and the violet one, are just as you left them, Mama.

LYUBOV ANDREYEVNA. The nursery . . . my dear, lovely nursery. . . . I used to sleep here when I was little. . . . *(Weeps.)* And now, like a child, I . . . *(Kisses her brother, Varya, then her brother again.)* Varya hasn't changed; she still looks like a nun. And I recognized Dunyasha. . . . *(Kisses Dunyasha.)*

GAYEV. The train was two hours late. How's that? What kind of management is that?

CHARLOTTA *(to Pishchik)*. My dog even eats nuts.

PISHCHIK *(amazed)*. Think of that now!

(They all go out except Anya and Dunyasha.)

DUNYASHA. We've been waiting and waiting for you. . . . *(Takes off Anya's coat and hat.)*

ANYA. I didn't sleep for four nights on the road . . . now I feel cold.

DUNYASHA. It was Lent when you went away, there was snow and frost then, but now? My darling! *(Laughs and kisses her.)* I've waited so long for you, my joy, my precious . . . I must tell you at once, I can't wait another minute. . . .

ANYA *(listlessly)*. What now?

DUNYASHA. The clerk, Yepikhodov, proposed to me just after Easter.

ANYA. You always talk about the same thing. . . . *(Straightening her hair.)* I've lost all my hairpins. . . . *(She is so exhausted she can hardly stand.)*

DUNYASHA. I really don't know what to think. He loves me—he loves me so!

ANYA *(looking through the door into her room, tenderly)*. My room, my windows . . . it's just as though I'd never been away. I am home! Tomorrow morning I'll get up and run into the orchard. . . . Oh, if I could only

[1] kvas beer

sleep! I didn't sleep during the entire journey, I was so tormented by anxiety.

DUNYASHA. Pyotr Sergeich arrived the day before yesterday.

ANYA (*joyfully*). Petya!

DUNYASHA. He's asleep in the bathhouse, he's staying there. "I'm afraid of being in the way," he said. (*Looks at her pocket watch.*) I ought to wake him up, but Varvara Mikhailovna told me not to. "Don't you wake him," she said.

(*Enter Varya with a bunch of keys at her waist.*)

VARYA. Dunyasha, coffee, quickly . . . Mama's asking for coffee.

DUNYASHA. This very minute. (*Goes out.*)

VARYA. Thank God, you've come! You're home again. (*Caressing her.*) My little darling has come back! My pretty one is here!

ANYA. I've been through so much.

VARYA. I can imagine!

ANYA. I left in Holy Week, it was cold then. Charlotta never stopped talking and doing her conjuring tricks the entire journey. Why did you saddle me with Charlotta?

VARYA. You couldn't have traveled alone, darling. At seventeen!

ANYA. When we arrived in Paris, it was cold, snowing. My French is awful. . . . Mama was living on the fifth floor, and when I got there, she had all sorts of Frenchmen and ladies with her, and an old priest with a little book, and it was full of smoke, dismal. Suddenly I felt sorry for Mama, so sorry. I took her head in my arms and held her close and couldn't let her go. Afterward she kept hugging me and crying. . . .

VARYA (*through her tears*). Don't talk about it, don't talk about it. . . .

ANYA. She had already sold her villa near Mentone, and she had nothing left, nothing. And I hadn't so much as a kopeck left, we barely managed to get there. But Mama doesn't understand! When we had dinner in a station restaurant, she always ordered the most expensive dishes and tipped each of the waiters a ruble. Charlotta is the same. And Yasha also ordered a dinner, it was simply awful. You know, Yasha is Mama's footman; we brought him with us.

VARYA. I saw the rogue.

ANYA. Well, how are things? Have you paid the interest?

VARYA. How could we?

ANYA. Oh, my God, my God!

VARYA. In August the estate will be put up for sale.

ANYA. My God!

(*Lopakhin peeps in at the door and moos like a cow.*)

LOPAKHIN. Moo-o-o! (*Disappears.*)

VARYA (*through her tears*). What I couldn't do to him! (*Shakes her fist.*)

ANYA (*embracing Varya, softly*). Varya, has he proposed to you? (*Varya shakes her head.*) But he loves you. . . . Why don't you come to an understanding, what are you waiting for?

VARYA. I don't think anything will ever come of it. He's too busy, he has no time for me . . . he doesn't even notice me. I've washed my hands of him, it makes me miserable to see him. . . . Everyone talks of our wedding, they all congratulate me, and actually there's nothing to it—it's like a dream. . . . (*In a different tone.*) You have a brooch like a bee.

ANYA (*sadly*). Mama bought it. (*Goes into her own room; speaks gaily, like a child.*) In Paris I went up in a balloon!

VARYA. My darling is home! My pretty one has come back!

(*Dunyasha has come in with the coffeepot and prepares coffee.*)

VARYA (*stands at the door of Anya's room*). You know, darling, all day long I'm busy looking after the house, but I keep dreaming. If we could marry you to a rich man I'd be at peace. I could go into a hermitage, then to Kiev, to Moscow, and from one holy place to another. . . . I'd go on and on. What a blessing!

ANYA. The birds are singing in the orchard. What time is it?

VARYA. It must be after two. Time you were asleep, darling. (*Goes into Anya's room.*) What a blessing!

(*Yasha enters with a lap robe and a traveling bag.*)

YASHA (*crosses the stage mincingly*). May one go through here?

DUNYASHA. A person would hardly recognize you, Yasha. Your stay abroad has done wonders for you.

YASHA. Hm. . . . And who are you?

DUNYASHA. When you left here I was only that high— (*indicating with her hand*). I'm Dunyasha, Fyodor Kozoyedov's daughter. You don't remember?

YASHA. Hm. . . . A little cucumber! (*Looks around, then embraces her; she cries out and drops a saucer. He quickly goes out.*)

VARYA (*in a tone of annoyance, from the doorway*). What's going on here?

DUNYASHA (*tearfully*). I broke a saucer.

VARYA. That's good luck.

ANYA. We ought to prepare Mama: Petya is here. . . .

VARYA. I gave orders not to wake him.

ANYA (*pensively*). Six years ago Father died, and a month later brother Grisha drowned in the river . . . a pretty little seven-year-old boy. Mama couldn't bear it and went away . . . went without looking back. . . . (*Shudders.*) How I understand her, if she only knew! (*Pause.*) And Petya Trofimov was Grisha's tutor, he may remind her. . . .

(*Enter Firs wearing a jacket and a white waistcoat.*)

FIRS (*goes to the coffeepot, anxiously*). The mistress will have her coffee here. (*Puts on white gloves.*) Is the coffee ready? (*To Dunyasha, sternly.*) You! Where's the cream?

DUNYASHA. Oh, my goodness! (*Quickly goes out.*)

FIRS (*fussing over the coffeepot*). Ah, what an addlepate! (*Mutters to himself.*) They've come back from Paris. . . . The master used to go to Paris . . . by carriage. . . . (*Laughs.*)

VARYA. What is it, Firs?

FIRS. If you please? (*Joyfully.*) My mistress has come home! At last! Now I can die. . . . (*Weeps with joy.*)

(*Enter Lyubov Andreyevna, Gayev, and Semyonov-Pishchik, the last wearing a sleeveless peasant coat of fine cloth and full trousers. Gayev, as he comes in, goes through the motions of playing billiards.*)

LYUBOV ANDREYEVNA. How does it go? Let's see if I can remember . . . cue ball into the corner! Double the rail to center table.

GAYEV. Cut shot into the corner! There was a time, sister, when you and I used to sleep here in this very room, and now I'm fifty-one, strange as it may seem. . . .

LOPAKHIN. Yes, time passes.

GAYEV. How's that?

LOPAKHIN. Time, I say, passes.

GAYEV. It smells of patchouli here.

ANYA. I'm going to bed. Good night, Mama. (*Kisses her mother.*)

LYUBOV ANDREYEVNA. My precious child. (*Kisses her hands.*) Are you glad to be home? I still feel dazed.

ANYA. Good night, Uncle.

GAYEV (*kisses her face and hands*). God bless you. How like your mother you are! (*To his sister.*) At her age you were exactly like her, Lyuba.

(*Anya shakes hands with Lopakhin and Pishchik and goes out, closing the door after her.*)

LYUBOV ANDREYEVNA. She's exhausted.

PISHCHIK. Must have been a long journey.

VARYA. Well, gentlemen? It's after two, high time you were going.

LYUBOV ANDREYEVNA (*laughs*). You haven't changed, Varya. (*Draws Varya to her and kisses her.*) I'll just drink my coffee and then we'll all go. (*Firs places a cushion under her feet.*) Thank you, my dear. I've got used to coffee. I drink it day and night. Thanks, dear old man. (*Kisses him.*)

VARYA. I'd better see if all the luggage has been brought in.

LYUBOV ANDREYEVNA. Is this really me sitting here? (*Laughs.*) I feel like jumping about and waving my arms. (*Buries her face in her hands.*) What if it's only a dream! God knows I love my country, love it dearly. I couldn't look out the train window, I was crying so! (*Through tears.*) But I must drink my coffee. Thank you, Firs, thank you, my dear old friend. I'm so glad you're still alive.

FIRS. The day before yesterday.

GAYEV. He's hard of hearing.

LOPAKHIN. I must go now, I'm leaving for Kharkov about five o'clock. It's so annoying! I wanted to have a good look at you, and have a talk. You're as splendid as ever.

PISHCHIK (*breathing heavily*). Even more beautiful. . . . Dressed like a Parisienne. . . . There goes my wagon, all four wheels!

LOPAKHIN. Your brother here, Leonid Andreich, says I'm a boor, a moneygrubber, but I don't mind. Let him talk. All I want is that you should trust me as you used to, and that your wonderful, touching eyes should look at me as they did then. Merciful God! My father was one of your father's serfs, and your grandfather's, but you yourself did so much for me once, that I've forgotten all that and love you as if you were my own kin—more than my kin.

LYUBOV ANDREYEVNA. I can't sit still, I simply cannot. (*Jumps up and walks about the room in great excitement.*) I cannot bear this joy. . . . Laugh at me, I'm silly. . . . My dear little bookcase . . . (*kisses bookcase*) my little table . . .

GAYEV. Nurse died while you were away.

LYUBOV ANDREYEVNA (*sits down and drinks coffee*). Yes, God rest her soul. They wrote me.

GAYEV. And Anastasy is dead. Petrushka Kosoi left me and is now with the police inspector in town. (*Takes a box of hard candies from his pocket and begins to suck one.*)

PISHCHIK. My daughter, Dashenka . . . sends her regards . . .

LOPAKHIN. I wish I could tell you something very pleasant and cheering. (*Glances at his watch.*) I must go directly, there's no time to talk, but . . . well, I'll say it in a couple of words. As you know, the cherry orchard is to be sold to pay your debts. The auction is set for August twenty-second, but you need not worry, my dear, you can sleep in peace, there is a way out. This is my plan. Now, please listen! Your estate is only twenty versts[2] from town, the railway runs close by, and if the cherry orchard and the land along the river were cut up into lots and leased for summer cottages, you'd have, at the very least, an income of twenty-five thousand a year.

GAYEV. Excuse me, what nonsense!

LYUBOV ANDREYEVNA. I don't quite understand you, Yermolai Alekseich.

LOPAKHIN. You will get, at the very least, twenty-five rubles a year for a two-and-half-acre lot, and if you advertise now, I guarantee you won't have a single plot of ground left by autumn, everything will be snapped up. In short, I congratulate you, you are saved. The site is splendid, the river is deep. Only, of course, the ground must be cleared . . . you must tear down all the old outbuildings, for instance, and this house, which is worthless, cut down the old cherry orchard—

LYUBOV ANDREYEVNA. Cut it down? Forgive me, my dear, but you don't know what you are talking about. If there is one thing in the whole province that is interesting, not to say remarkable, it's our cherry orchard.

LOPAKHIN. The only remarkable thing about this orchard is that it is very big. There's a crop of cherries every other year, and then you can't get rid of them, nobody buys them.

GAYEV. This orchard is even mentioned in the *Encyclopedia.*

LOPAKHIN (*glancing at his watch*). If we don't think of something and come to a decision, on the twenty-second of August the cherry orchard, and the entire estate, will be sold at auction. Make up your minds! There is no other way out, I swear to you. None whatsoever.

FIRS. In the old days, forty or fifty years ago, the cherries were dried, soaked, marinated, and made into jam, and they used to—

GAYEV. Be quiet, Firs.

FIRS. And they used to send cartloads of dried cherries to Moscow and Kharkov. And that brought in money! The dried cherries were soft and juicy in those days, sweet, fragrant. . . . They had a method then . . .

[2]**versts** A verst is a little more than half a mile.

LYUBOV ANDREYEVNA. And what has become of that method now?

FIRS. Forgotten. Nobody remembers. . . .

PISHCHIK. How was it in Paris? What's it like there? Did you eat frogs?

LYUBOV ANDREYEVNA. I ate crocodiles.

PISHCHIK. Think of that now!

LOPAKHIN. There used to be only the gentry and the peasants living in the country, but now these summer people have appeared. All the towns, even the smallest ones, are surrounded by summer cottages. And it is safe to say that in another twenty years these people will multiply enormously. Now the summer resident only drinks tea on his porch, but it may well be that he'll take to cultivating his acre, and then your cherry orchard will be a happy, rich, luxuriant—

GAYEV (*indignantly*). What nonsense!

(*Enter Varya and Yasha.*)

VARYA. There are two telegrams for you, Mama. (*Picks out a key and with a jingling sound opens an old-fashioned bookcase.*) Here they are.

LYUBOV ANDREYEVNA. From Paris. (*Tears up the telegrams without reading them.*) That's all over. . . .

GAYEV. Do you know, Lyuba, how old this bookcase is? A week ago I pulled out the bottom drawer, and what do I see? Some figures burnt into it. The bookcase was made exactly a hundred years ago. What do you think of that? Eh? We could have celebrated its jubilee. It's an inanimate object, but nevertheless, for all that, it's a bookcase.

PISHCHIK. A hundred years . . . think of that now!

GAYEV. Yes . . . that is something. . . . (*Feeling the bookcase.*) Dear, honored bookcase. I salute thy existence, which for over one hundred years has served the glorious ideals of goodness and justice; thy silent appeal to fruitful endeavor, unflagging in the course of a hundred years, tearfully sustaining through generations of our family, courage and faith in a better future, and fostering in us ideals of goodness and social consciousness. . . .

(*A pause.*)

LOPAKHIN. Yes . . .

LYUBOV ANDREYEVNA. You are the same as ever, Lyonya.

GAYEV (*somewhat embarrassed*). Carom into the corner, cut shot to center table.

LOPAKHIN (*looks at his watch*). Well, time for me to go.

YASHA (*hands medicine to Lyubov Andreyevna*). Perhaps you will take your pills now.

PISHCHIK. Don't take medicaments, dearest lady, they do neither harm nor good. Let me have them, honored lady. (*Takes the pillbox, shakes the pills into his hand, blows on them, puts them into his mouth, and washes them down with kvas.*) There!

LYUBOV ANDREYEVNA (*alarmed*). Why, you must be mad!

PISHCHIK. I've taken all the pills.

LOPAKHIN. What a glutton!

(*Everyone laughs.*)

FIRS. The gentleman stayed with us during Holy Week . . . ate half a bucket of pickles. . . . (*Mumbles.*)

LYUBOV ANDREYEVNA. What is he saying?

VARYA. He's been muttering like that for three years now. We've grown used to it.

YASHA. He's in his dotage.

(*Charlotta Ivanovna, very thin, tightly laced, in a white dress with a lorgnette at her belt, crosses the stage.*)

LOPAKHIN. Forgive me, Charlotta Ivanovna, I haven't had a chance to say how do you do to you. (*Tries to kiss her hand.*)

CHARLOTTA (*pulls her hand away*). If I permit you to kiss my hand you'll be wanting to kiss my elbow next, then my shoulder.

LOPAKHIN. I have no luck today. (*Everyone laughs.*) Charlotta Ivanovna, show us a trick!

LYUBOV ANDREYEVNA. Charlotta, show us a trick!

CHARLOTTA. No. I want to sleep. (*Goes out.*)

LOPAKHIN. In three weeks we'll meet again. (*Kisses Lyubov Andreyevna's hand.*) Good-bye till then. Time to go. (*To Gayev.*) Good-bye. (*Kisses Pishchik.*) Good-bye. (*Shakes hands with Varya, then with Firs and Yasha.*) I don't feel like going. (*To Lyubov Andreyevna.*) If you make up your mind about the summer cottages and come to a decision, let me know; I'll get you a loan of fifty thousand or so. Think it over seriously.

VARYA (*angrily*). Oh, why don't you go!

LOPAKHIN. I'm going, I'm going. (*Goes out.*)

GAYEV. Boor. Oh, pardon. Varya's going to marry him, he's Varya's young man.

VARYA. Uncle dear, you talk too much.

LYUBOV ANDREYEVNA. Well, Varya, I shall be very glad. He's a good man.

PISHCHIK. A man, I must truly say . . . most worthy. . . . And my Dashenka . . . says, too, that . . . says all sorts of things. (*Snores but wakes up at once.*) In any case, honored lady, oblige me . . . a loan of two hundred and forty rubles . . . tomorrow the interest on my mortgage is due. . . .

VARYA (*in alarm*). We have nothing, nothing at all!

LYUBOV ANDREYEVNA. I really haven't any money.

PISHCHIK. It'll turn up. (*Laughs.*) I never lose hope. Just when I thought everything was lost, that I was done for, lo and behold—the railway line ran through my land . . . and they paid me for it. And before you know it, something else will turn up, if not today—tomorrow. . . . Dashenka will win two hundred thousand . . . she's got a lottery ticket.

LYUBOV ANDREYEVNA. The coffee is finished, we can go to bed.

FIRS (*brushing Gayev's clothes, admonishingly*). You've put on the wrong trousers again. What am I to do with you?

VARYA (*softly*). Anya's asleep. (*Quietly opens the window.*) The sun has risen, it's no longer cold. Look, Mama dear, what wonderful trees! Oh, Lord, the air! The starlings are singing!

GAYEV (*opens another window*). The orchard is all white. You haven't forgotten, Lyuba? That long avenue there that runs straight—straight as a stretched-out strap; it gleams on moonlight nights. Remember? You've not forgotten?

LYUBOV ANDREYEVNA (*looking out the window at the orchard*). Oh, my childhood, my innocence! I used to sleep in this nursery, I looked out from here into the orchard, happiness awoke with me each morning, it was just as it is now, nothing has changed. (*Laughing with joy.*) All, all white! Oh, my orchard! After the dark, rainy autumn and the cold winter, you are young again, full of happiness, the heavenly angels have not forsaken you. . . . If I could cast off this heavy stone weighing on my breast and shoulders, if I could forget my past!

GAYEV. Yes, and the orchard will be sold for our debts, strange as it may seem. . . .

LYUBOV ANDREYEVNA. Look, our dead mother walks in the orchard . . . in a white dress! (*Laughs with joy.*) It is she!

GAYEV. Where?

VARYA. God be with you, Mama dear.

LYUBOV ANDREYEVNA. There's no one there, I just imagined it. To the right, as you turn to the summerhouse, a slender white sapling is bent over . . . it looks like a woman.

(*Enter Trofimov wearing a shabby student's uniform and spectacles.*)

LYUBOV ANDREYEVNA. What a wonderful orchard! The white masses of blossoms, the blue sky—

TROFIMOV. Lyubov Andreyevna! (*She looks around at him.*) I only want to pay my respects, then I'll go at once. (*Kisses her hand ardently.*) I was told to wait until morning, but I hadn't the patience.

(*Lyubov Andreyevna looks at him, puzzled.*)

VARYA (*through tears*). This is Petya Trofimov.

TROFIMOV. Petya Trofimov, I was Grisha's tutor. . . . Can I have changed so much?

(*Lyubov Andreyevna embraces him, quietly weeping.*)

GAYEV (*embarrassed*). There, there, Lyuba.

VARYA (*crying*). Didn't I tell you, Petya, to wait till tomorrow?

LYUBOV ANDREYEVNA. My Grisha . . . my little boy . . . Grisha . . . my son. . . .

VARYA. What can we do, Mama dear? It's God's will.

TROFIMOV (*gently, through tears*). Don't, don't. . . .

LYUBOV ANDREYEVNA (*quietly weeping*). My little boy dead, drowned. . . . Why? Why, my friend? (*In a lower voice.*) Anya is sleeping in there, and I'm talking loudly . . . making all this noise. . . . But Petya, why do you look so bad? Why have you grown so old?

TROFIMOV. A peasant woman in the train called me a mangy gentleman.

LYUBOV ANDREYEVNA. You were just a boy then, a charming little student, and now your hair is thin— and spectacles! Is it possible you are still a student? (*Goes toward the door.*)

TROFIMOV. I shall probably be an eternal student.

LYUBOV ANDREYEVNA (*kisses her brother, then Varya*). Now, go to bed. . . . You've grown older too, Leonid.

PISHCHIK (*follows her*). Well, seems to be time to sleep. . . . Oh, my gout! I'm staying the night. Lyubov Andreyevna, my soul, tomorrow morning . . . two hundred and forty rubles. . . .

GAYEV. He keeps at it.

PISHCHIK. Two hundred and forty rubles . . . to pay the interest on my mortgage.

LYUBOV ANDREYEVNA. I have no money, my friend.

PISHCHIK. My dear, I'll pay it back. . . . It's a trifling sum.

LYUBOV ANDREYEVNA. Well, all right, Leonid will give it to you. . . . Give it to him, Leonid.

GAYEV. Me give it to him! . . . Hold out your pocket!

LYUBOV ANDREYEVNA. It can't be helped, give it to him. . . . He needs it. . . . He'll pay it back.

(*Lyubov Andreyevna, Trofimov, Pishchik, and Firs go out. Gayev, Varya, and Yasha remain.*)

GAYEV. My sister hasn't yet lost her habit of squandering money. (*To Yasha.*) Go away, my good fellow, you smell of the henhouse.

YASHA (*with a smirk*). And you, Leonid Andreyevich, are just the same as ever.

GAYEV. How's that? (*To Varya.*) What did he say?

VARYA. Your mother has come from the village; she's been sitting in the servants' room since yesterday, waiting to see you. . . .

YASHA. Let her wait, for God's sake!

VARYA. Aren't you ashamed?

YASHA. A lot I need her! She could have come tomorrow. (*Goes out.*)

VARYA. Mama's the same as ever, she hasn't changed a bit. She'd give away everything, if she could.

GAYEV. Yes. . . . (*A pause.*) If a great many remedies are suggested for a disease, it means that the disease is incurable. I keep thinking, racking my brains, I have many remedies, a great many, and that means, in effect, that I have none. It would be good to receive a legacy from someone, good to marry our Anya to a very rich man, good to go to Yaroslav and try our luck with our aunt, the Countess. She is very, very rich, you know.

VARYA (*crying*). If only God would help us!

GAYEV. Stop bawling. Auntie's very rich, but she doesn't like us. In the first place, sister married a lawyer, not a nobleman . . . (*Anya appears in the doorway.*) She married beneath her, and it cannot be said that she has conducted herself very virtuously. She is good, kind, charming, and I love her dearly, but no matter how much you allow for extenuating circumstances, you must admit she leads a sinful life. You feel it in her slightest movement.

VARYA (*in a whisper*). Anya is standing in the doorway.

GAYEV. What? (*Pause.*) Funny, something got into my right eye . . . I can't see very well. And Thursday, when I was in the district court . . .

(*Anya enters.*)

VARYA. Why aren't you asleep, Anya?

ANYA. I can't get to sleep. I just can't.

GAYEV. My little one! (*Kisses Anya's face and hands.*) My child. . . . (*Through tears.*) You are not my niece, you are my angel, you are everything to me. Believe me, believe . . .

ANYA. I believe you, Uncle. Everyone loves you and respects you, but, Uncle dear, you must keep quiet, just keep quiet. What were you saying just now about my mother, about your own sister? What made you say that?

GAYEV. Yes, yes. . . . (*Covers his face with her hand.*) Really, it's awful! My God! God help me! And today I made a speech to the bookcase . . . so stupid! And it was only when I had finished that I realized it was stupid.

VARYA. It's true, Uncle dear, you ought to keep quiet. Just don't talk, that's all.

ANYA. If you could keep from talking, it would make things easier for you, too.

GAYEV. I'll be quiet. (*Kisses Anya's and Varya's hands.*) I'll be quiet. Only this is about business. On Thursday I was in the district court, well, a group of us gathered together and began talking about one thing and another, this and that, and it seems it might be possible to arrange a loan on a promissory note to pay the interest at the bank.

VARYA. If only God would help us!

GAYEV. On Tuesday I'll go and talk it over again. (*To Varya.*) Stop bawling. (*To Anya.*) Your mama will talk to Lopakhin; he, of course, will not refuse her. . . . And as soon as you've rested, you will go to Yaroslav to the Countess, your great-aunt. In that way we shall be working from three directions—and our business is in the hat. We'll pay the interest, I'm certain of it. . . . (*Puts a candy in his mouth.*) On my honor, I'll swear by anything you like, the estate shall not be sold. (*Excitedly.*) By my happiness, I swear it! Here's my hand on it, call me a worthless, dishonorable man if I let it come to auction! I swear by my whole being!

ANYA (*a calm mood returns to her, she is happy*). How good you are, Uncle, how clever! (*Embraces him.*) Now I am at peace! I'm at peace! I'm happy!

(*Enter Firs.*)

FIRS (*reproachfully*). Leonid Andreich, have you no fear of God? When are you going to bed?

GAYEV. Presently, presently. Go away, Firs. I'll . . . all right, I'll undress myself. Well, children, bye-bye. . . . Details tomorrow, and now go to sleep. (*Kisses Anya and Varya.*) I am a man of the eighties. . . . They don't think much of that period today, nevertheless, I can say that in the course of my life I have suffered not a little for my convictions. It is not for nothing that the peasant loves me. You have to know the peasant! You have to know from what—

ANYA. There you go again, Uncle!

VARYA. Uncle dear, do be quiet.

FIRS (*angrily*). Leonid Andreich!

GAYEV. I'm coming, I'm coming. . . . Go to bed. A clean double rail shot to center table. . . . (*Goes out; Firs hobbles after him.*)

ANYA. I'm at peace now. I would rather not go to Yaroslav, I don't like my great-aunt, but still, I'm at peace, thanks to Uncle. (*She sits down.*)

VARYA. We must get some sleep. I'm going now. Oh, something unpleasant happened while you were away. In the old servants' quarters, as you know, there are only the old people: Yefimushka, Polya, Yevstignei, and, of course, Karp. They began letting in all sorts of rogues to spend the night—I didn't say anything. But then I heard they'd been spreading a rumor that I'd given an order for them to be fed nothing but dried peas. Out of stinginess, you see. . . . It was all Yevstignei's doing. . . . Very well, I think, if that's how it is, you just wait. I send for Yevstignei . . . (*yawning*) he comes. . . . "How is it, Yevstignei," I say, "that you could be such a fool. . . ." (*Looks at Anya.*) She's fallen asleep. (*Takes her by the arm.*) Come to your little bed. . . . Come along. (*Leading her.*) My little darling fell asleep. Come. . . . (*They go.*)

(*In the distance, beyond the orchard, a shepherd is playing on a reed pipe. Trofimov crosses the stage and, seeing Varya and Anya, stops.*)

VARYA. Sh! She's asleep . . . asleep. . . . Come along, darling.

ANYA (*softly, half-asleep*). I'm so tired. . . . Those bells . . . Uncle . . . dear . . . Mama and Uncle . . .

VARYA. Come, darling, come along. (*They go into Anya's room.*)

TROFIMOV (*deeply moved*). My sunshine! My spring!

ACT II

(*A meadow. An old, lopsided, long-abandoned little chapel; near it a well, large stones that apparently were once tombstones, and an old bench. A road to the Gayev manor house can be seen. On one side, where the cherry orchard begins, tall poplars loom. In the distance a row of telegraph poles, and far, far away, on the horizon, the faint outline of a large town, which is visible only in very fine, clear weather. The sun will soon set. Charlotta, Yasha, and Dunyasha are sitting on the bench; Yepikhodov stands near playing something sad on the guitar. They are all lost in thought. Charlotta wears an old forage cap; she has taken a gun from her shoulder and is addressing the buckle on the sling.*)

CHARLOTTA (*reflectively*). I haven't got a real passport, I don't know how old I am, but it always seems to me that I'm quite young. When I was a little girl, my father and mother used to travel from one fair to another giving performances—very good ones. And I did the *salto mortale* and all sorts of tricks. Then when Papa and Mama died, a German lady took me to live with her and began teaching me. Good. I grew up and became a governess. But where I come from and who

I am—I do not know. . . . Who my parents were—perhaps they weren't even married—I don't know. (*Takes a cucumber out of her pocket and eats it.*) I don't know anything. (*Pause.*) One wants so much to talk, but there isn't anyone to talk to . . . I have no one.

YEPIKHODOV (*plays the guitar and sings*). "What care I for the clamorous world, what's friend or foe to me?" . . . How pleasant it is to play a mandolin!

DUNYASHA. That's a guitar, not a mandolin. (*Looks at herself in a hand mirror and powders her face.*)

YEPIKHODOV. To a madman, in love, it is a mandolin. . . . (*Sings.*) "Would that the heart were warmed by the flame of requited love . . ."

(*Yasha joins in.*)

CHARLOTTA. How horribly these people sing? . . . Pfui! Like jackals!

DUNYASHA (*to Yasha*). Really, how fortunate to have been abroad!

YASHA. Yes, to be sure. I cannot but agree with you there. (*Yawns, then lights a cigar.*)

YEPIKHODOV. It stands to reason. Abroad everything has long since been fully constituted.

YASHA. Obviously.

YEPIKHODOV. I am a cultivated man, I read all sorts of remarkable books, but I am in no way able to make out my own inclinations, what it is I really want, whether, strictly speaking, to live or to shoot myself; nevertheless, I always carry a revolver on me. Here it is. (*Shows revolver.*)

CHARLOTTA. Finished. Now I'm going. (*Slings the gun over her shoulder.*) You're a very clever man, Yepikhodov, and quite terrifying; women must be mad about you. Brrr! (*Starts to go.*) These clever people are all so stupid, there's no one for me to talk to. . . . Alone, always alone, I have no one . . . and who I am, and why I am, nobody knows. . . . (*Goes out unhurriedly.*)

YEPIKHODOV. Strictly speaking, all else aside, I must state regarding myself, that fate treats me unmercifully, as a storm does a small ship. If, let us assume, I am mistaken, then why, to mention a single instance, do I wake up this morning, and there on my chest see a spider of terrifying magnitude? . . . Like that. (*Indicates with both hands.*) And likewise, I take up some kvas to quench my thirst, and there see something in the highest degree unseemly, like a cockroach. (*Pause.*) Have you read Buckle?[3] (*Pause.*) If I may

[3]**Buckle** Thomas Henry Buckle (1821–62), a historian; he formulated a scientific basis for history emphasizing the interrelationship of climate, food production, population, and wealth.

trouble you, Avdotya Fedorovna, I should like to have a word or two with you.

DUNYASHA. Go ahead.

YEPIKHODOV. I prefer to speak with you alone. . . . (*Sighs.*)

DUNYASHA (*embarrassed*). Very well . . . only first bring me my little cape . . . you'll find it by the cupboard. . . . It's rather damp here. . . .

YEPIKHODOV. Certainly, ma'am . . . I'll fetch it, ma'am. . . . Now I know what to do with my revolver. . . . (*Takes the guitar and goes off playing it.*)

YASHA. Two-and-twenty Troubles! Between ourselves, a stupid fellow. (*Yawns.*)

DUNYASHA. God forbid that he should shoot himself. (*Pause.*) I've grown so anxious, I'm always worried. I was only a little girl when I was taken into the master's house, and now I'm quite unused to the simple life, and my hands are white as can be, just like a lady's. I've become so delicate, so tender and ladylike, I'm afraid of everything. . . . Frightfully so. And, Yasha, if you deceive me, I just don't know what will become of my nerves.

YASHA (*kisses her*). You little cucumber! Of course, a girl should never forget herself. What I dislike above everything is when a girl doesn't conduct herself properly.

DUNYASHA. I'm passionately in love with you, you're educated, you can discuss anything. (*Pause.*)

YASHA (*yawns*). Yes. . . . As I see it, it's like this: If a girl loves somebody, that means she's immoral. (*Pause.*) Very pleasant smoking a cigar in the open air. . . . (*Listens.*) Someone's coming this way. . . . It's the masters. (*Dunyasha impulsively embraces him.*) You go home, as if you'd been to the river to bathe; take that path, otherwise they'll see you and suspect me of having a rendezvous with you. I can't endure that sort of thing.

DUNYASHA (*with a little cough*). My head is beginning to ache from your cigar. . . . (*Goes out.*)

(*Yasha remains, sitting near the chapel. Lyubov Andreyevna, Gayev, and Lopakhin enter.*)

LOPAKHIN. You must make up your mind once and for all—time won't stand still. The question, after all, is quite simple. Do you agree to lease the land for summer cottages or not? Answer in one word: Yes or no? Only one word!

LYUBOV ANDREYEVNA. Who is it that smokes those disgusting cigars out here? (*Sits down.*)

GAYEV. Now that the railway line is so near, it's made things convenient. (*Sits down.*) We went to town and had lunch . . . cue ball to the center! I feel like going to the house first and playing a game.

LYUBOV ANDREYEVNA. Later.

LOPAKHIN. Just one word! (*Imploringly.*) Do give me an answer.

GAYEV (*yawning*). How's that?

LYUBOV ANDREYEVNA (*looks into her purse*). Yesterday I had a lot of money, and today there's hardly any left. My poor Varya tries to economize by feeding everyone milk soup, and in the kitchen the old people get nothing but dried peas, while I squander money foolishly. . . . (*Drops the purse, scattering gold coins.*) There they go. . . . (*Vexed.*)

YASHA. Allow me, I'll pick them up in an instant. (*Picks up the money.*)

LYUBOV ANDREYEVNA. Please do, Yasha. And why did I go to town for lunch? . . . That miserable restaurant of yours with its music, and tablecloths smelling of soap. . . . Why drink so much, Lyonya? Why eat so much? Why talk so much? Today in the restaurant again you talked too much, and it was all so pointless. About the seventies, about the decadents. And to whom? Talking to waiters about the decadents!

LOPAKHIN. Yes.

GAYEV (*waving his hand*). I'm incorrigible, that's evident. . . . (*Irritably to Yasha.*) Why do you keep twirling about in front of me?

YASHA (*laughs*). I can't help laughing when I hear your voice.

GAYEV (*to his sister*). Either he or I—

LYUBOV ANDREYEVNA. Go away, Yasha, run along.

YASHA (*hands Lyubov Andreyevna her purse*). I'm going, right away. (*Hardly able to contain his laughter.*) This very instant. . . . (*Goes out.*)

LOPAKHIN. That rich man, Deriganov, is prepared to buy the estate. They say he's coming to the auction himself.

LYUBOV ANDREYEVNA. Where did you hear that?

LOPAKHIN. That's what they're saying in town.

LYUBOV ANDREYEVNA. Our aunt in Yaroslav promised to send us something, but when and how much, no one knows.

LOPAKHIN. How much do you think she'll send? A hundred thousand? Two hundred?

LYUBOV ANDREYEVNA. Oh . . . ten or fifteen thousand, and we'll be thankful for that.

LOPAKHIN. Forgive me, but I have never seen such frivolous, such queer, unbusinesslike people as you, my friends. You are told in plain language that your estate is to be sold, and it's as though you don't understand it.

LYUBOV ANDREYEVNA. But what are we to do? Tell us what to do.

LOPAKHIN. I tell you every day. Every day I say the same thing. Both the cherry orchard and the land must be leased for summer cottages, and it must be done now, as quickly as possible—the auction is close at hand. Try to understand! Once you definitely decide on the cottages, you can raise as much money as you like, and then you are saved.

LYUBOV ANDREYEVNA. Cottages, summer people—forgive me, but it's so vulgar.

GAYEV. I agree with you, absolutely.

LOPAKHIN. I'll either burst into tears, start shouting, or fall into a faint! I can't stand it! You've worn me out! (*To Gayev.*) You're an old woman!

GAYEV. How's that?

LOPAKHIN. An old woman! (*Starts to go.*)

LYUBOV ANDREYEVNA (*alarmed*). No, don't go, stay, my dear. I beg you. Perhaps we'll think of something!

LOPAKHIN. What is there to think of?

LYUBOV ANDREYEVNA. Don't go away, please. With you here it's more cheerful somehow. . . . (*Pause.*) I keep expecting something to happen, like the house caving in on us.

GAYEV (*in deep thought*). Double rail shot into the corner. . . . Cross table to the center. . . .

LYUBOV ANDREYEVNA. We have sinned so much. . . .

LOPAKHIN. What sins could you have—

GAYEV (*puts a candy into his mouth*). They say I've eaten up my entire fortune in candies. . . . (*Laughs.*)

LYUBOV ANDREYEVNA. Oh, my sins. . . . I've always squandered money recklessly, like a madwoman, and I married a man who did nothing but amass debts. My husband died from champagne—he drank terribly—then, to my sorrow, I fell in love with another man, lived with him, and just at that time—that was my first punishment, a blow on the head—my little boy was drowned . . . here in the river. And I went abroad, went away for good, never to return, never to see this river. . . . I closed my eyes and ran, beside myself, and *he* after me . . . callously, without pity. I bought a villa near Mentone, because he fell ill there, and for three years I had no rest, day or night. The sick man wore me out, my soul dried up. Then last year, when the villa was sold to pay my debts, I went to Paris, and there he stripped me of everything, and left me for another woman; I tried to poison myself. . . . So stupid, so shameful. . . . And suddenly I felt a longing for Russia, for my own country, for my little girl. . . . (*Wipes away her tears.*) Lord, Lord, be merciful, forgive my sins! Don't punish me anymore! (*Takes a telegram out of her pocket.*) This came today from Paris. . . . He asks my forgiveness, begs me to return. . . . (*Tears up telegram.*) Do I hear music? (*Listens.*)

GAYEV. That's our famous Jewish band. You remember, four violins, a flute, and double bass.

LYUBOV ANDREYEVNA. It's still in existence? We ought to send for them sometime and give a party.

LOPAKHIN (*listens*). I don't hear anything. . . . (*Sings softly.*) "The Germans, for pay, will turn Russians into Frenchmen, they say." (*Laughs.*) What a play I saw yesterday at the theater—very funny!

LYUBOV ANDREYEVNA. There was probably nothing funny about it. Instead of going to see plays you ought to look at yourselves a little more often. How drab your lives are, how full of futile talk!

LOPAKHIN. That's true. I must say, this life of ours is stupid. . . . (*Pause.*) My father was a peasant, an idiot; he understood nothing, taught me nothing; all he did was beat me when he was drunk, and always with a stick. As a matter of fact, I'm as big a blockhead and idiot as he was. I never learned anything, my handwriting's disgusting, I write like a pig—I'm ashamed to have people see it.

LYUBOV ANDREYEVNA. You ought to get married, my friend.

LOPAKHIN. Yes . . . that's true.

LYUBOV ANDREYEVNA. To our Varya. She's a nice girl.

LOPAKHIN. Yes.

LYUBOV ANDREYEVNA. She's a girl who comes from simple people, works all day long, but the main thing is she loves you. Besides, you've liked her for a long time now.

LOPAKHIN. Well? I've nothing against it. . . . She's a good girl. (*Pause.*)

GAYEV. I've been offered a place in the bank. Six thousand a year. . . . Have you heard?

LYUBOV ANDREYEVNA. How could you! You stay where you are. . . .

(*Firs enters carrying an overcoat.*)

FIRS (*to Gayev*). If you please, sir, put this on, it's damp.

GAYEV (*puts on the overcoat*). You're a pest, old man.

FIRS. Never mind. . . . You went off this morning without telling me. (*Looks him over.*)

LYUBOV ANDREYEVNA. How you have aged, Firs!

FIRS. What do you wish, madam?

LOPAKHIN. She says you've grown very old!

FIRS. I've lived a long time. They were arranging a marriage for me before your papa was born. . . . (*Laughs.*) I was already head footman when the emancipation came. At that time I wouldn't consent to my freedom, I stayed with the masters. . . . (*Pause.*) I remember, everyone was happy, but what they were happy about, they themselves didn't know.

LOPAKHIN. It was better in the old days. At least they flogged them.

FIRS (*not hearing*). Of course. The peasants kept to the masters, the masters kept to the peasants; but now they have all gone their own ways, you can't tell about anything.

GAYEV. Be quiet, Firs. Tomorrow I must go to town. I've been promised an introduction to a certain general who might let us have a loan.

LOPAKHIN. Nothing will come of it. And you can rest assured, you won't even pay the interest.

LYUBOV ANDREYEVNA. He's raving. There is no such general.

(*Enter Trofimov, Anya, and Varya.*)

GAYEV. Here come our young people.

ANYA. There's Mama.

LYUBOV ANDREYEVNA (*tenderly*). Come, come along, my darlings. (*Embraces Anya and Varya.*) If you only knew how I love you both! Sit here beside me—there, like that.

(*They all sit down.*)

LOPAKHIN. Our eternal student is always with the young ladies.

TROFIMOV. That's none of your business.

LOPAKHIN. He'll soon be fifty, but he's still a student.

TROFIMOV. Drop your stupid jokes.

LOPAKHIN. What are you so angry about, you queer fellow?

TROFIMOV. Just leave me alone.

LOPAKHIN (*laughs*). Let me ask you something: What do you make of me?

TROFIMOV. My idea of you, Yermolai Alekseich, is this: You're a rich man, you will soon be a millionaire. Just as the beast of prey, which devours everything that crosses its path, is necessary in the metabolic process, so are you necessary.

(*Everybody laughs.*)

VARYA. Petya, you'd better tell us something about the planets.

LYUBOV ANDREYEVNA. No, let's go on with yesterday's conversation.

TROFIMOV. What was it about?

GAYEV. About the proud man.

TROFIMOV. We talked a long time yesterday, but we didn't get anywhere. In the proud man, in your sense of the word, there's something mystical. And you may be right from your point of view, but if you look at it simply, without being abstruse, why even talk about pride? Is there any sense in it if, physiologically, man is poorly constructed, if, in the vast majority of cases, he is coarse, ignorant, and profoundly unhappy? We should stop admiring ourselves. We should just work, and that's all.

GAYEV. You die, anyway.

TROFIMOV. Who knows? And what does it mean—to die? It may be that man has a hundred senses, and at his death only the five that are known to us perish, and the other ninety-five go on living.

LYUBOV ANDREYEVNA. How clever you are, Petya!

LOPAKHIN (*ironically*). Terribly clever!

TROFIMOV. Mankind goes forward, perfecting its powers. Everything that is now unattainable will some day be comprehensible and within our grasp, only we must work, and help with all our might those who are seeking the truth. So far, among us here in Russia, only a very few work. The great majority of the intelligentsia that I know seek nothing, do nothing, and as yet are incapable of work. They call themselves the intelligentsia, yet they belittle their servants, treat the peasants like animals, are wretched students, never read anything serious, and do absolutely nothing; they only talk about science and know very little about art. They all look serious, have grim expressions, speak of weighty matters, and philosophize; and meanwhile anyone can see that the workers eat abominably, sleep without pillows, thirty or forty to a room, and everywhere there are bedbugs, stench, dampness, and immorality. . . . It's obvious that all our fine talk is merely to delude ourselves and others. Show me the day nurseries they are always talking about—and where are the reading rooms? They only write about them in novels, but in reality they don't exist. There is nothing but filth, vulgarity, asiaticism.[4] . . . I'm afraid of those very serious countenances, I don't like them, I'm afraid of serious conversations. We'd do better to remain silent.

LOPAKHIN. You know, I get up before five in the morning, and I work from morning to night; now, I'm always handling money, my own and other people's, and I see what people around me are like. You have only to start doing something to find out how few honest, decent people there are. Sometimes, when I can't sleep, I think: "Lord, Thou gavest us vast forests, boundless fields, broad horizons, and living in their midst we ourselves ought truly to be giants. . . ."

[4]**asiaticism** Trofimov is referring to Asian apathy, a common Russian prejudice of the time.

LYUBOV ANDREYEVNA. Now you want giants! They're good only in fairy tales, otherwise they're frightening.

(*Yepikhodov crosses at the rear of the stage, playing the guitar.*)

LYUBOV ANDREYEVNA (*pensively*). There goes Yepikhodov . . .

ANYA (*pensively*). There goes Yepikhodov . . .

GAYEV. The sun has set, ladies and gentlemen.

TROFIMOV. Yes.

GAYEV (*in a low voice, as though reciting*). Oh, Nature, wondrous Nature, you shine with eternal radiance, beautiful and indifferent; you, whom we call mother, unite within yourself both life and death, giving life and taking it away. . . .

VARYA (*beseechingly*). Uncle dear!

ANYA. Uncle, you're doing it again!

TROFIMOV. You'd better cue ball into the center.

GAYEV. I'll be silent, silent.

(*All sit lost in thought. The silence is broken only by the subdued muttering of Firs. Suddenly a distant sound is heard, as if from the sky, like the sound of a snapped string mournfully dying away.*)

LYUBOV ANDREYEVNA. What was that?

LOPAKHIN. I don't know. Somewhere far off in a mine shaft a bucket's broken loose. But somewhere very far away.

GAYEV. It might be a bird of some sort . . . like a heron.

TROFIMOV. Or an owl . . .

LYUBOV ANDREYEVNA (*shudders*). It's unpleasant somehow. . . . (*Pause.*)

FIRS. The same thing happened before the troubles: An owl hooted and the samovar hissed continually.

GAYEV. Before what troubles?

FIRS. Before the emancipation.

LYUBOV ANDREYEVNA. Come along, my friends, let us go, evening is falling. (*To Anya.*) There are tears in your eyes—what is it, my little one?

(*Embraces her.*)

ANYA. It's all right, Mama. It's nothing.

TROFIMOV. Someone is coming.

(*A Stranger appears wearing a shabby white forage cap and an overcoat. He is slightly drunk.*)

STRANGER. Permit me to inquire, can I go straight through here to the station?

GAYEV. You can follow the road.

STRANGER. I am deeply grateful to you. (*Coughs.*) Splendid weather. . . . (*Reciting.*) "My brother, my suffering brother . . . come to the Volga, whose groans" . . . (*To Varya.*) Mademoiselle, will you oblige a hungry Russian with thirty kopecks?

(*Varya, frightened, cries out.*)

LOPAKHIN (*angrily*). There's a limit to everything.

LYUBOV ANDREYEVNA (*panic-stricken*). Here you are—take this . . . (*Fumbles in her purse.*) I have no silver. . . . Never mind, here's a gold piece for you. . . .

STRANGER. I am deeply grateful to you. (*Goes off.*)

(*Laughter.*)

VARYA (*frightened*). I'm leaving . . . I'm leaving. . . . Oh, Mama, dear, there's nothing in the house for the servants to eat, and you give him a gold piece!

LYUBOV ANDREYEVNA. What's to be done with such a silly creature? When we get home I'll give you all I've got. Yermolai Alekseyevich, you'll lend me some more!

LOPAKHIN. At your service.

LYUBOV ANDREYEVNA. Come, my friends, it's time to go. Oh, Varya, we have definitely made a match for you. Congratulations!

VARYA (*through tears*). Mama, that's not something to joke about.

LOPAKHIN. "Aurelia, get thee to a nunnery . . . "[5]

GAYEV. Look, my hands are trembling: It's a long time since I've played a game of billiards.

LOPAKHIN. "Aurelia, O Nymph, in thy orisons, be all my sins remember'd!"

LYUBOV ANDREYEVNA. Let us go, my friends, it will soon be suppertime.

VARYA. He frightened me. My heart is simply pounding.

LOPAKHIN. Let me remind you, ladies and gentlemen: On the twenty-second of August the cherry orchard is to be sold. Think about that!—Think!

(*All go out except Trofimov and Anya.*)

ANYA (*laughs*). My thanks to the stranger for frightening Varya, now we are alone.

TROFIMOV. Varya is so afraid we might suddenly fall in love with each other that she hasn't left us alone for days. With her narrow mind she can't understand that we are above love. To avoid the petty and the illusory, which prevent our being free and happy— that is the aim and meaning of life. Forward! We are moving irresistibly toward the bright star that burns in the distance! Forward! Do not fall behind, friends!

[5]**"Aurelia . . . nunnery"** Lopakhin misquotes Hamlet's famous line rejecting Ophelia. His next line is also from *Hamlet*.

ANYA (*clasping her hands*). How well you talk! (*Pause.*) It's marvelous here today!

TROFIMOV. Yes, the weather is wonderful.

ANYA. What have you done to me, Petya, that I no longer love the cherry orchard as I used to? I loved it so tenderly, it seemed to me there was no better place on earth than our orchard.

TROFIMOV. All Russia is our orchard. It is a great and beautiful land, and there are many wonderful places in it. (*Pause.*) Just think, Anya: Your grandfather, your great-grandfather, and all your ancestors were serf-owners, possessors of living souls. Don't you see that from every cherry tree, from every leaf and trunk, human beings are peering out at you? Don't you hear their voices? To possess living souls—that has corrupted all of you, those who lived before and you who are living now, so that your mother, you, your uncle, no longer perceive that you are living in debt, at someone else's expense, at the expense of those whom you wouldn't allow to cross your threshold. . . . We are at least two hundred years behind the times, we have as yet absolutely nothing, we have no definite attitude toward the past, we only philosophize, complain of boredom, or drink vodka. Yet it's quite clear that to begin to live we must first atone for the past, be done with it, and we can atone for it only by suffering, only by extraordinary, unceasing labor. Understand this, Anya.

ANYA. The house we live in hasn't really been ours for a long time, and I shall leave it, I give you my word.

TROFIMOV. If you have the keys of the household, throw them into the well and go. Be as free as the wind.

ANYA (*ecstasy*). How well you put that!

TROFIMOV. Believe me, Anya, believe me! I am not yet thirty, I am young, still a student, but I have already been through so much! As soon as winter comes, I am hungry, sick, worried, poor as a beggar, and—where has not fate driven me! Where have I not been? And yet always, every minute of the day and night, my soul was filled with inexplicable premonitions. I have a premonition of happiness, Anya, I can see it . . .

ANYA. The moon is rising.

(*Yepikhodov is heard playing the same melancholy song on the guitar. The moon rises. Somewhere near the poplars Varya is looking for Anya and calling: "Anya, where are you?"*)

TROFIMOV. Yes, the moon is rising. (*Pause.*) There it is— happiness . . . it's coming, nearer and nearer, I can hear its footsteps. And if we do not see it, if we do not recognize it, what does it matter? Others will see it.

VARYA'S VOICE. Anya! Where are you?

TROFIMOV. That Varya again! (*Angrily.*) It's revolting!

ANYA. Well? Let's go down to the river. It's lovely there.

TROFIMOV. Come on. (*They go.*)

VARYA'S VOICE. Anya! Anya!

ACT III

(*The drawing room, separated by an arch from the ballroom. The chandelier is lighted. The Jewish band that was mentioned in Act II is heard playing in the hall. It is evening. In the ballroom they are dancing a grand rond. The voice of Semyonov-Pishchik: "Promenade à une paire!"*[6] *They all enter the drawing room: Pishchik and Charlotta Ivanovna are the first couple, Trofimov and Lyubov Andreyevna the second, Anya and the Post-Office Clerk the third, Varya and the Stationmaster the fourth, etc. Varya, quietly weeping, dries her tears as she dances. Dunyasha is in the last couple. As they cross the drawing room Pishchik calls: "Grand rond, balancez!" and "Les cavaliers à genoux et remercier vos dames!"*[7] *Firs, wearing a dress coat, brings in a tray with seltzer water. Pishchik and Trofimov come into the drawing room.*)

PISHCHIK. I'm a full-blooded man, I've already had two strokes, and dancing's hard work for me, but as they say, "If you run with the pack, you can bark or not, but at least wag your tail." At that, I'm as strong as a horse. My late father—quite a joker he was, God rest his soul—used to say, talking about our origins, that the ancient line of Semyonov-Pishchik was descended from the very horse that Caligula had seated in the Senate.[8] . . . (*Sits down.*) But the trouble is— no money! A hungry dog believes in nothing but meat. . . . (*Snores but wakes up at once.*) It's the same with me—I can think of nothing but money. . . .

TROFIMOV. You know, there really is something equine about your figure.

PISHCHIK. Well, a horse is a fine animal. . . . You can sell a horse.

(*There is the sound of a billiard game in the next room. Varya appears in the archway.*)

TROFIMOV (*teasing her*). Madame Lopakhina! Madame Lopakhina!

VARYA (*angrily*). Mangy gentleman!

TROFIMOV. Yes, I am a mangy gentleman, and proud of it!

VARYA (*reflecting bitterly*). Here we've hired musicians, and what are we going to pay them with? (*Goes out.*)

TROFIMOV (*to Pishchik*). If the energy you have expended in the course of your life trying to find money to pay interest had gone into something else, ultimately, you might very well have turned the world upside down.

PISHCHIK. Nietzsche . . . the philosopher . . . the greatest, most renowned . . . a man of tremendous intellect . . . says in his works that it is possible to forge banknotes.

TROFIMOV. And have you read Nietzsche?

PISHCHIK. Well . . . Dashenka told me. I'm in such a state now that I'm just about ready for forging. . . . The day after tomorrow I have to pay three hundred and ten rubles . . . I've got a hundred and thirty. . . . (*Feels in his pocket, grows alarmed.*) The money is gone! I've lost the money! (*Tearfully.*) Where is my money? (*Joyfully.*) Here it is, inside the lining. . . . I'm all in a sweat. . . .

(*Lyubov Andreyevna and Charlotta Ivanovna come in.*)

LYUBOV ANDREYEVNA (*humming a Lezginka*).[9] Why does Leonid take so long? What is he doing in town? (*To Dunyasha.*) Dunyasha, offer the musicians some tea.

TROFIMOV. In all probability, the auction didn't take place.

LYUBOV ANDREYEVNA. It was the wrong time to have the musicians, the wrong time to give a dance. . . . Well, never mind. . . . (*Sits down and hums softly.*)

CHARLOTTA (*gives Pishchik a deck of cards*). Here's a deck of cards for you. Think of a card.

PISHCHIK. I've thought of one.

CHARLOTTA. Now shuffle the pack. Very good. And now, my dear Mr. Pishchik, hand it to me. *Ein, zwei, drei!* Now look for it—it's in your side pocket.

PISHCHIK (*takes the card out of his side pocket*). The eight of spades—absolutely right! (*Amazed.*) Think of that, now!

CHARLOTTA (*holding the deck of cards in the palm of her hand, to Trofimov*). Quickly, tell me, which card is on top?

TROFIMOV. What? Well, the queen of spades.

CHARLOTTA. Right! (*To Pishchik.*) Now which card is on top?

PISHCHIK. The ace of hearts.

---

[6]**"Promenade à une paire!"** "Promenade in pairs!"

[7]**"Grand rond . . . dames!"** "Large circle!" and "Gentlemen, kneel down and thank our ladies!"

[8]**Caligula . . . Senate** Caligula (A.D. 12–41), a Roman cavalry soldier; Roman emperor (A.D. 37–41) said to have appointed a horse to the Senate.

[9]**Lezginka** a lively Russian tune for a dance

CHARLOTTA. Right! (*Claps her hands and the deck of cards disappears.*) What lovely weather we're having today! (*A mysterious feminine voice, which seems to come from under the floor, answers her: "Oh, yes, splendid weather, madam."*) You are so nice, you're my ideal. . . . (*The voice: "And I'm very fond of you, too, madam."*)

STATIONMASTER (*applauding*). Bravo, Madame Ventriloquist!

PISHCHIK (*amazed*). Think of that, now! Most enchanting Charlotta Ivanovna . . . I am simply in love with you. . . .

CHARLOTTA. In love? (*Shrugs her shoulders.*) Is it possible that you can love? *Guter Mensch, aber schlechter Musikant.*[10]

TROFIMOV (*claps Pishchik on the shoulder*). You old horse, you!

CHARLOTTA. Attention, please! One more trick. (*Takes a lap robe from a chair.*) Here's a very fine lap robe; I should like to sell it. (*Shakes it out.*) Doesn't anyone want to buy it?

PISHCHIK (*amazed*). Think of that, now!

CHARLOTTA. *Ein, zwei, drei!* (*Quickly raises the lap robe; behind it stands Anya, who curtsies, runs to her mother, embraces her, and runs back into the ballroom amid the general enthusiasm.*)

LYUBOV ANDREYEVNA (*applauding*). Bravo, bravo!

CHARLOTTA. Once again! *Ein, zwei, drei.* (*Raises the lap robe; behind it stands Varya, who bows.*)

PISHCHIK (*amazed*). Think of that, now!

CHARLOTTA. The end! (*Throws the robe at Pishchik, makes a curtsy, and runs out of the room.*)

PISHCHIK (*hurries after her*). The minx! . . . What a woman! What a woman! (*Goes out.*)

LYUBOV ANDREYEVNA. And Leonid still not here. What he is doing in town so long, I do not understand! It must be all over by now. Either the estate is sold, or the auction didn't take place—but why keep us in suspense so long!

VARYA (*trying to comfort her*). Uncle has bought it, I am certain of that.

TROFIMOV (*mockingly*). Yes.

VARYA. Great-aunt sent him power of attorney to buy it in her name and transfer the debt. She's doing it for Anya's sake. And I am sure, with God's help, Uncle will buy it.

LYUBOV ANDREYEVNA. Our great-aunt in Yaroslav sent fifteen thousand to buy the estate in her name—she doesn't trust us—but that's not even enough to pay

the interest. (*Covers her face with her hands.*) Today my fate will be decided, my fate . . .

TROFIMOV (*teasing Varya*). Madame Lopakhina!

VARYA (*angrily*). Eternal student! Twice already you've been expelled from the university.

LYUBOV ANDREYEVNA. Why are you so cross, Varya? If he teases you about Lopakhin, what of it? Go ahead and marry Lopakhin if you want to. He's a nice man, he's interesting. And if you don't want to, don't. Nobody's forcing you, my pet.

VARYA. To be frank, Mama dear, I regard this matter seriously. He is a good man, I like him.

LYUBOV ANDREYEVNA. Then marry him. I don't know what you're waiting for!

VARYA. Mama, I can't propose to him myself. For the last two years everyone's been talking to me about him; everyone talks, but he is either silent or he jokes. I understand. He's getting rich, he's absorbed in business, he has no time for me. If I had some money, no matter how little, if it were only a hundred rubles, I'd drop everything and go far away. I'd go into a nunnery.

TROFIMOV. A blessing!

VARYA (*to Trofimov*). A student ought to be intelligent! (*In a gentle tone, tearfully.*) How homely you have grown, Petya, how old! (*To Lyubov Andreyevna, no longer crying.*) It's just that I cannot live without work, Mama. I must be doing something every minute.

(*Yasha enters.*)

YASHA (*barely able to suppress his laughter*). Yepikhodov has broken a billiard cue! (*Goes out.*)

VARYA. But why is Yepikhodov here? Who gave him permission to play billiards? I don't understand these people. . . . (*Goes out.*)

LYUBOV ANDREYEVNA. Don't tease her, Petya. You can see she's unhappy enough without that.

TROFIMOV. She's much too zealous, always meddling in other people's affairs. All summer long she's given Anya and me no peace—afraid a romance might develop. What business is it of hers? Besides, I've given no occasion for it, I am far removed from such banality. We are above love!

LYUBOV ANDREYEVNA. And I suppose I am beneath love. (*In great agitation.*) Why isn't Leonid here? If only I knew whether the estate had been sold or not! The disaster seems to me so incredible that I don't even know what to think, I'm lost. . . . I could scream this very instant . . . I could do something foolish. Save me, Petya. Talk to me, say something. . . .

TROFIMOV. Whether or not the estate is sold today— does it really matter? That's all done with long ago;

---

[10] *Guter Mensch, aber schlechter Musikant.* "Good man, but poor musician."

there's no turning back, the path is overgrown. Be calm, my dear. One must not deceive oneself; at least once in one's life one ought to look the truth straight in the eye.

LYUBOV ANDREYEVNA. What truth? You can see where there is truth and where there isn't, but I seem to have lost my sight, I see nothing. You boldly settle all the important problems, but tell me, my dear boy, isn't it because you are young and have not yet had to suffer for a single one of your problems? You boldly look ahead, but isn't it because you neither see nor expect anything dreadful, since life is still hidden from your young eyes? You're bolder, more honest, deeper than we are, but think about it, be just a little bit magnanimous, and spare me. You see, I was born here, my mother and father lived here, and my grandfather. I love this house, without the cherry orchard my life has no meaning for me, and if it must be sold, then sell me with the orchard. . . . (*Embraces Trofimov and kisses him on the forehead.*) And my son was drowned here. . . . (*Weeps.*) Have pity on me, you good, kind man.

TROFIMOV. You know I feel for you with all my heart.

LYUBOV ANDREYEVNA. But that should have been said differently, quite differently. . . . (*Takes out her handkerchief and a telegram falls to the floor.*) My heart is heavy today, you can't imagine. It's so noisy here, my soul quivers at every sound, I tremble all over, and yet I can't go to my room. When I am alone the silence frightens me. Don't condemn me, Petya . . . I love you as if you were my own. I would gladly let you marry Anya, I swear it, only you must study, my dear, you must get your degree. You do nothing, fate simply tosses you from place to place—it's so strange. . . . Isn't that true? Isn't it? And you must do something about your beard, to make it grow somehow. . . . (*Laughs.*) You're so funny!

TROFIMOV (*picks up the telegram*). I have no desire to be an Adonis.

LYUBOV ANDREYEVNA. That's a telegram from Paris. I get them every day. One yesterday, one today. That wild man has fallen ill again, he's in trouble again. . . . He begs my forgiveness, implores me to come, and really, I ought to go to Paris to be near him. Your face is stern, Petya, but what can one do, my dear? What am I to do? He is ill, he's alone and unhappy, and who will look after him there, who will keep him from making mistakes, who will give him his medicine on time? And why hide it or keep silent, I love him, that's clear. I love him, love him. . . . It's a millstone round my neck, I'm sinking to the bottom with it, but

I love that stone, I cannot live without it. (*Presses Trofimov's hand.*) Don't think badly of me, Petya, and don't say anything to me, don't say anything. . . .

TROFIMOV (*through tears*). For Gods sake, forgive my frankness: You know that he robbed you!

LYUBOV ANDREYEVNA. No, no, no, you mustn't say such things! (*Covers her ears.*)

TROFIMOV. But he's a scoundrel! You're the only one who doesn't know it! He's a petty scoundrel, a nonentity—

LYUBOV ANDREYEVNA (*angry, but controlling herself*). You are twenty-six or twenty-seven years old, but you're still a schoolboy!

TROFIMOV. That may be!

LYUBOV ANDREYEVNA. You should be a man, at your age you ought to understand those who love. And you ought to be in love yourself. (*Angrily.*) Yes, yes! It's not purity with you, it's simply prudery, you're a ridiculous crank, a freak—

TROFIMOV (*horrified*). What is she saying!

LYUBOV ANDREYEVNA. "I am above love!" You're not above love, you're just an addlepate, as Firs would say. Not to have a mistress at your age!

TROFIMOV (*in horror*). This is awful! What is she saying! . . . (*Goes quickly toward the ballroom.*) This is awful . . . I can't . . . I won't stay here. . . . (*Goes out, but immediately returns.*) All is over between us! (*Goes out to the hall.*)

LYUBOV ANDREYEVNA (*calls after him*). Petya, wait! You absurd creature, I was joking! Petya!

(*In the hall there is the sound of someone running quickly downstairs and suddenly falling with a crash. Anya and Varya scream, but a moment later laughter is heard.*)

LYUBOV ANDREYEVNA. What was that?

(*Anya runs in.*)

ANYA (*laughing*). Petya fell down the stairs! (*Runs out.*)

LYUBOV ANDREYEVNA. What a funny boy that Petya is!

(*The Stationmaster stands in the middle of the ballroom and recites A. Tolstoy's[11] "The Sinner." Everyone listens to him, but he has no sooner spoken a few lines than the sound of a waltz is heard from the hall and the recitation is broken off. They all dance. Trofimov, Anya, Varya, and Lyubov Andreyevna come in from the hall.*)

---

[11]**A. Tolstoy** Aleksey Konstantinovich Tolstoy (1817–75), Russian novelist, dramatist, and poet

LYUBOV ANDREYEVNA. Come, Petya . . . come, you pure soul . . . please, forgive me. . . . Let's dance. . . . (*They dance.*)

(*Anya and Varya dance. Firs comes in, puts his stick by the side door. Yasha also comes into the drawing room and watches the dancers.*)

YASHA. What is it, grandpa?

FIRS. I don't feel well. In the old days, we used to have generals, barons, admirals, dancing at our balls, but now we send for the post office clerk and the stationmaster, and even they are none too eager to come. Somehow I've grown weak. The late master, their grandfather, dosed everyone with sealing wax, no matter what ailed them. I've been taking sealing wax every day for twenty years or more; maybe that's what's kept me alive.

YASHA. You bore me, grandpa. (*Yawns.*) High time you croaked.

FIRS. Ah, you . . . addlepate! (*Mumbles.*)

(*Trofimov and Lyubov Andreyevna dance from the ballroom into the drawing room.*)

LYUBOV ANDREYEVNA. *Merci.* I'll sit down a while. (*Sits.*) I'm tired.

(*Anya comes in.*)

ANYA (*excitedly*). There was a man in the kitchen just now saying that the cherry orchard was sold today.

LYUBOV ANDREYEVNA. Sold to whom?

ANYA. He didn't say. He's gone. (*Dances with Trofimov; they go into the ballroom.*)

YASHA. That was just some old man babbling. A stranger.

FIRS. Leonid Andreich is not back yet, still hasn't come. And he's wearing the light, between-seasons overcoat; like enough he'll catch cold. Ah, when they're young they're green.

LYUBOV ANDREYEVNA. This is killing me. Yasha, go and find out who it was sold to.

YASHA. But that old man left long ago. (*Laughs.*)

LYUBOV ANDREYEVNA (*slightly annoyed*). Well, what are you laughing at? What are you so happy about?

YASHA. That Yepikhodov is very funny! Hopeless! Two-and-twenty Troubles.

LYUBOV ANDREYEVNA. Firs, if the estate is sold, where will you go?

FIRS. Wherever you tell me to go, I'll go.

LYUBOV ANDREYEVNA. Why do you look like that? Aren't you well? You ought to go to bed.

FIRS. Yes. . . . (*With a smirk.*) Go to bed, and without me who will serve, who will see to things? I'm the only one in the whole house.

YASHA (*to Lyubov Andreyevna*). Lyubov Andreyevna! Permit me to make a request, be so kind! If you go back to Paris again, do me the favor of taking me with you. It is positively impossible for me to stay here. (*Looking around, then in a low voice.*) There's no need to say it, you can see for yourself, it's an uncivilized country, the people have no morals, and the boredom! The food they give us in the kitchen is unmentionable, and besides, there's this Firs who keeps walking about mumbling all sorts of inappropriate things. Take me with you, be so kind!

(*Enter Pishchik.*)

PISHCHIK. May I have the pleasure of a waltz with you, fairest lady? (*Lyubov Andreyevna goes with him.*) I really must borrow a hundred and eighty rubles from you, my charmer . . . I really must. . . . (*Dancing.*) Just a hundred and eighty rubles. . . . (*They pass into the ballroom.*)

YASHA (*softly sings*). "Wilt thou know my soul's unrest . . ."

(*In the ballroom a figure in a gray top hat and checked trousers is jumping about, waving its arms; there are shouts of "Bravo, Charlotta Ivanovna!"*)

DUNYASHA (*stopping to powder her face*). The young mistress told me to dance—there are lots of gentlemen and not enough ladies—but dancing makes me dizzy, and my heart begins to thump. Firs Nikolayevich, the post office clerk just said something to me that took my breath away.

(*The music grows more subdued.*)

FIRS. What did he say to you?

DUNYASHA. "You," he said, "are like a flower."

YASHA (*yawns*). What ignorance. . . . (*Goes out.*)

DUNYASHA. Like a flower. . . . I'm such a delicate girl, I just adore tender words.

FIRS. You'll get your head turned.

(*Enter Yepikhodov.*)

YEPIKHODOV. Avdotya Fyodorovna, you are not desirous of seeing me. . . . I might also be some sort of insect. (*Sighs.*) Ah, life!

DUNYASHA. What is it you want?

YEPIKHODOV. Indubitably, you may be right. (*Sighs.*) But, of course, if one looks at it from a point of view, then, if I may so express myself, and you will forgive my frankness, you have completely reduced me to a state of mind. I know my fate, every day some misfortune befalls me, but I have long since grown accustomed to that; I look upon my fate with a smile. But you gave me your word, and although I—

DUNYASHA. Please, we'll talk about it later, but leave me in peace now. Just now I'm dreaming.... (*Plays with her fan.*)

YEPIKHODOV. Every day, a misfortune, and yet, if I may so express myself, I merely smile, I even laugh.

(*Varya enters from the ballroom.*)

VARYA. Are you still here, Semyon? What a disrespectful man you are, really! (*To Dunyasha.*) Run along, Dunyasha. (*To Yepikhodov.*) First you play billiards and break a cue, then you wander about the drawing room as though you were a guest.

YEPIKHODOV. You cannot, if I may so express myself, penalize me.

VARYA. I am not penalizing you, I'm telling you. You do nothing but wander from one place to another, and you don't do your work. We keep a clerk, but for what, I don't know.

YEPIKHODOV (*offended*). Whether I work, or wander about, or eat, or play billiards, these are matters to be discussed only by persons of discernment, and my elders.

VARYA. You dare say that to me! (*Flaring up.*) You dare? You mean to say I have no discernment? Get out of here! This instant!

YEPIKHODOV (*intimidated*). I beg you to express yourself in a more delicate manner.

VARYA (*beside herself*). Get out, this very instant! Get out! (*He goes to the door, she follows him.*) Two-and-twenty Troubles! Don't let me set eyes on you again!

YEPIKHODOV (*goes out, his voice is heard behind the door*). I shall lodge a complaint against you!

VARYA. Oh, you're coming back? (*Seizes the stick left near the door by Firs.*) Come, come on.... Come, I'll show you.... Ah, so you're coming, are you? Then take that—(*Swings the stick just as Lopakhin enters.*)

LOPAKHIN. Thank you kindly.

VARYA (*angrily and mockingly*). I beg your pardon.

LOPAKHIN. Not at all. I humbly thank you for your charming reception.

VARYA. Don't mention it. (*Walks away, then looks back and gently asks.*) I didn't hurt you, did I?

LOPAKHIN. No, it's nothing. A huge bump coming up, that's all.

(*Voices in the ballroom: "Lopakhin has come! Yermolai Alekseich!" Pishchik enters.*)

PISHCHIK. As I live and breathe! (*Kisses Lopakhin.*) There is a whiff of cognac about you, dear soul. And we've been making merry here, too.

(*Enter Lyubov Andreyevna.*)

LYUBOV ANDREYEVNA. Is that you, Yermolai Alekseich? What kept you so long? Where's Leonid?

LOPAKHIN. Leonid Andreich arrived with me, he's coming ...

LYUBOV ANDREYEVNA (*agitated*). Well, what happened? Did the sale take place? Tell me!

LOPAKHIN (*embarrased, fearing to reveal his joy*). The auction was over by four o'clock.... We missed the train, had to wait till half past nine. (*Sighing heavily.*) Ugh! My head is swimming....

(*Enter Gayev; he carries his purchases in one hand and wipes away his tears with the other.*)

LYUBOV ANDREYEVNA. Lyonya, what happened? Well, Lyonya? (*Impatiently, through tears.*) Be quick, for God's sake!

GAYEV (*not answering her, simply waves his hand. To Firs, weeping*). Here, take these.... There's anchovies, Kerch herrings.... I haven't eaten anything all day.... What I have been through! (*The click of billiard balls is heard through the open door to the billiard room, and Yasha's voice: "Seven and eighteen!" Gayev's expression changes, he is no longer weeping.*) I'm terribly tired. Firs, help me change. (*Goes through the ballroom to his own room, followed by Firs.*)

PISHCHIK. What happened at the auction? Come on, tell us!

LYUBOV ANDREYEVNA. Is the cherry orchard sold?

LOPAKHIN. It's sold.

LYUBOV ANDREYEVNA. Who bought it?

LOPAKHIN. I bought it. (*Pause.*)

(*Lyubov Andreyevna is overcome; she would fall to the floor if it were not for the chair and table near which she stands. Varya takes the keys from her belt and throws them on the floor in the middle of the drawing room and goes out.*)

LOPAKHIN. I bought it! Kindly wait a moment, ladies and gentlemen, my head is swimming. I can't talk.... (*Laughs.*) We arrived at the auction, Deriganov was already there. Leonid Andreich had only fifteen thousand, and straight off Deriganov bid thirty thousand over and above the mortgage. I saw how the land lay, so I got into the fight and bid forty. He bid forty-five. I bid fifty-five. In other words, he kept raising it by five thousand, and I by ten. Well, it finally came to an end. I bid ninety thousand above the mortgage, and it was knocked down to me. The cherry orchard is now mine! Mine! (*Laughs uproariously.*) Lord! God in heaven! The cherry orchard is mine! Tell me I'm drunk, out of my mind, that I imagine it. . . . (*Stamps his feet.*) Don't laugh at me! If my father and my grandfather could only rise from their graves and see all that has happened, how their Yermolai, their beaten, half-literate Yermolai, who used to run about barefoot in winter, how that same Yermolai has bought an estate, the most beautiful estate in the whole world! I bought the estate where my father and grandfather were slaves, where they weren't even allowed in the kitchen. I'm asleep, this is just some dream of mine, it only seems to be. . . . It's the fruit of your imagination, hidden in the darkness of uncertainty. . . . (*Picks up the keys, smiling tenderly.*) She threw down the keys, wants to show that she's not mistress here anymore. . . . (*Jingles the keys.*) Well, no matter. (*The orchestra is heard tuning up.*) Hey, musicians, play, I want to hear you! Come on, everybody, and see how Yermolai Lopakhin will lay the ax to the cherry orchard, how the trees will fall to the ground! We're going to build summer cottages and our grandsons and great-grandsons will see a new life here. . . . Music! Strike up!

(*The orchestra plays. Lyubov Andreyevna sinks into a chair and weeps bitterly.*)

LOPAKHIN (*reproachfully*). Why didn't you listen to me, why? My poor friend, there's no turning back now. (*With tears.*) Oh, if only all this could be over quickly, if somehow our discordant, unhappy life could be changed!

PISHCHIK (*takes him by the arm; speaks in an undertone*). She's crying. Let's go into the ballroom, let her be alone. . . . Come on. . . . (*Leads him into the ballroom.*)

LOPAKHIN. What's happened? Musicians, play so I can hear you! Let everything be as I want it! (*Ironically.*) Here comes the new master, owner of the cherry orchard! (*Accidentally bumps into a little table, almost upsetting the candelabrum.*) I can pay for everything! (*Goes out with Pishchik.*)

(*There is no one left in either the drawing room or the ballroom except Lyubov Andreyevna, who sits huddled up and weeping bitterly. The music plays softly. Anya and Trofimov enter hurriedly. Anya goes to her mother and kneels before her. Trofimov remains in the doorway of the ballroom.*)

ANYA. Mama! . . . Mama, you're crying! Dear, kind, good Mama, my beautiful one, I love you . . . I bless you. The cherry orchard is sold, it's gone, that's true, true, but don't cry, Mama, life is still before you, you still have your good, pure soul. . . . Come with me, come,

darling, we'll go away from here! . . . We'll plant a new orchard, more luxuriant than this one. You will see it and understand; and joy, quiet, deep joy, will sink into your soul, like the evening sun, and you will smile, Mama! Come, darling, let us go. . . .

ACT IV

(*The scene is the same as Act I. There are neither curtains on the windows nor pictures on the walls, and only a little furniture piled up in one corner, as if for sale. There is a sense of emptiness. Near the outer door, at the rear of the stage, suitcases, traveling bags, etc., are piled up. Through the open door on the left the voices of Varya and Anya can be heard. Lopakhin stands waiting. Yasha is holding a tray with little glasses of champagne. In the hall, Yepikhodov is tying up a box. Offstage, at the rear, there is a hum of voices. It is the peasants who have come to say good-bye. Gayev's voice: "Thanks, brothers, thank you."*)

YASHA. The peasants have come to say good-bye. In my opinion, Yermolai Alekseich, peasants are good-natured, but they don't know much.

(*The hum subsides. Lyubov Andreyevna enters from the hall with Gayev. She is not crying, but she is pale, her face twitches, and she cannot speak.*)

GAYEV. You gave them your purse, Lyuba. That won't do! That won't do!

LYUBOV ANDREYEVNA. I couldn't help it! I couldn't help it! (*They both go out.*)

LOPAKHIN (*in the doorway, calls after them*). Please, do me the honor of having a little glass at parting. I didn't think of bringing champagne from town, and at the station I found only one bottle. Please! What's the matter, friends, don't you want any? (*Walks away from the door.*) If I'd known that, I wouldn't have bought it. Well, then I won't drink any either. (*Yasha carefully sets the tray down on a chair.*) At least you have a glass, Yasha.

YASHA. To those who are departing! Good luck! (*Drinks.*) This champagne is not the real stuff, I can assure you.

LOPAKHIN. Eight rubles a bottle. (*Pause.*) It's devilish cold in here.

YASHA. They didn't light the stoves today; it doesn't matter, since we're leaving. (*Laughs.*)

LOPAKHIN. Why are you laughing?

YASHA. Because I'm pleased.

LOPAKHIN. It's October, yet it's sunny and still outside, like summer. Good for building. (*Looks at his watch, then calls through the door.*) Bear in mind, ladies and gentlemen, only forty-six minutes till train time! That means leaving for the station in twenty minutes. Better hurry up!

(*Trofimov enters from outside wearing an overcoat.*)

TROFIMOV. Seems to me it's time to start. The carriages are at the door. What the devil has become of my rubbers? They're lost. (*Calls through the door.*) Anya, my rubbers are not here. I can't find them.

LOPAKHIN. I've got to go to Kharkov. I'm taking the same train you are. I'm going to spend the winter in Kharkov. I've been hanging around here with you, and I'm sick and tired of loafing. I can't live without work, I don't know what to do with my hands; they dangle in some strange way, as if they didn't belong to me.

TROFIMOV. We'll soon be done, then you can take up your useful labors again.

LOPAKHIN. Here, have a little drink.

TROFIMOV. No, I don't want any.

LOPAKHIN. So you're off for Moscow?

TROFIMOV. Yes, I'll see them into town, and tomorrow I'll go to Moscow.

LOPAKHIN. Yes. . . . Well, I expect the professors haven't been giving any lectures: They're waiting for you to come!

TROFIMOV. That's none of your business.

LOPAKHIN. How many years is it you've been studying at the university?

TROFIMOV. Can't you think of something new? That's stale and flat. (*Looks for his rubbers.*) You know, we'll probably never see each other again, so allow me to give you one piece of advice at parting: Don't wave your arms about! Get out of that habit—of arm-waving. And another thing, building cottages and counting on the summer residents in time becoming independent farmers—that's just another form of arm-waving. Well, when all's said and done, I'm fond of you anyway. You have fine, delicate fingers, like an artist; you have a fine delicate soul.

LOPAKHIN (*embraces him*). Good-bye, my dear fellow. Thank you for everything. Let me give you some money for the journey, if you need it.

TROFIMOV. What for? I don't need it.

LOPAKHIN. But you haven't any!

TROFIMOV. I have. Thank you. I got some money for a translation. Here it is in my pocket. (*Anxiously.*) But where are my rubbers?

VARYA (*from the next room*). Here, take the nasty things! (*Flings a pair of rubbers onto the stage.*)

TROFIMOV. What are you so cross about, Varya? Hm. . . . But these are not my rubbers.

LOPAKHIN. In the spring I sowed three thousand acres of poppies, and now I've made forty thousand rubles clear. And when my poppies were in bloom, what a picture it was! So, I'm telling you, I've made forty thousand, which means I'm offering you a loan because I can afford to. Why turn up your nose? I'm a peasant—I speak bluntly.

TROFIMOV. Your father was a peasant, mine was a pharmacist—which proves absolutely nothing. (*Lopakhin takes out his wallet.*) No, don't—even if you gave me two hundred thousand I wouldn't take it. I'm a free man. And everything that is valued so highly and held so dear by all of you, rich and poor alike, has not the slightest power over me—it's like a feather floating in the air. I can get along without you, I can pass you by, I'm strong and proud. Mankind is advancing toward the highest truth, the highest happiness attainable on earth, and I am in the front ranks!

LOPAKHIN. Will you get there?

TROFIMOV. I'll get there. (*Pause.*) I'll either get there or I'll show others the way to get there.

(*The sound of axes chopping down trees is heard in the distance.*)

LOPAKHIN. Well, good-bye, my dear fellow. It's time to go. We turn up our noses at one another, but life goes on just the same. When I work for a long time without stopping, my mind is easier, and it seems to me that I, too, know why I exist. But how many there are in Russia, brother, who exist nobody knows why. Well, it doesn't matter, that's not what makes the wheels go round. They say Leonid Andreich has taken a position in the bank, six thousand a year. . . . Only, of course, he won't stick it out, he's too lazy. . . .

ANYA (*in the doorway*). Mama asks you not to start cutting down the cherry orchard until she's gone.

TROFIMOV. Yes, really, not to have had the tact . . . (*Goes out through the hall.*)

LOPAKHIN. Right away, right away. . . . Ach, what people. . . . (*Follows Trofimov out.*)

ANYA. Has Firs been taken to the hospital?

YASHA. I told them this morning. They must have taken him.

ANYA (*to Yepikhodov, who is crossing the room*). Semyon Panteleich, please find out if Firs has been taken to the hospital.

YASHA (*offended*). I told Yegor this morning. Why ask a dozen times?

YEPIKHODOV. It is my conclusive opinion that the venerable Firs is beyond repair; it's time he was gathered to his fathers. And I can only envy him. (*Puts a suitcase down on a hatbox and crushes it.*) There you are! Of course! I knew it! (*Goes out.*)

YASHA (*mockingly*). Two-and-twenty Troubles!

VARYA (*through the door*). Has Firs been taken to the hospital?

ANYA. Yes, he has.

VARYA. Then why didn't they take the letter to the doctor?

ANYA. We must send it on after them. . . . (*Goes out.*)

VARYA (*from the adjoining room*). Where is Yasha? Tell him his mother has come to say good-bye to him.

YASHA (*waves his hand*). They really try my patience.

(*Dunyasha has been fussing with the luggage; now that Yasha is alone she goes up to him.*)

DUNYASHA. You might give me one little look, Yasha. You're going away . . . leaving me. . . . (*Cries and throws herself on his neck.*)

YASHA. What's there to cry about? (*Drinks champagne.*) In six days I'll be in Paris again. Tomorrow we'll take the express, off we go, and that's the last you'll see of us. I can hardly believe it. *Vive la France!* This place is not for me, I can't live here. . . . It can't be helped. I've had enough of this ignorance—I'm fed up with it. (*Drinks champagne.*) What are you crying for? Behave yourself properly, then you won't cry.

DUNYASHA (*looks into a small mirror and powders her face*). Send me a letter from Paris. You know, I love you, Yasha, how I loved you! I'm such a tender creature, Yasha!

YASHA. Here they come. (*Busies himself with the luggage, humming softly.*)

(*Enter Lyubov Andreyevna, Gayev, Charlotta Ivanovna.*)

GAYEV. We ought to be leaving. There's not much time now. (*Looks at Yasha.*) Who smells of herring?

LYUBOV ANDREYEVNA. In about ten minutes we should be getting into the carriages. (*Glances around the room.*) Good-bye, dear house, old grandfather. Winter will pass, spring will come, and you will no longer be here, they will tear you down. How much these walls have seen! (*Kisses her daughter warmly.*) My treasure, you are radiant, your eyes are sparkling like two diamonds. Are you glad? Very?

GAYEV (*cheerfully*). Yes, indeed, everything is all right now. Before the cherry orchard was sold we were all worried and miserable, but afterward, when the question was finally settled once and for all, everybody calmed down and felt quite cheerful. . . . I'm in a bank now, a financier . . . cue ball into the center . . . and you, Lyuba, say what you like, you look better, no doubt about it.

LYUBOV ANDREYEVNA. Yes. My nerves are better, that's true. (*Her hat and coat are handed to her.*) I sleep well. Carry out my things, Yasha, it's time. (*To Anya.*) My little girl, we shall see each other soon. . . . I shall go to Paris and live there on the money your great-aunt sent to buy the estate—long live Auntie!—but that money won't last long.

ANYA. You'll come back soon, Mama, soon . . . won't you? I'll study hard and pass my high school examinations, and then I can work and help you. We'll read all sorts of books together, Mama. . . . Won't we? (*Kisses her mother's hand.*) We'll read in the autumn evenings, we'll read lots of books, and a new and wonderful world will open up before us. . . . (*Dreaming.*) Mama, come back. . . .

LYUBOV ANDREYEVNA. I'll come, my precious. (*Embraces her.*)

(*Enter Lopakhin, Charlotta Ivanovna is softly humming a song.*)

GAYEV. Happy Charlotta: She's singing!

CHARLOTTA (*picks up a bundle and holds it like a baby in swaddling clothes*). Bye, baby, bye. . . . (*A baby's crying is heard, "Wah Wah!"*) Be quiet, my darling, my dear little boy. (*"Wah! Wah!"*) I'm so sorry for you! (*Throws the bundle down.*) You will find me a position, won't you? I can't go on like this.

LOPAKHIN. We'll find something, Charlotta Ivanovna, don't worry.

GAYEV. Everyone is leaving us, Varya's going away . . . all of a sudden nobody needs us.

CHARLOTTA. I have nowhere to go in town. I must go away. (*Hums.*) It doesn't matter . . .

(*Enter Pishchik.*)

LOPAKHIN. Nature's wonder!

PISHCHIK (*panting*). Ugh! Let me catch my breath. . . . I'm exhausted. . . . My esteemed friends. . . . Give me some water. . . .

GAYEV. After money, I suppose? Excuse me, I'm fleeing from temptation. . . . (*Goes out.*)

PISHCHIK. It's a long time since I've been to see you . . . fairest lady. . . . (*To Lopakhin*) So you're here. . . . Glad to see you, you intellectual giant. . . . Here . . . take it . . . four hundred rubles . . . I still owe you eight hundred and forty . . .

LOPAKHIN (*shrugs his shoulders in bewilderment*). I must be dreaming. . . . Where did you get it?

PISHCHIK. Wait . . . I'm hot. . . . A most extraordinary event. Some Englishmen came to my place and discovered some kind of white clay on my land. (*To Lyubov Andreyevna*) And four hundred for you . . . fairest, most wonderful lady. . . . (*Hands her the money.*) The rest later. (*Takes a drink of water.*) Just now a young man in the train was saying that a certain . . . great philosopher recommends jumping off roofs. . . . "Jump!" he says, and therein lies the whole problem. (*In amazement.*) Think of that, now! . . . Water!

LOPAKHIN. Who were those Englishmen?

PISHCHIK. I leased them the tract of land with the clay on it for twenty-four years. . . . And now, excuse me, I have no time . . . I must be trotting along . . . I'm going to Znoikov's . . . to Kardamanov's . . . I owe everybody. (*Drinks.*) Keep well . . . I'll drop in on Thursday . . .

LYUBOV ANDREYEVNA. We're just moving into town, and tomorrow I go abroad . . .

PISHCHIK. What? (*Alarmed.*) Why into town? That's why I see the furniture . . . suitcases. . . . Well, never mind. . . . (*Through tears.*) Never mind. . . . Men of the greatest intellect, those Englishmen. . . . Never mind. . . . Be happy . . . God will help you. . . . Never mind. . . . Everything in this world comes to an end. . . . (*Kisses Lyubov Andreyevna's hand.*) And should the news reach you that my end has come, just remember this old horse, and say: "There once lived a certain Semyonov-Pishchik, God rest his soul." . . . Splendid weather. . . . Yes. . . . (*Goes out greatly disconcerted, but immediately returns and speaks from the doorway.*) Dashenka sends her regards. (*Goes out.*)

LYUBOV ANDREYEVNA. Now we can go. I am leaving with two things on my mind. First—that Firs is sick. (*Looks at her watch.*) We still have about five minutes. . . .

ANYA. Mama, Firs has already been taken to the hospital. Yasha sent him there this morning.

LYUBOV ANDREYEVNA. My second concern is Varya. She's used to getting up early and working, and now, with no work to do, she's like a fish out of water. She's grown pale and thin, and cries all the time, poor girl. . . . (*Pauses.*) You know very well, Yermolai Alekseich, that I dreamed of marrying her to you, and everything pointed to your getting married. (*Whispers to Anya, who nods to Charlotta, and they both go out.*) She loves you, you are fond of her, and I don't know—I don't know why it is you seem to avoid each other. I can't understand it!

LOPAKHIN. To tell you the truth, I don't understand it myself. The whole thing is strange, somehow. . . . If there's still time, I'm ready right now. . . . Let's finish it up—and *basta*,[12] but without you I feel I'll never be able to propose to her.

LYUBOV ANDREYEVNA. Splendid! After all, it only takes a minute. I'll call her in at once. . . .

LOPAKHIN. And we even have the champagne. (*Looks at the glasses.*) Empty! Somebody's already drunk it. (*Yasha coughs.*) That's what you call lapping it up.

LYUBOV ANDREYEVNA (*animatedly*). Splendid! We'll leave you. . . . Yasha, *allez!*[13] I'll call her. . . . (*At the door.*) Varya, leave everything and come here. Come! (*Goes out with Yasha.*)

LOPAKHIN (*looking at his watch*). Yes. . . . (*Pause.*)

(*Behind the door there is smothered laughter and whispering; finally Varya enters.*)

VARYA (*looking over the luggage for a long time*). Strange, I can't seem to find it . . .

LOPAKHIN. What are you looking for?

VARYA. I packed it myself, and I can't remember . . . (*Pause.*)

LOPAKHIN. Where are you going now, Varya Mikhailovna?

VARYA. I? To the Ragulins'. . . . I've agreed to go there to look after the house . . . as a sort of housekeeper.

LOPAKHIN. At Yashnevo? That would be about seventy versts from here. (*Pause.*) Well, life in this house has come to an end. . . .

VARYA (*examining the luggage*). Where can it be? . . . Perhaps I put it in the trunk. . . . Yes, life in this house has come to an end . . . there'll be no more . . .

LOPAKHIN. And I'm off for Kharkov . . . by the next train. I have a lot to do. I'm leaving Yepikhodov here . . . I've taken him on.

VARYA. Really!

LOPAKHIN. Last year at this time it was already snowing, if you remember, but now it's still and sunny. It's cold though . . . About three degrees of frost.

VARYA. I haven't looked. (*Pause.*) And besides, our thermometer's broken. (*Pause.*)

(*A voice from the yard calls: "Yermolai Alekseich!"*)

LOPAKHIN (*as if he had been waiting for a long time for the call*). Coming! (*Goes out quickly.*)

---

[12]***basta*** "enough" in Italian
[13]***allez*** "go" in French

(Varya sits on the floor, lays her head on a bundle of clothes, and quietly sobs. The door opens and Lyubov Andreyevna enters cautiously.)

LYUBOV ANDREYEVNA. Well? *(Pause.)* We must be going.

VARYA *(no longer crying, dries her eyes).* Yes, it's time, Mama dear. I can get to the Ragulins' today, if only we don't miss the train.

LYUBOV ANDREYEVNA *(in the doorway).* Anya, put your things on!

(Enter Anya, then Gayev and Charlotta Ivanovna. Gayev wears a warm overcoat with a hood. The servants and coachmen come in. Yepikhodov bustles about the luggage.)

LYUBOV ANDREYEVNA. Now we can be on our way.

ANYA *(joyfully).* On our way!

GAYEV. My friends, my dear, cherished friends! Leaving this house forever, can I pass over in silence, can I refrain from giving utterance, as we say farewell, to those feelings that now fill my whole being—

ANYA *(imploringly).* Uncle!

VARYA. Uncle dear, don't!

GAYEV *(forlornly).* Double the rail off the white to center table . . . yellow into the side pocket. . . . I'll be quiet. . . .

(Enter Trofimov, then Lopakhin.)

TROFIMOV. Well, ladies and gentlemen, it's time to go!

LOPAKHIN. Yepikhodov, my coat!

LYUBOV ANDREYEVNA. I'll sit here just one more minute. It's as though I had never before seen what the walls of this house were like, what the ceilings were like, and now I look at them hungrily, with such tender love . . .

GAYEV. I remember when I was six years old, sitting on this windowsill on Whitsunday, watching my father going to church . . .

LYUBOV ANDREYEVNA. Have they taken all the things?

LOPAKHIN. Everything, I think. *(Puts on his overcoat.)* Yepikhodov, see that everything is in order.

YEPIKHODOV *(in a hoarse voice).* Rest assured, Yermolai Alekseich!

LOPAKHIN. What's the matter with your voice?

YEPIKHODOV. Just drank some water . . . must have swallowed something.

YASHA *(contemptuously).* What ignorance!

LYUBOV ANDREYEVNA. When we go—there won't be a soul left here. . . .

LOPAKHIN. Till spring.

VARYA *(pulls an umbrella out of a bundle as though she were going to hit someone; Lopakhin pretends to be frightened).* Why are you—I never thought of such a thing!

TROFIMOV. Ladies and gentlemen, let's get into the carriages—it's time now! The train will soon be in!

VARYA. Petya, there they are—your rubbers, by the suitcase. *(Tearfully.)* And what dirty old things they are!

TROFIMOV *(putting on his rubbers).* Let's go, ladies and gentlemen!

GAYEV *(extremely upset, afraid of bursting into tears).* The train . . . the station. . . . Cross table to the center, double the rail . . . on the white into the corner.

LYUBOV ANDREYEVNA. Let us go!

GAYEV. Are we all here? No one in there? *(Locks the side door on the left.)* There are some things stored in there, we must lock up. Let's go!

ANYA. Good-bye, house! Good-bye, old life!

TROFIMOV. Hail to the new life! *(Goes out with Anya.)*

(Varya looks around the room and slowly goes out. Yasha and Charlotta with her dog go out.)

LOPAKHIN. And so, till spring. Come along, my friends. . . . Till we meet! *(Goes out.)*

(Lyubov Andreyevna and Gayev are left alone. As though they had been waiting for this, they fall onto each other's necks and break into quiet, restrained sobs, afraid of being heard.)

GAYEV *(in despair).* My sister, my sister. . . .

LYUBOV ANDREYEVNA. Oh, my dear, sweet, lovely orchard! . . . My life, my youth, my happiness, good-bye! . . . Good-bye!

ANYA'S VOICE *(gaily calling).* Mama!

TROFIMOV'S VOICE *(gay and excited).* Aa-oo!

LYUBOV ANDREYEVNA. One last look at these walls, these windows. . . . Mother loved to walk about in this room. . . .

GAYEV. My sister, my sister!

ANYA'S VOICE. Mama!

TROFIMOV'S VOICE. Aa-oo!

LYUBOV ANDREYEVNA. We're coming! *(They go out.)*

(The stage is empty. There is the sound of doors being locked, then of the carriages driving away. It grows quiet. In the stillness there is the dull thud of an ax on a tree, a forlorn, melancholy sound. Footsteps are heard. From the door on the right Firs appears. He is dressed as always in a jacket and white waistcoat, and wears slippers. He is ill.)

FIRS *(goes to the door and tries the handle).* Locked. They have gone. . . . *(Sits down on the sofa.)* They've forgotten me. . . . Never mind. . . . I'll sit here awhile. . . . I expect Leonid Andreich hasn't put on his fur coat and has gone off in his overcoat. *(Sighs anxiously.)*

And I didn't see to it. . . . When they're young, they're green! (*Mumbles something which cannot be understood.*) I'll lie down awhile. . . . There's no strength left in you, nothing's left, nothing. . . . Ach, you . . . addlepate! (*Lies motionless.*)

(*A distant sound is heard that seems to come from the sky, the sound of a snapped string mournfully dying away. A stillness falls, and nothing is heard but the thud of an ax on a tree far away in the orchard.*)

COMMENTARY

Note: The following essay represents a single interpretation of the play. For other perspectives on The Cherry Orchard, *consult the essays listed below.*

The Breaking String (Maurice Valency, 1966) remains among the finest studies of Chekhov's dramaturgy. The title is taken from a stage direction found in Act II of *The Cherry Orchard*:

> *All sit lost in thought. The silence is broken only by the subdued muttering of Firs. Suddenly a distant sound is heard, as if from the sky, like the sound of a snapped string mournfully dying away.*

Valency selects this moment for his title because it crystallizes the whole of Chekhov's drama. Here we see a cluster of people on a remote Russian estate, so typical of the "ensemble pathos" that marks Chekhov's style. Though they sit together, each is very much alone "lost in thought." In the distance we see telegraph poles (the new technology) and beyond them, the skyline of a growing city. Clearly the landscape of Mother Russia is changing, for it, too, is "mournfully dying away." The play premiered the year of the first of two great revolutions that transformed Russia between 1904 and 1917. Significantly, old Firs is a link to the 1862 revolution that overthrew feudalism. Though Chekhov was not a political writer in the manner of Ibsen or Shaw, *The Cherry Orchard* resonates with the social tensions of its time. The orchard itself, which is being chopped down as the final curtain falls, is emblematic of the aristocratic order that is outmoded.

Whatever its social relevance in 1904, the play—like each of Chekhov's major works—transcends the particulars of time and place and remains among the most universal studies of the human dilemma, even a century after its composition. *The Cherry Orchard* is a four-act study of frustrated human aspirations, the dominant theme in each of the playwright's four masterpieces. His characters consistently demonstrate an uncanny ability to desire most that which they are least likely to obtain, and they do little to help themselves realize their dreams. Lopakhin is perhaps the most notable exception to this Chekhovian law. While he does indeed attain the estate and its revered orchard, upon which his ancestors had toiled, he never quite gets around to marrying Varya, the object of his affection.

As detached observers, we see the absurdity of his characters' futile quests for the unachievable. Unlike Cervantes' similarly delusional Don Quixote, who also chased impossible dreams, Chekhov's characters are trapped by their own inertia (and folly) as much as by any external forces. Thus Chekhov's plays are simultaneously amusing and pathetic, even nearly tragic. Real lives are surely "being smashed up," but there is invariably something oddly absurd, even silly, about the characters' dilemmas. Evidence of such folly abounds throughout *The Cherry Orchard*.

- Madame Ranevskaya desperately wants to retain her estate, but she fritters away her money, most notably by throwing a lavish ball even as the estate is being sold to the very man (Lopakhin) who has provided sound business advice that would permit her to salvage the cherry orchard. Of her mother's profligacy, Anya says, "Dear Mother, the same as ever. Hasn't changed a bit. If you let her, she'd give everything away."
- Gayev, Madame Ranevskaya's silly, sentimental brother, clings to the past while refusing to adjust to the present. He is too settled into a way of life in which "I wrack my brains [to] come up with all sorts of solutions, all sorts, and that means, actually none."
- In contrast to Gayev, Trofimov expounds loftily about his visions for the future, but his credibility is undermined as we learn that he is little more than a professional student who will not venture out into the "real" world.
- Madame Ranevskaya's daughter, Anya, and Varya, her ward, are ineffectual in their pursuit of love—the former too eager to involve herself in irresponsible relationships, the latter too bound by her work to feel genuine emotions.

- Even the maid Dunyasha falls in love with the one person least likely to return her love: the self-absorbed valet, Yasha.
- And there is Yepikhodov, the bumbling bookkeeper whose very nickname epitomizes Chekhovian pathos: "Two-and-twenty Troubles."

It is perhaps natural for us to assign blame for the various predicaments of Chekhov's characters. In the tradition of melodrama in which the family estate is lost, Lopakhin, the newly rich landowner, might be something of a villain. But here we are actually pleased that he gains the estate because it affirms his family's progress from serfdom to respectability. In Chekhov's world, however, there is truly only one villain: time. In the world of Sophocles or Ibsen, time abets change, reveals truths, and ultimately liberates (and frequently vindicates) protagonists from their ordeals. In time, Oedipus learns his identity and is thus liberated from the lie of his past; and in time, Nora Helmer realizes that "I must stand on my feet to find out the truth about myself and my life." But in Chekhov's world, time only further entraps the characters because past, present, and future are virtually interchangeable. Note that Lopakhin opens the play with the question: "What time is it?" And throughout the action, such as there is in this drama of "inaction," each character dwells on the inexorable passage of time, most notably in Uncle Gayev's famed speech to the bookcase in Act I. But perhaps the most telling reference to time is found in the play's finale. As the family leaves the estate for the last time, and as Firs settles onto the sofa for a nap—or death?—we again hear the sound of the breaking string, backed by the metronomic thud of an ax on the cherry trees, much like the ticking of a cosmic clock.

Samuel Beckett (the dramatist most often aligned with Chekhov by modern critics) also meditates upon the villainy of time and perhaps best captures the essential Chekhovian dilemma in his masterpiece, *Waiting for Godot*: "Time! Time! Will you not stop tormenting me with your cursed Time? One day we are born, one day we die . . . that's how it is on this bitch of an earth." Compare this speech with the exchange about death between Trofimov and Gayev near the end of Act II. The inexorable march of time invests Chekhov's plays with their characteristic melancholy, far more than any of the lamentations of the characters. And it is here that Chekhov emerges as the most unflinchingly realistic of dramatists.

Other perspectives on *The Cherry Orchard*:

Fergusson, Francis. "*Ghosts* and *The Cherry Orchard*." In Francis Fergusson, *The Idea of a Theatre*. Princeton, NJ: Princeton Paperbacks, 1949, 146–77.

Kramer, Karl D. "Love and Comic Insatiability in *The Cherry Orchard*." In Kenneth N. Brostrom (ed.), *Russian Literature and American Critics*. Ann Arbor, MI: MCI, 1984, 295–307.

Chekhov's plays on video/film:

The Sea Gull. Dir. Nichos Psacharopolous. Perf. Frank Langella, Blythe Danner, and Olympia Dukakis. Kultur, 118 min., 1975.

Uncle Vanya. Dir. Laurence Olivier and Stuart Burge. Perf. Laurence Olivier, Joan Plowright, and Michael Redgrave. Insight Media, 90 min., 1962.

The Three Sisters. Dir. Paul Bogart and Lee Strasberg. Perf. Sandy Dennis, Geraldine Page, Kim Stanley, and Shelley Winters. Hen's Tooth Video, 166 min., 1965.

About Chekhov:
Chekhov. Films for the Humanities, 53 min., 1993.

SHOWCASE — THE STANISLAVSKY SYSTEM AND THE MOSCOW ART THEATRE

In the West, actor training—and therefore acting styles—have changed considerably over the roughly twenty-six centuries since Thespis established the profession in ancient Greece. Traditionally, most approaches to acting fall into one of two broad categories: *external* (vocal and physical) technique and *internal* (emotion-centered) technique. Today a third designation is evolving: *integrated* actors who fuse the external and internal approaches. Whatever their technique, the goal remains constant for actors: to create memorable characters that engage audiences.

External actors work largely "from the outside in," that is, they begin with rigorous physical and vocal training since the body and especially the voice are the actor's primary tools. Some actors are famous for their obsession with external details. Virtually all of pre-twentieth-century drama necessitated an external approach. Enormous theaters, scripts whose poetry and songs demanded an exceptional vocal range, conventions such as men playing women's roles, few or no rehearsals, an oratorical acting tradition, and many other factors demanded an external or "technical" style. Voice, breathing, and elocution exercises were compulsory, as was training in dance, mime, acrobatics, juggling, swordplay, posture, and balance. Today many Western actors have added to their physical regimen martial arts and yoga, longtime staples of Asian training.

If the accounts of eyewitnesses are reasonably accurate, a basically external approach to acting in the West produced two thousand years of admirable actors from Thespis in ancient Greece to Henry Irving in the late nineteenth century. However, there were times when external technique approached the ludicrous. Consider these instructions from *The Thespian Preceptor, or, A Full Display of the Scenic Art*, an 1810 acting text that promised "ample and easy instructions for treading the stage." When playing anger a male actor produces "a violent and sudden shake" and then he

. . . *opens the eyes and mouth very wide, draws down the eye brows, gives the countenance an air of wildness, draws back the elbows parallel with the sides, lifts up the open hand (his fingers together) to the height of the breast so that the palms face the dreadful object, as shields opposed against it. The heart beats violently; the breath is fetched quick and short, and the whole is thrown in a general tremor.*

For women anger was simply indicated "by a violent shriek, which produces fainting." Strangely, this advice was intended to ensure truthfulness and naturalness in performance. "Truthful," "natural," and especially "lifelike" are always relative terms when applied to acting and must be considered in light of the age in which they are used. Do you think that the acting style of a 1920s silent movie is as "natural" as that of a recent film with Denzel Washington or Jodie Foster?

External acting does not preclude strongly felt inner emotion or truth. Aristotle believed that "those who feel emotion are most convincing through natural sympathy with the characters they represent." Hamlet counsels his actors to "use all gently. . . . let your own discretion be your tutor: suit the action to the word, the word to the action, with this special observance, that you o'erstep not the modesty of nature."

These comments by Aristotle and Shakespeare point the way toward *internal* acting that is largely a modern and Western approach to performance. The plays of Ibsen, Chekhov, and their contemporaries demanded an intimacy in playing style (as well as new playing spaces). Thus a subtler, internally based style emerged, largely under the teaching of Constantin Stanislavsky (1863–1938), cofounder of the Moscow Art Theatre in 1897. Stanislavsky saw the more naturalistic style employed by the Meiningen Company (see earlier Showcase, "The Rise of the

Director and Germany's Meiningen Players") and believed it to be the antidote to the excessively melodramatic style that dominated the stages of Russia. Another young artist, Vladimir Nemerovich-Danchenko (1858–1943), shared his vision. The two met at a Moscow tearoom in 1897 to discuss a new theater devoted to the new drama, as well as a new approach to acting. And discuss they did: eighteen hours later they emerged with a plan for the Moscow Public Art Theatre, arguably the single most important theater in the modern West.

The MAT, as it is now known, opened in 1898, first with a popular Russian tragedy (*Tsar Fyodor*), a Shakespeare play (*The Merchant of Venice*), and a comic drama by Anton Chekhov (*The Sea Gull*). Chekhov's play had been an indisputable failure two years earlier when it was performed at Alexandrevsky Theater, largely because the cast—trained in the melodramatic style of the age—was incapable of handling Chekhov's subtle style. However, under Stanislavsky's tutelage *The Sea Gull* was an immediate success with Moscow audiences who were enthralled by a style of acting they had not seen. The play and the theater in which it was performed have become long-lasting institutions among the Russian people. Fittingly, the MAT still features an insignia of a sea gull on its act curtain.

The actors employed by the MAT, including Olga Knipper (Chekhov's wife), were taught by Stanislavsky to carefully study their parts to glean all pertinent information about their characters; Stanislavsky referred to such information as "the given circumstances." Actors were also told to break scripts into a series of *beats* in which they defined the moment-to-moment intentions (or "objectives") of their characters, the external and internal obstacle(s) that might keep them from achieving the goal, and the tactics characters might use to overcome them. ("Beat," by the way, actually derived from Stanislavsky's mispronunciation of the word "bit," meaning "a little piece of the whole.") Beats evolve into "units" (usually a section of a scene), units become scenes, and scenes become acts, the whole of which is defined by an overall intention. Stanislavsky called this "the super objective," which he defined as "the whole stream of individual, minor objectives, all the imaginative thoughts, feelings and actions of an actor." (Director Harold Clurman uses an anatomical metaphor—"the spine"—to denote the super objective.) In *Death of a Salesman* Willy Loman's spine might be "to preserve my dignity" or "to make my sons love me," while Linda's may be "to save Willy."

Having completed this careful analysis, Stanislavky then asked his actors to consider what they would do "if" they were in the situation they had analyzed. This "Magic IF" is the cornerstone of Stanislavsky's approach to acting—a technique he derived from watching children play games of make-believe. Stanislavsky's famous "System," as it became known, took many years to develop, as he constantly modified his approach.

Consider, as an actor might, a beat (the smallest unit of a scene) from *Death of a Salesman*. These lines open Act II and, at first glance, there appears to be little conflict in the dialogue between Willy and his wife.

WILLY. Wonderful coffee. Meal in itself.
LINDA. Can I make you some eggs?
WILLY. No. Take a breath.
LINDA. You look so rested, dear.

Early morning chitchat, no conflict, nothing happening, right? True, this is a moment of repose in the otherwise tempestuous Loman household. It signals the start of what Willy hopes will be a brighter day, and it suggests precisely the kind of home life Linda wants. But consider the given circumstances: the previous night ended in a noisy argument between Willy and his son, Biff; Willy has cursed Linda; Biff has discovered a length of rubber hose with which Willy perhaps intends to

kill himself. Given these circumstances, the small talk is loaded with subtext. Willy's intentions are to placate Linda, to apologize for his gruff behavior. The compliment about the coffee is his way of saying, "Listen, I was out of line last night." As we see elsewhere in the play, he is a proud man and apologies don't come easily. Thus his text ("Wonderful coffee") implies a subtext: "You're a good wife. I know it's been hard for you." In these lines Willy must overcome not only Linda's hurt feelings but also his own self-doubts. The kind words are his tactics for doing so. Linda is motivated to save the Loman household. Her obstacles? His despondent behavior, his low self-esteem, she is "only" a woman in a male-dominated household. Her tactics? To get his mind off the problems, to make his favorite breakfast, to feed his ego ("You look so rested"). The subtext here says: "Everything will be all right. No need for you to kill yourself." There is enormous urgency to Linda's tactics, as there must be in all well-written scenes. One of the challenges of acting is that there are so many possible answers for these questions. This is where actors must finally make "choices" to define their characters.

Stanislavsky also encouraged the MAT actors to tap their inner resources by using *emotion memory*, among other things, to project themselves into the characters they play. Though the process is complex and often misunderstood, emotion memory asks actors to summon up memories of personal experiences and the attendant emotions that are comparable to those of the scripted characters. For instance, an actor who plays Willy Loman should recall the pain and perhaps humiliation he experienced when he was denied an important role he coveted. Theoretically, this triggers the appropriate response when he must react to being fired by Howard. At times internal actors can place too much emphasis on inner feeling, which can lead to self-indulgence and a breakdown of the vocal and physical demands of perfor-

mance. In truth, Stanislavsky (and, it is important to note, Lee Strasberg, who later mentored both the Group Theatre and the Actors Studio) stressed that actors must first develop the voice and body before advancing to the internal aspects of performance. The Russian master told his pupils, "You must have a strong, well-trained voice of pleasant, expressive timbre, perfect diction, plasticity of movement—without being a poseur—a face that is beautiful and mobile, a good figure, and expressive hands."

This combination of actors grounded in physical and vocal technique and a well-motivated approach to their characters created an ensemble that worked closely as a unit. Gone was the old "star system," and each play produced at the MAT benefited from scrupulous attention to detail. The finished product was a more lifelike presentation of people in dilemmas, however minute, that audiences had not seen before.

Stanislavsky's System excited a young generation of American actors in the 1930s, first with the Group Theatre (1931–41) and later with the Actors Studio (1947–present) where the System became known as "the Method." (See Showcase, "The Group Theatre and the Actors Studio: American Acting Matures," in Part II.) Today you may see the legacy of work begun at the MAT in the early twentieth century in the realistic acting that dominates such contemporary films as *Training Day*, which features Denzel Washington and Ethan Hawke, each of whom regularly uses techniques conceived by Stanislavsky and his MAT actors. The MAT, by the way, still produces plays and remains among the oldest continuously running theaters in the world; it is revered as a national treasure by the Russian people.

A video about Stanislavsky and the Moscow Art Theatre:

The Stanislavsky Century (3 parts). Insight Media, 180 min., 1993.

RIDERS TO THE SEA

JOHN MILLINGTON SYNGE

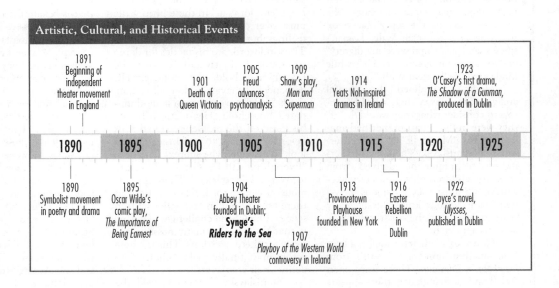

Artistic, Cultural, and Historical Events

1891
Beginning of
independent
theater movement
in England

1901
Death of
Queen Victoria

1905
Freud
advances
psychoanalysis

1909
Shaw's play,
*Man and
Superman*

1914
Yeats Noh-inspired
dramas in Ireland

1923
O'Casey's first drama,
The Shadow of a Gunman,
produced in Dublin

| 1890 | 1895 | 1900 | 1905 | 1910 | 1915 | 1920 | 1925 |

1890
Symbolist movement
in poetry and drama

1895
Oscar Wilde's
comic play,
*The Importance of
Being Earnest*

1904
Abbey Theater
founded in Dublin;
**Synge's
Riders to the Sea**

1907
Playboy of the Western World
controversy in Ireland

1913
Provincetown
Playhouse
founded in New York

1916
Easter
Rebellion
in
Dublin

1922
Joyce's novel,
Ulysses,
published in Dublin

JOHN MILLINGTON SYNGE (1871–1909)

Although he was not the leader of the "Irish Renaissance," the turn-of-the-century movement that gave birth to the modern Irish theater, no artist likely had more influence on the development of contemporary drama in Ireland. Actually, Synge (pronounced "sing") was in Paris when, in 1899, William Butler Yeats and Lady Augusta Gregory, aided by George Moore and Edward Martyn, envisioned an Irish national theater that would, in the words of their manifesto, "build up a Celtic and Irish school of dramatic literature" and "bring upon the stage the deeper thoughts and emotions of Ireland." Furthermore, these artists wanted to eradicate the centuries-old perception, fostered by the British, that Ireland was the "home of buffoonery and of easy entertainment." In short, the new Irish Literary Theatre wanted to cultivate a native drama about local life and problems, spoken in the native idiom.

In 1904 the group, now known as the Irish National Theatre Society, opened the Abbey Theatre in Dublin, which remains the oldest continuous national theater in Europe. While the Abbey met with some success with the works of Yeats and Lady Gregory, it was not until 1907, when it produced Synge's *The Playboy of the Western World*, that the theater became the center of national attention. Many Irish felt that Synge's raucous portrait of Irish peasants was blasphemous, yet Synge was merely depicting his countrymen and women with an uncompromising honesty, born of a genuine love of Ireland and its people. Such candor would become the hallmark of subsequent Abbey productions. The *Playboy* controversy sparked a national debate about the work of the Abbey and catapulted it to the forefront of Irish culture.

Synge was educated at Trinity College in Dublin, Ireland's foremost university and the spawning ground of Irish literati. Yet, like so many Irishmen, Synge fled this native home in 1894 seeking a literary career in Paris. In 1896 Yeats met Synge in Paris and counseled the young writer to return to Ireland. "Give up Paris," he urged, "you will never create anything by reading Racine. . . . Go to the Aran Islands. Live there as if you were one of the people themselves; express a life that has never found expression." Synge, haunted by Yeats's admonition, gradually abandoned his Parisian quest and returned to Ireland, and from 1898 to 1902 Synge spent each summer among the rugged peasant stock of the Aran Isles west of Galway. Here he found source material for his best work, especially *Riders to the Sea*. He also learned the dialect of the common people, a language he turned into the poetic idiom that characterizes his plays. He filled notebooks with observations about life among the fishermen and farmers, and he particularly noted phrases, sayings, and other linguistic peculiarities. He also collected folk songs and dances that he used in his plays. Synge was himself an accomplished violinist, a talent that endeared him to his Aran hosts.

In 1902 Synge was invited by Yeats to join the emerging Irish National Theatre Society, and during the remaining seven years of his life (cut short by Hodgkin's disease), he wrote six plays that would establish him as the first great playwright of the Abbey Theatre. In addition to *Riders to the Sea* and *The Playboy of the Western World*, Synge's best works include *In the Shadow of the Glen*, *The Well of the Saints*, and *Deirdre of the Sorrows*. The latter was produced posthumously in 1910 and, like *Riders to the Sea*, remains among Ireland's finest tragedies.

As You Read *Riders to the Sea*

Historically, *Riders to the Sea* is a significant work because it is among the earliest and most successful modern attempts to use the folk idiom as a vehicle for serious drama. In his preface to *The Playboy of the Western World*, Synge argued that modern drama must use a rich language that grows out of the folk imagination of the peasant people: "In Ireland . . . we have a popular imagination that is fiery and magnificent and tender, so that those of us who wish to write start with a chance that is not given to writers in places where the springtime of the local life has been forgotten." Don't be lulled by the prose format in which Synge wrote the play: this is poetic drama at its most eloquent. As you read this short play, "hear" the soft Irish accents.

RIDERS TO THE SEA

——J OHN M ILLINGTON S YNGE——

L IST OF C HARACTERS
MAURYA, *an old woman*
BARTLEY, *her son*
CATHLEEN, *her daughter*
NORA, *a younger daughter*
MEN *and* WOMEN

Scene: An island off the West of Ireland.

Cottage kitchen, with nets, oil-skins, spinning-wheel, some new boards standing by the wall, etc. Cathleen, a girl of about twenty, finishes kneading cake, and puts it down in the pot-oven by the fire; then wipes her hands, and begins to spin at the wheel. Nora, a young girl, puts her head in at the door.

NORA (*in a low voice*). Where is she?

CATHLEEN. She's lying down, God help her, and may be sleeping, if she's able.

Nora comes in softly, and takes a bundle from under her shawl.

CATHLEEN (*spinning the wheel rapidly*). What is it you have?

NORA. The young priest is after bringing them. It's a shirt and a plain stocking were got off a drowned man in Donegal.

Cathleen stops her wheel with a sudden movement, and leans out to listen.

NORA. We're to find out if it's Michael's they are, some time herself will be down looking by the sea.

CATHLEEN. How would they be Michael's, Nora? How would he go the length of that way to the far north?

NORA. The young priest says he's known the like of it. "If it's Michael's they are," says he, "you can tell herself he's got a clean burial by the grace of God, and if

they're not his, let no one say a word about them, for she'll be getting her death," says he, "with crying and lamenting."

The door which Nora half-closed is blown open by a gust of wind.

CATHLEEN (*looking out anxiously*). Did you ask him would he stop Bartley going this day with the horses to the Galway fair?

NORA. "I won't stop him," says he, "but let you not be afraid. Herself does be saying prayers half through the night, and the Almighty God won't leave her destitute," says he, "with no son living."

CATHLEEN. Is the sea bad by the white rocks, Nora?

NORA. Middling bad, God help us. There's a great roaring in the west, and it's worse it'll be getting when the tide's turned to the wind. (*She goes over to the table with the bundle.*) Shall I open it now?

CATHLEEN. Maybe she'd wake up on us, and come in before we'd done. (*Coming to the table.*) It's a long time we'll be, and the two of us crying.

NORA (*goes to the inner door and listens*). She's moving about on the bed. She'll be coming in a minute.

CATHLEEN. Give me the ladder, and I'll put them up in the turf-loft, the way she won't know of them at all, and maybe when the tide turns she'll be going down to see would he be floating from the east.

They put the ladder against the gable of the chimney; Cathleen goes up a few steps and hides the bundle in the turf-loft. Maurya comes from the inner room.

MAURYA (*looking up at Cathleen and speaking querulously*). Isn't it turf enough you have for this day and evening?

CATHLEEN. There's a cake baking at the fire for a short space (*throwing down the turf*) and Bartley will want it when the tide turns if he goes to Connemara.

Nora picks up the turf and puts it round the pot-oven.

MAURYA (*sitting down on a stool at the fire*). He won't go this day with the wind rising from the south and west. He won't go this day, for the young priest will stop him surely.

NORA. He'll not stop him, Mother, and I heard Eamon Simon and Stephen Pheety and Colum Shawn saying he would go.

MAURYA. Where is he itself?

NORA. He went down to see would there be another boat sailing in the week, and I'm thinking it won't be long till he's here now, for the tide's turning at the green head, and the hooker's[1] tacking from the east.

CATHLEEN. I hear some one passing the big stones.

NORA (*looking out*). He's coming now, and he in a hurry.

BARTLEY (*comes in and looks round the room. Speaking sadly and quietly*). Where is the bit of new rope, Cathleen, was bought in Connemara?

CATHLEEN (*coming down*). Give it to him, Nora; it's on a nail by the white boards. I hung it up this morning, for the pig with the black feet was eating it.

NORA (*giving him a rope*). Is that it, Bartley?

MAURYA. You'd do right to leave that rope, Bartley, hanging by the boards. (*Bartley takes the rope.*) It will be wanting in this place, I'm telling you, if Michael is washed up to-morrow morning, or the next morning, or any morning in the week, for it's a deep grave we'll make him by the grace of God.

BARTLEY (*beginning to work with the rope*). I've no halter the way I can ride down on the mare, and I must go now quickly. This is the one boat going for two weeks or beyond it, and the fair will be a good fair for horses I heard them saying below.

MAURYA. It's a hard thing they'll be saying below if the body is washed up and there's no man in it to make the coffin, and I after giving a big price for the finest white boards you'd find in Connemara.

She looks round at the boards.

BARTLEY. How would it be washed up, and we after looking each day for nine days, and a strong wind blowing a while back from the west and south?

MAURYA. If it wasn't found itself, that wind is raising the sea, and there was a star up against the moon, and it rising in the night. If it was a hundred horses, or a thousand horses you had itself, what is the price of a thousand horses against a son where there is one son only?

BARTLEY (*working at the halter, to Cathleen*). Let you go down each day, and see the sheep aren't jumping in on the rye, and if the jobber comes you can sell the pig with the black feet if there is a good price going.

MAURYA. How would the like of her get a good price for a pig?

BARTLEY (*to Cathleen*). If the west wind holds with the last bit of the moon let you and Nora get up weed enough for another cock for the kelp.[2] It's hard set we'll be from this day with no one in it but one man to work.

MAURYA. It's hard set we'll be surely the day you're drownd'd with the rest. What way will I live and the girls with me, and I an old woman looking for the grave?

Bartley lays down the halter, takes off his old coat, and puts on a newer one of the same flannel.

BARTLEY (*to Nora*). Is she coming to the pier?

NORA (*looking out*). She's passing the green head and letting fall her sails.

BARTLEY (*getting his purse and tobacco*). I'll have half an hour to go down, and you'll see me coming again in two days, or in three days, or maybe in four days if the wind is bad.

MAURYA (*turning round to the fire, and putting her shawl over her head*). Isn't it a hard and cruel man won't hear a word from an old woman, and she holding him from the sea?

CATHLEEN. It's the life of a young man to be going on the sea, and who would listen to an old woman with one thing and she saying it over?

BARTLEY (*taking the halter*). I must go now quickly. I'll ride down on the red mare, and the gray pony'll run behind me. . . . The blessing of God on you.

He goes out.

MAURYA (*crying out as he is in the door*). He's gone now, God spare us, and we'll not see him again. He's gone now, and when the black night is falling I'll have no son left me in the world.

CATHLEEN. Why wouldn't you give him your blessing and he looking round in the door? Isn't it sorrow enough is on every one in this house without your sending him out with an unlucky word behind him, and a hard word in his ear?

Maurya takes up the tongs and begins raking the fire aimlessly without looking round.

---

[1]**hooker** boat

[2]**kelp** seaweed used as fertilizer

NORA (*turning towards her*). You're taking away the turf from the cake.

CATHLEEN (*crying out*). The Son of God forgive us, Nora, we're after forgetting his bit of bread.

She comes over to the fire.

NORA. And it's destroyed he'll be going till dark night, and he after eating nothing since the sun went up.

CATHLEEN (*turning the cake out of the oven*). It's destroyed he'll be, surely. There's no sense left on any person in a house where an old woman will be talking for ever.

Maurya sways herself on her stool.

CATHLEEN (*cutting off some of the bread and rolling it in a cloth; to Maurya*). Let you go down now to the spring well and give him this and he passing. You'll see him then and the dark word will be broken, and you can say "God speed you," the way he'll be easy in his mind.

MAURYA (*taking the bread*). Will I be in it as soon as himself?

CATHLEEN. If you go now quickly.

MAURYA (*standing up unsteadily*). It's hard set I am to walk.

CATHLEEN (*looking at her anxiously*). Give her the stick, Nora, or maybe she'll slip on the big stones.

NORA. What stick?

CATHLEEN. The stick Michael brought from Connemara.

MAURYA (*taking a stick Nora gives her*). In the big world the old people do be leaving things after them for their sons and children, but in this place it is the young men do be leaving things behind for them that do be old.

She goes out slowly. Nora goes over to the ladder.

CATHLEEN. Wait, Nora, maybe she'd turn back quickly. She's that sorry, God help her, you wouldn't know the thing she'd do.

NORA. Is she gone around by the bush?

CATHLEEN (*looking out*). She's gone now. Throw it down quickly, for the Lord knows when she'll be out of it again.

NORA (*getting the bundle from the loft*). The young priest said he'd be passing to-morrow, and we might go down and speak to him below if it's Michael's they are surely.

CATHLEEN (*taking the bundle*). Did he say what way they were found?

NORA (*coming down*). "There were two men," says he, "and they rowing round with poteen[3] before the cocks crowed, and the oar of one of them caught the body, and they passing the black cliffs of the north."

CATHLEEN (*trying to open the bundle*). Give me a knife, Nora, the strings perished with the salt water, and there's a black knot on it you wouldn't loosen in a week.

NORA (*giving her a knife*). I've heard tell it was a long way to Donegal.

CATHLEEN (*cutting the string*). It is surely. There was a man in here a while ago—the man sold us that knife—and he said if you set off walking from the rock beyond, it would be seven days you'd be in Donegal.

NORA. And what time would a man take, and he floating?

Cathleen opens the bundle and takes out a bit of a stocking. They look at them eagerly.

CATHLEEN (*in a low voice*). The Lord spare us, Nora! isn't it a queer hard thing to say if it's his they are surely?

NORA. I'll get his shirt off the hook the way we can put the one flannel on the other. (*She looks through some clothes hanging in the corner.*) It's not with them, Cathleen, and where will it be?

CATHLEEN. I'm thinking Bartley put it on him in the morning, for his own shirt was heavy with the salt in it. (*Pointing to the corner.*) There's a bit of a sleeve was of the same stuff. Give me that and it will do.

Nora brings it to her and they compare the flannel.

CATHLEEN. It's the same stuff, Nora; but if it is itself aren't there great rolls of it in the shops of Galway, and isn't it many another man may have a shirt of it as well as Michael himself?

NORA (*who has taken up the stocking and counted the stitches, crying out*). It's Michael, Cathleen, it's Michael; God spare his soul, and what will herself say when she hears this story, and Bartley on the sea?

CATHLEEN (*taking the stocking*). It's a plain stocking.

NORA. It's the second one of the third pair I knitted, and I put up three score stitches, and I dropped four of them.

CATHLEEN (*counts the stitches*). It's that number is in it. (*Crying out.*) Ah, Nora, isn't it a bitter thing to think of him floating that way to the far north, and no one to keen[4] him but the black hags that do be flying on the sea?

NORA (*swinging herself round, and throwing out her arms on the clothes*). And isn't it a pitiful thing when there is nothing left of a man who was a great rower and fisher, but a bit of an old shirt and a plain stocking?

[3]**poteen** whiskey

[4]**keen** lament; a mournful, soft wailing

CATHLEEN (*after an instant*). Tell me is herself coming, Nora? I hear a little sound on the path.

NORA (*looking out*). She is, Cathleen. She's coming up to the door.

CATHLEEN. Put these things away before she'll come in. Maybe it's easier she'll be after giving her blessing to Bartley, and we won't let on we've heard anything the time he's on the sea.

NORA (*helping Cathleen to close the bundle*). We'll put them here in the corner.

They put them into a hole in the chimney corner. Cathleen goes back to the spinning-wheel.

NORA. Will she see it was crying I was?

CATHLEEN. Keep your back to the door the way the light'll not be on you.

Nora sits down at the chimney corner, with her back to the door. Maurya comes in very slowly, without looking at the girls, and goes over to her stool at the other side of the fire. The cloth with the bread is still in her hand. The girls look at each other, and Nora points to the bundle of bread.

CATHLEEN (*after spinning for a moment*). You didn't give him his bit of bread?

Maurya begins to keen softly, without turning round.

CATHLEEN. Did you see him riding down?

Maurya goes on keening.

CATHLEEN (*a little impatiently*). God forgive you; isn't it a better thing to raise your voice and tell what you seen, than to be making lamentation for a thing that's done? Did you see Bartley, I'm saying to you.

MAURYA (*with a weak voice*). My heart's broken from this day.

CATHLEEN (*as before*). Did you see Bartley?

MAURYA. I seen the fearfulest thing.

CATHLEEN (*leaves her wheel and looks out*). God forgive you; he's riding the mare now over the green head, and the gray pony behind him.

MAURYA (*starts, so that her shawl falls back from her head and shows her white tossed hair. With a frightened voice*). The gray pony behind him.

CATHLEEN (*coming to the fire*). What is it ails you, at all?

MAURYA (*speaking very slowly*). I've seen the fearfulest thing any person has seen, since the day Bride Dara seen the dead man with the child in his arms.

CATHLEEN AND NORA. Uah.

They crouch down in front of the old woman at the fire.

NORA. Tell us what it is you seen.

MAURYA. I went down to the spring well, and I stood there saying a prayer to myself. Then Bartley came along, and he riding on the red mare with the gray pony behind him. (*She puts up her hands, as if to hide something from her eyes.*) The Son of God spare us, Nora!

CATHLEEN. What is it you seen?

MAURYA. I seen Michael himself.

CATHLEEN (*speaking softly*). You did not, mother; it wasn't Michael you seen, for his body is after being found in the far north, and he's got a clean burial by the grace of God.

MAURYA (*a little defiantly*). I'm after seeing him this day, and he riding and galloping. Bartley came first on the red mare; and I tried to say "God speed you," but something choked the words in my throat. He went by quickly; and "the blessing of God on you," says he, and I could say nothing. I looked up then, and I crying, at the gray pony, and there was Michael upon it—with fine clothes on him, and new shoes on his feet.

CATHLEEN (*begins to keen*). It's destroyed we are from this day. It's destroyed, surely.

NORA. Didn't the young priest say the Almighty God wouldn't leave her destitute with no son living?

MAURYA (*in a low voice, but clearly*). It's little the like of him knows of the sea. . . . Bartley will be lost now, and let you call in Eamon and make me a good coffin out of the white boards, for I won't live after them. I've had a husband, and a husband's father, and six sons in this house—six fine men, though it was a hard birth I had with every one of them and they coming to the world—and some of them were found and some of them were not found, but they're gone now the lot of them. . . . There were Stephen, and Shawn, were lost in the great wind, and found after in the Bay of Gregory of the Golden Mouth, and carried up the two of them on the one plank, and in by that door.

She pauses for a moment, the girls start as if they heard something through the door that is half open behind them.

NORA (*in a whisper*). Did you hear that, Cathleen? Did you hear a noise in the north-east?

CATHLEEN (*in a whisper*). There's some one after crying out by the seashore.

MAURYA (*continues without hearing anything*). There was Sheamus and his father, and his own father again, were lost in a dark night, and not a stick or sign was seen of them when the sun went up. There was Patch

117

after was drowned out of a curagh[5] that turned over. I was sitting here with Bartley, and he a baby, lying on my two knees, and I seen two women, and three women, and four women coming in, and they crossing themselves, and not saying a word. I looked out then, and there were men coming after them, and they holding a thing in the half of a red sail, and water dripping out of it—it was a dry day, Nora—and leaving a track to the door.

She pauses again with her hand stretched out towards the door. It opens softly and old women begin to come in, crossing themselves on the threshold, and kneeling down in front of the stage with red petticoats over their heads.

MAURYA (*half in a dream, to Cathleen*). Is it Patch, or Michael, or what is it at all?

CATHLEEN. Michael is after being found in the far north, and when he is found there how could he be here in this place?

MAURYA. There does be a power of young men floating round in the sea, and what way would they know if it was Michael they had, or another man like him, for when a man is nine days in the sea, and the wind blowing, it's hard set his own mother would be to say what man was it.

CATHLEEN. It's Michael, God spare him, for they're after sending us a bit of his clothes from the far north.

She reaches out and hands Maurya the clothes that belonged to Michael. Maurya stands up slowly and takes them in her hand. Nora looks out.

NORA. They're carrying a thing among them and there's water dripping out of it and leaving a track by the big stones.

CATHLEEN (*in a whisper to the women who have come in*). Is it Bartley it is?

ONE OF THE WOMEN. It is surely, God rest his soul.

Two younger women come in and pull out the table. Then men carry in the body of Bartley, laid on a plank, with a bit of sail over it, and lay it on the table.

CATHLEEN (*to the women, as they are doing so*). What way was he drowned?

ONE OF THE WOMEN. The gray pony knocked him into the sea, and he was washed out where there is a great surf on the white rocks.

Maurya has gone over and knelt down at the head of the table. The women are keening softly and sway-

ing *themselves with a slow movement. Cathleen and Nora kneel at the other end of the table. The men kneel near the door.*

MAURYA (*raising her head and speaking as if she did not see the people around her*). They're all gone now, and there isn't anything more the sea can do to me.... I'll have no call now to be up crying and praying when the wind breaks from the south, and you can hear the surf is in the east, and the surf is in the west, making a great stir with the two noises, and they hitting one on the other. I'll have no call now to be going down and getting Holy Water in the dark nights after Samhain,[6] and I won't care what way the sea is when the other women will be keening. (*To Nora.*) Give me the Holy Water, Nora, there's a small sup still on the dresser.

Nora gives it to her.

MAURYA (*drops Michael's clothes across Bartley's feet, and sprinkles the Holy Water over him*). It isn't that I haven't prayed for you, Bartley, to the Almighty God. It isn't that I haven't said prayers in the dark night till you wouldn't know what I'd be saying; but it's a great rest I'll have now, and it's time surely. It's a great rest I'll have now, and great sleeping in the long nights after Samhain, if it's only a bit of wet flour we do have to eat, and maybe a fish that would be stinking.

She kneels down again, crossing herself, and saying prayers under her breath.

CATHLEEN (*to an old man*). Maybe yourself and Eamon would make a coffin when the sun rises. We have fine white boards herself bought, God help her, thinking Michael would be found, and I have a new cake you can eat while you'll be working.

THE OLD MAN (*looking at the boards*). Are there nails with them?

CATHLEEN. There are not, Colum; we didn't think of the nails.

ANOTHER MAN. It's a great wonder she wouldn't think of the nails, and all the coffins she's seen made already.

CATHLEEN. It's getting old she is, and broken.

Maurya stands up again very slowly and spreads out the pieces of Michael's clothes beside the body, sprinkling them with the last of the Holy Water.

NORA (*in a whisper to Cathleen*). She's quiet now and easy; but the day Michael was drowned you could

[5]**curagh** an unstable canoe-like boat

[6]**Samhain** November 1, All Saints' Day

hear her crying out from this to the spring well. It's fonder she was of Michael, and would any one have thought that?

CATHLEEN (*slowly and clearly*). An old woman will be soon tired with anything she will do, and isn't it nine days herself is after crying and keening, and making great sorrow in the house?

MAURYA (*puts the empty cup mouth downwards on the table, and lays her hands together on Bartley's feet*). They're all together this time, and the end is come. May the Almighty God have mercy on Bartley's soul, and on Michael's soul, and on the souls of Sheamus and Patch, and Stephen and Shawn (*bending her head*);

and may He have mercy on my soul, Nora, and on the soul of every one is left living in the world.

She pauses, and the keen rises a little more loudly from the women, then sinks away.

MAURYA (*continuing*). Michael has a clean burial in the far north, by the grace of the Almighty God. Bartley will have a fine coffin out of the white boards, and a deep grave surely. What more can we want than that? No man at all can be living for ever, and we must be satisfied.

She kneels down again and the curtain falls slowly.

COMMENTARY

Note: The following essay represents a single interpretation of the play. For other perspectives on Riders to the Sea, *consult the essays listed below.*

Although it is thoroughly Irish in its language, customs, and specific subject matter (the death of Aran Islanders at the hands of the raging Western sea), *Riders to the Sea* evokes the memories of two ancient forms of drama: Greek tragedy and Noh drama. Synge, who graduated with high honors in Greek at Trinity College, creates a modern equivalent of Attic tragedy both in mood and style. First, there is the inexorable presence of death here. Maurya has already lost a husband and five sons to the sea, and Bartley's fateful journey is cast with a tragic inevitability. Just as the ancient oracles foretold a character's fate, Maurya's dream about red and gray ponies shapes the play's ending. Cathleen and Nora function as a chorus, slowly revealing Michael's fate. Importantly, at the end of the play they are joined by the larger chorus of women, keening a lament as old as Aran's rocks. The dirge sung by these Irish women, the sea's ultimate victims who are left with little but "a bit of wet flour . . . and maybe a fish that would be stinking," echoes the cry of Euripides's chorus in *The Trojan Women*.

Ultimately, however, it is the extraordinary dignity with which Maurya bears her sorrow that makes *Riders to the Sea* memorable. Tragic heroes since Oedipus have met their fate with a calm and certitude that transcends mortal comprehension. Maurya, who has endured the very worst that life can offer, defiantly notes "there isn't anything more the sea can do to me," and in the play's last speech addresses life's ultimate certainty: "No man at all can be living for ever, and we must be satisfied." This realization aligns her with other tragic heroes, like Hamlet who similarly noted of death that "there is a special providence in the fall of a sparrow. If it be now, 'tis not to come. If it be not to come, it will be now; if it be not now, yet it will come. The readiness is all." Indeed, life on the Aran Isles taught Synge and the characters he admired that the readiness is all.

Though it was Yeats whose writing was more obviously indebted to the Noh theater of Japan, Synge's short drama here begs comparison with Japan's stately drama. First, the play is—as noted—a dirge in which the surviving women "keen" (i.e., chant mournfully) in memory of the dead men. The keening, coupled with the lyrical language (not to mention the absolute simplicity of staging it requires), invests the drama with a meditative quality not unlike that of the Noh theater. Most importantly, the impulse behind Synge's play aligns it with our most ancient dramatic impulses: the observance of the life cycle. Though death apparently triumphs on Aran's isles, the life force manifests itself in Maurya's heroic perseverance.

Still, Synge's play is from the modern era, and at a time when Ibsen, Shaw, and others were presenting women as protagonists of Europe's new drama, Synge has rendered a hugely sympathetic—as opposed to merely sentimental—portrait of women as the victims of a society in which they have no recourse. Long after the men have been buried in "fine coffins out of white boards and a deep grave surely," it is the women who must survive. As Maurya asks Bartley, "What way will I live and the girls with me, and I an old woman looking for the grave?" Although Synge would never have considered himself a social dramatist in the mold of Ibsen or Shaw ("The drama, like the symphony, does not have to teach or prove anything," he wrote in response to the new Naturalism), he nonetheless defines the plight of women entering the twentieth century in this simple folk tragedy. Denied work beyond their peasant huts, they could only "bear and bury" the men who supported them.

Other perspectives on *Riders to the Sea*:

Casey, Daniel J. "An Aran Requiem: Setting in *Riders to the Sea*." In Daniel J. Casey (ed.), *Critical Essays on John Millington Synge*. New York: Maxwell Macmillan Canada, 1994, 88–97.

Durbach, Errol. "Synge's Tragic Vision of the Old Mother and the Sea." *Modern Drama* 14:4 (February 1972): 363–72.

Other plays by Synge on video/film:

The Playboy of the Western World. Perf. Abbey Theatre Company. Insight Media, 140 min., 1985.

The Well of the Saints. 45 min., 1975.

About Irish drama:

Irish Theater and Juno and the Paycock. Insight Media, 16 min., 1983.

Irish Theater: Raw Bones and Poetry. Films for the Humanities, 51 min., 2000.

SHOWCASE THE IRISH RENAISSANCE

Although Ireland is a small country, home to fewer than four million people, it has produced one of the world's great literatures, especially in twentieth-century drama. For centuries the island was home to Celtic bards whose power was second only to that of their chieftains and whose oral tradition was handed down in native Irish long before the island was colonized and finally subdued by the British in 1601. For two centuries after the forced introduction of English, a series of Anglo-Irish writers, born and educated in Ireland, contributed significant comedies to the repertory of English drama. Among these writers were Richard Brinsley Sheridan (*The Rivals, The School for Scandal*) and his mother, Frances Chamberlaine, before him; William Congreve, whose *The Way of the World* proved the culmination of English Restoration comedy; George Farquhar (*The Recruiting Officer*); and Oliver Goldsmith (*She Stoops to Conquer*). This expatriate dramatic tradition continued in the late nineteenth century as George Bernard Shaw (see *Heartbreak House* later in Part I) and Oscar Wilde, both Dublin writers, eagerly attempted to make their marks in more sophisticated London. But at the turn of the twentieth century, another group of Irishmen, some from native families, some from the Anglo-Irish Ascendancy, joined together in a conscious attempt to create a specifically Irish literature, centered in the drama and headquartered after 1904 at the Abbey Theatre.

The women of the Aran Isles on the western shore of Ireland mourn the loss of their men in Synge's folk tragedy, Riders to the Sea, *performed in 1988 by the Royal Shakespeare Company.*

In *A Portrait of the Artist as a Young Man*, Stephan Dedaelus, the alter ego of Irish author James Joyce, set out to "forge in the smithy of my soul the uncreated conscience of my race." Joyce chose to do so in exile, far from the Church-dominated Irish whose nationalism he sometimes feared would be no more liberating than English colonialism. But while Joyce (and Samuel Beck-

ett much later) wrote from exile, the Abbey dramatists were determined to forge this new conscience at home. Two of the founding members of the Abbey—Lady Augusta Gregory and the poet William Butler Yeats—were playwrights. Yeats had written a book of folk and supernatural writings, *The Celtic Twilight*, in 1893, claiming for the residual Celts a special vision, which, he implied, the Anglo-Irish settlers had lost, even destroyed. This idea became one of the defining elements of the cultural nationalism, which characterized the Irish literary revival, and the work of its first generation of playwrights. The Abbey, under the direction of Lennox Robinson, soon was acknowledged as Ireland's national theater and became the English-speaking world's first state-subsidized theater in 1924. This Irish Renaissance and its drama (including plays by Yeats, Gregory, John Millington Synge, and Sean O'Casey) have been recently studied, initially by historian Declan Kiberd, as the first body of postcolonial literature and as a model for the writers emerging from colonial domination in both Africa (see *Death and the King's Horseman* in Part III) and the Caribbean and Latin America (see *Pantomime* and *Paper Flowers* in Part III).

While Yeats wrote poetic dramas centering on the Celtic past, few of which are still produced, and Lady Gregory (born Augusta Persse, 1852–1932) contributed more tragic works anatomizing earlier colonial times, John

Millington Synge (1871–1909) based his characters and plots on the real peasantry of the West of Ireland. Following in the Gaelic tradition of the bards, all three writers emphasized the lore of Irish places. Synge had spent much of his childhood walking and cycling in County Wicklow and learned Irish at the School of Divinity of Trinity College Dublin. After a period of literary dabbling in Paris, he was encouraged by Yeats to visit the Aran Islands off the Western coast of Ireland, a rugged place where Irish was still spoken and where he gathered material for what became *In the Shadow of a Glen*, his poetic *Riders to the Sea*, and his most famous work, the riot-provoking *The Playboy of the Western World* (1907). While rioters cried out that Synge blasphemed against the Catholic Church and the peasantry by depicting their adulation for a man who killed his father, critic Kiberd suggests that Synge actually depicted the inevitability of Irish Home Rule and saw "so profoundly into the culture [of peasants in County Mayo] that their future" became clear.

The next generation of Irish playwrights came to maturity after the Easter Rebellion of 1916, against the backdrop of the drive for Home Rule. Sean O'Casey (1880–1964) was born in Dublin of working-class Protestant parents, and his dramatic work did for the slum-dwellers of the city what Synge did for the peasants of Connacht and Wicklow, creating a back-street poetry that still sings to contemporary audiences. O'Casey's trilogy *The Shadow of a Gunman* (1923), *Juno and the Paycock* (1924), and especially *The Plough and the Stars* (1926) proved shocking to Abbey patrons because the underclass onstage spoke with an eloquence and urban wit that were new. O'Casey's plays proved too honest for the self-conscious nationalism of the evolving state, especially his treatment of the Easter Rising, a quixotic and bloody Dublin standoff with British troops which made martyrs of such rebels as the poet Patrick Pearse and which launched the era of Irish independence. During the riotous Abbey opening of *The Plough and the Stars*, one angry patron shouted, "There are no prostitutes in Ireland," to which Yeats replied, "You have disgraced yourselves again."

Other Abbey playwrights included its director Lennox Robinson, the poet AE, and Padraic Colum. The Abbey opened a second theater, The Peacock, which stages mainly experimental plays, and the Dublin scene has been enriched by the opening of the classics-oriented Gate Theatre in 1930 and the establishment of the Dublin International Theatre Festival in 1957. Also significant is the Druid Theatre in Galway, founded and directed by Garry Hines, who in 1998 became the first woman to win a Tony Award for directing. The tradition of Irish playwriting remains vigorous to this day, with the much-produced international writers Brian Friel and Tom Murphy leading the current older generation of writers. Friel's brilliant ear for dialogue and his Chekhovian sense of the tears behind the joy in things, and Murphy's starker, keenly tragic vision, continue traditions begun in the early twentieth century. Among the younger, sometimes sardonic, playwrights are Martin McDonagh, Colin McPherson, Marina Carr, and Marie Jones, all of whom have had works successfully produced on Broadway and throughout the United States.

For further study:

Hogan, Patrick Colm. *Irish Identity and the Literary Revival: Synge, Yeats, Joyce and O'Casey*. Dublin: College Literature, 1996.

Kiberd, Declan. *Inventing Ireland: The Literature of the Modern Nation*. London: Vintage, 1996.

THE GHOST SONATA
AUGUST STRINDBERG

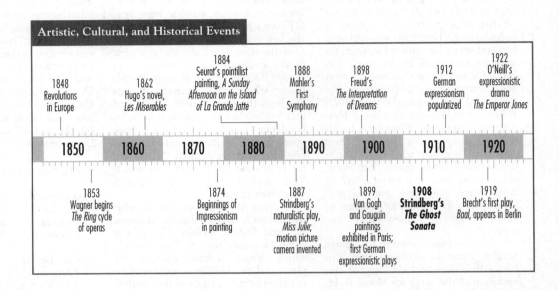

Artistic, Cultural, and Historical Events

1848 Revolutions in Europe	1862 Hugo's novel, Les Miserables	1884 Seurat's pointillist painting, A Sunday Afternoon on the Island of La Grande Jatte	1888 Mahler's First Symphony	1898 Freud's The Interpretation of Dreams	1912 German expressionism popularized	1922 O'Neill's expressionistic drama The Emperor Jones	

| 1850 | 1860 | 1870 | 1880 | 1890 | 1900 | 1910 | 1920 |

| 1853 Wagner begins The Ring cycle of operas | 1874 Beginnings of Impressionism in painting | 1887 Strindberg's naturalistic play, Miss Julie; motion picture camera invented | 1899 Van Gogh and Gauguin paintings exhibited in Paris; first German expressionistic plays | 1908 Strindberg's The Ghost Sonata | 1919 Brecht's first play, Baal, appears in Berlin |

AUGUST STRINDBERG (1849–1912)

Strindberg's plays, particularly those described as naturalistic (and even in expressionistic plays like *The Ghost Sonata*), are noted for their violent confrontations, especially between men and women. Considering the circumstances of his childhood and three painful failed marriages, this contentiousness is understandable. Born in Stockholm out of wedlock to a tyrannical father and a weak-willed mother, Strindberg was one of a dozen children. His family lived in the kind of cramped quarters and squalor often depicted by late-nineteenth-century Naturalists. His mother died when he was 13, but his family life only worsened when his father remarried. Consequently, Strindberg was a melancholy, irritable youth who quarreled with his teachers and subsequently lost his scholarship to Uppsala University.

He found work as a teacher and journalist, and eventually he attracted some fame with the publication of a small novel, *The Red Room* (1879). Strindberg traveled extensively and chose to live abroad because of his discontent with Swedish puritanism (he was once censured for "unseemly" material in his short stories). From 1882 through 1897 he lived in Switzerland, Germany, Austria, Denmark, and particularly France, where he was inspired by many of the new European dramas at the Théâtre Libre. In 1907 Strindberg founded the Intimate Theatre in Stockholm, among the most important "little theaters" that proliferated in Europe and America in the new century. (See Showcase, "Independent and Intimate Theaters.")

Strindberg was a multitalented figure who excelled in areas other than literature; he was a painter, a photographer (who did much to raise the medium to an art form), and a noted amateur chemist. He is, however, remembered for his plays and some fine novels, especially *The Inferno* (1897), written from the depths of a mental illness that institutionalized him for several years. Of the early Modernists, Strindberg was the boldest experimenter with form and subject matter. With Emile Zola, Strindberg is credited with advancing Naturalism, both as a theatrical style and as a philosophy. Despite the intensely real settings, situations, dialogue, and especially the psychological portraiture of his naturalistic plays, Strindberg was still too much the poet not to incorporate symbolism and ritual into his work, and his plays exhibit a remarkable theatricality. Not only did he write naturalistic plays, of which *The Father* (1886), *Miss Julie* (1888), and *The Dance of Death* (1901, successfully revived in London and New York in 2001) are the finest, but he also wrote 20 chronicle plays based on Nordic history (e.g., *Queen Christina*, 1903). His expressionistic dramas, typified by the trilogy *The Road to Damascus* (1898–1901), *A Dream Play* (1906), and *The Ghost Sonata* (1907), legitimized the style and exerted a profound influence on Eugene O'Neill, Elmer Rice, and particularly the German Expressionists. In the two-year period following Strindberg's death in 1912, over 1,000 performances of his plays, especially the expressionistic works, could be seen in some 60 German cities.

Even the briefest survey of Strindberg's life must address his alleged misogyny. It is tempting to believe that Strindberg loathed women, especially given his tempestuous marriages. Lines culled from his plays only reinforce the notion that he hated women and that women hated him. Miss Julie asserts that her mother taught her "to distrust and hate all men—you've heard how she hated men—and I swore never to be slave to any man." Still, Strindberg is too complicated to be reduced to a single psychological state (interestingly, his life has inspired several case studies by psychologists). Like so many of his characters, he vacillated wildly in his feelings, especially where the sexes were concerned. The old cliché about the fine line between love and hate is particularly applicable to Strindberg and the lost souls of his dramas. The most tormented of contemporary American dramatists, O'Neill, said of the man who inspired his works: "Strindberg was the precursor of all modernity in the modern theatre . . . the greatest interpreter of the characteristic spiritual conflicts which constitute drama—the blood—of our lives today."

AS YOU READ *THE GHOST SONATA*

Sometimes translated as *The Spook Sonata* (*Spoksonaten*), this short play typifies the new expressionistic drama that Strindberg helped create. Perhaps it is best understood in light of the playwright's 1906 comments about *A Dream Play* (1906), an earlier (and longer) experiment with Expressionism. Strindberg's words echo those of Freud, whose *Interpretation of Dreams* (1902) was given theatrical form by the Swede and later the German Expressionists:

> [I have] tried to imitate the disjointed but apparently logical form of a dream. Anything may happen: everything is possible and probable. Time and space do not exist. The characters are split, doubled and multiplied; they evaporate and are condensed, are diffused and concentrated. But a single consciousness holds sway over them all—that of the dreamer; and before it there are no secrets, no incongruities, no scruples, no laws.

You may better appreciate Strindberg's comments here, and *The Ghost Sonata* itself, by substituting "nightmare" for "dream." The play may seem less perplexing if you consider the many MTV videos that employ techniques typical of the expressionistic dramas of the early twentieth century. Note, however, that the playwright sets his nightmare in a seemingly realistic setting—a fashionable home, the kind that could be seen in the plays of Strindberg's contemporaries such as Ibsen, Shaw, and Chekov. It is this clash between the realistic and the hallucinatory that provides much of the play's impact. Read the play as if it were a realistic piece, but see the play in your mind's eye as if it were a macabre nightmare.

THE GHOST SONATA

AUGUST STRINDBERG

Translated by Elizabeth Sprigge

CHARACTERS

THE OLD MAN (HUMMEL), a Company Director
THE STUDENT (ARKENHOLTZ)
THE MILKMAID, an apparition
THE CARETAKER'S WIFE
THE CARETAKER
THE LADY IN BLACK, the daughter of the Caretaker's Wife and
    the Dead Man. Also referred to as the Dark Lady
THE COLONEL
THE MUMMY (AMELIA), the Colonel's wife
THE GIRL (ADÈLE), the Colonel's daughter, actually the daugh-
    ter of the Old Man
THE ARISTOCRAT (BARON SKANSKORG), engaged to the Lady
    in Black
JOHANSSON, the Old Man's servant
BENGTSSON, the Colonel's servant
THE FIANCÉE (BEATRICE VON HOLSTEINKRONA), a white-
    haired old woman, once betrothed to the Old Man
THE COOK
A MAIDSERVANT
BEGGARS

SCENE 1

*Outside the house. The corner of the façade of a modern
house, showing the ground floor above, and the street in
front. The ground floor terminates on the right in the
Round Room, above which, on the first floor, is a balcony
with a flagstaff. The windows of the Round Room face the
street in front of the house, and at the corner look on to the
suggestion of a side-street running toward the back. At the
beginning of the scene the blinds of the Round Room are
down. When, later, they are raised, the white marble
statue of a young woman can be seen, surrounded with
palms and brightly lighted by rays of sunshine.*

*To the left of the Round Room is the Hyacinth Room; its
window filled with pots of hyacinths, blue, white, and pink.*

*Further left, at the back, is an imposing double front door
with laurels in tubs on either side of it. The doors are wide
open, showing a staircase of white marble with a banister
of mahogany and brass: To the left of the front door is another ground-floor window, with a window-mirror.[1] On
the balcony rail in the corner above the Round Room are a
blue silk quilt and two white pillows. The windows to the
left of this are hung with white sheets.[2]*

*In the foreground, in front of the house, is a green
bench; to the right a street drinking-fountain, to the left
an advertisement column.*

*It is a bright Sunday morning, and as the curtain rises
the bells of several churches, some near, some far away,
are ringing.*

On the staircase the Lady in Black stands motionless.

*The Caretaker's Wife sweeps the doorstep, then polishes
the brass on the door and waters the laurels.*

*In a wheel-chair by the advertisement column sits the
Old Man, reading a newspaper. His hair and beard are
white and he wears spectacles.*

*The Milkmaid comes round the corner on the right, car-
rying milk bottles in a wire basket. She is wearing a summer dress with brown shoes, black stockings and a white
cap. She takes off her cap and hangs it on the fountain,
wipes the perspiration from her forehead, washes her
hands and arranges her hair, using the water as a mirror.*

*A steamship bell is heard, and now and then the silence is
broken by the deep notes of an organ in a nearby church.*

---

[1]Set at an angle inside the window, so as to show what is going on in
the street.—Tr.
[2]Sign of mourning.—Tr.

After a few moments, when all is silent and the Milk-maid has finished her toilet, the Student enters from the left. He has had a sleepless night and is unshaven. He goes straight up to the fountain. There is a pause before he speaks.

STUDENT. May I have the cup? (*The Milkmaid clutches the cup to her*) Haven't you finished yet?

(*The Milkmaid looks at him with horror*)

OLD MAN (*to himself*). Who's he talking to? I don't see anybody. Is he crazy?

(*He goes on watching them in great astonishment*)

STUDENT (*To the Milkmaid*). What are you staring at? Do I look so terrible? Well, I've had no sleep, and of course you think I've been making a night of it . . . (*The Milkmaid stays just as she is*) You think I've been drinking, eh? Do I smell of liquor? (*The Milk-maid does not change*) I haven't shaved, I know. Give me a drink of water, girl. I've earned it. (*Pause*) Oh well, I suppose I'll have to tell you. I spent the whole night dressing wounds and looking after the injured. You see, I was there when that house col-lapsed last night. Now you know. (*The Milkmaid rinses the cup and gives him a drink*) Thanks. (*The Milkmaid stands motionless. Slowly*) Will you do me a great favor? (*Pause*) The thing is, my eyes, as you can see, are inflamed, but my hands have been touching wounds and corpses, so it would be dan-gerous to put them near my eyes. Will you take my handkerchief—it's quite clean—and dip it in the fresh water and bathe my eyes? Will you do this? Will you play the good Samaritan? (*The Milkmaid hesitates, but does as he bids*) Thank you, my dear. (*He takes out his purse. She makes a gesture of refusal*) Forgive my stupidity, but I'm only half-awake. . . .

(*The Milkmaid disappears*)

OLD MAN (*To the Student*). Excuse me speaking to you, but I heard you say you were at the scene of the acci-dent last night. I was just reading about it in the paper.

STUDENT. Is it in the paper already?

OLD MAN. The whole thing, including your portrait. But they regret that they have been unable to find out the name of the splendid young student. . . .

STUDENT. Really? (*Glances at the paper*) Yes, that's me. Well I never!

OLD MAN. Who was it you were talking to just now?

STUDENT. Didn't you see? (*Pause*)

OLD MAN. Would it be impertinent to inquire—what in fact your name is?

STUDENT. What would be the point? I don't care for pub-licity. If you get any praise, there's always disapproval too. The art of running people down has been devel-oped to such a pitch. . . . Besides, I don't want any re-ward.

OLD MAN. You're well off, perhaps.

STUDENT. No, indeed. On the contrary, I'm very poor.

OLD MAN. Do you know, it seems to me I've heard your voice before. When I was young I had a friend who pronounced certain words just as you do. I've never met anyone else with quite that pronunciation. Only him—and you. Are you by any chance related to Mr. Arkenholtz, the merchant?

STUDENT. He was my father.

OLD MAN. Strange are the paths of fate. I saw you when you were an infant, under very painful circumstances.

STUDENT. Yes, I understand I came into the world in the middle of a bankruptcy.

OLD MAN. Just that.

STUDENT. Perhaps I might ask your name.

OLD MAN. I am Mr. Hummel.

STUDENT. Are you the? . . . I remember that . . .

OLD MAN. Have you often heard my name mentioned in your family?

STUDENT. Yes.

OLD MAN. And mentioned perhaps with a certain aver-sion? (*The Student is silent*) Yes, I can imagine it. You were told, I suppose, that I was the man who ruined your father? All who ruin themselves through foolish speculations consider they were ruined by those they couldn't fool. (*Pause*) Now these are the facts. Your father robbed me of seventeen thousand crowns— the whole of my savings at that time.

STUDENT. It's queer that the same story can be told in two such different ways.

OLD MAN. You surely don't believe I'm telling you what isn't true?

STUDENT. What am I to believe? My father didn't lie.

OLD MAN. That is so true. A father never lies. But I too am a father, and so it follows . . .

STUDENT. What are you driving at?

OLD MAN. I saved your father from disaster, and he repaid me with all the frightful hatred that is born of an obligation to be grateful. He taught his family to speak ill of me.

STUDENT. Perhaps you made him ungrateful by poisoning your help with unnecessary humiliation.

OLD MAN. All help is humiliating, sir.

STUDENT. What do you want from me?

OLD MAN. I'm not asking for the money, but if you will render me a few small services, I shall consider myself well paid. You see that I am a cripple. Some say it is my own fault; others lay the blame on my parents. I prefer to blame life itself, with its pitfalls. For if you escape one snare, you fall headlong into another. In any case, I am unable to climb stairs or ring doorbells, and that is why I am asking you to help me.

STUDENT. What can I do?

OLD MAN. To begin with, push my chair so that I can read those playbills. I want to see what is on tonight.

STUDENT (*Pushing the chair*). Haven't you got an attendant?

OLD MAN. Yes, but he has gone on an errand. He'll be back soon. Are you a medical student?

STUDENT. No, I am studying languages, but I don't know at all what I'm going to do.

OLD MAN. Aha! Are you good at mathematics?

STUDENT. Yes, fairly.

OLD MAN. Good. Perhaps you would like a job.

STUDENT. Yes, why not?

OLD MAN. Splendid. (*He studies the playbills*) They are doing *The Valkyrie* for the matinée. That means the Colonel will be there with his daughter, and as he always sits at the end of the sixth row, I'll put you next to him. Go to that telephone kiosk please and order a ticket for seat eighty-two in the sixth row.

STUDENT. Am I to go to the Opera in the middle of the day?

OLD MAN. Yes. Do as I tell you and things will go well with you. I want to see you happy, rich, and honored. Your début last night as the brave rescuer will make you famous by tomorrow and then your name will be worth something.

STUDENT (*Going to the telephone kiosk*). What an odd adventure!

OLD MAN. Are you a gambler?

STUDENT. Yes, unfortunately.

OLD MAN. We'll make it fortunately. Go on now, telephone. (*The Student goes. The Old Man reads his paper. The Lady in Black comes out on to the pavement and talks to the Caretaker's Wife. The Old Man listens, but the audience hears nothing. The Student returns*) Did you fix it up?

STUDENT. It's done.

OLD MAN. You see that house?

STUDENT. Yes, I've been looking at it a lot. I passed it yesterday when the sun was shining on the windowpanes, and I imagined all the beauty and elegance there must be inside. I said to my companion: "Think of living up there in the top flat, with a beautiful young wife, two pretty little children and an income of twenty thousand crowns a year."

OLD MAN. So that's what you said. That's what you said. Well, well! I too am very fond of this house.

STUDENT. Do you speculate in houses?

OLD MAN. Mm—yes. But not in the way you mean.

STUDENT. Do you know the people who live here?

OLD MAN. Every one of them. At my age one knows everybody, and their parents and grandparents too, and one's always related to them in some way or other. I am just eighty, but no one knows me—not really. I take an interest in human destiny. (*The blinds of the Round Room are drawn up. The Colonel is seen, wearing mufti. He looks at the thermometer outside one of the windows, then turns back into the room and stands in front of the marble statue*) Look, that's the Colonel, whom you will sit next to this afternoon.

STUDENT. Is he—the Colonel? I don't understand any of this, but it's like a fairy story.

OLD MAN. My whole life's like a book of fairy stories, sir. And although the stories are different, they are held together by one thread, and the main theme constantly recurs.

STUDENT. Who is that marble statue of?

OLD MAN. That, naturally, is his wife.

STUDENT. Was she such a wonderful person?

OLD MAN. Er . . . yes.

STUDENT. Tell me.

OLD MAN. We can't judge people, young man. If I were to tell you that she left him, that he beat her, that she returned to him and married him a second time, and that now she is sitting inside there like a mummy, worshipping her own statue—then you would think me crazy.

STUDENT. I don't understand.

OLD MAN. I didn't think you would. Well, then we have the window with the hyacinths. His daughter lives there. She has gone out for a ride, but she will be home soon.

STUDENT. And who is the dark lady talking to the caretaker?

OLD MAN. Well, that's a bit complicated, but it is connected with the dead man, up there where you see the white sheets.

STUDENT. Why, who was he?

OLD MAN. A human being like you or me, but the most conspicuous thing about him was his vanity. If you were a Sunday child, you would see him presently come out of that door to look at the Consulate flag flying at half-mast. He was, you understand, a Consul, and he reveled in coronets and lions and plumed hats and colored ribbons.

STUDENT. Sunday child, you say? I'm told I was born on a Sunday.

OLD MAN. No, were you really? I might have known it. I saw it from the color of your eyes. Then you can see what others can't. Have you noticed that?

STUDENT. I don't know what others do see, but at times. . . . Oh, but one doesn't talk of such things!

OLD MAN. I was almost sure of it. But you can talk to me, because I understand such things.

STUDENT. Yesterday, for instance . . . I was drawn to that obscure little street where later on the house collapsed. I went there and stopped in front of that building which I had never seen before. Then I noticed a crack in the wall. . . . I heard the floor boards snapping. . . . I dashed over and picked up a child that was passing under the wall. . . . The next moment the house collapsed. I was saved, but in my arms, which I thought held the child, was nothing at all.

OLD MAN. Yes, yes, just as I thought. Tell me something. Why were you gesticulating that way just now by the fountain? And why were you talking to yourself?

STUDENT. Didn't you see the milkmaid I was talking to?

OLD MAN (in horror). Milkmaid?

STUDENT. Surely. The girl who handed me the cup.

OLD MAN. Really? So that's what was going on. Ah well, I haven't second sight, but there are things I can do. (The Fiancée is now seen to sit down by the window which has the window-mirror.) Look at that old woman in the window. Do you see her? Well, she was my fiancée once, sixty years ago. I was twenty. Don't be alarmed. She doesn't recognize me. We see one another every day, and it makes no impression on me, although once we vowed to love one another eternally. Eternally!

STUDENT. How foolish you were in those days! We never talk to our girls like that.

OLD MAN. Forgive us, young man. We didn't know any better. But can you see that old woman was once young and beautiful?

STUDENT. It doesn't show. And yet there's some charm in her looks. I can't see her eyes.

(The Caretaker's Wife comes out with a basket of chopped fir branches)[3]

OLD MAN. Ah, the caretaker's wife! That dark lady is her daughter by the dead man. That's why her husband was given the job of caretaker. But the dark lady has a suitor, who is an aristocrat with great expectations. He is in the process of getting a divorce—from his

[3]It was customary in Sweden to strew the ground with these for a funeral.—Tr.

present wife, you understand. She's presenting him with a stone mansion in order to be rid of him. This aristocratic suitor is the son-in-law of the dead man, and you can see his bedclothes being aired on the balcony upstairs. It is complicated, I must say.

STUDENT. It's fearfully complicated.

OLD MAN. Yes, that it is, internally and externally, although it looks quite simple.

STUDENT. But then who was the dead man?

OLD MAN. You asked me that just now, and I answered. If you were to look round the corner, where the tradesmen's entrance is, you would see a lot of poor people whom he used to help—when it suited him.

STUDENT. He was a kind man then.

OLD MAN. Yes—sometimes.

STUDENT. Not always?

OLD MAN. No-o. That's the way of people. Now, sir, will you push my chair a little, so that it gets into the sun. I'm horribly cold. When you're never able to move about, the blood congeals. I'm going to die soon, I know that, but I have a few things to do first. Take my hand and feel how cold I am.

STUDENT (Taking it). Yes, inconceivably. (He shrinks back, trying in vain to free his hand)

OLD MAN. Don't leave me. I am tired now and lonely, but I haven't always been like this, you know. I have an enormously long life behind me, enormously long. I have made people unhappy and people have made me unhappy—the one cancels out the other—but before I die I want to see you happy. Our fates are entwined through your father—and other things.

STUDENT. Let go of my hand. You are taking all my strength. You are freezing me. What do you want with me?

OLD MAN (Letting go). Be patient and you shall see and understand. Here comes the young lady.

(They watch the Girl approaching, though the audience cannot yet see her)

STUDENT. The Colonel's daughter?

OLD MAN. His daughter—yes. Look at her. Have you ever seen such a masterpiece?

STUDENT. She is like the marble statue in there.

OLD MAN. That's her mother, you know.

STUDENT. You are right. Never have I seen such a woman of woman born. Happy the man who may lead her to the altar and his home.

OLD MAN. You can see it. Not everyone recognizes her beauty. So, then, it is written.

(The Girl enters, wearing an English riding habit. Without noticing anyone she walks slowly to the *door, where she stops to say a few words to the Care-taker's Wife. Then she goes into the house. The Student covers his eyes with his hand)*

OLD MAN. Are you weeping?

STUDENT. In the face of what's hopeless there can be nothing but despair.

OLD MAN. I can open doors and hearts, if only I find an arm to do my will. Serve me and you shall have power.

STUDENT. Is it a bargain? Am I to sell my soul?

OLD MAN. Sell nothing. Listen. All my life I have *taken.* Now I have a craving to give—give. But no one will accept. I am rich, very rich, but I have no heirs, except for a good-for-nothing who torments the life out of me. Become my son. Inherit me while I am still alive. Enjoy life so that I can watch, at least from a distance.

STUDENT. What am I to do?

OLD MAN. First go to *The Valkyrie.*

STUDENT. That's settled. What else?

OLD MAN. This evening you must be in there—in the Round Room.

STUDENT. How am I to get there?

OLD MAN. By way of *The Valkyrie.*

STUDENT. Why have you chosen me as your medium? Did you know me before?

OLD MAN. Yes, of course. I have had my eye on you for a long time. But now look up there at the balcony. The maid is hoisting the flag to half-mast for the Consul. And now she is turning the bedclothes. Do you see that blue quilt? It was made for two to sleep under, but now it covers only one. (*The Girl, having changed her dress, appears in the window and waters the hy-acinths)* There is my little girl. Look at her, look! She is talking to the flowers. Is she not like that blue hy-acinth herself? She gives them drink—nothing but pure water, and they transform the water into color and fragrance. Now here comes the Colonel with the newspaper. He is showing her the bit about the house that collapsed. Now he's pointing to your portrait. She's not indifferent. She's reading of your brave deed. . . .

I believe it's clouding over. If it turns to rain I shall be in a pretty fix, unless Johansson comes back soon. (*It grows cloudy and dark. The Fiancée at the window-mirror closes her window)* Now my fi-ancée is closing the window. Seventy-nine years old. The window-mirror is the only mirror she uses, because in it she sees not herself, but the world out-side—in two directions. But the world can see her;

she hasn't thought of that. Anyhow she's a hand-some old woman.

(*Now the Dead Man, wrapped in a winding sheet, comes out of the door)*

STUDENT. Good God, what do I see?

OLD MAN. What do you see?

STUDENT. Don't *you* see? There, in the doorway, the dead man?

OLD MAN. I see nothing, but I expected this. Tell me.

STUDENT. He is coming out into the street. (*Pause*) Now he is turning his head and looking up at the flag.

OLD MAN. What did I tell you? You may be sure he'll count the wreaths and read the visiting cards. Woe to him who's missing.

STUDENT. Now he's turning the corner.

OLD MAN. He's gone to count the poor at the back door. The poor are in the nature of a decoration, you see. "Followed by the blessings of many." Well, he's not going to have my blessing. Between ourselves he was a great scoundrel.

STUDENT. But charitable.

OLD MAN. A charitable scoundrel, always thinking of his grand funeral. When he knew his end was near, he cheated the State out of fifty thousand crowns. Now his daughter has relations with another woman's hus-band and is wondering about the will. Yes, the scoundrel can hear every word we're saying, and he's welcome to it. Ah, here comes Johansson! (*Johansson enters*) Report! (*Johansson speaks, but the audience does not hear*) Not at home, eh? You are an ass. And the telegram? Nothing? Go on. . . . At six this evening? That's good. Special edition, you say? With his name in full. Arkenholtz, a student, born . . . par-ents . . . That's splendid. . . . I think it's beginning to rain. . . . What did he say about it? So—so. He wouldn't? Well, he must. Here comes the aristocrat. Push me round the corner, Johanson, so I can hear what the poor are saying. And, Arkenholtz, you wait for me here. Understand? (*To Johansson*) Hurry up now, hurry up.

(*Johansson wheels the chair round the corner. The Student remains watching the Girl, who is now loosening the earth round the hyacinths. The Aris-tocrat, wearing mourning, comes in and speaks to the Dark Lady, who has been walking to and fro on the pavement)*

ARISTOCRAT. But what can we do about it? We shall have to wait.

LADY. I can't wait.

ARISTOCRAT. You can't? Well then, go into the country.

LADY. I don't want to do that.

ARISTOCRAT. Come over here or they will hear what we are saying.

(*They move toward the advertisement column and continue their conversation inaudibly. Johansson returns*)

JOHANSSON (*To the Student*). My master asks you not to forget that other thing, sir.

STUDENT (*Hesitating*). Look here . . . first of all tell me . . . who is your master?

JOHANSSON. Well, he's so many things, and he has been everything.

STUDENT. Is he a wise man?

JOHANSSON. Depends what that is. He says all his life he's been looking for a Sunday child, but that may not be true.

STUDENT. What does he want? He's grasping, isn't he?

JOHANSSON. It's power he wants. The whole day long he rides round in his chariot like the god Thor himself. He looks at houses, pulls them down, opens up new streets, builds squares. . . . But he breaks into houses too, sneaks through windows, plays havoc with human destinies, kills his enemies—and never forgives. Can you imagine it, sir? This miserable cripple was once a Don Juan—although he always lost his women.

STUDENT. How do you account for that?

JOHANSSON. You see he's so cunning he makes the women leave him when he's tired of them. But what he's most like now is a horse-thief in the human market. He steals human beings in all sorts of different ways. He literally stole me out of the hands of the law. Well, as a matter of fact I'd made a slip—hm, yes—and only he knew about it. Instead of getting me put in jail, he turned me into a slave. I slave—for my food alone, and that's none of the best.

STUDENT. Then what is it he means to do in this house?

JOHANSSON. I'm not going to talk about that. It's too complicated.

STUDENT. I think I'd better get away from it all.

(*The Girl drops a bracelet out the window*)

JOHANSSON. Look! The young lady has dropped her bracelet out of the window. (*The Student goes slowly over, picks up the bracelet and returns it to the Girl, who thanks him stiffly. The Student goes back to Johansson*) So you mean to get away. That's not so easy as you think, once he's got you in his net. And he's afraid of nothing between heaven and earth—yes, of one thing he is—of one person rather. . . .

STUDENT. Don't tell me. I think perhaps I know.

JOHANSSON. How can you know?

STUDENT. I'm guessing. Is it a little milkmaid he's afraid of?

JOHANSSON. He turns his head the other way whenever he meets a milk cart. Besides, he talks in his sleep. It seems he was once in Hamburg. . . .

STUDENT. Can one trust this man?

JOHANSSON. You can trust him—to do anything.

STUDENT. What's he doing now round the corner?

JOHANSSON. Listening to the poor. Sowing a little word, loosening one stone at a time, till the house falls down—metaphorically speaking. You see I'm an educated man. I was once a book-seller. . . . Do you still mean to go away?

STUDENT. I don't like to be ungrateful. He saved my father once, and now he only asks a small service in return.

JOHANSSON. What is that?

STUDENT. I am to go to *The Valkyrie*.

JOHANSSON. That's beyond me. But he's always up to new tricks. Look at him now, talking to that policeman. He is always thick with the police. He uses them, gets them involved in his interests, holds them with false promises and expectations, while all the time he's pumping them. You'll see that before the day is over he'll be received in the Round Room.

STUDENT. What does he want there? What connection has he with the Colonel?

JOHANSSON. I think I can guess, but I'm not sure. You'll see for yourself once you're in there.

STUDENT. I shall never be in there.

JOHANSSON. That depends on yourself. Go to *The Valkyrie*.

STUDENT. Is that the way?

JOHANSSON. Yes, if he said so. Look. Look at him in his war chariot, drawn in triumph by the beggars, who get nothing for their pains but the hint of a treat at his funeral.

(*The Old Man appears standing up in his wheelchair, drawn by one of the beggars and followed by the rest*)

OLD MAN. Hail the noble youth who, at the risk of his own life, saved so many others in yesterday's accident. Three cheers for Arkenholtz! (*The Beggars bare their heads but do not cheer. The Girl at the window waves her handkerchief. The Colonel gazes from the window of the Round Room. The Old Woman rises at her window. The Maid on the balcony hoists the flag to the top*) Clap your hands, citizens. True, it is Sunday, but the ass in the pit and the ear in the corn field will absolve us. And although I am not a Sunday child, I have the gift of prophecy and also that of healing. Once I brought a drowned person back to life. That was in Hamburg on a Sunday morning just like this. . . .

(*The Milkmaid enters, seen only by the Student and the Old Man. She raises her arms like one who is drowning and gazes fixedly at the Old Man. He sits down, then crumples up, stricken with horror*)

Johansson! Take me away! Quick! . . . Arkenholtz, don't forget *The Valkyrie*.
STUDENT. What is all this?
JOHANSSON. We shall see. We shall see.

SCENE 2

Inside the Round Room. At the back is a white porcelain stove. On either side of it are a mirror, a pendulum clock, and candelabra. On the right of the stove is the entrance to the hall beyond which is a glimpse of a room furnished in green and mahogany. On the left of the stove is the door to a cupboard, papered like the wall. The statue, shaded by palms, has a curtain which can be drawn to conceal it.

A door to the left leads into the Hyacinth Room, where the Girl sits reading.

The back of the Colonel can be seen, as he sits in the Green Room, writing.

Bengtsson, the Colonel's servant, comes in from the hall. He is wearing livery, and is followed by Johansson, dressed as a waiter.

BENGTSSON. Now you'll have to serve the tea, Johansson, while I take the coats. Have you ever done it before?
JOHANSSON. It's true I push a war chariot in the daytime, as you know, but in the evenings I go as a waiter to receptions and so forth. It's always been my dream to get into this house. They're queer people here, aren't they?
BENGTSSON. Ye-es. A bit out of the ordinary anyhow.
JOHANSSON. Is it to be a musical party or what?
BENGTSSON. The usual ghost supper, as we call it. They drink tea and don't say a word—or else the Colonel does all the talking. And they crunch their biscuits, all at the same time. It sounds like rats in an attic.
JOHANSSON. Why do you call it the ghost supper?
BENGTSSON. They look like ghosts. And they've kept this up for twenty years, always the same people saying the same things or saying nothing at all for fear of being found out.

JOHANSSON. Isn't there a mistress of the house?
BENGTSSON. Oh yes, but she's crazy. She sits in a cupboard because her eyes can't bear the light. (*He points to the papered door*) She sits in there.
JOHANSSON. In there?
BENGTSSON. Well, I told you they were a bit out of the ordinary.
JOHANSSON. But then—what does she look like?
BENGTSSON. Like a mummy. Do you want to have a look at her? (*He opens the door*) There she is.

(*The figure of the Colonel's Wife is seen, white and shriveled into a Mummy.*)

JOHANSSON. Oh my God!
MUMMY (*Babbling*). Why do you open the door? Haven't I told you to keep it closed?
BENGTSSON (*In a wheedling tone*). Ta, ta, ta, ta. Be a good girl now, then you'll get something nice. Pretty Polly.
MUMMY (*Parrot-like*). Pretty Polly. Are you there, Jacob? Currrr!
BENGTSSON. She thinks she's a parrot, and maybe she's right. (*To the Mummy*) Whistle for us, Polly.

(*The Mummy whistles*)

JOHANSSON. Well, I've seen a few things in my day, but this beats everything.
BENGTSSON. You see, when a house gets old, it grows moldy, and when people stay a long time together and torment each other they go mad. The mistress of the house—shut up, Polly!—that mummy there, has been living here for forty years—same husband, same furniture, same relatives, same friends. (*He closes the papered door*) And the goings-on in this house—well, they're beyond me. Look at that statue—that's her when she was young.
JOHANSSON. Good Lord! Is that the mummy?
BENGTSSON. Yes. It's enough to make you weep. And somehow, carried away by her own imagination or something, she's got to be a bit like a parrot—the way she talks and the way she can't stand cripples or sick people. She can't stand the sight of her own daughter, because she's sick.
JOHANSSON. Is the young lady sick?
BENGTSSON. Didn't you know that?
JOHANSSON. No. And the Colonel, who is he?
BENGTSSON. You'll see.
JOHANSSON (*Looking at the statue*). It's horrible to think that . . . How old is she now?
BENGTSSON. Nobody knows. But it's said that when she was thirty-five she looked nineteen, and that's what she made the Colonel believe she was—here in this

very house. Do you know what that black Japanese screen by the couch is for? They call it the death-screen, and when someone's going to die, they put it round—same as in a hospital.

JOHANSSON. What a horrible house! And the student was longing to get in, as if it were paradise.

BENGTSSON. What student? Oh, I know. The one who's coming here this evening. The Colonel and the young lady happened to meet him at the Opera, and both of them took a fancy to him. Hm. Now it's my turn to ask questions. Who is your master—the man in the wheelchair?

JOHANSSON. Well, he er . . . Is he coming here too?

BENGTSSON. He hasn't been invited.

JOHANSSON. He'll come uninvited—if need be.

(*The Old Man apapears in the hall on crutches, wearing a frock-coat and top-hat. He steals forward and listens*)

BENGTSSON. He's a regular old devil, isn't he?

JOHANSSON. Up to the ears.

BENGTSSON. He looks like Old Nick himself.

JOHANSSON. And he must be a wizard too, for he goes through locked doors.

(*The Old Man comes forward and takes hold of Johansson by the ear*)

OLD MAN. Rascal—take care! (*To Bengtsson*) Tell the Colonel I am here.

BENGTSSON. But we are expecting guests.

OLD MAN. I know. But my visit is as good as expected, if not exactly looked forward to.

BENGTSSON. I see. What name shall I say? Mr. Hummel?

OLD MAN. Exactly. Yes. (*Bengtsson crosses the hall to the Green Room, the door of which he closes behind him. To Johansson*) Get out! (*Johansson hesitates*) Get out! (*Johansson disappears into the hall. The Old Man inspects the room and stops in front of the statue in much astonishment*) Amelia! It is she—she!

MUMMY (*From the cupboard*). Prrr-etty Polly. (*The Old Man starts*)

OLD MAN. What was that? Is there a parrot in the room? I don't see it.

MUMMY. Are you there, Jacob?

OLD MAN. The house is haunted.

MUMMY. Jacob!

OLD MAN. I'm scared. So these are the kind of secrets they guard in this house. (*With his back turned to the cupboard he stands looking at a portrait*) There he is—he! (*The Mummy comes out behind the Old Man and gives a pull at his wig*)

MUMMY. Currrrr! Is it . . . ? Currrrr!

OLD MAN (*Jumping out of his skin*). God in heaven! Who is it?

MUMMY (*In a natural voice*). Is it Jacob?

OLD MAN. Yes, my name is Jacob.

MUMMY (*With emotion*). And my name is Amelia.

OLD MAN. No, no, no . . . Oh my God!

MUMMY. That's how I look. Yes. (*Pointing to the statue*) And that's how I *did* look. Life opens one's eyes, does it not? I live mostly in the cupboard to avoid seeing and being seen. . . . But, Jacob, what do you want here?

OLD MAN. My child. Our child.

MUMMY. There she is.

OLD MAN. Where?

MUMMY. There—in the Hyacinth Room.

OLD MAN (*Looking at the Girl*). Yes, that is she. (*Pause*) And what about her father—the Colonel, I mean—your husband?

MUMMY. Once, when I was angry with him, I told him everything.

OLD MAN. Well . . . ?

MUMMY. He didn't believe me. He just said: "That's what all wives say when they want to murder their husbands." It was a terrible crime none the less. It has falsified his whole life—his family tree too. Sometimes I take a look in the Peerage, and then I say to myself: Here she is, going about with a false birth certificate like some servant girl, and for such things people are sent to the reformatory.

OLD MAN. Many do it. I seem to remember your own date of birth was given incorrectly.

MUMMY. My mother made me do that. I was not to blame. And in our crime, *you* played the biggest part.

OLD MAN. No. Your husband caused that crime, when he took my fiancée from me. I was born one who cannot forgive until he has punished. That was to me an imperative duty—and is so still.

MUMMY. What are you expecting to find in this house? What do you want? How did you get in? Is it to do with my daughter? If you touch her, you shall die.

OLD MAN. I mean well by her.

MUMMY. Then you must spare her father.

OLD MAN. No.

MUMMY. Then you shall die. In this room, behind that screen.

OLD MAN. That may be. But I can't let go once I've got my teeth into a thing.

MUMMY. You want to marry her to that student. Why? He is nothing and has nothing.

OLD MAN. He will be rich, through me.

MUMMY. Have you been invited here tonight?

OLD MAN. No, but I propose to get myself an invitation to this ghost supper.

MUMMY. Do you know who is coming?

OLD MAN. Not exactly.

MUMMY. The Baron. The man who lives up above—whose father-in-law was buried this afternoon.

OLD MAN. The man who is getting a divorce in order to marry the daughter of the Caretaker's wife . . . The man who used to be—your lover.

MUMMY. Another guest will be your former fiancée, who was seduced by my husband.

OLD MAN. A select gathering.

MUMMY. Oh God, if only we might die, might die!

OLD MAN. Then why have you stayed together?

MUMMY. Crime and secrets and guilt bind us together. We have broken our bonds and gone our own ways, times without number, but we are always drawn together again.

OLD MAN. I think the Colonel is coming.

MUMMY. Then I will go in to Adèle. (*Pause*) Jacob, mind what you do. Spare him. (*Pause. She goes into the Hyacinth Room and disappears*)

(*The Colonel enters, cold and reserved, with a letter in his hand.*)

COLONEL. Be seated, please. (*Slowly the Old Man sits down. Pause. The Colonel stares at him*) You wrote this letter, sir?

OLD MAN. I did.

COLONEL. Your name is Hummel?

OLD MAN. It is. (*Pause*)

COLONEL. As I understand, you have bought in all my unpaid promissory notes. I can only conclude that I am in your hands. What do you want?

OLD MAN. I want payment, in one way or another.

COLONEL. In what way?

OLD MAN. A very simple one. Let us not mention the money. Just bear with me in your house as a guest.

COLONEL. If so little will satisfy you . . .

OLD MAN. Thank you.

COLONEL. What else?

OLD MAN. Dismiss Bengtsson.

COLONEL. Why should I do that? My devoted servant, who has been with me a lifetime, who has the national medal for long and faithful service—why should I do that?

OLD MAN. That's how you see him—full of excellent qualities. He is not the man he appears to be.

COLONEL. Who is?

OLD MAN (*Taken aback*). True. But Bengtsson must go.

COLONEL. Are you going to run my house?

OLD MAN. Yes. Since everything here belongs to me—furniture, curtains, dinner service, linen . . . and more too.

COLONEL. How do you mean—more?

OLD MAN. Everything. I own everything here. It is mine.

COLONEL. Very well, it is yours. But my family escutcheon and my good name remain my own.

OLD MAN. No, not even those. (*Pause*) You are not a nobleman.

COLONEL. How dare you!

OLD MAN (*Producing a document*). If you read this extract from *The Armorial Gazette*, you will see that the family whose name you are using has been extinct for a hundred years.

COLONEL. I have heard rumors to this effect, but I inherited the name from my father. (*Reads*) It is true. You are right. I am not a nobleman. Then I must take off my signet ring. It is true, it belongs to you. (*Gives it to him*) There you are.

OLD MAN (*Pocketing the ring*). Now we will continue. You are not a Colonel either.

COLONEL. I am not . . . ?

OLD MAN. No. You once held the temporary rank of Colonel in the American Volunteer Force, but after the war in Cuba and the reorganization of the Army, all such titles were abolished.

COLONEL. Is this true?

OLD MAN (*Indicating his pocket*). Do you want to read it?

COLONEL. No, that's not necessary. Who are you, and what right have you to sit there stripping me in this fashion?

OLD MAN. You will see. but as far as stripping you goes . . . do you know who you are?

COLONEL. How dare you?

OLD MAN. Take off that wig and have a look at yourself in the mirror. But take your teeth out at the same time and shave off your moustache. Let Bengtsson unlace your metal stays and perhaps a certain X.Y.Z., a lackey, will recognize himself. The fellow who was a cupboard lover in a certain kitchen . . . (*The Colonel reaches for the bell on the table, but Hummel checks him*) Don't touch that bell, and don't call Bengtsson. If you do, I'll have him arrested. (*Pause*) And now the guests are beginning to arrive. Keep your composure and we will continue to play our old parts for a while.

COLONEL. Who are you? I recognize your voice and eyes.

OLD MAN. Don't try to find out. Keep silent and obey.

(*The Student enters and bows to the Colonel*)

STUDENT. How do you do, sir.

COLONEL. Welcome to my house, young man. Your splendid behavior at that great disaster has brought your name to everybody's lips, and I count it an honor to receive you in my home.

STUDENT. My humble descent, sir . . . Your illustrious name and noble birth . . .

COLONEL. May I introduce Mr. Arkenholtz—Mr. Hummel. If you will join the ladies in here, Mr. Arkenholtz—I must conclude my conversation with Mr. Hummel. (*He shows the Student into the Hyacinth Room, where he remains visible, talking shyly to the Girl*) A splendid young man, musical, sings, writes poetry. If he only had blue blood in him, if he were of the same station, I don't think I should object . . .

OLD MAN. To what?

COLONEL. To my daughter . . .

OLD MAN. *Your* daughter! But apropos of that, why does she spend all her time in there?

COLONEL. She insists on being in the Hyacinth Room except when she is out-of-doors. It's a peculiarity of hers. Ah, here comes Miss Beatrice von Holsteinkrona—a charming woman, a pillar of the Church, with just enough money of her own to suit her birth and position.

OLD MAN (*To himself*). My fiancée.

(*The Fiancée enters, looking a little crazy*)

COLONEL. Miss Holsteinkrona—Mr. Hummel. (*The Fiancée curtseys and takes a seat. The Aristocrat enters and seats himself. He wears mourning and looks mysterious*) Baron Skanskorg . . .

OLD MAN (*Aside, without rising*). That's the jewel-thief, I think. (*To the Colonel*) If you bring in the Mummy, the party will be complete.

COLONEL (*At the door of the Hyacinth Room*). Polly!

MUMMY (*Entering*). Currrrr . . . !

COLONEL. Are the young people to come in too?

OLD MAN. No, not the young people. They shall be spared.

(*They all sit silent in a circle*)

COLONEL. Shall we have the tea brought in?

OLD MAN. What's the use? No one wants tea. Why should we pretend about it?

COLONEL. Then shall we talk?

OLD MAN. Talk of the weather, which we know? Inquire about each other's health, which we know just as well. I prefer silence—then one can hear thoughts and see the past. Silence cannot hide anything—but words can. I read the other day that differences of language originated among savages for the purpose of keeping one tribe's secrets hidden from another.

Every language therefore is a code, and he who finds the key can understand every language in the world. But this does not prevent secrets from being exposed without a key, specially when there is a question of paternity to be proved. Proof in a Court of Law is another matter. Two false witnesses suffice to prove anything about which they are agreed, but one does not take witnesses along on the kind of explorations I have in mind. Nature herself has instilled in human beings a sense of modesty which tries to hide what should be hidden, but we slip into situations unintentionally, and by chance sometimes the deepest secret is divulged—the mask torn from the imposter, the villain exposed. . . . (*Pause. All look at each other in silence*) What a silence there is now! (*Long silence*) Here, for instance, in this honorable house, in this elegant home, where beauty, wealth and culture are united. . . . (*Long silence*) All of us now sitting here know who we are—do we not? There's no need for me to tell you. And you know me, although you pretend ignorance. (*He indicates the Hyacinth Room*) In there is my daughter. *Mine*—you know that too. She had lost the desire to live, without knowing why. The fact is she was withering away in this air charged with crime and deceit and falseness of every kind. That is why I looked for a friend for her in whose company she might enjoy the light and warmth of noble deeds. (*Long silence*) That was my mission in this house: to pull up the weeds, to expose the crimes, to settle all accounts, so that those young people might start afresh in this home, which is my gift to them. (*Long silence*) Now I am going to grant safe-conduct, to each of you in his and her proper time and turn. Whoever stays I shall have arrested. (*Long silence*) Do you hear the clock ticking like a death-watch beetle in the wall? Do you hear what it says? "It's time, it's time, it's time." When it strikes, in a few moments, your time will be up. Then you can go, but not before. It's raising its arm against you before it strikes. Listen! It is warning you. "The clock can strike." And I can strike too. (*He strikes the table with one of his crutches*) Do you hear?

(*Silence. The Mummy goes up to the clock and stops it, then speaks in a normal and serious voice*)

MUMMY. But I can stop time in its course. I can wipe out the past and undo what is done. But not with bribes, not with threats—only through suffering and repentance. (*She goes up to the Old Man*) We are miserable human beings, that we know. We have erred and we have sinned, we like all the rest. We are not what we seem, because at bottom we are better than ourselves, since we detest our sins. But when you, Jacob Hummel, with your false name, choose to sit in judgmemt over us, you prove yourself worse than us miserable sinners. For you are not the one you appear to be. You are a thief of human souls. You stole me once with false promises. You murdered the Consul who was buried today; you strangled him with debts. You have stolen the student, binding him by the pretence of a claim on his father, who never owed you a farthing. (*Having tried to rise and speak, the Old Man sinks back in his chair and crumples up more and more as she goes on*) But there is one dark spot in your life which I am not quite sure about, although I have my suspicions. I think Bengtsson knows. (*She rings the bell on the table.*)

OLD MAN. No, not Bengtsson, not him.

MUMMY. So he does know. (*She rings again. The Milkmaid appears in the hallway door, unseen by all but the Old Man, who shrinks back in horror. The Milkmaid vanishes as Bengtsson enters*) Do you know this man, Bengtsson?

BENGTSSON. Yes, I know him and he knows me. Life, as you are aware, has its ups and downs. I have been in his service; another time he was in mine. For two whole years he was a sponger in my kitchen. As he had to be away by three, the dinner was got ready at two, and the family had to eat the warmed-up leavings of that brute. He drank the soup stock, which the cook then filled up with water. He sat out there like a vampire, sucking the marrow out of the house, so that we became like skeletons. And he nearly got us put in prison when we called the cook a thief. Later I met this man in Hamburg under another name. He was a usurer than, a blood-sucker. But while he was there he was charged with having lured a young girl out on to the ice so as to drown her, because she had seen him commit a crime he was afraid would be discovered. . . .

(*The Mummy passes her hand over the Old Man's face*)

MUMMY. *This* is you. Now give up the notes and the will. (*Johansson appears in the hallway door and watches the scene with great interest, knowing he is now to be freed from slavery. The Old Man produces a bundle of papers and throws it on the table. The Mummy goes over and strokes his back*) Parrot. Are you there, Jacob?

OLD MAN (*Like a parrot*). Jacob is here. Pretty Polly. Currrrr!

MUMMY. May the clock strike?

OLD MAN (*With a clucking sound*). The clock may strike. (*Imitating a cuckoo clock*) *Cuckoo, cuckoo, cuckoo. . . .*

(*The Mummy opens the cupboard door*)

MUMMY. Now the clock has struck. Rise, and enter the cupboard where I have spent twenty years repenting our crime. A rope is hanging there, which you can take as the one with which you strangled the Consul, and with which you meant to strangle your benefactor. . . . Go! (*The Old Man goes in to the cupboaard. The Mummy closes the door*) Bengtsson! Put up the screen—the death-screen. (*Bengtsson places the screen in front of the door*) It is finished. God have mercy on his soul.

ALL. Amen. (*Long silence*)

(*The Girl and the Student appear in the Hyacinth Room. She has a harp, on which she plays a prelude, and then accompanies the Student's recitation*)

STUDENT.
I saw the sun. To me it seemed
that I beheld the Hidden.
Men must reap what they have sown;
blest is he whose deeds are good.
Deeds which you have wrought in fury,
cannot in evil find redress.
Comfort him you have distressed
with loving-kindness—this will heal.
No fear has he who does no ill.
Sweet is innocence.

SCENE 3

Inside the Hyacinth Room. The general effect of the room is exotic and oriental. There are hyacinths everywhere, of every color, some in pots, some with the bulbs in glass vases and the roots going down into the water.

On top of the tiled stove is a large seated Buddha, in whose lap rests a bulb from which rises the stem of a shallot (Allium ascalonicum), bearing its globular cluster of white, starlike flowers.

On the right is an open door, leading into the Round Room, where the Colonel and the Mummy are seated, inactive and silent. A part of the death-screen is also visible.

On the left is a door to the pantry and kitchen.

The Student and the Girl (Adèle) are beside the table; he standing, she seated with her harp.

GIRL. Now sing to my flowers.

STUDENT. Is this the flower of your soul?

GIRL. The one and only. Do you too love the hyacinth?

STUDENT. I love it above all other flowers—its virginal shape rising straight and slender out of the bulb, resting on the water and sending its pure white roots down into the colorless fluid. I love its colors: the snow-white, pure as innocence, the yellow honey-sweet, the youthful pink, the ripe red, but best of all the blue—the dewy blue, deep-eyed and full of faith. I love them all, more than gold or pearls. I have loved them ever since I was a child, have worshipped them because they have all the fine qualities I lack. . . . And yet . . .

GIRL. Go on.

STUDENT. My love is not returned, for these beautiful blossoms hate me.

GIRL. How do you mean?

STUDENT. Their fragrance, strong and pure as the early winds of spring which have passed over melting snows, confuses my senses, deafens me, blinds me, thrusts me out of the room, bombards me with poisoned arrows that wound my heart and set my head on fire. Do you know the legend of that flower?

GIRL. Tell it to me.

STUDENT. First its meaning. The bulb is the earth, resting on the water or buried in the soil. Then the stalk rises, straight as the axis of the world, and at the top are the six-pointed star-flowers.

GIRL. Above the earth—the stars. Oh, that is wonderful! Where did you learn this? How did you find it out?

STUDENT. Let me think . . . In your eyes. And so, you see, it is an image of the Cosmos. This is why Buddha is holding the earth-bulb, his eyes brooding as he watches it grow, outward and upward, transforming itself into a heaven. This poor earth will become a heaven. It is for this that Buddha waits.

GIRL. I see it now. Is not the snowflake six-pointed too like the hyacinth flower?

STUDENT. You are right. The snowflakes must be falling stars.

GIRL. And the snowdrop is a snow-star, grown out of snow.

STUDENT. But the largest and most beautiful of all the stars in the firmament, the golden-red Sirius, is the narcissus with its gold and red chalice and its six white rays.

GIRL. Have you seen the shallot in bloom?

STUDENT. Indeed I have. It bears its blossoms within a ball, a globe like the celestial one, strewn with white stars.

GIRL. Oh how glorious! Whose thought was that?

STUDENT. Yours.

GIRL. Yours.

STUDENT. Ours. We have given birth to it together. We are wedded.

GIRL. Not yet.

STUDENT. What's still to do?

GIRL. Waiting, ordeals, patience.

STUDENT. Very well. Put me to the test. (*Pause*) Tell me. Why do your parents sit in there so silently, not saying a single word?

GIRL. Because they have nothing to say to each other, and because neither believes what the other says. This is how my father puts it: What's the point of talking, when neither of us can fool the other?

STUDENT. What a horrible thing to hear!

GIRL. Here comes the Cook. Look at her, how big and fat she is. (*They watch the Cook, although the audience cannot yet see her*)

STUDENT. What does she want?

GIRL. To ask me about the dinner. I have to do the housekeeping as my mother's ill.

STUDENT. What have we to do with the kitchen?

GIRL. We must eat. Look at the Cook. I can't bear the sight of her.

STUDENT. Who is that ogress?

GIRL. She belongs to the Hummel family of vampires. She is eating us.

STUDENT. Why don't you dismiss her?

GIRL. She won't go. We have no control over her. We've got her for our sins. Can't you see that we are pining and wasting away?

STUDENT. Don't you get enough to eat?

GIRL. Yes, we get many dishes, but all the strength has gone. She boils the nourishment out of the meat and gives us the fibre and water, while she drinks the stock herself. And when there's a roast, she first boils out the marrow, eats the gravy and drinks the juices herself. Everything she touches loses its savor. It's as if she sucked with her eyes. We get the grounds when she has drunk the coffee. She drinks the wine and fills the bottles up with water.

STUDENT. Send her packing.

GIRL. We can't.

STUDENT. Why not?

GIRL. We don't know. She won't go. No one has any control over her. She has taken all our strength from us.

STUDENT. May I get rid of her?

GIRL. No. It must be as it is. Here she is. She will ask me what is to be for dinner. I shall tell her. She will make objections and get her own way.

STUDENT. Let her do the ordering herself then.

GIRL. She won't do that.

STUDENT. What an extraordinary house! It is bewitched.

GIRL. Yes. But now she is turning back, because she has seen you.

THE COOK (*In the doorway*). No, that wasn't the reason. (*She grins, showing all her teeth*)

STUDENT. Get out!

COOK. When it suits me. (*Pause*) It does suit me now. (*She disappears*)

GIRL. Don't lose your temper. Practice patience. She is one of the ordeals we have to go through in this house. You see, we have a housemaid too, whom we have to clean up after.

STUDENT. I am done for. *Cor in œthere*.[4] Music!

GIRL. Wait.

STUDENT. Music!

GIRL. Patience. This room is called the room of ordeals. It looks beautiful, but it is full of defects.

STUDENT. Really? Well, such things must be seen to. It is very beautiful, but a little cold. Why don't you have a fire?

GIRL. Because it smokes.

STUDENT. Can't you have the chimney swept?

GIRL. It doesn't help. You see that writing-desk there?

STUDENT. An unusually fine piece.

GIRL. But it wobbles. Every day I put a piece of cork under that leg, and every day the housemaid takes it away when she sweeps and I have to cut a new piece. The penholder is covered with ink every morning and so is the inkstand. I have to clean them up every morning after that woman, as sure as the sun rises. (*Pause*) What's the worst job you can think of?

STUDENT. To count the washing. Ugh!

GIRL. That I have to do. Ugh!

STUDENT. What else?

GIRL. To be waked in the middle of the night and have to get up and see to the window, which the housemaid has left banging.

STUDENT. What else?

GIRL. To get up on a ladder and tie the cord on the damper to the big stove, which the housmaid has torn off.

STUDENT. What else?

GIRL. To sweep after her, to dust after her, to light the fire in the stove when all she's done is throw in some wood. To see to the damper, to wipe the glasses, to lay the table over again, to open the bottles, to see that the rooms are aired, to remake my bed, to rinse the water-bottle when it's green with sediment, to buy matches and soap which are always lacking, to

wipe the chimneys and trim the wicks to keep the lamps from smoking—and so that they don't go out when we have company, I have to fill them myself. . . .

STUDENT. Music!

GIRL. Wait. The labor comes first. The labor of keeping the dirt of life at a distance.

STUDENT. But you are wealthy and have two servants.

GIRL. It doesn't help. Even if we had three. Living is hard work, and sometimes I grow tired. (*Pause*) Think then if there were a nursery as well.

STUDENT. The greatest of joys.

GIRL. And the costliest. Is life worth so much hardship?

STUDENT. That must depend on the reward you expect for your labors. I would not shrink from anything to win your hand.

GIRL. Don't say that. You can never have me.

STUDENT. Why not?

GIRL. You mustn't ask. (*Pause*)

STUDENT. You dropped your bracelet out of the window. . . .

GIRL. Because my hand has grown so thin. (*Pause*)

(*The Cook appears with a Japanese bottle in her hand*)

There she is—the one who devours me and all of us.

STUDENT. What has she in her hand?

GIRL. It is the bottle of coloring matter that has letters like scorpions on it. It is the soy which turns water into soup and takes the place of gravy. She makes cabbage soup with it—and mock-turtle soup too.

STUDENT (*to Cook*). Get out!

COOK. You drain us of sap, and we drain you. We take the blood and leave you the water, but colored . . . colored. I am going now, but all the same I shall stay, as long as I please.

(*She goes out*)

STUDENT. Why did Bengtsson get a medal?

GIRL. For his great merits.

STUDENT. Has he no defects?

GIRL. Yes, great ones. But you don't get a medal for them.

(*They smile*)

STUDENT. You have many secrets in this house.

GIRL. As in all others. Permit us to keep ours.

STUDENT. Don't you approve of candor?

GIRL. Yes—within reason.

STUDENT. Sometimes I'm seized with a raging desire to say all I think. But I know the world would go to pieces if one were completely candid. (*Pause*) I went to a funeral the other day . . . in church. It was very solemn and beautiful.

GIRL. Was it Mr. Hummel's?

[4]Lift up your heart.

138

STUDENT. My false benefactor's—yes. At the head of the coffin stood an old friend of the deceased. He carried the mace. I was deeply impressed by the dignified manner and moving words of the clergyman. I cried. We all cried. Afterward we went to a tavern, and there I learned that the man with the mace had been in love with the dead man's son. . . . (*The girl stares at him, trying to understand*) And that the dead man had borrowed money from his son's admirer. (*Pause*) Next day the clergyman was arrested for embezzling the church funds. A pretty story.

GIRL. Oh . . . ! (*Pause*)

STUDENT. Do you know how I am thinking about you now?

GIRL. Don't tell me, or I shall die.

STUDENT. I must, or I shall die.

GIRL. It is in asylums that people say everything they think.

STUDENT. Exactly. My father finished up in an asylum.

GIRL. Was he ill?

STUDENT. No, he was well, but he was mad. You see, he broke out once—in these circumstances. Like all of us, he was surrounded with a circle of acquaintances; he called them friends for short. They were a lot of rotters, of course, as most people are, but he had to have some society—he couldn't get on all alone. Well, as you know, in everyday life no one tells people what he thinks of them, and he didn't either. He knew perfectly well what frauds they were—he'd sounded the depths of their deceit—but as he was a wise and well-bred man, he was always courteous to them. Then one day he gave a big party. It was in the evening and he was tired by the day's work and by the strain of holding his tongue and at the same time talking rubbish with his guests. . . . (*The girl is frightened*) Well, at the dinner table he rapped for silence, raised his glass, and began to speak. Then something loosed the trigger. He made an enormous speech in which he stripped the whole company naked, one after the other, and told them of all their treachery. Then, tired out, he sat down on the table and told them all to go to hell.

GIRL. Oh!

STUDENT. I was there, and I shall never forget what happened then. Father and Mother came to blows, the guests rushed for the door . . . and my father was taken to a madhouse, where he died. (*Pause*) Water that is still too long stagnates, and so it is in this house too. There is something stagnating here. And yet I thought it was paradise itself that first time I saw you coming in here. There I stood that Sunday morning, gazing in. I saw a Colonel who was no Colonel. I had a benefactor who was a thief and had to hang himself. I saw a mummy who was not a mummy and an old maid—what of the maidenhood, by the way? Where is beauty to be found? In nature, and in my own mind, when it is in its Sunday clothes. Where are honor and faith? In fairy-tales and children's fancies. Where is anything that fulfills its promise? In my imagination. Now your flowers have poisoned me and I have given the poison back to you. I asked you to become my wife in a home full of poetry and song and music. Then the Cook came. . . . *Sursum Corda!*[5] Try once more to strike fire and glory out of the golden harp. Try, I beg you, I implore you on my knees. (*Pause*) Then I will do it myself. (*He picks up the harp, but the strings give no sound*) It is dumb and deaf. To think that the most beautiful flowers are so poisonous, are the most poisonous. The curse lies over the whole of creation, over life itself. Why will you not be my bride? Because the very life-spring within you is sick . . . now I can feel that vampire in the kitchen beginning to suck me. I believe she is a Lamia, one of those that suck the blood of children. It is always in the kitchen quarters that the seed-leaves of the children are nipped, if it has not already happened in the bedroom. There are poisons that destroy the sight and poisons that open the eyes. I seem to have been born with the latter kind, for I cannot see what is ugly as beautiful, nor call evil good. I cannot. Jesus Christ descended into hell. That was His pilgrimage on earth—to this mad-house, this prison, this charnel-house, this earth. And the madmen killed Him when He wanted to set them free; but the robber they let go. The robber always gets the sympathy. Woe! Woe to us all. Saviour of the world, save us! We perish.

(*And now the girl has drooped, and it is seen that she is dying. She rings*)

(*Bengtsson enters*)

GIRL. Bring the screen. Quick. I am dying.

(*Bengtsson comes back with the screen, opens it and arranges it in front of the girl*)

STUDENT. The Liberator is coming. Welcome, pale and gentle one. Sleep, you lovely, innocent, doomed creature, suffering for no fault of your own. Sleep without dreaming, and when you wake again . . . may you be greeted by a sun that does not burn, in a home

[5]Lift up your hearts.

without dust, by friends without stain, by a love without flaw. You wise and gentle Buddha, sitting there waiting for a Heaven to sprout from the earth, grant us patience in our ordeal and purity of will, so that this hope may not be confounded. (*The strings of the harp hum softly and a white light fills the room*)

> I saw the sun. To me it seemed
> that I beheld the Hidden.
> Men must reap what they have sown;
> blest is he whose deeds are good.
> Deeds which you have wrought in fury,
> cannot in evil find redress.
> Comfort him you have distressed
> with loving-kindness—this will heal.
> No fear has he who does no ill.
> Sweet is innocence.

(*A faint moaning is heard behind the screen*) You poor little child, child of this world of illusion, guilt, suffering and death, this world of endless change, disappointment, and pain. May the Lord of Heaven be merciful to you upon your journey.

(*The room disappears. Böcklin's picture,* The Island of the Dead, *is seen in the distance,*[6] *and from the island comes music, soft, sweet, and melancholy*)

Curtain

---

[6] Arnold Böcklin (1827–1901) was a Swiss painter noted for landscape and mythological frescoes. *The Island of the Dead (Die Toteninsel)* is his most famous work.

COMMENTARY

Note: The following essay represents a single interpretation of the play. For other perspectives on The Ghost Sonata, *consult the essays listed below.*

In Scene 3 the Hyacinth Girl, the product of the illicit love between the vampire Hummel and the Colonel's wife, dies a victim of the bloodsucking world in which she was doomed to be born. Her death occurs behind a large screen, which dissolves into the painting *The Island of the Dead* (*Die Toteninsel*) by the Swiss Romantic artist Arnold Böcklin (1827–1901). The girl's death is, of course, a liberation from the cruel, lifeless existence of this world "of illusion, guilt, suffering and death, this world of endless change, disappointment, and pain." Strindberg no doubt chose Böcklin's painting (in which a white-robed priest steers a skiff carrying a coffin to an island that is as mysterious and foreboding as it is strangely beautiful and serene) because it seems to suggest a "safe haven" far removed from the world depicted in the play.

Although the painting is central to our understanding of this perplexing drama, it is perhaps another art form—music—that best illuminates Strindberg's intentions. Both the title of the play (*Sonata*) and the style of theater in which it was written (chamber piece) are borrowed from the world of music, which was itself undergoing enormous change at the dawn of the twentieth century. Composers such as Arnold Schoenberg were redefining the possibilities of their art, as were painters (Pablo Picasso), novelists (Franz Kafka), and poets (T.S. Eliot). Schoenberg—like Freud, from Vienna—introduced dissonance and atonality in musical composition, techniques that promoted extraordinary leaps from one tone to another, fragments of melody that were not necessarily connected, interrupted rhythms, and violent contrasts—all for the purpose of showing the chaos, pain, and anguish of the world. Schoenberg's music might well have been composed as a soundtrack for *The Ghost Sonata*. In truth, it was likely Beethoven's *Geistertrio*, Opus 70, No. 1 (a three-piece work about the spirit world) that inspired Strindberg. And we cannot ignore the repeated references in Scene 1 to *The Valkyrie*; in Norse mythology the Valkyrie, so prominent in Richard Wagner's operas, chose young warriors to be slain in battle and accompanied them to Valhalla, the Viking version of heaven.

The three scenes of the play correspond to the three movements of a sonata ("little sound"). Scene 1 is an *allegro*, a "lively" (how ironic!) melody. We gather before "the façade of a modern house," ostensibly for a pleasant dinner that reunites the Old Man (Hummel), a once-successful businessman, with the Colonel and his wife. Hummel asks a young student-artist to accompany him into the house, specifically to engage the beautiful and mysterious daughter of the house. Strindberg's use of the word "façade" in the opening stage direction is quite deliberate, for as we enter the house (the sense of journey is central to the play) we understand that all is a façade; little is respectable in this house of respectability. In "counterpoint" to the first movement, the second is a *largo*, a slow, stately scene in which appearances are stripped away and terrifying realities become apparent. The seemingly frail, wheelchair-bound Hummel is in actuality a murderer, a vampire who is described as "a thief of human souls." The once-beautiful Colonel's wife (and Hummel's former lover) is now a shrieking mummy, the proud Colonel is reduced to a whimpering lackey. Only the Student, the sole character associated with life-giving forces, remains constant; fittingly, it is he who intones Hummel's dismal eulogy as Scene 2 ends.

Scene 3 is an *andante*, a musical term denoting a "moderately slow" rhythm. We begin with hope that the love of the Student for the Hyacinth Girl will overcome the pitiable condition in which they find themselves. The scene takes place in the Round Room, an apparent sanctum in the chamber of horrors. But as the Girl says, "The room is called the room of ordeals. It looks beautiful, but it is full of deceits." It is Strindberg's metaphor for the world itself. Death, in the guise of an obese cook, enters to give the Girl a vial with "letters like scorpions on it." As the Student recounts his strange journey through "this madhouse, this prison, this charnel-house, this earth," the Girl dies while "from the island [of Böcklin's painting] comes music, soft, sweet, and melancholy."

Like dreams, especially nightmares, the play defies an absolute interpretation. It does seem to suggest, however, that there is little room in the world for innocence, that the walking dead will ultimately corrupt those with "purity of will." But the play is not without its hint of optimism: beyond the Island of the Dead exists another world, guarded by Christ and the gentle Buddha (Strindberg was among the first Western writers to embrace Eastern religion), where the "sun . . . does not burn, in a home without dust, by friends without stain, by a love without flaw." In the final analysis, this utopian view is the ultimate counterpoint to the grotesqueries of Strindberg's world.

Other perspectives on *The Ghost Sonata:*

May, Milton A. "Strindberg's *Ghost Sonata*: Parodied Fairy Tale on Original Sin." *Modern Drama* 10 (September 1967): 189–94.

Rothwell, Brian. "The Chamber Plays." In Otto Reinert (ed.), *Strindberg*. Englewood Cliffs, NJ: Prentice-Hall, 1971, 152–163.

Other plays by Strindberg on video/film:

The Father (in Swedish, with subtitles). Dir. Bo Wilderberg. Insight Media, 120 min., 1988.

Strindberg's Miss Julie. Dir. Robin Philips. Perf. The Royal Shakespeare Company. Insight Media, 100 min., 1988.

SHOWCASE   INDEPENDENT AND INTIMATE THEATERS

Realism and other new-wave dramas of the 1880s necessitated changes in theatrical architecture, as well as performance styles. Nineteenth-century playhouses across Europe and in America were cavernous because they were designed to house the elaborate scenery and special effects required by the melodrama and to ensure enough seats to generate revenues to pay for the spectacles. Accordingly, actors were forced to use large gestures, to speak in thundering tones, and, in general, to portray characters in larger-than-life dimensions. (You can still see this style in many of the early silent movies that featured actors trained in the older methods.) New theater spaces provided intimacy so actors could sit and talk in the natural tones necessitated by the scripts. Furthermore, the controversial nature of the new works meant smaller audiences and the threat of censorship. Consequently, there sprang up a number of intimate theaters that placed audiences, now numbering perhaps a hundred, closer to the actors, who could speak naturally and who no longer needed grand gestures and grimaces. Strindberg's own theater in Stockholm was aptly named the Intimate Theatre.

The prototype of such theaters was the Théâtre Libre ("Free Theater"), founded in Paris in May 1887 by Andre Antoine (1858–1941), a French civil servant whose interest in the new social dramas led him to transform performance modes. Antoine named his enterprise after Victor Hugo's romantic essay, "A Theater Set Free." Like Hugo, Antoine wanted to free the theater from its old constraints by creating a new drama for commoners who could see plays addressing relevant social problems. To finance his venue, he sold season subscriptions to his "theater club" (a move to avoid censorship), where he produced the new works of such dramatists as Zola, Ibsen, Strindberg, Tolstoy, and Hauptmann. Not only were the new scripts revolutionary in content and form, the style in which they were presented was also innovative. Antoine insisted on new three-dimensional scenery for each production, and he advocated the use of natural light sources. He often brought "the real thing" on stage (he used actual beef carcasses in Fernand Icres's *The Butchers*). His actors stood with their backs to the audience and spoke in conversational tones. Everything about an Antoine production was calculated to suggest that the audience was watching the play through an invisible fourth wall of an actual room.

The integrity and success of the Théâtre Libre inspired imitators across Europe and, eventually, the United States and Latin America. In Germany, Otto Brahm created the Frei Buhne ("Free Theater") in 1889, while in London J. T. Grein opened the Independent Theatre in March 1891 with a production of Ibsen's *Ghosts*. He soon persuaded one of London's most thoughtful critics and social thinkers, George Bernard Shaw, to write plays for his *avant-garde* enterprise. In 1904 the Abbey Theatre opened in Dublin to encourage native voices, speaking in purely Irish accents. The poet-playwright William Butler Yeats, Lady Augusta Gregory (herself an excellent dramatist), and John Millington Synge founded the Abbey, which still flourishes today.

August Strindberg founded the Intimate Theatre in Stockholm in 1907 for productions of his "chamber plays," of which *The Ghost Sonata* is perhaps the most famous. Strindberg modeled his enterprise after two prominent European theaters: Antoine's Théâtre Libre, which ironically had rejected his early works (*Miss Julie*, however, was performed there in 1893, the first of his plays to be performed in Paris), and Max Reinhardt's Kammerspeilhaus in Berlin. The German director also referred to his theater as a "chamber theater," and fittingly many of Strindberg's works were performed there. Although the Intimate Theatre held only 161 patrons and was closed in 1910, in its short history this tiny stage hosted some of the most innovative dramas of the modern theater.

The "little theater" movement arrived in the United States in 1915 when George Cram Cook and his wife, Susan Glaspell, founded the Provincetown Players on Cape Cod. In the Greenwich Village section of New York City, Cook and his company converted a stable at 139 Macdougal Street into the Playwright's Theater. Here the 29 founding members of the Provincetown Players would, in Cook's words, "give American playwrights a chance to work out their ideas in freedom." Eugene O'Neill saw his first plays, particularly the collection of one-act plays known as "the sea plays," produced here. Glaspell's *Trifles* also enjoyed its premiere here. In 1918 it became the Provincetown Playhouse (and relocated to 133 Macdougal Street, where it still exists); it is traditionally recognized as the birthplace of the modern American theater. Not only did it spawn important new playwrights, but also other artists such as director Kenneth McGowan and scene designer Robert Edmund Jones began their theater careers on Macdougal Street.

Closer to our time, the Market Theatre (founded in 1976) in Johannesburg, South Africa, has captured the spirit of the independent theater; you may read about its inception and purpose in the Showcase following the discussion of Athol Fugard's *"MASTER HAROLD" . . . and the boys.* The Market has produced the work of Fugard and many of the most important contemporary African dramatists.

Whether in Paris, Berlin, Stockholm, Dublin, or Greenwich Village, the new independent theaters created between 1888 and 1918 had common goals. All were committed to new works concerned with contemporary society. All were drawn to the new production style that sought to give the illusion of real life on stage, though they also experimented with Expressionism and symbolist drama. Perhaps most importantly, all disdained the commercial theater. In some cases, however, the daring work of those who toiled in the independent theaters was moved into the commercial theaters and actually contributed to the demise of the former enterprises. The Provincetown Players, for instance, disbanded in 1929, partly because of the onset of the Great Depression, but largely because its leading artists (e.g., O'Neill and Jones) found larger audiences in the commercial theater.

HEARTBREAK HOUSE

BERNARD SHAW

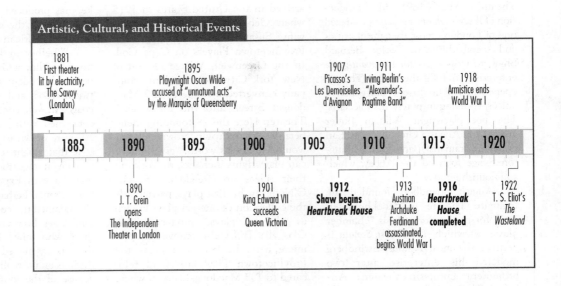

Artistic, Cultural, and Historical Events

1881
First theater
lit by electricity,
The Savoy
(London)

1895
Playwright Oscar Wilde
accused of "unnatural acts"
by the Marquis of Queensberry

1907
Picasso's
Les Demoiselles
d'Avignon

1911
Irving Berlin's
"Alexander's
Ragtime Band"

1918
Armistice ends
World War I

1885	1890	1895	1900	1905	1910	1915	1920

1890
J. T. Grein
opens
The Independent
Theater in London

1901
King Edward VII
succeeds
Queen Victoria

**1912
Shaw begins
Heartbreak House**

1913
Austrian
Archduke
Ferdinand
assassinated,
begins World War I

**1916
Heartbreak
House
completed**

1922
T. S. Eliot's
The
Wasteland

[GEORGE] BERNARD SHAW (1856–1950)

Only Shakespeare eclipses Shaw's importance to the British theater, both in critical material written about him and in productions of his plays. Indeed, there are numerous Shaw Festivals, the most prominent of which is in Niagara, Canada. Shaw is the most prodigious writer of English drama; his collected plays (53) fill almost forty volumes. His essays—such as "The Revolutionist's Handbook," which accompanies *Man and Superman*—make inspired reading for their wit and the breadth of subject matter. There is scarcely a topic on which Shaw has not written, and he remains among the most quoted writers in world literature.

Shaw's long life spanned a period of profound change. He was born amidst the Industrial Revolution and Victorianism, he matured as a writer as Europe entered World War I, he saw revolution in Russia and the economic collapse of Europe and America, and his last years witnessed World War II, the birth of the atomic age, and the beginning of the Cold War. Little wonder his plays are repositories of Western discourse during one of its most tumultuous eras. If any playwright has the most pronounced social voice in this collection, it must be Shaw, whose very name is synonymous with "soapbox" drama.

Shaw's early years provided the preface to his plays. Like John Gay and Richard Brindsley Sheridan before him, like his contemporary Oscar Wilde, and like Samuel Beckett after him, Shaw was Irish. His status as an outsider in English society gave him license to observe and comment satirically on the deficiencies of the Empire. His father, a drunkard, had a ready quip for every adversity, and his mother, a would-be opera singer, fled from life's difficulties into art. A stream of literary artists, elocution experts, and musicians flowed through the Shaw household and provided the youthful Shaw with the education that would serve him as a writer. (He proclaimed the Dublin school system "a prison.") His nanny frequently took him to visit her family in the slums of Dublin, where he developed a lifelong hatred of poverty ("the greatest crime") and human suffering. For Shaw, however, life was "too horrible to weep bitter tears: I must retreat to my shelter and indulge in a laugh at myself over it."

Shaw immigrated to England in 1876 where he attempted a series of novels, all quite unsuccessful. We still see the hand of the novelist at work in his prodigious stage directions. Shaw's first literary successes were as an arts critic for London's newspapers, and he excelled in his commentary on music, especially the opera and its offshoots. Though nonmusical, Shaw's plays attest to his profound musical knowledge; in *Heartbreak House* he purposefully designates his protagonists as tenor, baritone, bass, soprano because he customarily cast his plays for the harmony of voices that spoke his great verbal arias. Furthermore, the many nights Shaw spent in the theater watching musical plays, so steeped in melodrama, served him well as a playwright. He inverts well-established dramatic forms to challenge his audience's assumptions about thematic, as well as theatrical, issues in his plays.

The year 1882 was pivotal in Shaw's literary and personal life. He heard the socialist land-reformer Henry George speak, an event that provoked him to read a French edition of Karl Marx in the reading room of the British Museum. In 1889 Shaw edited and contributed a number of essays to one of England's most influential socialist documents, *Fabian Essays in Socialism*. In many ways his plays are an extension of the ideas he formulated therein. Not only did he write about socialism, he was also a powerful and entertaining orator who spoke from every platform, pulpit, and soapbox that would have him.

In 1891 J. T. Grein, whose Independent Theatre was London's version of Antoine's Théâtre Libre, encouraged Shaw to provide plays for his new enterprise. Shaw responded with *Widower's House*, a comedic look at the shortcomings of capitalism. When Shaw revised that play, he was careful to include detailed stage directions for his actors so that there was little doubt about his intentions. These became the forerunner of the so-called "Shavian Preface," the witty and philosophical essays that precede, follow, or accompany the majority of his plays. Over the next twelve years Shaw scripted eleven plays, culminating with *Man and Superman* (1903), which Eric Bentley calls "the supreme triumph of Shaw's dramaturgical dialectics." All were comedies, but for Shaw, "comedy is essentially a serious business." Shaw had a simple philosophy for getting laughs: "Tell the truth. It's the funniest joke in the world." Shaw's comedy is ironic because it forces audiences to reconsider long-held values and conventions, which he subverts to expose their hollowness. Where most playwrights attack a character for failing to live up to the ideals of society, Shaw attacks the ideals themselves. For him, "Civilization is a disease produced by the practice of building societies with rotten material," that is, outmoded ideas that preserve poverty, war, slavery (of all kinds, including that of the marriage contract), and power. Shaw's solution to the ills of civilization? Follow the word's of Dick Dudgeon, the rascally hero of *The Devil's Disciple* (1896–97): "Live by the law of [one's] own nature."

In addition to his prolific literary output of plays and essays, Shaw was a remarkable critic. His analysis of Ibsen's dramaturgy is still among the best of its kind, and his commentary on Shakespeare remains as fresh as it was almost a century ago. Of note are the many letters he wrote to actors, such as Mrs. Patrick Campbell and Ellen Terry, which contain both superb advice for performers and perceptive analyses of dramatic characters. Shaw staged many of his plays (often using a chessboard and figures to devise movement patterns) and left behind copious notes that are models of directorial insight. In short, Shaw was the complete man of the theater, as well as the complete man of the world.

AS YOU READ *HEARTBREAK HOUSE*

Shaw subtitled *Heartbreak House* "a fantasia in the Russian manner on English themes," clearly a reference to the Chekhov-like elements in the play. Like the Russian's major works, *Heartbreak House* is set on a remote estate in a country that is rapidly changing. Like Chekhov's plays (see *The Cherry Orchard* earlier in Part I), the playwright focuses on a variety of individuals rather than a single protagonist, each caught up in his or her own world, each living a life of self-deception. There seems to be little overt action (until the extraordinary ending), as the play consists of a series of conversations, each manifesting Shaw's wit. And like the best Chekhovian drama, the play swiftly shifts from the comedic to the pathetic. As you read the play, identify specific moments that are clearly Chekhovian, and those that are Shavian. Is the play an ingenious imitation—parody?—of Chekhov, or is it another of Shaw's witty discussion dramas? Is it possible that the typically optimistic Shaw, who was thoroughly disillusioned by World War I, could only turn to Chekhov's melancholic fatalism? Does he suggest that the old Ibsen discussion drama, which he defined in *The Quintessence of Ibsenism* the very year he began to write *Heartbreak House*, was no longer able to provide solutions to society's ills in a world gone mad? In this play, Shaw, the self-assured man who typically issued answers, seems to ask more questions than even he is able to answer.

One more thought on Shaw's writing: he followed the then British custom of not using punctuation as we do today. There are (usually) no apostrophes in contracted words (e.g., "dont"), nor periods after titles (e.g., Mr or Mrs). He also spells some words in an older style, especially "Shakespear" and "shew" (i.e., "show"). Shaw customarily refers to a character who makes an entrance only by his or her generic title (e.g., "The Man," or "The Burglar") until that character has been called by his or her name (e.g., Billy Dunn) by another character. This may confuse you at first, but it is part of Shaw's eccentric nature.

HEARTBREAK HOUSE

A Fantasia in the Russian Manner on English Themes

BERNARD SHAW

CHARACTERS

ELLIE DUNN	LADY UTTERWORD (*Ariadne*)
CAPTAIN SHOTOVER	MAZZINI DUNN
HESIONE HUSHABYE	RANDALL UTTERWORD
HECTOR HUSHABYE	THE BURGLAR
BOSS MANGAN	NURSE GUINNESS

ACT I

The hilly country in the middle of the north edge of Sussex, looking very pleasant on a fine evening at the end of September, is seen through the windows of a room which has been built so as to resemble the after part of an old-fashioned high-pooped ship with a stern gallery; for the windows are ship built with heavy timbering, and run right across the room as continuously as the stability of the wall allows. A row of lockers under the windows provides an unupholstered window-seat interrupted by twin glass doors, respectively halfway between the stern post and the sides. Another door strains the illusion a little by being apparently in the ship's port side, and yet leading, not to the open sea, but to the entrance hall of the house. Between this door and the stern gallery are bookshelves. There are electric light switches beside the door leading to the hall and the glass doors in the stern gallery. Against the starboard wall is a carpenter's bench. The vice has a board in its jaws; and the floor is littered with shavings, overflowing from a waste-paper basket. A couple of planes and a centrebit are on the bench. In the same wall, between the bench and the windows, is a narrow doorway with a half door, above which a glimpse of the room beyond shews[1] that it is a shelved pantry with bottles and kitchen crockery.

[1]**shews** shows.

On the starboard side, but close to the middle, is a plain oak drawing-table with a drawing-board, T-square, straightedges, set squares, mathematical instruments, saucers of water color, a tumbler of discolored water, Indian ink, pencils, and brushes on it. The drawing-board is set so that the draughtsman's chair has the window on its left hand. On the floor at the end of the table, on his right, is a ship's fire bucket. On the port side of the room, near the bookshelves, is a sofa with its back to the windows. It is a sturdy mahogany article, oddly upholstered in sailcloth, including the bolster, with a couple of blankets hanging over the back. Between the sofa and the drawing-table is a big wicker chair, with broad arms and a low sloping back, with its back to the light. A small but stout table of teak, with a round top and gate legs, stands against the port wall between the door and the bookcase. It is the only article in the room that suggests (not at all convincingly) a woman's hand in the furnishing. The uncarpeted floor of narrow boards is caulked and holystoned like a deck.

The garden to which the glass doors lead dips to the south before the landscape rises again to the hills. Emerging from the hollow is the cupola of an observatory. Between the observatory and the house is a flagstaff on a little esplanade, with a hammock on the east side and a long garden seat on the west.

A young lady, gloved and hatted, with a dust coat on, is sitting in the window-seat with her body twisted to enable her to look out at the view. One hand props her chin: the other hangs down with a volume of the Temple Shakespear in it, and her finger stuck in the page she has been reading.

A clock strikes six.

The young lady turns and looks at her watch. She rises with an air of one who waits and is almost at the end of her patience. She is a pretty girl, slender, fair, and intelligent looking, nicely but not expensively dressed, evidently not a smart idler.

With a sigh of weary resignation she comes to the draughtsman's chair; sits down; and begins to read Shakespear. Presently the book sinks to her lap; her eyes close; and she dozes into a slumber.

An elderly womanservant comes in from the hall with three unopened bottles of rum on a tray. She passes through and disappears in the pantry without noticing the young lady. She places the bottles on the shelf and fills her tray with empty bottles. As she returns with these, the young lady lets her book drop, awakening herself, and startling the womanservant so that she all but lets the tray fall.

THE WOMANSERVANT. God bless us! [*The Young Lady picks up the book and places it on the table*] Sorry to wake you, miss, I'm sure; but you are a stranger to me. What might you be waiting here for now?

THE YOUNG LADY. Waiting for somebody to shew some signs of knowing that I have been invited here.

THE WOMANSERVANT. Oh, youre invited, are you? And has nobody come? Dear! dear!

THE YOUNG LADY. A wild-looking old gentleman came and looked in at the window; and I heard him calling out 'Nurse: there is a young and attractive female waiting in the poop. Go and see what she wants.' Are you the nurse?

THE WOMANSERVANT. Yes, miss: I'm Nurse Guinness. That was old Captain Shotover, Mrs Hushabye's father. I heard him roaring; but I thought it was for something else. I suppose it was Mrs Hushabye that invited you, ducky?

THE YOUNG LADY. I understood her to do so. But really I think I'd better go.

NURSE GUINNESS. Oh, dont think of such a thing, miss. If Mrs Hushabye has forgotten all about it, it will be a pleasant surprise for her to see you, won't it?

THE YOUNG LADY. It has been a very unpleasant surprise to me to find that nobody expects me.

NURSE GUINNESS. You'll get used to it, miss: this house is full of surprises for them that dont know our ways.

CAPTAIN SHOTOVER [*Looking in from the hall suddenly: an ancient but still hardy man with an immense white beard, in a reefer jacket with a whistle hanging from his neck*]. Nurse: there is a hold-all and a handbag on the front steps for everybody to fall over. Also a tennis racquet. Who the devil left them there?

THE YOUNG LADY. They are mine, I'm afraid.

THE CAPTAIN [*Advancing to the drawing-table*]. Nurse: who is this misguided and unfortunate young lady?

NURSE GUINNESS. She says Miss Hessy invited her, sir.

THE CAPTAIN. And had she no friend, no parents, to warn her against my daughter's invitations? This is a pretty sort of house, by heavens! A young and attractive lady is invited here. Her luggage is left on the steps for hours; and she herself is deposited in the poop and abandoned, tired and starving. This is our hospitality. These are our manners. No room ready. No hot water. No welcoming hostess. Our visitor is to sleep in the toolshed, and to wash in the duckpond.

NURSE GUINNESS. Now it's all right, Captain: I'll get the lady some tea; and her room shall be ready before she has finished it. [*To The Young Lady*] Take off your hat, ducky; and make yourself at home. [*She goes to the door leading to the hall*]

THE CAPTAIN [*As she passes him*]. Ducky! Do you suppose, woman, that because this young lady has been insulted and neglected, you have the right to address her as you address my wretched children, whom you have brought up in ignorance of the commonest decencies of social intercourse?

NURSE GUINNESS. Never mind him, doty. [*Quite unconcerned, she goes out into the hall on her way to the kitchen*]

THE CAPTAIN. Madam: will you favor me with your name? [*He sits down in the big wicker chair*]

THE YOUNG LADY. My name is Ellie Dunn.

THE CAPTAIN. Dunn! I had a boatswain whose name was Dunn. He was originally a pirate in China. He set up as a ship's chandler with stores which I have every reason to believe he stole from me. No doubt he became rich. Are you his daugher?

ELLIE [*Indignant*]. No: certainly not. I am proud to be able to say that though my father has not been a successful man, nobody has ever had one word to say against him. I think my father is the best man I have ever known.

THE CAPTAIN. He must be greatly changed. Has he attained the seventh degree of concentration?

ELLIE. I dont understand.

THE CAPTAIN. But how could he, with a daughter! I, madam, have two daughers. One of them is Hesione Hushabye, who invited you here. I keep this house: she upsets it. I desire to attain the seventh degree of concentration: she invites visitors and leaves me to entertain them. [*Nurse Guinness returns with the tea-tray, which she places on the teak table*] I have a second daughter who is, thank God, in a remote part of the Empire with her numskull of a husband. As a child she thought the figure-head of my ship, the Dauntless, the most beautiful thing on earth. He resembled it. He had the same expression: wooden yet enterprising. She married him, and will never set foot in this house again.

NURSE GUINNESS [*Carrying the table, with the tea things on it, to Ellie's side*]. Indeed you never were more mistaken. She is in England this very moment. You have been told three times this week that she is coming home for a year for her health. And very glad you should be to see your own daughter again after all these years.

THE CAPTAIN. I am not glad. The natural term of the affection of the human animal for its offspring is six years. My daughter Ariadne was born when I was forty-six. I am now eighty-eight. If she comes, I am not at home. If she wants anything, let her take it. If she asks for me, let her be informed that I am extremely old, and have totally forgotten her.

NURSE GUINNESS. Thats no talk to offer to a young lady. Here, ducky, have some tea; and dont listen to him. [*She pours out a cup of tea*]

THE CAPTAIN [*Rising wrathfully*]. Now before high heaven they have given this innocent child Indian tea: the stuff they tan their own leather insides with. [*He seizes the cup and the tea-pot and empties both into the leathern bucket*]

ELLIE [*Almost in tears*]. Oh, please! I am so tired. I should have been glad of anything.

NURSE GUINNESS. Oh, what a thing to do! The poor lamb is ready to drop.

THE CAPTAIN. You shall have some of my tea. Do not touch that fly-blown cake: nobody eats it here except the dogs.

[*He disappears into the pantry*]

NURSE GUINNESS. Theres a man for you! They say he sold himself to the devil in Zanzibar before he was a captain; and the older he grows the more I believe them.

A WOMAN'S VOICE [*In the hall*]. Is anyone at home? Hesione! Nurse! Papa! Do come, somebody; and take in my luggage.

[*Thumping heard, as of an umbrella, on the wainscot*]

NURSE GUINNESS. My gracious! It's Miss Addie, Lady Utterword, Mrs Hushabye's sister: the one I told the Captain about. [*Calling*] Coming, Miss, coming.

[*She carries the table back to its place by the door, and is hurrying out when she is intercepted by Lady Utterword, who bursts in much flustered. Lady Utterword, a blonde, is very handsome, very well dressed, and so precipitate in speech and action that the first impression (erroneous) is one of comic silliness*]

LADY UTTERWORD. Oh, is that you, Nurse? How are you? You dont look a day older. Is nobody at home? Where is Hesione? Doesnt she expect me? Where are the servants? Whose luggage is that on the steps? Where's Papa? Is everybody asleep? [*Seeing Ellie*] Oh! I beg your pardon. I suppose you are one of my nieces. [*Approaching her with outstretched arms*] Come and kiss your aunt, darling.

ELLIE. I'm only a visitor. It is my luggage on the steps.

NURSE GUINNESS. I'll go get you some fresh tea, ducky. [*She takes up the tray*]

ELLIE. But the old gentleman said he would make some himself.

NURSE GUINNESS. Bless you! he's forgotten what he went for already. His mind wanders from one thing to another.

LADY UTTERWORD. Papa, I suppose?

NURSE GUINNESS. Yes, Miss.

LADY UTTERWORD [*Vehemently*]. Dont be silly, nurse. Dont call me Miss.

NURSE GUINNESS [*Placidly*]. No, lovey. [*She goes out with the tea-tray*]

LADY UTTERWORD [*Sitting down with a flounce on the sofa*]. I know what you must feel. Oh, this house, this house! I come back to it after twenty-three years; and it is just the same: the luggage lying on the steps, the servants spoilt and impossible, nobody at home to receive anybody, no regular meals, nobody ever hungry because they are always gnawing bread and butter or munching apples, and, what is worse, the same disorder in ideas, in talk, in feeling. When I was a child I was used to it: I had never known anything better, though I was unhappy, and longed all the time—oh, how I longed!—to be respectable, to be a lady, to live as others did, not to have to think of everything for myself. I married at nineteen to escape from it. My husband is Sir Hastings Utterword, who has been governor of all the crown colonies in succession. I have always been the mistress of Government House. I have been so happy: I had forgotten that people could live like this. I wanted to see my father, my sister, my nephews and nieces (one ought to, you know), and I was looking forward to it. And now the state of the house! the way I'm received! the casual impudence of that woman Guinness, our old nurse! really Hesione might at least have been here; some preparation might have been made for me. You must excuse my going on in this way; but I am really very much hurt and annoyed and disillusioned: and if I had realized it was to be like this, I wouldnt have come. I have a great mind to go away without another word. [*She is on the point of weeping*]

ELLIE [*Also very miserable*]. Nobody has been here to receive me either. I thought I ought to go away too. But how can I, Lady Utterword? My luggage is on the steps; and the station fly has gone.

[*The Captain emerges from the pantry with a tray of Chinese lacquer and a very fine tea-set on it. He rests it provisionally on the end of the table; snatches away the drawing-board, which he stands on the floor against the table legs; and puts the tray in the space thus cleared. Ellie pours out a cup greedily*]

THE CAPTAIN. Your tea, young lady. What! another lady! I must fetch another cup. [*He makes for the pantry*]

LADY UTTERWORD [*Rising from the sofa, suffused with emotion*]. Papa! Dont you know me? I'm your daughter.

THE CAPTAIN. Nonsense! my daughter's upstairs asleep. [*He vanishes through the half door*]

[*Lady Utterword retires to the window to conceal her tears*]

ELLIE [*Going to her with the cup*]. Dont be so distressed. Have this cup of tea. He is very old and very strange: he has been just like that to me. I know how dreadful it must be: my own father is all the world to me. Oh, I'm sure he didn't mean it.

[*The Captain returns with another cup.*]

THE CAPTAIN. Now we are complete. [*He places it on the tray*]

LADY UTTERWORD [*Hysterically*]. Papa: you cant have forgotten me. I am Ariadne. I'm little Paddy Patkins. Wont you kiss me? [*She goes to him and throws her arms round his neck*]

THE CAPTAIN [*Woodenly enduring her embrace*]. How can you be Ariadne? You are a middle-aged woman: well preserved, madam, but no longer young.

LADY UTTERWORD. But think of all the years and years I have been away, Papa. I have had to grow old, like other people.

THE CAPTAIN [*Disengaging himself*]. You should grow out of kissing strange men: they may be striving to attain the seventh degree of concentration.

LADY UTTERWORD. But I'm your daughter. You haven't seen me for years.

THE CAPTAIN. So much the worse! When our relatives are at home, we have to think of all their good points or it would be impossible to endure them. But when they are away, we console ourselves for their absence by dwelling on their vices. That is how I have come to think my absent daughter Ariadne a perfect fiend: so do not try to ingratiate yourself here by impersonating her. [*He walks firmly away to the other side of the room*]

LADY UTTERWORD. Ingratiating myself indeed! [*With dignity*] Very well, papa. [*She sits down at the drawing-table and pours out tea for herself*]

THE CAPTAIN. I am neglecting my social duties. You remember Dunn? Billy Dunn?

LADY UTTERWORD. Do you mean that villainous sailor who robbed you?

THE CAPTAIN [*Introducing Ellie*]. His daughter. [*He sits down on the sofa*]

ELLIE [*Protesting*]. No—

[*Nurse Guinness returns with fresh tea*]

THE CAPTAIN. Take that hogwash away. Do you hear?

NURSE. Youve actually remembered about the tea! [*To Ellie*] O, miss, he didnt forget you after all! You have made an impression.

THE CAPTAIN [*Gloomily*]. Youth! beauty! novelty! They are badly wanted in this house. I am excessively old. Hesione is only moderately young. Her children are not youthful.

LADY UTTERWORD. How can childen be expected to be youthful in this house? Almost before we could speak we were filled with notions that might have been all very well for pagan philosophers of fifty, but were certainly quite unfit for respectable people of any age.

NURSE. You were always for respectability, Miss Addy.

LADY UTTERWORD. Nurse: will you please remember that I am Lady Utterword, and not Miss Addy, nor lovey, nor darling, nor doty? Do you hear?

NURSE. Yes, ducky: all right, I'll tell them all they must call you my lady. [*She takes her tray out with undisturbed placidity*]

LADY UTTERWORD. What comfort? what sense is there in having servants with no manners?

ELLIE [*Rising and coming to the table to put down her empty cup*]. Lady Utterword: do you think Mrs Hushabye really expects me?

LADY UTTERWORD. Oh, don't ask me. You can see for yourself that Ive just arrived; her only sister, after twenty-three years absence! and it seems that *I* am not expected.

THE CAPTAIN. What does it matter whether the young lady is expected or not? She is welcome. There are beds: there is food. I'll find a room for her myself. [*He makes for the door*]

ELLIE [*Following him to stop him*]. Oh please—[*He goes out*] Lady Utterword: I dont know what to do. Your father persists in believing that my father is some sailor who robbed him.

LADY UTTERWORD. You had better pretend not to notice it. My father is a very clever man; but he always forgot things; and now that he is old, of course he is worse. And I must warn you that it is sometimes very hard to feel quite sure that he really forgets.

[*Mrs Hushabye bursts into the room tempestuously, and embraces Ellie. She is a couple of years older than Lady Utterword and even better looking. She has magnificent black hair, eyes like the fishpools of Heshbon, and a nobly modelled neck, short at the back and low between her shoulders in front. Unlike her sister she is uncorseted and dressed anyhow in a rich robe of black pile that shews off her white skin and statuesque contour.*]

MRS HUSHABYE. Ellie, my darling, my pettikins [*Kissing her*]: how long have you been here? I've been at home all the time: I was putting flowers and things in your room; and when I just sat down for a moment to try how comfortable the armchair was I went off to sleep. Papa woke me and told me you were here. Fancy you finding no one, and being neglected and abandoned. [*Kissing her again*] My poor love! [*She deposits Ellie on the sofa. Meanwhile Ariadne has left the table and come over to claim her share of attention*] Oh! youve brought someone with you. Introduce me.

LADY UTTERWORD. Hesione: is it possible that you dont know me?

MRS HUSHABYE [*Conventionally*]. Of course I remember your face quite well. Where have we met?

LADY UTTERWORD. Didnt Papa tell you I was here? Oh! this is really too much. [*She throws herself sulkily into the big chair*]

MRS HUSHABYE. Papa!

LADY UTTERWORD. Yes: Papa. Our papa, you unfeeling wretch. [*Rising angrily*] I'll go straight to a hotel.

MRS HUSHABYE [*Seizing her by the shoulders*]. My goodness gracious goodness, you don't mean to say that youre Addy!

LADY UTTERWORD. I certainly am Addy; and I dont think I can be so changed that you would not have recognized me if you had any real affection for me. And Papa didn't think me even worth mentioning!

MRS HUSHABYE. What a lark! Sit down. [*She pushes her back into the chair instead of kissing her, and posts herself behind it*] You do look a swell. Youre much handsomer than you used to be. Youve made the acquaintance of Ellie of course. She is going to marry a perfect hog of a millionaire for the sake of her father, who is as poor as a church mouse; and you must help me to stop her.

ELLIE. Oh please, Hesione.

MRS HUSHABYE. My pettikins, the man's coming here today with your father to begin persecuting you; and everybody will see the state of the case in ten minutes; so whats the use of making a secret of it?

ELLIE. He is not a hog, Hesione. You don't know how wonderfully good he was to my father, and how deeply grateful I am to him.

MRS HUSHABYE [*To Lady Utterword*]. Her father is a very remarkable man, Addy. His name is Mazzini Dunn. Mazzini was a celebrity of some kind who knew Ellie's grandparents. They were both poets, like the Brownings; and when her father came into the world Mazzini said 'Another soldier born for freedom!' So they christened him Mazzini; and he has been fighting for freedom in his quiet way ever since. That's why he is so poor.

ELLIE. I am proud of his poverty.

MRS HUSHABYE. Of course you are, pettikins. Why not leave him in it, and marry someone you love?

LADY UTTERWORD [*Rising suddenly and explosively*]. Hesione: are you going to kiss me or are you not?

MRS HUSHABYE. What do you want to be kissed for?

LADY UTTERWORD. I don't want to be kissed; but I do want you to behave properly and decently. We are sisters. We have been separated for twenty-three years. You ought to kiss me.

MRS HUSHABYE. Tomorrow morning, dear, before you make up. I hate the smell of powder.

LADY UTTERWORD. Oh! you unfeeling—[*She is interrupted by the return of The Captain*]

THE CAPTAIN [*To Ellie*]. Your room is ready. [*Ellie rises*] The sheets were damp; but I have changed them. [*He makes for the garden door on the port side*]

LADY UTTERWORD. Oh! What about my sheets?

THE CAPTAIN [*Halting at the door*]. Take my advice: air them; or take them off and sleep in blankets. You shall sleep in Ariadne's old room.

LADY UTTERWORD. Indeed I shall do nothing of the sort. That little hole! I am entitled to the best spare room.

THE CAPTAIN [*Continuing unmoved*]. She married a numskull. She told me she would marry anyone to get away from home.

LADY UTTERWORD. You are pretending not to know me on purpose. I will leave the house.

[Mazzine Dunn enters from the hall. He is a little elderly man with bulging credulous eyes and an earnest manner. He is dressed in a blue serge jacket with an unbuttoned mackintosh over it, and carries a soft black hat of clerical cut]

ELLIE. At last! Captain Shotover: here is my father.

THE CAPTAIN. This! Nonsense! not a bit like him. [He goes away through the garden, shutting the door sharply behind him]

LADY UTTERWORD. I will not be ignored and pretended to be somebody else. I will have it out with papa now, this instant. [To Mazzini] Excuse me. [She follows the Captain out, making a hasty bow to Mazzini, who returns it]

MRS HUSHABYE [Hospitably, shaking hands]. How good of you to come, Mr Dunn! You dont mind papa, do you? He is as mad as a hatter, you know, but quite harmless, and extremely clever. You will have some delightful talks with him.

MAZZINI. I hope so. [To Ellie] So here you are, Ellie dear. [He draws her arm affectionately through his] I must thank you, Mrs Hushabye, for your kindness to my daughter. I'm afraid she would have had no holiday if you had not invited her.

MRS HUSHABYE. Not at all. Very nice of her to come and attract young people to the house for us.

MAZZINI [Smiling]. I'm afraid Ellie is not interested in young men, Mrs Hushabye. Her taste is on the graver, solider side.

MRS HUSHABYE [With a sudden rather hard brightness in her manner]. Wont you take off your overcoat, Mr Dunn? You will find a cupboard for coats and hats and things in the corner of the hall.

MAZZINI [Hastily releasing Ellie]. Yes—Thank you I had better—[He goes out]

MRS HUSHABYE [Emphatically]. The old brute!

ELLIE. Who?

MRS HUSHABYE. Who! Him. He. It. [Pointing after Mazzini] 'Graver, solider tastes,' indeed!

ELLIE [Aghast]. You dont mean that you were speaking like that of my father!

MRS HUSHABYE. I was. You know I was.

ELLIE [With dignity]. I will leave your house at once. [She turns to the door]

MRS HUSHABYE. If you attempt it, I'll tell your father why.

ELLIE [Turning again]. Oh! How can you treat a visitor like this, Mrs Hushabye?

MRS HUSHABYE. I thought you were going to call me Hesione.

ELLIE. Certainly not now!

MRS HUSHABYE. Very well: I'll tell your father.

ELLIE [Distressed]. Oh!

MRS HUSHABYE. If you turn a hair—if you take his part against me and against your own heart for a moment, I'll give that born soldier of freedom a piece of my mind that will stand him on his selfish old head for a week.

ELLIE. Hesione! My father selfish! How little you know—

[She is interrupted by Mazzini, who returns, excited and perspiring]

MAZZINI. Ellie: Mangan has come: I thought youd like to know. Excuse me, Mrs Hushabye: the strange old gentleman—

MRS HUSHABYE. Papa. Quite so.

MAZZINI. Oh, I beg your pardon: of course: I was a little confused by his manner. He is making Mangan help him with something in the garden; and he wants me too—

[A powerful whistle is heard]

THE CAPTAIN'S VOICE. Bosun ahoy! [The whistle is repeated]

MAZZINI [Flustered]. Oh dear! I believe he is whistling for me.

[He hurries out]

MRS HUSHABYE. Now my father is a wonderful man if you like.

ELLIE. Hesione: listen to me. You dont understand. My father and Mr Mangan were boys together. Mr Ma—

MRS HUSHABYE. I don't care what they were: we must sit down if you are going to begin as far back as that. [She snatches at Ellie's waist, and makes her sit down on the sofa beside her] Now, pettikins: tell me all about Mr Mangan. They call him Boss Mangan, dont they? He is a Napoleon of industry and disgustingly rich, isnt he? Why isnt your father rich?

ELLIE. My poor father should never have been in business. His parents were poets; and they gave him the noblest ideas; but they could not afford to give him a profession.

MRS HUSHABYE. Fancy your grandparents, with their eyes in fine frenzy rolling! And so your poor father had to go into business. Hasnt he succeeded in it?

ELLIE. He always used to say he could succeed if he only had some capital. He fought his way along, to keep a roof over our heads and bring us up well; but it was always a struggle: always the same difficulty of not having capital enough. I dont know how to describe it to you.

MRS HUSHABYE. Poor Ellie! I know. Pulling the devil by the tail.

ELLIE [*Hurt*]. Oh no. Not like that. It was at least dignified.

MRS HUSHABYE. That made it all the harder, didnt it? *I* shouldnt have pulled the devil by the tail with dignity. I should have pulled hard—[*Between her teeth*] hard. Well? Go on.

ELLIE. At last it seemed that all our troubles were at an end. Mr Mangan did an extraordinarily noble thing out of pure friendship for my father and respect for his character. He asked him how much capital he wanted, and gave it to him. I dont mean that he lent it to him, or that he invested it in his business. He just simply made him a present of it. Wasnt that splendid of him?

MRS HUSHABYE. On condition that you married him?

ELLIE. Oh no, no, no. This was when I was a child. He had never even seen me: he never came to our house. It was absolutely disinterested. Pure generosity.

MRS HUSHABYE. Oh! I beg the gentleman's pardon. Well, what became of the money?

ELLIE. We all got new clothes and moved into another house. And I went to another school for two years.

MRS HUSHABYE. Only two years?

ELLIE. That was all; for at the end of two years my father was utterly ruined.

MRS HUSHABYE. How?

ELLIE. I dont know. I never could understand. But it was dreadful. When we were poor my father had never been in debt. But when he launched out into business on a large scale, he had to incur liabilities. When the business went into liquidation he owed more money than Mr Mangan had given him.

MRS HUSHABYE. Bit off more than he could chew, I suppose.

ELLIE. I think you are a little unfeeling about it.

MRS HUSHABYE. My pettikins: you mustnt mind my way of talking. I was quite as sensitive and particular as you once; but I have picked up so much slang from the children that I am really hardly presentable. I suppose your father had no head for business, and made a mess of it.

ELLIE. Oh, that just shews how entirely you are mistaken about him. The business turned out a great success. It now pays forty-four per cent after deducting the excess profits tax.

MRS HUSHABYE. Then why arnt you rolling in money?

ELLIE. I dont know. It seems very unfair to me. You see, my father was made bankrupt. It nearly broke his

heart, because he had persuaded several of his friends to put money into the business. He was sure it would succeed; and events proved that he was quite right. But they all lost their money. It was dreadful. I dont know what we should have done but for Mr Mangan.

MRS HUSHABYE. What! Did the Boss come to the rescue again, after all his money being thrown away?

ELLIE. He did indeed, and never uttered a reproach to my father. He bought what was left of the business—the buildings and the machinery and things—from the official trustee for enough money to enable my father to pay six and eight-pence in the pound and get his discharge. Everyone pitied papa so much, and saw so plainly that he was an honorable man, that they let him off at six-and-eight-pence instead of ten shillings. Then Mr Mangan started a company to take up the business, and made my father a manager in it to save us from starvation; for I wasnt earning anything then.

MRS HUSHABYE. Quite a romance. And when did the Boss develop the tender passion?

ELLIE. Oh, that was years after, quite lately. He took the chair one night at a sort of people's concert. I was singing there. As an amateur, you know; half a guinea for expenses and three songs with three encores. He was so pleased with my singing that he asked might he walk home with me. I never saw anyone so taken aback as he was when I took him home and introduced him to my father: his own manager. It was then that my father told me how nobly he had behaved. Of course it was considered a great chance for me, as he is so rich. And—and—we drifted into a sort of understanding—I suppose I should call it an engagement—[*She is distressed and cannot go on*]

MRS HUSHABYE [*Rising and marching about*]. You may have drifted into it; but you will bounce out of it, my pettikins, if I am to have anything to do with it.

ELLIE [*Hopelessly*]. No: it's no use. I am bound in honor and gratitude. I will go through with it.

MRS HUSHABYE [*Behind the sofa, scolding down at her*]. You know, of course, that it's not honorable or grateful to marry a man you don't love. Do you love this Mangan man?

ELLIE. Yes. At least—

MRS HUSHABYE. I dont want to know about 'the least': I want to know the worst. Girls of your age fall in love with all sorts of impossible people, especially old people.

ELLIE. I like Mr Mangan very much; and I shall always be—

MRS HUSHABYE. [*Impatiently completing the sentence and prancing away intolerantly to starboard*]. —grateful to him for his kindness to dear father. I know. Anybody else?

ELLIE. What do you mean?

MRS HUSHABYE. Anybody else? Are you in love with anybody else?

ELLIE. Of course not.

MRS HUSHABYE. Humph! [*The book on the drawing-table catches her eye. She picks it up, and evidently finds the title very unexpected. She looks at Ellie, and asks, quaintly*] Quite sure youre not in love with an actor?

ELLIE. No, no. Why? What put such a thing into your head?

MRS HUSHABYE. This is yours, isn't it? Why else should you be reading Othello?

ELLIE. My father taught me to love Shakespear.

MRS HUSHABYE [*Flinging the book down on the table*]. Really! Your father does seem to be about the limit.

ELLIE [*Naïvely*]. Do you never read Shakespear, Hesione? That seems to me so extraordinary. I like Othello.

MRS HUSHABYE. Do you indeed? He was jealous, wasn't he?

ELLIE. Oh, not that. I think all the part about jealousy is horrible. But dont you think it must have been a wonderful experience for Desdemona, brought up so quietly at home, to meet a man who had been out in the world doing all sorts of brave things and having terrible adventures, and yet finding something in her that made him love to sit and talk with her and tell her about them?

MRS HUSHABYE. Thats your idea of romance, is it?

ELLIE. Not romance, exactly. It might really happen.

[*Ellie's eyes shew that she is not arguing, but in a daydream. Mrs Hushabye, watching her inquisitively, goes deliberately back to the sofa and resumes her seat beside her*]

MRS HUSHABYE. Ellie, darling: have you noticed that some of those stories that Othello told Desdemona couldnt have happened?

ELLIE. Oh no. Shakespear thought they could have happened.

MRS HUSHABYE. Hm! Desdemona thought they could have happened. But they didnt.

ELLIE. Why do you look so enigmatic about it? You are such a sphinx: I never know what you mean.

MRS HUSHABYE. Desdemona would have found him out if she had lived, you know. I wonder was that why he strangled her!

ELLIE. Othello was not telling lies.

MRS HUSHABYE. How do you know?

ELLIE. Shakespear would have said if he was. Hesione: there are men who have done wonderful things: men like Othello, only, of course, white, and very handsome, and—

MRS HUSHABYE. Ah! Now we're coming to it. Tell me all about him. I knew there must be somebody, or youd never have been so miserable about Mangan: youd have thought it quite a lark to marry him.

ELLIE [*Blushing vividly*]. Hesione: you are dreadful. But I dont want to make a secret of it, though of course I dont tell everybody. Besides, I dont know him.

MRS HUSHABYE. Dont know him! What does that mean?

ELLIE. Well, of course I know him to speak to.

MRS HUSHABYE. But you want to know him ever so much more intimately, eh?

ELLIE. No no: I know him quite—almost intimately.

MRS HUSHABYE. You dont know him; and you know him almost intimately. How lucid!

ELLIE. I mean that he does not call on us. I—I got into conversation with him by chance at a concert.

MRS HUSHABYE. You seem to have rather a gay time at your concerts, Ellie.

ELLIE. Not at all: we talk to everyone in the green-room waiting for our turns. I thought he was one of the artists: he looked so splendid. But he was only one of the committee. I happened to tell him that I was copying a picture at the National Gallery. I make a little money that way. I cant paint much; but as it's always the same picture I can do it pretty quickly and get two or three pounds for it. It happened that he came to the National Gallery one day.

MRS HUSHABYE. One student's day. Paid sixpence to stumble about through a crowd of easels, when he might have come in next day for nothing and found the floor clear! Quite by accident?

ELLIE [*Triumphantly*]. No. On purpose. He liked talking to me. He knows lots of the most splendid people. Fashionable women who are all in love with him. But he ran away from them to see me at the National Gallery and persuade me to come with him for a drive round Richmond Park in a taxi.

MRS HUSHABYE. My pettikins, you have been going it. It's wonderful what you good girls can do without anyone saying a word.

ELLIE. I am not in society, Hesione. If I didn't make acquaintances in that way I shouldnt have any at all.

MRS HUSHABYE. Well, no harm if you know how to take care of yourself. May I ask his name?

ELLIE [*Slowly and musically*]. Marcus Darnley.

MRS HUSHABYE [*Echoing the music*]. Marcus Darnley! What a splendid name!

ELLIE. Oh, I'm so glad you think so. I think so too; but I was afraid it was only a silly fancy of my own.

MRS HUSHABYE. Hm! Is he one of the Aberdeen Darnleys?

ELLIE. Nobody knows. Just fancy! He was found in an antique chest—

MRS HUSHABYE. A what?

ELLIE. An antique chest, one summer morning in a rose garden, after a night of the most terrible thunderstorm.

MRS HUSHABYE. What on earth was he doing in the chest? Did he get into it because he was afraid of the lightning?

ELLIE. Oh no, no: he was a baby. The name Marcus Darnley was embroidered on his babyclothes. And five hundred pounds in gold.

MRS HUSHABYE [*Looking hard at her*]. Ellie!

ELLIE. The garden of the Viscount—

MRS HUSHABYE. —de Rougemont?

ELLIE [*Innocently*]. No: de Larochejaquelin. A French family. A vicomte. His life has been one long romance. A tiger—

MRS HUSHABYE. Slain by his own hand?

ELLIE. Oh no: nothing vulgar like that. He saved the life of the tiger from a hunting party; one of King Edward's hunting parties in India. The King was furious: that was why he never had his military services properly recognized. But he doesnt care. He is a Socialist and despises rank, and has been in three revolutions fighting on the barricades.

MRS HUSHABYE. How can you sit there telling me such lies? You, Ellie, of all people! And I thought you were a perfectly simple, straightforward good girl.

ELLIE [*Rising, dignified but very angry*]. Do you mean to say you dont believe me?

MRS HUSHABYE. Of course I dont believe you. Youre inventing every word of it. Do you take me for a fool?

[*Ellie stares at her. Her candor is so obvious that Mrs Hushabye is puzzled*]

ELLIE. Goodbye, Hesione. I'm very sorry. I see now that it sounds very improbable as I tell it. But I cant stay if you think that way about me.

MRS HUSHABYE [*Catching her dress*]. You shant go. I couldnt be so mistaken: I know too well what lies are like. Somebody has really told you all this.

ELLIE [*Flushing*]. Hesione: dont say that you dont believe him. I couldnt bear that.

MRS HUSHABYE [*Soothing her*]. Of course I believe him, dearest. But you should have broken it to me by degrees. [*Drawing her back to the seat*] Now tell me all about him. Are you in love with him?

ELLIE. Oh no, I'm not so foolish. I dont fall in love with people. I'm not so silly as you think.

MRS HUSHABYE. I see. Only something to think about—to give some interest and pleasure to life.

ELLIE. Just so. Thats all, really.

MRS HUSHABYE. It makes the hours go fast, doesnt it? No tedious waiting to go to sleep at nights and wondering whether you will have a bad night. How delightful it makes waking up in the morning! How much better than the happiest dream! All life transfigured! No more wishing one had an interesting book to read, because life is so much happier than any book! No desire but to be alone and not to have to talk to anyone: to be alone and just think about it.

ELLIE [*Embracing her*]. Hesione: you are a witch. How do you know? Oh, you are the most sympathetic woman in the world.

MRS HUSHABYE [*Caressing her*]. Pettikins, my pettikins: how I envy you! and how I pity you!

ELLIE. Pity me! Oh, why?

[*A very handsome man of fifty, with mousquetaire moustaches, wearing a rather dandified curly brimmed hat, and carrying an elaborate walking-stick, comes into the room from the hall, and stops short at sight of the women on the sofa*]

ELLIE [*Seeing him and rising in glad surprise*]. Oh! Hesione: this is Mr Marcus Darnley.

MRS HUSHABYE [*Rising*]. What a lark! He is my husband.

ELLIE. But how—[*She stops suddenly; then turns pale and sways*]

MRS HUSHABYE [*Catching her and sitting down with her on the sofa*]. Steady, my pettikins.

THE MAN [*With a mixture of confusion and effrontery, depositing his hat and stick on the teak table*]. My real name, Miss Dunn, is Hector Hushabye. I leave you to judge whether that is a name any sensitive man would care to confess to. I never use it when I can possibly help it. I have been away for nearly a month; and I had no idea you knew my wife, or that you were coming here. I am none the less delighted to find you in our little house.

ELLIE [*In great distress*]. I dont know what to do. Please, may I speak to papa? Do leave me. I cant bear it.

MRS HUSHABYE. Be off, Hector.

HECTOR. I—

MRS HUSHABYE. Quick, quick. Get out.

HECTOR. If you think it better—[*He goes out, taking his hat with him but leaving the stick on the table*]

MRS HUSHABYE [*Laying Ellie down at the end of the sofa*]. Now, pettikins, he is gone. Theres nobody but me. You can let yourself go. Dont try to control yourself. Have a good cry.

ELLIE [*Raising her head*]. Damn!

MRS HUSHABYE. Splendid! Oh, what a relief! I thought you were going to be broken-hearted. Never mind me. Damn him again.

ELLIE. I am not damning him: I am damning myself for being such a fool. [*Rising*] How could I let myself be taken in so? [*She begins prowling to and fro, her bloom gone, looking curiously older and harder*]

MRS HUSHABYE [*Cheerfully*]. Why not, pettikins? Very few young women can resist Hector. I couldnt when I was your age. He is really rather splendid, you know.

ELLIE [*Turning on her*]. Splendid! Yes: splendid looking, of course. But how can you love a liar?

MRS HUSHABYE. I dont know. But you can, fortunately. Otherwise there wouldnt be much love in the world.

ELLIE. But to lie like that! To be a boaster! a coward!

MRS HUSHABYE [*Rising in alarm*]. Pettikins: none of that, if you please. If you hint the slightest doubt of Hector's courage, he will go straight off and do the most horribly dangerous things to convince himself that he isnt a coward. He has a dreadful trick of getting out of one third-floor window and coming in at another, just to test his nerve. He has a whole drawerful of Albert Medals for saving people's lives.

ELLIE. He never told me that.

MRS HUSHABYE. He never boasts of anything he really did: he cant bear it; and it makes him shy if anyone else does. All his stories are made-up stories.

ELLIE [*Coming to her*]. Do you mean that he is really brave, and really has adventures, and yet tells lies about things that he never did and that never happened?

MRS HUSHABYE. Yes, Pettikins, I do. People dont have their virtues and vices in sets: they have them anyhow: all mixed.

ELLIE [*Staring at her thoughtfully*]. Theres something odd about this house, Hesione, and even about you. I dont know why I'm talking to you so calmly. I have a horrible fear that my heart is broken, but that heartbreak is not like what I thought it must be.

MRS HUSHABYE [*Fondling her*]. It's only life educating you, pettikins. How do you feel about Boss Mangan now?

ELLIE [*Disengaging herself with an expression of distaste*]. Oh, how can you remind me of him, Hesione?

MRS HUSHABYE. Sorry, dear. I think I hear Hector coming back. You dont mind now, do you dear?

ELLIE. Not in the least,. I am quite cured.

[*Mazzini Dunn and Hector come in from the hall*]

HECTOR [*As he opens the door and allows Mazzini to pass in*]. One second more, and she would have been a dead woman!

MAZZINI. Dear! dear! what an escape! Ellie, my love: Mr Hushabye has just been telling me the most extraordinary—

ELLIE. Yes: I've heard it. [*She crosses to the other side of the room*]

HECTOR [*Following her*]. Not this one: I'll tell it to you after dinner. I think youll like it. The truth is, I made it up for you, and was looking forward to the pleasure of telling it to you. But in a moment of impatience at being turned out of the room, I threw it away on your father.

ELLIE [*Turning at bay with her back to the carpenter's bench, scornfully self-possessed*]. It was not thrown away. He believes it. I should not have believed it.

MAZZINI [*Benevolently*]. Ellie is very naughty, Mr Hushabye. Of course she does not really think that. [*He goes to the bookshelves, and inspects the titles of the volumes*]

[*Boss Mangan comes in from the hall, followed by the Captain. Mangan, carefully frock-coated as for church or for a director's meeting, is about fifty-five, with a careworn, mistrustful expression, standing a little on an entirely imaginary dignity, and with a dull complexion, straight, lustreless hair, and features so entirely commonplace that it is impossible to describe them*]

CAPTAIN SHOTOVER [*To Mrs Hushabye, introducing the newcomer*]. Says his name is Mangan. Not ablebodied.

MRS HUSHABYE [*Graciously*]. How do you do, Mr Mangan?

MANGAN [*Shaking hands*]. Very pleased.

CAPTAIN SHOTOVER. Dunn's lost his muscle, but recovered his nerve. Men seldom do after three attacks of delirium tremens. [*He goes into the pantry*]

MRS HUSHABYE. I congratulate you, Mr Dunn.

MAZZINI [*Dazed*]. I am a lifelong teetotaler.

MRS HUSHABYE. You will find it far less trouble to let papa have his own way than try to explain.

MAZZINI. But three attacks of delirium tremens, really!

MRS HUSHABYE [*To Mangan*]. Do you know my husband, Mr Mangan: [*She indicates Hector*]

MANGAN [*Going to Hector, who meets him with outstretched hand*]. Very pleased. [*Turning to Ellie*] I hope, Miss Ellie, you have not found the journey down too fatiguing. [*They shake hands*]

MRS HUSHABYE. Hector: shew Mr Dunn his room.

HECTOR. Certainly. Come along, Mr Dunn. [*He takes Mazzini out*]

ELLIE. You havnt shewn me my room yet, Hesione.

MRS HUSHABYE. How stupid of me! Come along. Make yourself at home, Mr Mangan. Papa will entertain you. [*She calls to the Captain in the pantry*] Papa: come and explain the house to Mr Mangan.

[*She goes out with Ellie. The Captain comes from the pantry.*]

CAPTAIN SHOTOVER. Youre going to marry Dunn's daughter. Dont. Youre too old.

MANGAN [*Staggered*]. Well! Thats fairly blunt, Captain.

CAPTAIN SHOTOVER. It's true.

MANGAN. She doesnt think so.

CAPTAIN SHOTOVER. She does.

MANGAN. Older men than I have—

CAPTAIN SHOTOVER [*Finishing the sentence for him*]. —made fools of themselves. That, also, is true.

MANGAN [*Asserting himself*]. I dont see that this is any business of yours.

CAPTAIN SHOTOVER. It is everybody's business. The stars in their courses are shaken when such things happen.

MANGAN. I'm going to marry her all the same.

CAPTAIN SHOTOVER. How do you know?

MANGAN [*Playing the strong man*]. I intend to. I mean to. See? I never made up my mind to do a thing yet that I didnt bring it off. Thats the sort of man I am; and there will be a better understanding between us when you make up your mind to that, Captain.

CAPTAIN SHOTOVER. You frequent picture palaces.

MANGAN. Perhaps I do. Who told you?

CAPTAIN SHOTOVER. Talk like a man, not like a movy. You mean that you make a hundred thousand a year.

MANGAN. I dont boast. But when I meet a man that makes a hundred thousand a year, I take off my hat to that man, and stretch out my hand to him and call him brother.

CAPTAIN SHOTOVER. Then you also make a hundred thousand a year, hey?

MANGAN. No. I cant say that. Fifty thousand, perhaps.

CAPTAIN SHOTOVER. His half brother only. [*He turns away from Mangan with his usual abruptness, and collects the empty tea-cups on the Chinese tray*]

MANGAN [*Irritated*]. See here, Captain Shotover. I dont quite understand my position here. I came here on your daughter's invitation. Am I in her house or in yours?

CAPTAIN SHOTOVER. You are beneath the dome of heaven, in the house of God. What is true within these walls is true outside them. Go out on the seas; climb the mountains; wander through the valleys. She is still too young.

MANGAN [*Weakening*]. But I'm very little over fifty.

CAPTAIN SHOTOVER. You are still less under sixty. Boss Mangan: you will not marry the pirate's child. [*He carries the tray away into the pantry*]

MANGAN [*Following him to the half door*]. What pirate's child? What are you talking about?

CAPTAIN SHOTOVER [*In the pantry*]. Ellie Dunn. You will not marry her.

MANGAN. Who will stop me?

CAPTAIN SHOTOVER [*Emerging*]. My daughter. [*He makes for the door leading to the hall*]

MANGAN [*Following him*]. Mrs Hushabye! Do you mean to say she brought me down here to break it off?

CAPTAIN SHOTOVER [*Stopping and turning to him*]. I know nothing more than I have seen in her eye. She will break it off. Take my advice: marry a West Indian negress: they make excellent wives. I was married to one myself for two years.

MANGAN. Well, I am damned!

CAPTAIN SHOTOVER. I thought so. I was, too, for many years. The negress redeemed me.

MANGAN [*Feebly*]. This is queer. I ought to walk out of this house.

CAPTAIN SHOTOVER. Why?

MANGAN. Well, many men would be offended by your style of talking.

CAPTAIN SHOTOVER. Nonsense! It's the other sort of talking that makes quarrels. Nobody ever quarrels with me.

[*A gentleman, whose firstrate tailoring and frictionless manners proclaim the wellbred West Ender, comes in from the hall. He has an engaging air of being young and unmarried, but on close inspection is found to be at least over forty*]

THE GENTLEMAN. Excuse my intruding in this fashion; but there is no knocker on the door; and the bell does not seem to ring.

CAPTAIN SHOTOVER. Why should there be a knocker? Why should the bell ring? The door is open.

THE GENTLEMAN. Precisely. So I ventured to come in.

CAPTAIN SHOTOVER. Quite right. I will see about a room for you. [*He makes for the door*]

THE GENTLEMAN [*Stopping him*]. But I'm afraid you don't know who I am.

CAPTAIN SHOTOVER. Do you suppose that at my age I make distinctions between one fellow creature and another? [*He goes out. Mangan and the newcomer stare at one another*]

MANGAN. Strange character, Captain Shotover, sir.

THE GENTLEMAN. Very.

CAPTAIN SHOTOVER [*Shouting outside*]. Hesione: another person has arrived and wants a room. Man about town, well dressed, fifty.

THE GENTLEMAN. Fancy Hesione's feelings! May I ask are you a member of the family?

MANGAN. No.

THE GENTLEMAN. I am. At least a connexion.

[Mrs Hushabye comes back]

MRS HUSHABYE. How do you do? How good of you to come!

THE GENTLEMAN. I am very glad indeed to make your acquaintance, Hesione. [Insted of taking her hand he kisses her. At the same moment the Captain appears in the doorway] You will excuse my kissing your daughter, Captain, when I tell you that—

CAPTAIN SHOTOVER. Stuff! Everyone kisses my daughter. Kiss her as much as you like. [He makes for the pantry]

THE GENTLEMAN. Thank you. One moment. Captain. [The Captain halts and turns. The Gentleman goes to him affably] Do you happen to remember—but probably you dont, as it occurred many years ago—that your younger daughter married a numskull.

CAPTAIN SHOTOVER. Yes. She said she'd marry anybody to get away from this house. I should not have recognized you: your head is no longer like a walnut. Your aspect is softened. You have been boiled in bread and milk for years and years, like other married men. Poor devil! [He disappears into the pantry]

MRS HUSHABYE [Going past Mangan to the gentleman and scrutinizing him]. I dont believe you are Hastings Utterword.

THE GENTLEMAN. I am not.

MRS HUSHABYE. Then what business had you to kiss me?

THE GENTLEMAN. I thought I would like to. The fact is, I am Randall Utterword, the unworthy younger brother of Hastings. I was abroad diplomatizing when he was married.

LADY UTTERWORD [Dashing in]. Hesione: where is the key of the wardrobe in my room? My diamonds are in my dressing-bag: I must lock it up—[Recognizing the stranger with a shock] Randall: how dare you? [She marches at him past Mrs Hushabye, who retreats and joins Mangan near the sofa]

RANDALL. How dare I what? I am not doing anything.

LADY UTTERWORD. Who told you I was here?

RANDALL. Hastings. You had just left when I called on you at Claridge's; so I followed you down here. You are looking extremely well.

LADY UTTERWORD. Dont presume to tell me so.

MRS HUSHABYE. What is wrong with Mr Randall, Addy?

LADY UTTERWORD [Recollecting herself]. Oh, nothing. But he has no right to come bothering you and papa without being invited. [She goes to the windowseat and sits down, turning away from them ill-humoredly and looking into the garden, where Hector and Ellie are now seen strolling together]

MRS HUSHABYE. I think you have not met Mr Mangan, Addy.

LADY UTTERWORD [Turning her head and nodding coldly to Mangan]. I beg your pardon. Randall: you have flustered me so: I made a perfect fool of myself.

MRS HUSHABYE. Lady Utterword. My sister. My younger sister.

MANGAN [Bowing]. Pleased to meet you, Lady Utterword.

LADY UTTERWORD [With marked interest]. Who is that gentleman walking in the garden with Miss Dunn?

MRS HUSHABYE. I dont know. She quarrelled mortally with my husband only ten minutes ago; and I didnt know anyone else had come. It must be a visitor. [She goes to the window to look] Oh, it is Hector. Theyve made it up.

LADY UTTERWORD. Your husband! That handsome man?

MRS HUSHABYE. Well, why shouldnt my husband be a handsome man?

RANDALL [Joining them at the window]. One's husband never is, Ariadne. [He sits by Lady Utterword, on her right]

MRS HUSHABYE. One's sister's husband always is, Mr Randall.

LADY UTTERWORD. Dont be vulgar, Randall. And you, Hesione, are just as bad.

[Ellie and Hector come in from the garden by the starboard door. Randall rises. Ellie retires into the corner near the pantry. Hector comes forward; and Lady Utterword rises looking her very best]

MRS HUSHABYE. Hector: this is Addy.

HECTOR [Apparently surprised]. Not this lady.

LADY UTTERWORD [Smiling]. Why not?

HECTOR [Looking at her with a piercing glance of deep but respectful admiration, his moustache bristling]. I thought— [Pulling himself together] I beg your pardon, Lady Utterword. I am extremely glad to welcome you at last under our roof. [He offers his hand with grave courtesy]

MRS HUSHABYE. She wants to be kissed, Hector.

LADY UTTERWORD. Hesione! [But she still smiles]

MRS HUSHABYE. Call her Addy; and kiss her like a good brother-in-law; and have done with it. [She leaves them to themselves]

HECTOR. Behave yourself, Hesione. Lady Utterword is entitled not only to hospitality but to civilization.

LADY UTTERWORD [Gratefully]. Thank you, Hector. [They shake hands cordially]

[Mazzini Dunn is seen crossing the garden from starboard to port]

CAPTAIN SHOTOVER [*Coming from the pantry and addressing Ellie*]. Your father has washed himself.

ELLIE [*Quite selfpossessed*]. He often does, Captain Shotover.

CAPTAIN SHOTOVER. A strange conversion! I saw him through the pantry window.

[*Mazzini Dunn enters through the port window door, newly washed and brushed, and stops, smiling benevolently, between Mangan and Mrs Hushabye*]

MRS HUSHABYE [*Introducing*]. Mr Mazzini Dunn, Lady Ut—oh, I forgot: youve met. [*Indicating Ellie*] Miss Dunn.

MAZZINI [*Walking across the room to take Ellie's hand, and beaming at his own naughty irony*]. I have met Miss Dunn also. She is my daughter. [*He draws her arm through his caressingly*]

MRS HUSHABYE. Of course: how stupid! Mr Utterword, my sister's—er—

RANDALL [*Shaking hands agreeably*]. Her brother-in-law, Mr Dunn. How do you do?

MRS HUSHABYE. This is my husband.

HECTOR. We have met, dear. Dont introduce us any more. [*He moves away to the big chair, and adds*] Wont you sit down, Lady Utterword? [*She does so very graciously*]

MRS HUSHABYE. Sorry. I hate it: it's like making people shew their tickets.

MAZZINI [*Sententiously*]. How little it tells us, after all! The great question is, not who we are, but what we are.

CAPTAIN SHOTOVER. Ha! What are you?

MAZZINI [*Taken aback*]. What am I?

CAPTAIN SHOTOVER. A thief, a pirate, and a murderer.

MAZZINI. I assure you you are mistaken.

CAPTAIN SHOTOVER. An adventurous life; but what does it end in? Respectability. A ladylike daughter. The language and appearance of a city missionary. Let it be a warning to all of you. [*He goes out through the garden*]

DUNN. I hope nobody here believes that I am a thief, a pirate, or a murderer. Mrs Hushabye: will you excuse me a moment? I must really go and explain. [*He follows the Captain*]

MRS HUSHABYE [*As he goes*]. It's no use. Youd really better —[*But Dunn has vanished*] We had better all go out and look for some tea. We never have regular tea; but you can always get some when you want: the servants keep it stewing all day. The kitchen veranda is the best place to ask. May I shew you? [*She goes to the starboard door*]

RANDALL [*Going with her*]. Thank you, I dont think I'll take any tea this afternoon. But if you will shew me the garden—?

MRS HUSHABYE. Theres nothing to see in the garden except papa's observatory, and a gravel pit with a cave where he keeps dynamite and things of that sort. However, it's pleasanter out of doors; so come along.

RANDALL. Dynamite! Isnt that rather risky?

MRS HUSHABYE. Well, we dont sit in the gravel pit when theres a thunderstorm.

LADY UTTERWORD. Thats something new. What is the dynamite for?

HECTOR. To blow up the human race if it goes too far. He is trying to discover a psychic ray that will explode all the explosives at the will of a Mahatma.

ELLIE. The Captain's tea is delicious, Mr Utterword.

MRS HUSHABYE [*Stopping in the doorway*]. Do you mean to say that youve had some of my father's tea? that you got round him before you were ten minutes in the house?

ELLIE. I did.

MRS HUSHABYE. You little devil! [*She goes out with Randall*]

MANGAN. Wont you come, Miss Ellie?

ELLIE. I'm too tired. I'll take a book up to my room and rest a little. [*She goes to the bookshelf*]

MANGAN. Right. You cant do better. But I'm disappointed. [*He follows Randall and Mrs Hushabye*]

[*Ellie, Hector, and Lady Utterword are left. Hector is close to Lady Utterword. They look at Ellie, waiting for her to go*]

ELLIE [*Looking at the title of a book*]. Do you like stories of adventure, Lady Utterword?

LADY UTTERWORD [*Patronizingly*]. Of course, dear.

ELLIE. Then I'll leave you to Mr Hushabye. [*She goes out through the hall*]

HECTOR. That girl is mad about tales of adventure. The lies I have to tell her!

LADY UTTERWORD [*Not interested in Ellie*]. When you saw me what did you mean by saying that you thought, and then stopping short? What did you think?

HECTOR [*Folding his arms and looking down at her magnetically*]. May I tell you?

LADY UTTERWORD. Of course.

HECTOR. It will not sound very civil. I was on the point of saying 'I thought you were a plain woman.'

LADY UTTERWORD. Oh for shame, Hector! What right had you to notice whether I am plain or not?

HECTOR. Listen to me, Ariadne. Until today I have seen only photographs of you; and no photograph can give the strange fascination of the daughters of that super-natural old man. There is some damnable quality in them that destroys men's moral sense, and carries them beyond honor and dishonor. You know that, dont you?

LADY UTTERWORD. Perhaps I do, Hector. But let me warn you once for all that I am a rigidly conventional woman. You may think because I'm a Shotover that I'm a Bohemian, because we all are so horribly Bohemian. But I'm not. I hate and loathe Bohemianism. No child brought up in a strict Puritan household ever suffered from Puritanism as I suffered from our Bohemianism.

HECTOR. Our childen are like that. They spend their holidays in the houses of their respectable schoolfellows.

LADY UTTERWORD. I shall invite them for Christmas.

HECTOR. Their absence leaves us both without our natural chaperons.

LADY UTTERWORD. Children are certainly very inconvenient sometimes. But intelligent people can always manage, unless they are Bohemians.

HECTOR. You are no Bohemian; but you are no Puritan either: your attraction is alive and powerful. What sort of woman do you count yourself?

LADY UTTERWORD. I am a woman of the world, Hector; and I can assure you that if you will only take the trouble always to do the perfectly correct thing, and to say the perfectly correct thing, you can do just what you like. An ill-conducted, careless woman gets simply no chance. An ill-conducted, careless man is never allowed within arm's length of any woman worth knowing.

HECTOR. I see. You are neither a Bohemian woman nor a Puritan woman. You are a dangerous woman.

LADY UTTERWORD. On the contrary, I am a safe woman.

HECTOR. You are a most accursedly attractive woman. Mind: I am not making love to you. I do not like being attracted. But you had better know how I feel if you are going to stay here.

LADY UTTERWORD. You are an exceedingly clever ladykiller, Hector. And terribly handsome. I am quite a good player, myself, at that game. Is it quite understood that we are only playing?

HECTOR. Quite. I am deliberately playing the fool, out of sheer worthlessness.

LADY UTTERWORD [Rising brightly]. Well, you are my brother-in-law. Hesione asked you to kiss me. [He seizes her in his arms, and kisses her strenuously] Oh! that was a little more than play, brother-in-law. [She pushes him suddenly away] You shall not do that again.

HECTOR. In effect, you got your claws deeper into me than I intended.

MRS HUSHABYE [Coming in from the garden]. Dont let me disturb you: I only want a cap to put on daddiest. The sun is setting; and he'll catch cold. [She makes for the door leading to the hall]

LADY UTTERWORD. Your husband is quite charming, darling. He has actually condescended to kiss me at last. I shall go into the garden: it's cooler now. [She goes out by the port door]

MRS HUSHABYE. Take care, dear child. I dont believe any man can kiss Addy without falling in love with her. [She goes into the hall]

HECTOR [Striking himself on the chest]. Fool! Goat!

[Mrs Hushabye comes back with the Captain's cap]

HECTOR. Your sister is an extremely enterprising old girl. Wheres Miss Dunn!

MRS HUSHABYE. Mangan says she has gone up to her room for a nap. Addy wont let you talk to Ellie: she has marked you for her own.

HECTOR. She has the diabolical family fascination. I began making love to her automatically. What am I to do? I cant fall in love; and I cant hurt a woman's feelings by telling her so when she falls in love with me. And as women are always falling in love with my moustache I get landed in all sorts of tedious and terrifying flirtations in which I'm not a bit in earnest.

MRS HUSHABYE. Oh, neither is Addy. She has never been in love in her life, though she has always been trying to fall in head over ears. She is worse than you, because you had one real go at least, with me.

HECTOR. That was a confounded madness. I cant believe that such an amazing experience is common. It has left its mark on me. I believe that is why I have never been able to repeat it.

MRS HUSHABYE [Laughing and caressing his arm]. We were frightfully in love with one another, Hector. It was such an enchanting dream that I have never been able to grudge it to you or anyone else since. I have invited all sorts of pretty women to the house on the chance of giving you another turn. But it has never come off.

HECTOR. I dont know that I want it to come off. It was damned dangerous. You fascinated me; but I loved you; so it was heaven. This sister of yours fascinates me; but I hate her, so it is hell. I shall kill her if she persists.

MRS HUSHABYE. Nothing will kill Addy: she is as strong as a horse. [Releasing him] Now I am going off to fascinate somebody.

HECTOR. The Foreign Office toff? Randall?

MRS HUSHABYE. Goodness gracious, no! Why should I fascinate him?

HECTOR. I presume you dont mean the bloated capitalist, Mangan?

MRS HUSHABYE. Hm! I think he had better be fascinated by me than by Ellie. [*She is going into the garden when the Captain comes in from it with some sticks in his hand*] What have you got there, daddiest?

CAPTAIN SHOTOVER. Dynamite.

MRS HUSHABYE. Youve been to the gravel pit. Dont drop it about the house: theres a dear. [*She goes into the garden, where the evening light is now very red*]

HECTOR. Listen, O sage. How long dare you concentrate on a feeling without risking having it fixed in your consciousness all the rest of your life?

CAPTAIN SHOTOVER. Ninety minutes. An hour and a half. [*He goes into the pantry*]

[*Hector, left alone, contracts his brows, and falls into a daydream. He does not move for some time. Then, throwing his hands behind him, and gripping one with the other, he strides tragically once to and fro. Suddenly he snatches his walking-stick from the teak table, and draws it; for it is a sword-stick. He fights a desperate duel with an imaginary antagonist, and after many vicissitudes runs him through the body up to the hilt. He sheathes his sword and throws it on the sofa, falling into another reverie as he does so. He looks straight into the eyes of an imaginary woman; seizes her by the arms; and says in a deep and thrilling tone 'Do you love me!' The Captain comes out of the pantry at this moment; and Hector, caught with his arms stretched out and his fists clenched, has to account for his attitude by going through a series of gymnastic exercises*]

CAPTAIN SHOTOVER. That sort of strength is no good. You will never be as strong as a gorilla.

HECTOR. What is the dynamite for?

CAPTAIN SHOTOVER. To kill fellows like Mangan.

HECTOR. No use. They will always be able to buy more dynamite than you.

CAPTAIN SHOTOVER. I will make a dynamite that he cannot explode.

HECTOR. And that you can, eh?

CAPTAIN SHOTOVER. Yes: when I have attained the seventh degree of concentration.

HECTOR. Whats the use of that? You never do attain it.

CAPTAIN SHOTOVER. What then is to be done? Are we to be kept for ever in the mud by these hogs to whom the universe is nothing but a machine for greasing their bristles and filling their snouts?

HECTOR. Are Mangan's bristles worse than Randall's lovelocks?

CAPTAIN SHOTOVER. We must win powers of life and death over them both. I refuse to die until I have invented the means.

HECTOR. Who are we that we should judge them?

CAPTAIN SHOTOVER. What are they that they should judge us? Yet they do, unhesitatingly. There is an enmity between our seed and their seed. They know it and act on it, strangling our souls. They believe in themselves. When we believe in ourselves, we shall kill them.

HECTOR. It is the same seed. You forget that your pirate has a very nice daughter. Mangan's son may be a Plato: Randall's a Shelley. What was my father?

CAPTAIN SHOTOVER. The damndest scoundrel I ever met. [*He replaces the drawing-board; sits down at the table; and begins to mix a wash of color*]

HECTOR. Precisely. Well, dare you kill his innocent grandchildren?

CAPTAIN SHOTOVER. They are mine also.

HECTOR. Just so. We are members one of another. [*He throws himself carelessly on the sofa*] I tell you I have often thought of this killing of human vermin. Many men have thought of it. Decent men are like Daniel in the lion's den: their survival is a miracle; and they do not always survive. We live among the Mangans and Randalls and Billie Dunns as they, poor devils, live among the disease germs and the doctors and the lawyers and the parsons and the restaurant chefs and the tradesmen and the servants and all the rest of the parasites and blackmailers. What are our terrors to theirs? Give me the power to kill them; and I'll spare them in sheer—

CAPTAIN SHOTOVER [*Cutting in sharply*]. Fellow feeling?

HECTOR. No. I should kill myself if I believed that. I must believe that my spark, small as it is, is divine, and that the red light over their door is hell fire. I should spare them in simple magnanimous pity.

CAPTAIN SHOTOVER. You cant spare them until you have the power to kill them. At present they have the power to kill you. There are millions of blacks over the water for them to train and let loose on us. Theyre going to do it. Theyre doing it already.

HECTOR. They are too stupid to use their power.

CAPTAIN SHOTOVER [*Throwing down his brush and coming to the end of the sofa*]. Do not deceive yourself: they do use it. We kill the better half of ourselves every day to propitiate them. The knowledge that these people are there to render all our aspirations barren prevents us having the aspirations. And when we are tempted to seek their destruction they bring forth demons to delude us, disguised as pretty daughters, and singers and poets and the like, for whose sake we spare them.

HECTOR [*Sitting up and leaning towards him*]. May not Hesione be such a demon, brought forth by you lest I should slay you?

CAPTAIN SHOTOVER. That is possible. She has used you up, and left you nothing but dreams, as some women do.

HECTOR. Vampire women, demon women.

CAPTAIN SHOTOVER. Men think the world well lost for them, and lose it accordingly. Who are the men that do things? The husbands of the shrew and of the drunkard, the men with the thorn in the flesh. [*Walking distractedly away towards the pantry*] I must think these things out. [*Turning suddenly*] But I go on with the dynamite none the less. I will discover a ray mightier than any X-ray: a mind ray that will explode the ammunition in the belt of my adversary before he can point his gun at me. And I must hurry. I am old: I have no time to waste in talk. [*He is about to go into the pantry, and Hector is making for the hall, when Hesione comes back*]

MRS HUSHABYE. Daddiest: you and Hector must come and help me to entertain all these people. What on earth were you shouting about?

HECTOR [*Stopping in the act of turning the door-handle*]. He is madder than usual.

MRS HUSHABYE. We all are.

HECTOR. I must change. [*He resumes his door opening*]

MRS HUSHABYE. Stop, stop. Come back, both of you. Come back. [*They return, reluctantly*] Money is running short.

HECTOR. Money! Where are my April dividends?

MRS HUSHABYE. Where is the snow that fell last year?

CAPTAIN SHOTOVER. Where is all the money you had for that patent lifeboat I invented?

MRS HUSHABYE. Five hundred pounds; and I have made it last since Easter!

CAPTAIN SHOTOVER. Since Easter! Barely four months! Monstrous extravagance! I could live for seven years on £500.

MRS HUSHABYE. Not keeping open house as we do here, daddiest.

CAPTAIN SHOTOVER. Only £500 for that lifeboat! I got twelve thousand for the invention before that.

MRS HUSHABYE. Yes, dear; but that was for the ship with the magnetic keel that sucked up submarines. Living at the rate we do, you cannot afford life-saving inventions. Cant you think of something that will murder half Europe at one bang?

CAPTAIN SHOTOVER. No. I am ageing fast. My mind does not dwell on slaughter as it did when I was a boy. Why doesnt your husband invent something? He does nothing but tell lies to women.

HECTOR. Well, that is a form of invention, is it not? However, you are right: I ought to support my wife.

MRS HUSHABYE. Indeed you shall do nothing of the sort: I should never see you from breakfast to dinner. I want my husband.

HECTOR [*Bitterly*]. I might as well be your lapdog.

MRS HUSHABYE. Do you want to be my breadwinner, like the other poor husbands?

HECTOR. No, by thunder! What a damned creature a husband is anyhow!

MRS HUSHABYE [*To the Captain*]. What about that harpoon cannon?

CAPTAIN SHOTOVER. No use. It kills whales, not men.

MRS HUSHABYE. Why not? You fire the harpoon out of a cannon. It sticks in the enemy's general; you wind him in; and there you are.

HECTOR. You are your father's daughter, Hesione.

CAPTAIN SHOTOVER. There is something in it. Not to wind in generals: they are not dangerous. But one could fire a grapnel and wind in a machine gun or even a tank. I will think it out.

MRS HUSHABYE [*Squeezing the Captain's arm affectionately*]. Saved! You are a darling, daddiest. Now we must go back to these dreadful people and entertain them.

CAPTAIN SHOTOVER. They have had no dinner. Dont forget that.

HECTOR. Neither have I. And it is dark: it must be all hours.

MRS HUSHABYE. Oh, Guinness will produce some sort of dinner for them. The servants always take jolly good care that there is food in the house.

CAPTAIN SHOTOVER [*Raising a strange wail in the darkness*]. What a house! What a daughter!

MRS HUSHABYE [*Raving*]. What a father!

HECTOR [*Following suit*]. What a husband!

CAPTAIN SHOTOVER. Is there no thunder in heaven?

HECTOR. Is there no beauty, no bravery, on earth?

MRS HUSHABYE. What do men want? They have their food, their firesides, their clothes mended, and our love at the end of the day. Why are they not satisfied? Why do they envy us the pain with which we bring them into the world, and make strange dangers and torments for themselves to be even with us?

CAPTAIN SHOTOVER [*Weirdly chanting*].
  I built a house for my daughters, and
      opened the doors thereof,
  That men might come for their choosing, and
      their betters spring from their love;
  But one of them married a numskull;

HECTOR [*Taking up the rhythm*].
  The other a liar wed;

MRS HUSHABYE [*Completing the stanza*].
 And now must she lie beside him, even as she
  made her bed.
LADY UTTERWORD [*Calling from the garden*]. Hesione! Hes-
 ione! Where are you?
HECTOR. The cat is on the tiles.
MRS HUSHABYE. Coming, darling, coming. [*She goes
 quickly into the garden*]
 [*The Captain goes back to his place at the table*]
HECTOR [*Going into the hall*]. Shall I turn up the lights for
 you?
CAPTAIN SHOTOVER. No. Give me deeper darkness.
 Money is not made in the light.

ACT II

*The same room, with the lights turned up and the cur-
tains drawn. Ellie comes in, followed by Mangan. Both
are dressed for dinner. She strolls to the drawing-table.
He comes between the table and the wicker chair.*

MANGAN. What a dinner! I dont call it a dinner: I call it
 a meal.
ELLIE. I am accustomed to meals, Mr Mangan, and very
 lucky to get them. Besides, the Captain cooked some
 macaroni for me.
MANGAN [*Shuddering liverishly*]. Too rich; I cant eat such
 things. I suppose it's because I have to work so much
 with my brain. Thats the worst of being a man of
 business: you are always thinking, thinking, thinking. By the way, now that we are alone, may I take
 the opportunity to come to a little understanding
 with you?
ELLIE [*Settling into the draughtsman's seat*]. Certainly. I
 should like to.
MANGAN [*Taken aback*]. Should you? That surprises me;
 for I thought I noticed this afternoon that you
 avoided me all you could. Not for the first time either.
ELLIE. I was very tired and upset. I wasnt used to the ways
 of this extraordinary house. Please forgive me.
MANGAN. Oh, thats all right: I dont mind. But Captain
 Shotover has been talking to me about you. You and
 me, you know.
ELLIE [*Interested*]. The Captain! What did he say?
MANGAN. Well, he noticed the difference between our
 ages.
ELLIE. He notices everything.
MANGAN. You dont mind, then?
ELLIE. Of course I know quite well that our engagement—
MANGAN. Oh! you call it an engagement.
ELLIE. Well, isn't it?

MANGAN. Oh, yes, yes: no doubt it is if you hold to it.
 This is the first time youve used the word; and I didnt
 quite know where we stood: thats all. [*He sits down in
 the wicker chair; and resigns himself to allow her to lead
 the conversation*] You were saying—?
ELLIE. Was I? I forget. Tell me. Do you like this part of the
 country? I heard you ask Mr Hushabye at dinner
 whether there are any nice houses to let down here.
MANGAN. I like the place. The air suits me. I shouldnt be
 surprised if I settled down here.
ELLIE. Nothing would please me better. The air suits me
 too. And I want to be near Hesione.
MANGAN [*With growing uneasiness*]. The air may suit us;
 but the question is, should we suit one another? Have
 you thought about that?
ELLIE. Mr Mangan: we must be sensible, mustnt we? It's
 no use pretending that we are Romeo and Juliet. But
 we can get on very well together if we choose to
 make the best of it. Your kindness of heart will make
 it easy for me.
MANGAN [*Leaning forward, with the beginning of something
 like deliberate unpleasantness in his voice*]. Kindness of
 heart, eh? I ruined your father, didn't I?
ELLIE. Oh, not intentionally.
MANGAN. Yes, I did. Ruined him on purpose.
ELLIE. On purpose!
MANGAN. Not out of ill-nature, you know. And youll
 admit that I kept a job for him when I had finished
 with him. But business is business; and I ruined him
 as a matter of business.
ELLIE. I dont understand how that can be. Are you trying
 to make me feel that I need not be grateful to you, so
 that I may choose freely?
MANGAN [*Rising aggressively*]. No. I mean what I say.
ELLIE. But how could it possibly do you any good to ruin
 my father? The money he lost was yours.
MANGAN [*With a sour laugh*]. Was mine! It is mine, Miss
 Ellie, and all the money the other fellows lost too.
 [*He shoves his hands into his pockets and shews his teeth*]
 I just smoked them out like a hive of bees. What do
 you say to that? A bit of a shock, eh?
ELLIE. It would have been, this morning. Now! you cant
 think how little it matters. But it's quite interesting.
 Only, you must explain it to me. I dont understand it.
 [*Propping her elbows on the drawing-board and her chin
 on her hands, she composes herself to listen with a combination of conscious curiosity with unconscious contempt
 which provokes him to more and more unpleasantness,
 and an attempt at patronage of her ignorance*]
MANGAN. Of course you dont understand: what do you
 know about business? You just listen and learn. Your

father's business was a new business; and I dont start new businesses: I let other fellows start them. They put all their money and their friends' money into starting them. They wear out their souls and bodies trying to make a success of them. Theyre what you call enthusiasts. But the first dead lift of the thing is too much for them; and they havnt enough financial experience. In a year or so they have either to let the whole show go bust, or sell out to a new lot of fellows for a few deferred ordinary shares: that is, if theyre lucky enough to get anything at all. As likely as not the very same thing happens to the new lot. They put in more money and a couple of years more work; and then perhaps they have to sell out to a third lot. If it's really a big thing the third lot will have to sell out too, and leave their work and their money behind them. And thats where the real business man comes in: where I come in. But I'm cleverer than some: I dont mind dropping a little money to start the process. I took your father's measure. I saw that he had a sound idea, and that he would work himself silly for it if he got the chance. I saw that he was a child in business, and was dead certain to outrun his expenses and be in too great a hurry to wait for his market. I knew that the surest way to ruin a man who doesnt know how to handle money is to give him some. I explained my idea to some friends in the city, and they found the money; for I take no risks in ideas, even when theyre my own. Your father and the friends that ventured their money with him were no more to me than a heap of squeezed lemons. Youve been wasting your gratitude: my kind heart is all rot. I'm sick of it. When I see your father beaming at me with his moist, grateful eyes, regularly wallowing in gratitude, I sometimes feel I must tell him the truth or burst. What stops me is that I know he wouldnt belive me. He'd think it was my modesty, as you did just now. He'd think anything rather than the truth, which is that he's a blamed fool, and I am a man that knows how to take care of himself. [*He throws himself back into the big chair with large self-approval*] Now what do you think of me, Miss Ellie?

ELLIE [*Dropping her hands*]. How strange! that my mother, who knew nothing at all about business, should have been quite right about you! She always said—not before papa, of course, but to us children—that you were just that sort of man.

MANGAN [*Sitting up, much hurt*]. Oh! did she? And yet she'd have let you marry me.

ELLIE. Well, you see, Mr Mangan, my mother married a very good man—for whatever you may think of my fa-

ther as a man of business, he is the soul of goodness—and she is not at all keen on my doing the same.

MANGAN. Anyhow, you dont want to marry me now, do you?

ELLIE [*Very calmly*]. Oh, I think so. Why not?

MANGAN [*Rising aghast*]. Why not!

ELLIE. I dont see why we shouldnt get on very well together.

MANGAN. Well, but look here, you know—[*He stops, quite at a loss*]

ELLIE [*Patiently*]. Well?

MANGAN. Well, I thought you were rather particular about people's characters.

ELLIE. If we women were particular about men's characters, we should never get married at all, Mr Mangan.

MANGAN. A child like you talking of 'we women'! What next! Youre not in earnest?

ELLIE. Yes I am. Arnt you?

MANGAN. You mean to hold me to it?

ELLIE. Do you wish to back out of it?

MANGAN. Oh no. Not exactly back out of it.

ELLIE. Well?

[*He has nothing to say. With a long whispered whistle, he drops into the wicker chair and stares before him like a beggared gambler. But a cunning look soon comes into his face. He leans over towards her on his right elbow, and speaks in a low steady voice*]

MANGAN. Suppose I told you I was in love with another woman!

ELLIE [*Echoing him*]. Suppose I told you I was in love with another man!

MANGAN [*Bouncing angrily out of his chair*]. I'm not joking.

ELLIE. Who told you I was?

MANGAN. I tell you I'm serious. Youre too young to be serious; but youll have to believe me. I want to be near your friend Mrs Hushabye. I'm in love with her. Now the murder's out.

ELLIE. I want to be near your friend Mr Hushabye. I'm in love with him. [*She rises and adds with a frank air*] Now we are in one another's confidence, we shall be real friends. Thank you for telling me.

MANGAN [*Almost beside himself*]. Do you think I'll be made a convenience of like this?

ELLIE. Come, Mr Mangan! You made a business convenience of my father. Well, a woman's business is marriage. Why shouldnt I make a domestic convenience of you?

MANGAN. Because I dont choose, see? Because I'm not a silly gull like your father. Thats why.

ELLIE [*With serene contempt*]. You are not good enough to clean my father's boots, Mr Mangan; and I am paying you a great compliment in condescending to make a convenience of you, as you call it. Of course you are free to throw over our engagement if you like; but, if you do, youll never enter Hesione's house again: I will take care of that.

MANGAN [*Gasping*]. You little devil, youve done me. [*On the point of collapsing into the big chair again he recovers himself*] Wait a bit, though: youre not so cute as you think. You cant beat Boss Mangan as easy as that. Suppose I go straight to Mrs Hushabye and tell her that youre in love with her husband.

ELLIE. She knows it.

MANGAN. You told her!!!

ELLIE. She told me.

MANGAN [*Clutching at his bursting temples*]. Oh, this is a crazy house. Or else I'm going clean off my chump. Is she making a swop with you—she to have your husband and you to have hers?

ELLIE. Well, you dont want us both, do you?

MANGAN [*Throwing himself into the chair distractedly*]. My brain wont stand it. My head's going to split. Help! Help me to hold it. Quick: hold it: squeeze it. Save me. [*Ellie comes behind his chair; clasps his head hard for a moment; then begins to draw her hands from his forehead back to his ears*] Thank you. [*Drowsily*] Thats very refreshing. [*Waking a little*] Dont you hypnotize me, though. Ive seen men made fools of by hypnotism.

ELLIE [*Steadily*]. Be quiet. Ive seen men made fools of without hypnotism.

MANGAN [*Humbly*]. You dont dislike touching me, I hope. You never touched me before, I noticed.

ELLIE. Not since you fell in love naturally with a grown-up nice woman, who will never expect you to make love to her. And I will never expect him to make love to me.

MANGAN. He may, though.

ELLIE [*Making her passes rhythmically*]. Hush. Go to sleep. Do you hear? You are to go to sleep, go to sleep, go to sleep; be quiet, deeply deeply quiet; sleep, sleep, sleep, sleep, sleep.

[*He falls asleep. Ellie steals away; turns the light out; and goes into the garden*]

[*Nurse Guinness opens the door and is seen in the light which comes in from the hall*]

GUINNESS [*Speaking to someone outside*]. Mr Mangan's not here, ducky: theres no one here. It's all dark.

MRS HUSHABYE [*Without*]. Try the garden. Mr Dunn and I will be in my boudoir. Shew him the way.

GUINNESS. Yes, ducky. [*She makes for the garden door in the dark; stumbles over the sleeping Mangan; and screams*] Ahoo! Oh Lord, sir! I beg your pardon, I'm sure: I didnt see you in the dark. Who is it? [*She goes back to the door and turns on the light*] Oh, Mr Mangan, sir, I hope I havnt hurt you plumping into your lap like that. [*Coming to him*] I was looking for you, sir. Mrs Hushabye says will you please—[*Noticing that he remains quite insensible*] Oh, my good Lord, I hope I havnt killed him. Sir! Mr Mangan! Sir! [*She shakes him; and he is rolling inertly off the chair on the floor when she holds him up and props him against the cushion*] Miss Hessy! Miss Hessy! Quick, doty darling. Miss Hessy! [*Mrs Hushabye comes in from the hall, followed by Mazzini Dunn*] Oh, Miss Hessy, Ive been and killed him.

[*Mazzini runs round the back of the chair to Mangan's right hand, and sees that the nurse's words are apparently only too true*]

MAZZINI. What tempted you to commit such a crime, woman?

MRS HUSHABYE [*Trying not to laugh*]. Do you mean you did it on purpose?

GUINNESS. Now is it likely I'd kill any man on purpose. I fell over him in the dark; and I'm a pretty tidy weight. He never spoke nor moved until I shook him; and then he would have dropped dead on the floor. Isnt it tiresome?

MRS HUSHABYE [*Going past the nurse to Mangan's side, and inspecting him less credulously than Mazzini*]. Nonsense! He is not dead: he is only asleep. I can see him breathing.

GUINNESS. But why wont he wake?

MAZZINI [*Speaking very politely into Mangan's ear*]. Mangan! My dear Mangan! [*He blows into Mangan's ear*]

MRS HUSHABYE. Thats no good. [*She shakes him vigorously*] Mr Mangan: wake up. Do you hear? [*He begins to roll over*] Oh! Nurse, nurse: he's falling: help me.

[*Nurse Guinness rushes to the rescue. With Mazzini's assistance, Mangan is propped safely up again*]

GUINNESS [*Behind the chair; bending over to test the case with her nose*]. Would he be drunk, do you think, pet?

MRS HUSHABYE. Had he any of papa's rum?

MAZZINI. It cant be that: he is most abstemious. I am afraid he drank too much formerly, and has to drink too little now. You know, Mrs Hushabye, I really think he has been hypnotized.

GUINNESS. Hip no what, sir?

MAZZINI. One evening at home, after we had seen a hypnotizing performance, the children began playing at it; and Ellie stroked my head. I assure you I went off dead asleep; and they had to send for a professional to wake me up after I had slept eighteen hours. They had to carry me upstairs; and as the poor children were not very strong, they let me slip; and I rolled right down the whole flight and never woke up. [*Mrs Hushabye splutters*] Oh, you may laugh, Mrs Hushabye; but I might have been killed.

MRS HUSHABYE. I couldnt have helped laughing even if you had been, Mr Dunn. So Ellie has hypnotized him. What fun!

MAZZINI. Oh no, no, no. It was such a terrible lesson to her: nothing would induce her to try such a thing again.

MRS HUSHABYE. Then who did it? *I* didn't.

MAZZINI. I thought perhaps the Captain might have done it unintentionally. He is so fearfully magnetic: I feel vibrations whenever he comes close to me.

GUINNESS. The Captain will get him out of it anyhow, sir: I'll back him for that. I'll go fetch him. [*She makes for the pantry*]

MRS HUSHABYE. Wait a bit. [*To Mazzini*] You say he is all right for eighteen hours?

MAZZINI. Well, *I* was asleep for eighteen hours.

MRS HUSHABYE. Were you any the worse for it?

MAZZINI. I dont quite remember. They had poured brandy down my throat, you see; and—

MRS HUSHABYE. Quite. Anyhow, you survived. Nurse, darling: go and ask Miss Dunn to come to us here. Say I want to speak to her particularly. You will find her with Mr Hushabye probably.

GUINNESS. I think not, ducky: Miss Addy is with him. But I'll find her and send her to you. [*She goes out into the garden*]

MRS HUSHABYE [*Calling Mazzini's attention to the figure on the chair*]. Now, Mr Dunn, look. Just look. Look hard. Do you still intend to sacrifice your daughter to that thing?

MAZZINI [*Troubled*]. You have completely upset me, Mrs Hushabye, by all you have said to me. That anyone could imagine that I—I, a consecrated soldier of freedom, if I may say so—could sacrifice Ellie to anybody or anyone, or that I should ever have dreamed of forcing her inclinations in any way, is a most painful blow to my—well, I suppose you would say to my good opinion of myself.

MRS HUSHABYE [*Rather stolidly*]. Sorry.

MAZZINI [*Looking forlornly at the body*]. What is your objection to poor Mangan, Mrs Hushabye? He looks all right to me. But then I am so accustomed to him.

MRS HUSHABYE. Have you no heart? Have you no sense? Look at the brute! Think of poor weak innocent Ellie

in the clutches of this slavedriver, who spends his life making thousands of rough violent workmen bend to his will and sweat for him: a man accustomed to have great masses of iron beaten into shape for him by steam-hammers! to fight with women and girls over a halfpenny an hour ruthlessly! a captain of industry, I think you call him, dont you? Are you going to fling your delicate, sweet, helpless child into such a beast's claws just because he will keep her in an expensive house and make her wear diamonds to shew how rich he is?

MAZZINI [*Staring at her in wide-eyed amazement*]. Bless you, dear Mrs Hushabye, what romantic ideas of business you have! Poor dear Mangan isnt a bit like that.

MRS HUSHABYE [*Scornfully*]. Poor dear Mangan indeed!

MAZZINI. But he doesnt know anything about machinery. He never goes near the men: he couldnt manage them: he is afraid of them. I never can get him to take the least interest in the works: he hardly knows more about them than you do. People are cruelly unjust to Mangan: they think he is all rugged strength just because his manners are bad.

MRS HUSHABYE. Do you mean to tell me he isnt strong enough to crush poor little Ellie?

MAZZINI. Of course it's very hard to say how any marriage will turn out; but speaking for myself, I should say that he wont have a dog's chance against Ellie. You know, Ellie has remarkable strength of character. I think it is because I taught her to like Shakespear when she was very young.

MRS HUSHABYE [*Contemptuously*]. Shakespear! The next thing you will tell me is that you could have made a great deal more money than Mangan. [*She retires to the sofa, and sits down at the port end of it in the worst of humors.*]

MAZZINI [*Following her and taking the other end*]. No: I'm no good at making money. I dont care enough for it, somehow. I'm not ambitious! that must be it. Mangan is wonderful about money: he thinks of nothing else. He is so dreadfully afraid of being poor. I am always thinking of other things: even at the works I think of the things we are doing and not of what they cost. And the worst of it is, poor Mangan doesnt know what to do with his money when he gets it. He is such a baby that he doesnt know even what to eat and drink: he has ruined his liver eating and drinking the wrong things; and now he can hardly eat at all. Ellie will diet him splendidly. You will be surprised when you come to know him better: he is really the most helpless of mortals. You get quite a protective feeling towards him.

MRS HUSHABYE. Then who manages his business, pray?

MAZZINI. I do. And of course other people like me.

MRS HUSHABYE. Footling people, you mean.

MAZZINI. I suppose youd think us so.

MRS HUSHABYE. And pray why dont you do without him if youre all so much cleverer?

MAZZINI. Oh, we couldnt: we should ruin the business in a year. I've tried; and I know. We should spend too much on everything. We should improve the quality of the goods and make them too dear. We should be sentimental about the hard cases among the workpeople. But Mangan keeps us in order. He is down on us about every extra halfpenny. We could never do without him. You see, he will sit up all night thinking of how to save sixpence. Wont Ellie make him jump, though, when she takes his house in hand!

MRS HUSHABYE. Then the creature is a fraud even as a captain of industry!

MAZZINI. I am afraid all the captains of industry are what you call frauds, Mrs Hushabye. Of course there are some manufacturers who really do understand their own works; but they dont make as high a rate of profit as Mangan does. I assure you Mangan is quite a good fellow in his way. He means well.

MRS HUSHABYE. He doesnt look well. He is not in his first youth, is he?

MAZZINI. After all, no husband is in his first youth for very long, Mrs Hushabye. And men cant afford to marry in their first youth nowadays.

MRS HUSHABYE. Now if *I* said that, it would sound witty. Why cant you say it wittily? What on earth is the matter with you? Why dont you inspire everybody with confidence? with respect?

MAZZINI [*Humbly*]. I think that what is the matter with me is that I am poor. You dont know what that means at home. Mind: I dont say they have ever complained. Theyve all been wonderful: theyve been proud of my poverty. Theyve even joked about it quite often. But my wife has had a very poor time of it. She has been quite resigned—

MRS HUSHABYE [*Shuddering involuntarily*]. !!

MAZZINI. There! You see, Mrs Hushabye. I dont want Ellie to live on resignation.

MRS HUSHABYE. Do you want her to have to resign herself to living with a man she doesnt love?

MAZZINI [*Wistfully*]. Are you sure that would be worse than living with a man she did love, if he was a footling person?

MRS HUSHABYE [*Relaxing her contemptuous attitude, quite interested in Mazzini now*]. You know, I really think you must love Ellie very much; for you become quite clever when you talk about her.

MAZZINI. I didnt know I was so very stupid on other subjects.

MRS HUSHABYE. You are, sometimes.

MAZZINI [*Turning his head away; for his eyes are wet*]. I have learnt a good deal about myself from you, Mrs Hushabye; and I'm afraid I shall not be the happier for your plain speaking. But if you thought I needed it to make me think of Ellie's happiness you were very much mistaken.

MRS HUSHABYE [*Leaning towards him kindly*]. Have I been a beast?

MAZZINI [*Pulling himself together*]. It doesnt matter about me, Mrs Hushabye. I think you like Ellie; and that is enough for me.

MRS HUSHABYE. I'm beginning to like you a little. I perfectly loathed you at first. I thought you the most odious, self-satisfied, boresome elderly prig I ever met.

MAZZINI [*Resigned, and now quite cheerful*]. I daresay I am all that. I never have been a favorite with gorgeous women like you. They always frighten me.

MRS HUSHABYE [*Pleased*]. Am I a gorgeous woman, Mazzini? I shall fall in love with you presently.

MAZZINI [*With placid gallantry*]. No you wont, Hesione. But you would be quite safe. Would you believe it that quite a lot of women have flirted with me because I am quite safe? But they get tired of me for the same reason.

MRS HUSHABYE [*Mischievously*]. Take care. You may not be so safe as you think.

MAZZINI. Oh yes, quite safe. You see, I have been in love really: the sort of love that only happens once. [*Softly*] Thats why Ellie is such a lovely girl.

MRS HUSHABYE. Well, really, you are coming out. Are you quite sure you wont let me tempt you into a second grand passion?

MAZZINI. Quite. It wouldnt be natural. The fact is, you dont strike on my box, Mrs Hushabye; and I certainly dont strike on yours.

MRS HUSHABYE. I see. Your marriage was a safety match.

MAZZINI. What a very witty application of the expression I used! I should never have thought of it.

[*Ellie comes in from the garden, looking anything but happy*]

MRS HUSHABYE [*Rising*]. Oh! here is Ellie at last. [*She goes behind the sofa*]

ELLIE [*On the threshold of the starboard door*]. Guinness said you wanted me: you and papa.

MRS HUSHABYE. You have kept us waiting so long that it almost came to—well, never mind. Your father is a very wonderful man [*She ruffles his hair affectionately*]: the only one I ever met who could resist me when I made myself really agreeable. [*She comes to the big chair, on Mangan's left*] Come here. I have something to shew you. [*Ellie strolls listlessly to the other side of the chair*] Look.

ELLIE [*Contemplating Mangan without interest*]. I know. He is only asleep. We had a talk after dinner; and he fell asleep in the middle of it.

MRS HUSHABYE. You did it, Ellie. You put him asleep.

MAZZINI [*Rising quickly and coming to the back of the chair*]. Oh, I hope not. Did you, Ellie?

ELLIE [*Wearily*]. He asked me to.

MAZZINI. But it's dangerous. You know what heppened to me.

ELLIE [*Utterly indifferent*]. Oh, I daresay I can wake him. If not, somebody else can.

MRS HUSHABYE. It doesnt matter, anyhow, because I have at last persuaded your father than you dont want to marry him.

ELLIE [*Suddenly coming out of her listlessness, much vexed*]. But why did you do that, Hesione? I do want to marry him. I fully intend to marry him.

MAZZINI. Are you quite sure, Ellie? Mrs Hushabye has made me feel that I may have been thoughtless and selfish about it.

ELLIE [*Very clearly and steadily*]. Papa. When Mrs Hushabye takes it on herself to explain to you what I think or dont think, shut yours ears tight; and shut your eyes too. Hesione knows nothing about me: she hasnt the least notion of the sort of person I am, and never will. I promise you I wont do anything I dont want to do and mean to do for my own sake.

MAZZINI. You are quite, quite sure?

ELLIE. Quite, quite sure. Now you must go away and leave me to talk to Mrs Hushabye.

MAZZINI. But I should like to hear. Shall I be in the way?

ELLIE [*Inexorable*]. I had rather talk to her alone.

MAZZINI [*Affectionately*]. Oh, well, I know what a nuisance parents are, dear. I will be good and go. [*He goes to the garden door*] By the way, do you remember the address of that professional who woke me up? Dont you think I had better telegraph to him.

MRS HUSHABYE [*Moving towards the safe*]. It's too late to telegraph tonight.

MAZZINI. I suppose so. I do hope he'll wake up in the course of the night. [*He goes out into the garden*]

ELLIE [*Turning vigorously on Hesione the moment her father is out of the room*]. Hesione: what the devil do you mean by making mischief with my father about Mangan?

MRS HUSHABYE [*promptly losing her temper*]. Dont you dare speak to me like that, you little minx. Remember that you are in my house.

ELLIE. Stuff! Why dont you mind your own business? What is it to you whether I choose to marry Mangan or not?

MRS HUSHABYE. Do you suppose you can bully me, you miserable little matrimonial adventurer?

ELLIE. Every woman who hasnt any money is a matrimonial adventurer. It's easy for you to talk: you have never known what it is to want money; and you can pick up men as if they were daisies. I am poor and respectable—

MRS HUSHABYE [*Interrupting*]. Ho! respectable! How did you pick up Mangan? How did you pick up my husband? You have the audacity to tell me that I am a—a—a—

ELLIE. A siren. So you are. You were born to lead men by the nose: if you werent, Marcus would have waited for me, perhaps.

MRS HUSHABYE [*Suddenly melting and half laughing*]. Oh, my poor Ellie, my pettikins, my unhappy darling! I am so sorry about Hector. But what can I do? It's not my fault: I'd give him to you if I could.

ELLIE. I dont blame you for that.

MRS HUSHABYE. What a brute I was to quarrel with you and call you names! Do kiss me and say youre not angry with me.

ELLIE [*Fiercely*]. Oh, dont slop and gush and be sentimental. Dont you see that unless I can be hard—as hard as nails—I shall go mad. I dont care a damn about your calling me names: do you think a woman in my situation can feel a few hard words?

MRS HUSHABYE. Poor little woman! Poor little situation!

ELLIE. I suppose you think youre being sympathetic. You are just foolish and stupid and selfish. You see me getting a smasher right in the face that kills a whole part of my life: the best part that can never come again; and you think you can help me over it by a little coaxing and kissing. When I want all the strength I can get to lean on: something iron, something stony, I dont care how cruel it is, you go all mushy and want to slobber over me. I'm not angry; I'm not unfriendly; but for God's sake do pull yourself together; and dont think that because youre on velvet and always have been, women who are in hell can take it as easily as you.

MRS HUSHABYE [*Shrugging her shoulders*]. Very well. [*She sits down on the sofa in her old place*] But I warn you that when I am neither coaxing and kissing nor laughing, I am just wondering how much longer I can stand living in this cruel, damnable world. You object to the siren: well, I drop the siren. You want to rest your wounded bosom against a grindstone. Well [*Folding her arms*], here is the grindstone.

ELLIE [*Sitting down beside her, appeased*]. Thats better: you really have the trick of falling in with everyone's mood; but you dont understand, because you are not the sort of woman for whom there is only one man and only one chance.

MRS HUSHABYE. I certainly dont understand how your marrying that object [*Indicating Mangan*] will console you for not being able to marry Hector.

ELLIE. Perhaps you dont understand why I was quite a nice girl this morning, and am now neither a girl nor particularly nice.

MRS HUSHABYE. Oh yes I do. It's because you have made up your mind to do something despicable and wicked.

ELLIE. I dont think so, Hesione. I must make the best of my ruined house.

MRS HUSHABYE. Pooh! Youll get over it. Your house isnt ruined.

ELLIE. Of course I shall get over it. You dont suppose I'm going to sit down and die of a broken heart, I hope, or be an old maid living on a pittance from the Sick and Indigent Roomkeepers' Association. But my heart is broken, all the same. What I mean by that is that I know that what has happened to me with Marcus will not happen to me ever again. In the world for me there is Marcus and a lot of other men of whom one is just the same as another. Well, if I cant have love, thats no reason why I should have poverty. If Mangan has nothing else, he has money.

MRS HUSHABYE. And are there no young men with money?

ELLIE. Not within my reach. Besides, a young man would have the right to expect love from me, and would perhaps leave me when he found I could not give it to him. Rich young men can get rid of their wives, you know, pretty cheaply. But this object, as you call him, can expect nothing more from me than I am prepared to give him.

MRS HUSHABYE. He will be your owner, remember. If he buys you, he will make the bargain pay him and not you. Ask your father.

ELLIE [*Rising and strolling to the chair to contemplate their subject*]. You need not trouble on that score, Hesione. I have more to give Boss Mangan than he has to give me: it is I who am buying him, and at a pretty good price too, I think. Women are better at that sort of bargain than men. I have taken the Boss's measure; and ten Boss Mangans shall not prevent me doing far more as I please as his wife than I have ever been able to do as a poor girl. [*Stooping to the recumbent figure*] Shall they, Boss? I think not. [*She passes on to the drawing-table, and leans against*

the end of it, facing the windows] I shall not have to spend most of my time wondering how long my gloves will last, anyhow.

MRS HUSHABYE [*Rising superbly*]. Ellie: you are a wicked sordid little beast. And to think that I actually condescended to fascinate that creature there to save you from him! Well, let me tell you this: if you make this disgusting match, you will never see Hector again if I can help it.

ELLIE [*Unmoved*]. I nailed Mangan by telling him that if he did not marry me he should never see you again. [*She lifts herself on her wrists and seats herself on the end of the table*]

MRS HUSHABYE [*Recoiling*]. Oh!

ELLIE. So you see I am not unprepared for your playing that trump against me. Well, you just try it: thats all. I should have made a man of Marcus, not a household pet.

MRS HUSHABYE [*Flaming*]. You dare!

ELLIE [*Looking almost dangerous*]. Set him thinking about me if you dare.

MRS HUSHABYE. Well, of all the impudent little fiends I ever met! Hector says there is a certain point at which the only answer you can give to a man who breaks all the rules is to knock him down. What would you say if I were to box your ears?

ELLIE [*Calmly*]. I should pull your hair.

MRS HUSHABYE. [*Mischievously*]. That wouldnt hurt me. Perhaps it comes off at night.

ELLIE [*So taken aback that she drops off the table and runs to her*]. Oh, you dont mean to say, Hesione, that your beautiful black hair is false?

MRS HUSHABYE [*Patting it*]. Dont tell Hector. He believes in it.

ELLIE [*Groaning*]. Oh! Even the hair that ensnared him false! Everything false!

MRS HUSHABYE. Pull it and try. Other women can snare men in their hair; but I can swing a baby on mine. Aha! you cant do that, Goldylocks.

ELLIE [*Heartbroken*]. No. You have stolen my babies.

MRS HUSHABYE. Pettikins: dont make me cry. You know, what you said about my making a household pet of him is a little true. Perhaps he ought to have waited for you. Would any other women on earth forgive you?

ELLIE. Oh, what right had you to take him all for yourself! [*Pulling herself together*] There! You couldnt help it: neither of us could help it. He couldnt help it. No: dont say anything more; I cant bear it. Let us wake the object. [*She begins stroking Mangan's head, reversing the movement with which she put him to sleep*] Wake up, do you hear? You are to wake up at once. Wake up, wake up, wake—

MANGAN [*Bouncing out of the chair in a fury and turning on them*]. Wake up! So you think Ive been asleep, do you? [*He kicks the chair violently out of his way, and gets between them*] You throw me into a trance so that I cant move hand or foot—I might have been buried alive! it's a mercy I wasnt—and then you think I was only asleep. If youd let me drop the two times you rolled me about, my nose would have been flattened for life against the floor. But Ive found you all out, anyhow. I know the sort of people I'm among now. Ive heard every word youve said, you and your precious father, and [*To Mrs Hushabye*] you too. So I'm an object, am I? I'm a thing, am I? I'm a fool that hasnt sense enough to feed myself properly, am I? I'm afraid of the men that would starve if it werent for the wages I give them, am I? I'm nothing but a disgusting old skinflint to be made a convenience of by designing women and fool managers of my works, am I? I'm—

MRS HUSHABYE [*With the most elegant aplomb*]. Sh-sh-sh-sh-sh! Mr Mangan: you are bound in honor to obliterate from your mind all you heard while you were pretending to be asleep. It was not meant for you to hear.

MANGAN. Pretending to be asleep! Do you think if I was only pretending that I'd have sprawled there helpless, and listened to such unfairness, such lies, such injustice and plotting and backbiting and slandering of me, if I could have up and told you what I thought of you! I wonder I didnt burst.

MRS HUSHABYE [*Sweetly*]. You dreamt it all, Mr Mangan. We were only saying how beautifully peaceful you looked in your sleep. That was all, wasnt it, Ellie? Believe me, Mr Mangan, all those unpleasant things came into your mind in the last half second before you woke. Ellie rubbed your hair the wrong way; and the disagreeable sensation suggested a disagreeable dream.

MANGAN [*Doggedly*]. I believe in dreams.

MRS HUSHABYE. So do I. But they go by contraries, dont they?

MANGAN [*Depths of emotion suddenly welling up in him*]. I shant forget, to my dying day, that when you gave me the glad eye that time in the garden, you were making a fool of me. That was a dirty low mean thing to do. You had no right to let me come near you if I disgusted you. It isnt my fault if I'm old and havnt a moustache like a bronze candlestick as your husband has. There are things no decent woman would do to a man—like a man hitting a women in the breast.

[*Hesione, utterly shamed, sits down on the sofa and covers her face with her hands. Mangan sits down*

also on his chair and begins to cry like a child. Ellie stares at them. Mrs Hushabye, at the distressing sound he makes, takes down her hands and looks at him. She rises and runs to him]

MRS HUSHABYE. Dont cry: I cant bear it. Have I broken your heart? I didnt know you had one. How could I?

MANGAN. I'm a man aint I?

MRS HUSHABYE [*Half coaxing, half rallying, altogether tenderly*]. Oh no: not what I call a man. Only a Boss: just that and nothing else. What business has a Boss with a heart?

MANGAN. Then youre not a bit sorry for what you did, nor ashamed?

MRS HUSHABYE. I was ashamed for the first time in my life when you said that about hitting a woman in the breast, and I found out what I'd done. My very bones blushed red. Youve had your revenge, Boss. Arnt you satisfied?

MANGAN. Serve you right! Do you hear? Serve you right! Youre just cruel. Cruel.

MRS HUSHABYE. Yes: cruelty would be delicious if one could only find some sort of cruelty that didnt really hurt. By the way [*Sitting down beside him on the arm of the chair*], whats your name? It's not really Boss, is it?

MANGAN [*Shortly*]. If you want to know, my name's Alfred.

MRS HUSHABYE [*Springing up*]. Alfred!! Ellie: he was christened after Tennyson!!!

MANGAN [*Rising*]. I was christened after my uncle, and never had a penny from him, damn him! What of it?

MRS HUSHABYE. It comes to me suddenly that you are a real person: that you had a mother, like anyone else. [*Putting her hands on his shoulders and surveying him*] Little Alf!

MANGAN. Well, you have a nerve.

MRS HUSHABYE. And you have a heart, Alfy, a whimpering little heart, but a real one. [*Releasing him suddenly*] Now run and make it up with Ellie. She has had time to think what to say to you, which is more than I had. [*She goes out quickly into the garden by the port door*]

MANGAN. That woman has a pair of hands that go right through you.

ELLIE. Still in love with her, in spite of all we said about you?

MANGAN. Are all women like you two? Do they never think of anything about a man except what they can get out of him? You werent even thinking that about me. You were only thinking whether your gloves would last.

ELLIE. I shall not have to think about that when we are married.

MANGAN. And you think I am going to marry you after what I heard there!

ELLIE. You heard nothing from me that I did not tell you before.

MANGAN. Perhaps you think I cant do without you.

ELLIE. I think you would feel lonely without us all now, after coming to know us so well.

MANGAN [*With something like a yell of despair*]. Am I never to have the last word?

CAPTAIN SHOTOVER [*Appearing at the starboard garden door*]. There is a soul in torment here. What is the matter?

MANGAN. This girl doesnt want to spend her life wondering how long her gloves will last.

CAPTAIN SHOTOVER [*Passing through*]. Dont wear any. I never do. [*He goes into the pantry*]

LADY UTTERWORD [*Appearing at the port garden door, in a handsome dinner dress*]. Is anything the matter?

ELLIE. This gentleman wants to know is he never to have the last word?

LADY UTTERWORD [*Coming forward to the sofa*]. I should let him have it, my dear. The important thing is not to have the last word, but to have your own way.

MANGAN. She wants both.

LADY UTTERWORD. She wont get them, Mr Mangan. Providence always has the last word.

MANGAN [*Desperately*]. Now you are going to come religion over me. In this house a man's mind might as well be a football. I'm going. [*He makes for the hall, but is stopped by a hail from the Captain, who has just emerged from his pantry*]

CAPTAIN SHOTOVER. Whither away, Boss Mangan?

MANGAN. To hell out of this house: let that be enough for you and all here.

CAPTAIN SHOTOVER. You were welcome to come: you are free to go. The wide earth, the high seas, the spacious skies are waiting for you outside.

LADY UTTERWORD. But your things, Mr Mangan. Your bags, your comb and brushes, your pyjamas—

HECTOR [*Who has just appeared in the port doorway in a handsome Arab costume*]. Why should the escaping slave take his chains with him?

MANGAN. Thats right, Hushabye. Keep the pyjamas, my lady; and much good may they do you.

HECTOR [*Advancing to Lady Utterword's left hand*]. Let us all go out into the night and leave everything behind us.

MANGAN. You stay where you are, the lot of you. I want no company, especially female company.

ELLIE. Let him go. He is unhappy here. He is angry with us.

CAPTAIN SHOTOVER. Go, Boss Mangan; and when you have found the land where there is happiness and where there are no women, send me its latitude and longitude; and I will join you there.

LADY UTTERWORD. You will certainly not be comfortable without your luggage, Mr Mangan.

ELLIE [*Impatient*]. Go, go: why dont you go? It is a heavenly night: you can sleep on the heath. Take my waterproof to lie on: it is hanging up in the hall.

HECTOR. Breakfast at nine, unless you prefer to breakfast with the Captain at six.

ELLIE. Good night, Alfred.

HECTOR. Alfred! [*He runs back to the door and calls into the garden*] Randall: Mangan's Christian name is Alfred.

RANDALL [*Appearing in the starboard doorway in evening dress*]. Then Hesione wins her bet.

[*Mrs Hushabye appears in the port doorway. She throws her left arm round Hector's neck; draws him with her to the back of the sofa; and throws her right arm around Lady Utterword's neck*]

MRS HUSHABYE. They wouldnt believe me, Alf.

[*They contemplate him*]

MANGAN. Is there any more of you coming in to look at me, as if I was the latest thing in a menagerie?

MRS HUSHABYE. You are the latest thing in this menagerie.

[*Before Mangan can retort, a fall of furniture is heard from upstairs; then a pistol shot, and a yell of pain. The staring group breaks up in consternation*]

MAZZINI'S VOICE [*From above*]. Help! A burglar! Help!

HECTOR [*His eyes blazing*]. A burglar!!!

MRS HUSHABYE. No, Hector: you'll be shot [*But it is too late: he has dashed out past Mangan, who hastily moves towards the bookshelves out of his way*]

CAPTAIN SHOTOVER [*Blowing his whistle*]. All hands aloft! [*He strides out after Hector*]

LADY UTTERWORD. My diamonds! [*She follows the Captain*]

RANDALL [*Rushing after her*]. No, Ariadne. Let me.

ELLIE. Oh, is papa shot? [*She runs out*]

MRS HUSHABYE. Are you frightened, Alf?

MANGAN. No. It aint my house, thank God.

MRS HUSHABYE. If they catch a burglar, shall we have to go into court as witnesses, and be asked all sorts of questions about our private lives?

MANGAN. You wont be believed if you tell the truth.

[*Mazzini, terribly upset, with a duelling pistol in his hand, comes from the hall, and makes his way to the drawing-table*]

MAZZINI. Oh, my dear Mrs Hushabye, I might have killed him. [*He throws the pistol on the table and staggers round to the chair*] I hope you wont believe I really intended to.

[*Hector comes in, marching an old and villainous looking man before him by the collar. He plants him in the middle of the room and releases him*]

[*Ellie follows, and immediately runs across to the back of her father's chair, and pats his shoulders*]

RANDALL [*Entering with a poker*]. Keep your eye on this door, Mangan. I'll look after the other. [*He goes to the starboard door and stands on guard there*]

[*Lady Utterword comes in after Randall, and goes between Mrs Hushabye and Mangan*]

[*Nurse Guinness brings up the rear, and waits near the door, on Mangan's left*]

MRS HUSHABYE. What has happened?

MAZZINI. Your housekeeper told me there was somebody upstairs, and gave me a pistol that Mr Hushabye had been practising with. I thought it would frighten him; but it went off at a touch.

THE BURGLAR. Yes, and took the skin off my ear. Precious near took the top off my head. Why dont you have a proper revolver instead of a thing like that, that goes off if you as much as blow on it?

HECTOR. One of my duelling pistols. Sorry.

MAZZINI. He put his hands up and said it was a fair cop.

THE BURGLAR. So it was. Send for the police.

HECTOR. No, by thunder! It was not a fair cop. We were four to one.

MRS HUSHABYE. What will they do to him?

THE BURGLAR. Ten years. Beginning with solitary. Ten years off my life. I shant serve it all: I'm too old. It will see me out.

LADY UTTERWORD. You should have thought of that before you stole my diamonds.

THE BURGLAR. Well, youve got them back, lady: havnt you? Can you give me back the years of my life you are going to take from me?

MRS HUSHABYE. Oh, we cant bury a man alive for ten years for a few diamonds.

THE BURGLAR. Ten little shining diamonds! Ten long black years!

LADY UTTERWORD. Think of what it is for us to be dragged through the horrors of a criminal court, and have all our family affairs in the papers! If you were a native, and Hastings could order you a good beating and send you away, I shouldn't mind; but here in England there is no real protection for any respectable person.

THE BURGLAR. I'm too old to be giv a hiding, lady. Send for the police and have done with it. It's only just and right you should.

RANDALL [*Who has relaxed his vigilance on seeing the burglar so pacifically disposed, and comes forward swinging the poker between his fingers like a well-folded umbrella*]. It is neither just nor right that we should be put to a lot of inconvenience to gratify your moral enthusiasm, my friend. You had better get out, while you have the chance.

THE BURGLAR [*Inexorably*]. No. I must work my sin off my conscience. This has come as a sort of call to me. Let me spend the rest of my life repenting in a cell. I shall have my reward above.

MANGAN [*Exasperated*]. The very burglars cant behave naturally in this house.

HECTOR. My good sir: you must work out your salvation at somebody else's expense. Nobody here is going to charge you.

THE BURGLAR. Oh, you wont charge me, wont you?

HECTOR. No. I'm sorry to be inhospitable; but will you kindly leave the house?

THE BURGLAR. Right. I'll go to the police station and give myself up. [*He turns resolutely to the door; but Hector stops him*]

HECTOR. } Oh no. You mustnt do that.

RANDALL. } No, no. Clear out, man, cant you; and dont be a fool.

Mrs HUSHABYE. } Dont be so silly. Cant you repent at home?

LADY UTTERWORD. You will have to do as you are told.

THE BURGLAR. It's compounding a felony, you know.

MRS HUSHABYE. This is utterly ridiculous. Are we to be forced to prosecute this man when we dont want to?

THE BURGLAR. Am I to be robbed of my salvation to save you the trouble of spending a day at the sessions? Is that justice? Is it right? Is it fair to me?

MAZZINI [*Rising and leaning across the table persuasively as if it were a pulpit desk or a shop counter*]. Come, come! Let me shew you how you can turn your very crimes to account. Why not set up as a locksmith? You must know more about locks than most honest men?

THE BURGLAR. Thats true, sir. But I couldnt set up as a locksmith under twenty pounds.

RANDALL. Well, you can easily steal twenty pounds. You will find it in the nearest bank.

THE BURGLAR [*Horrified*]. Oh what a thing for a gentleman to put into the head of a poor criminal scrambling out of the bottomless pit as it were! Oh, shame on you, sir! Oh, God forgive you! [*He throws himself into the big chair and covers his face as if in prayer*]

LADY UTTERWORD. Really, Randall!

HECTOR. It seems to me that we shall have to take up a collection for this inopportunely contrite sinner.

LADY UTTERWORD. But twenty pounds is ridiculous.

THE BURGLAR [*Looking up quickly*]. I shall have to buy a lot of tools, lady.

LADY UTTERWORD. Nonsense: you have your burgling kit.

THE BURGLAR. Whats a jemmy and a centrebit and an acetylene welding plant and a bunch of skeleton keys? I shall want a forge, and a smithy, and a shop, and fittings. I cant hardly do it for twenty.

HECTOR. My worthy friend, we havnt got twenty pounds.

THE BURGLAR [*Now master of the situation*]. You can raise it among you, cant you?

MRS HUSHABYE. Give him a sovereign, Hector; and get rid of him.

HECTOR [*Giving him a pound*]. There! Off with you.

THE BURGLAR [*Rising and taking the money very ungratefully*]. I wont promise nothing. You have more on you than a quid: all the lot of you, I mean.

LADY UTTERWORD [*Vigorously*]. Oh, let us prosecute him and have done with it. I have a conscience too, I hope; and I do not feel at all sure that we have any right to let him go, especially if he is going to be greedy and impertinent.

THE BURGLAR [*Quickly*]. All right, lady, all right. I've no wish to be anything but agreeable. Good evening, ladies and gentlemen; and thank you kindly.

[*He is hurrying out when he is confronted in the doorway by Captain Shotover*]

CAPTAIN SHOTOVER [*Fixing The Burglar with a piercing regard*]. What's this? Are there two of you?

THE BURGLAR [*Falling on his knees before the Captain in abject terror*]. Oh my good Lord, what have I done? Dont tell me it's your house I've broken into, Captain Shotover.

[*The Captain seizes him by the collar; drags him to his feet; and leads him to the middle of the group, Hector falling back beside his wife to make way for them*]

CAPTAIN SHOTOVER [*Turning him towards Ellie*]. Is that your daughter? [*He releases him*]

THE BURGLAR. Well, how do I know, Captain? You know the sort of life you and me has led. Any young lady of that age might be my daughter anywhere in the wide world, as you might say.

CAPTAIN SHOTOVER [*To Mazzini*]. You are not Billy Dunn. This is Billy Dunn. Why have you imposed on me?

THE BURGLAR [*Indignantly to Mazzini*]. Have you been giving yourself out to be me? You, that nigh blew my head off! Shooting yourself, in a manner of speaking!

MAZZINI. My dear Captain Shotover, ever since I came into this house I have done hardly anything else but assure you that I am not Mr William Dunn, but Mazzini Dunn, a very different person.

THE BURGLAR. He dont belong to my branch, Captain. Theres two sets in the family: the thinking Dunns and the drinking Dunns, each going their own ways. I'm a drinking Dunn: he's a thinking Dunn. But that didn't give him any right to shoot me.

CAPTAIN SHOTOVER. So youve turned burglar, have you?

THE BURGLAR. No, Captain: I wouldnt disgrace our old sea calling by such a thing. I am no burglar.

LADY UTTERWORD. What were you doing with my diamonds?

GUINNESS. What did you break into the house for if youre no burglar?

RANDALL. Mistook the house for your own and came in by the wrong window, eh?

THE BURGLAR. Well, it's no use my telling you a lie: I can take in most captains, but not Captain Shotover, because he sold himself to the devil in Zanzibar, and can divine water, spot gold, explode a cartridge in your pocket with a glance of his eye, and see the truth hidden in the heart of man. But I'm no burglar.

CAPTAIN SHOTOVER. Are you an honest man?

THE BURGLAR. I dont set up to be better than my fellow-creatures, and never did, as you well know, Captain. But what I do is innocent and pious. I enquire about for houses where the right sort of people live. I work it on them same as I worked it here. I break into the house; put a few spoons or diamonds in my pocket; make a noise; get caught; and take up a collection. And you wouldnt believe how hard it is to get caught when youre actually trying to. I have knocked over all the chairs in a room without a soul paying any attention to me. In the end I have had to walk out and leave the job.

RANDALL. When that happens, do you put back the spoons and diamonds?

THE BURGLAR. Well, I dont fly in the face of Providence, if thats what you want to know.

CAPTAIN SHOTOVER. Guinness: you remember this man?

GUINNESS. I should think so, seeing I was married to him, the blackguard!

HESIONE.   } *Exclaiming* { Married to him!
LADY UTTERWORD. } *together* { Guinness!!

THE BURGLAR. It wasnt legal. I've been married to no end of women. No use coming that over me.

CAPTAIN SHOTOVER. Take him to the forecastle. [*He flings him to the door with a strength beyond his years*]

GUINNESS. I suppose you mean the kitchen. They wont have him there. Do you expect servants to keep company with thieves and all sorts?

CAPTAIN SHOTOVER. Land-thieves and water-thieves are the same flesh and blood. I'll have no boatswain on my quarter-deck. Off with you both.

THE BURGLAR. Yes, Captain. [*He goes out humbly*]

MAZZINI. Will it be safe to have him in the house like that?

GUINNESS. Why didn't you shoot him, sir? If I'd known who he was, I'd have shot him myself. [*She goes out*]

MRS HUSHABYE. Do sit down, everybody. [*She sits down on the sofa*]

[*They all move except Ellie. Mazzini resumes his seat. Randall sits down in the window seat near the starboard door, again making a pendulum of his poker, and studying it as Galileo might have done. Hector sits on his left, in the middle. Mangan, forgotten, sits in the port corner. Lady Utterword takes the big chair. Captain Shotover goes into the pantry in deep abstraction. They all look after him; and Lady Utterword coughs unconsciously.*]

MRS HUSHABYE. So Billy Dunn was poor nurse's little romance. I knew there had been somebody.

RANDALL. They will fight their battles over again and enjoy themselves immensely.

LADY UTTERWORD [*Irritably*]. You are not married; and you know nothing about it, Randall. Hold your tongue.

RANDALL. Tyrant!

MRS HUSHABYE. Well, we have had a very exciting evening. Everything will be an anticlimax after it. We'd better all go to bed.

RANDALL. Another burglar may turn up.

MAZZINI. Oh, impossible! I hope not.

RANDALL. Why not? There is more than one burglar in England.

MRS HUSHABYE. What do you say, Alf?

MANGAN [*Huffily*]. Oh, I dont matter. I'm forgotten. The burglar has put my nose out of joint. Shove me into a corner and have done with me.

MRS HUSHABYE [*Jumping up mischievously, and going to him*]. Would you like a walk on the heath, Alfred? With me?

ELLIE. Go, Mr Mangan. It will do you good. Hesione will soothe you.

MRS HUSHABYE [*Slipping her arm under his and pulling him upright*]. Come, Alfred. There is a moon: it's like the night in Tristan and Isolde. [*She caresses his arm and draws him to the port garden door*]

MANGAN [*Writhing but yielding*]. How can you have the face—the heart—[*He breaks down and is heard sobbing as she takes him out*]

LADY UTTERWORD. What an extraordinary way to behave! What is the matter with the man?

ELLIE [*In a strangely calm voice, staring into an imaginary distance*]. His heart is breaking: that is all. [*The Captain appears in the pantry door, listening*] It is a curious sensation: the sort of pain that goes mercifully beyond our powers of feeling. When your heart is broken, your boats are burned; nothing matters any more. It is the end of happiness and the beginning of peace.

LADY UTTERWORD [*Suddenly rising in rage, to the astonishment of the rest*]. How dare you?

HECTOR. Good heavens! Whats the matter?

RANDALL [*In a warning whisper*]. Tch—tch—tch! Steady.

ELLIE [*Surprised and haughty*]. I was not addressing you particularly, Lady Utterword. And I am not accustomed to be asked how dare I.

LADY UTTERWORD. Of course not. Anyone can see how badly you have been brought up.

MAZZINI. Oh, I hope not, Lady Utterword. Really!

LADY UTTERWORD. I know very well what you meant. The impudence!

ELLIE. What on earth do you mean?

CAPTAIN SHOTOVER [*Advancing to the table*]. She means that her heart will not break. She has been longing all her life for someone to break it. At last she has become afraid she has none to break.

LADY UTTERWORD [*Flinging herself on her knees and throwing her arms round him*]. Papa: dont say you think Ive no heart.

CAPTAIN SHOTOVER [*Raising her with grim tenderness*]. If you had no heart how could you want to have it broken, child?

HECTOR [*Rising with a bound*]. Lady Utterword: you are not to be trusted. You have made a scene. [*He runs out into the garden through the starboard door*]

LADY UTTERWORD. Oh! Hector, Hector! [*She runs out after him*]

RANDALL. Only nerves, I assure you. [*He rises and follows her, waving the poker in his agitation*] Ariadne! Ariadne! For God's sake be careful. You will— [*He is gone*]

MAZZINI [*Rising*]. How distressing! Can I do anything, I wonder?

CAPTAIN SHOTOVER [*Promptly taking his chair and setting to work at the drawing-board*]. No. Go to bed. Goodnight.

MAZZINI [*Bewildered*]. Oh! Perhaps you are right.

ELLIE. Goodnight, dearest. [*She kisses him*]

MAZZINI. Goodnight, love. [*He makes for the door, but turns aside to the bookshelves*] I'll just take a book. [*He takes one*] Goodnight. [*He goes out, leaving Ellie alone with the Captain*]

[*The Captain is intent on his drawing. Ellie, standing sentry over his chair, contemplates him for a moment*]

ELLIE. Does nothing ever disturb you, Captain Shotover?

CAPTAIN SHOTOVER. I've stood on the bridge for eighteen hours in a typhoon. Life here is stormier; but I can stand it.

ELLIE. Do you think I ought to marry Mr Mangan?

CAPTAIN SHOTOVER [*Never looking up*]. One rock is as good as another to be wrecked on.

ELLIE. I am not in love with him.

CAPTAIN SHOTOVER. Who said you were?

ELLIE. You are not surprised?

CAPTAIN SHOTOVER. Surprised! At my age!

ELLIE. It seems to be quite fair. He wants me for one thing: I want him for another.

CAPTAIN SHOTOVER. Money?

ELLIE. Yes.

CAPTAIN SHOTOVER. Well, one turns the cheek: the other kisses it. One provides the cash: the other spends it.

ELLIE. Who will have the best of the bargain, I wonder?

CAPTAIN SHOTOVER. You. These fellows live in an office all day. You will have to put up with him from dinner to breakfast; but you will both be asleep most of that time. All day you will be quit of him; and you will be shopping with his money. If that is too much for you, marry a seafaring man: you will be bothered with him only three weeks in the year, perhaps.

ELLIE. That would be best of all, I suppose.

CAPTAIN SHOTOVER. It's a dangerous thing to be married right up to the hilt, like my daughter's husband. The man is at home all day, like a damned soul in hell.

ELLIE. I never thought of that before.

CAPTAIN SHOTOVER. If youre marrying for business, you cant be too businesslike.

ELLIE. Why do women always want other women's husbands?

CAPTAIN SHOTOVER. Why do horse-thieves prefer a horse that is broken-in to one that is wild?

ELLIE [*With a short laugh*]. I suppose so. What a vile world it is!

CAPTAIN SHOTOVER. It doesnt concern me. I'm nearly out of it.

ELLIE. And I'm only just beginning.

CAPTAIN SHOTOVER. Yes: so look ahead.

ELLIE. Well, I think I am being very prudent.

CAPTAIN SHOTOVER. I didnt say prudent. I said look ahead.

ELLIE. Whats the difference?

CAPTAIN SHOTOVER. It's prudent to gain the whole world and lose your own soul. But dont forget that your soul sticks to you if you stick to it; but the world has a way of slipping through your fingers.

ELLIE [*Wearily, leaving him and beginning to wander restlessly about the room*]. I'm sorry, Captain Shotover; but it's no use talking like that to me. Old-fashioned people are no use to me. Old-fashioned people think you can have a soul without money. They think the less money you have, the more soul you have. Young people nowadays know better. A soul is a very expensive thing to keep: much more so than a motor car.

CAPTAIN SHOTOVER. Is it? How much does your soul eat?

ELLIE. Oh, a lot. It eats music and pictures and books and mountains and lakes and beautiful things to wear and nice people to be with. In this country you cant have them without lots of money: that is why our souls are so horribly starved.

CAPTAIN SHOTOVER. Mangan's soul lives on pigs' food.

ELLIE. Yes: money is thrown away on him. I suppose his soul was starved when he was young. But it will not be thrown away on me. It is just because I want to save my soul that I am marrying for money. All the women who are not fools do.

CAPTAIN SHOTOVER. There are other ways of getting money. Why dont you steal it?

ELLIE. Because I dont want to go to prison.

CAPTAIN SHOTOVER. Is that the only reason? Are you quite sure honesty has nothing to do with it?

ELLIE. Oh, you are very very old-fashioned, Captain. Does any modern girl believe that the legal and illegal ways of getting money are the honest and dishonest ways? Mangan robbed my father and my father's friends. I should rob all the money back from Mangan if the police would let me. As they wont, I must get it back by marrying him.

CAPTAIN SHOTOVER. I cant argue: I'm too old: my mind is made up and finished. All I can tell you is that, old-fashioned or new-fashioned, if you sell yourself, you deal your soul a blow that all the books and pictures and concerts and scenery in the world wont heal. [*He gets up suddenly and makes for the pantry*]

ELLIE [*Running after him and seizing him by the sleeve*]. Then why did you sell yourself to the devil in Zanzibar?

CAPTAIN SHOTOVER [*Stopping, startled*]. What?

ELLIE. You shall not run away before you answer. I have found out that trick of yours. If you sold yourself, why shouldn't I?

175

CAPTAIN SHOTOVER. I had to deal with men so degraded that they wouldnt obey me unless I swore at them and kicked them and beat them with my fists. Foolish people took young thieves off the streets; flung them into a training ship where they were taught to fear the cane instead of fearing God; and thought theyd made men and sailors of them by private subscription. I tricked these thieves into believing I'd sold myself to the devil. It saved my soul from the kicking and swearing that was damning me by inches.

ELLIE [*Releasing him*]. I shall pretend to sell myself to Boss Mangan to save my soul from the poverty that is damning me by inches.

CAPTAIN SHOTOVER. Riches will damn you ten times deeper. Riches wont save even your body.

ELLIE. Old-fashioned again. We know now that the soul is the body, and the body the soul. They tell us they are different because they want to persuade us that we can keep our souls if we let them make slaves of our bodies. I am afraid you are no use to me, Captain.

CAPTAIN SHOTOVER. What did you expect? A Savior, eh? Are you old-fashioned enough to believe in that?

ELLIE. No. But I thought you were very wise, and might help me. Now I have found you out. You pretend to be busy, and think of fine things to say, and run in and out to surprise people by saying them, and get away before they can answer you.

CAPTAIN SHOTOVER. It confuses me to be answered. It discourages me. I cannot bear men and women. I have to run away. I must run away now. [*He tries to*]

ELLIE [*Again seizing his arm*]. You shall not run away from me. I can hypnotize you. You are the only person in the house I can say what I like to. I know you are fond of me. Sit down. [*She draws him to the sofa*]

CAPTAIN SHOTOVER [*Yielding*]. Take care: I am in my dotage. Old men are dangerous: it doesnt matter to them what is going to happen to the world.

[*They sit side by side on the sofa. She leans affectionately against him with her head on his shoulder and her eyes half closed*]

ELLIE [*Dreamily*]. I should have thought nothing else mattered to old men. They cant be very interested in what is going to happen to themselves.

CAPTAIN SHOTOVER. A man's interest in the world is only the overflow from his interest in himself. When you are a child your vessel is not yet full; so you care for nothing but your own affairs. When you grow up, your vessel overflows; and you are a politician, a philosopher, or an explorer adventurer. In old age the vessel dries up: there is no overflow: you are a child

again. I can give you the memories of my ancient wisdom: mere scraps and leavings; but I no longer really care for anything but my own little wants and hobbies. I sit here working out my old ideas as a means of destroying my fellow-creatures. I see my daughters and their men living foolish lives of romance and sentiment and snobbery. I see you, the younger generation, turning from their romance and sentiment and snobbery to money and comfort and hard common sense. I was ten times happier on the bridge in the typhoon, or frozen into Arctic ice for months in darkness, than you or they have ever been. You are looking for a rich husband. At your age I looked for hardship, danger, horror, and death, that I might feel the life in me more intensely. I did not let the fear of death govern my life; and my reward was, I had my life. You are going to let the fear of poverty govern your life; and your reward will be that you will eat, but you will not live.

ELLIE [*Sitting up impatiently*]. But what can I do? I am not a sea captain: I cant stand on bridges in typhoons, or go slaughtering seals and whales in Greenland's icy mountains. They wont let women be captains. Do you want me to be a stewardess?

CAPTAIN SHOTOVER. There are worse lives. The stewardesses could come ashore if they liked; but they sail and sail and sail.

ELLIE. What could they do ashore but marry for money? I dont want to be a stewardess: I am too bad a sailor. Think of something else for me.

CAPTAIN SHOTOVER. I cant think so long and continuously. I am too old. I must go in and out. [*He tries to rise*]

ELLIE [*Pulling him back*]. You shall not. You are happy here, arnt you?

CAPTAIN SHOTOVER. I tell you it's dangerous to keep me. I cant keep awake and alert.

ELLIE. What do you run away for? To sleep?

CAPTAIN SHOTOVER. No. To get a glass or rum.

ELLIE [*Frightfully disillusioned*]. Is that it? How disgusting! Do you like being drunk?

CAPTAIN SHOTOVER. No: I dread being drunk more than anything in the world. To be drunk means to have dreams; to go soft; to be easily pleased and deceived; to fall into the clutches of women. Drink does that for you when you are young. But when you are old: very very old, like me, the dreams come by themselves. You dont know how terrible that is: you are young: you sleep at night only, and sleep soundly. But later on you will sleep in the afternoon. Later still you will sleep even in the morning; and you will awake tired, tired of life. You will never be free from dozing and dreams; the dreams will steal upon your work every ten minutes unless you can awaken yourself with rum. I drink now to keep sober; but the dreams are conquering: rum is not what it was: I have had ten glasses since you came; and it might be so much water. Go get me another: Guinness knows where it is. You had better see for yourself the horror of an old man drinking.

ELLIE. You shall not drink. Dream. I like you to dream. You must never be in the real world when we talk together.

CAPTAIN SHOTOVER. I am too weary to resist or too weak. I am in my second childhood. I do not see you as you really are. I cant remember what I really am. I feel nothing but the accursed happiness I have dreaded all my life long: the happiness that comes as life goes, the happiness of yielding and dreaming instead of resisting and doing, the sweetness of the fruit that is going rotten.

ELLIE. You dread it almost as much as I used to dread losing my dreams and having to fight and do things. But that is all over for me: my dreams are dashed to pieces. I should like to marry a very old, very rich man. I should like to marry you. I had much rather marry you than marry Mangan. Are you very rich?

CAPTAIN SHOTOVER. No. Living from hand to mouth. And I have a wife somewhere in Jamaica: a black one. My first wife. Unless she's dead.

ELLIE. What a pity! I feel so happy with you. [*She takes his hand, almost unconsciously, and pats it*] I thought I should never feel happy again.

CAPTAIN SHOTOVER. Why?

ELLIE. Dont you know?

CAPTAIN SHOTOVER. No.

ELLIE. Heartbreak. I fell in love with Hector, and didn't know he was married.

CAPTAIN SHOTOVER. Heartbreak? Are you one of those who are so sufficient to themselves that they are only happy when they are stripped of everything, even of hope?

ELLIE [*Gripping the hand*]. It seems so; for I feel now as if there was nothing I could not do, because I want nothing.

CAPTAIN SHOTOVER. Thats the only real strength. Thats genius. Thats better than rum.

ELLIE [*Throwing away his hand*]. Rum! Why did you spoil it?

[*Hector and Randall come in from the garden through the starboard door*]

HECTOR. I beg your pardon. We did not know there was anyone here.

ELLIE [*Rising*]. That means that you want to tell Mr Randall the story about the tiger. Come, Captain: I want to talk to my father; and you had better come with me.

CAPTAIN SHOTOVER [*Rising*]. Nonsense! the man is in bed.

ELLIE. Aha! I've caught you. My real father has gone to bed; but the father you gave me is in the kitchen. You knew quite well all along. Come. [*She draws him out into the garden with her through the port door*]

HECTOR. Thats an extraordinary girl. She has the Ancient Mariner on a string like a Pekinese dog.

RANDALL. Now that they have gone, shall we have a friendly chat?

HECTOR. You are in what is supposed to be my house. I am at your disposal.

[*Hector sits down in the draughtsman's chair, turning it to face Randall, who remains standing, leaning at his ease against the carpenter's bench*]

RANDALL. I take it that we may be quite frank. I mean about Lady Utterword.

HECTOR. You may. I have nothing to be frank about. I never met her until this afternoon.

RANDALL [*Straightening up*]. What! But you are her sister's husband.

HECTOR. Well, if you come to that, you are her husband's brother.

RANDALL. But you seem to be on intimate terms with her.

HECTOR. So do you.

RANDALL. Yes; but I am on intimate terms with her. I have known her for years.

HECTOR. It took her years to get to the same point with you that she got to with me in five minutes, it seems.

RANDALL [*Vexed*]. Really, Ariadne is the limit. [*He moves away huffishly towards the windows*]

HECTOR [*Coolly*]. She is, as I remarked to Hesione, a very enterprising woman.

RANDALL [*Returning, much troubled*]. You see, Hushabye, you are what women consider a good-looking man.

HECTOR. I cultivated that appearance in the days of my vanity; and Hesione insists on my keeping it up. She makes me wear these ridiculous things [*Indicating his Arab costume*] because she thinks me absurd in evening dress.

RANDALL. Still, you do keep it up, old chap. Now, I assure you I have not an atom of jealousy in my disposition—

HECTOR. The question would seem to be rather whether your brother has any touch of that sort.

RANDALL. What! Hastings! Oh, dont trouble about Hastings. He has the gift of being able to work sixteen hours a day at the dullest detail, and actually likes it. That gets him to the top wherever he goes. As long as Ariadne takes care that he is fed regularly, he is only too thankful to anyone who will keep her in good humor for him.

HECTOR. And as she has all the Shotover fascination, there is plenty of competition for the job, eh?

RANDALL [*Angrily*]. She encourages them. Her conduct is perfectly scandalous. I assure you, my dear fellow, I havnt an atom of jealousy in my composition; but she makes herself the talk of every place she goes to by her thoughtlessness. It's nothing more; she doesnt really care for the men she keeps hanging about her; but how is the world to know that? It's not fair to Hastings. It's not fair to me.

HECTOR. Her theory is that her conduct is so correct—

RANDALL. Correct! She does nothing but make scenes from morning til night. You be careful, old chap. She will get you into trouble: that is she would if she really cared for you.

HECTOR. Doesn't she?

RANDALL. Not a scrap. She may want your scalp to add to her collection; but her true affection has been engaged years ago. You had really better be careful.

HECTOR. Do you suffer much from this jealousy?

RANDALL. Jealousy! I jealous! My dear fellow, havnt I told you that there is not an atom of—

HECTOR. Yes. And Lady Utterword told me she never made scenes. Well, dont waste your jealousy on my moustache. Never waste jealousy on a real man: it is the imaginary hero that supplants us all in the long run. Besides, jealousy does not belong to your easy man-of-the-world pose, which you carry so well in other respects.

RANDALL. Really, Hushabye, I think a man may be allowed to be a gentleman without being accused of posing.

HECTOR. It is a pose like any other. In this house we know all the poses: our game is to find out the man under the pose. The man under your pose is apparently Ellie's favorite, Othello.

RANDALL. Some of the games in this house are damned annoying, let me tell you.

HECTOR. Yes: I have been their victim for many years. I used to writhe under them at first; but I became accustomed to them. At last I learned to play them.

RANDALL. If it's all the same to you, I had rather you didnt play them on me. You evidently dont quite understand my character, or my notions of good form.

HECTOR. Is it your notion of good form to give away Lady Utterword?

RANDALL [*A childishly plaintive note breaking into his huff*]. I have not said a word against Lady Utterword. This is just the conspiracy over again.

HECTOR. What conspiracy?

RANDALL. You know very well, sir. A conspiracy to make me out to be pettish and jealous and childish and everything I am not. Everyone knows I am just the opposite.

HECTOR [*Rising*]. Something in the air of the house has upset you. It often does have that effect. [*He goes to the garden door and calls Lady Utterword with commanding emphasis*] Ariadne!

LADY UTTERWORD [*At some distance*]. Yes.

RANDALL. What are you calling her for? I want to speak—

LADY UTTERWORD [*Arriving breathless*]. Yes. You really are a terribly commanding person. Whats the matter?

HECTOR. I do not know how to manage your friend Randall. No doubt you do.

LADY UTTERWORD. Randall: have you been making yourself ridiculous, as usual? I can see it in your face. Really, you are the most pettish creature.

RANDALL. You know quite well, Ariadne, that I have not an ounce of pettishness in my disposition. I have made myself perfectly pleasant here. I have remained absolutely cool and imperturbable in the face of a burglar. Imperturbability is almost too strong a point of mine. But [*Putting his foot down with a stamp, and walking angrily up and down the room*] I insist on being treated with a certain consideration. I will not allow Hushabye to take liberties with me. I will not stand your encouraging people as you do.

HECTOR. The man has a rooted delusion that he is your husband.

LADY UTTERWORD. I know. He is jealous. As if he had any right to be! He compromises me everywhere. He makes scenes all over the place. Randall: I will not allow it. I simply will not allow it. You had no right to discuss me with Hector. I will not be discussed by men.

HECTOR. Be reasonable, Ariadne. Your fatal gift of beauty forces men to discuss you.

LADY UTTERWORD. Oh indeed! what about your fatal gift of beauty?

HECTOR. How can I help it?

LADY UTTERWORD. You could cut off your moustache: I cant cut off my nose. I get my whole life messed up with people falling in love with me. And then Randall says I run after men.

RANDALL. I—

LADY UTTERWORD. Yes you do: you said it just now. Why cant you think of something else than women? Napoleon was quite right when he said that women are the occupation of the idle man. Well, if ever there was an idle man on earth, his name is Randall Utterword.

RANDALL. Ariad—

LADY UTTERWORD [*Overwhelming him with a torrent of words*]. Oh yes you are: it's no use denying it. What have you ever done? What good are you? You are as much trouble in the house as a child of three. You couldnt live without your valet.

RANDALL. That is—

LADY UTTERWORD. Laziness! You are laziness incarnate. You are selfishness itself. You are the most uninteresting man on earth. You cant even gossip about anything but yourself and your grievances and your ailments and the people who have offended you. [*Turning to Hector*] Do you know what they call him, Hector?

HECTOR. ⎰ *speaking* ⎱ Please dont tell me.
RANDALL. ⎰ *together* ⎱ I'll not stand it—

LADY UTTERWORD. Randall the Rotter: that is his name in good society.

RANDALL [*Shouting*]. I'll not bear it, I tell you. Will you listen to me, you infernal—[*He chokes*]

LADY UTTERWORD. Well: go on. What were you going to call me? An infernal what? Which unpleasant animal is it to be this time?

RANDALL [*Foaming*]. There is no animal in the world so hateful as a woman can be. You are a maddening devil. Hushabye: you will not believe me when I tell you that I have loved this demon all my life; but God knows I have paid for it. [*He sits down in the draughtsman's chair, weeping*]

LADY UTTERWORD [*Standing over him with triumphant contempt*]. Cry-baby!

HECTOR [*Gravely, coming to him*]. My friend: the Shotover sisters have two strange powers over men. They can make them love; and they can make them cry. Thank your stars that you are not married to one of them.

LADY UTTERWORD [*Haughtily*]. And pray, Hector—

HECTOR [*Suddenly catching her round the shoulders; swinging her right around him and away from Randall; and gripping her throat with the other hand*]. Ariadne: If you attempt to start on me, I'll choke you: do you hear? The cat-and-mouse game with the other sex is a good game; but I can play your head off at it. [*He throws her, not at all gently, into the big chair, and proceeds, less fiercely but firmly*] It is true that Napoleon said that woman is the occupation of the idle man. But he added that she is the relaxation of the warrior. Well, I am the warrior. So take care.

LADY UTTERWORD [*Not in the least put out, and rather pleased by his violence*]. My dear Hector: I have only done what you asked me to do.

HECTOR. How do you make that out, pray?

LADY UTTERWORD. You called me in to manage Randall, didnt you? You said you couldnt manage him yourself.

HECTOR. Well, what if I did? I did not ask you to drive the man mad.

LADY UTTERWORD. He isnt mad. Thats the way to manage him. If you were a mother, youd understand.

HECTOR. Mother! What are you up to now?

LADY UTTERWORD. It's quite simple. When the children got nerves and were naughty, I smacked them just enough to give them a good cry and a healthy nervous shock. They went to sleep and were quite good afterwards. Well, I cant smack Randall: he is too big; so when he gets nerves and is naughty, I just rag him till he cries. He will be all right now. Look: he is half asleep already. [*Which is quite true*]

RANDALL [*Waking up indignantly*]. I'm not. You are most cruel, Ariadne. [*Sentimentally*] But I suppose I must forgive you as usual. [*He checks himself in the act of yawning*]

LADY UTTERWORD [*To Hector*]. Is the explanation satisfactory, dread warrior?

HECTOR. Some day I shall kill you, if you go too far. I thought you were a fool.

LADY UTTERWORD [*Laughing*]. Everybody does, at first. But I am not such a fool as I look. [*She rises complacently*] Now, Randall: go to bed. You will be a good boy in the morning.

RANDALL [*Only very faintly rebellious*]. I'll go to bed when I like. It isnt ten yet.

LADY UTTERWORD. It is long past ten. See that he goes to bed at once, Hector. [*She goes into the garden*]

HECTOR. Is there any slavery on earth viler than this slavery of men to women?

RANDALL [*Rising resolutely*]. I'll not speak to her tomorrow. I'll not speak to her for another week. I'll give her such a lesson. I'll go straight to bed without bidding her goodnight. [*He makes for the door leading to the hall*]

HECTOR. You are under a spell, man. Old Shotover sold himself to the devil in Zanzibar. The devil gave him a black witch for a wife; and these two demon daughters are their mystical progeny. I am tied to Hesione's apron-string; but I'm her husband; and if I did go stark staring mad about her, at least we became man and wife. But why should you let yourself be dragged about and beaten by Ariadne as a toy donkey is dragged about and beaten by a child? What do you get by it? Are you her lover?

RANDALL. You must not misunderstand me. In a higher sense—in a Platonic sense—

HECTOR. Psha! Platonic sense! She makes you her servant; and when pay-day comes around, she bilks you: that is what you mean.

RANDALL [*Feebly*]. Well, if I dont mind, I dont see what business it is of yours. Besides, I tell you I am going to punish her. You shall see: *I* know how to deal with women. I'm really very sleepy. Say goodnight to Mrs Hushabye for me, will you, like a good chap. Goodnight. [*He hurries out*]

HECTOR. Poor wretch! Oh women! women! women! [*He lists his fists in invocation to heaven*] Fall. Fall and crush. [*He goes out into the garden*]

ACT III

In the garden, Hector, as he comes out through the glass door of the poop, finds Lady Utterword lying voluptuously in the hammock on the east side of the flagstaff, in the circle of light cast by the electric arc, which is like a moon in its opal globe. Beneath the head of the hammock, a capstool. On the other side of the flagstaff, on the long garden seat, Captain Shotover is asleep, with Ellie beside him, leaning affectionately against him on his right hand. On his left is a deck chair. Behind them in the gloom, Hesione is strolling about with Mangan. It is a fine still night, moonless.

LADY UTTERWORD. What a lovely night! It seems made for us.

HECTOR. The night takes no interest in us. What are we to the night? [*He sits down moodily in the deck chair*]

ELLIE [*Dreamily, nestling against the Captain*]. Its beauty soaks into my nerves. In the night there is peace for the old and hope for the young.

HECTOR. Is that remark your own?

ELLIE. No. Only the last thing the Captain said before he went to sleep.

CAPTAIN SHOTOVER. I'm not asleep.

HECTOR. Randall is. Also Mr Mazzini Dunn. Mangan too, probably.

MANGAN. No

HECTOR. Oh, you are there. I thought Hesione would have sent you to bed by this time.

MRS HUSHABYE [*Coming to the back of the garden seat, into the light, with Mangan*]. I think I shall. He keeps telling me he has a presentiment that he is going to die. I never met a man so greedy for sympathy.

MANGAN [*Plaintively*]. But I have a presentiment. I really have. And you wouldnt listen.

MRS HUSHABYE. I was listening for something else. There was a sort of splendid drumming in the sky. Did none of you hear it? It came from a distance and then died away.

MANGAN. I tell you it was a train.

MRS HUSHABYE. And *I* tell you, Alf, there is no train at this hour. The last is nine fortyfive.

MANGAN. But a goods train.

MRS HUSHABYE. Not on our little line. They tack a truck on to the passenger train. What can it have been, Hector?

HECTOR. Heaven's threatening growl of disgust at us useless futile creatures. [*Fiercely*] I tell you, one of two things must happen. Either out of that darkness some new creation will come to supplant us as we have supplanted the animals, or the heavens will fall in thunder and destroy us.

LADY UTTERWORD [*In a cool instructive manner, wallowing comfortably in her hammock*]. We have not supplanted the animals, Hector. Why do you ask heaven to destroy this house, which could be made quite comfortable if Hesione had any notion of how to live? Dont you know what is wrong with it?

HECTOR. We are wrong with it. There is no sense in us. We are useless, dangerous, and ought to be abolished.

LADY UTTERWORD. Nonsense! Hastings told me the very first day he came here, nearly twentyfour years ago, what is wrong with the house.

CAPTAIN SHOTOVER. What! The numskull said there was something wrong with my house!

LADY UTTERWORD. I said Hastings said it; and he is not in the least a numskull.

CAPTAIN SHOTOVER. Whats wrong with my house?

LADY UTTERWORD. Just what is wrong with a ship, papa. Wasnt it clever of Hastings to see that?

CAPTAIN SHOTOVER. The man's a fool. Theres nothing wrong with a ship.

LADY UTTERWORD. Yes there is.

MRS HUSHABYE. But what is it? Dont be aggravating, Addy.

LADY UTTERWORD. Guess.

HECTOR. Demons. Daughters of the witch of Zanzibar. Demons.

LADY UTTERWORD. Not a bit. I assure you, all this house needs to make it a sensible, healthy, pleasant house, with good appetites and sound sleep in it, is horses.

MRS HUSHABYE. Horses! What rubbish!

LADY UTTERWORD. Yes: horses. Why have we never been able to let this house? Because there are no proper stables. Go anywhere in England where there are natural, wholesome, contented, and really nice English people; and what do you always find? That the stables are the real centre of the household; and that if any visitor wants to play the piano the whole room has to be upset before it can be opened, there are so many things piled on it. I never lived until I learned to ride; and I shall never ride really well because I didnt begin as a child. There are only two classes in good society in England: the equestrian classes and the neurotic classes. It isnt mere convention: everybody can see that the people who hunt are the right people and the people who dont are the wrong ones.

CAPTAIN SHOTOVER. There is some truth in this. My ship made a man of me; and a ship is the horse of the sea.

LADY UTTERWORD. Exactly how Hastings explained your being a gentleman.

CAPTAIN SHOTOVER. Not bad for a numskull. Bring the man here with you next time: I must talk to him.

LADY UTTERWORD. Why is Randall such an obvious rotter? He is well bred; he has been at a public school and a university; he has been in the Foreign Office; he knows the best people and has lived all his life among them. Why is he so unsatisfactory, so contemptible? Why cant he get a valet to stay with him longer than a few months? Just because he is too lazy and pleasure-loving to hunt and shoot. He strums the piano, and sketches, and runs after married women, and reads literary books and poems. He actually plays the flute; but I never let him bring it into my house. If he would only—[*She is interrupted by the melancholy strains of a flute coming from an open window above. She raises herself indignantly in the hammock*] Randall: You have not gone to bed. Have you been listening? [*The flute replies pertly:*]

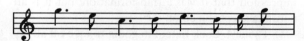

How vulgar! Go to bed instantly, Randall: how dare you? [*The window is slammed down. She subsides*] How can anyone care for such a creature!

MRS HUSHABYE. Addy: do you think Ellie ought to marry poor Alfred merely for his money?

MANGAN [*Much alarmed*]. Whats that? Mrs Hushabye: are my affairs to be discussed like this before everybody?

LADY UTTERWORD. I dont think Randall is listening now.

MANGAN. Everybody is listening. It isnt right.

MRS HUSHABYE. But in the dark, what does it matter? Ellie doesnt mind. Do you Ellie?

ELLIE. Not in the least. What is your opinion, Lady Utterword? You have so much good sense.

MANGAN. But it isnt right. It—[*Mrs Hushabye puts her hand on his mouth*] Oh, very well.

LADY UTTERWORD. How much money have you, Mr Mangan?

MANGAN. Really—No: I cant stand this.

LADY UTTERWORD. Nonsense, Mr Mangan! It all turns on your income, doesn't it?

MANGAN. Well, if you come to that, how much money has she?

ELLIE. None.

LADY UTTERWORD. You are answered, Mr Mangan. And now, as you have made Miss Dunn throw her cards on the table, you cannot refuse to shew your own.

MRS HUSHABYE. Come, Alf! out with it! How much?

MANGAN [*Baited out of all prudence*]. Well, if you want to know, I have no money and never had any.

MRS HUSHABYE. Alfred: you mustnt tell naughty stories.

MANGAN. I'm not telling you stories, I'm telling you the raw truth.

LADY UTTERWORD. Then what do you live on, Mr Mangan?

MANGAN. Travelling expenses. And a trifle of commission.

CAPTAIN SHOTOVER. What more have any of us but travelling expenses for our life's journey?

MRS HUSHABYE. But you have factories and capital and things?

MANGAN. People think I have. People think I'm an industrial Napoleon. Thats why Miss Ellie wants to marry me. But I tell you I have nothing.

ELLIE. Do you mean that the factories are like Marcus's tigers? That they dont exist?

MANGAN. They exist all right enough. But theyre not mine. They belong to syndicates and shareholders and all sorts of lazy good-for-nothing capitalists. I get money from such people to start the factories. I find people like Miss Dunn's father to work them, and keep a tight hand so as to make them pay. Of course I make them keep me going pretty well; but it's a dog's life; and I dont own anything.

MRS HUSHABYE. Alfred, Alfred: you are making a poor mouth of it to get out of marrying Ellie.

MANGAN. I'm telling the truth about my money for the first time in my life; and it's the first time my word has ever been doubted.

LADY UTTERWORD. How sad! Why dont you go in for politics, Mr Mangan?

MANGAN. Go in for politics! Where have you been living? I am in politics.

LADY UTTERWORD. I'm sure I beg your pardon. I never heard of you.

MANGAN. Let me tell you, Lady Utterword, that the Prime Minister of this country asked me to join the Government without even going through the nonsense of an election, as the dictator of a great public department.

LADY UTTERWORD. As a Conservative or a Liberal?

MANGAN. No such nonsense. As a practical business man. [*They all burst out laughing*] What are you all laughing at?

MRS HUSHABYE. Oh Alfred, Alfred!

ELLIE. You! who have to get my father to do everything for you?

MRS HUSHABYE. You! who are afraid of your own workmen!

HECTOR. You! with whom three women have been playing cat and mouse all the evening!

LADY UTTERWORD. You must have given an immense sum to the party funds, Mr Mangan.

MANGAN. Not a penny out of my own pocket. The syndicate found the money: they knew how useful I should be to them in the Government.

LADY UTTERWORD. This is most interesting and unexpected, Mr Mangan. And what have your administrative achievements been, so far?

MANGAN. Achievements? Well, I dont know what you call achievements; but Ive jolly well put a stop to the games of the other fellows in the other departments. Every man of them thought he was going to save the country all by himself, and do me out of the credit and out of my chance of a title. I took good care that if they wouldnt let me do it they shouldnt do it themselves either. I may not know anything about my own machinery; but I know how to stick a ramrod into the other fellow's. And now they all look the biggest fools going.

HECTOR. And in heaven's name, what do you look like?

MANGAN. I look like the fellow that was too clever for all the others, dont I? If that isnt a triumph of practical business, what is?

HECTOR. Is this England, or is it a madhouse?

LADY UTTERWORD. Do you expect to save the country, Mr Mangan?

MANGAN. Well, who else will? Will your Mr Randall save it?

LADY UTTERWORD. Randall the Rotter! Certainly not.

MANGAN. Will your brother-in-law save it with his moustache and his fine talk?

HECTOR. Yes, if they will let me.

MANGAN [Sneering]. Ah! Will they let you?

HECTOR. No. They prefer you.

MANGAN. Very well then, as youre in a world where I'm appreciated and youre not, youd best be civil to me, hadnt you? Who else is there but me?

LADY UTTERWORD. There is Hastings. Get rid of your ridiculous sham democracy; and give Hastings the necessary powers, and a good supply of bamboo to bring the British native to his senses: he will save the country with the greatest ease.

CAPTAIN SHOTOVER. It had better be lost. Any fool can govern with a stick in his hand. I could govern that way. It is not God's way. The man is a numskull.

LADY UTTERWORD. The man is worth all of you rolled into one. What do you say, Miss Dunn?

ELLIE. I think my father would do very well if people did not put upon him and cheat him and despise him because he is so good.

MANGAN [Contemptuously]. I think I see Mazzini Dunn getting into parliament or pushing his way into the Government. Weve not come to that yet, thank God! What do you say, Mrs Hushabye?

MRS HUSHABYE. Oh, I say it matters very little which of you governs the country so long as we govern you.

HECTOR. We? Who is we, pray?

MRS HUSHABYE. The devil's granddaughters, dear. The lovely women.

HECTOR [Raising his hands as before]. Fall, I say; and deliver us from the lures of Satan!

ELLIE. There seems to be nothing real in the world except my father and Shakespear. Marcus's tigers are false; Mr Mangan's millions are false; there is nothing really strong and true about Hesione but her beautiful black hair; and Lady Utterword's is too pretty to be real. The one thing that was left to me was the Captain's seventh degree of concentration; and that turns out to be—

CAPTAIN SHOTOVER. Rum.

LADY UTTERWORD [Placidly]. A good deal of my hair is quite genuine. The Duchess of Dithering offered me fifty guineas for this [Touching her forehead] under the impression that it was a transformation; but it is all natural except the color.

MANGAN [Wildly]. Look here: I'm going to take off all my clothes. [He begins tearing off his coat]

LADY UTTERWORD. ⎫   ⎧ Mr Mangan!
CAPTAIN SHOTOVER. ⎬ [In   ⎨ Whats that?
HECTOR. ⎪ conster-   ⎪ Ha! Ha! Do. Do.
ELLIE. ⎭ nation]   ⎩ Please dont.

MRS HUSHABYE [Catching his arm and stopping him]. Alfred: for shame! Are you mad?

MANGAN. Shame! What shame is there in this house? Let's all strip stark naked. We may as well do the thing thoroughly when we're about it. Weve stripped ourselves morally naked; well, let us strip ourselves physically naked as well, and see how we like it. I tell you I cant bear this. I was brought up to be respectable. I dont mind the women dyeing their hair and the men drinking: it's human nature. But it's not human nature to tell everybody about it. Every time one of you opens your mouth I go like this [He cowers as if to avoid a missile] afraid of what will come next. How are we to have any self-respect if we dont keep it up that we're better than we really are?

LADY UTTERWORD. I quite sympathize with you, Mr Mangan. I have been through it all; and I know by experience that men and women are delicate plants and must be cultivated under glass. Our family habit of throwing stones in all directions and letting the air in is not only unbearably rude, but positively dangerous. Still, there is no use catching physical colds as well as moral ones; so please keep your clothes on.

MANGAN. I'll do as I like: not what you tell me. Am I a child or a grown man? I wont stand this mothering tyranny. I'll go back to the city, where I'm respected and made much of.

MRS HUSHABYE. Goodbye, Alf. Think of us sometimes in the city. Think of Ellie's youth!

ELLIE. Think of Hesione's eyes and hair!

CAPTAIN SHOTOVER. Think of this garden in which you are not a dog barking to keep the truth out!

HECTOR. Think of Lady Utterword's beauty! her good sense! her style!

LADY UTTERWORD. Flatterer. Think, Mr Mangan, whether you can really do any better for yourself elsewhere: that is the essential point, isnt it?

MANGAN [Surrendering]. All right: all right. I'm done. Have it your own way. Only let me alone. I dont know whether I'm on my head or my heels when you all start on me like this. I'll stay. I'll marry her. I'll do anything for a quiet life. Are you satisfied now?

ELLIE. No. I never really intended to make you marry me, Mr Mangan. Never in the depths of my soul. I only wanted to feel my strength: to know that you could not escape if I chose to take you.

MANGAN [Indignantly]. What! Do you mean to say you are going to throw me over after my acting so handsome?

LADY UTTERWORD. I should not be too hasty, Miss Dunn. You can throw Mr Mangan over at any time up to the last moment. Very few men in his position go bankrupt. You can live very comfortably on his reputation for immense wealth.

ELLIE. I cannot commit bigamy, Lady Utterword.

MRS HUSHABYE.		Bigamy! Whatever on earth are you talking about, Ellie?
LADY UTTERWORD.	[Exclaiming all together]	Bigamy! What do you mean, Miss Dunn?
MANGAN.		Bigamy! Do you mean to say youre married already?
HECTOR.		Bigamy! This is some enigma.

ELLIE. Only half an hour ago I became Captain Shotover's white wife.

MRS HUSHABYE. Ellie! What nonsense! Where?

ELLIE. In heaven, where all true marriages are made.

LADY UTTERWORD. Really, Miss Dunn! Really, papa!

MANGAN. He told me I was too old! And him a mummy!

HECTOR [Quoting Shelley].
    Their altar the grassy earth outspread,
    And their priest the muttering wind.

ELLIE. Yes: I, Ellie Dunn, give my broken heart and my strong sound soul to its natural captain, my spiritual husband and second father.

[She draws the Captain's arm through hers, and pats his hand. The Captain remains fast asleep]

MRS HUSHABYE. Oh, thats very clever of you, pettikins. Very clever. Alfred: you could never have lived up to Ellie. You must be content with a little share of me.

MANGAN [Sniffing and wiping his eyes]. It isnt kind—[His emotion chokes him]

LADY UTTERWORD. You are well out of it, Mr Mangan. Miss Dunn is the most conceited young woman I have met since I came back to England.

MRS HUSHABYE. Oh, Ellie isnt conceited. Are you, pettikins?

ELLIE. I know my strength now, Hesione.

MANGAN. Brazen, I call you. Brazen.

MRS HUSHABYE. Tut tut, Alfred: dont be rude. Dont you feel how lovely this marriage night is, made in heaven? Arnt you happy, you and Hector? Open your eyes: Addy and Ellie look beautiful enough to please the most fastidious man: we live and love and have not a care in the world. We women have managed all that for you. Why in the name of common sense do you go on as if you were two miserable wretches?

CAPTAIN SHOTOVER. I tell you happiness is no good. You can be happy when you are only half alive. I am happier now I am half dead than ever I was in my prime. But there is no blessing on my happiness.

ELLIE [Her face lighting up]. Life with a blessing! that is what I want. Now I know the real reason why I couldnt marry Mr Mangan: there would be no blessing on our marriage. There is a blessing on my broken heart. There is a blessing on your beauty, Hesione. There is a blessing on your father's spirit. Even on the lies of Marcus there is a blessing; but on Mr Mangan's money there is none.

MANGAN. I dont understand a word of that.

ELLIE. Neither do I. But I know it means something.

MANGAN. Dont say there was any difficulty about the blessing. I was ready to get a bishop to marry us.

MRS HUSHABYE. Isnt he a fool, pettikins?

HECTOR [*Fiercely*]. Do not scorn the man. We are all fools.

[*Mazzini, in pyjamas and a richly colored silk dressing-gown, comes from the house, on Lady Utterword's side*]

MRS HUSHABYE. Oh! here comes the only man who ever resisted me. Whats the matter, Mr Dunn? Is the house on fire?

MAZZINI. Oh no: nothing's the matter; but really it's impossible to go to sleep with such an interesting converstion going on under one's window, and on such a beautiful night too. I just had to come down and join you all. What has it all been about?

MRS HUSHABYE. Oh, wonderful things, soldier of freedom.

HECTOR. For example, Mangan, as a practical business man, has tried to undress himself and has failed ignominiously; whilst you, as an idealist, have succeeded brilliantly.

MAZZINI. I hope you dont mind my being like this, Mrs Hushabye. [*He sits down on the campstool*]

MRS HUSHABYE. On the contrary, I could wish you always like that.

LADY UTTERWORD. Your daughter's match is off, Mr Dunn. It seems that Mr Mangan, whom we all supposed to be a man of property, owns absolutely nothing.

MAZZINI. Well of course I knew that, Lady Utterword. But if people believe in him and are always giving him money, whereas they dont believe in me and never give me any, how can I ask poor Ellie to depend on what I can do for her?

MANGAN. Dont you run away with this idea that I have nothing. I—

HECTOR. Oh, dont explain. We understand. You have a couple of thousand pounds in exchequer bills, 50,000 shares worth tenpence a dozen, and half a dozen tabloids of cyanide of potassium to poison yourself with when you are found out. Thats the reality of your millions.

MAZZINI. Oh no, no, no. He is quite honest: the businesses are genuine and perfectly legal.

HECTOR [*Disgusted*]. Yah! Not even a great swindler!

MANGAN. So you think. But Ive been too many for some honest men for all that.

LADY UTTERWORD. There is no pleasing you, Mr Mangan. You are determined to be neither rich nor poor, honest nor dishonest.

MANGAN. There you go again. Ever since I came into this silly house I have been made to look like a fool, though I'm as good a man in this house as in the city.

ELLIE [*Musically*]. Yes: this silly house, this strangely happy house, this agonizing house, this house without foundations. I shall call it Heartbreak House.

MRS HUSHABYE. Stop, Ellie; or I shall howl like an animal.

MANGAN [*Breaks into a low sniveling*]. !!!

MRS HUSHABYE. There! You have set Alfred off.

ELLIE. I like him best when he is howling.

CAPTAIN SHOTOVER. Silence! [*Mangan subsides into silence*] I say, let the heart break in silence.

HECTOR. Do you accept that name for your house?

CAPTAIN SHOTOVER. It is not my house: it is only my kennel.

HECTOR. We have been too long here. We do not live in this house: we haunt it.

LADY UTTERWORD [*Heart torn*]. It is dreadful to think how you have been here all these years while I have gone round the world. I escaped young; but it has drawn me back. It wants to break my heart too. But it shant. I have left you and it behind. It was silly of me to come back. I felt sentimental about papa and Hesione and the old place. I felt them calling to me.

MAZZINI. But what a very natural and kindly and charming human feeling, Lady Utterword!

LADY UTTERWORD. So I thought, Mr Dunn. But I know now that it was only the last of my influenza. I found that I was not remembered and not wanted.

CAPTAIN SHOTOVER. You left because you did not want us. Was there no heartbreak in that for your father? You tore yourself up by the roots; and the ground healed up and brought forth fresh plants and forgot you. What right had you to come back and probe old wounds?

MRS HUSHABYE. You were a complete stranger to me at first, Addy; but now I feel as if you had never been away.

LADY UTTERWORD. Thank you, Hesione; but the influenza is quite cured. The place may be Heartbreak House to you, Miss Dunn, and to this gentleman from the city who seems to have so little self-control; but to me it is only a very ill-regulated and rather untidy villa without any stables.

HECTOR. Inhabited by—?

ELLIE. A crazy old sea captain and a young singer who adores him.

MRS HUSHABYE. A sluttish female, trying to stave off a double chin and an elderly spread, vainly wooing a born soldier of freedom.

MAZZINI. Oh, really, Mrs Hushabye—

MANGAN. A member of His Majesty's Government that everybody sets down as a nincompoop: dont forget him, Lady Utterword.

LADY UTTERWORD. And a very fascinating gentleman whose chief occupation is to be married to my sister.

HECTOR. All heartbroken imbeciles.

MAZZINI. Oh no. Surely, if I may say so, rather a favorable specimen of what is best in our English culture. You are very charming people, most advanced, unprejudiced, frank, humane, unconventional, democratic, free-thinking, and everything that is delightful to thoughtful people.

MRS HUSHABYE. You do us proud, Mazzini.

MAZZINI. I am not flattering, really. Where else could I feel perfectly at ease in my pyjamas? I sometimes dream that I am in very distinguished society, and suddenly I have nothing on but my pyjamas! Sometimes I havnt even pyjamas. And I always feel overwhelmed with confusion. But here, I dont mind in the least: it seems quite natural.

LADY UTTERWORD. An infallible sign that you are not now in really distinguished society, Mr Dunn. If you were in my house, you would feel embarrassed.

MAZZINI. I shall take particular care to keep out of your house, Lady Utterword.

LADY UTTERWORD. You will be quite wrong, Mr Dunn. I should make you very comfortable; and you would not have the trouble and anxiety of wondering whether you should wear your purple and gold or your green and crimson dressing-gown at dinner. You complicate life instead of simplifying it by doing these ridiculous things.

ELLIE. Your house is not Heartbreak House: is it, Lady Utterword?

HECTOR. Yet she breaks hearts, easy as her house is. That poor devil upstairs with his flute howls when she twists his heart, just as Mangan howls when my wife twists his.

LADY UTTERWORD. That is because Randall has nothing to do but have his heart broken. It is a change from having his head shampooed. Catch anyone breaking Hastings' heart!

CAPTAIN SHOTOVER. The numskull wins, after all.

LADY UTTERWORD. I shall go back to my numskull with the greatest satisfaction when I am tired of you all, clever as you are.

MANGAN [Huffily]. I never set up to be clever.

LADY UTTERWORD. I forgot you, Mr Mangan.

MANGAN. Well, I dont see that quite, either.

LADY UTTERWORD. You may not be clever, Mr Mangan; but you are successful.

MANGAN. But I dont want to be regarded merely as a successful man. I have an imagination like anyone else. I have a presentiment—

MRS HUSHABYE. Oh, you are impossible, Alfred. Here I am devoting myself to you; and you think of nothing but your ridiculous presentiment. You bore me. Come and talk poetry to me under the stars. [She drags him away into the darkness]

MANGAN [Tearfully, as he disappears]. Yes: it's all very well to make fun of me; but if you only knew—

HECTOR [Impatiently]. How is all this going to end?

MAZZINI. It wont end, Mr Hushabye. Life doesnt end: it goes on.

ELLIE. Oh, it cant go on for ever. I'm always expecting something. I dont know what it is; but life must come to a point sometime.

LADY UTTERWORD. The point for a young woman of your age is a baby.

HECTOR. Yes, but damn it, I have the same feeling; and I cant have a baby.

LADY UTTERWORD. By deputy, Hector.

HECTOR. But I have children. All that is over and done with for me: and yet I too feel that this cant last. We sit here talking, and leave everything to Mangan and to chance and to the devil. Think of the powers of destruction that Mangan and his mutual admiration gang wield! It's madness: it's like giving a torpedo to a badly brought up child to play at earthquakes with.

MAZZINI. I know. I used often to think about that when I was young.

HECTOR. Think! Whats the good of thinking about it? Why didnt you do something?

MAZZINI. But I did. I joined societies and made speeches and wrote pamphlets. That was all I could do. But, you know, though the people in the societies thought they knew more than Mangan, most of them wouldnt have joined if they had known as much. You see they had never had any money to handle or any men to manage. Every year I expected a revolution, or some frightful smash-up; it seemed impossible that we could blunder and muddle on any longer. But nothing happened, except, of course, the usual poverty and crime and drink that we are used to. Nothing ever does happen. It's amazing how well we get along, all things considered.

LADY UTTERWORD. Perhaps, somebody cleverer than you and Mr Mangan was at work all the time.

MAZZINI. Perhaps so. Though I was brought up not to believe in anything, I often feel that there is a great deal to be said for the theory of an over-ruling Providence, after all.

LADY UTTERWORD. Providence! I meant Hastings.

MAZZINI. Oh, I beg your pardon, Lady Utterword.

CAPTAIN SHOTOVER. Every drunken skipper trusts to Providence. But one of the ways of Providence with drunken skippers is to run them on the rocks.

MAZZINI. Very true, no doubt, at sea. But in politics, I assure you, they only run into jellyfish. Nothing happens.

CAPTAIN SHOTOVER. At sea nothing happens to the sea. Nothing happens to the sky. The sun comes up from the east and goes down to the west. The moon grows from a sickle to an arc lamp, and comes later and later until she is lost in the light as other things are lost in the darkness. After the typhoon, the flying-fish glitter in the sunshine like birds. It's amazing how they get along, all things considered. Nothing happens, except something not worth mentioning.

ELLIE. What is that, O Captain, my captain?

CAPTAIN SHOTOVER [*Savagely*]. Nothing but the smash of the drunken skipper's ship on the rocks, the splintering of her rotten timbers, the tearing of her rusty plates, the drowning of the crew like rats in a trap.

ELLIE. Moral: dont take rum.

CAPTAIN SHOTOVER [*Vehemently*]. That is a lie, child. Let a man drink ten barrels of rum a day, he is not a drunken skipper until he is a drifting skipper. Whilst he can lay his course and stand on his bridge and steer it, he is no drunkard. It is the man who lies drinking in his bunk and trusts to Providence that I call the drunken skipper, though he drank nothing but the waters of the River Jordan.

ELLIE. Splendid! And you havnt had a drop for an hour. You see you dont need it: your own spirit is not dead.

CAPTAIN SHOTOVER. Echoes: nothing but echoes. The last shot was fired years ago.

HECTOR. And this ship we are all in? This soul's prison we call England?

CAPTAIN SHOTOVER. The captain is in his bunk, drinking bottled ditch-water; and the crew is gambling in the forecastle. She will strike and sink and split. Do you think the laws of God will be suspended in favor of England because you were born in it?

HECTOR. Well, I dont mean to be drowned like a rat in a trap. I still have the will to live. What am I to do?

CAPTAIN SHOTOVER. Do? Nothing simpler. Learn your business as an Englishman.

HECTOR. And what may my business as an Englishman be, pray?

CAPTAIN SHOTOVER. Navigation. Learn it and live; or leave it and be damned.

ELLIE. Quiet, quiet; youll tire yourself.

MAZZINI. I thought all that once, Captain; but I assure you nothing will happen.

[*A dull distant explosion is heard*]

HECTOR [*Starting up*]. What was that?

CAPTAIN SHOTOVER. Something happening. [*He blows his whistle*] Breakers ahead!

[*The light goes out*]

HECTOR [*Furiously*]. Who put that light out? Who dared put that light out?

NURSE GUINNESS [*Running in from the house to the middle of the esplanade*]. I did, sir. The police have telephoned to say we'll be summoned if we dont put that light out: it can be seen for miles.

HECTOR. It shall be seen for a hundred miles. [*He dashes into the house*]

NURSE GUINNESS. The rectory is nothing but a heap of bricks, they say. Unless we can give the rector a bed he has nowhere to lay his head this night.

CAPTAIN SHOTOVER. The Church is on the rocks, breaking up. I told him it would unless it headed for God's open sea.

NURSE GUINNESS. And you are all to go down to the cellars.

CAPTAIN SHOTOVER. Go there yourself, you and all the crew. Batten down the hatches.

NURSE GUINNESS. And hide beside the coward I married! I'll go on the roof first. [*The lamp lights up again*] There! Mr Hushabye's turned it on again.

THE BURGLAR [*Hurrying in and appealing to Nurse Guinness*]. Here: wheres the way to that gravel pit? The boot-boy says theres a cave in the gravel pit. Them cellars is no use. Wheres the gravel pit, Captain?

NURSE GUINNESS. Go straight on past the flagstaff until you fall into it and break your dirty neck. [*She pushes him contemptuously towards the flagstaff, and herself goes to the foot of the hammock and waits there, as it were by Ariadne's cradle*]

[*Another and louder explosion is heard. The burglar stops and stands trembling*]

ELLIE [*Rising*]. That was nearer.

CAPTAIN SHOTOVER. The next one will get us. [*He rises*] Stand by, all hands, for judgment.

THE BURGLAR. Oh my Lordy God! [*He rushes away frantically past the flagstaff into the gloom*]

MRS HUSHABYE [*Emerging panting from the darkness*]. Who was that running away? [*She comes to Ellie*] Did you hear the explosions? And the sound in the sky: it's splendid: it's like an orchestra: it's like Beethoven.

ELLIE. By thunder, Hesione: it is Beethoven.

[*She and Hesione throw themselves into one another's arms in wild excitement. The light increases*]

MAZZINI [*Anxiously*]. The light is getting brighter.

NURSE GUINNESS [*Looking up at the house*]. It's Mr Hushabye turning on all the lights in the house and tearing down the curtains.

RANDALL [*Rushing in in his pyjamas, distractedly waving a flute*]. Ariadne: my soul, my precious, go down to the cellars: I beg and implore you, go down to the cellars!

LADY UTTERWORD [*Quite composed in her hammock*]. The governor's wife in the cellars with the servants! Really, Randall!

RANDALL. But what shall I do if you are killed?

LADY UTTERWORD. You will probably be killed, too, Randall. Now play your flute to shew that you are not afraid; and be good. Play us Keep the home fires burning.

NURSE GUINNESS [*Grimly*]. Theyll keep the home fires burning for us: them up there.

RANDALL [*Having tried to play*]. My lips are trembling. I cant get a sound.

MAZZINI. I hope poor Mangan is safe.

MRS HUSHABYE. He is hiding in the cave in the gravel pit.

CAPTAIN SHOTOVER. My dynamite drew him there. It is the hand of God.

HECTOR [*Returning from the house and striding across to his former place*]. There is not half light enough. We should be blazing to the skies.

ELLIE [*Tense with excitement*]. Set fire to the house, Marcus.

MRS HUSHABYE. My house! No.

HECTOR. I thought of that; but it would not be ready in time.

CAPTAIN SHOTOVER. The judgment has come. Courage will not save you; but it will shew that your souls are still alive.

MRS HUSHABYE. Sh-sh! Listen: do you hear it now? It's magnificent.

[*They all turn away from the house and look up, listening*]

HECTOR [*Gravely*]. Miss Dunn: you can do no good here. We of this house are only moths flying into the candle. You had better go down to the cellar.

ELLIE [*Scornfully*]. I dont think.

MAZZINI. Ellie, dear, there is no disgrace in going to the cellar. An officer would order his soldiers to take cover. Mr Hushabye is behaving like an amateur. Mangan and the burglar are acting very sensibly; and it is they who will survive.

ELLIE. Let them. I shall behave like an amateur. But why should you run any risk?

MAZZINI. Think of the risk those poor fellows up there are running!

NURSE GUINNESS. Think of them, indeed, the murdering blackguards! What next?

[*A terrific explosion shakes the earth. They reel back into their seats, or clutch the nearest support. They hear the falling of the shattered glass from the windows*]

MAZZINI. Is anyone hurt?

HECTOR. Where did it fall?

NURSE GUINNESS [*In hideous triumph*]. Right in the gravel pit: I seen it. Serve un right! I seen it. [*She runs away towards the gravel pit, laughing harshly*]

HECTOR. One husband gone.

CAPTAIN SHOTOVER. Thirty pounds of good dynamite wasted.

MAZZINI. Oh, poor Mangan!

HECTOR. Are you immortal that you need pity him? Our turn next.

[*They wait in silence and intense expectation. Hesione and Ellie hold each other's hand tight*]

[*A distant explosion is heard*]

MRS HUSHABYE [*Relaxing her grip*]. Oh! They have passed us.

LADY UTTERWORD. The danger is over, Randall. Go to bed.

CAPTAIN SHOTOVER. Turn in, all hands. The ship is safe. [*He sits down and goes asleep*]

ELLIE [*Disappointedly*]. Safe!

HECTOR [*Disgustedly*]. Yes, safe. And how damnably dull the world has become again suddenly! [*He sits down*]

MAZZINI [*Sitting down*]. I was quite wrong, after all. It is we who have survived; and Mangan and the burglar—

HECTOR. —the two burglars—

LADY UTTERWORD. —the two practical men of business—

MAZZINI. —both gone. And the poor clergyman will have to get a new house.

MRS HUSHABYE. But what a glorious experience! I hope theyll come again tomorrow night.

ELLIE [*Radiant at the prospect*]. Oh, I hope so.

[*Randall at last succeeds in keeping the home fires burning on his flute*]

COMMENTARY

Note: The following essay represents a single interpretation of the play. For other perspectives on Heartbreak House, *consult the essays listed below.*

Shaw began writing *Heartbreak House* in 1913, literally on the eve of World War I, ironically known as "the war to end all wars," but the normally productive playwright did not complete the play until 1916 during the darkest hours of the great conflagration. The play's lengthy evolution may explain, in part, the bizarre ending in which the "cream" of upper-crust British society stands amidst falling bombs from airplanes (the new technology rendered by World War I) and pray, even joyfully, that "they'll come again tomorrow night." "Oh, I hope so," reiterates Ellie Dunn, the play's most sympathetic character. It is Shaw's most terrifying and uncharacteristic climax, and it places *Heartbreak House* squarely in the midst of modern drama—even postmodern—in its tone. This is the same Shaw who argued, however whimsically, in *Major Barbara* (1905) that munitions-makers rendered a greater service to humanity than Christians because, at least, they provided work for the masses.

As Shaw began to write the play in 1913, war, especially on the scale of World War I, was a theoretical construct, and it was fought largely according to the old standards of "gentlemen's agreements." But the carnage of the war (more people died during World War I than during all the previous wars combined) and the impersonal nature by which it was fought (long guns, aircraft, and gas canisters left in trenches) meant the rules had indeed changed. And England was proving itself to be a fading empire: note that the Shotover house resembles "an old-fashioned high-pooped ship" that is clearly floundering upon the rocks of modern civilization, a metaphor Shaw pursues in more than a few conversations in the play (see especially Act III). The play's disturbing finale suggests that the great ship, which once had ruled the seas, was splitting, despite its captain's declaration that "the ship is safe."

Consider the steps that Shaw takes to lead us to the final page of his drama (which, although it has comedic moments, is Shaw's *dramatic* masterpiece). Although *Heartbreak House* maintains the trappings of the eighteenth-century comedy of manners perfected by Richard Brinsley Sheridan and Oliver Goldsmith, the play is more akin to the much older medieval morality play. Into this strange world of temptations enters Ellie Dunn, an Everywoman who learns the ways of the world. She is an innocent who must be taught, and thus she typifies a favorite device employed by Shaw, the didactic playwright who used the stage to instruct even as he delighted his audiences. In each of the play's three acts Ellie is tempted by a character who represents three modes of life. In Act I the romantic Hector Hushabye (a.k.a. Marcus Darnley) teaches her that love is rarely what it appears to be. In Act II, she encounters Boss Mangan, the capitalist whose fortune is as illusory as Hector/Marcus's declarations of love (note how Shaw contrasts Mangan with the likeable thief, Billie; and note especially how the playwright dispatches Boss Mangan). In the final act Ellie turns to the venerable prophet-philosopher, Captain Shotover, only to discover that his fabled seventh degree of concentration is merely "rum." Thus Ellie learns too well that love, commerce, and philosophy are mere illusions, and that no one can be trusted in this world. Little wonder Shaw begins the play with "a sigh of weary resignation" from Ellie; by the play's conclusion her sigh has understandably become a lamentation. Certainly the play is a requiem for modern Europe. Its skepticism and the lack of a satisfactory resolution make this Shaw's most contemporary play, one closer to the spirit of John Osborne and Harold Pinter than Oscar Wilde and the long line of playwrights who believed that British pluck and intelligence would eventually save the day.

For a theater artist's perspective on *Heartbreak House*, see director Harold Clurman's analysis of the play in the accompanying Showcase.

Other perspectives on Heartbreak House:

Freeburn, Richard. "A Shavian Fantasia in the Russian Manner: Chekhov's Last Play." *The Shavian* 8:7 (Winter 1999/2000): 6–9.

Peters, Sally. "*Heartbreak House*: Shaw's Ship of Fools." *Modern Drama* 21:3 (1978): 267–86.

See *Heartbreak House* on video:

Heartbreak House. Dir. Anthony Page. Perf. Rex Harrison, Rosemary Harris, and Amy Irving. Educational Broadcasting Corporation, 118 min., 1987.

Other plays by Shaw on film/video:

Caesar and Cleopatra. Dir. Gabriel Pascal. Perf. Vivian Leigh and Claude Rains. VidAmerica, Inc., 134 min., 1948.

Major Barbara. Dir. Gabriel Pascal. Perf. Rex Harrison and Deborah Kerr. Home Vision Entertainment, 90 min., 1940.

About Shaw:

George Bernard Shaw and His Times. Films for the Humanities, 38 min., 1984.

Harold Clurman Directs Shaw

In 1959 Harold Clurman (see Showcase in Part II, "The Group Theatre and the Actors Studio: American Acting Matures") directed a popular production of Shaw's Heartbreak House *on Broadway. His notes—written without regard to style and format—offer an extraordinary insight into both the director's mind and the play itself. These notes have been abridged but may be found in their entirety in his book,* On Directing *(New York: Collier Macmillan Publishers, 1972), pp. 229–41.*

FIRST NOTES

This *crazy house* is a truth house—for adults.

There is a certain "child-ishness" in this play.

The play [is about] a bunch of brilliant kids not as old as the people they impersonate—much wiser and gayer and more cracklingly articulate than such people would "nor-mally" (naturalistically!) be.

A charming, surprising *harlequinade.* (An intellectual vaudeville.)

Make them funnier—"nuttier"—than Shavian "re-alism" (or literalism) usually permits.

"The house is full of surprises," the Nurse says. The Captain's whistle, the sudden entrances and exits are Shaw's clues to this.

Another character says "something odd about this house." The style tends toward a bright-minded wackiness. A puppet show! (Shaw jokes about bow-ings, introductions, greetings, etc.)

Sound—"a sort of splendid drum-ming in the air." Later the air raid is com-pared to Beethoven. Ideally the air raid should be orchestrated—use musical in-struments—on a Beethoven annunciatory theme—but not the motto of the 5th!

In 1959 Harold Clurman, a founding member of the Group Theatre, directed Shaw's dark comedy, Heartbreak House, *at the Billy Rose Theater in New York. Clurman's directorial notes, written as he prepared for the production, also serve as a valuable piece of dramatic criticism about the play and especially its characters.*

SECOND NOTES (*on further reading*)

Shaw's characters are ideas, concep-tions of people, theatrically and comi-cally colored. The adverse criticism of certain critics who say that Shaw's char-acters are merely puppets spouting ideas should be made a positive element of the production style.

They may be made as puppet-like as the nature of the play's dramatic structure and the audience's taste will allow. Mangan says he wants to get "the hell out of this house." Everyone in the play wants somehow to escape his or her condition. All are dissatisfied with it . . . it's a crazy house, driving them crazy!

All in a sense are "crazy," not true to themselves, not what he or she seems or pretends to be. So that everyone is some-how odd, a clown-disguised, masked . . . "The trick is to find the man under the pose."

This is the director's job as well:

  a. What is the pose?
  b. What is the man or woman under the pose?

MORE RANDOM NOTES
(*after still further readings*)

These English in *Heartbreak House* do not behave as Eng-lish people do: an Irishman has rendered them! They are more impish, more extrovert, more devilish, devilishly comic. Hes-ione is a "serpent"—she has mischief in her—not a "proper" lady. She's the cat who swal-lowed the canary, an intelli-gent minx. Mentally speaking she winks.

They are all aware that they are living in a loony world, which they are ex-pected to take seriously—but can't. As they progress they be-come aware of the need to act mad in order to approximate reality. To achieve their libera-tion, their world must be destroyed.

RANDOM NOTES CONTINUED

The movement of the play is not placid, polite (or Chekhovian!). It is rapid, hectic, almost "wild." (The actors are asked by Shaw to sit on tables, etc.)

SPINE (*or Main Action*)

To get the hell out of this place.

This "hell" suggests some of the ex-plosive quality desired in the playing—the element of *opera-boufje* involved.

THE CHARACTERS

Shotover: The Sage of Heartbreak House.

This "sage" has fed himself on rum, worked hard with his body, his fists, and his wits. The rugged person on whose hard work and tough life the house was built. But this sage has a mask—a pose—as important for the actor as his wisdom—indeed more important. It is the mask of the Drinking Devil. . . .

His dismissal of everything secondary comes from his urge to get at fundamental reality—to run the ship—to find the means to set the boat on its due course. This requires the "seventh degree of concentration."

To drive toward *that* goal (the seventh degree, etc.) is his spine—his prime motive or action. (To scare people into doing what he wants, or to be free of their nonsense, their blather). . . .

Ellie: The new life or youth in Heartbreak House.

She wants to find a port. (A goal for her life.)

The pose is the Sweet Young Thing: the well-bred ingenue.

The real person is eager, intelligent, with a strong will and capacity to fight.

The House is bewildering, heartbreaking: all the facts she learns are upsetting. . . . She encounters hidden or masked wisdom in the Devil—the ogre Shotover. So she ends bravely in a sort of exaltation—"greater than happiness."

In the transition between these two aspects of her character, she is miserable, hard, calculating.

Then she "falls in love"—differently—with life itself, in all its danger in the person or symbol of Shotover.

Hesione: Heartbreak House is *her* house.

The Eternal Woman! (And an "actress" by nature.)

She wants to make life beautiful, to keep it romantically beautiful.

She wants to get out of the house too (they all do) because she knows its madness . . . yet she likes it here—the adventure, the uncertainty, the fun . . . like an actress who understands the theatre's absurdity and deception but at the same time enjoys its warm charm.

She is loving but so intelligent that she occasionally is sharp in the face of hypocrisy or stuffiness. . . .

She has temperament and temper, too—like an actress! She is changeable, with swift alternations of mood.

Lady Utterword (Addy): The Fine Lady of Horseback Hall. Conventionality is her mask and protection—the sense of "form" in the "Colonel's lady" manner.

Her reality beneath the mask is a hunger for experience . . . her desire to escape the prison of her class convention. This expresses itself secretly, stealthily, unobserved . . . except in unguarded moments of hysteria. . . .

Her way out of Heartbreak House is to run off to India, to the garden, to tea, to fashionable behavior. . . .

Hector: The Intelligent Man without Employment in Heartbreak House.

He wants to get out—somehow . . . but there's no place to go. He cannot see the goal. Therefore he wants everything destroyed! He has no task. For this reason he dreams up exploits, philanders, plays "parts," dresses up (in "crazy" costumes), becomes decorative . . . even in his intelligence.

Like Ellie he's trying to find port, but he knows of none, foresees none.

"I am deliberately playing the fool," but not out of worthlessness, out of aimlessness. . . .

Debonair and cool like a practical madman. A bit of a show-off. This gives him an identity. . . .

But this is his pose . . . the real man is dissatisfied, unhappy. . . . He curses women because they are the only thing left for him to deal with . . . yet he knows they are only distractions to him. . . .

The "saddest" character in the play and he behaves like an ass and a liar . . . though he often speaks honestly and even wisely.

Mangan: The "Strong Man" of Heartbreak House ("Not a well man").

He wants to get in everywhere—and to get the hell out, too.

The big "capitalist"; the sharper, the practical man, the man who counts in business and in politics. All of this is the pose. The real man is wistful, twisted, rather frightened and a somewhat resentful child . . . the most "cheated" or frustrated person in the house.

He's "aggressive" . . . yet he is always caught off guard. He's sure an aggressive manner is the way to success, but he becomes unsure when his success is challenged or his aggressiveness doesn't impress.

Except in a very limited sphere, he's always out of his element, shaky—unhappy.

So he's always forced to pose—except when he believes it's particularly clever of him to tell the truth about himself.

"I don't quite understand my position here" is the keynote. He never does—anywhere outside his office. . . .

The craziness (or "unusual circumstances") of this house bursts the bubble of his pose . . . he collapses into tears, a hurt boy.

Mazzini Dunn: The Ineffectual Intellectual in Heartbreak House.

To be helpful to all (in Heartbreak House) is the "spine." Mazzini has "moist eyes," always smiling—except for moments of total consternation, and even then there's a little smile. He is obliging to everybody.

He feels a bit inferior, insufficient, guilty. Thus he wants to make up for it by being helpful. He regards everyone as somehow better, cleverer, stronger than he. He admires everyone.

He is credulous, gullible . . . the world is always a surprise to him; he smiles with wonder and admiration. He really doesn't understand evil.

He thinks all one has to have are the right influences and inspirations to become good, loyal, strong.

(Key lines: "How distressing! Can I do anything I wonder?". . . .)

Randall.

To act as if he were the one proper, immovable person. The "imperturbably," the superb English gentleman. Ornament of all diplomatic circles.

That is the Pose. Unruffled, exquisite, the last word in smoothness. Narcissistic.

The real man: a bundle of ragged nerves, a spoiled almost hysterical baby.

He believes himself a romantic character, so impressive in bearing that no matter what he does he must somehow appear dashing and right. . . .

The most absurd of all the characters. . . the most "typically" British—in the old-fashioned comic sense. A "cultured" dandy, super-sophisticated. He will still look and be a kid at sixty-five. . . .

Billy Dunn.

He reverses all values in Heartbreak House.

To get out, make out—any way he can.

Shaw's intention with this character is to illustrate the total topsy-turvydom of Heartbreak House. A sense of guilt hovers over Heartbreak House. Its inhabitants no longer believe in the old justice. The criminal no longer believes in his crime: it's just another way of earning a living. . . .

Nurse Guinness: The Leveler.

To wait it out—with a minimum of worry.

She's an "anarchist"—she doesn't care because she does get along.

A CONCLUDING STATEMENT
[from Clurman's "Director's Note" in the souvenir program]

. . . What was Shaw's purpose and why did he write *Heartbreak House* in this peculiar way? The play exemplifies a typical Shavian "trick." *Heartbreak House* is all carefree talk and horseplay, apparently devoid of dark portent; then it bursts for a moment into a scene of shock and ends ironically on a note of almost languid peace. "Nothing will happen," one of the guests says. Something does happen and something more fatal may yet happen—expected, almost hoped for, by certain of the characters.

These "charming people, most advanced, unprejudiced, frank, humane, unconventional, free thinking and everything that is delightful," are content to drift. No matter what inner qualms they may have, no matter what emptiness or discontent they occasionally experience, they have settled for the happiness of dreams and daily pastimes. For all his sharp teasing, Shaw is tolerant with them. Only, says he, in earnest jest, if you go on like this without "navigation"—that is without plan, purpose and preparative action—your ship will "strike and sink and split."

The thought or warning which informs the play—stated in a frolic of entertaining words and postures—is wholly appropriate to our day and our theatre. Though the people of *Heartbreak House* are English, it is not merely a play about a certain class or a certain country. Time has turned it into a play about practically all of us, everyone.

PART II

Late Modern Drama: 1920–63

Jo Mielziner's scene design for the original production of Death of a Salesman *in 1949 remains one of the most admired designs in the American theater. The sagging roofline, which is dwarfed by the New York skyline, reflects Willy's mental state. You may read Mielziner's discussion of the design in the Showcase in Part II.*

PART II:
LATE
MODERN
DRAMA:
1920–63

The Aftermath of World War I

Prior to World War I, thanks largely to advances in science and an increased democratization of the West, the spirit of liberal optimism encouraged people to think that a utopian world in which social problems were eradicated—or at least minimized—was possible.

However, the Great War of 1914–18, originally referred to as "the war to end all wars," altered that perception irrevocably. The great cities of Europe were devastated, the economy lay in ruins (despite an apparent surge in wealth during the "Roaring Twenties"), and the population was decimated. The war not only destroyed lives and cities but also ravaged old beliefs and traditional values as people, especially in central Europe, felt betrayed. War itself was no longer a gentleman's game fought according to codes of honor. The new war killed indiscriminately as people died horribly in trenches from gas or were killed by long guns and bombs from airplanes that could not be seen. No longer could old values—"How sweet and beautiful it is to die for one's country"—hold true, as the English war poet Wilfred Owen (1893–1918) suggested in his antiwar poem, "Dulce et Docorum Est." Ironically, Owen was killed two days before the armistice; his poetry about the horrors of World War I epitomizes the disillusionment of the young generation victimized by the war. Bernard Shaw, as we saw in *Heartbreak House*, was similarly disillusioned by the war, as were the German Expressionists and Bertolt Brecht.

A decade after the war, the Great Depression (1929–c. 1935) challenged old assumptions about economic systems and laissez-faire government. Angered and frightened, people turned to new forms of government such as socialism and fascism (Germany, Italy, Spain) and communism (Russia and, later, China), which eventually led to some of the most repressive regimes in the history of the world. Personal freedoms were destroyed as men of extraordinary power seized lands and peoples without regard to previously held tenets of civilization. The Western world was plunged into World War II (1939–45) and what poets called "the Age of Anxiety" (W. H. Auden) and "the Wasteland" (T. S. Eliot). Later came the Cold War and its threat of nuclear annihilation.

The (apparent) certainty of earlier ages was replaced by *Relativism*, a belief that truths rest with individuals and groups—as opposed to universal systems—holding them. In Part I you learned that Einstein's theory of relativity provided a scientific impetus for Relativism. In 1922 an Austrian philosopher, Ludwig Wittgenstein (1889–1951), wrote a treatise (*Tractatus Logico-Philophicus*) in which he argued that classical philosophy was suspect because it relied on a language that was imprecise and subject to individual interpretation based on one's reality in the world. He argued that mathematics and science were better equipped to render "truth" (and Einstein's theory seemed to support his claims). Wittgenstein's belief led to the philosophy of Logical Positivism—in which terms and statements had to be clarified and qualified—and influenced much of the literature of the late modern and especially postmodern ages (see Part III). Harold Pinter and Tom Stoppard are but two of the many playwrights influenced by Wittgenstein's theories of language.

Another philosopher, the German Martin Heidegger (1889–1976), further advanced notions of Relativism by defining *Existentialism* as the dominant mode of thought during the middle years of the twentieth century. Heidegger, whose country was decimated during World War I, believed that human existence (hence the term) was precarious, that there no longer seemed a fixed system to order the world. Thus individuals were obliged to define themselves *authentically* (a key term) by making correct and creative choices instead of immersing themselves in trivial activities. Existentialist notions permeate twentieth-century drama, particularly in the plays of the Absurdists (see below and the Showcase, "Forerunners of the Absurd").

Luigi Pirandello's *Six Characters in Search of an Author* (1921) is the prototype of the relativist play and is a fitting prelude to many of the remaining plays in this anthology. The brief synopsis of the play and a critical discussion of its themes may be found in the accompanying Showcase: "The Prototype of the Relativist Drama: Pirandello's *Six Characters in Search of an Author*."

Pirandello's *Six Characters in Search of an Author*

Although it was written in 1921, Luigi Pirandello's *Six Characters in Search of an Author* is arguably the first postmodern play. Like so many dramas written in the late 20th century, *Six Characters* is concerned with defining reality by considering the multiple perspectives that constitute reality. It employs the "play-within-the-play," or metatheatric, structure so prevalent in postmodern plays. It is tempting to say that Pirandello (1867–1936) created metatheatric drama —or Pirandellian drama— but Shakespeare and his contemporaries often employed such devices. Because of the play's length and space constraints within this text, we can only offer a brief commentary on Pirandello's seminal drama to prepare you to understand such works as Tom Stoppard's *Rosencrantz and Guildenstern Are Dead* and other postmodern plays.

Pirandello's troubled life influenced his writing and especially his philosophy. The son of a wealthy owner of sulfur mines in Sicily, the young Pirandello failed in the business world. He then enrolled at the University of Rome to prepare for a career in philology (the uses of language).

To accommodate their father's wishes Pirandello married a young woman from his hometown in 1894, and after ten years of a happy marriage disaster struck. The family sulfur mines were flooded, bringing financial ruin to both families and the onset of a mental illness that plagued his wife until her death. To care for his family, Pirandello accepted a teaching position at a college for women in Rome, which unfortunately elicited fits of jealous rage from his wife. Although he was encouraged to institutionalize her, he continued to care for his

Real life intrudes upon life in the theater as Pirandello's Six Characters interrupt a rehearsal of the melodrama, "Mixing It Up." Six Characters in Search of an Author was performed by the Jean Cocteau Repertory Company in New York. Note that the theater lighting and rehearsal props are visible to remind the audience that they are watching a play.

wife at home for fifteen years. In her mind he was a philandering scoundrel, yet in reality he was a caring, devoted husband. Here we see a central theme of Pirandello's drama, epitomized in the title of his other best-known work *Right You Are—If You Think You Are*, or *It Is So, If You Think So* (1916). The title articulates a basic Pirandellian tenet: there can be no truth because truth varies with the individual and the circumstance.

In most of his 40 plays, Pirandello challenged the validity of scientific or objective observation as a means of ascertaining truth. Invariably his characters are placed in situations where they question the fine line between illusion and reality as they search for truth, themes that obsessed a new generation of writers in the aftermath of World War I. Pirandello also explored the connection between art and nature. Because he saw nature as a process of continual change, he created a theater that would accurately depict this dynamic. He believed that art, to truly

reflect the world in which we live, must be rooted in a philosophy and style that intermingle the two. For him, art should be nearly indistinguishable from life. As the Step Daughter in *Six Characters in Search of an Author* exclaims: "How shall I play [life], how shall I live it?"

Most analyses of dramatic literature often begin with style and genre, a logical starting point for traditional discussion. However, Pirandello's "logic" is not traditional. For him, following a traditional, uncomplicated structure was an insufficient means of holding "the mirror up to nature." Realism was inadequate because it was— in Pirandello's estimation— too simple. So too were the traditional generic classifications of comedy, tragedy, farce, and melodrama that told the audience what to expect as they entered the theater. By accepting as truth the simple action of a traditional plot, the audience members remained outside the drama. Pirandello wanted the spectator not only to witness the action but also to be caught up in it, to share the characters' anxiety as they struggled to understand their essence. To accomplish this Pirandello fabricated an intricate metatheatrical structure. And *Six Characters in Search of an Author* is nothing if "metatheatric," a term variously defined as "a dramatic genre that does go beyond drama. . . . becoming a kind of anti-form in which the boundaries between the play as a work of self-contained art and life are dissolved." The playwright uses the characters' awareness of their existence *as characters* as a metaphor for the audience's conscious or unconscious awareness of their own participation in the "drama" of life. Just as Pirandello's six characters seek an author to give them understanding, we also seek knowledge of our reason for being.

The action of *Six Characters* exists on at least three levels. On the first level we have the "actors" rehearsing a tawdry melodrama titled "Mixing It Up." On the second level we see six characters interrupt them as they search for an author. Finally, we have the "actors" and "characters" from the first two levels, playing or, in the case of the six characters, replaying the scene that occurs in Madam Pace's shop. To complicate matters, both the "actors" and the "characters" are conscious of the roles they play. All of this, of course, manifests the essential Pirandellian dilemma (and that of so many postmodern writers): our inability as humans to come to grips with the "truth" and to distinguish illusion from reality. Fittingly, the form of the play reflects Pirandello's complicated view of human awareness.

Pirandello presents the action of his play through a series of surprises. As the players rehearse "Mixing It Up," they are, without warning, confronted by the Six Characters, who are, in turn, surprised not only by the inability of the "actors" to convincingly play the scene but also by their own lack of success in finding an author. In what more likely environs than a theater could they have expected to find their "savior"? And we, the audience, are surprised by the multilayered interaction between the "actors" and the "characters" in the colliding worlds of the theater and life.

By the end of the play we do not find a conclusion in the traditional sense. The actors in "Mixing It Up" have neither completed their own play nor succeeded in portraying the "Madam Pace" scene from the Six Characters' lives. The Six Characters continue their fruitless search for an author. The audience is left without a resolution to either plot. Thus Pirandello would have us actually experience the perplexing lives of his "actors" and "characters," which parallels our own lives because we, too, are all "actors" playing different roles we do not understand. With no certain knowledge of what is illusion and what is reality, we are also left in search of meaning in our lives. No matter how carefully we prepare ourselves for life's inevitabilities, we are constantly surprised by what happens. Just when we think we have our lives under control, new "characters" seeking authors and answers enter our lives.

Such were Pirandello's circumstances as he created *Six Characters in Search of an Author*. Thanks to the "nimble little maidservant" he called "Fantasy," Pirandello claims that: "without having made any effort to seek them out, I found before me, alive . . . the six characters now seen on the stage." And when these Six Characters *appeared* to him, Pirandello said to himself, "I have already afflicted my readers with hundreds and hundreds of stories. Why should I afflict them now by narrating the sad entanglements of these six unfortunates?" Why, indeed? Perhaps because their plight was the ideal illustration of Pirandello's view of our complicated lives, or, as he said, "Born alive, they wished to live." Or as the Step Daughter in the play says, "What is the stage? It's a place, baby, you know, where people play at being serious, a place where they act comedies. We've got to act a comedy now, dead serious, you know. . . ."

Thus, it is not by chance that Pirandello entitles his play within the play "Mixing It Up." It is, after all, Pirandello who is "mixing it up." Is this play "a comedy in the making" as he subtitled it? Or is it "the bursting forth of . . . passions seeking . . . to overwhelm each other with a tragic, lacerating fury," as he says in his Preface? The answer is, of course, "both" and "neither." By including the various levels and by obliterating traditional styles and genres, Pirandello gives us an art form that approximates reality. The Father (Pirandello's *raisonneur?*) characterizes it best: "Reality is a mere transitory and fleeting illusion, taking this form today and that tomorrow, according to your will, your sentiments which in turn are controlled by an intellect that shows them to you today in one manner and tomorrow . . . who knows how?"

See *Six Characters in Search of an Author* on video:
Six Characters in Search of an Author. Dir. Stacy Keach. Perf. Andy Griffith, John Houseman, and Beverly Todd. Kulture, 90 min., 1976.

A video about Pirandello:
"Luigi Pirandello: In Search of an Author." BBC, 96 min.

Other "Isms"

Although Expressionism (as discussed in Part I) developed into a major theatrical style that can yet be found in recent dramas (e.g., Tony Kushner's two-play epic, *Angels in America*), other movements challenged the primacy of Realism and also returned the theater to its metaphorical roots. Among the most significant antirealist styles were Surrealism, Futurism, and Constructivism.

Surrealism

We are inclined to think of Surrealism first in the paintings of Salvador Dali and René Magritte, and it certainly flourished in the painterly arts. But it was also a theatrical movement that may be regarded as an extension of Expressionism. It was a playwright, Guilliame Appollinaire (1880–1918), who coined the term *"drame surréaliste"* and appended it to the title of his play *The Breasts of Tiresias* (1917), in which the heroine, Euryidice, opens her dress to expose two balloon-like breasts floating to the heavens even as she is transformed into a man! In 1924 André Breton (1896–1966), the artist most associated with Surrealism, issued a manifesto (and a second five years later) in which he glorified the work of Freud and defined Surrealism as "psychic automatism" that would reveal the process of thought. That is to say, artists need only project those things that appear on the landscape of their minds, regardless of the logic behind them.

If the Expressionists sought to portray subjective experience (e.g., dreams and hallucinations) through objective means, it might be said that the Surrealists, who believed in the primacy of the subconscious, sought to portray subjective experience through subjective means. They freely juxtaposed familiar objects with the bizarre. Dali's most famous painting, *The Persistence of Memory* (1931), perhaps best illustrates this concept. Ordinary pocket watches, bent like melted rubber, dot a barren landscape. Surrealism had perhaps a more profound effect on design than playwriting, but it furthered the notion that plays no longer had to be ruled by an absolute logic. The French were particularly enamored with Surrealism, and Jean Cocteau (1892–1963) remains the most performed of the surrealistic dramatists; *The Infernal Machine* (1932), a retelling of the Oedipus legend (with material borrowed from *Hamlet*), is his most performed work. The Theater of the Absurd is indebted to the work of the Surrealists and a parallel movement, Dadaism, which is discussed later in conjunction with the Absurd.

Futurism

An Italian poet, Filippo Marinetti (1876–1944), reacted quite differently to the advances of science and technology. Rather than condemn them as the Romantics and the Expressionists often did, he virtually deified technology and speed. In his famous 1909 manifesto he referred to himself and his youthful sympathizers as "living Futurists" who sought to redefine the arts—including theater—in the new, machine-age century. In a variety of subsequent essays, Marinetti and his colleagues implored playwrights to invent new forms, a *synthetic* drama, drawn from a variety of media. Their idolatry of speed caused them to create plays that were short. In one typical piece performed in 1915, the audience saw a curtain rise to reveal a deserted road at night. Seconds later a gunshot was heard in the distance as the curtain fell. In another play, four actors performed four unrelated pantomimes before a white wall to illustrate the simultaneity of life, a concern of many modern and postmodern dramatists. Futurist actors mimicked machines in their movements, and rather than use words, they created sounds to communicate. All was intended to denigrate the traditional theater elements of plot, character, and diction—and, of course, thought or theme—which were considered passé and old-fashioned.

Such gimmicks were short-lived as their novelty waned and lost the capacity to engage audiences. However, some Futurists introduced techniques that enhanced the lasting drama of the early- to mid-twentieth century. Among these were the use of new technologies to create multimedia productions; the Germans Erwin Piscator and Bertolt Brecht are especially noted for this. Barriers between the arts were removed, and words were often replaced by other forms of communication. Perhaps most importantly, the "fourth wall" was shattered as performers often confronted spectators and freely moved among them. Pirandello wrote *Six Characters in Search of an Author* precisely at the time when Futurism was fashionable in Italy. It is more coherent than most Futurist works, yet its extraordinary conceit in which "real characters" enter from the audience to confront the actors of a melodrama is very much in the spirit of Futurism.

Constructivism

Even as Russia was establishing itself as the epicenter of Realism in the theater, largely because of Stanislavsky's productions at the Moscow Art Theatre, there were significant antirealist movements evolving in that country. Vsevolod Meyerhold (1874–1940) was the foremost exponent of experimental theater and is remembered for pioneering Biomechanics and Constructivism, both of which were inspired by scientific advancements. Biomechanics—a mechanistic approach to acting that fused the older technique of the *commedia dell'arte* with the then-new work of the Futurists—is discussed in the Showcase ("Theater in the Industrial Age") that accompanies *Machinal* later in Part II.

Constructivism was not an approach to acting, although it provided a physical setting on which actors could work. Meyerhold envisioned a stage that functioned much like a machine. Indeed, he referred to his stage as a "machine for acting" that was devoid of superfluous decoration; each object on Meyerhold's "machine" was meant to be practical, and his actors were merely extensions of that machine, which was itself part of the larger machine that served society. At Meyerhold's theater audiences saw a stage stripped of all but simple platforms and steps; lighting instruments (which did not use colored filters) were exposed, as was the back wall of the theater. Objects were devised to accommodate a particular play—e.g., a windmill-like device that turned with rhythmic precision like a cog in a factory machine was the centerpiece for his noted production of *The Magnificent Cuckold* (1922). Like the Futurists, Meyerhold and other Constructivists used modern technology to create backgrounds for a production: slides, film, screens, projections. Actors wore everyday clothing: "One must not waste time with costumes," Meyerhold wrote. "The modern actor will wear overalls and no make up." These are techniques that Erwin Piscator and especially Bertolt Brecht would use, as would subsequent generations of artists attempting to redefine theater. In later years such techniques became known as "Total Theater" and included television monitors as the new technology. We can imagine a time when some future Meyerhold will use holographs and other virtual-reality devices as part of twenty-first-century theater. Like other of the antirealistic "Isms," Constructivism emphasized the symbolic, even the abstract, to challenge assumptions about what was "real."

Popular Culture

Although popular—as opposed to "high"—culture has always appealed to common people, the first half of the twentieth century has been referred to as "The Age of the Masses" because a worldwide mass culture developed, led by the commercialism of the United States. By the end of World War II the United States was clearly the arbiter of culture throughout the world, thanks largely to the ubiquitous presence of film, radio, phonographs, the print media, and (although in its infancy) television. Within the decade after World War II, television transformed the world into what the Canadian cultural commentator Marshall McLuhan called "the global village."

Certainly popular novels in the nineteenth century helped precipitate a mass culture in that epoch. Melodramas were popular not only on European and American stages but also in the "penny dreadfuls" of Europe and the "dime novels" of the United States. Cheap novels often provided scripts for the stage—and eventually the screen, both silent and sounded, which craved fast-paced action that could be photographed for "moving pictures." Thomas Edison invented the phonograph in 1877 and the motion picture camera in 1888; just eight years later (1896) the first commercial films were exhibited. By the second decade of the twentieth century film had become a legitimate "art" form (e.g., W. D. Griffith's *The Birth of a Nation*, 1914), and in 1927 the world listened in awe as the motion picture "talked" and sang. *The Jazz Singer*, starring the popular vaudeville artist Al Jolson, is regarded as the first "talkie."

And how fitting that that film's subject matter was jazz, arguably the United States' most significant contribution to world culture. In actuality jazz evolved from the rhythms of Africa, as the descendents of slaves fused music from their homelands with popular European and American melodies. Ragtime, the blues, Dixieland, and soon myriad other musical styles quickly evolved to meet the demands of a new generation of people who eschewed older traditions (in no small part because they believed they were aligned with the elitists who had led them into the Great War and the Depression). By the 1930s jazz artists such as Louis "Satchmo" Armstrong, Duke Ellington, Billie Holliday, and Ella Fitzgerald were as important in world culture as Igor Stravinsky, Pablo Picasso, and T. S. Eliot. The Cotton Club in New York's Harlem district was as much a temple of culture as Milan's La Scala Opera or London's Covent Garden Theatre.

Recordings by jazz and other musicians sold as quickly as movie tickets and novels. Radio abetted the rise of popular music since average workers could afford the price of a Philco, even during the Depression. By the 1950s radios and phonographs (now called "stereos") were as ubiquitous as stoves in homes, as was the newest form of musical expression: rock 'n' roll, an energetic hybrid of jazz, blues, pop, and country musical styles. Although not the first rock 'n' roll musician, Elvis Presley soon became "King" and presided over one of the most far-reaching transformations of popular culture in the world. One might say that Elvis's first appearance (1956) on *The Ed Sullivan Show*, a vaudeville-style television program that was the showcase of pop culture in the 1950s, was the culminating moment of the popular culture revolution of the first half of the twentieth century. Eight years later (1964), the Sullivan show would help launch a second revolution (the counter-cultural revolution) when the Beatles first appeared. No artists in any media influenced all aspects of culture more than the longhaired Beatles, whose experiments with far Eastern philosophy and antiestablishment lifestyles radically altered the way the world saw itself. In Part III we shall return to the Beatles and their influence on the arts in the 1960s.

Because it is essentially a populist medium that depends on large audiences for its existence, the theater was quick to adapt elements from popular culture. In the 1920s Erwin Piscator (see below and the Showcase, "Theater in the Industrial Age") used film and photographic slides as the scenic backdrop for his experimental productions. His countryman, Bertolt Brecht (see below), was himself a popular Berlin cabaret singer who wrote "pop music" for his satirical songs about postwar German life. In the United States John Howard Lawson, a leftist playwright of the 1930s, wrote jazz operas, and George Gershwin's *Porgy and Bess* (1933) is arguably America's finest opera, an extraordinary fusion of folk, pop, and especially jazz music. From the 1920s through the 1950s the American theater was dominated by the musical, a blend of comedy, drama, and popular musical styles. From *Oklahoma!* (1943) to *Camelot* (1962) America enjoyed a "golden age" of musicals, and one—*West Side Story* (1957)—was instrumental in awakening the country's social conscience in its portrait of racial tensions among disaffected youth. Some of America's most admired playwrights—Tennessee Williams and Sam Shepard—freely used jazz and rock 'n' roll in their plays. (Shepard was himself at one time a rock 'n' roll drummer with the Holy Modal Rounders, who provided the soundtrack for the antiestablishment cult film *Easy Rider*.)

As significant as historical, political, and social events may be, popular culture has invariably had an effect on the theater. Brecht, who began his performance career in the cabarets of Berlin, knew this and fused social issues with popular entertainment.

The Epic Theatre

Of all the experiments undertaken in theaters in Europe and America during the first half of the twentieth century, none so completely fused social concerns, politics, and populist sentiments as did the Epic Theatre of Bertolt Brecht (1898–1956), who most transformed the German and consequently Western theater. It may be argued that Brecht is the most influential artist in the modern theater. He radically altered the means by which artists use the theater as a political instrument. Today we frequently employ the term "Brechtian" to denote a particular style that can be found in both Western (e.g., *Angels in America*) and non-Western dramas (e.g., see Showcase, "South African Township Theater," in Part III), musical theater (e.g., *Cabaret*), and even opera (e.g., *Nixon in China*). Classical plays have also been presented in a Brechtian style (e.g., the Royal Shakespeare Company's acclaimed 1963 production of *The War of the Roses*). Although it might be argued with good reason that Brecht initiated postmodern theater (see Part III), he was—like Ibsen and Shaw—committed to transforming society through didactic theater, and he is discussed within the context of modern drama.

Brecht was inspired not only by the work of the Expressionists but also by the bold experiments of Erwin Piscator (1893–1966), whose work at Berlin's Volksbuhne (People's Theater) from 1924 to 1927 laid much of the foundation for the Epic Theatre. Piscator was committed to bringing theater to the working class, which had been decimated in the aftermath of World War I. An antirealist, Piscator used film and slide projections, poster boards, life-size cartoons, and fragmented scenery in such strident productions as *The Good Soldier Schweick* (1927), which he adapted from a popular antiwar novel. Brecht also wrote a play about the hapless soldier and employed similar devices to achieve his alienation effects (see below). As importantly, Piscator borrowed events from the past as his subject matter to comment on current social and political problems, and "historification" became

The Berliner Ensemble of Bertolt Brecht: 1949–99

Bertolt Brecht emerged as arguably the leading voice in the development of Western dramatic and theatrical theory in the twentieth century. Brecht's dramatic and theatrical vision was extraordinary as he continued, throughout his entire career, to alter radically the Aristotelian sense of the dramatic narrative, and the realistic, illusionary approach to acting derived from Stanislavsky. Basically, Brecht faced two potent forces in the development of Western dramatic and theatrical theory. Single-handedly, Brecht confronted and questioned the validity of Aristotle's *The Poetics* as the foundation for writing "proper" drama. Furthermore, he determined that Stanislavsky's naturalistic approach to acting was remote from twentieth-century values. What Brecht accomplished, therefore, was the development of a theater capable of mirroring a new industrial and modern world, which he believed was proficient at destroying itself in a matter of hours, thanks to the misapplication of scientific discoveries. Recall that he participated in World War I, which killed more people than all previous wars combined.

In 1949, together with his wife, the renowned actor Helene Weigel, Brecht founded the Berliner Ensemble, a company of actors, directors, designers, and musicians dedicated to his theories of the Epic Theatre—an artistic and philosophical exploration of what the theater could achieve if the spectator could view dramatic action through the exploration of socioeconomic and political themes. By writing *Lehrstucke* (teaching dramas), Brecht and the Berliner Ensemble were able to combine a visual aesthetic rooted in the *verfrumdungseffekt* ("alienation effect"). The Ensemble's *mise en scène* was dedicated to a didactic and dialectic theatrical experience. By separating yet collectively unifying a production's acting, directing, visual, and aural components, Brecht hoped to achieve a theater devoid of realistic illusion and emotional empathy in favor of an objective examination of what occurs in the playing arena.

Since company members often enjoyed the luxury of a long rehearsal process (sometimes up to nine months), the Berliner Ensemble produced effective and polished results, as evidenced by the written and photographic documentation of the rehearsal and performance experience. Together with his insightful essays on modern theater and drama, this documentation is the foundation for our understanding of Brecht's attempt to define his concept for an Epic Theatre. Concisely, Brecht's vision included:

- A *playwright* who would avoid a plot-driven drama in favor of an episodic one; a play that would speak of a historical past in relationship to what is occurring in the current socioeconomic structure of modern society. Such events (or scenes) would distance the spectators from any type of emotional involvement.
- A *stage director* who, through scrupulous staging patterns, would paint a stage picture capable of emphasizing the character's place within the socioeconomic world of the play.
- An *actor* who would demonstrate a socioeconomic presence rather than to imitate (or emotionally act out) an action. The task of the actor would always be to speak to the audience directly, physically and intellectually, so that the spectator could ponder the message of the *Lehrstucke*.
- A *designer* of sets and lights who would essentially create a stark visual background, lacking in mood-creating effects. Brecht always suggested that a stage, free of imposing scenic clutter, would drive the message forward to the spectator. When minor set pieces had to be placed or removed following a particular scene, it would occur in full view of the audience. Likewise, the lighting (mostly a white wash) had to demonstrate the veracity of the environment, rather than create illusion through mood or color enhancement.
- A *musician/composer* who would create an aural background made to comment on the situation, rather than to create an emotional additive; the lyrics and music, therefore, had to juxtapose the action taking place on stage. Like contemporary rap music, lyrics should comment on the scene's social significance.

Through the work of the members of the Berliner Ensemble, Brecht was able to bring to life his vision for an industrial, socialist theater. Originally housed in 1949 at the Deutsches Theatre in East Berlin, the company found its permanent home in 1954 at the Theatre am Schiffbauerdamm. There such commemorative productions of *The Threepenny Opera*, *The Caucasian Chalk Circle*, and *The Life of Galileo* influenced a Western theater in search of a modern sensibility. Significant contributors to the work of the Berliner Ensemble were actors Helene Weigel, Peter Lorree, and Harald Paulsen; directors Benno Besson and Manfred Wekwerth; designer Caspar Neher; composers Kurt Weill and Hanns Eisler; and the postmodern playwright and Brecht's protégé, Heiner Müller (see Part III).

In 1954 the Ensemble performed in Paris to exceptional acclaim, and it spent the summer of 1956 in London. (See Showcase, "Britain's Theater Revolution of 1956," later in Part II.) Unfortunately, the Berliner Ensemble was disbanded in 1999, the fiftieth anniversary of its founding. The reunification of Germany after the fall of Communism contributed to the Ensemble's demise as German audiences no longer felt the urgency of Brecht's vision. Still, the legacy of the Berliner Ensemble is permanent as few theater companies in the twentieth century can claim to have had such a profound impact on theater production.

For further reading:

Brecht, Bertolt. *Brecht on Theatre.* Trans. John Willet. New York: Hill and Wang, 1964.

Brecht and the Berliner Ensemble on video:

Bertolt Brecht. Dir. Kurt Tetzlaf. Films for the Humanities, 53 min., 1995.

a central premise of the Epic Theatre. Piscator immigrated to the United States at the outbreak of World War II and produced plays for New York's New School of Social Research until 1951; he was thus instrumental in bringing the Epic Theatre to North America.

Brecht began writing for the theater at the height of the German expressionistic movement in 1922. He was not so much an antirealist as he was against any form of drama that sought to appeal primarily to an audience's emotions. For Brecht, this traditional approach—which he called the "Aristotelian" or "Dramatic" Theater—erred on two counts.

1. An audience aroused to an emotional state might not make rational decisions that could amend the problem presented in the play.
2. By solving the problem on stage, the audience might not feel compelled to attack the problem in the streets.

Brecht's solution was an Epic Theatre, which

> . . . not only releases the feelings, insights, and impulses possible within the particular historical field of human relations in which the action takes place, but employs and encourages those thoughts and feelings which help transform the field itself.

The Epic Theatre rejected the Aristotelian catharsis, which implied a release of emotions as the problem was resolved. Instead, Brecht sought to use the stage to provoke audiences into action. Specifically, he argued that the theater must "criticize constructively from a social point of view." In the preface of *The Rise and Fall of the City of Mahagonny* (1930), Brecht constructed the following comparison between his Epic Theatre and the Dramatic Theater of Aristotle:

Dramatic Theater	Epic Theatre
plot	narrative
implicates spectator in stage situation	turns spectator into an observer
wears down his capacity for action	arouses his capacity for action
provides him with sensations	forces him to make decisions
experience	picture of the world
spectator is involved in something	spectator is made to face something
suggestion	argument
instinctive feelings are preserved	brought to point of recognition
spectator is in the thick of it, shares the experience	spectator stands outside, studies the experience
human being is taken for granted	human being is the subject of inquiry
eyes on the finish	eyes on the course
one scene makes another	each scene for itself
growth	montage
linear development	in curves (ups/downs)
evolutionary determinism	jumps
man as a fixed point	man as a process
thought determines being	social being determines thought
feeling	reason

To discourage the audience from becoming emotionally involved with the characters, Brecht developed the *verfrumdungseffekt* ("alienation effect"), derived from the German verb *verfrumdung* ("to make strange"). In Brechtian terms, the A-effect (as it is called) challenges audiences to see a social problem as if for the first time, evaluate the issues, and devise solutions to correct it. Hence, the Epic Theatre is didactic because it educates and arouses an audience to action, however entertaining its means.

To achieve the A-effect, Brecht resorted to a calculated theatricality that reminded audiences that they were watching only a play, not real life. He admitted an influence of such diverse and nonrealistic entertainment as folk plays, medieval dramas, the cabaret and vaudeville, the films of Charlie Chaplin, Elizabethan stagecraft, court trials, and even boxing matches. Brecht returned the theater to the art of storytelling, frequently using narrators or singers to tell episodic tales. Between episodes, Brecht inserted speeches, songs, and visual devices such as Piscator-like signboards to instruct audiences about the play's intent. He rejected romantic lighting for the harsh, white lighting of the boxing arena to "illuminate" the action; he rejected pretty scenery in favor of curtains that merely suggested locale and ambience; and he rejected beautiful costumes for worn, used clothing made by the proletariat. Ironically, his costumes were often quite realistic looking.

Primarily, Brecht set his plays in remote times and places; this *historification* reminded audiences that time and people can change societies and institutions. In *The Good Woman of Setzuan* Brecht placed his exposé of modern capitalism in provincial China. In every case he asked his audiences to judge the "pastness" of an action that clearly paralleled a modern situation. Brecht was, of course, borrowing from earlier theater traditions, most notably the medieval and Elizabethan theaters, which also used history as a parallel for contemporary social problems.

Not only did Brecht and those whom he inspired revolutionize playwriting, he also offered an alternative to realistic acting. Whereas Stanislavsky's actors sought to identify with their characters through introspection and psychological motivation, Brechtian actors were taught to "quote" their characters's social essence (a boss, a worker, the oppressed, a soldier, etc.). The Stanislavskian actor used a superobjective to get at a character's soul; the Brechtian actor defined a character in terms of its *gestus* (i.e., social function). Brecht was influenced by Chinese actors he saw in Moscow in 1935, especially the great Mei Lan-fang, a man whose specialty was female roles. Brecht noted that Chinese actors never attempted to become their characters, but rather manifested the social essence of their characters.

Brecht has often been accused of being antiemotional, yet a look at his plays (especially *Mother Courage*, in which a mother loses three children to war) suggests that he could summon up an audience's emotions as well as any "dramatic" playwright. Brecht frequently employed traditional devices, particularly those of the melodrama, to arouse emotions in his audience. However, he short-circuited the emotional response to keep audiences from achieving the catharsis of the Aristotelian theater, which Brecht called "barbaric" because it allowed the slaughter of noble beings like Oedipus and Hamlet. At an emotional crest, Brecht inserted one of his A-effects—a speech, joke, or signboard—to challenge audiences to evaluate why they felt so strongly about the issues. He asked them to consider alternatives to the social problems that created the dilemma. As you read *The Good Woman of Setzuan*, *Zoot Suit*, *Top Girls*, and sections of *Angels in America* you will observe these theories in practice; the Academy Award–winning film *Chicago* (2002) features many techniques we now call "Brechtian."

The Second Generation of Realists

Although the Epic Theatre, like the experiments of the Futurists, Constructivists, and others, did much to alter drama, Realism and Naturalism still flourished in the West throughout much of the first half of the twentieth century, particularly in the United States, where the Group Theatre and Actors Studio fostered actors and playwrights who were especially adept at Realism. (See Showcase, "The Group Theatre and the Actors Studio: American Acting Matures" later in Part II.) However, even so-called realistic playwrights employed techniques associated with Expressionism and other antirealistic styles. The period from

1915 through the 1950s might be considered as the "Golden Age" of realistic drama in the United States. Eugene O'Neill, Susan Glaspell, Lillian Hellman, Clifford Odets, Tennessee Williams, Arthur Miller, and William Inge were at the height of their powers. In turn, they influenced a new generation of American playwrights, including Edward Albee, Sam Shepard, David Mamet, Marsha Norman, and even commercial playwrights such as Neil Simon. Yet even as these major playwrights wrote for the major segment of American society, the white middle-class, minority drama was becoming an integral part of the theater.

African-American Theater

As might be expected, a vibrant African-American theater, a by-product of the African diaspora that uprooted people from their homelands, also emerged in the 1950s as a significant force in American culture in response to problems created by segregation and racism. To be sure, theater performed by—and often for—people of African origin had existed in the United States since the early nineteenth century. To seek solace from their slavery and to maintain an indigenous culture, Africans in America performed folktales, songs, music, and dance in cabins and camp meetings, even in town parks such as Congo Square in New Orleans. Such performances eventually melded with and were transformed by the Euro-American culture. In 1821 William Henry Brown established the African Theatre in New York, an enterprise modeled after the white playhouses. Brown's company performed traditional European faire, particularly Shakespeare, but Brown also authored *The Drama of King Shotaway*, based on slavery; it is the first play written by someone of African descent in the United States. In 1915 the Lafayette Players were founded in New York and became the preeminent outlet for African-American dramatists in the early twentieth century. That year also saw the emergence of the Provincetown Players (see Part I), which produced Eugene O'Neill's *The Emperor Jones* in 1922. Charles Gilpin played Brutus Jones to great acclaim and became the first prominent African-American actor on Broadway.

In 1923 Willis Richardson's *The Chip Woman's Fortune* was the first nonmusical play written by an African-American staged on Broadway. However, Lorraine Hansberry's drama, *A Raisin in the Sun* (1959), is generally cited as the first play written by an African-American to become a Broadway "hit." There were, however, notable antecedents to *A Raisin in the Sun*. The title of that play was taken from a poem by Langston Hughes who, in the 1920s and 1930s, was a leader of the Harlem Renaissance, an outpouring of poetry, fiction, and plays by and for African-Americans. Hughes's own play, *Mulatto* (1935), was among the finest achievements of the Harlem Renaissance. The play, which portrayed the lynching of a young man of mixed race, ran for almost 400 performances on Broadway, a testimony to the power of Hughes's writing and to the acting of Rose McClendon, among the first black women to achieve stardom in the New York theater. The play was later turned into an opera, *The Barrier* (1950). The American Negro Theatre, founded by Abram Hill and Frederick O'Neill in 1940, provided more opportunities for dramatists and actors to work in the American mainstream. Its most successful production, *Anna Lucasta* (1944), played for 957 performances on Broadway and became an international hit.

The civil rights movement in postwar America fostered more African-American and integrated theater companies, most notably the Free Southern Theater, founded by Gilbert Moses to develop African-American drama "as unique to the Negro people as blues and jazz." Based in New Orleans, the Free Southern Theater was the first integrated theater company to perform in the American South; it produced both European dramas (e.g., *Waiting for Godot*) and works written expressly for African-Americans (e.g., Ossie Davis's rousing comedy, *Purlie Victorious*). African-American theater, however, found its footing in the 1960s. Part III discusses this movement further and presents important plays by August Wilson and Suzan-Lori Parks.

England and Europe

England, too, produced a number of significant Realists, none more important than John Osborne (1929–95) whose scathing social drama, *Look Back in Anger* (1956), reinvigo-

Contrary to popular belief, *A Raisin in the Sun* was not the first play by and about African-Americans produced on Broadway. In 1923 Willis Richardson's *The Chip Woman's Fortune* claimed the distinction of becoming the first non-musical African-American play to be produced on Broadway. *A Raisin in the Sun*, however, is rightly recognized as the first commercially successful play written by an African-American and performed on Broadway. There are two outstanding film versions of the play, an early film based on the Broadway production with Sidney Poitier, and a made-for-television film (1990, available on video) with Danny Glover. The play represents a significant moment in American theater history, and you should familiarize yourself with it.

The play was written by Lorraine Hansberry (1930–65) who was born into a prominent, middle-class African-American family in Chicago (her father helped found one of the first banks for people of color in that city). However, the Hansberry world was not idyllic. Her father became disillusioned with the treatment of African-Americans in the United States and migrated to Mexico to seek a more color-blind existence; his quest for interracial harmony instilled in his daughter a similar passion.

Hansberry attended the University of Wisconsin and Roosevelt College in Chicago, but her real education came when she moved to New York in 1950. She married a songwriter–music publisher (Bob Nemiroff) and lived in Greenwich Village, where liberal politics and an intellectual environment kindled her aspirations to become a writer. In 1955 she began to write *A Raisin in the Sun*. Because plays by and about African-Americans were virtually nonexistent, it was difficult to raise funds for the play, but after successful out-of-town tryouts, which encouraged the producers, the play eventually premiered at the Ethel Barrymore Theater on March 11, 1959. It was directed by a young African-American, Lloyd Richards (noted for his long-time association with August Wilson), and it starred an unknown Poitier as Walter Lee. Audiences embraced the play, and Hansberry was awarded the New York Drama Critics' Circle Award for the best play of the season. It was the first time an African-American woman received this prestigious award. Despite her short life and the small output of works, Hansberry is recognized as a major force in the shaping of minority theater in the United States. Yet she always argued that she was not a black playwright. She maintained that she wrote about people, "some of whom happened to be black."

There are many reasons for the success of *A Raisin in the Sun*. First, it is useful to look at the play in terms of its historical context. The legitimacy of African-American literature and arts was established by the Harlem Renaissance of the 1930s, a movement that encouraged young African-American writers and artists to cultivate work that reflected the American experience from the black point of view. Its leader was Langston Hughes, a fine playwright and a superb poet. It was Hughes who provided Hansberry with the title of her play in his most famous poem, which asked:

What happens to a dream deferred?
Does it wither like a raisin in the sun?
....
Or does it explode?

Hughes anticipated the "black rage" that erupted in America in the 1960s when anger at social injustices literally exploded in the streets of Watts, Detroit, and Newark.

But while there is a repressed anger lurking beneath *A Raisin in the Sun*, it is not an angry play in the confrontational manner of many of the Black Power dramatists of the 1960s. And that is precisely one of the reasons the play was embraced by Broadway audiences in 1959. White audiences entering the Barrymore Theater were far more sympathetic to the injustices suffered by African-Americans than perhaps at any time in the nation's history. In April 1947, Jackie Robinson showed that African-Americans could perform magnificently in a previously all-white world when he broke baseball's color barrier. Soon other African-Americans followed Robinson in baseball, as well as other sports. The nation had a new host of African-American heroes to admire.

In 1954 the Supreme Court desegregated schools, a move that emboldened the emerging civil rights movement. Even as Hansberry's play moved to Broadway, the Reverend Martin Luther King, Jr., was leading marches through the South; his famous "I Have a Dream" speech was delivered just four years after *Raisin* opened. Rosa Parks defiantly refused to "move to the back of the bus" in Mobile, Alabama. Such events were duly recorded on television, a relatively new medium that allowed middle-class America to see firsthand the problems and poverty spawned by racism. A new consciousness about race relations was developing. Mama's eloquent reflection on her husband's dreams engaged Broadway audiences on a more personal level than was possible for previous generations: "Big Walter used to say . . . 'Seem like God didn't see fit to give the black man nothing but dreams—but He did give us children to make them dreams worthwhile.'"

Actually, the dreams that most affected audiences at the Barrymore—and in the theaters throughout the country that added *Raisin* to their repertory—was the American Dream of owning a house. Mama's argument that "it makes a difference in a man when he can walk on floors that belong to *him*" echoed any number of lines that had become the staple of American drama. In 1943 *Oklahoma* expressed the sentiment that "we know we belong to the land, and the land we belong to is grand." *Tobacco Road*, the longest running Broadway play during the Great Depression, presented a dirt-poor farmer, Jeeter Lester, who eloquently defended his property to a banker who was attempting to evict him:

This was my Daddy's place and his Daddy's before him, and I don't know how many Lesters before that. There wasn't nothing here but the whole country before they came . . . Now I don't own it and it belongs to a durn bank that ain't never had nothing to do with it even. By God, that ain't right, I tell you. God won't stand for such cheating much longer. He ain't so liking of the rich as people think He is. God, he likes the poor.

Or "plain people," to use Mama Younger's term.

Despite its status as a seminal African-American drama, *A Raisin in the Sun* is actually a rather conventional play. At its heart it is a mid-twentieth-century version of the German *familenstucke*, a brand of melodrama pioneered by August Iffland early in the nineteenth century. Such plays—in which families were threatened by eviction if they did not raise money for the mortgage—became a staple of the American melodrama. Audiences understood the sanctity of the "old homestead." The irony of Hansberry's play, however, is that the Younger family actually has the mortgage money. It is not the greed of the heartless banker that threatens their new home; rather, it is the incipient racism expressed by Mr. Linder, the spokesman for the Home-owners Association: ". . . our Negro families are happier when they live in their *own* communities." Ironically, the greedy thief of the old melodrama is Walter Lee's friend, Willy Harris, who dashes the Younger dream when he absconds with the insurance money, a plot element that elevates Hansberry's play above the level of mere polemic.

Beneatha, Mama's daughter, offered white audiences an occasion to see a newly emerging phenomenon among African-Americans: the quest to recapture the pride and dignity of their cultural roots. (Less than two decades after *Raisin*, Arthur Hailey's epic novel *Roots* became the most popular mini-series in the history of American television.) She proclaims proudly and defiantly that she is looking for her identity. Furthermore, she is not an assimilationist, that is, one who gives up her cultural roots in favor of those of the country in which she lives. Hansberry invents Joseph Asagai, the immigrant student with aspirations to the American Dream, to underscore Beneatha's plight. He retains his "old country" prejudices against women ("For a woman [love and a family] should be enough"), and ironically Beneatha must fight biases among her own people as much as those of the white society. Again Hansberry raised issues beyond racial intolerance.

Despite its status as a groundbreaking work, *A Raisin in the Sun* has fallen into disrepute among some African-Americans. It has been criticized for not being militant enough. Mama's dependence on religion ("There'll always be a God in this house!") has caused her to be seen as passive; she relies on divine guidance rather than actively working to change her circumstances. These issues and others have been addressed by George C. Wolfe, the playwright and director who now heads the New York Free Shakespeare Theatre and the Public Theatre. Wolfe wrote *The Colored Museum* (1988), a collection of sketches, some fiercely satirical, others poignant vignettes, which attack stereotypical views of African-Americans enshrined in "the colored museum" of white consciousness. One sketch, "The Last Mama on the Couch Play," parodies *A Raisin in the Sun* (and Poitier's mannered acting). Because it critiques Hansberry's work from the perspective of African-Amerians in the late twentieth century, Wolfe's sketch creates a dialogue between his generation and that represented by Hansberry.

However much subsequent events in the civil rights movement may have altered the status of *A Raisin in the Sun*, it nonetheless remains among the most significant plays in the history of the American theater. It was an urgent play in 1959 and a necessary step in the evolution of African-American literature and performance.

See *A Raisin in the Sun* on video:

A Raisin in the Sun. Dir. Daniel Petrie. Perf. Sidney Poitier and Claudia McNeil. Columbia Tri-Star, 128 min., 1961.

A Raisin in the Sun. Dir. Bill Duke. Perf. Danny Glover and Esther Rolle. Monterey Home Video, 171 min., 1990.

---

rated the British theater and yielded a new generation of angry young men and women such as John Arden, Edward Bond, Sheilah Delaney, and Caryl Churchill. Like their predecessor in social drama, Bernard Shaw, they questioned those institutions and social conventions that limited an individual's freedom and growth. (See Showcase, "Britain's Theater Revolution of 1956," later in Part II.) Curiously, realistic drama has not been a part of the Continent's modern repertory. Although small pockets of the social realist drama can be found in France, Germany, Italy, Spain, and especially Russia, the vast majority of Continental drama has been rendered in other of the "Isms," especially Expressionism (Germany), the Absurd (France), and Symbolism (Italy and Spain).

Frequently, however, the social dramas at mid-century were driven by a cynicism and hopelessness (prompted by the Cold War and atomic weapons) that set them apart from the earlier Realism of Ibsen, Shaw, and Odets. Compare two speeches by leading Realists. In Odets's *Awake and Sing* (1936), a Depression-era youth vows to fight for a better world:

> Get teams [of workers] together all over. Spit on your hands and get to work. And with enough teams together maybe we'll get steam in the warehouse so our fingers don't freeze off. Maybe we'll fix it so life won't be printed on dollar bills.

In Osborne's drama, written only 20 years later, a spokesman for the postwar generation of disaffected youth laments that:

> . . . there aren't any good, brave causes left. If the big bang does come, and we all get killed off, it won't be in aid of the old-fashioned grand design. It'll just be for the Brave New-nothing-very-much-thank-you. About as pointless and inglorious as stepping in front of a bus.

As you read the varied social dramas herein, note those in which change seems possible and those in which the protagonists feel trapped by time and circumstance.

Asia, Africa, and Latin America

By contrast, Asia has remained conspicuously nonrealistic in its drama, though the plays of India's Nobel Laureate, Rabindranath Tagore (1861–1941), reflected some of the social criticism, usually in a satirical mode, that was emanating from the West. Japan and China have seen the emergence of some realistic dramas, but for the most part contemporary social problems are addressed in more traditional—or at least nonrealistic—terms. In Japan, for example, Shigure Hasegawa has used the forms of Kabuki theater in such plays as *Wavering Traces* to address the problems of being a woman in contemporary Japan. In China, the Maoist government sponsored spectacular operas, such as *The White-Haired Girl*, to validate the Communist regime and to attack the feudal system that precipitated the revolution. (See Showcase, "The Conventions of Chinese Theater," later in Part II.) *The Bus Stop*, by Chinese dissident Gao Xingjian (who won the Nobel Prize for literature), is included in Part III to represent a new strain of drama emerging from China.

The history of the theater in Africa, particularly that of the sub-Sahara, is complex. While its theatrical roots are ancient, drama written by black Africans is largely a twentieth-century phenomenon. Prior to this time, formal drama was largely the product of European colonists, but since the late 1950s, native black Africans (as opposed to Africans of European descent, such as Athol Fugard, included in Part III) have used drama as a political tool. Accordingly, the evolution of contemporary African theater parallels the political emancipation of much of the continent. As European colonists have relinquished control of Africa back to its indigenous peoples, African drama has reasserted its own cultural and linguistic integrity by returning to its theatrical roots.

We do not find plays published by native black Africans until the 1930s, and there is little significant publication and production of black African plays until the 1950s. The drama of black Africans developed in three significant stages:

1. Plays in which black Africans attempt to show they have assimilated the culture of the colonists; these dramas are clearly indebted to European dramaturgy. Popular European plays, such as those by Oscar Wilde, Bernard Shaw, and the operettas of Gilbert and Sullivan, were often the staples of colonial African theater, whether performed by Europeans or black Africans.
2. Plays in which the colonized dramatists display an uncertainty about their status and attempt to recover their native past and its forms. Because of a Eurocentric educational system, plays still rely on an essentially Old World dramaturgy.
3. Plays that revolt against colonization, both politically and aesthetically. Here dramatists purposefully employ traditional African theater modes as they write plays designed to rouse the people against colonization. In 1956 the West African playwright Aime Cesaire wrote a play in which a central character tells his oppressors: "Leave me alone, leave me to shout enough to intoxicate myself with that cry of revolt, I wish to be alone under my skin, I recognize no one's right to live in me."

The Rollin' Theater of Puerto Rico and Rene Marques's *The Oxcart*

If historical accounts are accurate, we are told that in the month of March 534 BCE, an itinerant performer named Thespis was ordered by the ruler of Athens to perform as part of the artistic festivities of the City Dionysia. Thespis took his act into the streets, carrying his presentational garments and props in a four-wheeled wagon. Here lies, perhaps, the first recorded evidence of the migratory professional performer, seeking social acceptance and economic survival.

During England's Middle Ages, the cycle of the York mystery plays were staged on decorative wagons to enlighten mostly illiterate audiences about the meaning of the Bible. These elaborate pageant wagons were, in effect, movable stages housing actors who played principal biblical characters. They were often surrounded by evocative settings symbolizing Satan's hell mouth or Noah's Ark. On a more secular note, the popular *commedia dell'arte* of the sixteenth century traveled Europe's provinces in carts, improvising impressions of everyday life through acting, song, and dance. Theirs was a theater closely connected to the people as they performed in city squares or in the streets.

Closer to our time, the influence of the Industrial Revolution clearly impacted the productivity of the duke of Saxe-Meiningen's professional company (see Showcase in Prologue) as he transported by train ninety-plus actors, large sets, and a vast collection of historically accurate costumes and props. His privately owned locomotive pulled approximately sixteen railway cars throughout the German provinces to bring epic productions to eager nineteenth-century spectators across Europe.

With the advent of the automobile in the early twentieth century, many of the companies discussed in this text were able to disseminate their artistic vision via cars, trucks, buses, and vans. During the so-called alternative American theater movement of the 1960s and early 70s, companies such as The Living Theater, The San Francisco Mime Troupe, The Open Theatre, Bread and Puppet Theatre, and The Performance Group reached the masses as they traveled from gymnasiums, to auditoriums, to streets and parks, in search of an audience willing to radically transform a society in social, economic, and political transition. In 1965, Luis Valdez, the founder and artistic director of El Teatro Campesino, took his actors to the fields of Central California where they performed—often on open bed trucks—short plays that exposed the exploitation of Mexican migrant workers. In 1970 the Phoenix Theatre created The Phoenix Theatre Touring Bus to transport live theater to the public in the streets of New York City. Conceptualized by the environmental scenographer Jerry Rojo, The Touring Bus was a 1967 GMC school bus, externally equipped with collapsible platforms, stairs units, and ladders that folded onto the sides of the bus following each performance. The interior of the bus was gutted in order to make room for lighting and sound equipment, as well as a storage space for tools.

In 1967, The Puerto Rican Traveling Theatre, under the leadership of the respected actor Miriam Colón, toured Rene Marques's *The Oxcart*, utilizing a school bus, truck and automobiles, to bring this important play to large Puerto Rican audiences in New York City. The film actor Raul Julia began his theater career with the Puerto Rican Traveling Theatre. Colon's enterprise was modeled after Teatro Rodante Universitario (The Rollin University Theatre) of the University of Puerto Rico. From 1946 to 1973, the Teatro Rodante educated Puerto Ricans across the island by presenting an eclectic repertoire of classical and contemporary dramas—often after hours of driving over muddy, nearly impassable roads. Fittingly, Teatro Rodante Universitario was itself influenced by the 1930s Spanish traveling theater of Federico García Lorca's *La Barraca* (see *Blood Wedding*).

The Oxcart (*La Carreta*)[1] was written in 1953 by a young Puerto Rican playwright, Rene Marques, and it is generally regarded as the most important play in the modern Puerto Rican theater. In this pioneer work, which influenced subsequent generations of Hispanic and Caribbean playwrights, such as Eduardo Machado and Dolores Prieda, Marques depicts the plight of a poor farm family from the mountains of Puerto Rico. The failure of the coffee crop drives them from their land into San Juan, where they live in a slum known as La Perla. This shantytown perched on the ocean sits in the shadows of the old Spanish colonial fortress, the symbol of the imperialism that has confounded Puerto Rico since the sixteenth century. A young girl in the family is raped in La Perla and her brother turns to crime to survive. Desperate for a better life, the family migrates to New York City, but there they also meet poverty and exploitation. After Luis, the idealistic eldest son, is killed in a factory accident, the stoic mother gathers her children to return to Puerto Rico. The play concludes with a rousing speech by the daughter, Juanita, that serves as a manifesto for subsequent Caribbean and Latino drama:

> Now we know the world don't change by itself. We're the ones who change the world. And we're gonna help change it. We're gonna go like people with dignity, like grandpa used to say. With our heads high. Knowin' there are things to fight for. Knowin' that all God's children are equal. And my children will learn things I didn't learn, things they don't teach in

[1] Because permission to publish this play was not received by press time, the play was, regrettably, omitted from this anthology.

school. That's how we'll go back home! You and I, mama, as firm as ausubo trees above our land . . .

In 1957, just four years after *The Oxcart* premiered in Puerto Rico and the United States, *West Side Story* opened on Broadway (its film version won the Academy Award as best film in 1961). *West Side Story* depicted the problems of urban youth, Anglos and Puerto Ricans, living on New York's tough upper west side, the very setting Marques chose for his play. It was among the first stage shows to awaken general audiences to racial and economic strife suffered by Puerto Rican immigrants, an issue raised by Marques and taken to the streets of New York by Colón's Puerto Rican Traveling Theatre, which still thrives today.

Modern society often demands an awareness based on commonality, on an immediate sharing of information, and often in the belief that we can reinvent our reality by declaring our independence in a variety of ways. Rapid transportation continues to inform our imaginations with the notion that if we can travel from town to town, then certainly we can satisfy our curiosity through international travel, or even journeys into the depths of the solar system. Yet the magnificent discovery of the wheel continues to mystify us, and it is this pure and simple invention that has allowed the theater to exist by breaking social, political, economic, and linguistic barriers.

Hubert Ogunde (Nigeria), Ngugiwa Thiong'o (Kenya), and Herbert Dholmo (South Africa) were among the first black African playwrights to achieve international respect for dramas about the liberation of Africa.

In 1966 the First World Festival of Negro Arts was held in Dakar, Senegal (formerly French West Africa), and in 1977 a Black and African Festival of Arts and Culture (FESTAC) convened in Lagos, Nigeria. In many ways, these events signaled the arrival of contemporary black African theater and its arts as entities liberated from the Eurocentric tradition that dominated African stages for over a century. Unfortunately, there yet exists relatively few outlets for contemporary African drama in the West because of translation and publication problems. The best-known work comes from Nigeria and South Africa, though playwrights such as Jacob Hemvi in Uganda are enjoying international publication and production. We may now expect to see greater accessibility to contemporary African drama and theater.

Latin American and Caribbean playwrights, especially Mexico's Rudolfo Usigli (1905–79), often combined fantasy and psychological realism to their advantage as they probed the social dilemmas of their nations as they emerged from colonialism to independence. René Marques, Puerto Rico's foremost naturalistic playwright, wrote *The Oxcart* (*La Carreta*) in 1953, and it remains arguably the most important play to come from the Caribbean. *Paper Flowers*, by Chile's Egon Wolff (see Part III), works on two levels—as psychological realism and as grotesque fantasy—in its symbolic depiction of the revolt against the old monied order by the oppressed. In one relevant speech, an impoverished young man tells the wealthy woman that "I only know I am what I seem and not that I am what I don't seem. In other words, you have your fantasy and I have only reality, which is much poorer, much sadder, much more disillusioning."

The Theater of the Absurd

Whether they used realistic or other means in their exploration of social issues, most writers and artists in the modern theater shared the optimistic belief that change is possible, that social dilemmas can be solved if people are made aware of the problems that create them. Others, however, were less hopeful. Like Chekhov, they believed that time and institutions are indifferent to the human condition and that we are trapped by our circumstances and inertia. One of the most famous plays of the mid-twentieth century, Jean-Paul Sartre's *No Exit* (*Huis Clos*, 1944) argues that there is no escape from the pain of being human. (See Showcase, "Forerunners of the Absurd.")

Out of the ashes of the two great wars of this century arose a philosophy and a related theater movement that challenged optimistic assumptions about people and institutions. The philosophy was *Existentialism* as fostered by Heidegger (discussed earlier). Osborne's *Look Back in Anger* depicts Jimmy Porter's existential dilemma: how does a common man

SHOWCASE THE THEATER OF THE ABSURD

Forerunners of the Absurd: Alfred Jarry's *Ubu Roi* and Jean-Paul Sartre's *No Exit*

While we generally date the advent of the Theater of the Absurd from the late 1940s (Ionesco's *The Bald Soprano*, 1949) and the early 1950s (Beckett's *Waiting for Godot*, 1953), there were plays written earlier that presaged the coming of the Absurd at mid-century. Buchner's *Woyzeck* (1836), discussed in the Prologue, certainly belongs in this category, as do the many works of the Futurists, the Surrealists, and especially the Dadaists. However, two plays from France—the incubator of the Theater of the Absurd—merit attention here: Alfred Jarry's *Ubu Roi* and Jean-Paul Sartre's *No Exit*. Each had a profound impact on the Absurd.

Ubu Roi (1896)

Between 1830 and 1953 three plays premiered in Paris, each of which was marked by a turbulent opening, yet each altered the French (and thereby Western) theater for decades to come:

- Victor Hugo's *Hernani* in 1830 (see Showcase in the Prologue)
- Alfred Jarry's *Ubu Roi* in 1896
- Samuel Beckett's *Waiting for Godot* in 1953 (see Showcase later in Part II)

On December 11, 1896, *Ubu Roi* (translated as *King Turd*) opened at Paris's Theatre de l'Oeuvre, with a stellar actor (Fermin Gemier) in the leading role. It was directed by the *enfant terrible* of Parisian theater at the turn of the century: Aurelien F. Lugne-Pole. Its author, Alfred Jarry (1873–1907), was an *avant-garde* playwright who began his career as a puppeteer in the *gran guignol* (i.e., "grotesque") tradition. In fact, *Ubu Roi* was originally designed as a puppet play in 1888, but its author kept revising it. This bitterly comic play is about a stupid, cowardly, and ineffectual Polish king (equal parts Oedipus and Macbeth) who maintains power by killing and maiming all those who oppose him with his infamous "disem-

braining" machine. (Forty mannequins were beheaded during the production.) He massacres indiscriminately for sausages and umbrellas, and—most importantly—for "*phynances*" (money). Eventually he is driven from his country, but he promises to return, a symbol of the permanence of random evil in Jarry's world. Consequently Jarry wrote sequels: *Ubu Bound* and *Ubu the Cuckhold*, neither of which is particularly memorable.

Jarry intended the play as a denunciation of all that is vulgar and inhumane in a world that was on the verge of the First World War. The playwright declared that he wanted his stage to become a mirror "in which the vicious see themselves with bull's horns and a dragon's body" because he regarded his bourgeois audience as carriers of "eternal human imbecility, eternal lust, eternal gluttony, baseness of instinct which takes over completely." To illustrate the inhumanity of the characters, the acting was mechanistic and the lines were recited monotonously, with equal stress on all syllables (including normally silent ones). The play opened with the word "*Merde*"—or "shit"—theretofore unheard in French theaters. (The King's wife, a horrific parody of Lady Macbeth, was named Dame Merde.) The word sparked a fifteen-minute riot and others followed when the vulgarity was repeated. The Irish playwright and poet William Butler Yeats, who sat in that first audience, declared that Jarry was the harbinger of a "savage god." The play remains among the most caustic renderings of human depravity and waste of spirit; it is still performed with some regularity, and a film version exists (see below). Despite a mere two performances in 1896, *Ubu Roi* was entrenched in the psyches of young French writers, and Jarry became, in the words of theater historian Oscar Brockett, "virtually a patron saint of the Absurdists." Antonin Artaud, progenitor of the Theater of Cruelty (see Part III),

began his theater career at the Théâtre du Alfred Jarry.

No Exit (1944)

Though its plot, dialogue, and characters are not overtly in the style we associate with the Absurd, *No Exit* (*Huis Clos*) nonetheless embodies a central premise of most absurdist plays in its depiction of helpless characters trapped in a void over which they have no control. It was written by Jean-Paul Sartre (1905–80), among the most controversial philosophers of the twentieth century. Sartre, who wrote nine plays, novels, and volumes of philosophical essays, was the primary literary spokesman (with Albert Camus) of Existentialism, more specifically, a nihilistic branch of that philosophy that saw the modern, Godless world devoid of meaning, purpose, or order. (Sartre and his colleagues lived in Paris during the Nazi occupation; he was a member of the Resistance.) Humans could give meaning and order to the chaos of the world by making responsible choices that shape their destinies: "Man is what he wills himself to be," Sartre wrote in *No Exit*. Irresponsible choices doomed one to an ignominy from which there was no escape—or "no exit." Thus, in Sartre's estimation, humans are "condemned" to be free, that is, to make responsible choices or face the consequences of their ill-advised choices. Despair, angst, and "nausea" (the title of Sartre's best-known philosophical tract) were the by-products of both bad choices and the condition in which humans found themselves. *No Exit* illustrates this conundrum.

At first reading *No Exit* seems to be a tawdry melodrama in which a man, Garcin, and two women, Inez and Estelle, find themselves in a room. Each has committed a crime (cowardice in war, infanticide, illicit love), but each knows that the crime is not a total representation of his or her true character. Still the others treat one another with disdain. To their horror, each learns that he or she is in hell—and is therefore condemned to spend eternity with the people who most despise themselves, even as they desperately seek love from one another. Truly, as Sartre says in the most quoted line of the play, "Hell is other people." But "hell is other people" precisely because "other people" become mirrors that show one's true self (and Sartre specifies that there are no actual mirrors in this strange room). Inez attests to this grim view when she says, "Each of us will act as torturer to the others." Such sentiments are the very stuff of Albee's

plays, most famously *Who's Afraid of Virginia Woolf?*

Sartre's play is a grim parody of the social comedy made famous by his countryman, Eugene Scribe; indeed it has elements of the well-made play in its many reversals and especially in its withheld secret that is made known only on the last page of the script. Its dialogue and characterization seem products of the psychological-realist dramas of the early twentieth century. Still, *No Exit* is a precursor to the Theater of the Absurd—and myriad other dramas of the latter twentieth century—in its exploration of the futility of human ac-

tion. If life is by its very nature futile and without hope, then it is indeed absurd that we persevere in our personal hells, alone or with other people. Less than a decade after Sartre wrote his finest play, Beckett would shift the locus of hell from a room from which there is no exit to a sterile landscape where two tramps wait under a barren tree forever—for Godot.

See *Ubu Roi* on video:

Ubu Roi. Dir. Paul Kafno. Perf. Donald Pleasance and Brenda Bruce. Films for the Humanities. 50 min., 1999.

---

educated by the establishment survive in a social system that is still rooted in the old class structure? "He doesn't," in Jimmy's estimation, and there is a fundamental absurdity to his dilemma. But the inherent rationality of the realistic theater was dismissed as an inadequate means of portraying the senselessness of contemporary society. Consequently, the Theater of the Absurd, as much a philosophical worldview as a theatrical style, developed primarily in France, which had been scarred by years of Nazi occupation. Importantly, the theater of Latin America, especially South America, has also been a fertile source of absurdist and grotesque drama as its artists (such as Griselda Gambaro) turned to bleak humor to depict the senselessness of their existence in an oppressive society.

We often find moments that an Absurdist would recognize in the plays of Aristophanes, the clowning of *commedia dell'arte* actors, and even in the plays of Shakespeare; the Polish critic Jan Kott makes a compelling argument that there are moments in *King Lear* that might have been written by Samuel Beckett. However, there are more recent antecedents to the Theater of the Absurd. Recall that Georg Buchner wrote *Woyzeck* (1836) to illustrate that humans are trapped in intolerable situations from which there is no escape. Some have called *Woyzeck* the first truly absurdist work, while others cite Alfred Jarry's *Ubu Roi* (1896), a grotesque version of the *Macbeth* story that exposes all that the playwright found irrational about the bourgeois society in which he lived. It is among the darkest comedies composed in the preabsurdist era.

There also existed an antiart movement—*Dadaism*—that was a legitimate precursor to Absurdism. In Zurich in 1916 the original Dadaists, a group of artists disillusioned by the futility of World War I, conceived of a "negative art" that would destroy the apparently senseless values, promulgated by literature and art, of modern society. To create poetry they selected random words from a dictionary, wrote them on slips of paper, and cast them to the wind. The term "*dada*" itself was randomly picked from a French dictionary; it is a word used by infants to describe horses. Paintings were created by randomly tossing paint at a canvas. And theater was represented, in one famous French example, by a bicycle wheel, a clothesline on which signs were hung, and a series of insults exchanged between actors and audience. By 1922 Dadaism had lost much of its appeal, but it planted the seeds of an antiart skepticism that would resurface in the 1940s as the Theater of the Absurd.

During and immediately after World War II a group of international writers and philosophers flourished in Paris: Sartre and Albert Camus (from France), Eugene Ionesco (from Romania), and Samuel Beckett (from Ireland; see Showcase, "*Waiting for Godot*: The Modern Masterpiece" later in Part II). Appalled by German atrocities, they embraced Existentialism, which argued that there was no longer a system of order in the world (how else could one explain the Holocaust?) and that one was responsible for defining one's existence through personal choices. Disillusioned by the horrors of war, the economic depression of the 1930s, and other modern catastrophes, these nihilistic Existentialists asserted that "the world is irrational and the truth unknowable."

If the world was indeed senseless, then it followed that art itself should mirror that senselessness. Traditional theater had to be transformed to reflect this condition. Conventional plots, dependent on causality and resolution, were abandoned in favor of cyclic plots that rarely resolved conflicts. Borrowing from the Expressionists and Symbolists, the Absurdists drew characters who were poetic abstractions. They were given generalized names (A and B, He and She, Gogo and Didi) and placed in unspecified time and space, often against dark curtains symbolizing the black void of existence. To illustrate the lack of communication, language was frequently reduced to nonsensical utterings, non sequiturs, or mechanically repeated phrases. This dialogue from Ionesco's *The Bald Soprano* (1950) parodies the discussion drama of polite society. The speakers are intentionally indistinguishable from one another:

MR. MARTIN.	One doesn't polish spectacles with black wax.
MRS. SMITH.	Yes, but with money one can buy anything.
MR. MARTIN.	I'd rather kill a rabbit than sing in the garden.
MR. SMITH.	Cockatoos, cockatoos, cockatoos, cockatoos, cockatoos, cockatoos, cockatoos, cockatoos, cockatoos, cockatoos.
MR. MARTIN.	Such caca, such caca, such caca, such caca, such caca, such caca, such caca, such caca, such caca.
MR. MARTIN.	Such cascades of caca, such cascades of caca. . . . [etc.]

Traditional distinctions among the genres blur in the absurdist world: the comic frequently becomes serious, even near tragic, while the serious becomes laughable. Most absurdist plays are essentially comic, partly because they are satirical and partly because we do not engage in the dramatic life of the characters. We laugh, albeit uncomfortably, at the enormous gap between human aspirations and the reality of existence. Edward Albee, whose early plays (e.g., *The American Dream*) are often categorized as absurdist, is perhaps the most successful playwright to have fused the philosophical concerns of the Absurdists with traditional dramatic forms. His assessment of Absurdism identifies the movement's concerns:

As I get it, the Theater of the Absurd is an absorption-in-art of certain existentialist and post-existentialist philosophical concepts having to do, in the main, with man's attempts to make sense of his senseless position in a world which makes no sense—which makes no sense because the moral, religious, political and social structures man has erected to "illusion" himself have collapsed.

In short, the Theater of the Absurd attempts to "make sense through nonsense." Unlike Ibsen, Shaw, and Brecht, absurdist playwrights refuse to suggest solutions to human problems. Meaning in this senseless world is placed squarely on the audience; in the Theater of the Absurd the discussion takes place long after the inevitable fade to black.

Dramatists soon became adept at fusing seemingly polar styles to create yet another form. Harold Pinter (*The Birthday Party*), Sam Shepard (*True West*), and Egon Wolff (*Paper Flowers*) have written enigmatic works that are apparently realistic in style yet absurdist in tone. This collision of styles creates an unsettling ambiguity in their works that—by design—discomforts audiences, who enter the theater already discomforted by the memories of two world wars, the Depression, the threat of atomic annihilation, and myriad other anxieties. Such anxieties were compounded in November 1963, when a young American president, who represented hopes for a new and positive era sometimes referred to as Camelot (after the successful Broadway musical that opened during his presidency), was assassinated on the streets of Dallas. The ensuing decade, from the mid-1960s through the mid-1970s, radically altered the political, social, and especially the cultural foundations of the West and gave way to a more truly global world.

MACHINAL

SOPHIE TREADWELL

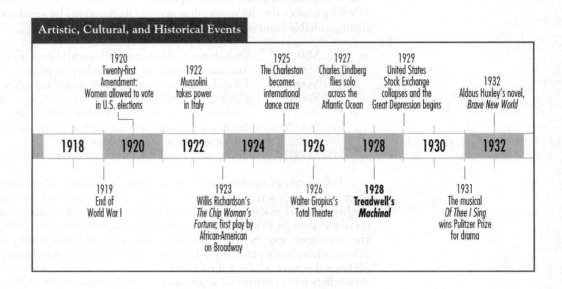

Artistic, Cultural, and Historical Events

1920 — Twenty-first Amendment: Women allowed to vote in U.S. elections

1922 — Mussolini takes power in Italy

1925 — The Charleston becomes international dance craze

1927 — Charles Lindberg flies solo across the Atlantic Ocean

1929 — United States Stock Exchange collapses and the Great Depression begins

1932 — Aldous Huxley's novel, *Brave New World*

1918 — 1920 — 1922 — 1924 — 1926 — 1928 — 1930 — 1932

1919 — End of World War I

1923 — Willis Richardson's *The Chip Woman's Fortune*; first play by African-American on Broadway

1926 — Walter Gropius's Total Theater

1928 — Treadwell's *Machinal*

1931 — The musical *Of Thee I Sing* wins Pulitzer Prize for drama

SOPHIE TREADWELL (1885–1970)

Sophie Treadwell was a crusading journalist, novelist, playwright, and occasional director and producer. She is best known in the theater world for one extraordinary play—*Machinal*. Born in California, Treadwell began writing and acting at the University of California in 1906. Trained as a reporter, she hoped to be an actress, although her career onstage was short-lived. She worked instead for newspapers in San Francisco, covering everything from theater events to sports, before setting off to research investigative stories (on homeless women, for instance) and to conduct exclusive interviews (e.g., with Mexican revolutionary Pancho Villa) that sealed her reputation as a hard-hitting journalist. She reported from the European battle zones during World War I and served as a special correspondent in Mexico during World War II.

Like Eugene O'Neill's adventures at sea and around the New York docks, Treadwell's travels also fed her material for some thirty plays, providing stories, subjects, and settings that ranged from Mexico to Moscow. Beginning with *Gringo* (1922), based on her experiences in Mexico, and *O Nightingale* (1924), a comedy about a stage-struck young woman, Treadwell persisted in getting her dramas staged. Sometimes she directed and even produced her own work—an unusual accomplishment in the male-dominated American commercial theater, especially for a playwright based on the West Coast. Just seven of her plays were produced in New York. Treadwell also paralleled O'Neill in exploring dramatic form and style. Even more than O'Neill's expressionist plays *The Emperor Jones* and *The Hairy Ape*, Treadwell's *Machinal* (1928) follows German expressionist practice by presenting its dramatic world through the subjective lens of its main character, Helen, who lives in a mechanistic, materialistic world. By validating her subjectivity, the play protests the oppressive structure of authoritarian families and a capitalistic system that views even intimate relationships in economic terms.

Among Treadwell's hundreds of reportorial assignments was the trial of Ruth Snyder who, with her lover Judd Gray, had murdered her husband. She was convicted and executed in the electric chair. The playwright loosely based the story of Helen in *Machinal* upon that real-life crime. Treadwell does not emphasize the sensational story, however, but instead focuses on the dependent status of women and the nightmare of a loveless, sexually repugnant marriage.

Stylistically, *Machinal* employs all the key ingredients of the expressionist project. The characters are flat, rather than fully rounded, with Helen a kind of Everywoman figure force-marched through life. Sound effects are harsh. Dialogue and action are repetitive, suggesting clichés mechanically repeated or machine-like reactions rather than spontaneously felt human responses. And, as in Strindberg's *The Ghost Sonata*, interior and exterior action is sometimes indistinguishable. A feminist critique as well, *Machinal* uses images of entrapment to express Helen's domination by male figures and by male-identified women such as her mother.

Later in her career, notes theater historian Judith E. Barlow, Treadwell became embittered by the lukewarm reception of *Hope for a Harvest* (1941), an autobiographical play exposing environmental destruction in her beloved California. Foreshadowing much later work by women artists, *Harvest* anatomized the relationship between prejudice against women and exploitation of the environment. That same year, writes Barlow, the eminent critic George Jean Nathan "sneered that 'even the best of our [American] women playwrights falls immeasurably short of the mark of our best masculine' because women 'by nature' lack 'complete objectivity' and the emotional control of their male counterparts." It was in such an atmosphere that Sophie Treadwell attempted to be heard, and it was then that she stopped producing her work in New York.

Treadwell was married for twenty years to fellow journalist William O. McGeehan, though she maintained her own name and sometimes her own home. She marched in favor of the vote for women. In the political engagement of her life and work, she forecast many social currents of the 1960s. *Machinal* premiered successfully on Broadway in 1928 with Clark Gable as the lover. It was performed in 1930 in London and proved a sensation when it was directed by Alexander Tairov at Moscow's Kamerny Theatre in 1933. The play—and Treadwell—was largely forgotten until two high-profile productions in the early 1990s. Director Michael Greif (who later directed the hit musical *Rent*) revived *Machinal* for the off-Broadway Public Theater in New York; then a scenically monumental 1993 production at the Royal National Theatre starred Fiona Shaw and brought international attention to the neglected playwright. That revival, acclaimed by critics, was directed by Stephen Daldry. Since then, *Machinal* has been performed often, especially on university campuses. As New York critics have pointed out in reviewing recent revivals of her work, Treadwell's dramatic universe is uncomfortably like our own technology-saturated world, and her clipped dialogue calls to mind such contemporary playwrights as Harold Pinter and David Mamet.

As You Read *Machinal*

You will almost immediately note that the action is divided into short, sometimes almost wordless scenes and that Treadwell's stage directions call for exact images and sounds: typewriters, an adding machine, telephones, a radio, a jazz band. Against this cacophonous urban backdrop, we often hear Helen thinking out loud. Episode 1, for instance, ends with such an interior monologue. Paying close attention to such stage directions and stylistic cues will help you imagine the play onstage. That imagining is particularly important with such expressionistic drama, for its emotional effect resides very much in its sound and its visual images.

MACHINAL

S O P H I E T R E A D W E L L

The Plot: *The story of a woman who murders her husband—an ordinary young woman, any woman.*

The Plan: *To tell this story by showing the different phases of life that the woman comes in contact with, and in none of which she finds any place, any peace. The woman is essentially soft, tender, and the life around her is essentially hard, mechanized. Business, home, marriage, having a child, seeking pleasure—all are difficult for her—mechanical, nerve nagging. Only in an illicit love does she find anything with life in it for her, and when she loses this, the desperate effort to win free to it again is her undoing.*

The story is told in nine scenes. In the dialogue of these scenes there is the attempt to catch the rhythm of our common city speech, its brassy sound, its trick of repetition, etc.

Then there is, also, the use of many different sounds chosen primarily for their inherent emotional effect (steel riveting, a priest chanting, a Negro singing, jazz band, etc.), but contributing also to the creation of a background, an atmosphere.

The Hope: *To create a stage production that will have 'style', and at the same time, by the story's own innate drama, by the directness of its telling, by the variety and quick changingness of its scenes, and the excitement of its sounds, to create an interesting play.*

Scenically: *This play is planned to be handled in two basic sets (or in one set with two backs).*

The first division—the first Four Episodes—needs an entrance at one side, and a back having a door and a large window. The door gives, in

Episode 1—to Vice President's office.
Episode 2—to hall.
Episode 3—to bathroom.
Episode 4—to corridor.

And the window shows, in

Episode 1—An opposite office.
Episode 2—An inner apartment court.
Episode 3—Window of a dance casino opposite.
Episode 4—Steel girders. (Of these, only the casino window is important. Sky could be used for the others.)

The second division—the last Five Episodes—has the same side entrance, but the back has only one opening—for a small window (barred).

Episode 5—window is masked by electric piano.
Episode 6—window is disclosed (sidewalk outside).
Episode 7—window is curtained.
Episode 8—window is masked by Judge's bench.
Episode 9—window is disclosed (sky outside).

There is a change of furniture, and props for each episode—only essential things, full of character. For Episode 9, the room is closed in from the sides, and there is a place with bars and a door in it, put straight across stage down front (back far enough to leave a clear passageway in front of it).

Lighting concentrated and intense.—Light and shadow—bright light and darkness.—This darkness, already in the scene, grows and blacks out the light for dark stage when the scene changes are made.

Offstage Voices: *Characters in the Background Heard, but Unseen:*

A Janitor
A Baby
A Boy and a Girl
A Husband and Wife
A Husband and Wife
A Radio Announcer
A Negro Singer

Mechanical Offstage Sounds:
A small jazz band
A hand organ
Steel riveting
Telegraph insruments
Aeroplane engine

Mechanical Onstage Sounds:
Office Machines (typewriters, telephones, etc.)
Electric piano.

Characters: *in the Background Seen, Not Heard (Seen, off the main set, i.e., through a window or door)*

Couples of men and women dancing
A Woman in a bathrobe
A Woman in a wheel chair
A Nurse with a covered basin
A Nurse with a tray
The feet of men and women passing in the street

EPISODE 1

TO BUSINESS

SCENE: *An office: a switchboard, filing cabinet, adding machine, typewriter and table, manifold machine.*
SOUNDS: *Office machines: typewriters, adding machine, manifold, telephone bells, buzzers.*
CHARACTERS AND THEIR MACHINES: *A Young woman (typewriter); A Stenographer (typewriter); A Filing Clerk (filing cabinet and manifold); An Adding Clerk (adding machine); Telephone Operator (switchboard); Jones*

BEFORE THE CURTAIN: *Sounds of machines going. They continue throughout the scene, and accompany the Young Woman's thoughts after the scene is blacked out.*

AT THE RISE OF THE CURTAIN: *All the machines are disclosed, and all the characters with the exception of the Young Woman.*

Of these characters, the Young Woman, going any day to any business. Ordinary. The confusion of her own inner thoughts, emotions, desires, dreams cuts her off from any actual adjustment to the routine of work. She gets through this routine with a very small surface of her consciousness. She is not homely and she is not pretty. She is preoccupied with herself—with her person. She has well kept hands, and a trick of constantly arranging her hair over her ears.

The Stenographer is the faded, efficient woman office worker. Drying, dried.

The Adding Clerk is her male counterpart.

The Filing Clerk is a boy not grown, callow adolescence.

The Telephone Girl, young, cheap and amorous.

Lights come up on office scene. Two desks right and left.

Telephone booth back right center. Filing cabinet back of center. Adding machine back left center.

ADDING CLERK (*in the monotonous voice of his monotonous thoughts; at his adding machine*). 2490, 28, 76, 123, 36842, 1, 1/4, 37, 804, 23 1/2, 982.

FILING CLERK (*in the same way—at his filing desk*). Accounts—A. Bonds—B. Contracts—C. Data—D. Earnings—E.

STENOGRAPHER (*in the same way—left*). Dear Sir—in re—your letter—recent date—will state—

TELEPHONE GIRL. Hello—Hello—George H. Jones Company good morning—hello hello—George H. Jones Company good morning—hello.

FILING CLERK. Market—M. Notes—N. Output—O. Profits—P.—! (*Suddenly*) What's the matter with Q?

TELEPHONE GIRL. Matter with it—Mr. J.—Mr. K. wants you—What you mean matter? Matter with what?

FILING CLERK. Matter with Q.

TELEPHONE GIRL. Well—what is? Spring 1726?

FILING CLERK. I'm asking yuh—

TELEPHONE GIRL. Well?

FILING CLERK. Nothing filed with it—

TELEPHONE GIRL. Well?

FILING CLERK. Look at A. Look at B. What's the matter with Q?

TELEPHONE GIRL. Ain't popular. Hello—Hello—George H. Jones Company.

FILING CLERK. Hot dog! Why ain't it?

ADDING CLERK. Has it personality?

STENOGRAPHER. Has it Halitosis?

TELEPHONE GIRL. Has it got it?

FILING CLERK. Hot dog!

TELEPHONE GIRL. What number do you want? (*Recognizing but not pleased.*) Oh—hello—sure I know who it is—tonight? Uh, uh—(*Negative, but each with a different inflection.*) You heard me—No!

FILING CLERK. Don't you like him?

STENOGRAPHER. She likes 'em all.

TELEPHONE GIRL. I do not!

STENOGRAPHER. Well—pretty near all!

TELEPHONE GIRL. What number do you want? Wrong number. Hello—hello—George H. Jones Company. Hello, hello—

STENOGRAPHER. Memorandum—attention Mr. Smith—at a conference of—

ADDING CLERK. 125—83 3/4—22—908—34—l/4—28593.

FILING CLERK. Report—R, Sales—S, Trade—T.

TELEPHONE GIRL. Shh—! Yes, Mr. J.—? No—Miss A. ain't in yet—I'll tell her, Mr. J.—just the minute she gets in.

STENOGRAPHER. She's late again, huh?

TELEPHONE GIRL. Out with her sweetie last night, huh?

FILING CLERK. Hot dog.

ADDING CLERK. She ain't got a sweetie.

STENOGRAPHER. How do you know?

ADDING CLERK. I know.

FILING CLERK. Hot dog.

ADDING CLERK. She lives alone with her mother.

TELEPHONE GIRL. Spring 1876? Hello—Spring 1876. Spring! Hello, Spring 1876? 1876! Wrong number! Hello! Hello!

STENOGRAPHER. Director's meeting semi-annual report card.

FILING CLERK. Shipments—Sales—Schedules—S.

ADDING CLERK. She doesn't belong in an office.

TELEPHONE GIRL. Who does?

STENOGRAPHER. I do!

ADDING CLERK. You said it!

FILING CLERK. Hot dog!

TELEPHONE GIRL. Hello—hello—George H. Jones Company—hello—hello—

STENOGRAPHER. I'm efficient. She's inefficient.

FILING CLERK. She's inefficient.

TELEPHONE GIRL. She's got J. going.

STENOGRAPHER. Going?

TELEPHONE GIRL. Going and coming.

FILING CLERK. Hot dog.

Enter Jones.

JONES. Good morning, everybody.

TELEPHONE GIRL. Good morning.

FILING CLERK. Good morning.

ADDING CLERK. Good morning.

STENOGRAPHER. Good morning, Mr. J.

JONES. Miss A. isn't in yet?

TELEPHONE GIRL. Not yet, Mr. J.

FILING CLERK. Not yet.

ADDING CLERK. Not yet.

STENOGRAPHER. She's late.

JONES. I just wanted her to take a letter.

STENOGRAPHER. I'll take the letter.

JONES. One thing at a time and that done well.

ADDING CLERK (*yessing*). Done well.

STENOGRAPHER. I'll finish it later.

JONES. Hew to the line.

ADDING CLERK. Hew to the line.

STENOGRAPHER. Then I'll hurry.

JONES. Haste makes waste.

ADDING CLERK. Waste.

STENOGRAPHER. But if you're in a hurry.

JONES. I'm never in a hurry—That's how I get ahead! (*Laughs. They all laugh.*) First know you're right—then go ahead.

ADDING CLERK. Ahead.

JONES (*to Telephone Girl*). When Miss A. comes in tell her I want her to take a letter. (*Turns to go in—then.*) It's important.

TELEPHONE GIRL (*making a note*). Miss A.—important.

JONES (*starts up—then*). And I don't want to be disturbed.

TELEPHONE GIRL. You're in conference?

JONES. I'm in conference. (*Turns—then.*) Unless it's A.B.—of course.

TELEPHONE GIRL. Of course—A.B.

JONES (*starts—turns again; attempts to be facetious*). Tell Miss A. the early bird catches the worm.

Exit Jones.

TELEPHONE GIRL. The early worm gets caught.

ADDING CLERK. He's caught.

TELEPHONE GIRL. Hooked.

ADDING CLERK. In the pan.

FILING CLERK. Hot dog.

STENOGRAPHER. We beg leave to announce—

Enter Young Woman. Goes behind telephone booth to desk right.

STENOGRAPHER. You're late!

FILING CLERK. You're late.

ADDING CLERK. You're late.

STENOGRAPHER. And yesterday!

FILING CLERK. The day before.

ADDING CLERK. And the day before.

STENOGRAPHER. You'll lose your job.

YOUNG WOMAN. No!

STENOGRAPHER. No?

Workers exchange glances.

YOUNG WOMAN. I can't!

STENOGRAPHER. Can't?

Same business.

FILING CLERK. Rent—bills—installments—miscellaneous.

ADDING CLERK. A dollar ten—ninety-five—3.40—35—12.60.

STENOGRAPHER. Then why are you late?

YOUNG WOMAN. Why?

STENOGRAPHER. Excuse!

ADDING CLERK. Excuse!

FILING CLERK. Excuse.

TELEPHONE GIRL. Excuse it, please.

STENOGRAPHER. Why?

YOUNG WOMAN. The subway?

TELEPHONE GIRL. Long distance?

FILING CLERK. Old stuff!

ADDING CLERK. That stall!

STENOGRAPHER. Stalled?

YOUNG WOMAN. No—

STENOGRAPHER. What?

YOUNG WOMAN. I had to get out!

ADDING CLERK. Out!

FILING CLERK. Out?

STENOGRAPHER. Out where?

YOUNG WOMAN. In the air!

STENOGRAPHER. Air?

YOUNG WOMAN. All those bodies pressing.

FILING CLERK. Hot dog!

YOUNG WOMAN. I thought I would faint! I had to get out in the air!

FILING CLERK. Give her the air.

ADDING CLERK. Free air—

STENOGRAPHER. Hot air—

YOUNG WOMAN. Like I'm dying.

STENOGRAPHER. Same thing yesterday. (*Pause*). And the day before.

YOUNG WOMAN. Yes—what am I going to do?

ADDING CLERK. Take a taxi! (*They laugh*).

FILING CLERK. Call a cop!

TELEPHONE GIRL. Mr. J. wants you.

YOUNG WOMAN. Me?

TELEPHONE GIRL. You!

YOUNG WOMAN (*rises*). Mr. J.!

STENOGRAPHER. Mr. J.

TELEPHONE GIRL. He's bellowing for you!

Young Woman gives last pat to her hair—goes off into door—back.

STENOGRAPHER (*after her*). Get it just right.

FILING CLERK. She's always doing that to her hair.

TELEPHONE GIRL. It gives a line—it gives a line—

FILING CLERK. Hot dog.

ADDING CLERK. She's artistic.

STENOGRAPHER. She's inefficient.

FILING CLERK. She's inefficient.

STENOGRAPHER. Mr. J. knows she's inefficient.

ADDING CLERK. 46—23—84—2—2—2—1,492—678.

TELEPHONE GIRL. Hello—hello—George H. Jones Company—hello—Mr. Jones? He's in conference.

STENOGRAPHER (*sarcastic*). Conference!

ADDING CLERK. Conference.

FILING CLERK. Hot dog!

TELEPHONE GIRL. Do you think he'll marry her?

ADDING CLERK. If she'll have him.

STENOGRAPHER. If she'll have him!

FILING CLERK. Do you think she'll have him?

TELEPHONE GIRL. How much does he get?

ADDING CLERK. Plenty—5,000—10,000—15,000—20,000—25,000.

STENOGRAPHER. And plenty put away.

ADDING CLERK. Gas Preferred—4's—steel—5's—oil—6's.

FILING CLERK. Hot dog.

STENOGRAPHER. Will she have him? Will she have him? This agreement entered into—party of the first part—party of the second part—will he have her?

TELEPHONE GIRL. Well, I'd hate to get into bed with him. (*Familiar melting voice.*) Hello—humhum—hum—hum—hold the line a minute—will you—hum hum. (*Professional voice.*) Hell, hello—A.B., just a minute. Mr. A.B.—Mr. J.? Mr. A.B.—go ahead, Mr. A.B. (*Melting voice.*) We were interrupted—huh—huh—huh—huh-huh—hum—hum.

Enter Young Woman—she goes to her chair, sits with folded hands.

FILING CLERK. That's all you ever say to a guy—

STENOGRAPHER. Hum—hum—or uh huh—(*Negative.*)

TELEPHONE GIRL. That's all you have to. (*To phone.*) Hum—hum—hum hum—hum hum.

STENOGRAPHER. Mostly hum hum.

ADDING CLERK. You've said it!

FILING CLERK. Hot dog.

TELEPHONE GIRL. Hum hum huh hum humhumhum—tonight? She's got a date—she told me last night—humhumhuh—hum—all right. (*Disconnects*) Too bad—my boy friend's got a friend—but my girl friend's got a date.

YOUNG WOMAN. You have a good time.

TELEPHONE GIRL. Big time.

STENOGRAPHER. Small time.

ADDING CLERK. A big time on the small time.

TELEPHONE GIRL. I'd ask you, kid, but you'd be up to your neck!

STENOGRAPHER. Neckers!

ADDING CLERK. Petters!

FILING CLERK. Sweet papas.

TELEPHONE GIRL. Want to come?

YOUNG WOMAN. Can't.

TELEPHONE GIRL. Date?

YOUNG WOMAN. My mother.

STENOGRAPHER. Worries?

TELEPHONE GIRL. Nags—hello—George H. Jones Company—Oh hello—

Young Woman sits before her machine—hands in lap, looking at them.

STENOGRAPHER. Why don't you get to work?

YOUNG WOMAN (*dreaming*). What?

ADDING CLERK. Work!

YOUNG WOMAN. Can't.

STENOGRAPHER. Can't?

YOUNG WOMAN. My machine's out of order.

STENOGRAPHER. Well, fix it!

YOUNG WOMAN. I can't—got to get somebody.

STENOGRAPHER. Somebody! Somebody! Always somebody! Here, sort the mail, then!

YOUNG WOMAN (*rises*). All right.

STENOGRAPHER. And hurry! You're late.

YOUNG WOMAN (*sorting letters*). George H. Jones and Company—George H. Jones Inc. George H. Jones—

STENOGRAPHER. You're always late.

ADDING CLERK. You'll lose your job.

YOUNG WOMAN (*hurrying*). George H. Jones—George H. Jones Personal—

TELEPHONE GIRL. Don't let 'em get your goat, kid—tell 'em where to get off.

YOUNG WOMAN. What?

TELEPHONE GIRL. Ain't it all set?

YOUNG WOMAN. What?

TELEPHONE GIRL. You and Mr. J.

STENOGRAPHER. You and the boss.

FILING CLERK. You and the big chief.

ADDING CLERK. You and the big cheese.

YOUNG WOMAN. Did he tell you?

TELEPHONE GIRL. I told you!

ADDING CLERK. I told you!

STENOGRAPHER. I don't believe it.

ADDING CLERK. 5,000—10,000—15,000.

FILING CLERK. Hot dog.

YOUNG WOMAN. No—it isn't so.

STENOGRAPHER. Isn't it?

YOUNG WOMAN. No.

TELEPHONE GIRL. Not yet.

ADDING CLERK. But soon.

FILING CLERK. Hot dog.

Enter Jones.

TELEPHONE GIRL (*busy*). George H. Jones Company—Hello—Hello.

STENOGRAPHER. Awaiting your answer—

ADDING CLERK. 5,000—10,000—15,000—

JONES (*crossing to Young Woman—puts hand on her shoulder, all stop and stare*). That letter done?

YOUNG WOMAN. No. (*She pulls away.*)

JONES. What's the matter?

STENOGRAPHER. She hasn't started.

JONES. O.K.—want to make some changes.

YOUNG WOMAN. My machine's out of order.

JONES. O.K.—use the one in my room.

YOUNG WOMAN. I'm sorting the mail.

STENOGRAPHER (*sarcastic*). One thing at a time!

JONES (*retreating—goes back center*). O.K. (*To Young Woman.*) When you're finished. (*Starts back to his room.*)

STENOGRAPHER. Haste makes waste.

JONES (*at door*). O.K.—don't hurry.

Exits.

STENOGRAPHER. Hew to the line!

TELEPHONE GIRL. He's hewing.

FILING CLERK. Hot dog.

TELEPHONE GIRL. Why did you flinch, kid?

YOUNG WOMAN. Flinch?

TELEPHONE GIRL. Did he pinch?

YOUNG WOMAN. No.

TELEPHONE GIRL. Then what?

YOUNG WOMAN. Nothing!—Just his hand.

TELEPHONE GIRL. Oh—just his hand—(*Shakes her head thoughtfully.*) Uhhuh. (*Negative.*) Uhhuh. (*Decisively.*) No! Tell him no.

STENOGRAPHER. If she does she'll lose her job.

ADDING CLERK. Fired.

FILING CLERK. The sack!

TELEPHONE GIRL (*on the defensive*). And if she doesn't?

ADDING CLERK. She'll come to work in a taxi!

TELEPHONE GIRL. Work?

FILING CLERK. No work.

STENOGRAPHER. No worry.

ADDING CLERK. Breakfast in bed.

STENOGRAPHER (*sarcastic*). Did Madame ring?

FILING CLERK. Lunch in bed!

TELEPHONE GIRL. A double bed! (*In phone.*) Yes, Mr. J. (*To Young Woman.*) J. wants you.

YOUNG WOMAN (*starts to get to her feet—but doesn't*). I can't—I'm not ready—in a minute. (*Sits staring ahead of her.*)

ADDING CLERK. 5,000—10,000—15,000—

FILING CLERK. Profits—plans—purchase—

STENOGRAPHER. Call your attention our prices are fixed.

TELEPHONE GIRL. Hello—hello—George H. Jones Company—hello—hello—

YOUNG WOMAN (*thinking her thoughts aloud—to the subdued accompaniment of the office sounds and voices*). Marry me—wants to marry me—George H. Jones—George H. Jones and Company—Mrs. George H. Jones—Mrs. George H. Jones. Dear Madame—marry—do you take this man to be your wedded husband—I do—to love, honor and to love—kisses—no—I can't—George H. Jones—How would you like to marry me—What do you say—Why Mr. Jones I—let

me look at your little hands—you have such pretty little hands—let me hold your pretty little hands—George H. Jones—Fat hands—flabby hands—don't touch me—please—fat hands are never weary—please don't—married—all girls—most girls—married—babies—a baby—curls—little curls all over its head—George H. Jones—straight—thin—bald—don't touch me—please—no—can't—must—somebody—something—no rest—must rest—no rest—must rest—no rest—late today—yesterday—before—late—subway—air—pressing—bodies pressing—bodies—trembling—air—stop—air—late—job—no job—fired—late—alarm clock—alarm clock—alarm clock—hurry—job—ma—nag—nag—nag—ma—hurry—job—no job—no money—installments due—no money—money—George H. Jones—money—Mrs. George H. Jones—money—no work—no worry—free!—rest—sleep till nine—sleep till ten—sleep till noon—now you take a good rest this morning—don't get up till you want to—thank you—oh thank you—oh don't!—please don't touch me—I want to rest—no rest—earn—got to earn—married—earn—no—yes—earn—all girls—most girls—ma—pa—ma—all women—most women—I can't—must—maybe—must—somebody—something—ma—pa—ma—can I, ma? Tell me, ma—something—somebody.

The scene blacks out. The sounds of the office machines continue until the scene lights into Episode 2—and the office sounds become the sound of a radio, offstage.

EPISODE 2

AT HOME

SCENE: *A kitchen: table, chairs, plates and food, garbage can, a pair of rubber gloves. The door at the back now opens on a hall—the window, on an apartment house court.*

SOUNDS: *Buzzer, radio (voice of announcer; music and singer).*

CHARACTERS: *Young Woman; Mother*

OUTSIDE VOICES: *characters heard, but not seen: A Janitor; A Baby; A Mother and a Small Boy; A Young Boy and Young Girl; A Husband and a Wife; Another Husband and a Wife*

AT RISE: *Young Woman and Mother eating—radio offstage—radio stops.*

YOUNG WOMAN. Ma—I want to talk to you.
MOTHER. Aren't you eating a potato?
YOUNG WOMAN. No.
MOTHER. Why not?
YOUNG WOMAN. I don't want one.
MOTHER. That's no reason. Here! Take one.
YOUNG WOMAN. I don't want it.
MOTHER. Potatoes go with stew—here!
YOUNG WOMAN. Ma, I don't want it!
MOTHER. Want it! Take it!
YOUNG WOMAN. But I—oh, all right. (*Takes it—then.*) Ma, I want to ask you something.
MOTHER. Eat your potato.
YOUNG WOMAN (*takes a bite—then*). Ma, there's something I want to ask you—something important.
MOTHER. Is it mealy?
YOUNG WOMAN. S'all right. Ma—tell me.
MOTHER. Three pounds for a quarter.
YOUNG WOMAN. Ma—tell me(*Buzzer.*)
MOTHER (*her dull voice brightening*). There's the garbage. (*Goes to door—or dumbwaiter—opens it. Stop radio.*)
JANITOR'S VOICE (*offstage*). Garbage.
MOTHER (*pleased—busy*). All right. (*Gets garbage can—puts it out. Young Woman walks up and down.*) What's the matter now?
YOUNG WOMAN. Nothing.
MOTHER. That jumping up from the table every night the garbage is collected! You act like you're crazy.
YOUNG WOMAN. Ma, do all women—
MOTHER. I suppose you think you're too nice for anything so common! Well, let me tell you, my lady, that it's a very important part of life.
YOUNG WOMAN. Oh, Ma!
MOTHER. Well, are you?
YOUNG WOMAN. Am I what?
MOTHER. Glad! Grateful.
YOUNG WOMAN. Yes!
MOTHER. You don't act like it!
YOUNG WOMAN. Oh, Ma, don't talk!
MOTHER. You just said you wanted to talk.
YOUNG WOMAN. Well now—I want to think. I got to think.
MOTHER. Aren't you going to finish your potato?
YOUNG WOMAN. Oh, Ma!
MOTHER. Is there anything the matter with it?
YOUNG WOMAN. No—
MOTHER. Then why don't you finish it?
YOUNG WOMAN. Because I don't want it.
MOTHER. Why don't you?
YOUNG WOMAN. Oh, Ma! Let me alone!
MOTHER. Well, you've got to eat! If you don't eat—

YOUNG WOMAN. Ma! Don't nag!
MOTHER. Nag! Just because I try to look out for you—nag! Just because I try to care for you—nag! Why, you haven't sense enought to eat! What should become of you I'd like to know—if I didn't nag!

Offstage—a sound of window opening—all these offstage sounds come in through the court window at the back.

WOMAN'S VOICE. Johnny—Johnny—come in now!
A SMALL BOY'S VOICE. Oh, Ma!
WOMAN'S VOICE. It's getting cold.
A SMALL BOY'S VOICE. Oh, Ma!
WOMAN'S VOICE. You heard me! (*Sound of window slamming.*)
YOUNG WOMAN. I'm grown up, Ma.
MOTHER. Grown up! What do you mean by that?
YOUNG WOMAN. Nothing much—I guess. (*Offstage sound of baby crying. Mother rises, clatters dishes.*) Let's not do the dishes right away, Ma. Let's talk—I gotta.
MOTHER. Well, I can't talk with dirty dishes around—you may be able to but—(*Clattering—clattering.*)
YOUNG WOMAN. Ma! Listen! Listen!—There's a man wants to marry me.
MOTHER (*stops clattering—sits*). What man?
YOUNG WOMAN. He says he fell in love with my hands.
MOTHER. In love! Is that beginning again! I thought you were over that!

Offstage Boy's voice—whistles—Girls's voice answers.

BOY'S VOICE. Come on out.
GIRL'S VOICE. Can't.
BOY'S VOICE. Nobody'll see you.
GIRL'S VOICE. I can't.
BOY'S VOICE. It's dark now—come on.
GIRL'S VOICE. Well——just for a minute.
BOY'S VOICE. Meet you round the corner.
YOUNG WOMAN. I got to get married, Ma.
MOTHER. What do you mean?
YOUNG WOMAN. I gotta.
MOTHER. You haven't got in trouble, have you?
YOUNG WOMAN. Don't talk like that!
MOTHER. Well, you say you got to get married—what do you mean?
YOUNG WOMAN. Nothing.
MOTHER. Answer me!
YOUNG WOMAN. All women get married, don't they?
MOTHER. Nonsense!
YOUNG WOMAN. You got married, didn't you?
MOTHER. Yes, I did!

Offstage voices.

WOMAN'S VOICE. Where you going?
MAN'S VOICE. Out.
WOMAN'S VOICE. You were out last night.
MAN'S VOICE. Was I?
WOMAN'S VOICE. You're always going out.
MAN'S VOICE. Am I?
WOMAN'S VOICE. Where you going?
MAN'S VOICE. Out.

End of offstage voices.

MOTHER. Who is he? Where did you come to know him?
YOUNG WOMAN. In the office.
MOTHER. In the office!
YOUNG WOMAN. It's Mr. J.
MOTHER. Mr. J.?
YOUNG WOMAN. The Vice-President.
MOTHER. Vice-President! His income must be—Does he know you've got a mother to support?
YOUNG WOMAN. Yes.
MOTHER. What does he say?
YOUNG WOMAN. All right.
MOTHER. How soon you going to marry him?
YOUNG WOMAN. I'm not going to.
MOTHER. Not going to!
YOUNG WOMAN. No! I'm not going to.
MOTHER. But you just said—
YOUNG WOMAN. I'm not going to.
MOTHER. Are you crazy?
YOUNG WOMAN. I can't, Ma! I can't!
MOTHER. Why can't you?
YOUNG WOMAN. I don't love him.
MOTHER. Love!—what does that amount to! Will it clothe you? Will it feed you? Will it pay the bills?
YOUNG WOMAN. No! But it's real just the same!
MOTHER. Real!
YOUNG WOMAN. If it isn't—what can you count on in life?
MOTHER. I'll tell you what you can count on! You can count that you've got to eat and sleep and get up and put clothes on your back and take 'em off again—that you got to get old—and that you got to die. That's what you can count on! All the rest is in your head!
YOUNG WOMAN. But Ma—didn't you love Pa?
MOTHER. I suppose I did—I don't know—I've forgotten—what difference does it make—now?
YOUNG WOMAN. But then!—oh Ma, tell me!
MOTHER. Tell you what?
YOUNG WOMAN. About all that—love!

Offstage voices.

WIFE'S VOICE. Don't.
HUSBAND'S VOICE. What's the matter—don't you want me to kiss you?
WIFE'S VOICE. Not like that.
HUSBAND'S VOICE. Like what?
WIFE'S VOICE. That silly kiss!
HUSBAND'S VOICE. Silly kiss?
WIFE'S VOICE. You look so silly—oh I know what's coming when you look like that—and kiss me like that—don't—go away—

End of offstage voices.

MOTHER. He's a decent man, isn't he?
YOUNG WOMAN. I don't know. How should I know—yet.
MOTHER. He's a Vice-President—of course he's decent.
YOUNG WOMAN. I don't care whether he's decent or not. I won't marry him.
MOTHER. But you just said you wanted to marry—
YOUNG WOMAN. Not him.
MOTHER. Who?
YOUNG WOMAN. I don't know—I don't know—I haven't found him yet!
MOTHER. You talk like you're crazy!
YOUNG WOMAN. Oh, Ma—tell me!
MOTHER. Tell you what?
YOUNG WOMAN. Tell me—(*Words suddenly pouring out.*) Your skin oughtn't to curl—ought it—when he just comes near you—ought it? That's wrong, ain't it? You don't get over that, do you—ever, do you or do you? How is it, Ma—do you?
MOTHER. Do you what?
YOUNG WOMAN. Do you get used to, it—so after a while it doesn't matter? Or don't you? Does it always matter? You ought to be in love, oughtn't you, Ma? You must be in love, mustn't you, Ma? That changes everything, doesn't it—or does it? Maybe if you just like a person it's all right—is it? When he puts a hand on me, my blood turns cold. But your blood oughtn't to run cold, ought it? His hands are—his hands are fat, Ma—don't you see—his hands are fat—and they sort of press—and they're fat—don't you see?—Don't you see?
MOTHER (*stares at her bewildered*). See what?
YOUNG WOMAN (*rushing on*). I've always thought I'd find somebody—somebody young—and—and attractive—with wavy hair—wavy hair—I always think of children with curls—little curls all over their head—somebody young—and attractive—that I'd like—that I'd love—But I haven't found anybody like that yet—I haven't found anybody—I've hardly known anybody—you'd never let me go with anybody and—

MOTHER. Are you throwing it up to me that—

YOUNG WOMAN. No—let me finish, Ma! No—let me finish! I just mean I've never found anybody—anybody—nobody's ever asked me—till now—he's the only man that's ever asked me—And I suppose I got to marry somebody—all girls do—

MOTHER. Nonsense.

YOUNG WOMAN. But, I can't go on like this, Ma—I don't know why—but I can't—it's like I'm all tight inside—sometimes I feel like I'm stifling!—You don't know—stifling. (*Walks up and down.*) I can't go on like this much longer—going to work—coming home—going to work—coming home—I can't—Sometimes in the subway I think I'm going to die—sometimes even in the office if something don't happen—I got to do something—I don't know—it's like I'm all tight inside.

MOTHER. You're crazy.

YOUNG WOMAN. Oh, Ma!

MOTHER. You're crazy.

YOUNG WOMAN. Ma—if you tell me that again I'll kill you! I'll kill you!

MOTHER. If that isn't crazy!

YOUNG WOMAN. I'll kill you—Maybe I am crazy—I don't know. Sometimes I think I am—the thoughts that go on in my mind—sometimes I think I am—I can't help it if I am—I do the best I can—I do the best I can and I'm nearly crazy! (*Mother rises and sits.*) Go away! Go away! You don't know anything about anything! And you haven't got any pity—no pity—you just take it for granted that I go to work every day—and come home every night and bring my money every week—and just take it for granted—you'd let me go on forever—and never feel any pity—

Offstage radio—a voice singing a sentimental mother song or popular home song. Mother begins to cry—crosses to chair left—sits.

Oh Ma—forgive me! Forgive me!

MOTHER. My own child! To be spoken to like that by my own child!

YOUNG WOMAN. I didn't mean it, Ma—I didn't mean it! (*She goes to her mother—crosses to left.*)

MOTHER (*clinging to her hand*). You're all I've got in the world—and you don't want me—you want to kill me.

YOUNG WOMAN. No—no, I don't, Ma! I just said that!

MOTHER. I've worked for you and slaved for you!

YOUNG WOMAN. I know, Ma.

MOTHER. I brought you into the world.

YOUNG WOMAN. I know, Ma.

MOTHER. You're flesh of my flesh and—

YOUNG WOMAN. I know, Ma, I know.

MOTHER. And—

YOUNG WOMAN. You rest now, Ma—you rest—

MOTHER (*struggling*). I got to do the dishes.

YOUNG WOMAN. I'll do the dishes—You listen to the music, Ma—I'll do the dishes.

Ma sits. Young Woman crosses to behind screen. Takes a pair of rubber gloves and begins to put them on. The Mother sees them—they irritate her—there is a return of her characteristic mood.

MOTHER. Those gloves! I've been washing dishes for forty years and I never wore gloves! But my lady's hands! My lady's hands!

YOUNG WOMAN. Sometimes you talk to me like you're jealous, Ma.

MOTHER. Jealous?

YOUNG WOMAN. It's my hands got me a husband.

MOTHER. A husband? So you're going to marry him now?

YOUNG WOMAN. I suppose so.

MOTHER. If you ain't the craziest—

The scene blacks out. In the darkness, the mother song goes into jazz—very faint—as the scene lights into

EPISODE 3

H O N E Y M O O N

SCENE: *Hotel bedroom: bed, chair, mirror. The door at the back now opens on a bathroom; the window, on a dancing casino opposie.*

SOUNDS: *A small jazz band (violin, piano, saxophone—very dim, at first, then louder).*

CHARACTERS: *Young Woman; Husband; Bellboy*

OFFSTAGE: *Seen not not heard, Men and Women dancing in couples.*

AT RISE: *Set dark Bellboy, Husband, and Young Woman enter. Bellboy carries luggage. He switches on light by door. Stop music.*

HUSBAND. Well, here we are. (*Throws hat on bed; Bellboy puts luggage down, crosses to window; raises shade three inches. Opens window three inches. Sounds of jazz music louder. Offstage.*)

BELLBOY (*comes to man for tip*). Anything else, Sir? (*Receives tip. Exits.*)

HUSBAND. Well, here we are.

YOUNG WOMAN. Yes, here we are.

HUSBAND. Aren't you going to take your hat off—stay a while? (*Young Woman looks around as though looking for a way out, then takes off her hat, pulls the hair automatically around her ears.*) This is all right, isn't it? Huh? Huh?

YOUNG WOMAN. It's very nice.

HUSBAND. Twelve bucks a day! They know how to soak you in these pleasure resorts. Twelve bucks! (*Music.*) Well—we'll get our money's worth out of it all right. (*Goes toward bathroom.*) I'm going to wash up. (*Stops at door.*) Don't you want to wash up?

Young Woman shakes head 'No'.

I do! It was a long trip! I want to wash up!

Goes off—closes door; sings in bathroom. Young Woman goes to window—raises shade—sees the dancers going round and round in couples. Music is louder. Re-enter Husband.

Say, pull that blind down! They can see in!

YOUNG WOMAN. I thought you said there'd be a view of the ocean!

HUSBAND. Sure there is.

YOUNG WOMAN. I just see people—dancing.

HUSBAND. The ocean's beyond.

YOUNG WOMAN (*desperately*). I was counting on seeing it!

HUSBAND. You'll see it tomorrow—what's eating you? We'll take in the boardwalk—Don't you want to wash up?

YOUNG WOMAN. No!

HUSBAND. It was a long trip. Sure you don't? (*Young Woman shakes her head 'No'. Husband takes off his coat—puts it over chair.*) Better make yourself at home. I'm going to. (*She stares at him—moves away from the window.*) Say, pull down that blind! (*Crosses to chair down left—sits.*)

YOUNG WOMAN. It's close—don't you think it's close?

HUSBAND. Well—you don't want people looking in, do you? (*Laughs.*) Huh—Huh?

YOUNG WOMAN. No.

HUSBAND (*laughs*). I guess not. Huh? (*Takes off shoes. Young Woman leaves the window, and crosses down to the bed.*) Say—you look a little white around the gills! What's the matter?

YOUNG WOMAN. Nothing.

HUSBAND. You look like you're scared.

YOUNG WOMAN. No.

HUSBAND. Nothing to be scared of. You're with your husband, you know. (*Takes her to chair, left.*)

YOUNG WOMAN. I know.

HUSBAND. Happy?

YOUNG WOMAN. Yes.

HUSBAND (*sitting*). Then come here and give us a kiss. (*He puts her on his knee.*) That's the girlie. (*He bends her head down, and kisses her along the back of her neck.*) Like that? (*She tries to get to her feet.*) Say—stay there! What you moving for?—You know—you got to learn to relax, little girl—(*Dancers go off. Dim lights. Pinches her above knee.*) Say, what you got under there?

YOUNG WOMAN. Nothing.

HUSBAND. Nothing! (*Laughs.*) That's a good one! Nothing, huh? Huh? That reminds me of the story of the pullman porter and the—what's the matter—did I tell you that one? (*Music dims off and out.*)

YOUNG WOMAN. I don't know.

HUSBAND. The pullman porter and the tart?

YOUNG WOMAN. No.

HUSBAND. It's a good one—well—the train was just pulling out and the tart—

YOUNG WOMAN. You did tell that one!

HUSBAND. About the—

YOUNG WOMAN. Yes! Yes! I remember now!

HUSBAND. About the—

YOUNG WOMAN. Yes!

HUSBAND. All right—if I did. You're sure it was the one about the—

YOUNG WOMAN. I'm sure.

HUSBAND. When he asked her what she had underneath her seat and she said—

YOUNG WOMAN. Yes! Yes! That one!

HUSBAND. All right—But I don't believe I did. (*She tries to get up again, and he holds her.*) You know you have got something under there—what is it?

YOUNG WOMAN. Nothing—just—just my garter.

HUSBAND. Your garter! Your garter! Say did I tell you the one about—

YOUNG WOMAN. Yes! Yes!

HUSBAND (*with dignity*). How do you know which one I mean?

YOUNG WOMAN. You told me them all!

HUSBAND (*pulling her back to his knee*). No, I didn't! Not by a jugful! I got a lot of 'em up my sleeve yet—that's part of what I owe my success to—my ability to spring a good story—You know—you got to learn to relax, little girl—haven't you?

YOUNG WOMAN. Yes.

HUSBAND. That's one of the biggest things to learn in life. That's part of what I owe my success to. Now you go and get those heavy things off—and relax.

YOUNG WOMAN. They're not heavy.

HUSBAND. You haven't got much on—have you? But you'll feel better with 'em off. (*Gets up.*) Want me to help you?

YOUNG WOMAN. No.

HUSBAND. I'm your husband, you know.

YOUNG WOMAN. I know.

HUSBAND. You aren't afraid of your husband, are you?

YOUNG WOMAN. No—of course not—but I thought maybe—can't we go out for a little while?

HUSBAND. Out? What for?

YOUNG WOMAN. Fresh air—walk—talk.

HUSBAND. We can talk here—I'll tell you all about myself. Go along now. (*Young Woman goes toward bathroom door. Gets bag.*) Where are you going?

YOUNG WOMAN. In here.

HUSBAND. I thought you'd want to wash up.

YOUNG WOMAN. I just want to—get ready.

HUSBAND. You don't have to go in there to take your clothes off!

YOUNG WOMAN. I want to.

HUSBAND. What for?

YOUNG WOMAN. I always do.

HUSBAND. What?

YOUNG WOMAN. Undress by myself.

HUSBAND. You've never been married till now—have you? (*Laughs.*) Or have you been pulling something over on me?

YOUNG WOMAN. No.

HUSBAND. I understand—kind of modest—huh? Huh?

YOUNG WOMAN. Yes.

HUSBAND. I understand women—(*Indulgently.*) Go along.

She goes off—starts to close door. Young Woman exits.

Don't close the door—thought you wanted to talk.

He looks around the room with satisfaction—after a pause—rises—takes off his collar.

You're awful quiet—what are you doing in there?

YOUNG WOMAN. Just—getting ready—

HUSBAND (*still in his mood of satisfaction*). I'm going to enjoy life from now on—I haven't had such an easy time of it. I got where I am by hard work and self denial—now I'm going to enjoy life—I'm going to make up for all I missed—aren't you about ready?

YOUNG WOMAN. Not yet.

HUSBAND. Next year maybe we'll go to Paris. You can buy a lot of that French underwear—and Switzerland—all my life I've wanted a Swiss watch—that I bought right there—I coulda' got a Swiss watch here, but I always wanted one that I bought right there—Isn't that funny—huh? Isn't it? Huh? Huh?

YOUNG WOMAN. Yes.

HUSBAND. All my life I've wanted a Swiss watch that I bought right there. All my life I've counted on having that some day—more than anything—except one thing—you know what?

YOUNG WOMAN. No.

HUSBAND. Guess.

YOUNG WOMAN. I can't.

HUSBAND. Then I'm coming in and tell you.

YOUNG WOMAN. No! Please! Please don't.

HUSBAND. Well hurry up then! I thought you women didn't wear much of anything these days—huh? Huh? I'm coming in!

YOUNG WOMAN. No—no! Just a minute!

HUSBAND. All right. Just a minute. (*Young Woman is silent. Husband laughs and takes out watch.*)13—14—I'm counting the seconds on you—that's what you said, didn't you—just a minute!—49—50—51—52—53—

Enter Young Woman.

YOUNG WOMAN (*at the door*). Here I am. (*She wears a little white gown that hangs very straight. She is very still, but her eyes are wide with a curious, helpless, animal terror.*)

HUSBAND (*starts toward her—stops. The room is in shadow except for one dim light by the bed. Sound of girl weeping*).You crying? (*Sound of weeping.*) What are you crying for? (*Crosses to her.*)

YOUNG WOMAN (*crying out*). Ma! Ma! I want my mother!

HUSBAND. I thought you were glad to get away from her.

YOUNG WOMAN. I want her now—I want somebody.

HUSBAND. You got me, haven't you?

YOUNG WOMAN. Somebody—somebody—

HUSBAND. There's nothing to cry about. There's nothing to cry about.

The scene blacks out. The music continues until the lights go up for Episode 4. Rhythm of the music is gradually replaced by the sound of steel riveting for Episode 4.

EPISODE 4

MATERNAL

SCENE: A room in a hospital: bed, chair. The door in the back now opens on a corridor; the window on a tall building going up.

SOUNDS: Outside window—riveting.

CHARACTERS IN THE SCENE: *Young Woman; Doctors; Nurses; Husband*

CHARACTERS SEEN BUT NOT HEARD: *Woman in Wheel Chair; Woman in Bathrobe; Stretcher Wagon; Nurse with Tray; Nurse with Covered Basin*

AT RISE: *Young Woman lies still in bed. The door is open. In the corridor, a stretcher wagon goes by. Enter Nurse.*

NURSE. How are you feeling today? (*No response from Young Woman.*) Better? (*No response.*) No pain? (*No response. Nurse takes her watch in one hand, Young Woman's wrist in the other—stands, then goes to chart at foot of bed—writes.*) You're getting along fine. (*No response.*) Such a sweet baby you have, too. (*No response.*) Aren't you glad it's a girl? (*Young Woman makes sign with her head 'No'.*) You're not! Oh, my! That's no way to talk! Men want boys—woman ought to want girls. (*No response.*) Maybe you didn't want either, eh? (*Young Woman signs 'No'. Riveting machine.*) You'll feel different when it begins to nurse. You'll just love it then. Your milk hasn't come yet—has it? (*Sign—'No'.*) It will! (*Sign—'No'.*) Oh, you don't know Doctor! (*Goes to door—turns.*) Anything else you want? (*Young Woman points to window.*) Draft? (*Sign—'No'.*) The noise? (*Young Woman signs 'Yes'.*) Oh, that can't be helped. Hospital's got to have a new wing. We've the biggest Maternity Hospital in the world. I'll close the window, though. (*Young Woman signs 'No'.*) No?

YOUNG WOMAN (*whispers*). I smell everything then.

NURSE (*starting out the door—riveting machine*). Here's your man!

Enter Husband with large bouquet. Crosses to bed.

HUSBAND. Well, how are we today? (*Young Woman—no response.*)

NURSE. She's getting stronger!

HUSBAND. Of course she is!

NURSE (*taking flowers*). See what your husband brought you.

HUSBAND. Better put 'em in water right away. (*Exit nurse.*) Everything O.K.? (*Young Woman signs 'No'.*) Now see here, my dear, you've got to brace up, you know! And—and face things! Everybody's got to brace up and face things! That's what makes the world go round. I know all you've been through but—(*Young Woman signs 'No'.*) Oh, yes I do! I know all about it! I was right outside all the time! (*Young*

Woman makes violent gestures of 'No'. Ignoring.) Oh yes! But you've got to brace up now! Make an effort! Pull yourself together! Start the up-hill climb! Oh I've been down—but I haven't stayed down. I've been licked but I haven't stayed licked! I've pulled myself up by my own bootstraps, and that's what you've got to do! Will power! That's what conquers! Look at me! Now you've got to brace up! Face the music! Stand the gaff! Take life by the horns! Look it in the face!—Having a baby's natural! Perfectly natural thing—why should—

Young Woman chokes—points wildly to door. Enter Nurse with flowers in a vase.

NURSE. What's the matter?

HUSBAND. She's got that gagging again—like she had the last time I was here.

Young Woman gestures him out.

NURSE. Better go, sir.

HUSBAND (*at door*). I'll be back.

Young Woman gasping and gesturing.

NURSE. She needs rest.

HUSBAND. Tomorrow then. I'll be back tomorrow—tomorrow and every day—goodbye. (*Exits.*)

NURSE. You got a mighty nice husband, I guess you know that? (*Writes on chart.*) Gagging.

Corridor life—Woman in a Bathrobe passes door. Enter Doctor, Young Doctor, Nurse, wheeling surgeon's wagon with bottles, instruments, etc.

DOCTOR. How's the little lady today? (*Crosses to bed.*)

NURSE. She's better, Doctor.

DOCTOR. Of course she's better! She's all right—aren't you? (*Young Woman does not respond.*) What's the matter? Can't you talk? (*Drops her hand. Takes chart.*)

NURSE. She's a little weak yet, Doctor.

DOCTOR (*at chart*). Milk hasn't come yet?

NURSE. No, Doctor.

DOCTOR. Put the child to breast. (*Young Woman—'No—no'!—Riveting machine.*) No? Don't you want to nurse your baby? (*Young Woman signs 'No'.*) Why not? (*No response.*) These modern neurotic women, eh, Doctor? What are we going to do with 'em? (*Young Doctor laughs. Nurse smiles.*) Bring the baby!

YOUNG WOMAN. No!

DOCTOR. Well—that's strong enough. I thought you were too weak to talk—that's better. You don't want your baby?

YOUNG WOMAN. No.

DOCTOR. What do you want?

YOUNG WOMAN. Let alone—let alone.

DOCTOR. Bring the baby.

NURSE. Yes, Doctor—she's behaved very badly every time, Doctor—very upset—maybe we better not.

DOCTOR. I decide what we better and better not here, Nurse!

NURSE. Yes, doctor.

DOCTOR. Bring the baby.

NURSE. Yes, Doctor.

DOCTOR (*with chart*). Gagging—you mean nausea.

NURSE. Yes, Doctor, but—

DOCTOR. No buts, nurse.

NURSE. Yes, Doctor.

DOCTOR. Nausea!—Change the diet!—What is her diet?

NURSE. Liquids.

DOCTOR. Give her solids.

NURSE. Yes, Doctor. She says she can't swallow solids.

DOCTOR. Give her solids.

NURSE. Yes, Doctor. (*Starts to go—riveting machine.*)

DOCTOR. Wait—I'll change her medicine. (*Takes pad and writes prescription in Latin. Hands it to Nurse.*) After meals. (*To door.*) Bring her baby.

Exit Doctor, followed by Young Doctor and Nurse with surgeon's wagon.

NURSE. Yes, Doctor.

Exits.

YOUNG WOMAN (*alone*). Let me alone—let me alone—let me alone—I've submitted to enough—I won't submit to any more—crawl off—crawl off in the dark—Vixen crawled under the bed—way back in the corner under the bed—they were all drowned—puppies don't go to heaven—heaven—golden stairs—long stairs—long—too long—long golden stairs—climb those golden stairs—stairs—stairs—climb—tired—too tired—dead—no matter—nothing matters—dead—stairs—long stairs—all the dead going up—going up—to be in heaven—heaven—golden stairs—all the children coming down—coming down to be born—dead going up—children coming down—going up—coming down—going up—coming down—going up—coming down—going up—stop—stop—no—no traffic cop—no—no traffic cop in heaven—traffic cop—traffic cop—can't you give us a smile—tired—too tired—no matter—it doesn't matter—St. Peter—St. Peter at the gate—you can't come in—no matter—it doesn't matter—I'll rest—I'll lie down—down—all written down—down in a big book—no matter—it doesn't matter—I'll lie down—it weighs me—it's over me—it weighs—weighs—it's heavy—it's a heavy book—no matter—lie still—don't move—can't move—rest—forget—they say you forget—a girl—aren't you glad it's a girl—a little girl—with no hair—none—little curls all over his head—a little bald girl—curls—curls all over his head—what kind of hair had God? No matter—it doesn't matter—everybody loves God—they've got to—got to—got to love God—God is love—even if he's bad they got to love him—if he's got fat hands—fat hands—no no—he wouldn't be God—His hands make you well—He lays on his hands—well—and happy—no matter—doesn't matter—far—too far—tired—too tired Vixen crawled off under bed—eight—there were eight—a woman crawled off under the bed—a woman has one—two three four—one two three four—one two three four—two plus two is four—two times two is four—two times four is eight—Vixen had eight—one two three four five six seven eight—eight—Puffie had eight—all drowned—drowned—drowned in blood—blood—Oh God! God—God never had one—Mary had one—in a manger—the lowly manger—God's on a high throne—far—too far—no matter—it doesn't matter—God Mary Mary God Mary—Virgin Mary—Mary had one—the Holy Ghost—the Holy Ghost—George H. Jones—oh don't—please don't! Let me rest—now I can rest—the weight is gone—inside the weight is gone—it's only outside—outside—all around—weight—I'm under it—Vixen crawled under the bed—there were eight—I'll not submit any more—I'll not submit—I'll not submit—

The scene blacks out. The sound of riveting continues until it goes into the sound of an electric piano and the scene lights up for Episode 5.

EPISODE 5

PROHIBITED

SCENE: *Bar: bottles, tables, chairs, electric piano.*

SOUND: *Electric piano.*

CHARACTERS: *Man behind the bar; Policeman at bar; Waiter; At Table 1: a Man and a Woman; at Table 2: a Man and a Boy; at Table 3: Two Men waiting for Two Girls, who are; Telephone Girl of Episode 1 and Young Woman.*

AT RISE: *Everyone except the Girls on. Of the characters, the Man and Woman at Table 1 are an ordinary man and woman. The man at Table 2 is a middle-aged fairy; the Boy is young, untouched. At Table 3, First Man is pleasing, common, vigorous. He has coarse wavy hair. Second Man is an ordinary salesman type.*

At Table 3.

FIRST MAN. I'm going to beat it.
SECOND MAN. Oh, for the love of Mike.
FIRST MAN. They ain't going to show.
SECOND MAN. Sure they'll show.
FIRST MAN. How do you know they'll show?
SECOND MAN. I tell you you can't keep that baby away from me—just got to—(*Snaps fingers.*)—She comes running.
FIRST MAN. Looks like it.
SECOND MAN (*to Waiter makes sign '2' with his fingers*). The same. (*Waiter goes to the bar.*)

At Table 2.

MAN. Oh, I'm sorry I brought you here.
BOY. Why?
MAN. This Purgatory of noise! I brought you here to give you pleasure—let you taste pleasure. This sherry they have here is bottled—heaven. Wait till you taste it.
BOY. I don't drink.
MAN. Drink! This isn't drink! Real amontillado is sunshine and orange groves—it's the Mediterranean and blue moonlight and—love? Have you ever been in love?
BOY. No.
MAN. Never in love with—a woman?
BOY. No—not really.
MAN. What do you mean really?
BOY. Just—that.
MAN. Ah! (*Makes sign to Waiter.*) To—you know what I want—Two. (*Waiter goes to the bar.*)

At Table 1.

MAN. Well, are you going through with it, or ain't you?
WOMAN. That's what I want to do—go through with it.
MAN. But you can't.
WOMAN. Why can't I?
MAN. How can yuh? (*Silence.*) It's nothing—most women don't think anything about it—they just—Bert told me a doctor to go to—gave me the address—
WOMAN. Don't talk about it!
MAN. Got to talk about it—you got to get out of this. (*Silence—Man makes sign to Waiter.*) What you having?

WOMAN. Nothing—I don't want anything. I had enough.
MAN. Do you good. The same?
WOMAN. I suppose so.
MAN (*makes sign '2' to Waiter*). The same. (*Waiter goes to the bar.*)

At Table 3.

FIRST MAN. I'm going to beat it.
SECOND MAN. Oh say, listen! I'm counting on you to take the other one off my hands.
FIRST MAN. I'm going to beat it.
SECOND MAN. For the love of Mike have a heart! Listen—as a favor to me—I got to be home by six—I promised my wife—sure. That don't leave me no time at all if we got to hang around—entertain some dame. You got to take her off my hands.
FIRST MAN. Maybe she won't fall for me.
SECOND MAN. Sure she'll fall for you! They all fall for you—even my wife likes you—tries to kid herself it's your brave exploits, but I know what it is—sure she'll fall for you.

Enter two girls—Telephone Girl and Young Woman.

GIRL (*coming to table*). Hello—
SECOND MAN (*grouch*). Good night.
GIRL. Good night? What's eatin' yuh?
SECOND MAN (*same*). Nothin's eatin' me—thought somethin' musta swallowed you.
GIRL. Why?
SECOND MAN. You're late!
GIRL (*unimpressed*). Oh—(*Brushing it aside.*) Mrs. Jones—Mr. Smith.
SECOND MAN. Meet my friend, Mr. Roe. (*They all sit. To the Waiter.*) The same and two more. (*Waiter goes.*)
GIRL. So we kept you waiting, did we?
SECOND MAN. Only about an hour.
YOUNG WOMAN. Was it that long?
SECOND MAN. We been here that long—ain't we Dick?
FIRST MAN. Just about, Harry.
SECOND MAN. For the love of God what delayed yuh?
GIRL. Tell Helen that one.
SECOND MAN (*to Young Woman*). The old Irish woman that went to her first race? Bet on the skate that came in last—she went up to the jockey and asked him, 'For the love of God, what delayed yuh'.

All laugh.

YOUNG WOMAN. Why, that's kinda funny!
SECOND MAN. Kinda!—What do you mean kinda?
YOUNG WOMAN. I just mean there are not many of 'em that are funny at all.

SECOND MAN. Not if you haven't heard the funny ones.

YOUNG WOMAN. Oh I've heard 'em all.

FIRST MAN. Not a laugh in a carload, eh?

GIRL. Got a cigarette?

SECOND MAN (*with package*). One of these?

GIRL (*taking one*). Uhhuh.

He offers the package to Young Woman.

YOUNG WOMAN (*taking one*). Uhhuh.

SECOND MAN (*to First Man*). One of these?

FIRST MAN (*showing his own package*). Thanks—I like these.

He lights Young Woman's cigarette.

SECOND MAN (*lighting Girl's cigarette*). Well—baby—how they comin', huh?

GIRL. Couldn't be better.

SECOND MAN. How's every little thing?

GIRL. Just great.

SECOND MAN. Miss me?

GIRL. I'll say so—when did you get in?

SECOND MAN. Just a coupla hours ago.

GIRL. Miss me?

SECOND MAN. Did I? You don't know the half of it.

YOUNG WOMAN (*interrupting restlessly*). Can we dance here?

SECOND MAN. Not here.

YOUNG WOMAN. Where do we go from here?

SECOND MAN. Where do we go from here! You just got here!

FIRST MAN. What's the hurry?

SECOND MAN. What's the rush?

YOUNG WOMAN. I don't know.

GIRL. Helen wants to dance.

YOUNG WOMAN. I just want to keep moving.

FIRST MAN (*smiling*). You want to keep moving, huh?

SECOND MAN. You must be one of those restless babies! Where do we go from here!

YOUNG WOMAN. It's only some days—I want to keep moving.

FIRST MAN. You want to keep moving, huh? (*He is staring at her smilingly.*)

YOUNG WOMAN (*nods*). Uhhuh.

FIRST MAN (*quietly*). Stick around a while.

SECOND MAN. Where do we go from here! Say, what kind of a crowd do you run with, anyway?

GIRL. Helen don't run with any crowd—do you, Helen?

YOUNG WOMAN (*embarrassed*). No.

FIRST MAN. Well, I'm not a crowd—run with me.

SECOND MAN (*gratified*). All set, huh?—Dick was about ready to beat it.

FIRST MAN. That's before I met the little lady.

Waiter serves drinks.

FIRST MAN. Here's how.

SECOND MAN. Here's to you.

GIRL. Here's looking at you.

YOUNG WOMAN. Here's—happy days.

They all drink.

FIRST MAN. That's good stuff!

SECOND MAN. Off a boat.

FIRST MAN. Off a boat?

SECOND MAN. They get all their stuff here—off a boat.

GIRL. That's what *they* say.

SECOND MAN. No! Sure! Sure they do! Sure!

GIRL. It's all right with me.

SECOND MAN. But they do! Sure!

GIRL. I believe you, darling!

SECOND MAN. Did you miss me?

GIRL. Uhhuh. (*Affirmative.*)

SECOND MAN. Any other daddies?

GIRL. Uhhuh. (*Negative.*)

SECOND MAN. Love any daddy but daddy?

GIRL. Uhhuh. (*Negative.*)

SECOND MAN. Let's beat it!

GIRL (*a little self-conscious before Young Woman*). We just got here.

SECOND MAN. Don't I know it—Come on!

GIRL. But—(*Indicates Young Woman.*)

SECOND MAN (*not understanding*). They're all set—aren't you?

FIRST MAN (*to Young Woman.*) Are we? (*She doesn't answer.*)

SECOND MAN. I got to be out to the house by six—come on—(*Rising—to Girl.*) Come on, kid—let's us beat it! (*Girl indicates Young Woman. Now understanding—very elaborate.*) Business is business, you know! I got a lot to do yet this afternoon—thought you might go along with me—help me out—how about it?

GIRL (*rising, her dignity preserved.*) Sure—I'll go along with you—help you out. (*Both rise.*)

SECOND MAN. All right with you folks?

FIRST MAN. All right with me.

SECOND MAN. All right with you? (*To Young Woman.*)

YOUNG WOMAN. All right with me.

SECOND MAN. Come on, kid. (*They rise.*) Where's the damage?

FIRST MAN. Go on!

SECOND MAN. No!

FIRST MAN. Go on!

SECOND MAN. I'll match you.

YOUNG WOMAN. Heads win!

GIRL. Heads I win—tails you lose.

SECOND MAN (*impatiently*). He's matching me.

FIRST MAN. Am I matching you or are you matching me?

SECOND MAN. I'm matching you. (*They match.*) You're stung!

FIRST MAN (*contentedly*). Not so you can notice it. (*Smiles at Young Woman.*)

GIRL. That's for you, Helen.

SECOND MAN. She ain't dumb! Come on.

GIRL (*to First Man*). You be nice to her now. She's very fastidious.—Goodbye.

Exit Second Man and Girl.

YOUNG WOMAN. I know what business is like.

FIRST MAN. You do—do yuh?

YOUNG WOMAN. I used to be a business girl myself before—

FIRST MAN. Before what?

YOUNG WOMAN. Before I quit.

FIRST MAN. What did you quit for?

YOUNG WOMAN. I just quit.

FIRST MAN. You'e married, huh?

YOUNG WOMAN. Yes—I am.

FIRST MAN. All right with me.

YOUNG WOMAN. Some men don't seem to like a woman after she's married—

Waiter comes to the table.

FIRST MAN. What's the difference?

YOUNG WOMAN. Depends on the man, I guess.

FIRST MAN. Depends on the woman, I guess. (*To Waiter, makes sign of '2'.*) The same. (*Waiter goes to the bar.*)

At Table 1.

MAN. It don't amount to nothing. God! Most women just—

WOMAN. I know—I know—I know.

MAN. They don't think nothing of it. They just—

WOMAN. I know—I know—I know.

Re-enter Second Man and Girl. They go to Table 3.

SECOND MAN. Say, I forgot—I want you to do something for me, will yuh?

FIRST MAN. Sure—what is it?

SECOND MAN. I want you to telephone me out home to-morrow—and ask me to come into town—will yuh?

FIRST MAN. Sure—why not?

SECOND MAN. You know—business—get me?

FIRST MAN. I get you.

SECOND MAN. I've worked the telegraph gag to death—and my wife likes you.

FIRST MAN. What's your number?

SECOND MAN. I'll write it down for you. (*Writes.*)

FIRST MAN. How is your wife?

SECOND MAN. She's fine.

FIRST MAN. And the kid?

SECOND MAN. Great. (*Hands him the card. To Girl.*) Come on, kid. (*Turns back to Young Woman.*) Get this bird to tell you about himself.

GIRL. Keep him from it.

SECOND MAN. Get him to tell you how he killed a couple of spig down in Mexico.

GIRL. You been in Mexico?

SECOND MAN. He just came up from there.

GIRL. Can you teach us the tango?

YOUNG WOMAN. You killed a man?

SECOND MAN. Two of 'em! With a bottle! Get him to tell you—with a bottle. Come on, kid. Goodbye.

Exit Second Man and Girl.

YOUNG WOMAN. Why did you?

FIRST MAN. What?

YOUNG WOMAN. Kill 'em?

FIRST MAN. To get free.

YOUNG WOMAN. Oh.

At Table 2.

MAN. You really must taste this—just taste it. It's a real amontillado, you know.

BOY. Where do they get it here?

MAN. It's always down the side streets one finds the real pleasures, don't you think?

BOY. I don't know.

MAN. Learn. Come, taste this! Amontillado! Or don't you like amontillado?

BOY. I don't know. I never had any before.

MAN. Your first taste! How I envy you! Come, taste it! Taste it! And die.

Boy tastes wine—finds it disappointing.

MAN (*gliding it*). Poe was a lover of amontillado. He returns to it continually, you remember—or are you a lover of Poe?

BOY. I've read a lot of him.

MAN. But are you a lover?

At Table 3.

FIRST MAN. There were a bunch of bandidos—bandits, you know, took me into the hills—holding me there—what was I to do? got the two birds that guarded me drunk one night, and then I filled the empty bottle with small stones—and let 'em have it!

YOUNG WOMAN. Oh!

FIRST MAN. I had to get free, didn't I? I let 'em have it—
YOUNG WOMAN. Oh—then what did you do?
FIRST MAN. Then I beat it.
YOUNG WOMAN. Where to—?
FIRST MAN. Right here. (*Pause.*) Glad?
YOUNG WOMAN (*nods*). Yes.
FIRST MAN (*makes sign to Waiter of '2'*). The same. (*Waiter goes to the bar.*)

At Table 1.

MAN. You're just scared because this is the first time and—
WOMAN. I'm not scared.
MAN. Then what are you for Christ's sake?
WOMAN. I'm not scared. I want it—I want to have it— that ain't being scared, is it?
MAN. It's being goofy.
WOMAN. I don't care.
MAN. What about your folks?
WOMAN. I don't care.
MAN. What about your job? (*Silence.*) You got to keep your job, haven't you? (*Silence.*) Haven't you?
WOMAN. I suppose so.
MAN. Well—there you are!
WOMAN (*silence—then*). All right—let's go now—You got the address?
MAN. Now you're coming to.

They get up and go off. Exit Man and Woman.

At Table 3.

YOUNG WOMAN. A bottle like that? (*She picks it up.*)
FIRST MAN. Yeah—filled with pebbles.
YOUNG WOMAN. What kind of pebbles?
FIRST MAN. Pebbles! Off the ground.
YOUNG WOMAN. Oh.
FIRST MAN. Necessity, you know, mother of invention. (*As Young Woman handles the bottle.*) Ain't a bad weapon—first you got a sledge hammer—then you got a knife.
YOUNG WOMAN. Oh. (*Puts bottle down.*)
FIRST MAN. Women don't like knives, do they? (*Pours drink.*)
YOUNG WOMAN. No.
FIRST MAN. Don't mind a hammer so much, though, do they?
YOUNG WOMAN. No—
FIRST MAN. I didn't like it myself—any of it—but I had to get free, didn't I? Sure I had to get free, didn't I? (*Drinks.*) Now I'm damn glad I did.
YOUNG WOMAN. Why?
FIRST MAN. You know why. (*He puts his hand over hers.*)

At Table 2.

MAN. Let's go to my rooms—and I'll show them to you— I have a first edition of Verlaine that will simply make your mouth water. (*They stand up.*) Here— there's just a sip at the bottom of my glass—

Boy takes it.

That last sip's the sweetest—Wasn't it?
BOY (*laughs*). And I always thought that was dregs. (*Exit Man followed by Boy.*)

At Table 3.

The Man is holding her hand across the table.

YOUNG WOMAN. When you put your hand over mine! When you just touch me!
FIRST MAN. Yeah? (*Pause.*) Come on, kid, let's go!
YOUNG WOMAN. Where?
FIRST MAN. You haven't been around much, have you, kid?
YOUNG WOMAN. No.
FIRST MAN. I could tell that just to look at you.
YOUNG WOMAN. You could?
FIRST MAN. Sure I could. What are you running around with a girl like that other one for?
YOUNG WOMAN. I don't know. She seems to have a good time.
FIRST MAN. So that's it?
YOUNG WOMAN. Don't she?
FIRST MAN. Don't you?
YOUNG WOMAN. No.
FIRST MAN. Never?
YOUNG WOMAN. Never.
FIRST MAN. What's the matter?
YOUNG WOMAN. Nothing—just me, I guess.
FIRST MAN. You're all right.
YOUNG WOMAN. Am I?
FIRST MAN. Sure. You just haven't met the right guy— that's all—girl like you—you got to meet the right guy.
YOUNG WOMAN. I know.
FIRST MAN. You're different from girls like that other one—any guy'll do her. You're different.
YOUNG WOMAN. I guess I am.
FIRST MAN. You didn't fall for that business gag—did you—when they went off?
YOUNG WOMAN. Well, I thought they wanted to be alone probably, but—
FIRST MAN. And how!
YOUNG WOMAN. Oh—so that's it.
FIRST MAN. That's it. Come along—let's go—
YOUNG WOMAN. Oh, I couldn't ! Like this?

FIRST MAN. Don't you like me?

YOUNG WOMAN. Yes

FIRST MAN. Then what's the matter?

YOUNG WOMAN. Do—you—like me?

FIRST MAN. Like yuh? You don't know the half of it—listen—you know what you seem like to me?

YOUNG WOMAN. What?

FIRST MAN. An angel. Just like an angel.

YOUNG WOMAN. I do?

FIRST MAN. That's what I said! Let's go!

YOUNG WOMAN. Where?

FIRST MAN. Where do you live?

YOUNG WOMAN. Oh, we can't go to my place.

FIRST MAN. Then come to my place.

YOUNG WOMAN. Oh I couldn't—is it far?

FIRST MAN. Just a step—come on—

YOUNG WOMAN. Oh I couldn't—what is it—a room?

FIRST MAN. No—an apartment—a one room apartment.

YOUNG WOMAN. That's different.

FIRST MAN. On the ground floor—no one will see you—coming or going.

YOUNG WOMAN (getting up). I couldn't.

FIRST MAN (rises). Wait a minute—I got to pay the damage—and I'll get a bottle of something to take along.

YOUNG WOMAN. No—don't.

FIRST MAN. Why not?

YOUNG WOMAN. Well—don't bring any pebbles.

FIRST MAN. Say—forget that! Will you?

YOUNG WOMAN. I just meant I don't think I'll need anything to drink.

FIRST MAN (leaning to her eagerly). You like me—don't you, kid?

YOUNG WOMAN. Do you me?

FIRST MAN. Wait!

He goes to the bar. She remains, her hands outstretched on the table, staring ahead. Enter a Man and a Girl. They go to one of the empty tables. The Waiter goes to them.

MAN (to Girl). What do you want?

GIRL. Same old thing.

MAN (to the Waiter). The usual. (Makes a sign '2'.)

The First Man crosses to Young Woman with a wrapped bottle under his arm. She rises and starts out with him. As they pass the piano, he stops and puts in a nickel—the music starts as they exit. The scene blacks out.

The music of the electric piano continues until the lights go up for Episode 6, and the music has become the music of a hand organ, very very faint.

EPISODE 6

INTIMATE

SCENE: A dark room.

SOUNDS. A hand organ; footbeats, of passing feet.

CHARACTERS: Man; Young Woman

AT RISE: Darkness. Nothing can be discerned. From the outside comes the sound of a hand organ, very faint, and the irregular rhythm of passing feet. The hand organ is playing Cielito Lindo, that Spanish song that has been on every hand organ lately.

MAN. You're awful still, honey. What you thinking about?

WOMAN. About sea shells. (The sound of her voice is beautiful.)

MAN. Sheshells? Gee! I can't say it!

WOMAN. When I was little my grandmother used to have a big pink sea shell on the mantle behind the stove. When we'd go to visit her they'd let me hold it, and listen. That's what I was thinking about now.

MAN. Yeah?

WOMAN. You can hear the sea in 'em, you know.

MAN. Yeah, I know.

WOMAN. I wonder why tht is?

MAN. Search me. (Pause.)

WOMAN. You going? (He has moved.)

MAN. No. I just want a cigarette.

WOMAN (glad, relieved). Oh.

MAN. Want one?

WOMAN. No. (Taking the match.) Let me light it for you.

MAN. You got mighty pretty hands, honey. (The match is out.) This little pig went to market. This little pig stayed home. This little pig went—

WOMAN (laughs). Diddle diddle dee. (Laughs again.)

MAN. You got awful pretty hands.

WOMAN. I used to have. But I haven't taken much care of them lately. I will now—(Pause. The music gets clearer.) What's that?

MAN. What?

WOMAN. That music?

MAN. A dago hand organ. I gave him two bits the first day I got here—so he comes every day.

WOMAN. I mean—what's that he's playing?

MAN. Cielito Lindo.

WOMAN. What does that mean?

MAN. Little Heaven.

WOMAN. Little Heaven?

MAN. That's what lovers call each other in Spain.

WOMAN. Spain's where all the castles are, ain't it?

MAN. Yeah.

WOMAN. Little Heaven—sing it!

MAN (*singing to the music of the hand organ*). Da la sierra morena viene, bajando viene, bajando; un par de ojitos negros—cielito lindo—da contrabando.

WOMAN. What does it mean?

MAN. From the high dark mountains.

WOMAN. From the high dark mountains—?

MAN. Oh it doesn't mean anything. It doesn't make sense. It's love. (*Taking up the song.*) Ay-ay-ay-ay.

WOMAN. I know what that means.

MAN. What?

WOMAN. Ay-ay-ay-ay. (*They laugh.*)

MAN (*taking up the song*). Canta non llores—Sing don't cry—

WOMAN (*taking up the song*). La-la-la-la-la-la-la-la-la-la—Little Heaven!

MAN. You got a nice voice, honey.

WOMAN. Have I? (*Laughs—tickles him.*)

MAN. You bet you have—hey!

WOMAN (*laughing*). You ticklish?

MAN. Sure I am! Hey! (*They laugh.*) Go on, honey, sing something.

WOMAN. I couldn't.

MAN. Go on—you got a fine voice.

WOMAN (*laughs and sings*). Hey, diddle, diddle, the cat and the fiddle, The cow jumped over the moon, The little dog laughed to see the sport, And the dish ran away with the spoon—

Both laugh.

I never thought that had any sense before—now I get it.

MAN. You got me beat.

WOMAN. It's you and me—La-lalalalala—lalalalalala—Little Heaven. You're the dish and I'm the spoon.

MAN. You're a little spoon all right.

WOMAN. And I guess I'm the little cow that jumped over the moon. (*A pause.*) Do you believe in sorta guardian angels?

MAN. What?

WOMAN. Guardian angels?

MAN. I don't know. Maybe.

WOMAN. I do. (*Taking up the song again.*) Lalalalala—lalalalala—lalalala—Little Heaven. (*Talking.*) There must be something that looks out for you and brings you your happiness, at last—look at us! How did we both happen to go to that place today if there wasn't something!

MAN. Maybe you're right.

WOMAN. Look at us!

MAN. Everything's us to you, kid—ain't it?

WOMAN. Ain't it?

MAN. All right with me.

WOMAN. We belong together! We belong together! And we're going to stick together, ain't we?

MAN. Sing something else.

WOMAN. I tell you I can't sing!

MAN. Sure you can!

WOMAN. I tell you I hadn't thought of singing since I was a little bit of a girl.

MAN. Well sing anyway.

WOMAN (*singing*). And every little wavelet had its night cap on—its night cap on—its night cap on—and every little wave had its night cap on—so very early in the morning. (*Talking.*) Did you used to sing that when you were a little kid?

MAN. Nope.

WOMAN. Didn't you? We used to—in the first grade—little kids—we used to go round and round in a ring—and flop our hands up and down—supposed to be the waves. I remember it used to confuse me—because we did just the same thing to be little angels.

MAN. Yeah?

WOMAN. You know why I came here?

MAN. I can make a good guess.

WOMAN. Because you told me I looked like an angel to you! That's why I came.

MAN. Jeez, honey, all women look like angels to me—all white women. I ain't been seeing nothing but Indians, you know for the last couple a years. Gee, when I got off the boat here the other day—and saw all the women—gee I pretty near went crazy—talk about looking like angels—why—

WOMAN. You've had a lot of women, haven't you?

MAN. Not so many—real ones.

WOMAN. Did you—like any of 'em—better than me?

MAN. Nope—there wasn't one of 'em any sweeter than you, honey—not as sweet—no—not as sweet.

WOMAN. I like to hear you say it. Say it again—

MAN (*protesting good humoredly*). Oh—

WOMAN. Go on—tell me again!

MAN. Here! (*Kisses her.*) Does that tell you?

WOMAN. Yes. (*Pause.*) We're going to stick together—always—aren't we?

MAN (*honestly*). I'll have to be moving on, kid—some day, you know.

WOMAN. When?

MAN. Quien sabe?

WOMAN. What does that mean?

MAN. Quien sabe? You got to learn that, kid, if you're figuring on coming with me. It's the answer to everything—below the Rio Grande.

WOMAN. What does it mean?

MAN. It means—who knows?

WOMAN. Keen sabe?

MAN. Yep—don't forget it—now.

WOMAN. I'll never forget it!

MAN. Quien sabe.

WOMAN. And I'll never get used to it.

MAN. Quien sabe.

WOMAN. I'll never get—below the Rio Grande—I'll never get out of here.

MAN. Quien sabe.

WOMAN (*change of mood*). That's right! Keen sabe? Who knows?

MAN. That's the stuff.

WOMAN. You must like it down there.

MAN. I can't live anywhere else—for long.

WOMAN. Why not?

MAN. Oh—you're free down there! You're free!

A street light is lit outside. The outlines of a window take form against this light. There are bars across it, and from outside it, the sidewalk cuts across almost at the top. It is a basement room. The constant going and coming of passing feet, mostly feet of couples, can be dimly seen. Inside, on the ledge, there is a lily blooming in a bowl of rocks and water.

WOMAN. What's that?

MAN. Just the street light going on.

WOMAN. Is it as late as that?

MAN. Late as what?

WOMAN. Dark.

MAN. It's been dark for hours—didn't you know that?

WOMAN. No!—I must go! (*Rises.*)

MAN. Wait—the moon will be up in a little while—full moon.

WOMAN. It isn't that! I'm late! I must go!

She comes into the light. She wears a white chemise that might be the tunic of a dancer, and as she comes into the light she fastens about her waist a little skirt. She really wears almost exactly the clothes that women wear now, but the finesse of their cut, and the grace and ease with which she puts them on, must turn this episode of her dressing into a personification, an idealization of a woman clothing herself. All her gestures must be unconscious, innocent, relaxed, sure and full of natural grace. As she sits facing the window pulling on a stocking.

What's that?

MAN. What?

WOMAN. On the window ledge.

MAN. A flower.

WOMAN. Who gave it to you?

MAN. Nobody gave it to me. I bought it.

WOMAN. For yourself?

MAN. Yeah—Why not?

WOMAN. I don't know.

MAN. In Chinatown—made me think of Frisco where I was a kid—so I bought it.

WOMAN. Is that where you were born—Frisco?

MAN. Yep. Twin Peaks.

WOMAN. What's that?

MAN. A couple of hills—together.

WOMAN. One for you and one for me.

MAN. I bet you'd like Frisco.

WOMAN. I knew a woman went out there once!

MAN. The bay and the hills! Jeez, that's the life! Every Saturday we used to cross the Bay—get a couple nags and just ride—over the hills. One would have a blanket on the saddle—the other, the grub. At night, we'd make a little fire and eat—and then roll up in the old blanket and—

WOMAN. Who? Who was with you?

MAN (*indifferently*). Anybody. (*Enthusiastically.*) Jeez, that dry old grass out there smells good at night—full of tar weed—you know—

WOMAN. Is that a good smell?

MAN. Tar weed? Didn't you ever smell it? (*She shakes her head 'No'.*) Sure it's a good smell! The Bay and the hills.

She goes to the mirror of the dresser, to finish dressing. She has only a dress to put on that is in one piece—with one fastening on the side. Before slipping it on, she stands before the mirror and stretches. Appreciatively but indifferently.

You look in good shape, kid. A couple of months riding over the mountains with me, you'd be great.

WOMAN. Can I?

MAN. What?

WOMAN. Some day—ride mountains with you?

MAN. Ride mountains? Ride donkeys!

WOMAN. It's the same thing!—with you!—Can I—some day? The high dark mountains?

MAN. Who knows?

WOMAN. It must be great!

MAN. You ever been off like that, kid?—high up? On top of the world?

WOMAN. Yes.

MAN. When?

WOMAN. Today.

MAN. You're pretty sweet.

WOMAN. I never knew anything like this way! I never knew that I could feel like this! So,—so purified! Don't laugh at me!

MAN. I ain't laughing, honey.

WOMAN. Purified.

MAN. It's a hell of a word—but I know what you mean. That's the way it is—sometimes.

WOMAN (*she puts on a little hat, then turns to him*). Well—goodbye.

MAN. Aren't you forgetting something? (*Rises.*)

She looks toward him, then throws her head slowly back, lifts her right arm—this gesture that is in so many statues of women—Volupte. He comes out of the shadow, puts his arm around her, kisses her. Her head and arm go further back—then she brings her arm around with a wide encircling gesture, her hand closes over his head, her fingers spread. Her fingers are protective, clutching. When he releases her, her eyes are shining with tears. She turns away. She looks back at him—and the room—and her eyes fasten on the lily.

WOMAN. Can I have that?

MAN. Sure—why not?

She takes it—goes. As she opens the door, the music is louder. The scene blacks out.

WOMAN. Goodbye. And—(*Hesitates.*) And—thank you.

Curtain

The music continues until the curtain goes up for Episode 7. It goes up on silence.

EPISODE 7

D O M E S T I C

SCENE: *A sitting room: a divan, a telephone, a window.*

CHARACTERS: *Husband; Young Woman*

They are seated on opposie ends of the divan. They are both reading papers—to themselves.

HUSBAND. Record production.

YOUNG WOMAN. Girl turns on gas.

HUSBAND. Sale hits a millions—

YOUNG WOMAN. Woman leaves all for love—

HUSBAND. Market trend steady—

YOUNG WOMAN. Young wife disappears—

HUSBAND. Owns a life interest—

Phone rings. Young Woman looks toward it.

That's for me. (*In phone.*) Hello—oh hello, A.B. It's all settled?—Everything signed? Good. Good! Tell R.A. to call me up. (*Hangs up phone—to Young Woman.*) Well, it's all settled. They signed!—aren't you interested? Aren't you going to ask me?

YOUNG WOMAN (*by rote*). Did you put it over?

HUSBAND. Sure I put it over.

YOUNG WOMAN. Did you swing it?

HUSBAND. Sure I swung it.

YOUNG WOMAN. Did they come through?

HUSBAND. Sure they came through.

YOUNG WOMAN. Did they sign?

HUSBAND. I'll say they signed.

YOUNG WOMAN. On the dotted line?

HUSBAND. On the dotted line.

YOUNG WOMAN. The property's yours?

HUSBAND. The property's mine. I'll put a first mortgage. I'll put a second mortage and the property's mine. Happy?

YOUNG WOMAN (*by rote*). Happy.

HUSBAND (*going to her*). The property's mine! It's not all that's mine! (*Pinching her cheek—happy and playful.*) I got a first mortgage on her—I got a second mortgage on her—and she's mine!

Young Woman pulls away swiftly.

What's the matter?

YOUNG WOMAN. Nothing—what?

HUSBAND. You flinched when I touched you.

YOUNG WOMAN. No.

HUSBAND. You haven't done that in a long time.

YOUNG WOMAN. Haven't I?

HUSBAND. You used to do it every time I touched you.

YOUNG WOMAN. Did I?

HUSBAND. Didn't know that, did you?

YOUNG WOMAN (*unexpectedly*). Yes. Yes, I know it.

HUSBAND. Just purity.

YOUNG WOMAN. No.

HUSBAND. Oh, I liked it. Purity.

YOUNG WOMAN. No.

HUSBAND. You're one of the purest women that ever lived.

YOUNG WOMAN. I'm just like anybody else only—(*Stops.*)

HUSBAND. Only what?

YOUNG WOMAN (*pause*). Nothing.

HUSBAND. It must be something.

Phone rings. She gets up and goes to window.

HUSBAND (*in phone*). Hello—hello, R.A.—well, I put it over—yeah, I swung it—sure they came through—

did they sign? On the dotted line! The property's mine. I made the proposition. I sold them the idea. Now watch me. Tell D.D. to call me up. (*Hangs up.*) That was R.A. What are you looking at?

YOUNG WOMAN. Nothing.

HUSBAND. You must be looking at something.

YOUNG WOMAN. Nothing—the moon.

HUSBAND. The moon's something, isn't it?

YOUNG WOMAN. Yes.

HUSBAND. What's it doing?

YOUNG WOMAN. Nothing.

HUSBAND. It must be doing something.

YOUNG WOMAN. It's moving—moving—(*She comes down restlessly.*)

HUSBAND. Pull down the shade, my dear.

YOUNG WOMAN. Why?

HUSBAND. People can look in.

Phone rings.

Hello—hello D.D.—Yes—I put it over—they came across—I put it over on them—yep—yep—yep—I'll say I am—yep—on the dotted line—Now you watch me—yep. Yep yep. Tell B.M. to phone me. (*Hangs up.*) That was D.D. (*To Young Woman who has come down to davenport and picked up a paper.*) Aren't you listening?

YOUNG WOMAN. I'm reading.

HUSBAND. What you reading?

YOUNG WOMAN. Nothing.

HUSBAND. Must be something. (*He sits and picks up his paper.*)

YOUNG WOMAN (*reading*). Prisoner escapes—lifer breaks jail—shoots way to freedom—

HUSBAND. Don't read that stuff—listen—here's a first rate editorial. I agree with this. I agree absolutely. Are you listening?

YOUNG WOMAN. I'm listening.

HUSBAND (*importantly*). All men are born free and entitled to the pursuit of happiness. (*Young Woman gets up.*) My, you're nervous tonight.

YOUNG WOMAN. I try not to be.

HUSBAND. You inherit that from your mother. She was in the office today.

YOUNG WOMAN. Was she?

HUSBAND. To get her allowance.

YOUNG WOMAN. Oh—

HUSBAND. Don't you know it's the *first*.

YOUNG WOMAN. Poor Ma.

HUSBAND. What would she do without me?

YOUNG WOMAN. I know. You're very good.

HUSBAND. One thing—she's grateful.

YOUNG WOMAN. Poor Ma—poor Ma.

HUSBAND. She's got to have care.

YOUNG WOMAN. Yes. She's got to have care.

HUSBAND. A mother's a very precious thing—a good mother.

YOUNG WOMAN (*excitedly*). I try to be a good mother.

HUSBAND. Of course you're a good mother.

YOUNG WOMAN. I try! I try!

HUSBAND. A mother's a very precious thing—(*Resuming his paper.*) And a child's a very precious thing. Precious jewels.

YOUNG WOMAN (*reading*). Sale of jewels and precious stones.

Young Woman puts her hand to throat.

HUSBAND. What's the matter?

YOUNG WOMAN. I feel as though I were drowning.

HUSBAND. Drowning?

YOUNG WOMAN. With stones around my neck.

HUSBAND. You just imagine that.

YOUNG WOMAN. Stifling.

HUSBAND. You don't breathe deep enough—breathe now—look at me. (*He breathes.*) Breath is life. Life is breath.

YOUNG WOMAN (*suddenly*). And what is death?

HUSBAND (*smartly*). Just—no breath!

YOUNG WOMAN (*to herself*). Just no breath.

Takes up paper.

HUSBAND. All right?

YOUNG WOMAN. All right.

HUSBAND (*reads as she stares at her paper. Looks up after a pause.*) I feel cold air, my dear.

YOUNG WOMAN. Cold air?

HUSBAND. Close the window, will you?

YOUNG WOMAN. It isn't open.

HUSBAND. Don't you feel cold air?

YOUNG WOMAN. No—you just imagine it.

HUSBAND. I never imagine anything. (*Young Woman is staring at the paper.*) What are you reading?

YOUNG WOMAN. Nothing.

HUSBAND. You must be reading something.

YOUNG WOMAN. Woman finds husband dead.

HUSBAND (*uninterested*). Oh. (*Interested.*) Here's a man says 'I owe my success to a yeast cake a day—my digestion is good—I sleep very well—and—(*His wife gets up, goes toward door.*) Where you going?

YOUNG WOMAN. No place.

HUSBAND. You must be going some place.

YOUNG WOMAN. Just—to bed.

HUSBAND. It isn't even eleven yet. Wait.

YOUNG WOMAN. Wait?

HUSBAND. It's only ten-forty-six—wait! (*Holds out his arms to her.*) Come here!

YOUNG WOMAN (*takes a step toward him—recoils*). Oh—I want to go away!

HUSBAND. Away? Where?

YOUNG WOMAN. Anywhere—away.

HUSBAND. Why, what's the matter?

YOUNG WOMAN. I'm scared.

HUSBAND. What of?

YOUNG WOMAN. I can't sleep—I haven't slept.

HUSBAND. That's nothing.

YOUNG WOMAN. And the moon—when it's full moon.

HUSBAND. That's nothing.

YOUNG WOMAN. I can't sleep.

HUSBAND. Of course not. It's the light.

YOUNG WOMAN. I don't see it! I feel it! I'm afraid.

HUSBAND (*kindly*). Nonsense—come here.

YOUNG WOMAN. I want to go away.

HUSBAND. But I can't get away now.

YOUNG WOMAN. Alone!

HUSBAND. You've never been away alone.

YOUNG WOMAN. I know.

HUSBAND. What would you do?

YOUNG WOMAN. Maybe I'd sleep.

HUSBAND. Now you wait.

YOUNG WOMAN (*desperately*). Wait?

HUSBAND. We'll take a trip—we'll go to Europe—I'll get my watch—I'll get my Swiss watch—I've always wanted a Swiss watch that I bought right there—isn't that funny? Wait—wait. (*Young Woman comes down to davenport—sits. Husband resumes his paper.*) Another revolution below the Rio Grande.

YOUNG WOMAN. Below the Rio Grande?

HUSBAND. Yes—another—

YOUNG WOMAN. Anyone—hurt?

HUSBAND. No.

YOUNG WOMAN. Any prisoners?

HUSBAND. No.

YOUNG WOMAN. All free?

HUSBAND. All free.

He resumes his paper. Young Woman sits, staring ahead of her. The music of the hand organ sounds off very dimly, playing Cielito Lindo. Voices begin to sing it—'Ay-ay-ay-ay'—and then the words—the music and voices get louder.

THE VOICE OF HER LOVER. They were a bunch of bandidos—bandits you know—holding me there—what was I to do—I had to get free—didn't I? I had to get free—

VOICES. Free—free—free—

LOVER. I filled an empty bottle with small stones—

VOICES. Stones—stones—precious stones—millstones—stones—stones—millstones

LOVER. Just a bottle with small stones.

VOICES. Stones—stones—small stones—

VOICE OF A HUCKSTER. Stones for sale—stones—stones—small stones—precious stones—

VOICES. Stones—stones—precious stones—

LOVER. Had to get free, didn't I? Free!

VOICES. Free? Free?

LOVER. Quien sabe? Who knows? Who knows?

VOICES. Who'd know? Who'd know? Who'd know?

HUCKSTER. Stones—stones—small stones—big stones—millstones—cold stones—head stones—

VOICES. Head stones—head stones—head stones.

The music—the voices—mingle—increase—the Young Woman flies from her chair and cries out in terror.

YOUNG WOMAN. Oh! Oh!

The scene blacks out—the music and the dim voices, 'Stones—stones—stones,' continue until the scene lights for Episode 8.

EPISODE 8

THE LAW

SCENE: *Courtroom*

SOUNDS: *Clicking of telegraph instruments offstage.*

CHARACTERS: *Judge; Jury; Lawyers; Spectators; Reporters; Messenger Boys; Law Clerks; Bailiff; Court Reporter; Young Woman*
    The words and movements of all these people except the Young Woman are routine—mechanical. Each is going through the motions of his own game.

AT RISE: *All assembled, except Judge.*

Enter Judge

BAILIFF (*mumbling*). Hear ye—hear ye—! (*All rise. Judge sits. All sit. Lawyer for Defense gets to his feet—He is the verbose, 'eloquent' typical criminal defense lawyer. Judge signs to him to wait—turns to Law Clerks, grouped at foot of the bench.*

FIRST CLERK (*handing up a paper—routine voice*). State versus Kling—stay of execution.

JUDGE. Denied.

First Clerk goes.

SECOND CLERK. Bing vs. Ding—demurrer.

Judge signs. Second Clerk goes.

THIRD CLERK. Case of John King—habeas corpus.

Judge signs. Third Clerk goes. Judge signs to Bailiff.

BAILIFF (*mumbling*). People of the State of ———— versus Helen Jones.

JUDGE (*to Lawyer for Defense*). Defense ready to proceed?

LAWYER FOR DEFENSE. We're ready, your Honor.

JUDGE. Proceed.

LAWYER FOR DEFENSE. Helen Jones.

BAILIFF. Helen Jones!

Young Woman rises.

LAWYER FOR DEFENSE. Mrs. Jones, will you take the stand?

Young Woman goes to witness stand.

FIRST REPORTER (*writing rapidly*). The defense sprang a surprise at the opening of court this morning by putting the accused woman on the stand. The prosecution was swept off its feet by this daring defense strategy and—(*Instruments get louder.*)

SECOND REPORTER. Trembling and scarcely able to stand, Helen Jones, accused murderess, had to be almost carried to the witness stand this morning when her lawyer—

BAILIFF (*mumbling—with Bible*). Do you swear to tell the truth, the whole truth and nothing but the truth—so help you God?

YOUNG WOMAN. I do.

JUDGE. You may sit.

She sits in witness chair.

COURT REPORTER. What is your name?

YOUNG WOMAN. Helen Jones.

COURT REPORTER. Your age?

YOUNG WOMAN (*hesitates—then*). Twenty-nine.

COURT REPORTER. Where do you live?

YOUNG WOMAN. In prison.

LAWYER FOR DEFENSE. This is my client's legal address.

Hands a scrap of paper.

LAWYER FOR PROSECUTION (*jumping to his feet*). I object to this insinuation on the part of counsel of any illegality in the holding of this defendant in jail when the law—

LAWYER FOR DEFENSE. I made no such insinuation.

LAWYER FOR PROSECUTION. You implied it—

LAWYER FOR DEFENSE. I did not!

LAWYER FOR PROSECUTION. You're a—

JUDGE. Order!

BAILIFF. Order!

LAWYER FOR DEFENSE. Your Honor, I object to counsel's constant attempt to—

LAWYER FOR PROSECUTION. I protest—I—

JUDGE. Order!

BAILIFF. Order!

JUDGE. Proceed with the witness.

LAWYER FOR DEFENSE. Mrs. Jones, you are the widow of the late George H. Jones, are you not?

YOUNG WOMAN. Yes.

LAWYER FOR DEFENSE. How long were you married to the late George H. Jones before his demise?

YOUNG WOMAN. Six years.

LAWYER FOR DEFENSE. Six years! And it was a happy marriage, was it not? (*Young Woman hesitates.*) Did you quarrel?

YOUNG WOMAN. No sir.

LAWYER FOR DEFENSE. Then it was a happy marriage, wasn't it?

YOUNG WOMAN. Yes, sir.

LAWYER FOR DEFENSE. In those six years of married life with your late husband, the late George H. Jones, did you EVER have a quarrel?

YOUNG WOMAN. No, sir.

LAWYER FOR DEFENSE. Never one quarrel?

LAWYER FOR PROSECUTION. The witness has said—

LAWYER FOR DEFENSE. Six years without one quarrel! Six years! Gentlemen of the jury, I ask you to consider this fact! Six years of married life without a quarrel. (*The Jury grins.*) I ask you to consider it seriously! Very seriously! Who of us—and this is not intended as any reflection on the sacred institution of marriage—no—but!

JUDGE. Proceed with your witness.

LAWYER FOR DEFENSE. You have one child—have you not, Mrs. Jones?

YOUNG WOMAN. Yes, sir.

LAWYER FOR DEFENSE. A little girl, is it not?

YOUNG WOMAN. Yes, sir.

LAWYER FOR DEFENSE. How old is she?

YOUNG WOMAN. She's five—past five.

LAWYER FOR DEFENSE. A little girl of past five. Since the demise of the late Mr. Jones you are the only parent she has living, are you not?

YOUNG WOMAN. Yes, sir.

LAWYER FOR DEFENSE. Before your marriage to the late Mr. Jones, you worked and supported your mother, did you not?

LAWYER FOR PROSECUTION. I object, your honor! Irrelevant—immaterial—and—

JUDGE. Objection sustained!

LAWYER FOR DEFENSE. In order to support your mother and yourself as a girl, you worked, did you not?

YOUNG WOMAN. Yes, sir.

LAWYER FOR DEFENSE. What did you do?

YOUNG WOMAN. I was a stenographer.

LAWYER FOR DEFENSE. And since your marriage you have continued as her sole support, have you not?

YOUNG WOMAN. Yes, sir.

LAWYER FOR DEFENSE. A devoted daughter, gentlemen of the jury! As well as a devoted wife and a devoted mother!

LAWYER FOR PROSECUTION. Your Honor!

LAWYER FOR DEFENSE (*quickly*). And now, Mrs. Jones, I will ask you—the law expects me to ask you—it demands that I ask you—did you—or did you not—on the night of June 2nd last or the morning of June 3rd last—kill your husand, the late George H. Jones— did you, or did you not?

YOUNG WOMAN. I did not.

LAWYER FOR DEFENSE. You did not?

YOUNG WOMAN. I did not.

LAWYER FOR DEFENSE. Now, Mrs. Jones, you have heard the witnesses for the State—They were not many— and they did not have much to say—

LAWYER FOR PROSECUTION. I object.

JUDGE. Sustained.

LAWYER FOR DEFENSE. You have heard some police and you have heard some doctors. None of whom was present! The prosecution could not furnish any witness to the crime—not one witness!

LAWYER FOR PROSECUTION. Your Honor!

LAWYER FOR DEFENSE. Nor one motive.

LAWYER FOR PROSECUTION. Your Honor—I protest! I—

JUDGE. Sustained.

LAWYER FOR DEFENSE. But such as these witnesses were, you have heard them try to accuse you of deliberately murdering your own husband, this husband with whom, by your own statement, you had never had a quarrel—not one quarrel in six years of married life, murdering him, I say, or rather—they say, while he slept, by brutally hitting him over the head with a bottle—a bottle filled with small stones—Did you, I repeat this, or did you not?

YOUNG WOMAN. I did not.

LAWYER FOR DEFENSE. You did not! Of course you did not! (*Quickly.*) Now, Mrs. Jones, will you tell the jury in your own words exactly what happened on the night of June 2nd or the morning of June 3rd last, at the time your husband was killed.

YOUNG WOMAN. I was awakened by hearing somebody— something—in the room, and I saw two men standing by my husband's bed.

LAWYER FOR DEFENSE. Your husband's bed—that was also your bed, was it not, Mrs. Jones?

YOUNG WOMAN. Yes.

LAWYER FOR DEFENSE. You hadn't the modern idea of separate beds, had you, Mrs. Jones?

YOUNG WOMAN. Mr. Jones objected.

LAWYER FOR DEFENSE. I mean you slept in the same bed, did you not?

YOUNG WOMAN. Yes.

LAWYER FOR DEFENSE. Then explain just what you mean by saying 'my husband's bed'.

YOUNG WOMAN. Well—I—

LAWYER FOR DEFENSE. You meant his side of the bed, didn't you?

YOUNG WOMAN. Yes, His side.

LAWYER FOR DEFENSE. That is what I thought, but I wanted the jury to be clear on that point. (*To the Jury.*) Mr. and Mrs. Jones slept in the same bed. (*To her.*) Go on, Mrs. Jones. (*As she is silent.*) You heard a noise and—

YOUNG WOMAN. I heard a noise and I awoke and saw two men standing beside my husband's side of the bed.

LAWYER FOR DEFENSE. Two men?

YOUNG WOMAN. Yes.

LAWYER FOR DEFENSE. Can you describe them?

YOUNG WOMAN. Not very well—I couldn't see them very well.

LAWYER FOR DEFENSE. Could you say whether they were big or small—light or dark, thin or—

YOUNG WOMAN. They were big dark looking men.

LAWYER FOR DEFENSE. Big dark looking men?

YOUNG WOMAN. Yes.

LAWYER FOR DEFENSE. And what did you do, Mrs. Jones, when you suddenly awoke and saw two big dark looking men standing beside your bed?

YOUNG WOMAN. I didn't do anything!

LAWYER FOR DEFENSE. You didn't have time to do anything—did you?

YOUNG WOMAN. No. Before I could do anything—one of them raised—something in his hand and struck Mr. Jones over the head with it.

LAWYER FOR DEFENSE. And what did Mr. Jones do?

Spectators laugh.

JUDGE. Silence.

BAILIFF. Silence.

LAWYER FOR DEFENSE. What did Mr. Jones do, Mrs. Jones?

YOUNG WOMAN. He gave a sort of groan and tried to raise up.

LAWYER FOR DEFENSE. Tried to raise up!

YOUNG WOMAN. Yes!

LAWYER FOR DEFENSE. And then what happened?

YOUNG WOMAN. The man struck him again and he fell back.

LAWYER FOR DEFENSE. I see. What did the men do then? The big dark looking men.

YOUNG WOMAN. They turned and ran out of the room.

LAWYER FOR DEFENSE. I see. What did you do then, Mrs. Jones?

YOUNG WOMAN. I saw Mr. Jones was bleeding from the temple. I got towels and tried to stop it, and then I realized he had—passed away.

LAWYER FOR DEFENSE. I see. What did you do then?

YOUNG WOMAN. I didn't know what to do. But I thought I'd better call the police. So I went to the telephone and called the police.

LAWYER FOR DEFENSE. What happened then?

YOUNG WOMAN. Nothing. Nothing happened.

LAWYER FOR DEFENSE. The police came, didn't they?

YOUNG WOMAN. Yes—they came.

LAWYER FOR DEFENSE (quickly). And that is all you know concerning the death of your husband in the late hours of June 2nd or the early hours of June 3rd last, isn't it?

YOUNG WOMAN. Yes sir.

LAWYER FOR DEFENSE. All?

YOUNG WOMAN. Yes sir.

LAWYER FOR DEFENSE (to Lawyer for Prosecution). Take the witness.

FIRST REPORTER (writing). The accused woman told a straightforward story of—

SECOND REPORTER. The accused woman told a rambling, disconnected story of—

LAWYER FOR PROSECUTION. You made no effort to cry out, Mrs. Jones, did you, when you saw those two big dark men standing over your helpless husband, did you?

YOUNG WOMAN. No sir. I didn't. I—

LAWYER FOR PROSECUTION. And when they turned and ran out of the room, you made no effort to follow them or cry out after them, did you?

YOUNG WOMAN. No sir.

LAWYER FOR PROSECUTION. Why didn't you?

YOUNG WOMAN. I saw Mr. Jones was hurt.

LAWYER FOR PROSECUTION. Ah! You saw Mr. Jones was hurt! You saw this—how did you see it?

YOUNG WOMAN. I just saw it.

LAWYER FOR PROSECUTION. Then there was a light in the room?

YOUNG WOMAN. A sort of light.

LAWYER FOR PROSECUTION. What do you mean—a sort of light? A bed light?

YOUNG WOMAN. No. No, there was no light on.

LAWYER FOR PROSECUTION. They where did it come from—this sort of light?

YOUNG WOMAN. I don't know.

LAWYER FOR PROSECUTION. Perhaps—from the window.

YOUNG WOMAN. Yes—from the window.

LAWYER FOR PROSECUTION. Oh, the shade was up!

YOUNG WOMAN. No—no, the shade was down.

LAWYER FOR PROSECUTION. You're sure of that?

YOUNG WOMAN. Yes. Mr. Jones always wanted the shade down.

LAWYER FOR PROSECUTION. The shade was down—there was no light in the room—but the room was light—how do you explain this?

YOUNG WOMAN. I don't know.

LAWYER FOR PROSECUTION. You don't know!

YOUNG WOMAN. I think where the window was open—under the shade—light came in.

LAWYER FOR PROSECUTION. There is a street light there?

YOUNG WOMAN. No—there's no street light.

LAWYER FOR PROSECUTION. Then where did this light come from—that came in under the shade?

YOUNG WOMAN (desperately). From the moon!

LAWYER FOR PROSECUTION. The moon!

YOUNG WOMAN. Yes! It was a bright moon!

LAWYER FOR PROSECUTION. It was a bright moon—you are sure of that!

YOUNG WOMAN. Yes.

LAWYER FOR PROSECUTION. How are you sure?

YOUNG WOMAN. I couldn't sleep—I never can sleep in the bright moon. I never can.

LAWYER FOR PROSECUTION. It was bright moon. Yet you could not see two big dark looking men—but you could see your husband bleeding from the temple.

YOUNG WOMAN. Yes sir.

LAWYER FOR PROSECUTION. And did you call a doctor?

YOUNG WOMAN. No.

LAWYER FOR PROSECUTION. Why didn't you?

YOUNG WOMAN. The police did.

LAWYER FOR PROSECUTION. But you didn't?

YOUNG WOMAN. No.

LAWYER FOR PROSECUTION. Why didn't you? (No answer.) Why didn't you?

YOUNG WOMAN (whispers). I saw it was—useless.

LAWYER FOR PROSECUTION. Ah! You saw that! You saw that—very clearly.

YOUNG WOMAN. Yes.

LAWYER FOR PROSECUTION. And you didn't call a doctor.

YOUNG WOMAN. It was—useless.

LAWYER FOR PROSECUTION. What did you do?

YOUNG WOMAN. It was useless—there was no use of anything.

LAWYER FOR PROSECUTION. I asked you what you did?

YOUNG WOMAN. Nothing.

LAWYER FOR PROSECUTION. Nothing!

YOUNG WOMAN. I just sat there.

LAWYER FOR PROSECUTION. You sat there! A long while, didn't you?

YOUNG WOMAN. I don't know.

LAWYER FOR PROSECUTION. You don't know? (*Showing her the neck of a broken bottle.*) Mrs. Jones, did you ever see this before?

YOUNG WOMAN. I think so.

LAWYER FOR PROSECUTION. You think so.

YOUNG WOMAN. Yes.

LAWYER FOR PROSECUTION. What do you think it is?

YOUNG WOMAN. I think it's the bottle that was used against Mr. Jones.

LAWYER FOR PROSECUTION. Used against him—yes—that's right. You've guessed right. This neck and these broken pieces and these pebbles were found on the floor and scattered over the bed. There were no fingerprints, Mrs. Jones, on this bottle. None at all. Doesn't that seem strange to you?

YOUNG WOMAN. No.

LAWYER FOR PROSECUTION. It doesn't seem strange to you that this bottle held in the big dark hand of one of those big dark men left no mark! No print! That doesn't seem strange to you?

YOUNG WOMAN. No.

LAWYER FOR PROSECUTION. You are in the habit of wearing rubber gloves at night, Mrs. Jones—are you not? To protect—to soften your hands—are you not?

YOUNG WOMAN. I used to.

LAWYER FOR PROSECUTION. Used to—when was that?

YOUNG WOMAN. Before I was married.

LAWYER FOR PROSECUTION. And after your marriage you gave it up?

YOUNG WOMAN. Yes.

LAWYER FOR PROSECUTION. Why?

YOUNG WOMAN. Mr. Jones did not like the feeling of them.

LAWYER FOR PROSECUTION. You always did everything Mr. Jones wanted?

YOUNG WOMAN. I tried to—Anyway I didn't care any more—so much—about my hands.

LAWYER FOR PROSECUTION. I see—so after your marriage you never wore gloves at night any more?

YOUNG WOMAN. No.

LAWYER FOR PROSECUTION. Mrs. Jones, isn't it true that you began wearing your rubber gloves again—in spite of your husband's expressed dislike—about a year ago—a year ago this spring?

YOUNG WOMAN. No.

LAWYER FOR PROSECUTION. You did not suddenly begin to care particularly for your hands again—about a year ago this spring?

YOUNG WOMAN. No.

LAWYER FOR PROSECUTION. You're quite sure of that?

YOUNG WOMAN. Yes.

LAWYER FOR PROSECUTION. Quite sure?

YOUNG WOMAN. Yes.

LAWYER FOR PROSECUTION. Then you did not have in your possession, on the night of June 2nd last, a pair of rubber gloves?

YOUNG WOMAN (*shakes her head*). No.

LAWYER FOR PROSECUTION (*to Judge*). I'd like to introduce these gloves as evidence at this time, your Honor.

JUDGE. Exhibit 24.

LAWYER FOR PROSECUTION. I'll return to them later—now, Mrs. Jones—this nightgown—you recognize it, don't you?

YOUNG WOMAN. Yes.

LAWYER FOR PROSECUTION. Yours, is it not?

YOUNG WOMAN. Yes.

LAWYER FOR PROSECUTION. The one you were wearing the night your husband was murdered, isn't it?

YOUNG WOMAN. The night he died—yes.

LAWYER FOR PROSECUTION. Not the one you wore under your peignoir—I believe that it's what you call it, isn't it? A peignoir? When you received the police—but the one you wore before that—isn't it?

YOUNG WOMAN. Yes.

LAWYER FOR PROSECUTION. This was found—not where the gloves were found—no—but at the bottom of the soiled clothes hamper in the bathroom—rolled up and wet—why was it wet, Mrs. Jones?

YOUNG WOMAN. I had tried to wash it.

LAWYER FOR PROSECUTION. Wash it? I thought you had just sat?

YOUNG WOMAN. First—I tried to make things clean.

LAWYER FOR PROSECUTION. Why did you want to make this—clean—as you say?

YOUNG WOMAN. There was blood on it.

LAWYER FOR PROSECUTION. Spattered on it?

YOUNG WOMAN. Yes.

LAWYER FOR PROSECUTION. How did that happen?

YOUNG WOMAN. The bottle broke—and the sharp edge cut.

LAWYER FOR PROSECUTION. Oh, the bottle broke and the sharp edge cut!

YOUNG WOMAN. Yes. That's what they told me afterwards.

LAWYER FOR PROSECUTION. Who told you?

YOUNG WOMAN. The police—that's what they say happened.

LAWYER FOR PROSECUTION. Mrs. Jones, why did you try so deperately to wash that blood away—before you called the police?

LAWYER FOR DEFENSE. I object!

JUDGE. Objection overruled.

LAWYER FOR PROSECUTION. Why, Mrs. Jones?

YOUNG WOMAN. I don't know. It's what anyone would have done, wouldn't they?

LAWYER FOR PROSECUTION. That depends, doesn't it? (*Suddenly taking up bottle.*) Mrs. Jones—when did you first see this?

YOUNG WOMAN. The night my husband was—done away with.

LAWYER FOR PROSECUTION. Done away with! You mean killed?

YOUNG WOMAN. Yes.

LAWYER FOR PROSECUTION. Why don't you say killed?

YOUNG WOMAN. It sounds so brutal.

LAWYER FOR PROSECUTION. And you never saw this before then?

YOUNG WOMAN. No sir.

LAWYER FOR PROSECUTION. You're quite sure of that?

YOUNG WOMAN. Yes.

LAWYER FOR PROSECUTION. And these stones—when did you first see them?

YOUNG WOMAN. The night my husband was done away with.

LAWYER FOR PROSECUTION. Before that night your husband was murdered—you never saw them? Never before then?

YOUNG WOMAN. No sir.

LAWYER FOR PROSECUTION. You are quite sure of that!

YOUNG WOMAN. Yes.

LAWYER FOR PROSECUTION. Mrs. Jones, do you remember about a year ago, a year ago this spring, bringing home to your house—a lily, a Chinese water lily?

YOUNG WOMAN. No—I don't think so.

LAWYER FOR PROSECUTION. You don't think you remember bringing home a water lily growing in a bowl filled with small stones?

YOUNG WOMAN. No—No I don't.

LAWYER FOR PROSECUTION. I'll show you this bowl, Mrs. Jones. Does that refresh your memory?

YOUNG WOMAN. I remember the bowl—but I don't remember—the lily.

LAWYER FOR PROSECUTION. You recognize the bowl then?

YOUNG WOMAN. Yes.

LAWYER FOR PROSECUTION. It is yours, isn't it?

YOUNG WOMAN. It was in my house—yes.

LAWYER FOR PROSECUTION. How did it come there?

YOUNG WOMAN. How did it come there?

LAWYER FOR PROSECUTION. Yes—where did you get it?

YOUNG WOMAN. I don't remember.

LAWYER FOR PROSECUTION. You don't remember?

YOUNG WOMAN. No.

LAWYER FOR PROSECUTION. You don't remember about a year ago bringing this bowl into your bedroom filled with small stones and some water and a lily? You don't remember tending very carefully that lily till it died? And when it died you don't remember hiding the bowl full of little stones away on the top shelf of your closet—and keeping it there until—you don't remember?

YOUNG WOMAN. No, I don't remember.

LAWYER FOR PROSECUTION. You may have done so?

YOUNG WOMAN. No—no—I didn't! I didn't! I don't know anything about all that.

LAWYER FOR PROSECUTION. But you do remember the bowl?

YOUNG WOMAN. Yes. It was in my house—you found it in my house.

LAWYER FOR PROSECUTION. But you don't remember the lily or the stones?

YOUNG WOMAN. No—No I don't!

(*Lawyer for Prosecution turns to look among his papers in a brief case.*)

FIRST REPORTER (*writing*). Under the heavy artillery fire of the State's attorney's brilliant cross-questioning, the accused woman's defense was badly riddled. Pale and trembling she—

SECOND REPORTER (*writing*). Undaunted by the Prosecution's machine-gun attack, the defendant was able to maintain her position of innocence in the face of rapid-fire questioning that threatened, but never seriously menaced her defense. Flushed but calm she—

LAWYER FOR PROSECUTION (*producing paper*). Your Honor, I'd like to introduce this paper in evidence at this time.

JUDGE. What is it?

LAWYER FOR PROSECUTION. It is an affidavit taken in the State of Guanajato, Mexico.

LAWYER FOR DEFENSE. Mexico? Your Honor, I protest. A Mexican affidavit! Is this the United States of America or isn't it?

LAWYER FOR PROSECUTION. It's properly executed—sworn to before a notary—and certified by an American Consul.

LAWYER FOR DEFENSE. Your Honor! I protest! In the name of this great United States of America—I protest—are we to permit our sacred institutions to be thus—

JUDGE. What is the purpose of this document—who signed it?

LAWYER FOR PROSECUTION. It is signed by one Richard Roe, and its purpose is to refresh the memory of the witness on the point at issue—and incidentally supply a motive for this murder—this brutal and cold-blooded murder of a sleeping man by—

LAWYER FOR DEFENSE. I protest, your Honor! I object!

JUDGE. Objection sustained. Let me see the document. (*Takes paper which is handed to him—looks at it.*) Perfectly regular. Do you offer this affidavit as evidence at this time for the purpose of refreshing the memory of the witness at this time?

LAWYER FOR PROSECUTION. Yes, your Honor.

JUDGE. You may introduce the evidence.

LAWYER FOR DEFENSE. I object! I object to the introduction of this evidence at this time as irrelevant, immaterial, illegal, biased, prejudicial, and—

JUDGE. Objection overruled.

LAWYER FOR DEFENSE. Exception.

JUDGE. Exception noted. Proceed.

LAWYER FOR PROSECUTION. I wish to read the evidence to the jury at this time.

JUDGE. Proceed.

LAWYER FOR DEFENSE. I object.

JUDGE. Objection overruled.

LAWYER FOR DEFENSE. Exception.

JUDGE. Noted.

LAWYER FOR DEFENSE. Why is this witness himself not brought into court—so he can be cross-questioned?

LAWYER FOR PROSECUTION. The witness is a resident of the Republic of Mexico and as such not subject to subpoena as a witness to this court.

LAWYER FOR DEFENSE. If he was out of the jurisdiction of this court how did you get this affidavit out of him?

LAWYER FOR PROSECUTION. This affidavit was made voluntarily by the deponent in the furtherance of justice.

LAWYER FOR DEFENSE. I suppose you didn't threaten him with extradition on some other trumped-up charge so that—

JUDGE. Order!

BAILIFF. Order!

JUDGE. Proceed with the evidence.

LAWYER FOR PROSECUTION (*reading*). In the matter of the State of ———— vs. Helen Jones, I Richard Roe, being of sound mind, do herein depose and state that I know the accused, Helen Jones, and have known her for a period of over one year immediately preceding the date of the signature on this affidavit. That I first met the said Helen Jones in a so-called speakeasy somewhere in the West 40s in New York City. That on the day I met her, she went with me to my

room, also somewhere in the West 40s in New York City, where we had intimate relations—

YOUNG WOMAN (*moans*). Oh!

LAWYER FOR PROSECUTION (*continues reading*). —and where I gave her a bowl filled with pebbles, also containing a flowering lily. That from the first day we met until I departed for Mexico in the Fall, the said Helen Jones was an almost daily visitor to my room where we continued to—

YOUNG WOMAN. No! No! (*Moans.*)

LAWYER FOR PROSECUTION. What is it, Mrs. Jones—what is it?

YOUNG WOMAN. Don't read any more! No more!

LAWYER FOR PROSECUTION. Why not?

YOUNG WOMAN. I did it! I did it! I did it!

LAWYER FOR PROSECUTION. You confess?

YOUNG WOMAN. Yes—I did it!

LAWYER FOR DEFENSE. I object, your Honor.

JUDGE. You confess you killed your husband?

YOUNG WOMAN. I put him out of the way—yes.

JUDGE. Why?

YOUNG WOMAN. To be free.

JUDGE. To be free? Is that the only reason?

YOUNG WOMAN. Yes.

JUDGE. If you just wanted to be free—why didn't you divorce him?

YOUNG WOMAN. Oh I couldn't do that!! I couldn't hurt him like that!

Burst of laughter from all in the court. The Young Woman stares out at them, and then seems to go rigid.

JUDGE. Silence!

BAILIFF. Silence!

(There is a gradual silence.)

JUDGE. Mrs. Jones, why—

Young Woman begins to moan—suddenly—as though the realization of the enormity of her isolation had just come upon her. It is a sound of desolation, of agony, of human woe. It continues until the end of the scene.

Why—?

(Young Woman cannot speak.)

LAWYER FOR DEFENSE. Your Honor, I ask a recess to—

JUDGE. Court's adjourned.

Spectators begin to file out. The Young Woman continues in the witness box, unseeing, unheeding.

FIRST REPORTER. Murderess confesses.
SECOND REPORTER. Paramour brings confession.
THIRD REPORTER. I did it! Woman cries!

There is a great burst of speed from the telegraphic instruments. They keep up a constant accompaniment to the Woman's moans. The scene blacks out as the courtroom empties, and two policemen go to stand by the woman. The sound of the telegraph instruments continues until the scene lights into Episode 9—and the prayers of the Priest.

EPISODE 9

A MACHINE

SCENE: *A prison room. The front bars face the audience. They are set back far enough to permit a clear passageway across the stage.*

SOUNDS: *The voice of a Negro singing; the whir of an aeroplane flying.*

CHARACTERS: *Young Woman; A Priest; A Jailer; Two Barbers; A Matron; Mother; Two Guards*

AT RISE: *In front of the bars, at one side, sits a Man; at the opposite side, a Woman—the Jailer and the Matron.*

Inside the bars, a Man and a Woman—the Young Woman and a Priest. The Young Woman sits still with folded hands. The Priest is praying.

PRIEST. Hear, oh Lord, my prayer; and let my cry come to Thee. Turn not away Thy face from me; in the day when I am in trouble, incline thy ear to me. In what day soever I shall call upon Thee, hear me speedily. For my days are vanished like smoke; and my bones are grown dry, like fuel for the fire. I am smitten as grass, and my heart is withered; because I forgot to eat my bread. Through the voice of my groaning, my bone hath cleaved to my flesh. I am become like to a pelican of the wilderness. I am like a night raven in the house. I have watched and become as a sparrow all alone on the housetop. All the day long my enemies reproach me; and they that praised me did swear against me. My days have declined like a shadow, and I am withered like grass. But Thou, oh Lord, end rest forever. Thou shalt arise and have mercy, for it is time to have mercy. The time is come.

Voice of Negro offstage—begins to sing a Negro spiritual.

PRIEST. The Lord hath looked upon the earth, that He might hear the groans of them that are in fetters, that He might release the children of—

Voice of Negro grown louder.

JAILER. Stop that nigger yelling.
YOUNG WOMAN. No, let him sing. He helps me.
MATRON. You can't hear the Father.
YOUNG WOMAN. He helps me.
PRIEST. Don't I help you, daughter?
YOUNG WOMAN. I understand him. He is condemned. I understand him.

The voice of the Negro goes on louder, drowning out the voice of the Priest.

PRIEST (*chanting in Latin*). Gratiam tuum, quaesumus, Domine, metibus nostris infunde, ut qui, angelo nuntiante, Christifilii tui incarnationem cognovimus, per passionem eius et crucem ad ressurectionis gloriam perducamus. Per eudem Christum Dominum nostrum.

Enter Two Barbers. There is a rattling of keys.

FIRST BARBER. How is she?
MATRON. Calm.
JAILER. Quiet.
YOUNG WOMAN (*rising*). I am ready.
FIRST BARBER. Then sit down.
YOUNG WOMAN (*in a steady voice*). Aren't you the death guard come to take me?
FIRST BARBER. No, we ain't the death guard. We're the barbers.
YOUNG WOMAN. The barbers.
MATRON. Your hair must be cut.
JAILER. Must be shaved.
BARBER. Just a patch.

The Barbers draw near her.

YOUNG WOMAN. No!
PRIEST. Daughter, you're ready. You know you are ready.
YOUNG WOMAN (*crying out*). Not for this! Not for this!
MATRON. The rule.
JAILER. Regulations.
BARBER. Routine.

The Barbers take her by the arms.

YOUNG WOMAN. No! No! Don't touch me—touch me!

(*They take her and put her down in the chair, cut a patch from her hair.*)

I will not be submitted—this indignity! No! I will not be submitted!—Leave me alone! Oh my God am I never to be let alone! Always to have to submit—to

245

submit! No more—not now—I'm going to die—I won't submit! Not now!

BARBER (*finishing cutting a patch from her hair*). You'll submit, my lady. Right to the end, you'll submit! There, and a neat job too.

JAILER. Very neat.

MATRON. Very neat.

Exit Barbers.

YOUNG WOMAN (*her calm shattered*). Father, Father! Why was I born?

PRIEST. I came forth from the Father and have come into the world—I leave the world and go onto the Father.

YOUNG WOMAN (*weeping*). Submit! Submit! Is nothing mine? The hair on my head! The very hair on my head—

PRIEST. Praise God.

YOUNG WOMAN. Am I never to be let alone! Never to have peace! When I'm dead, won't I have peace?

PRIEST. Ye shall indeed drink of my cup.

YOUNG WOMAN. Won't I have peace tomorrow?

PRIEST. I shall raise Him up at the last day.

YOUNG WOMAN. Tomorrow! Father! Where shall I be tomorrow?

PRIEST. Behold the hour cometh. Yea, is now come. Ye shall be scattered every man to his own.

YOUNG WOMAN. In Hell! Father! Will I be in Hell!

PRIEST. I am the Resurrection and the Life.

YOUNG WOMAN. Life has been hell to me, Father!

PRIEST. Life has been hell to you, daughter, because you never knew God! Gloria in excelsis Deo.

YOUNG WOMAN. How could I know Him, Father? He never was around me.

PRIEST. You didn't seek Him, daughter. Seek and ye shall find.

YOUNG WOMAN. I sought something—I was always seeking something.

PRIEST. What? What were you seeking?

YOUNG WOMAN. Peace. Rest and peace. Will I find it tonight, Father? Will I find it?

PRIEST. Trust in God.

A shadow falls across the passage in the front of the stage—and there is a whirring sound.

YOUNG WOMAN. What is that? Father! Jailer! What is that?

JAILER. An aeroplane.

MATRON. Aeroplane.

PRIEST. God in his Heaven.

YOUNG WOMAN. Look, Father! A man flying! He has wings! But he is not an angel!

JAILER. Hear his engine.

MATRON. Hear the engine.

YOUNG WOMAN. He has wings—but he isn't free! I've been free, Father! For one moment—down here on earth—I have been free! When I did what I did I was free! Free and not afraid! How is that, Father? How can that be? A great sin—a mortal sin—for which I must die and go to hell—but it made me free! One moment I was free! How is that, Father? Tell me that?

PRIEST. Your sins are forgiven.

YOUNG WOMAN. And that other sin—the other sin—that sin of love—That's all I ever knew of Heaven—heaven on earth! How is that, Father? How can that be—a sin—a mortal sin—all I know of heaven?

PRIEST. Confess to Almighty God.

YOUNG WOMAN. Oh, Father, pray for me—a prayer—that I can understand!

PRIEST. I will pray for you, daughter, the prayer of desire. Behind the King of Heaven, behold thy Redeemer and God, Who is even now coming; prepare thyself to receive Him with love, invite him with the ardor of thy desire; come, oh my Jesus, come to thy soul which desires Thee! Before Thou givest Thyself to me, I desire to give Thee my miserable heart. Do Thou accept it, and come quickly to take possession of it! Come my God, hasten! Delay no longer! My only and Infinite Good, my Treasure, my Life, my Paradise, my Love, my all, my wish is to receive thee with the love with which—

Enter the Mother. She comes along the passageway and stops before the bars.

YOUNG WOMAN (*recoiling*). Who's that woman?

JAILER. Your Mother

MATRON. Your Mother.

YOUNG WOMAN. She's a stranger—take her away—she's a stranger.

JAILER. She's come to say goodbye to you—

MATRON. To say goodbye.

YOUNG WOMAN. But she's never known me—never known me—ever—(*To the Mother.*) Go away! You're a stranger! Stranger! Stranger! (*Mother turns and starts away. Reaching out her hands to her.*) Oh Mother! Mother! (*They embrace through the bars.*)

Enter Two Guards.

PRIEST. Come, daughter.

FIRST GUARD. It's time.

SECOND GUARD. Time

YOUNG WOMAN. Wait! Mother, my child; my little strange child! I never knew her! She'll never know me! Let her live, Mother. Let her live! Live! Tell her—

PRIEST. Come, daughter.

YOUNG WOMAN. Wait! Wait! Tell her—

The Jailer takes the Mother away.

GUARD. It's time.

YOUNG WOMAN. Wait! Wait! Tell her! Wait! Just a minute more! There's so much I want to tell her—Wait—

The Jailer takes the Mother off. The Two Guards take the Young Woman by the arms, and start through the door in the bars and down the passage, across stage and off: the Priest follows; the Matron follows the Priest; the Priest is praying. The scene blacks out. The voice of the Priest gets dimmer and dimmer.

PRIEST. Lord have mercy—Christ have mercy—Lord have mercy—Christ hear us! God the Father of Heaven! God the Son, Redeemer of the World, God the Holy Ghost—Holy Trinity one God—Holy Mary—Holy Mother of God—Holy Virgin of Virgins—St. Michael—St. Gabriel—St. Raphael—

His voice dies out. Out of the darkness come the voices of Reporters.

FIRST REPORTER. What time is it now?

SECOND REPORTER. Time now.

THIRD REPORTER. Hush.

FIRST REPORTER. Here they come.

THIRD REPORTER. Hush.

PRIEST (*his voice sounds dimly—gets louder—continues until the end*). St. Peter pray for us—St. Paul pray for us—St. James pray for us—St. John pray for us—all ye holy Angels and Archangels—all ye blessed orders of holy spirits—St. Joseph—St. John the Baptist—St. Thomas—

FIRST REPORTER. Here they are!

SECOND REPORTER. How little she looks! She's gotten smaller.

THIRD REPORTER. Hush.

PRIEST. St. Phillip pray for us. All you Holy Patriarchs and prophets—St. Phillip—St. Matthew—St. Simon—St. Thaddeus—All ye holy apostles—all ye holy disciples—all ye holy innocents—Pray for us—Pray for us—Pray for us—

FIRST REPORTER. Suppose the machine shouldn't work!

SECOND REPORTER. It'll work!—It always works!

THIRD REPORTER. Hush!

PRIEST. Saints of God make intercession for us—Be merciful—Spare us, oh Lord—be merciful—

FIRST REPORTER. Her lips are moving—what is she saying?

SECOND REPORTER. Nothing.

THIRD REPORTER. Hush!

PRIEST. Oh Lord deliver us from all evil—from all sin—from Thy wrath—from the snares of the devil—from anger and hatred and every evil will—from—

FIRST REPORTER. Did you see that? She fixed her hair under the cap—pulled her hair out under the cap.

THIRD REPORTER. Hush!

PRIEST. —Beseech Thee—hear us—that Thou would'st spare us—that Thou would'st pardon us—Holy Mary—pray for us—

SECOND REPORTER. There—

YOUNG WOMAN (*calling out*). Somebody! Somebod—

Her voice is cut off.

PRIEST. Christ have mercy—Lord have mercy—Christ have mercy—

Curtain

COMMENTARY

Note: The following essay represents a single interpretation of the play. For other perspectives on Machinal, *consult the essays listed below.*

"Is nothing mine?" Helen asks in Treadwell's trenchant, episodic play. The answer, unfortunately, is "No." Even the death of this unhappy Everywoman is stage-managed by the state that executes her for murder. Helen arrives in the first scene late for work, a dreamer amidst her gossipy coworkers and rigid boss, already feeling claustrophobic from her subway ride and soon unable to begin working because her "machine is broken." When her boss George Jones uses that as a reason to take her into his office, hold her "pretty little hands," and ask her to marry him, Helen returns with a disturbing stream-of-consciousness monologue suggesting both her repulsion and her fascination with the freedom he seems to represent.

Treadwell's nine scenes move this young woman from one crushing expectation to another as her mother—in the next scene with its rejected potato, its rubber gloves, and radio—urges her to embrace the man's proposal for purely economic reasons: "He's a Vice-President—of course he's decent." On her honeymoon, when her new husband tells dirty jokes hoping to excite his innocent young wife, Helen is already desperate to get away. Even the birth of her first child, instead of bringing joy, furthers her sense of entrapment as she falls into a death-haunted depression remembering her dog who died after giving birth and whose puppies were drowned.

In the fifth scene, Treadwell depicts a nightclub that resembles one of today's singles bars. With jazz music in the background, we listen in on various conversations. Treadwell telegraphs information about several erotic relationships: one couple seems to be discussing sex or an abortion; an older man is seducing a young man; a couple contemplates getting stylishly drunk; and Helen is slowly swept off her feet by a man who had lived in Mexico and murdered a man there. Treadwell creates a sensuous, openly feminine and eventually sexually fulfilled Helen in these scenes with her lover. The hand images, which had been frightening, almost grotesque, in scenes with her husband, become lyrical here. After their first afternoon of lovemaking in Episode 6, Helen asks her free-spirited new lover for the lily rooted in stones which she admires in his room and which figures as both a symbol of Helen's innocence and a plot device when we learn later of her husband's murder. Treadwell next contrasts Helen's openness with her lover to a typical evening at home with her husband, creating counterpointed (and comical) monologues for the two disconnected souls. When he demands that she play the good wife and act interested in his business dealings, Helen talks to her husband in clichés. And he, meanwhile, calls his mortgages and stocks "her" as if they, too, were women he owned.

Treadwell's most dramatic (and challenging to stage) scene comes in the courtroom where the voices of journalists taking notes mix with questions from lawyers and decisions by the judge, all their words circling about the murder of George Jones. In one satiric moment, the newspaper scribes report contradictory stories about the trial. The lawyers, of course, are trying to reach contradictory verdicts. And it appears Helen is innocent—or at least may be acquitted—until a lawyer who has deposed her lover in Mexico reports a final betrayal by this man Helen loves. The sounds of typewriters and court stenographers become deafening as Helen acknowledges her crime and senses now her complete and ultimate isolation. With a priest chanting and praying for her soul, Helen prepares to accept the death penalty, although she protests the terrible indignity of having her hair shaved before she dies. In her final moments, she rejects her mother, whom she says never knew her. She seeks futilely to speak wisely with her own daughter, and dies still trying—and failing—to connect with another human being. Her end has neither sentimental pathos nor tragic grandeur: she is simply one more victim of an unfeeling social machine.

Early reviewers of *Machinal* compared it thematically to Theodore Dreiser's naturalistic novel, *An American Tragedy*, with which it shares the theme of a young, inexperienced

SHOWCASE | THEATER IN THE INDUSTRIAL AGE

Just as Realism necessitated new approaches to acting and playing spaces, so, too, was the stage refashioned to reflect the reality of an age when science and industry affected virtually every facet of life in the West. While many visionaries could be cited for their bold experimentation with performance spaces, scenery, and even performance styles in the Industrial Age, four in particular merit attention here: Vsevolod Meyerhold, Leopold Jessner, Erwin Piscator, and Walter Gropius.

Ironically, the Russian Meyerhold (1874–1940) began his assault on the realistic theater by staging Ibsen's most realistic psychological drama, *Hedda Gabbler*. In 1906 he staged the play in an intimate space where the audience was seated only seven feet from the actors. Dissatisfied with the naturalistic acting techniques, Meyerhold first used a style that was almost robotic to force audiences to see the inner truth of characters stripped of outer realism. From this boldly experimental approach, Meyerhold developed *Biomechanics*, a style in which actors performed either on an empty stage or, more likely, on a space reflecting the machinery fostered by the Industrial Revolution. To encourage his actors to distance themselves from realistic techniques, Meyerhold adapted styles drawn from a variety of theatrical performance modes: the Renaissance-era Italian *commedia dell'arte* and pantomime, cabaret, modern dance, ballet, and frozen tableaux. Think, for instance, of break-dancing or Michael Jackson's "moon walk"—both of which use techniques that Meyerhold would recognize.

Jessner (1878–1945), a German director, created a scenic structure—*jessnerstreppen* (*Jessner-steps*)—that manipulated both the playing arena and the acting style. He fashioned enormous steps leading from the forestage to the rear wall of the theater to create dynamic and impressive compositions. Jessner's actors had to learn to use these steps horizontally and vertically in order to appear in three-dimensional positions. Like Meyerhold, Jessner forced the actors into a style that was antithetical to the principles set forth by Realism and Naturalism. The styles reflected the modern industrial world in which workers were robotic parts of a great machine.

In Germany Piscator and Gropius did much to transform theater spaces, production methods, and acting styles to create a total theater experience beyond the boundaries of Realism and Naturalism. Piscator (1893–1966), who influenced Brecht, designed a playing space that incorporated large projection screens and revolving, nonrealistic sets using noisy machinery. He introduced film and slide projections to create "Total Theater," a presentational style that appealed to all of the audience's senses.

The concept of Total Theater actually originated as a part of a Bauhaus experiment. *Bauhaus* refers to a post–World War I architectural school founded by Gropius (1883–1969) that synthesized technology, craftsmanship, and design aesthetics. In consultation with Piscator, Gropius designed a theater that brought together audience, actor, designer, and technician in a brave new world of surprises and possibilities. Both artists migrated to the United States where their "high-tech" experiments influenced both theater architecture and production practices after World War II. Postmodernism (see Part III) is among the significant developments of the work begun by Gropius and others. Central Europeans, especially the Czechs and Romanians, are especially accomplished in their work with Bauhaus-influenced Total Theater.

---

woman drawn toward a sexual relationship that will end in betrayal and abandonment. And like Elmer Rice's expressionistic drama *The Adding Machine* (1922), Treadwell's play creates a mechanistic environment that becomes part of its theatrical technique. But Treadwell's critique goes farther than either Dreiser's or Rice's, extending to medicine, law, journalism, and religion as complicit in the subjugation of women. Helen's attempts to find financial security and a loving family life, to control her own body and realize her own dreams, may be thwarted, but Treadwell's own voice, distinctive and powerful, is still being heard.

Other perspectives on *Machinal*:

Wynn, Nancy. *Sophie Treadwell: The Career of a Twentieth Century Feminist*. Ann Arbor, MI: UMI, 1982.

———. "Sophie Treadwell: Author of *Machinal*." *Journal of American Drama and Theater* 3:1 (Winter 1991): 29–47.

BLOOD WEDDING

FEDERICO GARCÍA LORCA

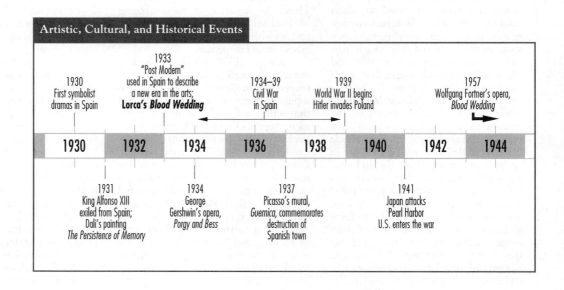

FEDERICO GARCÍA LORCA (1898–1936)

When Lorca was senselessly and cruelly executed on the morning of August 19, 1936, at the hands of the Black Squad, Spain's fascist police force, the theatrical world lost one of its most eclectic and original artists. A gifted poet, musician, dramatist, literary critic, actor, and stage director, Lorca's contributions to the development of modern drama are extraordinary—from a keen understanding of the mechanisms of tragedy to the agile repartee of his comic characters. His distinctive style was heavily influenced by Surrealism, the *avant-garde*, cinema, and the social and political upheavals of his native land.

Fashioned at a very early age by his elevated social status and classical education, his intellectual and artistic curiosity were deeply influenced by the surrealist painter Salvador Dali and the filmmaker Luis Buñuel, both of whom were Lorca's close associates while living at the Residéncia de Estudiántes (Student Residence) in Madrid. Although Lorca's university studies commenced at the University of Granada, where he studied philosophy and law, the departure from his native city proved to be a pivotal turning point as he immersed himself in a more cosmopolitan environment. In Madrid, Lorca flourished as a poet and dramatist as public readings of his work brought about a deep interest among the city's literary intelligentsia. In 1927, the staging of his first full-length play, *Mariana Pineda*, brought him considerable attention, while the publication of his poetic work, *Romancero gitano* (Gypsy Ballads), in 1928 established Lorca as a serious writer.

In 1929, given Spain's political turmoil, Lorca traveled to New York City, where he found residence at Columbia University. New York found itself amidst an economic debacle brought about by the stock market crash. The Great Depression influenced the writing of his eloquent and highly regarded work, *Poeta en Nueva York* (*Poet in New York*), a masterful vision of human despair in a century consumed by materialistic impulses. After a brief visit to Cuba in 1930, Lorca returned to Europe to continue his work in the theater. His creation of the traveling theater company, *La Barraca* (The Caravan; see Showcase "Wheels in Motion" in Part II), surely impacted his artistic vision as he journeyed throughout the Spanish provinces, presenting to illiterate and impoverished workers plays by the most distinguished classical Spanish dramatists: Calderón de la Barca, Tirso de Molina, Lope de Vega, and Cervantes. These efforts, coupled with the achievement of his rural tragedies, *Bodas de sangre* (*Blood Wedding*, 1933), *Yerma* (1934), and *La casa de Bernarda Alba* (*The House of Bernarda Alba*, 1936), established Lorca as a leading innovator of modern Western drama.

Lorca's fusion of verse, prose, and descriptions of settings akin to a surrealistic painting, together with his power to move an audience through melodic repartee, created a new theater in contrast to the stilted, historical morality plays of early-twentieth-century Spanish drama. Lorca's finest works are bathed in the aural and visual power of music and dance, as his theater, rooted in the classical and romantic tradition, broke the barriers of realistic drama in order to create a theatrical language reminiscent of the Spanish Golden Age masters.

Lorca died while fighting the fascist troops of Generalissimo Franco and today remains not only one of Spain's most admired literary artists but also a martyr to the Spanish people.

As You Read *Blood Wedding*

Lorca changed the modern Spanish theater by making poetic drama accessible to mass audiences; he was always regarded as the people's poet. His extensive travels with his company, *La Barraca*, taught him that the power of the word reached the hearts and minds of the uneducated. As an iconoclast, he questioned the moral tenor of his time by exploring the hidden social issues of the Spanish provincial landscape and by delving into the unconscious of his characters. His was a theater filled with Freudian overtones, bathed in Surrealism and Expressionism. Thus, as you read the play, rid yourself of the realistic dramatic formula, and envision the play in a cinematic format. Here are some questions you might wish to explore: Do you consider the plot of *Blood Wedding* to be a linear one? How do the scenic descriptions resemble a painted canvas? Why does the author mix realistic and allegorical characters? How does the use of music advance the rhythm of the play?

BLOOD WEDDING

FEDERICO GARCÍA LORCA

Translated from the Spanish by Richard L. O'Connell and James Graham-Luján

CHARACTERS

THE MOTHER
THE NEIGHBOR WOMAN
THE MOON
THE BRIDE
YOUNG GIRLS
DEATH (*as a Beggar Woman*)
THE MOTHER-IN-LAW
LEONARDO
WOODCUTTERS
LEONARDO'S WIFE
THE BRIDEGROOM
YOUNG MEN
THE SERVANT WOMAN
THE BRIDE'S FATHER

ACT I, SCENE 1

A room painted yellow.

BRIDEGROOM [*Entering*]. Mother.

MOTHER. What?

BRIDEGROOM. I'm going.

MOTHER. Where?

BRIDEGROOM. To the vineyard. [*He starts to go*]

MOTHER. Wait.

BRIDEGROOM. You want something?

MOTHER. Your breakfast, son.

BRIDEGROOM. Forget it. I'll eat grapes. Give me the knife.

MOTHER. What for?

BRIDEGROOM [*Laughing*]. To cut the grapes with.

MOTHER [*Muttering as she looks for the knife*]. Knives, knives. Cursed be all knives, and the scoundrel who invented them.

BRIDEGROOM. Let's talk about something else.

MOTHER. And guns and pistols and the smallest little knife—and even hoes and pitchforks.

BRIDEGROOM. All right.

MOTHER. Everything that can slice a man's body. A handsome man, full of young life, who goes out to the vineyards or to his own olive groves—his own because he's inherited them . . .

BRIDEGROOM [*Lowering his head*]. Be quiet.

MOTHER. . . . and then that man doesn't come back. Or if he does come back it's only for someone to cover him over with a palm leaf or a plate of rock salt so he won't bloat. I don't know how you dare carry a knife on your body—or how I let this serpent [*She takes a knife from a kitchen chest*] stay in the chest.

BRIDEGROOM. Have you had your say?

MOTHER. If I lived to be a hundred I'd talk of nothing else. First your father; to me he smelled like a carnation and I had him for barely three years. Then your brother. Oh, is it right—how can it be—that a small thing like a knife or a pistol can finish off a man—a bull of a man? No. I'll never be quiet. The months pass and the hopelessness of it stings in my eyes and even to the roots of my hair.

BRIDEGROOM [*Forcefully*]. Let's quit this talk!

MOTHER. No. No. Let's not quit this talk. Can anyone bring me your father back? Or your brother? Then there's the jail. What do they mean, jail? They eat there, smoke there, play music there! My dead men choking with weeds, silent, turning to dust. Two men like two beautiful flowers. The killers in jail, carefree, looking at the mountains.

BRIDEGROOM. Do you want me to go kill them?

MOTHER. No . . . If I talk about it it's because . . . Oh, how can I help talking about it, seeing you go out that door? It's . . . I don't like you to carry a knife.

It's just that . . . that I wish you wouldn't go out to the fields.

BRIDEGROOM [*Laughing*]. Oh, come now!

MOTHER. I'd like it if you were a woman. Then you wouldn't be going out to the arroyo now and we'd both of us embroider flounces and little woolly dogs.

BRIDEGROOM [*He puts his arm around his mother and laughs*]. Mother, what if I should take you with me to the vineyards?

MOTHER. What would an old lady do in the vineyards? Were you going to put me down under the young vines?

BRIDEGROOM [*Lifting her in his arms*]. Old lady, old lady—you little old, little old lady!

MOTHER. Your father, he used to take me. That's the way with men of good stock; good blood. Your grandfather left a son on every corner. That's what I like. Men, men; wheat, wheat.

BRIDEGROOM. And I, Mother?

MOTHER. You, what?

BRIDEGROOM. Do I need to tell you again?

MOTHER [*Seriously*]. Oh!

BRIDEGROOM. Do you think it's bad?

MOTHER. No.

BRIDEGROOM. Well, then?

MOTHER. I don't really know. Like this, suddenly, it always surprises me. I know the girl is good. Isn't she? Well behaved. Hard working. Kneads her bread, sews her skirts, but even so when I say her name I feel as though someone had hit me on the forehead with a rock.

BRIDEGROOM. Foolishness.

MOTHER. More than foolishness. I'll be left alone. Now only you are left me—I hate to see you go.

BRIDEGROOM. But you'll come with us.

MOTHER. No. I can't leave your father and brother here alone. I have to go to them every morning and if I go away it's possible one of the Félix family, one of the killers, might die—and they'd bury him next to ours. And that'll never happen! Oh, no! That'll never happen! Because I'd dig them out with my nails and, all by myself, crush them against the wall.

BRIDEGROOM [*Sternly*]. There you go again.

MOTHER. Forgive me. [*Pause*] How long have you known her?

BRIDEGROOM. Three years. I've been able to buy the vineyard.

MOTHER. Three years. She used to have another sweetheart, didn't she?

BRIDEGROOM. I don't know. I don't think so. Girls have to look at what they'll marry.

MOTHER. Yes. I looked at nobody. I looked at your father, and when they killed him I looked at the wall in front of me. One woman with one man, and that's all.

BRIDEGROOM. You know my girl's good.

MOTHER. I don't doubt it. All the same, I'm sorry not to have known what her mother was like.

BRIDEGROOM. What difference does it make now?

MOTHER [*Looking at him*]. Son.

BRIDEGROOM. What is it?

MOTHER. That's true! You're right! When do you want me to ask for her?

BRIDEGROOM [*Happily*]. Does Sunday seem all right to you?

MOTHER [*Seriously*]. I'll take her the bronze earrings, they're very old—and you buy her . . .

BRIDEGROOM. You know more about that . . .

MOTHER. . . . you buy her some open-work stockings—and for you, two suits—three! I have no one but you now!

BRIDEGROOM. I'm going. Tomorrow I'll go see her.

MOTHER. Yes, yes—and see if you can make me happy with six grandchildren—or as many as you want, since your father didn't live to give them to me.

BRIDEGROOM. The first-born for you!

MOTHER. Yes, but have some girls. I want to embroider and make lace, and be at peace.

BRIDEGROOM. I'm sure you'll love my wife.

MOTHER. I'll love her. [*She starts to kiss him but changes her mind*] Go on. You're too big now for kisses. Give them to your wife. [*Pause. To herself*] When she is your wife.

BRIDEGROOM. I'm going.

MOTHER. And that land around the little mill—work it over. You've not taken good care of it.

BRIDEGROOM. You're right. I will

MOTHER. God keep you. [*The Son goes out. The Mother remains seated—her back to the door. A Neighbor Woman with a 'kerchief on her head appears in the door*] Come in.

NEIGHBOR. How are you?

MOTHER. Just as you see me.

NEIGHBOR. I came down to the store and stopped in to see you. We live so far away!

MOTHER. It's twenty years since I've been up to the top of the street.

NEIGHBOR. You're looking well.

MOTHER. You think so?

NEIGHBOR. Things happen. Two days ago they brought in my neighbor's son with both arms sliced off by the machine.

[*She sits down*]

MOTHER. Rafael?

NEIGHBOR. Yes. And there you have him. Many times I've thought your son and mine are better off where they are—sleeping, resting—not running the risk of being left helpless.

MOTHER. Hush. That's all just something thought up—but no consolation.

NEIGHBOR [Sighing]. Ay!

MOTHER [Sighing]. Ay! [Pause]

NEIGHBOR [Sadly]. Where's your son?

MOTHER. He went out.

NEIGHBOR. He finally bought the vineyard!

MOTHER. He was lucky.

NEIGHBOR. Now he'll get married.

MOTHER [As though reminded of something, she draws her chair near The Neighbor]. Listen.

NEIGHBOR [In a confidential manner]. Yes. What is it?

MOTHER. You know my son's sweetheart?

NEIGHBOR. A good girl!

MOTHER. Yes, but . . .

NEIGHBOR. But who knows her really well? There's nobody. She lives out there alone with her father—so far away—fifteen miles from the nearest house. But she's a good girl. Used to being alone.

MOTHER. And her mother?

NEIGHBOR. Her mother I did know. Beautiful. Her face glowed like a saint's—but I never liked her. She didn't love her husband.

MOTHER [Sternly]. Well, what a lot of things certain people know!

NEIGHBOR. I'm sorry. I didn't mean to offend—but it's true. Now, whether she was decent or not nobody said. That wasn't discussed. She was haughty.

MOTHER. There you go again

NEIGHBOR. You asked me.

MOTHER. I wish no one knew anything about them—either the live one or the dead one—that they were like two thistles no one even names but cuts of at the right moment.

NEIGHBOR. You're right. Your son is worth a lot.

MOTHER. Yes—a lot. That's why I look after him. They told me the girl had a sweetheart some time ago.

NEIGHBOR. She was about fifteen. He's been married two years now—to a cousin of hers, as a matter of fact. But nobody remembers about their engagement.

MOTHER. How do you remember it

NEIGHBOR. Oh, what questions you ask!

MOTHER. We like to know all about the things that hurt us. Who was the boy?

NEIGHBOR. Leonardo.

MOTHER. What Leonardo?

NEIGHBOR. Leonardo Félix.

MOTHER. Félix!

NEIGHBOR. Yes, but—how is Leonardo to blame for anything? He was eight years old when those things happened.

MOTHER. That's true. But I hear that name—Félix—and it's all the same. [Muttering] Félix, a slimy mouthful. [She spits] It makes me spit—spit so I won't kill!

NEIGHBOR. Control yourself. What good will it do?

MOTHER. No good. But you see how it is.

NEIGHBOR. Don't get in the way of your son's happiness. Don't say anything to him. You're old. So am I. It's time for you and me to keep quiet.

MOTHER. I'll say nothing to him.

NEIGHBOR [Kissing her]. Nothing.

MOTHER [Calmly]. Such things . . . !

NEIGHBOR. I'm going. My men will soon be coming in from the fields.

MOTHER. Have you ever known such a hot sun?

NEIGHBOR. The children carrying water out to the reapers are black with it. Goodbye, woman.

MOTHER. Goodbye.

[The Mother starts toward the door at the left. Halfway there she stops and slowly crosses herself]

Curtain

SCENE 2

A room painted rose with copperware and wreaths of common flowers. In the center of the room is a table with a tablecloth. It is morning.

Leonardo's Mother-in-law sits in one corner holding a child in her arms and rocking it. His Wife is in the other corner mending stockings.

MOTHER-IN-LAW.
Lullaby, my baby
once there was a big horse
who didn't like water.
The water was black there
under the branches.
When it reached the bridge
it stopped and it sang.
Who can say, my baby,
what the stream holds
with its long tail
in its green parlor?

WIFE [Softly].
Carnation, sleep and dream,
the horse won't drink from the stream.

MOTHER-IN-LAW.
> My rose, asleep now lie,
> the horse is starting to cry.
> His poor hooves were bleeding,
> his long mane was frozen,
> and deep in his eyes
> stuck a silvery dagger.
> Down he went to the river,
> Oh, down he went down!
> And his blood was running,
> Oh, more than the water.

WIFE.
> Carnation, sleep and dream,
> the horse won't drink from the stream.

MOTHER-IN-LAW.
> My rose, asleep now lie,
> the horse is starting to cry.

WIFE.
> He never did touch
> the dank river shore
> though his muzzle was warm
> and with silvery flies.
> So, to the hard mountains
> he could only whinny
> just when the dead stream
> coverd his throat.
> Ay-y-y, for the big horse
> who didn't like water!
> Ay-y-y, for the snow-wound
> big horse of the dawn!

MOTHER-IN-LAW.
> Don't come in! Stop him
> and close up the window
> with branches of dreams
> and a dream of branches.

WIFE.
> My baby is sleeping.

MOTHER-IN-LAW.
> My baby is quiet.

WIFE.
> Look, horse, my baby
> has him a pillow.

MOTHER-IN-LAW.
> His cradle is metal.

WIFE.
> His quilt is a fine fabric.

MOTHER-IN-LAW.
> Lullaby, my baby.

WIFE.
> Ay-y-y, for the big horse
> who didn't like water!

MOTHER-IN-LAW.
> Don't come near, don't come in!
> Go away to the mountains
> and through the grey valleys,
> that's where your mare is.

WIFE [*Softly*].
> Carnation, sleep and dream,
> The horse won't drink from the stream.

MOTHER-IN-LAW [*Getting up, very softly*].
> My rose, asleep now lie
> for the horse is starting to cry.

[*She carries the child out. Leonardo enters*]

LEONARDO. Where's the baby?

WIFE. He's sleeping.

LEONARDO. Yesterday he wasn't well. He cried during the night.

WIFE. Today he's like a dahlia. And you? Were you at the blacksmith's?

LEONARDO. I've just come from there. Would you believe it? For more than two months he's been putting new shoes on the horse and they're always coming off. As far as I can see he pulls them off on the stones.

WIFE. Couldn't it just be that you use him so much?

LEONARDO. No. I almost never use him.

WIFE. Yesterday the neighbors told me they'd seen you on the far side of the plains.

LEONARDO. Who said that?

WIFE. The women who gather capers. It certainly surprised me. Was it you?

LEONARDO. No. What would I be doing there, in that wasteland?

WIFE. That's what I said. But the horse was streaming sweat.

LEONARDO. Did you see him?

WIFE. No. Mother did.

LEONARDO. Is she with the baby?

WIFE. Yes. Do you want some lemonade?

LEONARDO. With good cold water.

WIFE. And then you didn't come to eat!

LEONARDO. I was with the wheat weighers. They always hold me up.

WIFE [*Very tenderly, while she makes the lemonade*]. Did they pay you a good price?

LEONARDO. Fair.

WIFE. I need a new dress and the baby a bonnet with ribbons.

LEONARDO [*Getting up*]. I'm going to take a look at him.

WIFE. Be careful. He's asleep.

MOTHER-IN-LAW. Well! Who's been racing the horse that way? He's down there, worn out, his eyes popping from their sockets as though he'd come from the ends of the earth.

LEONARDO [*Acidly*]. I have.

MOTHER-IN-LAW. Oh, excuse me! He's your horse.

WIFE [*Timidly*]. He was at the wheat buyers.

MOTHER-IN-LAW. He can burst for all of me! [*She sits down. Pause*]

WIFE. Your drink. Is it cold?

LEONARDO. Yes.

WIFE. Did you hear they're going to ask for my cousin?

LEONARDO. When?

WIFE. Tomorrow. The wedding will be within a month. I hope they're going to invite us.

LEONARDO [*Gravely*]. I don't know.

MOTHER-IN-LAW. His mother, I think, wasn't very happy about the match.

LEONARDO. Well, she may be right. She's a girl to be careful with.

WIFE. I don't like to have you thinking bad things about a good girl.

MOTHER-IN-LAW [*Meaningfully*]. If he does, it's because he knows her. Didn't you know he courted her for three years?

LEONARDO. But I left her. [*To his Wife*] Are you going to cry now? Quit that![*He brusquely pulls her hands away from her face*] Let's go see the baby.

[*They go in with their arms around each other. A Girl appears. She is happy. She enters running*]

GIRL. Señora.

MOTHER-IN-LAW. What is it?

GIRL. The groom came to the store and he's bought the best of everything they had.

MOTHER-IN-LAW. Was he alone?

GIRL. No. With his mother. Stern, tall. [*She imitates her*] And such extravagance!

MOTHER-IN-LAW. They have money.

GIRL. And they bought some open-work stockings! Oh, such stockings! A woman's dream of stockings! Look: a swallow here. [*She points to her ankle*] a ship here [*She points to her calf*] and here [*She points to her thigh*] a rose!

MOTHER-IN-LAW. Child!

GIRL. A rose with seeds and the stem! Oh! All in silk.

MOTHER-IN-LAW. Two rich families are being brought together. [*Leonardo and his Wife appear*]

GIRL. I came to tell you what they're buying.

LEONARDO [*Loudly*]. We don't care.

WIFE. Leave her alone.

MOTHER-IN-LAW. Leonardo, it's not that important.

GIRL. Please excuse me. [*She leaves, weeping*]

MOTHER-IN-LAW. Why do you always have to make trouble with people?

LEONARDO. I didn't ask for your opinion. [*He sits down*]

MOTHER-IN-LAW. Very well. [*Pause*]

WIFE [*To Leonardo*]. What's the matter with you? What idea've you got boiling there inside your head? Don't leave me like this, not knowing anything.

LEONARDO. Stop that.

WIFE. No. I want you to look at me and tell me.

LEONARDO. Let me alone. [*He rises*]

WIFE. Where you are going, love?

LEONARDO [*Sharply*]. Can't you shut up?

MOTHER-IN-LAW [*Energetically, to her daughter*]. Be quiet! [*Leonardo goes out*] The baby!

[*She goes into the bedroom and comes out again with the baby in her arms. The Wife has remained standing unmoving*]

MOTHER-IN-LAW.
    His poor hooves were bleeding,
    his long mane was frozen,
    and deep in his eyes
    stuck a silvery dagger.
    Down he went to the river,
    Oh, down he went down!
    And his blood was running,
    oh, more than the water.

WIFE [*Turning slowly, as though dreaming*].
    Carnation, sleep and dream,
    the horse is drinking from the stream.

MOTHER-IN-LAW.
    My rose, asleep now lie
    the horse is starting to cry.

WIFE.
    Lullaby, my baby.

MOTHER-IN-LAW.
    Ay-y-y, for the big horse
    who didn't like water!

WIFE [*Dramatically*].
    Don't come near, don't come in!
    Go away to the mountains!
    Ay-y-y, for the snow-wound,
    big horse of the dawn!

MOTHER-IN-LAW [*Weeping*].
    My baby is sleeping . . .

WIFE [*Weeping, as she slowly moves closer*].
    My baby is resting . . .

MOTHER-IN-LAW.
    Carnation, sleep and dream,
    the horse won't drink from the stream.

WIFE [*Weeping, and leaning on the table*].
    My rose, asleep now lie,
    the horse is starting to cry.

Curtain

SCENE 3

Interior of the cave where The Bride lives. At the back is a cross of large rose-colored flowers. The round doors have lace curtains with rose-colored ties. Around the walls, which are of a white and hard material, are round fans, blue jars, and little mirrors.

SERVANT. Come right in . . . [*She is very affable, full of humble hypocrisy. The Bridegroom and his Mother enter. The Mother is dressed in black satin and wears a lace mantilla; The Bridegroom in black corduroy with a great golden chain*] Won't you sit down? They'll be right here. [*She leaves. The Mother and Son are left sitting motionless as statues. Long pause*]

MOTHER. Did you wear the watch?

BRIDEGROOM. Yes. [*He takes it out and looks at it*]

MOTHER. We have to be back on time. How far away these people live!

BRIDEGROOM. But this is good land.

MOTHER. Good; but much too lonesome. A four hour trip and not one house, not one tree.

BRIDEGROOM. This is the wasteland.

MOTHER. Your father would have covered it with trees.

BRIDEGROOM. Without water?

MOTHER. He would have found some. In the three years we were married he planted ten cherry trees. [*Remembering*] Those three walnut trees by the mill, a whole vineyard and a plant called Jupiter which had scarlet flowers—but it dried up. [*Pause.*]

BRIDEGROOM [*Referring to The Bride*]. She must be dressing.

[*The Bride's Father enters. He is very old, with shining white hair. His head is bowed. The Mother and the Bridegroom rise. They shake hands in silence*]

FATHER. Was it a long trip?

MOTHER. Four hours. [*They sit down*]

FATHER. You must have come the longest way.

MOTHER. I'm too old to come along the cliffs by the river.

BRIDEGROOM. She gets dizzy. [*Pause.*]

FATHER. A good hemp harvest.

BRIDEGROOM. A really good one.

FATHER. When I was young this land didn't even grow hemp. We've had to punish it, even weep over it, to make it give us anything useful.

MOTHER. But now it does. Don't complain. I'm not here to ask you for anything.

FATHER [*Smiling*]. You're richer than I. Your vineyards are worth a fortune. Each young vine is a silver coin. But—do you know?—what bothers me is that our lands are separated. I like to have everything together. One thorn I have in my heart, and that's the little orchard there, stuck in between my fields—and they won't sell it to me for all the gold in the world.

BRIDEGROOM. That's the way it always is.

FATHER. If we could just take twenty teams of oxen and move your vineyards over here, and put them down on that hillside, how happy I'd be!

MOTHER. But why?

FATHER. What's mine is hers and what's yours is his. That's why. Just to see it all together. How beautiful it is to bring things together!

BRIDEGROOM. And it would be less work.

MOTHER. When I die, you could sell ours and buy here, right alongside.

FATHER. Sell? Sell! Bah! Buy, my friend, buy everything. If I had had sons I would have bought all this mountainside right up to the part with the stream. It's not good land, but strong arms can make it good, and since no people pass by, they don't steal your fruit and you can sleep in peace. [*Pause*]

MOTHER. You know what I'm here for.

FATHER. Yes.

MOTHER. And?

FATHER. It seems all right to me. They have talked it over.

MOTHER. My son has money and knows how to manage it.

FATHER. My daughter too.

MOTHER. My son is handsome. He's never known a woman. His good name cleaner than a sheet spread out in the sun.

FATHER. No need to tell you about my daughter. At three, when the morning star shines, she prepares the bread. She never talks: soft as wool, she embroiders all kinds of fancy work and she can cut a strong cord with her teeth.

MOTHER. God bless her house.

FATHER. May God bless it.

[*The Servant appears with two trays. One with drinks and the other with sweets*]

MOTHER [*To The Son*]. When would you like the wedding?

BRIDEGROOM. Next Thursday.

FATHER. The day on which she'll be exactly twenty-two years old.

MOTHER. Twenty-two! My oldest son would be that age if he were alive. Warm and manly as he was, he'd be living now if men hadn't invented knives.

FATHER. One mustn't think about that.

MOTHER. Every minute. Always a hand on your breast.

FATHER. Thursday, then? Is that right?

BRIDEGROOM. That's right.

FATHER. You and I and the bridal couple will go in a carriage to the church which is very far from here; the wedding party on the carts and horses they'll bring with them.

MOTHER. Agreed. [*The Servant passes through*]

FATHER. Tell her she may come in now. [*To The Mother*] I shall be much pleased if you like her.

[*The Bride appears. Her hands fall in a modest pose and her head is bowed*]

MOTHER. Come here. Are you happy?

BRIDE. Yes, señora.

FATHER. You shouldn't be so solemn. After all, she's going to be your mother.

BRIDE. I'm happy. I've said "yes" because I wanted to.

MOTHER. Naturally. [*She takes her by the chin*] Look at me.

FATHER. She resembles my wife in every way.

MOTHER. Yes? What a beautiful glance! Do you know what it is to be married, child?

BRIDE [*Seriously*]. I do.

MOTHER. A man, some children and a wall two yards thick for everything else.

BRIDEGROOM. Is anything else needed?

MOTHER. No. Just that you live—that's it! Live long!

BRIDE. I'll know how to keep my word.

MOTHER. Here are some gifts for you.

BRIDE. Thank you.

FATHER. Shall we have something?

MOTHER. Nothing for me. [*To The Son*] But you?

BRIDEGROOM. Yes, thank you. [*He takes one sweet, The Bride another*]

FATHER. [*To The Bridegroom*] Wine?

MOTHER. He doesn't touch it.

FATHER. All the better. [*Pause. All are standing*]

BRIDEGROOM. [*To The Bride*] I'll come tomorrow.

BRIDE. What time?

BRIDEGROOM. Five.

BRIDE. I'll be waiting for you.

BRIDEGROOM. When I leave your side I feel a great emptiness, and something like a knot in my throat.

BRIDE. When you are my husband you won't have it any more.

BRIDEGROOM. That's what I tell myself.

MOTHER. Come. The sun doesn't wait. [*To The Father*] Are we agreed on everything?

FATHER. Agreed.

MOTHER [*To The Servant*]. Goodbye, woman.

SERVANT. God go with you!

[*The Mother kisses The Bride and they begin to leave in silence*]

MOTHER [*At the door*]. Goodbye, daughter. [*The Bride answers with her hand*]

FATHER. I'll go out with you. [*They leave*]

SERVANT. I'm bursting to see the presents.

BRIDE [*Sharply*]. Stop that!

SERVANT. Oh, child, show them to me.

BRIDE. I don't want to.

SERVANT. At least the stockings. They say they're all open work. Please!

BRIDE. I said no.

SERVANT. Well, my Lord. All right then. It looks as if you didn't want to get married.

BRIDE [*Biting her hand in anger*]. Ay-y-y!

SERVANT. Child, child! What's the matter with you? Are you sorry to give up your queen's life? Don't think of bitter things. Have you any reason to? None. Let's look at the presents. [*She takes the box*]

BRIDE [*Holding her by the wrists*]. Let go.

SERVANT. Ay-y-y, girl!

BRIDE. Let go, I said.

SERVANT. You're stronger than a man.

BRIDE. Haven't I done a man's work? I wish I were.

SERVANT. Don't talk like that.

BRIDE. Quiet, I said. Let's talk about something else.

[*The light is fading from the stage. Long pause*]

SERVANT. Did you hear a horse last night?

BRIDE. What time?

SERVANT. Three.

BRIDE. It might have been a stray horse—from the herd.

SERVANT. No. It carried a rider.

BRIDE. How do you know?

SERVANT. Because I saw him. He was standing by your window. It shocked me greatly.

BRIDE. Maybe it was my fiancé. Sometimes he comes by at that time.

SERVANT. No.

BRIDE. You saw him?

SERVANT. Yes.

BRIDE. Who was it?

SERVANT. It was Leonardo.

BRIDE [*Strongly*]. Liar! You liar! Why should he come here?

SERVANT. He came.

BRIDE. Shut up! Shut your cursed mouth.

[*The sound of a horse is heard*]

SERVANT [*At the window*]. Look. Lean out. Was it Leonardo?

BRIDE. It was!

Quick Curtain

ACT II, SCENE 1

The entrance hall of The Bride's house. A large door in the back. It is night. The Bride enters wearing ruf-fled white petticoats full of laces and embroidered bands, and a sleeveless white bodice. The Servant is dressed the same way.

SERVANT. I'll finish combing your hair out here.

BRIDE. It's too warm to stay in there.

SERVANT. In this country it doesn't even cool off at dawn.

[*The Bride sits on a low chair and looks into a little hand mirror. The Servant combs her hair*]

BRIDE. My mother came from a place with lots of trees— from a fertile country.

SERVANT. And she was so happy!

BRIDE. But she wasted away here.

SERVANT. Fate.

BRIDE. As we're all wasting away here. The very walls give off heat. Ay-y-y! Don't pull so hard.

SERVANT. I'm only trying to fix this wave better. I want it to fall over your forehead. [*The Bride looks at herself in the mirror*] How beautiful you are! Ay-y-y! [*She kisses her passionately*]

BRIDE [*Seriously*]. Keep right on combing.

SERVANT [*Combing*]. Oh, lucky you—going to put your arms around a man; and kiss him; and feel his weight.

BRIDE. Hush.

SERVANT. And the best part will be when you'll wake up and you'll feel him at your side and when he caresses your shoulders with his breath, like a little nightin-gale's feather.

BRIDE [*Sternly*]. Will you be quiet.

SERVANT. But, child! What *is* a wedding? A wedding is just that and nothing more. Is it the sweets—or the bouquets of flowers? No. It's a shining bed and a man and a woman.

BRIDE. But you shouldn't talk about it.

SERVANT. Oh, *that's* something else again. But fun enough too.

BRIDE. Or bitter enough.

SERVANT. I'm going to put the orange blossoms on from here to here, so the wreath will shine out on top of your hair. [*She tries on the sprigs of orange blossom*]

BRIDE [*Looking at herself in the mirror*]. Give it to me. [*She takes the wreath, looks at it and lets her head fall in dis-couragement*]

SERVANT. Now what's the matter?

BRIDE. Leave me alone.

SERVANT. This is not time for you to start feeling sad. [*En-couragingly*] Give me the wreath. [*The Bride takes the wreath and hurls it away*] Child! You're just asking God to punish you, throwing the wreath on the floor like that. Raise your head! Don't you want to get married? Say it. You can still withdraw. [*The Bride rises*]

BRIDE. Storm clouds. A chill wind that cuts through my heart. Who hasn't felt it?

SERVANT. You love your sweetheart, don't you?

BRIDE. I love him.

SERVANT. Yes, yes. I'm sure you do.

BRIDE. But this is a very serious step.

SERVANT. You've got to take it.

BRIDE. I've already given my word.

SERVANT. I'll put on the wreath.

BRIDE [*She sits down*]. Hurry. They should be arriving by now.

SERVANT. They've already been at least two hours on the way.

BRIDE. How far is it from here to the church?

SERVANT. Five leagues by the stream, but twice that by the road. [*The Bride rises and The Servant grows excited as she looks at her*]

SERVANT.

Awake, O Bride, awaken,
On your wedding morning waken!
The world's rivers may all
Bear along your bridal Crown!

BRIDE [*Smiling*]. Come now.

SERVANT [*Enthusiastically kissing her and dancing around her*].

Awake
with the fresh bouquet
of flowering laurel.
Awake,
by the trunk and branch
of the laurels!

[*The banging of the front door latch is heard*]

BRIDE. Open the door! That must be the first guests. [*She leaves. The Servant opens the door*]

SERVANT [*In astonishment*]. You!

LEONARDO. Yes, me. Good morning.

SERVANT. The first one!

LEONARDO. Wasn't I invited?

SERVANT. Yes.

LEONARDO. That's why I'm here.

SERVANT. Where's your wife?

LEONARDO. I came on my horse. She's coming by the road.

SERVANT. Didn't you meet anyone?

LEONARDO. I *passed* them on my horse.

SERVANT. You're going to kill that horse with so much racing.

LEONARDO. When he dies, he's dead! [*Pause*]

SERVANT. Sit down. Nobody's up yet.

LEONARDO. Where's the bride?

SERVANT. I'm just on my way to dress her.

LEONARDO. The bride! She ought to be happy!

SERVANT [*Changing the subject*]. How's the baby?

LEONARDO. What baby?

SERVANT. Your son.

LEONARDO [*Remembering, as though in a dream*]. Ah!

SERVANT. Are they bringing him?

LEONARDO. No. [*Pause. Voices sing distantly*]

VOICES.
> Awake, O Bride, awaken,
> On your wedding morning waken!

LEONARDO.
> Awake, O Bride, awaken,
> On your wedding morning waken!

SERVANT. It's the guests. They're still quite a way off.

LEONARDO. The bride's going to wear a big wreath, isn't she? But it ought not to be so large. One a little smaller would look better on her. Has the groom already brought her the orange blossom that must be worn on the breast?

BRIDE [*Appearing, still in petticoats and wearing the wreath*]. He brought it.

SERVANT [*Sternly*]. Don't come out like that.

BRIDE. What does it matter? [*Seriously*] Why do you ask if they brought the orange blossom? Do you have something in mind?

LEONARDO. Nothing. What would I have in mind? [*Drawing near her*] You, you know me; you know I don't. Tell me so. What have I ever meant to you? Open your memory, refresh it. But two oxen and an ugly little hut are almost nothing. That's the thorn.

BRIDE. What have you come here to do?

LEONARDO. To see your wedding.

BRIDE. Just as I saw yours!

LEONARDO. Tied up by you, done with your two hands. Oh, they can kill me but they can't spit on me. But even money, which shines so much, spits sometimes.

BRIDE. Liar!

LEONARDO. I don't want to talk. I'm hot-blooded and I don't want to shout so all these hills will hear me.

BRIDE. My shouts would be louder.

SERVANT. You'll have to stop talking like this. [*To The Bride*] You don't have to talk about what's past. [*The Servant looks around uneasily at the doors*]

BRIDE. She's right. I shouldn't even talk to you. But it offends me to the soul that you come here to watch me, and spy on my wedding, and ask about the orange blossom with something on your mind. Go and wait for your wife at the door.

LEONARDO. But, can't you and I even talk?

SERVANT [*with rage*]. No! No, you can't talk.

LEONARDO. Ever since I got married I've been thinking night and day about whose fault it was, and every time I think about it, out comes a new fault to eat up the old one; but always there's a fault left!

BRIDE. A man with a horse knows a lot of things and can do a lot to ride roughshod over a girl stuck out in the desert. But I have my pride. And that's why I'm getting married. I'll lock myself in with my husband and then I'll have to love him above everyone else.

LEONARDO. Pride won't help you a bit. [*He draws near to her*]

BRIDE. Don't come near me!

LEONARDO. To burn with desire and keep quiet about it is the greatest punishment we can bring on ourselves. What good was pride to me—and not seeing you, and letting you lie awake night after night? No good! It only served to bring the fire down on me! You think that time heals and walls hide things, but it isn't true, it isn't true! When things get that deep inside you there isn't anybody can change them.

BRIDE [*Trembling*]. I can't listen to you. I can't listen to your voice. It's as though I'd drunk a bottle of anise and fallen asleep wrapped in a quilt of roses. It pulls me along, and I know I'm drowning—but I go on down.

SERVANT [*Seizing Leonardo by the lapels*]. You've got to go right now!

LEONARDO. This is the last time I'll ever talk to her. Don't you be afraid of anything.

BRIDE. And I know I'm crazy and I know my breast rots with longing; but here I am—calmed by hearing him, by just seeing him move his arms.

LEONARDO. I'd never be at peace if I didn't tell you these things. I got married. Now you get married.

SERVANT. But she *is* getting married!

[*Voices are heard singing, nearer*]

VOICES.
>   Awake, O Bride, awaken,
>   On your wedding morning waken!

BRIDE.
>   Awake, O Bride, awaken,

[She goes out, running toward her room]

SERVANT. The people are here now. [*To Leonardo*] Don't
>   you come near her again.

LEONARDO. Don't worry. [*He goes out to the left. Day begins
>   to break*]

FIRST GIRL [*Entering*].
>   Awake, O Bride, awaken,
>   the morning you're to marry;
>   sing round and dance round;
>   balconies a wreath must carry.

VOICES.
>   Bride, awaken!

SERVANT [*Creating enthusiasm*].
>   Awake,
>   with the green bouquet
>   of love in flower.
>   Awake,
>   by the trunk and the branch
>   of the laurels!

SECOND GIRL [*Entering*].
>   Awake,
>   with her long hair,
>   snowy sleeping gown,
>   patent leather boots with silver—
>   her forehead jasmines crown.

SERVANT.
>   Oh, shepherdess,
>   the moon begins to shine!

FIRST GIRL.
>   Oh, gallant.
>   leave your hat beneath the vine!

FIRST YOUNG MAN [*Entering, holding his hat on high*].
>   Bride, awaken,
>   for over the fields
>   the wedding draws nigh
>   with trays heaped with dahlias
>   and cakes piled high.

VOICES.
>   Bride, awaken!

SECOND GIRL.
>   The bride
>   has set her white wreath in place
>   and the groom
>   ties it on with a golden lace.

SERVANT.
>   By the orange tree,
>   sleepless the bride will be.

THIRD GIRL [*Entering*].
>   By the citron vine,
>   gifts from the groom will shine.

[Three Guests come in]

FIRST YOUTH.
>   Dove, awaken!
>   In the dawn
>   shadowy bells are shaken.

GUEST.
>   The bride, the white bride
>   today a maiden,
>   tomorrow a wife.

FIRST GIRL.
>   Dark one, come down
>   trailing the train of your silken gown.

GUEST.
>   Little dark one, come down,
>   cold morning wears a dewy crown.

FIRST GUEST.
>   Awaken, wife, awake,
>   orange blossoms the breezes shake.

SERVANT.
>   A tree I would embroider her
>   with garnet sashes wound
>   And on each sash a cupid,
>   with "Long Live" all around.

VOICES.
>   Bride, awaken.

FIRST YOUTH.
>   The morning you're to marry!

GUEST.
>   The morning you're to marry
>   how elegant you'll seem;
>   worthy, mountain flower,
>   of a captain's dream.

FATHER [*Entering*].
>   A captain's wife
>   the groom will marry.
>   He comes with his oxen the treasure to carry!

THIRD GIRL.
>   The groom
>   is like a flower of gold.
>   When he walks,
>   blossoms at his feet unfold.

SERVANT.
>   Oh, my lucky girl!

SECOND YOUTH.
　　Bride, awaken.
SERVANT.
　　Oh, my elegant girl!
FIRST GIRL.
　　Through the windows
　　hear the wedding shout.
SECOND GIRL.
　　Let the bride come out.
FIRST GIRL.
　　Come out, come out!
SERVANT.
　　Let the bells
　　ring and ring out clear!
　　For here she comes!
　　For now she's near!
SERVANT.
　　Like a bull, the wedding
　　is arising here!

[*The Bride appears. She wears a black dress in the style of 1900, with a bustle and large train covered with pleated gauzes and heavy laces. Upon her hair, brushed in a wave over her forehead, she wears an orange blossom wreath. Guitars sound. The Girls kiss The Bride*]

THIRD GIRL. What scent did you put on your hair?
BRIDE [*Laughing*]. None at all.
SECOND GIRL [*Looking at her dress*]. This cloth is what you
　　can't get.
FIRST YOUTH. Here's the groom!
BRIDEGROOM. Salud!
FIRST GIRL [*Putting a flower behind his ear*].
　　The groom
　　is like a flower of gold.
SECOND GIRL.
　　Quiet breezes
　　from his eyes unfold.

[*The Groom goes to The Bride*]

BRIDE. Why did you put on those shoes?
BRIDEGROOM. They're gayer than the black ones.
LEONARDO'S WIFE [*Entering and kissing The Bride*]. Salud!
　　[*They all speak excitedly*]
LEONARDO [*Entering, as one who performs a duty*].
　　The morning you're to marry
　　We give you a wreath to wear.
LEONARDO'S WIFE.
　　So the fields may be made happy
　　with the dew dropped from your hair!
MOTHER [*To The Father*]. Are those people here, too?

FATHER. They're part of the family. Today is a day of for-
　　giveness!
MOTHER. I'll put up with it, but I don't forgive.
BRIDEGROOM. With your wreath, it's a joy to look at you!
BRIDE. Let's go to the church quickly.
BRIDEGROOM. Are you in a hurry?
BRIDE. Yes. I want to be your wife right now so that I can
　　be with you alone, not hearing any voice but yours.
BRIDEGROOM. That's what I want!
BRIDE. And not seeing any eyes but yours. And for you
　　to hug me so hard, that even though my dead
　　mother should call me, I wouldn't be able to draw
　　away from you.
BRIDEGROOM. My arms are strong. I'll hug you for forty
　　years without stopping.
BRIDE [*Taking his arm, dramatically*]. Forever!
FATHER. Quick now! Round up the teams and carts! The
　　sun's already out.
MOTHER. And go along carefully! Let's hope nothing goes
　　wrong.

[*The great door in the background opens*]

SERVANT [*Weeping*].
　　As you set out from your house.
　　oh, maiden white,
　　remember you leave shining
　　with a star's light.
FIRST GIRL.
　　Clean of body, clean of clothes
　　from her home to church she goes.

[*They start leaving*]

SECOND GIRL.
　　Now you leave your home
　　for the church!
SERVANT.
　　The wind sets flowers
　　on the sands.
THIRD GIRL.
　　Ah, the white maid!
SERVANT.
　　Dark winds are the lace
　　of her mantilla.

[*They leave. Guitars, castanets and tambourines are heard. Leonardo and his Wife are left alone*]

WIFE. Let's go.
LEONARDO. Where?
WIFE. To the church. But not on your horse. You're com-
　　ing with me.
LEONARDO. In the cart?

WIFE. Is there anything else?

LEONARDO. I'm not the kind of man to ride in a cart.

WIFE. Nor I the wife to go to a wedding without her husband. I can't stand any more of this!

LEONARDO. Neither can I!

WIFE. And why do you look at me that way? With a thorn in each eye.

LEONARDO. Let's go!

WIFE. I don't know what's happening. But I think, and I don't want to think. One thing I do know. I'm already cast off by you. But I have a son. And another coming. And so it goes. My mother's fate was the same. Well, I'm not moving from here.

[Voices outside]

VOICES.
As you set out from your home
and to the church go
remember you leave shining
with a star's glow.

WIFE [Weeping].
Remember you leave shining
with a star's glow!
I left my house like that too. They could have stuffed the whole countryside in my mouth. I was that trusting.

LEONARDO [Rising]. Let's go!

WIFE. But you with me!

LEONARDO. Yes. [Pause] Start moving! [They leave]

VOICES.
As you set out from your home
and to the church go,
remember you leave shining
with a star's glow.

Slow Curtain

SCENE 2

The exterior of The Bride's Cave Home, in white gray and cold blue tones. Large cactus trees. Shadowy and silver tones. Panoramas of light tan tablelands, everything hard like a landscape in popular ceramics.

SERVANT [Arranging glasses and trays on a table].
A-turning,
the wheel was a-turning,
and the water was flowing,
for the wedding night comes.
May the branches part

and the moon be arrayed
at her white balcony rail.

[In a loud voice]

Set out the tablecloths!

[In a pathetic voice]

A-singing,
bride and groom were singing
and the water was flowing
for their wedding night comes.
Oh, rime-frost, flash!—
and almonds bitter
fill with honey!

[In a loud voice]

Get the wine ready!

[In a poetic tone]

Elegant girl,
most elegant in the world,
see the way the water is flowing,
for your wedding night comes.
Hold your skirts close in
under the bridegroom's wing
and never leave your house,
for the Bridegroom is a dove
with his breast a firebrand
and the fields wait for the whisper
of spurting blood.
A-turning
the wheel was a-turning
and the water was flowing
and your wedding night comes.
Oh, water, sparkle!

MOTHER [Entering]. At last!

FATHER. Are we the first ones?

SERVANT. No, Leonardo and his wife arrived a while ago. They drove like demons. His wife got here dead with fright. They made the trip as though they'd come on horseback.

FATHER. That one's looking for trouble. He's not of good blood.

MOTHER. What blood would you expect him to have? His whole family's blood. It comes down from his great grandfather, who started in killing, and it goes on down through the whole evil breed of knife wielding and false smiling men.

FATHER. Let's leave it at that!

SERVANT. But how can she leave it at that?

MOTHER. It hurts me to the tips of my veins. On the forehead of all of them I see only the hand with which they killed what was mine. Can you really see me? Don't I seem mad to you? Well, it's the madness of not having shrieked out all my breast needs to. Always in my breast there's a shriek standing tiptoe that I have to beat down and hold in under my shawls. But the dead are carried off and one has to keep still. And then, people find fault. [*She removes her shawl*]

FATHER. Today's not the day for you to be remembering these things.

MOTHER. When the talk turns on it, I have to speak. And more so today. Because today I'm left alone in my house.

FATHER. But with the expectation of having someone with you.

MOTHER. That's my hope: grandchildren. [*They sit down*]

FATHER. I want them to have a lot of them. This land needs hands that aren't hired. There's a battle to be waged against weeds, the thistles, the big rocks that come from one doesn't know where. And those hands have to be the owner's, who chastises and dominates, who makes the seeds grow. Lots of sons are needed.

MOTHER. And some daughters! Men are like the wind! They're forced to handle weapons. Girls never go out into the street.

FATHER [*Happily*]. I think they'll have both.

MOTHER. My son will cover her well. He's of good seed. His father could have had many sons with me.

FATHER. What I'd like is to have all this happen in a day. So that right away they'd have two or three boys.

MOTHER. But it's not like that. It takes a long time. That's why it's so terrible to see one's own blood spilled out on the ground. A fountain that spurts for a minute, but costs us years. When I got to my son, he lay fallen in the middle of the street. I wet my hands with his blood and licked them with my tongue—because it was my blood. You don't know what that's like. In a glass and topaze shrine I'd put the earth moistened by his blood.

FATHER. Now you must hope. My daughter is wide-hipped and your son is strong.

MOTHER. That's why I'm hoping. [*They rise*]

FATHER. Get the wheat trays ready!

SERVANT. They're all ready.

LEONARDO'S WIFE [*Entering*]. May it be for the best!

MOTHER. Thank you.

LEONARDO. Is there going to be a celebration?

FATHER. A small one. People can't stay long.

SERVANT. Here they are!

[*Guests begin entering in gay groups. The Bride and Groom come in arm-in-arm. Leonardo leaves*]

BRIDEGROOM. There's never beeen a wedding with so many people!

BRIDE [*Sullen*]. Never.

FATHER. It was brilliant.

MOTHER. Whole branches of families came.

BRIDEGROOM. People who never went out of the house.

MOTHER. Your father sowed well, and now you're reaping it.

BRIDEGROOM. There were cousins of mine whom I no longer knew.

MOTHER. All the people from the seacoast.

BRIDEGROOM [*Happily*]. They were frightened of the horses. [*They talk*]

MOTHER [*To The Bride*]. What are you thinking about?

BRIDE. I'm not thinking about anything.

MOTHER. Your blessings weigh heavily. [*Guitars are heard*]

BRIDE. Like lead.

MOTHER [*Stern*]. But they shouldn't weigh so. Happy as a dove you'd ought to be.

BRIDE. Are you staying here tonight?

MOTHER. No. My house is empty.

BRIDE. You'd ought to stay!

FATHER [*To The Mother*]. Look at the dance they're forming. Dances of the faraway seashore.

[*Leonardo enters and sits down. His Wife stands rigidly behind him*]

MOTHER. They're my husband's cousins. Stiff as stones at dancing.

FATHER. It makes me happy to watch them. What a change for this house! [*He leaves*]

BRIDEGROOM [*To The Bride*]. Did you like the orange blossom?

BRIDE [*Looking at him fixedly*]. Yes.

BRIDEGROOM. It's all of wax. It will last forever. I'd like you to have had them all over your dress.

BRIDE. No need of that. [*Leonardo goes off to the right*]

FIRST GIRL. Let's go and take out your pins.

BRIDE [*To The Groom*]. I'll be right back.

LEONARDO'S WIFE. I hope you'll be happy with my cousin!

BRIDEGROOM. I'm sure I will.

LEONARDO'S WIFE. The two of you here; never going out; building a home. I wish I could live far away like this, too!

BRIDEGROOM. Why don't you buy land? The mountainside is cheap and children grow up better.

LEONARDO'S WIFE. We don't have any money. And at the rate we're going . . . !

BRIDEGROOM. Your husband is a good worker.

LEONARDO'S WIFE. Yes, but he likes to fly around too much; from one thing to another. He's not a patient man.

SERVANT. Aren't you having anything? I'm going to wrap up some wine cakes for your mother. She likes them so much.

BRIDEGROOM. Put up three dozen for her.

LEONARDO'S WIFE. No, no. A half-dozen's enough for her!

BRIDEGROOM. But today's a day!

LEONARDO'S WIFE [*To The Servant*]. Where's Leonardo?

BRIDEGROOM. He must be with the guests.

LEONARDO'S WIFE. I'm going to go see. [*She leaves*]

SERVANT [*Looking off at the dance*]. That's beautiful there.

BRIDEGROOM. Aren't you dancing?

SERVANT. No one will ask me.

[*Two Girls pass across the back of the stage; during this whole scene the background should be an animated crossing of figures*]

BRIDEGROOM [*Happily*]. They just don't know anything. Lively old girls like you dance better than the young ones.

SERVANT. Well! Are you tossing me a compliment, boy? What a family yours is! Men among men! As a little girl I saw your grandfather's wedding. What a figure! It seemed as if a mountain were getting married.

BRIDEGROOM. I'm not as tall.

SERVANT. But there's the same twinkle in your eye. Where's the girl?

BRIDEGROOM. Taking off her wreath.

SERVANT. Ah! Look. For midnight, since you won't be sleeping, I have prepared ham for you, and some large glasses of old wine. On the lower shelf of the cupboard. In case you need it.

BRIDEGROOM [*Smiling*]. I won't be eating at midnight.

SERVANT [*Slyly*]. If not you, maybe the bride. [*She leaves*]

FIRST YOUTH [*Entering*]. You've got to come have a drink with us!

BRIDEGROOM. I'm waiting for the bride.

SECOND YOUTH. You'll have her at dawn!

FIRST YOUTH. That's when it's best!

SECOND YOUTH. Just for a minute.

BRIDEGROOM. Let's go. [*They leave. Great excitement is heard. The Bride enters. From the opposite side Two Girls come running to meet her.*]

FIRST GIRL. To whom did you give the first pin; me or this one?

BRIDE. I don't remember.

FIRST GIRL. To me, you gave it to me here.

SECOND GIRL. To me, in front of the altar.

BRIDE [*Uneasily, with a great inner struggle*]. I don't know anything about it.

FIRST GIRL. It's just that I wish you'd . . .

BRIDE [*Interrupting*]. Nor do I care. I have a lot to think about.

SECOND GIRL. Your pardon. [*Leonardo crosses at the rear of the stage*]

BRIDE [*She sees Leonardo*]. And this is an upsetting time.

FIRST GIRL. We wouldn't know anything about that!

BRIDE. You'll know about it when your time comes. This step is a very hard one to take.

FIRST GIRL. Has she offended you?

BRIDE. No. You must pardon me.

SECOND GIRL. What for? But *both* the pins are good for getting married, aren't they?

BRIDE. Both of them.

FIRST GIRL. Maybe now one will get married before the other.

BRIDE. Are you so eager?

SECOND GIRL [*Shyly*]. Yes.

BRIDE. Why?

FIRST GIRL. Well . . . [*She embraces The Second Girl. Both go running off. The Groom comes in very slowly and embraces The Bride from behind*]

BRIDE [*In sudden fright*]. Let go of me!

BRIDEGROOM. Are you frightened of me?

BRIDE. Ay-y-y! It's you?

BRIDEGROOM. Who else would it be? [*Pause*] Your father or me.

BRIDE. That's true!

BRIDEGROOM. Of course, your father would have hugged you more gently.

BRIDE [*Darkly*]. Of course!

BRIDEGROOM [*Embracing her strongly and a litttle bit brusquely*]. Because he's old.

BRIDE [*Curtly*]. Let me go!

BRIDEGROOM. Why? [*He lets her go*]

BRIDE. Well . . . the people. They can see us.

[*The Servant crosses at the back of the stage again without looking at The Bride and Bridegroom*]

BRIDEGROOM. What of it? It's consecrated now.

BRIDE. Yes, but let me be . . . Later.

BRIDEGROOM. What's the matter with you? You look frightened!

BRIDE. I'm all right. Don't go.

[*Leonardo's Wife enters*]

LEONARDO'S WIFE. I don't mean to intrude . . .

BRIDEGROOM. What is it?

LEONARDO'S WIFE. Did my husband come through here?

BRIDEGROOM. No.

LEONARDO'S WIFE. Because I can't find him, and his horse isn't in the stable either.

BRIDEGROOM [*Happily*]. He must be out racing it.

[*The Wife leaves, troubled. The Servant enters*]

SERVANT. Aren't you two proud and happy with so many good wishes?

BRIDEGROOM. I wish it were over with. The bride is a little tired.

SERVANT. That's no way to act, child.

BRIDE. It's as though I'd been struck on the head.

SERVANT. A bride from these mountains must be strong. [*To The Groom*] You're the only one who can cure her, because she's yours. [*She goes running off*]

BRIDEGROOM [*Embracing The Bride*]. Let's go dance a little. [*He kisses her*]

BRIDE [*Worried*]. No. I'd like to stretch out on my bed a little.

BRIDEGROOM. I'll keep you company.

BRIDE. Never! With all these people here? What would they say? Let me be quiet for a moment.

BRIDEGROOM. Whatever you say! But don't be like that tonight!

BRIDE [*At the door*]. I'll be better tonight.

BRIDEGROOM. That's what I want. [*The Mother appears*]

MOTHER. Son.

BRIDEGROOM. Where've you been?

MOTHER. Out there—in all that noise. Are you happy?

BRIDEGROOM. Yes.

MOTHER. Where's your wife?

BRIDEGROOM. Resting a little. It's a bad day for brides!

MOTHER. A bad day? The only good one. To me it was like coming into my own. [*The Servant enters and goes toward The Bride's room*] Like the breaking of new ground; the planting of new trees.

BRIDEGROOM. Are you going to leave?

MOTHER. Yes. I'd ought to be at home.

BRIDEGROOM. Alone.

MOTHER. Not alone. For my head is full of things: of men, and fights.

BRIDEGROOM. But now the fights are no longer fights.

[*The Servant enters quickly; she disappears at the rear of the stage, running*]

MOTHER. While you live, you have to fight.

BRIDEGROOM. I'll always obey you!

MOTHER. Try to be loving with your wife, and if you see she's acting foolish or touchy, caress her in a way that will hurt her a little: a strong hug, a bite and then a soft kiss. Not so she'll be angry, but just so she'll feel you're the man, the boss, the one who gives orders. I learned that from your father. And since you don't have him, I have to be the one to tell you about these strong defenses.

BRIDEGROOM. I'll always do as you say.

FATHER [*Entering*]. Where's my daughter?

BRIDEGROOM. She's inside. [*The Father goes to look for her*]

FIRST GIRL. Get the bride and groom! We're going to dance a round!

FIRST YOUTH [*To The Bridegroom*]. You're going to lead it.

FATHER [*Entering*]. She's not there.

BRIDEGROOM. No?

FATHER. She must have gone up to the railing.

BRIDEGROOM. I'll go see! [*He leaves. A hubbub of excitement and guitars is heard*]

FIRST GIRL. They've started it already! [*She leaves*]

BRIDEGROOM [*Entering*]. She isn't there.

MOTHER [*Uneasily*]. Isn't she?

FATHER. But where could she have gone?

SERVANT [*Entering*]. But where's the girl, where is she?

MOTHER [*Seriously*]. That we don't know. [*The Bridegroom leaves. Three guests enter*]

FATHER [*Dramatically*]. But, isn't she in the dance?

SERVANT. She's not in the dance.

FATHER [*With a start*]. There are a lot of people. Go look!

SERVANT. I've already looked.

FATHER [*Tragically*]. Then where is she?

BRIDEGROOM [*Entering*]. Nowhere. Not anywhere.

MOTHER [*To The Father*]. What does this mean? Where is your daughter?

[*Leonardo's Wife enters*]

LEONARDO'S WIFE. They've run away! They've run away! She and Leonardo. On the horse. With their arms round each other, they rode off like a shooting star!

FATHER. That's not true! Not my daughter!

MOTHER. Yes, your daughter. Spawn of a wicked mother, and he, he too. But now she's my son's wife!

BRIDEGROOM [*Entering*]. Let's go after them! Who has a horse?

MOTHER. Who has a horse? Right away! Who has a horse? I'll give him all I have—my eyes, my tongue even. . . .

VOICE. Here's one.

MOTHER [*To The Son*]. Go! After them! [*He leaves with two young men*] No. Don't go. Those people kill quickly and well . . . but yes, run, and I'll follow!

FATHER. It couldn't be my daughter. Perhaps she's thrown herself in the well.

MOTHER. Decent women throw themselves in water; not that one! But now she's my son's wife. Two groups. There are two groups here. [*They all enter*] My family and yours. Everyone set out from here. Shake the dust from your heels! We'll go help my son. [*The people separate in two groups*] For he has his family: his cousins from the sea, and all who came from inland.

Out of here! On all roads. The hour of blood has come again. Two groups! You with yours and I with mine. After them! After them!

Curtain

ACT III, SCENE 1

A forest. It is nighttime. Great moist tree trunks. A dark atmosphere. Two violins are heard. Three Woodcutters enter.

FIRST WOODCUTTER. And have they found them?

SECOND WOODCUTTER. No. But they're looking for them everywhere.

THIRD WOODCUTTER. They'll find them.

SECOND WOODCUTTER. Sh-h-h!

THIRD WOODCUTTER. What?

SECOND WOODCUTTER. They seem to be coming closer on all the roads at once.

FIRST WOODCUTTER. When the moon comes out they'll see them.

SECOND WOODCUTTER. They'd ought to let them go.

FIRST WOODCUTTER. The world is wide. Everybody can live in it.

THIRD WOODCUTTER. But they'll kill them.

SECOND WOODCUTTER. You have to follow your passion. They did right to run away.

FIRST WOODCUTTER. They were deceiving themselves but at the last blood was stronger.

THIRD WOODCUTTER. Blood!

FIRST WOODCUTTER. You have to follow the path of your blood.

SECOND WOODCUTTER. But blood that sees the light of day is drunk up by the earth.

FIRST WOODCUTTER. What of it? Better dead with the blood drained away than alive with it rotting.

THIRD WOODCUTTER. Hush!

FIRST WOODCUTTER. What? Do you hear something?

THIRD WOODCUTTER. I hear the crickets, the frogs, the night's ambush.

FIRST WOODCUTTER. But not the horse.

THIRD WOODCUTTER. No.

FIRST WOODCUTTER. By now he must be loving her.

SECOND WOODCUTTER. Her body for him; his body for her.

THIRD WOODCUTTER. They'll find them and they'll kill them.

FIRST WOODCUTTER. But by then they'll have mingled their bloods. They'll be like two empty jars, like two dry arroyos.

SECOND WOODCUTTER. There are many clouds and it would be easy for the moon not to come out.

THIRD WOODCUTTER. The bridegroom will find them with or without the moon. I saw him set out. Like a raging star. His face the color of ashes. He looked the fate of all his clan.

FIRST WOODCUTTER. His clan of dead men lying in the middle of the street.

SECOND WOODCUTTER. There you have it!

THIRD WOODCUTTER. You think they'll be able to break through the circle?

SECOND WOODCUTTER. It's hard to. There are knives and guns for ten leagues 'round.

THIRD WOODCUTTER. He's riding a good horse.

SECOND WOODCUTTER. But he's carrying a woman.

FIRST WOODCUTTER. We're close by now.

SECOND WOODCUTTER. A tree with forty branches. We'll soon cut it down.

THIRD WOODCUTTER. The moon's coming out now. Let's hurry.

[From the left shines a brightness]

FIRST WOODCUTTER.
　　Oh rising moon!
　　Moon among the great leaves.

SECOND WOODCUTTER.
　　Cover the blood with jasmines!

FIRST WOODCUTTER.
　　O lonely moon!
　　Moon among the great leaves.

SECOND WOODCUTTER.
　　Silver on the bride's face.

THIRD WOODCUTTER.
　　O evil moon!
　　Leave for their love a branch in shadow.

FIRST WOODCUTTER.
　　O sorrowing moon!
　　Leave for their love a branch in shadow!

[They go out. The Moon appears through the shining brightness at the left. The Moon is a young woodcutter with a white face. The stage takes on an intense blue radiance]

MOON.
　　Round swan in the river
　　and a cathedral's eye,
　　false dawn on the leaves,
　　they'll not escape; these things am I!
　　Who is hiding? And who sobs
　　in the thornbrakes of the valley?
　　The moon sets a knife

abandoned in the air
which being a leaden threat
yearns to be blood's pain.
Let me in! I am freezing
down to walls and windows!
Open roofs, open breasts
where I may warm myself!
I'm cold! My ashes
of somnolent metals
seek the fire's crest
on mountains and streets.
But the snow carries me
upon its mottled back
and pools soak me
in their water, hard and cold.
But this night there will be
red blood for my cheeks,
and for the reeds that cluster
at the wide feet of the wind.
Let there be neither shadow nor bower,
and then they can't get away!
O let me enter a breast
where I may get warm!
A heart for me!
Warm! That will spurt
over the mountains of my chest;
let me come in, oh let me!

[To the branches]

I want no shadows. My rays
must get in everywhere,
even among the dark trunks I want
the whisper of gleaming lights,
so that this night there will be
sweet blood for my cheeks,
and for the reeds that cluster
at the wide feet of the wind.
Who is hiding? Out, I say!
No! They will not get away!
I will light up the horse
with a fever bright as diamonds.

[He disappears among the trunks, and the stage goes back to its dark lighting. An Old Woman comes out completely covered by thin green cloth. She is bare-footed. Her face can barely be seen among the folds. This character does not appear in the cast]

BEGGAR WOMAN.
    That moon's going away, just when they're near.
    They won't get past here. The river's whisper
    and the whispering tree trunks will muffle

the torn flight of their shrieks.
It has to be here, and soon. I'm worn out.
The coffins are ready, and white sheets
wait on the floor of the bedroom
for heavy bodies with torn throats.
Let not one bird awake, let the breeze,
gathering their moans in her skirt,
fly with them over black tree tops
or bury them in soft mud.

[Impatiently]

Oh, that moon! That moon!

[The Moon appears. The intense blue light returns]

MOON. They're coming. One band through the ravine
    and the other along the river. I'm going to light up
    the boulders. What do you need?
BEGGAR WOMAN. Nothing.
MOON. The wind blows hard now, with a double edge.
BEGGAR WOMAN. Light up the waistcoat and open the
    buttons; the knives will know the path after that.
MOON.
    But let them be a long time a-dying. So the blood
    will slide its delicate hissing between my fingers.
    Look how my ashen valleys already are waking
    in longing for this fountain of shuddering gushes!
BEGGAR WOMAN. Let's not let them get past the arroyo.
    Silence!
MOON. There they come! *[He goes. The stage is left dark]*
BEGGAR WOMAN. Quick! Lots of light! Do you hear me?
    They can't get away!

[The Bridegroom and the First Youth enter. The Beggar Woman sits down and covers herself with her cloak]

BRIDEGROOM. This way.
FIRST YOUTH. You won't find them.
BRIDEGROOM *[Angrily]*. Yes, I'll find them!
FIRST YOUTH. I think they've taken another path.
BRIDEGROOM. No. Just a moment ago I felt the galloping.
FIRST YOUTH. It could have been another horse.
BRIDEGROOM *[Intensely]*. Listen to me. There's only one
    horse in the whole world, and this one's it. Can't you
    understand that? If you're going to follow me, follow
    me without talking.
FIRST YOUTH. It's only that I want to . . .
BRIDEGROOM. Be quiet. I'm sure of meeting them here. Do
    you see this arm? Well, it's not my arm. It's my
    brother's arm, and my father's, and that of all the dead
    ones in my family. And it has so much strength that it
    can pull this tree up by the roots, if it wants to. And
    let's move on, because here I feel the clenched teeth
    of all my people in me so that I can't breathe easily.

BEGGAR WOMAN [*Whining*]. Ay-y-y!
FIRST YOUTH. Did you hear that?
BRIDEGROOM. You go that way and then circle back.
FIRST YOUTH. This is a hunt.
BRIDEGROOM. A hunt. The greatest hunt there is.

[*The Youth goes off. The Bridegroom goes rapidly to the left and stumbles over The Beggar Woman, Death*]

BEGGAR WOMAN. Ay-y-y!
BRIDEGROOM. What do you want?
BEGGAR WOMAN. I'm cold.
BRIDEGROOM. Which way are you going?
BEGGAR WOMAN [*Always whining like a beggar*]. Over there, far away . . .
BRIDEGROOM. Where are you from?
BEGGAR WOMAN. Over there . . . very far away.
BRIDEGROOM. Have you seen a man and a women running away on a horse?
BEGGAR WOMAN [*Awakening*]. Wait a minute . . . [*She looks at him*] Handsome young man. [*She rises*] But you'd be much handsomer sleeping.
BRIDEGROOM. Tell me; answer me. Did you see them?
BEGGAR WOMAN. Wait a minute . . . What broad shoulders! How would you like to be laid out on them and not have to walk on the soles of your feet which are so small?
BRIDEGROOM [*Shaking her*]. I asked you if you saw them! Have they passed through here?
BEGGAR WOMAN [*Energetically*]. No. They haven't passed; but they're coming from the hill. Don't you hear them?
BRIDEGROOM. No.
BEGGAR WOMAN. Do you know the road?
BRIDEGROOM. I'll go, whatever it's like!
BEGGAR WOMAN. I'll go along with you. I know this country.
BRIDEGROOM [*Impatiently*]. Well, let's go! Which way?
BEGGAR WOMAN [*Dramatically*]. This way!

[*They go rapidly out. Two violins, which represent the forest, are heard distantly. The Woodcutters return. They have their axes on their shoulders. They move slowly among the tree trunks*]

FIRST WOODCUTTER.
    O rising death!
    Death among the great leaves.
SECOND WOODCUTTER.
    Don't open the gush of blood!
FIRST WOODCUTTER.
    O lonely death!
    Death among the dried leaves.
THIRD WOODCUTTER.
    Don't lay flowers over the wedding!

SECOND WOODCUTTER.
    O sad death!
    Leave for their love a green branch.
FIRST WOODCUTTER.
    O evil death!
    Leave for their love a branch of green!

[*They go out while they are talking. Leonardo and The Bride appear*]

LEONARDO.
    Hush!
BRIDE.
    From here I'll go on alone.
    You go now! I want you to turn back.
LEONARDO.
    Hush, I said!
BRIDE.
    With your teeth, with your hands, anyway you can,
    take from my clean throat
    the metal of this chain,
    and let me live forgotten
    back there in my house in the ground.
    And if you don't want to kill me
    as you would kill a tiny snake,
    set in my hands, a bride's hands,
    the barrel of your shotgun.
    Oh, what lamenting, what fire,
    sweeps upward through my head!
    What glass splinters are stuck in my tongue!
LEONARDO.
    We've taken the step now; hush!
    because they're close behind us,
    and I must take you with me.
BRIDE.
    Then it must be by force!
LEONARDO.
    By force? Who was it first
    went down the stairway?
BRIDE.
    I went down it.
LEONARDO.
    And who was it put
    a new bridle on the horse?
BRIDE.
    I myself did it. It's true.
LEONARDO.
    And whose were the hands
    strapped spurs to my boots?
BRIDE.
    The same hands, these that are yours,
    but which when they see you would like

to break the blue branches
and sunder the purl of your veins.
I love you! I love you! But leave me!
For if I were able to kill you
I'd wrap you 'round in a shroud
with the edges bordered in violets.
Oh, what lamenting, what fire,
sweeps upward through my head!

LEONARDO.
What glass splinters are stuck in my tongue!
Because I tried to forget you
and put a wall of stone
between your house and mine.
It's true. You remember?
And when I saw you in the distance
I threw sand in my eyes.
But I was riding a horse
and the horse went straight to your door.
And the silver pins of your wedding
turned my red blood black.
And in me our dream was choking
my flesh with its poisoned weeds.
Oh, it isn't my fault—
the fault is the earth's—
and this fragrance that you exhale
from your breasts and your braids.

BRIDE.
Oh, how untrue! I want
from you neither bed nor food,
yet there's not a minute each day
that I don't want to be with you,
because you drag me, and I come,
then you tell me to go back
and I follow you,
like chaff blown on the breeze.
I have left a good, honest man,
and all his people,
with the wedding feast half over
and wearing my bridal wreath.
But you are the one who will be punished
and that I don't want to happen.
Leave me alone now! You run away!
There is no one who will defend you.

LEONARDO.
The birds of early morning
are calling among the trees.
The night is dying
on the stone's ridge.
Let's go to a hidden corner
where I may love you forever,
for to me the people don't matter,
nor the venom they throw on us.

[*He embraces her strongly*]

BRIDE.
And I'll sleep at your feet,
to watch over your dreams.
Naked, looking over the fields,
as though I were a bitch.
Because that's what I am! Oh, I look at you
and your beauty sears me.

LEONARDO.
Fire is stirred by fire.
The same tiny flame
will kill two wheat heads together.
Let's go!

BRIDE.
Where are you taking me?

LEONARDO.
Where they cannot come,
these men who surround us.
Where I can look at you!

BRIDE [*Sarcastically*].
Carry me with you from fair to fair,
a shame to clean women,
so that people will see me
with my wedding sheets
on the breeze like banners.

LEONARDO.
I, too, would want to leave you
if I thought as men should.
But wherever you go, I go.
You're the same. Take a step. Try.
Nails of moonlight have fused
my waist and your chains.

[*This whole scene is violent, full of great sensuality*]

BRIDE.
Listen!

LEONARDO.
They're coming.

BRIDE.
                    Run!
It's fitting that I should die here,
with water over my feet,
with thorns upon my head.
And fitting the leaves should mourn me,
a woman lost and virgin.

LEONARDO.
Be quiet. Now they're appearing.

BRIDE.
                Go now!
LEONARDO.
        Quiet. Don't let them hear us.

[The Bride hesitates]

BRIDE.
        Both of us!
LEONARDO *[Embracing her]*.
                        Any way you want!
        If they separate us, it will be
        because I am dead.
BRIDE.
                        And I dead too.

[They go out in each other's arms]

*[The Moon appears very slowly. The stage takes on
a strong blue light. The two violins are heard. Suddenly two long, ear-splitting shrieks are heard, and
the music of the two violins is cut short. At the second shriek The Beggar Woman appears and stands
with her back to the audience. She opens her cape
and stands in the center of the stage like a great bird
with immense wings. The Moon halts. The curtain
comes down in absolute silence]*

Curtain

SCENE 2

The Final Scene

*A white dwelling with arches and thick walls. To the
right and left, are white stairs. At the back, a great
arch and a wall of the same color. The floor also
should be shining white. This simple dwelling should
have the monumental feeling of a church. There
should not be a single gray nor any shadow, not even
what is necessary for perspective. Two Girls dressed
in dark blue are winding a red skein.*

FIRST GIRL.
        Wool, red wool,
        what would you make?
SECOND GIRL.
        Oh, jasmine for dresses,
        fine wool like glass.
        At four o'clock born,
        At ten o'clock dead.
        A thread from this wool yarn,
        a chain 'round your feet

        a knot that will tighten
        the bitter white wreath.
LITTLE GIRL *[Singing]*.
        Were you at the wedding?
FIRST GIRL.
        No.
LITTLE GIRL.
        Well, neither was I!
        What could have happened
        'midst the shoots of the vineyards?
        What could have happened
        'neath the branch of the olive?
        What really happened
        that no one came back?
        Were you at the wedding?
SECOND GIRL.
        We told you once, no.
LITTLE GIRL *[Leaving]*.
        Well, neither was I!
SECOND GIRL.
        Wool, red wool,
        what would you sing?
FIRST GIRL.
        Their wounds turning waxen,
        balm-myrtle for pain.
        Asleep in the morning,
        and watching at night.
LITTLE GIRL *[In the doorway]*.
        And then, the thread stumbled
        on the flinty stones,
        but mountains, blue mountains,
        are letting it pass.
        Running, running, running,
        and finally to come
        to stick in a knife blade,
        to take back the bread.

        [She goes out]

SECOND GIRL.
        Wool, red wool,
        what would you tell?
FIRST GIRL.
        The lover is silent,
        crimson the groom,
        at the still shoreline
        I saw them laid out.

        [She stops and looks at the skein]

LITTLE GIRL *[Appearing in the doorway]*.
        Running, running, running,
        the thread runs to here.

All covered with clay
I feel them draw near.
Bodies stretched stiffly
in ivory sheets!

[*The Wife and Mother-in-law of Leonardo appear.
They are anguished*]

FIRST GIRL.
　　Are they coming yet?
MOTHER-IN-LAW [*Harshly*].
　　We don't know.
SECOND GIRL.
　　What can you tell us about the wedding?
FIRST GIRL.
　　Yes, tell me.
MOTHER-IN-LAW [*Curtly*]. Nothing.
LEONARDO'S WIFE. I want to go back and find out all
　　about it.
MOTHER-IN-LAW [*Sternly*].
　　You, back to your house.
　　Brave and alone in your house.
　　To grow old and to weep.
　　But behind closed doors.
　　Never again. Neither dead nor alive.
　　We'll nail up our windows
　　and let rains and nights
　　fall on the bitter weeds.
LEONARDO'S WIFE.
　　What could have happened?
MOTHER-IN-LAW.
　　It doesn't matter what.
　　Put a veil over your face.
　　Your children are yours,
　　that's all. On the bed
　　put a cross of ashes
　　where his pillow was.

[*They go out*]

BEGGAR WOMAN [*At the door*].
　　A crust of bread, little girls.
LITTLE GIRL.
　　Go away!

[*The Girls huddle close together*]

BEGGAR WOMAN.
　　Why?
LITTLE GIRL.
　　Because you whine; go away!
FIRST GIRL.
　　Child!

BEGGAR WOMAN.
　　I might have asked for your eyes! A cloud
　　of birds is following me. Will you have one?
LITTLE GIRL.
　　I want to get away from here!
SECOND GIRL [*To the Beggar Woman*].
　　Don't mind her!
FIRST GIRL.
　　Did you come by the road through the arroyo?
BEGGAR WOMAN.
　　I came that way!
FIRST GIRL [*Timidly*].
　　Can I ask you something?
BEGGAR WOMAN.
　　I saw them: they'll be here soon; two torrents
　　still at last, among the great boulders,
　　two men at the horse's feet.
　　Two dead men in the night's splendor.

[*With pleasure*]

　　Dead, yes, dead.
FIRST GIRL.
　　Hush, old woman, hush!
BEGGAR WOMAN.
　　Crushed flowers for eyes, and their teeth
　　two fistfuls of hard-frozen snow.
　　Both of them fell, and the Bride returns
　　with bloodstains on her skirt and hair.
　　And they come covered with two sheets
　　carried on the shoulders of two tall boys.
　　That's how it was; nothing more. What
　　　　was fitting.
　　Over the golden flower, dirty sand.

[*She goes. The Girls bow their heads and start going
out rhythmically*]

FIRST GIRL.
　　Dirty sand.
SECOND GIRL.
　　Over the golden flower.
LITTLE GIRL.
　　Over the golden flower
　　they're bringing the dead from the arroyo.
　　Dark the one,
　　dark the other.
　　What shadowy nightingale flies and weeps
　　over the golden flower!

[*She goes. The stage is left empty. The Mother and a
Neighbor Woman appear. The Neighbor is weeping*]

MOTHER. Hush.

NEIGHBOR. I can't.

MOTHER. Hush, I said. [*At the door*] Is there nobody here? [*She puts her hands to her forehead*] My son ought to answer me. But now my son is an armful of shrivelled flowers. My son is a fading voice beyond the mountains now. [*With rage, to The Neighbor*] Will you shut up? I want no wailing in this house. Your tears are only tears from your eyes, but when I'm alone mine will come—from the soles of my feet, from my roots—burning more than blood.

NEIGHBOR. You come to my house; don't you stay here.

MOTHER. I want to be here. Here. In peace. They're all dead now: and at midnight I'll sleep, sleep without terror of guns or knives. Other mothers will go to their windows, lashed by rain, to watch for their sons' faces. But not I. And of my dreams I'll make a cold ivory dove that will carry camellias of white frost to the graveyard. But no; not graveyard, not graveyard: the couch of earth, the bed that shelters them and rocks them in the sky. [*A woman dressed in black enters, goes toward the right, and there kneels. To The Neighbor*] Take your hands from your face. We have terrible days ahead. I want to see no one. The earth and I. My grief and I. And these four walls. Ay-y-y! Ay-y-y! [*She sits down, overcome*]

NEIGHBOR. Take pity on yourself!

MOTHER [*Pushing back her hair*]. I must be calm. [*She sits down*] Because the neighbor women will come and I don't want them to see me so poor. So poor! A woman without even one son to hold to her lips.

[*The Bride appears. She is without her wreath and wears a black shawl*]

NEIGHBOR [*With rage, seeing the Bride*]. Where are you going?

BRIDE. I'm coming here.

MOTHER [*To The Neighbor*]. Who is it?

NEIGHBOR. Don't you recognize her?

MOTHER. That's why I asked who it was. Because I don't want to recognize her, so I won't sink my teeth in her throat. You snake! [*She moves wrathfully on The Bride, then stops. To The Neighbor*] Look at her! There she is, and she's crying, while I stand here calmly and don't tear her eyes out. I don't understand myself. Can it be I didn't love my son? But, where's his good name? Where is it now? Where is it? [*She beats The Bride who drops to the floor*]

NEIGHBOR. For God's sake! [*She tries to separate them*]

BRIDE [*To The Neighbor*]. Let her; I came here so she'd kill me and they'd take me away with them. [*To The Mother*] But not with her hands; with grappling hooks, with a sickle—and with force—until they break on my bones. Let her! I want her to know I'm clean, that I may be crazy, but that they can bury me without a single man ever having seen himself in the whiteness of my breasts.

MOTHER. Shut up, shut up; what do I care about that?

BRIDE. Because I ran away with the other one; I ran away! [*With anguish*] You would have gone, too. I was a woman burning with desire, full of sores inside and out, and your son was a little bit of water from which I hoped for children, land, health; but the other one was a dark river, choked with brush, that brought near me the undertone of its rushes and its whispered song. And I went along with your son who was like a little boy of cold water—and the other sent against me hundreds of birds who got in my way and left white frost on my wounds, my wounds of a poor withered woman, of a girl caressed by fire. I didn't want to; remember that! I didn't want to. Your son was my destiny and I have not betrayed him, but the other one's arm dragged me along like the pull of the sea, like the head toss of a mule, and he would have dragged me always, always, always—even if I were an old woman and all your son's sons held me by the hair!

[*A Neighbor enters*]

MOTHER. She is not to blame; nor am I! [*Sarcastically*] Who is, then? It's a delicate, lazy, sleepless woman who throws away an orange blossom wreath and goes looking for a piece of bed warmed by another woman!

BRIDE. Be still! Be still! Take your revenge on me; here I am! See how soft my throat is; it would be less work for you than cutting a dahlia in your garden. But never that! Clean, clean as a new-born little girl. And strong enough to prove it to you. Light the fire. Let's stick our hands in; you, for your son, I, for my body. *You'll* draw yours out first.

[*Another Neighbor enters*]

MOTHER. But what does your good name matter to me? What does your death matter to me? What does anything about anything matter to me? Blessèd be the wheat stalks, because my sons are under them; blessèd be the rain, because it wets the face of the dead. Blessèd be God, who stretches us out together to rest.

[*Another Neighbor enters*]

BRIDE. Let me weep with you.

MOTHER. Weep. But at the door. [*The Girl enters. The Bride stays at the door. The Mother is at the center of the stage*]

LEONARDO'S WIFE [*Entering and going to the left*].
      He was a beautiful horseman,
      now he's a heap of snow.

He rode to fairs and mountains
and women's arms.
Now, the night's dark moss
crowns his forehead.

MOTHER.
A sunflower to your mother,
a mirror of the earth.
Let them put on your breast
the cross of bitter rosebay;
and over you a sheet
of shining silk;
between your quiet hands
let water form its lament.

WIFE.
Ay-y-y, four gallant boys
come with tired shoulders!

BRIDE.
Ay-y-y, four gallant boys
carry death on high!

MOTHER.
Neighbors.

Little GIRL [At the door].
They're bringing them now.

MOTHER.
It's the same thing.
Always the cross, the cross.

WOMEN.
Sweet nails,
cross adored,
sweet name
of Christ our Lord.

BRIDE. May the cross protect both the quick and the dead.

MOTHER.
Neighbors: with a knife,
with a little knife,
on their appointed day, between two and three,
these two men killed each other for love.
With a knife,
with a tiny knife
that barely fits the hand,
but that slides in clean
through the astonished flesh
and stops at the place
where trembles, enmeshed,
the dark root of a scream.

BRIDE.
And this is a knife,
a tiny knife
that barely fits the hand;
fish without scales, without river,
so that on their appointed day, between two and three,
with this knife,
two men are left stiff,
with their lips turning yellow.

MOTHER.
And it barely fits the hand
but it slides in clean
through the astonished flesh
and stops there, at the place
where trembles enmeshed
the dark root of a scream.

[The Neighbors, kneeling on the floor, sob]

Curtain

COMMENTARY

Note: The following essay represents a single interpretation of the play. For other perspectives on Blood Wedding, *consult the essays listed below.*

"A DIRECTOR DISCUSSES *BLOOD WEDDING* WITH HIS CAST"

Roberto D. Pomo directed Blood Wedding *at California State University-Sacramento in the fall of 2001. Here you may read his commentary to the cast at the first rehearsal. In the Showcase that accompanies this play, you may also read how the scenic designer, Haibo Yu, approached this challenging work.*

Act I, Scene 1

The play begins at a heightened, climatic point as the Bridegroom attempts to flee the immediate reality that imprisons him: yellow walls, a maternal hold, nights spent in mental flight. The scene is a musical crescendo because, after all, Lorca crafted his play in approximately fifteen days while listening to recordings of Bach cantatas. These produced a prolonged surge of energy as the poet and dramatist became one. The Bridegroom and the Mother clash violently after only eleven brief lines—as the play begins, they are already at the point of no return. Symbols of death and violence abound: knives, guns, pistols, pitch forks. We are told of the murder of the Mother's son and her husband. All is laid out, within the first three minutes into the tragedy—and it is much more than foreshadowing. It is the coming of the storm; the angel of death is already present. Distrust is in the air as the Bridegroom announces his desire to marry—the birth of a new life is already clouded by memories of horrific deaths.

The Mother and the Neighbor are overheard in a confidential exchange. Clearly, there are two worlds involved on this Spanish landscape: the spheres of violent men; and that of women subjugated by the violence of men. It is Lorca's warning: be aware of social structures based on class, rights of birth, paranoia and guilt derived from religious superstition, of never uttering aloud the whisperings of the psyche. Silence and inner turmoil are best.

The opening moments of *Blood Wedding* are reminiscent of classical Greek tragedy, particularly as envisioned by Euripides. It is a pessimistic view of life, without harmony, in its collision of unrestrained human desires. Furthermore, the spirit of John Millington Synge prevails, for Lorca read and admired Synge's *Riders to the Sea*—the harshness of an isolated existence, surrounded by an expansive arid landscape; again we witness the role of women in constant desperation.

Throughout the play we see recurring symbols: the symbols of fertility (blood); Eros (blood); death (blood); the baptismal water as the cleanser of sins; light, as it attempts to guide the way out of perdition, but to no avail. Clearly the image of blood as lineage, as a consequence of violent acts, as the essence of life is the dominant image.

Act I, Scene 2

The play's structure shifts radically to an operatic motif as the Mother-in-Law's lullaby becomes a metaphor for the play's forthcoming events. The use of music in *Blood Wedding* is quite distinct from anything written in the history of Spanish drama. Although the poetry/lyrics are not written in verse, they are driven by a strong musical thrust that merges literature and music. In a curious way, the music emotionally detaches the audience from the play's dramatic structure because they have to listen to the lyrics in order to understand its symbolic meaning.

The Mother-in-Law is the voice of reason; she's fully aware of Leonardo's earthy and irrational impulses. She's the ominous power of the scene. By contrast, the Wife is meek, non-confrontational, and totally aware of Leonardo's thirst for freedom, but she cannot escape her social condition. Her life is one of servitude; her maternal duties her only responsibility. Significantly, Leonardo is the only character who has a name. His psychological state of mind, his impetuousness and capricious attitude represent the male-dominated sphere of *Blood Wedding*. His is the erotic quality of the play, manifested in act 3, scene 1. His is an uncontrolled passion and lust. In the words of the lullaby, he is "the big horse who didn't like water." He's a caged animal out of control.

Act I, Scene 3

The Bride's home is a symbol of obedience and social control. The scene is a slow and calculated social contract that is sealed on obedience and accepting the status quo. It is the omnipotent power of generational control through an arranged wedding. The Mother and the Bride's Father are the landowners; they control humanity in the same manner that they oversee the management and cultivation of the land. Thus, the Father is only preoccupied with the status quo, and his vineyards as a provider for material fortune. His only desire is the acquisition of additional land, itself a wilderness representing the spirit of the play.

The scene between the Bride and the Servant suddenly reveals the Bride's repression, her lust for Leonardo, her uncontrolled impulses. She is Leonardo personified, and as calculating as the male-oriented existence of *Blood Wedding*. The conclusion is a musical crescendo of emotional chaos. As in Greek tragedy, the audience is warned that destiny may not be avoided because the characters are caught in a circumfusion of frustration.

Act II, Scene 1

As in act 1, we begin with a clash of emotions. In an open discussion about sexual impulses, the Bride and the Servant reveal a world all too distant and rare in early twentieth century Spanish drama. In a realistic, almost comedic fashion, the women explore their physical desires. Off stage voices in song remind the audience of the scene's festive occasion, that of the impending wedding. Again, Lorca mixes musical and choral elements in order to increase the play's structural tension. Leonardo and the Bride confront each other: their past is revealed and their erotic impulses are clearly unfolded. Immediately, the audience realizes that they are creatures of their secluded environment. Like Lorca himself, they want to break free of topography burdened by economic and social constraints. They are now two caged animals in search of personal freedom.

Scene 1 concludes in discord and confrontation. In juxtaposition, the act reveals two realities:

- images of the continuation of the life cycle through marriage and/or tradition;
- the terrestrial and psychological human impulses capable of disrupting a peaceful existence.

Act II, Scene 2

Here we experience the play's symphonic crescendo, structured in a quick succession of events—a cinematic unfolding of events in quick montage. As the wedding festivities continue, confusion increases. The Bride, unable to celebrate the occasion, asks to be excused; the Bridegroom also departs in preparation for his wedding night. Suddenly, as the Bride cannot be located, Leonardo's Wife enters the stage to announce that her husband and the Bride have run away, on a horse "like a shooting star!" It is a powerful, almost melodramatic ending. In addition, it contains the essential elements of classical tragedy: reversal (things are no longer what they were) and recognition.

Act III, Scene 1

Once again, the structure of *Blood Wedding* shifts radically. It is now a surrealistic journey into the realm of the unconscious. The act is a combination of opera, modern styles (Surrealism, Expressionism), and cinematic panoramas (e.g., the panorama of the forest). There is nothing realistic in this particular scene. Even the erotic sequence between Leonardo and the Bride takes place under the shadows of the moonlight, engulfed by the choral recitatives and violin sounds. The Woodcutters are allegorical figures, reminiscent of the classical Greek chorus. They become seers and revelators as they recount the "union" between Leonardo and the Bride. The symbolic character of the Moon sings a death hymn, and the allegorical nature of its character reinforces the theme that death is forthcoming.

Leonardo and the Bride, through their impulsive union in the forest, destroy yet another generation. The ancient Beggar Woman is the angel of death who symbolically and metaphorically guides the Bridegroom into the valley of death. The final tableaux of the scene contains one of the most powerful images in modern drama as the Beggar Woman, now Death, ". . . appears and stands with her back to the audience. She opens her cape and stands in the center of the stage like a great bird with immense wings." This was Lorca's favorite scene as he was able to combine his artistic strengths: poetry, musical composition, ethereal sound, and scenic descriptions that are, in essence, expressionistic paintings.

Act III, Scene 2

The final scene completes the circle of physical and spiritual death. The scene is stylistically realistic, as the women congregate in a classical choral manner. The Mother, Leonardo's Wife and the Bride form a triangle of solace and emptiness; they will remain unfulfilled, trapped forever in this cyclical pattern of existence. Surely, this final tableau reminds us why Lorca's folk play became the first tragedy in the development of Spain's modern drama. And although *Blood Wedding* is a masterful poetic drama, nonetheless, it contains a strong statement with regard to the social conditions of its time, as Spain saw herself embroiled in a chaotic political whirlwind that culminated in a bloody civil war. The violence in the play reflected the blood that stained the ground of that ancient country. Accordingly, this "folk play" is an apt symbol for Spain in the 1930s.

Other perspectives on *Blood Wedding*:

Anderson, Andrews A. "Some Shakespearean Reminiscences in Garcia Lorca's Drama." *Comparative Literature Studies* 22:2 (Summer 1985): 187–210.

Hewitt, Bernard (ed.). "Lorca Discusses His Plays." *Tulane Drama Review* 7:2 (Winter 1962): 111–19.

See *Blood Wedding* on video:

Bodas de sangre (*Blood Wedding*). Dir. Emiliano Piedra. Perf. Antonio Gades, Cristina Hoyos, and Marisol. Media Home Entertainment, 71 min., 1986. (Note: This is a flamenco music and dance version of the play in Spanish, with English subtitles.)

Another Lorca play on video:

The House of Bernarda Alba. Dir. Nuria Espert and Stuart Burge. Perf. Glenda Jackson. Films for the Humanities, 100 min., 1991.

A video about Lorca:

Federico García Lorca: Remembering the Earth. Dir. Enrique Nicanor. Films for the Humanities, 59 min., 1999.

SHOWCASE   DESIGNING THE SCENERY FOR *BLOOD WEDDING*

In 2001 Haibo Yu, who was born in Beijing and educated in London, designed the scenery for a production of Blood Wedding *at California State University-Sacramento. Here he discusses the design process with the play's director.*

Describe your research process as you began conceptualizing the design element for the production of *Blood Wedding*.

Having designed for Lorca's *Blood Wedding* before, I didn't have to spend much time on preliminary script analysis and background research. I spent two to three weeks collecting visual materials. To broaden the appeal of the play to a more diverse audience, I expanded the search zone from the original rural Spain setting to South America. Despite the different cultural and geographical identities, I found many similarities. For example, the texture of the buildings is exactly the same, earthy and primitive, even though the Spanish structures appear to be slightly more delicate. In my final design, nothing was a subjective invention. Everything was carefully selected and refined from my research. Yet the whole design style was not that realistic, as this was more consistent with the director's and my vision.

Haibo Yu's sketch for the setting of Blood Wedding, *and the set as it was realized at California State University-Sacramento. In keeping with the poetic nature of Lorca's folk tragedy, the rustic setting is not realistic but merely evokes the feeling of a village in remote Spain.*

ful Spanish culture and have a huge admiration for its fantastic arts tradition, from the cave paintings at Altamira two thousand years ago to the contemporary Guggenheim Museum at Bilbao. You are very lucky to have such a vast historic and cultural heritage to support your design, but on the other hand, it could be a burden. You must choose from the immense number of interesting images. The artistic instinct is important here. It is not deep thought but a trust in one's instinct that is involved. I encountered this early in my design. Based on my understanding of the director's vision, focusing on the north mountain area as specified in the play was not so significant. We decided to place the story under a much larger scope to confront some basic human issues. This required my design to provide the audience with an imaginative landscape. Therefore, I abandoned all of the geographical details and only kept the dryness, which was caught by my instinct from the first minute of my research as the essential component of the landscape.

How did the historical and geographical landscape of Lorca's *Blood Wedding* influence your vision of the design?

I have always been amazed by the color-

How did Lorca's use of dialogue and poetic imagery influence your design process?

It is a bonus for a designer to work on a

play that does not require merely a realistic environment. The poetic quality in Lorca's *Blood Wedding* liberates the imagination. The crisp dialogue and the symbolic imagery Lorca used, such as the moon, the horse, the dagger, and different kinds of flowers in various scenes, mark instantly the direction of the non-realistic visual approach. I believe poetic writing and non-realistic visual arts share certain principles and esthetic values: subjectivity, symbolization and exaggeration among others. These principles led me to use the simplified, exaggerated and magnified wall units as the basic image to echo the play's beautifully refined poetic characteristic.

You are truly a product of a twentieth century multicultural upbringing—from your early days living in China, to your training in Great Britain, to your professional work in the United States. How has your background influenced your design work?

The different cultures have given me different philosophical methodologies. The Eastern culture makes a person think along a non-linear path, so that you handle patchy images more flexibly in the early design stages. The training I received from the West provides a more logical approach and strict discipline. The result is a combination of sense and sensibility. I always hope that my design provides a director with not only what the play requires but also great flexibility.

You were a painter before you became a full-time scenographer. How has your background in the visual fine arts impacted your theatrical design?

There is an interesting description of a stage designer: a person with a dramatist's head, an artist's eyes, and a craftsman's hands. A scenographer, first of all, should be a visual artist. An artist's vision is about shape, color and texture. The same is true for a scenographer. Look into the design history, and you will find that many design masters had been intensively trained in the fine arts.

In the visual arts, the basic esthetic principles are the same, no matter what the medium and form. In fact, stage designers have never stopped searching for inspirations from the fine arts. This is true for me. Art books are an important part of my research. I also paint when I have time. I find this discipline indispensable in my design work.

Describe your imaginative process as you read *Blood Wedding* for the very first time.

When I first read the stage descriptions, I found them rather disturbing. The existing images such as the pink room and the yellow room didn't make much sense to me. I had to struggle to make my own way and ignore the descriptions in the script. Soon enough, my nerve was hit by the mother's line in Scene 3: "Do you know what the marriage is? . . . One man, children, and a wall two feet thick between you and everything else." The Wall, the thick wall, instantaneously struck me as a metaphor of the alienation and oppressiveness in the female characters' lives and became the prime scenic element of the design.

Talk to us about your perception of color in *Blood Wedding*.

Color carries some conventional perceptions and can cause some common responses, yet is also very personal in many aspects. While I would reject the use of bright colors in *Blood Wedding*, others may love them. For this production, I visualized the colors as black and white—highly contrasting and minimalist. Red, the color of blood, I would use for emphasis and only once in a delicate and subtle way. In the opening of the final scene, the audience sees against the white wall and with all women in black, a piece of striking red wool. As this is the first time the audience catches a bright color, the symbolic meaning of red as blood is more starkly felt.

How did you communicate your design vision to the director? What

was your "starting point"? Did the final design shift from your original concept?

We started our first meeting by sharing some patchy ideas. I found my approach tended to be too stylized and abstract for the director's more historic and folksy vision. But within less than an hour, we came closer and reached a conceptual agreement according to the poetic quality of this play. I began to understand the director's conceptual direction and acting styles, and even some of his visions for the stage compositions. His overall grasp of the script and the basic visual requirements for staging gave me a clear guideline. However, he also trusted my vision and did not ask for any specific structures. This mutual trust and open communication were the corner stone of our collaboration.

Once you conceptualize your design ideas, as a scenographer, what comes first: drawings, renderings, or the three-dimensional model?

I usually start with doing free sketches and drawings. At the early stages you might have dozens of new ideas a day. Like most designers, I cannot think without a pencil in hand. Then I might play with a white working model to explore the physical spaces before making the scaled color model. As for renderings, sometimes I make them but often I do not, depending on whether I need to build a serious presentation package. I personally think the real value of a nice rendering is for display and collection. A rendering is much less useful to the production team than a three-dimensional model, because it does not carry enough basic information such as dimensions. Most directors and actors also prefer visualizing the actual space directly from a three-dimensional model box rather than from a pretty two-dimensional rendering.

What inspires you as an artist?
The pursuit of freedom.

THE GOOD WOMAN OF SETZUAN

BERTOLT BRECHT

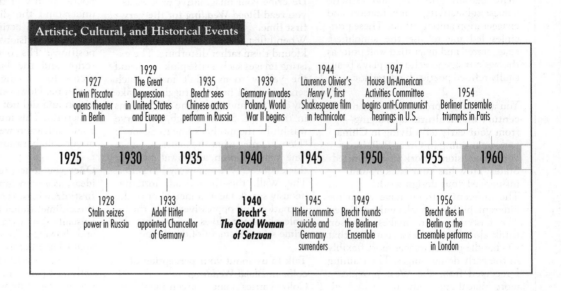

Artistic, Cultural, and Historical Events

1927 Erwin Piscator opens theater in Berlin

1929 The Great Depression in United States and Europe

1935 Brecht sees Chinese actors perform in Russia

1939 Germany invades Poland, World War II begins

1944 Laurence Olivier's *Henry V*, first Shakespeare film in technicolor

1947 House Un-American Activities Committee begins anti-Communist hearings in U.S.

1954 Berliner Ensemble triumphs in Paris

1925 1930 1935 1940 1945 1950 1955 1960

1928 Stalin seizes power in Russia

1933 Adolf Hitler appointed Chancellor of Germany

1940 Brecht's *The Good Woman of Setzuan*

1945 Hitler commits suicide and Germany surrenders

1949 Brecht founds the Berliner Ensemble

1956 Brecht dies in Berlin as the Ensemble performs in London

BERTOLT BRECHT (1898–1956)

The son of a prosperous manager of a factory in Augsberg, Bavaria, Bertolt Brecht established himself as a controversial writer at an early age. As a high school student during World War I, he was nearly expelled for writing antiwar poetry. His intentions to pursue a medical career were cut short when he was conscripted into the German army in 1918 to serve as a medic. He observed firsthand the carnage and misery created by war, and his subsequent writings—poetry, drama, song lyrics, and essays—were devoted to the eradication of all institutions that contributed to human suffering and indignity. In addition to war and the governments that wage it, Brecht's political satires expose corrupt social, economic, spiritual, and cultural institutions that oppress the common man. In this sense, Brecht is properly a romantic, however modern and "anti-emotional" the methods he employs.

Like so many young artists who lived in economically depressed postwar Germany, Brecht was cynical, even nihilistic, in his view of society. And like many of his contemporaries, he gravitated to Communism, whose philosophy of dialectical materialism provided him with both the subject matter and the methodology for his plays. Brecht's plays transcend mere propaganda, and he is the most admired and imitated Marxist playwright of the twentieth century. Brecht was too much the humanist to write only ideological tracts, and his plays manifest a universality that transcends the particulars of Marxism. Ever the individualist who was owned by no country or party, Brecht spent much of World War II writing film scripts in Santa Monica, California. When he returned to East Berlin in 1948 he obtained Austrian citizenship to skirt state censorship, and he retained a publisher in the West to protect the copyrights on his literary work. When he received the Stalin Peace Prize shortly before his death, he quickly invested the financial portion of his award in a Swiss bank account.

Brecht's first attempts at playwriting were in the expressionistic mode popular among young Germans during the war years. Such works as *Baal* (1918) and *Drums in the Night* (1918) are among his darkest efforts and reflect the angst of young Germans who realized that "the Great War" was not worth fighting. Gradually he turned to satire to vent his anger, and in the early 1920s Brecht gained a reputation as a witty cabaret artist who sang politically caustic songs to the accompaniment of his own guitar. His subsequent plays are liberally sprinkled with such songs, which play an integral part of his *verfrumdungseffekt*. "Song of the Smoke" in Scene 1 of *The Good Woman of Setzuan* is a representative example.

In 1928 Brecht collaborated with composer Kurt Weill to write *The Threepenny Opera*, a contemporary retelling of John Gay's 1728 ballad opera, *The Beggar's Opera*. Largely because of its musical comedy nature, it is Brecht's most performed work and was made into a film starring Raul Julia as the notorious Macheath, about whom the popular song "Mack the Knife" was written. (Sting played the role in a New York revival in 1992.) You have probably heard "Mack the Knife" in either the Bobby Darrin or Louis Armstrong versions, neither of which is like the Brecht-Weill arrangement. The point is made here because the song was intended to be dissonant and even unpleasant, quite unlike the catchy, up-tempo recording heard in pop music venues. Brecht wanted his music to be much like the plays he wrote—unsettling, antiromantic, emotionally "cool"—so that audiences would listen to the message rather than the melody.

As he was defining his methodology for an "Epic Theatre," Brecht discovered the Japanese Noh theater and found in this ancient masked drama, like the Chinese drama he saw in Russia in 1935, an acting style that accommodated his performance theory. Brecht wanted his actors to portray the social status (or "gestus") of his dramatic creations rather than become one with the emotional life of a character. This synthesis of an antirealistic approach to playwriting and performance can be found in his masterworks: *Mother Courage and Her Children* (1938), *Galileo* (1938), *The Good Woman of Setzuan* (1940), and *The Caucasian Chalk Circle* (1944).

Between 1933 and 1948 Brecht lived in exile because his anti-Fascist politics made him a target of the Nazi Party. He first fled to Switzerland and subsequently spent time in Finland, Sweden, Denmark, Russia, and ultimately the United States. The anti-Communist purges of the McCarthy era forced him to return to Germany in 1948, but not before he was called before the House Un-American Activities Commission, a Senate committee charged with identifying Communists in the United States. True to form, the playwright turned his hearing into a comical piece of theater as he bantered wittily with his interrogators.

In East Berlin Brecht founded the Berliner Ensemble, a state-supported theater dedicated to the production of his works and those of similar ideology. (See Showcase, "The Berliner Ensemble of Bertolt Brecht," earlier in Part II.) The Ensemble's production of *Mother Courage* in January 1949 (in which Brecht's wife, Helene Weigel, played the title role to great acclaim) made the Ensemble one of Europe's most respected theater companies. In 1954 the Berliner Ensemble performed in Paris; two years later they spent the summer in London. (See Showcase, "The British Revolution of 1956," later in Part II.) These engagements captivated the postwar generation of theater artists. The Ensemble became the model for mainstream companies (e.g., the Royal Shakespeare Company) and also many of the alternative theater collectives that proliferated during the 1950s and 1960s. Both as playwright and performance theorist, Brecht remains among the most imitated artists of the twentieth century. It is likely that no single artist has exerted as much influence on the antirealist movement as Brecht has.

AS YOU READ *THE GOOD WOMAN OF SETZUAN*

Brecht structures the play in ten scenes and a prologue. Although there is a discernable plot line, it is not based on causality in the traditional sense. Rather, the ten scenes exist independently of one another and are bound by a thematic unity that explores the play's central question: To what extent is morality defined by one's economic status? Most scenes are followed by a short sub-scene (e.g., 1A, 3A, etc.) in which a comical water seller, Wong, engages the three gods in satiric banter. The water seller is a variant on the "story teller" that Brecht favored in his works. Wong provides a critical context from which to judge the story of Shen Te. Note that he frequently addresses the audience directly (as does Shen Te); his speeches are elaborate, Westernized versions of the *yin tzu* of the ancient Chinese opera in which a character describes his social status and dramatic purpose to the audience. Brecht, the old cabaret balladeer, interpolates a half-dozen songs throughout the play, each commenting satirically on the action and themes. That the final scene takes place in a courtroom is no accident. The trial was among Brecht's favorite devices because, he argued, the theater itself should function as a court in which the jury (or audience/reader) dispassionately examines evidence, hears opposing arguments, and renders a judgment.

Throughout the play Brecht uses techniques central to his Epic Theatre. First, he purposefully sets the action of his "parable" in remote and distant Setzuan, which for him stands "for all places where men are exploited by men." This typifies Brecht's concept of "historification"—that is, removing a play's action from contemporary life so that audiences may compare their circumstances with those of the past. Furthermore, Setzuan is an intriguing choice for locale: because it is identifiable with ancient China, it encourages his actors to use the acting techniques from the Chinese opera that influenced his methodology. (See Showcase, "The Conventions of Chinese Theater.") The fact that the actor who plays Shen Te must also play Shui Ta in a mask creates a "distancing" effect.

THE GOOD WOMAN OF SETZUAN

BERTOLT BRECHT

Translated by Eric Bentley

LIST OF CHARACTERS

WONG, *a water seller*
THREE GODS
SHEN TE, *a prostitute, later a shopkeeper*
MRS. SHIN, *former owner of Shen Te's shop*
A FAMILY OF EIGHT (*husband, wife, brother, sister-in-law, grandfather, nephew, niece, boy*)
AN UNEMPLOYED MAN
A CARPENTER
MRS. MI TZU, *Shen Te's landlady*
YANG SUN, *an unemployed pilot, later a factory manager*
AN OLD WHORE
A POLICEMAN
AN OLD MAN
AN OLD WOMAN, *his wife*
MR. SHU FU, *a barber*
MRS. YANG, *mother of Yang Sun*
GENTLEMEN, VOICES, CHILDREN (*three*), etc.

PROLOGUE

(*At the gates of the half-westernized city of Setzuan.* Evening. Wong the Water Seller introduces himself to the audience.*)

WONG. I sell water here in the city of Setzuan. It isn't easy. When water is scarce, I have long distances to go in search of it, and when it is plentiful, I have no income. But in our part of the world there is nothing unusual about poverty. Many people think only the gods can save the situation. And I hear from a cattle merchant—who travels a lot—that some of the highest gods are on their way here at this very moment. Informed sources have it that heaven is quite disturbed at all the complaining. I've been coming out here to the city gates for three days now to bid these gods welcome. I want to be the first to greet them. What about those fellows over there? No, no, they *work.* And that one there has ink on his fingers, he's no god, he must be a clerk from the cement factory. *Those* two are another story. They look as though they'd like to beat you. But gods don't need to beat you, do they? (*Enter Three Gods.*) What about those three? Old-fashioned clothes—dust on their feet—they *must* be gods! (*He throws himself at their feet.*) Do with me what you will, illustrious ones!

FIRST GOD (*with an ear trumpet*). Ah! (*He is pleased.*) So we were expected?

WONG (*giving them water*). Oh, yes. And I *knew* you'd come.

FIRST GOD. We need somewhere to stay the night. You know of a place?

WONG. The whole town is at your service, illustrious ones! What sort of a place would you like?

(*The Gods eye each other.*)

FIRST GOD. Just try the first house you come to, my son.

WONG. That would be Mr. Fo's place.

FIRST GOD. Mr. Fo.

WONG. One moment! (*He knocks at the first house.*)

VOICE FROM MR. FO'S. No!

(*Wong returns a little nervously.*)

WONG. It's too bad. Mr. Fo isn't in. And his servants don't dare do a thing without his consent. He'll have a fit when he finds out who they turned away, won't he?

---

*"So Brecht's first manuscript. Brecht must later have learned that Setzuan (usually spelled Szechwan) is not a city but a province, and he adjusted the printed German text. I have kept the earlier reading since such mythology seems to me more Brechtian than Brecht's own second thoughts."—E.B.

FIRST GOD (*smiling*). He will, won't he?

WONG. One moment! The next house is Mr. Cheng's. Won't he be thrilled?

FIRST GOD. Mr. Cheng.

(*Wong knocks.*)

VOICE FROM MR. CHENG'S. Keep your gods. We have our own troubles!

WONG (*back with the Gods*). Mr. Cheng is very sorry, but he has a houseful of relations. I think some of them are a bad lot, and naturally, he wouldn't like you to see them.

THIRD GOD. Are we so terrible?

WONG. Well, only with bad people, of course. Everyone knows the province of Kwan is always having floods.

SECOND GOD. Really? How's *that*?

WONG. Why, because they're so irreligious.

SECOND GOD. Rubbish. It's because they neglected the dam.

FIRST GOD (*to Second*). Sh! (*To Wong.*) You're still in hopes, aren't you, my son?

WONG. Certainly. All Setzuan is competing for the honor! What happened up to now is pure coincidence. I'll be back. (*He walks away, but then stands undecided.*)

SECOND GOD. What did I tell you?

THIRD GOD. It *could* be pure coincidence.

SECOND GOD. The same coincidence in Shun, Kwan, and Setzuan? People just aren't religious any more, let's face the fact. Our mission has failed!

FIRST GOD. Oh come, we might run into a good person any minute.

THIRD GOD. How did the resolution read? (*Unrolling a scroll and reading from it.*) "The world can stay as it is if enough people are found living lives worthy of human beings." Good people, that is. Well, what about this Water Seller himself? *He's* good, or I'm very much mistaken.

SECOND GOD. You're very much mistaken. When he gave us a drink, I had the impression there was something odd about the cup. Well, look! (*He shows the cup to the First God.*)

FIRST GOD. A false bottom!

SECOND GOD. The man is a swindler.

FIRST GOD. Very well, count *him* out. That's one man among millions. And as a matter of fact, we only need one on *our* side. These atheists are saying, "The world must be changed because no one can *be* good and *stay* good." No one, eh? I say: let us find one—just one—and we have those fellows where we want them!

THIRD GOD (*to Wong*). Water Seller, is it so hard to find a place to stay?

WONG. Nothing could be easier. It's just me. I don't go about it right.

THIRD GOD. Really? (*He returns to the others. A Gentleman passes by.*)

WONG. Oh dear, they're catching on. (*He accosts the Gentleman.*) Excuse the intrusion, dear sir, but three Gods have just turned up. Three of the very highest. They need a place for the night. Seize this rare opportunity—to have real gods as your guests!

GENTLEMAN (*laughing*). A new way of finding free rooms for a gang of crooks.

(*Exit Gentleman.*)

WONG (*shouting at him*). Godless rascal! Have you no religion, gentlemen of Setzuan? (*Pause.*) Patience, illustrious ones! (*Pause.*) There's only one person left. Shen Te, the prostitute. She can't say no. (*Calls up to a window.*) Shen Te!

(*Shen Te opens the shutters and looks out.*)

WONG. *They're* here, and nobody wants them. Will you take them?

SHEN TE. Oh, no, Wong, I'm expecting a gentleman.

WONG. Can't you forget about him for tonight?

SHEN TE. The rent has to be paid by tomorrow or I'll be out on the street.

WONG. This is no time for calculation, Shen Te.

SHEN TE. Stomachs rumble even on the Emperor's birthday, Wong.

WONG. Setzuan is one big dung hill!

SHEN TE. Oh, very well! I'll hide till my gentleman has come and gone. Then I'll take them. (*She disappears.*)

WONG. They mustn't see her gentleman or they'll know what she is.

FIRST GOD (*who hasn't heard any of this*). I think it's hopeless.

(*They approach Wong.*)

WONG (*jumping, as he finds them behind him*). A room has been found, illustrious ones! (*He wipes sweat off his brow.*)

SECOND GOD. Oh, good.

THIRD GOD. Let's see it.

WONG (*nervously*). Just a minute. It has to be tidied up a bit.

THIRD GOD. Then we'll sit down here and wait.

WONG (*still more nervous*). No, no! (*Holding himself back.*) Too much traffic, you know.

THIRD GOD (*with a smile*). Of course, if you *want* us to move.

(They retire a little. They sit on a doorstep. Wong sits on the ground.)

WONG *(after a deep breath).* You'll be staying with a single girl—the finest human being in Setzuan!

THIRD GOD. That's nice.

WONG *(to the audience).* They gave me such a look when I picked up my cup just now.

THIRD GOD. You're worn out, Wong.

WONG. A little, maybe.

FIRST GOD. Do people here have a hard time of it?

WONG. The good ones do.

FIRST GOD. What about yourself?

WONG. You mean I'm not good. That's true. And I don't have an easy time either!

(During this dialogue, a Gentleman has turned up in front of Shen Te's house, and has whistled several times. Each time Wong has given a start.)

THIRD GOD *(to Wong, softly).* Psst! I think he's gone now.

WONG *(confused and surprised).* Ye-e-es.

(The Gentleman has left now, and Shen Te has come down to the street.)

SHEN TE *(softly).* Wong!

(Getting no answer, she goes off down the street. Wong arrives just too late, forgetting his carrying pole.)

WONG *(softly).* Shen Te! Shen Te! *(To himself.)* So she's gone off to earn the rent. Oh dear, I can't go to the gods again with no room to offer them. Having failed in the service of the gods, I shall run to my den in the sewer pipe down by the river and hide from their sight!

(He rushes off. Shen Te returns, looking for him, but finding the gods. She stops in confusion.)

SHEN TE. You are the illustrious ones? My name is Shen Te. It would please me very much if my simple room could be of use to you.

THIRD GOD. Where is the Water Seller, Miss . . . Shen Te?

SHEN TE. I missed him, somehow.

FIRST GOD. Oh, he probably thought you weren't coming, and was afraid of telling us.

THIRD GOD *(picking up the carrying pole).* We'll leave this with you. He'll be needing it.

(Led by Shen Te, they go into the house. It grows dark, then light. Dawn. Again escorted by Shen Te, who leads them through the half-light with a little lamp, the Gods take their leave.)

FIRST GOD. Thank you, thank you, dear Shen Te, for your elegant hospitality! We shall not forget! And give our thanks to the Water Seller—he showed us a good human being.

SHEN TE. Oh, *I'm* not good. Let me tell you something: when Wong asked me to put you up, I hesitated.

FIRST GOD. It's all right to hesitate if you then go ahead! And in giving us that room you did much more than you knew. You proved that good people still exist, a point that has been disputed of late—even in heaven. Farewell!

SECOND GOD. Farewell!

THIRD GOD. Farewell!

SHEN TE. Stop, illustrious ones! I'm not sure you're right. I'd like to be good, it's true, but there's the rent to pay. And that's not all: I sell myself for a living. Even so I can't make ends meet, there's too much competition. I'd like to honor my father and mother and speak nothing but the truth and not covet my neighbor's house. I should love to stay with one man. But how? How is it done? Even breaking only a *few* of your commandments, I can hardly manage.

FIRST GOD *(clearing his throat).* These thoughts are but, um, the misgivings of an unusually good woman!

THIRD GOD. Goodbye, Shen Te! Give our regards to the Water Seller!

SECOND GOD. And above all: be good! Farewell!

FIRST GOD. Farewell!

THIRD GOD. Farewell!

(They start to wave good-bye.)

SHEN TE. But everything is so expensive, I don't feel sure I can do it!

SECOND GOD. That's not in our sphere. We never meddle with economics.

THIRD GOD. One moment.

(They stop.)

Isn't it true she might do better if she had more money?

SECOND GOD. Come, come! How could we ever account for it Up Above?

FIRST GOD. Oh, there are ways.

(They put their heads together and confer in dumb show.)

(To Shen Te, with embarrassment.) As you say you can't pay your rent, well, um, we're not paupers, so of course we insist on paying for our room. *(Awkwardly thrusting money into her hands.)* There!

(*Quickly.*) But don't tell anyone! The incident is open to misinterpretation.

SECOND GOD. It certainly is!

FIRST GOD (*defensively*). But there's no law against it! It was never decreed that a god mustn't pay hotel bills!

(*The Gods leave.*)

SCENE 1

(*A small tobacco shop. The shop is not as yet completely furnished and hasn't started doing business.*)

SHEN TE (*to the audience*). It's three days now since the gods left. When they said they wanted to pay for the room, I looked down at my hand, and there was more than a thousand silver dollars! I bought a tobacco shop with the money, and moved in yesterday. I don't own the building, of course, but I can pay the rent, and I hope to do a lot of good here. Beginning with Mrs. Shin, who's just coming across the square with her pot. She had the shop before me, and yesterday she dropped in to ask for rice for her children.

(*Enter Mrs. Shin. Both women bow.*)

How do you do, Mrs. Shin.

MRS. SHIN. How do you do, Miss Shen Te. You like your new home?

SHEN TE. Indeed, yes. Did your children have a good night?

MRS. SHIN. In that hovel? The youngest is coughing already.

SHEN TE. Oh, dear!

MRS. SHIN. You're going to learn a thing or two in these slums.

SHEN TE. Slums? That's not what you said when you sold me the shop!

MRS. SHIN. Now don't start nagging! Robbing me and my innocent children of their home and then calling it a slum! That's the limit! (*She weeps.*)

SHEN TE (*tactfully*). I'll get your rice.

MRS. SHIN. And a little cash while you're at it.

SHEN TE. I'm afraid I haven't sold anything yet.

MRS. SHIN (*screeching*). I've got to have it. Strip the clothes from my back and then cut my throat, will you? I know what I'll do: I'll leave my children on your doorstep! (*She snatches the pot out of Shen Te's hands.*)

SHEN TE. Please don't be angry. You'll spill the rice.

(*Enter an elderly Husband and Wife with their shabbily-dressed Nephew.*)

WIFE. Shen Te, dear! You've come into money, they tell me. And we haven't a roof over our heads! A tobacco shop. We had one too. But it's gone. Could we spend the night here, do you think?

NEPHEW (*appraising the shop*). Not bad!

WIFE. He's our nephew. We're inseparable!

MRS. SHIN. And who are these . . . ladies and gentlemen?

SHEN TE. They put me up when I first came in from the country. (*To the audience.*) Of course, when my small purse was empty, they put me out on the street, and they may be afraid I'll do the same to them. (*To the newcomers, kindly.*) Come in, and welcome, though I've only one little room for you—it's behind the shop.

HUSBAND. That'll do. Don't worry.

WIFE (*bringing Shen Te some tea*). We'll stay over here, so we won't be in your way. Did you make it a tobacco shop in memory of your first real home? We can certainly give you a hint or two! That's one reason we came.

MRS. SHIN (*to Shen Te*). Very nice! As long as you have a few customers too!

HUSBAND. Sh! A customer!

(*Enter an Unemployed Man, in rags.*)

UNEMPLOYED MAN. Excuse me. I'm unemployed.

(*Mrs. Shin laughs.*)

SHEN TE. Can I help you?

UNEMPLOYED MAN. Have you any damaged cigarettes? I thought there might be some damage when you're unpacking.

WIFE. What nerve, begging for tobacco! (*Rhetorically.*) Why don't they ask for bread?

UNEMPLOYED MAN. Bread is expensive. One cigarette butt and I'll be a new man.

SHEN TE (*giving him cigarettes*). That's very important— to be a new man. You'll be my first customer and bring me luck.

(*The Unemployed Man quickly lights a cigarette, inhales, and goes off, coughing.*)

WIFE. Was that right, Shen Te, dear?

MRS. SHIN. If this is the opening of a shop, you can hold the closing at the end of the week.

HUSBAND. I bet he had money on him.

SHEN TE. Oh, no, he said he hadn't!

NEPHEW. How d'you know he wasn't lying?

SHEN TE (*angrily*). How do you know he was?

WIFE (*wagging her head*). You're too good, Shen Te, dear. If you're going to keep this shop, you'll have to learn to say No.

HUSBAND. Tell them the place isn't yours to dispose of. Belongs to . . . some relative who insists on all accounts being strictly in order . . .

MRS. SHIN. That's right! What do you think you are—a philanthropist?

SHEN TE (*laughing*). Very well, suppose I ask you for my rice back, Mrs. Shin?

WIFE (*combatively, at Mrs. Shin*). So that's *her* rice?

(*Enter the Carpenter, a small man.*)

MRS. SHIN (*who, at the sight of him, starts to hurry away*). See you tomorrow, Miss Shen Te! (*Exit Mrs. Shin.*)

CARPENTER. Mrs. Shin, it's you I want!

WIFE (*to Shen Te*). Has she some claim on you?

SHEN TE. She's hungry. That's a claim.

CARPENTER. Are you the new tenant? And filling up the shelves already? Well, they're not yours, till they're paid for, ma'am. I'm the carpenter, so I should know.

SHEN TE. I took the shop "furnishings included."

CARPENTER. You're in league with that Mrs. Shin, of course. All right: I demand my hundred silver dollars.

SHEN TE. I'm afraid I haven't got a hundred silver dollars.

CARPENTER. Then you'll find it. Or I'll have you arrested.

WIFE (*whispering to Shen Te*). That relative: make it a cousin.

SHEN TE. Can't it wait till next month?

CARPENTER. No!

SHEN TE. Be a little patient, Mr. Carpenter, I can't settle all claims at once.

CARPENTER. Who's patient with me? (*He grabs a shelf from the wall.*) Pay up—or I take the shelves back!

WIFE. Shen Te! Dear! Why don't you let your . . . cousin settle this affair? (*To Carpenter.*) Put your claim in writing. Shen Te's cousin will see you get paid.

CARPENTER (*derisively*). Cousin, eh?

HUSBAND. Cousin, yes.

CARPENTER. I know these cousins!

NEPHEW. Don't be silly. He's a personal friend of mine.

HUSBAND. What a man! Sharp as a razor!

CARPENTER. All right. I'll put my claim in writing. (*Puts shelf on floor, sits on it, writes out bill.*)

WIFE (*to Shen Te*). He'd tear the dress off your back to get his shelves. Never recognize a claim! That's my motto.

SHEN TE. He's done a job, and wants something in return. It's shameful that I can't give it to him. What will the gods say?

HUSBAND. You did your bit when you took *us* in.

(*Enter the Brother, limping, and the Sister-in-Law, pregnant.*)

BROTHER (*to Husband and Wife*). So this is where you're hiding out! There's family feeling for you! Leaving us on the corner!

WIFE (*embarrassed, to Shen Te*). It's my brother and his wife. (*To them.*) Now stop grumbling, and sit quietly in that corner. (*To Shen Te.*) It can't be helped. She's in her fifth month.

SHEN TE. Oh, yes. Welcome!

WIFE (*to the couple*). Say thank you.

(*They mutter something.*)

The cups are there. (*To Shen Te.*) Lucky you bought this shop when you did!

SHEN TE (*laughing and bringing tea*). Lucky indeed!

(*Enter Mrs. Mi Tzu, the landlady.*)

MRS. MI TZU. Miss Shen Te? I am Mrs. Mi Tzu, your landlady. I hope our relationship will be a happy one? I like to think I give my tenants modern, personalized service. Here is your lease. (*To the others, as Shen Te reads the lease.*) There's nothing like the opening of a little shop, is there? A moment of true beauty! (*She is looking around.*) Not very much on the shelves, of course. But everything in the gods' good time! Where are your references, Miss Shen Te?

SHEN TE. Do I *have* to have references?

MRS. MI TZU. After all, I haven't a notion who you are!

HUSBAND. Oh, *we'd* be glad to vouch for Miss Shen Te! We'd go through fire for her!

MRS. MI TZU. And who may *you* be?

HUSBAND (*stammering*). Ma Fu, tobacco dealer.

MRS. MI TZU. Where is your shop, Mr. . . . Ma Fu?

HUSBAND. Well, um, I haven't a shop—I've just sold it.

MRS. MI TZU. I see. (*To Shen Te.*) Is there no one else that knows you?

WIFE (*whispering to Shen Te*). Your cousin! Your cousin!

MRS. MI TZU. This is a respectable house, Miss Shen Te. I never sign a lease without certain assurances.

SHEN TE (*slowly, her eyes downcast*). I have . . . a cousin.

MRS. MI TZU. On the square? Let's go over and see him. What does he do?

SHEN TE (*as before*). He lives . . . in another city.

WIFE (*prompting*). Didn't you say he was in Shung?

SHEN TE. That's right. Shung.

HUSBAND (*prompting*). I had his name on the tip of my tongue. Mr. . . .

SHEN TE (*with an effort*). Mr. . . . Shui . . . Ta.

HUSBAND. That's it! Tall, skinny fellow!

SHEN TE. Shui Ta!

NEPHEW (*to Carpenter*). You were in touch with him, weren't you? About the shelves?

CARPENTER (*surlily*). Give him this bill. (*He hands it over.*) I'll be back in the morning. (*Exit Carpenter.*)

NEPHEW (*calling after him, but with his eyes on Mrs. Mi Tzu*). Don't worry! Mr. Shui Ta pays on the nail!

MRS. MI TZU (*looking closely at Shen Te*). I'll be happy to make his acquaintance, Miss Shen Te. (*Exit Mrs. Mi Tzu.*)

(*Pause.*)

WIFE. By tomorrow morning she'll know more about you than you do yourself.

SISTER-IN-LAW (*to Nephew*). This thing isn't built to last.

(*Enter Grandfather.*)

WIFE. It's Grandfather! (*To Shen Te.*) Such a good old soul!

(*The Boy enters.*)

BOY (*over his shoulder*). Here they are!

WIFE. And the boy, how he's grown! But he always could eat enough for ten.

(*Enter the Niece.*)

WIFE (*to Shen Te*). Our little niece from the country. There are more of us now than in your time. The less we had, the more there were of us; the more there were of us, the less we had. Give me the key. We must protect ourselves from unwanted guests. (*She takes the key and locks the door.*) Just make yourself at home. I'll light the little lamp.

NEPHEW (*a big joke*). I hope her cousin doesn't drop in tonight! The strict Mr. Shui Ta!

(*Sister-in-Law laughs.*)

BROTHER (*reaching for a cigarette*). One cigarette more or less . . .

HUSBAND. One cigarette more or less.

(*They pile into the cigarettes. The Brother hands a jug of wine round.*)

NEPHEW. Mr. Shui Ta'll pay for it!

GRANDFATHER (*gravely, to Shen Te*). How do you do?

(*Shen Te, a little taken aback by the belatedness of the greeting, bows. She has the Carpenter's bill in one hand, the landlady's lease in the other.*)

WIFE. How about a bit of a song? To keep Shen Te's spirits up?

NEPHEW. Good idea. Grandfather: you start!

SONG OF THE SMOKE

GRANDFATHER.
> I used to think (before old age beset me)
>> That brains could fill the pantry of the poor.
> But where did all my cerebration get me?
>> I'm just as hungry as I was before.
>>> So what's the use?
>>>> See the smoke float free
>>>> Into ever colder coldness!
>>>>> It's the same with me.

HUSBAND.
> The straight and narrow path leads to disaster
>> And so the crooked path I tried to tread.
> That got me to disaster even faster.
>> (They say we shall be happy when we're dead.)
>>> So what's the use, etc.

NIECE.
> You older people, full of expectation,
>> At any moment now you'll walk the plank!
> The future's for the younger generation!
>> Yes, even if that future is a blank.
>>> So what's the use, etc.

NEPHEW (*to the Brother*). Where'd you get that wine?

SISTER-IN-LAW (*answering for the Brother*). He pawned the sack of tobacco.

HUSBAND (*stepping in*). What? That tobacco was all we had to fall back on! You pig!

BROTHER. *You'd* call a man a pig because your wife was frigid! Did you refuse to drink it?

(*They fight. The shelves fall over.*)

SHEN TE (*imploringly*). Oh, don't! Don't break everything! Take it, take it all, but don't destroy a gift from the gods!

WIFE (*disparagingly*). This shop isn't big enough. I should never have mentioned it to Uncle and the others. When *they* arrive, it's going to be disgustingly overcrowded.

SISTER-IN-LAW. And did you hear our gracious hostess? She cools off quick!

(*Voices outside. Knocking at the door.*)

UNCLE'S VOICE. Open the door!

WIFE. Uncle? Is that you, Uncle?

UNCLE'S VOICE. Certainly, it's me. Auntie says to tell you she'll have the children here in ten minutes.

WIFE (*to Shen Te*). I'll have to let him in.

SHEN TE (*who scarcely hears her*).
> The little lifeboat is swiftly sent down
> Too many men too greedily
> Hold on to it as they drown.

SCENE 1A

(Wong's den in a sewer pipe.)

WONG *(crouching there).* All quiet! It's four days now since I left the city. The gods passed this way on the second day. I heard their steps on the bridge over there. They must be a long way off by this time, so I'm safe.

(Breathing a sigh of relief, he curls up and goes to sleep. In his dream the pipe becomes transparent, and the Gods appear.)

(Raising an arm, as if in self-defense.) I know, I know, illustrious ones! I found no one to give you a room—not in all Setzuan! There, it's out. Please continue on your way!

FIRST GOD *(mildly).* But you did find someone. Someone who took us in for the night, watched over us in our sleep, and in the early morning lighted us down to the street with a lamp.

WONG. It was . . . Shen Te, that took you in?

THIRD GOD. Who else?

WONG. And I ran away! "She isn't coming," I thought, "she just can't afford it."

GODS *(singing).*
   O you feeble, well-intentioned, and yet feeble chap!
   Where there's need the fellow thinks there is no
      goodness!
   When there's danger he thinks courage starts to ebb
      away!
   Some people only see the seamy side!
   What hasty judgment! What premature desperation!

WONG. I'm *very* ashamed, illustrious ones.

FIRST GOD. Do us a favor, Water Seller. Go back to Setzuan. Find Shen Te, and give us a report on her. We hear that she's come into a little money. Show interest in her goodness—for no one can be good for long if goodness is not in demand. Meanwhile we shall continue the search, and find other good people. After which, the idle chatter about the impossibility of goodness will stop!

(The Gods vanish.)

SCENE 2

(A knocking.)

WIFE. Shen Te! Someone at the door. Where is she anyway?

NEPHEW. She must be getting the breakfast. Mr. Shui Ta will pay for it.

(The Wife laughs and shuffles to the door. Enter Mr. Shui Ta and the Carpenter.)

WIFE. Who is it?

SHUI TA. I am Miss Shen Te's cousin.

WIFE. What?

SHUI TA. My name is Shui Ta.

WIFE. Her cousin?

NEPHEW. Her cousin?

NIECE. But that was a joke. She hasn't got a cousin.

HUSBAND. So early in the morning?

BROTHER. What's all the noise?

SISTER-IN-LAW. This fellow says he's her cousin.

BROTHER. Tell him to prove it.

NEPHEW. Right. If you're Shen Te's cousin, prove it by getting the breakfast.

SHUI TA *(whose regime begins as he puts out the lamp to save oil. Loudly, to all present, asleep or awake).* Would you all please get dressed! Customers will be coming! I wish to open my shop!

HUSBAND. *Your* shop? Doesn't it belong to our good friend Shen Te?

(Shui Ta shakes his head.)

SISTER-IN-LAW. So we've been cheated. Where *is* the little liar?

SHUI TA. Miss Shen Te has been delayed. She wishes me to tell you there will be nothing she can do—now I am here.

WIFE *(bowled over).* I thought she was *good!*

NEPHEW. Do you have to believe *him?*

HUSBAND. *I* don't.

NEPHEW. Then do something.

HUSBAND. Certainly! I'll send out a search party at once. You, you, you, and you, go out and look for Shen Te.

(As the Grandfather rises and makes for the door.)

Not you, Grandfather, you and I will hold the fort.

SHUI TA. You won't find Miss Shen Te. She has suspended her hospitable activity for an unlimited period. There are too many of you. She asked me to say: this is a tobacco shop, not a gold mine.

HUSBAND. Shen Te never said a thing like that. Boy, food! There's a bakery on the corner. Stuff your shirt full when they're not looking!

SISTER-IN-LAW. Don't overlook the raspberry tarts.

HUSBAND. And don't let the policeman see you.

(The Boy leaves.)

SHUI TA. Don't you depend on this shop now? Then why give it a bad name, by stealing from the bakery?

NEPHEW. Don't listen to him. Let's find Shen Te. She'll give him a piece of her mind.

SISTER-IN-LAW. Don't forget to leave us some breakfast.

(*Brother, Sister-in-Law, and Nephew leave.*)

SHUI TA (*to the Carpenter*). You see, Mr. Carpenter, nothing has changed since the poet, eleven hundred years ago, penned these lines:

> A governor was asked what was needed
> To save the freezing people in the city.
> He replied:
> "A blanket ten thousand feet long
> To cover the city and all its suburbs."

(*He starts to tidy up the shop.*)

CARPENTER. Your cousin owes me money. I've got witnesses. For the shelves.

SHUI TA. Yes, I have your bill. (*He takes it out of his pocket.*) Isn't a hundred silver dollars rather a lot?

CARPENTER. No deductions! I have a wife and children.

SHUI TA. How many children?

CARPENTER. Three.

SHUI TA. I'll make you an offer. Twenty silver dollars.

(*The Husband laughs.*)

CARPENTER. You're crazy. Those shelves are real walnut.

SHUI TA. Very well. Take them away.

CARPENTER. What?

SHUI TA. They cost too much. Please take them away.

WIFE. Not bad! (*And she, too, is laughing.*)

CARPENTER (*a little bewildered*). Call Shen Te, someone! (*To Shui Ta.*) She's good!

SHUI TA. Certainly. She's ruined.

CARPENTER (*provoked into taking some of the shelves*). All right, you can keep your tobacco on the floor.

SHUI TA (*to the Husband*). Help him with the shelves.

HUSBAND (*grins and carries one shelf over to the door where the Carpenter now is*). Goodbye, shelves!

CARPENTER (*to the Husband*). You dog! You want my family to starve?

SHUI TA. I repeat my offer. I have no desire to keep my tobacco on the floor. Twenty silver dollars.

CARPENTER (*with desperate aggressiveness*). One hundred!

(*Shui Ta shows indifference, looks through the window. The Husband picks up several shelves.*)

(*To Husband.*) You needn't smash them against the doorpost, you idiot! (*To Shui Ta.*) These shelves were made to measure. They're no use anywhere else!

SHUI TA. Precisely.

(*The Wife squeals with pleasure.*)

CARPENTER (*giving up, sullenly*). Take the shelves. Pay what you want to pay.

SHUI TA (*smoothly*). Twenty silver dollars.

(*He places two large coins on the table. The Carpenter picks them up.*)

HUSBAND (*brings the shelves back in*). And quite enough too!

CARPENTER (*slinking off*). Quite enough to get drunk on.

HUSBAND (*happily*). Well, we got rid of *him!*

WIFE (*weeping with fun, gives a rendition of the dialogue just spoken*). "Real walnut," says he. "Very well, take them away," says his lordship. "I have children," says he. "Twenty silver dollars," says his lordship. "They're no use anywhere else," says he. "Precisely," said his lordship!

(*She dissolves into shrieks of merriment.*)

SHUI TA. And now: go!

HUSBAND. What's that?

SHUI TA. You're thieves, parasites. I'm giving you this chance. Go!

HUSBAND (*summoning all his ancestral dignity*). That sort deserves no answer. Besides, one should never shout on an empty stomach.

WIFE. Where's that boy?

SHUI TA. Exactly. The boy. I want no stolen goods in this shop. (*Very loudly.*) I strongly advise you to leave! (*But they remain seated, noses in the air. Quietly.*) As you wish.

(*Shui Ta goes to the door. A Policeman appears. Shui Ta bows.*)

I am addressing the officer in charge of this precinct?

POLICEMAN. That's right, Mr., um . . . what was the name, sir?

SHUI TA. Mr. Shui Ta.

POLICEMAN. Yes, of course, sir.

(*They exchange a smile.*)

SHUI TA. Nice weather we're having.

POLICEMAN. A little on the warm side, sir.

SHUI TA. Oh, a little on the warm side.

HUSBAND (*whispering to the Wife*). If he keeps it up till the boy's back, we're done for. (*Tries to signal Shui Ta.*)

SHUI TA (*ignoring the signal*). Weather, of course, is one thing indoors, another out on the dusty street!

POLICEMAN. Oh, quite another, sir!

WIFE (*to the Husband*). It's all right as long as he's standing in the doorway—the boy will see him.

SHUI TA. Step inside for a moment! It's quite cool indoors. My cousin and I have just opened the place. And we attach the greatest importance to being on good terms with the, um, authorities.

POLICEMAN (*entering*). Thank you, Mr. Shui Ta. It *is* cool!

HUSBAND (*whispering to the Wife*). And now the boy *won't* see him.

SHUI TA (*showing Husband and Wife to the Policeman*). Visitors, I think my cousin knows them. They were just leaving.

HUSBAND (*defeated*). Ye-e-es, we were . . . just leaving.

SHUI TA. I'll tell my cousin you couldn't wait.

(*Noise from the street. Shouts of "Stop, thief!"*)

POLICEMAN. What's that?

(*The Boy is in the doorway with cakes and buns and rolls spilling out of his shirt. The Wife signals desperately to him to leave. He gets the idea.*)

No, you don't! (*He grabs the Boy by the collar.*) Where's all this from?

BOY (*vaguely pointing*). Down the street.

POLICEMAN (*grimly*). So that's it. (*Prepares to arrest the Boy.*)

WIFE (*stepping in*). And *we* knew nothing about it. (*To the Boy.*) Nasty little thief!

POLICEMAN (*dryly*). Can you clarify the situation, Mr. Shui Ta?

(*Shui Ta is silent.*)

POLICEMAN (*who understands silence*). Aha. You're all coming with me—to the station.

SHUI TA. I can hardly say how sorry I am that *my* establishment . . .

WIFE. Oh, he saw the boy leave not ten minutes ago!

SHUI TA. And to conceal the theft asked a policeman in?

POLICEMAN. Don't listen to her, Mr. Shui Ta, I'll be happy to relieve you of their presence one and all! (*To all three.*) Out! (*He drives them before him.*)

GRANDFATHER (*leaving last. Gravely*). Good morning!

POLICEMAN. Good morning!

(*Shui Ta, left alone, continues to tidy up. Mrs. Mi Tzu breezes in.*)

MRS. MI TZU. *You're* her cousin, are you? Then have the goodness to explain what all this means—police dragging people from a respectable house! By what right does your Miss Shen Te turn my property into a house of assignation?—Well, as you see, I know all!

SHUI TA. Yes. My cousin has the worst possible reputation: that of being poor.

MRS. MI TZU. No sentimental rubbish, Mr. Shui Ta. Your cousin was a common . . .

SHUI TA. Pauper. Let's use the uglier word.

MRS. MI TZU. I'm speaking of her conduct, not her earnings. But there must have *been* earnings, or how did she buy all this? Several elderly gentlemen took care of it, I suppose. I repeat: this is a respectable house! I have tenants who prefer not to live under the same roof with such a person.

SHUI TA (*quietly*). How much do you want?

MRS. MI TZU (*he is ahead of her now*). I beg your pardon.

SHUI TA. To reassure yourself. To reassure your tenants. How much will it cost?

MRS. MI TZU. You're a cool customer.

SHUI TA (*picking up the lease*). The rent is high. (*He reads on.*) I assume it's payable by the month?

MRS. MI TZU. Not in her case.

SHUI TA (*looking up*). What?

MRS. MI TZU. Six months rent payable in advance. Two hundred silver dollars.

SHUI TA. Six . . . ! Sheer usury! And where am I to find it?

MRS. MI TZU. You should have thought of that before.

SHUI TA. Have you no heart, Mrs. Mi Tzu? It's true Shen Te acted foolishly, being kind to all those people, but she'll improve with time. I'll see to it she does. She'll work her fingers to the bone to pay her rent, and all the time be as quiet as a mouse, as humble as a fly.

MRS. MI TZU. Her social background . . .

SHUI TA. Out of the depths! She came out of the depths! And before she'll go back there, she'll work, sacrifice, shrink from nothing. . . . Such a tenant is worth her weight in gold, Mrs. Mi Tzu.

MRS. MI TZU. It's silver we were talking about, Mr. Shui Ta. Two hundred silver dollars or . . .

(*Enter the Policeman.*)

POLICEMAN. Am I intruding, Mr. Shui Ta?

MRS. MI TZU. This tobacco shop is well-known to the police, I see.

POLICEMAN. Mr. Shui Ta has done us a service, Mrs. Mi Tzu. I am here to present our official felicitations!

MRS. MI TZU. That means less than nothing to me, sir. Mr. Shui Ta, all I can say is: I hope your cousin will find my terms acceptable. Good day, gentlemen. (*Exit.*)

SHUI TA. Good day, ma'am.

(*Pause.*)

POLICEMAN. Mrs. Mi Tzu a bit of a stumbling block, sir?

SHUI TA. She wants six months' rent in advance.

POLICEMAN. And you haven't got it, eh?

(*Shui Ta is silent.*)

But surely you can get it, sir? A man like you?

SHUI TA. What about a woman like Shen Te?

POLICEMAN. You're not staying, sir?

SHUI TA. No, and I won't be back. Do you smoke?

POLICEMAN (*taking two cigars, and placing them both in his pocket*). Thank you, sir—I see your point. Miss Shen Te—let's mince no words—Miss Shen Te lived by selling herself. "What else could she have done?" you ask. "How else was she to pay the rent?" True. But the fact remains, Mr. Shui Ta, it is not respectable. Why not? A very deep question. But, in the first place, love—love isn't bought and sold like cigars, Mr. Shui Ta. In the second place, it isn't respectable to go waltzing off with someone that's paying his way, so to speak—it must be for love! Thirdly and lastly, as the proverb has it: not for a handful of rice but for love! (*Pause. He is thinking hard.*) "Well," you may say, "and what good is all this wisdom if the milk's already spilt?" Miss Shen Te is what she is. Is *where* she is. We have to face the fact that if she doesn't get hold of six months' rent pronto, she'll be back on the streets. The question then as I see it—everything in this world is a matter of opinion—the question as I see it is: *how* is she to get hold of this rent? How? Mr. Shui Ta: I don't know. (*Pause.*) I take that back, sir. It's just come to me. A husband. We must find her a husband!

(*Enter a little Old Woman.*)

OLD WOMAN. A good cheap cigar for my husband, we'll have been married forty years tomorrow and we're having a little celebration.

SHUI TA. Forty years? And you still want to celebrate?

OLD WOMAN. As much as we can afford to. We have the carpet shop across the square. We'll be good neighbors, I hope?

SHUI TA. I hope so too.

POLICEMAN (*who keeps making discoveries*). Mr. Shui Ta, you know what we need? We need capital. And how do we acquire capital? We get married.

SHUI TA (*to Old Woman*). I'm afraid I've been pestering this gentleman with my personal worries.

POLICEMAN (*lyrically*). We can't pay six months' rent, so what do we do? We marry money.

SHUI TA. That might not be easy.

POLICEMAN. Oh, I don't know. She's a good match. Has a nice, growing business. (*To the Old Woman.*) What do you think?

OLD WOMAN (*undecided*). Well—

POLICEMAN. Should she put an ad in the paper?

OLD WOMAN (*not eager to commit herself*). Well, if *she* agrees—

POLICEMAN. I'll write it for her. *You* lend us a hand, and *we* write an ad for you! (*He chuckles away to himself, takes out his notebook, wets the stump of a pencil between his lips, and writes away.*)

SHUI TA (*slowly*). Not a bad idea.

POLICEMAN. "What . . . *respectable* . . . man . . . with small capital . . . widower . . . not excluded . . . desires . . . marriage . . . into flourishing . . . tobacco shop?" And now let's add: "am . . . pretty . . ." No! . . . "Prepossessing appearance."

SHUI TA. If you don't think that's an exaggeration?

OLD WOMAN. Oh, not a bit. I've seen her.

(*The Policeman tears the page out of his notebook, and hands it over to Shui Ta.*)

SHUI TA (*with horror in his voice*). How much luck we need to keep our heads above water! How many ideas! How many friends! (*To the Policeman.*) Thank you, sir. I think I see my way clear.

SCENE 3

(*Evening in the municipal park. Noise of a plane overhead. Yang Sun, a young man in rags, is following the plane with his eyes: one can tell that the machine is describing a curve above the park. Yang Sun then takes a rope out of his pocket, looking anxiously about him as he does so. He moves toward a large willow. Enter Two Prostitutes, one old, the other the Niece whom we have already met.*)

NIECE. Hello. Coming with me?

YANG SUN (*taken aback*). If you'd like to buy me a dinner.

OLD WHORE. Buy you a dinner! (*To the Niece.*) Oh, we know him—it's the unemployed pilot. Waste no time on him!

NIECE. But he's the only man left in the park. And it's going to rain.

OLD WHORE. Oh, how do you know?

(*And they pass by. Yang Sun again looks about him, again takes his rope, and this time throws it round a branch of the willow tree. Again he is interrupted. It is the Two Prostitutes returning—and in such a hurry they don't notice him.*)

NIECE. It's going to pour!

(Enter Shen Te.)

OLD WHORE. There's that *gorgon* Shen Te! That *drove* your family out into the cold!

NIECE. It wasn't her. It was that cousin of hers. She offered to *pay* for the cakes. I've nothing against her.

OLD WHORE. I have, though. *(So that Shen Te can hear.)* Now where could the little lady be off to? She may be rich now but that won't stop her snatching our young men, will it?

SHEN TE. I'm going to the tearoom by the pond.

NIECE. Is it true what they say? You're marrying a widower—with three children?

SHEN TE. Yes. I'm just going to see him.

YANG SUN *(his patience at breaking point)*. Move on there! This is a park, not a whorehouse!

OLD WHORE. Shut your mouth!

(But the Two Prostitutes leave.)

YANG SUN. Even in the farthest corner of the park, even when it's raining, you can't get rid of them! *(He spits.)*

SHEN TE *(overhearing this)*. And what right have you to scold them? *(But at this point she sees the rope.)* Oh!

YANG SUN. Well, what are you staring at?

SHEN TE. That rope. What is it for?

YANG SUN. Think! Think! I haven't a penny. Even if I had, I wouldn't spend it on you. I'd buy a drink of water.

(The rain starts.)

SHEN TE *(still looking at the rope)*. What is the rope for? You mustn't!

YANG SUN. What's it to you? Clear out!

SHEN TE *(irrelevantly)*. It's raining.

YANG SUN. Well, don't try to come under this tree.

SHEN TE. Oh, no. *(She stays in the rain.)*

YANG SUN. Now go away. *(Pause.)* For one thing, I don't like your looks, you're bow-legged.

SHEN TE *(indignantly)*. That's not true!

YANG SUN. Well, don't show 'em to me. Look, it's raining. You better come under this tree.

(Slowly, she takes shelter under the tree.)

SHEN TE. Why did you want to do it?

YANG SUN. You really want to know? *(Pause.)* To get rid of you! *(Pause.)* You know what a flyer is?

SHEN TE. Oh yes, I've met a lot of pilots. At the tearoom.

YANG SUN. You call *them* flyers? Think they know what a machine *is*? Just 'cause they have leather helmets? They gave the airfield director a bribe, that's the way *those* fellows got up in the air! Try one of them out sometime. "Go up to two thousand feet," tell him,

"then let it fall, then pick it up again with a flick of the wrist at the last moment." Know what he'll say to that? "It's not in my contract." Then again, there's the landing problem. It's like landing on your own backside. It's no different, planes are human. Those fools don't understand. *(Pause.)* And I'm the biggest fool for reading the book on flying in the Peking school and skipping the page where it says: "We've got enough flyers and we don't need you." I'm a mail pilot and no mail. You understand that?

SHEN TE *(shyly)*. Yes, I do.

YANG SUN. No, you don't. You'd never understand that.

SHEN TE. When we were little we had a crane with a broken wing. He made friends with us and was very good-natured about our jokes. He would strut along behind us and call out to stop us going too fast for him. But every spring and autumn when the cranes flew over the villages in great swarms, he got quite restless. *(Pause.)* I understood that. *(She bursts out crying.)*

YANG SUN. Don't!

SHEN TE *(quieting down)*. No.

YANG SUN. It's bad for the complexion.

SHEN TE *(sniffing)*. I've stopped.

(She dries her tears on her big sleeve. Leaning against the tree, but not looking at her, he reaches for her face.)

YANG SUN. You can't even wipe your own face. *(He is wiping it for her with his handkerchief. Pause.)*

SHEN TE *(still sobbing)*. I don't know *anything!*

YANG SUN. You interrupted me! What for?

SHEN TE. It's such a rainy day. You only wanted to do . . . *that* because it's such a rainy day.

(To the audience.)

> In our country
> The evenings should never be somber
> High bridges over rivers
> The grey hour between night and morning
> And the long, long winter:
> Such things are dangerous
> For, with all the misery,
> A very little is enough
> And men throw away an unbearable life.

(Pause.)

YANG SUN. Talk about yourself for a change.

SHEN TE. What about me? I have a shop.

YANG SUN *(incredulous)*. You have a shop, do you? Never thought of walking the streets?

SHEN TE. I *did* walk the streets. Now I have a shop.

YANG SUN (*ironically*). A gift of the gods, I suppose!

SHEN TE. How did you know?

YANG SUN (*even more ironical*). One fine evening the gods turned up saying: here's some money!

SHEN TE (*quickly*). One fine morning.

YANG SUN (*fed up*). This isn't much of an entertainment.

(*Pause.*)

SHEN TE. I can play the zither a little. (*Pause.*) And I can mimic men. (*Pause.*) I got the shop, so the first thing I did was to give my zither away. I can be as stupid as a fish now, I said to myself, and it won't matter.

I'm rich now, I said
I walk alone, I sleep alone
For a whole year, I said
I'll have nothing to do with a man.

YANG SUN. And now you're marrying one! The one at the tearoom by the pond?

(*Shen Te is silent.*)

YANG SUN. What do you know about love?

SHEN TE. Everything.

YANG SUN. Nothing. (*Pause.*) Or d'you just mean you enjoyed it?

SHEN TE. No.

YANG SUN (*again without turning to look at her, he strokes her cheek with his hand*). You like that?

SHEN TE. Yes.

YANG SUN (*breaking off*). You're easily satisfied, I must say. (*Pause.*) What a town!

SHEN TE. You have no friends?

YANG SUN (*defensively*). Yes, I have! (*Change of tone.*) But they don't want to hear I'm still unemployed. "What?" they ask. "Is there still water in the sea?" You have friends?

SHEN TE (*hesitating*). Just a . . . cousin.

YANG SUN. Watch him carefully.

SHEN TE. He only came once. Then he went away. He won't be back.

(*Yang Sun is looking away.*)

But to be without hope, they say, is to be without goodness!

(*Pause.*)

YANG SUN. Go on talking. A voice is a voice.

SHEN TE. Once, when I was a little girl, I fell, with a load of brushwood. An old man picked me up. He gave me a penny too. Isn't it funny how people who don't have very much like to give some of it away? They must like to show what they can do, and how could they show it better than by being kind? Being wicked is just like being clumsy. When we sing a song, or build a machine, or plant some rice, we're being kind. You're kind.

YANG SUN. You make it sound easy.

SHEN TE. Oh, no. (*Little pause.*) Oh! A drop of rain!

YANG SUN. Where'd you feel it?

SHEN TE. Between the eyes.

YANG SUN. Near the right eye? Or the left?

SHEN TE. Near the left eye.

YANG SUN. Oh, good. (*He is getting sleepy.*) So you're through with men, eh?

SHEN TE (*with a smile*). But I'm not bow-legged.

YANG SUN. Perhaps not.

SHEN TE. Definitely not.

(*Pause.*)

YANG SUN (*leaning wearily against the willow*). I haven't had a drop to drink all day, I haven't eaten anything for *two* days. I couldn't love you if I tried.

(*Pause.*)

SHEN TE. I like it in the rain.

(*Enter Wong the Water Seller, singing.*)

THE SONG OF THE WATER SELLER IN THE RAIN
"Buy my water," I am yelling
And my fury restraining
For no water I'm selling
'Cause it's raining, 'cause it's raining!
    I keep yelling: "Buy my water!"
    But no one's buying
    Athirst and dying
    And drinking and paying!
    Buy water!
    Buy water, you dogs!
Nice to dream of lovely weather!
Think of all the consternation
Were there no precipitation
Half a dozen years together!
Can't you hear them shrieking: "Water!"
Pretending they adore me!
They all would go down on their knees before me!
Down on your knees!
Go down on your knees, you dogs!
What are lawns and hedges thinking?
What are fields and forests saying?
"At the cloud's breast we are drinking!
And we've no idea who's paying!"

I keep yelling: "Buy my water!"
But no one's buying
A thirst and dying
And drinking and paying!
Buy water!
Buy water, you dogs!

(*The rain has stopped now. Shen Te sees Wong and runs toward him.*)

SHEN TE. Wong! You're back! Your carrying pole's at the shop.

WONG. Oh, thank you, Shen Te. And how is life treating *you?*

SHEN TE. I've just met a brave and clever man. And I want to buy him a cup of your water.

WONG (*bitterly*). Throw back your head and open your mouth and you'll have all the water you need—

SHEN TE (*tenderly*).

I want *your* water, Wong
The water that has tired you so
The water that you carried all this way
The water that is hard to sell because it's been raining
I need it for the young man over there—he's a flyer!

A flyer is a bold man:
Braving the storms
In company with the clouds
He crosses the heavens
And brings to friends in far-away lands
The friendly mail!

(*She pays Wong, and runs over to Yang Sun with the cup. But Yang Sun is fast asleep.*)

(*Calling to Wong, with a laugh.*) He's fallen asleep! Despair and rain and I have worn him out!

SCENE 3A

(*Wong's den. The sewer pipe is transparent, and the Gods again appear to Wong in a dream.*)

WONG (*radiant*). I've seen her, illustrious ones! And she hasn't changed!

FIRST GOD. That's good to hear.

WONG. She loves someone.

FIRST GOD. Let's hope the experience gives her the strength to stay good!

WONG. It does. She's doing good deeds all the time.

FIRST GOD. Ah? What sort? What sort of good deeds, Wong?

WONG. Well, she has a kind word for everybody.

FIRST GOD (*eagerly*). And then?

WONG. Hardly anyone leaves her shop without tobacco in his pocket—even if he can't pay for it.

FIRST GOD. Not bad at all. Next?

WONG. She's putting up a family of eight.

FIRST GOD (*gleefully, to the Second God*). Eight! (*To Wong.*) And that's not all, of course!

WONG. She bought a cup of water from me even though it was raining.

FIRST GOD. Yes, yes, yes, all these smaller good deeds!

WONG. Even they run into money. A little tobacco shop doesn't make so much.

FIRST GOD (*sententiously*). A prudent gardener works miracles on the smallest plot.

WONG. She hands out rice every morning. That eats up half her earnings.

FIRST GOD (*a little disappointed*). Well, as a beginning . . .

WONG. They call her the Angel of the Slums—whatever the Carpenter may say!

FIRST GOD. What's this? A carpenter speaks ill of her?

WONG. Oh, he only says her shelves weren't paid for in full.

SECOND GOD (*who has a bad cold and can't pronounce his n's and m's*). What's this? Not paying a carpenter? Why was that?

WONG. I suppose she didn't have the money.

SECOND GOD (*severely*). One pays what one owes, that's in our book of rules! First the letter of the law, then the spirit!

WONG. But it wasn't Shen Te, illustrious ones, it was her cousin. She called *him* in to help.

SECOND GOD. Then her cousin must never darken her threshold again!

WONG. Very well, illustrious ones! But in fairness to Shen Te, let me say that her cousin is a businessman.

FIRST GOD. Perhaps we should inquire what is customary? I find business quite unintelligible. But everybody's doing it. Business! Did the Seven Good Kings do business? Did Kung the Just sell fish?

SECOND GOD. In any case, such a thing must not occur again!

(*The Gods start to leave.*)

THIRD GOD. Forgive us for taking this tone with you, Wong, we haven't been getting enough sleep. The rich recommend us to the poor, and the poor tell us they haven't enough room.

SECOND GOD. Feeble, feeble, the best of them!

FIRST GOD. No great deeds! No heroic daring!

THIRD GOD. On such a *small* scale!

SECOND GOD. Sincere, yes, but what is actually *achieved?*
(*One can no longer hear them.*)

WONG (*calling after them*). I've thought of something, illustrious ones: Perhaps you shouldn't ask—too—much—all—at—once!

SCENE 4

(*The square in front of Shen Te's tobacco shop. Beside Shen Te's place, two other shops are seen: the carpet shop and a barber's. Morning. Outside Shen Te's the Grandfather, the Sister-in-Law, the Unemployed Man, and Mrs. Shin stand waiting.*)

SISTER-IN-LAW. She's been out all night again.

MRS. SHIN. No sooner did we get rid of that crazy cousin of hers than Shen Te herself starts carrying on! Maybe she does give us an ounce of rice now and then, but can you depend on her? Can you depend on her?

(*Loud voices from the Barber's.*)

VOICE OF SHU FU. What are you doing in my shop? Get out—at once!

VOICE OF WONG. But sir. They all let me sell . . .

(*Wong comes staggering out of the barber's shop pursued by Mr. Shu Fu, the barber, a fat man carrying a heavy curling iron.*)

SHU FU. Get out, I said! Pestering my customers with your slimy old water! Get out! Take your cup!

(*He holds out the cup. Wong reaches out for it. Mr. Shu Fu strikes his hand with the curling iron, which is hot. Wong howls.*)

You had it coming, my man!

(*Puffing, he returns to his shop. The Unemployed Man picks up the cup and gives it to Wong.*)

UNEMPLOYED MAN. You can report that to the police.

WONG. My hand! It's smashed up!

UNEMPLOYED MAN. Any bones broken?

WONG. I can't move my fingers.

UNEMPLOYED MAN. Sit down. I'll put some water on it.

(*Wong sits.*)

MRS. SHIN. The water won't cost you anything.

SISTER-IN-LAW. You might have got a bandage from Miss Shen Te till she took to staying out all night. It's a scandal.

MRS. SHIN (*despondently*). If you ask me, she's forgotten we ever existed!

(*Enter Shen Te down the street, with a dish of rice.*)

SHEN TE (*to the audience*). How wonderful to see Setzuan in the early morning! I always used to stay in bed with my dirty blanket over my head afraid to wake up. This morning I saw the newspapers being delivered by little boys, the streets being washed by strong men, and fresh vegetables coming in from the country on ox carts. It's a long walk from where Yang Sun lives, but I feel lighter at every step. They say you walk on air when you're in love, but it's even better walking on the rough earth, on the hard cement. In the early morning, the old city looks like a great rubbish heap. Nice, though—with all its little lights. And the sky, so pink, so transparent, before the dust comes and muddies it! What a lot you miss if you never see your city rising from its slumbers like an honest old craftsman pumping his lungs full of air and reaching for his tools, as the poet says! (*Cheerfully, to her waiting guests.*) Good morning, everyone, here's your rice! (*Distributing the rice, she comes upon Wong.*) Good morning, Wong, I'm quite lightheaded today. On my way over, I looked at myself in all the shop windows. I'd love to be beautiful.

(*She slips into the carpet shop. Mr. Shu Fu has just emerged from his shop.*)

SHU FU (*to the audience*). It surprises me how beautiful Miss Shen Te is looking today! I never gave her a passing thought before. But now I've been gazing upon her comely form for exactly three minutes! I begin to suspect I am in love with her. She is overpoweringly attractive! (*Crossly, to Wong.*) Be off with you, rascal!

(*He returns to his shop. Shen Te comes back out of the carpet shop with the Old Man, its proprietor, and his wife—whom we have already met—the Old Woman. Shen Te is wearing a shawl. The Old Man is holding up a looking glass for her.*)

OLD WOMAN. Isn't it lovely? We'll give you a reduction because there's a little hole in it.

SHEN TE (*looking at another shawl on the Old Woman's arm*). The other one's nice too.

OLD WOMAN (*smiling*). Too bad there's no hole in that!

SHEN TE. That's right. My shop doesn't make very much.

OLD WOMAN. And your good deeds eat it all up! Be more careful, my dear . . .

SHEN TE (*trying on the shawl with the hole*). Just now, I'm lightheaded! Does the color suit me?

OLD WOMAN. You'd better ask a man.

SHEN TE (*to the Old Man*). Does the color suit me?

OLD MAN. You'd better ask your young friend.

SHEN TE. I'd like to have your opinion.

OLD MAN. It suits you, very well. But wear it this way: the dull side out.

(*Shen Te pays up.*)

OLD WOMAN. If you decide you don't like it, you can exchange it. (*She pulls Shen Te to one side.*) Has he got money?

SHEN TE (*with a laugh*). Yang Sun? Oh, no.

OLD WOMAN. Then how're you going to pay your rent?

SHEN TE. I'd forgotten about that.

OLD WOMAN. And next Monday is the first of the month! Miss Shen Te, I've got something to say to you. After we (*indicating her husband*) got to know you, we had our doubts about that marriage ad. We thought it would be better if you'd let *us* help you. Out of our savings. We reckon we could lend you two hundred silver dollars. We don't need anything in writing—you could pledge us your tobacco stock.

SHEN TE. You're prepared to lend money to a person like me?

OLD WOMAN. It's folks like you that need it. We'd think twice about lending anything to your cousin.

OLD MAN (*coming up*). All settled, my dear?

SHEN TE. I wish the gods could have heard what your wife was just saying, Mr. Ma. They're looking for good people who're happy—and helping me makes you happy because you know it was love that got me into difficulties!

(*The old couple smile knowingly at each other.*)

OLD MAN. And here's the money, Miss Shen Te.

(*He hands her an envelope. Shen Te takes it. She bows. They bow back. They return to their shop.*)

SHEN TE (*holding up her envelope*). Look, Wong, here's six months' rent! Don't you believe in miracles now? And how do you like my new shawl?

WONG. For the young fellow I saw you with in the park?

(*Shen Te nods.*)

MRS. SHIN. Never mind all that. It's time you took a look at his hand!

SHEN TE. Have you hurt your hand?

MRS. SHIN. That barber smashed it with his hot curling iron. Right in front of our eyes.

SHEN TE (*shocked at herself*). And I never noticed! We must get you to a doctor this minute or who knows what will happen?

UNEMPLOYED MAN. It's not a doctor he should see, it's a judge. He can ask for compensation. The barber's filthy rich.

WONG. You think I have a chance?

MRS. SHIN (*with relish*). If it's really good and smashed. But is it?

WONG. I think so. It's very swollen. Could I get a pension?

MRS. SHIN. You'd need a witness.

WONG. Well, you all saw it. You could all testify.

(*He looks round. The Unemployed Man, the Grandfather, and the Sister-in-Law are all sitting against the wall of the shop eating rice. Their concentration on eating is complete.*)

SHEN TE (*to Mrs. Shin*). You saw it yourself.

MRS. SHIN. I want nothin' to do with the police. It's against my principles.

SHEN TE (*to Sister-in-Law*). What about you?

SISTER-IN-LAW. Me? I wasn't looking.

SHEN TE (*to the Grandfather, coaxingly*). Grandfather, you'll testify, won't you?

SISTER-IN-LAW. And a lot of good that will do. He's simple-minded.

SHEN TE (*to the Unemployed Man*). You seem to be the only witness left.

UNEMPLOYED MAN. My testimony would only hurt him. I've been picked up twice for begging.

SHEN TE. Your brother is assaulted, and you shut your eyes?

He is hit, cries out in pain, and you are silent?
The beast prowls, chooses and seizes his victim, and
     you say:
"Because we showed no displeasure, he has spared us."
If no one present will be a witness, I will. I'll say I saw it.

MRS. SHIN (*solemnly*). The name for that is perjury.

WONG. I don't know if I can accept that. Though maybe I'll have to. (*Looking at his hand.*) Is it swollen enough, do you think? The swelling's not going down?

UNEMPLOYED MAN. No, no, the swelling's holding up well.

WONG. Yes. It's *more* swollen if anything. Maybe my wrist is broken after all. I'd better see a judge at once.

(*Holding his hand very carefully, and fixing his eyes on it, he runs off. Mrs. Shin goes quickly into the barber's shop.*)

UNEMPLOYED MAN (*seeing her*). She is getting on the right side of Mr. Shu Fu.

SISTER-IN-LAW. You and I can't change the world, Shen Te.

SHEN TE. Go away! Go away all of you!

(*The Unemployed Man, the Sister-in-Law, and the Grandfather stalk off, eating and sulking.*)

(*To the audience.*)

> They've stopped answering
> They stay put
> They do as they're told
> They don't care
> Nothing can make them look up
> But the smell of food.

(*Enter Mrs. Yang, Yang Sun's mother, out of breath.*)

MRS. YANG. Miss. Shen Te. My son has told me everything. I am Mrs. Yang, Sun's mother. Just think. He's got an offer. Of a job as a pilot. A letter has just come. From the director of the airfield in Peking!

SHEN TE. So he can fly again! Isn't that wonderful!

MRS. YANG (*less breathlessly all the time*). They won't give him the job for nothing. They want five hundred silver dollars.

SHEN TE. We can't let money stand in his way, Mrs. Yang!

MRS. YANG. If only you could help him out!

SHEN TE. I have the shop. I can try! (*She embraces Mrs. Yang.*) I happen to have two hundred with me now. Take it. (*She gives her the old couple's money.*) It was a loan but they said I could repay it with my tobacco stock.

MRS. YANG. And they were calling Sun the Dead Pilot of Setzuan! A friend in need!

SHEN TE. We must find another three hundred.

MRS. YANG. How?

SHEN TE. Let me think. (*Slowly.*) I know someone who can help. I didn't want to call on his services again, he's hard and cunning. But a flyer must fly. And I'll make this the last time.

(*Distant sound of a plane.*)

MRS. YANG. If the man you mentioned can do it. . . . Oh, look, there's the morning mail plane, heading for Peking!

SHEN TE. The pilot can see us, let's wave!

(*They wave. The noise of the engine is louder.*)

MRS. YANG. You know that pilot up there?

SHEN TE. Wave, Mrs. Yang! I know the pilot who *will* be up there. He gave up hope. But he'll do it now. One man to raise himself above the misery, above us all.

(*To the audience.*)

> Yang Sun, my lover:
> Braving the storms
> In company with the clouds
> Crossing the heavens
> And bringing to friends in far-away lands
> The friendly mail!

SCENE 4A

(*In front of the inner curtain. Enter Shen Te, carrying Shui Ta's mask. She sings.*)

THE SONG OF DEFENSELESSNESS

> In our country
> A useful man needs luck
> Only if he finds strong backers can he prove himself useful
> The good can't defend themselves and
> Even the gods are defenseless.
>
> Oh, why don't the gods have their own ammunition
> And launch against badness their own expedition
> Enthroning the good and preventing sedition
> And bringing the world to a peaceful condition?
>
> Oh, why don't the gods do the buying and selling
> Injustice forbidding, starvation dispelling
> Give bread to each city and joy to each dwelling?
> Oh, why don't the gods do the buying and selling?

(*She puts on Shui Ta's mask and sings in his voice.*)

> You can only help one of your luckless brothers
> By trampling down a dozen others
>
> Why is it the gods do not feel indignation
> And come down in fury to end exploitation
> Defeat all defeat and forbid desperation
> Refusing to tolerate such toleration?
> Why is it?

SCENE 5

(*Shen Te's tobacco shop. Behind the counter, Mr. Shui Ta, reading the paper. Mrs. Shin is cleaning up. She talks and he takes no notice.*)

MRS. SHIN. And when certain' rumors get about, what *happens* to a little place like this? It goes to pot. *I* know. So, if you want my advice, Mr. Shui Ta, find out just what exactly has been going on between Miss Shen Te and that Yang Sun from Yellow Street.

And remember: a certain interest in Miss Shen Te has been expressed by the barber next door, a man with twelve houses and only one wife, who, for that matter, is likely to drop off at any time. A certain interest has been expressed. (*She relishes the phrase.*) He was even inquiring about her means and, if *that* doesn't prove a man is getting serious, what would? (*Still getting no response, she leaves with her bucket.*)

YANG SUN'S VOICE. Is that Miss Shen Te's tobacco shop?

MRS. SHIN'S VOICE. Yes, it is, but it's Mr. Shui Ta who's here today.

(*Shui Ta runs to the looking glass with the short, light steps of Shen Te, and is just about to start primping, when he realizes his mistake, and turns away, with a short laugh. Enter Yang Sun. Mrs. Shin enters behind him and slips into the back room to eavesdrop.*)

YANG SUN. I am Yang Sun.

(*Shui Ta bows.*)

Is Miss Shen Te in?

SHUI TA. No.

YANG SUN. I guess you know our relationship? (*He is inspecting the stock.*) Quite a place! And I thought she was just talking big. I'll be flying again, all right. (*He takes a cigar, solicits and receives a light from Shui Ta.*) You think we can squeeze the other three hundred out of the tobacco stock?

SHUI TA. May I ask if it is your intention to sell at once?

YANG SUN. It was decent of her to come out with the two hundred but they aren't much use with the other three hundred still missing.

SHUI TA. Shen Te was overhasty promising so much. She might have to sell the shop itself to raise it. Haste, they say, is the wind that blows the house down.

YANG SUN. Oh, she isn't a girl to keep a man waiting. For one thing or the other, if you take my meaning.

SHUI TA. I take your meaning.

YANG SUN (*leering*). Uh, huh.

SHUI TA. Would you explain what the five hundred silver dollars are for?

YANG SUN. Trying to sound me out? Very well. The director of the Peking airfield is a friend of mine from flying school. I give him five hundred: he gets me the job.

SHUI TA. The price is high.

YANG SUN. Not as these things go. He'll have to fire one of the present pilots—for negligence. Only the man he has in mind isn't negligent. Not easy, you understand. You needn't mention that part of it to Shen Te.

SHUI TA (*looking intently at Yang Sun*). Mr. Yang Sun, you are asking my cousin to give up her possessions, leave her friends, and place her entire fate in your hands. I presume you intend to marry her?

YANG SUN. I'd be prepared to.

(*Slight pause.*)

SHUI TA. Those two hundred silver dollars would pay the rent here for six months. If you were Shen Te wouldn't you be tempted to continue in business?

YANG SUN. What? Can you imagine Yang Sun the Flyer behind a counter? (*In an oily voice.*) "A strong cigar or a mild one, worthy sir?" Not in this century!

SHUI TA. My cousin wishes to follow the promptings of her heart, and, from her own point of view, she may even have what is called the right to love. Accordingly, she has commissioned me to help you to this post. There is nothing here that I am not empowered to turn immediately into cash. Mrs. Mi Tzu, the landlady, will advise me about the sale.

(*Enter Mrs. Mi Tzu.*)

MRS. MI TZU. Good morning, Mr. Shui Ta, you wish to see me about the rent? As you know it falls due the day after tomorrow.

SHUI TA. Circumstances have changed, Mrs. Mi Tzu: my cousin is getting married. Her future husband here, Mr. Yang Sun, will be taking her to Peking. I am interested in selling the tobacco stock.

MRS. MI TZU. How much are you asking, Mr. Shui Ta?

YANG SUN. Three hundred sil—

SHUI TA. Five hundred silver dollars.

MRS. MI TZU. How much did she pay for it, Mr. Shui Ta?

SHUI TA. A thousand. And very little has been sold.

MRS. MI TZU. She was robbed. But I'll make you a special offer if you'll promise to be out by the day after tomorrow. Three hundred silver dollars.

YANG SUN (*shrugging*). Take it, man, take it.

SHUI TA. It is not enough.

YANG SUN. Why not? Why not? Certainly, it's enough.

SHUI TA. Five hundred silver dollars.

YANG SUN. But why? We only need three!

SHUI TA (*to Mrs. Mi Tzu*). Excuse me. (*Takes Yang Sun on one side.*) The tobacco stock is pledged to the old couple who gave my cousin the two hundred.

YANG SUN. Is it in writing?

SHUI TA. No.

YANG SUN (*to Mrs. Mi Tzu*). Three hundred will do.

MRS. MI TZU. Of course, I need an assurance that Miss Shen Te is not in debt.

YANG SUN. Mr. Shui Ta?

SHUI TA. She is not in debt.

YANG SUN. When can you let us have the money?

MRS. MI TZU. The day after tomorrow. And remember: I'm doing this because I have a soft spot in my heart for young lovers! (*Exit.*)

YANG SUN (*calling after her*). Boxes, jars and sacks— three hundred for the lot and the pain's over! (*To Shui Ta.*) Where else can we raise money by the day after tomorrow?

SHUI TA. Nowhere. Haven't you enough for the trip and the first few weeks?

YANG SUN. Oh, certainly.

SHUI TA. How much, exactly?

YANG SUN. Oh, I'll dig it up, if I have to steal it.

SHUI TA. I see.

YANG SUN. Well, don't fall off the roof. I'll get to Peking somehow.

SHUI TA. Two people can't travel for nothing.

YANG SUN (*not giving Shui Ta a chance to answer*). I'm leaving *her* behind. No millstones round *my* neck!

SHUI TA. Oh.

YANG SUN. Don't look at me like that!

SHUI TA. How precisely is my cousin to live?

YANG SUN. Oh, you'll think of something.

SHUI TA. A small request, Mr. Yang Sun. Leave the two hundred silver dollars here until you can show me two tickets for Peking.

YANG SUN. You learn to mind your own business, Mr. Shui Ta.

SHUI TA. I'm afraid Miss Shen Te may not wish to sell the shop when she discovers that . . .

YANG SUN. You don't know women. She'll want to. Even then.

SHUI TA (*a slight outburst*). She is a human being, sir! And not devoid of common sense!

YANG SUN. Shen Te is a woman: she *is* devoid of common sense. I only have to lay my hand on her shoulder, and church bells ring.

SHUI TA (*with difficulty*). Mr. Yang Sun!

YANG SUN. Mr. Shui Whatever-it-is!

SHUI TA. My cousin is devoted to you . . . because . . .

YANG SUN. Because I have my hands on her breasts. Give me a cigar. (*He takes one for himself, stuffs a few more in his pocket, then changes his mind and takes the whole box.*) Tell her I'll marry her, then bring me the three hundred. Or let her bring it. One or the other. (*Exit.*)

MRS. SHIN (*sticking her head out of the back room*). Well, he has your cousin under his thumb, and doesn't care if all Yellow Street knows it!

SHUI TA (*crying out*). I've lost my shop! And he doesn't love me! (*He runs berserk through the room, repeating*

these lines incoherently. Then stops suddenly, and addresses Mrs. Shin.) Mrs. Shin, you grew up in the gutter, like me. Are we lacking in hardness? I doubt it. If you steal a penny from me, I'll take you by the throat till you spit it out! You'd do the same to me. The times are bad, this city is hell, but we're like ants, we keep coming, up and up the walls, however smooth! Till bad luck comes. Being in love, for instance. *One* weakness is enough, and love is the deadliest.

MRS. SHIN (*emerging from the back room*). You should have a little talk with Mr. Shu Fu the Barber. He's a real gentleman and just the thing for your cousin. (*She runs off.*)

SHUI TA.

> A caress becomes a stranglehold
> A sigh of love turns to a cry of fear
> Why are there vultures circling in the air?
> A girl is going to meet her lover.

(*Shui Ta sits down and Mr. Shu Fu enters with Mrs. Shin.*)

Mr. Shu Fu?

SHU FU. Mr. Shui Ta.

(*They both bow.*)

SHUI TA. I am told that you have expressed a certain interest in my cousin Shen Te. Let me set aside all propriety and confess: she is at this moment in grave danger.

SHU FU. Oh, dear!

SHUI TA. She has lost her shop, Mr. Shu Fu.

SHU FU. The charm of Miss Shen Te, Mr. Shui Ta, derives from the goodness, not of her shop, but of her heart. Men call her the Angel of the Slums.

SHUI TA. Yet her goodness has cost her two hundred silver dollars in a single day: we must put a stop to it.

SHU FU. Permit me to differ, Mr. Shui Ta. Let us rather, open wide the gates to such goodness! Every morning, with pleasure tinged by affection, I watch her charitable ministrations. For they are hungry, and she giveth them to eat! Four of them, to be precise. Why only four? I ask. Why not four hundred? I hear she has been seeking shelter for the homeless. What about my humble cabins behind the cattle run? They are at her disposal. And so forth. And so on. Mr. Shui Ta, do you think Miss Shen Te could be persuaded to listen to certain ideas of mine? Ideas like these?

SHUI TA. Mr. Shu Fu, she would be honored.

(*Enter Wong and the Policeman. Mr. Shu Fu turns abruptly away and studies the shelves.*)

WONG. Is Miss Shen Te here?

SHUI TA. No.

WONG. I am Wong the Water Seller. You are Mr. Shui Ta?

SHUI TA. I am.

WONG. I am a friend of Shen Te's.

SHUI TA. An intimate friend, I hear.

WONG (to the Policeman). You see? (To Shui Ta.) It's because of my hand.

POLICEMAN. He hurt his hand, sir, that's a fact.

SHUI TA (quickly). You need a sling, I see. (He takes a shawl from the back room, and throws it to Wong.)

WONG. But that's her new shawl!

SHUI TA. She has no more use for it.

WONG. But she bought it to please someone!

SHUI TA. It happens to be no longer necessary.

WONG (making the sling). She is my only witness.

POLICEMAN. Mr. Shui Ta, your cousin is supposed to have seen the Barber hit the Water Seller with a curling iron.

SHUI TA. I'm afraid my cousin was not present at the time.

WONG. But she was, sir! Just ask her! Isn't she in?

SHUI TA (gravely). Mr. Wong, my cousin has her own troubles. You wouldn't wish her to add to them by committing perjury?

WONG. But it was she that told me to go to the judge!

SHUI TA. Was the judge supposed to heal your hand?

(Mr. Shu Fu turns quickly around. Shui Ta bows to Shu Fu, and vice versa.)

WONG (taking the sling off, and putting it back). I see how it is.

POLICEMAN. Well, I'll be on my way. (To Wong.) And you be careful. If Mr. Shu Fu wasn't a man who tempers justice with mercy, as the saying is, you'd be in jail for libel. Be off with you!

(Exit Wong, followed by Policeman.)

SHUI TA. Profound apologies, Mr. Shu Fu.

SHU FU. Not at all, Mr. Shui Ta. (Pointing to the shawl.) The episode is over?

SHUI TA. It may take her time to recover. There are some fresh wounds.

SHU FU. We shall be discreet. Delicate. A short vacation could be arranged . . .

SHUI TA. First, of course, you and she would have to talk things over.

SHU FU. At a small supper in a small, but high-class, restaurant.

SHUI TA. I'll go and find her. (Exit into back room.)

MRS. SHIN (sticking her head in again). Time for congratulations, Mr. Shu Fu?

SHU FU. Ah, Mrs. Shin! Please inform Miss Shen Te's guests they may take shelter in the cabins behind the cattle run!

(Mrs. Shin nods, grinning.)

(To the audience.) Well? What do you think of me, ladies and gentlemen? What could a man do more? Could he be less selfish? More farsighted? A small supper in a small but . . . Does that bring rather vulgar and clumsy thoughts into your mind? Ts, ts, ts. Nothing of the sort will occur. She won't even be touched. Not even accidentally while passing the salt. An exchange of ideas only. Over the flowers on the table— white chrysanthemums, by the way (He writes down a note of this.)—yes, over the white chrysanthemums, two young souls will . . . shall I say "find each other"? We shall NOT exploit the misfortune of others. Understanding? Yes. An offer of assistance? Certainly. But quietly. Almost inaudibly. Perhaps with a single glance. A glance that could also—mean more.

MRS. SHIN (coming forward). Everything under control, Mr. Shu Fu?

SHU FU. Oh, Mrs. Shin, what do you know about this worthless rascal Yang Sun?

MRS. SHIN. Why, he's the most worthless rascal . . .

SHU FU. Is he really? You're sure? (As she opens her mouth.) From now on, he doesn't exist! Can't be found anywhere!

(Enter Yang Sun.)

YANG SUN. What's been going on here?

MRS. SHIN. Shall I call Mr. Shui Ta, Mr. Shu Fu? He wouldn't want strangers in here!

SHU FU. Mr. Shui Ta is in conference with Miss Shen Te. Not to be disturbed!

YANG SUN. Shen Te here? I didn't see her come in. What kind of conference?

SHU FU (not letting him enter the back room). Patience, dear sir! And if by chance I have an inkling who you are, pray take note that Miss Shen Te and I are about to announce our engagement.

YANG SUN. What?

MRS. SHIN. You didn't expect that, did you?

(Yang Sun is trying to push past the barber into the back room when Shen Te comes out.)

SHU FU. My dear Shen Te, ten thousand apologies! Perhaps you . . .

YANG SUN. What is it, Shen Te? Have you gone crazy?

SHEN TE (*breathless*). My cousin and Mr. Shu Fu have come to an understanding. They wish me to hear Mr. Shu Fu's plans for helping the poor.

YANG SUN. Your cousin wants to part us.

SHEN TE. Yes.

YANG SUN. And you've agreed to it?

SHEN TE. Yes.

YANG SUN. They told you I was bad.

(*Shen Te is silent.*)

And suppose I am. Does that make me need you less? I'm low, Shen Te, I have no money, I don't do the right thing but at least I put up a fight! (*He is near her now, and speaks in an undertone.*) Have you no eyes? Look at him. Have you forgotten already?

SHEN TE. No.

YANG SUN. How it was raining?

SHEN TE. No.

YANG SUN. How you cut me down from the willow tree? Bought me water? Promised me money to fly with?

SHEN TE (*shakily*). Yang Sun, what do you want?

YANG SUN. I want you to come with me.

SHEN TE (*in a small voice*). Forgive me, Mr. Shu Fu, I want to go with Mr. Yang Sun.

YANG SUN. We're lovers you know. Give me the key to the shop.

(*Shen Te takes the key from around her neck. Yang Sun puts it on the counter. To Mrs. Shin.*)

Leave it under the mat when you're through. Let's go, Shen Te.

SHU FU. But this is rape! Mr. Shui Ta!!

YANG SUN (*to Shen Te*). Tell him not to shout.

SHEN TE. Please don't shout for my cousin, Mr. Shu Fu. He doesn't agree with me, I know, but he's wrong. (*To the audience.*)

I want to go with the man I love
I don't want to count the cost
I don't want to consider if it's wise
I don't want to know if he loves me
I want to go with the man I love.

YANG SUN. That's the spirit.

(*And the couple leave.*)

SCENE 5A

(*In front of the inner curtain. Shen Te in her wedding clothes, on the way to her wedding.*)

SHEN TE. Something terrible has happened. As I left the shop with Yang Sun, I found the old carpet dealer's wife waiting in the street, trembling all over. She told me her husband had taken to his bed—sick with all the worry and excitement over the two hundred silver dollars they lent me. She said it would be best if I gave it back now. Of course, I had to say I would. She said she couldn't quite trust my cousin Shui Ta or even my fiancé Yang Sun. There were tears in her eyes. With my emotions in an uproar, I threw myself into Yang Sun's arms, I couldn't resist him. The things he'd said to Shui Ta had taught Shen Te nothing. Sinking into his arms, I said to myself:

To let no one perish, not even oneself
To fill everyone with happiness, even oneself
Is so good

How could I have forgotten those two old people? Yang Sun swept me away like a small hurricane. But he's not a bad man, and he loves me. He'd rather work in the cement factory than owe his flying to a crime. Though, of course, flying is a great passion with Sun. Now, on the way to my wedding, I waver between fear and joy.

SCENE 6

(*The "private dining room" on the upper floor of a cheap restaurant in a poor section of town. With Shen Te: the Grandfather, the Sister-in-Law, the Niece, Mrs. Shin, the Unemployed Man. In a corner, alone, a Priest. A Waiter pouring wine. Downstage, Yang Sun talking to his mother. He wears a dinner jacket.*)

YANG SUN. Bad news, Mamma. She came right out and told me she can't sell the shop for me. Some idiot is bringing a claim because he lent her the two hundred she gave you.

MRS. YANG. What did *you* say? Of course, you can't marry her now.

YANG SUN. It's no use saying anything to *her*. I've sent for her cousin, Mr. Shui Ta. He said there was nothing in writing.

MRS. YANG. Good idea. I'll go out and look for him. Keep an eye on things.

(*Exit Mrs. Yang. Shen Te has been pouring wine.*)

SHEN TE (*to the audience, pitcher in hand*). I wasn't mistaken in him. He's bearing up well. Though it must have been an awful blow—giving up flying. I do love him so. (*Calling across the room to him.*) Sun, you haven't drunk a toast with the bride!

YANG SUN. What do we drink to?

SHEN TE. Why, to the future!

YANG SUN. When the bridegroom's dinner jacket won't be a hired one!

SHEN TE. But when the bride's dress will still get rained on sometimes!

YANG SUN. To everything we ever wished for!

SHEN TE. May all our dreams come true!

(*They drink.*)

YANG SUN (*with loud conviviality*). And now, friends, before the wedding gets under way, I have to ask the bride a few questions. I've no idea what kind of a wife she'll make, and it worries me. (*Wheeling on Shen Te.*) For example. Can you make five cups of tea with three tea leaves?

SHEN TE. No.

YANG SUN. So I won't be getting very much tea. Can you sleep on a straw mattress the size of that book? (*He points to the large volume the Priest is reading.*)

SHEN TE. The two of us?

YANG SUN. The one of you.

SHEN TE. In that case, no.

YANG SUN. What a wife! I'm shocked!

(*While the audience is laughing, his mother returns. With a shrug of her shoulders, she tells Yang Sun the expected guest hasn't arrived. The Priest shuts the book with a bang, and makes for the door.*)

MRS. YANG. Where are *you* off to? It's only a matter of minutes.

PRIEST (*watch in hand*). Time goes on, Mrs. Yang, and I've another wedding to attend to. Also a funeral.

MRS. YANG (*irately*). D'you think we planned it this way? I was hoping to manage with one pitcher of wine, and we've run through two already. (*Points to empty pitcher. Loudly.*) My dear Shen Te, I don't know where your cousin can be keeping himself!

SHEN TE. My cousin?

MRS. YANG. Certainly. I'm old fashioned enough to think such a close relative should attend the wedding.

SHEN TE. Oh, Sun, is it the three hundred silver dollars?

YANG SUN (*not looking her in the eye*). Are you deaf? Mother says she's old fashioned. And I say I'm considerate. We'll wait another fifteen minutes.

HUSBAND. Another fifteen minutes.

MRS. YANG (*addressing the company*). Now you all know, don't you, that my son is getting a job as a mail pilot?

SISTER-IN-LAW. In Peking, too, isn't it?

MRS. YANG. In Peking, too! The two of us are moving to Peking!

SHEN TE. Sun, tell your mother Peking is out of the question now.

YANG SUN. Your cousin'll tell her. If he agrees. I don't agree.

SHEN TE (*amazed, and dismayed*). Sun!

YANG SUN. I hate this godforsaken Setzuan. What people! Know what they look like when I half close my eyes? Horses! Whinnying, fretting, stamping, screwing their necks up! (*Loudly.*) And what is it the thunder says? They are su-per-flu-ous! (*He hammers out the syllables.*) They've run their last race! They can go trample themselves to death! (*Pause.*) I've got to get out of here.

SHEN TE. But I've promised the money to the old couple.

YANG SUN. And since you always do the wrong thing, it's lucky your cousin's coming. Have another drink.

SHEN TE (*quietly*). My cousin can't be coming.

YANG SUN. How d'you mean?

SHEN TE. My cousin can't be where I am.

YANG SUN. Quite a conundrum!

SHEN TE (*desperately*). Sun, I'm the one that loves you. Not my cousin. He was thinking of the job in Peking when he promised you the old couple's money—

YANG SUN. Right. And that's why he's bringing the three hundred silver dollars. Here—to my wedding.

SHEN TE. He is not bringing the three hundred silver dollars.

YANG SUN. Huh? What makes you think that?

SHEN TE (*looking into his eyes*). He says you only bought one ticket to Peking.

(*Short pause.*)

YANG SUN. That was yesterday. (*He pulls two tickets part way out of his inside pocket, making her look under his coat.*) Two tickets. I don't want Mother to know. She'll get left behind. I sold her furniture to buy these tickets, so you see . . .

SHEN TE. But what's to become of the old couple?

YANG SUN. What's to become of me? Have another drink. Or do you believe in moderation? If I drink, I fly again. And if you drink, you may learn to understand me.

SHEN TE. You want to fly. But I can't help you.

YANG SUN. "Here's a plane, my darling—but it's only got one wing!"

(*The Waiter enters.*)

WAITER. Mrs. Yang! Mrs. Yang!

MRS. YANG. Yes?

WAITER. Another pitcher of wine, ma'am?

MRS. YANG. We have enough, thanks. Drinking makes
me sweat.

WAITER. Would you mind paying, ma'am?

MRS. YANG (to everyone). Just be patient a few moments
longer, everyone, Mr. Shui Ta is on his way over! (To
the Waiter.) Don't be a spoilsport.

WAITER. I can't let you leave till you've paid your bill,
ma'am.

MRS. YANG. But they know me here!

WAITER. That's just it.

PRIEST (ponderously getting up). I humbly take my leave.
(And he does.)

MRS. YANG (to the others, desperately). Stay where you are,
everybody! The priest says he'll be back in two minutes!

YANG SUN. It's no good, Mamma. Ladies and gentlemen,
Mr. Shui Ta still hasn't arrived and the priest has
gone home. We won't detain you any longer.

(They are leaving now.)

GRANDFATHER (in the doorway, having forgotten to put his
glass down). To the bride! (He drinks, puts down the
glass, and follows the others.)

(Pause.)

SHEN TE. Shall I go too?

YANG SUN. You? Aren't you the bride? Isn't this your
wedding? (He drags her across the room, tearing her
wedding dress.) If we can wait, you can wait. Mother
calls me her falcon. She wants to see me in the
clouds. But I think it may be St. Nevercome's Day
before she'll go to the door and see my plane thunder
by. (Pause. He pretends the guests are still present.)
Why such a lull in the conversation, ladies and gentlemen? Don't you like it here? The ceremony is only
slightly postponed—because an important guest is
expected at any moment. Also because the bride
doesn't know what love is. While we're waiting, the
bridegroom will sing a little song. (He does so.)

THE SONG OF ST. NEVERCOME'S DAY
On a certain day, as is generally known,
One and all will be shouting: Hooray, hooray!
For the beggar maid's son has a solid-gold throne
And the day is St. Nevercome's Day
On St. Nevercome's, Nevercome's, Nevercome's
    Day
He'll sit on his solid-gold throne

Oh, hooray, hooray! That day goodness will pay!
That day badness will cost you your head!
And merit and money will smile and be funny
While exchanging salt and bread

On St. Nevercome's, Nevercome's, Nevercome's Day
While exchanging salt and bread

And the grass, oh, the grass will look down at the sky
And the pebbles will roll up the stream
And all men will be good without batting an eye
They will make of our earth a dream
On St. Nevercome's, Nevercome's, Nevercome's Day
They will make of our earth a dream

And as for me, that's the day I shall be
A flyer and one of the best
Unemployed man, you will have work to do
Washerwoman, you'll get your rest
On St. Nevercome's, Nevercome's, Nevercome's Day
Washerwoman, you'll get your rest.

MRS. YANG. It looks like he's not coming.

(The three of them sit looking at the door.)

SCENE 6A

(Wong's den. The sewer pipe is again transparent
and again the Gods appear to Wong in a dream.)

WONG. I'm so glad you've come, illustrious ones. It's
Shen Te. She's in great trouble from following the
rule about loving thy neighbor. Perhaps she's too
good for this world!

FIRST GOD. Nonsense! You are eaten up by lice and
doubts!

WONG. Forgive me, illustrious one, I only meant you
might deign to intervene.

FIRST GOD. Out of the question! My colleague here in-
tervened in some squabble or other only yesterday.
(He points to the Third God who has a black eye.) The
results are before us!

WONG. She had to call on her cousin again. But not
even he could help. I'm afraid the shop is done for.

THIRD GOD (a little concerned). Perhaps we should help
after all?

FIRST GOD. The gods help those that help themselves.

WONG. What if we can't help ourselves, illustrious ones?

(Slight pause.)

SECOND GOD. Try, anyway! Suffering ennobles!

FIRST GOD. Our faith in Shen Te is unshaken!

THIRD GOD. We certainly haven't found any other good
people. You can see where we spend our nights from
the straw on our clothes.

WONG. You might help her find her way by—

FIRST GOD. The good man finds his own way here below!

SECOND GOD. The good woman too.

FIRST GOD. The heavier the burden, the greater her strength!

THIRD GOD. We're only onlookers, you know.

FIRST GOD. And everything will be all right in the end, O ye of little faith!

(*They are gradually disappearing through these last lines.*)

SCENE 7

(*The yard behind Shen Te's shop. A few articles of furniture on a cart. Shen Te and Mrs. Shin are taking the washing off the line.*)

MRS. SHIN. If you ask me, you should fight tooth and nail to keep the shop.

SHEN TE. How can I? I have to sell the tobacco to pay back the two hundred silver dollars today.

MRS. SHIN. No husband, no tobacco, no house and home! What are you going to live on?

SHEN TE. I can work. I can sort tobacco.

MRS. SHIN. Hey, look, Mr. Shui Ta's trousers! He must have left here stark naked!

SHEN TE. Oh, he may have another pair, Mrs. Shin.

MRS. SHIN. But if he's gone for good as you say, why has he left his pants behind?

SHEN TE. Maybe he's thrown them away.

MRS. SHIN. Can I take them?

SHEN TE. Oh, no.

(*Enter Mr. Shu Fu, running.*)

SHU FU. Not a word! Total silence! I know all. You have sacrificed your own love and happiness so as not to hurt a dear old couple who had put their trust in you! Not in vain does this district—for all its malevolent tongues!—call you the Angel of the Slums! That young man couldn't rise to your level, so you left him. And now, when I see you closing up the little shop, that veritable haven of rest for the multitude, well, I cannot, I cannot let it pass. Morning after morning I have stood watching in the doorway not unmoved—while you graciously handed out rice to the wretched. Is that never to happen again? Is the good woman of Setzuan to disappear? If only you would allow *me* to assist you! Now don't say anything! No assurances, no exclamations of gratitude! (*He has taken out his check book.*) Here! A blank check. (*He places it on the cart.*) Just my signature. Fill it out as you wish. Any sum in the world. I herewith

retire from the scene, quietly, unobtrusively, making no claims, on tiptoe, full of veneration, absolutely selflessly . . . (*He has gone.*)

MRS. SHIN. Well! You're saved. There's always some idiot of a man . . . Now hurry! Put down a thousand silver dollars and let me fly to the bank before he comes to his senses.

SHEN TE. I can pay you for the washing without any check.

MRS. SHIN. What? You're not going to cash it just because you might have to marry him? Are you crazy? Men like him *want* to be led by the nose! Are you still thinking of that flyer? All Yellow Street knows how he treated you!

SHEN TE.
When I heard his cunning laugh, I was afraid
But when I saw the holes in his shoes, I loved him dearly.

MRS. SHIN. Defending that good for nothing after all that's happened!

SHEN TE (*staggering as she holds some of the washing*). Oh!

MRS. SHIN (*taking the washing from her, dryly*). So you feel dizzy when you stretch and bend? There couldn't be a little visitor on the way? If that's it, you can forget Mr. Shu Fu's blank check: it wasn't meant for a christening present!

(*She goes to the back with a basket. Shen Te's eyes follow Mrs. Shin for a moment. Then she looks down at her own body, feels her stomach, and a great joy comes into her eyes.*)

SHEN TE. O joy! A new human being is on the way. The world awaits him. In the cities the people say: he's got to be reckoned with, this new human being! (*She imagines a little boy to be present, and introduces him to the audience.*)
This is my son, the well-known flyer!
Say: Welcome
To the conqueror of unknown mountains and unreachable regions
Who brings us our mail across the impassable deserts!

(*She leads him up and down by the hand.*) Take a look at the world, my son. That's a tree. Tree, yes. Say: "Hello, tree!" And bow. Like this. (*She bows.*) Now you know each other. And, look, here comes the Water Seller. He's a friend, give him your hand. A cup of fresh water for my little son, please. Yes, it is a warm day. (*Handing the cup.*) Oh dear, a policeman, we'll have to make a circle round him. Perhaps we can pick a few cherries over there in the rich Mr. Pung's garden. But we mustn't be seen. You want cherries? Just like children with fathers. No, no, you can't go straight at them like that. Don't pull. We must learn to be reasonable. Well, have it your own way. (*She has let him make for the cherries.*) Can you reach? Where to put them? Your mouth is the best place. (*She tries one herself.*) Mmm, they're good. But the policeman, we must run! (*They run.*) Yes, back to the street. Calm now, so no one will notice us. (*Walking the street with her child, she sings.*)

> Once a plum—'twas in Japan—
> Made a conquest of a man
> But the man's turn soon did come
> For he gobbled up the plum

(*Enter Wong, with a Child by the hand. He coughs.*)

SHEN TE. Wong!

WONG. It's about the Carpenter, Shen Te. He's lost his shop, and he's been drinking. His children are on the streets. This is one. Can you help?

SHEN TE (*to the child*). Come here, little man. (*Takes him down to the footlights. To the audience.*)

> You there! A man is asking you for shelter!
> A man of tomorrow says: what about today?
> His friend the conqueror, whom you know,
> Is his advocate!

(*To Wong.*) He can live in Mr. Shu Fu's cabins. I may have to go there myself. I'm going to have a baby. That's a secret—don't tell Yang Sun—we'd only be in his way. Can you find the Carpenter for me?

WONG. I knew you'd think of something. (*To the Child.*) Goodbye, son, I'm going for your father.

SHEN TE. What about your hand, Wong? I wanted to help, but my cousin . . .

WONG. Oh, I can get along with one hand, don't worry. (*He shows how he can handle his pole with his left hand alone.*)

SHEN TE. But your right hand! Look, take this cart, sell everything that's on it, and go to the doctor with the money . . .

WONG. She's still good. But first I'll bring the Carpenter. I'll pick up the cart when I get back. (*Exit Wong.*)

SHEN TE (*to the Child*). Sit down over here, son, till your father comes.

(*The Child sits crosslegged on the ground. Enter the Husband and Wife, each dragging a large, full sack.*)

WIFE (*furtively*). You're alone, Shen Te, dear?

(*Shen Te nods. The Wife beckons to the Nephew offstage. He comes on with another sack.*)

Your cousin's away?

(*Shen Te nods.*)

He's not coming back?

SHEN TE. No. I'm giving up the shop.

WIFE. That's why we're here. We want to know if we can leave these things in your new home. Will you do us this favor?

SHEN TE. Why, yes, I'd be glad to.

HUSBAND (*cryptically*). And if anyone asks about them, say they're yours.

SHEN TE. Would anyone ask?

WIFE (*with a glance back at her Husband*). Oh, someone might. The police, for instance. They don't seem to like us. Where can we put it?

SHEN TE. Well, I'd rather not get in any more trouble . . .

WIFE. Listen to her! The good woman of Setzuan!

(*Shen Te is silent.*)

HUSBAND. There's enough tobacco in those sacks to give us a new start in life. We could have our own tobacco factory!

SHEN TE (*slowly*). You'll have to put them in the back room.

(*The sacks are taken offstage, where the Child is left alone. Shyly glancing about him, he goes to the garbage can, starts playing with the contents, and eating some of the scraps. The others return.*)

WIFE. We're counting on you, Shen Te!

SHEN TE. Yes. (*She sees the Child and is shocked.*)

HUSBAND. We'll see you in Mr. Shu Fu's cabins.

NEPHEW. The day after tomorrow.

SHEN TE. Yes. Now, go. Go! I'm not feeling well.

(*Exeunt all three, virtually pushed off.*)

> He is eating the refuse in the garbage can!
> Only look at his little grey mouth!

(*Pause. Music.*)

> As this is the world my son will enter
> I will study to defend him.
> To be good to you, my son,
> I shall be a tigress to all others
> If I have to.
> And I shall have to.

(*She starts to go.*) One more time, then. I hope really the last.

(*Exit Shen Te, taking Shui Ta's trousers. Mrs. Shin enters and watches her with marked interest. Enter the Sister-in-Law and the Grandfather.*)

SISTER-IN-LAW. So it's true, the shop has closed down. And the furniture's in the back yard. It's the end of the road!

MRS. SHIN (*pompously*). The fruit of high living, selfishness, and sensuality! Down the primrose path to Mr. Shu Fu's cabins—with you!

SISTER-IN-LAW. Cabins? Rat holes! He gave them to us because his soap supplies only went mouldy there!

(*Enter the Unemployed Man.*)

UNEMPLOYED MAN. Shen Te is moving?

SISTER-IN-LAW. Yes. She was sneaking away.

MRS. SHIN. She's ashamed of herself, and no wonder!

UNEMPLOYED MAN. Tell her to call Mr. Shui Ta or she's done for this time!

SISTER-IN-LAW. Tell her to call Mr. Shui Ta or *we're* done for this time!

(*Enter Wong and Carpenter, the latter with a Child on each hand.*)

CARPENTER. So we'll have a roof over our heads for a change!

MRS. SHIN. Roof? Whose roof?

CARPENTER. Mr. Shu Fu's cabins. And we have little Feng to thank for it. (*Feng, we find, is the name of the child already there; his Father now takes him. To the other two.*) Bow to your little brother, you two! (*The Carpenter and the two new arrivals bow to Feng.*)

(*Enter Shui Ta.*)

UNEMPLOYED MAN. Sst! Mr. Shui Ta!

(*Pause.*)

SHUI TA. And what is this crowd here for, may I ask?

WONG. How do you do, Mr. Shui Ta? This is the Carpenter. Miss Shen Te promised him space in Mr. Shu Fu's cabins.

SHUI TA. That will not be possible.

CARPENTER. We can't go there after all?

SHUI TA. All the space is needed for other purposes.

SISTER-IN-LAW. You mean we have to get out? But we've got nowhere to go.

SHUI TA. Miss Shen Te finds it possible to provide employment. If the proposition interests you, you may stay in the cabins.

SISTER-IN-LAW (*with distaste*). You mean *work*? Work for Miss Shen Te?

SHUI TA. Making tobacco, yes. There are three bales here already. Would you like to get them?

SISTER-IN-LAW (*trying to bluster*). We have our own tobacco! We were in the tobacco business before you were born!

SHUI TA (*to the Carpenter and the Unemployed Man*). You *don't* have your own tobacco. What about you?

(*The Carpenter and the Unemployed Man get the point, and go for the sacks. Enter Mrs. Mi Tzu.*)

MRS. MI TZU. Mr. Shui Ta? I've brought you your three hundred silver dollars.

SHUI TA. I'll sign your lease instead. I've decided not to sell.

MRS. MI TZU. What? You don't need the money for that flyer?

SHUI TA. No.

MRS. MI TZU. And you can pay six months' rent?

SHUI TA (*takes the barber's blank check from the cart and fills it out*). Here is a check for ten thousand silver dollars. On Mr. Shu Fu's account. Look! (*He shows her the signature on the check.*) Your six months' rent will be in your hands by seven this evening. And now, if you'll excuse me.

MRS. MI TZU. So it's Mr. Shu Fu now. The flyer has been given his walking papers. These modern girls! In my day they'd have said she was flighty. That poor, deserted Mr. Yang Sun!

(*Exit Mrs. Mi Tzu. The Carpenter and the Unemployed Man drag the three sacks back on the stage.*)

CARPENTER (*to Shui Ta*). I don't know why I'm doing this for you.

SHUI TA. Perhaps your children want to eat, Mr. Carpenter.

SISTER-IN-LAW (*catching sight of the sacks*). Was my brother-in-law here?

MRS. SHIN. Yes, he was.

SISTER-IN-LAW. I thought as much. I know those sacks! That's our tobacco!

SHUI TA. Really? I thought it came from my back room? Shall we consult the police on the point?

SISTER-IN-LAW (*defeated*). No.

SHUI TA. Perhaps you will show me the way to Mr. Shu Fu's cabins?

(*Shui Ta goes off, followed by the Carpenter and his two older children, the Sister-in-Law, the Grandfather, and the Unemployed Man. Each of the last three drags a sack. Enter Old Man and Old Woman.*)

MRS. SHIN. A pair of pants—missing from the clothes line one minute—and next minute on the honorable backside of Mr. Shui Ta!

OLD WOMAN. We thought Miss Shen Te was here.

MRS. SHIN (*preoccupied*). Well, she's not.

OLD MAN. There was something she was going to give us.

WONG. She was going to help me too. (*Looking at his hand.*) It'll be too late soon. But she'll be back. This cousin has never stayed long.

MRS. SHIN (*approaching a conclusion*). No, he hasn't, has he?

SCENE 7A

(*The sewer pipe: Wong asleep. In his dream, he tells the Gods his fears. The Gods seem tired from all their travels. They stop for a moment and look over their shoulders at the Water Seller.*)

WONG. Illustrious ones, I've been having a bad dream. Our beloved Shen Te was in great distress in the rushes down by the rivers—the spot where the bodies of suicides are washed up. She kept staggering and holding her head down as if she was carrying something and it was dragging her down into the mud. When I called out to her, she said she had to take your Book of Rules to the other side, and not get it wet, or the ink would all come off. You had talked to her about the virtues, you know, the time she gave you shelter in Setzuan.

THIRD GOD. Well, but what do you suggest, my dear Wong?

WONG. Maybe a little relaxation of the rules, Benevolent One, in view of the bad times.

THIRD GOD. As for instance?

WONG. Well, um, good-will, for instance, might do instead of love?

THIRD GOD. I'm afraid that would create new problems.

WONG. Or, instead of justice, good sportsmanship?

THIRD GOD. That would only mean more work.

WONG. Instead of honor, outward propriety?

THIRD GOD. Still more work! No, no! The rules will have to stand, my dear Wong!

(*Wearily shaking their heads, all three journey on.*)

SCENE 8

(*Shui Ta's tobacco factory in Shu Fu's cabins. Huddled together behind bars, several families, mostly women and children. Among these people the Sister-in-Law, the Grandfather, the Carpenter, and his three children. Enter Mrs. Yang followed by Yang Sun.*)

MRS. YANG (*to the audience*). There's something I just *have* to tell you: strength and wisdom are wonderful things. The strong and wise Mr. Shui Ta has transformed my son from a dissipated good-for-nothing into a model citizen. As you may have heard, Mr. Shui Ta opened a small tobacco factory near the cattle runs. It flourished. Three months ago—I shall never forget it—I asked for an appointment, and Mr. Shui Ta agreed to see us—me and my son. I can see him now as he came through the door to meet us . . .

(*Enter Shui Ta, from a door.*)

SHUI TA. What can I do for you, Mrs. Yang?

MRS. YANG. This morning the police came to the house. We find you've brought an action for breach of promise of marriage. In the name of Shen Te. You also claim that Sun came by two hundred silver dollars by improper means.

SHUI TA. That is correct.

MRS. YANG. Mr. Shui Ta, the money's all gone. When the Peking job didn't materialize, he ran through it all in three days. I know he's a good-for-nothing. He sold my furniture. He was moving to Peking without me. Miss Shen Te thought highly of him at one time.

SHUI TA. What do *you* say, Mr. Yang Sun?

YANG SUN. The money's gone.

SHUI TA (*to Mrs. Yang*). Mrs. Yang, in consideration of my cousin's incomprehensible weakness for your son, I am prepared to give him another chance. He can have a job—here. The two hundred silver dollars will be taken out of his wages.

YANG SUN. So it's the factory or jail?

SHUI TA. Take your choice.

YANG SUN. May I speak with Shen Te?

SHUI TA. You may not.

(*Pause.*)

YANG SUN (*sullenly*). Show me where to go.

MRS. YANG. Mr. Shui Ta, you are kindness itself: the gods will reward you! (*To Yang Sun.*) And honest work will make a man of you, my boy.

(*Yang Sun follows Shui Ta into the factory. Mrs. Yang comes down again to the footlights.*)

Actually, honest work didn't agree with him—at first. And he got no opportunity to distinguish himself till—in the third week—when the wages were being paid. . . .

(*Shui Ta has a bag of money. Standing next to his foreman—the former Unemployed Man—he counts out the wages. It is Yang Sun's turn.*)

UNEMPLOYED MAN (*reading*). Carpenter, six silver dollars. Yang Sun, six silver dollars.

YANG SUN (*quietly*). Excuse me, sir. I don't think it can be more than five. May I see? (*He takes the foreman's list.*) It says six working days. But that's a mistake, sir. I took a day off for court business. And I won't take what I haven't earned, however miserable the pay is!

UNEMPLOYED MAN. Yang Sun. Five silver dollars. (*To Shui Ta.*) A rare case, Mr. Shui Ta!

SHUI TA. How is it the book says six when it should say five?

UNEMPLOYED MAN. I must've made a mistake, Mr. Shui Ta. (*With a look at Yang Sun.*) It won't happen again.

SHUI TA (*taking Yang Sun aside*). You don't hold back, do you? You give your all to the firm. You're even honest. Do the foreman's mistakes always favor the workers?

YANG SUN. He does have . . . friends.

SHUI TA. Thank you. May I offer you any little recompense?

YANG SUN. Give me a trial period of one week, and I'll prove my intelligence is worth more to you than my strength.

MRS. YANG (*still down at the footlight*). Fighting words, fighting words! That evening, I said to Sun: "If you're a flyer, then fly, my falcon! Rise in the world!" And he got to be foreman. Yes, in Mr. Shui Ta's tobacco factory, he worked real miracles.

(*We see Yang Sun with his legs apart standing behind the workers who are handing along a basket of raw tobacco above their heads.*)

YANG SUN. Faster! Faster! You there, d'you think you can just stand around now you're not foreman any more? It'll be your job to lead us in song. Sing!

(*Unemployed Man starts singing. The others join in the refrain.*)

SONG OF THE EIGHTH ELEPHANT
Chang had seven elephants—all much the same—
But then there was Little Brother
The seven, they were wild, Little Brother, he was tame
And to guard them Chang chose Little Brother
Run faster!
Mr. Chang has a forest park
Which must be cleared before tonight
And already it's growing dark!

When the seven elephants cleared that forest park
Mr. Chang rode high on Little Brother
While the seven toiled and moiled till dark
On his big behind sat Little Brother
Dig faster!
Mr. Chang has a forest park
Which must be cleared before tonight
And already it's growing dark!

And the seven elephants worked many an hour
Till none of them could work another
Old Chang, he looked sour, on the seven, he did glower
But gave a pound of rice to Little Brother
What was that?
Mr. Chang has a forest park
Which must be cleared before tonight
And already it's growing dark!

And the seven elephants hadn't any tusks
The one that had the tusks was Little Brother!
Seven are no match for one, if the one has a gun!
How old Chang did laugh at Little Brother!
Keep on digging!
Mr. Chang has a forest park
Which must be cleared before tonight
And already it's growing dark!

(*Smoking a cigar, Shui Ta strolls by. Yang Sun, laughing, has joined in the refrain of the third stanza and speeded up the tempo of the last stanza by clapping his hands.*)

MRS. YANG. And that's why I say: strength and wisdom are wonderful things. It took the strong and wise Mr. Shui Ta to bring out the best in Yang Sun. A real superior man is like a bell. If you ring it, it rings, and if you don't, it don't, as the saying is.

SCENE 9

(*Shen Te's shop, now an office with club chairs and fine carpets. It is raining. Shui Ta, now fat, is just dismissing the Old Man and Old Woman. Mrs. Shin, in obviously new clothes, looks on, smirking.*)

SHUI TA. No! I can NOT tell you when we expect her back.

OLD WOMAN. The two hundred silver dollars came today. In an envelope. There was no letter, but it must be from Shen Te. We want to write and thank her. May we have her address?

SHUI TA. I'm afraid I haven't got it.

OLD MAN (*pulling Old Woman's sleeve*). Let's be going.

OLD WOMAN. She's got to come back some time! (*They move off, uncertainly, worried. Shui Ta bows.*)

MRS. SHIN. They lost the carpet shop because they couldn't pay their taxes. The money arrived too late.

SHUI TA. They could have come to me.

MRS. SHIN. People don't like coming to you.

SHUI TA (*sits suddenly, one hand to his head*). I'm dizzy.

MRS. SHIN. After all, you *are* in your seventh month. But old Mrs. Shin will be there in your hour of trial! (*She cackles feebly.*)

SHUI TA (*in a stifled voice*). Can I count on that?

MRS. SHIN. We all have our price, and mine won't be too high for the great Mr. Shui Ta! (*She opens Shui Ta's collar.*)

SHUI TA. It's for the child's sake. All of this.

MRS. SHIN. "All for the child," of course.

SHUI TA. I'm so fat. People must notice.

MRS. SHIN. Oh no, they think it's 'cause you're rich.

SHUI TA (*more feelingly*). What will happen to the child?

MRS. SHIN. You ask that nine times a day. Why, it'll have the best that money can buy!

SHUI TA. He must never see Shui Ta.

MRS. SHIN. Oh, no. Always Shen Te.

SHUI TA. What about the neighbors? There are rumors, aren't there?

MRS. SHIN. As long as Mr. Shu Fu doesn't find out, there's nothing to worry about. Drink this.

(*Enter Yang Sun in a smart business suit, and carrying a businessman's brief case. Shui Ta is more or less in Mrs. Shin's arms.*)

YANG SUN (*surprised*). I seem to be in the way.

SHUI TA (*ignoring this, rises with an effort*). Till tomorrow, Mrs. Shin.

(*Mrs. Shin leaves with a smile, putting her new gloves on.*)

YANG SUN. Gloves now! She couldn't be fleecing you? And since when did *you* have a private life? (*Taking a paper from the brief case.*) You haven't been at your best lately, and things are getting out of hand. The police want to close us down. They say that at the most they can only permit twice the lawful number of workers.

SHUI TA (*evasively*). The cabins are quite good enough.

YANG SUN. For the workers maybe, not for the tobacco. They're too damp. We must take over some of Mrs. Mi Tzu's buildings.

SHUI TA. Her price is double what I can pay.

YANG SUN. Not unconditionally. If she has me to stroke her knees she'll come down.

SHUI TA. I'll never agree to that.

YANG SUN. What's wrong? Is it the rain? You get so irritable whenever it rains.

SHUI TA. Never! I will never . . .

YANG SUN. Mrs. Mi Tzu'll be here in five minutes. *You* fix it. And Shu Fu will be with her. . . . What's all that noise?

(*During the above dialogue, Wong is heard off stage calling: "The good Shen Te, where is she? Which of you has seen Shen Te, good people? Where is Shen Te?" A knock. Enter Wong.*)

WONG. Mr. Shui Ta, I've come to ask when Miss Shen Te will be back, it's six months now . . . There are rumors. People say something's happened to her.

SHUI TA. I'm busy. Come back next week.

WONG (*excited*). In the morning there was always rice on her doorstep—for the needy. It's been there again lately!

SHUI TA. And what do people conclude from this?

WONG. That Shen Te is still in Setzuan! She's been . . . (*He breaks off.*)

SHUI TA. She's been what? Mr. Wong, if you're Shen Te's friend, talk a little less about her, that's my advice to you.

WONG. I don't want your advice! Before she disappeared, Miss Shen Te told me something very important— she's pregnant!

YANG SUN. What? What was that?

SHUI TA (*quickly*). The man is lying.

WONG. A good woman isn't so easily forgotten. Mr. Shui Ta.

(*He leaves. Shui Ta goes quickly into the back room.*)

YANG SUN (*to the audience*). Shen Te pregnant? So that's why. Her cousin sent her away, so I wouldn't get wind of it. I have a son, a Yang appears on the scene, and what happens? Mother and child vanish into thin air! That scoundrel, that unspeakable . . . (*The sound of sobbing is heard from the back room.*) What was that? Someone sobbing? Who was it? Mr. Shui Ta the Tobacco King doesn't weep his heart out. And where does the rice come from that's on the doorstep in the morning?

(*Shui Ta returns. He goes to the door and looks out into the rain.*)

Where is she?

SHUI TA. Sh! It's nine o'clock. But the rain's so heavy, you can't hear a thing.

YANG SUN. What do you want to hear?

SHUI TA. The mail plane.

YANG SUN. What?

SHUI TA. I've been told *you* wanted to fly at one time. Is that all forgotten?

YANG SUN. Flying mail is night work. I prefer the daytime. And the firm is very dear to me—after all it belongs to my ex-fiancée, even if she's not around. And she's not, is she?

SHUI TA. What do you mean by that?

YANG SUN. Oh, well, let's say I haven't altogether—lost interest.

SHUI TA. My cousin might like to know that.

YANG SUN. I might not be indifferent—if I found she was being kept under lock and key.

SHUI TA. By whom?

YANG SUN. By you.

SHUI TA. What could you do about it?

YANG SUN. I could submit for discussion—my position in the firm.

SHUI TA. You are now my Manager. In return for a more appropriate position, you might agree to drop the enquiry into your ex-fiancée's whereabouts?

YANG SUN. I might.

SHUI TA. What position *would* be more appropriate?

YANG SUN. The one at the top.

SHUI TA. My own? (*Silence.*) And if I preferred to throw you out on your neck?

YANG SUN. I'd come back on my feet. With suitable escort.

SHUI TA. The police?

YANG SUN. The police.

SHUI TA. And when the police found no one?

YANG SUN. I might ask them not to overlook the back room. (*Ending the pretense.*) In short, Mr. Shui Ta, my interest in this young woman has not been officially terminated. I should like to see more of her. (*Into Shui Ta's face.*) Besides, she's pregnant and needs a friend. (*He moves to the door.*) I shall talk about it with the Water Seller.

(*Exit.*)

(*Shui Ta is rigid for a moment, then he quickly goes into the back room. He returns with Shen Te's belongings: underwear, etc. He takes a long look at the shawl of the previous scene. He then wraps the things in a bundle which, upon hearing a noise, he hides under the table. Enter Mrs. Mi Tzu and Mr. Shu Fu. They put away their umbrellas and galoshes.*)

MRS. MI TZU. I thought your manager was here, Mr. Shui Ta. He combines charm with business in a way that can only be to the advantage of all of us.

SHU FU. You sent for us, Mr. Shui Ta?

SHUI TA. The factory is in trouble.

SHU FU. It always is.

SHUI TA. The police are threatening to close us down unless I can show that the extension of our facilities is imminent.

SHU FU. Mr. Shui Ta, I'm sick and tired of your constantly expanding projects. I place cabins at your cousin's disposal; you make a factory of them. I hand your cousin a check; you present it. Your cousin disappears and you find the cabins too small and talk of yet more . . .

SHUI TA. Mr. Shu Fu, I'm authorized to inform you that Miss Shen Te's return is now imminent.

SHU FU. Imminent? It's becoming his favorite word.

MRS. MI TZU. Yes, what does it mean?

SHUI TA. Mrs. Mi Tzu, I can pay you exactly half what you asked for your buildings. Are you ready to inform the police that I am taking them over?

MRS. MI TZU. Certainly, if I can take over your manager.

SHU FU. What?

MRS. MI TZU. He's so efficient.

SHUI TA. I'm afraid I need Mr. Yang Sun.

MRS. MI TZU. So do I.

SHUI TA. He will call on you tomorrow

SHU FU. So much the better. With Shen Te likely to turn up at any moment, the presence of that young man is hardly in good taste.

SHUI TA. So we have reached a settlement. In what was once the good Shen Te's little shop we are laying the foundations for the great Mr. Shui Ta's twelve magnificent super tobacco markets. You will bear in mind that though they call me the Tobacco King of Setzuan, it is my cousin's interests that have been served . . .

VOICES (*off*). The police, the police! Going to the tobacco shop! Something must have happened! (*et cetera.*)

(*Enter Yang Sun, Wong, and the Policeman.*)

POLICEMAN. Quiet there, quiet, quiet! (*They quiet down.*) I'm sorry, Mr. Shui Ta, but there's a report that you've been depriving Miss Shen Te of her freedom. Not that I believe all I hear, but the whole city's in an uproar.

SHUI TA. That's a lie.

POLICEMAN. Mr. Yang Sun has testified that he heard someone sobbing in the back room.

SHU FU. Mrs. Mi Tzu and myself will testify that no one here has been sobbing.

MRS. MI TZU. We have been quietly smoking our cigars.

POLICEMAN. Mr. Shui Ta, I'm afraid I shall have to take a look at that room. (*He does so. The room is empty.*) No one there, of course, sir.

YANG SUN. But I hear sobbing. What's that? (*He finds the clothes.*)

WONG. Those are Shen Te's things. (*To crowd.*) Shen Te's clothes are here!

VOICES (*Off. In sequence*). Shen Te's clothes! They've been found under the table! Body of murdered girl still missing! Tobacco King suspected!

POLICEMAN. Mr. Shui Ta, unless you can tell us where the girl is, I'll have to ask you to come along.

SHUI TA. I do not know.

POLICEMAN. I can't say how sorry I am, Mr. Shui Ta. (*He shows him the door.*)

SHUI TA. Everything will be cleared up in no time. There are still judges in Setzuan.

YANG SUN. I heard sobbing!

SCENE 9A

(*Wong's den. For the last time, the Gods appear to the Water Seller in his dream. They have changed and show signs of a long journey, extreme fatigue, and plenty of mishaps. The First no longer has a hat; the Third has lost a leg; all Three are barefoot.*)

WONG. Illustrious ones, at last you're here. Shen Te's been gone for months and today her cousin's been arrested. They think he murdered her to get the shop. But I had a dream and in this dream Shen Te said her cousin was keeping her prisoner. You must find her for us, illustrious ones!

FIRST GOD. We've found very few good people anywhere, and even they didn't keep it up. Shen Te is still the only one that stayed good.

SECOND GOD. If she *has* stayed good.

WONG. Certainly she has. But she's vanished.

FIRST GOD. That's the last straw. All is lost!

SECOND GOD. A little moderation, dear colleague!

FIRST GOD (*plaintively*). What's the good of moderation now? If she can't be found, we'll have to resign! The world is a terrible place! Nothing but misery, vulgarity, and waste! Even the countryside isn't what it used to be. The trees are getting their heads chopped off by telephone wires, and there's such a noise from all the gunfire, and I can't stand those heavy clouds of smoke, and—

THIRD GOD. The place is absolutely unlivable! Good intentions bring people to the brink of the abyss, and

good deeds push them over the edge. I'm afraid our book of rules is destined for the scrap heap—

SECOND GOD. It's people! They're a worthless lot!

THIRD GOD. The world is too cold!

SECOND GOD. It's people! They are too weak!

FIRST GOD. Dignity, dear colleagues, dignity! Never despair! As for this world, didn't we agree that we only have to find one human being who can stand the place? Well, we found her. True, we lost her again. We must find her again, that's all! And at once!

(*They disappear.*)

SCENE 10

(*Courtroom. Groups: Shu Fu and Mrs. Mi Tzu; Yang Sun and Mrs. Yang; Wong, the Carpenter, the Grandfather, the Niece, the Old Man, the Old Woman; Mrs. Shin, the Policeman; the Unemployed Man, the Sister-in-Law.*)

OLD MAN. So much power isn't good for one man.

UNEMPLOYED MAN. And he's going to open twelve super tobacco markets!

WIFE. One of the judges is a friend of Mr. Shu Fu's.

SISTER-IN-LAW. Another one accepted a present from Mr. Shui Ta only last night. A great fat goose.

OLD WOMAN (*to Wong*). And Shen Te is nowhere to be found.

WONG. Only the gods will ever know the truth.

POLICEMAN. Order in the court! My lords the judges!

(*Enter the Three Gods in judges' robes. We overhear their conversation as they pass along the footlights to their bench.*)

THIRD GOD. We'll never get away with it, our certificates were so badly forged.

SECOND GOD. My predecessor's "sudden indigestion" will certainly cause comment.

FIRST GOD. But he *had* just eaten a whole goose.

UNEMPLOYED MAN. Look at that! *New* judges!

WONG. New judges. And what good ones!

(*The Third God hears this, and turns to smile at Wong. The Gods sit. The First God beats on the bench with his gavel. The Policeman brings in Shui Ta who walks with lordly steps. He is whistled at.*)

POLICEMAN (*to Shui Ta*). Be prepared for a surprise. The judges have been changed.

(*Shui Ta turns quickly round, looks at them, and staggers.*)

NIECE. What's the matter now?

WIFE. The great Tobacco King nearly fainted.

HUSBAND. Yes, as soon as he saw the new judges.

WONG. Does *he* know who they are?

(Shui Ta picks himself up, and the proceedings open.)

FIRST GOD. Defendant Shui Ta, you are accused of doing away with your cousin Shen Te in order to take possession of her business. Do you plead guilty or not guilty?

SHUI TA. Not guilty, my lord.

FIRST GOD (*thumbing through the documents of the case*). The first witness is the Policeman. I shall ask him to tell us something of the respective reputations of Miss Shen Te and Mr. Shui Ta.

POLICEMAN. Miss Shen Te was a young lady who aimed to please, my lord. She liked to live and let live, as the saying goes. Mr. Shui Ta, on the other hand, is a man of principle. Though the generosity of Miss Shen Te forced him at times to abandon half measures, unlike the girl, he was always on the side of the law, my lord. One time, he even unmasked a gang of thieves to whom his too trustful cousin had given shelter. The evidence, in short, my lord, proves that Mr. Shui Ta was *incapable* of the crime of which he stands accused!

FIRST GOD. I see. And are there others who could testify along, shall we say, the same lines?

(Shu Fu rises.)

POLICEMAN (*whispering to Gods*). Mr. Shu Fu—a very important person.

FIRST GOD (*inviting him to speak*). Mr. Shu Fu!

SHU FU. Mr. Shui Ta is a businessman, my lord. Need I say more?

FIRST GOD. Yes.

SHU FU. Very well, I will. He is Vice President of the Council of Commerce and is about to be elected a Justice of the Peace. (*He returns to his seat.*)

WONG. Elected! *He* gave him the job!

(With a gesture the First God asks who Mrs. Mi Tzu is.)

POLICEMAN. Another very important person. Mrs. Mi Tzu.

FIRST GOD (*inviting her to speak*). Mrs. Mi Tzu!

MRS. MI TZU. My lord, as Chairman of the Committee on Social Work, I wish to call attention to just a couple of eloquent facts: Mr. Shui Ta not only has erected a model factory with model housing in our city, he is a regular contributor to our home for the disabled. (*She returns to her seat.*)

POLICEMAN (*whispering*). And she's a great friend of the judge that ate the goose!

FIRST GOD (*to the* Policeman). Oh, thank you. What next? (*To the Court, genially.*) Oh, yes. We should find out if any of the evidence is less favorable to the Defendant.

(Wong, the Carpenter, the Old Man, the Old Woman, the Unemployed Man, the Sister-in-Law, and the Niece come forward.)

POLICEMAN (*whispering*). Just the riff raff, my lord.

FIRST GOD (*addressing the "riff raff"*). Well, um, riff raff— do you know anything of the Defendant, Mr. Shui Ta?

WONG. Too much, my lord.

UNEMPLOYED MAN. What don't we know, my lord?

CARPENTER. He ruined us.

SISTER-IN-LAW. He's a cheat.

NIECE. Liar.

WIFE. Thief.

BOY. Blackmailer.

BROTHER. Murderer.

FIRST GOD. Thank you. We should now let the Defendant state his point of view.

SHUI TA. I only came on the scene when Shen Te was in danger of losing what I had understood was a gift from the gods. Because I did the filthy jobs which someone had to do, they hate me. My activities were held down to the minimum, my lord.

SISTER-IN-LAW. He had us arrested!

SHUI TA. Certainly. You stole from the bakery!

SISTER-IN-LAW. Such concern for the bakery! You didn't want the shop for yourself, I suppose!

SHUI TA. I didn't want the shop overrun with parasites.

SISTER-IN-LAW. We had nowhere else to go.

SHUI TA. There were too many of you.

WONG. What about this old couple: Were *they* parasites?

OLD MAN. We lost our shop because of you!

SISTER-IN-LAW. And we gave your cousin money!

SHUI TA. My cousin's fiancé was a flyer. The money had to go to *him*.

WONG. Did you care whether he flew or not? Did you care whether she married him or not? You wanted her to marry someone else! (*He points at Shu Fu.*)

SHUI TA. The flyer unexpectedly turned out to be a scoundrel.

YANG SUN (*jumping up*). Which was the reason you made him your Manager?

SHUI TA. Later on he improved.

WONG. And when he improved, you sold him to her? (*He points out Mrs. Mi Tzu.*)

SHUI TA. She wouldn't let me have her premises unless she had him to stroke her knees!

MRS. MI TZU. What? The man's a pathological liar. (*To him.*) Don't mention my property to me as long as you live! Murderer! (*She rustles off, in high dudgeon.*)

YANG SUN (*pushing in*). My lord, I wish to speak for the Defendant.

SISTER-IN-LAW. Naturally. He's your employer.

UNEMPLOYED MAN. And the worst slave driver in the country.

MRS. YANG. That's a lie! My lord, Mr. Shui Ta is a great man. He . . .

YANG SUN. He's this and he's that, but he is not a murderer, my lord. Just fifteen minutes before his arrest I heard Shen Te's voice in his own back room.

FIRST GOD. Oh? Tell us more!

YANG SUN. I heard sobbing, my lord!

FIRST GOD. But lots of women sob, we've been finding.

YANG SUN. Could I fail to recognize her voice?

SHU FU. No, you made her sob so often yourself, young man!

YANG SUN. Yes. But I also made her happy. Till he (*pointing at Shui Ta*) decided to sell her to you!

SHUI TA. Because you didn't love her.

WONG. Oh, no: it was for the money, my lord!

SHUI TA. And what was the money for, my lord? For the poor! And for Shen Te so she could go on being good!

WONG. For the poor? That he sent to his sweatshops? And why didn't you let Shen Te be good when you signed the big check?

SHUI TA. For the child's sake, my lord.

CARPENTER. What about *my* children? What did he do about them?

(*Shui Ta is silent.*)

WONG. The shop was to be a fountain of goodness. That was the gods' idea. You came and spoiled it!

SHUI TA. If I hadn't, it would have run dry!

MRS. SHIN. There's a lot in that, my lord.

WONG. What have you done with the good Shen Te, bad man? She *was* good, my lords, she was, I swear it! (*He raises his hand in an oath.*)

THIRD GOD. What's happened to your hand, Water Seller?

WONG (*pointing to Shui Ta*). It's all his fault, my lord, *she* was going to send me to a doctor—(*To Shui Ta.*) You were her worst enemy!

SHUI TA. I was her only friend!

WONG. Where is she then? Tell us where your good friend is!

(*The excitement of this exchange has run through the whole crowd.*)

ALL. Yes, where is she? Where is Shen Te? (*et cetera.*)

SHUI TA. Shen Te had to go.

WONG. Where? Where to?

SHUI TA. I cannot tell you! I cannot tell you!

ALL. Why? Why did she have to go away? (*et cetera.*)

WONG (*into the din with the first words, but talking on beyond the others*). Why not, why not? Why did she have to go away?

SHUI TA (*shouting*). Because you'd all have torn her to shreds, that's why! My lords, I have a request. Clear the court! When only the judges remain, I will make a confession.

ALL (*except Wong, who is silent, struck by the new turn of events*). So he's guilty? He's confessing! (*et cetera.*)

FIRST GOD (*using the gavel*). Clear the court!

POLICEMAN. Clear the court!

WONG. Mr. Shui Ta has met his match this time.

MRS. SHIN (*with a gesture toward the judges*). You're in for a little surprise.

(*The court is cleared. Silence.*)

SHUI TA. Illustrious ones!

(*The Gods look at each other, not quite believing their ears.*)

SHUI TA. Yes, I recognize you!

SECOND GOD (*taking matters in hand, sternly*). What have you done with our good woman of Setzuan?

SHUI TA. I have a terrible confession to make: I am she! (*He takes off his mask, and tears away his clothes. Shen Te stands there.*)

SECOND GOD. Shen Te!

SHEN TE. Shen Te, yes. Shui Ta *and* Shen Te. Both.
  Your injunction
  To be good and yet to live
  Was a thunderbolt:
  It has torn me in two
  I can't tell how it was
  But to be good to others
  And myself at the same time
  I could not do it
  Your world is not an easy one, illustrious ones!
  When we extend our hand to a beggar, he tears it off
    for us
  When we help the lost, we are lost ourselves.
  And so
  Since not to eat is to die
  Who can long refuse to be bad?

As I lay prostrate beneath the weight of good
    intentions
Ruin stared me in the face
It was when I was unjust that I ate good meat
And hobnobbed with the mighty
Why?
Why are bad deeds rewarded?
Good ones punished?
I enjoyed giving
I truly wished to be the Angel of the Slums
But washed by a foster-mother in the water of the
    gutter
I developed a sharp eye
The time came when pity was a thorn in my side
And, later, when kind words turned to ashes in my
    mouth
And anger took over
I became a wolf
Find me guilty, then, illustrious ones,
But know:
All that I have done I did
To help my neighbor
To love my lover
And to keep my little one from want
For your great, godly deeds, I was too poor, too
    small.

(*Pause.*)

FIRST GOD (*shocked*). Don't go on making yourself mis-
    erable, Shen Te! We're overjoyed to have found
    you!
SHEN TE. I'm telling you I'm the bad man who commit-
    ted all those crimes!
FIRST GOD (*using—or failing to use—his ear trumpet*). The
    good woman who did all those good deeds?
SHEN TE. Yes, but the bad man too!
FIRST GOD (*as if something had dawned*). Unfortunate co-
    incidences! Heartless neighbors!
THIRD GOD (*shouting in his ear*). But how is she to continue?
FIRST GOD. Continue? Well, she's a strong, healthy
    girl . . .
SECOND GOD. You didn't hear what she said!
FIRST GOD. I heard every word! She is confused, that's
    all! (*He begins to bluster.*) And what about this book
    of rules—we can't renounce our rules, can we? (*More
    quietly.*) Should the world be changed? How? By
    whom? The world should *not* be changed! (*At a sign
    from him, the lights turn pink, and music plays.*)
    And now the hour of parting is at hand.
    Dost thou behold, Shen Te, yon fleecy cloud?
    It is our chariot. At a sign from me

'Twill come and take us back from whence we came
Above the azure vault and silver stars . . .
SHEN TE. No! Don't go, illustrious ones!
FIRST GOD.
    Our cloud has landed now in yonder field
    From whence it will transport us back to heaven.
    Farewell, Shen Te, let not thy courage fail thee . . .

(*Exeunt Gods.*)

SHEN TE. What about the old couple? They've lost their
    shop! What about the Water Seller and his hand?
    And I've got to defend myself against the barber, be-
    cause I don't love him! And against Sun, because I
    do love him! How? How?

(*Shen Te's eyes follow the Gods as they are imagined
to step into a cloud which rises and moves forward
over the orchestra and up beyond the balcony*)

FIRST GOD (*from on high*). We have faith in you, Shen
    Te!
SHEN TE. There'll be a child. And he'll have to be fed. I
    can't stay here. Where shall I go?
FIRST GOD. Continue to be good, good woman of Setzuan!
SHEN TE. I need my bad cousin!
FIRST GOD. But not very often!
SHEN TE. Once a week at least!
FIRST GOD. Once a month will be quite enough!
SHEN TE (*shrieking*). No, no! Help!

(*But the cloud continues to recede as the Gods sing.*)

VALEDICTORY HYMN
What rapture, oh, it is to know
A good thing when you see it
And having seen a good thing, oh,
What rapture 'tis to flee it
Be good, sweet maid of Setzuan
Let Shui Ta be clever
Departing, we forget the man
Remember your endeavor
Ò Because through all the length of days
Her goodness faileth never
Sing hallelujah! May Shen Te's
Good name live on forever!

SHEN TE. Help!

Epilogue

You're thinking, aren't you, that this is no right
Conclusion to the play you've seen tonight?
After a tale, exotic, fabulous,

315

A nasty ending was slipped up on us.
We feel deflated too. We too are nettled
To see the curtain down and nothing settled.
How could a better ending be arranged?
Could one change people? Can the world be
  changed?

Would new gods do the trick? Will atheism?
Moral rearmament? Materialism?
It is for you to find a way, my friends,
To help good men arrive at happy ends.
You write the happy ending to the play!
There must, there must, there's got to be a way!

COMMENTARY

Note: The following essay represents a single interpretation of the play. For other perspectives on
The Good Woman of Setzuan, *consult the essays listed below.*

Most anthologies title this play *The Good* Woman *of Setzuan*, largely because its central
character, Shen Te, is indeed a good and honest woman who struggles to survive in a corrupt
world. However, Brecht's German title was *Der Gute Mensch von Setzuan*. "Mensch" is derived from an Old High German word (*mennisco*) which means "man" in the most generic
sense, that is, "humanity" or "human being." Hence, "person" is more accurate than
"woman." It is also worth noting that a *mensch* in the Yiddish idiom is "a person of integrity
and honor"; Brecht may have known this meaning since Yiddish (an amalgam of Hebrew
and German) was commonly spoken in Germany. More accurately, a *mensch* is often used
cynically to refer to "the little guy" whose integrity is constantly challenged by the un-
scrupulous. In this sense, a *mensch* is a "sucker" who is easily preyed upon by con artists.

These distinctions are significant because they help us understand Brecht's intentions. Shen Te is more than a former prostitute who comes into some money and opens a
small tobacco shop to earn an honest living. (Brecht frequently uses such irony in his
plays: the prostitute is ultimately the most moral person in the society.) To her dismay
Shen Te soon discovers that she can survive in her honest trade only when she assumes
the role of a nefarious male cousin, Shui Ta, who is as ruthless as he is callous. In this sense
Shen Te is neither woman nor man, and the generic *mensch*—a person, irrespective of
gender—is appropriate.

Mensch, in its Yiddish sense, is also applicable because Shen Te, without her mean-
spirited alter ego, is very much a "sucker." Her innate goodness and her propensity to see
others as honest first earns her money (when she provides shelter to the three gods who
seek an honest human), but later brings her misery. She is exploited by the wealthy, by her
poor neighbors, and most importantly by her lover, the penniless pilot who is after her
money. Only in the guise of Shui Ta can she protect herself, her fortune, and finally her
child. Her confession in the final scene crystallizes her dilemma:

> But to be good to others
> And myself at the same time
> I could not do it
> Your world is not an easy one, illustrious ones!
> When we extend our hand to a beggar, he tears it off for us
> When we help the lost, we are lost ourselves.

That Brecht indicts ruthless exploiters like the factory owner Shui Ta and his equally
corrupt manager Yang Sun is to be expected; they epitomize the capitalist bosses who were
skewered in many agitprop dramas of the 1930s. But Brecht is also as acid in his treatment
of the poor. Mrs. Shin, although comical, is every bit as greedy and exploitive as Shui Ta.
Brecht is not indifferent to the plight of the poor and oppressed; rather, he scolds them
(and audiences who identify with them) for not taking matters into their own hands to
create the changes to improve their lot.

The Good Woman of Setzuan, however, seems to suggest that change is impossible in
this world. The play ends without a satisfactory resolution as the very gods who can effect
change abandon Shen Te and float back to heaven on a pink cloud with the admonition
that "The world should *not* be changed!" This ending, a perverse parody of the ancient
deus ex machina ending in which gods were literally lowered onto the stage to resolve
human problems, further complicates the situation. Little wonder Shen Te can only
scream "Help!" as the curtain falls.

Brecht's artificial and purposefully unresolved ending for *The Good Woman of Setzuan*
is as contrived as those of the old nineteenth-century melodrama that dispensed poetic
justice to all. Like Shaw, with whom he is a kindred spirit, Brecht also borrowed well-

known theater forms and subverted them to challenge audiences' attitudes. *The Good Woman of Setzuan* is a parody of the "rags-to-riches" melodrama, with elements of the "damsel in distress" generously incorporated. That his refashioned melodrama ends unsatisfactorily should not imply pessimism on Brecht's part. Rather, the ending represents the quintessentially Brechtian technique of depriving the audience of a catharsis in order to provoke them, instead, to action. He believed that the theater was not the place to solve worldly problems by punishing transgressors, which is why he condemned the old Aristotelian theater as "barbaric." His purpose was to identify social ills and arouse audiences' indignation at them. He challenges them to return to the streets to eradicate injustice through political action. Herein we find the optimism of Brecht's works, however cynical they may appear. Although the gods refuse to issue a verdict or "renounce the rules" that permit the Shui Ta's of the world to hold sway, in Brecht's estimation, the gods sitting in the seats beyond the stage can—and must.

Other perspectives on *The Good Woman of Setzuan*:

Lennox, Sue. "Women in Brecht's Works." *New German Critique* 14 (1978): 83–96.

Morley. Michael. "The Exceptional Individual." In Michael Morley, *Brecht: A Study*. London: Roman and Littlefield, 1977, 46–66.

Another play by Brecht on video/film:

Mack the Knife (*The Threepenny Opera*). Dir. Menahem Golen. Perf. Raul Julia, Richard Harris, and Julie Waters. Highlight Communications, 148 min., 1989.

Video about Brecht:

Bertolt Brecht. Films for the Humanities, 53 min., 1986.

SHOWCASE   THE CONVENTIONS OF CHINESE THEATER

The Chinese theater has not (until only recently) conspicuously attempted to portray life in realistic terms on its stages. It is a symbolic, exquisitely stylized theater that uses a sophisticated system of gestures, poses, stage properties, costumes, and musical accompaniment. It was precisely these antirealistic devices that attracted Bertolt Brecht, who saw in them the means to achieve his "alienation effects." Though there are specific differences among the many styles of Chinese theater, there are general conventions that may help you understand this venerable theater form. Of more immediate concern, they will provide you with another useful perspective from which to view Brecht's work.

The Peking Opera of China is among the most colorful forms of theater in the world. In this photo we can see its roots in martial arts and dance, as well as music and storytelling. Since the mid-twentieth century, the theater of Asia has had an important influence on Western theater.

deliberately shapes the ending of *The Good Woman of Setzuan* to undercut any notion of poetic justice; he believed it is the audience, not the dramatist, who must bring justice to the world.

Staging Devices

Traditionally, the Chinese theater—like that of Brecht—uses a minimum of scenery. Most stories are told with the aid of a couple of wooden chairs and a large box or table that is either painted in red and gold or covered by a bright cloth. These few stage properties are all that are needed to tell even the most complex tales. A chair may be sat upon, but it can also be jumped off to suggest a leap from a high place; or it might be leapt over to suggest a suicide (e.g., jumping into a river or into a well). At other times the chair can suggest locale: the slats of the chair back can suggest a prison; tilted sideways it can represent a gate. The box serves as a desk, a throne, or a rock; it may also be a hiding place or a large object such as a wall. *The Good Woman of Setzuan* invites such inventive staging, and in another Brecht play (*The Caucasian Chalk Circle*), the playwright actually asks that a bridge be built by placing a board between two chairs.

More importantly, actors use movement and gesture to define locale. Perhaps the best known of these is the "threshold" effect (*k'ua men chien*): when actors want to suggest that they are entering a building, they lift their legs ceremoniously to step over the doorsill, which is customarily about eight inches high in Chinese houses. If they are moving from one locale to another, actors merely circle the stage; they circle it twice for longer

Playwriting

Chinese audiences have not lost their fascination with plays that are centuries old, and consequently there is a relatively small number of works in the repertory. In fact, it is not uncommon for Chinese theater troupes to perform a series of acts taken from a variety of famous plays in an evening. Because the plots are well known, playwrights do not need to obey the laws of strict logic. Time and place are manipulated freely for dramatic effect, plays may contain scores of scenes (cf. the Epic Theatre), historical accuracy is not obligatory, and soliloquies, asides, and other presentational modes are commonplace. These are elements central to Brecht's dramaturgy. The plays of Chinese opera represent dramatic storytelling at its most flexible as readers and audiences alike are, according to Chinese scholar Harold Acton, "translated into the Kingdom of the Imagination."

Confucianism is inherent in the Chinese culture and its literature. At the risk of oversimplifying a complex issue, Confucianism is a moralistic ideology that teaches correct codes of behavior. There is a well-defined sense of right and wrong which gives rise to the principles of poetic justice. Virtue must be rewarded, particularly patience, the paramount virtue of Confucianism; vice must be punished. Such beliefs are also embodied in the teachings of China's most notable spiritual movements, Buddhism and Taoism. Thus it is not surprising that retribution plays should be integral to Chinese drama. There is not, however, a well-defined sense of tragedy in the Chinese theater, for it was the duty of the playwright to see that the truly good were rewarded and that the transgressors were punished by the final curtain. Liu Wu-chi notes that from the Chinese point of view "it would be a blemish in a literary work not to give its [audience] a sense of satisfaction in the ultimate vindication and triumph of the good and virtuous." Recall that Brecht journeys. A rider defines his horse by use of a whip and a ceremoniously lifted leg to suggest mounting the horse. An oar or long pole is sufficient to suggest the entirety of a boat; in fact, it was this specific technique that attracted Brecht when he saw Mei Lan-fang perform in Russia, and it inspired his famous essay, "Alienation Effects in Chinese Acting."[1]

Actors also employ simple yet highly effective emblems to further the color and invention of the Chinese theater. Black-clad actors (who are therefore not "seen" by the audience) wave blue silk scarves rhythmically to suggest water. Snowstorms are defined by tossing white confetti, while thunderstorms are created by billowing black cloth. Two yellow flags held horizontally define a chariot or cart; its passengers merely walk between the flags. Ghosts are identified by long strips of white paper affixed to an actor's right ear (and by the cacophony of fireworks set off by stagehands). Gods carry a horsehair switch and enter to the sound of a reverent gong. A yellow cloth over the face denotes a sick person; the dead wear a red cloth. Each of these devices, and many more, contribute to the alienation effect, as audiences are reminded that they are watching a metaphorical, as opposed to actual, representation of life.

A 1925 visitor to an opera in Peking recalls a particularly imaginative illustration of the power of Chinese staging conventions. The play required the slaughter of a pig on stage. An actor with a black cloth over his head mimed the movement of a pig, driven by another actor carrying a swineherd's stick. The actor-pig placed his head on the chair while the butcher mimed the beheading, after which the cloth was removed from the man's head. Now neither actor nor pig, the man simply walked upright off stage to conclude the scene.

Acting Technique

In addition to the many pantomimic gestures employed by actors, Chinese performers are bound by a number of highly refined body movements that denote

[1]Brecht wrote a note on the manuscript of his essay: "This essay arose out of a performance by Mei Lan-fang's company in Moscow in spring [May] 1935."

character. To illustrate, consider hand gestures. Female roles (whether played by a woman or a man) require specialized pointing gestures; never is "she" permitted to expose her thumb, which is hidden by the middle finger. A male juvenile (the *hsiao-sheng*) keeps his thumb as inconspicuous as possible, while the *lao-sheng* (a "painted face" depicting a warrior or bandit-hero) sticks his thumb up and extends both middle and index finger before him. There are also a wide variety of walks and foot movements for specific character types that must be mastered. There is even a popular comic character known exclusively by his walk—the mischievous "hobbler" who drags a withered leg about the stage.

In addition to these essentially mimetic techniques, Chinese actors must learn to manipulate costumes and accessories. To cite but a single example, imagine the various uses of the "water sleeves" (*shui hsui*—because their movement suggests rippling water). The sleeves, which adorn traditional costumes, are about two feet long. They denote a variety of symbolic meanings, and they signal the orchestra that the actor will begin singing. Sleeve movements, performed rhythmically to the musical accompaniment, suggest a variety of emotional states. For instance, when both arms are used simultaneously, the movement suggests worry. There are similar movements for hats, fans, and warrior feathers.

Even stranger to non-Chinese audiences than the physical actions, which are usually recognizable to the most naive visitor, are the vocal techniques. There is a specific vocal signature for the major character types. The dignified male roles (*lao-sheng*) are softer and more pleasant to listen to, being neither too high-pitched nor too harsh. By contrast, the young man (*hsiao-sheng*) must have a shrill, high-pitched voice to suggest the voice change of adolescence. The women's roles (*tan*) are divided into a half-dozen types, each with a recognizable vocal quality. The virtuous woman (*ching i*) has a pure, high-pitched voice, while the flirtatious *hua-tan* sings in a nasal voice. Thus Chinese actors do not attempt to identify with their characters but rather play the "type." Brecht's concept of "gestus" (i.e., playing one's social type) is a variant on this age-old tradition.

Because the Chinese language is tonal (i.e., the meaning of a word is determined by the voice inflection), there is an extraordinary musicality in Chinese speech. It is heightened in the theater by the use of meter and rhyme. Actors must learn some thirteen different rhyming formulas for their work. Among the most popular is the *shu pan*, a comic tour de force. The *shu pan* is a gigantic tongue twister requiring accelerated speech and body movement. Specialized vocal effects mark entrances and exits. Upon entrance, all principal roles perform the *yin tzu*, a two- to four-line poem that is half sung, half recited, to introduce a character. *The Good Woman of Setzuan* provides examples of this tradition, particularly in the sequences involving Wong, the Water Seller. Given the rigorous physical and vocal techniques demanded by the traditions of the Chinese theater, actors must spend up to seven years training for their profession.

Music and Sound

Perhaps no aspect of Chinese theater is more daunting to untrained ears than the cacophony of sound produced by the small orchestra (seven to nine musicians) who sit in "The Den of the Seven Dragons," a screened area "off left." Banging cymbals and gongs, the sharp retort of drums and percussive sticks (*pan*), and the shrill wail of the two-stringed fiddle (*hu ch'in*) can indeed be overwhelming to the uninitiated. Chinese opera music is built not on Western harmonic scales but on those introduced by the Mongols in the eleventh century. Music and Chinese theater are inseparable: without music the actors cannot function. Entrances and exits are ceremoniously heralded by music that defines the character. The orchestra punctuates every piece of stage business, whether by a simple, reverent gong or a crescendo of all instruments. The musicians, by the way, do not use sheet music: they have memorized the entire repertory of the company of which they are indispensable members. As with the acting and staging devices, music in the Chinese theater is used to emphasize the artificiality of the performance. Brecht himself used music throughout his plays, much of it as dissonant as that of the Chinese opera.

A MOON FOR THE MISBEGOTTEN

EUGENE O'NEILL

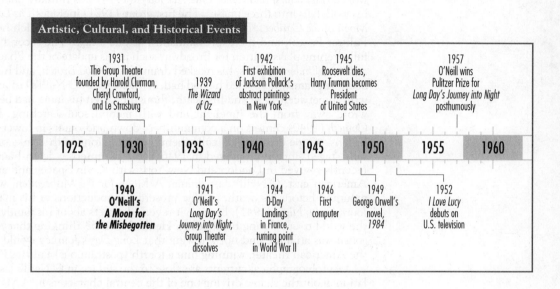

Artistic, Cultural, and Historical Events

1931 The Group Theater founded by Harold Clurman, Cheryl Crawford, and Le Strasburg	**1939** *The Wizard of Oz*	**1942** First exhibition of Jackson Pollack's abstract paintings in New York		**1945** Roosevelt dies, Harry Truman becomes President of United States			**1957** O'Neill wins Pulitzer Prize for *Long Day's Journey into Night* posthumously

1925	1930	1935	1940	1945	1950	1955	1960

1940 O'Neill's *A Moon for the Misbegotten*	**1941** O'Neill's *Long Day's Journey into Night*; Group Theater dissolves	**1944** D-Day Landings in France, turning point in World War II	**1946** First computer	**1949** George Orwell's novel, *1984*	**1952** *I Love Lucy* debuts on U.S. television	

EUGENE O'NEILL (1888–1953)

Eugene O'Neill, one of the most significant figures in the history of the American theater, was the first U.S.-born playwright to achieve an international reputation. During much of his career he experimented restlessly with style and form, bringing to American audiences Expressionism (*The Hairy Ape*), the stream-of-consciousness monologue (*Strange Interlude*), domesticated Greek tragedy (*Mourning Becomes Electra*), the new psychological realism (*Long Day's Journey into Night*), and other innovations explored by European writers. As a founding playwright of the Provincetown Players, he became the architect of an American tradition in theater, introducing techniques that are now staples of drama in the United States and creating with the Provincetown group and at the Theater Guild in New York an art theater that later became the model for America's regional theater movement.

O'Neill was the son of a leading nineteenth-century Irish-American actor, James Tyrone O'Neill. The father traded his artistic potential in a varied repertory for the chance to tour for many years in a single star vehicle: he played the swashbuckling title role in the romantic melodrama, *The Count of Monte Cristo*. Eugene was born in a New York hotel, and his early itinerant childhood was a hardship on his mother, a beautiful convent girl who became addicted to morphine. The playwright's difficult family life—a penny-pinching alcoholic father, a depressed mother, and a hard-drinking actor brother, James—as well as his passionate love-hate relationship with all three became the material for two of his finest, most profoundly truthful plays: *Long Day's Journey into Night*, produced after his death, and *A Moon for the Misbegotten*, first staged in 1944.

321

The young O'Neill enrolled for a time at Princeton University, but he failed there and left on a gold-prospecting expedition to Honduras, which ended in illness. He then became a stage manager, a tramp, an actor, a sailor, and a reporter, sometimes working on cattle steamers and around the docks, gaining the experience of men and manners that fed a linked series of early one-acts, the sea plays. O'Neill began writing when he was bedridden for six months in 1912, recovering in a sanatorium from tuberculosis. By then he knew not only the simple melodramas of his father's time but also the works of Shakespeare, the dramas of Ibsen, the depth psychology of Strindberg, and something of the experimental trends in Germany and Ireland.

By 1914, O'Neill had written twelve one-acts and two longer plays. Of these early works, only *Thirst and Other One-Act Plays* (1914) was initially published. From then on, his work falls into three phases. The first group (1921) includes *The Long Voyage Home, The Moon of the Caribbees, Beyond the Horizon, Anna Christie* (for which he won his first of four Pulitzer Prizes), and the expressionistic *The Hairy Ape*. The second phase includes many full-evening plays written for Broadway such as his update of the Phaedra-Hippolytus myth as *Desire Under the Elms*, his masked drama *Great God Brown*, and his only comedy, a play about the family he wished he had had, *Ah Wilderness!* O'Neill's last and greatest plays were written between 1938 and his death, though by then his fame had begun to recede and he wrote away from the limelight and with painful soul-searching. His epic *The Iceman Cometh* (1940) centers on a community of down-and-outers in lower New York and the illusions—"pipe dreams," he calls them—which, along with drink, sustain them. Successfully staged since it premiered in 1946, the long, intense, death-haunted drama was most recently revived in London and New York with Kevin Spacey and an all-star English and American cast. O'Neill's last drama, *A Moon for the Misbegotten*, was never successfully mounted before his death, and he proscribed productions of his masterpiece, *Long Day's Journey into Night* (1941), because it revealed secrets about his family that he did not want the world to see during his lifetime. He died in 1953 thinking that *A Moon for the Misbegotten* was a failure and not knowing that *Long Day's Journey* would become a bulwark of the American theater, winning him a fourth (posthumous) Pulitzer Prize for drama.

Autobiographical currents are close to the surface in O'Neill's last dramas. A key revelation about the shame driving one of the central characters in *A Moon for the Misbegotten*, James Tyrone, Jr., derives from the real life of O'Neill's brother "Jamie," who accompanied their mother's corpse from California just after she died on February 28, 1922. Jamie and the coffin arrived by train from the West Coast on the night *The Hairy Ape* opened on Broadway. O'Neill neither met the train nor attended the opening, though both the death and the critically acclaimed play proved pivotal. *The Hairy Ape*, about the tormented stoker Yank, is generally considered a watershed for O'Neill, the drama that led to his mature period. So, too, did the death of his mother, Ella, prove a turning point, leading the playwright inward to the psychological landscape explored in his plays from 1922 until his death.

O'Neill is the only American playwright to win the Nobel Prize for literature, and although some theater historians still point to the limitations of his works—a lack of control, a certain awkwardness of expression, and a diffuse rather than compact structure—he remains the preeminent force who revolutionized American drama. He's also one of the few twentieth-century playwrights anywhere whose work has theatrical immediacy, emotional intensity, and a truly tragic dimension.

AS YOU READ *A MOON FOR THE MISBEGOTTEN*

Jose Quintero, who directed a landmark revival of *A Moon for the Misbegotten* in New York in 1973, wrote that it deals with "two people who can't possibly believe they are worthy of love; who can't possibly believe that they can create a tender feeling in anyone. . . . O'Neill creates a moon which sheds a healing glow into the numerous hidden caves of their hearts." As you read the play you might look for these "hidden caves of the heart" to see what secrets Jim Tyrone and Josie Hogan keep there and what healing happens (or doesn't) over the course of their evening under the moon.

A MOON FOR THE MISBEGOTTEN

EUGENE O'NEILL

CHARACTERS

JOSIE HOGAN
PHIL HOGAN, *her father*
MIKE HOGAN, *her brother*

JAMES TYRONE, JR.
T. STEDMAN HARDER

SCENES

Act I: The farmhouse. Around noon. Early September, 1923.

Act II: The same, but with the interior of sitting room revealed—11 o'clock that night.

Act III: The same as Act I. No time elapses between Acts II and III.

Act IV: The same—Dawn of the following morning.

SCENE OF THE PLAY

The play takes place in Connecticut at the home of tenant farmer, Phil Hogan, between the hours of noon on a day in early September, 1923, and sunrise of the following day.

The house is not, to speak mildly, a fine example of New England architecture, placed so perfectly in its setting that it appears a harmonious part of the landscape, rooted in the earth. It has been moved to its present site, and looks it. An old box-like, clapboarded affair, with a shingled roof and brick chimney, it is propped up about two feet above ground by layers of timber blocks. There are two windows on the lower floor of this side of the house which faces front, and one window on the floor above. These windows have no shutters, curtains or shades. Each has at least one pane missing, a square of cardboard taking its place.

The house had once been painted a repulsive yellow with brown trim, but the walls now are a blackened and weathered gray, flaked with streaks and splotches of dim lemon. Just around the left corner of the house, a flight of steps leads to the front door.

To make matters worse, a one-story, one-room addition has been tacked on at right. About twelve feet long by six high, this room, which is Josie Hogan's bedroom, is evidently homemade. Its walls and sloping roof are covered with tarpaper, faded to dark gray. Close to where it joins the house, there is a door with a flight of three unpainted steps leading to the ground. At right of door is a small window.

From these steps is a footpath going around an old pear tree, at right-rear, through a field of hay stubble to a patch of woods. The same path also extends left to join a dirt road which leads up from the county highway (about a hundred yards off left) to the front door of the house, and thence back through a scraggly orchard of apple trees to the barn. Close to the house, under the window next to Josie's bedroom, there is a big boulder with a flat top.

ACT I

Scene: As described. It is just before noon. The day is clear and hot.

The door of Josie's bedroom opens and she comes out on the steps, bending to avoid bumping her head.

Josie is twenty-eight. She is so oversize for a woman that she is almost a freak—five feet eleven in her stockings and weighs around one hundred and eighty. Her sloping shoulders are broad, her chest deep with large, firm breasts, her waist wide but *slender by contrast with her hips and thighs. She has long smooth arms, immensely strong, although no muscles show. The same is true of her legs.*

She is more powerful than any but an exceptionally strong man, able to do the manual labor of two ordinary men. But there is no mannish quality about her. She is all woman.

The map of Ireland is stamped on her face, with its long upper lip and small nose, thick black eyebrows, black hair as coarse as a horse's mane, freckled, sunburned fair skin, high cheekbones and heavy jaw. It is not a pretty face, but her large dark-blue eyes give it a note of beauty, and her smile, revealing even white teeth, gives it charm.

She wears a cheap, sleeveless, blue cotton dress. Her feet are bare, the soles earth-stained and tough as leather.

She comes down the steps and goes left to the corner of the house and peers around it toward the barn. Then she moves swiftly to the right of the house and looks back.

JOSIE. Ah, thank God. (*She goes back toward the steps as her brother, Mike, appears hurrying up from right-rear.*)

(*Mike Hogan is twenty, about four inches shorter than his sister. He is sturdily built, but seems almost puny compared to her. He has a common Irish face, its expression sullen, or slyly cunning, or primly self-righteous. He never forgets that he is a good Catholic, faithful to all the observances, and so is one of the élite of Almighty God in a world of damned sinners composed of Protestants and bad Catholics. In brief, Mike is a New England Irish Catholic Puritan, Grade B, and an extremely irritating youth to have around.*)

(*Mike wears dirty overalls, a sweat-stained brown shirt. He carries a pitchfork.*)

JOSIE. Bad luck to you for a slowpoke. Didn't I tell you half-past eleven?

MIKE. How could I sneak here sooner with him peeking around the corner of the barn to catch me if I took a minute's rest, the way he always does? I had to wait till he went to the pig pen. (*He adds viciously*) Where he belongs, the old hog! (*Josie's right arm strikes with surprising swiftness and her big hand lands on the side of his jaw. She means it to be only a slap, but his head jerks back and he stumbles, dropping the pitchfork, and pleads cringingly.*) Don't hit me, Josie! Don't now!

JOSIE (*Quietly*). Then keep your tongue off him. He's my father, too, and I like him, if you don't.

MIKE (*Out of her reach—sullenly*). You're two of a kind, and a bad kind.

JOSIE (*Good-naturedly*). I'm proud of it. And I didn't hit you, or you'd be flat on the ground. It was only a love tap to waken your wits, so you'll use them. If he catches you running away, he'll beat you half to death. Get your bag now. I've packed it. It's inside the door of my room with your coat laid over it. Hurry now, while I see what he's doing. (*She moves quickly to peer around the corner of the house at left. He goes up the steps into her room and returns carrying an old coat and a cheap bulging satchel. She comes back.*) There's no sight of him. (*Mike drops the satchel on the ground while he puts on the coat.*) I put everything in the bag. You can change to your Sunday suit in the can at the station or in the train, and don't forget to wash your face. I know you want to look your best when our brother, Thomas, sees you on his doorstep. (*Her tone becomes derisively amused.*) And him way up in the world, a noble sergeant of the Bridgeport police. Maybe he'll get you on the force. It'd suit you. I can see you leading drunks to the lockup while you give them a lecture on temperance. Or if Thomas can't get you a job, he'll pass you along to our brother, John, the noble barkeep in Meriden. He'll teach you the trade. You'll make a nice one, who'll never steal from the till, or drink, and who'll tell customers they've had enough and better go home just when they're beginning to feel happy. (*She sighs regretfully.*) Ah, well, Mike, you was born a priest's pet, and there's no help for it.

MIKE. That's right! Make fun of me again, because I want to be decent.

JOSIE. You're worse than decent. You're virtuous.

MIKE. Well, that's a thing nobody can say about—(*He stops, a bit ashamed, but mostly afraid to finish.*)

JOSIE. (*Amused*). About me? No, and what's more, they don't. (*She smiles mockingly.*) I know what a trial it's been to you, Mike, having a sister who's the scandal of the neighborhood.

MIKE. It's you that's saying it, not me. I don't want to part with hard feelings. And I'll keep on praying for you.

JOSIE (*Roughly*). Och! To hell with your prayers!

MIKE (*Stiffly*). I'm going. (*He picks up his bag.*)

JOSIE (*Her manner softening*). Wait. (*She comes to him.*) Don't mind my rough tongue, Mike. I'm sorry to see you go, but it's the best thing for you. That's why I'm helping you, the same as I helped Thomas and John. You can't stand up to the Old Man any more than

Thomas or John could, and the old divil would always keep you a slave. I wish you all the luck in the world, Mike. I know you'll get on—and God bless you. (*Her voice has softened, and she blinks back tears. She kisses him—then fumbling in the pocket of her dress, pulls out a little roll of one-dollar bills and presses it in his hand.*) Here's a little present over your fare. I took it from his little green bag, and won't he be wild when he finds out! But I can handle him.

MIKE (*Enviously*). You can. You're the only one. (*Gratefully moved for a second*) Thank you, Josie. You've a kind heart. (*Then virtuously*) But I don't like taking stolen money.

JOSIE. Don't be a bigger jackass than you are already. Tell your conscience it's a bit of the wages he's never given you.

MIKE. That's true, Josie. It's rightfully mine. (*He shoves the money into his pocket.*)

JOSIE. Get along now, so you won't miss the trolley. And don't forget to get off the train at Bridgeport. Give my love to Thomas and John. No, never mind. They've not written me in years. Give them a boot in the tail for me.

MIKE. That's nice talk for a woman. You've a tongue as dirty as the Old Man's.

JOSIE (*Impatiently*). Don't start preaching, like you love to, or you'll never go.

MIKE. You're as bad as he is, almost. It's his influence made you what you are, and him always scheming how he'll cheat people, selling them a broken-down nag or a sick cow or a pig that he's doctored up to look good for a day or two. It's no better than stealing, and you help him.

JOSIE. I do. Sure, it's grand fun.

MIKE. You ought to marry and have a home of your own away from this shanty and stop your shameless ways with men. (*He adds, not without moral satifaction.*) Though it'd be hard to find a decent man who'd have you now.

JOSIE. I don't want a decent man, thank you. They're no fun. They're all sticks like you. And I wouldn't marry the best man on earth and be tied down to him alone.

MIKE (*With a cunning leer*). Not even Jim Tyrone, I suppose? (*She stares at him.*) You'd like being tied to money, I know that, and he'll be rich when his mother's estate is settled. (*Sarcastically*) I suppose you've never thought of that? Don't tell me! I've watched you making sheep's eyes at him.

JOSIE (*Contemptuously*). So I'm leading Jim on to propose, am I?

MIKE. I know it's crazy, but maybe you're hoping if you got hold of him alone when he's mad drunk—Anyway, talk as you please to put me off, I'll bet my last penny you've cooked up some scheme to hook him, and the Old Man put you up to it. Maybe he thinks if he caught you with Jim and had witnesses to prove it, and his shotgun to scare him—

JOSIE (*Controlling her anger*). You're full of bright thoughts. I wouldn't strain my brains any more, if I was you.

MIKE. Well, I wouldn't put it past the Old Man to try any trick. And I wouldn't put it past you, God forgive you. You've never cared about your virtue, or what man you went out with. You've always been brazen as brass and proud of your disgrace. You can't deny that, Josie.

JOSIE. I don't. (*Then ominously*) You'd better shut up now. I've been holding my temper, because we're saying good-bye. (*She stands up.*) But I'm losing patience.

MIKE (*Hastily*). Wait till I finish and you won't be mad at me. I was going to say I wish you luck with your scheming, for once. I hate Jim Tyrone's guts, with his quotin' Latin and his high-toned Jesuit College education, putting on airs as if he was too good to wipe his shoes on me, when he's nothing but a drunken bum who never done a tap of work in his life, except acting on the stage while his father was alive to get him the jobs. (*Vindictively*) I'll pray you'll find a way to nab him, Josie, and skin him out of his last nickel!

JOSIE (*Makes a threatening move toward him*). One more word out of you—(*Then contemptuously*) You're a dirty tick and it'd serve you right if I let you stay gabbing until Father came and beat you to a jelly, but I won't. I'm too anxious to be rid of you. (*Roughly*) Get out of here, now! Do you think he'll stay all day with the pigs, you gabbing fool? (*She goes left to peer around the corner of the house—with real alarm.*) There he is, coming up to the barn. (*Mike grabs the satchel, terrified. He slinks swiftly around the corner and disappears along the path to the woods, right-rear. She keeps watching her father and does not notice Mike's departure.*) He's looking toward the meadow. He sees you're not working. He's running down there. He'll come here next. You'd better run for your life! (*She turns and sees he's gone—contemptuously.*) I might have known. I'll bet you're a mile away by now, you rabbit! (*She peeks around the corner again—with amused admiration.*) Look at my poor old father pelt. He's as spry on his stumpy legs as a yearling—and as full of rage as a nest of wasps! (*She laughs and comes back to look along the path to the woods.*) Well, that's the last of you, Mike, and good riddance. It was the little boy you used to be that I had to mother, and not you, I stole the money for. (*This dis-*

misses him. *She sighs*.) Well, himself will be here in a minute. I'd better be ready. (*She reaches in her bedroom corner by the door and takes out a sawed-off broom handle*.) Not that I need it, but it saves his pride. (*She sits on the steps with the broom handle propped against the steps near her right hand. A moment later, her father, Phil Hogan, comes running up from left-rear and charges around the corner of the house, his arms pumping up and down, his fists clenched, his face full of fighting fury*.)

(*Hogan is fifty-five, about five feet six. He has a thick neck, lumpy, sloping shoulders, a barrel-like trunk, stumpy legs, and big feet. His arms are short and muscular, with large hairy hands. His head is round with thinning sandy hair. His face is fat with a snub nose, long upper lip, big mouth, and little blue eyes and bleached lashes and eyebrows that remind one of a white pig's. He wears heavy brogans, filthy overalls, and a dirty short-sleeved undershirt. Arms and face are sunburned and freckled. On his head is an old wide-brimmed hat of coarse straw that would look more becoming on a horse. His voice is high-pitched with a pronounced brogue.*)

HOGAN (*Stops as he turns the corner and sees her— furiously*). Where is he? Is he hiding in the house? I'll wipe the floors with him, the lazy bastard! (*Turning his anger against her*) Haven't you a tongue in your head, you great slut you?

JOSIE (*With provoking calm*). Don't be calling me names, you bad-tempered old hornet, or maybe I'll lose my temper, too.

HOGAN. To hell with your temper, you overgrown cow!

JOSIE. I'd rather be a cow than an ugly little buck goat. You'd better sit down and cool off. Old men shouldn't run around raging in the noon sun. You'll get sunstroke.

HOGAN. To hell with sunstroke! Have you seen him?

JOSIE. Have I seen who?

HOGAN. Mike! Who else would I be after, the Pope? He was in the meadow, but the minute I turned my back he sneaked off. (*He sees the pitchfork*.) There's his pitchfork! Will you stop your lying!

JOSIE. I haven't said I didn't see him.

HOGAN. Then don't try to help him hide from me, or— Where is he?

JOSIE. Where you'll never find him.

HOGAN. We'll soon see! I'll bet he's in your room under the bed, the cowardly lump! (*He moves toward the steps.*)

JOSIE. He's not. He's gone like Thomas and John before him to escape your slave-driving.

HOGAN (*Stares at her incredulously*). You mean he's run off to make his own way in the world?

JOSIE. He has. So make up your mind to it, and sit down.

HOGAN (*Baffled, sits on the boulder and takes off his hat to scratch his head—with a faint trace of grudging respect*). I'd never dream he had that much spunk. (*His temper rising again*) And I know damned well he hadn't, not without you to give him the guts and help him, like the great soft fool you are!

JOSIE. Now don't start raging again, Father.

HOGAN (*Seething*). You've stolen my satchel to give him, I suppose, like you did before for Thomas and John?

JOSIE. It was my satchel, too. Didn't I help you in the trade for the horse, when you got the Crowleys to throw in the satchel for good measure? I was up all night fixing that nag's forelegs so his knees wouldn't buckle together till after the Crowleys had him a day or two.

HOGAN (*Forgets his anger to grin reminiscently*). You've a wonderful way with animals, God bless you. And do you remember the two Crowleys came back to give me a beating, and I licked them both?

JOSIE (*With calculating flattery*). You did. You're a wonderful fighter. Sure, you could give Jack Dempsey himself a run for his money.

HOGAN (*With sharp suspicion*). I could, but don't try to change the subject and fill me with blarney.

JOSIE. All right. I'll tell the truth then. They were getting the best of you till I ran out and knocked one of them tail over tin cup against the pigpen.

HOGAN (*Outraged*). You're a liar! They was begging for mercy before you came. (*Furiously*) You thief, you! You stole my fine satchel for that lump! And I'll bet that's not all. I'll bet, like when Thomas and John sneaked off, you—(*He rises from the boulder threateningly.*) Listen, Josie, if you found where I hid my little green bag, and stole my money to give to that lousy altar boy, I'll—

JOSIE (*Rises from the steps with the broom handle in her right hand*). Well, I did. So now what'll you do? Don't be threatening me. You know I'll beat better sense in your skull if you lay a finger on me.

HOGAN. I never yet laid hands on a woman—not when I was sober—but if it wasn't for that club—(*Bitterly*) A fine curse God put on me when he gave me a daughter as big and strong as a bull, and as vicious and disrespectful. (*Suddenly his eyes twinkle and he grins admiringly.*) Be God, look at you standing there with the club! If you ain't the damnedest daughter in Connecticut, who is? (*He chuckles and sits on the boulder again.*)

JOSIE (*Laughs and sits on the steps, putting the club away*). And if you ain't the damnedest father in Connecticut, who is?

HOGAN (*Takes a clay pipe and plug of tobacco and knife from his pocket. He cuts the plug and stuffs his pipe—without rancor*). How much did you steal, Josie?

JOSIE. Six dollars only.

HOGAN. *Only!* Well, God grant someone with wits will see that dopey gander at the depot and sell him the railroad for the six. (*Grumbling*) It isn't the money I mind, Josie—

JOSIE. I know. Sure, what do you care for money? You'd give your last penny to the first beggar you met—if he had a shotgun pointed at your heart!

HOGAN. Don't be teasing. You know what I mean. It's the thought of that pious lump having my money that maddens me. I wouldn't put it past him to drop it in the collection plate next Sunday, he's that big a jackass.

JOSIE. I knew when you'd calmed down you'd think it worth six dollars to see the last of him.

HOGAN (*Finishes filling his pipe*). Well, maybe I do. To tell the truth, I never liked him. (*He strikes a match on the seat of his overalls and lights his pipe.*) And I never liked Thomas and John, either.

JOSIE (*Amused*). You've the same bad luck in sons I have in brothers.

HOGAN (*Puffs ruminatively*). They all take after your mother's family. She was the only one in it had spirit, God rest her soul. The rest of them was a pious lousy lot. They wouldn't dare put food in their mouths before they said grace for it. They was too busy preaching temperance to have time for a drink. They spent so much time confessing their sins, they had no chance to do any sinning. (*He spits disgustedly.*) The scum of the earth! Thank God, you're like me and your mother.

JOSIE. I don't know if I should thank God for being like you. Sure, everyone says you're a wicked old tick, as crooked as a corkscrew.

HOGAN. I know. They're an envious lot, God forgive them. (*They both chuckle. He pulls on his pipe reflectively.*) You didn't get much thanks from Mike, I'll wager, for your help.

JOSIE. Oh, he thanked me kindly. And then he started to preach about my sins—and yours.

HOGAN. Oho, did he? (*Exploding*) For the love of God, why didn't you hold him till I could give him one good kick for a father's parting blessing!

JOSIE. I near gave him one myself.

HOGAN. When I think your poor mother was killed bringing that crummy calf into life! (*Vindictively*) I've never set foot in a church since, and never will. (*A pause. He speaks with a surprising sad gentleness.*) A

sweet woman. Do you remember her, Josie? You were only a little thing when she died.

JOSIE. I remember her well. (*With a teasing smile which is half sad*) She was the one could put you in your place when you'd come home drunk and want to tear down the house for the fun of it.

HOGAN (*With admiring appreciation*). Yes, she could do it, God bless her. I only raised my hand to her once— just a slap because she told me to stop singing, it was after daylight. The next moment I was on the floor thinking a mule had kicked me. (*He chuckles.*) Since you've grown up, I've had the same trouble. There's no liberty in my own home.

JOSIE. That's lucky—or there wouldn't be any home.

HOGAN (*After a pause of puffing on his pipe*). What did that donkey, Mike, preach to you about?

JOSIE. Oh, the same as ever—that I'm the scandal of the countryside, carrying on with men without a marriage license.

HOGAN (*Gives her a strange, embarrassed glance and then looks away. He does not look at her during the following dialogue. His manner is casual*). Hell roast his soul for saying it. But it's true enough.

JOSIE (*Defiantly*). It is, and what of it? I don't care a damn for the scandal.

HOGAN. No. You do as you please and to hell with everyone.

JOSIE. Yes, and that goes for you, too, if you are my father. So don't you start preaching too.

HOGAN. Me, preach? Sure, the divil would die laughing. Don't bring me into it. I learned long since to let you go your own way because there's no controlling you.

JOSIE. I do my work and I earn my keep and I've a right to be free.

HOGAN. You have. I've never denied it.

JOSIE. No. You've never. I've often wondered why a man that likes fights as much as you didn't grab at the excuse of my disgrace to beat the lights out of the men.

HOGAN. Wouldn't I look a great fool, when everyone knows any man who tried to make free with you, and you not willing, would be carried off to the hospital? Anyway, I wouldn't want to fight an army. You've had too many sweethearts.

JOSIE (*With a proud toss of her head—boastfully*). That's because I soon get tired of any man and give him his walking papers.

HOGAN. I'm afraid you were born to be a terrible wanton woman. But to tell the truth, I'm well satisfied you're what you are, though I shouldn't say it, because if you was the decent kind, you'd have married some fool long ago, and I'd have lost your company and your help on the farm.

JOSIE (*With a trace of bitterness*). Leave it to you to think of your own interest.

HOGAN (*Puffs on his pipe*). What else did my beautiful son, Mike, say to you?

JOSIE. Oh, he was full of stupid gab, as usual. He gave me good advice—

HOGAN (*Grimly*). That was kind of him. It must have been good—

JOSIE. I ought to marry and settle down—if I could find a decent man who'd have me, which he was sure I couldn't.

HOGAN (*Beginning to boil*). I tell you, Josie, it's going to be the saddest memory of my life I didn't get one last swipe at him!

JOSIE. So the only hope, he thought, was for me to catch some indecent man, who'd have money coming to him I could steal.

HOGAN (*Gives her a quick, probing side glance—casually*). He meant Jim Tyrone?

JOSIE. He did. And the dirty tick accused you and me of making up a foxy scheme to trap Jim. I'm to get him alone when he's crazy drunk and lead him on to marry me. (*She adds in a hard, scornful tone.*) As if that would ever work. Sure, all the pretty little tarts on Broadway, New York, must have had a try at that, and much good it did them.

HOGAN (*Again with a quick side glance—casually*). They must have, surely. But that's in the city where he's suspicious. You never can tell what he mightn't do here in the country, where he's innocent, with a moon in the sky to fill him with poetry and a quart of bad hootch inside of him.

JOSIE (*Turns on him angrily*). Are you taking Mike's scheme seriously, you old goat?

HOGAN. I'm not. I only thought you wanted my opinion. (*She regards him suspiciously, but his face is blank, as if he hadn't a thought beyond enjoying his pipe.*)

JOSIE (*Turning away*). And if that didn't work, Mike said maybe we had a scheme that I'd get Jim in bed with me and you'd come with witnesses and a shotgun, and catch him there.

HOGAN. Faith, me darlin' son never learnt that from his prayer book! He must have improved his mind on the sly.

JOSIE. The dirty tick!

HOGAN. Don't call him a tick: I don't like ticks but I'll say this for them, I never picked one off me yet was a hypocrite.

JOSIE. Him daring to accuse us of planning a rotten trick like that on Jim!

HOGAN (*As if he misunderstood her meaning*). Yes, it's as old as the hills. Everyone's heard of it. But it still works now and again, I'm told, and sometimes an old trick is best because it's so ancient no one would suspect you'd try it.

JOSIE (*Staring at him resentfully*). That's enough out of you, Father. I never can tell to this day, when you put that dead mug on you, whether you're joking or not, but I don't want to hear any more—

HOGAN (*Mildly*). I thought you wanted my honest opinion on the merits of Mike's suggestion.

JOSIE. Och, shut up, will you? I know you're only trying to make game of me. You like Jim and you'd never play a dirty trick on him, not even if I was willing.

HOGAN. No—not unless I found he was playing one on me.

JOSIE. Which he'd never.

HOGAN. No, I wouldn't think it, but my motto in life is never trust anyone too far, not even myself.

JOSIE. You've reason for the last. I've often suspected you sneak out of bed in the night to pick your own pockets.

HOGAN. I wouldn't call it a dirty trick on him to get you for a wife.

JOSIE (*Exasperatedly*). God save us, are you off on that again?

HOGAN. Well, you've put marriage in my head and I can't help considering the merits of the case, as they say. Sure, you're two of a kind, both great disgraces. That would help make a happy marriage because neither of you could look down on the other.

JOSIE. Jim mightn't think so.

HOGAN. You mean he'd think he was marrying beneath his station? He'd be a damned fool if he had that notion, for his Old Man who'd worked up from nothing to be rich and famous didn't give a damn about station. Didn't I often see him working on his grounds in clothes I wouldn't put on a scarecrow, not caring who saw him? (*With admiring affection*) God rest him, he was a true Irish gentleman.

JOSIE. He was, and didn't you swindle him, and make me help you at it? I remember when I was a slip of a girl, and you'd get a letter saying his agent told him you were a year behind in the rent, and he'd be damned if he'd stand for it, and he was coming here to settle the matter. You'd make me dress up, with my hair brushed and a ribbon in it, and leave me to soften his heart before he saw you. So I'd skip down the path to meet him, and make a courtesy, and hold on to his hand, and bat my eyes at him and lead him in the house, and offer him a drink of the good whiskey you didn't keep for company, and gape at him and tell him he was the handsomest man in the world, and the fierce expression he'd put on for you woud go away.

HOGAN (*Chuckles*). You did it wonderful. You should have gone on the stage.

JOSIE (*Dryly*). Yes, that's what he'd tell me, and he'd reach in his pocket and take out a half dollar, and ask me if you hadn't put me up to it. So I'd say yes, you had.

HOGAN (*Sadly*). I never knew you were such a black traitor, and you only a child.

JOSIE. And then you'd come and before he could get a word out of him, you'd tell him you'd vacate the premises unless he lowered the rent and painted the house.

HOGAN. Be God, that used to stop him in his tracks.

JOSIE. It didn't stop him from saying you were the damnedest crook ever came out of Ireland.

HOGAN. He said it with admiration. And we'd start drinking and telling stories, and singing songs, and by the time he left we were both too busy cursing England to worry over the rent. (*He grins affectionately.*) Oh, he was a great man entirely.

JOSIE. He was. He always saw through your tricks.

HOGAN. Didn't I know he would? Sure, all I wanted was to give him the fun of seeing through them so he couldn't be hard-hearted. That was the real trick.

JOSIE (*Stares at him*). You old devil, you've always a trick hidden behind your tricks, so no one can tell at times what you're after.

HOGAN. Don't be so suspicious. Sure, I'd never try to fool you. You know me too well. But we've gone off the track. It's Jim we're discussing, not his father. I was telling you I could see the merit in your marrying him.

JOSIE (*Exasperatedly*). Och, a cow must have kicked you in the head this morning.

HOGAN. I'd never give it a thought if I didn't know you had a soft spot in your heart for him.

JOSIE (*Resentfully*). Well, I haven't! I like him, if that's what you mean, but it's only to talk to, because he's educated and quiet-spoken and has politeness even when he's drunkest, and doesn't roar around cursing and singing, like some I could name.

HOGAN. If you could see the light in your eyes when he blarneys you—

JOSIE (*Roughly*). The light in me foot! (*Scornfully*) I'm in love with him, you'll be saying next!

HOGAN (*Ignores this*). And another merit of the case is, he likes you.

JOSIE. Because he keeps dropping in here lately? Sure, it's only when he gets sick of the drunks at the Inn, and it's more to joke with you than see me.

HOGAN. It's your happiness I'm considering when I recommend your using your wits to catch him, if you can.

JOSIE (*Jeeringly*). If!

HOGAN. Who knows? With all the sweethearts you've had, you must have a catching way with men.

JOSIE (*Boastfully*). Maybe I have. But that doesn't mean—

HOGAN. If you got him alone tonight—there'll be a beautiful moon to fill him with poetry and loneliness, and—

JOSIE. That's one of Mike's dirty schemes.

HOGAN. Mike be damned! Sure, that's every woman's scheme since the world was created. Without it there'd be no population. (*Persuasively*) There'd be no harm trying it, anyway.

JOSIE. And no use, either. (*Bitterly*) Och, Father, don't play the jackass with me. You know, and I know, I'm an ugly overgrown lump of a woman, and the men that want me are no better than stupid bulls. Jim can have all the pretty, painted little Broadway girls he wants—and dancers on the stage, too—when he comes into his estate. That's the kind he likes.

HOGAN. I notice he's never married one. Maybe he'd like a fine strong handsome figure of a woman for a change, with beautiful eyes and hair and teeth and a smile.

JOSIE (*Pleased, but jeering*). Thank you kindly for your compliments. Now I know a cow kicked you in the head.

HOGAN. If you think Jim hasn't been taking in your fine points, you're a fool.

JOSIE. You mean you've noticed him? (*Suddenly furious*) Stop your lying!

HOGAN. Don't fly in a temper. All I'm saying is, there may be a chance in it to better yourself.

JOSIE (*Scornfully*). Better myself by being tied down to a man who's drunk every night of his life? No, thank you!

HOGAN. Sure, you're strong enough to reform him. A taste of that club you've got, when he came home to you paralyzed, and in a few weeks you'd have him a dirty prohibitionist.

JOSIE (*Seriously*). It's true, if I was his wife, I'd cure him of drinking himself to death, if I had to kill him. (*Then angrily*) Och, I'm sick of your crazy gab, Father! Leave me alone!

HOGAN. Well, let's put it another way. Don't tell me you couldn't learn to love the estate he'll come into.

JOSIE (*Resentfully*). Ah, I've been waiting for that. That's what Mike said again. Now we've come to the truth behind all your blather of my liking him or him liking me. (*Her manner changing—defiantly*) All right then. Of course I'd love the money. Who wouldn't? And why shouldn't I get my hands on it, if I could? He's bound to be swindled out of it, anyway. He'll go back to the Broadway he thinks is heaven, and by the time the pretty little tarts, and the barroom sponges and racetrack touts and gamblers are through with him he'll be picked clean. I'm no saint, God knows, but I'm decent and deserving compared to those scum.

HOGAN (*Eagerly*). Be God, now you're using your wits. And where there's a will there's a way. You and me have never been beat when we put our brains together. I'll keep thinking it over, and you do the same.

JOSIE (*With illogical anger*). Well, I won't! And you keep your mad scheming to yourself. I won't listen to it.

HOGAN (*As if he were angry, too*). All right. The divil take you. It's all you'll hear from me. (*He pauses—then with great seriousness, turning toward her.*) Except one thing—(*As she starts to shut him up—sharply*) I'm serious, and you'd better listen, because it's about this farm, which is home to us.

JOSIE (*Surprised, stares at him*). What about the farm?

HOGAN. Don't forget, if we have lived on it twenty years, we're only tenants and we could be thrown out on our necks any time. (*Quickly*) Mind you, I don't say Jim would ever do it, rent or no rent, or let the executors do it, even if they wanted, which they don't, knowing they'd never find another tenant.

JOSIE. What's worrying you, then?

HOGAN. This. I've been afraid lately the minute the estate is out of probate, Jim will sell the farm.

JOSIE (*Exasperatedly*). Of course he will! Hasn't he told us and promised you can buy it on easy time payments at the small price you offered?

HOGAN. Jim promises whatever you like when he's full of whiskey. He might forget a promise as easy when he's drunk enough.

JOSIE (*Indignantly*). He'd never! And who'd want it except us? No one ever has in all the years—

HOGAN. Someone has lately. The agent got an offer last month, Jim told me, bigger than mine.

JOSIE. Och, Jim loves to try and get your goat. He was kidding you.

HOGAN. He wasn't. I can tell. He said he told the agent to tell whoever it was the place wasn't for sale.

JOSIE. Of course he did. Did he say who'd made the offer?

HOGAN. He didn't know. It came through a real-estate man who wouldn't tell who his client was. I've been trying to guess, but I can't think of anyone crazy enough unless it'd be some damn fool of a millionaire buying up land to make a great estate for himself, like our beautiful neighbor, Harder, the Standard Oil thief, did years ago. (*He adds with bitter fervency.*) May he roast in hell and his Limey superintendent with him!

JOSIE. Amen to that. (*Then scornfully*) This land for an estate? And if there was an offer, Jim's refused it, and that ends it. He wouldn't listen to any offer, after he's given his word to us.

HOGAN. Did I say he would—when he's in his right mind? What I'm afraid of is, he might be led into it sometime when he has one of his sneering bitter drunks on and talks like a Broadway crook himself, saying money is the only thing in the world, and everything and anyone can be bought if the price is big enough. You've heard him.

JOSIE. I have. But he doesn't fool me at all. He only acts like he's hard and shameless to get back at life when it's tormenting him—and who doesn't? (*He gives her a quick, curious side glance which she doesn't notice.*)

HOGAN. Or take the other kind of queer drunk he gets on sometimes when, without any reason you can see, he'll suddenly turn strange, and look sad, and stare at nothing as if he was mourning over some ghost inside him, and—

JOSIE. I think I know what comes over him when he's like that. It's the memory of his mother comes back and his grief for her death. (*Pityingly*) Poor Jim.

HOGAN (*Ignoring this*). And whiskey seems to have no effect on him, like water off a duck's back. He'll keep acting natural enough, and you'd swear he wasn't bad at all, but the next day you find his brain was so paralyzed he don't remember a thing until you remind him. He's done a lot of mad things, when he was that way, he was sorry for after.

JOSIE (*Scornfully*). What drunk hasn't? But he'd never— (*Resentfully*) I won't have you suspecting Jim without any cause, d'you hear me!

HOGAN. I don't suspect him. All I've said is, when a man gets as queer drunk as Jim, he doesn't know himself what he mightn't do, and we'd be damned fools if we didn't fear the possibility, however small it is, and do all we can to guard against it.

JOSIE. There's no possibility! And how could we guard against it, if there was?

HOGAN. Well, you can put yourself out to be extra nice to him, for one thing.

JOSIE. How nice is extra nice?

HOGAN. You ought to know. But here's one tip. I've noticed when you talk rough and brazen like you do to other men, he may grin like they do, as if he enjoyed it, but he don't. So watch your tongue.

JOSIE (*With a defiant toss of her head*). I'll talk as I please, and if he don't like it he can lump it! (*Scornfully*) I'm to pretend I'm a pure virgin, I suppose? That would fool him, wouldn't it, and him hearing all about me from the men at the Inn? (*She gets to her feet, abruptly changing the subject.*) We're wasting the day, blathering. (*Then her face hardening.*) If he ever went back on his word, no matter how drunk he was, I'd be with you in any scheme you made against him, no matter how dirty. (*Hastily*) But it's all your nonsense. I'd never believe it. (*She comes and picks up the pitchfork.*) I'll go to the meadow and finish Mike's work. You needn't fear you'll miss his help on the farm.

HOGAN. A hell of a help! A weak lazy back and the appetite of a drove of starving pigs! (*As she turns to go—suddenly bellicose*) Leaving me, are you? When it's dinner time? Where's my dinner, you lazy cow?

JOSIE. There's stew on the stove, you bad-tempered runt. Go in and help yourself. I'm not hungry. Your gab has bothered my mind. I need hard work in the sun to clear it. (*She starts to go off toward rear-right.*)

HOGAN (*Glancing down the road, off left-front*). You'd better wait. There's a caller coming to the gate—and if I'm not mistaken, it's the light of your eyes himself.

JOSIE (*Angrily*). Shut up! (*She stares off—her face softens and grows pitying.*) Look at him when he thinks no one is watching, with his eyes on the ground. Like a dead man walking slow behind his own coffin. (*Then roughly*) Faith, he must have a hangover. He sees us now. Look at the bluff he puts up, straightening himself and grinning. (*Resentfully*) I don't want to meet him. Let him make jokes with you and play the old game about a drink you both think is such fun. That's all he comes for, anyway. (*She starts off again.*)

HOGAN. Are you running away from him? Sure, you must be afraid you're in love. (*Josie halts instantly and turns back defiantly. He goes on.*) Go in the house now, and wash your face, and tidy your dress, and give a touch to your hair. You want to look decent for him.

JOSIE (*Angrily*). I'll go in the house, but only to see the stew ain't burned, for I supposed you'll have the foxiness to ask him to have a bite to eat to keep in his good graces.

HOGAN. Why shouldn't I ask him? I know damned well he has no appetite this early in the day, but only a thirst.

JOSIE. Och, you make me sick, you sly miser! (*She goes through her bedroom, slamming the door behind her. Hogan refills his pipe, pretending he doesn't notice Tyrone approaching, his eyes bright with droll expectation. Jim Tyrone enters along the road from the highway, left.*)

(*Tyrone is in his early forties, around five feet nine, broad-shouldered and deep-chested. His naturally fine physique has become soft and soggy from dissipation, but his face is still good-looking despite its unhealthy puffiness and the bags under the eyes. He has thinning dark hair, parted and brushed back to cover a bald spot. His eyes are brown, the whites congested and yellowish. His nose, big and aquiline, gives his face a certain Mephistophelian quality which is accentuated by his habitually cynical expression. But when he smiles without sneering, he still has the ghost of a former youthful irresponsible Irish charm—that of the beguiling ne'er-do-well, sentimental and romantic. It is his humor and charm which have kept him attractive to women, and popular with men as a drinking companion. He is dressed in an expensive dark-brown suit, tight-fitting and drawn in at the waist, dark-brown made-to-order shoes and silk socks, a white silk shirt, silk handkerchief in breast pocket, a dark tie. This get-up suggests that he follows a style set by well-groomed Broadway gamblers who would like to be mistaken for Wall Street brokers.*)

(*He has had enough pick-me-ups to recover from morning-after nausea and steady his nerves. During the following dialogue, he and Hogan are like players at an old familiar game where each knows the other's moves, but which still amuses them.*)

TYRONE (*Approaches and stands regarding Hogan with sardonic relish. Hogan scratches a match on the seat of his overalls and lights his pipe, pretending not to see him. Tyrone recites with feeling*).

"Fortunate senex, ergo tua rura manebunt,
et tibi magna saatis, quamvis lapis omnia nudus."

HOGAN (*Mutters*). It's the landlord again, and my shotgun not handy. (*He looks up at Tyrone.*) Is it Mass you're saying, Jim? That was Latin. I know it by ear. What the hell—insult does it mean?

TYRONE. Translated very freely into Irish English, something like this. (*He imitates Hogan's brogue.*) "Ain't you the lucky old bastard to have this beautiful farm, if it is full of nude rocks."

HOGAN. I like that part about the rocks. If cows could eat them this place would make a grand dairy farm. (*He spits.*) It's easy to see you've a fine college education. It must be a big help to you, conversing with whores and barkeeps.

TYRONE. Yes, a very valuable worldly asset. I was once offered a job as office boy—until they discovered I wasn't qualified because I had no Bachelor of Arts diploma. There had been a slight misunderstanding just before I was to graduate.

HOGAN. Between you and the Fathers? I'll wager!

TYRONE. I made a bet with another Senior I could get a tart from the Haymarket to visit me, introduce her to the Jebs as my sister—and get away with it.

HOGAN. But you didn't?

TYRONE. Almost. It was a memorable day in the halls of learning. All the students were wise and I had them rolling in the aisles as I showed Sister around the grounds, accompanied by one of the Jebs. He was a bit suspicious at first, but Dutch Maisie—her professional name—had no make-up on, and was dressed in black, and had eaten a pound of Sen-Sen to kill the gin on her breath, and seemed such a devout girl that he forgot his suspicions. (*He pauses.*) Yes, all would have been well, but she was a mischievous minx, and had her own ideas of improving on my joke. When she was saying good-bye to Father Fuller, she added innocently: "Christ, Father, it's nice and quiet out here away from the damned Sixth Avenue El. I wish to hell I could stay here!" (*Dryly*) But she didn't, and neither did I.

HOGAN (*Chuckles delightedly*). I'll bet you didn't! God bless Dutch Maisie! I'd like to have known her.

TYRONE (*Sits down on the steps—with a change of manner*). Well, how's the Duke of Donegal this fine day?

HOGAN. Never better.

TYRONE. Slaving and toiling as usual, I see.

HOGAN. Hasn't a poor man a right to his noon rest without being sneered at by his rich landlord?

TYRONE. "Rich" is good. I would be, if you'd pay up your back rent.

HOGAN. You ought to pay me, instead, for occupying this rockpile, miscalled a farm. (*His eyes twinkling*) But I have fine reports to give you of a promising harvest. The milkweed and the thistles is in thriving condition, and I never saw the poison ivy so bounteous and beautiful. (*Tyrone laughs. Without their noticing, Josie appears in the doorway behind Tyrone. She has tidied up and arranged her hair. She smiles down at Jim, her face softening, pleased to hear him laugh.*)

TYRONE. You win. Where did Josie go, Phil? I saw her here—

HOGAN. She ran in the house to make herself beautiful for you.

JOSIE (*Breaks in roughly*). You're a liar. (*To Tyrone, her manner one of bold, free-and-easy familiarity*) Hello, Jim.

TYRONE (*Starts to stand up*). Hello, Josie.

JOSIE (*Puts a hand on his shoulder and pushes him down*). Don't get up. Sure, you know I'm no lady. (*She sits on the top step—banteringly.*) How's my fine Jim this beautiful day? You don't look so bad. You must have stopped at the Inn for an eye-opener—or ten of them.

TYRONE. I've felt worse (*He looks up at her sardonically.*) And how's my Virgin Queen of Ireland?

JOSIE. Yours, is it? Since when? And don't be miscalling me a virgin. You'll ruin my reputation, if you spread that lie about me. (*She laughs. Tyrone is staring at her. She goes on quickly.*) How is it you're around so early? I thought you never got up till afternoon.

TYRONE. Couldn't sleep. One of those heebie-jeebie nights when the booze keeps you awake instead of— (*He catches her giving him a pitying look—irritably.*) But what of it!

JOSIE. Maybe you had no woman in bed with you, for a change. It's a terrible thing to break the habit of years.

TYRONE (*Shrugs his shoulders*). Maybe.

JOSIE. What's the matter with the tarts in town, they let you do it? I'll bet the ones you know on Broadway, New York, wouldn't neglect their business.

TYRONE (*Pretends to yawn boredly*). Maybe not. (*Then irritably*) Cut out the kidding, Josie. It's too early.

HOGAN (*Who has been taking everything in without seeming to*). I told you not to annoy the gentleman with your rough tongue.

JOSIE. Sure I thought I was doing my duty as hostess making him feel at home.

TYRONE (*Stares at her again*). Why all the interest lately in the ladies of the profession, Josie?

JOSIE. Oh, I've been considering joining their union. It's easier living than farming, I'm sure. (*Then resentfully*) You think I'd starve at it, don't you, because your fancy is for dainty dolls of women? But other men like—

TYRONE (*With sudden revulsion*). For God's sake, cut out that kind of talk, Josie! It sounds like hell.

JOSIE (*Stares at him startedly—then resentfully*). Oh, it does, does it? (*Forcing a scornful smile*) I'm shocking you, I suppose? (*Hogan is watching them both, not missing anything in their faces, while he seems intent on his pipe.*)

TYRONE (*Looking a bit sheepish and annoyed at himself for his interest—shrugs his shoulders*). No. Hardly. Forget it. (*He smiles kiddingly.*) Anyway, who told you I fall for the dainty dolls? That's all a thing of the past. I like them tall and strong and voluptuous, now, with beautiful big breasts. (*She blushes and looks confused and is furious with herself for doing so.*)

HOGAN. There you are, Josie, darlin'. Sure he couldn't speak fairer than that.

JOSIE (*Recovers herself*). He couldn't, indeed. (*She pats Tyrone's head—playfully.*) You're a terrible blarneying liar, Jim, but thank you just the same. (*Tyrone turns his attention to Hogan. He winks at Josie and begins in an exaggeratedly casual manner.*)

TYRONE. I don't blame you, Mr. Hogan, for taking it easy on such a blazing hot day.

HOGAN (*Doesn't look at him. His eyes twinkle*). Hot, did you say? I find it cool, meself. Take off your coat if you're hot, Mister Tyrone.

TYRONE. One of the most stifling days I've ever known. Isn't it, Josie?

JOSIE (*Smiling*). Terrible. I know you must be perishing.

HOGAN. I wouldn't call it a damned bit stifling.

TYRONE. It parches the membranes in your throat.

HOGAN. The what? Never mind. I can't have them, for my throat isn't parched at all. If yours is, Mister Tyrone, there's a well full of water at the back.

TYRONE. Water? That's something people wash with, isn't it? I mean, some people.

HOGAN. So I've heard. But, like you, I find it hard to believe. It's a dirty habit. They must be foreigners.

TYRONE. As I was saying, my throat is parched after the long dusty walk I took just for the pleasure of being your guest.

HOGAN. I don't remember inviting you, and the road is hard macadam with divil a speck of dust, and it's less than a quarter mile from the Inn here.

TYRONE. I didn't have a drink at the Inn. I was waiting until I arrived here, knowing that you—

HOGAN. Knowing I'd what?

TYRONE. Your reputation as a generous host—

HOGAN. The world must be full of liars. So you didn't have a drink at the Inn? Then it must be the air itself smells of whiskey today, although I didn't notice it before you came. You've gone on the water-wagon, I suppose? Well, that's fine, and I ask pardon for misjudging you.

TYRONE. I've wanted to go on the wagon for the past twenty-five years, but the doctors have strictly forbidden it. It would be fatal—with my weak heart.

HOGAN. So you've a weak heart? Well, well, and me thinking all along it was your head. I'm glad you told me. I was just going to offer you a drink, but whiskey is the worst thing—

TYRONE. The Docs say it's a matter of life and death. I must have a stimulant—one big drink, at least, whenever I strain my heart walking in the hot sun.

HOGAN. Walk back to the Inn, then, and give it a good strain, so you can buy yourself two big drinks.

JOSIE (*Laughing*). Ain't you the fools, playing that old game between you, and both of you pleased as punch!

Tyrone (*Gives up with a laugh*). Hasn't he ever been known to loosen up, Josie?

JOSIE. You ought to know. If you need a drink you'll have

to buy it from him or die of thirst.

TYRONE. Well, I'll bet this is one time he's going to treat.

HOGAN. Be God, I'll take that bet!

TYRONE. After you've heard the news I've got for you, you'll be so delighted you won't be able to drag out the old bottle quick enough.

HOGAN. I'll have to be insanely delighted.

JOSIE (*Full of curiosity*). Shut up, Father. What news, Jim?

TYRONE. I have it off the grapevine that a certain exalted personage will drop in on you before long.

HOGAN. It's the sheriff again. I know by the pleased look on your mug.

TYRONE. Not this time. (*He pauses tantalizingly.*)

JOSIE. Bad luck to you, can't you tell us who?

TYRONE. A more eminent grafter than the sheriff—(*Sneeringly*) A leading aristocrat in our Land of the Free and Get-Rich-Quick, whose boots are licked by one and all—and one of the Kings of our Republic by Divine Right of Inherited Swag. In short, I refer to your good neighbor, T. Stedman Harder, Standard Oil's sappiest child, whom I know you both love so dearly. (*There is a pause after this announcement. Hogan and Josie stiffen, and their eyes begin to glitter. But they can't believe their luck at first.*)

HOGAN (*In an ominous whisper*). Did you say Harder is coming to call on us, Jim?

JOSIE. It's too good to be true.

TYRONE (*Watching them with amusement*). No kidding. The great Mr. Harder intends to stop here on his way back to lunch from a horseback ride.

JOSIE. How do you know?

TYRONE. Simpson told me. I ran into him at the Inn.

HOGAN. That English scum of a superintendent!

TYRONE. He was laughing himself sick. He said he suggested the idea to Harder—told him you'd be overwhelmed with awe if he deigned to interview you in person.

HOGAN. Overwhelmed isn't the word. Is it, Josie?

JOSIE. It isn't indeed, Father.

TYRONE. For once in his life, Simpson is cheering for you. He doesn't like his boss. In fact, he asked me to tell you he hopes you kill him.

HOGAN (*Disdainfully*). To hell with the Limey's good wishes. I'd like both of them to call together.

JOSIE. Ah, well, we can't have everything. (*To Tyrone*) What's the reason Mr. Harder decided to notice poor, humble scum the like of us?

TYRONE (*Grinning*). That's right, Josie. Be humble. He'll expect you to know your place.

HOGAN. Will he now? Well, well. (*With a great happy sigh*) This is going to be a beautiful day entirely.

JOSIE. But what's Harder's reason, Jim?

TYRONE. Well, it seems he has an ice pond on his estate.

HOGAN. Oho! So that's it!

TYRONE. Yes. That's it. Harder likes to keep up the good old manorial customs. He clings to his ice pond. And your pigpen isn't far from his ice pond.

HOGAN. A nice little stroll for the pigs, that's all.

TYRONE. And somehow Harder's fence in that vicinity has a habit of breaking down.

HOGAN. Fences are queer things. You can't depend on them.

TYRONE. Simpson says he's had it repaired a dozen times, but each time on the following night it gets broken down again.

JOSIE. What a strange thing! It must be the bad fairies. I can't imagine who else could have done it. Can you, Father?

HOGAN. I can't, surely.

TYRONE. Well, Simpson can. He knows you did it and he told his master so.

HOGAN (*Disdainfully*). Master is the word. Sure, the English can't live unless they have a lord's backside to kiss, the dirty slaves.

TYRONE. The result of those breaks in the fence is that your pigs stroll—as you so gracefully put it—stroll through to wallow happily along the shores of the ice pond.

HOGAN. Well, why not? Sure, they're fine ambitious American-born pigs and they don't miss any opportunities. They're like Harders' father who made the money for him.

TYRONE. I agree, but for some strange reason Harder doesn't look forward to the taste of pig in next summer's ice water.

HOGAN. He must be delicate. Remember he's delicate, Josie, and leave your club in the house. (*He bursts into joyful menacing laughter.*) Oh, be God and be Christ in the mountains! I've pined to have a quiet word with Mr. Harder for years, watching him ride past in his big shiny automobile with his snoot in the air, and being tormented always by the complaints of his Limey superintendent. Oh, won't I welcome him!

JOSIE. Won't *we*, you mean. Sure, I love him as much as you.

HOGAN. I'd kiss you, Jim, for this beautiful news, if you wasn't so damned ugly. Maybe Josie'll do it for me. She has a stronger stomach.

JOSIE. I will! He's earned it. (*She pulls Tyrone's head back and laughingly kisses him on the lips. Her expression changes. She looks startled and confused, stirred and at the same time frightened. She forces a scornful laugh.*) Och, there's no spirit in you! It's like kissing a corpse.

TYRONE (*Gives her a strange surprised look—mockingly*). Yes? (*Turning to Hogan*) Well, how about that drink, Phil? I'll leave it to Josie if drinks aren't on the house.

HOGAN. I won't leave it to Josie. She's prejudiced, being in love.

JOSIE (*Angrily*). Shut up, you old liar! (*Then guiltily, forcing a laugh*) Don't talk nonsense to sneak out of treating Jim.

HOGAN (*Sighing*). All right, Josie. Go get the bottle and one small glass, or he'll never stop nagging me. I can turn my back, so the sight of him drinking free won't break my heart. (*Josie gets up, laughing, and goes in the house. Hogan peers at the road off left.*) On his way back to lunch, you said? Then it's time—(*Fervently*) O Holy Joseph, don't let the bastard change his mind!

TYRONE (*Beginning to have qualms*). Listen, Phil. Don't get too enthusiastic. He has a big drag around here, and he'll have you pinched, sure as hell, if you beat him up.

HOGAN. Och, I'm no fool. (*Josie comes out with a bottle and a tumbler.*) Will you listen to this, Josie. He's warning me not to give Harder a beating—as if I'd dirty my hands on the scum.

JOSIE. As if we'd need to. Sure, all we want is a quiet chat with him.

HOGAN. That's all. As neighbor to neighbor.

JOSIE (*Hands Tyrone the bottle and tumbler*). Here you are, Jim. Don't stint yourself.

HOGAN (*Mournfully*). A fine daughter! I tell you a small glass and you give him a bucket. (*As Tyrone pours a big drink, grinning at him, he turns away with a comic shudder.*) That's a fifty-dollar drink, at least.

TYRONE. Here's luck, Phil.

HOGAN. I hope you drown. (*Tyrone drinks and makes a wry face.*)

TYRONE. The best chicken medicine I've ever tasted.

HOGAN. That's gratitude for you! Here, pass me the bottle. A drink will warm up my welcome for His Majesty. (*He takes an enormous swig from the bottle.*)

JOSIE (*Looking off to left*). There's two horseback riders on the county road now.

HOGAN. Praise be to God! It's him and a groom. (*He sets the bottle on top of the boulder.*)

JOSIE. That's McCabe. An old sweetheart of mine. (*She glances at Tyrone provokingly—then suddenly worried and protective.*) You get in the house, Jim. If Harder sees you here, he'll lay the whole blame on you.

TYRONE. Nix, Josie. You don't think I'm going to miss this, do you?

JOSIE. You can sit inside by my window and take in everything. Come on, now, don't be stubborn with me.

(*She puts her hands under his arms and lifts him to his feet as easily as if he was a child—banteringly.*) Go into my beautiful bedroom. It's a nice place for you.

TYRONE (*Kiddingly*). Just what I've been thinking for some time, Josie.

JOSIE (*Boldly*). Sure, you've never given me a sign of it. Come up tonight and we'll spoon in the moonlight and you can tell me your thoughts.

TYRONE. That's a date. Remember, now.

JOSIE. It's you who'll forget. Get inside now, before it's too late. (*She gives him a shove inside and closes the door.*)

HOGAN (*Has been watching the visitor approach*). He's dismounting—as graceful as a scarecrow, and his poor horse longing to give him a kick. Look at Mac grinning at us. Sit down, Josie. (*She sits on the steps, he on the boulder.*) Pretend you don't notice him. (*T. Stedman Harder appears at left. They act as if they didn't see him. Hogan knocks out his pipe on the palm of his hand.*)

(*Harder is in his late thirties but looks younger because his face is unmarked by worry, ambition, or any of the common hazards of life. No matter how long he lives, his four undergraduate years will always be for him the most significant in his life, and the moment of his highest achievement the time he was tapped for an exclusive Senior Society at the Ivy university to which his father had given millions. Since that day he has felt no need for further aspiring, no urge to do anything except settle down on his estate and live the life of a country gentleman, mildly interested in saddle horses and sport models of foreign automobiles. He is not the blatantly silly, playboy heir to millions whose antics make newspaper headlines. He doesn't drink much except when he attends his class reunion every spring—the most exciting episode of each year for him. He doesn't give wild parties, doesn't chase after musical-comedy cuties, is a mildly contented husband and father of three children. A not unpleasant man, affable, goodlooking in an ordinary way, sunburnt and healthy, beginning to take on fat, he is simply immature, naturally lethargic, a bit stupid. Coddled from birth, everything arranged and made easy for him, deferred to because of his wealth, he usually has the self-confident attitude of acknowledged superiority, but assumes a supercilious insecure air when dealing with people beyond his ken. He is dressed in a beautifully tailored English tweed coat and whipcord riding breeches, immaculately polished English riding boots with spurs, and carries a riding crop in his hand.*)

(*It would be hard to find anyone more ill-equipped for combat with the Hogans. He has never come in contact with anyone like them. To make matters easier for them he is deliberate in his speech, slow on the uptake, and has no sense of humor. The experienced strategy of the Hogans in verbal battle is to take the offensive at once and never let an opponent get set to hit back. Also, they use a beautifully coordinated, bewildering change of pace, switching suddenly from jarring shouts to low, confidential vituperation. And they exaggerate their Irish brogues to confuse an enemy still further.*)

HARDER (*Walks toward Hogan—stiffly*). Good morning. I want to see the man who runs this farm.

HOGAN (*Surveys him deliberately, his little pig eyes gleaming with malice*). You do, do you? Well, you've seen him. So run along now and play with your horse, and don't bother me. (*He turns to Josie, who is staring at Harder, much to his discomfiture, as if she had discovered a cockroach in her soup.*) D'you see what I see, Josie? Be God, you'll have to give that damned cat of yours a spanking for bringing it to our doorstep.

HARDER (*Determined to be authoritative and command respect—curtly*). Are you Hogan?

HOGAN (*Insultingly*). I am *Mister* Philip Hogan—to a gentleman.

JOSIE (*Glares at Harder*). Where's your manners, you spindle-shanked jockey? Were you brought up in a stable?

HARDER (*Does not fight with ladies, and especially not with this lady—ignoring her*). My name is Harder. (*He obviously expects them to be immediately impressed and apologetic.*)

HOGAN (*Contemptuously*). Who asked you your name, me little man?

JOSIE. Sure, who in the world cares who the hell you are?

HOGAN. But if you want to play politeness, we'll play with you. Let me introduce you to my daughter, Harder—Miss Josephine Hogan.

JOSIE (*Petulantly*). I don't want to meet him, Father. I don't like his silly sheep's face, and I've no use for jockeys, anyway. I'll wager he's no damned good to a woman. (*From inside her bedroom comes a burst of laughter. This revelation of an unseen audience startles Harder. He begins to look extremely unsure of himself.*)

HOGAN. I don't think he's a jockey. It's only the funny pants he's wearing. I'll bet if you asked his horse, you'd find he's no cowboy either. (*To Harder, jeeringly*) Come, tell us the truth, me honey. Don't you kiss your horse each time you mount and beg him, please don't throw me today, darlin', and I'll give you an extra bucket of oats. (*He bursts into an extravagant roar of laugher, slapping his thigh, and Josie guffaws with him, while they watch the disconcerting effect of this theatrical mirth on Harder.*)

HARDER (*Beginning to lose his temper*). Listen to me, Hogan! I didn't come here—(*He is going to add "to listen to your damned jokes" or something like that, but Hogan silences him.*)

HOGAN (*Shouts*). What? What's that you said? (*He stares at the dumbfounded Harder with droll amazement, as if he couldn't believe his ears.*) You didn't come here? (*He turns to Josie—in a whisper.*) Did you hear that, Josie? (*He takes off his hat and scratches his head in comic bewilderment.*) Well, that's a puzzle, surely. How d'you suppose he got here?

JOSIE. Maybe the stork brought him, bad luck to it for a dirty bird. (*Again Tyrone's laughter is heard from the bedroom.*)

HARDER (*So off balance now he can only repeat angrily*). I said I didn't come here—

HOGAN (*Shouts*). Wait! Wait, now! (*Threateningly*) We've had enough of that. Say it a third time and I'll send my daughter to telephone the asylum.

HARDER (*Forgetting he's a gentleman*). Damn you, I'm the one who's had enough—!

JOSIE (*Shouts*). Hold your dirty tongue! I'll have no foul language in my presence.

HOGAN. Och, don't mind him, Josie. He's said he isn't here, anyway, so we won't talk to him behind his back. (*He regards Harder with pitying contempt.*) Sure, ain't you the poor crazy creature? Do you want us to believe you're your own ghost?

HARDER (*Notices the bottle on the boulder for the first time—tries to be contemptuously tolerant and even to smile with condescending disdain*). Ah! I understand now. You're drunk. I'll come back sometime when you're sober—or send Simpson—(*He turns away, glad of an excuse to escape.*)

JOSIE (*Jumps up and advances on him menacingly*). No, you don't! You'll appologize first for insulting a lady—insinuating I'm drunk this early in the day—or I'll knock some good breeding in you!

HARDER (*Actually frightened now*). I—I said nothing about you—

HOGAN (*Gets up to come between them*). Aisy now, Josie. He didn't mean it. He don't know what he means, the poor loon. (*To Harder—pityingly*) Run home, that's a good lad, before your keeper misses you.

HARDER (*Hastily*). Good day. (*He turns eagerly toward left but suddenly Hogan grabs his shoulder and spins him around—then shifts his grip to the lapel of Harder's coat.*)

HOGAN (*Grimly*). Wait now, me Honey Boy. I'll have a word with you, if you plaze. I'm beginning to read some sense into this. You mentioned that English bastard, Simpson. I know who you are now.

HARDER (*Outraged*). Take your hands off me, you drunken fool. (*He raises his riding crop.*)

JOSIE (*Grabs it and tears it from his hand with one powerful twist—fiercely*). Would you strike my poor infirm old father, you coward, you!

HARDER (*Calling for help*). McCabe!

HOGAN. Don't think McCabe will hear you, if you blew Gabriel's horn. He knows I or Josie can lick him with one hand. (*Sharply*) Josie! Stand between us and the gate. (*Josie takes her stand where the path meets the road. She turns her back for a moment, shaking with suppressed laughter, and waves her hand at McCabe and turns back. Hogan releases his hold on Harder's coat.*) There now. Don't try running away or my daughter will knock you senseless. (*He goes on grimly before Harder can speak.*) You're the blackguard of a millionaire that owns the estate next to ours, ain't you? I've been meaning to call on you, for I've a bone to pick with you, you bloody tyrant! But I couldn't bring myself to set foot on land bought with Standard Oil money that was stolen from the poor it ground in the dust beneath its dirty heel—land that's watered with the tears of starving widows and orphans—(*He abruptly switches from this eloquence to a matter-of-fact tone.*) But never mind that, now. I won't waste words trying to reform a born crook. (*Fiercely, shoving his dirty unshaven face almost into Harder's.*) What I want to know is, what the hell d'you mean by your contemptible trick of breaking down your fence to entice my poor pigs to take their death in your ice pond? (*There is a shout of laughter from Josie's bedroom, and Josie doubles up and holds her sides. Harder is so flabbergasted by this mad accusation he cannot even sputter. But Hogan acts as if he'd denied it—savagely.*) Don't lie, now! None of your damned Standard Oil excuses, or be Jaysus, I'll break you in half! Haven't I mended that fence morning after morning, and seen the footprints where you had sneaked up in the night to pull it down again. How many times have I mended that fence, Josie?

JOSIE. If it's once, it's a hundred, Father.

HOGAN. Listen, me little millionaire! I'm a peaceful, mild man that believes in live and let live, and as long as the neighboring scum leaves me alone, I'll let them alone, but when it comes to standing by and seeing my poor pigs murthered one by one—! Josie! How many pigs is it caught their death of cold in his damned ice pond and died of pneumonia?

JOSIE. Ten of them, Father. And ten more died of cholera after drinking the dirty water in it.

HOGAN. All prize pigs, too! I was offered two hundred dollars apiece for them. Twenty pigs at two hundred, that's four thousand. And a thousand to cure the sick and cover funeral expenses for the dead. Call it four thousand you owe me. (*Furiously*) And you'll pay it, or I'll sue you, so help me Christ! I'll drag you in every court in the land! I'll paste your ugly mug on the front page of every newspaper as a pig-murdering tyrant! Before I'm through with you, you'll think you're the King of England at an Irish wake! (*With a quick change of pace to a wheedling confidential tone*) Tell me now, if it isn't a secret, whatever made you take such a savage grudge against pigs? Sure, it isn't reasonable for a Standard Oil man to hate hogs.

HARDER (*Manages to get in three sputtering words*). I've had enough—!

HOGAN (*With a grin*). Be God, I believe you! (*Switching to fierceness and grabbing his lapel again*) Look out, now! Keep your place and be soft-spoken to your betters! You're not in your shiny automobile now with your funny nose cocked so you won't smell the poor people. (*He gives him a shake.*) And let me warn you! I have to put up with a lot of pests on this heap of boulders some joker once called a farm. There's a cruel skinflint of a landlord who swindles me out of my last drop of whiskey, and there's poison ivy, and ticks and potato bugs, and there's snakes and skunks! But, be God, I draw the line somewhere, and I'll be damned if I'll stand for a Standard Oil man trespassing! So will you kindly get the hell out of here before I plant a kick on your backside that'll land you in the Atlantic Ocean! (*He gives Harder a shove.*) Beat it now! (*Harder tries to make some sort of disdainfully dignified exit. But he has to get by Josie.*)

JOSIE (*Leers at him idiotically*). Sure, you wouldn't go without a word of good-bye to me, would you, darlin'? Don't scorn me just because you have on your jockey's pants. (*In a hoarse whisper*) Meet me tonight, as usual, down by the pigpen. (*Harder's retreat becomes a rout. He disappears on left, but a second later his voice, trembling with anger, is heard calling back threateningly.*)

HARDER. If you dare touch that fence again, I'll put this matter in the hands of the police!

HOGAN (*Shouts derisively*). And I'll put it in my lawyer's hands and in the newspapers! (*He doubles up with glee.*) Look at him fling himself on his nag and spur the poor beast! And look at McCabe behind him! He can hardly stay in the saddle for laughing! (*He slaps his thigh.*) O Jaysus, this is a great day for the poor and oppressed! I'll do no more work! I'll go down to the Inn and spend money and get drunk as Moses!

JOSIE. Small blame to you. You deserve it. But you'll have your dinner first, to give you a foundation. Come on now. (*They turn back toward the house. From inside another burst of laughter from Tyrone is heard. Josie smiles.*) Listen to Jim still in stitches. It's good to hear him laugh as if he meant it. (*Tyrone appears in the doorway of her bedroom.*)

TYRONE. O God, my sides are sore. (*They all laugh together. He joins them at the left corner of the house.*)

JOSIE. It's dinner time. Will you have a bit to eat with us, Jim? I'll boil you some eggs.

HOGAN. Och, why do you have to mention eggs? Don't you know it's the one thing he might eat? Well, no matter. Anything goes today. (*He gets the bottle of whiskey.*) Come in, Jim. We'll have a drink while Josie's fixing the grub. (*They start to go in the front door, Hogan in the lead.*)

TYRONE (*Suddenly—with sardonic amusement*). Wait a minute. Let us pause to take a look at this very valuable property. Don't you notice the change, Phil? Every boulder on the place has turned to solid gold.

HOGAN. What the hell—? You didn't get the D.T.'s from my whiskey, I know that.

TYRONE. No D.T.'s about it. This farm has suddenly become a gold mine. You know that offer I told you about? Well, the agent did a little detective work and he discovered it came from Harder. He doesn't want the damned place but he dislikes you as a neighbor and he thinks the best way to get rid of you would be to become your landlord.

HOGAN. The sneaking skunk! I'm sorry I didn't give him that kick.

TYRONE. Yes. So am I. That would have made the place even more valuable. But as it is, you did nobly. I expect him to double or triple his first offer. In fact, I'll bet the sky is the limit now.

HOGAN (*Gives Josie a meaningful look*). I see your point! But we're not worrying you'd ever forget your promise to us for any price.

TYRONE. Promise? What promise? You know what Kipling wrote: (*Paraphrasing the "Rhyme of the Three Sealers"*) There's never a promise of God or man goes north of ten thousand bucks.

HOGAN. D'you hear him, Josie? We can't trust him.

JOSIE. Och, you know he's kidding.

HOGAN. I don't! I'm becoming suspicious.

TYRONE (*A trace of bitterness beneath his amused tone*). That's wise dope, Phil. Trust and be a sucker. If I were you, I'd be seriously worried. I've always wanted to own a gold mine—so I could sell it.

JOSIE (*Bursts out*). Will you shut up your rotten Broadway blather!

TYRONE (*Stares at her in surprise*). Why so serious and indignant, Josie? You just told your unworthy Old Man I was kidding. (*To Hogan*) At last, I've got you by the ears, Phil. We must have a serious chat about when you're going to pay that back rent.

HOGAN (*Groans*). A landlord who's a blackmailer! Holy God, what next! (*Josie is smiling with relief now.*)

TYRONE. And you, Josie, please remember when I keep that moonlight date tonight I expect you to be very sweet to me.

JOSIE (*With a bold air*). Sure, you don't have to blackmail me, I'd be that to you, anyway.

HOGAN. Are you laying plots in my presence to seduce my only daughter? (*Then philosophically*) Well, what can I do? I'll be drunk at the Inn, so how could I prevent it? (*He goes up the steps.*) Let's eat, for the love of God. I'm starving. (*He disappears inside the house.*)

JOSIE (*With an awkward playful gesture, takes Tyrone by the hand*). Come along, Jim.

TYRONE (*Smiles kiddingly*). Afraid you'll lose me? Swell chance! (*His eyes fix on her breasts—with genuine feeling*). You have the most beautiful breasts in the world, do you know it, Josie?

JOSIE (*Pleased—shyly*). I don't—but I'm happy if you think—(*Then quickly*) But I've no time now to listen to your kidding, with my mad old father waiting for his dinner. So come on. (*She tugs at his hand and he follows her up the steps. Her manner changes to worried solicitude.*) Promise me you'll eat something, Jim. You've got to eat. You can't go on the way you are, drinking and never eating, hardly. You're killing yourself.

TYRONE (*Sardonically*). That's right. Mother me, Josie, I love it.

JOSIE (*Bullyingly*). I will, then. You need one to take care of you. (*They disappear inside the house.*)

Curtain

ACT II

Scene: The same, with the wall of the living room removed. It is a clear warm moonlight night, around eleven o'clock.

Josie is sitting on the steps before the front door. She has changed to her Sunday best, a cheap dark-blue dress, black stockings and shoes. Her hair is care-fully arranged, and by way of adornment a white flower is pinned on her bosom. She is hunched up, elbows on knees, her chin in her hands. There is an expression on her face we have not seen before, a look of sadness and loneliness and humiliation.

She sighs and gets slowly to her feet, her body stiff from sitting long in the same position. She goes into the living room, fumbles for a box of matches, and lights a kerosene lamp on the table.

The living room is small, low-ceilinged, with faded, fly-specked wallpaper, a floor of bare boards. It is cluttered up with furniture that looks as it it had been picked up at a fire sale. There is a table at center, a disreputable old Morris chair beside it; two ugly sideboards, one at left, the other at right-rear; a porch rocking-chair, painted green, with a hole in its cane bottom; a bureau against the rear wall, with two chairs on either side of a door to the kitchen. On the bureau is an alarm clock which shows the time to be five past eleven. At right-front is the door to Josie's bedroom.

JOSIE (*Looks at the clock—dully*). Five past eleven, and he said he'd be here around nine. (*Suddenly in a burst of humiliated anger, she tears off the flower pinned to her bosom and throws it in the corner.*) To hell with you, Jim Tyrone! (*From down the road, the quiet of the night is shattered by a burst of melancholy song. It is unmistakably Hogan's voice wailing an old Irish lament at the top of his lungs. Josie starts—then frowns irritably.*) What's bringing him home an hour before the Inn closes? He must be more paralyzed than ever I've known him. (*She listens to the singing—grimly.*) Ah, here you come, do you, as full as a tick! I'll give you a welcome, if you start cutting up! I'm in no mood to put up with you. (*She goes into her bedroom and returns with her broomstick club. Outside the singing grows louder as Hogan approaches the house. He only remembers one verse of the song and he has been repeating it.*)

HOGAN.

*Oh the praties they grow small
Over here, over here,
Oh, the praties they grow small
Over here
Oh the praties they grow small
And we dig them in the fall
And we eat them skins and all
Over here, over here.*

(*He enters left-front, weaving and lurching a bit. But he is not as drunk as he appears. Or rather, he is one of those people who can drink an enormous amount and be absolutely plastered when they want to be for their own pleasure, but at the same time are able to pull themselves together when they wish and be cunningly clear-headed. Just now, he is letting himself go and getting great satisfaction from it. He pauses and bellows belligerently at the house.)* Hurroo! Down with all tyrants, male and female! To hell with England, and God damn Standard Oil!

JOSIE (*Shouts back*). Shut up your noise, you crazy old billy goat!

HOGAN (*Hurt and mournful*). A sweet daughter and a sweet welcome home in the dead of night. (*Beginning to boil*) Old goat! There's respect for you! (*Angrily—starting for the front door*) Crazy billy goat, is it? Be God, I'll learn you manners! (*He pounds on the door with his fist.*) Open the door! Open this door, I'm saying, before I drive a fist through it, or kick it into flinders! (*He gives it a kick.*)

JOSIE. It's not locked, you drunken old loon! Open it yourself!

HOGAN (*Turns the knob and stamps in*). Drunken old loon, am I? Is that the way to address your father?

JOSIE. No. It's too damned good for him.

HOGAN. It's time I taught you a lesson. Be Jaysus, I'll take you over my knee and spank your tail, if you are as big as a cow! (*He makes a lunge to grab her.*)

JOSIE. Would you, though! Take that, then! (*She raps him smartly, but lightly, on his bald spot with the end of her broom handle.*)

HOGAN (*With an exaggerated howl of pain*). Ow! (*His anger evaporates and he rubs the top of his head ruefully—with bitter complaint.*) God forgive you, it's a great shame to me I've raised a daughter so cowardly she has to use a club.

JOSIE (*Puts her club on the table—grimly*). Now I've no club.

HOGAN (*Evades the challenge*). I never thought I'd see the day when a daughter of mine would be such a coward as to threaten her old father when he's helpless drunk and can't hit back. (*He slumps down on the Morris chair.*)

JOSIE. Ah, that's better. Now that little game is over. (*Then angrily*) Listen to me, Father. I have no patience left, so get up from that chair, and go in your room, and go to bed, or I'll take you by the scruff of your neck and the seat of your pants and throw you in and lock the door on you! I mean it, now! (*On the verge of angry tears*) I've had all I can bear this night, and I want some peace and sleep, and not to listen to an old lush!

HOGAN (*Appears drunker, his head wagging, his voice thick, his talk rambling*). That's right. Fight with me. My

own daughter has no feelings or sympathy. As if I hadn't enough after what's happened tonight.

JOSIE (*With angry disgust*). Och, don't try—(*Then curiously*) What's happened? I thought something must be queer, you coming home before the Inn closed, but then I thought maybe for once you'd drunk all you could hold. (*Scathingly*) And, God pity you, if you ain't that full, you're damned close to it.

HOGAN. Go on. Make fun of me. Old lush! You wouldn't feel so comical, if—(*He stops, mumbling to himself.*)

JOSIE. If what?

HOGAN. Never mind. Never mind. I didn't come home to fight, but seek comfort in your company. And if I was singing coming along the road, it was only because there's times you have to sing to keep from crying.

JOSIE. I can see you crying!

HOGAN. You will. And you'll see yourself crying, too, when—(*He stops again and mumbles to himself.*)

JOSIE. When what? (*Exasperatedly*) Will you stop your whiskey drooling and talk plain?

HOGAN (*Thickly*). No matter. No matter. Leave me alone.

JOSIE (*Angrily*). That's good advice. To hell with you! I know your game. Nothing at all has happened. All you want is to keep me up listening to your guff. Go to your room, I'm saying, before—

HOGAN. I won't. I couldn't sleep with my thoughts tormented the way they are. I'll stay here in this chair, and you go to your room and let me be.

JOSIE (*Snorts*). And have you singing again in a minute and smashing the furniture—

HOGAN. Sing, is it? Are you making fun again? I'd give a keen of sorrow or howl at the moon like an old mangy hound in his sadness if I knew how, but I don't. So rest aisy. You won't hear a sound from me. Go on and snore like a pig to your heart's content. (*He mourns drunkenly.*) A fine daughter! I'd get more comfort from strangers.

JOSIE. Och, for God's sake, dry up! You'll sit in the dark then. I won't leave the lamp lit for you to tip over and burn down the house. (*She reaches out to turn down the lamp.*)

HOGAN (*Thickly*). Let it burn to the ground. A hell of a lot I care if it burns.

JOSIE (*In the act of turning down the lamp, stops and stares at him, puzzled and uneasy*). I never heard you talk that way before, no matter how drunk you were. (*He mumbles. Her tone becomes persuasive.*) What's happened to you, Father?

HOGAN (*Bitterly*). Ah it's "Father" now, is it, not old billy goat? Well, thank God for small favors. (*With heavy sarcasm*) Oh, nothing's happened to me at all, at all.

A trifle, only. I wouldn't waste your time mentioning it, or keep you up when you want sleep so bad.

JOSIE (*Angrily*). Och, you old loon, I'm sick of you. Sleep it off till you get some sense. (*She reaches for the lamp again.*)

HOGAN. Sleep it off? We'll see if you'll sleep it off when you know—(*He lapses into drunken mumbling.*)

JOSIE (*Again stares at him*). Know what, Father?

HOGAN (*Mumbles*). The son of a bitch!

JOSIE (*Trying a light tone*). Sure, there's a lot of those in the neighborhood. Which one do you mean? Is Harder on your mind again?

HOGAN (*Thickly*). He's one and a prize one, but I don't mean him. I'll say this for Harder, you know what to expect from him. He's no wolf in sheep's clothing, nor a treacherous snake in the grass who stabs you in the back with a knife—

JOSIE (*Apprehensive now—forces a joke*). Sure, if you've found a snake who can stab you with a knife, you'd better join the circus with him and make a pile of money.

HOGAN (*Bitterly*). Make jokes, God forgive you! You'll soon laugh from the wrong end of your mouth! (*He mumbles.*) Pretending he's our friend! The lying bastard!

JOSIE (*Bristles resentfully*). Is it Jim Tyrone you're calling hard names?

HOGAN. That's right. Defend him, you big soft fool! Faith, you're a prize dunce! You've had a good taste of believeing his word, waiting hours for him dressed up in your best like a poor sheep without pride or spirit—

JOSIE (*Stung*). Shut up! I was calling him a lying bastard myself before you came, and saying I'd never speak to him again. And I knew all along he'd never remember to keep his date after he got drunk.

HOGAN. He's not so drunk he forgot to attend to business.

JOSIE (*As if she hadn't heard—defiantly*). I'd have stayed up anyway a beautiful night like this to enjoy the moonlight, if there wasn't a Jim Tyrone in the world.

HOGAN (*With heavy sarcasm*). In your best shoes and stockings? Well, well. Sure, the moon must feel flattered by your attentions.

JOSIE (*Furiously*). You won't feel flattered if I knock you tail over cup out of that chair! And stop your whiskey gabble about Jim. I see what you're driving at with your dark hints and curses, and if you think I'll believe—(*With forced assurance*) Sure, I know what's happened as well as if I'd been there. Jim saw you'd got drunker than usual and you were an easy mark for a joke, and he's made a goat of you!

HOGAN (*Bitterly*). Goat, again! (*He struggles from his chair and stands swaying unsteadily—with offended dignity.*)

All right, I won't say another word. There's no use telling the truth to a bad-tempered woman in love.

JOSIE. Love be damned! I hate him now!

HOGAN. Be Christ, you have me stumped. A great proud slut who's played games with half the men around here, and now you act like a numbskull virgin that can't believe a man would tell her a lie!

JOSIE (*Threateningly*). If you're going to your room, you'd better go quick!

HOGAN (*Fixes his eyes on the door at rear—with dignity*). That's where I'm going, yes—to talk to meself so I'll know someone with brains is listening. Good night to you, Miss Hogan. (*He starts—swerves left—tries to correct this and lurches right and bumps against her, clutching the supporting arm she stretches out.*)

JOSIE. God help you, if you try to go upstairs now, you'll end up in the cellar.

HOGAN (*Hanging on to her arm and shoulder—maudlinly affectionate now*). You're right. Don't listen to me. I'm wrong to bother you. You've had sorrow enough this night. Have a good sleep, while you can, Josie, darlin'—and good night and God bless you. (*He tries to kiss her, but she wards him off and steers him back to the chair.*)

JOSIE. Sit down before you split in pieces on the floor and I have to get a wheelbarrow to collect you. (*She dumps him in the chair where he sprawls limply, his chin on his chest.*)

HOGAN (*Mumbles dully*). It's too late. It's all settled. We're helpless, entirely.

JOSIE (*Really worried now*). How is it all settled? If you're helpless, I'm not. (*Then as he doesn't reply—scornfully*) It's the first time I ever heard you admit you were licked. And it's the first time I ever saw you so paralyzed you couldn't shake the whiskey from your brains and get your head clear when you wanted. Sure, that's always been your pride—and now look at you, the stupid object you are, mumbling and drooling!

HOGAN (*Struggles up in his chair—angrily*). Shut up your insults! Be God, I can get my head clear if I like! (*He shakes his head violently.*) There! It's clear. I can tell you each thing that happened tonight as clear as if I'd not taken a drop, if you'll listen and not keep calling me a liar.

JOSIE. I'll listen, now I see you have hold of your wits.

HOGAN. All right, then. I'll begin at the beginning when him and me left here, and you gave him a sweet smile, and rolled your big beautiful cow's eyes at him, and wiggled your backside, and stuck out your beautiful breasts you know he admires, and said in a sick sheep's voice: "Don't forget our moonlight date, Jim."

JOSIE (*With suppressed fury*). You're a—! I never—! You old—!

HOGAN. And he said: "You bet I won't forget, Josie."

JOSIE. The lying crook!

HOGAN (*His voice begins to sink into a dejected monotone*). We went to the Inn and started drinking whiskey. And I got drunk.

JOSIE (*Exasperatedly*). I guessed that! And Jim got drunk, too. And then what?

HOGAN (*Dully*). Who knows how drunk he got? He had one of his queer fits when you can't tell. He's the way I told you about this morning, when he talks like a Broadway crook, who'd sell his soul for a price, and there's a sneering divil in him, and he loves to pick out the weakness in people and say cruel, funny things that flay the hide off them, or play cruel jokes on them. (*With sudden rage*) God's curse on him, I'll wager he's laughing to himself this minute, thinking it's the cutest joke in the world, the fools he's made of us. You in particular. Be God, I had my suspicions, at least, but your head was stuffed with mush and love, and you wouldn't—

JOSIE (*Furiously*). You'll tell that lie about my love once too often! And I'll play a joke on him yet that'll make him sorry he—

HOGAN (*Sunk in drunken defeatism again*). It's too late. You shouldn't have let him get away from you to the Inn. You should have kept him here. Then maybe, if you'd got him drunk enough you could have—(*His head nodding, his eyes blinking—thickly*) But it's no good talking now—no good at all—no good—

JOSIE (*Gives him a shake*). Keep hold of your wits or I'll give you a cuff on both ears! Will you stop blathering like an old woman and tell me plainly what he's done!

HOGAN. He's agreed to sell the farm, that's what! Simpson came to the Inn to see him with a new offer from Harder. Ten thousand, cash.

JOSIE (*Overwhelmed*). Ten thousand! Sure, three is all it's worth at most. And two was what you offered that Jim promised—

HOGAN. What's money to Harder? After what we did to him, all he wants is revenge. And here's where he's foxy. Simpson must have put him up to it knowing how Jim hates it here living on a small allowance, and he longs to go back to Broadway and his whores. Jim won't have to wait for his half of the cash till the estate's settled. Harder offers to give him five thousand cash as a loan against the estate the second the sale is made. Jim can take the next train to New York.

JOSIE (*Tensely, on the verge of tears*). And Jim accepted? I don't believe it!

HOGAN. Don't then. Be God, you'll believe it tomorrow. Harder proposed that he meet with Jim and the executors in the morning and settle it, and Jim promised Simpson he would.

JOSIE (*Desperately*). Maybe he'll get so drunk he'll never remember—

HOGAN. He won't. Harder's coming in his automobile to pick him up and make sure of him. Anyway don't think because he forgot you were waiting—in the moonlight, eating your heart out, that he'd ever miss a date with five thousand dollars, and all the pretty whores of Broadway he can buy with it.

JOSIE (*Distractedly*). Will you shut up! (*Angrily*) And where were you when all this happened? Couldn't you do anything to stop it, you old loon?

HOGAN. I couldn't. Simpson came and sat at the table with us—

JOSIE. And you let him!

HOGAN. Jim invited him. Anyway, I wanted to find out what trick he had up his sleeve, and what Jim would do. When it was all over, I got up and took a swipe at Simpson, but I missed him. (*With drunken sadness*) I was too drunk—too drunk—too drunk—I missed him, God forgive me! (*His chin sinks on his chest and his eyes shut.*)

JOSIE (*Shakes him*). If you don't keep awake, be God, I won't miss you!

HOGAN. I was going to take a swipe at Jim, too, but I couldn't do it. My heart was too broken with sorrow. I'd come to love him like a son—a real son of my heart!—to take the place of that jackass, Mike, and me two other jackasses.

JOSIE (*Her face hard and bitter*). I think now Mike was the only one in this house with sense.

HOGAN. I was too drowned in sorrow by his betraying me— and you he'd pretended to like so much. So I only called him a dirty lying skunk of a treacherous bastard, and I turned my back on him and left the Inn, and I made myself sing on the road so he'd hear, and they'd all hear in the Inn, to show them I didn't care a damn.

JOSIE (*Scathingly*). Sure, wasn't you the hero! A hell of a lot of good—

HOGAN. Ah, well, I suppose the temptation was too great. He's weak, with one foot in the grave from whiskey. Maybe we shouldn't blame him.

JOSIE (*Her eyes flashing*). Not blame him? Well, I blame him, God damn him! Are you making excuses for him, you old fool!

HOGAN. I'm not. He's a dirty snake! But I was thinking how do I know what I wouldn't do for five thousand cash, and how do you know what you wouldn't do?

JOSIE. Nothing could make me betray him! (*Her face grows hard and bitter.*) Or it couldn't before. There's nothing I wouldn't do now. (*Hogan suddenly begins to chuckle.*) Do you think I'm lying? Just give me a chance—

HOGAN. I remembered something. (*He laughs drunkenly.*) Be Christ, Josie, for all his Broadway wisdom about women, you've made a prized damned fool of him and that's some satisfaction!

JOSIE (*Bewildered*). How'd you mean?

HOGAN. You'll never believe it. Neither did I, but he kept on until, be God, I saw he really meant it.

JOSIE. Meant what?

HOGAN. It was after he'd turned queer—early in the night before Simpson came. He started talking about you, as if you was on his mind, worrying him—and before he finished I take my oath I began to hope you could really work Mike's first scheme on him, if you got him alone in the moonlight, because all his gab was about his great admiration for you.

JOSIE. Och! The liar!

HOGAN. He said you had great beauty in you that no one appreciated but him.

JOSIE (*Shakenly*). You're lying.

HOGAN. Great strength you had, and great pride, he said—and great goodness, no less! But here's where you've made a prize jackass of him, like I said. (*With a drunken leer*) Listen now, darlin', and don't drop dead with amazement. (*He leans toward her and whispers.*) He believes you're a virgin! (*Josie stiffens as if she'd been insulted. Hogan goes on.*) He does, so help me! He means it, the poor dunce! He thinks you're a poor innocent virgin! He thinks it's all boasting and pretending you've done about being a slut. (*He chuckles.*) A virgin, no less! You!

JOSIE (*Furiously*). Stop saying it! Boasting and pretending, am I? The dirty liar!

HOGAN. Faith, you don't have to tell me. (*Then he looks at her in drunken surprise—thickly.*) Are you taking it as an insult? Why the hell don't you laugh? Be God, you ought to see what a stupid sheep that makes him.

JOSIE (*Forces a laugh*). I do see it.

HOGAN (*Chuckling drunkenly*). Oh, be God, I've just remembered another thing, Josie. I know why he didn't keep his date with you. It wasn't that he'd forgot. He remembered well enough, for he talked about it—

JOSIE. You mean he deliberately, knowing I'd be waiting—(*Fiercely*) God damn him!

HOGAN. He as much as told me his reason, though he wouldn't come out with it plain, me being your father. His conscience was tormenting him. He's going

to leave you alone and not see you again—for your sake, because he loves you! (*He chuckles.*)

JOSIE (*Looks stricken and bewildered—her voice trembling*). Loves me? You're making it up.

HOGAN. I'm not. I know it sounds crazy but—

JOSIE. What did he mean, for my sake?

HOGAN. Can't you see? You're a pure virgin to him, but all the same there's things besides your beautiful soul he feels drawn to, like your beautiful hair and eyes, and—

JOSIE (*Strickenly*). Och, don't, Father! You know I'm only a big—

HOGAN (*As if she hadn't spoken*). So he'll keep away from temptation because he can't trust himself, and it'd be a sin on his conscience if he was to seduce you. (*He laughs drunkenly.*) Oh, be God! If that ain't rich!

JOSIE (*Her voice trembles*). So that was his reason—(*Then angrily*) So he thinks all he has to do is crook a finger and I'll fall for him, does he, the vain Broadway crook!

HOGAN (*Chuckling*). Be Jaysus, it was the maddest thing in the world, him gabbing like a soft loon about you—and there at the bar in plain sight was two of the men you've been out with, the gardener at Smith's and Regan, the chauffeur for Driggs, having a drink together!

JOSIE (*With a twitching smile*). It must have been mad, surely. I wish I'd been there to laugh up my sleeve. (*Angry*) But what's all his crazy lying blather got to do with him betraying us and selling the place?

HOGAN (*At once hopelessly dejected again*). Nothing at all. I only thought you'd like to know you'd had that much revenge.

JOSIE. A hell of a revenge! I'll have a better one than that on him—or I'll try to! I'm not like you, owning up I'm beaten and crying wurra-wurra like a coward and getting hopeless drunk! (*She gives him a shake.*) Get your wits about you and answer me this: Did Simpson get him to sign a paper?

HOGAN. No, but what good is that? In the morning he'll sign all they shove in front of him.

JOSIE. It's this good. It means we still have a chance. Or I have.

HOGAN. What chance? Are you going to beg him to take pity on us?

JOSIE. I'll see him in hell first! There's another chance, and a good one. But I'll need your help—(*Angrily*) And look at you, your brains drowned in whiskey, so I can't depend on you!

HOGAN (*Rousing himself*). You can, if there's any chance. Be God, I'll make myself as sober as a judge for you in the wink of an eye! (*Then dejectedly*) But what can you do now, darlin'? You haven't even got him here. He's down at the Inn sitting alone, drinking and dreaming of the little whores he'll be with tomorrow night on Broadway.

JOSIE. I'll get him here! I'll humble my pride and go down to the Inn for him! And if he doesn't want to come I've a way to make him. I'll raise a scene and pretend I'm in a rage because he forgot his date. I'll disgrace him till he'll be glad to come with me to shut me up. I know his weakness, and it's his vanity about his women. If I was a dainty, pretty tart he'd be proud I'd raise a rumpus about him. But when it's a big, ugly hulk like me—(*She falters and forces herself to go on.*) If he ever was tempted to want me, he'd be ashamed of it. That's the truth behind the lies he told you of his conscience and his fear he might ruin me, God damn him!

HOGAN. No, he meant it, Josie. But never mind that now. Let's say you've got him here. Then what will you do?

JOSIE. I told you this morning if he ever broke his promise to us I'd do anything and not mind how crooked it was. And I will! Your part in it is to come at sunrise with witnesses and catch us in—(*She falters.*)

HOGAN. In bed, is it? Then it's Mike's second scheme you're thinking about?

JOSIE. I told you I didn't care how dirty a trick—(*With a hard bitter laugh*) The dirtier the better now!

HOGAN. But how'll you get him in bed, with all his honorable scruples, thinking you're a virgin? But I'm forgetting he stayed away because he was afraid he'd be tempted. So maybe—

JOSIE (*Tensely*). For the love of God, don't harp on his lies. He won't be tempted at all. But I'll get him so drunk he'll fall asleep and I'll carry him in and put him in bed—

HOGAN. Be God, that's the way! But you'll have to get a pile of whiskey down him. You'll never do it unless you're more sociable and stop looking at him, the way you do, whenever he takes a drink, as if you was praying Almighty God to forgive a poor drunkard. You've got to encourage him. The best way would be for you to drink with him. It would put him at his ease and unsuspecting, and it'd give you courage, too, so you'd act bold for a change instead of giving him brazen talk he's tired of hearing, while you act shy as a mouse.

JOSIE (*Gives her father a bitter, resentful look*). You're full of sly advice all of a sudden, ain't you? You dirty little tick!

HOGAN (*Angrily*). Didn't you tell me to get hold of my wits? Be God if you want me drunk, I've only to let go. That'd suit me. I want to forget my sorrow, and I've no faith in your scheme because you'll be too

full of scruples. Like the drinking. You're such a virtuous teetotaller—

JOSIE. I've told you I'd do anything now! (*Then confusedly*) All I meant was, it's not right, a father to tell his daughter how to—(*Then angrily*) I don't need your advice. Haven't I had every man I want around here?

HOGAN. Ah, thank God, that sounds natural! Be God, I thought you'd started playing virgin with me just because the Broadway sucker thinks you're one.

JOSIE (*Furiously*). Shut up! I'm not playing anything. And don't worry I can't do my part of the trick.

HOGAN. That's the talk! But let me get it all clear. I come at sunrise with my witnesses, and you've forgot to lock your door, and we walk in, and there's the two of you in bed, and I raise the roof and threaten him if he don't marry you—

JOSIE. Marry him? After what he's done to us? I wouldn't marry him now if he was the last man on earth! All we want is a paper signed by him with witnesses that he'll sell the farm to you for the price you offered, and not to Harder.

HOGAN. Well, that's justice, but that's all it is. I thought you wanted to make him pay for his black treachery against us, the dirty bastard!

JOSIE. I do want! (*She again gives him a bitter resentful glance.*) It's the estate money you're thinking of, isn't it? Leave it to you! (*Hastily*) Well, so am I! I'd like to get my hooks on it! (*With a hard, brazen air*) Be God, if I'm to play whore, I deserve my pay! We'll make him sign a paper he owes me ten thousand dollars the minute the estate is settled. (*She laughs.*) How's that? I'll bet none of his tarts on Broadway ever got a thousandth part of that out of him, no matter how dainty and pretty! (*Laughing again*) And here's what'll be the greatest joke to teach him a lesson. He'll pay it for nothing! I'll get him in bed but I'll never let him—

HOGAN (*With delighted admiration*). Och, by Jaysus, Josie, that's the best yet! (*He slaps his thigh enthusiastically.*) Oh, that'll teach him to double-cross his friends! That'll show him two can play at tricks! And him believing you so innocent! Be God, you'll make him the prize sucker of the world! Won't I roar inside me when I see his face in the morning! (*He bursts into coarse laughter.*)

JOSIE (*Again with illogical resentment*). Stop laughing! You're letting yourself be drunk again (*Then with a hard, business-like air*) We've done enough talking. Let's start—

HOGAN. Wait, now. There's another thing. Just what do you want me to threaten him with when I catch you? That we'll sue him for outraging your virtue? Sure, his lawyer would have all your old flames in the witness box, till the jury would think you'd been faithful to the male inhabitants of America. So what threat—I can't think of any he wouldn't laugh at.

JOSIE (*Tensely*). Well, I can! Do I have to tell you his weakness again? It's his vanity about women, and his Broadway pride he's so wise no woman could fool him. It's the disgrace to his vanity—being caught with the likes of me—(*Falteringly, but forcing herself to go on*) My mug beside his in all the newspapers—the New York papers, too—he'll see the whole of Broadway splitting their sides laughing at him—and he'll give anything to keep us quiet, I tell you. He will! I know him! So don't worry—(*She ends up on the verge of bitter humiliated tears.*)

HOGAN (*Without looking at her—enthusiastic again*). Be God, you're right!

JOSIE (*Gives him a bitter glance—fiercely*). Then get the hell out of that chair and let's start it! (*He gets up. She surveys him resentfully.*) You're steady on your pins, ain't you, you scheming old thief, now there's the smell of money around! (*Quickly*) Well, I'm glad. I know I can depend on you now. You'll walk down to the Inn with me and hide outside until you see me come out with him. Then you can sneak in the Inn yourself and pick the witnesses to stay up with you. But mind you don't get drunk again, and let them get too drunk.

HOGAN. I won't, I take my oath! (*He pats her on the shoulder approvingly.*) Be God, you've got the proud, fighting spirit in you that never says die, and you make me ashamed of my weakness. You're that eager now, be damned if I don't almost think you're glad of the excuse!

JOSIE (*Stiffens*). Excuse for what, you old—

HOGAN. To show him no man can get the best of you— what else?—like you showed all the others.

JOSIE. I'll show him to his sorrow! (*Then abruptly, starting for the screen door at left*) Come on. We've no time to waste. (*But when she gets to the door, she appears suddenly hesitant and timid—hurriedly*) Wait. I'd better give a look at myself in the mirror. (*In a brazen tone*) Sure, those in my trade have to look their best!

(*She hurries back across the room into her bedroom and closes the door. Hogan stares after her. Abruptly he ceases to look like a drunk who, by an effort, is keeping himself half-sober. He is a man who has been drinking a lot but is still clear-headed and has complete control of himself.*)

HOGAN (*Watches the crack under Josie's door and speaks half-aloud to himself, shaking his head pityingly*). A look

in the mirror and she's forgot to light her lamp! (*Remorsefully*) God forgive me, it's bitter medicine. But it's the only way I can see that has a chance now. (*Josie's door opens. At once, he is as he was. She comes out, a fixed smile on her lips, her head high, her face set defiantly. But she has evidently been crying.*)

JOSIE (*Brazenly*). There, now. Don't I look ten thousand dollars' worth to any drunk?

HOGAN. You look a million, darlin'!

JOSIE (*Goes to the screen door and pushes it open with the manner of one who has burned all bridges*). Come along, then. (*She goes out. He follows close on her heels. She stops abruptly on the first step—startledly.*) Look! There's someone on the road—

HOGAN (*Pushes past her down the steps—peering off left-front—as if aloud to himself, in dismay*). Be God, it's him! I never thought—

JOSIE (*As if aloud to herself*). So he didn't forget—

HOGAN (*Quickly*). Well, it proves he can't keep away from you, and that'll make it easier for you—(*Then furiously*) Oh, the dirty, double-crossing bastard! The nerve of him! Coming to call on you, after making you wait for hours, thinking you don't know what he's done to us this night, and it'll be a fine cruel joke to blarney you in the moonlight, and you trusting him like a poor sheep, and never suspecting—

JOSIE (*Stung*). Shut up! I'll teach him who's the joker! I'll let him go on as if you hadn't told me what he's done—

HOGAN. Yes, don't let him suspect it, or you wouldn't fool him. He'd know you were after revenge. But he can see me here now. I can't sneak away or he'd be suspicious. We've got to think of a new scheme quick to get me away—

JOSIE (*Quickly*). I know how. Pretend you're as drunk as when you came. Make him believe you're so drunk you don't remember what he's done, so he can't suspect you told me.

HOGAN. I will. Be God, Josie, damned if I don't think he's so queer drunk himself he don't remember, or he'd never come here.

JOSIE. The drunker he is the better! (*Lowering her voice— quickly*) He's turned in the gate where he can hear us. Pretend we're fighting and I'm driving you off till you're sober. Say you won't be back tonight. It'll make him sure he'll have the night alone with me. You start the fight.

HOGAN (*Becomes at once very drunk. He shouts*). Put me out of my own home, will you, you undutiful slut!

JOSIE. Celebration or not, I'll have no drunks cursing and singing all night. Go back to the Inn.

HOGAN. I will! I'll get a room and two bottles and stay drunk as long as I please!

JOSIE. Don't come back till you've slept it off, or I'll wipe the floor with you! (*Tyrone enters, left-front. He does not appear to be drunk—that is, he shows none of the usual syumptoms. He seems much the same as in Act I. The only perceptible change is that his eyes have a peculiar fixed, glazed look, and there is a certain vague quality in his manner and speech, as if he were a bit hazy and absent-minded.*)

TYRONE (*Dryly*). Just in time for the Big Bout. Or is this the final round?

HOGAN (*Whirls on him unsteadily*). Who the hell—(*Peering at him.*) Oh, it's you, is it?

TYRONE. What was the big idea, Phil, leaving me flat?

HOGAN. Leave you flat? Be Jaysus, that reminds me I owe you a swipe on the jaw for something. What was it? Be God, I'm too drunk to remember. But here it is, anyway. (*He turns loose a round-house swing that misses Tyrone by a couple of feet, and reels away. Tyrone regards him with vague surprise.*)

JOSIE. Stop it, you damned old fool, and get out of here!

HOGAN. Taking his side against your poor old father, are you? A hell of a daughter! (*He draws himself up with drunken dignity.*) Don't expect me home tonight, Miss Hogan, or tomorrow either, maybe. You can take your bad temper out on your sweetheart here. (*He starts off down the road, left-front, with a last word over his shoulder.*) Bad luck to you both. (*He disappears. A moment later he begins to bawl his mournful Irish song.*) "Oh, the praties they grow small, Over here, over here," etc. (*During a part of the following scene the song continues to be heard at intervals, receding as he gets farther off on his way to the Inn.*)

JOSIE. Well, thank God. That's good riddance. (*She comes to Tyrone, who stands staring after Hogan with a puzzled look.*)

TYRONE. I've never seen him that stinko before. Must have got him all of a sudden. He didn't seem so lit up at the Inn, but I guess I wasn't paying much attention.

JOSIE (*Forcing a playful air*). I should think, if you were a real gentleman, you'd be apologizing to me, not thinking of him. Don't you know you're two hours and a half late? I oughtn't to speak to you, if I had any pride.

TYRONE (*Stares at her curiously*). You've got too damn much pride, Josie. That's the trouble.

JOSIE. And just what do you mean by that, Jim?

TYRONE (*Shrugs his shoulders*). Nothing. Forget it. I do apologize, Josie. I'm damned sorry. Haven't any excuse. Can't think up a lie. (*Staring at her curiously*

again) Or, now I think of it, I had a damned good honorable excuse, but—(*He shrugs.*) Nuts. Forget it.

JOSIE. Holy Joseph, you're full of riddles tonight. Well, I don't need excuses. I forgive you, anyway, now you're here. (*She takes his hand—playfully.*) Come on now and we'll sit on my bedroom steps and be romantic in the moonlight, like we planned to. (*She leads him there. He goes along in an automatic way, as if only half-conscious of what he is doing. She sits on the top step and pulls him down on the step beneath her. A pause. He stares vaguely at nothing. She bends to give him an uneasy appraising glance.*)

TYRONE (*Suddenly, begins to talk mechanically*). Had to get out of the damned Inn. I was going batty alone there. The old heebie-jeebies. So I came to you. (*He pauses—then adds with strange, wondering sincerity.*) I've really begun to love you a lot, Josie.

Josie (*Blurts out bitterly*). Yes, you've proved that tonight, haven't you? (*Hurriedly regaining her playful tone*) But never mind. I said I'd forgive you for being so late. So go on about love. I'm all ears.

TYRONE (*As if he hadn't listened*). I thought you'd have given me up and gone to bed. I remember I had some nutty idea I'd get in bed with you—just to lie with my head on your breast.

Josie (*Moved in spite of herself—but keeps her bold, playful tone*). Well, maybe I'll let you—(*Hurriedly*) Later on, I mean. The night's young yet, and we'll have it all to ourselves. (*Boldly again*) But here's for a starter. (*She puts her arms around him and draws him back till his head is on her breast.*) There, now.

TYRONE (*Relaxes—simply and gratefully*). Thanks, Josie. (*He closes his eyes. For a moment she forgets everything and stares down at his face with a passionate, possessive tenderness. A pause. From far-off on the road to the Inn, Hogan's mournful song drifts back through the moonlight quiet: "Oh, the praties they grow small, Over here, over here." Tyrone rouses himself and straightens up. He acts embarrassed, as if he felt he'd been making a fool of himself—mockingly.*) Hark, Hark, the Donegal lark! "Thou wast not born for death, immortal bird." Can't Phil sing anything but that damned dirge, Josie? (*She doesn't reply. He goes on hazily.*) Still, it seems to belong tonight—in the moonlight—or in my mind—(*He quotes.*)

"Now more than ever seems it rich to die,
To cease upon the midnight with no pain.
In such an ecstasy!"

(*He has recited this with deep feeling. Now he sneers.*) Good God! Ode to Phil the Irish Nightingale! I must have the D.T.'s.

JOSIE (*Her face grown bitter*). Maybe it's only your bad conscience.

TYRONE (*Starts guiltily and turns to stare into her face—suspiciously*). What put that in your head? Conscience about what?

JOSIE (*Quickly*). How would I know, if you don't? (*Forcing a playful tone*) For the sin of wanting to be in bed with me. Maybe that's it.

TYRONE (*With strange relief*). Oh. (*A bit shamefacedly*) Forget that stuff, Josie. I was half nutty.

Josie (*Bitterly*). Och, for the love of God, don't apologize as if you was ashamed of—(*She catches herself.*)

TYRONE (*With a quick glance at her face*). All right. I certainly won't apologize—if you're not kicking. I was afraid I might have shocked your modesty.

JOSIE (*Roughly*). My modesty? Be God, I didn't know I had any left.

TYRONE (*Draws away from her—irritably*). Nix, Josie. Lay off that line, for tonight at least. (*He adds slowly.*) I'd like tonight to be different.

JOSIE. Different from what? (*He doesn't answer. She forces a light tone.*) All right. I'll be different as you please.

TYRONE (*Simply*). Thanks, Josie. Just be yourself. (*Again as if he were ashamed, or afraid he had revealed some weakness—off-handedly.*) This being out in the moonlight instead of the lousy Inn isn't a bad bet, at that. I don't know why I hang out in that dump, except I'm even more bored in the so-called good hotels in this hick town.

JOSIE (*Trying to examine his face without his knowing*). Well, you'll be back on Broadway soon now, won't you?

TYRONE. I hope so.

JOSIE. Then you'll have all the pretty little tarts to comfort you when you get your sorrowful spell on.

TYRONE. Oh, to hell with the rough stuff, Josie! You promised you'd can it tonight.

JOSIE (*Tensely*). You're a fine one to talk of promises!

TYRONE (*Vaguely surprised by her tone*). What's the matter? Still sore at me for being late?

JOSIE (*Quickly*). I'm not. I was teasing you. To prove there's no hard feelings, how would you like a drink? But I needn't ask. (*She gets up.*) I'll get a bottle of his best.

TYRONE (*Mechanically*). Fine. Maybe that will have some kick. The booze at the Inn didn't work tonight.

JOSIE. Well, this'll work. (*She starts to go into her bedroom. He sits hunched up on the step, staring at nothing. She pauses in the doorway to glance back. The hard, calculating expression on her face softens. For a second she stares at him, bewildered by her conflicting feelings. Then she goes inside, leaving the door open. She opens the door*

from her room to the lighted living room, and is seen going to the kitchen on the way to the cellar. She has left the door from the living room to her bedroom open and the light reveals a section of the bedroom framed in the doorway behind Tyrone. The foot of the bed which occupies most of the room can be seen, and that is all except that the walls are unpainted pine boards. Tyrone continues to stare at nothing, but becomes restless. His hands and mouth twitch.)

TYRONE (*Suddenly, with intense hatred*). You rotten bastard! (*He springs to his feet—fumbles in his pockets for cigarettes—strikes a match which lights up his face, on which there is now an expression of miserable guilt. His hand is trembling so violently he cannot light the cigarette.*)

ACT III

(*Scene: The living-room wall has been replaced and all we see now of its lighted interior is through the two windows. Otherwise, everything is the same, and this Act follows the preceding without any lapse of time. Tyrone is still trying with shaking hands to get his cigarette lighted. Finally he succeeds, and takes a deep inhale, and starts pacing back and forth a few steps, as if in a cell of his own thought. He swears defensively.*) God damn it. You'll be crying in your beer in a minute. (*He begins to sing sneeringly half under his breath a snatch from an old sob song, popular in the Nineties.*)

"And baby's cries can't waken her
In the baggage coach ahead."

(*His sneer changes to a look of stricken guilt and grief*) Christ! (*He seems about to break down and sob but he fights this back.*) Cut it out, you drunken fool! (*Josie can be seen through the windows, returning from the kitchen. He turns with a look of relief and escape.*) Thank God! (*He sits on the boulder and waits. Josie stops by the table in the living room to turn down the lamp until only a dim light remains. She has a quart of whiskey under her arm, two tumblers, and a pitcher of water. She goes through her bedroom and appears in the outer doorway. Tyrone gets up.*) Ah! At last the old booze! (*He relieves her of the pitcher and tumblers as she comes down the steps.*)

JOSIE (*With a fixed smile*). You'd think I'd been gone years. You didn't seem so perishing for a drink.

TYRONE (*In his usual, easy, kidding way*). It's you I was perishing for. I've been dying of loneliness—

JOSIE. You'll die of lying some day. But I'm glad you're alive again. I thought when I left you really were dying on me.

TYRONE. No such luck.

JOSIE. Och, don't talk like that. Come have a drink. We'll use the boulder for a table and I'll be barkeep. (*He puts the pitcher and tumblers on the boulder and she uncorks the bottle. She takes a quick glance at his face—startledly.*) What's come over you, Jim? You look as if you've seen a ghost.

TYRONE (*Looks away—dryly*). I have. My own. He's punk company.

JOSIE. Yes, it's the worst ghost of all, your own. Don't I know? But this will keep it in place. (*She pours a tumbler half full of whiskey and hands it to him.*) Here. But wait till I join you. (*She pours the other tumbler half full.*)

TYRONE (*Surprised*). Hello! I thought you never touched it.

JOSIE (*Glibly*). I have on occasion. And this is one. I don't want to be left out altogether from celebrating our victory over Harder. (*She gives him a sharp bitter glance. Meeting his eyes, which are regarding her with puzzled wonder, she forces a laugh.*) Don't look at me as if I was up to some game. A drink or two will make me better company, and help me enjoy the moon and the night with you. Here's luck. (*She touches his glass with hers.*)

TYRONE (*Shrugs his shoulders*). All right. Here's luck. (*They drink. She gags and sputters. He pours water in her glass. She drinks it. He puts his glass and the pitcher back on the boulder. He keeps staring at her with a puzzled frown.*)

JOSIE. Some of it went down the wrong way.

TYRONE. So I see. That'll teach you to pour out baths instead of drinks.

JOSIE. It's the first time I ever heard you complain a drink was too big.

TYRONE. Yours was too big.

JOSIE. I'm my father's daughter. I've a strong head. So don't worry I'll pass out and you'll have to put me to bed. (*She gives a little bold laugh.*) Sure, that's a beautiful notion. I'll have to pretend I'm—

TYRONE (*Irritably*). Nix on the raw stuff, Josie. Remember you said—

JOSIE (*Resentment in her kidding*). I'd be different? That's right. I'm forgetting it's your pleasure to have me pretend I'm an innocent virgin tonight.

TYRONE (*In a strange tone that is almost threatening*). If you don't look out, I'll call you on that bluff, Josie. (*He stares at her with a deliberate sensualist's look that undresses her.*) I'd like to. You know that, don't you?

JOSIE (*Boldly*). I don't at all. You're the one who's bluffing.

TYRONE (*Grabs her in his arms—with genuine passion*). Josie! (*Then as suddenly lets her go*) Nix. Let's cut it out. (*He turns away. Her face betrays the confused conflict within her of fright, passion, happiness, and bitter resentment. He goes on with an abrupt change of tone.*) How about another drink? That's honest-to-God old bonded Bourbon. How the devil did Phil get hold of it?

JOSIE. Tom Lombardo, the bootlegger, gave him a case for letting him hide a truckload in our barn when the agents were after him. He stole it from a warehouse on faked permits. (*She pours out drinks as she speaks, a half tumblerful for him, a small one for herself.*) Here you are. (*She gives him his drink—smiles at him coquettishly, beginning to show the effect of her big drink by her increasingly bold manners.*) Let's sit down where the moon will be in our eye and we'll see romance. (*She takes his arm and leads him to her bedroom steps. She sits on the top step, pulling him down beside her but on the one below. She raises her glass.*) Here's hoping before the night's out you'll have more courage and kiss me at least.

TYRONE (*Frowns—then kiddingly*). That's a promise. Here's how. (*He drains his tumbler. She drinks half of hers. He puts his glass on the ground beside him. A pause. She tries to read his face without his noticing. He seems to be lapsing again into vague preoccupation.*)

JOSIE. Now don't sink back half-dead-and-alive in dreams the way you were before.

TYRONE (*Quickly*). I'm not. I had a good final dose of heebie-jeebies when you were in the house. That's all for tonight. (*He adds a bit maudlinly, his two big drinks beginning to affect him.*) Let the dead past bury its dead.

JOSIE. That's the talk. There's only tonight, and the moon, and us—and the bonded Bourbon. Have another drink, and don't wait for me.

TYRONE. Not now, thanks. They're coming too fast. (*He gives her a curious, cynically amused look.*) Trying to get me soused, Josie?

JOSIE (*Starts—quickly*). I'm not. Only to get you feeling happy, so you'll forget all sadness.

TYRONE (*Kiddingly*). I might forget all my honorable intentions, too. So look out.

JOSIE. I'll look forward to it—and I hope that's another promise, like the kiss you owe me. If you're suspicious I'm trying to get you soused—well, here goes. (*She drinks what is left in her glass.*) There, now. I must be scheming to get myself soused, too.

TYRONE. Maybe you are.

JOSIE (*Resentfully*). If I was, it'd be to make you feel at home. Don't all the pretty little Broadway tarts get soused with you?

TYRONE (*Irritably*). There you go again with that old line!

JOSIE. All right, I won't! (*Forcing a laugh*) I must be eaten up with jealousy for them, that's it.

TYRONE. You needn't be. They don't belong.

JOSIE. And I do?

TYRONE. Yes. You do.

JOSIE. For tonight only, you mean?

TYRONE. We've agreed there is only tonight—and it's to be different from any past night—for both of us.

JOSIE (*In a forced, kidding tone*). I hope it will be. I'll try to control my envy for your Broadway flames. I suppose it's because I have a picture of them in my mind as small and dainty and pretty—

TYRONE. They're just gold-digging tramps.

JOSIE (*As if he hadn't spoken*). While I'm only a big, rough, ugly cow of a woman.

TYRONE. Shut up! You're beautiful.

JOSIE (*Jeeringly, but her voice trembles*). God pity the blind!

TYRONE. You're beautiful to me.

JOSIE. It must be the Bourbon—

TYRONE. You're real and healthy and clean and fine and warm and strong and kind—

JOSIE. I have a beautiful soul, you mean?

TYRONE. Well, I don't know much about ladies' souls— (*He takes her hand.*) But I do know you're beautiful. (*He kisses her hand.*) And I love you a lot—in my fashion.

JOSIE (*Stammers*). Jim—(*Hastily forcing her playful tone*) Sure, you're full of fine compliments all of a sudden, and I ought to show you how pleased I am. (*She pulls his head back and kisses him on the lips—a quick, shy kiss.*) That's for my beautiful soul.

TYRONE (*The kiss arouses his physical desire. He pulls her head down and stares into her eyes*). You have a beautiful strong body, too, Josie—and beautiful eyes and hair, and a beautiful smile and beautiful warm breasts. (*He kisses her on the lips. She pulls back frightenedly for a second—then returns his kiss. Suddenly he breaks away—in a tone of guilty irritation.*) Nix! Nix! Don't be a fool, Josie. Don't let me pull that stuff.

JOSIE (*Triumphantly for a second*). You mean it! I know you mean it! (*Then with resentful bitterness—roughly*) Be God, you're right I'm a damned fool to let you make me forget you're the greatest liar in the world! (*Quickly*) I mean, the greatest kidder. And now, how about another drink?

TYRONE (*Staring at nothing—vaguely*). You don't get me, Josie. You don't know—and I hope you never will know—

JOSIE (*Blurts out bitterly*). Maybe I know more than you think.

TYRONE (*As if she hadn't spoken*). There's always the aftermath that poisons you. I don't want you to be poisoned—

JOSIE. Maybe you know what you're talking about—

TYRONE. And I don't want to be poisoned myself—not again—not with you. (*He pauses—slowly.*) There have been too many nights—and dawns. This must be different. I want—(*His voice trails off into silence.*)

JOSIE (*Trying to read his face—uneasily*). Don't get in one of your queer spells, now. (*She gives his shoulder a shake—forcing a light tone.*) Sure, I don't think you know what you want. Except another drink. I'm sure you want that. And I want one, too.

TYRONE (*Recovering himself*). Fine! Grand idea. (*He gets up and brings the bottle from the boulder. He picks up his tumbler and pours a big drink. She is holding out her tumbler but he ignores it.*)

JOSIE. You're not polite, pouring your own first.

TYRONE. I said a drink was a grand idea—for me. Not for you. You skip this one.

JOSIE (*Resentfully*). Oh, I do, do I? Are you giving me orders?

TYRONE. Yes. Take a big drink of moonlight instead.

JOSIE (*Angrily*). You'll pour me a drink, if you please, Jim Tyrone, or—

TYRONE (*Stares at her—then shrugs his shoulders*). All right, if you want to take it that way, Josie. It's your funeral. (*He pours a drink into her tumbler.*)

JOSIE (*Ashamed but defiant—stiffly*). Thank you kindly. (*She raises her glass—mockingly.*) Here's to tonight. (*Tyrone is staring at her, a strange bitter disgust in his eyes. Suddenly he slaps at her hand, knocking the glass to the ground.*)

TYRONE (*His voice hard with repulsion*). I've slept with drunken tramps on too many nights!

Josie (*Stares at him, too startled and bewildered to be angry. Her voice trembles with surprising meekness*). All right, Jim, if you don't want me to—

TYRONE (*Now looks as bewildered by his action as she does*). I'm sorry, Josie. Don't know what the drink got into me. (*He picks up her glass.*) Here, I'll pour you another.

JOSIE (*Still meek*). No, thank you. I'll skip this one. (*She puts the glass on the ground.*) But you drink up.

TYRONE. Thanks. (*He gulps down his drink. Mechanically, as if he didn't know what he was doing, he pours, another. Suddenly he blurts out with guilty loathing.*) That fat blonde pig on the train—I got her drunk! That's why—(*He stops guiltily.*)

JOSIE (*Uneasily*). What are you talking about? What train?

TYRONE. No train. Don't mind me. (*He gulps down the drink and pours another with the same strange air of acting unconsciously.*) Maybe I'll tell you—later, when I'm—That'll cure you—for all time! (*Abruptly he re-*

alizes what he is saying. He gives the characteristic shrug of shoulders—cynically.) Nuts! The Brooklyn boys are talking again. I guess I'm more stewed than I thought—in the center of the old bean, at least. (*Dully*) I better beat it back to the Inn and go to bed and stop bothering you, Josie.

JOSIE (*Bullyingly—and pityingly*). Well, you won't, not if I have to hold you. Come on now, bring your drink and sit down like you were before. (*He does so. She pats his cheek—forcing a playful air.*) That's a good boy. And I won't take any more whiskey. I've all the effect from it I want already. Everything is far away and doesn't matter—except the moon and its dreams—and you are, too. (*She adds with a rueful little laugh.*) I keep forgetting the thing I've got to remember. I keep hoping it's a lie, even though I know I'm a damned fool.

TYRONE (*Hazily*). Damned fool about what?

JOSIE. Never mind. (*Forcing a laugh*) I've just had a thought. If my poor old father had seen you knocking his prize whiskey on the ground—Holy Joseph, he'd have had three paralytic strokes!

TYRONE (*Grins*). Yes, I can picture him. (*He pauses—with amused affection.*) But that's all a fake. He loves to play tightwad, but the people he likes know better. He'd give them his shirt. He's a grand old scout, Josie. (*A bit maudlin*) The only real friend I've got left—except you. I love his guts.

JOSIE (*Tensely—sickened by his hypocrisy*). Och, for the love of God—!

TYRONE (*Shrugs his shoulders*). Yes, I suppose that does sound like moaning-at-the-bar stuff. But I mean it.

JOSIE. Do you? Well, I know my father's virtues without you telling me.

TYRONE. You ought to appreciate him because he worships the ground you walk on—and he knows you a lot better than you think. (*He turns to smile at her teasingly.*) As well as I do—almost.

JOSIE (*Defensively*). That's not saying much. Maybe I can guess what you think you know—(*Forcing a contemptuous laugh*) If it's that, God pity you, you're a terrible fool.

TYRONE (*Teasingly*). If it's what? I haven't said anything.

JOSIE. You'd better not, or I'll die laughing at you. (*She changes the subject abruptly.*) Why don't you drink up? It makes me nervous watching you hold it as if you didn't know it was there.

TYRONE. I didn't, at that. (*He drinks.*)

JOSIE. And have another.

TYRONE (*A bit drunkenly*). Will a whore go to a picnic? Real bonded Bourbon. That's my dish. (*He goes to the boulder for the bottle. He is as steady on his feet as if he were completely sober.*)

JOSIE (*In a light tone*). Bring the bottle back so it'll be handy and you won't have to leave me. I miss you.

TYRONE (*Comes back with the bottle. He smiles at her cynically*). Still trying to get me soused, Josie?

JOSIE. I'm not such a fool—with your capacity.

TYRONE. You better watch your step. It might work—and then think of how disgusted you'd feel with me lying beside you, probably snoring, as you watched the dawn come. You don't know—

JOSIE (*Defiantly*). The hell I don't! Isn't that the way I've felt with every one of them, after?

TYRONE (*As if he hadn't heard—bitterly*). But take it from me, I know. I've seen too God-damned many dawns creeping grayly over too many dirty windows.

JOSIE (*Ignores this—boldly*). But it might be different with you. Love could make it different. And I've been head over heels in love ever since you said you loved my beautiful soul. (*Again he doesn't seem to have heard, resentfully.*) Don't stand there like a loon, mourning over the past. Why don't you pour yourself a drink and sit down?

TYRONE (*Looks at the bottle and tumbler in his hands, as if he'd forgotten them—mechanically*). Sure thing. Real bonded Bourbon. I ought to know. If I had a dollar for every drink of it I had before Prohibition, I'd hire our dear bully, Harder, for a valet. (*Josie stiffens and her face hardens. Tyrone pours a drink and sets the bottle on the ground. He looks up suddenly into her eyes—warningly.*) You'd better remember I said you had beautiful eyes and hair—and breasts.

JOSIE. I remember you did. (*She tries to be calculatingly enticing.*) So sit down and I'll let you lay your head—

TYRONE. No. If you won't watch your step, I've got to. (*He sits down but doesn't lean back.*) And don't let me get away with pretending I'm so soused I don't know what I'm doing. I always know. Or part of me does. That's the trouble. (*He pauses—then bursts out in a strange threatening tone.*) You better look out, Josie. She was tickled to death to get me pie-eyed. Had an idea she could roll me, I guess. She wasn't so tickled about it—later on.

JOSIE. What she? (*He doesn't reply. She forces a light tone.*) I hope you don't think I'm scheming to roll you.

TYRONE (*Vaguely*). What? (*Coming to—indignantly*) Of course not. What are you talking about? For God's sake, you're not a tart.

JOSIE (*Roughly*). No, I'm a fool. I'm always giving it away.

TYRONE (*Angrily*). That lousy bluff again, eh? You're a liar! For Christ's sake, quit the smut stuff, can't you!

JOSIE (*Stung*). Listen to me, Jim! Drunk or not, don't you talk that way to me or—

TYRONE. How about your not talking the old smut stuff to me? You promised you'd be yourself. (*Pauses—vaguely*) You don't get it, Josie. You see, she was one of the smuttiest talking pigs I've ever listened to.

JOSIE. What she? Do you mean the blonde on the train?

TYRONE (*Starts—sharply*). Train? Who told you—? (*Quickly*) Oh—that's right—I did say—(*Vaguely*) What blonde? What's the difference? Coming back from the Coast. It was long ago. But it seems like tonight. There is no present or future—only the past happening over and over again—now. You can't get away from it. (*Abruptly*) Nuts! To hell with that crap.

JOSIE. You came back from the Coast about a year ago after—(*She checks herself.*)

TYRONE (*Dully*). Yes. After Mama's death. (*Quickly*) But I've been to the Coast a lot of times during my career as a third-rate ham. I don't remember which time—or anything much—except I was pie-eyed in a drawing room for the whole four days. (*Abruptly*) What were we talking about before? What a grand guy Phil is. You ought to be glad you've got him for a father. Mine was an old bastard.

JOSIE. He wasn't! He was one of the finest, kindest gentlemen ever lived.

TYRONE (*Sneeringly*). Outside the family, sure. Inside, he was a lousy tightwad bastard.

JOSIE (*Repelled*). You ought to be ashamed!

TYRONE. To speak ill of the dead? Nuts! He can't hear, and he knows I hated him, anyway—as much as he hated me. I'm glad he's dead. So is he. Or he ought to be. Everyone ought to be, if they have any sense. Out of a bum racket. At peace. (*He shrugs his shoulders.*) Nuts! What of it?

JOSIE (*Tensely*). Don't Jim. I hate you when you talk like that. (*Forcing a light tone.*) Do you want to spoil our beautiful moonlight night! And don't be telling me of your old flames, on trains or not. I'm too jealous.

TYRONE (*With a shudder of disgust*). Of that pig? (*He drinks his whiskey as if to wash a bad taste from his mouth—then takes one of her hands in both of his—simply.*) You're a fool to be jealous of anyone. You're the only woman I care a damn about.

JOSIE (*Deeply stirred, in spite of herself—her voice trembling*). Jim, don't—(*Forcing a tense little laugh*) All right, I'll try and believe that—for tonight.

TYRONE (*Simply*). Thanks, Josie. (*A pause. He speaks in a tone of random curiosity.*) Why did you say a while ago I'd be leaving for New York soon?

JOSIE (*Stiffens—her face hardening*). Well, I was right, wasn't I? (*Unconsciously she tries to pull her hand away.*)

TYRONE. Why are you pulling your hand away?

JOSIE (*Stops*). Was I? (*Forcing a smile*) I suppose because it seems crazy for you to hold my big ugly paw so tenderly. But you're welcome to it, if you like.

TYRONE. I do like. It's strong and kind and warm—like you. (*He kisses it.*)

JOSIE (*Tensely*). Och, for the love of God—! (*She jerks her hand away—then hastily forces a joking tone.*) Wasting kisses on my hand! Sure, even the moon is laughing at us.

TYRONE. Nuts for the moon! I'd rather have one light on Broadway than all the moons since Rameses was a pup. (*He takes cigarettes from his pocket and lights one.*)

JOSIE (*Her eyes searching his face, lighted up by the match*). You'll be taking a train back to your dear old Broadway tomorrow night, won't you?

TYRONE (*Still holding the burning match, stares at her in surprise*). Tomorrow night? Where did you get that?

JOSIE. A little bird told me.

TYRONE (*Blows out the match in a cloud of smoke*). You'd better give that bird the bird. By the end of the week, is the right dope. Phil got his dates mixed.

JOSIE (*Quickly*). He didn't tell me. He was too drunk to remember anything.

TYRONE. He was sober when I told him. I called up the executors when we reached the Inn after leaving here. They said the estate would be out of probate within a few days. I told Phil the glad tidings and bought drinks for all and sundry. There was quite a celebration. Funny, Phil wouldn't remember that.

JOSIE (*Bewildered—not knowing what to believe*). It is—funny.

TYRONE (*Shrugs his shoulders*). Well, he's stewed to the ears. That always explains anything. (*Then strangely*) Only sometimes it doesn't.

JOSIE. No—sometimes it doesn't.

TYRONE (*Goes on without real interest, talking to keep from thinking*). Phil certainly has a prize bun on tonight. He never took a punch at me before. And that drivel he talked about owing me one—What got into his head, I wonder.

JOSIE (*Tensely*). How would I know, if you don't?

TYRONE. Well, I don't. Not unless—I remember I did try to get his goat. Simpson sat down with us. Harder sent him to see me. You remember after Harder left here I said the joke was on you, that you'd made this place a gold mine. I was kidding, but I had the right dope. What do you think he told Simpson to offer? Ten grand! On the level, Josie.

JOSIE (*Tense*). So you accepted?

TYRONE. I told Simpson to tell Harder I did. I decided the best way to fix him was to let him think he'd got away with it, and then when he comes tomorrow morning to drive me to the executor's office, I'll tell him what he can do with himself, his bankroll, and tin oil tanks.

JOSIE (*Knows he is telling the truth—so relieved she can only stammer stupidly*). So that's—the truth of it.

TYRONE (*Smiles*). Of course, I did it to kid Phil, too. He was right there, listening. But I know I didn't fool him.

JOSIE (*Weakly*). Maybe you did fool him, for once. But I don't know.

TYRONE. And that's why he took a swing at me? (*He laughs, but there is a forced note to it.*) Well, if so, it's one hell of a joke on him. (*His tone becomes hurt and bitter.*) All the same, I'll be good and sore, Josie. I promised this place wouldn't be sold except to him. What the hell does he think I am? He ought to know I wouldn't double-cross you and him for ten million!

JOSIE (*Giving away at last to her relief and joy*). Don't I know! Oh, Jim, darling! (*She hugs him passionately and kisses him on the lips.*) I knew you'd never—I told him—(*She kisses him again.*) Oh, Jim, I love you.

TYRONE (*Again with a strange, simple gratitude*). Thanks, Josie. I mean, for not believing I'm a rotten louse. Everyone else believes it—including myself—for a damned good reason. (*Abruptly changing the subject*) I'm a fool to let this stuff about Phil get under my skin, but—Why, I remember telling him tonight I'd even written my brother and got his okay on selling the farm to him. And Phil thanked me. He seemed touched and grateful. You wouldn't think he'd forget that.

JOSIE (*Her face hard and bitter*). I wouldn't, indeed. There's a lot of things he'll have to explain when he comes at sun—(*Hastily*) When he comes back. (*She pauses—then bursts out.*) The damned old schemer, I'll teach him to—(*Again checking herself*) to act like a fool.

TYRONE (*Smiles*). You'll get out the old club, eh? What a bluff you are, Josie. (*Teasingly*) You and your lovers, Messalina—when you've never—

JOSIE (*With a faint spark of her old defiance*). You're a liar.

TYRONE. "Pride is the sin by which the angels fell." Are you going to keep that up—with me?

JOSIE (*Feebly*). You think I've never because no one would—because I'm a great ugly cow—

TYRONE (*Gently*). Nuts! You could have had any one of them. You kidded them till you were sure they wanted you. That was all you wanted. And then you slapped them groggy when they tried for more. But you had to keep convincing yourself—

JOSIE (*Tormentedly*). Don't, Jim.

TYRONE. You can take the truth, Josie—from me. Because you and I belong to the same club. We can kid the world but we can't fool ourselves, like most people, no matter what we do—nor escape ourselves no matter where we run away. Whether it's the bottom of a bottle, or a South Sea Island, we'd find our own ghosts there waiting to greet us—"sleepless with pale commemorative eyes," as Rossetti wrote. (*He sneers to himself.*) The old poetic bull, eh? Crap! (*Reverting to a teasing tone*) You don't ask how I saw through your bluff, Josie. You pretend too much. And so do the guys. I've listened to them at the Inn. They all lie to each other. No one wants to admit all he got was a slap in the puss, when he thinks a lot of other guys made it. You can't blame them. And they know you don't give a damn how they lie. So—

JOSIE. For the love of God, Jim! Don't!

TYRONE. Phil is wise to you, of course, but although he knew I knew, he would never admit it until tonight.

JOSIE (*Startled—vindictively*). So he admitted it, did he? Wait till I get hold of him!

TYRONE. He'll never admit it to you. He's afraid of hurting you.

JOSIE. He is, is he? Well—(*Almost hysterically*) For the love of God, can't you shut up about him!

TYRONE (*Glances up at her, surprised—then shrugs his shoulders*). Oh, all right. I wanted to clear things up, that's all—for Phil's sake as well as yours. You have a hell of a license to be sore. He's the one who ought to be. Don't you realize what a lousy position you've put him in with your brazen-trollop act?

JOSIE (*Tensely*). No. He doesn't care, except to use me in his scheming. He—

TYRONE. Don't be a damned fool. Of course he cares. And so do I. (*He turns and pulls her head down and kisses her on the lips.*) I care, Josie. I love you.

JOSIE (*With pitiful longing*). Do you, Jim? Do you? (*She forces a trembling smile—faintly.*) Then I'll confess the truth to you. I've been a crazy fool. I am a virgin. (*She begins to sob with a strange forlorn shame and humiliation.*) And now you'll never—and I want you to—now more than ever—because I love you more than ever, after what's happened—(*Suddenly she kisses him with fierce passion.*) But you will! I'll make you! To hell with your honorable scruples! I know you want me! I couldn't believe that until tonight—but now I know. It's in your kisses! (*She kisses him again—with passionate tenderness.*) Oh, you great fool! As if I gave a damn what happened after! I'll have had tonight and your love to remember for the rest of my days!

(*She kisses him again.*) Oh, Jim darling, haven't you said yourself there's only tonight? (*She whispers tenderly.*) Come. Come with me. (*She gets to her feet, pulling at his arm—with a little self-mocking laugh.*) But I'll have to make you leave before sunrise. I mustn't forget that.

TYRONE (*A strange change has come over his face. He looks her over now with a sneering cynical lust. He speaks thickly as if he was suddenly very drunk*). Sure thing, Kiddo. What the hell else do you suppose I came for? I've been kidding myself. (*He steps up beside her and puts his arm around her and presses his body to hers.*) You're the goods, Kid. I've wanted you all along. Love, nuts! I'll show you what love is. I know what you want, Bright Eyes. (*She is staring at him now with a look of frightened horror. He kisses her roughly.*) Come on, Baby Doll, let's hit the hay. (*He pushes her back in the doorway.*)

JOSIE (*Strickenly*). Jim! Don't! (*She pulls his arms away so violently that he staggers back and would fall down the steps if she didn't grab his arm in time. As it is he goes down on one knee. She is on the verge of collapse herself—brokenly.*) Jim! I'm not a whore.

TYRONE (*Remains on one knee—confusedly, as if he didn't know what had happened*). What the hell? Was I trying to rape you, Josie? Forget it. I'm drunk—not responsible. (*He gets to his feet, staggering a bit, and steps down to the ground.*)

JOSIE (*Covering her face with her hands*). Oh, Jim! (*She sobs.*)

TYRONE (*With vague pity*). Don't cry. No harm done. You stopped me, didn't you? (*She continues to sob. He mutters vaguely, as if talking to himself.*) Must have drawn a blank for a while. Nuts! Cut out the faking. I knew what I was doing. (*Slowly, staring before him.*) But it's funny, I *was* seeing things. That's the truth, Josie. For a moment I thought you were that blonde pig— (*Hastily*) The old heebie-jeebies. Hair of the dog. (*He gropes around for the bottle and his glass.*) I'll have another shot—

JOSIE (*Takes her hands from her face—fiercely*). Pour the whole bottle down your throat, if you like! Only stop talking! (*She covers her face with her hands and sobs again.*)

TYRONE (*Stares at her with a hurt and sad expression—dully*). Can't forgive me, eh? You ought to. You ought to thank me for letting you see—(*He pauses, as if waiting for her to say something, but she remains silent. He shrugs his shoulders, pours out a big drink mechanically.*) Well, here's how. (*He drinks and puts the bottle and glass on the ground—dully.*) That was a nightcap. Our moonlight romance seems to be a flop, Josie. I guess I'd better go.

JOSIE (*Dully*). Yes. You'd better go. Good night.

TYRONE. Not good night. Good-bye.

JOSIE (*Lifts her head*). Good-bye?

TYRONE. Yes. I won't see you again before I leave for New York. I was a damned fool to come tonight. I hoped—But you don't get it. How could you? So what's the good—(*He shrugs his shoulders hopelessly and turns toward the road.*)

JOSIE. Jim!

TYRONE (*Turning back—bitter accusation in his tone now*). Whore? Who said you were a whore? But I warned you, didn't I, if you kept on—Why did you have to act like one, asking me to come to bed? That wasn't what I came here for. And you promised tonight would be different. Why the hell did you promise that, if all you wanted was what all the others want, if that's all love means to you? (*Then guiltily*) Oh, Christ, I don't mean that, Josie. I know how you feel, and if I could give you happiness—But it wouldn't work. You don't know me. I'd poison it for myself and for you. I've poisoned it already, haven't I, but it would be a million times worse after—No matter how I tried not to. I'd make it like all the other nights—for you, too. You'd lie awake and watch the dawn come with disgust, with nausea retching your memory, and the wine of passion poets blab about, a sour aftertaste in your mouth of Dago red ink! (*He gives a sneering laugh.*)

JOSIE (*Distractedly*). Oh, Jim, don't! Please don't!

TYRONE. You'd hate me and yourself—not for a day or two but for the rest of your life. (*With a perverse, jeering note of vindictive boastfulness in his tone*) Believe me, Kid, when I poison them, they stay poisoned!

JOSIE (*With dull bitterness*). Good-bye, Jim.

TYRONE (*Miserably hurt and sad for a second—appealingly*). Josie—(*Gives the characteristic shrug of his shoulders—simply*) Good-bye. (*He turns toward the road—bitterly.*) I'll find it hard to forgive, too. I came here asking for love—just for this one night, because I thought you loved me. (*Dully*) Nuts. To hell with it. (*He starts away.*)

JOSIE (*Watches him for a second, fighting the love that, in spite of her, responds to his appeal—then she springs up and runs to him—with fierce, possessive, maternal tenderness*). Come here to me, you great fool, and stop your silly blather. There's nothing to hate you for. There's nothing to forgive. Sure, I was only trying to give you happiness, because I love you. I'm sorry I was so stupid and didn't see—But I see now, and you'll find I have all the love you need. (*She gives him a hug and kisses him. There is passion in her kiss but it is a tender, protective maternal passion, which he responds to with an instant grateful yielding.*)

TYRONE (*Simply*). Thanks, Josie. You're beautiful. I love you. I knew you'd understand.

JOSIE. Of course I do. Come, now. (*She leads him back, her arm around his waist.*)

TYRONE. I didn't want to leave you. You know that.

JOSIE. Indeed I know it. Come now. We'll sit down. (*She sits on the top step and pulls him down on the step below her.*) That's it—with my arm around you. Now lay your head on my breast—the way you said you wanted to do—(*He lets his head fall back on her breast. She hugs him—gently.*) There, now. Forget all about my being a fool and forgive—(*Her voice trembles—but she goes on determinedly.*) Forgive my selfishness, thinking only of myself. Sure, if there's one thing I owe you tonight, after all my lying and scheming, it's to give you the love you need, and it'll be my pride and my joy—(*Forcing a trembling echo of her playful tone*) It's easy enough, too, for I have all kinds of love for you—and maybe this is the greatest of all—because it costs so much. (*She pauses, looking down at his face. He has closed his eyes and his haggard, dissipated face looks like a pale mask in the moonlight—at peace as a death mask is at peace. She becomes frightened.*) Jim! Don't look like that!

TYRONE (*Opens his eyes—vaguely*). Like what?

JOSIE (*Quickly*). It's the moonlight. It makes you look so pale, and with your eyes closed—

TYRONE (*Simply*). You mean I looked dead?

JOSIE. No! As if you'd fallen asleep.

TYRONE (*Speaks in a tired, empty tone, as if he felt he ought to explain something to her—something which no longer interests him*). Listen, and I'll tell you a little story, Josie. All my life I had just one dream. From the time I was a kid, I loved race-horses. I thought they were the most beautiful things in the world. I liked to gamble, too. So the big dream was that some day I'd have enough dough to play a cagey system of betting on favorites, and follow the horses south in the winter, and come back north with them in the spring, and be at the track every day. It seemed that would be the ideal life—for me. (*He pauses.*)

JOSIE. Well, you'll be able to do it.

TYRONE. No. I won't be able to do it, Josie. That's the joke. I gave it a try-out before I came up here. I borrowed some money on my share of the estate, and started going to tracks. But it didn't work. I played my system, but I didn't care if I won or lost. The horses were beautiful, but I found myself saying to myself, what of it? Their beauty didn't mean anything. I found that every day I was glad when the last race was over, and I could go back to the hotel—and

the bottle in my room. (*He pauses, staring into the moonlight with vacant eyes.*)

JOSIE (*Uneasily*). Why did you tell me this?

TYRONE (*In the same listless monotone*). You said I looked dead. Well, I am.

JOSIE. You're not! (*She hugs him protectively.*) Don't talk like that!

TYRONE. Ever since Mama died.

JOSIE (*Deeply moved—pityingly*). I know. I've felt all along it was that sorrow was making you—(*She pauses—gently.*) Maybe if you talked about your grief for her, it would help you. I think it must be all choked up inside you, killing you.

TYRONE (*In a strange warning tone*). You'd better look out, Josie.

JOSIE. Why?

TYRONE (*Quickly, forcing his cynical smile*). I might develop a crying jag, and sob on your beautiful breast.

JOSIE (*Gently*). You can sob all you like.

TYRONE. Don't encourage me. You'd be sorry. (*A deep conflict shows in his expression and tone. He is driven to go on in spite of himself.*) But if you're such a glutton for punishment—After all, I said I'd tell you later, didn't I?

JOSIE (*Puzzled*). You said you'd tell me about the blonde on the train.

TYRONE. She's part of it. I lied about that. (*He pauses—then blurts out sneeringly.*) You won't believe it could have happened. Or if you did believe, you couldn't understand or forgive—(*Quickly*) But you might. You're the one person who might. Because you really love me. And because you're the only woman I've ever met who understands the lousy rotten things a man can do when he's crazy drunk, and draws a blank—especially when he's nutty with grief to start with.

JOSIE (*Hugging him tenderly*). Of course I'll understand, Jim, darling.

TYRONE (*Stares into the moonlight—hauntedly*). But I didn't draw a blank. I tried to. I drank enough to knock out ten men. But it didn't work. I knew what I was doing. (*He pauses—dully.*) No, I can't tell you, Josie. You'd loathe my guts, and I couldn't blame you.

JOSIE. No! I'll love you no matter what—

TYRONE (*With strange triumphant harshness*). All right! Remember that's a promise! (*He pauses—starts to speak—pauses again.*)

JOSIE (*Pityingly*). Maybe you'd better not—if it will make you suffer.

TYRONE. Trying to welch now, eh? It's too late. You've got me started. Suffer? Christ, I ought to suffer! (*He pauses. Then he closes his eyes. It is as if he had to hide from sight before he can begin. He makes his face expres-*

sionless. His voice becomes impersonal and objective, as though what he told concerned some man he had known, but had nothing to do with him. This is the only way he can start telling the story.) When Mama died, I'd been on the wagon for nearly two years. Not even a glass of beer. Honestly. And I know I would have stayed on. For her sake. She had no one but me. The Old Man was dead. My brother had married—had a kid—had his own life to live. She'd lost him. She had only me to attend to things for her and take care of her. She'd always hated my drinking. So I quit. It made me happy to do it. For her. Because she was all I had, all I cared about. Because I loved her. (*He pauses.*) No one would believe that now, who knew—But I did.

JOSIE (*Gently*). I know how much you loved her.

TYRONE. We went out to the Coast to see about selling a piece of property the Old Man had bought three years ago. And one day she suddenly became ill. Got rapidly worse. Went into a coma. Brain tumor. The docs said, no hope. Might never come out of coma. I went crazy. Couldn't face losing her. The old booze yen got me. I got drunk and stayed drunk. And I began hoping she'd never come out of the coma, and see I was drinking again. That was my excuse, too—that she'd never know. And she never did. (*He pauses—then sneeringly.*) Nix! Kidding myself again. I know damned well just before she died she recognized me. She saw I was drunk. Then she closed her eyes so she couldn't see, and was glad to die! (*He opens his eyes and stares into the moonlight as if he saw this deathbed scene before him.*)

JOSIE (*Soothingly*). Ssshh. You only imagine that because you feel guilty about drinking.

TYRONE (*As if he hadn't heard, closes his eyes again*). After that, I kept so drunk I did draw a blank most of the time, but I went through the necessary motions and no one guessed how drunk—(*He pauses.*) But there are things I can never forget—the undertakers, and her body in a coffin with her face made up. I couldn't hardly recognize her. She looked young and pretty like someone I remembered meeting long ago. Practically a stranger. To whom I was a stranger. Cold and indifferent. Not worried about me any more. Free at last. Free from worry. From pain. From me. I stood looking down at her, and something happened to me. I found I couldn't feel anything. I knew I ought to be heartbroken but I couldn't feel anything. I seemed dead, too. I knew I ought to cry. Even a crying jag would look better than just standing there. But I couldn't cry. I cursed to myself, "You dirty bastard, it's Mama. You loved her, and now she's dead. She's gone away from you forever. Never, never again—" But it

had no effect. All I did was try to explain to myself, "She's dead. What does she care now if I cry or not, or what I do? It doesn't matter a damn to her. She's happy to be where I can't hurt her ever again. She's rid of me at last. For God's sake, can't you leave her alone even now? For God's sake, can't you let her rest in peace?" (*He pauses—then sneeringly.*) But there were several people around and I knew they expected me to show something. Once a ham, always a ham! So I put on an act. I flopped on my knees and hid my face in my hands and faked some sobs and cried, "Mama! Mama! My dear mother!" But all the time I kept saying to myself, "You lousy ham! You God-damned lousy ham! Christ, in a minute you'll start singing 'Mother Macree'!" (*He opens his eyes and gives a tortured, sneering laugh, staring into the moonlight.*)

JOSIE (*Horrified, but still deeply pitying*). Jim! Don't! It's past. You've punished yourself. And you were drunk. You didn't mean—

TYRONE (*Again closes his eyes*). I had to bring her body East to be buried beside the Old Man. I took a drawing room and hid in it with a case of booze. She was in her coffin in the baggage car. No matter how drunk I got, I couldn't forget that for a minute. I found I couldn't stay alone in the drawing room. It became haunted. I was going crazy. I had to go out and wander up and down the train looking for company. I made such a public nuisance of myself that the conductor threatened if I didn't quit, he'd keep me locked in the drawing room. But I'd spotted one passenger who was used to drunks and could pretend to like them, if there was enough dough in it. She had parlor house written all over her—a blonde pig who looked more like a whore than twenty-five whores, with a face like an over-grown doll's and a come-on smile as cold as a polar bear's feet. I bribed the porter to take a message to her and that night she sneaked into my drawing room. She was bound for New York, too. So every night—for fifty bucks a night—(*He opens his eyes and now he stares torturedly through the moonlight into the drawing room.*)

JOSIE (*Her face full of revulsion—stammers*). Oh, how could you! (*Instinctively she draws away, taking her arms from around him.*)

TYRONE. How could I? I don't know. But I did. I suppose I had some mad idea she could make me forget—what was in the baggage car ahead.

JOSIE. Don't. (*She draws back again so he has to raise his head from her breast. He doesn't seem to notice this.*)

TYRONE. No, it couldn't have been that. Because I didn't seem to want to forget. It was like some plot I had to carry out. The blonde—she didn't matter. She was only something that belonged in the plot. It was as if I wanted revenge—because I'd been left alone—because I knew I was lost, without any hope left—that all I could do would be drink myself to death, because no one was left who could help me. (*His face hardens and a look of cruel vindictiveness comes into it—with a strange horrible satisfaction in his tone.*) No, I didn't forget even in that pig's arms! I remembered the last two lines of a lousy tear-jerker song I'd heard when I was a kid kept singing over and over in my brain.

> *"And baby's cries can't waken her*
> *In the baggage coach ahead."*

JOSIE (*Distractedly*). Jim!

TYRONE. I couldn't stop it singing. I didn't want to stop it!

JOSIE. Jim! For the love of God. I don't want to hear!

TYRONE (*After a pause—dully*). Well, that's all—except I was too drunk to go to her funeral.

JOSIE. Oh! (*She has drawn away from him as far as she can without getting up. He becomes aware of this for the first time and turns slowly to stare at her.*)

TYRONE (*Dully*). Don't want to touch me now, eh? (*He shrugs his shoulders mechanically.*) Sorry. I'm a damned fool. I shouldn't have told you.

JOSIE (*Her horror ebbing as her love and protective compassion return—moves nearer him—haltingly*). Don't, Jim. Don't say—I don't want to touch you. It's—a lie. (*She puts a hand on his shoulder.*)

TYRONE (*As if she hadn't spoken—with hopeless longing*). Wish I could believe in the spiritualists' bunk. If I could tell her it was because I missed her so much and couldn't forgive her for leaving me—

JOSIE. Jim! For the love of God—!

TYRONE (*Unheeding*). She'd understand and forgive me, don't you think? She always did. She was simple and kind and pure of heart. She was beautiful. You're like her deep in the heart. That's why I told you. I thought—(*Abruptly his expression becomes sneering and cynical—harshly.*) My mistake. Nuts! Forget it. Time I got a move on. I don't like your damned moon, Josie. It's an ad for the past. (*He recites mockingly.*)

> *"It is the very error of the moon:*
> *She comes more nearer earth than she was wont,*
> *And makes men mad."*

(*He moves*) I'll grab the last trolley for town. There'll be a speak open, and some drunk laughing. I need a laugh. (*He starts to get up.*)

JOSIE (*Throws her arms around him and pulls him back—tensely*). No! You won't go! I won't let you! (*She hugs him close—gently.*) I understand now, Jim, darling, and I'm proud you came to me as the one in the world you know loves you enough to understand and forgive—and I do forgive!

TYRONE (*Lets his head fall back on her breast—simply*). Thanks, Josie. I knew you—

JOSIE. As *she* forgives, do you hear me! As *she* loves and understands and forgives!

TYRONE (*Simply*). Yes, I know she—(*His voice breaks.*)

JOSIE (*Bends over him with a brooding maternal tenderness*). That's right. Do what you came for, my darling. It isn't drunken laughter in a speakeasy you want to hear at all, but the sound of yourself crying your heart's repentance against her breast. (*His face is convulsed. He hides it on her breast and sobs rackingly. She hugs him more tightly and speaks softly, staring into the moonlight.*) She hears. I feel her in the moonlight, her soul wrapped in it like a silver mantle, and I know she understand and forgives me, too, and her blessing lies on me. (*A pause. His sobs begin to stop exhaustedly. She looks down at him again and speaks soothingly as she would to a child.*) There. There, now. (*He stops. She goes on in a gentle, bullying tone.*) You're a fine one, wanting to leave me when the night I promised I'd give you has just begun, our night that'll be different from all the others, with a dawn that won't creep over dirty windowpanes but will wake in the sky like a promise of God's peace in the soul's dark sadness. (*She smiles a little amused smile.*) Will you listen to me, Jim! I must be a poet. Who would have guessed it? Sure, love is a wonderful mad inspiration! (*A pause. She looks down. His eyes are closed. His face against her breast looks pale and haggard in the moonlight. Calm with the drained, exhausted peace of death. For a second she is frightened. Then she realizes and whispers softly.*) Asleep. (*In a tender crooning tone like a lullaby.*) That's right. Sleep in peace, my darling. (*Then with sudden anguished longing.*) Oh, Jim, Jim, maybe my love could still save you, if you could want it enough! (*She shakes her head.*) No. That can never be. (*Her eyes leave his face to stare up at the sky. She looks weary and stricken and sad. She forces a defensive, self-derisive smile.*) God forgive me, it's a fine end to all my scheming, to sit here with the dead hugged to my breast, and the silly mug of the moon grinning down, enjoying the joke!

Curtain

ACT IV

Scene: Same as Act III. It is dawn. The first faint streaks of color, heralding the sunrise, appear in the eastern sky at left.

Josie sits in the same position on the steps, as if she had not moved, her arms around Tyrone. He is still asleep, his head on her breast. His face has the same exhausted, death-like repose. Josie's face is set in an expression of numbed, resigned sadness. Her body sags tiredly. In spite of her strength, holding herself like this for hours, for fear of waking him, is becoming too much for her.

The two make a strangely tragic picture in the wan dawn light—this big sorrowful woman hugging a haggard-faced, middle-aged drunkard against her breast, as if he were a sick child.

Hogan appears at left-rear, coming from the barn. He approaches the corner of the house stealthily on tiptoe. Wisps of hay stick to his clothes and his face is swollen and sleepy, but his little pig's eyes are sharply wide awake and sober. He peeks around the corner, and takes in the two on the steps. His eyes fix on Josie's face in a long, probing stare.

JOSIE (*Speaks in a low grim tone.*). Stop hiding, Father. I heard you sneak up. (*He comes guiltily around the corner. She keeps her voice low, but her tone is commanding.*) Come here, and be quiet about it. (*He obeys meekly, coming as far as the boulder silently, his eyes searching her face, his expression becoming guilty and miserable at what he sees. She goes on in the same tone, without looking at him.*) Talk low, now. I don't want him wakened—(*She adds strangely.*) Not until the dawn has beauty in it.

HOGAN (*Worriedly*). What? (*He decides it's better for the present to ask no questions. His eyes fall on Tyrone's face. In spite of himself, he is startled—in an awed, almost frightened whisper.*) Be god, he looks dead!

JOSIE (*Strangely*). Why wouldn't he? He is.

HOGAN. Is?

JOSIE. Don't be a fool. Can't you see him breathing? Dead asleep, I mean. Don't stand there gawking. Sit down. (*He sits meekly on the boulder. His face betrays a guilty dread of what is coming. There is a pause in which she doesn't look at him, but he keeps glancing at her, growing visibly more uneasy. She speaks bitterly.*) Where's your witnesses?

HOGAN (*Guiltily*). Witnesses? (*Then forcing an amused grin*) Oh, be God, if that ain't a joke on me! Sure, I got so

blind drunk at the Inn I forgot all about our scheme and came home and went to sleep in the hayloft.

JOSIE (*Her expression harder and more bitter*). You're a liar.

HOGAN. I'm not. I just woke up. Look at the hay sticking to me. That's proof.

JOSIE. I'm not thinking of that, and well you know it. (*With bitter voice*) So you just woke up—did you?—and then came sneaking here to see if the scheme behind your scheme had worked!

HOGAN (*Guiltily*). I don't know what you mean.

JOSIE. Don't lie any more, Father. This time, you've told one too many. (*He starts to defend himself but the look on her face makes him think better of it and he remains uneasily silent. A pause.*)

HOGAN (*Finally has to blurt out*). Sure, if I'd brought the witnesses, there's nothing for them to witness that—

JOSIE. No. You're right there. There's nothing. Nothing at all. (*She smiles strangely.*) Except a great miracle they'd never believe, or you either.

HOGAN. What miracle?

JOSIE. A virgin who bears a dead child in the night, and the dawn finds her still a virgin. If that isn't a miracle, what is?

HOGAN (*Uneasily*). Stop talking so queer. You give me the shivers. (*He attempts a joking tone.*) Is it you who's the virgin? Faith, that *would* be a miracle, no less! (*He forces a chuckle.*)

JOSIE. I told you to stop lying, Father.

HOGAN. What lie? (*He stops and watches her face worriedly. She is silent, as if she were not aware of him now. Her eyes are fixed on the wanton sky.*)

JOSIE (*As if to herself*). It'll be beautiful soon, and I can wake him.

HOGAN (*Can't retain his anxiety any longer*). Josie, darlin'! For the love of God, can't you tell me what happened to you?

JOSIE (*Her face hard and bitter again*). I've told you once. Nothing.

HOGAN. Nothing? If you could see the sadness in your face—

JOSIE. What woman doesn't sorrow for the man she loved who has died? But there's pride in my heart, too.

HOGAN (*Tormentedly*). Will you stop talking as if you'd gone mad in the night! (*Raising his voice—with revengeful anger*) Listen to me! If Jim Tyrone has done anything to bring you sorrow—(*Tyrone stirs in his sleep and moans, pressing his face against her breast as if for protection. She looks down at him and hugs him close.*)

JOSIE (*Croons softly*). There, there, my darling. Rest in peace a while longer. (*Turns on her father angrily and whispers*) Didn't I tell you to speak low and not wake him! (*She pauses—then quietly.*) He did nothing to bring me sorrow. It was my mistake. I thought there was still hope. I didn't know he'd died already—that it was a damned soul coming to me in the moonlight, to confess and be forgiven and find peace for a night—

HOGAN. Josie! Will you stop!

JOSIE (*After a pause—dully*). He'd never do anything to hurt me. You know it. (*Self-mockingly*) Sure, hasn't he told me I'm beautiful to him and he loves me—in his fashion. (*Then matter-of-factly*) All that happened was that he got drunk and he had one of his crazy notions he wanted to sleep the way he is, and I let him sleep. (*With forced roughness*) And, be God, the night's over. I'm half dead with tiredness and sleepiness. It's that you see in my face, not sorrow.

HOGAN. Don't try to fool me, Josie. I—

JOSIE (*Her face hard and bitter—grimly*). Fool you, is it? It's you who made a fool of me with your lies, thinking you'd use me to get your dirty greasy paws on the money he'll have!

HOGAN. No! I swear by all the saints—

JOSIE. You'd swear on a Bible while you were stealing it! (*Grimly*) Listen to me, Father. I didn't call you here to answer questions about what's none of your business. I called you here to tell you I've seen through all the lies you told last night to get me to—(*As he starts to speak*) Shut up! I'll do the talking now. You weren't drunk. You were only putting it on as part of your scheme—

HOGAN (*Quietly*). I wasn't drunk, no. I admit that, Josie. But I'd had slews of drinks and they were in my head or I'd never have the crazy dreams—

JOSIE (*With biting scorn*). Dreams, is it? The only dream you've ever had, or will have, is of yourself counting a fistful of dirty money, and divil a care how you got it, or who you robbed or made suffer!

HOGAN (*Winces—pleadingly*). Josie!

JOSIE. Shut up! (*Scathingly*) I'm sure you've made up a whole new set of lies and excuses. You're that cunning and clever, but you can save your breath. They wouldn't fool me now. I've been fooled once too often. (*He gives her a frightened look, as if something he had dreaded has happened. She goes on, grimly accusing.*) You lied about Jim selling the farm. You knew he was kidding. You knew the estate would be out of probate in a few days, and he'd go back to Broadway, and you had to do something quick or you'd lose the last chance of getting your greedy hooks on his money.

HOGAN (*Miserably*). No. It wasn't that, Josie.

JOSIE. You saw how hurt and angry I was because he'd kept me waiting here, and you used that. You knew I loved him and wanted him and you used that. You used all you knew about me—Oh, you did it clever! You ought to be proud! You worked it so it was me who did all the dirty scheming—You knew I'd find out from Jim you'd lied about the farm, but not before your lie had done its work—made me go after him, get him drunk, get drunk myself so I could be shameless—and when the truth did come out, wouldn't it make me love him all the more and be more shameless and willing! Don't tell me you didn't count on that, and you such a clever schemer! And if he once had me, knowing I was a virgin, didn't you count on his honor and remorse, and his loving me in his fashion, to make him offer to marry me? Sure, why wouldn't he, you thought. It wouldn't hold him. He'd go back to Broadway just the same and never see me again. But there'd be money in it, and when he'd finished killing himself, I'd be his legal widow and get what's left.

HOGAN (*Miserably*). No! It wasn't that.

JOSIE. But what's the good of talking? It's all over. I've only one more word for you, Father, and it's this: I'm leaving you today, like my brothers left. You can live alone and work alone your cunning schemes on yourself.

HOGAN (*After a pause—slowly*). I knew you'd be bitter against me, Josie, but I took the chance you'd be so happy you wouldn't care how—

JOSIE (*As if she hadn't heard, looking at the eastern sky which is now glowing with color*). Thank God, it's beautiful. It's time. (*To Hogan*) Go in the house and stay there till he's gone. I don't want you around to start some new scheme. (*He looks miserable, starts to speak, thinks better of it, and meekly tiptoes past her up the steps and goes in, closing the door quietly after him. She looks down at Tyrone. Her face softens with a maternal tenderness—sadly.*) I hate to bring you back to life, Jim, darling. If you could have died in your sleep, that's what you would have liked, isn't it? (*She gives him a gentle shake.*) Wake up, Jim. (*He moans in his sleep and presses more closely against her. She stares at his face.*) Dear God, let him remember that one thing and forget the rest. That will be enough for me. (*She gives him a more vigorous shake.*) Jim! Wake up, don't you hear? It's time.

TYRONE (*Half wakens without opening his eyes—mutters*). What the hell? (*Dimly conscious of a woman's body—cynically.*) Again, eh? Same old stuff. Who the hell are you, sweetheart? (*Irritably*) What's the big idea, waking me up? What time is it?

JOSIE. It's dawn.

TYRONE (*Still without opening his eyes*). Dawn? (*He quotes drowsily.*)

> "But I was desolate and sick of an old passion,
> When I awoke and found the dawn was gray."

(*Then with a sneer*) They're all gray. Go to sleep, Kid—and let me sleep. (*He falls asleep again.*)

JOSIE (*Tensely*). This one isn't gray, Jim. It's different from all the others—(*She sees he is asleep—bitterly.*) He'll have forgotten. He'll never notice. And I'm the whore on the train to him now, not—(*Suddenly she pushes him away from her and shakes him roughly.*) Will you wake up, for God's sake! I've had all I can bear—

TYRONE (*Still half asleep*). Hey! Cut out the rough stuff, Kid. What? (*Awake now, blinking his eyes—with dazed surprise.*) Josie.

JOSIE (*Still bitter*). That's who, and none of your damned tarts. (*She pushes him.*) Get up now, so you won't fall asleep again. (*He does so with difficulty, still in a sleepy daze, his body stiff and cramped. She conquers her bitter resentment and puts on her old free-and-easy kidding tone with him, but all the time waiting to see how much he will remember.*) You're stiff and cramped, and no wonder. I'm worse from holding you, if that's any comfort. (*She stretches and rubs her numbed arms, groaning comicallly.*) Holy Joseph, I'm a wreck entirely. I'll never be the same. (*Giving him a quick glance*) You look as if you'd drawn a blank and were wondering how you got here. I'll bet you don't remember a thing.

TYRONE (*Moving his arms and legs gingerly—sleepily*). I don't know. Wait till I'm sure I'm still alive.

JOSIE. You need an eye-opener. (*She picks up the bottle and glass and pours him a drink.*) Here you are.

TYRONE (*Takes the glass mechanically*). Thanks, Josie. (*He goes and sits on the boulder, holding the drink as if he had no interest in it.*)

JOSIE (*Watching him*). Drink up or you'll be asleep again.

TYRONE. No, I'm awake now, Josie. Funny. Don't seem to want a drink. Oh, I've got a head all right. But no heebie-jeebies—yet.

JOSIE. That's fine. It must be a pleasant change—

TYRONE. It is. I've got a nice, dreamy peaceful hangover for once—as if I'd had a sound sleep without nightmares.

JOSIE. So you did. Divil a nightmare. I ought to know. Wasn't I holding you and keeping them away?

TYRONE. You mean you—(*Suddenly*) Wait a minute. I remember now I was sitting alone at a table in the Inn, and I suddenly had a crazy notion I'd come up here and sleep with my head on your—So that's why I woke up in your arms. (*Shame-facedly*) And you let me get away with it. You're a nut, Josie.

JOSIE. Oh, I didn't mind.

TYRONE. You must have seen how blotto I was, didn't you?

JOSIE. I did. You were as full as a tick.

TYRONE. They why didn't you give me the bum's rush?

JOSIE. Why would I? I was glad to humor you.

TYRONE. For God's sake, how long was I cramped on you like that?

JOSIE. Oh, a few hours, only.

TYRONE. God, I'm sorry, Josie, but it's your own fault for letting me—

JOSIE. Och, don't be apologizing. I was glad of the excuse to stay awake and enjoy the beauty of the moon.

TYRONE. Yes, I can remember what a beautiful night it was.

JOSIE. Can you? I'm glad of that, Jim. You seemed to enjoy it the while we were sitting here together before you fell asleep.

TYRONE. How long a while was that?

JOSIE. Not long. Less than an hour, anyway.

TYRONE. I suppose I bored the hell out of you with a lot of drunken drivel.

JOSIE. Not a lot, no. But some. You were full of blarney, saying how beautiful I was to you.

TYRONE (*Earnestly*). That wasn't drivel, Josie. You were. You are. You always will be.

JOSIE. You're a wonder, Jim. Nothing can stop you, can it? Even me in the light of dawn, looking like something you'd put in the field to scare the crows from the corn. You'll kid at the Day of Judgment.

TYRONE (*Impatiently*). You know damned well it isn't kidding. You're not a fool. You can tell.

JOSIE (*Kiddingly*). All right, then, I'm beautiful and you love me—in your fashion.

TYRONE. "In my fashion," eh? Was I reciting poetry to you? That must have been hard to take.

JOSIE. It wasn't. I liked it. It was all about beautiful nights and the romance of the moon.

TYRONE. Well, there was some excuse for that, anyway. It sure was a beautiful night. I'll never forget it.

JOSIE. I'm glad, Jim.

TYRONE. What other bunk did I pull on you—or I mean, did old John Barleycorn pull?

JOSIE. Not much. You were mostly quiet and sad—in a kind of daze, as if the moon was in your wits as well as whiskey.

TYRONE. I remember I was having a grand time at the Inn, celebrating with Phil, and then suddenly, for no reason, all the fun went out of it, and I was more melancholy than ten Hamlets. (*He pauses.*) Hope I didn't tell the sad story of my life and weep on your bosom, Josie.

JOSIE. You didn't. The one thing you talked a lot about was that you wanted the night with me to be different from all the other nights you'd spent with women.

TYRONE (*With revulsion*). God, don't make me think of those tramps now! (*Then with deep, grateful feeling*) It sure was different, Josie. I may not remember much, but I know how different it was from the way I feel now. None of my usual morning-after stuff—the damned sick remorse that makes you wish you'd died in your sleep so you wouldn't have to face the rotten things you're afraid you said and did the night before, when you were so drunk you didn't know what you were doing.

JOSIE. There's nothing you said or did last night for you to regret. You can take my word for it.

TYRONE (*As if he hadn't heard—slowly*). It's hard to describe how I feel. It's a new one on me. Sort of at peace with myself and this lousy life—as if all my sins had been forgiven—(*He becomes self-conscious—cynically.*) Nuts with that sin bunk, but you know what I mean.

JOSIE (*Tensely*). I do, and I'm happy you feel that way, Jim. (*A pause. She goes on.*) You talked about how you'd watched too many dawns come creeping grayly over dirty windowpanes, with some tart snoring beside you—

TYRONE (*Winces*). Have a heart. Don't remind me of that now, Josie. Don't spoil this dawn! (*A pause. She watches him tensely. He turns slowly to face the east, where the sky is now glowing with all the colors of an exceptionally beautiful sunrise. He stares, drawing a deep breath. He is profoundly moved but immediately becomes self-conscious and tries to sneer it off—cynicallly.*) God seems to be putting on quite a display. I like Belasco better. Rise of curtain, Act-Four stuff. (*Her face has fallen into lines of bitter hurt, but he adds quickly and angrily.*) God, it's beautiful, Josie! I—I'll never forget it—here with you.

JOSIE (*Her face clearing—simply*). I'm glad, Jim. I was hoping you'd feel beauty in it—by way of a token.

TYRONE (*Watching the sunrise—mechanically*). Token of what?

JOSIE. Oh, I don't know. Token to me that—never mind. I forget what I meant. (*Abruptly changing the subject*) Don't think I woke you just to admire the sunrise. You're on a farm, not Broadway, and it's time for me to start work, not go to bed. (*She gets to her feet and stretches. There is a growing strain behind her free-and-easy manner.*) And that's a hint, Jim. I can't stay entertaining you. So go back to the Inn, that's a good boy. I know you'll understand the reason, and not think I'm tired of your company. (*She forces a smile.*)

TYRONE (*Gets up*). Of course, I understand. (*He pauses—then blurts out guiltily.*) One more question. You're sure I didn't get out of order last night—and try to make you, or anything like that.

JOSIE. You didn't. You kidded back when I kidded you, the way we always do. That's all.

TYRONE. Thank God for that. I'd never forgive myself if—I wouldn't have asked you except I've pulled some pretty rotten stuff when I was drawing a blank. (*He becomes conscious of the forgotten drink he has in his hand.*) Well, I might as well drink this. The bar at the Inn won't be open for hours. (*He drinks—then looks pleasantly surprised.*) I'll be damned! That isn't Phil's rotgut. That's real, honest-to-God bonded Bourbon. Where—(*This clicks in his mind and suddenly he remembers everything and Josie sees that he does. The look of guilt and shame and anguish settles over his face. Instinctively he throws the glass away, his first reaction one of loathing for the drink which brought back memory. He feels Josie staring at him and fights desperately to control his voice and expression.*) Real Bourbon. I remember now you said a bootlegger gave it to Phil. Well, I'll run along and let you do your work. See you later, Josie. (*He turns toward the road.*)

JOSIE (*Strickenly*). No! Don't, Jim! Don't go like that! You won't see me later. You'll never see me again now, and I know that's best for both of us, but I can't bear to have you ashamed you wanted my love to comfort your sorrow—when I'm so proud I could give it. (*Pleadingly*) I hoped, for your sake, you wouldn't remember, but now you do, I want you to remember my love for you gave you peace for a while.

TYRONE (*Stares at her, fighting with himself. He stammers defensively*). I don't know what you're talking about. I don't remember—

JOSIE (*Sadly*). All right, Jim. Neither do I then. Good-bye, and God bless you. (*She turns as if to go up the steps into the house.*)

TYRONE (*Stammers*). Wait, Josie! (*Coming to her*) I'm a liar! I'm a louse! Forgive me, Josie. I do remember! I'm glad I remember! I'll never forget your love! (*He kisses her on the lips.*) Never! (*Kissing her again*) Never, do you hear! I'll always love you, Josie. (*He kisses her again.*) Good-bye—and God bless you! (*He turns away and walks quickly down the road off left without looking back. She stands, watching him go, for a moment, then she puts her hands over her face, her head bent, and sobs. Hogan comes out of her room and stands on top of the steps. He looks after Tyrone and his face is hard with bitter anger.*)

JOSIE (*Sensing his presence, stops crying and lifts her head—dully*). I'll get your breakfast in a minute, Father.

HOGAN. To hell with my breakfast! I'm not a pig that has no other thought but eating! (*Then pleadingly*) Listen, darlin'. All you said about my lying and scheming, and what I hoped would happen, is true. But it wasn't his money, Josie. I did see it was the last chance—the only one left to bring the two of you to stop your damned pretending, and face the truth that you loved each other. I wanted you to find happiness—by hook or crook, one way or another, what did I care how? I wanted to save him, and hoped he'd see that only your love could—It was his talk of the beauty he saw in you that made me hope—And I knew he'd never go to bed with you even if you'd let him unless he married you. And if I gave a thought to his money at all, that was the least of it, and why shouldn't I want to have you live in ease and comfort for a change, like you deserve, instead of in this shanty on a lousy farm, slaving for me? (*He pauses—miserably.*) Can't you believe that's the truth, Josie, and not feel so bitter against me?

JOSIE (*Her eyes still following Tyrone—gently*). I know it's the truth, Father. I'm not bitter now. Don't be afraid I'm going to leave you. I only said it to punish you for a while.

HOGAN (*With humble gratitude*). Thank God for that, darlin'.

JOSIE (*Forces a teasing smile and a little of her old manner*). A ginger-haired, rooked old goat like you to be playing Cupid!

HOGAN (*His face lights up joyfully. He is almost himself again—ruefully*). You had me punished, that's sure. I was thinking after you'd gone I'd drown myself in Harder's ice pond. There was this consolation in it, I knew that the bastard would never look at a piece of ice again without remembering me. (*She doesn't hear this. Her thoughts are on the receding figure of Tyrone again. Hogan looks at her sad face worriedly—gently.*) Don't darlin'. Don't be hurting yourself.

(*Then as she still doesn't hear, he puts on his old, fuming irascible tone.*) Are you going to moon at the sunrise forever, and me with the sides of my stomach knocking togther?

JOSIE (*Gently*). Don't worry about me, Father. It's over now. I'm not hurt. I'm only sad for him.

HOGAN. For him? (*He bursts out in a fit of smoldering rage.*) May the blackest curse from the pit of hell—

JOSIE (*With an anguished cry*). Don't, Father! I love him!

HOGAN (*Subsides, but his face looks sorrowful and old—dully*). I didn't mean it. I know whatever happened he meant no harm to you. It was life I was cursing—(*With a trace of his natural manner.*) And, be God, that's a waste of breath, if it does deserve it. (*Then as she remains silent—miserably*) Or maybe I was cursing myself for a damned old scheming fool, like I ought to.

JOSIE (*Turns to him, forcing a teasing smile*). Look out, I might say Amen to that. (*Gently*) Don't be sad, Father. I'm all right—and I'm well content here with you. (*Forcing her teasing manner again*) Sure, living with you has spoilt me for any other man, anyway. There'd never be the same fun or excitement.

HOGAN (*Plays up to this—in his fuming manner*). There'll be excitement if I don't get my breakfast soon, but it won't be fun, I'm warning you!

JOSIE (*Forcing her usual reaction to his threats*). Och, don't be threatening me, you bad-tempered old tick. Let's go in the house and I'll get your damned breakfast.

HOGAN. Now you're talking. (*He goes in the house through her room. She follows him as far as the door—then turns for a last look down the road.*)

JOSIE (*Her face sad, tender and pitying—gently*). May you have your wish and die in your sleep soon, Jim, darling. May you rest forever in forgiveness and peace. (*She turns slowly and goes into the house.*)

Curtain

COMMENTARY

Note: The following essay represents a single interpretation of the play. For other perspectives on A Moon for the Misbegotten, *consult the essays listed below.*

The setting of the play is the shabby New England farmhouse of tenant farmer Phil Hogan in 1923. As this last of O'Neill's dramas opens, the last of Hogan's sons is leaving. The hard-drinking old Irish father wishes the boy good riddance but will do anything to protect his daughter and his land, including tricking his landlord, James Tyrone, Jr., on both counts. James is the same doomed James Tyrone, Jr., of O'Neill's autobiographical *Long Day's Journey into Night,* the masterpiece to which *Moon* is the coda. In May 1923, the year after his mother's death, O'Neill's brother Jamie, the model for James Tyrone, Jr., had nearly drunk himself to an early grave. He was carried to a sanatorium in a straitjacket. His hair had turned white. He had lost his eyesight. And by fall, he was dead.

In transforming his brother's end in *A Moon for the Misbegotten,* O'Neill gave his fictional James Tyrone, Jr., an evening of conversation with Josie Hogan. Like him, she has masked a gentle and generous spirit. Strong as a man and unbridled in her exuberance, she has talked and behaved as if she were the neighborhood slut, when actually she is a virgin. During the long, often hilarious banter of the first act, father Phil Hogan seems to hate his own sons, driving them off his pitiful, rock-strewn farm, though in performance, the drunken Phil should twinkle with wit as he calls the last one to leave "that big pious lump" and lets us in on his desire that his children be better than he. And for none does he wish this more than for Josie, despite calling her "a big overgrown cow" and worse during the bantering buildup. Of a previous visit by Jim, he brags: "By the time he left, we were both too busy cursing England to bother about the rent." Josie remains skeptical; she thinks Jim's obvious attraction to her when she appears dressed up for him in the moonlight could be simply part of a trick to divest the Hogans of their property. But at the beginning of Act II, Jim's confession begins. Josie tells him, "You look like you've seen a ghost," and he answers quietly, "I have. Me."

The ensuing scene moves through false starts and true intimacies, with Josie twice leaving to hear Jim's protestations through a window in the shanty door. Josie and Jim confess their feelings for one another in a climactic end to the third act. They bless each other in ways that illuminate and redeem them, with her sitting against a rock to enfold him, in a Pieta image. And however much a reader/viewer might want Jim to drop his "honorable scruples" and bed this woman who's loved him all her life, the weary, worldly wise man shows this cannot be. Plumbing the depths of his conscience-stricken, guilt-driven addictions, Jim needs rest, the one night of peace Josie can give him. And then he leaves, probably to die.

Director John Rando, who staged the play in 1997 for San Diego's Old Globe Theatre, contends that "James knows what he wants to do before he dies is to speak to someone who has some understanding of him, so he can admit the wrong he's done. This is where the play is very religious in its way, looking toward death for absolution. O'Neill really does believe in the soul, the human spirit. He understands that when people face their death, they need a sense of peace." Peace comes to Jim after a self-lacerating monologue near the end of this harrowing and also pointedly funny drama.

O'Neill wrote the play while living at Tao House, his Chinese-style mansion on an estate in Contra Costa County, California. He began drafting it soon after he completed *Long Day's Journey* in 1941. His wife, Carlotta Monterey O'Neill, wrote that the effort to confront and exorcise his family past aged him: "He was tortured every day by his own writing. He would come out of his study at the end of a day gaunt and sometimes weeping. His eyes would be all red and he looked 10 years older than when he went in the morning." After the Japanese attack on Pearl Harbor, O'Neill stopped writing, but by early 1944 he had completed the play.

The first production was at the Hartman Theater in Columbus, Ohio; badly cast and not well directed, this Theatre Guild production never made it to New York. In Pittsburgh the play was damned by the Chamber of Commerce, and in Detroit it was closed on the night of the second performance by a policeman who considered it a slander on motherhood: the words "prostitute" and "mother" were uttered in the same sentence. When the cop was told O'Neill had won the Nobel Prize, he reportedly answered: "Lady, I don't care what kind of prize he's won, he can't put on a dirty show in my town."

This failure ended O'Neill's life in theater, as the tremors of Parkinson's disease and his deteriorating condition made writing generally impossible for him. In the last known example of his handwriting, O'Neill inscribed a copy of *A Moon for the Misbegotten* to Carlotta in 1952, calling it "a poor thing . . . which I have come to loathe . . . my last." On November 27 of the following year he died, as he had been born, in a hotel.

Revivals of the play continued in the 1950s and 1960s, but it was not until Quintero's 1973 breakthrough production at the Morosco Theatre on Broadway that the play found its true theatrical form. With Jason Robards as James and Colleen Dewhurst as what critics called the "definitive" Josie, *A Moon for the Misbegotten* ran for two years and has been frequently performed in regional theaters and abroad since then. Public television aired a solid video production starring Kate Nelligan, and a 2000 Broadway revival, directed by Daniel Sullivan, brought potent performances from film star Gabriel Byrne as Jim, Cherry Jones as Josie, and Royal Shakespeare Company veteran Roy Dotrice as the trickster Phil Hogan.

Other perspectives on *A Moon for the Misbegotten*:

Brustein, Robert. *The Theater of Revolt*. Boston: Little, Brown. 1966.

Tornqvist, Egil. "From *A Wife for a Life* to *A Moon for the Misbegotten*: On O'Neill's Play Titles." In Marc Maufort (ed.), *Eugene O'Neill and the Emergence of American Drama*. Amsterdam: Rodopi, 1989, 97–106.

See *A Moon for the Misbegotten* on video:

A Moon for the Misbegotten. Dir. José Quintero. Perf. Jason Robards and Colleen Dewhurst. Kultur, 150 min., 1975.

Other O'Neill plays on video/film:

Ah, Wilderness! Dir. Clarence Brown. Perf. Wallace Beery, Mickey Rooney, and Lionel Barrymore. Turner Home Video, 101 min., 1935.

Ah, Wilderness! Dir. Arvin Brown at the Long Wharf Theater. Perf. Geraldine Fitzgerald and Swoosie Kurtz. Kultur, 120 min., 1976.

Beyond the Horizon. Dir. Michael Kahn. Perf. Geraldine Fitzgerald, John Houseman, and Maria Tucci. Kultur, 90 min., 1976.

Desire Under the Elms. Dir. Delbert Mann. Perf. Anthony Perkins, Sophia Loren, and Burl Ives. Paramount Studio, 114 min., 1958.

The Iceman Cometh. Dir. Sidney Lumet. Perf. Jason Robards and Robert Redford. Kultur, 240 min., 1960.

Mourning Becomes Electra. Dir. Nick Havinga. Perf. Bruce Davison, John Hackett, and Roberta Maxwell. Kultur, 5 episodes, 58 min. each, 1975.

Long Day's Journey into Night. Dir. Sidney Lumet. Perf. Ralph Richardson, Katherine Hepburn, and Jason Robards. Republic Studios, 170 min., 1962.

Long Day's Journey into Night. Dir. Nick Havinga. Perf. William Hutt, Martha Henry, and Peter Donaldson. Kultur, 180 min., 1996.

SHOWCASE — A GREAT AMERICAN PLAY

Arthur Miller and *Death of a Salesman*

(You may read Death of a Salesman *in the Penguin edition of the play, which may be included with this text. Because the permission rights for reprinting the play were prohibitive, we include a brief biography of Miller and a short commentary on the play. We also urge you to see one of the video versions listed below.)*

While Eugene O'Neill was the first American playwright to be widely accepted outside the United States, Arthur Miller is better know internationally and is the most widely produced American playwright. The son of Jewish immigrants, Miller's early life provided much of the thematic material for his plays. Achieving financial success and then losing it in the stock market crash of 1929, his father epitomized the roller coaster world of the free enterprise system. Miller's playwriting career began while he was a student at the University of Michigan, and in 1937 he won the Theater Guild National Award, which he shared with the man who was to become his chief rival from 1945 until the early 1960s—Tennessee Williams. Following a brief stint with the Federal Theatre Project, he wrote his first Broadway play, ironically titled *The Man Who Had All the Luck* (1944)—it closed after four performances (but enjoyed a moderately successful revival on Broadway in 2002). His next play, *All My Sons* (1947) proved more successful both commercially and critically. His most famous play, *Death of a Salesman* (1949), earned him not only his second New York Drama Critics' Circle Award but the Tony Award for best play and the Pulitzer Prize. *Death of a Salesman* is Miller's most produced play, staged not only throughout the United States and Canada but also frequently in Latin America, and it remains a popular example of American drama in Europe. In 1982 it was directed by Miller himself in the People's Republic of China.

As a playwright, Miller is an exceptional craftsman. His plays are marked by well-constructed plots, complex characters, and brutally honest social themes. However, his work is not limited to this traditional, realistic form. In *Death of a Salesman, After the Fall,* and *American Clock* he combines Realism and Expressionism as his characters freely bound, sometimes in their own minds and sometimes in ours, from one time and place to another. (*The Inside of His Head* was actually Miller's working title for *Death of a Salesman.*) Thematically, Miller displays two basic concerns: the disaster precipitated by materialistic evils and the individual's struggle with conscience. Invariably the family father lives a life of lies and delusions as he struggles to obtain the materialistic aspects of "the American Dream" for his family.

Death of a Salesman embodies nearly all the components of Miller's writing style: a tightly constructed plot reminiscent of the well-made play; believable characters drawn from the American middle class; and a seamless blending of Realism and Expressionism. Thematically, it relies on most of Miller's recurring concerns: a secret past action that plants the seeds for the destruction of the dysfunctional family and its individual members; a father who lives a lie; and the struggle of facing one's responsibility to family and society. Miller accomplishes this by creating a play that is based, in both content and form, on seeming contradictions. While using what in 1949 may have been regarded as antithetical styles—Realism and Expressionism—Miller portrays the simultaneous development and destruction of the American family and American Dream. These contradictions are exemplified by the most powerful image in the play—that of Willy and his sample cases. The play opens with one of the most pathetic images in the modern theater: a defeated Willy lugging his worn and shabby sample cases back into the house after yet another failed day on the road. He is a traveling salesman who can no longer travel and who can no longer sell. What does Willy sell? We are never told.

What is in the cases? Willy Loman himself. The cases contain the many contradictory aspects of his life. Contained in one case is what he says and in the other is what he does. In one case are his dreams and in the other is his reality. In one case is the disappearing pastoral environment for which he longs and in the other the encroaching urban society which is driving him to his grave. In one case are the sons whose potential has been the joy of his life, while in the other the sons whose failures have become the bane of his existence. Together, the cases and their contents become Willy's coffin—the means of his livelihood has become the means of his death. He has spent his life living a lie, yet he goes to his death believing another lie. Why do these cases contain so many contradictions? Willy himself is a constant contradiction.

Within minutes of the opening curtain we hear Willy ask Linda, "Why am I always being contradicted?" He is contradicted because those around him are reflecting what is happening on "the inside of his head," Miller's original title of the play. His contradictory nature permeates the play. He describes Biff as "a lazy bum!" and within minutes, he claims, "There's one thing about Biff—he's not lazy." Regarding his car he says, the "Chevrolet, Linda, is the greatest car ever built!"; a moment later he castigates the same vehicle, "They ought to prohibit the manufacture of that automobile." And, when schooling Biff to request a business loan from Bill Oliver, Willy first cautions his son not "to crack any jokes" because "everybody likes a kidder but nobody lends him money." In the next breath he advises him to "walk in with a big laugh" and "start off with a couple of your best stories."

Such dichotomies reflect the chasm between his dreams of success and the reality of his mediocrity. In both the past and the present episodes his dreams of prosperity are countered by the reality of his failure. In the "old days" he dreamed of having "Knocked 'em cold in Providence" and "slaughtered 'em in Boston!", yet it is clear that he was always struggling to make ends meet.

His family's impressions of him are not much better. At the moment when Willy needs him most, his son Happy acknowledges Willy, not as his father, but as "just a guy." Biff, the son he worshiped, is so repulsed by him that he returns home only on rare occasions, reunions which end in quarrels. Even Linda, while noting that "attention must be finally paid to such a person," concedes that "he's not easy to get along with" and that "no one knows him any more, no one welcomes him."

These contradictions between Willy's words and his actions, his dreams and his reality, the past and the present are more easily understood if we remember that the play depicts the death of two antithetical salesmen. The first is the "salesman's salesman," the man Willy would like to be—Dave Singleman. The other is the mediocre salesman, the man Willy cannot escape being—Willy Loman. As their names imply, one is a "Singleman," a man who is "one in a million," while the other is a "Lo[w]man," a man who is "a dime a dozen." The death and funeral of the former is a "singular" event attended by

hundreds, while the funeral of the other is a common affair attended only by the family, only one of whom is brought to tears by the death of a salesman.

Willy's preoccupation with being another "Singleman" is symbolic of Miller's exploration of the American Dream. To Willy, Dave Singleman and his brother, Ben, personify the American Dream, and he envisions himself raising a family that will inhabit this dream world. Realizing that he will never achieve this dream, Willy projects this vision onto his sons who represent the two parts of their father. Biff, the laborer, appreciates the beauty of nature and bygone days, while Happy, the businessman, possesses an "overdeveloped sense of competition." These young men, whom Willy regarded as "Adonises" when they were teens, are now disappointments to him. One is a philanderer and the other a kleptomaniac. Though Willy claims, "I never in my life told [them] anything but decent things," it is he who is responsible for their lifestyles. He not only condoned their thievery but bragged about it in front of them. As a result, Happy has become another Willy, a man with no awareness of his plight. Because he is his father's son, Happy's pursuit of the American Dream is as blind and fruitless as his attempts to gain his father's attention. "I'm losing weight, Pop!" and "I'm gonna get married, Mom!" are hollow echoes of Willy's "knocked 'em cold in Providence . . . slaughtered 'em in Boston." While Biff at first appears

headed in the same direction, it is he who evolves into the realist by virtue of two discoveries. First, he realizes that "all I want is out there, waiting for me the minute I say I know who I am!" And equally important is the revelation that not only did Willy have "all the wrong dreams," but that the Loman family was itself "a dime a dozen" and "a dollar an hour"; all "hard working drummers who landed in the ash can like all the rest of them."

Other perspectives on *Death of a Salesman*:

Stanton, Kay. "Women and the American Dream of *Death of a Salesman.*" In Jane Schleuter (ed.), *Feminist Readings of Modern American Drama.* Rutherford, NJ: Fairleigh Dickenson Press, 1989, 67–102.

Vogel, Nan. "Willy Tyrranos." In Vogel, *The Three Masks of American Tragedy.* Baton Rouge, LA: Louisiana State University Press, 1974, 91–102.

Death of a Salesman on video:

Death of a Salesman. Dir. Elia Kazan. Perf. Lee J. Cobb, Mildred Dunnock, George Segal, and Gene Wilder. Kultur, 120 min., 1967.

Death of a Salesman. Dir. Volker Schlondorff. Perf. Dustin Hoffman, Kate Reid, and John Malkovich. Image Entertainment, 135 min., 1986.

Designing a Play: *Death of a Salesman*

Jo Mielziner

My four months of living with *Death of a Salesman* began with a telephone call. . . .

Bloomgarden was sitting back from his desk, his feet up, deep in a manuscript. He removed a cigar from his mouth and said that he was rereading the script of an extraordinary play just completed by Arthur Miller. He called it a real "toughie." "At the end of his forty-odd scenes Miller says, 'The scenic solution to this production will have to be an imaginative and simple one. I don't know the answer, but the designer must work out something which makes the script flow easily.'"

Bloomgarden went on to say that they hoped to go into rehearsal in two weeks; Elia Kazan, who had read the script, had just called from Boston, where he was directing a new musical, *Love Life*, to say that he was anxious to take on the direction as soon as he was free. I took the script and went home to read.

I had previously had a fine time designing Tennessee Williams's *A Streetcar Named Desire* for Kazan, so I knew that if *Death of a Salesman* proved to be a tough job, I would have the support of a director with a strong visual imagination and a mind of his own. . . .

I started reading the Miller manuscript late that afternoon, and after supper I picked it up again. Script reading is always a slow process for me, but this time it was particularly laborious. It was not that the manuscript was overlong; I simply found it difficult to stick to the rule I had established many years before. This was to read a manuscript as if I were a member of an audience sitting out front, not as a scenic artist or as a director or even as a theatre man. I often go so far as to skip descriptions of scenes or business in these first readings. With *Death of a Salesman* I couldn't stick to my rule; the stage action was too complicated, and to follow the story line demanded an understanding of the sequence of scenes.

I began to understand what Bloomgarden had meant when he called it a "toughie." It was not only that there were so many different scenic locations but that the action demanded instantaneous time changes from the present to the past and back again. Actors playing a contemporaneous scene suddenly went back fifteen years in exactly the same setting—the Salesman's house. . . .

. . . a good scenic artist, without lacking respect for his author's contribution, should first make his own "breakdown" of the action, either in his mind or on paper. I always do mine on paper, as I did in rough form this night for *Death of a Salesman*. The designer should discover for himself what the author is saying in terms of the flow of action; he must examine the story as it unfolds and determine on his own where the most important scenes should be played. After these key scenes are fully identified, an intelligent design can begin to develop.

SEPTEMBER 25, 1948

Early the next morning I glanced through the breakdown I had made. One thought came to me: in the scenes where the Salesman mentally goes back to the early years of his marriage, when his boys were young and the house was surrounded by trees and open country, I had to create something visually that would make these constant transitions in time immediately clear to the audience. My next thought was that, even if we ended up with a big stage, with plenty of stagehands, and I was able to design some mechanism for handling the large number of individual scenes, the most important visual symbol in the play—the real background of the story—was the Salesman's house. Therefore, why should that house not be the main set, with all the other scenes—the corner of a graveyard, a hotel room in Boston, the corner of a

business office, a lawyer's consultation room,[1] and so on—played on a forestage? If I designed these little scenes in segments and fragments, with easily moved props and fluid lighting effects, I might be able, without ever lowering the curtain, to achieve the easy flow that the author clearly wanted.

By ten o'clock I had Bloomgarden on the telephone and we arranged to meet with Miller and Kazan later in the day. My calendar worried me. Kermit wanted *Death of a Salesman* to go into rehearsal in two weeks. This would leave me only six weeks in which to design and execute an extremely complex production. . . . But it wasn't other jobs that made me uneasy as much as it was my instinct that the new script would require a great deal of work by everyone if my basic idea for the setting proved to be acceptable. From long experience I knew that to delay an opening is usually too expensive for a producer even to consider; in addition, it sometimes means losing the services of important actors or of a topnotch director like Kazan.

Just the same, after we had gathered in Bloomgarden's office, I described the way I envisioned the production design and the method of its operation. When I finished, there was a long—a much too long—pause. Then Kazan spoke up and said to Miller, "Art, this means a hell of a lot of work for me, and even more for you." And Kermit broke in with, "It means we can't possibly go into rehearsal in two weeks. I'll have to cancel my bookings out of town and in

---

[1]There is no scene in *Salesman* that takes place in a lawyer's consultation room. Perhaps Mielziner is thinking of the scene between Willy and Bernard that takes place in Charley's outer office. Since Mielziner began work with an early version of Miller's play, it is possible that he is referring to a scene that was later discarded. Similarly, his reference to a nonexistent character, Mr. Heizer, may stem from an early script.

New York. It's up to you fellows to make the decisions. I'll go along if you feel you really need the time."

A long discussion followed. To Arthur Miller, a design scheme allowing him as author to blend scenes at will without even the shortest break for physical changes was a significant decision. To Kazan, with his strong sense of movement, stimulated by his already proven genius as a film director, the scheme would permit use of some of the best cinematic techniques. The decision to be made was not just a visual one; it would set the style in direction and performance, as well as in design.

Kazan had immediate commitments: he had to fly back to Boston that afternoon to a tryout of his musical. Miller had a great deal of rewriting to do, and felt that he didn't want to go ahead without constant conference with his director. Bloomgarden had complex financial and booking adjustments to make. But they all finally agreed to postpone and, provided my ideas worked out, to rewrite. . . .

SEPTEMBER 29, 1948

. . . In the five days that followed, I prepared about twenty sketches for *Death of a Salesman*. I decided to dispense with color at this time because it was more important to get the mood—the light and dark—and the feeling of isolation that lighting only a small segment of the setting would evoke. John Harvey[2] and his assistant went to work with my little ground plans, enlarging them to one half an inch to the foot. They were also going to build a model: the skeletonized version of the Salesman's house—the focal point of the whole design—was of the utmost importance and had to be developed three-dimensionally in a model, even if no one but the director ever looked at it. I was careful to start each sketch with the figures of Willy Loman, the Salesman, of his sons, or his wife, not only to intensify the dramatic mood of the sketch, but to control the interrelation of all the elements of the stage picture including the all-important human figure.

[2]Mielziner's assistant.

OCTOBER 4, 1948

. . . The greatest conundrum was in the scene in which the Salesman's two sons, as adults, go to bed in their attic bedroom in full view of the audience and then must appear elsewhere on the set a moment later as they were in their youth, entering downstage dressed in football togs. How were we going to get them out of bed and offstage without their being seen, when both the beds and their own bodies under the covers were completely visible to the audience, and also provide for an instantaneous costume change?

I said, "Let me try this out: We can build an inner frame in the beds that can act as an elevator. It can lower the boys quietly from the attic bedroom down some seven feet to the stage in a spot hidden from the audience by the set. From there they can sneak backstage, make their changes, and appear in time." "But," someone asked, "what's going to happen if the audience sees their pillows and blankets suddenly flatten out?"

. . . I finally found the solution: the heads of the beds in the attic room were to face the audience; the pillows, in full view since there were to be no solid headboards, would be made of papier mâché. A depression in each pillow would permit the heads of the boys to be concealed from the audience, and they would lie under the blankets that had been stiffened to stay in place. We could then lower them and still retain the illusion of their being in bed.

Whenever I use a special mechanism of this sort, I always demonstrate it in full light at one of the early technical rehearsals. When I tried out this device, John Harvey was the demonstrator; he is a good six feet one and probably weighed more than either Arthur Kennedy or Cameron Mitchell, who were to play the sons. He got into position in one of the beds, and we signaled the master property man, Joe Lynn, to lower the elevator. Engineers had recommended that the mechanism be electrically driven, but both Joe and John advised me that it would be safer to have a hand-driven winch that could be instantly stopped or reversed if anything went wrong. We had already determined that signals would be necessary: a red light, controlled by a button under the pillow on each bed, enabled each boy to indicate when he was in position, ready for the stagehand below to turn the crank of the winch that would lower the inner frame of the bed.

The mechanism worked perfectly in the first demonstration. Then Arthur Kennedy asked to try it. He climbed into the bed and, on cue, flashed his red light. As Joe Lynn worked the winch, we suddenly heard a frightening crunching and grinding noise. Kazan cried, "My God, I hope that isn't Kennedy's skull!" Fortunately for both the actor and the play, it turned out to be the papier-mâché pillow, which was half an inch too large and had jammed in the elevator. This was soon fixed, and on the next try we did it with stage lighting. The effect worked magnificently. Theatrical illusion had been achieved. . . .

OCTOBER 15, 1948

. . . Anticipating the many lighting difficulties in *Death of a Salesman*, particularly in the scenes that used projections, I decided to have a preliminary checkup with my friend [Edward] Kook [of Century Lighting Company]. I outlined my problem: There must be a transformation of the Salesman's home from a house closely encircled by tenement buildings, which cut out all sunlight and view of the sky, to a vista of the same house years earlier, surrounded by open air and sunlit trees giving a feeling of leafy airiness. I showed him my design for the backdrop; instead of the customary rather opaque linen, I planned to use unbleached muslin, a much lighter material. On it I intended to have the surrounding buildings painted in translucent colors, particularly the windows, which would appear rather bright when lit from the rear. When the transformations to earlier times were to occur, I planned to use a number of projection units, like magic lanterns, both from the auditorium and from backstage, throwing leaf patterns on the backdrop and on parts of the house. As the lights behind the backdrop were faded out, the painted buildings on the front would, I hoped, virtually disappear as images of light, spring-like leaves and fresh greens were superimposed, liberating the house from the oppression of the surrounding structures and giving the stage a feeling of the free outdoors. This was an integral part of the Salesman's life story and had to be an easily recognized symbol of the springtime of that life. . . .[3]

OCTOBER 19, 1948

. . . I had reduced the Salesman's home to a series of three levels, with the frame outline of the house forming an open skeleton. Some of the doors were simply open framework; arches and windows were cut-outs of wood, but were drawn and painted with a good deal of quality in their line. Given this rather stark background, whatever props there would have to be highly significant in character. One thing in particular loomed large: the icebox.

One of the best references in my library is not a work on theatre history or the fine arts; it is a torn and tattered collection of old Sears, Roebuck catalogues. One of the difficulties of research into period costumes or furnishings is that the illustrators of most of the books show what the upper crust was wearing or sitting on; when a designer wants to know about *hoi polloi*, it usually takes some concentrated digging. In 1929, which was the year I needed for the icebox, Sears, Roebuck was not attracting customers from Fifth Avenue or Newport, and so, in looking through the catalogues for that year, I found a picture of what I had remembered as a refrigerator typical of the time—cast-iron Chippendale-type legs that were rather thin and ridiculous-looking, and condensation coils covered in white enamel and perched on top of the cabinet, looking for all the world like a mechanistic wedding cake.

Joe said he remembered the type very well, but added that they were hard to find, even in the best junkyards. However, he told me not to worry: "We'll

allow ourselves enough time so that if we can't find one, we can make it. . . ."

NOVEMBER 1, 1948

. . . [Kazan's] chief concern after studying my model for *Salesman* was whether his actors would have enough room on the forestage to play the considerable number of scenes that we had placed there. We had agreed that the scenic effects for these episodes would have to be simple, but they would obviously involve a prop or two, and props have a way of taking up valuable playing space. Each scene would have to have enough of them to make it identifiable. The model showed only five feet of space between the footlight area and the beginning of the Salesman's house. This worried Kazan.

I had previously discussed, and was still seriously working on, the idea of extending the working stage beyond the footlights. This, of course, meant losing valuable seats in the first two rows, and both the producer and the general manager were concerned about the economics of the suggestion. . . .

DECEMBER 8, 1948

I was still to face the possible battle over the lighting equipment, but, first, the time had come to pin down exactly what we were going to do about the forestage. Bloomgarden, Kazan, Miller, Max Allentuck, the general manager, and I met at the Morosco.

Del Hughes, the production stage manager, had been given my blueprint of the ground plan and had marked the stage floor with tape, indicating the location of the steps, platforms, exits, and entrances in relation to the footlight area. Kazan spent a silent half-hour moving thoughtfully around the stage, taking various positions, his head held down much of the time as he examined the marks on the floor; occasionally he would take a quick glance toward the forestage, mentally estimating where other actors would be when an actor was standing in the position that he, Kazan, was holding at the moment.

Suddenly he said, "Fine. But the real headache is out here," and he pointed to the space far downstage that I had

asked for. He jumped over the footlights and landed in the aisle. He said, "Kerm, I'm afraid I'm going to kill at least a row and a half of doomed seats." I could see Max Allentuck concernedly counting the doomed seats. We experimented back and forth, and then Kazan offered a compromise. He decided that we would have to eliminate only the center section of the first row, a total of eleven seats. This meant a loss of $323.40 per week in receipts, which can mount up over a year. But the request was urgent, and Bloomgarden readily agreed. I was to build a forestage in this area.

With some nervousness I next brought up the high costs of the lighting equipment. After an hour of talk we settled on two special follow-spots and, necessarily, two extra men to operate them. As Bloomgarden pointed out, it was like a director saying, "I need two more good actors for this scene." And his reply to my request was the same as it would have been to his hypothetical director: "If it's important, you shall have them."

DECEMBER 10, 1948

. . . Bloomgarden asked me if I would meet with Alex North, the composer who had been engaged to do the music for *Death of a Salesman*. Everyone had agreed that the sound must be controlled with as much subtlety and care as the lights, increasing and diminishing almost imperceptibly. Since we had already planned to cover the orchestra pit with the forestage, where would the music be played, and what would the controlling mechanism be?

Using the blueprint of the ground plan, I reviewed the limitations with North and we concluded that we would use a dressing room as a control center and pipe the sound into the auditorium mechanically. Using headphones and a control speaker, the stage manager could then coordinate lighting cues with sound cues, for these two elements had to be in perfect harmony.

DECEMBER 15, 1948

. . . During the previous weeks I had been receiving from Arthur Miller, scene by scene, the final version of the

[3]For Mielziner's conception of the house, before and after the transformation, see the color paintings in *Designing for the Theatre*, pp. 146–147. The volume also contains (pp. 28–29) reproductions of some of Mielziner's black-and-white sketches.

rehearsal script. Although he had done the basic rewriting, he had made no attempt to say how the transitions from one scene to another would be made. This was a problem for the director and the designer to work out together as we studied the model, the ground plan, and the cut-out cardboard symbols representing the props.

I pointed out to Kazan how difficult it would be in an office scene, for instance, to remove two desks, two chairs, and a hatrack (which the present script called for) and at the same time have an actor walk quickly across the stage and appear in "a hotel room in Boston where he meets a girl." I urged him to do even more cutting, not in the text but in the props called for in this latest version of the script. We finally got the office pared down to one desk and one chair. Then I suggested going so far as to use the same desk for both office scenes—first in Heiser's[4] office and then, with a change of other props, in Charley's office. As usual, Kazan's imagination rose to the suggestion. He replied, "Sure, let's cut this down to the bone—we can play on practically anything." This is effective abstraction, giving the spectator the opportunity to "fill in."

I had felt from the outset that the cemetery scene at the end of the play would be done on the forestage, and I had actually drawn up a design for a trick trapdoor out of which would rise the small gravestone that we thought necessary for this scene. I had shown Kazan the working drawing for the gravestone, explained how it would operate, and mentioned that because of union rules the man operating this mechanism would be doing this and nothing else, thereby adding a member to the crew for the sake of one effect. I

[4]Heiser may simply be a slip of Mielziner's pen, but it may also be a name given at one stage of the writing to Howard Wagner, the only character other than Charley who has an office in the play.

had also mentioned that since the trap would be very close to the audience the sound of its opening might disturb the solemnity of the scene.

With some malice aforethought, I had also done a drawing showing the Salesman's widow sitting on the step leading to the forestage, with her two sons standing behind her, their heads bowed; on the floor at her feet was a small bouquet of flowers. The whole scene was bathed in a magic-lantern projection of autumn leaves. Here, again, leaves were symbolic. With this kind of lighting I thought I could completely obliterate the house in the background and evoke a sense of sadness and finality that might enable us to eliminate the gravestone itself.

My hints were not lost. "I get your point," Kazan said. "Let's do it without the gravestone. No matter how quietly you move it into place, everybody nearby is going to be so busy thinking, 'How is that done?' that they'll miss the mood of the scene."

. . . When we came to the scene in the Boston hotel room, Kazan said, "I don't need anything; just give me the feeling of a hotel room." I showed him a sketch of a panel of cheap wallpaper which I planned to project from the theatre balcony onto a background that was really a section of the trellis at one side of the Salesman's house. Projected images used in conjunction with scenery can be very valuable. In this case, the associations evoked by faded old wallpaper gave the audience a complete picture. Both the house and the exterior trellis faded away. The audience saw the Salesman in the cheap hotel room with that woman. I stress the phrase "in that room." Actors should never play against a scenic background but within the setting.

Kazan felt that the right actress cast in the role of the girl who visits Willy Loman in the hotel room, dressed in the right costume, plus the visual image of the wallpaper, would be enough to

make this short scene come alive. There is no question that when a good actor is backed up by simple scenic treatment, his strong qualities are stressed. Of course, this can work in reverse, but Arthur Miller was lucky in the casting of *Salesman*; even the bit roles were played by vivid actors. . . .

DECEMBER 24, 1948

. . . One example was the kitchen table for the Loman house. It would have been cheaper to buy one at a department store or a secondhand shop, but its color had to be right. I felt that in the Salesman's kitchen an old-fashioned oilcloth would have covered this table. But oilcloth is impossible to use on the stage because its shiny surface reflects too much light; and the moment the surface is sprayed down to kill the glare, the look of the oilcloth is lost. I knew from experience that glazed chintz with the right pattern plus a little over-painting by hand gives the impression of oilcloth. . . .

FEBRUARY 10, 1949

I was relaxed at the Broadway opening of *Death of a Salesman*. Here was a strong play. Audiences in Philadelphia had been tremendously enthusiastic. To me it was simply a question of how big a success the play would achieve. More than four months had passed since the initial phone call from Bloomgarden, and I felt I had done everything I was capable of doing to make the production visually effective and mechanically smooth-running. The performance *was* technically perfect. Artistically, the cast was superb, and they received a thunderous ovation. This type of reception is sometimes followed the next morning by cool reviews; but in this case the press was enthusiastic too. Contrary to custom, I even stayed up that night and went to a party. . . .

CAT ON A HOT TIN ROOF
TENNESSEE WILLIAMS

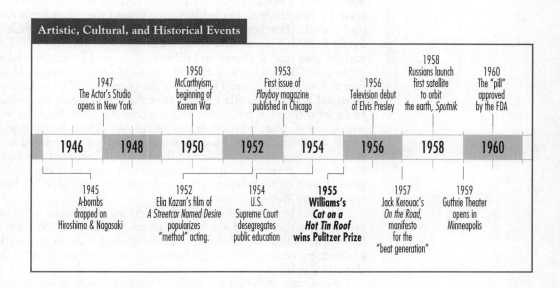

Artistic, Cultural, and Historical Events

1947
The Actor's Studio
opens in New York

1950
McCarthyism,
beginning of
Korean War

1953
First issue of
Playboy magazine
published in Chicago

1956
Television debut
of Elvis Presley

1958
Russians launch
first satellite
to orbit
the earth, *Sputnik*

1960
The "pill"
approved
by the FDA

1946 1948 1950 1952 1954 1956 1958 1960

1945
A-bombs
dropped on
Hiroshima & Nagasaki

1952
Elia Kazan's film of
A Streetcar Named Desire
popularizes
"method" acting.

1954
U.S.
Supreme Court
desegregates
public education

1955
**Williams's
Cat on a
Hot Tin Roof
wins Pulitzer Prize**

1957
Jack Kerouac's
On the Road,
manifesto
for the
"beat generation"

1959
Guthrie Theater
opens in
Minneapolis

TENNESSEE WILLIAMS (1911–83)

Despite his status as one of the twentieth-century's preeminent playwrights, Tennessee Williams is not regarded as a social dramatist in the manner of such contemporaries as Clifford Odets, Lillian Hellman, and especially Arthur Miller, whose own playwriting career virtually parallels that of Williams. Whereas these artists and their peers might be properly considered "the sons and daughters of Ibsen," Williams is much more a "son of Chekhov" (or Strindberg). His plays portray the loneliness of life, especially from the perspective of those who are outsiders by virtue of their personality, sexual orientation, or some flaw considered aberrant by society. However, these disturbing, often shocking, portraits of marginalized victims of a cruel society make Williams among the most eloquent of America's social voices. The central question of Williams's dramas—"Is there no mercy left in the world anymore?"—is perhaps the most urgent query of the modern world.

The story of Williams's life reads much like one of his scripts, which is fitting because he was the most intensely subjective of the major American playwrights. He was born Thomas Lanier Williams in Mississippi, the site of *Cat on a Hot Tin Roof*. Although his Southern roots are evident throughout his works, he is more than a regional playwright. His father, an abusive traveling shoe salesman, cruelly teased his son about his lack of masculinity (Williams was gay), frequently calling him "Miss Lucy." His mother, the daughter of a clergyman who schooled her in Southern gentility, suffered from bouts of mental illness. His sister, Rose, was sickly, delicate, and retiring (the paradigm of the Williams heroine), and he sympathized with her loneliness and unhappiness. His unhappy youth and fractured family life can be seen in his first playwriting success, *The Glass Menagerie* (1944), which was originally written as a screenplay (*The Gentleman Caller*) for MGM, to whom Williams was contracted.

Williams attended the University of Missouri for two years and ultimately graduated from the University of Iowa, where he studied theater and playwriting. An odyssey across America provided him with odd jobs and experiences for his short stories and plays. Williams settled into a career as a dramatist after he won a playwriting contest sponsored by the Group Theatre (out of which would grow the Actors Studio with which Williams's name is inextricably linked). His one-act plays caught the attention of a literary agent, Audrey Wood, who championed his writing. The success of *The Glass Menagerie* in 1944 and the triumph of *A Streetcar Named Desire* (1947), for which he received a Pulitzer Prize, made him (with Miller) the preeminent American playwright at mid-century. His best works, written between 1944 and 1962, include *Summer and Smoke* (1948); *Camino Real* (1953); *Cat on a Hot Tin Roof* (1955, Pulitzer Prize winner and the play that Williams, in his *Memoirs*, named his best work because it comes "closest to being both a work of art and a work of craft"); *Orpheus Descending* (1957); *Sweet Bird of Youth* (1959); and *The Night of the Iguana* (1962). His later plays—which suffered a critical backlash mostly because they failed to surpass his earlier works—are marked by experimentation with form and content. In 1999 Williams was back on Broadway with a "new" play, a prison drama called *Not About Nightingales*, which had been recently discovered among his early manuscripts. It was produced in a joint effort between the Alley Theatre of Houston and the Moving Theatre of London (founded by Vanessa Redgrave to promote political drama). The production, directed by Trevor Nunn, was greeted with such enthusiasm in London that it transferred to Broadway, where it won several Tony Awards.

Like his heroes and heroines, Williams was plagued by substance abuse, bouts of depression and illness, and sexual indulgence. His death in 1983 was a grotesque parody of his own dramas: alone in a hotel room, he choked to death on a medicine bottle cap while his partner, unaware of his predicament, remained in an adjoining room as Williams gasped for help.

Alma, one of Williams's troubled women, speaks a line in *Summer and Smoke* that serves as a universal description of the principal characters in his collected works: "My little company of the faded and frightened and difficult and odd and lonely." These include alcoholics and addicts, the sexually promiscuous, defrocked ministers, expatriates and foreigners, the mentally and physically ill, and—importantly—even the artist. Shakespeare, in *A Midsummer Night's Dream* (5.1.7-ff.), noted that "lunatics, lovers, and poets" share a common imagination, and Williams frequently creates characters with an artistic sensibility that permits them to articulate the pain they suffer by virtue of being different. For instance, Blanche Du Bois, the deluded heroine of *A Streetcar Named Desire*, once taught poetry and fancies herself as possessed of an artistic spirit. It is the alienated artist in Williams's world who reminds the Philistines—such as Stanley Kowalski and Gooper Pollitt—that "we are all civilized, which means that we are all savages at heart but observing the amenities of civilized behavior."

Because he writes such extraordinary psychological portraits, and because his plays are customarily placed in naturalistic settings (one's environment is a significant character in a Williams play), it is easy to align Williams with those playwrights we call "realists." But like Blanche Du Bois, who says, "I don't want realism, I want magic," Williams couples his realism with a superb theatricality, much of it derived from Expressionism. The action of Williams's plays is set against a bold array of sounds, lighting effects, and choric characters. Moments of crisis are almost always marked by a spectacular visual image. Williams's language is also theatrical. While his plays are written in prose and seem at first reading to be entirely naturalistic, Williams elevates Southern colloquialisms to a poetic level that transcends ordinary speech. The playwright once cited Big Daddy in *Cat on a Hot Tin Roof* as possessing "a crude eloquence" that he "managed to give no other character" in his canon. This extraordinary fusion of theatricality, heightened speech, and an abundance of verbal and visual symbols has earned Williams the title of "poetic realist." When Williams died, Walter Kerr, then America's foremost drama critic, simply said, "We have lost our greatest playwright."

AS YOU READ *CAT ON A HOT TIN ROOF*

At first glance *Cat on a Hot Tin Roof* seems Williams's most naturalistic play, partly because it conspicuously maintains the neoclassical unities of time, place, and action. Williams, in perhaps the boldest experiment of this play, insists that the action portrayed on stage occupy "precisely the time of its performance." That is, the running time of the play is exactly the time (two intermissions notwithstanding) it takes the Pollitts to confront the many "mendacities" that have destroyed this once-proud family. The founders of Naturalism, Zola and Strindberg, called for exactly such "true time" chronologies to portray truthfully "a slice of life" on stage. The play is also naturalistic in that heredity (heritage and familial loyalties dominate the play) and environment (the Old South) contribute to the dramatic action and its themes.

Ironically, this play—which is obsessed with obliterating falsity—is not truly a naturalistic play; that stylistic veneer is a subterfuge. *Cat on a Hot Tin Roof* is a grandly theatrical work that supercedes its apparent Naturalism. Williams's description of the setting he envisioned, as rendered in his "Note to the Designer" (Jo Mielziner, who designed both *A Streetcar Named Desire* and Miller's *Death of a Salesman* on Broadway), suggests a theatrical motif with "walls that dissolve mysteriously into the air." As much as the patently antirealistic scenery (which was actually made simpler and thereby more theatrical by Mielziner and director Elia Kazan; see endnote), it is the many lengthy speeches that give the play its theatrical resonance: Act I is virtually a monologue for Maggie the Cat. You may find it useful to consider these extraordinary speeches as the equivalent of the Elizabethan soliloquy (in which a character shared his innermost thoughts with the audience), the French tirade (lengthy, passionate outbursts that dominated Parisian stages in the seventeenth century), or, better yet, operatic arias that test the range and skill of the actors who sing them. (Williams actually refers to Maggie's speeches as "recitatives"—a term borrowed from the opera—in a stage direction late in Act II.)

Here, then, we find a case of the structure of a play reflecting its content: what seems on the surface to be one kind of play (a naturalistic family drama) is actually another (a theatrical tour de force by its playwright and for its actors). As you read the play, look for the artful "mendacities" Williams has created as he tries to "snare . . . the truth of human experience."

CAT ON A HOT TIN ROOF

TENNESSEE WILLIAMS

CHARACTERS

LACEY
SONNY
SOOKEY
TRIXIE
MARGARET
BIG DADDY
BRICK
REVEREND TOOKER
MAE
DOCTOR BAUGH
COOPER
DAISY
BIG MAMA
BRIGHTIE
DIXIE
SMALL
BUSTER

ACT I

Notes for the Designer

The set is the bed-sitting room of a plantation home in the Mississippi Delta. It is along an upstairs gallery which probably runs around the entire house; it has two pairs of very wide doors opening onto the gallery, showing white balustrades against a fair summer sky that fades into dusk and night during the course of the play, which occupies precisely the time of its performance, excepting, of course, the fifteen minutes of intermission.

Perhaps the style of the room is not what you would expect in the home of the Delta's biggest cotton-planter. It is Victorian with a touch of the Far East. It hasn't changed much since it was occupied by the original owners of the place, Jack Straw and Peter Ochello, a pair of old bachelors who shared this room all their lives together. In other words, the room must evoke some ghosts; it is gently and poetically haunted by a relationship that must have involved a tenderness which was uncommon. This may be irrelevant or unnecessary, but I once saw a reproduction of a faded photograph of the verandah of Robert Louis Stevenson's home on that Samoan Island where he spent his last years, and there was a quality of tender light on weathered wood, such as porch furniture made of bamboo and wicker, exposed to tropical suns and tropical rains, which came to mind when I thought about the set for this play, bringing also to mind the grace and comfort of light, the reassurance it gives, on a late and fair afternoon in summer, the way that no matter what, even dread of death, is gently touched and soothed by it. For the set is the background for a play that deals with human extremities of emotion, and it needs that softness behind it.

The bathroom door, showing only pale-blue tile and silver towel racks, is in one side wall; the hall door in the opposite wall. Two articles of furnitures need mention: a big double bed which staging should make a functional part of the set as often as suitable, the surface of which should be slightly raked to make figures on it seen more easily; and against the wall space between the two huge double doors upstage: a monumental monstrosity peculiar to our times, a huge console combination of radio-phonograph (Hi-Fi with three speakers) TV set and liquor cabinet, bearing and containing many glasses and bottles, all in one piece, which is a composition of muted silver tones, and the opalescent tones of reflecting glass, a chromatic link, this thing, between the sepia (tawny gold) tones of the interior and the cool (white and *blue) tones of the gallery and sky. This piece of furniture (?!), this little shrine to virtually all the comforts and illusions behind which we hide from such things as the characters in the play are faced with. . . .*

The set should be far less realistic than I have so far implied in this description of it. I think the walls below the ceiling should dissolve mysteriously into air; the set should be roofed by the sky; stars and moon suggested by traces of milky pallor, as if they were observed through a telescope lens out of focus.

Anything else I can think of? Oh, yes, fanlights (transoms shaped like an open glass fan) above all the doors in the set, with panes of blue and amber, and above all, the designer should take as many pains to give the actors room to move about freely (to show their restlessness, their passion for breaking out) as if it were a set for a ballet.

An evening in summer. The action is continuous, with two intermissions.

At the rise of the curtain someone is taking a shower in the bathroom, the door of which is half open. A pretty young woman, with anxious lines in her face, enters the bedroom and crosses to the bathroom door.

MARGARET (*Shouting above roar of water*). One of those no-neck monsters hit me with a hot buttered biscuit so I have t' change! (*Margaret's voice is both rapid and drawling. In her long speeches she has the vocal tricks of a priest delivering a liturgical chant, the lines are almost sung, always continuing a little beyond her breath so she has to gasp for another. Sometimes she intersperses the lines with a little wordless singing, such as "Da-da-daaaa!"*)

(*Water turns off and Brick calls out to her, but is still unseen. A tone of politely feigned interest, masking indifference, or worse, is characteristic of his speech with Margaret.*)

BRICK. What'd you say, Maggie? Water was on s' loud I couldn't hearya. . . .

MARGARET. Well, I!—just remarked that!—one of th' no-neck monsters messed up m' lovely lace dress so I got t'—cha-a-ange. . . . (*She opens and kicks shut drawers of the dresser.*)

BRICK. Why d'ya call Gooper's kiddies no-neck monsters?

MARGARET. Because they've got no necks! Isn't that a good enough reason?

BRICK. Don't they have any necks?

MARGARET. None visible. Their fat little heads are set on their fat little bodies without a bit of connection.

BRICK. That's too bad.

MARGARET. Yes, it's too bad because you can't wring their necks if they've got no necks to wring! Isn't that right, honey? (*She steps out of her dress, stands in a slip of ivory satin and lace.*) Yep, they're no-neck monsters, all no-neck people are monsters . . . (*Children shriek downstairs.*) Hear them? Hear them screaming? I don't know where their voice-boxes are located since they don't have necks. I tell you I got so nervous at that table tonight I thought I would throw back my head and utter a scream you could hear across the Arkansas border an' parts of Louisiana an' Tennessee. I said to your charming sister-in-law, Mae, honey, couldn't you feed those precious little things at a separate table with an oilcloth cover? They make such a mess an' the lace cloth looks *so* pretty! She made enormous eyes at me and said, "Ohhh, noooooo! On Big Daddy's birthday? Why, he would never forgive me!" Well, I want you to know, Big Daddy hadn't been at the table two minutes with those five no-neck monsters slobbering and drooling over their food before he threw down his fork an' shouted, "Fo' God's sake, Gooper, why don't you put them pigs at a trough in th' kitchen?"—Well, I swear, I simply could have di-ieed!

Think of it, Brick, they've got five of them and number six is coming. They've brought the whole bunch down here like animals to display at a county fair. Why, they have those children doin' tricks all the time! "Junior, show Big Daddy how you do this, show Big Daddy how you do that, say your little piece fo' Big Daddy, Sister. Show your dimples, Sugar. Brother, show Big Daddy how you stand on your head!"—It goes on all the time, along with constant little remarks and innuendos about the fact that you and I have not produced any children, are totally childless and therefore totally useless!—Of course it's comical but it's also disgusting since it's so obvious what they're up to!

BRICK (*without interest*). What are they up to, Maggie?

MARGARET. Why, you know what they're up to!

BRICK (*appearing*). No, I don't know what they're up to. (*He stands there in the bathroom doorway drying his hair with a towel and hanging onto the towel rack because one ankle is broken, plastered and bound. He is still slim and firm as a boy. His liquor hasn't started tearing him down outside. He has the additional charm of that cool air of detachment that people have who have given up the struggle. But now and then, when disturbed, something flashes behind it, like lighting in a fair sky, which shows that at some deeper level he is far from peaceful. Perhaps in a stronger light he would show some signs of deliquescence, but the fading, still warm, light from the gallery treats him gently.*)

MARGARET. I'll tell you what they're up to, boy of mine!—They're up to cutting you out of your father's estate, and—(*She freezes momentarily before her next remark. Her voice drops as if it were somehow a personally embarrassing admission.*)—Now we know that Big Daddy's dyin' of—cancer.... (*There are voices on the lawn below: long-drawn calls across distance. Margaret raises her lovely bare arms and powders her armpits with a light sigh. She adjusts the angle of a magnifying mirror to straighten an eyelash, then rises fretfully saying:*) There's so much light in the room it—

BRICK (*softly but sharply*). Do we?

MARGARET. Do we what?

BRICK. Know Big Daddy's dyin' of cancer?

MARGARET. Got the report today.

BRICK. Oh . . .

MARGARET (*letting down bamboo blinds which cast long, gold-fretted shadows over the room*). Yep, got th' report just now . . . it didn't surprise me, Baby. . . . (*Her voice has range, and music; sometimes it drops low as a boy's and you have a sudden image of her playing boys' games as a child.*) I recognized the symptoms soon's we got here last spring and I'm willin' to bet you that Brother Man and his wife were pretty sure of it, too. That more than likely explains why their usual summer migration to the coolness of the Great Smokies was passed up this summer in favor of—hustlin' down here ev'ry whip-stitch with their whole screamin' tribe! And why so many allusions have been made to Rainbow Hill lately. You know what Rainbow Hill is? Place that's famous for treatin' alcoholics an' dope fiends in the movies!

BRICK. I'm not in the movies.

MARGARET. No, and you don't take dope. Otherwise you're a perfect candidate for Rainbow Hill, Baby, and that's where they aim to ship you—over my dead body! Yep, over my dead body they'll ship you there, but nothing would please them better. Then Brother Man could get a-hold of the purse strings and dole out remittances to us, maybe get power-of-attorney and sign checks for us and cut off our credit wherever, whenever he wanted! Son-of-a-bitch!—How'd you like that, Baby?—Well, you've been doin' just about ev'rything in your power to bring it about, you've just been doin' ev'rything you can think of to aid and abet them in this scheme of theirs! Quittin' work, devoting yourself to the occupation of drinkin'!—Breakin' your ankle last night on the high school athletic field: doin' what? Jumpin' hurdles? At

two or three in the morning? Just fantastic! Got in the paper. *Clarksdale Register* carried a nice little item about it, human interest story about a well-known former athlete stagin' a one-man track meet on the Glorious Hill High School athletic field last night, but was slightly out of condition and didn't clear the first hurdle! Brother Man Gooper claims he exercised his influence t' keep it from goin' out over AP or UP or every goddam "P."

But, Brick? You still have one big advantage!

(*During the above swift flood of words, Brick has reclined with contrapuntal leisure on the snowy surface of the bed and has rolled over carefully on his side or belly.*)

BRICK (*wryly*). Did you *say* something, Maggie?

MARGARET. Big Daddy dotes on you, honey. And he can't stand Brother Man and Brother Man's wife, that monster of fertility, Mae; she's downright odious to him! Know how I know? By little expressions that flicker over his face when that woman is holding fo'th on one of her choice topics such as—how she refused twilight sleep!—when the twins were delivererd! Because she feels motherhood's an experience that a woman ought to experience fully!—in order to fully appreciate the wonder and beauty of it! HAH! (*This loud "HAH!" is accompanied by a violent action such as slamming a drawer shut.*)—and how she made Brother Man come in an' stand beside her in the delivery room so he would not miss out on the "wonder and beauty" of it either!—producin' those no-neck monsters. . . . (*A speech of this kind would be antipathetic from almost anybody but Margaret; she makes it oddly funny, because her eyes constantly twinkle and her voice shakes with laughter which is basically indulgent.*)—Big Daddy shares my attitude toward those two! As for me, well—I give him a laugh now and then and he tolerates me. In fact!—I sometimes suspect that Big Daddy harbors a little unconscious "lech" fo' me. . . .

BRICK. What makes you think that Big Daddy has a lech for you, Maggie?

MARGARET. Way he always drops his eyes down my body when I'm talkin' to him, drops his eyes to my boobs an' licks his old chops! Ha ha!

BRICK. That kind of talk is disgusting.

MARGARET. Did anyone ever tell you that you're an ass-aching Puritan, Brick?

I think it's mighty fine that the ole fellow, in the doorstep of death, still takes in my shape with what I think is deserved appreciation!

And you wanta know something else? Big Daddy didn't know how many little Maes and Goopers had been produced! "How many kids have you got?" he asked at the taable, just like Brother Man and his wife were new acquaintances to him! Big Mama said he was jokin', but that old boy wasn't jokin', Lord, no!

And when they infawmed him that they had five already and were turning out number six!—the news seemed to come as a sort of unpleasant surprise . . . (*Children yell below.*) Scream, monsters! (*Turns to Brick with a sudden, gay, charming smile which fades as she notices that he is not looking at her but into fading gold space with a troubled expression.*)

(*It is constant rejection that makes her humor "bitchy."*) Yes, you should of been at that supper-table, Baby. (*Whenever she calls him "baby" the word is a soft caress.*) Y'know, Big Daddy, bless his old sweet soul, he's the dearest ole thing in the world, but he does hunch over his food as if he preferred not to notice anything else. Well, Mae an' Gooper were side by side at the table, direckly across from Big Daddy, watchin' his face like hawks while they jawed an' jabbered about the cuteness an' brilliance of th' no-neck monsters! (*She giggles with a hand fluttering at her throat and her breast and her long throat arched.*)

(*She comes downstage and recreates the scene with voice and gesture.*) And the no-neck monsters were ranged around the table, some in high chairs and some on th' *Books of Knowledge,* all in fancy little paper caps in honor of Big Daddy's birthday, and all through dinner, well, I want you to know that Brother Man an' his partner never once, for one moment, stopped exchanging pokes an' pinches an' kicks an' signs an' signals!—Why, they were like a couple of cardsharps fleecing a sucker.—Even Big Mama, bless her old sweet soul, she isn't th' quickest an' brightest thing in the world, she finally noticed, at last, an' said to Gooper, "Gooper, what are you an' Mae makin' all these signs at each other about?"—I swear t' goodness, I nearly choked on my chicken! (*Margaret, back at the dressing-table, still doesn't see Brick. He is watching her with a look that is not quite definable.—Amused? shocked? contemptuous?—part of those and part of something else.*) Y'know—your brother Gooper still cherishes the illusion he took a giant step up on the social ladder when he married Miss Mae Flynn of the Memphis Flynns. (*Margaret moves about the room as she talks, stops before the mirror, moves on.*) But I have a piece of Spanish news for Gooper. The Flynns never had a thing in this world but money and they lost that, they were nothing at all but fairly successful climbers. Of course, Mae Flynn came out of Memphis eight years before I made my debut in Nashville, but I had friends at Ward-Belmont who came from Memphis and they used to come to see me and I used to go to see them for Christmas and spring vacations, and so I know who rates an' who doesn't rate in Memphis society. Why, y'know ole Papa Flynn, he barely escaped doing time in the Federal pen for shady manipulations on th' stock market when his chain stores crashed, and as for Mae having been a cotton carnival queen, as they remind us so often, lest we forget, well, that's one honor that I don't envy her for!—Sit on a brass throne on a tacky float an' ride down Main Street, smilin', bowin', and blowin' kisses to all the trash on the street—(*She picks out a pair of jeweled sandals and rushes to the dressing-table.*) Why, year before last, when Susan McPheeters was singled out fo' that honor, y'know what happened to her? Y'know what happened to poor little Susie McPheeters?

BRICK (*absently*). No. What happened to little Susie McPheeters?

MARGARET. Somebody spit tobacco juice in her face.

BRICK (*dreamily*). Somebody spit tobacco juice in her face?

MARGARET. That's right, some old drunk leaned out of a window in the Hotel Gayoso and yelled, "Hey, Queen, hey, hey, there, Queenie!" Poor Susie looked up and flashed him a radiant smile and he shot out a squirt of tobacco juice right in poor Susie's face.

BRICK. Well, what d'you know about that.

MARGARET (*gaily*). What do I know about it? I was there, I saw it!

BRICK (*absently*). Must have been kind of funny.

MARGARET. Susie didn't think so. Had hysterics. Screamed like a banshee. They had to stop th' parade an' remove her from her throne and' go on with— (*She catches sight of him in the mirror, gasps slightly, wheels about to face him. Count ten.*)—Why are you looking at me like that?

BRICK (*whistling softly, now*). Like what, Maggie?

MARGARET (*intensely, fearfully*). The way y' were lookin' at me just now, befo' I caught your eye in the mirror and you started t' whistle! I don't know how t' describe it but it froze my blood!—I've caught you lookin' at me like that so often lately. What are you thinkin' of when you look at me like that?

BRICK. I wasn't conscious of lookin' at you, Maggie.

MARGARET. Well, I was conscious of it! What were you thinkin'?

BRICK. I don't remember thinking of anything, Maggie.

MARGARET. Don't you think I know that—? Don't you—? —Think I know that—?

BRICK (*coolly*). Know *what*, Maggie?

MARGARET (*struggling for expression*). That I've gone through this—*hideous!*—transformation, become—hard! Frantic! (*Then she adds, almost tenderly:*)—cruel!! That's what you've been observing in me lately. How could y' help but observe it? That's all right. I'm not—thin-skinned any more, can't afford t' be thin-skinned any more. (*She is now recovering her power.*)—But Brick? Brick?

BRICK. Did you say something?

MARGARET. I was goin' t' say something: that I get—lonely. Very!

BRICK. Ev'rybody gets that . . .

MARGARET. Living with someone you love can be lonelier—than living entirely *alone!*—if the one that y' love doesn't love you. . . . (*There is a pause. Brick hobbles downstage and asks, without looking at her.*)

BRICK. Would you like to live alone, Maggie?

(*Another pause: then—after she has caught a quick, hurt breath:*)

MARGARET. *No!—God!—I wouldn't!* (*Another gasping breath. She forcibly controls what must have been an impulse to cry out. We see her deliberately, very forcibly, going all the way back to the world in which you can talk about ordinary matters.*) Did you have a nice shower?

BRICK. Uh-huh.

MARGARET. Was the water cool?

BRICK. No.

MARGARET. But it made y' feel fresh, huh?

BRICK. Fresher. . . .

MARGARET. I know something would make y' feel *much* fresher!

BRICK. What?

MARGARET. An alcohol rub. Or cologne, a rub with cologne!

BRICK. That's good after a workout but I haven't been workin' out, Maggie.

MARGARET. You've kept in good shape, though.

BRICK (*indifferently*). You think so, Maggie?

MARGARET. I always thought drinkin' men lost their looks, but I was plainly mistaken.

BRICK (*wryly*). Why, thanks, Maggie.

MARGARET. You're the only drinkin' man I know that it never seems t' put fat on.

BRICK. I'm gettin' softer, Maggie.

MARGARET. Well, sooner or later it's bound to soften you up. It was just beginning to soften up Skipper when—(*She stops short.*) I'm sorry. I never could keep my fingers off a sore—I wish you *would* lose your looks. If you did it would make the martyrdom of Saint Maggie a little more bearable. But no such goddam luck. I actually believe you've gotten better looking since you've gone on the bottle. Yeah, a person who didn't know you would think you'd never had a tense nerve in your body or a strained muscle. (*There are sounds of croquet on the lawn below: the click of mallets, light voices, near and distant.*) Of course, you always had that detached quality as if you were playing a game without much concern over whether you won or lost, and now that you've lost the game, not lost but just quit playing, you have that rare sort of charm that usually only happens in very old or hopelessly sick people, the charm of the defeated.—You look so cool, so cool, so enviably cool. (*Music is heard.*) They're playing croquet. The moon has appeared and it's white, just beginning to turn a little bit yellow. . . .

You were a wonderful lover. . . .

Such a wonderful person to go to bed with, and I think mostly because you were really indifferent to it. Isn't that right? Never had any anxiety about it, did it naturally, easily, slowly, with absolute confidence and perfect calm, more like opening a door for a lady or seating her at a table than giving expression to any longing for her. Your indifference made you wonderful at lovemaking—*strange?*—but true. . . .

You know, if I thought you would never, never, *never* make love to me again—I would go downstairs to the kitchen and pick out the longest and sharpest knife I could find and stick it straight into my heart, I swear that I would!

But one thing I don't have is the charm of the defeated, my hat is still in the ring, and I am determined to win! (*There is the sound of croquet mallets hitting croquet balls.*)—What is the victory of a cat on a hot tin roof?—I wish I knew. . . .

Just staying on it, I guess, as long as she can. . . . (*More croquet sounds.*) Later tonight I'm going to tell you I love you an' maybe by that time you'll be drunk enough to believe me. Yes, they're playing croquet. . . .

Big Daddy is dying of cancer. . . .

What were you thinking of when I caught you looking at me like that? Were you thinking of Skipper? (*Brick takes up his crutch, rises.*) Oh, excuse me, forgive me, but laws of silence don't work! No, laws of silence don't work. . . . (*Brick crosses to the bar, takes a quick drink, and rubs his head with a towel.*) Laws of silence don't work. . . .

When something is festering in your memory or your imagination, laws of silence don't work, it's just like shutting a door and locking it on a house on fire in hope of forgetting that the house is burning. But not facing a fire doesn't put it out. Silence about a thing just magnifies it. It grows and festers in silence, becomes malignant. . . . Get dressed, Brick.

(*He drops his crutch.*)

BRICK. I've dropped my crutch. (*He has stopped rubbing his hair dry but still stands hanging onto the towel rack in a white towel-cloth robe.*)

MARGARET. Lean on me.

BRICK. No, just give me my crutch.

MARGARET. Lean on my shoulder.

BRICK. *I don't want to lean on your shoulder, I want my crutch!* (*This is spoken like sudden lightning.*) Are you going to give me my crutch or do I have to get down on my knees on the floor and—

MARGARET. *Here, here, take it, take it!* (*She has thrust the crutch at him.*)

BRICK (*hobbling out*). Thanks . . .

MARGARET. We mustn't scream at each other, the walls in this house have ears. . . . (*He hobbles directly to liquor cabinet to get a new drink.*)—but that's the first time I've heard you raise your voice in a long time, Brick. A crack in the wall?—Of composure?

—I think that's a good sign. . . .

A sign of nerves in a player on the defensive!

(*Brick turns and smiles at her coolly over his fresh drink.*)

BRICK. It just hasn't happened yet, Maggie.

MARGARET. What?

BRICK. The click I get in my head when I've had enough of this stuff to make me peaceful. . . . Will you do me a favor?

MARGARET. Maybe I will. What favor?

BRICK. Just, just keep your voice down!

MARGARET (*in a hoarse whisper*). I'll do you that favor, I'll speak in a whisper, if not shut up completely, if *you* will do *me* a favor and make that drink your last one till after the party.

BRICK. What party?

MARGARET. Big Daddy's birthday party.

BRICK. Is this Big Daddy's birthday?

MARGARET. You know this is Big Daddy's birthday!

BRICK. No, I don't, I forgot it.

MARGARET. Well, I remembered it for you. . . .

(*They are both speaking as breathlessly as a pair of kids after a fight, drawing deep exhausted breaths and looking at each other with faraway eyes, shaking and panting together as if they had broken apart from a violent struggle.*)

BRICK. Good for you, Maggie.

MARGARET. You just have to scribble a few lines on this card.

BRICK. You scribble something, Maggie.

MARGARET. It's got to be your handwriting; it's your present, I've given him my present; it's got to be your handwriting!

(*The tension between them is building again, the voices becoming shrill once more.*)

BRICK. I didn't get him a present.

MARGARET. I got one for you.

BRICK. All right. You write the card, then.

MARGARET. And have him know you didn't remember his birthday?

BRICK. I didn't remember his birthday.

MARGARET. You don't have to prove you didn't!

BRICK. I don't want to fool him about it.

MARGARET. Just write "Love, Brick!" for God's—

BRICK. No.

MARGARET. You've *got* to!

BRICK. I don't have to do anything I don't want to do. You keep forgetting the conditions on which I agreed to stay on living with you.

MARGARET (*out before she knows it*). I'm not living with you. We occupy the same cage.

BRICK. You've got to remember the conditions agreed on.

MARGARET. They're impossible conditions!

BRICK. Then why don't you—?

MARGARET. HUSH! Who is out there? Is somebody at the door?

(*There are footsteps in hall.*)

MAE (*outside*). May I enter a moment?

MARGARET. Oh, *you*! Sure. Come in, Mae.

(*Mae enters bearing aloft the bow of a young lady's archery set.*)

MAE. Brick, is this thing yours?

MARGARET. Why, Sister Woman—that's my Diana Trophy. Won it at the inter-collegiate archery contest on the Ole Miss campus.

MAE. It's a mighty dangerous thing to leave exposed round a house full of nawmal rid-blooded childen attracted t'weapons.

MARGARET. "Nawmal rid-blooded children attracted t'weapons" ought t'be taught to keep their hands off things that don't belong to them.

MAE. Maggie, honey, if you had children of your own you'd know how funny that is. Will you please lock this up and put the key out of reach?

MARGARET. Sister Woman, nobody is plotting the destruction of your kiddies.—Brick and I still have our special archers' license. We're goin' deer-huntin' on Moon Lake as soon as the season starts. I love to run with dogs through chilly woods, run, run leap over obstructions—(*She goes into the closet carrying the bow.*)

MAE. How's the injured ankle, Brick?

BRICK. Doesn't hurt. Just itches.

MAE. Oh, my! Brick—Brick, you should've been downstairs after supper! Kiddies put on a show. Polly played the piano, Buster an' Sonny drums, an' then they turned out the lights an' Dixie an' Trixie puhfawmed a toe dance in fairy costume with *spahkluhs!* Bid Daddy just beamed! He just beamed!

MARGARET (*From the closet with a sharp laugh*). Oh, I bet. It breaks my heart that we missed it! (*She reenters.*) But Mae? Why did y' give dawgs' names to all your kiddies?

MAE. *Dog's* names?

(*Margaret has made this observation as she goes to raise the bamboo blinds, since the sunset glare has diminished. In crossing she winks at Brick.*)

MARGARET (*sweetly*). Dixie, Trixie, Buster, Sonny, Polly!—Sounds like four dogs and a parrot . . . animal act in a circus!

MAE. Maggie? (*Margaret turns with a smile*). Why are you so catty?

MARGARET. Cause I'm a cat! But why can't *you* take a joke, Sister Woman?

MAE. Nothin' pleases me more than a joke that's funny. You know the real names of our kiddies. Buster's real name is Robert. Sonny's real name is Saunders. Trixie's real name is Marlene and Dixie's—(*Someone downstairs calls for her, "Hey, Mae!"—She rushes to door, saying.*) Intermission is over!

MARGARET (*as Mae closes door*). I wonder what Dixie's real name is?

BRICK. Maggie, being catty doesn't help things any . . .

MARGARET. I know! WHY!—Am I so catty?—Cause I'm consumed with envy an' eaten up with longing?—Brick, I've laid out your beautiful Shantung silk suit from Rome and one of your monogrammed silk shirts. I'll put your cuff-links in it, those lovely star sapphires I get you to wear so rarely. . . .

BRICK. I can't get trousers on over this plaster cast.

MARGARET. Yes, you can, I'll help you.

BRICK. I'm not going to get dressed, Maggie.

MARGARET. Will you just put on a pair of white silk pajamas?

BRICK. Yes, I'll do that, Maggie.

MARGARET. *Thank* you, thank you so *much!*

BRICK. Don't mention it.

MARGARET. *Oh, Brick!* How long does it have t' go on? This punishment? Haven't I done time enough, haven't I served my term, can't I apply for a—pardon?

BRICK. Maggie, you're spoiling my liquor. Lately your voice always sounds like you'd been running upstairs to warn somebody that the house was on fire!

MARGARET. Well, no wonder, no wonder. Y'know what I feel like, Brick? (*Children's and grownups' voices are blended, below, in a loud but uncertain rendition of "My Wild Irish Rose."*) I feel all the time like a cat on a hot tin roof!

BRICK. Then jump off the roof, jump off it, cats can jump off roofs and land on their four feet uninjured!

MARGARET. Oh, yes!

BRICK. Do it!—fo' God's sake, do it . . .

MARGARET. Do what?

BRICK. Take a lover!

MARGARET. I can't see a man but you! Even with my eyes closed, I just see you! Why don't you get ugly, Brick, why don't you please get fat or ugly or something so I could stand it? (*She rushes to hall door, opens it, listens.*) The concert is still going on! Bravo, no-necks, bravo! (*She slams and locks door fiercely.*)

BRICK. What did you lock the door for?

MARGARET. To give us a little privacy for a while.

BRICK. You know better, Maggie.

MARGARET. No, I don't know better. . . . (*She rushes to gallery doors, draws the rose-silk drapes across them.*)

BRICK. Don't make a fool of yourself.

MARGARET. I don't mind makin' a fool of myself over you!

BRICK. I mind, Maggie. I feel embarrassed for you.

MARGARET. Feel embarrassed! But don't continue my torture. I can't live on and on under these circumstances.

BRICK. You agreed to—

MARGARET. I know but—

BRICK. —Accept that condition!

MARGARET. *I CAN'T! CAN'T! CAN'T!* (*She seizes his shoulder*)

BRICK. Let go! (*He breaks away from her and seizes the small boudoir chair and raises it like a lion-tamer facing a big circus cat.*)

(*Count five. She stares at him with her fist pressed to her mouth, then bursts into shrill, almost hysterical laughter. He remains grave for a moment, then grins and puts the chair down. Big Mama calls through closed door.*)

BIG MAMA. Son? Son? Son?

BRICK. What is it, Big Mama?

BIG MAMA (*outside*). Oh, son! We got the most wonderful news about Big Daddy. I just had t' run up an' tell you right this—(*She rattles the knob.*)—What's this door doin', locked, faw? You all think there's robbers in the house?

MARGARET. Big Mama, Brick is dressin', he's not dressed yet.

BIG MAMA. That's all right, it won't be the first time I've seen Brick not dressed. Come on, open this door!

(*Margaret, with a grimace, goes to unlock and open the hall door, as Brick hobbles rapidly to the bathroom and kicks the door shut. Big Mama has disappeared from the hall.*)

MARGARET. Big Mama?

(*Big Mama appears through the opposite gallery doors behind Margaret, huffing and puffing like an old bulldog. She is a short, stout woman: her sixty years and 170 pounds have left her somewhat breathless most of the time; she's always tensed like a boxer, or rather, a Japanese wrestler. Her "family" was maybe a little superior to Big Daddy's, but not much. She wears a black or silver lace dress and at least half a million in flashy gems. She is very sincere.*)

BIG MAMA (*loudly, startling Margaret*). Here—I come through Gooper's and Mae's gall'ry door. Where's Brick? *Brick*—Hurry on out of there, son, I just have a second and want to give you the news about Big Daddy.—I hate locked doors in a house. . . .

MARGARET (*with affected lightness*). I've noticed you do, Big Mama, but people have got to have *some* moments of privacy, don't they?

BIG MAMA. No, ma'am, not in *my* house. (*Without pause*) Whacha took off you' dress faw? I thought that little lace dress was so sweet on yuh, honey.

MARGARET. I thought it looked sweet on me, too, but one of m' cute little table-partners used it for a napkin so—!

BIG MAMA (*Picking up stockings on floor*). What?

MARGARET. You know, Big Mama, Mae and Gooper's so touchy about those children—thanks, Big Mama . . . (*Big Mama has thrust the picked-up stockings in Margaret's hand with a grunt.*)—that you just don't dare to suggest there's any room for improvement in their—

BIG MAMA. Brick, hurry out!—Shoot, Maggie, you just don't like children.

MARGARET. I do SO like childen! Adore them!—well brought up!

BIG MAMA (*gentle—loving*). Well, why don't you have some and bring them up well, then, instead of all the time pickin' on Gooper's an' Mae's?

GOOPER (*shouting up the stairs*). Hey, hey, Big Mama, Betsy an' Hugh got to go, waitin' to tell yuh g'by!

BIG MAMA. Tell 'em to hold their hawses, I'll be right down in a jiffy! (*She turns to the bathroom door and calls out.*) Son? Can you hear me in there? (*There is a muffled answer.*) We just got the full report from the laboratory at the Ochsner Clinic, completely negative, son, ev'rything negative, right on down the line! Nothin' a-tall's wrong with him but some little functional thing called a spastic colon. Can you hear me, son?

MARGARET. He can hear you, Big Mama.

BIG MAMA. Then why don't he say something? God Almighty, a piece of news like that should make him shout. It made *me* shout, I can tell you. I shouted and sobbed and fell right down on my knees!—Look! (*She pulls up her skirt.*) See the bruises where I hit my kneecaps? Took both doctors to haul me back on my feet! (*She laughs—she always laughs like hell at herself.*) Big Daddy was furious with me! But ain't that wonderful news? (*Facing bathroom again, she continues.*) After all the anxiety we been through to git a report like that on Big Daddy's birthday? Big Daddy tried to hide how much of a load that news took off his mind, but didn't fool *me*. He was mighty close to crying about it *himself*! (*Good-bys are shouted downstairs, and she rushes to door.*) Hold those people down there, don't let them go!—Now, git dressed, we're all comin' up to this room fo' Big Daddy's birthday party because of your ankle.—How's his ankle, Maggie?

MARGARET. Well, he broke it, Big Mama.

BIG MAMA. I know he broke it. (*A phone is ringing in hall. A Negro voice answers: "Mistuh Polly's res'dence."*) I mean does it hurt him much still.

MARGARET. I'm afraid I can't give you that information, Big Mama. You'll have to ask Brick if it hurts much still or not.

SOOKEY (*in the hall*). It's Memphis, Mizz Polly, it's Miss Sally in Memphis.

BIG MAMA. Awright, Sookey. (*Big Mama rushes into the hall and is heard shouting on the phone.*) Hello, Miss Sally. How are you, Miss Sally?—Yes, well, I was just gonna call you about it. Shoot!—(*She raises her voice to a bellow.*) Miss Sally? Don't ever call me from the Gayoso Lobby, too much talk goes on in that hotel lobby, no wonder you can't hear me! Now listen, Miss Sally. They's nothin' serious wrong with Big Daddy. We got the report just now, they's nothin' wrong but a thing called a—spastic! SPASTIC!—colon . . . (*She appears at the hall door and calls to Margaret.*)—Maggie, come out here and talk to that fool on the phone. I'm shouted breathless!

MARGARET (*goes out and is heard sweetly at phone*). Miss Sally? This is Brick's wife, Maggie. So nice to hear your voice. Can you hear *mine?* Well, *good!*—Big Mama just wanted you to know that they've got the report from the Ochsner Clinic and what Big Daddy has is a spastic colon. Yes. Spastic colon, Miss Sally. That's right, spastic colon. *G'by, Miss Sally, hope I'll see you real soon! (Hangs up a little before Miss Sally was probably ready to terminate the talk. She returns through the hall door.)* She heard me perfectly. I've discovered with deaf people the thing to do is not shout at them but just enunciate clearly. My rich old aunt Cornelia was deaf as the dead but I could make her hear me just by sayin' each word slowly, distinctly, close to her ear. I read her the *Commercial Appeal* ev'ry night, read her the classified ads in it, even, she never missed a word of it. But was she a mean ole thing! Know what I got when she died? Her unexpired subscriptions to five magazines and the Book-of-the-Month Club and a LIBRARY full of ev'ry dull book ever written! All else went to her hellcat of a sister . . . meaner than she was, even!

(Big Mama has been straightening things up in the room during this speech.)

BIG MAMA (*Closing closet door on discarded clothes*). Miss Sally sure is a case! Big Daddy says she's always got her hand out fo' something. He's not mistaken. That poor ole thing always has her hand out fo' somethin'. I don't think Big Daddy gives her as much as he should. (*Somebody shouts for her downstairs and she shouts.*) I'm comin'! (*She starts out. At the hall door, turns and jerks a forefinger, first toward the bathroom door, then toward the liquor cabinet, meaning: "Has Brick been drinking?" Margaret pretends not to understand, cocks her head and raises her brows as if the pantomimic performance was completely mystifying to her. Big Mama rushes back to Margaret.*) Shoot! Stop playin' so dumb!—I mean has he been drinkin' that stuff much yet?

MARGARET (*with a little laugh*). Oh! I think he had a high-ball after supper.

BIG MAMA. Don't laugh about it!—some single men stop drinkin' when they git married and others start! Brick never touched liquor before he—!

MARGARET (*crying out*). *THAT'S NOT FAIR!*

BIG MAMA. Fair or not fair I want to ask you a question, one question: D'you make Brick happy in bed?

MARGARET. Why don't you ask if he makes *me* happy in bed?

BIG MAMA. Because I know that—

MARGARET. *It works both ways!*

BIG MAMA. Something's not right! You're childless and my son drinks! (*Someone has called her downstairs and*

she has rushed to the door on the line above. She turns at the door and points at the bed.)—When a marriage goes on the rocks, the rocks are *there*, right *there!*

MARGARET. *That's*—(*Big Mama has swept out of the room and slammed the door.*)—not—*fair . . .*

(Margaret is alone, completely alone, and she feels it. She draws in, hunches her shoulders, raises her arms with fists clenched, shuts her eyes tight as a child about to be stabbed with a vaccination needle. When she opens her eyes again, what she sees is the long oval mirror and she rushes straight to it, stares into it with a grimace and says: "Who are you?"— Then she crouches a little and answers herself in a diffferent voice which is high, then, mocking: "I am Maggie the Cat!"—Straightens quickly as bathroom door opens a little and Brick calls out to her.)

BRICK. Has Big Mama gone?

MARGARET. She's gone. (*He opens the batharoom door and hobbles out, with his liquor glass now empty, straight to the liquor cabinet. He is whistling softly. Margaret's head pivots on her long, slender throat to watch him. She raises a hand uncertainly to the base of her throat, as if it was difficult for her to swallow, before she speaks.*) You know, our sex life didn't just peter out in the usual way, it was cut off short, long before the natural time for it to, and it's going to revive again, just as sudden as that. I'm confident of it. That's what I'm keeping myself attractive for. For the time when you'll see me again like other men see me. Yes, like other men see me. They still see me, Brick, and they like what they see. Uh-huh. Some of them would give their—

Look, Brick! (*She stands before the long oval mirror, touches her breast and then her hips with her two hands.*) How high my body stays on me!—Nothing has fallen on me—not a fraction. . . . (*Her voice is soft and trembling: a pleading child's. At this moment as he turns to glance at her—a look which is like a player passing a ball to another player, third down and goal to go— she has to capture the audience in a grip so tight that she can hold it till the first intermission without any lapse of attention.*) Other men still want me. My face looks strained, sometimes, but I've kept my figure as well as you've kept yours, and men admire it. I still turn heads on the street. Why, last week in Memphis everywhere that I went men's eyes burned holes in my clothes, at the country club and in restaurants and department stores, there wasn't a man I met or walked by that didn't just eat me up with his eyes and turn around when I passed him and look back at me. Why, at Alice's party for her New York cousins, the best lookin' man in the crowd—followed me upstairs and tried to force his way in the powder room with me, followed me to the door and tried to force his way in!

BRICK. Why didn't you let him, Maggie?

MARGARET. Because I'm not that common, for one thing. Not that I wasn't almost tempted to. You like to know who it was? It was Sonny Boy Maxwell, that's who!

BRICK. Oh, yeah, Sonny Boy Maxwell, he was a good end-runner but had a little injury to his back and had to quit.

MARGARET. He has no injury now and has no wife and still has a lech for me!

BRICK. I see no reason to lock him out of a powder room in that case.

MARGARET. And have someone catch me at it? I'm not that stupid. Oh, I might sometime cheat on you with someone, since you're so insultingly eager to have me do it!—But if I do, you can be damned sure it will be in a place and a time where no one but me and the man could possibly know. Because I'm not going to give you any excuse to divorce me for being unfaithful or anything else. . . .

BRICK. Maggie, I wouldn't divorce you for being unfaithful or anything else. Don't you know that? Hell. I'd be relieved to know that you'd found yourself a lover.

MARGARET. Well, I'm taking no chances. No, I'd rather stay on in this hot tin roof.

BRICK. A hot tin roof's 'n uncomfo'table place t' stay on. . . . (*He starts to whistle softly.*)

MARGARET (*through his whistle*). Yeah, but I can stay on it just as long as I have to.

BRICK. You could leave me, Maggie. (*He resumes whistle. She wheels about to glare at him.*)

MARGARET. *Don't want to and will not!* Besides if I did, you don't have a cent to pay for it but what you get from Big Daddy and he's dying of cancer! (*For the first time a realization of Big Daddy's doom seems to penetrate to Brick's consciousness, visibly, and he looks at Margaret.*)

BRICK. Big Mama just said he *wasn't*, that the report was okay.

MARGARET. That's what she thinks because she got the same story that they gave Big Daddy. And was just as taken in by it as he was, poor ole things. . . .

But tonight they're going to tell her the truth about it. When Big Daddy goes to bed, they're going to tell her that he is dying of cancer. (*She slams the dresser drawer.*)—It's malignant and it's terminal.

BRICK. Does Big Daddy know it?

MARGARET. Hell, do they *ever* know it? Nobody says, "You're dying." You have to fool them. They have to fool *themselves*.

BRICK. Why?

MARGARET. *Why?* Because human beings dream of life everlasting, that's the reason! But most of them want it on earth and not in heaven. (*He gives a short, hard laugh at her touch of humor.*) Well. . . . (*She touches up her mascara.*) That's how it is, anyhow. . . . (*She looks about.*) Where did I put down my cigarette? Don't want to burn up the home-place, at least not with Mae and Gooper and their five monsters in it! (*She has found it and sucks at it greedily. Blows out smoke and continues.*) So this is Big Daddy's last birthday. And Mae and Gooper, they know it, oh, *they* know it, all right. They got the first information from the Ochsner Clinic. That's why they rushed down here with their no-neck monsters. Because. Do you know something? Big Daddy's made no will? Big Daddy's never made out any will in his life, and so this campaign's afoot to impress him, forcibly as possible, with the fact that you drink and I've borne no children!

(*He continues to stare at her a moment, then mutters something sharp but not audible and hobbles rather rapidly out onto the long gallery in the fading, much faded, gold light.*)

MARGARET (*continuing her liturgical chant*). Y'know, I'm fond of Big Daddy. I am genuinely fond of that old man, I really *am*, you know . . . .

BRICK (*faintly, vaguely*). Yes, I know you are. . . .

MARGARET. I've always sort of admired him in spite of his coarseness, his four-letter words and so forth. Because Big Daddy *is* what he *is*, and he makes no bones about it. He hasn't turned gentleman farmer, he's still a Mississippi red neck, as much of a red neck as he must have been when he was just overseer here on the old Jack Straw and Peter Ochello place. But he got hold of it an' built it into th' biggest an' finest plantation in the Delta.—I've always *liked* Big Daddy. . . . (*She crosses to the proscenium.*) Well, this is Big Daddy's last birthday. I'm sorry about it. But I'm facing the facts. It takes money to take care of a drinker and that's the office that I've been elected to lately.

BRICK. You don't have to take care of me.

MARGARET. Yes, I do. Two people in the same boat have got to take care of each other. At least you want money to buy more Echo Spring when this supply is exhausted, or will you be satisfied with a ten-cent beer?

Mae an' Gooper are plannin' to freeze us out of Big Daddy's estate because you drink and I'm childless. But we can defeat that plan. We're *going* to defeat that plan!

Brick, y'know, I've been so God damn disgustingly poor all my life!—That's *the truth,* Brick!

BRICK. I'm not sayin' it isn't.

MARGARET. Always had to suck up to people I couldn't stand because they had money and I was poor as Job's turkey. You don't know what that's like. Well, I'll tell you, it's like you would feel a thousand miles away from Echo Spring!—And had to get back to it on that broken ankle . . . without a crutch!

That's how it feels to be as poor as Job's turkey and have to suck up to relatives that you hated because they had money and all you had was a bunch of hand-me-down clothes and a few old moldy three per cent government bonds. My daddy loved his liquor, he fell in love with his liquor the way you've fallen in love with Echo Spring!—And my poor mama, having to maintain some semblance of social position, to keep appearances up, on an income of one hunded and fifty dollars a month on those old government bonds!

When I came out, the year that I made my debut, I had just two evening dresses! One Mother made me from a pattern in *Vogue,* the other a hand-me-down from a snotty rich cousin I hated!

—The dress that I married you in was my grandmother's weddin' gown. . . .

So that's why I'm like a cat on a hot tin roof!

(Brick is still on the gallery. Someone below calls up to him in a warm Negro voice. "Hiya, Mistuh Brick, how yuh feelin'?" Brick raises his liquor glass as if that answered the question.)

MARGARET. You can be young without money but you can't be old without it. You've got to be old *with* money because to be old without it is just too awful, you've got to be one or the other, either *young* or *with money,* you can't be old and *without* it.—That's the *truth,* Brick. . . . *(Brick whistles softly, vaguely.)* Well, now I'm dressed, I'm all dressed, there's nothing else for me to do. *(Forlornly, almost fearfully.)* I'm dressed, all dressed, nothing else for me to do. . . . *(She moves about restlessly, aimlessly, and speaks, as if to herself.)* I know when I made my mistake.—What am I—? Oh!—my bracelets. . . . *(She starts working a collection of bracelets over her hands onto her wrists, about six on each, as she talks.)* I've thought a whole lot about it and now I know when I made my mistake. Yes, I made my mistake when I told you the truth about that thing with Skipper. Never should have con-

fessed it, a fatal error, tellin' you about that thing with Skipper.

BRICK. Maggie, shut up about Skipper. I mean it, Maggie; you got to shut up about Skipper.

MARGARET. You ought to understand that Skipper and I—

BRICK. You don't think I'm serious, Maggie? You're fooled by the fact that I am saying this quiet? Look, Maggie. What you're doing is a dangerous thing to do. You're—you're—you're—foolin' with something that—nobody ought to fool with.

MARGARET. This time I'm going to finish what I have to say to you. Skipper and I made love, if love you could call it, because it made both of us feel a little bit closer to you. You see, you son of a bitch, you asked too much of people, of me, of him, of all the unlucky poor damned sons of bitches that happen to love you, and there was a whole pack of them, yes, there was a pack of them besides me and Skipper, you asked too goddam much of people that loved you, you—superior creature!—you godlike being!—And so we made love to each other to dream it was you, both of us! Yes, yes, yes! Truth, truth! What's so awful about it? I like it, I think the truth is—yeah! I shouldn't have told you. . . .

BRICK *(holding his head unnaturally still and uptilted a bit).* It was Skipper that told me about it. Not you, Maggie.

MARGARET. I told you!

BRICK After he told me!

MARGARET. What does it matter who—? *(Brick turns suddenly out upon the gallery and calls.)*

BRICK. Little girl! Hey, little girl!

LITTLE GIRL *(at a distance).* What, Uncle Brick?

BRICK. Tell the folks to come up!—Bring everybody upstairs!

MARGARET. I can't stop myself! I'd go on telling you this in front of them all, if I had to!

BRICK. Little girl! Go on, go on, will you? Do what I told you, call them!

MARGARET. Because it's got to be told and you, you!—you never let me! *(She sobs, then controls herself, and continues almost calmly.)* It was one of those beautiful, ideal things they tell about in the Greek legends, it couldn't be anything else, you being you, and that's what made it so sad, that's what made it so awful, because it was love that never could be carrried through to anything satisfying or even talked about plainly. Brick, I tell you, you got to believe me, Brick, I *do* understand all about! I—I think it was—*noble!* Can't you tell I'm sincere when I say I respect it? My only point, the only point that I'm making, is life has got to be allowed to continue even after the *dream of life is—all—over*. . . . (*Brick is without his crutch. Leaning on furniture, he crosses to pick it up as she continues as if possessed by a will outside herself.*) Why I remember when we double-dated at college, Gladys Fitzgerald and I and you and Skipper, it was more like a date between you and Skipper. Gladys and I were just sort of tagging along as if it was necessary to chaperone you!—to make a good public impression—

BRICK (*turns to face her, half lifting his crutch*). Maggie, you want me to hit you with this crutch? Don't you know I could kill you with this crutch?

MARGARET. Good Lord, man, d' you think I'd care if you did?

BRICK. One man has one great good true thing in his life. One great good thing which is true!—I had friendship with Skipper.—You are naming it dirty!

MARGARET. I'm not naming it dirty! I am naming it clean.

BRICK. Not love with you, Maggie, but friendship with Skipper was that one great true thing, and you are naming it dirty!

MARGARET. Then you haven't been listenin', not understood what I'm saying! I'm naming it so damn clean that it killed poor Skipper!—You two had something that had to be kept on ice, yes, incorruptible, yes!—and death was the only icebox where you could keep it. . . .

BRICK. I married you, Maggie. Why would I marry you, Maggie, if I was—?

MARGARET. Brick, don't brain me yet, let me finish!—I know, believe me I know, that it was only Skipper that harbored even any *unconscious* desire for anything not perfectly pure between you two!—Now let me skip a little. You married me early that summer we graduated out of Ole Miss, and we were happy, weren't we, we were blissful, yes, hit heaven together ev'ry time that we loved! But that fall you an' Skipper turned down wonderful offers of jobs in order to keep on bein' football heroes—pro-football heroes. You organized the Dixie stars that fall, so you could keep on bein' team-mates forever! But somethin' was not right with it!—*Me included!*—between you. Skipper began hittin' the bottle . . . you got a spinal injury—couldn't play the Thanksgivin' game in Chicago, watched it on TV from a traction bed in Toledo. I joined Skipper. The Dixie Stars lost because poor Skipper was drunk. We drank togther that night all night in the bar of the Blackstone and when cold day was comin' up over the Lake an' we were comin' out drunk to take a dizzy look at it, I said, "SKIPPER! STOP LOVIN' MY HUSBAND OR

TELL HIM HE'S GOT TO LET YOU ADMIT IT TO HIM!"—one way or another!

HE SLAPPED ME HARD ON THE MOUTH!— then turned and ran without stopping once, I am sure, all the way back into his room at the Blackstone. . . .

—When I came to his room that night, with a little scratch like a shy little mouse at his door, he made that pitiful, ineffectual little attempt to prove that what I had said wasn't true. . . . (*Brick strikes at her with crutch, a blow that shatters the gemlike lamp on the table.*)—In this way, I destroyed him, by telling him truth that he and his world which he was born and raised in, yours and his world, had told him could not be told?

—From then on Skipper was nothing at all but a receptacle for liquor and drugs. . . .

—*Who shot cock-robin? I with my*—(*She throws back her head with tight-shut eyes.*)—*merciful arrow!* (*Brick strikes at her; misses.*) Missed me!—Sorry,—I'm not tryin' to whitewash my behavior, Christ, no! Brick, I'm not good. I don't know why people have to pretend to be good, nobody's good. The rich or the well-to-do can afford to respect moral patterns, conventional moral patterns, but I could never afford to, yeah, but—I'm honest! Give me credit for just that, will you *please?*—Born poor, raised poor, expect to die poor unless I manage to get us something out of what Big Daddy leaves when he dies of cancer! But Brick?!—*Skipper is dead! I'm alive!* Maggie the cat is— (*Brick hops awkwardly forward and strikes at her again with his crutch.*)—alive! I am alive, alive! I am . . . (*He hurls the crutch at her, across the bed she took refuge behind, and pitches forward on the floor as she completes her speech.*)—alive! (*A little girl, Dixie, bursts into the room, wearing an Indian war bonnet and firing a cap pistol at Margaret and shouting: "Bang, bang, bang!" Laughter downstairs floats through the open hall door. Margaret had crouched gasping to bed at child's entrance. She now rises and says with cool fury:*) Little girl, your mother or someone should teach you—(*Gasping*)—to knock at a door before you come into a room. Otherwise people might think that you—lack—good breeding. . . .

DIXIE. Yanh, yanh, yanh, what is Uncle Brick doin' on th' floor?

BRICK. I tried to kill your Aunt Maggie, but I failed—and I fell. Little girl, give me my crutch so I can get up off th' floor.

MARGARET. Yes, give your uncle his crutch, he's a cripple, honey, he broke his ankle last night jumping hurdles on the high school athletic field!

DIXIE. What were you jumping hurdles for, Uncle Brick?

BRICK. Because I used to jump them, and people like to do what they used to do, even after they've stopped being able to do it. . . .

MARGARET. That's right, that's your answer, now go away, little girl. (*Dixie fires cap pistol at Margaret three times.*) Stop, you stop that, monster! You little no-neck monster! (*She seizes the cap pistol and hurls it through gallery doors.*)

DIXIE (*with a precocious instinct for the cruelest thing*). You're jealous!—You're just jealous because you can't have babies! (*She sticks out her tongue at Margaret as she sashays past her with her stomach struck out, to the gallery. Margaret slams the gallery doors and leans panting against them. There is a pause. Brick has replaced his spilt drink and sits, faraway, on the great four-poster bed.*)

MARGARET. You see?—they gloat over us being childless, even in front of their five little no-neck monsters! (*Pause. Voices on the stairs.*) Brick?—I've been to a doctor in Memphis, a—a gynecologist. . . . I've been completely examined, and there is no reason why we can't have a child whenever we want one. And this is my time by the calendar to conceive. Are you listening to me? Are you? Are you LISTENING TO ME!

BRICK. Yes. I hear you, Maggie. (*His attention returns to her inflamed face.*)—how in hell on earth do you imagine—that you're going to have a child by a man that can't stand you?

MARGARET. That's a problem that I will have to work out. (*She wheels about to face the hall door.*) Here they come!

(*The lights dim.*)

Curtain

ACT II

There is no lapse of time. Margaret and Brick are in the same positions they held at the end of Act I.

MARGARET (*at door*). Here they come!

(*Big Daddy appears first, a tall man with a fierce, anxious look, moving carefully not to betray his weakness even, or especially, to himself.*)

BIG DADDY. Well, Brick.

BRICK. Hello, Big Daddy.—Congratulations!

BIG DADDY. —Crap. . . .

(*Some of the people are approaching through the hall, others along the gallery: voices from both directions. Gooper and Reverend Tooker become visible outside gallery doors, and their voices come in clearly. They pause outside as Gooper lights a cigar.*)

REVERAND TOOKER (*vivaciously*). Oh, but St. Paul's in Grenada has three memorial windows, and the latest one is a Tiffany stained-glass window that cost twenty-five hundred dollars, a picture of Christ the Good Shepherd with a Lamb in His arms.

GOOPER. Who give that window, Preach?

REVEREND TOOKER. Clyde Fletcher's widow. Also presented St. Pauls with a baptismal font.

GOOPER. Y'know what somebody ought t' give your church is a *coolin'* system, Preach.

REVEREND TOOKER. Yes, siree, Bob! And y'know what Gus Hamma's family gave in his memory to the church at Two Rivers? A complete new stone parish-house with a basketball court in the basement and a—

BIG DADDY (*uttering a loud barking laugh which is far from truly mirthful*). Hey, Preach! What's all this talk about memorials, Preach? Y' think somebody's about t' kick off around here? 'S that it?

(*Startled by this interjection, Reverend Tooker decides to laugh at the question almost as loud as he can. How he would answer the question we'll never know, as he's spared that embarrassment by the voice of Gooper's wife, Mae, rising high and clear as she appears with "Doc" Baugh, the family doctor, through the hall foor.*)

MAE (*almost religiously*). —Let's see now, they've had their *tyyy*-phoid shots, and their tetanus shots, their diphtheria shots and their hepatitis shots and their polio shots, they got *those* shots every month from May through September, and—Gooper? Hey! Gooper!—What all have the kiddies been shot faw?

MARGARET (*overlapping a bit*). Turn on the Hi-Fi, Brick! Let's have some music t' start off th' party with!

(*The talk becomes so general that the room sounds like a great aviary of chattering birds. Only Brick remains unengaged, leaning upon the liquor cabinet with his faraway smile, an ice cube in a paper napkin with which he now and then rubs his forehead. He doesn't respond to Margaret's command. She bounds forward and stoops over the instrument panel of the console.*)

GOOPER. We gave 'em that thing for a third anniversary present, got three speakers in it. (*The room is suddenly blasted by the climax of a Wagnerian opera or a Beethoven symphony.*)

BIG DADDY. *Turn that damn thing off!*

(*Almost instant silence, almost instantly broken by the shouting charge of Big Mama, entering through hall door like a charging rhino.*)

BIG MAMA. *Wha's my Brick, wha's mah precious baby!!*
BIG DADDY. *Sorry! Turn it back on!*

(*Everyone laughs very loud. Big Daddy is famous for his jokes at Big Mama's expense, and nobody laughs louder at these jokes than Big Mama herself, though sometimes they're pretty cruel and Big Mama has to pick up or fuss with something to cover the hurt that the loud laugh doesn't quite cover.*)

(*On this occasion, a happy occasion because the dread in her heart has also been lifted by the false report on Big Daddy's condition, she giggles, grotesquely, coyly, in Big Daddy's direction and bears down upon Brick, all very quick and alive.*)

BIG MAMA. Here he is, here's my precious baby! What's that you've got in your hand? You put that liquor down, son, your hand was made fo' holdin' somethin' better than that!
GOOPER. Look at Brick put it down!

(*Brick has obeyed Big Mama by draining the glass and handing it to her. Again everyone laughs, some high, some low.*)

BIG MAMA. Oh, you bad boy, you, you're my bad little boy. Give Big Mama a kiss, you bad boy, you!—Look at him shy away, will you? Brick never liked bein' kissed or made a fuss over, I guess because he's always had too much of it!
      Son, you turn that thing off! (*Brick has switched on the TV set.*) I can't stand TV, radio was bad enough, but TV has gone it one better, I mean— (*Plops wheezing in chair*)—one worse, ha ha! Now what'm I sittin' down here faw? I want t' sit next to my sweetheart on the sofa, hold hands with him and love him up a little! (*Big Mama has on a black and white figured chiffon. The large irregular patterns, like the markings of some massive animal, the luster of her great diamonds and many pearls, the brilliants set in the silver frames of her glasses, her riotous voice, booming laugh, have dominated the room since she entered. Big Daddy has been regarding her with a steady grimace of chronic annoyance. Still louder.*) Preacher, Preacher, hey, Preach! Give me you' hand an' help me up from this chair!
REVEREND TOOKER. None of your tricks, Big Mama!
BIG MAMA. What tricks? You give me you' hand so I can get up an'—(*Reverend Tooker extends her his hand. She grabs it and pulls him into her lap with a shrill laugh that*

spans an octave in two notes.*) Ever seen a preacher in a fat lady's lap? Hey, hey, folks! Ever seen a preacher in a fat lady's lap? (*Big Mama is notorious throughout the Delta for this sort of inelegant horseplay. Margaret looks on with indulgent humor, sipping Dubonnet "on the rocks" and watching Brick, but Mae and Gooper exchange signs of humorless anxiety over these antics, the sort of behavior which Mae thinks may account for their failure to quite get in with the smartest young married set in Memphis, despite all. One of the Negroes, Lacey or Sookey, peeks in, cackling. They are waiting for a sign to bring in the cake and champagne. But Big Daddy's not amused. He doesn't understand why, in spite of the infinite mental relief he's received from the doctor's report, he still has these same old fox teeth in his guts. "This spastic thing sure is something," he says to himself, but aloud he roars at Big Mama:*)

BIG DADDY. BIG MAMA, WILL YOU QUIT HORSIN'?—You're too old an' too fat fo' that sort of crazy kid stuff an' besides a woman with your blood-pressure—she had two hundred last spring!—is riskin' a stroke when you mess around like that. . . .
BIG MAMA. *Here comes Big Daddy's birthday!*

(*Negroes in white jackets enter with an enormous birthday cake ablaze with candles and carrying buckets of champagne with satin ribbons about the bottle necks.*)

(*Mae and Gooper strike up song, and everybody, including the Negroes and children, joins in. Only Brick remains aloof.*)

EVERYONE.
      Happy birthday to you.
      Happy birthday to you.
      Happy birthday, Big Daddy—

(*Some sing: "Dear, Big Daddy!"*)

      Happy birthday to you.

(*Some sing: "How old are you?"*)

(*Mae has come down center and is organizing her children like a chorus. She gives them a barely audible: "One, two, three!" and they are off in the new tune.*)

CHILDREN.
      Skinamarinka—dinka—dink
      Skinamarinka—do
      We love you.
      Skinamarinka—dinka—dink
      Skinamarinka—do.

(*All together, they turn to Big Daddy.*)

    Big Daddy, you!

(*They turn back front, like a musical comedy chorus.*)

    We love you in the morning;
    We love you in the night.
    We love you when we're with you.
    And we love you out of sight.
    Skinamarinka—dinka—dink
    Skinamarinka—do.

(*Mae turns to Big Mama.*)

    Big Mama, too!

(*Big Mama bursts into tears. The Negroes leave.*)

BIG DADDY. Now Ida, what the hell is the matter with you?

MAE. She's just so happy.

BIG MAMA. I'm just so happy, Big Daddy, I have to cry or something. (*Sudden and loud in the hush:*) Brick, do you know the wonderful news that Doc Baugh got from the clinic about Big Daddy? Big Daddy's one hundred per cent!

MARGARET. Isn't that wonderful?

BIG MAMA. He's just one hundred per cent. Passed the examination with flying colors. Now that we know there's nothing wrong with Big Daddy but a spastic colon, I can tell you something. I was worried sick, half out of my mind, for fear that Big Daddy might have a thing like—

(*Margaret cuts through this speech, jumping up and exclaiming shrilly:*)

MARGARET. Brick, honey, aren't you going to give Big Daddy his birthday present? (*Passing by him, she snatches his liquor glass from him. She picks up a fancily wrapped package.*) Here it is, Big Daddy, this is from Brick!

BIG MAMA. This is the biggest birthday Big Daddy's ever had, a hundred presents and bushels of telegrams from—

MAE (*at same time*). What is it, Brick?

GOOPER. I bet 500 to 50 that Brick don't know what it is.

BIG MAMA. The fun of presents is not knowing what they are till you open the package. Open your present, Big Daddy.

BIG DADDY. Open it you'self. I want to ask Brick somethin! Come here, Brick.

MARGARET. Big Daddy's callin' you, Brick. (*She is opening the package.*)

BRICK. Tell Big Daddy I'm crippled.

BIG DADDY. I see you're crippled. I want to know how you got crippled.

MARGARET (*making diversionary tactics*). Oh, look, oh, look, why, it's a cashmere robe! (*She holds the robe up for all to see.*)

MAE. You sound surprised, Maggie.

MARGARET. I never saw one before.

MAE. That's funny.—Hah!

MARGARET (*turning on her fiercely, with a brilliant smile*). Why is it funny? All my family ever had was family—and luxuries such as cashmere robes still surprise me!

BIG DADDY (*ominously*). Quiet!

MAE (*heedless in her fury*). I don't see how you could be so surprised when you bought it yourself at Loewenstein's in Memphis last Saturday. You know how I know?

BIG DADDY. I said, Quiet!

MAE. —I know because the salesgirl that sold it to you waited on me and said, Oh, Mrs. Pollitt, your sister-in-law just bought a cashmere robe for your husband's father!

MARGARET. Sister Woman! Your talents are wasted as a housewife and mother, you really ought to be with the FBI or—

BIG DADDY. QUIET!

(*Reverend Tooker's reflexes are slower than the others'. He finishes a sentence after the bellow.*)

REVEREND TOOKER (*to Doc Baugh*). —the Stork and the Reaper are running neck and neck! (*He starts to laugh gaily when he notices the silence and Big Daddy's glare. His laugh dies falsely.*)

BIG DADDY. Preacher, I hope I'm not butting in on more talk about memorial stained-glass windows, am I, Preacher? (*Reverend Tooker laughs feebly, then coughs dryly in the embarrassed silence.*) Preacher?

BIG MAMA. Now, Big Daddy, don't you pick on Preacher!

BIG DADDY (*raising his voice*). You ever hear that expression all hawk and no spit? You bring that expression to mind with that little dry cough of yours, all hawk an' no spit. . . .

(*The pause is broken only by a short startled laugh from Margaret, the only one there who is conscious of and amused by the grotesque.*)

MAE (*raising her arms and jangling her bracelets*). I wonder if the mosquitoes are active tonight?

BIG DADDY. What's that, Little Mama? Did you make some remark?

MAE. Yes, I said I wondered if the mosquitoes would eat us alive if we went out on the gallery for a while.

BIG DADDY. Well, if they do, I'll have your bones pulverized for fertilizer!

BIG MAMA (*quickly*). Last week we had an airplane spraying the place and I think it done some good, at least I haven't had a—

BIG DADDY (*cutting her speech*). Brick, they tell me, if what they tell me is true, that you done some jumping last night on the high school athletic field?

BIG MAMA. Brick, Big Daddy is talking to you, son.

BRICK (*smiling vaguely over his drink*). What was that, Big Daddy?

BIG DADDY. They said you done some jumping on the high school track field last night.

BRICK. That's what they told me, too.

BIG DADDY. Was it jumping or humping that you were doing out there? What were you doing out there at three A.M., layin' a woman on that cinder track?

BIG MAMA. Big Daddy, you are off the sick-list, now, and I'm not going to excuse you for talkin' so—

BIG DADDY. Quiet!

BIG MAMA. —*nasty* in front of Preacher and—

BIG DADDY. QUIET!—I ast you, Brick, if you was cuttin' you'self a piece o' poon-tang last night on that cinder track? I thought maybe you were chasin' poon-tang on that track an' tripped over something in the heat of the chase—'sthat it?

(*Gooper laughs, loud and false, others nervously following suit. Big Mama stamps her foot, and purses her lips, crossing to Mae and whispering something to her as Brick meets his father's hard, intent, grinning stare with a slow, vague smile that he offers all situations from behind the screen of his liquor.*)

BRICK. No, sir. I don't think so. . . .

MAE (*at the same time, sweetly*). Reverend Tooker, let's you and I take a stroll on the widow's walk. (*She and the preacher go out on the gallery as Big Daddy says:*)

BIG DADDY. Then what the hell were you doing out there at three o'clock in the morning?

BRICK. Jumping the hurdles, Big Daddy, runnin' and jumpin' the hurdles, but those high hurdles have gotten too high for me, now.

BIG DADDY. Cause you was drunk?

BRICK (*his vague smile fading a little*). Sober I wouldn't have tried to jump the low ones. . . .

BIG MAMA (*quickly*). Big Daddy, blow out the candles on your birthday cake!

MARGARET (*at the same time*). I want to propose a toast to Big Daddy Pollitt on his sixty-fifth birthday, the biggest cotton-planter in—

BIG DADDY (*bellowing with fury and disgust*). *I told you to stop it, now stop it, quit this—!*

BIG MAMA (*coming in front of Big Daddy with the cake*). Big Daddy, I will not allow you to talk that way, not even on your birthday, I—

BIG DADDY. I'll talk like I want to on my birthday, Ida, or any other goddam' day of the year and anybody here that don't like it knows what they can do!

BIG MAMA. You don't mean that!

BIG DADDY. What makes you think I don't mean it?

(*Meanwhile various discreet signals have been exchanged and Gooper has also gone out on the gallery.*)

BIG MAMA. I just know you don't mean it.

BIG DADDY. You don't know a goddam thing and you never did!

BIG MAMA. Big Daddy, you don't mean that.

BIG DADDY. Oh, yes, I do, oh, yes, I do, I mean it! I put up with a whole lot of crap around here because I thought I was dying. And you thought I was dying and you started taking over, well, you can stop taking over now, Ida, because I'm not gonna die, you can just stop now this business of taking over because you're not taking over because I'm not dying, I went through the laboratory and the goddam exploratory operation and there's nothing wrong with me but a spastic colon. And I'm not dying of cancer which you thought I was dying of. Ain't that so? Didn't you think that I was dying of cancer, Ida? (*Almost everybody is out on the gallery but the two old people glaring at each other across the blazing cake. Big Mama's chest heaves and she presses a fat fist to her mouth. Big Daddy continues, hoarsely.*) Ain't that so, Ida? Didn't you have an idea I was dying of cancer and now you could take control of this place and everything on it? I got that impression, I seemed to get that impression. Your loud voice everywhere, your fat old body butting in here and there!

BIG MAMA. Hush! The Preacher!

BIG DADDY. Rut the goddam preacher! (*Big Mama gasps loudly and sits down on the sofa which is almost too small for her.*) Did you hear what I said? I said rut the goddam preacher!

(*Somebody closes the gallery doors from ouside just as there is a burst of fireworks and excited cries from the children.*)

BIG MAMA. I never seen you act like this before and I can't think what's got in you!

BIG DADDY. I went through all that laboratory and operation and all just so I would know if you or me was boss here! Well, now it turns out that I am and you ain't—and that's my birthday present—and my cake and champagne!—because for three years now you been gradually taking over. Bossing. Talking. Sashaying your fat old body around the place I made! I made this place! I was overseer on it! I was the overseer on the old Straw and Ochello plantation. I quit school at ten! I quit school at ten years old and went to work like a nigger in the fields. And I rose to be overseer of the Straw and Ochello plantation. And old Straw died and I was Ochello's partner and the place got bigger and bigger and bigger and bigger and bigger! I did all that myself with no goddam help from you, and now you think you're just about to take over. Well, I am just about to tell you that you are not just about to take over, you are not just about to take over a God damn thing. Is that clear to you, Ida? Is that very plain to you, now? Is that understood completely? I been through the laboratory from A to Z. I've had the goddam exploratory operation, and nothing is wrong with me but a spastic colon—made spastic, I guess, by *disgust!* By all the goddam lies and liars that I have had to put up with, and all the goddam hypocrisy that I lived with all these forty years that we been livin' together!

Hey, Ida!! Blow out the candles on the birthday cake! Purse up your lips and draw a deep breath and blow out the goddam candles on the cake!

BIG MAMA. Oh, Big Daddy, oh, oh, oh, Big Daddy!

BIG DADDY. What's the matter with you?

BIG MAMA. *In all these years you never believed that I loved you??*

BIG DADDY. Huh?

BIG MAMA. *And I did, I did so much, I did love you!*—I even loved your hate and your hardness, Big Daddy! (*She sobs and rushes awkwardly out onto the gallery.*)

BIG DADDY (*to himself*). *Wouldn't it be funny if that was true. . . .* (*A pause is followed by a burst of light in the sky from the fireworks.*) BRICK! HEY, BRICK! (*He stands over his blazing birthday cake. After some moments, Brick hobbles in on his crutch, holding his glass. Margaret follows him with a bright, anxious smile.*) I didn't call you, Maggie. I called Brick.

MARGARET. I'm just delivering him to you.

(*She kisses Brick on the mouth which he immediately wipes with the back of his hand. She flies girlishly back out. Brick and his father are alone.*)

BIG DADDY. Why did you do that?

BRICK. Do what, Big Daddy?

BIG DADDY. Wipe her kiss off your mouth like she'd spit on you.

BRICK. I don't know. I wasn't conscious of it.

BIG DADDY. That woman of yours has a better shape on her than Gooper's but somehow or other they got the same look about them.

BRICK. What sort of look is that, Big Daddy?

BIG DADDY. I don't know how to describe it but it's the same look.

BRICK. They don't look peaceful, do they?

BIG DADDY. No, they sure in hell don't.

BRICK. They look nervous as cats?

BIG DADDY. That's right, they look nervous as cats.

BRICK. Nervous as a couple of cats on a hot tin roof?

BIG DADDY. That's right, boy, they look like a couple of cats on a hot tin roof. It's funny that you and Gooper being so different would pick out the same type of woman.

BRICK. Both of us married into society, Big Daddy.

BIG DADDY. Crap . . . I wonder what gives them both that look?

BRICK. Well. They're sittin' in the middle of a big piece of land, Big Daddy, twenty-eight thousand acres is a pretty big piece of land and so they're squaring off on it, each determined to knock off a bigger piece of it than the other whenever you let it go.

BIG DADDY. I got a surprise for those women. I'm not gonna let it go for a long time yet if that's what they're waiting for.

BRICK. That's right, Big Daddy. You just sit tight and let them scratch each other's eyes out. . . .

BIG DADDY. You bet your life I'm going to sit tight on it and let those sons of bitches scratch their eyes out, ha ha ha. . . .

But Gooper's wife's a good breeder, you got to admit she's fertile. Hell, at supper tonight she had them all at the table and they had to put a couple of extra leafs in the table to make room for them, she's got five head of them now, and another one's comin'.

BRICK. Yep, number six is comin'. . . .

BIG DADDY. Brick, you know, I swear to God, I don't know the way it happens?

BRICK. The way what happens, Big Daddy?

BIG DADDY. You git you a piece of land, by hook or crook, an' things start growin' on it, things accumulate on it, and the first thing you know it's completely out of hand, completely out of hand!

BRICK. Well, they say nature hates a vacuum, Big Daddy.

BIG DADDY. That's what they say, but sometimes I think that a vacuum is a hell of a lot better than some of the stuff that nature replaces it with.

Is someone out there by that door?

BRICK. Yep.

BIG DADDY. Who? (*He has lowered his voice.*)

BRICK. Someone int'rested in what we say to each other.

BIG DADDY. Gooper?—GOOPER! (*After a discreet pause, Mae appears in the gallery door.*)

MAE. Did you call Gooper, Big Daddy?

BIG DADDY. Aw, it was you.

MAE. Do you want Gooper, Big Daddy?

BIG DADDY. No, and I don't want you. I want some privacy here, while I'm having a confidential talk with my son Brick. Now it's too hot in here to close them doors, but if I have to close those rotten doors in order to have a private talk with my son Brick, just let me know and I'll close 'em. Because I hate eavesdroppers, I don't like any kind of sneakin' an' spyin'.

MAE. Why, Big Daddy—

BIG DADDY. You stood on the wrong side of the moon, it threw your shadow!

MAE. I was just—

BIG DADDY. You was just nothing but *spyin'* an' you know it!

MAE (*begins to sniff and sob*). Oh, Big Daddy, you're so unkind for some reason to those that really love you!

BIG DADDY. Shut up, shut up, shut up! I'm going to move you and Gooper out of that room next to this! It's none of your goddam business what goes on in here at night between Brick an' Maggie. You listen at night like a couple of rutten peek-hole spies and go and give a report on what you hear to Big Mama an' she comes to me and says they say such and such and so and so about what they heard goin' on between Brick an' Maggie, and Jesus, it makes me sick. I'm goin' to move you an' Gooper out of that room, I can't stand sneakin' an' spyin', it makes me sick. . . .

(*Mae throws her head and rolls her eyes heavenward and extends her arms as if invoking God's pity for this unjust martyrdom; then she presses a handkerchief to her nose and flies form the room with a loud swish of skirts.*)

BRICK (*now at the liquor cabinet*). They listen, do they?

BIG DADDY. Yeah. They listen and give reports to Big Mama on what goes on in here between you and Maggie. They say that—(*He stops as if embarrassed.*)—You won't sleep with her, that you sleep on the sofa. Is that true or not true? If you don't like Maggie, get rid of Maggie!—What are you doin' there now?

BRICK. Fresh'nin' up my drink.

BIG DADDY. Son, you know you got a real liquor problem?

BRICK. Yes, sir, yes, I know.

BIG DADDY. Is that why you quit sports-announcing, because of this liquor problem?

BRICK. Yes, sir, yes, sir. I guess so. (*He smiles vaguely and amiably at his father across his replenished drink.*)

BIG DADDY. Son, don't guess about it, it's too important.

BRICK (*vaguely*). Yes, sir.

BIG DADDY. And listen to me, don't look at the damn chandelier. . . . (*Pause. Big Daddy's voice is husky.*)—Somethin' else we picked up at th' big fire-sale in Europe. (*Another pause.*) Life is important. There's nothing else to hold onto. A man that drinks is throwing his life away. Don't do it, hold onto your life. There's nothing else to hold onto. . . .
    Sit down over here so we don't have to raise our voices, the walls have ears in this place.

BRICK (*hobbling over to sit on the sofa beside him*). All right, Big Daddy.

BIG DADDY. Quit!—how'd that come about? Some disappointment?

BRICK. I don't know. Do you?

BIG DADDY. I'm askin' you, God damn it! How in hell would I know if you don't?

BRICK. I just got out there and found that I had a mouth full of cotton. I was always two or three beats behind what was goin' on on the field and so I—

BIG DADDY. Quit!

BRICK (*amiably*). Yes, quit.

BIG DADDY. Son?

BRICK. Huh?

BIG DADDY (*inhales loudly and deeply from his cigar; then bends suddenly a little forward, exhaling loudly and raising a hand to his forehead*). —Whew!—ha ha!—I took in too much smoke, it made me a little light-headed. . . (*The mantel clock chimes.*) Why is it so damn hard for people to talk?

BRICK. Yeah. . . . (*The clock goes on sweetly chiming till it has completed the stroke of ten.*)—Nice peaceful-soundin' clock, I like to hear it all night. . . . (*He slides low and comfortable on the sofa; Big Daddy sits up straight and rigid with some unspoken anxiety. All his gestures are tense and jerky as he talks. He wheezes and pants and sniffs through his nervous speech, glancing quickly, shyly, from time to time, at his son.*)

BIG DADDY. We got that clock the summer we wint to Europe, me an' Big Mama on that damn Cook's Tour, never had such an awful time in my life, I'm tellin' you, son, those gooks over there, they gouge your eyeballs out in their grand hotels. And Big Mama bought more stuff than you could haul in a couple of boxcars, that's no crap. Everywhere she wint on this whirlwind tour, she bought, bought, bought. Why, half that stuff she bought is still crated up in the cellar, under water last spring! (*He laughs.*) That Europe is nothin' on earth but a great big auction, that's all it is, that bunch of old worn-out places, it's just a big fire-sale, the whole rutten thing, an' Big Mama wint wild in it, why, you couldn't hold that woman with a mule's harness! Bought, bought, bought!—lucky I'm a rich man, yes siree, Bob, an' half that stuff is mildewin' in th' basement. It's lucky I'm a rich man, it sure is lucky, well, I'm a rich man, Brick, yep, I'm a mighty rich man. (*His eyes light up for a moment.*) Y'know how much I'm worth? Guess, Brick! Guess how much I'm worth! (*Brick smiles vaguely over his drink.*) Close on ten million in cash an' blue chip stocks. Outside, mind you, of twenty-eight thousand acres of the richest land this side of the valley Nile! (*A puff and crackle and the night sky blooms with an eerie greenish glow. Children shriek on the gallery.*) But a man can't buy his life with it, he can't buy back his life with it when his life has been spent, that's one thing not offered in the Europe fire-sale or in the American markets or any markets on earth, a man can't buy his life with it, he can't buy back his life when his life is finished. . . .

That's a sobering thought, a very sobering thought, and that's a thought that I was turning over in my head, over and over and over—until today. . . .

I'm wiser and sadder, Brick, for this experience which I just gone through. They's one thing else that I remember in Europe.

BRICK. What is that, Big Daddy?

BIG DADDY. The hills around Barcelona in the country of Spain and the children running over those bare hills in their bare skins beggin' like stavin' dogs with howls and screeches, and how fat the priests are on the streets of Barcelona, so many of them and so fat and so pleasant, ha ha!—Y'know I could feed that country? I got money enough to feed that goddam country, but the human animal is a selfish beast and I don't reckon the money I passed out there to those howling children in the hills around Barcelona would more than upholster one of the chairs in this room, I mean pay to put a new cover on this chair!

Hell, I threw them money like you'd scatter feed corn for chickens, I threw money at them just to get rid of them long enough to climb back into th' car and—drive away. . . .

And then in Morocco, them Arabs, why, prostitution begins at four or five, that's no exaggeration, why, I remember one day in Marrakech, that old walled Arab city, I set on a broken-down wall to have a cigar, it was fearful hot there and this Arab woman stood in the road and looked at me till I was embar-

rassed, she stood stock still in the dusty hot road and looked at me till I was embarrassed. But listen to this. She had a naked child with her, a little naked girl with her, barely able to toddle, and after a while she set this child on the ground and give her a push and whispered something to her.

This child come toward me, barely able t' walk, come toddling up to me and—

Jesus, it makes you sick t' remember a thing like this! It stuck out its hand and tried to unbutton my trousers!

That child was not yet five! Can you believe me? Or do you think that I am making this up? I wint back to the hotel and said to Big Mama, Git packed! We're clearing out of this country. . . .

BRICK. Big Daddy, you're on a talking jag tonight.

BIG DADDY (*ignoring this remark*). Yes, sir, that's how it is, the human animal is a beast that dies but the fact that he's dying don't give him pity for others, no, sir, it—Did you say something?

BRICK. Yes.

BIG DADDY. What?

BRICK. Hand me over that crutch so I can get up.

BIG DADDY. Where you goin'?

BRICK. I'm takin' a little short trip to Echo Spring.

BIG DADDY. To where?

BRICK. Liquor cabinet. . . .

BIG DADDY. Yes, sir, boy—(*He hands Brick the crutch.*)—the human animal is a beast that dies and if he's got money he buys and buys and buys and I think the reason he buys everything he can buy is that in the back of his mind he has the crazy hope that one of his purchases will be life everlasting!—Which it never can be. . . . The human animal is a beast that—

BRICK. (*at the liquor cabinet*). Big Daddy, you sure are shootin' th' breeze here tonight.

(*There is a pause and voices are heard outside.*)

BIG DADDY. I been quiet here lately, spoke not a word, just sat and stared into space. I had something heavy weighing on my mind but tonight that load was took off me. That's why I'm talking.—The sky looks diff'rent to me. . . . Brick. You know what I like to hear most?

BIG DADDY. What?

BRICK. Solid quiet. Perfect unbroken quiet.

BIG DADDY. Why?

BRICK. Because it's more peaceful.

BIG DADDY. Man, you'll hear a lot of that in the grave. (*He chuckles agreeably.*)

BRICK. Are you through talkin' to me?

BIG DADDY. Why are you so anxious to shut me up?

BRICK. Well, sir, ever so often you say to me, Brick, I want to have a talk with you, but when we talk, it never materializes. Nothing is said. You sit in a chair and gas about this and that and I look like I listen. I try to look like I listen, but I don't listen, not much. Communication is—awful hard between people an'—somehow between you and me, it just don't—

BIG DADDY. Have you ever been scared? I mean have you ever felt downright terror of something? (*He gets up.*) Just one moment. I'm going to close these doors. . .

(*He closes doors on gallery as if he were going to tell an important secret.*)

BRICK. What?

BIG DADDY. Brick?

BRICK. Huh?

BIG DADDY. Son, I thought I had it!

BRICK. Had what? Had what, Big Daddy?

BIG DADDY. Cancer!

BRICK. Oh . . .

BIG DADDY. I thought the old man made out of bones had laid his cold and heavy hand on my shoulder!

BRICK. Well, Big Daddy, you kept a tight mouth about it.

BIG DADDY. A pig squeals. A man keeps a tight mouth about it, in spite of a man not having a pig's advantage.

BRICK. What advantage is that?

BIG DADDY. Ignorance—of mortality—is a comfort. A man don't have that comfort, he's the only living thing that conceives of death, that knows what it is. The others go without knowing which is the way that anything living should go, go without knowing, without any knowledge of it, and yet a pig squeals, but a man sometimes, he can keep a tight mouth about it. Sometimes he—(*There is a deep, smoldering ferocity in the old man.*)—can you keep a tight mouth about it. I wonder if—

BRICK. What, Big Daddy?

BIG DADDY. A whiskey highball would injure this spastic condition?

BRICK. No, sir, it might do it good.

BIG DADDY (*grins suddenly, wolfishly*). Jesus, I can't tell you! The sky is open! Christ, it's open again! It's open, boy, it's open!

(*Brick looks down at his drink.*)

BRICK. You feel better, Big Daddy?

BIG DADDY. Better? Hell! I can breathe!—All of my life I been like a doubled up fist. . . . (*He pours a drink.*)—Poundin', smashin', drivin'!—now I'm going to loosen these doubled up hands and touch things *easy*

with them. . . . (*He spreads his hands as if caressing the air.*) You know what I'm contemplating?

BRICK (*vaguely*). No, sir. What are you contemplating?

BIG DADDY. Ha ha!—*Pleasure!*—pleasure with *women!* (*Brick's smile fades a little but lingers.*) Brick, this stuff burns me!—Yes, boy. I'll tell you something that you might not guess. I still have desire for women and this is my sixty-fifth birthday.

BRICK. I think that's mighty remarkable, Big Daddy.

BIG DADDY. Remarkable?

BRICK. *Admirable*, Big Daddy.

BIG DADDY. You're damn right it is, remarkable and admirable both. I realize now that I never had me enough. I let many chances slip by because of scruples about it, scruples, convention—crap. . . . All that stuff is bull, bull, bull!—It took the shadow of death to make me see it. Now that shadow's lifted, I'm going to cut loose and have, what is it they call it, have me a—ball!

BRICK. A ball, huh?

BIG DADDY. That's right, a ball, a ball! Hell!—I slept with Big Mama till, let's see, five years ago, till I was sixty and she was fifty-eight, and never even liked her, never did!

(*The phone has been ringing down the hall. Big Mama enters, exclaiming:*)

BIG MAMA. Don't you men hear that phone ring? I heard it way out on the gall'ry.

BIG DADDY. There's five rooms off this front gall'ry that you could go through. Why do you go through this one? (*Big Mama makes a playful face as she bustles out the hall door.*) Hunh!—Why, when Big Mama goes out of a room, I can't remember what that woman looks like, but when Big Mama comes back into the room, boy, then I see what she looks like, and I wish I didn't! (*Bends over laughing at his joke till it hurts his guts and he straightens with a grimace. The laugh subsides to a chuckle as he puts the liquor glass a little distrustfully down on the table. Brick has risen and hobbled to the gallery doors.*) Hey! Where you goin'?

BRICK. Out for a breather.

BIG DADDY. Not yet you ain't. Stay here till this talk is finished, young fellow.

BRICK. I thought it was finished, Big Daddy.

BIG DADDY. It ain't even begun.

BRICK. My mistake. Excuse me. I just wanted to feel that river breeze.

BIG DADDY. Turn on the ceiling fan and set back down in that chair.

(*Big Mama's voice rises, carrying down the hall.*)

BIG MAMA. Miss Sally, you're a case! You're a caution, Miss Sally. Why didn't you give me a chance to explain it to you?

BIG DADDY. Jesus, she's talking to my old maid sister again.

BIG MAMA. Well, good-by, now, Miss Sally. You come down real soon, Big Daddy's dying to see you! Yaisss, good-by, Miss Sally. . . . (*She hangs up and bellows with mirth. Big Daddy groans and covers his ears as she approaches. Bursting in:*) Big Daddy, that was Miss Sally callin' from Memphis again! You know what she done, Big Daddy? She called her doctor in Memphis to git him to tell her what that spastic thing is! Ha-HAAAA!—And called back to tell me how relieved she was that—Hey! Let me in! (*Big Daddy has been holding the door half-closed against her.*)

BIG DADDY. Naw I ain't. I told you not to come and go through this room. You just back out and go through those five other rooms.

BIG MAMA. Big Daddy? Big Daddy? Oh, Big Daddy!—You didn't mean those things you said to me, did you? (*He shuts door firmly against her but she still calls.*) Sweetheart? Sweetheart? Big Daddy? You didn't mean those awful things you said to me?—I know you didn't. I know you didn't mean those things in your heat. . . . (*The childlike voice fades with a sob and her heavy footsteps retreat down the hall. Brick has risen once more on his crutches and starts for the gallery again.*)

BIG DADDY. All I ask of that woman is that she leave me alone. But she can't admit to herself that she makes me sick. That comes of having slept with her too many years. Should of quit much sooner but that old woman she never got enough of it—and I was good in bed . . . I never should of wasted so much of it on her. . . . They say you got just so many and each one is numbered. Well, I got a few left in me, a few, and I'm going to pick me a good one to spend 'em on! I'm going to pick me a choice one, I don't care how much she costs, I'll smother her in—minks! Ha! ha! I'll strip her naked and smother her in minks and choke her with diamonds! Ha ha! I'll strip her naked and choke her with diamonds and smother her with minks and hump her from hell to breakfast. *Ha aha ha ha ha!*

MAE. (*gaily at door*). Who's that laughin' in there?

GOOPER. Is Big Daddy laughin' in there?

BIG DADDY. Crap!—them two—drips. . . . (*He goes over and touches Brick's shoulder.*) Yes, son. Brick, boy.—I'm—happy! I'm happy, son, I'm happy! (*He chokes a little and bites his under lip, pressing his head quickly, shyly against his son's head and then, coughing with embarrassment, goes uncertainly back to the table where he*

set down the glass. He drinks and makes a grimace as it burns his guts. Brick sighs and rises with effort.*) What makes you so restless? Have you got ants in your britches?

BRICK. Yes, sir . . .

BIG DADDY. Why?

BRICK. —Something—hasn't—happened. . . .

BIG DADDY. Yeah? What is that!

BRICK (*sadly*). —the click. . . .

BIG DADDY. Did you say click?

BRICK. Yes, click.

BIG DADDY. What click?

BRICK. A click that I get in my head that makes me peaceful.

BIG DADDY. I sure in hell don't know what you're talking about, but it disturbs me.

BRICK. It's just a mechanical thing.

BIG DADDY. What is a mechanical thing?

BRICK. This click that I get in my head that makes me peaceful. I got to drink till I get it. It's just a mechanical thing, something like a—like a—like a—

BIG DADDY. Like a—

BRICK. Switch clicking off in my head, turning the hot light off and the cool night on and—(*He looks up, smiling sadly.*)—all of a sudden there's—peace!

BIG DADDY (*whistles long and soft with astonishment; he goes back to Brick and clasps his son's two shoulders*). Jesus! I didn't know it had gotten that bad with you. Why, boy, you're—alcoholic!

BRICK. That's the truth, Big Daddy. I'm alcoholic.

BIG DADDY. This shows how I—let things go!

BRICK. I have to hear that little click in my head that makes me peaceful. Usually I hear it sooner than this, sometimes as early as—noon, but—today it's—dilatory. . . . —I just haven't got the right level of alcohol in my bloodstream yet! (*This last statement is made with energy as he freshens his drink.*)

BIG DADDY. Uh—huh. Expecting death made me blind. I didn't have no idea that a son of mine was turning into a drunkard under my nose.

BRICK (*gently*). Well, now you do, Big Daddy, the news has penetrated.

BIG DADDY. UH-huh, yes, now I do, the news has—penetrated. . . .

BRICK. And so if you'll excuse me—

BIG DADDY. No, I won't excuse you.

BRICK. —I'd better sit by myself till I hear that click in my head, it's just a mechanical thing but it don't happen except when I'm alone or talking to no one. . . .

BIG DADDY. You got a long, long time to sit still, boy, and talk to no one, but now you're talkin' to me. At least

I'm talking to you. And you set there and listen until I tell you the conversation is over!

BRICK. But this talk is like all the others we've ever had together in our lives! It's nowhere, nowhere!—it's—it's *painful*, Big Daddy. . . .

BIG DADDY. All right, then let it be painful, but don't you move from that chair!—I'm going to remove that crutch. . . . (*He seizes the crutch and tosses it across room.*)

BRICK. I can hop on one foot, and if I fall, I can crawl!

BIG DADDY. If you ain't careful you're gonna crawl off this plantation and then, by Jesus, you'll have to hustle your drinks along Skid Row!

BRICK. That'll come, Big Daddy.

BIG DADDY. Naw, it won't. You're my son and I'm going to straighten you out; now that *I'm* straightened out, I'm going to straighten out you!

BRICK. Yeah?

BIG DADDY. Today the report come in from Ochsner Clinic. Y'know what they told me? (*His face glows with triumph.*) The only thing that they could detect with all the instruments of science in that great hospital is a little spastic condition of the colon! And nerves torn to pieces by all that worry about it. (*A little girl bursts into room with a sparkler clutched in each fist, hops and shrieks like a monkey gone mad and rushes back out again as Big Daddy strikes at her. Silence. The two men stare at each other. A woman laughs gaily outside.*) I want you to know I breathed a sigh of relief almost as powerful as the Vicksburg tornado!

BRICK. You weren't ready to go?

BIG DADDY. GO WHERE?—crap. . . . —When you are gone from here, boy, you are long gone and no where! The human machine is not no different from the animal machine or the fish machine or the bird machine or the reptile machine or the insect machine! It's just a whole God damn lot more complicated and consequently more trouble to keep together. Yep. I thought I had it. The earth shook under my foot, the sky come down like the black lid of a kettle and I couldn't breathe!—Today!!—that lid was lifted, I drew my first free breath in—how many years?—God—*three*. . . . (*There is laughter outside, running footsteps, the soft, plushy sound and light of exploding rockets. Brick stares at him soberly for a long moment; then makes a sort of startled sound in his nostrils and springs up on one foot and hops across the room to grab his crutch, swinging on the furniture for support. He gets the crutch and flees as if in horror for the gallery. His father seizes him by the sleeve of his white silk pajamas.*) Stay here, you son of a bitch!—till I say go!

BRICK. I can't.

BIG DADDY. You sure in hell will, God damn it.

BRICK. No, I can't. We talk, you talk, in—circles! We get nowhere, nowhere! It's always the same, you say you want to talk to me and don't have a ruttin' thing to say to me!

BIG DADDY. Nothin' to say when I'm tellin' you I'm going to live when I thought I was dying?!

BRICK. Oh—*that*—Is that what you have to say to me?

BIG DADDY. Why, you son of a bitch! Ain't that, ain't that—*important?!*

BRICK. Well, you said that, that's said, and now I—

BIG DADDY. Now you set back down.

BRICK. You're all balled up, you—

BIG DADDY. I ain't balled up!

BRICK. You are, you're all balled up!

BIG DADDY. Don't tell me what I am, you drunken whelp! I'm going to tear this coat sleeve off if you don't set down!

BRICK. Big Daddy—

BIG DADDY. Do what I tell you! I'm the boss here, now! I want you to know I'm back in the driver's seat now! (*Big Mama rushes in, clutching her great heaving bosom.*) What in hell do you want in here, Big Mama?

BIG MAMA. Oh, Big Daddy! Why are you shouting like that? I just cain't *stainnnnnnnd—it*. . . .

BIG DADDY (*raising the back of his hand above his head*). GIT!—outa here.

(*She rushes back out, sobbing.*)

BRICK (*softly, sadly*). Christ. . . .

BIG DADDY (*fiercely*). Yeah! Christ!—is right . . . (*Brick breaks loose and hobbles toward the gallery. Big Daddy jerks his crutch from under Brick so he steps with the injured ankle. He utters a hissing cry of anguish, clutches a chair and pulls it over on top of him on the floor.*) Son of a—tub of—hog fat. . . .

BRICK. Big Daddy! Give me my crutch. (*Big Daddy throws the crutch out of reach.*) Give me that crutch, Big Daddy.

BIG DADDY. Why do you drink?

BRICK. Don't know, give me my crutch!

BIG DADDY. You better think why you drink or give up drinking!

BRICK. Will you please give me my crutch so I can get up off this floor?

BIG DADDY. First you answer my question. Why do you drink? Why are you throwing your life away, boy, like somethin' disgusting you picked up on the street?

BRICK (*getting onto his knees*). Big Daddy, I'm in pain, I stepped on that foot.

BIG DADDY. Good! I'm glad you're not too numb with the liquor in you to feel some pain!

BRICK. You—spilled my—drink . . .

BIG DADDY. I'll make a bargain with you. You tell me why you drink and I'll hand you one. I'll pour you the liquor myself and hand it to you.

BRICK. Why do I drink?

BIG DADDY. Yeah! Why?

BRICK. Give me a drink and I'll tell you.

BIG DADDY. Tell me first!

BRICK. I'll tell you in one word.

BIG DADDY. What word?

BRICK. DISGUST! (*The clock chimes softly, sweetly. Big Daddy gives it a short, outraged glance.*) Now how about that drink?

BIG DADDY. What are you disgusted with? You got to tell me that, first. Otherwise being disgusted don't make no sense!

BRICK. Give me my crutch.

BIG DADDY. You heard me, you got to tell me what I asked you first.

BRICK. I told you, I said to kill my disgust!

BIG DADDY. DISGUST WITH WHAT!

BRICK. You strike a hard bargain.

BIG DADDY. What are you disgusted with?—an' I'll pass you the liquor.

BRICK. I can hop on one foot, and if I fall, I can crawl.

BIG DADDY. You want liquor that bad?

BRICK (*dragging himself up, clinging to bedstead*). Yeah, I want it that bad.

BIG DADDY. If I give you a drink, will you tell me what it is you're disgusted with, Brick?

BRICK. Yes, sir, I will try to. (*The old man pours him a drink and solemnly passes it to him. There is silence as Brick drinks.*) Have you ever heard the word "mendacity"?

BIG DADDY. Sure. Mendacity is one of them five dollar words that cheap politicians throw back and forth at each other.

BRICK. You know what it means?

BIG DADDY. Don't it mean lying and liars?

BRICK. Yes, sir, lying and liars.

BIG DADDY. Has someone been lying to you?

CHILDREN (*chanting in chorus offstage*).
We want Big Dad-dee!
We want Big Dad-dee!

(*Gooper appears in the gallery door.*)

GOOPER. Big Daddy, the kiddies are shouting for you out there.

BIG DADDY (*fiercely*). Keep out, Gooper!

GOOPER. 'Scuse *me!*

(*Big Daddy slams the doors after Gooper.*)

BIG DADDY. Who's been lying to you, has Margaret been lying to you, has your wife been lying to you about something, Brick?

BRICK. Not her. That wouldn't matter.

BIG DADDY. Then who's been lying to you, and what about?

BRICK. No one single person and no one lie. . . .

BIG DADDY. Then what, what then, for Christ's sake?

BRICK. —The whole, the whole—thing. . . .

BIG DADDY. Why are you rubbing your head? You got a headache?

BRICK. No, I'm tryin to—

BIG DADDY. —Concentrate, but you can't because your brain's all soaked with liquor, is that the trouble? Wet brain? (*He snatches the glass from Brick's hand.*) What do you know about this menadacity thing? Hell! I could write a book on it! Don't you know that? I could write a book on it and still not cover the subject? Well, I could, I could write a goddam book on it and still not cover the subject anywhere near enough!!—Think of all the lies I got to put up with!—Pretenses! Ain't that mendacity? Having to pretend stuff you don't think or feel or have any idea of? Having for instance to act like I care for Big Mama!—I haven't been able to stand the sight, sound, or smell of that woman for forty years now!— even when I *laid* her!—regular as a piston. . . .

Pretend to love that son of a bitch of a Gooper and his wife Mae and those five same screechers out there like parrots in a jungle? Jesus! Can't stand to look at 'em!

Church!—it bores the Bejesus out of me but I go!—I go an' sit there and listen to the fool preacher!

Clubs!—Elks! Masons! Rosary!—*crap!*

(*A spasm of pain makes him clutch his belly. He sinks into a chair and his voice is softer and hoarser.*) You I do like for some reason, did always have some kind of real feeling for—affection—respect—yes, always. . . .

You and being a success as a planter is all I ever had any devotion to in my whole life!—and that's the truth. . . . I don't know why, but it is!

I've lived with menadcity!—Why can't *you* live with it? Hell, you *got* to live with it, there's nothing *else* to *live* with except menadacity, is there?

BRICK. Yes, sir. Yes, sir there is something else that you can live with!

BIG DADDY. What?

BRICK (*lifting his glass*). This!—Liquor. . . .

BIG DADDY. That's not living, that's dodging away from life.

BRICK. I want to dodge away from it.

BIG DADDY. Then why don't you kill yourself, man?

BRICK. I like to drink. . . .

BIG DADDY. Oh, God, I can't talk to you. . . .

BRICK. I'm sorry, Big Daddy.

BIG DADDY. Not as sorry as I am. I'll tell you something. A little while back when I thought my number was up—(*This speech should have torrential pace and fury.*)—before I found out it was just this—spastic—colon. I thought about you. Should I or should I not, if the jig was up, give you this place when I go—since I hate Gooper an' Mae know that they hate me, and since all five same monkeys are little Maes an' Goopers.—And I thought, No!—Then I thought, Yes!—I couldn't make up my mind. I hate Gooper and his five same monkeys and that bitch Mae! Why should I turn over twenty-eight thousand acres of the richest land this side of the valley Nile to not my kind?—But why in hell, on the other hand, Brick—should I subsidize a goddam fool on the bottle?—Liked or not liked, well, maybe even—*loved!*—Why should I do that?—Subsidize worthless behavior? Rot? Corruption?

BRICK (*smiling*). I understand.

BIG DADDY. Well, if you do, you're smarter than I am, God damn it, because I don't understand. And this I will tell you frankly. I didn't make up my mind at all on that question and still to this day I ain't made out no will!—Well, now I don't *have* to. The pressure is gone. I can just wait and see if you pull yourself togther or if you don't.

BRICK. That's right, Big Daddy.

BIG DADDY. You sound like you thought I was kidding.

BRICK (*rising*). No, sir. I know you're not kidding.

BIG DADDY. But you don't care—?

BRICK (*hobbling toward the gallery door*). No sir, I don't care. . . . Now how about taking a look at your birthday fireworks and getting some of that cool breeze off the river? (*He stands in the gallery doorway as the night sky turns pink and green and gold with successive flashes of light.*)

BIG DADDY. WAIT—Brick. . . . (*His voice drops. Suddenly there is something shy, almost tender, in his restraining gesture.*) Don't let's—leave it like this, like them other talks we've had, we've always—talked around things, we've—just talked around things for some rutten reason. I don't know what, it's always like something was left not spoken, something avoided because neither of us was honest enough with the—other. . .

BRICK. I never lied to you, Big Daddy.

BIG DADDY. Did I ever to *you?*

BRICK. No, sir. . . .

BIG DADDY. Then there is at least two people that never lied to each other.

BRICK. But we've never *talked* to each other.

BIG DADDY. We can *now*.

BRICK. Big Daddy, there don't seem to be anything much to say.

BIG DADDY. You say that you drink to kill your disgust with lying.

BRICK. You said to give you a reason.

BIG DADDY. Is liquor the only thing that'll kill this disgust?

BRICK. Now. Yes.

BIG DADDY. But not once, huh?

BRICK. Not when I was stilll young an' believing. A drinking man's someone who wants to forget he isn't still young an' believing.

BIG DADDY. Believing what?

BRICK. Believing. . . .

BIG DADDY. Believing *what?*

BRICK (*stubbornly evasive*). Believing. . . .

BIG DADDY. I don't know what the hell you mean by believing and I don't think you know what you mean by believing, but if you still got sports in your blood, go back to sports announcing and—

BRICK. Sit in a glass box watching games I can't play? Describing what I can't do while players do it? Sweating out their disgust and confusion in contests I'm not fit for? Drinkin' a coke, half bourbon, so I can stand it? That's no goddam good any more, no help—time just outran me, Big Daddy—got there first. . .

BIG DADDY. I think you're passing the buck.

BRICK. You know many drinkin' men?

BIG DADDY (*with a slight, charming smile*). I have known a fair number of that species.

BRICK. Could any of them tell you why he drank?

BIG DADDY. Yep, you're passin' the buck to things like time and disgust with "mendacity" and—crap!—if you got to use that kind of language about a thing, it's ninety-proof bull, and I'm not buying any.

BRICK. I had to give you a reason to get a drink!

BIG DADDY. You started drinkin' when your friend Skipper died.

(*Silence for five beats. Then Brick makes a startled movement, reaching for his crutch.*)

BRICK. What are you suggesting?

BIG DADDY. I'm suggesting nothing. (*The shuffle and clop of Brick's rapid hobble away from his father's steady, grave attention.*)—But Gooper an' Mae suggested that there was something not right exactly in your—

BRICK. (*stopping short downstage as if backed to a wall*). "Not right?"

BIG DADDY. Not, well, exactly *normal* in your friendship with—

BRICK. They suggested that, too? I thought that was Maggie's suggestion. (*Brick's detachment is at last broken through. His heart is accelerated; his forehead sweat-beaded; his breath becomes more rapid and his voice hoarse. The thing they're discussing, timidly and painfully on the side of Big Daddy, fiercely, violently on Brick's side, is the inadmissable thing that Skipper died to disavow between them. The fact that if it existed it had to be disavowed to "keep face" in the world they lived in, may be at the heart of the "mendacity" that Brick drinks to kill his disgust with. It may be the root of his collapse. Or maybe it is only a single manifestation of it, not even the most important. The bird that I hope to catch in the net of this play is not the solution of one man's psychological problem. I'm trying to catch the true quality of experience in a group of people, that cloudy, flickering, evanescent—fiercely charged!—interplay of live human beings in the thundercloud of a common crisis. Some mystery should be left in the revelation of character in a play, just as a great deal of mystery is always left in the revelation of character in life, even in one's own character to himself. This does not absolve the playwright of his duty to observe and probe as clearly and deeply as he legimately can: but it should steer him away from "pat" conclusions, facile definitions which make a play just a play, not a snare for the truth of human experience. The following scene should be played with great concentration, with most of the power leashed but palpable in what is left unspoken.*) Who else's suggestion is it, is it yours? How many others thought that Skipper and I were—

BIG DADDY (*gently*). Now, hold on, hold on a minute, son.—I knocked around in my time.

BRICK. What's that got to do with—

BIG DADDY. I said "Hold on!"—I bummed, I bummed this country till I was—

BRICK. Whose suggestion, who else's suggestion is it?

BIG DADDY. Slept in hobo jungles and railroad Y's and flophouses in all cities before I—

BRICK. Oh, *you* think so, too, you call me your son and a queer. Oh! Maybe that's why you put Maggie and me in this room that was Jack Straw's and Peter Ochello's, in which that pair of old sisters slept in a double bed where both of 'em died!

BIG DADDY. *Now just don't go throwing rocks at*—(*Suddenly Reverend Tooker appears in the gallery doors, his head slightly, playfully, fatuously cocked, with a practised clergyman's smile, sincere as a bird-call blown on a hunter's whis-*

tle, the living embodiment of the pious, conventional lie. Big Daddy gasps a little at this perfectly timed, but incongruous, apparition.)—What're you lookin' for, Preacher?

REVEREND TOOKER. The gentleman's lavatory, ha ha!—heh, heh . . .

BIG DADDY (*with strained courtesy*). —Go back out and walk down to the other end of the gallery, Reverend Tooker, and use the bathroom connected with my bedroom, and if you can't find it, ask them where it is!

REVEREND TOOKER. Ah, thanks. (*He goes out with a deprecatory chuckle.*)

BIG DADDY. It's hard to talk in this place . . .

BRICK. Son of a—!

BIG DADDY (*leaving a lot unspoken*). —I seen all things and understood a lot of them, till 1910. Christ, the year that—I had worn my shoes through, hocked my—I hopped off a yellow dog freight car half a mile down the road, slept in a wagon of cotton outside the gin—Jack Straw an' Peter Ochello took me in. Hired me to manage this place which grew into this one.—When jack Straw died—why, old Peter Ochello quit eatin' like a dog does when its master's dead, and died, too!

BRICK. Christ!

BIG DADDY. I'm just saying I understand such—

BRICK (*violently*). Skipper is dead. I have not quit eating!

BIG DADDY. No, but you started drinking.

(*Brick wheels on his crutch and hurls his glass across the room shouting.*)

BRICK. YOU THINK SO, TOO?

BIG DADDY. *Shhh!* (*Footsteps run on the gallery. There are women's calls. Big Daddy goes toward the door.*) Go way!—Just broke a glass. . . .

(*Brick is transformed, as if a quiet mountain blew suddenly up in volcanic flame.*)

BRICK. You think so, too? You think so, too? You think me an' Skipper did, did, did!—*sodomy!*—together?

BIG DADDY. Hold—!

BRICK. That what you—

BIG DADDY. —ON—a minute!

BRICK. You think we did dirty things between us, Skipper an'—

BIG DADDY. Why are you shouting like that? Why are you—

BRICK. —Me, is that what you think of Skipper, is that—

BIG DADDY. —so excited? I don't think nothing. I don't know nothing. I'm simply telling you what—

BRICK. You think that Skipper and me were a pair of dirty old men?

BIG DADDY. Now that's—

BRICK. Straw? Ochello? A couple of—

BIG DADDY. Now just—

BRICK. —ducking sissies? Queers? Is that what you—

BIG DADDY. Shhh.

BRICK. —think? (*He loses his balance and pitches to his knees without noticing the pain. He grabs the bed and drags himself up.*)

BIG DADDY. Jesus!—Whew. . . . Grab my hand!

BRICK. Naw, I don't want your hand. . . .

BIG DADDY. Well, I want yours. Git up! (*He draws him up, keeps an arm about him with concern and affection.*) You broken out in a sweat! You're panting like you'd run a race with—

BRICK (*freeing himself from his father's hold*). Big Daddy, you shock me, Big Daddy, you, you—*shock* me! Talkin' so—(*He turns away from his father.*)—casually!—about a—thing like that . . .

   —Don't you know how people *feel* about things like that? How, how *disgusted* they are by things like that? Why, at Ole Miss when it was discovered a pledge to our fraternity, Skipper's and mine, did a, *attempted* to do a, unnatural thing with—

   We not only dropped him like a hot rock!—We told him to git off the campus, and he did, he got!—All the way to—(*He halts, breathless.*)

BIG DADDY. —Where?

BRICK. —North Africa, last I heard!

BIG DADDY. Well, I have come back from further away than that, I have just now returned from the other side of the moon, death's country, son, and I'm not easy to shock by anything here. (*He comes downstage and faces out.*)

   Always, anyhow, lived with too much space around me to be infected by ideas of other people. One thing you can grow on a big place more important than cotton!—is *tolerance!*—I grown it. (*He returns toward Brick.*)

BRICK. Why can't exceptional friendship, *real, real, deep, deep friendship!* beween two men be respected as something clean and decent without being thought of as—

BIG DADDY. It can, it is, for God's sake.

BRICK. —*Fairies.* . . . (*In his utterance of this word, we gauge the wide and profound reach of the conventional mores he got from the world that crowned him with early laurel.*)

BIG DADDY. I told Mae an' Gooper—

BRICK. Frig Mae and Gooper, frig all dirty lies and liars!—Skipper and me had a clean, true thing between us!—had a clean friendship, practically all our lives, till Maggie got the idea you're talking about. Normal? No!—It was too rare to be normal, any true thing between two people is too rare to be normal.

Oh, once in a while he put his hand on my shoulder or I'd put mine on his, oh, maybe even, when we were touring the country in pro-football an' shared hotel-rooms we'd reach across the space between the two beds and shake hands to say good-night, yeah, one or two times we—

BIG DADDY. Brick, nobody thinks that that's not normal!

BRICK. Well, they're mistaken, it was! It was a pure an' true thing an' that's not normal.

(*They both stare straight at each other for a long moment. The tension breaks and both turn away as if tired.*)

BIG DADDY. Yeah, it's—hard t'—talk. . . .

BRICK. All right, then, let's—let it go. . . .

BIG DADDY. Why did Skipper crack up? Why have you?

(*Brick looks back at his father again. He has already decided, without knowing that he has made this decision, that he is going to tell his father that he is dying of cancer. Only this could even the score between them: one inadmissible thing in return for another.*)

BRICK (*ominously*). All right. You're asking for it, Big Daddy. We're finally going to have that real true talk you wanted. It's too late to stop it, now, we got to carry it through and cover every subject. (*He hobbles back to the liquor cabinet.*) Uh-huh. (*He opens the ice bucket and picks up the silver tongs with slow admiration of their frosty brightness.*) Maggie declares that Skipper and I went into pro-football after we left "Ole Miss" because we were scared to grow up . . . (*He moves downstage with the shuffle and clop of a cripple on a crutch. As Margaret did when her speech became "recitative," he looks out into the house, commanding its attention by his direct, concentrated gaze—a broken, "tragically elegant" figure telling simply as much as he knows of "the Truth.")*—Wanted to—keep on tossing—those long, long!—high, high!—passes that—couldn't be intercepted except by time, the serial attack that made us famous! And so we did, we did, we kept it up for one season, that aerial attack, we held it high!—Yeah, but—

   —that summer, Maggie, she laid the law down to me, said, Now or never, and so I married Maggie. . . .

BIG DADDY. How was Maggie in bed?

BRICK (*wryly*). Great! the greatest! (*Big Daddy nods as if he thought so.*) She went on the road that fall with the Dixie Stars. Oh, she made a great show of being the world's best sport. She wore a—wore a—tall bearskin cap! A shako, they call it, a dyed moleskin coat, a moleskin coat dyed red!—Cut up crazy! Rented hotel ballrooms for victory celebrations, wouldn't cancel them when it—turned out—defeat. . . .

MAGGIE THE CAT! Ha ha! (*Big Daddy nods.*)—But Skipper, he had some fever which came back on him which doctors couldn't explain and I got that injury—turned out to be just a shadow on the X-ray plate—and a touch of bursitis. . . . I lay in a hospital bed, watched our games on TV, saw Maggie on the bench next to Skipper when he was hauled out of a game for stumbles, fumbles!—Burned me up the way she hung on his arm!—Y'know, I think that Maggie had always felt sort of left out because she and me never got any closer together than two people just get in bed, which is not much closer than two cats on a—fence humping. . .

So! She took this time to work on poor dumb Skipper. He was a less than average student at Ole Miss, you know that, don't you?!—Poured in his mind the dirty, false idea that what we were, him and me, was a frustrated case of that ole pair of sisters that lived in this room, Jack Straw and Peter Ochello!—He, poor Skipper, went to bed with Maggie to prove it wasn't true, and when it didn't work out, he thought it *was* true!—Skipper broke in two like a rotten stick—nobody ever turned so fast to a lush—or died of it so quick. . . .

—Now are you satisfied?

(*Big Daddy has listened to this story, dividing the grain from the chaff. Now he looks at his son.*)

BIG DADDY. Are *you* satisfied?
BRICK. With what?
BIG DADDY. That half-ass story!
BRICK. What's half-ass about it?
BIG DADDY. Something's left out of that story. What did you leave out?

(*The phone has started ringing in the hall. As if it reminded him of something, Brick glances suddenly toward the sound and says.*)

BRICK. Yes!—I left out a long-distance call which I had from Skipper, in which he made a drunken confession to me and on which I hung up!—last time we spoke to each other in our lives. . . .

(*Muted ring stops as someone answers phone in a soft, indistinct voice in hall.*)

BIG DADDY. You hung up?
BRICK. Hung up. Jesus! Well—
BIG DADDY. Anyhow now!—we have tracked down the lie with which you're disgusted and which you are

drinking to kill your disgust with, Brick. You been passing the buck. This disgust with mendacity is disgust with yourself.

You!—dug the grave of your friend and kicked him in it!—before you'd face truth with him!
BRICK. *His* truth, not *mine!*
BIG DADDY. His truth, okay! But you wouldn't face it with him!
BRICK. Who *can* face truth? Can *you?*
BIG DADDY. Now don't start passin' the rotten buck again, boy!
BRICK. *How about these birthday congratulations, these many, many happy returns of the day, when ev'rybody but you knows there won't be any!* (*Whoever has answered the hall phone lets out a high, shrill laugh; the voice becomes audible saying:* "No, no, you got it all wrong! Upside down! Are you crazy?")

(*Brick suddenly catches his breath as he realizes that he has made a shocking disclosure. He hobbles a few paces, then freezes, and without looking at his father's shocked face, says:*) Let's, let's—go out, now, and— (*Big Daddy moves suddenly forward and grabs hold of the boy's crutch like it was a weapon for which they were fighting for possession.*)

BIG DADDY. Oh, no, no! No one's going out! What did you start to say?
BRICK. I don't remember.
BIG DADDY. "Many happy returns when they know there won't be any"?
BRICK. Aw, hell, Big Daddy, forget it. Come on out on the gallery and look at the fireworks they're shooting off for your birthday. . . .
BIG DADDY. First you finish that remark you were makin' before you cut off. "Many happy returns when they know there won't be any"?—Ain't that what you just said?
BRICK. Look, now. I can get around without that crutch if I have to but it would be a lot easier on the furniture an' glassware if I didn't have to go swinging along like Tarzan of th'—
BIG DADDY. FINISH! WHAT YOU WAS SAYIN'!

(*An eerie green glow shows in sky behind him.*)

BRICK (*sucking the ice in his glass, speech becoming thick*). Leave th' place to Gooper and Mae an' their five little same little monkeys. All I want is—
BIG DADDY. "LEAVE TH' PLACE," did you say?
BRICK (*vaguely*). All twenty-eight thousand acres of the richest land this side of the valley Nile.
BIG DADDY. Who said I was "leaving the place" to Gooper or anybody? This is my sixty-fifth birthday! I

got fifteen years or twenty years left in me! I'll outlive *you!* I'll bury you an' have to pay for your coffin!

BRICK. Sure. Many happy returns. Now let's go watch the fireworks, come on, let's—

BIG DADDY. Lying, have they been lying? About the report from th'—clinic? Did they, did they—find something?—*Cancer. Maybe?*

BRICK. Mendacity is a system that we live in. Liquor is one way out an' death's the other. . . . (*He takes the crutch from Big Daddy's loose grip and swings out on the gallery leaving the doors open.*)

(*A song, "Pick a Bale of Cotton," is heard.*)

MAE (*appearing in door*). Oh, Big Daddy, the field-hands are singin' fo' you!

BIG DADDY (*shouting hoarsely*). BRICK! BRICK!

MAE. He's outside drinkin', Big Daddy.

BIG DADDY. *BRICK!*

(*Mae retreats, awed by the passion of his voice. Children call Brick in tones mocking Big Daddy. His face crumbles like broken yellow plaster about to fall into dust.*)

(*There is a glow in the sky. Brick swings back through the doors, slowly, gravely, quite soberly.*)

BRICK. I'm sorry, Big Daddy. My head don't work any more and it's hard for me to understand how anybody could care if he lived or died or was dying or cared about anything but whether or not there was liquor left in the botttle and so I said what I said without thinking. In some ways I'm no better than the others, in some ways worse because I'm less alive. Maybe it's being alive that makes them lie, and being almost *not* alive makes me sort of accidentally truthful—I don't know but—anyway—we've been friends . . . And being friends is telling each other the truth. . . . (*There is a pause.*) You told *me!* I told *you!*

(*A child rushes into the room and grabs a fistful of firecrackers and runs out again.*)

CHILD (*screaming*). Bang, bang, bang, bang, bang, bang, bang, bang, bang!

BIG DADDY (*slowly and passionately*). CHRIST—DAMN—ALL—LYING SONS OF—LYING BITCHES! (*He straightens at last and crosses to the inside door. At the door he turns and looks back as if he had some desperate question he couldn't put into words. Then he nods reflectively and says in a hoarse voice.*) Yes, all liars, all liars, all lying dying liars! (*This is said slowly, slowly, with a fierce revulsion. He goes on out.*)—Lying! Dying!

Liars! (*His voice dies out. There is the sound of a child being slapped. It rushes, hideously bawling, through room and out the hall door.*)

(*Brick remains motionless as the lights dim out and the curtain falls.*)

Curtain

* * *

Williams originally wrote a version of Act III that is quite different from that which is published here. The original, the so-called "published version" (i.e., the text Williams wrote in 1954), was replaced by the "Broadway version," which Williams drastically revised per Elia Kazan's suggestions for the production at the Morosco Theater in March 1955. We intended to publish both versions so you might see how a playwright, in effect, critiques his own work when revising the play. Regrettably, there is not space in this volume to include both versions; we have selected the version that is usually performed and have included Williams's brief "Note of Explanation" concerning his rewrite of the act. We urge you to read Williams's original draft, which is included in *Tennessee Williams: Eight Plays* (1979).

In the original Act III, Big Daddy does not appear. Dr. Baugh tells the gathered family that the recent tests confirm that Big Daddy has terminal cancer. Big Mama at first refuses to acknowledge the truth concerning Big Daddy's illness, even as Gooper and Mae maneuver to gain control of the plantation. Gooper produces a legal document that gives him a legal claim, but Maggie trumps him by announcing that she is pregnant with Brick's child. Big Mama is ecstatic because she knows Big Daddy has always wanted Brick and his heir to have the plantation. This domestic squabble is cut short by "a long drawn cry of agony and rage" from Big Daddy, who is feeling the effects of the cancer. As the others rush to tend to Big Daddy, Brick and Maggie are left alone. She admits that she is not pregnant, but that it is an opportune time for her to conceive. She withholds Brick's liquor until he promises to make love to her. As the curtain falls, she swears she loves him, to which Brick responds (*"smiling with charming sadness"*), "Wouldn't it be funny if that were true?"

—*Eds.*

NOTE OF EXPLANATION

Some day when time permits I would like to write a piece about the influence, its dangers and its values, of a powerful and highly imaginative director upon the development of a play, before and during production. It does have dangers, but it has them only if the playwright is excessively malleable or submissive, or the director is excessively insistent on ideas or interpretations of his own. Elia Kazan and I have enjoyed the advantages and avoided the dangers of this highly explosive relationship because of the deepest mutual respect for each other's creative function: we have worked together three times with a phenomenal absence of friction between us and each occasion has increased the trust.

If you don't want a director's influence on your play, there are two ways to avoid it, and neither is good. One way is to arrive at an absolutely final draft of your play before you let your director see it, then hand it to him saying, Here it is, take it or leave it! The other way is to select a director who is content to put your play on the stage precisely as you conceived it with no ideas of his own. I said neither is a good way, and I meant it. No living playright, that I can think of, hasn't something valuable to learn about his own work from a director so keenly perceptive as Elia Kazan. It so happened that in the case of *Streetcar*, Kazan was given a script that was completly finished. In the case of *Cat*, he was shown the first typed version of the play, and he was excited by it, but he had definite reservations about it which were concentrated in the third act. The gist of his reservations can be listed as three points: one, he felt that Big Daddy was too vivid and important a character to disappear from the play except as an offstage cry after the second act curtain; two, he felt that the character of Brick should undergo some apparent mutation as a result of the virtual vivisection that he undergoes in his interview with his father in Act II. Three, he felt that the character of Margaret, while he understood that I sympathized with her and liked her myself, should be, if possible, more clearly sympathetic to an audience.

It was only the third of these suggestions that I embraced wholeheartedly from the outset, because it so happened that Maggie the Cat had become steadily more charming to me as I worked on her characterization. I didn't want Big Daddy to reappear in Act III and I felt that the moral paralysis of Brick was a root thing in his tragedy, and to show a dramatic progression would obscure the meaning of that tragedy in him and because I don't believe that a conversation, however revelatory, ever effects so immediate a change in the heart or even conduct of a person in Brick's state of spiritual disrepair.

However, I wanted Kazan to direct the play, and though these suggestions were not made in the form of an ultimatum, I was fearful that I would lose his interest if I didn't

re-examine the script from his point of view. I did. And you will find included in this published script the new third act that resulted from his creative influence on the play. The reception of the playing-script has more than justified, in my opinion, the adjustments made to that influence. A failure reaches fewer people, and touches fewer, than does a play that succeeds.

It may be that *Cat* number one would have done just as well, or nearly, as *Cat* number two; it's an interesting question.

TENNESSEE WILLIAMS

ACT III

As played in New York Production
Big Daddy is seen leaving as at the end of Act II.

BIG DADDY (*shouts, as he goes out DR on gallery*). ALL—LYIN'—DYIN'—LIARS! LIARS! LIARS!

(*After Big Daddy has gone, Margaret enters from DR on gallery, into room through DS door. She X to Brick at LC.*)

MARGARET. Brick, what in the name of God was goin' on in this room?

(*Dixie and Trixie rush through the room from the hall, L to gallery R, brandishing cap pistols, which they fire repeatedly, as they shout: "Bang! Bang! Bang!" Mae appears from DR gallery entrance, and turns the children back UL, along gallery. At the same moment, Gooper, Reverend Tooker and Dr. Baugh enter from L in the hall.*)

MAE. Dixie! You quit that! Gooper, will y'please git these kiddies t'baid? Right now?

(*Gooper and Reverend Tooker X along upper gallery. Dr. Baugh holds, UC, near hall door. Reverend Tooker X to Mae near section of gallery just outside doors, R.*)

GOOPER (*urging the children along*). Mae—you seen Big Mama?

MAE. Not yet.

(*Dixie and Trixie vanish through hall, L.*)

REVEREND TOOKER (*to Mae*). Those kiddies are so full of vitality, I think I'll have to be startin' back to town.

(*Margaret turns to watch and listen.*)

MAE. Not yet, Preacher. You know we regard you as a member of this fam'ly, one of our closest an' dearest, so you just got t'be with us when Doc Baugh gives Big Mama th' actual truth about th' report from th' clinic. (*Calls through door.*) Has Big Daddy gone to bed, Brick?

(*Gooper has gone out DR at the beginning of the exchange between Mae and Reverend Tooker.*)

MARGARET (*replying to Mae*). Yes, he's gone to bed. (*To Brick.*) Why'd Big Daddy shout "liars"?

GOOPER (*off DR*). Mae!

(*Mae exits DR. Reverend Tooker drifts along upper gallery*).

BRICK. I didn't lie to Big Daddy. I've lied to nobody, nobody but myself, just lied to myself. The time has come to put me in Rainbow Hill, put me in Rainbow Hill, Maggie, I ought to go there.

MARGARET. Over my dead body! (*Brick starts R. She holds him.*) Where do you think you're goin'?

(*Mae enters from DR on gallery, X to Reverend Tooker, who comes to meet her.*)

BRICK (*X below to C*). Out for some air, I want air—

GOOPER (*entering from DR to Mae, on gallery*). Now, where is that old lady?

MAE. Cantcha find her, Gooper?

(*Reverend Tooker goes out DR.*)

GOOPER (*X to Doc above hall door*). She's avoidin' this talk.

MAE. I think she senses somethin'.

GOOPER (*calls off L*). Sookey! Go find Big Mama an' tell her Doc Baugh an' the Preacher've got to go soon.

MAE. Don't let Big Daddy hear yuh! (*Brings Dr. Baugh to R on gallery.*)

REVEREND TOOKER (*off DR, calls*). Big Mama.

SOOKEY AND DAISY (*running from L to R in lawn, calling*) Miss Ida! Miss Ida! (*They go out UR.*)

GOOPER (*calling off upper gallery*). Lacey, you look downstairs for Big Mama!

MARGARET. Brick, they're going to tell Big Mama the truth now, an' she needs you!

(*Reverend Tooker appears in lawn area, UR, X C.*)

DOCTOR BAUGH (*to Mae, on R gallery*). This is going to be painful.

MAE. Painful things can't always be avoided.

DOCTOR BAUGH. That's what I've noticed about 'em, Sister Woman.

REVEREND TOOKER (*on lawn, points off R*). I see Big mama! (*Hurries off L and reappears shortly in hall.*)

GOOPER (*hurrying into hall*). She's gone round the gall'ry to Big Daddy's room. Hey, Mama! (*Off.*) Hey, Big Mama! Come here!

MAE (*calls*). Hush, Gooper! Don't holler, go to her!

(*Gooper and Reverend Tooker now appear together in hall. Big Mama runs in from DR, carrying a glass of milk. She X past Dr. Baugh to Mae, on R gallery. Dr. Baugh turns away.*)

BIG MAMA. Here I am! What d'you all want with me?

GOOPER (*steps toward Big Mama*). Big Mama, I told you we got to have this talk.

BIG MAMA. What talk you talkin' about? I saw the light go on in Big Daddy's bedroom an' took him his glass of milk, an' he just shut the shutters right in my face. (*Steps into room through R door.*) When old couples have been together as long as me an' Big Daddy, they, they get irritable with each other just from too much—devotion! Isn't that so? (*X below wicker seat to RC area.*)

MARGARET (*X to Big Mama, embracing her*). Yes, of course it's so.

(*Brick starts out UC through hall, but sees Gooper and Reverend Tooker entering, so he hobbles through C out DS door and onto gallery.*)

BIG MAMA. I think Big Daddy was just worn out. He loves his fam'ly. He loves to have 'em around him, but it's a strain on his nerves. He wasn't himself tonight, Brick—(*XC toward Brick. Brick passes her on his way out, DS.*) Big Daddy wasn't himself, I could tell he was all worked up.

REVEREND TOOKER (*USC*). I think he's remarkable.

BIG MAMA. Yaiss! Just remarkable. (*Faces US, turns, X to bar, puts down glass of milk.*) Did you notice all the food he ate at that table? (*XR a bit.*) Why he ate like a hawss!

GOOPER (*USC*). I hope he don't regret it.

BIG MAMA (*turns US toward Gooper*). What! Why that man ate a huge piece of cawn bread with molasses on it! Helped himself twice to hoppin' john!

MARGARET (*X to Big Mama*). Big Daddy loves hoppin' john. We had a real country dinner.

BIG MAMA. Yais, he simply adores it! An' candied yams. Son—(*X to DS door, looking out at Brick. Margaret X above Big Mama to her L.*) That man put away enough food at that table to stuff a fieldhand.

GOOPER. I hope he don't have to pay for it later on.

BIG MAMA (*turns US*). What's that, Gooper?

MAE. Gooper says he hopes Big Daddy doesn't suffer tonight.

BIG MAMA (*turns to Margaret, DC*). Oh, shoot, Gooper says, Gooper says! Why should Big Daddy suffer for satisfyin' a nawmal appetite? There's nothin' wrong with that man but nerves; he's sound as a dollar! An' now he knows he is, an' that's why he ate such a supper. He had a big load off his mind, knowin' he wasn't doomed to—what—he thought he was—doomed t'—(*She wavers.*)

(*Margaret puts her arms around Big Mama.*)

GOOPER (*urging Mae forward*). MAE!

(*Mae runs forward below wicker seat. She stands below Big Mama, Margaret above Big Mama. They help her to the wicker seat. Big Mama sits. Margaret sits above her. Mae stands behind her.*)

MARGARET. Bless his ole sweet soul.

BIG MAMA. Yes—bless his heart.

BRICK (*DS on gallery, looking out front*). Hello, moon, I envy you, you cool son of a bitch.

BIG MAMA. I want Brick!

MARGARET. He just stepped out for some fresh air.

BIG MAMA. Honey! I want Brick!

MAE. Bring li'l Brother in here so we cin talk. (*Margaret rises, X through DS door to Brick on gallery.*)

BRICK (*to the moon*). I envy you—you cool son of a bitch.

MARGARET. Brick, what're you don' out here on the gall'ry, Baby?

BRICK. Admirin' an' complimentin' th' man in the moon.

(*Mae X to Dr. Baugh on R gallery. Reverend Tooker and Gooper move R UC, looking at Big Mama.*)

MARGARET (*to Brick*). Come in, Baby. They're gettin' ready to tell Big Mama the truth.

BRICK. I can't witness that thing in there.

MAE. Doc Baugh, d' you think those vitamin B_{12} injections are all they're cracked up t'be? (*Enters room to upper side, behind wicker seat.*)

DOCTOR BAUGH (*X to below wicker seat*). Well, I guess they're as good t'be stuck with as anything else. (*Looks at watch; X through to LC.*)

MARGARET (*to Brick*). Big Mama needs you!

BRICK. I can't witness that thing in there!

BIG MAMA. What's wrong here? You all have such long faces, you sit here waitin' for somethin' like a bomb—to go off.

GOOPER. We're waitin' for Brick an' Maggie to come in for this talk.

MARGARET (*X above Brick, to his R*). Brother Man an' Mae have got a trick up their sleeves, an' if you don't go in there t'help Big Mama, y'know what I'm goin' to do—?

BIG MAMA. Talk. Whispers! Whispers! (*Looks out DR.*) Brick! . . .

MARGARET (*answering Big Mama's call*). Comin', Big Mama! (*To Brick:*) I'm goin' to take every dam' bottle on this place an' pitch it off th' levee into th' river!

BIG MAMA. Never had this sort of atmosphere here before.

MAE (*sits above Big Mama on wicker seat*). Before what, Big Mama?

BIG MAMA. This occasion. What's Brick an' Maggie doin' out there now?

GOOPER (*X DC, looks out*). They seem to be havin' some little altercation.

(*Brick X toward DS step. Maggie moves R above him to portal DR. Reverend Tooker joins Dr. Baugh, LC.*)

BIG MAMA (*taking a pill from pill box on chain at her wrist*). Give me a little somethin' to wash this tablet down with. Smell of burnt fireworks always makes me sick.

(*Mae X to bar to pour glass of water. Dr. Baugh joins her. Gooper X to Reverend Tooker, LC.*)

BRICK (*to Maggie*). You're a live cat, aren't you?

MARGARET. You're dam' right I am!

BIG MAMA. Gooper, will y'please open that hall door— an' let some air circulate in this stiflin' room?

(*Gooper starts US, but is restrained by Mae who X through C with glass of water. Gooper turns to men DLC.*)

MAE (*X to Big Mama with water, sits above her*). Big Mama, I think we ought to keep that door closed till after we talk.

BIG MAMA. I swan! (*Drinks water. Washes down pill.*)

MAE. I just don't think we ought to take any chance of Big Daddy hearin' a word of this discussion.

BIG MAMA (*hands glass to Mae.*) What discussion of what? Maggie! Brick! Nothin' is goin to be said in th' house of Big Daddy Pollitt that he can't hear if he wants to!

(*Mae rises, X to bar, puts down glass, joins Gooper and the two men, LC.*)

BRICK. How long are you goin' to stand behind me, Maggie?

MARGARET. Forever, if necessary.

(*Brick X US to R gallery door.*)

BIG MAMA. *Brick!*

(*Mae rises, looks out DS, sits.*)

GOOPER. That boy's gone t'pieces—he's just gone t'pieces.

DOCTOR BAUGH. Y'know, in my day they used to have somethin' they called the Keeley cure for drinkers.

BIG MAMA. Shoot!

DOCTOR BAUGH. But nowadays, I understand they take some kind of tablets that kill their taste for the stuff.

GOOPER (*turns to Dr. Baugh*). Call 'em anti-bust tablets.

BIG MAMA. Brick don't need to take nothin'. That boy is just broken up over Skipper's death. You know how poor Skipper died. They gave him a big, big dose of that sodium amytal stuff at his home an' then they called the ambulance an' give him another big, big dose of it at th' hospital an' that an' all the alcohol in his system fo' months an' months just proved too much for his heart an' his heart quit beatin'. I'm scared of needles! I'm more scared of a needle than th' knife—

(*Brick has entered the room to behind the wicker seat. He rests his hand on Big Mama's head. Gooper has moved a bit URC, facing Big Mama.*)

BIG MAMA. Oh! Here's Brick! My precious baby!

(*Dr. Baugh X to bar, puts down drink. Brick X below Big Mama through C to bar.*)

BRICK. Take it, Gooper!

MAE (*rising.*) What?

BRICKER. Gooper knows what. Take it, Gooper!

(*Mae turns to Gooper URC. Dr. Baugh X to Reverend Tooker. Margaret, who has followed Brick US on R gallery befoe he entered the room, now enters room, to behind wicker seat.*)

BIG MAMA (*to Brick*). You just break my heart.

BRICK (*at bar*). Sorry—anyone else?

MARGARET. Brick, sit with Big Mama an' hold her hand while we talk.

BRICK. You do that, Maggie. I'm a restless cripple. I got to stay on my crutch.

(*Mae sits above Big Mama. Gooper moves in front, below, and sits on couch, facing Big Mama. Reverend Tooker closes in to RC. Dr. Baugh XDC faces upstage, smoking cigar. Margaret turns away to R doors.*)

BIG MAMA. Why're you all *surroundin'* me?—like this? Why're you all starin' at me like this an' makin' signs at each other? (*Brick hobbles out hall door and X along R gallery.*) I don't need nobody to hold my hand. Are you all crazy? Since when did Big Daddy or me need anybody—?

(*Reverend Tooker moves behind wicker seat.*)

MAE. Calm yourself, Big Mama.

BIG MAMA. Calm you'self *you'self*, Sister Woman! How could I calm myself with everyone starin' at me as if big drops of blood had broken out on m'face? What's this all about Annh! What?

GOOPER. Doc Baugh—(*Mae rises.*) Sit down, Mae—(*Mae sits.*)—Big Mama wants to know the complete truth about th' report we got today from the Ochsner Clinic!

(*Dr. Baugh buttons his coat, faces group at RC.*)

BIG MAMA. Is there somethin'—somethin' that I don't know?

DOCTOR BAUGH. Yes—well . . .

BIG MAMA (*rises*). I—want to— knowwwww! (*X to Dr. Baugh.*) Somebody must be lyin' *I want to know!*

(*Mae, Gooper, Reverend Tooker surround Big Mama.*)

MAE. Sit down, Big Mama, sit down on this sofa!

(*Brick has passed Margaret Xing DR on gallery.*)

MARGARET. Brick! Brick!

BIG MAMA. *What is it; what is it?* (*Big Mama drives Dr. Baugh a bit DLC. Others follow, surrounding Big Mama.*)

DOCTOR BAUGH. I never have seen a more thorough examination than Big Daddy Pollitt was given in all my experience at the Ochsner Clinic.

GOOPER. It's one of th' best in th' country.

MAE. It's *THE* best in th' country—bar none!

DOCTOR BAUGH. Of course they were ninety-nine and nine-tenths per cent certain before they even started.

BIG MAMA. Sure of what, sure of what, sure of what— *WHAT?*

MAE. Now, Mommy, be a brave girl!

BRICK (*on DR gallery, covers his ears, sings*). "By the light, by the light, of the silvery moon!"

GOOPER (*breaks DR. Calls out to Brick*). Shut up, Brick! (*Returns to group LC.*)

BRICK. Sorry . . . (*Continues singing.*)

DOCTOR BAUGH. But now, you see, Big Mama, they cut a piece off this growth, a specimen of the tissue, an'—

BIG MAMA. Growth? You told Big Daddy—

DOCTOR BAUGH. Now, wait—

BIG MAMA. You told me an' Big Daddy there wasn't a thing wrong with him but—

MAE. Big Mama, they always—

GOOPER. Let Doc Baugh talk, will yuh?

BIG MAMA. —little spastic condition of—

REVEREND TOOKER (*throughout all this*). Shh! Shh! Shh!

(*Big Mama breaks UC, they all follow.*)

DOCTOR BAUGH. Yes, that's what we told Big Daddy. But we had this bit of tissue run through the laboratory an' I'm sorry t'say the test was positive on it. It's malignant.

(*Pause.*)

BIG MAMA. *Cancer! Cancer!*

MAE. Now, now, Mommy—

GOOPER (*at the same time*). You had to know, Big Mama.

BIG MAMA. *Why didn't they cut it out of him? Hanh? Hannh?*

DOCTOR BAUGH. Involved too much, Big Mama, too many organs affected.

MAE. Big Mama, the liver's affected, an' so's the kidneys, both. It's gone way past what they call a—

GOOPER. —a surgical risk.

(*Big Mama gasps.*)

REVEREND TOOKER. Tch, tch, tch.

DOCTOR BAUGH. Yes, it's gone past the knife.

MAE. That's why he's turned yellow!

(*Brick stops singing, turns away UR on gallery.*)

BIG MAMA (*pushes Mae DS*). Git away from me, git away from me, Mae! (*XDSR*) I want Brick! Where's Brick! *Where's my only son?*

MAE (*a step after Big Mama*). Mama! Did she say "only" son?

GOOPER (*following Big Mama*). What does that make me?

MAE (*above Gooper*). A sober responsible man with five precious children—*six!*

BIG MAMA. I want Brick! Brick! Brick!

MARGARET (*a step to Big Mama above couch*). Mama, let *me* tell you.

BIG MAMA (*pushing her aside*). No, no, leave me alone, you're not my blood! (*She rushes onto the DS gallery.*)

GOOPER (*X to Big Mama on gallery*). Mama! I'm your son! Listen to me!

MAE. Gooper's your son, Mama, he's your first-born!

BIG MAMA. Gooper never liked Daddy!

MAE. That's not true!

REVEREND TOOKER (*UC*). I think I'd better slip away at this point. Good night, good night everybody, and God bless you all—on this place. (*Goes out through hall.*)

DOCTOR BAUGH (*XDR to above DS door*). Well, Big Mama—

BIG MAMA (*leaning against Gooper, on lower gallery*). It's all a mistake, I know it's just a bad dream.

DOCTOR BAUGH. We're gonna keep Big Daddy as comfortable as we can.

BIG MAMA. Yes, it's just a bad dream, that's all it is, it's just an awful dream.

GOOPER. In my opinion Big Daddy is havin' some pain but won't admit that he has it.

BIG MAMA. Just a dream, a bad dream.

DOCTOR BAUGH. That's what lots of 'em do, they think if they don't admit they're havin' the pain they can sort of escape th' fact of it.

(*Brick X US on R gallery. Margaret watches him from R doors.*)

GOOPER. Yes, they get sly about, get real sly about it.

MAE (*X to R of Dr. Baugh*). Gooper an' I think—

GOOPER. Shut up, Mae—Big Mama, I really do think Big Daddy should be started on morphine.

BIG MAMA (*pulling away from Gooper*) Nobody's goin' give Big Daddy morphine!

DOCTOR BAUGH. Now, Big Mama, when that pain strikes it's goin' to strike mighty hard an' Big Daddy's goin' t'need the needle to bear it.

BIG MAMA (*X to Dr. Baugh*). I tell you, nobody's goin' to give him morphine!

MAE. Big Mama, you don't want to see Big Daddy suffer, y'know y'—

DOCTOR BAUGH (*X to bar*). Well, I'm leavin' this stuff here (*Puts packet of morphine, etc., on bar.*) so if there's a sudden attack you won't have to send out for it. (*Big Mama hurries to L side bar.*)

MAE (*X C, below Dr. Baugh*). I know how to give a hypo.

BIG MAMA. Nobody's goin' to give Big Daddy morphine!

GOOPER (*X C*). Mae took a course in nursin' durin' th' war.

MARGARET. Somehow I don't think Big Daddy would want Mae t' give him a hypo.

MAE (*to Margaret*). You think he'd want *you* to do it?

DOCTOR BAUGH. Well—

GOOPER. Well, Doc Baugh is goin'—.

DOCTOR BAUGH. Yes, I got to be goin'. Well, keep your chin up, Big Mama. (*X to hall.*)

GOOPER (*as he and Mae follow Dr. Baugh into the hall. She's goin' to keep her ole chin up, aren't you, Big Mama? (*They go out L.*) Well, Doc, we sure do appreciate all you've done. I'm tellin you, we're obligated—

BIG MAMA. Margaret! (*XRC.*)

MARGARET (*meeting Big Mama in front of wicker seat*). I'm right here, Big Mama.

BIG MAMA. Margaret, you've got to cooperate with me an' big Daddy to straighten Brick out now—

GOOPER (*off L, returning with Mae*). I guess that Doctor has got a lot on his mind, but it wouldn't hurt him to act a little more human—

BIG MAMA. —because it'll break Big Daddy's heart if Brick don't pull himself together an' take hold of things here.

(*Brick XDSR on gallery.*)

MAE (*UC, overhearing*). Take hold of what things, Big Mama?

BIG MAMA (*sits in wicker chair, Margaret standing behind chair*). The place.

GOOPER (*UC*). Big Mama, you've had a shock.

MAE (*X with Gooper to Big Mama*). Yais, we've all had a shock, but—

GOOPER. Let's be realistic—

MAE. Big Daddy would not, would *never*, be foolish enough to—

GOOPER. —put this place in irresponsible hands!

BIG MAMA. Big Daddy ain't goin' t'put th' place in anybody's hands, Big Daddy is *not* goin' t'die! I want you to git that into your haids, all of you!

(*Mae sits above Big Mama, Margaret turns R to door, Gooper X L C a bit.*)

MAE. Mommy, Mommy, Big Mama, we're just as hopeful an' optimistic as you are about Big Daddy's prospects, we have faith in prayer—but nevertheless there are certain matters that have to be discussed an' dealt with, because otherwise—

GOOPER. Mae, will y'please get my briefcase out of our room?

MAE. Yes, honey. (*Rises, goes out through hall L.*)

MARGARET (*X to Brick on DS gallery*). Hear them in there? (*X back to R gallery door.*)

GOOPER (*stands above Big Mama. Leaning over her*). Big Mama, what you said just now was not at all true, an' you know it. I've always loved Big Daddy in my own quiet way. I never made a show of it. I know that Big Daddy has always been fond of me in a quiet way, too.

(*Margaret drifts UR on gallery. Mae returns, X to Gooper's L with briefcase.*)

MAE. Here's your briefcase, Gooper, honey. (*Hands it to him.*)

GOOPER (*hands briefcase back to Mae*). Thank you. Of ca'use, my relationship with Big Daddy is different from Brick's.

MAE. You're eight years older'n Brick an' always had t'carry a bigger load of th' responsibilities than Brick ever had t'carry; he never carried a thing in his life but a football or a highball.

GOOPER. Mae, will y'let me talk, please?

MAE. Yes, honey.

GOOPER. Now a twenty-eight thousand acre plantation's a mighty big thing t'run.

MAE. Almost single-handed!

BIG MAMA. You never had t'run this place, Brother Man, what're you talkin' about, as if Big Daddy was dead an' in his grave, you had to run it? Why, you just had t'help him out with a few business details an' had your law practice at the same time in Memphis.

MAE. Oh, Mommy, Mommy, Mommy! Let's be fair! Why, Gooper has given himself body an' soul t'keepin' this place up fo' the past five years since Big Daddy's health started fallin'. Gooper won't say it. Gooper never thought of it as a duty, he just did it. An' what did Brick do? Brick kep' livin' in his past glory at college!

(*Gooper places a restraining hand on Mae's leg; Margaret drifts DS in gallery.*)

GOOPER. Still a football player at twenty-seven!

MARGARET (*bursts into UR door*). Who are you talkin' about now? Brick? A football player? He isn't a football player an' you know it! Brick is a sports announcer on TV an' one of the best-known ones in the country!

MAE (*breaks UC*). I'm talkin' about what he was!

MARGARET (*X to above lower gallery door*). Well, I wish you would just stop talkin' about my husband!

GOOPER (*X to above Margaret*). Listen, Margaret, I've got a right to discuss my own brother with other members of my own fam'ly, which don't include *you*! (*Pokes finger at her; she slaps his finger away.*) Now, why don't you go on out there an' drink with Brick?

MARGARET. I've never seen such malice toward a brother.

GOOPER. How about his for me? Why he can't stand to be in the same room with me!

BRICK (*on lower gallery*). That's the truth!

MARGARET. This is a delibrate campaign of vilification for the most disgusting and sordid reason on earth, and I know what it is! *It's avarice, avarice, greed, greed!*

BIG MAMA. Oh, I'll scream, I will scream in a moment unless this stops! Margaret, child, come here, sit next to Big Mama.

MARGARET (*X to Big Mama, sits above her*). Precious Mommy. (*Gooper X to bar.*)

MAE. How beautiful, how touchin' this display of devotion! Do you know why she's childless? She's childless because that big, beautiful athlete husband of hers won't go to bed with her, that's why! (*X to L of bed, looks at Gooper.*)

GOOPER. You just won't let me do this the nice way, will yuh? Aw right—(*X to above wicker seat.*) I don't give a goddam if Big Daddy likes me or don't like me or did or never did or will or will never! I'm just appealin' to a sense of common decency an' fair play! I'm tellin' you th' truth—(*X DS through lower door to Brick on DR gallery*). I've resented Big Daddy's partiality to Brick ever since th' goddam day you were born, son, an' th' way I've been treated, like I was just barely good enough to spit on, an' sometimes not even good enough for that. (*X back through room to above wicker seat.*) Big Daddy is dyin' of cancer an' it's spread all through him an' it's attacked all his vital organs includin' the kidneys an' right now he is sinkin' into uremia, an' you all know what uremia is, it's poisonin' of the whole system due to th' failure of th' body to eliminate its poisons.

MARGARET. Poisons, poisons, venomous thoughts and words! In hearts and minds! That's poisons!

GOOPER. I'm askin' for a square deal an' by God I expect to get one. But if I don't get one, if there's any peculiar shenanigans goin' on around here behind my back, well I'm not a corporation lawyer for nothin! (*XDS toward lower gallery door, on apex.*) I know how to protect my own interests. (*Rumble of distant thunder.*)

BRICK (*entering the room through DS door*). Storm comin' up.

GOOPER. Oh, a late arrival!

MAE (*X through C to below bar, LCO*). Behold, the conquerin' hero comes!

GOOPER (*X through C to bar, following Brick, imitating his limp*).The fabulous Brick Pollitt! Remember him? Who could forget him?

MAE. He looks like he's been injured in a game!

GOOPER. Yep, I'm afraid you'll have to warm th' bench at the Sugar Bowl this year, Brick! Or was it the Rose Bowl that he made his famous run in. (*Another rumble of thunder, sound of wind rising.*)

MAE (*X to L of Brick, who has reached the bar*). The punch bowl, honey, it was the punch bowl, the cut-glass punch bowl!

GOOPER. That's right! I'm always gettin' the boy's *bowls* mixed up! (*Pats Brick on the butt.*)

MARGARET (*rushes at Gooper, striking him*). Stop that! You stop that!

(*Thunder. Mae X toward Margaret from L of Gooper, flails at Margaret; Gooper keeps the women apart. Lacey runs through the US lawn area in a raincoat.*)

DAISY AND SOOKEY (*off UL*). Storm! Storm comin! Storm! Storm!

LACEY (*running out UR*). Brightie, close them shutters!

GOOPER (*X onto R gallery, calls after Lacey*). Lacey, put the top up on my Cadillac, will yuh?

LACEY (*off R*). Yes, sur, Mistah Pollitt!

GOOPER (*X to above Big Mama*). Big Mama, you know it's goin' to be necessary for me t' go back to Memphis in th' mornin' t'represent the Paker estate in a lawsuit.

(*Mae sits on L side bed, arranges papers she removes from brief case.*)

BIG MAMA. Is it, Gooper?

MAE. Yaiss.

GOOPER. That's why I'm forced to—to bring up a problem that—

MAE. Somethin' that's too important t' be put off!

GOOPER. If Brick was sober, he ought to be in on this. I think he ought to be present when I present this plan.

MARGARET (*UC*). Brick is present, we're present!

GOOPER. Well, good. I will now give you this outline my patner, Tom Bullit, an' me have drawn up—a sort of dummy—trusteeship!

MARGARET. Oh, that's it! You'll be in charge an' dole out remittances, will you?

GOOPER. This we did as soon as we got the report on Big Daddy from th' Ochsner Laboratories. We did this thing, I mean we drew up this dummy outline with the advice and assistance of the Chairman of the Boa'd of Directors of th' Southern Plantuhs Bank and Trust Company in Memphis, C. C. Bellowes, a man who handles estates for all th' prominent families in West Tennessee an th' Delta!

BIG MAMA. Gooper?

GOOPER (*X behind seat to below Big Mama*). Now this is not—not final, or anything like it, this is just a preliminary outline. But it does provide a—basis—a design—a—possible, feasible—plan! (*He waves papers Mae has thrust into his hand, US.*)

MARGARET (*XDL*). Yes, I'll bet it's a plan! (*Thunder rolls. Interior lighting dims.*)

MAE. It's a plan to protect the biggest estate in the Delta from irresponsibility an'—

BIG MAMA. Now you listen to me, all of you, you listen here! They's not goin' to be no more catty talk in my house! And Gooper, you put that away before I grab it out of your hand and tear it right up! I don't know what the hell's in it, and I don't want to know what the hell's in it. I'm talkin' in Big Daddy's language now, I'm his *wife*, not his *widow*, I'm still his *wife*! And I'm talkin' to you in his language an'—

GOOPER. Big Mama, what I have here is—

MAE. Gooper explained that it's just a plan. . . .

BIG MAMA. I don't care what you got there, just put it back where it come from an' don't let me see it again, not even the outside of the envelope of it! Is that understood? Basis! Plan! Preliminary! Design!—I say—what is it that Big Daddy always says when he's disgusted? (*Storm clouds race across sky.*)

BRICK (*from bar*). Big Daddy says "crap" when he is disgusted.

BIG MAMA (*rising*). That's right—CRAPPPP! I say CRAP too, like Big Daddy!

(*Thunder rolls.*)

MAE. Coarse language don't seem called for in this—
GOOPER. Somethin' in me is *deeply outraged* by this.
BIG MAMA. *Nobody's goin' to do nothin'!* till Big Daddy lets go of it, and maybe just possibly not—not even then! No, not even then!

(*Thunder clap. Glass crash, off L. Off UR, children commence crying. Many storm sounds, L and R: barnyard animals in terror, papers crackling, shutters rattling. Sookey and Daisy hurry from L to R in lawn area. Inexplicably, Daisy hits together two leather pillows. They cry, "Storm! Storm!" Sookey waves a piece of wrapping paper to cover lawn furniture. Mae exits to hall and upper gallery. Strange man runs across lawn, R to L. Thunder rolls repeatedly.*)

MAE. Sookey, hurry up an' git that po'ch fu'niture cov-ahed; want th' paint to come off? (*Starts DR on gallery. Gooper runs through hall to R gallery.*)
GOOPER (*yells to Lacey, who appears from R*). Lacey, put mah car away!
LACEY. Cain't, Mistah Pollitt, you got the keys! (*Exit US.*)
GOOPER. Naw, you got 'em, man. (*Exit DR. Reappears UR, calls to Mae.*) Where th' keys to th' car, honey? (*Runs C.*)
MAE (*DR on gallery*). You got 'em in your pocket! (*Exit DR. Gooper exits UR. Dog howls. Daisy and Sookey sing off UR to comfort children. Mae is heard placating the children. Storm fades away. During the storm, Margaret X and sits on couch, DR. Big Mama X DC.*)
BIG MAMA. BRICK! Come here, Brick, I need you.

(*Thunder distantly. Children whimper, off L Mae consoles them. Brick X to R of Big Mama.*)

BIG MAMA. Tonight Brick looks like he used to look when he was a little boy just like he did when he played wild games in the orchard back of the house and used to come home when I hollered myself hoarse for him! all—sweaty—and pink-cheeked—an' sleepy with his curls shinin'—(*Thunder distantly. Children whimper, off L. Mae consoles them. Dog howls, off.*) Time goes by so fast. Nothin' can outrun it. Death commences too early—almost before you're half-acquainted with life—you meet with the other. Oh, you know we just got to love each other, an' stay togther all of us just as close as we can, specially now that such a *black* thing has come and moved into this place without invita-tion. (*Dog howls, off.*) Oh, Brick, son of Big Daddy, Big Daddy does so love you. Y'know what would be his fondest dream come true? If before he passed on, if Big Daddy has to pass on . . . (*Dog howls, off.*) You

give him a child of yours, a grandson as much like his son as his son is like Big Daddy. . . .
MARGARET. I know that's Big Daddy's dream.
BIG MAMA. That's his dream.
BIG DADDY (*off DR on gallery*). Looks like the wind was takin' liberties with this place.

(*Lacey appears UL, X to UC in lawn area: Brightie and Small appear UR on lawn. Big Daddy X onto the UR gallery.*)

LACEY. Evenin', Mr. Pollitt.
BRIGHTIE AND SMALL. Evenin', Cap'n. Hello, Cap'n.
MARGARET (*X to R door*). Big Daddy's on the gall'ry.
BIG DADDY. Stawm crossed th' river, Lacey?
LACEY. Gone to Arkansas, Cap'n.

(*Big Mama has turned toward the hall door at the sound of Big Daddy's voice on the gallery. Now she X's DSR and out the DS door onto the gallery.*)

BIG MAMA. I can't stay here. He'll see somethin' in my eyes.
BIG DADDY (*on upper gallery, to the boys*). Stawm done any damage around here?
BRIGHTIE. Took the po'ch off ole Aunt Crawley's house.
BIG DADDY. Ole Aunt Crawley should of been settin' on it. It's time fo' th' wind to blow that ole girl away! (*Field-hands laugh, exit, UR. Big Daddy enters room, UC, hall door.*) Can I come in? (*Puts his cigar in ash tray on bar. Mae and Gooper hurry along the upper gallery and stand behind Big Daddy in hall door.*)
MARGARET. Did the storm wake you up, Big Daddy?
BIG DADDY. Which stawm are you talkin' about—th' one outside or th' hullaballoo in here? (*Gooper squeezes past Big Daddy.*)
GOOPER (*X toward bed, where legal papers are strewn*). 'Scuse me, sir . . . (*Mae tries to squeeze past Big Daddy to join Gooper, but Big Daddy puts his arm firmly around her.*)
BIG DADDY. I heard some mighty loud talk. Sounded like somethin' important was bein' discussed. What was the pow-wow about?
MAE (*flustered*). Why—nothin', Big Daddy . . .
BIG DADDY (*XDLC, taking Mae with him*). What is that pregnant-lookin' envelope you're puttin' back in your briefcase, Gooper?
GOOPER (*at foot of bed, caught, as he stuffs papers into enve-lope*).That? Nothin', suh—nothin' much of anythin' at all . . .
BIG DADDY. Nothin'? It looks like a whole lot of nothing! (*Turns US to group.*) You all know th' story about th' young married couple—

GOOPER. Yes, sir!

BIG DADDY. Hello, Brick—

BRICK. Hello, Big Daddy.

(The group is arranged in a semi-circle above Big Daddy, Margaret at the extreme R, then Mae and Gooper, then Big Mama, with Brick at L.)

BIG DADDY. Young married couple took Junior out to th' zoo one Sunday, inspected all of God's creatures in their cages, with satisfaction.

GOOPER. Satisfaction.

BIG DADDY (*XUSC, face front*). This afternoon was a warm afternoon in spring an' that ole elephant had somethin' else on his mind which was bigger'n peanuts. You know this story, Brick? (*Gooper nods.*)

BRICK. No, sir, I don't know it.

BIG DADDY. Y'see, in th' cage adjoinin' they was a young female elephant in heat!

BIG MAMA (*at Big Daddy's shoulder*). Oh, Big Daddy!

BIG DADDY. What's the matter, preacher's gone, ain't he? All right. That female elephant in the next cage was permeatin' the atmosphere about her with a powerful and excitin' odor of female fertility! Huh! Ain't that a nice way to put it, Brick?

BRICK. Yes, sir, nothin' wrong with it.

BIG MAMA. Oh, Big Daddy!

BIG DADDY (*XDSC*). So this ole bull elephant still had a couple of fornications left in him. He reared back his trunk an' got a whiff of that elephant lady next door!—began to paw at the dirt in his cage an' butt his head against the separatin' partition and, first thing y'know, there was a conspicuous change in his *profile*—very *conspicuous*! Ain't I tellin' this story in decent language, Brick?

BRICK. Yes, sir, too ruttin' decent!

BIG DADDY. So, the little boy pointed at it and said, "What's that?" His Mam said, "Oh, that's— nothin'!"—His Papa said, "She's spoiled!"

(Field-hands sing off R, featuring Sookey: "I Just Can't Stay Here by Myself," through following scene. Big Daddy X to Brick at L.)

BIG DADDY. You didn't laugh at that story, Brick.

(Big Mama X DRC crying. Margaret goes to her. Mae and Gooper hold URC.)

BRICK. No, sir, I didn't laugh at that story.

(On the lower gallery, Big Mama sobs. Big Daddy looks toward her.)

BIG DADDY. What's wrong with that long, thin woman over there, loaded with diamonds? Hey, what's-your- name, what's the matter with you?

MARGARET (*X toward Big Daddy*). She had a slight dizzy spell, Big Daddy.

BIG DADDY (*ULC*). You better watch that, Big Mama. A stroke is a bad way to go.

MARGARET (*X to Big Daddy at C*). Oh, Brick, Big Daddy has on your birthday present to him, Brick, he has on your cashmere robe, the softest material I have ever felt.

BIG DADDY. Yeah, this is my soft birthday, Maggie. . . . Not my gold or my silver birthday, but my soft birth- day, everything's got to be soft for Big Daddy on this soft birthday.

(Maggie kneels before Big Daddy C. As Gooper and Mae speak, Big Mama X USRC in front of them, hushing them with a gesture.)

GOOPER. Maggie, I hate to make such a crude observation, but there is somethin' a little indecent about your—

MAE. Like a slow-motion football tackle—

MARGARET. Big Daddy's got on his Chinese slippers that I gave him, Brick. Big Daddy, I haven't given you my big present yet, but now I will, now's the time for me to present it to you! I have an announcement to make!

MAE. What? What kind of annoucement?

GOOPER. A sports announcement, Maggie?

MARGARET. Announcement of life beginning! A child is coming, sired by Brick, and out of Maggie the Cat! I have Brick's child in my body, an' that's my birthday present to Big Daddy on this birthday! (*Big Daddy looks at Brick who X behind Big Daddy to DLS portal, L.*)

BIG DADDY. Get up, girl, get up off your knees, girl. (*Big Daddy helps Margaret rise. He X above her, to her R, bites off the end of a fresh cigar, taken from his bathrobe pocket, as he studies Margaret.*) Uh-huh, this girl has life in her body, that's no lie!

BIG MAMA. BIG DADDY'S DREAM COME TRUE!

BRICK. *JESUS!*

BIG DADDY (*XR below wicker seat*). Gooper, I want my lawyer in the mornin'.

BRICK. Where are you goin', Big Daddy?

BIG DADDY. Son, I'm goin' up on the roof to the belvedere on th' roof to look over my kingdom before I give up my kingdom—twenty-eight thousand acres of th' richest land this side of the Valley Nile! (*Exit through R doors, and DR on gallery.*)

BIG MAMA (*following*). Sweetheart, sweetheart, sweet- heart—can I come with you? (*Exits DR. Margaret is DSC in mirror area.*)

GOOPER (*X to bar.*) Brick, could you possibly spare me one small shot of that liquor?

BRICK (*DLC*). Why, help yourself, Gooper boy.

GOOPER. I will.

MAE (*X forward*). Of course we know that this is a lie!

GOOPER (*drinks*). Be still, Mae!

MAE (*X to Gooper at bar*). I won't be still! I know she's made this up!

GOOPER. God damn it, I said to shut up!

MAE. That woman isn't pregnant!

GOOPER. Who said she was?

MAE. She did!

GOOPER. The doctor didn't. Doc Baugh didn't.

MARGARET (*X R to above couch*). I haven't gone to Doc Baugh.

GOOPER (*X through to L of Margaret*). Then who'd you go to, Maggie? (*Offstage song finishes.*)

MARGARET. One of the best gynecologists in the South.

GOOPER. Uh-huh, I see—(*Foot on end of couch, trapping Margaret.*) May we have his name please?

MARGARET. No, you may not, Mister—Prosecutin' Attorney!

MAE (*X to R of Margaret, above*). He doesn't have any name, he doesn't exist!

MARGARET. He does so exist, and so does my baby, Brick's baby!

MAE. You can't conceive a child by a man that won't sleep with you unless you think you're—(*Forces Margaret onto couch, turns away C. Brick starts C for Mae.*) He drinks all the time to be able to tolerate you! Sleeps on the sofa to keep out of contact with you!

GOOPER (*X above Margaret, who lies face down on couch*). Don't try to kid us, Margaret—

MAE (*X to bed, L side, rumpling pillows*). How can you conceive a child by a man that won't sleep with you? How can you conceive? How can you? How can you!

GOOPER (*sharply*). MAE!

BRICK (*X below Mae to her R, takes hold of her*). Mae, sister Woman, how d'you know that I don't sleep with Maggie?

MAE. We occupy the next room an' th' wall between isn't soundproof.

BRICK. Oh . . .

MAE. We hear the nightly pleadin' and the nightly refusal. So don't imagine you're goin' t'put a trick over on us, to fool a dyin' man with—a—

BRICK. Mae, Sister Woman, not everybody makes much noise about love. Oh, I know some people are huffers an' puffers, but others are silent lovers.

GOOPER (*behind seat, R*). This talk is pointless, completely.

BRICK. How d'y'know that we're not silent lovers? Even if y'got a peep-hole drilled in the wall, how can y'tell if sometime when Gooper's got business in Memphis an' you're playin' scrabble at the country club with other ex-queens of cotton, Maggie and I don't come to some temporary agreements? How do you know that—? (*He X above wicker seat to above R end couch.*)

MAE. Brick, I never thought that you would stoop to her level, I just never dreamed that you would stoop to her level.

GOOPER. I don't think Brick will stoop to her level.

BRICK (*sits R of Margaret on couch*). What is your level? Tell me your level so I can sink or rise to it. (*Rises.*) You heard what Big Daddy said. This girl has life in her body.

MAE. That is a lie!

BRICK. No, truth is something desperate, an' she's got it. Believe me, it's somethin' desperate, an' she's got it. (*X below seat to below bar.*) An' now if you will stop actin' as if Brick Pollitt was dead an' buried, invisible, not heard, an' go on back to your peep-hole in the wall—I'm drunk, and sleepy—not as alive as Maggie, but still alive. . . . (*Pours drink, drinks.*)

GOOPER (*picks up briefcase from R foot of bed*). Come on, Mae. We'll leave these love birds together in their nest.

MAE. Yeah, nest of lice! Liars!

GOOPER. Mae—Mae, you jes' go on back to our room—

MAE. Liars! (*Exits through hall.*)

GOOPER (*DR above Margaret*). We're jest goin' to wait an' see. Time will tell. (*X to R of bar.*) Yes, sir, little brother, we're just goin' to wait an' see! (*Exit, hall. The clock strikes twelve.*)

(*Maggie and Brick exchange a look. He drinks deeply, puts his glass on the bar. Gradually, his expression changes. He utters a sharp exhalation. The exhalation is echoed by the singers, off UR, who commence vocalizing with "Gimme a Cool Drink of Water Fo' I Die," and continue till end of act.*)

MARGARET (*as she hears Brick's exhalation*). The click?

(*Brick looks toward the singers, happily, almost gratefully. He XR to bed, piks up his pillow, and starts toward head of couch, DR, Xing wicker seat. Margaret seizes the pillow from his grasp, rises, stands facing C, holding the pillow close. Brick watches her with growing admiration. She moves quickly USC, throwing pillow onto bed. She X to bar. Brick counters below wicker seat, watching her. Margaret grabs all the bottles from the bar. She goes into the hall, pitches the bottles, one after the other,*) *off the platform into the UL lawn area. Bottles break, off L. Margaret reenters the room, stands UC, facing Brick.*) Echo Spring has gone dry, and no one but me could drive you to town for more.

BRICK. Lacey will get me—
MARGARET. Lacey's been told not to!
BRICK. I could drive—
MARGARET. And you lost your driver's license! I'd phone ahead and have you stopped on the highway before you got halfway to Ruby Lightfoot's gin mill. I told a lie to Big Daddy, but we can make that lie come true. And then I'll bring you liquor, and we'll get drunk together, here, tonight, in this place that death has come into! What do you say? What do you say, baby?

BRICK (*X to L side bed*). I admire you, Maggie.

(*Brick sits on edge of bed. He looks up at the over-head light, then at Margaret. She reaches for the light, turns it out; then she kneels quickly beside Brick at foot of bed.*)

MARGARET. Oh, you weak, beautiful people who give up with such grace. What you need is someone to take hold of you—gently, with love, and hand your life back to you, like something gold you let go of—and I can! I'm determined to do it—and nothing's more determined than a cat on a tin roof—is there? Is there, baby? (*She touches his cheek, gently.*)

Curtain

COMMENTARY

Note: The following essay represents a single interpretation of the play. For other perspectives on Cat on a Hot Tin Roof, *consult the essays listed below.*

In Part I we included director Harold Clurman's thoughtful analysis of Shaw's *Heartbreak House*, another play about false fronts, which—like *Cat on a Hot Tin Roof*—is set in a venerable home presided over by a seemingly invincible patriarch (cf. Captain Shotover and Big Daddy Pollitt). Although Clurman did not direct Williams's play on Broadway as he did *Heartbreak House*, his practitioner's assessment of the drama (written as the Preface to *Tennessee Williams: Eight Plays* in 1979) crystallizes its thematic emphasis:

> In *Cat on a Hot Tin Roof*, Williams focuses on the hidden and disguised disease of our society: The avoidance of truth, the failure to face the real state of our condition—the sordid chicanery, the greed, the pseudo-religious flimflam, resistance to acknowledge natural fact, the fraudulence of our social action. It is the cancer of our civilization, the abstract counterpart of Big Daddy's fatal disease.

If Big Daddy's cancer, which most in the household refuse to acknowledge until late in the play, is the "abstract counterpart" of the mendacities that permeate this Mississippi mansion, then the central visual image—the enormous bed that dominates the stage—is its concrete essence. Importantly, Williams places the action of his play in an upstairs bed-sitting room, not, as we might expect, the family sitting room downstairs. Visually and verbally much is made of the importance of the bed and the events that have (or, in Brick's case, have not) occurred thereon. Note the history of the bed and its former occupants, the former plantation owners, Jack Straw and Peter Ochello, for whom Big Daddy once managed the 28,000-acre plantation. In the Old South, the very "buckle of the Bible Belt," it would have been unthinkable for two wealthy men, pillars of their community, to live openly in a homosexual relationship; thus those two "old sisters" survived by playing the role of genteel Southern gentlemen. And how fitting that the Pollitts, themselves consummate role-players, now infest this old house, a stage upon which they act out the roles they have created for themselves as they, too, attempt to survive in a world of "god damn lies and liars . . . and all the god damn hypocrisy" attacked by Big Daddy in his Act II tirade to Brick. In the lengthy (and poetic) stage direction in the midst of this confrontation, Williams notes that what Big Daddy calls an "unnatural" relationship between Brick and Skipper (who is never seen, yet always present) is

> . . . the inadmissible thing that Skipper died to disavow between them. The fact that it had to be disavowed to "keep face" in the world they lived in, may be at the heart of the "mendacity" that Brick drinks to kill his disgust with. . . . The bird that I hope to catch in the net of this play is not the solution of one man's psychological problems. I'm trying to catch the true quality of experience in a group of people, that cloudy, flickering, evanescent—fiercely charged!—interplay of live human beings in the thundercloud of a common crisis.

The operative phrase in this revealing stage direction is "keep face," or better yet, "putting on a face," to mask the truth. Here it may be useful to recall Clurman's analysis of Shaw's play (see Showcase in Part I), for it is no less applicable to *Cat on a Hot Tin Roof*:

> All in a sense are "crazy," not true to themselves, not what he or she seems or pretends to be. So that everyone is somehow odd, a clown-disguised, masked . . . "The trick is to find the man under the pose."
> This is the director's job as well:
> a. What is the pose?
> b. What is the man or woman under the pose?

Having read the play, you can identify the pose (e.g., Brick's drinking) assumed by each of the Pollitts, and even that of the lecherous old Reverend Tooker (there is a pun in his name!), whose very presence is, as Williams says in a stage direction, "the living embodiment of the pious, conventional lie." (In one of the play's funniest moments, the Reverend enters searching for the "gentleman's lavatory" precisely when Brick reveals the truth about the "old sisters." Williams described the entrance as "perfectly timed, but incongruous," a coy mendacity that suggests that the playwright was not above providing some comic relief during the play's most emotionally wrenching scene.)

Actors, of course, need props and a stage to enhance the illusions they create. We may consider that huge double bed a "prop," although in the final moments of Act III (either version) Maggie turns it into a stage for her finest performance: the seductress who must lure her own husband to the bed/stage to validate his masculinity and to make true the lie that she and Brick are expecting a child, an heir to Big Daddy's empire. Kazan, whom Williams adamantly wanted to direct the play despite their creative differences about the draft of the play, argued for a conspicuously theatrical staging of this manifestly naturalistic play. In his autobiography (*Elia Kazan: A Life*, 1988), the director recalls that neither he nor Mielziner saw the play as realistic: "We saw its great merit was its brilliant rhetoric and its theatricality. . . . If it were done realistically, I would have to contrive stage business to keep [Big Daddy] talking those great second-act speeches turned out front and pretend that it was just another day in the life of the Pollitt family." Kazan wanted a stage that would allow both actors and audience "to glory in the author's language."

Despite Williams's reservations, Kazan and Mielziner finally settled upon a "large, triangular platform, tipped toward the audience and holding only one piece of furniture, an ornate bed." (There were also an armchair and night table to allow for some stage business.) Mielziner's own memoir (1965) describes the finished product as "steeply raked toward the audience with one corner actually jutting out over the footlights. In its final form it turned out to be a sort of thrust stage." Kazan believed this design, as opposed to the more elaborate set described in Williams's draft, would make it impossible to act the play "realistically;" rather, it reinforced the theatricality of the script's majestic language and, as importantly, the notion that the characters—Maggie and Big Daddy in particular—were "performers." Follow-spots were also used to enhance the theatricality of the production and, of course, to further isolate the central characters as they directed their arias to the audience. Kazan believed this more fully presentational approach, one that goes back to the very origins of the theater in distant lands, "sucks the audience into the experience and emotion of that moment." Audiences agreed with Kazan's concept, for as Williams noted in his memoirs, it became "my biggest and longest-running play." And how ironic that this "naturalistic" play would help audiences rediscover the power of the truly theatrical—a lone actor speaking directly to a live audience—that had been, by and large, missing from Broadway stages for several decades.

For other perspectives on *Cat on a Hot Tin Roof*:

Cafgna, Dianne. "Blanche Du Bois and Maggie the Cat: Illusion and Reality in Tennessee Williams." In Robert A. Martin (ed.), *Critical Essays on Tennessee Williams*. New York: Prentice Hall, 1997, 119–31.

Tischler, Nancy M. "On Creating *Cat*." *Tennessee Williams Journal* 2:2 (1991–92): 9–16.

See *Cat on a Hot Tin Roof* on video:

Cat on a Hot Tin Roof. Dir. Richard Brooks. Perf. Paul Newman, Elizabeth Taylor, and Burl Ives. CBS Home Video, 180 min., 1958.

Cat on a Hot Tin Roof. Dir. Jack Hofsiss. Perf. Tommy Lee Jones and Jessica Lange. Monterey Home Video, 144 min., 1994.

Other plays by Tennessee Williams on film/video:

Eccentricities of a Nightingale. Dir. Glenn Jordan. Perf. Blythe Danner and Frank Langella. Kultur, 120 min., 1976.

The Fugitive Kind. Dir. Sidney Lumet. Perf. Marlon Brando. MGM/UA Studios, 121 min., 1960.

The Glass Menagerie. Dir. Anthony Harvey. Perf. Katherine Hepburn, Sam Waterston, and Joanna Miles. Kultur, 120 min., 1973.

The Glass Menagerie. Dir. Paul Newman. Perf. Joann Woodward, John Malkovich, and Karen Allen. MCA Home Video, 134 min., 1987.

The Night of the Iguana. Dir. John Huston. Perf. Richard Burton, Ava Gardner, and Debra Kerr. Warner Studios, 117 min., 1964.

The Rose Tatoo. Dir. Daniel Mann. Perf. Anna Magnani and Burt Lancaster. Paramount, 116 min., 1955.

A Streetcar Named Desire: The Director's Cut. Dir. Elia Kazan. Perf. Marlon Brando and Vivien Leigh. Warner Home Video, 125 min., 1951.

A Streetcar Named Desire. Dir. John Emen. Perf. Ann-Margaret, Treat Williams, and Randy Quaid. Republic Studios, 96 min., 1984.

A Streetcar Named Desire. Dir. Glenn Jordan. Perf. Jessica Lange, Alec Baldwin, and John Goodman. Twentieth Century Fox, 156 min., 1995.

Suddenly Last Summer. Dir. Joseph Mankiewicz. Perf. Elizabeth Taylor. Columbia/Tristar, 114 min., 1959.

Summer and Smoke. Dir. Peter Glenville. Perf. Laurence Harvey and Geraldine Page. Paramount Studios, 118 min., 1961.

Sweet Bird of Youth. Dir. Richard Brooks. Perf. Paul Newman. Warner Studios, 120 min., 1962.

Ten Blocks on the Camino Real. Dir. Jack Landau. Perf. Martin Sheen, Lottie Lenya, and Carrie Nye. Kultur, 69 min., 1966.

This Property Is Condemned. Dir. Sidney Pollack. Perf. Robert Redford. Paramount Studio, 109 min., 1966.

Videos about Tennessee Williams:

Tennessee Williams—Biography. A&E Insight Media, 50 min., 1998.

Tennessee Williams and the American South. Films for Humanities, 45 min., 1989.

Tennessee Williams: Orpheus on the American Stage. Films for Humanities, 97 min., 1994.

The Group Theatre and the Actors Studio

While the Provincetown Players are traditionally credited with having given birth to the modern American drama in 1915 (see related Showcase in Part I), it was the Group Theatre that brought it to its maturity. From its founding in 1931 through its dissolution ten years later, the Group Theatre not only produced many new plays and cultivated some of the country's foremost playwrights, directors, and actors, it also established an ensemble acting style that was as discernibly "American" as Stanislavsky's Moscow Art Theatre was "Russian."

The Group Theatre was actually spawned by a disciple of Stanislavsky, Richard Boleslavsky, who founded the American Laboratory Theatre in 1922. Stanislavsky's company visited New York that year and Boleslavsky remained in the United States to teach the acting system developed at the Moscow Art Theatre. Inspired by their contact with the Russians, a new generation of theater artists wanted to abandon an actor-training system based mostly on an external approach that had served American actors well as they performed melodramas in large theaters. But the New Drama that was being imported from Europe—as well as the work of Eugene O'Neill, Susan Glaspell, Elmer Rice, and other young American playwrights—demanded a more internal and realistic style.

Three young actors—Harold Clurman, Cheryl Crawford, and Lee Strasberg—who worked for the Theatre Guild (the preeminent producing agency for New York theaters in the 1920s) attended Boleslavsky's workshops and talked enthusiastically about forming a theater company that would, in Clurman's words, "give voice to the essential moral and social preoccupations of our time." They envisioned a permanent acting company (as opposed to one that hired actors for a specific production) that would create theater as a communal enterprise. They were eager to test the Stanislavsky-Boleslavsky system, particularly in the areas of improvisation, emotion memory, and exploring the "given circumstances" of a text. Clurman himself coined the term "spine" to describe the primary motivation that controlled a character's actions (cf. Stanislavsky's "superobjective").

Soon other artists joined this trio, inspired by Clurman's messianic talks backstage at the Theatre Guild. Among them were Sanford Meisner, Franchot Tone, Jules (John) Garfield, Morris Carnovsky, and Stella Adler, all of whom made significant contributions to American theater and cinema. Clurman persuaded the Theatre Guild to underwrite a production as part of its Sunday afternoon experimental program. In 1929 the young actors performed *Red Dust*, a Marxist play that would haunt ex-members of the Group twenty years later when they were called before Senator Joseph McCarthy's House Un-American Activities Committee.

For two years these artists continued to work as a unit, meeting virtually every Friday night to hear Clurman describe his vision for the theater. In 1931 Clurman told the Guild that he and his colleagues wanted to form their own production company. A $1,000 gift from the Guild enabled "the Group," as it became formally known, to spend the summer at the Brookfield Center in Connecticut. There the 30 charter members of the company worked, played, rehearsed, and experimented together under the tutelage of Strasberg, who had become the company's primary acting teacher. At night the Group gathered in the lodge where Clurman passionately delivered hours-long speeches to fuel their collective "fervor to create a new theater." Clurman's lively memoir, *The Fervent Years*, remains the best account of the Group Theatre's decade of excellence and allows us to eavesdrop on those Connecticut sessions.

In the fall of 1931 the Group returned to New York, where it opened its first official production, Paul Green's *The House of Connolly*. The Group's ensemble acting received exceptional reviews, enthusiastic audiences grew in number, and new plays by gifted dramatists such as Maxwell Anderson, Sidney Kingsley, and John Howard Lawson were quickly added to the repertory. In 1934 Stella Adler, the Group's finest actress, worked with Stanislavsky for five weeks in Paris and returned to the company to revitalize its work. Looking back on this experience, Adler recalled, "My return from work with Stanislavsky was the most important moment in the Group's work [because] the actors for the first time understood what Stanislavsky really meant and they applied it to their work."

In January 1935 the Group produced *Waiting for Lefty*, an agitprop drama about a recent taxi drivers' strike in New York. It was written by Clifford Odets, a quiet young actor who had been on the fringe of the Group for several years. The play was a defining moment not only for the Group Theatre but also for the political drama of the Depression era. One of the actors in *Waiting for Lefty* was Elia Kazan, who would later direct the Broadway productions (and then the films) of Tennessee Williams's *A Streetcar Named Desire* and Arthur Miller's *Death of a Salesman*. The following year the Group produced Odets's *Awake and Sing*, arguably the finest play in the Group's ten-year history. The play, about a Jewish family struggling to survive during the Great Depression, provided the Group—indeed, the generation of the 1930s—with its motto: "Life shouldn't be printed on dollar bills."

The Group continued to produce important plays, including Odets's *Golden Boy* (1937) and William Saroyan's *My Heart Is in the Highlands* (1938), still staples of American drama. In a nod toward its Russian heritage, it also produced the work of Chekhov. In ten years the Group produced 25 plays, many by Odets, the company's premiere playwright. More importantly, the Group set a standard for acting, particularly as an ensemble, unseen before in the history of the American theater.

The Group dissolved in the winter of 1940–41, partly because of the success of its members in film and the commercial theater. Unfortunately, there was dissension among the company. In 1937 Crawford and Strasberg resigned, and Clurman was left to rally the remaining members of the company. Adler recalls that the company was plagued by "[T]rouble. Conflict. Lack of peace and quiet . . . struggle" during its ten-year history. Carnovsky explains some of the reasons for the conflict: "We were ruthless in tearing ourselves apart in order to build ourselves up again." Much of the dissension was aimed at Strasberg, whose teaching methods and—in the minds of some Group actors—misapplication of Stanislavsky's principles (particularly with regard to emotion memory) were challenged. The controversy would continue to plague Strasberg at the Actors Studio in the 1950s.

The Studio was founded in 1947 when Group Theatre alumni Crawford, Kazan, and Robert Lewis sought to revive the actor training developed by the Group. (Note that Strasberg, whose name is most associated with the Studio, was not a founding member; he became a teacher in 1948 and the artistic director in 1951.) Fittingly, the first meeting—October 5, 1947—of the 85 charter members of the Studio took place in the same building where Boleslavsky taught the Stanislavsky System a quarter-century earlier. Significantly, Tennessee Williams and Arthur Miller were also present at the inaugural meeting. The fundamental premise of the Studio was that actors would perform short scenes that would be criticized by their peers, under the supervision of master teachers such as Strasberg, Meisner, Lewis, and Kazan. The Studio was not a school or training academy (although it now offers training and issues degrees) but a place where professional actors could show their work to their peers and receive constructive criticism. The Studio became a place where new plays were cultivated (e.g.,

Williams's *Ten Blocks on the Camino Real*) and directors could test their skills by working with young actors.

While actors at the Studio employed elements of Stanislavsky's System, they soon became known as "Method" actors because they were grounded in the style of the defunct Group Theatre, which had been trained by Strasberg, who explained the difference between the System and his Method:

I do not believe that anyone but Stanislavsky himself has the right to talk of the Stanislavsky System. I have therefore stressed the use of the word "Method" as against "System" to suggest that while we [the Studio] obviously are influenced by Stanislavsky's ideas and practices, we used it within the limitations of our own knowledge and experience. . . . We emphasized elements that he had not emphasized and disregarded elements which he might have considered of greater importance. . . . I therefore feel it both theoretically wise and practically sound to talk of the work done by the Group Theatre and the Actors Studio as being "An Adaptation of the Stanislavsky System." The "Method" is therefore our version of the System.

Rightly or wrongly, "emotion memory"—through which actors draw upon personal experiences—is usually regarded as the cornerstone of the Method. Among the chief criticisms aimed at Strasberg's teaching and Method actors is that they relied heavily (too heavily?) on psychological soul searching, which often produced idiosyncratic "private moments" on stage at the expense of the fundamental techniques of good diction, projection, and physical control. Marlon Brando's much discussed and influential performance as Stanley Kowalski in both the stage and film versions of *A Streetcar Named Desire* has often been cited as the exemplar of the Method's excesses. Some even refer to it as "the scratch-and-mumble" school of acting. The criticism is not entirely fair, as Strasberg and others at the Studio in fact emphasized both external

technique (voice, diction, movement) and internal analysis.

The Studio, thanks largely to the notoriety it achieved with *A Streetcar Named Desire* (which actually opened several weeks before the Studio was formed), soon became America's foremost training ground for actors, and it solidified the so-called "American style" of realism that yet dominates film acting. Studio alumni are among the most respected actors in American theater, film, and television:

Anne Bancroft, Marlon Brando, Ellen Burstyn, James Dean, Robert DiNero, Robert Duval, Gene Hackman, Dustin Hoffman, Harvey Keitel, Steve McQueen, Marilyn Monroe (who did her best work under Strasberg's tutelage), Paul Newman, Patricia Neal, Jack Nicholson, Carroll O'Connor, Al Pacino, Sidney Poitier, Jerome Robbins (the acclaimed choreographer), Eli Wallach, Gene Wilder, Shelley Winters, and Joanne Woodward

Barbara Streisand was briefly a member of the Studio; she performed in only one scene—as Juliet in Shakespeare's *Romeo and Juliet*. Duval, Hackman, and Hoffman actually roomed together while attending the Studio.

In truth, however, the Studio's legacy was begun almost twenty years earlier when Clurman exhorted the founding members of the Group Theatre to develop their craft and to accept the responsibility to use the theater as an instrument of social change: ". . . craft is very important; without craft nothing can be accomplished. But what are we going to say with our craft? What's it going to be for? How are we going to contribute to our society, to our audience? What are we going to tell them? There are things that should be said." Today the Actors Studio is still a vital part of American theater and film; it is located at 432 West 44th Street, appropriately in the heart of the Broadway theater district. There is an excellent video on the history of the Studio ("Miracle on 44th Street"), hosted by Studio alums Paul Newman and Joanne Woodward (American Masters, 1991).

THE BIRTHDAY PARTY
HAROLD PINTER

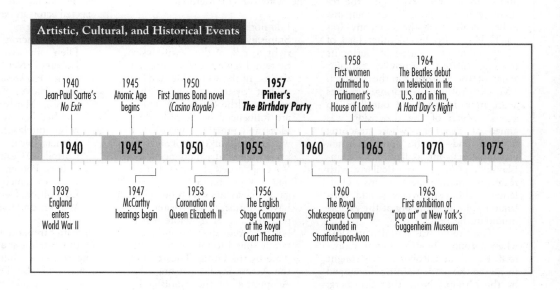

Artistic, Cultural, and Historical Events

| 1940 | 1945 | 1950 | 1955 | 1960 | 1965 | 1970 | 1975 |

Above timeline:
- **1940** Jean-Paul Sartre's *No Exit*
- **1945** Atomic Age begins
- **1950** First James Bond novel (*Casino Royale*)
- **1957** Pinter's *The Birthday Party*
- **1958** First women admitted to Parliament's House of Lords
- **1964** The Beatles debut on television in the U.S. and in film, *A Hard Day's Night*

Below timeline:
- **1939** England enters World War II
- **1947** McCarthy hearings begin
- **1953** Coronation of Queen Elizabeth II
- **1956** The English Stage Company at the Royal Court Theatre
- **1960** The Royal Shakespeare Company founded in Stratford-upon-Avon
- **1963** First exhibition of "pop art" at New York's Guggenheim Museum

HAROLD PINTER (1933–)

As a writer for both stage and screen, Harold Pinter is among the most prolific dramatists of the post–World War II era. Subsequently he has inspired numerous young writers who have imitated his cryptic style, as well as his message that no one is safe from the terrors of the unknown in this nuclear age. Furthermore, few playwrights better illustrate the modern notion that truth is relative, that each of us constructs our version of "the truth" to fit our needs.

Pinter was born in the tough East End of London, the son of Portuguese Jews who Anglicized their name (Da Pinta) to protect themselves from anti-Semitic prejudices. His status as an outsider in British society provided him with subject matter for his dramas. After high school, where he acted and wrote poetry, Pinter enrolled in London's Royal Academy of Dramatic Art (RADA) where he was introduced to classical acting and Stanislavsky's System. The latter influenced Pinter's playwriting, particularly in its emphasis on subtext. A Pinter play is virtually all subtext as his characters desperately hide behind a cloud of words to protect themselves from malevolent forces they cannot understand. Feigning a nervous breakdown, Pinter left RADA, however, because he was terrified that he could not compete with his more sophisticated peers. Pinter then ran afoul of the British government when he refused to enter military service because he was a conscientious objector; subsequently, he was fined and reprimanded for his pacifist sentiments. Two short plays, "One for the Road" (1984) and "Mountain Language" (1985), evidence his long-standing hostility toward governments, and he remains a human rights activist and spokesman for humanitarian causes. Though his earlier plays do not seem political, Pinter has admitted that his works have always been indictments of oppression.

Pinter eventually attended the Central School of Speech and Drama, where he became further acquainted with Stanislavsky's theories. He also was influenced by Rudolf Laban, the respected dance and mime teacher. Building on the legacy of Chekhov and Beckett, Pinter writes plays noted for their "pauses" and "silences," and he relies on the actor's body language and subtlety of gesture. For example, *The Birthday Party* requires that the actor playing Stanley rely on discreet physical reactions in response to the brutal verbal assaults by Goldberg and McCann.

Pinter first worked professionally in the theater as an actor, touring Ireland with Anew McMaster's company. Under the name of David Baron, he also acted in British films, many of which were of the gangster variety. These, too, provided Pinter with material for his plays, especially in the manner in which characters use words as weapons in their assault on one another. His scripts are rife with threatening innuendoes and the possibility of explosive violence. One other influence bears mention: Pinter was—like so many of his generation—captivated by Franz Kafka's novel *The Trial* (1925), in which a young man is inexplicably arrested for no apparent crime, subjected to psychological terrors by his interrogators, and sentenced at a mock trial that is designed to humiliate him. The novel was Kafka's metaphor for the uncertainty of a modern world in which nothing, particularly the truth, is verifiable. It is clearly an inspiration for *The Birthday Party*.

Like Samuel Beckett, Pinter depicts the absurdity and virtual hopelessness of modern life, although he sets his plays in a more recognizable world. Though his plays have the patina of Naturalism in both setting and speech, they avoid the strict logic of Realism. To convey the "unknown" (which is always the villain of a Pinter play), the playwright rarely provides exposition about situation or characters, and he customarily refuses to script denouements that neatly resolve his conflicts. Like the absurdist playwrights with whom he is aligned, he places the burden of meaning squarely on the audience. Pinter has, in fact, quite coyly said that even he does not always understand his characters's motivations or the strange twists of plot. Generically, his plays are often referred to as "the theater of menace" because there invariably exists a threat that both the characters and audience do not quite fathom. Characteristically, his plays are quite funny—at least at the outset—but they gradually give way to silent terrors. His skillful use of silence has ingrained the term "the Pinter pause" in the postmodern theater's lexicon. In a 1962 essay, "Writing for the Theatre," Pinter explains his fascination with silence in the theater:

> So often, below the word spoken, is the thing unknown and unspoken . . . a language where under what is said, another thing is being said. It is in the silence that my characters are most evident to me. There are two silences. One when no word is spoken. The other when perhaps a torrent of language is being employed. The speech is an indication of that which we don't hear. It is a necessary avoidance, a violent, sly, anguished or mocking smoke screen which keeps the other in its place. . . . One way of looking at speech is to say that it is a constant stratagem to cover nakedness.

Pinter's best-known works include the one-acts "The Room" (1957), "The Dumb Waiter" (1957), "The Dwarfs" (1961), "The Collection" (1962), "One for the Road" (1984), and "Mountain Language" (1985). His full-length plays include *The Birthday Party* (1957), *The Caretaker* (1960), *The Homecoming* (1965), *No Man's Land* (1970), *Old Times* (1971), *Betrayal* (1977), and *Moonlight* (1994). Pinter's many screenplays include *The Pumpkin Eater*, *The Servant*, *The French Lieutenant's Woman*, and *The Turtle Diaries*. Pinter also directs his own work and that of other playwrights; when Great Britain opened its National Theatre in 1976, Pinter directed Noel Coward's *Blithe Spirit* to inaugurate the Lyttleton Theatre.

AS YOU READ *THE BIRTHDAY PARTY*

Typically a Pinter play such as *The Birthday Party* uses the recurring motif in which a "room" is invaded by an outside force about which the insiders know little (an early work was simply titled *The Room*). The action proceeds through a series of ambiguous conversations in which the invader attempts to uncover a hidden truth about the victim, while the victim struggles against being "found out." Like Josef K in Kafka's *The Trial*, victims rarely know why they are being scrutinized, but there is always the nagging insinuation (induced by a latent guilt for some past transgression?) that they must protect themselves at all costs. Frequently, the victims uncover some hidden truth about the invader, which only increases the precariousness of their dilemma. Pinter's plays most often end without the secret being revealed, and the audience is left to assign "truth" to the situation—although Pinter's plays seem to suggest that "truth" is unverifiable in our absurd and dangerous world. As you read *The Birthday Party*, don't be alarmed by the many ambiguities; they are very much part of the "fun" in this theater of menace.

THE BIRTHDAY PARTY

HAROLD PINTER

CHARACTERS

PETEY, *a man in his sixties*
MEG, *a woman in her sixties*
STANLEY, *a man in his late thirties*
LULU, *a girl in her twenties*
GOLDBERG, *a man in his fifties*
MCCANN, *a man of thirty*

ACT I

The living-room of a house in a seaside town. A door leading to the hall down left. Back door and small window up left. Kitchen hatch, centre back. Kitchen door up right. Table and chairs, centre.

    Petey enters from the door on the left with a paper and sits at the table. He begins to read. Meg's voice comes through the kitchen hatch.

MEG. Is that you, Petey?

    Pause

    Petey, is that you?

    Pause.

    Petey?
PETEY. What?
MEG. Is that you?
PETEY. Yes, it's me.
MEG. What? (*Her face appears at the hatch.*) Are you back?
PETEY. Yes.
MEG. I've got your cornflakes ready. (*She disappears and reappears.*) Here's your cornflakes.

    He rises and takes the plate from her, sits at the table, props up the paper and begins to eat. Meg enters by the kitchen door.

    Are they nice?
PETEY. Very nice.
MEG. I thought they'd be nice. (*She sits at the table.*) You got your paper?

PETEY. Yes.
MEG. Is it good?
PETEY. Not bad.
MEG. What does it say?
PETEY. Nothing much.
MEG. You read me out some nice bits yesterday.
PETEY. Yes, well, I haven't finished this one yet.
MEG. Will you tell me when you come to something good?
PETEY. Yes.

    Pause.

MEG. Have you been working hard this morning?
PETEY. No. Just stacked a few of the old chairs. Cleaned up a bit.
MEG. Is it nice out?
PETEY. Very nice.

    Pause.

MEG. Is Stanley up yet?
PETEY. I don't know. Is he?
MEG. I don't know. I haven't seen him down yet.
PETEY. Well then, he can't be up.
MEG. Haven't you seen him down?
PETEY. I've only just come in.
MEG. He must be still asleep.

    She looks round the room, stands, goes to the sideboard and takes a pair of socks from a drawer, collects wool and a needle and goes back to the table.

    What time did you go out this morning, Petey?
PETEY. Same time as usual.
MEG. Was it dark?
PETEY. No, it was light.
MEG (*beginning to darn*). But sometimes you go out in the morning and it's dark.
PETEY. That's in the winter.
MEG. Oh, in winter.
PETEY. Yes, it gets light later in winter.
MEG. Oh.

419

Pause.

What are you reading?

PETEY. Someone's just had a baby.

MEG. Oh, they haven't! Who?

PETEY. Some girl.

MEG. Who, Petey, who?

PETEY. I don't think you'd know her.

MEG. What's her name?

PETEY. Lady Mary Splatt.

MEG. I don't know her.

PETEY. No.

MEG. What is it?

PETEY (*studying the paper*). Er—a girl.

MEG. Not a boy?

PETEY. No.

MEG. Oh, what a shame. I'd be sorry. I'd much rather have a little boy.

PETEY. A little girl's all right.

MEG. I'd much rather have a little boy.

Pause . . . Vaguely.

PETEY. I've finished my cornflakes.

MEG. Were they nice?

PETEY. Very nice.

MEG. I've got something else for you.

PETEY. Good.

She rises, takes his plate and exits into the kitchen. She then appears at the hatch with two pieces of fried bread on a plate.

MEG. Here you are, Petey.

He rises, collects the plate, looks at it, sits at the table. Meg re-enters.

Is it nice?

PETEY. I haven't tasted it yet.

MEG. I bet you don't know what it is.

PETEY. Yes, I do.

MEG. What is it, then?

PETEY. Fried bread.

MEG. That's right.

He begins to eat.

She watches him eat.

PETEY. Very nice.

MEG. I knew it was.

Petey (*turning to her*). Oh, Meg, two men came up to me on the beach last night.

MEG. Two men?

PETEY. Yes. They wanted to know if we could put them up for a couple of nights.

MEG. Put them up? Here?

PETEY. Yes.

MEG. How many men?

PETEY. Two.

MEG. What did you say?

PETEY. Well, I said I didn't know. So they said they'd come round to find out.

MEG. Are they coming?

PETEY. Well, they said they would.

MEG. Had they heard about us, Petey?

PETEY. They must have done.

MEG. Yes, they must have done. They must have heard this was a very good boarding house. It is. This house is on the list.

PETEY. It is.

MEG. I know it is.

PETEY. They might turn up today. Can you do it?

MEG. Oh, I've got that lovely room they can have.

PETEY. You've got a room ready?

MEG. I've got the room with the armchair all ready for visitors.

PETEY. You're sure?

MEG. Yes, that'll be all right then, if they come today.

PETEY. Good.

She takes the socks etc. back to the sideboard drawer.

MEG. I'm going to wake that boy.

PETEY. There's a new show coming to the Palace.

MEG. On the pier?

PETEY. No. The Palace, in the town.

MEG. Stanley could have been in it, if it was on the pier.

PETEY. This is a straight show.

MEG. What do you mean?

PETEY. No dancing or singing.

MEG. What do they do then?

PETEY. They just talk.

Pause.

MEG. Oh.

PETEY. You like a song, eh, Meg.?

MEG. I like listening to the piano. I used to like watching Stanley play the piano. Of course, he didn't sing. (*Looking at the door.*) I'm going to call that boy.

PETEY. Didn't you take him up his cup of tea?

MEG. I always take him up his cup of tea. But that was a long time ago.

PETEY. Did he drink it?

MEG. I made him. I stood there till he did. I'm going to call him. (*She goes to the door.*) Stan! Stanny! (*She listens.*) Stan! I'm coming up to fetch you if you don't come down! I'm coming up! I'm going to count three! One! Two! Three! I'm coming to get you! (*She exits and goes upstairs. In a moment, shouts from Stanley, wild laughter from Meg. Petey takes his plate to the hatch. Shouts. Laughter. Petey sits at the table. Silence. She returns.*) He's coming down. (*She is panting and arranges her hair.*) I told him if he didn't hurry up he'd get no breakfast.

PETEY. That did it, eh?

MEG. I'll get his cornflakes.

Meg exits to the kitchen. Petey reads the paper. Stanley enters. He is unshaven, in his pyjama jacket and wears glasses. He sits at the table.

PETEY. Morning, Stanley.

STANLEY. Morning.

Silence. Meg enters with a bowl of cornflakes, which she sets on the table.

MEG. So he's come down at last, has he? He's come down at last for his breakfast. But he doesn't deserve any, does he, Petey? (*Stanley stares at the cornflakes.*) Did you sleep well?

STANLEY. I didn't sleep at all.

MEG. You didn't sleep at all? Did you hear that, Petey? Too tired to eat your breakfast, I suppose? Now you eat up those cornflakes like a good boy. Go on.

He begins to eat.

STANLEY. What's it like out today?

PETEY. Very nice.

STANLEY. Warm?

PETEY. Well, there's a good breeze blowing.

STANLEY. Cold?

PETEY. No, no, I wouldn't say it was cold.

MEG. What are the cornflakes like, Stan?

STANLEY. Horrible.

MEG. Those flakes? Those lovely flakes? You're a liar, a little liar. They're refreshing. It says so. For people when they get up late.

STANLEY. The milk's off.

MEG. It's not. Petey ate his, didn't you, Petey?

PETEY. That's right.

MEG. There you are then.

STANLEY. All right, I'll go on to the second course.

MEG. He hasn't finished the first course and he wants to go on to the second course!

STANLEY. I feel like something cooked.

MEG. Well, I'm not going to give it to you.

PETEY. Give it to him.

MEG (*sitting at the table, right*). I'm not going to.

Pause.

STANLEY. No breakfast.

Pause.

All night long I've been dreaming about this breakfast.

MEG. I thought you said you didn't sleep.

STANLEY. Day-dreaming. All night long. And now she won't give me any. Not even a crust of bread on the table.

Pause.

Well, I can see I'll have to go down to one of those smart hotels on the front.

MEG (*rising quickly*). You won't get a better breakfast there than here.

She exits to the kitchen. Stanley yawns broadly. Meg appears at the hatch with a plate.

Here you are. You'll like this.

Petey rises, collects the plate, brings it to the table, puts it in front of Stanley, and sits.

STANLEY. What's this?

PETEY. Fried bread.

MEG (*entering*). Well, I bet you don't know what it is.

STANLEY. Oh yes, I do.

MEG. What?

STANLEY. Fried bread.

MEG. He knew.

STANLEY. What a wonderful surprise.

MEG. You didn't expect that, did you?

STANLEY. I bloody well didn't.

PETEY (*rising*). Well, I'm off.

MEG. You going back to work?

PETEY. Yes.

MEG. Your tea! You haven't had your tea!

PETEY. That's all right. No time now.

MEG. I've got it made inside.

PETEY. No, never mind. See you later. Ta-ta, Stan.

STANLEY. Ta-ta.

Petey exits, left.

Tch, tch, tch, tch.

MEG (*defensively*). What do you mean?

STANLEY. You're a bad wife.

MEG. I'm not. Who said I am?

STANLEY. Not to make your husband a cup of tea. Terrible.

MEG. He knows I'm not a bad wife.

STANLEY. Giving him sour milk instead.

MEG. It wasn't sour.

STANLEY. Disgraceful.

MEG. You mind your own business, anyway. (*Stanley eats.*) You won't find many better wives than me, I can tell you. I keep a very nice house and I keep it clean.

STANLEY. Whoo!

MEG. Yes! And this house is very well known, for a very good boarding house for visitors.

STANLEY. Visitors? Do you know how many visitors you've had since I've been here?

MEG. How many?

STANLEY. One.

MEG. Who?

STANLEY. Me! I'm your visitor.

MEG. You're a liar. This house is on the list.

STANLEY. I bet it is.

MEG. I know it is.

He pushes his plate away and picks up the paper.

Was it nice?

STANLEY. What?

MEG. The fried bread.

STANLEY. Succulent.

MEG. You shouldn't say that word.

STANLEY. What word?

MEG. That word you said.

STANLEY. What, succulent—?

MEG. Don't say it!

STANLEY. What's the matter with it?

MEG. You shouldn't say that word to a married woman.

STANLEY. Is that a fact?

MEG. Yes.

STANLEY. Well, I never knew that.

MEG. Well, it's true.

STANLEY. Who told you that?

MEG. Never you mind.

STANLEY. Well, if I can't say it to a married woman who can I say it to?

MEG. You're bad.

STANLEY. What about some tea?

MEG. Do you want some tea? (*Stanley reads the paper.*) Say please.

STANLEY. Please.

MEG. Say sorry first.

STANLEY. Sorry first.

MEG. No. Just sorry.

STANLEY. Just sorry!

MEG. You deserve the strap.

STANLEY. Don't do that!

She takes his plate and ruffles his hair as she passes. Stanley exclaims and throws her arm away. She goes

into the kitchen. He rubs his eyes under his glasses and picks up the paper. She enters.

MEG. I brought the pot in.

STANLEY (*absently*). I don't know what I'd do without you.

MEG. You don't deserve it though.

STANLEY. Why not?

MEG (*pouring the tea, coyly*). Go on. Calling me that.

STANLEY. How long has that tea been in the pot?

MEG. It's good tea. Good strong tea.

STANLEY. This isn't tea. It's gravy!

MEG. It's not.

STANLEY. Get out of it. You succulent old washing bag.

MEG. I am not! And it isn't your place to tell me if I am!

STANLEY. And it isn't your place to come into a man's bedroom and—wake him up.

MEG. Stanny! Don't you like your cup of tea of a morning—the one I bring you?

STANLEY. I can't drink this muck. Didn't anyone ever tell you to warm the pot, at least?

MEG. That's good strong tea, that's all.

STANLEY (*putting his head in his hands*). Oh God, I'm tired.

Silence. Meg goes to the sideboard, collects a duster, and vaguely dusts the room, watching him. She comes to the table and dusts it.

Not the bloody table!

Pause.

MEG. Stan?

STANLEY. What?

MEG (*shyly*). Am I really succulent?

STANLEY. Oh, you are. I'd rather have you than a cold in the nose any day.

MEG. You're just saying that.

STANLEY (*violently.*) Look, why don't you get this place cleared up! It's a pigsty. And another thing, what about my room? It needs sweeping. It needs papering. I need a new room!

MEG (*sensual, stroking his arm*). Oh, Stan, that's a lovely room. I've had some lovely afternoons in that room.

He recoils from her hand in disgust, stands and exits quickly by the door on the left. She collects his cup and the teapot and takes them to the hatch shelf. The street door slams. Stanley returns.

MEG. Is the sun shining? (*He crosses to the window, takes a cigarette and matches from his pyjama jacket, and lights his cigarette.*) What are you smoking?

STANLEY. A cigarette.

MEG. Are you going to give me one?

STANLEY. No.

MEG. I like cigarettes. (*He stands at the window, smoking. She crosses behind him and tickles the back of his neck.*) Tickle, tickle.

STANLEY (*pushing her*). Get away from me.

MEG. Are you going out?

STANLEY. Not with you.

MEG. But I'm going shopping in a minute.

STANLEY. Go.

MEG. You'll be lonely, all by yourself.

STANLEY. Will I?

MEG. Without your old Meg. I've got to get things in for the two gentlemen.

A pause. Stanley slowly raises his head. He speaks without turning.

STANLEY. What two gentlemen?

MEG. I'm expecting visitors.

He turns.

STANLEY. What?

MEG. You didn't know that, did you?

STANLEY. What are you talking about?

MEG. Two gentlemen asked Petey if they could come and stay for a couple of nights. I'm expecting them. (*She picks up the duster and begins to wipe the cloth on the table.*)

STANLEY. I don't believe it.

MEG. It's true.

STANLEY (*moving to her*). You're saying it on purpose.

MEG. Petey told me this morning.

STANLEY (*grinding his cigarette*). When was this? When did he see them?

MEG. Last night.

STANLEY. Who are they?

MEG. I don't know.

STANLEY. Didn't he tell you their names?

MEG. No.

STANLEY (*pacing the room*). Here? They wanted to come here?

MEG. Yes, they did. (*She takes the curlers out of her hair.*)

STANLEY. Why?

MEG. This house is on the list.

STANLEY. But who are they?

MEG. You'll see when they come.

STANLEY (*decisively*). They won't come.

MEG. Why not?

STANLEY (*quickly*). I tell you they won't come. Why didn't they come last night, if they were coming?

MEG. Perhaps they couldn't find the place in the dark. It's not easy to find in the dark.

STANLEY. They won't come. Someone's taking the Michael. Forget all about it. It's a false alarm. A false alarm. (*He sits at the table.*) Where's my tea?

MEG. I took it away. You didn't want it.

STANLEY. What do you mean, you took it away?

MEG. I took it away.

STANLEY. What did you take it away for?

MEG. You didn't want it!

STANLEY. Who said I didn't want it?

MEG. You did!

STANLEY. Who gave you the right to take away my tea?

MEG. You wouldn't drink it.

Stanley stares at her.

STANLEY (*quietly*). Who do you think you're talking to?

MEG (*uncertainly*). What?

STANLEY. Come here.

MEG. What do you mean?

STANLEY. Come over here.

MEG. No.

STANLEY. I want to ask you something. (*Meg fidgets nervously. She does not go to him.*) Come on. (*Pause.*) All right. I can ask it from here just as well. (*Deliberately.*) Tell me, Mrs. Boles, when you address yourself to me, do you ever ask yourself who exactly you are talking to? Eh?

Silence. He groans, his trunk falls forward, his head falls into his hands.

MEG (*in a small voice*). Didn't you enjoy your breakfast, Stan? (*She approaches the table.*) Stan? When are you going to play the piano again? (*Stanley grunts.*) Like you used to? (*Stanley grunts.*) I used to like watching you play the piano. When are you going to play it again?

STANLEY. I can't, can I?

MEG. Why not?

STANLEY. I haven't got a piano, have I?

MEG. No, I meant like when you were working. That piano.

STANLEY. Go and do your shopping.

MEG. But you wouldn't have to go away if you got a job, would you? You could play the piano on the pier.

He looks at her, then speaks airily.

STANLEY. I've . . . er . . . I've been offered a job, as a matter of fact.

MEG. What?

STANLEY. Yes. I'm considering a job at the moment.

MEG. You're not.

STANLEY. A good one, too. A night club. In Berlin.

MEG. Berlin?

STANLEY. Berlin. A night club. Playing the piano. A fabulous salary. And all found.

MEG. How long for?

STANLEY. We don't stay in Berlin. Then we go to Athens.

MEG. How long for?

STANLEY. Yes. Then we pay a flying visit to . . . er . . . whatsisname. . . .

MEG. Where?

STANLEY. Constantinople. Zagreb. Vladivostock. It's a round the world tour.

MEG (*sitting at the table*). Have you played the piano in those places before?

STANLEY. Played the piano? I've played the piano all over the world. All over the country. (*Pause.*) I once gave a concert.

MEG. A concert?

STANLEY (*reflectively*). Yes. It was a good one, too. They were all there that night. Every single one of them. It was a great success. Yes. A concert. At Lower Edmonton.

MEG. What did you wear?

STANLEY (*to himself*). I had a unique touch. Absolutely unique. They came up to me. They came up to me and said they were grateful. Champagne we had that night, the lot. (*Pause.*) My father nearly came down to hear me. Well, I dropped him a card anyway. But I don't think he could make it. No, I—I lost the address, that was it. (*Pause.*) Yes. Lower Edmonton. Then after that, you know what they did? They carved me up. It was all arranged, it was all worked out. My next concert. Somewhere else it was. In winter. I went down there to play. Then, when I got there, the hall was closed, the place was shuttered up, not even a caretaker. They'd locked it up. (*Takes off his glasses and wipes them on his pyjama jacket.*) A fast one. They pulled a fast one. I'd like to know who was responsible for that. (*Bitterly.*) All right, Jack, I can take a tip. They want me to crawl down on my bended knees. Well I can take a tip . . . any day of the week. (*He replaces his glasses, then looks at Meg.*) Look at her. You're just an old piece of rock cake, aren't you? (*He rises and leans across the table to her.*) That's what you are, aren't you?

MEG. Don't you go away again, Stan. You stay here. You'll be better off. You stay with your old Meg. (*He groans and lies across the table*) Aren't you feeling well this morning, Stan. Did you pay a visit this morning?

He stiffens, then lifts himself slowly, turns to face her and speaks lightly, casually.

STANLEY. Meg. Do you know what?

MEG. What?

STANLEY. Have you heard the latest?

MEG. No.

STANLEY. I'll bet you have.

MEG. I haven't.

STANLEY. Shall I tell you?

MEG. What latest?

STANLEY. You haven't heard it?

MEG. No.

STANLEY (*advancing*). They're coming today.

MEG. Who?

STANLEY. They're coming in a van.

MEG. Who?

STANLEY. And do you know what they've got in that van?

MEG. What?

STANLEY. They've got a wheelbarrow in that van.

MEG (*breathlessly*). They haven't.

STANLEY. Oh yes they have.

MEG. You're a liar.

STANLEY (*advancing upon her*). A big wheelbarrow. And when the van stops they wheel it out, and they wheel it up the garden path, and then they knock at the front door.

MEG. They don't.

STANLEY. They're looking for someone.

MEG. They're not.

STANLEY. They're looking for someone. A certain person.

MEG (*hoarsely*). No, they're not!

STANLEY. Shall I tell you who they're looking for?

MEG. No!

STANLEY. You don't want me to tell you?

MEG. You're a liar!

A sudden knock on the front door. Lulu's voice: Ooh-ooh! Meg edges past Stanley and collects her shopping bag. Meg goes out. Stanley sidles to the door and listens.

VOICE (*through letter box*). Hullo, Mrs. Boles . . .

MEG. Oh, has it come?

VOICE. Yes, it's just come.

MEG. What, is that it?

VOICE. Yes. I thought I'd bring it round.

MEG. Is it nice?

VOICE. Very nice. What shall I do with it?

MEG. Well, I don't . . . (*Whispers.*)

VOICE. No, of course not . . . (*Whispers.*)

MEG. All right, but . . . (*Whispers.*)

VOICE. I won't . . . (*Whispers.*) Ta-ta, Mrs. Boles.

Stanley quickly sits at the table. Enter Lulu.

LULU. Oh, hullo.

STANLEY. Ay-ay.

LULU. I just want to leave this in here.

STANLEY. Do. (*Lulu crosses to the sideboard and puts a solid, round parcel upon it.*) That's a bulky object.

LULU. You're not to touch it.

STANLEY. Why would I want to touch it?

LULU. Well, you're not to, anyway.

Lulu walks upstage.

LULU. Why don't you open the door? It's all stuffy in here.

She opens the back door.

STANLEY (*rising*). Stuffy? I disinfected the place this morning.

LULU (*at the door*). Oh, that's better.

STANLEY. I think it's going to rain to-day. What do you think?

LULU. I hope so. You could do with it.

STANLEY. Me! I was in the sea at half past six.

LULU. Were you?

STANLEY. I went right out to the headland and back before breakfast. Don't you believe me!

She sits, takes out a compact and powders her nose.

LULU (*offering him the compact*). Do you want to have a look at your face? (*Stanley withdraws from the table.*) You could do with a shave, do you know that? (*Stanley sits, right, at the table.*) Don't you ever go out? (*He does not answer.*) I mean, what do you do, just sit around the house like this all day long? (*Pause.*) Hasn't Mrs. Boles got enough to do without having you under her feet all day long?

STANLEY. I always stand on the table when she sweeps the floor.

LULU. Why don't you have a wash? You look terrible.

STANLEY. A wash wouldn't make any difference.

LULU (*rising*). Come out and get a bit of air. You depress me, looking like that.

STANLEY. Air? Oh, I don't know about that.

LULU. It's lovely out. And I've got a few sandwiches.

STANLEY. What sort of sandwiches?

LULU. Cheese.

STANLEY. I'm a big eater, you know.

LULU. That's all right. I'm not hungry.

STANLEY (*abruptly*). How would you like to go away with me?

LULU. Where.

STANLEY. Nowhere. Still, we could go.

LULU. But where could we go?

STANLEY. Nowhere. There's nowhere to go. So we could just go. It wouldn't matter.

LULU. We might as well stay here.

STANLEY. No. It's no good here.

LULU. Well, where else is there?

STANLEY. Nowhere.

LULU. Well, that's a charming proposal. (*He gets up.*) Do you have to wear those glasses?

STANLEY. Yes.

LULU. So you're not coming out for a walk?

STANLEY. I can't at the moment.

LULU. You're a bit of a washout, aren't you?

She exits, left. Stanley stands. He then goes to the mirror and looks in it. He goes into the kitchen, takes off his glasses and begins to wash his face. A pause. Enter, by the back door, Goldberg and McCann. McCann carries two suitcases, Goldberg a briefcase. They halt inside the door, then walk downstage. Stanley, wiping his face, glimpses their backs through the hatch. Goldberg and McCann look round the room. Stanley slips on his glasses, sidles through the kitchen door and out of the back door.

McCANN. Is this it?

GOLDBERG. This is it.

McCANN. Are you sure?

GOLDBERG. Sure I'm sure.

Pause.

McCANN. What now?

GOLDBERG. Don't worry yourself, McCann. Take a seat.

McCANN. What about you?

GOLDBERG. What about me?

McCANN. Are you going to take a seat?

GOLDBERG. We'll both take a seat. (*McCann puts down the suitcases and sits at the table, left.*) Sit back, McCann. Relax. What's the matter with you? I bring you down for a few days to the seaside. Take a holiday. Do yourself a favour. Learn to relax, McCann, or you'll never get anywhere.

McCANN. Ah sure, I do try, Nat.

GOLDBERG (*sitting at the table, right*). The secret is breathing. Take my tip. It's a well-known fact. Breathe in, breathe out, take a chance, let yourself go, what can you lose? Look at me. When I was an apprentice yet, McCann, every second Friday of the month my Uncle Barney used to take me to the seaside, regular as clockwork. Brighton, Canvey Island, Rottingdean—Uncle Barney wasn't particular. After lunch on Shabbuss we'd go and sit in a couple of deck chairs—you know, the ones with canopies—we'd have a little paddle, we'd watch the tide coming in, going out, the sun coming down—golden days, believe me, McCann. (*Reminiscent.*) Uncle

Barney. Of course, he was an impeccable dresser. One of the old school. He had a house just outside Basingstoke at the time. Respected by the whole community. Culture? Don't talk to me about culture. He was an all-round man, what do you mean? He was a cosmopolitan.

MCCANN. Hey, Nat. . . .

GOLDBERG (*reflectively*). Yes. One of the old school.

MCCANN. Nat. How do we know this is the right house?

GOLDBERG. What?

MCCANN. How do we know this is the right house?

GOLDBERG. What makes you think it's the wrong house?

MCCANN. I didn't see a number on the gate.

GOLDBERG. I wasn't looking for a number.

MCCANN. No?

GOLDBERG (*settling in the armchair*). You know one thing Uncle Barney taught me? Uncle Barney taught me that the word of a gentleman is enough. That's why, when I had to go away on business I never carried any money. One of my sons used to come with me. He used to carry a few coppers. For a paper, perhaps, to see how the M.C.C. was getting on overseas. Otherwise my name was good. Besides, I was a very busy man.

MCCANN. What about this, Nat? Isn't it about time someone came in?

GOLDBERG. McCann, what are you so nervous about? Pull yourself together. Everywhere you go these days it's like a funeral.

MCCANN. That's true.

GOLDBERG. True? Of course it's true. It's more than true. It's a fact.

MCCANN. You may be right.

GOLDBERG. What is it, McCann? You don't trust me like you did in the old days?

MCCANN. Sure I trust you, Nat.

GOLDBERG. But why is it that before you do a job you're all over the place, and when you're doing the job you're as cool as a whistle?

MCCANN. I don't know, Nat. I'm just all right once I know what I'm doing. When I know what I'm doing, I'm all right.

GOLDBERG. Well, you do it very well.

MCCANN. Thank you, Nat.

GOLDBERG. You know what I said when this job came up. I mean naturally they approached me to take care of it. And you know who I asked for?

MCCANN. Who?

GOLDBERG. You.

MCCANN. That was very good of you, Nat.

GOLDBERG. No, it was nothing. You're a capable man, McCann.

MCCANN. That's a great compliment, Nat, coming from a man in your position.

GOLDBERG. Well, I've got a position, I won't deny it.

MCCANN. You certainly have.

GOLDBERG. I would never deny that I had a position.

MCCANN. And what a position!

GOLDBERG. It's not a thing I would deny.

MCCANN. Yes, it's true, you've done a lot for me. I appreciate it.

GOLDBERG. Say no more.

MCCANN. You've always been a true Christian.

GOLDBERG. In a way.

MCCANN. No, I just thought I'd tell you that I appreciate it.

GOLDBERG. It's unnecessary to recapitulate.

MCCANN. You're right there.

GOLDBERG. Quite unnecessary.

Pause. McCann leans forward.

MCCANN. Hey Nat, just one thing. . . .

GOLDBERG. What now?

MCCANN. This job—no, listen—this job, is it going to be like anything we've ever done before?

GOLDBERG. Tch, tch, tch.

MCCANN. No, just tell me that. Just that, and I won't ask any more.

Goldberg sighs, stands, goes behind the table, ponders, looks at McCann, and then speaks in a quiet, fluent, official tone.

GOLDBERG. The main issue is a singular issue and quite distinct from your previous work. Certain elements, however, might well approximate in points of procedure to some of your other activities. All is dependent on the attitude of our subject. At all events, McCann, I can assure you that the assignment will be carried out and the mission accomplished with no excessive aggravation to you or myself. Satisfied?

MCCANN. Sure. Thank you, Nat.

Meg enters, left.

GOLDBERG. Ah, Mrs. Boles?

MEG. Yes?

GOLDBERG. We spoke to your husband last night. Perhaps he mentioned us? We heard that you kindly let rooms for gentlemen. So I brought my friend along with me. We were after a nice place, you understand. So we came to you. I'm Mr. Goldberg and this is Mr. McCann.

MEG. Very pleased to meet you.

They shake hands.

GOLDBERG. We're pleased to meet you, too.

MEG. That's very nice.

GOLDBERG. You're right. How often do you meet someone it's a pleasure to meet?

McCANN. Never.

GOLDBERG. But today it's different. How are you keeping, Mrs. Boles?

MEG. Oh, very well, thank you.

GOLDBERG. Yes? Really?

MEG. Oh yes, really.

GOLDBERG. I'm glad.

Goldberg sits at the table, right.

GOLDBERG. Well, so what do you say? You can manage to put us up, eh, Mrs. Boles?

MEG. Well, it would have been easier last week.

GOLDBERG. It woud, eh?

MEG. Yes.

GOLDBERG. Why? How many have you got here at the moment?

MEG. Just one at the moment.

GOLDBERG. Just one?

MEG. Yes. Just one. Until you came.

GOLDBERG. And your husband, of course?

MEG. Yes, but he sleeps with me.

GOLDBERG. What does he do, your husband?

MEG. He's a deck-chair attendant.

GOLDBERG. Oh, very nice.

MEG. Yes, he's out in all weathers.

She begins to take her purchases from her bag.

GOLDBERG. Of course. And your guest? Is he a man?

MEG. A man?

GOLDBERG. Or a woman?

MEG. No. A man.

GOLDBERG. Been here long?

MEG. He's been here about a year now.

GOLDBERG. Oh yes. A resident. What's his name?

MEG. Stanley Webber.

GOLDBERG. Oh yes? Does he work here?

MEG. He used to work. He used to be a pianist. In a concert party on the pier.

GOLDBERG. Oh yes? On the pier, eh? Does he play a nice piano?

MEG. Oh, lovely. (*She sits at the table.*) He once gave a concert.

GOLDBERG. Oh? Where?

MEG (*falteringly*). In . . . a big hall. His father gave him champagne. But then they locked the place up and he couldn't get out. The caretaker had gone home. So he had to wait until the morning before he could get out. (*With confidence.*) They were very grateful. (*Pause.*) And then they all wanted to give him a tip. And so he took the tip. And then he got a fast train and he came down here.

GOLDBERG. Really?

MEG. Oh yes. Straight down.

Pause.

MEG. I wish he could have played tonight.

GOLDBERG. Why tonight?

MEG. It's his birthday today.

GOLDBERG. His birthday?

MEG. Yes. Today. But I'm not going to tell him until tonight.

GOLDBERG. Doesn't he know it's his birthday?

MEG. He hasn't mentioned it.

GOLDBERG (*thoughtfully*). Ah! Tell me. Are you going to have a party?

MEG. A party?

GOLDBERG. Weren't you going to have one?

MEG (*her eyes wide*). No.

GOLDBERG. Well, of course, you must have one. (*He stands.*) We'll have a party, eh? What do you say?

MEG. Oh yes!

GOLDBERG. Sure. We'll give him a party. Leave it to me.

MEG. Oh, that's wonderful, Mr. Gold—

GOLDBERG. Berg.

MEG. Berg.

GOLDBERG. You like the idea?

MEG. Oh, I'm so glad you came today.

GOLDBERG. If we hadn't come today we'd have come tomorrow. Still, I'm glad we came today. Just in time for his birthday.

MEG. I wanted to have a party. But you must have people for a party.

GOLDBERG. And now you've got McCann and me. McCann's the life and soul of any party.

McCANN. What?

GOLDBERG. What do you think of that, McCann? There's a gentleman living here. He's got a birthday today, and he's forgotten all about it. So we're going to remind him. We're going to give him a party.

McCANN. Oh, is that a fact?

MEG. Tonight.

GOLDBERG. tonight.

MEG. I'll put on my party dress.

GOLDBERG. And I'll get some bottles.

MEG. And I'll invite Lulu this afternoon. Oh, this is going to cheer Stanley up. It will. He's been down in the dumps lately.

GOLDBERG. We'll bring him out of himself.

MEG. I hope I look nice in my dress.

GOLDBERG. Madam, you'll look like a tulip.

MEG. What colour?

GOLDBERG. Er—well, I'll have to see the dress first.

MCCANN. Could I go up to my room?

MEG. Oh, I've put you both together. Do you mind being both together?

GOLDBERG. I don't mind. Do you mind, McCann?

MCCANN. No.

MEG. What time shall we have the party?

GOLDBERG. Nine o'clock.

MCCANN (*at the door*). Is this the way?

MEG (*rising*). I'll show you. If you don't mind coming upstairs.

GOLDBERG. With a tulip? It's a pleasure.

Meg and Goldberg exit laughing, followed by McCann. Stanley at the window. He enters by the back door. He goes to the door on the left, opens it and listens. Silence. He walks to the table. He stands. He sits, as Meg enters. She crosses and hangs her shopping bag on a hook. He lights a match and watches it burn.

STANLEY. Who is it?

MEG. The two gentlemen.

STANLEY. What two gentlemen?

MEG. The ones that were coming. I just took them to their room. They were thrilled with their room.

STANLEY. They've come?

MEG. They're very nice, Stan.

STANLEY. Why didn't they come last night?

MEG. They said the beds were wonderful.

STANLEY. Who are they?

MEG (*sitting*). They're very nice, Stanley.

STANLEY. I said, who are they?

MEG. I've told you, the two gentlemen.

STANLEY. I didn't think they'd come.

He rises and walks to the window.

MEG. They have. They were here when I came in.

STANLEY. What do they want here?

MEG. They want to stay.

STANLEY. How long for?

MEG. They didn't say.

STANLEY (*turning*). But why here? Why not somewhere else?

MEG. This house is on the list.

STANLEY (*coming down*). What are they called? What are their names?

MEG. Oh, Stanley, I can't remember.

STANLEY. They told you, didn't they? Or didn't they tell you?

MEG. Yes, they. . . .

STANLEY. Then what are they? Come on. Try to remember.

MEG. Why, Stan? Do you know them?

STANLEY. How do I know if I know them until I know their names?

MEG. Well . . . he told me, I remember.

STANLEY. Well?

She thinks.

MEG. Gold—something.

STANLEY. Goldsomething?

MEG. Yes. Gold. . . .

STANLEY. Yes?

MEG. Goldberg.

STANLEY. Goldberg?

MEG. That's right. That was one of them.

Stanley slowly sits at the table, left.

Do you know them?

Stanley does not answer.

Stan, they won't wake you up, I promise. I'll tell them they must be quiet.

Stanley sits still.

They won't be here long, Stan. I'll still bring you up your early morning tea.

Stanley sits still.

You mustn't be sad today. It's your birthday.

A pause.

STANLEY (*dumbly*). Uh?

MEG. It's your birthday, Stan. I was going to keep it a secret until tonight.

STANLEY. No.

MEG. It is. I've brought you a present. (*She goes to the sideboard, picks up the parcel, and places it on the table in front of him.*) Here. Go on. Open it.

STANLEY. What's this?

MEG. It's your present.

STANLEY. This isn't my birthday, Meg.

MEG. Of course it is. Open your present.

He stares at the parcel, slowly stands, and opens it. He takes out a boy's drum.

STANLEY (*flatly*). It's a drum. A boy's drum.

MEG (*tenderly*). It's because you haven't got a piano. (*He stares at her, then turns and walks towards the door, left.*) Aren't you going to give me a kiss? (*He turns sharply, and stops. He walks back towards her slowly.*

He stops at her chair, looking down upon her. Pause. His shoulders sag, he bends and kisses her on the cheek.) There are some sticks in there. *(Stanley looks into the parcel. He takes out two drumsticks. He taps them together. He looks at her.)*
STANLEY. Shall I put it round my neck?

She watches him, uncertainly. He hangs the drum around his neck, taps it gently with the sticks, then marches round the table, beating it regularly. Meg, pleased, watches him. Still beating it regularly, he begins to go round the table a second time. Halfway round the beat becomes erratic, uncontrolled. Meg expresses dismay. He arrives at her chair, banging the drum, his face and the drumbeat now savage and possessed.

Curtain

ACT II

McCann is sitting at the table tearing a sheet of newspaper into five equal strips. It is evening. After a few moments Stanley enters from the left. He stops upon seeing McCann, and watches him. He then walks towards the kitchen, stops, and speaks.

STANLEY. Evening.
McCANN. Evening.

Chuckles are heard from outside the back door, which is open.

STANLEY. Very warm tonight. *(He turns towards the back door, and back.)* Someone out there?

McCann tears another length of paper. Stanley goes into the kitchen and pours a glass of water. He drinks it looking through the hatch. He puts the glass down, comes out of the kitchen and walks quickly towards the door, left. McCann rises and intercepts him.

McCANN. I don't think we've met.
STANLEY. No, we haven't.
McCANN. My name's McCann.
STANLEY. Staying here long?
McCANN. Not long. What's your name?
STANLEY. Webber.
McCANN. I'm glad to meet you, sir. *(He offers his hand. Stanley takes it, and McCann holds the grip.)* Many happy returns of the day. *(Stanley withdraws his hand. They face each other.)* Were you going out?

STANLEY. Yes.
McCANN. On your birthday?
STANLEY. Yes. Why not?
McCANN. But they're holding a party here for you tonight.
STANLEY. Oh really? That's unfortunate.
McCANN. Ah no. It's very nice.

Voices from outside the back door.

STANLEY. I'm sorry. I'm not in the mood for a party tonight.
McCANN. Oh, is that so? I'm sorry.
STANLEY. Yes, I'm going out to celebrate quietly, on my own.
McCANN. That's a shame.

They stand.

STANLEY. Well, if you'd move out of my way—
McCANN. But everything's laid on. The guests are expected.
STANLEY. Guests? What guests?
McCANN. Myself for one. I had the honour of an invitation.

McCann begins to whistle "The Mountains of Morne".

STANLEY *(moving away)*. I wouldn't call it an honour, would you? It'll just be another booze-up.

Stanley joins McCann in whistling "The Mountains of Morne". During the next five lines the whistling is continuous, one whistling while the other speaks, and both whistling together.

McCANN. But it is an honour.
STANLEY. I'd say you were exaggerating.
McCANN. Oh no. I'd say it was an honour.
STANLEY. I'd say that was plain stupid.
McCANN. Ah no.

They stare at each other.

STANLEY. Who are the other guests?
McCANN. A young lady.
STANLEY. Oh yes? And. . . . ?
McCANN. My friend.
STANLEY. Your friend?
McCANN. That's right. It's all laid on.

Stanley walks round the table towards the door. McCann meets him.

STANLEY. Excuse me.
McCANN. Where are you going?
STANLEY. I want to go out.

McCann. Why don't you stay here?

Stanley moves away, to the right of the table.

Stanley. So you're down here on holiday?

McCann. A short one. (*Stanley picks up a strip of paper. McCann moves in.*) Mind that.

Stanley. What is it?

McCann. Mind it. Leave it.

Stanley. I've got a feeling we've met before.

McCann. No we haven't.

Stanley. Ever been anywhere near Maidenhead?

McCann. No.

Stanley. There's a Fuller's teashop. I used to have my tea there.

McCann. I don't know it.

Stanley. And a Boots Library. I seem to connect you with the High Street.

McCann. Yes?

Stanley. A charming town, don't you think?

McCann. I don't know it.

Stanley. Oh no. A quiet, thriving community. I was born and brought up there. I lived well away from the main road.

McCann. Yes?

Pause.

Stanley. You're here on a short stay?

McCann. That's right.

Stanley. You'll find it very bracing.

McCann. Do you find it bracing?

Stanley. Me? No. But you will. (*He sits at the table.*) I like it here, but I'll be moving soon. Back home. I'll stay there too, this time. No place like home. (*He laughs.*) I wouldn't have left, but business calls. Business called, and I had to leave for a bit. You know how it is.

McCann (*sitting at the table, left*). You in business?

Stanley. No. I think I'll give it up. I've got a small private income, you see. I think I'll give it up. Don't like being away from home. I used to live very quietly—played records, that's about all. Everything delivered to the door. Then I started a little private business, in a small way, and it compelled me to come down here—kept me longer than I expected. You never get used to living in someone else's house. Don't you agree? I lived so quietly. You can only appreciate what you've had when things change. That's what they say, isn't it? Cigarette?

McCann. I don't smoke.

Stanley lights a cigarette. Voices from the back.

Stanley. Who's out there?

McCann. My friend and the man of the house.

Stanley. You know what? To look at me, I bet you wouldn't think I'd led such a quiet life. The lines on my face, eh? It's the drink. Been drinking a bit down here. But what I mean is . . . you know how it is . . . away from your own . . . all wrong, of course . . . I'll be all right when I get back . . . but what I mean is, the way some people look at me you'd think I was a different person. I suppose I have changed, but I'm still the same man that I always was. I mean, you wouldn't think, to look at me, really . . . I mean, not really, that I was the sort of bloke to—to cause any trouble, would you? (*McCann looks at him.*) Do you know what I mean?

McCann. No. (*As Stanley picks up a strip of paper.*) Mind that.

Stanley (*quickly*). Why are you down here?

McCann. A short holiday.

Stanley. This is a ridiculous house to pick on. (*He rises.*)

McCann. Why?

Stanley. Because it's not a boarding house. It never was.

McCann. Sure it is.

Stanley. Why did you choose this house?

McCann. You know, sir, you're a bit depressed for a man on his birthday.

Stanley (*sharply*). Why do you call me sir?

McCann. You don't like it?

Stanley (*to the table*). Listen. Don't call me sir.

McCann. I won't, if you don't like it.

Stanley (*moving away*). No. Anyway, this isn't my birthday.

McCann. No?

Stanley. No. It's not till next month.

McCann. Not according to the lady.

Stanley. Her? She's crazy. Round the bend.

McCann. That's a terrible thing to say.

Stanley (*to the table*). Haven't you found that out yet? There's a lot you don't know. I think someone's leading you up the garden path.

McCann. Who would do that?

Stanley (*leaning across the table*). That woman is mad!

McCann. That's slander.

Stanley. And you don't know what you're doing.

McCann. Your cigarette is near that paper.

Voices from the back.

Stanley. Where the hell are they? (*Stubbing his cigarette.*) Why don't they come in? What are they doing out there?

McCann. You want to steady yourself.

Stanley crosses to him and grips his arm.

Stanley (*urgently*). Look—

MCCANN. Don't touch me.

STANLEY. Look. Listen a minute.

MCCANN. Let go my arm.

STANLEY. Look. Sit down a minute.

MCCANN (*savagely, hitting his arm*). Don't do that!

Stanley backs across the stage, holding his arm.

STANLEY. Listen. You knew what I was talking about before, didn't you?

MCCANN. I don't know what you're at at all.

STANLEY. It's a mistake! Do you understand?

MCCANN. You're in a bad state, man.

STANLEY (*whispering, advancing*). Has he told you anything? Do you know what you're here for? Tell me. You needn't be frightened of me. Or hasn't he told you?

MCCANN. Told me what?

STANLEY (*hissing*). I've explained to you, damn you, that all those years I lived in Basingstoke I never stepped outside the door.

MCCANN. You know, I'm flabbergasted with you.

STANLEY (*reasonably*). Look. You look an honest man. You're being made a fool of, that's all. You understand? Where do you come from?

MCCANN. Where do you think?

STANLEY. I know Ireland very well. I've many friends there. I love that country and I admire and trust its people. I trust them. They respect the truth and they have a sense of humour. I think their policemen are wonderful. I've ben there. I've never seen such sunsets. What about coming out to have a drink with me? There's a pub down the road serves draught Guinness. Very difficult to get in these parts—(*He breaks off. The voices draw nearer. Goldberg and Petey enter from the back door.*)

GOLDBERG (*as he enters*). A mother in a million. (*He sees Stanley.*) Ah.

PETEY. Oh hullo, Stan. You haven't met Stanley, have you, Mr. Goldberg?

GOLDBERG. I haven't had the pleasure.

PETEY. Oh well, this is Mr. Goldberg, this is Mr. Webber.

GOLDBERG. Pleased to meet you.

PETEY. We were just getting a bit of air in the garden.

GOLDBERG. I was telling Mr. Boles about my old mum. What days. (*He sits at the table, right.*) Yes. When I was a youngster, of a Friday, I used to go for a walk down the canal with a girl who lived down my road. A beautiful girl. What a voice that bird had! A nightingale, my word of honour. Good? Pure? She wasn't a Sunday school teacher for nothing. Anyway, I'd leave her with a little kiss on the cheek—I never took liberties—we weren't like the young men these days in those days. We knew the meaning of respect. So I'd give her a peck and I'd bowl back home. Humming away I'd be, past the children's playground. I'd tip my hat to the toddlers, I'd give a helping hand to a couple of stray dogs, everything came natural. I can see it like yesterday. The sun falling behind the dog stadium. Ah! (*He leans back contentedly.*)

MCCANN. Like behind the town hall.

GOLDBERG. What town hall?

MCCANN. In Carrikmacross.

GOLDBERG. There's no comparison. Up the street, into my gate, inside the door, home. "Simey!" my old mum used shout, "quick before it gets cold." And there on the table what would I see? The nicest piece of gefilte fish you could wish to find on a plate.

MCCANN. I thought your name was Nat.

GOLDBERG. She called me Simey.

PETEY. Yes, we all remembr our childhood.

GOLDBERG. Too true. Eh, Mr. Webber, what do you say? Childhood. Hot water bottles. Hot milk, Pancakes. Soap suds. What a life.

Pause.

PETEY (*rising from the table*). Well, I'll have to be off.

GOLDBERG. Off?

PETEY. It's my chess night.

GOLDBERG. You're not staying for the party?

PETEY. No, I'm sorry, Stan. I didn't know about it till just now. And we've got a game on. I'll try and get back early.

GOLDBERG. We'll save some drink for you, all right? Oh, that reminds me. You'd better go and collect the bottles.

MCCANN. Now?

GOLDBERG. Of course, now. Time's getting on. Round the corner, remember? Mention my name.

PETEY. I'm coming your way.

GOLDBERG. Beat him quick and come back, Mr. Boles.

PETEY. Do my best. See you later, Stan.

Petey and McCann go out, left. Stanley moves to the centre.

GOLDBERG. A warm night.

STANLEY (*turning*). Don't mess me about!

GOLDBERG. I beg your pardon?

STANLEY (*moving downstage*). I'm afraid there's been a misake. We're booked out. Your room is taken. Mrs. Boles forgot to tell you. You'll have to find somewhere else.

GOLDBERG. Are you the manager here?

STANLEY. That's right.

GOLDBERG. Is it a good game?

STANLEY. I run the house. I'm afraid you and your friend will have to find other accommodation.

GOLDBERG (*rising*). Oh, I forgot, I must congratulate you on your birthday. (*Offering his hand.*) Congratulations.

STANLEY (*ignoring hand*). Perhaps you're deaf.

GOLDBERG. No, what makes you think that? As a matter of fact, every single one of my senses is at its peak. Not bad going, eh? For a man past fifty. But a birthday, I always feel, is a great occasion, taken too much for granted these days. What a thing to celebrate— birth! Like getting up in the morning. Marvellous! Some people don't like the idea of getting up in the morning. I've heard them. Getting up in the morning, they say, what is it? Your skin's crabby, you need a shave, your eyes are full of muck, your mouth is like a boghouse, the palms of your hands are full of sweat, your nose is clogged up, your feet stink, what are you but a corpse waiting to be washed? Whenever I hear that point of view I feel cheerful. Because I know what it is to wake up with the sun shining, to the sound of the lawnmower, all the little birds, the smell of the grass, church bells, tomato juice—

STANLEY. Get out.

Enter McCann, with bottles.

Get that drink out. These are unlicensed premises.

GOLDBERG. You're in a terrible humour today, Mr. Webber. And on your birthday too, with the good lady getting her strength up to give you a party.

McCann puts the bottles on the sideboard.

STANLEY. I told you to get those bottles out.

GOLDBERG. Mr. Webber, sit down a minute.

STANLEY. Let me—just make this clear. You don't bother me. To me, you're nothing but a dirty joke. But I have a responsibility towards the people in this house. They've been down here too long. They've lost their sense of smell. I haven't. And nobody's going to take advanatage of them while I'm here. (*A little less forceful.*) Anyway, this house isn't your cup of tea. There's nothing here for you, from any angle, any angle. So why don't you just go, without any more fuss?

GOLDBERG. Mr. Webber, sit down.

STANLEY. It's no good starting any kind of trouble.

GOLDBERG. Sit down.

STANLEY. Why should I?

GOLDBERG. If you want to know the truth, Webber, you're beginning to get on my breasts.

STANLEY. Really? Well, that's —

GOLDBERG. Sit down.

STANLEY. No.

Goldberg sighs, and sits at the table right.

GOLDBERG. McCann.

MCCANN. Nat?

GOLDBERG. Ask him to sit down.

MCCANN. Yes, Nat. (*McCann moves to Stanley.*) Do you mind sitting down?

STANLEY. Yes, I do mind.

MCCANN. Yes now, but—it'd be better if you did.

STANLEY. Why don't you sit down?

MCCANN. No, not me—you.

STANLEY. No thanks.

Pause.

MCCANN. Nat.

GOLDBERG. What?

MCCANN. He won't sit down.

GOLDBERG. Well, ask him.

MCCANN. I've asked him.

GOLDBERG. Ask him again.

MCCANN (*to Stanley*). Sit down.

STANLEY. Why?

MCCANN. You'd be more comfortable.

STANLEY. So would you.

Pause.

MCCANN. All right. If you will I will.

STANLEY. You first.

McCann slowly sits at the table, left.

MCCANN. Well?

STANLEY. Right. Now you've both had a rest you can get out!

MCCANN (*rising*). That's a dirty trick! I'll kick the shite out of him!

GOLDBERG (*rising*). No! I have stood up.

MCCANN. Sit down again!

GOLDBERG. Once I'm up I'm up.

STANLEY. Same here.

MCCANN (*moving to Stanley*). You've made Mr. Goldberg stand up.

STANLEY (*his voice rising*). It'll do him good!

MCCANN. Get in that seat.

GOLDBERG. McCann.

MCCANN. Get down in that seat!

GOLDBERG (*crossing to him*). Webber. (*Quietly.*) SIT DOWN. (*Silence. Stanley begins to whistle "The Mountains of Morne". He strolls casually to the chair at*

the table. They watch him. He stops whistling. Silence.
He sits.)

STANLEY. You'd better be careful.

GOLDBERG. Webber, what were you doing yesterday?

STANLEY. Yesterday?

GOLDBERG. And the day before. What did you do the day before that?

STANLEY. What do you mean?

GOLDBERG. What are you wasting evrybody's time, Webber? Why are you getting in everybody's way?

STANLEY. Me? What are you—

GOLDBERG. I'm telling you, Webber. You're a washout. Why are you getting on everybody's wick? Why are you driving that old lady off her conk?

McCANN. He likes to do it!

GOLDBERG. Why do you behave so badly, Webber? Why do you force that old man out to play chess?

STANLEY. Me?

GOLDBERG. Why do you treat that young lady like a leper? She's not the leper, Webber!

STANLEY. What the—

GOLDBERG. What did you wear last week, Webber? Where do you keep your suits?

McCANN. Why did you leave the organization?

GOLDBERG. What would your old mum say, Webber?

McCANN. Why did you betray us?

GOLDBERG. You hurt me, Webber. You're playing a dirty game.

McCANN. That's a Black and Tan fact.

GOLDBERG. Who does he think he is?

McCANN. Who do you think you are?

STANLEY. You're on the wrong horse.

GOLDBERG. When did you come to this place?

STANLEY. Last year.

GOLDBERG. Where did you come from?

STANLEY. Somewhere else.

GOLDBERG. Why did you come here?

STANLEY. My feet hurt!

GOLDBERG. Why did you stay?

STANLEY. I had a headache!

GOLDBERG. Did you take anything for it?

STANLEY. Yes.

GOLDBERG. What?

STANLEY. Fruit salts!

GOLDBERG. Enos or Andrews?

STANLEY. En—An—

GOLDBERG. Did you stir properly? Did they fizz?

STANLEY. Now, now, wait, you—

GOLDBERG. Did they fizz? Did they fizz or didn't they fizz?

McCANN. He doesn't know!

GOLDBERG. You don't know. When did you last have a bath?

STANLEY. I have one every—

GOLDBERG. Don't lie.

McCANN. You betrayed the organization. I know him!

STANLEY. You don't!

GOLDBERG. What can you see without your glasses?

STANLEY. Anything.

GOLDBERG. Take off his glasses.

McCann snatches his glasses and as Stanley rises,
reaching for them, takes his chair downstage centre,
below the table, Stanley stumbling as he follows.
Stanley clutches the chair and stays bent over it.

Webber, you're a fake. (*They stand on each side of*
the chair.) When did you last wash up a cup?

STANLEY. The Christmas before last.

GOLDBERG. Where?

STANLEY. Lyons Corner House.

GOLDBERG. Which one?

STANLEY. Marble Arch.

GOLDBERG. Where was your wife?

STANLEY. In—

GOLDBERG. Answer.

STANLEY (*turning, crouched*). What wife?

GOLDBERG. What have you done with your wife?

McCANN. He's killed his wife!

GOLDBERG. Why did you kill your wife?

STANLEY (*sitting, his back to the audience*). What wife?

McCANN. How did he kill her?

GOLDBERG. How did you kill her?

McCANN. You throttled her.

GOLDBERG. With arsenic.

McCANN. There's your man!

GOLDBERG. Where's your old mum?

STANLEY. In the sanatorium.

McCANN. Yes!

GOLDBERG. Why did you never get married?

McCANN. She was waiting at the porch.

GOLDBERG. You skedaddled from the wedding.

McCANN. He left her in the lurch.

GOLDBERG. You left her in the pudding club.

McCANN. She was waiting at the church.

GOLDBERG. Webber! Why did you change your name?

STANLEY. I forgot the other one.

GOLDBERG. What's your name now?

STANLEY. Joe Soap.

GOLDBERG. You stink of sin.

McCANN. I can smell it.

GOLDBERG. Do you recognise an external force?

STANLEY. What?

GOLDBERG. Do you recognise an external force?

McCANN. That's the question!

GOLDBERG. Do you recognise an external force, responsible for you, suffering for you?
STANLEY. It's late.
GOLDBERG. Late! Late enough! When did you last pray?
McCANN. He's sweating!
GOLDBERG. When did you last pray?
McCANN. He's sweating!
GOLDBERG. Is the number 846 possible or necessary?
STANLEY. Neither.
GOLDBERG. Wrong! Is the numbr 846 possible or necessary?
STANLEY. Both.
GOLDBERG. Wrong! It's necessary but not possible.
STANLEY. Both
GOLDBERG. Wrong! Why do you think the number 846 is necessarily possible?
STANLEY. Must be.
GOLDBERG. Wrong! It's only necessarily necessary! We admit possibility only after we grant necessity. It is possible because necessary but by no means necessary through possibility. The possibility can only be assumed after the proof of necessity.
McCANN. Right!
GOLDBERG. Right? Of course right! We're right and you're wrong, Webber, all along the line.
McCANN. All along the line!
GOLDBERG. Where is your lechery leading you?
McCANN. You'll pay for this.
GOLDBERG. You stuff yourself with dry toast.
McCANN. You contaminate womankind.
GOLDBERG. Why don't you pay the rent?
McCANN. Mother defiler!
GOLDBERG. Why do you pick your nose?
McCANN. I demand justice!
GOLDBERG. What's your trade?
McCANN. What about Ireland?
GOLDBERG. What's your trade?
STANLEY. I play the piano.
GOLDBERG. How many fingers do you use?
STANLEY. No hands!
GOLDBERG. No society would touch you. Not even a building society.
McCANN. You're a traitor to the cloth.
GOLDBERG. What do you use for pyjamas?
STANLEY. Nothing.
GOLDBERG. You verminate the sheet of your birth.
McCANN. What about the Albigensenist heresy?
GOLDBERG. Who watered the wicket in Melbourne?
McCANN. What about the blessed Oliver Plunkett?
GOLDBERG. Speak up Webber. Why did the chicken cross the road?
STANLEY. He wanted to—he wanted to—he wanted to. . . .

McCANN. He doesn't know!
GOLDBERG. Why did the chicken cross the road?
STANLEY. He wanted to—he wanted to. . . .
GOLDBERG. Why did the chicken cross the road?
STANLEY. He wanted. . . .
McCANN. He doesn't know. He doesn't know which came first!
GOLDBERG. Which came first?
McCANN. Chicken? Egg? Which came first?
GOLDBERG and McCANN. Which came first? Which came first? Which came first?

Stanley screams.

GOLDBERG. He doesn't know. Do you know your own face?
McCANN. Wake him up. Stick a needle in his eye.
GOLDBERG. You're a plague, Webber. You're an overthrow.
McCANN. You're what's left!
GOLDBERG. But we've got the answer to you. We can sterilise you.
McCANN. What about Drogheda?
GOLDBERG. Your bite is dead. Only your pong is left.
McCANN. You betrayed our land.
GOLDBERG. You betray our breed.
McCANN. Who are you, Webber?
GOLDBERG. What makes you think you exist?
McCANN. You're dead.
GOLDBERG. You're dead. You can't live, you can't think, you can't love. You're dead. You're a plague gone bad. There's no juice in you. You're nothing but an odour!

Silence. They stand over him. He is crouched in the chair. He looks up slowly and kicks Goldberg in the stomach. Goldberg falls. Stanley stands. McCann seizes a chair and lifts it above his head. Stanley seizes a chair and covers his head with it. McCann and Stanley circle.

GOLDBERG. Steady, McCann.
STANLEY (*circling*). Uuuuuuhhhhh!
McCANN. Right, Judas.
GOLDBERG (*rising*). Steady, McCann.
McCANN. Come on!
STANLEY. Uuuuuuuhhhhh!
McCANN. He's sweating.
STANLEY. Uuuuuuhhhhh!
GOLDBERG. Easy, McCann.
McCANN. The bastard sweatpig is sweating.

A loud drumbeat off left, descending the stairs. Goldberg takes the chair from Stanley. They put the chairs down. They stop still. Enter Meg, in evening dress, holding sticks and drum.

MEG. I brought the drum down. I'm dressed for the party.

GOLDBERG. Wonderful.

MEG. You like my dress?

GOLDBERG. Wonderful. Out of this world.

MEG. I know. My father gave it to me. (*Placing drum on table.*) Doesn't it make a beautiful noise?

GOLDBERG. It's a fine piece of work. Maybe Stan'll play us a little tune afterwards.

MEG. Oh yes. Will you, Stan?

STANLEY. Could I have my glasses?

GOLDBERG. Ah yes. (*He holds his hand out to McCann. McCann passes him his glasses.*) Here they are. (*Stanley takes them.*) Now. What have we got here? Enough to scuttle a liner. We've got four bottles of Scotch and one bottle of Irish.

MEG. Oh, Mr. Goldberg, what should I drink?

GOLDBERG. Glasses, glasses first. Open the Scotch, McCann.

MEG (*at the sideboard*). Here's my very best glasses in here.

MCCANN. I don't drink Scotch.

GOLDBERG. You've got the Irish.

MEG (*bringing the glasses*). Here they are.

GOLDBERG. Good. Mrs. Boles, I think Stanley should pour the toast, don't you?

MEG. Oh yes. Come on, Stanley. (*Stanley walks slowly to the table.*) Do you like my dress, Mr. Goldberg?

GOLDBERG. It's out on its own. Turn yourself round a minute. I used to be in the business. Go on, walk up there.

MEG. Oh no.

GOLDBERG. Don't be shy. (*He slaps her bottom.*)

MEG. Oooh!

GOLDBERG. Walk up the boulevard. Let's have a look at you. What a carriage. What's your opinion, McCann? Like a Countess, nothing less. Madam, now turn around and promenade to the kitchen. What a deportment!

MCCANN (*to Stanley*). You can pour my Irish too.

GOLDBERG. You look like a Gladiola.

MEG. Stan, what about my dress?

GOLDBERG. One for the lady, one for the lady. Now madam—your glass.

MEG. Thank you.

GOLDBERG. Lift your glasses, ladies and gentlemen. We'll drink a toast.

MEG. Lulu isn't here.

GOLDBERG. It's past the hour. Now—who's going to propose the toast? Mrs. Boles, it can only be you.

MEG. Me?

GOLDBERG. Who else?

MEG. But what do I say?

GOLDBERG. Say what you feel. What you honestly feel. (*Meg looks uncertain.*) It's Stanley's birthday. Your

Stanley. Look at him. Look at him and it'll come. Wait a minute, the light's too strong. Let's have proper lighting. McCann, have you got your torch?

MCCANN (*bringing a small torch from his pocket.*) Here.

GOLDBERG. Switch out the light and put on your torch. (*McCann goes to the door, switches off the light, comes back, shines the torch on Meg. Outside the window there is still a faint light.*) Not on the lady, on the gentleman! You must shine it on the birthday boy. (*McCann shines the torch in Stanley's face.*) Now, Mrs. Boles, it's all yours.

Pause.

MEG. I don't know what to say.

GOLDBERG. Look at him. Just look at him.

MEG. Isn't the light in his eyes?

GOLDBERG. No, no. Go on.

MEG. Well—it's very, very nice to be here tonight, in my house, and I want to propose a toast to Stanley, because it's his birthday, and he's lived here for a long while now, and he's my Stanley now. And I think he's a good boy, although sometimes he's bad. (*An appreciative laugh from Goldberg.*) And he's the only Stanley I know, and I know him better than all the world, although he doesn't think so. (*"Hear—hear" from Goldberg.*) Well, I could cry because I'm so happy, having him here and not gone away, on his birthday, and there isn't anything I wouldn't do for him, and all you good people here tonight. . . . (*She sobs.*)

GOLDBERG. Beautiful! A beautiful speech. Put the light on, McCann. (*McCann goes to the door. Stanley remains still.*) That was a lovely toast. (*The light goes on. Lulu enters from the door, left. Goldberg comforts Meg.*) Buck up now. Come on, smile at the birdy. That's better. Ah, look who's here.

MEG. Lulu.

GOLDBERG. How do you do, Lulu? I'm Nat Goldberg.

LULU. Hallo.

GOLDBERG. Stanley, a drink for your guest. You just missed the toast, my dear, and what a toast.

LULU. Did I?

GOLDBERG. Stanley, a drink for your guest. Stanley. (*Stanley hands a glass to Lulu.*) Right. Now raise your glasses. Everyone standing up? No, not you, Stanley. You must sit down.

MCCANN. Yes, that's right. He must sit down.

GOLDBERG. You don't mind sitting down a minute? We're going to drink to you.

MEG. Come on!

LULU. Come on!

Stanley sits in a chair at the table.

GOLDBERG. Right. Now Stanley's sat down. (*Taking the stage.*) Well, I want to say first that I've never been so touched to the heart as by the toast we've just heard. How often, in this day and age, do you come across real, true warmth? Once in a lifetime. Until a few minutes ago, ladies and gentlemen, I, like all of you, was asking the same question. What's happened to the love, the bonhomie, the unashamed expression of affection of the day before yesterday, that our mums taught us in the nursery?

McCANN. Gone with the wind.

GOLDBERG. That's what I thought, until today. I believe in a good laugh, a day's fishing, a bit of gardening. I was very proud of my old greenhouse, made out of my own spit and faith. That's the sort I am. Not size but quality. A little Austin, tea in Fullers, a library book from Boots, and I'm satisfied. But just now, I say just now, the lady of the house said her piece and I for one am knocked over by the sentiments she expressed. Lucky is the man who's at the receiving end, that's what I say. (*Pause.*) How can I put it to you? We all wander on our tod through this world. It's a lonely pillow to kip on. Right!

LULU (*admiringly*). Right!

GOLDBERG. Agreed. But tonight, Lulu, McCann, we've known a great fortune. We've heard a lady extend the sum total of her devotion, in all its pride, plume and peacock, to a member of her own living race. Stanley, my heartfelt congratulations. I wish you, in behalf of us all, a happy birthday. I'm sure you've never been a prouder man than you are today. Mazaltov! And may we only meet at Simchahs! (*Lulu and Meg applaud.*) Turn out the light, McCann, while we drink the toast.

LULU. That was a wonderful speech.

McCann switches out the light, comes back, and shines the torch in Stanley's face. The light outside the window is fainter.

GOLDBERG. Lift your glasses. Stanley—happy birthday.

McCANN. Happy birthday.

LULU. Happy birthday.

MEG. Many happy returns of the day, Stan.

GOLDBERG. And well over the fast.

They all drink.

MEG (*kissing him*). Oh, Stanny. . . .

GOLDBERG. Lights!

McCANN. Right! (*He switches on the lights.*)

MEG. Clink my glass, Stan.

LULU. Mr. Goldberg—

GOLDBERG. Call me Nat.

MEG (*to McCann*). You clink my glass.

LULU (*to Goldberg*). You're empty. Let me fill you up.

GOLDBERG. It's a pleasure.

LULU. You're a marvellous speaker, Nat, you know that? Where did you learn to speak like that?

GOLDBERG. You liked it, eh?

LULU. Oh yes!

GOLDBERG. Well, my first chance to stand up and give a lecture was at the Ethical Hall, Bayswater. A wonderful opportunity. I'll never forget it. They were all there that night. Charlotte Street was empty. Of course, that's a good while ago.

LULU. What did you speak about?

GOLDBERG. The Necessary and the Possible. It went like a bomb. Since then I always speak at weddings.

Stanley is still. Goldberg sits left of the table. Meg joins McCann downstage, right, Lulu is downstage, left. McCann pours more Irish from the bottle, which he carries, into his glass.

MEG. Let's have some of yours.

McCANN. In that?

MEG. Yes.

McCANN. Are you used to mixing them?

MEG. No.

McCANN. Give me your glass.

Meg sits on a shoe-box, downstage, right. Lulu, at the table, pours more drink for Goldberg and herself, and gives Goldberg his glass.

GOLDBERG. Thank you.

MEG (*to McCann*). Do you think I should?

GOLDBERG. Lulu, you're a big bouncy girl. Come and sit on my lap.

McCANN. Why not?

LULU. Do you think I should?

GOLDBERG. Try it.

MEG (*sipping*). Very nice.

LULU. I'll bounce up to the ceiling.

McCANN. I don't know how you can mix that stuff.

GOLDBERG. Take a chance.

MEG (*to McCann*). Sit down on this stool.

Lulu sits on Goldberg's lap.

McCANN. This?

GOLDBERG. Comfortable?

LULU. Yes, thanks.

McCANN (*sitting*). It's comfortable.

GOLDBERG. You know, there's a lot in your eyes.

LULU. And in yours, too.

GOLDBERG. Do you think so?

LULU (giggling). Go on!

McCANN (to Meg). Where'd you get it?

MEG. My father gave it to me.

LULU. I didn't know I was going to meet you here tonight.

McCANN (to Meg). Ever been to Carrikmacross?

MEG (drinking). I've been to King's Cross.

LULU. You came right out of the blue, you know that?

GOLDBERG (as she moves). Mind how you go. You're cracking a rib.

MEG (standing). I want to dance! (Lulu and Goldberg look into each other's eyes. McCann drinks. Meg crosses to Stanley.) Stanley. Dance. (Stanley sits still. Meg dances round the room alone, then comes back to McCann, who fills her glass. She sits.)

LULU (to Goldberg). Shall I tell you something?

GOLDBERG. What?

LULU. I trust you.

GOLDBERG (lifting his glass). Gesundheit.

LULU. Have you got a wife?

GOLDBERG. I had a wife. What a wife. Listen to this. Friday, of an afternoon, I'd take myself for a little constitutional, down over the park. Eh, do me a favour, just sit on the table a minute, will you? (Lulu sits on the table. He stretches and continues.) A little constitutional. I'd say hullo to the little boys, the little girls—I never made distinctions—and then back I'd go, back to my bangalow with the flat roof. "Simey," my wife would shout, "quick, before it gets cold!" And there on the table what would I see? The nicest piece of rollmop and pickled cucumber you could wish to find on a plate.

LULU. I thought your name was Nat.

GOLDBERG. She called me Simey.

LULU. I bet you were a good husband.

GOLDBERG. You should have seen her funeral.

LULU. Why?

GOLDBERG (draws in his breath and wags head). What a funeral.

MEG (to McCann). My father was going to take me to Ireland once. But then he went away by himself.

LULU (to Goldberg). Do you think you knew me when I was a little girl?

GOLDBERG. Were you a nice little girl?

LULU. I was.

MEG. I don't know if he went to Ireland.

GOLDBERG. Maybe I played piggy-back with you.

LULU. Maybe you did.

MEG. He didn't take me.

GOLDBERG. Or pop goes the weasel.

LULU. Is that a game?

GOLDBERG. Sure it's a game!

McCANN. Why didn't he take you to Ireland?

LULU. You're tickling me!

GOLDBERG. You should worry.

LULU. I've always liked older men. They can soothe you.

They embrace.

McCANN. I know a place. Roscrea. Mother Nolan's.

MEG. There was a night-light in my room, when I was a little girl.

McCANN. One time I stayed there all night with the boys. Singing and drinking all night.

MEG. And my Nanny used to sit up with me, and sing songs to me.

McCANN. And a plate of fry in the morning. Now where am I?

MEG. My little room was pink. I had a pink carpet and pink curtains, and I had musical boxes all over the room. And they played me to sleep. And my father was a very big doctor. That's why I never had any complaints. I was cared for, and I had little sisters and brothers in other rooms, all different colours.

McCANN. Tullamore, where are you?

MEG (to McCann). Give us a drop more.

McCANN (filling her glass and singing). Glorio, Glorio, to the bold Fenian men!

MEG. Oh. what a lovely voice.

GOLDBERG. Give us a song, McCann.

LULU. A love song!

McCANN (reciting). The night that poor Paddy was stretched, the boys they all paid him a visit.

GOLDBERG. A love song!

McCANN (in a full voice, sings).

> Oh, the Garden of Eden has vanished, they say,
> But I know the lie of it still.
> Just turn to the left at the foot of Ben Clay
> And stop when halfway to Coote Hill.
> It's there you will find it, I know sure enough,
> And it's whispering over to me:
> Come back, Paddy Reilly, to Bally-James-Duff,
> Come home, Paddy Reilly, to me!

LULU (to Goldberg). You're the dead image of the first man I ever loved.

GOLDBERG. It goes without saying.

MEG (rising). I want to play a game!

GOLDBERG. A game?

LULU. What game?

MEG. Any game.

LULU (jumping up). Yes, let's play a game.

GOLDBERG. What game?

McCANN. Hide and seek.

LULU. Blind man's buff.

MEG. Yes!

GOLDBERG. You want to play blind man's buff?

LULU AND MEG. Yes!

GOLDBERG. All right. Blind man's buff. Come on! Every-one up! (*Rising.*) McCann. Stanley—Stanley!

MEG. Stanley. Up.

GOLDBERG. What's the matter with him?

MEG (*bending over him*). Stanley, we're going to play a game. Oh, come on, don't be sulky, Stan.

LULU. Come on.

Stanley rises. McCann rises.

GOLDBERG. Right! Now—who's going to be blind first?

LULU. Mrs. Boles.

MEG. Not me.

GOLDBERG. Of course you.

MEG. Who, me?

LULU (*taking her scarf from her neck*). Here you are.

McCANN. How do you play this game?

LULU (*tying her scarf round Meg's eyes*). Haven't you ever played blind man's buff? Keep still, Mrs. Boles. You mustn't be touched. But you can't move after she's blind. You must stay where you are after she's blind. And if she touches you then you become blind. Turn round. How many fingers am I holding up?

MEG. I can't see.

LULU. Right.

GOLDBERG. Right! Everyone move about. McCann. Stanley. Now stop. Now still. Off you go!

Stanley is downstage, right, Meg moves about the room. Goldberg fondles Lulu at arm's length. Meg touches McCann.

MEG. Caught you!

LULU. Take off your scarf.

MEG. What lovely hair!

LULU (*untying the scarf*). There.

MEG. It's you!

GOLDBERG. Put it on, McCann.

LULU (*tying it on McCann*). There. Turn round. How many fingers am I holding up?

McCANN. I don't know.

GOLDBERG. Right! Everyone move about. Right. Stop! Still!

McCann begins to move.

MEG. Oh, this is lovely!

GOLDBERG. Quiet! Tch, tch, tch. Now—all move again. Stop! Still!

McCann moves about. Goldberg fondles Lulu at arm's length. McCann draws near Stanley. He stretches his arm and touches Stanley's glasses.

MEG. It's Stanley!

GOLDBERG (*to Lulu*). Enjoying the game?

MEG. It's your turn, Stan.

McCann takes off the scarf.

McCANN (*to Stanley*). I'll take your glasses.

McCann takes Stanley's glasses.

MEG. Give me the scarf.

GOLDBERG (*holding Lulu*). Tie his scarf, Mrs. Boles.

MEG. That's what I'm doing. (*To Stanley.*) Can you see my nose?

GOLDBERG. He can't. Ready? Right! Everyone move. Stop! And still!

Stanley stands blindfold. McCann backs slowly across the stage to the left. He breaks Stanley's glasses, snapping the frames. Meg is downstage, left, Lulu and Goldberg upstage centre, close together. Stanley begins to move, very slowly, across the stage to the left. McCann picks up the drum and places it sideways in Stanley's path. Stanley walks into the drum and falls over with his foot caught in it.

MEG. Ooh!

GOLDBERG. Sssh!

Stanley rises. He begins to move towards Meg, drag-ging the drum on his foot. He reaches her and stops. His hands move towards her and they reach her throat. He begins to strangle her. McCann and Goldberg rush forward and throw him off.

BLACKOUT

There is now no light at all through the window. The stage is in darkness.

LULU. The lights!

GOLDBERG. What's happened?

LULU. The lights!

McCANN. Wait a minute.

GOLDBERG. Where is he?

McCANN. Let go of me!

GOLDBERG. Who's this?

LULU. Someone's touching me!

McCANN. Where is he?

MEG. Why has the light gone out?

GOLDBERG. Where's your torch? (*McCann shines the torch in Goldberg's face.*) Not on me! (*McCann shifts the torch. It is knocked from his hand and falls. It goes out.*)

MCCANN. My torch!

LULU. Oh God!

GOLDBERG. Where's your torch? Pick up your torch!

MCCANN. I can't find it.

LULU. Hold me. Hold me.

GOLDBERG. Get down on your knees. Help him find the torch.

LULU. I can't.

MCCANN. It's gone.

MEG. Why has the light gone out?

GOLDBERG. Everyone quiet! Help him find the torch.

Silence. Grunts from McCann and Goldberg on their knees. Suddenly there is a sharp, sustained rat-a-tat with a stick on the side of the drum from the back of the room. Silence. Whimpers from Lulu.

GOLDBERG. Over here. McCann!

MCCANN. Here.

GOLDBERG. Come to me, come to me. Easy. Over there.

Goldberg and McCann move up left of the table. Stanley moves down right of the table. Lulu suddenly perceives him moving towards her, screams and faints. Goldberg and McCann turn and stumble against each other.

GOLDBERG. What is it?

MCCANN. Who's that?

GOLDBERG. What is it?

In the darkness Stanley picks up Lulu and places her on the table.

MEG. It's Lulu!

Goldberg and McCann move downstage, right.

GOLDBERG. Where is she?

MCCANN. She fell.

GOLDBERG. Where?

MCCANN. About here.

GOLDBERG. Help me pick her up.

MCCANN (*moving downstage, left*). I can't find her.

GOLDBERG. She must be somewhere.

MCCANN. She's not here.

GOLDBERG (*moving downstage, left*). She must be.

MCCANN. She's gone.

McCann finds the torch on the floor, shines it on the table and Stanley. Lulu is lying spread-eagled on the table, Stanley bent over her. Stanley, as soon as the torchlight hits him, begins to giggle. Goldberg and McCann move towards him. He backs, giggling, the torch on his face. They follow him upstage, left.

He backs against the hatch, giggling. The torch draws closer. His giggle rises and grows as he flattens himself against the wall. Their figures converge upon him.

Curtain

ACT III

The next morning, Petey enters, left, with a newspaper and sits at the table. He begins to read. Meg's voice comes through the kitchen hatch.

MEG. Is that you, Stan? (*Pause.*) Stanny?

PETEY. Yes?

MEG. Is that you?

PETEY. It's me.

MEG (*appearing at the hatch*). Oh, it's you. I've run out of cornflakes.

PETEY. Well, what else have you got?

MEG. Nothing.

PETEY. Nothing?

MEG. Just a minute. (*She leaves the hatch and enters by the kitchen door.*) You got your paper?

PETEY. Yes.

MEG. Is it good?

PETEY. Not bad.

MEG. The two gentlemen had the last of the fry this morning.

PETEY. Oh, did they?

MEG. There's some tea in the pot though. (*She pours tea for him.*) I'm going out shopping in a minute. Get you something nice.

MEG. I've got a splitting headache.

PETEY (*reading*). You slept like a log last night.

MEG. Did I?

PETEY. Dead out.

MEG. I must have been tired. (*She looks about the room and sees the broken drum in the fireplace.*) Oh, look. (*She rises and picks it up.*) The drum's broken. (*Petey looks up.*) Why is it broken?

PETEY. I don't know.

She hits it with her hand.

MEG. It still makes a noise.

PETEY. You can always get another one.

MEG (*sadly*). It was probably broken in the party. I don't remember it being broken though, in the party. (*She puts it down.*) What a shame.

PETEY. You can always get another one, Meg.

MEG. Well, at least he did have it on his birthday, didn't he? Like I wanted him to.

PETEY (*reading*). Yes.

MEG. Have you seen him down yet? (*Petey does not answer.*) Petey.

PETEY. What?

MEG. Have you seen him down?

PETEY. Who?

MEG. Stanley.

PETEY. No.

MEG. Nor have I. That boy should be up. He's late for his breakfast.

PETEY. There isn't any breakfast.

MEG. Yes, but he doesn't know that. I'm going to call him.

PETEY (*quickly*). No don't do that, Meg. Let him sleep.

MEG. But you say he stays in bed too much.

PETEY. Let him sleep . . . this morning. Leave him.

MEG. I've been up once, with his cup of tea. But Mr. McCann opened the door. He said they were talking. He said he'd made him one. He must have been up early. I don't know what they were talking about. I was surprised. Because Stanley's usually fast asleep when I wake him. But he wasn't this morning. I heard him talking. (*Pause.*) Do you think they know each other? I think they're old friends. Stanley had a lot of friends. I know he did. (*Pause.*) I didn't give him his tea. He'd already had one. I came down again and went on with my work. Then, after a bit, they came down to breakfast. Stanley must have gone to sleep again.

Pause.

PETEY. When are you going to do your shopping, Meg?

MEG. Yes, I must. (*Collecting the bag.*) I've got a rotten headache. (*She goes to the back door, stops suddenly and turns.*) Did you see what's outside this morning?

PETEY. What?

MEG. That big car.

PETEY. Yes.

MEG. It wasn't there yesterday. Did you . . . did you have a look inside it?

PETEY. I had a peep.

MEG (*coming down tensely, and whispering*). Is there anything in it?

PETEY. In it?

MEG. Yes.

PETEY. What do you mean, in it?

MEG. Inside it.

PETEY. What sort of thing?

MEG. Well . . . I mean . . . is there . . . is there a wheelbarrow in it?

PETEY. A wheelbarrow?

MEG. Yes.

PETEY. I didn't see one.

MEG. You didn't? Are you sure?

PETEY. What would Mr. Goldberg want with a wheelbarrow?

MEG. Mr. Goldberg?

PETEY. It's his car.

MEG (*relieved*). His car? Oh, I didn't know it was his car.

PETEY. Of course it's his car.

MEG. Oh, I feel better.

PETEY. What are you on about?

MEG. Oh, I do feel better.

PETEY. You go and get a bit of air.

MEG. Yes, I will. I will. I'll go and get the shopping. (*She goes towards the back door. A door slams upstairs. She turns.*) It's Stanley! He's coming down—what am I going to do about his breakfast? (*She rushes into the kitchen.*) Petey, what shall I give him? (*She looks through the hatch.*) There's no cornflakes. (*They both gaze at the door. Enter Goldberg. He halts at the door, as he meets their gaze, then smiles.*)

GOLDBERG. A reception committee!

MEG. Oh, I thought it was Stanley.

GOLDBERG. You find a resemblance?

MEG. Oh no. You look quite different.

GOLDBERG (*coming into the room*). Different build, of course.

MEG (*entering from the kitchen*). I thought he was coming down for his breakfast. He hasn't had his breakfast yet.

GOLDBERG. Your wife makes a very nice cup of tea, Mr. Boles, you know that?

PETEY. Yes, she does sometimes. Sometimes she forgets.

MEG. Is he coming down?

GOLDBERG. Down? Of course he's coming down. On a lovely sunny day like this he shouldn't come down? He'll be up and about in next to no time. (*He sits at the table.*) And what a breakfast he's going to get.

MEG. Mr. Goldberg.

GOLDBERG. Yes?

MEG. I didn't know that was your car outside.

GOLDBERG. You like it?

MEG. Are you going to go for a ride?

GOLDBERG (*to Petey*). A smart car, eh?

PETEY. Nice shine on it all right.

GOLDBERG. What is old is good, take my tip. There's room there. Room in the front, and room in the back. (*He strokes the teapot.*) The pot's hot. More tea, Mr. Boles?

PETEY. No thanks.

GOLDBERG (*pouring tea*). That car? That car's never let me down.

MEG. Are you going to go for a ride?

GOLDBERG (*ruminatively*). And the boot. A beautiful boot. There's just room . . . for the right amount.

MEG. Well, I'd better be off now. (*She moves to the back door, and turns.*) Petey, when Stanley comes down. . . .

PETEY. Yes?

MEG. Tell him I won't be long.

PETEY. I'll tell him.

MEG (*vaguely*). I won't be long. (*She exits.*)

GOLDBERG (*sipping his tea*). A good woman. A charming woman. My mother was the same. My wife was identical.

PETEY. How is he this morning?

GOLDBERG. Who?

PETEY. Stanley, is he any better?

GOLDBERG (*a little uncertainly*). Oh . . . a little better, I think, a little better. Of course, I'm not really qualified to say, Mr. Boles. I mean, I haven't got the . . . the qualifications. The best thing would be if someone with the proper . . . mnn . . . qualifications . . . was to have a look at him. Someone with a few letters after his name. It makes all the difference.

PETEY. Yes.

GOLDBERG. Anyway, Dermot's with him at the moment. He's . . . keeping him company.

PETEY. Dermot?

GOLDBERG. Yes.

PETEY. It's a terrible thing.

GOLDBERG (*sighs*). Yes. The birthday celebration was too much for him.

PETEY. What came over him?

GOLDBERG (*sharply*). What came over him? Breakdown, Mr. Boles. Pure and simple. Nervous breakdown.

PETEY. But what brought it on so suddenly?

GOLDBERG (*rising, and moving upstage*). Well, Mr. Boles, it can happen in all sorts of ways. A friend of mine was telling me about it only the other day. We'd both been concerned with another case—not entirely similar, of course, but . . . quite alike, quite alike. (*He pauses.*) Anyway, he was telling me, you see, this friend of mine, that sometimes it happens gradual—day by day it grows and grows and grows . . . day by day. And then other times it happens all at once. Poof! Like that! The nerves break. There's no guarantee how it's going to happen, but with certain people . . . it's a foregone conclusion.

PETEY. Really?

GOLDBERG. Yes. This friend of mine—he was telling me about it—only the other day. (*He stands uneasily for a moment, then brings out a cigarette case and takes a cigarette.*) Have an Abdullah.

PETEY. No, no, I don't take them.

GOLDBERG. Once in a while I treat myself to a cigarette. An Abdullah, perhaps, or a . . . (*He snaps his fingers.*)

PETEY. What a night. (*Goldberg lights his cigarette with a lighter.*) Came in the front door and all the lights were out. Put a shilling in the slot, came in here and the party was over.

GOLDBERG (*coming downstage*). You put a shilling in the slot?

PETEY. Yes.

GOLDBERG. And the lights came on.

PETEY. Yes, then I came in here.

GOLDBERG (*with a short laugh*). I could have sworn it was a fuse.

PETEY (*continuing*). There was dead silence. Couldn't hear a thing. So I went upstairs and your friend—Dermot—met me on the landing. And he told me.

GOLDBERG (*sharply*). Who?

PETEY. Your friend—Dermot.

GOLDBERG (*heavily*). Dermot. Yes. (*He sits.*)

PETEY. They get over it sometimes though, don't they? I mean, they can recover from it, can't they?

GOLDBERG. Recover? Yes, sometimes they recover, in one way or another.

PETEY. I mean, he might have recovered by now, mightn't he?

GOLDBERG. It's conceivable. Conceivable.

Petey rises and picks up the teapot and cup.

PETEY. Well, if he's no better by lunchtime I'll go and get hold of a doctor.

GOLDBERG (*briskly*). It's all taken care of, Mr. Boles. Don't worry yourself.

PETEY (*dubiously*). What do you mean? (*Enter McCann with two suitcases.*) All packed up?

Petey takes the teapot and cups into the kitchen. McCann crosses left and puts down the suitcases. He goes up to the window and looks out.

GOLDBERG. Well? (*McCann does not answer.*) McCann. I asked you well.

McCANN (*without turning*). Well what?

GOLDBERG. What's what? (*McCann does not answer*).

McCANN (*turning to look at Goldberg, grimly*). I'm not going up there again.

GOLDBERG. Why not?

McCANN. I'm not going up there again.

GOLDBERG. What's going on now?

McCANN (*moving down*). He's quiet now. He stopped all that. . . . talking a while ago.

Petey appears at the kitchen hatch, unnoticed.

GOLDBERG. When will he be ready?

MCCANN (*sullenly*). You can go up yourself next time.

GOLDBERG. What's the matter with you?

MCCANN (*quietly*). I gave him. . . .

GOLDBERG. What?

MCCANN. I gave him his glasses.

GOLDBERG. Wasn't he glad to get them back?

MCCANN. The frames are bust.

GOLDBERG. How did that happen?

MCCANN. He tried to fit the eyeholes into his eyes. I left him doing it.

PETEY (*at the kitchen door*). There's some Sellotape somewhere. We can stick them together.

Goldberg and McCann turn to see him. Pause.

GOLDBERG. Sellotape? No, no, that's all right, Mr. Boles. It'll keep him quiet for the time being, keep his mind off other things.

PETEY (*moving downstage*). What about a doctor?

GOLDBERG. It's all taken care of.

McCann moves over right to the shoe-box, and takes out a brush and brushes his shoes.

PETEY (*moves to the table*). I think he needs one.

GOLDBERG. I agree with you. It's all taken care of. We'll give him a bit of time to settle down, and then I'll take him to Monty.

PETEY. You're going to take him to a doctor?

GOLDBERG (*staring at him*). Sure. Monty.

Pause. McCann brushes his shoes.

So Mrs. Boles has gone out to get us something nice for lunch?

PETEY. That's right.

GOLDBERG. Unfortunately we may be gone by then.

PETEY. Will you?

GOLDBERG. By then we may be gone.

Pause.

PETEY. Well, I think I'll see how my peas are getting on, in the meantime.

GOLDBERG. The meantime?

PETEY. While we're waiting.

GOLDBERG. Waiting for what? (*Petey walks towards the back door.*) Aren't you going back to the beach?

PETEY. No, not yet. Give me a call when he comes down, will you, Mr. Goldberg?

GOLDBERG (*earnestly*). You'll have a crowded beach today . . . on a day like this. They'll be lying on their backs, swimming out to sea. My life. What about the deck-chairs? Are the deck-chairs ready?

PETEY. I put them all out this morning.

GOLDBERG. But what about the tickets? Who's going to take the tickets?

PETEY. That's all right. That'll be all right, Mr. Goldberg. Don't you worry about that. I'll be back.

He exits. Goldberg rises, goes to the window and looks after him. McCann crosses to the table, left, sits, picks up the paper and begins to tear it into strips.

GOLDBERG. Is everything ready?

MCCANN. Sure.

Goldberg walks heavily, brooding, to the table. He sits right of it noticing what McCann is doing.

GOLDBERG. Stop doing that!

MCCANN. What?

GOLDBERG. Why do you do that all the time? It's childish, it's pointless. It's without a solitary point.

MCCANN. What's the matter with you today?

GOLDBERG. Questions, questions. Stop asking me so many questions. What do you think I am?

McCann studies him. He then folds the paper, leaving the strips inside.

MCCANN. Well?

Pause. Goldberg leans back in the chair, his eyes closed.

MCCANN. Well?

GOLDBERG (*with fatigue*). Well what?

MCCANN. Do we wait or do we go and get him?

GOLDBERG (*slowly*). You want to go and get him?

MCCANN. I want to get it over.

GOLDBERG. That's understandable.

McCANAN. So do we wait or do we go and get him?

GOLDBERG (*interrupting*). I don't know why, but I feel knocked out. I feel a bit . . . It's uncommon for me.

MCCANN. Is that so?

GOLDBERG. It's unusual.

MCCANN (*rising swiftly and going behind Goldberg's chair. Hissing*). Let's finish and go. Let's get it over and go. Get the thing done. Let's finish the bloody thing. Let's get the thing done and go!

Pause.

Will I go up?

Pause.

Nat!

Goldberg sits humped. McCann slips to his side.

Simey!

GOLDBERG (*opening his eyes, regarding McCann*). What—did—you—call—me?

McCANN. Who?

GOLDBERG (*murderously*). Don't call me that! (*He seizes McCann by the throat.*) NEVER CALL ME THAT!

McCANN (*writhing*). Nat, Nat, Nat, NAT! I called you Nat. I was asking you, Nat. Honest to God. Just a question that's all, just a question, do you see, do you follow me?

GOLDBERG (*jerking him away*). What question?

McCANN. Will I go up?

GOLDBERG (*violently*). Up? I thought you weren't going to go up there again?

McCANN. What do you mean? Why not?

GOLDBERG. You said so!

McCANN. I never said that!

GOLDBERG. No?

McCANN (*from the floor, to the room at large*). Who said that? I never said that! I'll go up now!

He jumps up and rushes to the door, left.

GOLDBERG. Wait!

He stretches his arms to the arms of the chair.

Come here.

McCann approaches him very slowly.

I want your opinion. Have a look in my mouth.

He opens his mouth wide.

Take a good look.

McCann looks.

You know what I mean?

McCann peers.

You know what? I've never lost a tooth. Not since the day I was born. Nothing's changed. (*He gets up.*) That's why I've reached my position, McCann. Because I've always been as fit as a fiddle. All my life I've said the same. Play up, play up, and play the game. Honour thy father and thy mother. All along the line. Follow the line, the line, McCann, and you can't go wrong. What do you think, I'm a self-made man? No! I sat where I was told to sit. I kept my eye on the ball. School? Don't talk to me about school. Top in all subjects. And for why? Because I'm telling you, I'm telling you, follow my line? Follow my mental? Learn by heart. Never write down a thing. And don't go too near the water.

And you'll find—that what I say is true. Because I believe that the world . . . (*Vacant.*). . . . Because I believe that the world . . . (*Desperate.*). . . . BECAUSE I BELIEVE THAT THE WORLD . . . (*Lost.*). . . .

He sits in chair.

Sit down, McCann, sit here where I can look at you.

McCann kneels in front of the table.

(*Intensely, with growing certainty.*) My father said to me, Benny, Benny, he said, come here. He was dying. I knelt down. By him day and night. Who else was there? Forgive, Benny, he said, and let live. Yes, Dad. Go home to your wife. I will, Dad. Keep an eye open for low-lives, for schnorrers and for layabouts. He didn't mention names. I lost my life in the service of others, he said, I'm not ashamed. Do your duty and keep your observations. Always bid good morning to the neighbours. Never, never forget your family, for they are the rock, the constitution and the core! If you're ever in any difficulties Uncle Barney will see you in the clear. I knelt knwn. (*He kneels, facing McCann:*) I swore on the good book. And I knew the word I had to remember—Respect! Because McCann— (*Gently.*) Seamus—who came before your father? His father? And who came before him? Before him? . . . (*Vacant—triumphant.*) Who came before your father's father but your father's father's mother! Your great-gran-granny.

Silence. He slowly rises.

And that's why I've reached my position, McCann. Because I've always been as fit as a fiddle. My motto. Work hard and play hard. Not a day's illness.

Goldberg sits.

GOLDBERG. All the same, give me a blow. (*Pause.*) Blow in my mouth.

McCann stands, puts his hands on his knees, bends, and blows in Goldberg's mouth.

One for the road.

McCann blows again in his mouth. Goldberg breathes deeply, smiles.

GOLDBERG. Right!

Enter Lulu. McCann looks at them, and goes to the door.

McCANN (*at the door*). I'll give you five minutes. (*He exits with the expander.*)

GOLDBERG. Come over here.

LULU. What's going to happen?

GOLDBERG. Come over here.

LULU. No, thank you.

GOLDBERG. What's the matter? You got the needle to Uncle Natey?

LULU. I'm going.

GOLDBERG. Have a game of pontoon first, for old time's sake.

LULU. I've had enough games.

GOLDBERG. A girl like you, at your age, at your time of health, and you don't take to games?

LULU. You're very smart.

GOLDBERG. Anyway, who says you don't take to them?

LULU. Do you think I'm like all the other girls?

GOLDBERG. Are all the other girls like that, too?

LULU. I don't know about any other girls.

GOLDBERG. Nor me. I've never touched another woman.

LULU (distressed). What would my father say, if he knew? And what would Eddie say?

GOLDBERG. Eddie?

LULU. He was my first love, Eddie was. And whatever happened, it was pure. With him! He didn't come into my room at night with a briefcase!

GOLDBERG. Who opened the briefcase, me or you? Lulu, schmulu, let bygones be bygones, do me a turn. Kiss and make up.

LULU. I wouldn't touch you.

GOLDBERG. And today I'm leaving.

LULU. You're leaving?

GOLDBERG. Today.

LULU (with growing anger). You used me for a night. A passing fancy.

GOLDBERG. Who used who?

LULU. You made use of me by cunning when my defences were down.

GOLDBERG. Who took them down?

LULU. That's what you did. You quenched your ugly thirst. You taught me things a girl shouldn't know before she's been married at least three times!

GOLDBERG. Now you're a jump ahead! What are you complaining about?

Enter McCann quickly.

LULU. You didn't appreciate me for myself. You took all those liberties only to satisfy your appetite. Oh Nat, why did you do it?

GOLDBERG. You wanted me to do it, Lulula, so I did it.

McCANN. That's fair enough. (*Advancing.*) You had a long sleep, Miss.

LULU (backing upstage left). Me?

McCANN. Your sort, you spend too much time in bed.

LULU. What do you mean?

McCANN. Have you got anything to confess?

LULU. What?

McCANN (savagely). Confess!

LULU. Confess what?

McCANN. Down on your knees and confess!

LULU. What does he mean?

GOLDBERG. Confess. What can you lose?

LULU. What, to him?

GOLDBERG. He's only been unfrocked six months.

McCANN. Kneel down, woman, and tell me the latest!

LULU (retreating to the back door). I've seen everything that's happened. I know what's going on. I've got a pretty shrewd idea.

McCANN (advancing). I've seen you hanging about the Rock of Cashel, profaning the soil with your goings-on. Out of my sight!

LULU. I'm going.

She exits. McCann goes to the door, left, and goes out. He ushers in Stanley, who is dressed in a dark well cut suit and white collar. He holds his broken glasses in his hand. He is clean-shaven. McCann follows and closes the door. Goldberg meets Stanley, seats him in a chair.

GOLDBERG. How are you, Stan?

Pause.

Are you feeling any better?

Pause.

What's the matter with your glasses?

Goldberg bends to look.

They're broken. A pity.

Stanley stares blankly at the floor.

McCANN (at the table). He looks better, doesn't he?

GOLDBERG. Much better.

McCANN. A new man.

GOLDBERG. You know what we'll do?

McCANN. What?

GOLDBERG. We'll buy him another pair.

They begin to woo him, gently and with relish. During the following sequence Stanley shows no reaction. He remains, with no movement, where he sits.

McCANN. Out of our own pockets.

GOLDBERG. It goes without saying. Between you and me, Stan, it's about time you had a new pair of glasses.

MCCANN. You can't see straight.

GOLDBERG. It's true. You've been cockeyed for years.

MCCANN. Now you're even more cockeyed.

GOLDBERG. He's right. You've gone from bad to worse.

MCCANN. Worse than worse.

GOLDBERG. You need a long convalescence.

MCCANN. A change of air.

GOLDBERG. Somewhere over the rainbow.

MCCANN. Where angels fear to tread.

GOLDBERG. Exactly.

MCCANN. You're in a rut.

GOLDBERG. You look anaemic.

MCCANN. Rheumatic.

GOLDBERG. Myopic.

MCCANN. Epileptic.

GOLDBERG. You're on the verge.

MCCANN. You're a dead duck.

GOLDBERG. But we can save you.

MCCANN. From a worse fate.

GOLDBERG. True.

MCCANN. Undeniable.

GOLDBERG. From now on, we'll be the hub of your wheel.

MCCANN. We'll renew your season ticket.

GOLDBERG. We'll take tuppence off your morning tea.

MCCANN. We'll give you a discount on all inflammable goods.

GOLDBERG. We'll watch over you.

MCCANN. Advise you.

GOLDBERG. Give you proper care and treatment.

MCCANN. Let you use the club bar.

GOLDBERG. Keep a table reserved.

MCCANN. Help you acknowledge the fast days.

GOLDBERG. Bake you cakes.

MCCANN. Help you kneel on kneeling days.

GOLDBERG. Give you a free pass.

MCCANN. Take you for constitutionals.

GOLDBERG. Give you hot tips.

MCCANN. We'll provide the skipping rope.

GOLDBERG. The vest and pants.

MCCANN. The ointment.

GOLDBERG. The hot poultice.

MCCANN. The fingerstall.

GOLDBERG. The abdomen belt.

MCCANN. The ear plugs.

GOLDBERG. The baby powder.

MCCANN. The back scratcher.

GOLDBERG. The spare tyre.

MCCANN. The stomach pump.

GOLDBERG. The oxygen tent.

MCCANN. The prayer wheel.

GOLDBERG. The plaster of Paris.

MCCANN. The crash helmet.

GOLDBERG. The crutches.

MCCANN. A day and night service.

GOLDBERG. All on the house.

MCCANN. That's it.

GOLDBERG. We'll make a man of you.

MCCANN. And a woman.

GOLDBERG. You'll be re-orientated.

MCCANN. You'll be rich.

GOLDBERG. You'll be adjusted.

MCCANN. You'll be our pride and joy.

GOLDBERG. You'll be a mensch.

MCCANN. You'll be a success.

GOLDBERG. You'll be integrated.

MCCANN. You'll give orders.

GOLDBERG. You'll make decisions.

MCCANN. You'll be a magnate.

GOLDBERG. A statesman.

MCCANN. You'll own yachts.

GOLDBERG. Animals.

MCCANN. Animals

Goldberg looks at McCann.

GOLDBERG. I said animals. (*He turns back to Stanley.*) You'll be able to make or break, Stan. By my life. (*Silence. Stanley is still.*) Well? What do you say?

Stanley's head lifts very slowly and turns in Goldberg's direcion.

GOLDBERG. What do you think? Eh, boy?

Stanley begins to clench and unclench his eyes.

MCCANN. What's your opinion, sir? Of this prospect, sir?

GOLDBERG. Prospect. Sure. Sure it's a prospect.

Stanley's hands clutching his glasses begin to tremble.

What's your opinion of such a prospect? Eh, Stanley?

Stanley concentrates, his mouth opens, he attempts to speak, fails and emits sounds from his throat.

STANLEY. Uh-gug . . . uh-gug . . . eeehhh-gag . . . (*On the breath.*) *Caahh . . . caahh. . . .*

They watch him. He draws a long breath which shudders down his body. He concentrates.

GOLDBERG. Well, Stanny boy, what do you say, eh?

They watch. He concentrates. His head lowers, his chin draws into his chest, he crouches.

STANLEY. Uh-gughh . . . uh-gughhh. . . .

MCCANN. What's your opinion, sir?

STANLEY. Caaahhh . . . caaahhh. . . .

McCANN. Mr. Webber! What's your opinion?

GOLDBERG. What do you say, Stan? What do you think of the prospect?

McCANN. What's your opinion of the prospect?

Stanley's body shudders, relaxes, his head drops, he becomes still again, stooped. Petey enters from door, downstage, left.

GOLDBERG. Still the same old Stan. Come with us. Come on, boy.

McCANN. Come along with us.

PETEY. Where are you taking him?

They turn. Silence.

GOLDBERG. We're taking him to Monty.

PETEY. He can stay here.

GOLDBERG. Don't be silly

PETEY. We can look after him here.

GOLDBERG. Why do you want to look after him?

PETEY. He's my guest.

GOLDBERG. He needs special treatment.

PETEY. We'll find someone.

GOLDBERG. No. Monty's the best there is. Bring him, McCann.

They help Stanley out of the chair. Goldberg puts the bowler hat on Stanley's head. They all three move towards the door, left.

PETEY. Leave him alone!

They stop. Goldberg studies him.

GOLDBERG (*insidiously*). Why don't you come with us, Mr. Boles?

McCANN. Yes, why don't you come with us?

GOLDBERG. Come with us to Monty. There's plenty of room in the car.

Petey makes no move. They pass him and reach the door. McCann opens the door and picks up the suitcases.

PETEY (*broken*). Stan, don't let them tell you what to do!

They exit.

Silence. Petey stands. The front door slams. Sound of a car starting. Sound of a car going away. Silence. Petey slowly goes to the table. He sits on a chair, left. He picks up the paper and opens it. The strips fall to the floor. He looks down at them. Meg comes

past the window and enters by the back door. Petey studies the front page of the paper.

MEG (*coming downstage*). The car's gone.

PETEY. Yes.

MEG. Have they gone?

PETEY. Yes.

MEG. Won't they be in for lunch?

PETEY. No.

MEG. Oh, what a shame. (*She puts her bag on the table.*) It's hot out. (*She hangs her coat on a hook.*) What are you doing?

PETEY. Reading.

MEG. Is it good?

PETEY. All right.

She sits by the table.

MEG. Where's Stan?

Pause.

Is Stan down yet, Petey?

PETEY. No . . . he's. . . .

MEG. Is he still in bed?

PETEY. Yes, he's . . . still asleep.

MEG. Still? He'll be late for his breakfast.

PETEY. Let him . . . sleep.

Pause.

MEG. Wasn't it a lovely party last night?

PETEY. I wasn't there.

MEG. Weren't you?

PETEY. I came in afterwards.

MEG. Oh.

Pause.

It was a lovely party. I haven't laughed so much for years. We had dancing and singing. And games. You should have been there.

PETEY. It was good, eh?

Pause.

MEG. I was the belle of the ball.

PETEY. Were you?

MEG. Oh yes. They all said I was.

PETEY. I bet you were, too.

MEG. Oh, it's true. I was.

Pause.

I know I was.

Curtain

COMMENTARY

Note: The following essay represents a single interpretation of the play. For other perspectives on The Birthday Party, *consult the essays listed below.*

The characteristics of Pinter's early work are epitomized in *The Birthday Party*, in which he adroitly creates a mood of warmth in a domestic situation that is shattered by the arrival of menacing intruders who, using implied violence and intimidation, succeed in shifting the once-placid atmosphere to one of ambiguous apprehension.

As the curtain rises we find ourselves voyeurs of an early-morning routine in a naturalistic environment. As Meg prepares breakfast for Petey and Stanley, she chats with Petey about the mundane—his corn flakes, his newspaper, and his morning walk—all the while preening in anticipation of Stanley's entrance. Upon Stanley's arrival at the breakfast table, Meg shifts into high gear as she brazenly flirts with him. While the dialogue is not that of a Neal Simon or Alan Ayckbourn comedy, it is essentially lighthearted and playful, precisely as we might expect for the opening of a play named after one of the world's most widely observed celebrations—a birthday party.

As the Act I curtain comes down, however, the jovial mood has evolved into one of anxiety, even fear. What began as a rather mundane day for some very mundane people evolves into an extraordinarily eventful day. And the best (or worst!) is yet to come as the anxiety continues to build through the climactic ending of Stanley's grotesque "birthday party" at the end of Act II. By the close of the play any sense of the ordinary has vanished and, as Meg and Petey once again begin their daily routines, they behave as if nothing has happened.

The impetus for this convulsive change in atmosphere is another ingredient of Pinter's work: the menacing intruder(s). In this case we witness Goldberg and McCann who, they say, are there "for Stanley's own good." While Stanley is alarmed by their arrival, Meg and Petey treat them with the hospitality usually reserved for prospective boarders. Insinuating themselves into the family-like situation at Meg and Petey's boardinghouse with the flair of the best of con men, they succeed in ingratiating themselves not only to their hosts but to Lulu as well. In fact, so successful are they in their duping of "the family" that they become the "insiders," and Stanley is reduced to an outsider. But what is the key to Goldberg's and McCann's power over not only the family but also Stanley? This mystery has intrigued the Pinter playgoer since his works were first presented in the late 1950s.

Witness this exchange of letters in *The Times* (London) after the opening of *The Birthday Party*:

Dear Sir [Harold Pinter]:
I would be obliged if you would kindly explain to me the meaning of your play *The Birthday Party*. These are the points which I do not understand: 1. Who are the two men? 2. Where did Stanley come from? 3. Were they all supposed to be normal? You will appreciate that without the answers to my questions I cannot fully understand your play.

Sincerely,
[Jane Doe]

Dear Madam:
I would be obliged if you would kindly explain to me the meaning of your letter. These are the points which I do not understand: 1. Who are you? 2. Where do you come from? 3. Are you supposed to be normal? You will appreciate that without the answers to my questions I cannot fully understand your letter.

Sincerely,
Harold Pinter

Among the keys to Pinter's intriguing plots is his manipulation of the menacing invaders. Goldberg and McCann are men of ambiguous backgrounds. "Who are they? From where do they come?" are indeed the questions we would likely ask ourselves. With the exception of Stanley, however, Pinter's characters don't find these to be important questions—they accept Goldberg and McCann as rather ordinary people. Stanley, on the other hand, sees menace in their every word and action. And as a result of his paranoia and the others' commentary, we are nearly clueless about Stanley's past and his relationship with them. So confused are we, they, and he, that what has happened in the past, if anything, is obscure at best. As Anna, a character in a later Pinter play, *Old Times*, declares: "There are some things one remembers even though they may never have happened." But is it Goldberg and McCann who are remembering events that never really happened, or is it Stanley who, selective in his memory, recalls certain events and conveniently forgets others? Once again it is Pinter's use of the ambiguous that not only engages our curiosity but keeps us riveted to the action.

Also typical of early Pinter is the absence of nearly all physical violence, Stanley's inept and pitiful attempted rape of Lulu in Act II notwithstanding. However, for the most part violence in Pinter's world is intellectual, imagined, or insinuated. Goldberg and McCann, the perceived threats to Stanley's well-being, lay nary a hand on Stanley nor any of the other characters. In fact, having become part of "the family" they seem intent on not only celebrating Stanley's birthday but also being the life of that party as they eagerly participate in the games. Having had so much fun, Goldberg and McCann succeed in driving Stanley to the brink of his sanity—all through the use of language and intimidation, thus proving what we all come to realize as we grow older: the old adage, "Sticks and stones may break my bones, but words will never hurt me!" is not only an untruth but is, in fact, one of the greatest lies told to children. With words alone, Goldberg and McCann reduce Stanley to a quivering mass.

The ambiguity of Goldberg and McCann's intimidation of Stanley is complemented by the ambiguity of the communication within the play. It has been said that in Pinter subtext is all and that a Pinter play "is like an Ibsen play . . . with one-third of the dialogue missing." In Pinter, only the essentials are part of the text. Much of the meaning lies in the subtext which Pinter, perhaps for the sake of intriguing us, conveniently indicates by the most often used word in his texts—*pause*. It is during these silences that the play's real action transpires. Not only is the subtext expressed but a great deal of nonverbal communication is exchanged as well.

How does Pinter accomplish this? A partial answer rests on his exceptional craftsmanship. First, drawing on the dramatic structure of the Greeks, the Neoclassicists, and some of the twentieth-century realistic and naturalistic writers, Pinter adheres strictly to the three unities of time, place, and action. By confining the play not only to the single locale and to "a single revolution of the sun" but also to a single action (i.e., stripping Stanley of his dignity and sense of being), Pinter intensifies both the 180-degree mood swing and the menace and power of Goldberg and McCann. The action happens so quickly in production that audiences become disoriented and unable to fathom motivations.

Second, Pinter deftly blends the comic and the serious to the point where they become indistinguishable. Precisely that which evokes our laughter in the early scenes induces our fear in the latter episodes. For example, Stanley's Act I mischievous yet hilarious teasing of Meg about the van and wheelbarrow "coming to take her away" loses its humor when, in Act III, it is Stanley who is "taken away." By the final curtain, those early sources of humor—Stanley's whereabouts, one's daily nourishment, Stanley's career, and, of course "the birthday party" itself—are no longer part of "the claustrophobic theatricality," as one critic described the play, but sources of fear, anxiety, and apprehension.

Finally, and not the least important, is Pinter's use of seemingly innocent actions to induce suspense and menace. The play's title itself conjures up an afternoon of good spirits as opposed to the nearly macabre climax of Stanley's birthday party. Surely McCann's careful, almost ritualistic tearing of the newspaper into strips, the whistling of the little "duet" by the mysterious intruders, and the playing of blind man's buff are harmless endeavors, but in the hands of the skilled playwright they become terrifyingly unnerving. Like Stanley, each of us sitting in what we thought was the comfort of our seats in the theater knows that at any moment someone could knock on our door and say to us, "I know what you did and now you must come with me." That is the ultimate menace that lurks in the shadows of Pinter's strange world.

Other perspectives on *The Birthday Party*:

Dukore, Bernard F. "The Theatre of Harold Pinter." *Tulane Drama Review* 6:3 (March 1962): 23–30.

Esslin, Martin. *The Peopled Wound: The Work of Harold Pinter*. Garden City, NJ: Doubleday Anchor, 1970, 74–86.

See *The Birthday Party* on video:

The Birthday Party. Dir. William Friedkin. Perf. Robert Shaw and Patrick McGee. Anchor Bay Entertainment, 128 min., 1968.

SHOWCASE   BRITAIN'S THEATER REVOLUTION OF 1956

During a roughly ten-week period in the late spring and summer of 1956, the British theater was transformed from a rather conventional, staid, and "safe" medium into an often-angry and politically vigorous forum. Although the social and political satires of Bernard Shaw and Oscar Wilde tweaked the noses of the British establishment—as did the operettas of Gilbert and Sullivan—the majority of plays written in the first half of the twentieth century reflected the stereotypical notion of the English: stodgy and "propah." Plays were admired for their craftsmanship, and the well-made play was a staple of English drama. Even when it addressed social concerns, all was discussed in witty, elegant dialogue and tied up neatly by the final curtain.

The center of the British commercial theater was (and still is) located in "the West End," a roughly 15-square-block area just north of Trafalgar Square. Its chief patron was "Aunt Edna," a mythical Every Audience who expected well-written, crisply acted plays that did not make extraordinary demands on the British sense of propriety, especially where the class system and sexual morality were concerned. Gifted actors (John Gielgud and Joan Plowright) and playwrights (Noel Coward and Terrence Rattigan) graced West End stages, and audiences were satisfied.

In 1956 Oscar Lewenstein and Ronald Duncan took a 34-year lease on the venerable Royal Court Theatre on Sloan Square in Chelsea, where Shaw and Harley Granville Barker had modernized the British theater in the early years of the twentieth century. George Devine, a precocious young director, was named artistic director of the newly formed English Stage Company and charged with the task of challenging the commercial theater's monopoly on British audiences. (England, it must be noted, was in the waning days of its 400-year Empire, and British youth of all classes were seeking a voice as the country redefined itself.) Devine enlisted young writers, actors, and directors and gave them—as he proudly noted years later—"the right to fail," that is, a place where they could experiment with new theatrical forms and especially content.

On May 8, 1956, a new play by John Osborne, then 26, opened at the Royal Court. *Look Back in Anger*, both a searing indictment of England's class system and a dirge for the dying Empire, launched a generation of "angry young men" (and later women) who transformed the British theater. Its caustic antihero, Jimmy Porter, was educated in England's new public-supported universities but remained condemned to a life as a candy salesman because of his lower-class status. He verbally, even sadistically, abuses his wife (Alison) and closest friend (Cliff), sleeps with his wife's best friend (Helen), and spends much of the play lamenting that "there are no brave causes anymore." The play found its young audience and may rightly be considered the first shot in the counterculture movement that would flower in Europe and the United States in the mid-1960s. Later British playwrights—John Arden, Edward Bond, Howard Brenton, Caryl Churchill, Pam Gems, David Hare—produced plays that surpassed Osborne's in their audacity and political commitment. To cite but one famous example, Bond's *Saved* (1965) shocked audiences when a band of disenfranchised youth savagely stoned a baby to death as it lay in its perambulator (the play sparked a revision of British censorship laws).

A month later in a small theater located in the tough waterfront docks of London's East End, Joan Littlewood, whose artistry was weaned on Depression-era politics, directed a gritty production of *The Quare Fellow* by a controversial Irish playwright, Brendan Behan. The drama, about a death-row inmate in a Dublin prison, argued that we are all prisoners of the state (a popular theme of many 1960s dramas). To prepare her actors, Littlewood coached them through Stanislavsky-like improvisations on the roof of the Theatre Royal at Stratford East, home of the director's Theatre Workshop. The production caught the attention of uptown London audiences who were fascinated by actors who no longer had to speak in polished tones, stand dutifully erect, or move with dignified grace and charm. Colloquial speech in natural cadences and a rough-hewn physicality captivated audiences as much as Behan's iconoclastic wit. Henceforth, regional dialects and slovenly posture became as commonplace on English stages as the Queen's English and ramrod-straight stances had been for the previous generation. When the Royal Shakespeare Company (RSC) was founded just four years later, the new breed of Shakespearean actors (David Warner, Ian Holm) displayed an indebtedness to the decidedly unpolished style of Littlewood's Theatre Workshop.

During one of the hottest Julys on record, Brecht's internationally acclaimed Berliner Ensemble (which had captivated Paris audiences in 1954) was contracted for an eight-week residency in the West End. While most theater patrons generally ignored the Ensemble—the Palace Theatre had no air-conditioning, while language barriers and old wartime animosities conspired against the Germans—the "next generation" of British theater artists were very much in attendance. Peter Hall, fresh out of Cambridge University (and the director of the London premiere of Beckett's *Waiting for Godot* at the Arts Theatre in 1955) was there, as was John Barton, Hall's Cambridge theater colleague. In 1960 Hall and Barton founded the RSC, using the Berliner Ensemble as its model. Indeed, the RSC's "house style" for Shakespeare in its early years was decidedly Brechtian, most notably the critically admired *The War of the Roses* (1963). Brecht's dramaturgy also influenced the style of the angry young writers spawned at the Royal Court; Bond has been called "the British Brecht."

This extraordinary convergence of work at the Royal Court, at Littlewood's Workshop, and by Europe's preeminent acting company in 1956 encouraged:

- The development of new plays about previously taboo subjects
- An antiromantic acting style that was applied to classical works as well as new dramas
- The formation of theater companies committed to an ideology and ensemble.

Furthermore, British audiences accustomed to opulent scenery and costumes saw plays mounted in sparse settings and performed by actors in workaday clothing. Although the Empire was dead (as depicted in Osborne's second Royal Court play, *The Entertainer*, about a pathetic British music hall performer), the theater that arose from its ashes remains among the most vital and urgent in the world today.

KRAPP'S LAST TAPE

SAMUEL BECKETT

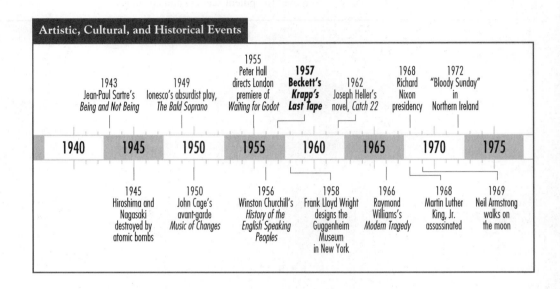

Artistic, Cultural, and Historical Events

1943 Jean-Paul Sartre's *Being and Not Being*

1949 Ionesco's absurdist play, *The Bald Soprano*

1955 Peter Hall directs London premiere of *Waiting for Godot*

1957 Beckett's *Krapp's Last Tape*

1962 Joseph Heller's novel, *Catch 22*

1968 Richard Nixon presidency

1972 "Bloody Sunday" in Northern Ireland

1940　1945　1950　1955　1960　1965　1970　1975

1945 Hiroshima and Nagasaki destroyed by atomic bombs

1950 John Cage's avant-garde *Music of Changes*

1956 Winston Churchill's *History of the English Speaking Peoples*

1958 Frank Lloyd Wright designs the Guggenheim Museum in New York

1966 Raymond Williams's *Modern Tragedy*

1968 Martin Luther King, Jr. assassinated

1969 Neil Armstrong walks on the moon

SAMUEL BECKETT (1906–89)

Perhaps no writer in the second half of the twentieth century has been as influential and imitated as Samuel Beckett. Harold Pinter, Tom Stoppard, and Edward Albee—to name the most prominent examples—have cited Beckett as the inspiration for their earliest works. In a 1974 interview (*Theatre Quarterly* IV:15, p. 18) Sam Shepard recalls that reading *Waiting for Godot* when he was a teenager in California motivated his subsequent writing career: "I didn't understand it at all, but the words and the language amazed me. I had no place to put it in, no category, but once I started writing plays, I felt a connection." And no other twentieth-century playwright has generated so many critical assessments of his work; there is even an academic journal devoted exclusively to Beckett's drama, poetry, and novels.

Beckett was another transplanted Irishman who fled his homeland. He wanted partly to escape oppressive Catholicism (though he was Protestant) and to experience the robust intellectual life of Europe's capitals between the wars. After receiving a degree in languages at Dublin's Trinity College (where he also taught briefly), he traveled throughout the Continent. In Paris he met James Joyce, his countryman, whose writing he helped translate into French. Beckett's writing clearly shows the influence of Joyce, particularly in its inventive word play and in the stream-of-consciousness style found in such plays as *Krapp's Last Tape*. Beckett settled permanently in Paris in 1938, declaring that he would "rather live in France during war than in Ireland during peace." After 1946 he wrote the bulk of his work in French and later translated it into his native English. Consequently, he is claimed by both French and English literati, though in truth he is the most international of modern playwrights because his works are conspicuously free of the specifics of time and place.

By the 1940s Paris had become the nexus for such existential writer-philosophers as Jean-Paul Sartre and Albert Camus, and Beckett's writing echoes many of the darker elements of these thinkers who argued that the world lacks a cohesive system to guide it. Beckett's plays are peopled with characters trapped both by a universe they cannot comprehend and, equally importantly, by their own inability to change their circumstances. Consider Gogo and Didi, the tramps who wait futilely under the barren tree in *Waiting for Godot*, or Nagg and Nell, the old couple who spend *Endgame* encased in ashbins. Like the old man imprisoned in his squalid room in *Krapp's Last Tape*, they are victims of their own inertia as much as the world's indifference to their existence. "There is no escape from the days and the hours," Beckett wrote in echo of Proust.

While Beckett wrote in the absurdist tradition—as much as any writer he gave it credibility—his dramatic works transcend Absurdism's limitations. Beckett is a minimalist (he actually titled one of his pieces "Lessness") who has shown us how little it takes to create an effective, poetic theater. *Krapp's Last Tape* is the exemplar of Beckett's minimalist technique: a lonely man sits, immobile, in his chair awaiting his inevitable death. His language is as sparse as his stage settings, and like his simple, deftly chosen set pieces (e.g., a tape recorder that becomes a ghost of a man's past), it is ripe with possibilities. In the very ambiguity of his language there exist multiple layers of meaning. Beckett once said that the most important word in his plays was "perhaps," which suggests virtually all possibilities of meaning—or none.

Beckett was not only an admired playwright who won the Nobel Prize for Literature in 1969 but also a superb director of his works; his marginal notes provide valuable critical insights into his themes and dramaturgy. Curiously, in his later years he allowed only schoolchildren to attend his rehearsals. Beckett's most significant dramatic works include *Waiting for Godot* (1952), *All That Fall* (1957), *Endgame* (1958), *Krapp's Last Tape* (1960), *Happy Days* (1962), *Not I* (1973), *That Time* and *Footfalls* (1976), *Ghost Trio* (1977), and *Rockaby* (1981). His novels include *Malloy* (1951), *Malone Dies* (1951), and *The Unnamable* (1953). He also wrote numerous poems, as well as an admired study of Proust.

AS YOU READ *KRAPP'S LAST TAPE*

With perhaps only the exception of Griselda Gambaro's *Personal Effects* (Part III)—which itself was influenced by Beckett's style and thematic concerns—no play in this collection is as spare as *Krapp's Last Tape*. Do not look for elaborate scenery, for here you get only a nearly bare room. Do not look for extravagant props, for here you get only an antique tape recorder (yet it is one of the most profound symbols on the modern stage). Do not look for a cast of colorful characters in fashionable costumes, for here you get a solitary old man in the shabbiest of clothes. Do not look for crackling dialogue, for here you find no true dialogue but some of the saddest of speeches uttered in twentieth-century theater. And those speeches are not spoken by an actor but by a machine. In this short play the human being has become absolutely superfluous—and that is precisely Beckett's point.

KRAPP'S LAST TAPE

SAMUEL BECKETT

(A late evening in the future.)

(Krapp's den.)

(Front center a small table, the two drawers of which open toward audience.)

(Sitting at the table, facing front, i.e., across from the drawers, a wearish* old man: Krapp.)

(Rusty black narrow trousers too short for him. Rusty black sleeveless waistcoat, four capacious pockets. Heavy silver watch and chain. Grimy white shirt open at neck, no collar. Surprising pair of dirty white boots, size ten at least, very narrow and pointed.)

(White face. Purple nose. Disordered gray hair. Unshaven.)

(Very near-sighted [but unspectacled]. Hard of hearing.)

(Cracked voice. Distinctive intonation.)

(Laborious walk.)

(On the table a tape recorder with microphone and a number of cardboard boxes containing reels of recorded tapes.)

(Table and immediately adjacent area in strong white light. Rest of stage in darkness.)

(Krapp remains a moment motionless, heaves a great sigh, looks at his watch, fumbles in his pockets, takes out an envelope, puts it back, fumbles, takes out a small bunch of keys, raises it to his eyes, chooses a key, gets up and moves to front of table. He stoops, unlocks first drawer, peers into it, feels about inside it, takes out a reel of tape, peers at it, puts it back, locks drawer, unlocks second drawer, peers into it, feels about inside it, takes out a large banana, peers at it, locks drawer, puts keys back in his pocket. He turns, advances to edge of stage, halts, strokes banana, peels it, drops skin at his feet, puts end of banana in his mouth, and remains mo-

tionless, staring vacuously before him. Finally he bites off the end, turns aside, and begins pacing to and fro at edge of stage, in the light, i.e., not more than four or five paces either way, meditatively eating banana. He treads on skin, slips, nearly falls, recovers himself, stoops and peers at skin and finally pushes it, still stooping, with his foot over the edge of stage into pit. He resumes his pacing, finishes banana, returns to table, sits down, remains a moment motionless, heaves a great sigh, takes keys from his pockets, raises them to his eyes, chooses key, gets up and moves to front of table, unlocks second drawer, takes out a second large banana, peers at it, locks drawer, puts back keys in his pocket, turns, advances to edge of stage, halts, strokes banana, peels it, tosses skin into pit, puts end of banana in his mouth, and remains motionless, staring vacuously before him. Finally he has an idea, puts banana in his waistcoat pocket, the end emerging, and goes with all the speed he can muster backstage into darkness. Ten seconds. Loud pop of cork. Fifteen seconds. He comes back into light carrying an old ledger and sits down at table. He lays ledger on table, wipes his mouth, wipes his hands on the front of his waistcoat, brings them smartly together and rubs them.)

KRAPP (briskly). Ah! (He bends over ledger, turns the pages, finds the entry he wants, reads.) Box . . . thrree . . . spool . . . five. (He raises his head and stares front. With relish.) Spool! (Pause.) Spooool! (Happy smile. Pause. He bends over table, starts peering and poking at the boxes.) Box . . . thrree . . . thrree . . . four . . . two . . . (with surprise) nine! good God! . . . seven . . . ah! the little rascal! (He takes up box, peers at it.) Box thrree. (He lays it on table, opens it and peers at spools inside.) Spool . . . (he peers at ledger) . . . five . . . (he peers at spools) . . . five . . . five . . . ah! the little scoundrel!

---

*wearish: Sickly, withered

(He takes out a spool, peers at it.) Spool five. *(He lays it on table, closes box three, puts it back with the others, takes up the spool.)* Box thrree, spool five. *(He bends over the machine, looks up. With relish.)* Spooool! *(Happy smile. He bends, loads spool on machine, rubs his hands.)* Ah! *(He peers at ledger, reads entry at foot of page.)* Mother at rest at last . . . Hm . . . The black ball . . . *(He raises his head, stares blankly front. Puzzled.)* Black ball? . . . *(He peers again at ledger, reads.)* The dark nurse . . . *(He raises his head, broods, peers again at ledger, reads.)* Slight improvement in bowel condition . . . Hm . . . Memorable . . . what? *(He peers closer.)* Equinox, memorable equinox. *(He raises his head, stares blankly front. Puzzled.)* Memorable equinox? . . . *(Pause. He shrugs his shoulders, peers again at ledger, reads.)* Farewell to—*(he turns the page)*—love.

(He raises his head, broods, bends over machine, switches on and assumes listening posture, i.e., leaning forward, elbows on table, hand cupping ear toward machine, face front.)

TAPE *(strong voice, rather pompous, clearly Krapp's at a much earlier time).* Thirty-nine today, sound as a— *(Settling himself more comfortably he knocks one of the boxes off the table, curses, switches off, sweeps boxes and ledger violently to the ground, winds tape back to beginning, switches on, resumes posture.)* Thirty-nine today, sound as a bell, apart from my old weakness, and intellectually I have now every reason to suspect at the . . . *(hesitates)* . . . crest of the wave—or thereabouts. Celebrated the awful occasion, as in recent years, quietly at the Wine-house. Not a soul. Sat before the fire with closed eyes, separating the grain from the husks. Jotted down a few notes, on the back of an envelope. Good to be back in my den, in my old rags. Have just eaten I regret to say three bananas and only with difficulty refrained from a fourth. Fatal things for a man with my condition. *(Vehemently.)* Cut 'em out! *(Pause.)* The new light above my table is a great improvement. With all this darkness round me I feel less alone. *(Pause.)* In a way. *(Pause.)* I love to get up and move about in it, then back here to . . . *(hesitates)* . . . me. *(Pause.)* Krapp.

(Pause.)

The grain, now what I wonder do I mean by that, I mean . . . *(hesitates)* . . . I suppose I mean those things worth having when all the dust has—when all *my* dust has settled. I close my eyes and try and imagine them.

(Pause. Krapp closes his eyes briefly.)

Extraordinary silence this evening. I strain my ears and do not hear a sound. Old Miss McGlome always sings at this hour. But not tonight. Songs of her girl-hood, she says. Hard to think of her as a girl. Wonderful woman though. Connaught, I fancy. *(Pause.)* Shall I sing when I am her age, if I ever am? No. *(Pause.)* Did I sing as a boy? No. *(Pause.)* Did I ever sing? No.

(Pause.)

Just been listening to an old year, passages at random. I did not check in the book, but it must be at least ten or twelve years ago. At that time I think I was still living on and off with Bianca in Kedar Street. Well out of that, Jesus yes! Hopeless business. *(Pause.)* Not much about her, apart from a tribute to her eyes. Very warm. I suddenly saw them again. *(Pause.)* Incomparable! *(Pause.)* Ah well . . . *(Pause.)* These old P.M.s are gruesome, but I often find them—*(Krapp switches off, broods, switches on)*—a help before embarking on a new . . . *(hesitates)* . . . retrospect. Hard to believe I was ever that young whelp. The voice! Jesus! And the aspirations! *(Brief laugh in which Krapp joins.)* And the resolutions! *(Brief laugh in which Krapp joins.)* To drink less, in particular. *(Brief laugh of Krapp alone.)* Statistics. Seventeen hundred hours, out of the preceding eight thousand odd, consumed on licensed premises alone. More than 20%, say 40% of his waking life. *(Pause.)* Plans for a less . . . *(hesitates)* . . . engrossing sexual life. Last illness of his father. Flagging pursuit of happiness. Unattainable laxation. Sneers at what he calls his youth and thanks to God that it's over. *(Pause.)* False ring there. *(Pause.)* Shadows of the opus . . . magnum. Closing with a—*(brief laugh)*—yelp to Providence. *(Prolonged laugh in which Krapp joins.)* What remains of all that misery? A girl in a shabby green coat, on a railway-station platform? No?

(Pause.)

When I look—

(Krapp switches off, broods, looks at his watch, gets up, goes backstage into darkness. Ten seconds, Pop of cork. Ten seconds. Second cork. Ten seconds. Third cork. Ten seconds. Brief burst of quavering song.)

KRAPP *(sings).* Now the day is over,
Night is drawing nigh-igh,
Shadows—

(Fit of coughing. He comes back into light, sits down, wipes his mouth, switches on, resumes his listening posture.)

TAPE. —back on the year that is gone, with what I hope is perhaps a glint of the old eye to come, there is of course the house of the canal where mother lay a-dying, in the late autumn, after her long viduity *(Krapp gives a start)*, and the—*(Krapp switches off, winds back tape a little, bends his ear closer to machine, switches on)*—a-dying, after her long viduity, and the—

(Krapp switches off, raises his head, stares blankly before him. His lips move in the syllables of "viduity." No sound. He gets up, goes backstage into darkness, comes back with an enormous dictionary, lays it on table, sits down and looks up the word.)

KRAPP *(reading from dictionary)*. State—or condition of being—or remaining—a widow—or widower. *(Looks up. Puzzled.)* Being—or remaining? . . . *(Pause. He peers again at dictionary. Reading.)* "Deep weeds of viduity" . . . Also of an animal, especially a bird . . . the vidua or weaver-bird . . . Black plumage of male . . . *(He looks up. With relish.)* The vidua-bird!

(Pause. He closes dictionary, switches on, resumes listening posture.)

TAPE. —bench by the weir from where I could see her window. There I sat, in the biting wind, wishing she were gone. *(Pause.)* Hardly a soul, just a few regulars, nursemaids, infants, old men, dogs. I got to know them quite well—oh by appearance of course I mean! One dark young beauty I recollect particularly, all white and starch, incomparable bosom, with a big black hooded perambulator, most funereal thing. Whenever I looked in her direction she had her eyes on me. And yet when I was bold enough to speak to her—not having been introduced—she threatened to call a policeman. As if I had designs on her virtue! *(Laugh. Pause.)* The face she had! The eyes! Like . . . *(hesitates)* . . . chrysolite! *(Pause.)* Ah well . . . *(Pause.)* I was there when—*(Krapp switches off, broods, switches on again)*—the blind went down, one of those dirty brown roller affairs, throwing a ball for a little white dog, as chance would have it. I happened to look up and there it was. All over and done with, at last. I sat on for a few moments with the ball in my hand and the dog yelping and pawing at me. *(Pause.)* Moments. Her moments, my moments. *(Pause.)* The dog's moments. *(Pause.)* In the end I held it out to him and he took it in his mouth, gently,

gently. A small, old, black, hard, solid rubber ball. *(Pause.)* I shall feel it, in my hand, until my dying day. *(Pause.)* I might have kept it. *(Pause.)* But I gave it to the dog.

(Pause.)

Ah well . . .

(Pause.)

Spiritually a year of profound gloom and indigence until that memorable night in March, at the end of the jetty, in the howling wind, never to be forgotten, when suddenly I saw the whole thing. The vision, at last. This I fancy is what I have chiefly to record this evening, against the day when my work will be done and perhaps no place left in my memory, warm or cold, for the miracle that . . . *(hesitates)* . . . for the fire that set it alight. What I suddenly saw then was this, that the belief I had been going on all my life, namely—*(Krapp switches off impatiently, winds tape forward, switches on again)*—great granite rocks the foam flying up in the light of the lighthouse and the wind-gauge spinning like a propellor, clear to me at last that the dark I have always struggled to keep under is in reality my most—*(Krapp curses, switches off, winds tape forward, switches on again)*—unshatterable association until my dissolution of storm and night with the light of the understanding and the fire—*(Krapp curses louder, switches off, winds tape forward, switches on again)*—my face in her breasts and my hand on her. We lay there without moving. But under us all moved, and moved us, gently, up and down, and from side to side.

(Pause.)

Past midnight. Never knew such silence. The earth might be uninhabited.

(Pause.)

Here I end—

(Krapp switches off, winds tape back, switches on again.)

—upper lake, with the punt, bathed off the bank, then pushed out into the stream and drifted. She lay stretched out on the floorboards with her hands under her head and her eyes closed. Sun blazing down, bit of a breeze, water nice and lively. I noticed a scratch on her thigh and asked her how she came by it. Picking gooseberries, she said. I said again I thought it was hopeless and no good going on, and she agreed, without opening her eyes. (*Pause.*) I asked her to look at me and after a few moments—(*pause*)—after a few moments she did, but the eyes just slits, because of the glare. I bent over her to get them in the shadow and they opened. (*Pause. Low.*) Let me in. (*Pause.*) We drifted in among the flags and stuck. The way they went down, sighing, before the stem! (*Pause.*) I lay down across her with my face in her breasts and my hand on her. We lay there without moving. But under us all moved, and moved us, gently, up and down, and from side to side.

(*Pause.*)

Past midnight. Never knew—

(*Krapp switches off, broods. Finally he fumbles in his pockets, encounters the banana, takes it out, peers at it, puts it back, fumbles, brings out the envelope, fumbles, puts back envelope, looks at his watch, gets up and goes backstage into darkness. Ten seconds. Sound of bottle against glass, then brief siphon. Ten seconds. Bottle against glass alone. Ten seconds. He comes back a little unsteadily into light, goes to front of table, takes out keyes, raises them to his eyes, chooses key, unlocks first drawer, peers into it, feels about inside, takes out reel, peers at it, locks drawer, puts keys back in his pocket, goes and sits down, takes reel off machine, lays it on dictionary, loads virgin reel on machine, takes envelope from his pocket, consults back of it, lays it on table, switches on, clears his throat, and begins to record.*)

KRAPP. Just been listening to that stupid bastard I took myself for thirty years ago, hard to believe I was ever as bad as that. Thank God that's all done with anyway. (*Pause.*) The eyes she had! (*Broods, realizes he is recording silence, switches off, broods. Finally.*) Everything there, everything, all the—(*Realizes this is not being recorded, switches on.*) Everything there, everything on this old muckball, all the light and dark and famine and feasting of . . . (*hesitates*) . . . the ages! (*In a shout.*) Yes! (*Pause.*) Let that go! Jesus! Take his mind off his homework! Jesus! (*Pause. Weary.*) Ah well, maybe he was right. (*Pause.*) Maybe he was right. (*Broods. Realizes. Switches off. Consults envelope.*) Pah! (*Crumples it and throws it away. Broods. Switches on.*) Nothing to say, not a squeak. What's a year now? The sour cud and the iron stool. (*Pause.*) Reveled in the word spool. (*With relish.*) Spoooool! Happiest moment of the past half million. (*Pause.*) Seventeen copies sold, of which

eleven at trade price to free circulating libraries beyond the seas. Getting known. (*Pause.*) One pound six and something, eight I have little doubt. (*Pause.*) Crawled out once or twice, before the summer was cold. Sat shivering in the park, drowned in dreams and burning to be gone. Not a soul. (*Pause.*) Last fancies. (*Vehemently.*) Keep 'em under! (*Pause.*) Scalded the eyes out of me reading *Effie* again, a page a day, with tears again. Effie . . . (*Pause.*) Could have been happy with her, up there on the Baltic, and the pines, and the dunes. (*Pause.*) Could I? (*Pause.*) And she? (*Pause.*) Pah! (*Pause.*) Fanny came in a couple of times. Bony old ghost of a whore. Couldn't do much, but I suppose better than a kick in the crotch. The last time wasn't so bad. How do you manage it, she said, at your age? I told her I'd been saving up for her all my life. (*Pause.*) Went to Vespers once, like when I was in short trousers. (*Pause. Sings.*)

> Now the day is over,
> Night is drawing nigh-igh,
> Shadows—(*coughing, then almost inaudible*)—of the evening
> Steal across the sky.

(*Gasping.*) Went to sleep and fell off the pew. (*Pause.*) Sometimes wondered in the night if a last effort mightn't—(*Pause.*) Ah finish your booze now and get to your bed. Go on with this drivel in the morning. Or leave it at that. (*Pause.*) Leave it at that. (*Pause.*) Lie propped up in the dark—and wander. Be again in the dingle on a Christmas Eve, gathering holly, the red-berried. (*Pause.*) Be again on Croghan on a Sunday morning, in the haze, with the bitch, stop and listen to the bells. (*Pause.*) And so on. (*Pause.*) Be again, be again. (*Pause.*) All that old misery. (*Pause.*) Once wasn't enough for you. (*Pause.*) Lie down across her.

(*Long pause. He suddenly bends over machine, switches off, wrenches off tape, throws it away, puts on the other, winds it forward to the passage he wants, switches on, listens staring front.*)

TAPE. —gooseberries, she said. I said again I thought it was hopeless and no good going on, and she agreed, without opening her eyes. (*Pause.*) I asked her to look at me and after a few moments—(*pause*)—after a few moments she did, but the eyes just slits, because of the glare. I bent over her to get them in the shadow and they opened. (*Pause. Low.*) Let me in. (*Pause.*) We drifted in among the flags and stuck. The way they went down, sighing, before the stem!

(*Pause.*) I lay down across her with my face in her breasts and my hand on her. We lay there without moving. But under us all moved, and moved us, gently, up and down, and from side to side.

(*Pause. Krapp's lips move. No sound.*)

Past midnight. Never knew such silence. The earth might be uninhabited.

(*Pause.*)

Here I end this reel. Box—(*pause*)—three, spool—(*pause*)—five. (*Pause.*) Perhaps my best years are gone. When there was a chance of happiness. But I wouldn't want them back. Not with the fire in me now. No, I wouldn't want them back.

(*Krapp motionless staring before him. The tape runs on in silence.*)

COMMENTARY

Note: The following essay represents a single interpretation of the play. For other perspectives on Krapp's Last Tape, *consult the essays listed below.*

Despite its brevity, *Krapp's Last Tape* actually encompasses a lifetime. A man with "white face . . . purple nose" (the clown image is intentional; see below) sits before a tape recorder on his sixty-ninth birthday listening to his voice as it was recorded exactly thirty years earlier. His voice from his past drones on to create a world of experience that succinctly defines the futility of human endeavor. On one hand, Krapp craves contact, even if it is only a mechanical voice in the distance, yet the "rerun" of the tape emphasizes his inability to change in this unyielding world. True, Krapp is not the man he was at 39 ("that stupid bastard I took myself for thirty years ago"), but he remains every bit the alienated being he was. For Krapp, as for all Beckett's characters, habit is indeed "the great deadener" (*Waiting for Godot*). Finally he sits "motionless, staring before him [as] the tape runs on in silence." The final word, "silence"—the most terrifying in Beckett's universe—encapsulates Krapp's life. For all his meticulous record keeping, whether in journals or on the metallic tapes that fill his boxes, ultimately Krapp's life comes down to "silence." The absence of meaningful sound, the lack of being. Krapp's former self—for he is not now the man he once was—even laments that he "never knew such silence. The earth might be uninhabited."

Krapp's Last Tape offers an uncompromising picture of loneliness and alienation. It is told in the simplest of terms and in the least amount of action imaginable. Yet by the end of the play, we feel as if we have participated in the totality of the man's life. We know he has loved (or at least made love to a woman in the punt), that he had aspirations, that at one time his life held promise. And now sadly and ironically, Krapp—alone, friendless, and without apparent accomplishment—can only gloat that he would not want these years "when there was a chance of happiness" back. How immeasurably hollow that line is.

Yet for all its austerity and the ultimate pessimism of its portrait of a human lost in his own despair, *Krapp's Last Tape* has a comedic, even farcical, side that cannot be ignored. This is typical of so much contemporary theater in general, and of the Theater of the Absurd in particular. Indeed, Beckett is the exemplar of this ironic fusion of the profoundly sad (even the near tragic) and the comic. The majority of Beckett's protagonists—Gogo and Didi in *Waiting for Godot* remain the prototypes—are essentially clowns who remind us that (in Shaw's words) "laughter is essentially a serious business." The playwright's initial description of Krapp (whose very name suggests scatological humor: the human as excrement) identifies him as a clown in white face, purple nose, baggy trousers, and silly shoes. (Interestingly, in subsequent productions in Berlin and London in the 1970s, Beckett the Director [as opposed to Beckett the Playwright] toned down Krapp's more overtly clownish characteristics.) Even before he speaks, Krapp slips on a banana peel in that oldest of circus gags. However, the only time Krapp seems truly happy—even giddy—is when he plays, childlike, with the spool of tape, both the object itself and the very word that names it. Initially we are asked to laugh at Krapp, but as that "infernal machine" (to use a term popular with *avant-garde* artists) continues to roll on and on without cessation, much like the very years that diminish Krapp's life, our laughter turns to tears. We realize that the man before us is dying the loneliest of deaths imaginable, with only his former self sounding from the tape. For him, there is "no exit" from his hell in that hovel. For him hell is not other people, as Sartre, Beckett's existentialist colleague, argued. (See Showcase, "Forerunners of the Absurd," earlier in Part II.) In Beckett's grim world, "hell is oneself."

Other perspectives on *Krapp's Last Tape*:

Brustein, Robert. "Listening to the Past." In Brustein, *Season of Discontent*. New York: Simon and Schuster, 1965, 26–29.

Dukore, Bernard F. "*Krapp's Last Tape* as Tragicomedy." *Modern Drama* (1973): 351–54.

See *Krapp's Last Tape* on video:

Krapp's Last Tape. Dir. Alan Schneider. Perf. Jack MacGowran. Pennebaker Assoc., 54 min., 1971.

Other Beckett plays on video and film:

Endgame. Dir. Toby Cole. BBC, 90 min., 1992.

Happy Days. Perf. Irene Worth and George Voscovek. BBC, 90 min., 1980.

Rockaby. Dir. Alan Schneider. Perf. Billie Whitelaw. Pennebaker Assoc., 58 min., 1982.

Samuel Beckett: Three Plays. (Contains *Eh Joe*, *Footfalls*, and *Rockaby*.) Perf. Billie Whitelaw. Films for the Humanities, 79 min., 1988.

Waiting for Godot. Dir. Alan Schneider. Perf. Zero Mostel and Burgess Meredith. Films for the Humanities, 102 min., 1976.

Videos about Beckett:

Between Beckett and Brecht: Looking In, Looking Out. Films for the Humanities, 51 min., 2000.

Samuel Beckett: As the Story Was Told. BBC, 110 min., 1996.

Samuel Beckett: Silence to Silence. Dir. Sean O'Mordha. Films for the Humanities, 80 min., 1986.

Waiting for Beckett: A Portrait of Samuel Beckett. Perf. Jack MacGowran, Billie Whitelaw, and Zero Mostel. Insight Media, 86 min., 1993.

SHOWCASE   A MODERN MASTERPIECE

Waiting for Godot

Samuel Beckett's *Waiting for Godot* is among the most remarkable plays in the history of world theater. Nothing quite like it preceded its arrival in Paris in 1953, and it has since become among the most imitated (if indirectly) and analyzed plays of the twentieth century. It stands as the epitome of the Theater of the Absurd, yet it has transcended the limitations of the Absurd and remains a metaphysical landmark of the late twentieth century. Ironically, its status as a masterwork has curtailed its publication rights, so we may offer only this brief synopsis of the play and a brief assessment of its impact on the modern theater.

The story of *Waiting for Godot* is as sparse as the landscape on which it takes place: two tramps (Gogo and Didi) wait under a barren tree for a "Mr. Godot." They "improvise life" as they wait, and we watch them quarreling about seemingly insignificant matters, eating carrots and chicken bones, adjusting their ill-fitted shoes, and attempting suicide (which fails, how fittingly for a play about futility!). Their wait is interrupted by two strangers, Pozzo (a master) and Lucky (his slave). The tramps engage in pseudo-philosophic discourse with Pozzo, who proclaims that we live on a "bitch of an earth." The tree sprouts a few leaves between acts, and Pozzo and Lucky return, this time blind and dumb. Finally, a boy arrives to inform the tramps that Godot will not come, and they continue to wait "in the midst of nothingness." The mundane routines with which Gogo and Didi occupy themselves as they wait reinforce the play's most quoted line: "Habit is the great deadener."

While "nothing" seems to happen during the play and in its seemingly in-

Since its premiere in 1953 Waiting for Godot *has been among the most performed plays in the world. Here South African actors Winston Ntshona and John Kani perform the roles of Beckett's famous tramps at the Long Wharf Theater in 1981.*

coherent conversations, in actuality everything happens. Virtually every aspect of the human condition is addressed—birth, death, suffering, redemption, salvation, loss, freedom, slavery, free will, isolation, companionship, hope, and despair. Midway through the play, Lucky (who speaks only once) delivers a long monologue in the stream-of-consciousness style of Beckett's countryman, James Joyce which seems to summarize the history of humanity as it sits perched "astride of a grave and a difficult birth":

. . . but time will tell I resume alas alas on on in short in fine on on

abode of stones who can doubt it I resume but not so fast I resume the skull fading fading fading and concurrently simultaneously what is more for reasons unknown in spite of the tennis on on the beard the flames the tears the stones so blue so calm alas alas on on the skull the skull the skull the skull in Connemara in spite of the tennis the labors abandoned left unfinished graver still abode of stones in a word I resume alas alas abandoned unfinished. . . .

So what does *Godot* mean? Indeed, who/what is Godot? Until his dying day Beckett steadfastly refused to reveal his intentions, saying only that "perhaps" is the most important word in the play. In the spirit of the Theater of the Absurd, the playwright thus forces audiences—as they have since 1953—to assign meaning to the play, if there is indeed meaning. Critics, scholars, philosophers, directors, actors, and general audiences have each attempted assign meaning to Beckett's enigmatic play:

- It portrays humanity's fruitless search for someone or something that gives meaning to life.
- It attempts to bridge the gap between human hopes and human futility.
- It is a modern myth, grounded in archetypal characters and situations, about "the suffering of being."
- It shows that humans "act out" life rather than live it; that is, we are actors in a cosmic drama, yet we do not know our lines, much less the character we are asked to play.
- It is a meaningless exercise that mirrors the meaningless of all human activity.

Despite its cryptic themes, *Godot* has transformed the contemporary theater by loosening the grip of realism and absolute logic on dramaturgy. It returned the language of the theater to the realm of the evocative and symbolic, rather than the literal, and it released characterization from the particulars of psychology and sociology, thus making stage characters again mythic. Gogo and Didi, by the way, are rooted in that most elemental theater character: the hapless clown. For all its modernity, *Godot* is theater at its most essential—an empty space, a universal question, and skilled actors who bring it to life.

Godot was first staged by Roger Blin at the Théâtre de Babylon in Paris, where it ran for over 400 performances. Like *Hernani* in 1830, it also provoked heated discussion; some in the audience on opening night felt they had been duped by this "nonplay." Like Gogo, they, too, believed the play was an event in which "nothing happens, nobody comes, nobody goes, it's awful." Others saw it as a theatrical "Second Coming" that would free the theater from the snares of realism, just as *Hernani* had overthrown the neoclassic codes 120 years earlier. News of Beckett's audacious work spread, and the play was performed at the Arts Theatre in London in 1955. It was directed by Peter Hall, fresh out of Cambridge University, who would found the Royal Shakespeare Company five years later. Harold Pinter and Tom Stoppard would be among the prominent British playwrights drawn to Beckett's new style; Edward Albee and Sam Shepard have both admitted their indebtedness to Beckett's *Godot*. *Rosencrantz and Guildenstern Are Dead* (see Part III) is a dark comedy in which *Hamlet*'s Rosencrantz and Guildenstern resemble Beckett's tramps more than Shakespeare's creations.

The American premiere of *Godot* was also provocative, but for quite different reasons. Hearing that the play was a popular French comedy, an impresario booked it into a tourist's resort theater in Florida, where it was a disaster. It has since played in hundreds of theaters and featured some of the American theater's most important actors: Bert Lahr, E. G. Marshall, and George C. Scott, to name but a few. A recent production at New York's Lincoln Center featured two of the United States' most popular comedians, Steve Martin and Robin Williams. *Godot* has been performed throughout the world. In 1979 Gogo and Didi were played at the Australian Academy of Dramatic Art by then-student actors Mel Gibson and Geoffrey Rush. In 2002 the Gate Theatre in Dublin issued a DVD collection of nineteen of Beckett's plays in performance, including *Waiting for Godot*.

For almost a half-century actors, audiences, and critics have responded to Beckett's central question, spoken here by Didi: "What are we doing here, *that* is the question? And we are blessed in this, that we happen to know the answer. Yes, in the immense confusion one thing alone is clear. We are waiting for Godot to come."

THE AMERICAN DREAM

EDWARD ALBEE

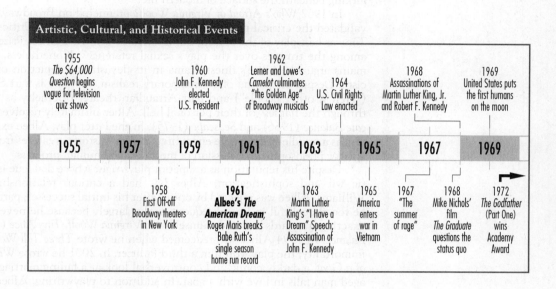

Artistic, Cultural, and Historical Events

1955
The $64,000 Question begins vogue for television quiz shows

1960
John F. Kennedy elected U.S. President

1962
Lerner and Lowe's *Camelot* culminates "the Golden Age" of Broadway musicals

1964
U.S. Civil Rights Law enacted

1968
Assassinations of Martin Luther King, Jr. and Robert F. Kennedy

1969
United States puts the first humans on the moon

| 1955 | 1957 | 1959 | 1961 | 1963 | 1965 | 1967 | 1969 |

1958
First Off-off Broadway theaters in New York

1961
Albee's *The American Dream*; Roger Maris breaks Babe Ruth's single season home run record

1963
Martin Luther King's "I Have a Dream" Speech; Assassination of John F. Kennedy

1965
America enters war in Vietnam

1967
"The summer of rage"

1968
Mike Nichols' film *The Graduate* questions the status quo

1972
The Godfather (Part One) wins Academy Award

EDWARD ALBEE (1928–)

The winner of three Pulitzer Prizes for drama, Edward Albee is one of the most admired American playwrights of the twentieth century. He stands between the early generation of playwrights (Eugene O'Neill, Arthur Miller, Tennessee Williams) and the current one (Sam Shepard, August Wilson, Tony Kushner). No playwright dominated the American theater in the 1960s as did Albee. He pioneered American Absurdism in *The American Dream* and *The Sandbox*. After his initial exploration of absurdist drama, Albee took psychological realism to uncommon heights, tempering it with an almost surrealistic overlay. And he has emerged as one of the most articulate and candid spokesmen for the arts in America.

It is fitting that Albee should have pursued a life in the theater. His adoptive parents were heirs to the fortune amassed by Edward Franklin Albee II and B. F. Keith, who founded in 1885 a vaudeville empire that eventually stretched across America. Upon his adoption from a home for foundlings in Washington, D.C., Albee was christened Edward F. Albee III in memory of his adoptive grandfather. Though Albee's early life seems to have been charmed, his childhood was troubled and rancorous. His antipathy to his parents, especially his domineering mother, has been well publicized, and it appears that the domestic battles of the Albee household have provided him with material for such plays as *Who's Afraid of Virginia Woolf?* and *The American Dream*, both of which are concerned with the disintegration of the contemporary family.

His parent's prosperity allowed Albee to attend the finest prep schools in the East, including Choate, followed by a brief stint at Trinity College in 1946–47. His grandmother—who was a model for the Grandmother in *The Sandbox* and *The American Dream*—bequeathed him money so he could escape his tempestuous home life. After a series of odd jobs, Albee achieved his first playwriting success when *The Zoo Story* was performed in New York (but only after proving itself in a West Berlin production in 1959). Performed on a bill with Beckett's *Krapp's Last Tape*, *The Zoo Story* was generously praised by Tennessee Williams. In May 1960 Albee wrote a short one-act, *The Sandbox*, whose principal characters reappeared the following year in *The American Dream*. In these works we see several Albee motifs: the impossibility of honest, open communication; emasculated father figures embattled in a war of words with overbearing wives; the callous rejection of the older generation; reality masked with illusions (or delusions); and violence lurking beneath the surface of modern life.

In 1962 *Who's Afraid of Virginia Woolf?* premiered on Broadway, and its two-year run validated the critical praise it earned. It received the Drama Critics Circle Award and a Tony as best play of the season, but it failed to win the Pulitzer Prize because of a dispute among the trustees over the play's sexual references. Nonetheless, this lengthy play remains arguably Albee's finest drama in its devastating depiction of psychological exorcism. Despite its patina of contemporary realism, the play is part Sartian existentialism ("Hell is other people") and part Artaudian theater of cruelty as its characters "signal through the flames" of their personal hell. Albee ultimately received Pulitzers for *A Delicate Balance* (1966) and *Seascape* (1975). In the latter play, Albee experimented with fantasy as a middle-aged couple encounters two prehistoric creatures from the sea; the play is a witty, philosophical discussion of mortality and human progress.

Despite his reputation as a superior playwright whose dialogue is admired for its caustic wit and sophistication, Albee has had a curious relationship with critics. Like Williams, Albee was rejected by critics after his initial successes, partly because he tried to be too thoughtful in his subsequent works, largely because he never measured up to the exacting standards he set for himself with *Virginia Woolf*, *Tiny Alice* (1964), and *A Delicate Balance*. In 1994 Albee was redeemed when he wrote *Three Tall Women*, a poetic look at immortality; the play won him a third Pulitzer. In 2001 he wrote *Who Is Sylvia? The Story of a Goat*, a darkly comic and controversial look at a failing marriage in which a middle-aged man falls in love with a goat. In addition to playwriting, Albee also directs his own works. When not in New York, he teaches playwriting at the University of Houston and is an associate artist at Houston's Alley Theater.

AS YOU READ *THE AMERICAN DREAM*

On its most elemental level, Albee's play typifies absurdist drama, the kind that emanated from Europe in the late 1940s and throughout the 1950s. In spirit and content, it is indebted to Eugene Ionesco's seminal comedy of the Absurd, *The Bald Soprano* (1949). As in Ionesco's parody of banal small talk that precludes meaningful communication, *The American Dream* also relies on hilarious non-sequiturs, the inversion of normal social exchanges (e.g., "What a dreadful apartment you have here," followed by "Yes, but you don't know what trouble it is"), gross violations of decorum (e.g., when Mrs. Barker removes her dress at Mommy's too polite invitation), and the reduction of adult conversation to infantile prattling ("Try to get the leak in the johnny fixed"). Furthermore, there are self-canceling statements ("She's just a dreadful woman . . . so naturally I'm terribly fond of her"), and the most trivial elements of human endeavors (e.g., the color of a hat) are elevated to nearly cosmic significance. These were very much the arsenal of early Absurdists who lamented the impossibility of communication in an increasingly illogical world; for them, language is reduced to a mechanical process of thoughtless noncommunication. So do not be put off if the dialogue seems illogical: that is precisely the point (or "a" point) of the play.

THE AMERICAN DREAM

A Play in One Scene (1959–60)

EDWARD ALBEE

FOR DAVID DIAMOND

THE PLAYERS
MOMMY
DADDY
GRANDMA
MRS. BARKER
YOUNG MAN

The Scene: A living room. Two armchairs, one toward either side of the stage, facing each other diagonally out toward the audience. Against the rear wall, a sofa. A door, leading out from the apartment, in the rear wall, far stage-right. An archway, leading to other rooms, in the side wall, stage-left.

At the beginning, Mommy and Daddy are seated in the armchairs, Daddy in the armchair stage-left, Mommy in the other.

Curtain up. A silence. Then:

MOMMY. I don't know what can be keeping them.

DADDY. They're late, naturally.

MOMMY. Of course, they're late; it never fails.

DADDY. That's the way things are today, and there's nothing you can do about it.

MOMMY. You're quite right.

DADDY. When we took this apartment, they were quick enough to have me sign the lease; they were quick enough to take my check for two months' rent in advance . . .

MOMMY. And one month's security . . .

DADDY. . . . and one month's security. They were quick enough to check my references; they were quick enough about all that. But now! But now, try to get the icebox fixed, try to get the doorbell fixed, try to get the leak in the johnny fixed! Just try it . . . they aren't so quick about *that*.

MOMMY. Of course not; it never fails. People think they can get away with anything these days . . . and, of course they can. I went to buy a new hat yesterday.

(Pause)

I said, I went to buy a new hat yesterday.

DADDY. Oh! Yes . . . yes.

MOMMY. Pay attention.

DADDY. I *am* paying attention, Mommy.

MOMMY. Well, be sure you do.

DADDY. Oh, I am.

MOMMY. All right, Daddy; now listen.

DADDY. I'm listening, Mommy.

MOMMY. You're sure!

DADDY. Yes . . . yes, I'm sure, I'm all ears.

MOMMY (*Giggles at the thought; then*). All right, now. I went to buy a new hat yesterday and I said, "I'd like a new hat, please." And so, they showed me a few hats, green ones and blue ones, and I didn't like any of them, not one bit. What did I say? What did I just say?

DADDY. You didn't like any of them, not one bit.

MOMMY. That's right; you just keep paying attention. And then they showed me one that I did like. It was a lovely little hat, and I said, "Oh, this is a lovely little hat; I'll take this hat; oh my, it's lovely. What color is it?" And they said, "Why, this is beige; isn't it a lovely little beige hat?" And I said, "Oh, it's just lovely." And so, I bought it.

(Stops, looks at Daddy)

DADDY (*To show he is paying attention*). And so you bought it.

465

MOMMY. And so I bought it, and I walked out of the store with the hat right on my head, and I ran spang into the chairman of our woman's club, and she said, "Oh, my dear, isn't that a lovely little hat? Where did you get that lovely little hat? It's the loveliest little hat; I've always wanted a wheat-colored hat *myself*." And, I said, "Why, no, my dear; this hat is beige; beige." And she laughed and said, "Why no, my dear, that's a wheat-colored hat . . . wheat. I know beige from wheat." And I said, "Well, my dear, I know beige from wheat, too." What did I say? What did I just say?

DADDY (*Tonelessly*). Well, my dear, I know beige from wheat, too.

MOMMY. That's right. And she laughed, and she said, "Well, my dear, they certainly put one over on you. That's wheat if I ever saw wheat. But it's lovely, just the same." And then she walked off. She's a dreadful woman, you don't know her; she has dreadful taste, two dreadful children, a dreadful house, and an absolutely adorable husband who sits in a wheel chair all the time. You don't know him. You don't know anybody, do you? She's just a dreadful woman, but she *is* chairman of our woman's club, so naturally I'm terribly fond of her. So, I went right back into the hat shop, and I said, "Look here; what do you mean selling me a hat that you say is beige, when it's wheat all the time . . . wheat! I can tell beige from wheat any day in the week, but not in this artificial light of yours." They have artificial light, Daddy.

DADDY. Have they!

MOMMY. And I said, "The minute I got outside I could tell that it wasn't a beige hat at all; it was a wheat hat." And they said to me, "How could you tell that when you had the hat on the top of your head?" Well, that made me angry, and so I made a scene right there; I screamed as hard as I could; I took my hat off and I threw it down on the counter, and oh, I made a terrible scene. I said, I made a terrible scene.

DADDY (*Snapping to*). Yes . . . yes . . . good for you!

MOMMY. And I made an absolutely terrible scene; and they became frightened, and they said, "Oh, madam; oh, madam." But I kept right on, and finally they admitted that they might have made a mistake; so they took my hat into the back, and then they came out again with a hat that looked exactly like it. I took one look at it, and I said, "This hat is wheat-colored; wheat." Well, of course, they said, "Oh, no, madam, this hat is beige; you go outside and see." So, I went outside, and lo and behold, it *was* beige. So I bought it.

DADDY (*Clearing his throat*). I would imagine that it was the same hat they tried to sell you before.

MOMMY (*With a little laugh*). Well, of course it was!

DADDY. That's the way things are today; you just can't get satisfaction; you just try.

MOMMY. Well, *I* got satisfaction.

DADDY. That's right, Mommy. *You did* get satisfaction, didn't you?

MOMMY. Why are they so late? I don't know what can be keeping them.

DADDY. I've been trying for two weeks to have the leak in the johnny fixed.

MOMMY. You can't get satisfaction; just try. *I* can get satisfaction, but you can't.

DADDY. I've been trying for two weeks and it isn't so much for my sake; I can always go to the club.

MOMMY. It isn't so much for my sake, either; I can always go shopping.

DADDY. It's really for Grandma's sake.

MOMMY. Of course it's for Grandma's sake. Grandma cries every time she goes to the johnny as it is; but now that it doesn't work it's even worse, it makes Grandma think she's getting feeble-headed.

DADDY. Grandma *is* getting feeble-headed.

MOMMY. Of course Grandma is getting feeble-headed, but not about her johnny-do's.

DADDY. No; that's true. I must have it fixed.

MOMMY. WHY are they so late? I don't know what can be keeping them.

DADDY. When they came here the first time, they were ten minutes early; they were quick enough about it then.

(*Enter Grandma from the archway, stage left. She is loaded down with boxes, large and small, neatly wrapped and tied.*)

MOMMY. Why Grandma, look at you! What *is* all that you're carrying?

GRANDMA. They're boxes. What do they look like?

MOMMY. Daddy! Look at Grandma; look at all the boxes she's carrying!

DADDY. My goodness, Grandma; look at those boxes.

GRANDMA. Where'll I put them?

MOMMY. Heavens! I don't know. Whatever are they for?

GRANDMA. That's nobody's damn business.

MOMMY. Well, in that case, put them down next to Daddy; there.

GRANDMA (*Dumping the boxes down, on and around Daddy's feet*). I sure wish you'd get the john fixed.

DADDY. Oh, I do wish they'd come and fix it. We hear you . . . for hours . . . whimpering away . . .

MOMMY. Daddy! What a terrible thing to say to Grandma!

GRANDMA. Yeah. For shame, talking to me that way.

DADDY. I'm sorry, Grandma.

MOMMY. Daddy's sorry, Grandma.

GRANDMA. Well, all right. In that case I'll go get the rest of the boxes. I suppose I deserve being talked to that way. I've gotten so old. Most people think that when you get so old, you either freeze to death or you burn up. But you don't. When you get so old, all that happens is that people talk to you that way.

DADDY (*Contrite*). I said I'm sorry, Grandma.

MOMMY. Daddy said he was sorry.

GRANDMA. Well, that's all that counts. People being sorry. Makes you feel better; gives you a sense of dignity, and that's all that's important . . . a sense of dignity. And it doesn't matter if you don't care, or not, either. You got to have a sense of dignity, even if you don't care, 'cause, if you don't have that, civilization's doomed.

MOMMY. You've been reading my book club selections again!

DADDY. How dare you read Mommy's book club selections, Grandma!

GRANDMA. Because I'm old! When you're old you gotta do something. When you get old, you can't talk to people because people snap at you. When you get so old, people talk to you that way. That's why you become deaf, so you won't be able to hear people talking to you that way. And that's why you go and hide under the covers in the big soft bed, so you won't feel the house shaking from people talking to you that way. That's why old people die, eventually. People talk to them that way. I've got to go and get the rest of the boxes.

(*Grandma exits.*)

DADDY. Poor Grandma, I didn't mean to hurt her.

MOMMY. Don't you worry about it; Grandma doesn't know what she means.

DADDY. She knows what she says, though.

MOMMY. Don't you worry about it; she won't know that soon. I love Grandma.

DADDY. I love her, too. Look how nicely she wrapped these boxes.

MOMMY. Grandma has always wrapped boxes nicely. When I was a little girl, I was very poor, and Grandma was very poor, too, because Grandpa was in heaven. And every day, when I went to school, Grandma used to wrap a box for me, and I used to take it with me to school; and when it was lunchtime, all the little boys and girls used to take out their boxes of lunch, and they weren't wrapped nicely at all, and they used to open them and eat their chicken legs and chocolate cakes; and I used to say, "Oh, look at my lovely lunch box; it's so nicely wrapped it would break my heart to open it." And so, I wouldn't open it.

DADDY. Because it was empty.

MOMMY. Oh no. Grandma always filled it up, because she never ate the dinner she cooked the evening before; she gave me all her food for my lunch box the next day. After school, I'd take the box back to Grandma, and she'd open it and eat the chicken legs and chocolate cake that was inside. Grandma used to say, "I love day-old cake." That's where the expression day-old cake came from. Grandma always ate everything a day late. I used to eat all the other little boys' and girls' food at school, because they thought my lunch box was empty. They thought my lunch box was empty, and that's why I wouldn't open it. They thought I suffered from the sin of pride, and since that made them better than me, they were very generous.

DADDY. You were a very deceitful little girl.

MOMMY. We were very poor! But then I married you, Daddy, and now we're very rich.

DADDY. Grandma isn't rich.

MOMMY. No, but you've been so good to Grandma she feels rich. She doesn't know you'd like to put her in a nursing home.

DADDY. I wouldn't!

MOMMY. Well, heaven knows, *I* would! I can't stand it, watching her do the cooking and the housework, polishing the silver, moving the furniture. . . .

DADDY. She likes to do that. She says it's the least she can do to earn her keep.

MOMMY. Well, she's right. You can't live off people. I can live off you, because I married you. And aren't you lucky all I brought with me was Grandma. A lot of women I know would have brought their whole families to live off you. All I brought was Grandma. Grandma is all the family I have.

DADDY. I feel very fortunate.

MOMMY. You should. I have a right to live off of you because I married you, and because I used to let you get on top of me and bump your uglies; and I have a right to all your money when you die. And when you do, Grandma and I can live by ourselves . . . if she's still here. Unless you have her put away in a nursing home.

DADDY. I have no intention of putting her in a nursing home.

MOMMY. Well, I wish somebody would do something with her!

DADDY. At any rate, you're very well provided for.

MOMMY. You're my sweet Daddy; that's very nice.

DADDY. I love my Mommy.

(Enter Grandma again, laden with more boxes)

GRANDMA *(Dumping the boxes on and around Daddy's feet)*. There; that's the lot of them.

DADDY. They're wrapped so nicely.

GRANDMA *(To Daddy)*. You won't get on my sweet side that way . . .

MOMMY. Grandma!

GRANDMA. . . . telling me how nicely I wrap boxes. Not after what you said: how I whimpered for hours. . . .

MOMMY. Grandma!

GRANDMA *(To Mommy)*. Shut up!

(To Daddy)

You don't have any feelings, that's what's wrong with you. Old people make all sorts of noises, half of them they can't help. Old people whimper, and cry, and belch, and make great hollow rumbling sounds at the table; old people wake up in the middle of the night screaming, and find out they haven't even been asleep; and when old people *are* asleep, they try to wake up, and they can't . . . not for the longest time.

MOMMY. Homilies, homilies!

GRANDMA. And there's more, too.

DADDY. I'm really very sorry, Grandma.

GRANDMA. I know you are, Daddy; it's Mommy over there makes all the trouble. If you'd listened to me, you wouldn't have married her in the first place. She was a tramp and a trollop and a trull to boot, and she's no better now.

MOMMY. Grandma!

GRANDMA *(To Mommy)*. Shut up!

(To Daddy)

When she was no more than eight years old she used to climb up on my lap and say, in a sickening little voice, "When I gwo up, I'm going to mahwy a wich old man; I'm going to set my wittle were end right down in a tub o' butter, that's what I'm going to do." And I warned you, Daddy; I told you to stay away from her type. I told you to. I did.

MOMMY. You stop that! You're my mother, not his!

GRANDMA. I am?

DADDY. That's right, Grandma. Mommy's right.

GRANDMA. Well, how would you expect somebody as old as I am to remember a thing like that? You don't make allowances for people. I want an allowance. I want an allowance!

DADDY. All right, Grandma; I'll see to it.

MOMMY. Grandma! I'm ashamed of you.

GRANDMA. Humf! It's a fine time to say that. You should have gotten rid of me a long time ago if that's the way you feel. You should have had Daddy set me up in business somewhere . . . I could have gone into the fur business, or I could have been a singer. But no; not you. You wanted me around so you could sleep in my room when Daddy got fresh. But now it isn't important, because Daddy doesn't want to get fresh with you any more, and I don't blame him. You'd rather sleep with me, wouldn't you, Daddy?

MOMMY. Daddy doesn't want to sleep with anyone. Daddy's been sick.

DADDY. I've been sick. I don't even want to sleep in the apartment.

MOMMY. You see? I told you.

DADDY. I just want to get everything over with.

MOMMY. That's right. Why are they so late? Why can't they get here on time?

GRANDMA *(An owl)*. Who? Who? . . . Who? Who?

MOMMY. You know, Grandma.

GRANDMA. No, I don't.

MOMMY. Well, it doesn't really matter whether you do or not.

DADDY. Is that true?

MOMMY. Oh, more or less. Look how pretty Grandma wrapped these boxes.

GRANDMA. I didn't really like wrapping them; it hurt my fingers, and it frightened me. But it had to be done.

MOMMY. Why, Grandma?

GRANDMA. None of your damn business.

MOMMY. Go to bed.

GRANDMA. I don't want to go to bed. I just got up. I want to stay here and watch. Besides . . .

MOMMY. Go to bed.

DADDY. Let her stay up, Mommy; it isn't noon yet.

GRANDMA. I want to watch; besides . . .

DADDY. Let her watch, Mommy.

MOMMY. Well all right, you can watch; but don't you dare say a word.

GRANDMA. Old people are very good at listening; old people don't like to talk; old people have colitis and lavender perfume. Now I'm going to be quiet.

DADDY. She never mentioned she wanted to be a singer.

MOMMY. Oh, I forgot to tell you, but it was ages ago.

(The doorbell rings.)

Oh, goodness! Here they are!

GRANDMA. Who? Who?

MOMMY. Oh, just some people.

GRANDMA. The van people? Is it the van people? Have you finally done it? Have you called the van people to come and take me away?

DADDY. Of course not, Grandma!

GRANDMA. Oh, don't be too sure. She'd have you carted off too, if she thought she could get away with it.

MOMMY. Pay no attention to her, Daddy.

(An aside to Grandma)

My God, you're ungrateful!

(The doorbell rings again.)

DADDY *(Wringing his hands)*. Oh dear; oh dear.

MOMMY *(Still to Grandma)*. Just you wait; I'll fix your wagon.

(Now to Daddy)

Well, go let them in Daddy. What are you waiting for?

DADDY. I think we should talk about it some more. Maybe we've been hasty . . . a little hasty, perhaps.

(Doorbell rings again.)

I'd like to talk about it some more.

MOMMY. There's no need. You made up your mind; you were firm; you were masculine and decisive.

DADDY. We might consider the pros and the . . .

MOMMY. I won't argue with you; it has to be done; you were right. Open the door.

DADDY. But I'm not sure that . . .

MOMMY. Open the door.

DADDY. Was I firm about it?

MOMMY. Oh, so firm; so firm.

DADDY. And was I decisive?

MOMMY. SO decisive! Oh, I shivered.

DADDY. And masculine? Was I really masculine?

MOMMY. Oh, Daddy, you were so masculine; I shivered and fainted.

GRANDMA. Shivered and fainted, did she? Humf!

MOMMY. You be quiet.

GRANDMA. Old people have a right to talk to themselves; it doesn't hurt the gums, and it's comforting.

(Doorbell rings again.)

DADDY. I shall now open the door.

MOMMY. WHAT a masculine Daddy! Isn't he a masculine Daddy?

GRANDMA. Don't expect me to say anything. Old people are obscene.

MOMMY. Some of your opinions aren't so bad. You know that?

DADDY *(Backing off from the door)*. Maybe we can send them away.

MOMMY. Oh, look at you! You're turning into jelly; you're indecisive; you're a woman.

DADDY. All right. Watch me now; I'm going to open the door. Watch. Watch!

MOMMY. We're watching; we're watching.

GRANDMA. *I'm* not.

DADDY. Watch now; it's opening.

(He opens the door.)

It's open!

(Mrs. Barker steps into the room.)

Here they are!

MOMMY. Here they are!

GRANDMA. Where?

DADDY. Come in. You're late. But, of course, we expected you to be late; we were saying that we expected you to be late.

MOMMY. Daddy, don't be rude! We were saying that you just can't get satisfaction these days, and we were talking about you, of course. Won't you come in?

MRS. BARKER. Thank you. I don't mind if I do.

MOMMY. We're very glad that you're here, late as you are. You do remember us, don't you? You were here once before. I'm Mommy, and this is Daddy, and that's Grandma, doddering there in the corner.

MRS. BARKER. Hello, Mommy; hello, Daddy; and hello there, Grandma.

DADDY. Now that you're here, I don't suppose you could go away and maybe come back some other time.

MRS. BARKER. Oh no; we're much too efficient for that. I said, hello there, Grandma.

MOMMY. Speak to them, Grandma.

GRANDMA. I don't see them.

DADDY. For shame, Grandma; they're here.

MRS. BARKER. Yes, we're here, Grandma. I'm Mrs. Barker. I remember you; don't you remember me?

GRANDMA. I don't recall. Maybe you were younger, or something.

MOMMY. Grandma! What a terrible thing to say!

MRS. BARKER. Oh no, don't scold her, Mommy; for all she knows she may be right.

DADDY. Uh . . . Mrs. Barker, is it? Won't you sit down?

MRS. BARKER. I don't mind if I do.

MOMMY. Would you like a cigarette, and a drink, and would you like to cross your legs?

MRS. BARKER. You forget yourself, Mommy; I'm a professional woman. But I will cross my legs.

DADDY. Yes, make yourself comfortable.

MRS. BARKER. I don't mind if I do.

GRANDMA. Are they still here?

MOMMY. Be quiet, Grandma.

MRS. BARKER. Oh, we're still here. My, what an unattractive apartment you have!

MOMMY. Yes, but you don't know what a trouble it is. Let me tell you . . .

DADDY. I was saying to Mommy . . .

MRS. BARKER. Yes, I know. I was listening outside.

DADDY. About the icebox, and . . . the doorbell . . . and the . . .

MRS. BARKER. . . . and the johnny. Yes, we're very efficient; we have to know everything in our work.

DADDY. Exactly what do you do?

MOMMY. Yes, what is your work?

MRS. BARKER. Well, my dear, for one thing, I'm chairman of your woman's club.

MOMMY. Don't be ridiculous. I was talking to the chairman of my woman's club just yester—Why, so you are. You remember, Daddy, the lady I was telling you about? The lady with the husband who sits in the *swing*? Don't you remember?

DADDY. No . . . no.

MOMMY. Of course you do. I'm sorry, Mrs. Barker. I would have known you anywhere, except in this artificial light. And look! You have a hat just like the one I bought yesterday.

MRS. BARKER (*With a little laugh*). No, not really; this hat is cream.

MOMMY. Well, my dear, that may look like a cream hat to you, but I can . . .

MRS. BARKER. Now, now; you seem to forget who I am.

MOMMY. Yes, I do, don't I? Are you sure you're comfortable? Won't you take off your dress.

MRS. BARKER. I don't mind if I do.

(*She removes her dress.*)

MOMMY. There. You must feel a great deal more comfortable.

MRS. BARKER. Well, I certainly *look* a great deal more comfortable.

DADDY. I'm going to blush and giggle.

MOMMY. Daddy's going to blush and giggle.

MRS. BARKER (*Pulling the hem of her slip above her knees*). You're lucky to have such a man for a husband.

MOMMY. Oh, don't I know it!

DADDY. I just blushed and giggled and went sticky wet.

MOMMY. Isn't Daddy a caution, Mrs. Barker?

MRS. BARKER. Maybe if I smoked . . . ?

MOMMY. Oh, that isn't necessary.

MRS. BARKER. I don't mind if I do.

MOMMY. No; no, don't. Really.

MRS. BARKER. I don't mind . . .

MOMMY. I won't have you smoking in my house, and that's that! You're a professional woman.

DADDY. Grandma drinks AND smokes; don't you, Grandma?

GRANDMA. No.

MOMMY. Well, now, Mrs. Barker; suppose you tell us why you're here.

GRANDMA (*As Mommy walks through the boxes*). The boxes . . . the boxes . . .

MOMMY. Be quiet, Grandma.

DADDY. What did you say, Grandma?

GRANDMA (*As Mommy steps on several of the boxes*). The boxes, damn it!

MRS. BARKER. Boxes; she said boxes. She mentioned the boxes.

DADDY. What about the boxes, Grandma? Maybe Mrs. Barker is here because of the boxes. Is that what you meant, Grandma?

GRANDMA. I don't know if that's what I meant or not. It's certainly not what I *thought* I meant.

DADDY. Grandma is of the opinion that . . .

MRS. BARKER. Can we assume that the boxes are for us? I mean, can we assume that you had us come here for the boxes?

MOMMY. Are you in the habit of receiving boxes?

DADDY. A very good question.

MRS. BARKER. Well, that would depend on the reason we're here. I've got my fingers in so many little pies, you know. Now, I can think of one of my little activities in which we are in the habit of receiving *baskets*; but more in a literary sense than really. We *might* receive boxes, though, under very special circumstances. I'm afraid that's the best answer I can give you.

DADDY. It's a very interesting answer.

MRS. BARKER. *I* thought so. But, does it help?

MOMMY. No; I'm afraid not.

DADDY. I wonder if it might help us any if I said I feel misgivings, that I have definite qualms.

MOMMY. Where, Daddy?

DADDY. Well, mostly right here, right around where the stitches were.

MOMMY. Daddy had an operation, you know.

MRS. BARKER. Oh, you poor Daddy! I didn't know; but then, how could I?

GRANDMA. You might have asked; it wouldn't have hurt you.

MOMMY. Dry up, Grandma.

GRANDMA. There you go. Letting your true feelings come out. Old people aren't dry enough, I suppose.

My sacks are empty, the fluid in my eyeballs is all caked on the inside edges, my spine is made of sugar candy, I breathe ice; but you don't hear me complain. Nobody hears old people complain because people think that's all old people do. And *that's* because old people are gnarled and sagged and twisted into the shape of a complaint.

(*Signs off*)

That's all.

MRS. BARKER. What was wrong, Daddy?

DADDY. Well, you know how it is: the doctors took out something that was there and put in something that wasn't there. An operation.

MRS. BARKER. You're very fortunate, I should say.

MOMMY. Oh, he is; he is. All his life. Daddy has wanted to be a United States Senator; but now . . . why now he's changed his mind, and for the rest of his life he's going to want to be Governor . . . it would be nearer the apartment, you know.

MRS. BARKER. You *are* fortunate, Daddy.

DADDY. Yes, indeed; except that I get these qualms now and then, definite ones.

MRS. BARKER. Well, it's just a matter of things settling; you're like an old house.

MOMMY. Why Daddy, thank Mrs. Barker.

DADDY. Thank you.

MRS. BARKER. Ambition! That's the ticket. I have a brother who's very much like you, Daddy . . . ambitious. Of course, he's a great deal younger than you; he's even younger than I am . . . if such a thing is possible. He runs a little newspaper. Just a little newspaper . . . but he runs it. He's chief cook and bottle washer of that little newspaper, which he calls *The Village Idiot*. He has such a sense of humor; he's so self-deprecating, so modest. And he'd never admit it himself, but he *is* the Village Idiot.

MOMMY. Oh, I think that's just grand. Don't you think so, Daddy?

DADDY. Yes, just grand.

MRS. BARKER. My brother's a dear man, and he has a dear little wife, whom he loves, dearly. He loves her so much he just can't get a sentence out without mentioning her. He wants everybody to know he's married. He's really a stickler on that point; he can't be introduced to anybody and say hello without adding, "Of course, I'm married." As far as I'm concerned, he's the chief exponent of Women Love in this whole country; he's even been written up in psychiatric journals because of it.

DADDY. Indeed!

MOMMY. Isn't that lovely.

MRS. BARKER. Oh, I think so. There's too much woman hatred in this country, and that's a fact.

GRANDMA. Oh, I don't know.

MOMMY. Oh, I think that's just grand. Don't you think so, Daddy?

DADDY. Yes, just grand.

GRANDMA. In case anybody's interested . . .

MOMMY. Be quiet, Grandma.

GRANDMA. Nuts!

MOMMY. Oh, Mrs. Barker, you *must* forgive Grandma. She's rural.

MRS. BARKER. I don't mind if I do.

DADDY. Maybe Grandma has something to say.

MOMMY. Nonsense. Old people have nothing to say; and if old people *did* have something to say, nobody would listen to them.

(*To Grandma*)

You see? I can pull that stuff just as easy as you can.

GRANDMA. Well, you got the rhythm, but you don't really have the quality. Besides, you're middle-aged.

MOMMY. I'm proud of it.

GRANDMA. Look. I'll show you how it's really done. Middle-aged people think they can do anything, but the truth is that middle-aged people can't do most things as well as they used to. Middle-aged people think they're special because they're like everybody else. We live in the age of deformity. You see? Rhythm *and* content. You'll learn.

DADDY. I do wish I weren't surrounded by women; I'd like some men around here.

MRS. BARKER. You can say that again!

GRANDMA. I don't hardly count as a woman, so can I say my piece?

MOMMY. Go on. Jabber away.

GRANDMA. It's very simple; the fact is, these boxes don't have anything to do with why this good lady is come to call. Now, if you're interested in knowing why these boxes *are* here . . .

DADDY. I'm sure that must be all very true, Grandma, but what does it have to do with why . . . pardon me, what is that name again?

MRS. BARKER. Mrs. Barker.

DADDY. Exactly. What does it have to do with why . . . that name again?

MRS. BARKER. Mrs. Barker.

DADDY. Precisely. What does it have to do with why what's-her-name is here?

MOMMY. They're here because we asked them.

MRS. BARKER. Yes. That's why.

GRANDMA. Now if you're interested in knowing why these boxes *are* here . . .

MOMMY. Well, nobody *is* interested!

GRANDMA. You can be as snippety as you like for all the good it'll do you.

DADDY. You two will have to stop arguing.

MOMMY. I don't argue with her.

DADDY. It will just have to stop.

MOMMY. Well, why don't you call a van and have her taken away?

GRANDMA. Don't bother; there's no need.

DADDY. No, now, perhaps I can go away myself. . . .

MOMMY. Well, one or the other; the way things are now it's impossible. In the first place, it's too crowded in this apartment.

(To Grandma)

And it's you that takes up all the space, with your enema bottles, and your Pekinese, and God-only-knows-what-else . . . and now all these boxes . . .

GRANDMA. These boxes are . . .

MRS. BARKER. I've never heard of enema *bottles*. . . .

GRANDMA. She means enema bags, but she doesn't know the difference. Mommy comes from extremely bad stock. And besides, when Mommy was born . . . well, it was a difficult delivery, and she had a head shaped like a banana.

MOMMY. You ungrateful—Daddy? Daddy, you see how ungrateful she is after all these years, after all the things we've done for her?

(To Grandma)

One of these days you're going away in a van; that's what's going to happen to you!

GRANDMA. Do tell!

MRS. BARKER. Like a banana?

GRANDMA. Yup, just like a banana.

MRS. BARKER. My word!

MOMMY. You stop listening to her; she'll say anything. Just the other night she called Daddy a hedgehog.

MRS. BARKER. She didn't!

GRANDMA. That's right, baby; you stick up for me.

MOMMY. I don't know where she gets the words; on the television, maybe.

MRS. BARKER. Did you really call him a hedgehog?

GRANDMA. Oh look; what difference does it make whether I did or not?

DADDY. Grandma's right. Leave Grandma alone.

MOMMY *(To Daddy)*. How dare you!

GRANDMA. Oh, leave her alone, Daddy; the kid's all mixed up.

MOMMY. You see? I told you. It's all those television shows. Daddy, you go right into Grandma's room and take her television and shake all the tubes loose.

DADDY. Don't mention tubes to me.

MOMMY. Oh! Mommy forgot!

(To Mrs. Barker)

Daddy has tubes now, where he used to have tracts.

MRS. BARKER. Is that a fact!

GRANDMA. I know why this dear lady is here.

MOMMY. You be still.

MRS. BARKER. Oh, I do wish you'd tell me.

MOMMY. No! No! That wouldn't be fair at all.

DADDY. Besides, she knows why she's here; she's here because we called them.

MRS. BARKER. La! But that still leaves me puzzled. I know I'm here because you called us, but I'm such a busy girl, with this committee and that committee, and the Responsible Citizens Activities I indulge in.

MOMMY. Oh my; busy, busy.

MRS. BARKER. Yes, indeed. So I'm afraid you'll have to give me some help.

MOMMY. Oh, no. No, you must be mistaken. I can't believe we asked you here to give you any help. With the way taxes are these days, and the way you can't get satisfaction in ANYTHING . . . no, I don't believe so.

DADDY. And if you need help . . . why, I should think you'd apply for a Fulbright Scholarship.

MOMMY. And if not that . . . why, then a Guggenheim Fellowship. . . .

GRANDMA. Oh, come on; why not shoot the works and try for the Prix de Rome.

(Under her breath to Mommy and Daddy)

Beasts!

MRS. BARKER. Oh, what a jolly family. But let me think. I'm knee-deep in work these days; there's the Ladies' Auxiliary Air Raid Committee, for one thing; how do you feel about air raids?

MOMMY. Oh, I'd say we're hostile.

DADDY. Yes, definitely; we're hostile.

MRS. BARKER. Then, you'll be no help there. There's too much hostility in the world these days as it is; but I'll not badger you! There's a surfeit of badgers as well.

GRANDMA. While we're at it, there's been a run on old people, too. The Department of Agriculture, or maybe it wasn't the Department of Agriculture—anyway, it was some department that's run by a girl—put out figures showing that ninety per cent of the adult population of the country is over eighty years old . . . or eighty percent is over ninety years old . . .

MOMMY. You're such a liar! You just finished saying that everyone is middle-aged.

GRANDMA. I'm just telling you what the government says . . . that doesn't have anything to do with what . . .

MOMMY. It's that television! Daddy, go break her television.

GRANDMA. You won't find it!

DADDY (*Wearily getting up*). If I must . . . I must.

MOMMY. And don't step on the Pekinese; it's blind.

DADDY. It may be blind, but Daddy isn't.

(*He exits, through the archway, stage-left.*)

GRANDMA. You won't find *it*, either.

MOMMY. Oh, I'm so fortunate to have such a husband. Just think; I could have a husband who was poor, or argumentative, or a husband who sat in a wheel chair all day . . . OOOOHHHH! *What* have I said? What *have* I said?

GRANDMA. You said you could have a husband who sat in a wheel . . .

MOMMY. I'm mortified! I could die! I could cut my tongue out! I could . . .

MRS. BARKER (*Forcing a smile*). Oh, now . . . now . . . don't think about it . . .

MOMMY. I could . . . why, I could . . .

MRS. BARKER. . . . don't think about it . . . really. . . .

MOMMY. You're quite right. I won't think about it, and that way I'll forget that I ever said it, and that way it will be all right.

(*Pause*)

There . . . I've forgotten. Well, now, now that Daddy is out of the room we can have some girl talk.

MRS. BARKER. I'm not sure that I . . .

MOMMY. You *do* want to have some girl talk, don't you?

MRS. BARKER. I was going to say I'm not sure that I wouldn't care for a glass of water. I feel a little faint.

MOMMY. Grandma, go get Mrs. Barker a glass of water.

GRANDMA. Go get it yourself. I quit.

MOMMY. Grandma loves to do little things around the house; it gives her a false sense of security.

GRANDMA. I quit! I'm through!

MOMMY. Now, you be a good Grandma, or you know what will happen to you. You'll be taken away in a van.

GRANDMA. You don't frighten me. I'm too old to be frightened. Besides . . .

MOMMY. WELL! I'll tend to you later. I'll hide your teeth . . . I'll . . .

GRANDMA. Everything's hidden.

MRS. BARKER. I *am* going to faint. I *am*.

MOMMY. Good heavens! I'll go myself.

(*As she exits, through the archway, stage-left*)

I'll fix you, Grandma. I'll take care of you later.

(*She exits.*)

GRANDMA. Oh, go soak your head.

(*To Mrs. Barker*)

Well, dearie, how do you feel?

MRS. BARKER. A little better, I think. Yes, much better, thank you, Grandma.

GRANDMA. That's good.

MRS. BARKER. But . . . I feel so lost . . . not knowing why I'm here . . . and, on top of it, they say I was here before.

GRANDMA. Well, you were. You weren't *here*, exactly, because we've moved around a lot, from one apartment to another, up and down the social ladder like mice, if you like similes.

MRS. BARKER. I don't . . . particularly.

GRANDMA. Well, then, I'm sorry.

MRS. BARKER (*Suddenly*). Grandma, I feel I can trust you.

GRANDMA. Don't be too sure; it's every man for himself around this place. . . .

MRS. BARKER. Oh . . . is it? Nonetheless, I really do feel that I can trust you. *Please* tell me why they called and asked us to come. I implore you!

GRANDMA. Oh my; that feels good. It's been so long since anybody implored me. Do it again. Implore me some more.

MRS. BARKER. You're your daughter's mother, all right!

GRANDMA. Oh, I don't mean to be hard. If you won't implore me, then beg me, or ask me, or entreat me . . . just anything like that.

MRS. BARKER. You're a dreadful old woman!

GRANDMA. You'll understand some day. Please!

MRS. BARKER. Oh, for heaven's sake! . . . I implore you . . . I beg you . . . I beseech you!

GRANDMA. Beseech! Oh, that's the nicest word I've heard in ages. You're a dear, sweet woman. . . . You . . . beseech . . . me. I can't resist that.

MRS. BARKER. Well, then . . . please tell me why they asked us to come.

GRANDMA. Well, I'll give you a hint. That's the best I can do, because I'm a muddleheaded old woman. Now listen, because it's important. Once upon a time, not too very long ago, but a long enough time ago . . . oh, about twenty years ago . . . there was a man very much like Daddy, and a woman very much like Mommy, who were married to each other, very much like Mommy and Daddy are married to each other; and they lived in an apartment very much like one that's very much like this one, and they lived there with an old woman who was very much like yours truly, only younger, because it was some time ago; in fact, they were all somewhat younger.

MRS. BARKER. How fascinating!

GRANDMA. Now, at the same time, there was a dear lady very much like you, only younger then, who did all sorts of Good Works.... And one of the Good Works this dear lady did was in something very much like a volunteer capacity for an organization very much like the Bye-Bye Adoption Service, which is nearby and which was run by a terribly deaf old lady very much like the Miss Bye-Bye who runs the Bye-Bye Adoption Service nearby.

MRS. BARKER. How enthralling!

GRANDMA. Well, be that as it may. Nonetheless, one afternoon this man, who was very much like Daddy, and this woman who was very much like Mommy came to see this dear lady who did all the Good Works, who was very much like you, dear, and they were very sad and very hopeful, and they cried and smiled and bit their fingers, and they said all the most intimate things.

MRS. BARKER. How spellbinding! What did they say?

GRANDMA. Well, it was very sweet. The woman, who was very much like Mommy, said that she and the man who was very much like Daddy had never been blessed with anything very much like a bumble of joy.

MRS. BARKER. A what?

GRANDMA. A bumble; a bumble of joy.

MRS. BARKER. Oh, like bundle.

GRANDMA. Well, yes; very much like it. Bundle, bumble; who cares? At any rate, the woman, who was very much like Mommy, said that they wanted a bumble of their own, but that the man, who was very much like Daddy, couldn't have a bumble; and the man, who was very much like Daddy, said that yes, they had wanted a bumble of their own, but that the woman, who was very much like Mommy, couldn't have one, and that now they wanted to buy something very much like a bumble.

MRS. BARKER. How engrossing!

GRANDMA. Yes. And the dear lady, who was very much like you, said something that was very much like, "Oh, what a shame; but take heart ... I think we have just the bumble *for* you." And, well, the lady, who was very much like Mommy, and the man, who was very much like Daddy, cried and smiled and bit their fingers, and said some more intimate things, which were totally irrelevant but which were pretty hot stuff, and so the dear lady, who was very much like you, and who had something very much like a

penchant for pornography, listened with something very much like enthusiasm. "Whee," she said. "Whoooopeeeeee!" But that's beside the point.

MRS. BARKER. I suppose *so*. But how gripping!

GRANDMA. Anyway ... they *bought* something very much like a bumble, and they took it away with them. But ... things didn't work out very well.

MRS. BARKER. You mean there was trouble?

GRANDMA. You got it.

(With a glance through the archway)

But, I'm going to have to speed up now because I think I'm leaving soon.

MRS. BARKER. Oh. Are you really?

GRANDMA. Yup.

MRS. BARKER. But old people don't go anywhere; they're either taken places, or put places.

GRANDMA. Well, this old person is different. Anyway ... things started going badly.

MRS. BARKER. Oh yes. Yes.

GRANDMA. Weeeeelllll ... in the first place, it turned out the bumble didn't look like either one of its parents. That was enough of a blow, but things got worse. One night, it cried its heart out, if you can imagine such a thing.

MRS. BARKER. Cried its heart out! Well!

GRANDMA. But that was only the beginning. Then it turned out it only had eyes for its Daddy.

MRS. BARKER. For its Daddy! Why, any self-respecting woman would have gouged those eyes right out of its head.

GRANDMA. Well, she did. That's exactly what she did. But then, it kept its nose up in the air.

MRS. BARKER. Ufggh! How disgusting!

GRANDMA. That's what they thought. But *then*, it began to develop an interest in its you-know-what.

MRS. BARKER. In its you-know-what! Well! I hope they cut its hands off at the wrists!

GRANDMA. Well, yes, they did that eventually. But first, they cut off its you-know-what.

MRS. BARKER. A much better idea!

GRANDMA. That's what they thought. But after they cut off its you-know-what, it *still* put its hands under the covers, *looking* for its you-know-what. So, finally, they *had* to cut off its hands at the wrists.

MRS. BARKER. Naturally!

GRANDMA. And it was such a resentful bumble. Why, one day it called its Mommy a dirty name.

MRS. BARKER. Well, I hope they cut its tongue out!

GRANDMA. Of course. And then, as it got bigger, they found out all sorts of terrible things about it, like: it didn't have a head on its shoulders, it had no guts, it was spineless, its feet were made of clay . . . just dreadful things.

MRS. BARKER. Dreadful!

GRANDMA. So you can understand how they became discouraged.

MRS. BARKER. I certainly can! And what did they do?

GRANDMA. What did they do? Well, for the last straw, it finally up and died; and you can imagine how *that* made them feel, their having paid for it, and all. So, they called up the lady who sold them the bumble in the first place and told her to come right over to their apartment. They wanted satisfaction; they wanted their money back. That's what they wanted.

MRS. BARKER. My, my, my.

GRANDMA. How do you like *them* apples?

MRS. BARKER. My, my, my.

DADDY (*Off stage*). Mommy! I can't find Grandma's television, and I can't find the Pekinese, either.

MOMMY (*Off stage*). Isn't that funny! And I can't find the water.

GRANDMA. Heh, heh, heh. I told them everything was hidden.

MRS. BARKER. Did you hide the water, too?

GRANDMA (*Puzzled*). No. No, I didn't do *that*.

DADDY (*Off stage*). The truth of the matter is, I can't even find Grandma's room.

GRANDMA. Heh, heh, heh.

MRS. BARKER. My! You certainly did hide things, didn't you?

GRANDMA. Sure, kid, sure.

MOMMY (*Sticking her head in the room*). Did you ever hear of such a thing, Grandma? Daddy can't find your television, and he can't find the Pekinese, and the truth of the matter is he can't even find your room.

GRANDMA. I told you. I hid everything.

MOMMY. Nonsense, Grandma! Just wait until I get my hands on you. You're a troublemaker . . . that's what you are.

GRANDMA. Well, I'll be out of here pretty soon, baby.

MOMMY. Oh, you don't know how right you are! Daddy's been wanting to send you away for a long time now, but I've been restraining him. I'll tell you one thing, though . . . I'm getting sick and tired of this fighting, and I might just let him have his way. Then you'll see what'll happen. Away you'll go; in a van, too. I'll let Daddy call the van man.

GRANDMA. I'm away ahead of you.

MOMMY. How can you be so old and so smug at the same time? You have no sense of proportion.

GRANDMA. You just answered your own question.

MOMMY. Mrs. Barker, I'd much rather you came into the kitchen for that glass of water, what with Grandma out here, and all.

MRS. BARKER. I don't see what Grandma has to do with it; and besides, I don't think you're very polite.

MOMMY. You seem to forget that you're a guest in this house . . .

GRANDMA. Apartment!

MOMMY. Apartment! And that you're a professional woman. So, if you'll be so good as to come into the kitchen, I'll be more than happy to show you where the water is, and where the glass is, and then you can put two and two together, if you're clever enough.

(*She vanishes.*)

MRS. BARKER. (*After a moment's consideration*). I suppose she's right.

GRANDMA. Well, that's how it is when people call you up and ask you over to do something for them.

MRS. BARKER. I suppose you're right, too. Well, Grandma, it's been very nice talking to you.

GRANDMA. And I've enjoyed listening. Say, don't tell Mommy or Daddy that I gave you that hint, will you?

MRS. BARKER. Oh, dear me, the hint! I'd forgotten about it, if you can imagine such a thing. No, I won't breathe a word of it to them.

GRANDMA. I don't know if it helped you any . . .

MRS. BARKER. I can't tell, yet. I'll have to . . . what *is* the word I want? . . . I'll have to relate it . . . that's it . . . I'll have to relate it to certain things that I *know*, and . . . draw . . . conclusions. . . . What I'll really have to do is to see if it applies to anything. I mean, after all, I *do* do volunteer work for an adoption service, but it isn't very much *like* the Bye-Bye Adoption Service . . . it *is* the Bye-Bye Adoption Service . . . and while I can remember Mommy and Daddy coming to see me, oh, about twenty years ago, about buying a bumble, I can't quite remember anyone very much *like* Mommy and Daddy coming to see me about buying a bumble. Don't you see? It really presents quite a problem. . . . I'll have to think about it . . . mull it . . . but at any rate, it was truly first-class of you to try to help me. Oh, will you still be here after I've had my drink of water?

GRANDMA. Probably . . . I'm not as spry as I used to be.

MRS. BARKER. Oh. Well, I won't say good-by then.

GRANDMA. No. Don't.

(*Mrs. Barker exits through the archway.*)

People don't say good-by to old people because they think they'll frighten them. Lordy! If they only knew how awful "hello" and "My, you're looking chipper" sounded, they wouldn't say those things either. The truth is, there isn't much you *can* say to old people that doesn't sound just terrible.

(*The doorbell rings.*)

Come on in!

(*The Young Man enters. Grandma looks him over.*)

Well, now, aren't you a breath of fresh air!

YOUNG MAN. Hello there.

GRANDMA. My, my, my. Are you the van man?

YOUNG MAN. The what?

GRANDMA. The van man. The van man. Are you coming to take me away?

YOUNG MAN. I don't know what you're talking about.

GRANDMA. Oh.

(*Pause*)

Well.

(*Pause*)

My, my, aren't you something!

YOUNG MAN. Hm?

GRANDMA. I said, my, my, aren't you something.

YOUNG MAN. Oh. Thank you.

GRANDMA. You don't sound very enthusiastic.

YOUNG MAN. Oh, I'm . . . I'm used to it.

GRANDMA. Yup . . . yup. You know, if I were about a hundred and fifty years younger I could go for you.

YOUNG MAN. Yes, I imagine so.

GRANDMA. Unh-hunh . . . will you look at those muscles!

YOUNG MAN (*Flexing his muscles*). Yes, they're quite good, aren't they?

GRANDMA. Boy, they sure are. They natural?

YOUNG MAN. Well the basic structure was there, but I've done some work, too . . . you know, in a gym.

GRANDMA. I'll bet you have. You ought to be in the movies, boy.

YOUNG MAN. I know.

GRANDMA. Yup! Right up there on the old silver screen. But I suppose you've heard that before.

YOUNG MAN. Yes, I have.

GRANDMA. You ought to try out for them . . . the movies.

YOUNG MAN. Well, actually, I may have a career there yet. I've lived out on the West coast almost all my life . . . and I've met a few people who . . . might be able to help me. I'm not in too much of a hurry, though. I'm almost as young as I look.

GRANDMA. Oh, that's nice. And will you look at that face!

YOUNG MAN. Yes, it's quite good, isn't it? Clean-cut, midwest farm boy type, almost insultingly good-looking in a typically American way. Good profile, straight nose, honest eyes, wonderful smile . . .

GRANDMA. Yup. Boy, you know what you are, don't you? You're the American Dream, that's what you are. All those other people, they don't know what they're talking about. You . . . *you* are the American Dream.

YOUNG MAN. Thanks.

MOMMY (*Off stage*). Who rang the doorbell?

GRANDMA (*Shouting off-stage*). The American Dream!

MOMMY (*Off stage*). What? What was that, Grandma?

GRANDMA (*Shouting*). The American Dream! The American Dream! Damn it!

DADDY (*Off stage*). How's that, Mommy?

MOMMY (*Off stage*). Oh, some gibberish; pay no attention. Did you find Grandma's room?

DADDY (*Off stage*). No. I can't even find Mrs. Barker.

YOUNG MAN. What was all that?

GRANDMA. Oh, that was just the folks, but let's not talk about them, honey; let's talk about you.

YOUNG MAN. All right.

GRANDMA. Well, let's see. If you're not the van man, what are you doing here?

YOUNG MAN. I'm looking for work.

GRANDMA. Are you! Well, what kind of work?

YOUNG MAN. Oh, almost anything . . . almost anything that pays. I'll do almost anything for money.

GRANDMA. Will you . . . will you? Hmmmm. I wonder if there's anything you could do around here?

YOUNG MAN. There might be. It looked to be a likely building.

GRANDMA. It's always looked to be a rather unlikely building to me, but I suppose you'd know better than I.

YOUNG MAN. I can sense these things.

GRANDMA. There *might* be something you could do around here. Stay there! Don't come any closer.

YOUNG MAN. Sorry.

GRANDMA. I don't mean I'd *mind*. I don't know whether I'd mind, or not. . . . But it wouldn't look well; it would look just *awful*.

YOUNG MAN. Yes; I suppose so.

GRANDMA. Now, stay there, let me concentrate. What could you do? The folks have been in something of a quandary around here today, sort of a dilemma, and I wonder if you mightn't be some help.

YOUNG MAN. I hope so . . . if there's money in it. Do you have any money?

GRANDMA. Money! Oh, there's more money around here than you'd know what to do with.

YOUNG MAN. I'm not so sure.

GRANDMA. Well, maybe not. Besides, I've got money of my own.

YOUNG MAN. You have?

GRANDMA. Sure. Old people quite often have lots of money; more often than most people expect. Come here, so I can whisper to you . . . not too close. I might faint.

YOUNG MAN. Oh, I'm sorry.

GRANDMA. It's all right, dear. Anyway . . . have you ever heard of that big baking contest they run? The one where all the ladies get together in a big barn and bake away?

YOUNG MAN. I'm . . . not . . . sure. . . .

GRANDMA. Not so close. Well, it doesn't matter whether you've heard of it or not. The important thing is— and I don't want anybody to hear this . . . the folks think I haven't been out of the house in eight years—the important thing is that I won first prize in that baking contest this year. Oh, it was in all the papers; not under my own name, though. I used a *nom de boulangère*; I called myself Uncle Henry.

YOUNG MAN. Did you?

GRANDMA. Why not? I didn't see any reason not to. I look just as much like an old man as I do like an old woman. And you know what I called it . . . what I won for?

YOUNG MAN. No. What did you call it?

GRANDMA. I called it Uncle Henry's Day-Old Cake.

YOUNG MAN. That's a very nice name.

GRANDMA. And it wasn't any trouble, either. All I did was go out and get a store-bought cake, and keep it around for a while, and then slip it in, unbeknownst to anybody. Simple.

YOUNG MAN. You're a very resourceful person.

GRANDMA. Pioneer stock.

YOUNG MAN. Is all this true? Do you want me to believe all this?

GRANDMA. Well, you can believe it or not . . . it doesn't make any difference to me. All *I* know is, Uncle Henry's Day-Old Cake won me twenty-five thousand smackerolas.

YOUNG MAN. Twenty-five thou—

GRANDMA. Right on the old loggerhead. Now . . . how do you like them apples?

YOUNG MAN. Love 'em.

GRANDMA. I thought you'd be impressed.

YOUNG MAN. Money talks.

GRANDMA. Hey! You look familiar.

YOUNG MAN. Hm? Pardon?

GRANDMA. I said you look familiar.

YOUNG MAN. Well, I've done some modeling.

GRANDMA. No . . . no. I don't mean that. You look familiar.

YOUNG MAN. Well, I'm a type.

GRANDMA. Yup; you sure are. Why do you say you'd do anything for money . . . if you don't mind my being nosy?

YOUNG MAN. No, no. It's part of the interviews. I'll be happy to tell you. It's that I have no talents at all, except what you see . . . my person; my body, my face. In every other way I am incomplete, and I must therefore . . . compensate.

GRANDMA. What do you mean, incomplete? You look pretty complete to me.

YOUNG MAN. I think I can explain it to you, partially because you're very old, and very old people have perceptions they keep to themselves, because if they expose them to other people . . . well, you know what ridicule and neglect are.

GRANDMA. I do, child, I do.

YOUNG MAN. Then listen. My mother died the night that I was born, and I never knew my father; I doubt my mother did. But, I wasn't alone, because lying with me . . . in the placenta . . . there was someone else . . . my brother . . . my twin.

GRANDMA. Oh, my child.

YOUNG MAN. We were identical twins . . . he and I . . . not fraternal . . . identical; we were derived from the same ovum; and in *this*, in that we were twins not from separate ova but from the same one, we had a kinship such as you cannot imagine. We . . . we felt each other breathe . . . his heartbeats thundered in my temples . . . mine in his . . . our stomachs ached and we cried for feeding at the same time . . . are you old enough to understand?

GRANDMA. I think so, child; I think I'm nearly old enough.

YOUNG MAN. I hope so. But we were separated when we were still very young, my brother, my twin and I . . . inasmuch as you can separate one being. We were torn apart . . . thrown to opposite ends of the continent. I don't know what became of my brother . . . to the rest of myself . . . except that, from time to time, in the years that have passed, I have suffered losses . . . that I can't explain. A fall from grace . . . a departure of innocence . . . loss . . . loss. How can I put it to you? All right; like this: Once . . . it was as if all at once my heart . . . became numb . . . almost as though I . . . almost as though . . . just like that . . . it had been wrenched from my body . . . and from that time I have been unable to love. Once . . . I was asleep at the time . . . I awoke, and my eyes were burning. And since that time I have been unable to see anything, *anything*, with pity, with affection . . . with anything but . . . cool disinterest. And my groin . . . even there . . . since one time . . . one specific agony . . . since then I

Edward Albee

have not been able to *love* anyone with my body. And even my hands . . . I cannot touch another person and feel love. And there is more . . . there are more losses, but it all comes down to this: I no longer have the capacity to feel anything. I have no emotions. I have been drained, torn asunder . . . disemboweled. I have, now, only my person . . . my body, my face. I use what I have . . . I let people love me . . . I accept the syntax around me, for while I know I cannot relate . . . I know I must be related *to*. I let people love me . . . I let people touch me . . . I let them draw pleasure from my groin . . . from my presence . . . from the fact of me . . . but, that is all it comes to. As I told you, I am incomplete . . . I can feel nothing. I can feel nothing. And so . . . here I am . . . as you see me. I am . . . but this . . . what you see. And it will always be thus.

GRANDMA. Oh, my child; my child.

(Long pause; then)

I was mistaken . . . before. I don't know you from somewhere, but I knew . . . once . . . someone very much like you . . . or, very much as perhaps you were.

YOUNG MAN. Be careful; be very careful. What I have told you may not be true. In my profession . . .

GRANDMA. Shhhhhh.

(The Young Man bows his head, in acquiescence.)

Someone . . . to be more precise . . . who might have turned out to be very much like you might have turned out to be. And . . . unless I'm terribly mistaken . . . you've found yourself a job.

YOUNG MAN. What are my duties?

MRS. BARKER *(Off stage)*. Yoo-hoo! Yoo-hoo!

GRANDMA. Oh-oh. You'll . . . you'll have to play it by ear, my dear . . . unless I get a chance to talk to you again. I've got to go into my act, now.

YOUNG MAN. But, I . . .

GRANDMA. Yoo-hoo!

MRS. BARKER *(Coming through archway)*. Yoo-hoo . . . oh, there you are, Grandma. I'm glad to see somebody. I can't find Mommy or Daddy.

(Double takes)

Well . . . who's this?

GRANDMA. This? Well . . . uh . . . oh, this is the . . . uh . . . the van man. That's who it is . . . the van man.

MRS. BARKER. So! It's true! They *did* call the van man. They *are* having you carted away.

GRANDMA *(Shrugging)*. Well, you know. It figures.

MRS. BARKER *(To Young Man)*. How dare you cart this poor old woman away!

YOUNG MAN *(After a quick look at Grandma, who nods)*. I do what I'm paid to do. I don't ask any questions.

MRS. BARKER *(After a brief pause)*. Oh.

(Pause)

Well, you're quite right, of course, and I shouldn't meddle.

GRANDMA *(To Young Man)*. Dear, will you take my things out to the van? *(She points to the boxes)*

YOUNG MAN *(After only the briefest hesitation)*. Why, certainly.

GRANDMA *(As the Young Man takes up half the boxes, exits by the front door)*. Isn't that a nice young van man?

MRS. BARKER *(Shaking her head in disbelief, watching the Young Man exit)*. Unh-hunh . . . some things have changed for the better. I remember when I had *my* mother carted off . . . the van man who came for her wasn't anything near as nice as this one.

GRANDMA. Oh, did you have your mother carted off, too?

MRS. BARKER *(Cheerfully)*. Why certainly! Didn't you?

GRANDMA *(Puzzling)*. No . . . no, I didn't. At least, I can't remember. Listen dear; I got to talk to you for a second.

MRS. BARKER. Why certainly, Grandma.

GRANDMA. Now, listen.

MRS. BARKER. Yes, Grandma. Yes.

GRANDMA. Now listen carefully. You got this dilemma here with Mommy and Daddy . . .

MRS. BARKER. Yes! I wonder where they've gone to?

GRANDMA. They'll be back in. Now, LISTEN!

MRS. BARKER. Oh, I'm sorry.

GRANDMA. Now, you got this dilemma here with Mommy and Daddy, and I think I got the way out for you.

(The Young Man re-enters through the front door.)

Will you take the rest of my things out now, dear?

(To Mrs. Barker, while the Young Man takes the rest of the boxes, exits again by the front door)

Fine. Now listen, dear.

(She begins to whisper in Mrs. Barker's ear.)

MRS. BARKER. Oh! Oh! Oh! I don't think I could . . . do you really think I could? Well, why not? What a wonderful idea . . . what an absolutely wonderful idea!

GRANDMA. Well, yes, I thought it was.

MRS. BARKER. And you so old!

GRANDMA. Heh, heh, heh.

MRS. BARKER. Well, I think it's absolutely marvelous, anyway. I'm going to find Mommy and Daddy right now.

GRANDMA. Good. You do that.

MRS. BARKER. Well, now. I think I will say good-by. I can't thank you enough.

(*She starts to exit through the archway.*)

GRANDMA. You're welcome. Say it!

MRS. BARKER. Huh? What?

GRANDMA. Say good-by.

MRS. BARKER. Oh. Good-by.

(*She exits.*)

Mommy! I say, Mommy! Daddy!

GRANDMA. Good-by.

(*By herself now, she looks about.*)

Ah me.

(*Shakes her head*)

Ah me.

(*Takes in the room*)

Good-by.

(*The Young Man re-enters.*)

GRANDMA. Oh, hello, there.

YOUNG MAN. All the boxes are outside.

GRANDMA (*A little sadly*). I don't know why I bother to take them with me. They don't have much in them . . . some old letters, a couple of regrets . . . Pekinese . . . blind at that . . . the television . . . my Sunday teeth . . . eighty-six years of living . . . some sounds . . . a few images, a little garbled by now . . . and, well . . .

(*She shrugs.*)

. . . you know . . . the things one accumulates.

YOUNG MAN. Can I get you . . . a cab, or something?

GRANDMA. Oh no, dear . . . thank you just the same. I'll take it from here.

YOUNG MAN. And what shall I do now?

GRANDMA. Oh, you stay here, dear. It will all become clear to you. It will be explained. You'll understand.

YOUNG MAN. Very well.

GRANDMA (*After one more look about*). Well . . .

YOUNG MAN. Let me see you to the elevator.

GRANDMA. Oh . . . that *would* be nice, dear.

(*They both exit by the front door, slowly.*)

(*Enter Mrs. Barker, followed by Mommy and Daddy*)

MRS. BARKER. . . . and I'm happy to tell you that the whole thing's settled. Just like that.

MOMMY. Oh, we're so glad. We were afraid there might be a problem, what with delays, and all.

DADDY. Yes, we're very relieved.

MRS. BARKER. Well, now; that's what professional women are for.

MOMMY. Why . . . where's Grandma? Grandma's not here! Where's Grandma? And look! The boxes are gone, too. Grandma's gone, and so are the boxes. She's taken off, and she's stolen something! Daddy!

MRS. BARKER. Why, Mommy, the van man was here.

MOMMY (*Startled*). The what?

MRS. BARKER. The van man. The van man was here.

(*The lights might dim a little, suddenly.*)

MOMMY (*Shakes her head*). No, that's impossible.

MRS. BARKER. Why, I saw him with my own two eyes.

MOMMY (*Near tears*). No, no, that's impossible. No. There's no such thing as the van man. There is no van man. We . . . we made him up. Grandma? Grandma?

DADDY (*Moving to Mommy*). There, there, now.

MOMMY. Oh Daddy . . . where's Grandma?

DADDY. There, there, now.

(*While Daddy is comforting Mommy, Grandma comes out, stage right, near the footlights.*)

GRANDMA (*To the audience*). Shhhhhh! I want to watch this.

(*She motions to Mrs. Barker who, with a secret smile, tiptoes to the front door and opens it. The Young Man is framed therein. Lights up full again as he steps into the room.*)

MRS. BARKER. Surprise! Surprise! Here we are!

MOMMY. What? What?

DADDY. Hm? What?

MOMMY (*Her tears merely sniffles now*). What surprise?

MRS. BARKER. Why, I told you. The surprise I told you about.

DADDY. You . . . you know, Mommy.

MOMMY. Sur . . . prise?

DADDY (*Urging her to cheerfulness*). You remember, Mommy; why we asked . . . uh . . . what's-her-name to come here?

MRS. BARKER. Mrs. Barker, if you don't mind.

DADDY. Yes. Mommy? You remember now? About the bumble . . . about wanting satisfaction?

MOMMY (*Her sorrow turning into delight*). Yes. Why yes! Of course! Yes! Oh, how wonderful!

MRS. BARKER (*To the Young Man*). This is Mommy.

YOUNG MAN. How . . . how do you do?

MRS. BARKER (*Stage whisper*). Her name's Mommy.

YOUNG MAN. How . . . how do you do, Mommy?

MOMMY. Well! Hello there!

MRS. BARKER (*To the Young Man*). And that is Daddy.

YOUNG MAN. How do you do, sir?

DADDY. How do you do?

MOMMY (*Herself again, circling the Young Man, feeling his arm, poking him*). Yes, sir! Yes, sirree! Now this is more like it. Now this is a great deal more like it! Daddy! Come see. Come see if this isn't a great deal more like it.

DADDY. I . . . I can see from here, Mommy. It does look a great deal more like it.

MOMMY. Yes, sir. Yes sirree! Mrs. Barker, I don't know *how* to thank you.

MRS. BARKER. Oh, don't worry about that. I'll send you a bill in the mail.

MOMMY. What this really calls for is a celebration. It calls for a drink.

MRS. BARKER. Oh, what a nice idea.

MOMMY. There's some sauterne in the kitchen.

YOUNG MAN. I'll go.

MOMMY. Will you? Oh, how nice. The kitchen's through the archway there.

(*As the Young Man exits: to Mrs. Barker*)

He's very nice. Really top notch; much better than the other one.

MRS. BARKER. I'm glad you're pleased. And I'm glad everything's all straightened out.

MOMMY. Well, at least we know why we sent for you. We're glad that's cleared up. By the way, what's his name?

MRS. BARKER. Ha! Call him whatever you like. He's yours. Call him what you called the other one.

MOMMY. Daddy? What did we call the other one?

DADDY (*Puzzles*). Why . . .

YOUNG MAN (*Re-entering with a tray on which are a bottle of sauterne and five glasses*). Here we are!

MOMMY. Hooray! Hooray!

MRS. BARKER. Oh, good!

MOMMY (*Moving to the tray*). So, let's—Five glasses? Why five? There are only four of us. Why five?

YOUNG MAN (*Catches Grandma's eye; Grandma indicates she is not there*). Oh, I'm sorry.

MOMMY. You must learn to count. We're a wealthy family, and you must learn to count.

YOUNG MAN. I will.

MOMMY. Well, everybody take a glass.

(*They do.*)

And we'll drink to celebrate. To satisfaction! Who says you can't get satisfaction these days!

MRS. BARKER. What dreadful sauterne!

MOMMY. Yes, isn't it?

(*To Young Man, her voice already a little fuzzy from the wine*)

You don't know how happy I am to see you! Yes sirree. Listen, that time we had with . . . with the other one. I'll tell you about it some time.

(*Indicates Mrs. Barker*)

After she's gone. She was responsible for all the trouble in the first place. I'll tell you all about it.

(*Sidles up to him a little*)

Maybe . . . maybe later tonight.

YOUNG MAN (*Not moving away*). Why yes. That would be very nice.

MOMMY (*Puzzles*). Something familiar about you . . . you know that? I can't quite place it.

GRANDMA (*Interrupting . . . to audience*). Well, I guess that just about wraps it up. I mean, for better or worse, this is a comedy, and I don't think we'd better go any further. No, definitely not. So, let's leave things as they are right now . . . while everybody's happy . . . while everybody's got what he wants . . . or everybody's got what he thinks he wants. Good night, dears.

Curtain

COMMENTARY

Note: The following essay represents a single interpretation of the play. For other perspectives on The American Dream, *consult the essays listed below.*

Because the centerpiece of this play is a lengthy story (an Albee trademark) about the adoption of "a little bumble of joy" by overbearing parents, it is tempting to regard *The American Dream* as an autobiographical piece in which the playwright exorcises the demons of his troubled youth. While this reading has some validity, the play transcends the particulars of Albee's life and remains among the most disturbing depictions of American culture in the postwar era. Furthermore, it provides insights into Albee's more mature, full-length works, such as *Who's Afraid of Virginia Woolf?* and *A Delicate Balance*. It may be argued that this one-act was a "first draft" of *Virginia Woolf*, just as *The Sandbox* was a precursor to *The American Dream*.

Typical of the early absurdist plays, the characters in Albee's bitter comedy are ciphers, nonentities unto themselves, but provocative symbols of the world at large. Only Mrs. Barker is given an actual name, yet in the context of this play it seems thoroughly generic. The bland box set described in the opening stage direction is peopled by the prototypical antiheroes of Albee's urban, WASPish wasteland. Daddy is the archetypal Albee male: emasculated, ineffectual, unable to commit himself to anything. Mommy is predictably domineering, stifling, sexually repressed. These are the parents of the American household at mid-century. In *Who's Afraid of Virginia Woolf?* the playwright fleshes them out with greater psychological complexity and, ominously, names them "George" and "Martha," a macabre joke about the "first parents" of America. Only Grandma is presented sympathetically, yet she is just another discard in our disposable society. Like an animal, she is allowed to live only in a box behind the stove (which may be a progress of sorts: in *The Sandbox* she is left to die in a child's sandbox). Here Albee seems less interested in exposing the plight of the elderly than in examining America's preoccupation with "the cult of youth." Even as Albee wrote the play in 1960, America was electing its youngest President (Kennedy) and the Baby Boomer generation was entering teenhood.

Enter the Young Man, a virile, narcissistic youth who, we are told, is "the American Dream." Who is he, this identical twin of a child earlier adopted (and subsequently destroyed) by Mommy and Daddy? Is he the "American Dream"—i.e., the handsome, charming youth who seems immortal? Is he "the Angel of Death"—as Albee called virtually the same character in *The Sandbox*? (Albee returned to the Angel of Death in his 1979 play, *The Lady from Dubuque*.) Albee challenges the audience to ascertain the symbolic value of this enigmatic character. Whatever he represents, the Young Man's most compelling line captures the ultimate dilemma in Albee's world. He tells Grandma, with whom he has a sympathetic covenant, that "I have been unable to love." The Young Man, it needs saying, is one of the first sympathetic portraits of a homosexual in the American theater as he recounts his plight as a male prostitute. Here Albee opened vistas for a subsequent generation of playwrights, including Harvey Fierstein and Tony Kushner.

Despite its grim view of contemporary life, the play is a comedy in its satirical portrait of the manners of a bourgeois family. In this sense it is kin to the works of late-seventeenth- and eighteenth-century comedies from France (Molière's *Tartuffe*) and England (Sheridan's *The School for Scandal*). Significantly, Albee ends his play with the staple of comedies since Aristophanes: the *komos*, or "joyful ending," in which opposing parties unite to celebrate a new order. Albee's absurdly dysfunctional family, joined by Mrs. Barker and the mysterious Young Man, gather together "while everybody's happy" to drink "dreadful sauterne" in what appears to be a harmonious conclusion. Grandma breaks the illusion of the fourth wall to tell the audience that it is time to end the comedy "while everybody's got what he wants . . . or what he thinks he wants." And getting what one "wants" is, of course, the American Dream. For Albee, the American Dream seems to be as hollow and artificial as the contrived and sentimental ending of his play.

Other perspectives on *The American Dream*:

Miller, Jordan Y. "Myth and the American Dream: O'Neill to Albee." *Modern Drama* (1964): 190–98.

Way, Brian. "Albee and the Absurd: *The American Dream* and *The Zoo Story*." In Harold Bloom (ed.), *Edward Albee: Modern Critical Views*. New York: Cheslea House Publishers, 1987, 9–37.

Another play by Albee on video/film:

Who's Afraid of Virginia Woolf? Dir. Mike Nichols. Perf. Richard Burton, Elizabeth Taylor, George Segal, and Sandy Dennis. Warner Home Video, 131 min., 1966.

Videos about Albee:

Edward Albee. Films for the Humanities, 52 min., 1995.

PART III

Contemporary and Postmodern Drama:

1964–The Present

Robert Wilson's postmodern staging of Ibsen's realistic drama,
When We Dead Awaken, *was created at the Alley Theater in
Houston, Texas. Note the strong use of visual and poetic images, a
stark contrast to the realistic setting used for the original production
of* A Doll's House *(see Part I).*

PART III: CONTEMPORARY AND POSTMODERN DRAMA: 1964—THE PRESENT

A New Theater for a New World

As we enter the new millennium, the world itself has provided extraordinary scenarios that reflect a new reality.

- Late at night in a provincial Chinese village, where running water and indoor toilets are rare, flickering lights emanate from virtually every small house and store. The lights are produced by 13-inch color television sets that show John Forsythe apparently speaking fluent Mandarin on *Falcon Crest*.
- Baseball, that most American of sports, now regularly features players from Japan, South Korea, Australia, the Caribbean, and Latin America. Between innings fans—many of whom were born in Asia, Africa, and Latin America—rise to dance the "Macarena" from South America while their pictures are projected onto a giant television screen made in Japan. Many listen to the game they are watching on transistor radios manufactured under the new capitalism of Communist China. American fans now clap Korean "thunder sticks" together to show their support for their team, much as earlier generations used pennants and cowbells to root for the home team.
- In June 2002 the Queen of England, Elizabeth II, celebrated the fiftieth anniversary of her coronation with a parade through the streets of London, where over a million people of all nationalities and ethnic backgrounds gathered. The parade included marching bands, dancers, and circus acts from Asia, Africa, Latin America, and the Caribbean. In addition to an evening of classical music to mark the event, she was feted at a pop music concert that featured such diverse artists as Paul McCartney, the Beach Boys, Ozzie Osborne, and Queen. The events were shared with a worldwide audience via satellite television; the telecast was underwritten, in part, by commercials for products made in nations that once were part of the British Empire, many of which are now more financially sound than England itself.

Our rapidly changing world is becoming—in Marshall McLuhan's words—"a global village," and the tension between beliefs in an older, more absolute order and one that is more pluralistic, democratic, and ambiguous can be found in the theater as well as politics, commerce, and education. Contemporary thought has been shaped by any number of thinkers and historical events, which have prompted us to reevaluate the way we perceive the world. Global capitalism and religious fundamentalism represent just two extremes vying for dominance in today's complex political, economic, and cultural struggles.

Influences on Contemporary Thought

Ironically, we can actually find the roots of the changes in contemporary thought in the challenges to the Enlightenment and its emphasis on rationality and absolute values. In the eighteenth century the universe was viewed as a great, ordered machine bound by well-defined, fixed laws. In Sir Isaac Newton's world an apple fell because it obeyed the law of gravity; but we now know that an apple can actually float upward because there is no gravity twelve miles above the earth. Thinkers such as the Scottish empiricist David Hume (1711–76) showed the limits of reason—and the absolutism it encouraged in much Western thought—by challenging the inviolability of the principle of cause and effect. In the theater, causality was the foundation for Scribe's well-made play and the Naturalists' belief that social problems were caused by one's heredity and environment.

Even as Ibsen was writing his social dramas questioning the old absolute order, Freidrich Nietzsche (1844–1900) argued that an absolute "truth" does not exist, that a search for the truth is an "artificial burden," and ultimately that societies change their belief systems (or "perspectives") over time without arriving at an absolute view of the world. Fittingly, Nietzsche—who has been called the first philosopher with a truly postmodern view—developed his theories while trying to discover the original text of a tragedy by Sophocles; he found only various conflicting copies of the original which had been filtered through the perspectives of subsequent cultures. He argued that a fixed interpretation of a literary work does not and cannot exist and that one person's subjective response is as "truthful" as any other is.

World events have been as forceful in altering our beliefs as any philosophical writing. In the past century two world wars, the Holocaust, a global depression, the threat of nuclear annihilation, the decline of the so-called superpowers, and terrorist acts leading to the mass destruction of life and property have taught us, often through painful experience, that the old absolutes are no longer necessarily operable. Thinkers and artists have challenged other apparent certainties about language, social organisms, gender, and race. Such challenges have also been made *in* theaters—and *about* the very way theater is written and performed. And as we saw during our survey of modern drama (i.e., that of Ibsen and his successors), philosophers, social scientists, and critics created an intellectual atmosphere that inspired yet another revolution in the arts.

In Austria, Ludwig Wittgenstein (1889–1951) argued that the West was in decline largely because our instrument of communication (i.e., language) was faulty and imprecise. Or as the Player in Tom Stoppard's *Rosencrantz and Guildenstern Are Dead* notes wryly: our language "makes up in obscurity what it lacks in style." (And that from men—both Stoppard and the Player—who make their living using words!) In particular, philosophy was suspect because it relied on such ambiguous terms as "good" and "moral," words whose meanings were relative to particular cultures and times. Therefore, the limits and liabilities of language necessarily redefined human perceptions of the world. Each person was, in essence, free to define "reality" according to her or his perceptions of the truth behind the language. Perception became reality, a concept that is summarized by the title of Luigi Pirandello's play *It Is So! If You Think So* (1917). Playwrights, notably Harold Pinter and Sam Shepard, applied these principles to dramaturgy. Classical texts have been given new, ironic readings by actors and directors versed in new language theories represented by the French critic-philosopher, Jacques Derrida, who argues that "there is nothing outside the text." This proposition encourages the reader/interpreter/viewer to participate actively in creating whatever meaning or message one finds in the text, whatever the author's intentions. Other stage artists, such as Robert Wilson and Heiner Müller, discussed elsewhere in this section, have virtually abandoned language as an integral part of the theater experience and use an almost exclusively visual vocabulary.

Not only has language been reassessed in contemporary thought but so have human institutions. In 1966 Peter Berger and Thomas Luckmann wrote *The Social Construction of Reality* in which they argued that society, culture, and even the roles we play in our daily lives are created by humans. We routinely forget that we have created these things and live in a world we have forgotten we made. We err by assuming that our social organizations, our culture and its myths, and especially the societal roles we play cannot be recreated. Not only was it possible to recreate social institutions but individuals were challenged to recreate themselves. The feminist and civil rights movements sought to redefine the roles imposed upon women and minorities by traditional social systems.

In 1949 Simone de Beauvoir (1908–86) wrote *The Second Sex* to argue that women were treated as "the Other," an anthropological term used to describe those who are different from—or who are not included in—a majority culture. She claimed that men often accord women a different and inferior existence than themselves, and she advised women to seek independence from the old patriarchy by creating their own identity. Betty Friedan (1921–) initiated the modern American feminist movement with the publication of *The Feminine Mystique* (1963), which articulated the politics of gender.

Coincidentally, 1963 was the year in which the African-American civil rights movement experienced a triumphant moment as Martin Luther King, Jr., led hundreds of thousands of activists into Washington, D.C., where he delivered his famous "I Have a Dream" speech. Perhaps the most famous example of how language, social structures, and individual worth were redefined is the "Black Is Beautiful" slogan created by the civil rights movement. Though they do not eradicate racism, such reconfigurations of language encouraged people of all colors to think—and perhaps act—more positively about people of

African descent. Social change precipitated by the feminist and the civil rights movements gave new voices and power to other previously marginalized groups of Western society: Latinos, Asians, indigenous peoples, lesbians and gay men.

Note that several of the books cited here, as well as many of the major events of the civil and women's rights movements, gained popularity in the mid-1960s. Probably no decade in the twentieth century conjures such specific images as does the Sixties, with the antiwar movement, civil demonstrations (both peaceful and violent), hippies, love-ins—in short, the so-called Countercultural Revolution. The British rock group, the Beatles, became the emblem of this radical change in many facets of society: fashion, musical tastes, irreverence for the old order, experimentation with mind-altering substances, and the exploration of other cultures and religions. The Beatles introduced Eastern philosophy, religion, and music to Western youth, and it is perhaps no accident that the mainstream theater itself became more involved with and influenced by the artistry of non-Western cultures, especially those from Asia and Africa, during the mid-1960s. To be sure, Brecht had evidenced an influence of Chinese theater in their works in the 1930s, but never to the degree that was seen in post-1960s theater.

Correspondingly, the theater has become a major outlet through which the new pluralism expresses itself. In this section you will find a variety of recent dramas that reflect the diversity of the voices and ideologies of the pluralistic culture in which we now live.

Postmodernism and the Theater

Though we think of this as the "contemporary era," it is often referred to as *postmodern* (i.e., "after the modern"), an often controversial term which describes a less Euro-centered culture than that which dominated the world for the past 400 years. Contemporary culture is decidedly more pluralistic and multicultural than at any time in human history.

In keeping with this shift in thought, there has emerged a postmodern style in the arts that is characterized by irony, that is, a detached view that sees the world from perspectives heretofore unexplored. Whether Postmodernism will survive and become a long-lived artistic movement or whether it is merely a transitional period (such as those that typically appear at the turn of a century) remains to be seen.

Though the concept of "Postmodernism" was first defined in the 1930s (by Federico de Onis in his 1934 study of Spanish-language poetry, then in 1938 in Arnold Toynbee's *A Study of History*), Postmodernism as a *bona fide* movement in the arts evolved from architects who rebelled against the stark, sterile, purely functional, and thereby "inhuman" designs of the so-called Modernists. The new school of architects, exemplified by Robert Venturi (1925–), who favored "messy vitality over obvious unity," playfully fused elements taken from contemporary "pop" (or "democratic" as opposed to the old "aristocratic") culture with traditional styles. In a spirit of global unity encouraged by the founding of the United Nations in 1948, architects looked to the Third World for inspiration. For example, they fronted a neoclassic building with the silhouette of an African hut. These deliberate contraries of style are hallmarks of Postmodernism, and words such as *pastiche*, *collage*, and *eclecticism* are central to its vocabulary and its practice. (Architects, by the way, write the term as "Post-Modern," with the hyphen. "Postmodern" is usually applied to literature and the other arts. This quibble suggests that the term is still being defined and that there is appreciable disagreement among Postmodernism's practitioners as well as its critics.) The commercial theater's populist equivalent of eclectic postmodern architecture may well be *The Lion King*. The simple, cartoon-based story—an amalgam of archetypes from many cultures—is set in Africa and uses traditional music and dance from that continent. Portions of the score were written by British pop artist Elton John, American director Julie Taymor used staging techniques she learned in Indonesia, and the cast is comprised of artists from several nations.

Contraries in artworks can create a playful irony that encourages people to look at the world from new perspectives. The imaginative blend of materials drawn from cultures beyond Europe and America is integral to Postmodernists who, like the early Modernists, seek a more equitable world. Richard Rorty, an American philosopher (e.g., *Contingency, Irony, Solidarity*, 1989), envisions a truly democratic world committed to universal freedom, creativity, and the elimination of cruelty. This new utopia is achieved by "poeticizing" human experience rather than "rationalizing" it. By recasting traditional forms through the inclusion of material drawn from a truly pluralistic society, new-wave creator-artists shatter what they perceive as an oppressive power aligned with the older Eurocentric order. The Canadian Jean-Francois Lyotard, whose study *The Post-Modern Condition: A Report on Knowledge* (1979) laid the foundation for much of the critical thinking of the phenomenon, describes what he considers the appeal of Postmodernism: "One listens to reggae [music], watches a Western, eats McDonald's food for lunch and local cuisine for dinner, wears Paris perfume in Tokyo and 'retro' clothes in Hong Kong." Similarly, Peter Sellars, the theater and opera director whose work is unmistakably postmodern, told the *New York Times* in 1984:

> We're living in a culture that is incredibly multifaceted. I grew up with [*avant-garde* composer] John Cage and [modern dancer] Merce Cunningham as old masters. But while they were giving birth to something, [painter] Norman Rockwell was also in his prime. With the push of a button we can choose some 18th-century Chinese lute music, the Mahler 6th [symphony], or [the artist formerly known as] Prince.

In *Post-Modernism in the Social Sciences* Pauline Marie Rosenau identifies two approaches to Postmodernism. First, there is Skeptical Postmodernism, inspired by Nietzsche and akin to the Absurdist movement, which is pessimistic and steeped in malaise. In general, these skeptics are Europeans, scarred by the memories of World War II and Communism. There is also Affirmative Postmodernism, more indigenous to the Anglo–North American culture, which seeks a harmonious world in which traditional distinctions between genders, races, nations, and cultural biases are analyzed as relative constructs. Rorty typifies the latter strain in his belief that freedom means the individual can live and create without being obsessed by universal truths and rules that all rational beings must follow.

In addition to Lyotard's "healthy pluralism," there is also a spiritualism underlying some postmodern thinking, though it is not necessarily rooted in traditional Judeo-Christian religions. Whereas Modernists looked to science and technology as means to eradicate social ills, many Postmodernists distrust unbridled technology, which, they argue, gave the world the atomic age and its threat of instant annihilation, pollution, and a greater disparity between the "haves" and the "have nots." In its place they have turned to ancient religions (such as Taoism), the occult, and mysticism to fill the void left by the "religion of science." Though it borrows freely from ancient religions, rituals, and musical practices, "New Age" is the term most associated with the new spiritualism. Nonetheless, it suggests a deeply rooted quest for something that transcends the particulars of sociology, psychology, politics, and contemporary mass-produced culture. The theories of the French anthropologist Claude Levi-Strauss (1908–99) helped define this worldview, which maintains that innate—archetypal—mental patterns of all humans, irrespective of historical period or social setting, cause humans to interact with nature and one another in recurring ways. In particular, Levi-Strauss examined ritual activities around the world, and his findings have influenced Western theater practice, which in many instances has returned to a ritualistic (as opposed to realistic) depiction of human activity. Most theater in Asia, Africa, and much of Latin America never completely abandoned its ritual heritage.

Postmodernism in the theater and other arts has at times been criticized, partly because it energetically and often irreverently challenges old systems, partly because it is perceived to be a license for indulgence among artists who—some would say—can now do anything they want and call it art. Walter D. Bannard, writing for *Arts Magazine* in 1983, dismissed Postmodernism as "aimless, anarchic, amorphous, self-indulgent, inclusive, horizontally structured, and aim[ing] for the popular." It can be, and it has done so. Yet Postmodernism, a constellation of many legitimate styles, seems to be the prevailing style of our age. To put Bannard's critique in perspective (or to "relativize" it), his comments might well have been penned by a member of the French Academy in 1830 as a response to Hugo's *Hernani*.

Artaud and the Theatre of Cruelty

Such attitudes concerning cultural diversity have affected the theater and drama. The recreation of ritual has been espoused as a primary component of the contemporary theater experience. Antonin Artaud (1895–1948) foreshadowed the new theater practice with his bold visions and experiments in Paris. Theater historian Margaret Croyden has written that "more than any other theorist of his generation, Artaud set the tone for the theater of the 1960s" and the first generation of postmodern theater artists. It must be said that Artaud's theater is emotionally charged, and Postmodernism employs, by and large, a much "cooler" style in its ironic assessment of the world's events. Still Artaud, like Brecht (see Part II), was in the vanguard of what we now recognize as the postmodern style.

In 1933 Artaud, an actor frustrated by the limitations of the realistic theater, and its emphasis on a rational depiction of life, saw a Balinese theater company performing a centuries-old trance dance at an international exhibition in Paris. This Barong dance portrayed a universal battle between good and evil.

> Rangda is an evil witch that opposes the Barong, a life-giving lion who defends the Balinese against her destructive powers. Balinese farmers carry short swords (*kris*) to expel Rangda's evil powers, while an entire village gathers under an enormous banyan tree in front of the temple honoring Banaspati Radja, king of the benevolent spirits. The drama is underscored by the hypnotic beat of drums and bamboo xylophones played by the *gamelan*, the sacred musicians. The climax is riveting: Rangda casts a spell on the attacking dancers whose swords are turned violently toward their chests. However, those who believe in the goodness of the Barong are not harmed, and the sharp swords bend grotesquely against the men's breastbones. The dancers fall into a deep trance and eventually awaken, exhausted from their encounter with the Evil One. The village celebrates its liberation from evil as girls, each named after a flower, dance the *sang hyang* to celebrate life. An old priest pours a libation on the ground to purify it, while smoke from a sacred brazier is wafted into the faces of the congregation as they return to their homes, purified by their experience at the *Barong* (or "trance") dance.

Based on this experience, Artaud envisioned a Theatre of Cruelty that would, in his words,

> . . . link the theater to the expressive possibilities of forms, to everything in the domain of gestures, noises, colors, movements [in order] to restore it to its original direction, to reinstate it in its religious and metaphysical aspect, to reconcile it with the universe.

By "cruelty" Artaud meant that artists should force audiences to confront their basest instincts and crimes, which, he believed, promoted the horrors of modern civilization. The theater, he argued, must compel humans to unmask themselves through "cries, groans, apparitions, surprises, theatricalities of all kinds, resplendent lighting, sudden changes of lights, masks, and effigies." Artaud's theater assaulted the senses of its audience to break down their defenses and force them to confront the "plague," his metaphor for modern atrocities. Whereas the Romantics sought an intensely emotional reaction to societal ills, and Brecht encouraged his spectators to view a play with an intellectual detachment, Artaud craved a thoroughly visceral response that transcends sentiment and rationality.

Though Artaud's own theater work failed to achieve his ends, he has had a pronounced influence on production style, playwrights, and theater companies. In its early

Peter Weiss's *Marat/Sade*

"Shocked," "Stunned," "Exhilarated," "Thrilled," "Provoked," and "Spellbound"! So exclaimed the London theater critics about the opening of *The Persecution and Assassination of Jean Paul Marat as Performed by the Inmates of the Asylum of Charenton under the Direction of the Marquis de Sade* (*Marat/Sade*). The play, by Peter Weiss, then a little-known German playwright living in Sweden, was directed by Peter Brook for the Royal Shakespeare Company (RSC) in 1964. Culminating a year of what was described as "experiments in the Theatre of Cruelty," Brook's production has been widely acknowledged as among the seminal pieces of theater of the twentieth century. The innovative Brook (and his codirector, Charles Marowitz) was weary of "the deadly theatre," his term for London's commercial West End. Stimulated by the theories of Antonin Artaud and Bertolt Brecht, and working with collages of sight, movement and sound, fragmented montages, visual and aural images, happenings, and other nontraditional forms, the RSC spent months investigating, improvising, and experimenting with style, text, and spectacle. But it was not until they began work with *Marat/Sade* that they discovered the ideal vehicle for their vision. In Weiss's script they found the nearly perfect fusion of the rough intellect of Brecht and the cruel sensibility of Artaud. Here was a text that included song and language, music and movement, Naturalism and Surrealism, with hints of Pirandello and ritual. At last, here was a "total play" that permitted the RSC to explore "total theater." According to Brook, in an interview with *Plays and Players*, his intention was to fuse the Brechtian overtones with the Artaudian cruelty: "With Artaud it's a complete involvement of the spectator by performances of such intensity that all his intellectual barriers are smashed," claimed Brook, who continued: "In Brecht, it's the *exact* opposite . . . pour-ing cold water all the time on emotional involvement so that the audience's critical faculties can come into play." All this culminated in the fusion of the cerebral Brecht with the sensory Artaud.

As its title indicates, the play presents de Sade's play as a play-within-the-play that is enacted in a lunatic asylum. The French Revolution, Charlotte Corday's murder of Marat, the political dialectic, and the debate between Marat and de Sade provide intriguing material for the inmates, whose varied mental illnesses parallel the historical characters they are portraying. Brook presented Coulmier (the Director of the asylum), his wife, and his daughter watching the spectacle while we, in turn, simultaneously watch them watch the spectacle. The theatrical device of the insane asylum not only offered a provocative metaphor for our social and political world but also provided Brook and his company a rare opportunity to exercise their imaginations freely while remaining within a prescribed text. After all, anything and everything can be justified and believable in a "madhouse." According to critic Margaret Croyden, whose book *Lunatics, Lover and Poets: The Contemporary Experimental Theater* (1974) is among the best studies of the *avant-garde* theater:

> . . . [Weiss's] montages could move instantaneously and jaggedly, not as super-imposed theatrical devices, but because the inmates' inner rhythms dictated it. Odd voices, exaggerated sounds, unconventional speech patterns, or peculiar movements could be justified; the inner and outer mind of the inmate could be separated, merged, pushed to its extreme. In fact, various acting techniques that often have been compared to certain symptoms of madness,

could be tested to the limits in Brook's production. Naturalism was appropriately used to depict the specific physical characteristics of various forms of madness; surrealism, for the Herald and the Quartet of clowns and Marat's dream sequence; expressionistic German cabaret for the songs and music; ritual for the trials and killings; the Brechtian "alienation" for the dialectic between Sade and Marat. Further, Brook's and Weiss's overall conception served as an ironic Artaudian metaphor. Artaud claimed that theatre as therapy could "cure" audiences by "cruelty" techniques.

The production was an explosion of sights and sounds—some hilarious, some poignant, some disgusting, some electrifying—but all gripping and riveting. Confronting the audience was RSC designer Sally Jacobs's drab and dreary asylum bathhouse, which proved to be appropriately functional and repulsive. In a filthy old bathtub on one side of the stage, draped in soggy bandages, forever scratching, writing, talking, and waiting, sat the naked, psoriasis-ridden Marat. Perched opposite him in a Louis XIV chair sat the aloof, weary, and infinitely sad Marquis de Sade. In a box to the side of the stage sat Coulmier and his family, while on the other side sat the psychotic musicians who played Richard Peaslee's bitter music (patterned after that of Brecht and Kurt Weill) to accompany the action.

As they entered the theater the audience was presented with a vast array of misshapen, bulging-eyed, disjointed "lunatics." Among the filthy and lice-ridden were the giggling, drooling, scab-picking spastic; the thumb-sucker; the baby-rocker; the nymphomaniac; the paranoid; the schizophrenic; the catatonic; and the manic-depressive. Surrounding and moving carefully among the inmates were gray-garbed guards, nuns in black habits, and overpoweringly sinister-looking men in coarse butcher aprons. To all of this was added a bizarre, surrealist quartet of zany lunatics in *commedia*-like costumes—the clown-faced singers whose not-so-zany songs were mimed by the other inmates. The quartet became a cynical chorus that steered the audience through Weiss's labyrinth-like text.

Slowly the ensemble drifted onstage and, with the Herald's traditional thumping of his staff to signal the beginning of the performance, the play began. Simultaneously portraying their own illnesses as well as those of the characters they played, the lunatics, stammering, stumbling, and here and there forgetting their lines, enacted the assassination of Marat under the ever-watchful eye of de Sade. Intertwining the past, present and future, the play-within-the-play moved backward and forward in time as images and events were ritualistically repeated. With the exception of Marat and de Sade, the lunatics integrated their individual madnesses with their roles. As actors, they portrayed the proletariat and aristoc-

racy in an ever-expanding class struggle. They played Marat's parents, as well as French citizens, judges, witnesses, and executioners of mass trials during the "reign of terror." As the play progressed, the "actors" grew more and more aggressive and had to be controlled by male nurses.

As the performance continued, the inmates' belief in their own acting became so adamant that they could no longer distinguish illusion from reality. Having furiously called for "liberty, equality, and fraternity," the lunatics, in a savagely vicious revolt, took over the asylum. They toppled the stage furniture and decorations and stormed their oppressors, even while attempting to rape the nuns and kill the guards. But at Coulmier's command, the guards fought back and a violent battle ensued—a revolution grew out of a revolution. All appeared to have lost control as the inmates marched menacingly downstage toward the increasingly uncertain and fearful London audiences. Then a whistle was heard; the ensemble halted; the stage manager appeared and took control of the production and saved the audience. Relieved that it was really only the end of the play, the audience broke

into applause. But then the "actors," stimulated by the applause, began to parody the response and the rhythmic, ironic clapping crescendoed as the "actors," poised for immediate attack, stood at the edge of the stage, smirking sardonically, even viciously. Finally, as the "actors" continued their thunderous applause, a few of the spectators began to leave while others sat and seemingly contemplated the identity of and the distinction between the sane and the insane and the meaning of revolution. All the while, de Sade looked on triumphantly.

Most who saw that production left the Aldwych Theatre shaken (the Artaudian response) yet pensive (the Brechtian ideal). They had witnessed the immense power of the Theatre of Cruelty to strip an audience of its emotional defenses, even as it forced them to ponder the atrocities that humans can render to one another.

See *Marat/Sade* on video:

Marat/Sade. Dir. Peter Brook. Perf. the Royal Shakespeare Company. I. S. Productions, 115 min., 1989.

years, for instance, the Royal Shakespeare Company devoted its 1962–63 season to an exploration of Artaud's theories on both classical and modern texts. Peter Brook directed the "cruelty season," staging *King Lear* and Peter Weiss's *The Persecution and Assassination of Jean-Paul Marat as Performed by the Inmates of the Asylum of Charenton under the Direction of the Marquis de Sade* (or *Marat/Sade*; see Showcase). Even Broadway and London musicals, such as *Hair* (1967) and *Jesus Christ Superstar* (1970), employed techniques espoused by Artaud. Curiously, among the most successful derivatives of Artaud's theories, whether by design or accident, have been modern rock concerts and MTV videos. Pulsing lights, heavily amplified music, scenic effects such as towers of flame, stage actions such as smashing cars and guitars, and—in the case of videos—rapid cutting and overlapping of highly sensory images all are techniques espoused by Artaud, though they lack the spiritual foundation of his visionary theater.

In addition to Artaud's encounter with the Balinese dancers, other postmodern theater artists have looked to the East in their attempts to return the theater to its spiritual roots. Arianne Mnouchkine's Theatre du Soliel regularly employs Asian dance and gesture in her refashioning of classical Western myths, as did Brook's eight-hour multinational production of India's sacred *Mahabharata* (1983). Stylized gesture and dance are central to many contemporary plays and productions of earlier works. The diminution of language, the new spirituality, and—just as significantly—music videos as typified by MTV have all conspired to return theater to many of its original performance modes. Ironically, through rituals, through dance and gesture, and especially through powerful and provocative images that transcend purely intellectual and emotional responses, the theater has to some degree come full circle by returning to its most elemental means of communication.

However well intended contemporary theater artists may be as they turn to other cultures for inspiration, such actions have occasioned some controversy, particularly concerning "appropriation." Those—particularly Europeans and Americans—who borrow, or "appropriate," material and performance modes from non-Western cultures are often considered by their critics to be engaging in a form of "cultural imperialism." Taymor's staging of *The Lion King* is perhaps the most prominent example of this practice in the contemporary theater and has been denounced by some critics because it has turned African rituals into a commercial enterprise. In reality, the practice is not a late-twentieth-century phenomenon. In the 1930s Orson Welles, among the most respected stage and film directors of the twentieth century, set *Macbeth* in Haiti and incorporated voodoo rites in his production, which was performed by an African-American cast. *The Voodoo Macbeth* (as it became known) was praised for its daring innovation, and there was virtually no criticism that Welles had "appropriated" material from a non-Western culture. That *The Lion King* received some criticism (although minimal) over 60 years later is but another indicator of how much the world has changed and how artists must be more sensitive to the values of previously marginalized and colonized cultures.

Theater Collectives and Alternative Theater

Inspired by the theories and practices of Brecht and Artaud (both of whom are legitimate precursors of the postmodern theater), the *theater collective* has become one of the most notable phenomena of theater since the 1960s. Collectives are companies that frequently live together and share a sociopolitical ideology; they experiment with theater forms and collectively create a play and its production. There is a degree to which the modern theater collective functions much like the "tribe" of older civilizations in that its members are bound spiritually (though not necessarily religiously) by common beliefs and goals that transcend commercialism and even art itself. Theodore Shank, who has studied collectives at length, offers a useful description of both the philosophy and the techniques of these experimental (or alternative) theater companies in *American Alternative Theater* (1982):

> The artists who comprise alternative theater explore the relationship of the artist and the performance to the spectator. They attempt to discover the possibilities of live theater, and they seek ways of extending the uses of theater beyond its entertainment and financial functions. . . . They set out to articulate what they know about being alive in changing times, about society, about perceiving, feeling, and knowing. Of necessity, they find new materials, develop new techniques, and create new forms to hold and express this knowledge because the theatrical conventions cannot express the concepts they consider important.

If this sounds familiar, it may be because Dumas *fils*, Ibsen, Strindberg, Shaw, Brecht, and so many of the other social revolutionaries in the theater have said much the same thing at various times.

The prototype of the modern theater collective in the West was the Group Theatre (discussed in Part II; see Showcase, "The Group Theatre and the Actors Studio"), which inspired subsequent generations of artists who also experimented with theater forms, especially those that are nonrealistic.

In the West, two companies merit particular attention because of their influence: the Living Theatre of Judith Malina (1926–) and Julian Beck (1925–94) and the Polish Laboratory Theatre of Jerzy Grotowski. The Living Theatre (see related Showcase) was founded in 1948, ostensibly to perform poetic dramas such as Federico García Lorca's *Blood Wedding*. After a period in the late 1950s when they experimented with improvisational realism (*The Connection*, 1959), the Living Theatre turned to the work for which it was best known: highly ritualized performance pieces critical of institutions that the com-

SHOWCASE | THE LIVING THEATRE AND OTHER THEATER COLLECTIVES

Impacted by thunderous national social and political changes, the American theater in the mid-twentieth century witnessed the emergence of a new theatrical language that altered an entire dramatic landscape that had been created by Realism, Naturalism, and especially Hollywood. By the 1950s, the American suburban family was suddenly confronted by left-wing political movements, the possibility of nuclear annihilation, rapid political shifts in underdeveloped nations, and the realization that the traditional North American and Euro-centric political, military, and economic influences were no longer central to a prosperous existence.

Nowhere was this sentiment more discernable than in the commercial theater, film, and television mass-produced for American popular culture. President Eisenhower's "vanilla America" quickly journeyed from Elvis Presley's rockabilly to the musical tremors of the Beatles, the Rolling Stones, acid rock, experimentation with mind-altering substances, the sexual revolution, flower children, and a subculture radically opposed to the core values of white, middle-class America. Out of these cultural changes evolved a handful of theater collectives eager to confront the status quo through imaginative approaches that altered the American theater. These so-called alternative performance groups expanded the perimeters established by the (mostly) anticommercial Off-Off Broadway theater movement to include a highly physical and experimental, non-text-based performance aesthetic. Significantly, these artists were committed to the elimination of an illusionary, realistic drama.

More importantly, these socially and politically minded performance collectives, such as the Living Theatre, the Open Theatre, the Performance and Garage Group, the San Francisco Mime Troupe, El Teatro Campesino (see Luis Valdez's *Zoot Suit*), and the Bread and Puppet Theatre, shared a similar vision: to obliterate the separa-

tion between audience and performer. These revolutionary artists envisioned theatrical experiences that would direct the spectator's consciousness away from an authoritarian political and economic system that, in their estimation, had been marginalized by "the establishment." Often influenced by the artistic shouts of the *avant-garde* and visions prescribed by poets, choreographers, composers, cultural anthropologists, behavioral psychologists, and the like, these performing guerrilla "tribes" expanded the possibilities of both physical and spoken language. Additionally, each collective attracted and nurtured audiences willing to take risks and experience new modes of theatrical performance.

Consider the work of several of the most representative of these collectives. Joseph Chaikin's Open Theatre (1963–73) provided a forum whereby the actor, through improvisation and rigorous physical training (often referred to as Transformational Acting), was capable of creating a metaphoric experience, visually and aurally, intended to make audiences aware of human violence, rampant materialism, and consumption. The Performance and Garage Group (1967–80), under the artistic direction of Richard Schechner, experimented with unconventional performance spaces and staging techniques unifying the audience and actor as a collective entity. With scenic designer Jerry Rojo, Schechner explored the theoretical principles of environmental theatre, which used "found" spaces such as a garage or storefront rather than conventional theaters. Such politically charged groups as the San Francisco Mime Troupe (1959–present; R. G. Davis, Artistic Director) and Luis Valdez's El Teatro Campesino (1965–present) promoted social activism through their critiques of economic oppression. Peter Schumann's Bread and Puppet Theatre (1961–74) advocated a humanity unified by a spiritualism that fostered the coexistence of all people. The Bread

and Puppet Theatre created large (some over 20 feet high) puppets, banners, and masks and used live music, singing, stylized movement, and dance to approximate the feel and look of a traveling circus eager to include spectators as active participants.

However, it is the work and theatrical aesthetic of the Living Theatre that inspired many of the theatrical innovations by these groups. Created in 1948 by Julian Beck and Judith Malina, the Living Theatre established a framework that radically expanded twentieth-century experimental performance theories. Highly influenced by the theories of Vsevold Meyerhold, Erwin Piscator, Bertolt Brecht, and Antonin Artaud, the nomadic Living Theatre Company abandoned the traditional theater in favor of an anarchistic, "in your face," physical performance style. From their beginnings in a New York City apartment, to their self-exiled wanderings throughout Europe in the 1960s, to their arrest and subsequent deportation from Brazil in 1971, the members of the Living Theatre steadfastly remained committed, as critic Theodore Shank states, to "eliminating the separation between art and life, between dramatic action and social action, between living and acting, between spectator and performer, and between revolution and theatre."

The ritualistic productions of the Living Theatre mirrored the American political upheavals of the 1960s and early 1970s. *The Brig* (1963), for example, coincided with an American nation torn apart by the assassination of its President, John F. Kennedy, while the company's mounting of *Frankenstein* (1965) took place at a time of U.S. military intervention in Vietnam. *Paradise Now* (1968), its most significant endeavor, was conceived during the year that witnessed the assassinations of Martin Luther King, Jr., and Senator Robert F. Kennedy. These momentous events fueled the Living Theatre's performance aesthetic, which consisted of:

- Extensive improvisation
- The complete avoidance of formal, linear plot structures
- The elimination of most scenic elements and costumes
- The inclusion of audiences as part of the performance activity
- The abandonment of conventional and realistic acting techniques
- An emphasis on thematic issues involving an anarchic distrust of government, capitalism, social class structure, and international boundaries

In keeping with the social vogue of the times, the Living Theatre's performance style encouraged the acceptance of uninhibited sexual freedom, public nudity, marijuana, and the collective sharing of human resources. Its actors used a ritualistic and confrontational vocal style, as well as a heightened physicality, to numb the senses while simultaneously awakening the audience to the realization that a nonviolent existence could occur only by stripping away social and economic masks imposed by a political system.

The Living Theatre's legacy inspired other American theater collectives to adopt unique performance methodologies tailored to meet their own aesthetic and political visions. Chaikin's Open Theatre formulated a nonverbal, stylized psychological approach to acting as exhibited in its 1967 production of *The Serpent*. Schechner's Performance and Garage Group altered the theatrical physical environment,

unifying audience and performers, as the Group produced, among others, such collective creations as *Dionysus in 69* (1968), *Commune* (1969), and an adaptation of Brecht's *Mother Courage and Her Children* (1974). Less concerned with performance-centered experimentation, the works of the San Francisco Mime Troupe, El Teatro Campesino, and the Bread and Puppet Theatre contained a more overt political ideology. Like the Living Theatre, these ensembles dedicated themselves to social and economic change by exposing racism, stereotypes, and economic and/or political oppression. Shying away from formal theatrical spaces, members of these collectives became guerrilla performers and occupied found environments such as streets, parks, fields, and the steps of courthouses and capitols. The San Francisco Mime Troupe's *commedia dell' arte* production of *L'Amant Militaire* (1967), El Teatro Campesino's *Los Vendidos* (*The Sellouts*, 1967), and the Bread and Puppet Theatre's *A Man Says Goodbye to His Mother* (1968) remain the most representative examples of plays developed during their many years of collective creativity.

Together, as they traveled the American heartland, on foot, in old buses, or in dilapidated trucks, these alternative collectives radically changed the American theater. The cries of a newly emerging culture on the road to uncertainty reached Broadway even as Camelot was shattered on the streets of Dallas. While many collectives have disbanded, several of these groups—in-

cluding their successors, the San Francisco Mime Troupe, Mabou Mines, and the Wooster Group—continue to perform into the new millennium.

Videos about theater collectives:

The Bread and Puppet Theatre

Brother Bread, Sister Puppet. Dir. Jeff Farber. Cinema Guild, 59 min., 1995.

The Living Theatre

The Connection. Dir. Shirley Clark. Mystic Fire Video, 105 min., 1961.

Paradise Now. Dir. Sheldon Rochlin. Mystic Fire Video, 95 min., 1970.

Signals through the Flames. Dir. Sheldon Rochlin. Mystic Fire Video, 97 min., 1983.

The Open Theatre

Joseph Chaikin and the Open Theatre. (Contains *Nightwalk*, with Sam Shepard.) Insight Media, 55 min., 1977.

The Open Theatre: Fable. Insight Media, 28 min., 1975.

The Open Theatre: Terminal. Dir. Joseph Chaikin and Roberta Sklar. Insight Media, 27 min., 1971.

The Serpent. Dir. Joseph Chaikin. Insight Media, 80 min., 1969.

El Teatro Campesino: See Luis Valdez and *Zoot Suit* (later in Part III)

pany considered "antihuman." Most of the alternative companies emphasized physicality, rhythm, and chanting (among other things) instead of characterization and literary scripts. They perhaps came closest to realizing Artaud's vision for a modern theater steeped in ritual and archetypal images to exorcise modern demons.

In Poland, Jerzy Grotowski (1933–) founded the Polish Laboratory Theatre in Wroclaw in 1965. His company experimented with performance styles while addressing totalitarianism and the many social issues that have plagued Poland for hundreds of years. Out of this work came Grotowski's vision of a "Poor Theatre," perhaps the most influential concept for the many socially conscious theater collectives in the 1960s and 1970s. In essence Grotowski wanted to return the theater to its spiritual roots by creating a ceremonial experience in which spectators and performers together could achieve a "collective introspection" of the social and philosophical problems confronting society. To achieve these ends, Grotowski and his colleagues reduced the theater experience to its most essential elements—actors in a space before an audience. The motto "*Via negativa*" ("to refrain from doing") dictated the Poor Theatre's production choices. Grotowski and his disciples avoided all elaborate lighting effects and performed in intimate spaces that were created for each play. The audience members were invariably interspersed in the acting area to reinforce their roles as "privileged participants in a ritual." There was no scenery as such, and all props were multifunctional and made of "found" objects. Actors wore no makeup but learned to transform their faces into masks through arduous physical training. Productions such as *Akropolis* (about Nazi concentration camps) and an adaptation of Calderon's *The Constant Prince* became renowned for their ritualistic simplicity and the physical discipline of Grotowski's superbly trained actors. For Grotowski, actors were the equivalent of modern shamans who took on the suffering of the community; hence, they were trained as artist-priests who practiced self-denial and physical hardship for the good of the community.

Much of the most compelling experimental theater was produced in Third World countries where the lack of economic resources necessarily promoted creative, as opposed to monetary, solutions to problems. In South Africa, Mbogeni Ngema founded Committed Artists in 1984 to develop scripts about the problems of apartheid and township life. Township theater (see Showcase, "South African Township Theater," later in Part III) has by its very nature used many of the ideas espoused by Grotowski; "found" objects such as old tires, corrugated tin panels, and packing crates customarily form the scenic backdrop for the plays. *Woza Albert!* is typical of the work produced by Committed Artists, as was the 1993 film featuring Whoopi Goldberg, *Sarafina!*, based on an Ngema musical.

In Latin America, Augusto Boal's Teatro de Arena (Brazil) has produced socially relevant works that could, due to their ingenuity and simplicity, be taken into remote villages to educate people, much like Sergio Corrieri's Groupo Teatro Escambray in Cuba. Like Brecht, Boal rejects the Aristotelian theater because he perceives it as coercive in its punishment of wrongdoers, whom he regards as oppressed. Boal actually takes Brecht a step further by actively engaging members of his audiences and prompting them to discover how they might rectify social problems. In the United States a similar phenomenon occurred with the founding of El Teatro Campesino by Luis Valdez in 1965. Valdez's accomplishments are discussed later in Part III with *Zoot Suit*, a play that vividly illustrates the incorporation of ancient religions and rituals (in this case, those of the Aztecs) with contemporary social issues.

In the final quarter of the twentieth century there was a proliferation of theaters that targeted specific audiences who have traditionally been separated from the mainstream. An admittedly random sampling of such enterprises will give you some sense of the scope of the theater's newest constituencies: The Women's Playwright Project and Women's Interart, among others, have provided a theatrical platform for feminist issues. In 1974 a women's theater collective called At the Foot of the Mountain was formed in Minneapolis, Minnesota, to create new, ritual-based works drawn from the personal experiences (e.g., abuse) of the members and the issues that confronted them (e.g., the challenges of motherhood). Audience members were invited to assist in the creation of a piece, which, naturally, changed from one performance to another. Gay men and lesbian issues are argued by such companies as Rhinoceros, the Cockettes, and Split Britches. The AIDS crisis has quite understandably been a central concern of many theater companies, both gay and straight. Such companies as The National Theatre of the Deaf (NTD), which employs both hearing and hearing-impaired actors, depict the needs of the physically disadvantaged. The NTD also creates extraordinary productions of classical and poetic texts such as Ben Jonson's *Volpone* and Dylan Thomas's *Under Milkwood*; some members speak the lines while others "sign" them with a physicality that is as poetic as the spoken word.

Contemporary Playwriting

All of this discussion of visionary directors (now sometimes referred to as *auteurs* because their roles are more creative than interpretative) and theater collectives suggests a diminution of the role of the playwright. Playwrights are still very much the cornerstone of the theater process, though the lure of the television and film industries (and their lucrative contracts) has created something of a crisis. Nonetheless, plays are still being commissioned, written, and produced although their forms have diversified considerably since Scribe's well-made play and Ibsen's discussion drama. Because of the reassessment of purely rational communication (i.e., language and the well-structured plot), "ambiguity"—some even say "incomprehensibility"—is a term sometimes applied to much contemporary theater. Plot, character, and meaning cannot be readily fathomed because we lack a single, consistent perspective from which to view them. Contemporary artists, both playwrights and collectives, develop new "myths" or "metanarratives" (a term preferred by Postmodernists) that reflect the pluralism of the world. Lyotard, in fact, defined Postmodernism as an "incredulity towards metanarratives" while suggesting that the old myths lost their legitimacy in a world in which traditional truths were challenged. Irony is thus an essential tool of postmodern thought and style, as myths and historical contexts are reframed (or "recontextualized") to allow audiences to consider them from a fresh perspective.

As we have seen often throughout our study of the theater, the form of a play often reflects its content. The Greeks and Neoclassicists believed in a harmonious universe, and their plays were carefully structured affairs in which problems were resolved (although not always happily) in five compact acts. By contrast, the Absurdists wrote about the great "rut of existence" and devised cyclic plots to show the meaninglessness of our actions. Because they see the world as a series of artificial constructs whose meanings change according to time, circumstance, and personal experience, many contemporary dramatists resist a single explanation for issues, characters, and plots, and thus *fragmentation* is often a characteristic of postmodern plays.

Plots are rarely linear, and instead of lengthy acts with a well-defined beginning, middle, and end, we are given a series of scenes, often in markedly contrasting styles and moods (a technique used by Brecht and even Shakespeare, though for different reasons). Native American playwright Diane Glancy makes particular note of this practice in the introduction to her play, *The Woman Who Was a Red Deer Dressed for the Deer Dance* (see later in Part III); her short play is typical of the structure of many postmodern plays. Many plays, in fact, are bereft of traditional exposition and denouements to heighten their ambiguity. The plays of Pinter and Shepard are particularly representative of this technique. ("I write stories without endings," says Shepard.) All is calculated to encourage audience members to assign meanings based on their own particular perceptions of reality. This is sometimes whimsically referred to as the MYOM ("Make Your Own Meaning") syndrome.

Some theorists, especially those aligned with Postmodernism, argue that originality in art is a romantic myth and that all art—indeed, all human endeavor—is influenced by myriad cultures and consciousness. Hence, art in our postmodern age is achieved by freely integrating styles and subject matter from across the spectrum of time and place. To achieve this spirit of *pastiche* (or *collage*), scripts frequently incorporate (or "quote") material from other periods and pieces of literature. Because of its pervasive influence on world culture and economics, material drawn from America's pop culture is especially popular. This often contradictory, purposefully disorienting style of playwriting is intended to challenge our beliefs about the way we perceive the world and the manner in which artists can represent it. In Kushner's *Angels in America, Part One: Millennium Approaches*, for instance, AIDS sufferer Prior Walter is visited in his hallucinations by ancestors from plague years in previous centuries. As with all art, reinventing forms can have both salutary and controversial effects. Shepard regularly intersperses pop icons, such as comic book characters and cowboy heroes, with "real" characters throughout his innovative and much-praised work. In one of the most controversial examples of the pastiche script, Arthur Miller sued Elizabeth LeCompte and the Wooster Group, among New York's most controversial experimental theater companies, for using material from his play *The Crucible* in their 1984 collectively created "inter-textual" work, *L.S.D.* (or *Just the High Points*).

Time can be nonlinear and space malleable in postmodern plays, an outgrowth of the argument that history is suspect because it has been written by those in power to protect their base; like literature, history itself must be deconstructed. Scripts freely commingle

SHOWCASE   DARIO FO: NOBEL LAUREATE, ANARCHIST, AND CLOWN

In this anthology you may read the works of almost every dramatist who has won the world's highest honor for writers, the Nobel Prize for Literature: Eugene O'Neill (United States); Samuel Beckett (Ireland); Wole Soyinka (Nigeria); Derek Walcott (Trinidad-Tobago); and Gao Xingjian (China). The 1997 Nobel Laureate—Italy's Dario Fo (1926–)—is not included herein, although he is recognized as the world's most performed living playwright since 1964. Fo's farcical dramas "play" better than they read and require superb comic actors (such as Fo himself) for their effect; also, they generally depend on an audience knowledgeable about Italian and European politics. Strange criteria for one who holds the world's premiere literary award. The Italian press, literati, and politicians shared this concern; the critic Geno Pampeloni scoffed, "The Nobel Prize? A joke!" when he heard the news of Fo's Nobel.

The iconoclastic Fo, of course, appreciated "the joke," for he has been making Italians—and audiences in 41 countries—laugh at those in power, whether they be politicians or intellectuals, since he began performing in postwar Italy. Bernard Shaw once said that the purpose of comedy is to "stick pins into pigs," and surely no theater artist in the last half-century has performed this act with more relish—and success—than Fo. Consequently, his own life has been a frightful melodrama that borders on the tragic: he has been arrested numerous times, been rebuked by the Vatican, had his house firebombed twice; he suffered at the hands of neo-fascists who kidnapped and raped his actress-wife (Franca Rame) in 1973; and he was denied entry to the United States in 1980. (He was finally allowed to enter after prominent artists protested, including Arthur Miller and filmmaker Martin Scorsese.) Despite these tribulations he has kept his irreverent sense of humor and still enjoys the enthusiastic following of common workers and students. If anyone has earned the accolade "The People's Playwright," it is Dario Fo.

On what merits did Fo receive the Nobel award? An answer to that question provides an understanding of Fo's approach to drama, as well as the the atrical tradition in which he works. The citation of the Swedish Academy, which named Fo as the recipient of its prize, read:

> Dario Fo . . . emulates the jesters of the Middle Ages in scourging authority and upholding the dignity of the downtrodden. For many years Fo has been performed all over the world, perhaps more than any other contemporary dramatist, and his influence has been considerable. He, if anyone, merits the epithet of "jester" in the true meaning of that word. With a blend of laughter and gravity he opens our eyes to abuses and injustices in society and also the wider historical perspectives in which they are placed.

Fo's acceptance speech (which included projections of cartoons to illustrate his points) further illuminates the importance of his award in the evolution of international culture:

> This Nobel is not only for me, but for all the people of the theater. It is the first time that the prize has been given to an author who was also an actor. The first time that they have recognized the value of not only the written word . . . and so this Nobel rings out like an extraordinary vendetta, the revenge of the actor who is always banished from power, suddenly brought to the table of the king. The power of the *giullare* [a medieval mime] is now with this prize rehabilitated. . . . And even more ex-

traordinary is that this Nobel goes to a comic, one who makes people laugh and has the audacity to write. A scandalous combination.

Fo found his theater roots in the small town near Lake Maggiore, near the Swiss border, where he was born in 1926. He recalls that the town was filled with "characters," most of whom were anarchists involved in smuggling. There he also saw *fabulatori*, itinerant storytellers, who traveled throughout the region telling tales that were "simple hyperboles based on an observation of everyday life, but behind these 'absurd' stories they hid a bitterness . . . of a disappointed people and a biting satire against the official world." Fo's description of the *fabulatori* is as applicable to his plays and performance pieces.

Fo attended the Brera Art Academy in Milan—still his home base—to study architecture; here he became enamored of the work of simple, ignorant craftsmen who, like Fo himself, "have always been the pariahs of official culture." At Brera he began writing plays modeled on the material he learned from the *fabulatori*. He was conscripted into Mussolini's fascist army in World War II, but he deserted and worked with his father in the Resistance to help smuggle enemies of the state, including Jews, into Switzerland. After the war he continued to study architecture, even as he wrote and performed farcical plays. After a nervous breakdown in 1950, he took up acting professionally, and by 1953 established his reputation when he founded *I Dritti* (The Standups), which produced his first hit play (*A Finger in the Eye*). In 1954 he married Franca Rame, an outstanding actress, who has been his collaborator for almost fifty years. Rame and Fo founded the Collettivo Teatrale La Commune (or simply La Commune) in Milan, among Europe's most important alternative theaters.

For the next fifteen years Fo continued to write farcical political plays (e.g., *Seventh Commandment: Thou Shalt Steal a Bit Less*, 1964). In 1969 he first performed the work that defines him as writer and performer: *Mistero Bufo*, a blasphemous parody of the sacred mystery plays of the medieval church into which Fo inserted topical material about politics and a large dose of Marxist ideology. Fo performed the dozen pieces alone, on a bare stage with few props, yet captivated his audiences. It has been estimated that over three million Italians have seen *Mistero Bufo*, which was censured by the Vatican for its coarse humor at the expense of the Church. One of the most intriguing features of *Mistero Bufo*, which Fo has used in other works, are the *grammelot*: onomatopoeic patter that hints at foreign languages (this was a staple of the medieval jesters and the actors of the sixteenth-century *commedia dell'arte* who mocked the language of others). In *Mistero Bufo* Christ instills this mock language in a poor peasant whose wife has been raped so that he may speak "in a language that will cut like a knife." For a half-century Fo's outrageous comedies have done precisely that.

Because few actors other than Fo have the skills required of *Mistero Bufo*, Fo's best-known works beyond Italy are *Non Si Paga? Non Si Paga!* (*Can't Pay? Won't Pay!*, 1974), about a workers' strike in Milan, and *The Accidental Death of an Anarchist* (1970), which the playwright describes in his subtitle as "a grotesque farce about a tragic farce." In the late 1960s, a popular Italian anarchist, Pino Pinelli, was killed by the police, who claimed the man jumped from a fourth-story window in an attempt to escape their interrogation. In Fo's play a "maniac" (played brilliantly by Fo) comes to the Milan Police Station and assumes a variety of hilarious identities (including a bishop) to extract the truth from the police. At one point he manages to convince the police that they, too, should leap from the window. The play is a surrealistic farce, yet it is filled with unflinching anger and political discourse. In his introduction (and a subsequent postscript) to the play—which has enjoyed success in many countries, most notably in England, where it had a long run in the West End—Fo states his intentions for the play and for others in his vast repertory:

> Popular theater has always used the grotesque and farce—which was invented by the people—to develop dramatic arguments. Anger and hatred must become conscious action in collaboration with others, and not just the individual letting off steam in an impotent way. . . . what has been the reason for the show's success? . . . the indignation which can be relieved by a little burp in the form of scandal; scandal as a liberating catharsis of the system. But luckily for [the State], they will have to realize that there are a lot of us, and this time their burp is going to stick in their throats.

Although Dario Fo is rooted in the much older traditions of the medieval *guillari* (jesters) and the *commedia dell' arte* of the Renaissance, he is as much a Postmodernist in the playful and ironic way in which he subverts older forms and myths for contemporary political purposes. His works fuse a variety of seemingly dissonant styles to form a brash new style "that is new within the traditional." Fo calls this "the throwaway theater" (*un teatro da bruciare*) that "won't go down in bourgeois history, but which is useful, like a newspaper article, a debate or a political discussion." In truth, Fo has earned a place in the pantheon of bourgeois history (the Academy of Nobel Laureates) because he transcends the particulars of time and place in his unyielding—and hilarious—commentary on the folly of the powerful.

Read about Dario Fo:

Jenkins, Ron. *Dario Fo and Franca Rame: Artful Laughter*. New York: Aperture, 2001.

See a video about Dario Fo:

Dario Fo and Franca Rame: A Nobel for Two. Insight Media, 55 min., 1998.

---

historical periods and even reconstruct time lines. Caryl Churchill's *Top Girls* (see later in Part III) portrays women from five different historical periods who meet a contemporary Margaret Thatcher–style "top girl" for lunch; the play ends with a scene that takes place one year *before* the first scene.

Whatever quibbles some may have about contemporary dramatic literature, there is considerable agreement that the movement has reenergized theater. By emphasizing the visual aspects of performance, the theater has been revitalized and reestablished as "the seeing place," its original Greek term. Ironically, much of this has been accomplished by the very technology that Postmodernists disdain. The realistic setting and the overused box set are now passé and best left to film and television, which handle the realistic style more convincingly. The conceptually stunning and purely theatrical images created by such directors as Peter Brook, Peter Stein, Anne Bogart, Tadashi Suzuki, Joanne Akalitis, Julie Taymor, and especially Robert Wilson reaffirm that the theater can create idiosyncratic effects live and before a living audience in imaginative ways that film cannot. After years of stark, minimalist designs reflecting the modernist preoccupation with a "less is more" philosophy, the designs of Joseph Svoboda, Ming Cho Lee, Maria Bjornson, and Bob Crowley commonly blend multiple styles, periods, and media to create haunting, archetypal images that transcend time and place.

Acting in Contemporary Plays

With its current focus on the multiple roles we play in our lives, as well as the "game playing" that is required to survive in this world of artificial constructs, the theater itself has become a leading metaphor for contemporary philosophy. (Shakespeare notwithstanding: proclaiming that "All the world's a stage," he used the "play-life" metaphor in virtually every play he wrote.) The "actor" has become a favorite metaphor for artists. In 1922 Luigi Pirandello defined this theme in *Six Characters in Search of an Author* (see Showcase in Part II), which remains the prototype of the life-as-theater play script. Even though it was written in 1922, many scholars and critics have called it the first postmodern play. The English social satirist Tom Stoppard echoes Pirandello in *Rosencrantz and Guildenstern Are Dead* (1967), a retelling of *Hamlet* from the bit-players' point of view. In that play he reminds us that in our day-to-day existence, "every entrance is an exit, and every exit is an entrance." How adroitly we shift from one role to another as we make those entrances and exits is a predominant theme of the contemporary theater.

Actors themselves have had to adjust to the texts of contemporary scripts. Like the characters they portray, actors are often required to play multiple roles, literally and figuratively. It is not uncommon—as in Churchill's *Top Girls*—for an actor to play several roles in a single play to underscore the fragmentation of personality (and, of course, to save producers money in a competitive and costly business). Often actors cross-dress to call attention to gender issues; Tony Kushner's *Angels in America, Part One: Millennium Approaches* provides an innovative example. Anna Deavere Smith's *Twilight, L.A.* (see Showcase, "Docudrama," later in this section) is more than a "one-woman show" in which she skillfully plays more than 30 different women and men of many races. Hers is the quintessential postmodern performance, resulting in a dazzling mosaic of voices reflecting multiple perspectives on truth. Even when an actor plays a single character, the old notion of the Stanislavskian "spine" or "through line"—which suggests a consistency of character and motivation and a linear movement toward a univalent truth—is now less applicable. In the postmodern theater, characters are often the sum of their inconsistencies, each determined by the many roles they play in society. The postmodern actor must be extraordinarily versatile and able to mix styles (e.g., Realism with the New Vaudeville, or the classical with Expressionism) in a heartbeat. Furthermore, postmodern actors are more frequently required to perform in a presentational style derived from Brecht, unlike method actors who are grounded in an essentially representational style that draws from their personal emotions and ignores the presence of the audience.

Contemporary Dramatic Criticism: Deconstruction, Theory, New Approaches

Postmodernism in the arts has fostered and also influenced many new approaches to criticism and to literary theory. The so-called New Criticism of the mid-twentieth century focused on literary and dramatic texts as self-contained units to be scrutinized closely and analyzed formally for technique, structure, imagery, and style as keys to meaning. "Form is content" was the motto of such analyses, which began, in the 1960s, to give way to other types of interdisciplinary and contextual work, much of it originating in France. The work of Jacques Derrida on *deconstruction* and the ideas of Jacques Lacan in *psychosemiotics* brought these fields to the forefront as tools of critical analysis. Lacan argued that in order to achieve mastery of language, a child relinquishes a sensuous, experiential access to the world and moves into a more abstract understanding mediated by language, the symbolic.

SHOWCASE | PERFORMANCE ART

Musician Laurie Anderson is one. So are the writers Spalding Gray and Eric Bogosian. So are environmental activist Rachel Rosenthal and Mexican-American policy critic Guillermo Gomez-Peña. But attempting to define the border-crossing forms created by these artists under the rubric "performance art" creates the same problem that confronted the blind men describing an elephant: the field is so big and varied, the definition depends upon where you're standing.

Performance art earned notoriety during the culture wars of the 1980s and the political battles over funding the National Endowment for the Arts during the 1990s, but its antecedents stretch back to the Dadaists with their visual paradoxes and chance approach to making art (see Introduction to Part II), and certainly to the American protest movements of the early 1960s. During the latter period, artists from many disciplines—painting, theater, dance, music—gathered to stage deliberately provocative and evanescent events, documented on video but not meant to be repeated. Such events, organized by painter Allan Kaprow, for instance, or sculptor Claes Oldenberg, were called "Happenings." Their purpose, aside from self-expression, was to provide a forum for spontaneous creation, separate from the commodity culture and the museum system of the art world. Such events could not be bought and sold. They were not scripted, and thus they contested the manufacture of creative "products" marketed in an increasingly commercialized international art scene. "I was looking for a way of being genial, inventive. I thought being real might involve being very different. The model of everyday life was substituted for the model of the history of art," said Kaprow, known as the father of performance art. The free-form, performative nature of such events appealed especially to artists also involved in the growing counterculture—the Vietnam, civil rights, gay, and feminist protest movements. When they took their performance works indoors, private galleries or artist-run spaces, not traditional theaters, became the main venues for performance art.

The content of such work tended to jab at social norms, subvert societal prejudices, and often fell outside the taste of mainstream audiences, for the subject matter ranged from intimate and personal life stories (sometimes involving homosexuality, homelessness, or sexual abuse framed in such a way that "the personal is the political") to lighter, more comical spectacles closer in spirit to parades or a new form of vaudeville. Eventually, such artists as Rosenthal, who began her artistic life as a painter, picked up theatrical skills that helped make the content and issues raised by such work more legible to audiences. She began publishing her performance texts side-by-side with those of playwrights. Monologuist David Cale publishes his dramatic monologues, just as Eric Bogosian does his (e.g., *Sex, Drugs, and Rock 'n' Roll*). Comic Lily Tomlin and Jane Wagner published their script for Tomlin's multicharacter solo, *The Search for Signs of Intelligent Life in the Universe*.

Several traits distinguish true contemporary performance art from theater, however. Narrative time tends to be fractured and discontinuous in these pieces. More media than words are usually involved in the presentation—film, video, music, slide projections, sometimes painted canvases. Many such artists are disinterested in slick production values; they create highly personal works without much artifice. Very often, the texts are so personal they cannot be performed effectively by an artist or actor other than their creator. And most importantly, the performer's relationship to the audience is more direct and presentational than in most drama which, despite Brecht, still tends to represent the illusion of a reality toward which we suspend our disbelief.

David Antin, a performer/writer who teaches in the visual arts department at the University of California–San Diego, calls the area in which contemporary performance art happens "the genre-free zone." His is a useful though broad description because when you enter the genre-free zone, you enter a place without borders where anything can happen.

Over the last two decades, some performance artists, even those who disdained prevailing social values, became relatively popular, actually a part of the mainstream. Monologuists and writers such as Spalding Gray, Eric Bogosian, David Cale, and Whoopi Goldberg moved from alternative spaces to mainstream theaters, television, even Hollywood. In cases such as Goldberg's the work has been radically compromised. More often, however, as with Gray's film *Swimming to Cambodia* or Bogosian's televised version of his anatomy of addiction, *Drinking in America*, success has simply brought a wider audience to the same work. But the variety and increasing marketability of performance pieces are only two aspects of the form—the ear and trunk, perhaps, of the proverbial elephant.

In 1990, four performance artists became the crux of a debate over the role of the National Endowment for the Arts (NEA) as arbiter of national taste. Holly Hughes, Tim Miller, Karen Finley, and John Fleck all had grants personally rescinded by then-NEA chief John Frohenmayer, an appointee of the first President George Bush. The work of Hughes and Miller often deals with their own homosexuality and their experiences in the dominant heterosexual culture, while Finley's often sexually explicit work deals with issues of abuse and victimization in an incantatory mode that summons great power in performance. The defunding of these four artists led to other political actions by members of the same conservative wing of Congress who had been speaking out against such artists as photographer Robert Mapplethorpe and installation maker Andres Serrano. In the ensuing uproar, which the four "defundos" pursued to the Supreme Court and lost, Sen. Jesse Helms of North Carolina led a floor fight that slashed the NEA budget by half (a sum not yet restored as of the 2002–03 budget), while the NEA itself dropped the grant categories for individual artists and for touring—the precise areas that had opened the door to federal money making its way to such solo performers.

Despite the cutbacks and the closure of several high-profile urban performance spaces, the impulse to create such personally inventive work still finds expression in the international touring of Anderson and Rosenthal, the ongoing politically charged pieces of Miller, Finley, and Gomez-Peña, and the discovery of such new voices as the Italian Laura Curino and Londoner Victoria Worsley. Among the most important performance spaces still thriving in the United States are P.S. 122 in New York, Highways in Los Angeles, and Theatre Artaud in San Francisco.

Lacan and Derrida both contended that language itself "privileges" some people and experiences over others. Their newer philosophical approaches, therefore, construct new meanings through the analysis and "destruction" of traditional interpretations, viewed as erroneous perceptions of language, the result of hierarchical thinking, and false categories.

Detractors of Deconstructionism viewed it less as a critical tool than as an ideological movement that, intentionally or not, undermined Western orthodoxy and at an extreme led to "political correctness" and the culture wars of the 1980s and 1990s in major American universities. However, new poststructuralist impulses such as deconstruction and psychosemiotics do represent a radical departure from Euro-American humanism and have made their way into many scholarly articles, have transformed certain academic disciplines, and behind the scenes have invigorated many theatrical productions. Because "theory" has reoriented literary and theatrical history and has opened up and complicated the meanings of that history, theater studies are no longer viewed as separate from the histories of politics, economics, race relations, and the roles of women and minorities in society. Such new contextual approaches have become both subject and strategy for theater artists.

Although Derrida's ideas have lost some of the potency they first had, they have left two important legacies, both crucial to understanding contemporary theater. First, deconstructionist thought made possible, and even respectable, ironic readings of texts. A theater director, for instance, could argue with the text in a program essay and/or in a production by playing against the work's traditional historical and cultural meaning. This technique of framing a text with distancing irony encouraged a debate between contemporary society and the one that originally generated the work. For instance, Peter Zadek, an Austrian director known for provocative interpretations of classical texts, applied deconstructionist theory and practice to his treatment of *Othello* in 1976. Othello was played by a Caucasian actor in black face to underscore his obvious ethnicity and perhaps subliminally to refer to the American tradition of blackface minstrelsy; by design, the actor's makeup rubbed off on all with whom he came into contact. Desdemona was dressed in a bikini to suggest that Shakespeare represented her as little more than an object over whom men fought. Much of the play was acted as a cheap vaudeville sketch to undercut its idealized romantic foundation. These directorial choices were at variance with our usual perceptions of Shakespeare's intentions, but their audacity forced audiences to reconsider the racism and sexism inherent in our culture—and in Shakespeare's.

Second, Deconstructionism carried an "openness to the other," that is, an acceptance of the multiplicity of perspectives, that has enlarged the arena for criticism and therefore expanded the canon of respected literature worldwide. Derrida argues that this is Deconstructionism's most affirmative project. Evolving with Deconstructionism and psychosemiotics—and in part because of them—are other kinds of specialized analysis that have led to women's studies, gender studies, queer theory, and various perspectives (Chicano, African-American, Asian-American) grouped together as multicultural studies. All share the common impulse to expand the literary (and theatrical) canon and theatrical criticism from the once-dominant viewpoint of traditional white male thought. Differences of sex, race, class, ethnicity, and sexual preference, these critics write, give us a sense of personal identity, which has often been marginalized, distorted, or rendered invisible onstage and in academic culture.

In the late 1960s, the women's movement gained momentum in the United States, and after Kate Millett's groundbreaking study *Sexual Politics* (1968), feminist critics realized that the classical canon of literature and the plays produced by most theaters were written neither for women nor by them. Roles for male stage actors still outnumber those for females by three to one. Similarly, as the various civil rights movements of the 1960s gathered force, scholars began to analyze the ways in which African-Americans, Latinos, and other ethnic groups (as well as gay men and lesbian women) were historically depicted and, more important, how and why their images were distorted and their creative output underrepresented onstage and in the academy. Until the late 1960s, drama anthologies such as this one would have contained very few, if any, plays by women, by people of color, or by openly gay men and lesbians.

The new scholarship began theorizing the social, political, and cultural reasons for these distortions, and by framing and critiquing the inherited body of dramatic literature it began clearing a space in the canon for the voices (and truths) of these invisible "others" to be heard. Arguing that gender and race are constructed by representational forms such as theater and film, feminist scholars such as Jill Dolan, Sandra Gilbert, and Susan Gubar showed that the requirements of an academic curriculum or of a not-for-profit theater season have led to the subtle oppression of "difference." Their studies encouraged theater directors whose interpretations of existing texts supported new ways of staging them to question or foreground their portrayals of women. Other sympathetic directors, such as Lee Breuer at Mabou Mines, subverted canonical texts; Breuer's feminized *King Lear*, for instance, starred Ruth Maleczich as Shakespeare's aging monarch and Karen Kandel as Edgar/Edna. Others used cross-generational, cross-gender, and color-blind casting to subvert theater practice. Many who were interested in "difference" but who wished to forge a new, more inclusive commonality created their own texts (as Anna Deavere Smith does from interviews and Holly Hughes does from her own experience as a lesbian and comic writer). Inquiries into issues of race, gender, and sexual preference became thematic threads in such work.

As the feminist movement evolved and split during the theoretical ferment of the 1980s, critics came to realize that they needed to study gender and sexual differences not only in literature but also in science and in history. Thus came the field of gender studies and, eventually, queer theory, which rescued homosexual literature from the outskirts of literature and analysis. Representations of homophobia, for instance, could become tools for understanding the gender system as a whole. Similarly, black writers created alternative myths in order to counter the destructive impact of white myths on the black psyche. Once-marginalized experiences now serve as the thematic thrust not only for feminist theater groups and projects but also for such successful mainstream plays as Tony Kushner's *Angels in America, Part One: Millennium Approaches*, Suzan-Lori Parks's *Topdog/Underdog*, and Moises Kaufman's *The Laramie Project*.

Some ethnic as well as feminist and gay critics argue that when whites attempt to speak for nonwhites (or men for women, or straights for gays), they are engaging in "ventriloquism," which is, like appropriation, another form of cultural imperialism. To cite a prominent example: when pop singer Paul Simon and Derek Walcott wrote *The Capeman* (1997), a musical drama about a Puerto Rican murder scandal in New York, Simon was criticized by some Latinos for appropriating their music and culture. Critic and director Robert Brustein has often written of his fears that a cultural revolution could replace "an old elite system with a populist agenda through egalitarian leveling." But neither he nor most critics reject pluralism itself, with the expansion of possibilities it brings to the creative experience.

As the theater continues to address fundamental human concerns with social and political as well as psychological and aesthetic awareness, it will continue to evolve and open itself to a wide spectrum of voices and viewpoints. The advantage we have today is that we are especially well equipped—intellectually, imaginatively, and technologically—to portray the triumphs, the sufferings, and the shortcomings of all the human race by such truly global means.

SHOWCASE   DOCUDRAMA

Anna Deavere Smith played 36 roles in her docudrama of the 1992 Los Angeles riots in Twilight: Los Angeles, 1992. *She played people of both genders, a variety of ages, and many ethnicities in the production in one of the most remarkable performances in the contemporary theater.*

Long before "Real TV" and Fox TV and MTV turned cameras on lives stranger than fiction, theater artists made drama from interviews, transcripts, and testimony, from the voices of real people who trusted and talked, then talked some more until they gave voice to themselves. During the 1990s, when public violence intersected private lives, Anna Deavere Smith listened to scores of those voices and with her *Fires in the Mirror: Crown Heights, Brooklyn and Other Identities* (1991) and her *Twilight: Los Angeles, 1992* (1993) became the most celebrated docudramatist of our time. These two works, both of them dazzling, multicharacter solos, culminated a more than 20-year-long series of interview-based pieces which together Smith called "On the Road: In Search of the American Character."

Smith is one of many theater artists, including Moises Kaufman and Emily Mann, who make drama from documentary material. Though Living Newspaper performances were a standard novelty during the Depression years, the more recent documentary work began with an unlikely source: Chicago's barstool bard, Studs Terkel. A radio and television host and social com-

mentator, Terkel held the microphone to countless people before creating fourteen books of oral history, three of which, including *Working*, were adapted for the stage. Princeton playwright Mann borrowed Terkel's documentary techniques, hearing hundreds of hours of talk and poring over stacks of clippings and trial documents for her *Execution of Justice* about the 1978 murders of San Francisco Mayor George Moscone and gay Councilman Harvey Milk, as well as for *Still Life*, a courtroom drama about domestic violence triggered by an out-of-control Vietnam veteran.

Extending the tradition into 2002, San Francisco Mime Troupe writer Joan Holden adapted Barbara Ehrenreich's popular and wrenching first-person account of living among the working poor, *Nickel and Dimed*, as a stage show that played the Intiman Theatre in Seattle and the Mark Taper Forum in Los Angeles under the direction of Bartlett Sher.

Smith writes in her book *Talk to Me* that her "On the Road" project was an attempt to get beyond the fragmentation of a multicultural society toward the wider embrace of a pluralistic national "we" as in "we the people." The

drama of "burning bras, the Panthers' guns, Woodstock, etcetera, may have been short lived," she writes. "However, a conversation reverberated for three decades in schools and universities and popular culture about who could speak for whom. Women wanted to speak for themselves, people of color wanted to think for themselves. In this cacophony of sound, where does 'we' come from?" She set out to find what she calls the soul of the culture by interviewing people whose words would be the doorway into their individual souls. "My search was specifically to find America in its language. I interview people and communities about the events of our time, in the hope that I will be able to absorb America. . . . This is a country of many tongues, even if we stick to English. Placing myself in other people's words, as in placing myself in other people's shoes, has given me the opportunity to get below the surface—to get 'real'."

Smith was in New York City in May 1992 performing her *Fires in the Mirror: Crown Heights, Brooklyn and Other Identities* about murderous ethnic clashes there when the Rodney King verdicts came in and South Central Los

Angeles erupted in violence. The Mark Taper Forum, a regional theater noted for supporting new work, commissioned her to record the aftermath. So she interviewed 200 people, among them Simi Valley jurors, Rodney King's Aunt Angela, trucker Reginald Denny, a paranoid Hollywood agent, and gun-collecting former police chief Daryl Gates. She listened and transcribed, waiting for that moment in the interview when she found what she calls the "diamond" of the conversation. "People will talk themselves into a frenzy until they achieve that moment of clarity," she told a San Diego critic before performances there. Smith, who teaches acting at Stanford University, notes that her interviewing techniques are paralleled by psycholinguistic theory, which describes the "speech act as the process by which people talk and talk and talk until they have an experience of themselves . . . and then they're silent." Smith then listens to the silences too.

Terkel has said that he also guides his subjects toward that same moment when they have an experience of themselves. Often, he has written, people will realize they have never experienced themselves talking: "There's always something of discovery for them." Similarly, Leigh Fondakowski, a member of Kaufman's Tectonic Theater Project and author of the docudrama about lesbian experience, *I Think I Like Girls*, said that the whole interviewing process is about "pulling the poetry from people's vernacular, and just putting a highlight on it."

As these artists begin shaping the material they've gathered, they adhere to a key tenet of postmodern thinking: truth emerges not from a single interpreter but from multiple points of view. The list of characters in these shows is usually very long. Smith herself played

36 people of divergent races, ages, and genders in *Twilight L.A.*, segueing smoothly with a change of voice, a wig, or body language. In their series of place-inspired satiric docudramas the Chicano comedy trio Culture Clash impersonate dozens of people they've interviewed. In the Terkel-based musical *Working*, nine singing actors take on 35 roles.

Finding the connections, shaping the interviews into a coherent evening is a key task for such writers/performers. When the piece (and the people interviewed) are responding to an event as Smith's, Mann's, and Kaufman's works do, it's possible to build suspense into the storytelling because of the nature of the subject. But when the show centers on a place (as Culture Clash does) or a theme (as Fondakowski and Terkel have), there's no narrative to organize the evening. "Trying to make the work flow from one person to the next is the first challenge," said Culture Clash actor/writer Ric Salinas. "Juxtaposition is the easiest method because it lets the people comment upon one another and leaves it up to the audience to decide." In the Clash's *Radio Mambo*, for instance, the trio juxtaposed the words of an environmentalist trying to save the Everglades with those of a colorful local who dumps refuse into the same national swamp. Smith also works by contrasts, letting points of view collide, sparks of conflict ignite, in hopes that audiences will develop tolerance by working their way through antithetical points of view. By showing that each person onstage has a "moral imagination," Smith said she tries to suggest that "every 'other' can be as empathetic as the self."

As a craftsman, Smith said she does not manipulate her subjects to make political points, nor does she edit

the interviews to support a particular point of view. "I am shaping, building something. That's not unconsciously done. The failure of the work would be if it became manipulation. Manipulation is a step beyond awareness."

Because the actors (except in Mann's more conventionally performed dramas) must play multiple roles and move in and out of them quickly in these docudramas, their style veers away from naturalistic method acting toward the Brechtian. Audiences remain aware that the actor is both an actor and the character he or she represents. Fondakowski, who was the head writer on *The Laramie Project*, told the *San Diego Union-Tribune* that in that play and her own *I Think I Like Girls*, the "actor is always present. Their challenge is to figure out how little they can use to create the character."

Terkel and his heir, Smith, strive for a compassionate breadth of democratic vision, and in their wake, Kaufman intentionally shaped *The Laramie Project* not as an indictment of a crime but as a portrait of a people. "The human race is bigger than the issues and the human race has shown over and over that people have great potential. It's circumstances that limit potential," Smith said, explaining a deep optimism about commonalities that infuses her work and that of the many others she has inspired.

For further reading:

Smith, Anna Deavere. *Fires in the Mirror: Crown Heights, Brooklyn and Other Identities.* New York: Anchor, 1993.

Smith, Anna Deavere. *Twilight: Los Angeles, 1992.* In *On the Road: A Search for American Character.* New York: Anchor, 1994.

ROSENCRANTZ AND GUILDENSTERN ARE DEAD

TOM STOPPARD

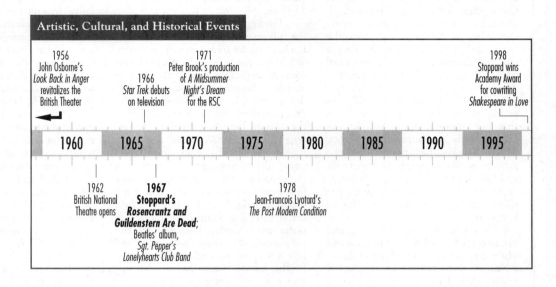

Artistic, Cultural, and Historical Events

1956
John Osborne's
Look Back in Anger
revitalizes the
British Theater

1966
Star Trek debuts
on television

1971
Peter Brook's production
of *A Midsummer
Night's Dream*
for the RSC

1998
Stoppard wins
Academy Award
for cowriting
Shakespeare in Love

1960 | 1965 | 1970 | 1975 | 1980 | 1985 | 1990 | 1995

1962
British National
Theatre opens

1967
**Stoppard's
*Rosencrantz and
Guildenstern Are Dead*;**
Beatles' album,
*Sgt. Pepper's
Lonelyhearts Club Band*

1978
Jean-Francois Lyotard's
The Post Modern Condition

TOM STOPPARD (1937–)

Perhaps no contemporary English-language playwright is more admired for his verbal dexterity and wit than Tom Stoppard, and very few possess the sweeping intellect and erudition for which he is noted. He is the legitimate successor of the great wits of the modern British theater: Bernard Shaw, Oscar Wilde, and Noel Coward. Stoppard, however, is not British by birth, nor is English his first language. And this most sophisticated and well read of playwrights spent exactly one day as a university student. His standing as the reigning intellect of the contemporary theater is thus all the more remarkable.

Stoppard was born Tomas Straussler in Zlin, Czechoslovakia, the son of a physician; Stoppard learned only recently his family was Jewish on both sides. In 1938 the Straussler family moved to Singapore, where his father was the staff doctor at a Czech-owned shoe factory. When the Japanese invaded Southeast Asia in 1942, Tomas and his mother fled to India (then a British colony), while his father remained behind, only to be killed by Japanese soldiers. Stoppard began school at a multiracial English-speaking school in Darjeeling, where his mother managed a shoe store. She married an English army officer, Kenneth Stoppard, and in 1946 the family moved to England. There young Tom (he anglicized his first name and took his stepfather's surname) was educated at prep schools in Nottingham and Yorkshire.

In 1954 Stoppard entered the University of Bristol, which he attended for one day. He left school when he secured a job as a reporter for the *Western Daily Press*, for whom he wrote features stories and—most importantly—theater and film reviews. He excelled as a theater critic, and by 1963 he was chief reviewer for London's *Scene* magazine. Within a seven-month period he saw over 130 plays, which laid the foundation for his subsequent career as one of England's (indeed, the world's) most prolific and successful playwrights.

Stoppard's plays are often labeled "pastiches" because he fashions new works by ingeniously parodying a variety of established theater and playwriting styles, the kind he saw nightly in his role as critic. For instance, *Rosencrantz and Guildenstern Are Dead* is Shakespeare's *Hamlet* as if it were written by Samuel Beckett and Luigi Pirandello (see below); *The Real Thing* (1982) is equal parts Noel Coward and Pirandello, with a little John Osborne tossed in. And several of his most recent plays (e.g., *Arcadia*, 1993, and *The Invention of Love*, 2000) have been simultaneously set in two distinct time periods that require a mixture of peformance styles.

In the early 1960s Stoppard began writing short plays, some for radio (e.g., *Albert's Bridge*) and television (*A Walk on the Water*, later revised as *Enter a Free Man*). It was, however, the success of *Rosencrantz and Guildenstern Are Dead* in 1966 that brought him international recognition. Students from Oxford University first performed the play at the Edinburgh (Scotland) Festival, where it received favorable attention from theater producers and critics. In 1967 the first London production of the play by the National Theatre of Great Britain won several prestigious awards as best new play. Other plays and awards followed with regularity, including *The Real Inspector Hound* (1968); *Jumpers* (1972); *Travesties* (1974); *Every Good Boy Deserves Favour* (1977); *Night and Day* (1978); *The Real Thing* (1982); *Hapgood* (1988); *Arcadia* (1993); and, most recently, *The Invention of Love* (2000). His latest work is a trilogy of plays collectively titled *The Coast of Utopia* (2002). Given his family history and Czech-Jewish heritage, Stoppard has written a number of political comedies that expose the absurdity of government-controlled institutions; *Dirty Linen* and *New Found Land* (1976) and *Cahoot's Macbeth* (1979) are among the best of these. He won the Academy Award for cowriting the popular film *Shakespeare in Love*, which itself received the best picture award of 1998.

Stoppard's "style" is, as we have suggested, taking a well-known literary or dramatic form, juxtaposing it with another, and thereby creating a world that seems disjointed on first inspection. In *Travesties*, perhaps his brashest play, Stoppard fuses Oscar Wilde's comedy of manners, *The Importance of Being Ernest*, with Marxist philosophy and Dadaist aesthetics. By doing so, he challenges audiences to examine their preconceptions about art and the world as he explores the central theme that permeates his work: the relationship between truth and the appearance of truth, between knowledge and what is "knowable." Or, to use the title of one of his most conventional plays: how do we know what "the real thing" is? Although the plays are essentially comic because of the dizzying confusion they create, they border on the tragic (as does *Rosencrantz and Guildenstern Are Dead*) because we find people hopelessly trapped in circumstances they cannot control. And in the tradition of the British comedy of manners, Stoppard's plays are noted for their epigrams; the Player in *Rosencrantz and Guildenstern Are Dead* affirms that tragedy occurs when "things have gone about as far as they can possibly go when things have got about as bad as they reasonably get."

As You Read *Rosencrantz and Guildenstern Are Dead*

Although it is possible to enjoy the play without an intimate knowledge of *Hamlet*, *Waiting for Godot*, or Pirandello's dramaturgy, you will find Stoppard's play a richer—and much funnier—experience if you know something about them. We have provided a brief synopsis and commentary on *Hamlet* for your convenience. Better yet, see one of the fine films of the play, particularly Kenneth Branagh's uncut version, which perhaps is most successful in its treatment of the Rosencrantz (Ros) and Guildenstern (Guil) subplot. Also, review the brief essay on *Waiting for Godot* in Part II. Although Stoppard coyly denies that Pirandello and Beckett inspired his play, you will better appreciate both Stoppard's intentions and the humor of the play armed with an understanding of these seminal playwrights and their themes. Furthermore, you will note a number of lengthy one-line exchanges between Ros and Guil. Much of this parodies the banter between Beckett's tramps in *Godot*; but remember that Beckett (like Stoppard) was influenced by British music hall comedians. It will help to think of these rapid-fire exchanges being performed by first-rate vaudevillians such as Abbot and Costello in their famous "Who's on First" routine.

ROSENCRANTZ AND GUILDENSTERN ARE DEAD

TOM STOPPARD

CAST OF CHARACTERS
ROSENCRANTZ
GUILDENSTERN
THE PLAYER
ALFRED
TRAGEDIANS
HAMLET
OPHELIA
CLAUDIUS
GERTRUDE
POLONIUS
SOLDIER
HORATIO
COURTIERS, AMBASSADORS, SOLDIERS, AND ATTENDANTS

ACT I

Two Elizabethans passing the time in a place without any visible character.

They are well dressed—hats, cloaks, sticks and all.

Each of them has a large leather money bag.

Guildenstern's bag is nearly empty.

Rosencrantz's bag is nearly full.

The reason being: they are betting on the toss of a coin, in the following manner: Guildenstern (hereafter "Guil") takes a coin out of his bag, spins it, letting it fall. Rosencrantz (hereafter "Ros") studies it, announces it as "heads" (as it happens) and puts it into his own bag. Then they repeat the process. They have apparently been doing this for some time.

The run of "heads" is impossible, yet Ros betrays no surprise at all—he feels none. However, he is nice enough to feel a little embarrassed at taking so much money off his friend. Let that be his character note.

Guil is well alive to the oddity of it. He is not worried about the money, but he is worried by the implications; aware but not going to panic about it—his character note.

Guil sits. Ros stands (he does the moving, retrieving coins).

Guil spins. Ros studies coin.

Ros. Heads.

He picks it up and puts it in his bag. The process is repeated.

Heads.

Again.

Heads.

Again.

Heads.

Again.

Heads.

GUIL (*flipping a coin*). There is an art to the building up of suspense.
Ros. Heads.
GUIL (*flipping another*). Though it can be done by luck alone.
Ros. Heads.
GUIL. If that's the word I'm after.
Ros (*raises his head at Guil*). Seventy-six—love.

Guil gets up but has nowhere to go. He spins another coin over his shoulder without looking at it, his attention being directed at his environment or lack of it.

Heads.

508

GUIL. A weaker man might be moved to re-examine his faith, if in nothing else at least in the law of probability. (*He slips a coin over his shoulder as he goes to look upstage.*)

ROS. Heads.

Guil, examining the confines of the stage, flips over two more coins as he does so, one by one of course. Ros announces each of them as "heads."

GUIL (*musing*). The law of probability, it has been oddly asserted, is something to do with the proposition that if six monkeys (*he has surprised himself*) . . . if six monkeys were . . .

ROS. Game?

GUIL. Were they?

ROS. Are you?

GUIL (*understanding*). Game. (*Flips a coin.*) The law of averages, if I have got this right, means that if six monkeys were thrown up in the air for long enough they would land on their tails about as often as they would land on their ——

ROS. Heads. (*He picks up the coin.*)

GUIL. Which even at first glance does not strike one as particularly rewarding speculation, in either sense, even without the monkeys. I mean you wouldn't *bet* on it. I mean *I* would, but *you* wouldn't. . . . (*As he flips a coin.*)

ROS. Heads.

GUIL. Would you? (*Flips a coin.*)

ROS. Heads.

Repeat.

Heads. (*He looks up at Guil—embarrassed laugh.*) Getting a bit of a bore, isn't it?

GUIL (*coldly*). A bore?

ROS. Well . . .

GUIL. What about the suspense?

ROS (*innocently*). What suspense?

Small pause.

GUIL. It must be the law of diminishing returns. . . . I feel the spell about to be broken. (*Energizing himself somewhat. He takes out a coin, spins it high, catches it, turns it over on to the back of his other hand, studies the coin— and tosses it to Ros. His energy deflates and he sits.*) Well, it was an even chance . . . if my calculations are correct.

ROS. Eighty-five in a row—beaten the record!

GUIL. Don't be absurd.

ROS. Easily!

GUIL (*angry*). Is that *it*, then? Is that all?

ROS. What?

GUIL. A new record? Is that as far as you are prepared to go?

ROS. Well . . .

GUIL. No questions? Not even a pause?

ROS. You spun them yourself.

GUIL. Not a flicker of doubt?

ROS (*aggrieved, aggressive*). Well, I won—didn't I?

GUIL (*approaches him—quieter*). And if you'd lost? If they'd come down against you, eighty-five times, one after another, just like that?

ROS (*dumbly*). Eighty-five in a row? *Tails?*

GUIL. Yes! What would you think?

ROS (*doubtfully*). Well. . . . (*Jocularly.*) Well, I'd have a good look at your coins for a start!

GUIL (*retiring*). I'm relieved. At least we can still count on self-interest as a predictable factor. . . . I suppose it's the last to go. Your capacity for trust made me wonder if perhaps . . . you, alone . . . (*He turns on him suddenly, reaches out a hand.*) Touch.

Ros clasps his hand. Guil pulls him up to him.

GUIL (*more intensely*). We have been spinning coins together since—— (*He releases him almost as violently.*) This is not the first time we have spun coins!

ROS. Oh no—we've been spinning coins for as long as I remember.

GUIL. How long is that?

ROS. I forget. Mind you—eighty-five times!

GUIL. Yes?

ROS. It'll take some beating, I imagine.

GUIL. Is *that* what you imagine? Is that it? No *fear?*

ROS. Fear?

GUIL (*in fury—flings a coin on the ground*). Fear! The crack that might flood your brain with light!

ROS. Heads. . . . (*He puts it in his bag.*)

Guil sits despondently. He takes a coin, spins it, lets it fall between his feet. He looks at it, picks it up, throws it to Ros, who puts it in his bag.

Guil takes another coin, spins it, catches it, turns it over on to his other hand, looks at it, and throws it to Ros, who puts it in his bag.

Guil takes a third coin, spins it, catches it in his right hand, turns it over onto his left wrist, lobs it in the air, catches it with his left hand, raises his left leg, throws the coin up under it, catches it and turns it over on the top of his head, where it sits. Ros comes, looks at it, puts it in his bag.

ROS. I'm afraid——

GUIL. So am I.

ROS. I'm afraid it isn't your day.

GUIL. I'm afraid it is.

Small pause.

ROS. Eighty-nine.

GUIL. It must be indicative of something, besides the redistribution of wealth. (*He muses.*) List of possible explanations. One: I'm willing it. Inside where nothing shows, I am the essence of a man spinning double-headed coins, and betting against himself in private atonement for an unremembered past. (*He spins a coin at Ros.*)

ROS. Heads.

GUIL. Two: time has stopped dead, and the single experience of one coin being spun once has been repeated ninety times. . . . (*He flips a coin, looks at it, tosses it to Ros.*) On the whole, doubtful. Three: divine intervention, that is to say, a good turn from above concerning him, cf. children of Israel, or retribution from above concerning me, cf. Lot's wife. Four: a spectacular vindication of the principle that each individual coin spun individually (*he spins one*) is as likely to come down heads as tails and therefore should cause no surprise each individual time it does. (*It does. He tosses it to Ros.*)

ROS. I've never known anything like it!

GUIL. And a syllogism: One, he has never known anything like it. Two, he has never known anything to write home about. Three, it is nothing to write home about. . . . Home . . . What's the first thing you remember?

ROS. Oh, let's see. . . . the first thing that comes into my head, you mean?

GUIL. No—the first thing you remember.

ROS. Ah. (*Pause.*) No, it's no good, it's gone. It was a long time ago.

GUIL (*patient but edged*). You don't get my meaning. What is the first thing after all the things you've forgotten?

ROS. Oh I see. (*Pause.*) I've forgotten the question.

Guil leaps up and paces.

GUIL. Are you happy?

ROS. What?

GUIL. Content? At ease?

ROS. I suppose so.

GUIL. What are you going to do now?

ROS. I don't know. What do you want to do?

GUIL. I have no desires. None. (*He stops pacing dead.*) There was a messenger . . . that's right. We were sent for. (*He wheels at Ros and raps out:*) Syllogism the second: One, probability is a factor which operates within natural forces. Two, probability is not operating as a factor. Three, we are now within un-, sub- or supernatural forces. Discuss. (*Ros is suitably startled. Acidly.*) Not too heatedly.

ROS. I'm sorry I—What's the matter with you?

GUIL. The scientific approach to the examination of phenomena is a defence against the pure emotion of fear. Keep tight hold and continue while there's time. Now—counter to the previous syllogism: tricky one, follow me carefully, it may prove a comfort. If we postulate, and we just have, that within un-, sub- or supernatural forces *the probability is* that the law of probability will not operate as a factor, then we must accept that the probability of the *first* part will not operate as a factor, in which case the law of probability *will* operate as a factor within un, sub- or supernatural forces. And since it obviously hasn't been doing so, we can take it that we are not held within un-, sub- or supernatural forces after all; in all probability, that is. Which is a great relief to me personally. (*Small pause.*) Which is all very well, except that—— (*He continues with tight hysteria, under control.*) We have been spinning coins together since I don't know when, and in all that time (if it *is* all that time) I don't suppose either of us was more than a couple of gold pieces up or down. I hope that doesn't sound surprising because its very unsurprisingness is something I am trying to keep hold of. The equanimity of your average tosser of coins depends upon a law, or rather a tendency, or let us say a probability, or at any rate a mathematically calculable chance, which ensures that he will not upset himself by losing too much nor upset his opponent by winning too often. This made for a kind of harmony and a kind of confidence. It related the fortuitous and the ordained into a reassuring union which we recognized as nature. The sun came up about as often as it went down, in the long run, and a coin showed heads about as often as it showed tails. Then a messenger arrived. We had been sent for. Nothing else happened. Ninety-two coins spun consecutively have come down heads ninety-two consecutive times . . . and for the last three minutes on the wind of a windless day I have heard the sound of drums and flute. . . .

ROS (*cutting his fingernails*). Another curious scientific phenomenon is the fact that the fingernails grow after death, as does the beard.

GUIL. What?

ROS (*loud*). Beard!

GUIL. But you're not dead.

Ros (*irritated*). I didn't say they *started* to grow after death! (*Pause, calmer.*) The fingernails also grow before birth, though *not* the beard.

Guil. *What?*

Ros (*shouts*). Beard! What's the matter with you? (*Reflectively.*) The toenails, on the other hand, never grow at all.

Guil (*bemused*). The toenails never grow at all?

Ros. Do they? It's a funny thing—I cut my fingrnails all the time, and every time I think to cut them, they need cutting. Now, for instance. And yet, I never, to the best of my knowledge, cut my toenails. They ought to be curled under my feet by now, but it doesn't happen. I never think about them. Perhaps I cut them absent-mindedly, when I'm thinking of something else.

Guil (*tensed up by this rambling*). Do you remember the first thing that happened today?

Ros (*promptly*). I woke up, I suppose. (*Triggered.*) Oh— I've got it now—that man, a foreigner, he woke us up——

Guil. A messenger. (*He relaxes, sits.*)

Ros. That's it—pale sky before dawn, a man standing on his saddle to bang on the shutters—shouts—What's all the row about?! Clear off!—But then he called our names. You remember that—this man woke us up.

Guil. Yes.

Ros. We were sent for.

Guil. Yes.

Ros. That's why we're here. (*He looks round, seems doubtful, then the explanation.*) Travelling.

Guil. Yes.

Ros (*dramatically*). It was urgent—a matter of extreme urgency, a royal summons, his very words: official business and no questions asked—lights in the stableyard, saddle up and off headlong and hotfoot across the land, our guides outstripped in breakneck pursuit of our duty! Fearful lest we come too late!!

Small pause.

Guil. Too late for what?

Ros. How do I know? We haven't got there yet.

Guil. Then what are we doing here, I ask myself.

Ros. You might well ask.

Guil. We better get on.

Ros. You might well think.

Guil. We better get on.

Ros (*actively*). Right! (*Pause.*) On where?

Guil. Forward.

Ros (*forward to footlights*). Ah. (*Hesitates.*) Which way do we——(*He turns round.*) Which way did we——?

Guil. Practically starting from scratch. . . . An awakening, a man standing on his saddle to bang on the shutters, our names shouted in a certain dawn, a message, a summons . . . A new record for heads and tails. We have not been . . . picked out . . . simply to be abandoned . . . set loose to find our own way. We are entitled to some direction. . . . I would have thought.

Ros (*alert, listening*). I say——! I say——

Guil. Yes?

Ros. I can hear—I thought I heard—music.

Guil raises himself.

Guil. Yes?

Ros. Like a band. (*He looks around, laughs embarrassedly, expiating himself.*) It sounded like—a band. Drums.

Guil. Yes.

Ros (*relaxes*). It couldn't have been real.

Guil. "The colours red, blue and green are real. The colour yellow is a mystical experience shared by everybody"—demolish.

Ros (*at edge of stage*). It must have been thunder. Like drums . . .

By the end of the next speech, the band is faintly audible.

Guil. A man breaking his journey between one place and another at a third place of no name, character, population or significance, sees a unicorn cross his path and disappear. That in itself is startling, but there are precedents for mystical encounters of various kinds, or to be less extreme, a choice of persuasions to put it down to fancy; until—"My God," says a second man, "I must be dreaming, I thought I saw a unicorn." At which point, a dimension is added that makes the experience as alarming as it will ever be. A third witness, you understand, adds no further dimension but only spreads it thinner, and a fourth thinner still, and the more witnesses there are the thinner it gets and the more reasonable it becomes until it is as thin as reality, the name we give to the common experience. . . . "Look, look!" recites the crowd. "A horse with an arrow in its forehead! It must have been mistaken for a deer."

Ros (*eagerly*). I knew all along it was a band.

Guil (*tiredly*). He knew all along it was a band.

Ros. Here they come!

Guil (*at the last moment before they enter—wistfully*). I'm sorry it wasn't a unicorn. It would have been nice to have unicorns.

The Tragedians are six in number, including a small Boy (Alfred). Two pull and push a cart piled with props and belongings. There is also a Drummer, a Horn-Player and a Flautist. The Spokesman ("the Player") has no instrument. He brings up the rear and is the first to notice them.

PLAYER. Halt!

The group turns and halts.

(*Joyously.*) An audience!

Ros and Guil half rise.

Don't move!

They sink back. He regards them fondly.

Perfect! A lucky thing we came along.

ROS. For us?

PLAYER. Let us hope so. But to meet two gentlemen on the road—we would not hope to meet them off it.

ROS. No?

PLAYER. Well met, in fact, and just in time.

ROS. Why's that?

PLAYER. Why, we grow rusty and you catch us at the very point of decadence—by this time tomorrow we might have forgotten everything we ever knew. That's a thought, isn't it (*He laughs generously.*) We'd be back where we started—improvising.

ROS. Tumblers, are you?

PLAYER. We can give you a tumble if that's your taste, and times being what they are. . . . Otherwise, for a jingle of coin we can do you a selection of gory romances, full of fine cadence and corpses, pirated from the Italian; and it doesn't take much to make a jingle—even a single coin has music in it.

They all flourish and bow, raggedly.

Tragedians, at your command.

Ros and Guil have got to their feet.

ROS. My name is Guildenstern, and this is Rosencrantz.

Guil confers briefly with him.

(*Without embarrassment.*) I'm sorry—*his* name's Guildenstern, and *I'm* Rosencrantz.

PLAYER. A pleasure. We've played to bigger, of course, but quality counts for something. I recognized you at once—

ROS. And who are we?

PLAYER. —as fellow artists.

ROS. I thought we were gentlemen.

PLAYER. For some of us it is performance, for others, patronage. They are two sides of the same coin, or, let us say, being as there are so many of us, the same side of two coins. (*Bows again.*) Don't clap too loudly—it's a very old world.

ROS. What is your line?

PLAYER. Tragedy, sir. Deaths and disclosures, universal and particular, denouements both unexpected and inexorable, transvestite melodrama on all levels including the suggestive. We transport you into a world of intrigue and illusion . . . clowns, if you like, murderers—we can do you ghosts and battles, on the skirmish level, heroes, villains, tormented lovers—set pieces in the poetic vein; we can do you rapiers or rape or both, by all means, faithless wives and ravished virgins—*flagrante delicto* at a price, but that comes under realism for which there are special terms. Getting warm, am I?

ROS (*doubtfully*). Well, I don't know. . . .

PLAYER. It costs little to watch, and little more if you happen to get caught up in the action, if that's your taste and times being what they are.

ROS. What are they?

PLAYER. Indifferent.

ROS. Bad?

PLAYER. Wicked. Now what precisely is your pleasure? (*He turns to the Tragedians.*) Gentlemen, disport yourselves.

The Tragedians shuffle into some kind of line.

There! See anything you like?

ROS (*doubtful, innocent*). What do they do?

PLAYER. Let your imagination run riot. They are beyond surprise.

ROS. And how much?

PLAYER. To take part?

ROS. To watch.

PLAYER. Watch what?

ROS. A private performance.

PLAYER. How private?

ROS. Well, there are only two of us. Is that enough?

PLAYER. For an audience, disappointing. For voyeurs, about average.

ROS. What's the difference?

PLAYER. Ten guilders.

ROS (*horrified*). Ten *guilders!*

PLAYER. I mean eight.

ROS. Together?

PLAYER. Each. I don't think you understand—

ROS. What are you *saying?*

PLAYER. What am I saying—seven.

ROS. Where have you *been?*

PLAYER. Roundabout. A nest of children carries the custom of the town. Juvenile companies, they are the fashion. But they cannot match our repertoire . . . we'll stoop to anything if that's your bent. . . .

He regards Ros meaningly but Ros returns the stare blankly.

ROS. They'll grow up.
PLAYER (*giving up*). There's one born every minute. (*To Tragedians:*) On-ward!

The Tragedians start to resume their burdens and their journey. Guil stirs himself at last.

GUIL. Where are you going?
PLAYER. Ha-alt!

They halt and turn.

Home, sir.
GUIL. Where from?
PLAYER. Home. We're travelling people. We take our chances where we find them.
GUIL. It was chance, then?
PLAYER. Chance?
GUIL. You found us.
PLAYER. Oh yes.
GUIL. You were looking?
PLAYER. Oh no.
GUIL. Chance, then.
PLAYER. Or fate.
GUIL. Yours or ours?
PLAYER. It could hardly be one without the other.
GUIL. Fate, then.
PLAYER. Oh, yes. We have no control. Tonight we play to the court. Or the night after. Or to the tavern. Or not.
GUIL. Perhaps I can use my influence.
PLAYER. At the tavern?
GUIL. At the court. I would say I have some influence.
PLAYER. Would you say so?
GUIL. I have influence yet.
PLAYER. Yet what?

Guil seizes the Player violently.

GUIL. I have influence!

The Player does not resist. Guil loosens his hold.

(*More calmly.*) You said something—about getting caught up in the action——
PLAYER (*gaily freeing himself*). I did!—I did!—You're quicker than your friend. . . . (*Confidingly.*) Now for a handful of guilders I happen to have a private and uncut performance of *The Rape of the Sabine Women*—or rather woman, or rather Alfred—(*Over his shoulder.*) Get your skirt on, Alfred——

The Boy starts struggling into a female robe.

. . . and for eight you can participate.

Guil backs, Player follows.

. . . taking either part.

Guil backs.

. . . or both for ten.

Guil tries to turn away, Player holds his sleeve.

. . . with encores——

Guil smashes the Player across the face. The Player recoils. Guil stands trembling.

(*Resigned and quiet.*) Get your skirt off, Alfred. . . .

Alfred struggles out of his half-on robe.

GUIL (*shaking with rage and fright*). It could have been—it didn't have to be *obscene*. . . . It could have been—a bird out of season, dropping bright-feathered on my shoulder. . . . It could have been a tongueless dwarf standing by the road to point the way. . . . I was *pre-pared*. But it's this, is it? No enigma, no dignity, nothing classical, portentous, only this—a comic pornographer and a rabble of prostitutes. . . .
PLAYER (*acknowledging the description with a sweep of his hat, bowing; sadly*). You should have caught us in bet-ter times. We were purists then. (*Straightens up.*) On-ward.

The Players make to leave.

ROS (*his voice has changed: he has caught on*). Excuse me!
PLAYER. Ha-alt!

They halt.

A-al-l-fred!

Alfred resumes the struggle. The Player comes for-ward.

ROS. You're not—ah—exclusively players, then?
PLAYER. We're inclusively players, sir.
ROS. So you give—exhibitions?
PLAYER. Performances, sir.
ROS. Yes, of course. There's more money in that, is there?
PLAYER. There's more trade, sir.
ROS. Times being what they are.
PLAYER. Yes.
ROS. Indifferent.
PLAYER. Completely.
ROS. You know I'd no idea——
PLAYER. No——

ROS. I mean, I've *heard* of—but I've never actually——
PLAYER. No.
ROS. I mean, what exactly do you *do*?
PLAYER. We keep to our usual stuff, more or less, only inside out. We do on stage the things that are supposed to happen off. Which is a kind of integrity, if you look on every exit being an entrance somewhere else.
ROS (*nervy, loud*). Well, I'm not really the type of man who—no, but don't hurry off—sit down and tell us about some of the things people ask you to do——

The Player turns away.

PLAYER. On-ward!
ROS. Just a minute!

They turn and look at him without expression.

Well, all right—I wouldn't mind seing—just an idea of the kind of—(*Bravely.*) What will you do for that? (*And tosses a single coin on the ground between them.*)

The Player spits at the coin, from where he stands.

The Tragedians demur, trying to get at the coin. He kicks and cuffs them back.

On!

Alfred is still half in and out of his robe. The Player cuffs him.

(*To Alfred:*) What are you playing at?

Ros is shamed into fury.

ROS. Filth! Disgusting—I'll report you to the authorities—*perverts!* I know your game all right, it's all filth!

The Players are about to leave. Guil has remained detached.

GUIL (*casually*). Do you like a bet?

The Tragedians turn and look interested. The Player comes forward.

PLAYER. What kind of bet did you have in mind?

Guil walks half the distance towards the Player, stops with his foot over the coin.

GUIL. Double or quits.
PLAYER. Well . . . heads.

Guil raises his foot. The Player bends. The Tragedians crowd round. Relief and congratulations. The Player picks up the coin. Guil throws him a second coin.

GUIL. Again?

Some of the Tragedians are for it, others against.

GUIL. Evens.

The Player nods and tosses the coin.

GUIL. Heads.

It is. He picks it up.

Again.

Guil spins coin.

PLAYER. Heads.

It is. Player picks up coin. He has two coins again. He spins one.

GUIL. Heads.

It is. Guil picks it up. Then tosses it immediately.

PLAYER (*fractional hesitation*). Tails.

But it's heads. Guil picks it up. Player tosses down his last coin by way of paying up, and turns away. Guil doesn't pick it up; he puts his foot on it.

GUIL. Heads.
PLAYER. No!

Pause. The Tragedians are against this.

(*Apologetically.*) They don't like the odds.
GUIL (*lifts his foot, squats; picks up the coin still squatting; looks up*). You were right—heads. (*Spins it, slaps his hand on it, on the floor.*) Heads I win.
PLAYER. No.
GUIL (*uncovers coin*). Right again. (*Repeat.*) Heads I win.
PLAYER. No.
GUIL (*uncovers coin*). And right again. (*Repeat.*) Heads I win.
PLAYER. No!

He turns away, the Tragedians with him. Guil stands up, comes close.

GUIL. Would you believe it? (*Stands back, relaxes, smiles.*) Bet me the year of my birth doubled is an odd number.
PLAYER. *Your* birth——!
GUIL. If you don't trust me don't bet with me.
PLAYER. Would you trust *me*?
GUIL. *Bet* me then.
PLAYER. My birth?
GUIL. Odd numbers you win.
PLAYER. You're on——

The Tragedians have come forward, wide awake.

GUIL. Good. Year of your birth. Double it. Even numbers I win, odd numbers I lose.

Silence. An awful sigh as the Tragedians realize that any number doubled is even. Then a terrible row as they object. Then a terrible silence.

PLAYER. We have no money.

Guil turns to him.

GUIL. Ah. Then what *have* you got?

The Player silently brings Alfred forward. Guil regards Alfred sadly.

Was it for this?

PLAYER. It's the best we've got.

GUIL (*looking up and around*). Then the times are bad indeed.

The Player starts to speak, protestation, but Guil turns on him viciously.

The very *air* stinks.

The Player moves back. Guil moves down to the footlights and turns.

Come here, Alfred.

Alfred moves down and stands, frightened and small.

(*Gently.*) Do you lose often?

ALFRED. Yes, sir.

GUIL. Then what could you have left to lose?

ALFRED. Nothing, sir.

Pause. Guil regards him.

GUIL. Do you like being . . . an actor?

ALFRED. No, sir.

Guil looks around, at the audience.

GUIL. You and I, Alfred—we could create a dramatic precedent here.

And Alfred, who has been near tears, starts to sniffle.

Come, come, Alfred, this is no way to fill the theatres of Europe.

The Player has moved down, to remonstrate with Alfred. Guil cuts him off again.

(*Viciously.*) Do you know any good plays?

PLAYER. Plays?

ROS (*coming forward, faltering shyly*). Exhibitions. . . .

GUIL. I thought you said you were actors.

PLAYER (*dawning*). Oh. Oh well, we *are*. We are. But there hasn't been much call——

GUIL. You lost. Well then—one of the Greeks, perhaps? You're familiar with the tragedies of antiquity, are you? The great homicidal classics? Matri, patri, fratri, sorrori, uxori and it goes without saying——

ROS. Saucy——

GUIL. —Suicidal—hm? Maidens aspiring to godheads——

ROS. And vice versa——

GUIL. Your kind of thing, is it?

PLAYER. Well, no, I can't say it is, really. We're more of the blood, love and rhetoric school.

GUIL. Well, I'll leave the choice to you, if there is anything to choose between them.

PLAYER. They're hardly divisible, sir—well, I can do you blood and love without the rhetoric, and I can do you blood and rhetoric without the love, and I can do you all three concurrent or consecutive, but I can't do you love and rhetoric without the blood. Blood is compulsory—they're all blood, you see.

GUIL. Is that what people want?

PLAYER. It's what we do. (*Small pause. He turns away.*)

Guil touches Alfred on the shoulder.

GUIL (*wry, gentle*). Thank you; we'll let you know.

The Player has moved upstage. Alfred follows.

PLAYER (*to Tragedians*). Thirty-eight!

ROS (*moving across, fascinated and hopeful*). Position?

PLAYER. Sir?

ROS. One of your—tableaux?

PLAYER. No, sir.

ROS. Oh.

PLAYER (*to the Tragedians, now departing with their cart, already taking various props off it*). Entrances there and there (*indicating upstage*).

The Player has not moved his position for his last four lines. He does not move now. Guil waits.

GUIL. Well . . . aren't you going to change into your costume?

PLAYER. I never change out of it, sir.

GUIL. Always in character.

PLAYER. That's it.

Pause.

GUIL. Aren't you going to—come on?

PLAYER. I *am* on.

GUIL. But if you *are* on, you can't *come* on. Can you?

PLAYER. I *start* on.

515

GUIL. But it hasn't *started*. Go on. We'll look out for you.

PLAYER. I'll give you a wave.

> *He does not move. His immobility is now pointed, and getting awkward. Pause. Ros walks up to him till they are face to face.*

ROS. Excuse me.

> *Pause. The Player lifts his downstage foot. It was covering Guil's coin. Ros puts his foot on the coin. Smiles.*

Thank you.

> *The Player turns and goes. Ros has bent for the coin.*

GUIL (*moving out*). Come on.

ROS. I say—that was slucky.

GUIL (*turning*). What?

ROS. It was tails.

> *He tosses the coin to Guil who catches it. Simultaneously—a lighting change sufficient to alter the exterior mood into interior, but nothing violent.*

> *And Ophelia runs on in some alarm, holding up her skirts—followed by Hamlet.*

> *Ophelia has been sewing and she holds the garment. They are both mute. Hamlet, with his doublet all unbraced, no hat upon his head, his stockings fouled, ungartered and downgyved to his ankle, pale as his shirt, his knees knocking each other . . . and with a look so piteous, he takes her by the wrist and holds her hard, then he goes to the length of his arm, and with his other hand over his brow, falls to such perusal of her face as he would draw it. . . . At last, with a little shaking of his arm, and thrice his head waving up and down, he raises a sign so piteous and profound that it does seem to shatter all his bulk and end his being. That done he lets her go, and with his head over his shoulder turned, he goes out backwards without taking his eyes off her . . . she runs off in the opposite direction.*

> *Ros and Guil have frozen. Guil unfreezes first. He jumps at Ros.*

GUIL. Come on!

> *But a flourish—enter Claudius and Gertrude, attended.*

CLAUDIUS. Welcome, dear Rosencrantz . . . (*he raises a hand at Guil while Ros bows—Guil bows late and hurriedly*) . . . and Guildenstern.

> *He raises a hand at Ros while Guil bows to him—Ros is still straightening up from his previous bow and halfway up he bows down again. With his head down, he twists to look at Guil, who is on the way up.*

Moreover that we did much long to see you,
The need we have to use you did provoke
Our hasty sending.

> *Ros and Guil still adjusting their clothing for Claudius's presence.*

Something have you heard
Of Hamlet's transformation, so call it,
Sith nor th'exterior nor the inward man
Resembles that it was. What it should be,
More than his father's death, that thus hath put him,
So much from th'undersanding of himself,
I cannot dream of. I entreat you both
That, being of so young days brought up with him
And sith so neighboured to his youth and haviour
That you vouchsafe your rest here in our court
Some little time, so by your companies
To draw him on to pleasures, and to gather
So much as from occasion you may glean,
Whether aught to us unknown afflicts him thus,
That opened lies within our remedy.

GERTRUDE. Good (*fractional suspense*) gentlemen . . .

> *They both bow.*

He hath much talked of you,
And sure I am, two men there is not living
To whom he more adheres. If it will please you
To show us so much gentry and goodwill
As to expand your time with us awhile
For the supply and profit of our hope,
Your visitation shall receive such thanks
As fits a king's remembrance.

ROS. Both your majesties
Might, by the sovereign power you have of us,
Put your dread pleasures more into command
Than to entreaty.

GUIL. But we both obey,
And here give up ourselves in the full bent
To lay our service freely at your feet,
To be commanded.

CLAUDIUS. Thanks, Rosencrantz (*turning to Ros who is caught unprepared, while Guil bows*) and gentle Guildenstern (*turning to Guil who is bent double*).

GERTRUDE (*correcting*). Thanks Guildenstern (*turning to Ros, who bows as Guil checks upward movement to bow too—both bent double, squinting at each other*) . . . and

gentle Rosencrantz (*turning to Guil, both straightening up—Guil checks again and bows again*).
And I beseech you instantly to visit
My too much changed son. Go, some of you,
And bring these gentlemen where Hamlet is.

Two Attendants exit backwards, indicating that Ros and Guil should follow.

GUIL. Heaven make our presence and our practices
    Pleasant and helpful to him.
GERTRUDE. Ay, amen!

Ros and Guil move towards a downstage wing. Before they get there, Polonius enters. They stop and bow to him. He nods and hurries upstage to Claudius. They turn to look at him.

POLONIUS. The ambassadors from Norway, my good lord,
    are joyfully returned.
CLAUDIUS. Thou still hast been the father of good news.
POLONIUS. Have I, my lord? Assure you, my good liege,
    I hold my duty as I hold my soul,
    Both to my God and to my gracious King;
    And I do think, or else this brain of mine
    Hunts not the trail of policy so sure
    As it hath used to do, that I have found
    The very cause of Hamlet's lunacy. . . .

Exeunt—leaving Ros and Guil.

ROS. I want to go home.
GUIL. Don't let them confuse you.
ROS. I'm out of my step here——
GUIL. We'll soon be home and high—dry and home—
    I'll——
ROS. It's all over my *depth*——
GUIL. —I'll hie you home and——
ROS. —out of my head——
GUIL. —dry you high and——
ROS (*cracking, high*). —over my step over my head body!—I tell you it's all stopping to a death, it's boding to a depth, stepping to a head, it's all heading to a dead stop——
GUIL (*the nursemaid*). There! . . . and we'll soon be home and dry . . . and *high* and dry. . . . (*Rapidly.*) Has it ever happened to you that all of a sudden and for no reason at all you haven't the faintest idea how to spell the word—"wife"—or "house"—because when you write it down you just can't remember ever having seen those letters in that order before . . . ?
ROS. I remember——
GUIL. Yes?
ROS. I remember when there were no questions.

GUIL. There were always questions. To exchange one set for another is no great matter.
ROS. Answers, yes. There were answers to everything.
GUIL. You've forgotten.
ROS (*flaring*). I haven't forgotten—how I used to remember my own name—and yours, oh *yes*! There were answers everywhere you *looked*. There was no question about it—people knew who I was and if they didn't they asked and I told them.
GUIL. You did, the trouble is, each of them is . . . plausible, without being instinctive. All your life you live so close to truth, it becomes a permanent blur in the corner of your eye, and when something nudges it into outline it is like being ambushed by a grotesque. A man standing in his saddle in the half-lit half-alive dawn banged on the shutters and called two names. He was just a hat and a cloak levitating in the grey plume of his own breath, but when he called we came. That much is certain—we came.
ROS. Well I can tell you I'm sick to death of it. I don't care one way or another, so why don't you make up your mind.
GUIL. We can't afford anything quite so arbitrary. Nor did we come all this way for a christening. All *that*—preceded us. But we are comparatively fortunate; we might have been left to sift the whole field of human nomenclature, like two blind men looting a bazaar for their own portraits. . . . At least we are presented with alternatives.
ROS. Well as from now——
GUIL. —But not choice.
ROS. You made me look ridiculous in there.
GUIL. I looked just as ridiculous as you did.
ROS (*an anguished cry*). Consistency is all I ask!
GUIL (*low, wry rhetoric*). Give us this day our daily mask.
ROS (*a dying fall*). I want to go home. (*Moves.*) Which way did we come in? I've lost my sense of direction.
GUIL. The only beginning is birth and the only end is death—if you can't count on that, what can you count on?

They connect again.

ROS. We don't owe anything to anyone.
GUIL. We've been caught up. Your smallest action sets off another somewhere else, and is set off by it. Keep an eye open, an ear cocked. Tread warily, follow instructions. We'll be all right.
ROS. For how long?
GUIL. Till events have played themselves out. There's a logic at work—it's all done for you, don't worry. Enjoy it. Relax. To be taken in hand and led, like

being a child again, even without the innocence, a child—it's like being given a prize, an extra slice of childhood when you least expect it, as a prize for being good, or compensation for never having had one. . . . Do I contradict myself?

Ros. I can't remember . . . . What have we got to go on?

Guil. We have been briefed. Hamlet's transformation. What do you recollect?

Ros. Well, he's changed, hasn't he? The exterior and inward man fails to resemble——

Guil. Draw him on to pleasures—glean what afflicts him.

Ros. Something more than his father's death——

Guil. He's always talking about us—there aren't two people living whom he dotes on more than us.

Ros. We cheer him up—find out what's the matter——

Guil. Exactly, it's a matter of asking the right questions and giving away as little as we can. It's a game.

Ros. And then we can go?

Guil. And receive such thanks as fits a king's remembrance.

Ros. I like the sound of that. What do you think he means by remembrance?

Guil. He doesn't forget his friends.

Ros. Would you care to estimate?

Guil. Difficult to say, really—some kings tend to be amnesiac, others I suppose—the opposite, whatever that is. . . .

Ros. Yes—but——

Guil. Elephantine . . . ?

Ros. Not how long—how much?

Guil. *Retentive*—he's a very retentive king, a royal retainer. . . .

Ros. What are you playing at?

Guil. Words, words. They're all we have to go on.

Pause.

Ros. Shouldn't we be doing something—constructive?

Guil. What did you have in mind? . . . A short, blunt human pyramid . . . ?

Ros. We could go.

Guil. Where?

Ros. After him.

Guil. Why? They've got us placed now—if we start moving around, we'll all be chasing each other all night.

Hiatus.

Ros (*at footlights*). How very intriguing! (*Turns.*) I feel like a spectator—an appalling business. The only thing that makes it bearable is the irrational belief that somebody interesting will come on in a minute. . . .

Guil. See anyone?

Ros. No. You?

Guil. No. (*At footlights.*) What a fine persecution—to be kept intrigued without ever quite being enlightened. . . . (*Pause.*) We've had no practice.

Ros. We could play at questions.

Guil. What good would that do?

Ros. Practice!

Guil. Statement! One—love.

Ros. Cheating!

Guil. How?

Ros. I hadn't started yet.

Guil. Statement. Two—love.

Ros. Are you counting that?

Guil. What?

Ros. Are you counting that?

Guil. Foul! No repetitions. Three—love. First game to . . .

Ros. I'm not going to play if you're going to be like that.

Guil. Whose serve?

Ros. Hah?

Guil. Foul! No grunts. Love—one.

Ros. Whose go?

Guil. Why?

Ros. Why not?

Guil. What for?

Ros. Foul! No synonyms! One—all.

Guil. What in God's name is going on?

Ros. Foul! No rhetoric. Two—one.

Guil. What does it all add up to?

Ros. Can't you guess?

Guil. Were you addressing me?

Ros. Is there anyone else?

Guil. Who?

Ros. How would I know?

Guil. Why do you ask?

Ros. Are you serious?

Guil. Was that rhetoric?

Ros. No.

Guil. Statement! Two—all. Game point.

Ros. What's the matter with you today?

Guil. When?

Ros. What?

Guil. Are you deaf?

Ros. Am I dead?

Guil. Yes or no?

Ros. Is there a choice?

Guil. Is there a God?

Ros. Foul! No *non sequiturs*, three—two, one game all.

Guil (*seriously*). What's your name?

Ros. What's yours?

Guil. I asked you first.

Ros. Statement. One—love.

GUIL. What's your name when you're at home?

ROS. What's yours?

GUIL. When I'm at home?

ROS. Is it different at home?

GUIL. What home?

ROS. Haven't you got one?

GUIL. Why do you ask?

ROS. What are you driving at?

GUIL (*with emphasis*). What's your name?!

ROS. Repetition. Two—love. Match point to me.

GUIL (*seizing him violently*). WHO DO YOU THINK YOU ARE?

ROS. Rhetoric! Game and match! (*Pause.*) Where's it going to end?

GUIL. That's the question.

ROS. It's *all* questions.

GUIL. Do you think it matters?

ROS. Doesn't it matter to you?

GUIL. Why should it matter?

ROS. What does it matter why?

GUIL (*teasing gently*). Doesn't it *matter* why it matters?

ROS (*rounding on him*). What's the *matter* with you?

Pause.

GUIL. It doesn't matter.

ROS (*voice in the wilderness*). . . . What's the game?

GUIL. What are the rules?

Enter Hamlet behind, crossing the stage, reading a book—as he is about to disappear Guil notices him.

GUIL (*sharply*). Rosencrantz!

ROS (*jumps*). What!

Hamlet goes. Triumph dawns on them, they smile.

GUIL. There! How was that?

ROS. Clever!

GUIL. Natural?

ROS. Instinctive.

GUIL. Got it in your head?

ROS. I take my hat off to you.

GUIL. Shake hands.

They do.

ROS. Now I'll try you—Guil——!

GUIL. —Not yet—catch me unawares.

ROS. Right.

They separate. Pause. Aside to Guil.

Ready?

GUIL (*explodes*). Don't be stupid.

ROS. Sorry.

Pause.

GUIL (*snaps*). Guildenstern!

ROS (*jumps*). What?

He is immediately crestfallen. Guil is disgusted.

GUIL. Consistency is all I ask!

ROS (*quietly*). Immortality is all I seek. . . .

GUIL (*dying fall*). Give us this day our daily week. . . .

Beat.

ROS. Who was that?

GUIL. Didn't you know him?

ROS. He didn't know me.

GUIL. He didn't see you.

ROS. I didn't see him.

GUIL. We shall see. I *hardly* knew him, he's changed.

ROS. You could see that?

GUIL. Transformed.

ROS. How do you know?

GUIL. Inside and out.

ROS. I see.

GUIL. He's not himself.

ROS. He's changed.

GUIL. I could see that.

Beat.

Glean what afflicts him.

ROS. Me?

GUIL. Him.

ROS. How?

GUIL. Question and answer. Old ways are the best ways.

ROS. He's afflicted.

GUIL. You question, I'll answer.

ROS. He's not himself, you know.

GUIL. I'm him, you see.

Beat.

ROS. Who am I then?

GUIL. You're yourself.

ROS. And he's you?

GUIL. Not a bit of it.

ROS. Are you afflicted?

GUIL. That's the idea. Are you ready?

ROS. Let's go back a bit.

GUIL. I'm afflicted.

ROS. I see.

GUIL. Glean what afflicts me.

ROS. Right.

GUIL. Question and answer.

ROS. How should I begin?

GUIL. Address me.

Ros. My dear Guildenstern!

Guil (*quietly*). You've forgotten—haven't you?

Ros. My dear Rosencrantz!

Guil (*great control*). I don't think you quite understand. What we are attempting is a hypothesis in which *I* answer for *him*, while *you* ask me questions.

Ros. Ah! Ready?

Guil. You know what to do?

Ros. What?

Guil. Are you stupid?

Ros. Pardon?

Guil. Are you deaf?

Ros. Did you speak?

Guil (*admonishing*). Not now——

Ros. Statement.

Guil (*shouts*). Not now! (*Pause.*) If I had any doubts, or rather hopes, they are dispelled. What could we possibly have in common except our situation? (*They separate and sit.*) Perhaps he'll come back this way.

Ros. Should we go?

Guil. Why?

Pause.

Ros (*starts up. Snaps fingers*). Oh! You mean—you pretend to be *him*, and *I* ask you questions!

Guil (*dry*). Very good.

Ros. You had me confused.

Guil. I could see I had.

Ros. How should I begin?

Guil. Address me.

They stand and face each other, posing.

Ros. My honoured Lord!

Guil. My dear Rosencrantz!

Pause.

Ros. Am I pretending to be you, then?

Guil. Certainly not. If you like. Shall we continue?

Ros. Question and answer.

Guil. Right.

Ros. Right. My honoured lord!

Guil. My dear fellow!

Ros. How are you?

Guil. Afflicted!

Ros. Really? In what way?

Guil. Transformed.

Ros. Inside or out?

Guil. Both.

Ros. I see. (*Pause.*) Not much new there.

Guil. Go into details. *Delve.* Probe the background, establish the situation.

Ros. So—so your uncle is the king of Denmark?!

Guil. And my father before him.

Ros. His father before him?

Guil. No, my father before him.

Ros. But surely——

Guil. You might well ask.

Ros. Let me get it straight. Your father was king. You were his only son. Your father dies. You are of age. Your uncle becomes king.

Guil. Yes.

Ros. Unorthodox.

Guil. Undid me.

Ros. Undeniable. Where were you?

Guil. In Germany.

Ros. Usurpation, then.

Guil. He slipped in.

Ros. Which reminds me.

Guil. Well, it would.

Ros. I don't want to be personal.

Guil. It's common knowledge.

Ros. Your mother's marriage.

Guil. He slipped in.

Beat.

Ros (*lugubriously*). His body was still warm.

Guil. So was hers.

Ros. Extraordinary.

Guil. Indecent.

Ros. Hasty.

Guil. Suspicious.

Ros. It makes you think.

Guil. Don't think I haven't thought of it.

Ros. And with her husband's brother.

Guil. They were close.

Ros. She went to him——

Guil. —Too close——

Ros. —for comfort.

Guil. It looks bad.

Ros. It adds up.

Guil. Incest to adultery.

Ros. Would you go so far?

Guil. Never.

Ros. To sum up: your father, whom you love, dies, you are his heir, you come back to find that hardly was the corpse cold before his young brother popped onto his throne and into his sheets, thereby offending both legal and natural practice. Now why exactly are you behaving in this extraordinary manner?

Guil. I can't imagine! (*Pause.*) But all that is well known, common property. Yet he sent for us. And we did come.

Ros (*alert, ear cocked*). I say! I heard music——
Guil. We're here.
Ros. —Like a band—I thought I heard a band.
Guil. Rosencrantz . . .
Ros (*absently, still listening*). What?

> *Pause, short.*

Guil (*gently wry*). Guildenstern . . .
Ros (*irritated by the repetition*). What?
Guil. Don't you discriminate at all?
Ros (*turning dumbly*). What?

> *Pause.*

Guil. Go and see if he's there.
Ros. Who?
Guil. There.

> *Ros goes to an upstage wing, looks, returns, formally making his report.*

Ros. Yes.
Guil. What is he doing?

> *Ros repeats movement.*

Ros. Talking.
Guil. To himself?

> *Ros starts to move. Guil cuts in impatiently.*

Is he alone?
Ros. No.
Guil. Then he's not talking to himself, is he?
Ros. Not *by* himself. . . . Coming this way, I think. (*Shiftily.*) Should we go?
Guil. Why? We're marked now.

> *Hamlet enters, backwards, talking, followed by Polonius, upstage. Ros and Guil occupy the two downstage corners looking upstage.*

Hamlet. . . . for you yourself, sir, should be as old as I am if like a crab you could go backward.
Polonius (*aside*). Though this be madness, yet there is method in it. Will you walk out of the air, my lord?
Hamlet. Into my grave.
Polonius. Indeed, that's out of the air.

> *Hamlet crosses to upstage exit, Polonius asiding unintelligibly until——*

My lord, I will take my leave of you.
Hamlet. You cannot take from me anything that I will more willingly part withal—except my life, except my life, except my life. . . .
Polonius (*crossing downstage*). Fare you well, my lord. (*To Ros:*) You go to seek Lord Hamlet? There he is.

Ros (*to Polonius*). God save you sir.

> *Polonius goes.*

Guil (*calls upstage to Hamlet*). My honoured Lord!
Ros. My most dear lord!

> *Hamlet centred upstage, turns to them.*

Hamlet. My excellent good friends! How dost thou Guildenstern? (*Coming downstage with an arm raised to Ros, Guil meanwhile bowing to no greeting. Hamlet corrects himself. Still to Ros:*) Ah Rosencrantz!

> *They laugh good-naturedly at the mistake. They all meet midstage, turn upstage to walk, Hamlet in the middle, arm over each shoulder.*

Hamlet. Good lads how do you both?

> *Blackout*

ACT II

> *Hamlet, Ros and Guil talking, the continuation of the previous scene. Their conversation, on the move, is indecipherable at first. The first intelligible line is Hamlet's, coming at the end of a short speech—see Shakespeare Act II, scene ii.*

Hamlet. S'blood, there is something in this more than natural, if philosophy could find it out.

> *A flourish from the Tragedians' band.*

Guil. There are the players.
Hamlet. Gentlemen, you are welcome to Elsinore. Your hands, come then. (*He takes their hands.*) The appurtenance of welcome is fashion and ceremony. Let me comply with you in this garb, lest my extent to the players (which I tell you must show fairly outwards) should more appear like entertainment than yours. You are welcome. (*About to leave.*) But my uncle-father and aunt-mother are deceived.
Guil. In what, my dear lord?
Hamlet. I am but mad north north-west; when the wind is southerly I know a hawk from a handsaw.

> *Polonius enters as Guil turns away.*

Polonius. Well be with you gentlemen.
Hamlet (*to Ros*). Mark you, Guildenstern (*uncertainly to Guil*) and you too; at each ear a hearer. That great baby you see there is not yet out of his swaddling clouts. . . . (*He takes Ros upstage with him, talking together.*)

POLONIUS. My Lord! I have news to tell you.

HAMLET (*releasing Ros and mimicking*). My Lord, I have news to tell you. . . . When Roscius was an actor in Rome . . .

Ros comes downstage to rejoin Guil.

POLONIUS (*as he follows Hamlet out*). The actors are come hither my lord.

HAMLET. Buzz, buzz.

Exeunt Hamlet and Polonius.

Ros and Guil ponder. Each reluctant to speak first.

GUIL. Hm?

ROS. Yes?

GUIL. What?

ROS. I thought you . . .

GUIL. No.

ROS. Ah.

Pause.

GUIL. I think we can say we made some headway.

ROS. You think so?

GUIL. I think we can say that.

ROS. I think we can say he made us look ridiculous.

GUIL. We played it close to the chest of course.

ROS (*derisively*). "Question and answer. Old ways are the best ways"! He was scoring off us all down the line.

GUIL. He caught us on the wrong foot once or twice, perhaps, but I thought we gained some ground.

ROS (*simply*). He murdered us.

GUIL. He might have had the edge.

ROS (*roused*). Twenty-seven—three, and you think he might have had the edge?! He *murdered* us.

GUIL. He had six rhetoricals——

ROS. It was question and answer, all right. Twenty-seven questions he got out in ten minutes, and answered three. I was waiting for you to *delve*. "When is he going to start *delving?*" I asked myself.

GUIL. —And two repetitions.

ROS. Hardly a leading question between us.

GUIL. We got his *symptoms*, didn't we?

ROS. Half of what he said meant something else, and the other half didn't mean anything at all.

GUIL. Thwarted ambition—a sense of grievance, that's my diagnosis.

ROS. Six rhetorical and two repetition, leaving nineteen, of which we answered fifteen. And what did we get in return? He's depressed! . . . Denmark's a prison and he'd rather live in a nutshell; some shadow-play about the nature of ambition, which never got down

to cases, and finally one direct question which might have led somewhere, and led in face to his illuminating claim to tell a hawk from a handsaw.

Pause.

GUIL. When the wind is southerly.

ROS. And the weather's clear.

GUIL. And when it isn't he can't.

ROS. He's at the mercy of the elements. (*Licks his finger and holds it up—facing audience.*) Is that southerly?

They stare at audience.

GUIL. It doesn't *look* southerly. What made you think so?

ROS. I didn't *say* I think so. It could be northerly for all I know.

GUIL. I wouldn't have thought so.

ROS. Well, if you're going to be dogmatic.

GUIL. Wait a minute—we came from roughly south according to a rough map.

ROS. I see. Well, which way did we come in? (*Guil looks round vaguely.*) Roughly.

GUIL (*clears his throat*). In the morning the sun would be easterly. I think we can assume that.

ROS. That it's morning?

GUIL. If it is, and the sun is over *there* (*his right as he faces the audience*) for instance, *that* (*front*) would be northerly. On the other hand, if it is not morning and the sun is over *there* (*his left*) . . . *that* . . . (*lamely*) would *still* be northerly. (*Picking up.*) To put it another way, if we came from down there (*front*) and it is morning, the sun would be up there (*his left*), and if it is actually over there (*his right*) and it's still morning, we must have come from up *there* (*behind him*), and if *that* is southerly (*his left*) and the sun is really over *there* (*front*), then it's the afternoon. However, if none of these is the case——

ROS. Why don't you go and have a look?

GUIL. Pragmatism?!—is that all you have to offer? You seem to have no conception of where we stand! You won't find the answer written down for you in the bowl of a compass—I can tell you that. (*Pause.*) Besides, you can never tell this far north—it's probably dark out there.

ROS. I merely suggest that the position of the sun, if it is out, would give you a rough idea of the time; alternatively, the clock, if it is going, would give you a rough idea of the position of the sun. I forget which you're trying to establish.

GUIL. I'm trying to establish the direction of the wind.

ROS. There isn't any wind. *Draught*, yes.

GUIL. In that case, the origin. Trace it to its source and it might give us a rough idea of the way we came in—which might give us a rough idea of south, for further reference.

ROS. It's coming up through the floor. (*He studies the floor.*) That can't be south, can it?

GUIL. That's not a direction. Lick your toe and wave it around a bit.

Ros considers the distance of his foot.

ROS. No, I think you'd have to lick it for me.

Pause.

GUIL. I'm prepared to let the whole matter drop.

ROS. Or I could lick yours, of course.

GUIL. No thank you.

ROS. I'll even wave it around for you.

GUIL (*down Ros's throat*). What in God's name is the matter with you?

ROS. Just being friendly.

GUIL (*retiring*). Somebody might come in. It's what we're counting on, after all. Ultimately.

Good pause.

ROS. Perhaps they've all trampled each other to death in the rush. . . . Give them a shout. Something provocative. *Intrigue* them.

GUIL. Wheels have been set in motion, and they have their own pace, to which we are . . . condemned. Each move is dictated by the previous one—that is the meaning of order. If we start being arbitrary it'll just be a shambles: at least, let us hope so. Because if we happened, just happened to discover, or even suspect, that our spontaneity was part of their order, we'd know that we were lost. (*He sits.*) A Chinaman of the T'ang Dynasty—and, by which definition, a philosopher—dreamed he was a butterfly, and from that moment he was never quite sure that he was not a butterfly dreaming it was a Chinese philosopher. Envy him; in his two-fold security.

A good pause. Ros leaps up and bellows at the audience.

ROS. Fire!

Guil jumps up.

GUIL. Where?

ROS. It's all right—I'm demonstrating the misuse of free speech. To prove that it exists. (*He regards the audience, that is the direction, with contempt—and other directions, then front again.*) Not a move. They should

burn to death in their shoes. (*He takes out one of his coins. Spins it. Catches it. Looks at it. Replaces it.*)

GUIL. What was it?

ROS. What?

GUIL. Heads or tails?

ROS. Oh. I didn't look.

GUIL. Yes you did.

ROS. Oh, did I? (*He takes out a coin, studies it.*) Quite right—it rings a bell.

GUIL. What's the last thing you remember?

ROS. I don't wish to be reminded of it.

GUIL. We cross our bridges when we come to them and burn them behind us, with nothing to show for our progress except a memory of the smell of smoke, and a presumption that once our eyes watered.

Ros approaches him brightly, holding a coin between finger and thumb. He covers it with his other hand, draws his fists apart and holds them for Guil. Guil considers them. Indicates the left hand, Ros opens it to show it empty.

ROS. No.

Repeat process. Guil indicates left hand again. Ros shows it empty.

Double bluff!

Repeat process—Guil taps one hand, then the other hand, quickly. Ros inadvertently shows that both are empty. Ros laughs as Guil turns upstage. Ros stops laughing, looks around his feet, pats his clothes, puzzled.

Polonius breaks that up by entering upstage followed by the Tragedians and Hamlet.

POLONIUS (*entering*). Come sirs.

HAMLET. Follow him, friends. We'll hear a play tomorrow. (*Aside to the Player, who is the last of the Tragedians:*) Dost thou hear me, old friend? Can you play *The Murder of Gonzago?*

PLAYER. Ay, my lord.

HAMLET. We'll ha't tomorrow night. You could for a need study a speech of some dozen or sixteen lines which I would set down and insert in't, could you not?

PLAYER. Ay, my lord.

HAMLET. Very well. Follow that lord, and look you mock him not.

The Player crossing downstage, notes Ros and Guil. Stops. Hamlet crossing downstage addresses them without pause.

HAMLET. My good friends, I'll leave you till tonight. You are welcome to Elsinore.

ROS. Good, my lord.

Hamlet goes.

GUIL. So you've caught up.

PLAYER (*coldly*). Not yet, sir.

GUIL. Now mind your tongue, or we'll have it out and throw the rest of you away, like a nightingale at a Roman feast.

ROS. Took the very words out of my mouth.

GUIL. You'd be *lost* for words.

ROS. You'd be tongue-tied.

GUIL. Like a mute in a monologue.

ROS. Like a nightingale at a Roman feast.

GUIL. Your diction will go to pieces.

ROS. Your lines will be cut.

GUIL. To dumbshows.

ROS. And dramatic pauses.

GUIL. You'll never *find* your tongue.

ROS. Lick your lips.

GUIL. Taste your tears.

ROS. Your breakfast.

GUIL. You won't know the difference.

ROS. There won't be any.

GUIL. We'll take the very words out of your mouth.

ROS. So you've caught on.

GUIL. So you've caught up.

PLAYER (*tops*). Not yet! (*Bitterly.*) You left us.

GUIL. Ah! I'd forgotten—you performed a dramatic spectacle on the way. Yes, I'm sorry we had to miss it.

PLAYER (*bursts out*). We can't look each other in the face! (*Pause, more in control.*) You don't understand the humiliation of it—to be tricked out of the single assumption which makes our existence viable—that somebody is *watching*. . . . The plot was two corpses gone before we caught sight of ourselves, stripped naked in the middle of nowhere and pouring ourselves down a bottomless well.

ROS. Is *that* thirty-eight?

PLAYER (*lost*). There we were—demented children mincing about in clothes that no one ever wore, speaking as no man ever spoke, swearing love in wigs and rhymed couplets, killing each other with wooden swords, hollow protestations of faith hurled after empty promises of vengeance—and every gesture, every pose, vanishing into the thin unpopulated air. We ransomed our dignity to the clouds, and the uncomprehending birds listened. (*He rounds on them.*) Don't you see?! We're *actors*—we're the opposite of people! (*They recoil nonplussed, his voice calms.*)

Think, in your head, *now*, think of the most . . . *private* . . . *secret* . . . *intimate* thing you have ever done secure in the knowledge of its privacy. . . . (*He gives them—and the audience—a good pause. Ros takes on a shifty look.*) Are you thinking of it? (*He strikes with his voice and his head.*) Well, I saw you do it!

Ros leaps up, dissembling madly.

ROS. You never! It's a lie! (*He catches himself with a giggle in a vacuum and sits down again.*)

PLAYER. We're actors. . . . We pledged our identities, secure in the conventions of our trade, that someone would be watching. And then, gradually, no one was. We were caught, high and dry. It was not until the murderer's long soliloquy that we were able to look around; frozen as we were in profile, our eyes searched you out, first confidently, then hesitantly, then desperately as each patch of turf, each log, every exposed corner in every direction proved uninhabited, and all the while the murderous King addressed the horizon with his dreary interminable guilt. . . . Our heads began to move, wary as lizards, the corpse of unsullied Rosalinda peeped through his fingers, and the King faltered. Even then, habit and a stubborn trust that our audience spied upon us from behind the nearest bush, forced our bodies to blunder on long after they had emptied of meaning, until like runaway carts they dragged to a halt. No one came forward. No one shouted at us. The silence was unbreakable, it imposed itself upon us; it was obscene. We took off our crowns and swords and cloth of gold and moved silent on the road to Elsinore.

Silence. Then Guil claps solo with slow measured irony.

GUIL. Brilliantly re-created—if these eyes could weep! . . . Rather strong on metaphor, mind you. No criticism—only a matter of taste. And so here you are—with a vengeance. That's a figure of speech . . . isn't it? Well let's say we've made up for it, for you may have no doubt whom to thank for your performance at the court.

ROS. We are counting on you to take him out of himself. You are the pleasures which we draw him on to—(*he escapes a fractional giggle but recovers immediately*) and by that I don't mean your usual filth; you can't treat royalty like people with normal perverted desires. They know nothing of that and you know nothing of them, to your mutual survival. So give him a good clean show suitable for all the family, or you can rest assured you'll be playing the tavern tonight.

GUIL. Or the night after.

ROS. Or not.

PLAYER. We already have an entry here. And always have had.

GUIL. You've played for him before?

PLAYER. Yes, sir.

ROS. And what's *his* bent?

PLAYER. Classsical.

ROS. Saucy!

GUIL. What will you play?

PLAYER. *The Murder of Gonzago.*

GUIL. Full of fine cadence and corpses.

PLAYER. Pirated from the Italian. . . .

ROS. What is it about?

PLAYER. It's about a King and Queen. . . .

GUIL. Escapism! What else?

PLAYER. Blood——

GUIL. —Love and rhetoric.

PLAYER. Yes. (*Going.*)

GUIL. Where are you going?

PLAYER. I can come and go as I please.

GUIL. You're evidently a man who knows his way around.

PLAYER. I've been here before.

GUIL. We're still finding our feet.

PLAYER. I should concentrate on not losing your heads.

GUIL. Do you speak from knowledge?

PLAYER. Precedent.

GUIL. You've been here before.

PLAYER. And I know which way the wind is blowing.

GUIL. Operating on two levels, are we?! How clever! I expect it comes naturally to you, being in the business so to speak.

The Player's grave face does not change. He makes to move off again. Guil for the second time cuts him off.

The truth is, we value your company, for want of any other. We have been left so much to our own devices—after a while one welcomes the uncertainty of being left to other people's.

PLAYER. Uncertainty is the normal state. You're nobody special.

He makes to leave again. Guil loses his cool.

GUIL. But for God's sake what are we supposed to *do*?!

PLAYER. Relax. Respond. That's what people do. You can't go through life questioning your situation at every turn.

GUIL. But we don't know what's going on, or what to do with ourselves. We don't know how to *act*.

PLAYER. Act natural. You know why you're here at least.

GUIL. We only know what we're told, and that's little enough. And for all we know it isn't even true.

PLAYER. For all anyone knows, nothing is. Everything has to be taken on trust; truth is only that which is taken to be true. It's the currency of living. There may be nothing behind it, but it doesn't make any difference so long as it is honoured. One acts on assumptions. What do you assume?

ROS. Hamlet is not himself, outside or in. We have to glean what afflicts him.

GUIL. He doesn't give much away.

PLAYER. Who does, nowadays?

GUIL. He's—melancholy.

PLAYER. Melancholy?

ROS. Mad.

PLAYER. How is he mad?

ROS. Ah. (*To Guil:*) How is he mad?

GUIL. More morose than mad, perhaps.

PLAYER. Melancholy.

GUIL. Moody.

ROS. He has moods.

PLAYER. Of moroseness?

GUIL. Madness. And yet.

ROS. Quite.

GUIL. For instance.

ROS. He talks to himself, which might be madness.

GUIL. If he didn't talk sense, which he does.

ROS. Which suggests the opposite.

PLAYER. Of what?

Small pause.

GUIL. I think I have it. A man talking sense to himself is no madder than a man talking nonsense not to himself.

ROS. Or just as mad.

GUIL. Or just as mad.

ROS. And he does both.

GUIL. So there you are.

ROS. Stark raving sane.

Pause.

PLAYER. Why?

GUIL. Ah. (*To Ros:*) Why?

ROS. Exactly.

GUIL. Exactly what?

ROS. Exactly why.

GUIL. Exactly why *what*?

ROS. What?

GUIL. *Why?*

ROS. Why what, exactly?

GUIL. Why is he mad?!

ROS. *I don't know!*

Beat.

PLAYER. The old man thinks he's in love with his daughter.

ROS (*appalled*). Good God! We're out of our depth here.

PLAYER. No, no, no—*he* hasn't got a daughter—the old man thinks he's in love with *his* daughter.

ROS. The old man is?

PLAYER. Hamlet, in love with the old man's daughter, the old man thinks.

ROS. Ha! It's beginning to make sense! Unrequited passion!

The Player moves.

GUIL (*fascist*). Nobody leaves this room! (*Pause, lamely.*) Without a *very* good reason.

PLAYER. Why not?

GUIL. All this strolling about is getting too arbitrary by half—I'm rapidly losing my grip. From now on reason will prevail.

PLAYER. I have lines to learn.

GUIL. Pass!

The Player passes into one of the wings. Ros cups his hands and shouts into the opposite one.

ROS. Next!

But no one comes.

GUIL. What did you expect?

ROS. Something . . . someone . . . nothing.

They sit facing front.

Are you hungry?

GUIL. No, are you?

ROS (*thinks*). No. You remember that coin?

GUIL. No.

ROS. I think I lost it.

GUIL. What coin?

ROS. I don't remember exactly.

Pause.

GUIL. Oh, that coin . . . clever.

ROS. I can't remember how I did it.

GUIL. It probably comes natural to you.

ROS. Yes, I've got a show-stopper there.

GUIL. Do it again.

Slight pause.

ROS. We can't afford it.

GUIL. Yes, one must think of the future.

ROS. It's the normal thing.

GUIL. To have one. One is, after all, having it all the time . . . now . . . and now . . . and now. . . .

ROS. I could go on for ever. Well, not for *ever*, I suppose. (*Pause.*) Do you ever think of yourself as actually *dead*, lying in a box with a lid on it?

GUIL. No.

ROS. Nor do I, really. . . . It's silly to be depressed by it. I mean one thinks of it like being *alive* in a box, one keeps forgetting to take into account the fact that one is *dead* . . . which should make all the difference . . . shouldn't it? I mean, you'd never *know* you were in a box, would you? It would be just like being *asleep* in a box. Not that I'd like to sleep in a box, mind you, not without any air—you'd wake up dead, for a start, and then where would you be? Apart from inside a box. That's the bit I don't like, frankly. That's why I don't think of it. . . .

Guil stirs restlessly, pulling his cloak round him.

Because you'd be helpless, wouldn't you? Stuffed in a box like that, I mean you'd be in there for ever. Even taking into account the fact that you're dead, it isn't a pleasant thought. *Especially* if you're dead, really . . . *ask* yourself, if I asked you straight off—I'm going to stuff you in this box now, would you rather be alive or dead? Naturally, you'd prefer to be alive. Life in a box is better than no life at all. I expect. You'd have a chance at least. You could lie there thinking—well, at least I'm not dead! In a minute someone's going to bang on the lid and tell me to come out. (*Banging the floor with his fists.*) "Hey you, whatsyername! Come out of there!"

GUIL (*jumps up savagely*). You don't have to flog it to death!

Pause.

ROS. I wouldn't think about it, if I were you. You'd only get depressed. (*Pause.*) Eternity is a terrible thought. I mean, where's it going to end? (*Pause, then brightly.*) Two early Christians chanced to meet in Heaven. "Saul of Tarsus yet!" cried one. "What are *you* doing here?!" . . . "Tarsus-Schmarsus," replied the other, "I'm Paul already." (*He stands up restlessly and flaps his arms.*) They don't care. We count for nothing. We could remain silent till we're green in the face, they wouldn't come.

GUIL. Blue, red.

ROS. A Christian, a Moslem and a Jew chanced to meet in a closed carriage. . . . "Silverstein!" cried the Jew. "Who's your friend?" . . . "His name's Abdullah," replied the Moslem, "but he's no friend of mine since he became a convert." (*He leaps up again, stamps his foot and shouts into the wings.*) All right, we know you're in there! Come out talking! (*Pause.*) We have no control. None at all . . . (*He paces.*) Whatever be-came of the moment when one first knew about death? There must have been one, a moment, in childhood when it first occurred to you that you don't go on for ever. It must have been shattering—stamped into one's memory. And yet I can't remember it. It never occurred to me at all. What does one make of that? We must be born with an intuition of mortality. Before we know the words for it, before we know that there are words, out we come, bloodied and squalling with the knowledge that for all the compasses in the world, there's only one direction, and time is its only measure. (*He reflects, getting more desperate and rapid.*) A Hindu, a Buddhist and a lion-tamer chanced to meet, in a circus on the Indo-Chinese border. (*He breaks out.*) They're taking us for granted! Well, I won't stand for it! In future, notice will be taken. (*He wheels again to face into the wings.*) Keep out, then! I forbid anyone to enter! (*No one comes. Breathing heavily.*) That's better. . . .

Immediately, behind him a grand procession enters, principally Claudius, Gertrude, Polonius and Ophelia. Claudius takes Ros's elbow as he passes and is immediately deep in conversation: the context is Shakespeare Act III, scene i. Guil still faces front as Claudius, Ros, etc., pass upstage and turn.

GUIL. Death followed by eternity . . . the worst of both worlds. It *is* a terrible thought.

He turns upstage in time to take over the conversation with Claudius. Gertrude and Ros head downstage.

GERTRUDE. Did he receive you well?

ROS. Most like a gentleman.

GUIL (*returning in time to take it up*). But with much forcing of his disposition.

ROS (*a flat lie and he knows it and shows it, perhaps catching Guil's eye*). Niggard of question, but of our demands most free in his reply.

GERTRUDE. Did you assay him to any pastime?

ROS. Madam, it so fell out that certain players
   We o'erraught on the way: of these we told him
   And there did seem in him a kind of joy
   To hear of it. They are here about the court,
   And, as I think, they have already order
   This night to play before him.

POLONIUS. 'Tis most true
   And he beseeched me to entreat your Majesties
   To hear and see the matter.

CLAUDIUS. With all my heart, and it doth content me
   To hear him so inclined.
   Good gentlemen, give him a further edge
   And drive his purpose into these delights.

ROS. We shall, my lord.

CLAUDIUS (*leading out procession*).
   Sweet Gertrude, leave us, too,
   For we have closely sent for Hamlet hither,
   That he, as t'were by accident, may here
   Affront Ophelia. . . .

Exeunt Claudius and Gertrude.

ROS (*peevish*). Never a moment's peace! In and out, on and off, they're coming at us from all sides.

GUIL. You're never satisfied.

ROS. Catching us on the trot. . . . Why can't *we* go by *them*?

GUIL. What's the difference?

ROS. I'm going.

Ros pulls his cloak round him. Guil ignores him. Without confidence Ros heads upstage. He looks out and comes back quickly.

He's coming.

GUIL. What's he doing?

ROS. Nothing.

GUIL. He must be doing something.

ROS. Walking.

GUIL. On his hands?

ROS. No, on his feet.

GUIL. Stark naked?

ROS. Fully dressed.

GUIL. Selling toffee apples?

ROS. Not that I noticed.

GUIL. You could be wrong?

ROS. I don't think so.

Pause.

GUIL. I can't for the life of me see how we're going to get into conversation.

Hamlet enters upstage, and pauses, weighing up the pros and cons of making his quietus.

Ros and Guil watch him.

ROS. Nevertheless, I suppose one might say that this was a chance. . . . One might well . . . accost him. . . . Yes, it definitely looks like a chance to me. . . . Something on the lines of a direct informal approach . . . man to man . . . straight from the shoulder. . . . Now look here, what's it all about . . . sort of thing. Yes. Yes, this looks like one to be grabbed with both hands, I should say . . . if I were asked. . . . No point in looking at a gift horse till you see the whites of its eyes, etcetera. (*He has moved towards Hamlet but his nerve fails. He returns.*)

We're overawed, that's our trouble. When it comes to the point we succumb to their personality. . . .

Ophelia enters, with prayerbook, a religious procession of one.

HAMLET. Nymph, in thy orisons be all my sins remembered.

At his voice she has stopped for him, he catches her up.

OPHELIA. Good my lord, how does your honour for this many a day?

HAMLET. I humbly thank you—well, well, well.

They disappear talking into the wing.

ROS. It's like living in a public park!

GUIL. Very impressive. Yes, I thought your direct informal approach was going to stop this thing dead in its tracks there. If I might make a suggestion—shut up and sit down. Stop being perverse.

ROS (*near tears*). I'm not going to stand for it!

A Female Figure, ostensibly the Queen, enters. Ros marches up behind her, puts his hands over her eyes and says with a desperate frivolity.

ROS. Guess who?!

PLAYER (*having appeared in a downstage corner*). Alfred!

Ros lets go, spins around. He has been holding Alfred, in his robe and blond wig. Player is in the downstage corner still. Ros comes down to that exit. The Player does not budge. He and Ros stand toe to toe.

ROS. Excuse me.

The Player lifts his downstage foot. Ros bends to put his hand on the floor. The Player lowers his foot. ROS screams and leaps away.

PLAYER (*gravely*). I beg your pardon.

GUIL (*to Ros*). What did he do?

PLAYER. I put my foot down.

ROS. My hand was on the floor!

GUIL. You put your hand under his foot?

ROS. I——

GUIL. What for?

ROS. I thought——(*Grabs Guil.*) Don't leave me!

He makes a break for an exit. A Tragedian dressed as a King enters. Ros recoils, breaks for the opposite wing. Two cloaked Tragedians enter. Ros tries again but another Tragedian enters, and Ros retires to midstage. The Player claps his hands matter-of-factly.

PLAYER. Right! We haven't got much time.

GUIL. What are you doing?

PLAYER. Dress rehearsal. Now if you two wouldn't mind just moving back . . . there . . . good. . . . (*To Tragedians:*) Everyone ready? And for goodness' sake, remember what we're doing. (*To Ros and Guil:*) We always use the same costumes more or less, and they forget what they are supposed to be *in* you see. . . . Stop picking your nose, Alfred. When Queens have to they do it by a cerebral process passed down in the blood. . . . Good. Silence! Off we go!

PLAYER-KING. Full thirty times hath Phoebus' cart——

Player jumps up angrily.

PLAYER. No, no, no! Dumbshow first, your confounded majesty! (*To Ros and Guil:*) They're a bit out of practice, but they always pick up wonderfully for the deaths—it brings out the poetry in them.

GUIL. How nice.

PLAYER. There's nothing more unconvincing than an unconvincing death.

GUIL. I'm sure.

Player claps his hands.

PLAYER. Act One—moves now.

The mime. Soft music from a recorder. Player-King and Player-Queen embrace. She kneels and makes a show of protestation to him. He takes her up, declining his head upon her neck. He lies down. She, seeing him asleep, leaves him.

GUIL. What is the dumbshow for?

PLAYER. Well, it's a device, really—it makes the action that follows more or less comprehensible; you understand, we are tied down to a language which makes up in obscurity what it lacks in style.

The mime (continued)—enter another. He takes off the Sleeper's crown, kisses it. He has brought in a small bottle of liquid. He pours the poison in the Sleeper's ear, and leaves him. The Sleeper convulses heroically, dying.

ROS. Who was that?

PLAYER. The King's brother and uncle to the Prince.

GUIL. Not exactly fraternal.

PLAYER. Not exactly avuncular, as time goes on.

The Queen returns, makes passionate action, finding the King dead. The Poisoner comes in again, attended by two others (the two in cloaks.) The Poisoner seems to console with her. The dead body is carried away. The Poisoner woos the Queen with gifts. She seems harsh awhile but in the end accepts his love. End of mime, at which point, the wail of a woman in torment and Ophelia appears, wailing, closely followed by Hamlet in a hysterical state, shouting at her, circling her, both midstage.

HAMLET. Go to, I'll no more on't; it hath made me mad!

She falls on her knees weeping.

I say we will have no more marriage! (*His voice drops to include the Tragedians, who have frozen.*) Those that are married already (*he leans close to the Player-Queen and Poisoner, speaking with quiet edge*) all but one shall live. (*He smiles briefly at them without mirth, and starts to back out, his parting shot rising again.*) The rest shall keep as they are. (*As he leaves, Ophelia tottering upstage, he speaks into her ear a quick clipped sentence.*) To a nunnery, go.

He goes out. Ophelia falls on to her knees upstage, her sobs barely audible. A slight silence.

PLAYER-KING. Full thirty times hath Phoebus' cart——

Claudius enters with Polonius and goes over to Ophelia and lifts her to her feet. The Tragedians jump back with heads inclined.

CLAUDIUS. Love? His affections do not that way tend,
Or what he spake, though it lacked form a little,
Was not like madness. There's something
In his soul o'er which his melancholy sits on
Brood, and I do doubt the hatch and the
Disclose will be some danger; which for to
Prevent I have in quick determination thus set
It down: he shall with speed to England . . .

Which carries the three of them—Claudius, Polonius, Ophelia—out of sight. The Player moves, clapping his hands for attention.

PLAYER. Gentlemen! (*They look at him.*) It doesn't seem to be coming. We are not getting it at all. (*To Guil:*) What did you think?

GUIL. What was I supposed to think?

PLAYER (*to Tragedians*). You're not getting across!

Ros had gone halfway up to Ophelia; he returns.

ROS. That didn't look like love to me.

GUIL. Starting from scratch again . . .

PLAYER (*to Tragedians*). It was a *mess*.

ROS (*to Guil*). It's going to be chaos on the night.

GUIL. Keep back—we're spectators.

PLAYER. Act Two! Positions!

GUIL. Wasn't that the end?

PLAYER. Do you call that an ending?—with practically everyone on his feet? My goodness no—over your dead body.

GUIL. How am I supposed to take that?

PLAYER. Lying down. (*He laughs briefly and in a second has never laughed in his life.*) There's a design at work in all art—surely you know that? Events must play themselves out to aesthetic, moral and logical conclusion.

GUIL. And what's that, in this case?

PLAYER. It never varies—we aim at the point where everyone who is marked for death dies.

GUIL. Marked?

PLAYER. Between "just desserts" and "tragic irony" we are given quite a lot of scope for our particular talent. Generally speaking, things have gone about as far as they can possibly go when things have got about as bad as they reasonably get. (*He switches on a smile.*)

GUIL. Who decides?

PLAYER (*switching off his smile*). Decides? It is *written*.

He turns away. Guil grabs him and spins him back violently.

(*Unflustered.*) Now if you're going to be subtle, we'll miss each other in the dark. I'm referring to oral tradition. So to speak.

Guil releases him.

We're tragedians, you see. We follow directions—there is no *choice* involved. The bad end unhappily, the good unluckily. That is what tragedy means. (*Calling.*) Positions!

The Tragedians have taken up positions for the continuation of the mime: which in this case means a love scene, sexual and passionate, between the Queen and the Poisoner/King.

PLAYER. Go!

The lovers begin. The Player contributes a breathless commentary for Ros and Guil.

Having murdered his brother and wooed the widow—the poisoner mounts the throne! Here we see him and his queen give rein to their unbridled passion! She little knowing that the man she holds in her arms——!

ROS. Oh, I say—here—really! You can't do that!

PLAYER. Why not?

ROS. Well, really—I mean, people want to be *entertained*—they don't come expecting sordid and gratuitous filth.

529

PLAYER. You're wrong—they do! Murder, seduction and incest—what do you want—*jokes*?

ROS. I want a good story, with a beginning, middle and end.

PLAYER (*to Guil*). And you?

GUIL. I'd prefer art to mirror life, if it's all the same to you.

PLAYER. It's all the same to me, sir. (*To the grappling Lovers:*) All right, no need to indulge yourselves. (*They get up. To Guil:*) I come on in a minute. Lucianus, nephew to the king! (*Turns his attention to the Tragedians.*) Next!

They disport themselves to accommodate the next piece of mime, which consists of the Player himself exhibiting an excitable anguish (choreographed, stylized) leading to an impassioned scene with the Queen (cf. "The Closet Scene," Shakespeare Act III, scene iv) and a very stylized reconstruction of a Polonius figure being stabbed behind the arras (the murdered King to stand in for Polonius) while the Player himself continues his breathless commentary for the benefit of Ros and Guil.

PLAYER. Lucianus, nephew to the king . . . usurped by his uncle and shattered by his mother's incestuous marriage . . . loses his reason . . . throwing the court into turmoil and disarray as he alternates between bitter melancholy and unrestricted lunacy . . . staggering from the suicidal (*a pose*) to the homicidal (*here he kills "Polonius"*) . . . he at last confronts his mother and in a scene of provocative ambiguity—(*a somewhat oedipal embrace*) begs her to repent and recant——(*He springs up, still talking.*) The King—(*he pushes forward the Poisoner/King*) tormented by guilt—haunted by fear—decides to despatch his nephew to England—and entrusts this underaking to two smiling accomplices—friends—courtiers—to two spies——

He has swung round to bring together the Poisoner/King and the two cloaked Tragedians; the latter kneel and accept a scroll from the King.

—giving them a letter to present to the English court——! And so they depart—on board ship——

The two Spies position themselves on either side of the Player, and the three of them sway gently in unison, the motion of a boat; and then the Player detaches himself.

—and they arrive——

One Spy shades his eyes at the horizon.

—and disembark—and present themselves before the English king——(*He wheels round.*) The English king——

An exchange of headgear creates the English King from the remaining player—that is, the Player who played the original murdered king.

But where is the Prince? Where indeed? The plot has thickened—a twist of fate and cunning has put into their hands a letter that seals their deaths!

The two Spies present their letter; the English King reads it and orders their deaths. They stand up as the Player whips off their cloaks preparatory to execution.

Traitors hoist by their own petard?—or victims of the gods?—we shall never know!

The whole mime has been fluid and continuous but now Ros moves forward and brings it to a pause. What brings Ros forward is the fact that under their cloaks the two Spies are wearing coats identical to those worn by Ros and Guil, whose coats are now covered by their cloaks. Ros approaches "his" Spy doubtfully. He does not quite understand why the coats are familiar. Ros stands close, touches the coat, thoughtfully. . . .

ROS. Well, if it isn't——! No, wait a minute, don't tell me—it's a long time since—where was it? Ah, this is taking me back to—when was it? I know you, don't I? I never forget a face—(*he looks into the Spy's face*) . . . not that I know yours, that is. For a moment I thought—no, I don't know you, do I? Yes, I'm afraid you're quite wrong. You must have mistaken me for someone else.

Guil meanwhile has approached the other Spy, brow creased in thought.

PLAYER (*to Guil*). Are you familiar with this play?

GUIL. No.

PLAYER. A slaughterhouse—eight corpses all told. It brings out the best in us.

GUIL (*tense, progressively rattled during the whole mime and commentary*). You!—What do *you* know about *death*?

PLAYER. It's what the actors do best. They have to exploit whatever talent is given to them, and their talent is dying. They can die heroically, comically, ironically, slowly, suddenly, disgustingly, charmingly, or from a great height. My own talent is more general. I extract significance from melodrama, a significance which it does not in fact contain; but occasionally, from out of this matter, there escapes a thin beam of light that, seen at the right angle, can crack the shell of mortality.

ROS. Is that all they can do—die?

PLAYER. No, no—they kill beautifully. In fact some of them kill even better than they die. The rest die better than they kill. They're a team.

ROS. Which ones are which?

PLAYER. There's not much in it.

GUIL (*fear, derision*). Actors! The mechanics of cheap melodrama! That isn't *death!* (*More quietly.*) You scream and choke and sink to your knees, but it doesn't bring death home to anyone—it doesn't catch them unawares and start the whisper in their skulls that says—"One day you are going to die." (*He straightens up.*) You die so many times; how can you expect them to believe in your death?

PLAYER. On the contrary, it's the only kind they do believe. They're conditioned to it. I had an actor once who was condemned to hang for stealing a sheep—or a lamb, I forget which—so I got permission to have him hanged in the middle of a play—had to change the plot a bit but I thought it would be effective, you know—and you wouldn't believe it, he just *wasn't* convincing! It was impossible to suspend one's disbelief—and what with the audience jeering and throwing peanuts, the whole thing was a *disaster!*—he did nothing but cry all the time—right out of character—just stood there and cried. . . . Never again.

In good humour he has already turned back to the mime: the two Spies awaiting execution at the hands of the Player, who takes his dagger out of his belt.

Audiences know what to expect, and that is all that they are prepared to believe in. (*To the Spies:*) Show!

The Spies die at some length, rather well.

The light has begun to go, and it fades as they die, and as Guil speaks.

GUIL. No, no, no . . . you've got it all wrong . . . you can't act death. The *fact* of it is nothing to do with seeing it happen—it's not gasps and blood and falling about—that isn't what makes it death. It's just a man failing to reappear, that's all—now you see him, now you don't, that's the only thing that's real: here one minute and gone the next and never coming back—an exit, unobtrusive and unannounced, a disappearance gathering weight as it goes on, until, finally, it is heavy with death.

The two Spies lie still, barely visible. The Player comes forward and throws the Spies' cloaks over their bodies. Ros starts to clap, slowly.

Blackout.

A second of silence, then much noise. Shouts . . . "The King rises!" . . . "Give o'er the play!" . . . and cries for "Lights, lights, lights!"

When the light comes, after a few seconds, it comes as a sunrise.

The stage is empty save for two cloaked figures sprawled on the ground in the approximate positions last held by the dead Spies. As the light grows, they are seen to be Ros and Guil, and to be resting quite comfortably. Ros raises himself on his elbows and shades his eyes as he stares into the auditorium. Finally:

ROS. That must be east, then. I think we can assume that.

GUIL. I'm assuming nothing.

ROS. No, it's all right. That's the sun. East.

GUIL (*looks up*). Where?

ROS. I watched it come up.

GUIL. No . . . it was light all the time, you see, and you opened your eyes very, very slowly. If you'd been facing back there you'd be swearing that was east.

ROS (*standing up*). You're a mass of prejudice.

GUIL. I've been taken in before.

ROS (*looks out over the audience*). Rings a bell.

GUIL. They're waiting to see what we're going to do.

ROS. Good old east.

GUIL. As soon as we make a move they'll come pouring in from every side, shouting obscure instructions, confusing us with ridiculous remarks, messing us about from here to breakfast and getting our names wrong.

Ros starts to protest but he has hardly opened his mouth before:

CLAUDIUS (*off stage—with urgency*). Ho, Guildenstern!

Guil is still prone. Small pause.

ROS AND GUIL. You're wanted. . . .

Guil furiously leaps to his feet as Claudius and Gertrude enter. They are in some desperation.

CLAUDIUS. Friends both, go join you with some further aid: Hamlet in madness hath Polonius slain, and from his mother's closet hath he dragged him. Go seek him out; speak fair and bring the body into the chapel. I pray you haste in this. (*As he and Gertrude are hurrying out.*) Come Gertrude, we'll call up our wisest friends and let them know both what we mean to do. . . .

They've gone. Ros and Guil remain quite still.

GUIL. Well . . .

ROS. Quite . . .

GUIL. Well, well.

ROS. Quite, quite. (*Nods with spurious confidence.*) Seek him out. (*Pause.*) Etcetera.

GUIL. Quite.

ROS. Well. (*Small pause.*) Well, that's a step in the right direction.

GUIL. You didn't like him?

ROS. Who?

GUIL. Good God, I hope more tears are shed for *us*! . . .

ROS. Well, it's *progress*, isn't it? Something positive. Seek him out. (*Looks round without moving his feet.*) Where does one begin . . . ? (*Takes one step towards the wings and halts.*)

GUIL. Well, that's a step in the right direction.

ROS. You think so? He could be anywhere.

GUIL. All right—you go that way, I'll go this way.

ROS. Right.

They walk towards opposite wings. Ros halts.

No.

Guil halts.

You go this way—I'll go that way.

GUIL. All right.

They march towards each other, cross. Ros halts.

ROS. Wait a minute.

Guil halts.

I think we should stick together. He might be violent.

GUIL. Good point. I'll come with you.

Guil marches across to Ros. They turn to leave. Ros halts.

ROS. No, I'll come with you.

GUIL. Right.

They turn, march across to the opposite wing. Ros halts. Guil halts.

ROS. I'll come with *you*, my way.

GUIL. All right.

They turn again and march across. Ros halts. Guil halts.

ROS. I've just thought. If we both go, he could come *here*. That would be stupid, wouldn't it?

GUIL. All right—I'll stay, you go.

ROS. Right.

Guil marches to midstage.

I say.

Guil wheels and carries on marching back towards Ros, who starts marching downstage. They cross. Ros halts.

I've just thought.

Guil halts.

We ought to stick together; he might be violent.

GUIL. Good point.

Guil marches down to join Ros. They stand still for a moment in their original positions.

Well, at last we're getting somewhere.

Pause.

Of course, he might not come.

ROS (*airily*). Oh, he'll come.

GUIL. We'd have some explaining to do.

ROS. He'll come. (*Airily wanders upstage.*) Don't worry— take my word for it—(*Looks out—is appalled.*) He's coming!

GUIL. What's he doing?

ROS. Walking.

GUIL. Alone?

ROS. No.

GUIL. Not walking?

ROS. No.

GUIL. Who's with him?

ROS. The old man.

GUIL. Walking?

ROS. No.

GUIL. Ah. That's an opening if ever there was one. (*And is suddenly galvanized into action.*) Let him walk into the trap!

ROS. What trap?

GUIL. You stand there! Don't let him pass!

He positions Ros with his back to one wing, facing Hamlet's entrance.

Guil positions himself next to Ros, a few feet away, so that they are covering one side of the stage, facing the opposite side. Guil unfastens his belt. Ros does the same. They join the two belts, and hold them taut between them. Ros's trousers slide slowly down.

Hamlet enters opposite, slowly, dragging Polonius's body. He enters upstage, makes a small arc and leaves by the same side, a few feet downstage.

Ros and Guil, holding the belts taut, stare at him in some bewilderment.

Hamlet leaves, dragging the body. They relax the strain on the belts.

ROS. That was close.

GUIL. There's a limit to what two people can do.

They undo the belts: Ros pulls up his trousers.

ROS (*worriedly—he walks a few paces towards Hamlet's exit*). He *was* dead.

GUIL. Of course he's dead!

ROS (*turns to Guil*). Properly.

GUIL (*angrily*). Death's death, isn't it?

Ros falls silent. Pause.

Perhaps he'll come back this way.

Ros starts to take off his belt.

No, no, no!—If we can't learn by experience, what else have we got?

Ros desists.

Pause.

ROS. Give him a shout.

GUIL. I thought we'd been into all that.

ROS (*shouts*). Hamlet!

GUIL. Don't be sbsurd.

ROS (*shouts*). Lord Hamlet!

Hamlet enters. Ros is a little dismayed.

What have you done, my lord, with the dead body?

HAMLET. Compounded it with dust, whereto 'tis kin.

ROS. Tell us where 'tis, that we may take it thence and bear it to the chapel.

HAMLET. Do not believe it.

ROS. Believe what?

HAMLET. That I can keep your counsel and not mine own. Besides, to be demanded of a sponge, what replication should be made by the son of a king?

ROS. Take you me for a sponge, my lord?

HAMLET. Ay, sir, that soaks up the King's countenance, his rewards, his authorities. But such officers do the King best service in the end. He keeps them, like an ape, in the corner of his jaw, first mouthed, to be last swallowed. When he needs what you have gleaned, it is but squeezing you and, sponge, you shall be dry again.

ROS. I understand you not, my lord.

HAMLET. I am glad of it: a knavish speech sleeps in a foolish ear.

ROS. My lord, you must tell us where the body is and go with us to the King.

HAMLET. The body is with the King, but the King is not with the body. The King is a thing——

GUIL. A thing, my lord——?

HAMLET. Of nothing. Bring me to him.

Hamlet moves resolutely towards one wing. They move with him, shepherding. Just before they reach the exit, Hamlet, apparently seeing Claudius approaching from off stage, bends low in a sweeping bow. Ros and Guil, cued by Hamlet, also bow deeply—a sweeping ceremonial bow with their cloaks swept round them. Hamlet, however, continues the movement into an about-turn and walks off in the opposite direction. Ros and Guil, with their heads low, do not notice.

No one comes on. Ros and Guil squint upwards and find that they are bowing to nothing.

Claudius enters behind them. At first words they leap up and do a double-take.

CLAUDIUS. How now? What hath befallen?

ROS. Where the body is bestowed, my lord, we cannot get from him.

CLAUDIUS. But where is he?

ROS (*fractional hesitation*). Without, my lord; guarded to know your pleasure.

CLAUDIUS (*moves*). Bring him before us.

This hits Ros between the eyes but only his eyes show it. Again his hesitation is fractional. And then with great deliberation he turns to Guil.

ROS. Ho! Bring in the lord.

Again there is a fractional moment in which Ros is smug, Guil is trapped and betrayed. Guil opens his mouth and closes it.

The situation is saved: Hamlet, escorted, is marched in just as Claudius leaves. Hamlet and his escort cross the stage and go out, following Claudius.

Lighting changes to Exterior.

ROS (*moves to go*). All right, then?

GUIL (*does not move, thoughtfully*). And yet it doesn't seem enough; to have breathed such significance. Can that be all? And why us?—anybody would have done. And we have contributed nothing.

ROS. It was a trying episode while it lasted, but they've done with us now.

GUIL. Done what?

ROS. I don't pretend to have understood. Frankly, I'm not very interested. If they won't tell us, that's their affair. (*He wanders upstage towards the exit.*) For my part, I'm only glad that that's the last we've seen of him—(*And he glances off stage and turns front, his face betraying the fact that Hamlet is there.*)

GUIL. I knew it wasn't the end. . . .

Ros (*high*). What else?!
Guil. We're taking him to England. What's he doing?

Ros goes upstage and returns.

Ros. Talking.
Guil. To himself?

Ros makes to go, Guil cuts him off.

Is he alone?
Ros. No, he's with a soldier.
Guil. Then he's not talking to himself, is he?
Ros. Not *by* himself. . . . Should we go?
Guil. Where?
Ros. Anywhere.
Guil. Why?

Ros puts up his head listening.

Ros. There it is again. (*In anguish.*) All I ask is a change of ground!
Guil (*coda*). Give us this day our daily round. . . .

Hamlet enters behind them, talking with a soldier in arms. Ros and Guil don't look round.

Ros. They'll have us hanging about till we're dead. At least. And the weather will change. (*Looks up.*) The spring can't last for ever.
Hamlet. Good sir, whose powers are these?
Soldier. They are of Norway, sir.
Hamlet. How purposed, sir, I pray you?
Soldier. Against some part of Poland.
Hamlet. Who commands them, sir?
Soldier. The nephew to old Norway, Fortinbras.
Ros. We'll be cold. The summer won't last.
Guil. It's autumnal.
Ros (*examining the ground*). No leaves.
Guil. Autumnal—nothing to do with leaves. It is to do with a certain brownness at the edges of the day. . . . Brown is creeping up on us, take my word for it. . . . Russets and tangerine shades of old gold flushing the very outside edge of the senses . . . deep shining ochres, burnt umber and parchments of baked earth—reflecting on itself and through itself, filtering the light. At such times, perhaps, coincidentally, the leaves might fall, somewhere, by repute. Yesterday was blue, like smoke.
Ros (*head up, listening*). I got it again then.

They listen—faintest sound of Tragedians' band.

Hamlet. I humbly thank you, sir.
Soldier. God by you, sir. (*Exit.*)

Ros gets up quickly and goes to Hamlet.

Ros. Will it please you go, my lord?
Hamlet. I'll be with you straight. Go you a little before.

Hamlet turns to face upstage. Ros returns down. Guil faces front, doesn't turn.

Guil. Is he there?
Ros. Yes.
Guil. What's he doing?

Ros looks over his shoulder.

Ros. Talking.
Guil. To himself?
Ros. Yes.

Pause. Ros makes to leave.

Ros. He *said* we can go. Cross my heart.
Guil. I like to know where I am. Even if I don't know where I am, I like to know *that*. If we go there's no knowing.
Ros. No knowing what?
Guil. If we'll ever come back.
Ros. We don't want to come back.
Guil. That may very well be true, but do we want to go?
Ros. We'll be free.
Guil. I don't know. It's the same sky.
Ros. We've come this far.

He moves toward exit. Guil follows him.

And besides, anything could happen yet.

They go.

Blackout

ACT III

Opens in pitch darkness. Soft sea sounds.

After several seconds of nothing, a voice from the dark . . .

Guil. Are you there?
Ros. Where?
Guil (*bitterly*). A flying start. . . .

Pause.

Ros. Is that you?
Guil. Yes.
Ros. How do you know?
Guil (*explosion*). Oh-for-God's-sake!
Ros. We're not finished, then?
Guil. Well, we're here, aren't we?

Ros. Are we? I can't see a thing.
Guil. You can still *think*, can't you?
Ros. I think so.
Guil. You can still *talk*.
Ros. What should I say?
Guil. Don't bother. You can *feel*, can't you?
Ros. Ah! There's life in me yet!
Guil. What are you feeling?
Ros. A leg. Yes, it feels like my leg.
Guil. How does it feel?
Ros. Dead.
Guil. Dead?
Ros (*panic*). I can't feel a thing!
Guil. Give it a pinch! (*Immediately he yelps.*)
Ros. Sorry.
Guil. Well, that's cleared that up.

Longer pause: the sound builds a little and identifies itself—the sea. Ship timbers, wind in the rigging, and then shouts of sailors calling obscure but inescapably nautical instructions from all directions, far and near: A short list:

>   Hard a larboard!
>   Let go the stays!
>   Reef down me hearties!
>   Is that you, cox'n?
>   Hel-llo! Is that you?
>   Hard a port!
>   Easy as she goes!
>   Keep her steady on the lee!
>   Haul away, lads!
>   (*Snatches of sea shanty maybe.*)
>   Fly the jib!
>   Tops'l up, me maties!

When the point has been well made and more so.

Ros. We're on a boat. (*Pause.*) Dark, isn't it?
Guil. Not for night.
Ros. No, not for *night*.
Guil. Dark for day.

Pause.

Ros. Oh yes, it's dark for *day*.
Guil. We must have gone north, of course.
Ros. Off course?
Guil. Land of the midnight sun, that is.
Ros. Of course.

Some sailor sounds.

A lantern is lit upstage—in fact by Hamlet.

The stage lightens disproportionately—

Enough to see:

Ros and Guil sitting downstage.

Vague shapes of rigging, etc., behind.

I think it's getting light.
Guil. Not for night.
Ros. This far north.
Guil. Unless we're off course.
Ros (*small pause*). Of course.
A better light—Lantern? Moon? . . . Light.

Revealing, among other things, three large man-sized casks on deck, upended, with lids. Spaced but in line. Behind and above—a gaudy striped umbrella, on a pole stuck into the deck, tilted so that we do not see behind it—one of those huge six-foot-diameter jobs. Still dim upstge. Ros and Guil still facing front.

Ros. Yes, it's lighter than it was. It'll be night soon. This far north. (*Dolefully.*) I suppose we'll have to go to sleep. (*He yawns and stretches.*)
Guil. Tired?
Ros. No . . . I don't think I'd take to it. Sleep all night, can't see a thing all day. . . . Those eskimos must have a quiet life.
Guil. Where?
Ros. What?
Guil. I thought you——(*Relapses.*) I've lost all capacity for disbelief. I'm not sure that I could even rise to a little gentle scepticism.

Pause.

Ros. Well, shall we stretch our legs?
Guil. I don't feel like stretching my legs.
Ros. I'll stretch them for you, if you like.
Guil. No.
Ros. We could stretch each other's. That way we wouldn't have to go anywhere.
Guil (*pause*). No, somebody might come in.
Ros. In where?
Guil. Out here.
Ros. In out here?
Guil. On deck.

Ros considers the floor: slaps it.

Ros. Nice bit of planking, that.
Guil. Yes, I'm very fond of boats myself. I like the way they're—contained. You don't have to worry about which way to go, or whether to go at all—the question doesn't arise, because you're on a *boat*, aren't you? Boats are safe areas in the game of tag . . . the

players will hold their positions until the music starts. . . . I think I'll spend most of my life on boats.

ROS. Very healthy.

Ros inhales with expectation, exhales with boredom. Guil stands up and looks over the audience.

GUIL. One is free on a boat. For a time. Relatively.

ROS. What's it like?

GUIL. Rough.

Ros joins him. They look out over the audience.

ROS. I think I'm going to be sick.

Guil licks a finger, holds it up experimentally.

GUIL. Other side, I think.

Ros goes upstage: Ideally a sort of upper deck joined to the downstage lower deck by short steps. The umbrella being on the upper deck. Ros pauses by the umbrella and looks behind it. Guil meanwhile has been resuming his own theme—looking out over the audience—

Free to move, speak, extemporise, and yet. We have not been cut loose. Our truancy is defined by one fixed star, and our drift represents merely a slight change of angle to it: we may seize the moment, toss it around while the moments pass, a short dash here, an exploration there, but we are brought round full circle to face again the single immutable fact—that we, Rosencrantz and Guildenstern, bearing a letter from one king to another, are taking Hamlet to England.

By which time, Ros has returned, tiptoeing with great import, teeth clenched for secrecy, gets to Guil, points surreptitiously behind him—and a tight whisper:

ROS. I say—*he's there!*

GUIL (*unsurprised*). What's he doing?

ROS. Sleeping.

GUIL. It's all right for him.

ROS. What is?

GUIL. He can sleep.

ROS. It's all right for him.

GUIL. He's got us now.

ROS. He can sleep.

GUIL. It's all done for him.

ROS. He's got us.

GUIL. And we've got nothing. (*A cry.*) All I ask is our common due!

ROS. For those in peril on the sea. . . .

GUIL. Give us this day our daily cue.

Beat, pause. Sit. Long pause.

ROS (*after shifting, looking around*). What now?

GUIL. What do you mean?

ROS. Well, nothing is happening.

GUIL. We're on a boat.

ROS. I'm aware of that.

GUIL (*angrily*). Then what do you expect? (*Unhappily.*) We act on scraps of information . . . sifting half-remembered directions that we can hardly separate from instinct.

Ros puts a hand into his purse, then both hands behind his back, then holds his fists out.

Guil taps one fist.

Ros opens it to show a coin.

He gives it to Guil.

He puts his hand back into his purse. Then both hands behind his back, then holds his fists out.

Guil taps one.

Ros opens it to show a coin. He gives it to Guil.

Repeat.

Repeat.

Guil getting tense. Desperate to lose.

Repeat.

Guil taps a hand, changes his mind, taps the other, and Ros inadvertently reveals that he has a coin in both fists.

GUIL. You had money in both hands.

ROS (*embarassed*). Yes.

GUIL. Every time?

ROS. Yes.

GUIL. What's the point of that?

ROS (*pathetic*). I wanted to make you happy.

Beat.

GUIL. How much did he give you?

ROS. Who?

GUIL. The King. He gave us some money.

ROS. How much did he give you?

GUIL. I asked you first.

ROS. I got the same as you.

GUIL. He wouldn't discriminate between us.

ROS. How much did you get?

GUIL. The same.

ROS. How do you know?

GUIL. You just told me—how do *you* know?

ROS. He wouldn't discriminate between us.

GUIL. Even if he could.

ROS. Which he never could.

GUIL. He couldn't even be sure of mixing us up.

ROS. Without mixing us up.

GUIL (*turning on him furiously*). Why don't you say something original! No wonder the whole thing is so stagnant! You don't take me up on anything—you just repeat it in a different order.

ROS. I can't think of anything original. I'm only good in support.

GUIL. I'm sick of making the running.

ROS (*humbly*). It must be your dominant personality. (*Almost in tears.*) Oh, what's going to become of us!

And Guil comforts him, all harshness gone.

GUIL. Don't cry . . . it's all right . . . there . . . there, I'll see we're all right.

ROS. But we've got nothing to go on, we're out on our own.

GUIL. We're on our way to England—we're taking Hamlet there.

ROS. What for?

GUIL. What for? Where have you been?

ROS. When? (*Pause.*) We won't know what to do when we get there.

GUIL. We take him to the King.

ROS. Will *he* be there?

GUIL. No—the king of England.

ROS. He's expecting us?

GUIL. No.

ROS. He won't know what we're playing at. What are we going to *say*?

GUIL. We've got a letter. You remember the letter.

ROS. Do I?

GUIL. Everything is explained in the letter. We count on that.

ROS. Is that it, then?

GUIL. What?

ROS. We take Hamlet to the English king, we hand over the letter—what then?

GUIL. There may be something in the letter to keep us going a bit.

ROS. And if not?

GUIL. Then that's it—we're finished.

ROS. At a loose end?

GUIL. Yes.

Pause.

ROS. Are there likely to be loose ends? (*Pause.*) Who is the English king?

GUIL. That depends on when we get there.

ROS. What do you think it says?

GUIL. Oh . . . greetings. Expressions of loyalty. Asking of favours, calling in of debts. Obscure promises balanced by vague threats. . . . Diplomacy. Regards to the family.

ROS. And about Hamlet?

GUIL. Oh yes.

ROS. And us—the full background?

GUIL. I should say so.

Pause.

ROS. So we've got a letter which explains everything.

GUIL. You've got it.

Ros takes that literally. He starts to pat his pockets, etc.

What's the matter?

ROS. The letter.

GUIL. Have you got it?

ROS (*rising fear*). Have I? (*Searches frantically.*) Where would I have put it?

GUIL. You can't have lost it.

ROS. I must have!

GUIL. That's odd—I thought he gave it to me.

Ros looks at him hopefully.

ROS. Perhaps he did.

GUIL. But you seemed so sure it was *you* who hadn't got it.

ROS (*high*). It *was* me who hadn't got it!

GUIL. But if he gave it to me there's no reason why you should have had it in the first place, in which case I don't see what all the fuss is about you *not* having it.

ROS (*pause*). I admit it's confusing.

GUIL. This is all getting rather undisciplined. . . . The boat, the night, the sense of isolation and uncertainty . . . all these induce a loosening of the concentration. We must not lose control. Tighten up. Now. Either you have lost the letter or you didn't have it to lose in the first place, in which case the King never gave it to you, in which case he gave it to me, in which case I would have put it into my inside top pocket, in which case (*calmly producing the letter*) . . . it will be . . . here. (*They smile at each other.*) We mustn't drop off like that again.

Pause. Ros takes the letter gently from him.

ROS. Now that we have found it, why were we looking for it?

GUIL (*thinks*). We thought it was lost.

ROS. Something else?

GUIL. No.

Deflation.

ROS. Now we've lost the tension.

GUIL. What tension?

ROS. What was the last thing I said before we wandered off?

GUIL. When was that?

ROS. (*helplessly*). I can't remember.

GUIL (*leaping up*). What a shambles! We're just not getting anywhere.

ROS (*mournfully*). Not even England. I don't believe in it anyway.

GUIL. What?

ROS. England.

GUIL. Just a conspiracy of cartographers, you mean?

ROS. I mean I don't believe it! (*Calmer.*) I have no image. I try to picture us arriving, a little harbour perhaps . . . roads . . . inhabitants to point the way . . . horses on the road . . . riding for a day or a fortnight and then a palace and the English king. . . . That would be the logical kind of thing. . . . But my mind remains a blank. No. We're slipping off the map.

GUIL. Yes . . . yes. . . . (*Rallying.*) But you don't believe anything till it happens. And it *has* all happened. Hasn't it?

ROS. We drift down time, clutching at straws. But what good's a brick to a drowning man?

GUIL. Don't give up, we can't be long now.

ROS. We might as well be dead. Do you think death could possibly be a boat?

GUIL. No, no, no . . . Death is . . . not. Death isn't. You take my meaning. Death is the ultimate negative. Not-being. You can't not-be on a boat.

ROS. I've frequently not been on boats.

GUIL. No, no, no—what you've been is not on boats.

ROS. I wish I was dead. (*Considers the drop.*) I could jump over the side. That would put a spoke in their wheel.

GUIL. Unless they're counting on it.

ROS. I shall remain on board. That'll put a spoke in their wheel. (*The futility of it, fury.*) All right! We don't question, we don't doubt. We perform. But a line must be drawn somewhere, and I would like to put it on record that I have no confidence in England. Thank you. (*Thinks about this.*) And even if it's true, it'll just be another shambles.

GUIL. I don't see why.

ROS (*furious*). He won't know what we're talking about.—What are we going to *say*?

GUIL. We say—Your majesty, we have arrived!

ROS (*kingly*). And who are you?

GUIL. We are Rosencrantz and Guildenstern.

ROS (*barks*). Never heard of you!

GUIL. Well, we're nobody special——

ROS (*regal and nasty*). What's your game?

GUIL. We've got our instructions——

ROS. First I've heard of it——

GUIL (*angry*): Let me finish——(*Humble.*) We've come from Denmark.

ROS. What do you want?

GUIL. Nothing—we're delivering Hamlet——

ROS. Who's he?

GUIL (*irritated*). You've heard of *him*——

ROS. Oh, I've heard of him all right and I want nothing to do with it.

GUIL. But——

ROS. You march in here without so much as a by-your-leave and expect me to take in every lunatic you try to pass off with a lot of unsubstantiated——

GUIL. We've got a letter——

Ros snatches it and tears it open.

ROS (*efficiently*). I see . . . I see . . . well, this seems to support your story such as it is—it is an exact command from the king of Denmark, for several different reasons, importing Denmark's health and England's too, that on the reading of this letter, without delay, I should have Hamlet's head cut off——!

Guil snatches the letter. Ros, double-taking, snatches it back. Guil snatches it half back. They read it together, and separate.

Pause.

They are well downstage looking front.

ROS. The sun's going down. It will be dark soon.

GUIL. Do you think so?

ROS. I was just making conversation. (*Pause.*) We're his *friends.*

GUIL. How do you know?

ROS. From our young days brought up with him.

GUIL. You've only got their word for it.

ROS. But that's what we depend on.

GUIL. Well, yes, and then again no. (*Airily.*) Let us keep things in proportion. Assume, if you like, that they're going to kill him. Well, he is a man, he is mortal, death comes to us all, etcetera, and consequently he would have died anyway, sooner or later. Or to look at it from the social point of view—he's just one man among many, the loss would be well within reason and convenience. And then again, what is so terrible about death? As Socrates so philosophically put it, since we don't know what death is, it is illogical to fear it. It might be . . . very nice. Certainly it is a release from the burden of life, and, for the godly, a haven and a reward. Or to look at it another way—we are little men, we don't know the ins and outs of the matter, there are wheels within wheels, etcetera—it would be presumptuous of us to interfere with the designs of fate or even of kings. All in all, I think we'd be well advised to leave well alone. Tie up the letter—there—neatly—like that.—They won't notice the broken seal, assuming you were in character.

ROS. But what's the point?

GUIL. Don't apply logic.

ROS. He's done nothing to us.

GUIL. Or justice.

ROS. It's awful.

GUIL. But it could have been worse. I was beginning to think it was. (*And his relief comes out in a laugh.*)

Behind them Hamlet appears from behind the umbrella. The light has been going. Slightly. Hamlet is going to the lantern.

ROS. The position as I see it, then. We, Rosencrantz and Guildenstern, from our young days brought up with him, awakened by a man standing on his saddle, are summoned, and arrive, and are instructed to glean what afflicts him and draw him on to pleasures, such as a play, which unfortunately, as it turns out, is abandoned in some confusion owing to certain nuances outside our appreciation—which, among other causes, results in, among other effects, a high, not to say, homicidal, excitement in Hamlet, whom we, in consequence, are escorting, for his own good, to England. Good. We're on top of it now.

Hamlet blows out the lantern. The stage goes pitch black. The black resolves itself to moonlight, by which Hamlet approaches the sleeping Ros and Guil. He extracts the letter and takes it behind his umbrella; the light of his lantern shines through the fabric, Hamlet emerges again with a letter, and replaces it, and retires, blowing out his lantern.

Morning comes.

Ros watches it coming—from the auditorium. Behind him is a gay sight. Beneath the re-tilted umbrella, reclining in a deck-chair, wrapped in a rug, reading a book, possibly smoking, sits Hamlet.

Ros watches the morning come, and brighten to high noon.

ROS. I'm assuming nothing. (*He stands up. Guil wakes.*) The position as I see it, then. That's west unless we're off course, in which case it's night; the King gave me the same as you, the King gave you the same as me; the King never gave me the letter, the King gave you the letter, we don't know what's in the letter; we take Hamlet to the English king, it depending on when we get there who he is, and we hand over the letter, which may or may not have something in it to keep us going, and if not, we are finished and at a loose end, if they have loose ends. We could have done worse. I don't think we missed any chances. . . . Not that we're getting much help. (*He sits down again. They lie down—prone.*) If we stopped breathing we'd vanish.

The muffled sound of a recorder. They sit up with disproportionate interest.

GUIL. Here we go.

ROS. Yes, but what?

They listen to the music.

GUIL (*excitedly*). Out of the void, finally, a sound; while on a boat (admittedly) outside the action (admittedly) the perfect and absolute silence of the wet lazy slap of water against water and the rolling creak of timber—breaks; giving rise at once to the speculation or the assumption or the hope that something is about to happen; a pipe is heard. One of the sailors has pursed his lips against a woodwind, his fingers and thumb governing, shall we say, the ventages, whereupon, giving it breath, let us say, with his mouth, it, the pipe, discourses, as the saying goes, most eloquent music. A thing like that, it could change the course of events. (*Pause.*) Go and see what it is.

ROS. It's someone playing on a pipe.

GUIL. Go and find him.

ROS. And then what?

GUIL. I don't know—request a tune.

ROS. What for?

GUIL. Quick—before we lose our momentum.

ROS. Why!—something is happening. It had quite escaped my attention!

He listens: Makes a stab at an exit. Listens more carefully: Changes direction.

Guil takes no notice.

Ros wanders about trying to decide where the music comes from. Finally he tracks it down—unwillingly—to the middle barrel. There is no getting away from it. He turns to Guil who takes no notice. Ros, during this whole business, never quite breaks into articulate speech. His face and his hands indicate his incredulity. He stands gazing at the middle barrel. The pipe plays on within. He kicks the barrel. The pipe stops. He leaps back towards Guil. The pipe starts up again. He approaches the barrel cautiously. He lifts the lid. The music is louder. He slams down the lid. The music is softer. He goes back towards Guil. But a drum starts, muffled. He freezes. He turns. Considers the left-hand barrel. The drumming goes on within, in time to the flute. He walks back to Guil. He opens his mouth to speak. Doesn't make it. A lute is heard. He spins round at the third barrel. More instruments join in. Until it is quite inescapable that inside the three barrels, distributed, playing together a familiar tune which has been heard three times before, are the Tragedians.

They play on.

Ros sits beside Guil. They stare ahead.

The tune comes to an end.

Pause.

Ros. I thought I heard a band. (*In anguish.*) Plausibility is all I presume!

Guil (*coda*). Call us this day our daily tune. . . .

The lid of the middle barrel flies open and the Player's head pops out.

PLAYER. Aha! All in the same boat, then! (*He climbs out. He goes round banging on the barrels.*)

Everybody out!

Impossibly, the Tragedians climb out of the barrels. With their instruments, but not their cart. A few bundles. Except Alfred. The Player is cheerful.

(*To Ros:*) Where are we?

Ros. Travelling.

PLAYER. Of course, we haven't got there yet.

Ros. Are we all right for England?

PLAYER. You look all right to me. I don't think they're very particular in England. Al-l-fred!

Alfred emerges from the Player's barrel.

GUIL. What are you doing here?

PLAYER. Travelling. (*To Tragedians:*) Right—blend into the background!

The Tragedians are in costume (from the mime): A King with crown, Alfred as Queen, Poisoner and the two cloaked figures.

They blend.

(*To Guil:*) Pleased to see us? (*Pause.*) You've come out of it very well, so far.

GUIL. And you?

PLAYER. In disfavour. Our play offended the King.

GUIL. Yes.

PLAYER. Well, he's a second husband himself. Tactless, really.

Ros. It was quite a good play nevertheless.

PLAYER. We never really got going—it was getting quite interesting when they stopped it.

Looks up at Hamlet.

That's the way to travel. . . .

GUIL. What were you doing in there?

PLAYER. Hiding. (*Indicating costumes.*) We had to run for it just as we were.

Ros. Stowaways.

PLAYER. Naturally—we didn't get paid, owing to circumstances ever so slightly beyond our control, and all the money we had we lost betting on certainties. Life is a gamble, at terrible odds—if it was a bet you wouldn't take it. Did you know that any number doubled is even?

Ros. Is it?

PLAYER. We learn something every day, to our cost. But we troupers just go on and on. Do you know what happens to old actors?

Ros. What?

PLAYER. Nothing. They're still acting. Surprised, then?

GUIL. What?

PLAYER. Surprised to see us?

GUIL. I knew it wasn't the end.

PLAYER. With practically everyone on his feet. What do you make of it, so far?

GUIL. We haven't got much to go on.

PLAYER. You speak to him?

Ros. It's possible.

GUIL. But it wouldn't make any difference.

Ros. But it's possible.

GUIL. Pointless.

Ros. It's allowed.

GUIL. Allowed, yes. We are not restricted. No boundaries have been defined, no inhibitions imposed. We have, for the while, secured, or blundered into, our release, for the while. Spontaneity and whim are the order of the day. Other wheels are turning but they are not our concern. We can breathe. We can relax. We can do what we like and say what we like to whomever we like, without restriction.

ROS. Within limits, of course.
GUIL. Certainly within limits.

*Hamlet comes down to footlights and regards the au-
dience. The others watch but don't speak. Hamlet
clears his throat noisily and spits into the audience.
A split second later he claps his hand to his eye and
wipes himself. He goes back upstage.*

ROS. A compulsion towards philosophical introspection
is his chief characteristic, if I may put it like that. It
does not mean he is mad. It does not mean he isn't.
Very often, it does not mean anything at all. Which
may or may not be a kind of madness.

GUIL. It really boils down to symptoms. Pregnant replies,
mystic allusions, mistaken identities, arguing his father is his mother, that sort of thing; intimations of
suicide, forgoing of exercise, loss of mirth, hints of
claustrophobia not to say delusions of imprisonment;
invocations of camels, chameleons, capons, whales,
weasels, hawks, handsaws—riddles, quibbles and
evasions; amnesia, paranoia, myopia; day-dreaming,
hallucinations; stabbing his elders, abusing his parents, insulting his lover, and appearing hatless in
public—knock-kneed, drop-stockinged and sighing
like a love-sick schoolboy, which at his age is coming
on a bit strong.

ROS. And talking to himself.
GUIL. And talking to himself.

Ros and Guil move apart togther.

Well, where has that got us?
ROS. He's the Player.
GUIL. His play offended the King——
ROS. —offended the King——
GUIL. —who orders his arrest——
ROS. —orders his arrest——
GUIL. —so he escapes to England——
ROS. On the boat to which he meets——
GUIL. Guildenstern and Rosencrantz taking Hamlet——
ROS. —who also offended the King——
GUIL. —and killed Polonius——
ROS. —offended the King in a variety of ways——
GUIL. —to England. (*Pause.*) That seems to be it.

Ros jumps up.

ROS. Incidents! All we get is incidents! Dear God, is it
too much to expect a little sustained action?!

*And on the word, the Pirates attack. That is to say:
Noise and shouts and rushing about. "Pirates."*

*Everyone visible goes frantic. Hamlet draws his
sword and rushes downstage. Guil, Ros and Player*

*draw swords and rush upstage. Collision. Hamlet
turns back up. They turn back down. Collision. By
which time there is general panic right upstage. All
four charge upstage with Ros, Guil and Player
shouting:*

At last!
To arms!
Pirates!
Up there!
Down there!
To my sword's length!
Action!

*All four reach the top, see something they don't like,
waver, run for their lives downstage:*

*Hamlet, in the lead, leaps into the left barrel. Player
leaps into the right barrel. Ros and Guil leap into the
middle barrel. All closing the lids after them.*

*The lights dim to nothing while the sound of fighting
continues. The sound fades to nothing. The lights come
up. The middle barrel (Ros's and Guil's) is missing.*

*The lid of the right-hand barrel is raised cautiously,
the heads of Ros and Guil appear.*

*The lid of the other barrel (Hamlet's) is raised. The
head of the Player appears.*

All catch sight of each other and slam down lids.

Pause.

Lids raised cautiously.

ROS (*relief*). They've gone. (*He starts to climb out.*) That
was close. I've never thought quicker.

*They are all three out of barrels. Guil is wary and
nervous. Ros is light-headed. The Player is phleg-
matic. They note the missing barrel.*

Ros looks round.

ROS. Where's——?

The Player takes off his hat in mourning.

PLAYER. Once more, alone—on our own resources.
GUIL (*worried*). What do you mean? Where is he?
PLAYER. Gone.
GUIL. Gone where?
PLAYER. Yes, we were dead lucky there. If that's the word
I'm after.
ROS (*not a pick up*). Dead?
PLAYER. Lucky.

ROS (*he means*). Is he dead?

PLAYER. Who knows?

GUIL (*rattled*). He's not coming back?

PLAYER. Hardly.

ROS. He's dead then. He's dead as far as we're concerned.

PLAYER. Or we are as far as he is. (*He goes and sits on the floor to one side.*) Not too bad, is it?

GUIL (*rattled*). But he can't—we're supposed to be—we've got a *letter*—we're going to England with a letter for the King——

PLAYER. Yes, that much seems certain. I congratulate you on the unambiguity of your situation.

GUIL. But you don't understand—it contains—we've had our instructions——the whole thing's pointless without him.

PLAYER. Pirates could happen to anyone. Just deliver the letter. They'll send ambassadors from England to explain. . . .

GUIL (*worked up*). Can't you see—the pirates left us home and high—dry and home—drome——(*Furiously.*) The pirates left us high and dry!

PLAYER (*comforting*). There . . .

GUIL (*near tears*). Nothing will be resolved without him. . . .

PLAYER. There . . . !

GUIL. We need Hamlet for our release!

PLAYER. There!

GUIL. What are we supposed to do?

PLAYER. This.

He turns away, lies down if he likes. Ros and Guil apart.

ROS. Saved again.

GUIL. Saved for what?

Ros sighs.

ROS. The sun's going down. (*Pause.*) It'll be night soon. (*Pause.*) If that's west. (*Pause.*) Unless we've——

GUIL (*shouts*). Shut up! I'm sick of it! Do you think conversation is going to help us now?

ROS (*hurt, desperately ingratiating*). I—I bet you all the money I've got the year of my birth doubled is an odd number.

GUIL (*moan*): No-o.

ROS. Your birth!

Guil smashes him down.

GUIL (*broken*). We've travelled too far, and our momentum has taken over; we move idly towards eternity, without possibility of reprieve or hope of explanation.

ROS. Be happy—if you're not even *happy* what's so good about surviving? (*He picks himself up.*) We'll be all right. I suppose we just go on.

GUIL. Go where?

ROS. To England.

GUIL. England! *That's* a dead end. I never believed in it anyway.

ROS. All we've got to do is make our report and that'll be that. Surely.

GUIL. I don't *believe* it—a shore, a harbour, say—and we get off and we stop someone and say—Where's the King?—And he says, Oh, you follow that road there and take the first left and——(*Furiously.*) I don't believe any of it!

ROS. It doesn't sound very plausible.

GUIL. And even if we came face to face, what do we say?

ROS. We say—We've arrived!

GUIL (*kingly*). And who are you?

ROS. We are Guildenstern and Rosencrantz.

GUIL. Which is which?

ROS. Well, I'm—You're——

GUIL. What's it all about?——

ROS. Well, we were bringing Hamlet—but then some pirates——

GUIL. I don't begin to understand. Who are all these people, what's it got to do with me? You turn up out of the blue with some cock and bull story——

ROS (*with letter*). We have a letter——

GUIL (*snatches it, opens it*). A letter—yes—that's true. That's something . . . a letter . . . (*Reads.*) "As England is Denmark's faithful tributary . . . as love between them like the palm might flourish, etcetera . . . that on the knowing of this contents, without delay of any kind, should those bearers, Rosencrantz and Guildenstern, put to sudden death——"

He double-takes. Ros snatches the letter. Guil snatches it back. Ros snatches it half back. They read it again and look up.

The Player gets to his feet and walks over to his barrel and kicks it and shouts into it.

PLAYER. They've gone! It's all over!

One by one the Players emerge, impossibly, from the barrel, and form a casually menacing circle round Ros and Guil, who are still appalled and mesmerised.

GUIL (*quietly*). Where we went wrong was getting on a boat. We can move, of course, change direction, rattle about, but our movement is contained within a larger one that carries us along as inexorably as the wind and current. . . .

ROS. They had it in for us, didn't they? Right from the beginning. Who'd have thought that we were so important?

GUIL. But why? Was it all for this? Who are we that so much should converge on our little deaths? (*In anguish to the Player:*) Who are *we*?

PLAYER. You are Rosencrantz and Guildenstern. That's enough.

GUIL. No—it is not enough. To be told so little—to such an end—and still, finally, to be denied an explanation——

PLAYER. In our experience, most things end in death.

GUIL (*fear, vengeance, scorn*): Your experience!—Actors!

He snatches a dagger from the Player's belt and holds the point at the Player's throat: the Player backs and Guil advances, speaking more quietly.

I'm talking about death—and you've never experienced *that*. And you cannot *act* it. You die a thousand casual deaths—with none of that intensity which squeezes out life . . . and no blood runs cold anywhere. Because even as you die you know that you will come back in a different hat. But no one gets up after *death*—there is no applause—there is only silence and some second-hand clothes, and that's—*death*——

And he pushes the blade in up to the hilt. The Player stands with huge, terrible eyes, clutches at the wound as the blade withdraws: he makes small weeping sounds and falls to his knees, and then right down.

While he is dying, Guil, nervous, high, almost hysterical, wheels on the Tragedians——

If we have a destiny, then so had he—and if this is ours, then that was his—and if there are no explanations for us, then let there be none for him——

The Tragedians watch the Player die: they watch with some interest. The Player finally lies still. A short moment of silence. Then the Tragedians start to applaud with genuine admiration. The Player stands up, brushing himself down.

PLAYER (*modestly*). Oh, come, come, gentlemen—no flattery—it was merely competent——

The Tragedians are still congratulating him. The Player approaches Guil, who stands rooted, holding the dagger.

PLAYER. What did you think? (*Pause.*) You see, it *is* the kind they do believe in—it's what is expected.

He holds his hand out for the dagger. Guil slowly puts the point of the dagger on to the Player's hand, and pushes . . . the blade slides back into the handle. The Player smiles, reclaims the dagger.

For a moment you thought I'd—cheated.

Ros relieves his own tension with loud nervy laughter.

ROS. Oh, very good! Very good! Took me in completely—didn't he take you in completely—(*claps his hands*). Encore! Encore!

PLAYER (*activated, arms spread, the professional*): Deaths for all ages and occasions! Deaths by suspension, convulsion, consumption, incision, execution, asphyxiation and malnutrition—! Climactic carnage, by poison and by steel—! Double deaths by duel—! Show!—

Alfred, still in his Queen's costume, dies by poison: the Player, with rapier, kills the "King" and duels with a fourth Tragedian, inflicting and receiving a wound. The two remaining Tragedians, the two "Spies" dressed in the same coats as Ros and Guil, are stabbed, as before. And the light is fading over the deaths which take place right upstage.

(*Dying amid the dying—tragically; romantically.*) So there's an end to that—it's commonplace: light goes with life, and in the winter of your years the dark comes early. . . .

GUIL (*tired, drained, but still an edge of impatience; over the mime*). No . . . no . . . not for *us*, not like that. Dying is not romantic, and death is not a game which will soon be over . . . Death is not anything . . . death is not . . . It's the absence of presence, nothing more . . . the endless time of never coming back . . . a gap you can't see, and when the wind blows through it, it makes no sound. . . .

The light has gone upstage. Only Guil and Ros are visible as Ros's clapping falters to silence.

Small pause.

ROS. That's it, then, is it?

No answer. He looks out front.

The sun's going down. Or the earth's coming up, as the fashionable theory has it.

Small pause.

Not that it makes any difference.

Pause.

What was it all about? When did it begin?

Pause. No answer.

Couldn't we just stay put? I mean no one is going to come on and drag us off. . . . They'll just have to wait. We're still young . . . fit . . . we've got years. . . .

Pause. No answer.

(*A cry.*) We've done nothing wrong! We didn't harm anyone. Did we?
GUIL. I can't remember.

Ros pulls himself together.

ROS. All right, then. I don't care. I've had enough. To tell you the truth, I'm relieved.

And he disappears from view. Guil does not notice.

GUIL. Our names shouted in a certain dawn . . . a message . . . a summons . . . There must have been a moment, at the beginning, where we could have said—no. But somehow we missed it. (*He looks round and sees he is alone.*)

Rosen—?
Guil—?

He gathers himself.

Well, we'll know better next time. Now you see me, now you—(*and disappears*).

Immediately the whole stage is lit up, revealing, up-stage, arranged in the approximate positions last held by the dead Tragedians, the tableau of court and corpses which is the last scene of Hamlet.

That is: The King, Queen, Laertes and Hamlet all dead. Horatio holds Hamlet. Fortinbras is there.

So are two Ambassadors from England.

AMBASSADOR. The sight is dismal;
and our affairs from England come too late.
The ears are senseless that should give us hearing
to tell him his commandment is fulfilled,
that Rosencrantz and Guildenstern are dead.
Where should we have our thanks?
HORATIO. Not from his mouth,
had it the ability of life to thank you:
He never gave commandment for their death.
But since, so jump upon this bloody question,
you from the Polack wars, and you from England,
are here arrived, give order that these bodies
high on a stage be placed to the view;
and let me speak to the yet unknowing world
how these things came about: so shall you hear
of carnal, bloody and unnatural acts,
of accidental judgments, casual slaughters,
of deaths put on by cunning and forced cause,
and, in this upshot, purposes mistook
fallen on the inventors' heads: all this I
truly deliver.

But during the above speech, the play fades out, overtaken by dark and music.

COMMENTARY

Notes: The following essay represents a single interpretation of the play. For other perspectives on Rosencrantz and Guildenstern Are Dead, *consult the essays listed below.*

In 1917 T. S. Eliot wrote "The Love Song of J. Alfred Prufrock," which some have labeled "the first modern poem" because it portrays both comically and sadly the loneliness of the insignificant, even superfluous, little man (cf. Buchner's drama, *Woyzeck,* in the Prologue). Late in the poem Prufrock laments that—"No!"—he is

> . . . not Prince Hamlet, nor was meant to be;
> Am an attendant lord, one that will do
> To swell a progress, start a scene or two,
> Advise the prince; no doubt an easy tool,
> Deferential, glad to be of use,
> Politic, cautious, and meticulous;
> Full of high sentence, but a bit obtuse,
> At times, indeed, almost ridiculous—
> Almost, at times, the Fool.

Stoppard's invention (and there seem to be no precedents for the kind of play he has written here) is to make Ros and Guil, those quintessential "attendant lords," the heroes of a Shakespeare-like tragedy. Here we get a much closer look at perhaps the two least consequential supporting roles in Shakespeare's canon. On closer inspection they seem to be two characters from a Beckett play in search of an author. (Indeed, Stoppard nods to their Beckettian roots in the final act when he stuffs Ros and Guil in barrels, a parody of the characters who spend that play confined to ash cans in Beckett's *Endgame.*)

Like Hamlet, Ros and Guil pass time meditating on death as they wander to and through Elsinore's deadly castle. And as they do for Hamlet, the traveling actors, led by the loquacious Player King, help Ros and Guil understand their dilemma—sort of. In actuality, the Player, who is the third most important character in the play and its raisonneur, mostly manages to muddy the waters for them. His version of reality, which depends on the ingenuity of a playwright, does not always square with the reality Ros and Guil experience when they are not characters in Shakespeare's plays and have to live "real life."

Keep in mind that we observe two sets of Ros and Guils in this play:

- Those that Shakespeare created, who are, at best, attendant lords and easy tools for the machinations at Elsinore's court
- Those that Stoppard created, who are witty, philosophical, and engaging in ways that Shakespeare did not envision (nor should he have)

In Shakespeare's play Hamlet tells his other school chum, Horatio, that he has sent Ros and Guil to their deaths in the English court without remorse ("They are not near my conscience . . . they did make love to their employment," he tells Horatio). However, thanks to Stoppard's ingenuity, Ros and Guil are very near our consciences when they "disappear" into darkness in Act III. We know them intimately through their many conversations with one another and the Player. They emerge as likeable flesh-and-blood human beings who were only tangential to Shakespeare's play. We enjoy them for their witty, thoughtful musings on life, death, literature (the play also functions as a piece of dramatic criticism), and a host of other topics. Mostly we are attracted to them because we often find ourselves in their position. They've been thrust into a game they must play, but they do not know the rules or even the object of the game. At one point early in the play, Ros cries out (a *"voice in the wilderness,"* says the stage direction): "What's the game?" To which Guil responds forlornly, "What are the rules?" This is precisely the dilemma of contemporary humans: we must often play a game we cannot comprehend because there are no discernible rules (ever had an IRS audit?). Or to use the other metaphor upon which

Stoppard builds his Pirandello-like play: Ros and Guil are cast in a comic drama called "Life," but they don't have a script from which to work; they are not even sure what characters they play (note they, too, have trouble distinguishing themselves from one another). Thus they can only improvise their way through the unfathomable twists and turns of the plot, theirs as well as that of *Hamlet* (the play), "asking the right questions and giving away as little as we can." Significantly, the questions they ask, as well as the improvisations they devise to pass the time between meetings with the King and the Prince, constitute a kind of dramatic criticism of *Hamlet*. (Says Ros of the Danish Prince: "A compulsion towards philosophical introspection is his chief characteristic. . . . It does not mean he is mad. It does not mean he isn't. Very often, it doesn't mean anything at all. Which may or may not be a kind of madness.")

Are Ros and Guil, therefore, merely victims of the cruel game/play in which they are forced to participate? Yes. And no. True, they are victimized by the machinations of Claudius and Hamlet in their titanic struggle for control of Elsinore. In another age and country Ros and Guil might have been called "good Germans" who blindly follow the commands of their leaders. On the other hand, Stoppard—unlike Shakespeare—actually gives Ros and Guil an "out" of the existential dilemma in which they find themselves. In the final act, while on the boat to England, they discover the letter that Claudius has written to the English king demanding the death of Hamlet. (Stoppard, by the way, wrote an earlier version of this play, *Rosencrantz and Guildenstern Meet King Lear*, because he surmised Lear may well have been the English king at the time of Hamlet.) They debate whether to warn Hamlet, whom they judge to be a friend who has "done nothing to us." But Guil, ever the rationalist of this duo, delivers a lengthy speech in which he callously rejects Hamlet, noting that (a) Hamlet "is a man, he is mortal, death comes to us all, etcetera" and (b) they are only "little men [who] don't know the ins and outs of the matter." He concludes that "it would be presumptuous of us to interfere with the designs of fate or even of kings." Like Hamlet, who callously decides not to kill Claudius as he kneels praying in order to dispatch him to hell (thereby precipitating the chain of events that lead to his death and that of others), Ros and Guil also make a choice that seals their fate. They die—or, as they say, become "the absence of presence."

Unlike Hamlet, who ultimately recognizes that there is a divinity in the fall of a sparrow and that one must therefore be ready for death ("for it will come"), Ros and Guil never understand the design of the world any more than they understand that there is indeed a probability that a coin can come up "heads" 80-plus times under precisely the right circumstances. Sadly, yet comically, these "intellects" actually witness their own executions during the Players' rehearsal for the Mousetrap, failing to note that the doomed courtiers are dressed as they are. In their final moments they can only ruminate that "there must have been a moment . . . where we could have said—no. But somehow we missed it." Much like Sartre's trio in *No Exit* (see "Forerunners of the Absurd" Showcase in Part II) who are fixed forever by ill-chosen actions, this duo is doomed to be remembered as ineffectual cowards who "never received an explanation." Truly they are "obtuse . . . at times ridiculous, at times the Fools." Samuel Taylor Coleridge, the theater critic and poet, once said of Hamlet's appeal to generations of theatergoers: "I have a little smack of Hamlet in me." So, too, do we have "a little smack of Ros and Guil in us" as we improvise our way through the play called "Life."

Other perspectives on *Rosencrantz and Guildenstern Are Dead*:

Egan, Robert. "A Thin Beam of Light: The Purpose of Playing in *Rosencrantz and Guildenstern Are Dead*." *Theatre Journal* 31 (March 1979): 59–69.

Kelly, Katherine E. "At the Boundary: *Rosencrantz and Guildenstern Are Dead*." In Kelly, *Tom Stoppard and the Craft of Comedy*. Ann Arbor: University of Michigan Press, 1991, 71–81.

See *Rosencrantz and Guildenstern Are Dead* on video:

Rosencrantz and Guildenstern Are Dead. Dir. Tom Stoppard. Perf. Tim Roth and Gary Oldham. Buena Vista Home Video, 118 min., 1988.

SUPPLEMENT   A *HAMLET* PRIMER

Shakespeare's *Hamlet* (1601) may well be the most performed play in the world, and it is unquestionably the most dissected and critiqued play ever written. Stoppard's play is, in effect, yet another piece of dramatic criticism about the enigmatic prince of Denmark. Interestingly, the two plays are often performed in tandem, usually at summer Shakespeare festivals. Actors often play the same character in each play.

In case you are not already familiar with *Hamlet*, we present a brief synopsis of its plot, with specific reference to the scenes in which Rosencrantz and Guildenstern appear.

The Story

Hamlet, the Prince of Denmark, is a student at Wittenberg University when he learns that his father, the King, has suddenly died. He returns to Elsinore Castle for the funeral to discover that his mother, the Queen, intends to marry Claudius, Hamlet's uncle and the brother of the dead king. The ghost of Old Hamlet (who likely was played by Shakespeare himself at the Globe Theatre) appears to some soldiers and Horatio, Hamlet's friend from Wittenberg. They tell Hamlet of the strange apparition, even as Hamlet is despondently reacting to his mother's "o'er hasty marriage" to Claudius. The Prince seeks out the Ghost, who says that he was murdered by Claudius and commands his son to revenge "this most foul and unnatural murder." Hamlet adopts a pose of madness to keep the King and court off guard while he seeks the truth about his father's murder. The King and Queen, troubled by Hamlet's strange behavior, summon two more of his schoolmates, Rosencrantz and Guildenstern, to Elsinore to report on Hamlet's behavior.

At first Hamlet is glad to see his friends, and the trio exchanges some light banter about current theater conditions. Ros and Guil talk about the problems that boys' acting companies (the "little Eyases") are creating for adult theater companies (a problem Shakespeare's own company faced in 1601). Hamlet becomes suspicious of their motives but is heartened when Ros and Guil tell him that traveling actors are approaching Elsinore to entertain the court. Hamlet immediately concocts a plan whereby the actors will recreate the murder of his royal father so that he may "catch the conscience of the king."

Not only have Ros and Guil been employed to spy on Hamlet, however unwittingly, but so has Ophelia, Hamlet's love and the daughter of Polonius, the counselor to Claudius. When Hamlet catches Ophelia lying to him about her father's whereabouts (even as Polonius and the King are themselves spying on Hamlet), the Prince becomes even more suspicious—perhaps even paranoid—of those around him, especially Ros and Guil. After the traveling actors perform their play (which Hamlet has dubbed "The Mousetrap") to expose Claudius, Hamlet turns viciously against Ros and Guil and threatens them. Hamlet, now armed with the truth, kills Polonius, who is hiding behind a curtain to spy on Hamlet and his mother. Hamlet berates his mother for her adultery and threatens Claudius. The King, fearing for his life, sends Hamlet, accompanied by Ros and Guil, to England, ostensibly to collect money from the English king; however, he sends a letter with Ros and Guil instructing the English to kill Hamlet.

While Hamlet, Ros, and Guil are en route to England via ship, Ophelia goes mad and drowns herself. Her brother, Laertes, returns from Paris to seek revenge for Polonius's death and that of his sister. He and Claudius devise a plan to kill Hamlet during a "rigged" duel when they learn that the Prince has suddenly returned to Denmark after boldly (and miraculously?) boarding a pirate's vessel and securing passage back to Elsinore.

As Hamlet prepares for the duel with Laertes, he confides to Horatio that he discovered the letter demanding his death. Hamlet says he rewrote the letter so that its bearers—Ros and Guil—would be sentenced to death. Hamlet fights Laertes, and each man is mortally wounded, even as the Queen dies from drinking a poisoned cup of wine the King had set out for Hamlet. Before he dies, Hamlet kills Claudius and thus avenges his father's murder. Messengers from England arrive with the news that "Rosencrantz and Guildenstern are dead." Only Horatio lives to tell this sad tale to young Fortinbras, son of the Norwegian king whom Old Hamlet had killed years earlier. Fortinbras becomes the king of Denmark and commands that Hamlet be given a royal burial.

The Function of Rosencrantz and Guildenstern in *Hamlet*

Of the named characters in *Hamlet*, Ros and Guil are the least developed, least interesting participants in this extraordinary tragedy. Shakespeare himself underscores their "facelessness" when Claudius confuses one for the other, only to be corrected by the Queen. (Or is it the Queen who is confused? Stoppard continues this joke in his own play.) Ros and Guil have been created primarily to advance a major motif Shakespeare uses throughout the play: spying. This is a play in which everyone spies, eavesdrops, observes everyone else; in effect, each character is both an actor and an audience, one who performs while others watch or watches while others perform. This reinforces the play-life metaphor Shakespeare employs in virtually all of his plays; this is the man who wrote "All the world's a stage" in *As You Like It*.

Ros and Guil also give us a glimpse of Hamlet's lighter side. We get to see him as he might have been at Wittenberg, exchanging bawdy jokes with his buddies, talking about current events and theater practice. We also see how vicious Hamlet can be when he has been crossed by those whom he once trusted. In short, Ros and Guil allow Shakespeare to paint a more complex portrait of the Prince, just as Stoppard does with the two courtiers in his play. And, as is often the case with such characters who appear briefly in a play, they ask all the right questions of Hamlet and create exposition in their dialogue. (As one critic noted: imagine how many more soliloquies *Hamlet* would require were not the three lads from Wittenberg come to Elsinore!)

Finally, Ros and Guil fall victim to the pervasive evil that destroys Elsinore. In the Elizabethan schema, evil would finally devour itself, as it does Claudius, who himself introduces all of the devices that lead to his death in Act V. But

evil is indiscriminate and kills the innocent as well as the guilty. Whether Ros and Guil are entirely guiltless, we shall leave you to judge as you read Stoppard's ingenious play.

See *Hamlet* on video:

There are over two dozen film versions of *Hamlet*; three of the most accessible are listed below.

Hamlet. Dir. Laurence Olivier. Perf. Laurence Olivier and Jean Simmons. MGM/UA Video, 157 min., 1948.

Hamlet. Dir. Franco Zeffirelli. Perf. Mel Gibson, Alan Bates, Glenn Close, and Helen Bonham-Carter. Warner, 135 min., 1992.

Hamlet. Dir. Kenneth Branagh. Perf. Kenneth Branagh, Kate Winslett, Derek Jacobi, and Julie Christie. Castle Rock, 280 min., 1996. *Note:* This version contains the complete text of Shakespeare's play and the most comprehensive treatment of the Rosencrantz and Guildenstern subplot.

Some of the most provocative and powerful theater works of the late twentieth and early twenty-first centuries have fused ancient texts with contemporary sensibilities. Playwright Naomi Iizuka calls this process "jostling." Scholar Marianne McDonald calls it "reinterpreting." Critic Bonnie Marranca terms it "layering." And the influential Japanese theater director Tadashi Suzuki names his three potent adaptations from Greek tragedy "reconstructions" intended to explore how the classic drama intersects with Japan's decadent, post–World War II society. Such fusions have been as popularly appealing as Mary Zimmerman's shimmering, pool-set, visually striking *Metamorphoses*, a riff on the Latin poet Ovid, which moved from American regional theaters to Broadway and won its creator a 2002 Tony Award for directing. The spoiled, sun-loving Icarus, in this interpretation, floats about a Beverly Hills pool wearing a gold swimsuit and sunglasses. Or the fusions can maintain the emotional intensity and harrowing spirit of source material in Greek tragedy: Suzuki's post-nuclear *Clytemnestra* and *The Trojan Women* with towering, primal performances by Kayoko Shiraishi reimagined the already modern and despairing spirit of Euripides for our age. So, too, did the wordless, preapocalyptic Euripides-based stage works of Heiner Müller such as *Medeaplay*. As directed by Sir Peter Hall, John Barton's eight-hour-long *Tantalus* (2000)—an epic cycle of plays based on the legends of the Trojan wars—even used classically derived masks and other devices from ancient drama to intermittently weave a theatrical spell.

Still other writers play fast and loose with their sources, achieving a mixed, contemporary tone, as Charles L. Mee, Jr., did in his punk-and-pop-inflected *Big Love*, an update on Aeschylus's *The Suppliant Women*, which spliced passages from popular magazines and Motown songs into the ancient text. Similarly free-form in her approach is playwright Kelly Stuart, who conflated the three parts of Aeschylus's *Orestia* into a sex-and-violence family drama called *Fierce Blood* (1999). One of the more effective of these updates was D. W. Jacobs and Scott Feldsher's *The Whole World Is Watching* (1995), which reconceived Sophocles's *Oedipus Tyrannos* in talk show format, with the citizens of Thebes as a Jerry Springer–like audience demanding answers about the plague decimating their city.

Clearly these works range widely in depth, significance, and quality. But the preponderance of such fusions suggests both the universal relevance of the classical stories and the global interest in the roots of drama in ancient Greece and Rome. The American director Peter Sellars is one of the more astute students of ancient drama. With writer Robert Auletta, he adapted the earliest surviving Greek tragedy, *The Persians*, a play centering on the defeated rather than the victors, and created in 1994 a kind of cautionary tale after the Gulf War. The production, seen in several American cities and many European drama festivals, proved an intense meditation upon the causes and consequences of war, an exploration of the resources of theater, a thought-provoking, if sometimes muddled comment on the U.S. military adventure in the Persian Gulf, and in the end, a thrilling, intractable, irreducible work of theatrical art.

Though adapted in the same spirit of empathy, *The Persians* of Auletta and Sellars barely resembles the play that won Aeschylus the first prize for tragedy at the Great Dionysa in 472 B.C., the play that scholars consider the first known Western drama. When the production opened at the Mark Taper Forum in Los Angeles, the light trickle of walkouts became something of a stream when the extraordinary Howie Seago, the gestural (because deaf) actor, began signing his passionate "speeches" as the ghost of the Persian King Darius. Still, at its best Sellars' production reenvisioned the tragic cadence and ritual spirit of early Greek theater in contemporary terms, while at its most gnawingly specific in its textual updating *The Persians* sank to a political tirade.

Seago and Ben Halley, Jr., in a ceremonial, declamatory role as the first Chorus, had worked with Sellars and Auletta before on their powerful, more floridly postmodern production of *Ajax* at the La Jolla Playhouse in 1986, a stunning production pointedly asking whether any successful soldier inured to killing (Americans after Vietnam, especially) could adjust to civilian life. In one of its most striking images, Ajax stood in a Plexiglas box that gradually filled with blood. Since then, Sellars has been stripping his means toward a more elemental—and therefore, classical—approach to theatrical expression, as demonstrated in *The Persians*.

Such has also been the transformation of Suzuki's vision; the Japanese director initially created works based on the realism of foreign models from a progressive point of view. Over time, his understanding of Japan's classic Noh drama and of Greek tragedy, as well as his association with Shiraishi, led him to create more monumental and abstract drama. He also acquired in 1976 a unique performing space in the countryside village of Toga, and there he created a method of physical training and a spirit of ensemble among his actors that give his reconstructions of classics their singular intensity, beauty, and communal energy.

Interestingly, Sellars made similar though less consistent use of a physical vocabulary of movement in his production of *The Persians*. Halley and Seago are both immense physical and dramatic presences; joined with Joseph Haj as the second Chorus, they physically embodied a view of "male" political power. The consequences of their actions were literally embodied in three "female" characters: the queen Atossa played by diminutive, vulnerable Cordelia Gonzalez, the third Chorus by Javanese classical dancer Martinus Miroto, and the bold, androgynous

Xerxes by John Ortiz. The casting—in its physical and vocal details and its multiculturalism—proved nearly perfect for Sellars' dramatic purposes, while scenically *The Persians* was spare and ascetic, in the tradition of Asian dance theater. Against the curved, white back wall of the Taper Forum were just two black chairs facing a central microphone where, after the long choric opening, the Persian queen Atossa stood to address the chorus. She speaks through a microphone, which Sellars here uses for characters in their public roles; they drop the mike when they speak from the heart. Underscoring and unifying the whole was the heart-piercing music of the Nubian composer-performer Hamza El Din.

The internationalism of the cast and staging techniques in *The Persians* suggested that the best of these classic fusions, such as Peter Brooks's landmark stage adaptation of the Indian epic *Mahabharata*, are becoming a matrix for artistic expression across national and language boundaries. The Attis Theater of Greece has brought stunningly physical and visual stagings of Heiner Müller works inspired by Euripides to the United States. When a work such as Attis Theater's "Despoiled Shore/*Medea*material/Landscape with Argonauts" in Greek is embraced by Americans, artistic globalization begins to reveal new and shared dimensions of reality.

PAPER FLOWERS

("Flores de Papel")

EGON WOLFF

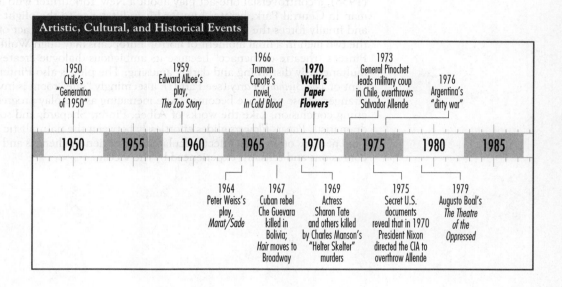

Artistic, Cultural, and Historical Events

1950 Chile's "Generation of 1950"	1959 Edward Albee's play, *The Zoo Story*	1966 Truman Capote's novel, *In Cold Blood*	**1970 Wolff's Paper Flowers**	1973 General Pinochet leads military coup in Chile, overthrows Salvador Allende	1976 Argentina's "dirty war"

1950   1955   1960   1965   1970   1975   1980   1985

1964 Peter Weiss's play, *Marat/Sade*	1967 Cuban rebel Che Guevara killed in Bolivia; *Hair* moves to Broadway	1969 Actress Sharon Tate and others killed by Charles Manson's "Helter Skelter" murders	1975 Secret U.S. documents reveal that in 1970 President Nixon directed the CIA to overthrow Allende	1979 Augusto Boal's *The Theatre of the Oppressed*

EGON WOLFF (1926–)

Although a chemical engineer by training, Egon Wolff has emerged as a leading voice in South American drama, particularly when *Paper Flowers* won the coveted *Casa de las Americas* Prize in 1970 as Latin America's best new play. *The Latin American Theatre Review* called the play "among the top three or four plays from all of Spanish America" in its Spring 1983 edition.

Wolff first wrote plays as an avocation largely because he wished to address the social, political, and economic problems facing his native Chile. In 1963 he achieved national recognition for his play *The Invaders*, an expressionistic work in which a rich industrialist dreams that his estate is invaded by the poor—a dream that becomes frighteningly true. Chileans considered the play prophetic when in 1970 Salvador Allende Gossens was elected president, the first Marxist to be elected democratically in the Western Hemisphere. Allende, who promised to turn Chile into a socialist state, was driven from office just three years later by a right-wing military coup, led by Augusto Pinochet Ugarte.

As might be expected, Wolff's plays reflect the bitter and often violent struggles between Chile's wealthy and the poor. He maintains his emphasis on class conflict because "people aren't listening." His plays are directed at the upper class, which—according to Wolff—has the responsibility and the power to change social circumstances in Chile (and elsewhere in Latin America). However, he does not write overt political drama because, he says, "it doesn't interest me."

Wolff admits that his work has become increasingly darker, less hopeful. When he was younger he felt he had answers for the social problems he depicted. "I write for the present of Chile and that is enough. 'Future' is a word that sometimes terrifies me." He continues to write and to work as an engineer. His works have been produced throughout Latin America, the United States, and Great Britain, frequently in both Spanish and English productions.

As You Read *Paper Flowers*

Paper Flowers may remind North American audiences of Edward Albee's *The Zoo Story* (1958), a controversial one-act play about a New York drifter who accosts a middle-class man in Central Park, berates him for his indifference to the plight of the less fortunate, and finally forces the hapless bourgeois to commit a shocking act of violence that melds the two men in a final moment of horror. Europeans may align Wolff's drama with Harold Pinter's "theatre of menace" because its ambiguous dialogue creates a tension that is simultaneously disturbing and darkly amusing. The plot is also Pinteresque, even reminiscent of *The Birthday Party* (see Part II): a seemingly "safe" room is invaded by a mysterious stranger whose presence becomes more menacing as the play progresses toward its frightening conclusion. Like the works of Albee, Pinter, Shepard, and so many contemporary dramatists, *Papers Flowers* glides effortlessly between the naturalistic and surrealistic styles (and perhaps others), an effect calculated to disorient audiences and make them sense the confusions and tensions experienced by the victim.

PAPER FLOWERS

A Play in Six Scenes

EGON WOLFF

Translated by Margaret Sayers Peden

The hake is a fish of the Chilean seacoast. It is long and thin-bodied, its large, acute-nosed mouth set with sharp teeth. It hunts the deep waters of the Pacific to feed its voracious appetite.

SCENE 1

The living room of a small suburban apartment, carefully arranged, revealing a feminine hand. Comfortable. Intimate. Three doors in addition to the entrance. One to the bedroom; one to the bathroom; the third to the kitchen.

One window.

A canary in a cage.

Somewhere, an easel with a half-finished painting. A box of oils.

Also, straw figures: fish, heads of animals, roosters, etc.

The stage is empty. Then Eva and The Hake enter. Eva, forty, is well dressed, with conscious elegance. The Hake, thirty, dirty, his hair uncombed, thin, pale. Eva, who opens the door, enters resolutely. She walks toward the kitchen. The Hake stands in the doorway. He carries two large paper bags. He is trembling visibly. He looks at the room with timid curiosity.

EVA (*returning from the kitchen*). Well, come in! Come in! Leave those in there, in the kitchen!

The Hake enters with respectful caution. Never taking his eyes from the objects in the room, he places the bags on the floor, in the middle of the room.

Not there! (*She points to the kitchen.*) In the kitchen. Next to the stove, please!

The Hake does as she says. He returns without the bags. Eva has gone into the bedroom. She comes out brushing her hair. She takes a bill from her wallet, which has been lying on a small table, and hands it to him.

EVA. Here you are, and . . . thanks very much.

The Hake refuses the bill she hands him. Take it! You're not going to tell me you carried my packages for nothing?

The Hake stares at her.

Well, then . . . thanks very much. You've been very kind.

The Hake continues to stare at her.

Very pleasant. There was no reason for you to do it. Thank you very much.

THE HAKE (*in an impersonal, painful voice*). I would rather you gave me a cup . . . of tea.

EVA (*a little surprised*). Tea?

THE HAKE. You do have some, don't you?

EVA. Yes, I do, but . . . I don't have time. (*She offers him the bill once more.*) You can buy yourself some tea anywhere with this. There's a drugstore on the corner.

THE HAKE. "Anywhere" wouldn't be the same.

EVA (*interested, amused*). Oh, no? Why?

553

THE HAKE. It wouldn't be the same.

He stares at her, continuously.

EVA. Well . . . but I don't have time, I already told you. Take this and go on. I have things to do.

THE HAKE. They're waiting for me down there.

EVA. Who's waiting for you?

THE HAKE. Miguel and "Birdy."

EVA. The two that were following us?

The Hake nods.

What do they want? Why are they waiting for you?

THE HAKE. To get me.

EVA. Well, what do you want me to do? (*Annoyed.*) Take this. I have things to do.

THE HAKE. They're going to kill me.

EVA. That's your affair. Don't bother me any more, I tell you. Go away!

THE HAKE. I didn't think you'd be so hard. You don't look it.

EVA. Well, then, you were mistaken.

THE HAKE. Since the first time I saw you, last year, painting those flowers in the Botanical Garden. I've thought you were different.

A pause.

EVA. The Botanical Garden? You saw me?

THE HAKE. You were behind the parrot's cage, painting some clumps of laurel. . . . (*He stares at her.*) You had on a light straw hat with a green ribbon. And a kerchief with some scenes of Venice.

EVA. You're a good observer, aren't you?

THE HAKE. I observe certain things.

EVA. So your offer today, to carry the packages for me. . . . (*Perturbed.*) What did you say you wanted?

THE HAKE. A cup of tea.

EVA. Wouldn't you rather have a bowl of soup? I'll bet you haven't eaten today.

THE HAKE. Anything you want to give me.

EVA. I have some soup from last night. Shall I warm it for you?

THE HAKE. If you want to.

EVA. Well, sit down while I fix it.

She goes into the kitchen. One hears the clatter of pots and pans. The Hake, meanwhile, stands fixed where he is, not moving a millimeter. Eva comes back after a while.

Sit down. Surely you're not going to stand there all day.

THE HAKE. Not in these clothes.

EVA (*from the kitchen*). I don't think the furniture will mind.

The Hake takes a newspaper from an inside pocket of his coat, doubles it carefully, scrupulously, and places it on one of the armchairs. He sits upon it. Eva watches his actions and smiles. She props open the kitchen door with a chair so she will be able to talk through the open door.

Do you go often to the Botanical Garden?

THE HAKE. Sometimes.

EVA. To look at the flowers?

THE HAKE. No, to give peanuts to the monkeys.

EVA. Do you like the monkeys?

The Hake shrugs his shoulders.

I think they're dirty . . . gross! I can't bear them. To watch them . . . there . . . picking their fleas in front of everybody. I can't stand them!

THE HAKE. They do what they can.

EVA. Do you have time for that?

THE HAKE. For what?

EVA. To go to the Garden?

THE HAKE. I arrange it.

EVA. I wish I had more!

At that moment The Hake is struck by uncontrollable spasms. They rack his entire body. They contort his face. He must hold on to the table to maintain his upright position. He turns his back to the door of the kitchen and clamps his arms between his legs. It concerns him that Eva not see him in this state. Nevertheless, Eva notices. Finally, he masters the spasms.

How do you do at the supermarket? Do you find many clients?

THE HAKE. There's always someone who finds his packages too heavy.

Eva comes out of the kitchen carrying soup and table service for them both. She places it all on the small table. As she does this, The Hake rises.

EVA. It isn't very warm, but I suppose you'd like it better that way. Sit down!

THE HAKE. I'm fine.

EVA. Sit down and help yourself.

The Hake takes the bowl and begins to take spoonfuls standing up.

But sit down, for Heaven's sake!

She returns to the kitchen and comes out again car-
rying a hard-boiled egg, a tomato, and a glass of
milk. She places them on the table.

I'm not going to begin if you go on standing there
like that.

THE HAKE. It's . . . considerate enough of you to invite
me to have this. I wouldn't take advantage and sit
down with you—where I don't belong.

EVA (*openly*). And if I tell you it doesn't matter to me?

THE HAKE. I thought you were saying it to make it
seem . . . easy. (*He sits down.*) It isn't good to go too
far. (*Indicating the soup.*) Is it because of your figure?

EVA (*laughing*). Yes. Because of my figure! If it weren't for
this, I'd be big as a balloon! I have a terrible tendency
to gain weight. I eat a piece of bread and I gain a
pound.

THE HAKE. That's a shame.

EVA. Yes. And a nuisance.

THE HAKE. It's just the opposite with Mario.

EVA. Who's Mario?

THE HAKE. A friend. Every time he eats a piece of bread
he loses half a pound. He's skin and bones. It comes
from stubbornness. The doctors tell him he should
eat more, but he's stubborn.

He looks in her eyes with an expressionless, concen-
trated look.

You shouldn't do that.

EVA. Do what?

THE HAKE. Eat so little. It might harm you. You might
die.

EVA. Does it matter? Does it matter to anyone?

THE HAKE. It matters to me.

They eat a moment, in silence, each one concentrat-
ing on his soup. The Hake spoons his, but never takes
his eyes off Eva. After a while, Eva rises nervously.

EVA (*half laughing*). So that's how you kill your time?
Going to the Botanical Garden to see how a lonely
old woman kills *her* time painting the laurel in
bloom?

She goes into the kitchen. She returns with salt and a
napkin.

Because that's how I seem to you, isn't it? A lonely
old woman? Killing time?

The Hake looks at her; he does not respond.

Let's see. Tell me! What do you think I am?

THE HAKE. A woman.

EVA. No, no! What I mean is: married or single?

THE HAKE. Married.

EVA (*with coquettish curiosity*). Why?

THE HAKE. From the way you cross your legs.

Eva laughs.

EVA. Oh, how amusing! And why? How do old maids
cross their legs?

THE HAKE (*expressionless*). They don't cross them.

Eva laughs nervously.

EVA. How amusing you are! (*Always half laughing.*) Tell
me. Do you always stare at people?

The Hake immediately lowers his glance to his soup.

Well, you guessed (*touched; excited*). I'm married.
Doesn't that worry you? What if my husband should
enter suddenly and find me here with you?

THE HAKE (*low*). What *could* he think?

EVA (*still coquettish*). Why not?

THE HAKE. You shouldn't joke about being poor.

A moment of embarrassment. The Hake is struck by
another attack, which he can scarcely suppress.

EVA (*doesn't know what to do*). Eat something, man. You
haven't eaten a thing.

The Hake gestures that it doesn't matter.

A drink? Is that it? (*Pause.*) Do you need a drink to
calm that trembling?

The Hake makes a vague gesture. Eva goes toward
the kitchen and returns with a glass of wine, which
The Hake grabs from her hands and drinks avidly.
This finally calms him.

Almost, mmmm?

THE HAKE. Almost what?

EVA. Well . . . almost. I didn't mean to offend you. I
wasn't amusing myself at your expense; it's just that
it seems so . . . well, so strange, that you remember
me. Among others. . . . There are other people who
paint in the Garden. For instance, the old man in
the blue corduroy hat. Have you seen him? The one
who comes in the afternoons with his little cane
stool. Sometimes with a dog, sometimes without.
(*Laughs.*) One day he got angry with me because of
the way I use green tones. He practically yelled at
me that it wasn't academic. I never knew what he
meant by that. He walked around and around me,
shaking his cane. I thought he was going to knock
over my easel!

During this monologue, The Hake is almost doubled over.

Are you in pain?

THE HAKE. No.

EVA. Well, then, what's the matter?

THE HAKE. After my "dance," my stomach always knots up.

EVA. I have some tranquilizers. Do you want one?

THE HAKE. No, thank you.

EVA. Then, do you need a drink?

The Hake looks at her.

I mean, the trembling comes because of that, doesn't it?

There is no response. An embarrassing moment. Eva looks toward the kitchen.

Well, you'd better hurry because I have to leave soon. I open the store at two.

The Hake renews his slow spooning of soup. Eva returns with two peeled peaches. She places one in front of The Hake. She eats hers.

These peaches don't have the flavor they used to. I don't know what they do to them now. I remember when I was a child. We used to go with Mamma and Papa to a farm near the river where for practically nothing they let us go to the orchard and eat our fill of peaches and strawberries. What we could throw down! Those peaches really had flavor! Today they export the best ones and leave the leftovers for us. I remember that while Papa and Mamma sat down to eat at some tables that had been set under the trees, Alfredo and I—Alfredo is my brother—would go play in a barn that was close by. Climbing over the baler. . . . My brother Alfredo! He had a real obsession for doing the heroic thing. I remember he would hoist a handkerchief tied like a flag and we'd play "Take the Brigantine"! (*Laughs.*) He was the glorious captain, and I was the accursed corsair! Oh, what times! Silly, happy kids!

THE HAKE. If you throw me out, Miguel and "Birdy" will kill me.

EVA. And what do you want me to do? Leave you here?

THE HAKE. They're waiting for me around the corner, behind the pharmacy.

Eva goes to the window and looks out, barely raising the curtain.

EVA. There they are. They're looking up here.

She turns toward him.

Well. . . . What shall we do? I can't leave you here! (*Hardening herself.*) I have to go to the store . . . soon. I've already told you.

The Hake suddenly explodes, a spurting, agitated, machine-gun rattle of words. The tone is monotonous, mournful, almost a litany. As he finishes, he has a new onslaught of trembling.

THE HAKE. "Birdy" has a meathook under his coat! He has a meathook and he's been waiting all morning for me to kill me! Because last night I won a few bucks from him shooting craps and he says I cheated on him! And it isn't true, because I won fair and square. Playing fair and square. He came to Julia's house this morning to look for me, but I saw him hide behind the oven and got past him and ran toward the river. All morning I hid in the bushes down by the tannery, until I went to the supermarket, and if you hadn't helped me, he'd have killed me! If you don't help me and hide me, he'll kill me! If you don't help me hide, I'll die, and I don't want to die! I don't want to die! I don't want to die!

EVA. There, it's all right. It's all right! Calm yourself. No one's going to do anything to you.

She doesn't know what to do.

I could notify the police. Do you want me to? So they'll arrest those men?

The Hake shakes his head.

Ah, yes. That's true. The code of honor, umm? You don't denounce each other.

The Hake is bent over. He shivers. Eva considers the situation a while.

I'll have to lock you up in here.

The Hake looks at her.

Because you understand, don't you? I don't know you. And besides, the lock and chain are on the outside. I'll have to lock you inside until I come back.

THE HAKE. I understand.

EVA. I'll lock the other rooms, too. You'll have to wait for me here.

THE HAKE. More than logical.

EVA. You have some magazines. Today's paper . . .

THE HAKE. Thank you. . . .

He smiles for the first time—a broad, open smile—that says nothing.

It's as if everything had been . . . well, prepared. . . . Ready. . . . The newspapers, I mean, and the magazines. I couldn't ask for anything more, to tell the truth. Anything else would be, well . . . ungrateful, I'd say.

EVA. Yes.

Eva removes the bowls. She goes into the bathroom and then walks around combing her hair. The Hake eats a little of the peach. Then he gets up and walks toward the canary's cage.

THE HAKE. A pretty little bird. What's its name?

EVA. Goldie.

THE HAKE. Goldie, eh? (*He plays with it.*) Ps, ps, ps, ps! (*He gives it a piece of peach.*) You like that, eh? Ps, ps, ps, ps! You like to eat ripe fruit under the trees, eh, little glutton? (*Gives it another piece.*) Here, take it! That's it!

Eva closes the door to the bathroom. The Hake is alone.

You have quite a gullet, eh, you little queer? (*His voice takes on a tone of harshness.*) Did you know that I'm the cursed captain and you're the glorious corsair? Didn't you know that, you fuck-up? (*He shakes the cage.*) Didn't you know that? That I'm the cursed captain and you're the glorious corsair, you freaking bird? (*With a wounded voice.*) I don't know you! (*He shakes the cage again.*) I'll have to lock you up, because I don't know you, son-of-a-bitch bird. I'll have to chain you . . . !

Eva comes from the bathroom. She is ready to leave.

Ps, ps, ps, ps! Little canary . . . !

Eva turns on the radio.

EVA. I'll leave you this. Change it if you want.

THE HAKE. Thank you.

Eva walks toward the door.

Ma'am . . .

EVA (*turns*). Yes?

THE HAKE. I knew. The thousand times I've seen you, I knew that you were what your eyes say you are. . . .

EVA. I'll be back at six. (*Points to the kitchen.*) If you want to help yourself to anything. . . .

She exits.

One hears the noise of the lock and the rattle of the chain.

The Hake shakes the cage.

THE HAKE. Eat your little peaches! Eat, you shit! Eat, you fruity corsair!

He is shaking the cage as the curtain falls.

SCENE 2

The same evening, a little after six o'clock. The Hake is making a paper basket from doubled strips of newspaper. A paper bird hangs from the light fixture, a kind of gull, tied by a thread. The Hake is kneeling on the floor, surrounded by piles of scattered, disordered newspapers. The radio is playing a dance tune. Offstage, the sound of an automobile's brakes and the closing of its door. The Hake goes to the window to look, peering out from behind the curtain. Then he returns to his work.

After the sound of the key in the lock and the rattle of the chain, Eva enters. She is carrying a paper bag from which the neck of a bottle protrudes.

EVA (*nervous; appearing to be casual*). You see? Three minutes after six. Not a minute before or a minute after!

She closes the door. She bumps into the bird.

And this? What is it? Did you make it?

THE HAKE. Nobody else has been here.

EVA. It's precious! You're quite an artist, you know? A gull?

THE HAKE. Do you think it is?

EVA. Yes, of course! A gull! Precious!

THE HAKE. Then it is.

EVA (*about the basket*). And that? A basket?

The Hake nods.

That's precious, too. Where did you learn the art?

THE HAKE. It's for you. . . .

EVA. What? The basket.

THE HAKE. Everything.

EVA. Oh, thank you!

THE HAKE. Providing it doesn't bother you. . . .

EVA. No. Why should it bother me?

THE HAKE. The newspapers, I mean. Because I have spread out all the papers this way. Everything messed up.

He begins hastily to pick up the papers. He folds them carefully.

EVA. No, it doesn't matter. . . .

She goes toward the kitchen.

But, where did you learn this?

THE HAKE. Around. I worked for a guy who worked with wicker. But he was a moron. He only knew how to make chairs. I know how to make flowers, too.

EVA. Flowers?

THE HAKE. Camellias.

EVA (*from the kitchen*). But . . . for Heaven's sake! The dishes! Who washed them?

The Hake does not respond. Eva enters from the kitchen.

You didn't have to do that.

The Hake shrugs his shoulders.

I'll bet you scrubbed the floor, too? It wasn't this shiny when I left.

THE HAKE. There was some wax here, and I thought a little polish wouldn't hurt it any.

EVA (*smiling*). I don't dare go into the bedroom. What might I find there?

THE HAKE. Nothing. How could I go in there without your permission?

Eva goes into the kitchen again and returns with a salami and some cheese and a few packages of cigarettes.

EVA. Speaking of surprises, don't think I forgot you. I thought, since the nights are cold and "a full stomach is one's best friend" . . . a few snacks. A little paté. And cheese. Gruyère. Very rich. It was especially recommended by the owner of the store, who's a friend of mine.

The Hake scarcely looks at what Eva is showing him. He has finished gathering up the newspapers in a carefully folded stack and is going to carry them to the kitchen. He runs into Eva, and this produces a brief business of getting into each other's way.

Where are you going?

THE HAKE (*referring to the papers*). I took them from the kitchen.

EVA. Leave them. It doesn't matter.

THE HAKE. Everything's going to be messy.

EVA (*a little impatient; nervous*). It doesn't matter, I tell you. (*Smiles.*) Put them down there. (*Always with a small, nervous smile that looks strange, almost as if she were laughing to herself.*) When I went into the store, I was so wild to get there, thinking about buying this, that I completely forgot to invent an . . . excuse, because the question was bound to come up, and it did. "Who are you buying all this for, dear? Don't tell me

it's all for you?" At first, I didn't know what to say. I stammered out a couple of silly things, and then, when I was about out of breath, it occurred to me to say that it was for a picnic! (*Laughs.*) A picnic with some friends. Imagine! Me, on a picnic!

The Hake, kneeling on the floor again, folds and smooths the stack of newspapers with exaggerated care.

Because if I told her the truth. . . . Who do you think would have believed me?

THE HAKE. Nobody.

EVA. Yes. That's what I thought, too.

THE HAKE. In these cases you always offer a bowl of warm soup. (*Indicating the snacks.*) That would never occur to anyone. It's not necessary.

EVA (*laughs nervously*). Do you like it?

THE HAKE. What?

EVA. The salami? The cheese?

THE HAKE. You always ask two questions at once. I never know which to answer first.

EVA (*confused*). The salami?

THE HAKE. It turns my stomach.

EVA. You don't like it?

THE HAKE. It isn't that. It must be because my stomach isn't used to it. When you're only given rice soup and things like that, you develop a weak stomach. Once the sisters at the charity kitchen gave me roast meat with mushroom and I vomited for two days.

EVA. I should have thought of that. I shouldn't have bought it.

THE HAKE (*looks at her for the first time, with the look so typical of him—it says nothing*). Eat it with your friends on the picnic.

EVA. What friends? I don't have any friends.

THE HAKE. Tough luck for you.

Resumes his task.

EVA (*lively*). Well, I think I should start preparing dinner. That's my life. Eat, and then eat some more. A meal in the morning. A meal at noon. A meal at night! Sometimes I get to the point I think that's all life is: one big continuous meal, with an occasional pause for boredom, and then we begin eating again. And happiness too, naturally! Like a thin powdery dusting of sugar over the whole affair!

While speaking, she has gone from the kitchen to the bedroom, putting on and taking off a wool jacket, putting on and taking off some slippers, opening and closing closets, always with The Hake watching her imperturbably.

What foolish things one does. . . . Opening and closing closets . . . and putting clothes on and off . . . If you add up the days, the hours, you lose doing useless things . . .

She goes to the kitchen, where she can be heard working with the pans. She drops a glass. The noise of breaking glass.

Oh! How stupid I am! What's the matter with me today!

She comes out of the kitchen winding a handkerchief around her finger and walks toward the bedroom.

I cut myself! The day never passes that I don't have to go to my medicine chest!

The Hake rises.

THE HAKE. May I help you?

EVA (*from the bedroom*). No, let it be. I'm used to it. I told you. My fingers are covered with scars! The quarts of blood I've spilled! Not that I do it on purpose!

She comes out of the bedroom.

But a person wouldn't do a thing like that on purpose, do you think?

She hands him a pair of scissors and gauze.

Cut it here, will you, please?

The Hake cuts the gauze skillfully.

THE HAKE. Iodine, do you have any?

EVA. Yes.

She goes to the bedroom and returns with a little bottle of iodine that The Hake also uses with agility and skill. He paints the wound with iodine, places the gauze on it, and secures it with adhesive. Eva observes his movements. The Hake ostensively avoids all physical contact with her. He avoids her with prudent and delicate caution. Eva, on the other hand, doesn't show the same reticence; rather, curious sympathy, in contrast to his timidity. When The Hake finishes, he starts to tremble again. He sits down. He clasps his arms between his knees in his characteristic gesture. Eva goes to the kitchen and returns with a glass of wine. The Hake drinks avidly. The trembling subsides. He coughs.

Is that better?

The Hake nods.

It seems you have learned a little of everything around, haven't you? The only thing you don't seem to have learned is to talk. . . . Are you always so frugal with your words?

THE HAKE. Where I live there isn't much interest in listening.

EVA (*with irony*). I don't think where I live there is, either.

THE HAKE. Put on the jacket.

EVA. What did you say?

THE HAKE. The jacket and the slippers. . . .

EVA. Oh, that! No, I'm all right this way. . . .

THE HAKE. You were going to put them on.

EVA. Yes, but I'm fine. . . .

THE HAKE. Well, you were going to put them on. . . .

EVA. Yes, but . . . not now . . . and don't look at me like that! (*Laughs nervously.*) Don't look at me so much. Good Lord, what a starer you are! What a starer of a man! Do you always stare like that, tell me?

The Hake lowers his glance.

You're capable of making one completely . . .

She goes toward the kitchen.

Let's see, but I want to hear your story! Come on, tell me. Where did you learn to use your hands so well? In putting on gauze and adhesive, I mean?

From the kitchen.

You give the impression of being very familiar with them.

THE HAKE. I learned from an orderly, a sergeant.

EVA. Were you in the Army?

THE HAKE. In the hospital.

EVA. Ill?

THE HAKE. Something like that.

EVA. Like what? What was the matter?

THE HAKE. I can't talk like this. . . .

Eva comes out of the kitchen.

I can't talk like this . . . with you in the kitchen and me here, shouting. I can't talk if I don't see the other person's face. You'll forgive me, won't you? But I think you don't allow yourself sufficient . . . repose.

EVA (*her curiosity piqued*). Why do you say that?

THE HAKE. Because you're always going back and forth . . . up and down . . . moving things . . . changing things around . . . with no apparent reason. Since I came in here, you haven't once stopped moving around. Have you looked, for example, at the basket I'm making?

EVA. I looked at it, yes . . .

THE HAKE. No, but really . . . looked at it?

EVA. Yes, I looked at it, I already told you.

THE HAKE. Thought about it?

EVA. Well . . .

THE HAKE. Do you like it?

EVA. Yes. I like it. I told you already.

THE HAKE. Why?

EVA (*anguished*). It's only a . . . basket.

THE HAKE. It's more than that.

Moment of embarrassment.

EVA. Yes. You're right. Forgive me. I told you, I'm a machine. I think it's because of the kind of life I have to lead.

THE HAKE. I could show you how I make the flowers, for example. Paper flowers.

EVA (*more than necessarily interested*). Yes. Let's see, show me!

She kneels down next to him.

THE HAKE (*taking a sheet of newspaper*). You take a sheet of newspaper, like this, and you double it from the corner, like this, you see? (*He does it.*) And it isn't an ordinary sheet of paper, as you will see. You take a piece of paper that has a lot of printing, or a large photograph, or a lot of photographs without any printing, you see? Like this. So that the flower has some meaning. Some continuity. Some beauty.

While he works and speaks, something is changing in him. Something that possesses and absorbs him.

For some people the paper of newspapers is just that. A strip of worthless paper that's only good to wrap meat, to plug holes, or to line suitcases. But it isn't that. Those who think so, it's clear, are marked, and you can recognize them by other superficial features. The paper from newspapers has a world of things to say. It takes whatever form you want to give it. It folds submissively. It allows itself to be handled without resistance. It occupies very little space in your pocket. And it is a faithful companion on winter nights. It keeps you company . . . tranquilly . . . silently . . . always ready, there it is, for any use whatever.

The flower is ready.

There it is! A camellia, you see?

He places it at Eva's brow.

To adorn the beautiful.

EVA. Who are you?

THE HAKE. I also make carnations and chrysanthemums, but that's a little more difficult, because you need scissors, and scissors aren't something they let you have, ordinarily. Even less on winter nights, down by the river.

His excitement continues to increase.

I also make fish and butterflies of paper! But that's much more difficult, because once you have them made, no one wants them. Because everyone wants fish in beautifully lighted fishbowls, and butterflies mounted on pins in little mahogany boxes. But made from dirty newspapers that are only good for lining suitcases, no! No one wants dirty paper butterflies, dirty from wrapping meat, mounted in lighted mahogany boxes! Nor does anyone want to dirty her brow with flowers of dirty paper!

As he finishes he is panting.

At least, that's what the bourgeois say . . . who are the arbiters of style . . . in everything . . . including the way you work . . . the paper . . . the newspapers.

He coughs. Brief pause.

EVA. Who are you?

THE HAKE. They call me "The Hake."

EVA. I mean . . . your name?

THE HAKE. I don't know. A name, one loses it around here in the streets, down a crack . . .

EVA. But you must have some name. I can't call you "The Hake."

THE HAKE (*with an expressionless face*). Why not?

EVA (*confused*). Well . . . because . . .

THE HAKE (*with the same lack of expression*). Because it's the name the gang uses.

EVA. It isn't a Christian name.

THE HAKE. And you're not part of the gang.

EVA (*with certain defiance*). No, no I'm not, if you want to put it like that. Among my friends we call each other by Christian names.

THE HAKE. I thought you told me you didn't have any friends.

EVA. It's a way of speaking.

THE HAKE. It must be, then, that between us—who aren't friends—we call each other by names that *aren't* Christian. (*Smiles, pacifying her.*) My mother calls me Robert.

EVA. That's better. I'll call you Robert, then.

THE HAKE. And Bobby.

EVA. Bobby?

THE HAKE. And pig. Pig before we ate. I had two mothers. She called me pig before we ate, Bobby, after.

EVA. Did she die?

THE HAKE. Something like that.

Eva rises, and with exaggerated vivacity goes to a piece of furniture and takes out some scissors and hands them to him.

EVA. Well! Here we're not on the shore of the river; we have scissors! Show me how you make the chrysanthemums!

THE HAKE (*rises*). I think it's time for me to go.

EVA (*hadn't thought about this*). Oh, yes! Of course! But, those men? Don't you think you're still in danger?

Eva rises and goes to the window.

There they are! They're still waiting for you!

THE HAKE. What do you think? That they're playing?

EVA. Well, what do they want? You haven't done anything except win a couple of dollars from them shooting dice! Isn't winning allowed among you?

THE HAKE. It's allowed. But you pay for it.

EVA. I don't understand! How can they be so vengeful?

THE HAKE. From watching how dogs fight over a piece of meat.

EVA. So, as soon as you leave the building they'll assault you?

THE HAKE. Their pulse won't miss a beat.

EVA. I can't allow them to do that.

THE HAKE. Shall I show you how I make paper chrysanthemums?

EVA. You stay here until those men go away.

The Hake begins to cut up pieces of paper. He is contained at first, but then goes about it with increasing fury.

THE HAKE. You take a piece of paper and you cut it from the corners, you see?

He does it.

You make some long cuts along the printed lines, you see? Until you make shreds of paper, the thinnest possible . . . with the finest points . . . until the whole sheet of paper, which originally was a newspaper, . . . looks like a big piece of shredded paper! As if a dog had made it his prey! Or a falcon! Or any rabid animal! Like when in the bus someone runs his razor along the seats and leaves his mark of stupor and rage there! Or when in the hospital the orderly pours iodine on a back shredded by the whip.

EVA. Bobby . . .

The Hake looks at her.

Do you mind if I call you Bobby?

The Hake continues to stare at her with eyes that express nothing.

Does it seem like a good idea . . . for you to sleep here? Tonight? In this big chair? I'll lend you some blankets. It doesn't matter to me.

THE HAKE. But you brought me salami and cheese so I'd leave.

EVA. Not now, Bobby. You can't go like this.

THE HAKE. If I stay I'll have to . . . take a bath, naturally?

EVA. Have I said that?

The Hake laughs and looks for laughter in Eva's face.

THE HAKE (*laughing*). No, no! Say it! "It would be better if you took a bath, Bobby!"

EVA. I already told you: it's just the same to me.

THE HAKE (*always laughing*). No, no! It isn't the same! Go on, say it! Confess! I want to hear how you say it! "It would be better if you took a bath, Bobby, because like that, with those clothes and that filth . . . ," mmh? Come on!

EVA. All right, if you insist. "It would be better if you took a bath, Bobby."

THE HAKE (*suddenly serious*). But . . . I can't use your bathroom. How could such a thing ever occur to me?

EVA. Go ahead and use it! Did I say not to?

THE HAKE. No, naturally not. That's true, you didn't tell me! What ideas I have! How could you say such a thing to me?

Suddenly.

Shall I show you how I make paper chrysanthemums?

EVA. You already showed me.

THE HAKE (*never taking his eyes off her*). But you didn't look.

EVA (*protests*). Yes, I . . .

THE HAKE. No, you never looked.

EVA. Well, show me.

The Hake takes another sheet of paper and begins to cut it the same way he did the first.

THE HAKE. You take a sheet of paper and you cut it with the scissors from the corners, you see? You make some long cuts along the printed lines until you make shreds of paper, the thinnest possible . . . with the finest points . . . until the whole sheet of paper, which originally was a newspaper, . . . looks like a big piece of shredded paper! Or like a dog had made it his prey! Or a falcon! Or any rabid animal!

His voice has become tense. The words are squeezed from his mouth.

Or like in the bus when somebody runs a razor . . .

Curtain

SCENE 3

The following day, early morning. The Hake is already up. It is obvious he has bathed and combed his hair. His clothing is folded on a chair. Next to it, his shoes. He has put on one of Eva's bathrobes, which is obviously short and tight on him. He is moving around the room, cleaning with a broom and a dustcloth. He opens the curtains. He runs the dustcloth over the furniture. From the kitchen, the noise of a teakettle. He hums a tune while he cleans. The sun floods in. The straw figures are no longer in view. In their place on the walls, and hanging from threads stretched from wall to wall, some paper flowers and a few butterflies. After a while.

EVA (*from the bedroom*). Good morning!

THE HAKE. Good morning.

EVA. How did you sleep?

THE HAKE. Couldn't be better!

EVA. Up so early?

THE HAKE. It's a beautiful morning!

EVA. What are you doing?

THE HAKE. A little cleaning!

EVA. But why?

She opens the bedroom door, which obviously has been locked. She enters, in a bathrobe, combing her hair.

You didn't have to . . .

She notices the appearance of The Hake. She cannot repress an expression of stupefied amusement.

THE HAKE (*gesturing to the bathrobe*). It was in the bathroom. It doesn't bother you, I suppose?

EVA. No, no. Why should it bother me?

THE HAKE. The soapsuds were so fragrant it must have gone to my head. I didn't know what I was doing. This morning I woke with this on.

EVA. That's fine.

THE HAKE. And then I said to myself: "Hake, you have to do something useful!" I looked around and I saw the blossoms of the mimosa and the beautiful swallows swooping after each other around the General's statue, and I said to myself: "Hake, you have to do something useful!" (*Laughs his characteristic laugh; a*

laugh that covers his whole face, but says nothing.) On a day like this, even the river rats would like to come out dressed in lace! How do you like your eggs?

EVA. Eggs?

THE HAKE. Yes, eggs.

EVA. But, Bobby, I don't . . .

THE HAKE. Fried or boiled?

EVA (*resigned*). Boiled.

THE HAKE. I guessed! They're already boiling. That doesn't bother you, I suppose?

EVA. What?

THE HAKE. That I took the eggs like that, without permission?

EVA. Why should it bother me?

THE HAKE. You told me the same thing yesterday.

EVA. What?

THE HAKE. "Why should it bother me?" Curious how one always repeats himself, isn't it?

While he speaks, he has been straightening his improvised bed. He collects the blankets. He folds them carefully. Eva goes into the bathroom.

I used to have a friend, down south in a sawmill where I was working for a while, who had a little refrain too. "I'm innocent," he used to say all the time. When he got up, at breakfast, on the job . . . persistently. It was an obsession that made a martyr of him. "I'm innocent! I'm innocent!" He drove us out of our minds! One day a few of us grabbed him and hung him up by his feet, so he wouldn't go on talking. No use! Even hanging upside down that way he kept on: "I'm innocent! . . . I'm innocent!" No one ever knew what he was innocent of! Simply, the poor man thought he was innocent of something, and that gave him strength to go on living! Curious things, refrains, aren't they? Sometimes they seem meaningless!

Eva comes out of the bathroom, tying a ribbon in her combed hair.

EVA. You woke up loquacious this morning, didn't you? You weren't, last night. I love to see you this way.

The Hake shrugs his shoulders, lifts the corner of the rug, sweeps.

THE HAKE. I already told you. The mimosa in bloom.

Eva looks at him.

EVA. Your face, too. You look different today.

THE HAKE (*smiles happily*). The bath . . .

Eva sees that the straw figures are not there.

EVA. And my figures?

THE HAKE. Mmh?

EVA. My straw figures? The burro's head? The rooster?

THE HAKE. I put them in the kitchen cabinet.

EVA (*surprised*). And why?

THE HAKE (*indicating the flowers*). I thought that these would look better.

EVA (*doesn't know what to say*). Oh, yes . . .

THE HAKE. It doesn't bother you, I suppose?

THE TWO IN CHORUS. No, why should it bother me?

The Hake laughs, then Eva.

EVA. Well, anyway, one of these days I was going to take them down. You just saved me the effort.

THE HAKE. Why? Didn't you like them?

EVA. Horrible.

THE HAKE. Why? I didn't think they were so bad.

EVA. Why did you take them down, then?

THE HAKE. Because I thought these would look better. That's all. Don't you agree?

EVA. Oh, yes.

THE HAKE. You shouldn't belittle your own work. Because . . . you made them yourself, didn't you?

EVA. In a weak moment.

THE HAKE. That's bad, that you expect so much of yourself.

He leaps toward the kitchen.

Those eggs must be well cooked by now!

From the kitchen.

By the way . . . the little bird . . . I gave him some seeds. Was that all right?

EVA (*goes to the cage; plays with the canary*). Yes, that's fine!

THE HAKE. I was going to give him some bread balls, but I remembered that he's a pet! That's a habit from feeding pigeons!

EVA. Bobby!

THE HAKE. Yes?

EVA. I heard voices last night.

THE HAKE. Voices?

EVA. Arguments! It seemed to me they were coming from the corridor! Did you hear anything?

THE HAKE. Arguments? No!

EVA. Like people arguing heatedly!

THE HAKE. I slept like a log! I couldn't hear a thing!

EVA. Strange! Then I heard something like a door being slammed! It must have been the neighbors. Some Italians who work in a cabaret. Sometimes they bring friends home with them in the middle of the night. They forget this is a building where people are . . .

THE HAKE. Quiet and unassuming.

EVA. What did you say?

THE HAKE. Quiet, unassuming people.

EVA. Well, yes . . . something like that! You always take the words out of my mouth!

THE HAKE. People who don't know how to act! I always say they should go live down by the river to learn how not to do it!

He comes out of the kitchen with a tray on which are two eggs in egg cups, two cups, a teapot, a creamer, a napkin, a butter dish, and biscuits, all very tastefully arranged in the clean, neat manner of an upper-class hotel. He has doubled the towel over his arm to serve as his napkin. He puts everything down with great skill and elegance.

EVA. Don't tell me you worked in a hotel, too?

THE HAKE (*very efficient; with a bow*). *Comment ditesvous, madame?*

Eva laughs.

The Hake is now serious.

Préférez-vous le beurre salé ou sans sel, madame?

Eva laughs good-naturedly.

EVA. Who are you, Bobby? Where did you learn to do that? You are diverse! Really diverse!

THE HAKE (*always serious*). One does what one can.

Both begin to eat their eggs.

EVA. Did you work in a hotel? Really?

THE HAKE. Mmh.

EVA. As a . . . waiter?

THE HAKE (*with his mouth full of egg*). As a thief.

Eva laughs.

It's true. It was a snobbish hotel; because of that I had to go in the back door so the public wouldn't see me, you understand?

Eva understands.

I had a contract as a washer. A dishwasher. It really wasn't a real contract. Just a slap on the back by the fat guy who ran the kitchen. A guy who liked to make himself important. (*He imitates.*) "All right, stupid, go stand over there by one of those sinks. Let's see if you can wash a plate!" He told me he'd give me a penny for every washed plate. He was tricky. He didn't tell me he'd deduct for all the ones I broke. In the evening when I went to pick up my money, I owed him two dollars.

EVA. You owed him?

THE HAKE. I owed him.

EVA. And the French?

THE HAKE. What about it?

EVA. Where did you learn it? There?

THE HAKE. I had to stay six days to pay my debt. Actually I never did pay it, because every day that passed, my debt was bigger. You understand, don't you?

EVA. Yes.

THE HAKE. After a week I realized that wasn't the way to get ahead. That's when I decided to steal a calculating machine, and I lifted . . .

EVA. That seems fair to me.

THE HAKE. Do you think so? They didn't.

EVA. But . . . the French? Where did you learn it? In another hotel?

THE HAKE. Painting some incubators for a guy in Saint Andrews.

EVA. Was he French?

THE HAKE. No, Yugoslavian. Do you know I can make silhouettes with my hands?

EVA. Silhouettes?

THE HAKE. Yes. (*He spoons the bottom of his cup.*) Dogs . . . foxes . . .

EVA. Let's see.

The Hake goes to close the curtains. He turns on the lamp that's on the table. He spreads the leaves of a magazine so it will stand on edge.

THE HAKE. Look! What do you see?

He throws the silhouette of a figure on the magazine.

EVA. A dog!

THE HAKE. And now?

EVA. A rabbit!

THE HAKE. And this?

EVA. A deer? Let's see, let me do it!

She tries.

No. It doesn't come out. How do you do it?

THE HAKE. The forefinger up. The thumb like this.

EVA (*holds out her hands to him*). You do it for me!

The Hake hesitates in taking her hands.

Come on!

THE HAKE (*taking her fingers with care*). Like this. No. This finger's stuck out.

EVA. A deer! (*Enthusiastic.*) Come on . . . another!

The Hake moves close to her. He holds her hands. This produces a brief, embarrassed paralysis of

movement during which they look in each other's eyes. Then The Hake, confused, goes to the window and opens the curtains again. He turns off the lamp.

Bobby, there's no reason to be timid with me. (*Laughs.*) I'm not going to eat you, don't you know. (*Agitated.*) After all, having spent the night here together, gives us a right to . . . a certain familiarity, don't you think?

THE HAKE. Don't play with me, please.

EVA. But, Bobby, it's ridiculous. Just because you brushed my hand . . . it doesn't matter to me.

THE HAKE. One ought to keep his distance.

EVA. What distance?

THE HAKE (*indicating the bathrobe*). It's because you see me in this, and washed, that you forget.

EVA. What have I forgotten?

The Hake points to his clothes.

Don't be ridiculous. Have I shown in any way that it matters to me?

THE HAKE. It can't be.

EVA. If you insist.

THE HAKE. I'll have to go right now.

EVA. I'm not saying you should go.

The Hake rises and moves away from her. He turns his back.

THE HAKE (*suspiciously*). Why?

EVA. Why, what?

THE HAKE. Why do you want me to stay?

EVA. I haven't said you should stay. I've only said you don't have to go.

THE HAKE (*complaining*). Why is it my fault, I say?

EVA. But Bobby . . .

THE HAKE. Why is it my fault I was born as I was. I didn't ask my mother to be born where I was!

Eva rises.

EVA. But, Bobby, for Heaven's sake!

THE HAKE. I'm a simple man, but I have my pride!

EVA. Of course you have! Who says you don't?

She approaches him. To his back.

Bobby! I'm not the woman I seem to be. I'm just a woman filled with a need for kindness! Perhaps it doesn't seem so, because I look so forceful, so . . . fulfilled. (*Smiles.*) But you see, I paint alone, laurel in bloom, Saturday afternoons in the Botanical Garden. Doesn't that seem . . . odd?

THE HAKE. I'll need new pants. If I stay here any longer, I'll need new pants. I can't put those back on.

Eva looks at him without speaking.

Because if I put those on, I can't stay here, isn't that right?

EVA. I hadn't thought about that.

THE HAKE (*never looking at her*). But now you think about it, isn't it true?

EVA. Well, perhaps . . .

THE HAKE (*his tone changes; he returns to his earlier manner of speaking, anxious, intense*). Because what if suddenly, someone came in here? Yes, suddenly, some friend of yours came in here, what explanation could we give them? If they see me here, with this on (*indicating the bathrobe*), or those (*indicating his pants*), sitting on one of your chairs like a king in his castle? Don't you see? They might think I'm a beggar from down by the river that you picked up out of pity to prevent the poor devil's turning up his paws before God meant him to, offering him something . . . some warm soup or salami. . . . It wouldn't be very correct, do you think? Sad, instead, don't you think? A sad, hopeless situation that neither you, nor I, could stand for very long, don't you agree? Because that would mean that you know as well as I . . . how could we avoid it? That you as well as I knew the sad reality. It would establish a situation of moral misery between us that would be very difficult . . . to disguise. Don't you think so?

EVA. And do you think a new pair of pants will change all that?

THE HAKE. We could play at it a little, deceive ourselves. Don't you think so?

EVA. You'll have to overcome that . . . that obsession, Bobby. I've noticed how it makes you suffer.

The Hake whirls around. A broad smile illuminates his face.

THE HAKE. Blue pants with a white stripe. A white stripe an inch wide, no more, no less. That's the kind I've always dreamed of.

EVA. We'll look for something you like.

THE HAKE (*like a happy child*). Will you do it? Really? Will you go yourself from store to store, looking for what I ask?

EVA. Why not?

The Hake takes her hands and pulls her up. He whirls her around.

THE HAKE. You're an angel. You're an angel! An angel!

EVA. Oh, for Heaven's sake, Bobby!

They stop. Eva is breathless.

What I meant is I find it meaningless! Really meaningless, Bobby! I don't notice things like that!

THE HAKE (*laughing in amusement; teasing slyly*). Yes, yes, you notice!

EVA. No, really, no.

THE HAKE (*reprimands her with a finger*). Yes, you notice! You notice!

EVA. Why do you say that to me? Why are you laughing?

The Hake laughs as if he were telling a funny and rather embarrassing story.

THE HAKE. Yesterday evening, when you arrived here, a friend brought you in her car and you didn't want to let her come up!

EVA (*denying effusively*). No . . .

THE HAKE. Yes, yes! I saw the gestures she was making. As if she wanted to come up with you, but you told her, with signs, too, that you were fine . . . that you didn't need anything, or something like that! It was amusing, extremely amusing, to see how you were trying to think of something . . . how you cast about, almost desperately, for some explanation!

Choked with laughter.

Waving your arms like this! Gasping for air!

EVA. No, no. That wasn't the reason . . .

THE HAKE. Yes, yes! But don't get mad. I understand! I understand! If you only knew how well I understand!

Suddenly becoming serious.

What did you tell your friend?

EVA. Well, I told her that . . .

THE HAKE. When I have new pants, we'll be free from embarrassment, you see. We can say I'm your cousin. A distant cousin who dropped in from the country, how does that seem? A cousin, or an uncle? Which seems better? More plausible?

A pause.

EVA. You're going to have to get that obsession out of your head, Bobby.

The Hake drops his arms, discouraged.

THE HAKE. Yes. Perhaps that comes from wandering around by the river so much, looking for things under the stones. From so much crawling around, looking for things, scratching for food. Finally, the world gets you right around the ankles. It's a little tiny world, the one you see, and in this tiny little world, we're the tiniest of all! Not even as high as a toad. You get a kind of subservient personality. Sub-something, anyway. (*He*

smiles again with an empty smile, radiant, meaningless.)
A "sub" personality . . . sub-normal . . . sub-ordinant . . .
sub-jugated . . . sub-versive!

He stands before her, smiling happily.

A white stripe an inch wide. No more, no less. Will
you buy them for me as I asked?

EVA (*worried*). I'll do what I can.

The Hake kisses her hands.

THE HAKE. You're an angel!

Eva pours herself some coffee.

EVA. If this means anything to you, Bobby, I should tell
you that I've become very fond of you. In my opinion, you have a tremendous potential for becoming a
. . . fulfilled man.

*As she says "fulfilled," The Hake starts to tremble
again. Eva wants to help him, but he waves her
away. He calms down again.*

I don't know what it is that torments you.

*The Hake picks up the papers and begins to make
flowers again.*

Drink your coffee.

Eva walks to the kitchen.

This needs sugar.

Suddenly a scream from the kitchen.

What's this?

*She enters. She is carrying the straw rooster and
burro. One is hanging grotesquely from each hand;
their necks are broken.*

Why did you throw these into the trash can? And
their necks . . . why did you break them?

THE HAKE. They didn't fit in the trash can.

EVA. But throw them away. You told me yourself you'd
put them in the cabinet.

THE HAKE. But they didn't fit there either. (*Innocently
protesting.*) But you told me yourself they were horrible!

EVA. Yes, but . . .

THE HAKE. I'll make you one of paper! I swear that when
you come back this evening I'll have a rooster and a
burro made of paper for you! Mmh? What do you say?
With strong, red feet, and a great golden comb! A
strong powerful rooster! Mmh? Is that all right?

EVA (*doesn't know what to say*). Well, I . . .

THE HAKE (*with his broad smile; playful, vacant*). It won't
bother you if I do it, will it?

THE TWO IN CHORUS. No. Why should it bother me!

*The Hake laughs loudly. Eva enters in chorus.
Both laugh with all their hearts. The Hake's, fi-
nally, with exaggeration, out of tune, drowning out
Eva's laughter.*

Curtain

SCENE 4

*Evening of the same day. The arrangement of all the
pieces of furniture has been changed. The canary
cage, its door open, is empty. The shade of the floor
lamp has been taken off. It serves now as a vase for
three enormous paper flowers with wire stems. In
addition, there are flowers hanging from the walls
and from the lamp.*

*The Hake, his legs wrapped in a blanket of Scotch
wool, a bottle of cognac at his side, is lounging in the
big chair, watching television. One can see he has
just washed his hair, because he has a towel wrapped
around his head. He is apparently happy. The television entertains him enormously. The sound of shots
from the screen, which cannot be seen. The shouting
of Indians. Little by little The Hake becomes involved in the action. He imitates the movements he
sees. He hides behind the chair. He shoots toward
the set. He jumps on top of the chair. He shoots
again. A bullet gets him. He "dies" ostentatiously in
the middle of the living room floor.*

*He's lying there, sprawled on the floor, when the
door opens and Eva enters. She is carrying several
packages.*

EVA. Bobby!

The Hake doesn't move.

Bobby! What's the matter?

*She drops the packages on the floor. She kneels next
to him.*

What's the matter with you? (*She touches him.*) My
God! (*She touches his face.*) Bobby. . . . (*She shakes
him.*) Wake up! Bobby, for God's sake!

*She looks around desperately. She goes into the
kitchen. She runs back with a glass of water. She*

gives him a drink while she holds his head. The Hake opens one eye.

THE HAKE. Did you bring the pants?
EVA. Oh, God, Bobby! What did you do? You frightened me so!
THE HAKE. Blue? With white stripes?

Eva hands him a package, which The Hake opens eagerly, ripping the paper.

They're gray!
EVA. Yes. I couldn't find the ones you wanted.
THE HAKE (*injured*). But I asked you for blue ones!
EVA. I'm telling you. I couldn't find what you wanted.
THE HAKE (*screams*). Blue, with a white stripe! An inch wide! And you bring me gray! What do you want me to do with these?
EVA. I looked in all the stores, but . . .
THE HAKE. You didn't look enough.
EVA. Yes, I looked Bobby. I looked, but . . .
THE HAKE. You didn't look. Yesterday I saw three pairs in different stores.

He holds the pants up.

What am I going to look like in these? What will Mario say to me when he sees me dressed like this? That I'm one of those playboys from España Square, that's what he's going to say I look like. One of those playboys from the apartments in España Square, who aren't good for anything except to warm their women's beds! Playboys in skirts! Playboys with soft bellies! That's what he'll say I look like!

He throws them away.

I don't want them!

Eva picks them up dejectedly. She wraps them up again.

EVA. I didn't think it would matter so much.
THE HAKE. No, of course not. For a guy who goes around in rags, anything is good enough.
EVA. I wasn't thinking that when I did it.

A long embarrassing pause. The Hake turns off the television.

THE HAKE. Do you like the way I arranged the furniture?
EVA (*distraught*). Oh, yes . . . fine.
THE HAKE. Is it better this way?
EVA. Better, yes.
THE HAKE. And the flowers? Do you like them?
EVA. Pretty, yes.

THE HAKE. The canary got out.

Eva turns toward the cage.

EVA. Goldie! Oh, God! How did it happen?
THE HAKE (*in the middle of the room: the very picture of innocence*). I opened the door to give him some seeds, and zap! he got away!
EVA. And where is he?
THE HAKE. I don't know.

Eva goes to the window and looks outside.

It was when I opened the door to give him some seeds that he got away. He flew around the room a while; he went into the bedroom, into the kitchen, and then flew over my head again. I tried to catch him with a towel. I got a towel from the bathroom and tried to catch him. For a minute I thought I'd caught him. It was when he lighted on the frame of that picture. I stopped in front of him, waiting for the minute to throw the towel over him, but that's when I realized that he didn't *want* me to get him.

Eva turns toward him.

It was all up to me. I couldn't miss. It was a question of throwing the towel, zap! he would have been mine. But that's when I realized he didn't want me to catch him. Something in his attitude, you understand?
EVA. So you let him get away?
THE HAKE. I don't know. It was just that for a minute, I couldn't do anything. I think that's when he started to fly again; he flew around the whole apartment and, finally, went out that window . . . toward the mimosa blossoms. It must be my fault. I think that bird never liked me. From the first day, he always looked at me out of the corner of his eye, a little suspicious. It must be that he realized, before I did, that there wasn't room enough for both of us here.

His smile—that says nothing—returns.

Little creatures have tremendous insight in these matters. It's lucky that he left first, because if not, suddenly, it could have been me . . .

Eva disappears into the bedroom.

Did you know I'd given him a nickname? "Corsair." A strange name for a canary, I know, but it's just that that name reminds me of something! Maybe that it's necessary to be very brave to be able to bear a cage! "Corsair." Poor little thing.

He waits a while.

Do you want me to go?

Eva enters, putting on a robe over her dress. She can't help smiling at the appearance of The Hake standing in the middle of the room, his arms by his sides, wrapped up in the blanket, his head wrapped in the towel, his legs bare—guilty, abject, contrite.

EVA. And why should I want you to go?

THE HAKE. Because of the bird. Ever since I've come I haven't done anything but cause confusion.

EVA. You're just a spoiled child, Bobby.

THE HAKE. To be so unpleasant to you when I refused the beautiful pants you brought me.

Eva takes his hand.

EVA. Come on, you big baby. I've been thinking we need to talk about something. Clear something up.

THE HAKE. After all your affection . . .

Eva sits him beside her in the chair. She places a finger on his lips.

EVA. What were you doing in the Botanical Garden, the day I was painting the laurel, spoiled child?

THE HAKE. Well . . . wandering around.

EVA. Come on, tell me the truth.

The Hake maintains his distance from her.

THE HAKE. You talk to me as if you've known me for a long time.

EVA. You can treat me the same way if you want. I won't break because of it, you know.

THE HAKE. There you go again, laughing at me.

EVA (*impatient*). Oh, Bobby, come on! Why don't you drop it? We're not going to spend a lifetime this way, you so sensitive, and I not knowing how to take you. I know you're not what you seem or what you pretend to be. Some error, some slip "along life's road" (*She makes a gesture as if entertained at her own cliché.*) brought you where you find yourself now, but I know you aren't what you seem . . . or you don't seem to be what you *are* . . . None of that matters to me; you see I don't even ask you. Can you accuse me of that? Of having asked you?

The Hake shakes his head.

No, isn't that true? Then why don't you be yourself? Hmm? Shall we talk as equal to equal?

THE HAKE. As equal to what?

EVA. Well, as equal to equal, as I said.

THE HAKE. And if I weren't what I seem to be, or I didn't seem to be what I am, we wouldn't be speaking like this, isn't that right? As equal to equal . . .

EVA. Well, maybe not.

THE HAKE. Why?

EVA. Because your sensitivity would be in the way, preventing it. (*She moves a little closer to him.*) Come on, silly, tell me . . . what were you doing in the Garden?

THE HAKE. Looking at the parrots.

EVA. No, really? What were you doing?

THE HAKE. Mario had sent me to pick up cigarette butts in front of Orfeon kiosk, so we could grind up the tobacco and sell it at the Marquesa's brothel.

Pause.

EVA. So you don't want to confess, eh?

THE HAKE. Also Chancha, the deaf old woman who sells newspapers in front of the Congress, had asked me to pull some feathers out of the parrot's tail to make a decoration for her hat.

EVA. Yesterday, just after you arrived, you told me that you remembered me a year ago painting the blooming laurels in the Garden in my straw hat with a green ribbon. Unless you're terribly observant and have a very special memory, no one would believe that you'd remember those details so long, if it weren't for a very special reason.

THE HAKE. Special reason?

EVA. Special inclination.

THE HAKE. Special inclination?

He is standing far away from her, his back turned.

EVA. Oh, Bobby, don't be so . . . timid!

The Hake rises.

THE HAKE. It's just that it can't be!

EVA (*from her place*). Why?

THE HAKE. Where would all this lead?

EVA. Who cares? It's strange that you, with the life you lead, should worry about tomorrow. As if you had spent all your life looking ahead. I'll bet you've never worried about anything in your life. Why worry now? Am I worried, for example?

THE HAKE. It's different with you.

EVA. Why with me?

THE HAKE. Because you know what I don't know.

EVA. And what do I know?

THE HAKE. That I'm not what I seem or I don't seem to be what I am. On the other hand, I only know I am what I seem and not that I am not what I don't seem. In other words, you have your fantasy and I have only reality, which is much poorer, much sadder, much more disillusioning. . . . (*In a clipped voice*.) That's the advantage you have over me, although you tell me not to worry . . . what happens is that one worries so much about worrying that in the end he doesn't worry any more about worrying.

EVA. Bobby, Bobby, turn around!

The Hake turns. He doesn't look at her, however.

If you were only the poor vagabond you seem to be, we wouldn't even be able to have this conversation, don't you see? It would all have been over between us a long time ago. Yesterday perhaps. After I gave you your warm soup, I would have sent you away, because it's certain you would have ended up . . . boring me. There's nothing more boring than the conversation of the poor when they're complaining. Don't you agree?

The Hake thinks so. He nods his head, looking at the floor. Eva approaches him and takes his arm.

From the first moment I saw you, I knew who you were. I understand that your shyness must be a consequence of the bad treatment you've had from life. Things that have happened to you have made you pull into your shell. I want you to believe that I'm completely sincere when I tell you that doesn't matter to me. I place no false barriers between us, do you understand?

The Hake understands.

Do you believe I'm your friend, Bobby?

The Hake believes.

Then . . . ?

Eva waits.

THE HAKE. Then we'll have to change the furniture here.

EVA (*surprised*). The furniture? Why?

THE HAKE. I don't like it.

EVA. You don't like it?

THE HAKE. That's what I said.

EVA. Well . . . (*Doesn't know what to say.*) What do we . . . ?

THE HAKE. It has no class.

EVA. Class?

THE HAKE. Style. It has no style. (*With irritation.*) Trash you find by the thousands in any second-class junk store! Just looking at it makes me want to scream! It has no imagination, no fantasy, no dream of any kind!

Eva is stunned. The Hake whirls toward her.

Let's see! How much time did you spend choosing it?

EVA. Well, I . . .

THE HAKE. Not five minutes, I'll bet! You went in the store like someone going in to buy some aspirin and you pointed to the first piece of junk that met your eyes, I'll bet! Anything that would serve to throw your body on and fall asleep! Well, you're mistaken! You need to be a poet to choose furniture and give it the tone it deserves! All the nerve cells that decide taste must be aroused when the moment comes to decide! You're like that crazy old Fabian from the other side of the bay who'll set his ass down on anything he finds . . . an old paraffin tin . . . a rickety old suitcase . . . his shoes . . . on the chest of the old syphilitic Sandilla who bums around with him stealing railroad ties, anything at all. . . . As if one could resolve the problem that way! Choosing furniture is a liturgical act!

His excitement increases as he acts out what he has been describing. His concentration absorbs him completely. He concludes as if debating with another being that is within himself, as if arguing with someone whom he should convince.

You have to raise the chair skirt and see if the framework is made of poplar or of mahogany, because there is always some wretch who wants to trade you a cat for a hare and pass off poplar for mahogany, and that wouldn't be good, because your visitors might notice! Then, it's also important that all the nails be in place! All the nails, or rather all the glue, because it could be that it isn't satin fringe but only tufts of ordinary cloth some son-of-a-bitch wants to palm off! And it's also important, very important, of *primary* importance, to concern yourself with the form, the color, the design, whether it's brocade or velvet, whether the style today is an oblong silhouette or square design, whether the pegs are concave or convex, whether the sons-of-bitches have put in nails—nails, and not screws! Because when visitors sit down they shouldn't simply fall into a chair, but instead, when they bend their knees they should encounter . . . that's it, they should encounter the anatomy of a chair adjusted to their rumps. All of that should be taken into account! All of that should be considered with the greatest care! Because all of it is of maximum importance! Of primary importance! Of the *most* primary importance. (*He concludes, exhausted.*) You must put life into it, life . . . if necessary . . . that's what that stupid Fabian can't understand! (*Pause.*) We have to change this furniture. We owe it to our visitors.

EVA. Well, we'll change it. You choose. Is that all right with you?

THE HAKE. When?

EVA. Tomorrow?

THE HAKE. I won't be here tomorrow.

EVA. Don't you understand, silly, that starting from today you'll be here tomorrow and all the days you want to?

THE HAKE. We'll have to go out.

EVA. For what?

THE HAKE. To choose the furniture.

EVA. Well, what about it? We'll go out, then.

THE HAKE. In what clothes?

EVA. I'll buy you a suit.

THE HAKE. Gray.

EVA. I thought you wanted blue with white stripes.

THE HAKE. That's for the pants. The suit I want gray. Gray with little white flecks, hardly visible. Better invisible than visible . . . better . . .

EVA. Whatever you say. Is that all right with you?

The Hake looks at her out of the corner of his eye. Distrustful. Icy.

THE HAKE. No, not unless you tell me what it will be like?

EVA. How *what* will be like?

THE HAKE. Walking through the streets.

EVA. I don't understand.

THE HAKE. Will I walk in front of you or behind you?

EVA. There you go again. Beside me, if you want to.

THE HAKE. How far away? A foot? Two? Have you thought about it? And what will we tell the store owner?

Eva looks at him. She does not answer.

Because there are suspicious types, tremendously suspicious. They see rags and they imagine a world of things. Just a simple glance at some rags awakens a whole mythological fantasy.

He turns toward Eva.

Do you understand what I mean? We have to be extremely careful. (*His face completely blank.*) Do you think it would be a good idea if we say I play . . . tennis?

EVA. Tennis? Why that?

THE HAKE. Doesn't your husband play tennis?

EVA. Yes. How did you know?

THE HAKE (*points toward the bedroom*). The pants and the racket there in the closet.

EVA. Curious, hmm?

THE HAKE. Do you think I could pass?

EVA. You could pass for anything at all!

The Hake's blank smile.

THE HAKE. Even for a gigolo, hmm?

EVA. Tonight you'll sleep here in the chair, but I won't lock my bedroom door. I no longer distrust you, you see?

The Hake takes her hands.

If you feel lonely, don't hesitate to call me. I sleep very lightly.

Very close to him.

Unless you're not attracted by ladies over forty who paint out of desperation, or for nostalgia's sake keep the clothes of a man who left his nest centuries ago. A woman alone who doesn't even know how to buy the right kind of furniture.

THE HAKE (*rigid again*). Will I have to . . . take a bath again?

Eva leans her head on his chest.

EVA. Oh, Bobby! Give up! Relax. (*After a while.*) Resting my head on your chest is like resting it on a rock. What has life done to you to make you like this?

THE HAKE. *Comment dîtes-vous, madame?*

EVA (*looks at him; kisses his cheek*). Oh, my love!

The Hake looks straight ahead. He is a rock. A sphinx.

THE HAKE. Yes. It is of the greatest importance, of absolutely primary importance, to choose appropriate words to say what one wishes to say. It involves a complete process of selection carefully prearranged by the spirit. A process that has nothing to do with one's own will. The fundamental thing is to believe in the beauty of one's own expression, since without the contribution of one's delivery, words, thrown out by pure whim, acquire a false dimension in which not even one's self, and certainly not others, can find anything that evokes even a lie. The important thing, then, is to say what one wants to say without saying it, so that others contribute the entire weight of their own . . . deception. Only this way may one be happy.

EVA. Oh, God!

The Hake begins to make little figures with his hands that he projects upon the front wall.

THE HAKE. A rabbit, see? An owl. A child. A frightened child. (*He looks at her.*) Do you have a hatchet?

EVA. Yes.

THE HAKE. And a saw? And a hammer?

EVA. Yes.

THE HAKE. Give them to me. Tonight I'll make the kind of furniture I like.

EVA. They're in the kitchen.

Eva goes into the kitchen. A scream.

What's this! What happened to Goldie!

She comes in with the dead canary hanging from her hand.

Who did this to him?

THE HAKE (*disconsolate; very rapidly, like a child caught doing something wrong*). I told you! I wanted to catch him, but he wouldn't let me. From the beginning he took a dislike to me! From the first glance, he looked at me out of the corner of his eye! I followed him all over the room! I begged him, I implored him to let me catch him, but he insisted on flying! He didn't want to hear my pleas. . . . (*Pause.*) When finally he couldn't fly any more, he was too worn out to understand the meaning of my pleas. He expired without giving me the opportunity to explain to him. (*Another pause.*) I could have loved that little bird. (*Sobs.*) I could have really loved him if he had only let me.

(*He looks at Eva.*)

Poor Goldie. Poor son-of-a-bitch.

Curtain

SCENE 5

The following morning. The radio is playing "The Waltz of the Dragon-Flies." The Hake, in tennis clothes, is kneeling in the middle of the living room, nailing together a rustic chair, or rather what seems to be a chair, from the remains of a torn-up chair. Of the original chair all that remains is a scattered pile of cotton and feathers, springs and ripped cloth. The wood frame, too, has been violently torn apart as if a bird of prey had seized upon it.

The pictures are no longer there. In their places hang pages from newspapers. There are more paper flowers scattered around. The flowers are larger now, more carelessly made. Simulacrums of flowers, as if made from whole pages of wadded newspapers, at-

tached in the center to wire stems. The Hake hums happily to the music as he works.

After a while Eva appears, in her bathrobe, in the doorway. For a moment she watches The Hake working, then . . .

EVA. I heard you working all night long. It sounded as if a big rat had been trapped in my apartment.

She looks at the room.

You can't say you haven't been busy.

THE HAKE. Do you like it?

EVA. Good work.

THE HAKE. The fever got me. When I get the fever it's like seeing double. I see one thing to do, and then another to be done. When I attack one, there's already another asking me to persist, and so on . . . Mario has never given me credit for being a carpenter.

EVA. He ought to come see now.

THE HAKE. He says I'm good for taking things apart . . . breaking them, but as for carpentry, real carpentry . . . doing it really right, you understand?

EVA. Yes.

THE HAKE. He says I'm no good. "You're a vandal," he tells me. He's continually telling me that. Perhaps because he's always seen me do just this: rebuilding scattered pieces, putting scraps together. Don't you think?

Eva has gone to sit down in the only remaining chair.

EVA. It must be because of that.

THE HAKE. That's the bad thing about Mario. He only has the imagination about a posteriori things. He doesn't have any imagination about a priori things. I think he ought to see me doing this now, don't you think?

EVA. That's what I told you.

THE HAKE. That would shut his big yap. Don't you think?

He doesn't wait for an answer. He holds on high, in triumph, the chair he has just finished.

Louis XV! What do you think? Or Louis XVI perhaps?

EVA. Restoration.

He finds the idea amusing. He laughs.

THE HAKE. Restoration, yes! That's funny, you know? Restoration. I hadn't thought about that. (*Still laughing.*) That's what I like about you, you know? You have a sense of humor. From the first moment I stuck my dirty paws into your kingdom. I come in here and I break all your furniture . . . I let your canary loose . . . I turn your closets inside out . . . I fill your room with horrible papers flowers and you're still . . . complacent! Always smiling!

EVA. So? What else is there for me to do?

THE HAKE. Yes. The force of circumstances?

EVA. Of destiny.

THE HAKE (*abruptly serious*). Destiny is cirrhosis of the liver or a lung punctured by a stupid life squandered in drunkenness. Don't confuse it with anything else. I'm here strictly because of some warm soup. Don't forget it.

He shows her again the chair on which he has been working.

Do you like it now?

Eva goes to the radio and turns it off.

EVA. Bobby . . . I left the door open last night. You didn't come in. (*The Hake concentrates on his work.*) I waited for you. (*Pause; uncertain smile.*) Since you didn't come in, you couldn't know that I even put on a special nightgown last night. The nightgown I wore my first night of . . . love. (*She laughs.*) Afterwards, my husband made me wear it on our anniversaries. A long gown, celestial blue, with two rosettes here on the yoke. A gown that still has the odor of the pines at Saint Stephens. My husband thought so anyway. That it retained the odor of our first night under the pines at Saint Stephens . . . with the waves of the sea breaking nearby . . . almost at our feet . . . and the moon . . . the eternal moon. (*Smiles.*) An intrusive, friendly moon, witnessing our . . . passion.

She waits.

Would you believe it, Bobby? That I would be capable of that? Of a night of passion beneath the pines, with only the moon as witness, and the blue nightgown as a pillow?

She presses her hand to her forehead.

It doesn't seem possible to you, does it? That's what makes you so unjust, that you think that it isn't possible . . . or that it isn't possible any more. Because you *do* think that it isn't possible, don't you?

The Hake works.

Isn't that right? You think that it's no longer possible?

A vague evasive gesture; and an uncertain smile; brief dizziness.

That a woman like me, alone, oh God! . . . could strip herself of her prudery and open her arms to love, with only the aroma of the pines as witness . . . and the intrusive moon . . .

She looks at him.

Answer me. You don't even hear what I'm saying! Answer me! Do you think it's possible?

The Hake has finished his chair. He holds it in the air. He shakes it in triumph.

THE HAKE. I finished it! I finished it! Now I'd like to invite Mario to come see it! That would shut the old pessimist's trap! Firm structure, well assembled! Strong back, as ordered! Firmness in the line! Solid! Resistant! Do you like it?

EVA. Yes. I like it.

THE HAKE. A lie! You say it for some secret motive locked up in that head of yours. You say it out of compassion! I know the symptoms of the voice. I know each inflection of the voice when somebody speaks out of compassion. It's the voice of one who lowers his hand to give something, which is distinct from the voice of someone who raises his hand to receive something. Let's hear you say, "I like your chair."

EVA. I like your chair.

The Hake gives a cry of triumph.

THE HAKE. There, that's it! You see? That inflection in the voice! That uncertain tremble! That painful quiver! YOU HAVE COMPASSION FOR ME!

The Hake shakes the chair. He looks at it with disgust.

This chair is horrible. Bad taste. Badly put together. Badly structured. Badly conceived. The risers don't fit. The back's coming apart.

He begins to tear it apart.

The pieces don't fit. You can see the hand that made it had no class.

With every word a piece of the chair is torn off.

No refinement, stubby, primitive, ordinary, shiftless, dumb, of a concept . . . made . . . by a man . . . of the . . . PEOPLE!

He shatters on the floor the few pieces that remain.

It was a chair that deserved to sit near a campfire of filthy trash by the shore of a river, not in a beautiful apartment on España Square.

He rests, finally.

The end of a dream. (*Looks at Eva.*) You should have told me, though.

EVA (*with the greatest naturalness possible*). Why should I tell you something I don't feel?

THE HAKE. Because this establishes an abyss between you and me, you understand? An abyss as wide as the distance around the world.

Declamatory, impersonal, once again sententious. Light.

Pity is the broken, hanging bridge that joins wrath to a full belly!

He smiles a vacant smile that covers his whole face.

Did you like that?

EVA. Oh, God, Bobby! How shall I take you?

The Hake looks at her, desolated.

I swear I don't know. As soon as you arrived I opened the door of my house to you; I received you in it with all my affection. I tried to give you everything I have, but you persist in . . . ignoring me.

The Hake stands in the middle of the room. As Eva speaks, everything in him takes on a desolate air, like a guilty child receiving a reprimand for something he's done, that he cannot now repair.

I speak to you with affection and you respond with irony. I want to be sincere with you and you reject me, saying that I'm lying. I do everything possible to erase between us any sign that recalls your . . . poverty, but you insist on recalling it.

The Hake begins to tremble. He is a child without shelter who is cold, who is afraid. The smallest expression, diminished and sad, of the child of the ruins, hungry, abandoned, frozen.

I'm not the rich, cruel, and frivolous woman you think you see in me. I am a poor lonely woman, very lonely . . . hungry for friendship and affection. I offer you my love, Bobby.

She walks toward him and takes his face. His whole body shivers. A trembling that racks him, which he cannot control.

Oh, my love, be calm, be calm! I am here with you. Your woman is here with you and she's going to help you! Your woman is here with you and she's going to give you all the warmth you've been denied.

The Hake looks before him into the emptiness.

Bobby! Bobby! Look at me! I'm here! I love you! Do you hear me? I love you, Bobby, look at me! Bobby . . .

She shakes him.

Look at me! For the love of God, look at me!

She shakes him violently.

I'm speaking to you! Listen to me!

Still shaking him.

Listen to me, you damned fool! Look at me!

Nothing. She falls at his feet. Slowly The Hake ceases trembling. A long pause. The "Waltz of the Dragon-Flies" sounds in the emptiness.

THE HAKE (*after the pause*). You still haven't told me how I look in the tennis outfit.

He says it without looking at her, his cold eyes staring into the emptiness straight ahead of him. Eva screams.

EVA. Oh! You don't want me to help you! Your arrogance, your pride, is so great you don't want me to help you!

She rises, wrathful.

So nobody can get near your precious body, huh? Well, I'm going to tell you what you look like in that outfit!

She moves away from him. She picks up the paper flowers and other paper objects and throws them at him as she screams.

Do you know what you look like? A puppet! A ridiculous, deformed puppet! You don't even have any chest! You don't have any shoulders. You don't have the carriage to wear an outfit like that! How dare you put it on!

She awaits his reaction, which doesn't come.

Do you know what you have to have to walk around in something like that? You have to have smooth muscles! Long, smooth, springy muscles! Sure and decisive movements! Not muscles like yours, twisted and starved, that are only fit for scarecrows!

She waits another moment. She moves closer to him. In his face.

You don't have shoulders! You have a hump!

She drops sobbing at his feet, her voice barely discernible.

You don't have muscles . . . you have . . . lumps!

THE HAKE (*distant; very lightly; as if reciting*). And then out of the thicket flew a little bird. He flew for an instant above the green foliage . . .

EVA. Oh . . .

THE HAKE. Over the scenery bathed in light! Fly, little Corsair, I told him . . .

Eva covers her ears.

Fly, little bird!

The Hake looks at her with smiling compassion. He sits down beside her. He is sententious.

Love is a truce between periods of exhaustion. Love is broken teeth in a hungry mouth. What do you say? Did you like it?

EVA (*looks at him through tearful eyes*). Go away.

The Hake looks at her, perplexed.

THE HAKE (*genuinely desolate*). Are your throwing me out?

EVA. Yes! Yes! Yes! Yes! Yes!

THE HAKE. And what am I going to do?

EVA. It doesn't matter to me! Get out!

THE HAKE. I told Mario . . . I told him: these rich people give up in a hurry. At the first opposition they throw the whole thing over. (*Laughs.*) They forget themselves in a good symphony or by giving up something for Lent.

He looks at her.

Do you know what I saw a monkey in a circus do once? That monkey was trying to reach his mate, but he couldn't because they had put them in two separate cages and there were bars between them. It must have been about one o'clock in the afternoon when I saw him try to reach her for the first time. That night he hadn't succeeded, but he was still trying. His chest was all bloody and his teeth were broken from the iron bars, but still he kept trying. It was the following day that he succeeded in getting close to her, when they carried the female monkey to his burial. Sad, isn't it?

He wants to talk. He sits down on the floor at Eva's feet, crossing his legs in the position of a Hindu.

That is, naturally, always considering that love still exists. Saint Simon, the fool of Constitution Bridge, says that it doesn't. Actually, he doesn't even say that any more. One can only deduce it, given his . . . peculiar attitude. Do you know what he does, or what he *doesn't* do? He sits there night and day, on the railing of the bridge, watching the water go by. If anyone speaks to him: nothing. If anyone pokes him: nothing. If anyone shouts at him: (*He shouts.*) Ahhhhhh! Nothing! It's just that nothing interests him any more. He's arrived at a state of complete renunciation of life, where not even struggle is possible any longer. They say that one day a dove made a nest in his hat and he wasn't even aware of it. It's a legend, naturally, but it illustrates the situation, don't you think? Don't you think it illustrates it?

EVA. Didn't you hear what I asked you?

THE HAKE. What?

EVA. That you leave?

THE HAKE. Do you believe that? That we've arrived at the point of spiritual starvation where not even struggle is possible?

Eva rises to her feet. She screams and flees toward the bedroom. She locks herself in. The Hake watches her flee, halfway between stupefaction and amusement.

Do you believe that, Corsair? That we've arrived at a point of lack of love where love is no longer possible?

He approaches the cage. He talks to it, as he hits it, amuses himself. The cage almost hits the ceiling. The blows grow more violent as he speaks as in an interview; making the clichés ridiculous.

"Do you believe that, Mr. Happy?" . . . "That the human soul, deprived of all consolation, finds itself in a lamentable stage of spiritual prostration, where not even mutual confidence is possible?" "Do you believe it, Miss Smile?"

A violent blow.

Do you believe it, you fruity bird? Umm? What do you say? Do you believe it, you son-of-a-bitching bird? Don't you think that flying around the room that way without even saying goodbye was really a fruity thing to do, you pig of a bird? Umm? What do you say? What do you say, you shit? (*Screams.*) Speak, you queer! SPEAK!

The cage shatters against the wall.

Curtain

SCENE 6

The night of the same day.

Nothing of the original décor remains in the room.

Everything is turned upside down.

There are no longer any curtains. In their place hang men's pants.

From corner to corner are draped garlands made from men's shirts tied together by the sleeves, interwoven with others made of women's underwear.

Furniture has been constructed from pieces of the original furniture tied together with strips of wool jackets, torn blankets, and spreads.

The lamps that were hanging are now on the floor. Those that were on the floor are hanging.

The walls are covered with childish figures and drawings, made with burnt cork; "the cat," "the bad man," "the hand," etc. There are also sayings: "I am good" . . . "Christ is King" . . . "God is at my right hand" . . . "Long live me!"

In essence, nothing is in its rightful place. A cyclone has passed through the room. The only things that retain any appearance of premeditated arrangement are the paper flowers. Many new large paper flowers hang in profuse garlands from the walls and are distributed here and there on the floor.

Eva, standing in the midst of the disorder, is allowing herself to serve as model for a bridal gown, which The Hake is fitting to her body with careful solicitude.

THE HAKE (*pinning; making pleats*). Do you see? You see that with a little hope, a little good will, this was worth digging into the old trunk for? It's a little tight, it's true, . . . a little wrinkled, but we must concede that you never . . . suspected that sometime you would have "a second chance," umm?

He moves away, looking at his work.

Or was it for a first time that never was? Umm?

He adjusts a pleat.

There you are! That's it! A little tight through the hips, perhaps. The fault of too much starch, or the years . . . or carelessness, but it passes the test, doesn't it?

He adjusts another pleat. He is the tailor who speaks to his client, intimately, suggestively.

We oughtn't to have put it so far down in the trunk. I understand: because of a passing streetcar, a hand waving suggestively as it moves out of sight, or a word that was left unsaid, or all, all, all the imagination now passed under the bridge, we condemned it to the depths of the trunk, but what about the bells? The little bells? And the laughter at the entrance of the church? And the furtive kiss on the cheek? "Goodbye, Mary, I hope you'll be very happy!" "Good luck!" Doesn't that count, too? We shouldn't be so harsh with time. Objects, too, have a right to take revenge. We shouldn't expect that everything will take its just place, if we don't help it a little, don't you agree?

He moves away, he approaches again. Something about the total appearance displeases him. He rips one side of the dress.

Perhaps it's a question of ripping the cloth a little, in order to see the flesh.

He tears off a piece of the cretonne from the chair by his feet, and with it patches a piece of the torn dress. He smiles.

Sweet little brides! I've observed them! Crouched under the crepe myrtle in the park opposite the church; I've seen them, I've watched them. Not that I had any twisted feeling, like envy or anything like that! No! Why should I, when I had enough paper and scissors at hand?

He tears another piece of the dress and patches it with another strip of cretonne cloth.

They come walking through the high grass, their feet scarcely touching the ground, as if they were floating above the spikes of rye grass . . . they come shimmering over in the damp meadows . . . cadenced steps . . . radiant . . . in smooth white undulations, moving sinuously among the trunks of the oaks . . . straight toward the steps radiant in the sun . . . straight toward the gloved hand!

He speaks into her ear.

And there, at the same moment, before the lascivious glances of all the horrible dwarfs hidden behind the brick walls, hidden under the shadowy atrium, I have seen them . . . I have seen them!

He chokes. Trembles.

I have seen them! Open . . . ! The petals of their bodies! And offer . . . imagine! Offer! (*He shouts.*) Offer!

(*He calms himself.*) . . . Their virgin corollas to the consummation of love.

A choked cry.

Oh, God!

He controls himself. He regains his festive tone. He rips a sleeve. He replaces it with another sleeve made from a scrap of paper.

There are some naturally who have a different version of the affair, Fabian, for example. One day I was with him under the crepe myrtle. He had lifted some tinned smoked oysters, and we were preparing to enjoy them . . .

He slashes the hem of the skirt with the scissors.

I should warn you that Fabian has an especially noisy way of moving his mouth when he eats, a manner like this, holding his food in his mouth . . . as if he were afraid it would get to his intestines too fast, or that he might finish too soon, or that it might end too soon the pleasure of his de-gus-ta-tion! The fact is that I don't know if it was his way of chewing, I mean, or my particular state of tension that day, or the stone under my elbow—because a stone had got under my elbow, a damned stone under my elbow! The fact is I don't know if it was that way of his of chewing, like I said, or the stone, or my particular state of tension . . . the fact is that Fabian irritates me! He drives me to madness, I must confess! I don't know if it were that, I say, or the other . . . the insolence of his type, you understand me? His brutal, his bestial insensitivity, or his way of chewing, or the stone, or my particular state of tension. The fact is that, looking toward the church, I suddenly say, "Look!" And he answers me, "Those bitches! Those bitches." Imagine. I looked at his puss and I saw the oil of the smoked oysters dribbling from the corners of his mouth . . . and his bloodshot eyes, you understand me? And his noisy, disagreeable, embarrassing, repugnant way of chewing! The fact is that *something* produced in me, you understand me, a particular state of uncontrollable tension . . . and I grabbed the other tin of oysters that was open, but not eaten, you understand me . . . ? And I pushed it . . . I ground it . . . I shoved it into his filthy puss!

The preceding in screams; he calms himself. Now angelical.

In that moment the church bells rang, and I felt that I had done something that had to be done, you understand? That I had fulfilled my duty! Because guys like Fabian don't know, can't imagine, can't conceive . . . the scope . . . the complete miracle signified by the sur-ren-der-of-one's-vir-gi-ni-ty!

Accentuating the words with false pronunciation, he completely vitiates the meaning.

THE . . . MOST . . . SPLEN-DID . . . OFFERING OF LOVE!

He is amused by his own idea.

Love is a broken bridge with a broken tooth with a broken crank that whirls beyond its four confines breaking heads! Love is a dog with three feet! A tramp with only one hand and two bananas.

He has torn most of the skirt and is replacing it with pieces of the curtain and pieces of his own shirt he has torn into strips. He looks at her.

What's the matter with you? Are you shivering?

Eva shivers, with the same trembling as The Hake.

Are you cold? Are you hot? What is it?

Pause. He waits.

Do you want to go for a stroll on the beach with the happy bridegroom? Gathering shells? Hand in hand, gathering sand dollars? Discussing the number, and the sex, and the number, and the names, and the number, and the sex, of the children that the splendid future will give you? Discussing the arrangement of the furniture . . . of the cretonne . . . of the colors . . . of the "No it's better here," "No it's better there," of the sizes . . . of the cretonne . . . of the furniture . . . (*His voice is growing louder, faster.*) of the positions of the cretonnes! Of the sizes! Of the numbers, of the children, of the furniture . . . of the sizes . . . of the children? Spea-king-of-love! Love with an L, an O, an E, an X, a U, a tongue, everything, with strength, without strength! The possibilities . . . of being! Of achieving! Of fleeing! Of love! Of solitude! Of death! With a tongue! Arriving! Arriving! Arriving!

He screams.

ARRIVING! ARRIVING! AR . . . RI . . . VING!

He pants.

Is that it? Is that the secret the refrigerator hides?

Of the original bride's dress, only the veil remains. The rest is a ragbag.

That's funny. Now we're two little brothers.

He rips off the rest of his shirt. He covers his head with a paper rosette in the manner of a crown from which hang long strips of paper that reach to his waist. He takes a board from a piece of furniture in the manner of a lance and brandishes it.

I am Ukelele, the Simba Warrior!

He circles around Eva, making grotesque contortions and amusing grimaces.

Uku! Azahanba! Humba! Tekeke! Takamba! Tumba!

He looks at her as a curious orangutan might regard his prey, with simian curiosity. He puts his face right up to hers.

Comment allez-vous, madame? Did you say something?

EVA (*with an effort*). I . . .

THE HAKE. Yes?

EVA. I . . .

THE HAKE. Yes?

EVA. I only . . .

THE HAKE. You only, yes . . . ? You already said that. You only . . .

EVA. I only . . .

THE HAKE. Yes?

Eva tries to speak, but can't. Once or twice she makes an effort that frustrates her, then gives up. A pause.

You only wanted to love me and for me to love you. Is that it?

Eva nods weakly.

Yes. But it's too late for that. Ukelele has his guts in his hands and now he doesn't know what to do with them.

He places one of the big paper flowers in the bodice of Eva's dress. It is so large it completely covers her face. He takes her arm in his.

Shall we go?

Someone is knocking at the door.

Yes! (*He yells.*) We're coming.

He looks at Eva with solicitude, like a very considerate sweetheart.

Are you ready?

His expression changes suddenly to the one we are accustomed to seeing. Sententious. Vacant.

As you see, it is of the greatest importance to have understood the game. To believe in each other. To confide mutually. To renounce your own identity, to the benefit of the identity of the other, until your own identity and the identity of the other, and your own identity . . . own . . . identity . . . of the other . . . identity . . . own . . . don't you think so?

Eva weakly agrees.

Mendelssohn's Wedding March. Their march begins. "Ukelele," very stiff, pathetic almost in his dignity, nude, covered only in rags; on his head is a crown of shredded paper. Eva by his side, her arm in his, absent, lost, beneath the immensity of her paper flower. The only real thing about her is the beautiful veil.

Before we arrive there, I think I should inform you about the geography of the river, of the dangers it offers. There are, out there, some dangerous depths, where on nights of the full moon—when the river flows swollen with broken furniture—many people, falling, have broken their necks.

They exit. In the room now, total disorder reigns. Everything is broken, undone. There remains in it only the new beauty. The dark, enormous, ragged paper flowers.

Curtain

COMMENTARY

Note: The following essay represents a single interpretation of the play. For other perspectives on Paper Flowers, *consult the essays listed below.*

While Wolff may have absorbed both plot and stylistic elements from the likes of Albee and Pinter, his work—particularly *Paper Flowers*—reflects the social and political realities that shaped Latin American drama in the 1970s. Wolff's native Chile was perhaps the most notorious example of a country run by an oppressive military dictatorship committed to the preservation of wealth by the few at the expense of the many. The Hake's debasement and eventual conquest of the middle-class Eva reflects the restless, revolutionary spirit among Latin America's poor. Woolf's antipathy toward the middle-class's complacency, which he believes contributes to anarchy and revolution among the oppressed, has been well documented. *Paper Flowers* is, in one respect, a dramatic working out of a manifesto issued by the Coordinating Committee of the Revolutionary Imagination in Buenos Aires in 1969:

> Art as produced by our society will always be absorbed and rendered useless by the bourgeois. . . . What is it we want to transform? The Latin American man— ourselves: victims of neocolonial exploitation, of our native oligarchy, of all the forms of degradation and humiliation, conscious and unconscious, which shape our human and cultural values, our very existence.

It was in this spirit that many theater companies and collectives were formed throughout Latin America. And it is in this spirit that the Hake tells Eva that "I only know I am what I seem and not that I am not what I don't seem. In other words, you have your fantasy and I have only reality, which is much poorer, much sadder, much more disillusioning." The destruction he wreaks upon her well-ordered bourgeois home manifests Wolff's vision of the anarchy that awaits Chile—indeed, much of South America—if the disparity between social classes is not addressed. The apocalyptic finale (a mock wedding between the warring classes) is Wolff's darkest resolution and suggests that the hope for reconciliation he expressed in a similar play (*The Invaders*, 1963) is impossible.

But *Paper Flowers* is a more intriguing play than so many of the political tracts that emerged throughout Latin America during this tumultuous period. On one hand, the play is a taut psychological thriller in which the Hake methodically destroys Eva's personality and absorbs it into his own, which is filled with self-loathing. We are simultaneously fascinated and repulsed by the audacity of his mischief. The skilled yet destructive tempter is among the oldest archetypes known to humanity. It is no accident that Wolff names his heroine Eva and makes a point of having the Hake discover her in the Botanical Garden painting picture-perfect flowers. The Hake—whose name in Spanish is *El Merluza*—is named after a predatory fish of the Chilean seacoast noted for its sharp teeth and voracious appetite. He is a cousin of the infamous serpent in the Garden of Genesis, a seducer of the impressionable. Thus the playwright marries mythology with sociology, noting that because the hake is a staple of the diet of Chile's poor, it is an apt symbol of the socioeconomic conflict of the play.

On another level, *Paper Flowers* joins a rich treasury of literature devoted to "the battle of the sexes." The Hake's conquest is as much one of sexual domination as it is sociopolitical or psychological. He takes over not only Eva's habitat but her clothing as well (e.g., he wears her bathrobe in Scene 3). And throughout the play his language is fraught with sexual innuendo that is simultaneously erotic and degrading (its ambiguity becomes a weapon by which he destroys Eva). Such phrases as "anything you want to give me," "the way you cross your legs," and "you have to raise the chair skirt" abet the Hake's multilevel seductions of Eva.

Although Wolff has said he did not know Strindberg's one-act play, *Miss Julie* (1888), when he wrote *Paper Flowers*, there are nonetheless extraordinary similarities between the two works. The brutal killing of Eva's pet canary (cf. Julie's green finch) is an obvious parallel. However, *Miss Julie* was a naturalistic drama that explored the hereditary forces leading to the countess's destruction, even as it reflected Strindberg's much-discussed misogyny. But Wolff is no misogynist, and the Hake's degradation of Eva reflects the unfortunate reality of the subjugation of women throughout the world. In Latin America the problem is particularly exacerbated by the cult of *machismo* (or *macho*) by which one's manhood is validated by "owning" a woman. Note that the Hake refers (with his usual ambiguity) to the "macho" world of the streets, gangs, and violence. (Curiously, he is terrified by the ominous specter of Mario, who may or may not exist.) The converse of *machismo* is *mariannismo*, a term used by psychotherapists Rosa Maria Gil and Carmen Inoa Vazquez to describe a situation in which Latinas enable men by remaining faithful and submissive, regardless of how they are treated. Among the most frequently asked questions about the play is: Why does Eva allow the Hake to treat her so inhumanely? It is the question, unfortunately, that we must ask ourselves when we read about battered women. *Paper Flowers* may be read as a condemnation of *machismo* as well as *mariannismo*, both of which contribute to the loss of human dignity.

Finally, Wolff's play explores one of the literature's most archetypal conflicts: the battle between rationality and raw passion. Our first impressions of Eva's apartment (neat, orderly), her art (realistic, classical), and her language (lucid and in ordered paragraphs) all suggest a rational mind. By contrast, the Hake lives in makeshift slums and speaks in halting, often incomplete sentences (marked by a disturbing lack of specificity); he creates art of trash (mostly old newspapers, the most transitory and disposable means of communication). We therefore think of him as "raw," "primitive," even "uncivilized." As each scene progresses we note that his attempts at restraint give way to unbridled passion. Each outburst becomes more violent and destructive. Eventually, it is the Hake's modes of expression that triumph. Eva's furniture, artwork, and ultimately her language are destroyed. In the end she "tries to speak, but can't. Once or twice she makes an effort that frustrates her, then gives up." The Hake speaks, but in disjointed, often unintelligible gibberish ("Humba! Tekeke! Takamba!"), and when he does make sense, his message is terrifying ("many people, falling, have broken their necks"). His art—"dark, enormous, ragged paper flowers"—provides the play's final image, and the flowers dominate a landscape in which "total disorder reigns."

Wolff is not, of course, advocating the superiority of the Hake's "primitive" art. Hardly. Rather, he seems to indict the old order, the Aristotelian imitation of the beautiful, because its indifference to the oppressed contributes to a world in which anarchy reigns. His ultimate message, in this play of many messages, seems to be that art has the responsibility to produce more than pretty pictures of pretty flowers, or it may be replaced by "paper flowers" and all that they imply.

Other perspectives on *Paper Flowers*:

Lopez, David. "Ambiguity in *Flores de Papel* [*Paper Flowers*]." *Latin American Theatre Review* 12:2 (Spring 1978): 43–49.

Taylor, Diana. "Art and Anti-Art in Egon Wolff's *Flores de Papel* [*Paper Flowers*]." *Latin American Theatre Review* 18:1 (Fall 1984): 22–28.

Latin American Theater Under the Gun

But the theatre of the people cannot be the "finished" show; it has to be the "rehearsal," because the people do not yet know how their world is going to evolve. You have to make the kind of theatre in which everything is tested.

—Augusto Boal,
The Theatre of the Oppressed

The evolution of twentieth-century Latin American theater is marked by a long tradition of political turmoil aimed at controlling populations unwilling to accept mandates dictated by the ruling ideology. In a region rich in cultural traditions and natural resources, it is often paradoxical to survey the many historical accounts that have often altered the progress of southern nations in social and economic transition. Regardless of the many national upheavals, the emergence of a viable modern and contemporary Latin American independent theater movement forged a radically new aesthetic capable of transforming the theatrical and dramatic identity of individual nations as it denounced the heinous abuses perpetrated by political figureheads eager to silence a unified majority.

From the southern tip of Argentina to the Caribbean Basin, Latin America has produced a distinguished number of playwrights, directors, and performance ensembles reflecting a new and distinct artistry wrapped in an intellectual, experimental, and activist perspective. Argentina, the second largest South American nation, produced Osvaldo Dragún (1929–99), one of Latin America's most prolific contemporary dramatists, and his collective group, Fray Mocho Theatre. In 1955, Dragún recalled being in Buenos Aires with the members of the Fray Mocho company witnessing an army parade—a parade of the very forces which had just overthrown the president of Argentina, Juan Domingo Perón. This particular experience changed his approach to

drama. As he stood on a corner, he became aware that men dressed in suits and women in fur coats were happily welcoming the new powers with shouts of joy and victory signs. According to Dragún, suddenly everything became ridiculous and grotesque. A day before, these same individuals had been hoping for a more stable government, one that would be an improvement over a president accused of being ineffective and dishonest. But they had also been witnesses of a destructive revolution that had claimed a large number of human lives. Nevertheless, in their best apparel, they were now welcoming the authors of that destruction.

As Dragún and his company walked back to the theater for a rehearsal of Gorky's *The Smug Citizens*, they realized that the work would no longer have meaning. After all, Gorky's play is based on cause and effect; it is a piece that explores social transition, not chaos. But after that moment in the streets, the company's own reality could no longer be founded on cause and effect. On the contrary, their reality had been shattered; there was no equilibrium. If before they had abhorred Peronism, they now found themselves, as Vladimir in Samuel Beckett's *Waiting for Godot* puts it, "in the midst of nothingness."

This "nothingness" is what many Latin American nations experienced during the course of the twentieth century. These were lands in continuous conflict, housing societies that attempted to survive military regimes imposed by a handful of corrupt army officials. They ruled by means of the machine gun, the military police, abductions, and murder. Someone who became a threat to the existing system could disappear without a trace. Torture was not new in many Latin American countries. It came in many forms: psychological pressures, blacklists, confinement, and, of course, physical abuse. However, under the shadow of this sinister and brutal existence, the theater

continued to exist, often finding ways to express itself in layers of coded voices or by directly confronting the audience in an agit-prop, didactic manner. Collective performance groups such as Fray Mocho Theatre (Teatro Fray Mocho) of Argentina, the Theatre Escambray (Grupo Teatro Escambray) of Cuba, the Experimental Theatre of Cali (Teatro Experimental de Cali, or TEC), of Colombia, and the experimental university theaters of Chile, to name just a few, impacted the development of Latin American theater by condemning these human brutalities while simultaneously engendering a performance aesthetic that transformed the theater into a forum for direct collaborative communication between audience members and performers. Likewise, these groups shared a stylistic blueprint that essentially altered their performance methodology. As a general rule, they mapped a terrain in which the work of the actors and director served as a catalyst for the playwright's finished product—an ensemble theater in the truest sense of the word. Given the lack of financial support, these companies rehearsed and performed in small or found spaces, where the playing arena became a symbol for physical and psychological freedom. For Osvaldo Dragún's Fray Mocho Theatre, for instance, a stage cluttered with scenery and costumes could present only a type of illusionist experience that had nothing to do with their current socioeconomic and political surroundings. An empty stage, therefore, was certainly more appropriate.

The Theatre Escambray of Cuba was formed in 1967 amidst international tensions between two superpowers: the United States and the Soviet Union (now Russia). Amidst American predominance and Eastern European expansion, the Theatre Escambray, under the leadership of renowned film actor Sergio Corrieri (b. 1938), together with a handful of professional actors, left the urban environment of

Havana for the central Cuban mountains of Escambray, where they searched for an identity solidly rooted in socialist revolutionary ideology. Following Fidel Castro's mandate ("For the Revolution, everything is possible, but against the Revolution, nothing is"), the company's goal was to fuse artistry with original research on the lives of Cuban citizens who inhabited Escambray. Whereas Fray Mocho could exist only in a cosmopolitan reality, the Theatre Escambray found refuge away from urban cacophony, nestling in the words and experiences of soil tillers and dairy farmers. With a modest subsidy from the local Communist fraternity, the Escambray actors befriended, mingled with, and interviewed members of the community in order to assess the population's social and economic changes following the Cuban Revolution of 1959. The company's approach was collective in nature, gathering the research and interviews into a script format as they improvised and constructed scenes along the way. Often, a public presentation was accompanied by audience participation so that the spectator could become a part of the action. Additionally, performances included postproduction audience discussions that often led to rearranging or rewriting specific dramatic sequences.

If the Theatre Escambray was a product of a politically successful Socialist revolution, the Experimental Theatre of Cali, founded by Enrique Buenaventura (b. 1925), was the result of a search for a new dramatic discourse capable of modifying the contemporary Latin American theater. According to scholar Maida Watson Espener, "Buenaventura's commitment is to the solution of Latin American social problems, especially the problem of cultural dependency, through the creation of a theatre which will inspire its audience to change the structure of society." Highly influenced by the theories of Bertolt Brecht, Enrique Buenaventura set out to create a "collective" working environment—scripts were written in a collective manner, while the rehearsal process evolved through collective improvisations. Resembling the Theatre Escambray, Buenaventura's company incorporated in-depth actor/audience discussions as part of their working technique. These open forums delved into the anatomy of Colombia's turbulent politics in relationship to the company's ideological objective: to change the government's violent tendencies. From the 1940s to the 1960s, Colombia saw the annihilation of approximately 300,000 of its own citizens caught in the cauldron of terrorism, civil uprisings, collisions between indigenous people and the military police, and numerous guerrilla uprisings. While providing his audiences with a theatrical experience bathed in historical occurrences, Buenaventura developed an extensive assortment of theoretical writings outlining his sociopolitical and intellectual voice, as well as providing detailed descriptions for a new performance aesthetic.

Chile's search for a new national theater throughout the middle decades of the twentieth century began within the walls of the country's educational structure: the university theaters. Fatigued by a bourgeois and escapist national drama, the University of Chile and the Catholic University of Chile witnessed the evolution of a new popular theater by encouraging the writing of new domestic dramas in a period of agitated political activity. During the 1950s and 1960s, as Chile confronted a period of massive inflation coupled with an active political shift toward Communism and Socialism, the nation's cultural landscape created a new forum for sustaining viable intellectual and artistic expression. Highly committed to maintaining an active theatrical identity, the University of Chile launched a program to promote the staging of original dramatic works as part of its versatile year-round production repertoire. The Catholic University of Chile, on the other hand, sustained a dynamic theatrical vitality by offering classical European plays while nurturing young playwrights. Fundamentally, these university theaters provided an enterprising artistic panorama by attracting not only middle-class Chileans but also the working classes by generating affordable ticket prices. Additionally, these and other university theater ensembles toured the countryside to bring live theater to populations that otherwise would rely on television or commercial films for the sole purpose of mindless entertainment. It must be noted that these university-based theaters were also responsible for training professionals in all areas of the performing arts. The violent 1973 military coup d'état that removed the democratically elected government of Salvador Allende created a central shift in Chile's political history. As thousands of citizens were abducted, tortured, or jailed for political or ideological views contrary to the newly established military oligarchy, many Chilean artists, writers, and intellectuals went into exile, thus curtailing a vibrant national artistic, theatrical, and dramatic presence.

The most prolific and distinctive voice in the development of twentieth-century Latin American theater is that of Augusto Boal, a Brazilian-born director, theorist, and author of the acclaimed text, *The Theatre of the Oppressed* (1979). Boal's theater, the Arena Theatre (Teatro de Arena) manifests his artistic vision: to remind Brazilians, and all Latin Americans for that matter, that they live in a state of continual political and socioeconomic subjugation. Imprisoned and tortured for his artistic and ideological commitment to the theater, Boal continued to develop his theories, even in exile:

> In Argentina, we would board a train and then, once inside the train, the actors would take over the car. No one would know that we were actors performing and the scene would be done as if it were actually happening. We went to a market place to discuss problems of inflation. We prepared a scene and there in front of the stands where they were selling goods the scene "exploded." This is what we call "invisible theater." But we also use other forms of theater for the purpose of interpreting news from a newspaper. This we call "newspaper theater." There are lots of techniques in which the reading public can take material

from the newspapers and create theatrical scenes.

Boal's artistic impulses have always been drawn to the cries of the socially disadvantaged; in Brazil, for instance, he found his audience among factory workers or people working within the black slums of São Paulo. In Perú, Boal contributed to the establishment of a literacy program through acting techniques and physical action practiced by the dispossessed. Influenced by the writings of Aristotle (whom he actually rejects), Hegel, and Brecht, Boal's commitment to the theater continues to be based on a highly sociopolitical and intellectual thrust. Boal's personal engagement with the acting process was, and still is, a clear metaphor for the plight of the Latin American condition: through the act of performance one is able to change the social fiber for the benefit of an entire nation, regardless of one's social birthright. In describing his methodology for teaching acting to nonprofessional performers, he states:

We found that the people had to practice the art of portraying animals and even "professions" (lawyers and so forth). Then we would go to forms of theater in which the audience tells the actors what they have to do, and the actors do nothing unless the audience says, "Do this and do that." So the political solutions of the play's problems are offered by the audience. We go from there to another form of theater in which the people must use the bodies of the actors much as a sculptor would, to show what they think of reality.

Yet this was no different than what Dragún's Fray Mocho Theatre was attempting to do with professionally trained actors: to present a Latin American reality based on the past, the present, and the unreality of the future. Like Dragún's actors, Boal's performers were trained to work physically in order to make up for the lack of costumes, scenery, and illusionist lighting. Actors became animals, trees, a river, and their voices replaced the electronic sound effects of a more technologically dependent theater.

The artistic accomplishments of Argentina's Fray Mocho Theatre, Cuba's Theatre Escambray, Colombia's Experimental Theatre of Cali, and the vibrant university theater of Chile ushered in a people's collective theater aesthetic, rooted in a political and ideological reality. The combination of an empty space and versatility in the acting process created a dual freedom: freedom of expression for the artist and freedom of expression for the audience. It was a type of psychological freedom sorely absent in the daily clashes artists and audiences found on the streets of Latin America.

DEATH AND THE KING'S HORSEMAN

WOLE SOYINKA

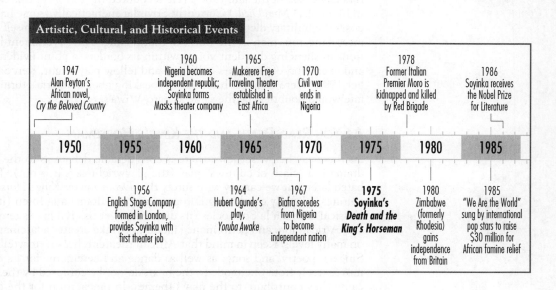

Artistic, Cultural, and Historical Events

1947 Alan Peyton's African novel, *Cry the Beloved Country*

1960 Nigeria becomes independent republic; Soyinka forms Masks theater company

1965 Makerere Free Traveling Theater established in East Africa

1970 Civil war ends in Nigeria

1978 Former Italian Premier Moro is kidnapped and killed by Red Brigade

1986 Soyinka receives the Nobel Prize for Literature

| 1950 | 1955 | 1960 | 1965 | 1970 | 1975 | 1980 | 1985 |

1956 English Stage Company formed in London, provides Soyinka with first theater job

1964 Hubert Ogunde's play, *Yoruba Awake*

1967 Biafra secedes from Nigeria to become independent nation

1975 Soyinka's *Death and the King's Horseman*

1980 Zimbabwe (formerly Rhodesia) gains independence from Britain

1985 "We Are the World" sung by international pop stars to raise $30 million for African famine relief

WOLE SOYINKA (1934–)

Born into the Yoruba culture of Abeokuta, Nigeria, Akinwande Oluwole Soyinka has emerged as Africa's most noteworthy playwright, as well as an accomplished poet, novelist, short story writer, and literary theorist. He received his initial education at St. Peter's School and the Abeokuta Grammar School in his native city, then went to Nigeria's capital of Ibadan to study at both the Government College and University College. From 1954 to 1957 he was a student at Leeds University in central England, where he earned honors in English and some renown as a short story writer.

In 1957 he was attached to the newly founded Royal Court Theatre in London as a play reader, and it was there that his unpublished play *The Invention* was first performed in 1959. The Royal Court has continued to produce many of Soyinka's works, including *The Lion and the Jewel* (1963), *A Dance in the Forest* (1963), *The Road* (1965), *Kongi's Harvest* (1967), an adaptation of Euripides's *The Bacchae* (1973), *Death and the King's Horseman* (1975), *A Play of Giants* (1984), and most recently *From Zia with Love* (1992). His novels include *The Interpreters* (1965) and *Seasons of Agony* (1973), while his poetry is collected under such titles as *Indare and Other Poems* (1967), *Ogun Abibiman* (1976), and *Mandela's Earth* (1988). Soyinka has written several autobiographical works, including *Ake: The Years of Childhood* (1981) and *Ibadan* (1994). He has excelled in critical writing, most notably *Myth, Literature, and the African World* (1976) and *Art, Dialogue, and Outrage* (1988). This prodigious outpouring of literature, which has inspired both praise and controversy, earned Soyinka the Nobel Prize in 1986; he was the first African writer to receive the world's most prestigious literary award.

Soyinka's critics—primarily Marxists and neo-Negritudists—have attacked him on the grounds that his work lacks a specific political direction. Generally, such claims are accurate: Soyinka himself has frequently spoken out forcefully against imposing constraints on artistic exploration in favor of the hegemonic goals of a particular group. Yet Soyinka is anything but apolitical. As early as 1965 he was arrested for "pirating" a radio broadcast made from the Nigerian Broadcasting Corporation subsequent to the disputed elections in Nigeria's Western Regions. Though he was acquitted of this crime, he was later arrested and placed in solitary confinement for not being demonstrably anti-Biafran during Nigeria's Civil War of the late 1960s. (He recounted the terrors of this two-year imprisonment in his book *A Man Died*.) Currently, Soyinka energetically (some have said recklessly) opposes the military dictatorship that rules Nigeria and claims himself to be one of the three most dangerous men in the world to that regime. The government has shown no reservations in silencing dissident voices within its borders, a point evidenced by the mock trial and execution of Soyinka's colleague and fellow playwright, Ken Saro-Wiwa, in November 1995. Were Soyinka himself not speaking about Nigeria's turmoil while in exile, his fate would doubtless be the same as Saro-Wiwa's.

AS YOU READ *DEATH AND THE KING'S HORSEMAN*

As the essay below suggests, there is considerable debate as to the degree that Soyinka's drama is a "clash of cultures" play (the playwright says it is not). That point will be debated later, but we can say with surety that *Death and the King's Horseman* is a "synthesis of cultures" play. By combining European realistic drama à la Ibsen (it is a discussion play), classical drama à la Sophocles (its divine law versus civil law is reminiscent of *Antigone*), and African lore and performance modes, Soyinka creates a fascinating hybrid that works on many levels. Keep in mind that African theater relies on storytellers (here it is a Praise-Singer), poetry, and song, as well as dance and ceremony, for its effects. Soyinka's play moves freely from one mode to the next; do not be confused by these sudden changes because they contribute to the play's themes. In preparation for the play, you may want to read the accompanying Showcase, which introduces you to Yoruba thought and theater.

DEATH AND THE KING'S HORSEMAN

WOLE SOYINKA

CHARACTERS

PRAISE-SINGER
ELESIN, *Horseman of the King*
IYALOJA, *'Mother' of the market*
SIMON PILKINGS, *District Officer*
JANE PILKINGS, *his wife*
SERGEANT AMUSA
JOSEPH, *houseboy to the Pilkingses*
BRIDE
H.R.H. THE PRINCE
THE RESIDENT
AIDE-DE-CAMP
OLUNDE, *eldest son of Elesin*
DRUMMERS, WOMEN, YOUNG GIRLS, DANCERS AT THE BALL

AUTHOR'S NOTE

This play is based on events which took place in Oyo, ancient Yoruba city of Nigeria, in 1946. That year, the lives of Elesin (Olori Elesin), his son, and the Colonial District Officer intertwined with the disastrous results set out in the play. The changes I have made are in matters of detail, sequence and of course characterisation. The action has also been set back two or three years to while the war was still on, for minor reasons of dramaturgy.

The factual account still exists in the archives of the British Colonial Administration. It has already inspired a fine play in Yoruba (*Oba Wàjà*) by Duro Ladipo. It has also misbegotten a film by some German television company.

The bane of themes of this genre is that they are no sooner employed creatively than they acquire the facile tag of 'clash of cultures', a prejudicial label which, quite apart from its frequent misapplication, presupposes a potential equality *in every given situation* of the alien culture and the indigenous, on the actual soil of the latter. (In the area of misapplication, the overseas prize for illiteracy and mental conditioning undoubtedly goes to the blurb-writer for the American edition of my novel *Seasons of Agony* who unblushingly declares that this work portrays the 'clash between old values and new ways, between western methods and African traditions'!) It is thanks to this kind of perverse mentality that I find it necessary to caution the would-be producer of this play against a sadly familiar reductionist tendency, and to direct his vision instead to the far more difficult and risky task of eliciting the play's threnodic essence.

One of the more obvious alternative structures of the play would be to make the District Officer the victim of a cruel dilemma. This is not to my taste and it is not by chance that I have avoided dialogue or situation which would encourage this. No attempt should be made in production to suggest it. The Colonial Factor is an incident, a catalytic incident merely. The confrontation in the play is largely metaphysical, contained in the human vehicle which is Elesin and the universe of the Yoruba mind—the world of the living, the dead and the unborn, and the numinous passage which links all: transition. *Death and the King's Horseman* can be fully realised only through an evocation of music from the abyss of transition.

W.S.

SCENE 1

A passage through a market in its closing stages. The stalls are being emptied, mats folded. A few women pass through on their way home, loaded with baskets. On a cloth-stand, bolts of cloth are taken down, display pieces folded and piled on a tray. Elesin Oba enters along a passage before the market, pursued by his drummers and praise-singers. He is a man of enormous vitality, speaks, dances and sings with that infectious enjoyment of life which accompanies all his actions.

PRAISE-SINGER. Elesin o! Elesin Oba! Howu! What tryst is this the cockerel goes to keep with such haste that he must leave his tail behind?

ELESIN (*slows down a bit, laughing*). A tryst where the cockerel needs no adornment.

PRAISE-SINGER. O-oh, you hear that my companions? That's the way the world goes. Because the man approaches a brand-new bride he forgets the long faithful mother of his children.

ELESIN. When the horse sniffs the stable does he not strain at the bridle? The market is the long-suffering home of my spirit and the women are packing up to go. That Esu-harrassed day slipped into the stewpot while we feasted. We ate it up with the rest of the meat. I have neglected my women.

PRAISE-SINGER. We know all that. Still it's no reason for shedding your tail on this day of all days. I know the women will cover you in damask and *alari* but when the wind blows cold from behind, that's when the fowl knows his true friends.

ELESIN. Olohun-iyo!

PRAISE-SINGER. Are you sure there will be one like me on the other side?

ELESIN. Olohun-iyo!

PRAISE-SINGER. Far be it for me to belittle the dwellers of that place but, a man is either born to his art or he isn't. And I don't know for certain that you'll meet my father, so who is going to sing these deeds in accents that will pierce the deafness of the ancient ones? I have prepared my going—just tell me: Olohun-iyo, I need you on this journey and I shall be behind you.

ELESIN. You're like a jealous wife. Stay close to me, but only on this side. My fame, my honour are legacies to the living; stay behind and let the world sip its honey from your lips.

PRAISE-SINGER. Your name will be like the sweet berry a child places under his tongue to sweeten the passage of food. The world will never spit it out.

ELESIN. Come then. This market is my roost. When I come among the women I am a chicken with a hundred mothers. I become a monarch whose palace is built with tenderness and beauty.

PRAISE-SINGER. They love to spoil you but beware. The hands of women also weaken the unwary.

ELESIN. This night I'll lay my head upon their lap and go to sleep. This night I'll touch feet with their feet in a dance that is no longer of this earth. But the smell of their flesh, their sweat, the smell of indigo on their cloth, this is the last air I wish to breathe as I go to meet my great forebears.

PRAISE-SINGER. In their time the world was never tilted from its groove, it shall not be in yours.

ELESIN. The gods have said No.

PRAISE-SINGER. In their time the great wars came and went, the little wars came and went; the white slavers came and went, they took away the heart of our race, they bore away the mind and muscle of our race. The city fell and was rebuilt; the city fell and our people trudged

through mountain and forest to found a new home but—Elesin Oba do you hear me?

ELESIN. I hear your voice Olohun-iyo.

PRAISE-SINGER. Our world was never wrenched from its true course.

ELESIN. The gods have said No.

PRAISE-SINGER. There is only one home to the life of a river-mussel; there is only one home to the life of a tortoise; there is only one shell to the soul of man: there is only one world to the spirit of our race. If that world leaves its course and smashes on boulders of the great void, whose world will give us shelter?

ELESIN. It did not in the time of my forebears, it shall not in mine.

PRAISE-SINGER. The cockerel must not be seen without his feathers.

ELESIN. Nor will the Not-I bird be much longer without his nest.

PRAISE-SINGER (*stopped in his lyric stride*). The Not-I bird, Elesin?

ELESIN. I said, the Not-I bird.

PRAISE-SINGER. All respect to our elders but, is there really such a bird?

ELESIN. What! Could it be that he failed to knock on your door?

PRAISE-SINGER (*smiling*). Elesin's riddles are not merely the nut in the kernel that breaks human teeth; he also buries the kernel in hot embers and dares a man's fingers to draw it out.

ELESIN. I am sure he called on you, Olohun-iyo. Did you hide in the loft and push out the servant to tell him you were out?

(*Elesin executes a brief, half-taunting dance. The drummer moves in and draws a rhythm out of his steps. Elesin dances towards the market-place as he chants the story of the Not-I bird, his voice changing dexterously to mimic his characters. He performs like a born raconteur, infecting his retinue with his humour and energy. More women arrive during his recital, including Iyaloja.*)

Death came calling.
Who does not know his rasp of reeds?
A twilight whisper in the leaves before
The great araba falls? Did you hear it?

Not I! swears the farmer! He snaps
His fingers round his head, abandons
A hard-worn harvest and begins
A rapid dialogue with his legs.

'Not I,' shouts the fearless hunter, 'but—
It's getting dark, and this night-lamp
Has leaked out all it soil. I think
It's best to go home and resume my hunt

Another day.' But now he pauses, suddenly
Lets out a wail: 'Oh foolish mouth, calling
Down a curse on your own head!
  Your lamp
Has leaked out all its oil, has it?'
Forwards or backwards now he dare not move.
To search for leaves and make *etutu*
On that spot? Or race home to the safety
Of his hearth? Ten market-days have passed
My friends, and still he's rooted there
Rigid as the plinth of Orayan.

The mouth of the courtesan barely
Opened wide enough to take a ha'penny *robo*
When she wailed: 'Not I.' All dressed she was
To call upon my friend the Chief Tax Officer.
But now she sends her go-between instead:
'Tell him I'm ill: my period has come suddenly
But not—I hope—my time.'

Why is the pupil crying?
His hapless head was made to taste
The knuckles of my friend the Mallam:
'If you were then reciting the Koran
Would you have ears for idle noises
Darkening the trees, you child of ill omen?'
He shuts down school before its time
Runs home and rings himself with amulets.

And take my good kinsman Ifawomi.
His hands were like a carver's, strong
And true. I saw them
Tremble like wet wings of a fowl
One day he cast his time-smoothed *opele*
Across the divination board. And all because
The suppliant looked him in the eye and asked,
'Did you hear that whisper in the leaves?'
'Not I,' was his reply; 'perhaps I'm growing deaf—
Good-day.' And Ifa spoke no more that day
The priest locked fast his doors,
Sealed up his leaking roof—but wait!
This sudden care was not for Fawomi
But for Osanyin, courier-bird of Ifa's
Heart of wisdom. I did not know a kite
Was hovering in the sky
And Ifa now a twittering chicken in
The brood of Fawomi the Mother Hen.

Ah, but I must not forget my evening
Courier from the abundant palm, whose groan
Became Not I, as he constipated down
A wayside bush. He wonders if Elegbara
Has tricked his buttocks to discharge
Against a sacred grove. Hear him
Mutter spells to ward off penalties
For an abomination he did not intend.

If any here
Stumbles on a gourd of wine, fermenting
Near the road, and nearby hears a stream
Of spells issuing from a crouching form,
Brother to a *sigidi*, bring home my wine,
Tell my tapper I have ejected
Fear from home and farm. Assure him,
All is well.

PRAISE-SINGER. In your time we do not doubt the peace of
  farmstead and home, the peace of road and hearth, we
  do not doubt the peace of the forest.

ELESIN. There was fear in the forest too.
  Not-I was lately heard even in the lair
  Of beasts. The hyena cackled loud Not I,
  The civet twitched his fiery tail and glared:
  Not I. Not-I became the answering-name
  Of the restless bird, that little one
  Whom Death found nesting in the leaves
  When whisper of his coming ran
  Before him on the wind. Not-I
  Has long abandoned home. This same dawn
  I heard him twitter in the gods' abode.
  Ah, companions of this living world
  What a thing this is, that even those
  We call immortal
  Should fear to die.

IYALOJA. But you, husband of multitudes?

ELESIN. I, when that Not-I bird perched
  Upon my roof, bade him seek his nest again,
  Safe, without care or fear. I unrolled
  My welcome mat for him to see. Not-I
  Flew happily away, you'll hear his voice
  No more in this lifetime—You all know
  What I am.

PRAISE-SINGER. That rock which turns its open lodes
  Into the path of lightning. A gay
  Thoroughbred whose stride disdains
  To falter through an adder reared
  Suddenly in his path.

ELESIN. My rein is loosened.
  I am master of my Fate. When the hour comes
  Watch me dance along the narrowing path
  Glazed by the soles of my great precursors.
  My soul is eager. I shall not turn aside.

WOMEN. You will not delay?

ELESIN. Where the storm pleases, and when, it directs
  The giants of the forest. When friendship summons
  Is when the true comrade goes.

WOMEN. Nothing will hold you back?

ELESIN. Nothing. What! Has no one told you yet?
  I go to keep my friend and master company.
  Who says the mouth does not believe in
  'No, I have chewed all that before?' I say I have.
  The world is not a constant honey-pot.
  Where I found little I made do with little.

Where there was plenty I gorged myself.
My master's hands and mine have always
Dipped together and, home or sacred feast,
The bowl was beaten bronze, the meats
So succulent our teeth accused us of neglect.
We shared the choicest of the season's
Harvest of yams. How my friend would read
Desire in my eyes before I knew the cause—
However rare, however precious, it was mine.

WOMEN. The town, the very land was yours.

ELESIN. The world was mine. Our joint hands
Raised houseposts of trust that withstood
The siege of envy and the termites of time.
But the twilight hour brings bats and rodents—
Shall I yield them cause to foul the rafters?

PRAISE-SINGER. Elesin Oba! Are you not that man who
Looked out of doors that stormy day
The god of luck limped by, drenched
To the very lice that held
His rags together? You took pity upon
His sores and wished him fortune.
Fortune was footloose this dawn, he replied,
Till you trapped him in a heartfelt wish
That now returns to you. Elesin Oba!
I say you are that man who
Chanced upon the calabash of honour
You thought it was palm wine and
Drained its contents to the final drop.

ELESIN. Life has an end. A life that will outlive
Fame and friendship begs another name.
What elder takes his tongue to his plate,
Licks it clean of every crumb? He will encounter
Silence when he calls on children to fulfill
The smallest errand! Life is honour.
It ends when honour ends.

WOMEN. We know you for a man of honour.

ELESIN. Stop! Enough of that!

WOMEN (puzzled, they whisper among themselves, turning
mostly to Iyaloja). What is it? Did we say something to
give offence? Have we slighted him in some way?

ELESIN. Enough of that sound I say. Let me hear no more in
that vein. I've heard enough.

IYALOJA. We must have said something wrong. (Comes
forward a little.) Elesin Oba, we ask forgiveness before
you speak.

ELESIN. I am bitterly offended.

IYALOJA. Our unworthiness has betrayed us. All we can do is
ask your forgiveness. Correct us like a kind father.

ELESIN. This day of all days . . .

IYALOJA. It does not bear thinking. If we offend you now we
have mortified the gods. We offend heaven itself.
Father of us all, tell us where we went astray. (She kneels,
the other women follow.)

ELESIN. Are you not ashamed? Even a tear-veiled
Eye preserves its function of sight.

Because my mind was raised to horizons
Even the boldest man lowers his gaze
In thinking of, must my body here
Be taken for a vagrant's?

IYALOJA. Horseman of the King, I am more baffled than ever.

PRAISE-SINGER. The strictest father unbends his brow when
the child is penitent, Elesin. When time is short, we do
not spend it prolonging the riddle. Their shoulders are
bowed with the weight of fear lest they have marred
your day beyond repair. Speak now in plain words and
let us pursue the ailment to the home of remedies.

ELESIN. Words are cheap. 'We know you for
A man of honour.' Well tell me, is this how
A man of honour should be seen?
Are these not the same clothes in which
I came among you a full half-hour ago?

(He roars with laughter and the women, relieved,
rise and rush into stalls to fetch rich cloths.)

WOMAN. The gods are kind. A fault soon remedied is soon
forgiven. Elesin Oba, even as we match our words with
deed, let your heart forgive us completely.

ELESIN. You who are breath and giver of my being
How shall I dare refuse you forgiveness
Even if the offence were real.

IYALOJA (dancing round him. Sings).
He forgives us. He forgives us.
What a fearful thing it is when
The voyager sets forth
But a curse remains behind.

WOMEN. For a while we truly feared
Our hands had wrenched the world adrift
In emptiness.

IYALOJA. Richly, richly, robe him richly
The cloth of honour is alari
Sanyan is the band of friendship
Boa-skin makes slippers of esteem

WOMEN. For a while we truly feared
Our hands had wrenched the world adrift
In emptiness.

PRAISE-SINGER. He who must, must voyage forth
The world will not roll backwards
It is he who must, with one
Great gesture overtake the world.

WOMEN. For a while we truly feared
Our hands had wrenched the world
In emptiness.

PRAISE-SINGER. The gourd you bear is not for shirking.
The gourd is not for setting down
At the first crossroad or wayside grove.
Only one river may know its contents

WOMEN. We shall all meet at the great market
We shall all meet at the great market
He who goes early takes the best bargains
But we shall meet, and resume our banter.

(Elesin stands resplendent in rich clothes, cap, shawl, etc. His sash is of a bright red alari cloth. The women dance round him. Suddenly, his attention is caught by an object off-stage.)

ELESIN. The world I know is good.
WOMEN. We know you'll leave it so.
ELESIN. The world I know is the bounty
Of hives after bees have swarmed.
No goodness teems with such open hands
Even in the dreams of deities.
WOMEN. And we know you'll leave it so.
ELESIN. I was born to keep it so. A hive
Is never known to wander. An anthill
Does not desert its roots. We cannot see
The still great womb of the world—
No man beholds his mother's womb—
Yet who denies it's there? Coiled
To the navel of the world is that
Endless cord that links us all
To the great origin. If I lose my way
The trailing cord will bring me to the roots.
WOMEN. The world is in your hands.

(The earlier distraction, a beautiful young girl, comes along the passage through which Elesin first made his entry.)

ELESIN. I embrace it. And let me tell you, women—
I like this farewell that the world designed,
Unless my eyes deceive me, unless
We are already parted, the world and I,
And all that breeds desire is lodged
Among our tireless ancestors. Tell me friends,
Am I still earthed in that beloved market
Of my youth? Or could it be my will
Has outleapt the conscious act and I have come
Among the great departed?
PRAISE-SINGER. Elesin-Oba why do your eyes roll like a bushrat who sees his fate like his father's spirit, mirrored in the eye of a snake? And all these questions! You're standing on the same earth you've always stood upon. This voice you hear is mine, Oluhun-iyo, not that of an acolyte in heaven.
ELESIN. How can that be? In all my life
As Horseman of the King, the juiciest
Fruit on every tree was mine. I saw,
I touched, I wooed, rarely was the answer No.
The honour of my place, the veneration I
Received in the eye of man or woman
Prospered my suit and
Played havoc with my sleeping hours.
And they tell me my eyes were a hawk
In perpetual hunger. Split an iroko tree
In two, hide a woman's beauty in its heartwood
And seal it up again—Elesin, journeying by,

Would make his camp beside that tree
Of all the shades in the forest.
PRAISE-SINGER. Who would deny your reputation, snake-on-the-loose in dark passages of the market! Bed-bug who wages war on the mat and receives the thanks of the vanquished! When caught with his bride's own sister he protested—but I was only prostrating myself to her as becomes a grateful in-law. Hunter who carries his powder-horn on the hips and fires crouching or standing! Warrior who never makes that excuse of the whining coward—but how can I go to battle without my trousers?—trouserless or shirtless it's all one to him. Oka-rearing-from-a-camouflage-of-leaves, before he strikes the victim is already prone! Once they told him, Howu, a stallion does not feed on the grass beneath him: he replied, true, but surely he can roll on it!
WOMEN. Ba-a-a-ba O!
PRAISE-SINGER. Ah, but listen yet. You know there is the leaf-knibbling grub and there is the cola-chewing beetle; the leaf-nibbling grub lives on the leaf, the cola-chewing beetle lives in the colanut. Don't we know what our man feeds on when we find him cocooned in a woman's wrapper?
ELESIN. Enough, enough, you all have cause
To know me well. But, if you say this earth
Is still the same as gave birth to those songs,
Tell me who was that goddess through whose lips
I saw the ivory pebbles of Oya's riverbed.
Iyaloja, who is she? I saw her enter
Your stall; all your daughters I know well.
No, not even Ogun-of-the-farm toiling
Dawn till dusk on his tuber patch
Not even Ogun with the finest hoe he ever
Forged at the anvil could have shaped
That rise of buttocks, not though he had
The richest earth between his fingers.
Her wrapper was no disguise
For thighs whose ripples shamed the river's
Coils around the hills of Ilesi. Her eyes
Were new-laid eggs glowing in the dark.
Her skin . . .
IYALOJA. Elesin Oba . . .
ELESIN. What! Where do you all say I am?
IYALOJA. Still among the living.
ELESIN. And that radiance which so suddenly
Lit up this market I could boast
I knew so well?
IYALOJA. Has one step already in her husband's home. She is betrothed.
ELESIN *(irritated)*. Why do you tell me that?

(Iyaloja falls silent. The women shuffle uneasily.)

IYALOJA. Not because we dare give you offence Elesin. Today is your day and the whole world is yours. Still, even those who leave town to make a new dwelling elsewhere like to be remembered by what they leave behind.

ELESIN. Who does not seek to be remembered?
Memory is Master of Death, the chink
In his armour of conceit. I shall leave
That which makes my going the sheerest
Dream of an afternoon. Should voyagers
Not travel light? Let the considerate traveller
Shed, of his excessive load, all
That may benefit the living.

WOMEN (*relieved*). Ah Elesin Oba, we knew you for a man of honour.

ELESIN. Then honour me. I deserve a bed of honour to lie upon.

IYALOJA. The best is yours. We know you for a man of honour. You are not one who eats and leaves nothing on his plate for children. Did you not say it yourself? Not one who blights the happiness of others for a moment's pleasure.

ELESIN. Who speaks of pleasure? O women, listen!
Pleasure palls. Our acts should have meaning.
The sap of the plantain never dries.
You have seen the young shoot swelling
Even as the parent stalk begins to wither.
Women, let my going be likened to
The twilight hour of the plantain.

WOMEN. What does he mean Iyaloja? This language is the language of our elders, we do not fully grasp it.

IYALOJA. I dare not understand you yet Elesin.

ELESIN. All you who stand before the spirit that dares
The opening of the last door of passage,
Dare to rid my going of regrets! My wish
Transcends the blotting out of thought
In one mere moment's tremor of the senses.
Do me credit. And do me honour.
I am girded for the route beyond
Burdens of waste and longing.
Then let me travel light. Let
Seed that will not serve the stomach
On the way remain behind. Let it take root
In the earth of my choice, in this earth
I leave behind.

IYALOJA (*turns to women*). The voice I hear is already touched by the waiting fingers of our departed. I dare not refuse.

WOMAN. But Iyaloja . . .

IYALOJA. The matter is no longer in our hands.

WOMAN. But she is betrothed to your own son. Tell him.

IYALOJA. My son's wish is mine. I did the asking for him, the loss can be remedied. But who will remedy the blight of closed hands on the day when all should be openness and light? Tell him, you say! You wish that I burden him with knowledge that will sour his wish and lay regrets on the last moments of his mind. You pray to him who is your intercessor to the other world—don't set this world

adrift in your own time; would you rather it was my hand whose sacrilege wrenched it loose?

WOMAN. Not many men will brave the curse of a dispossessed husband.

IYALOJA. Only the curses of the departed are to be feared. The claims of one whose foot is on the threshold of their abode surpasses even the claims of blood. It is impiety even to place hindrances in their ways.

ELESIN. What do my mothers say? Shall I step
Burdened into the unknown?

IYALOJA. Not we, but the very earth says No. The sap in the plantain does not dry. Let grain that will not feed the voyagers at his passage drop here and take root as he steps beyond this earth and us. Oh you who fill the home from hearth to threshold with the voices of children, you who now bestride the hidden gulf and pause to draw the right foot across and into the resting-home of the great forebears, it is good that your loins be drained into the earth we know, that your last strength be ploughed back into the womb that gave you being.

PRAISE-SINGER. Iyaloja, mother of multitudes in the teeming market of the world, how your wisdom transfigures you!

IYALOJA (*smiling broadly, completely reconciled*). Elesin, even at the narrow end of the passage I know you will look back and sigh a last regret for the flesh that flashed past your spirit in flight. You always had a restless eye. Your choice has my blessing. (*To the women.*) Take the good news to our daughter and make her ready. (*Some women go off.*)

ELESIN. Your eyes were clouded at first.

IYALOJA. Not for long. It is those who stand at the gateway of the great change to whose cry we must pay heed. And then, think of this—it makes the mind tremble. The fruit of such a union is rare. It will be neither of this world nor of the next. Nor of the one behind us. As if the timelessness of the ancestor world and the unborn have joined spirits to wring an issue of the elusive being of passage . . . Elesin!

ELESIN. I am here. What is it?

IYALOJA. Did you hear all I said just now?

ELESIN. Yes.

IYALOJA. The living must eat and drink. When the moment comes, don't turn the food to rodents' droppings in their mouth. Don't let them taste the ashes of the world when they step out at dawn to breathe the morning dew.

ELESIN. This doubt is unworthy of you Iyaloja.

IYALOJA. Eating the awusa nut is not so difficult as drinking water afterwards.

ELESIN. The waters of the bitter stream are honey to a man
Whose tongue has savoured all.

IYALOJA. No one knows when the ants desert their home; they leave the mound intact. The swallow is never seen to peck holes in its nest when it is time to move with the season. There are always throngs of humanity behind the leave-taker. The rain should not come through the roof for them, the wind must not blow through the walls at night.

ELESIN. I refuse to take offence.

IYALOJA. You wish to travel light. Well, the earth is yours. But be sure the seed you leave in it attracts no curse.

ELESIN. You really mistake my person Iyaloja.

IYALOJA. I said nothing. Now we must go prepare your bridal chamber. Then these same hands will lay your shrouds.

ELESIN (*exasperated*). Must you be so blunt? (*Recovers.*) Well, weave your shrouds, but let the fingers of my bride seal my eyelids with earth and wash my body.

IYALOJA. Prepare yourself Elesin.

(*She gets up to leave. At that moment the women return, leading the Bride. Elesin's face glows with pleasure. He flicks the sleeves of his agbada with renewed confidence and steps forward to meet the group. As the girl kneels before Iyaloja, lights fade out on the scene.*)

SCENE 2

The verandah of the District Officer's bungalow. A tango is playing from an old hand-cranked gramophone and, glimpsed through the wide windows and doors which open onto the forestage verandah are the shapes of Simon Pilkings and his wife, Jane, tangoing in and out of shadows in the living-room. They are wearing what is immediately apparent as some form of fancy-dress. The dance goes on for some moments and then the figure of a 'Native Administration' policeman emerges and climbs up the steps onto the verandah. He peeps through and observes the dancing couple, reacting with what is obviously a long-standing bewilderment. He stiffens suddenly, his expression changes to one of disbelief and horror. In his excitement he upsets a flower-pot and attracts the attention of the couple. They stop dancing.

PILKINGS. Is there anyone out there?

JANE. I'll turn off the gramophone.

PILKINGS (*approaching the verandah*). I'm sure I heard something fall over. (*The constable retreats slowly, open-mouthed as Pilkings approaches the verandah.*) Oh it's you Amusa. Why didn't you just knock instead of knocking things over?

AMUSA (*stammers badly and points a shaky finger at his dress*). Mista Pirinkin . . . Mista Pirinkin . . .

PILKINGS. What is the matter with you?

JANE (*emerging*). Who is it dear? Oh, Amusa . . .

PILKINGS. Yes its Amusa, and acting most strangely.

AMUSA (*his attention now transferred to Mrs Pilkings*). Mammadam . . . you too!

PILKINGS. What the hell is the matter with you man!

JANE. Your costume darling. Our fancy dress.

PILKINGS. Oh hell, I'd forgotten all about that. (*Lifts the face mask over his head showing his face. His wife follows suit.*)

JANE. I think you've shocked his big pagan heart bless him.

PILKINGS. Nonsense, he's a Moslem. Come on Amusa, you don't believe in all this nonsense do you? I thought you were a good Moslem.

AMUSA. Mista Pirinkin, I beg you sir, what you think you do with that dress? It belong to dead cult, not for human being.

PILKINGS. Oh Amusa, what a let down you are. I swear by you at the club you know—thank God for Amusa, he doesn't believe in any mumbo-jumbo. And now look at you!

AMUSA. Mista Pirinkin, I beg you, take it off. Is no good for man like you to touch that cloth.

PILKINGS. Well, I've got it on. And what's more Jane and I have bet on it we're taking first prize at the ball. Now, if you can just pull yourself together and tell me what you wanted to see me about . . .

AMUSA. Sir, I cannot talk this matter to you in that dress. I no fit.

PILKINGS. What's that rubbish again?

JANE. He is dead earnest too Simon. I think you'll have to handle this delicately.

PILKINGS. Delicately my . . . ! Look here Amusa, I think this little joke has gone far enough hm? Let's have some sense. You seem to forget that you are a police officer in the service of His Majesty's Government. I order you to report your business at once or face disciplinary action.

AMUSA. Sir, it is a matter of death. How can man talk against death to person in uniform of death? Is like talking against government to person in uniform of police. Please sir, I go and come back.

PILKINGS (*roars*). Now! (*Amusa switches his gaze to the ceiling suddenly, remains mute.*)

JANE. Oh Amusa, what is there to be scared of in the costume? You saw it confiscated last month from those *egungun* men who were creating trouble in town. You helped arrest the cult leaders yourself—if the juju didn't harm you at the time how could it possibly harm you now? And merely by looking at it?

AMUSA (*without looking down*). Madam, I arrest the ringleaders who make trouble but me I no touch *egungun*. That *egungun* itself, I no touch. And I no abuse 'am. I arrest ringleader but I treat *egungun* with respect.

PILKINGS. It's hopeless. We'll merely end up missing the best part of the ball. When they get this way there is nothing you can do. It's simply hammering against a brick wall. Write your report or whatever it is on that pad Amusa and take yourself out of here. Come on Jane. We only upset his delicate sensibilities by remaining here.

(*Amusa waits for them to leave, then writes in the notebook, somewhat laboriously. Drumming from the direction of the town wells up. Amusa listens, makes a movement as if he wants to recall Pilkings but changes his mind. Completes his note and goes. A few moments later Pilkings emerges, picks up the pad and reads.)*

PILKINGS. Jane!

JANE (*from the bedroom*). Coming darling. Nearly ready.

PILKINGS. Never mind being ready, just listen to this.

JANE. What is it?

PILKINGS. Amusa's report. Listen. 'I have to report that it come to my information that one prominent chief, namely, the Elesin Oba, is to commit death tonight as a result of native custom. Because this is criminal offence I await further instruction at charge office. Sergeant Amusa.'

(*Jane comes out onto the verandah while he is reading.*)

JANE. Did I hear you say commit death?

PILKINGS. Obviously he means murder.

JANE. You mean a ritual murder?

PILKINGS. Must be. You think you've stamped it all out but it's always lurking under the surface somewhere.

JANE. Oh. Does it mean we are not getting to the ball at all?

PILKINGS. No-o. I'll have the man arrested. Everyone remotely involved. In any case there may be nothing to it. Just rumours.

JANE. Really? I thought you found Amusa's rumours generally reliable.

PILKINGS. That's true enough. But who knows what may have been giving him the scare lately. Look at his conduct tonight.

JANE (*laughing*). You have to admit he had his own peculiar logic. (*Deepens her voice.*) How can man talk against death to person in uniform of death? (*Laughs.*) Anyway, you can't go into the police station dressed like that.

PILKINGS. I'll send Joseph with instructions. Damn it, what a confounded nuisance!

JANE. But don't you think you should talk first to the man, Simon?

PILKINGS. Do you want to go to the ball or not?

JANE. Darling, why are you getting rattled? I was only trying to be intelligent. It seems hardly fair just to lock up a man—and a chief at that—simply on the er . . . what is that legal word again?—uncorroborated word of a sergeant.

PILKINGS. Well, that's easily decided. Joseph!

JOSEPH (*from within*). Yes master.

PILKINGS. You're quite right of course, I am getting rattled. Probably the effect of those bloody drums. Do you hear how they go on and on?

JANE. I wondered when you'd notice. Do you suppose it has something to do with this affair?

PILKINGS. Who knows? They always find an excuse for making a noise . . . (*Thoughtfully.*) Even so . . .

JANE. Yes Simon?

PILKINGS. It's different Jane. I don't think I've heard this particular—sound—before. Something unsettling about it.

JANE. I thought all bush drumming sounded the same.

PILKINGS. Don't tease me now Jane. This may be serious.

JANE. I'm sorry. (*Gets up and throws her arms around his neck. Kisses him. The houseboy enters, retreats and knocks.*)

PILKINGS (*wearily*). Oh, come in Joseph! I don't know where you pick up all these elephantine notions of tact. Come over here.

JOSEPH. Sir?

PILKINGS. Joseph, are you a Christian or not?

JOSEPH. Yessir.

PILKINGS. Does seeing me in this outfit bother you?

JOSEPH. No sir, it has no power.

PILKINGS. Thank God for some sanity at last. Now Joseph, answer me on the honour of a Christian—what is supposed to be going on in town tonight?

JOSEPH. Tonight sir? You mean that chief who is going to kill himself?

PILKINGS. What?

JANE. What do you mean, kill himself?

PILKINGS. You do mean he is going to kill somebody don't you?

JOSEPH. No master. He will not kill anybody and no one will kill him. He will simply die.

JANE. But why Joseph?

JOSEPH. It is native law and custom. The King die last month. Tonight is his burial. But before they can bury him, the Elesin must die so as to accompany him to heaven.

PILKINGS. I seem to be fated to clash more often with that man than with any of the other chiefs.

JOSEPH. He is the King's Chief Horseman.

PILKINGS (*in a resigned way*). I know.

JANE. Simon, what's the matter?

PILKINGS. It would have to be him!

JANE. Who is he?

PILKINGS. Don't you remember? He's that chief with whom I had a scrap some three or four years ago. I helped his son get to a medical school in England, remember? He fought tooth and nail to prevent it.

JANE. Oh now I remember. He was that very sensitive young man. What was his name again?

PILKINGS. Olunde. Haven't replied to his last letter come to think of it. The old pagan wanted him to stay and carry on some family tradition or the other. Honestly I couldn't understand the fuss he made. I literally had to help the boy escape from close confinement and load him onto the next boat. A most intelligent boy, really bright.

JANE. I rather thought he was much too sensitive you know. The kind of person you feel should be a poet munching rose petals in Bloomsbury.

PILKINGS. Well, he's going to make a first-class doctor. His mind is set on that. And as long as he wants my help he is welcome to it.

JANE (*after a pause*). Simon.

PILKINGS. Yes?

JANE. This boy, he was his eldest son wasn't he?

PILKINGS. I'm not sure. Who could tell with that old ram?

JANE. Do you know, Joseph?

JOSEPH. Oh yes madam. He was the eldest son. That's why Elesin cursed master good and proper. The eldest son is not supposed to travel away from the land.

JANE (*giggling*). Is that true Simon? Did he really curse you good and proper?

PILKINGS. By all accounts I should be dead by now.

JOSEPH. Oh no, master is white man. And good Christian. Black man juju can't touch master.

JANE. If he was his eldest, it means that he would be the Elesin to the next king. It's a family thing isn't it Joseph?

JOSEPH. Yes madam. And if this Elesin had died before the King, his eldest son must take his place.

JANE. That would explain why the old chief was so mad you took the boy away.

PILKINGS. Well it makes me all the more happy I did.

JANE. I wonder if he knew.

PILKINGS. Who? Oh, you mean Olunde?

JANE. Yes. Was that why he was so determined to get away? I wouldn't stay if I knew I was trapped in such a horrible custom.

PILKINGS (*thoughtfully*). No, I don't think he knew. At least he gave no indication. But you couldn't really tell with him. He was rather close you know, quite unlike most of them. Didn't give much away, not even to me.

JANE. Aren't they all rather close, Simon?

PILKINGS. These natives here? Good gracious. They'll open their mouths and yap with you about their family secrets before you can stop them. Only the other day . . .

JANE. But Simon, do they really give anything away? I mean, anything that really counts. This affair for instance, we didn't know they still practised that custom did we?

PILKINGS. Ye-e-es, I suppose you're right there. Sly, devious bastards.

JOSEPH (*stiffly*). Can I go now master? I have to clean the kitchen.

PILKINGS. What? Oh, you can go. Forgot you were still here.

(*Joseph goes.*)

JANE. Simon, you really must watch your language. Bastard isn't just a simple swear-word in these parts, you know.

PILKINGS. Look, just when did you become a social anthropologist, that's what I'd like to know.

JANE. I'm not claiming to know anything. I just happen to have overheard quarrels among the servants. That's how I know they consider it a smear.

PILKINGS. I thought the extended family system took care of all that. Elastic family, no bastards.

JANE (*shrugs*). Have it your own way.

(*Awkward silence. The drumming increases in volume. Jane gets up suddenly, restless.*)

That drumming Simon, do you think it might really be connected with this ritual? It's been going on all evening.

PILKINGS. Let's ask our native guide. Joseph! Just a minute Joseph. (*Joseph re-enters.*) What's the drumming about?

JOSEPH. I don't know master.

PILKINGS. What do you mean you don't know? It's only two years since your conversion. Don't tell me all that holy water nonsense also wiped out your tribal memory.

JOSEPH (*visibly shocked*). Master!

JANE. Now you've done it.

PILKINGS. What have I done now?

JANE. Never mind. Listen Joseph, just tell me this. Is that drumming connected with dying or anything of that nature?

JOSEPH. Madam, this is what I am trying to say: I am not sure. It sounds like the death of a great chief and then, it sounds like the wedding of a great chief. It really mix me up.

PILKINGS. Oh get back to the kitchen. A fat lot of help you are.

JOSEPH. Yes master. (*Goes.*)

JANE. Simon . . .

PILKINGS. Alright, alright. I'm in no mood for preaching.

JANE. It isn't my preaching you have to worry about, it's the preaching of the missionaries who preceded you here. When they make converts they really convert them. Calling holy water nonsense to our Joseph is really like insulting the Virgin Mary before a Roman Catholic. He's going to hand in his notice tomorrow you mark my word.

PILKINGS. Now you're being ridiculous.

JANE. Am I? What are you willing to bet that tomorrow we are going to be without a steward-boy? Did you see his face?

PILKINGS. I am more concerned about whether or not we will be one native chief short by tomorrow. Christ! Just listen to those drums. (*He strides up and down, undecided.*)

JANE (*getting up*). I'll change and make up some supper.

PILKINGS. What's that?

JANE. Simon, it's obvious we have to miss this ball.

PILKINGS. Nonsense. It's the first bit of real fun the European club has managed to organise for over a year, I'm damned if I'm going to miss it. And it is a rather special occasion. Doesn't happen every day.

JANE. You know this business has to be stopped Simon. And you are the only man who can do it.

PILKINGS. I don't have to stop anything. If they want to throw themselves off the top of a cliff or poison themselves for the sake of some barbaric custom what is that to me? If it were ritual murder or something like that I'd be duty-bound to do something. I can't keep an eye on all the potential suicides in this province. And as for that man—believe me it's good riddance.

JANE (*laughs*). I know you better than that Simon. You are going to have to do something to stop it—after you've finished blustering.

PILKINGS (*shouts after her*). And suppose after all it's only a wedding. I'd look a proper fool if I interrupted a chief on his honeymoon, wouldn't I? (*Resumes his angry stride, slows down.*) Ah well, who can tell what those chiefs actually do on their honeymoon anyway? (*He takes up the pad and scribbles rapidly on it.*) Joseph! Joseph! Joseph! (*Some moments later Joseph puts in a sulky appearance.*) Did you hear me call you? Why the hell didn't you answer?

JOSEPH. I didn't hear master.

PILKINGS. You didn't hear me! How come you are here then?

JOSEPH (*stubbornly*). I didn't hear master.

PILKINGS (*controls himself with an effort*). We'll talk about it in the morning. I want you to take this note directly to Sergeant Amusa. You'll find him at the charge office. Get on your bicycle and race there with it. I expect you back in twenty minutes exactly. Twenty minutes, is that clear?

JOSEPH. Yes master. (*Going.*)

PILKINGS. Oh er . . . Joseph.

JOSEPH. Yes master?

PILKINGS (*between gritted teeth*). Er . . . forget what I said just now. The holy water is not nonsense. *I* was talking nonsense.

JOSEPH. Yes master. (*Goes.*)

JANE (*pokes her head round the door*). Have you found him?

PILKINGS. Found who?

JANE. Joseph. Weren't you shouting for him?

PILKINGS. Oh yes, he turned up finally.

JANE. You sounded desperate. What was it all about?

PILKINGS. Oh nothing. I just wanted to apologise to him. Assure him that the holy water isn't really nonsense.

JANE. Oh? And how did he take it?

PILKINGS. Who the hell gives a damn! I had a sudden vision of our Very Reverend Macfarlane drafting another letter of complaint to the Resident about my unchristian language towards his parishioners.

JANE. Oh I think he's given up on you by now.

PILKINGS. Don't be too sure. And anyway, I wanted to make sure Joseph didn't 'lose' my note on the way. He looked sufficiently full of the holy crusade to do some such thing.

JANE. If you've finished exaggerating, come and have something to eat.

PILKINGS. No, put it all way. We can still get to the ball.

JANE. Simon . . .

PILKINGS. Get your costume back on. Nothing to worry about. I've instructed Amusa to arrest the man and lock him up.

JANE. But that station is hardly secure Simon. He'll soon get his friends to help him escape.

PILKINGS. A-ah, that's where I have out-thought you. I'm not having him put in the station cell. Amusa will bring him right here and lock him up in my study. And he'll stay with him till we get back. No one will dare come here to incite him to anything.

JANE. How clever of you darling. I'll get ready.

PILKINGS. Hey.

JANE. Yes darling.

PILKINGS. I have a surprise for you. I was going to keep it until we actually got to the ball.

JANE. What is it?

PILKINGS. You know the Prince is on a tour of the colonies don't you? Well, he docked in the capital only this morning but he is already at the Residency. He is going to grace the ball with his presence later tonight.

JANE. Simon! Not really.

PILKINGS. Yes he is. He's been invited to give away the prizes and he has agreed. You must admit old Engleton is the best Club Secretary we ever had. Quick off the mark that lad.

JANE. But how thrilling.

PILKINGS. The other provincials are going to be damned envious.

JANE. I wonder what he'll come as.

PILKINGS. Oh I don't know. As a coat-of-arms perhaps. Anyway it won't be anything to touch this.

JANE. Well that's lucky. If we are to be presented I won't have to start looking for a pair of gloves. It's all sewn on.

PILKINGS (*laughing*). Quite right. Trust a woman to think of that. Come on, let's get going.

JANE (*rushing off*). Won't be a second. (*Stops.*) Now I see why you've been so edgy all evening. I thought you weren't handling this affair with your usual brilliance— to begin with that is.

PILKINGS (*his mood is much improved*). Shut up woman and get your things on.

JANE. Alright boss, coming.

(*Pilkings suddenly begins to hum the tango to which they were dancing before. Starts to execute a few practice steps. Lights fade.*)

SCENE 3

A swelling, agitated hum of women's voices rises immediately in the background. The lights come on and we see the frontage of a converted cloth stall in the market. The floor leading up to the entrance is covered in rich velvets and woven cloth. The women come on stage, borne backwards by the determined progress of Sergeant Amusa and his two constables who already have their batons out and use them as a pressure against the women. At the edge of the cloth-covered floor however the women take a determined stand and block all further progress of the men. They begin to tease them mercilessly.

AMUSA. I am tell you women for last time to commot my road. I am here on official business.

WOMAN. Official business you white man's eunuch? Official business is taking place where you want to go and it's a business you wouldn't understand.

WOMAN (*makes a quick tug at the constable's baton*). That doesn't fool anyone you know. It's the one you carry under your government knickers that counts. (*She bends low as if to peep under the baggy shorts. The embarrassed constable quickly puts his knees together. The women roar.*)

WOMAN. You mean there is nothing there at all?

WOMAN. Oh there was something. You know that handbell which the whiteman uses to summon his servants . . . ?

AMUSA (*he manages to preserve some dignity throughout*). I hope you women know that interfering with officer in execution of his duty is criminal offence.

WOMAN. Interfere? He says we're interfering with him. You foolish man we're telling you there's nothing there to interfere with.

AMUSA. I am order you now to clear the road.

WOMAN. What road? The one your father built?

WOMAN. You are a Policeman not so? Then you know what they call trespassing in court. Or—(*Pointing to the cloth-lined steps*)—do you think that kind of road is built for every kind of feet?

WOMAN. Go back and tell the white man who sent you to come himself.

AMUSA. If I go I will come back with reinforcement. And we will all return carrying weapons.

WOMAN. Oh, now I understand. Before they can put on those knickers the white man first cuts off their weapons.

WOMAN. What a cheek! You mean you come here to show power to women and you don't even have a weapon.

AMUSA (*shouting above the laughter*). For the last time I warn you women to clear the road.

WOMAN. To where?

AMUSA. To that hut. I know he dey dere.

WOMAN. Who?

AMUSA. The chief who call himself Elesin Oba.

WOMAN. You ignorant man. It is not he who calls himself Elesin Oba, it is his blood that says it. As it called out to his father before him and will to his son after him. And that is in spite of everything your white man can do.

WOMAN. Is it not the same ocean that washes this land and the white man's land? Tell your white man he can hide our son away as long as he likes. When the time comes for him, the same ocean will bring him back.

AMUSA. The government say dat kin' ting must stop.

WOMAN. Who will stop it? You? Tonight our husband and father will prove himself greater than the laws of strangers.

AMUSA. I tell you nobody go prove anyting tonight or anytime. Is ignorant and criminal to prove dat kin' prove.

IYALOJA (*entering, from the hut. She is accompanied by a group of young girls who have been attending the Bride*). What is it Amusa? Why do you come here to disturb the happiness of others?

AMUSA. Madame Iyaloja, I glad you come. You know me. I no like trouble but duty is duty. I am here to arrest Elesin for criminal intent. Tell these women to stop obstructing me in the performance of my duty.

IYALOJA. And you? What gives you the right to obstruct our leader of men in the performance of his duty?

AMUSA. What kin' duty be dat one Iyaloja?

IYALOJA. What kin' duty? What kin' duty does a man have to his new bride?

AMUSA (*bewildered, looks at the women and at the entrance to the hut*). Iyaloja, is it wedding you call dis kin' ting?

IYALOJA. You have wives haven't you? Whatever the white man has done to you he hasn't stopped you having wives. And if he has, at least he is married. If you don't know what a marriage is, go and ask him to tell you.

AMUSA. This no to wedding.

IYALOJA. And ask him at the same time what he would have done if anyone had come to disturb him on his wedding night.

AMUSA. Iyaloja, I say dis no to wedding.

IYALOJA. You want to look inside the bridal chamber? You want to see for yourself how a man cuts the virgin knot?

AMUSA. Madam . . .

WOMAN. Perhaps his wives are still waiting for him to learn.

AMUSA. Iyaloja, make you tell dese women make den no insult me again. If I hear dat kin' insult once more . . .

GIRL (*pushing her way through*). You will do what?

GIRL. He's out of his mind. It's our mothers you're talking to, do you know that? Not to any illiterate villager you can bully and terrorise. How dare you intrude here anyway?

GIRL. What a cheek, what impertinence!

GIRL. You've treated them too gently. Now let them see what it is to tamper with the mothers of this market.

GIRLS. Your betters dare not enter the market when the women say no!

GIRL. Haven't you learnt that yet, you jester in khaki and starch?

IYALOJA. Daughters . . .

GIRL. No no Iyaloja, leave us to deal with him. He no longer knows his mother, we'll teach him.

(*With a sudden movement they snatch the batons of the two constables. They begin to hem them in.*)

GIRL. What next? We have your batons? What next? What are you going to do?

(*With equally swift movements they knock off their hats.*)

GIRL. Move if you dare. We have your hats, what will you do about it? Didn't the white man teach you to take off your hats before women?

IYALOJA. It's a wedding night. It's a night of joy for us. Peace . . .

GIRL. Not for him. Who asked him here?

GIRL. Does he dare go to the Residency without an invitation?

GIRL. Not even where the servants eat the left-overs.

GIRLS (*in turn. In an 'English' accent*). Well well it's Mister Amusa. Were you invited? (*Play-acting to one another. The older women encourage them with their titters.*)

—Your invitation card please?

—Who are you? Have we been introduced?

—And who did you say you were?

—Sorry, I didn't quite catch your name.

—May I take your hat?

—If you insist. May I take yours? (*Exchanging the policeman's hats.*)

—How very kind of you.

—Not at all. Won't you sit down?

—After you.

—Oh no.

—I insist.

—You're most gracious.

—And how do you find the place?

—The natives are alright.

—Friendly?

—Tractable.

—Not a teeny-weeny bit restless?

—Well, a teeny-weeny bit restless.

—One might even say, difficult?

—Indeed one might be tempted to say, difficult.

—But you do manage to cope?

—Yes indeed I do. I have a rather faithful ox called Amusa.

—He's loyal?

—Absolutely.

—Lay down his life for you what?

—Without a moment's thought.

—Had one like that once. Trust him with my life.

—Mostly of course they are liars.

—Never known a native tell the truth.

—Does it get rather close around here?

—It's mild for this time of the year.

—But the rains may still come.

—They are late this year aren't they?

—They are keeping African time.

—Ha ha ha ha

—Ha ha ha ha

—The humidity is what gets me.

—It used to be whisky.

—Ha ha ha ha

—Ha ha ha ha

—What's your handicap old chap?

—Is there racing by golly?

—Splendid golf course, you'll like it.

—I'm beginning to like it already.

—And a European club, exclusive.

—You've kept the flag flying.

—We do our best for the old country.

—It's a pleasure to serve.

—Another whisky old chap?

—You are indeed too too kind.

—Not at all sir. Where is that boy? (*With a sudden bellow.*) Sergeant!

AMUSA (*snaps to attention*). Yessir!

(*The women collapse with laughter.*)

GIRL. Take your men out of here.

AMUSA (*realising the trick, he rages from loss of face*). I'm give you warning . . .

GIRL. Alright then. Off with his knickers! (*They surge slowly forward.*)

IYALOJA. Daughters, please.

AMUSA (*squaring himself for defence*). The first woman wey touch me . . .

IYALOJA. My children, I beg of you . . .

GIRL. Then tell him to leave this market. This is the home of our mothers. We don't want the eater of white left-overs at the feast their hands have prepared.

IYALOJA. You heard them Amusa. You had better go.

GIRLS. Now!

AMUSA (*commencing his retreat*). We dey go now, but make you no say we no warn you.

GIRL. Now!

GIRL. Before we read the riot act—you should know all about that.

AMUSA. Make we go. (*They depart, more precipitately.*)

(*The women strike their palms across in the gesture of wonder.*)

WOMAN. Do they teach you all that at school?

WOMAN. And to think I nearly kept Apinke away from the place.

WOMAN. Did you hear them? Did you see how they mimicked the white man?

WOMAN. The voices exactly. Hey, there are wonders in this world!

IYALOJA. Well, our elders have said it: Dada may be weak, but he has a younger sibling who is truly fearless.

WOMAN. The next time the white man shows his face in this market I will set Wuraola on his tail.

(*A woman bursts into song and dance of euphoria— 'Tani l'awa o l'ogbeja? Kayi! A l'ogbeja. Omo Kekere l'ogbeja.* The rest of the women join in, some placing the girls on their back like infants, other dancing round them. The dance becomes general, mounting in excitement. Elesin appears, in wrapper only. In his hands a white velvet cloth folded loosely as if it held some delicate object. He cries out.*)

ELESIN. Oh you mothers of beautiful brides! (*The dancing stops. They turn and see him, and the object in his hands. Iyaloja approaches and gently takes the cloth from him.*)

*Who says we haven't a defender? Silence! We have our defenders. Little children are our champions.

Take it. It is no mere virgin stain, but the union of life and the seeds of passage. My vital flow, the last from this flesh is intermingled with the promise of future life. All is prepared. Listen! (*A steady drum-beat from the distance.*) Yes. It is nearly time. The King's dog has been killed. The King's favourite horse is about to follow his master. My brother chiefs know their task and perform it well. (*He listens again.*)

(*The Bride emerges, stands shyly by the door. He turns to her.*)

Our marriage is not yet wholly fulfilled. When earth and passage wed, the consummation is complete only when there are grains of earth on the eyelids of passage. Stay by me till then. My faithful drummers, do me your last service. This is where I have chosen to do my leave-taking, in this heart of life, this hive which contains the swarm of the world in its small compass. This is where I have known love and laughter away from the palace. Even the richest food cloys when eaten days on end; in the market, nothing ever cloys. Listen. (*They listen to the drums.*) They have begun to seek out the heart of the King's favourite horse. Soon it will ride in its bolt of raffia with the dog at its feet. Together they will ride on the shoulders of the King's grooms through the pulse centres of the town. They know it is here I shall await them. I have told them. (*His eyes appear to cloud. He passes his hand over them as if to clear his sight. He gives a faint smile.*) It promises well; just then I felt my spirit's eagerness. The kite makes for wide spaces and the wind creeps up behind its tail; can the kite say less than— thank you, the quicker the better? But wait a while my spirit. Wait. Wait for the coming of the courier of the King. Do you know friends, the horse is born to this one destiny, to bear the burden that is man upon its back. Except for this night, this night alone when the spotless stallion will ride in triumph on the back of man. In the time of my father I witnessed the strange sight. Perhaps tonight also I shall see it for the last time. If they arrive before the drums beat for me, I shall tell him to let the Alafin know I follow swiftly. If they come after the drums have sounded, why then, all is well for I have gone ahead. Our spirits shall fall in step along the great passage. (*He listens to the drums. He seems again to be falling into a state of semi-hypnosis; his eyes scan the sky but it is in a kind of daze. His voice is a little breathless.*) The moon has fed, a glow from its full stomach fills the sky and air, but I cannot tell where is that gateway through which I must pass. My faithful friends, let our feet touch together this last time, lead me into the other market with sounds that cover my skin with down yet make my limbs strike earth like a thoroughbred. Dear mothers, let me dance into the passage even as I have lived beneath your roofs. (*He comes down progressively among them. They make a way for him, the drummers playing. His dance is one of solemn, regal motions, each gesture of the body is*

made with a solemn finality. The women join him, their steps a somewhat more fluid version of his. Beneath the Praise-Singer's exhortation the women dirge 'Alẹ, lẹ lẹ, awo mil lọ'.)

PRAISE-SINGER. Elesin Alafin, can you hear my voice?

ELESIN. Faintly, my friend, faintly.

PRAISE-SINGER. Elesin Alafin, can you hear my call?

ELESIN. Faintly my king, faintly.

PRAISE-SINGER. Is your memory sound Elesin?
Shall my voice be a blade of grass and
Tickle the armpit of the past?

ELESIN. My memory needs no prodding but
What do you wish to say to me?

PRAISE-SINGER. Only what has been spoken. Only
what concerns
The dying wish of the father of all.

ELESIN. It is buried like seed-yam in my mind
This is the season of quick rains, the harvest
Is this moment due for gathering.

PRAISE-SINGER. If you cannot come, I said, swear
You'll tell my favourite horse. I shall
Ride on through the gates alone.

ELESIN. Elesin's message will be read
Only when his loyal heart no longer beats.

PRAISE-SINGER. If you cannot come Elesin, tell my dog.
I cannot stay the keeper too long
At the gate.

ELESIN. A dog does not outrun the hand
That feeds it meat. A horse that throws its rider
Slows down to a stop. Elesin Alafin
Trusts no beasts with messages between
A king and his companion.

PRAISE-SINGER. If you get lost my dog will track
The hidden path to me.

ELESIN. The seven-way crossroads confuses
Only the stranger. The Horseman of the King
Was born in the recesses of the house.

PRAISE-SINGER. I know the wickedness of men. If there is
Weight on the loose end of your sash, such weight
As no mere man can shift; if your sash is earthed
By evil minds who mean to part us at the last . . .

ELESIN. My sash is of the deep purple *alari*;
It is no tethering-rope. The elephant
Trails no tethering-rope; that king
Is not yet crowned who will peg an elephant—
Not even you my friend and King.

PRAISE-SINGER. And yet this fear will not depart from me
The darkness of this new abode is deep—
Will your human eyes suffice?

ELESIN. In a night which falls before our eyes
However deep, we do not miss our way.

PRAISE-SINGER. Shall I now not acknowledge I have stood
Where wonders met their end? The elephant deserves
Better than that we say 'I have caught
A glimpse of something'. If we see the tamer
Of the forest let us say plainly, we have seen
An elephant.

ELESIN (*his voice is drowsy*).
    I have freed myself of earth and now
    It's getting dark. Strange voices guide my feet.
PRAISE-SINGER. The river is never so high that the eyes
    Of a fish are covered. The night is not so dark
    That the albino fails to find his way. A child
    Returning homewards craves no leading by the hand.
    Gracefully does the mask regain his
    grove at the end of day . . .
    Gracefully. Gracefully does the mask dance
    Homeward at the end of day, gracefully . . .

(*Elesin's trance appears to be deepening, his steps heavier.*)

IYALOJA. It is the death of war that kills the valiant,
    Death of water is how the swimmer goes
    It is the death of markets that kills the trader
    And death of indecision takes the idle away
    The trade of the cutlass blunts its edge
    And the beautiful die the death of beauty.
    It takes an Elesin to die the death of death . . .
    Only Elesin . . . dies the unknowable death of death . . .
    Gracefully, gracefully does the horseman regain
    The stables at the end of day, gracefully . . .
PRAISE-SINGER. How shall I tell what my eyes have seen? The Horseman gallops on before the courier, how shall I tell what my eyes have seen? He says a dog may be confused by new scents of beings he never dreamt of, so he must precede the dog to heaven. He says a horse may stumble on strange boulders and be lamed, so he races on before the horse to heaven. It is best, he says, to trust no messenger who may falter at the outer gate; oh how shall I tell what my ears have heard? But do you hear me still Elesin, do you hear your faithful one?

(*Elesin in his motions appears to feel for a direction of sound, subtly, but he only sinks deeper into his trance-dance.*)

Elesin, Alafin, I no longer sense your flesh. The drums are changing now but you have gone far ahead of the world. It is not yet noon in heaven; let those who claim it is begin their own journey home. So why must you rush like an impatient bride: why do you race to desert your Olohun-iyo?

(*Elesin is now sunk fully deep in his trance, there is no longer sign of any awareness of his surroundings.*)

Does the deep voice of *gbedu* cover you then, like the passage of royal elephants? Those drums that brook no rivals, have they blocked the passage to your ears that my voice passes into wind, a mere leaf floating in the night? Is your flesh lightened Elesin, is that lump of earth I slid between your slippers to keep you longer slowly sifting from your feet? Are the drums on the other side no tuning skin to skin with ours in osugbo?

Are there sounds there I cannot hear, do footsteps surround you which pound the earth like *gbedu*, roll like thunder round the dome of the world? Is the darkness gathering in your head Elesin? Is there now a streak of light at the end of the passage, a light I dare not look upon? Does it reveal whose voices we often heard, whose touches we often felt, whose wisdoms come suddenly into the mind when the wisest have shaken their heads and murmured; It cannot be done? Elesin Alafin, don't think I do not know why your lips are heavy, why your limbs are drowsy as palm oil in the cold of harmattan. I would call you back but when the elephant heads for the jungle, the tail is too small a handhold for the hunter that would pull him back. The sun that heads for the sea no longer heeds the prayers of the farmer. When the river begins to taste the salt of the ocean, we no longer know what deity to call on, the river-god or Olokun. No arrow flies back to the string, the child does not return through the same passage that gave it birth. Elesin Oba, can you hear me at all? Your eyelids are glazed like a courtesan's, is it that you see the dark groom and master of life? And will you see my father? Will you tell him that I stayed with you to the last? Will my voice ring in your ears awhile, will you remember Olohun-iyo even if the music on the other side surpasses his mortal craft? But will they know you over there? Have they eyes to gauge your worth, have they the heart to love you, will they know what thoroughbred prances towards them in caparisons of honour? If they do not Elesin, if any there cuts your yam with a small knife, or pours you wine in a small calabash, turn back and return to welcoming hands. If the world were not greater than the wishes of Olohun-iyo, I would not let you go . . .

(*He appears to break down. Elesin dances on, completely in a trance. the dirge wells up louder and stronger. Elesin's dance does not lose its elasticity but his gestures become, if possible, even more weighty. Lights fade slowly on the scene.*)

SCENE 4

A Masque. The front side of the stage is part of a wide corridor around the great hall of the Residency extending beyond vision into the rear and wings. It is redolent of the tawdry decadence of a far-flung but key imperial frontier. The couples in a variety of fancy-dress are ranged around the walls, gazing in the same direction. The guest-of-honour is about to make an appearance. A portion of the local police brass band with its white conductor is just visible. At last, the entrance of Royalty. The band plays 'Rule Britannia', badly, beginning long before he is visible. The couples bow and curtsey as he passes by them. Both he and his companions are dressed in seventeenth century European costume. Following behind are the Resident and his partner similarly attired. As they gain the end of the hall where the orchestra dais begins the music comes to an end. The Prince bows to the guests. The bank strikes up a Viennese waltz and the Prince formally opens the floor. Several bars later the Resident and his companion follow suit. Others follow in appropriate pecking order. The orchestra's waltz rendition is not of the highest musical standard.

Some time later the Prince dances again into view and is settled into a corner by the Resident who then proceeds to select couples as they dance past for introduction, sometimes threading his way through the dancers to tap the lucky couple on the shoulder. Desperate efforts from many to ensure that they are recognised in spite of, perhaps, their costume. The ritual of introductions soon takes in Pilkings and his wife. The Prince is quite fascinated by their costume and they demonstrate the adaptations they have made to it, pulling down the mask to demonstrate how the egungun normally appears, then showing the various press-button controls they have innovated for the face flaps, the sleeves, etc. They demonstrate the dance steps and the guttural sounds made by the egungun, harass other dancers in the hall, Mrs Pilkings playing the 'restrainer' to Pilkings' manic darts. Everyone is highly entertained, the Royal Party especially who lead the applause.

At this point a liveried footman comes in with a note on a salver and is intercepted almost absent-mindedly by the Resident who takes the note and reads it. After polite coughs he succeeds in excusing the Pilkingses from the Prince and takes them aside. The Prince considerately offers the Resident's wife his hand and dancing is resumed.

On their way out the Resident gives an order to his Aide-De-Camp. They come into the side corridor where the Resident hands the note to Pilkings.

RESIDENT. As you see it says 'emergency' on the outside. I took the liberty of opening it because His Highness was obviously enjoying the entertainment. I didn't want to interrupt unless really necessary.

PILKINGS. Yes, yes of course sir.

RESIDENT. Is it really as bad as it says? What's it all about?

PILKINGS. Some strange custom they have sir. It seems because the King is dead some important chief has to commit suicide.

RESIDENT. The King? Isn't it the same one who died nearly a month ago?

PILKINGS. Yes sir.

RESIDENT. Haven't they buried him yet?

PILKINGS. They take their time about these things sir. The pre-burial ceremonies last nearly thirty days. It seems tonight is the final night.

RESIDENT. But what has it got to do with the market women? Why are they rioting? We've waived that troublesome tax haven't we?

PILKINGS. We don't quite know that they are exactly rioting yet sir. Sergeant Amusa is sometimes prone to exaggerations.

RESIDENT. He sounds desperate enough. That comes out even in his rather quaint grammar. Where is the man anyway? I asked my aide-de-camp to bring him here.

PILKINGS. They are probably looking in the wrong verandah. I'll fetch him myself.

RESIDENT. No no you stay here. Let your wife go and look for them. Do you mind my dear . . . ?

JANE. Certainly not, your Excellency. (*Goes.*)

RESIDENT. You should have kept me informed Pilkings. You realise how disastrous it would have been if things had erupted while His Highness was here.

PILKINGS. I wasn't aware of the whole business until tonight sir.

RESIDENT. Nose to the ground Pilkings, nose to the ground. If we all let these little things slip past us where would the empire be eh? Tell me that. Where would we all be?

PILKINGS (*low voice*). Sleeping peacefully at home I bet.

RESIDENT. What did you say Pilkings?

PILKINGS. It won't happen again sir.

RESIDENT. It mustn't Pilkings. It mustn't. Where is that damned sergeant? I ought to get back to His Highness as quickly as possible and offer him some plausible explanation for my rather abrupt conduct. Can you think of one Pilkings?

PILKINGS. You could tell him the truth sir.

RESIDENT. I could? No no no no Pilkings, that would never do. What! Go and tell him there is a riot just two miles away from him? This is supposed to be a secure colony of His Majesty, Pilkings.

PILKINGS. Yes sir.

RESIDENT. Ah, there they are. No, these are not our native police. Are these the ring-leaders of the riot?

PILKINGS. Sir, these are my police officers.

RESIDENT. Oh, I beg your pardon officers. You do look at little . . . I say, isn't there something missing in their uniform? I think they used to have some rather colourful sashes. If I remember rightly I recommended them myself in my young days in the service. A bit of colour always appeals to the natives, yes, I remember putting that in my report. Well well well, where are we? Make your report man.

PILKINGS (*moves close to Amusa, between his teeth*). And let's have no more superstitious nonsense from your Amusa or I'll throw you in the guardroom for a month and feed you pork!

RESIDENT. What's that? What has pork to do with it?

PILKINGS. Sir, I was just warning him to be brief. I'm sure you are most anxious to hear his report.

RESIDENT. Yes yes yes of course. Come on man, speak up. Hey, didn't we give them some colourful fez hats with all those wavy things, yes, pink tassells . . .

PILKINGS. Sir, I think if he was permitted to make his report we might find that he lost his hat in the riot.

RESIDENT. Ah yes indeed. I'd better tell His Highness that. Lost his hat in the riot, ha ha. He'll probably say well, as long as he didn't lose his head. (*Chuckles to himself.*) Don't forget to send me a report first thing in the morning young Pilkings.

PILKINGS. No sir.

RESIDENT. And whatever you do, don't let things get out of hand. Keep a cool head and—nose to the ground Pilkings. (*Wanders off in the general direction of the hall.*)

PILKINGS. Yes sir.

AIDE-DE-CAMP. Would you be needing me sir?

PILKINGS. No thanks Bob. I think His Excellency's need of you is greater than ours.

AIDE-DE-CAMP. We have a detachment of soldiers from the capital sir. They accompanied His Highness up here.

PILKINGS. I doubt if it will come to that but, thanks, I'll bear it in mind. Oh, could you send an orderly with my cloak.

AIDE-DE-CAMP. Very good sir. (*Goes.*)

PILKINGS. Now Sergeant.

AMUSA. Sir . . . (*Makes an effort, stops dead. Eyes to the ceiling.*)

PILKINGS. Oh, not again.

AMUSA. I cannot against death to dead cult. This dress get power of dead.

PILKINGS. Alright, let's go. You are relieved of all further duty Amusa. Report to me first thing in the morning.

JANE. Shall I come Simon?

PILKINGS. No, there's no need for that. If I can get back later I will. Otherwise get Bob to bring you home.

JANE. Be careful Simon . . . I mean, be clever.

PILKINGS. Sure I will. You two, come with me. (*As he turns to go, the clock in the Residency begins to chime. Pilkings looks at his watch then turns, horror-stricken, to stare at his wife. The same thought clearly occurs to her. He swallows hard. An orderly brings his cloak.*) It's midnight. I had no idea it was that late.

JANE. But surely . . . they don't count the hours the way we do. The moon, or something . . .

PILKINGS. I am . . . not so sure.

(*He turns and breaks into a sudden run. The two constables follow, also at a run. Amusa, who has kept his eyes on the ceiling throughout waits until the last of the footsteps has faded out of hearing. He salutes suddenly, but without once looking in the direction of the woman.*)

AMUSA. Goodnight madam.

JANE. Oh. (*She hesitates.*) Amusa . . . (*He goes off without seeming to have heard.*) Poor Simon . . . (*A figure emerges from the shadows, a young black man dressed in a sober western suit. He peeps into the hall, trying to make out the figures of the dancers.*) Who is that?

OLUNDE (*emerging into the light*). I didn't mean to startle you madam. I am looking for the District Officer.

JANE. Wait a minute . . . don't I know you? Yes, you are Olunde, the young man who . . .

OLUNDE. Mrs Pilkings! How fortunate. I came here to look for your husband.

JANE. Olunde! Let's look at you. What a fine young man you've become. Grand but solemn. Good God, when did you return? Simon never said a word. But you do look well Olunde. Really!

OLUNDE. You are . . . well, you look quite well yourself Mrs Pilkings. From what little I can see of you.

JANE. Oh, this. It's caused quite a stir I assure you, and not all of it very pleasant. You are not shocked I hope?

OLUNDE. Why should I be? But don't you find it rather hot in there? Your skin must find it difficult to breathe.

JANE. Well, it is a little hot I must confess, but it's all in a good cause.

OLUNDE. What cause Mrs Pilkings?

JANE. All this. The ball. And His Highness being here in person and all that.

OLUNDE (*mildly*). And that is the good cause for which you desecrate an ancestral mask?

JANE. Oh, so you are shocked after all. How disappointing.

OLUNDE. No I am not shocked Mrs Pilkings. You forget that I have now spent four years among your people. I discovered that you have no respect for what you do not understand.

JANE. Oh. So you've returned with a chip on your shoulder. That's a pity Olunde. I am sorry.

(*An uncomfortable silence follows.*)

I take it then that you did not find your stay in England altogether edifying.

OLUNDE. I don't say that. I found your people quite admirable in many ways, their conduct and courage in this war for instance.

JANE. Ah yes the war. Here of course it is all rather remote. From time to time we have a black-out drill just to remind us that there is a war on. And the rare convoy passes through on its way somewhere or on manoeuvres. Mind you there is the occasional bit of excitement like that ship that was blown up in the harbour.

OLUNDE. Here? Do you mean through enemy action?

JANE. Oh no, the war hasn't come that close. The captain did it himself. I don't quite understand it really. Simon tried to explain. The ship had to be blown up because it had become dangerous to the other ships, even to the city itself. Hundreds of the coastal population would have died.

OLUNDE. Maybe it was loaded with ammunition and had caught fire. Or some of those lethal gases they've been experimenting on.

JANE. Something like that. The captain blew himself up with it. Deliberately. Simon said someone had to remain on board to light the fuse.

OLUNDE. It must have been a very short fuse.

JANE (shrugs). I don't know much about it. Only that there was no other way to save lives. No time to devise anything else. The captain took the decision and carried it out.

OLUNDE. Yes . . . I quite believe it. I met men like that in England.

JANE. Oh just look at me! Fancy welcoming you back with such morbid news. Stale too. It was at least six months ago.

OLUNDE. I don't find it morbid at all. I find it rather inspiring. It is an affirmative commentary on life.

JANE. What is?

OLUNDE. That captain's self-sacrifice.

JANE. Nonsense. Life should never be thrown deliberately away.

OLUNDE. And the innocent people round the harbour?

JANE. Oh, how does one know? The whole thing was probably exaggerated anyway.

OLUNDE. That was a risk the captain couldn't take. But please Mrs Pilkings, do you think you could find your husband for me? I have to talk to him.

JANE. Simon? Oh. (As she recollects for the first time the full significance of Olunde's presence.) Simon is . . . there is a little problem in town. He was sent for. But . . . when did you arrive? Does Simon know you're here?

OLUNDE (suddenly earnest). I need your help Mrs Pilkings. I've always found you somewhat more understanding than your husband. Please find him for me and when you do, you must help me talk to him.

JANE. I'm afraid I don't quite . . . follow you. Have you seen my husband already?

OLUNDE. I went to your house. Your houseboy told me you were here. (He smiles.) He even told me how I would recognise you and Mr Pilkings.

JANE. Then you must know what my husband is trying to do for you.

OLUNDE. For me?

JANE. For you. For your people. And to think he didn't even know you were coming back! But how do you happen to be here? Only this evening we were talking about you. We thought you were still four thousand miles away.

OLUNDE. I was sent a cable.

JANE. A cable? Who did? Simon? The business of your father didn't begin till tonight.

OLUNDE. A relation sent it weeks ago, and it said nothing about my father. All it said was, Our King is dead. But I knew I had to return home at once so as to bury my father. I understood that.

JANE. Well, thank God you don't have to go through that agony. Simon is going to stop it.

OLUNDE. That's why I want to see him. He's wasting his time. And since he has been so helpful to me I don't want him to incur the enmity of our people. Especially over nothing.

JANE (sits down open-mouthed). You . . . you Olunde!

OLUNDE. Mrs Pilkings, I came home to bury my father. As soon as I heard the news I booked my passage home. In fact we were fortunate. We travelled in the same convoy as your Prince, so we had excellent protection.

JANE. But you don't think your father is also entitled to whatever protection is available to him?

OLUNDE. How can I make you understand? He has protection. No one can undertake what he does tonight without the deepest protection the mind can conceive. What can you offer him in place of his peace of mind, in place of the honour and veneration of his own people? What would you think of your Prince if he had refused to accept the risk of losing his life on this voyage? This . . . showing-the-flag tour of colonial possessions.

JANE. I see. So it isn't just medicine you studied in England.

OLUNDE. Yet another error into which your people fall. You believe that everything which appears to make sense was learnt from you.

JANE. Not so fast Olunde. You have learnt to argue I can tell that, but I never said you made sense. However cleverly you try to put it, it is still a barbaric custom. It is even worse—it's feudal! The king dies and a chieftain must be buried with him. How feudalistic can you get!

OLUNDE (waves his hand towards the background. The Prince is dancing past again—to a different step—and all the guests are bowing and curtseying as he passes). And this? Even in the midst of a devastating war, look at that. What name would you give to that?

JANE. Therapy, British style. The preservation of sanity in the midst of chaos.

OLUNDE. Others would call it decadence. However, it doesn't really interest me. You white races know how to survive; I've seen proof of that. By all logical and natural laws this war should end with all the white races wiping out one another, wiping out their so-called civilisation for all time and reverting to a state of primitivism the like of which has so far only existed in your imagination when you thought of us. I thought all that at the beginning. Then I slowly realised that your greatest art is the art of survival. But at least have the humility to let others survive in their own way.

JANE. Through ritual suicide?

OLUNDE. Is that worse than mass suicide? Mrs Pilkings, what do you call what those young men are sent to do by their generals in this war? Of course you have also mastered the art of calling things by names which don't remotely describe them.

JANE. You talk! You people with your long-winded, roundabout way of making conversation.

OLUNDE. Mrs Pilkings, whatever we do, we never suggest that a thing is the opposite of which it really is. In your newsreels I heard defeats, thorough, murderous defeats described as strategic victories. No wait, it wasn't just on your newsreels. Don't forget I was attached to hospitals all the time. Hordes of your wounded passed through those wards. I spoke to them. I spent long evenings by their bedside while they spoke terrible truths of the realities of that war. I know now how history is made.

JANE. But surely, in a war of this nature, for the morale of the nation you must expect . . .

OLUNDE. That a disaster beyond human reckoning be spoken of as a triumph? No. I mean, is there no mourning in the home of the bereaved that such blasphemy is permitted?

JANE (*after a moment's pause*). Perhaps I can understand you now. The time we picked for you was not really one for seeing us at our best.

OLUNDE. Don't think it was just the war. Before that even started I had plenty of time to study your people. I saw nothing, finally, that gave you the right to pass judgement on other peoples and their ways. Nothing at all.

JANE (*hesitantly*). Was it the . . . colour thing? I know there is some discrimination.

OLUNDE. Don't make it so simple, Mrs Pilkings. You make it sound as if when I left, I took nothing at all with me.

JANE. Yes . . . and to tell the truth, only this evening, Simon and I agreed that we never really knew what you left with.

OLUNDE. Neither did I. But I found out over there. I am grateful to your country for that. And I will never give it up.

JANE. Olunde, please . . . promise me something. Whatever you do, don't throw away what you have started to do. You want to be a doctor. My husband and I believe you will make an excellent one, sympathetic and competent. Don't let anything make you throw away your training.

OLUNDE (*genuinely surprised*). Of course not. What a strange idea. I intend to return and complete my training. Once the burial of my father is over.

JANE. Oh, please . . . !

OLUNDE. Listen! Come outside. You can't hear anything against that music.

JANE. What is it?

OLUNDE. The drums. Can you hear the change? Listen.

(*The drums come over, still distant but more distinct. There is a change of rhythm, it rises to a crescendo and then, suddenly, it is cut off. After a silence, a new beat begins, slow and resonant.*)

There. It's all over.

JANE. You mean he's . . .

OLUNDE. Yes Mrs Pilkings, my father is dead. His willpower has always been enormous; I know he is dead.

JANE (*screams*). How can you be so callous! So unfeeling! You announce your father's own death like a surgeon looking down on some strange . . . stranger's body! You're just a savage like all the rest.

AIDE-DE-CAMP (*rushing out*). Mrs Pilkings. Mrs Pilkings. (*She breaks down, sobbing.*) Are you alright, Mrs Pilkings?

OLUNDE. She'll be alright. (*Turns to go.*)

AIDE-DE-CAMP. Who are you? And who the hell asked your opinion?

OLUNDE. You're quite right, nobody. (*Going.*)

AIDE-DE-CAMP. What the hell! Did you hear me ask you who you were?

OLUNDE. I have business to attend to.

AIDE-DE-CAMP. I'll give you business in a moment you impudent nigger. Answer my question!

OLUNDE. I have a funeral to arrange. Excuse me. (*Going.*)

AIDE-DE-CAMP. I said stop! Orderly!

JANE. No no, don't do that. I'm alright. And for heaven's sake don't act so foolishly. He's a family friend.

AIDE-DE-CAMP. Well he'd better learn to answer civil questions when he's asked them. These natives put a suit on and they get high opinions of themselves.

OLUNDE. Can I go now?

JANE. No no don't go. I must talk to you. I'm sorry about what I said.

OLUNDE. It's nothing Mrs Pilkings. And I'm really anxious to go. I couldn't see my father before, it's forbidden for me, his heir and successor to set eyes on him from the moment of the king's death. But now . . . I would like to touch his body while it is still warm.

JANE. You will. I promise I shan't keep you long. Only, I couldn't possibly let you go like that. Bob, please excuse us.

AIDE-DE-CAMP. If you're sure . . .

JANE. Of course I'm sure. Something happened to upset me just then, but I'm alright now. Really.

(*The Aide-De-Camp goes, somewhat reluctantly.*)

OLUNDE. I mustn't stay long.

JANE. Please, I promise not to keep you. It's just that . . . oh you saw yourself what happens to one in this place. The Resident's man thought he was being helpful, that's the way we all react. But I can't go in among that crowd just now and if I stay by myself somebody will come looking for me. Please, just say something for a few moments and then you can go. Just so I can recover myself.

OLUNDE. What do you want me to say?

JANE. Your calm acceptance for instance, can you explain that? It was so unnatural. I don't understand that at all. I feel a need to understand all I can.

OLUNDE. But you explained it yourself. My medical training perhaps. I have seen death too often. And the soldiers who returned from the front, they died on our hands all the time.

JANE. No. It has to be more than that. I feel it has to do with the many things we don't really grasp about your people. At least you can explain.

OLUNDE. All these things are part of it. And anyway, my father has been dead in my mind for nearly a month. Ever since I learnt of the King's death. I've lived with my bereavement so long now that I cannot think of him alive. On that journey on the boat, I kept my mind on my duties as the one who must perform the rites over his body. I went through it all again and again in my mind as he himself had taught me. I didn't want to do anything wrong, something which might jeopardise the welfare of my people.

JANE. But he had disowned you. When you left he swore publicly you were no longer his son.

OLUNDE. I told you, he was a man of tremendous will. Sometimes that's another way of saying stubborn. But among our people, you don't disown a child just like that. Even if I had died before him I would still be buried like his eldest son. But it's time for me to go.

JANE. Thank you. I feel calmer. Don't let me keep you from your duties.

OLUNDE. Goodnight Mrs Pilkings.

JANE. Welcome home. (*She holds out her hand. As he takes it footsteps are heard approaching the drive. A short while later a woman's sobbing is also heard.*)

PILKINGS (*off*). Keep them here till I get back. (*He strides into view, reacts at the sight of Olunde but turns to his wife.*) Thank goodness you're still here.

JANE. Simon, what happened?

PILKINGS. Later Jane, please. Is Bob still here?

JANE. Yes, I think so. I'm sure he must be.

PILKINGS. Try and get him out here as quietly as you can. Tell him it's urgent.

JANE. Of course. Oh Simon, you remember . . .

PILKINGS. Yes yes. I can see who it is. Get Bob out here. (*She runs off.*) At first I thought I was seeing a ghost.

OLUNDE. Mr Pilkings, I appreciate what you tried to do. I want you to believe that. I can only tell you it would have been a terrible calamity if you'd succeeded.

PILKINGS (*opens his mouth several times, shuts it*). You . . . said what?

OLUNDE. A calamity for us, the entire people.

PILKINGS (*sighs*). I see. Hm.

OLUNDE. And now I must go. I must see him before he turns cold.

PILKINGS. Oh ah . . . em . . . but this is a shock to see you. I mean er thinking all this while you were in England and thanking God for that.

OLUNDE. I came on the mail boat. We travelled in the Prince's convoy.

PILKINGS. Ah yes, a-ah, hm . . . er well . . .

OLUNDE. Goodnight. I can see you are shocked by the whole business. But you must know by now there are things you cannot understand—or help.

PILKINGS. Yes. Just a minute. There are armed policemen that way and they have instructions to let no one pass. I suggest you wait a little. I'll er . . . yes, I'll give you an escort.

OLUNDE. That's very kind of you. But do you think it could be quickly arranged.

PILKINGS. Of course. In fact, yes, what I'll do is send Bob over with some men to the er . . . place. You can go with them. Here he comes now. Excuse me a minute.

AIDE-DE-CAMP. Anything wrong sir?

PILKINGS (*takes him to one side*). Listen Bob, that cellar in the disused annex of the Residency, you know, where the slaves were stored before being taken down to the coast . . .

AIDE-DE-CAMP. Oh yes, we use it as a storeroom for broken furniture.

PILKINGS. But it's still got the bars on it?

AIDE-DE-CAMP. Oh yes, they are quite intact.

PILKINGS. Get the keys please. I'll explain later. And I want a strong guard over the Residency tonight.

AIDE-DE-CAMP. We have that already. The detachment from the coast . . .

PILKINGS. No, I don't want them at the gates of the Residency. I want you to deploy them at the bottom of the hill, a long way from the main hall so they can deal with any situation long before the sound carries to the house.

AIDE-DE-CAMP. Yes of course.

PILKINGS. I don't want His Highness alarmed.

AIDE-DE-CAMP. You think the riot will spread here?

PILKINGS. It's unlikely but I don't want to take a chance. I made them believe I was going to lock the man up in my house, which was what I had planned to do in the first place. They are probably assailing it by now. I took a roundabout route here so I don't think there is any danger at all. At least not before dawn. Nobody is to leave the premises of course—the native employees I mean. They'll soon smell something is up and they can't keep their mouths shut.

AIDE-DE-CAMP. I'll give instructions at once.

PILKINGS. I'll take the prisoner down myself. Two policemen will stay with him throughout the night. Inside the cell.

AIDE-DE-CAMP. Right sir. (*Salutes and goes off at the double.*)

PILKINGS. Jane. Bob is coming back in a moment with a detachment. Until he gets back please stay with Olunde. (*He makes an extra warning gesture with his eyes.*)

OLUNDE. Please Mr Pilkings . . .

PILKINGS. I hate to be stuffy old son, but we have a crisis on our hands. It has to do with your father's affair if you must know. And it happens also at a time when we have His Highness here. I am responsible for security so you'll simply have to do as I say. I hope that's understood. (*Marches off quickly, in the direction from which he made his first appearance.*)

OLUNDE. What's going on? All this can't be just because he failed to stop my father killing himself.

JANE. I honestly don't know. Could it have sparked off a riot?

OLUNDE. No. If he'd succeeded that would be more likely to start the riot. Perhaps there were other factors involved. Was there a chieftaincy dispute?

JANE. None that I know of.

ELESIN (*an animal bellow from off*). Leave me alone! Is it not enough that you have covered me in shame! White man, take your hand from my body!

(*Olunde stands frozen on the spot. Jane understanding at last, tries to move him.*)

JANE. Let's go in. It's getting chilly out here.

PILKINGS (*off*). Carry him.

ELESIN. Give me back the name you have taken away from me you ghost from the land of the nameless!

PILKINGS. Carry him! I can't have a disturbance here. Quickly! stuff up his mouth.

JANE. Oh God! Let's go in. Please Olunde. (*Olunde does not move.*)

ELESIN. Take your albino's hand from me you . . .

(*Sounds of a struggle. His voice chokes as he is gagged.*)

OLUNDE (*quietly*). That was my father's voice.

JANE. Oh you poor orphan, what have you come home to?

(*There is a sudden explosion of rage from off-stage and powerful steps come running up the drive.*)

PILKINGS. You bloody fools, after him!

(*Immediately Elesin, in handcuffs, comes pounding in the direction of Jane and Olunde, followed some moments afterwards by Pilkings and the constables. Elesin, confronted by the seeming statue of his son, stops dead. Olunde stares above his head into the distance. The constables try to grab him. Jane screams at them.*)

JANE. Leave him alone! Simon, tell them to leave him alone.

PILKINGS. All right, stand aside you. (*Shrugs.*) Maybe just as well. It might help to calm him down.

For several moments they hold the same position. Elesin moves a few steps forward, almost as if he's still in doubt.

ELESIN. Olunde! (*He moves his head, inspecting him from side to side.*) Olunde! (*He collapses slowly at Olunde's feet.*) Oh son, don't let the sight of your father turn you blind!

OLUNDE (*he moves for the first time since he heard his voice, brings his head slowly down to look on him*). I have no father, eater of left-overs.

(*He walks slowly down the way his father had run. Light fades out on Elesin, sobbing into the ground.*)

SCENE 5

A wide iron-barred gate stretches almost the whole width of the cell in which Elesin is imprisoned. His wrists are encased in thick iron bracelets, chained together; he stands against the bars, looking out. Seated on the ground to one side on the outside is his recent bride, her eyes bent perpetually to the ground. Figures of the two guards can be seen deeper inside the cell, alert to every movement Elesin makes. Pilkings now in a police officer's uniform enters noiselessly, observes him for a while. Then he coughs ostentatiously and approaches. Leans against the bars near a corner, his back to Elesin. He is obviously trying to fall in mood with him. Some moments' silence.

PILKINGS. You seem fascinated by the moon.

ELESIN (*after a pause*). Yes, ghostly one. Your twin-brother up there engages my thoughts.

PILKINGS. It is a beautiful night.

ELESIN. Is that so?

PILKINGS. The light on the leaves, the peace of the night . . .

ELESIN. The night is not at peace, District Officer.

PILKINGS. No? I would have said it was. You know, quiet . . .

ELESIN. And does quiet mean peace for you?

PILKINGS. Well, nearly the same thing. Naturally there is a subtle difference . . .

ELESIN. The night is not at peace ghostly one. The world is not at peace. You have shattered the peace of the world for ever. There is no sleep in the world tonight.

PILKINGS. It is still a good bargain if the world should lose one night's sleep as the price of saving a man's life.

ELESIN. You did not save my life District Officer. You destroyed it.

PILKINGS. Now come on . . .

ELESIN. And not merely my life but the lives of many. The end of the night's work is not over. Neither this year nor the next will see it. If I wished you well, I would pray that you do not stay long enough on our land to see the disaster you have brought upon us.

PILKINGS. Well, I did my duty as I saw it. I have no regrets.

ELESIN. No. The regrets of life always come later.

(*Some moments' pause.*)

You are waiting for dawn white man. I hear you saying to yourself: only so many hours until dawn and then the danger is over. All I must do is keep him alive tonight. You don't quite understand it all but you know that tonight is when what ought to be must be brought about. I shall ease your mind even more, ghostly one. It is not an entire night but a moment of the night, and that moment is past. The moon was my messenger and guide. When it reached a certain gateway in the sky, it touched that moment for which my whole life has been spent in blessings. Even I do not know the gateway. I have stood here and scanned the sky for a glimpse of that door but, I cannot see it. Human eyes are useless for a search of this nature. But in the house of osugbo, those who keep watch through the spirit recognised the moment, they sent word to me through the voice of our sacred drums to prepare myself. I heard them and I shed all thoughts of earth. I began to follow the moon to the abode of gods . . . servant of the white king, that was when you entered my chosen place of departure on feet of desecration.

PILKINGS. I'm sorry, but we all see our duty differently.

ELESIN. I no longer blame you. You stole from me my firstborn, sent him to your country so you could turn him into something in your own image. Did you plan it all beforehand? There are moments when it seems part of a larger plan. He who must follow my footsteps is taken from me, sent across the ocean. Then, in my turn, I am stopped from fulfilling my destiny. Did you think it all out before, this plan to push our world from its course and sever the cord that links us to the great origin?

PILKINGS. You don't really believe that. Anyway, if that was my intention with your son, I appear to have failed.

ELESIN. You did not fail in the main thing ghostly one. We know the roof covers the rafters, the cloth covers blemishes; who would have known that the white skin covered our future, preventing us from seeing the death our enemies had prepared for us. The world is set adrift and its inhabitants are lost. Around them, there is nothing but emptiness.

PILKINGS. Your son does not take so gloomy a view.

ELESIN. Are you dreaming now white man? Were you not present at my reunion of shame? Did you not see when the world reversed itself and the father fell before his son, asking forgiveness?

PILKINGS. That was in the heat of the moment. I spoke to him and . . . if you want to know, he wishes he could cut out his tongue for uttering the words he did.

ELESIN. No. What he said must never be unsaid. The contempt of my own son rescued something of my shame at your hands. You may have stopped me in my duty but I know now that I did give birth to a son. Once I mistrusted him for seeking the companionship of those my spirit knew as enemies of our race. Now I understand. One should seek to obtain the secrets of his enemies. He will avenge my shame, white one. His spirit will destroy you and yours.

PILKINGS. That kind of talk is hardly called for. If you don't want my consolation . . .

ELESIN. No white man, I do not want your consolation.

PILKINGS. As you wish. Your son anyway, sends his consolation. He asks your forgiveness. When I asked him not to despise you his reply was: I cannot judge him, and if I cannot judge him, I cannot despise him. He wants to come to you to say goodbye and to receive your blessing.

ELESIN. Goodbye? Is he returning to your land?

PILKINGS. Don't you think that's the most sensible thing for him to do? I advised him to leave at once, before dawn, and he agrees that is the right course of action.

ELESIN. Yes, it is best. And even if I did not think so, I have lost the father's place of honour. My voice is broken.

PILKINGS. Your son honours you. If he didn't he would not ask your blessing.

ELESIN. No. Even a thoroughbred is not without pity for the turf he strikes with his hoof. When is he coming?

PILKINGS. As soon as the town is a little quieter. I advised it.

ELESIN. Yes white man, I am sure you advised it. You advise all our lives although on the authority of what gods, I do not know.

PILKINGS (*opens his mouth to reply, then appears to change his mind. Turns to go. Hesitates and stops again*). Before I leave you, may I ask just one thing of you?

ELESIN. I am listening.

PILKINGS. I wish to ask you to search the quiet of your heart and tell me—do you not find great contradictions in the wisdom of your own race?

ELESIN. Make yourself clear, white one.

PILKINGS. I have lived among you long enough to learn a saying or two. One came to my mind tonight when I stepped into the market and saw what was going on. You were surrounded by those who egged you on with song and praises. I thought, are these not the same people who say: the elder grimly approaches heaven and you ask him to bear your greetings yonder; do you really think he makes the journey willingly? After that, I did not hesitate.

(*A pause. Elesin sighs. Before he can speak a sound of running feet is heard.*)

JANE (*off*). Simon! Simon!

PILKINGS. What on earth . . . ! (*Runs off.*)

(*Elesin turns to his new wife, gazes on her for some moments.*)

ELESIN. My young bride, did you hear the ghostly one? You sit and sob in your silent heart but say nothing to all this. First I blamed the white man, then I blamed my gods for deserting me. Now I feel I want to blame you for the mystery of the sapping of my will. But blame is a strange peace offering for a man to bring a world he has deeply wronged, and to its innocent dwellers. Oh little mother, I have taken countless women in my life but you were more than a desire of the flesh. I needed you as the abyss across which my body must be drawn, I filled it with earth and dropped my seed in it at the moment of preparedness for my crossing. You were the final gift of the living to their emissary to the land of the ancestors, and perhaps your warmth and youth brought new insights of this world to me and turned my feet leaden on this side of the abyss. For I confess to you, daughter, my weakness came not merely from the abomination of the white man who came violently into my fading presence, there was also a weight of longing on my earth-held limbs. I would have shaken it off, already my foot had begun to lift but then, the white ghost entered and all was defiled.

(*Approaching voices of Pilkings and his wife.*)

JANE. Oh Simon, you will let her in won't you?
PILKINGS. I really wish you'd stop interfering.

(*They come in view. Jane is in a dressing-gown. Pilkings is holding a note to which he refers from time to time.*)

JANE. Good gracious, I didn't initiate this. I was sleeping quietly, or trying to anyway, when the servant brought it. It's not my fault if one can't sleep undisturbed even in the Residency.
PILKINGS. He'd have done the same if we were sleeping at home so don't sidetrack the issue. He knows he can get round you or he wouldn't send you the petition in the first place.
JANE. Be fair Simon. After all he was thinking of your own interests. He is grateful you know, you seem to forget that. He feels he owes you something.
PILKINGS. I just wish they'd leave this man alone tonight, that's all.
JANE. Trust him Simon. He's pledged his word it will all go peacefully.
PILKINGS. Yes, and that's the other thing. I don't like being threatened.
JANE. Threatened? (*Takes the note.*) I didn't spot any threat.
PILKINGS. It's there. Veiled, but it's there. The only way to prevent serious rioting tomorrow—what a cheek!
JANE. I don't think he's threatening you Simon.
PILKINGS. He's picked up the idiom alright. Wouldn't surprise me if he's been mixing with commies or anarchists over there. The phrasing sounds too good to be true. Damn! If only the Prince hadn't picked this time for his visit.
JANE. Well, even so Simon, what have you got to lose? You don't want a riot on your hands, not with the Prince here.
PILKINGS (*going up to Elesin*). Let's see what he has to say. Chief Elesin, there is yet another person who wants to see you. As she is not a next-of-kin I don't really feel obliged to let her in. But your son sent a note with her, so it's up to you.

ELESIN. I know who that must be. So she found out your hiding-place. Well, it was not difficult. My stench of shame is so strong, it requires no hunter's dog to follow it.
PILKINGS. If you don't want to see her, just say so and I'll send her packing.
ELESIN. Why should I not want to see her? Let her come. I have no more holes in my rag of shame. All is laid bare.
PILKINGS. I'll bring her in. (*Goes off.*)
JANE (*hesitates, then goes to Elesin*). Please, try and understand. Everything my husband did was for the best.
ELESIN (*he gives her a long strange stare, as if he is trying to understand who she is*). You are the wife of the District Officer?
JANE. Yes. My name is Jane.
ELESIN. That is my wife sitting down there. You notice how still and silent she sits? My business is with your husband.

(*Pilkings returns with Iyaloja.*)

PILKINGS. Here she is. Now first I want your word of honour that you will try nothing foolish.
ELESIN. Honour? White one, did you say you wanted my word of honour?
PILKINGS. I know you to be an honourable man. Give me your word of honour you will receive nothing from her.
ELESIN. But I am sure you have searched her clothing as you would never dare touch your own mother. And there are these two lizards of yours who roll their eyes even when I scratch.
PILKINGS. And I shall be sitting on that tree trunk watching even how you blink. Just the same I want your word that you will not let her pass anything to you.
ELESIN. You have my honour already. It is locked up in that desk in which you will put away your report of the night's events. Even the honour of my people you have taken already; it is tied together with those papers of treachery which make you masters in this land.
PILKINGS. Alright. I am trying to make things easy but if you must bring in politics we'll have to do it the hard way. Madam, I want you to remain along this line and move no nearer to that cell door. Guards! (*They spring to attention.*) If she moves beyond this point, blow your whistle. Come on Jane. (*They go off.*)
IYALOJA. How boldly the lizard struts before the pigeon when it was the eagle itself he promised us he would confront.
ELESIN. I don't ask you to take pity on me Iyaloja. You have a message for me or you would not have come. Even if it is the curses of the world, I shall listen.
IYALOJA. You made so bold with the servant of the white king who took your side against death. I must tell your brother chiefs when I return how bravely you waged war against him. Especially with words.
ELESIN. I more than deserve your scorn.

IYALOJA (*with sudden anger*). I warned you, if you must leave a seed behind, be sure it is not tainted with the curses of the world. Who are you to open a new life when you dared not open the door to a new existence? I say who are you to make so bold? (*The Bride sobs and Iyaloja notices her. Her contempt noticeably increases as she turns back to Elesin.*) Oh you self-vaunted stem of the plantain, how hollow it all proves. The pith is gone in the parent stem, so how will it prove with the new shoot? How will it go with that earth that bears it? Who are you to bring this abomination on us!

ELESIN. My powers deserted me. My charms, my spells, even my voice lacked strength when I made to summon the powers that would lead me over the last measure of earth into the land of the fleshless. You saw it, Iyaloja. You saw me struggle to retrieve my will from the power of the stranger whose shadow fell across the doorway and left me floundering and blundering in a maze I had never before encountered. My senses were numbed when the touch of cold iron came upon my wrists. I could do nothing to save myself.

IYALOJA. You have betrayed us. We fed you sweetmeats such as we hoped awaited you on the other side. But you said No, I must eat the world's left-overs. We said you were the hunter who brought the quarry down; to you belonged the vital portions of the game. No, you said, I am the hunter's dog and I shall eat the entrails of the game and the faeces of the hunter. We said you were the hunter returning home in triumph, a slain buffalo pressing down on his neck; you said wait, I first must turn up this cricket hole with my toes. We said yours was the doorway at which we first spy the tapper when he comes down from the tree, yours was the blessing of the twilight wine, the purl that brings night spirits out of doors to steal their portion before the light of day. We said yours was the body of wine whose burden shakes the tapper like a sudden gust on his perch. You said, No, I am content to lick the dregs from each calabash when the drinkers are done. We said, the dew on earth's surface was for you to wash your feet along the slopes of honour. You said No, I shall step in the vomit of cats and the droppings of mice; I shall fight them for the left-overs of the world.

ELESIN. Enough Iyaloja, enough.

IYALOJA. We called you leader and oh, how you led us on. What we have no intention of eating should not be held to the nose.

ELESIN. Enough, enough. My shame is heavy enough.

IYALOJA. Wait. I came with a burden.

ELESIN. You have more than discharged it.

IYALOJA. I wish I could pity you.

ELESIN. I need neither your pity nor the pity of the world. I need understanding. Even I need to understand. You were present at my defeat. You were part of the beginnings. You brought about the renewal of my tie to earth, you helped in the binding of the cord.

IYALOJA. I gave you warning. The river which fills up before our eyes does not sweep us away in its flood.

ELESIN. What were warnings beside the moist contact of living earth between my fingers? What were warnings beside the renewal of famished embers lodged eternally in the heart of man? But even that, even if it overwhelmed one with a thousandfold temptations to linger a little while, a man could overcome it. It is when the alien hand pollutes the source of will, when a stranger force of violence shatters the mind's calm resolution, this is when a man is made to commit the awful treachery of relief, commit in his thought the unspeakable blasphemy of seeing the hand of the gods in this alien rupture of his world. I know it was this thought that killed me, sapped my powers and turned me into an infant in the hands of unnamable strangers. I made to utter my spells anew but my tongue merely rattled in my mouth. I fingered hidden charms and the contact was damp; there was no spark left to sever the life-strings that should stretch from every finger-tip. My will was squelched in the spittle of an alien race, and all because I had committed this blasphemy of thought— that there might be the hand of the gods in a stranger's intervention.

IYALOJA. Explain it how you will, I hope it brings you peace of mind. The bush-rat fled his rightful cause, reached the market and set up a lamentation. 'Please save me!'—are these fitting words to hear from an ancestral mask? 'There's a wild beast at my heels' is not becoming language from a hunter.

ELESIN. May the world forgive me.

IYALOJA. I came with a burden I said. It approaches the gates which are so well guarded by those jackals whose spittle will from this day be on your food and drink. But first, tell me, you who were once Elesin Oba, tell me, you who know so well the cycle of the plantain: is it the parent shoot which withers to give sap to the younger or, does your wisdom see it running the other way?

ELESIN. I don't see your meaning Iyaloja?

IYALOJA. Did I ask you for a meaning? I asked a question. Whose trunk withers to give sap to the other? The parent shoot or the younger?

ELESIN. The parent.

IYALOJA. Ah. So you do know that. There are sights in this world which say different Elesin. There are some who choose to reverse this cycle of our being. Oh you emptied bark that the world once saluted for a pith-laden being, shall I tell you what the gods have claimed of you?

(*In her agitation she steps beyond the line indicated by Pilkings and the air is rent by piercing whistles. The two Guards also leap forward and place safe-guarding hands on Elesin. Iyaloja stops, astonished. Pilkings comes racing in, followed by Jane.*)

PILKINGS. What is it? Did they try something?

GUARD. She stepped beyond the line.

ELESIN (*in a broken voice*). Let her alone. She meant no harm.

IYALOJA. Oh Elesin, see what you've become. Once you had no need to open your mouth in explanation because evil-smelling goats, itchy of hand and foot had lost their senses. And it was a brave man indeed who dared lay hands on you because Iyaloja stepped from one side of the earth onto another. Now look at the spectacle of your life. I grieve for you.

PILKINGS. I think you'd better leave. I doubt you have done him much good by coming here. I shall make sure you are not allowed to see him again. In any case we are moving him to a different place before dawn, so don't bother to come back.

IYALOJA. We foresaw that. Hence the burden I trudged here to lay beside your gates.

PILKINGS. What was that you said?

IYALOJA. Didn't our son explain? Ask that one. He knows what it is. At least we hope the man we once knew as Elesin remembers the lesser oaths he need not break.

PILKINGS. Do you know what she is talking about?

ELESIN. Go to the gates, ghostly one. Whatever you find there, bring it to me.

IYALOJA. Not yet. It drags behind me on the slow, weary feet of women. Slow as it is Elesin, it has long overtaken you. It rides ahead of your laggard will.

PILKINGS. What is she saying now? Christ! Must your people forever speak in riddles?

ELESIN. It will come white man, it will come. Tell your men at the gates to let it through.

PILKINGS (*dubiously*). I'll have to see what it is.

IYALOJA. You will. (*Passionately*.) But this is one oath he cannot shirk. White one, you have a king here, a visitor from your land. We know of his presence here. Tell me, were he to die would you leave his spirit roaming restlessly on the surface of earth? Would you bury him here among those you consider less than human? In your land have you no ceremonies of the dead?

PILKINGS. Yes. But we don't make our chiefs commit suicide to keep him company.

IYALOJA. Child, I have not come to help your understanding. (*Points to Elesin.*) This is the man whose weakened understanding holds us in bondage to you. But ask him if you wish. He knows the meaning of a king's passage; he was not born yesterday. He knows the peril to the race when our dead father, who goes as intermediary, waits and waits and knows he is betrayed. He knows when the narrow gate was opened and he knows it will not stay for laggards who drag their feet in dung and vomit, whose lips are reeking of the left-overs of lesser men. He knows he has condemned our king to wander in the void of evil with beings who are enemies of life.

PILKINGS. Yes er . . . but look here . . .

IYALOJA. What we ask is little enough. Let him release our King so he can ride on homewards alone. The messenger is on his way on the backs of women. Let him send word through the heart that is folded up within the bolt. It is the least of all his oaths, it is the easiest fulfilled.

(*The Aide-De-Camp runs in.*)

PILKINGS. Bob?

AIDE-DE-CAMP. Sir, there's a group of women chanting up the hill.

PILKINGS (*rounding on Iyaloja*). If you people want trouble . . .

JANE. Simon, I think that's what Olunde referred to in his letter.

PILKINGS. He knows damned well I can't have a crowd here! Damn it, I explained the delicacy of my position to him. I think it's about time I got him out of town. Bob, send a car and two or three soldiers to bring him in. I think the sooner he takes his leave of his father and gets out the better.

IYALOJA. Save your labour white one. If it is the father of your prisoner you want, Olunde, he who until this night we knew as Elesin's son, he comes soon himself to take his leave. He has sent the women ahead, so let them in.

(*Pilkings remains undecided.*)

AIDE-DE-CAMP. What do we do about the invasion? We can still stop them far from here.

PILKINGS. What do they look like?

AIDE-DE-CAMP. They're not many. And they seem quite peaceful.

PILKINGS. No men?

AIDE-DE-CAMP. Mm, two or three at the most.

JANE. Honestly, Simon, I'd trust Olunde. I don't think he'll deceive you about their intentions.

PILKINGS. He'd better not. Alright, let them in Bob. Warn them to control themselves. Then hurry Olunde here. Make sure he brings his baggage because I'm not returning him into town.

AIDE-DE-CAMP. Very good sir. (*Goes.*)

PILKINGS (*to Iyaloja*). I hope you understand that if anything goes wrong it will be on your head. My men have orders to shoot at the first sign of trouble.

IYALOJA. To prevent one death you will actually make other deaths? Ah, great is the wisdom of the white race. But have no fear. Your Prince will sleep peacefully. So at long last will ours. We will disturb you no further, servant of the white king. Just let Elesin fulfil his oath and we will retire home and pay homage to our King.

JANE. I believe her Simon, don't you?

PILKINGS. Maybe.

ELESIN. Have no fear ghostly one. I have a message to send my King and then you have nothing more to fear.

IYALOJA. Olunde would have done it. The chiefs asked him to speak the words but he said no, not while you lived.

ELESIN. Even from the depths to which my spirit has sunk, I find some joy that this little has been left to me.

(The women enter, intoning the dirge 'Ọ̀lẹ̀ lẹ̀ lẹ̀' and swaying from side to side. On their shoulders is borne a longish object roughly like a cylindrical bolt, covered in cloth. They set it down on the spot where Iyaloja had stood earlier, and form a semi-circle round it. The Praise-Singer and Drummer stand on the inside of the semi-circle but the drum is not used at all. The Drummer intones under the Praise-Singer's invocations.)

PILKINGS *(as they enter)*. What is *that*?

IYALOJA. The burden you have made white one, but we bring it in peace.

PILKINGS. I said *what* is it?

ELESIN. White man, you must let me out. I have a duty to perform.

PILKINGS. I most certainly will not.

ELESIN. There lies the courier of my King. Let me out so I can perform what is demanded of me.

PILKINGS. You'll do what you need to do from inside there or not at all. I've gone as far as I intend to with this business.

ELESIN. The worshipper who lights a candle in your church to bear a message to his god bows his head and speaks in a whisper to the flame. Have I not seen it ghostly one? His voice does not ring out to the world. Mine are no words for anyone's ears. They are not words even for the bearers of this load. They are words I must speak secretly, even as my father whispered them in my ears and I in the ears of my first-born. I cannot shout them to the wind and the open night-sky.

JANE. Simon . . .

PILKINGS. Don't interfere. Please!

IYALOJA. They have slain the favourite horse of the king and slain his dog. They have borne them from pulse to pulse centre of the land receiving prayers for their king. But the rider has chosen to stay behind. Is it too much to ask that he speak his heart to heart of the waiting courier? *(Pilkings turns his back on her.)* So be it. Elesin Oba, you see how even the mere leavings are denied you. *(She gestures to the Praise-Singer.)*

PRAISE-SINGER. Elesin Oba! I call you by that name only this last time. Remember when I said, if you cannot come, tell my horse! *(Pause.)* What? I cannot hear you! I said, if you cannot come, whisper in the ears of my horse. Is your tongue severed from the roots Elesin? I can hear no response. I said, if there are boulders you cannot climb, mount my horse's back, this spotless black stallion, he'll bring you over them. *(Pauses.)* Elesin Oba, once you had a tongue that darted like a drummer's stick. I said, if you get

lost my dog will track a path to me. My memory fails me but I think you replied: My feet have found the path, Alafin.

(The dirge rises and falls.)

I said at the last, if evil hands hold you back, just tell my horse there is weight on the hem of your smock. I dare not wait too long.

(The dirge rises and falls.)

There lies the swiftest ever messenger of a king, so set me free with the errand of your heart. There lie the head and heart of the favourite of the gods, whisper in his ears. Oh my companion, if you had followed when you should, we would not say that the horse preceded its rider. If you had followed when it was time, we would not say the dog has raced beyond and left his master behind. If you had raised your will to cut the thread of life at the summons of the drums, we would not say your mere shadow fell across the gateway and took its owner's place at the banquet. But the hunter, laden with a slain buffalo, stayed to root in the cricket's hole with his toes. What now is left? If there is a dearth of bats, the pigeon must serve us for the offering. Speak the words over your shadow which must now serve in your place.

ELESIN. I cannot approach. Take off the cloth. I shall speak my message from heart to heart of silence.

IYALOJA *(moves forward and removes the covering)*. Your courier Elesin, cast your eyes on the favoured companion of the King.

(Rolled up in the mat, his head and feet showing at either end is the body of Olunde.)

There lies the honour of your household and of our race. Because he could not bear to let honour fly out of doors, he stopped it with his life. The son has proved the father Elesin, and there is nothing left in your mouth to gnash but infant gums.

PRAISE-SINGER. Elesin, we placed the reins of the world in your hands yet you watched it plunge over the edge of the bitter precipice. You sat with folded arms while evil strangers tilted the world from its course and crashed it beyond the edge of emptiness—you muttered, there is little that one man can do, you left us floundering on a blind future. Your heir has taken the burden on himself. What the end will be, we are not gods to tell. But this young shoot has poured its sap into the parent stalk, and we know this is not the way of life. Our world is tumbling in the void of strangers, Elesin.

(Elesin has stood rock-still, his knuckles taut on the bars, his eyes glued to the body of his son. The still-ness seizes and paralyses everyone, including Pilk-ings who has turned to look. Suddenly Elesin flings

*one arm round his neck, once, and with the loop of
the chain, strangles himself in a swift, decisive pull.
The guards rush forward to stop him but they are
only in time to let his body down. Pilkings has leapt
to the door at the same time and struggles with the
lock. He rushes within, fumbles with the handcuffs
and unlocks them, raises the body to a sitting position while he tries to give resuscitation. The women
continue their dirge, unmoved by the sudden event.)*

IYALOJA. Why do you strain yourself? Why do you labour at
tasks for which no one, not even the man lying there
would give you thanks? He is gone at last into the
passage but oh, how late it all is. His son will feast on
the meat and throw him bones. The passage is clogged
with droppings from the King's stallion; he will arrive
all stained in dung.

PILKINGS *(in a tired voice)*. Was this what you wanted?

IYALOJA. No child, it is what you brought to be, you who
play with strangers' lives, who even usurp the vestments
of our dead, yet believe that the stain of death will not
cling to you. The gods demanded only the old expired
plantain but you cut down the sap-laden shoot to feed
your pride. There is your board, filled to overflowing.

Feast on it. *(She screams at him suddenly, seeing that
Pilkings is about to close Elesin's staring eyes.)* Let him
alone! However sunk he was in debt he is no pauper's
carrion abandoned on the road. Since when have
strangers donned clothes of indigo before the bereaved
cries out his loss?

*(She turns to the Bride who has remained motionless
throughout.)*

CHILD.

*(The girl takes up a little earth, walks calmly into the
cell and closes Elesin's eyes. She then pours some
earth over each eyelid and comes out again.)*

Now forget the dead, forget even the living. Turn your
mind only to the unborn.

*(She goes off, accompanied by the Bride. The dirge
rises in volume and the women continue their sway.
Lights fade to a black-out.)*

The End

COMMENTARY

Note: The following essay represents a single interpretation of the play. For other perspectives on Death and the King's Horseman, *consult the essays listed below.*

Soyinka's "Author's Note" to *Death and the King's Horseman* has received much attention from critics—though there is little consensus about its meaning. To the Yoruba (or to many peoples whose religious life is animistic and therefore not separated from the natural world), Soyinka's instructions seem superfluous. But the playwright does not level his warnings to those who already understand them; rather, he admonishes those areas of Western consciousness that he sees as ultimately prohibitive to the apprehension of Yoruba tragedy. For the Western reader steeped in "modernist" sensibilities, perhaps Soyinka's note should appear at the end of the play. Reading it subsequent to the actual text might prove an efficacious means of measuring the extent to which Soyinka is accurate in his assessment of how the play must be interpreted. Should readers ignore the "Author's Note" as a prologue (as some critics have suggested it is) and instead read it afterward as a commentary on a specific type of work, they may discover the very trap that Soyinka identifies as "the bane of themes of this genre." That is to say, such plays acquire the facile tag of a "clash of cultures" play. In fact, a real clash of cultures does occur when the Western mind attempts to analyze drama that does not conform to traditional forms or content. It is at precisely this point where Soyinka's poetic imagination comes into conflict with the Western-trained critic.

Soyinka's approach to tragic myth within the context of the Yoruba worldview (see the related Showcase) can be found in his essay "The Fourth Stage," a piece heavily influenced by Friedrich Nietzsche's *The Birth of Tragedy* (1872). Nietzsche's work, among the most important in dramatic theory, explores the manner in which Greek tragedy developed through a marriage between the Apollonian (i.e., rational) art of the sculptor and the nonvisual Dionysian (i.e., emotional) art of music. Though these two creative urges are often in violent opposition to one another, they ultimately coupled to form tragedy, which was for Nietzsche the perfect synthesis of the Apollonian and Dionysian impulses in humans. Certainly Yoruba tragedy, as discussed in Soyinka's "Fourth Stage," is not intended as a copy of Greek tragedy. Yet these Nietzschean images and those of the Yoruba myth lend themselves to a comparison that may lead us to an understanding of *Death and the King's Horseman.*

The same sense of duality that is found in Nietzsche's tragic schema can be found in the dyadic, self-contradictory nature of Ogun—a god seeking to rejoin himself to man. At the same time, humans attempt to elevate themselves to the stature of a god, as demonstrated by Elesin's desire to follow his King in death. Both god and humans reach for knowledge they do not possess, a daring and hubristic quest that challenges Nature itself. Thus Soyinka sees Ogun as the embodiment of not only the Apollonian and Dionysian but also of the Promethean virtues. The tragic hero is one who confronts nature (often on his own) and thereby dares to enter the great abyss—what Soyinka calls "the gulf of transition"—and suffers whatever agony awaits him before achieving the ultimate reward: cosmic oneness. To the Yoruba and Soyinka, Ogun is the embodiment of the Will which originally overcame the forces of this abyss between Being and Non-Being, and it is Ogun who reunited the gods with humans. When humans, in the world of the living, face a challenge of tragic proportion, it is seen as a vital manifestation, not merely a representation, of Ogun's self-sacrifice. Elesin's obsession with meeting his death as "the King's (first) Horseman" is best understood in this light: the horseman is recreating Ogun's own act.

Ogun's tragic heroism restored the inseparability of the gods and man in nature (as seen in animism: Elesin, the rider, is an extension of the horse itself). It is in this that Ogun earned his most revered title, The Lord of the Road—the "road" being the means by which peoples of all times are connected. Consequently, there is no separation among the ancestors, the living, and the unborn. After Ogun's sacrifice, "the gulf of transition" continuously connects the three realms of the dead, the living, and the unborn. But in order to pass from one realm to the next, one must brave the abyss after the manner of the hero-god Ogun. Thus, all transitions become rites of passage. Braving the abyss, as Prince Olunde does, demands the Will of a true tragic hero. Soyinka's "Fourth Stage" is the abyss itself, the chthonic realm of the immediate, physical, and animistic world of the Yoruba for whom all things are potentially sacred.

In the "Author's Note" Soyinka insists that the play's "threnodic essence" be stressed. This relates to the rhythm and music of the dirge that provides the aural backdrop for *Death and the King's Horseman.* Music is an immediate and necessary element in tragedy, and for Soyinka music is inseparable from the Will. The contemporary mind cannot fully appreciate this concept of Music-as-Will without first shedding all notions of music as merely a diversion or commercial enterprise. To those for whom tragedy is a living product of natural forces, such as Soyinka and Nietzsche, music is the mournful lament (i.e., the threnody) as well as the solitary companion of the tragic hero at the moment of "self-individuation" on the brink of the abyss. Soyinka says that "if we agree that, in the European sense, music is the direct copy or the direct expression of the Will, it is only because nothing rescues man (ancestral, living, or unborn) from loss of self within this abyss but a titanic resolution of the Will whose ritual summons, response, and expression is the strange alien sound to which we give the name of Music." Music, then, is the creative essence, the Will itself, and it both drives and accompanies the tragic hero—Ogun, Elesin, Olunde—into the abyss of transition. Ironically, the means by which Soyinka illustrates this in *Death and the King's Horseman* is largely Apollonian: words, symbols, argument. Herein we find the play's true "clash of cultures."

Allen Alford
Louisiana State University

Other perspectives on *Death and the King's Horseman*:

Booth, James. "Self Sacrifice in Soyinka's *Death and the King's Horseman*." In James Gibbs and Bernth Lundford (eds.), *Research on Wole Soyinka.* Trenton, NJ: African World Press, 1993, 127–48.

Ralph-Bowman, Mark. "Leaders and Left-overs: A Reading of Soyinka's *Death and the King's Horseman*." *Research in African Literature* 14 (1983): 81–97.

Another Soyinka play on video:

The Swampdwellers. Dir. Norman Florence. Phoenix Films and Video, 40 min., 1973.

Though their roots are thousands of years old, Yoruba festivals have been continuously celebrated in late January in many Nigerian villages since the seventeenth century. The Yoruba use rituals to mark seasonal rhythms, religious beliefs, and cultural heritage. For the Yoruba contemporary theater remains directly related to the rituals and dance dramas from which it sprang. An understanding of their theology helps us understand why theater remains an intensely spiritual activity for the Yoruba.

The Yoruba Worldview

As one of Africa's most resilient people, the Yoruba can be traced throughout the Western world of the sub-Saharan Diaspora. The Yoruba are also unusual among Africans because they have successfully adapted to large urban centers. Both Lagos and Ibadan lie within that part of southwest Nigeria known as Yorubaland, where currently thirteen million Yoruba live.

The Yoruba are animistic; that is, their existence is governed by a religion that abounds with gods and spirits that interact—usually in animal form—with humans. The actual number of deities within the Yoruba pantheon is virtually impossible to ascertain because the people within various regions in Yorubaland have gods that are unique only to them. There are, however, several major gods who are recognized and worshipped by all Yoruba in varying forms.

According to Yoruba myth, the gods and humans once dwelt on earth and shared the joys of comradeship and thereby a sense of wholeness. Each needed the other to exist. A "cosmic totality" (to apply Soyinka's phrase) can exist only when gods and humans share this wholeness; only when each seeks an interaction with the essential character of the other can either claim a complete personality. This bond was broken (either through sin or sacrilege, as various interpreters have suggested), and the gods sought new residence in the ethereal regions. Humans were then separated from the gods by death. It was the god Ogun, who is given to imperfection, as are all Yoruba gods, who felt the "anguish of incompleteness" and broke away from the other deities. In order to bridge "the gulf of transition" between gods and humans, Ogun plunged hubristically into the chthonic realm. This act of self-sacrifice gives Ogun a heroic status that sets him apart from all other Yoruba deities.

In addition to being the god of iron and metallurgy, Ogun is also "The Creative Essence" (similar to the Greek Dionysus) and "The Lord of the Road" because he leads humans over the "way" that bridges the "gulf of transition." He is perhaps the favorite god of the Yoruba, and Soyinka identifies most with him because Ogun, by becoming human again, is "the first actor" (i.e., one who assumes an identity other than his own). Ogun was the first to confront nature and bend it to his will, even while suffering the pain of disintegration within the abyss of Being and Non-Being. The communicant chorus in the ritual reenactments of Ogun's heroic act (the Ogun Mysteries) is, in itself, a physical manifestation of the god's spiritual reincarnation.

The Yoruba Festival

Thus, the Obatala Festival in Ede is an intense spiritual experience that employs such common ritualistic devices as symbolic sacrifice, prayers, drumming, singing, dancing, and storytelling that encourage worshippers to come closer to their gods through the enactment of their myths. After a day of sacred songs and dances, the second day of the festival features heroic epics handed down from generation to generation. The performance lasts for almost two weeks as solo maskers often take an entire day to tell stories of superhuman deeds that nourish the Yoruba. The festival begins with the women dancing into the playing space as they carry sacred masks (eba) to symbolize fertility and harmony. The men tell stories through songs, using bananas and oils derived from native plants to lubricate their throats and facilitate their incantations. The action is mimed by dancers in colorful costumes and enormous headpieces that not only disguise their human form but also transform them into god-like beings. Nonperformers are forbidden to touch these "gods" who sing and dance, or even to imitate their sounds.

The performers and their audience collectively relive the fabled battle between Ajagemo, the incarnation of Obatala, and another priest, Olunwi. Ajagemo is captured by Olunwi and carried off from the palace. The Oba (King), however, seeks his release. He pays ransom to Olunwi, and Ajagemo is freed and returns to the palace. His triumph is marked by a magnificent procession in which the performers and audience unite in celebration. Death and the King's Horseman is a contemporary play that retains elements of Yoruba ritual in its use of the Praise-Singer and especially in the costumes worn by the Pilkings to their masquerade.

For a full account of Yoruba art and myth:

Euba, Femi. Archetypes, Imprecators, and Victims of Fate. New York: Greenwood Press, 1989.

Yoruba drama on video:

Oba Koso: Nigerian Drama. Dir. Merrill Brockway. Intro. Margaret Croyden. Creative Arts Television, 28 min., 1996.

HAMLETMACHINE (HAMLETMASCHINE)

HEINER MÜLLER

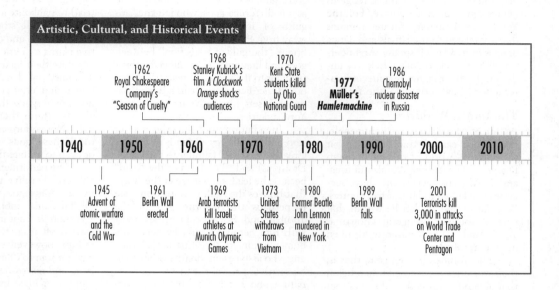

Artistic, Cultural, and Historical Events

1962 Royal Shakespeare Company's "Season of Cruelty"

1968 Stanley Kubrick's film *A Clockwork Orange* shocks audiences

1970 Kent State students killed by Ohio National Guard

1977 Müller's *Hamletmachine*

1986 Chernobyl nuclear disaster in Russia

1940 1950 1960 1970 1980 1990 2000 2010

1945 Advent of atomic warfare and the Cold War

1961 Berlin Wall erected

1969 Arab terrorists kill Israeli athletes at Munich Olympic Games

1973 United States withdraws from Vietnam

1980 Former Beatle John Lennon murdered in New York

1989 Berlin Wall falls

2001 Terrorists kill 3,000 in attacks on World Trade Center and Pentagon

HEINER MÜLLER (1929–1995)

Heiner Müller, among the most important playwrights in the contemporary German theater since Brecht, is also among the most controversial and outspoken artists of the postmodern era. Consider the following comment taken from an interview shortly before his death:

> The worst experience I had during my stay in the United States was a film I saw called *Fantasia*, by Walt Disney. I had never heard of it and actually ended up watching it by mistake. There were three films playing at the same movie house and I went to the wrong one. The most barbaric thing about this film, something I learned later, was that almost every American child between the ages of six and eight gets to view it. Which means that these people will never again be able to hear specific works by Beethoven, Bach, Handel, Tchaikovsky, etc., without seeing the Disney figures and images. The horrifying thing for me in this is the occupation of the imagination by cliches and images which will never go away; the use of images to prevent experiences, to prevent the having of experiences.

Born on January 9, 1929, in Eppendorf, Saxony, Müller was a journalist, critic, philosopher, poet, and playwright. The recipient of many literary prizes, in 1975 he was awarded the Lessing Prize, Germany's highest literary honor, and in 1979 received the prestigious *Mulheimer Dramatikerpreis* for excellence in dramatic writing.

Müller's creative genius emanated from the destruction of Europe in World War II and the rubble of postwar political and economic decay. At the age of four his reality was radically altered as he witnessed the apprehension and lengthy incarceration of his father by the German Fascist political system. Müller himself became a prisoner of war in 1945; for two days he was imprisoned by the Allied liberation army, which actually allowed him to escape and return to his home on foot. The division of Germany, the violent strike by Berlin construction workers in 1953 (which forced the Soviet army to intercede), the Hungarian Revolution of 1956, the Cold War, and the erection of the Berlin Wall in 1961 were also important events that contributed to his literary output. The Wall, literally and symbolically, isolated Müller from the rest of Germany and his European sensibility. Müller was unable to travel freely until the 1970s, and then only thanks to the international reputation his artistic achievements had earned him. Yet he always returned to Berlin, conspicuously choosing to be a comfortable product of German isolationism.

In addition to Shakespeare and Brecht, Müller's theatrical models were the classical Greek tragedians, especially the cynical Euripides. His dramatic themes concern human beings in a state of flux because of sociopolitical displacement. Carl Weber, the foremost scholar and translator of Müller's works, defines the playwright's purpose:

> The reader will discover certain threads which connect most, if not all, of Müller's thinking and writing. There is the conflict of the individual's desire for fulfillment . . . the pursuit of happiness, which clashes with the crushing demands history and its social upheavals force upon humankind. Müller has kept struggling with and writing about this conflict for forty years. The conviction that individuals are beholden to history and social forces which are forged by it is never forgotten by Müller. He may investigate and question the individual's commitment, he may discuss and distrust ideologies which enforce such a commitment, but he always maintains that the individual cannot escape responsibility for humankind's present and future.

Although his early dramatic works were influenced by Brecht and the early Realists, Müller's greatest contribution to the theater came after the early 1970s, when his drama emphasized "synthetic fragment." He coined the term to define a postmodern, image-driven, often surrealistic approach to a radically new performance aesthetic intended to disintegrate the "fourth wall" of the social realists. Many of his pieces, in particular *Hamletmachine* (1977), *The Task* (1980), and *Heartpiece* (1981), are nonlinear, devoid of conflict, and tension free. They are intellectual and ideological explorations of humans attempting to explain their present condition in a preapocalyptic world. Written in an almost hieroglyphic manner, Müller's plays create an audience response rarely experienced in the contemporary theater. Thematically, they manifest the playwright's sensitivity for the oppressed and the individual caught in historical schisms. His is not a theater of illusion but one that penetrates both the conscious and particularly the unconscious. Like Brecht, Müller wants his audiences to ponder, to think, and to choose if necessary—but never to remain inert in the face of destiny.

As You Read *Hamletmachine*

Müller's literary canon, whether in the form of prose, poetry, or drama, defies the structure of linear narrative. Both in the actual writing and in the superb crafting of theatrical landscapes, Müller attempted to escape the predictability of the classic realistic dramatic text in order to create a cognitive theatrical experience capable of piercing the senses. As you read the play, keep in mind that *Hamletmachine* is a drama of images to be altered by the vision of a director willing to stage, let us say, a three-hour extravaganza. If you were the director, how would you stage *Hamletmachine*? Would you use live actors? Giant puppets? A combination of both? You decide how you would go about designing Müller's scenic descriptions. Would you use advanced technology? If so, on what type of technology would you rely? Would you incorporate music? What kind of music? Would you stage this piece in an enclosed environment? Outdoors? Somewhere in the Rocky Mountains? By the shores of a calm river? On an expansive beach?

HAMLETMACHINE

HEINER MÜLLER

Translated by Carl Weber

FRAGMENT I
FAMILY SCRAPBOOK

I was Hamlet. I stood at the shore and talked with the surf BLABLA, the ruins of Europe in back of me. The bells tolled the state-funeral, murderer and widow a couple, the councillors goose-stepping behind the highranking carcass' coffin, bawling with badly paid grief WHO IS THE CORPSE IN THE HEARSE / ABOUT WHOM THERE'S SUCH A HUE AND CRY / 'TIS THE CORPSE OF A GREAT / GIVER OF ALMS the lane formed by the populace, creation of his statecraft HE WAS A MAN HE TOOK THEM ALL FOR ALL. I stopped the funeral procession, I pried open the coffin with my sword, the blade broke, yet with the blunt reminder I succeeded, and I dispensed my dead procreator FLESH LIKES TO KEEP THE COMPANY OF FLESH among the bums around me. The mourning turned into rejoicing, the rejoicing into lip-smacking, on top of the empty coffin the murderer humped the widow LET ME HELP YOU UP, UNCLE, OPEN YOUR LEGS, MAMA. I laid down on the ground and listened to the world doing its turns in step with the putrefaction.

I'M GOOD HAMLET GI'ME A CAUSE FOR GRIEF*

AH THE WHOLE GLOBE FOR A REAL SORROW*

RICHARD THE THIRD I THE PRINCE-KILLING KING*

OH MY PEOPLE WHAT HAVE I DONE UNTO THEE*

*The lines with an asterisk are in English in the German text.

I'M LUGGING MY OVERWEIGHT BRAIN LIKE A HUNCHBACK

CLOWN NUMBER TWO IN THE SPRING OF COMMUNISM

SOMETHING IS ROTTEN IN THIS AGE OF HOPE*

LET'S DELVE IN EARTH AND BLOW HER AT THE MOON*

Here comes the ghost who made me, the ax still in his skull. Keep your hat on, I know you've got one hole too many. I would my mother had one less when you were still of flesh: I would have been spared myself. Women should be sewed up—a world without mothers. We could butcher each other in peace and quiet, and with some confidence, if life gets too long for us or our throats too tight for our screams. What do you want of me? Is one state-funeral not enough for you? You old sponger. Is there no blood on your shoes? What's your corpse to me? Be glad the handle is sticking out, maybe you'll go to heaven. What are you waiting for? All the cocks have been butchered. Tomorrow morning has been cancelled.

SHALL I

AS IS THE CUSTOM STICK A PIECE OF IRON INTO

THE NEAREST FLESH OR THE SECOND BEST

TO LATCH UNTO IT SINCE THE WORLD IS SPINNING

LORD BREAK MY NECK WHILE I'M FALLING FROM AN ALEHOUSE BENCH

Enters Horatio. Confidant of my thoughts so full of blood since the morning is curtained by the empty sky. YOU'LL BE TOO LATE MY FRIEND FOR

YOUR PAYCHECK / NO PART FOR YOU IN THIS MY TRAGEDY. Horatio, do you know me? Are you my friend, Horatio? If you know me how can you be my friend? Do you want to play Polonius who wants to sleep with his daughter, the delightful Ophelia, here she enters right on cue, look how she shakes her ass, a tragic character. Horatio Polonius. I knew you're an actor. I am too, I'm playing Hamlet. Denmark is a prison, a wall is growing between the two of us. Look what's growing from that wall. Exit Polonius. My mother the bride. Her breasts a rosebed, her womb the snakepit. Have you forgotten your lines, mama. I'll prompt you. WASH THE MURDER OFF YOUR FACE MY PRINCE / AND OFFER THE NEW DENMARK YOUR GLAD EYE. I'll change you back into a virgin mother, so your king will have a bloodwedding. A MOTHER'S WOMB IS NOT A ONE-WAY STREET. Now, I tie your hands on your back with your bridal veil since I'm sick of your embrace. Now, I tear the wedding dress. Now, I smear the shreds of the wedding dress with the dust my father turned into, and with the soiled shreds your face your belly your breasts. Now, I take you, my mother, in his, my father's invisible tracks. I stifle your scream with my lips. Do you recognize the fruit of your womb? Now go to your wedding, whore, in the broad Danish sunlight which shines on the living and the dead. I want to cram the corpse down the latrine so the palace will choke in royal shit. Then let me eat your heart, Ophelia, which weeps my tears.

FRAGMENT II
THE EUROPE OF WOMEN

Enormous room.* Ophelia. Her heart is a clock.

OPHELIA (*Chorus/Hamlet*). I am Ophelia. The one the river didn't keep. The woman dangling from the rope. The woman with her arteries cut open. The woman with the overdose. SNOW ON HER LIPS. The woman with her head in the gas stove. Yesterday I stopped killing myself. I'm alone with my breasts my thighs my womb. I smash the tools of my captivity, the chair the table the bed. I destroy the battlefield that was my home. I fling open the doors so the wind gets in and the scream of the world. I smash the window. With my bleeding hands I tear the photos of the men I loved and who used me on the bed on the table on the chair on the ground. I set fire to my

prison. I throw my clothes into the fire. I wrench the clock that was my heart out of my breast. I walk into the street clothed in my blood.

FRAGMENT III
SCHERZO

The university of the dead. Whispering and muttering. From their gravestones (lecterns), the dead philosophers throw their books at Hamlet. Gallery (ballet) of the dead women. The woman dangling from the rope. The woman with her arteries cut open, etc. . . . . Hamlet views them with the attitude of a visitor in a museum (theatre). The dead women tear his clothes off his body. Out of an upended coffin, labeled HAMLET I, step Claudius and Ophelia, the latter dressed and made up like a whore. Striptease by Ophelia.

OPHELIA. Do you want to eat my heart, Hamlet? (*Laughs.*)
HAMLET (*Face in his hands*). I want to be a woman.

(Hamlet dresses in Ophelia's clothes, Ophelia puts the make-up of a whore on his face, Claudius—now Hamlet's father—laughs without uttering a sound, Ophelia blows Hamlet a kiss and steps with Claudius/Hamlet's Father back into the coffin. Hamlet poses as a whore. An Angel, his face at the back of his head: Horatio. He dances with Hamlet.)

VOICES (*From the coffin*). What thou killed thou shalt love.

(The dance grows faster and wilder. Laughter from the coffin. On a swing, the madonna with breast cancer. Horatio opens an umbrella, embraces Hamlet. They freeze under the umbrella, embracing. The breast cancer radiates like a sun.)

FRAGMENT IV
PEST IN BUDA / BATTLE FOR GREENLAND

Space 2, as destroyed by Ophelia. An empty armor, an ax stuck in the helmet.

HAMLET. The stove is smoking in quarrelsome October
A BAD COLD HE HAD OF IT JUST THE WORST TIME*
JUST THE WORST TIME OF THE YEAR FOR A REVOLUTION*

Cement in bloom walks through the slums
Doctor Zhivago weeps
For his wolves
SOMETIMES IN WINTER THEY CAME INTO
THE VILLAGE
AND TORE APART A PEASANT

(He takes off make-up and costume.)

THE ACTOR PLAYING HAMLET. I'm not Hamlet. I don't take part any more. My words have nothing to tell me anymore. My thoughts suck the blood out of the images. My drama doesn't happen anymore. Behind me the set is put up. By people who aren't interested in my drama, for people to whom it means nothing. I'm not interested in it anymore either. I won't play along anymore. (Unnoticed by the Actor Playing Hamlet, Stagehands place a refrigerator and three TV-sets on the stage. Humming of the refrigerator. Three TV-channels without sound.) The set is a monument. It presents a man who made history, enlarged a hundred times. The petrification of a hope. His name is interchangeable, the hope has not been fulfilled. The monument is toppled into the dust, razed by those who succeeded him in power three years after the state funeral of the hated and most honored leader. The stone is inhabited. In the spacy nostrils and auditory canals, in the creases of skin and uniform of the demolished monument, the poorer inhabitants of the capital are dwelling. After an appropriate period, the uprising follows the toppling of the monument. My drama, if it still would happen, would happen in the time of the uprising. The uprising starts with a stroll. Against the traffic rules, during the working hours. The street belongs to the pedestrians. Here and there, a car is turned over. Nightmare of a knife thrower: Slowly driving down a one-way street towards an irrevocable parking space surrounded by armed pedestrians. Policemen, if in the way, are swept to the curb. When the procession approaches the government district it is stopped by a police line. People form groups, speakers arise from them. On the balcony of a government building, a man in badly fitting mufti appears and begins to speak too. When the first stone hits him, he retreats behind the double doors of bullet-proof glass. The call for more freedom turns into the cry for the overthrow of the government. People begin to disarm the policemen, to storm two, three buildings, a prison a police precinct an office of the secret police, they string up a dozen henchmen of the rulers by their heels, the govern-

ment brings in troops, tanks. My place, if my drama would still happen, would be on both sides of the front, between the frontlines, over and above them. I stand in the stench of the crowd and hurl stones at policemen soldiers tanks bullet-proof glass. I look through the double doors of bullet-proof glass at the crowd pressing forward and smell the sweat of my fear. Choking with nausea, I shake my fist at myself who stands behind the bullet-proof glass. Shaking with fear and contempt, I see myself in the crowd pressing forward, foaming at the mouth, shaking my fist at myself. I string up my uniformed flesh by my own heels. I am the soldier in the gun turret, my head is empty under the helmet, the stifled scream under the tracks. I am the typewriter. I tie the noose when the ringleaders are strung up, I pull the stool from under their feet, I break my own neck. I am my own prisoner. I feed my own data into the computers. My parts are the spittle and the spittoon the knife and the wound the fang and the throat the neck and the rope. I am the data bank. Bleeding in the crowd. Breathing again behind the double doors. Oozing wordslime in my soundproof blurb over and above the battle. My drama didn't happen. The script has been lost. The actors put their faces on the rack in the dressing room. In his box, the prompter is rotting. The stuffed corpses in the house don't stir a hand. I go home and kill the time, at one with my undivided self.

Television The daily nausea Nausea
Of prefabricated babble Of decreed cheerfulness
How do you spell GEMÜTLICHKEIT
Give us this day our daily murder
Since thine is nothingness Nausea
Of the lies which are believed
By the liars and nobody else
Nausea
Of the lies which are believed Nausea
Of the mugs of the manipulators marked
By their struggle for positions votes bank accounts
Nausea A chariot armed with scythes sparkling with
    punchlines
I walk through street stores Faces
Scarred by the consumers battle Poverty
Without dignity Poverty without the dignity
Of the knife the knuckleduster the clenched fist
The humiliated bodies of women
Hope of generations
Stifled in blood cowardice stupidity
Laughter from dead bellies

Hail Coca Cola
A kingdom
For a murderer
I WAS MACBETH
THE KING HAD OFFERED HIS THIRD MISTRESS
TO ME
I KNEW EVERY MOLE ON HER HIPS
RASKOLNIKOV CLOSE TO THE
HEART UNDER THE ONLY COAT THE AX FOR
THE
ONLY
SKULL OF THE PAWNBROKER
In the solitude of airports
I breathe again I am
A privileged person My nausea
Is a privilege
Protected by torture
Barbed wire Prisons

(*Photograph of the author.*)

I don't want to eat drink breathe love a woman a man a child an animal anymore. I don't want to die anymore. I don't want to kill anymore.

(*Tearing of the author's photograph.*)

I force open my sealed flesh. I want to dwell in my veins, in the marrow of my bones, in the maze of my skull. I retreat into my entrails. I take my seat in my shit, in my blood. Somewhere bodies are torn apart so I can dwell in my shit. Somewhere bodies are opened so I can be alone with my blood. My thoughts are lesions in my brain. My brain is a scar. I want to be a machine. Arms for grabbing Legs to walk on, no pain no thoughts.

(*TV screens go black. Blood oozes from the refrigerator. Three naked women: Marx, Lenin, Mao. They speak simultaneously, each one in his own language, the text:*)

THE MAIN POINT IS TO OVERTHROW ALL
EXISTING CONDITIONS... †

(*The Actor of Hamlet puts on make-up and costume.*)

HAMLET THE DANE PRINCE AND MAGGOTS FODDER STUMBLING FROM HOLE TO HOLE TOWARDS THE FINAL HOLE LISTLESS IN HIS BACK THE GHOST THAT ONCE MADE HIM GREEN LIKE OPHELIA'S FLESH IN CHILDBED AND SHORTLY ERE THE THIRD COCK'S CROW A CLOWN WILL TEAR THE FOOL'S CAP OFF THE PHILOSOPHER A BLOATED BLOODHOUND'LL CRAWL INTO THE ARMOR

(*He steps into the armor, splits with the ax the heads of Marx, Lenin, Mao. Snow. Ice Age.*)

F R A G M E N T   V
F I E R C E L Y   E N D U R I N G
M I L L E N N I U M S   I N   T H E
F E A R F U L   A R M O R

The deep sea. Ophelia in a wheelchair. Fish, debris, dead bodies and limbs drift by.

OPHELIA (*While two men in white smocks wrap gauze around her and the wheelchair, from bottom to top*). This is Electra speaking. In the heart of darkness. Under the sun of torture. To the capitals of the world. In the name of the victims. I eject all the sperm I have received. I turn the milk of my breasts into lethal poison. I take back the world I gave birth to. I choke between my thighs the world I gave birth to. I bury it in my womb. Down with the happiness of submission. Long live hate and contempt, rebellion and death. When she walks through your bedrooms carrying butcher knives you'll know the truth.

(*The men exit. Ophelia remains on stage, motionless in her white wrappings.*)

---

†English-language productions could use the entire quote from Karl Marx: Introduction to *Critique of Hegel's Philosophy of Law*.

COMMENTARY

Note: The following essay represents a single interpretation of the play. For other perspectives on Hamletmachine, *consult the essays listed below.*

In his deconstructionist adaptation of Shakespeare's tragedy, Müller modeled the character of Ophelia after Ulrike Meinhof, a member of the Red Army Faction, a German terrorist guerilla group responsible for the kidnapping and murder of various German officials throughout the politically turbulent 1960s and 1970s. This preoccupation with his nation's sociopolitical occurrences, coupled with Müller's own personal encounters with a German political system that has shifted the paradigm of a global political and economic reality, is at the core of his thematic literary canon. From his journalistic writings to his poetry and ultimately in his groundbreaking antilinear theater, Müller transformed the structure of twentieth-century dramatic composition. As a disciple of Brecht, Müller crystallized and refined the Epic Theatre in order to create one of the most stunningly vivid and mesmerizing pictorial landscapes in the history of Western theater.

Müller's apocalyptic and phenomenological theater examines the historical and cultural ashes of a Western society gone amok through two world wars, a myriad of international political upheavals, and the destabilization of global economic foundations. Surely, his theater is rooted in the identity of his own nation, having witnessed, from his early years, a leading political infrastructure collapse at the heels of a major world war, specifically the defeat of Adolf Hitler's Nazi imperialism. Concomitantly, the 1949 division of Germany into two separate states, the Federal Republic of Germany (West) and the German Democratic Republic (East), altered Müller's psychological, intellectual, and political sensibility. Although *Hamletmachine* was completed in 1977, its conceptual framework was rooted in yet another major European geopolitical event, the 1956 Hungarian Revolution. As a liberal Socialist, Müller was appalled by the excesses of the Soviet Communist regime. The combination, therefore, of the sociopolitical and economic ramifications of his Eastern European experience, together with a unique and distinct theatrical imagination, influenced the meticulous crafting of *Hamletmachine*.

When asked to define the essence of his theatrical *mise en scène*, Müller stated, "I have no message, I just want conflicts, even between the audience and the text." This six-page manuscript, in five fragments, is a complex, nonlinear assemblage of epic-like settings, scattered dialogue, narrative passages, and stage directions bathed in Artaudian effects:

> *The university of the dead. Whispering and muttering. From their gravestones (lecterns), the dead philosophers throw their books at Hamlet. Gallery (ballet) of dead women. The woman dangling from the rope. The woman with her arteries cut open, etc. . . .*

Müller's disregard for anything naturalistic in the areas of dramatic writing, acting, and stage images propelled him to construct a *montage* of tightly woven sequences, depicting the plight of the easily identified Western tragic character, as a metaphor for the illnesses inherited by our Westernized condition. But in *Hamletmachine*, gone are the traits of classical tragedy where formal and moral order is shattered by the actions of a sole individual. In Müller's cosmology, we as citizens of the world are communally responsible for our own destruction, for in the current era there are no cosmic sanctions left. Instead, we have become "products" of an industrialized, mechanized society in which value systems are based on sheer quantity, speed, and the knowledge that we can annihilate an entire civilization in the twinkling of an eye. In fact, in Fragment 4 the narrative, as uttered by The Actor Playing Hamlet, exemplifies Müller's view that we have forged our destiny by allowing our identities to be manipulated by the forces of political control. Müller sees the process of history as a repetitive pattern of violence and chaos, while simultaneously suggesting that our cultural traditions have been appropriated by the banalities of a frivolous existence (review his comments about Disney's *Fantasia* in the biography above).

Müller's scenic descriptions mirror his intellectual vision of a world in constant flux; they become signifiers, collapsing the past, present, and future into one collective reality. His stage directions are often not directions at all but rather a guide, a map for the director to interpret according to her or his own vision and understanding of the work. While in rehearsal for his 1986 production of *Hamletmachine* at New York University, Robert Wilson, the iconoclastic American director (see Showcase, "From *The Theater of Images*"), made a decision not to stage some of the vivid stage directions found in the actual script, while choosing instead to have the actor speak such descriptions as lines of dialogue. When asked why he accepted Wilson's directorial interpretation, Müller swiftly replied, "Why should he do the stage directions? It's in the text." As Müller's drama blends factual life occurrences with excerpts from the Shakespearean text and narratives borrowed from statements uttered by contemporary populace, his dramatic characters are a mixture of spoken dialogue, textual descriptions, and directions, embodied by Müller's outlandish, epic settings. The characters, therefore, are only microscopic entities in the ebb and flow of historical continuity, to be reinterpreted by the hands of the stage director; Wilson's meticulously precise 1986 Obie Award–winning production lasted two-and-a-half hours.

If Müller is often regarded as the most prominent German playwright since Brecht, perhaps it is safe to assume that Müller brought a twenty-first-century postmodernist sensibility to the theater of the West, as Georg Buchner's dramatic works ushered in twentieth-century modernism. Like Shakespeare, Müller was a visionary with an insightful understanding of the human condition. When asked in the 1980s where he would prefer to stage or witness the production of his plays, Müller replied, "I would like to stage *Macbeth* on top of the World Trade Center for an audience in helicopters." In the writing of *Hamletmachine*, even Müller's preoccupation with terrorism could never anticipate the horrific events of September 11, 2001, as his imaginary playing space for a play about ambition was obliterated by a terrorist act never before experienced in the history of the United States.

Other perspectives on *Hamletmachine*:

Blau, Herbert. "Ideology and Performance." *Theatre Journal* 35:4 (1983): 441–60.

Zurbrugg, Nicholas. "Post-Modern and the Multi-Media Sensibility: Heiner Müller's *Hamletmachine* and the Art of Robert Wilson." *Modern Drama* 31:3 (1988): 439–53.

SHOWCASE   FROM *THE THEATRE OF IMAGES*

by Bonnie Marranca

Bonnie Marranca is among the foremost chroniclers of contemporary theater trends; she has written numerous books and articles on the principal trendsetters in the theater of the 1980s and 1990s. In this introduction to her book, The Theatre of Images, *she summarizes the shift to a visual, less verbal theater as created by Robert Wilson, Richard Foreman, and Lee Breuer.*

In the last dozen years the American avant-garde theater has emerged as a dynamic voice in the international arts scene. From its crude beginnings in out-of-the-way lofts, churches, private clubs and renovated spaces, it has become for many the liveliest, most creative center of theatrical activity in the West. This is due partly to the help of grant monies, but primarily to the emergence of a number of highly imaginative and gifted theater artists.

Experimental groups of the sixties and early seventies broke down traditional parameters of theatrical experience by introducing new approaches to acting, playwriting and the creation of theatrical environments; they reorganized audience and performing space relationships, and eliminated dialogue from drama. Collaborative creation became the rule.

Value came increasingly to be placed on performance with the result that the new theater never became a literary theater, but one dominated by images—visual and aural. This is the single most important feature of contemporary American theater, and it is characteristic of the works of groups *and* playwrights. As early as eight years ago Richard Kostelanetz pointed out the non-literary character of the American theater when he wrote in *The Theatre of Mixed Means:*

. . . the new theatre contributes to the contemporary cultural revolt against the predominance of the word; for it is definitely a theatre for a post-literate (which is not the same as illiterate) age. . . .[1]

If this theatre refused to believe in the supremacy of language as a critique of reality, it offered a multiplicity of images in its place. Kostelanetz's McLuhanesque statement clarifies the direction that the American theater has steadily followed since the Happenings. It has now culminated in a Theater of Images—the generic term I have chosen to define a particular style of the American avant-garde which is represented here by Richard Foreman (Ontological-Hysteric Theater), Robert Wilson (Byrd Hoffman School of Byrds) and Lee Breuer (Mabou Mines).

The works of Foreman, Wilson and Breuer represent the climactic point of a movement in the American avant-garde that extends from The Living Theatre, The Open Theatre, The Performance Group, The Manhattan Project and the Iowa Theatre Lab, to the "show and tell" styles of political groups like El Teatro Campesino, The San Francisco Mime Troupe and The Bread and Puppet Theatre. (And it is continued in the current proliferation of art-performances.) Today it is demonstrated in the image-oriented Structuralist Workshop of Michael Kirby and in the works of younger artists: *Sakonnet Point* by Spalding Gray and Elizabeth LeCompte; the "spectacles" of Stuart Sherman. All of the productions and groups mentioned above exclude dialogue or use words minimally in favor of aural, visual and verbal imagery that calls for alternative modes of perception on the part of the audience. This break from a theatrical structure founded on dialogue marks a watershed

in the history of American theatre, a *rite de passage.*

The intention of this [essay] is to demonstrate the significance of the Theatre of Images, its derivation from theatrical and non-theatrical sources, its distinctively American roots in the avant-garde, its embodiment of a certain contemporary sensibility and its impact on audiences.

This essay, which first isolates characteristics of the Theatre of Images, and then deals at length with the specific pieces published here, will perhaps suggest an attitude to bring to this theatre. Hopefully, it will also offer helpful, new tools of analysis—an alternative critical vocabulary—with which to view contemporary theatre.

The absence of dialogue leads to the predominance of the stage picture in the Theatre of Images. This voids all considerations of theatre as it is conventionally understood in terms of plot, character, setting, language and movement. Actors do not create "roles." They function instead as media through which the playwright expresses his ideas; they serve as icons and images. Text is merely a pretext—a scenario.

The texts as published here (less so in the case of *The Red Horse Animation* which offers a comic book as a textual alternative) remain incomplete documents of a theatre that must be seen to be understood; one cannot talk about the works of Foreman, Wilson and Breuer without talking about their productions. Attending a theatrical performance is always an experience apart

---

[1]Richard Kostelanetz, *Theatre of Mixed Means* (N.Y.: Dial Press, 1968), p. 33.

from reading a dramatic text; but a playscript *does* generally stand on its own merits as a pleasurable experience, indicating what it is about and usually giving a clue as to how it is staged. Conversely, reading Wilson's *A Letter for Queen Victoria* can be frustrating for readers attuned to theme, character, story, genre and logical language structure. There is scarcely a clue to its presentation in a script composed of bits and pieces of overheard conversations, television and films. Similarly, in Foreman's work, which insists on demonstrating what the words say (in Wittgensteinian-styled language games), to read the text alone is to lose the sensual delight and intellectual exchange of his theatre. And *The Red Horse Animation* is not a play at all.

Just as the Happenings had no immediate theatrical antecedents, the Theatre of Images, though not quite so renegade, has developed aesthetically from numerous non-theatrical roots. This is not to say that this movement disregards theatrical practices of the past: It is the application of them that makes the difference. More directly, the avant-garde must use the past in order to create a dialogue with it.

Foreman's work shows the influence (and the radicalization) of Brechtian technique; Breuer has acknowledged his attempt to synthesize the acting theories of Stanislavsky, Brecht and Grotowski; the productions of Wilson descend from Wagner. However, in their work, spatial, temporal and linguistic concepts are non-theatrically conditioned. Extra-theatrical influences have had a more formative impact. Cagean aesthetics, new dance, popular cultural forms, painting, sculpture and the cinema are important forces that have shaped the Theatre of Images. It is also logical that America, a highly technological society dominated by aural and visual stimuli, should produce this kind of theatre created, almost exclusively, by a generation of artists who grew up with television and movies.

The proliferation of images, ideas and forms availaible to the artist in such a culture leads to a crisis in the artist's choice of creative materials, and in his relationship to the art object. It is not suprising, then, that all of the pieces collected here are metatheatrical: They are about the making of art. In *Pandering to the Masses: A Misrepresentation* Foreman speaks directly to the audience (on tape) concerning the "correct" interpretation of events *as they occur*. The actors relate the formal "Outline" of the production at intervals in *Red Horse*. The result is a high degree of focus on process. How one sees is as important as what one sees.

This focus on process—the producedness, or seams-showing quality of a work—is an attempt to make the audience more conscious of events in the theatre than they are accustomed to. It is the idea of *being there* in the theatre that is the impulse behind Foreman's emphasis on immediacy in the relationship of the audience to the theatrical event.

The importance given to consciousness in the Theatre of Images is also manifest in its use of individual psychologies: Foreman in his psychology of art; Wilson in his collaboration with Christopher Knowles, an autistic teenager whose personal psychology is used as creative material (not as a psychology of the disturbed); and in Breuer's interest in motivational acting. In *Pandering*, life and theatre merge as Foreman incorporates his thoughts into the written text. In *Queen Victoria*, Wilson adapts, if only partially, autistic behavior as an alternative, positive mode of perceiving life. Through Breuer's use of interior monologue, the consciousness of the Horse is explored in *Red Horse*.

Each artist refrains from developing character in a predictable, narrative framework which would evoke conditioned patterns of intellectual and emotional response. Like all modernist experiments, which necessarily suggest a new way to perceive familiar objects and events, their works agitate for radical, alternative modes of perception.

In the Theatre of Images the painterly and sculptural qualities of performance are stressed, transforming this theatre into a spatially dominated one activated by sense impressions, as opposed to a time-dominated one ruled by linear narrative. Like modern painting, the Theatre of Images is timeless (*Queen Victoria* could easily be expanded or contracted), abstract and presentational (in *Red Horse*, images are both abstract and anthropomorphic), often static (the principle of duration rules the work of Foreman and Wilson); frequently the stage picture is framed two-dimensionally (in *Pandering* the actors are often poised in frontal positions). Objects are dematerialized, functioning in their natural rhythmic context. The body of the actor is malleable and pictorial—like the three actors who form multiple images of an Arabian steed lying *on* the performing space (*Red Horse*). It is flattening of the image (stage picture) that characterizes the Theatre of Images, just as it does modern painting.

If the acting is pictorial, it's also nonvirtuosic, an inheritance from the new dance which emphasizes natural movement. This is an aesthetic quality of the particular branch of the avant-garde dealt with here. What I wish to suggest is that the Theatre of Images in performance demonstrates a radical refunctioning of naturalism. It uses the performer's natural, individual movements as a starting point in production. Of the artists featured in this anthology, Foreman is the most thoroughly naturalistic. He allows performers (untrained) a personal freedom of expression while at the same time making them appear highly stylized in slow-motion, speeded-up, noninflectional patterns of speech or movement. He also pays a great deal of attention to actual situation and detail and the factor of time. Foreman's work is stylized yet naturalistic as are Alain Resnais's *Last Year at Marienbad* and Marguerite Duras's *India Song*.

The naturalism of nontraditional theatre is a curious phenomenon but one worth paying attention to because of its prevalence and diversity; it is also quite a paradox to admit that the avant-garde, in 1976, is naturalistic. In addition to being characteristic of the scripts printed here, it has shown itself in the production of David Gaard's *The Marilyn Project* directed last year by Richard Schechner, in Scott Burton's recent art-performance *Pair Behavior Tableaux*, as well as in Peter Handke's play without words, *My Foot My Tutor*. In these works there is a high degree of stylization by performers who "naturally" engage in an activity which is presented pictorially.

623

Perhaps that is why, in the Theatre of Images, tableau is so often the chief unit of composition. Tableau, in fact, has been a dominant structure in the work of twentieth-century innovators: the Cubists, Gertrude Stein, Bertolt Brecht, Jean-Luc Godard, Alain Robbe-Grillet, Philip Glass, to name a few. It is evident in the work of Foreman, Wilson and Breuer as well. Tableau has the multiple function of compelling the spectator to analyze its specific placement in the artistic framework, stopping time by throwing a scene into relief, expanding time and framing scenes. In *Pandering*, the tableaux function as objects in a cubist space, very often confusing perception by the intrusion of a single kinetic element. The cinematic "cuts" of *Red Horse* frequently focus the actors in close-up; "frames" are duplicated in the actual comic book documentation of the performance.

The stillness of tableau sequences suspends time, causing the eye to focus on an image, and slows down the process of input. This increases the critical activity of the mind. For Foreman it represents the ideal moment to impart taped directives to the audience; it also regulates the dialectical interplay of word and image.

Neither time nor space are bound by conventional law. Time is slowed-down, speeded up—experienced as duration. It is never clocked time. Likewise, spatial readjustment is frequent in all of the pieces published here. *Red Horse* is played in multiple viewing perspectives: The actors perform both lying on the floor and standing on it, and up against a back wall of the performing space. *Pandering* alternates easily from flat perspective to linear perspective; the actors continually rearrange the drapes and flats of the set during performance. In *Queen Victoria* space is divided, cut apart and blackened—usually by means of light—leaving the actors to serve as images or silhouettes in a surreal landscape.

If time and space are dysynchronous in the Theatre of Images, so is language broken apart and disordered. The language of *Queen Victoria* is "throw-away," devoid of content. In *Red Horse* choral narrative is correlated with the image in space as interior monologue substitutes for dialogue. *Pandering* is ruled by the distributive principle of sound: Actors speak parts of sentences which are completed either by other actors or Foreman's voice on tape.

Sound is used sculpturally, just as the actors are. Aural tableaux complement or work dialectically with visual tableaux. In *Pandering* the audience, surrounded by stereo speakers, is bombarded with sound. Sound and visual images dominate in performance in an attempt to expand normal capabilities for experiencing sense stimuli. Because of the sophisticated sound equipment used in the productions of Foreman, Wilson and Breuer it is reasonable to conclude that the Theatre of Images would not exist without the benefit of advanced technology. Perhaps experiments with holography may lead in the future to a theatre of total images and recorded sound.

The significance of the Theatre of Images is its expansion of the audience's capacity to perceive. It is a theatre devoted to the creation of a new stage language, a visual grammar "written" in sophisticated perceptual codes. To break these codes is to enter the refined sensual worlds this theatre offers. . . .

FEFU AND HER FRIENDS

MARIA IRENE FORNES

Artistic, Cultural, and Historical Events

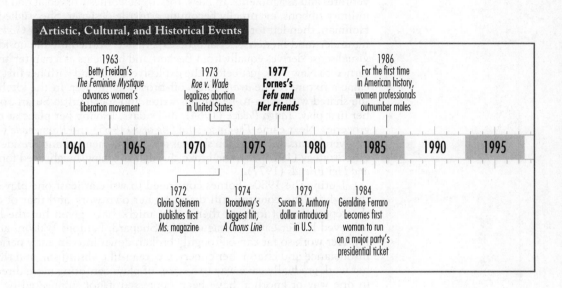

1963
Betty Freidan's
The Feminine Mystique
advances women's
liberation movement

1973
Roe v. Wade
legalizes abortion
in United States

**1977
Fornes's
*Fefu and
Her Friends***

1986
For the first time
in American history,
women professionals
outnumber males

| 1960 | 1965 | 1970 | 1975 | 1980 | 1985 | 1990 | 1995 |

1972
Gloria Steinem
publishes first
Ms. magazine

1974
Broadway's
biggest hit,
A Chorus Line

1979
Susan B. Anthony
dollar introduced
in U.S.

1984
Geraldine Ferraro
becomes first
woman to run
on a major party's
presidential ticket

MARIA IRENE FORNES (1930–)

Alone among the off-Broadway playwrights who came to prominence in the 1960s, Maria Irene Fornes has retained her bohemian credentials, her joyous taste for radical transformations of style and content. Because her work resists formal and generic classification, Fornes is also America's most significant under-produced playwright. Pulitzer-winner Tony Kushner contends that "America has produced no dramatist of greater importance than Maria Irene Fornes," ranking her with Edward Albee, with the late Heiner Müller of Germany, and with England's Caryl Churchill. Scores of playwrights such as Cherrie Moraga and Eduardo Machado, many of whom were her students at the Padua Hills Playwrights Festival outside Los Angeles or at the International Arts Relations (INTAR) Hispanic Theater Project in New York, acknowledge Fornes's profound influence. *Angels in America* author Kushner wrote in the anthology *Conducting a Life* that Fornes altered "my understanding of what theater is, what it aims at accomplishing, what it may demand of its audiences . . . and the role that beauty plays in the political, redemptive, transformative power of art."

Fornes's plays mix Realism, Absurdism, and Surrealism, shifting planes of perception and moving across social classes and time periods, as she focuses on those moments when characters reveal themselves coming into themselves or on what Ross Wetzsteon calls "the psychological pivot" of a relationship rather than on its causes or consequences. Fornes often directs her own work, as she did a ravishing and romantic *Abingdon Square* at the San Diego Repertory Theatre in 1992, employing her matchless pictorial sense to make each image and grouping evocative as in a meticulously composed painting. The tenderness and lyricism that infuse even her darkest works are unusual in contemporary drama. Unabashedly intimate as well, her plays stand in a complex relationship to feminism, for Fornes creates women—and men—characters who are truly subjects, not mouthpieces. Bonnie Marranca writes of Fornes's *Mud* (1984) that her work is "imbued with a feminism of the most subtle order, an understanding based on the idea that a free woman is one who has autonomy of thought."

Fornes was born in 1930 in Havana, Cuba, to a poor and artistically colorful family. She was educated only through the sixth grade and came to the United States in 1945 with her widowed mother, Carmen, who accompanied her daughter on many of her adventures and assignments. In New York Irene Fornes worked at odd jobs, making dolls and military ribbons, eventually becoming a textile designer. She studied painting with Hans Hoffman, then left for Paris, where she saw Beckett's *Waiting for Godot*. Although she didn't understand French, she said the experience "turned my life upside down." Her strong visual sense derives equally from Beckett and her years as a painter and movie fan. She returned to New York just before the explosive 1960s and with her first few plays quickly became a fixture in the *avant-garde*, off-Broadway theater. In the kitchen of the apartment she shared with soon-to-be-famous writer and social critic Susan Sontag, Fornes penned her first play, *Tango Palace* (1964), in 19 days, leaving her place at the table only to buy groceries. Next came *The Successful Life of 3* (1965) and *Promenade* (1967). After a hiatus of several years during which she was a founding member and president of New York Theatre Strategy (1973–78), she broke through to a new, heightened form of Realism in *Fefu and Her Friends* (1977).

During the 1980s, Fornes continued to write at least one play a year, still teaching throughout the country, still directing her own work and that of others, still resisting the repetitions of form or theme that might have given her the higher-profile career achieved by her early colleagues Sam Shepard, Lanford Wilson, and Terrence McNallay. Her work so far can be roughly broken down into an early period during which her insouciance and charm, her cheery, Cocteau-like absurdism, and the wry dark humor of her work gradually gave way to a series of plays centering more directly on women who, in one way or another, have been oppressed if not subjugated by civilization and the male attitudes that shape it. *Fefu and Her Friends*, her New York–set Latina play-with-music *Sarita* (1984), her lower-depths *Mud* (1983), and the Latin America–set *The Conduct of Life* (1985) all deal with women—whether from the upper or lower classes—who have been unable to think and therefore to act, to *be* fully themselves. Many of her plays since the late 1980s have been more epic in scope. Her *Terra Incognita* (1992) proved an ironic contribution to the 500th anniversary of Columbus's "discovery" of the New World, as Fornes layered the conversation of a man and women in a café over the voice of a man at a nearby table reading from a missionary's horrific report of torture by the Spanish invaders.

A Latina and a lesbian, Fornes cannot be pigeonholed politically any more than she can be artistically. Though almost documentary in their starkness, the emotional richness and complexity of her best dramas derive from their emphasis on the sensual and imagistic rather than on intellectual argument, as we see real bodies and carefully selected objects bump up against one another in theatrical space. During the famed Angry Arts Week in downtown New York in 1967, for instance, while other artists created shrill or satiric works directly protesting the Vietnam War, Fornes contributed *A Vietnamese Wedding*. Four members of the audience played the bride and groom and their parents, while four actors guided them through rituals with symbolic objects related to Southeast Asian myths; Fornes directed the actors to be "casual, gracious, unobtrusive." Tender empathy, not rhetorical argument, became the agent of enlightenment for the audience. That tenderness and grace reappear in unexpected dramatic, often domestic contexts, becoming one strong unifying element in Fornes's shape-shifting dramatic world.

AS YOU READ *FEFU AND HER FRIENDS*

One of Fornes's best-known works, *Fefu and Her Friends* (pronounced Feh-foo) is set in the mid-1930s and presents a first image of three women who call to mind the leisured women of Chekhov's *Three Sisters*. From the immediate openness of their conversation about women's "loathsomeness," we know that the play will be concerned with women's issues, with how they think they are viewed by men, how they talk together, how they eat and dress, how they empower or thwart one another, as they reunite to prepare a theatrically staged fundraiser for an educational cause. One aspect of the play's originality is the site-specific nature of the writing and dramaturgy, especially for Part II. Here, the audience divides into four groups, each visiting a different setting as the characters dissolve into smaller units and carry on their conversations (or monologues) in the kitchen, the bedroom, the study, or, in the case of Emma and Fefu, outdoors. The audience then reassembles in the main auditorium as the eight characters come together to rehearse for their fundraiser. Another startling element is the character Julia, a woman who was mysteriously "shot" when a nearby deer was hunted and killed; she took on the bleeding bullet hole, a kind of stigmata she displays from her wheelchair. The ending of the play repeats this kind of surreal event, though in a different key. As you hear Julia's hallucinated speeches and watch her interact with Fefu, try to imagine her wound and her death-haunted pain without reducing it to a single simple interpretation.

FEFU AND HER FRIENDS

MARIA IRENE FORNES

CHARACTERS
FEFU
CINDY
CHRISTINA
JULIA
EMMA
PAULA
SUE
CECILIA

New England, Spring 1935.

Part I: Noon. The living room. The entire audience watches from the main auditorium.

Part II: Afternoon. The lawn, the study, the bedroom, the kitchen. The audience is divided into four groups. Each group is led to the spaces. These scenes are performed simultaneously. When the scenes are completed the audience moves to the next space and the scenes are performed again. This is repeated four times until each group has seen all four scenes. Then the audience is led back to the main auditorium.

Part III: Evening. The living room. The entire audience watches from the main auditorium.

Author's Note: Fefu is pronounced Feh-foo.

PART I

The living room of a country house in New England. The decor is a tasteful mixture of styles. To the right is the foyer and the main door. To the left, French doors leading to a terrace, the lawn and a pond. At the rear, there are stairs that lead to the upper floor, the entrance to the kitchen, and the entrance to other rooms on the ground floor. A couch faces the audience. There is a coffee table, two chairs on each side of the table. Upstage right there is a piano. Against the right wall there is an open liquor cabinet. Besides bottles of liquor there are glasses, an ice bucket, and a seltzer bottle. A double barrel shotgun leans on the wall near the French doors. On the table there is a dish with chocolates. On the couch there is a throw. Fefu stands on the landing. Cindy lies on the couch. Christina sits on the chair to the right.

FEFU. My husband married me to have a constant reminder of how loathsome women are.
CINDY. What?
FEFU. Yup.
CINDY. That's just awful.
FEFU. No, it isn't.
CINDY. It isn't awful?
FEFU. No.
CINDY. I don't think anyone would marry for that reason.
FEFU. He did.
CINDY. Did he say so?
FEFU. He tells me constantly.
CINDY. Oh, dear.
FEFU. I don't mind. I laugh when he tells me.
CINDY. You laugh?
FEFU. I do.
CINDY. How can you?
FEFU. It's funny.—And it's true. That's why I laugh.
CINDY. What is true?
FEFU. That women are loathsome.
CINDY. . . . . Fefu!
FEFU. That shocks you.
CINDY. It does. I don't feel loathsome.
FEFU. I don't mean that you're loathsome.
CINDY. You don't mean that I'm loathsome.

FEFU. No . . . It's something to think about. It's a thought.
CINDY. It's a hideous thought.
FEFU. I take it all back.
CINDY. Isn't she incredible?
FEFU. Cindy, I'm not talking about anyone in particular. It's something to think about.
CINDY. No one in particular, just women.
FEFU. Yes.
CINDY. In that case I am relieved. I thought you were referring to us.
FEFU (*Affectionately*). You are being stupid.
CINDY. Stupid and loathsome. (*To Christina*). Have you ever heard anything so outrageous.
CHRISTINA. I am speechless.
FEFU. Why are you speechless?
CHRISTINA. I think you are outrageous.
FEFU. Don't be offended. I don't take enough care to be tactful. I know I don't. But don't be offended. Cindy is not offended. She pretends to be, but she isn't really. She understands what I mean.
CINDY. I do not.
FEFU. Yes, you do.—I like exciting ideas. They give me energy.
CHRISTINA. And how is women being loathsome an exciting idea?
FEFU (*With mischief*). It revolts me.
CHRISTINA. You find revulsion exciting?
FEFU. Don't you?
CHRISTINA. No.
FEFU. I do. It's something to grapple with.—What do you do with revulsion?
Christina; I avoid anything that's revolting to me.
FEFU. Hmmm. (*To Cindy*). You too?
CINDY. Yes.
FEFU. Hmm. Have you ever turned a stone over in damp soil?
CHRISTINA. Ahm.
FEFU. And when you turn it there are worms crawling on it?
CHRISTINA. Ahm.
FEFU. And it's damp and full of fungus?
CHRISTINA. Ahm.
FEFU. Were you revolted?
CHRISTINA. Yes.
FEFU. Were you fascinated?
CHRISTINA. I was.
FEFU. There you have it! You too are fascinated with revulsion.
CHRISTINA. Hmm.
FEFU. You see, that which is exposed to the exterior . . . is smooth and dry and clean. That which is not . . . underneath, is slimy and filled with fungus and crawling with worms. It is another life that is parallel to the one we manifest. It's there. the way worms are underneath the stone. If you don't recognize it . . . (*Whispering.*) it eats you. That is my opinion. Well, who is ready for lunch?
CINDY. I'll have some fried worms with lots of pepper.
FEFU (*To Christina*). You?
CHRISTINA. I'll have mine in a sandwich with mayonnaise.
FEFU. And to drink?
CHRISTINA. Just some dirty dishwater in a tall glass with ice.

(*Fefu looks at Cindy.*)

CINDY. That sounds fine.
FEFU. I'll go dig them up. (*Fefu walks to the French doors. Beckoning Christina.*) Pst! (*Fefu gets the gun as Christina goes to the French doors.*) You haven't met Phillip. Have you?
CHRISTINA. No.
FEFU. That's him.
CHRISTINA. Which one?
FEFU (*Aims and shoots*). That one!

(*Christina and Cindy scream. Fefu smiles proudly. She blows on the mouth of the barrel. She puts down the gun and looks out again.*)

CINDY. Christ, Fefu.
FEFU. There he goes. He's up. It's a game we play. I shoot and he falls. Whenever he hears the blast he falls. No matter where he is, he falls. One time he fell in a puddle of mud and his clothes were a mess. (*She looks out.*) It's not too bad. He's just dusting off some stuff. (*She waves to Phillip and starts to go upstairs.*) He's all right. Look.
CINDY. A drink?
CHRISTINA. Yes.

(*Cindy goes to the liquor cabinet.*)

CINDY. What would you like?
CHRISTINA. Bourbon and soda . . . (*Cindy puts ice and bourbon in a glass. As she starts to squirt the soda . . .*) lots of soda. Just soda. (*Cindy starts with a fresh glass. She starts to squirt soda just as Christina speaks.*) Wait. (*Cindy stops squirting, but not soon enough.*) I'll have an ice cube with a few drops of bourbon. (*Cindy starts with a fresh glass.*)
CINDY. One or two ice cubes?
CHRISTINA. One. Something to suck on.
CINDY. She's unique. There's no one like her.
CHRISTINA. Thank God.

(*Cindy gives the drink to Christina.*)

CINDY. But she is lovely you know. She really is.

CHRISTINA. She's crazy.

CINDY. A little. She has a strange marriage.

CHRISTINA. Strange? It's revolting.—What is he like?

CINDY. He's crazy too. They drive each other crazy. They are not crazy really. They drive each other crazy.

CHRISTINA. Why do they stay together?

CINDY. They love each other.

CHRISTINA. Love?

CINDY. It's love.

CHRISTINA. Who are the other two men?

CINDY. Fefu's younger brother, John. And the gardener. His name is Tom.—The gun is not loaded.

CHRISTINA. How do you know?

CINDY. It's not. Why should it be loaded?

CHRISTINA. It seemed to be loaded a moment ago.

CINDY. That was just a blank.

CHRISTINA. It sounded like a cannon shot.

CINDY. That was just gun powder. There's no bullet in a blank.

CHRISTINA. The blast alone could kill you. One can die of fright, you know.

CINDY. True.

CHRISTINA. My heart is still beating.

CINDY. That's just fright. You're being a scaredy cat.

CHRISTINA. Of course it's just fright. It's fright.

CINDY. I mean, you were just scared. You didn't get hurt.

CHRISTINA. Just scared. I guess I was lucky I didn't get shot.

CINDY. Fefu won't shoot you. She only shoots Phillip.

CHRISTINA. That's nice of her. Put the gun away, I don't like looking at it.

FEFU (As she appears on the landing). I just fixed the toilet in your bathroom.

CINDY. You did?

FEFU. I did. The water stopper didn't work. It drained. I adjusted it. I'm waiting for the tank to fill up. Make sure it all works.

CHRISTINA. You do your own plumbing?

FEFU. I just had to bend the metal that supports the rubber stopper so it falls right over the hole. What happened was it fell to the side so the water wouldn't stop running into the bowl. (Fefu sits near Cindy.) He scared me this time, you know. He looked like he was really hurt.

CINDY. I thought the guns were not loaded.

FEFU. I'm never sure.

CHRISTINA. What?

CINDY. Fefu, what do you mean?

FEFU. He told me one day he'll put real bullets in the guns. He likes to make me nervous. (There is a mo-ment's silence.) I have upset you . . . I don't mean to upset you. That's the way we are with each other. We always go to extremes but it's not anything to be upset about.

CHRISTINA. You scare me.

FEFU. That's all right. I scare myself too, sometimes. But there's nothing wrong with being scared . . . it makes you stronger.—It does me.—He won't put real bullets in the guns.—It suits our relationship . . . the game, I mean. If I didn't shoot him with blanks, I might shoot him for real. Do you see the sense of it?

CHRISTINA. I think you're crazy.

FEFU. I'm not. I'm sane.

CHRISTINA (Gently). You're very stupid.

FEFU. I'm not. I'm very bright.

CHRISTINA (Gently). You depress me.

FEFU. Don't be depressed. Laugh at me if you don't agree with me. Say I'm ridiculous. I know I'm ridiculous. Come on, laugh. I hate to think I'm depressing to you.

CHRISTINA. All right. I'll laugh.

FEFU. I'll make you a drink.

CHRISTINA. No, I'm just sucking on the ice.

FEFU. Don't you feel well?

CHRISTINA. I'm all right.

FEFU. What are you drinking?

CHRISTINA. Bourbon.

FEFU (Getting Christina's glass and going to the liquor cabinet). Would you like some more? I'll get you some.

CHRISTINA. Just a drop.

FEFU (With great care pours a single drop of bourbon on the ice cube). Like that?

CHRISTINA. Yes, thank you.

FEFU (Gives Christina the drink and watches her put the cube to her lips). That's the cutest thing I've ever seen. It's cold. (Christina nods.) You need a stick in the ice, like a popsicle stick. You hold the stick and your fingers won't get cold. I have some sticks. I'll do some for you.

CHRISTINA. Don't trouble yourself.

FEFU. It won't be any trouble. You might want some later.—I'm strange, Christina. But I am fortunate in that I don't mind being strange. It's hard on others sometimes. But not that hard. Is it, Cindy? Those who love me, love me precisely because I am the way I am. (To Cindy.) Isn't that so? (Cindy smiles and nods.)

CINDY. I would love you even if you weren't the way you are.

FEFU. You wouldn't know it was me if I weren't the way I am.

CINDY. I would still know it was you underneath.
FEFU (*To Christina*). You see?—There are some good things about me.—I'm never angry, for example.
CHRISTINA. But you make everyone else angry.

(*Fefu thinks a moment.*)

FEFU. No.
CHRISTINA. You've made me furious.
FEFU. I know. And I might make you angry again. Still I would like it if you liked me.—You think it's unlikely.
CHRISTINA. I don't know.
FEFU. . . . We'll see. (*Fefu goes to the doors. She stands there briefly and speaks reflectively.*) I still like men better than women.—I envy them. I like being like a man. Thinking like a man. Feeling like a man.—They are well together. Women are not. Look at them. They are checking the new grass mower. . . . Out in the fresh air and the sun, while we sit here in the dark. . . . Men have natural strength. Women have to find their strength, and when they do find it, it comes forth with bitterness and it's erratic. . . . Women are restless with each other. They are like live wires . . . either chattering to keep themselves from making contact, or else, if they don't chatter, they avert their eyes . . . like Orpheus . . . as if a god once said "and if they shall recognize each other, the world will be blown apart." They are always eager for the men to arrive. When they do, they can put themselves at rest, tranquilized and in a mild stupor. With the men they feel safe. The danger is gone. That's the closest they can be to feeling wholesome. Men are muscle that cover the raw nerve. They are the insulators. The danger is gone, but the price is the mind and the spirit. . . . High price.—I've never understood it. Why?—What is feared?—Hmm. Well . . .—Do you know? Perhaps the heavens would fall.—Have I offended you again?
CHRISTINA. No. I too have wished for that trust men have for each other. The faith the world puts in them and they in turn put in the world. I know I don't have it.
FEFU. Hmm. Well, I have to see how my toilet is doing.
(*Fefu goes to the landing and exits. She puts her head out. She smiles.*) Plumbing is more important than you think.

(*Christina falls off her chair in a mock faint. Cindy goes to her.*)

CINDY. What do you think?
CHRISTINA. Think? I hurt. I'm all shreds inside.
CINDY. Anything I can do?
CHRISTINA. Sing.

(*Cindy sings "Winter Wonderland." Christina harmonizes. There is the sound of a horn. Fefu enters.*)

FEFU. It's Julia. (*To Christina, who is on the floor.*) Are you all right?
CHRISTINA. Yes. (*Fefu exits through the foyer.*) Darn it!
(*Christina starts to stand.*)
FEFU (*Off-stage*). Julia . . . let me help you.
JULIA. I can manage. I'm much stronger now.
FEFU. There you go.
JULIA. You have my bag.
FEFU. Yes.

(*Julia and Fefu enter. Julia is in a wheelchair.*)

JULIA. Hello Cindy.
CINDY. Hello darling. How are you?
JULIA. I'm very well now. I'm driving now. You must see my car. It's very clever the way they worked it all out. You might want to drive it. It's not hard at all. (*Turning to Christina.*) Christina.
CHRISTINA. Hello Julia.
JULIA. I'm glad to see you.
FEFU. I'll take this to your room. You're down here, if you want to wash up.

(*Fefu exits through the upstage exit. Julia follows her.*)

CINDY. I can't get used to it.
CHRISTINA. She's better. Isn't she?
CINDY. Not really.
CHRISTINA. Was she actually hit by the bullet?
CINDY. No . . . I was with her.
CHRISTINA. I know.
CINDY. I thought the bullet hit her, but it didn't.—How do you know if a person is hit by a bullet?
CHRISTINA. Cindy . . . there's a wound and . . . there's a bullet.
CINDY. Well, the hunter aimed . . . at the deer. He shot.
CHRISTINA. He?
CINDY. Yes.
CHRISTINA (*Pointing in the direction of Fefu*). It wasn't? . . .
CINDY. Fefu? . . . No. She wasn't even there. She used to hunt but she doesn't hunt any more. She loves animals.
CHRISTINA. Go on.
CINDY. He shot. Julia and the deer fell. The deer was dead . . . dying. Julia was unconscious. She had convulsions . . . like the deer. He died and she didn't. I screamed for help and the hunter came and examined Julia. He said, "She is not hurt." Julia's forehead was bleeding. He said, "It is a surface wound. I didn't

hurt her." I know it wasn't he who hurt her. It was someone else. He went for help and Julia started talking. She was delirious.—Apparently there was a spinal nerve injury. She hit her head and she suffered a concussion. She blanks out and that is caused by the blow on the head. It's a scar in the brain. It's called the petit mal.

(*Fefu enters.*)

CHRISTINA. What was it she said?
CINDY. Hmm? . . .
CHRISTINA. When she was delirious.
CINDY. When she was delirious? That she was persecuted.—That they tortured her. . . . That they had tried her and that the shot was her execution. That she recanted because she wanted to live. . . . That if she talked about it . . . to anyone . . . she would be tortured further and killed. And I have not mentioned this before because . . . I fear for her.
CHRISTINA. It doesn't make any sense, Cindy.
CINDY. It makes sense to me. You heard? (*Fefu goes to Cindy and holds her.*)
FEFU. Who hurt her?
CINDY. I don't know.
FEFU (*To Christina*). Did you know her?
CHRISTINA. I met her once years ago.
FEFU. You remember her then as she was. . . . She was afraid of nothing. . . . Have you ever met anyone like that? . . . She knew so much. She was so young and yet she knew so much. . . . How did she learn all that? . . . (*To Cindy.*) Did you ever wonder? Well, I still haven't checked my toilet. Can you believe that. I still haven't checked it. (*Fefu goes upsairs.*)
CHRISTINA. How long ago was the accident?
CINDY. A year . . . a little over a year.
CHRISTINA. Is she in pain?
CINDY. I don't think so.
CHRISTINA. We are made of putty. Aren't we?

(*There is the sound of a car. Car doors opening and closing. A house window opening.*)

FEFU (*Off-stage*). Emma! What is that you're wearing. You look marvelous.
EMMA (*Off-stage*). I got it in Turkey.
FEFU. Hi Paula, Sue.
PAULA. Hi.
SUE. Hi.

(*Cindy goes out to greet them. Julia enters. She wheels herself to the downstage area.*)

FEFU. I'll be right down! Hey, my toilet works.

EMMA. Stephany. Mine does too.
FEFU. Don't be funny.
EMMA. Come down.

(*Fefu enters as Emma, Sue, and Paula enter. Emma and Fefu embrace.*)

FEFU. How are you?
EMMA. Good . . . good . . . good . . . (*Still embracing Fefu, Emma sees Julia.*) Julia! (*She runs to Julia and sits on her lap.*)
FEFU. Emma!
JULIA. It's all right.
EMMA. Take me for a ride. (*Julia wheels the chair in a circle. Emma waves as they ride.*) Hi, Cindy, Paula, Sue, Fefu.
JULIA. Do you know Christina?
EMMA. How do you do.
CHRISTINA. How do you do.
EMMA (*Pointing*). Sue . . . Paula . . .
SUE. Hello.
PAULA. Hello.
CHRISTINA. Hello.
PAULA (*To Fefu*). I liked your talk at Flossie Crit.
FEFU. Oh god, don't remind me. I thought I was awful. Come, I'll show you your rooms. (*She starts to go up.*)
PAULA. I thought you weren't. I found it very stimulating.
EMMA. When was that? . . . What was it on?
FEFU. Aviation.
PAULA. It wasn't on aviation. It was on Voltairine de Cleyre.
JULIA. I wish I had known.
FEFU. It wasn't important.
JULIA. I would have gone, Fefu.
FEFU. Really, it wasn't worth the trouble.
EMMA. Now you'll have to tell Julia and me all about Voltairine de Cleyre.
FEFU. You know all about Voltairine de Cleyre.
EMMA. I don't.
FEFU. I'll tell you at lunch.
EMMA. I had lunch.
JULIA. You can sit and listen while we eat.
EMMA. I will. When do we start our meeting?
FEFU. After lunch. We'll have something to eat and then we'll have our meeting. Who's ready for lunch?

(*The following lines are said almost simultaneously.*)

CINDY. I am.
JULIA. I'm not really hungry.
CHRISTINA. I could eat now.
PAULA. I'm ready.
SUE. I'd rather wait.

632

EMMA. I'll have coffee.

FEFU. . . . Well . . . we'll take a vote later.

CINDY. What are we doing exactly?

FEFU. About lunch?

CINDY. That too, but I meant the agenda.

SUE. Well, I thought we should first discuss what each of us is going to talk about, so we don't duplicate what someone else is saying, and then we have a review of it, a sort of rehearsal, so we know in what order we should speak and how long it's going to take.

EMMA. We should do a rehearsal in costume. What color should each wear. It matters. Do you know what you're wearing?

PAULA. I haven't thought about it. What color should I wear?

EMMA. Red.

PAULA. Red!

EMMA. Cherry red or white.

SUE. And I?

EMMA. Dark green.

CINDY. The treasurer should wear green.

EMMA. It suits her too.

SUE. And then we'll speak in order of color.

EMMA. Right. Who else wants to know? (*Cindy and Julia raise their hands. To Cindy.*) For you lavender. (*To Julia.*) Purpurra. (*Fefu raises her hand.*) For you, all the gold in Persia.

FEFU. There is no gold in Persia.

EMMA. In Peru. I brought my costume. I'll put it on later.

FEFU. You're not in costume?

EMMA. No. This is just a dress. My costume is . . . dramatic. I won't tell you any more about it. You'll see it.

SUE. I had no idea we were going to do theatre.

EMMA. Life is theatre. Theatre is life. If we're showing what life is, can be, we must do theatre.

SUE. Will I have to act?

EMMA. It's not acting. It's being. It's springing forth with the powers of the spirit. It's breathing.

JULIA. I'll do a dance.

EMMA. I'll stage a dance for you.

JULIA. Sitting?

EMMA. On a settee.

JULIA. I'm game.

EMMA (*Takes a deep breath and walks through the French doors*). Phillip! What are you doing?—Hello.—Hello, John.—What? I'm staging a dance for Julia!

FEFU. We'll never see her again.—Come.

(*Fefu, Paula, and Sue go upstairs. Julia goes to the gun, takes it and smells the mouth of the barrel. She looks at Cindy.*)

CINDY. It's a blank.

(*Julia takes the remaining slug out of the gun. She lets it fall on the floor.*)

JULIA. She's hurting herself. (*Julia looks blank and is motionless. Cindy picks up the slug. She notices Julia's condition.*)

CINDY. Julia. (*To Christina.*) She's absent.

CHRISTINA. What do we do?

CINDY. Nothing, she'll be all right in a moment. (*She takes the gun from Julia. Julia comes to.*)

JULIA. It's a blank . . .

CINDY. It is.

JULIA. She's hurting herself. (*Julia lets out a strange whimper. She goes to the coffee table, takes a piece of chocolate, puts it in her mouth and goes toward her room. After she crosses the threshold, she stops.*) I must lie down a while.

CINDY. Call me if you need anything.

JULIA. I will. (*She exits. Cindy tries to put the slug in the rifle. There is the sound of a car, a car door opening, closing.*)

CINDY. Do you know how to do this?

CHRISTINA. Of course not.

(*Cindy succeeds in putting the slug in the gun. Cecilia stands in the threshold of the foyer.*)

CECILIA. I am Cecilia Johnson. Do I have the right place?

CINDY. Yes.

(*Cindy locks the gun. Lights fade all around Cecilia. Only her head is lit. The light fades.*)

PART II

ON THE LAWN

There is a bench or a tree stump. Fefu and Emma bring boxes of potatoes, carrots, beets, winter squash, and other vegetables from a root cellar and put them in a small wagon. Fefu wears a hat and gardening gloves.

EMMA (*Re-enters carrying a box as Fefu exits*). Do you think about genitals all the time?

FEFU. Genitals? No, I don't think about genitals all the time.

EMMA (*Starting to exit*). I do, and it drives me crazy. Each person I see in the street, anywhere at all . . . I keep thinking of their genitals, what they look like, what position they are in. I think it's odd that everyone has them. Don't you?

FEFU (*Crossing Emma*). No, I think it'd be odder if they didn't have them.

(*Emma laughs. Fefu re-enters.*)

EMMA. I mean, people act as if they don't have genitals.

FEFU. How do people with genitals act?

EMMA. I mean, how can business men and women stand in a room and discuss business without even one reference to their genitals. I mean everybody has them. They just pretend they don't.

FEFU. I see. (*Shifting her glance from left to right with a fiendish look.*) You mean they should do this all the time.

(*Emma laughs.*)

EMMA. No, I don't mean that. Think of it. Don't you think I'm right?

FEFU. Yes, I think you're right. (*Fefu sits.*) Oh, Emma, EmmaEmmaEmma.

EMMA. That's m'name.—Well, you see, it's generally believed that you go to heaven if you are good. If you are bad you go to hell. That is correct. However, in heaven they don't judge goodness the way we think. They don't. They have a divine registry of sexual performance. In that registry they mark down every little sexual activity in your life. If your faith is not entirely in it, if you just perform as an obligation and you don't feel the most profound devotion, if your spirit, your heart, and your flesh is not religiously delivered to it, you are condemned. They put you down in the black list and you don't go to heaven. Heaven is populated with divine lovers. And in hell live the duds.

FEFU. That's probably true.

EMMA. I knew you'd see it that way.

FEFU. Oh, I do. I do. You see, on earth we are judged by public acts, and sex is a private act. The partner cannot be said to be the public, since both partners are engaged. So naturally, it stands to reason that it's angels who judge our sexual life.

EMMA. Naturally.

(*Pause.*)

FEFU. You always bring joy to me.

EMMA. Thank you.

FEFU. I thank you. (*Fefu becomes distressed. She sits.*) I am in constant pain. I don't want to give in to it. If I do I am afraid I will never recover. . . . It's not physical, and it's not sorrow. It's very strange Emma, I can't describe it, and it's very frightening. . . . It is as if normally there is a lubricant . . . not in the body . . . a spiritual lubricant . . . it's hard to describe . . . and without it, life is a nightmare, and everything is distorted.—A black cat started coming to my kitchen. He's awfully mangled and big. He is missing an eye and his skin is diseased. At first I was repelled by him, but then, I thought, this is a monster that has been sent to me and I must feed him. And I fed him. One day he came and shat all over my kitchen. Foul diarrhea. He still comes and I still feed him.—I am afraid of him. (*Emma kisses Fefu.*) How about a little lemonade?

EMMA. Yes.

FEFU. How about a game of croquet?

EMMA. Fine.

(*Fefu exits. Emma improvises an effigy of Fefu. She puts Fefu's hat and gloves on it.*)

Not from the stars do I my judgment pluck.
And yet methinks I have astronomy;
But not to tell of good or evil luck,
Of plagues, of dearths, or seasons' quality;
Nor can I fortune to brief minutes tell,
Pointing to each his thunder, rain, and wind,
Or say with princes if it shall go well
By oft predict that I in heaven find.
But from thine eyes my knowledge I derive.
And, constant stars, in them I read such art
As truth and beauty shall together thrive
If from thyself to store thou wouldst convert:
    Or else of thee this I prognosticate,
    Thy end is truth's and beauty's doom and date.

(*If Fefu's entrance is delayed, Emma will sing a popular song of the period. Fefu re-enters with a pitcher and two glasses.*)

IN THE STUDY

There are books on the walls, a desk, Victorian chairs, a rug on the floor. Christina sits behind the desk. She reads a French text book. She mumbles French sentences. Cindy sits to the left of the desk with her feet up on a chair. She looks at a magazine. A few moments pass.

CHRISTINA (*Practicing*). Etes-vous externe ou demi-pensionnaire? La cuisine de votre cantine est-elle bonne, passable ou mauvaise? (*She continues reading almost inaudibly. A moment passes.*)

CINDY (*Reading*). A lady in Africa divorced her husband because he was a cheetah.

CHRISTINA. Oh, dear. (*They laugh. They go back to their reading. A moment passes.*) Est-ce que votre professeur interroge souvant les eleves? (*They go back to their reading. A moment passes.*)

CINDY. I suppose . . . when a person is swept off their feet . . . the feet remain and the person goes off . . . with the broom.

CHRISTINA. No . . . when a person is swept off their feet . . . there is no broom.

CINDY. What does the sweeping?

CHRISTINA. An emotion . . . a feeling.

CINDY. Then emotions have bristles?

CHRISTINA. Yes.

CINDY. Now I understand. Do the feet remain?

CHRISTINA. No, the feet fly also . . . but separate from the body. At the end of the leap, just before the landing, they join the ankles and one is complete again.

CINDY. Oh, that sounds nice.

CHRISTINA. It is. Being swept off your feet is nice. Anything else?

CINDY. Not for now. (*They go back to their reading. A moment passes.*) Are you having a good time?

CHRISTINA. Yes, I'm very glad I came.

CINDY. Do you like everybody?

CHRISTINA. Yes.

CINDY. Do you like Fefu?

CHRISTINA. I do . . . She confuses me a little.—I try to be honest . . . and I wonder if she is . . . I don't mean that she doesn't tell the truth. I know she does. I mean a kind of integrity. I know she has integrity too. . . . But I don't know if she's careful with life . . . something bigger than the self . . . I suppose I don't mean with life but more with convention. I think she is an adventurer in a way. Her mind is adventurous. I don't know if there is dishonesty in that. But in adventure there is taking chances and risks, and then one has to, somehow, have less regard or respect for things as they are. That is, regard for a kind of convention, I suppose. I am probably ultimately a conformist, I think. And I suppose I do hold back for fear of being disrespectful or destroying something—and I admire those who are not. But I also feel they are dangerous to me. I don't think they are dangerous to the world; they are more useful than I am, more important, but I feel some of my life is endangered by their way of thinking. Do you understand?

CINDY. Yes, I do.

CHRISTINA. I guess I am proud and I don't like thinking that I am thoughtful of things that have no value.—I like her.

CINDY. I had a terrible dream last night.

CHRISTINA. What was it?

CINDY. I was at a dance. And there was a young doctor I had seen in connection with my health. We all danced in a circle and he identified himself and said that he had spoken to Mike about me, but that it was all right, that he had put it so that it was all right. I was puzzled as to why Mike would mind and why he had spoken to him. Then, suddenly everybody sat down on the floor and pretended they were having singing lessons and one person was practicing Italian. The singing professor was being tested by two secret policemen. They were having him correct the voice of someone they had brought. He apparently didn't know how to do it. Then, one of the policemen put his hands on his vocal cords and kicked him out the door. Then he grabbed me and felt my throat from behind with his thumbs while he rubbed my nipples with his pinkies. Then, he pushed me out the door. Then, the young doctor started cursing me. His mouth moved like the mouth of a horse. I was on an upper level with a railing and I said to him, "Stop and listen to me." I said it so strongly that he stopped. Everybody turned to me in admiration because I had made him stop. Then, I said to him, "Restrain yourself." I wanted to say respect me. I wasn't sure whether the words coming out of my mouth were what I wanted to say. I turned to ask my sister. The young man was bending over and trembling in mad rage. Another man told me to run before the young man tried to kill me. Meg and I ran downstairs. She asked me if I wanted to go to her place. We grabbed a taxi, but before the taxi got enough speed he came out and ran to the taxi and was on the verge of opening the door when I woke up.

(*The door opens. Fefu looks in. Her entrance may interrupt Cindy's speech at any point according to how long it takes her to reach the kitchen.*)

FEFU. Who's for a game of croquet?

CINDY. In a little while.

FEFU. See you outside.

CHRISTINA. That was quite a dream.

CINDY. What do you think it means?

CHRISTINA. I think it means you should go to a different doctor.

CINDY. He's not my doctor. I never saw him before.

CHRISTINA. Well good. I'm sure he's not a good doctor.

(*At the end of the fourth repeat, when Fefu invites them for croquet, Cindy says, "Oh let's play croquet" and they follow Fefu.*)

IN THE BEDROOM

A plain unpainted room. Perhaps a room that was used for storage and was set up as a sleeping place for Julia. There is a mattress on the floor. To the right of the mattress there is a small table, to the left is Julia's wheelchair. There is a sink on the wall. There are dry leaves on the floor although the time is not fall. The sheets are linen. Julia lies in bed covered to her shoulders. She wears a white hospital gown. Julia hallucinates. However, her behavior should not be the usual behavior attributed to a mad person. It should be rather still and luminuous. There will be aspects of her hallucination that frighten her, but hallucinating itself does not.

JULIA. They clubbed me. They broke my head. They broke my will. They broke my hands. They tore my eyes out. They took my voice away. They didn't do anything to my heart because I didn't bring my heart with me. They clubbed me again, but my head did not fall off in pieces. That was because they were so good and they felt sorry for me. The judges. You didn't know the judges?—I was good and quiet. I never dropped my smile. I smiled to everyone. If I stopped smiling I would get clubbed because they love me. They say they love me. I go along with that because if I don't . . .

(With her finger she indicates her throat being cut and makes the sound that usually accompanies that gesture.)

I told them the stinking parts of the body are the important ones: the genitals, the anus, the mouth, the armpit. All important parts except the armpits. And who knows, maybe the armpits are important too. That's what I said. (*Her voice becomes gravelly and tight in imitation of the judges.*) He said that all those parts must be kept clean and put away. He said that women's entrails are heavier than anything on earth and to see a woman running creates a disparate and incongruous image in the mind. It's antiaesthetic. Therefore women should not run. Instead they should strike positions that take into account the weight of their entrails. Only if they do, can they be aesthetic. He said, for example, Goya's Maja. He said Ruben's women are not aesthetic. Flesh. He said that a woman's bottom should be in a cushion, otherwise it's revolting. He said there are exceptions. Ballet dancers are exceptions. They can run and lift their legs because they

have no entrails. Isadora Duncan had entrails, that's why she should not have danced. But she danced and for this reason became crazy. (*Her voice is back to normal.*) She wasn't crazy.

(She moves her hand as if guarding from a blow.)

She was. He said that I had to be punished because I was getting too smart. I'm not smart. I never was. Neither is Fefu smart. They are after her too. Well, she's still walking!

(She guards from a blow. Her eyes close.)

Wait! I'll say my prayers. I'm saying it.

(She mumbles. She opens her eye with caution.)

You don't think I'm going to argue with them, do you? I repented. I told they exactly what they wanted to hear. They killed me. I was dead. The bullet didn't hit me. It hit the deer. But I died. He didn't. Then I repented and the deer died and I lived. (*With a gravelly voice.*) They said, "Live but crippled. And if you tell . . ."

(She repeats the throat cutting gesture.)

Why do you have to kill Fefu, for she's only a joker? (*With a gravelly voice.*) "Not kill, cure. Cure her." Will it hurt?

(She whimpers.)

Oh, dear, dear, my dear, they want your light. Your light my dear. Your precious light. Oh dear, my dear.

(Her head moves as if slapped.)

Not cry. I'll say my prayer. I'll say it. Right now. Look.

(She sits up as if pulled by an invisible force.)

The human being is of the masculine gender. The human being is a boy as a child and grown up he is a man. Everything on earth is for the human being, which is man. To nourish him.—There are evil things on earth, and noxious things. Evil and noxious things are on earth for man also. For him to fight with, and conquer and turn its evil into good. So that it too can nourish him.—There are Evil Plants, Evil Animals, Evil Minerals, and Women are evil.—Woman is not a human being. She is: 1— A mystery. 2—Another species. 3—As yet undefined. 4—Unpredictable; therefore wicked and gentle and evil and good which is evil.—If a man commits an evil act, he must be pitied. The evil comes from outside him, through him and into the act. Woman generates the evil herself.—God gave man no other mate but woman. The oxen is good but it is not a mate for man. The sheep is good but it is not a mate for man. The mate for man is woman and that is the cross man must bear.—Man is not spiritually sexual, he therefore can enjoy sexuality. His sexuality is physical which means his spirit is pure. Woman's spirit is sexual. That is why after coitus they dwell in nefarious feelings. Because that is their natural habitat. That is why it is difficult for them to return to the human world. Their sexual feelings remain with them till they die. And they take those feelings with them to the afterlife where they corrupt the heavens, and they are sent to hell where through suffering they may shed those feelings and return to earth as man.

(Her head moves as if slapped.)

Don't hit me. Didn't I just say my prayer?

(A smaller slap.)

I believe it.

(She lies back.)

They say when I believe the prayer I will forget the judges. And when I forget the judges I will believe the prayer. They say both happen at once. And all women have done it. Why can't I?

(Sue enters with a bowl of soup on a tray.)

SUE. Julia, are you asleep?

(Short pause.)

JULIA. No.
SUE. I brought your soup.
JULIA. Put it down. I'm getting up in a moment.

(Sue puts the soup down.)

SUE. Do you want me to help you?
JULIA. No, I can manage. Thank you, Sue.

(Sue goes to the door.)

SUE. You're all right?
JULIA. Yes.
SUE. I'll see you later.
JULIA. Thank you, Sue.

(Sue exits. Julia closes her eyes. As soon as each audience group leaves, the tray is removed, if possible through a back door.)

IN THE KITCHEN

A fully equipped kitchen. There is a table and chairs and a high cutting table. On a counter next to the stove there is a tray with a soup dish and a spoon. There is also a ladle. On the cutting table there are two empty glasses. Soup is heating on a burner. A kettle with water sits on an unlit burner. In the refrigerator there is an ice tray with wooden sticks in each cube. The sticks should rest on the edge of the tray forming two parallel rows, like a caterpillar lying on its back. In the refrigerator there are also two pitchers, one with water, one with lemonade. Paula sits at the table She is writing on a pad. Sue waits for the soup to heat.

PAULA. I have it all figured out.
SUE. What?
PAULA. A love affair lasts seven years and three months.
SUE. It does?
PAULA *(Reading)*. 3 months of love. 1 year saying: It's all right. This is just a passing disturbance. 1 year trying to to understand what's wrong. 2 years knowing the end had come. 1 year finding the way to end it. After the separation, 2 years trying to understand what happened. 7 years, 3 months. *(No longer reading.)* At any point the sequence might be interrupted by another love affair that has the same sequence. That is, it's not really interrupted, the new love affair relegates the first one to a second plane and both continue their sequence at the same time.

(Sue looks over Paula's shoulder.)

SUE. You really added it up.
PAULA. Sure.
SUE. What do you want to drink?
PAULA. Water. The old love affair may fade, so you are not aware the process goes on. A year later it may surface and you might find yourself figuring out what's wrong with the new one while trying to end the old one.
SUE. So how do you solve the problem?
PAULA. Celibacy?
SUE *(Going to the refrigerator)*. Celibacy doesn't solve anything.
PAULA. That's true.
SUE *(Taking out the ice tray with the sticks)*. What's this? *(Paula shakes her head.)* Dessert. *(Paula shrugs her shoulders. Sue takes an ice cube and places it against her forehead.)* For a headache. *(She takes another cube and moves her arms in a Judo style.)* Eskimo wrestling. *(She*

places one stick behind her ear.) Brain cooler. That's when you're thinking too much. You could use one. (*She tries to put the ice cube behind Paula's ear. They wrestle and laugh. She puts the stick in her own mouth. She takes it out to speak.*) This is when you want to keep chaste. No one will kiss you. (*She puts it back in to demonstrate. Then takes it out.*) That's good for celibacy. If you walk around with one of these in your mouth for seven years you can keep all your sequences straight. Finish one before you start the other. (*She puts the ice cube in the tray and looks at it.*) A frozen caterpillar. (*She puts the tray away.*)

PAULA. You're leaving that ice cube in there?

SUE. I'm clean. (*Looking at the soup.*) So what else do you have on love? (*Sue places a bowl and spoon on the table and sits as she waits for the soup to heat.*)

PAULA. Well, the break-up takes place in parts. The brain, the heart, the body, mutual things, shared things. The mind leaves but the heart is still there. The heart has left but the body wants to stay. The body leaves but the things are still at the apartment. You must come back. You move everything out of the apartment but the mind stays behind. Memory lingers in the place. Seven years later, perhaps seven years later, it doesn't matter any more. Perhaps it takes longer. Perhaps it never ends.

SUE. It depends.

PAULA. Yup. It depends.

SUE (*Pouring soup in the bowl*). Something's bothering you.

PAULA. No.

SUE (*Taking the tray*). I'm going to take this to Julia.

PAULA. Go ahead.

(*As Sue exits, Cecilia enters.*)

CECILIA. May I come in?

PAULA. Yes . . . Would you like something to eat?

CECILIA. No, I ate lunch.

PAULA. I didn't eat lunch. I wasn't very hungry.

CECILIA. I know.

PAULA. Would you like some coffee?

CECILIA. I'll have tea.

PAULA. I'll make some.

CECILIA. No, you sit. I'll make it. (*Cecilia looks for tea.*)

PAULA. Here it is. (*She gets the tea and gives it to Cecilia.*)

CECILIA (*As she lights the burner*). I've been meaning to call you.

PAULA. It doesn't matter. I know you're busy.

CECILIA. Still I would have called you but I really didn't find the time.

PAULA. Don't worry.

CECILIA. I wanted to see you again. I want to see you often.

PAULA. There's no hurry. Now we know we can see each other.

CECILIA. Yes, I'm glad we can.

PAULA. I have thought a great deal about my life since I saw you. I have questioned my life. I can't help doing that. It's been many years and I wondered how you see me now.

CECILIA. You're the same.

PAULA. I felt small in your presence . . . I haven't done all that I could have. All I wanted to do. Our lives have gone in such different directions I cannot help but review what those years have been for me. I gave up, almost gave up. I missed you in my life. . . . I became lazy. I lost the drive. You abandoned me and I kept going. But after a while I didn't know how to. I didn't know how to go on. I knew why when I was with you. To give you pleasure. So we could laugh together. So we could rejoice together. To bring beauty to the world. . . . Now we look at each other like strangers. We are guarded. I speak and you don't understand my words. I remember every day.

(*Fefu enters. She takes the lemonade pitcher from the refrigerator and two glasses from the top of the refrigerator.*)

FEFU. Emma and I are going to play croquet. You want to join us? . . . No. You're having a serious conversation.

PAULA. Very serious. (*Paula smiles at Cecilia in a conciliatory manner.*) Too serious.

FEFU (*As she exits*). Come.

PAULA. I'm sorry. Let's go play croquet.—I'm not reproaching you.

CECILIA (*Reaching for Paula's hand*). I know. I've missed you too.

(*They exit. As soon as the audience leaves the props are reset.*)

PART III

The living room. It is dusk. As the audience enters, two or three of the women are around the piano playing and singing Schubert's "Who is Silvia." They exit. Emma enters, checks the lights in the room on her hand, looks around the room and goes upstairs. The rest enter through the rear. Cecilia enters speaking.

CECILIA. Well, we each have our own system of receiving information, placing it, responding to it. (*She*

sits in the center of the couch; the rest sit around her.)
That system can function with such a bias that it
could take any situation and translate it into one
formula. That is, I think, the main reason for stupidity or even madness, not being able to tell the
difference between things.

SUE. Like?

CECILIA. Like . . . this person is screaming at me. He's a
bully. I don't like being screamed at. Another person
or the same person screams in a different situation.
But you know you have done something that provokes him to scream. He has a good reason. They are
two different things, the screaming of one and the
screaming of the other. Often that distinction is not
made. We cannot survive in a vacuum. We must be
part of a community, perhaps 10, 100, 1000. It depends on how strong you are. But even the strongest
will need a dozen, three, even one who sees, thinks,
and feels as he does. The greater the need for that
kind of reassurance, the greater the number that he
needs to identify with. Some need to identify with
the whole nation. Then, the greater the number the
more limited the number of responses and thoughts.
A common denominator must be reached. Thoughts,
emotions that fit all, have to be limited to a small
number. That is, I feel, the concern of the educator—to teach how to be sensitive to the differences
in ourselves as well as outside ourselves, not to super-
vise the memorization of facts. (*Emma's head appears
in the doorway to the stairs.*) Otherwise the unusual in
us will perish. As we grow we feel we are strange and
fear any thought that is not shared with everyone.

JULIA. As I feel I am perishing. My hallucinations are
madness, of course, but I wish I could be with others
who hallucinate also. I would still know I am mad
but I would not feel so isolated.—Hallucinations are
real, you know. They are not like dreams. They are as
real as all of you here. I have actually asked to be hospitalized so I could be with other nuts. But the doctors don't want to. They can't diagnose me. That
makes me even more isolated. (*There is a moment's silence.*) You see, right now, it's an awful moment because you don't know what to say or do. If I were with
other people who hallucinate, they would say, "Oh
yeah. Sure. It's awful. Those dummies, they don't see
anything." (*The others begin to relax.*) It's not so bad,
really. I can laugh at it. . . . Emma is ready. We should
start. (*The others are hesitant. Julia speaks to Fefu.*)
Come on.

FEFU. Sure. (*Fefu begins to move the table. Others help move
the table and enough furniture to clear a space in the cen-*

*ter. They sit in a semicircle downstage on the floor facing
upstage. Cecilia sits on a chair to the left of the semicircle.*) All right. I start. Right?

CINDY. Right.

(*Fefu goes to the center and faces the others. Emma
sits on the steps. Only her head and legs are visible.*)

FEFU. I talk about the stifling conditions of primary school
education, etc. . . . etc. . . . The project . . . I know
what I'm going to say but I don't want to bore you
with it. We all know it by heart. Blah blah blah blah.
And so on and so on. And so on and so on. Then I
introduce Emma . . . And now Miss Emma Blake.
(*They applaud. Emma shakes her head.*) What.

EMMA. Paula goes next.

FEFU. Does it matter?

EMMA. Of course it matters. Dra-ma-tics. It has to build.
I'm in costume.

FEFU. Oh. And now, ladies and gentlemen, Miss Paula
Cori will speak on Art as a Tool for Learning. And I
tell them the work you have done at the Institute,
community centers, essays, etc. Miss Paula Cori.

(*They applaud. Paula goes to center.*)

PAULA. Ladies and gentlemen, I, like my fellow educator
and colleague, Stephany Beckmann . . .

FEFU. I am not an educator.

PAULA. What are you?

FEFU. . . . a do gooder, a girl scout.

PAULA. Well, I, like my fellow girl scout Stephany Beckmann say blah blah blah blah, blah blah blah blah and I
offer the jewels of my wisdom and experience, which
I will write down and memorize, otherwise I would
just stand there and stammer and go blank. And
even after I memorize it I'm sure I will just stand
there and stammer and go blank.

EMMA. I'll work with you on it.

PAULA. However, after our other colleague Miss Emma
Blake works with me on it . . . (*In imitation of Emma
she brings her hands together and opens her arms as she
moves her head back and speaks.*) My impulses will
burst forth through a symphony of eloquence.

EMMA. Breathe . . . in . . . (*Paula inhales slowly.*) And bow.
(*Paula bows. They applaud.*)

PAULA (*Coming up from the bow*). Oh, I liked that. (*She
sits.*)

EMMA. Good . . .

(*They applaud . . .*)

FEFU. And now, ladies and gentlemen, the one and only,
the incomparable, our precious, dear Emma Blake.

(*Emma walks to center. She wears a robe which hangs from her arms to the floor.*)

EMMA. From the prologue to "The Science of Educational Dramatics" by Emma Sheridan Fry. (*She takes a dramatic pose and starts. The whole speech is dramatized by interpretive gestures and movements that cover the stage area.*)

Environment knocks at the gateway of the senses. A rain of summons beats upon us day and night. . . . We do not answer. Everything around us shouts against our deafness, struggles with our unwillingness, batters our walls, flashes into our blindness, strives to sieve through us at every pore, begging, fighting, insisting. It shouts, "Where are you? Where are you?" But we are deaf. The signals do not reach us.

Society restricts us, school straight jackets us, civilization submerges us, privation wrings us, luxury feather-beds us. The Divine Urge is checked. The Winged Horse balks on the road, and we, discouraged, defeated, dismount and burrow into ourselves. The gates are closed and Divine Urge is imprisoned at Center. Thus we are taken by indifference that is death. Environment finding the gates closed tries to break in. Turned away, it comes another way. Kept back, it stretches its hands to us. Always scheming to reach us. Never was suitor more insistent than Environment, seeking admission, claiming recognition, signaling to be seen, shouting to be heard. And through the ages we sit inside ourselves deaf, dumb and blind, and will not stir. . . .

. . . Maybe you are not deaf. . . . Perhaps signals reach you. Maybe you stir. . . . The gates give. . . . Eternal Urge pushes through the stupor of our senses, making paths to meet the challenging suitor, windows through which to see him, ears through which to hear him. Environment shouting, "Where are you?" and Center battering at the inner side of the wall crying, "Here I am," and dragging down bars, wrenching gates, prying at port-holes. Listening at cracks, reaching everywhere, and demanding that sense gates be flung open. The gates are open! Eternal Urge stands at the threshold signaling with venturous flag. An imperious instinct lets us know that "all" is ours, and that whatever anyone has ever known, or may ever have or know, we will call and claim. A sense of life universal surges through our life individual. We attack the feast of this table with an insatiable appetite that cries for all.

What are we? A creation of God's consciousness coming now slowly and painfully into recognition of ourselves.

What is Personality? A small part of us. The whole of us is behind that hungry rush at the gates of Senses.

What is Civilization? A circumscribed order in which the whole has not entered.

What is Environment? Our mate, our true mate that clamors for our reunion.

We will meet him. We will seize all, learn all, know all here, that we may fare further on the great quest! The task of Now is only a step toward the task of the Whole! Let us then seek the laws governing real life forces, that coming into their own, they may create, develop and reconstruct. Let us awaken life dormant! Let us, boldly, seizing the star of our intent, lift it as the lantern of our necessity, and let it shine over the darkness of our compliance. Come! The light shines. Come! It brightens our way. Come! Don't let its glorious light pass you by! Come! The day has come!

(*Emma throws herself on the couch. Paula embraces her.*) Oh, it's so beautiful.

JULIA. It is, Emma. It is.

(*They applaud.*)

CINDY. Encore! Encore!

(*Emma stands.*)

EMMA. Environment knocks at the gateway . . . (*She laughs and joins the others in the semi-circle. Paula remains seated on the couch.*) What's next.

FEFU (*Going center*). I introduce Cecilia. I don't think I should introduce Cecilia. She should just come after Emma. Now things don't need introduction. (*Imitating Emma as she goes to her seat.*) They are happening.

EMMA. Right!

(*Cecilia goes to center.*)

CECILIA. Well, as we say in the business, that's a very hard act to follow.

EMMA. Not *very* hard. It's a hard act to follow.

CECILIA. Right. I should say my name first.

FEFU. Yes.

CECILIA. I should breathe too. (*She takes a breath. All except Paula start singing "Cecilia." Cecilia is perplexed and walks backwards till she sits on the couch. She is next to Paula. Unaware of who she is next to, she puts her hand on Paula's leg. At the end of the song Cecilia realizes she is next to Paula and stands.)* I should go before Emma. I don't think anyone should speak after Emma.

CINDY. Right. It should be Fefu, Paula, Cecilia, then Emma, and then Sue explaining the finances and asking for pledges. And the money should roll in. It's very good. *(They applaud.)* Sue . . . *(Sue goes to center.)*

SUE. Yes, blahblahblahblah, pledges and money. *(She does a few balletic moves and bows. They applaud.)*

FEFU *(As Sue returns to her seat)*. Who's ready for coffee?

CINDY *(As she stands)*. And dishes.

CHRISTINA *(As she stands)*. I'll help.

EMMA *(As she stands)*. Me too.

FEFU. Don't all come. Sit. Sit. You have done enough, relax.

(They put the furniture back as Emma and Sue jump over the couch making loud warlike sounds. As they exit to the kitchen, Sue tries to get ahead of Emma. Emma speeds ahead of her. All except Julia jump over the couch. All except Cindy and Julia exit.)

JULIA. I should go do the dishes. I haven't done anything.

CINDY. You can do them tomorrow.

JULIA. True.—So how have you been?

CINDY. Hmm.

JULIA. Let me see. I can tell by looking at your face. Not so bad.

CINDY. Not so bad.

(There is the sound of laughter from the kitchen. Christina runs in.)

CHRISTINA. They're having a water fight over who's going to do the dishes.

CINDY. Emma?

CHRISTINA. And Paula, and Sue, all of them. Fefu was getting into it when I left. Cecilia got out the back door.

(Christina walks back to the kitchen with some caution. She runs back and lies on the couch covering her head with the throw. Emma enters with a pan of water in her hand. She is wet. Cindy and Julia point to the lawn. Emma runs to the lawn. There is the sound of knocking from upstairs. While the following conversation goes on, Emma, Sue, Cindy, and Julia engage in water fights in and out of the living room. The screams, laughter, and water splashing may drown the words.)

PAULA. Open up.

FEFU. There's no one here.

PAULA. Open up you coward.

FEFU. I can't. I'm busy.

PAULA. What are you doing?

FEFU. I have a man here. Ah ah ah ah ah.

PAULA. O.K. I'll wait. Take your time.

FEFU. It's going to take quite a while.

PAULA. It's all right. I'll wait.

FEFU. Do me a favor?

PAULA. Sure. Open up and I'll do you a favor.

(There is the sound of a pot falling, a door slamming.)

FEFU. Fill it up for me.

PAULA. O.K.

FEFU. Thank you.

PAULA. Here's water. Open up.

FEFU. Leave it there. I'll come out in a minute.

PAULA. O.K. Here it is. I'm leaving now.

(Loud steps. Paula comes down with a filled pan. Emma hides by the entrance to the steps. Emma splashes water on Paula. Paula splashes water on Emma. Sue appears with a full pan.)

PAULA. Truce!

SUE. Who's the winner?

PAULA. You are. You do the dishes.

SUE. I'm the winner. You do the dishes.

FEFU *(From the landing)*. Line up!

SUE. Psst. *(Paula and Emma look. Sue splashes water on them.)* Gotcha!

EMMA. Please don't.

PAULA. Truce. Truce.

FEFU. O.K. Line up. *(Pointing to the kitchen.)* Get in there! *(They all go to the kitchen.)* Start doing those dishes. *(There is a moment's pause.)*

JULIA. It's over.

CINDY. We're safe.

JULIA *(To Christina)*. You can come up now. *(Christina stays down.)* You rather wait a while.

(Christina nods.)

CHRISTINA *(Playful)*. I feel danger lurking.

CINDY. She's been hiding all day.

(Fefu enters. She is wet.)

FEFU. I won. I got them working.

JULIA. I thought the fight was over who'd do the dishes.

FEFU. Yes. *(Starting to go.)* I have to change. I'm soaked.

CHRISTINA. They forgot what the fight was about.

FEFU. We did?

JULIA. That's usually the way it is.

FEFU (*Going to Christina and lifting the cover from her face*). Are you ready for an ice cube?

(*Fefu exits upstairs. Christina runs upstairs. There is silence.*)

CINDY. So.—And how have you been?

JULIA. All right. I've been taking care of myself.

CINDY. You look well.

JULIA. I do not. . . . Have you seen Mike?

CINDY. No, not since Christmas.

JULIA. I'm sorry.

CINDY. I'm O.K.—And how's your love life?

JULIA. Far away. . . . I have no need for it.

CINDY. I'm sorry.

JULIA. Don't be. I'm very morbid these day. I think of death all the time.

PAULA (*Standing in the doorway*). Anyone for coffee? (*They raise their hands.*) Anyone take milk? (*They raise their hands.*)

JULIA. Should we go in?

PAULA. I'll bring it out. (*Paula exits.*)

JULIA. I feel we are constantly threatened by death, every second, every instant, it's there. And every moment something rescues us. Something rescues us from death every moment of our lives. For every moment we live we have to thank something. We have to be grateful to something that fights for us and saves us. I have felt lifeless and in the face of death. Death is not anything. It's being lifeless and I have felt lifeless sometimes for a brief moment, but I have been rescued by these . . . guardians. I am not sure who these guardians are. I only know they exist because I have felt their absence. I think we have come to know them as life, and we have become familiar with certain forms they take. Our sight is a form they take. That is why we take pleasure in seeing things, and we find some things beautiful. The sun is a guardian. Those things we take pleasure in are usually guardians. We enjoy looking at the sunlight when it comes through the window. Don't we? We, as people, are guardians to each other when we give love. And then of course we have white cells and antibodies protecting us. Those moments when I feel lifeless have occurred, and I am afraid one day the guardians won't come in time and I will be defenseless. I will die . . . for no apparent reason.

(*Pause. Paula stands in the doorway with a bottle of milk.*)

PAULA (*In a low-keyed manner*). Anyone take rotten milk? (*Pause.*) I'm kidding. This one is no good but there's more in there . . . (*Remaining in good spirits.*) Forget it. It's not a good joke.

JULIA. It's good.

PAULA. In there it seemed funny but here it isn't. (*As she exits and shrugging her shoulders.*) It's a kitchen joke. Bye.

JULIA (*After her*). It is funny, Paula. (*To Cindy.*) It was funny.

CINDY. It's all right, Paula doesn't mind.

JULIA. I'm sure she minds. I'll go see . . . (*Julia starts to go. Paula appears in the doorway.*)

PAULA (*In a low-keyed manner*). Hey, who was that lady I saw you with?—That was no lady. That was my rotten wife. That one wasn't good either, was it? (*Exiting.*) Emma. . . . That one was no good either.

(*Sue starts to enter carrying a tray with sugar, milk, and two cups of coffee. She stops at the doorway to look at Paula and Emma who are behind the wall.*)

SUE (*Whispering*). What are you doing?—What?—O.K., O.K. (*She enters whispering. Sue puts the tray down.*) They're plotting something.

(*Paula appears in the doorway.*)

PAULA (*In a low-keyed manner*). Ladies and gentlemen. Ladies, since our material is too shocking and avant-garde, we have decided to uplift our subject matter so it's more palatable to the sensitive public. (*Paula takes a pose. Emma enters. She lifts an imaginary camera to her face.*)

EMMA. Say cheese.

PAULA. Cheese. (*They both turn front and smile. The others applaud.*) Ah, success, success. Make it clean and you'll succeed.—Coffee's in the kitchen.

SUE. Oh, I brought theirs out.

PAULA. Oh, shall we have it here?

JULIA. We can all go in the kitchen. (*They each take their coffee and go to the kitchen. Sue takes the tray to the kitchen. The sugar remains on the table.*)

PAULA. Either here or there. (*She sits on the couch.*) I'm exhausted.

(*Cecilia enters from the lawn.*)

CECILIA. Is the war over?

PAULA. Yes.

CECILIA. It's nice out. (*Paula nods in agreement.*) Where's everybody?

PAULA. In the kitchen, having coffee.

CECILIA. We must talk. (*Paula starts to speak.*) Not now. I'll call you. (*Cecilia starts to go.*)
PAULA. When?
CECILIA. I don't know.
PAULA. I don't want you, you know.
CECILIA. I know.
PAULA. No, you don't. I'm not lusting after you.
CECILIA. I know that. (*She starts to go.*) I'll call you.
PAULA. When?
CECILIA. As soon as I can.
PAULA. I won't be home then.
CECILIA. When will you be home?
PAULA. I'll check my book and let you know.
CECILIA. Do that.—I'll be leaving after coffee. I'll say goodbye now.
PAULA. Goodbye. (*Cecilia goes towards the kitchen. Paula starts towards the steps. Fefu comes down the steps.*)
FEFU. You're still wet.
PAULA. I'm going to change now.
FEFU. Do you need anything?
PAULA. No, I have something I can change to. Thank you.

(*Paula goes upstairs. Fefu stands by the steps. She is downcast. As the lights shift to an eerie tone, Julia enters in slow motion, walking. She goes to the coffee table, gets the sugar bowl, lifts it in Fefu's direction, takes the cover off, puts it back on and walks to the kitchen. As soon as Julia exits, Sue's voice is heard speaking the following lines. Immediately after, Julia re-enters wheeled by Sue. Cindy, Christina, Emma, and Cecilia are with them. On the arms of the wheelchair rests a tray with a coffee pot and cups. As they reach the couch and chairs they sit. Sue puts the tray on the table. Fefu stares at Julia.*)

SUE. I was terribly exhausted and run down. I lived on coffee so I could stay up all night and do my work. And they used to give us these medical check-ups all the time. But all they did was ask how we felt and we'd say "Fine," and they'd check us out. In the meantime I looked like a ghost. I was all bones. Remember Susan Austin? She was very naive and when they asked her how she felt, she said she was nervous and she wasn't sleeping well. So she had to see a psychiatrist from then on.
EMMA. Well, she was crazy.

(*Fefu exits.*)

SUE. No, she wasn't.—Oh god, those were awful days. . . . Remember Julie Brooks?

EMMA. Sure.
SUE. She was a beautiful girl.
EMMA. Ah yes, she was gorgeous.

(*Paula comes down the stairs as soon as she has changed. She sits on the steps half way down.*)

SUE. At the end of the first semester they called her in because she had been out with 28 men and they thought that was awful. And the worst thing was that after that, she thought there was something wrong with her.
CINDY (*Jokingly*). She was a nymphomaniac, that's all.
SUE. She was not. She was just very beautiful so all the boys wanted to go out with her. And if a boy asked her to go have a cup of coffee she'd sign out and write in the name of the boy. None of us did of course. All she did was go for coffee or go to a movie. She was really very innocent.
EMMA. And Gloria Schuman? She wrote a psychology paper the faculty decided she didn't write and they called her in to try to make her admit she hadn't written it. She insisted she wrote it and they sent her to a psychiatrist also.
JULIA. Everybody ended going to the psychiatrist.

(*Fefu enters through the foyer.*)

EMMA. After a few visits the psychiatrist said: Don't you think you know me well enough now that you can tell me the truth about the paper? He almost drove her crazy. They just couldn't believe she was so smart.
SUE. Those were difficult times.
PAULA. We were young. That's why it was difficult. On my first year I thought you were all very happy. I had been so deprived in my childhood that I believed the rich were all happy. During the summer you spent your vacations in Europe or the Orient. I went to work and I resented that. But then I realized that many lives are ruined by poverty and many lives are ruined by wealth. I was always able to manage. And I think I enjoyed myself as much when I went to Revere Beach on my day off as you did when you visited the Taj Mahal. (*Cecilia enters from the foyer. She stands there and listens. Paula doesn't acknowledge her.*) Then, when I stopped feeling envy, I started noticing the waste. I began feeling contempt for those who, having everything a person can ask for, make such a mess of it. I resented them because they were not better than the poor. If you have all you need you should be generous. If you can afford to go to school your mind should be better. If you didn't have to fight for your place on earth you should be nobler. But I saw

them cheating and grabbing like the kids in the slums, or wasting away with self-indulgence. And I saw them be plain stupid. If there is a reason why some are rich while others starve it must be so they put everything they have at the service of others. They should take the responsibility of everything that happens in the world. They are the only ones who can influence things. The poor don't have the power to change things. I think we should teach the poor and let the rich take care of themselves. I'm sorry, I know that's what we're doing. That's what Emma has been doing. I'm sorry . . . I guess I feel it's not enough. (*Paula sobs.*) I'll wash my face. I'll be right back. (*She starts to go towards the kitchen.*) I think highly of all of you.

(*Cecilia follows her. Paula turns. Cecilia opens her arms and puts them around Paula, engulfing her. She kisses Paula on the lips. Paula steps back. She is fearful. Cecilia follows her. Fefu enters from the lawn.*)

FEFU. Have you been out? The sky is full of stars.

(*Emma, Sue, Christina, and Cindy exit.*)

JULIA. What's the matter?

(*Fefu shakes her head. Julia starts to go toward the door.*)

FEFU. Stay a moment, will you?
JULIA. Of course.
FEFU. Did you have enough coffee?
JULIA. Yes.
FEFU. Did you find the sugar?
JULIA. Yes. There was sugar in the kitchen. What's the matter?
FEFU. Can you walk? (*Julia is hurt. She opens her arms implying she hides nothing.*) I am sorry, my dear.
JULIA. What is the matter?
FEFU. I don't know, Julia. Every breath is painful for me. I don't know. (*Fefu turns Julia's head to look into her eyes.*) I think you know.

(*Julia breaks away from Fefu.*)

JULIA (*Avoiding Fefu's glance*). No, I don't know. I haven't seen much of you lately. I have thought of you a great deal. I always think of you. Cindy tells me how you are. I always ask her. How is Phillip? Things are not well with Phillip?
FEFU. No.
JULIA. What's wrong?
FEFU. A lot is wrong.
JULIA. He loves you.

FEFU. He can't stand me.
JULIA. He loves you.
FEFU. He's left me. His body is here but the rest is gone. I exhaust him. I torment him and I torment myself. I need him, Julia.
JULIA. I know you do.
FEFU. I need his touch. I need his kiss. I need the person he is. I can't give him up. (*She looks into Julia's eyes.*) I look into your eyes and I know what you see. (*Julia closes her eyes.*) It's death. (*Julia shakes her head.*) Fight!
JULIA. I can't.
FEFU. I saw you walking.
JULIA. No. I can't walk.
FEFU. You came for sugar, Julia. You came for sugar. Walk!
JULIA. You know I can't walk.
FEFU. Why not? Try! Get up! Stand up!
JULIA. What is wrong with you?
FEFU. You have given up!
JULIA. I get tired! I get exhausted! I am exhausted!
FEFU. What is it you see? (*Julia doesn't answer.*) What is it you see! Where is it you go that tires you so?
JULIA. I can't spend time with others! I get tired!
FEFU. What is it you see!
JULIA. You want to see it too?
FEFU. No, I don't. You're nuts, and willingly so.
JULIA. You know I'm not.
FEFU. And you're contagious. I'm going mad too.
JULIA. I try to keep away from you.
FEFU. Why?
JULIA. I might be harmful to you.
FEFU. Why?
JULIA. I am contagious. I can't be what I used to be.
FEFU. You have no courage.
JULIA. You're being cruel.
FEFU. I want to rest, Julia. How does a person rest. I want to put my mind at rest. I am frightened. (*Julia looks at Fefu.*) Don't look at me. (*She covers Julia's eyes with her hand.*) I lose my courage when you look at me.
JULIA. May no harm come to your head.
FEFU. Fight!
JULIA. May no harm come to your will.
FEFU. Fight, Julia!

(*Fefu starts shaking the wheelchair and pulling Julia off the wheelchair.*)

JULIA. I have no life left.
FEFU. Fight, Julia!
JULIA. May no harm come to your hands.
FEFU. I need you to fight.
JULIA. May no harm come to your eyes.

FEFU. Fight with me!

JULIA. May no harm come to your voice.

FEFU. Fight with me!

JULIA. May no harm come to your heart.

(Christina enters. Fefu sees Christina, releases Julia. To Christina.)

FEFU. Now I have done it. Haven't I. You think I'm a monster. *(She turns to Julia and speaks to her with kindness.)* Forgive me if you can. *(Julia nods.)*

JULIA. I forgive you.

(Fefu gets the gun.)

CHRISTINA. What in the world are you doing with that gun!

FEFU. I'm going to clean it!

CHRISTINA. I think you better not!

FEFU. You're silly!

(Cecilia appears on the landing.)

CHRISTINA. I don't care if you shoot yourself! I just don't like the mess you're making!

(Fefu starts to go to the lawn and turns.)

FEFU. I enjoy betting it won't be a real bullet! You want to bet!

CHRISTINA. No! *(Fefu exits. Christina goes to Julia.)* Are you all right?

JULIA. Yes.

CHRISTINA. Can I get you anything?

JULIA. Water. *(Cecilia goes to the liquor cabinet for water.)* Put some sugar in it. Could I have a damp cloth for my forehead? *(Christina goes toward the kitchen. Julia speaks front.)* I didn't tell her anything. Did I? I didn't.

CECILIA *(Going to Julia with the water)*. About what?

JULIA. She knew.

(There is the sound of a shot. Christina and Cecilia run out. Julia puts her hand to her forehead. Her hand goes down slowly. There is blood on her forehead. Her head falls back. Fefu enters holding a dead rabbit.)

FEFU. I killed it . . . I just shot . . . and killed it. . . . Julia . . .

(Dropping the rabbit, Fefu walks to Julia and stands behind the chair as she looks at Julia. Sue and Cindy enter from the foyer, Emma and Paula from the kitchen, Christina and Cecilia from the lawn. They surround Julia. The lights fade.)

COMMENTARY

Note: The following essay offers one interpretation of the play. For other perspectives on Fefu and Her Friends, *consult the essays listed below.*

Although *Fefu* is a realistic play, it is riddled with mystery and menace, as if violence—which has afflicted Julia with hallucinations and paralysis and soon will appear in Cindy's nightmare of a malevolent doctor as well as Fefu's gun-shooting game with her husband—could erupt at any moment. Yet against this undertow of danger, there is a stronger current of positive warmth and female support as the women conduct their conversations, have their lunch and tea, worry about one another and especially about Julia, all with real tenderness and affection. The presence of Fefu's husband Phillip outside on the lawn is one source of potential violence, for it is he, Fefu says, who believes women to be "loathsome" and who, she says, she has already left "in the mind" though not the body. Julia's long, hallucinatory speech in Part II takes this idea much farther as she remembers being tortured in terms of dismemberment, with her inquisitors demanding she rid herself of all the "stinking parts" of her body. Ballerinas, she decides, are acceptable because they have no "entrails," but the trailblazer of modern dance, Isadora Duncan, proves disgusting because, she does not hide her sexuality or gender.

Two of the women—the steady, clear-headed Paula and the cool, unemotional Cecilia—are lesbians who once had an affair. Cecilia crudely tries to resume the relationship, but neither woman is subject to the horrible doubts that bring the heterosexual Fefu close to madness, Julia closer to death, and Cindy coping by day but fearful at night. The ebullient, often comical Emma is obsessed with genitals and imagines a sexual heaven in which fully committed performance (a theme picked up in her later speech about educating through theatrical performance) can bring bliss. Sue, the treasurer of this group, is the least troubled of the eight, while Christina, who fears Fefu's male-identified strength, is the least interesting. Critic Elinor Fuchs views the play as an exploration of the differences between male and female gender roles and self-images. The outdoors (where Phillip is situated, along with Fefu's brother and their gardener) is the male sphere, while indoors, where it's dark, is the female world, an increasingly intimate place in Part II as the audience moves from the auditorium into real rooms with four walls and the actors up close. Fuchs cogently analyzes the key confrontation between Fefu and the death-haunted, wheelchair-bound Julia whom Fefu has seen walking and believes can put her hysterical paralysis and seeming self-hatred behind her. Early in Part I, Fefu invokes the myth of Orpheus to explain that women avert their eyes from one another, as if a god had once said "and if they shall recognize each other the world will be blown apart." Toward the end, Julia averts her eyes from Fefu's strong gaze, and later, Fefu turns her gaze away from Julia, who understands her unhappiness. Lost is their opportunity to "blow the world apart." Fefu returns to her shooting game with the rifle and returns with the kill (a rabbit); nearby, the parallel victim Julia is now in a stupor, or perhaps dead, though certainly not healed.

Typically for Fornes, the final scene has its comic, almost burlesque elements. The field rabbit is a far cry from the more noble and symbolic deer described in the first Julia-related shooting. But even Julia's speeches when she's back in reality—her offhanded longing to "be with others who also hallucinate"—have a wit never far from the pain in the most harrowing moments of any Fornes plays.

Fornes herself has written enigmatically that the play "is not fighting anything, not negating anything. My intention has not been to confront anything. I felt as I wrote the play that I was surrounded by friends. I felt very happy to have such good and interesting friends. Is it a feminist play? . . . Yes, it is." Bonnie Marranca most clearly states the artistic effect of Fornes's treatment of her characters as "good friends." The playwright makes "no attempt to tell the whole story of a life, only to distill its essence. Fornes brings a much needed intimacy to drama, and her economy of approach suggests another vision of theatricality. She has lifted the burden of psychology, declamation, morality and sentimentality from the concept of character. She has freed characters from explaining themselves in a way that attempts to suggest interpretations." And perhaps most distinctively, Fornes's "authorial voice does not demand power over the theatrical experience." In this womanly delicacy, more than any other American playwright, Fornes resembles the Russian Realist with a delicate touch, Anton Chekhov.

Other perspectives on *Fefu and Her Friends*:

Cummings, Scott. "Seeing with Clarity: The Visions of Maria Irene Fornes." *Yale Theater* 17 (Winter 1985): 51–56.

Moroff, Diane Lynn. *Fefu and Her Friends*. In Moroff, *Fornes: Theatre in the Present Tense*. Ann Arbor: University of Michigan Press, 1966, 33–55.

FROM *ACTING OUT: FEMINIST PERFORMANCES*

by Lynda Hart and Peggy Phelan

Dull Gret confronts a modern "top girl," Marlene, as Pope Joan and others look on; the New York Shakespeare Festival produced the American premiere of Caryl Churchill's play, Top Girls, *among the most inventive of feminist works in the contemporary theater.*

Acting Out: Feminist Performances, edited by Lynda Hart and Peggy Phelan, provides an overview of contemporary feminist theater, both its traditional plays and experimental work, such as performance art. The introduction to their book, reprinted here, outlines the early history of feminist performance and identifies key artists within the movement.

I got the kind of madness Socrates talked about, "A divine release of the soul from the yoke of custom and convention." I refuse to be intimidated by reality anymore. After all, what is reality anyway? Nothin' but a collective hunch.

—Jane Wagner,
The Search for Signs of Intelligent Life in the Universe

"Reality" is a fantasy-construction which enables us to mask the Real of our desire.

—Jacques Lacan

Jane Wagner's "bag lady" Trudy speaks her subjectivity from the far margins of the social order as well as the borderlands of psychic space. Wagner thus neatly connects the material circumstances of her heroine with her psychic determination. Lily Tomlin's one-woman performance processes a series of rapidly mutating personae, all traversed by the consciousness of Trudy, whose madness affords her a motility that might be read as evidence of the primordial splitting of the antihumanistic subject. Trudy inhabits a spatiotemporal order—the spaced-out time of her extraterrestrial chums—disconsonant with the linear time of humanistic narrative. Miming the unconscious, where the subject is not consonant with the self, where the "I" is multiple, shifting, and subject and object positions are endlessly mutable, this subject-without-a-fixed-identity created in the fissure of a radical split would be in need of a therapeutic restoration of wholeness for the humanist spectator. Trudy is "acting out," transgressing the boundary between the imaginary and the real. Catherine Clément points out that acting out, "however dangerous it might be, is also therapeutic, monstrously so."[1] Wagner both calls attention to and reinforces the impossibility of her female speaker's rejection of the symbolic as Trudy reports: "I never could've done stuff like that when I was in my *right* mind. I'd be worried people would think I was *crazy*."[2]

By translating her madness into divinity, Trudy attempts to make the best of a bad situation. Her dilemma is not unlike that of women in general. If "there can be nothing *human* that pre-exists or exists outside the law represented by the father; [if] there is only either its denial (psychosis) or the fortunes and misfortunes ('normality' and neurosis) of its terms,"[3] then we can better understand why *Search for Signs*, a materialist-feminist performance that satirizes the misfortunes of women caught within the sociosymbolic order dominated by the law of the Father, seeks escape in madness and communion with extrahuman space chums. Wagner and Tomlin deviously address the problem but nonetheless appeal to the model. There is no easy way out for Trudy and her multiple incarnations. She attempts to manipulate her world, but, Cassandra-like, no one will believe her. Her madness relegates her to an aberrant individuality; thus isolated, she cannot speak for a credible community. It is nonetheless in these moments of "acting out" that the "factious identity of the subject disappears."[4] Clément speaks of identity as a prosthesis or an armor that one must wear in order to be understood. Identities are necessary if we are to live in reality, but they mask our desire. Feminist identities embrace the monstrous possibilities of acting out. Cutting ourselves off from "reality" can be a way to escape our inundation in *a* masculine imaginary that passes as *the* symbolic order.

If *Search for Signs* managed to squeak some subversive moments past the patriarchal censors and still gain wide popularity as well as commercial success, what the theatrical establishment usually authorizes under the name "women's," and occasionally even "feminist," theater is recently best represented by Wendy Wasserstein's *Heidi Chronicles*. Wasserstein herself as well as her main character, Heidi Holland, eschew a feminist identity in deference to a humanist one, and thereby become spokeswomen for a feminism that failed, that left women like Heidi "stranded." The play's most highly charged moment occurs when Dr. Heidi Holland is invited to address Miss Crain's School East Coast Alumnae Association as a distinguished alumna. Her topic is "Women, Where Are We Going?" "Nowhere" is her answer. She sums up the history of the feminist movement in an iconic aerobics class locker room scene, in which she finds herself alienated from, envious of, and superior to the young women wearing purple and green leather who bring their own heavier weights, the mothers with pressed blue jeans who know where to purchase Zeus sneakers, the gray-haired woman who talks about brown rice and women's fiction, and whom Heidi imagines is having "a bisexual relationship with a female dock worker."[5] Heidi realizes at this moment that she is not happy and hasn't been for a long time. Her speech ends with this spontaneous, nostalgic lament: "I don't blame the ladies in the locker room for how I feel. I don't blame any of us. We're all concerned, intelligent, good women. (Pause). It's just that I feel stranded. And I thought the whole point was that I wouldn't feel stranded. I thought the point was that we were all in this together. Thank you. (She walks off.)"[6]

The Heidi Chronicles is a valuable commodity in this increasingly conservative political climate. Feminism, it insists, has woefully failed "women." The play's realism offers nothing in the way of commentary on the fact that the conceptual space it carves out for "women" is occupied by a white, middle-class, heterosexual woman who finds her fulfillment in motherhood and considers herself a humanist. For those women who have contributed to the demise of such a monolithic feminism, Heidi's "failure" is our triumph. This play fulfills the fantasy that the divi-

sions within contemporary feminism signal a dissolve, rather than productive disassembling. . . .

. . . There is a moment in the U.S. lesbian-feminist Split Britches and London's gay duo Bloolips collaboration, *Belle Reprieve*, that addresses this emphasis. Frustrated with this postmodern pastiche of Tennessee William's *A Streetcar Named Desire*, Bloolips Bette (Blanche) demands a story. Stamping his feet and whining his complaints with hyperbolic distress, Bette insists that the cast stop all this "romping about in the avant-garde and I don't know what else,"[7] and allow him to memorize his lines, don a pair of pretty pumps, and play a real part, a part his seventy-three-year-old mother, who is still hoping to see him play Romeo one day, can understand. Lois Weaver (Stella) menacingly challenges Bette to a realistic scene. Peggy Shaw (Stanley) attempts to play it with him—straight—from *A Streetcar Named Desire*:

BLANCHE: "Just let me get by you."
STANLEY: "Get by me? Sure, go ahead."
BLANCHE: "You stand over there."
STANLEY: "You got plenty of room, go ahead."
BLANCHE: "Not with you there! I've got to get by somehow!"

Bette is a drag queen, which offers him a way out of sliding too easily into patriarchal womanhood, and he refuses to play the scene. When he realizes what is about to happen to him, he interrupts the action by reminding Stanley that he is not a real man. No, Shaw admits, if I were a real man I would say: "Come to think of it, maybe you wouldn't be so bad to interfere with. . . . If you want to play a woman, the woman in this play gets raped and goes crazy."[8] Bette says that he didn't plan on getting raped and going crazy; he only wanted a chance to wear a nice frock. This is one moment in which the "reprieve," a temporary escape from pain or trouble, occurs. This performance of bodies and drives and violence upends any expectation for realism. If spectators are frustrated in their desire for identification, Bette (Blanche) finally gives them the moment described above in which they might enter this show. Laura Mulvey's claim that "sadism demands a story" has never seemed so incandescent.[9] Getting raped, going crazy, and, of course, dying—this is what women appear to do most often in realistic theater. The recurrence of these actions is often enough thematic, but it also indicates the space of representation for the feminine subject position. Within the psychosemiotics of theatrical realism, the "death-space," space of absence, negativity, unrepresentability, is where femininity most often takes a place. Realism, like/as ideology, needs subjects, and subjects are constituted through divisions and losses that are always already gendered.

One response to the impossibility of the feminine taking a place within the symbolic has been an effort to recover, or postulate, a prediscursive body, a critical effort to free the female body from its overdeterminations as a body saturated with sex, site of pleasure for (an)other, subjected and devoid of subjectivity. This issue has a particular valence in performance studies, where the female body on stage is easily received as iconic, seemingly less arbitrary than a linguistic sign, and even more so than photographic or televisual images, exceptionally susceptible to naturalization. Indeed, the female body on stage appears to be the "thing itself," incapable of mimesis, afforded not only no distance between sign and referent but, indeed, taken for the referent.

In his discussion of the reception of televisual broadcasts Stuart Hall retains the distinction "denotation/connotation"—a conceptual pairing that he recognizes as rather outmoded in linguistic theory—but which continues to hold a certain "analytic value." The distinction is useful for thinking about the female body in performance, for, as Hall outlines it, the connotative level of the sign is the site where "'meanings' are *not* apparently fixed in natural perception (that is, they are not fully naturalized), and their fluidity of meaning and association can be more fully exploited and transformed."[10] By contrast the denotative level of the sign (understood here as an analytic category and not a literal transcription) is the site where "its ideological value is strongly *fixed*—because it has become so fully universal and

'natural.'"[11] Elin Diamond has cautioned us against "leap[ing] to examples of performance art where, supposedly, the body's texts displace the conventional mimesis of the text-performance structure."[12] Certainly the work represented here does not simply and effortlessly evade the body/text conflation of conventional mimesis, but I do envision this collection as an antidote to the virtual hegemony of realism in Anglo-American theater.

Most of the performance [art] texts . . . do not have the status of "plays," nor do they aspire to such categorization. They do not, however, by virtue of operating on the level of the connotative sign—where, according to Hall's schema, "situational ideologies alter and transform signification"—produce meanings that are *outside* of ideology. But perhaps they could be said to have a certain advantage that is produced alongside their marginalized status. In that sense they are in limited but important ways "unbound," achieving a fluidity of movement simultaneously inside and outside dominant discourses. . . .

Collective authorship was an extremely important concept in early feminist companies of the 1970s and 1980s. As the utopian fervor of such collectivities gave way to a realization that they were, to some extent, based on a vision of feminist homogeneity that could not fully take into account the divisions and productive conflicts between and among feminists, the "idea" of a collective suffered fragmentations, largely in response to women of color and lesbians, who began calling attention to the inadequacies of the model. Nevertheless, today we may yet have something to learn from the history of these collectives; certainly the problem of authorship and textual ownership has become even more pressing in the last few decades. Julie Malnig and Judy Rosenthal map the history of the Women's Experimental Theatre Company (WET), an emblematic company founded in 1975. The optimism of the 1970s, in which feminist theater companies were operating with the idea that presenting "positive" images of women could counteract the misogyny of masculinist representations of women, gave way to

the realization that differences between, among, and within women precluded any direct access to what constitutes "positivity." WET dissolved in 1985, but its ten-year history is marked with the conflicts that many women in performance grappled with during this period. In the histories of these collectives we can observe the process of feminists wrestling with what Derrida has called "women as truth" and "women as untruth," both remaining "within the economy of truth's system, in the phallogocentric space."[13] Such oscillation between competing claims for a definition of "women" raises the problem of essentialism and the necessity of performing gender and sexuality in a register that disrupts a metaphysics of presence. . . .

The three-woman troupe Split Britches has been one of the most influential groups in feminist performance. Its productions have been the subject of excitement, controversy, and much provocative writing in feminist performance studies. . . . As a single feminist performance artist, Karen Finley probably has the highest profile of any woman working in the field today. Her notoriety as centerpiece for the National Endowment for the Arts (NEA) controversies has propelled her into a refractive and projective spotlight, which . . . has taken quite a toll on her. Long before the NEA debates began, however, Finley's performances elicited heated reactions. . . . Finley's work excites a multiplicity of spectatorial identifications that illuminate the complexities of seeing. She is both susceptible to assimilation and co-optation by the dominant gaze that decries her representations and a model for subversive transgressions.[14]

The question of identity formations is crucial to feminist theorizing. As the work of the collectives exemplifies, the last decade has been one of struggle between competing identities. Whereas earlier feminist theorists were enabled by constituting "women" as a group opposed to a dominant patriarchy, they also came to realize that such a position presumed a hegemonic Other that was by no means monolithic. Such an "us-them" stance was not only reductive, but it also precluded making coalitions across gender, race, and sexual borders. It relegated "us" to victims and gave "them" a hegemonic power that left no way out for feminist subjectivities. And, most important, it erased the differences between, among, and within "women," who presumably constituted the category. This has been a central issue in feminist theory for some time now, and its ongoing political importance is addressed by many writers in this collection. Yvonne Yarbro-Bejarano evokes the Chicana "speaking for ourselves" but is quick to problematize the expression in Cherríe Moraga's work that permits no simplistic access to a unified Chicana identity or experience. Moraga is one of the leading figures in representing and historicizing the imbrication of gender, race, and sexuality as both multiple sites of oppression and spaces of contradiction in which different subjectivities can be constructed. Yarbo-Bejarano shows that the "familia" is a crucial concept to maintain for Chicano/a ethnic identity—but it must be refigured by ending the social construct of "man." . . .

Anna Deavere Smith's one-woman "On the Road" performances make patent the way in which feminist poststructuralists theorize formations of subjectivity. I particularly like Sandra Richard's description of Smith's work as "solo carnival," a provocative paradox that neatly captures Smith's "imitations" of her interviewees. If the "selves" that Smith performs are a series of ego identifications, she shows that these are dialogic formations that constantly mutate. Smith does not simply capture the people she interviews and reproduce their images; she also shows us the more unsettling

process of their subjectivities being formed in the act of exchange with her, then among the spectators who witness the multiple incarnations. Such a "kaleidoscope of often contradictory positions" both addresses the problematics of community building and, ironically perhaps, facilitates their formation. . . .

I am concerned that feminists will retreat in the face of the deeply reactionary times in which we are mired. Will the progress we have made in fracturing monumental, exclusionary, totalizing constructs of women lose its force as we seek ways to mobilize our defenses? This seems to me to be a most urgent threat. Is greater visibility our best offense and defense? Acting out, acting up, coming out—these have been the strategies most frequently deployed to resist the swell of the New Right's agenda. They have produced some astonishing successes but have also been compromising in complex ways that bear close scrutiny.

Notes

1 Catherine Clément, *The Lives and Legends of Jacques Lacan*, trans. Arther Goldhammer (New York: Columbia University Press, 1983), 71.

2 Jane Wagner, *The Search for Signs of Intelligent Life in the Universe* (New York: Harper and Row, 1986), 18.

3 Juliet Mitchell, "Introduction—I," *Feminine Sexuality: Jacques Lacan and the école freudienne*, trans. Jacqueline Rose (New York: W. W. Norton, 1985), 23.

4 Clément, *Lives and Legends*, 92.

5 Wendy Wasserstein, *The Heidi Chronicles* (New York: Dramatists Play Services,

1990), 61. *The Heidi Chronicles* won not only the 1989 Pulitzer Prize for drama but also the 1989 best play distinction from the Drama Desk, the New York Drama Critics' Circle, the Outer Critics' Circle, as well as the Dramatists Guild's Hull Warriner Award and the Susan Smith Blackburn Prize.

6 Ibid., 62.

7 *Belle Reprieve* is a collaborative work by Split Britches and Bloolips. It will be published in *Gay and Lesbian Plays Today*, ed. Terry Helbing (Portsmouth, N.H.: Heinemann). My quotations are taken from proof pages.

8 Ibid.

9 Laura Mulvey, "Visual Pleasure and Narrative Cinema," *Visual and Other Pleasures* (Bloomington: Indiana University Press, 1989), 22.

10 Stuart Hall, "Encoding/decoding," *Culture, Media, Language*, ed. Stuart Hall (London: Hutchinson, 1980), 133.

11 Ibid.

12 Elin Diamond, "Mimesis, Mimicry, and the 'True-Real,'" *Modern Drama* 32, no. 1 (March 1989): 68.

13 Jacques Derrida, *Spurs: Nietzche's Styles*, trans. Barbara Harlow (Chicago: University of Chicago Press, 1978), 97 and passim.

14 I have discussed Finley's work at length elsewhere. See Lynda Hart, "Motherhood according to Karen Finley: The Theory of Total Blame," *Drama Review* 36, no. 1 (Spring 1992): 124–34; and "Karen Finley's Dirty Work: Homophobia, Censorship, and the NEA," *Genders* 14 (Fall 1992): 1–15.

ZOOT SUIT

LUIS VALDEZ

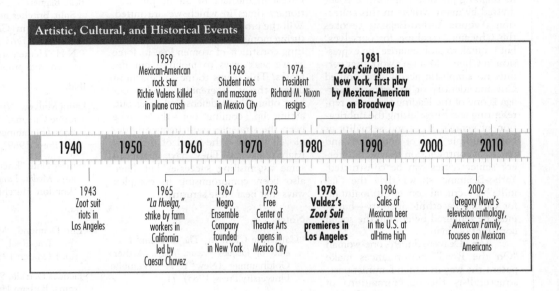

Artistic, Cultural, and Historical Events

1959
Mexican-American
rock star
Richie Valens killed
in plane crash

1968
Student riots
and massacre
in Mexico City

1974
President
Richard M. Nixon
resigns

1981
Zoot Suit opens in
New York, first play
by Mexican-American
on Broadway

1940 | 1950 | 1960 | 1970 | 1980 | 1990 | 2000 | 2010

1943
Zoot suit
riots in
Los Angeles

1965
"La Huelga,"
strike by farm
workers in
California
led by
Caesar Chavez

1967
Negro
Ensemble
Company
founded
in New York

1973
Free
Center of
Theater Arts
opens in
Mexico City

1978
**Valdez's
Zoot Suit
premieres in
Los Angeles**

1986
Sales of
Mexican beer
in the U.S. at
all-time high

2002
Gregory Nava's
television anthology,
American Family,
focuses on Mexican
Americans

LUIS VALDEZ (1940–)

No individual is more responsible for the development of Mexican-American drama than Luis Valdez, and no Chicano in any art medium has had more written about him and his work. From simple beginnings in farm fields in California's Central Valley in the 1960s, Valdez's theatrical and now film work has become truly mainstream. *Zoot Suit* (1981) was the first play by a Mexican-American to be produced on Broadway, and his 1987 film *La Bamba* (about Chicano rock star Richie Valens) was admired by critics and the public.

Valdez was born in Delano, California, in 1940, the son of *campesinos*, migrant farm workers who picked grapes and other crops from the citrus groves of Southern California to the apple orchards of Washington State. Because of their transient lifestyle, the children of *campesinos* often do not do well in school and frequently drop out. Valdez, however, persevered and graduated from high school, even while working as a ventriloquist on a local television station. He earned a scholarship to San Jose State College (now University), where he took theater classes and eventually wrote his first play, *The Shrunken Head of Pancho Villa*. A surrealistic work about a young Mexican-American without a head (who represents "faceless" Chicanos struggling for recognition in mainstream America), the play received a lengthy standing ovation at its premiere at San Jose State College and has been reworked to become an integral part of Valdez's canon.

After college Valdez joined the San Francisco Mime Troupe, a politically committed band of artists in the Bay Area who fused a *commedia dell'arte* style with social activism. When he returned to his home in Delano in 1965, he met Caesar Chávez, who was organizing the United Farm Workers (UFW) in an attempt to gain better working conditions, wages, health care, and education for the *campesinos*. Valdez worked as a UFW recruiter for two years. Applying what he had learned from the Mime Troupe, Valdez began a theater company, El Teatro Campesino, that performed short plays (*actos*) in fields, at union halls, in churches, even on flatbed trucks. The *actos* were an inventive combination of satirical clowning, Brechtian theater, folk-plays, and agit-prop designed to educate farm workers about their rights and to provoke them into action (specifically, to "strike" against the growers). Valdez also refers to these early *actos* as *huelguistas* ("strike plays") because they were performed during the period of *La Huelga*, the historical grape boycott which eventually led to a victory for the UFW. It was the beginning of the civil rights movement for Hispanic-Americans, and El Teatro Campesino's plays were as instrumental in its success as Martin Luther King, Jr.'s speeches were for the African-American movement. Many of the *actos* end with the actors get-

Edward James Olmos played El Pachuco in the original Los Angeles and New York productions of Luis Valdez's Zoot Suit *and in the film. The large newspaper image in the background is typical of the theater of Piscator and Brecht (see Part II), which influenced Valdez's political theater.*

ting the audience to rise and shout "*La raza*" ("the race"), "*La huelga*" ("strike"), and "Chicano power" in the best agit-prop fashion.

Valdez himself defines the purpose of *actos*:

Inspire the audience to social action. Illuminate specific points about social problems. Satirize the opposition. Show or hint at a solution. Express what people are feeling.

The *actos* performed by El Teatro Campesino epitomize "the Rough Theatre" as defined by Sir Peter Brook in *The Empty Space* (1968): "The Rough Theatre is close to the people . . . the theatre that's not a theatre, the theatre on carts, on wagons, on trestles, audiences standing, drinking, sitting round tables, audiences joining in, answering back." To further the bond between actors and performers, the *actos* were frequently accompanied by *corridos* and *rancheras*, popular songs that served as a kind of "living newspaper" to keep audiences informed about current events. Valdez's actors, it must be noted, were not trained professionals (though many became professional actors) but were taken from the ranks of the farm workers themselves. Their presence lent a compelling authenticity to the message of the plays.

Among Valdez's best-known *actos* is *Los Vendidos* (1967), a satirical portrait of Mexican-American "sellouts" who contribute to the stereotypical notions Anglos have about

Hispanics or who try to "pass" as Anglos. *The Dark Root of a Scream* (1967) and *Soldado Raza* (1970) are *actos* about the victimization of Hispanics during the Vietnam War. After the success of *La Huelga*, Valdez turned to mythological themes extolling the virtues of Aztlan, the sacred kingdom of the Aztecs and the repository of the greatness of "*la raza.*" *Bernabe* (1970) is an especially poignant portrait of a young Chicano with learning disabilities who quests after La Tierra, the mythical goddess of the land.

El Teatro Campesino is still based in San Juan Bautista, California. In addition to its stage work, it has contributed films and several television shows to contemporary culture. Each Christmas season, PBS broadcasts *La Pastorela*, a Chicano version of the Nativity story featuring such well-known Mexican-American performers as Linda Rondstadt, Paul Rodriguez, Cheech Marin, and the Texas Tornados. Valdez continues to write plays (e.g., *Bandido*, 1999) and screenplays.

AS YOU READ *ZOOT SUIT*

Because *Zoot Suit* is based on two historical incidents, it draws on specific elements of Mexican-American culture. In his program note for the New York production, Valdez stressed that the play is not "a documentary but an imaginative dramatization." Nonetheless, there are several things you need to know as you read the play.

- In 1942 seventeen young Mexican-American men were put on trial for the murder of a Hispanic male in the Sleepy Lagoon section of Los Angeles. The trial was a sham and increased distrust between the Mexican-American community and the Anglo establishment. (Note that "Sleepy Lagoon" was also the title of a Big Band hit during the 1940s; the play derives much of its tension from the clash of salsa and Big Band music.)
- In June 1943 Los Angeles witnessed a ten-day period of violence and protests after a group of U.S. servicemen and civilians attacked a group of Mexican-American youths; with a police escort protecting them, Marines went into the *barrios* to beat young men. This event and the infamous Sleepy Lagoon Trial galvanized the Mexican-American community and promoted a greater pride in "*la Raza.*"
- The young Mexican-American males were known as "zoot-suiters" because of the extravagant clothing they wore as a sign of their ethnic pride. The snap-brimmed hat ("lid") and the brightly colored zoot suits (which may have been patterned after the costume Rhett Butler wore in *Gone with the Wind*) were worn by youths of various ethnicities and had actually inspired pop songs in the early 1940s (e.g., "I Wanna Zoot Suit"). Young Mexican-American men adopted the suit (*el tacuche*) as a badge of honor, and some Anglos looked upon the extravagantly dressed men in their fingertip-length coats, baggy pants, gold chains, and "lids" as anarchistic threats because they were "different." America was at war and there was considerable animosity against those who did not readily appear to be "American."
- The play is narrated by El Pachuco, Valdez's mythic embodiment of the glory of the Aztec race from which many Mexicans descended. A *pachuco* was a street-smart youth who lived on the edge of the law; the term is still used today, although *vato* (a variant on *bato*, a soldier in Pancho Villa's revolutionary army in 1916) and "lowrider" are near-synonyms.
- *Pachucos* spoke *Calo*—a fanciful blend of Spanish and English used on the streets—which Valdez uses to poetic effect in this play. You needn't understand every word of Calo, which is used to create an aura of authenticity for the play. It also may be regarded as a "tribal language" that *pachucos* used to promote their identity.
- Hispanic theater in general, and Mexican theater in particular, is distinguished by its fanciful blend of styles (known as *rasquachi* or *rasquachismo*) to create a "magic realism" (*majico realismo*) that encourages artists and audiences to transcend the limitations of day-to-day existence by undertaking a spiritual journey that illuminates truths about the human condition. Therefore, do not look for a consistency of style in this play, as its appeal—and its themes—depend on a calculated blend of dissonant styles.

ZOOT SUIT

LUIS VALDEZ

CHARACTERS

EL PACHUCO
HENRY REYNA

HIS FAMILY:
ENRIQUE REYNA
DOLORES REYNA
LUPE REYNA
RUDY REYNA

HIS FRIENDS:
GEORGE SHEARER
ALICE BLOOMFIELD

HIS GANG:
DELLA BARRIOS
SMILEY TORRES
JOEY CASTRO
TOMMY ROBERTS
ELENA TORRES
BERTHA VILLARREAL

THE DOWNEY GANG:
RAFAS
RAGMAN
HOBO
CHOLO
ZOOTER
GÜERA
HOBA
BLONDIE
LITTLE BLUE

DETECTIVES:
LIEUTENANT EDWARDS
SERGEANT SMITH

THE PRESS:
PRESS
CUB REPORTER
NEWSBOY

THE COURT:
JUDGE F.W. CHARLES
BAILIFF

THE PRISON:
GUARD

THE MILITARY:
BOSUN'S MATE
SAILORS
MARINE
SWABBIE
MANCHUKA
SHORE PATROLMAN

OTHERS:
GIRLS
PIMP
CHOLO

SETTING

The giant facsimile of a newpaper fromt page serves as a drop curtain. The huge masthead reads: LOS ANGELES HERALD EXPRESS Thursday, June 3, 1943. A headline cries out: ZOOT-SUITER HORDES INVADE LOS ANGELES. US NAVY AND MARINES ARE CALLED IN. Behind this are black drapes creating a place of haunting shadows larger than life. The somber shapes and outlines of pachuco images hang subtly, black on black, against a back-ground of heavy fabric evoking memories and feelings like an old suit hanging forgotten in the depths of a closet somewhere, sometime . . . Below this is a sweeping, curving place of levels and rounded corners with the hard, ingrained brilliance of countless spit shines, like the memory of a dance hall.

ACT I

PROLOGUE

A switchblade plunges through the newspaper. It slowly cuts a rip to the bottom of the drop. To the sounds of "Perdido" by Duke Ellington, El Pachuco emerges from the slit. He adjusts his clothing, meticulously fussing with his collar, suspenders, cuffs. He tends to his hair, combing back every strand into a long luxurious ducktail, with infinite loving pains. Then he reaches into the slit and pulls out his coat and hat. He dons them. His fantastic costume is complete. It is a zoot suit. He is transformed into the very image of the pachuco myth, from his portk-pie hat to the tip of his four-foot watch chain. Now he turns to the audience. His three-soled shoes with metal taps click-clack as he proudly, slovenly, defiantly makes his way downstage. He stops and assumes a pachuco stance.

PACHUCO.
    ¿Que le watcha a mis trapos, ese?
    ¿Sabe qué, carnal?
    Estas garras me las planté porque
    Vamos a dejarnos caer un play, ¿sabe?

(He crosses to center stage, models his clothes.)

Watcha mi tacuche, ese. Aliviánese con mis calcos, tando,
    lisa, tramos, y carlango, ese.

(Pause.)

Nel, sabe qué, usted está muy verdolaga. Como se me hace que es puro square.

(El Pachuco breaks character and addresses the audience in perfect English.)

Ladies and gentlemen
the play you are about to see
is a construct of fact and fantasy.
The Pachuco Style was an act in Life
and his language a new creation.
His will to be was an awesome force
eluding all documentation . . .
A mythical, quizzical, frightening being
precursor of revolution
Or a piteous, hideous heroic joke
deserving of absolution?
I speak as an actor on the stage.
The Pachuco was existential
for he was an Actor in the streets
both profane and reverential.
It was the secret fantasy of every bato
in or out of the Chicanada
to put on a Zoot Suit and play the Myth
más chucote que la chingada.

    (Puts hat back on and turns.)

¡Pos órale!

(Music. The newspaper drop flies. El Pachuco begins his chuco stroll upstage, swinging his watch chain.)

1. ZOOT SUIT

The scene is a barrio dance in the forties. Pachucos and Pachucas in zoot suits and pompadours.

They are members of the 38th Street Gang, led by Henry Reyna, 21, dark, Indian-looking, older than his years, and Della Barrios, 20, his girlfriend in miniskirt and finger-tip coat. A Sailor called Swabbie dances with his girlfriend Manchuka among the Couples. Movement. Animation. El Pachuco sings.

PACHUCO.
    PUT ON A ZOOT SUIT, MAKES YOU FEEL
        REAL ROOT
    LOOK LIKE A DIAMOND, SPARKLING, SHIN-
        ING
    READY FOR DANCING
    READY FOR THE BOOGIE TONIGHT!

(The Couples, dancing, join the Pachuco in exclaiming the last term of each line in the next verse.)

    THE HEPCATS UP IN HARLEM WEAR THAT
        DRAPE SHAPE
    COMO LOS PACHUCONES DOWN IN L.A.
    WHERE HUISAS IN THEIR POMPADOURS
        LOOK REAL KEEN
    ON THE DANCE FLOOR OF THE BALL-
        ROOMS
    DONDE BAILAN SWING.

    YOU BETTER GET HEP TONIGHT
    AND PUT ON THAT ZOOT SUIT!

(The Downey Gang, a rival group of pachucos enters upstage left. Their quick dance step becomes a challenge to 38th Street.)

DOWNEY GANG. Downey . . . ¡Rifa!
HENRY *(Gesturing back)*. ¡Toma! *(The music is hot. El Pachuco slides across the floor and momentarily breaks the tension. Henry warns Rafas, the leader of the Downey Gang, when he sees him push his brother Rudy.)* ¡Rafas!

PACHUCO (*Sings*).

> TRUCHA, ESE LOCO, VAMOS AL BORLO
> WEAR THAT CARLANGO, TRAMOS Y TANDO
> DANCE WITH YOUR HUISA
> DANCE TO THE BOOGIE TONIGHT!
>
> 'CAUSE THE ZOOT SUIT IS THE STYLE IN
>   CALIFORNIA
> TAMBIÉN EN COLORADO Y ARIZONA
> THEY'RE WEARING THAT TACUCHE EN EL
>   PASO
> Y EN TODOS LOS SALONES DE CHICAGO
>
> YOU BETTER GET HEP TONIGHT
> AND PUT ON THAT ZOOT SUIT!

2. THE MASS ARRESTS

We hear a siren, then another, and another. It sounds like gangbusters. The dance is interrupted. Couples pause on the dance floor.

PACHUCO. Trucha, la jura. ¡Pélenle! (*Pachucos start to run out, but Detectives leap onstage with drawn guns. A Cub Reporter takes flash pictures.*)

SGT. SMITH. Hold it right there, kids!

LT. EDWARDS. Everybody get your hands up!

RUDY. Watcha! This way! (*Rudy escapes with some others.*)

LT. EDWARDS. Stop or I'll shoot! (*Edwards fires his revolver into the air. A number of pachucos and their girlfriends freeze. The cops round them up. Swabbie, an American sailor, and Manchuka, a Japanese-American dancer, are among them.*)

SGT. SMITH. ¡Ándale! (*Sees Swabbie.*) You! Get out of here.

SWABBIE. What about my girl?

SGT. SMITH. Take her with you. (*Swabbie and Manchuka exit.*)

HENRY. What about my girl?

LT. EDWARDS. No dice, Henry. Not this time. Back in line.

SGT. SMITH. Close it up!

LT. EDWARDS. Spread! (*The Pachucos turn upstage in a line with their hands up. The sirens fade and give way to the sound of a teletype. The Pachucos turn and form a lineup, and the Press starts shooting pictures as he speaks.*)

PRESS. The City of the Angels, Monday, August 2, 1942. The Los Angeles Examiner, Headline:

THE LINEUP (*In chorus*). Death Awakens Sleepy Lagoon (*Breath.*) LA Shaken by Lurid "Kid" Murder.

PRESS. The City of the Angels, Monday August 2, 1942. The Los Angeles Times Headline:

THE LINEUP. One Killed, Ten Hurt in Boy Wars: (*Breath.*) Mexican Boy Gangs Operating Within City.

PRESS. The City of the Angels, August 2, 1942. Los Angeles Herald Express Headline:

THE LINEUP. Police Arrest Mexican Youths. Black Widow Girls in Boy Gangs.

PRESS. The City of the Angels . . .

PACHUCO (*Sharply*). El Pueblo de Nuestra Señora la Reina de los Ángeles de Porciúncula, pendejo.

PRESS (*Eyeing the Pachuco cautiously*). The Los Angeles Daily News Headline:

BOYS IN THE LINEUP. Police Nab 300 in Roundup.

GIRLS IN THE LINEUP. Mexican Girls Picked Up in Arrests.

LT. EDWARDS. Press Release, Los Angeles Police Department: A huge showup of nearly 300 boys and girls rounded up by the police and sheriff's deputies will be held tonight at eight o'clock in Central Jail at First and Hill Street. Victims of assault, robbery, purse snatching, and similar crimes are asked to be present for the identification of suspects.

PRESS. Lieutenant . . . ? (*Edwards poses as the Press snaps a picture.*)

LT. EDWARDS. Thank you.

PRESS. Thank you. (*Smith gives a signal, and the lineup moves back, forming a straight line in the rear, leaving Henry up front by himself.*)

LT. EDWARDS. Move! Turn! Out! (*As the rear line moves off to the left following Edwards, Smith takes Henry by the arm and pulls him downstage, shoving him to the floor.*)

3. PACHUCO YO

SGT. SMITH. Okay, kid, you wait here till I get back. Think you can do that? Sure you can. You pachucos are regular tough guys. (*Smith exits. Henry sits up on the floor. El Pachuco comes forward.*)

HENRY. Bastards. (*He gets up and paces nervously. Pause.*) ¡Ese? ¡Ese?

PACHUCO (*Behind him*). ¿Qué pues, nuez?

HENRY (*Turning*). Where the hell you been, ese?

PACHUCO. Checking out the barrio. Qué desmadre, ¿no?

HENRY. What's going on, ese? This thing is big.

PACHUCO. The city's cracking down on pachucos, carnal. Don't you read the newspapers? They're screaming for blood.

HENRY. All I know is they got nothing on me. I didn't do anything.

PACHUCO. You're Henry Reyna, ese—Hank Reyna! The snarling juvenile delinquent. The zootsuiter. The bitter young pachuco gang leader of 38th Street. That's what they got on you.

HENRY. I don't like this, ese (*Suddenly intense.*) I DON'T LIKE BEING LOCKED UP!

PACHUCO. Calmantes montes, chicas patas. Haven't I taught you to survive? Play it cool.

HENRY. They're going to do it again, ese! They're going to charge me with some phony rap and keep me until they make something stick.

PACHUCO. So what's new?

HENRY (*Pause*). I'm supposed to report for the Navy tomorrow. (*The Pachuco looks at him with silent disdain.*) You don't want me to go, do you?

PACHUCO. Stupid move, carnal.

HENRY (*Hurt and angered by Pachuco's disapproval*). I've got to do something.

PACHUCO. Then hang tough. Nobody's forcing you to do shit.

HENRY. I'm forcing me, ese—ME, you understand?

PACHUCO. Muy patriotic, eh?

HENRY. Yeah.

PACHUCO. Off to fight for your country.

HENRY. Why not?

PACHUCO. Because this ain't your country. Look what's happening all around you. The Japs have sewed up the Pacific. Rommel is kicking ass in Egypt but the Mayor of L.A. has declared all-out war on Chicanos. On you! ¡Te curas?

HENRY. Órale.

PACHUCO. Qué mamada, ¿no? Is that what you want to go out and die for? Wise up. These bastard paddy cops have it in for you. You're a marked man. They think you're the enemy.

HENRY (*Refusing to accept it*). Screw them bastard cops!

PACHUCO. And as soon as the Navy finds out you're in jail again, ya estuvo, carnal. Unfit for military duty because of your record. Think about it.

HENRY (*Pause*). You got a frajo?

PACHUCO. Simón. (*He pulls out a cigarette, hands it to Henry, lights it for him. Henry is pensive.*)

HENRY (*Smokes, laughs ironically*). I was all set to come back a hero, see? Me la rayo. For the first time in my life I really thought Hank Reyna was going someplace.

PACHUCO. Forget the war overseas, carnal. Your war is on the homefront.

HENRY (*With new resolve*). What do you mean?

PACHUCO. The barrio needs you, carnal. Fight back! Stand up to them with some style. Show the world a Chicano has balls. Hang tough. You can take it. Remember, Pachuco Yo!

HENRY (*Assuming the style*). Con safos, carnal.

4. THE INTERROGATION

The Press enters, followed by Edwards and Smith.

PRESS (*To the audience*). Final Edition; The Los Angeles Daily News. The police have arrested twenty-two members of the 38th Street Gang, pending further investigation of various charges.

LT. EDWARDS. Well, son, I was hoping I wouldn't see you in here again.

HENRY. Then why did you arrest me?

LT. EDWARDS. Come on, Hank, you know why you're here.

HENRY. Yeah. I'm a Mexican.

LT. EDWARDS. Don't give me that. How long have I known you? Since '39?

HENRY. Yeah, when you got me for stealing a car, remember?

LT. EDWARDS. All right. That was a mistake. I didn't know it was your father's car. I tried to make it up to you. Didn't I help you set up the youth club?

SGT. SMITH. They turned it into a gang, Lieutenant. Everything they touch turns to shit.

LT. EDWARDS. I remember a kid just a couple of years back. Head boy at the Catholic Youth Center. His idea of fun was going to the movies. What happened to that nice kid, Henry?

PRESS. He's "Gone With The Wind," trying to look like Clark Gable.

SGT. SMITH. Now he thinks he's Humphrey Bogart.

PACHUCO. So who are you, puto? Pat O'Brien?

LT. EDWARDS. This is the wrong time to be anti-social, son. This country's at war, and we're under strict orders to crack down on all malcontents.

SGT. SMITH. Starting with all pachucos and draft dodgers.

HENRY. I ain't no draft dodger.

LT. EDWARDS. I know you're not. I heard you got accepted by the Navy. Congratulations. When do you report?

HENRY. Tomorrow?

SGT. SMITH. Tough break!

LT. EDWARDS. It's still not too late, you know. I could still release you in time to get sworn in.

HENRY. If I do what?

LT. EDWARDS. Tell me, Henry, what do you know about a big gang fight last Saturday night, out at Sleepy Lagoon?

PACHUCO. Don't tell 'em shit.

HENRY. Which Sleepy lagoon?

LT. EDWARDS. You mean there's more than one? Come on, Hank, I know you were out there. I've got a statement from your friends that says you were beaten up. Is that true? Were you and your girl attacked?

HENRY. I don't know anything about it. Nobody's ever beat me up.

SGT. SMITH. That's a lie and you know it. Thanks to your squealer friends, we've got enough dope on you to indict for murder right now.

HENRY. Murder?

SGT. SMITH. Yeah, murder. Another greaser named José Williams.

HENRY. I never heard of the bato.

SGT. SMITH. Yeah, sure.

LT. EDWARDS. I've been looking at your record, Hank. Petty theft, assault, burglary, and now murder. Is that what you want? The gas chamber? Play square with me. Give me a statement as to what happened at the Lagoon, and I'll go to bat for you with the Navy. I promise you.

PACHUCO. If that ain't a line of gabacho bullshit, I don't know what is.

LT. EDWARDS. Well?

PACHUCO. Spit in his pinche face.

SGT. SMITH. Forget it, Lieutenant. You can't treat these animals like people.

LT. EDWARDS. Shut up! I'm thinking of your family, Hank. your old man would be proud to see you in the Navy. One last chance, son. What do you say?

HENRY. I ain't your son, cop.

LT. EDWARDS. All right, Reyna, have it your way. (Edwards and Press exit.)

PACHUCO. You don't deserve it, ese, but your going to get it anyway.

SGT. SMITH. All right, muchacho, it's just me and you now. I hear tell you pachucos wear these monkey suits as a kind of armor. Is that right? How's it work? This is what you zooters need—a little old-fashioned discipline.

HENRY. Screw you, flatfoot.

SGT. SMITH. You greasy son of a bitch. What happened at the Sleepy Lagoon? Talk! Talk! Talk! (Smith beats Henry with a rubber sap. Henry passes out and falls to the floor, with his hands still handcuffed behind his back. Dolores his mother appears in a spot upstage, as he falls.)

DOLORES. Henry! (Lights change. Four Pachuco Couples enter, dancing a 40's pasodoble (two-step) around Henry on the floor, as they swing in a clothesline of newspaper sheets. Music.)

PACHUCO.
Get up and escape, Henry . . .
leave reality behind
with your buenas garras
muy chamberlain
escape through the barrio streets of your mind
through a neighborhood of memories
all chuckhole lined
and the love
and the pain
as fine as wine . . .

(Henry sits up, seeing his mother Dolores folding newspaper sheets like clothes on a clothesline.)

DOLORES. Henry?

PACHUCO. It's a lifetime ago, last Saturday night . . . before Sleepy Lagoon and the big bad fight.

DOLORES. Henry!

PACHUCO. Tu mamá, carnal. (He recedes into the background.)

DOLORES (At the clothesline). Henry, ¿hijo? Ven a cenar.

HENRY (Gets up off the floor). Sorry, jefita, I'm not hungry. Besides, I got to pick up Della. We're late for the dance.

DOLORES. Dance? In this heat? Don't you muchachos ever think of anything else? God knows I suffer la pena negra seeing you go out every night.

HENRY. This isn't just any night, jefa. It's my last chance to use my tacuche.

DOLORES. Tacuche? Pero tu padre . . .

HENRY (Revealing a stubborn streak). I know what mi 'apá said, 'amá. I'm going to wear it anyway.

DOLORES (Sighs, resigns herself). Mira, hijo. I know you work hard for your clothes. And I know how much they mean to you. Pero por diosito santo, I just don't know what you see en esa cochinada de "soot zoot."

HENRY (Smiling). Drapes, 'amá, we call them drapes.

DOLORES (Scolding playfully). Ay sí, drapes, muy funny, ¿verdad? And what do the police call them, eh? They've put you in jail so many times. ¿Sabes qué? I'm going to send them all your clothes!

HENRY. A qué mi 'amá. Don't worry. By this time next week, I'll be wearing my Navy blues. Okay?

DOLORES. Bendito sea Dios. I still can't believe you're going off to war. I almost wish you were going back to jail.

HENRY. ¡Órale! (Lupe Reyna, 16, enters dressed in a short skirt and baggy coat. She is followed by Della Barrios, 17, dressed more modestly. Lupe hides behind a newspaper sheet on the line.)

LUPE. Hank! Let's go, carnal. Della's here.

HENRY. Della . . . Órale, esa. What are you doing here? I told you I was going to pick you up at your house.

DELLA. You know how my father gets.

HENRY. What happened?

DELLA. I'll tell you later.

DOLORES. Della, hija, buenas noches. How pretty you look.

DELLA. Buenas noches. (Dolores hugs Della, then spots Lupe hiding behind the clothesline.)

DOLORES (To Lupe). ¿Oye y tú? What's wrong with you? What are you doing back there.

LUPE. Nothing, 'amá.

DOLORES. Well, come out then.

LUPE. We're late, 'amá.

DOLORES. Come out, te digo. (*Lupe comes out exposing her extremely short skirt. Dolores gasps.*) ¡Válgame Dios! Guadalupe, are you crazy? Why bother to wear anything?

LUPE. Ay, 'amá, it's the style. Short skirt and fingertip coat. Huh, Hank?

HENRY. Uh, yeah, 'amá.

DOLORES. ¿Oh sí? And how come Della doesn't get to wear the same style?

HENRY. No . . . that's different. No, chale.

ENRIQUE (*Off*). ¡VIEJA!

DOLORES. Ándale. Go change before your father sees you.

ENRIQUE. I'm home. (*Coming into the scene.*) Buenas noches, everybody. (*All respond. Enrique sees Lupe.*) ¡Ay, jijo! Where's the skirt?!

LUPE. It's here.

ENRIQUE. Where's the rest of it?

DOLORES. She's going to the dance.

ENRIQUE. ¿Y a mí qué me importa? Go and change those clothes. Ándale.

LUPE. Please, 'apá?

ENRIQUE. No, señorita.

LUPE. Chihuahua, I don't want to look like a square.

ENRIQUE. ¡Te digo que no! I will not have my daughter looking like a . . .

DOLORES. Like a puta . . . I mean, a pachuca.

LUPE (*Pleading for help*). Hank . . .

HENRY. Do what they say, sis.

LUPE. But you let Henry wear his drapes.

ENRIQUE. That's different. He's a man. Es hombre.

DOLORES. Sí, that's different. You men are all alike. From such a stick, such a splinter. De tal palo, tal astillota.

ENRIQUE. Natural, muy natural, and look how he came out. ¡Bien macho! Like his father. ¿Verdad, m'ijo?

HENRY. If you say so, jefito.

ENRIQUE (*To Della*). Buenas noches.

DELLA. Buenas noches.

HENRY. 'Apá, this is Della Barrios.

ENRIQUE. Mira, mira . . . So this is your new girlfriend, eh? Muy bonita. Quite a change from the last one.

DOLORES. Ay, señor.

ENRIQUE. It's true. What was her name?

DELLA. Bertha?

ENRIQUE. That's the one. The one with the tattoo.

DOLORES. Este hombre. We have company.

ENRIQUE. That reminds me. I invited the compadres to the house mañana.

DOLORES. ¿Que qué?

ENRIQUE. I'm buying a big keg of cerveza to go along with the menudo.

DOLORES. Oye, ¿cuál menudo?

ENRIQUE (*Cutting her off*). ¡Qué caray, mujer! It isn't every day a man's son goes off to fight for his country. I should know. Della, m'ija, when I was in the Mexican Revolution, I was not even as old as my son is.

DOLORES. N'ombre, don't start with your revolution. We'll be here all night.

HENRY. Yeah, jefe, we've got to go.

LUPE (*Comes forward. She has rolled down her skirt*). 'Apá, is this better?

ENRIQUE. Bueno. And you leave it that way.

HENRY. Órale, pues. It's getting late. Where's Rudy?

LUPE. He's still getting ready. Rudy! (*Rudy Reyna, 19, comes downstage in an old suit made into a tachuche.*)

RUDY. Let's go everybody. I'm ready.

ENRIQUE. Oye, oye, ¿y tú? What are you doing with my coat?

RUDY. It's my tachuche, 'apá.

ENRIQUE. ¡Me lleva la chingada!

DOLORES. Enrique . . . ¡por el amor de Dios!

ENRIQUE (*To Henry*). You see what you're doing? First that one and now this one. (*To Rudy.*) Hijo, don't go out like that. Por favor. You look like an idiot, pendejo.

RUDY. Órale, Hank. Don't I look all right?

HENRY. Nel, ese, you look fine. Watcha. Once I leave for the service, you can have my tachuche. Then you can really be in style. ¿Cómo la ves?

RUDY. Chale. Thanks, carnal, but if I don't join the service myself, I'm gonna get my own tachuche.

HENRY. You sure? I'm not going to need it where I'm going. ¿Tú sabes?

RUDY. Are you serious?

HENRY. Simón.

RUDY. I'll think about it.

HENRY. Pos, no hay pedo, ese.

ENRIQUE. ¿Cómo que pedo? Nel, ¿Simón? Since when did we stop speaking Spanish in this house? Have you no respect?

DOLORES. Muchachos, muchachos, go to your dance. (*Henry starts upstage.*)

HENRY. Buenas Noches . . . (*Enrique holds out his hand. Henry stops, looks, and then returns to kiss his father's hand. Then he moves to kiss his Mother and Rudy in turn kisses Enrique's hand. Enrique says "Buenas Noches" to each of his sons.*)

HENRY. Órale, we'd better get going . . . (*General "goodbyes" from everybody.*)

ENRIQUE (*As Rudy goes past him*). Henry! Don't let your brother drink beer.

RUDY. Ay, 'apá. I can take care of myself.

DOLORES. I'll believe that when I see it. (*She kisses him on the nose.*)

LUPE. Ahí te watcho, 'amá.

ENRIQUE. ¿Que qué?

LUPE. I mean, I'll see you later. (*Henry, Della, Lupe and Rudy turn upstage. Music starts.*)

ENRIQUE. Mujer, why didn't you let me talk?

DOLORES (*Sighing*). Talk, señor, talk all you want. I'm listening. (*Enrique and Dolores exit up right. Rudy and Lupe exit up left. Lights change. We hear hot dance music. Henry and Della dance at center stage. El Pachuco sings.*)

PACHUCO.

CADA SÁBADO EN LAS NOCHE
YO ME VOY A BORLOTEAR
CON MI LINDA PACHUCONA
LAS CADERAS A MENEAR

ELLA LE HACE MUY DE AQUELLAS
CUANDO EMPIEZA A GUARACHAR
AL COMPÁS DE LOS TIMBALES
YO ME SIENTO PETATEAR

(*From upstage right, three pachucos now enter in a line, moving to the beat. They are Joey Castro, 17; Smiley Torres, 23; and Tommy Roberts, 19, Anglo. They all come downstage left in a diagonal.*)

LOS CHUCOS SUAVES BAILAN RUMBA
BAILAN LA RUMBA Y LE ZUMBAN
BAILAN GUARACHA SABROSÓN
EL BOTECITO Y EL DANZÓN!

(*Chorus repeats, the music fades. Henry laughs and happily embraces Della.*)

5. THE PRESS

Lights change. El Pachuco escorts Della off right. The Press appears at upstage center.

PRESS. Los Angeles Times: August 8, 1942.

A Newsboy enters, lugging in two more bundles of newspapers, hawking them as he goes. People of various walks of life enter at intervals and buy newspapers. They arrange themselves in the background reading.

NEWSBOY. EXTRA! EXTRAAA! READ ALL ABOUT IT. SPECIAL SESSION OF L.A. COUNTY GRAND JURY CONVENES. D.A. CHARGES CONSPIRACY IN SLEEPY LAGOON MURDER. EXTRAAA! (*A Cub Reporter emerges and goes to the Press, as Lieutenant Edwards enters.*)

CUB REPORTER. Hey, here comes Edwards! (*Edwards is beseiged by the Press, joined by Alice Bloomfield, 26, a woman reporter.*)

PRESS. How about it, Lieutenant? What's the real scoop on the Sleepy Lagoon? Sex, violence . . .

CUB REPORTER. Marijuana?

NEWSBOY. Read all about it! Mexican Crime Wave Engulfs L.A.

LT. EDWARDS. Slums breed crime, fellas. That's your story.

ALICE. Lieutenant. What exactly is the Sleepy Lagoon?

CUB REPORTER. A great tune by Harry James, doll. Wanna dance? (*Alice ignores the Cub.*)

LT. EDWARDS. It's a reservoir. An old abandoned gravel pit, really. It's on a ranch between here and Long Beach. Serves as a swimming hole for the younger Mexican kids.

ALICE. Because they're not allowed to swim in the public plunges?

PRESS. What paper are you with, lady? The Daily Worker?

LT. EDWARDS. It also doubles as a sort of lovers' lane at night—which is why the gangs fight over it. Now they've finally murdered somebody.

NEWSBOY. EXTRA! EXTRA! ZOOT-SUITED GOONS OF SLEEPY LAGOON!

LT. EDWARDS. But we're not going to mollycoddle these youngsters any more. And you can quote me on that.

PRESS. One final question, Lieutenant. What about the 38th Street Gang—weren't you the first to arrest Henry Reyna?

LT. EDWARDS. I was. And I noticed right away the kid had great leadership potential. However . . .

PRESS. Yes?

LT. EDWARDS. You can't change the spots on a leopard.

PRESS. Thank you, sir. (*People with newspapers crush them and throw them down as they exit. Edwards turns and exits. Alice turns towards Henry for a moment.*)

NEWSBOY. EXTRA, EXTRA. READ ALL ABOUT THE MEXICAN BABY GANGSTERS. EXTRA, EXTRA.

The Press and Cub Reporter rush out happily to file their stories. The Newsboy leaves, hawking his papers. Alice exits, with determination. Far upstage, Enrique enters with a rolling garbage can. He is a street sweeper. During the next scene he silently sweeps up the newspapers, pausing at the last to read one of the news stories.

6. THE PEOPLE'S LAWYER

JOEY. ¡Chale, ese, chale! Qué pinche agüite.

SMILEY. Mexican Baby Gangsters?!

TOMMY. Zoot-suited goons! I knew it was coming. Every time the D.A. farts, they throw us in the can.

SMILEY. Pos, qué chingados, Hank. I can't believe this. Are they really going to pin us with a murder rap? I've got a wife and kid, man!

JOEY. Well, there's one good thing anyway. I bet you know that we've made the headlines. Everbody knows we got the toughest gang in town.

TOMMY. Listen to this, pip squeak. The biggest heist he ever pulled was a Tootsie Roll.

JOEY (*Grabbing his privates*). Here's your Tootsie Roll, ese.

TOMMY. What, that? Get my microscope, Smiley.

JOEY. Why don't you come here and take a little bite, joto.

TOMMY. Joto? Who you calling a joto, maricón?

JOEY. You, white boy. Did I ever tell you, you got the finest little duck ass in the world.

TOMMY. No, you didn't tell me that, culero. (*Joey and Tommy start sparring.*)

SMILEY (*Furious*). Why don't you batos knock it off?

HENRY (*Cool*). Cálmenla.

SMILEY. ¡Pinches chavalos! (*The batos stop.*)

JOEY. We're just cabuliando, ese.

TOMMY. Simón, ese. Horsing around. (*He gives Joey a final punch.*)

SMILEY (*With deep self-pity*). I'm getting too old for this pedo, Hank. All this farting around con esos chavalillos.

HENRY. Relax, carnal. No te agüites.

SMILEY. You and me have been through a lot, Hank. Parties, chingazos, jail. When you said let's join the pachucada, I joined the pachucada. You and me started the 38th, bato. I followed you even after my kid was born, but what now, carnal? This pinche pedo is serious.

TOMMY. He's right, Hank. They indicted the whole gang.

JOEY. Yeah, you know the only one who ain't here is Rudy. (*Henry turns sharply.*) He was at the Sleepy Lagoon too, ese. Throwing chingazos.

HENRY. Yeah, but the cops don't know that, do they? Unless one of us turned stoolie.

JOEY. Hey, ese, don't look at me. They beat the shit out of me, but that's all they got. Shit.

TOMMY. That's all you got to give. (*Laughs.*)

HENRY. Okay! Let's keep it that way. I don't want my carnalillo pulled into this. And if anybody asks about him, you batos don't know nothing. You get me?

SMILEY. Simón.

TOMMY. Crazy.

JOEY (*Throwing his palms out*). Say, Jackson, I'm cool. You know that.

HENRY. There's not a single paddy we can trust.

TOMMY. Hey, ese, what about me?

HENRY. You know what I mean.

TOMMY. No, I don't know what you mean. I'm here with the rest of yous.

JOEY. Yeah, but you'll be the first one out, cabrón.

TOMMY. Gimme a break, maníaco. ¡Yo soy pachuco!

HENRY. Relax, ese. Nobody's getting personal with you. don't I let you take out my carnala? Well, don't I?

TOMMY. Simón.

HENRY. That's because you respect my family. The rest of them paddies are after our ass.

PACHUCO. Talk about paddies, ese, you got company. (*George Shearer enters upstage right and comes down. He is a middle-aged lawyer, strong and athletic, but with the slightly frazzled look of a people's lawyer.*)

GEORGE. Hi, boys.

HENRY. Trucha!

GEORGE. My name is George Shearer. I've been retained by your parents to handle your case. Can we sit and talk for a little bit? (*Pause. The Boys eye George suspiciously. He slides a newspaper bundle a few feet upstage.*)

PACHUCO. Better check him out, ese. He looks like a cop.

HENRY (*To the Guys, sotto voce*). Pónganse al alba. Este me huele a chota.

GEORGE. What was that? Did you say I could sit down? Thank you. (*He pulls a bundle upstage. He sits.*) Okay, let me get your names straight first. Who's José Castro?

JOEY. Right here, ese. What do you want to know?

GEORGE. We'll get to that. Ismael Torres?

SMILEY (*Deadpan*). That's me. But they call me Smiley.

GEORGE (*A wide grin*). Smiley? I see. You must be Thomas Roberts.

TOMMY. I ain't Zoot Suit Yokum.

GEORGE. Which means you must be Henry Reyna.

HENRY. What if I am. Who are you?

GEORGE. I already told you, my name's George Shearer. Your parents asked me to come.

HENRY. Oh yeah? Where did they get the money for a lawyer?

GEORGE. I'm a People's Lawyer, Henry.

SMILEY. People's Lawyer?

JOEY. Simón, we're people.

TOMMY. At least they didn't send no animal's lawyer.

HENRY. So what does that mean? You doing this for free or what?

GEORGE (*Surprise turning to amusement*). I try not to work for free, if I can help it, but I do sometimes. In this case, I expect to be paid for my services.

HENRY. So who's paying you? For what? And how much?

GEORGE. Hey, hey, hold on there. I'm supposed to ask the questons. You're the one going on trial, not me.

PACHUCO. Don't let him throw you, ese.

GEORGE. I sat in on part of the Grand Jury. It was quite a farce, wasn't it? Murder one indictment and all.

SMILEY. You think we stand a chance?

GEORGE. There's always a chance, Smiley. That's what trials are for.

PACHUCO. He didn't answer your question, ese.

HENRY. You still didn't answer my question, mister. Who's paying you? And how much?

GEORGE (*Getting slightly peeved*). Well, Henry, it's really none of your damned business. (*The Boys react.*) But for whatever it's worth, I'll tell you a little story. The first murder case I ever tried, and won incidentally, was for a Filipino. I was paid exactly three dollars and fifty cents plus a pack of Lucky Strike cigarettes, and a note for a thousand dollars—never redeemed. Does that answer your question?

HENRY. How do we know you're really a lawyer?

GEORGE. How do I know you're Henry Reyna? What do you really mean, son? Do you think I'm a cop?

HENRY. Maybe.

GEORGE. What are you trying to hide from the cops? Murder? (*The Boys react.*) All right! Aside from your parents, I've been called into this case by a citizens committee that's forming in your behalf, Henry. In spite of evidence to the contrary, there are some people out there who don't want to see you get the shaft.

HENRY. ¿Sabes qué, mister? Don't do us any favors.

GEORGE (*Starting to leave*). All right, you want another lawyer? I'll talk to the Public Defender's office.

JOEY (*Grabbing his briefcase*). Hey, wait a minute, ese. Where are you going?

TOMMY. De cincho se le va a volar la tapa.

JOEY. Nel, este bolillo no sabe nada.

GEORGE (*Exploding*). All right, kids, cut the crap!

SMILEY (*Grabs his briefcase and crosses to Henry*). Let's give him a break, Hank. (*Smiley hands the briefcase to George.*)

GEORGE. Thank you. (*He starts to exit. Stops.*) You know, you're making a big mistake. I wonder if you know who your friends are? You boys are about to get a mass trial. You know what that is? Well, it's a new one on me too. The Grand Jury has indicted you all on the same identical crime. Not just you four. The whole so-called 38th Street Gang. And you know who the main target is? You, Henry, because they're saying you're the ringleader. (*Looks around at the Guys.*) And I suppose you are. But you're leading your buddies here down a dead-end street. The

D.A.'s coming after you, son, and he's going to put you and your whole gang right into the gas chamber. (*George turns to leave. Smiley panics. Joey and Tommy react with him.*)

SMILEY/JOEY/TOMMY (*All together*). Gas chamber! But we didn't do nothing! We're innocent!

HENRY. ¡Cálmenla! (*The batos stop in their tracks.*) Okay. Say we believe you're a lawyer, what does that prove? The press has already tried and convicted us. Think you can change that?

GEORGE. Probably not. But then, public opinion comes and goes, Henry. What matters is our system of justice. I believe it works, however slowly the wheels may grind. It could be a long uphill fight, fellas, but we can make it. I know we can. I've promised your parents the best defense I'm capable of. The question is, Henry, will you trust me?

HENRY. Why should I? You're a gringo.

GEORGE (*Calmly, deliberately*). ¡Cómo sabes!

TOMMY (*Shocked*). Hey, you speak Spanish?

GEORGE. Más o menos.

JOEY. You mean you understood us a while ago?

GEORGE. More or less.

JOEY (*Embarrassed*). ¡Híjole, qué gacho, ese!

GEORGE. Don't worry. I'm not much on your pachuco slang. The problem seems to be that I look like an Anglo to you. What if I were to tell you that I had Spanish blood in my veins? That my roots go back to Spain, just like yours? What if I'm an Arab? What if I'm a Jew? What difference does it make? The question is, will you let me help you? (*Pause. Henry glances at the Pachuco.*)

PACHUCO. ¡Chale!

HENRY (*Pause*). Okay!

SMILEY. Me too!

JOEY. Same here!

TOMMY. ¡Órale!

GEORGE (*Eagerly*). Okay! Let's go to work. I want to know exactly what happened right from the beginning. (*George sits down and opens his briefcase.*)

HENRY. Well, I think the pedo really started at the dance last Saturday night . . . (*El Pachuco snaps his fingers and we hear dance music. Lights change. George exits.*)

7. THE SATURDAY NIGHT DANCE

Swabbie and Manchuka come running onstage as the barrio dance begins to take shape. Henry and the batos move upstage to join other Pachucos and Pachucas coming in. Henry joins Della Barrios; Joey

teams up with Bertha Villarreal, Tommy picks up Lupe Reyna; and Smiley escorts his wife Elena Torres. They represent the 38th Street neighborhood. Also entering the dance comes the Downey Gang, looking mean. Rudy stands upstage, in the background, drinking a bottle of beer. El Pachuco sings.

PACHUCO.
CUANDO SALGO YO A BAILAR
YO ME PONGO MUY CATRÍN
LAS HUISITAS TODAS GRITAN, DADDY
VAMOS A BAILAR EL SWING!

(The Couples dance. A lively swing number. The music comes to a natural break and shifts into a slow number. Bertha approaches Henry and Della downstage on the dance floor.)

BERTHA. Ese, ¡surote! How about a dance for old time's sake? No te hagas gacho.

HENRY (*Slow dancing with Della*). Sorry, Bertha.

BERTHA. Is this your new huisa? This little fly chick?

DELLA. Listen, Bertha . . .

HENRY (*Stops her*). Chale. She's just jealous. Beat it, Bertha.

BERTHA. Beat it yourself. Mira. You got no hold on me, cabrón. Not any more. I'm as free as a bird.

SMILEY (*Coming up*). Ese, Hank, that's the Downey Gang in the corner. You think they're looking for trouble?

HENRY. There's only a couple of them.

BERTHA. That's all we need.

SMILEY. Want me to alert the batos?

HENRY. Nel, be cool.

BERTHA. Be cool? Huy, yu, yui. Forget it, Smiley. Since he joined the Navy, this bato forgot the difference between being cool and being cool-O. (*She laughs and turns but Henry grabs her angrily by the arm. Bertha pulls free and walks away cool and tough. The music changes and the beat picks up. El Pachuco sings as the Couples dance.*)

PACHUCO.
CUANDO VOY AL VACILÓN
Y ME METO YO A UN SALÓN
LAS CHAVALAS GRITAN, PAPI VENTE
VAMOS A BAILAR DANSÓN!

(The dance turns Latin. The music comes to another natural break and holds. Lupe approaches Henry on the dance floor.)

LUPE. Hank. Rudy's at it again. He's been drinking since we got here.

HENRY (*Glancing over at Rudy*). He's okay, sis, let the carnal enjoy himself.

RUDY (*Staggering over*). ¡Ese, carnal!

HENRY. What you say, brother?

RUDY. I'm flying high, Jackson. Feeling good.

LUPE. Rudy, if you go home drunk again, mi 'apá's going to use you for a punching bag. (*Rudy kisses her on the cheek and moves on.*)

DELLA. How are you feeling?

HENRY. Okay.

DELLA. Still thinking about Bertha?

HENRY. Chale, ¿qué traes? Listen, you want to go out to the Sleepy Lagoon? I've got something to tell you.

DELLA. What?

HENRY. Later, later.

LUPE. You better tell Rudy to stop drinking.

HENRY. Relax, sis. If he gets too drunk, I'll carry him home.

(Music picks up again. El Pachuco sings a third verse.)

PACHUCO.
TOCAN MAMBO SABROSÓN
SE ALBOROTA EL CORAZÓN
Y CON UNA CHAVALONA VAMOS
VAMOS A BAILAR EL MAMBO

(The Couples do the mambo. In the background, Rudy gets into an argument with Rafas, the leader of the Downey Gang. A fight breaks out as the music comes to a natural break. Rafas pushes Rudy, half drunk, onto the floor.)

RAFAS. ¡Y a ti qué te importa, puto!

RUDY (*He falls*). ¡Cabrón!

HENRY (*Reacting immediately*). Hey! (*The whole dance crowd tenses up immediately, splitting into separate camps. Batos from 38th clearly outnumber the Guys from Downey.*)

RAFAS. He started it, ese. El comenzó a chingar conmigo.

RUDY. You chicken shit, ese! Tú me haces la puñeta, ¡pirujo!

RAFAS. Come over here and say that, puto!

HENRY (*Pulling Rudy behind him*). ¡Agüítala, carnal! (*Faces Rafas.*) You're a little out of your territory, ¿que no Rafas?

RAFAS. It's a barrio dance, ese. We're from the barrio.

HENRY. You're from Downey.

RAFAS. Vale madre. ¡Downey Rifa!

DOWNEY GANG. ¡SIMÓN!

RAFAS. What are you going to do about it?

HENRY. I'm going to kick your ass. (*The Two Sides start to attack each other.*) ¡Cálmenla! (*All stop.*)

RAFAS (*Pulls out a switchblade*). You and how many batos?

HENRY. Just me and you, cabrón. That's my carnalillo you started pushing around, see? And nobody chinga con mi familia without answering to me, ese! Hank Reyna! (*He pulls out another switchblade.*)

BERTHA. ALL-RIGHT!

HENRY. Let's see if you can push me around like you did my little brother, ese. Come on . . . COME ON! (*They knife fight. Henry moves in fast. Recoiling, Rafas falls to the floor. Henry's blade is at his throat. El Pachuco snaps his fingers. Everyone freezes.*)

PACHUCO. Qué mamada, Hank. That's exactly what the play needs right now. Two more Mexicans killing each other. Watcha . . . Everbody's looking at you.

HENRY (*Looks out at the audience*). Don't give me that bullshit. Either I kill him or he kills me.

PACHUCO. That's exactly what they paid to see. Think about it. (*El Pachuco snaps again. Everybody unfreezes.*)

HENRY (*Kicks Rafas*). Get out of here. ¡Píntate!

BERTHA. What?

GÜERA (*Rafas' girlfriend runs forward*). Rafas. ¡Vámonos! (*She is stopped by other Downey Batos.*)

RAFAS. Está suave. I'll see you later.

HENRY. Whenever you want, cabrón. (*The Downey Gang retreats, as the 38th razzes them all the way out. Insults are exchanged. Bertha shouts "!Chinga tu madre!" and they are gone. The 38th whoops in victory.*)

SMILEY. Órale, you did it, ese! ¡Se escamaron todos!

TOMMY. We sure chased those jotos out of here.

BERTHA. I could have beat the shit out of those two rucas.

JOEY. That pinche Rafas is yellow without his gang, ese.

LUPE. So why didn't you jump out there?

JOEY. Chale, Rudy ain't my baby brother.

RUDY (*Drunk*). Who you calling a baby, pendejo? I'll show you who's a baby!

JOEY. Be cool, ese.

TOMMY. Man, you're lucky your brother was here.

BERTHA. Why? He didn't do nothing. The old Hank would have slit Rafas' belly like a fat pig.

HENRY. Shut your mouth, Bertha!

RUDY. ¿Por qué, carnal? You backed down, ese. I could have taken that sucker on by myself.

HENRY. That's enough, Rudy. You're drunk.

DELLA. Hank, what if Rafas comes back with all his gang?

HENRY (*Reclaiming his leadership*). We'll kill the sons of bitches.

JOEY. ¡Órale! ¡La 38th rifa! (*Music. Everybody gets back with furious energy. El Pachuco sings.*)

PACHUCO.
DE LOS BAILES QUE MENTÉ
Y EL BOLERO Y EL BEGUÍN
DE TODOS LOS BAILES JUNTOS
ME GUSTA BAILAR EL SWING! HEY!
(*The dance ends with a group exclamation: HEY!*)

8. EL DÍA DE LA RAZA

The Press enters upstage level, pushing a small hand truck piled high with newspaper bundles. The batos and rucas on the dance floor freeze in their final dance positions. El Pachuco is the only one who relaxes and moves.

PRESS. October 12, 1942: Columbus Day. Four Hundred and Fiftieth Anniversary of the Discovery of America. Headlines!

(In their places, the Couples now stand straight and recite a headline before exiting. As they do so, the Press moves the bundles of newspapers on the floor to outline the four corners of a jail cell.)

SMILEY/ELENA. President Roosevelt Salutes Good Neighbors in Latin America. (*Smiley and Elena exit.*)

TOMMY/LUPE. British Begin Drive to Oust Rommel From North Africa. (*Tommy and Lupe exit.*)

RUDY/CHOLO. Japs In Death Grip On Pacific Isles. (*Rudy and Cholo exit. Press tosses another bundle.*)

ZOOTER/LITTLE BLUE. Web Of Zoot Crime Spreads. (*Zooter and Little Blue exit.*)

MANCHUKA/SWABBIE. U.S. Marines Land Bridgehead On Guadalcanal. (*Manchuka and Swabbie exit.*)

JOEY/BERTHA. First Mexican Braceros Arrive In U.S.A. (*Joey and Bertha exit.*)

DELLA. Sleepy Lagoon Murder Trial Opens Tomorrow. (*Della and the Press exit. As they exit, George and Alice enter upstage left. Henry is center, in a "cell" outlined by four newspaper bundles left by the Press.*)

GEORGE. Henry? How you doing, son? Listen, I've brought somebody with me that wants very much to meet you. I thought you wouldn't mind. (*Alice crosses to Henry.*)

ALICE. Hello! My name is Alice Bloomfield and I'm a reporter from the Daily People's World.

GEORGE. And . . . And, I might add, a red hot member of the ad hoc committee that's fighting for you guys.

ALICE. Oh, George! I'd hardly call it fighting, for Pete's sake. This struggle has just barely begun. But we're sure going to win it, aren't we, Henry?

HENRY. I doubt it.

GEORGE. Oh come on, Henry. How about it, son? You all set for tomorrow? Anything you need, anything I can get for you?

HENRY. Yeah. What about the clean clothes you promised me? I can't go to court looking like this.

GEORGE. You mean they didn't give them to you?

HENRY. What?

GEORGE. Your mother dropped them off two days ago. Clean pants, shirt, socks, underwear, the works. I cleared it with the Sheriff last week.

HENRY. They haven't given me mothing.

GEORGE. I'm beginning to smell something around here.

HENRY. Look, George, I don't like being like this. I ain't dirty. Go do something, man!

GEORGE. Calm down. Take it easy, son. I'll check on it right now. Oh! Uh, Alice?

ALICE. I'll be okay, George.

GEORGE. I'll be right back. (*He exits.*)

ALICE (*Pulling out a pad and pencil*). Now that I have you all to myself, mind if I ask you a couple of questions?

HENRY. I got nothing to say.

ALICE. How do you know? I haven't asked you anything yet. Relax. I'm from the progressive press. Okay? (*Henry stares at her, not knowing quite how to react. Alice sits on a bundle and crosses her goodlooking legs. Henry concentrates on that.*) Now. The regular press is saying the Pachuco Crime Wave is fascist inspired— any thoughts about that?

HENRY (*Bluntly*). No.

ALICE. What about the American Japanese? Is it true they are directing the subversive activities of the pachucos from inside the relocation camps? (*Henry turns to the Pachuco with a questioning look.*)

PACHUCO. This one's all yours, ese.

HENRY. Look, lady, I don't know what the hell you're talking about.

ALICE. I'm talking about you, Henry Reyna. And what the regular press has been saying. Are you aware you're in here just because some bigshot up in San Simeon wants to sell more papers? It's true.

HENRY. So?

ALICE. So, he's the man who started this Mexican Crime Wave stuff. Then the police got into the act. Get the picture? Somebody is using you as a patsy.

HENRY (*His machismo insulted*). Who you calling a patsy?

ALICE. I'm sorry, but it's true.

HENRY (*Backing her up*). What makes you so goddamned smart?

ALICE (*Starting to get scared and trying not to show it*). I'm a reporter. It's my business to know.

PACHUCO. Puro pedo. She's just a dumb broad only good for you know what.

HENRY. Look, Miss Bloomfield, just leave me alone, all right? (*Henry moves away. Alice takes a deep breath.*)

ALICE. Look, let's back up and start all over, okay? Hello. My name is Alice Bloomfield, and I'm not a reporter. I'm just somebody that wants very much to be your friend. (*Pause. With sincere feeling.*) Can you believe that?

HENRY. Why should I?

ALICE. Because I'm with you.

HENRY. Oh, yeah? Then how come you ain't in jail with me?

ALICE (*Holding her head up*). We are all in jail, Henry. Some of us just don't know it.

PACHUCO. Mmm, pues. No comment. (*Pause. Henry stares at her, trying to figure her out. Alice tries a softer approach.*)

ALICE. Believe it nor not, I was born in Los Angeles just like you. But for some strange reason I grew up here, not knowing very much about Mexicans at all. I'm just trying to learn.

HENRY (*Intrigued, but cynical*). What?

ALICE. Little details. Like that tattooed cross on your hand. Is that the sign of the pachuco? (*Henry covers his right hand with an automatic reflex, then he realizes what he has done.*)

HENRY (*Smiles to himself, embarrassed*). Órale.

ALICE. Did I embarrass you? I'm sorry. Your mother happened to mention it.

HENRY (*Surprised*). My mother? You talked to my jefita?

ALICE (*With enthusiasm*). Yes! And your father and Lupe and Rudy. The whole family gave me a helluva interview. But your mother was sensational. I especially liked her story about the midnight raid. How the police rushed into your house with drawn guns, looking for you on some trumped up charge, and how your father told them you were already in jail . . . God, I would have paid to have seen the cops' faces.

HENRY (*Hiding his sentiment*). Don't believe anything my jefa tells you. (*Then quickly.*) There's a lot she doesn't know. I'm no angel.

ALICE. I'll just bet you're not. But you have been taken in for suspicion a dozen times, kept in jail for a few days, then released for lack of evidence. And it's all stayed on your juvenile record.

HENRY. Yeah, well I ain't no punk, see.

ALICE. I know. You're an excellent mechanic. And you fix all the guys' cars. Well, at least you're not one of the lumpen proletariat.

HENRY. The lumpen what?

ALICE. Skip it. Let's just say you're a classic social victim.

HENRY. Bullshit.

ALICE (*Pause. A serious queston*). Are you saying you're guilty?

HENRY. Of what?

ALICE. The Sleepy Lagoon Murder.

HENRY. What if I am?

ALICE. Are you?

HENRY (*Pause, a serious answer*). Chale. I've pulled a lot of shit in my time, but I didn't do that. (*George re-enters flushed and angry, trying to conceal his frustration.*)

GEORGE. Henry, I'm sorry, but dammit, something's coming off here, and the clothes have been withheld. I'll have to bring it up in court.

HENRY. In court?

GEORGE. They've left me no choice.

ALICE. What's going on?

HENRY. It's a set up, George. Another lousy set up!

GEORGE. It's just the beginning, son. Nobody said this was going to be a fair fight. Well, if they're going to fight dirty, so am I. Legally, but dirty. Trust me.

ALICE (*Passionately*). Henry, no matter what happens in the trial, I want you to know I believe you're innocent. Remember that when you look out, and it looks like some sort of lynch mob. Some of us . . . a lot of us . . . are right there with you.

GEORGE. Okay, Alice, let's scram. I've got a million things to do. Henry, see you tomorrow under the big top, son. Good luck, son.

ALICE. Thumbs up, Henry, we're going to beat this rap! (*Alice and George exit. El Pachuco watches them go, then turns to Henry.*)

PACHUCO. "Thumbs up, Henry, we're going to beat this rap." You really think you're going to beat this one, ese?

HENRY. I don't want to think about it.

PACHUCO. You've got to think about it, Hank. Everbody's playing you for a sucker. Wake up, carnal!

HENRY. Look, bato, what the hell do you expect me to do?

PACHUCO. Hang tough. (*Grabs his scrotum.*) Stop going soft.

HENRY. Who's going soft?

PACHUCO (*Incisively*). You're hoping for something that isn't going to happen, ese. These paddies are leading you by the nose. Do you really believe you stand a chance?

HENRY (*Stubborn all the more*). Yeah. I think I got a chance.

PACHUCO. Just because that white broad says so?

HENRY. Nel, ese, just because Hank Reyna says so.

PACHUCO. The classic social victim, eh?

HENRY (*Furious but keeping his cool*). Mira, ese. Hank Reyna's no loser. I'm coming out of this on top. ¡Me entiendes, Mendez? (*He walks away with a pachuco gait.*)

PACHUCO (*Forcefully*). Don't try to out-pachuco ME, ese! We'll see who comes out on top. (*He picks up a bundle of newspapers and throws it upstage center. It lands with a thud.*) Let's go to court!

9. OPENING OF THE TRIAL

Music. The Judge's bench, made up of more newspaper bundles piled squarely on a four-wheeled hand truck, is pushed in by the batos. The Press rides it in, holding the State and Federal Flags. A Bailiff puts in place a hand cart: the Judge's throne. From the sides, spectators enter, including Henry's family and friends: Alice, Della, Bertha, Elena.

PRESS. The largest mass trial in the history of Los Angeles County opens this morning in the Superior Court at ten A.M. The infamous Sleepy Lagoon Murder case involves sity-six charges against twenty-two defendants with seven lawyers pleading for the defense, two for the prosecution. The District Attorney estimates that over a hundred witnesses will be called and has sworn—I quote—"to put an end to Mexican baby gangsterism." End quote.

BAILIFF (*Bangs a gavel on the bench*). The Superior Court of the State of California. In and For the County of Los Angeles. Department forty-three. The honorable F. W. Charles, presiding. All rise! (*Judge Charles enters. All rise. El Pachuco squats. The Judge is played by the same actor that portrays Edwards.*)

JUDGE. Please be seated. (*All sit. Pachuco stands.*) Call this case, Bailiff.

BAILIFF (*Reading from a sheet*). The people of the State of California Versus Henry Reyna, Ismael Torres, Thomas Roberts, José Castro and eighteen other . . . (*Slight hesitation.*) . . . pa-coo-cos.

JUDGE. Is Counsel for the Defense present?

GEORGE (*Rises*). Yes, Your Honor.

JUDGE. Please proceed. (*Signals the Press.*)

PRESS. Your Honor . . .

GEORGE (*Moving in immediately*). If the Court please, it was reported to me on Friday that the District Attorney has absolutely forbidden the Sheriff's Office to permit these boys to have clean clothes or haircuts. Now, it's been three months since the boys were arrested . . .

PRESS (*Jumping in*). Your Honor, there is testimony we expect to develop that the 38th Street Gang are characterized by their style of haircuts . . .

GEORGE. Three months, Your Honor.

PRESS. . . . the thick heavy heads of hair, the ducktail comb, the pachuco pants . . .

GEORGE. Your Honor, I can only infer that the Prosecution . . . is trying to make these boys look disreputable, like mobsters.

PRESS. Their appearance is distinctive, Your Honor. Essential to the case.

GEORGE. You are trying to exploit the fact that these boys look foreign in appearance! Yet clothes like these are being worn by kids all over America.

PRESS. Your Honor . . .

JUDGE (*Bangs the gavel*). I don't believe we will have any difficulty if their clothing becomes dirty.

GEORGE. What about the haircuts, Your Honor?

JUDGE (*Ruling*). The zoot haircuts will be retained throughout the trial for purposes of identification of defendants by witnesses.

PACHUCO. You hear that one, ese? Listen to it again. (*Snaps. Judge repeats automatically.*)

JUDGE. The zoot haircuts will be retained throughout the trial for purposes of identification of defendants by witnesses.

PACHUCO. He wants to be sure we know who you are.

JUDGE. It has been brought to my attention the Jury is having trouble telling one boy from another, so I am going to rule the defendants stand each time their names are mentioned.

GEORGE. I object. If the Prosecution makes an accusation, it will mean self-incrimination.

JUDGE (*Pause*). Not necessarily. (*To Press.*) Please proceed.

GEORGE (*Still trying to set the stage*). Then if the Court please, might I request that my clients be allowed to sit with me during the trial so that I might consult with them?

JUDGE. Request denied.

GEORGE. May I inquire of Your Honor, if the defendant Thomas Robert might rise from his seat and walk over to counsel table so as to consult with me during the trial?

JUDGE. I certainly will not permit it.

GEORGE. You will not?

JUDGE. No. This is a small courtroom, Mr. Shearer. We can't have twenty-two defendants all over the place.

GEORGE. Then I object. On the grounds that that is denial of the rights guaranteed all defendants by both the Federal and State constitutions.

JUDGE. Well, that is your opinion. (*Gavel.*) Call your first witness.

PRESS. The prosecution calls Lieutenant Sam Edwards of the Los Angeles Police Department.

PACHUCO (*Snaps. Does double take on Judge*). You know what. We've already heard from that bato. Let's get on with the defense. (*Snaps. Press sits. George stands.*)

GEORGE. The defense calls Adela Barrios.

BAILIFF (*Calling out*). Adeela Barreeos to the stand. (*Della Barrios comes forth out of the spectators. Bertha leans forward.*)

BERTHA (*Among the spectators*). Don't tell 'em nothing. (*The Bailiff swears in Della silently.*)

PACHUCO. Look at your gang. They do look like mobsters. Se watchan bien gachos. (*Henry looks at the batos, who are sprawled out in their places.*)

HENRY (*Under his breath*). Come on, Batos, sit up.

SMILEY. We're tired, Hank.

JOEY. My butt is sore.

TOMMY. Yeah, look at the soft chairs the jury's got.

HENRY. What did you expect? They're trying to make us look bad. Come on! Straighten up.

SMILEY. Simón, batos, Hank is right.

JOEY. ¡Más alba nalga!

TOMMY. Put some class on your ass.

HENRY. Sit up! (*They all sit up.*)

GEORGE. State your name please.

DELLA. Adela Barrios. (*She sits.*)

GEORGE. Miss Barrios, were you with Henry Reyna on the night of August 1, 1942?

DELLA. Yes.

JUDGE (*To Henry*). Please stand. (*Henry stands.*)

GEORGE. Please tell the court what transpired that night.

DELLA (*Pause. Takes a breath*). Well, after the dance that Saturday night, Henry and I drove out to the Sleepy Lagoon about eleven-thirty.

10. SLEEPY LAGOON

Music: The Harry James Theme. El Pachuco creates the scene. The light changes. We see a shimmering pattern of light on the floor growing to the music. It becomes the image of the Lagoon. As the music soars to a trumpet solo, Henry reaches out to Della, and she glides to her feet.

DELLA. There was a full moon that night, and as we drove up to the Lagoon we noticed right away the place was empty . . . (*A pair of headlights silently pulls in from the black background upstage center.*) Henry parked the car on the bank of the reservoir and we relaxed. (*Headlights go off.*) It was such a warm, beautiful night, and the sky was so full of stars, we couldn't just sit in the car. So we got out, and Henry took my hand . . . (*Henry stands and takes Della's hand.*) We went for a walk around the Lagoon. Neither of us said anything at first, so the only sounds we could hear were the crickets and the frogs . . . (*Sounds of crickets and frogs, then music faintly in the background.*) When we got to the other side of the reservoir, we began to hear music, so I asked Henry, what's that?

HENRY. Sounds like they're having a party.

DELLA. Where?

HENRY. Over at the Williams' Ranch. See the house lights.

DELLA. Who lives there?

HENRY. A couple of families. Mexicanos. I think they work on the ranch. You know, their name used to be Gonzales, but they changed it to Williams.

DELLA. Why?

HENRY. I don't know. Maybe they think it gives 'em more class. (*We hear Mexican music.*) Ay, jijo. They're probably celebrating a wedding or something.

DELLA. As soon as he said wedding, he stopped talking and we both knew why. He had something on his mind, something he was trying to tell me without sounding like a square.

HENRY. Della . . . what are you going to do if I don't come back from the war?

DELLA. That wasn't the question I was expecting, so I answered something dumb, like I don't know, what's going to keep you from coming back?

HENRY. Maybe wanting too much out of life, see? Ever since I was kid, I've had this feeling like there's a big party going on someplace, and I'm invited, but I don't know how to get there. And I want to get there so bad, I'll even risk my life to make it. Sounds crazy, huh? (*Della and Henry kiss. They embrace and then Henry speaks haltingly.*) If I get back from the war . . . will you marry me?

DELLA. Yes! (*She embraces him and almost causes them to topple over.*)

HENRY. ¡Órale! You'll knock us into the Lagoon. Listen, what about your old man? He ain't going to like you marrying me.

DELLA. I know. But I don't care. I'll go to hell with you if you want me to.

HENRY. ¿Sabes qué? I'm going to give you the biggest Pachuco wedding L.A. has ever seen. (*Another pair of headlights comes in from the left. Della goes back to her narration.*)

DELLA. Just then another car pulled up to the Lagoon. It was Rafas and some drunk guys in a gang from Downey. They got out and started to bust the windows on Henry's car. Henry yelled at them, and they started cussing at us. I told Henry not to say anything, but he cussed them back!

HENRY. You stay here, Della.

DELLA. Henry, no! Don't go down there! Please don't go down there!

HENRY. Can't you hear what they're doing to my car?

DELLA. There's too many of them. They'll kill you!

HENRY. ¡Chale! (*Henry turns and runs upstage, where he stops in a freeze.*)

DELLA. Henry! Henry ran down the back of the Lagoon and attacked the gang by himself. Rafas had about ten guys with him and they jumped on Henry like a

pack of dogs. He fought them off as long as he could, then they threw him on the ground hard and kicked him until he passed out . . . (*Headlights pull off.*) After they left, I ran down to Henry and held him in my arms until he came to. And I could tell he was hurt, but the first thing he said was . . .

PACHUCO. Let's go into town and get the guys. (*Music: Glen Miller's "In the Mood." Henry turns to the batos and they stand. Smiley, Joey and Tommy are joined by Rudy, Bertha, Lupe and Elena, who enter from the side. They turn downstage in a body and freeze.*)

DELLA. It took us about an hour to go into town and come back. We got to the Lagoon with about eight cars, but the Downey gang wasn't there.

JOEY. Órale, ¿pos qué pasó? Nobody here.

SMILEY. Then let's go to Downey.

THE BOYS (*Ad lib*). Let's go!

HENRY. ¡Chale! ¡Chale! (*Pause. They all stop.*) Ya estuvo. Everybody go home. (*A collective groan from The Boys.*) Go home!

DELLA. That's when we heard music coming from the Williams' Ranch again. We didn't know Rafas and his gang had been there too, causing trouble. So when Joey said . . .

JOEY. Hey, there's a party! Bertha, let's crash it.

DELLA. We all went there yelling and laughing. (*The group of batos turns upstage in a mimetic freeze.*) At the Williams' Ranch they saw us coming and thought we were the Downey Gang coming back again . . . They attacked us. (*The group now mimes a series of tableaus showing the fight.*) An old man ran out of the house with a kitchen knife and Henry had to hit him. Then a girl grabbed me by the hair and in a second everybody was fighting! People were grabbing sticks from the fence, bottles, anything! It all happened so fast, we didn't know what hit us, but Henry said let's go!

HENRY. ¡Vámonos! Let's get out of here.

DELLA. And we started to back off . . . Before we got to the cars, I saw something out of the corner of my eye . . . It was a guy. He was hitting a man on the ground with a big stick. (*El Pachuco mimes this action.*) Henry called to him, but he wouldn't stop. He wouldn't stop . . . He wouldn't stop . . . He wouldn't stop . . . (*Della in tears, holds Henry in her arms. The batos and rucas start moving back to their places, quietly.*) Driving back in the car, everybody was quiet, like nothing had happened. We didn't know José Williams had died at the party that night and that the guys would be arrested the next day for murder. (*Henry separates from her and goes back to stand in his place. Della resumes the witness stand.*)

11. THE CONCLUSION OF
THE TRIAL

Lights change back to courtroom, as Judge Charles bangs his gavel. Everyone is seated back in place.

GEORGE. Your witness.

PRESS (*Springing to the attack*). You say Henry Reyna hit the man with his fist. (*Indicates Henry standing.*) Is this the Henry Reyna?

DELLA. Yes. I mean, no. He's Henry, but he didn't . . .

PRESS. Please be seated. (*Henry sits.*) Now, after Henry Reyna hit the old man with his closed fist, is that when he pulled the knife?

DELLA. The old man had the knife.

PRESS. So Henry pulled one out, too?

GEORGE (*Rises*). Your Honor, I object to counsel leading the witness.

PRESS. I am not leading the witness.

GEORGE. You are.

PRESS. I certainly am not.

GEORGE. Yes, you are.

JUDGE. I would suggest, Mr. Shearer, that you look up during the noon hour just what a leading question is?

GEORGE. If the Court please, I am going to assign that remark of Your Honor as misconduct.

JUDGE (*To Press*). Proceed. (*George crosses back to his chair.*)

PRESS. Where was Smiley Torres during all this? Is it not true that Smiley Torres grabbed a woman by the hair and kicked her to the ground? Will Smiley Torres please stand? (*Smiley stands.*) Is this the man?

DELLA. Yes, it's Smiley, but he . . .

PRESS. Please be seated. (*Smiley sits. Press picks up a two-by-four.*) Wasn't José Castro carrying a club of some kind?

GEORGE (*On his feet again*). Your Honor, I object! No such club was ever found. The prosecution is implying that this two-by four is associated with my client in some way.

PRESS. I'm not implying anything, Your Honor, I'm merely using this stick as an illustration.

JUDGE. Objection overruled.

PRESS. Will José Castro please stand? (*Joey stands.*) Is this the man who was carrying a club? (*Della refuses to answer.*) Answer the question please.

DELLA. I refuse.

PRESS. You are under oath. You can't refuse.

JUDGE. Answer the question, young lady.

DELLA. I refuse.

PRESS. Is this the man you saw hitting another man with a two-by-four? Your Honor . . .

JUDGE. I order you to answer the question.

GEORGE. Your Honor, I object. The witness is obviously afraid her testimony will be manipulated by the Prosecution.

PRESS. May I remind the court that we have a signed confession from one José Castro taken while in jail . . .

GEORGE. I object. Those were not confessions! Those are statements. They are false and untrue, Your Honor, obtained through beatings and coercion of the defendants by the police!

JUDGE. I believe the technical term is admissions, Mr. Prosecutor. Objection sustained. (*Applause from spectators.*) At the next outburst, I will clear this courtroom. Go on, Mr. Prosecutor.

PRESS. Sit down please. (*Joey sits. George goes back to his seat.*) Is Henry Reyna the leader of the 38th Street Gang? (*Henry stands.*)

DELLA. Not in the sense that you mean.

PRESS. Did Henry Reyna, pachuco ringleader of the 38th Street Gang, willfully murder José Williams?

DELLA. No. They attacked us first.

PRESS. I didn't ask for your comment.

DELLA. But they did, they thought we were the Downey gang.

PRESS. Just answer my questions.

DELLA. We were just defending ourselves so we could get out of there.

PRESS. Your Honor, will you instruct the witness to be cooperative.

JUDGE. I must caution you, young lady, answer the questions or I'll hold you in contempt.

PRESS. Was this the Henry Reyna who was carrying a three-foot lead pipe?

GEORGE. I object!

JUDGE. Overruled.

DELLA. No.

PRESS. Was it a two-foot lead pipe?

GEORGE. Objection!

JUDGE. Overruled.

DELLA. No!

PRESS. Did he kick a women to the ground?

DELLA. No, he was hurt from the beating.

PRESS. Sit down. (*Henry sits.*) Did Tommy Roberts rip stakes from a fence and hit a man on the ground?

GEORGE. Objection!

JUDGE. Overruled.

DELLA. I never saw him do anything.

PRESS. Did Joey Castro have a gun?

GEORGE. Objection!

JUDGE. Overruled. (*Joey stands.*)

PRESS. Sit down. (*Joey sits.*) Did Henry Reyna have a blackjack in his hand? (*Henry stands.*)

DELLA. No.

PRESS. A switchblade knife?

DELLA. No.

PRESS. A two-by-four?

DELLA. No.

PRESS. Did he run over to José Williams, hit him on the head and kill him?

DELLA. He could barely walk, how could he run to any place?

PRESS (*Moving in for the kill*). Did Smiley Torres? (*The batos stand and sit as their names are mentioned.*) Did Joey Castro? Did Tommy Roberts? Did Henry Reyna? Did Smiley Torres? Did Henry Reyna? Did Henry Reyna? Did Henry Reyna kill José Williams?!

DELLA. No, no, no!

GEORGE (*On his feet again*). Your Honor, I object! The Prosecution is pulling out objects from all over the place, none of which were found at Sleepy Lagoon, and none of which have been proven to be associated with my clients in any way.

JUDGE. Overruled.

GEORGE. If Your Honor please, I wish to make an assignment of misconduct!

JUDGE. We have only had one this morning. We might as well have another now.

GEORGE. You have it, Your Honor.

JUDGE. One more remark like that and I'll hold you in contempt. Quite frankly, Mr. Shearer, I am getting rather tired of your repeated useless objections.

GEORGE. I have not made useless objections.

JUDGE. I am sorry. Somebody is using ventriloquism. We have a Charlie McCarthy using Mr. Shearer's voice.

GEORGE. I am going to assign that remark of Your Honor as misconduct.

JUDGE. Fine. I would feel rather bad if you did not make an assignment of misconduct at least three times every session. (*Gavel.*) Witness is excused. (*Della stands.*) However, I am going to remand her to the custody of the Ventura State School for Girls for a period of one year . . .

HENRY. What?

JUDGE. . . . . to be held there as juvenile ward of the State. Bailiff?

GEORGE. If the court please . . . If the court please . . . (*Bailiff crosses to Della and takes her off left.*)

JUDGE. Court is in recess until tomorrow morning. (*Judge retires. Press exits. Henry meets George halfway across center stage. The rest of the batos stand and stretch in the background.*)

GEORGE. Now, Henry, I want you to listen to me, please. You've got to remember he's the judge, Hank. And this is his courtroom.

HENRY. But he's making jokes, George, and we're getting screwed!

GEORGE. I know. I can't blame you for being bitter, but believe me, we'll get him.

HENRY. I thought you said we had a chance.

GEORGE (*Passionately*). We do! This case is going to be won on appeal.

HENRY. Appeal? You mean you already know we're going to lose?

PACHUCO. So what's new?

GEORGE. Don't you see, Henry, Judge Charles is hanging himself as we go. I've cited over a hundred separate cases of misconduct by the bench, and it's all gone into the record. Prejudicial error, denial of due process, inadmissible evidence, hearsay . . .

HENRY. ¿Sabes qué, George? Don't tell me any more. (*Henry turns. Alice and Enrique approach him.*)

ALICE. Henry . . . ?

HENRY (*Turns furiously*). I don't want to hear it, Alice! (*Henry sees Enrique, but neither father nor son can think of anything to say. Henry goes back upstage.*)

ALICE. George, is there anything we can do?

GEORGE. No. He's bitter, and he has a right to be. (*Judge Charles pounds his gavel. All go back to their places and sit.*)

JUDGE. We'll now hear the Prosecution's concluding statement.

PRESS. Your Honor, ladies and gentlemen of the jury. What you have before you is a dilemma of our times. The City of Los Angeles is caught in the midst of the biggest, most terrifying crime wave in its history. A crime wave that threatens to engulf the very foundations of our civic wellbeing. We are not only dealing with the violent death of one José Williams in a drunken barrio brawl. We are dealing with a threat and danger to our children, our families, our homes. Set these pachucos free, and you shall unleash the forces of anarchy and destruction in our society. Set these pachucos free and you will turn them into heroes. Others just like them must be watching us at this very moment. What nefarious schemes can they be hatching in their twisted minds? Rape, drugs, assault, more violence? Who shall be their next innocent victim in some dark alley way, on some lonely street? You? You? Your loved ones? No! Henry Reyna and his Latin juvenile cohorts are not heroes. They are criminals, and they must be stopped. The specific details of this murder are irrelevant before the overwhelming danger of the pachuco in our midst. I ask you to find these zoot-suited gangsters guilty of murder and to put them in the gas chamber where they belong. (*The Press sits down. George rises and takes center stage.*)

GEORGE. Ladies and gentlemen of the jury, you have heard me object to the conduct of this trial. I have tried my best to defend what is most precious in our American society—a society now at war against the forces of racial intolerance and totalitarian injustice. The prosecution has not provided one witness that actually saw, with his own eyes, who actually murdered José Williams. These boys are not the Downey gang, yet the evidence suggests that they were attacked because the people at the ranch thought they were. Henry Reyna and Della Barrios were victims of the same bunch. Yes, they might have been spoiling for a revenge—who wouldn't under the circumstances—but not with the intent to conspire to commit murder. So how did José Williams die? Was it an accident? Was it manslaughter? Was it murder? Perhaps we may never know. All the prosecution has been able to prove is that these boys wear long hair and zoot suits. And all the rest has been circumstantial evidence, hearsay and war hysteria. The prosecution has tried to lead you to believe that they are some kind of inhuman gangsters. Yet they are Americans. Find them guilty of anything more serious than a juvenile bout of fisticuffs, and you will condemn all American youth. Find them guilty of murder, and you will murder the spirit of racial justice in America. (*George sits down.*)

JUDGE. The jury will retire to consider its verdict. (*The Press stands and starts to exit with the Bailiff. El Pachuco snaps. All freeze.*)

PACHUCO. Chale. Let's have it. (*Snaps again. The Press turns and comes back again.*)

JUDGE. Has the jury reached a verdict?

PRESS. We have, Your Honor.

JUDGE. How say you?

PRESS. We find the defendants guilty of murder in the first and second degrees.

JUDGE. The defendants will rise. (*The batos come to their feet.*) Henry Reyna, José Castro, Thomas Roberts, Ismael Torres, and so forth. You have been tried by a jury of your peers and found guilty of murder in the first and second degrees. The Law prescribes the capital punishment for this offense. However, in view of your youth and in consideration of your families, it is hereby the judgement of this court that you be sentenced to life imprisonment . . .

RUDY. No!

JUDGE. . . . and sent to the State Penitentiary at San Quentin. Court adjourned. (*Gavel. Judge exits. Do-*
lores, *Enrique and family go to Henry. Bertha crosses to Joey; Lupe goes to Tommy. Elena crosses to Smiley. George and Alice talk.*)

DOLORES. ¡Hijo mío! ¡Hijo de mi alma! (*Bailiff comes down with a pair of handcuffs.*)

BAILIFF. Okay, boys. (*He puts the cuffs on Henry. Rudy comes up.*)

RUDY. ¿Carnal? (*Henry looks at the Bailiff, who gives him a nod of permission to spend a moment with Rudy. Henry embraces him with the cuffs on. George and Alice approach.*)

GEORGE. Henry? I can't pretend to know how you feel, son. I just want you to know that our fight has just begun.

ALICE. We may have lost this decision, but we're going to appeal immediately. We're going to stand behind you until your name is absolutely clear. I swear it!

PACHUCO. What the hell are they going to do, ese? They just sent you to prison for life. Once a Mexican goes in, he never comes out.

BAILIFF. Boys? (*The Boys exit with the Bailiff. As they go Enrique calls after them.*)

ENRIQUE (*Holding back tears*). Hijo. Be a man, hijo. (*Then to his family.*) Vámonos . . . ¡Vámonos! (*The family leaves and El Pachuco slowly walks to center stage.*)

PACHUCO. We're going to take a short break right now, so you can all go out and take a leak, smoke a frajo. Ahí los watcho. (*He exits up center and the newspaper backdrop comes down.*)

ACT II

PROLOGUE

Lights up and El Pachuco emerges from the shadows. The newspaper drop is till down. Music.

PACHUCO.
Watchamos pachucos
los batos
the dudes
street-corner warriors who fought and moved
like unknown soldiers in wars of their own
El Pueblo de Los was the battle zone
from Sleepy Lagoon to the Zoot Suit wars
when Marines and Sailors made their scores
stomping like Nazis on East L.A. . . .
pero ¿saben qué?
That's later in the play. Let's pick it up in prison.
We'll begin this scene
inside the walls of San Quintín.

1. SAN QUENTIN

A bell rings as the drop rises. Henry, Joey, Smiley and Tommy enter accompanied by a Guard.

GUARD. All right, people, lock up. (*Boys move downstage in four directions. They step into "cells" simply marked by shadows of bars on the floor in their separate places. Newspaper handcarts rest on the floor as cots. Sound of cell doors clsing. The Guard paces back and forth upstage level.*)

HENRY.

San Quentin, California

March 3, 1943

Dear Family:

Coming in from the yard in the evening, we are quickly locked up in our cells. Then the clank and locking of the doors leaves one with a rather empty feeling. You are standing up to the iron door, waiting for the guard to come along and take the count, listening as his footsteps fade away in the distance. By this time there is a tense stillness that seems to crawl over the cellblock. You realize you are alone, so all alone.

PACHUCO. This all sound rather tragic, doesn't it?

HENRY. But here comes the guard again, and he calls out your number in a loud voice . . .

GUARD (*Calls numbers; Boys call name*). 24–545

HENRY. Reyna!

GUARD. 24–546

JOEY. Castro!

GUARD. 24–547

TOMMY. Roberts!

GUARD. 24–548

SMILEY. Torres! (*Guard passes through dropping letters and exits up left.*)

HENRY. You jump to your feet, stooping to pick up the letter . . .

JOEY (*Excited*). Or perhaps several letters . . .

TOMMY. You are really excited as you take the letters from the envelope.

SMILEY. The censor has already broken the seal when he reads it.

HENRY. You make a mental observation to see if you recognize the handwriting on the envelope.

SMILEY (*Anxious*). It's always nice to hear from home . . .

JOEY. Or a close comrade . . .

TOMMY. Friends that you know on the outside . . .

HENRY. Or perhaps it's from a stranger. (*Pause. Spotlight at upstage center. Alice walks in with casual clothes on. Her hair is in pigtails, and she wears a pair of drapes. She is cheerful.*)

2. THE LETTERS

Dear Boys,

Announcing the publication (mimeograph) of the Appeal News, your very own newsletter, to be sent to you twice a month for the purpose of keeping you reliably informed of everything—the progress of the Sleeping Lagoon Defense Committee (We have a name now) and, of course, the matter of your appeal.

Signed,
Your editor
Alice Bloomfield.

(*Music. "Perdido" by Duke Ellington. Alice steps down and sits on the lip of the upstage level. The Boys start swinging the bat, dribbling the basketball, shadow-boxing and exercising. Alice mimes typing movements and we hear the sounds of a typewriter. Music fades. Alice rises.*)

ALICE. The Appeal News Volume I, Number I, April 7, 1943.

Boys,

You can, you must, and you will help us on the outside by what you do on the inside. Don't forget, what you do affects others. You have no control over that. When the time comes, let us be proud to show the record.

Signed,
Your editor.

(*Music up again. The Boys go through their activities. Alice moves downstage center and the music fades.*)

SMILEY (*Stepping toward her*).

April 10, 1943

Dear Miss Bloomfield,

I have discovered from my wife that you are conducting door-to-door fund-raising campaigns in Los Angeles. She doesn't want to tell you, but she feels bad about doing such a thing. It's not our custom to go around the neighborhoods asking for money.

ALICE (*Turning toward Smiley*).

Dear Smiley,

Of course, I understand your feelings . . .

SMILEY (*Adamant*). I don't want my wife going around begging.

ALICE. It isn't begging—it's fund-raising.

SMILEY. I don't care what you call it. If that's what it's going to take, count me out.

ALICE. All right. I won't bother your wife if she really doesn't want me to. Okay? (*Smiley looks at her and turns back to his upstage position. Music. The batos move again. Tommy crosses to Alice. Another fade.*)

TOMMY.

April 18, 1943

Dear Alice,

Trying to find the words and expression to thank you for your efforts in behalf of myself and the rest of the batos makes me realize what a meager vocabulary I possess . . .

ALICE.

Dear Tommy,

Your vocabulary is just fine. Better than most.

TOMMY. Most what?

ALICE. People.

TOMMY (*Glances at Henry*). Uh, listen, Alice. I don't want to be treated any different than the rest of the batos, see? And don't expect me to talk to you like some square Anglo, some pinche gabacho. You just better find out what it means to be Chicano, and it better be pretty damn quick.

ALICE. Look, Tommy, I didn't . . .

TOMMY. I know what you're trying to do for us and that's reet, see? Shit. Most paddies would probably like to see us locked up for good. I been in jail a couple of times before, but never nothing this deep. Strange, ain't it, the trial in Los? I don't really know what happened or why. I don't give a shit what the papers said. We didn't do half the things I read about. I also know that I'm in here just because I hung around with Mexicans . . . or pachucos. Well, just remember this, Alicia . . . I grew up right alongside most of these batos, and I'm pachuco too. Simón, esa, you better believe it! (*Music up. Movement. Tommy returns to his position. Henry stands. Alice turns toward him, but he walks over to The Pachuco, giving her his back.*)

JOEY (*Stepping forward anxiously*).

May 1, 1943

Dear Alice . . . Darling!

I can't help but spend my time thinking about you. How about sending us your retra—that is, your photograph? Even though Tommy would like one of Rita Hayworth—he's always chasing Mexican skirts (Ha! Ha!)—I'd prefer to see your sweet face any day.

ALICE (*Directly to him*).

Dear Joey,

Thank you so much. I really appreciated receiving your letter.

JOEY. That's all reet, Grandma! You mind if I call you Grandma?

ALICE. Oh, no.

JOEY. Eres una ruca de aquellas.

ALICE. I'm a what?

JOEY. Ruca. A fine chick.

ALICE (*Pronounces the word*). Ruca?

JOEY. De aquellas. (*Makes a cool gesture, palms out at hip level.*)

ALICE (*Imitating him*). De aquellas.

JOEY. All reet! You got it. (*Pause.*) P.S. Did you forget the photograph?

ALICE (*She hands it to him*).

Dearest Joey,

Of course not. Here it is, attached to a copy of the Appeal News. I'm afraid it's not exactly a pin-up.

JOEY (*Kissing the photo*). Alice, honey, you're a doll! (*Joey shows the photo to Tommy then Smiley, who is curious enough to come into the circle. Alice looks at Henry, but he continues to ignore her.*)

ALICE (*Back at center*). The Appeal News, Volume I, Number 3, May 5, 1943.

Dear Boys,

Feeling that el Cinco de Mayo is a very appropriate day—the CIO radio program, "Our Daily Bread," is devoting the entire time this evening to a discussion of discrimination against Mexicans in general and against you guys in particular.

Music up. The repartee between Alice and the batos is now friendly and warm. Even Smiley is smiling with Alice. They check out her "drapes."

3 . THE INCORRIGIBLE PACHUCO

Henry stands at downstage left, looks at the group, then decides to speak.

HENRY.

> May 17, 1943
>
> Dear Miss Bloomfield,
>
> I understand you're coming up to Q this weekend, and I would like to talk to you—in private. Can you arrange it?

(The batos turn away, taking a hint.)

ALICE *(Eagerly)*. Yes, yes, I can. What can I do for you, Henry? *(Henry and Alice step forward toward each other. El Pachuco moves in.)*

HENRY. For me? ¡Ni madre!

ALICE *(Puzzled)*. I don't understand.

HENRY. I wanted you to be the first to know, Alice. I'm dropping out of the appeal.

ALICE *(Unbelieving)*. You're what?

HENRY. I'm bailing out, esa. Dropping out of the case, see?

ALICE. Henry, you can't!

HENRY. Why can't I?

ALICE. Because you'll destroy our whole case! If we don't present a united front, how can we ask the public to support us?

HENRY. That's your problem. I never asked for their support. Just count me out.

ALICE *(Getting nervous, anxious)*. Henry, please, think about what you're saying. If you drop out, the rest of the boys will probably go with you. How can you even think of dropping out of the appeal? What about George and all the people that have contributed their time and money in the past few months? You just can't quit on them!

HENRY. Oh no? Just watch me.

ALICE. If you felt this way, why didn't you tell me before?

HENRY. Why didn't you ask me? You think you can just move in and defend anybody you feel like? When did I ever ask you to start a defense committee for me? Or a newspaper? Or a fundraising drive and all that other shit? I don't need defending, esa. I can take care of myself.

ALICE. But what about the trial, the sentence. They gave you life imprisonment?

HENRY. It's my life!

ALICE. Henry, honestly—are you kidding me?

HENRY. You think so?

ALICE. But you've seen me coming and going. Writing to you, speaking for you, traveling up and down the state. You must have known I was doing it for you. Nothing has come before my involvement, my attachment, my passion for this case. My boys have been everything to me.

HENRY. My boys? My boys! What the hell are we—your personal property? Well, let me set you straight, lady, I ain't your boy.

ALICE. You know I never meant it that way.

HENRY. You think I haven't seen through your bullshit? Always so concerned. Come on, boys. Speak out, boys. Stand up for your people. Well, you leave my people out of this! Can't you understand that?

ALICE. No, I can't understand that.

HENRY. You're just using Mexicans to play politics.

ALICE. Henry, that's the worst thing anyone has ever said to me.

HENRY. Who are you going to help next—the Colored People?

ALICE. No, as a matter of fact, I've already helped the Colored People. What are you going to do next—go to the gas chamber?

HENRY. What the hell do you care?

ALICE. I don't!

HENRY. then get the hell out of here!

ALICE *(Furious)*. You think you're the only one who doesn't want to be bothered? You ought to try working in the Sleepy Lagoon defense office for a few months. All the haggling, the petty arguments, the lack of co-operation. I've wanted to quit a thousand times. What the hell am I doing here? They're coming at me from all sides. You're too sentimental and emotional about this, Alice. You're too cold hearted, Alice. You're collecting money and turning it over to the lawyers, while the families are going hungry. They're saying you can't be trusted because you're a Communist, because you're a Jew. Okay! If that's the way they feel about me, then to hell with them! I hate them too. I hate their language, I hate their enchiladas, and I hate their goddamned mariachi music! *(Pause. They look at each other. Henry smiles, then Alice—feeling foolish—and they both break out laughing.)*

HENRY. All right! Now you sound like you mean it.

ALICE. I do.

HENRY. Okay! Now we're talking straight.

ALICE. I guess I have been sounding like some square paddy chick. But, you haven't exactly been Mister Cool yourself . . . ese.

HENRY. So, let's say we're even Steven.

ALICE. Fair enough. What now?

HENRY. Why don't we bury the hatchet, you know what I mean?

ALICE. Can I tell George you'll go on with the appeal?

HENRY. Yeah. I know there's a lot of people out there who are willing and trying to help us. People who feel that our conviction was an injustice. People like George . . .

and you. Well, the next time you see them, tell them Hank Reyna sends his thanks.

ALICE. Why don't you tell them?

HENRY. You getting wise with me again?

ALICE. If you write an article—and I know you can—we'll publish it in the People's World. What do you say?

PACHUCO. Article! Pos who told you, you could write, ese?

HENRY (*Laughs*). Chale.

ALICE. I'm serious. Why don't you give it a try?

HENRY. I'll think about it. (*Pause.*) Listen, you think you and I could write each other . . . outside the newsletter?

ALICE. Sure.

HENRY. Then it's a deal. (*They shake hands.*)

ALICE. I'm glad we're going to be communicating. I think we're going to be very good friends. (*Alice lifts her hands to Henry's shoulder in a gesture of comradeship. Henry follows her hand, putting his on top of hers.*)

HENRY. You think so?

ALICE. I know so.

GUARD. Time, miss.

ALICE. I gotta go. Think about the article, okay? (*She turns to the Boys.*) I gotta go, boys.

JOEY. Goodbye, Grandma! Say hello to Bertha.

SMILEY. And to my wife!

TOMMY. Give my love to Lupe!

GUARD. Time!

ALICE. I've got to go. Goodbye, goodbye. (*Alice exits, escorted by the Guard upstage left. As she goes, Joey calls after her.*)

JOEY. See you, Grandma.

TOMMY (*Turning to Joey and Smiley*). She loves me.

PACHUCO. Have you forgotten what happened at the trial? You think the Appeals Court is any different? Some paddy judge sitting in the same fat-ass judgment of your fate.

HENRY. Come on, ese, give me a break!

PACHUCO. One break, coming up! (*He snaps his fingers. The Guard blows his whistle.*)

GUARD. Rec time! (*The batos move upstage to the upper level. Music. The Boys mime a game of handball against the backdrop. During the game, George enters at stage right and comes downstage carrying his briefcase. The Guard blows a whistle and stops the game.*)

GUARD. Reyna, Castro, Roberts, Torres!—You got a visitor.

4. MAJOR GEORGE

The Boys turn and see George. They come down enthusiastically.

JOEY. ¡Óra-leh! ¡Ese, Cheer!

SMILEY. George!

GEORGE. Hi, guys! (*The Boys shake his hand, pat him on the back. Henry comes to him last.*) How are you all doing? You boys staying in shape?

JOEY. Ese, you're looking at the hero of the San Quentin athletic program. Right, batos? (*He shadowboxes a little.*)

TOMMY. Ten rounds with a busted ankle.

JOEY. ¡Simón! And I won the bout, too. I'm the terror of the flyweights, ese. The killer fly!

TOMMY. They got us doing everything, Cheer. Baseball, basketball.

SMILEY. Watch repairing.

GEORGE (*Impressed*). Watch repairing?

SMILEY. I'm also learning to improve my English and arithmetic.

GEORGE. Warden Duffy has quite a program. I hear he's a good man?

JOEY. Simón, he's a good man. We've learned our lesson . . . Well, anyway, I've learned my lesson, boy. No more pachuquismo for me. Too many people depending on us to help out. The raza here in Los. The whole Southwest. Mexico, South America! Like you and Grandma say, this is the people's world. If you get us out of here, I figure the only thing I could do is become a union organizer. Or go into major league baseball.

GEORGE. Baseball?

JOEY. Simón, ese. You're looking at the first Mexican Babe Ruth. Or maybe, "Babe Root." Root! You get it?

TOMMY. How about "Baby Zoot"?

JOEY. Solid, Jackson.

GEORGE. Babe Zooter!

JOEY. Solid tudee, that's all reet, ese.

GEORGE. What about you, Henry? What have you been doing?

HENRY. Time, George, I've been doing time.

TOMMY. Ain't it the truth?

SMILEY. Yeah, George! When you going to spring us out of here, ese?

HENRY. How's the appeal coming?

GEORGE (*Getting serious*). Not bad. There's been a development I have to talk to you about. But other than that . . .

HENRY. Other than what?

SMILEY (*Pause*). Bad news?

GEORGE (*Hedging*). It all depends on how you look at it, Smiley. It really doesn't change anything. Work on the brief is going on practically day and night. The thing is, even with several lawyers on the case now, it'll still be several months before we file. I want to be honest about that.

HENRY (*Suspiciously*). Is that the bad news?

GEORGE. Not exactly. Sit down, boys. (*Pause. He laughs to himself.*) I really don't mean to make such a big deal out of this thing. Fact is I'm still not quite used to the idea myself. (*Pause.*) You see . . . I've been drafted.

JOEY. Drafted?

TOMMY. Into the Army?

SMILEY. You?

GEORGE. That's right. I'm off to war.

JOEY. But . . . you're old, Cheer.

HENRY (*A bitter edge*). Why you, George? Why did they pick on you?

GEORGE. Well, Henry, I wouldn't say they "picked" on me. There's lots of men my age overseas. After all, it is war time and . . .

HENRY. And you're handling our appeal.

GEORGE (*Pause*). We have other lawyers.

HENRY. But you're the one who knows the case!

GEORGE (*Pause*). I knew you were going to take this hard. Believe me, Henry, my being drafted has nothing to do with your case. It's just a coincidence.

HENRY. Like our being in here for life is a coincidence?

GEORGE. No, that's another . . .

HENRY. Like our being hounded every goddam day of our life is a coincidence?

GEORGE. Henry . . . (*Henry turns away furiously. There is a pause.*) It's useless anger, son, believe me. Actually, I'm quite flattered by your concern, but I'm hardly indispensable.

HENRY (*Deeply disturbed*). What the hell are you talking about, George?

GEORGE. I'm talking about all the people trying to get you out. Hundreds, perhaps thousands. Alice and I aren't the only ones. We've got a heck of a fine team of lawyers working on the brief. With or without me, the appeal will be won. I promise you that.

HENRY. It's no use, George.

GEORGE. I realize all that sounds pretty unconvincing under the circumstances, but it's true.

HENRY. Those bastard cops are never going to let us out of here. We're here for life and that's it.

GEORGE. You really believe that?

HENRY. What do you expect me to believe?

GEORGE. I wish I could answer that, son, but that's really for you to say.

GUARD. Time, Counselor.

GEORGE. Coming. (*Turns to the other Boys.*) Listen, boys, I don't know where in the world I'll be the day your appeal is won—and it will be won—whether it's in the Pacific somewhere or in Europe or in a hole in the ground . . . Take care of yourselves.

TOMMY. See you around, George.

SMILEY. So long, George.

JOEY. 'Bye, Cheer.

GEORGE. Yeah. See you around. (*Pause.*) Goodbye, Henry. Good luck and God bless you.

HENRY. God bless you, too, George. Take care of yourself.

TOMMY. Say, George, when you come back from the war, we're going to take you outa town and blast some weed.

JOEY. We'll get you a pair of buns you can hold in your hands!

GEORGE. I may just take you up on that. (*The Guard escorts George out, then turns back to the Boys.*)

GUARD. All right, new work assignments. Everybody report to the jute mill. Let's go. (*Smiley, Joey and Tommy start to exit. Henry hangs back.*) What's the matter with you, Reyna? You got lead in your pants? I said let's go.

HENRY. We're supposed to work in the mess hall.

GUARD. You got a new assignment.

HENRY. Since when?

GUARD. Since right now. Get going!

HENRY (*Hanging back*). The warden know about this?

GUARD. What the hell do you care? You think you're something special? Come on, greaseball. Move!

HENRY. Make me, you bastard!

GUARD. Oh yeah. (*The Guard pushes Henry. Henry pushes back. The batos react, as the Guard traps Henry with his club around the chest. The Boys move to Henry's defense.*) Back!

HENRY (*To the batos*). Back off! BACK OFF! Don't be stupid.

GUARD. Okay, Reyna, you got solitary! Bastard, huh? Into the hole! (*He pushes Henry onto center stage. Lights down. A single spot.*) Line, greaseballs. Move out! (*As they march.*) Quickly, quickly. You're too slow. Move, move, move. (*The Boys exit with the Guard.*)

5. SOLITARY

A lone saxophone sets the mood.

PACHUCO. Too bad, ese. He set you up again.

HENRY (*Long pause. He looks around*). Solitary, ese . . . they gave me solitary. (*He sits down on the floor, a forlorn figure.*)

PACHUCO. Better get used to it, carnal. That's what this stretch is going to be about, see? You're in here for life, bato.

HENRY. I can't accept it, ese.

PACHUCO.
You've go to, Hank . . .
only this reality is real now,

only this place is real,
sitting in the lonely cell of your will . . .

HENRY. I can't see my hands.

PACHUCO.
Then tell you eyes to forget the light, ese
Only the hard floor is there, carnal
Only the cold hard edge of this reality
and there is no time . . .
Each second is a raw drop of blood from your brain
that you must swallow
drop by drop
and don't even start counting
or you'll lose your mind . . .

HENRY. I've got to know why I'm here, ese! I've got to
have a reason for being here.

PACHUCO. You're here, Hank, because you chose to be—
because you protected your brother and your family.
And nobody knows the worth of that effort better
than you, ese.

HENRY. I miss them, ese . . . my jefitos, my carnalillo, my
sis . . . I miss Della.

PACHUCO (A spot illuminates Henry's family standing up-
stage; El Pachuco snaps it off).
Forget them!
Forget them all.
Forget your family and the barrio
beyond the wall.

HENRY. There's still a chance I'll get out.

PACHUCO. Fat chance.

HENRY. I'm talking about the appeal!

PACHUCO. And I'm talking about what's real! ¿Qué traes,
Hank? Haven't you learned yet?

HENRY. Learned what?

PACHUCO.
Not to expect justice when it isn't there.
No court in the land's going to set you free.
Learn to protect your loves by binding them
in hate, ese! Stop hanging on to false hopes.
The moment those hopes come crashing down,
you'll find yourself on the ground foaming at
the mouth. ¡Como loco!

HENRY (Turning on him furiously). ¿Sabes qué? Don't
tell me any more. I don't need you to tell me what
to do. Fuck off! FUCK OFF! (Henry turns away
from El Pachuco. Long pause. An anxious, intense
moment. El Pachuco shifts gears and breaks the tension with a satirical twist. He throws his arms out and
laughs.)

PACHUCO.
¡Órale pues!
Don't take the pinche play so seriously, Jesús!

Es puro vacilón!
Watcha.

(He snaps his fingers. Lights change. We hear the
sounds of the city.)

This is Los, carnal.
You want to see some justice for pachucos?
Check out what's happening back home today.
The Navy has landed, ese—
on leave with full pay
and war's breaking out in the streets of L.A.!

6. ZOOT SUIT RIOTS

We hear music: the bugle call from "Bugle Call
Rag." Suddenly the stage is awash in colored lights.
The city of Los Angeles appears in the background in
a panoramic vista of lights tapering into the night
horizon. Sailors and Girls jitterbug on the dance
floor. It is the Avalon Ballroom. The music is hot,
the dancing hotter. El Pachuco and Henry stand to
the side.
    The scene is in dance and mostly pantomime.
Occasionally words are heard over the music which
is quite loud. On the floor are two Sailors (Swabbie
is one.) and a Marine dancing with the Girls. A
Shore Patrolman speaks to the Cigarette Girl. A
Pimp comes on and watches the action. Little Blue
and Zooter are also on the floor. Rudy enters wearing Henry's zoot suit with Bertha and Lupe. Lupe
takes their picture, then all three move up center to
the rear of the ballroom. Cholo comes in down center, sees them and moves up stage. All four make an
entrance onto the dance floor.
    The Marine takes his girl aside after paying her.
She passes the money to the Pimp. The Sailors try to
pick up on Lupe and Bertha, and Cholo pushes one
back. The Sailors complain to the Shore Patrol, who
throws Cholo out the door down center. There is an
argument that Rudy joins. The Sailors go back to
Bertha and Lupe who resist. Cholo and Rudy go to
their defense and a fight develops. Zooter and Little
Blue split. Cholo takes the Girls out and Rudy pulls
a knife. He is facing the three Sailors and the Marine, when The Pachuco freezes the action.

PACHUCO (Forcefully). Órale, that's enough! (El Pachuco
takes Rudy's knife and with a tap sends him off-stage.
Rudy exits with the Girls. El Pachuco is now facing the
angry Servicemen. He snaps his fingers. The Press enters
quickly to the beeping sound of a radio broadcast.)

PRESS. Good evening, Mr. and Mrs. North and South America and all the ships at sea. Let's go to press. FLASH. Los Angeles, California, June 3, 1943. Serious rioting broke out here today as flying squadrons of Marines and soldiers joined the Navy in a new assault on zooter-infested districts. A fleet of twenty taxicabs carrying some two hundred servicemen pulled out of the Naval Armory in Chavez Ravine tonight and assembled a task force that invaded the eastside barrio. (*Unfreeze. The following speeches happen simultaneously.*)

MATE. You got any balls in them funny pants, boy?

SAILOR. He thinks he's tough . . .

SWABBIE. How about it, lardhead? You a tough guy or just a draft dodger?

PRESS. The Zoot Suiters, those gamin' dandies . . .

PACHUCO (*Cutting them off*). Why don't you tell them what I really am, ese, or how you've been forbidden to use the very word . . .

PRESS. We are complying in the interest of the war.

PACHUCO. How have you complied?

PRESS. We're using other terms.

PACHUCO. Like "pachuco" and "zoot suiter?"

PRESS. What's wrong with that? The Zoot Suit Crime Wave is even beginning to push the war news off the front page.

PACHUCO.
The Press distorted the very meaning of the word "zoot suit."
All it is for you guys is another way to say Mexican.
But the ideal of the original chuco
was to look like a diamond
to look sharp
hip
bonaroo
finding a style of urban survival
in the rural skirts and outskirts
of the brown metropolis of Los, cabrón.

PRESS. It's an afront to good taste.

PACHUCO. Like the Mexicans, Filipinos and blacks who wear them.

PRESS. Yes!

PACHUCO. Even the white kids and the Wops and the Jews are putting on the drape shape.

PRESS. You are trying to outdo the white man in exaggerated white man's clothes!

PACHUCO.
Because everybody knows
that Mexicans, Filipinos and Blacks
belong to the huarache
the straw hat and the dirty overall.

PRESS. You savages weren't even wearing clothes when the white man pulled you out of the jungle.

MARINE. My parents are going without collars and cuffs so you can wear that shit.

PRESS. That's going too far, too goddamned far and it's got to be stopped!

PACHUCO. Why?

PRESS. Don't you know there's a war on? Don't you fucking well know you can't get away with that shit? What are we fighting for if not to annihilate the enemies of the American way of life?

MATE. Let's tear it off his back!

SAILORS/MARINE. Let's strip him! Get him! (Etc.)

PRESS. KILL THE PACHUCO BASTARD! (*Music: "American Patrol" by Glenn Miller. The Press gets a searchlight from upstage center while the Four Servicemen stalk El Pachuco.*)

SAILOR. Heh, zooter. Come on, zooter!

SWABBIE. You think you're more important than the war, zooter?

MATE. let's see if you got any balls in them funny pants, boy.

SWABBIE. Watch out for the knife.

SAILOR. That's a real chango monkey suit he's got on.

MATE. I bet he's half monkey—just like the Filipinos and Niggers that wear them.

SWABBIE. You trying to outdo the white man in them glad rags, Mex? (*They fight now to the finish. El Pachuco is overpowered and stripped as Henry watches helplessly from his position. The Press and Servicemen exit with pieces of El Pachuco's zoot suit. El Pachuco stands. The only item of clothing on his body is a small loincloth. He turns and looks at Henry, with mystic intensity. He opens his arms as an Aztec conch blows, and he slowly exits backward with powerful calm into the shadows. Silence. Henry comes downstage. He absorbs the impact of what he has seen and falls to his knees at center stage, spent and exhausted. Lights down.*)

7. ALICE

The Guard and Alice enter from opposite sides of the stage. The Guard carries a handful of letters and is reading one of them.

GUARD. July 2, 1943.

ALICE.

Dear Henry,

I hope this letter finds you in good health and good spirits—but I have to assume you've heard about the riots in Los Angeles. It was a nightmare, and it lasted for a week. The city is still in a state of shock.

GUARD (*Folds letter back into envelope, then opens another*). August 5, 1943.

ALICE.

Dear Henry,

The riots here in L.A. have touched off race riots all over the country—Chicago, Detroit, even little Beaumont, Texas, for Christ's sake. But the one in Harlem was the worst. Millions of dollars worth of property damage. 500 people were hospitalized, and five Negroes were killed.

GUARD. Things are rough all over.

ALICE. Please write to me and tell me how you feel.

GUARD (*The Guard folds up the second letter, stuffs it back into its envelope and opens a third*). August 20, 1943.

ALICE.

Dear Henry,

Although I am disappointed not to have heard from you, I thought I would send you some good news for a change. Did you know we had a gala fund-raiser at the Mocambo?

GUARD. The Mocambo . . . Hotcha!

ALICE.

. . . and Rita Hayworth lent your sister Lupe a ball gown for the occasion. She got dressed at Cecil B. DeMille's house, and she looked terrific. Her escort was Anthony Quinn, and Orson Welles said . . .

GUARD. Orson Welles! Well! Sounds like Louella Parsons. (*He folds up the letter.*) September 1, 1943.

ALICE. Henry, why aren't you answering my letters?

GUARD. He's busy. (*He continues to stuff the envelope.*)

ALICE. Henry, if there's something I've said or done . . . ? (*The Guard shuffles the envelopes.*) Henry . . . (*Lights change. Guard crosses to center stage, where Henry is still doubled up on the floor.*)

GUARD. Welcome back to the living, Reyna. It's been a long hot summer. Here's your mail. (*The Guard tosses the letters to the floor directly in front of Henry's head. Henry looks up slowly and grabs one of the letters. He opens it, trying to focus. The Guard exits.*)

ALICE. Henry, I just found out you did ninety days in solitary. I'm furious at the rest of the guys for keeping it from me. I talked to Warden Duffy, and he said you struck a guard. Did something happen I should know about? I wouldn't ask if it wasn't so important, but a clean record . . . (*Henry rips up the letter he has been reading and scatters the others. Alarmed.*) Henry?

(*Henry pauses, his instant fury spent and under control. He sounds almost weary, but the anger is still there.*)

HENRY. You still don't understand, Alice.

ALICE (*Softly, compassionate*). But I do! I'm not accusing you of anything. I don't care what happened or why they sent you there. I'm sure you had your reasons. But you know the public is watching you.

HENRY (*Frustrated, a deep question*). Why do you do this, Alice?

ALICE. What?

HENRY. The appeal, the case, all the shit you do. You think the public gives a goddamn?

ALICE (*With conviction*). Yes! We are going to get you out of here, Henry Reyna. We are going to win!

HENRY (*Probing*). What if we lose?

ALICE (*Surprised but moving on*). We're not going to lose.

HENRY (*Forcefully, insistent, meaning more than he is saying*). What if we do? What if we get another crooked judge, and he nixes the appeal?

ALICE. Then we'll appeal again. We'll take it to the Supreme Court. (*A forced laugh.*) Hell, we'll take it all the way to President Roosevelt!

HENRY (*Backing her up—emotionally*). What if we still lose?

ALICE (*Bracing herself against his aggression*). We can't.

HENRY. Why can't we?

ALICE (*Giving a political response in spite of herself*). Because we've got too much support. You should see the kinds of people responding to us. Unions, Mexicans, Negroes, Oakies. It's fantastic.

HENRY (*Driving harder*). Why can't we lose, Alice?

ALICE. I'm telling you.

HENRY. No, you're not.

ALICE (*Starting to feel vulnerable*). I don't know what to tell you.

HENRY. Yes, you do!

ALICE (*Frightened*). Henry . . . ?

HENRY. Tell me why we can't lose, Alice!

ALICE (*Forced to fight back, with characteristic passion*). Stop it, Henry! Please stop it! I won't have you treat me this way. I never have been able to accept one person pushing another around . . . pushing me around! Can't you see that's why I'm here? Because I can't stand it happening to you. Because I'm a Jew, goddamnit! I have been there . . . I have been there! If you lose, I lose. (*Pause. The emotional tension is immense. Alice fights to hold back tears. She turns away.*)

HENRY. I'm sorry . . .

ALICE (*Pause*). It's stupid for us to fight like this. I look forward to coming here for weeks. Just to talk to you, to be with you, to see your eyes.

HENRY (*Pause*). I thought a lot about you when I was in the hole. Sometimes . . . sometimes I'd even see you walk in, in the dark, and talk to me. Just like you are right now. Same look, same smile, same perfume . . . (*He pauses.*) Only the other one never gave me so much lip. She just listened. She did say one thing. She said . . .

ALICE (*Trying to make light of it. Then more gently*). I can't say that to you, Henry. Not the way you want it.

HENRY. Why not?

ALICE (*She means it*). Because I can't allow myself to be used to fill in for all the love you've always felt and always received from all your women.

HENRY (*With no self-pity*). Give it a chance, Alice.

ALICE (*Beside herself*). Give it a chance? You crazy idiot. If I thought making love to you would solve all your problems, I'd do it in a second. Don't you know that? But it won't. It'll only complicate things. I'm trying to help you, goddammit. And to do that, I have to be your friend, not your white woman.

HENRY (*Getting angry*). What makes you think I want to go to bed with you. Because you're white? I've had more white pieces of ass than you can count, ¿sabes? Who do you think you are? God's gift to us brown animals.

ALICE (*Alice slaps him and stops, horrifies. A whirlpool of emotions*). Oh, Hank. All the love and hate it's taken to get us together in this lousy prison room. Do you realize only Hitler and the Second World War could have accomplished that? I don't know whether to laugh or cry. (*Alice folds into her emotional spin, her body shaking. Suddenly she turns, whipping herself out of it with a cry, both laughing and weeping. The come to each other and embrace. Then they kiss—passionately. The Guard enters. He frowns.*)

GUARD. Time, Miss.

ALICE (*Turning*). Already? Oh, my God, Henry, there's so many messages I was going to give you. Your mother and father send their love, of course. And Lupe and . . . Della. And . . . oh, yes. They want you to know Rudy's in the Marines.

HENRY. The Marines?

ALICE. I'll write you all about it. Will you write me?

HENRY (*A glance at the Guard*). Yes.

GUARD (*His tone getting harsher*). Let's go, lady.

HENRY. Goodbye, Licha.

ALICE. I'll see you on the outside . . . Hank. (*Alice gives Henry a thumb up gesture, and the Guard escorts her out. Henry turns downstage, full of thoughts. He addresses El Pachuco, who is nowhere to be seen.*)

HENRY. You were wrong, ese . . . There's something to hope for. I know now we're going to win the appeal.

Do you hear me, ese? Ese! (*Pause.*) Are you even there any more? (*The Guard re-enters at a clip.*)

GUARD. Okay, Reyna, come on.

HENRY. Where to?

GUARD. We're letting you go . . . (*Henry looks at him incredulously. The Guard smiles.*) . . . to Folsom Prison with all the rest of the hardcore cons. You really didn't expect to walk out of here a free man, did you? Listen, kid, your appeal stands about as much chance as the Japs and Krauts of winning the war. Personally, I don't see what that broad sees in you. I wouldn't give you the sweat off my balls. Come on! (*Henry and the Guard turn upstage to leave. Lights change. El Pachuco appears halfway up the backdrop, fully dressed again and clearly visible. Henry stops with a jolt as he sees him. El Pachuco lifts his arms. Lights go down as we hear the high sound of a bomb falling to earth.*)

8. THE WINNING OF THE WAR

The aerial bomb explodes with a reverberating sound and a white flash that illuminates the form of pachuco images in the black backdrop. Other bombs fall and all hell breaks loose. Red flashes, artillery, gunfire, ack-ack. Henry and the Guard exit. The Four Servicemen enter as an honor guard. Music: Glen Miller's "Saint Louis Blues March." As the Servicemen march on we see Rudy down left in his marine uniform, belt undone. Enrique, Dolores and Lupe join him. Dolores has his hat, Lupe her camera. Enrique fastens two buttons on the uniform as Rudy does up his belt. Dolores inspects his collar and gives him his hat. Rudy puts on his hat and all pose for Lupe. She snaps the picture and Rudy kisses them all and is off. He picks up the giant switchblade from behind a newspaper bundle and joins the Servicemen as they march down in drill formation. The family marches off, looking back sadly. The drill ends and Rudy and the Shore Patrol move to one side. As Rudy's interrogation goes on, People in the barrio come on with newspapers to mime daily tasks. The Press enters.

PRESS. The Los Angeles Examiner, July 1, 1943. Headline: WORLD WAR II REACHES TURNING POINT. If the late summer of 1942 was the low point, a year later the war for the Allies is pounding its way to certain victory.

SHORE PATROL. July 10!

RUDY. U.S., British and Canadian troops invade Sicily, Sir!

SHORE PATROL. August 6!

RUDY. U.S. troops occupy Solomon Island, Sir!

SHORE PATROL. September 5!

RUDY. MacArthur's forces land on New Guinea, Sir!

SHORE PATROL. October 1!

RUDY. U.S. Fifth Army enters Naples, Sir!

PRESS. On and on it goes. From Corsica to Kiev, from Tarawa to Anzio. The relentless advance of the Allied armies cannot be checked. (*One by one, Henry's family and friends enter, carrying newspapers. They tear the papers into small pieces.*) The Los Angeles Times, June 6, 1944. Headline: Allied forces under General Eisenhower land in Normandy.

SHORE PATROL. August 19!

RUDY. American First Army reaches Germany, Sir!

SHORE PATROL. October 17!

RUDY. MacArthur returns to the Philippines, Sir!

PRESS. On the homefront, Americans go on with their daily lives with growing confidence and relief, as the war pushes on toward inevitable triumph. (*Pause.*) The Los Angeles Daily News, Wednesday, November 8, 1944. Headline: District Court of Appeals decides in Sleepy Lagoon murder case . . . boys in pachuco murder given . . .

PEOPLE. FREEDOM!!! (*Music bursts forth as the joyous crowd tosses the shredded newspaper into the air like confetti. The Boys enter upstage center, and the crowd rushes to them, weeping and cheering. There are kisses and hugs and tears of joy. Henry is swept forward by the triumphal procession.*)

9. RETURN TO THE BARRIO

The music builds and people start dancing. Others just embrace. The tune is "Soldado Razo" played to a lively corrido beat. It ends with joyous applause, laughter and tears.

RUDY. ¡Ese carnal!

HENRY. Rudy!!

DOLORES. ¡Bendito sea Dios! Who would believe this day would ever come? Look at you—you're all home!

LUPE. I still can't believe it. We won! We won the appeal! (*Cheers.*)

ENRIQUE. I haven't felt like this since Villa took Zacatecas. (*Laughter, cheers.*) ¡Pero mira! Look who's here. Mis hijos. (*Puts his arm around Henry and Rudy.*) It isn't every day a man has two grown sons come home from so far away—one from the war, the other from . . . bueno, who cares? The Sleepy Lagoon is history, hombre. For a change, los Mexicanos have won! (*Cheers.*)

GEORGE. Well, Henry. I don't want to say I told you so, but we sure taught Judge Charles a lesson in misconduct, didn't we? (*More cheers.*) Do you realize this is the greatest victory the Mexican-American community has ever had in the history of this whole blasted country?

DOLORES. Yes, but if it wasn't for the unselfish thoughtfulness of people like you and this beautiful lady—and all the people who helped out, Mexicanos, Negros, all Americanos—our boys would not be home today.

GEORGE. I only hope you boys realize how important you are now.

JOEY. Pos, I realize it, ese. (*Laughter.*)

RUDY. I came all the way from Hawaii just to get here, carnal. I only got a few days, but I'm going to get you drunk.

HENRY. Pos, we'll see who gets who drunk, ese. (*Laughter and hoots. Henry spots El Pachuco entering from stage right.*)

DOLORES. Jorge, Licha, todos. Let's go into the house, eh? I've made a big pot of menudo, and it's for everybody.

ENRIQUE. There's ice-cold beer too. Vénganse, vamos todos.

GEORGE (*To Alice*). Alice . . . Menudo, that's Mexican chicken soup? (*Everybody exits, leaving Henry behind with El Pachuco.*)

HENRY. It's good to see you again, ese. I thought I'd lost you.

PACHUCO. H'm pues, it'd take more than the U.S. Navy to wipe me out.

HENRY. Where you been?

PACHUCO. Pos, here in the barrio. Welcome back.

HENRY. It's good to be home.

PACHUCO. No hard feelings?

HENRY. Chale—we won, didn't we?

PACHUCO. Simón.

HENRY. Me and the batos have been in a lot of fights together, ese. But we won this one, because we learned to fight in a new way.

PACHUCO. And that's the perfect way to end this play—happy ending y todo. (*Pachuco makes a sweeping gesture. Lights come down. He looks up at the lights, realizing something is wrong. He flicks his wrist, and the lights go back up again.*)

But life ain't that way, Hank.
The barrio's still out there, waiting and wanting.
The cops are still tracking us down like dogs.
The gangs are still killing each other,
Families are barely surviving,
And there in your own backyard . . . life goes on.

(*Soft music. Della enters.*)

DELLA. Hank? (*Henry goes to her and they embrace.*)

HENRY. Where were you? Why didn't you come to the Hall of Justice to see us get out?

DELLA. I guess I was a little afraid things had changed. So much has happened to both of us.

PACHUCO. Simón. She's living in your house.

DELLA. After I got back from Ventura, my parents gave me a choice. Forget about you or get out.

HENRY. Why didn't you write to me?

DELLA. You had your own problems. Your jefitos took care of me. Hey, you know what, Hank, I think they expect us to get married.

PACHUCO. How about it, ese? You still going to give her that big pachuco wedding you promised.

HENRY. I have to think about it.

ALICE (*Off-stage*). Henry?

PACHUCO (*Snaps fingers*). Wish you had the time. But here comes Licha.

ALICE (*Entering*). Henry, I've just come to say good night. (*Della freezes and Henry turns to Alice.*)

HENRY. Good night? Why are you leaving so soon?

ALICE. Soon? I've been here all afternoon. There'll be other times, Henry. You're home now, with your family, that's what matters.

HENRY. Don't patronize me, Alice.

ALICE (*Surprised*). Patronize you?

HENRY. Yeah. I learned a few words in the joint.

ALICE. Yo también, Hank. Te quiero. (*Pachuco snaps. Alice freezes, and Rudy enters.*)

RUDY. Ese, carnal, congratulations, the jefita just told me about you and Della. That's great, ese. But if you want me to be best man, you better do it in the next three days.

HENRY. Wait a minute, Rudy, don't push me.

RUDY. Qué pues, getting cold feet already? (*Henry is beginning to be surrounded by separate conversations.*)

DELLA. If you don't want me here, I can move out.

RUDY. Watcha. I'll let you and Della have our room tonight, bato. I'll sleep on the couch.

ALICE. You aren't expecting me to sleep here, are you?

HENRY. I'm not asking you to.

PACHUCO/ALICE/RUDY/DELLA. Why not?

RUDY. The jefitos will never know, ese.

ALICE. Be honest, Henry.

DELLA. What do you want me to do?

HENRY. Give me a chance to think about it. Give me a second!

PACHUCO. One second! (*Pachuco snaps. Enrique enters.*)

ENRIQUE. Bueno, bueno, pues, what are you doing out here, hijo? Aren't you coming in for menudo?

HENRY. I'm just thinking, jefito.

ENRIQUE. ¿De qué, hombre? Didn't you do enough of that in prison? Andale, this is your house. Come in and live again.

HENRY. 'Apá, did you tell Della I was going to marry her?

ENRIQUE. Yes, but only after you did.

RUDY. ¿Qué traes, carnal? Don't you care about Della anymore?

ALICE. If it was just me and you, Henry, it might be different. But you have to think of your family.

HENRY. I don't need you to tell me my responsibilities.

ALICE. I'm sorry.

RUDY. Sorry, carnal.

DELLA. I don't need anybody to feel sorry for me. I did what I did because I wanted to. All I want to know is what's going to happen now. If you still want me, órale, suave. If you don't, that's okay, too. But I'm not going to hang around like a pendeja all my life.

RUDY. Your huisa's looking finer than ever, carnal.

ALICE. You're acting as if nothing has happened.

ENRIQUE. You have your whole life ahead of you.

ALICE. You belong here, Henry. I'm the one that's out of place.

RUDY. If you don't pick up on her, I'm going to have to step in.

HENRY. That's bullshit. What about what we shared in prison? I've never been that close to anybody.

ALICE. That was in prison.

HENRY. What the hell do you think the barrio is?

RUDY. It's not bullshit!

HENRY. Shut up, carnalillo!

RUDY. Carnalillo? How can you still call me that? I'm not your pinche little brother no more.

GEORGE (*Entering*). You guys have got to stop fighting, Henry, or the barrio will never change. Don't you realize you men represent the hope of your people?

ALICE. Della was in prison too. You know you had thousands of people clamoring for your release, but you were Della's only hope.

HENRY. Look, esa, I know you did a year in Ventura. I know you stood up for me when it counted. I wish I could make it up to you.

DELLA. Don't give me your bullshit, Henry. Give it to Alice.

ALICE. I think it's time for Alice Bloomfield to go home.

HENRY. Don't be jealous, esa.

DELLA. Jealous? Mira, cabrón, I know I'm not the only one you ever took to the Sleepy Lagoon.

RUDY. The Sleepy Lagoon ain't shit. I saw real lagoons in those islands, ese—killing Japs! I saw some pachucos go out there that are never coming back.

DELLA. But I was always there when you came back, wasn't I?

DOLORES (*Entering*). Henry? Come back inside, hijo. Everybody's waiting for you.

RUDY. Why didn't you tell them I was there, Carnal? I was at the Sleepy Lagoon. Throwing chingazos with everybody!

HENRY. Don't you understand, Rudy? I was trying to keep you from getting a record. Those bastard cops are never going to leave us alone.

GEORGE. You've got to forget what happened, Henry.

HENRY. What can I give you, Della? I'm an ex-con.

DELLA. So am I!

SMILEY (*Entering*). Let's face it, Hank. There's no future for us in this town. I'm taking my wife and kid and moving to Arizona.

DOLORES (*Simultaneously*). I know what you are feeling, hijo, it's home again. I know inside you are afraid that nothing has changed. That the police will never leave you in peace. Pero no le hace. Everything is going to be fine now. Marry Della and fill this house with children. Just do one thing for me—forget the zoot suit clothes.

ENRIQUE. If there's one thing that will keep a man off the streets it's his own familia.

GEORGE. Don't let this thing eat your heart out for the rest of your . . .

ALICE. Sometimes the best thing you can do for someone you love is walk away.

DELLA. What do you want, Hank?

RUDY. It cost me more than it did you.

SMILEY. We started the 38th and I'll never forget you, carnal. But I got to think about my family.

HENRY. Wait a minute! I don't know if I'll be back in prison tomorrow or not! I have nothing to give you, Della. Not even a piece of myself.

DELLA. I have my life to live, too, Hank. I love you. I would even die for you. Pero me chingan la madre if I'm going to throw away my life for nothing.

HENRY. But I love you . . . (*Both Girls turn. Henry looks at Alice, then to the whole group upstage of him. Still turning. He looks at Della and goes to embrace her. The freeze ends and other people enter.*)

LUPE. ¡Órale, Hank! Watcha Joey. The crazy bato went all the way to his house and put on his drapes.

JOEY. ¡Esos, batooooooosss! ¡Esas, huisaaaaaass!

TOMMY. Look at this cat! He looks all reet.

LUPE. Yeah, like a parakeet!

HENRY. ¿Y tú, ese? How come you put on your tacuche? Where's the party?

JOEY. Pos, ain't the party here?

RUDY. Yeah, ese, but this ain't the Avalon Ballroom. The zoot suit died under fire here in Los. Don't you know that, cabrón?

ENRIQUE. Rudolfo!

LUPE. And he was supposed to get Henry drunk.

RUDY. Shut up, esa!

ENRIQUE. ¡Ya pues! Didn't you have any menudo? Vieja, fix him a great big bowl of menudo and put plenty of chile in it. We're going to sweat it out of him.

RUDY. I don't need no pinche menudo.

HENRY. Watch your language, carnal.

RUDY. And I don't need you! I'm a man. I can take care of myself!

JOEY. Muy marine el bato . . .

ENRIQUE. Rudy, hijo. Are you going to walk into the kitchen or do I have to drag you.

RUDY. Whatever you say, jefito.

GEORGE. Well, Alice. This looks like the place where we came in. I think it's about time we left.

ALICE. Say the word, George, just say the word.

DOLORES. No, no. You can't leave so soon.

JOEY. Chale, chale, chale. You can't take our Grandma. ¿Qué se trae, carnal? Póngase más abusado, ese. No se haga tan square.

GEORGE. Okay, square I got. What was the rest of it?

JOEY. Pos, le estoy hablando en chicas patas, ese. Es puro chicano.

RUDY. ¿Qué chicano? Ni que madre, cabrón. Why don't you grow up?

JOEY. Grow up, ese?

RUDY. Try walking downtown looking like that. See if the sailors don't skin your ass alive.

JOEY. So what? It's no skin off your ass. Come on, Bertha.

RUDY. She's staying with me.

JOEY. She's mine.

RUDY. Prove it, punk. (*Rudy attacks Joey and they fight. The Batos and Rucas take out Joey. Henry pacifies Rudy, who bursts out crying. Enrique, Della, Dolores, Alice, Lupe and George are the only ones left. Rudy in a flush of emotion.*) Cabrones, se amontonaron. They ganged up on me, carnal. You left me and they ganged up on me. You shouldn't have done it, carnal. Why didn't you take me with you. For the jefitos? The jefitos lost me anyway.

HENRY. Come on in the house, Rudy . . .

RUDY. No! I joined the Marines. I didn't have to join, but I went. ¿Sabes por qué? Because they got me, carnal. Me chingaron, ese. (*Sobs.*) I went to the pinche show with Bertha, all chingón in your tachuche, ese. I was wearing your zoot suit, and they got me. Twenty sailors, Marines. We were up in the balcony. They came down from behind. They grabbed me by the neck and dragged me down the stairs, kicking and punching and pulling my greña. They dragged me out into the streets . . . and all the people watched while they stripped me. (*Sobs.*) They stripped me, carnal. Bertha saw them strip me. Hijos de la chingada, they stripped me. (*Henry goes to Rudy and embraces him with fierce love and desperation. Pause. Tommy comes running in.*)

TOMMY. ¡Órale! There's cops outside. They're trying to arrest Joey. (*George crosses to Tommy.*)

GEORGE (*Bursting out*). Joey?

TOMMY. They got him up against your car. They're trying to say he stole it!

GEORGE. Oh, God. I'll take care of this.

ALICE. I'll go with you. (*George, Tommy and Alice exit.*)

HENRY. Those fucking bastards! (*He starts to exit.*)

DELLA. Henry, no!

HENRY. What the hell do you mean no? Don't you see what's going on outside?

DELLA. They'll get you again! That's what they want.

HENRY. Get out of my way! (*He pushes her out of the way, toward Dolores.*)

ENRIQUE (*Stands up before Henry*). ¡Hijo!

HENRY. Get out of my way, jefe!

ENRIQUE. You will stay here!

HENRY. Get out of my way! (*Enrique powerfully pushes him back and throws Henry to the floor and holds.*)

ENRIQUE. ¡TE DIGO QUE NO! (*Silent moment, Henry stands up and offers to strike Enrique. But something stops him. The realization that if he strikes back or even if he walks out the door, the family bond is irreparably broken. Henry tenses for a moment, then relaxes and embraces his father. Della goes to them and joins the embrace. Then Dolores, then Lupe, then Rudy. All embrace in a tight little group. Press enters right and comes down.*)

PRESS. Henry Reyna went back to prison in 1947 for robbery and assault with a deadly weapon. While incarcerated, he killed another inmate and he wasn't released until 1955, when he got into hard drugs. He died of the trauma of his life in 1972.

PACHUCO. That's the way you see it, ese. But there's other ways to end this story.

RUDY. Henry Reyna went to Korea in 1950. He was shipped across in a destroyer and defended the 38th Parallel until he was killed at Inchon in 1952, being posthumously awarded the Congressional Medal of Honor.

ALICE. Henry Reyna married Della in 1948 and they have five kids, three of them now going to the University, speaking calo and calling themselves Chicanos.

GEORGE. Henry Reyna, the born leader . . .

JUDGE. Henry Reyna, the social victim . . .

BERTHA. Henry Reyna, the street corner warrior . . .

SMILEY. Henry Reyna, el carnal de aquellas . . .

JOEY. Henry Reyna, the zoot suiter . . .

TOMMY. Henry Reyna, my friend . . .

LUPE. Henry Reyna, my brother . . .

ENRIQUE. Henry Reyna . . .

DOLORES. Our son . . .

DELLA. Henry Reyna, my love . . .

PACHUCO. Henry Reyna . . . El Pachuco . . . The man . . . the myth . . . still lives. (*Lights down and fade out.*)

COMMENTARY

Note: The following essay represents a single interpretation of the play. For other perspectives on Zoot Suit, *consult the essays listed below.*

Octavio Paz, Mexico's most celebrated literary figure in the twentieth century, wrote disparagingly about the *pachuco* and his spectacular zoot suit in *The Labyrinth of Solitude*, an admired commentary on the Latino character. For Paz, the zoot suit's appeal

> . . . consists in its exaggeration. . . . [The *pachuco*] takes an ordinary suit and turns it into something beautiful, something artful. In this way he can occupy a place in the world that previously ignored him and thus becomes one of society's wicked heroes. The *pachuco* becomes the prey of society, but instead of hiding he adorns himself to attract the hunter.

The *pachuco* was at once both hero and rebel in his fight against racism and victims of racist forces; he was the source of considerable controversy both within the Mexican-American community and outside it.

For Valdez he became an apt symbol of the new consciousness of the Mexican-American, a forerunner of the "Chicano" of the 1960s. In an interview with Chicano playwright Carlos Morton, Valdez explains his attraction to the zoot-suited *pachuco* of the 1940s:

> To me *pachiquismo* was the direct antecedent of what has come to be termed "Chicano-consciousness." In the 1940s *pachucos* were caught between two cultures, viewed with suspicion by both conservative Mexican-Americans and Anglos. The *pachucos* were the first to acknowledge their bicultural backgrounds and to create a subculture based on this circumstance. . . . The *pachuco* emerged as a cult figure for he was the first to take pride in the complexity of his origins, and to *resist* conformity.
>
> (*Latin American Theater Review*, 15/2: 75)

Valdez gives us two *pachucos* in *Zoot Suit*. In the opening moment we meet El Pachuco (played superbly by Edward James Olmos on Broadway and in the subsequent film; see below), the play's narrator who leads us through this "construct of fact and fantasy." Immaculately dressed in a red-and-black zoot suit (the colors are significant as they are associated with the Aztec nation that ruled central and northern Mexico until the Conquest of 1521), El Pachuco is a Chicano version of the Brechtian storyteller who leads us through this episodic tale, snapping his fingers stylishly to denote changes of time and locale. El Pachuco represents pride in *La Raza* and even is transformed into the specter of Moctezuma (erroneously spelled as Montezuma), the last Aztec emperor.

The other *pachuco* is Henry Reyna, a street-tough kid who becomes the central figure (and victim) in Valdez's account of the Sleepy Lagoon Case. In actuality, however, El Pachuco and Henry are a single entity—the former being an objectification of Henry's inner self. Their pointed and quarrelsome dialogue establishes the dialectic of the play (that and of course the racial tensions) as the *pachuco* of myth and the *pachuco* of reality clash. Frustrated during his quest for maturity, Henry lashes out at his other self:

> *Sabe que, ese.* [Know what, man?] I'd got you all figured out. I know who you are, *carnal.* You're the one who got me here [in prison]. You're my own worst enemy and my best friend. Myself. So get lost.

Here Valdez employs a technique popularized in the allegorical dramas of medieval Europe: *psychomachia*, that is, the externalization of an interior state of mind. Often this was accomplished by having a Good Angel and a Bad Angel engage an "everyman" in dialogue. El Pachuco is simultaneously a Good and Bad Angel who tempts Henry to a variety of behaviors as he learns to survive in an intolerant and hostile world.

Henry has another Good Angel at his side: Alice Bloomfield (in real life, Alice Greenfield McGrath). She and lawyer George Shearer become the "white saviors" of Henry and the other Mexican-Americans trapped in an absurd judicial system and pilloried by a racist press. (Note that Valdez has the actor who plays the Hearst reporter double as the prosecutor in the Sleepy Lagoon trial.) And Alice becomes a love interest for Henry, thereby giving the play a romantic dimension that seems to enhance the "happy ending" that theater audiences crave.

Valdez is, on the one hand, quite honest when he admits that his play is a "construct of fact and fantasy." On the other hand, this "fantasy" concerning Alice Bloomfield creates an unsettling "drama-within-the-drama" of *Zoot Suit*. Yes, Alice was a member of the Sleepy Lagoon Defense Committee, but she was hired *after* the trial was completed, and there is no evidence of any romantic relationship between Alice and Henry. And if that were the actual truth, we could accept it as a creative invention to add a human dimension to a play that borders on the polemic.

However, there were two extraordinary Mexican-American women, Josefina Fierro and Luisa Moreno, who actually spearheaded the Defense Committee. They campaigned throughout the country to "set the record straight" about the injustice done to the Sleepy Lagoon defendants by the legal system and the press. Bert Corona, a Chicano scholar (and an actual member of the Sleepy Lagoon Defense Committee in 1942), wrote that "it is to be deplored that Luis Valdez could find insufficient drama in the true facts about the Defense of the Sleepy Lagoon and Zoot Suit victims, that he had to rely upon Hollywood gimmicks . . . to tell his story." But such were the pressures of trying to write the first major Chicano drama and film. While "the industry" wanted to expose the problems facing Mexican-Americans in the late 1970s, the playwright felt it necessary to perpetuate the fantasy of the "white savior" at the expense of the fact that the Mexican-American community itself was the primary instrument of justice. This disturbing compromise likely says as much about problems facing Mexican-Americans and the larger Hispanic community as anything stated in the play.

Other perspectives on *Zoot Suit*:

Broyles-Gonzalez, Yolanda. "El Teatro Campesino: From Alternative Theater to Mainstream." In Broyles-Gonzalez, *El Teatro Campesino*. Austin: University of Texas Press, 1994. See especially pp. 174–213 for a history of and commentary on *Zoot Suit* as play and film.

Huerta, Jorge. "Luis Valdez' *Zoot Suit*: A New Direction for Chicano Theater?" *Latin American Theater Review* 13:2 (Summer 1980): 69–76.

See *Zoot Suit* on film/video:

Zoot Suit. Dir. Luis Valdez. Perf. Edward James Olmos and Danny Valdez. Universal Studios, 104 min., 1981.

See a video about El Teatro Campesino:

Luis Valdez and El Teatro Campesino. Interview with Bettina Gregory. Films for the Humanities, 26 min., 1993.

SHOWCASE   PRE-COLUMBIAN THEATER IN MESOAMERICA

The complex glyph writings, calendars, and buildings in the Central American jungles of Yucatan, Chiapas, and Guatemala verify the exceptional artistry of the Maya, among the most intellectual and artistic people of Mesoamerica. Curiously, however, the Maya had no word for "art" in their vocabulary because "art" was not an entity separate from other religious or social activities. Mayan art—including theatrical activity—was a functional tool that maintained order and harmony between individuals, within society, and especially between the world and the cosmos. Though enjoyed for its craftsmanship, Mayan art was not merely an object of aesthetic pleasure but a spiritual and social necessity.

Archaeologists have traced remnants of the Mayan culture to about 2000 B.C. By the first century A.D. the Maya had developed a variety of rituals performed by the principal social classes: peasants, priests, and nobles. They were bound by a common mythology set forth in the *Popul Vuh* ("People's Book"), a sacred tome that has been called the Old Testament of the Maya because it details the cosmogony, traditions, and history of the race. It was refined and passed from generation to generation orally or through the sacred glyphs. A version was preserved in the Quiche dialect of the Mayan language in the mid-sixteenth century A.D. Though this text was lost, Francisco Ximenez, a seventeenth-century priest working in Guatemala, transcribed the material when he borrowed a worn copy from one of his parishioners. The *Popul Vuh* is too complex to summarize here, but it glorifies the Solar Deity worshipped by the people of this warm-weather climate.

The Maya were an agricultural people who valued the harmony between the material and spiritual worlds. The majority of peasants worked as farmers who often achieved a degree of prosperity. Indeed, a recognizable "middle class" emerged, infusing the Mayan culture with a love of artistry and leisure time. Many Mayan peasants became prolific in their occupational tasks, particularly in the arts, as painters, potters, sculptors, musicians, and *tlaquetzque* (entertainers). The combination of artistry and religious ceremonies in honor of the Sun Deity and other Mayan gods spawned dances, popular entertainment, and rituals inspired by various intoxicants (recall that the Greeks drank wine in their homage to Dionysus). Through documents passed down by the Spanish conquistadors, we know the indigenous peoples had a repertoire of more than a thousand choreographed dances. Likewise, peasant-actors wore spectacular costumes and masks to perform mythical stories to the accompaniment of drums and musical instruments. Just as goats and deer were imitated in other cultures, the *tlaquetzque* dressed themselves as creatures of this jungle kingdom: ocelots, sacred snakes, and colorful birds.

The principal Mayan dramatic rituals were performed in mid-June when the sun is at its zenith. A fragment from a sixteenth-century Nahua manuscript recounts the invention of music at the command of the Tezcatlipoca, the god of heaven and the four quarters of the sky:

> Wind the earth is sick from silence.
> Though we possess light and color and
>   fruit,
> Yet we have no music.
> We must bestow music on all
>   creation.
> . . . life should be all music!

The Wind dutifully carries out the god's bidding and

> Thus music was born on the bosom of
>   the earth.
> Thus did all things learn to sing:
> the awakening dawn,
> the dreaming man,
> the awaiting mother,
> the passing water and the flying bird.
> Life was all music from then on.

Thus intertwined through the arts, the material world and the spiritual world are rendered inseparable in this great myth.

As evidenced by the glyphs, these rituals—in which the priests were both celebrants and mediators between the people and the orderly, often harsh, universe—were highly theatrical. Furthermore, sacrifices of both animals and humans were central events in the rituals. The Mayan theater space was a pyramid, its stage a stone altar, its people the audience, and the sacrificial offering itself was the sacred performance. To the Maya, sacrifice was not a barbaric act but a sacred duty that induced harmony between man and nature, manifestation of the belief that life naturally extended into death—and vice versa. "Life," according to the Mexican scholar and writer Octavio Paz, "had no higher function than to flow into death."

Like the dramas of classical Greece, Mayan rituals also assumed a social as well as spiritual dimension. The Maya were a hierarchical society, and the nobles enjoyed privilege, depending on familial lineage. Again, as evidenced by sculptural works of art, vases, and jade plaques, we see an elaborate pageantry among Mayan nobles who used art as a propagandistic vehicle to explain their social standing within the cosmos. Thus dance rituals as well as storytelling performances were common means of asserting one's status. In the fourteenth century a Mayan court, for instance, could easily be comprised of over a hundred artists whose sole purpose was to provide music, storytelling, and dance to aggrandize the aristocrat who presided over them. There was spirited competition among the nobles to produce the best work among their artists. The artifacts of the so-called Late Classic period (*Chichen Itza*, c. 1250–1400 A.D.) attest to the superiority of Mayan artistry. We may assume that performance also became as sophisticated as other artistry, but theater, alas, is temporal. Performance records are difficult to maintain, and we have virtually no "scripts" and little empirical evidence about Mayan drama. The *Rabinal Achi* remains the single drama from ancient Maya.

The Rabinal Achi

The *Rabinal Achi* is a pre–Spanish conquest drama *cum* dance of Aeschylean proportions; it was first transcribed in Guatemala in 1859 from a performance by Indians in a remote village. Like Aeschylus's *Prometheus Bound*, this pageant has to do with bondage, sacrifice, and transgressions by mythical characters chronicled in the *Popul Vuh*. Like so many tragedies, it dramatizes the conflict between fierce pride and the personal responsibility associated with political power. In short, the unknown storyteller of the *Rabinal Achi* matches Aeschylus in intellectual scope, but he goes beyond Aristotelian dramaturgy to create a mythic, magical world of tragic ecstasy.

Structured like the earliest Greek plays, the *Rabinal Achi* is composed of a series of alternating monologues, which clarify the character's actions, and choric dance sequences, which comment on the action. Its episodic plot dramatizes the religious, philosophical, and idealistic reasons why the Warrior Chief of the Quiche must meet his doom at the sacrificial altar. He has made choices that have affected his people and his captors. For this he must die. Unlike our own Greco-Roman dramatic tradition that has made us psychologically attached to guilt for our errors in judgment, the Mayan hero's misjudgment displaced a cosmic schema much too difficult to decipher. Thus sacrificial death—and not merely mutilation as in *Oedipus the King*—was the only way to restore tranquility to the world.

Lamentably, we know little about the performance of the *Rabinal Achi* in the preconquest era. We can only imagine that it was majestic, colorful, and epic in nature. Given the Maya emphasis on communion with their environment, it could only be satisfactorily played in the outdoors against a backdrop of the universe itself. The cast was large and probably splendidly dressed. In addition to the three great warriors (Kiche, Rabinal, and Fifth Rain), the cast consisted of twin choruses of twelve Yellow Eagles and twelve Yellow Jaguars, as well as assorted soldiers, peasants, barons, and priests. Only portions of the text remain, but a sample suggests its majesty. In the epic's final scene, the Quiche Warrior prepares for his sacrificial death by divesting himself of his worldly possessions:

> O my gold and silver, my bow and shield, my Toltec mace, my Yaqui axe! You are all that will remain of me! Even my sandals will be left! For here is what our lord and master will be saying by now: "It is far too long since my valor and courage went hunting the game we like to see upon our table." Our lord and master will be saying that, but he will never guess that I am only waiting my doom here between Heaven and Earth. Alas! . . . If I must die here, oh let me change places with that squirrel or with that bird! They die upon the branches or on the tender grass where they find all their needs.

Mesoamerican theatrical activity was subsumed by European dramaturgy. Spanish priests, for example, used liturgical dramas to convert native peoples, which is perhaps why the Yaqui Easter contains both preconquest and European dramatic elements. Its spirit is kept alive, however, in the late twentieth century by a number of socially conscious, politically active Hispanic-American theater companies. Luis Valdez's El Teatro Campesino is particularly active in this tradition. In 1974 Valdez's company performed *El Baile de los Gigantes* ("The Dance of the Giants") in Mexico City. Based on material taken from the *Popul Vuh*, it depicts Mayan gods before the first dawn and the creation of humans. Valdez, who narrated the play, intoned a contemporary version of a Mayan hymn to begin the performance:

> Dear god of the sky, we came to this place so that you can concentrate all your energy on this town. We came in the name of justice, in the name of love, in the name of unity, in homage to the Solar Deity.

It is a hymn—like the reenactment of creation that followed it—that would not seem strange to the Greek Thespis because it, like the sacred Dionysian dithyramb, speaks to those elemental human concerns that are often realized through acts of theater.

PANTOMIME

Derek Walcott

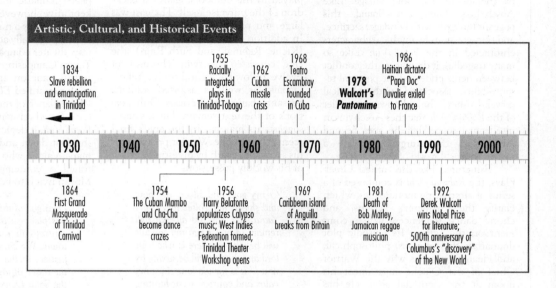

Artistic, Cultural, and Historical Events

1834 Slave rebellion and emancipation in Trinidad	1955 Racially integrated plays in Trinidad-Tobago
	1962 Cuban missile crisis
	1968 Teatro Escambray founded in Cuba
	1978 Walcott's Pantomime
	1986 Haitian dictator "Papa Doc" Duvalier exiled to France

1930 1940 1950 1960 1970 1980 1990 2000

1864 First Grand Masquerade of Trinidad Carnival	1954 The Cuban Mambo and Cha-Cha become dance crazes
	1956 Harry Belafonte popularizes Calypso music; West Indies Federation formed; Trinidad Theater Workshop opens
	1969 Caribbean island of Anguilla breaks from Britain
	1981 Death of Bob Marley, Jamaican reggae musician
	1992 Derek Walcott wins Nobel Prize for literature; 500th anniversary of Columbus's "discovery" of the New World

DEREK WALCOTT (1930–)

As a poet and a dramatist, Derek Walcott is among the most honored writers of the late twentieth century. In 1992—the five-hundredth anniversary of Columbus's first excursion into Walcott's native Caribbean region—Walcott achieved the world's highest literary award, the Nobel Prize, and thereby joined Pirandello, O'Neill, Beckett, Soyinka, Gao Xingjian, and Fo as the twentieth century's Nobel dramatists.

Walcott and his twin brother, Roderick (also a theater artist), were born on the island of St. Lucia and raised by their mother after their father died. Because his mother was the headmistress of the local Methodist Infant School, Walcott received an excellent education and an uncommonly fine grounding in English unavailable to other nonwhites on the island. His deceased father was a civil servant with a strong interest in the arts, particularly play reading and painting. The Walcott twins were encouraged by their mother and family friends to pursue these interests.

Walcott studied at University College of the West Indies in Jamaica, where he continued the classical education begun in St. Lucia. The tension between his Euro-centered education and his desire to create a theater representative of his native West Indies has created controversy for Walcott throughout his career. As a student Walcott distinguished himself as a poet, dramatist, and editor of a literary journal. He began writing plays in 1946, and his drama about Haiti's revolution, *Henri Christophe* (1949), earned him respect as a dramatist. In 1950 he cofounded the Arts Guild of Sta. Lucia as an outlet for native voices.

The Trinidad Theatre Workshop, which evolved from his work with Little Carib Theatre and the Basement Theatre, was founded in the mid-1950s and remains the legacy of Walcott's vision of a "little theater" devoted to the development of native Caribbean drama performed in a distinctive West Indian style. The Trinidad Theatre Workshop created works fusing native stories, music, and dance with such diverse non-Caribbean theater forms as Noh and Kabuki, classical European theater, American method acting, Brechtian Epic Theatre, and Grotowski's Poor Theatre. Walcott's best-known dramatic pieces include *Ti-Jean and His Brothers* (1958); *Dream on Monkey Mountain* (1968); *The Joker of Seville* (a work commissioned by the Royal Shakespeare Company in 1975); *O! Babylon!* (1976); *Pantomime* (1978); *Beef, No Chicken* (1981); and *A Branch of the Blue Nile* (1983). His works have been produced by the New York Free Shakespeare Festival, the Mark Taper Forum in Los Angeles, and the Boston Playwright's Theatre. Lowell Fiet, editor of the Caribbean's foremost literary journal, *Sargasso*, contends that Walcott's dramatic work "compares favorably to those of international contemporaries such as Dario Fo, Harold Pinter, Wole Soyinka, Heiner Müller, Athol Fugard, and Sam Shepard . . . as well as to major modern figures such as Shaw, O'Neill, Brecht and Beckett." In 1999 Walcott teamed with singer-writer Paul Simon to write the Broadway musical *The Capeman*, about a Puertoriqueno on death row. In addition to his plays, Walcott has written volumes of poetry, including his lengthy autobiographical poem, *Another Life*. He is among the most anthologized poets of the twentieth century.

AS YOU READ *PANTOMIME*

Pantomime belongs to the second period in Walcott's development as a playwright. His first works, the so-called "poetic plays" from the 1950s to the mid-1970s, were mostly based on folk tales from the Caribbean and Africa. They were exceptionally theatrical and made little pretense at realism. The second group is more realistic—at least on the surface—yet these plays retain a poetic quality, largely through the use of native dialects. The later plays are also social dramas, particularly as they address the problems of the Caribbean region's colonial past and the tension between those of European descent and those of multiethnic origins. We see this in *Pantomime* in the subject matter of the play Harry proposes to write as an entertainment at the seaside resort he runs: a retelling of the Robinson Crusoe story wrought by Daniel Defoe in 1719. (Trinidad-Tobago, by the way, is thought to be the setting of the novel.) Crusoe is one of two fictional characters created by European writers that have become symbols for the problems brought by colonialism; Caliban, from Shakespeare's *The Tempest*, is the other. *Pantomime* is, on the one hand, a rehearsal for the Crusoe play that emerges as an inventive theatrical piece despite its purported "realism." It is also an intimate drama that crystallizes the history and dilemmas of the Caribbean into the struggle between Crusoe and his man Friday (the first slave in the region?) and the struggle between the English actor and his serving man at the hotel located, significantly, on the edge of a cliff.

PANTOMIME

DEREK WALCOTT

For Wilbert Holder

CHARACTERS

HARRY TREWE, *English, mid-forties, owner of the Castaways Guest House, retired actor*

JACKSON PHILLIP, *Trinidadian, forty, his factotum, retired calypsonian*

The action takes place in a gazebo on the edge of a cliff, part of a guest house on the island of Tobago, West Indies.

ACT I

A small summerhouse or gazebo, painted white, with a few plants and a table set for breakfast. Harry Trewe enters—in white, carrying a tape recorder, which he rests on the table. He starts the machine.

HARRY (*Sings and dances*).
It's our Christmas panto,
it's called: Robinson Crusoe.
We're awfully glad that you've shown up,
it's for kiddies as well as for grown-ups.
Our purpose is to please:
so now with our magic wand . . .
        (*Dissatisfied with the routine, he switches off the machine. Rehearses his dance. Then presses the machine again*)
Just picture a lonely island
and a beach with its golden sand.
There walks a single man
in the beautiful Wet Indies!

(*He turns off the machine. Stands, staring out to sea. Then exits with the tape recorder. Stage empty for a few beats, then Jackson, in an open, white waiter's jacket and black trousers, but barefoot, en-*

ters *with a breakfast tray. He pus the tray down, looks around*)

JACKSON.
Mr. Trewe?
    (*English accent*)
Mr. Trewe, your scramble eggs is here! are here!
    (*Creole accent*)
You hear, Mr. Trewe? I here wid your eggs!
    (*English accent*)
Are you in there?
    (*To himself*)
And when his eggs get cold, is I to catch.
    (*He fans the eggs with one hand*)
What the hell I doing? That ain't go heat them. It go make them more cold. Well, he must be leap off the ledge. At long last. Well, if he ain't dead, he could call.

(*He exits with tray. Stage bare. Harry returns, carrying a hat made of goatskin and a goatskin parasol. He puts on the hat, shoulders the parasol, and circles the table. Then he recoils, looking down at the floor*)

HARRY (*Sings and dances*).
Is this the footprint of a naked man,
or is it the naked footprint of a man,
that startles me this morning on this bright and golden sand.
    (*To audience*)
There's no one here but I,
just the sea and lonely sky . . .
    (*Pauses*)
Yes . . . and how the hell did it go on?

(*Jackson enters, without the tray. Studies Harry*)

JACKSON. Morning, Mr. Trewe. Your breakfast ready.

HARRY. So how're you this morning, Jackson?

JACKSON. Oh, fair to fine, with seas moderate, with waves three to four feet in open water, and you, sir?

HARRY. Overcast with sunny periods, with the possibility of heavy showers by mid-afternoon, I'd say, Jackson.

JACKSON. Heavy showers, Mr. Trewe?

HARRY. Heavy showers. I'm so bloody bored I could burst into tears.

JACKSON. I bringing in breakfast.

HARRY. You do that, Friday.

JACKSON. Friday? It ain't go keep.

HARRY (*Gesturing*). Friday, you, bring Crusoe, me, breakfast now. Crusoe hungry.

JACKSON. Mr. Trewe, you come back with that same rake again? I tell you, I ain't no actor, and I ain't walking in front a set of tourists naked playing cannibal. Carnival, but not canni-bal.

HARRY. What tourists? We're closed for repairs. We're the only ones in the guest house. Apart from the carpenter, if he ever shows up.

JACKSON. Well, you ain't seeing him today, because he was out on a heavy lime last night . . . Saturday, you know? And with the peanuts you does pay him for overtime.

HARRY. All right, then. It's goodbye!

(*He climbs onto the ledge between the uprights, teetering, walking slowly*)

JACKSON. Get offa that ledge, Mr. Trewe! Is a straight drop to them rocks!

(*Harry kneels, arms extended, Jolson-style*)

HARRY. Hold on below there, sonny boooy! Daddy's a-coming. Your papa's a-coming, Sonnnnneee Booooooooy!
    (*To Jackson*)
You're watching the great Harry Trewe and his high-wire act.

JACKSON. You watching Jackson Phillip and his disappearing act.

(*Turning to leave*)

HARRY (*Jumping down*). I'm not a suicide, Jackson. It's a good act, but you never read the reviews. It would be too exasperating, anyway.

JACKSON. What, sir?

HARRY. Attempted suicide in a Third World country. You can't leave a note because the pencils break, you can't cut your wrist with the local blades . . .

JACKSON. We trying we best, sir, since all you gone.

HARRY. Doesn't matter if we're a minority group. Suicides are taxpayers, too, you know, Jackson.

JACKSON. Except it ain't going be suicide. They go say I push you. So, now the fun and dance done, sir, breakfast now?

HARRY. I'm rotting from insomnia, Jackson. I've been up since three, hearing imaginary guests arriving in the rooms, and I haven't slept since. I nearly came around the back to have a little talk. I started thinking about the same bloody problem, which is, What entertainment can we give the guests?

JACKSON. They ain't guests, Mr. Trewe. They's casualties.

HARRY. How do you mean?

JACKSON. This hotel like a hospital. The toilet catch asthma, the air-condition got ague, the front-balcony rail missing four teet', and every minute the fridge like it dancing the Shango . . . brrgudup . . . jukjuk . . . brrugudup. Is no wonder that the carpenter collapse. Termites jumping like steel band in the foundations.

HARRY. For fifty dollars a day they want Acapulco?

JACKSON. Try giving them the basics: Food. Water. Shelter. They ain't shipwrecked, they pay in advance for their vacation.

HARRY. Very funny. But the ad says, "Tours" and "Nightly Entertainment." Well, Christ, after they've seen the molting parrot in the lobby and the faded sea fans, they'll be pretty livid if there's no "nightly entertainment," and so would you, right? So, Mr. Jackson, it's your neck and mine. We open next Friday.

JACKSON. Breakfast, sir. Or else is overtime.

HARRY. I kept thinking about this panto I co-authored, man. *Robinson Crusoe*, and I picked up this old script. I can bring it all down to your level, with just two characters. Crusoe, Man Friday, maybe even the parrot, if that horny old bugger will remember his lines . . .

JACKSON. Since we on the subject, Mr. Trewe, I am compelled to report that parrot again.

HARRY. No, not again, Jackson?

JACKSON. Yes.

HARRY (*Imitating parrot*).
    Heinegger, Heinegger.
        (*In his own voice*)
    Correct?

JACKSON. Wait, wait! I know your explanation: that a old German called Herr Heinegger used to own this place, and that when that masquereau of a macaw keep cracking: "Heinegger, Heinegger," he remembring the Nazi and not heckling me, but it playing a little havoc with me nerves. This is my fifth report. I am marking them down. Language is ideas, Mr. Trewe. And I think that this pre-colonial parrot have the wrong idea.

HARRY. It's his accent, Jackson. He's a Creole parrot. What can I do?

JACKSON. Well, I am not saying not to give the bird a fair trial, but I see nothing wrong in taking him out the cage at dawn, blindfolding the bitch, giving him a last cigarette if he want it, lining him up against the garden wall, and perforating his arse by firing squad.

HARRY. The war's over, Jackson! And how can a bloody parrot be prejudiced?

JACKSON. The same damn way they corrupt a child. By their upbringing. That parrot survive from a pre-colonial epoch, Mr. Trewe, and if it want to last in Trinidad and Tobago, then it go have to adjust.

(Long pause)

HARRY (Leaping up). Do you think we could work him into the panto? Give him something to do? Crusoe had a parrot, didn't he? You're right, Jackson, let's drop him from the show.

JACKSON. Mr. Trewe, you are a truly, truly stubborn man. I am not putting that old goatskin hat on my head and making an ass of myself for a milion dollars, and I have said so already.

HARRY. You got it wrong. I put the hat on, I'm . . . Wait, wait a minute. Cut! Cut! You know what would be a heavy twist, heavy with irony?

JACKSON. What, Mr. Trewe?

HARRY. We reverse it.

(Pause)

JACKSON. You mean you prepared to walk round naked as your mother make you, in your jockstrap, play-ing a white cannibal in front of your own people? You're a real actor! And you got balls, too, excuse me, Mr. Trewe, to even consider doing a thing like that! Good. Joke finish. Breakfast now, eh? Be-cause I ha' to fix the sun deck since the carpenter ain't reach.

HARRY. All right, breakfast. Just heat it a little.

JACKSON. Right, sir. The coffee must be warm still. But I best do some brand-new scramble eggs.

HARRY. Never mind the eggs, then. Slip in some toast, butter, and jam.

JACKSON. How long you in this hotel business, sir? No butter. Marge. No sugar. Big strike. Island-wide shortage. We down to half a bag.

HARRY. Don't forget I've heard you sing calypsos, Jackson. Right back there in the kitchen.

JACKSON. Mr. Trewe, every day I keep begging you to stop trying to make an entertainer out of me. I finish with

show business. I finish with Trinidad. I come to To-bago for peace and quiet. I quite satisfy. If you ain't want me to resign, best drop the topic.

(Exits. Harry sits at the table, staring out to sea. He is reciting softly to himself, then more audibly)

HARRY.
"Alone, alone, all, all alone,
Alone on a wide wide sea . . .
I bit my arm, I sucked the blood,
And cried, A sail! a sail!"

(He removes the hat, then his shirt, rolls up his trousers, removes them, puts them back on, removes them again)

Mastah . . . Mastah . . . Friday sorry. Friday never do it again. Master.

(Jackson enters with breakfast tray, groans, turns to leave. Returns)

JACKSON. Mr. Trewe, what it is going on on this blessed Sunday morning, if I may ask?

HARRY. I was feeling what it was like to be Friday.

JACKSON. Well, Mr. Trewe, you ain't mind putting back on your pants?

HARRY. Why can't I eat breakfast like this?

JACKSON. Because I am here. I happen to be here. I am the one serving you, Mr. Trewe.

HARRY. There's nobody here.

JACKSON. Mr. Harry, you putting on back your pants?

HARRY. You're frightened of something?

JACKSON. You putting on back your pants?

HARRY. What're you afraid of? Think I'm bent? That's such a corny interpretation of the Crusoe-Friday re-lationship, boy. My son's been dead three years, Jack-son, and I'vn't had much interest in women since, but I haven't gone queer, either. And to be a flasher, you need an audience.

JACKSON. Mr. Trewe, I am trying to explain that I myself feel like a ass holding this tray in my hand while you standing up there naked, and that if anybody should happen to pass, my name is immediately mud. So, when you put back on your pants, I will serve your breakfast.

HARRY. Actors do this sort of thing. I'm getting into a part.

JACKSON. Don't bother getting into the part, get into the pants. Please.

HARRY. Why? You've got me worried now, Jackson.

JACKSON (Exploding). Put on your blasted pants, man! You like a blasted child, you know!

(Silence. Harry puts on his pants)

HARRY. Shirt, too?

(Jackson sucks his teeth)

There.

(Harry puts on his shirt)

You people are such prudes, you know that? What's it in you, Jackson, that gets so Victorian about a man in his own hotel deciding to have breakfast in his own underwear, on a totally deserted Sunday morning?

JACKSON. Manners, sir. Manners.

(He puts down the tray)

HARRY. Sit.

JACKSON. Sit? Sit where? How you mean, sit?

HARRY. Sit, and I'll serve breakfast. You can teach me manners. There's more manners in serving than in being served.

JACKSON. I ain't know what it is eating you this Sunday morning, you hear, Mr. Trewe, but I don't feel you have any right to mamaguy me, because I is a big man with three children, all outside. Now, being served by a white man ain't no big deal for me. It happen to me every day in New York, so it's not going to be any particularly thrilling experience. I would like to get breakfast finish with, wash up, finish my work, and go for my sea bath. Now I have worked here six months and never lost my temper, but it wouldn't take much more for me to fling this whole fucking tray out in that sea and get somebody more to your sexual taste.

HARRY *(Laughs)*. Aha!

JACKSON. Not aha, oho!

HARRY *(Drawing out a chair)*. Mr. Phillips . . .

JACKSON. Phillip. What?

HARRY. Your reservation.

JACKSON. You want me play this game, eh?

(He walks around, goes to a corner of the gazebo)

I'll tell you something, you hear, Mr. Trewe? And listen to me good, good. Once and for all. My sense of humor can stretch so far. Then it does snap. You see that sea out there? You know where I born? I born over there. Trinidad. I was a very serious steel-band man, too. And where I come from is a very serious place. I used to get into some serious trouble. A man keep bugging my arse once. A bad john called Boysie. Indian fellow, want to play nigger. Every day in that panyard he would come making joke with nigger boy this, and so on, and I used to just laugh and tell him stop, but he keep laughing and I keep laughing and he going on and I begging him to stop and two of us laughing, until . . .

(He turns, goes to the tray, and picks up a fork)

one day, just out of the blue, I pick up a ice pick and walk over to where he and two fellers was playing card, and I nail that ice pick through his hand to the table, and I laugh, and I walk away.

HARRY. Your table, Mr. Phillip.

(Silence. Jackson shrugs, sits at the table)

JACKSON. Okay, then. Until.

HARRY. You know, if you want to exchange war experiances, lad, I could bore you with a couple of mine. Want to hear?

JACKSON. My shift is seven-thirty to one.

(He folds his arms. Harry offers him a cigarette)

I don't smoke on duty.

HARRY. We put on a show in the army once. Ground crew. RAF. In what used to be Palestine. A Christmas panto. Another one. And yours truly here was the dame. The dame in a panto is played by a man. Well, I got the part. Wrote the music, the book, everything, whatever original music there was. *Aladdin and His Wonderful Vamp*. Very obscene, of course. I was the Wonderful Vamp. Terrific reaction all around. Thanks to me music-hall background. Went down great. Well, there was a party afterward. Then a big sergeant in charge of maintenance started this very boring business of confusing my genius with my life. Kept pinching my arse and so on. It got kind of boring after a while. Well, he was the size of a truck, mate. And there wasn't much I could do but keep blushing and pretending to be liking it. But the Wonderful Vamp was waiting outside for him, the Wonderful Vamp and a wrench this big, and after that, laddie, it took all of maintenance to put him back again.

JACKSON. That is white-man fighting. Anyway, Mr. Trewe, I feel the fun finish; I would like, with your permission, to get up now and fix up the sun deck. 'Cause when rain fall . . .

HARRY. Forget the sun deck. I'd say, Jackson, that we've come closer to a mutual respect, and that things need not get that hostile. Sit, and let me explain what I had in mind.

JACKSON. I take it that's an order?

HARRY. You want it to be an order? Okay, it's an order.

JACKSON. It didn't sound like no order.

HARRY. Look, I'm a liberal, Jackson. I've done the whole routine. Aldermaston, Suez, Ban the Bomb, Burn the Bra, Pity the Poor Pakis, et cetera. I've even tried jumping up to the steel band at Notting Hill Gate, and

I'd no idea I'd wind up in this ironic position of giving orders, but if the new script I've been given says: HARRY TREWE, HOTEL MANAGER, then I'm going to play Harry Trewe, Hotel Manager, to the hilt, damnit. So *sit* down! Please. Oh, goddamnit, *sit . . . down . . .*

(Jackson sits. Nods)

Good. Relax. Smoke. Have a cup of tepid coffee. I sat up from about three this morning, working out this whole skit in my head.

(Pause)

Mind putting that hat on for a second, it will help my point. Come on. It'll make things clearer.

(He gives Jackson the goatskin hat. Jackson, after a pause, puts it on)

JACKSON. I'll take that cigarette.

(Harry hands over a cigarette)

HARRY. They've seen that stuff, time after time. Limbo, dancing girls, fire-eating . . .
JACKSON. Light.
HARRY. Oh, sorry.

(He lights Jackson's cigarette)

JACKSON. I listening.
HARRY. We could turn this little place right here into a little cabaret, with some very witty acts. Build up the right audience. Get an edge on the others. So, I thought, Suppose I get this material down to two people. Me and . . . well, me and somebody else. Robinson Crusoe and Man Friday. We could work up a good satire, you know, on the master-servant—no offense—relationship. Labor-management, white-black, and so on . . . Making some trenchant points about topical things, you know. Add that show to the special dinner for the price of one ticket . . .
JACKSON. You have to have music.
HARRY. Pardon?
JACKSON. A show like that should have music. Just a lot of talk is very boring.
HARRY. Right. But I'd have to have somebody help me, and that's where I thought . . . Want to take the hat off?
JACKSON. It ain't bothering me. When you going make your point?
HARRY. We had that little Carnival contest with the staff and you knocked them out improvising, remember that? You had the bloody guests in stitches . . .
JACKSON. You ain't start to talk money yet, Mr. Harry.

HARRY. Just improvising with the quatro. And not the usual welcome to Port of Spain, I am glad to see you again, but I'll tell you, artist to artist, I recognized a real pro, and this is the point of the hat. I want to make a point about the hotel industry, about manners, conduct, to generally improve relations all around. So, whoever it is, you or whoever, plays Crusoe, and I, or whoever it is, get to play Friday, and imagine first of all the humor and then the impact of that. What you think?
JACKSON. You want my honest, professional opinion?
HARRY. Fire away.
JACKSON. I think is shit.
HARRY. I've never been in shit in my life, my boy.
JACKSON. It sound like shit to me, but I could be wrong.
HARRY. You could say things in fun about this place, about the whole Caribbean, that would hurt while people laughed. You get half the gate.
JACKSON. Half?
HARRY. What do you want?
JACKSON. I want you to come to your senses, let me fix the sun deck and get down to the beach for my sea bath. So, I put on this hat, I pick up this parasol, and I walk like a mama-poule up and down this stage and you have a black man playing Robinson Crusoe and then a half-naked, white, fish-belly man playing Friday, and you want to tell me it ain't shit?
HARRY. It could be hilarious!
JACKSON. Hilarious, Mr. Trewe? Supposing I wasn't a waiter, and instead of breakfast I was serving you communion, this Sunday morning on this propical island, and I turn to you, Friday, to teach you my faith, and I tell you, kneel down and eat this man. Well, kneel, nuh! What you think you would say, eh?

(Pause)

You, this white savage?
HARRY. No, that's cannibalism.
JACKSON. Is no more cannibalism than to eat a god. Suppose I make you tell me: For three hundred years I have made you my servant. For three hundred years . . .
HARRY. It's pantomime, Jackson, just keep it light . . . Make them laugh.
JACKSON. Okay.

(Giggling)

For three hundred years I served you. Three hundred years I served you breakfast in . . . in my white jacket on a white veranda, boss, bwana, effendi, bacra, sahib . . . in that sun that never set on your empire I was your shadow, I did what you did, boss, bwana, effendi, bacra, sahib . . . that was my pantomime. Every movement you made, your shadow copied . . .

(*Stops giggling*)

and you smiled at me as a child does smile at his shadow's helpless obedience, boss, bwana, effendi, bacra, sahib, Mr. Crusoe. Now . . .

HARRY. Now?

(*Jackson's speech is enacted in a trance-like drone, a zombie*)

JACKSON. But after a while the child does get frighten of the shadow he make. He say to himself, That is too much obedience, I better hads stop. But the shadow don't stop, no matter if the child stop playing that pantomime, and the shadow does follow the child everywhere; when he praying, the shadow pray too, when he turn round frighten, the shadow turn round too, when he hide under the sheet, the shadow hiding too. He cannot get rid of it, no matter what, and that is the power and black magic of the shadow, boss, bwana, effendi, bacra, sahib, until it is the shadow that start dominating the child, it is the servant that start dominating the master . . .

(*Laughs maniacally, like The Shadow*)

and that is the victory of the shadow, boss.

(*Normally*)

And that is why all them Pakistani and West Indians in England, all them immigrant Fridays driving all you so crazy. And they go keep driving you crazy till you go mad. In that sun that never set, they's your shadow, you can't shake them off.

HARRY. Got really carried away that time, didn't you? It's pantomime, Jackson, keep it light. Improvise!

JACKSON. You mean we making it up as we go along?

HARRY. Right!

JACKSON. Right! I in dat!

(*He assumes a stern stance and points stiffly*)

Robinson obey Thursday now. Speak Thursday language. Obey Thursday gods.

HARRY. Jesus Christ!

JACKSON (*Inventing language*). Amaka nobo sakamaka khaki pants kamaluma Jesus Christ! Jesus Christ kamalogo!

(*Pause. Then with a violent gesture*)

Kamalongo kaba!

(*Meaning: Jesus is dead!*)

HARRY. Sure.

(*Pause. Peers forward. Then speaks to an imaginary projectionist, while Jackson stands, feet apart, arms folded, frowning, in the usual stance of the Noble Savage*)

Now, could you run it with the subtitles, please?

(*He walks over to Jackson, who remains rigid. Like a movie director*)

Let's have another take, Big Chief.

(*To imaginary camera*)

Roll it. Sound!

(*Jackson shoves Harry aside and strides to the table. He bangs the heel of his palm on the tabletop*)

JACKSON. Patamba! Patamba! Yes?

HARRY. You want us to strike the prop? The patamba?

(*To cameraman*)

Cut!

JACKSON (*To cameraman*). Rogoongo! Rogoongo!

(*Meaning: Keep it rolling*)

HARRY. Cut!

JACKSON. Rogoongo, damnit!
  (*Defiantly, furiously, Jackson moves around, first signaling the camera to follow him, then pointing out the objects which he rechristens, shaking or hitting them violently. Slams table*)
Patamba!
  (*Rattles beach chair*)
Backaraka! Backaraka!
  (*Holds up cup, points with other hand*)
Banda!
  (*Drops cup*)
Banda karan!
  (*Puts his arm around Harry; points at him*)
Subu!
  (*Faster, pointing*)
Masz!
  (*Stamping the floor*)
Zohgooooor!
  (*Rests his snoring head on his closed palms*)
Oma! Omaaaa!
  (*Kneels, looking skyward. Pauses; eyes closed*)
Booora! Booora!
  (*Meaning the world. Silence. He rises*)
Cut!
And dat is what it was like, before you come here with your table this and cup that.

HARRY. All right. Good audition. You get twenty dollars a
day without dialogue.

JACKSON. But why?

HARRY. You never called anything by the same name
twice. What's a table?

JACKSON. I forget.

HARRY. I remember: patamba!

JACKSON. Patamba?

HARRY. Right. You fake.

JACKSON. That's a breakfast table. *Ogushi.* That's a dressing table. *Amanga ogushi.* I remember now.

HARRY. I'll tell you one thing, friend. If you want me to
learn your language, you'd better have a gun.

JACKSON. You best play Crusoe, chief. I surrender. All you
win.

(*Points wearily*)

Table. Chair. Cup. Man. Jesus. I accept. I accept. All
you win. Long time.

(*Smiles*)

HARRY. All right, then. Improvise, then. Sing us a song.
In your new language, mate. In English. Go ahead. I
challenge you.

JACKSON. You what?

(*Rises, takes up parasol, handling it like a guitar,
and strolls around the front row of the audience*)
(*Sings*)
I want to tell you 'bout Robinson Crusoe.
He tell Friday, when I do so, do so.
Whatever I do, you must do like me.
He make Friday a Good Friday Bohbolee;*
That was the first example of slavery,
'Cause I am still Friday and you ain't me.
Now Crusoe he was this Christian and all,
And Friday, his slave, was a cannibal,
But one day things bound to go in reverse,
With Crusoe the slave and Friday the boss.

HARRY. Then comes this part where Crusoe sings to the
goat. Little hint of animal husbandry:
(*Kneels, embraces an imaginary goat, to the melody of
"Swanee"*)
(*Sings*)
Nanny, how I love you,
How I love you,
My dear old nanny . . .

JACKSON. Is a li'l obscene.

HARRY (*Music-hall style*). Me wife thought so. Know
what I used to tell her? Obscene? Well, better to be
obscene than not heard. How's that? Harry Trewe,

*A Judas effigy beaten at Easter in Trinidad and Tobago.

I'm telling you again, the music hall's loss is calypso's gain.

(*Stops*)

(*Jackson pauses. Stares upward, muttering to himself. Harry turns. Jackson is signaling in the air with
a self-congratulatory smile*)

HARRY. What is it? What've we stopped for?

(*Jackson hisses for silence from Harry, then returns
to his reverie. Miming*)

Are you feeling all right, Jackson?

(*Jackson walks some distance away from Harry. An
imaginary guitar suddenly appears in his hand.
Harry circles him. Lifts one eyelid, listens to his
heartbeat. Jackson revolves, Harry revolves with
him. Jackson's whole body is now silently rocking in
rhythm. He is laughing to himself. We hear, very
loud, a calypso rhythm*)

Two can play this game, Jackson.

(*He strides around in imaginary straw hat, twirling
a cane. We hear, very loud, music hall. It stops.
Harry peers at Jackson*)

JACKSON. You see what you start?
(*Sings*)
Well, a Limey name Trewe came to Tobago.
He was in show business but he had no show,
so in desperation he turn to me
and said: "Mister Phillip" is the two o' we,
one classical actor, and one Creole . . .

HARRY. Wait! Hold it, hold it, man! Don't waste that. Try
and remember it. I'll be right back.

JACKSON. Where you going?

HARRY. Tape. Repeat it, and try and keep it. That's what I
meant, you see?

JACKSON. You start to exploit me already?

HARRY. That's right. Memorize it.

(*Exits quickly. Jackson removes his shirt and jacket,
rolls up his pants above the knee, clears the breakfast
tray to one side of the floor, overturns the table, and
sits in it, as it it were a boat, as Harry returns with
the machine*)

What's all this? I'm ready to tape. What're you up to?

(*Jackson sits in the upturned table, rowing calmly,
and from time to time surveying the horizon. He
looks up toward the sky, shielding his face from the
glare with one hand; then he gestures to Harry*)

What?

(Jackson flaps his arms around leisurely, like a large sea bird, indicating that Harry should do the same)

What? What about the song? You'll forget the bloody song. It was a fluke.

JACKSON (*Steps out from the table, crosses to Harry, irritated*). If I suppose to help you with this stupidness, we will have to cool it and collaborate a little bit. Now, I was in that boat, rowing, and I was looking up to the sky to see a storm gathering, and I wanted a big white sea bird beating inland from a storm. So what's the trouble, Mr. Trewe?

HARRY. Sea bird? What sea bird? I'm not going to play a fekking sea bird.

JACKSON. Mr. Trewe, I'm only asking you to play a white sea bird because I am supposed to play a black explorer.

HARRY. Well, I don't want to do it. Anyway, that's the silliest acting I've seen in a long time. And Robinson Crusoe wasn't *rowing* when he got shipwrecked; he was on a huge boat. I didn't come here to play a sea bird, I came to tape the song.

JACKSON. Well, then, is either the sea bird or the song. And I don't see any reason why you have to call my acting silly. We suppose to improvise.

HARRY. All right, Jackson, all right. After I do this part, I hope you can remember the song. Now you just tell me, before we keep stopping, what I am supposed to do, how many animals I'm supposed to play, and . . . you know, and so on, and so on, and then when we get all that part fixed up, we'll tape the song, all right?

JACKSON. That suits me. Now, the way I see it here: whether Robinson Crusoe was on a big boat or not, the idea is that he got . . . (*Pause*) shipwrecked. So I . . . if I am supposed to play Robinson Crusoe my way, then I will choose the way in which I will get shipwrecked. Now, as Robinson Crusoe is rowing, he looks up and he sees this huge white sea bird, which is making loud sea-bird noises, because a storm is coming. And Robinson Crusoe looks up toward the sky and sees that there is this storm. Then, there is a large wave, and Robinson Crusoe finds himself on the beach.

HARRY. Am I supposed to play the beach? Because that's white . . .

JACKSON. Hilarious! Mr. Trewe. Now look, you know, I am doing *you* a favor. On this beach, right? Then he sees a lot of goats. And, because he is naked and he needs clothes, he kills a goat, he takes off the skin, and he makes this parasol here and this hat, so he

doesn't go around naked for everybody to see. Now I *know* that there is nobody there, but there is an audience, so the sooner Robinson Crusoe puts on his clothes, then the better and happier we will all be. I am going to go back in the boat. I am going to look up toward the sky. You will, *please*, make the sea-bird noises. I will do the wave, I will crash onto the sand, you will come down like a goat, I will kill you, take off your skin, make a parasol *and* a hat, and after that, then I promise you that I will remember the song. And I will sing it to the best of my ability.

(Pause)

However shitty that is.

HARRY. I said "silly." Now listen . . .

JACKSON. Yes, Mr. Trewe?

HARRY. Okay, if you're a black explorer . . . Wait a minute . . . wait a minute. If you're really a white explorer but you're black, shouldn't I play a black sea bird because I'm white?

JACKSON. Are you . . . going to extend . . . the limits of prejudice to include . . . the flora and fauna of this island? I am entering the boat.

(He is stepping into the upturned table or boat, as Harry halfheartedly imitates a bird, waving his arms)

HARRY. Kekkkk, kekkkk,
Kekkk, kekkkk!

(Stops)

What's wrong?

JACKSON. What's wrong? Mr. Trewe, that is not a sea gull . . . that is some kind of . . . well, I don't know what it is . . . some kind of *jumbie* bird or something.

(Pause)

I am returning to the boat.

(He carefully enters the boat, expecting an interrupting bird cry from Harry, but there is none, so he begins to row)

HARRY. Kekk! Kekkk.

(He hangs his arms down. Pause)

Er, Jackson, wait a minute. Hold it a second. Come here a minute.

(Jackson patiently gets out of the boat, elaborately pantomiming lowering his body into shallow water, releasing his hold on the boat, swimming a little

distance toward shore, getting up from the shallows, shaking out his hair and hands, wiping his hands on his trousers, jumping up and down on one foot to unplug water from his clogged ear, seeing Harry, then walking wearily, like a man who has swum a tremendous distance, and collapsing at Harry's feet)

Er, Jackson. This is too humiliating. Now, let's just forget it and please don't continue, or you're fired.

(Jackson leisurely wipes his face with his hands)

JACKSON. It don't go so, Mr. Trewe. You know me to be a meticulous man. I didn't want to do this job. I didn't even want to work here. You convinced me to work here. I have worked as meticulously as I can, until I have been promoted. This morning I had no intention of doing what I am doing now; you have always admired the fact that whatever I begin, I finish. Now, I will accept my resignation, if you want me to, *after* we have finished this thing. But I am not leaving in the middle of a job, that has never been my policy. So you can sit down, as usual, and watch me work, but until I have finished this whole business of Robinson Crusoe being in the boat

(He rises and repeats the pantomime)

looking at an imaginary sea bird, being shipwrecked, killing a goat, making this hat *and* this parasol, walking up the beach and finding a naked footprint, which should take me into about another ten or twelve minutes, at the most, I will pack my things and I will leave, and you can play *Robinson Crusoe* all by yourself. My plans were, after this, to take the table like this . . .

(He goes to the table, puts it upright)

Let me show you: take the table, turn it all around, go under the table . . .

(He goes under the table)

and this would now have become Robinson Crusoe's hut.

(Emerges from under the table and, without looking at Harry, continues to talk)

Now, you just tell me if you think I am overdoing it, or if you think it's more or less what we agreed on?

(Pause)

Okay? But I am not resigning.

(Turns to Harry slowly)

You see, it's your people who introduced us to this culture: Shakespeare, *Robinson Crusoe*, the classics, and so on, and when we start getting as good as them, you can't leave halfway. So, I will continue? Please?

HARRY. No, Jackson. You will *not* continue. You will straighten this table, put back the tablecloth, take away the breakfast things, give me back the hat, put your jacket back on, and we will continue as normal and forget the whole matter. Now, I'm very serious, I've had enough of this farce. I would like to stop.

JACKSON. May I say what I think, Mr. Trewe? I think it's a matter of prejudice. I think that you cannot believe: one: that I can act, and two: that any black man should play Robinson Crusoe. A little while aback, I came out here quite calmly and normally with the breakfast things and find you almost stark naked, kneeling down, and you told me you were getting into your part. Here am I getting into *my* part and you object. This is the story . . . this is history. This moment that we are now acting here is the history of imperialism; it's nothing less than that. And I don't think that I can—should—concede my getting into a part halfway and abandoning things, just because you, as my superior, give me orders. People become independent. Now, I could go down to that beach by myself with this hat, and I could play Robinson Crusoe, I could play Columbus, I could play Sir Francis Drake, I could play anybody discovering anywhere, but I don't want you to tell me when and where to draw the line!

(Pause)

Or what to discover and when to discover it. All right?

HARRY. Look, I'm sorry to interrupt you again, Jackson, but as I—you know—was watching you, I realized it's much more profound than that; that it could get offensive. We're trying to do something light, just a little pantomime, a little satire, a little picong. But if you take this thing seriously, we might commit Art, which is a kind of crime in this society . . . I mean, there'd be a lot of things there that people . . . well, it would make them think too much, and well, we don't want that . . . we just want a little . . . entertainment.

JACKSON. How do you mean, Mr. Trewe?

HARRY. Well, I mean if you . . . well, I mean. If you did the whole thing in reverse . . . I mean, okay, well, all right . . . you've got this black man . . . no, no . . . all right. You've got this man who is black, Robinson

Crusoe, and he discovers this island on which there is this white cannibal, all right?

JACKSON. Yes. That is, after he has killed the goat . . .

HARRY. Yes, I know, I know. After he has killed the goat and made a . . . the hat, the parasol, and all of that . . . and, anyway, he comes across this man called Friday.

JACKSON. How do you know I mightn't choose to call him Thursday? Do I have to copy every . . . I mean, are we improvising?

HARRY. All right, so it's Thursday. He comes across this naked white cannibal called Thursday, you know. And then look at what would happen. He would have to start to . . . well, he'd have to, sorry . . . This cannibal, who is a Christian, would have to start unlearning his Christianity. He would have to be taught . . . I mean . . . he'd have to be taught by this—African . . . that everything was wrong, that what he was doing . . . I mean, for nearly two thousand years . . . was wrong. That his civilization, his culture, his whatever, was . . . *horrible*. Was all . . . wrong. Barbarous, I mean, you know. And Crusoe would then have to teach him things like, you know, about . . . Africa, his gods, patamba, and so on. . . . and it would get very, very complicated, and I suppose ultimately it would be very boring, and what we'd have on our hands would be . . . would be a play and not a little pantomime . . .

JACKSON. I'm too ambitious?

HARRY. No, no, the whole thing would have to be reversed; white would become black, you know . . .

JACKSON (*Smiling*). You see, Mr. Trewe, I don't see anything wrong with that, up to now.

HARRY. Well, I do. It's not the sort of thing I want, and I think you'd better clean up, and I'm going inside, and when I come back I'd like this whole place just as it was. I mean, just before everything started.

JACKSON. You mean you'd like it returned to its primal state? Natural? Before Crusoe finds Thursday? But, you see, that is not history. That is not the world.

HARRY. No, no, I don't give an Eskimo's fart about the world, Jackson. I just want this little place here *cleaned up*, and I'd like you to get back to fixing the sun deck. Let's forget the whole matter. Righto. Excuse me.

(*He is leaving. Jackson's tone will stop him*)

JACKSON. Very well, So I take it you don't want to hear the song, neither?

HARRY. No, no, I'm afraid not. I think really it was a silly idea, it's all my fault, and I'd like things to return to where they were.

JACKSON. The story of the British Empire, Mr. Trewe. However, it is too late. The history of the British Empire.

HARRY. Now, how do you get that?

JACKSON. Well, you come to a place, you find that place as God make it; like Robinson Crusoe, you civilize the natives; they try to do something, you turn around and you say to them: "You are not good enough, let's call the whole thing off, return things to normal, you go back to your position as slave or servant, I will keep mine as master, and we'll forget the whole thing ever happened." Correct? You would like me to acccept this.

HARRY. You're really making this very difficult, Jackson. Are you hurt? Have I offended you?

JACKSON. Hurt? No, no, no. I didn't expect any less. I am not hurt.

(*Pause*)

I am just . . .

(*Pause*)

HARRY. You're just what?

JACKSON. I am just ashamed . . . of making such a fool of myself.

(*Pause*)

I expected . . . a little respect. That is all.

HARRY. I respect you . . . I just, I . . .

JACKSON. No. It's perfectly all right.
    (*Harry goes to the table, straightens it*)
I . . . no . . . I'll fix the table myself.
    (*He doesn't move*)
I am all right, thank you. Sir.
    (*Harry stops fixing the table*)
    (*With the hint of a British accent*)
Thank you very much.

HARRY (*Sighs*).
    I . . . am sorry . . . er . . .

(*Jackson moves toward the table*)

JACKSON. It's perfectly all right, sir. It's perfectly all . . . right.
    (*Almost inaudibly*)
Thank you.
    (*Harry begins to straighten the table again*)
No, thank you very much, don't touch anything.
    (*Jackson is up against the table. Harry continues to straighten the table*)
Don't touch anything. . . Mr. Trewe. Please.
    (*Jackson rests one arm on the table, fist closed. They watch each other for three beats*)

Now that . . . is MY order. . .

(They watch each other for several beats as the lights fade)

ACT II

Noon. White glare. Harry, with shirt unbuttoned, in a deck chair reading a paperback thriller. Sound of intermittent hammering from stage left, where Jackson is repairing the sun-deck slats. Harry rises, decides he should talk to Jackson about the noise, decides against it, and leans back in the deck chair, eyes closed. Hammering has stopped for a long while. Harry opens his eyes, senses Jackson's presence, turns suddenly, to see him standing quite close, shirtless, holding a hammer. Harry bolts from his chair.

JACKSON. You know something, sir? While I was up there nailing the sun deck, I just stay so and start giggling all by myself.
HARRY. Oh, yes? Why?
JACKSON. No, I was remembering a feller, you know . . . ahhh, he went for audition once for a play, you know, and the way he, you know, the way he prop . . . present himself to the people, said . . . ahmm, "You know, I am an actor, you know. I do all kind of acting, classical acting, *Creole* acting." That's when I laugh, you know?
　　(Pause)
I going back and fix the deck, then.
　　(Moves off. Stops, turns)
The . . . the hammering not disturbing you?
HARRY. No, no, it's fine. You have to do it, right? I mean, you volunteered, the carpenter didn't come, right?
JACKSON. Yes. Creole acting. I wonder what kind o' acting dat is.

(Spins the hammer in the air and does or does not catch it)

Yul Brynner. *Magnificent Seven*. Picture, papa! A kind of Western Creole acting. It ain't have no English cowboys, eh, Mr. Harry? Something wrong, boy, something wrong.

(He exits. Harry lies back in the deck chair, the book on his chest, arms locked behind his head. Silence. Hammering violently resumes)

　　(Off)
Kekkk, kekkkekk, kekk!

Kekkekk, kekkkekk, ekkek!

(Harry rises, moves from the deck chair toward the sun deck)

HARRY. Jackson! What the hell are you doing? What's that noise?
JACKSON *(Off; loud)*. I doing like a black sea gull, suh!
HARRY. Well, it's very distracting.
JACKSON *(Off)*. Sorry, sir.

(Harry returns. Sits down on the deck chair. Waits for the hammering. Hammering resumes. Then stops. Silence. Then we hear)

(Singing loudly)
I want to tell you 'bout Robinson Crusoe.
He tell Friday, when I do so, do so.
Whatever I do, you must do like me,
He make Friday a Good Friday Bohbolee
　　(Spoken)
And the chorus:
　　(Sings)
Laide-die
Laidie, lay-day, de-day-de-die,
Laidee-doo-day-dee-day-dee-die
Laidee-day-doh-dee-day-dee-die

Now that was the first example of slavery,
'Cause I am still Friday and you ain't me,
Now Crusoe he was this Christian and all,
Friday, his slave, was a cannibal,
But one day things bound to go in reverse,
With Crusoe the slave and Friday the boss . . .
Caiso, boy! Caiso!

(Harry rises, goes toward the sun deck)

HARRY. Jackson, man! Jesus!

(He returns to the deck chair, is about to sit)

JACKSON *(Off)*. Two more lash and the sun deck finish, sir!
　　(Harry waits)
Stand by . . . here they come . . .
First lash . . .
　　(Sound)
Pow!
Second lash:
　　(Two sounds)
Pataow! Job complete! Lunch, Mr. Trewe? You want your lunch now? Couple sandwich or what?
HARRY *(Shouts without turning)*. Just bring a couple beers from the icebox, Jackson. And the Scotch.
　　(To himself)
What the hell, let's all get drunk.

(To Jackson)
Bring some beer for yourself, too, Jackson!

JACKSON *(Off)*. Thank you, Mr. Robinson . . . Thank you, Mr. Trewe, sir!
Cru-soe, Trewe-so!
    (Faster)
Crusoe-Trusoe, Robinson Trewe-so!

HARRY. Jesus, Jackson; cut that out and just bring the bloody beer!

JACKSON *(Off)*. Right! A beer for you and a beer for me! Now, what else is it going to be? A sandwich for you, but none for me.

(Harry picks up the paperback and opens it, removing a folded sheet of paper. He opens it and is reading it carefully, sometimes lifting his head, closing his eyes, as if remembering its contents, then reading again. He puts it into a pocket quickly as Jackson returns, carrying a tray with two beers, a bottle of Scotch, a pitcher of water, and two glasses. Jackson sets them down on the table.)

I'm here, sir. At your command.

HARRY. Sit down. Forget the sandwiches, I don't want to eat. Let's sit down, man to man, and have a drink. That was the most sarcastic hammering I've ever heard, and I know you were trying to get back at me with all those noises and that Uncle Tom crap. So let's have a drink, man to man, and try and work out what happened this morning, all right?

JACKSON. I've forgotten about this morning, sir.

HARRY. No, no, no, I mean, the rest of the day it's going to bother me, you know?

JACKSON. Well, I'm leaving at half-past one.

HARRY. No, but still . . . Let's . . . Okay. Scotch?

JACKSON. I'll stick to beer, sir, thank you.

(Harry pours a Scotch and water, Jackson serves himself a beer. Both are still standing)

HARRY. Sit over there, please, Mr. Phillip. On the deck chair.

(Jackson sits on the deck chair, facing Harry)

Cheers?

JACKSON. Cheers. Cheers. Deck chair and all.

(They toast and drink)

HARRY. All right. Look, I think you misunderstood me this morning.

JACKSON. Why don't we forget the whole thing, sir? Let me finish this beer and go for my sea bath, and you can spend the rest of the day all by yourself.

(Pause)

Well. What's wrong? What happen, sir? I said something wrong just now?

HARRY. This place isn't going to drive me crazy, Jackson. Not if I have to go mad preventing it. Not physically crazy; but you just start to think crazy thoughts, you know? At the beginning it's fine; there's the sea, the palm trees, monarch of all I survey and so on, all that postcard stuff. And then it just becomes another back yard. God, is there anything deadlier than Sunday afternoons in the tropics when you can't sleep? The horror and stillness of the heat, the shining, godforsaken sea, the bored and boring clouds? Especially in an empty boarding house. You sit by the stagnant pool counting the dead leaves drifting to the edge. I daresay the terror of emptiness made me want to act. I wasn't trying to humiliate you. I meant nothing by it. Now, I don't usually apologize to people. I don't do things to apologize for. When I do them, I mean them, but, in your case, I'd like to apologize.

JACKSON. Well, if you find here boring, go back home. Do something else, nuh?

HARRY. It's not that simple. It's a little more complicated than that. I mean, everything I own is sunk here, you see? There's a little matter of a brilliant actress who drank too much, and a car crash at Brighton after a panto . . . Well. That's neither here nor there now. Right? But I'm determined to make this place work. I gave up the theater for it.

JACKSON. Why?

HARRY. Why? I wanted to be the best. Well, among other things; oh, well, that's neither here nor there. Flopped at too many things, though. Including classical and Creole acting. I just want to make this place work, you know. And a desperate man'll try anything. Even at the cost of his sanity, maybe. I mean, I'd hate to believe that under everything else I was also prejudiced, as well. I wouldn't have any right here, right?

JACKSON. 'Tain't prejudice that bothering you, Mr. Trewe; you ain't no parrot to repeat opinion. No, is loneliness that sucking your soul as dry as the sun suck a crab shell. On a Sunday like this, I does watch you. The whole staff does study you. Walking round restless, staring at the sea. You remembering your wife and your son, not right? You ain't get over that yet?

HARRY. Jackson . . .

JACKSON. Is none of my business. But it really lonely here out of season. Is summer, and your own people gone, but come winter they go flock like sandpipers all down that beach. So you lonely, but I could make you forget all o' that. I could make H. Trewe, Esquire, a brand-new man. You come like a challenge.

HARRY. Think I keep to myself too much?

JACKSON. If! You would get your hair cut by phone. You drive so careful you make your car nervous. If you was in charge of the British Empire, you wouldn'ta lose it, you'da misplace it.

HARRY. I see, Jackson.

JACKSON. But all that could change if you do what I tell you.

HARRY. I don't want a new life, thanks.

JACKSON. Same life. Different man. But that stiff upper lip goin' have to quiver a little.

HARRY. What's all this? Obeah? "That old black magic"?

JACKSON. Nothing. I could have the next beer?

HARRY. Go ahead. I'm drinking Scotch.

(Jackson takes the other beer, swallows deep, smacks his lips, grins at Harry)

JACKSON. Nothing. We will have to continue from where we stop this morning. You will have to be Thursday.

HARRY. Aha, you bastard! It's a thrill giving orders, hey? But I'm not going through all that rubbish again.

JACKSON. All right. Stay as you want. But if you say yes, it go have to be man to man, and none of this boss-and-Jackson business, you see, Trewe . . . I mean, I just call you plain Trewe, for example, and I notice that give you a slight shock. Just a little twitch of the lip, but a shock all the same, eh, Trewe? You see? You twitch again. It would be just me and you, all right? You see, two of we both acting a role here we ain't really really believe, in, you know. I ent think you strong enough to give people orders, and I *know* I ain't the kind who like taking *them*. So both of we doesn't have to *improvise* so much as *exaggerate*. We faking, faking all the time. But, man to man, I mean . . .

(Pause)

that could be something else. Right, Mr. Trewe?

HARRY. Aren't we man to man now?

JACKSON. No, no. We having one of them "playing man-to-man" talks, where a feller does look a next feller in the eye and say, "Le' we settle this thing, man to man," and this time the feller who smiling and saying it, his whole honest intention is to take that feller by the crotch and rip out he stones, and dig out he eye and leave him for corbeaux to pick.

(Silence)

HARRY. You know, that thing this morning had an effect on me, man to man now. I didn't think so much

about the comedy of *Robinson Crusoe*, I thought what we were getting into was a little sad. So, when I went back to the room, I tried to rest before lunch, before you began all that vindictive hammering . . .

JACKSON. Vindictive?

HARRY. Man to man: that vindictive hammering and singing, and I thought, Well, maybe we could do it straight. Make a real straight thing out of it.

JACKSON. You mean like a tradegy. With one joke?

HARRY. Or a codemy, with none. You mispronounce words on purpose, don't you, Jackson?

(Jackson smiles)

Don't think for one second that I'm not up on your game, Jackson. You're playing the stage nigger with me. I'm an actor, you know. It's a smile in front and a dagger behind your back, right? Or the smile itself is the bloody dagger. I'm aware, chum. I'm aware.

JACKSON. The smile kinda rusty, sir, but it goes with the job. Just like the water in this hotel:

(Demonstrates)

I turn it on at seven and lock it off at one.

HARRY. Didn't hire you for the smile; I hired you for your voice. We've the same background. Old-time calypso, old-fashioned music hall:

(Sings)

Oh, me wife can't cook and she looks like a horse
And the way she makes coffee is grounds for divorce . . .
(Does a few steps)
But when love is at stake she's my Worcester sauce . . .
(Stops)

Used to wow them with that. All me own work. Ah, the lost glories of the old music hall, the old provincials, grimy brocade, the old stars faded one by one. The brassy pantomimes! Come from an old music-hall family, you know, Jackson. Me mum had this place she ran for broken-down actors. Had tea with the greats as a tot.
(Sings softly, hums)
Oh, me wife can't cook . . .
(Silence)
You married, Jackson?

JACKSON. I not too sure, sir.

HARRY. You're not sure?

JACKSON. That's what I said.

HARRY. I know what you mean. I wasn't sure I was when I was. My wife's remarried.

JACKSON. You showed me her photo. And the little boy own.

HARRY. But I'm not. Married. So there's absolutely no hearth for Crusoe to go home to. While you were up there, I rehearsed this thing

(Presents a folded piece of paper)

Want to read it?

JACKSON. What . . . er . . . what is it . . . a poetry?

HARRY. No, no, not a poetry. A thing I wrote. Just a speech in the play . . . that if . . .

JACKSON. Oho, we back in the play again?

HARRY. Almost. You want to read it?

(He offers the paper)

JACKSON. All right.

HARRY. I thought—no offense, now. Man to man. If you were doing Robinson Crusoe, this is what you'd read.

JACKSON. You want me to read this, right?

HARRY. Yeah.

JACKSON *(Reads slowly)*.

"O silent sea, O wondrous sunset that I've gazed on ten thousand times, who will rescue me from this complete desolation? . . . "

(Breaking)

All o' this?

HARRY. If you don't mind. Don't act it. Just read it.

(Jackson looks at him)

No offense.

JACKSON *(Reads)*.

"Yes, this is paradise, I know. For I see around me the splendors of nature . . . "

HARRY. Don't act it . . .

JACKSON *(Pauses, then continues)*. "How I'd like to fuflee this desolate rock."

(Pauses)

Fuflee? Pardon, but what is a fuflee, Mr. Trewe?

HARRY. A fuflee? I've got "fuflee" written there?

JACKSON *(Extends paper, points at word)*.

So, how you does fuflee, Mr. Harry? Is Anglo-Saxon English?

(Harry kneels down and peers at the word. He rises)

HARRY. It's F . . . then F-L-E-E—flee to express his hesitation. It's my own note as an actor. He quivers, he hesitates . . .

JACKSON. He quivers, he hesitates, but he still can't fuflee?

HARRY. Just leave that line out, Jackson.

JACKSON. I like it.

HARRY. *Leave it out!*

JACKSON. No fuflee?

HARRY. I said no.

JACKSON. Just because I read it wrong. I know the word "flee," you know. Like to take off. Flee. Faster than run. Is the extra *F* you put in there so close to flee that had me saying fuflee like a damn ass, but le' we leave it in, nuh? One fuflee ain't go kill anybody. Much less bite them.

(Silence)

Get it?

HARRY. Don't take this personally . . .

JACKSON. No fuflees on old Crusoe, boy . . .

HARRY. But, if you're going to do professional theater, Jackson, don't take this personally, more discipline is required. All right?

JACKSON. You write it. Why you don't read it?

HARRY. I wanted to hear it. Okay, give it back . . .

JACKSON *(Loudly, defiantly)*. "The ferns, the palms like silent sentinels, the wide and silent lagoons that briefly hold my passing, solitary reflection. The volcano . . . "

(Stops)

"The volcano." What?

HARRY. . . . "wreathed" . . .

JACKSON. Oho, oho . . . like a wreath? "The volcano *wreathed* in mist. But what is paradise without a woman? Adam in paradise!"

HARRY. Go ahead.

JACKSON *(Restrained)*. "Adam in paradise had his woman to share his loneliness, but I miss the voice of even one consoling creature, the touch of a hand, the look of kind eyes. Where is the wife from whom I vowed never to be sundered? How old is my little son? If he could see his father like this, mad with memories of them . . . Even Job had his family. But I am alone, alone, I am all alone."

(Pause)

Oho. You write this?

HARRY. Yeah.

JACKSON. Is good. Very good.

HARRY. Thank you.

JACKSON. Touching. Very sad. But something missing.

HARRY. What?

JACKSON. Goats. You leave out the goats.

HARRY. The goats. So what? What've you got with goats, anyway?

JACKSON. Very funny. Very funny, sir.

HARRY. Try calling me Trewe.

JACKSON. Not yet. That will come. Stick to the point. You ask for my opinion and I *gave* you my opinion. No doubt I don't have the brains. But *my* point is that this man ain't facing reality. *There are goats* all around him.

HARRY. You're full of shit.

JACKSON. The man is not facing reality. He is not a practical man *shipwrecked*.

HARRY. I suppose that's the difference between classical and Creole acting?

(He pours a drink and downs it furiously)

JACKSON. If he is not practical, he is not Robinson Crusoe. And yes, is Creole acting, yes. Because years afterward his litle son could look at the parasol and the hat and look at a picture of Daddy and boast: "My daddy smart, boy. He get shipwreck and first thing he do is he build a hut, then he kill a goat or two and makes clothes, a parasol and a hat." That way Crusoe *achieve* something, and his son could boast. . . .

HARRY. Only his son is dead.

JACKSON. Whose son dead?

HARRY. Crusoe's.

JACKSON. No, pardner. *Your* son dead. Crusoe wife and child waiting for him, and he is a practical man and he know somebody go come and save him . . .

HARRY *(Almost inaudibly)*.

"I bit my arm, I sucked the blood,

And cried, 'A sail! a sail!'"

How the hell does he know "somebody go come and save him"? That's shit. That's not in his character at that moment. How the hell can he know? You're a cruel bastard . . .

JACKSON *(Enraged)*. *Because, you fucking ass, he has faith!*

HARRY *(Laughing)*. Faith? What faith?

JACKSON. He not sitting on his shipwrecked arse bawling out . . . what it is you have here?

(Reads)

"O . . ." Where is it?

(Reads)

"O silent sea, O wondrous sunset," and all that shit. No. He shipwrecked. He desperate, he hungry. He look up and he see this fucking goat with its fucking beard watching him and smiling, this goat with its forked fucking beard and square yellow eye just like the fucking devil, standing up there . . .

(Pantomimes the goat and Crusoe in turn)

smiling at him, and putting out its tongue and letting go one fucking *bleeeeeh!* And Robbie ent thinking 'bout his wife and son and O silent sea and O wondrous sunset; no, Robbie is the First True Creole, so he watching the goat with his eyes narrow, narrow, and he say: *blehhh*, eh? You muther-fucker, I go show you *blehhh* in your goat-ass, and vam, vam, next thing is Robbie and the goat, *mano a mano*, man to man, man to goat, goat to man, wrestling on the sand, and next thing we know we hearing one last faint, feeble *bleeeeeeehhhhhhhhhhhhhh*, and Robbie is next seen walking up the beach with a goatskin hat and a goatskin umbrella, feeling like a million dollars because *he have faith!*

HARRY *(Applauds)*. Bravo! You're the Christian. I am the cannibal. Bravo!

JACKSON. If I does hammer sarcastic, you does clap sarcastic. Now I want to pee.

HARRY. I think I'll join you.

JACKSON. So because I go and pee, you must pee, too?

HARRY. Subliminal suggestion.

JACKSON. Monkey see, monkey do.

HARRY. You're the bloody ape, mate. You people just came down from the trees.

JACKSON. Say that again, please.

HARRY. I'm going to keep that line.

JACKSON. Oho! Rehearse you rehearsing? I thought you was serious.

HARRY. You go have your pee. I'll run over my monologue.

JACKSON. No, you best do it now, sir. Or it going to be on my mind while we rehearsing that what you really want to do is take a break and pee. We best go together, then.

HARRY. We'll call it the pee break. Off we go, then. How long will you be, then? You people take forever.

JACKSON. Maybe you should hold up a sign, sir, or give some sort of signal when you serious or when you joking, so I can know not to react. I would say five minutes.

HARRY. Five minutes? What is this, my friend, Niagara Falls?

JACKSON. It will take me . . . look, you want me to time it? I treat it like a ritual, I don't just pee for peeing's sake. It will take me about forty to fifty seconds to walk to the servants' toilets . . .

HARRY. Wait a second . . .

JACKSON. No, you wait, please, sir. That's almost one minute, take another fifty seconds to walk back, or even more, because after a good pee a man does be in a mood, both ruminative and grateful that the earth has received his libation, so that makes . . .

HARRY. Hold on, please.

JACKSON (*Voice rising*). Jesus, sir, give me a break, nuh? That is almost two minutes, and in between those two minutes it have such solemn and ruminative behavior as opening the fly, looking upward or downward, the ease and relief, the tender shaking, the solemn tucking in, like you putting a little baby back to sleep, the reverse zipping or buttoning, depending on the pants, then, with the self-congratulating washing of the hands, looking at yourself for at least half a minute in the mirror, then the drying of hands as if you were a master surgeon just finish a major operation, and the walk back . . .

HARRY. You said that. Any way you look at it, it's under five minutes, and I interrupted you because . . .

JACKSON. I could go and you could time me, to see if I on a go-slow, or wasting up my employer's precious time, but I know it will take at least five, unless, like most white people, you either don't flush it, a part I forgot, or just wipe your hands fast fast or not at all . . .

HARRY. Which white people, Jackson?

JACKSON. I was bathroom attendant at the Hilton, and I know men and races from their urinary habits, and most Englishmen . . .

HARRY. Most Englishmen . . . Look, I was trying to tell you, instead of going all the way round to the servants' lavatories, pop into my place, have a quick one, and that'll be under five bloody minutes in any circumstances and regardless of the capacity. Go on. I'm all right.

JACKSON. Use your bathroom, Mr. Harry?

HARRY. Go on, will you?

JACKSON. I want to get this. You giving me permission to go through your living room, with all your valuables lying about, with the picture of your wife watching me in case I should leave the bathroom open, and you are granting me the privilege of taking out my thing, doing my thing right there among all those lotions and expensive soaps, and . . . after I finish, wiping my hands on a clean towel?

HARRY. Since you make it so vividly horrible, why don't you just walk around to the servants' quarters and take as much time as you like? Five minutes won't kill me.

JACKSON. I mean, equality is equality and art is art, Mr. Harry, but to use those clean, rough Cannon towels . . . You mustn't rush things, people have to slide into independence. They give these islands independence so fast that people still ain't recover from the shock, so they pissing and wiping their hands indiscriminately. You don't want that to happen in this guest house, Mr. Harry. Let me take my little five minutes, as usual,

and if you have to go, you go to your place, and I'll go to mine, and let's keep things that way until I can feel I can use your towels without a profound sense of gratitude, and you could, if you wanted, a little later maybe, walk round the guest house in the dark, put your foot in the squelch of those who missed the pit by the outhouse, that charming old-fashioned outhouse so many tourists take Polaroids of, without feeling degraded, and we can then respect each other as artists. So, I appreciate the offer, but I'll be back in five. Kindly excuse me.

(He exits)

HARRY. You've got logorrhea, Jackson. You've been running your mouth like a parrot's arse. But don't get sarcastic with me, boy!

(Jackson returns)

JACKSON. You don't understand, Mr. Harry. My problem is, I really mean what I say.

HARRY. You've been pretending indifference to this game, Jackson, but you've manipulated it your way, haven't you? Now you can spew out all that bitterness in fun, can't you? Well, we'd better get things straight around here, friend. You're still on duty. And if you stay out there too long, your job is at stake. it's . . . *(consulting his watch)* five minutes to one now. You've got exactly three minutes to get in there and back, and two minutes left to finish straightening this place. It's a bloody mess.

(Silence)

JACKSON. Bloody mess, eh?

HARRY. That's correct.

JACKSON (*In exaggerated British accent*). I go try and make it back in five, bwana. If I don't, the mess could be bloodier. I saw a sign once in a lavatory in Mobile, Alabama. COLORED. But it didn't have no time limit. Funny, eh?

HARRY. Ape! Mimic! Three bloody minutes!

(Jackson exits, shaking his head. Harry recovers the sheet of paper from the floor and puts it back in his pants pocket. He pours a large drink, swallows it all in two large gulps, then puts the glass down. He looks around the gazebo, wipes his hands briskly. He removes the drinks tray with scotch, the two beer bottles, glasses, water pitcher, and sets them in a corner of the gazebo. He lifts up the deck chair and sets it, sideways, in another corner. He turns the table carefully over on its side; then, when it is on its back, he looks at it. He changes his mind and care-

fully tilts the table back upright. He removes his shirt and folds it and places it in another corner of the gazebo. He rolls up his trouser cuffs almost to the knee. He is now half-naked. He goes over to the drinks tray and pours the bowl of melted ice, now tepid water, over his head. He ruffles his hair, his face dripping; then he sees an ice pick. He picks it up)

JACKSON'S VOICE. "One day, just out of the blue, I pick up a ice pick and walk over to where he and two fellers was playing cards, and I nail that ice pick through his hand to the table, and I laugh . . ."

(Harry drives the ice pick hard into the tabletop, steps back, looking at it. Then he moves up to it, wrenches it out, and gets under the table, the ice pick at his feet. A few beats, then Jackson enters, pauses)

JACKSON *(Laughs)*. What you doing under the table, Mr. Trewe?

(Silence. Jackson steps nearer the table)

Trewe? You all right?

(Silence. Jackson crouches close to Harry)

Harry, boy, you cool?

(Jackson rises. Moves away some distance. He takes in the space. An arena. Then he crouches again)

Ice-pick time, then?
Okay. "Fee fi fo fum,
I smell the blood of an Englishman . . ."

(Jackson exits quickly. Harry waits a while, then crawls from under the table, straightens up, and places the ice pick gently on the tabletop. He goes to the drinks tray and has a sip from the Scotch; then replaces the bottle and takes up a position behind the table. Jackson returns dressed as Crusoe—goatskin hat, open umbrella, the hammer stuck in the waistband of his rolled-up trousers. He throws something across the room to Harry's feet. The dead parrot, in a carry-away box. Harry opens it)

One parrot, to go! Or you eating it here?
HARRY. You son of a bitch.
JACKSON. Sure.

(Harry picks up the parrot and hurls it into the sea)

First bath in five years.

(Jackson moves toward the table, very calmly)

HARRY. You're a bloody savage. Why'd you strangle him?

JACKSON *(As Friday)*. Me na strangle him, bwana. Him choke from prejudice.
HARRY. Prejudice? A bloody parrot. The bloody thing can't reason.

(Pause. They stare at each other. Harry crouches, tilts his head, shifts on his perch, flutters his wings like the parrot, squawks)

Heinegger. Heinegger.

(Jackson stands over the table and folds the umbrella)

You people create nothing. You imitate everything. It's all been done before, you see, Jackson. The parrot. Think that's something? It's from *The Seagull*. It's from *Miss Julie*. You can't ever be original, boy. That's the trouble with shadows, right? They can't think for themselves.

(Jackson shrugs, looking away from him)

So you take it out on a parrot. Is that one of your African sacrifices, eh?
JACKSON. Run your mouth, Harry, run your mouth.
HARRY *(Squawks)*.
Heinegger . . . Heinegger . . .

(Jackson folds the parasol and moves to enter the up-turned table)

I wouldn't go under there if I were you, Jackson.

(Jackson reaches into the back of his waistband and removes a hammer)

JACKSON. The first English cowboy.

(He turns and faces Harry)

HARRY. It's my property. Don't get in there.
JACKSON. The hut. That was my idea.
HARRY. The table's mine.
JACKSON. What else is yours, Harry?

(Gestures)

This whole fucking island? Dem days gone, boy.
HARRY. The costume's mine, too.

(He crosses over, almost nudging Jackson, and picks up the ice pick)

I'd like them back.
JACKSON. Suit yourself.

(Harry crosses to the other side, sits on the edge of the wall or leans against a post. Jackson removes the hat and throws it into the arena, then the parasol)

HARRY. The hammer's mine.
JACKSON. I feel I go need it.
HARRY. If you keep it, you're a bloody thief.

(*Jackson suddenly drops to the floor on his knees, letting go of the hammer, weeping and cringing, and advancing on his knees toward Harry*)

JACKSON. Pardon, master, pardon! Friday bad boy! Friday wicked nigger. Sorry. Friday nah t'ief again. Mercy, master. Mercy.

(*He rolls around on the floor, laughing*)

Oh, Jesus, I go dead! I go dead. Ay-ay.

(*Silence. Jackson on the floor, gasping, lying on his back. Harry crosses over, picks up the parasol, opens it, after a little difficulty, then puts on the goatskin hat. Jackson lies on the floor, silent*)

HARRY. I never hit any goddamned maintenance sergeant on the head in the service. I've never hit anybody in my life. Violence makes me sick. I don't believe in ownership. If I'd been more posssessive, more authoritative, I don't think she'd have left me. I don't think you ever drove an ice pick through anybody's hand, either. That was just the two of us acting.
JACKSON. Creole acting?

(*He is still lying on the floor*)

Don't be too sure about the ice pick.
HARRY. I'm sure. You're a fake. You're a kind man and you think you have to hide it. A lot of other people could have used that to their own advantage. That's the difference between master and servant.
JACKSON. That master-and-servant shit finish. Bring a beer for me.

(*He is still on his back*)

HARRY. There's no more beer. You want a sip of Scotch?
JACKSON. Anything.

(*Harry goes to the Scotch, brings over the bottle, stands over Jackson*)

HARRY. Here. To me bloody wife!

(*Jackson sits up, begins to move off*)

What's wrong, you forget to flush it?
JACKSON. I don't think you should bad-talk her behind her back.

(*He exits*)

HARRY. Behind her back? She's in England. She's a star.

Star? She's a bloody planet.

(*Jackson returns, holding the photograph of Harry's wife*)

JACKSON. If you going bad-talk, I think she should hear what you going to say, you don't think so, darling?
(*Addressing the photograph, which he puts down*)
If you have to tell somebody something, tell them to their face.
(*Addressing the photograph*)
Now, you know all you women, eh? Let the man talk his talk and don't interrupt.
HARRY. You're fucking bonkers, you know that? Before I hired you, I should have asked for a medical report.
JACKSON. Please tell your ex-wife good afternoon or something. The dame in the pantomime is always played by a man, right?
HARRY. Bullshit.

(*Jackson sits close to the photograph, wiggling as he ventriloquizes*)

JACKSON (*In an Englishwoman's voice*). Is not bullshit at all, Harold. Everything I say you always saying bullshit, bullshit. How can we conduct a civilized conversation if you don't give me a chance? What have I done, Harold, oh, Harold, for you to treat me so?
HARRY. Because you're a silly selfish bitch and you *killed our son!*
JACKSON (*Crying*). There, there, you see . . . ?

(*He wipes the eyes of the photograph*)

You're calling me names, it wasn't my fault, and you're calling me names. Can't you ever forgive me for that, Harold?
HARRY. Ha! You never told him that, did you? You neglected to mention that little matter, didn't you, love?
JACKSON (*Weeping*). I love you, Harold. I love you, and I loved him, too. Forgive me, O God, please, please forgive me . . .
(*As himself*)
So how it happen? Murder? A accident?
HARRY (*To the photograph*). Love me? You loved me so much you get drunk and you . . . ah, ah, what's the use? What's the bloody use?

(*Wipes his eyes. Pause*)

JACKSON (*As wife*). I'm crying too, Harold. Let bygones be bygones . . .
(*Harry lunges for the photograph, but Jackson whips it away*)
(*As himself*)

You miss, Harold.
(*Pause; as wife*)
Harold . . .
(*Silence*)
Harold . . . speak to me . . . please.
(*Silence*)
What do you plan to do next?
(*Sniffs*)
What'll you do now?

HARRY. What difference does it make? . . . All right. I'll tell you what I'm going to do next, Ellen: you're such a big star, you're such a luminary, I'm going to leave you to shine by yourself. I'm giving up this bloody rat race and I'm going to take up Mike's offer. I'm leaving "the thea-tuh," which destroyed my confidence, screwed up my marriage, and made you a star. I'm going somewhere where I can get pissed every day and watch the sun set, like Robinson bloody Crusoe. That's what I'm going to bloody do. You always said it's the only part I could play.

JACKSON (*As wife*). Take me with you, then. Let's get away together. I always wanted to see the tropics, the palm trees, the lagoons . . .

(*Harry grabs the photograph from Jackson, he picks up the ice pick and puts the photograph on the table, pressing it down with one palm*)

HARRY. All right, Ellen, I'm going to . . . You can scream all you like, but I'm going to . . .

(*He raises the ice pick*)

JACKSON (*As wife*). My face is my fortune.

(*He sneaks up behind Harry, whips the photograph away while Harry is poised with the ice pick*)

HARRY. Your face is your fortune, eh? I'll kill her, Jackson, I'll maim that smirking bitch . . .

(*He lunges toward Jackson, who leaps away, holding the photograph before his face, and runs around the gazebo, shrieking*)

JACKSON (*As wife*). Help! Help! British police! My husband trying to kill me! Help, somebody, help!

(*Harry chases Jackson with the ice pick, but Jackson nimbly avoids him*)

(*As wife*)

Harry! Have you gone mad?

(*He scrambles onto the ledge of the gazebo. He no longer holds the photograph to his face, but his voice is the wife's*)

HARRY. Get down off there, you melodramatic bitch. You're too bloody conceited to kill yourself. Get down from there, Ellen! Ellen, it's a straight drop to the sea!

JACKSON (*As wife*). Push me, then! Push me, Harry! You hate me so much, why you don't come and push me?

HARRY. Push yourself, then. You never needed my help. Jump!

JACKSON (*As wife*). Will you forgive me now, or after I jump?

HARRY. Forgive you? . . .

JACKSON (*As wife*). All right, then. Goodbye!

(*He turns, teetering, about to jump*)

HARRY (*Shouts*). Ellen! Stop! I forgive you!

(*Jackson turns on the ledge. Silence. Harry is now sitting on the floor*)

That's the real reason I wanted to do the panto. To do it better than you ever did. You played Crusoe in the panto, Ellen. I was Friday. Black bloody grease-paint that made you howl. You wiped the stage with me . . . Ellen . . . well. Why not? I was no bloody good.

JACKSON (*As himself*). Come back to the play, Mr. Trewe. Is Jackson. We was playing Robinson Crusoe, remember?
(*Silence*)
Master, Friday here . . .
(*Silence*)
You finish with the play? The panto? Crusoe must get up, he must make himself get up. He have to face a next day again.
(*Shouts*)
I tell you: man must live! Then, after many years, he see this naked footprint that is the mark of his salvation . . .

HARRY (*Recites*).
"The self-same moment I could pray;
and . . . tata tee-tum-tum
The Albatross fell off and sank
Like lead into the sea."
God, my memory . . .

JACKSON. That ain't Crusoe, that is "The Rime of the Ancient Mariner."

(*He pronounces it "Marina"*)

HARRY. Mariner.
JACKSON. Marina.
HARRY. Mariner.
JACKSON. "The Rime of the Ancient Marina." So I learn it in Fourth Standard.

HARRY. It's your country, mate.

JACKSON. Is your language, pardner. I stand corrected. Now, you ain't see English crazy? I could sit down right next to you and tell you I *stand* corrected.

HARRY. Sorry. Where were we, Mr. Phillip?

JACKSON. Tobago. Where are you? It was your cue, Mr. Trewe.

HARRY. Where was I, then?

JACKSON. Ahhhm . . . that speech you was reading . . . that speech . . .

HARRY. Speech?

JACKSON. "O silent sea and so on . . . wreathed in mist . . ." Shall we take it from there, then? The paper.

HARRY. I should know it. After all, I wrote it. But prompt . . .

(*Harry gives Jackson his copy of the paper, rises, walks around, looks toward the sea*)

Creole or classical?

JACKSON. Don't make joke.

(*Silence. Sea-gull cries*)

HARRY. Then Crusoe, in his desolation, looks out to the sea, for the ten thousandth time, and remembers England, his wife, his little son, and speaks to himself:

(*As Crusoe*)

"O silent sea, O wondrous sunset that I've gazed on ten thousand times, who will rescue me from this complete desolation? Yes, this is paradise, I know. For I see around me the splendors of nature. The ferns, the palms like silent sentinels, the wide and silent lagoons that briefly hold my passing, solitary reflection. The volcano wreathed in mist. But what is paradise without a woman? Adam in paradise had his woman to share his loneliness . . . loneliness . . .

JACKSON (*Prompts*). . . . but I miss the voice . . .

HARRY (*Remembering*). "But I miss the voice . . .

(*Weeping, but speaking clearly*)

of even one consoling creature, the touch . . . of a hand . . . the look of kind eyes . . . Where is the wife from whom I vowed . . . never to be sundered? How old is my little son? If he could see his father like this . . . dressed in goatskins and mad with memories of them?"

(*He breaks down, quietly sobbing. A long pause*)

JACKSON. You crying or you acting?

HARRY. Acting.

JACKSON. I think you crying. Nobody could act that good.

HARRY. How would you know? You an actor?

JACKSON. Maybe not. But I cry a'ready.

HARRY. Okay, I was crying.

JACKSON. For what?

HARRY (*Laughs*). For what? I got carried away. I'm okay now.

JACKSON. But you laughing now.

HARRY. It's the same sound. You can't tell the difference if I turn my back.

JACKSON. Don't make joke.

HARRY. It's an old actor's trick. I'm going to cry now, all right?

(*He turns, then sobs with laughter, covering and uncovering his face with his hands. Jackson stalks around, peers at him, then begins to giggle. They are now both laughing*)

JACKSON (*Through laughter*). So . . . so . . . next Friday . . . when the tourists come . . . Crusoe . . . Crusoe go be ready for them . . . Goat race . . .

HARRY (*Laughing*). Goat-roti!

JACKSON (*Laughing*). Gambling.

HARRY (*Baffled*). Gambling?

JACKSON. Goat-to-pack. Every night . . .

HARRY (*Laughing*). Before they goat-to-bed!

JACKSON (*Laughing*). So he striding up the beach with his little goat-ee . . .

HARRY (*Laughing*). E-goat-istical, again.

(*Pause*)

JACKSON. You get the idea. So, you okay, Mr. Trewe?

HARRY. I'm fine, Mr. Phillip. You know . . .

(*He wipes his eyes*)

An angel passes through a house and leaves no imprint of his shadow on its wall. A man's life slowly changes and he does not understand the change. Things like this have happened before, and they can happen again. You understand Jackson? You see what it is I'm saying?

JACKSON. You making a mole hill out of a mountain, sir. But I think I follow you. You know what all this make me decide, pardner?

HARRY. What?

(*Jackson picks up the umbrella, puts on the goatskin hat*)

JACKSON. I going back to the gift that's my God-given calling. I benignly resign, you fire me. With inspiration. Caiso is my true work, caiso is my true life.

(*Sings*)

Well, a Limey name Trewe come to Tobago.
He was in show business but he had no show,
so in desperation he turn to me
and said: "Mr. Phillip" is the two o' we,
one classical actor and one Creole,
let we act together with we heart and soul.
It go be man to man, and we go do it fine,
and we go give it the title of pantomime.
La da dee da da da
dee da da da da da . . .

(He is singing as if in a spotlight. Music, audience applause. Harry joins in)

Wait! Wait! Hold it!

(Silence: walks over to Harry)

Starting from Friday, Robinson, we could talk 'bout a raise?

(Fadeout)

COMMENTARY

Note: The following essay represents a single interpretation of the play. For other perspectives on Pantomime, *consult the essays listed below.*

The "play-within-the-play" is a favorite motif of playwrights from Shakespeare (*A Midsummer Night's Dream* and *Hamlet*) to Luigi Pirandello (*Six Characters in Search of an Author*; reread the Showcase on that play and its discussion of "metatheater") to Tom Stoppard (*Rosencrantz and Guildenstern Are Dead*). The device serves two purposes. First, it creates a metaphor for life: the world often casts us in roles we must play, although we do not always understand the drama in which we find ourselves. We therefore "improvise" to survive. Late in *Pantomime* Jackson, the native forced into a submissive role by race and economics, says in his poetic dialectic, "[B]oth of we doesn't have to *improvise* so much as *exaggerate*. We faking, faking all the time." Jackson has learned to survive by playing—to use Harry's ugly term—"the stage nigger" whose surface appearance is one of submission; beneath that surface, however, is the heart of a revolutionary. "It's a smile in front and a dagger behind your back," says Harry in a heated exchange.

Secondly, as with all good plays, the play-within-the-play is instructive and illuminates the issues of the "real-life drama" that surrounds it. The characters acting in the artificial drama, as well as the audience watching it from the security of their seats, often come to an understanding of their personal dilemmas that transcends the "pretend drama"in which they perform. The very artificiality of the play-within-the-play allows the playwright to proclaim ideas that otherwise might seem manipulated in the supposedly "real drama."

So it is with Walcott. *Pantomime* is a microcosm of the Caribbean experience, as is its companion piece, *Remembrance* (1977), which also uses metatheater in its modern retelling of the Ariel-Caliban story from *The Tempest*. The first line of the play—a snatch of a song sung by Harry, the English expatriate who owns the shabby guest house—alludes to a specific kind of play: the "Christmas panto." Although its name is derived from the abbreviated form of "pantomime," a "panto" is actually an extravagant pageant that traditionally uses large casts, colorful scenery, and spectacular costumes. Harry's characterization is, therefore, typical of the unrealistic way in which he views the world, an illusion that the rehearsal for the panto dispels.

Beyond their visual splendor, pantos are noted for two characteristics that Walcott exploits to his thematic advantage. The traditional panto, which may have derived from mid-winter mummings (medieval celebrations of life over death), uses role-reversal as a staple of its humor. It is notable that Trinidad-Tobago's most celebrated festival, the pre-Lenten Carnival, grew out of a revolution in 1830 and yet retains role-playing/reversal among its chief impulses. (See Showcase, "The Trinidad Carnival.") Much of the play's humor, as well as its searing drama, derives from the frequent switching of roles between Harry and Jackson. The former begins as a proud landowner, the latter a timid serving man. As the play progresses—actually both plays, the Harry-Jackson play as well as the Crusoe-Friday play—the two men often find themselves transformed into their opposite. Crusoe acts more like Friday, just as Jackson becomes much more "the boss" in the drama.

Among the most popular traditions in the English panto (which Harry-the-Colonialist has imported to the Caribbean to entertain the white guests at his resort) is the Betsy, a man dressed in female clothing. And Walcott deftly uses this device to reveal the reason for Harry's bitterness. Jackson assumes the role of Ellen, Harry's ex-wife, and in the process of acting out their relationship he extorts a shocking truth from his employer. For years Harry has lived with the resentment that Ellen was better at playing panto than he—that he, Harry, for years played Friday to Ellen's Crusoe. What may seem a tawdry moment from that quintessentially theatrical form, the melodrama, is actually an exposé of a truth beyond the stage: Harry, the emblem of Old World colonial superiority, is exposed as emasculated and ineffectual. The most boisterous and bawdy joke of the Old World panto is turned into a bitter truth about the actual state of affairs in this late-twentieth-century island paradise.

Pantos traditionally rely on myths and fairy tales for their subject matter; for instance, *Peter Pan* remains among the most popular Christmas pantos. Given the season and the disposition of audiences that attend them, pantos invariably end "happily ever after," even if it means promulgating a distorted picture of reality. For his panto, Walcott turns to one of the best-known novels in English literature, Dafoe's *Robinson Crusoe*, a mythic story of survival in which an Englishman is castaway on a tropical island. Dafoe's novel, despite its value as escapist entertainment, has been reinterpreted (or perhaps deconstructed) as a metaphor for the colonial exploitation of the Caribbean. And it is tempting, even as this essay has suggested, to see *Pantomime* in this context. But that is only one implication of this play with many implications.

To Walcott Crusoe was also "the third Adam" since the Fall in the Garden. Christ was the second, and Crusoe the third. Walcott scholar Paula Burnett explains in *Derek Walcott: Politics and Poetics* (2000) that Crusoe is, in the playwright's estimation, "the New World's Third Chance...the man of the islands." Crusoe, the naked man bereft of all civilized accoutrements, must start from scratch, must reinvent everything he needs to survive in a beautiful but potentially hostile world. In essence Crusoe, like Walcott who identifies with him, is a craftsman, an artist who can recreate a better world. In the preface to his 1965 poem, "The Castaway," Walcott says that "the stripped and naked man, however abused, however disabused of old beliefs, instinctually, even desperately begins again as a craftsman. [His art will have] real faith, mapless, Historyless." Thus as Harry and Jackson together create their new panto for a new world, they inevitably create a world that is ultimately stripped of illusions, even in their illusory drama, so they can move forward together, not as master and servant, white and black, but as coequals, a union marked by Jackson's final caiso (calypso) song:

> *let we act together with we heart and soul.*
> *It go be [i.e., "it has got to be"] man to man, and we go do it fine,*
> *and we go give it the title of pantomime. . . .*

Walcott's panto may end "happily" as "an angel passes through a house," but the "ever after" is yet to be written by that most demanding of dramatists: history and the course of human events.

Other perspectives on *Pantomime*:

Jones, Bridget. "With Crusoe the Slave and Friday the Boss: Derek Walcott's *Pantomime*." In Lieve Spaas and Brian Simpson (eds), *Robinson Crusoe: Myths and Metamorphoses*. Basingstroke, England: Macmillan, 1996, 128–42.

Taylor, Patrick. "Myth and Reality in Caribbean Narrative: Derek Walcott's *Pantomime*." *World Literature Written in English* 26:1 (1986): 17–25.

See scenes from *Pantomime* on video:

Pantomime. Dir. Paul Kafno. Films for the Humanities, 20 min., 1991.

SHOWCASE   THE TRINIDAD CARNIVAL

You got the great big long wall in China,
And in India the Taj Mahal,
I know the greatest wonder of them all
Is my Trinidad carnival.

Though perhaps not as familiar as Mardi Gras in New Orleans or Carnival in Rio de Janeiro, the Carnival in Trinidad, extolled here in the Mighty Douglas's calypso song, has been called "undoubtedly the greatest annual theatrical spectacle of all time," according to Erroll Hill in *The Trinidad Carnival* (1972). Annually over 100,000 people appear in striking masquerades, street dances, and stage shows during the week before Lent. Most Christian societies enjoy some form of pre-Lenten carnival, most of which were actually derived from pagan rites such as the Roman Saturnalia. Carnival is a period of indulgent merrymaking in which costumed revelers take to the streets to sing, dance, mime, perform, eat, drink, and carouse before entering into a somber period of abstinence for forty days. "Carnival" comes from a Latin phrase—*carne vale*—which means "flesh farewell," a bittersweet reminder that both eating meat and indulging in the pleasures of the flesh are forbidden for six weeks.

The essence of carnival is role-reversal, that is, a celebration of chaos in which normality is suspended for a few days. Streets conveying people to the workplace are sealed off and overrun with merrymakers whose thoughts are far from the workaday world. Men dress as animals or women; the poor caricature the wealthy. (Note that role-reversal is a significant thematic and plot component of Walcott's *Pantomime*.) Rationality, conventionality, and restraint give way to indulgence, fantasy, and play. The comic spirit reigns, as evidenced by the cartoon-like costumes, headpieces, and masks; the frenetic dancing; the bawdy and sensual music; the satiric plays improvised on makeshift stages and under

tents. Ash Wednesday is the time for solemnity and reflection, but on Mardi Gras ("Fat Tuesday") there is only time for giving oneself to the spirit of carnival.

Carnival in Trinidad is a fascinating hybrid of many cultures and ideologies: pagan and Christian, European and African, Indian and Spanish, Western and Eastern, ancient and modern, poor and wealthy. Trinidad dates the beginnings of its Carnival to 1783 and the arrival of French planters with their African slaves. Early Carnivals had a racist tone as the plantation owners imitated the dress and manners of the slaves and danced traditional African dances such as the *bamboula* and the *ghouba*. This typifies the role-reversal aspect so prominent in Carnivals. Today, the Carnival has a more salutary effect on the twin-island nation of Trinidad-Tobago: the ethnic and social divisions in this multiracial culture are united in a common will to make each new Carnival the greatest ever.

Trinidad's slaves were emancipated on August 1, 1834, an event that forever made the Carnival a symbol of freedom for the masses. It was never again a plaything for the elite as it became a celebration of deliverance. Not surprisingly, many popular costumes are comic reminders of the days of oppression: Moco Jumbie, a cult figure found throughout West Africa, dances atop ten-to-fifteen-foot stilts as he wears an Eton coat and Lord Admiral's hat to parody the European oppressor. Each Carnival begins with a *canboulay*, a military march mocking the imperial guards who subjugated the slaves. There is clearly a political dimension to this great Carnival that transcends its roots. Similarly, Walcott's dramas are equal parts island lore and political commentary; *Pantomime* merges the English "panto" (which is a remnant of ancient masquerades; see below) with an examination of the interracial frictions that

are the legacy of Trinidad-Tobago's colonial past.

Masquerades were once used to channel the dead into the souls of the living, but modern masquerades mirror societal concerns. A grand Masquerade, dating back to 1866, dominates the final two days of the festival. The maskers are transformed into possessed spirits on "the glorious Monday morning" that begins the Masquerade. At dawn, Act One begins; it is the *jouvay* (from a Creole expression, "Is it daybreak?") in which characters from island folklore are brought to life. Many are demonic (the *diablesse*); others are satiric, such as the popular Dame Lorraine, a "fashionable lady" played by men in gaudy female dress, an example of the cross-dressing phenomenon found throughout world theater. The masqueraders typify the spirit of mockery and misrule permeating Carnival. Act Two presents traditional masks such as the Wild Indian, the Clowns, Midnight Robbers, and others that are often portrayed for generations within a single family. The third act introduces the big bands and calypso music for which the island is famous. (It is significant that Jackson in *Pantomime* is a retired calypso musician. On the one hand it represents the "happy islander" so familiar in tourist commercials; on the other, calypso music is a means of disseminating political commentary among the people.) Act Four is devoted to historical pageantry, a blend of past events, fantasy, and imagination in which islanders imitate world leaders and conquering heroes. At dusk on Tuesday, the final act brings together the various performers and—very importantly—the spectators in an enormous, spontaneous street dance, songfest, and mimed combat.

Drum dance competitions are held in bamboo huts built especially for the Carnival. A Masquerade King and Queen in extravagant regalia preside over the dance competitions. A coronation ceremony is among the first orders of business; a *borokit* (from the Spanish *borriquito*, "little donkey"), i.e., a comic horse's costume, is placed on the King, who then dances around the room carrying a wooden sword. He is accompanied by his Queen, always a male in drag, who begs money to finance the spectacle. Shortly before midnight on Fat Tuesday (Mardi Gras),

the Masquerade concludes with a mock execution of the King of Carnival. The execution is accompanied by a chant as old as time:

And every year we dance and sing,
And every year we kill the king,
Because the old king must be slain
For the new king to rise again.

See a video about the Trindad Carnival:

Mas Fever. Dir. Glenn Micallef. University of California Center for Media and Independent Learning, 55 min., 1989.

TRUE WEST

SAM SHEPARD

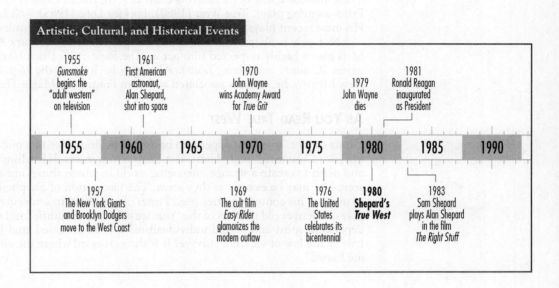

Artistic, Cultural, and Historical Events

1955 *Gunsmoke* begins the "adult western" on television	**1961** First American astronaut, Alan Shepard, shot into space		**1970** John Wayne wins Academy Award for *True Grit*		**1979** John Wayne dies	**1981** Ronald Reagan inaugurated as President	

| **1955** | **1960** | **1965** | **1970** | **1975** | **1980** | **1985** | **1990** |

1957 The New York Giants and Brooklyn Dodgers move to the West Coast			**1969** The cult film *Easy Rider* glamorizes the modern outlaw	**1976** The United States celebrates its bicentennial	**1980** **Shepard's** ***True West***	**1983** Sam Shepard plays Alan Shepard in the film *The Right Stuff*	

SAM SHEPARD (1943–)

Few American playwrights have received such critical attention by scholars in the past quarter-century as Sam Shepard, an oddity given that only one of his plays—*Buried Child*—has appeared on the Broadway stage (and then only as a revival in 1995). Like Beckett, who was his earliest inspiration, Shepard writes enigmatic dramas whose meanings are passionately debated by critics and scholars.

Shepard is a self-described "Air Force brat" whose family was constantly on the move, perhaps contributing to one of Shepard's thematic obsessions: the quest to find one's roots. As a teenager, his family settled in Duarte, California, located in the high desert east of Los Angeles. Not surprisingly, many of Shepard's plays (e.g., *True West*) are set on or adjacent to the desert. As a teen in Duarte, Shepard read his first play: Samuel Beckett's desolate tragicomedy, *Waiting for Godot*, which he claims has had the most influence on his writing.

In the early 1960s Shepard fled the high desert for New York City, where he waited tables while searching for work as a musician (he was the drummer for a rock band, the Holy Modal Rounders, who contributed music to the cult film *Easy Rider*). Shepard ran the streets of New York with the son of jazz great Charlie Mingus. His early plays attempted to create the theatrical equivalent of the improvisational jazz style, which reflects impressions of American life; he refers to these plays as "vibrations."

Shepard joined Joseph Chaikin's experimental theater company, the Open Theatre, for whom he both acted and wrote plays until 1973. The Open Theatre was especially noted for its work with transformations, acting exercises in which performers transformed themselves from one being into another. Transformation is a central theme of Shepard's dramatic works (note that Lee and Austin seem to transform into one another in *True West*), and his style requires that actors move effortlessly between naturalistic and stylistic modes of performance.

Shepard's canon can be divided into three phases: the early vibrations, almost exclusively one-acts (e.g., *Cowboy Mouth*, 1965), written as nonrealistic, experimental monologues; the middle plays (e.g., *Tooth of Crime*, 1968), which were fantasies that borrowed from western and gangster films, science fiction works, cartoons, and pop entertainment while exploring the isolation of the artist in a violent world; and the later, neorealistic plays, which collectively explore the disintegration of the family in the American West. These include *Curse of the Starving Class* (1978), *Buried Child* (1979—that year's Pulitzer Prize–winning play), *True West* (1980), *Fool for Love* (1983), and *Lie of the Mind* (1985). His most recent plays include *Simpatico* (1996) and *Eyes for Consuela* (1998).

Not only is Shepard among the finest late-twentieth-century American playwrights, he is also a highly respected film actor (*The Right Stuff, Black Hawk Down*) and screenwriter (*Country* and *Paris, Texas*). Although he lives in the high desert near Santa Fe, New Mexico, he remains associated with San Francisco's Magic Theatre.

AS YOU READ *TRUE WEST*

On its surface *True West* appears to be a realistic drama set in a middle-class home on the fringe of California's high desert. But Shepherd transcends Realism as he fuses Surrealism and myth to create a strange, menacing world in which things are apparently not as they seem—or may be exactly as they seem. The fascination of Shepherd's drama, like that of so many of his contemporaries (e.g., Pinter), stems from its ambiguity. The very title of the play challenges old notions of the "true west." Is it a romantic land that celebrates the independent spirit and rugged individualism? Is it an untamed land where only those who live by the law of violence survive? Is it the graveyard where the country's darkest secrets are buried?

TRUE WEST

SAM SHEPARD

CHARACTERS

AUSTIN: *early thirties, light blue sports shirt, light tan cardigan sweater, clean blue jeans, white tennis shoes*

LEE: *his older brother, early forties, filthy white t-shirt, tattered brown overcoat covered with dust, dark blue baggy suit pants from the Salvation Army, pink suede belt, pointed black forties dress shoes scuffed up, holes in the soles, no socks, no hat, long pronounced sideburns, "Gene Vincent" hairdo, two days' growth of beard, bad teeth*

SAUL KIMMER: *late forties, Hollywood producer, pink and white flower print sports shirt, white sports coat with matching polyester slacks, black and white loafers*

MOM: *early sixties, mother of the brothers, small woman, conservative white skirt and matching jacket, red shoulder bag, two pieces of matching red luggage*

SCENE: *All nine scenes take place on the same set; a kitchen and adjoining alcove of an older home in a Southern California suburb, about 40 miles east of Los Angeles. The kitchen takes up most of the playing area to stage left. The kitchen consists of a sink, upstage center, surrounded by counter space, a wall telephone, cupboards, and a small window just above it bordered by neat yellow curtains. Stage left of sink is a stove. Stage right, a refrigerator. The alcove adjoins the kitchen to stage right. There is no wall division or door to the alcove. It is open and easily accessible from the kitchen and defined only by the objects in it: a small round glass breakfast table mounted on white iron legs, two matching white iron chairs set across from each other. The two exterior walls of the alcove which prescribe a corner in the upstage right are composed of many small windows, beginning from a solid wall about three feet high and extending to the ceiling. The windows look out to bushes and citrus trees. The al-cove is filled with all sorts of house plants in various pots, mostly Boston ferns hanging in planters at different levels. The floor of the alcove is composed of green synthetic grass.*

All entrances and exits are made stage left from the kitchen. There is no door. The actors simply go off and come onto the playing area.

NOTE ON SET AND COSTUME: *The set should be constructed realistically with no attempt to distort its dimensions, shapes, objects, or colors. No objects should be introduced which might draw special attention to themselves other than the props demanded by the script. If a stylistic "concept" is grafted onto the set design it will only serve to confuse the evolution of the characters' situation, which is the most important focus of the play.*

Likewise, the costumes should be exactly representative of who the characters are and not added onto for the sake of making a point to the audience.

NOTE ON SOUND: *The Coyote of Southern California has a distinct yapping, dog-like bark, similar to a Hyena. This yapping grows more intense and maniacal as the pack grows in numbers, which is usually the case when they lure and kill pets from suburban yards. The sense of growing frenzy in the pack should be felt in the background, particularly in Scenes 7 and 8. In any case, these Coyotes never make the long, mournful, solitary howl of the Hollywood stereotype.*

The sound of Crickets can speak for itself.

These sounds should also be treated realistically even though they sometimes grow in volume and numbers.

719

ACT I

SCENE 1

Night. Sound of crickets in dark. Candlelight appears in alcove, illuminating Austin, seated at glass table hunched over a writing notebook, pen in hand, cigarette burning in ashtray, cup of coffee, typewriter on table, stacks of paper, candle burning on table.

Soft moonlight fills kitchen illuminting Lee, beer in hand, six-pack on counter behind him. He's leaning against the sink, mildly drunk; takes a slug of beer.

LEE. So, Mom took off for Alaska, huh?

AUSTIN. Yeah.

LEE. Sorta' left you in charge.

AUSTIN. Well, she knew I was coming down here so she offered me the place.

LEE. You keepin' the plants watered?

AUSTIN. Yeah.

LEE. Keepin' the sink clean? She don't like even a single tea leaf in the sink ya' know.

AUSTIN (*trying to concentrate on writing*). Yeah, I know.

(*pause*)

LEE. She gonna' be up there a long time?

AUSTIN. I don't know.

LEE. Kinda' nice for you, huh? Whole place to yourself.

AUSTIN. Yeah, it's great.

LEE. Ya' got crickets anyway. Tons a' crickets out there. (*looks around kitchen*) Ya' got groceries? Coffee?

AUSTIN (*looking up from writing*). What?

LEE. You got coffee?

AUSTIN. Yeah.

LEE. At's good. (*short pause*) Real coffee? From the bean?

AUSTIN. Yeah. You want some?

LEE. Naw. I brought some uh—(*motions to beer*)

AUSTIN. Help yourself to whatever's—(*motions to refrigerator*)

LEE. I will. Don't worry about me. I'm not the one to worry about. I mean I can uh—(*pause*) You always work by candlelight?

AUSTIN. No—uh—not always.

LEE. Just sometimes?

AUSTIN (*puts pen down, rubs his eyes*). Yeah. Sometimes it's soothing.

LEE. Isn't that what the old guys did?

AUSTIN. What old guys?

LEE. The Forefathers. You know.

AUSTIN. Forefathers?

LEE. Isn't that what they did? Candlelight burning into the night? Cabins in the wilderness.

AUSTIN (*rubs hand through his hair*). I suppose.

LEE. I'm not botherin' you am I? I mean I don't wanna break into yer uh—concentration or nothin'.

AUSTIN. No, it's all right.

LEE. That's good. I mean I realize that yer line a' work demands a lota' concentration.

AUSTIN. It's okay.

LEE. You probably think that I'm not fully able to comprehend somethin' like that, huh?

AUSTIN. Like what?

LEE. That stuff yer doin'. That art. You know. Whatever you call it.

AUSTIN. It's just a little research.

LEE. You may not know it but I did a little art myself once.

AUSTIN. You did?

LEE. Yeah! I did some a' that. I fooled around with it. No future in it.

AUSTIN. What'd you do?

LEE. Never mind what I did! Just never mind about that. (*pause*) It was ahead of its time.

(*pause*)

AUSTIN. So, you went out to see the old man, huh?

LEE. Yeah, I seen him.

AUSTIN. How's he doing?

LEE. Same. He's doin' just about the same.

AUSTIN. I was down there too, you know.

LEE. What d'ya' want, an award? You want some kinda' medal? You were down there. He told me all about you.

AUSTIN. What'd he say?

LEE. He told me. Don't worry.

(*pause*)

AUSTIN. Well—

LEE. You don't have to say nothin'.

AUSTIN. I wasn't.

LEE. Yeah, you were gonna' make somethin' up. Somethin' brilliant.

(*pause*)

AUSTIN. You going to be down here very long, Lee?

LEE. Might be. Depends on a few things.

AUSTIN. You got some friends down here?

LEE (*laughs*). I know a few people. Yeah.

AUSTIN. Well, you can stay here as long as I'm here.

LEE. I don't need your permission do I?

AUSTIN. No.

LEE. I mean she's my mother too, right?

AUSTIN. Right.

LEE. She might've just as easily asked me to take care of her place as you.

AUSTIN. That's right.

LEE. I mean I know how to water plants.

(long pause)

AUSTIN. So you don't know how long you'll be staying then?

LEE. Depends mostly on houses, ya' know.

AUSTIN. Houses?

LEE. Yeah. Houses. Electric devices. Stuff like that. I gotta' make a little tour first.

(short pause)

AUSTIN. Lee, why don't you just try another neighborhood, all right?

LEE (laughs). What'sa' matter with this neighborhood? This is a great neighborhood. Lush. Good class a' people. Not many dogs.

AUSTIN. Well, our uh—Our mother just happens to live here. That's all.

LEE. Nobody's gonna' know. All they know is somethin's missing. That's all. She'll never even hear about it. Nobody's gonna' know.

AUSTIN. You're going to get picked up if you start walking around here at night.

LEE. Me? I'm gonna' git picked up? What about you? You stick out like a sore thumb. Look at you. You think yer regular lookin'?

AUSTIN. I've got too much to deal with here to be worrying about—

LEE. Yer not gonna' have to worry about me! I've been doin' all right without you. I haven't been anywhere near you for five years! Now isn't that true?

AUSTIN. Yeah.

LEE. So you don't have to worry about me. I'm a free agent.

AUSTIN. All right.

LEE. Now all I wanna' do is borrow yer car.

AUSTIN. No!

LEE. Just fer a day. One day.

AUSTIN. No!

LEE. I won't take it outside a twenty mile radius. I promise ya'. You can check the speedometer.

AUSTIN. You're not borrowing my car! That's all there is to it.

(pause)

LEE. Then I'll just take the damn thing.

AUSTIN. Lee, look—I don't want any trouble, all right?

LEE. That's a dumb line. That is a dumb fuckin' line. You git paid fer dreamin' up a line like that?

AUSTIN. Look, I can give you some money if you need money.

(Lee suddenly lunges at Austin, grabs him violently by the shirt and shakes him with tremendous power)

LEE. Don't you say that to me! Don't you ever say that to me! (just as suddenly he turns him loose, pushes him away and backs off) You may be able to git away with that with the Old Man. Git him tanked up for a week! Buy him off with yer Hollywood blood money, but not me! I can git my own money my own way. Big money!

AUSTIN. I was just making an offer.

LEE. Yeah, well keep it to yourself!

(long pause)

Those are the most monotonous fuckin' crickets I ever heard in my life.

AUSTIN. I kinda' like the sound.

LEE. Yeah. Supposed to be able to tell the temperature by the number a' pulses. You believe that?

AUSTIN. The temperature?

LEE. Yeah. The air. How hot it is.

AUSTIN. How do you do that?

LEE. I don't know. Some woman told me that. She was a Botanist. So I believed her.

AUSTIN. Where'd you meet her?

LEE. What?

AUSTIN. The woman Botanist?

LEE. I met her on the desert. I been spendin' a lota' time on the desert.

AUSTIN. What were you doing out there?

LEE (pause, stares in space). I forgit. Had me a Pit Bull there for a while but I lost him.

AUSTIN. Pit Bull?

LEE. Fightin' dog. Damn I made some good money off that little dog. Real good money.

(pause)

AUSTIN. You could come up north with me, you know.

LEE. What's up there?

AUSTIN. My family.

LEE. Oh, that's right, you got the wife and kiddies now don't ya'. The house, the car, the whole slam. That's right.

AUSTIN. You could spend a couple days. See how you like it. I've got an extra room.

LEE. Too cold up there.

(*pause*)

AUSTIN. You want to sleep for a while?

LEE (*pause, stares at Austin*). I don't sleep.

(*lights to black*)

SCENE 2

Morning. Austin is watering plants with a vaporizer,
Lee sits at glass table in alcove drinking beer.

LEE. I never realized the old lady was so security-minded.

AUSTIN. How do you mean?

LEE. Made a little tour this morning. She's got locks on everything. Locks and double-locks and chain locks and—What's she got that's so valuable?

AUSTIN. Antiques I guess. I don't know.

LEE. Antiques? Brought everything with her from the old place, huh. Just the same crap we always had around. Plates and spoons.

AUSTIN. I guess they have personal value to her.

LEE. Personal value. Yeah. Just a lota' junk. Most of it's phony anyway. Idaho decals. Now who in the hell wants to eat offa' plate with the State of Idaho starin' ya' in the face. Every time ya' take a bite ya' get to see a little bit more.

AUSTIN. Well it must mean something to her or she wouldn't save it.

LEE. Yeah, well personally I don't wann' be invaded by Idaho when I'm eatin'. When I'm eatin' I'm home. Ya' know what I'm sayin'? I'm not driftin', I'm home. I don't need my thoughts swept off to Idaho. I don't need that!

(*pause*)

AUSTIN. Did you go out last night?

LEE. Why?

AUSTIN. I thought I heard you go out.

LEE. Yeah, I went out. What about it?

AUSTIN. Just wondered.

LEE. Damn coyotes kept me awake.

AUSTIN. Oh yeah, I heard them. They must've killed somebody's dog or something.

LEE. Yappin' their fool heads off. They don't yap like that on the desert. They howl! These are city coyotes here.

AUSTIN. Well, you don't sleep anyway do you?

(*pause, Lee stares at him*)

LEE. You're pretty smart aren't ya?

AUSTIN. How do you mean?

LEE. I mean you never had any more on the ball than I did. But here you are gettin' invited into prominent people's houses. Sittin' around talkin' like you know somethin'.

AUSTIN. They're not so prominent.

LEE. They're a helluva' lot more prominent than the houses I get invited into.

AUSTIN. Well you invite yourself.

LEE. That's right. I do. In fact I probably got a wider range a' choices than you do, come to think of it.

AUSTIN. I wouldn't doubt it.

LEE. In fact I been inside some pretty classy places in my time. And I never even went to an Ivy League school either.

AUSTIN. You want some breakfast or something?

LEE. Breakfast?

AUSTIN. Yeah. Don't you eat breakfast?

LEE. Look, don't worry about me pal. I can take care a' myself. You just go ahead as though I wasn't even here, all right?

(*Austin goes into kitchen, makes coffee*)

AUSTIN. Where'd you walk to last night?

(*pause*)

LEE. I went up in the foothills there. Up in the San Gabriels. Heat was driven' me crazy.

AUSTIN. Well, wasn't it hot out on the desert?

LEE. Different kinda' heat. Out there it's clean. Cools off at night. There's a nice little breeze.

AUSTIN. Where were you, the Mojave?

LEE. Yeah. The Mojave. That's right.

AUSTIN. I haven't been out there in years.

LEE. Out past Needles there.

AUSTIN. Oh yeah.

LEE. Up here it's different. This country's real different.

AUSTIN. Well, it's been built up.

LEE. Built up? Wiped out is more like it. I don't even hardly recognize it.

AUSTIN. Yeah. Foothills are the same though, aren't they?

LEE. Pretty much. It's funny goin' up in there. The smells and everything. Used to catch snakes up there, remember?

AUSTIN. You caught snakes.

LEE. Yeah. And you'd pretend you were Geronimo or some damn thing. You used to go right out to lunch.

AUSTIN. I enjoyed my imagination.

LEE. That what you call it? Looks like yer still enjoyin' it.

AUSTIN. So you just wandered around up there, huh?

LEE. Yeah. With a purpose.

AUSTIN. See any houses?

(pause)

LEE. Couple. Couple a' real nice ones. One of 'em didn't even have a dog. Walked right up and stuck my head in the window. Not a peep. Just a sweet kinda' surburban silence.

AUSTIN. What kind of a place was it?

LEE. Like a paradise. Kinda' place that sorta' kills ya' inside. Warm yellow lights. Mexican tile all around. Copper pots hangin' over the stove. Ya' know like they got in the magazines. Blonde people movin' in and outa' the rooms, talkin' to each other. (pause) Kinda' place you wish you sorta' grew up in, ya know.

AUSTIN. That's the kind of place you wish you'd grown up in?

LEE. Yeah, why not?

AUSTIN. I thought you hated that kind of stuff.

LEE. Yeah, well you never knew too much about me did ya'?

(pause)

AUSTIN. Why'd you go out to the desert in the first place?

LEE. I was on my way to see the old man.

AUSTIN. You mean you just passed through there?

LEE. Yeah. That's right. Three months of passin' through.

AUSTIN. Three months?

LEE. Somethin' like that. Maybe more. Why?

AUSTIN. You lived on the Mojave for three months?

LEE. Yeah. What'sa' matter with that?

AUSTIN. By yourself?

LEE. Mostly. Had a couple a' visitors. Had that dog for a while.

AUSTIN. Didn't you miss people?

LEE (laughs). People?

AUSTIN. Yeah. I mean I go crazy if I have to spend three nights in a motel by myself.

LEE. Yer not in a motel now.

AUSTIN. No, I know. But sometimes I have to stay in motels.

LEE. Well, they got people in motels don't they?

AUSTIN. Strangers.

LEE. Yer friendly aren't ya'? Aren't you the friendly type?

(pause)

AUSTIN. I'm going to have somebody coming by here later, Lee.

LEE. Ah! Lady friend?

AUSTIN. No, a producer.

LEE. Aha! What's he produce?

AUSTIN. Film. Movies. You know.

LEE. Oh, movies. Motion Pictures! A Big Wig huh?

AUSTIN. Yeah.

LEE. What's he comin' by here for?

AUSTIN. We have to talk about a project.

LEE. Whadya' mean, "a project"? What's "a project"?

AUSTIN. A script.

LEE. Oh. That's what yer doin' with all these papers?

AUSTIN. Yeah.

LEE. Well, what's the project about?

AUSTIN. We're uh—it's a period piece.

LEE. What's a "period piece"?

AUSTIN. Look, it doesn't matter. The main thing is we need to discuss this alone. I mean—

LEE. Oh, I get it. You want me outa' the picture.

AUSTIN. Not exactly. I just need to be alone with him for a couple of hours. So we can talk.

LEE. Yer afraid I'll embarrass ya' huh?

AUSTIN. I'm not afraid you'll embarass me!

LEE. Well, I tell ya' what—Why don't you just gimme the keys to yer car and I'll be back here around six o'clock or so. That give ya' enough time?

AUSTIN. I'm not loaning you my car, Lee.

LEE. You want me to just git lost huh? Take a hike? Is that it? Pound the pavement for a few hours while you bullshit yer way into a million bucks.

AUSTIN. Look, it's going to be hard enough for me to face this character on my own without—

LEE. You don't know this guy?

AUSTIN. No I don't know—He's a producer. I mean I've been meeting with him for months but you never get to know a producer.

LEE. Yer tryin' to hustle him? Is that it?

AUSTIN. I'm not trying to hustle him! I'm trying to work out a deal! It's not easy.

LEE. What kinda' deal?

AUSTIN. Convince him it's a worthwhile story.

LEE. He's not convinced? How come he's comin' over here if he's not convinced? I'll convince him for ya'.

AUSTIN. You don't understand the way things work down here.

LEE. How do things work down here?

(pause)

AUSTIN. Look, if I loan you my car will you have it back here by six?

LEE. On the button. With a full tank a' gas.

AUSTIN (digging in his pocket for keys). Forget about the gas.

LEE. Hey, these days gas is gold, old buddy.

(*Austin hands the keys to Lee*)

You remember that car I used to loan you?
AUSTIN. Yeah.
LEE. Forty Ford. Flathead.
AUSTIN. Yeah.
LEE. Sucker hauled ass didn't it?
AUSTIN. Lee, it's not that I don't want to loan you my car—
LEE. You are loanin' me yer car.

(*Lee gives Austin a pat on the shoulder, pause*)

AUSTIN. I know. I just wish—
LEE. What? You wish what?
AUSTIN. I don't know. I wish I wasn't—I wish I didn't have to be doing business down here. I'd like to just spend some time with you.
LEE. I thought it was "Art" you were doin'.

(*Lee moves across kitchen toward exit, tosses keys in his hand*)

AUSTIN. Try to get it back here by six, okay?
LEE. No sweat. Hey, ya' know, if that uh—story of yours doesn't go over with the guy—tell him I got a couple a' "projects" he might be interested in. Real commercial. Full a' suspense. True-to-life stuff.

(*Lee exits, Austin stares after Lee then turns, goes to papers at table, leafs through pages, lights fade to black*)

SCENE 3

Afternoon. Alcove, Saul Kimmer and Austin seated across from each other at table.

SAUL. Well, to tell you the truth Austin, I have never felt so confident about a project in quite a long time.
AUSTIN. Well, that's good to hear, Saul.
SAUL. I am absolutely convinced we can get this thing off the ground. I mean we'll have to make a sale to television and that means getting a major star. Somebody bankable. But I think we can do it. I really do.
AUSTIN. Don't you think we need a first draft before we approach a star?
SAUL. No, no, not at all. I don't think it's necessary. Maybe a brief synopsis. I don't want you to touch the typewriter until we have some seed money.
AUSTIN. That's fine with me.
SAUL. I mean it's a great story. Just the story alone. You've really managed to capture something this time.

AUSTIN. I'm glad you like it, Saul.

(*Lee enters abruptly into kitchen carrying a stolen television set, short pause*)

LEE. Aw shit, I'm sorry about that. I am really sorry Austin.
AUSTIN (*standing*). That's all right.
LEE (*moving toward them*). I mean I thought it was way past six already. You said to have it back here by six.
AUSTIN. We were just finishing up. (*to Saul*) This is my, uh—brother, Lee.
SAUL (*standing*). Oh, I'm very happy to meet you.

(*Lee sets T.V. on sink counter, shakes hands with Saul*)

LEE. I can't tell ya' how happy I am to meet you sir.
SAUL. Saul Kimmer.
LEE. Mr. Kipper.
SAUL. Kimmer.
AUSTIN. Lee's been living out on the desert and he just uh—
SAUL. Oh, that's terrific! (*to Lee*) Palm Springs?
LEE. Yeah. Yeah, right. Right around in that area. Near uh—Bob Hope Drive there.
SAUL. Oh I love it out there. I just love it. The air is wonderful.
LEE. Yeah. Sure is. Healthy.
SAUL. And the golf. I don't know if you play golf, but the golf is just about the best.
LEE. I play a lota' golf.
SAUL. Is that right?
LEE. Yeah. In fact I was hoping I'd run into somebody out here who played a little golf. I've been lookin' for a partner.
SAUL. Well, I uh—
AUSTIN. Lee's just down for a visit while our mother's in Alaska.
SAUL. Oh, your mother's in Alaska?
AUSTIN. Yes. She went up there on a little vacation. This is her place.
SAUL. I see. Well isn't that something. Alaska.
LEE. What kinda' handicap do ya' have, Mr. Kimmer?
SAUL. Oh I'm just a Sunday duffer really. You know.
LEE. That's good 'cause I haven't swung a club in months.
SAUL. Well we ought to get together sometime and have a little game. Austin, do you play?

(*Saul mimes a Johnny Carson golf swing for Austin*)

AUSTIN. No. I don't uh—I've watched it on T.V.
LEE (*to Saul*). How 'bout tomorrow morning? Bright and early. We could get out there and put in eighteen holes before breakfast.

SAUL. Well, I've got uh—I have several appointments—

LEE. No, I mean real early. Crack a'dawn. While the dew's still thick on the fairway.

SAUL. Sounds really great.

LEE. Austin could be our caddie.

SAUL. Now that's an idea. (*laughs*)

AUSTIN. I don't know the first thing about golf.

LEE. There's nothin' to it. Isn't that right, Saul? He'd pick it up in fifteen minutes.

SAUL. Sure. Doesn't take long. 'Course you have to play for years to find your true form. (*chuckles*)

LEE (*to Austin*). We'll give ya' a quick run-down on the club faces. The irons, the woods. Show ya' a couple pointers on the basic swing. Might even let ya' hit the ball a couple times. Whatya' think, Saul?

SAUL. Why not. I think it'd be great. I haven't had any exercise in weeks.

LEE. 'At's the spirit! We'll have a little orange juice right afterwards.

(*pause*)

SAUL. Orange juice?

LEE. Yeah! Vitamin C! Nothin' like a shot a' orange juice after a round a' golf. Hot shower. Snappin' towels at each others' privates. Real sense a' fraternity.

SAUL (*smiles at Austin*). Well, you make it sound very inviting, I must say. It really does sound great.

LEE. Then it's a date.

SAUL. Well, I'll call the country club and see if I can arrange something.

LEE. Great! Boy, I sure am sorry that I busted in on ya' all in the middle of yer meeting.

SAUL. Oh that's quite all right. We were just about finished anyway.

LEE. I can wait out in the other room if you want.

SAUL. No really—

LEE. Just got Austin's color T.V. back from the shop. I can watch a little amateur boxing now.

(*Lee and Austin exchange looks*)

SAUL. Oh—Yes.

LEE. You don't fool around in Television, do you Saul?

SAUL. Uh—I have in the past. Produced some T.V. Specials. Network stuff. But it's mainly features now.

LEE. That's where the big money is, huh?

SAUL. Yes. That's right.

AUSTIN. Why don't I call you tomorrow, Saul and we'll get together. We can have lunch or something.

SAUL. That'd be terrific.

LEE. Right after the golf.

(*pause*)

SAUL. What?

LEE. You can have lunch right after the golf.

SAUL. Oh, right.

LEE. Austin was tellin' me that yer interested in stories.

SAUL. Well, we develop certain projects that we feel have commercial potential.

LEE. What kinda' stuff do ya' go in for?

SAUL. Oh, the usual. You know. Good love interest. Lots of action. (*chuckles at Austin*)

LEE. Westerns?

SAUL. Sometimes.

AUSTIN. I'll give you a ring, Saul.

(*Austin tries to move Saul acrosss the kitchen but Lee blocks their way*)

LEE. I got a Western that'd knock yer lights out.

SAUL. Oh really?

LEE. Yeah. Contemporary Western. Based on a true story. 'Course I'm not a writer like my brother here. I'm not a man of the pen.

SAUL. Well—

LEE. I mean I can tell ya' a story off the tongue but I can't put it down on paper. That don't make any difference though does it?

SAUL. No, not really.

LEE. I mean plenty a' guys have stories don't they? True-life stories. Musta' been a lota' movies made from real life.

SAUL. Yes. I suppose so.

LEE. I haven't seen a good Western since "Lonely Are the Brave." You remember that movie?

SAUL. No, I'm afraid I—

LEE. Kirk Douglas. Helluva' movie. You remember that movie, Austin?

AUSTIN. Yes.

LEE (*to Saul*). The man dies for the love of a horse.

SAUL. Is that right.

LEE. Yeah. Ya' hear the horse screamin' at the end of it. Rain's comin' down. Horse is screamin'. Then there's a shot. BLAM! Just a single shot like that. Then nothin' but the sound of rain. And Kirk Douglas is ridin' in the ambulance. Ridin' away from the scene of the accident. And when he hears that shot he knows that his horse has died. He knows. And you see his eyes. And his eyes die. Right inside his face. And then his eyes close. And you know that he's died too. You know that Kirk Douglas has died from the death of his horse.

SAUL (*eyes Austin nervously*). Well, it sounds like a great movie. I'm sorry I missed it.

LEE. Yeah, you shouldn't a' missed that one.

SAUL. I'll have to try to catch it some time. Arrange a screening or something. Well, Austin, I'll have to hit the freeway before rush hour.

AUSTIN (*ushers him toward exit*). It's good seeing you, Saul.

(*Austin and Saul shake hands*)

LEE. So ya' think there's room for a real Western these days? A true-to-life Western?

SAUL. Well, I don't see why not. Why don't you uh—tell the story to Austin and have him write a little outline.

LEE. You'd take a look at it then?

SAUL. Yes. Sure. I'll give it a read-through. Always eager for new material. (*smiles at Austin*)

LEE. That's great! You'd really read it then huh?

SAUL. It would just be my opinion of course.

LEE. That's all I want. Just an opinion. I happen to think it has a lota' possibilities.

SAUL. Well, it was great meeting you and I'll—

(*Saul and Lee shake*)

LEE. I'll call you tomorrow about the golf.

SAUL. Oh. Yes, right.

LEE. Austin's got your number, right?

SAUL. Yes.

LEE. So long Saul. (*gives Saul a pat on the back*)

(*Saul exits, Austin turns to Lee, looks at T.V. then back to Lee*)

AUSTIN. Give me the keys.

(*Austin extends his hand toward Lee, Lee doesn't move, just stares at Austin, smiles, lights to black*)

SCENE 4

Night. Coyotes in distance, fade, sound of type-writer in dark, crickets, candlelight in alcove, dim light in kitchen, lights reveal Austin at glass table typing, Lee sits aross from him, foot on table, drinking beer and whiskey, the T.V. is still on sink counter, Austin types for a while, then stops.

LEE. All right, now read it back to me.

AUSTIN. I'm not reading it back to you, Lee. You can read it when we're finished. I can't spend all night on this.

LEE. You got better things to do?

AUSTIN. Let's just go ahead. Now what happens when he leaves Texas?

LEE. Is he ready to leave Texas yet? I didn't know we were that far along. He's not ready to leave Texas.

AUSTIN. He's right at the border.

LEE (*sitting up*). No, see this is one a' the crucial parts. Right here. (*taps paper with beer can*) We can't rush through this. He's not right at the border. He's a good fifty miles from the border. A lot can happen in fifty miles.

AUSTIN. It's only an outline. We're not writing an entire script now.

LEE. Well ya' can't leave things out even if it is an outline. It's one a' the most important parts. Ya' can't go leavin' it out.

AUSTIN. Okay, okay. Let's just—get it done.

LEE. All right. Now. He's in the truck and he's got his horse trailer and his horse.

AUSTIN. We've already established that.

LEE. And he sees this other guy comin' up behind him in another truck. And that truck is pullin' a gooseneck.

AUSTIN. What's a gooseneck?

LEE. Cattle trailer. You know the kind with a gooseneck, goes right down in the bed a' the pick-up.

AUSTIN. Oh. All right. (*types*)

LEE. It's important.

AUSTIN. Okay. I got it.

LEE. All these details are important.

(*Austin types as they talk*)

AUSTIN. I've got it.

LEE. And this other guy's got his horse all saddled up in the back a' the gooseneck.

AUSTIN. Right.

LEE. So both these guys have got their horses right along with 'em, see.

AUSTIN. I understand.

LEE. Then this first guy suddenly realizes two things.

AUSTIN. The guy in front?

LEE. Right. The guy in front realizes two things almost at the same time. Simultaneous.

AUSTIN. What were the two things?

LEE. Number one, he realizes that the guy behind him is the husband of the woman he's been—

(*Lee makes gesture of screwing by pumping his arm*)

AUSTIN (*sees Lee's gesture*). Oh. Yeah.

LEE. And number two, he realizes he's in the middle of Tornado Country.

AUSTIN. What's "Tornado Country"?

LEE. Panhandle.

AUSTIN. Panhandle?

LEE. Sweetwater. Around in that area. Nothin'. Nowhere. And number three—

AUSTIN. I thought there was only two.

LEE. There's three. There's a third unforseen realization.

AUSTIN. And what's that?

LEE. That he's runnin' outa' gas.

AUSTIN (*stops typing*). Come on, Lee.

(*Austin gets up, moves to kitchen, gets a glass of water*)

LEE. Whadya' mean, "come on"? That's what it is. Write it down! He's runnin' outa' gas.

AUSTIN. It's too—

LEE. What? It's too what? It's too real! That's what ya' mean isn't it? It's too much like real life!

AUSTIN. It's not like real life! It's not enough like real life. Things don't happen like that.

LEE. What! Men don't fuck other men's women?

AUSTIN. Yes. But they don't end up chasing each other across the Panhandle. Through "Tornado Country."

LEE. They do in this movie!

AUSTIN. And they don't have horses conveniently along with them when they run out of gas! And they don't run out of gas either!

LEE. These guys run outa' gas! This is my story and one a' these guys runs outa' gas!

AUSTIN. It's just a dumb excuse to get them into a chase scene. It's contrived.

LEE. It is a chase scene! It's already a chase scene. They been chasin' each other fer days.

AUSTIN. So now they're supposed to abandon their trucks, climb on their horses and chase each other into the mountains?

LEE (*standing suddenly*). There aren't any mountains in the Panhandle! It's flat!

(*Lee turns violently toward windows in alcove and throws beer can at them*)

LEE. Goddam these crickets! (*yells at crickets*) Shut up out there! (*pause, turns back toward table*) This place is like a fuckin' rest home here. How're you supposed to think!

AUSTIN. You wanna' take a break?

LEE. No, I don't wanna' take a break! I wanna' get this done! This is my last chance to get this done.

AUSTIN (*moves back into alcove*). All right. Take it easy.

LEE. I'm gonna' be leavin' this area. I don't have time to mess around here.

AUSTIN. Where are you going?

LEE. Never mind where I'm goin'! That's got nothin' to do with you. I just gotta' get this done. I'm not like you. Hangin' around bein' a parasite offa' other fools. I gotta' do this thing and get out.

(*pause*)

AUSTIN. A parasite? Me?

LEE. Yeah, you!

AUSTIN. After you break into people's houses and take their televisions?

LEE. They don't need their televisions! I'm doin' them a service.

AUSTIN. Give me back my keys, Lee.

LEE. Not until you write this thing! You're gonna' write this outline thing for me or that car's gonna' wind up in Arizona with a different paint job.

AUSTIN. You think you can force me to write this? I was doing you a favor.

LEE. Git off yer high horse will ya'! Favor! Big favor. Handin' down favors from the mountain top.

AUSTIN. Let's just write it, okay? Let's sit down and not get upset and see if we can just get through this.

(*Austin sits at typewriter*)

(*long pause*)

LEE. Yer not gonna' even show it to him, are ya'?

AUSTIN. What?

LEE. This outline. You got no intention of showin' it to him. Yer just doin' this 'cause yer afraid a' me.

AUSTIN. You can show it to him yourself.

LEE. I will, boy! I'm gonna' read it to him on the golf course.

AUSTIN. And I'm not afraid of you either.

LEE. Then how come yer doin' it?

AUSTIN (*pause*). So I can get my keys back.

(*pause as Lee takes keys out of his pocket slowly and throws them on table, long pause, Austin stares at keys*)

LEE. There. Now you got yer keys back.

(*Austin looks up at Lee but doesn't take keys*)

LEE. Go ahead. There's yer keys.

(*Austin slowly takes keys off table and puts them back in his own pocket*)

Now what're you gonna' do? Kick me out?

AUSTIN. I'm not going to kick you out, Lee.

LEE. You couldn't kick me out, boy.

AUSTIN. I know.

LEE. So you can't even consider that one. (*pause*) You could call the police. That'd be the obvious thing.

AUSTIN. You're my brother.

LEE. That don't mean a thing. You go down to the L.A. Police Department there and ask them what kinda' people kill each other the most. What do you think they'd say?

AUSTIN. Who said anything about killing?

LEE. Family people. Brothers. Brothers-in-law. Cousins. Real American-type people. They kill each other in the heat mostly. In the Smog-Alerts. In the Brush Fire Season. Right about this time a' year.

AUSTIN. This isn't the same.

LEE. Oh no? What makes it different?

AUSTIN. We're not insane. We're not driven to acts of violence like that. Not over a dumb movie script. Now sit down.

(long pause, Lee considers which way to go with it)

LEE. Maybe not. *(he sits back down at table across from Austin)* Maybe you're right. Maybe we're too intelligent, huh? *(pause)* We got our heads on our shoulders. One of us has even got a Ivy League diploma. Now that means somethin' don't it? Doesn't that mean somethin'?

AUSTIN. Look, I'll write this thing for you, Lee. I don't mind writing it. I just don't want to get all worked up about it. It's not worth it. Now, come on. Let's just get through it, okay?

LEE. Nah. I think there's easier money. Lotsa' places I could pick up thousands. Maybe millions. I don't need this shit. I could go up to Sacramento Valley and steal me a diesel. Ten thousand a week dismantling one a' those suckers. Ten thousand a week!

(Lee opens another beer, puts his foot back up on table)

AUSTIN. No, really, look, I'll write it out for you. I think it's a great idea.

LEE. Nah, you got yer own work to do. I don't wanna' interfere with yer life.

AUSTIN. I mean it'd be really fantastic if you could sell this. Turn it into a movie. I mean it.

(pause)

LEE. Ya' think so huh?

AUSTIN. Absolutely. You could really turn your life around, you know. Change things.

LEE. I could get me a house maybe.

AUSTIN. Sure you could get a house. You could get a whole ranch if you wanted to.

LEE *(laughs)*. A ranch? I could get a ranch?

AUSTIN. 'Course you could. You know what a screenplay sells for these days?

LEE. No. What's it sell for?

AUSTIN. A lot. A whole lot of money.

LEE. Thousands?

AUSTIN. Yeah. Thousands.

LEE. Millions?

AUSTIN. Well—

LEE. We could get the old man outa' hock then.

AUSTIN. Maybe.

LEE. Maybe? Whadya' mean, maybe?

AUSTIN. I mean it might take more than money.

LEE. You were just tellin' me it'd change my whole life around. Why wouldn't it change his?

AUSTIN. He's different.

LEE. Oh, he's of a different ilk huh?

AUSTIN. He's not gonna' change. Let's leave the old man out of it.

LEE. That's right. He's not gonna' change but I will. I'll just turn myself right inside out. I could be just like you then, huh? Sittin' around dreamin' stuff up. Gettin' paid to dream. Ridin' back and forth on the freeway just dreamin' my fool head off.

AUSTIN. It's not all that easy.

LEE. It's not, huh?

AUSTIN. No. There's a lot of work involved.

LEE. What's the toughest part? Deciding whether to jog or play tennis?

(long pause)

AUSTIN. Well, look. You can stay here—do whatever you want to. Borrow the car. Come in and out. Doesn't matter to me. It's not my house. I'll help you write this thing or—not. Just let me know what you want. You tell me.

LEE. Oh. So now suddenly you're at my service. Is that it?

AUSTIN. What do you want to do Lee?

(long pause, Lee stares at him then turns and dreams at windows)

LEE. I tell ya' what I'd do if I still had that dog. Ya' wanna' know what I'd do?

AUSTIN. What?

LEE. Head out to Ventura. Cook up a little match. God that little dog could bear down. Lota' money in dog fightin'. Big money.

(pause)

AUSTIN. Why don't we try to see this through, Lee. Just for the hell of it. Maybe you've really got something here. What do you think?

(pause, Lee considers)

LEE. Maybe so. No harm in tryin' I guess. You think it's such a hot idea. Besides, I always wondered what'd be like to be you.

AUSTIN. You did?

LEE. Yeah, sure. I used to picture you walkin' around some campus with yer arms fulla' books. Blondes chasin' after ya'.

AUSTIN. Blondes? That's funny.

LEE. What's funny about it?

AUSTIN. Because I always used to picture you somewhere.

LEE. Where'd you picture me?

AUSTIN. Oh, I don't know. Different places. Adventures. You were always on some adventure.

LEE. Yeah.

AUSTIN. And I used to say to myself, "Lee's got the right idea. He's out there in the world and here I am. What am I doing?"

LEE. Well you were settin' yourself up for somethin'.

AUSTIN. I guess.

LEE. We better get started on this thing then.

AUSTIN. Okay.

(Austin sits up at typewriter, puts new paper in)

LEE. Oh. Can I get the keys back before I forget?

(Austin hesitates)

You said I could borrow the car if I wanted, right? Isn't that what you said?

AUSTIN. Yeah. Right.

(Austin takes keys out of his pocket, sets them on table, Lee takes keys slowly, plays with them in his hand)

LEE. I could get a ranch, huh?

AUSTIN. Yeah. We have to write it first though.

LEE. Okay. Let's write it.

(lights start dimming slowly to end of scene as Austin types, Lee speaks)

So they take off after each other straight into an endless black prairie. The sun is just comin' down and they can feel the night on their backs. What they don't know is that each one of 'em is afraid, see. Each one separately thinks that he's the only one that's afraid. And they keep ridin' like that straight into the night. Not knowing. And the one who's chasin' doesn't know where the other one is taking him. And the one who's being chased doesn't know where he's going.

(lights to black, typing stops in the dark, crickets fade)

ACT II

SCENE 5

Morning. Lee at the table in alcove with a set of golf clubs in a fancy leather bag, Austin at sink washing a few dishes.

AUSTIN. He really liked it, huh?

LEE. He wouldn't a' gave me these clubs if he didn't like it.

AUSTIN. He gave you the clubs?

LEE. Yeah. I told ya' he gave me the clubs. The bag too.

AUSTIN. I thought he just loaned them to you.

LEE. He said it was part a' the advance. A little gift like. Gesture of his good faith.

AUSTIN. He's giving you an advance?

LEE. Now what's so amazing about that? I told ya' it was a good story. You even said it was a good story.

AUSTIN. Well that is really incredible Lee. You know how many guys spend their whole lives down here trying to break into this business? Just trying to get in the door?

LEE *(pulling clubs out of bag, testing them)*. I got no idea. How many?

(pause)

AUSTIN. How much of an advance is he giving you?

LEE. Plenty. We were talkin' big money out there. Ninth hole is where I sealed the deal.

AUSTIN. He made a firm commitment?

LEE. Absolutely.

AUSTIN. Well, I know Saul and he doesn't fool around when he says he likes something.

LEE. I thought you said you didn't know him.

AUSTIN. Well, I'm familiar with his tastes.

LEE. I let him get two up on me goin' into the back nine. He was sure he had me cold. You shoulda' seen his face when I pulled out the old pitching wedge and plopped it pin-high, two feet from the cup. He 'bout shit his pants. "Where'd a guy like you ever learn how to play golf like that?" he says.

(Lee laughs, Austin stares at him)

AUSTIN. 'Course there's no contract yet. Nothing's final until it's on paper.

LEE. It's final, all right. There's no way he's gonna' back out of it now. We gambled for it.

AUSTIN. Saul, gambled?

LEE. Yeah, sure. I mean he liked the outline already so he wasn't risking that much. I just guaranteed it with my short game.

(pause)

AUSTIN. Well, we should celebrate or something. I think Mom left a bottle of champagne in the refrigerator. We should have a little toast.

(Austin gets glasses from cupboard, goes to refrigerator, pulls out bottle of champagne)

LEE. You shouldn't oughta' take her champagne, Austin. She's gonna' miss that.

AUSTIN. Oh, she's not going to mind. She'd be glad we put it to good use. I'll get her another bottle. Besides, it's perfect for the occasion.

(pause)

LEE. Yer gonna' get a nice fee fer writin' the script a' course. Straight fee.

(Austin stops, stares at Lee, puts glasses and bottle on table, pause)

AUSTIN. I'm writing the script?

LEE. That's what he said. Said we couldn't hire a better screenwriter in the whole town.

AUSTIN. But I'm already working on a script. I've got my own project. I don't have time to write two scripts.

LEE. No, he said he was gonna' drop that other one.

(pause)

AUSTIN. What? You mean mine? He's going to drop mine and do yours instead?

LEE *(smiles)*. Now look, Austin, it's jest beginner's luck ya' know. I mean I sank a fifty foot putt for this deal. No hard feelings.

(Austin goes to phone on wall, grabs it, starts dialing)

He's not gonna' be in, Austin. Told me he wouldn't be in 'till late this afternoon.

AUSTIN *(stays on phone, dialing, listens)*. I can't believe this. I just can't believe it. Are you sure he said that? Why would he drop mine?

LEE. That's what he told me.

AUSTIN. He can't do that without telling me first. Without talking to me at least. He wouldn't just make a decision like that without talking to me!

LEE. Well I was kinda' surprised myself. But he was real enthusiastic about my story.

(Austin hangs up phone violently, paces)

AUSTIN. What'd he say! Tell me everything he said!

LEE. I been tellin' ya'! He said he liked the story a whole lot. It was the first authentic Western to come along in a decade.

AUSTIN. He liked that story! Your story?

LEE. Yeah! What's so surprisin' about that?

AUSTIN. It's stupid! It's the dumbest story I ever heard in my life.

LEE. Hey, hold on! That's my story yer talkin' about!

AUSTIN. It's a bullshit story! It's idiotic. Two lamebrains chasing each other across Texas! Are you kidding? Who do you think's going to go see a film like that?

LEE. It's not a film! It's a movie. There's a big difference. That's somethin' Saul told me.

AUSTIN. Oh he did, huh?

LEE. Yeah, he said, "In this business we make movies, American movies. Leave the films to the French."

AUSTIN. So you got real intimate with old Saul huh? He started pouring forth his vast knowledge of Cinema.

LEE. I think he liked me a lot, to tell ya' the truth. I think he felt I was somebody he could confide in.

AUSTIN. What'd you do, beat him up or something?

LEE *(stands fast)*. Hey, I've about had it with the insults buddy! You think yer the only one in the brain department here? Yer the only one that can sit around and cook things up? There's other people got ideas too, ya' know!

AUSTIN. You must've done something. Threatened him or something. Now what'd you do Lee?

LEE. I convinced him!

(Lee makes sudden menacing lunge toward Austin, wielding golf club above his head, stops himself, frozen moment, long pause, Lee lowers club)

AUSTIN. Oh, Jesus. You didn't hurt him did you?

(long silence, Lee sits back down at table)

Lee! Did you hurt him?

LEE. I didn't do nothin' to him! He liked my story. Pure and simple. He said it was the best story he's come across in a long, long time.

AUSTIN. That's what he told me about my story! That's the same thing he said to me.

LEE. Well, he musta' been lyin'. He musta' been lyin' to one of us anyway.

AUSTIN. You can't come into this town and start pushing people around. They're gonna' put you away!

LEE. I never pushed anybody around! I beat him fair and square. *(pause)* They can't touch me anyway. They can't put a finger on me. I'm gone. I can come in through the window and go out through the door. They never knew what hit 'em. You, yer stuck. Yer the one that's stuck. Not me. So don't be warnin' me what to do in this town.

(pause, Austin crosses to table, sits at typewriter, rests)

AUSTIN. Lee, come on, level with me will you? It doesn't make any sense that suddenly he'd throw my idea out the window. I've been talking to him for months. I've got too much at stake. Everything's riding on this project.

LEE. What's yer idea?

AUSTIN. It's just a simple love story.

LEE. What kinda' love story?

AUSTIN *(stands, crosses into kitchen)*. I'm not telling you!

LEE. Ha! 'Fraid I'll steal it huh? Competition's gettin' kinda' close to home isn't it?

AUSTIN. Where did Saul say he was going?

LEE. He was gonna' take my story to a couple studios.

AUSTIN. That's *my* outline you know! I wrote that outline! You've got no right to be peddling it around.

LEE. You weren't ready to take credit for it last night.

AUSTIN. Give me my keys!

LEE. What?

AUSTIN. The keys! I want my keys back!

LEE. Where you goin'?

AUSTIN. Just give me my keys! I gotta' take a drive. I gotta' get out of here for a while.

LEE. Where you gonna' go, Austin?

AUSTIN *(pause)*. I might just drive out to the desert for a while. I gotta' think.

LEE. You can think here just as good. This is the perfect setup for thinkin'. We got some writin' to do here, boy. Now let's just have us a little toast. Relax. We're partners now.

(Lee pops the cork of the champagne bottle, pours two drinks as the lights fade to black)

SCENE 6

Afternoon. Lee and Saul in kitchen, Austin in alcove

LEE. Now you tell him. You tell him, Mr. Kipper.

SAUL. Kimmer.

LEE. Kimmer. You tell him what you told me. He don't believe me.

AUSTIN. I don't want to hear it.

SAUL. It's really not a big issue, Austin. I was simply amazed by your brother's story and—

AUSTIN. Amazed? You lost a bet! You gambled with my material!

SAUL. That's really beside the point, Austin. I'm ready to go all the way with your brother's story. I think it has a great deal of merit.

AUSTIN. I don't want to hear about it, okay? Go tell it to the executives! Tell it to somebody who's going to turn it into a package deal or something. A T.V. series. Don't tell it to me.

SAUL. But I want to continue with your project too, Austin. It's not as though we can't do both. We're big enough for that aren't we?

AUSTIN. "We"? *I* can't do both! I don't know about "we."

LEE *(to Saul)*. See, what'd I tell ya'. He's totally unsympathetic.

SAUL. Austin, there's no point in our going to another screenwriter for this. It just doesn't make sense. You're brothers. You know each other. There's a familiarity with the material that just wouldn't be possible otherwise.

AUSTIN. There's no familiarity with the material! None! I don't know what "Tornado Country" is. I don't know what a "gooseneck" is. And I don't want to know! *(pointing to Lee)* He's a hustler! He's a bigger hustler than you are! If you can't see that, then—

LEE *(to Austin)*. Hey, now hold on. I didn't have to bring this bone back to you, boy. I persuaded Saul here that you were the right man for the job. You don't have to go throwin' up favors in my face.

AUSTIN. Favors! I'm the one who wrote the fuckin' outline! You can't even spell.

SAUL *(to Austin)*. Your brother told me about the situation with your father.

(pause)

AUSTIN. What? *(looks at Lee)*

SAUL. That's right. Now we have a clear-cut deal here, Austin. We have big studio money standing behind this thing. Just on the basis of your outline.

AUSTIN *(to Saul)*. What'd he tell you about my father?

SAUL. Well—that he's destitute. He needs money.

LEE. That's right. He does.

(Austin shakes his head, stares at them both)

AUSTIN *(to Lee)*. And this little assignment is supposed to go toward the old man? A charity project? Is that what this is? Did you cook this up on the ninth green too?

SAUL. It's a big slice, Austin.

AUSTIN *(to Lee)*. I gave him money! I already gave him money. You know that. He drank it all up!

LEE. This is a different deal here.

SAUL. We can set up a trust for your father. A large sum of money. It can be doled out to him in paracels so he can't misuse it.

AUSTIN. Yeah, and who's doing the doling?

SAUL. Your brother volunteered.

(Austin laughs)

LEE. That's right. I'll make sure he uses it for groceries.

AUSTIN *(to Saul)*. I'm not doing this script! I'm not writing this crap for you or anybody else. You can't blackmail me into it. You can't threaten me into it. There's no way I'm doing it. So just give it up. Both of you.

(long pause)

SAUL. Well, that's it then. I mean this is an easy three hundred grand. Just for a first draft. It's incredible, Austin. We've got three different studios all trying to cut each other's throats to get this material. In one morning. That's how hot it is.

AUSTIN. Yeah, well you can afford to give me a percentage on the outline then. And you better get the genius here an agent before he gets burned.

LEE. Saul's gonna' be my agent. Isn't that right, Saul?

SAUL. That's right. *(to Austin)* Your brother has really got something, Austin. I've been around too long not to recognize it. Raw talent.

AUSTIN. He's got a lota' balls is what he's got. He's taking you right down the river.

SAUL. Three hundred thousand, Austin. Just for a first draft. Now you've never been offered that kind of money before.

AUSTIN. I'm not writing it.

(pause)

SAUL. I see. Well—

LEE. We'll just go to another writer then. Right, Saul? Just hire us somebody with some enthusiasm. Somebody who can recognize the value of a good story.

SAUL. I'm sorry about this, Austin.

AUSTIN. Yeah.

SAUL. I mean I was hoping we could continue both things but now I don't see how it's posssible.

AUSTIN. So you're dropping my idea altogether. Is that it? Just trade horses in midstream? After all these months of meetings.

SAUL. I wish there was another way.

AUSTIN. I've got everything riding on this, Saul. You know that. It's my only shot. If this falls through—

SAUL. I have to go with what my instincts tell me—

AUSTIN. Your instincts!

SAUL. My gut reaction.

AUSTIN. You lost! That's your gut reaction. You lost a gamble. Now you're trying to tell me you like his story? How could you possibly fall for that story? It's

as phony as Hoppalong Cassidy. What do you see in it? I'm curious.

SAUL. It has the ring of truth, Austin.

AUSTIN *(laughs)*. Truth?

LEE. It is true.

SAUL. Something about the real West.

AUSTIN. Why? Because it's got horses? Because it's got grown men acting like little boys?

SAUL. Something about the land. Your brother is speaking from experience.

AUSTIN. So am I!

SAUL. But nobody's interested in love these days, Austin. Let's face it.

LEE. That's right.

AUSTIN *(to Saul)*. He's been camped out on the desert for three months. Talking to cactus. What's he know about what people wanna' see on the screen! I drive on the freeway every day. I swallow the smog. I watch the news in color. I shop in the Safeway. I'm the one who's in touch! Not him!

SAUL. I have to go now, Austin.

(Saul starts to leave)

AUSTIN. There's no such thing as the West anymore! It's a dead issue! It's dried up, Saul, and so are you.

(Saul stops and turns to Austin)

SAUL. Maybe you're right. But I have to take the gamble, don't I?

AUSTIN. You're a fool to do this, Saul.

SAUL. I've always gone on my hunches. Always. And I've never been wrong. *(to Lee)* I'll talk to you tomorrow, Lee.

LEE. All right, Mr. Kimmer.

SAUL. Maybe we could have some lunch.

LEE. Fine with me. *(smiles at Austin)*

SAUL. I'll give you a ring.

(Saul exits, lights to black as brothers look at each other from a distance)

SCENE 7

Night. Coyotes, crickets, sound of typewriter in dark, candlelight up on Lee at typewriter struggling to type with one finger system, Austin sits sprawled out on kitchen floor with whiskey bottle, drunk.

AUSTIN *(singing, from floor)*.
"Red sails in the sunset
Way out on the blue

Please carry my loved one
Home safely to me

Red sails in the sunset—"

LEE (*slams fist on table*). Hey! Knock it off will ya'! I'm tryin' to concentrate here.

AUSTIN (*laughs*). You're tryin' to concentrate?

LEE. Yeah. That's right.

AUSTIN. Now you're tryin' to concentrate.

LEE. Between you, the coyotes and the crickets a thought don't have much of a chance.

AUSTIN. "Between me, the coyotes and the crickets." What a great title.

LEE. I don't need a title! I need a thought.

AUSTIN (*laughs*). A thought! Here's a thought for ya'—

LEE. I'm not askin' fer yer thoughts! I got my own. I can do this thing on my own.

AUSTIN. You're going to write an entire script on your own?

LEE. That's right.

(*pause*)

AUSTIN. Here's a thought. Saul Kimmer—

LEE. Shut up will ya'!

AUSTIN. He thinks we're the same person.

LEE. Don't get cute.

AUSTIN. He does! He's lost his mind. Poor old Saul. (*giggles*) Thinks we're one and the same.

LEE. Why don't you ease up on that champagne.

AUSTIN (*holding up bottle*). This isn't champagne anymore. We went through the champagne a long time ago. This is serious stuff. The days of champagne are long gone.

LEE. Well, go outside and drink it.

AUSTIN. I'm enjoying your company, Lee. For the first time since your arrival I am finally enjoying your company. And now you want me to go outside and drink alone?

LEE. That's right.

(*Lee reads through paper in typewriter, makes an erasure*)

AUSTIN. You think you'll make more progress if you're alone? You might drive yourself crazy.

LEE. I could have this thing done in a night if I had a little silence.

AUSTIN. Well you'd still have the crickets to contend with. The coyotes. The sounds of the Police Helicopters prowling above the neighborhood. Slashing their searchlights down through the streets. Hunting for the likes of you.

LEE. I'm a screenwriter now! I'm legitimate.

AUSTIN (*laughing*). A screenwriter!

LEE. That's right. I'm on salary. That's more'n I can say for you. I got an advance coming.

AUSTIN. This is true. This is very true. An advance. (*pause*) Well, maybe I oughta' go out and try my hand at your trade. Since you're doing so good at mine.

LEE. Ha!

(*Lee attempts to type some more but gets the ribbon tangled up, starts trying to re-thread it as they continue talking*)

AUSTIN. Well why not? You don't think I've got what it takes to sneak into people's houses and steal their T.V.s?

LEE. You couldn't steal a toaster without losin' yer lunch.

(*Austin stands with a struggle, supports himself by the sink*)

AUSTIN. You don't think I could sneak into somebody's house and steal a toaster?

LEE. Go take a shower or somethin' will ya!

(*Lee gets more tangled up with the typewriter ribbon, pulling it out of the machine as though it was fishing line*)

AUSTIN. You really don't think I could steal a crumby toaster? How much you wanna' bet I can't steal a toaster! How much? Go ahead! You're a gambler aren't you? Tell me how much yer willing to put on the line. Some part of your big advance? Oh, you haven't got that yet have you. I forgot.

LEE. All right. I'll bet you your car that you can't steal a toaster without gettin' busted.

AUSTIN. You already got my car!

LEE. Okay, your house then.

AUSTIN. What're you gonna' give me! I'm not talkin' about my house and my car, I'm talkin' about what are you gonna' give me. You don't have nothin' to give me.

LEE. I'll give you—shared screen credit. How 'bout that? I'll have it put in the contract that this was written by the both of us.

AUSTIN. I don't want my name on that piece of shit! I want something of value. You got anything of value? You got any tidbits from the desert? Any Rattlesnake bones? I'm not a greedy man. Any little personal treasure will suffice.

LEE. I'm gonna' just kick yer ass out in a minute.

AUSTIN. Oh, so now you're gonna' kick me out! Now I'm the intruder. I'm the one who's invading your precious privacy.

LEE. I'm trying to do some screenwriting here!!

(*Lee stands, picks up typewriter, slams it down hard on table, pause, silence except for crickets*)

AUSTIN. Well, you got everything you need. You got plenty a' coffee? Groceries. You got a car. A contract. (*pause*) Might need a new typewriter ribbon but other than that you're pretty well fixed. I'll just leave ya' alone for a while.

(*Austin tries to steady himself to leave, Lee makes a move toward him*)

LEE. Where you goin'?

AUSTIN. Don't worry about me. I'm not the one to worry about.

(*Austin weaves toward exit, stops*)

LEE. What're you gonna' do? Just go wander out into the night?

AUSTIN. I'm gonna' make a little tour.

LEE. Why don't ya' just go to bed for Christ's sake. Yer makin' me sick.

AUSTIN. I can take care a' myself. Don't worry about me.

(*Austin weaves badly in another attempt to exit, he crashes to the floor, Lee goes to him but remains standing*)

LEE. You want me to call your wife for ya' or something?

AUSTIN (*from floor*). My wife?

LEE. Yeah. I mean maybe she can help ya' out. Talk to ya' or somethin'.

AUSTIN (*struggles to stand again*). She's five hundred miles away. North. North of here. Up in the North country where things are calm. I don't need any help. I'm gonna' go outside and I'm gonna' steal a toaster. I'm gonna' steal some other stuff too. I might even commit bigger crimes. Bigger than you ever dreamed of. Crimes beyond the imagination!

(*Austin manages to get himself vertical, tries to head for exit again*)

LEE. Just hang on a minute, Austin.

AUSTIN. Why? What for? You don't need my help, right? You got a handle on the project. Besides, I'm lookin' forward to the smell of the night. The bushes. Orange blossoms. Dust in the driveways. Rain bird sprinklers. Lights in people's houses. You're right about the lights, Lee. Everybody else is livin' the life. Indoors. Safe. This is a Paradise down here. You know that? We're livin' in a Paradise. We've forgotten about that.

LEE. You sound just like the old man now.

AUSTIN. Yeah, well we all sound alike when we're sloshed. We just sorta' echo each other.

LEE. Maybe if we could work on this together we could bring him back out here. Get him settled down some place.

(*Austin turns violently toward Lee, takes a swing at him, misses and crashes to the floor again, Lee stays standing*)

AUSTIN. I don't want him out here! I've had it with him! I went all the way out there! I went out of my way. I gave him money and all he did was play Al Jolson records and spit at me! I gave him money!

(*pause*)

LEE. Just help me a little with the characters, all right? You know how to do it, Austin.

AUSTIN (*on floor, laughs*). The characters!

LEE. Yeah. You know. The way they talk and stuff. I can hear it in my head but I can't get it down on paper.

AUSTIN. What characters?

LEE. The guys. The guys in the story.

AUSTIN. Those aren't characters.

LEE. Whatever you call 'em then. I need to write somethin' out.

AUSTIN. Those are illusions of characters.

LEE. I don't give a damn what ya' call 'em! You know what I'm talkin' about!

AUSTIN. Those are fantasies of a long lost boyhood.

LEE. I gotta' write somethin' out on paper!!

(*pause*)

AUSTIN. What for? Saul's gonna' get you a fancy screenwriter isn't he?

LEE. I wanna' do it myself!

AUSTIN. Then do it! Yer on your own now, old buddy. You bulldogged yer way into contention. Now you gotta' carry it through.

LEE. I will but I need some advice. Just a couple a' things. Come on, Austin. Just help me get 'em talkin' right. It won't take much.

AUSTIN. Oh, now you're having a little doubt huh? What happened? The pressure's on, boy. This is it. You gotta' come up with it now. You don't come up with a winner on your first time out they just cut your head off. They don't give you a second chance ya' know.

LEE. I got a good story! I know it's a good story. I just need a little help is all.

AUSTIN. Not from me. Not from yer little old brother. I'm retired.

LEE. You could save this thing for me, Austin. I'd give ya' half the money. I would. I only need half anyway. With this kinda' money I could be a long time down the road. I'd never bother ya' again. I promise. You'd never even see me again.

AUSTIN (*still on floor*). You'd disappear?

LEE. I would for sure.

AUSTIN. Where would you disappear to?

LEE. That don't matter. I got plenty a' places.

AUSTIN. Nobody can disappear. The old man tried that. Look where it got him. He lost his teeth.

LEE. He never had any money.

AUSTIN. I don't mean that. I mean his teeth! His real teeth. First he lost his real teeth, then he lost his false teeth. You never knew that did ya'? He never confided in you.

LEE. Nah, I never knew that.

AUSTIN. You wanna' drink?

(*Austin offers bottle to Lee, Lee takes it, sits down on kitchen floor with Austin, they share the bottle*)

Yeah, he lost his real teeth one at a time. Woke up every morning with another tooth lying on the mattress. Finally, he decides he's gotta' get 'em all pulled out but he doesn't have any money. Middle of Arizona with no money and no insurance and every morning another tooth is lying on the mattress. (*takes a drink*) So what does he do?

LEE. I dunno'. I never knew about that.

AUSTIN. He begs the government. G.I. Bill or some damn thing. Some pension plan he remembers in the back of his head. And they send him out the money.

LEE. They did?

(*they keep trading the bottle between them, taking drinks*)

AUSTIN. Yeah. They send him the money but it's not enough money. Costs a lot to have all yer teeth yanked. They charge by the individual tooth, ya' know. I mean one tooth isn't equal to another tooth. Some are more expensive. Like the big ones in the back—

LEE. So what happened?

AUSTIN. So he locates a Mexican dentist in Juarez who'll do the whole thing for a song. And he takes off hitchhiking to the border.

LEE. Hitchhiking?

AUSTIN. Yeah. So how long you think it takes him to get to the border? A man his age.

LEE. I dunno.

AUSTIN. Eight days it takes him. Eight days in the rain and the sun and every day he's droppin' teeth on the blacktop and nobody'll pick him up 'cause his mouth's full a' blood.

(*pause, they drink*)

So finally he stumbles into the dentist. Dentist takes all his money and all his teeth. And there he is, in Mexico, with his gums sewed up and his pockets empty.

(*long silence, Austin drinks*)

LEE. That's it?

AUSTIN. Then I go out to see him, see. I go out there and I take him out for a nice Chinese dinner. But he doesn't eat. All he wants to do is drink Martinis outa' plastic cups. And he takes his teeth out and lays 'em on the table 'cause he can't stand the feel of 'em. And we ask the waitress for one a' those doggie bags to take the Chop Suey home in. So he drops his teeth in the doggie bag along with the Chop Suey. And then we go out to hit all the bars up and down the highway. Says he wants to introduce me to all his buddies. And in one a' those bars, in one a' those bars up and down the highway, he left that doggie bag with his teeth laying in the Chop Suey.

LEE. You never found it?

AUSTIN. We went back but we never did find it. (*pause*) Now that's a true story. True to life.

(*they drink as lights fade to black*)

SCENE 8

Very early morning, between night and day. No crickets, coyotes yapping feverishly in distance before light comes up, a small fire blazes up in the dark from alcove area, sound of Lee smashing typewriter with a golf club, lights coming up, Lee seen smashing typewriter methodically then dropping pages of his script into a burning bowl set on the floor of alcove, flames leap up, Austin has a whole bunch of stolen toasters lined up on the sink counter along with Lee's stolen T.V., the toasters are of a wide variety of models, mostly chrome, Austin goes up and down the line of toasters, breathing on them and polishing them with a dish towel, both men are drunk, empty whiskey bottles and beer cans litter floor of kitchen, they share a half empty bottle on one of the chairs in the alcove, Lee keeps periodically taking deliberate ax-chops at the typewriter using a nine-iron as Austin speaks, all of their mother's house plants are dead and drooping.

AUSTIN (*polishing toasters*). There's gonna' be a general lack of toast in the neighborhood this morning. Many, many unhappy, bewildered breakfast faces. I guess it's best not to even think of the victims. Not to even entertain it. Is that the right psychology?

LEE (*pauses*). What?

AUSTIN. Is that the correct criminal psychology? Not to think of the victims?

LEE. What victims?

(*Lee takes another swipe at typewriter with nine-iron, adds pages to the fire*)

AUSTIN. The victims of crime. Of breaking and entering. I mean is it a prerequisite for a criminal not to have a conscience?

LEE. Ask a criminal.

(*pause, Lee stares at Austin*)

What're you gonna' do with all those toasters? That's the dumbest thing I ever saw in my life.

AUSTIN. I've got hundreds of dollars worth of household appliances here. You may not realize that.

LEE. Yeah, and how many hundreds of dollars did you walk right past?

AUSTIN. It was toasters you challenged me to. Only toasters. I ignored every other temptation.

LEE. I never challenged you! That's no challenge. Anybody can steal a toaster.

(*Lee smashes typewriter again*)

AUSTIN. You don't have to take it out on my typewriter ya' know. It's not the machine's fault that you can't write. It's a sin to do that to a good machine.

LEE. A sin?

AUSTIN. When you consider all the writers who never even had a machine. Who would have given an eyeball for a good typewriter. Any typewriter.

(*Lee smashes typewriter again*)

AUSTIN (*polishing toasters*). All the ones who wrote on matchbook covers. Paper bags. Toilet paper. Who had their writing destroyed by their jailers. Who persisted beyond all odds. Those writers would find it hard to understand your actions.

(*Lee comes down on typewriter with one final crushing blow of the nine-iron then collapses in one of the chairs, takes a drink from bottle, pause*)

AUSTIN (*after pause*). Not to mention demolishing a perfectly good golf club. What about all the struggling golfers? What about Lee Trevino? What do you think

he would've said when he was batting balls around with broomsticks at the age of nine. Impoverished.

(*pause*)

LEE. What time is it anyway?

AUSTIN. No idea. Time stands still when you're havin' fun.

LEE. Is it too late to call a woman? You know any women?

AUSTIN. I'm a married man.

LEE. I mean a local woman.

(*Austin looks out at light through window above sink*)

AUSTIN. It's either too late or too early. You're the nature enthusiast. Can't you tell the time by the light in the sky? Orient yourself around the North Star or something?

LEE. I can't tell anything.

AUSTIN. Maybe you need a little breakfast. Some toast! How 'bout some toast?

(*Austin goes to cupboard, pulls out loaf of bread and starts dropping slices into every toaster, Lee stays sitting, drinks, watches Austin*)

LEE. I don't need toast. I need a woman.

AUSTIN. A woman isn't the answer. Never was.

LEE. I'm not talkin' about permanent. I'm talkin' about temporary.

AUSTIN (*putting toast in toasters*). We'll just test the merits of these little demons. See which brands have a tendency to burn. See which one can produce a perfectly golden piece of fluffy toast.

LEE. How much gas you got in yer car?

AUSTIN. I haven't driven my car for days now. So I haven't had an opportunity to look at the gas gauge.

LEE. Take a guess. You think there's enough to get me to Bakersfield?

AUSTIN. Bakersfield? What's in Bakersfield?

LEE. Just never mind what's in Bakersfield! You think there's enough goddamn gas in the car!

AUSTIN. Sure.

LEE. Sure. You could care less, right. Let me run outa' gas on the Grapevine. You could give a shit.

AUSTIN. I'd say there was enough gas to get you just about anywhere, Lee. With your determination and guts.

LEE. What the hell time is it anyway?

(*Lee pulls out his wallet, starts going through dozens of small pieces of paper with phone numbers written on them, drops some on the floor, drops others in the fire*)

AUSTIN. Very early. This is the time of morning when the coyotes kill people's cocker spaniels. Did you hear them? That's what they were doing out there. Luring innocent pets away from their homes.

LEE (*searching through his papers*). What's the area code for Bakersfield? You know?

AUSTIN. You could always call the operator.

LEE. I can't stand that voice they give ya'.

AUSTIN. What voice?

LEE. That voice that warns you that if you'd only tried harder to find the number in the phone book you wouldn't have to be calling the operator to begin with.

(*Lee gets up, holding a slip of paper from his wallet, stumbles toward phone on wall, yanks receiver, starts dialing*)

AUSTIN. Well I don't understand why you'd want to talk to anybody else anyway. I mean you can talk to me. I'm your brother.

LEE (*dialing*). I wanna' talk to a woman. I haven't heard a woman's voice in a long time.

AUSTIN. Not since the Botanist?

LEE. What?

AUSTIN. Nothing. (*starts singing as he tends toast*)
"Red sails in the sunset
Way out on the blue
Please carry my loved one
Home safely to me"

LEE. Hey, knock it off will ya'! This is long distance here.

AUSTIN. Bakersfield?

LEE. Yeah, Bakersfield. It's Kern County.

AUSTIN. Well, what County are *we* in?

LEE. You better get yourself a 7-Up, boy.

AUSTIN. One County's as good as another.

(*Austin hums "Red Sails" softly as Lee talks on phone*)

LEE (*to phone*). Yeah, operator look—first off I wanna' know the area code for Bakersfield. Right. Bakersfield! Okay. Good. Now I wanna' know if you can help me track somebody down. (*pause*) No, no I mean a phone number. Just a phone number. Okay. (*holds a piece of paper up and reads it*) Okay, the name is Melly Ferguson. Melly. (*pause*) I dunno'. Melly. Maybe. Yeah. Maybe Melanie. Yeah. Melanie Ferguson. Okay. (*pause*) What? I can't hear ya' so good. Sounds like yer under the ocean. (*pause*) You got ten Melanie Fergusons? How could that be? Ten Melanie Fergusons in Bakersfield? Well gimme all of 'em then. (*pause*) What d'ya' mean? Gimmie all ten Melanie Fergusons! That's right. Just a second. (*to Austin*) Gimme a pen.

AUSTIN. I don't have a pen.

LEE. Gimme a pencil then!

AUSTIN. I don't have a pencil.

LEE (*to phone*). Just a second, operator. (*to Austin*) Yer a writer and ya' don't have a pen or a pencil!

AUSTIN. I'm not a writer. You're a writer.

LEE. I'm on the phone here! Get me a pen or a pencil.

AUSTIN. I gotta' watch the toast.

LEE (*to phone*). Hang on a second, operator.

(*Lee lets the phone drop then starts pulling all the drawers in the kitchen out on the floor and dumping the contents, searching for a pencil, Austin watches him casually*)

LEE (*crashing through drawers, throwing contents around kitchen*). This is the last time I try to live with people, boy! I can't believe it. Here I am! Here I am again in a desperate situation! This would never happen out on the desert. I would never be in this kinda' situation out on the desert. Isn't there a pen or a pencil in this house! Who lives in this house anyway!

AUSTIN. Our mother.

LEE. How come she don't have a pen or a pencil! She's a social person isn't she? Doesn't she have to make shopping lists? She's gotta' have a pencil. (*finds a pencil*) Aaha! (*he rushes back to phone, picks up receiver*) All right operator. Operator? Hey! Operator! Goddamnit!

(*Lee rips the phone off the wall and throws it down, goes back to chair and falls into it, drinks, long pause*)

AUSTIN. She hung up?

LEE. Yeah, she hung up. I knew she was gonna' hang up. I could hear it in her voice.

(*Lee starts going through his slips of paper again*)

AUSTIN. Well, you're probably better off staying here with me anyway. I'll take care of you.

LEE. I don't need takin' care off! Not by you anyway.

AUSTIN. Toast is almost ready.

(*Austin starts buttering all the toast as it pops up*)

LEE. I don't want any toast!

(*long pause*)

AUSTIN. You gotta' eat something. Can't just drink. How long have we been drinking, anyway?

LEE (*looking through slips of paper*). Maybe it was Fresno. What's the area code for Fresno? How could I have lost that number! She was beautiful.

(*pause*)

AUSTIN. Why don't you just forget about that, Lee. Forget about the woman.

LEE. She had green eyes. You know what green eyes do to me?

AUSTIN. I know but you're not gonna' get it on with her now anyway. It's dawn already. She's in Bakersfield for Christ's sake.

(*long pause, Lee considers the situation*)

LEE. Yeah. (*looks at windows*) It's dawn?

AUSTIN. Let's just have some toast and—

LEE. What is this bullshit with the toast anyway! You make it sound like salvation or something. I don't want any goddamn toast! How many times I gotta' tell ya'! (*Lee gets up, crosses upstage to windows in alcove, looks out, Austin butters toast*)

AUSTIN. Well it is like salvation sort of. I mean the smell. I love the smell of toast. And the sun's coming up. It makes me feel like anything's possible. Ya' know?

LEE (*back to Austin, facing windows upstage*). So go to church why don't ya'

AUSTIN. Like a beginning. I love beginnings.

LEE. Oh yeah. I've always been kinda' partial to endings myself.

AUSTIN. What if I come with you, Lee?

LEE (*pause as Lee turns toward Austin*). What?

AUSTIN. What if I come with you out to the desert?

LEE. Are you kiddin'?

AUSTIN. No. I'd just like to see what it's like.

LEE. You wouldn't last a day out there pal.

AUSTIN. That's what you said about the toasters. You said I couldn't steal a toaster either.

LEE. A toaster's got nothin' to do with the desert.

AUSTIN. I could make it, Lee. I'm not that helpless. I can cook.

LEE. Cook?

AUSTIN. I can.

LEE. So what! You can cook. Toast.

AUSTIN. I can make fires. I know how to get fresh water from condensation.

(*Austin stacks buttered toast up in a tall stack on plate*)

(*Lee slams table*)

LEE. It's not somethin' you learn out of a Boy Scout handbook!

AUSTIN. Well how do you learn it then! How're you supposed to learn it!

(*pause*)

LEE. Ya' just learn it, that's all. Ya' learn it 'cause ya' have to learn it. You don't *have* to learn it.

AUSTIN. You could teach me.

LEE (*stands*). What're you, crazy or somethin'? You went to college. Here, you are down here, rollin' in bucks. Floatin' up and down in elevators. And you wanna' learn how to live on the desert!

AUSTIN. I do, Lee. I really do. There's nothin' down here for me. There never was. When we were kids here it was different. There was a life here then. But now—I keep comin' down here thinkin' it's the fifties or somethin'. I keep finding myself getting off the freeway at familiar landmarks that turn out to be unfamiliar. On the way to appointments. Wandering down streets I thought I recognized that turn out to be replicas of streets I remember. Streets I misremember. Streets I can't tell if I lived on or saw in a postcard. Fields that don't even exist anymore.

LEE. There's no point cryin' about that now.

AUSTIN. There's nothin' real down here, Lee! Least of all me!

LEE. Well I can't save you from that!

AUSTIN. You can let me come with you.

LEE. No dice, pal.

AUSTIN. You could let me come with you, Lee!

LEE. Hey, do you actually think I chose to live out in the middle a' nowhere? Do ya'? Ya' think it's some kinda' philosophical decision I took or somethin'? I'm livin' out there 'cause I can't make it here! And yer bitchin' to me about all yer success!

AUSTIN. I'd cash it all in in a second. That's the truth.

LEE (*pause, shakes his head*). I can't believe this.

AUSTIN. Let me go with you.

LEE. Stop sayin' that will ya'! Yer worse than a dog.

(*Austin offers out the plate of neatly stacked toast to Lee*)

AUSTIN. You want some toast?

(*Lee suddenly explodes and knocks the plate out of Austin's hand, toast goes flying, long frozen moment where it appears Lee might go all the way this time when Austin breaks it by slowly lowering himself to his knees and begins gathering the scattered toast from the floor and stacking it back on the plate, Lee begins to circle Austin in a slow, predatory way, crushing pieces of toast in his wake, no words for a while, Austin keeps gathering toast, even the crushed pieces*)

LEE. Tell ya' what I'll do, little brother. I might just consider makin' you a deal. Little trade. (*Austin continues gathering toast as Lee circles him through this*) You write me up this screenplay thing just like I tell ya'. I mean you can use all yer usual tricks and stuff. Yer fancy language. Yer artistic hocus pocus. But ya' gotta' write everything like

I say. Every move. Every time they run outa' gas, they run outa' gas. Every time they wanna' jump on a horse, they do just that. If they wanna' stay in Texas, by God they'll stay in Texas! (*Keeps circling*) And you finish the whole thing up for me. Top to bottom. And you put my name on it. And I own all the rights. And every dime goes in my pocket. You do that and I'll sure enough take ya' with me to the desert. (*Lee stops, pause, looks down at Austin*) How's that sound?

(*pause as Austin stands slowly holding plate of demolished toast, their faces are very close, pause*)

AUSTIN. It's a deal.

(*Lee stares straight into Austin's eyes, then he slowly takes a piece of toast off the plate, raises it to his mouth and takes a huge crushing bite never taking his eyes off Austin's, as Lee crunches into the toast the lights black out*)

SCENE 9

Mid-day. No sound, blazing heat, the stage is ravaged; bottles, toasters, smashed typewriter, ripped out telephone, etc. All the debris from previous scene is now starkly visible in intense yellow light, the effect should be like a desert junkyard at high noon, the coolness of the preceding scenes is totally obliterated. Austin is seated at table in alcove, shirt open, pouring with sweat, hunched over a writing notebook, scribbling notes desperately with a ballpoint pen. Lee with no shirt, beer in hand, sweat pouring down his chest, is walking a slow circle around the table, picking his way through the objects, sometimes kicking them aside.

LEE (*as he walks*). All right, read it back to me. Read it back to me!

AUSTIN (*scribbling at top speed*). Just a second.

LEE. Come on, come on! Just read what ya' got.

AUSTIN. I can't keep up! It's not the same as if I had a typewriter.

LEE. Just read what we got so far. Forget about the rest.

AUSTIN. All right. Let's see—okay—(*wipes sweat from his face, reads as Lee circles*). Luke says uh—

LEE. Luke?

AUSTIN. Yeah.

LEE. His name's Luke? All right, all right—we can change the names later. What's he say? Come on, come on.

AUSTIN. He says uh—(*reading*) "I told ya' you were a fool to follow me in here. I know this prairie like the back a' my hand."

LEE. No, no, no! That's not what I said. I never said that.

AUSTIN. That's what I wrote.

LEE. It's not what I said. I never said "like the back a' my hand." That's stupid. That's one a' those—whadya' call it? Whatya' call that?

AUSTIN. What?

LEE. Whadya' call it when somethin's been said a thousand times before. Whadya' call that?

AUSTIN. Um—a cliché?

LEE. Yeah. That's right. Cliché. That's what that is. A cliché. "The back a' my hand." That's stupid.

AUSTIN. That's what you said.

LEE. I never said that! And even if I did, that's where yer supposed to come in. That's where yer supposed to change it to somethin' better.

AUSTIN. Well how am I supposed to do that and write down what you say at the same time?

LEE. Ya' just do, that's all! You hear a stupid line you change it. That's yer job.

AUSTIN. All right. (*makes more notes*)

LEE. What're you changin' it to?

AUSTIN. I'm not changing it. I'm just trying to catch up.

LEE. Well change it! We gotta' change that, we can't leave that in there like that. ". . . the back a' my hand." That's dumb.

AUSTIN (*stops writing, sits back*). All right.

LEE (*pacing*). So what'll we change it to?

AUSTIN. Um—How 'bout—"I'm on intimate terms with this prairie."

LEE (*to himself considering line as he walks*). "I'm on intimate terms with this prairie." Intimate terms, intimate terms. Intimate—that means like uh—sexual right?

AUSTIN. Well—yeah—or—

LEE. He's on sexual terms with the prairie? How dya' figure that?

AUSTIN. Well it doesn't necessarily have to mean sexual.

LEE. What's it mean then?

AUSTIN. It means uh—close—personal—

LEE. All right. How's it sound? Put it into the uh—the line there. Read it back. Let's see how it sounds. (*to himself*) "Intimate terms."

AUSTIN (*scribbles in notebook*). Okay. It'd go something like this: (*reads*) "I told ya' you were a fool to follow me in here. I'm on intimate terms with this prairie."

LEE. That's good. I like that. That's real good.

AUSTIN. You do?

LEE. Yeah. Don't you?

AUSTIN. Sure.

LEE. Sounds original now. "Intimate terms." That's good. Okay. Now we're cookin! That has a real ring to it.

(*Austin makes more notes, Lee walks around, pours beer on his arms and rubs it over his chest feeling good about the new progress, as he does this Mom enters unobtrusively down left with her luggage, she stops and stares at the scene still holding luggage as the two men continue, unaware of her presence, Austin absorbed in his writing, Lee cooling himself off with beer*)

LEE (*continues*). "He's on intimate terms with this prairie." Sounds real mysterious and kinda' threatening at the same time.

AUSTIN (*writing rapidly*). Good.

LEE. Now—(*Lee turns and suddenly sees Mom, he stares at her for a while, she stares back, Austin keeps writing feverishly, not noticing, Lee walks slowly over to Mom and takes a closer look, long pause*)

LEE. Mom?

(*Austin looks up suddenly from his writing, sees Mom, stands quickly, long pause, Mom surveys the damage*)

AUSTIN. Mom. What're you doing back?

MOM. I'm back.

LEE. Here, lemme take those for ya.

(*Lee sets beer on counter than takes both her bags but doesn't know where to set them down in the sea of junk so he just keeps holding them*)

AUSTIN. I wasn't expecting you back so soon. I thought uh—How was Alaska?

MOM. Fine.

LEE. See any igloos?

MOM. No. Just glaciers.

AUSTIN. Cold huh?

MOM. What?

AUSTIN. It must've been cold up there?

MOM. Not really.

LEE. Musta' been colder than this here. I mean we're havin' a real scorcher here.

MOM. Oh? (*she looks at damage*)

LEE. Yeah. Must be in the hundreds.

AUSTIN. You wanna' take your coat off, Mom?

MOM. No. (*pause, she surveys space*) What happened in here?

AUSTIN. Oh um—Me and Lee were just sort of celebrating and uh—

MOM. Celebrating?

AUSTIN. Yeah. Uh—Lee sold a screenplay. A story, I mean.

MOM. Lee did?

AUSTIN. Yeah.

MOM. Not you?

AUSTIN. No. Him.

MOM (*to Lee*). You sold a screenplay?

LEE. Yeah. That's right. We're just sorta' finishing it up right now. That's what we're doing here.

AUSTIN. Me and Lee are going out to the desert to live.

MOM. You and Lee?

AUSTIN. Yeah. I'm taking off with Lee.

MOM (*she looks back and forth at each of them, pause*). You gonna go live with your father?

AUSTIN. No. We're going to a different desert Mom.

MOM. I see. Well, you'll probably wind up on the same desert sooner or later. What're all these toasters doing here?

AUSTIN. Well—we had kind of a contest.

MOM. Contest?

LEE. Yeah.

AUSTIN. Lee won.

MOM. Did you win a lot of money, Lee?

LEE. Well not yet. It's comin' in any day now.

MOM (*to Lee*). What happened to your shirt?

LEE. Oh. I was sweatin' like a pig and I took it off.

(*Austin grabs Lee's shirt off the table and tosses it to him, Lee sets down suitcases and puts his shirt on*)

MOM. Well it's one hell of a mess in here isn't it?

AUSTIN. Yeah, I'll clean it up for you, Mom. I just didn't know you were coming back so soon.

MOM. I didn't either.

AUSTIN. What happened?

MOM. Nothing. I just started missing all my plants.

(*she notices dead plants*)

AUSTIN. Oh.

MOM. Oh, they're all dead aren't they. (*she crosses toward them, examines them closely*) You didn't get a chance to water I guess.

AUSTIN. I was doing it and then Lee came and—

LEE. Yeah I just distracted him a whole lot here, Mom. It's not his fault.

(*pause, as Mom stares at plants*)

MOM. Oh well, one less thing to take care of I guess. (*turns toward brothers*) Oh, that reminds me—You boys will probably never guess who's in town. Try and guess.

(*long pause, brothers stare at her*)

AUSTIN. Whadya' mean, Mom?

MOM. Take a guess. Somebody very important has come to town. I read it, coming down on the Greyhound.

LEE. Somebody very important?

MOM. See if you can guess. You'll never guess.

AUSTIN. Mom—we're trying to uh—(*points to writing pad*)

MOM. Picasso. (*pause*) Picasso's in town. Isn't that incredible? Right now.

(*pause*)

AUSTIN. Picasso's dead, Mom.

MOM. No, he's not dead. He's visiting the museum. I read it on the bus. We have to go down there and see him.

AUSTIN. Mom—

MOM. This is the chance of a lifetime. Can you imagine? We could all go down and meet him. All three of us.

LEE. Uh—I don't think I'm really up fer meetin' anybody right now. I'm uh—What's his name?

MOM. Picasso! Picasso! You've never heard of Picasso? Austin, you've heard of Picasso.

AUSTIN. Mom, we're not going to have time.

MOM. It won't take long. We'll just hop in the car and go down there. An opportunity like this doesn't come along every day.

AUSTIN. We're gonna' be leavin' here, Mom!

(*pause*)

MOM. Oh.

LEE. Yeah.

(*pause*)

MOM. You're both leaving?

LEE (*looks at Austin*). Well we were thinkin' about that before but now I—

AUSTIN. No, we are! We're both leaving. We've got it all planned.

MOM (*to Austin*). Well you can't leave. You have a family.

AUSTIN. I'm leaving. I'm getting out of here.

LEE (*to Mom*). I don't really think Austin's cut out for the desert do you?

MOM. No. He's not.

AUSTIN. I'm going with you, Lee!

MOM. He's too thin.

LEE. Yeah, he'd just burn up out there.

AUSTIN (*to Lee*). We just gotta' finish this screenplay and then we're gonna' take off. That's the plan. That's what you said. Come on, let's get back to work, Lee.

LEE. I can't work under these conditions here. It's too hot.

AUSTIN. Then we'll do it on the desert.

LEE. Don't be tellin' me what we're gonna' do!

MOM. Don't shout in the house.

LEE. We're just gonna' have to postpone the whole deal.

AUSTIN. I can't postpone it! It's gone past postponing! I'm doing everything you said. I'm writing down exactly what you tell me.

LEE. Yeah, but you were right all along see. It is a dumb story. "Two lamebrains chasin' each other across Texas." That's what you said, right?

AUSTIN. I never said that.

(*Lee sneers in Austin's face then turns to Mom*)

LEE. I'm gonna' just borrow some a' your antiques, Mom. You don't mind do ya'? Just a few plates and things. Silverware.

(*Lee starts going through all the cupboards in kitchen pulling out plates and stacking them on counter as Mom and Austin watch*)

MOM. You don't have any utensils on the desert?

LEE. Nah, I'm fresh out.

AUSTIN (*to Lee*). What're you doing?

MOM. Well some of those are very old. Bone China.

LEE. I'm tired of eatin' outa' my bare hands, ya' know. It's not civilized.

AUSTIN (*to Lee*). What're you doing? We made a deal!

MOM. Couldn't you borrow the plastic ones instead? I have plenty of plastic ones.

LEE (*as he stacks plates*). It's not the same. Plastic's not the same at all. What I need is somethin' authentic. Somethin' to keep me in touch. It's easy to get outa' touch out there. Don't worry I'll get 'em back to ya'.

(*Austin rushes up to Lee, grabs him by shoulders*)

AUSTIN. You can't just drop the whole thing, Lee!

(*Lee turns, pushes Austin in the chest knocking him backwards into the alcove, Mom watches numbly, Lee returns to collecting the plates, silverware, etc.*)

MOM. You boys shouldn't fight in the house. Go outside and fight.

LEE. I'm not fightin'. I'm leavin'.

MOM. There's been enough damage done already.

LEE (*his back to Austin and Mom, stacking dishes on counter*). I'm clearin' outa' here once and for all. All this town does is drive a man insane. Look what it's done to Austin there. I'm not lettin' that happen to me. Sell myself down the river. No sir. I'd rather be a hundred miles from nowhere than let that happen to me.

(*during this Austin has picked up the ripped-out phone from the floor and wrapped the cord tightly around both his hands, he lunges at Lee whose back is still to him, wraps the cord around Lee's back and pulls back on the cord, tightening it, Lee chokes desperately, can't speak and can't reach Austin with his arms, Austin keeps applying pressure on*

Lee's back with his foot, bending him into the sink, Mom watches)

AUSTIN *(tightening cord)*. You're not goin' anywhere! You're not takin' anything with you. You're not takin' my car! You're not takin' the dishes! You're not takin' anything! You're stayin' right here!

MOM. You'll have to stop fighting in the house. There's plenty of room outside to fight. You've got the whole outdoors to fight in.

(Lee tries to tear himself away, he crashes across the stage like an enraged bull dragging Austin with him, he snorts and bellows but Austin hangs on and manages to keep clear of Lee's attempts to grab him, they crash into the table, to the floor, Lee is face down thrashing wildly and choking, Austin pulls cord tighter, stands with one foot planted on Lee's back and the cord stretched taut)

AUSTIN *(holding cord)*. Gimme back my keys, Lee! Take the keys out! Take 'em out!

(Lee desperately tries to dig in his pockets, searching for the car keys, Mom moves closer)

MOM *(calmly to Austin)*. You're not killing him are you?

AUSTIN. I don't know. I don't know if I'm killing him. I'm stopping him. That's all. I'm just stopping him.

(Lee thrashes but Austin is relentless)

MOM. You oughta' let him breathe a little bit.

AUSTIN. Throw the keys out, Lee!

(Lee finally gets keys out and throws them on the floor but out of Austin's reach, Austin keeps pressure on cord, pulling Lee's neck back, Lee gets one hand to the cord but can't relieve the pressure)

Reach me those keys would ya', Mom.

MOM *(not moving)*. Why are you doing this to him?

AUSTIN. Reach me the keys!

MOM. Not until you stop choking him.

AUSTIN. I can't stop choking him! He'll kill me if I stop choking him!

MOM. He won't kill you. He's your brother.

AUSTIN. Just get me the keys would ya'!

(pause. Mom picks keys up off floor, hands them to Austin)

AUSTIN *(to Mom)*. Thanks.

MOM. Will you let him go now?

AUSTIN. I don't know. He's not gonna' let me get outa' here.

MOM. Well you can't kill him.

AUSTIN. I can kill him! I can easily kill him. Right now. Right here. All I gotta' do is just tighten up. See? *(he tightens cord, Lee thrashes wildly, Austin releases pressure a little, maintaining control)* Ya' see that?

MOM. That's a savage thing to do.

AUSTIN. Yeah well don't tell me I can't kill him because I can. I can just twist. I can just keep twisting. *(Austin twists the cord tighter, Lee weakens, his breathing changes to a short rasp)*

MOM. Austin!

(Austin relieves pressure, Lee breathes easier but Austin keeps him under control)

AUSTIN *(eyes on Lee, holding cord)*. I'm goin' to the desert. There's nothing stopping me. I'm going by myself to the desert.

(Mom moving toward her luggage)

MOM. Well, I'm going to go check into a motel. I can't stand this anymore.

AUSTIN. Don't go yet!

(Mom pauses)

MOM. I can't stay here. This is worse than being homeless.

AUSTIN. I'll get everything fixed up for you, Mom. I promise. Just stay for a while.

MOM *(picking up luggage)*. You're going to the desert.

AUSTIN. Just wait!

(Lee thrashes, Austin subdues him, Mom watches holding luggage, pause)

MOM. It was the worst feeling being up there. In Alaska. Staring out a window. I never felt so desperate before. That's why when I saw that article on Picasso I thought—

AUSTIN. Stay here, Mom. This is where you live.

(she looks around the stage)

MOM. I don't recognize it at all.

(she exits with luggage, Austin makes a move toward her but Lee starts to struggle and Austin subdues him again with cord, pause)

AUSTIN *(holding cord)*. Lee? I'll make ya' a deal. You let me get outa' here. Just let me get to my car. All right, Lee? Gimme a little headstart and I'll turn you loose. Just gimme a little headstart. All right?

(Lee makes no response, Austin slowly releases tension cord, still nothing from Lee)

AUSTIN. Lee?

(Lee is motionless, Austin very slowly begins to stand, still keeping a tenuous hold on the cord and his eyes riveted to Lee for any sign of movement, Austin slowly drops the cord and stands, he stares down at Lee who appears to be dead)

AUSTIN *(whispers)*. Lee?

(pause, Austin considers, looks toward exit, back to Lee, then makes a small movement as if to leave. Instantly Lee is on his feet and moves toward exit, blocking Austin's escape. They square off to each other, keeping a distance between them. Pause, a single coyote heard in distance, lights fade softly into moonlight, the figures of the brothers now appear to be caught in a vast desert-like landscape, they are very still but watchful for the next move, lights go slowly to black as the after-image of the brothers pulses in the dark, coyote fades)

COMMENTARY

Note: This essay represents one interpretation of the play. For other perspectives on True West, *consult the essays listed below.*

With *Curse of the Starving Class* Shepard began writing a series of five family plays which evolved into what may be collectively called "the Old Man Cycle"—five plays bound together by the real or implied specter of "the old man" whose sins weigh heavily on the heads of his children. The offspring of "the old man" are obsessed with recapturing a vision of America (represented by "the West") and the family, which may or may not have ever existed. Like Aeschylus's *Oresteia*, Shepard's plays explore the traditional mythic themes of guilt and expiation, blood pollution, regeneration, violence, and passion within the context of the family.

Myth . . . family . . . the West—the three essential ingredients of Shepard's drama. For Shepard myth is the means of coming to grips with the mystery of life because it "speaks to everything at once":

> Myth is a powerful medium because it talks to the emotions and not the head. It moves us into an area of mystery. . . . [Folk-rock singer Bob] Dylan creates a mythic atmosphere out of the land around us. The land we walk on everyday and never see until someone shows it to us.

Shepard's modern myths, as seen in *True West*, are created through a fusion of incantatory language that possesses "the capacity to evoke visions in the eye of the audience" and powerful stage pictures that conjure archetypal images. These cause audiences to view the world with the same sense of awe, mystery, and even terror as our ancient forbearers felt. *True West*, for instance, concludes with the unsettling image of the two brothers in a primitive dance of death as coyotes howl in the distance. (Take a moment to reread the final stage direction; it is the play in miniature.) Shepard's theater achieves in practice the theory of Artaud's Theatre of Cruelty, which called for incantation, archetypal images, and other primal means to force audiences to confront the plague of modern civilization. Of such images Shepard has said:

> The fantastic thing about theatre is that it can make something be seen that is invisible . . . that you can be watching this thing happening with actors and costumes and lights and set and language and even plot, and something emerges beyond that, and that's the image part I'm looking for.

It is this quest for the invisible, the mysterious, the other-worldly, even the spiritual that aligns Shepard with the most ancient impulses of world theater. (See Showcase, "Myth and the Theater.")

In *True West* Shepard returns us to one of the first myths created by humans—the Cain and Abel story, in which one brother jealously kills another. In literature we often refer to this myth and many like it as "blood pollution" myths because they deal with family feuds that end in death to its members and the destruction of the family line. Since Aeschylus in ancient Greece, our most "ancient formulae" (another definition of myth offered by Shepard) have shown that stories of intrafamily strife have best met our dramatic and thematic needs. Aristotle devoted a section of Chapter 15 of *The Poetics* to "blood pollution," and Shakespeare refers to it in *Hamlet* as "the primal eldest curse." In *True West* Shepard himself reminds us of this unfortunate truth during a heated exchange between the brothers. Lee, who has mysteriously appeared from the desert, says to Austin: ". . . You go down to the L.A. Police Department there and ask them what kinda' people kill each other the most. . . . Family people. Brothers. Brothers-in-law. Cousins. Real American-type people. They kill each other in the heat mostly. . . ."

Thus in *True West* the brothers, one ostensibly civilized (Austin), the other more primitive (Lee), combine to destroy the interior of their mother's home: what was the quintessential *Better Homes and Gardens* kitchen in the opening scene is reduced to "a desert junkyard" as it is littered with crushed beer cans, stolen toasters, and mindlessly emptied drawers and cabinets.

Is *True West*—and the other plays in "the Old Man Cycle"—a legitimate successor to O'Neill's, Miller's, Williams's tormented studies of the American family at war with itself? Shepard has certainly absorbed these vital links in the evolution of contemporary American drama, but he also transcends them by creating his own myths that go beyond sociology. He creates modern myths (or metanarratives, to use a popular term from postmodern criticism) by fusing his tales with those of such modern "Homers" as John Ford and Sam Peckinpah, whose films helped define the "true west." As many critics have noted, Shepard's family plays are the final chapter of an odyssey in which a young man returns to the family to recover his roots. Austin has returned to his mother's home to write the great American screenplay at precisely the same moment the slovenly Lee returns from a desert pilgrimage to see "the old man." In the play's most comic scene, the two attempt to create a new American myth as they haggle over the details of Austin's screenplay. Ironically, they metamorphose into one another as Austin becomes more violent in temperament, Lee more artistic in his vision. Note that once the brothers are in silhouette in the final moments of the play, they are truly indistinguishable.

It is in this debate about the nature of the "true west" to be depicted on the silver screen that perhaps we come closest to understanding the implications of the play's title. On one hand Shepard's West is primordial and pristine, the paradise envisioned by those who settled "God's country" in the nineteenth century. Austin tells Lee that they are "livin' in a Paradise. We've forgotten about that." This is surely the West that Shepard would like America to be, the West that was in the dreams of our forefathers (or "old men" of another generation): a land of unparalleled optimism and opportunity. It is the West envisioned in such films as *Shane* and *Red River*; indeed such films perpetuated this myth of the "true west."

But that myth was a fiction, as the reality of the West was its violence. The code of the West was survival at all costs, even if it meant abandoning those closest to you. One made one's own laws to survive, to acquire land (or TV sets in Lee's case), to acquire the wealth the new land promised. In January 1984 Shepard discussed his interest in western violence, which he found simultaneously "ugly" and "very moving" because "it has something to do with humiliation." He ascribed the violence, in part, to "the guilt of having gotten this country by wiping out a race of people." His historical reference to the genocide of Native Americans defines the "true west" and demythologizes the romantic heritage portrayed in the art of Fredrick Remington or the films of John Wayne. Thus the American West, a Janus-faced entity, is the ideal metaphor for Shepard's apocalyptic vision of the world: the Promised Land is also a Wasteland; the territory of the rugged individualist is also the prison of the lonely and isolated; the home on the range is also the house of the cursed.

Thus Shepard in *True West*—as in the other works in his canon—is a voice crying in the wilderness. He ventures into the desert to seek the demons of our past. But his enigmatic endings do not provide the comfort of catharsis, which, says the playwright, "gets rid of something. I'm not looking to get rid of something, I'm looking to find it. I'm not writing plays to vent demons. I want to shake hands with them."

Other perspectives on *True West*:

Chubb, Kenneth. "Sam Shepard: Metaphors, Mad Dogs and Old Time Cowboys." *Theatre Quarterly* 4:15 (August–October 1974): 16.

Kleb, William. "Sam Shepard's *True West*." *Theater* 12:1 (Fall/Winter 1980): 65–71.

See *True West* on video:

True West. Dir. Allan Goldstein. Perf. John Malkovich and Gary Sinese. Academy Home
 Entertainment, 110 min., 1987.

Other plays by Shepard on video:

Curse of the Starving Class. Dir. J. Michael McClary. Perf. James Woods, Kathy Bates,
 Randy Quaid, and Louis Gossett, Jr. Vidmark, 102 min., 1994.

Fool for Love. Dir. Robert Altman. Perf. Sam Shepard, Kim Bassinger, Harry Dean Staton,
 and Randy Quaid. MGM/UA Studios, 106 min., 1985.

A video about Sam Shepard:

Sam Shepard: Stalking Himself. Interviews with Sam Shepard, John Malkovich, Ed Harris,
 Gary Sinese, and Ethan Hawke. Insight Media, 60 min., 1997.

SHOWCASE   MYTH AND THE THEATER

Myth is a powerful medium because it talks to the emotions and not the head. It moves us into an area of mystery.

—Sam Shepard

As was suggested in the introduction to Part III, one of the salient features of theater since the 1960s—after almost a century of plays based on the particulars of individuals in a given society—has been a marked return to myth as an integral element of playwriting and performance. And that is as it should be, for in virtually every documented instance, drama evolved from myths and used the great stories of a culture as the source of its first plays. Consider some prominent examples.

- Some two thousand years before the Greeks created theater, Egyptians reenacted the myth of Osiris, a sun god, each spring at Abydos, a sacred spot on the Nile River. The Abydos Passion Play portrayed the death and resurrection of Osiris, whose mutilated body buried along the Nile brought life-sustaining crops to the Egyptians, and the pharaohs used the occasion to associate their power with the gods. Accounts of the Abydos Passion Play written by a participant named Ikernofret represent some of the first accounts of theater practice known to humans. (Notably, Shepard's 1979 Pulitzer Prize play, *Buried Child*, retains elements of the Osiris myth.)

- According to Aristotle, Greek drama evolved from hymns (dithyrambs) honoring Dionysus, the god of the grape, fertility, and passion. Like Osiris, Dionysus was buried in the earth and revived each spring, and the Greeks set aside a week at the beginning of the planting season to honor their god in hopes that he would grant them plentitude. As Greek drama matured in the fifth century BCE, playwrights created plays—both tragic and comic—that were de-

rived from ancient myths known to the people.

- According to Hindu mythology, theater was a gift to humans by the gods themselves. Shiva—"the Lord of the Dance"—and other gods (Brahma and Krishna) believed theater could enlighten people about the sacred mysteries of life, and Shiva inspired a monk, Bharata, to write a treatise (*The Natyasastra*) that defined theater practice in India. The book is a part of the holy Vedas, which may be compared to the Judeo-Christian Bible for its importance to Hindu belief. The earliest plays in India were based on that country's great myths, *The Ramayana* and *The Mahabharata*.

- The Yoruba of Nigeria believe that Ogun was "the first actor" because he returned to earth to help humans bridge the gap between the living and those who have crossed into the hereafter. (See Showcase, "The Yoruba Obatala Festival in Ede" earlier in Part III.)

- The venerable Noh theater of Japan is said to have evolved from a tale in Shinto mythology: the goddess Uzume danced to lure the goddess of darkness, Amaterasu, from the cave in which she hid for many years. When the latter emerged, the world was bathed in sunlight, and since its inception the Noh theater has sought to "illuminate" audiences from darkness to light, from ignorance to knowledge.

- In a medieval cathedral in c. 960 CE, priests performed the *Quem Queritas Trope*, a musical retelling of the Easter story in which the dead Christ was resurrected after his death on Good Friday. European drama was itself "reborn" in such church ceremonies (although there were folk plays and other secular works). We can trace the growth of secular drama from plays that reenacted tales from the Bible.

Thus, in whichever corner of the globe you choose to find the roots of theater, you are most likely to find the great myths of a culture as both the impetus for performance and the source of its earliest dramas.

Why myth? Myths may be defined as stories that evolve over centuries and are created by a culture to explain natural phenomena, to promote a worldview of that culture, and, importantly, to embody the ideals held sacred by its people. Myths also connect people with metaphysical forces greater than themselves, which is why gods are at the heart of myths. Unlike fables and folk tales, myths are initially believed as true and held sacred by the people who create them. For our purposes in the contemporary world, myths represent archetypal characters and situations that illustrate essential human behaviors. Thus myths have an instructive purpose: they help us understand our place in the world and explain recurring patterns of human actions such as passion, revenge, and jealousy. This is why, to cite perhaps the most famous case, Sigmund Freud identified the Oedipus complex in men (or the Electra complex in women) to explain the natural rivalry between a son and his father. Freud saw in the story of Oedipus, the Theban king who killed his father and married his mother, the quintessential metaphor for sexual jealousy of a son for his father. You may recall a recent case in Houston, Texas, in which a woman drowned her five children; she was referred to as "a modern Medea," a reference to the myth of the queen of Argos who killed her children as revenge for her husband's infidelity. Myths, it should be noted, usually deal with extreme behaviors and serve to remind us that humans (like our gods) are capable of extraordinary, often irrational, acts.

The world's greatest playwrights—England's Shakespeare, Spain's Calderon, Germany's Goethe, India's Kalidasa, Japan's Zeami, to name but a few pre-Ibsen dramatists—frequently used myth as inspiration for their works.

Shakespeare used and even added to the "myth" of English history in his chronicle plays. It is possible that a playwright can actually elevate a human to near-mythic status, as Shakespeare did with Henry V, "the mirror of all Christian kings."

Much of modern drama, especially in its earliest years, was grounded in the particulars of a given society and its contemporary problems. Human behavior was often ascribed to economic circumstances, environment, or a particular neurosis. In many ways, myth was relegated to a secondary position in the creation of drama. To be sure, even the early Realists retained some affinity for myth. Ibsen wrote plays like *The Lady from the Sea* and *The Master Builder* that, on closer examination, evidence mythic roots, whatever the particulars of the late-nineteenth-century society they depict.

Many modern dramatists of note have recast ancient myths in a contemporary setting. Eugene O'Neill wrote *Mourning Becomes Electra*, a massive retelling of Aeschylus's revenge cycle, *The Oresteia*; O'Neill set its action in the American Civil War. *Desire Under the Elms* is the Phaedra-Hippolytus myth played out on a New England farm. Note that such myths, whether ancient or modern, most often deal with titanic struggles within a family, a metaphor for our interconnectedness as humans. Aristotle noted in *The Poetics* that the greatest tragedies dealt with families and "blood pollution." Tennessee Williams wrote *Orpheus Descending*, a modern journey through the hell of alcohol and an indifferent world. Jean-Paul Sartre's *The Flies* is an existentialist account of the Oedipus legend. Edward Albee's newest play, *The Goat, or Who Is Sylvia*, can trace its roots to the myth of Dionysus himself, who, you may remember, was guarded by a race of satyrs (half-men, half-goats).

Many of the plays in this anthology, especially in this final section, exhibit a mythic quality. You have just read that Shepard's *True West* ends with the frightful specter of brothers locked in mortal combat, an evocation of the Cain and Abel story in Genesis. Caryl Churchill juxtaposes mythic characters (Lady Ninjo, Dull Gret) with more mundane ones in *Top Girls* to illustrate the struggles of the modern woman within a larger cultural context. In *Zoot Suit* Luis Valdez evokes the mythology of the Aztecs to comment on contemporary Chicano life; the playwright invests the street-wise *pachuco* with a mythic stature to instill racial pride in his audiences. Although in *Angels in America* Tony Kushner explores the reality of current national crises, such as the AIDS epidemic, he frames his discussion mythically: holy books mysteriously erupt from the earth, while a glorious Angel descends on the AIDS-afflicted hero in the play's memorable finale. Perhaps the moment remains memorable precisely because it taps into our sense of the very metaphysical forces that inspired myth. Great theater has done this since its inception, and perhaps if the theater and its drama are to survive in the new century, it will be because artists are turning again to the power of myth to move us in ways that purely sociological drama cannot.

"MASTER HAROLD" . . . and the boys

ATHOL FUGARD

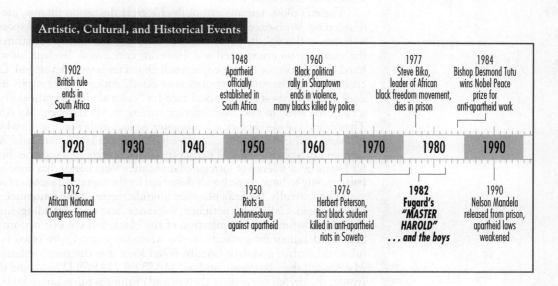

ATHOL FUGARD (1932–)

South African Harold Athol Lanning Fugard was born in Middleburg, Cape Province. When he was three, his family moved to Port Elizabeth in Eastern Province, where his mother was forced to be the family provider because of his father's heavy drinking and physical handicap. She ran the Jubilee Hotel and the Saint George's Park Tea Room. After graduation from the local technical high school, Fugard earned a scholarship at the University of Cape Town, where he studied philosophy for three years before dropping out to embark on a life as a sailor, journalist, and court clerk. In each job he was constantly confronted by the inequities, bigotry, and racism fostered by apartheid, South Africa's legal policy of racial separateness. As an adolescent he was subjected to his father's "pointless, unthought-out prejudices"; as the only white sailor on a voyage to Japan he gained intimate knowledge of the plight of many blacks and Asians; and as a court clerk he saw firsthand the cruel effects of apartheid.

Unsatisfied and at the urging of his wife, actress Sheila Meiring, he turned to playwriting. A voracious reader, he was influenced by British playwright John Osborne and the American novelist William Faulkner. Following Osborne's lead as the outspoken "angry young man" and Faulkner's "unashamedly regional" preoccupation, he developed into a passionate, regional playwright whose insight and sensitivity speak to both his native land and the world.

But it is not only life in South Africa that is portrayed in a Fugard play but also the life of the playwright himself. An autobiographical thread runs through his major plays, which include *No-Good Friday* (1958), *Blood Knot* (1961), *Bosman and Lena* (1968), *The Island* and

Sizwe Bansi Is Dead (1972, both written in collaboration with Winston Ntshona and John Kani), *Statements after an Arrest under the Immorality Act* (1974), *A Lesson from Aloes* (1978), *"MASTER HAROLD" . . . and the boys* (1982), *The Road to Mecca* (1984), *My Children! My Africa!* (1989), *Playland* (1992), *Valley Song* (1996), and *Sorrows and Rejoicings* (2002).

Fugard's work as a dramatist began in Port Elizabeth with the Serpent Players, a company including white, black, and "colored" South Africans, many of whom became his lifelong friends. Two of them, Zakes Mokae and John Kani—South Africa's leading black actors—have played many primary roles in his plays. His early works were developed as "pieces in progress" in which much of the action and the dialogue were created through improvisation. His later plays, though rooted in his apartheid experiences, are more the work of an individual voice.

Fugard's plots, reminiscent of Ibsen's great discussion dramas, are painstakingly slow in developing. With exceptional care, he meticulously lays out the exposition so that as the action moves through its complications, a tremendous sense of rhythm and momentum hurls the viewer to an unexpected and shattering conclusion. Because his works are usually populated by only two or three people, each character is well developed. Often the situations he creates reflect the mixed population of South Africa. For example, in *Blood Knot* there are Zack and Morrie—men of mixed race (or "coloreds," as apartheid classified them) who are sons of the same mother and different fathers; in *My Children! My Africa!* there are Mr. M., Thami, and Isabel—a black schoolmaster, a black male pupil, and a white female student; and in *"MASTER HAROLD" . . . and the boys* there are Hally, Sam, and Willie—a white adolescent and two older blacks. Whether his characters are tied together by a blood knot, a desire for learning, or a sense of surrogate family, they form bonds that cross racial and generational barriers only to have those bonds destroyed by the ingrained racism of which they are victims.

Thematically, Fugard's plays are an indictment of the ignorance and hatred that nourish apartheid. Calling for patience, tolerance, and understanding, his plays reveal not only the exploitation and victimization of the black and colored majority of South Africa but also the dehumanizing effects on the white minority. Quite often Fugard creates a peaceful world within a violent one. In *Blood Knot* it is the men's shanty hut; in *My Children! My Africa!*, the classroom; and in *"MASTER HAROLD" . . . and the boys*, the tea room. Inside, the dream of equality thrives and optimism rules; but outside, a nightmare of separateness and injustice flourishes while despair reigns supreme.

Fugard's two most recent works have taken him beyond the social realism of his apartheid era works. In *The Captain's Tiger* (1999), he dramatized, with not a little self-mockery, his early years as a writer and his relationship with his mother. In the less effective *Sorrows and Rejoicings* (2002), Fugard presented the ghost of a writer returning to his beloved desert, the Karoo.

Fugard now maintains a residence in the United States (Del Mar, California) and teaches at the University of California at San Diego.

AS YOU READ *"MASTER HAROLD" . . . and the boys*

For Fugard, the playwright's work begins not with ideas but with images. "From the very first, the generative—the seed of what energy's involved and goes on to produce a play—comes from images, not ideas," declares Fugard, ". . . something I have to see or hear, not think, but see or hear," that leads to crafting of the play. In *"MASTER HAROLD"* Fugard has created images of sublime memories juxtaposed with those of grotesque reality. Specifically, the play is composed of several central images—ballroom dancing, kite making and flying, and teaching—each presented to create in the tea room a microcosm of a bigoted world. And as is typical of Fugard's plays, things begin placidly with little sense of action; when this situation finally explodes, the shock is that much greater. The very structure of the play mirrors South Africa during white rule; underneath the apparent calm lies a festering wound that must suddenly explode. And it is useful to remember that this play is based on an actual incident from Fugard's youth. Here he presents an image of himself caught in emotional turmoil as he moved from innocence to the poisonous bigotry of adulthood.

"MASTER HAROLD" . . . and the boys

ATHOL FUGARD

The St. George's Park Tea Room on a wet and windy Port Elizabeth[1] afternoon.

Tables and chairs have been cleared and are stacked on one side except for one which stands apart with a single chair. On this table a knife, fork, spoon and side plate in anticipation of a simple meal, together with a pile of comic books.

Other elements: a serving counter with a few stale cakes under glass and a not very impressive display of sweets, cigarettes and cool drinks, etc.; a few cardboard advertising handouts—Cadbury's Chocolate, Coca-Cola—and a blackboard on which an untrained hand has chalked up the prices of Tea, Coffee, Scones, Milkshakes—all flavors—and Cool Drinks; a few sad ferns in pots; a telephone; an old-style jukebox.

There is an entrance on one side and an exit into a kitchen on the other.

Leaning on the solitary table, his head cupped in one hand as he pages through one of the comic books, is Sam. A black man in his mid-forties. He wears the white coat of a waiter. Behind him on his knees, mopping down the floor with a bucket of water and a rag, is Willie. Also black and about the same age as Sam. He has his sleeves and trousers rolled up.

The year: 1950

WILLIE (singing as he works).
"She was scandalizin' my name,
She took my money
She called me honey
But she was scandalizin' my name.
Called it love but was playin' a game . . ."

He gets up and moves the bucket. Stands thinking for a moment, then, raising his arms to hold an imaginary partner, he launches into an intricate ballroom dance step. Although a mildly comic figure, he reveals a reasonable degree of accomplishment.

[1]**Port Elizabeth** city in South Africa

Hey, Sam.

Sam, absorbed in the comic book, does not respond.

Hey, Boet[2] Sam!

Sam looks up.

I'm getting it. The quickstep. Look now and tell me. (He repeats the step.) Well?

SAM (encouragingly). Show me again.

WILLIE. Okay, count for me.

SAM. Ready?

WILLIE. Ready.

SAM. Five, six, seven, eight . . . (Willie starts to dance.) A-n-d one two three four . . . and one two three four. . . . (Ad libbing as Willie dances.) Your shoulders, Willie . . . your shoulders! Don't look down! Look happy, Willie! Relax, Willie!

WILLIE (desperate but still dancing). I am relax.

SAM. No, you're not.

WILLIE (he falters). Ag no man, Sam! Mustn't talk. You make me make mistakes.

SAM. But you're too stiff.

WILLIE. Yesterday I'm not straight . . . today I'm too stiff!

SAM. Well, you are. You asked me and I'm telling you.

WILLIE. Where?

SAM. Everywhere. Try to glide through it.

WILLIE. Glide?

SAM. Ja, make it smooth. And give it more style. It must look like you're enjoying yourself.

WILLIE (emphatically). I wasn't.

SAM. Exactly.

WILLIE. How can I enjoy myself? Not straight, too stiff and now it's also glide, give it more style, make it smooth. . . . Haai! Is hard to remember all those things, Boet Sam.

[2]**Boet** Buddy, Brother

Athol Fugard

SAM. That's your trouble. You're trying too hard.

WILLIE. I try hard because it *is* hard.

SAM. But don't let me see it. The secret is to make it look easy. Ballroom must look happy, Willie, not like hard work. It must . . . Ja! . . . it must look like romance.

WILLIE. Now another one! What's romance?

SAM. Love story with happy ending. A handsome man in tails, and in his arms, smiling at him, a beautiful lady in evening dress!

WILLIE. Fred Astaire, Ginger Rogers.

SAM. You got it. Tapdance or ballroom, it's the same. Romance. In two weeks' time when the judges look at you and Hilda, they must see a man and a woman who are dancing their way to a happy ending. What I saw was you holding her like you were frightened she was going to run away.

WILLIE. Ja! Because that is what she wants to do! I got no romance left for Hilda anymore, Boet Sam.

SAM. Then pretend. When you put your arms around Hilda, imagine she is Ginger Rogers.

WILLIE. With no teeth? You try.

SAM. Well, just remember, there's only two weeks left.

WILLIE. I know, I know! (*To the jukebox.*) I do it better with music. You got sixpence for Sarah Vaughan?[3]

SAM. That's a slow foxtrot. You're practicing the quickstep.

WILLIE. I'll practice slow foxtrot.

SAM (*shaking his head*). It's your turn to put money in the jukebox.

WILLIE. I only got bus fare to go home. (*He returns disconsolately to his work.*) Love story and happy ending! She's doing it all right, Boet Sam, but is not me she's giving happy endings. Fuckin' whore! Three nights now she doesn't come practice. I wind up gramophone, I get record ready and I sit and wait. What happens? Nothing. Ten o'clock I start dancing with my pillow. You try and practice romance by yourself, Boet Sam. Struesgod, she doesn't come tonight I take back my dress and ballroom shoes and I find me new partner. Size twenty-six. Shoes size seven. And now she's also making trouble for me with the baby again. Reports me to Child Wellfed, that I'm not giving her money. She lies! Every week I am giving her money for milk. And how do I know is my baby? Only his hair looks like me. She's fucking around all the time I turn my back. Hilda Samuels is a bitch! (*Pause.*) Hey, Sam!

SAM. Ja.

WILLIE. You listening?

SAM. Ja.

WILLIE. So what you say?

SAM. About Hilda?

WILLIE. Ja.

SAM. When did you last give her a hiding?

WILLIE (*reluctantly*). Sunday night.

SAM. And today is Thursday.

WILLIE (*he knows what's coming*). Okay.

SAM. Hiding on Sunday night, then Monday, Tuesday and Wednesday she doesn't come to practice . . . and you are asking me why?

WILLIE. I said okay, Boet Sam!

SAM. You hit her too much. One day she's going to leave you for good.

WILLIE. So? She makes me the hell-in too much.

SAM (*emphasizing his point*). *Too* much and *too* hard. You had the same trouble with Eunice.

WILLIE. Because she also make the hell-in, Boet Sam. She never got the steps right. Even the waltz.

SAM. Beating her up every time she makes a mistake in the waltz? (*Shaking his head.*) No, Willie! That takes the pleasure out of ballroom dancing.

WILLIE. Hilda is not too bad with the waltz, Boet Sam. Is the quickstep where the trouble starts.

SAM (*teasing him gently*). How's your pillow with the quickstep?

WILLIE (*ignoring the tease*). Good! And why? Because it got no legs. That's her trouble. She can't move them quick enough, Boet Sam. I start the record and before halfway Count Basie[4] is already winning. Only time we catch up with him is when gramophone runs down.

Sam laughs.

Haaikona, Boet Sam, is not funny.

SAM (*snapping his fingers*). I got it! Give her a handicap.

WILLIE. What's that?

SAM. Give her a ten-second start and then let Count Basie go. Then I put my money on her. Hot favorite in the Ballroom Stakes: Hilda Samuels ridden by Willie Malopo.

WILLIE (*turning away*). I'm not talking to you no more.

SAM (*relenting*). Sorry, Willie . . .

WILLIE. It's finish between us.

SAM. Okay, okay . . . I'll stop.

WILLIE. You can also fuck off.

SAM. Willie, listen! I want to help you!

WILLIE. No more jokes?

[3]**Sarah Vaughan** (1924–90) American jazz singer

[4]**Count Basie** William Basie (1904–84), American jazz pianist and band leader

752

SAM. I promise.

WILLIE. Okay. Help me.

SAM (*his turn to hold an imaginary partner*). Look and learn. Feet together. Back straight. Body relaxed. Right hand placed gently in the small of her back and wait for the music. Don't start worrying about making mistakes or the judges or the other competitors. It's just you, Hilda and the music, and you're going to have a good time. What Count Basie do you play?

WILLIE. "You the cream in my coffee, you the salt in my stew."

SAM. Right. Give it to me in strict tempo.

WILLIE. Ready?

SAM. Ready.

WILLIE. A-n-d . . . (*Singing.*)

"You the cream in my coffee.
You the salt in my stew.
You will always be my necessity.
I'd be lost without you. . . ." (etc.)

Sam launches into the quickstep. He is obviously a much more accomplished dancer than Willie. Hally enters. A seventeen-year-old white boy. Wet raincoat and school case. He stops and watches Sam. The demonstration comes to an end with a flourish. Applause from Hally and Willie.

HALLY. Bravo! No question about it. First place goes to Mr. Sam Semela.

WILLIE (*in total agreement*). You was gliding with style, Boet Sam.

HALLY (*cheerfully*). How's it, chaps?

SAM. Okay, Hally.

WILLIE (*springing to attention like a soldier and saluting*). At your service, Master Harold!

HALLY. Not long to the big event, hey!

SAM. Two weeks.

HALLY. You nervous?

SAM. No.

HALLY. Think you stand a chance?

SAM. Let's just say I'm ready to go out there and dance.

HALLY. It looked like it. What about you, Willie?

Willie groans.

What's the matter?

SAM. He's got leg trouble.

HALLY (*innocently*). Oh, sorry to hear that, Willie.

WILLIE. Boet Sam! You promised. (*Willie returns to his work.*)

Hally deposits his school case and takes off his raincoat. His clothes are a little neglected and untidy:

black blazer with school badge, gray flannel trousers in need of an ironing, khaki shirt and tie, black shoes. Sam has fetched a towel for Hally to dry his hair.

HALLY. God, what a lousy bloody day. It's coming down cats and dogs out there. Bad for business, chaps . . . (*Conspiratorial whisper.*) . . . but it also means we're in for a nice quiet afternoon.

SAM. You can speak loud. Your Mom's not here.

HALLY. Out shopping?

SAM. No. The hospital.

HALLY. But it's Thursday. There's no visiting on Thursday afternoons. Is my Dad okay?

SAM. Sounds like it. In fact, I think he's going home.

HALLY (*stopped short by Sam's remark*). What do you mean?

SAM. The hospital phoned.

HALLY. To say what?

SAM. I don't know. I just heard your Mom talking.

HALLY. So what makes you say he's going home?

SAM. It sounded as if they were telling her to come and fetch him.

Hally thinks about what Sam has said for a few seconds.

HALLY. When did she leave?

SAM. About an hour ago. She said she would phone you. Want to eat?

Hally doesn't respond.

Hally, want your lunch?

HALLY. I suppose so. (*His mood has changed.*) What's on the menu? . . . as if I don't know.

SAM. Soup, followed by meat pie and gravy.

HALLY. Today's?

SAM. No.

HALLY. And the soup?

SAM. Nourishing pea soup.

HALLY. Just the soup. (*The pile of comic books on the table.*) And these?

SAM. For your Dad. Mr. Kempston brought them.

HALLY. You haven't been reading them, have you?

SAM. Just looking.

HALLY (*examining the comics*). Jungle Jim . . . Batman and Robin . . . Tarzan . . . God, what rubbish! Mental pollution. Take them away.

Sam exits waltzing into the kitchen. Hally turns to Willie.

HALLY. Did you hear my Mom talking on the telephone, Willie?

WILLIE. No, Master Hally. I was at the back.

HALLY. And she didn't say anything to you before she left?

WILLIE. She said I must clean the floors.

HALLY. I mean about my Dad.

WILLIE. She didn't say nothing to me about him, Master Hally.

HALLY (*with conviction*). No! It can't be. They said he needed at least another three weeks of treatment. Sam's definitely made a mistake. (*Rummages through his school case, finds a book and settles down at the table to read.*) So, Willie!

WILLIE. Yes, Master Hally! Schooling okay today?

HALLY. Yes, okay.... (*He thinks about it.*) ... No, not really. Ag, what's the difference? I don't care. And Sam says you've got problems.

WILLIE. Big problems.

HALLY. Which leg is sore?

Willie groans.

Both legs.

WILLIE. There is nothing wrong with my legs. Sam is just making jokes.

HALLY. So then you will be in the competition.

WILLIE. Only if I can find me a partner.

HALLY. But what about Hilda?

SAM (*returning with a bowl of soup*). She's the one who's got trouble with her legs.

HALLY. What sort of trouble, Willie?

SAM. From the way he describes it, I think the lady has gone a bit lame.

HALLY. Good God! Have you taken her to see a doctor?

SAM. I think a vet would be better.

HALLY. What do you mean?

SAM. What do you call it again when a racehorse goes very fast?

HALLY. Gallop?

SAM. That's it!

WILLIE. Boet Sam!

HALLY. "A gallop down the homestretch to the winning post." But what's that got to do with Hilda?

SAM. Count Basie always gets there first.

Willie lets fly with his slop rag. It misses Sam and hits Hally.

HALLY (*furious*). For Christ's sake, Willie! What the hell do you think you're doing!

WILLIE. Sorry, Master Hally, but it's him. . . .

HALLY. Act your bloody age! (*Hurls the rag back at Willie.*) Cut out the nonsense now and get on with your work. And you too, Sam. Stop fooling around.

Sam moves away.

No. Hang on. I haven't finished! Tell me exactly what my Mom said.

SAM. I have. "When Hally comes, tell him I've gone to the hospital and I'll phone him."

HALLY. She didn't say anything about taking my Dad home?

SAM. No. It's just that when she was talking on the phone . . .

HALLY (*interrupting him*). No, Sam. They can't be discharging him. She would have said so if they were. In any case, we saw him last night and he wasn't in good shape at all. Staff nurse even said there was talk about taking more X-rays. And now suddenly today he's better? If anything, it sounds more like a bad turn to me . . . which I sincerely hope it isn't. Hang on . . . how long ago did you say she left?

SAM. Just before two . . . (*His wrist watch.*) . . . hour and a half.

HALLY. I know how to settle it. (*Behind the counter to the telephone. Talking as he dials.*) Let's give her ten minutes to get to the hospital, ten minutes to load him up, another ten, at the most, to get home and another ten to get him inside. Forty minutes. They should have been home for at least half an hour already. (*Pause—he waits with the receiver to his ear.*) No reply, chaps. And you know why? Because she's at his bedside in hospital helping him pull through a bad turn. You definitely heard wrong.

SAM. Okay.

As far as Hally is concerned, the matter is settled. He returns to his table, sits down and divides his attention between the book and his soup. Sam is at his school case and picks up a textbook "Modern Graded Mathematics for Standards Nine and Ten." Opens it at random and laughs at something he sees.

Who is this supposed to be?

HALLY. Old fart-face Prentice.

SAM. Teacher?

HALLY. Thinks he is. And believe me, that is not a bad likeness.

SAM. Has he seen it?

HALLY. Yes.

SAM. What did he say?

HALLY. Tried to be clever, as usual. Said I was no Leonardo da Vinci and that bad art had to be punished. So, six of the best, and his are bloody good.

SAM. On your bum?

HALLY. Where else? The days when I got them on my hands are gone forever, Sam.

SAM. With your trousers down!

HALLY. No. He's not quite that barbaric.

SAM. That's the way they do it in jail.

HALLY (*flicker of morbid interest*). Really?

SAM. Ja. When the magistrate sentences you to "strokes with a light cane."

HALLY. Go on.

SAM. They make you lie down on a bench. One policeman pulls down your trousers and holds your ankles, another one pulls your shirt over your head and holds your arms . . .

HALLY. Thank you! That's enough.

SAM. . . . and the one that gives you the strokes talks to you gently and for a long time between each one. (*He laughs.*)

HALLY. I've heard enough, Sam! Jesus! It's a bloody awful world when you come to think of it. People can be real bastards.

SAM. That's the way it is, Hally.

HALLY. It doesn't have to be that way. There is something called progress, you know. We don't exactly burn people at the stake anymore.

SAM. Like Joan of Arc.

HALLY. Correct. If she was captured today, she'd be given a fair trial.

SAM. And then the death sentence.

HALLY (*a world-weary sigh*). I know, I know! I oscillate between hope and despair for this world as well, Sam. But things will change, you wait and see. One day somebody is going to get up and give history a kick up the backside and get it going again.

SAM. Like who?

HALLY (*after thought*). They're called social reformers. Every age, Sam, has got its social reformer. My history book is full of them.

SAM. So where's ours?

HALLY. Good question. And I hate to say it, but the answer is: I don't know. Maybe he hasn't even been born yet. Or is still only a babe in arms at his mother's breast. God, what a thought.

SAM. So we just go on waiting.

HALLY. Ja, looks like it. (*Back to his soup and the book.*)

SAM (*reading from the textbook*). "Introduction: In some mathematical problems only the magnitude . . . " (*He mispronounces the word "magnitude."*)

HALLY (*correcting him without looking up*). Magnitude.

SAM. What's it mean?

HALLY. How big it is. The size of the thing.

SAM (*reading*). ". . . a magnitude of the quantities is of importance. In other problems we need to know whether these quantities are negative or positive.

For example, whether there is a debit or credit bank balance . . . "

HALLY. Whether you're broke or not.

SAM. ". . . whether the temperature is above or below zero . . . "

HALLY. Naught degrees. Cheerful state of affairs! No cash and you're freezing to death. Mathematics won't get you out of that one.

SAM. "All these quantities are called . . . " (*Spelling the word.*) . . . s-c-a-l . . .

HALLY. Scalars.

SAM. Scalars! (*Shaking his head with a laugh.*) You understand all that?

HALLY (*turning a page*). No. And I don't intend to try.

SAM. So what happens when the exams come?

HALLY. Failing a maths exam isn't the end of the world, Sam. How many times have I told you that examination results don't measure intelligence?

SAM. I would say about as many times as you've failed one of them.

HALLY (*mirthlessly*). Ha, ha, ha.

SAM (*simultaneously*). Ha, ha, ha.

HALLY. Just remember Winston Churchill didn't do particularly well at school.

SAM. You've also told me that one many times.

HALLY. Well, it just so happens to be the truth.

SAM (*enjoying the word*). Magnitude! Magnitude! Show me how to use it.

HALLY (*after thought*). An intrepid social reformer will not be daunted by the magnitude of the task he has undertaken.

SAM (*impressed*). Couple of jaw-breakers in there!

HALLY. I gave you three for the price of one. Intrepid, daunted and magnitude. I did that once in an exam. Put five of the words I had to explain in one sentence. It was half a page long.

SAM. Well, I'll put my money on you in the English exam.

HALLY. Piece of cake. Eighty percent without even trying.

SAM (*another textbook from Hally's case*). And history?

HALLY. So-so. I'll scrape through. In the fifties if I'm lucky.

SAM. You didn't do too badly last year.

HALLY. Because we had World War One. That at least had some action. You try to find that in the South African Parliamentary system.

SAM (*reading from the history textbook*). "Napoleon and the principle of equality." Hey! This sounds interesting. "After concluding peace with Britain in 1802, Napoleon used a brief period of calm to insti-tute . . . "

HALLY. Introduce.

SAM. "... many reforms. Napoleon regarded all people as equal before the law and wanted them to have equal opportunities for advancement. All ves-ti-ges of the feu-dal system with its oppression of the poor were abolished." Vestiges, feudal system and abolished. I'm all right on oppression.

HALLY. I'm thinking. He swept away ... abolished ... the last remains ... vestiges ... of the bad old days ... feudal system.

SAM. Ha! There's the social reformer we're waiting for. He sounds like a man of some magnitude.

HALLY. I'm not so sure about that. It's a damn good title for a book, though. A man of magnitude!

SAM. He sounds pretty big to me, Hally.

HALLY. Don't confuse historical significance with greatness. But maybe I'm being a bit prejudiced. Have a look in there and you'll see he's two chapters long. And hell! ... has he only got dates, Sam, all of which you've got to remember! This campaign and that campaign, and then, because of all the fighting, the next thing is we get Peace Treaties all over the place. And what's the end of the story? Battle of Waterloo, which he loses. Wasn't worth it. No, I don't know about him as a man of magnitude.

SAM. Then who would you say was?

HALLY. To answer that, we need a definition of greatness, and I suppose that would be somebody who ... somebody who benefited all mankind.

SAM. Right. But like who?

HALLY (*he speaks with total conviction*). Charles Darwin. Remember him? That big book from the library. *The Origin of the Species*.

SAM. Him?

HALLY. Yes. For his Theory of Evolution.

SAM. You didn't finish it.

HALLY. I ran out of time. I didn't finish it because my two weeks was up. But I'm going to take it out again after I've digested what I read. It's safe. I've hidden it away in the Theology section. Nobody ever goes in there. And anyway who are you to talk? You hardly even looked at it.

SAM. I tried. I looked at the chapters in the beginning and I saw one called "The Struggle for an Existence." Ah ha, I thought. At last! But what did I get? Something called the mistletoe which needs the apple tree and there's too many seeds and all are going to die except one ... ! No, Hally.

HALLY (*intellectually outraged*). What do you mean, No! The poor man had to start somewhere. For God's sake, Sam, he revolutionized science. Now we know.

SAM. What?

HALLY. Where we come from and what it all means.

SAM. And that's a benefit to mankind? Anyway, I still don't believe it.

HALLY. God, you're impossible. I showed it to you in black and white.

SAM. Doesn't mean I got to believe it.

HALLY. It's the likes of you that kept the Inquisition in business. It's called bigotry. Anyway, that's my man of magnitude. Charles Darwin! Who's yours?

SAM (*without hesitation*). Abraham Lincoln.

HALLY. I might have guessed as much. Don't get sentimental, Sam. You've never been a slave, you know. And anyway we freed your ancestors here in South Africa long before the Americans. But if you want to thank somebody on their behalf, do it to Mr. William Wilberforce.[5] Come on. Try again. I want a real genius. (*Now enjoying himself, and so is Sam. Hally goes behind the counter and helps himself to a chocolate.*)

SAM. William Shakespeare.

HALLY (*no enthusiasm*). Oh. So you're also one of them, are you? You're basing that opinion on only one play, you know. You've only read my *Julius Caesar* and even I don't understand half of what they're talking about. They should do what they did with the old Bible: bring the language up to date.

SAM. That's all you've got. It's also the only one you've read.

HALLY. I know. I admit it. That's why I suggest we reserve our judgment until we've checked up on a few others. I've got a feeling, though, that by the end of this year one is going to be enough for me, and I can give you the names of twenty-nine other chaps in the Standard Nine class of the Port Elizabeth Technical College who feel the same. But if you want him, you can have him. My turn now. (*Pacing.*) This is a damned good exercise, you know! It started off looking like a simple question and here it's got us really probing into the intellectual heritage of our civilization.

SAM. So who is it going to be?

HALLY. My next man ... and he gets the title on two scores: social reform and literary genius ... is Leo Nikolaevich Tolstoy.

SAM. That Russian.

HALLY. Correct. Remember the picture of him I showed you?

SAM. With the long beard.

HALLY (*trying to look like Tolstoy*). And those burning, visionary eyes. My God, the face of a social prophet if

[5]**William Wilberforce** (1759–1833) English abolitionist

ever I saw one! And remember my words when I showed it to you? Here's a *man*, Sam!

SAM. Those were words, Hally.

HALLY. Not many intellectuals are prepared to shovel manure with the peasants and then go home and write a "little book" called *War and Peace*. Incidentally, Sam, he was somebody else who, to quote, ". . . did not distinguish himself scholastically."

SAM. Meaning?

HALLY. He was also no good at school.

SAM. Like you and Winston Churchill.

HALLY (*mirthlessly*). Ha, ha, ha.

SAM (*simultaneously*). Ha, ha, ha.

HALLY. Don't get clever, Sam. That man freed his serfs of his own free will.

SAM. No argument. He was a somebody, all right. I accept him.

HALLY. I'm sure Count Tolstoy will be very pleased to hear that. Your turn. Shoot. (*Another chocolate from behind the counter.*) I'm waiting, Sam.

SAM. I've got him.

HALLY. Good. Submit your candidate for examination.

SAM. Jesus.

HALLY (*stopped dead in his tracks*). Who?

SAM. Jesus Christ.

HALLY. Oh, come on, Sam!

SAM. The Messiah.

HALLY. Ja, but still . . . No, Sam. Don't let's get started on religion. We'll just spend the whole afternoon arguing again. Suppose I turn around and say Mohammed?

SAM. All right.

HALLY. You can't have them both on the same list!

SAM. Why not? You like Mohammed, I like Jesus.

HALLY. I *don't* like Mohammed. I never have. I was merely being hypothetical. As far as I'm concerned, the Koran is as bad as the Bible. No. Religion is out! I'm not going to waste my time again arguing with you about the existence of God. You know perfectly well I'm an atheist . . . and I've got homework to do.

SAM. Okay, I take him back.

HALLY. You've got time for one more name.

SAM (*after thought*). I've got one I know we'll agree on. A simple straightforward great Man of Magnitude . . . and no arguments. And he really did benefit all mankind.

HALLY. I wonder. After your last contribution I'm beginning to doubt whether anything in the way of an intellectual agreement is possible between the two of us. Who is he?

SAM. Guess.

HALLY. Socrates? Alexandre Dumas? Karl Marx? Dostoevsky? Nietzsche?

Sam shakes his head after each name.

Give me a clue.

SAM. The letter P is important . . .

HALLY. Plato!

SAM. . . . and his name begins with an F.

HALLY. I've got it. Freud and Psychology.

SAM. No. I didn't understand him.

HALLY. That makes two of us.

SAM. Think of mouldy apricot jam.

HALLY (*after a delighted laugh*). Penicillin and Sir Alexander Fleming! And the title of the book: *The Microbe Hunters*. (*Delighted.*) Splendid, Sam! Splendid. For once we are in total agreement. The major breakthrough in medical science in the Twentieth Century. If it wasn't for him, we might have lost the Second World War. It's deeply gratifying, Sam, to know that I haven't been wasting my time in talking to you. (*Strutting around proudly.*) Tolstoy may have educated his peasants, but I've educated you.

SAM. Standard Four to Standard Nine.

HALLY. Have we been at it as long as that?

SAM. Yep. And my first lesson was geography.

HALLY (*intrigued*). Really? I don't remember.

SAM. My room there at the back of the old Jubilee Boarding House. I had just started working for your Mom. Little boy in short trousers walks in one afternoon and asks me seriously: "Sam, do you want to see South Africa?" Hey man! Sure I wanted to see South Africa!

HALLY. Was that me?

SAM. . . . So the next thing I'm looking at a map you had just done for homework. It was your first one and you were very proud of yourself.

HALLY. Go on.

SAM. Then came my first lesson. "Repeat after me, Sam: Gold in the Transvaal, mealies in the Free State, sugar in Natal and grapes in the Cape." I still know it!

HALLY. Well, I'll be buggered. So that's how it all started.

SAM. And your next map was one with all the rivers and the mountains they came from. The Orange, the Vaal, the Limpopo, the Zambezi . . .

HALLY. You've got a phenomenal memory!

SAM. You should be grateful. That is why you started passing your exams. You tried to be better than me.

They laugh together. Willie is attracted by the laughter and joins them.

HALLY. The old Jubilee Boarding House. Sixteen rooms with board and lodging, rent in advance and one week's notice. I haven't thought about it for donkey's years . . . and I don't think that's an accident. God, was I glad when we sold it and moved out. Those years are not remembered as the happiest ones of an unhappy childhood.

WILLIE (*knocking on the table and trying to imitate a woman's voice*). "Hally, are you there?"

HALLY. Who's that supposed to be?

WILLIE. "What you doing in there, Hally? Come out at once!"

HALLY (*to Sam*). What's he talking about?

SAM. Don't you remember?

WILLIE. "Sam, Willie . . . is he in there with you boys?"

SAM. Hiding away in our room when your mother was looking for you.

HALLY (*another good laugh*). Of course! I used to crawl and hide under your bed! But finish the story, Willie. Then what used to happen? You chaps would give the game away by telling her I was in there with you. So much for friendship.

SAM. We couldn't lie to her. She knew.

HALLY. Which meant I got another rowing for hanging around the "servants' quarters." I think I spent more time in there with you chaps than anywhere else in that dump. And do you blame me? Nothing but bloody misery wherever you went. Somebody was always complaining about the food, or my mother was having a fight with Micky Nash because she'd caught her with a petty officer in her room. Maud Meiring was another one. Remember those two? They were prostitutes, you know. Soldiers and sailors from the troopships. Bottom fell out of the business when the war ended. God, the flotsam and jetsam that life washed up on our shores! No joking, if it wasn't for your room, I would have been the first certified ten-year-old in medical history. Ja, the memories are coming back now. Walking home from school and thinking: "What can I do this afternoon?" Try out a few ideas, but sooner or later I'd end up in there with you fellows. I bet you I could still find my way to your room with my eyes closed. (*He does exactly that.*) Down the corridor . . . telephone on the right, which my Mom keeps locked because somebody is using it on the sly and not paying . . . past the kitchen and unappetizing cooking smells . . . around the corner into the backyard, hold my breath again because there are more smells coming when I pass your lavatory, then into that little passageway, first door on the right and into your room. How's that?

SAM. Good. But, as usual, you forgot to knock.

HALLY. Like that time I barged in and caught you and Cynthia . . . at it. Remember? God, was I embarrassed! I didn't know what was going on at first.

SAM. Ja, that taught you a lesson.

HALLY. And about a lot more than knocking on doors, I'll have you know, and I don't mean geography either. Hell, Sam, couldn't you have waited until it was dark?

SAM. No.

HALLY. Was it that urgent?

SAM. Yes, and if you don't believe me, wait until your time comes.

HALLY. No, thank you. I am not interested in girls. (*Back to his memories . . . Using a few chairs he recreates the room as he lists the items.*) A gray little room with a cold cement floor. Your bed against that wall . . . and I now know why the mattress sags so much! . . . Willie's bed . . . it's propped up on bricks because one leg is broken . . . that wobbly little table with the washbasin and jug of water . . . Yes! . . . stuck to the wall above it are some pin-up pictures from magazines. Joe Louis[6] . . .

WILLIE. Brown Bomber. World Title. (*Boxing pose.*) Three rounds and knockout.

HALLY. Against who?

SAM. Max Schmeling.

HALLY. Correct. I can also remember Fred Astaire and Ginger Rogers, and Rita Hayworth in a bathing costume which always made me hot and bothered when I looked at it. Under Willie's bed is an old suitcase with all his clothes in a mess, which is why I never hide there. Your things are neat and tidy in a trunk next to your bed, and on it there is a picture of you and Cynthia in your ballroom clothes, your first silver cup for third place in a competition and an old radio which doesn't work anymore. Have I left out anything?

SAM. No.

HALLY. Right, so much for the stage directions. Now the characters. (*Sam and Willie move to their appropriate positions in the bedroom.*) Willie is in bed, under his blankets with his clothes on, complaining nonstop about something, but we can't make out a word of what he's saying because he's got his head under the blankets as well. You're on your bed trimming your toenails with a knife—not a very edifying sight—and as for me . . . What am I doing?

SAM. You're sitting on the floor giving Willie a lecture about being a good loser while you get the checker

---

[6]**Joe Louis** (1914–81) African-American prizefighter known as the Brown Bomber

board and pieces ready for a game. Then you go to Willie's bed, pull off the blankets and make him play with you first because you know you're going to win, and that gives you the second game with me.

HALLY. And you certainly were a bad loser, Willie!

WILLIE. Haai!

HALLY. Wasn't he, Sam? And so slow! A game with you almost took the whole afternoon. Thank God I gave up trying to teach you how to play chess.

WILLIE. You and Sam cheated.

HALLY. I never saw Sam cheat, and mine were mostly the mistakes of youth.

WILLIE. Then how is it you two was always winning?

HALLY. Have you ever considered the possibility, Willie, that it was because we were better than you?

WILLIE. Every time better?

HALLY. Not every time. There were occasions when we deliberately let you win a game so that you would stop sulking and go on playing with us. Sam used to wink at me when you weren't looking to show me it was time to let you win.

WILLIE. So then you two didn't play fair.

HALLY. It was for your benefit, Mr. Malopo, which is more than being fair. It was an act of self-sacrifice. (*To Sam.*) But you know what my best memory is, don't you?

SAM. No.

HALLY. Come on, guess. If your memory is so good, you must remember it as well.

SAM. We got up to a lot of tricks in there, Hally.

HALLY. This one was special, Sam.

SAM. I'm listening.

HALLY. It started off looking like another of those useless nothing-to-do afternoons. I'd already been down to Main Street looking for adventure, but nothing had happened. I didn't feel like climbing trees in the Donkin Park or pretending I was a private eye and following a stranger . . . so as usual: See what's cooking in Sam's room. This time it was you on the floor. You had two thin pieces of wood and you were smoothing them down with a knife. It didn't look particularly interesting, but when I asked you what you were doing, you just said, "Wait and see, Hally. Wait . . . and see" . . . in that secret sort of way of yours, so I knew there was a surprise coming. You teased me, you bugger, by being deliberately slow and not answering my questions!

Sam laughs.

And whistling while you worked away! God, it was infuriating! I could have brained you! It was only

when you tied them together in a cross and put that down on the brown paper that I realized what you were doing. "Sam is making a kite?" And when I asked you and you said "Yes" . . . ! (*Shaking his head with disbelief.*) The sheer audacity of it took my breath away. I mean, seriously, what the hell does a black man know about flying a kite? I'll be honest with you, Sam, I had no hopes for it. If you think I was excited and happy, you got another guess coming. In fact, I was shit-scared that we were going to make fools of ourselves. When we left the boarding house to go up onto the hill, I was praying quietly that there wouldn't be any other kids around to laugh at us.

SAM (*enjoying the memory as much as Hally*). Ja, I could see that.

HALLY. I made it obvious, did I?

SAM. Ja. You refused to carry it.

HALLY. Do you blame me? Can you remember what the poor thing looked like? Tomato-box wood and brown paper! Flour and water for glue! Two of my mother's old stockings for a tail, and then all those bits and pieces of string you made me tie together so that we could fly it! Hell, no, that was now only asking for a miracle to happen.

SAM. Then the big argument when I told you to hold the string and run with it when I let go.

HALLY. I was prepared to run, all right, but straight back to the boarding house.

SAM (*knowing what's coming*). So what happened?

HALLY. Come on, Sam, you remember as well as I do.

SAM. I want to hear it from you.

Hally pauses. He wants to be as accurate as possible.

HALLY. You went a little distance from me down the hill, you held it up ready to let it go. . . . "This is it," I thought. "Like everything else in my life, here comes another fiasco." Then you shouted, "Go, Hally!" and I started to run. (*Another pause.*) I don't know how to describe it, Sam. Ja! The miracle happened! I was running, waiting for it to crash to the ground, but instead suddenly there was something alive behind me at the end of the string, tugging at it as if it wanted to be free. I looked back . . . (*Shakes his head.*) . . . I still can't believe my eyes. It was flying! Looping around and trying to climb even higher into the sky. You shouted to me to let it have more string. I did, until there was none left and I was just holding that piece of wood we had tied it to. You came up and joined me. You were laughing.

SAM. So were you. And shouting, "It works, Sam! We've done it!"

HALLY. And we had! I was so proud of us! It was the most splendid thing I had ever seen. I wished there were hundreds of kids around to watch us. The part that scared me, though, was when you showed me how to make it dive down to the ground and then just when it was on the point of crashing, swoop up again!

SAM. You didn't want to try yourself.

HALLY. Of course not! I would have been suicidal if anything had happened to it. Watching you do it made me nervous enough. I was quite happy just to see it up there with its tail fluttering behind it. You left me after that, didn't you? You explained how to get it down, we tied it to the bench so that I could sit and watch it, and you went away. I wanted you to stay, you know. I was a little scared of having to look after it by myself.

SAM (quietly). I had work to do, Hally.

HALLY. It was sort of sad bringing it down, Sam. And it looked sad again when it was lying there on the ground. Like something that had lost its soul. Just tomato-box wood, brown paper and two of my mother's old stockings! But, hell, I'll never forget that first moment when I saw it up there. I had a stiff neck the next day from looking up so much.

Sam laughs. Hally turns to him with a question he never thought of asking before.

Why did you make that kite, Sam?

SAM (evenly). I can't remember.

HALLY. Truly?

SAM. Too long ago, Hally.

HALLY. Ja, I suppose it was. It's time for another one, you know.

SAM. Why do you say that?

HALLY. Because it feels like that. Wouldn't be a good day to fly it, though.

SAM. No. You can't fly kites on rainy days.

HALLY (he studies Sam. Their memories have made him conscious of the man's presence in his life). How old are you, Sam?

SAM. Two score and five.

HALLY. Strange, isn't it?

SAM. What?

HALLY. Me and you.

SAM. What's strange about it?

HALLY. Little white boy in short trousers and a black man old enough to be his father flying a kite. It's not every day you see that.

SAM. But why strange? Because the one is white and the other black?

HALLY. I don't know. Would have been just as strange, I suppose, if it had been me and my Dad . . . cripple man and a little boy! Nope! There's no chance of me flying a kite without it being strange. (*Simple statement of fact—no self-pity.*) There's a nice little short story there. "The Kite-Flyers." But we'd have to find a twist in the ending.

SAM. Twist?

HALLY. Yes. Something unexpected. The way it ended with us was too straightforward . . . me on the bench and you going back to work. There's no drama in that.

WILLIE. And me?

HALLY. You?

WILLIE. Yes me.

HALLY. You want to get into the story as well, do you? I got it! Change the title: "Afternoons in Sam's Room" . . . expand it and tell all the stories. It's on its way to being a novel. Our days in the old Jubilee. Sad in a way that they're over. I almost wish we were still in that little room.

SAM. We're still together.

HALLY. That's true. It's just that life felt the right size in there . . . not too big and not too small. Wasn't so hard to work up a bit of courage. It's got so bloody complicated since then.

The telephone rings. Sam answers it.

SAM. St. George's Park Tea Room . . . Hello, Madam . . . Yes, Madam, he's here . . . Hally, it's your mother.

HALLY. Where is she phoning from?

SAM. Sounds like the hospital. It's a public telephone.

HALLY (relieved). You see! I told you. (*The telephone.*) Hello, Mom . . . Yes . . . Yes no fine. Everything's under control here. How's things with poor old Dad? . . . Has he had a bad turn? . . . What? . . . Oh, God! . . . Yes, Sam told me, but I was sure he'd made a mistake. But what's this all about, Mom? He didn't look at all good last night. How can he get better so quickly? . . . Then very obviously you must say no. Be firm with him. You're the boss. . . . You know what it's going to be like if he comes home. . . . Well, then, don't blame me when I fail my exams at the end of the year. . . . Yes! How am I expected to be fresh for school when I spend half the night massaging his gammy leg? . . . So am I! . . . So tell him a white lie. Say Dr. Colley wants more X-rays of his stump. Or bribe him. We'll sneak in double tots of brandy in future. . . . What? . . . Order him to get back into bed at once! If he's going to behave like a child, treat him like one. . . . All right, Mom! I was just trying to . . . I'm sorry. . . . I said I'm sorry. . . . Quick, give me your number. I'll phone you back. (*He hangs up and waits a few seconds.*) Here we go again! (*He dials.*) I'm sorry, Mom. . . . Okay . . . But now listen to me carefully. All it needs is for you to put your foot down. Don't take no for an answer. . . . Did you hear me? And whatever you do, don't discuss it with him. . . . Because I'm frightened you'll give in to him. . . . Yes, Sam gave me lunch. . . . I ate all of it! . . . No, Mom not a soul. It's still raining here. . . . Right, I'll tell them. I'll just do some homework and then lock up. . . . But remember now, Mom. Don't listen to anything he says. And phone me back and let me know what happens. . . . Okay. Bye, Mom. (*He hangs up. The men are staring at him.*) My Mom says that when you're finished with the floors you must do the windows. (*Pause.*) Don't misunderstand me, chaps. All I want is for him to get better. And if he was, I'd be the first person to say: "Bring him home." But he's not, and we can't give him the medical care and attention he needs at home. That's what hospitals are there for. (*Brusquely.*) So don't just stand there! Get on with it!

Sam clears Hally's table.

You heard right. My Dad wants to go home.

SAM. Is he better?

HALLY (*sharply*). No! How the hell can he be better when last night he was groaning with pain? This is not an age of miracles!

SAM. Then he should stay in hospital.

HALLY (*seething with irritation and frustration*). Tell me something I don't know, Sam. What the hell do you think I was saying to my Mom? All I can say is fuck-it-all.

SAM. I'm sure he'll listen to your Mom.

HALLY. You don't know what she's up against. He's already packed his shaving kit and pajamas and is sitting on his bed with his crutches, dressed and ready to go. I know him when he gets in that mood. If she tries to reason with him, we've had it. She's no match for him when it comes to a battle of words. He'll tie her up in knots. (*Trying to hide his true feelings.*)

SAM. I suppose it gets lonely for him in there.

HALLY. With all the patients and nurses around? Regular visits from the Salvation Army? Balls! It's ten times worse for him at home. I'm at school and my mother is here in the business all day.

SAM. He's at least got you at night.

HALLY (*before he can stop himself*). And we've got him! Please! I don't want to talk about it anymore. (*Unpacks his school case, slamming down books on the table.*) Life is just a plain bloody mess, that's all. And people are fools.

SAM. Come on, Hally.

HALLY. Yes, they are! They bloody well deserve what they get.

SAM. Then don't complain.

HALLY. Don't try to be clever, Sam. It doesn't suit you. Anybody who thinks there's nothing wrong with this world needs to have his head examined. Just when things are going along all right, without fail someone or something will come along and spoil everything. Somebody should write that down as a fundamental law of the Universe. The principle of perpetual disappointment. If there is a God who created this world, he should scrap it and try again.

SAM. All right, Hally, all right. What you got for homework?

HALLY. Bullshit, as usual. (*Opens an exercise book and reads.*) "Write five hundred words describing an annual event of cultural or historical significance."

SAM. That should be easy enough for you.

HALLY. And also plain bloody boring. You know what he wants, don't you? One of their useless old ceremonies. The commemoration of the landing of the 1820 Settlers, or if it's going to be culture, Carols by Candlelight every Christmas.

SAM. It's an impressive sight. Make a good description, Hally. All those candles glowing in the dark and the people singing hymns.

HALLY. And it's called religious hysteria. (*Intense irritation.*) Please, Sam! Just leave me alone and let me get on with it. I'm not in the mood for games this afternoon. And remember my Mom's orders . . . you're to help Willie with the windows. Come on now, I don't want any more nonsense in here.

SAM. Okay, Hally, okay.

Hally settles down to his homework; determined preparations . . . pen, ruler, exercise book, dictionary, another cake . . . all of which will lead to nothing. (Sam waltzes over to Willie and starts to replace tables and chairs. He practices a ballroom step while doing so. Willie watches. When Sam is finished, Willie tries.)

Good! But just a little bit quicker on the turn and only move in to her after she's crossed over. What about this one?

Another step. When Sam is finished, Willie again has a go.

Much better. See what happens when you just relax and enjoy yourself? Remember that in two weeks' time and you'll be all right.

WILLIE. But I haven't got partner, Boet Sam.

SAM. Maybe Hilda will turn up tonight.

WILLIE. No, Boet Sam. (*Reluctantly.*) I gave her a good hiding.

SAM. You mean a bad one.

WILLIE. Good bad one.

SAM. Then you mustn't complain either. Now you pay the price for losing your temper.

WILLIE. I also pay two pounds ten shilling entrance fee.

SAM. They'll refund you if you withdraw now.

WILLIE (*appalled*). You mean, don't dance?

SAM. Yes.

WILLIE. No! I wait too long and I practice too hard. If I find me new partner, you think I can be ready in two weeks? I ask Madam for my leave now and we practice every day.

SAM. Quickstep non-stop for two weeks. World record, Willie, but you'll be mad at the end.

WILLIE. No jokes, Boet Sam.

SAM. I'm not joking.

WILLIE. So then what?

SAM. Find Hilda. Say you're sorry and promise you won't beat her again.

WILLIE. No.

SAM. Then withdraw. Try again next year.

WILLIE. No.

SAM. Then I give up.

WILLIE. Haaikona, Boet Sam, you can't.

SAM. What do you mean, I can't? I'm telling you: I give up.

WILLIE (*adamant*). No! (*Accusingly.*) It was you who start me ballroom dancing.

SAM. So?

WILLIE. Before that I use to be happy. And is you and Miriam who bring me to Hilda and say here's partner for you.

SAM. What are you saying, Willie?

WILLIE. You!

SAM. But me what? To blame?

WILLIE. Yes.

SAM. Willie . . . ? (*Bursts into laughter.*)

WILLIE. And now all you do is make jokes at me. You wait. When Miriam leaves you is my turn to laugh. Ha! Ha! Ha!

SAM (*he can't take Willie seriously any longer*). She can leave me tonight! I know what to do. (*Bowing before an imaginary partner*). May I have the pleasure? (*He dances and sings.*)

"Just a fellow with his pillow . . .

Dancin' like a willow . . .

In an autumn breeze . . ."

WILLIE. There you go again!

Sam goes on dancing and singing.

Boet Sam!

SAM. There's the answer to your problem! Judges' announcement in two weeks' time: "Ladies and gentlemen, the winner in the open section . . . Mr. Willie Malopo and his pillow!"

This is too much for a now really angry Willie. He goes for Sam, but the latter is too quick for him and puts Hally's table between the two of them.

HALLY (*exploding*). For Christ's sake, you two!

WILLIE (*still trying to get at Sam*). I donner you, Sam! Struesgod!

SAM (*still laughing*). Sorry, Willie . . . Sorry . . .

HALLY. Sam! Willie! (*Grabs his ruler and gives Willie a vicious whack on the bum.*) How the hell am I supposed to concentrate with the two of you behaving like bloody children!

WILLIE. Hit him too!

HALLY. Shut up, Willie.

WILLIE. He started jokes again.

HALLY. Get back to your work. You too, Sam. (*His ruler.*) Do you want another one, Willie?

Sam and Willie return to their work. Hally uses the opportunity to escape from his unsuccessful attempt at homework. He struts around like a little despot, ruler in hand, giving vent to his anger and frustration.

Suppose a customer had walked in then? Or the Park Superintendent. And seen the two of you behaving like a pair of hooligans. That would have been the end of my mother's license, you know. And your jobs! Well, this is the end of it. From now on there will be no more of your ballroom nonsense in here. This is a business establishment, not a bloody New Brighton dancing school. I've been far too lenient with the two of you. (*Behind the counter for a green cool drink and a dollop of ice cream. He keeps up his tirade as he prepares it.*) But what really makes me bitter is that I allow you chaps a little freedom in here when business is bad and what do you do with it? The foxtrot! Specially you, Sam. There's more to life than trotting around a dance floor and I thought at least you knew it.

SAM. It's a harmless pleasure, Hally. It doesn't hurt anybody.

HALLY. It's also a rather simple one, you know.

SAM. You reckon so? Have you ever tried?

HALLY. Of course not.

SAM. Why don't you? Now.

HALLY. What do you mean? Me dance?

SAM. Yes. I'll show you a simple step—the waltz—then you try it.

HALLY. What will that prove?

SAM. That it might not be as easy as you think.

HALLY. I didn't say it was easy. I said it was simple—like in simple-minded, meaning mentally retarded. You can't exactly say it challenges the intellect.

SAM. It does other things.

HALLY. Such as?

SAM. Make people happy.

HALLY (*the glass in his hand*). So do American cream sodas with ice cream. For God's sake, Sam, you're not asking me to take ballroom dancing serious, are you?

SAM. Yes.

HALLY (*sigh of defeat*). Oh, well, so much for trying to give you a decent education. I've obviously achieved nothing.

SAM. You still haven't told me what's wrong with admiring something that's beautiful and then trying to do it yourself.

HALLY. Nothing. But we happen to be talking about a foxtrot, not a thing of beauty.

SAM. But that is just what I'm saying. If you were to see two champions doing, two masters of the art . . . !

HALLY. Oh, God, I give up. So now it's also art!

SAM. Ja.

HALLY. There's a limit, Sam. Don't confuse art and entertainment.

SAM. So then what is art?

HALLY. You want a definition?

SAM. Ja.

HALLY (*he realizes he has got to be careful. He gives the matter a lot of thought before answering*). Philosophers have been trying to do that for centuries. What is Art? What is Life? But basically I suppose it's . . . the giving of meaning to matter.

SAM. Nothing to do with beautiful?

HALLY. It goes beyond that. It's the giving of form to the formless.

SAM. Ja, well, maybe it's not art, then. But I still say it's beautiful.

HALLY. I'm sure the word you mean to use is entertaining.

SAM (*adamant*). No. Beautiful. And if you want proof, come along to the Centenary Hall in New Brighton in two weeks' time.

The mention of the Centenary Hall draws Willie over to them.

HALLY. What for? I've seen the two of you prancing around in here often enough.

SAM (*he laughs*). This isn't the real thing, Hally. We're just playing around in here.

HALLY. So? I can use my imagination.

SAM. And what do you get?

HALLY. A lot of people dancing around and having a so-called good time.

SAM. That all?

HALLY. Well, basically it is that, surely.

SAM. No, it isn't. Your imagination hasn't helped you at all. There's a lot more to it than that. We're getting ready for the championships, Hally, not just another dance. There's going to be a lot of people, all right, and they're going to have a good time, but they'll only be spectators, sitting around and watching. It's just the competitors out there on the dance floor. Party decorations and fancy lights all around the walls! The ladies in beautiful evening dresses!

HALLY. My mother's got one of those, Sam, and quite frankly, it's an embarrassment every time she wears it.

SAM (*undeterred*). Your imagination left out the excitement.

Hally scoffs.

Oh, yes. The finalists are not going to be out there just to have a good time. One of those couples will be the 1950 Eastern Province Champions. And your imagination left out the music.

WILLIE. Mr. Elijah Gladman Guzana and his Orchestral Jazzonions.

SAM. The sound of the big band, Hally. Trombone, trumpet, tenor and alto sax. And then, finally, your imagination also left out the climax of the evening when the dancing is finished, the judges have stopped whispering among themselves and the Master of Ceremonies collects their scorecards and goes up onto the stage to announce the winners.

HALLY. All right. So you make it sound like a bit of a do. It's an occasion. Satisfied?

SAM (*victory*). So you admit that!

HALLY. Emotionally yes, intellectually no.

SAM. Well, I don't know what you mean by that, all I'm telling you is that it is going to be the event of the year in New Brighton. It's been sold out for two weeks already. There's only standing room left. We've got competitors coming from Kingwilliamstown, East London, Port Alfred.

Hally starts pacing thoughtfully.

HALLY. Tell me a bit more.

SAM. I thought you weren't interested . . . intellectually.

HALLY (*mysteriously*). I've got my reasons.

SAM. What do you want to know?

HALLY. It takes place every year?

SAM. Yes. But only every third year in New Brighton. It's East London's turn to have the championships next year.

HALLY. Which, I suppose, makes it an even more significant event.

SAM. Ah ha! We're getting somewhere. Our "occasion" is now a "significant event."

HALLY. I wonder.

SAM. What?

HALLY. I wonder if I would get away with it.

SAM. But what?

HALLY (to the table and his exercise book). "Write five hundred words describing an annual event of cultural or historical significance." Would I be stretching poetic license a little too far if I called your ballroom championships a cultural event?

SAM. You mean . . . ?

HALLY. You think we could get five hundred words out of it, Sam?

SAM. Victor Sylvester has written a whole book on ballroom dancing.

WILLIE. You going to write about it, Master Hally?

HALLY. Yes, gentlemen, that is precisely what I am considering doing. Old Doc Bromely—he's my English teacher—is going to argue with me, of course. He doesn't like natives. But I'll point out to him that in strict anthropological terms the culture of a primitive black society includes its dancing and singing. To put my thesis in a nutshell: The war-dance has been replaced by the waltz. But it still amounts to the same thing: the release of primitive emotions through movement. Shall we give it a go?

SAM. I'm ready.

WILLIE. Me also.

HALLY. Ha! This will teach the old bugger a lesson. (Decision taken.) Right. Let's get ourselves organized. (This means another cake on the table. He sits.) I think you've given me enough general atmosphere, Sam, but to build the tension and suspense I need facts. (Pencil poised.)

WILLIE. Give him facts, Boet Sam.

HALLY. What you called the climax . . . how many finalists?

SAM. Six couples.

HALLY (making notes). Go on. Give me the picture.

SAM. Spectators seated right around the hall. (Willie becomes a spectator.)

HALLY. . . . and it's a full house.

SAM. At one end, on the stage, Gladman and his Orchestral Jazzonions. At the other end is a long table

with the three judges. The six finalists go onto the dance floor and take up their positions. When they are ready and the spectators have settled down, the Master of Ceremonies goes to the microphone. To start with, he makes some jokes to get the people laughing . . .

HALLY. Good touch! (As he writes.) ". . . creating a relaxed atmosphere which will change to one of tension and drama as the climax is approached."

SAM (onto a chair to act out the M.C.). "Ladies and gentlemen, we come now to the great moment you have all been waiting for this evening. . . . The finals of the 1950 Eastern Province Open Ballroom Dancing Championships. But first let me introduce the finalists! Mr. and Mrs. Welcome Tchabalala from Kingwilliamstown . . ."

WILLIE (he applauds after every name). Is when the people clap their hands and whistle and make a lot of noise, Master Hally.

SAM. "Mr. Mulligan Njikelane and Miss Nomhle Nkonyeni of Grahamstown; Mr. and Mrs. Norman Nchinga from Port Alfred; Mr. Fats Bokolane and Miss Dina Plaatjies from East London; Mr. Sipho Dugu and Mrs. Mable Magada from Peddie; and from New Brighton our very own Mr. Willie Malopo and Miss Hilda Samuels."

Willie can't believe his ears. He abandons his role as spectator and scrambles into position as a finalist.

WILLIE. Relaxed and ready to romance!

SAM. The applause dies down. When everybody is silent, Gladman lifts up his sax, nods at the Orchestral Jazzonions . . .

WILLIE. Play the jukebox please, Boet Sam!

SAM. I also only got bus fare, Willie.

HALLY. Hold it, everybody. (Heads for the cash register behind the counter.) How much is in the till, Sam?

SAM. Three shillings. Hally . . . your Mom counted it before she left.

Hally hesitates.

HALLY. Sorry, Willie. You know how she carried on the last time I did it. We'll just have to pool our combined imaginations and hope for the best. (Returns to the table.) Back to work. How are the points scored, Sam?

SAM. Maximum of ten points each for individual style, deportment, rhythm and general appearance.

WILLIE. Must I start?

HALLY. Hold it for a second, Willie. And penalties?

SAM. For what?

HALLY. For doing something wrong. Say you stumble or bump into somebody . . . do they take off any points?

SAM (*aghast*). Hally . . . !

HALLY. When you're dancing. If you and your partner collide into another couple.

Hally can get no further. Sam has collapsed with laughter. He explains to Willie.

SAM. If me and Miriam bump into you and Hilda . . .

Willie joins him in another good laugh.

Hally, Hally . . . !

HALLY (*perplexed*). Why? What did I say?

SAM. There's no collisions out there, Hally. Nobody trips or stumbles or bumps into anybody else. That's what that moment is all about. To be one of those finalists on that dance floor is like . . . like being in a dream about a world in which accidents don't happen.

HALLY (*genuinely moved by Sam's image*). Jesus, Sam! That's beautiful!

WILLIE (*can endure waiting no longer*). I'm starting! (*Willie dances while Sam talks.*)

SAM. Of course it is. That's what I've been trying to say to you all afternoon. And it's beautiful because that is what we want life to be like. But instead, like you said, Hally, we're bumping into each other all the time. Look at the three of us this afternoon: I've bumped into Willie, the two of us have bumped into you, you've bumped into your mother, she bumping into your Dad. . . . None of us knows the steps and there's no music playing. And it doesn't stop with us. The whole world is doing it all the time. Open a newspaper and what do you read? America has bumped into Russia, England is bumping into India, rich man bumps into poor man. Those are big collisions, Hally. They make for a lot of bruises. People get hurt in all that bumping, and we're sick and tired of it now. It's been going on for too long. Are we never going to get it right? . . . Learn to dance life like champions instead of always being just a bunch of beginners at it?

HALLY (*deep and sincere admiration of the man*). You've got a vision, Sam!

SAM. Not just me. What I'm saying to you is that everybody's got it. That's why there's only standing room left for the Centenary Hall in two weeks' time. For as long as the music lasts, we are going to see six couples get it right, the way we want life to be.

HALLY. But is that the best we can do, Sam . . . watch six finalists dreaming about the way it should be?

SAM. I don't know. But it starts with that. Without the dream we won't know what we're going for. And any-

way I reckon there are a few people who have got past just dreaming about it and are trying for something real. Remember that thing we read once in the paper about the Mahatma Gandhi? Going without food to stop those riots in India?

HALLY. You're right. He certainly was trying to teach people to get the steps right.

SAM. And the Pope.

HALLY. Yes, he's another one. Our old General Smuts as well, you know. He's also out there dancing. You know, Sam, when you come to think of it, that's what the United Nations boils down to . . . a dancing school for politicians!

SAM. And let's hope they learn.

HALLY (*a little surge of hope*). You're right. We mustn't despair. Maybe there's some hope for mankind after all. Keep it up, Willie. (*Back to his table with determination.*) This is a lot bigger than I thought. So what have we got? Yes, our title: "A World Without Collisions."

SAM. That sounds good! "A World Without Collisions."

HALLY. Subtitle: "Global Politics on the Dance Floor." No. A bit too heavy, hey? What about "Ballroom Dancing as a Political Vision"?

The telephone rings. Sam answers it.

SAM. St. George's Park Tea Room . . . Yes, Madam . . . Hally, it's your Mom.

HALLY (*back to reality*). Oh, God, yes! I'd forgotten all about that. Shit! Remember my words, Sam? Just when you're enjoying yourself, someone or something will come along and wreck everything.

SAM. You haven't heard what she's got to say yet.

HALLY. Public telephone?

SAM. No.

HALLY. Does she sound happy or unhappy?

SAM. I couldn't tell. (*Pause.*) She's waiting, Hally.

HALLY (*to the telephone*). Hello, Mom . . . No, everything is okay here. Just doing my homework. . . . What's your news? . . . You've what? . . . (*Pause. He takes the receiver away from his ear for a few seconds. In the course of Hally's telephone conversation, Sam and Willie discretely position the stacked tables and chairs. Hally places the receiver back to his ear.*) Yes, I'm still here. Oh, well, I give up now. Why did you do it, Mom? . . . Well, I just hope you know what you've let us in for. . . . (*Loudly.*) I said I hope you know what you've let us in for! It's the end of the peace and quiet we've been having. (*Softly.*) Where is he? (*Normal voice.*) He can't hear us from in there. But for God's sake, Mom, what happened? I told you to be firm with him. . . . Then you and the nurses should have held him down, taken his crutches away. . . . I know only too well he's my father! . . . I'm not being disrespectful, but I'm sick and tired of emptying stinking chamberpots full of phlegm and piss. . . . Yes, I do! When you're not there, he asks *me* to do it. . . . If you really want to know the truth, that's why I've got no appetite for my food. . . . Yes! There's a lot of things you don't know about. For your information, I still haven't got that science textbook I need. And you know why? He borrowed the money you gave me for it. . . . Because I didn't want to start another fight between you two. . . . He says that every time. . . . All right, Mom! (*Viciously.*) Then just remember to start hiding your bag away again, because he'll be at your purse before long for money for booze. And when he's well enough to come down here, you better keep an eye on the till as well, because that is also going to develop a leak. . . . Then don't complain to me when he starts his old tricks. . . . Yes, you do. I get it from you on one side and from him on the other, and it makes life hell for me. I'm not going to be the peacemaker anymore. I'm warning you now: when the two of you start fighting again, I'm leaving home. . . . Mom, if you start crying, I'm going to put down the receiver. . . . Okay . . . (*Lowering his voice to a vicious whisper.*) Okay, Mom. I heard you. (*Desperate.*) No. . . . Because I don't want to. I'll see him when I get home! Mom! . . . (*Pause. When he speaks again, his tone changes completely. It is not simply pretense. We sense a genuine emotional conflict.*) Welcome home, chum! . . . What's that? . . . Don't be silly, Dad. You being home is just about the best news in the world. . . . I bet you are. Bloody depressing there with everybody going on about their ailments, hey! . . . How you feeling? . . . Good . . . Here as well, pal. Coming down cats and dogs. . . . That's right. Just the day for a kip and a toss in your old Uncle Ned. . . . Everything's just hunky-dory on my side, Dad. . . . Well, to start with, there's a nice pile of comics for you on the counter. . . . Yes, old Kemple brought them in. *Batman and Robin, Submariner* . . . just your cup of tea . . . I will. . . . Yes, we'll spin a few yarns tonight. . . . Okay, chum, see you in a little while. . . . No, I promise. I'll come straight home. . . . (*Pause—his mother comes back on the phone.*) Mom? Okay. I'll lock up now. . . . What? . . . Oh, the brandy . . . Yes, I'll remember! . . . I'll put it in my suitcase now, for God's sake. I know well enough what will happen if he doesn't get it. . . . (*Places a bottle of brandy on the counter.*) I was kind to

him, Mom. I didn't say anything nasty! . . . All right. Bye. (*End of telephone conversation. A desolate Hally doesn't move. A strained silence.*)

SAM (*quietly*). That sounded like a bad bump, Hally.

HALLY (*having a hard time controlling his emotions. He speaks carefully*). Mind your own business, Sam.

SAM. Sorry. I wasn't trying to interfere. Shall we carry on? Hally? (*He indicates the exercise book. No response from Hally.*)

WILLIE (*also trying*). Tell him about when they give out the cups, Boet Sam.

SAM. Ja! That's another big moment. The presentation of the cups after the winners have been announced. You've got to put that in.

Still no response from Hally.

WILLIE. A big silver one, Master Hally, called floating trophy for the champions.

SAM. We always invite some big-shot personality to hand them over. Guest of honor this year is going to be His Holiness Bishop Jabulani of the All African Free Zionist Church.

Hally gets up abruptly, goes to his table and tears up the page he was writing on.

HALLY. So much for a bloody world without collisions.

SAM. Too bad. It was on its way to being a good composition.

HALLY. Let's stop bullshitting ourselves, Sam.

SAM. Have we been doing that?

HALLY. Yes! That's what all our talk about a decent world has been . . . just so much bullshit.

SAM. We did say it was still only a dream.

HALLY. And a bloody useless one at that. Life's a fuck-up and it's never going to change.

SAM. Ja, maybe that's true.

HALLY. There's no maybe about it. It's a blunt and brutal fact. All we've done this afternoon is waste our time.

SAM. Not if we'd got your homework done.

HALLY. I don't give a shit about my homework, so, for Christ's sake, just shut up about it. (*Slamming books viciously into his school case.*) Hurry up now and finish your work. I want to lock up and get out of here. (*Pause.*) And then go where? Home-sweet-fucking-home. Jesus, I hate that word.

Hally goes to the counter to put the brandy bottle and comics in his school case. After a moment's hesitation, he smashes the bottle of brandy. He abandons all further attempts to hide his feelings. Sam and Willie work away as unobtrusively as possible.

Do you want to know what is really wrong with your lovely little dream, Sam? It's not just that we are all bad dancers. That does happen to be perfectly true, but there's more to it than just that. You left out the cripples.

SAM. Hally!

HALLY (*now totally reckless*). Ja! Can't leave them out, Sam. That's why we always end up on our backsides on the dance floor. They're also out there dancing . . . like a bunch of broken spiders trying to do the quickstep! (*An ugly attempt at laughter.*) When you come to think of it, it's a bloody comical sight. I mean, it's bad enough on two legs . . . but one and a pair of crutches! Hell, no, Sam. That's guaranteed to turn that dance floor into a shambles. Why you shaking your head? Picture it, man. For once this afternoon let's use our imaginations sensibly.

SAM. Be careful, Hally.

HALLY. Of what? The truth? I seem to be the only one around here who is prepared to face it. We've had the pretty dream, it's time now to wake up and have a good long look at the way things really are. Nobody knows the steps, there's no music, the cripples are also out there tripping up everybody and trying to get into the act, and it's all called the All-Comers-How-to-Make-a-Fuckup-of-Life Championships. (*Another ugly laugh.*) Hang on, Sam! The best bit is still coming. Do you know what the winner's trophy is? A beautiful big chamber-pot with roses on the side, and it's full to the brim with piss. And guess who I think is going to be this year's winner.

SAM (*almost shouting*). Stop now!

HALLY (*suddenly appalled by how far he has gone*). Why?

SAM. Hally? It's your father you're talking about.

HALLY. So?

SAM. Do you know what you've been saying?

Hally can't answer. He is rigid with shame. Sam speaks to him sternly.

No, Hally, you mustn't do it. Take back those words and ask for forgiveness! It's a terrible sin for a son to mock his father with jokes like that. You'll be punished if you carry on. Your father is your father, even if he is a . . . cripple man.

WILLIE. Yes, Master Hally. Is true what Sam say.

SAM. I understand how you are feeling, Hally, but even so . . .

HALLY. No, you don't!

SAM. I think I do.

HALLY. And I'm telling you you don't. Nobody does. (*Speaking carefully as his shame turns to rage at Sam.*)

It's your turn to be careful, Sam. Very careful! You're treading on dangerous ground. Leave me and my father alone.

SAM. I'm not the one who's been saying things about him.

HALLY. What goes on between me and my Dad is none of your business!

SAM. Then don't tell me about it. If that's all you've got to say about him, I don't want to hear.

For a moment Hally is at loss for a response.

HALLY. Just get on with your bloody work and shut up.

SAM. Swearing at me won't help you.

HALLY. Yes, it does! Mind your own fucking business and shut up!

SAM. Okay. If that's the way you want it, I'll stop trying.

He turns away. This infuriates Hally even more.

HALLY. Good. Because what you've been trying to do is meddle in something you know nothing about. All that concerns you in here, Sam, is to try and do what you get paid for—keep the place clean and serve the customers. In plain words, just get on with your job. My mother is right. She's always warning me about allowing you to get too familiar. Well, this time you've gone too far. It's going to stop right now.

No response from Sam.

You're only a servant in here, and don't forget it.

Still no response. Hally is trying hard to get one.

And as far as my father is concerned, all you need to remember is that he is your boss.

SAM (*needled at last*). No, he isn't. I get paid by your mother.

HALLY. Don't argue with me, Sam!

SAM. Then don't say he's my boss.

HALLY. He's a white man and that's good enough for you.

SAM. I'll try to forget you said that.

HALLY. Don't! Because you won't be doing me a favor if you do. I'm telling you to remember it.

A pause. Sam pulls himself together and makes one last effort.

SAM. Hally, Hally . . . ! Come on now. Let's stop before it's too late. You're right. We are on dangerous ground. If we're not careful, somebody is going to get hurt.

HALLY. It won't be me.

SAM. Don't be so sure.

HALLY. I don't know what you're talking about, Sam.

SAM. Yes, you do.

HALLY (*furious*). Jesus, I wish you would stop trying to tell me what I do and what I don't know.

Sam gives up. He turns to Willie.

SAM. Let's finish up.

HALLY. Don't turn your back on me! I haven't finished talking.

He grabs Sam by the arm and tries to make him turn around. Sam reacts with a flash of anger.

SAM. Don't do that, Hally! (*Facing the boy.*) All right, I'm listening. Well? What do you want to say to me?

HALLY (*pause as Hally looks for something to say*). To begin with, why don't you also start calling me Master Harold, like Willie.

SAM. Do you mean that?

HALLY. Why the hell do you think I said it?

SAM. And if I don't.

HALLY. You might just lose your job.

SAM (*quietly and very carefully*). If you make me say it once, I'll never call you anything else again.

HALLY. So? (*The boy confronts the man.*) Is that meant to be a threat?

SAM. Just telling you what will happen if you make me do that. You must decide what it means to you.

HALLY. Well, I have. It's good news. Because that is exactly what Master Harold wants from now on. Think of it as a little lesson in respect, Sam, that's long overdue, and I hope you remember it as well as you do your geography. I can tell you now that somebody who will be glad to hear I've finally given it to you will be my Dad. Yes! He agrees with my Mom. He's always going on about it as well. "You must teach the boys to show you more respect, my son."

SAM. So now you can stop complaining about going home. Everybody is going to be happy tonight.

HALLY. That's perfectly correct. You see, you mustn't get the wrong idea about me and my Dad, Sam. We also have our good times together. Some bloody good laughs. He's got a marvelous sense of humor. Want to know what our favorite joke is? He gives out a big groan, you see, and says: "It's not fair, is it, Hally?" Then I have to ask: "What, chum?" And then he says: "A nigger's arse" . . . and we both have a good laugh.

The men stare at him with disbelief.

What's the matter, Willie? Don't you catch the joke? You always were a bit slow on the uptake. It's what is called a pun. You see, fair means both light in color and to be just and decent. (*He turns to Sam.*) I thought *you* would catch it, Sam.

SAM. Oh ja, I catch it all right.

HALLY. But it doesn't appeal to your sense of humor.

SAM. Do you really laugh?

HALLY. Of course.

SAM. To please him? Make him feel good?

HALLY. No, for heaven's sake! I laugh because *I* think it's a bloody good joke.

SAM. You're really trying hard to be ugly, aren't you? And why drag poor old Willie into it? He's done nothing to you except show you the respect you want so badly. That's also not being fair, you know . . . and *I* mean just or decent.

WILLIE. It's all right, Sam. Leave it now.

SAM. It's me you're after. You should just have said "Sam's arse" . . . because that's the one you're trying to kick. Anyway, how do you know it's not fair? You've never seen it. Do you want to? (*He drops his trousers and underpants and presents his backside for Hally's inspection.*) Have a good look. A real Basuto arse . . . which is about as nigger as they can come. Satisfied? (*Trousers up.*) Now you can make your Dad even happier when you go home tonight. Tell him I showed you my arse and he is quite right. It's not fair. And if it will give him an even better laugh next time, I'll also let him have a look. Come, Willie, let's finish up and go.

Sam and Willie start to tidy up the tea room. Hally doesn't move. He waits for a moment when Sam passes him.

HALLY (*quietly*). Sam . . .

Sam stops and looks expectantly at the boy. Hally spits in his face. A long and heartfelt groan from Willie. For a few seconds Sam doesn't move.

SAM (*taking out a handkerchief and wiping his face*). It's all right, Willie.

To Hally.

Ja, well, you've done it . . . Master Harold. Yes, I'll start calling you that from now on. It won't be difficult anymore. You've hurt yourself, Master Harold. I saw it coming. I warned you, but you wouldn't listen. You've just hurt yourself *bad*. And you're a coward, Master Harold. The face you should be spitting in is your father's . . . but you used mine, because you think you're safe inside your fair skin . . . and this time I don't mean just or decent. (*Pause, then moving violently towards Hally.*) Should I hit him, Willie?

WILLIE (*stopping Sam*). No, Boet Sam.

SAM (*violently*). Why not?

WILLIE. It won't help, Boet Sam.

SAM. I don't want to help! I want to hurt him.

WILLIE. You also hurt yourself.

SAM. And if he had done it to you, Willie?

WILLIE. Me? Spit at me like I was a dog? (*A thought that had not occurred to him before. He looks at Hally.*) Ja. Then I want to hit him. I want to hit him hard!

A dangerous few seconds as the men stand staring at the boy. Willie turns away, shaking his head.

But maybe all I do is go cry at the back. He's little boy, Boet Sam. Little *white* boy. Long trousers now, but he's still little boy.

SAM (*his violence ebbing away into defeat as quickly as it flooded*). You're right. So go on, then: groan again, Willie. You do it better than me. (*To Hally.*) You don't know all of what you've just done . . . Master Harold. It's not just that you've made me feel dirtier than I've ever been in my life . . . I mean, how do I wash off yours and your father's filth? . . . I've also failed. A long time ago I promised myself I was going to try and do something, but you've just shown me . . . Master Harold . . . that I've failed. (*Pause.*) I've also got a memory of a little white boy when he was still wearing short trousers and a black man, but they're not flying a kite. It was the old Jubilee days, after dinner one night. I was in my room. You came in and just stood against the wall, looking down at the ground, and only after I'd asked you what you wanted, what was wrong, I don't know how many times, did you speak and even then so softly I almost didn't hear you. "Sam, please help me to go and fetch my Dad." Remember? He was dead drunk on the floor of the Central Hotel Bar. They'd phoned for your Mom, but you were the only one at home. And do you remember how we did it? You went in first by yourself to ask permission for me to go into the bar. Then I loaded him onto my back like a baby and carried him back to the boarding house with you following behind carrying his crutches. (*Shaking his head as he remembers.*) A crowded Main Street with all the people watching a little white boy following his drunk father on a nigger's back! I felt for that little boy . . . Master Harold. I felt for him. After that we still had to clean him up, remember? He'd messed in his trousers, so we had to clean him up and get him into bed.

HALLY (*great pain*). I love him, Sam.

SAM. I know you do. That's why I tried to stop you from saying these things about him. It would have been so simple if you could have just despised him for being a weak man. But he's your father. You love him and you're ashamed of him. You're ashamed of so much! . . . And now that's going to include yourself. That was the promise I made to myself: to try and stop that happening. (*Pause.*) After we got him to bed you came back with me to my room and sat in a corner and carried on just looking down at the ground. And for days after that! You hadn't done anything wrong, but you went around as if you owed the world an apology for being alive. I didn't like seeing that! That's not the way a boy grows up to be a man! . . . But the one person who should have been teaching you what that means was the cause of your shame. If you really want to know, that's why I made you that kite. I wanted you to look up, be proud of something, of yourself . . . (*Bitter smile at the memory.*) . . . and you certainly were that when I left you with it up there on the hill. Oh, ja . . . something else! . . . If you ever do write it as a short story, there *was* a twist in our ending. I couldn't sit down there and stay with you. It was a "Whites Only" bench. You were too young, too excited to notice then. But not anymore. If you're not careful . . . Master Harold . . . you're going to be sitting up there by yourself for a long time to come, and there won't be a kite in the sky. (*Sam has got nothing more to say. He exits into the kitchen, taking off his waiter's jacket.*)

WILLIE. Is bad. Is all all bad in here now.

HALLY (*books into his school case, raincoat on*). Willie . . . (*It is difficult to speak.*) Will you lock up for me and look after the keys?

WILLIE. Okay.

Sam returns. Hally goes behind the counter and collects the few coins in the cash register. As he starts to leave . . .

SAM. Don't forget the comic books.

Hally returns to the counter and puts them in his case. He starts to leave again.

SAM (*to the retreating back of the boy*). Stop . . . Hally . . .

Hally stops, but doesn't turn to face him.

Hally . . . I've got no right to tell you what being a man means if I don't behave like one myself, and I'm not doing so well at that this afternoon. Should we try again, Hally?

HALLY. Try what?

SAM. Fly another kite, I suppose. It worked once, and this time I need it as much as you do.

HALLY. It's still raining, Sam. You can't fly kites on rainy days, remember.

SAM. So what do we do? Hope for better weather tomorrow?

HALLY (*helpless gesture*). I don't know. I don't know anything anymore.

SAM. You sure of that, Hally? Because it would be pretty hopeless if that was true. It would mean nothing has been learnt in here this afternoon, and there was a hell of a lot of teaching going on . . . one way or the other. But anyway, I don't believe you. I reckon there's one thing you know. You don't *have* to sit up there by yourself. You know what that bench means now, and you can leave it any time you choose. All you've got to do is stand up and walk away from it.

Hally leaves. Willie goes up quietly to Sam.

WILLIE. Is okay, Boet Sam. You see. Is . . . (*He can't find any better words.*) . . . is going to be okay tomorrow. (*Changing his tone.*) Hey, Boet Sam! (*He is trying hard.*) You right. I think about it and you right. Tonight I find Hilda and say sorry. And make promise I won't beat her no more. You hear me, Boet Sam?

SAM. I hear you, Willie.

WILLIE. And when we practice I relax and romance with her from beginning to end. Non-stop! You watch! Two weeks' time: "First prize for promising newcomers: Mr. Willie Malopo and Miss Hilda Samuels." (*Sudden impulse.*) To hell with it! I walk home. (*He goes to the jukebox, puts in a coin and selects a record. The machine comes to life in the gray twilight, blushing its way through a spectrum of soft, romantic colors.*) How did you say it, Boet Sam? Let's dream. (*Willie sways with the music and gestures for Sam to dance.*)

Sarah Vaughan sings.

"Little man you're crying,
I know why you're blue,
Someone took your kiddy car away;
Better go to sleep now,
Little man you've had a busy day." (*etc. etc.*)
You lead. I follow.

The men dance together.

"Johnny won your marbles,
Tell you what we'll do;
Dad will get you new ones right away;
Better go to sleep now,
Little man you've had a busy day."

COMMENTARY

Note: The following essay represents a single interpretation of the play. For other perspectives on "MASTER HAROLD" . . . and the boys, *consult the essays listed below.*

"Master Harold" (whose capitals in the title are intentional) is Hally, a precocious white South African teenager, and "the boys" (the lowercase type is also significant) are Willie and Sam, black men, both of whom work for Hally's family and are old enough to be his father. The action takes place in Port Elizabeth, South Africa, in 1950. On his way home from school, Hally stops by the family-owned tea room, where Willie and Sam are tidying up while they practice their ballroom dancing in preparation for the "event of the year"— the Eastern Province Open Ballroom Dancing Championships in New Brighton, a black township outside Port Elizabeth. A lifetime of camaraderie is apparent as Hally, Sam, and Willie talk, joke, and revel in fond memories. This cordial atmosphere is shattered, however, as Hally, via a telephone call from his mother, learns that his crippled, alcoholic father is about to be released from the hospital and will be home again, where his presence is painfully disruptive. Suddenly angry and afraid, Hally turns viciously on Willie and Sam. For the father whom he cannot strike, Hally substitutes the "fathers" who cannot retaliate. As Hally lashes out at his two lifelong African friends, we understand how the underlying realities of time and place define who we are and dominate our actions. Thus the play rests squarely in the naturalist tradition.

Among Fugard's most obvious images is that of life as a dance, a world in which accidents don't happen; a vision of "a world without collisions." The play presents simultaneous images of rituals in the tea room, one a figurative dance, the other a literal one. We immediately see the figurative dance—the boys preparing the dilapidated old tea room for the next business day. The establishment is a mess: chairs and tables piled atop one another, the floor half scrubbed, the windows dirty. As the action proceeds, they ritualistically clean the room. At the same time, the boys prepare for the ballroom dancing contest by taking turns dancing around the room with their invisible partners. The play ends with the tea room neatly prepared for the next day's business, while the boys continue their dance— gliding effortlessly through the clutter of the tea room, which represents their cluttered lives. And here Fugard invests his play with the metatheatric sensibility of the modern theater (discussed in conjunction with the *Six Characters in Search of an Author* Showcase in Part II).

Sam's image of the dance as "a world without collisions" is displayed as Hally, Sam, and Willie dance and reminisce. Just before the climax of the play, the tea room is partially cleaned and arranged, Sam explains "a world without collisions" to Hally, and Willie weaves his way through the clutter. When the dream world is interrupted by the "bump" from Hally's mother, the dancing ceases and their peace is destroyed.

While Fugard indicates that the boys are tidying the room and dancing, he mentions little specific action. He does imply, however, that in the course of rearranging the furniture, the boys have set up a difficult obstacle course that only experienced dancers could negotiate. The tea room resembles a crowded ballroom dance floor; it is a safe world inhabited only by the boys who, having violently bumped into Hally, continue to dream of a world without collisions. The final dance seems to be an image of harmony among men. Unfortunately, at the time the play is set (and even when it was composed), harmony existed only among black men. However, we now know it was the white man, Hally (Fugard himself), who went on to write about Sam's dream. It was Hally who in the end learned the lesson that was being taught on that rainy afternoon.

Images of a kite also appear throughout the play. Kite making and kite flying are presented as accomplishments. "I wanted you to look up," says Sam, "[and] be proud of something, of yourself." The remembered kite is not store-bought fresh from the factory but a "homemade" kite constructed from the refuse of their lives. The memory of that kite in flight conjures up the image of freedom and of Sam, a man who, surrounded by a constricting society, is free only in his mind. Sam relinquished control of the kite that fateful day in hopes that Hally might see the beauty of freedom. In addition to the freedom implied by a soaring kite, there is also the sense of communion between the kite and its handler. Neither one can be successful, nor can one exist, without the other. Their kite is, of course, a phoenix—it flew once and, as we see in postapartheid South Africa, it may fly again.

Closely aligned with the image of the kite is that of the "Whites Only" bench. While the kite signifies togetherness, the bench epitomizes separateness, or to use the Afrikaans term, apartheid. As long as the "Whites Only" bench exists and Hally continues to make use of it, the kite and its freedom will be only a vague memory of youth—a dream destined for oblivion. As Sam explains to Hally, ". . . you're going to be sitting up there by yourself for a long time to come, and there won't be a kite in the sky."

Throughout the play Hally seems to be the teacher and Sam the student. At the conclusion, we realize that while Hally has led Sam on a journey through books, it is Sam who has worked tirelessly to teach Hally "what being a man means." In the end Hally declares, "I don't know. I don't know anything anymore." Sam reassures him, saying, "You sure of that, Hally? Because it would be pretty hopeless if that was true. It would mean nothing has been learnt in here this afternoon, and there was a hell of a lot of teaching going on . . . one way or the other."

The characters move freely about the entire tea room, where, at least after hours, there are no "Whites Only" benches. Even as Sam and Willie dance, Hally stands behinds the counter to make an ice-cream soda. It is not until the final moments that they are separated, and we see an image of Sam and Willie as servants waiting to, in Hally's words, ". . . get on with [their] job[s]." But even this picture changes as Sam reaches out one last time to Hally. When he asks Hally if they "should try again . . . [to] fly another kite," it is more than forgiveness, more than turning the other cheek he represents. He is the epitome of generosity, the ultimate act of humanity, which makes Sam the "man of magnitude" referred to in Hally's school lesson.

The images of the dancing, the kite, the "Whites Only" bench, and the teaching are presented through a metatheatrical motif—everything is acted out. Fugard's few stage directions demand that the characters "perform" for one another. For example, as Hally conjures up the memory of the old Jubilee Boarding House he exclaims, "I bet you I could still find my way to your room with my eyes closed." To which Fugard adds, "(He does exactly that.)" Shortly thereafter, "Using a few chairs [Hally] recreates the room," and Willie, eager to partake in the drama, assumes the "boxing pose" of Joe Louis as Hally, now a director, works to bring the scene to life. Later, as Sam describes the finale to the ballroom dancing contest, Fugard places Sam "onto a chair to act out the M.C."

The "let's pretend" images of the play occur in the dialogue as well. As Hally completes his recreation of the old Jubilee Boarding House, he exclaims, "Right, so much for the stage directions. Now the characters." He proceeds to describe Sam and Willie, who "move to their appropriate positions in the bedroom." Certainly implied here are the directions for "Master Harold and the boys" to act out as much of the description in the text as possible—in short, to turn the narratives into dramatic performance.

The overriding reality of racism permeates the play's images, especially in Hally's dialogue. While his condescending "Don't try to be clever, Sam. It doesn't suit you," "what the hell does a black man know about flying a kite?" and "It's called bigotry," are attempts at humor, they are also signs of Hally's latent racism. Hally is his father's son, and the greatest irony of all is that while Hally is ashamed of his father's afflictions, his greatest disease is neither physical nor drug induced but his ignorant racism. The degrading racist lines we hear early in the play are actually figurative spits in the face as disturbing as the literal spit of the climax.

The world of the tea room is a microcosm of South Africa, which is itself a microcosm of the world. Fugard sees his hometown as representative of South Africa: "In Port Elizabeth, I think, you have a microcosm in a microcosm . . . black, white, Indian, Chinese, and Colored [people of mixed race]. It is also representative of South Africa in the range of its social strata, from total affluence on the white side to the extremist poverty of the non-white." Fugard has written that the circumstances of his life set him in opposition to apartheid and makes it clear that in his plays he is "judging my own people for what they have done to themselves, done to the Black people in that country, done to the Colored people in that country, done to the Indian people in that country, done to the Chinese people in that country. My sense of myself as judge came about without my realizing it; it came out of a sense of the common humanity of all people in that country." While apartheid has been "officially" banned in the Republic of South Africa and many other nations, a great deal of informal separateness lingers in our society breeding the same kind of racism we see in Hally.

Other perspectives on *"MASTER HAROLD"* . . . *and the boys*:

Jordan, John O. "Life in the Theatre: Politics and Romance in '*MASTER HAROLD*' . . . *and the boys*." *Twentieth Century Literature* 39:4 (1993): 461–72.

Vanderbroucke, Russell. "Fathers and Son: '*MASTER HAROLD*' . . . *and the boys*." In Vanderbroucke, *Truths the Hands Can Touch: The Theatre of Athol Fugard*. New York: TCG, 1985, 194–203.

See the play on video:

"MASTER HAROLD" . . . *and the boys*. Dir. Michael Lindsey-Hogg. Perf. Zakes Mokai, John Kani, and Matthew Broderick. Warner Studios, 85 min., 1986.

Other Fugard plays on video:

Blood Knot. Perf. James Earl Jones. Creative Arts Television, 28 min., 1964.

Boesman and Lena. Dir. John Berry. Perf. Danny Glover and Angela Bassett. Kino Video, 98 min., 2000.

Sizwe Bansi Is Dead. Dir. Andrew Martin. Perf. John Kani and Winston Nshona. Insight Media, 60 min., 1977.

SHOWCASE   SOUTH AFRICAN TOWNSHIP THEATER

South African township theater typifies Jerzy Grotowski's vision of a Poor Theatre because it is necessarily reduced to the essence of the theatrical act by stripping the performance of superfluous accoutrements. Grotowski argues and township theater proves that "theater *can* exist without make-up, without autonomic costume and scenography, without a separate performance area (stage), without lighting and sound effects, etc. It *cannot* exist without the actor-spectator relationship of perceptual, direct, live communion." The Polish artist envisioned a theater that becomes a "spiritual act," and South African township theater is that spiritual act. Its form develops out of the demands of its content and milieu, not a shaping of the content to fit an existing form. Township theater is about freedom. It is about poverty and oppression. It is about not only what is but also what could be. Township theater is presented with the barest essentials—the actor and the audience. It merely suggests scenery, properties, and costumes, all of which are usually "found" rather than "designed."

Township theater is, in the words of critic Keyan Tomaselli, "the most accessible and forceful medium . . . to articulate [black] ideology, expose the contradictions of apartheid, and communicate a more accurate portrayal of the actual conditions of existence." Playwright Matsemela Manaka says, "Our theater is here to search for the truth about the history of the dispossessed . . . [about] the liberation of the mind and the liberation of the body." In such a theater, David Coplan, author of *In the Township Tonight!*, declares: "The working class aesthetic of the township is that theater is a direct extension of the actual conditions of black existence, with no necessary boundaries between art and life, performer and audience."

Township theater, a relatively new form of South African entertainment, emerged within a decade of the formal establishment of apartheid in 1948.

This dauntless and dynamic theater was spawned in the "locations" or "township" (read "ghettos") established by the government. As Pretoria gradually tightened the noose of apartheid and the suffering of the indigenous population grew, both the form and content of this Poor Theatre evolved.

Its development passed through four stages, each lasting about ten years. The early plays, essentially those of the 1950s, were largely escapist entertainments depicting daily life in the townships. During the 1960s the plays developed into pictures of the suffering of the blacks of South Africa, presenting the plight of those who were physically and psychologically maimed by the system. As an awareness of history and bitterness against imperialism grew in the 1970s, township theater evolved into a medium for the expression of the rage that accompanied the rise in black consciousness. The final stage, which began in the late 1970s and continued throughout the 1980s to the present, is almost celebratory. It is an affirmation of the noble spirit, the undying optimism and the impending liberation of the people.

Township theater is truly a theater of the people. Although it exemplifies Grotowski's Poor Theatre, it also resembles other agit-prop and revolutionary theaters, most notably Bertolt Brecht's Epic Theatre (see Part II). Township theater first exposes the transgressions of the oppressors, and then it infuses the oppressed with a sense of beauty and self-worth and imbues them with political power. Declares Brecht, "There is only one ally against the growth of barbarism: the people on whom it imposes these sufferings. Only the people offer any prospects. Thus it is natural to turn to them."

The leaders of township theater are the playwrights and directors, who most often perform both duties. The popular term for this combined role is "playmaker." Playmakers work improvisationally with their companies to develop new works that rely on the people in the townships for their experiences and stories. In fact, the plays are often cast first, and then the script is developed based on the lives and observations of the actors. For example, when Mbongeni Ngema developed his company, Committed Artists, he gathered the homeless of Durban who knew firsthand the particulars of the rent strike. Their collective experience gave birth to the play *Asinamali!* ("We Have No Money!"). "If the actors didn't . . . get the spirit right," declares Ngema, "I would say, 'let's go to a funeral in Lamontville [where police were shooting people almost daily], so that we can experience running away from tear gas, how it is to be close to death.'"

This type of patchy, pieced-together playmaking, which is the heart and soul of township theater, has led to the development of what might be called a "Motley Theater"—motley venues, scripts, and performance style. The venues for these performances consist of "found spaces" because there are few or no theaters in the townships. For example, the township of Soweto, a community of a million people, is served by a single theater: Deipkloof Hall, a performance space that more closely approximates a small high school gymnasium than a theater. The most popular performance spaces are the local churches, school yards, community halls, garages, and streets.

The scripts consist of collages of images portraying township life. Farcical comedy combines with pathetic tragedy; poignant sentimentalism freely mixes with cold documentary; the surrealistic and expressionistic are superimposed on the realistic and naturalistic. This eclectic mix of styles bombards the senses with striking images of township life. These seemingly plotless, episodic, improvisational plays often offend traditional theater connoisseurs and critics.

These unique plays are often presented on a bare stage with little costuming. A packing crate or two, a couple of chairs, and whatever discarded clothes can be found are the visual staples of these dramas. The opening description of Ngema's *Woza Albert!* provides an excellent illustration.

> The set consists of two upended tea chests side by side about center stage. Further upstage an old wooden plank, about ten feet long, is suspended horizontally on ropes. From nails in the plank hang the ragged clothes that the actors will use for their transformation. The actors wear grey sweat-suits bottoms and running shoes. They are bare-chested.

Eclectic music is used to reinforce theme and mood. A single play may use music drawn from traditional African rhythms, Christian hymns, African choral songs, English secular compositions, Afro-American jazz, miners' chants, and *mbaquanga*—the music of the inner city so beautifully illustrated by the score for *Sarafina!*. The music, whether composed especially for the play or borrowed, is live, and the actors frequently sing *a cappella* in rich harmonies.

Township performers combine the skills of the actor, athlete, singer, dancer, mime, historian, impressionist, politician, and social commentator. In *Woza Albert!* the two actors appear on the stage as "themselves." These performers are specialists at "transformation"—the act of evolving spontaneously. Virtually an entire population can be played by a couple of actors using imaginative physical manipulation, clever vocal alteration, and a cacophony of sound effects. They create people ranging from the homeless to the Prime Minister; they create machines such as cement mixers, garbage trucks, and helicopters; and they create an airport, a prison, a TV studio, and a nuclear explosion. In later plays, such as Ngema's *Sarafina!* and *Township Fever!*, the casts are expanded and there is far less use of transformation. Such plays resemble a more traditional Western musical.

See township theater on video:

The Voices of Sarafina!. Dir. Nigel Noble. New Yorker Films, 82 min., 1996. (This video contains scenes from the Broadway production of *Sarafina!* and interviews with Ngema and his actors.)

THE DANCE AND THE RAILROAD

DAVID HENRY HWANG

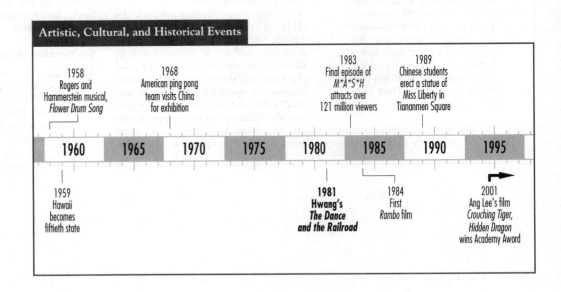

Artistic, Cultural, and Historical Events

1958
Rogers and
Hammerstein musical,
Flower Drum Song

1968
American ping pong
team visits China
for exhibition

1983
Final episode of
*M*A*S*H*
attracts over
121 million viewers

1989
Chinese students
erect a statue of
Miss Liberty in
Tiananmen Square

| 1960 | 1965 | 1970 | 1975 | 1980 | 1985 | 1990 | 1995 |

1959
Hawaii
becomes
fiftieth state

**1981
Hwang's
*The Dance
and the Railroad***

1984
First
Rambo film

2001
Ang Lee's film
*Crouching Tiger,
Hidden Dragon*
wins Academy Award

DAVID HENRY HWANG (1957–)

When Hwang's play M. *Butterfly* won the Tony Award (and a Pulitzer Prize nomination) in 1988, it marked the first time a playwright of Asian descent had won the American commercial theater's major award. Though there have been prominent Asian-Americans involved in the theater (e.g., the Shanghai-born designer Ming Cho Li and the *avant-garde* artist Ping Chong), Hwang is now a principal spokesman for Asian immigrants in the American theater.

Hwang was born in Los Angeles to an affluent family. An early play, *Family Devotions* (1981), is about a farcical encounter between an old uncle from mainland China visiting his wealthy family in the posh suburb of Bel Air. Typical of Hwang's work, it explores the clash between Eastern and Western value systems. Hwang was educated at Stanford University and then attended the Yale School of Drama. His first play, *F.O.B.* (1980), was developed in a playwriting seminar led by Sam Shepard. The title, an acronym for "fresh off the boat," suggests its theme: the problems faced by Chinese immigrants as they adapt to a new life in the West. Like *The Dance and the Railroad*, *F.O.B.* uses elements of Chinese opera, folk tales, and myth; Guan Gung, the god of warriors, writers, and prostitutes, is central to *F.O.B.*, just as he is to *The Dance and the Railroad*. Joseph Papp produced *F.O.B.* in New York, where the play won an Obie Award as the best Off-Broadway work of 1980. Its success led to other plays, such as *Rich Relations* (1986) and *Broken Promises* (1987), and an opera written with *avant-garde* composer Philip Glass, *A Thousand Airplanes on the Roof*. In 2002 Hwang revised the libretto for a Broadway revival of the Rogers and Hammerstein musical, *Flower Drum Song*; the new text deleted many of the stereotypes in the original and enhanced the dignity of Asian-Americans.

M. Butterfly, now a film, is among the more provocative plays in recent Broadway history. Based on the true story of a French diplomat and his Chinese lover (a beautiful opera singer who is revealed as not only a spy but also a transvestite), the play examines East-West relations and racial and sexual stereotyping. According to Hwang, the play is a critique of "Orientalism" (a term coined by Edward Said in his book of the same title), which refers to the West's erroneous notion that "the East is mysterious, inscrutable, and therefore ultimately inferior." Hwang's work, as typified by *M. Butterfly* and *The Dance and the Railroad*, often fuses Chinese theater practice and Western Realism.

As You Read *The Dance and the Railroad*

Hwang alternates realism and the theatricality of Chinese drama, among the most anti-realistic and ingeniously theatrical in the world. The realistic moments in which Lone and Ma discuss their plight and that of the Chinese workers (think "slaves") clash with those in which the two characters perform bits from the Peking opera. This contrast of markedly different theatrical styles parallels the clash of cultures—East and West—that defines the central conflict of the play. You will have little problem reading the realistic scenes, but you may find it useful to read (or review) the Showcase, "The Conventions of Chinese Theater," that accompanies the discussion of Brecht's play in Part II. Hwang's play may be considered to be in the Brechtian tradition; the Chinese theater scenes serve as "alienation effects" that force the audience to judge the social implications of the realistic scenes.

THE DANCE AND THE RAILROAD

—D A V I D   H E N R Y   H W A N G—

CHARACTERS
LONE, *twenty years old, ChinaMan railroad worker*
MA, *eighteen years old, ChinaMan railroad worker*

PLACE
A mountain top near the transcontinental railroad.

TIME
June, 1867.

SYNOPSIS OF SCENES
Scene 1: Afternoon.
Scene 2: Afternoon, a day later.
Scene 3: Late afternoon, four days later.
Scene 4: Late that night.
Scene 5: Just before the following dawn.

SCENE 1

A mountain top. Lone is practicing opera steps. He swings his pigtail around like a fan. Ma enters, cautiously, watches from a hidden spot. Ma approaches Lone.

LONE. So, there are insects hiding in the bushes.
MA. Hey, listen, we haven't met, but—
LONE. I don't spend time with insects.

(Lone whips his hair into Ma's face; Ma backs off; Lone pursues him, swiping at Ma with his hair.)

MA. What the . . . ? Cut it out!

(Ma pushes Lone away.)

LONE. Don't push me.
MA. What was that for?
LONE. Don't ever push me again.
MA. You mess like that, you're gonna get pushed.
LONE. Don't push me.
MA. You started it. I just wanted to watch.

LONE. You "just wanted to watch." Did you ask my permission?
MA. What?
LONE. Did you?
MA. C'mon.
LONE. You can't expect to get in for free.
MA. Listen. I got some stuff you'll wanna hear.
LONE. You think so?
MA. Yeah. Some advice.
LONE. Advice? How old are you, anyway?
MA. Eighteen!
LONE. A child.
MA. Yeah. Right. A child. But listen . . .
LONE. A child who tries to advise a grown man . . .
MA. Listen, you got this kind of attitude.
LONE. —is a child who will never grow up.
MA. You know, the ChinaMen down at camp, they can't stand it.
LONE. Oh?
MA. Yeah. You gotta watch yourself. You know what they say? They call you "Prince of the Mountain." Like you're too good to spend time with them.
LONE. Perceptive of them.
MA. After all, you never sing songs, never tell stories. They say you act like your spit is too clean for them, and they got ways to fix that.
LONE. Is that so?
MA. Like they're gonna bury you in the shitbuckets, so you'll have more to clean than your nails.
LONE. But I don't shit.
MA. Or they're gonna cut out your tongue, since you never speak to them.
LONE. There's no one here worth talking to.
MA. Cut it out, Lone. Look, I'm trying to help you, all right? I got a solution.
LONE. So young yet so clever.
MA. That stuff you're doing—it's beautiful. Why don't you do it for the guys at camp? Help us celebrate?

LONE. What will "this stuff" help celebrate?

MA. C'mon. The strike, of course. Guys on a railroad gang, we gotta stick together, you know.

LONE. This is something to celebrate?

MA. Yeah. Yesterday, the weak-kneed ChinaMen: they were running around like chickens without a head: "The white devils are sending their soldiers! Shoot us all!" But now, look—day four, see? Still in one piece. Those soldiers—we've never seen a gun or a bullet.

LONE. So you're all warrior-spirits, huh?

MA. They're scared of us, Lone—that's what it means.

LONE. I appreciate your advice. Tell you what—you go down—

MA. Yeah?

LONE. Down to the camp.

MA. Okay.

LONE. To where the men are—

MA. Yeah?

LONE. Sit there—

MA. Yeah?

LONE. And wait for me.

MA. Okay. (*Pause.*) That's it? What do you think I am?

LONE. I think you're an insect interrupting my practice. So fly away. Go home.

MA. Look, I didn't come here to get laughed at.

LONE. No, I suppose you didn't.

MA. So just stay up here. By yourself. You deserve it.

LONE. I do.

MA. And don't expect any more help from me.

LONE. I haven't gotten any yet.

MA. If one day, you wake up and your head is buried in the shit can—

LONE. Yes?

MA. You can't find your body, your tongue is cut out—

LONE. Yes.

MA. Don't worry 'cuz I'll be there.

LONE. Oh.

MA. To make sure your mother's head is sitting right next to yours.

(*Ma exits.*)

LONE. His head is too big for this mountain.

(*Returns to practicing.*)

SCENE 2

(*Mountaintop. Next day. Lone is practicing. Ma enters.*)

MA. Hey.

LONE. You? Again?

MA. I forgive you.

LONE. You . . . what?

MA. For making fun of me yesterday. I forgive you.

LONE. You can't—

MA. No. Don't thank me.

LONE. You can't forgive me.

MA. No. Don't mention it.

LONE. You—! I never asked for your forgiveness.

MA. I know. That's just the kinda guy I am.

LONE. This is ridiculous. Why don't you leave? Go down to your friends and play soldiers, sing songs, tell stories.

MA. Ah! See? That's just it. I got other ways I wanna spend my time. Will you teach me the opera?

LONE. What?

MA. I wanna learn it. I dreamt about it all last night.

LONE. No.

MA. The dance, the opera—I can do it.

LONE. You think so?

MA. Yeah. When I get outa here, I wanna go back to China and perform.

LONE. You want to become an actor?

MA. Well, I wanna perform.

LONE. Don't you remember the story about the three sons whose parents send them away to learn a trade? After three years, they return. The first one says, "I have become a coppersmith." The parents say, "Good. Second son, what have you become?" "I've become a silversmith." "Good . . . and youngest son . . . what about you?" "I have become an actor." When the parents hear that their son has become only an actor, they are very sad. The mother beats her head against the ground until the ground, out of pity, opens up and swallows her. The father is so angry, he can't even speak, and the anger builds up inside him until it blows his body to pieces—little bits of his skin are found hanging from trees days later. You don't know how you endanger your relatives by becoming an actor.

MA. Well, I don't wanna become an "actor." That sounds terrible. I just wanna perform. Look, I'll be rich by the time I get out of here, right?

LONE. Oh?

MA. Sure. By the time I go back to China, I'll ride in gold sedan chairs, with twenty wives fanning me all around.

LONE. Twenty wives? This boy is ambitious.

MA. I'll give out pigs on New Years and keep a stable of small birds to give to any woman who pleases me. And in my spare time, I'll perform.

LONE. Between your twenty wives and your birds, where will you find a free moment?

MA. I'll play Gwan Gung and tell stories of what life was like in the Gold Mountain.

LONE. Ma, just how long have you been in "America"?

MA. Huh? About four weeks.

LONE. You are a big dreamer.

MA. Well, all us ChinaMen here are—right? Men with little dreams have little brains to match. They walk with their eyes down, trying to find extra grains of rice on the ground.

LONE. So, you know all about "America"? Tell me, what kind of stories will you tell?

MA. I'll say, "We laid tracks like soldiers. Mountains? We hung from cliffs in baskets and the winds blew us like birds. Snow? We lived underground like moles for days at a time. Deserts? We—."

LONE. Wait. Wait. How do you know these things after only four weeks?

MA. They told me—the other ChinaMen on the gang. We've been telling stories ever since the strike began.

LONE. They make it sound like it's very enjoyable.

MA. They said it is.

LONE. Oh? And you believe them?

MA. They're my friends. Living underground in winter—sounds exciting, huh?

LONE. Did they say anything about the cold?

MA. Oh, I already know about that. They told me about the mild winters and the warm snow.

LONE. Warm snow?

MA. When I go home, I'll bring some back to show my brothers.

LONE. Bring some——On the boat?

MA. They'll be shocked—they never seen American snow before.

LONE. You can't. By the time you get snow to the boat, it'll have melted, evaporated, and returned as rain already.

MA. No.

LONE. No?

MA. Stupid.

LONE. Me?

MA. You been here awhile, haven't you?

LONE. Yes. Two years.

MA. Then how come you're so stupid? This is the Gold Mountain. The snow here doesn't melt. It's not wet.

LONE. That's what they told you?

MA. Yeah. It's true.

LONE. Did anyone show you any of this snow?

MA. No. It's not winter.

LONE. So where does it go?

MA. Huh?

LONE. Where does it go? If it doesn't melt, what happens to it?

MA. The snow? I dunno. I guess it just stays around.

LONE. So where is it? Do you see any?

MA. Here? Well, no, but . . . (Pause.) This is probably one of those places where it doesn't snow—even in winter.

LONE. Oh.

MA. Anyway, what's the use of me telling you what you already know? Hey, c'mon—teach me some of that stuff. Look—I've been practicing the walk—how's this? (Demonstrates)

LONE. You look like a duck in heat.

MA. Hey—it's a start, isn't it?

LONE. Tell you what—you want to play some *Die Siu*?

MA. *Die Siu*? Sure.

LONE. You know, I'm pretty good.

MA. Hey, I play with the guys at camp. You can't be any better than Lee—he's really got it down.

(*Lone pulls out a case with two dice*)

LONE. I used to play 'til morning.

MA. Hey, us too. We see the sun start to rise, and say, "Hey, if we go to sleep now, we'll never get up for work." So we just keep playing.

LONE (*Holding out dice*). *Die* or *Siu*?

MA. *Siu*.

LONE. You sure?

MA. Yeah!

LONE. All right. (*He rolls*) *Die*!

MA. *Siu*.

(*They see the result.*)

MA. *Siu*! Not bad.

(*They continue taking turns rolling through the following section; Ma always loses.*)

LONE. I haven't touched these in two years.

MA. I gotta practice more . . .

LONE. Have you lost much money?

MA. Huh? So what?

LONE. Oh, you have gold hidden in all your shirt linings, huh?

MA. Here in "America"—losing is no problem. You know—End of the Year Bonus?

LONE. Oh, right.

MA. After I get that, I'll laugh at what I lost.

LONE. Lee told you there was a bonus, right?

MA. How'd you know?

LONE. When I arrived here, Lee told me there was a bonus, too.

MA. Lee teach you how to play?

LONE. Him? He talked to me a lot.

MA. Look, why don't you come down and start playing with the guys again?

LONE. The "guys."

MA. Before we start playing, Lee uses a stick to write "Kill!" in the dirt.

LONE. You seem to live for your nights with "the guys."

MA. What's life without friends, huh?

LONE. Well, why do *you* think I stopped playing?

MA. Hey, maybe you were the one getting killed, huh?

LONE. What?

MA. Hey, just kidding.

LONE. Who's getting killed here?

MA. Just a joke.

LONE. That's not a joke, it's blasphemy.

MA. Look, obviously you stopped playing 'cause you wanted to practice the opera.

LONE. Do you understand that discipline?

MA. But, I mean, you don't have to overdo it either. You don't have to beat 'em like dirt. I mean, who are you trying to impress?

(Pause; Lone throws dice into the bushes.)

LONE. Ooooops. Better go see who won.

MA. Hey! C'mon! Help me look!

LONE. If you find them, they are yours.

MA. You serious?

LONE. Yes.

MA. Here.

(Finds the dice.)

LONE. Who won?

MA. I didn't check.

LONE. Well, no matter. Keep the dice. Take them, and go play with your friends.

MA. Here. *(He offers them to Lone)* A present.

LONE. A present? This isn't a present!

MA. They're mine, aren't they? You gave them to me, right?

LONE. Well, yes, but—

MA. So now I'm giving them to you.

LONE. You can't give me a present. I don't want them.

MA. You wanted them enough to keep them two years.

LONE. I'd forgotten I had them.

MA. See, I know, Lone. You wanna get rid of me. But you can't. I'm paying for lessons.

LONE. With my dice.

MA. Mine now. *(He offers them again)* Here.

(Pause; Lone runs Ma's hand across his forehead.)

LONE. Feel this.

MA. Hey!

LONE. Pretty wet, huh?

MA. Big deal.

LONE. Well, it's not from playing *Die Siu.*

MA. I know how to sweat. I wouldn't be here if I didn't.

LONE. Yes, but are you willing to sweat after you've finished sweating? Are you willing to come up after you've spent the whole day chipping half an inch off a rock, and punish your body some more?

MA. Yeah. Even after work, I still—

LONE. No, you don't. You want to gamble, and tell dirty stories, and dress up like women to do shows.

MA. Hey, I never did that.

LONE. You've only been here a month. *(Pause.)* And what about "the guys?" They're not going to treat you so well once you stop playing with them. Are you willing to work all day listening to them whisper, "That one—let's put spiders in his soup."

MA. They won't do that to me. With you, it's different.

LONE. Is it?

MA. You don't have to act that way.

LONE. What way?

MA. Like you're so much better than them.

LONE. No. You haven't even begun to understand. To practice every day, you must have a fear to force you up here.

MA. A fear? No—it's 'cause what you're doing is beautiful.

LONE. No.

MA. I've seen it.

LONE. It's ugly to practice when the mountain has turned your muscles to ice. When my body hurts too much to come here, I look at the other ChinaMen and think, "They are dead. Their muscles work only because the white man forces them." I live because I can still force my muscles to work for me." Say it. "They are dead."

MA. No. They're my friends.

LONE. Well, then, take your dice down to your friends.

MA. But I want to learn—

LONE. This is your first lesson.

MA. Look, it shouldn't matter—

LONE. It does.

MA. It shouldn't matter what I think.

LONE. Attitude is everything.

MA. But as long as I come up, do the exercises—

LONE. I'm not going to waste time on a quitter.

MA. I'm not!

LONE. Then say it—"They are dead men."

MA. I can't.

LONE. Then you will never have the dedication.

MA. That doesn't prove anything.

LONE. I will not teach a dead man.

MA. What?

LONE. If you can't see it, then you're dead too.

MA. Don't start pinning—

LONE. Say it!

MA. All right.

LONE. What?

MA. All right. I'm one of them. I'm a dead man too.

(Pause.)

LONE. I thought as much. So, go. You have your friends.

MA. But I don't have a teacher.

LONE. I don't think you need both.

MA. Are you sure?

LONE. I'm being questioned by a child.

(Lone returns to practicing; silence.)

MA. Look, Lone, I'll come up here every night—after work—I'll spend my time practicing, okay? *(Pause.)* But I'm not gonna say that they're dead. Look at them. They're on strike; dead men don't go on strike, Lone. The white devils—they try and stick us with a ten-hour day. We want a return to eight hours and also a fourteen-dollar-a-month raise. I learned the demon English—listen: "Eight hour a day good for white man, all same good for ChinaMan." These are the demands of live ChinaMen, Lone. Dead men don't complain.

LONE. All right, this is something new. But no one can judge the ChinaMen till after the strike.

MA. They say we'll hold out for months if we have to. The smart men will live on what we've hoarded.

LONE. A ChinaMan's mouth can swallow the earth. *(He takes the dice.)* While the strike is on, I'll teach you.

MA. And afterwards?

LONE. Afterwards—we'll decide then whether these are dead or live men.

MA. When can we start?

LONE. We've already begun. Give me your hand.

SCENE 3

(Lone and Ma are doing physical exercises.)

MA. How long will it be before I can play Gwan Gung?

LONE. How long before a dog can play the violin?

MA. Old Ah Hong—have you heard him play the violin?

LONE. Yes. Now he should take his violin and give it to a dog.

MA. I think he sounds okay.

LONE. I think he caused that avalanche last winter.

MA. He used to play for weddings back home.

LONE. Ah Hong?

MA. That's what he said.

LONE. You probably heard wrong.

MA. No.

LONE. He probably said he played for funerals.

MA. He's been playing for the guys down at camp.

LONE. He should play for the white devils—that will end this stupid strike.

MA. Yang told me for sure—it'll be over by tomorrow.

LONE. Eight days already. And Yang doesn't know anything.

MA. He said they're already down to an eight-hour day and five dollars raise at the bargaining sessions.

LONE. Yang eats too much opium.

MA. That doesn't mean he's wrong about this.

LONE. You can't trust him. One time—last year—he went around camp looking in everybody's eyes and saying, "Your nails are too long. They're hurting my eyes." This went on for a week. Finally, all the men clipped their nails, made a big pile, which they wrapped in leaves and gave to him. Yang used the nails to season his food—he put it in his soup, sprinkled it on his rice, and never said a word about it again. Now tell me—are you going to trust a man who eats other men's fingernails?

MA. Well, all I know is we won't go back to work until they meet all our demands. Listen, teach me some Gwan Gung steps.

LONE. I should have expected this. A boy who wants to have twenty wives is the type who demands more than he can handle.

MA. Just a few.

LONE. It takes years before an actor can play Gwan Gung.

MA. I can do it. I spend a lot of time watching the opera when it comes around. Every time I see Gwan Gung, I say, "Yeah. That's me. The god of fighters. The god of adventurers. We have the same kind of spirit."

LONE. I tell you, if you work very hard, when you return to China, you can perhaps be the Second Clown.

MA. Second Clown?

LONE. If you work hard.

MA. What's the Second Clown?

LONE. You can play the *p'i p'a*, and dance and jump all over.

MA. I'll buy them.

LONE. Excuse me?

MA. I'm going to be rich, remember? I'll buy a troupe and force them to let me play Gwan Gung.

LONE. I hope you have enough money, then, to pay audiences to sit through your show.

MA. You mean, I'm going to have to practice here every night—and in return, all I can play is the Second Clown?

LONE. If you work hard.

MA. Am I that bad? Maybe I shouldn't even try to do this. Maybe I should just go down.

LONE. It's not you. Everyone must earn the right to play Gwan Gung. I entered Opera school when I was ten years old. My parents decided to sell me for ten years to this Opera company. I lived with eighty other boys and we slept in bunks four beds high and hid our candy and rice cakes from each other. After eight years, I was studying to play Gwan Gung.

MA. Eight years?

LONE. I was one of the best in my class. One day, I was summoned by my master, who told me I was to go home for two days, because my mother had fallen very ill and was dying. When I arrived home, Mother was standing at the door waiting, not sick at all. Her first words to me, the son away for eight years, were, "You've been playing while your village has starved. You must go to the Gold Mountain and work."

MA. And you never returned to school?

LONE. I went from a room with eighty boys to a ship with three hundred men. So, you see, it does not come easily to play Gwan Gung.

MA. Did you want to play Gwan Gung?

LONE. What a foolish question!

MA. Well, you're better off this way.

LONE. What?

MA. Actors—they don't make much money. Here, you make a bundle, then go back and be an actor again. Best of both worlds.

LONE. "Best of both worlds."

MA. Yeah!

(Lone drops to the floor, begins imitating a duck, waddling and quacking.)

MA. Lone? What are you doing? *(Lone quacks)* You're a duck? *(Lone quacks)* I can see that. *(Lone quacks)* Is this an exercise? Am I supposed to do this? *(Lone quacks)* This is dumb. I never seen Gwan Gung waddle. *(Lone quacks)* Okay. All right I'll do it. *(Ma and Lone quack and waddle)* You know, I never realized before how uncomfortable a duck's life is. And you have to listen to yourself quacking all day. Go crazy! *(Lone stands up straight)* Now, what was that all about?

LONE. No, no. Stay down there, duck.

MA. What's the—

LONE *(prompting)*. Quack, quack, quack.

MA. I don't—

LONE. Act your species!

MA. I'm not a duck!

LONE. Nothing worse than a duck that doesn't know his place.

MA. All right. *(Mechanically)* Quack, quack.

LONE. More.

MA. Quack.

LONE. More!

MA. Quack, quack, quack!

(Ma now continues quacking, as Lone gives commands.)

LONE. Louder! It's your mating call! Think of your twenty duck wives! Good! Louder! Project! More! Don't slow down! Put your tail feathers into it! They can't hear you!

(Ma is now quacking up a storm. Lone exits, unnoticed by Ma)

MA. Quack! Quack! Quack! Quack. Quack . . . quack. *(He looks around)* Quack . . . quack . . . Lone? . . . Lone? *(He waddles around the stage looking)* Lone, where are you? Where'd you go? *(He stops, scratches his left leg with his right foot)* C'mon—stop playing around. What is this? *(Lone enters as a tiger, unseen by Ma)* Look, let's call it a day, okay? I'm getting hungry. *(Ma turns around, notices Lone right before Lone is to bite him)* Aaaaah! Quack, quack, quack!

(They face off, in character as animals. Duck-Ma is terrified.)

LONE. Grrrr!

MA *(as a cry for help)*. Quack, quack, quack!

(Lone pounces on Ma. They struggle, in character. Ma is quacking madly, eyes tightly closed. Lone stands up straight. Ma continues to quack)

LONE. Stand up.

MA *(eyes still closed)*. Quack, quack, quack!

LONE *(louder)*. Stand up!

MA *(opening his eyes)*. Oh.

LONE. What are you?

MA. Huh?

LONE. A ChinaMan or a duck?

MA. Huh? Gimme a second to remember.

LONE. You like being a duck?

MA. My feet fell asleep.

LONE. You change forms so easily.

MA. You said to.

LONE. What else could you turn into?

MA. Well, you scared me—sneaking up like that.

LONE. Perhaps a rock. That would be useful. When the men need to rest, they can sit on you.

MA. I got carried away.

LONE. Let's try . . . a locust. Can you become a locust?

MA. No. Let's cut this, okay?

LONE. Here. It's easy. You just have to know how to hop.

MA. You're not gonna get me—

LONE. Like this.

(He demonstrates.)

MA. Forget it, Lone.

LONE. I'm a locust.

(He begins jumping towards Ma)

MA. Hey! Get away!

LONE. I devour whole fields.

MA. Stop it.

LONE. I starve babies before they are born.

MA. Hey look, stop it!

LONE. I cause famines and destroy villages.

MA. I'm warning you! Get away!

LONE. What are you going to do? You can't kill a locust.

MA. You're not a locust.

LONE. You kill one, and another sits on your hand.

MA. Stop following me.

LONE. Locusts always trouble people. If not, we'd feel useless. Now, if you become a locust, too . . .

MA. I'm not going to become a locust.

LONE. Just stick your teeth! Out!

MA. I'm not gonna be a bug! It's stupid!

LONE. No man who's just been a duck has the right to call anything stupid.

MA. I thought you were trying to teach me something.

LONE. I am. Go ahead.

MA. All right. There. That look right?

LONE. Your legs should be a little lower. Lower! There. That's adequate. So, how does it feel to be a locust?

(Lone gets up.)

MA. I dunno. How long do I have to do this?

LONE. Could you do it for three years?

MA. Three years? Don't be—

LONE. You couldn't, could you? Could you be a duck for that long?

MA. Look, I wasn't born to be either of those.

LONE. Exactly. Well, I wasn't born to work on a railroad, either. "Best of both worlds." How can you be such an insect?

(Pause.)

MA. Lone . . .

LONE. Stay down there! Don't move! I've never told anyone my story—the story of my parents kidnapping me from school. All the time we were crossing the ocean, the last two years here—I've kept my mouth shut. To you, I finally tell it. And all you can say is, "Best of both worlds." You're a bug to me, a locust. You think you understand the dedication one must have to be in the opera? You think it's the same as working on a railroad?

MA. Lone, all I was saying is that you'll go back too, and—

LONE. You're no longer a student of mine.

MA. What?

LONE. You have no dedication.

MA. Lone, I'm sorry.

LONE. Get up.

MA. I'm honored that you told me that.

LONE. Get up.

MA. No.

LONE. No?

MA. I don't want to. I want to talk.

LONE. Well, I've learned from the past. You're stubborn. You don't go. All right. Stay there. If you want to prove to me that you're dedicated, be a locust 'til morning. I'll go.

MA. Lone, I'm really honored that you told me.

LONE. I'll return in the morning.

(Exits.)

MA. Lone? Lone, that's ridiculous. You think I'm gonna stay like this? If you do, you're crazy. Lone? Come back here.

SCENE 4

(Night. Ma, alone, as a locust.)

MA. Locusts travel in huge swarms, so large that when they cross the sky, they block out the sun, like a storm. Second Uncle—back home—when he was a young man, his whole crop got wiped out by locusts one year. In the famine that followed, Second Uncle lost his eldest son and his second wife—the one he married for love. Even to this day, we look around before saying the word "locust"—to make sure Second Uncle is out of hearing range. About eight years ago, my brother and I discovered Second Uncle's cave in back of the stream near our house. We saw him come out of it one day around noon. Later, just before the sun went down, we sneaked in. We only looked once. Inside, there must have been hundreds—maybe five hundred or more—grasshoppers in huge bamboo cages—and around them—stacks of grasshopper legs, grasshopper heads, grasshopper antennae, grasshoppers with one leg still trying to hop but toppling like trees coughing, grasshoppers wrapped around sharp branches rolling from side to side, grasshopper legs cut off grasshopper bodies then tied around grasshoppers and tightened till grasshoppers died. Every conceivable kind of grasshopper in every conceivable stage of life and death, subject to every conceivable grasshopper torture. We ran out quickly, my brother and I—we knew an evil place by the thickness of the air. Now, I think of Second Uncle. How sad that the locusts forced him to take out his agony on innocent grasshoppers. What if Second Uncle could see me now? Would he cut off my legs? He might as well. I can barely feel them. But then again, Second Uncle never tortured actual locusts, just weak grasshoppers.

SCENE 5

Night. Ma still as a locust.

LONE (*off, singing*).
    "Hit your hardest,
    Pound out your tears.
    The more you try,
    The more you'll cry
    At how little I've moved
    And how large I loom
    By the time the sun goes down."

MA. You look rested.

LONE. Me?

MA. Well, you sound rested.

LONE. No, not at all.

MA. Maybe I'm just comparing you to me.

LONE. I didn't even close my eyes all last night.

MA. Aw, Lone, you didn't have to stay up for me. You coulda just come up here and—

LONE. For you?

MA. —apologized and everything woulda' been—

LONE. I didn't stay up for you.

MA. Huh? You didn't?

LONE. No.

MA. Oh. You sure?

LONE. Positive. I was thinking, that's all.

MA. About me?

LONE. Well . . .

MA. Even a little?

LONE. I was thinking about the ChinaMen—and you. Get up, Ma.

MA. Aw, do I have to? I've gotten to know these grasshoppers real well.

LONE. Get up. I have a lot to tell you.

MA. What'll they think? They take me in even though I'm a little large, then they find out I'm a human being. I stepped on their kids. No trust. Gimme a hand, will you? (*Lone helps Ma up, but Ma's legs can't support him.*) Aw, shit. My legs are coming off.

(*He lies down and tries to straighten them out.*)

LONE. I have many surprises. First, you will play Gwan Gung.

MA. My legs will be sent home without me. What'll my family think? Come to port to meet me, and all they get is two legs.

LONE. Did you hear me?

MA. Hold on. I can't be in agony and listen to Chinese at the same time.

LONE. Did you hear my first surprise?

MA. No. I'm too busy screaming.

LONE. I said, you'll play Gwan Gung.

MA. Gwan Gung?

LONE. Yes.

MA. Me?

LONE. Yes.

MA. Without legs?

LONE. What?

MA. That might be good.

LONE. Stop that!

MA. I'll become a legend. Like the blind man who defended Amoy.

LONE. Did you hear?

MA. "The legless man who played Gwan Gung."

LONE. Isn't that what you want? To play Gwan Gung?

MA. No, I just wanna sleep.

LONE. No, you don't. Look. Here. I brought you something.

MA. Food?

LONE. Here. Some rice.

MA. Thanks, Lone. And duck?

LONE. Just a little.

MA. Where'd you get the duck?

LONE. Just bones and skin.

MA. We don't have duck. And the white devils have been blockading the food.

LONE. Sing—he had some left over.

MA. Sing? That thief?

LONE. And something to go with it.

MA. What? Lone, where did you find whiskey?

LONE. You know, Sing—he has almost anything.

MA. Yeah. For a price.

LONE. Once, even some thousand-day-old eggs.

MA. He's a thief. That's what they told me.

LONE. Not if you're his friend.

MA. Sing don't have any real friends. Everyone talks about him bein' tied in to the head of the klan in San Francisco. Lone, you didn't have to do this. Here. Have some.

LONE. I had plenty.

MA. Don't gimme that. This cost you plenty, Lone.

LONE. Well, I thought if we were going to celebrate, we should do it as well as we would at home.

MA. Celebrate? What for? Wait.

LONE. Ma, the strike is over.

MA. Shit, I knew it. And we won, right?

LONE. Yes, the ChinaMen have won. They can do more than just talk.

MA. I told you. Didn't I tell you?

LONE. Yes. Yes, you did.

MA. Yang told me it was gonna be done. He said—

LONE. Yes, I remember.

MA. Didn't I tell you? Huh?

LONE. Ma, eat your duck.

MA. Nine days, we civilized the white devils. I knew it, I knew we'd hold out till their ears started twitching. So that's where you got the duck, right? At the celebration?

LONE. No, there wasn't a celebration.

MA. Huh? You sure? The ChinaMen—they look for any excuse to party.

LONE. But I thought *we* should celebrate.

MA. Well, that's for sure.

LONE. So you will play Gwan Gung.

MA. God, nine days. Shit, it's finally done. Well, we'll show them how to party. Make noise. Jump off rocks. Make the mountain shake.

LONE. We'll wash your body, to prepare you for the role.

MA. What role?

LONE. Gwan Gung. I've been telling you.

MA. I don't wanna play Gwan Gung.

LONE. You've shown the dedication required to become my student, so—

MA. Lone, you think I stayed up last night 'cause I wanted to play Gwan Gung?

LONE. You said you were like him.

MA. I am. Gwan Gung stayed up all night once to prove his loyalty. Well, now I have too. Lone, I'm honored that you told me your story.

LONE. Yes . . . That is like Gwan Gung.

MA. Good. So let's do an opera about *me*.

LONE. What?

MA. You wanna party or what?

LONE. About you?

MA. You said I was like Gwan Gung, didn't you?

LONE. Yes, but—

MA. Well, look at the operas he's got. I ain't even got one.

LONE. Still, you can't—

MA. You tell me, is that fair?

LONE. You can't do an opera about yourself.

MA. I just won a victory, didn't I? I deserve an opera in my honor.

LONE. But, it's not traditional.

MA. Traditional? Lone, you gotta figure any way I could do Gwan Gung wasn't gonna be traditional anyway. I may be as good a guy as him, but he's a better dancer. (*sings*)

   Old Gwan Gung, just sits about
   Til the dime-store fighters have had it out.
   Then he pitches his peach pit
   Combs his beard
   Draws his sword
   And they scatter in fear

LONE. What are you talking about?

MA. I just won a great victory. I get—whatcha call it?— poetic license. C'mon. Hit the gongs. I'll immortalize my story.

LONE. I refuse. This goes against all my training. I try and give you your wish and—

MA. Do it. Gimme my wish. Hit the gongs.

LONE. I never—I can't.

MA. Can't what? Don't think I'm worth an opera? No. I guess not. I forgot—you think I'm just one of those dead men.

(*Silence. Lone pulls out a gong. Ma gets into position. Lone hits the gong. They do the following in a mock Chinese opera style.*)

MA. I am Ma. Yesterday, I was kicked out of my house by my three elder brothers, calling me the lazy dreamer of the family. I am sitting here in front of the temple trying to decide how I will avenge this indignity. Here comes the poorest beggar in this village. (*He cues Lone.*) He is called Fleaman because his body is the most popular meeting place for fleas from around the province.

LONE (*singing*).
   Fleas in love
   Find your happiness
   In the gray scraps of my suit

MA. Hello, Flea—

LONE (*Continuing*).
   Fleas in need,
   Shield your families
   In the gray hairs of my beard

MA. Hello, Flea—

(Lone cuts Ma off, continues an extended improvised aria)

MA. Hello, Fleaman.

LONE. Hello, Ma. Are you interested in providing a home for these fleas?

MA. No!

LONE. This couple here—seeking to start a new home. Housing today is so hard to find. How about your left arm.

MA. I may have plenty of my own fleas in time. I have been thrown out by my elder brothers.

LONE. Are you seeking revenge? A flea epidemic on your house? *(To a flea.)* Get back there. You should be asleep. Your mother will worry.

MA. Nothing would make my brothers angrier than seeing me rich.

LONE. Rich? After the bad crops of the last three years, even the fleas are thinking of moving north.

MA. I heard a white devil talk yesterday.

LONE. Oh—with hair the color of a sick chicken and eyes round as eggs? The fleas and I call him Chicken-Laying-an-Egg.

MA. He said we can make our fortunes on the Gold Mountain, where work is play and the sun scares off snow.

LONE. Don't listen to chicken-brains.

MA. Why not? He said gold grows like weeds.

LONE. I have heard that it is slavery.

MA. Slavery? What do you know, Fleaman? Who told you? The fleas? Yes, I will go to Gold Mountain.

(Gongs. Ma strikes a submissive pose to Lone)

LONE. "The one hundred twenty-five dollars passage money is to be paid to the said head of said Hong, who will make arrangements with the coolies, that their wages shall be deducted until the debt is absorbed."

(Ma bows to Lone. Gongs. They pick up fighting sticks and do a water-crossing dance. Dance ends. They stoop next to each other and rock)

MA. I have been in the bottom of this boat for thirty-six days now. Tang, how many have died?

LONE. Not me. I'll live through this ride.

MA. I didn't ask how you are.

LONE. But why's the Gold Mountain so far?

MA. We left with three hundred and three.

LONE. My family's depending on me.

MA. So tell me how many have died?

LONE. I'll be the last one alive.

MA. That's not what I wanted to know.

LONE. I'll find some fresh air in this hole.

MA. I asked, how many have died.

LONE. Is that a crack in the side?

MA. Are you listening to me?

LONE. If I had some air—

MA. I asked, don't you see—?

LONE. The crack—over there—

MA. Will you answer me please?

LONE. I need to get out.

MA. The rest here agree—

LONE. I can't stand the smell.

MA. That a hundred eighty—

LONE. I can't see the air.

MA. Of us will not see—

LONE. And I can't die.

MA. Our Gold Mountain dream.

(Lone/Tang dies; Ma throws his body overboard. The boat docks. Ma exits, walks through the streets. He picks up one of the fighting sticks, while Lone becomes the mountain.)

MA. I have been given my pickaxe. Now, I will attack the mountain.

(Ma does a dance of labor. Lone sings.)

LONE.

> Hit your hardest
> Pound out your tears
> The more you try
> The more you'll cry
> At how little I've moved
> And how large I loom
> By the time the sun goes down

(Dance stops)

MA. This Mountain is clever. But why shouldn't it be? It's fighting for its life, like we fight for ours.

(The Mountain picks up a stick. Ma and the Mountain do a battle dance. The dance ends)

MA. This Mountain not only defends itself—it also attacks. It turns our strength against us.

(Lone does Ma's labor dance, while Ma plants explosives in mid-air. Dance ends.)

MA. The Mountain has survived for millions of years. Its wisdom is immense.

(Lone and Ma begin a second battle dance. This one ends with them working the battle sticks together. Lone breaks away, does a warrior strut)

LONE. I am a white devil! Listen to my stupid language: "Wha che doo doo blah blah." Look at my wide eyes—like I have drunk seventy-two pots of tea. Look at my funny hair—twisting, turning, like a snake telling lies. (*To Ma.*) Bla bla doo doo tee tee.

MA. We don't understand English.

LONE (*angry*). Bla bla doo doo tee tee!

MA (*with Chinese accent*). Please you-ah speak-ah Chinese?

LONE. Oh. Work—uh—one—two—more—work—two—

MA. Two hours more? Stupid demons. As confused as your hair. We will strike!

(*Gongs. Ma is on strike*)

MA (*in broken English*). Eight hours day good for white man, alla same good for ChinaMan.

LONE. The strike is over! We've won!

MA. I knew we would.

LONE. We forced the white devil to act civilized.

MA. Tame the barbarians!

LONE. Did you think—

MA. Who woulda thought?

LONE. —it could be done?

MA. Who?

LONE. But who?

MA. Who could tame them?

MA AND LONE. Only a ChinaMan?

(*They laugh.*)

LONE. Well, c'mon.

MA. Let's celebrate!

LONE. We have.

MA. Oh.

LONE. Back to work.

MA. But we've won the strike.

LONE. I know. Congratulations. And now—

MA. —back to work?

LONE. Right.

MA. No.

LONE. But the strike is over.

(*Lone tosses Ma a stick; they resume their stick battle as before, but Ma is heard over Lone's singing.*)

LONE.	MA.
Hit your hardest,	Wait.
Pound out your tears.	I'm tired of this!
	How do we end it?
The more you try,	Let's stop now, all
The more you'll cry	right?
At how little I've moved	Look, I said enough!

And how large I
   loom
By the time the
   sun goes down.

(*Ma tosses his stick away, but Lone is already aiming a blow towards it, so that Lone hits Ma instead and knocks him down*)

MA. Oh! Shit . . .

LONE. I'm sorry! Are you all right?

MA. Yeah. I guess.

LONE. Why'd you let go? You can't just do that.

MA. I'm bleeding.

LONE. That was stupid—where?

MA. Here.

LONE. No.

MA. Ow!

LONE. There will probably be a bump.

MA. I dunno.

LONE. What?

MA. I dunno why I let go.

LONE. It was stupid.

MA. But how were we going to end the opera?

LONE. Here. (*He applies whiskey to Ma's bruise.*) I don't know.

MA. Why didn't we just end it with the celebration? Ow! Careful.

LONE. Sorry. But Ma, the celebration's not the end. We're returning to work. Today. At dawn.

MA. What?

LONE. We've already lost nine days of work. But we got eight hours.

MA. Today? That's terrible.

LONE. What do you think we're here for? But they listened to our demands. We're getting a raise.

MA. Right. Fourteen dollars.

LONE. No. Eight.

MA. What?

LONE. We had to compromise. We got an eight dollar raise.

MA. But we wanted fourteen! Why didn't we get fourteen?

LONE. It was the best deal they could get. Congratulations.

MA. Congratulations? Look, Lone, I'm sick of you making fun of the ChinaMen.

LONE. Ma, I'm not. For the first time. I was wrong. We got eight dollars.

MA. We wanted fourteen.

LONE. But we got eight hours.

MA. We'll go back on strike.

LONE. Why?

MA. We could hold out for months.

LONE. And lose all that work?

MA. But we just gave in.

LONE. You're being ridiculous. We got eight hours. Besides, it's already been decided.

MA. I didn't decide. I wasn't there. You made me stay up here.

LONE. The heads of the gangs decide.

MA. And that's it?

LONE. It's done.

MA. Back to work? That's what they decided? Lone, I don't want to go back to work.

LONE. Who does?

MA. I forgot what it's like.

LONE. You'll pick up the technique again soon enough.

MA. I mean, what it's like to have them telling you what to do all the time. Using up your strength.

LONE. I thought you said even after work, you still feel good.

MA. Some days. But others . . . (*Pause*) I get so frustrated sometimes. At the rock. The rock doesn't give in. It's not human. I wanna claw it with my fingers, but that would just rip them up. I wanna throw myself head first onto it, but it'd just knock my skull open. The rock would knock my skull open, then just sit there, smiling, still, like nothing had happened like a faceless Buddha. (*Pause*) Lone, when do I get out of here?

LONE. Well, the railroad may get finished—

MA. It'll never get finished.

LONE. —or you may get rich.

MA. Rich. Right. This is the Gold Mountain. (*Pause*) Lone, has anyone ever gone home rich from here?

LONE. Yes. Some.

MA. But most?

LONE. Most . . . do go home.

MA. Do you still have the fear?

LONE. The fear?

MA. That you'll become like them—dead men?

LONE. Maybe I was wrong about them.

MA. Well, I do. You wanted me to say it before, I can say it now: "They are dead men." Their greatest accomplishment was to win a strike that's gotten us nothing.

LONE. They're sending money home.

MA. No.

LONE. It's not much, I know, but it's something.

MA. Lone, I'm not even doing that. If I don't get rich here, I might as well die here. Let my brothers laugh in peace.

LONE. Ma, you're too soft to get rich here, naïve—you believed the snow was warm.

MA. I've got to change myself. Toughen up. Take no shit. Count my change. Learn to gamble. Learn to win. Learn to stare. Learn to deny. Learn to look at men with opaque eyes.

LONE. You want to do that?

MA. I will. 'Cause I've got the fear. You've given it to me.

(*Pause*)

LONE. Will I see you here tonight?

MA. Tonight?

LONE. I just thought I'd ask.

MA. I'm sorry, Lone. I haven't got time to be the Second Clown.

LONE. I thought you might not.

MA. Sorry.

LONE. You could have been a . . . fair actor.

MA. You coming down? I gotta get ready for work. This is gonna be a terrible day. My legs are sore and my arms are outa practice.

LONE. You go first. I'm going to practice some before work. There's still time.

MA. Practice? But you said you lost your fear. And you said that's what brings you up here.

LONE. I guess I was wrong about that, too. Today, I am dancing for no reason at all.

MA. Do whatever you want. See you down at camp.

LONE. Could you do me a favor?

MA. A favor?

LONE. Could you take this down so I don't have to take it all?

(*Lone points to a pile of props*)

MA. Well, okay. (*Pause*) But this is the last time.

LONE. Of course, Ma. (*Ma exits*) See you soon. The last time. I suppose so.

(*Lone resumes practicing. He twirls his hair around as in the beginning of the play. The sun begins to rise. It continues rising until Lone is moving and seen only in shadow.*)

COMMENTARY

Note: This essay presents one interpretation of the play. For other perspectives on The Dance and the Railroad, *consult the essays listed below.*

You may recall a scene in *The Godfather, Part II* in which the young Vito Corleone, himself "fresh off the boat" from Italy, seeks a bit of the "old country" in a small, colorful Italian-language theater in New York City's Little Italy. Immigrants frequently use the theater as a meeting place to share memories of the land they left behind as well as to discuss problems in adjusting to a new life in a strange land. Frequently, the plays themselves are used to ad-dress these problems, often satirically. In New York, for instance, the Yiddish theater for years provided a meeting place for displaced Jewish immigrants, just as the Bowery Theater courted Irish Americans. In Buenos Aires, Italian immigrants (who were, like Lone and Ma, imported to build railroads) laughed at the *cocoleche* plays about immigrants and their problems with language in a new country. Today, one can go to the Tricycle Theatre in North London and see plays staged by and for West Indian émigrés.

It was this impulse that led to the creation of *The Dance and the Railroad*. Based on a true incident in which Chinese rail workers went on strike in California in 1867, this one-act was developed by Hwang in collaboration with two actors trained in Chinese theater and dance, John Lone and Tzi Ma. Appropriately, Hwang named the play's characters after them because their own struggles as artists in a new culture mirror those of the immigrant workers. On its most obvious level, the play is about the conflict between "the dance" (the values of the East) versus "the railroad" (Western technology, built largely on the backs of immigrant workers and slaves). The railroad is an especially apt symbol as it was the means by which the country expanded in the nineteenth century. Furthermore, it is an ironic re-minder that workers like Ma have themselves traveled thousands of miles so that their sweat can provide a comfortable means of travel for others.

To tell his story Hwang uses a time-tested construct: the master-pupil relationship (a favorite ploy of Shaw: see the discussion of *Heartbreak House* in Part I). The device works well, especially for didactic drama, because as the pupil learns, so does the audience. In Hwang's play Lone, who trained in the Peking Opera for eight years before seeking his for-tune on Gold Mountain (a variant on the old "streets paved with gold" metaphor used by hopeful immigrants to describe America), is approached by Ma, newly arrived in Califor-nia. Ma ascends the mountain to ask Lone to be his instructor. The younger Chinese wants to learn the secrets of the opera, as well as how to survive in his new environment. Lone relies on the aesthetics and discipline of his opera training to escape from the drea-riness of the menial work at the foot of the mountain. "You think you understand the ded-ication one must have to be in the opera? You think it's the same as working on a rail-road?" he challenges his pupil.

As is often the case in education, it is the teacher who learns much from the student. In Ma's naivete—about the opera, about working conditions, about the American Dream—Lone ultimately sees himself. When he learns from Ma that the strike has been settled, though at no real advantage to the workers, he becomes aware that his dreams (delusions?) about the opera are as hollow as Ma's about working conditions. In the final moment of the play the teacher asks the pupil to help him take his stage props—symbols of his own unrealistic dreams—down the mountain. Reality waits in the "ChinaMan" camp at the foot of the mountain, while the mountain itself is as illusory as its name. There is no Gwan Gung, the Robin Hood–like warrior loved by devotees of the Peking Opera, to save Lone and Ma from their fate.

For all the play's talk about the "white devils" that exploit the workers, Hwang notes that there are enemies within the immigrant culture as well. We learn that "the heads of the gang" decide the fate of the rail workers; we learn that the "coolies" had to pay $125 "to the said head of said Hong" for their passage on the rotting ship from China because they were promised by Hong's minions that they could "make our fortunes on the Gold Mountain, where work is play and the sun scares off snow"; and we learn that a successful black market operation exploits newcomers in San Francisco. These are all references to a reality faced by immigrants that is as disturbing as any perpetrated by the majority culture: the "selling out" of immigrants by members of their own race. Not all of the devils Ma and Lone confront have "hair the color of a sick chicken and eyes round as eggs." Hwang's strength rests on his recognition that issues plaguing immigrants are more complex than racism.

We cannot, however, dismiss racism as a central issue of Hwang's play. Even though he is newly come to America, Ma quickly learns that he must play to racist stereotypes to survive. He speaks fluent "demon English": "Eight hour a day good for white man, all same good for ChinaMan." And both he and Lone can parody "demon English" as they play "white devils": "Wha che doo doo blah blah. . . . Bla bla doo doo tee tee." Ironically, to deal with the devil they must themselves adopt the same racist attitudes toward their bosses that the bosses have for them; note that they refer to whites in blatantly stereotypical terms. They have assimilated the customs of the country too well. Even behind their role playing within the opera motif, Ma and Lone are painfully aware that they are looked at as "different." When they play at being various animals, insects, and birds, Lone and Ma are reminded of intolerance. Ma discovers that he "never realized before how uncomfortable a duck's life is" as he squats and quacks; Lone tells his pupil that there is "Nothing worse than a duck [or a ChinaMan?] that doesn't know his place." Here art clearly imitates life for Lone.

Ma's lengthy speech in Scene 4 is a parable about one of the most disturbing problems facing immigrants—that is, various minorities are pitted against one another by the majority in a "divide and conquer" strategy. As he recounts his story about the locusts and the grasshoppers, he seems to suggest that one class of immigrants (the innocent grasshoppers) pays for the sins of another (the plague-bearing locusts) at the hands of the spiteful Second Uncle (Sam?). Is Ma suggesting that the Chinese are victims of prejudice against nonwhites, which in the California of his time (and today) would have been the Mexicans and their descendants? While we know that immigrants are too often and too easily blamed for any number of social and economic problems in their host country, Hwang lets us see yet another insidious aspect of "immigrant bashing," to use a current term: the resentment of one group of immigrants against another. History recently provided a concrete example of what seems to be one of Hwang's concerns in this play. In the Los Angeles riots following the Rodney King case in 1992 (in which white police officers were acquitted of beating King, an African-American, even though the ferocious beating was videotaped), it was Korean-Americans who suffered most at the hands of the black and Hispanic rioters.

In *The Dance and the Railroad*, Hwang offers a much bolder critique of intolerance and exploitation. By expanding his focus to include internal problems as well as the well-documented, much discussed external ones, he exposes "the cult of racism" (as opposed to only white racism) that is the blight on Gold Mountain.

Other perspectives on *The Dance and the Railroad*:

Di Gaetani, John L. "Interview with David Henry Hwang." *Drama Review* 33:3 (1989): 141–53.

Pace, Eric. "I Write Plays to Claim a Place for Asian-Americans." *New York Times*, 12 July, 1981, 4.

Another play by Hwang on video:

M. *Butterfly*. Dir. David Croneberg. Perf. Jeremy Irons, John Lone, Barbara Sukowa, and Ian Richardson. Warner Studios, 101 min., 1994.

TOP GIRLS
CARYL CHURCHILL

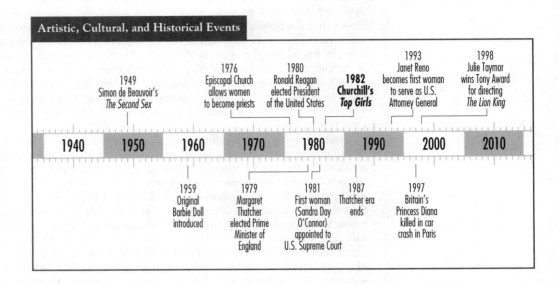

Artistic, Cultural, and Historical Events

1949
Simon de Beauvoir's
The Second Sex

1976
Episcopal Church
allows women
to become priests

1980
Ronald Reagan
elected President
of the United States

**1982
Churchill's
*Top Girls***

1993
Janet Reno
becomes first woman
to serve as U.S.
Attorney General

1998
Julie Taymor
wins Tony Award
for directing
The Lion King

| 1940 | 1950 | 1960 | 1970 | 1980 | 1990 | 2000 | 2010 |

1959
Original
Barbie Doll
introduced

1979
Margaret
Thatcher
elected Prime
Minister of
England

1981
First woman
(Sandra Day
O'Connor)
appointed to
U.S. Supreme Court

1987
Thatcher era
ends

1997
Britain's
Princess Diana
killed in car
crash in Paris

CARYL CHURCHILL (1938–)

Caryl Churchill is the most frequently produced and critically admired female playwright of our time. She has written for several of England's best political theaters, primarily the Royal Court. She has also been affiliated with the 7:84 Theatre Company (whose name refers to the fact that 7% of Britain's population controls 84% of its wealth), Joint Stock Company, and Monstrous Regiment, a major feminist company. In America, her works have been produced by Joseph Papp's Public Theatre (the U.S. equivalent of the Royal Court) and with regularity in Off-Broadway, Off-Off Broadway, and regional theaters. *Top Girls*, for instance, won several Obie Awards in 1982 as the best Off-Broadway work of that season.

Born in London, Churchill lived in Montreal, Canada, from 1949 to 1956 and then returned to England to study at Oxford University. Though her primary field was English literature, Churchill was introduced to Buddhism and other Eastern religions such as Taosim, Jain, and Hindu at Oxford. Eastern thought and spirituality have influenced many of the themes of her plays (e.g., illusions, historical cycles, and the transcendental nature of personality). The very structure of her plays also exhibits Eastern influences.

Churchill wrote several plays at Oxford, then several admired radio dramas in the 1960s. Though her first commercial stage play, *Owners*, was produced in 1972, it was not until 1979 that she became known internationally when the Royal Court produced *Cloud Nine*. Written as part of a collective exploration of sexual identities for the Joint Stock Company, *Cloud Nine* subsequently played in New York and other theater capitols. Her variegated works include *Top Girls* (1982), *Fen* (1983), *Softcops* (1984), *Serious Money* (1987), *Mad Forest* (1995), *Far Away* (2001), and *A Number* (2002).

Although she is generally accepted as a leading feminist playwright, Churchill describes herself as a socialist writer first who only later adopted the feminist cause. She now describes herself as a "socialist-feminist," noting that although "socialism and feminism aren't synonymous . . . I feel strongly about both and wouldn't be interested in a form of one that didn't include the other." Her later plays deal with feminist issues, but they are also framed by her critique of contemporary society, which she feels exploits its weakest individuals for monetary and political gain. Her plays often explore the friction between the traditional (i.e., colonial) system and a more pluralistic world in which women, gays, and people of color strive to overcome outmoded prejudice and inequities.

Churchill has adopted—and expanded on—many techniques associated with Brecht. She writes plays that thrive on dialectical arguments, which are often "historicized" to challenge modern assumptions about social, political, and economic issues. Act I of *Cloud Nine* is set in a nineteenth-century British colonial outpost, and in the second act both the characters and the play's issues are hurled into the late twentieth century. *Serious Money*, set amidst contemporary financial centers, is written as a mock Restoration comedy in rhymed couplets. *Top Girls*, perhaps Churchill's most innovative use of historification, opens with famous women of history and myth dining in a modern restaurant with the newly promoted executive of a personnel agency. The play's final scene takes place a year *prior* to the first scene as Churchill manipulates time to force her audiences to confront the play's deeper issues.

Churchill often supercedes Brecht's techniques, particularly in her use of social gestus as the foundation of an actor's character. Not only does Churchill typically assign multiple roles to actors (as in *Top Girls*), she also frequently specifies cross-gender casting (most notably in *Cloud Nine*) to subvert our preconceptions about sexual roles in society. Churchill wittily illustrates that history itself does this; Pope Joan in *Top Girls* personifies the ultimate example of cross-gender casting. In Churchill's boldly theatrical world, disorientation rules to shake audiences from their complacency. "Confusing" is a word often applied to her works by naive critics, but the confusion about time and history, sex and gender, and literary style itself is calculated to provoke the audience to find clarity in a world that confuses power and wealth with natural superiority.

As You Read *Top Girls*

Here we find a decidedly feminist play, yet it satirically indicts certain kinds of feminists, especially those who participate in their own oppression by "buying in" to the capitalist system during the Reagan-Thatcher era. Women, both modern and historical, who appear to be the exemplars of "the successful woman" prove each is flawed and unaware, thus diminishing the admiration we "thought" we had for them. The play opens with a fantasy about the past, yet it ends with a "flashback" that previews the future. Between these surreal sequences, Churchill scripts essentially realistic scenes from a contemporary society in which the only way to get ahead—whether man or woman—is to "play the game" ruthlessly. This free mixture of historical periods, contrary ideologies, and assorted theatrical styles typifies postmodern dramaturgy, and *Top Girls* represents some of the predominant impulses of contemporary experimental drama. More importantly, the meaning of Churchill's play is best found in its provocative contradictions. Note also Churchill's stage direction in which she indicates how the actor-characters are supposed to overlap lines, cut one another off, and speak contrapuntally to one another. This is part of her distinctive style; it makes great sense in performance (particularly in the hands of skilled actors), but it may prove a bit disconcerting to first-time readers.

TOP GIRLS

——— CARYL CHURCHILL ———

CHARACTERS
MARLENE
WAITRESS/KIT/SHONA
ISABELLA BIRD/JOYCE/MRS KIDD
LADY NIJO/WIN
DULL GRET/ANGIE
POPE JOAN/LOUISE
PATIENT GRISELDA/NELL/JEANINE

ACT I

Scene 1: A Restaurant.
Scene 2: Top Girls' Employment Agency, London.
Scene 3: Joyce's backyard in Suffolk.

ACT II

Scene 1: Top Girls' Employment Agency.
Scene 2: A Year Earlier. Joyce's kitchen.

Production Note: *The seating order for Act I, Scene 1 in the original production at the Royal Court was (from right) Gret, Nijo, Marlene, Joan, Griselda, Isabella.*

THE CHARACTERS
ISABELLA BIRD (1831–1904): *Lived in Edinburgh, traveled extensively between the ages of forty and seventy.*
LADY NIJO (b. 1258): *Japanese, was an Emperor's courtesan and later a Buddhist nun who traveled on foot through Japan.*
DULL GRET: *Is the subject of the Brueghel painting* Dulle Griet, *in which a woman in an apron and armor leads a crowd of women charging through hell and fighting the devils.*
POPE JOAN: *Disguised as a man, is thought to have been pope between 854 and 856.*

PATIENT GRISELDA: *Is the obedient wife whose story is told by Chaucer in "The Clerk's Tale" of* The Canterbury Tales.

THE LAYOUT

A speech usually follows the one immediately before it but:

(1) *When one character starts speaking before the other has finished, the point of interruption is marked* /. *e.g.,*

ISABELLA. This is the Emperor of Japan? / I once met the Emperor of Morocco.
NIJO. In fact he was the ex-Emperor.

(2) *A character sometimes continues speaking right through another's speech, e.g.,*

ISABELLA. When I was forty I thought my life was over. / Oh I was pitiful. I was
NIJO. I didn't say I felt it for twenty years. Not every minute.
ISABELLA. sent on a cruise for my health and I felt even worse. Pains in my bones, pins and needles . . . etc.

(3) *Sometimes a speech follows on from a speech marked earlier than the one immediately before it, and continuity is marked**. *e.g.,*

GRISELDA. I'd seen him riding by, we all had. And he'd seen me in the fields with the sheep.*
ISABELLA. I would have been well suited to minding sheep.
NIJO. And Mr. Nugent went riding by.
ISABELLA. Of course not, Nijo, I mean a healthy life in the open air.
JOAN. *He just rode up while you were minding the sheep and asked you to marry him?

where "in the fields with the sheep" is the cue to both "I would have been" and "He just rode up."

ACT I

SCENE 1

(Restaurant. Saturday night. There is a table with a white cloth set for dinner with six places. The lights come up on Marlene and the Waitress.)

MARLENE. Excellent, yes, table for six. One of them's going to be late but we won't wait. I'd like a bottle of Frascati straight away if you've got one really cold. *(The Waitress goes. Isabella Bird arrives.)* Here we are, Isabella.

ISABELLA. Congratulations, my dear.

MARLENE. Well, it's a step. It makes for a party. I haven't time for a holiday. I'd like to go somewhere exotic like you but I can't get away. I don't know how you could bear to leave Hawaii. / I'd like to lie

ISABELLA. I did think of settling.

MARLENE. in the sun forever, except of course I can't bear sitting still.

ISABELLA. I sent for my sister Hennie to come and join me. I said, Hennie we'll live here forever and help the natives. You can buy two sirloins of beef for what a pound of chops costs in Edinburgh. And Hennie wrote back, the dear, that yes, she would come to Hawaii if I wished, but I said she had far better stay where she was. Hennie was suited to life in Tobermory.

MARLENE. Poor Hennie.

ISABELLA. Do you have a sister?

MARLENE. Yes in fact.

ISABELLA. Hennie was happy. She was good. I did miss its face, my own pet. But I couldn't stay in Scotland. I loathed the constant murk.

(Lady Nijo arrives)

MARLENE *(seeing her.)*. Ah! Nijo! *(The Waitress enters with the wine.)*

NIJO. Marlene! *(To Isabella.)* So excited when Marlene told me / you were coming.

ISABELLA. I'm delighted / to meet you.

MARLENE. I think a drink while we wait for the others. I think a drink anyway. What a week. *(Marlene seats Nijo. The Waitress pours wine.)*

NIJO. It was always the men who used to get so drunk. I'd be one of the maidens, passing the sake.

ISABELLA. I've had sake.[1] Small hot drink. Quite fortifying after a day in the wet.

NIJO. One night my father proposed three rounds of three cups, which was normal, and then the Emperor should have said three rounds of three cups, but he said three rounds of nine cups, so you can imagine. Then the Emperor passed his sake cup to my father and said, "Let the wild goose come to me this spring."

MARLENE. Let the what?

NIJO. It's a literary allusion to a tenth-century epic, / His Majesty was very cultured.

ISABELLA. This is the Emperor of Japan? / I once met the Emperor of Morocco.

NIJO. In fact he was the ex-Emperor.

MARLENE. But he wasn't old? / Did you, Isabella?

NIJO. Twenty-nine.

ISABELLA. Oh it's a long story.

MARLENE. Twenty-nine's an excellent age.

NIJO. Well I was only fourteen and I knew he meant something but I didn't know what. He sent me an eight-layered gown and I sent it back. So when the time came I did nothing but cry. My thin gowns were badly ripped. But even that morning when he left / he'd a green

MARLENE. Are you saying he raped you?

NIJO. robe with a scarlet lining and very heavily embroidered trousers, I already felt different about him. It made me uneasy. No, of course not, Marlene, I belonged to him, it was what I was brought up for from a baby. I soon found I was sad if he stayed away. It was depressing day after day not knowing when he would come. I never enjoyed taking other women to him.

ISABELLA. I certainly never saw my father drunk. He was a clergyman. / And I didn't get married till I was fifty. *(The Waitress brings menus.)*

NIJO. Oh, my father was a very religious man. Just before he died he said to me, "Serve His Majesty, be respectful, if you lose his favour enter holy orders."

MARLENE. But he meant stay in a convent, not go wandering round the country.

NIJO. Priests were often vagrants, so why not a nun? You think I shouldn't? / I still did what my father wanted.

MARLENE. No, no, I think you should. / I think it was wonderful.

(Dull Gret arrives.)

ISABELLA. I tried to do what my father wanted.

MARLENE. Gret, good. Nijo. Gret / I know Griselda's going to be late, but should we wait for Joan? / Let's get you a drink.

ISABELLA. Hello Gret! *(She continues to Nijo:)* I tried to be a clergyman's daughter. Needlework, music, charitable schemes. I had a tumour removed from my

---

[1]**sake** a wine made from rice in Japan

spine and spent a great deal of time on the sofa. I studied the metaphysical poets and hymnology. / I thought I enjoyed intellectual pursuits.

NIJO. Ah, you like poetry. I come of a line of eight generations of poets. Father had a poem / in the anthology.

ISABELLA. My father taught me Latin although I was a girl. / But really I was

MARLENE. They didn't have Latin at my school.

ISABELLA. more suited to manual work. Cooking, washing, mending, riding horses. / Better than reading

NIJO. Oh but I'm sure you're very clever.

ISABELLA. books, eh Gret! A rough life in the open air.

NIJO. I can't say I enjoyed my rough life. What I enjoyed most was being the Emperor's favorite / and wearing thin silk.

ISABELLA. Did you have any horses, Gret?

GRET. Pig.

(Pope Joan arrives.)

MARLENE. Oh Joan, thank God, we can order. Do you know everyone? We were just talking about learning Latin and being clever girls. Joan was by way of an infant prodigy. Of course you were. What excited you when you were ten?

JOAN. Because angels are without matter they are not individuals. Every angel is a species.

MARLENE. There you are. (*They laugh. They look at menus.*)

ISABELLA. Yes, I forgot all my Latin. But my father was the mainspring of my life and when he died I was so grieved. I'll have the chicken, please, / and the soup.

NIJO. Of course you were grieved. My father was saying his prayers and he dozed off in the sun. So I touched his knee to rouse him. "I wonder what will happen," he said, and then he was dead before he finished the sentence. / If he'd

MARLENE. What a shock.

NIJO. died saying his prayers he would have gone straight to heaven. / Waldorf salad.

JOAN. Death is the return of all creatures to God.

NIJO. I shouldn't have woken him.

JOAN. Damnation only means ignorance of the truth. I was always attracted by the teachings of John the Scot, though he was inclined to confuse / God and the world.

ISABELLA. Grief always overwhelmed me at the time.

MARLENE. What I fancy is a rare steak. Gret?

ISABELLA. I am of course a member of the / Church of England.

MARLENE. Gret?

GRET. Potatoes.

MARLENE. I haven't been to church for years. / I like Christmas carols.

ISABELLA. Good works matter more than church attendance.

MARLENE. Make that two steaks and a lot of potatoes. Rare. But I don't do good works either.

JOAN. Canelloni, please, / and a salad.

ISABELLA. Well, I tried, but oh dear. Hennie did good works.

NIJO. The first half of my life was all sin and the second / all repentance.*

MARLENE. Oh what about starters?

GRET. Soup.

JOAN. *And which did you like best?

MARLENE. Were your travels just a penance? Avocado vinaigrette. Didn't you / enjoy yourself?

JOAN. Nothing to start with for me, thank you.

NIJO. Yes, but I was very unhappy. / It hurt to remember the past.

MARLENE. And the wine list.

NIJO. I think that was repentance.

MARLENE. Well I wonder.

NIJO. I might have just been homesick.

MARLENE. Or angry.

NIJO. Not angry, no, / why angry?

GRET. Can we have some more bread?

MARLENE. Don't you get angry? I get angry.

NIJO. But what about?

MARLENE. Yes let's have two more Frascati. And some more bread, please. (*The Waitress exits.*)

ISABELLA. I tried to understand Buddhism when I was in Japan but all this birth and death succeeding each other through eternities just filled me with the most profound melancholy. I do like something more active.

NIJO. You couldn't say I was inactive. I walked every day for twenty years.

ISABELLA. I don't mean walking. / I mean in the head.

NIJO. I vowed to copy five Mahayana sutras. / Do you know how long they are?

MARLENE. I don't think religious beliefs are something we have in common. Activity yes. (*Gret empties the bread basket into her apron.*)

NIJO. My head was active. / My head ached.

JOAN. It's no good being active in heresy.

ISABELLA. What heresy? She's calling the Church of England / a heresy.

JOAN. There are some very attractive / heresies.

NIJO. I had never heard of Christianity. Never / heard of it. Barbarians.

MARLENE. Well I'm not a Christian. / And I'm not a Buddhist.

ISABELLA. You have heard of it?

MARLENE. We don't all have to believe the same.

ISABELLA. I knew coming to dinner with a pope we should keep off religion.

JOAN. I always enjoy a theological argument. But I won't try to convert you, I'm not a missionary. Anyway I'm a heresy myself.

ISABELLA. There are some barbaric practices in the east.

NIJO. Barbaric?

ISABELLA. Among the lower classes.

NIJO. I wouldn't know.

ISABELLA. Well theology always made my head ache.

MARLENE. Oh good, some food. (*The Waitress brings the first course, serves it during the following, then exits.*)

NIJO. How else could I have left the court if I wasn't a nun? When father died I had only His Majesty. So when I fell out of favor I had nothing. Religion is a kind of nothing / and I dedicated what was left of me to nothing.

ISABELLA. That's what I mean about Buddhism. It doesn't brace.

MARLENE. Come on, Nijo, have some wine.

NIJO. Haven't you ever felt like that? You've all felt / like that. Nothing will ever happen again. I am dead already.

ISABELLA. You thought your life was over but it wasn't.

JOAN. You wish it was over.

GRET. Sad.

MARLENE. Yes, when I first came to London I sometimes . . . and when I got back from America I did. But only for a few hours. Not twenty years.

ISABELLA. When I was forty I thought my life was over. / Oh I was pitiful. I was sent

NIJO. I didn't say I felt it for twenty years. Not every minute.

ISABELLA. on a cruise for my health and I felt even worse. Pains in my bones, pins and needles in my hands, swelling behind the ears, and—oh, stupidity. I shook all over, indefinable terror. And Australia seemed to me a hideous country, the acacias stank like drains. / I

NIJO. You were homesick. (*Gret steals a bottle of wine.*)

ISABELLA. had a photograph taken for Hennie but I told her I wouldn't send it, my hair had fallen out and my clothes were crooked, I looked completely insane and suicidal.

NIJO. So did I, exactly, dressed as a nun. I was wearing walking shoes for the first time.

ISABELLA. I longed to go home, / but home to what? Houses are perfectly dismal.*

NIJO. I longed to go back ten years.

MARLENE. *I thought travelling cheered you both up.

ISABELLA. Oh it did / of course. It was on

NIJO. I'm not a cheerful person, Marlene. I just laugh a lot.

ISABELLA. the trip from Australia to the Sandwich Isles, I fell in love with the sea. There were rats in the cabin and ants in the food but suddenly it was like a new world. I woke up every morning happy, knowing there would be nothing to annoy me. No nervousness. No dressing.

NIJO. Don't you like getting dressed? I adored my clothes. / When I was chosen

MARLENE. You had prettier colours than Isabella.

NIJO. to give sake to His Majesty's brother, the Emperor Kameyana, on his formal visit, I wore raw silk pleated trousers and a seven-layered gown in shades of red, and two outer garments, / yellow lined with green

MARLENE. Yes, all that silk must have been very—

(*The Waitress enters, clears the first course and exits.*)

JOAN. I dressed as a boy when I left home.*

NIJO. and a light green jacket. Lady Betto had a five-layered gown in shades of green and purple.

ISABELLA. *You dressed as a boy?

MARLENE. Of course, / for safety.

JOAN. It was easy, I was only twelve. / Also women weren't allowed in the library. We wanted to study in Athens.

MARLENE. You ran away alone?

JOAN. No, not alone, I went with my friend. / He was

NIJO. Ah, an elopement.

JOAN. sixteen but I thought I knew more science than he did and almost as much philosophy.

ISABELLA. Well I always traveled as a lady and I repudiated strongly any suggestion in the press that I was other than feminine.

MARLENE. I don't wear trousers in the office. / I could but I don't.

ISABELLA. There was no great danger to a woman of my age and appearance.

MARLENE. And you got away with it, Joan?

JOAN. I did then. (*The Waitress brings the main course.*)

MARLENE. And nobody noticed anything?

JOAN. They noticed I was a very clever boy. / And

MARLENE. I couldn't have kept pretending for so long.

JOAN. when I shared a bed with my friend, that was ordinary—two poor students in a lodging house. I think I forgot I was pretending.

ISABELLA. Rocky Mountain Jim, Mr Nugent, showed me no disrespect. He found it interesting, I think, that I could make scones and also lasso cattle. Indeed he declared his love for me, which was most distressing.

NIJO. What did he say? / We always sent poems first.

MARLENE. What did you say?

ISABELLA. I urged him to give up whisky, / but he said it was too late.

MARLENE. Oh Isabella.

ISABELLA. He had lived alone in the mountains for many years.

MARLENE. But did you—? (*The Waitress goes.*)

ISABELLA. Mr Nugent was a man that any woman might love but none could marry. I came back to England.

NIJO. Did you write him a poem when you left? / Snow on the mountains. My sleeves

MARLENE. Did you never seen him again?

ISABELLA. No, never.

NIJO. are wet with tears. In England no tears, no snow.

ISABELLA. Well, I say never. One morning very early in Switzerland, it was a year later, I had a vision of him as I last saw him / in his trapper's clothes with his

NIJO. A ghost!

ISABELLA. hair round his face, and that was the day, / I learnt later, he died with a

NIJO. Ah!

ISABELLA. bullet in his brain. / He just bowed to me and vanished.

MARLENE. Oh Isabella.

NIJO. When your lover dies—One of my lovers died. / The priest Ariake.

JOAN. My friend died. Have we all got dead lovers?

MARLENE. Not me, sorry.

NIJO (*to Isabella*). I wasn't a nun, I was still at court, but he was a priest, and when he came to me he dedicated his whole life to hell. / He knew that when he died he would fall into one of the three lower realms. And he died, he did die.

JOAN (*to Marlene*). I'd quarrelled with him over the teachings of John the Scot, who held that our ignorance of God is the same as his ignorance of himself. He only knows what he creates because he creates everything he knows but he himself is above being—do you follow?

MARLENE. No, but go on.

NIJO. I couldn't bear to think / in what shape would he be reborn.*

JOAN. St. Augustine maintained that the Neo-Platonic Ideas are indivisible

ISABELLA. *Buddhism is really most uncomfortable.

JOAN. from God, but I agreed with John that the created world is essences derived from Ideas which derived from God. As Denys the Areopagite said—the pseudo-Denys—first we give God a name, then deny it / then reconcile the contradiction

NIJO. In what shape would he return?

JOAN. by looking beyond / those terms—

MARLENE. Sorry, what? Denys said what?

JOAN. Well we disagreed about it, we quarrelled. And next day he was ill, / I was so annoyed with him,

NIJO. Misery in this life and worse in the next, all because of me.

JOAN. all the time I was nursing him I kept going over the arguments in my mind. Matter is not a means of knowing the essence. The source of the species is the Idea. But then I realised he'd never understand my arguments again, and that night he died. John the Scot held that the individual disintegrates / and there is no personal immortality.

ISABELLA. I wouldn't have you think I was in love with Jim Nugent. It was yearning to save him that I felt.

MARLENE (*to Joan*). So what did you do?

JOAN. First I decided to stay a man. I was used to it. And I wanted to devote my life to learning. Do you know why I went to Rome? Italian men didn't have beards.

ISABELLA. The loves of my life were Hennie, my own pet, and my dear husband the doctor, who nursed Hennie in her last illness. I knew it would be terrible when Hennie died but I didn't know how terrible. I felt half of myself had gone. How could I go on my travels without that sweet soul waiting at home for my letters? It was Doctor Bishop's devotion to her in her last illness that made me decide to marry him. He and Hennie had the same sweet character. I had not.

NIJO. I thought his majesty had sweet character because when he found out about Ariake he was so kind. But really it was because he no longer cared for me. One night he even sent me out to a man who had been pursuing me. / He lay awake on the other side of the screens and listened.

ISABELLA. I did wish marriage had seemed more of a step. I tried very hard to cope with the ordinary drudgery of life. I was ill again with carbuncles on the spine and nervous prostration. I ordered a tricycle, that was my idea of adventure then. And John himself fell ill, with erysipelas and anemia. I began to love him with my whole heart but it was too late. He was a skeleton with transparent white hands. I wheeled him on various seafronts in a bathchair. And he faded and left me. There was nothing in my life. The doctors said I had gout / and my heart was much affected.

NIJO. There was nothing in my life, nothing, without the Emperor's favor. The Empress had always been my enemy, Marlene, she said I had no right to wear three-layered gowns. / But I was the adopted daughter of my grandfather the Prime Minister. I had been publicly granted permission to wear thin silk.

JOAN. There was nothing in my life except my studies. I was obsessed with pursuit of the truth. I taught at the Greek School in Rome, which St. Augustine had made famous. I was poor, I worked hard. I spoke apparently brilliantly, I was still very young, I was a stranger; suddenly I was quite famous, I was everyone's favorite. Huge crowds came to hear me. The day after they made me cardinal I fell ill and lay two weeks without speaking, full of terror and regret. / But then I got up determined to

MARLENE. Yes, success is very . . .

JOAN. go on. I was seized again / with a desperate longing for the absolute.

ISABELLA. Yes, yes, to go on. I sat in Tobermory among Hennie's flowers and sewed a complete outfit in Jaeger flannel. / I was fifty-six years old.

NIJO. Out of favor but I didn't die. I left on foot, nobody saw me go. For the next twenty years I walked through Japan.

GRET. Walking is good. (*Meanwhile, the Waitress enters, pours lots of wine, then shows Marlene the empty bottle.*)

JOAN. Pope Leo died and I was chosen. All right then. I would be Pope. I would know God. I would know everything.

ISABELLA. I determined to leave my grief behind and set off for Tibet.

MARLENE. Magnificent all of you. We need some more wine, please, two bottles I think, Griselda isn't even here yet, and I want to drink a toast to you all. (*The Waitress exits.*)

ISABELLA. To yourself surely, / we're here to celebrate your success.

NIJO. Yes, Marlene.

JOAN. Yes, what is it exactly, Marlene?

MARLENE. Well it's not Pope but it is managing director.*

JOAN. And you find work for people.

MARLENE. Yes, an employment agency.

NIJO. *Over all the women you work with. And the men.

ISABELLA. And very well deserved too. I'm sure it's just the beginning of something extraordinary.

MARLENE. Well it's worth a party.

ISABELLA. To Marlene.*

MARLENE. And all of us.

JOAN. *Marlene.

NIJO. Marlene.

GRET. Marlene.

MARLENE. We've all come a long way. To our courage and the way we changed our lives and our extraordinary achievements. (*They laugh and drink a toast.*)

ISABELLA. Such adventures. We were crossing a mountain pass at seven thousand feet, the cook was all to

pieces, the muleteers suffered fever and snow blindness. But even though my spine was agony I managed very well.*

MARLENE. Wonderful.

NIJO. Once I was ill for four months lying alone at an inn. Nobody to offer a horse to Buddha. I had to live for myself, and I did live.

ISABELLA. Of course you did. It was far worse returning to Tobermory. I always felt dull when I was stationary. / That's why I could never stay anywhere.

NIJO. Yes, that's it exactly. New sights. The shrine by the beach, the moon shining on the sea. The goddess had vowed to save all living things. / She would even save the fishes. I was full of hope.

JOAN. I had thought the Pope would know everything. I thought God would speak to me directly. But of course he knew I was a woman.

MARLENE. But nobody else even suspected? (*The Waitress brings more wine and then exits.*)

JOAN. In the end I did take a lover again.*

ISABELLA. In the Vatican?

GRET. *Keep you warm.

NIJO. *Ah, lover.

MARLENE. *Good for you.

JOAN. He was one of my chamberlains. There are such a lot of servants when you're a Pope. The food's very good. And I realized I did know the truth. Because whatever the Pope says, that's true.

NIJO. What was he like, the chamberlain?*

GRET. Big cock.

ISABELLA. Oh Gret.

MARLENE. *Did he fancy you when he thought you were a fella?

NIJO. What was he like?

JOAN. He could keep a secret.

MARLENE. So you did know everything.

JOAN. Yes, I enjoyed being Pope. I consecrated bishops and let people kiss my feet. I received the King of England when he came to submit to the church. Unfortunately there were earthquakes, and some village reported it had rained blood, and in France there was a plague of giant grasshoppers, but I don't think that can have been my fault, do you?* (*Laughter.*) The grasshoppers fell on the English Channel / and were washed up on shore

NIJO. I once went to sea. It was very lonely. I realised it made very little difference where I went.

JOAN. and their bodies rotted and poisoned the air and everyone in those parts died. (*Laughter.*)

ISABELLA. *Such superstition! I was nearly murdered in China by a howling mob. They thought the barbarians ate babies and put them under railway sleepers to make the tracks steady, and ground up their eyes to make the lenses of cameras. / So they were shouting,

MARLENE. And you had a camera!

ISABELLA. "child-eater, child-eater." Some people tried to sell girl babies to Europeans for cameras or stew! (*Laughter.*)

MARLENE. So apart from the grasshoppers it was a great success.

JOAN. Yes, if it hadn't been for the baby I expect I'd have lived to an old age like Theodora of Alexandria, who lived as a monk. She was accused by a girl / who fell in love with her of being the father of her child and—

NIJO. But tell us what happened to your baby. I had some babies.

MARLENE. Didn't you think of getting rid of it?

JOAN. Wouldn't that be a worse sin than having it? / But a Pope with a child was about as bad as possible.

MARLENE. I don't know, you're the Pope.

JOAN. But I wouldn't have known how to get rid of it.

MARLENE. Other Popes had children, surely.

JOAN. They didn't give birth to them.

NIJO. Well you were a woman.

JOAN. Exactly and I shouldn't have been a woman. Women, children and lunatics can't be Pope.

MARLENE. So the only thing to do / was to get rid of it somehow.

NIJO. You had to have it adopted secretly.

JOAN. But I didn't know what was happening. I thought I was getting fatter, but then I was eating more and sitting about, the life of a Pope is quite luxurious. I don't think I'd spoken to a woman since I was twelve. The chamberlain was the one who realized.

MARLENE. And by then it was too late.

JOAN. Oh I didn't want to pay attention. It was easier to do nothing.

NIJO. But you had to plan for having it. You had to say you were ill and go away.

JOAN. That's what I should have done I suppose.

MARLENE. Did you want them to find out?

NIJO. I too was often in embarrassing situations, there's no need for a scandal. My first child was His Majesty's, which unfortunately died, but my second was Akebono's. I was seventeen. He was in love with me when I was thirteen, he was very upset when I had to go to the Emperor, it was very romantic, a lot of poems. Now His Majesty hadn't been near me for two months so he thought I was four months pregnant when I was really six, so when I reached the ninth month / I announced I was seriously ill,

JOAN. I never knew what month it was.

NIJO. and Akebono announced he had gone on a religious retreat. He held me round the waist and lifted me up as the baby was born. He cut the cord with a short sword, wrapped the baby in white and took it away. It was only a girl but I was sorry to lose it. Then I told the Emperor that the baby had miscarried because of my illness, and there you are. The danger was past.

JOAN. But Nijo, I wasn't used to having a woman's body.

ISABELLA. So what happened?

JOAN. I didn't know of course that it was near the time. It was Rogation Day, there was always a procession. I was on the horse dressed in my robes and a cross was carried in front of me, and all the cardinals were following, and all the clergy of Rome, and a huge crowd of people. / We set off from St Peter's to go

MARLENE. Total Pope. (*Gret pours the wine and steals the bottle.*)

JOAN. to St John's. I had felt a slight pain earlier, I thought it was something I'd eaten, and then it came back, and came back more often. I thought when this is over I'll go to bed. There were still long gaps when I felt perfectly all right and I didn't want to attract attention to myself and spoil the ceremony. Then I suddenly realized what it must be. I had to last out till I could get home and hide. Then something changed, my breath started to catch, I couldn't plan things properly any more. We were in a little street that goes between St Clement's and the Colosseum, and I just had to get off the horse and sit down for a minute. Great waves of pressure were going through my body, I heard sounds like a cow lowing, they came out of my mouth. Far away I heard people screaming, "The Pope is ill, the Pope is dying." And the baby just slid out onto the road.*

MARLENE. The cardinals / won't have known where to put themselves.

NIJO. Oh dear, Joan, what a thing to do! In the street!

ISABELLA. *How embarrassing.

GRET. In a field, yah. (*They are laughing.*)

JOAN. One of the cardinals said, 'The Antichrist!' and fell over in a faint. (*They all laugh.*)

MARLENE. So what did they do? They weren't best pleased.

JOAN. They took me by the feet and dragged me out of town and stoned me to death. (*They stop laughing.*)

MARLENE. Joan, how horrible.

JOAN. I don't really remember.

NIJO. And the child died too?

JOAN. Oh yes, I think so, yes. (*The Waitress enters to clear the plates. They start talking quietly.*)

ISABELLA (*to Joan*). I never had any children. I was very fond of horses.

NIJO (*to Marlene*). I saw my daughter once. She was three years old. She wore a plum-red / small-sleeved gown. Akebono's wife

ISABELLA. Birdie was my favorite. A little Indian bay mare I rode in the Rocky Mountains.

NIJO. had taken the child because her own died. Everyone thought I was just a visitor. She was being brought up carefully so she could be sent to the palace like I was. (*Gret steals her empty plate.*)

ISABELLA. Legs of iron and always cheerful, and such a pretty face. If a stranger led her she reared up like a bronco.

NIJO. I never saw my third child after he was born, the son of Ariake the priest. Ariake held him on his lap the day he was born and talked to him as if he could understand, and cried. My fourth child was Ariake's too. Ariake died before he was born. I didn't want to see anyone, I stayed alone in the hills. It was a boy again, my third son. But oddly enough I felt nothing for him.

MARLENE. How many children did you have, Gret?

GRET. Ten.

ISABELLA. Whenever I came back to England I felt I had so much to atone for. Hennie and John were so good. I did no good in my life. I spent years in self-gratification. So I hurled myself into committees, I nursed the people of Tobermory in the epidemic of influenza, I lectured the Young Women's Christian Association on Thrift. I talked and talked explaining how the East was corrupt and vicious. My travels must do good to someone beside myself. I wore myself out with good causes.

MARLENE (*pause*). Oh God, why are we all so miserable?

JOAN (*pause*). The procession never went down that street again.

MARLENE. They rerouted it specially?

JOAN. Yes they had to go all round to avoid it. And they introduced a pierced chair.

MARLENE. A pierced chair?

JOAN. Yes, a chair made out of solid marble with a hole in the seat / and it was

MARLENE. You're not serious.

JOAN. in the Chapel of the Saviour, and after he was elected the Pope had to sit in it.

MARLENE. And someone looked up his skirts? / Not really?

ISABELLA. What an extraordinary thing.

JOAN. Two of the clergy / made sure he was a man.

NIJO. On their hands and knees!

MARLENE. A pierced chair!

GRET. Balls!

(*Griselda arrives unnoticed.*)

NIJO. Why couldn't he just pull up his robe?

JOAN. He had to sit there and look dignified.

MARLENE. You could have made all your chamberlains sit in it.*

GRET. Big one, small one.

NIJO. Very useful chair at court.

ISABELLA. *Or the laird of Tobermory in his kilt.

(*They are quite drunk. They get the giggles. Marlene notices Griselda and gets up to welcome her. The others go on talking and laughing. Gret crosses to Joan and Isabella and pours them wine from her stolen bottles. The Waitress gives out the menus.*)

MARLENE. Griselda! / There you are. Do you want to eat?

GRISELDA. I'm sorry I'm so late. No, no, don't bother.

MARLENE. Of course it's no bother. / Have you eaten?

GRISELDA. No really, I'm not hungry.

MARLENE. Well have some pudding.

GRISELDA. I never eat pudding.

MARLENE. Griselda, I hope you're not anorexic. We're having pudding, I am, and getting nice and fat.

GRISELDA. Oh if everyone is. I don't mind.

MARLENE. Now who do you know? This is Joan who was Pope in the ninth century, and Isabella Bird, the Victorian traveler, and Lady Nijo from Japan, Emperor's concubine and Buddhist nun, thirteenth century, nearer your own time, and Gret who was painted by Brueghel. Griselda's in Boccaccio and Petrarch and Chaucer because of her extraordinary marriage. I'd like profiteroles because they're disgusting.

JOAN. Zabaglione, please.

ISABELLA. Apple pie / and cream.

NIJO. What's this?

MARLENE. Zabaglione, it's Italian, it's what Joan's having, / it's delicious.

NIJO. A Roman Catholic / dessert? Yes please.

MARLENE. Gret?

GRET. Cake.

GRISELDA. Just cheese and biscuits, thank you. (*The Waitress exits.*)

MARLENE. Yes, Griselda's life is like a fairy story, except it starts with marrying the prince.

GRISELDA. He's only a marquis, Marlene.

MARLENE. Well everyone for miles around is his liege and he's absolute lord of life and death and you were the poor but beautiful peasant girl and he whisked you off. / Near enough a prince.

NIJO. How old were you?

GRISELDA. Fifteen.

NIJO. I was brought up in court circles and it was still a shock. Had you ever seen him before?

GRISELDA. I'd seen him riding by, we all had. And he'd seen me in the fields with the sheep.*

ISABELLA. I would have been well suited to minding sheep.

NIJO. And Mr. Nugent went riding by.

ISABELLA. Of course not, Nijo, I mean a healthy life in the open air.

JOAN. *He just rode up while you were minding the sheep and asked you to marry him?

GRISELDA. No, no, it was on the wedding day. I was waiting outside the door to see the procession. Everyone wanted him to get married so there'd be an heir to look after us when he died, / and at last he

MARLENE. I don't think Walter wanted to get married. It is Walter? Yes.

GRISELDA. announced a day for the wedding but nobody knew who the bride was, we thought it must be a foreign princess, we were longing to see her. Then the carriage stopped outside our cottage and we couldn't see the bride anywhere. And he came and spoke to my father.

NIJO. And your father told you to serve the Prince.

GRISELDA. My father could hardly speak. The Marquis said it wasn't an order, I could say not, but if I said yes I must always obey him in everything.

MARLENE. That's when you should have suspected.

GRISELDA. But of course a wife must obey her husband. / And of course I must obey the Marquis.*

ISABELLA. I swore to obey dear John, of course, but it didn't seem to arise. Naturally I wouldn't have wanted to go abroad while I was married.

MARLENE. *Then why bother to mention it at all? He'd got a thing about it, that's why.

GRISELDA. I'd rather obey the Marquis than a boy from the village.

MARLENE. Yes, that's a point.

JOAN. I never obeyed anyone. They all obeyed me.

NIJO. And what did you wear? He didn't make you get married in your own clothes? That would be perverse.*

MARLENE. Oh, you wait.

GRISELDA. *He had ladies with him who undressed me and they had a white silk dress and jewels for my hair.

MARLENE. And at first he seemed perfectly normal?

GRISELDA. Marlene, you're always so critical of him. / Of course he was normal, he was very kind.

MARLENE. But Griselda, come on, he took your baby.

GRISELDA. Walter found it hard to believe I loved him. He couldn't believe I would always obey him. He had to prove it.

MARLENE. I don't think Walter likes women.

GRISELDA. I'm sure he loved me, Marlene, all the time.

MARLENE. He just had a funny way / of showing it.

GRISELDA. It was hard for him too.

JOAN. How do you mean he took away your baby?

NIJO. Was it a boy?

GRISELDA. No, the first one was a girl.

NIJO. Even so it's hard when they take it away. Did you see it at all?

GRISELDA. Oh yes, she was six weeks old.

NIJO. Much better to do it straight away.

ISABELLA. But why did your husband take the child?

GRISELDA. He said all the people hated me because I was just one of them. And now I had a child they were restless. So he had to get rid of the child to keep them quiet. But he said he wouldn't snatch her, I had to agree and obey and give her up. So when I was feeding her a man came in and took her away. I thought he was going to kill her even before he was out of the room.

MARLENE. But you let him take her? You didn't struggle?

GRISELDA. I asked him to give her back so I could kiss her. And I asked him to bury her where no animals could dig her up. / It was Walter's child to do what he

ISABELLA. Oh my dear.

GRISELDA. liked with.*

MARLENE. Walter was bonkers.

GRET. Bastard.

ISABELLA. *But surely, murder.

GRISELDA. I had promised.

MARLENE. I can't stand this. I'm going for a pee.

(*Marlene goes out. The Waitress brings dessert, serves it during the following, then exits*)

NIJO. No, I understand. Of course you had to, he was your life. And were you in favor after that?

GRISELDA. Oh yes, we were very happy together. We never spoke about what had happened.

ISABELLA. I can see you were doing what you thought was your duty. But didn't it make you ill?

GRISELDA. No, I was very well, thank you.

NIJO. And you had another child?

GRISELDA. Not for four years, but then I did, yes, a boy.

NIJO. Ah a boy. / So it all ended happily.

GRISELDA. Yes he was pleased. I kept my son till he was two years old. A peasant's grandson. It made the people angry. Walter explained.

ISABELLA. But surely he wouldn't kill his children / just because—

GRISELDA. Oh it wasn't true. Walter would never give in to the people. He wanted to see if I loved him enough.

JOAN. He killed his children / to see if you loved him enough?

NIJO. Was it easier the second time or harder?

GRISELDA. It was always easy because I always knew I would do what he said. (*Pause. They start to eat.*)

ISABELLA. I hope you didn't have any more children.

GRISELDA. Oh no, no more. It was twelve years till he tested me again.

ISABELLA. So whatever did he do this time? / My poor John, I never loved him enough, and he would never have dreamt . . .

GRISELDA. He sent me away. He said the people wanted him to marry someone else who'd give him an heir and he'd got special permission from the Pope. So I said I'd go home to my father. I came with nothing / so I went with nothing. I took

NIJO. Better to leave if your master doesn't want you.

GRISELDA. off my clothes. He let me keep a slip so he wouldn't be shamed. And I walked home barefoot. My father came out in tears. Everyone was crying except me.

NIJO. At least your father wasn't dead. / I had nobody.

ISABELLA. Well it can be a relief to come home. I loved to see Hennie's sweet face again.

GRISELDA. Oh yes, I was perfectly content. And quite soon he sent for me again.

JOAN. I don't think I would have gone.

GRISELDA. But he told me to come. I had to obey him. He wanted me to help prepare his wedding. He was getting married to a young girl from France / and nobody except me knew how to arrange things the way he liked them.

NIJO. It's always hard taking him another woman. (*Marlene comes back.*)

JOAN. I didn't live a woman's life. I don't understand it.

GRISELDA. The girl was sixteen and far more beautiful than me. I could see why he loved her. / She had her younger brother with her as a page. (*The Waitress enters.*)

MARLENE. Oh God, I can't bear it. I want some coffee. Six coffees. Six brandies. / Double brandies. Straightaway. (*The Waitress exits.*)

GRISELDA. They all went in to the feast I'd prepared. And he stayed behind and put his arms round me and kissed me. / I felt half asleep with the shock.

NIJO. Oh, like a dream.

MARLENE. And he said, "This is your daughter and your son."

GRISELDA. Yes.

JOAN. What?

NIJO. Oh. Oh I see. You got them back.

ISABELLA. I did think it was remarkably barbaric to kill them but you learn not to say anything. / So he had them brought up secretly I suppose.

MARLENE. Walter's a monster. Weren't you angry? What did you do?

GRISELDA. Well I fainted. Then I cried and kissed the children. / Everyone was making a fuss of me.

NIJO. But did you feel anything for them?

GRISELDA. What?

NIJO. Did you feel anything for the children?

GRISELDA. Of course, I loved them.

JOAN. So you forgave him and lived with him?

GRISELDA. He suffered so much all those years.

ISABELLA. Hennie had the same sweet nature.

NIJO. So they dressed you again?

GRISELDA. Cloth of gold.

JOAN. I can't forgive anything.

MARLENE. You really are exceptional, Griselda.

NIJO. Nobody gave me back my children. (*She cries.*)

(*The Waitress brings the brandies and then exits. During the following, Joan goes to Nijo.*)

ISABELLA. I can never be like Hennie. I was always so busy in England, a kind of business I detested. The very presence of people exhausted my emotional reserves. I could not be like Hennie however I tried. I tried and was as ill as could be. The doctor suggested a steel net to support my head, the weight of my own head was too much for my diseased spine. It is dangerous to put oneself in depressing circumstances. Why should I do it?

JOAN (*to Nijo*). Don't cry.

NIJO. My father and the Emperor both died in the autumn. So much pain.

JOAN. Yes, but don't cry.

NIJO. They wouldn't let me into the palace when he was dying. I hid in the room with his coffin, then I couldn't find where I'd left my shoes, I ran after the funeral procession in bare feet, I couldn't keep up. When I got there it was over, a few wisps of smoke in the sky, that's all that was left of him. What I want to know is, if I'd still been at court, would I have been allowed to wear full mourning?

MARLENE. I'm sure you would.

NIJO. Why do you say that? You don't know anything about it. Would I have been allowed to wear full mourning?

ISABELLA. How can people live in this dim pale island and wear our hideous clothes? I cannot and will not live the life of a lady.

NIJO. I'll tell you something that made me angry. I was eighteen, at the Full Moon Ceremony. They make a special rice gruel and stir it with their sticks, and then they beat their women across the loins so they'll have sons and not daughters. So the Emperor beat us all / very hard as

MARLENE. What a sod. (*The Waitress enters with the coffees.*)

NIJO. usual—that's not it, Marlene, that's normal, what made us angry, he told his attendants they could beat us too. Well they had a wonderful time. / So Lady Genki and I made a plan, and the ladies

MARLENE. I'd like another brandy please. Better make it six. (*The Waitress exits.*)

NIJO. all hid in his rooms, and Lady Mashimizu stood guard with a stick at the door, and when His Majesty came in Genki seized him and I beat him till he cried out and promised he would never order anyone to hit us again. Afterward there was a terrible fuss. The nobles were horrified. "We wouldn't even dream of stepping on Your Majesty's shadow." And I had hit him with a stick. Yes, I hit him with a stick.

(*The Waitress brings the brandy bottle and tops up the glasses. Joan crosses in front of the table and back to her place while drunkenly reciting:*)

JOAN. Suave, mari magno turbantibus aequora
    ventis,
e terra magnum alterius spectare laborem;
non quia vexari quemquamst iucunda voluptas,
sed quibus ipse malis careas quia cernere suave
    est.
Suave etiam belli certamina magna tueri
per campos instructa tua sine parte pericli.
Sed nil dulcius est, bene quam munita tenere
edita doctrine sapientum templa serena, /
despicere uncle queas alios passimque videre
errare atque viam palantis quaerere vitae,

GRISELDA. I do think—I do wonder—it would have been nicer if Walter hadn't had to.

ISABELLA. Why should I? Why should I?

MARLENE. Of course not.

NIJO. I hit him with a stick.

JOAN. certare ingenio, contendere nobilitate,
noctes atque dies niti praestante labore
ad summas emergere opes retumque potiri.
O miseras hominum mentis, / o pectora caeca![2]

ISABELLA. Oh miseras!

NIJO. *Pectora caeca.

JOAN. qualibus in tenebris vitae quantisque periclis
degitur hoc aevi quodcumquest! / nonne videre

nil aliud sibi naturam latrare, nisi utqui
corpore seiunctus dolor absit, mente fruatur[3] . . .

(*She subsides.*)

GRET. We come to hell through a big mouth. Hell's black and red. / It's

MARLENE (*to Joan*). Shut up, pet.

GRISELDA. Hush, please.

ISABELLA. Listen, she's been to hell.

GRET. like the village where I come from. There's a river and a bridge and houses. There's places on fire like when the soldiers come. There's a big devil sat on a roof with a big hole in his arse and he's scooping stuff out of it with a big ladle and it's falling down on us, and it's money, so a lot of the women stop and get some. But most of us is fighting the devils. There's lots of little devils, our size, and we get them down all right and give them a beating. There's lots of funny creatures round your feet, you don't like to look, like rats and lizards, and nasty things, a bum with a face, and fish with legs, and faces on things that don't have faces on. But they don't hurt, you just keep going. Well we'd had worse, you see, we'd had the Spanish. We'd all had family killed. My big son die on a wheel. Birds eat him. My baby, a soldier run her through with a sword. I'd had enough, I was mad, I hate the bastards. I come out my front door that morning and shout till my neighbors come out and I said, "Come on, we're going where the evil come from and pay the bastards out." And they all come out just as they was / from baking or

NIJO. All the ladies come.

---

[2]**Suave, . . . o pectora caeca!** Joan is quoting a passage from Titus Lucretius Carus, a Roman philosopher, who wrote *On the Nature of Things* in the first century B.C.E. In English (by Cyril Bailey) the passage reads: Sweet it is, when on the great sea the winds are buffeting the waters, to gaze from the land on another's great struggles; not because it is pleasure or joy that any one should be distressed, but because it is sweet to perceive from what misfortune you yourself are free. Sweet is it too, to behold great contests of war in full array over the plains, when you have no part in the danger. But nothing is more gladdening than to dwell in the calm high places, firmly embattled on the heights by the teaching of the wise, whence you can look down on others, and see them wandering hither and thither, going astray as they seek the way of life, in strife matching their wits or rival claims of birth, struggling night and day by surpassing effort to rise up to the height of power and gain possession of the world. Ah! miserable minds of men, blind hearts! [3]**qualibus . . . fruatur** In what darkness of life, in what great dangers ye spend this little span of years! to think that ye should not see that nature cries aloud for nothing else but that pain may be kept far sundered from the body, and that, withdrawn from care and fear, she may enjoy in mind the sense of pleasure!

GRET. washing in their aprons, and we push down the street and the ground opens up and we go through a big mouth into a street just like ours but in hell. I've got a sword in my hand from somewhere and I fill a basket with gold cups they drink out of down there. You just keep running on and fighting / you didn't stop for nothing. Oh we give them devils such a beating.*

NIJO. Take that, take that.

JOAN. *Something something something mortisque timores

tum vacuum pectus[4]—damn.

Quod si ridicula—

something something on and on and on

and something splendorem purpureai.

ISABELLA. I thought I would have a last jaunt up the west river in China. Why not? But the doctors were so very grave. I just went to Morocco. The sea was so wild I had to be landed by ship's crane in a coal bucket. / My horse was a terror to me, a powerful black charger.

GRET. Coal bucket, good.

JOAN. nos in luce timemus

something

terrorem.[5]

(Nijo is laughing and crying. Joan gets up and is sick. Griselda looks after her.)

GRISELDA. Can I have some water, please? (*The Waitress exits.*)

ISABELLA. So off I went to visit the Berber sheikhs in full blue trousers and great brass spurs. I was the only European woman ever to have seen the Emperor of Morocco. I was (*the Waitress brings the water.*) seventy years old. What lengths to go to for a last chance of joy. I knew my return of vigour was only temporary, but how marvellous while it lasted.

---

[4]**Something . . . pectus.** From Lucretius: "the dread of death leaves your heart empty . . ." [5]**Quod . . . purpureai. . . . nos in luce . . . terrorem.** Also from Lucretius: But if we see that these thoughts are mere mirth and mockery, and in very truth the fears of men and the cares that dog them fear not the clash of arms nor the weapons of war, but pass boldly among kings and lords of the world, nor dread the glitter that comes from gold nor the bright sheen of the purple robe, can you doubt that all such power belongs to reason alone, above all when the whole of life is but a struggle in darkness? For even as children tremble and fear everything in blinding darkness, so we sometimes dread in the light things that are no whit more to be feared than what chidren shudder at in the dark.

SCENE 2

(*"Top Girls" Employment Agency. Monday morning. The lights come up on Marlene and Jeanine.*)

MARLENE. Right Jeanine, you are Jeanine aren't you? Let's have a look. O's and A's.[6] / No A's, all those

JEANINE. Six O's.

MARLENE. O's you probably could have got an A. / Speeds, not brilliant, not too bad.

JEANINE. I wanted to go to work.

MARLENE. Well, Jeanine, what's your present job like?

JEANINE. I'm a secretary.

MARLENE. Secretary or typist?

JEANINE. I did start as a typist but the last six months I've been a secretary.

MARLENE. To?

JEANINE. To three of them, really, they share me. There's Mr. Ashford, he's the office manager, and Mr. Philby / is sales, and—

MARLENE. Quite a small place?

JEANINE. A bit small.

MARLENE. Friendly?

JEANINE. Oh it's friendly enough.

MARLENE. Prospects?

JEANINE. I don't think so, that's the trouble. Miss Lewis is secretary to the managing director and she's been there forever, and Mrs. Bradford / is—

MARLENE. So you want a job with better prospects?

JEANINE. I want a change.

MARLENE. So you'll take anything comparable?

JEANINE. No, I do want prospects. I want more money.

MARLENE. You're getting—?

JEANINE. Hundred.

MARLENE. It's not bad you know. You're what? Twenty?

JEANINE. I'm saving to get married.

MARLENE. Does that mean you don't want a long-term job, Jeanine?

JEANINE. I might do.

MARLENE. Because where do the prospects come in? No kids for a bit?

JEANINE. Oh no, not kids, not yet.

MARLENE. So you won't tell them you're getting married?

JEANINE. Had I better not?

MARLENE. It would probably help.

JEANINE. I'm not wearing a ring. We thought we wouldn't spend on a ring.

---

[6]**O's and A's** Examinations given in British school. O-levels are for basic knowledge skills, while A-levels are for more advanced skills learned in secondary schools.

MARLENE. Saves taking it off.

JEANINE. I wouldn't take it off.

MARLENE. There's no need to mention it when you go for an interview. / Now Jeanine do you have a feel

JEANINE. But what if they ask?

MARLENE. for any particular kind of company?

JEANINE. I thought advertising.

MARLENE. People often do think advertising. I have got a few vacancies but I think they're looking for something glossier.

JEANINE. You mean how I dress? / I

MARLENE. I mean experience.

JEANINE. can dress different. I dress like this on purpose for where I am now.

MARLENE. I have a marketing department here of a knitwear manufacturer. / Marketing is near enough

JEANINE. Knitwear?

MARLENE. advertising secretary to the marketing manager, he's thirty-five, married, I've sent him a girl before and she was happy, left to have a baby, you won't want to mention marriage there. He's very fair I think, good at his job, you won't have to nurse him along. Hundred and ten, so that's better than you're doing now.

JEANINE. I don't know.

MARLENE. I've a fairly small concern here, father and two sons, you'd have more say potentially, secretarial and reception duties, only a hundred but the job's going to grow with the concern and then you'll be in at the top with new girls coming in underneath you.

JEANINE. What is it they do?

MARLENE. Lampshades. / This would be my first choice for you.

JEANINE. Just lampshades?

MARLENE. There's plenty of different kinds of lampshade. So we'll send you there, shall we, and the knitwear second choice. Are you free to go for an interview any day they call you?

JEANINE. I'd like to travel.

MARLENE. We don't have any foreign clients. You'd have to go elsewhere.

JEANINE. Yes I know. I don't really . . . I just mean . . .

MARLENE. Does your fiancé want to travel?

JEANINE. I'd like a job where I was here in London and with him and everything but now and then—I expect it's silly. Are there jobs like that?

MARLENE. There's personal assistant to a top executive in a multinational. If that's the idea you need to be planning ahead. Is that where you want to be in ten years?

JEANINE. I might not be alive in ten years.

MARLENE. Yes but you will be. You'll have children.

JEANINE. I can't think about ten years.

MARLENE. You haven't got the speeds anyway. So I'll send you to these two shall I? You haven't been to any other agency? Just so we don't get crossed wires. Now Jeanine I want you to get one of these jobs, all right? If I send you that means I'm putting myself on the line for you. Your presentation's OK, you look fine, just be confident and go in there convinced that this is the best job for you and you're the best person for the job. If you don't believe it they won't believe it.

JEANINE. Do you believe it?

MARLENE. I think you could make me believe it if you put your mind to it.

JEANINE. Yes, all right.

SCENE 3

(*Joyce's back yard. Sunday afternoon. The house with a back door is upstage. Downstage is a shelter made of junk, made by children. The lights come up on two girls, Angie and Kit, who are squashed together in the shelter. Angie is sixteen, Kit is twelve. They cannot be seen from the house.*)

JOYCE (*off, calling from the house*). Angie. Angie are you out there?

(*Silence. They keep still and wait. When nothing else happens they relax.*)

ANGIE. Wish she was dead.

KIT. Wanna watch *The Exterminator*?

ANGIE. You're sitting on my leg.

KIT. There's nothing on telly. We can have an ice cream. Angie?

ANGIE. Shall I tell you something?

KIT. Do you wanna watch *The Exterminator*?

ANGIE. It's X, innit.

KIT. I can get into Xs.

ANGIE. Shall I tell you something?

KIT. We'll go to something else. We'll go to Ipswich. What's on the Odeon?

ANGIE. She won't let me, will she?

KIT. Don't tell her.

ANGIE. I've no money.

KIT. I'll pay.

ANGIE. She'll moan though, won't she?

KIT. I'll ask her for you if you like.

ANGIE. I've no money, I don't want you to pay.

KIT. I'll ask her.

ANGIE. She don't like you.

KIT. I still got three pounds birthday money. Did she say she don't like me? I'll go by myself then.

ANGIE. Your mum don't let you. I got to take you.

KIT. She won't know.

ANGIE. You'd be scared who'd sit next to you.

KIT. No I wouldn't. She does like me anyway. Tell me then.

ANGIE. Tell you what?

KIT. It's you she doesn't like.

ANGIE. Well I don't like her so tough shit.

JOYCE (off). Angie. Angie. Angie. I know you're out there. I'm not coming out after you. You come in here. (Silence. Nothing happens.)

ANGIE. Last night when I was in bed. I been thinking yesterday could I make things move. You know, make things move by thinking about them without touching them. Last night I was in bed and suddenly a picture fell down off the wall.

KIT. What picture?

ANGIE. My gran, that picture. Not the poster. The photograph in the frame.

KIT. Had you done something to make it fall down?

ANGIE. I must have done.

KIT. But were you thinking about it?

ANGIE. Not about it, but about something.

KIT. I don't think that's very good.

ANGIE. You know the kitten?

KIT. Which one?

ANGIE. There only is one. The dead one.

KIT. What about it?

ANGIE. I heard it last night.

KIT. Where?

ANGIE. Out here. In the dark. What if I left you here in the dark all night?

KIT. You couldn't. I'd go home.

ANGIE. You couldn't.

KIT. I'd / go home.

ANGIE. No you couldn't, not if I said.

KIT. I could.

ANGIE. Then you wouldn't see anything. You'd just be ignorant.

KIT. I can see in the daytime.

ANGIE. No you can't. You can't hear it in the daytime.

KIT. I don't want to hear it.

ANGIE. You're scared that's all.

KIT. I'm not scared of anything.

ANGIE. You're scared of blood.

KIT. It's not the same kitten anyway. You just heard an old cat, / you just heard some old cat.

ANGIE. You don't know what I heard. Or what I saw. You don't know nothing because you're a baby.

KIT. You're sitting on me.

ANGIE. Mind my hair / you silly cunt.

KIT. Stupid fucking cow, I hate you.

ANGIE. I don't care if you do.

KIT. You're horrible.

ANGIE. I'm going to kill my mother and you're going to watch.

KIT. I'm not playing.

ANGIE. You're scared of blood. (Kit puts her hand under her dress, brings it out with blood on her finger.)

KIT. There, see, I got my own blood, so. (Angie takes Kit's hand and licks her finger.)

ANGIE. Now I'm a cannibal. I might turn into a vampire now.

KIT. That picture wasn't nailed up right.

ANGIE. You'll have to do that when I get mine.

KIT. I don't have to.

ANGIE. You're scared.

KIT. I'll do it, I might do it. I don't have to just because you say. I'll be sick on you.

ANGIE. I don't care if you are sick on me, I don't mind sick. I don't mind blood. If I don't get away from here I'm going to die.

KIT. I'm going home.

ANGIE. You can't go through the house. She'll see you.

KIT. I won't tell her.

ANGIE. Oh great, fine.

KIT. I'll say I was by myself. I'll tell her you're at my house and I'm going there to get you.

ANGIE. She knows I'm here, stupid.

KIT. Then why can't I go through the house?

ANGIE. Because I said not.

KIT. My mum don't like you anyway.

ANGIE. I don't want her to like me. She's a slag.

KIT. She is not.

ANGIE. She does it with everyone.

KIT. She does not.

ANGIE. You don't even know what it is.

KIT. Yes I do.

ANGIE. Tell me then.

KIT. We get it all at school, cleverclogs. It's on television. You haven't done it.

ANGIE. How do you know?

KIT. Because I know you haven't.

ANGIE. You know wrong then because I have.

KIT. Who with?

ANGIE. I'm not telling you / who with.

KIT. You haven't anyway.

ANGIE. How do you know?

KIT. Who with?

ANGIE. I'm not telling you.

KIT. You said you told me everything.

ANGIE. I was lying wasn't I?

KIT. Who with? You can't tell me who with because / you never—

ANGIE. Sh.

(*Joyce has come out of the house. She stops halfway across the yard and listens. They listen.*)

JOYCE. You there Angie? Kit? You there Kitty? Want a cup of tea? I've got some chocolate biscuits. Come on now I'll put the kettle on. Want a choccy biccy, Angie? (*They all listen and wait.*) Fucking rotten little cunt. You can stay there and die. I'll lock the door.

(*They all wait. Joyce goes back to the house. Angie and Kit sit in silence for a while.*)

KIT. When there's a war, where's the safest place?

ANGIE. Nowhere.

KIT. New Zealand is, my mum said. Your skin's burned right off. Shall we go to New Zealand?

ANGIE. I'm not staying here.

KIT. Shall we go to New Zealand?

ANGIE. You're not old enough.

KIT. You're not old enough.

ANGIE. I'm old enough to get married.

KIT. You don't want to get married.

ANGIE. No but I'm old enough.

KIT. I'd find out where they were going to drop it and stand right in the place.

ANGIE. You couldn't find out.

KIT. Better than walking round with your skin dragging on the ground. Eugh. / Would you like walking round with your skin dragging on the ground?

ANGIE. You couldn't find out, stupid, it's a secret.

KIT. Where are you going?

ANGIE. I'm not telling you.

KIT. Why?

ANGIE. It's a secret.

KIT. But you tell me all your secrets.

ANGIE. Not the true secrets.

KIT. Yes you do.

ANGIE. No I don't.

KIT. I want to go somewhere away from the war.

ANGIE. Just forget the war.

KIT. I can't.

ANGIE. You have to. It's so boring.

KIT. I'll remember it at night.

ANGIE. I'm going to do something else anyway.

KIT. What? Angie, come on. Angie.

ANGIE. It's a little secret.

KIT. It can't be worse than the kitten. And killing your mother. And the war.

ANGIE. Well I'm not telling you so you can die for all I care.

KIT. My mother says there's something wrong with you playing with someone my age. She says why haven't you got friends your own age. People your own age know there's something funny about you. She says you're a bad influence. She says she's going to speak to your mother. (*Angie twists Kit's arm till she cries out.*)

ANGIE. Say you're a liar.

KIT. She said it not me.

ANGIE. Say you eat shit.

KIT. You can't make me. (*Angie lets go.*)

ANGIE. I don't care anyway. I'm leaving.

KIT. Go on then.

ANGIE. You'll all wake up one morning and find I've gone.

KIT. Go on then.

ANGIE. You'll wake up one morning and find I've gone.

KIT. Good.

ANGIE. I'm not telling you when.

KIT. Go on then.

ANGIE. I'm sorry I hurt you.

KIT. I'm tired.

ANGIE. Do you like me?

KIT. I don't know.

ANGIE. You do like me.

KIT. I'm going home. (*She gets up.*)

ANGIE. No you're not.

KIT. I'm tired.

ANGIE. She'll see you.

KIT. She'll give me a chocolate biscuit.

ANGIE. Kitty.

KIT. Tell me where you're going.

ANGIE. Sit down.

KIT (*sitting down again*). Go on then.

ANGIE. Swear?

KIT. Swear.

ANGIE. I'm going to London. To see my aunt.

KIT. And what?

ANGIE. That's it.

KIT. I see my aunt all the time.

ANGIE. I don't see my aunt.

KIT. What's so special?

ANGIE. It is special. She's special.

KIT. Why?

ANGIE. She is.

KIT. Why?

ANGIE. She is.

KIT. Why?

ANGIE. My mother hates her.

KIT. Why?

ANGIE. Because she does.

KIT. Perhaps she's not very nice.

ANGIE. She is nice.

KIT. How do you know?

ANGIE. Because I know her.

KIT. You said you never see her.

ANGIE. I saw her last year. You saw her.

KIT. Did I?

ANGIE. Never mind.

KIT. I remember her. That aunt. What's so special?

ANGIE. She gets people jobs.

KIT. What's so special?

ANGIE. I think I'm my aunt's child. I think my mother's
     really my aunt.

KIT. Why?

ANGIE. Because she goes to America, now shut up.

KIT. I've been to London.

ANGIE. Now give us a cuddle and shut up because I'm
     sick.

KIT. You're sitting on my arm.

*(They curl up in each other's arms. Silence. Joyce
comes out and comes up to them quietly.)*

JOYCE. Come on.

KIT. Oh hello.

JOYCE. Time you went home.

KIT. We want to go to the Odeon.

JOYCE. What time?

KIT. Don't know.

JOYCE. What's on?

KIT. Don't know.

JOYCE. Don't know much do you?

KIT. That all right then?

JOYCE. Angie's got to clean her room first.

ANGIE. No I don't.

JOYCE. Yes you do, it's a pigsty.

ANGIE. Well I'm not.

JOYCE. Then you're not going. I don't care.

ANGIE. Well I am going.

JOYCE. You've no money, have you?

ANGIE. Kit's paying anyway.

JOYCE. No she's not.

KIT. I'll help you with your room.

JOYCE. That's nice.

ANGIE. No you won't. You wait here.

KIT. Hurry then.

ANGIE. I'm not hurrying. You just wait. *(Angie goes into
     the house. Silence.)*

JOYCE. I don't know. *(Silence.)* How's school then?

KIT. All right.

JOYCE. What are you now? Third year?

KIT. Second year.

JOYCE. Your mum says you're good at English. *(Silence.)*
     Maybe Angie should've stayed on.

KIT. She didn't like it.

JOYCE. I didn't like it. And look at me. If your face fits at
     school it's going to fit other places too. It wouldn't
     make no difference to Angie. She's not going to get a
     job when jobs are hard to get. I'd be sorry for anyone
     in charge of her. She'd better get married. I don't
     know who'd have her, mind. She's one of those girls
     might never leave home. What do you want to be
     when you grow up, Kit?

KIT. Physicist.

JOYCE. What?

KIT. Nuclear physicist.

JOYCE. Whatever for?

KIT. I could, I'm clever.

JOYCE. I know you're clever, pet. *(Silence.)* I'll make a cup
     of tea. *(Silence.)* Looks like it's going to rain. *(Si-
     lence.)* Don't you have friends your own age?

KIT. Yes.

JOYCE. Well then.

KIT. I'm old for my age.

JOYCE. And Angie's simple is she? She's not simple.

KIT. I love Angie.

JOYCE. She's clever in her own way.

KIT. You can't stop me.

JOYCE. I don't want to.

KIT. You can't, so.

JOYCE. Don't be cheeky, Kitty. She's always kind to little
     children.

KIT. She's coming so you better leave me alone.

*(Angie comes out. She has changed into an old best
dress, slightly small for her.)*

JOYCE. What you put that on for? Have you done your
     room? You can't clean your room in that.

ANGIE. I looked in the cupboard and it was there.

JOYCE. Of course it was there, it's meant to be there. Is
     that why it was a surprise, finding something in the
     right place? I should think she's surprised, wouldn't
     you Kit, to find something in her room in the right
     place.

ANGIE. I decided to wear it.

JOYCE. Not today, why? To clean your room? You're not
     going to the pictures till you've done your room. You
     can put your dress on after if you like. *(Angie picks up
     a brick.)* Have you done your room? You're not get-
     ting out of it, you know.

KIT. Angie, let's go.

JOYCE. She's not going till she's done her room.

KIT. It's starting to rain.

JOYCE. Come on, come on then. Hurry and do your room, Angie, and then you can go to the cinema with Kit. Oh it's wet, come on. We'll look up the time in the paper. Does your mother know, Kit, it's going to be a late night for you, isn't it? Hurry up, Angie. You'll spoil your dress. You make me sick. (*Joyce and Kit run into the house. Angie stays where she is. There is the sound of rain. Kit comes out of the house.*)

KIT (*shouting*). Angie. Angie, come on, you'll get wet. (*She comes back to Angie.*)

ANGIE. I put on this dress to kill my mother.

KIT. I suppose you thought you'd do it with a brick.

ANGIE. You can kill people with a brick. (*She puts the brick down.*)

KIT. Well you didn't, so.

ACT II

SCENE 1

(*"Top Girls" Employment Agency. Monday morning. There are three desks in the main office and a separate interviewing area. The lights come up in the main office on Win and Nell who have just arrived for work.*)

NELL. Coffee coffee coffee coffee / coffee.

WIN. The roses were smashing. / Mermaid.

NELL. Ohhh.

WIN. Iceberg. He taught me all their names. (*Nell has some coffee now.*)

NELL. Ah. Now then.

WIN. He has one of the finest rose gardens in West Sussex. He exhibits.

NELL. He what?

WIN. His wife was visiting her mother. It was like living together.

NELL. Crafty, you never said.

WIN. He rang on Saturday morning.

NELL. Lucky you were free.

WIN. That's what I told him.

NELL. Did you hell.

WIN. Have you ever seen a really beautiful rose garden?

NELL. I don't like flowers. / I like swimming pools.

WIN. Marilyn. Esther's Baby. They're all called after birds.

NELL. Our friend's late. Celebrating all weekend I bet you.

WIN. I'd call a rose Elvis. Or John Conteh.

NELL. Is Howard in yet?

WIN. If he is he'll be bleeping us with a problem.

NELL. Howard can just hang on to himself.

WIN. Howard's really cut up.

NELL. Howard thinks because he's a fella the job was his as of right. Our Marlene's got far more balls than Howard and that's that.

WIN. Poor little bugger.

NELL. He'll live.

WIN. He'll move on.

NELL. I wouldn't mind a change of air myself.

WIN. Serious?

NELL. I've never been a staying put lady. Pastures new.

WIN. So who's the pirate?

NELL. There's nothing definite.

WIN. Inquiries?

NELL. There's always inquiries. I'd think I'd got bad breath if there stopped being inquiries. Most of them can't afford me. Or you.

WIN. I'm all right for the time being. Unless I go to Australia.

NELL. There's not a lot of room upward.

WIN. Marlene's filled it up.

NELL. Good luck to her. Unless there's some prospects moneywise.

WIN. You can but ask.

NELL. Can always but ask.

WIN. So what have we got? I've got a Mr. Holden I saw last week.

NELL. Any use?

WIN. Pushy. Bit of a cowboy.

NELL. Good looker?

WIN. Good dresser.

NELL. High flyer?

WIN. That's his general idea certainly but I'm not sure he's got it up there.

NELL. Prestel wants six high flyers and I've only seen two and a half.

WIN. He's making a bomb on the road but he thinks it's time for an office. I sent him to IBM but he didn't get it.

NELL. Prestel's on the road.

WIN. He's not overbright.

NELL. Can he handle an office?

WIN. Provided his secretary can punctuate he should go far.

NELL. Bear Prestel in mind then, I might put my head round the door. I've got that poor little nerd I should never have said I could help. Tender heart me.

WIN. Tender like old boots. How old?

NELL. Yes well forty-five.

WIN. Say no more.

NELL. He knows his place, he's not after calling himself a manager, he's just a poor little bod wants a better commission and a bit of sunshine.

WIN. Don't we all.

NELL. He's just got to relocate. He's got a bungalow in Dymchurch.

WIN. And his wife says.

NELL. The lady wife wouldn't care to relocate. She's going through the change.

WIN. It's his funeral, don't waste your time.

NELL. I don't waste a lot.

WIN. Good weekend you?

NELL. You could say.

WIN. Which one?

NELL. One Friday, one Saturday.

WIN. Aye—aye.

NELL. Sunday night I watched telly.

WIN. Which of them do you like best really?

NELL. Sunday was best, I liked the Ovaltine.

WIN. Holden, Barker, Gardner, Duke.

NELL. I've a lady here thinks she can sell.

WIN. Taking her on?

NELL. She's had some jobs.

WIN. Services?

NELL. No, quite heavy stuff, electric.

WIN. Tough bird like us.

NELL. We could do with a few more here.

WIN. There's nothing going here.

NELL. No but I always want the tough ones when I see them. Hang onto them.

WIN. I think we're plenty.

NELL. Derek asked me to marry him again.

WIN. He doesn't know when he's beaten.

NELL. I told him I'm not going to play house, not even in Ascot.

WIN. Mind you, you could play house.

NELL. If I chose to play house I would play house ace.

WIN. You could marry him and go on working.

NELL. I could go on working and not marry him.

(*Marlene arrives.*)

MARLENE. Morning ladies. (*Win and Nell cheer and whistle.*) Mind my head.

NELL. Coffee coffee coffee.

WIN. We're tactfully not mentioning you're late.

MARLENE. Fucking tube.

WIN. We've heard that one.

NELL. We've used that one.

WIN. It's the top executive doesn't come in as early as the poor working girl.

MARLENE. Pass the sugar and shut your face, pet.

WIN. Well I'm delighted.

NELL. Howard's looking sick.

WIN. Howard is sick. He's got ulcers and heart. He told me.

NELL. He'll have to stop then won't he?

WIN. Stop what?

NELL. Smoking, drinking, shouting. Working.

WIN. Well, working.

NELL. We're just looking through the day.

MARLENE. I'm doing some of Pam's ladies. They've been piling up while she's away.

NELL. Half a dozen little girls and an arts graduate who can't type.

WIN. I spent the whole weekend at his place in Sussex.

NELL. She fancies his rose garden.

WIN. I had to lie down in the back of the car so the neighbours wouldn't see me go in.

NELL. You're kidding.

WIN. It was funny.

NELL. Fuck that for a joke.

WIN. It was funny.

MARLENE. Anyway they'd see you in the garden.

WIN. The garden has extremely high walls.

NELL. I think I'll tell the wife.

WIN. Like hell.

NELL. She might leave him and you could have the rose garden.

WIN. The minute it's not a secret I'm out on my ear.

NELL. Don't know why you bother.

WIN. Bit of fun.

NELL. I think it's time you went to Australia.

WIN. I think it's pushy Mr. Holden time.

NELL. If you've any really pretty bastards, Marlene, I want some for Prestel.

MARLENE. I might have one this afternoon. This morning it's all Pam's secretarial.

NELL. Not long now and you'll be upstairs watching over us all.

MARLENE. Do you feel bad about it?

NELL. I don't like coming second.

MARLENE. Who does?

WIN. We'd rather it was you than Howard. We're glad for you, aren't we Nell.

NELL. Oh yes. Aces.

(*Louise enters the interviewing area. The lights cross-fade to Win and Louise in the interviewing area. Nell exits.*)

WIN. Now Louise, hello, I have your details here. You've been very loyal to the one job I see.

LOUISE. Yes I have.

WIN. Twenty-one years is a long time in one place.

LOUISE. I feel it is. I feel it's time to move on.

WIN. And you are what age now?

LOUISE. I'm in my early forties.

WIN. Exactly?

LOUISE. Forty-six.

WIN. It's not necessarily a handicap, well it is of course we have to face that, but it's not necessarily a disabling handicap, experience does count for something.

LOUISE. I hope so.

WIN. Now between ourselves is there any trouble, any reason why you're leaving that wouldn't appear on the form?

LOUISE. Nothing like that.

WIN. Like what?

LOUISE. Nothing at all.

WIN. No long term understandings come to a sudden end, making for an insupportable atmosphere?

LOUISE. I've always completely avoided anything like that at all.

WIN. No personality clashes with your immediate superiors or inferiors?

LOUISE. I've always taken care to get on very well with everyone.

WIN. I only ask because it can affect the reference and it also affects your motivation, I want to be quite clear why you're moving on. So I take it the job itself no longer satisfies you. Is it the money?

LOUISE. It's partly the money. It's not so much the money.

WIN. Nine thousand is very respectable. Have you dependants?

LOUISE. No, no dependants. My mother died.

WIN. So why are you making a change?

LOUISE. Other people make changes.

WIN. But why are you, now, after spending most of your life in the one place?

LOUISE. There you are, I've lived for that company, I've given my life really you could say because I haven't had a great deal of social life, I've worked in the evenings. I haven't had office entanglements for the very reason you just mentioned and if you are committed to your work you don't move in many other circles. I had management status from the age of twenty-seven and you'll appreciate what that means. I've built up a department. And there it is, it works extremely well, and I feel I'm stuck there. I've spent twenty years in middle management. I've seen young men who I trained go on, in my own company or elsewhere, to higher things. Nobody notices me, I don't expect it, I don't attract attention by making mistakes, everybody takes it for granted that my work

is perfect. They will notice me when I go, they will be sorry I think to lose me, they will offer me more money of course, I will refuse. They will see when I've gone what I was doing for them.

WIN. If they offer you more money you won't stay?

LOUISE. No I won't.

WIN. Are you the only woman?

LOUISE. Apart from the girls of course, yes. There was one, she was my assistant, it was the only time I took on a young woman assistant, I always had my doubts. I don't care greatly for working with women, I think I pass as a man at work. But I did take on this young woman, her qualifications were excellent, and she did well, she got a department of her own, and left the company for a competitor where she's now on the board and good luck to her. She has a different style, she's a new kind of attractive well-dressed—I don't mean I don't dress properly. But there is a kind of woman who is thirty now who grew up in a different climate. They are not so careful. They take themselves for granted. I have had to justify my existence every minute, and I have done so, I have proved—well.

WIN. Let's face it, vacancies are going to be ones where you'll be in competition with younger men. And there are companies that will value your experience enough you'll be in with a chance. There are also fields that are easier for a woman, there is a cosmetic company here where your experience might be relevant. It's eight and a half, I don't know if that appeals.

LOUISE. I've proved I can earn money. It's more important to get away. I feel it's now or never. I sometimes / think—

WIN. You shouldn't talk too much at an interview.

LOUISE. I don't. I don't normally talk about myself. I know very well how to handle myself in an office situation. I only talk to you because it seems to me this is different, it's your job to understand me, surely. You asked the questions.

WIN. I think I understand you sufficiently.

LOUISE. Well good, that's good.

WIN. Do you drink?

LOUISE. Certainly not. I'm not a teetotaller, I think that's very suspect, it's seen as being an alcoholic if you're teetotal. What do you mean? I don't drink. Why?

WIN. I drink.

LOUISE. I don't.

WIN. Good for you.

(The lights crossfade to the main office with Marlene sitting at her desk. Win and Louise exit. Angie arrives in the main office.)

ANGIE. Hello.

MARLENE. Have you an appointment?

ANGIE. It's me. I've come.

MARLENE. What? It's not Angie?

ANGIE. It was hard to find this place. I got lost.

MARLENE. How did you get past the receptionist? The girl on the desk, didn't she try to stop you?

ANGIE. What desk?

MARLENE. Never mind.

ANGIE. I just walked in. I was looking for you.

MARLENE. Well you found me.

ANGIE. Yes.

MARLENE. So where's your mum? Are you up in town for the day?

ANGIE. Not really.

MARLENE. Sit down. Do you feel all right?

ANGIE. Yes thank you.

MARLENE. So where's Joyce?

ANGIE. She's at home.

MARLENE. Did you come up on a school trip then?

ANGIE. I've left school.

MARLENE. Did you come up with a friend?

ANGIE. No. There's just me.

MARLENE. You came up by yourself, that's fun. What have you been doing? Shopping? Tower of London?

ANGIE. No, I just came here. I came to you.

MARLENE. That's very nice of you to think of paying your aunty a visit. There's not many nieces make that the first port of call. Would you like a cup of coffee?

ANGIE. No thank you.

MARLENE. Tea, orange?

ANGIE. No thank you.

MARLENE. Do you feel all right?

ANGIE. Yes thank you.

MARLENE. Are you tired from the journey?

ANGIE. Yes, I'm tired from the journey.

MARLENE. You sit there for a bit then. How's Joyce?

ANGIE. She's all right.

MARLENE. Same as ever.

ANGIE. Oh yes.

MARLENE. Unfortunately you've picked a day when I'm rather busy, if there's ever a day when I'm not, or I'd take you out to lunch and we'd go to Madame Tussaud's. We could go shopping. What time do you have to be back? Have you got a day return?

ANGIE. No.

MARLENE. So what train are you going back on?

ANGIE. I came on the bus.

MARLENE. So what bus are you going back on? Are you staying the night?

ANGIE. Yes.

MARLENE. Who are you staying with? Do you want me to put you up for the night, is that it?

ANGIE. Yes please.

MARLENE. I haven't got a spare bed.

ANGIE. I can sleep on the floor.

MARLENE. You can sleep on the sofa.

ANGIE. Yes please.

MARLENE. I do think Joyce might have phoned me. It's like her.

ANGIE. This is where you work is it?

MARLENE. It's where I have been working the last two years but I'm going to move into another office.

ANGIE. It's lovely.

MARLENE. My new office is nicer than this. There's just the one big desk in it for me.

ANGIE. Can I see it?

MARLENE. Not now, no, there's someone else in it now. But he's leaving at the end of next week and I'm going to do his job.

ANGIE. Is that good?

MARLENE. Yes, it's very good.

ANGIE. Are you going to be in charge?

MARLENE. Yes I am.

ANGIE. I knew you would be.

MARLENE. How did you know?

ANGIE. I knew you'd be in charge of everything.

MARLENE. Not quite everything.

ANGIE. You will be.

MARLENE. Well we'll see.

ANGIE. Can I see it next week then?

MARLENE. Will you still be here next week?

ANGIE. Yes.

MARLENE. Don't you have to go home?

ANGIE. No.

MARLENE. Why not?

ANGIE. It's all right.

MARLENE. Is it all right?

ANGIE. Yes, don't worry about it.

MARLENE. Does Joyce know where you are?

ANGIE. Yes of course she does.

MARLENE. Well does she?

ANGIE. Don't worry about it.

MARLENE. How long are you planning to stay with me then?

ANGIE. You know when you came to see us last year?

MARLENE. Yes, that was nice wasn't it?

ANGIE. That was the best day of my whole life.

MARLENE. So how long are you planning to stay?

ANGIE. Don't you want me?

MARLENE. Yes yes, I just wondered.

ANGIE. I won't stay if you don't want me.

MARLENE. No, of course you can stay.

ANGIE. I'll sleep on the floor. I won't be any bother.

MARLENE. Don't get upset.

ANGIE. I'm not, I'm not. Don't worry about it.

(*Mrs Kidd comes in.*)

MRS KIDD. Excuse me.

MARLENE. Yes.

MRS KIDD. Excuse me.

MARLENE. Can I help you?

MRS KIDD. Excuse me bursting in on you like this but I have to talk to you.

MARLENE. I am engaged at the moment. / If you could go to reception—

MRS KIDD. I'm Rosemary Kidd, Howard's wife, you don't recognize me but we did meet, I remember you of course / but you wouldn't—

MARLENE. Yes of course, Mrs Kidd, I'm sorry, we did meet. Howard's about somewhere I expect, have you looked in his office?

MRS KIDD. Howard's not about, no. I'm afraid it's you I've come to see if I could have a minute or two.

MARLENE. I do have an appointment in five minutes.

MRS KIDD. This won't take five minutes. I'm very sorry. It is a matter of some urgency.

MARLENE. Well of course. What can I do for you?

MRS KIDD. I just wanted a chat, an informal chat. It's not something I can simply—I'm sorry if I'm interrupting your work. I know office work isn't like housework / which is all interruptions.

MARLENE. No, no, this is my niece. Angie. Mrs Kidd.

MRS KIDD. Very pleased to meet you.

ANGIE. Very well thank you.

MRS KIDD. Howard's not in today.

MARLENE. Isn't he?

MRS KIDD. He's feeling poorly.

MARLENE. I didn't know. I'm sorry to hear that.

MRS KIDD. The fact is he's in a state of shock. About what's happened.

MARLENE. What has happened?

MRS KIDD. You should know if anyone. I'm referring to you being appointed managing director instead of Howard. He hasn't been at all well all weekend. He hasn't slept for three nights. I haven't slept.

MARLENE. I'm sorry to hear that, Mrs Kidd. Has he thought of taking sleeping pills?

MRS KIDD. It's very hard when someone has worked all these years.

MARLENE. Business life is full of little setbacks. I'm sure Howard knows that. He'll bounce back in a day or two. We all bounce back.

MRS KIDD. If you could see him you'd know what I'm talking about. What's it going to do to him working for a woman? I think if it was a man he'd get over it as something normal.

MARLENE. I think he's going to have to get over it.

MRS KIDD. It's me that bears the brunt. I'm not the one that's been promoted. I put him first every inch of the way. And now what do I get? You women this, you women that. It's not my fault. You're going to have to be very careful how you handle him. He's very hurt.

MARLENE. Naturally I'll be tactful and pleasant to him, you don't start pushing someone round. I'll consult him over any decisions affecting his department. But that's no different, Mrs Kidd, from any of my other colleagues.

MRS KIDD. I think it is different, because he's a man.

MARLENE. I'm not quite sure why you came to see me.

MRS KIDD. I had to do something.

MARLENE. Well you've done it, you've seen me. I think that's probably all we've time for. I'm sorry he's been taking it out on you. He really is a shit, Howard.

MRS KIDD. But he's got a family to support. He's got three children. It's only fair.

MARLENE. Are you suggesting I give up the job to him then?

MRS KIDD. It had crossed my mind if you were unavailable after all for some reason, he would be the natural second choice I think, don't you? I'm not asking.

MARLENE. Good.

MRS KIDD. You mustn't tell him I came. He's very proud.

MARLENE. If he doesn't like what's happening here he can go and work somewhere else.

MRS KIDD. Is that a threat?

MARLENE. I'm sorry but I do have some work to do.

MRS KIDD. It's not that easy, a man of Howard's age. You don't care. I thought he was going too far but he's right. You're one of these ballbreakers, / that's what you

MARLENE. I'm sorry but I do have some work to do.

MRS KIDD. are. You'll end up miserable and lonely. You're not natural.

MARLENE. Could you please piss off?

MRS KIDD. I thought if I saw you at least I'd be doing something. (*Mrs Kidd goes.*)

MARLENE. I've got to go and do some work now. Will you come back later?

ANGIE. I think you were wonderful.

MARLENE. I've got to go and do some work now.

ANGIE. You told her to piss off.

MARLENE. Will you come back later?

ANGIE. Can't I stay here?
MARLENE. Don't you want to go sightseeing?
ANGIE. I'd rather stay here.
MARLENE. You can stay here I suppose, if it's not boring.
ANGIE. It's where I most want to be in the world.
MARLENE. I'll see you later then.

(Marlene goes. Shona and Nell enter the interviewing area. Angie sits at Win's desk. The lights crossfade to Nell and Shona in the interviewing area.)

NELL. Is this right? You are Shona?
SHONA. Yeh.
NELL. It says here you're twenty-nine.
SHONA. Yeh.
NELL. Too many late nights, me. So you've been where you are for four years, Shona, you're earning six basic and three commission. So what's the problem?
SHONA. No problem.
NELL. Why do you want a change?
SHONA. Just a change.
NELL. Change of product, change of area?
SHONA. Both.
NELL. But you're happy on the road?
SHONA. I like driving.
NELL. You're not after management status?
SHONA. I would like management status.
NELL. You'd be interested in titular management status but not come off the road?
SHONA. I want to be on the road, yeh.
NELL. So how many calls have you been making a day?
SHONA. Six.
NELL. And what proportion of those are successful?
SHONA. Six.
NELL. That's hard to believe.
SHONA. Four
NELL. You find it easy to get the initial interest do you?
SHONA. Oh yeh, I get plenty of initial interest.
NELL. And what about closing?
SHONA. I close, don't I?
NELL. Because that's what an employer is going to have doubts about with a lady as I needn't tell you, whether she's got the guts to push through to a closing situation. They think we're too nice. They think we listen to the buyer's doubts. They think we consider his needs and his feelings.
SHONA. I never consider people's feelings.
NELL. I was selling for six years, I can sell anything, I've sold in three continents, and I'm jolly as they come but I'm not very nice.
SHONA. I'm not very nice.

NELL. What sort of time do you have on the road with the other reps? Get on all right? Handle the chat?
SHONA. I get on. Keep myself to myself.
NELL. Fairly much of a loner are you?
SHONA. Sometimes.
NELL. So what field are you interested in?
SHONA. Computers.
NELL. That's a top field as you know and you'll be up against some very slick fellas there, there's some very pretty boys in computers, it's an American-style field.
SHONA. That's why I want to do it.
NELL. Video systems appeal? That's a high-flying situation.
SHONA. Video systems appeal OK.
NELL. Because Prestel has half a dozen vacancies I'm looking to fill at the moment. We're talking in the area of ten to fifteen thousand here and upwards.
SHONA. Sounds OK.
NELL. I've half a mind to go for it myself. But it's good money here if you've got the top clients. Could you fancy it do you think?
SHONA. Work here?
NELL. I'm not in a position to offer, there's nothing officially going just now, but we're always on the lookout. There's not that many of us. We could keep in touch.
SHONA. I like driving.
NELL. So the Prestel appeals?
SHONA. Yeh.
NELL. What about ties?
SHONA. No ties.
NELL. So relocation wouldn't be a problem.
SHONA. No problem.
NELL. So just fill me in a bit more could you about what you've been doing.
SHONA. What I've been doing. It's all down there.
NELL. The bare facts are down here but I've got to present you to an employer.
SHONA. I'm twenty-nine years old.
NELL. So it says here.
SHONA. We look young. Youngness runs in the family in our family.
NELL. So just describe your present job for me.
SHONA. My present job at present. I have a car. I have a Porsche. I go up the M1 a lot. Burn up the M1 a lot. Straight up the M1 in the fast lane to where the clients are, Staffordshire, Yorkshire, I do a lot in Yorkshire. I'm selling electric things. Like dishwashers, washing machines, stainless steel tubs are a feature and the reliability of the program. After sales service, we offer a very good after sales service, spare

parts, plenty of spare parts. And fridges, I sell a lot of fridges specially in the summer. People want to buy fridges in the summer because of the heat melting the butter and you get fed up standing the milk in a basin of cold water with a cloth over, stands to reason people don't want to do that in this day and age. So I sell a lot of them. Big ones with big freezers. Big freezers. And I stay in hotels at night when I'm away from home. On my expense account. I stay in various hotels. They know me, the ones I go to. I check in, have a bath, have a shower. Then I go down to the bar, have a gin and tonic, have a chat. Then I go into the dining room and have dinner. I usually have fillet steak and mushrooms, I like mushrooms. I like smoked salmon very much. I like having a salad on the side. Green salad. I don't like tomatoes.

NELL. Christ what a waste of time.

SHONA. Beg your pardon?

NELL. Not a word of this is true is it?

SHONA. How do you mean?

NELL. You just filled in the form with a pack of lies.

SHONA. Not exactly.

NELL. How old are you?

SHONA. Twenty-nine.

NELL. Nineteen?

SHONA. Twenty-one.

NELL. And what jobs have you done? Have you done any?

SHONA. I could though, I bet you.

(The lights crossfade to the main office with Angie sitting as before. Win comes in to the main office. Shona and Nell exit.)

WIN. Who's sitting in my chair?

ANGIE. What? Sorry.

WIN. Who's been eating my porridge?

ANGIE. What?

WIN. It's all right, I saw Marlene. Angie isn't it? I'm Win. And I'm not going out for lunch because I'm knackered. I'm going to set me down here and have a yogurt. Do you like yogurt?

ANGIE. No.

WIN. That's good because I've only got one. Are you hungry?

ANGIE. No.

WIN. There's a cafe on the corner.

ANGIE. No thank you. Do you work here?

WIN. How did you guess?

ANGIE. Because you look as if you might work here and you're sitting at the desk. Have you always worked here?

WIN. No I was headhunted. That means I was working for another outfit like this and this lot came and offered me more money. I broke my contract, there was a hell of a stink. There's not many top ladies about. Your aunty's a smashing bird.

ANGIE. Yes I know.

MARLENE. Fan are you? Fan of your aunty's?

ANGIE. Do you think I could work here?

WIN. Not at the moment.

ANGIE. How do I start?

WIN. What can you do?

ANGIE. I don't know. Nothing.

WIN. Type?

ANGIE. Not very well. The letters jump up when I do capitals. I was going to do a CSE[7] in commerce but I didn't.

WIN. What have you got?

ANGIE. What?

WIN. CSE's, O's.

ANGIE. Nothing, none of that. Did you do all that?

WIN. Oh yes, all that, and a science degree funnily enough. I started out doing medical research but there's no money in it. I thought I'd go abroad. Did you know they sell Coca-Cola in Russia and Pepsi-Cola in China? You don't have to be qualified as much as you might think. Men are awful bullshitters, they like to make out jobs are harder than they are. Any job I ever did I started doing it better than the rest of the crowd and they didn't like it. So I'd get unpopular and I'd have a drink to cheer myself up. I lived with a fella and supported him for four years, he couldn't get work. After that I went to California. I like the sunshine. Americans know how to live. This country's too slow. Then I went to Mexico, still in sales, but it's no country for a single lady. I came home, went bonkers for a bit, thought I was five different people, got over that all right, the psychiatrist said I was perfectly sane and highly intelligent. Got married in a moment of weakness and he's inside now, he's been inside four years, and I've not been to see him too much this last year. I like this better than sales, I'm not really that aggressive. I started thinking sales was a good job if you want to meet people, but you're meeting people that don't want to meet you. It's no good if you like being liked. Here your clients want to meet you because you're the one doing them some good. They hope. *(Angie has fallen asleep. Nell comes in.)*

NELL. You're talking to yourself, sunshine.

[7]**CSE** Certificate of Secondary Education

WIN. So what's new?

NELL. Who is this?

WIN. Marlene's little niece.

NELL. What's she got, brother, sister? She never talks about her family.

WIN. I was telling her my life story.

NELL. Violins?

WIN. No, success story.

NELL. You've heard Howard's had a heart attack?

WIN. No, when?

NELL. I heard just now. He hadn't come in, he was at home, he's gone to hospital. He's not dead. His wife was here, she rushed off in a cab.

WIN. Too much butter, too much smoke. We must send him some flowers. (*Marlene comes in.*) You've heard about Howard?

MARLENE. Poor sod.

NELL. Lucky he didn't get the job if that's what his health's like.

MARLENE. Is she asleep?

WIN. She wants to work here.

MARLENE. Packer in Tesco more like.

WIN. She's a nice kid. Isn't she?

MARLENE. She's a bit thick. She's a bit funny.

WIN. She thinks you're wonderful.

MARLENE. She's not going to make it.

SCENE 2

(*Joyce's kitchen. Sunday evening, a year earlier. The lights come up on Joyce, Angie, and Marlene. Marlene is taking presents out of bright carrier bag. Angie has already opened a box of chocolates.*)

MARLENE. Just a few little things. / I've

JOYCE. There's no need.

MARLENE. no memory for birthdays have I, and Christmas seems to slip by. So I think I owe Angie a few presents.

JOYCE. What do you say?

ANGIE. Thank you very much. Thank you very much, Aunty Marlene. (*She opens a present. It is the dress from Act I, new.*) Oh look, Mum, isn't it lovely?

MARLENE. I don't know if it's the right size. She's grown up since I saw her. / I knew she was always

ANGIE. Isn't it lovely?

MARLENE. tall for her age.

JOYCE. She's a big lump.

MARLENE. Hold it up, Angie, let's see.

ANGIE. I'll put it on, shall I?

MARLENE. Yes, try it on.

JOYCE. Go to your room then, we don't want / a strip show thank you.

ANGIE. Of course I'm going to my room, what do you think? Look Mum, here's something for you. Open it, go on. What is it? Can I open it for you?

JOYCE. Yes, you open it, pet.

ANGIE. Don't you want to open it yourself? / Go on.

JOYCE. I don't mind, you can do it.

ANGIE. It's something hard. It's—what is it? A bottle. Drink is it? No, it's what? Perfume, look. What a lot. Open it, look, let's smell it. Oh it's strong. It's lovely. Put it on me. How do you do it? Put it on me.

JOYCE. You're too young.

ANGIE. I can play wearing it like dressing up.

JOYCE. And you're too old for that. Here, give it here, I'll do it, you'll tip the whole bottle over yourself / and we'll have you smelling all summer.

ANGIE. Put it on you. Do I smell? Put it on Aunty too. Put it on Aunty too. Let's all smell.

MARLENE. I didn't know what you'd like.

JOYCE. There's no danger I'd have it already, / that's one thing.

ANGIE. Now we all smell the same.

MARLENE. It's a bit of nonsense.

JOYCE. It's very kind of you Marlene, you shouldn't.

ANGIE. Now I'll put on the dress and then we'll see. (*Angie goes.*)

JOYCE. You've caught me on the hop with the place in a mess. / If you'd let me

MARLENE. That doesn't matter.

JOYCE. know you was coming I'd have got something in to eat. We had our dinner dinnertime. We're just going to have a cup of tea. You could have an egg.

MARLENE. No, I'm not hungry. Tea's fine.

JOYCE. I don't expect you take sugar.

MARLENE. Why not?

JOYCE. You take care of yourself.

MARLENE. How do you mean you didn't know I was coming?

JOYCE. You could have written. I know we're not on the phone but we're not completely in the dark ages, / we do have a postman.

MARLENE. But you asked me to come.

JOYCE. How did I ask you to come?

MARLENE. Angie said when she phoned up.

JOYCE. Angie phoned up, did she?

MARLENE. Was it just Angie's idea?

JOYCE. What did she say?

MARLENE. She said you wanted me to come and see you. / It was a couple of

JOYCE. Ha.

817

MARLENE. weeks ago. How was I to know that's a ridiculous idea? My diary's always full a couple of weeks ahead so we fixed it for this weekend. I was meant to get here earlier but I was held up. She gave me messages from you.

JOYCE. Didn't you wonder why I didn't phone you myself?

MARLENE. She said you didn't like using the phone. You're shy on the phone and can't use it. I don't know what you're like, do I.

JOYCE. Are there people who can't use the phone?

MARLENE. I expect so.

JOYCE. I haven't met any.

MARLENE. Why should I think she was lying?

JOYCE. Because she's like what she's like.

MARLENE. How do I know / what she's like?

JOYCE. It's not my fault you don't know what she's like. You never come and see her.

MARLENE. Well I have now / and you don't seem over the moon.*

JOYCE. Good. *Well I'd have got a cake if she'd told me. (Pause.)

MARLENE. I did wonder why you wanted to see me.

JOYCE. I didn't want to see you.

MARLENE. Yes, I know. Shall I go?

JOYCE. I don't mind seeing you.

MARLENE. Great, I feel really welcome.

JOYCE. You can come and see Angie any time you like, I'm not stopping you. / You know where we are. You're the one went away, not me. I'm right here where I was. And will be a few years yet I shouldn't wonder.

MARLENE. All right. All right. (Joyce gives Marlene a cup of tea.)

JOYCE. Tea.

MARLENE. Sugar? (Joyce passes Marlene the sugar.) It's very quiet down here.

JOYCE. I expect you'd notice it.

MARLENE. The air smells different too.

JOYCE. That's the scent.

MARLENE. No, I mean walking down the lane.

JOYCE. What sort of air you get in London then?

(Angie comes in, wearing the dress. It fits.)

MARLENE. Oh, very pretty. / You do look pretty, Angie.

JOYCE. That fits all right.

MARLENE. Do you like the color?

ANGIE. Beautiful. Beautiful.

JOYCE. You better take it off, / you'll get it dirty.

ANGIE. I want to wear it. I want to wear it.

MARLENE. It is for wearing after all. You can't just hang it up and look at it.

ANGIE. I love it.

JOYCE. Well if you must you must.

ANGIE. If someone asks me what's my favorite colour I'll tell them it's this. Thank you very much, Aunty Marlene.

MARLENE. You didn't tell your mum you asked me down.

ANGIE. I wanted it to be a surprise.

JOYCE. I'll give you a surprise / one of these days.

ANGIE. I thought you'd like to see her. She hasn't been here since I was nine. People do see their aunts.

MARLENE. Is it that long? Doesn't time fly?

ANGIE. I wanted to.

JOYCE. I'm not cross.

ANGIE. Are you glad?

JOYCE. I smell nicer anyhow, don't I?

(Kit comes in without saying anything, as if she lived there.)

MARLENE. I think it was a good idea, Angie, about time. We are sisters after all. It's a pity to let that go.

JOYCE. This is Kitty, / who lives up the road. This is Angie's Aunty Marlene.

KIT. What's that?

ANGIE. It's a present. Do you like it?

KIT. It's all right. / Are you coming out?*

MARLENE. Hello, Kitty.

ANGIE. *No.

KIT. What's that smell?

ANGIE. It's a present.

KIT. It's horrible. Come on.*

MARLENE. Have a chocolate.

ANGIE. *No, I'm busy.

KIT. Coming out later?

ANGIE. No.

KIT (to Marlene). Hello. (Kit goes without a chocolate.)

JOYCE. She's a little girl Angie sometimes plays with because she's the only child lives really close. She's like a little sister to her really. Angie's good with little children.

MARLENE. Do you want to work with children, Angie? / Be a teacher or a nursery nurse?

JOYCE. I don't think she's ever thought of it.

MARLENE. What do you want to do?

JOYCE. She hasn't an idea in her head what she wants to do. / Lucky to get anything.

MARLENE. Angie?

JOYCE. She's not clever like you. (Pause.)

MARLENE. I'm not clever, just pushy.

JOYCE. True enough. (Marlene takes a bottle of whisky out of the bag.) I don't drink spirits.

ANGIE. You do at Christmas.

JOYCE. It's not Christmas, is it?

ANGIE. It's better than Christmas.

MARLENE. Glasses?

JOYCE. Just a small one then.

MARLENE. Do you want some, Angie?

ANGIE. I can't, can I?

JOYCE. Taste it if you want. You won't like it. (*Angie tastes it.*)

MARLENE. We got drunk together the night your grandfather died.

JOYCE. We did not get drunk.

MARLENE. I got drunk. You were just overcome with grief.

JOYCE. I still keep up the grave with flowers.

MARLENE. Do you really?

JOYCE. Why wouldn't I?

MARLENE. Have you seen Mother?

JOYCE. Of course I've seen Mother.

MARLENE. I mean lately.

JOYCE. Of course I've seen her lately, I go every Thursday.

MARLENE (*to Angie*). Do you remember your grandfather?

ANGIE. He got me out of the bath one night in a towel.

MARLENE. Did he? I don't think he ever gave me a bath. Did he give you a bath, Joyce? He probably got soft in his old age. Did you like him?

ANGIE. Yes of course.

MARLENE. Why?

ANGIE. What?

MARLENE. So what's the news? How's Mrs Paisley? Still going crazily? / And Dorothy. What happened to Dorothy?*

ANGIE. Who's Mrs Paisley?

JOYCE. *She went to Canada.

MARLENE. Did she? What to do?

JOYCE. I don't know. She just went to Canada.

MARLENE. Well / good for her.

ANGIE. Mr Connolly killed his wife.

MARLENE. What, Connolly at Whitegates?

ANGIE. They found her body in the garden. / Under the cabbages.

MARLENE. He was always so proper.

JOYCE. Stuck up git. Connolly. Best lawyer money could buy but he couldn't get out of it. She was carrying on with Matthew.

MARLENE. How old's Matthew then?

JOYCE. Twenty-one. / He's got a motorbike.

MARLENE. I think he's about six.

ANGIE. How can he be six? He's six years older than me. / If he was six I'd be nothing, I'd be just born this minute.

JOYCE. Your aunty knows that, she's just being silly. She means it's so long since she's been here she's forgotten about Matthew.

ANGIE. You were here for my birthday when I was nine. I had a pink cake. Kit was only five then, she was four, she hadn't started school yet. She could read already when she went to school. You remember my birthday? / You remember me?

MARLENE. Yes, I remember the cake.

ANGIE. You remember me?

MARLENE. Yes, I remember you.

ANGIE. And Mum and Dad was there, and Kit was.

MARLENE. Yes, how is your dad? Where is he tonight? Up the pub?

JOYCE. No, he's not here.

MARLENE. I can see he's not here.

JOYCE. He moved out.

MARLENE. What? When did he? / Just recently?*

ANGIE. Didn't you know that? You don't know much.

JOYCE. *No, it must be three years ago. Don't be rude, Angie.

ANGIE. I'm not, am I Aunty? What else don't you know?

JOYCE. You was in America or somewhere. You sent a postcard.

ANGIE. I've got that in my room. It's the Grand Canyon. Do you want to see it? Shall I get it? I can get it for you.

MARLENE. Yes, all right. (*Angie goes.*)

JOYCE. You could be married with twins for all I know. You must have affairs and break up and I don't need to know about any of that so I don't see what the fuss is about.

MARLENE. What fuss? (*Angie comes back with the postcard.*)

ANGIE. "Driving across the states for a new job in L. A. It's a long way but the car goes very fast. It's very hot. Wish you were here. Love from Aunty Marlene."

JOYCE. Did you make a lot of money?

MARLENE. I spent a lot.

ANGIE. I want to go to America. Will you take me?

JOYCE. She's not going to America, she's been to America, stupid.

ANGIE. She might go again, stupid. It's not something you do once. People who go keep going all the time, back and forth on jets. They go on Concorde and Laker and get jet lag. Will you take me?

MARLENE. I'm not planning a trip.

ANGIE. Will you let me know?

JOYCE. Angie, / you're getting silly.

ANGIE. I want to be American.

JOYCE. It's time you were in bed.

ANGIE. No it's not. / I don't have to go to bed at all tonight.

JOYCE. School in the morning.

ANGIE. I'll wake up.

JOYCE. Come on now, you know how you get.

ANGIE. How do I get? / I don't get anyhow.*

JOYCE. Angie. *Are you staying the night?

MARLENE. Yes, if that's all right. / I'll see you in the morning.

ANGIE. You can have my bed. I'll sleep on the sofa.

JOYCE. You will not, you'll sleep in your bed. / Think

ANGIE. Mum.

JOYCE. I can't see through that? I can just see you going to sleep / with us talking.

ANGIE. I would, I would go to sleep, I'd love that.

JOYCE. I'm going to get cross, Angie.

ANGIE. I want to show her something.

JOYCE. Then bed.

ANGIE. It's a secret.

JOYCE. Then I expect it's in your room so off you go. Give us a shout when you're ready for bed and your aunty'll be up and see you.

ANGIE. Will you?

MARLENE. Yes of course. (*Angie goes. Silence.*) It's cold tonight.

JOYCE. Will you be all right on the sofa? You can / have my bed.

MARLENE. The sofa's fine.

JOYCE. Yes the forecast said rain tonight but it's held off.

MARLENE. I was going to walk down to the estuary but I've left it a bit late. Is it just the same?

JOYCE. They cut down the hedges a few years back. Is that since you were here?

MARLENE. But it's not changed down the end, all the mud? And the reeds? We used to pick them up when they were bigger than us. Are there still lapwings?

JOYCE. You get strangers walking there on a Sunday. I expect they're looking at the mud and the lapwings, yes.

MARLENE. You could have left.

JOYCE. Who says I wanted to leave?

MARLENE. Stop getting at me then, you're really boring.

JOYCE. How could I have left?

MARLENE. Did you want to?

JOYCE. I said how, / how could I?

MARLENE. If you'd wanted to you'd have done it.

JOYCE. Christ.

MARLENE. Are we getting drunk?

JOYCE. Do you want something to eat?

MARLENE. No, I'm getting drunk.

JOYCE. Funny time to visit, Sunday evening.

MARLENE. I came this morning. I spent the day—

ANGIE (*off*). Aunty! Aunty Marlene!

MARLENE. I'd better go.

JOYCE. Go on then.

MARLENE. All right.

ANGIE (*off*). Aunty! Can you hear me? I'm ready.

(*Marlene goes. Joyce goes on sitting, clears up, sits again. Marlene comes back.*)

JOYCE. So what's the secret?

MARLENE. It's a secret.

JOYCE. I know what it is anyway.

MARLENE. I bet you don't. You always said that.

JOYCE. It's her exercise book.

MARLENE. Yes, but you don't know what's in it.

JOYCE. It's some game, some secret society she has with Kit.

MARLENE. You don't know the password. You don't know the code.

JOYCE. You're really in it, aren't you. Can you do the handshake?

MARLENE. She didn't mention a handshake.

JOYCE. I thought they'd have a special handshake. She spends hours writing that but she's useless at school. She copies things out of books about black magic, and politicians out of the paper. It's a bit childish.

MARLENE. I think it's a plot to take over the world.

JOYCE. She's been in the remedial class the last two years.

MARLENE. I came up this morning and spent the day in Ipswich. I went to see mother.

JOYCE. Did she recognize you?

MARLENE. Are you trying to be funny?

JOYCE. No, she does wander.

MARLENE. She wasn't wandering at all, she was very lucid thank you.

JOYCE. You were very lucky then.

MARLENE. Fucking awful life she's had.

JOYCE. Don't tell me.

MARLENE. Fucking waste.

JOYCE. Don't talk to me.

MARLENE. Why shouldn't I talk? Why shouldn't I talk to you? / Isn't she my mother too?

JOYCE. Look, you've left, you've gone away, / we can do without you.

MARLENE. I left home, so what, I left home. People do leave home / it is normal.

JOYCE. We understand that, we can do without you.

MARLENE. We weren't happy. Were you happy?

JOYCE. Don't come back.

MARLENE. So it's just your mother is it, your child, you never wanted me round, / you were jealous

JOYCE. Here we go.

MARLENE. of me because I was the little one and I was clever.

JOYCE. I'm not clever enough for all this psychology / if that's what it is.

MARLENE. Why can't I visit my own family / without

JOYCE. Aah.

MARLENE. all this?

JOYCE. Just don't go on about Mum's life when you haven't been to see her for how many years. / I go

MARLENE. It's up to me.

JOYCE. and see her every week.

MARLENE. Then don't go and see her every week.

JOYCE. Somebody has to.

MARLENE. No they don't. / Why do they?

JOYCE. How would I feel if I didn't go?

MARLENE. A lot better.

JOYCE. I hope you feel better.

MARLENE. It's up to me.

JOYCE. You couldn't get out of here fast enough. (Pause.)

MARLENE. Of course I couldn't get out of here fast enough. What was I going to do? Marry a dairyman who'd come home pissed? / Don't you fucking this

JOYCE. Christ.

MARLENE. fucking that fucking bitch fucking tell me what to fucking do fucking.

JOYCE. I don't know how you could leave your own child.

MARLENE. You were quick enough to take her.

JOYCE. What does that mean?

MARLENE. You were quick enough to take her.

JOYCE. Or what? Have her put in a home? Have some stranger / take her would you rather?

MARLENE. You couldn't have one so you took mine.

JOYCE. I didn't know that then.

MARLENE. Like hell, / married three years.

JOYCE. I didn't know that. Plenty of people / take that long.

MARLENE. Well it turned out lucky for you, didn't it?

JOYCE. Turned out all right for you by the look of you. You'd be getting a few less thousand a year.

MARLENE. Not necessarily.

JOYCE. You'd be stuck here / like you said.

MARLENE. I could have taken her with me.

JOYCE. You didn't want to take her with you. It's no good coming back now, Marlene, / and saying—

MARLENE. I know a managing director who's got two children, she breast feeds in the board room, she pays a hundred pounds a week on domestic help alone and she can afford that because she's an extremely high-powered lady earning a great deal of money.

JOYCE. So what's that got to do with you at the age of seventeen?

MARLENE. Just because you were married and had somewhere to live—

JOYCE. You could have lived at home. / Or live

MARLENE. Don't be stupid.

JOYCE. with me and Frank. / You

MARLENE. You never suggested.

JOYCE. said you weren't keeping it. You shouldn't have had it / if you wasn't

MARLENE. Here we go.

JOYCE. going to keep it. You was the most stupid, / for someone so clever you was the most stupid, get yourself pregnant, not go to the doctor, not tell.

MARLENE. You wanted it, you said you were glad, I remember the day, you said I'm glad you never got rid of it, I'll look after it, you said that down by the river. So what are you saying, sunshine, you don't want her?

JOYCE. Course I'm not saying that.

MARLENE. Because I'll take her, / wake her up and pack now.

JOYCE. You wouldn't know how to begin to look after her.

MARLENE. Don't you want her?

JOYCE. Course I do, she's my child.

MARLENE. Then why are you going on about / why did I have her?

JOYCE. You said I got her off you / when you didn't—

MARLENE. I said you were lucky / the way it—

JOYCE. Have a child now if you want one. You're not old.

MARLENE. I might do.

JOYCE. Good. (Pause.)

MARLENE. I've been on the pill so long / I'm probably sterile.

JOYCE. Listen when Angie was six months I did get pregnant and I lost it because I was so tired looking after your fucking baby / because she cried so

MARLENE. You never told me.

JOYCE. much—yes I did tell you— / and the doctor

MARLENE. Well I forgot.

JOYCE. said if I'd sat down all day with my feet up I'd've kept it / and that's the only chance I ever had because after that—

MARLENE. I've had two abortions, are you interested? Shall I tell you about them? Well I won't, it's boring, it wasn't a problem. I don't like messy talk about blood / and what a bad time we all had.

JOYCE. If I hadn't had your baby. The doctor said.

MARLENE. I don't want a baby. I don't want to talk about gynaecology.

JOYCE. Then stop trying to get Angie off of me.

MARLENE. I come down here after six years. All night you've been saying I don't come often enough. If I don't come for another six years she'll be twenty-one, will that be OK?

JOYCE. That'll be fine, yes, six years would suit me fine. (Pause.)

MARLENE. I was afraid of this. I only came because I thought you wanted . . . I just want . . . (*She cries.*)

JOYCE. Don't grizzle, Marlene, for God's sake. Marly? Come on, pet. Love you really. Fucking stop it, will you? (*She goes to Marlene.*)

MARLENE. No, let me cry. I like it. (*They laugh. Marlene begins to stop crying.*) I knew I'd cry if I wasn't careful.

JOYCE. Everyone's always crying in this house. Nobody takes any notice.

MARLENE. You've been wonderful looking after Angie.

JOYCE. Don't get carried away.

MARLENE. I can't write letters but I do think of you.

JOYCE. You're getting drunk. I'm going to make some tea.

MARLENE. Love you. (*Joyce gets up to make tea.*)

JOYCE. I can see why you'd want to leave. It's a dump here.

MARLENE. So what's this about you and Frank?

JOYCE. He was always carrying on, wasn't he? And if I wanted to go out in the evening he'd go mad, even if it was nothing, a class, I was going to go to an evening class. So he had this girlfriend, only twenty-two poor cow, and I said go on, off you go, hoppit. I don't think he even likes her.

MARLENE. So what about money?

JOYCE. I've always said I don't want your money.

MARLENE. No, does he send you money?

JOYCE. I've got four different cleaning jobs. Adds up. There's not a lot round here.

MARLENE. Does Angie miss him?

JOYCE. She doesn't say.

MARLENE. Does she see him?

JOYCE. He was never that fond of her to be honest.

MARLENE. He tried to kiss me once. When you were engaged.

JOYCE. Did you fancy him?

MARLENE. No, he looked like a fish.

JOYCE. He was lovely then.

MARLENE. Ugh.

JOYCE. Well I fancied him. For about three years.

MARLENE. Have you got someone else?

JOYCE. There's not a lot round here. Mind you, the minute you're on your own, you'd be amazed how your friends' husbands drop by. I'd sooner do without.

MARLENE. I don't see why you couldn't take my money.

JOYCE. I do, so don't bother about it.

MARLENE. Only got to ask.

JOYCE. So what about you? Good job?

MARLENE. Good for a laugh. / Got back

JOYCE. Good for more than a laugh I should think.

MARLENE. from the US of A a bit wiped out and slotted into this speedy employment agency and still there.

JOYCE. You can always find yourself work then.

MARLENE. That's right.

JOYCE. And men?

MARLENE. Oh there's always men.

JOYCE. No one special?

MARLENE. There's fellas who like to be seen with a high-flying lady. Shows they've got something really good in their pants. But they can't take the day to day. They're waiting for me to turn into the little woman. Or maybe I'm just horrible of course.

JOYCE. Who needs them?

MARLENE. Who needs them? Well I do. But I need adventures more. So on on into the sunset. I think the eighties are going to be stupendous.

JOYCE. Who for?

MARLENE. For me. / I think I'm going up up up.

JOYCE. Oh for you. Yes, I'm sure they will.

MARLENE. And for the country, come to that. Get the economy back on its feet and whosh. She's a tough lady, Maggie. I'd give her a job. / She just needs to hang

JOYCE. You voted for them, did you?

MARLENE. in there. This country needs to stop whining. / Monetarism is not

JOYCE. Drink your tea and shut up, pet.

MARLENE. stupid. It takes time, determination. No more slop. / And

JOYCE. Well I think they're filthy bastards.

MARLENE. who's got to drive it on? First woman prime minister. Terrifico. Aces. Right on. / You must admit. Certainly gets my vote.

JOYCE. What good's first women if it's her? I suppose you'd have liked Hitler if he was a woman. Ms. Hitler. Got a lot done, Hitlerina. / Great adventures.

MARLENE. Bosses still walking on the workers' faces? Still Dadda's little parrot? Haven't you learned to think for yourself? I believe in the individual. Look at me.

JOYCE. I am looking at you.

MARLENE. Come on, Joyce, we're not going to quarrel over politics.

JOYCE. We are through.

MARLENE. Forget I mentioned it. Not a word about the slimy unions will cross my lips. (*Pause.*)

JOYCE. You say Mother had a wasted life.

MARLENE. Yes I do. Married to that bastard.

JOYCE. What sort of life did he have? /

MARLENE. Violent life?

JOYCE. Working in the fields like an animal. / Why

MARLENE. Come off it.

JOYCE. wouldn't he want a drink? You want a drink. He couldn't afford whisky.

MARLENE. I don't want to talk about him.

JOYCE. You started, I was talking about her. She had a rotten life because she had nothing. She went hungry.

MARLENE. She was hungry because he drank the money. / He used to hit her.

JOYCE. It's not all down to him. / Their

MARLENE. She didn't hit him.

JOYCE. lives were rubbish. They were treated like rubbish. He's dead and she'll die soon and what sort of life / did they have?

MARLENE. I saw him one night. I came down.

JOYCE. Do you think I didn't? / They

MARLENE. I still have dreams.

JOYCE. didn't get to America and drive across it in a fast car. / Bad nights, they had bad days. I knew when I

MARLENE. America, America, you're jealous. / I had to get out,

JOYCE. Jealous?

MARLENE. was thirteen, out of their house, out of them, never let that happen to me, / never let him, make my own way, out.

JOYCE. Jealous of what you've done, you'd be ashamed of me if I came to your office, your smart friends, wouldn't you, I'm ashamed of you, think of nothing but yourself, you've got on, nothing's changed for most people / has it?

MARLENE. I hate the working class / which is what

JOYCE. Yes you do.

MARLENE. you're going to go on about now, it doesn't exist any more, it means lazy and stupid. / I don't

JOYCE. Come on, now we're getting it.

MARLENE. like the way they talk. I don't like beer guts and football vomit and saucy tits / and brothers and sisters—

JOYCE. I spit when I see a Rolls Royce, scratch it with my ring / Mercedes it was

MARLENE. Oh very mature—

JOYCE. I hate the cows I work for / and their dirty dishes with blanquette of fucking veau.

MARLENE. and I will not be pulled down to their level by a flying picket and I won't be sent to Siberia / or a loony bin just because I'm original. And I support

JOYCE. No, you'll be on a yacht, you'll be head of Coca-Cola and you wait, the eighties is going to be stupendous all right because we'll get you lot off our backs—

MARLENE. Reagan even if he is a lousy movie star because the reds are swarming up his map and I want to be free in a free world—

JOYCE. What? / What?

MARLENE. I know what I mean / by that—not shut up here.

JOYCE. So don't be round here when it happens because if someone's kicking you I'll just laugh. (*Silence.*)

MARLENE. I don't mean anything personal. I don't believe in class. Anyone can do anything if they've got what it takes.

JOYCE. And if they haven't.

MARLENE. If they're stupid or lazy or frightened, I'm not going to help them get a job, why should I?

JOYCE. What about Angie?

MARLENE. What about Angie?

JOYCE. She's stupid, lazy and frightened, so what about her?

MARLENE. You run her down too much. She'll be all right.

JOYCE. I don't expect so, no. I expect her children will say what a wasted life she had. If she has children. Because nothing's changed and it won't with them in.

MARLENE. Them, them. / Us and them?

JOYCE. And you're one of them.

MARLENE. And you're us, wonderful us, and Angie's us / and Mum and Dad's us.

JOYCE. Yes, that's right, and you're them.

MARLENE. Come on, Joyce, what a night. You've got what it takes.

JOYCE. I know I have.

MARLENE. I didn't really mean all that.

JOYCE. I did.

MARLENE. But we're friends anyway.

JOYCE. I don't think so, no.

MARLENE. Well it's lovely to be out in the country. I really must make the effort to come more often. I want to go to sleep. I want to go to sleep. (*Joyce gets blankets for the sofa.*)

JOYCE. Goodnight then. I hope you'll be warm enough.

MARLENE. Goodnight. Joyce—

JOYCE. No, pet. Sorry. (*Joyce goes. Marlene sits wrapped in a blanket and has another drink. Angie comes in.*)

ANGIE. Mum?

MARLENE. Angie? What's the matter?

ANGIE. Mum?

MARLENE. No. she's gone to bed. It's Aunty Marlene.

ANGIE. Frightening.

MARLENE. Did you have a bad dream? What happened in it? Well you're awake now, aren't you pet?

ANGIE. Frightening.

COMMENTARY

Note: The following essay represents a single interpretation of the play. For other perspectives on Top Girls, *consult the essays listed below.*

The play begins in that most mundane of modern meeting places—the chic restaurant (aptly named "La Prima Donna") known for its Frascati wine and avocado vinaigrette. Into this world comes Marlene, the successful woman, newly appointed to an executive position in the "Top Girls Employment Agency" (where, ironically, women are "ordered up" like items on a menu). Significantly, Marlene is the only role that is not subsequently "doubled" because she is unalterably the prototype of the "liberated woman." Marlene meets five celebrated women: Isabella Bird, the noted Victorian explorer who liberated herself from home and hearth as she trekked across the world; Lady Nijo, a medieval Japanese concubine who became a Buddhist nun; Dull Gret, an axe-wielding revolutionary from a painting by Breughel; Pope Joan, an actual woman who disguised herself as a man to ascend to the papacy in the ninth century; and Patient Griselda, the heroine of Chaucer's "Clerk's Tale."

Wryly, Churchill implies that Marlene thinks her promotion is the equivalent of the more grandiose exploits of her famous fore-sisters. ("Well it's not Pope but it is managing director," she says to aggrandize herself.) Here the playwright is mocking what has been called "bourgeois feminism," that is, the notion women succeed only when they assume the power and professional roles traditionally assigned to men. Yet in later scenes, we see that Marlene and her staff advise would-be employees to mute their female-ness. Tellingly, Marlene denigrates her own sister (Joyce) and her "niece" (Angie) as inferior because neither has risen above her class or intellectual ability. Marlene is especially cruel in her rejection of the slow-witted Angie. "She's not going to make it," she tells a coworker, a year after telling the sister Joyce who has raised the girl, "She'll be all right." Marlene epitomizes, in effect, the very aspects of the male-dominated, socioeconomic world condemned by socialists such as Churchill. Like Margaret Thatcher, the conservative Prime Minister of England when the play was written, Marlene is so comfortable in her position as a "Top Girl" (the sexual innuendo is thematically significant) that she will not attempt to change the exploitative, patriarchal structure of the corporate hierarchy. She has become one of the "old boys" who sustains the status quo by using, even abusing, others to get "on top."

Isabella Bird, Lady Nijo, Pope Joan, and Dull Gret represent historical myths of female success: each claims the superiority of the feminine principle, yet each is eventually seen as disaffected and alienated. Each seems to have charted her destiny in male-dominated worlds, and each has triumphed (more or less) over male prejudices, though several do so primarily by assuming a male identity (symbolized by clothing). Isabella seals herself off from the world to the extent that she is neither man nor woman but only a solitary Scot trekking across the world.

As strong and successful as these women are, each is limited by her socially created attitudes about race, class, and gender.

- Isabella is devoid of human feeling and she retains a colonialist's sense of superiority ("Buddhism is really most uncomfortable").
- Lady Nijo loves the "thin silk" too much, and she dismisses her dead child as "only a girl."
- Pope Joan wants the trappings of the papacy but none of its responsibilities.
- Dull Gret (who has raised ten children—and a pig) assaults the demons of hell not for herself or her oppressed "sisters" but to protect the men and children who made her daily existence a hell.

Significantly, Patient Griselda is the last to arrive at the dinner party. She has sacrificed her children and her life to prove her fealty to her abusive husband. The rapid-fire dinner conversation (note that lines overlap contrapuntally) shows the women to be self-centered egotists more interested in personal one-upsmanship than in the problems they face as women. Thus, when Marlene toasts the gathering—"To our courage and the way we changed our lives and our extraordinary achievements"—her words ring hollow. By the end of the first scene, all the women are drunk, including Lady Nijo, who had earlier mocked the men at court for being drunkards. The Waitress, a serving woman whose presence among these "top girls" is marked by an extraordinary silence, dutifully attends them.

Things are no better in the "real" world. Marlene's associates (Nell and Win) thrive on banality and are condescending to the women who seek employment (and empowerment). Marlene, we learn, has achieved her autonomy only by abandoning her roots and her literal and metaphorical sisters. She spurns Angie, her life's blood, as an unpleasant and unwanted memory of the past. Angie (played by the same actor who earlier played the battle-scarred Dull Gret) is socially maladjusted and homicidal, the by-product of Marlene's abandonment and that quintessential macho film, *The Terminator*. Marlene's best friend, Kit, will make it because she has charm and beauty—the requisites of a "top girl" in the old patriarchal society. Only Joyce shows true heroism when she agrees to raise her sister's illegitimate child. She is motivated by neither economic nor material gain but only by the will to do something "right" for her sister. Yet even Joyce is self-hating and oppressed. We might call her "Impatient Joyce" because of the way she wearily denigrates Angie in the ugliest of sexist terms. Indeed, Churchill presents us with a "frightening" world—to borrow the play's last line—in which the price of success for women in a patriarchal-capitalist system is much too high.

While Churchill is clearly sympathetic to the plight of women, she refuses to provide comfortable solutions to the problems of inequality for her sex. There is no preaching to the choir here. Rather, she raises questions, which may illuminate the greater problems created by a system in which women must become men—or at least male-like—to get "on top."

Other perspectives on *Top Girls*:

Brown, Janet. "Caryl Churchill's *Top Girls* Catches the Next Wave." In Phyllis R. Randall (ed.), *Caryl Churchill: A Casebook*. New York: Garland, 1988, 117–30.

Burk, Juli. "*Top Girls* and the Politics of Representation." In Ellen Donkin and Susan Clement (eds.), *Upstaging Big Daddy: Directing Theatre as if Gender and Race Matter*. Ann Arbor: University of Michigan Press, 1993, 67–78.

THE BUS STOP

GAO XINGJIAN

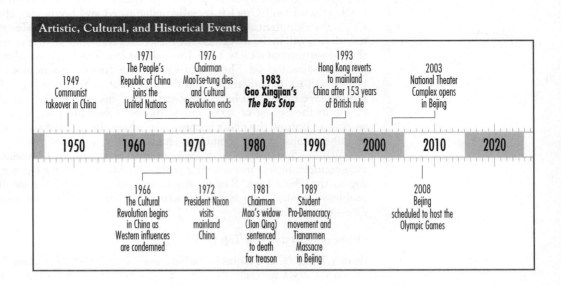

Artistic, Cultural, and Historical Events

1949
Communist
takeover in China

1971
The People's
Republic of China
joins the
United Nations

1976
Chairman
MaoTse-tung dies
and Cultural
Revolution ends

**1983
Gao Xingjian's
*The Bus Stop***

1993
Hong Kong reverts
to mainland
China after 153 years
of British rule

2003
National Theater
Complex opens
in Beijing

| 1950 | 1960 | 1970 | 1980 | 1990 | 2000 | 2010 | 2020 |

1966
The Cultural
Revolution begins
in China as
Western influences
are condemned

1972
President Nixon
visits
mainland
China

1981
Chairman
Mao's widow
(Jian Qing)
sentenced
to death
for treason

1989
Student
Pro-Democracy
movement and
Tiananmen
Massacre
in Beijing

2008
Beijing
scheduled to host the
Olympic Games

GAO XINGJIAN (1940–)

Gao Xingjian has been hailed as the first modern Chinese playwright to enter the world stage. His pioneering and experimental plays—inspired, in part, by Brecht, Artaud, and Beckett—were first produced at the People's Art Theatre of Beijing in the early 1980s. His debut, *Signal Alarm* (1982), was a tempestuous success, and the drama *The Bus Stop* (1981/1983), which established his reputation, proved both popular and highly contro- versial. The absurdist play about a varied group of contentious people waiting for a bus that never comes was condemned during the Chinese government's campaign against "in- tellectual pollution." One member of the Chinese Communist party described the play as the most "pernicious piece of writing since the foundation of the People's Republic of China." We must understand the backdrop of the Cultural Revolution to appreciate Gao Xingjian's literary accomplishments and his quest for freedom from the orthodoxies of both Marxist ideology and traditional Confucianism, and from the dramatic conventions of Chinese socialist Realism (see Showcase, "China's National Drama") and Western psy- chological Naturalism.

Gao Xingjian was born in 1940 in Guangzhou (formerly Canton) in southeastern China. His father was a bank official and his mother an amateur actress who encouraged her son's interest in theater and writing during the aftermath of the Japanese invasion and the Sino-Japanese war that followed (1937–45). He grew up under the Communist regime that took over China in 1949, receiving his basic education in the state schools of the People's Republic and taking a degree in French and literature in 1962 at the Institute of

Foreign Languages in Beijing. Although he worked for a time as a translator for the foreign language journal *China Reconstructs*, he was banished to the countryside during the Cultural Revolution (1967–77). There he worked beside peasants in a "reeducation camp" and felt it necessary to burn many of the manuscripts and drawings he had been working on since the age of ten. Nonetheless, under constant surveillance, he continued writing privately, attempting to understand himself and the value of human life despite the cruel realities he saw around him. Some of these manuscripts he has said he wrapped in plastic and buried in the ground.

After the Cultural Revolution ended, he was sent to southwest China as a schoolteacher. Not until 1979, when he was 38 years old, could he publish his work and travel abroad, which he did, first to France and Italy. Xingjian published several short stories and essays in literary magazines in China, as well as four books, including *The Art of Modern Fiction* and the *Search for a Modern Form of Dramatic Representation*, both of which gave rise to violent polemics in Beijing. In 1981, Xingjian was assigned to the Beijing People's Art Theatre and wrote *The Bus Stop*, which at first was rejected by the company because of its "nonrealistic tendencies." In 1982, he wrote *Signal Alarm*, which featured flashbacks, nonlinear sequences, and an almost musical counterpointing of objective and subjective points of view. Director Lin Zhou opted for a modernist staging with a minimum of props. When this breakthrough production moved to the theater's main auditorium, writes translator Gilbert C. F. Fong, it "aroused the authorities' suspicion and once again brought about a vehement war of words on modernism and realism."

The Bus Stop now intrigued the company and was given a short run in the banquet hall of the Beijing People's Art Theatre, but the new production was accused by one critic of imparting "a strong feeling of doubt and negativity against the existing way of life." Government authorities proscribed the play after thirteen performances and barred Xingjian from publication for one year. The proscription proved a turning point in the writer's life. Before he could be harassed or punished again with forced labor, he exiled himself to the mountains of southwestern China in order to preserve his "values, integrity and independence of spirit." He undertook a ten-month walking tour of the forest and mountain regions of Sichuan Province, searching for the traces of primitive cultures, age-old shamanistic rites, and Taoist notions that fueled the imaginations of traditional storytellers. When he returned to Beijing, he wrote *Wilderness Man*, about the destruction of nature and the environment by civilization; this experimental play has an epic structure, its thirty scenes set in timeless locales and including masked ceremonies, rituals, folk songs, and many dances. The work was well received but proved to be his last publicly performed in China. In 1986, after a trip to Europe, Xingjian completed *The Other Shore*, a complex, poetic, often dreamlike drama that questions the persecution of the individual by the collective rule of the group whose leader is a manipulator using brute force to assert his claim to power. Rehearsals of the play were ordered to stop after a month. Xingjian sensed his work would never again be performed in his native land and chose to go into exile in France in 1987.

Since then his theater works have been performed internationally, even as his emphasis has shifted from the more public subject matter of his early period to the more private and universal concerns of the plays after *The Other Shore*. Xingjian advocates what he calls a "cold literature" freed from politics, didacticism, even personal emotion. He espouses the idea of "none-ism," that is, skepticism of any authority, ideology, and prevailing artistic trend. He has written two heralded novels, *Soul Mountain* (1990), considered one of the foremost works of twentieth-century Chinese literature, and *One Man's Bible* (1999), a companion piece in which he reveals the three roles he played during the Cultural Revolution—as a leader of a rebel faction, as a victim, and as a silent observer. In 2000, he was awarded the writing world's highest honor, the Nobel Prize for Literature. "Gao Xingjian's plays are characterized by originality, in no way diminished by the fact that he has been influenced both by modern Western and traditional Chinese currents," said Professor Goran Malmqvist in presenting the prestigious award. "His greatness as a dramatist lies in the manner in which he has succeeded in enriching these fundamentally different elements and making them coalesce into something entirely new."

As You Read *The Bus Stop*

Like Wole Soyinka's *Death and the King's Horseman*, which melds traditional African and contemporary Western material, *The Bus Stop* exhibits traces of two worlds, as eight characters with generic names (Mother, Brash Young Man, Man with Glasses) pass the time waiting for a bus that never stops for them. Only one person—the elusive Silent Man—tires of the waiting game and moves away from the group, leaving behind a recurrent musical theme that wafts by "like the wind." Certain aspects of the action recall Beckett's *Waiting for Godot*. Like the tramps Didi and Gogo in the great drama by the Irishman (who also lived in exile in Paris), the characters in *The Bus Stop* toss a coin, play certain games, ask nonsensical questions, argue, and resolve to move forward, to do something about their predicament, when in fact they stand still.

As in some productions of Brecht, the actors are also instructed during certain moments in *The Bus Stop* to stop and speak directly to the audience, or to step out of their roles, breaking the dramatic illusion. This device is also common in Beijing Opera, the elaborate traditional form which Xingjian admired, especially for its technically complex, nonrealistic acting style. During certain moments in these mixed-genre opera performances, the actor freezes his movement to mark an entrance or the end of a display: he appears before the audience as neither himself nor the character. While the performance is suspended for a moment, the actor neutralizes his portrayal before taking up the role again. Other techniques you may remember from earlier playwrights are the use of overlapping monologues and simultaneous speeches that create a cacophony of human voices. Xingjian's dramaturgy here involves many sound effects for the invisible buses that roll past and for changes in the weather, but he demands a minimum of props and only a simple fence for a set. His is a theater of language with the actor paramount. Though written in Chinese when that nation was still largely cut off from the West, *The Bus Stop* is riddled with compassion and humor and ultimately hope; its themes are universal, and in this lively translation by Carla Kirkwood, it is not difficult to read or understand.

THE BUS STOP

GAO XINGJIAN

Translated by Carla Kirkwood

CHARACTERS
(In order of appearance)

A SILENT MAN	(Middle-aged)
AN OLD MAN	(In his sixties)
A YOUNG WOMAN	(Twenty-eight years old)
A BRASH YOUNG MAN	(Nineteen years old)
A MAN WEARING GLASSES	(In his thirties)
A MOTHER	(In her forties)
A MASTER CARPENTER	(Mid-forties)
MANAGER MA	(In his fifties)

(Characters should appear on stage as the age designated for them)

(At center stage stands a bus stop. Due to the wind and rain the writing appears faded. On either side of the bus stop there is a railing behind which passengers stand to form a line. The railing is in the shape of a cross, running from side to side and front to back, each in differing lengths. It suggests a crossroads, a point of intersection, a brief stopover on the road of life.)

(Characters appear on stage from various directions)

(The Silent Man comes on stage carrying a shoulder bag. He stands waiting for the bus. The Old Man enters empty-handed)

OLD MAN. Did a bus just pass?

(Silent Man nods)

OLD MAN. Are you going into town?

(Silent Man nods)

OLD MAN. You have to get here early if you're going to catch a bus on Saturday afternoon. You won't get on, if you wait until work's over.

(Silent Man smiles)

OLD MAN (*Turning to look*). No sign yet. Everyone wants to go into town on Saturday afternoon. But there are even fewer buses running and if you are a bit late you get caught in the "rush hour" traffic! Nothing you can do. As soon as everyone leaves work you should see rush of activity. Everyone packed together like sardines, pressing hard to get out. You've got to have the energy. Someone of my age hasn't got a chance! At least I have gotten here first. Those who have stopped work early have yet to make their move. I dare not even take a nap (*Yawns*). If I didn't have to go into town on business this evening I wouldn't go anywhere near the "rush hour". (*Pulls out a cigarette*) Do you smoke? (*Silent Man shakes his head*) Oh well, it is better not to. You spend money and all you end up with is cancer of the throat. I would like to smoke a really good brand, but you can't buy them. "Main Gate" is a good brand. As soon as it goes on sale people line up to buy them. The line goes all the way out into the street and wraps around a few corners. Each customer can only purchase two packs at a time. But when your time arrives, the sales clerk scowls and walks away. You ask for service, but they don't respond. Is this what they call "Serving The Customer"? It's all a front. "Main Gate" cigarettes have all gone out the "backdoor". Getting on the bus is the same thing. You follow the rules and wait in line, but someone slips ahead of you, waves to the driver and the front door opens. That's "having connections" for you. (*Snorting with contempt*) It always happens like that. When you finally get to the door it shuts with a bang! Is this what they call "Serving The Passenger"? And all you can do is stand back and watch. Everyone sees, but there is nothing you can do! (*Looking off stage*) You are first in line and I am behind you. That is the right order. In a moment, when the bus comes, this place will be a mess. Whoever has the strength to squeeze on will be the first to get a seat. That is how it usually goes.

(*Silent Man smiles*)

(*A Young Woman enters carrying a small hand bag. She stands a short distance from them*)

(*A Brash Young Man comes on stage, jumps up and sits on the railing. From his shirt pocket he pulls out a filtered cigarette, lighting it with a butane lighter*)

OLD MAN (*To Silent Man*). Look, didn't I tell you, this is how it always happens.

(*The Silent Man taps the railing with his fingers, showing agreement*)

BRASH YOUNG MAN. How long have you been waiting?

(*Old Man ignores him*)

BRASH YOUNG MAN. How often do the buses run?

OLD MAN (*Rudely*). Why don't you ask the Bus Company?

BRASH YOUNG MAN. Very funny. I was asking you.

(*The Silent Man takes out a book and reads it*)

OLD MAN. Why ask me? I am not the dispatcher.

BRASH YOUNG MAN. I asked YOU. How long have you been waiting?

OLD MAN. Young man, that is not the way to ask.

BRASH YOUNG MAN (*Realizing his mistake*). Oh, well, ah, granddad.

OLD MAN. I am not your granddad.

BRASH YOUNG MAN (*Mockingly*). Well, old boy . . .

OLD MAN. No need to call me that . . .

(*Brash Young Man disappointed, glances at the old man, starts whistling, and swings his legs back and forth*)

OLD MAN. This railing is for people to hold onto while they wait in line, it is not a place to sit.

BRASH YOUNG MAN. It's not made of rope. There's no problem if I sit here.

OLD MAN. Can't you see it is already bent?

BRASH YOUNG MAN. Because I sat on it?

OLD MAN. Isn't it bound to bend if everyone sits and rocks back and forth on it?

BRASH YOUNG MAN. Does this railing belong to you?

OLD MAN. I am only concerned because it is public property.

BRASH YOUNG MAN. Why don't you shut up? If you want to shoot off your mouth, go home to your old lady! (*Vigorously rocks the railing*)

OLD MAN (*Barely managing to remain patient, turns around sharply facing the Silent Man*). Just look at that . . . (*The Silent Man continues reading*)

(*A Man Wearing Glasses runs on stage*)

OLD MAN (*To the Young Woman*). Get in line. If you don't take your place others will get in front of you. In a minute this place will be a mess.

(*The Brash Young Man quickly jumps down from the railing, pushes forward and stands in front of the Young Woman*)

(*A Mother hurries on stage struggling with a large bag*)

OLD MAN. First come, first served.

YOUNG WOMAN (*To Old Man in a barely audible voice*). It doesn't matter. I'll just stand here.

(*The sound of a bus is heard. A Carpenter strides up carrying a tool bag. He takes his place at the end of the line. The sound of the bus is heard approaching rapidly. Everyone looks in the direction of the sound. The Silent Man puts away his book. Everyone moves forward*)

YOUNG WOMAN (*Turning around to Man Wearing Glasses*). Don't push!

OLD MAN. Get in line! Everyone get in line!

(*The sound of the bus is heard driving past. The Brash Young Man suddenly runs to the front of the line*)

EVERYONE (*Shouting at him*). Hey! Hey! Hey! (*The bus doesn't stop*) Stop! Stop! Why didn't it stop? Hey! (*The Brash Young Man chases the bus a few steps. The sound of the bus becomes faint*)

BRASH YOUNG MAN. Prick!

OLD MAN (*Furiously*). They never stop!

MOTHER. Hey! You in front, get in line.

MAN WEARING GLASSES (*To Brash Young Man*). Stand in line! Stand in line! Can't you hear?

BRASH YOUNG MAN. What's it to you? I'm in front of you.

MOTHER. There are only a few of us. It's best to line up properly.

MAN WEARING GLASSES (*To Brash Young Man*). You're behind them. (*Points to the Silent Man and the Old Man*)

OLD MAN (*To the Silent Man*). No upbringing.

BRASH YOUNG MAN. Did you have any upbringing?

MOTHER. Can't you be reasonable and wait in line?

OLD MAN (*Precisely and deliberately*). I said that if you cannot wait in line, you cannot have had any upbringing.

BRASH YOUNG MAN. Hey if you've got a itch, scratch it, don't hassle me.

MOTHER. It's not right that young people should behave this way.

MAN WEARING GLASSES. Everyone has asked you to get in line. Why can't you be sensible?

BRASH YOUNG MAN. Who isn't getting in line? The bus didn't stop. I pushed forward and called out. Why are you shouting at me?

MAN WEARING GLASSES. You are supposed to be behind the others!

BRASH YOUNG MAN. In front of you will do nicely.

OLD MAN (*Trembling with rage*). Get in line!

BRASH YOUNG MAN. What do you think you are doing? Do you think I am scared of you or somethin'?

OLD MAN. You want to hit me, is that it?

(*Silent Man walks over in front of the two men. The Brash Young Man sees that the Silent Man is strongly built. Being a bit scared he moves back a step and leans against the railing trying to act "cool"*)

BRASH YOUNG MAN. If you're so smart, why can't you stop the bus? (*Leans against the railing and rocks back and forth*)

OLD MAN. Young man, your education was a waste!

BRASH YOUNG MAN. What's it to you? If you're so educated and cultured how is it you don't ride in a car?

OLD MAN. There is no shame in standing in line for a bus. It shows public awareness. Weren't you taught that?

BRASH YOUNG MAN. I didn't get that lesson!

OLD MAN. What about your parents?

BRASH YOUNG MAN. Your mother taught you didn't she? So how come you didn't get on the bus?

(*Old Man is speechless for a moment. He looks at the Silent Man who has started reading again*)

BRASH YOUNG MAN (*Pleased with himself*). Old man, if you've never pushed onto a bus then everything you've learned is absolutely worthless!

MAN WEARING GLASSES. Everyone is waiting for the bus, be a bit more aware of that.

BRASH YOUNG MAN. Ain't I in line? In front of you.

MAN WEARING GLASSES. You came after her. (*Points to the Young Woman*)

BRASH YOUNG MAN. Okay, so she'll go first. But when the bus comes she'd better be able to push her way on.

YOUNG WOMAN (*Turning away*). Disgusting!

BRASH YOUNG MAN (*To Old Man*). If you can push your way on, that's okay with me. But, don't block those behind you who can. You are so sensible and cultured old man, but do you know how to squeeze onto a bus? I haven't had much schooling, but I know how to force my way onto a bus.

(*Sound of a bus heard*)

MOTHER. The bus is coming, everyone get in line.

BRASH YOUNG MAN (*Leaning on the railing, to the Young Woman*). I'm right behind you. But if you can't squeeze on don't blame me if I push you.

YOUNG WOMAN (*Frowning*). Just go in front of me.

(*The sound of the bus comes nearer. The Silent Man puts his book away. The Carpenter, who has been squatting on the ground, stands up. Everyone moves forward*)

MAN WEARING GLASSES (*To Young Woman*). To get on all you have to do, once the door opens, is grab onto the inside handle then pull yourself sideways up the steps.

(*The Young Woman looks at him without responding. Everyone moves forward in the direction of the bus. The Brash Young Man stands outside the railing, behind the Young Woman*)

OLD MAN. Stop! Stop!

MAN WEARING GLASSES. Hey! Stop!

MOTHER. We have been waiting a long time!

YOUNG WOMAN. The last one didn't stop either!

BRASH YOUNG MAN. You damned . . .

CARPENTER. Hey!

(*All the passengers chase the bus to one side of the stage. The Brash Young Man suddenly rushes forward. The Man Wearing Glasses grabs him. The Brash Young Man knocks his hand away. The Man Wearing Glasses catches the Brash Young Man's sleeve. The Brash Young Man turns around and hits him. The sound of the bus is heard disappearing in the distance*)

MAN WEARING GLASSES. How dare you hit me!

BRASH YOUNG MAN. Yeah. What are you going to do about it? (*They start fighting*)

OLD MAN. A fight, a fight!

MOTHER. I cannot believe how young men carry on nowadays!

YOUNG WOMAN (*To Man Wearing Glasses*). Just stay away from him.

MAN WEARING GLASSES. Hoodlum.

BRASH YOUNG MAN (*Rushing forward*). I'll kick your ass!

(*The Silent Man and the Carpenter separate the two men*)

CARPENTER. Stop it! Stop it! Haven't you had enough?

MAN WEARING GLASSES. Filthy hoodlum!

BRASH YOUNG MAN. You damned bastard!

MOTHER (*To Brash Young Man*). That is an awful thing to say. Don't you have any shame?

BRASH YOUNG MAN. What gives him the right to grab my clothes?

MAN WEARING GLASSES. I gave him a little tug. Why didn't you stay in line?

BRASH YOUNG MAN. You act pretty tough with everyone else around. But if you've got any guts, let's go somewhere else and see how tough you really are.

MAN WEARING GLASSES. Stinking hoodlum! I'm scared of you! (*The Brash Young Man pushes forward against him. The Carpenter grabs the Brash Young Man's wrist, preventing him from moving*)

CARPENTER. Why are you causing trouble? Get to the back of the line.

BRASH YOUNG MAN. What's it to you?

CARPENTER. Get to the back! (*Twisting his wrist he leads the Brash Young Man to the back of the line*)

OLD MAN. Right. Don't let him cause trouble and stop us from getting on. (*The Silent Man doesn't hear and continues to read*)

BRASH YOUNG MAN. I was near the front! So, you get to go into town but I don't, is that it?

MOTHER. No one is stopping you.

OLD MAN (*To Mother*). We're all going into town on business and he has to make trouble. We must be careful. Pickpockets always stir up trouble when you're getting onto a bus. (*Everyone quickly checks for their wallet, except for the Carpenter and Silent Man*)

BRASH YOUNG MAN. What makes you think you're so smart, you old fart?

(*The Young Woman and the Mother look at one another and grin. The Old Man glances at them disapprovingly*)

MOTHER (*Hurriedly changing the subject. To Man Wearing Glasses*). It is not worth it to tangle with him. Besides, if you did fight, you'd lose.

MAN WEARING GLASSES (*Acting heroically*). No one is going to get on the bus with troublemakers like him around. Are you going into town?

MOTHER. My husband and children live there. It's such a headache trying to catch a bus on Saturdays. It's like getting into a fight.

MAN WEARING GLASSES. Why don't you move into town?

MOTHER. Who wouldn't like to live and work in the city? But you have to have contacts to do that!

YOUNG WOMAN. Twice the bus has passed without stopping.

MAN WEARING GLASSES. The bus doesn't leave the terminal until it is full. (*To Young Woman*) Do you have any business in town? (*She nods her head*) Actually, if you want to catch the bus you'd best go to the terminal. Where do you live? (*She glances at him cautiously without replying. The Man Wearing Glasses, feeling put off, pushes his glasses higher up on his nose. The Silent Man, becoming impatient, closes his book, turns to look for the bus, then returns to his book*)

OLD MAN. It's infuriating. I must be at the Cultural Center promptly at seven.

MOTHER. You seem to be in high spirits. Are you going into town to see a play?

OLD MAN. No such luck. Plays are only for city folk, aren't they? I'm going in for a game of chess.

MOTHER. What?

OLD MAN. A game of chess. You know, the chariot, the horse, the cannon! Don't you recognize them? The general!

YOUNG WOMAN. Oh, you mean chess! You sound very excited about it.

OLD MAN. Young woman, I have played all my life.

MAN WEARING GLASSES. Everyone needs to have a special interest in life. If you don't have something you're enthusiastic about, what's the point of living.

OLD MAN. You are absolutely right! I have studied every book there is on chess, from Master Zhang's "Complete Secret Commentaries on Chinese Chess" to the newly published "One Hundred Ways to End a Chess Game". I can show you every move. Do you play?

MAN WEARING GLASSES. When I have the time I do.

OLD MAN. It's not just a game. It requires careful study and specialized skill.

MAN WEARING GLASSES. Yes, it is difficult to play well.

OLD MAN. Have you heard of Li Mo Sheng?

MOTHER (*Noticing that her bag is too close to the Carpenter's tool bag, she moves it nearer to her. To Carpenter*). Are you a carpenter?

CARPENTER. Yes.

MAN WEARING GLASSES (*To Old Man*). Which Li Mo Sheng?

MOTHER (*To Carpenter*). Do you work on Saturdays?

CARPENTER (*Unwilling to reply*). Hmmm.

OLD MAN. You play chess and you don't even know who Li Mo Sheng is?

MAN WEARING GLASSES (*Apologetically*). I don't seem to recall . . .

MOTHER (*To Carpenter*). Do you repair chair legs? At my house . . .

CARPENTER (*Interrupting her*). I am a cabinet maker!

OLD MAN. Don't you read the evening papers?

MAN WEARING GLASSES. I have been busy lately preparing for the university entrance exam.

OLD MAN (*Losing interest*). In that case you really don't know the "ins and outs" of the game.

MOTHER (*Turning to the Young Woman*). Do you live in the city?

YOUNG WOMAN. No. I have something to do there.

MOTHER (*Eyeing her up and down*). Meeting your boyfriend?

(*Young Woman nods shyly*)

MOTHER. Is he nice? What does he do? (*The Young Woman looks down and scrapes the ground with her toe*)

MOTHER. Are you going to get married soon?

YOUNG WOMAN. What a thing to say. (*Taking out her handkerchief from her bag, fans herself*) Why doesn't the bus come?

MAN WEARING GLASSES. The bus dispatcher is probably gossiping and has forgotten the time.

MOTHER. Is this any way to "Serve The Passenger"?

OLD MAN. It's the passengers that serve them! Obviously if no one ever waited at the bus stop, no one would know they exist! We'll just have to wait patiently.

MOTHER. I could have done a load of washing in the time that we've been waiting.

YOUNG WOMAN. Do you have to do the washing when you get home on Saturdays?

MOTHER. That's "Married Life" for you. My husband only knows how to read books, nothing else. He can't even wash a handkerchief clean. Don't have a bookworm as a boyfriend. If only my husband knew how to maneuver better, I would have had a job in town long ago.

OLD MAN. That's your own fault. Can't you get him to move out to the countryside? How can you bear this every week, waiting and pushing and shoving to get on a bus?

MOTHER. I've got a son to think of! My baby. Schools out here aren't very good. Very few children get into the university. The city schools are much better. (*Pointing her lips in the direction of the Brash Young Man*) I can't spoil my child's future and have him turn out like that.

(*Sound of a bus is heard*)

YOUNG WOMAN. The bus is coming!

MAN WEARING GLASSES. The bus is really coming, and it's empty!

MOTHER (*Picking up her bag*). Don't push! All of us can get on and we'll all get seats.

BRASH YOUNG MAN (*To Old Man*). You'd better watch your step. Don't fall over or lose your wallet. It would be pretty embarrassing if you couldn't find the money for your ticket.

OLD MAN. Don't be so ignorant young fellow! Sooner or later it will be your turn to cry! (*To Everyone*) No need to hurry. Everyone get in line.

(*Everyone looks lively and lines up in order. Sound of the bus coming is heard*)

(*Manager Ma hurries on, coat wide open swinging his arms, and goes directly to the front of the line*)

EVERYONE. Hey! Get in line. What's going on, don't you know the rules? Get to the end of the line!

MANAGER MA (*Objectively*). I just want to have a look. You stay in line.

MAN WEARING GLASSES. Haven't you ever seen a bus before?

MANAGER MA. I've never seen anyone like you before! (*Glares at him angrily*) I am looking for someone. (*The sound of the bus is heard passing by them without stopping. Manager Ma rushes forward*)

MANAGER MA (*Waving his hands in the air*). Hey! Hey! Wang! Mr. Wang! It's me! Old Ma from the Co-op Market! (*Everyone becomes disorganized and chases after the bus*)

MAN WEARING GLASSES. Why didn't it stop?

YOUNG WOMAN. Several have passed without stopping. Please stop!

MOTHER. There were only a few people on it, why didn't it stop?

MANAGER MA (*Pointing and shouting after the bus*). Take me. Open the front door. I am Manager Ma from the Co-op! Pick me up!

OLD MAN (*Pointing and cursing at the driver*). Have you ever seen a driver like this before? Does he care about the passengers?

CARPENTER. You old woman!

BRASH YOUNG MAN (*Picks up a stone and throws it at the bus*). I'll smash you! (*The sound of the bus becomes fainter. The Silent Man stares after it blankly*)

MANAGER MA. All right! You bus station employees better not ask me for a favor again!

OLD MAN. Are you the manager of the Co-op?

MANAGER MA (*Pretentiously*). What is it?

OLD MAN. Do you know that driver?

MANAGER MA. They've changed over. It's damned pragmaticism. Since I've never done him any favors he's not going to do me any. A boss's kindness is not appreciated.

OLD MAN. So you have no influence over him?

MANAGER MA. That's an end to those good relations. From now on if any of those station people come to me for anything, I'll do things by the rules! (*Pulls out a cigarette*) Cigarette?

OLD MAN (*Trying to make out the brand name*). No, thank you. I seem to have left my glasses at home.

MANAGER MA. "Main Gate".

OLD MAN. It is very hard to get those.

MANAGER MA. Sure! Why just the other day I let the bus station employees buy twenty cartons from me. I never thought they would treat me like this.

OLD MAN. Can you sell me a carton, wholesale?

MANAGER MA. It's not so easy with goods in short supply. They're very difficult to get.

OLD MAN. Oh, I see. All the "Main Gates" have disappeared through the "backdoor". No wonder the bus didn't stop.

MANAGER MA. What do you mean?

OLD MAN. Nothing.

MANAGER MA. What do you mean, "nothing"?

OLD MAN. Nothing at all

MANAGER MA. What do you mean, "nothing at all"?

OLD MAN. "Nothing at all" means "nothing at all".

MANAGER MA. Your "nothing at all" means "nothing at all" has some meaning.

OLD MAN. What do you mean?

MANAGER MA. Your "nothing at all" means "nothing at all" obviously has some meaning behind it! You mean that I, Manager Ma, take the lead in using the "backdoor". Don't you?

OLD MAN. That is what you say.

(*Silent Man impatiently paces back and forth*)

MAN WEARING GLASSES (*Reading aloud English word cards*). Book, pig, desk, dog, pig, dog, desk, book.

CARPENTER. Which country's English is that?

MAN WEARING GLASSES. English, it's just English. It doesn't belong to any country. This is American English. British and Americans both speak English, but their accents are different. Nowadays you have to take a foreign language examination in order to get into university. I never studied one before, so I must start from scratch. I can't waste precious time waiting at bus stops.

CARPENTER. You go ahead and read. Read.

(*The Mother and Young Woman speak separately but simultaneously toward the audience*)

MOTHER. My son is waiting for me to come home and prepare sweet dumplings . . .

YOUNG WOMAN. I promised to meet him at 7:15 this evening, at the park gate, opposite the main . . .

MOTHER. He doesn't like white sugar, sweetened bean paste or nutmeat centers . . .

YOUNG WOMAN. . . . road under the third lamppost. I was to take my red leather handbag . . .

MOTHER. . . . in his dumplings. He only likes the ones made with sesame . . .

YOUNG WOMAN. . . . with me. He said he'd be leaning against his "flying pigeon" bicycle.

MOTHER. . . . seed centers . . .

(*The Silent Man walks in front of the two women and looks at them gloomily. They stop talking*)

MANAGER MA (*To Old Man*). What do you call goods that are in short supply?

OLD MAN. Things you cannot buy.

MANAGER MA. Customers may refer to them as items that "cannot be bought" but for our commercial department they are referred to as goods "in short supply". This situation creates a contradiction between supply and demand. How would you resolve this contradiction?

OLD MAN. I am no manager.

MANAGER MA. True, but you are a customer! Can you give up smoking?

OLD MAN. I've tried several times.

MANAGER MA. Do you know that it is bad for your health?

OLD MAN. Yes, I know.

MANAGER MA. You know, but still you smoke? You see, it is all very well to have propaganda. We have family planning propaganda year after year don't we? But are the numbers of those who bear children reduced? The population as a whole has gone up. Adults who smoke don't seem to be able to give up and young people scarcely out of the womb are becoming addicted, one after the other. The numbers of those who smoke grow faster than the tobacco plants needed to make the cigarettes. Now, do you think that this conflict between supply and demand can be resolved?

(*The Silent Man slings his bag over his shoulder, starts to leave, then stops*)

MAN WEARING GLASSES (*Reading aloud*). Open your books! Open your pigs. Wrong! Open your dogs. Wrong! Wrong!

OLD MAN. Can't you produce more?

MANAGER MA. That's a reasonable question. But how can the commercial department resolve this? It's the production department's problem. I can only do favors for those who have some relationship to me. You criticize me for using the "backdoor", but you tell me how "Main Gate" can be opened up for wider sales? What do you say? There will always be people who can get them and people who can't. Now there wouldn't be any conflict if everyone could buy them, would there?

YOUNG WOMAN. I'm fed up.

MOTHER. Oh, you don't realize it now, but when you're a mother you'll have even more problems to deal with.

(*The Silent Man turns around. His eyes meet the Young Woman's. She immediately glances downward, shyly. The Silent Man doesn't notice, strides off stage without looking back. Light music begins to rise, music which sounds mournful and searching. It gradually fades out. The Young Woman looks in the direction of the Silent Man with a sense of loss*)

CARPENTER. Let me cut in for a minute. (*Manager Ma and the Old Man turn around.*) No, not you two, you go on with your little chitchat.

MANAGER MA. You think I am just chattering away? Well, I'll have you know that I am trying to explain something to a customer. (*Continuing to persuade the Old Man*) You have a lot of gloom, but you don't have any real knowledge as to how a commercial department functions. Do you admit that? Do you think it is really easy to be a manager? You should try it!

OLD MAN. I'm not capable.

MANAGER MA. Go on, give it a try.

OLD MAN. All right, I get your point! I give in!

MANAGER MA (*To Carpenter*). There, did you see? Did you see?

CARPENTER. See, what? You mean that teacher over there with the glasses on.

MAN WEARING GLASSES (*Making sentences*). Do you speak English? I speak a litter . . .

BRASH YOUNG MAN (*Imitating him in a strange tone*). ai——si——ke——a——ai——li——tu——r——

MAN WEARING GLASSES (*Indignantly*). Are you pig?

BRASH YOUNG MAN. Crap!

YOUNG WOMAN. Don't argue. I can't stand it!

CARPENTER (*To Man Wearing Glasses*). Teacher, what time is it by your watch?

MAN WEARING GLASSES (*Looks at his watch and is surprised*). What? How can that be?

CARPENTER. Has it stopped?

MAN WEARING GLASSES. Yes it has stopped . . . a year has gone by.

YOUNG WOMAN. You're kidding!

MAN WEARING GLASSES (*Looking at his watch again*). It's true. We have been waiting at this stop for a whole year! (*Brash Young Man puts his fingers in his mouth and whistles loudly*)

OLD MAN (*Glaring at them*). Nonsense!

MAN WEARING GLASSES. How is it nonsense? If you don't believe me, look at your watch.

CARPENTER. Hush. It's nothing.

MOTHER. Why, it's only 2:40 p.m. by my watch.

BRASH YOUNG MAN (*Walks over to her*). It's stopped.

CARPENTER. What are you shouting about? (*To Old Man*) Look at yours.

OLD MAN (*Trembling and with difficulty gets out his pocket watch*). How can it be wrong?

BRASH YOUNG MAN. You're probably looking at it upside down.

OLD MAN. Ten past . . . one. It's stopped.

BRASH YOUNG MAN (*Gloating*). It's not as good as the others. It's like you—old!

MANAGER MA (*Shaking his wrist and listening to the watch*). How come mine has stopped, too?

MOTHER. Look at the date. Does it have a calendar?

MANAGER MA (*Looking at it*). Month—the thirteenth, day—the forty-eighth. That's strange! But this is an imported Omega!

BRASH YOUNG MAN. Maybe it's insides are made of plastic.

MANAGER MA. Get out of here!

MAN WEARING GLASSES. My watch can't be wrong, it's quartz. Look, it's still running. I bought it last year and it has never stopped! It's a six function quartz watch: year, month, day, hour, minute and seconds. Look, a whole year has passed!

CARPENTER. You're making everyone nervous. What's so good about quartz watches? Some of them aren't all that accurate.

OLD MAN. We must trust science. Quartz watches are a product of science and science doesn't play tricks! This is the electronic age. Something must have gone wrong.

MOTHER. That would mean that we have been waiting for the bus for exactly one year.

MAN WEARING GLASSES. Yes, exactly one year. One year, three minutes and one second . . . two . . . three . . . four. There, look at it, it is still running.

BRASH YOUNG MAN. Hey, you guys. That's right. It's really a fuckin' year. (*Young Woman runs away covering her face with her hands. Everyone looks at her seriously*)

MOTHER (*Thinking aloud*). They won't have had a change of clothes for ages. He can't do anything. He can't mend clothes. My baby must be crying his heart out. My poor child.

(*The Young Woman squats down. Everyone slowly gathers around her*)

MAN WEARING GLASSES (*Speaking softly*). What's the matter?

CARPENTER. Maybe she's hungry. I have a corn biscuit in my bag.

OLD MAN. Do you have a stomach ache?

MANAGER MA (*To the audience in a loud voice*). Is there a doctor around? Could anyone with medical knowledge take a look at her?

MOTHER (*Taking control of herself. Walks over and bends down to the Young Woman*). Where does it hurt? Tell me. (*She strokes the Young Woman's head. The Young Woman buries her head in the Mother's chest, crying silently*) It's a female problem! The rest of you leave us alone. (*Everyone walks away*) Tell me. What is the matter?

YOUNG WOMAN. I feel ill.

MOTHER (*Stroking her*). Come on. (*She sits down on the ground. The Young Woman lays across her. She whispers questions in the Young Woman's ear*)

OLD MAN (*Looking very old*). The chess match must be over by now.

MANAGER MA. Were you only going into town for a game of chess?

OLD MAN. I have been waiting and waiting for this game. I have waited all my life.

YOUNG WOMAN. No! No! He won't wait for me any longer!

MOTHER. Silly girl. He'll wait.

YOUNG WOMAN. No, no! You don't understand.

MOTHER. How long have you known each other?

YOUNG WOMAN. This was to be our first date. At 7:15 pm. At the entrance to the park, opposite the main road, under the third lamppost.

MOTHER. You've never met him before?

YOUNG WOMAN. One of my classmates who works in town made the introduction.

MOTHER. Don't be upset. You'll find someone else. There are plenty of nice young men in the world.

YOUNG WOMAN. No one will ever wait for me again.

MANAGER MA (*Facing the audience. Thinking aloud*). I must go. Wasn't I only going into town to have something to eat and drink at the Tongqinglou Restaurant? I was invited by an "associate". It's not worth waiting a whole year for something like that. I have things to drink at home. Like that famous maotai in the white ceramic bottle with the red silk ribbon around the neck. All I need do is ask and it is mine. I don't even need to move, someone will fetch it for me. It's not worth the trip! It's not worth it!

OLD MAN (*Excitedly*). I must play in that chess match.

MANAGER MA (*To the audience*). He is a chess fanatic. There are all kinds of strange people in the world. Waiting a whole year at a bus stop for a game of chess. (*To Old Man sympathetically*) I often play chess, but I am certainly not as taken with it as you are. You are addicted to chess. Why don't you come to my house? We'll have a couple of drinks and I will help you satisfying your craving for drinking and playing and play-

ing and drinking. Now why is someone of your age hanging around at this bus stop? Come with me.

OLD MAN (*With contempt*). With you?

MANAGER MA. Old fellow, among the hundred or so people that work at the Co-op, including ten or so section and group leaders there is no one who can beat me in a game of chess. If you don't believe me go and ask them yourself.

MAN WEARING GLASSES (*Reading out loud*). PIG, BOOK—DESK—DOG . . . K . . . G . . . K . . .

OLD MAN (*Trembling with emotion*). Do you . . . Do you read the evening newspaper?

MANAGER MA. I never miss a day! I order the evening newspaper. It arrives at the Post Office around noontime and gets to the Co-op in the afternoon. I keep it to read after my evening meal. By the end of the evening I know everything that is going on in town.

OLD MAN. Have you heard of Li Mo Sheng?

MANAGER MA. Hey, you mean that famous new opera actor? He's great!

OLD MAN. You think you are a chess player. I am referring to the current national chess master.

MANAGER MA. Oh, do you mean the chess champion called Li something or other? He has the same surname as my wife's family.

OLD MAN. What do you mean, champion? He has a ways to go yet.

MANAGER MA. Does that mean that you could become the champion?

OLD MAN. All the moves of Li's championship game are printed in the evening newspaper. I've researched this. The only reason he does well is because he lives in town. If I lived in town . . .

MANAGER MA (*Smiling*). Then you would be champion?

OLD MAN. I didn't say that. Anyhow, I wrote a letter to Li Mo Sheng and fixed a game with him. That was to be tonight at the Cultural Center. Ha, tonight, one year ago. I made the appointment. I can't cancel it! I can't go back on my word!

MANAGER MA. That's true.

MAN WEARING GLASSES (*Trying hard to remember*). BIK, POOK,——This is very difficult!

BRASH YOUNG MAN. PiPi, PaPa. Are you still doing your western farts?

MAN WEARING GLASSES (*Impatiently*). I'm not like you. You hang around with nothing to do. I must get into the university. This is my last chance. If no bus comes, I will have passed the age limit for registration. Waiting and waiting. It's a shame to waste one's youth. You can't possibly understand that! Get out of here.

BRASH YOUNG MAN. I'm not stopping you.

MAN WEARING GLASSES (*Pleading*). Please go away! Just leave me alone, alright? There are lots of places for you to hang around.

BRASH YOUNG MAN. I can't in town! (*Walks away, totally bored, then bursts out*) Only the people in town can strut down city streets. I'm a person, aren't I? Aren't I? Why can't I go for a stroll in town? Well, I will!

CARPENTER (*Getting upset*). What in the hell are you shouting about? Can't you just sit down and have a rest? (*He squats down, tears off a piece of newspaper. From his bag he pulls out some tobacco, shreds it and rolls it into a cigarette. It is very quiet. The light slowly fades and the sound of a bus is heard in the distance. Music representing the Silent Man is heard. Everyone listens. It is like the wind, then fades out*)

MANAGER MA (*To the audience*). All of them are under an evil spell. (*To everyone*) Hey, haven't you given up? Aren't you going?

BRASH YOUNG MAN. Going where?

MANAGER MA. Going back.

BRASH YOUNG MAN. I thought you were going into town.

MANAGER MA. What do you think I am, crazy? Go all the way into town just for some rotten wine. I'm not that desperate.

BRASH YOUNG MAN (*Unhappily*). I want to go into town to eat some yogurt.

MANAGER MA. I am talking to someone! Why did you interrupt? (*To Old Man*) If you don't go, I'll go by myself. (*Everyone looks at each other. Pondering the idea*)

OLD MAN. Hmmmm. (*Looks at Manager Ma, stupefied*)

MOTHER (*Looking at Old Man*). You. . . .

YOUNG WOMAN (*Looking at Mother*). Oh . . .

MAN WEARING GLASSES (*To the Young Woman, sadly*). You . . .

CARPENTER (*Watching the actions of the Man Wearing Glasses*). Hey. (*Manager Ma walks over to the Carpenter, gestures to him, hinting that he follow him out. The Carpenter keeps watching the Man Wearing Glasses. Manager Ma lowers his head and stares at the Carpenter's tool bag. Ma kicks the tool bag. Everyone stops looking at each other.*)

BRASH YOUNG MAN. Hey, where is that guy? Did he sneak off?

OLD MAN. Who?

BRASH YOUNG MAN. You're senile. The guy that was standing here in front of you. He must've slipped off without telling anyone.

EVERYONE (*Except for the Young Woman, very excited*). Who? Who are you talking about? Who's gone?

OLD MAN (*Suddenly remembers, slaps his thigh*). Of course. I talked to him earlier. He left without saying anything.

MOTHER. Who? Who did you say left?

MAN WEARING GLASSES (*Remembering*). You mean the guy wearing the shoulder bag? He stood at the head of the line reading a book.

MOTHER. Yes. When you were fighting, he tried to stop you.

CARPENTER. Right. Now, why didn't I notice when he left?

MAN WEARING GLASSES. He could have gotten on the bus.

MANAGER MA. Did they open the door for him?

YOUNG WOMAN (*In the dark*). The bus didn't stop. He went into town alone.

MANAGER MA (*Pointing both ways*). Did he go this way, or that way?

YOUNG WOMAN. He went along the main road into town.

MANAGER MA. Did you see him?

YOUNG WOMAN (*Depressed*). He glanced at me, then walked away without looking back.

MAN WEARING GLASSES. He's probably already reached town.

BRASH YOUNG MAN. No shit!

OLD MAN (*To Young Woman*). Why didn't you say something earlier?

YOUNG WOMAN (*Terrified and nervous*). Wasn't everyone waiting for the bus . . .

OLD MAN. He planned that well.

YOUNG WOMAN. He didn't blink an eye when he looked at you as though he were looking through you.

MANAGER MA (*Nervously*). He couldn't be a cadre come to investigate from town? Did he pay any attention to what we were saying when I was doing my ideological work with the old man?

YOUNG WOMAN. He wasn't listening then, he paced back and forth. He seemed to have something on his mind.

MANAGER MA. He wasn't gathering information, was he? For example, my cigarette shortage solution—selling "Main Gate" through the backdoor!

YOUNG WOMAN. I didn't hear him say anything.

MANAGER MA. Why didn't you report the problem with the Bus Company to him? The public is very dissatisfied.

OLD MAN. In such times it's difficult to go out. (*Twisting the railing with his hand thoughtfully*) In this traffic it is hard to know what is what. I hope we are not standing at the wrong bus stop.

CARPENTER (*Uneasy*). What are you saying old man? Isn't this the stop for town?

OLD MAN. Maybe we should catch the bus on the other side.

MAN WEARING GLASSES (*Looking across the street*). That's the bus going the other way.

CARPENTER (*Relieved*). Oh, old man, you really had me worried. (*He squats down*)

OLD MAN (*Trembling, to the audience*). Are you waiting for the bus? (*To himself*) I can't hear. (*Speaking louder*) Are you waiting for the bus that goes into the countryside? (*Talking to himself*) Still can't hear me. (*To Man Wearing Glasses*) Young man, I'm hard of hearing. Could you please ask them if they are going to the countryside? If they're all waiting to go back, I won't bother going into town.

MANAGER MA (*Shakes his head and sighs*). The town is not paradise you know! Let's go back! My son is likely to be getting married soon. (*To Carpenter*) Are you a carpenter?

CARPENTER. Uh huh.

MANAGER MA. Could you make some furniture for my son? I promise I'll make it worth your while.

CARPENTER. No.

MANAGER MA. In addition to your payment, I'll throw in food and two foil wrapped packs of "Main Gate" cigarettes for each day of work. (*To himself*) Stop talking about those "Main Gate" cigarettes. If the control section investigator of the commercial bureau heard me, that would be bad. Hey, I still don't know about the quality of your workmanship.

CARPENTER. I am a cabinet maker. I work in hardwoods. I make traditional chairs carved out of rosewood. I make sitting room screens out of ebony. My skill was handed down from generation to generation. Do you really think that you can afford me?

MANAGER MA. Really fine talk. But let me tell you, the fashion in the city is to use sofas. Who wants your old-fashioned armchairs that are hard on the bum?

CARPENTER. My work is for people to look at, not to sit on.

MANAGER MA. Hmm. Interesting. I am always up with the newest things. You do work exclusively for decorative purposes, do you?

CARPENTER. I don't have to drum up business. These days you won't find people with my level of skill. The Export-Import Co. in town has asked me to take on apprentices.

MANAGER MA. You can wait here, go ahead and wait. Anyway, I am going back. Is anyone going with me?

(*Silence. The lights dim. The sound of a bus is heard in the distance. The Silent Man's music is heard, faintly but distinctly. Its probing rhythm becomes clearer*)

MAN WEARING GLASSES. Listen, listen. Do you hear that? (*Music fades out*) How come you didn't hear it? That man is already in town. We can't wait any longer. Pointless waiting, useless suffering.

OLD MAN. It's true. I have waited all my life, just like this. Waited and waited and now I am old.

MOTHER (*Simultaneously*). If I had known the journey was going to be so difficult I wouldn't have brought such a large bag. It's sesame seeds and red dates, a pity to throw them away.

YOUNG WOMAN (*Simultaneously*). I'm worn out. I'm probably as pale as a sheet, too. I don't want anything anymore. All I need is a good sleep.

BRASH YOUNG MAN. Stop all this bullshit! We could have crawled into town by now.

CARPENTER. Go ahead, crawl.

BRASH YOUNG MAN. You crawl and we'll follow.

CARPENTER. My hands are used for skilled work. I am not a sewer maggot!

MAN WEARING GLASSES (*To audience*). Hey! Are you still waiting for the bus? No sound. (*Louder*) Is anyone over there waiting for the bus?

YOUNG WOMAN. It's pitch dark, I can't see anything. It's night time. There won't be anymore buses.

CARPENTER. Then we'll wait for it til dawn. The bus stop is right here, they can't fool us.

MANAGER MA. What if it doesn't come? Will you wait for it like an idiot your entire life?

CARPENTER. I have my craft to offer. They want my skill in town. What have you got to offer?

MANAGER MA (*Hurt*). I won't go into town even though people have invited me for a meal!

CARPENTER. Why don't you just go home then?

MANAGER MA. I have been thinking about going back for a long time. (*Worried*) In this desolate place, "no village ahead, no inn behind". Why a dog could leap out at me from the darkness. Hey, who wants to go back with me?

OLD MAN. I want to go back, but the pitch dark road back makes it difficult. Aye!

BRASH YOUNG MAN (*Standing up slapping his thighs*). Are you ready to go?

MANAGER MA. Let's go together.

BRASH YOUNG MAN. Who wants to go with you? I'm going into town to get some yogurt.

CARPENTER. What can that possibly taste like? Turning good milk sour? It's like the beer they have in town, tastes like horse piss! Not everything in the city is so good.

BRASH YOUNG MAN. I like it. That's the only reason I'm going there. I can down five bottles in one sitting. (*To Man Wearing Glasses*) Let's not waste time with the rest of them. Let's you and me get out of here.

MAN WEARING GLASSES. What if the bus comes just after we're gone? (*Faces the audience, speaking out loud*) What if the bus comes but it doesn't stop? Logically, I feel I should go, but I am not sure. It just might come. I don't fear anything but I fear this I AM I. I am I! But you don't believe in yourself, instead you believe in this! (*Mockingly flips the coin*) Heads we wait, tails we go. We will decide it with one toss! (*Tosses the coin, it falls to the ground. He covers it with the palm of his hand*) Go or wait? Wait or go? Let's see what our fate is!

YOUNG WOMAN (*Pressing her hand against his*). I'm afraid! (*Realizing that she is touching him, quickly pulls back her hand*)

MAN WEARING GLASSES. Are you afraid of your own fate?

YOUNG WOMAN. I don't know, I don't know anything.

BRASH YOUNG MAN. These two are really great. Do you want to go or not?

CARPENTER. Is this ever going to end? Those who want to go, go! The bus stop is right here. We are all waiting, so why doesn't the bus come? How will the drivers get paid if they don't take our ticket money? (*Silence. The sound of a bus and the Silent Man's music rise up simultaneously. The music becomes clearer and the rhythm becomes distinct*)

MANAGER MA (*Waving his hand, as though he were driving away the distraction*). Hey, does anyone want to go? (*Music fades out. The Old Man is leaning against the sign dozing, he snores*)

OLD MAN (*Without opening his eyes*). Is the bus coming? (*No one replies*)

BRASH YOUNG MAN. This is boring, all of us hangin' around under this sign. (*He does a hand stand and dejectedly sits on the ground. Everyone squats or sits on the ground. The sound of a bus is heard but no one moves. They listen attentively. The sound of the bus increases. Lights come up*)

BRASH YOUNG MAN (*Lying on his stomach*). It's coming! Hey!

MOTHER. At long last. Old man, wake up now. It's daylight and the bus is coming!

OLD MAN. Is it coming? (*Stands up quickly*) It is!

YOUNG WOMAN. It won't just pass by again, will it?

MAN WEARING GLASSES. If it isn't going to stop this time, we will block the road!

YOUNG WOMAN. It won't stop.

OLD MAN. If it doesn't stop, they won't be doing their job.

MOTHER. But what if it doesn't stop?

BRASH YOUNG MAN (*Suddenly jumping to his feet*). Carpenter, do you have any large nails in your toolbag?

CARPENTER. What for?

BRASH YOUNG MAN. If it doesn't stop, I'm going to puncture its tires. Then no one will be able to go into town!

YOUNG WOMAN. Don't do that! It's against the law to sabotage the bus system.

MAN WEARING GLASSES. Let's form a line and stand in the road to block it!

CARPENTER. Alright!

BRASH YOUNG MAN (*Picks up a stick*). Hurry, the bus is coming!

(*Sound of the bus coming closer is heard. Everyone stands up*)

YOUNG WOMAN (*Shouting*). Stop!

MOTHER. We've already waited a whole year!

OLD MAN. Hey, hey—stop!

MANAGER MA. Hey—(*Everyone crowds around the front of the stage, blocking the road. The sound of the bus horn is heard*)

MAN WEARING GLASSES (*Directing Everyone*). Okay—one, two—

EVERYONE. Stop! Stop! Stop!

MAN WEARING GLASSES. We have been waiting here a whole year for no reason.

EVERYONE (*One after the other, shouting and waving their hands*). We can't wait any longer! Stop! Stop bus! Stop! Stop! Stop! (*The bus doesn't stop. The sound of the horn is heard*)

OLD MAN. Get out of the way! Hurry, move aside!

(*Everyone hurriedly moves aside and chases after the bus, shouting*)

BRASH YOUNG MAN (*Rushes forward waving a stick*). I'll get you!

MAN WEARING GLASSES (*Grabbing the Brash Young Man*). It'll run you over!

YOUNG WOMAN (*Frightened, closing her eyes*). Ahhh——

CARPENTER (*Running out, grabs the Brash Young Man*). Don't you want to live??

BRASH YOUNG MAN (*Struggling free, chases after the bus, then throws the stick*). Damn you! I hope you fall in the goddamn river and get eaten by turtles! (*The sound of the bus is heard in the distance. Silence*)

CARPENTER (*At a loss*). All of the passengers were foreigners!

MOTHER. It's a touring bus for foreigners.

MAN WEARING GLASSES. What is so impressive about that? Buses are not only for foreigners!

OLD MAN (*Muttering to himself*). It wasn't even full.

CARPENTER (*Sadly*). Wouldn't it be alright to stand? I'd pay for my ticket.

MANAGER MA. Do you have any foreign currency? They only take foreign currency.

OLD MAN (*Stomping his foot*). This is not a foreign country!

YOUNG WOMAN. I said that it wouldn't stop and it didn't.

(*At this point bus after bus passes in front of them. Some in one direction some in the other, some of different colors and with different sounds*)

MANAGER MA. This is too . . . too infuriating. They are just monkeying around with us. If they aren't going to stop they shouldn't put a sign here! If the bus company doesn't get organized, this traffic problem will not improve! You should write a letter of complaint and I will personally hand it to the transport authorities. (*Pointing to the Man Wearing Glasses*) You, write!

MAN WEARING GLASSES. What do I write?

MANAGER MA. What do you write? Like this. Like this and like this. Hey, you mean an intellectual like you doesn't even know how to write a letter of complaint?

MAN WEARING GLASSES. What good would that do? Won't we still be waiting?

MANAGER MA. Well, you can wait here if you like. Why should I worry? I decided a long time ago not to go into town for that meal. I was anxious for you. Wait then. It serves you right. Wait. (*Silence. The music of the Silent Man gently rises and then quickly changes to a quick three beat tempo. There is a sense of irony to it.*)

MAN WEARING GLASSES (*Looks at his watch, startled*). Oh, no!

(*The Young Woman moves closer to look at his watch. In the following sequence the rhythm of the music follows the months as they are read aloud*)

MAN WEARING GLASSES (*Repeatedly pressing the button, following the changes on the digital read out*). May, June, July, August, September, October, November, December . . .

YOUNG WOMAN. January, February, March, April——

MAN WEARING GLASSES. May, June, July, August——

YOUNG WOMAN. One year and eight months.

MAN WEARING GLASSES. Another year has passed.

YOUNG WOMAN. Two years and eight months.

MAN WEARING GLASSES. Two years and eight months, . . . No! That's wrong! It's three years and eight months. No! Wrong! Five years, six . . . no, seven months, eight months, nine months, ten months . . .

(*Everyone looks at each other startled*)

BRASH YOUNG MAN. Goddamn it, this is crazy!

MAN WEARING GLASSES. I am perfectly normal!

BRASH YOUNG MAN. I'm not talking about you. I was saying that, that thing is crazy.

MAN WEARING GLASSES. It can't be crazy. A watch is merely an instrument that measures time. Time cannot be affected by human madness.

YOUNG WOMAN. Please, please, don't talk, alright?

MAN WEARING GLASSES. Don't try and stop me. No. It has nothing to do with me. You can't stop time from slipping away. Look, all of you, look at my watch! (*Everyone crowds around him*)

MAN WEARING GLASSES. Six years, seven years——eight years, nine years——As we speak a full ten years have passed!

CARPENTER. Are you certain? (*Grabs him by the wrist, shakes it, listens and stares at the watch*)

BRASH YOUNG MAN (*Moves forward and pulls out the button on the watch*). Ah, ha! Why is there no number showing? Hey, it's blank! (*He grabs a hold of the Man Wearing Glasses's hand and holds it up in the air*) If you pull it out, it won't work! (*Pleased with himself*) This thing is just trying to scare all of us.

MAN WEARING GLASSES (*Seriously*). What do you know? Just because it's blank doesn't mean that time isn't passing by. Time has an objective reality! It can be calculated through mathematical formulas. T is equal to the square root of alpha plus beta times sigma, something something squared. This formula is part of Einstein's Theory of Relativity!

YOUNG WOMAN (*Hysterically*). I can't stand it! I can't stand it!

OLD MAN. Preposterous! (*Coughs*) They make us wait at this stop for no reason until we are old and gray . . . (*Immediately appears very old*) Ridiculous. Ridiculous . . .

CARPENTER (*Profoundly sad*). Can the Bus Company be deliberately plotting against us? But why I haven't done anything to them?

MOTHER (*In a state of utter exhaustion*). My baby, my poor child and husband. They have no clean clothes to change into. By now they must be too tattered to wear . . . He doesn't even know how to use a needle and thread . . . (*The Brash Young Man walks to one side kicking a stone back and forth. Then, depressed, sits on the ground, legs open, lost in thought*)

YOUNG WOMAN (*Stupefied*). I want to cry.

MOTHER. Go ahead and cry. There is no shame in it.

YOUNG WOMAN. The tears won't come.

MOTHER. Who meant us to be women? It is our fate to wait, to wait endlessly. First, we have to wait for a young man to seek us out and then have a hard time getting married. Then we must wait for a child to be born, then for the child to grow up. By then we are old ourselves . . .

YOUNG WOMAN. I have waited and now I am old . . . (*Leans on the Mother's shoulder*)

MOTHER. If you want to cry, let go and cry. You'll feel relieved if you do. I would like to fall into his arms and cry . . . For no reason . . . I can't say why . . .

MANAGER MA (*Sadly to the Old Man*). Old man, is it worth it? Why didn't you stay at home in comfortable retirement? You could have passed the time painting, playing music and chess. But you had to go into town and find yourself a match. Exposing your old self to the road for those knotty pieces of wood. Is it really worth it?

OLD MAN. What do you know? For you everything is business. Playing chess takes effort and spirit! In order to live in this world, you have to have a sense of spirit! (*The Brash Young Man, bored, walks behind the Man Wearing Glasses and pats him hard on the shoulder, disturbing the Man Wearing Glasses who is lost in thought*)

MAN WEARING GLASSES (*Indignantly*). You don't know what it is to suffer, that is why you are so insensitive! Life has cast us aside. The world has forgotten us. Life is just passing by in front of you. You don't understand! I can't live like this, I can't . . .

CARPENTER (*Unhappily*). I cannot go back. I work in finely crafted hardwoods. I am not going into town just to earn money. I have a skill. I can make a living in the countryside making beds, dining tables and cupboards. But how can I allow myself to do such simple work? My skill was handed down from my ancestors. You are a manager, you can't understand that.

MAN WEARING GLASSES (*Pushing the Brash Young Man away*). Go away! Leave me alone! (*Bursts out suddenly*) I need quiet! Do you understand? Quiet! Quiet! (*Brash Young Man leaves obediently, starts to whistle, then pulling his finger out of his mouth stopping himself*)

YOUNG WOMAN (*Towards the audience, speaking out loud*). I used to dream a lot . . . Some of them were wonderful . . .

MOTHER (*To audience, speaking out loud*). Sometimes I also wanted to dream.

(*The following sequences are spoken at the same time, overlapping, towards the audience*)

YOUNG WOMAN. I dreamt the moon could laugh . . .

MOTHER. But I always fell asleep as soon as I lay on the bed, always exhausted and sleepy, never getting enough sleep . . .

YOUNG WOMAN. I dreamt that he held my hand and whispered in my ear. I wanted to be near him . . .

MOTHER. As soon as I opened my eyes, I would see my son's socks worn through, his toes sticking out . . .

YOUNG WOMAN. Now I have no dreams . . .

MOTHER. His father's wool sweater unravelling at the sleeve . . .

YOUNG WOMAN. Now no black bear rushes after me . . .

MOTHER. My baby wanted a toy, a small battery powered car . . .

YOUNG WOMAN. There is no one ferociously chasing me . . .

MOTHER. It costs twenty cents to buy a pound of tomatoes . . .

YOUNG WOMAN. I won't dream anymore . . .

MOTHER. This is the heart of a mother. (*Turning towards the Young Woman*) I was not like this when I was your age.

(*The following is a dialogue between the two women*)

YOUNG WOMAN. You don't know. I have changed. I've become very narrow minded. I cannot stand to see other women wearing nice clothes. I know this isn't right. But when I see a girl from the city wearing high heeled shoes, I get upset. I feel that they are trampling down on me, that they are trying to irritate me. I know this isn't right.

MOTHER. I understand, you are not to blame. . . .

YOUNG WOMAN. You don't understand. I am jealous, really jealous . . .

MOTHER. Don't talk nonsense. It's not your fault.

YOUNG WOMAN. I have always wanted to wear a polka dot dress with a zip fastener around the waist. But I dare not make such a dress. It would be fine in the city, people wear them everywhere there. But I could never go out in one out here. What do you think?

MOTHER (*Stroking the girl's hair*). Wear what you want. Don't wait until you are my age. Your are still young. a young man will take a fancy to you and you will fall in love. You will have a child and his affection for you will grow.

YOUNG WOMAN. Go on, go on . . . Do I have any gray hair?

MOTHER (*Looking through her hair*). None, really!

YOUNG WOMAN. Don't lie to me!

MOTHER. Only one or two.

YOUNG WOMAN. Pull them out.

MOTHER. You can't really see them. You can't pull them out. The more you pull them, the more there will be.

YOUNG WOMAN. I beg you, please. (*The Mother pulls out the gray hair. Suddenly she embraces the Young Woman and starts crying*)

YOUNG WOMAN. What's wrong?

MOTHER. I have a lot of gray hair. Is it all gray?

YOUNG WOMAN. No, none . . . (*Embracing the Mother, they both cry*)

BRASH YOUNG MAN (*Sitting on the ground, slaps a bank note down on the ground. From his pocket he takes out three poker cards and tosses them on the ground*). Who wants to play? A five dollar bet! I'll play just this once.

(*The Old Man digs into his pocket*)

BRASH YOUNG MAN. Don't bother to check your pockets. I earned this workin' on the side. If you're lucky you can pick up something for nothing. I'm not waiting. (*The Old Man and Manager Ma crowd around*) Which of you is betting? In the left hand—three dollars, in the right—two dollars. I'll bet this five bucks, it was for my ticket into town and my yogurt.

MANAGER MA. You're young, why don't you learn something useful?

BRASH YOUNG MAN. Oh shut-up. Go back and teach your own son. Old man, why not try your luck? Choose two sides, you can't lose. It's only five dollars, isn't it? If you win you're in luck, if you lose, well then you are unlucky. A man of your age shouldn't care so much about a few dollars. If there were a wine shop near, why I would buy everyone some. (*Carpenter walks over*) Ace, King, Queen, take your pick. (*Carpenter hits him on the back*) Alright, I'm not going into town. I won't drink yogurt. (*Crying out loudly*) The streets in town are for the fuckin' city people to walk in!

OLD MAN. Pick them up! Young man, pick them up. (*The Brash Young Man wipes his eyes and nose with his dirty hand, picks up the money and cards. Bends his head down, sobbing. Silence. The sound of a bus in the distance is heard, mixed with the Silent Man's music. The music has a quick tempo which changes to a lively melody*)

MAN WEARING GLASSES. The bus won't come. (*Determined*) Let's leave the way that man did. For the time we have been waiting, he has not only arrived in town, but also has accomplished something. It's silly to wait here.

OLD MAN. You're right. Oh, young woman, don't cry. If you had gone with the silent man, you'd probably be married by now with a child, and your child would be walking. We've waited and waited. Now I am all hunched over. (*With difficulty*) Let's go. (*Staggers a bit. Man Wearing Glasses hastens to support him*) I am just afraid I won't be able to make it. (*To the Mother*) Are you going?

YOUNG WOMAN. Should I still go into town?

MOTHER (*Straightening the Young Woman's hair*). You have been treated unjustly. Is there no one who wants such a good girl? I'll introduce you to someone! (*Looking for her bag*) I shouldn't have brought such a heavy bag.

YOUNG WOMAN. I'll carry it for you.

MANAGER MA. Oh, is this your shopping?

OLD MAN. Are you going or not?

MANAGER MA. Old man, the town is not so great. (*Lost in thought*) As far as living is concerned, the village is more peaceful. All other things aside consider what it is like to cross the street in town. The red light and green light, in the blink of an eye, a car can run you over!

CARPENTER. I'm going!

BRASH YOUNG MAN (*His spirits restored*). You think you are so important. Do you want us to carry you in a big sedan chair?

MANAGER MA. Are you taking the piss? With my high blood pressure and hardened arteries. (*Indignantly*) I don't need this aggravation. I forgot to take my medicine. It has a double soaked compound of wolfberries and formalin. (*Turns back before exiting*) It calms my nerves, gives me energy and rejuvenates me.

(*Everyone watches as he exits*)

OLD MAN. He's gone back?

MOTHER (*Muttering to herself*). He's gone.

YOUNG WOMAN (*Weakly*). Don't go back!

BRASH YOUNG MAN. He'll go his way. We'll go ours.

CARPENTER (*To Man Wearing Glasses*). Why don't you go?

MAN WEARING GLASSES. I want to have one last look to see if the bus is coming or not. (*Takes off his glasses, wipes them and puts them back on. Everyone scatters in different directions. Then wander back and forth hesitantly. Some want to go, some stop abruptly, bumping into each other*)

OLD MAN. Get out of my way!

BRASH YOUNG MAN. You go your way.

MOTHER. This is really confusing

MAN WEARING GLASSES. Ah, life . . . life . . .

YOUNG WOMAN. What kind of life is this?

MAN WEARING GLASSES. This is life. Aren't we alive?

YOUNG WOMAN. Better to be dead.

MAN WEARING GLASSES. Then why don't you die?

YOUNG WOMAN. Come into the world and then just die. It's not worth it!

MAN WEARING GLASSES. Life should have meaning.

YOUNG WOMAN. Not dying, yet living like this is pointless! (*Everyone walks around in their original place, as if they are possessed*)

CARPENTER. Go!

YOUNG WOMAN. No——

MAN WEARING GLASSES. Aren't we going?

BRASH YOUNG MAN. Let's go!

MOTHER. Now

OLD MAN. Let's go! (*Silence. Sound of raindrops*)

OLD MAN. Is it raining?

BRASH YOUNG MAN. Old man, if you keep dawdling around like this it will start hailing.

CARPENTER (*Looks at sky*). The weather changes so quickly!

MOTHER. It's begun to rain. (*Sound of heavy rain falling*) What shall we do?

OLD MAN (*Mumbling to himself*). It would be best to find shelter.

YOUNG WOMAN (*Taking the Mother's hands*). Let's go. If we get soaked, so what?

BRASH YOUNG MAN (*Stripping to the waist*). If we don't go, we'll get drenched for nothin'. Spirit of the sky, rain down what you will, rain knives if you want.

MAN WEARING GLASSES (*To Young Woman*). It's no good if we catch cold. We'll get drenched.

CARPENTER. It's just a rain shower. It's nothing. When the clouds pass it will be over. (*From his toolbag he takes out a sheet of waterproof material and covers the Old Man and the Mother*)

MOTHER. This craftsman is very thoughtful.

CARPENTER. I spend most of my time outside. The wind and the rain are unavoidable. I am used to them. (*To the others*) Hey come take cover. (*Rain pours down. Man Wearing Glasses and Young Woman stand next to each other silently, under the waterproof sheet*)

CARPENTER (*To Brash Young Man*). Are you being foolish again? (*Brash Young Man slips under the rain cloth. Lights dim*)

OLD MAN. This autumn wind and cold rain don't bother you much when you are young, but when you get old and rheumatic, then you'll know how terrible it is.

MAN WEARING GLASSES (*To the Young Woman*). Are you cold?

YOUNG WOMAN (*Shivers*). A little.

MAN WEARING GLASSES. You have nothing on. Here, take my jacket.

YOUNG WOMAN. What about you?

MAN WEARING GLASSES. It doesn't matter. (*His teeth chatter from the cold*)

BRASH YOUNG MAN (*Pointing to the Man Wearing Glasses's watch*). Is it still working? Is it the year of the donkey, the month of the horse already?

YOUNG WOMAN. Don't look at it! Please!

MOTHER. We really don't know what year or month it is.

YOUNG WOMAN. It's better not to know.

(*Sound of the wind and rain. The following dialogue takes place against the background of the wind and rain. The voices mix together*)

BRASH YOUNG MAN. Ah, the water in the stream is rising up . . . we could catch some fish now . . . old man I'll have a bet with you . . .

YOUNG WOMAN (*Simultaneously*). . . . just sitting here like this . . . raining and raining. The wind is very cold . . . but my heart is warm and . . . leaning on his shoulder sitting together just like this . . .

MAN WEARING GLASSES (*Simultaneously*). . . . It's all right like this . . . foggy fields facing the hills, the future, life, all of it obscured . . . she is very gentle . . . honest . . . good . . .

OLD MAN. Young fellow, you are not so young. If you continue this way how will you ever have a family and make something of yourself?

YOUNG WOMAN (*Simultaneously*). Your glasses are fogged up.

MAN WEARING GLASSES (*Simultaneously*). She is so beautiful . . . How can I have only just now discovered it . . . ah, the fog, don't wipe it off, it makes everything dream like . . .

(*The following dialogue is divided into three overlapping groups. There is a contrast between strong and weak dialogue, as indicated. Sometimes one group is prominent, sometimes another*)

GROUP ONE

OLD MAN (*Forcefully*). You should learn a skill, otherwise no young woman will have you.

BRASH YOUNG MAN (*Forcefully*). Unless someone takes me on, it would be useless to . . .

OLD MAN (*Forcefully, glancing at the Carpenter*). Isn't he standing in front of you?

BRASH YOUNG MAN (*Forcefully, with confidence*). Craftsman, are you taking on apprentices?

CARPENTER (*Less forcefully*). That depends on what they are like.

BRASH YOUNG MAN (*Less forcefully*). What sort of apprentice do you require?

CARPENTER (*Less forcefully*). To take up a trade is different from going to school, you must be nimble fingered and hardworking.

BRASH YOUNG MAN (*Forcefully*). How about me?

CARPENTER (*Forcefully*). You have a bad attitude.

GROUP TWO

MAN WEARING GLASSES (*Less forcefully*). I've already lost my opportunity to go to university. I'm over the age limit. What else can I do? My youth has passed me by without my even knowing it.

YOUNG WOMAN (*Less forcefully, nudging him with her shoulder*). Why don't you go to night school? Correspondence school? You could qualify. You could.

MAN WEARING GLASSES (*Forcefully*). Do you think so?

YOUNG WOMAN (*Forcefully*). Yes I do. (*He squeezes her hand quietly*) That's not right. Don't do that. (*Young Woman draws back her hand, turns and takes a hold of the Mother's arm with both hands. He puts his hands around his knees and listens to their conversation*)

GROUP THREE

MOTHER (*Weakly*). Once, when I was walking along the road at night it was raining. It rained without stopping. I felt that someone was following me. I turned my head to look, the rain was so heavy, I couldn't see clearly. But I knew there was a person holding an umbrella, not far from me. When I sped up, they sped up. When I slowed down, so did they. I was frightened. My heart was beating quickly . . .

YOUNG WOMAN (*Less forcefully*). Then what?

MOTHER (*Less forcefully*). I finally managed to make it to my front door. (*At this point everyone begins talking together*) I stood still. The person following me walked over beneath a street light. I noticed that they were also female and frightened. She was afraid because she had no companion and frightened that she had come across an evil person.

CARPENTER. There aren't many bad people in the world. Nevertheless you must be on your guard. I do not scheme against others yet others may scheme against me.

OLD MAN. The horrible part is the scheming. I push you, you trample me. If everyone looked after each other life would be better.

MOTHER. We would all get along, if people cared more for each other.

CARPENTER (*The stage is quiet. The winter wind blows mournfully*). Let's move in . . .

OLD MAN. Closer together.

MAN WEARING GLASSES. Everybody, back to back.

MOTHER. It's warmer this way.

YOUNG WOMAN. I'm afraid I'll get tickled.

BRASH YOUNG MAN. Who's gonna tickle you? (*Everyone squeezes closer together. The loud winter wind carries in the voice of Manager Ma*)

CARPENTER (*To Brash Young Man*). What's that shouting over there? Go and look.

BRASH YOUNG MAN (*Sticking his head out from under the waterproof sheet*). It's Manager Ma from the Co-op.

MANAGER MA (*Offstage*). Wait—Wait, don't move! (*Manager Ma runs on shivering and hurriedly burrows beneath the rain cover*)

MOTHER. Your wet clothes will make you ill, hurry, take them off.

MANAGER MA. I didn't get very far before . . . (*Sneezing*) Ahhh choo . . .

OLD MAN. You were the one that wanted to go back. If you had stayed with us you wouldn't look like a chicken that fell into the soup.

MANAGER MA. Ah! You're still alive!

OLD MAN. I can't just give up half way. Are you still going into town for supper with your "associate"?

MANAGER MA. Are you still waiting to play that long finished game of chess?

OLD MAN. Can't I go into town to meet a chess partner?

MOTHER. Stop arguing.

MANAGER MA. It's his annoying mouth!

OLD MAN. Look to your own conduct.

MOTHER. We are all trying to keep dry together under this waterproof sheet.

MANAGER MA. He started it . . . ahhhh—ahhh (*Not being able to complete the sneeze*)

MOTHER. You'll feel better when the sun comes out.

MANAGER MA. Ah, this rain!

OLD MAN. This isn't rain, it's snow. (*Each person stretches out their hands and feet in a different direction checking for snow*)

YOUNG WOMAN. It's rain.

MAN WEARING GLASSES (*Sticking out his foot to test the ground*). It's snow.

BRASH YOUNG MAN (*Runs out and jumps around*). Goddamn, it's hailing.

CARPENTER. Are you crazy kid! Hold it up! (*The Brash Young Man obediently runs back and holds up the cover. The storm gains strength. Other sounds of cars starting and stopping and zooming past can be heard. The Silent Man's music starts again, this time louder and stronger than before*)

MOTHER. Anyway, we can't go anywhere. (*Tidying up her bag*) We don't know how many years or months we must wait until . . . This rain and snow will fall forever.

MAN WEARING GLASSES (*Head lowered, reciting from English flash cards*). IT IS RAIN, THAT IS SNOW.

OLD MAN (*Drawing a chess board on the ground*). The cannon at seven score equals eight, horse nine at score is five.

YOUNG WOMAN (*Lost in thought, she walks out towards the audience. With each step her character changes. By the time she has reached the audience she is completely out of character. The main stage lights gradually dim until they are completely dark*). It doesn't matter whether it is rain or snow, or if it is three years or five years or ten years. How many decades do you have in a lifetime?

(*The following characters speak in unison*)

YOUNG WOMAN. Your life has been held up, just like this.

MAN WEARING GLASSES (*Simultaneously, but weakly*). IT RAIN, IT RAINED.

OLD MAN (*Simultaneously but even weaker*). Horse at nine forward eight, cannon at four back three.

YOUNG WOMAN. Held up like this. But will we be held up like this forever?

MAN WEARING GLASSES. IT IS RAINING, IT WILL RAIN.

OLD MAN. Pawn at six score is equal to five, chariot at five forward one.

YOUNG WOMAN. Are you going to complain like this, suffer like this?

MAN WEARING GLASSES. IT SNOW, IT SNOWED.

OLD MAN. Guard at five back six, cannon at four score equals seven.

YOUNG WOMAN. Are you going to wait shamelessly forever, suffer shamelessly? Endlessly?

MAN WEARING GLASSES. IT IS SNOWING AND IT WILL SNOW.

OLD MAN. Chariot at three forward, five, ahhh—guard at five back six!

YOUNG WOMAN. The old are already old and the newly born are about to enter the world.

MAN WEARING GLASSES. RAIN IS RAIN, SNOW IS SNOW.

OLD MAN. Chariot at three forward two, cannon at four back one—

YOUNG WOMAN. After today there will still be a today. The future is always the future.

MAN WEARING GLASSES. RAIN IS NOT SNOW, SNOW IS NOT RAIN.

OLD MAN. Elephant five at ahh, back three, cannon at four back one.

YOUNG WOMAN. Are you going to go on waiting like this? Complaining all of your life?

MAN WEARING GLASSES. RAIN ISN'T SNOW AND SNOW ISN'T RAIN.

OLD MAN. Elephant at seven back five, chariot at three forward seven, the general!

(*Stage lights come up. Young Woman has already returned to the stage and her character. The sound of the wind and rain has stopped*)

CARPENTER (*Looking up at the sky*). I said the rain wouldn't last long. Isn't the sun coming out again? (*To the Brash Young Man*) Pack up the rain cloth.

BRASH YOUNG MAN. Okay! (*Promptly folds up the rain cloth*)

MOTHER. Are we going now?

YOUNG WOMAN (*Looking at Man Wearing Glasses*). Are we?

OLD MAN. Which way?

BRASH YOUNG MAN. Into town, eh craftsman?

CARPENTER. Just follow me.

OLD MAN. Into town? Will I be able to make it at my age?

MAN WEARING GLASSES. You'd have to walk back home, wouldn't you?

OLD MAN. You are right.

MOTHER. But my bag is so heavy.

MAN WEARING GLASSES. Ma'm, let me carry it for you! (*Picks up the large bag*)

MOTHER. Thank you very much. (*To Old Man*) Old man, be careful, watch your step. Don't slip in the water.

YOUNG WOMAN. Look out! (*Grabs the Old Man, supporting him*)

OLD MAN. You walk in front of me. Don't let an old man hold you back. If I lie down someplace, please take the time to dig a hole for me. Don't forget to place a plaque on it which reads: "Here lies a chess fanatic who, upon his death, had no regrets. He had no skill, he simply played chess his whole life. Always hoping to get the chance to go to the Cultural Center to display his talent. He waited and waited until he was old and useless. He died on the road into town."

YOUNG WOMAN. What are you saying?

OLD MAN. Good girl! (*Looking at Man Wearing Glasses, who appears uneasy and pushes his glasses up on his nose*) Manager Ma, are you going or not?

MANAGER MA. Yes I am! I am going into town to report the Bus Company! I will look for their manager and ask who in the hell are they driving the buses for? Is it for their personal convenience or to "Serve The Passengers"? They must be held responsible for making passengers suffer like this. I am going to sue them and ask that they pay for the aging of the passengers and their damaged health.

YOUNG WOMAN. Don't be funny, you can't sue for something like that.

MANAGER MA (*To Man Wearing Glasses*). Look at the sign, which stop is this? What time is it by your watch? Write it all down and then we will settle the account with the Bus Company.

MAN WEARING GLASSES (*Looking at the sign*). Why doesn't this sign have a name on it?

OLD MAN. Strange.

MANAGER MA. Why would they put a sign here with no name? Look at it again, more closely.

YOUNG WOMAN. It doesn't have one.

BRASH YOUNG MAN. Craftsman, we have waited here for nothing. They've cheated us.

OLD MAN. Look again, how can they have a sign with no name on it?

BRASH YOUNG MAN (*Walks over to the other side of the sign. To Man Wearing Glasses*). Come and have a look. It looks like a piece of paper has been pasted over this sign with only the mark remaining.

MAN WEARING GLASSES (*Looking carefully*). Maybe it was a notice.

MANAGER MA. Where did it go? Look for it!

YOUNG WOMAN (*Looking around the ground*). What with the rain and wind it will have long since disappeared. There's not even a trace left.

BRASH YOUNG MAN (*Climbing on the railing, looking at the sign*). The mark of the paste has turned gray.

MOTHER. Can it be that this stop has been removed? Just last Saturday I was . . .

YOUNG WOMAN. Which last Saturday?

MOTHER. Wasn't it last, last, last, last, last, last, last, last . . .

MAN WEARING GLASSES. Which last Saturday, of which month, of which year are you talking about? (*Lifts his watch up to look at it*)

BRASH YOUNG MAN. Don't look. It's blank. You should have changed the battery long ago!

CARPENTER. No wonder the bus didn't stop.

OLD MAN. Have we waited here for nothing?

MAN WEARING GLASSES. Yes, we have.

OLD MAN (*Upset*). Why is this sign still standing here? Isn't it cheating people?

YOUNG WOMAN. Let's go! Let's go!

MANAGER MA. No, we should sue them!

MAN WEARING GLASSES. Who will you sue?

MANAGER MA. The Bus Company. It won't do to mess passengers around like this! I will sue, even at the risk of losing my own managerial position!

MAN WEARING GLASSES. You should sue yourself then! Who made us not see things clearly? Who made us wait? Let's go, waiting is useless!

CARPENTER. Let's go!

EVERYONE (*Murmuring*). Let's go, let's go, let's go, let's go, let's go, let's go.

OLD MAN. Will we be able to reach the town?

MOTHER. Isn't it possible that the bridge has been destroyed by floodwaters and the road into town is blocked?

MAN WEARING GLASSES (*Impatiently*). With all the buses that have passed, how could it be blocked?

(*Again the sound of a bus is heard in the distance. Everyone silently looks toward it. Now the sounds are heard coming from all directions. Everyone appears to be at a loss as to what to do. The sound of a heavy, noisy bus is heard approaching. The music of the Silent Man encompasses them, like the universe. The music floats over the sounds of the heavy vehicles. Everyone stares straight ahead. Some walk toward the audience, some stay on stage. All of the actors step out of character. The light gradually changes as the actors drop their roles. The state is no longer bathed in light, but in different levels, some strong, some weak. The main lights fade out.*)

(*The following lines are spoken simultaneously by the seven actors. First person, second person, third person and so forth, speak alternately, linking together, forming a group, and resolving in complete sentences*)

ACTRESS PLAYING THE YOUNG WOMAN—FIRST PERSON. Why don't they go? Hasn't what needed to be said been said? . . . Then why don't these people go? Time has slipped away needlessly . . . I don't understand . . . I simply don't understand . . . Why don't any of them leave? . . . If you really wish to go, you must go . . . But tell them to go quickly! Why do they still not leave? . . . Let's all go, quickly . . .

ACTOR PLAYING MANAGER MA—SECOND PERSON. Sometimes people must wait. Have you ever had to wait in line to buy a fish? Oh, I see, you don't cook. Well you have probably waited in line to catch a bus, right? Waiting in a line is merely waiting. If you have been waiting in a line for a long time and it turns out that they aren't selling fish after all but washboards—[by the way the washboards made in the city are of the highest quality, they never destroy clothes], and you have a washing machine—well then you waited a long time for nothing. You can't help but be angry. So you can say it doesn't matter that you wait, what matters is that you know what you are waiting for. If you wait in line, wait half of your life in vain, perhaps even your whole life, well now isn't the joke on you?

ACTOR PLAYING THE CARPENTER—THIRD PERSON. . . . Waiting doesn't matter, people wait because they have hope. It would be sad if people had no hope . . . In the words of the man wearing glasses, it would be "desperate". Desperation is like drinking poison. Poison is used to kill mosquitos and flies. Why would someone drink it and suffer? Worse still, what if it doesn't kill you and you end up having to go to the hospital and get your stomach pumped? By the way, have you ever gone walking at night? In the huge wilderness where the sky is cloudy and it's pitch dark and it seems the more you walk the more you can't help but get lost, right? You must wait until daybreak, but aren't you the fool if daybreak comes and you are still found hanging around?

ACTRESS PLAYING THE MOTHER—FOURTH PERSON. . . . The mother says to her son: walk my dear child, walk. Children never learn to walk if you don't first let them crawl. Of course sometimes you must help them. Let them lean on the wall and walk from one corner to the other and then to the door . . . You must allow them to fall, then help them up. Small children don't learn to walk if they don't first stumble. A mother must have patience. Otherwise you are not fit to be called a mother. So, you see, it is difficult to be a mother. But then, it isn't easy to be human, is it?

ACTOR PLAYING THE OLD MAN—FIFTH PERSON. They always say that it is more difficult to play comedy than it is to play tragedy. If it is a tragedy the audience may not necessarily cry, but the actor must. This is not the case with comedy. If the audience doesn't laugh, you cannot very well laugh by yourself . . . What is more, if the audience doesn't laugh you can't make them laugh by reaching out and tickling them. So, it is more difficult to play comedy than tragedy. It is obvious when a play is a comedy, but you must appear to have a sad face and reveal one by one all the funny things in life to the audience. This is why it is said: performing comedy is much more difficult than tragedy.

ACTOR PLAYING THE BRASH YOUNG MAN—SIXTH PERSON. I don't understand . . . It seems they are waiting . . . Of course this isn't a bus stop . . . It isn't a terminal . . . They want to go . . . They should go . . . They have said all there is to say . . . We are waiting for them . . . Ahh, let's go . . .

ACTOR PLAYING MAN WEARING GLASSES—SEVENTH PERSON. . . . I don't understand why they are waiting . . . But time is not a bus stop . . . Life is also not a bus stop . . . I don't want to go . . . But let's go . . . What needed to be said has been said . . . We are waiting for them . . . Let's go!

(*From all different directions buses are heard rapidly approaching, mixed with the sound of the horns of different types of vehicles. At center stage the lights brighten. All the actors return to their characters. The music of the Silent Man changes into a grand but humorous marching tune*)

MAN WEARING GLASSES (*Looking at the Young Woman tenderly*). Let's go.

YOUNG WOMAN (*Nods*). Ah.

MOTHER. Where is my bag?

BRASH YOUNG MAN (*Cheerfully*). I'm carrying it.

MOTHER (*To Old Man*). Watch your step. (*Supporting the Old Man with her hand*)

OLD MAN. Thank you very much.

(*Everyone, looking after each other, starts off*)

MANAGER MA. Hey, hey wait! Wait! Wait! Wait! I've got to tie my shoelaces!

Blackout

First draft, July 1981—Beidaihe—Beijing

Second draft, January 1982—Beijing

First performed—Beijing People's Art Theatre

COMMENTARY

Note: The following essay represents a single interpretation of the play. For other perspectives on The Bus Stop, *consult the source listed below.*

Many years pass during the stage time of *The Bus Stop*. Early on, the Man Wearing Glasses notes that his watch has stopped and a year has gone by since he and the others began waiting for the Saturday afternoon bus to take them into town. Nonetheless, the Old Man, who realizes the chess game he wanted to play must be over by now, doesn't budge even when the Manager offers him a chess game at his home. The Manager, who at first seemed so competent and bold in his threats toward the irresponsible bus company, also stays where he is. The group accepts the condition of waiting as their fate, for they are fearful—each in a different way—to go back where they came from and unable to break their current pattern and perhaps walk to town. Long after the Silent Man leaves them, this group of waiters finally notices he is gone. "He glanced at me, then walked away without looking back," says the Young Woman, depressed now that she has missed two chances to connect: first with the date waiting for her in town, and later with the silent one whom she might have accompanied on his journey. The Silent Man clearly made a quiet individual decision to move forward on his own; he may represent the courageous individual breaking away from the timid collective. Certainly this is how the Chinese authorities "read" the play when they proscribed it for its negative depiction of life in 1980s China.

Many "criticisms" of the less than ideal state do emerge from the dialogue and debates staged by Xingjian in the play. The Old Man and the Manager argue about the black market cigarettes this bureaucrat lets out "the backdoor," making them unavailable to the common people in what is supposed to be a share-and-share-alike communist state. The Brash Young Man treats his elders and others with disrespect. The Mother whines about her unsatisfactory marriage and the poor quality of village schools. The Carpenter laments that his traditional craftsmanship, passed on from generation to generation, is no longer valued amidst the mass-produced goods in the marketplace of the city. The Man Wearing Glasses, who seeks an education and knowledge of English, wants the peace and quiet his fellows will not allow him. Eventually, the Man Wearing Glasses realizes that the sign at the bus stop has no name on it; a piece of paper had been pasted over the words and now has no mark left upon it. It is blank, as empty as the promises of the governmental "company" that runs the country.

But *The Bus Stop* is much more than a political allegory. As more time passes on stage—many years, in fact—the characters lay down their contentiousness and begin to acknowledge their common humanity. Each becomes aware of shifts in the weather and each allows the Carpenter to become a kind of caretaker protecting them from the elements. In one of the play's most beautiful moments of heightened speech, the Young Woman and the Mother describe their dreams and speak as if they were the same person in youth and old age. "I dreamt the Moon could laugh . . . he held my hand and whispered in my ear. I wanted to be near him . . ." But, says the Mother completing the refrain, "As soon as I opened my eyes, I would see my son's socks worn through, his toes sticking out . . . his father's wool sweater unravelling at the sleeve . . ." Such womanly lyricism and lament might be heard in any nation at any time. As Professor Malmqvist noted in his Nobel presentation (2000), Xingjian is one of a small number of "male writers who give the same weight to the truth of women as to his own."

Toward the end of *The Bus Stop*, the Young Woman makes helpful suggestions to the Man Wearing Glasses, and the Mother opens herself to the Carpenter and Old Man, all acknowledging that by caring for one another and moving closer together they can keep one another warm. A community has replaced the contentious collective of the opening scene. Without softening or sentimentalizing the ending, Xingjian leavens the last speeches with subtle humor and a dawning self-awareness. "You should sue yourself," the Man Wearing Glasses tells the Manager. "Who made us not see things clearly? Who made us wait? Let's go, waiting is useless!" And this time they do leave, though as actors stepping out of their roles to comment on the play, not as the characters they have been inhabiting. "Performing comedy is much more difficult than tragedy," says the Actor Playing the Old Man, echoing the timeless theatrical joke: "Dying is easy, comedy is hard." To go on living, to continue becoming human, to move forward despite the sufferings of every day, that is the overarching theme of *The Bus Stop*. It is a philosophy that has informed Xingjian's unflinching drama ever since, a literature in which there is no salvation—not even the political dissident's stance of superior morality—only acceptance of one's existential dilemma and of the flux that defines all life.

For another perspective on *The Bus Stop* and Gao Xingjian:

Zhao, Henry Y. H. *Towards a Modern Zen Theatre: Gao Xingjian and Chinese Theatre Experimentation*. London: School of Oriental and African Studies, 2000.

SHOWCASE — CHINA'S NATIONAL DRAMA: *THE WHITE-HAIRED GIRL*

Although Gao Xingjian's *The Bus Stop* represents China's dissident drama in its portrayal of life inside Communist China, it is not that country's most representative contemporary work. Rather, *The White-Haired Girl*, a crude melodrama written by He Jingzhi and Ding Yi in 1944, has emerged as China's national epic, particularly since 1965, when it was transformed into an operatic spectacle as part of Chairman Mao-Tse Tung's infamous Cultural Revolution.

Based on a true incident in Hebei province in 1940, which the Chinese raised to the status of myth to glorify the People's Army, *The White-Haired Girl* tells the story of Xier (Hsi-erh), a peasant girl who was raped by a villainous landowner who has also contributed to her father's suicide. Shamed and fearful for her life, she hid in a cave for many years, and the salty air in the cavern bleached her hair and skin white. She emerged only at night to find food, but her appearance caused those who saw her to believe she was a goddess. When Mao's Red Army discovered and liberated her during the Long March, she became an instant and revered symbol of the oppressed who were saved by the Communists. In his preface to the play He Jingzhi cited a line from his opera that defines an important change in the dramaturgy of the new order: "The old society changed men into ghosts, while the new society changes ghosts into men." Accordingly, the play ends with a song by the peasants who "stand proudly under the sun, countless arms held high":

We, who suffered in days bygone,
Shall be our own masters from now on!
Our—own—masters—from
now—on!

The five-act opera epitomized Mao's admonition (which echoes the sentiments of the Romantics and many of the early Realists) that "all of our literature and art for the masses of the people, and in the first place for the workers, peasants and soldiers; they are created for the workers, peasants and soldiers and are for their use." Providing, of course, that the state approved the art! *The Bus Stop* was created for the workers and peasants, but it would have hardly passed Mao's censors.

The White-Haired Girl was based on an ancient Chinese ritual, the *yangko*, a planting song chanted to relieve the hardship of rice planting. The *yangko*, which also celebrated courtship and fertility, can be traced to the Sung Dynasty (960–1279 C.E.). In 1937 the *yangko* was converted into propaganda drama when it was fused with political skits and popular folk songs and dances by students at Yenan University; they billed their work as "the People's Defense Corps on Guard." The students frequently borrowed folk tales rooted in superstitions of farmers as plot material for their works. The revitalized *yangko* thus became the ideal form for the revolutionary drama celebrating the liberation of the peasants by Mao's Eighth Route Army.

In 1965 the play, a staple of student productions across China for twenty years, was transformed into "a revolutionary modern ballet" at the Shanghai Dance School in May 1965. (Significantly, Mao's wife, once a Shanghai actress, became China's Minister of Culture and proclaimed *The White-Haired Girl* a national treasure.) The original plot was altered to make the landlord even more villainous and Xier more revolutionary. Its success was phenomenal: it ran for over a year in Shanghai and transferred to Beijing for a successful run in May and June 1966. This was the first year of the infamous Cultural Revolution, and the play-ballet became a touchstone for Mao's desire for Chinese-only art. It is performed regularly in the theater and on Chinese television and even radio.

FENCES

AUGUST WILSON

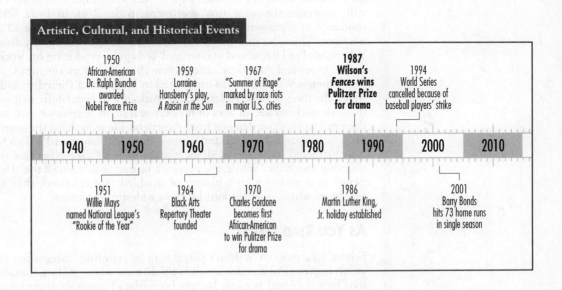

Artistic, Cultural, and Historical Events

1950
African-American
Dr. Ralph Bunche
awarded
Nobel Peace Prize

1959
Lorraine
Hansberry's play,
A Raisin in the Sun

1967
"Summer of Rage"
marked by race riots
in major U.S. cities

**1987
Wilson's
Fences wins
Pulitzer Prize
for drama**

1994
World Series
cancelled because of
baseball players' strike

| 1940 | 1950 | 1960 | 1970 | 1980 | 1990 | 2000 | 2010 |

1951
Willie Mays
named National League's
"Rookie of the Year"

1964
Black Arts
Repertory Theater
founded

1970
Charles Gordone
becomes first
African-American
to win Pulitzer Prize
for drama

1986
Martin Luther King,
Jr. holiday established

2001
Barry Bonds
hits 73 home runs
in single season

AUGUST WILSON (1945–)

Just as Arthur Miller and Tennessee Williams dominated the mainstream American theater in the years following World War II, August Wilson has joined the ranks of the United States' most decorated playwrights of the 1980s and 1990s. He has already won two Pulitzer Prizes (for *Fences*, 1987, and *The Piano Lesson*, 1990); virtually all of his other works (see below) have won a "best of season" award from the New York Drama Critics. Wilson will likely emerge as one of America's most honored playwrights before his playwriting career is concluded.

One intriguing aspect of his collected plays is their organizational principle. Each play of a proposed ten-play cycle is set in a different decade of the twentieth century, and each is framed against the backdrop of a peculiarly American cultural icon (1920s jazz for *Ma Rainey's Black Bottom*, 1950s baseball for *Fences*, and 1940s delta blues for *Seven Guitars*). Collectively the plays chronicle the evolution of an authentic African-American voice within the broader culture of the nation. Though the past Wilson depicts is painful in its dramatization of racism and the residue of slavery, there nonetheless remains an undercurrent of optimism in Wilson's work. He has talked about "exorcising the demons of memory" so that African-Americans can advance in the next century. (In *Joe Turner's Come and Gone* there is an actual exorcism that typifies his canon.)

Many of Wilson's plays are set in Pittsburgh, where he was born to a white father and a black mother; he was raised in the Hill district, a ghetto for African-Americans. His father was rarely around, and his strong-willed mother, determined that her son would succeed, moved the family to a mostly white suburb. But social realities deterred Wilson: he left a Catholic school because of racial slurs, he deemed a vocational school academically worthless, and his one attempt at a public high school embittered him when a teacher falsely accused him of plagiarizing a 20-page paper on Napoleon. Wilson's rage at such injustices drew him to the Black Power movement of the 1960s. In Pittsburgh he helped found the Black Horizon on the Hill, a theater company that staged the plays of LeRoi Jones (now Amiri Baraka), whose work inspired Wilson to take up playwriting. At first he was discouraged because he "wasn't any good at dialogue," an ironic assessment from a man whose plays are praised for their lyrical yet completely naturalistic language.

In 1978 Wilson accepted an invitation to move to St. Paul, Minnesota, to write plays for a theater company founded by a former Pittsburgh colleague. Despite his success, he still maintains the same tiny apartment in St. Paul. In 1982 Wilson was a fellow-in-residence at a playwright-development program at the Eugene O'Neill Center in Connecticut. There he met Lloyd Richards, an African-American director who headed the Yale School of Drama and encouraged Wilson by producing his works. Today his plays are toured to several American cities before their New York openings.

Though Wilson's works are rooted in Naturalism (heredity and environment clearly shape the lives of his characters), his works are so beautifully written that they transcend the style and assume an aura of mystery and myth. Again we turn to his comments about the need to exorcise demons from American life as perhaps the source of the mystic in his plays. Ultimately, his collected works—from *Ma Rainey* in 1983 to *King Hedley* in 2001— have attracted audiences of all races and economic classes because they speak of universal suffering and hope. While the plays are unmistakably about the African-American experience in a nation with a history of troubled race relations, they are also about human problems, which may account for their widespread success.

As You Read *Fences*

Fences, like most of Wilson's plays, may be rightfully categorized as naturalistic because environment (Pittsburgh's squalid Hill district, where Wilson himself grew up) and heredity (Troy is cursed because he was born black) motivate the plot and the play's various themes. You will note that Wilson has taken pains to recreate a specific world (the stage directions are especially important) and his characters speak in the distinct colloquialisms of African-Americans. However—as is also the case with Wilson's drama—the Naturalism coexists with the theatrical, thanks largely to his trademark use of jazz and American popular culture icons (baseball). And the speech, which seems so lifelike at first reading, manifests a poetic quality that transcends the ordinary. Wilson is perhaps the finest "poetic realist" in America since Tennessee Williams. As you read, note especially those moments when the naturalistic gives way to the theatrical and the poetic, for herein rests Wilson's power as a dramatist. Also, the specter of Josh Gibson looms heavily over "the Hill" and becomes an important, thought unseen, character in the Maxim story. Gibson was the greatest home run hitter in the old Negro Leagues before baseball's color line was broken in 1947 by Jackie Robinson (who is also mentioned throughout the play). Gibson was nicknamed "The Black Babe Ruth," but many argue that had he been allowed to play major league baseball he might have eclipsed Ruth's records.

FENCES

A U G U S T   W I L S O N

for Lloyd Richards,
who adds to whatever he touches.

When the sins of our fathers visit us
We do not have to play host.
We can banish them with forgiveness
As God, in His Largeness and Laws.

—*August Wilson*

C H A R A C T E R S

TROY MAXSON

JIM BONO, *Troy's friend*

ROSE, *Troy's wife*

LYONS, *Troy's oldest son by previous marriage*

GABRIEL, *Troy's brother*

CORY, *Troy and Rose's son*

RAYNELL, *Troy's daughter*

SETTING: *The setting is the yard which fronts the only entrance to the Maxson household, an ancient two-story brick house set back off a small alley in a big-city neighborhood. The entrance to the house is gained by two or three steps leading to a wooden porch badly in need of paint.*

A relatively recent addition to the house and running its full width, the porch lacks congruence. It is a sturdy porch with a flat roof. One or two chairs of dubious value sit at one end where the kitchen window opens onto the porch. An old-fashioned icebox stands silent guard at the opposite end.

The yard is a small dirt yard, partially fenced, except for the last scene, with a wooden saw horse, a pile of lumber, and other fence-building equipment set off to the side. Opposite is a tree from which hangs a ball made of rags. A baseball bat leans against the tree. Two oil drums serve as garbage receptacles and sit near the house at right to complete the setting.

THE PLAY: *Near the turn of the century, the destitute of Europe sprang on the city with tenacious claws and an honest and solid dream. The city devoured them. They swelled its belly until it burst into a thousand furnaces and sewing machines, a thousand butcher shops and bakers' ovens, a thousand churches and hospitals and funeral parlors and money-lenders. The city grew. It nourished itself and offered each man a partnership limited only by his talent, his guile, and his willingness and capacity for hard work. For the immigrants of Europe, a dream dared and won true.*

The descendants of African slaves were offered no such welcome or participation. They came from places called the Carolinas and the Virginias, Georgia, Alabama, Mississippi, and Tennessee. They came strong, eager, searching. The city rejected them and they fled and settled along the riverbanks and under bridges in shallow, ramshackle houses made of sticks and tarpaper. They collected rags and wood. They sold the use of their muscles and their bodies. They cleaned houses and washed clothes, they shined shoes, and in quiet desperation and vengeful pride, they stole, and lived in pursuit of their own dream. That they could breathe free, finally, and stand to meet life with the force of dignity and whatever eloquence the heart could call upon.

By 1957, the hard-won victories of the European immigrants had solidified the industrial might of America. War had been confronted and won with new energies that used loyalty and patriotism as its fuel. Life was rich, full, and flourishing. The Milwaukee Braves won the World Series, and the hot winds of change that would make the sixties a turbulent, racing, dangerous, and provocative decade had not yet begun to blow full.

ACT I

SCENE 1

It is 1957. Troy and Bono enter the yard, engaged in conversation. Troy is fifty-three years old, a large man with thick, heavy hands; it is this largeness that he strives to fill out and make an accommodation with. Together with his blackness, his largeness informs his sensibilities and the choices he has made in his life.

Of the two men, Bono is obviously the follower. His commitment to their friendship of thirty-odd years is rooted in his admiration of Troy's honesty, capacity for hard work, and his strength, which Bono seeks to emulate.

It is Friday night, payday, and the one night of the week the two men engage in a ritual of talk and drink. Troy is usually the most talkative and at times he can be crude and almost vulgar, though he is capable of rising to profound heights of expression. The men carry lunch buckets and wear or carry burlap aprons and are dressed in clothes suitable to their jobs as garbage collectors.

BONO. Troy, you ought to stop that lying!

TROY. I ain't lying! The nigger had a watermelon this big. (*He indicates with his hands.*) Talking about . . . "What watermelon, Mr. Rand?" I liked to fell out! "What watermelon, Mr. Rand?" . . . And it sitting there big as life.

BONO. What did Mr. Rand say?

TROY. Ain't said nothing. Figure if the nigger too dumb to know he carrying a watermelon, he wasn't gonna get much sense out of him. Trying to hide that great big old watermelon under his coat. Afraid to let the white man see him carry it home.

BONO. I'm like you . . . I ain't got no time for them kind of people.

TROY. Now what he look like getting mad cause he see the man from the union talking to Mr. Rand?

BONO. He come to me talking about . . . "Maxson gonna get us fired." I told him to get away from me with that. He walked away from me calling you a trouble-maker. What Mr. Rand say?

TROY. Ain't said nothing. He told me to go down the Commissioner's office next Friday. They called me down there to see them.

BONO. Well, as long as you got your complaint filed, they can't fire you. That's what one of them white fellows tell me.

TROY. I ain't worried about them firing me. They gonna fire me cause I asked a question? That's all I did. I went to Mr. Rand and asked him, "Why? Why you got the white mens driving and the colored lifting?" Told him, "what's the matter, don't I count? You think only white fellows got sense enough to drive a truck. That ain't no paper job! Hell, anybody can drive a truck. How come you got all whites driving and the colored lifting?" He told me "take it to the union." Well, hell, that's what I done! Now they wanna come up with this pack of lies.

BONO. I told Brownie if the man come and ask him any questions . . . just tell the truth! It ain't nothing but something they done trumped up on you cause you filed a complaint on them.

TROY. Brownie don't understand nothing. All I want them to do is change the job description. Give everybody a chance to drive the truck. Brownie can't see that. He ain't got that much sense.

BONO. How you figure he be making out with that gal be up at Taylor's all the time . . . that Alberta gal?

TROY. Same as you and me. Getting just as much as we is. Which is to say nothing.

BONO. It is, huh? I figure you doing a little better than me . . . and I ain't saying what I'm doing.

TROY. Aw, nigger, look here . . . I know you. If you had got anywhere near that gal, twenty minutes later you be looking to tell somebody. And the first one you gonna tell . . . that you gonna want to brag to . . . is me.

BONO. I ain't saying that. I see where you be eyeing her.

TROY. I eye all the women. I don't miss nothing. Don't never let nobody tell you Troy Maxson don't eye the women.

BONO. You been doing more than eyeing her. You done bought her a drink or two.

TROY. Hell yeah, I bought her a drink! What that mean? I bought you one, too. What that mean cause I buy her a drink? I'm just being polite.

BONO. It's all right to buy her one drink. That's what you call being polite. But when you wanna be buying two or three . . . that's what you call eyeing her.

TROY. Look here, as long as you known me . . . you ever known me to chase after women?

BONO. Hell yeah! Long as I done known you. You forgetting I knew you when.

TROY. Naw, I'm talking about since I been married to Rose?

BONO. Oh, not since you been married to Rose. Now, that's the truth, there. I can say that.

TROY. All right then! Case closed.

BONO. I see you be walking up around Alberta's house. You supposed to be at Taylors' and you be walking up around there.

TROY. What you watching where I'm walking for? I ain't watching after you.

BONO. I seen you walking around there more than once.

TROY. Hell, you liable to see me walking anywhere! That don't mean nothing cause you see me walking around there.

BONO. Where she come from anyway? She just kinda showed up one day.

TROY. Tallahassee. You can look at her and tell she one of them Florida gals. They got some big healthy women down there. Grow them right up out the ground. Got a little bit of Indian in her. Most of them niggers down in Florida got some Indian in them.

BONO. I don't know about that Indian part. But she damn sure big and healthy. Woman wear some big stockings. Got them great big old legs and hips as wide as the Mississippi River.

TROY. Legs don't mean nothing. You don't do nothing but push them out of the way. But them hips cushion the ride!

BONO. Troy, you ain't got no sense.

TROY. It's the truth! Like you riding on Goodyears!

Rose enters from the house. She is ten years younger than Troy, her devotion to him stems from her recognition of the possibilities of her life without him: a succession of abusive men and their babies, a life of partying and running the streets, the Church, or aloneness with its attendant pain and frustration. She recognizes Troy's spirit as a fine and illuminating one and she either ignores or forgives his faults, only some of which she recognizes. Though she doesn't drink, her presence is an integral part of the Friday night rituals. She alternates between the porch and the kitchen, where supper preparations are under way.

ROSE. What you all out here getting into?

TROY. What you worried about what we getting into for? This is men talk, woman.

ROSE. What I care what you all talking about? Bono, you gonna stay for supper?

BONO. No, I thank you, Rose. But Lucille say she cooking up a pot of pigfeet.

TROY. Pigfeet! Hell, I'm going home with you! Might even stay the night if you got some pigfeet. You got something in there to top them pigfeet, Rose?

ROSE. I'm cooking up some chicken. I got some chicken and collard greens.

TROY. Well, go on back in the house and let me and Bono finish what we was talking about. This is men talk. I got some talk for you later. You know what kind of talk I mean. You go on and powder it up.

ROSE. Troy Maxson, don't you start that now!

TROY (*puts his arm around her*). Aw, woman . . . come here. Look here, Bono . . . when I met this woman . . . I got out that place, say, "Hitch up my pony, saddle up my mare . . . there's a woman out there for me somewhere. I looked here. Looked there. Saw Rose and latched on to her." I latched on to her and told her— I'm gonna tell you the truth—I told her, "Baby, I don't wanna marry, I just wanna be your man." Rose told me . . . tell him what you told me, Rose.

ROSE. I told him if he wasn't the marrying kind, then move out the way so the marrying kind could find me.

TROY. That's what she told me. "Nigger, you in my way. You blocking the view! Move out the way so I can find me a husband." I thought it over two or three days. Come back—

ROSE. Ain't no two or three days nothing. You was back the same night.

TROY. Come back, told her . . . "Okay, baby . . . but I'm gonna buy me a banty rooster and put him out there in the backyard . . . and when he see a stranger come, he'll flap his wings and crow. . . ." Look here, Bono, I could watch the front door by myself . . . it was that back door I was worried about.

ROSE. Troy, you ought not talk like that. Troy ain't doing nothing but telling a lie.

TROY. Only thing is . . . when we first got married . . . forget the rooster . . . we ain't had no yard!

BONO. I hear you tell it. Me and Lucille was staying down there on Logan Street. Had two rooms with the outhouse in the back. I ain't mind the outhouse none. But when that goddamn wind blow through there in the winter . . . that's what I'm talking about! To this day I wonder why in the hell I ever stayed down there for six long years. But see, I didn't know I could do no better. I thought only white folks had inside toilets and things.

ROSE. There's a lot of people don't know they can do no better than they doing now. That's just something you got to learn. A lot of folks still shop at Bella's.

TROY. Ain't nothing wrong with shopping at Bella's. She got fresh food.

ROSE. I ain't said nothing about if she got fresh food. I'm talking about what she charge. She charge ten cents more than the A&P.

TROY. The A&P ain't never done nothing for me. I spends my money where I'm treated right. I go down to Bella, say, "I need a loaf of bread, I'll pay you Friday." She give it to me. What sense that make when I got money to go and spend it somewhere else and ignore the person who done right by me? That ain't in the Bible.

ROSE. We ain't talking about what's in the Bible. What sense it make to shop there when she overcharge?

TROY. You shop where you want to. I'll do my shopping where the people been good to me.

ROSE. Well, I don't think it's right for her to overcharge. That's all I was saying.

BONO. Look here . . . I got to get on. Lucille going be raising all kind of hell.

TROY. Where you going, nigger? We ain't finished this pint. Come here, finish this pint.

BONO. Well, hell, I am . . . if you ever turn the bottle loose.

TROY (hands him the bottle). The only thing I say about the A&P is I'm glad Cory got that job down there. Help him take care of his school clothes and things. Gabe done moved out and things getting tight around here. He got that job. . . . He can start to look out for himself.

ROSE. Cory done went and got recruited by a college football team.

TROY. I told that boy about that football stuff. The white man ain't gonna let him get nowhere with that football. I told him when he first come to me with it. Now you come telling me he done went and got more tied up in it. He ought to go and get recruited in how to fix cars or something where he can make a living.

ROSE. He ain't talking about making no living playing football. It's just something the boys in school do. They gonna send a recruiter by to talk to you. He'll tell you he ain't talking about making no living playing football. It's a honor to be recruited.

TROY. It ain't gonna get him nowhere. Bono'll tell you that.

BONO. If he be like you in the sports . . . he's gonna be all right. Ain't but two men ever played baseball as good as you. That's Babe Ruth and Josh Gibson.[1] Them's the only two men ever hit more home runs than you.

TROY. What it ever get me? Ain't got a pot to piss in or a window to throw it out of.

ROSE. Times have changed since you was playing baseball, Troy. That was before the war. Times have changed a lot since then.

TROY. How in hell they done changed?

ROSE. They got lots of colored boys playing ball now. Baseball and football.

BONO. You right about that, Rose. Times have changed, Troy. You just come along too early.

TROY. There ought not never have been no time called too early! Now you take that fellow . . . what's that fellow they had playing right field for the Yankees back then? You know who I'm talking about, Bono. Used to play right field for the Yankees.

ROSE. Selkirk?

TROY. Selkirk! That's it! Man batting .269, understand? .269. What kind of sense that make? I was hitting .432 with thirty-seven home runs! Man batting .269 and playing right field for the Yankees! I saw Josh Gibson's daughter yesterday. She walking around with raggedy shoes on her feet. Now I bet you Selkirk's daughter ain't walking around with raggedy shoes on the feet! I bet you that!

ROSE. They got a lot of colored baseball players now. Jackie Robinson[2] was the first. Folks had to wait for Jackie Robinson.

TROY. I done seen a hundred niggers play baseball better than Jackie Robinson. Hell, I know some teams Jackie Robinson couldn't even make! What you talking about Jackie Robinson. Jackie Robinson wasn't nobody. I'm talking about if you could play ball then they ought to have let you play. Don't care what color you were. Come telling me I come along too early. If you could play . . . then they ought to have let you play.

Troy takes a long drink from the bottle.

ROSE. You gonna drink yourself to death. You don't need to be drinking like that.

TROY. Death ain't nothing. I done seen him. Done wrassled with him. You can't tell me nothing about death. Death ain't nothing but a fastball on the outside corner. And you know what I'll do to that! Lookee here, Bono . . . am I lying? You get one of them fastballs, about waist high, over the outside corner of the plate where you can get the meat of the bat on it . . . and good god! You can kiss it goodbye. Now, am I lying?

BONO. Naw, you telling the truth there. I seen you do it.

TROY. If I'm lying . . . that 450 feet worth of lying! (Pause.) That's all death is to me. A fastball on the outside corner.

---

[1]**Josh Gibson** African-American ballplayer (1911–47), known as the Babe Ruth of the Negro leagues

[2]**Jackie Robinson** In 1947 Robinson (1919–72) became the first African-American to play baseball in the major leagues.

ROSE. I don't know why you want to get on talking about death.

TROY. Ain't nothing wrong with talking about death. That's part of life. Everybody gonna die. You gonna die, I'm gonna die. Bono's gonna die. Hell, we all gonna die.

ROSE. But you ain't got to talk about it. I don't like to talk about it.

TROY. You the one brought it up. Me and Bono was talking about baseball . . . you tell me I'm gonna drink myself to death. Ain't that right, Bono? You know I don't drink this but one night out of the week. That's Friday night. I'm gonna drink just enough to where I can handle it. Then I cuts it loose. I leave it alone. So don't you worry about me drinking myself to death. 'Cause I ain't worried about Death. I done seen him. I done wrestled with him.

Look here, Bono . . . I looked up one day and Death was marching straight at me. Like Soldiers on Parade! The Army of Death was marching straight at me. The middle of July, 1941. It got real cold just like it be winter. It seem like Death himself reached out and touched me on the shoulder. He touch me just like I touch you. I got cold as ice and Death standing there grinning at me.

ROSE. Troy, why don't you hush that talk.

TROY. I say . . . what you want, Mr. Death? You be wanting me? You done brought your army to be getting me? I looked him dead in the eye. I wasn't fearing nothing. I was ready to tangle. Just like I'm ready to tangle now. The Bible say be ever vigilant. That's why I don't get but so drunk. I got to keep watch.

ROSE. Troy was right down there in Mercy Hospital. You remember he had pneumonia? Laying there with a fever talking plumb out of his head.

TROY. Death standing there staring at me . . . carrying that sickle in his hand. Finally he say, "You want bound over for another year?" See, just like that . . . "You want bound over for another year?" I told him, "Bound over hell! Let's settle this now!"

It seem like he kinda fell back when I said that, and all the cold went out of me. I reached down and grabbed that sickle and threw it just as far as I could throw it . . . and me and him commenced to wrestling.

We wrestled for three days and three nights. I can't say where I found the strength from. Everytime it seemed like he was gonna get the best of me, I'd reach way down deep inside myself and find the strength to do him one better.

ROSE. Everytime Troy tell that story he find different ways to tell it. Different things to make up about it.

TROY. I ain't making up nothing. I'm telling you the facts of what happened. I wrestled with Death for three days and three nights and I'm standing here to tell you about it. (*Pause.*) All right. At the end of the third night we done weakened each other to where we can't hardly move. Death stood up, throwed on his robe . . . had him a white robe with a hood on it. He throwed on that robe and went off to look for his sickle. Say, "I'll be back." Just like that. "I'll be back." I told him, say, "Yeah, but . . . you gonna have to find me!" I wasn't no fool. I wasn't going looking for him. Death ain't nothing to play with. And I know he's gonna get me. I know I got to join his army . . . his camp followers. But as long as I keep my strength and see him coming . . . as long as I keep up my vigilance . . . he's gonna have to fight to get me. I ain't going easy.

BONO. Well, look here, since you got to keep up your vigilance . . . let me have the bottle.

TROY. Aw hell, I shouldn't have told you that part. I should have left out that part.

ROSE. Troy be talking that stuff and half the time don't even know what he be talking about.

TROY. Bono know me better than that.

BONO. That's right. I know you. I know you got some Uncle Remus[3] in your blood. You got more stories than the devil got sinners.

TROY. Aw hell, I done seen him too! Done talked with the devil.

ROSE. Troy, don't nobody wanna be hearing all that stuff.

Lyons enters the yard from the street. Thirty-four years old, Troy's son by a previous marriage, he sports a neatly trimmed goatee, sport coat, white shirt, tieless and buttoned at the collar. Though he fancies himself a musician, he is more caught up in the rituals and "idea" of being a musician than in the actual practice of the music. He has come to borrow money from Troy, and while he knows he will be successful, he is uncertain as to what extent his lifestyle will be held up to scrutiny and ridicule.

LYONS. Hey, Pop.

TROY. What you come "Hey, Popping" me for?

LYONS. How you doing, Rose? (*He kisses her.*) Mr. Bono. How you doing?

BONO. Hey, Lyons . . . how you been?

TROY. He must have been doing all right. I ain't seen him around here last week.

[3]**Uncle Remus** Narrator of traditional black tales in a book by Joel Chandler Harris

ROSE. Troy, leave your boy alone. He come by to see you and you wanna start all that nonsense.

TROY. I ain't bothering Lyons. (*Offers him the bottle.*) Here . . . get you a drink. We got an understanding. I know why he come by to see me and he know I know.

LYONS. Come on, Pop . . . I just stopped by to say hi . . . see how you was doing.

TROY. You ain't stopped by yesterday.

ROSE. You gonna stay for supper, Lyons? I got some chicken cooking in the oven.

LYONS. No, Rose . . . thanks. I was just in the neighborhood and thought I'd stop by for a minute.

TROY. You was in the neighborhood all right, nigger. You telling the truth there. You was in the neighborhood cause it's my payday.

LYONS. Well, hell, since you mentioned it . . . let me have ten dollars.

TROY. I'll be damned! I'll die and go to hell and play blackjack with the devil before I give you ten dollars.

BONO. That's what I wanna know about . . . that devil you done seen.

LYONS. What . . . Pop done seen the devil? You too much, Pops.

TROY. Yeah, I done seen him. Talked to him too!

ROSE. You ain't seen no devil. I done told you that man ain't had nothing to do with the devil. Anything you can't understand, you want to call it the devil.

TROY. Look here, Bono . . . I went down to see Hertzberger about some furniture. Got three rooms for two-ninety-eight. That what it say on the radio. "Three rooms . . . two-ninety-eight." Even made up a little song about it. Go down there . . . man tell me I can't get no credit. I'm working every day and can't get no credit. What to do? I got an empty house with some raggedy furniture in it. Cory ain't got no bed. He's sleeping on a pile of rags on the floor. Working every day and can't get no credit. Come back here— Rose'll tell you—madder than hell. Sit down . . . try to figure what I'm gonna do. Come a knock on the door. Ain't been living here but three days. Who know I'm here? Open the door . . . devil standing there bigger than life. White fellow . . . white fellow . . . got on good clothes and everything. Standing there with a clipboard in his hand. I ain't had to say nothing. First words come out of his mouth was . . . "I understand you need some furniture and can't get no credit." I liked to fell over. He say, "I'll give you all the credit you want, but you got to pay the interest on it." I told him, "Give me three rooms worth and charge whatever you want." Next day a truck pulled up here and two men unloaded them three rooms. Man what

drove the truck give me a book. Say send ten dollars, first of every month to the address in the book and every thing will be all right. Say if I miss a payment the devil was coming back and it'll be hell to pay. That was fifteen years ago. To this day . . . the first of the month I send my ten dollars, Rose'll tell you.

ROSE. Troy lying.

TROY. I ain't never seen that man since. Now you tell me who else that could have been but the devil? I ain't sold my soul or nothing like that, you understand. Naw, I wouldn't have truck with the devil about nothing like that. I got my furniture and pays my ten dollars the first of the month just like clockwork.

BONO. How long you say you been paying this ten dollars a month?

TROY. Fifteen years!

BONO. Hell, ain't you finished paying for it yet? How much the man done charged you?

TROY. Ah hell, I done paid for it. I done paid for it ten times over! The fact is I'm scared to stop paying it.

ROSE. Troy lying. We got that furniture from Mr. Glickman. He ain't paying no ten dollars a month to nobody.

TROY. Aw hell, woman. Bono know I ain't that big a fool.

LYONS. I was just getting ready to say . . . I know where there's a bridge for sale.

TROY. Look here, I'll tell you this . . . it don't matter to me if he was the devil. It don't matter if the devil give credit. Somebody has got to give it.

ROSE. It ought to matter. You going around talking about having truck with the devil . . . God's the one you gonna have to answer to. He's the one gonna be at the Judgment.

LYONS. Yeah, well, look here, Pop . . . Let me have that ten dollars. I'll give it back to you. Bonnie got a job working at the hospital.

TROY. What I tell you, Bono? The only time I see this nigger is when he wants something. That's the only time I see him.

LYONS. Come on, Pop, Mr. Bono don't want to hear all that. Let me have the ten dollars. I told you Bonnie working.

TROY. What that mean to me? "Bonnie working." I don't care if she working. Go ask her for the ten dollars if she working. Talking about "Bonnie working." Why ain't you working?

LYONS. Aw, Pop, you know I can't find no decent job. Where am I gonna get a job at? You know I can't get no job.

TROY. I told you I know some people down there. I can get you on the rubbish if you want to work. I told you that the last time you came by here asking me for something.

LYONS. Naw, Pop . . . thanks. That ain't for me. I don't wanna be carrying nobody's rubbish. I don't wanna be punching nobody's time clock.

TROY. What's the matter, you too good to carry people's rubbish? Where you think that ten dollars you talking about come from? I'm just supposed to haul people's rubbish and give my money to you cause you too lazy to work. You too lazy to work and wanna know why you ain't got what I got.

ROSE. What hospital Bonnie working at? Mercy?

LYONS. She's down at Passavant working in the laundry.

TROY. I ain't got nothing as it is. I give you that ten dollars and I got to eat beans the rest of the week. Naw . . . you ain't getting no ten dollars here.

LYONS. You ain't got to be eating no beans. I don't know why you wanna say that.

TROY. I ain't got no extra money. Gabe done moved over to Miss Pearl's paying her the rent and things done got tight around here. I can't afford to be giving you every payday.

LYONS. I ain't asked you to give me nothing. I asked you to loan me ten dollars. I know you got ten dollars.

TROY. Yeah, I got it. You know why I got it? Cause I don't throw my money away out there in the streets. You living the fast life . . . wanna be a musician . . . running around in them clubs and things . . . then, you learn to take care of yourself. You ain't gonna find me going and asking nobody for nothing. I done spent too many years without.

LYONS. You and me is two different people, Pop.

TROY. I done learned my mistake and learned to do what's right by it. You still trying to get something for nothing. Life don't owe you nothing. You owe it to yourself. Ask Bono. He'll tell you I'm right.

LYONS. You got your way of dealing with the world . . . I got mine. The only thing that matters to me is the music.

TROY. Yeah, I can see that! It don't matter how you gonna eat . . . where your next dollar is coming from. You telling the truth there.

LYONS. I know I got to eat. But I got to live too. I need something that gonna help me to get out of the bed in the morning. Make me feel like I belong in the world. I don't bother nobody. I just stay with the music cause that's the only way I can find to live in the world. Otherwise there ain't no telling what I might do. Now I don't come criticizing you and how you live. I just come by to ask you for ten dollars. I don't wanna hear all that about how I live.

TROY. Boy, your mamma did a hell of a job raising you.

LYONS. You can't change me, Pop. I'm thirty-four years old. If you wanted to change me, you should have been there when I was growing up. I come by to see you . . . ask for ten dollars and you want to talk about how I was raised. You don't know nothing about how I was raised.

ROSE. Let the boy have ten dollars, Troy.

TROY (*to Lyons*). What the hell you looking at me for? I ain't got no ten dollars. You know what I do with my money. (*To Rose.*) Give him ten dollars if you want him to have it.

ROSE. I will. Just as soon as you turn it loose.

TROY (*handing Rose the money*). There it is. Seventy-six dollars and forty-two cents. You see this, Bono? Now, I ain't gonna get but six of that back.

ROSE. You ought to stop telling that lie. Here, Lyons. (*She hands him the money.*)

LYONS. Thanks, Rose. Look . . . I got to run . . . I'll see you later.

TROY. Wait a minute. You gonna say, "thanks, Rose" and ain't gonna look to see where she got that ten dollars from? See how they do me, Bono?

LYONS. I know she got it from you, Pop. Thanks. I'll give it back to you.

TROY. There he go telling another lie. Time I see that ten dollars . . . he'll be owing me thirty more.

LYONS. See you, Mr. Bono.

BONO. Take care, Lyons!

LYONS. Thanks, Pop. I'll see you again.

Lyons exits the yard.

TROY. I don't know why he don't go and get him a decent job and take care of that woman he got.

BONO. He'll be all right, Troy. The boy is still young.

TROY. The *boy* is thirty-four years old.

ROSE. Let's not get off into all that.

BONO. Look here . . . I got to be going. I got to be getting on. Lucille gonna be waiting.

TROY (*puts his arm around Rose*). See this woman, Bono? I love this woman. I love this woman so much it hurts. I love her so much . . . I done run out of ways of loving her. So I got to go back to basics. Don't you come by my house Monday morning talking about time to go to work . . . 'cause I'm still gonna be stroking!

ROSE. Troy! Stop it now!

BONO. I ain't paying him no mind, Rose. That ain't nothing but gin-talk. Go on, Troy. I'll see you Monday.

TROY. Don't you come by my house, nigger! I done told you what I'm gonna be doing.

The lights go down to black.

SCENE 2

The lights come up on Rose hanging up clothes. She hums and sings softly to herself. It is the following morning.

ROSE (*sings*).

> Jesus, be a fence all around me every day
> Jesus, I want you to protect me as I travel on
>   my way.
> Jesus, be a fence all around me every day.

Troy enters from the house.

> Jesus, I want you to protect me
>   As I travel on my way.

(*To Troy.*) 'Morning. You ready for breakfast? I can fix it soon as I finish hanging up these clothes?

TROY. I got the coffee on. That'll be all right. I'll just drink some of that this morning.

ROSE. That 651 hit yesterday. That's the second time this month. Miss Pearl hit for a dollar . . . seem like those that need the least always get lucky. Poor folks can't get nothing.

TROY. Them numbers don't know nobody. I don't know why you fool with them. You and Lyons both.

ROSE. It's something to do.

TROY. You ain't doing nothing but throwing your money away.

ROSE. Troy, you know I don't play foolishly. I just play a nickel here and a nickel there.

TROY. That's two nickels you done thrown away.

ROSE. Now I hit sometimes . . . that makes up for it. It always comes in handy when I do hit. I don't hear you complaining then.

TROY. I ain't complaining now. I just say it's foolish. Trying to guess out of six hundred ways which way the number gonna come. If I had all the money niggers, these Negroes, throw away on numbers for one week—just one week—I'd be a rich man.

ROSE. Well, you wishing and calling it foolish ain't gonna stop folks from playing numbers. That's one thing for sure. Besides . . . some good things come from playing numbers. Look where Pope done bought him that restaurant off of numbers.

TROY. I can't stand niggers like that. Man ain't had two dimes to rub together. He walking around with his shoes all run over bumming money for cigarettes. All right. Got lucky there and hit the numbers . . .

ROSE. Troy, I know all about it.

TROY. Had good sense, I'll say that for him. He ain't throwed his money away. I seen niggers hit the numbers and go through two thousand dollars in four days. Man bought him that restaurant down there . . . fixed it up real nice . . . and then didn't want nobody to come in it! A Negro go in there and can't get no kind of service. I seen a white fellow come in there and order a bowl of stew. Pope picked all the meat out of the pot for him. Man ain't had nothing but a bowl of meat! Negro come behind him and ain't got nothing but the potatoes and carrots. Talking about what numbers do for people, you picked a wrong example. Ain't done nothing but make a worser fool out of him than he was before.

ROSE. Troy, you ought to stop worrying about what happened at work yesterday.

TROY. I ain't worried. Just told me to be down there at the Commissioner's office on Friday. Everybody think they gonna fire me. I ain't worried about them firing me. You ain't got to worry about that. (*Pause.*) Where's Cory? Cory in the house? (*Calls.*) Cory?

ROSE. He gone out.

TROY. Out, huh? He gone out 'cause he know I want him to help me with this fence. I know how he is. That boy scared of work.

Gabriel enters. He comes halfway down the alley and, hearing Troy's voice, stops.

TROY (*continues*). He ain't done a lick of work in his life.

ROSE. He had to go to football practice. Coach wanted them to get in a little extra practice before the season start.

TROY. I got his practice . . . running out of here before he get his chores done.

ROSE. Troy, what is wrong with you this morning? Don't nothing set right with you. Go on back in there and go to bed . . . get up on the other side.

TROY. Why something got to be wrong with me? I ain't said nothing wrong with me.

ROSE. You got something to say about everything. First it's the numbers . . . then it's the way the man runs his restaurant . . . then you done got on Cory. What's it gonna be next? Take a look up there and see if the weather suits you . . . or is it gonna be how you gonna put up the fence with the clothes hanging in the yard.

TROY. You hit the nail on the head then.

ROSE. I know you like I know the back of my hand. Go on in there and get you some coffee . . . see if that straighten you up. 'Cause you ain't right this morning.

Troy starts into the house and sees Gabriel. Gabriel starts singing. Troy's brother, he is seven years younger than Troy. Injured in World War II, he has a metal plate in his head. He carries an old trumpet tied around his waist and believes with every fiber of his being that he is the Archangel Gabriel. He carries a chipped basket with an assortment of discarded fruits and vegetables he has picked up in the strip district and which he attempts to sell.

GABRIEL (*singing*).
> Yes, ma'am I got plums
> You ask me how I sell them
> Oh ten cents apiece
> Three for a quarter
> Come and buy now
> 'Cause I'm here today
> And tomorrow I'll be gone

Gabriel enters.

Hey, Rose!
ROSE. How you doing Gabe?
GABRIEL. There's Troy . . . Hey, Troy!
TROY. Hey, Gabe.

Exit into kitchen.

ROSE (*to Gabriel*). What you got there?
GABRIEL. You know what I got, Rose. I got fruits and vegetables.
ROSE (*looking in basket*). Where's all these plums you talking about?
GABRIEL. I ain't got no plums today, Rose. I was just singing that. Have some tomorrow. Put me in a big order for plums. Have enough plums tomorrow for St. Peter and everybody.

Troy reenters from kitchen, crosses to steps.

(*To Rose.*) Troy's mad at me.
TROY. I ain't mad at you. What I got to be mad at you about? You ain't done nothing to me.
GABRIEL. I just moved over to Miss Pearl's to keep out from in your way. I ain't mean no harm by it.
TROY. Who said anything about that? I ain't said anything about that.
GABRIEL. You ain't mad at me, is you?
TROY. Naw . . . I ain't mad at you, Gabe. If I was mad at you I'd tell you about it.
GABRIEL. Got me two rooms. In the basement. Got my own door too. Wanna see my key? (*He holds up a key.*) That's my own key! My two rooms!
TROY. Well, that's good, Gabe. You got your own key . . . that's good.
ROSE. You hungry, Gabe? I was just fixing to cook Troy his breakfast.

GABRIEL. I'll take some biscuits. You got some biscuits? Did you know when I was in heaven . . . every morning me and St. Peter would sit down by the gate and eat some big fat biscuits? Oh, yeah! We had us a good time. We'd sit there and eat us them biscuits and then St. Peter would go off to sleep and tell me to wake him up when it's time to open the gates for the judgment.
ROSE. Well, come on . . . I'll make up a batch of biscuits.

Rose exits into the house.

GABRIEL. Troy . . . St. Peter got your name in the book. I seen it. It say . . . Troy Maxson. I say . . . I know him! He got the same name like what I got. That's my brother!
TROY. How many times you gonna tell me that, Gabe?
GABRIEL. Ain't got my name in the book. Don't have to have my name. I done died and went to heaven. He got your name though. One morning St. Peter was looking at his book . . . marking it up for the judgment . . . and he let me see your name. Got it in there under M. Got Rose's name . . . I ain't seen it like I seen yours . . . but I know it's in there. He got a great big book. Got everybody's name what was ever been born. That's what he told me. But I seen your name. Seen it with my own eyes.
TROY. Go on in the house there. Rose going to fix you something to eat.
GABRIEL. Oh, I ain't hungry. I done had breakfast with Aunt Jemimah. She come by and cooked me up a whole mess of flapjacks. Remember how we used to eat them flapjacks?
TROY. Go on in the house and get you something to eat now.
GABRIEL. I got to sell my plums. I done sold some tomatoes. Got me two quarters. Wanna see? (*He shows Troy his quarters.*) I'm gonna save them and buy me a new horn so St. Peter can hear me when it's time to open the gates. (*Gabriel stops suddenly. Listens.*) Hear that? That's the hellhounds. I got to chase them out of here. Go on get out of here! Get out!

Gabriel exits singing.

> Better get ready for the judgment
> Better get ready for the judgment
> My Lord is coming down

Rose enters from the house.

TROY. He's gone off somewhere.
GABRIEL (*offstage*).
> Better get ready for the judgment
> Better get ready for the judgment morning
> Better get ready for the judgment
> My God is coming down

ROSE. He ain't eating right. Miss Pearl say she can't get him to eat nothing.

TROY. What you want me to do about it, Rose? I done did everything I can for the man. I can't make him get well. Man got half his head blown away . . . what you expect?

ROSE. Seem like something ought to be done to help him.

TROY. Man don't bother nobody. He just mixed up from that metal plate he got in his head. Ain't no sense for him to go back into the hospital.

ROSE. Least he be eating right. They can help him take care of himself.

TROY. Don't nobody wanna be locked up, Rose. What you wanna lock him up for? Man go over there and fight the war . . . messin' around with them Japs, get half his head blow off . . . and they give him a lousy three thousand dollars. And I had to swoop down on that.

ROSE. Is you fixing to go into that again?

TROY. That's the only way I got a roof over my head . . . cause of that metal plate.

ROSE. Ain't no sense you blaming yourself for nothing. Gabe wasn't in no condition to manage that money. You done what was right by him. Can't nobody say you ain't done what was right by him. Look how long you took care of him . . . till he wanted to have his own place and moved over there with Miss Pearl.

TROY. That ain't what I'm saying, woman! I'm just stating the facts. If my brother didn't have that metal plate in his head . . . I wouldn't have a pot to piss in or a window to throw it out of. And I'm fifty-three years old. Now see if you can understand that!

Troy gets up from the porch and starts to exit the yard.

ROSE. Where you going off to? You been running out of here every Saturday for weeks. I thought you was gonna work on this fence?

TROY. I'm gonna walk down to Taylors'. Listen to the ball game. I'll be back in a bit. I'll work on it when I get back.

He exits the yard. The lights go to black.

SCENE 3

The lights come up on the yard. It is four hours later. Rose is taking down the clothes from the line. Cory enters carrying his football equipment.

ROSE. Your daddy like to had a fit with you running out of here this morning without doing your chores.

CORY. I told you I had to go to practice.

ROSE. He say you were supposed to help him with this fence.

CORY. He been saying that the last four or five Saturdays, and then he don't never do nothing, but go down to Taylors'. Did you tell him about the recruiter?

ROSE. Yeah, I told him.

CORY. What he say?

ROSE. He ain't said nothing too much. You get in there and get started on your chores before he gets back. Go on and scrub down them steps before he gets back here hollering and carrying on.

CORY. I'm hungry. What you got to eat, Mama?

ROSE. Go on and get started on your chores. I got some meat loaf in there. Go on and make you a sandwich . . . and don't leave no mess in there.

Cory exits into the house. Rose continues to take down the clothes. Troy enters the yard and sneaks up and grabs her from behind.

Troy! Go on, now. You liked to scared me to death. What was the score of the game? Lucille had me on the phone and I couldn't keep up with it.

TROY. What I care about the game? Come here, woman. (*He tries to kiss her.*)

ROSE. I thought you went down Taylors' to listen to the game. Go on, Troy! You supposed to be putting up this fence.

TROY (*attempting to kiss her again*). I'll put it up when I finish with what is at hand.

ROSE. Go on, Troy. I ain't studying you.

TROY (*chasing after her*). I'm studying you . . . fixing to do my homework!

ROSE. Troy, you better leave me alone.

TROY. Where's Cory? That boy brought his butt home yet?

ROSE. He's in the house doing his chores.

TROY (*calling*). Cory! Get your butt out here, boy!

Rose exits into the house with the laundry. Troy goes over to the pile of wood, picks up a board, and starts sawing. Cory enters from the house.

TROY. You just now coming in here from leaving this morning?

CORY. Yeah, I had to go to football practice.

TROY. Yeah, what?

CORY. Yessir.

TROY. I ain't but two seconds off you noway. The garbage sitting in there overflowing . . . you ain't done none of your chores . . . and you come in here talking about "Yeah."

CORY. I was just getting ready to do my chores now, Pop . . .

TROY. Your first chore is to help me with this fence on Saturday. Everything else come after that. Now get that saw and cut them boards.

Cory takes the saw and begins cutting the boards. Troy continues working. There is a long pause.

CORY. Hey, Pop . . . why don't you buy a TV?

TROY. What I want with a TV? What I want one of them for?

CORY. Everybody got one. Earl, Ba Bra . . . Jesse!

TROY. I ain't asked you who had one. I say what I want with one?

CORY. So you can watch it. They got lots of things on TV. Baseball games and everything. We could watch the World Series.

TROY. Yeah . . . and how much this TV cost?

CORY. I don't know. They got them on sale for around two hundred dollars.

TROY. Two hundred dollars, huh?

CORY. That ain't that much, Pop.

TROY. Naw, it's just two hundred dollars. See that roof you got over your head at night? Let me tell you something about that roof. It's been over ten years since that roof was last tarred. See now . . . the snow come this winter and sit up there on that roof like it is . . . and it's gonna seep inside. It's just gonna be a little bit . . . ain't gonna hardly notice it. Then the next thing you know, it's gonna be leaking all over the house. Then the wood rot from all that water and you gonna need a whole new roof. Now, how much you think it cost to get that roof tarred?

CORY. I don't know.

TROY. Two hundred and sixty-four dollars . . . cash money. While you thinking about a TV, I got to be thinking about the roof . . . and whatever else go wrong here. Now if you had two hundred dollars, what would you do . . . fix the roof or buy a TV?

CORY. I'd buy a TV. Then when the roof started to leak . . . when it needed fixing . . . I'd fix it.

TROY. Where you gonna get the money from? You done spent it for a TV. You gonna sit up and watch the water run all over your brand new TV.

CORY. Aw, Pop. You got money. I know you do.

TROY. Where I got it at, huh?

CORY. You got it in the bank.

TROY. You wanna see my bankbook? You wanna see that seventy-three dollars and twenty-two cents I got sitting up in there?

CORY. You ain't got to pay for it all at one time. You can put a down payment on it and carry it on home with you.

TROY. Not me. I ain't gonna owe nobody nothing if I can help it. Miss a payment and they come and snatch it right out of your house. Then what you got? Now, soon as I get two hundred dollars clear, then I'll buy a TV. Right now, as soon as I get two hundred and sixty-four dollars, I'm gonna have this roof tarred.

CORY. Aw . . . Pop!

TROY. You go on and get you two hundred dollars and buy one if ya want it. I got better things to do with my money.

CORY. I can't get no two hundred dollars. I ain't never seen two hundred dollars.

TROY. I'll tell you what . . . you get you a hundred dollars and I'll put the other hundred with it.

CORY. All right, I'm gonna show you.

TROY. You gonna show me how you can cut them boards right now.

Cory begins to cut the boards. There is a long pause.

CORY. The Pirates won today. That makes five in a row.

TROY. I ain't thinking about the Pirates. Got an all-white team. Got that boy . . . that Puerto Rican boy . . . Clemente. Don't even half-play him. That boy could be something if they give him a chance. Play him one day and sit him on the bench the next.

CORY. He gets a lot of chances to play.

TROY. I'm talking about playing regular. Playing every day so you can get your timing. That's what I'm talking about.

CORY. They got some white guys on the team that don't play every day. You can't play everybody at the same time.

TROY. If they got a white fellow sitting on the bench . . . you can bet your last dollar he can't play! The colored guy got to be twice as good before he get on the team. That's why I don't want you to get all tied up in them sports. Man on the team and what it get him? They got colored on the team and don't use them. Same as not having them. All them teams the same.

CORY. The Braves got Hank Aaron and Wes Covington. Hank Aaron hit two home runs today. That makes forty-three.

TROY. Hank Aaron ain't nobody. That what you supposed to do. That's how you supposed to play the game. Ain't nothing to it. It's just a matter of timing . . . getting the right follow-through. Hell, I can hit forty-three home runs right now!

CORY. Not off no major-league pitching, you couldn't.

TROY. We had better pitching in the Negro leagues. I hit seven home runs off of Satchel Paige.[4] You can't get no better than that!

CORY. Sandy Koufax. He's leading the league in strikeouts.

TROY. I ain't thinking of no Sandy Koufax.

CORY. You got Warren Spahn and Lew Burdette. I bet you couldn't hit no home runs off of Warren Spahn.

TROY. I'm through with it now. You go on and cut them boards. (*Pause.*) Your mama tell me you done got recruited by a college football team? Is that right?

CORY. Yeah. Coach Zellman say the recruiter gonna be coming by to talk to you. Get you to sign the permission papers.

TROY. I thought you supposed to be working down there at the A&P. Ain't you suppose to be working down there after school?

CORY. Mr. Stawicki say he gonna hold my job for me until after the football season. Say starting next week I can work weekends.

TROY. I thought we had an understanding about this football stuff? You suppose to keep up with your chores and hold that job down at the A&P. Ain't been around here all day on a Saturday. Ain't none of your chores done . . . and now you telling me you done quit your job.

CORY. I'm going to be working weekends.

TROY. You damn right you are! And ain't no need for nobody coming around here to talk to me about signing nothing.

CORY. Hey, Pop . . . you can't do that. He's coming all the way from North Carolina.

TROY. I don't care where he coming from. The white man ain't gonna let you get nowhere with that football noway. You go on and get your book-learning so you can work yourself up in that A&P or learn how to fix cars or build houses or something, get you a trade. That way you have something can't nobody take away from you. You go on and learn how to put your hands to some good use. Besides hauling people's garbage.

CORY. I get good grades, Pop. That's why the recruiter wants to talk with you. You got to keep up your grades to get recruited. This way I'll be going to college. I'll get a chance . . .

TROY. First you gonna get your butt down there to the A&P and get your job back.

CORY. Mr. Stawicki done already hired somebody else 'cause I told him I was playing football.

TROY. You a bigger fool than I thought . . . to let somebody take away your job so you can play some football. Where you gonna get your money to take out your girlfriend and whatnot? What kind of foolishness is that to let somebody take away your job?

CORY. I'm still gonna be working weekends.

TROY. Naw . . . naw. You getting your butt out of here and finding you another job.

CORY. Come on, Pop! I got to practice. I can't work after school and play football too. The team needs me. That's what Coach Zellman say . . .

TROY. I don't care what nobody else say. I'm the boss . . . you understand? I'm the boss around here. I do the only saying what counts.

CORY. Come on, Pop!

TROY. I asked you . . . did you understand?

CORY. Yeah . . .

TROY. What?!

CORY. Yessir.

TROY. You go on down there to that A&P and see if you can get your job back. If you can't do both . . . then you quit the football team. You've got to take the crookeds with the straights.

CORY. Yessir. (*Pause.*) Can I ask you a question?

TROY. What the hell you wanna ask me? Mr. Stawicki the one you got the questions for.

CORY. How come you ain't never liked me?

TROY. Liked you? Who the hell say I got to like you? What law is there say I got to like you? Wanna stand up in my face and ask a damn foolass question like that. Talking about liking somebody. Come here, boy, when I talk to you.

Cory comes over to where Troy is working. He stands slouched over and Troy shoves him on his shoulder.

Straighten up, goddammit! I asked you a question . . . what law is there say I got to like you?

CORY. None.

TROY. Well, all right then! Don't you eat every day? (*Pause.*) Answer me when I talk to you! Don't you eat every day?

CORY. Yeah.

TROY. Nigger, as long as you in my house, you put that sir on the end of it when you talk to me.

CORY. Yes . . . sir.

TROY. You eat every day.

CORY. Yessir!

TROY. Got a roof over your head.

CORY. Yessir!

TROY. Got clothes on your back.

4**Satchel Paige** (1906–82) was a pitcher in the Negro leagues.

CORY. Yessir.

TROY. Why you think that is?

CORY. Cause of you.

TROY. Ah, hell I know it's cause of me . . . but why do you think that is?

CORY (*hesitant*). Cause you like me.

TROY. Like you? I go out of here every morning . . . bust my butt . . . putting up with them crackers every day . . . cause I like you? You are the biggest fool I ever saw. (*Pause.*) It's my job. It's my responsibility! You understand that? A man got to take care of his family. You live in my house . . . sleep you behind on my bedclothes . . . fill you belly up with my food . . . cause you my son. You my flesh and blood. Not cause I like you! Cause it's my duty to take care of you. I owe a responsibility to you! Let's get this straight right here . . . before it go along any further . . . I ain't got to like you. Mr. Rand don't give me my money come payday cause he likes me. He gives me cause he owe me. I done give you everything I had to give you. I gave you your life! Me and your mama worked that out between us. And liking your black ass wasn't part of the bargain. Don't you try and go through life worrying about if somebody like you or not. You best be making sure they doing right by you. You understand what I'm saying boy?

CORY. Yessir.

TROY. Then get the hell out of my face, and get on down to that A&P.

Rose has been standing behind the screen door for much of the scene. She enters as Cory exits.

ROSE. Why don't you let the boy go ahead and play football, Troy? Ain't no harm in that. He's just trying to be like you with the sports.

TROY. I don't want him to be like me! I want him to move as far away from my life as he can get. You the only decent thing that ever happened to me. I wish him that. But I don't wish him a thing else from my life. I decided seventeen years ago that boy wasn't getting involved in no sports. Not after what they did to me in the sports.

ROSE. Troy, why don't you admit you was too old to play in the major leagues? For once . . . why don't you admit that?

TROY. What do you mean too old? Don't come telling me I was too old. I just wasn't the right color. Hell, I'm fifty-three years old and can do better than Selkirk's .269 right now!

ROSE. How's was you gonna play ball when you were over forty? Sometimes I can't get no sense out of you.

TROY. I got good sense, woman. I got sense enough not to let my boy get hurt over playing no sports. You been mothering that boy too much. Worried about if people like him.

ROSE. Everything that boy do . . . he do for you. He wants you to say "Good job, son." That's all.

TROY. Rose, I ain't got time for that. He's alive. He's healthy. He's got to make his own way. I made mine. Ain't nobody gonna hold his hand when he get out there in that world.

ROSE. Times have changed from when you was young, Troy. People change. The world's changing around you and you can't even see it.

TROY (*slow, methodical*). Woman . . . I do the best I can do. I come in here every Friday. I carry a sack of potatoes and a bucket of lard. You all line up at the door with your hands out. I give you the lint from my pockets. I give you my sweat and my blood. I ain't got no tears. I done spent them. We go upstairs in that room at night . . . and I fall down on you and try to blast a hole into forever. I get up Monday morning . . . find my lunch on the table. I go out. Make my way. Find my strength to carry me through to the next Friday. (*Pause.*) That's all I got, Rose. That's all I got to give. I can't give nothing else.

Troy exits into the house. The lights go down to black.

SCENE 4

It is Friday. Two weeks later. Cory starts out of the house with his football equipment. The phone rings.

CORY (*calling*). I got it! (*He answers the phone and stands in the screen door talking.*) Hello? Hey, Jesse. Naw . . . I was just getting ready to leave now.

ROSE (*calling*). Cory!

CORY. I told you, man, them spikes is all tore up. You can use them if you want, but they ain't no good. Earl got some spikes.

ROSE (*calling*). Cory!

CORY (*calling to Rose*). Mam? I'm talking to Jesse. (*Into phone.*) When she say that? (*Pause.*) Aw, you lying, man. I'm gonna tell her you said that.

ROSE (*calling*). Cory, don't you go nowhere!

CORY. I got to go to the game, Ma! (*Into the phone.*) Yeah, hey, look, I'll talk to you later. Yeah, I'll meet you over Earl's house. Later. Bye, Ma.

Cory exits the house and starts out the yard.

ROSE. Cory, where you going off to? You got that stuff all pulled out and thrown all over your room.

CORY (*in the yard*). I was looking for my spikes. Jesse wanted to borrow my spikes.

ROSE. Get up there and get that cleaned up before your daddy get back in here.

CORY. I got to go to the game! I'll clean it up *when I get back.*

Cory exits.

ROSE. That's all he need to do is see that room all messed up.

Rose exits into the house. Troy and Bono enter the yard. Troy is dressed in clothes other than his work clothes.

BONO. He told him the same thing he told you. Take it to the union.

TROY. Brownie ain't got that much sense. Man wasn't thinking about nothing. He wait until I confront them on it . . . then he wanna come crying seniority. (*Calls.*) Hey, Rose!

BONO. I wish I could have seen Mr. Rand's face when he told you.

TROY. He couldn't get it out of his mouth! Liked to bit his tongue! When they called me down there to the Commissioner's office . . . he thought they was gonna fire me. Like everybody else.

BONO. I didn't think they was gonna fire you. I thought they was gonna put you on the warning paper.

TROY. Hey, Rose! (*To Bono.*) Yeah, Mr. Rand like to bit his tongue.

Troy breaks the seal on the bottle, takes a drink, and hands it to Bono.

BONO. I see you run right down to Taylors' and told that Alberta gal.

TROY (*calling*). Hey Rose! (*To Bono.*) I told everybody. Hey, Rose! I went down there to cash my check.

ROSE (*entering from the house*). Hush all that hollering, man! I know you out here. What they say down there at the Commissioner's office?

TROY. You supposed to come when I call you, woman. Bono'll tell you that. (*To Bono.*) Don't Lucille come when you call her?

ROSE. Man, hush your mouth. I ain't no dog . . . talk about "come when you call me."

TROY (*puts his arm around Rose*). You hear this, Bono? I had me an old dog used to get uppity like that. You say, "C'mere, Blue!" . . . and he just lay there and look at you. End up getting a stick and chasing him away trying to make him come.

ROSE. I ain't studying you and your dog. I remember you used to sing that old song.

TROY (*he sings*).
    Hear it ring! Hear it ring! I had a dog his name was Blue.

ROSE. Don't nobody wanna hear you sing that old song.

TROY (*sings*).
    You know Blue was mighty true.

ROSE. Used to have Cory running around here singing that song.

BONO. Hell, I remember that song myself.

TROY (*sings*).
    You know Blue was a good old dog.
    Blue treed a possum in a hollow log.
    That was my daddy's song. My daddy made up that song.

ROSE. I don't care who made it up. Don't nobody wanna hear you sing it.

TROY (*makes a song like calling a dog*). Come here, woman.

ROSE. You come in here carrying on, I reckon they ain't fired you. What they say down there at the Commissioner's office?

TROY. Look here, Rose . . . Mr. Rand called me into his office today when I got back from talking to them people down there . . . it come from up top . . . he called me in and told me they was making me a driver.

ROSE. Troy, you kidding!

TROY. No I ain't. Ask Bono.

ROSE. Well, that's great, Troy. Now you don't have to hassle them people no more.

Lyons enters from the street.

TROY. Aw hell, I wasn't looking to see you today. I thought you was in jail. Got it all over the front page of the *Courier* about them raiding Sefus's place . . . where you be hanging out with all them thugs.

LYONS. Hey, Pop . . . that ain't got nothing to do with me. I don't go down there gambling. I go down there to sit in with the band. I ain't got nothing to do with the gambling part. They got some good music down there.

TROY. They got some rogues . . . is what they got.

LYONS. How you been, Mr. Bono? Hi, Rose.

BONO. I see where you playing down at the Crawford Grill tonight.

ROSE. How come you ain't brought Bonnie like I told you? You should have brought Bonnie with you, she ain't been over in a month of Sundays.

LYONS. I was just in the neighborhood . . . thought I'd stop by.

TROY. Here he come . . .

BONO. Your daddy got a promotion on the rubbish. He's gonna be the first colored driver. Ain't got to do nothing but sit up there and read the paper like them white fellows.

LYONS. Hey, Pop . . . if you knew how to read you'd be all right.

BONO. Naw . . . naw . . . you mean if the nigger knew how to drive he'd be all right. Been fighting with them people about driving and ain't even got a license. Mr. Rand know you ain't got no driver's license?

TROY. Driving ain't nothing. All you do is point the truck where you want it to go. Driving ain't nothing.

BONO. Do Mr. Rand know you ain't got no driver's license? That's what I'm talking about. I ain't asked if driving was easy. I asked if Mr. Rand know you ain't got no driver's license.

TROY. He ain't got to know. The man ain't got to know my business. Time he find out, I have two or three driver's licenses.

LYONS (going into his pocket). Say, look here, Pop . . .

TROY. I knew it was coming. Didn't I tell you, Bono? I know what kind of "Look here, Pop" that was. The nigger fixing to ask me for some money. It's Friday night. It's my payday. All them rogues down there on the avenue . . . the ones that ain't in jail . . . and Lyons is hopping in his shoes to get down there with them.

LYONS. See, Pop . . . if you give somebody else a chance to talk sometimes, you'd see that I was fixing to pay you back your ten dollars like I told you. Here . . . I told you I'd pay you when Bonnie got paid.

TROY. Naw . . . you go ahead and keep that ten dollars. Put it in the bank. The next time you feel like you wanna come by here and ask me for something . . . you go on down there and get that.

LYONS. Here's your ten dollars, Pop. I told you I don't want you to give me nothing. I just wanted to borrow ten dollars.

TROY. Naw . . . you go on and keep that for the next time you want to ask me.

LYONS. Come on, Pop . . . here go your ten dollars.

ROSE. Why don't you go on and let the boy pay you back, Troy?

LYONS. Here you go, Rose. If you don't take it I'm gonna have to hear about it for the next six months. (He hands her the money.)

ROSE. You can hand yours over here too, Troy.

TROY. You see this, Bono. You see how they do me.

BONO. Yeah, Lucille do me the same way.

Gabriel is heard singing off stage. He enters.

GABRIEL. Better get ready for the Judgment! Better get ready for . . . Hey! . . . Hey! . . . There's Troy's boy!

LYONS. How are you doing, Uncle Gabe?

GABRIEL. Lyons . . . The King of the Jungle! Rose . . . hey, Rose. Got a flower for you. (He takes a rose from his pocket.) Picked it myself. That's the same rose like you is!

ROSE. That's right nice of you, Gabe.

LYONS. What you been doing, Uncle Gabe?

GABRIEL. Oh, I been chasing hellhounds and waiting on the time to tell St. Peter to open the gates.

LYONS. You been chasing hellhounds, huh? Well . . . you doing the right thing, Uncle Gabe. Somebody got to chase them.

GABRIEL. Oh, yeah . . . I know it. The devil's strong. The devil ain't no pushover. Hellhounds snipping at everybody's heels. But I got my trumpet waiting on the judgment time.

LYONS. Waiting on the Battle of Armageddon, huh?

GABRIEL. Ain't gonna be too much of a battle when God get to waving that Judgment sword. But the people's gonna have a hell of a time trying to get into heaven if them gates ain't open.

LYONS (putting his arm around Gabriel). You hear this, Pop. Uncle Gabe, you all right!

GABRIEL (laughing with Lyons). Lyons! King of the Jungle.

ROSE. You gonna stay for supper, Gabe? Want me to fix you a plate?

GABRIEL. I'll take a sandwich, Rose. Don't want no plate. Just wanna eat with my hands. I'll take a sandwich.

ROSE. How about you, Lyons? You staying? Got some short ribs cooking.

LYONS. Naw, I won't eat nothing till after we finished playing. (Pause.) You ought to come down and listen to me play, Pop.

TROY. I don't like that Chinese music. All that noise.

ROSE. Go on in the house and wash up, Gabe . . . I'll fix you a sandwich.

GABRIEL (to Lyons, as he exits). Troy's mad at me.

LYONS. What you mad at Uncle Gabe for, Pop?

ROSE. He thinks Troy's mad at him cause he moved over to Miss Pearl's.

TROY. I ain't mad at the man. He can live where he want to live at.

LYONS. What he move over there for? Miss Pearl don't like nobody.

ROSE. She don't mind him none. She treats him real nice. She just don't allow all that singing.

TROY. She don't mind that rent he be paying . . . that's what she don't mind.

ROSE. Troy, I ain't going through that with you no more. He's over there cause he want to have his own place. He can come and go as he please.

TROY. Hell, he could come and go as he please here. I wasn't stopping him. I ain't put no rules on him.

ROSE. It ain't the same thing, Troy. And you know it.

Gabriel comes to the door.

Now, that's the last I wanna hear about that. I don't wanna hear nothing else about Gabe and Miss Pearl. And next week . . .

GABRIEL. I'm ready for my sandwich, Rose.

ROSE. And next week . . . when that recruiter come from that school . . . I want you to sign that paper and go on and let Cory play football. Then that'll be the last I have to hear about that.

TROY (*to Rose as she exits into the house*). I ain't thinking about Cory nothing.

LYONS. What . . . Cory got recruited? What school he going to?

TROY. That boy walking around here smelling his piss . . . thinking he's grown. Thinking he's gonna do what he want, irrespective of what I say. Look here, Bono . . . I left the Commissioner's office and went down to the A&P . . . that boy ain't working down there. He lying to me. Telling me he got his job back . . . telling me he working weekends . . . telling me he working after school . . . Mr. Stawicki tell me he ain't working down there at all!

LYONS. Cory just growing up. He's just busting at the seams trying to fill out your shoes.

TROY. I don't care what he's doing. When he get to the point where he wanna disobey me . . . then it's time for him to move on. Bono'll tell you that. I bet he ain't never disobeyed his daddy without paying the consequences.

BONO. I ain't never had a chance. My daddy came on through . . . but I ain't never knew him to see him . . . or what he had on his mind or where he went. Just moving on through. Searching out the New Land. That's what the old folks used to call it. See a fellow moving around from place to place . . . woman to woman . . . called it searching out the New Land. I can't say if he ever found it. I come along, didn't want no kids. Didn't know if I was gonna be in one place long enough to fix on them right as their daddy. I figured I was going searching too. As it turned out I been hooked up with Lucille near about as long as your daddy been with Rose. Going on sixteen years.

TROY. Sometimes I wish I hadn't known my daddy. He ain't cared nothing about no kids. A kid to him wasn't nothing. All he wanted was for you to learn how to walk so he could start you to working. When it come time for eating . . . he ate first. If there was anything left over, that's what you got. Man would sit down and eat two chickens and give you the wing.

LYONS. You ought to stop that, Pop. Everybody feed their kids. No matter how hard times is . . . everybody care about their kids. Make sure they have something to eat.

TROY. The only thing my daddy cared about was getting them bales of cotton in to Mr. Lubin. That's the only thing that mattered to him. Sometimes I used to wonder why he was living. Wonder why the devil hadn't come and got him. "Get them bales of cotton in to Mr. Lubin" and find out he owe him money . . .

LYONS. He should have just went on and left when he saw he couldn't get nowhere. That's what I would have done.

TROY. How he gonna leave with eleven kids? And where he gonna go? He ain't knew how to do nothing but farm. No, he was trapped and I think he knew it. But I'll say this for him . . . he felt a responsibility toward us. Maybe he ain't treated us the way I felt he should have . . . but without that responsibility he could have walked off and left us . . . made his own way.

BONO. A lot of them did. Back in those days what you talking about . . . they walk out their front door and just take on down one road or another and keep on walking.

LYONS. There you go! That's what I'm talking about.

BONO. Just keep on walking till you come to something else. Ain't you never heard of nobody having the walking blues? Well, that's what you call it when you just take off like that.

TROY. My daddy ain't had them walking blues! What you talking about? He stayed right there with his family. But he was just as evil as he could be. My mama couldn't stand him. Couldn't stand that evilness. She run off when I was about eight. She sneaked off one night after he had gone to sleep. Told me she was coming back for me. I ain't never seen her no more. All his women run off and left him. He wasn't good for nobody.

When my turn come to head out, I was fourteen and got to sniffing around Joe Canewell's daughter. Had us an old mule we called Greyboy. My daddy sent me out to do some plowing and I tied up Greyboy and went to fooling around with Joe Canewell's daughter. We done found us a nice little spot, got real cozy with each other. She about thirteen and we done figured we was grown anyway . . . so we down there enjoying ourselves . . . ain't thinking about nothing. We didn't know Greyboy had got loose and wandered back to the house and my daddy was looking for me. We down there by the creek enjoying ourselves when my daddy come up on us. Surprised us. He had them leather straps off the mule and commenced to whupping me like there was no tomorrow. I jumped up, mad and embarrassed. I was scared of my daddy. When he commenced to whupping on me . . . quite naturally I run to get out of the way. (*Pause.*) Now I thought he was mad cause I ain't done my work. But I see where he was chasing me off so he could have the gal for himself. When I see what the matter of it was, I lost all fear of my daddy. Right there is where I become a man . . . at fourteen years of age. (*Pause.*) Now it was my turn to run him off. I picked up them same reins that he had used on me. I picked up them reins and commenced to whupping on him. The gal jumped up and run off . . . and when my daddy turned to face me, I could see why the devil had never come to get him . . . cause he was the devil himself. I don't know what happened. When I woke up, I was laying right there by the creek, and Blue . . . this old dog we had . . . was licking my face. I thought I was blind. I couldn't see nothing. Both my eyes were swollen shut. I laid there and cried. I didn't know what I was gonna do. The only thing I knew was the time had come for me to leave my daddy's house. And right there the world suddenly got big. And it was a long time before I could cut it down to where I could handle it.

Part of that cutting down was when I got to the place where I could feel him kicking in my blood and knew that the only thing that separated us was the matter of a few years.

Gabriel enters from the house with a sandwich.

LYONS. What you got there, Uncle Gabe?
GABRIEL. Got me a ham sandwich. Rose gave me a ham sandwich.
TROY. I don't know what happened to him. I done lost touch with everybody except Gabriel. But I hope he's dead. I hope he found some peace.
LYONS. That's a heavy story, Pop. I didn't know you left home when you was fourteen.
TROY. And didn't know nothing. The only part of the world I knew was the forty-two acres of Mr. Lubin's land. That's all I knew about life.
LYONS. Fourteen's kinda young to be out on your own. (*Phone rings.*) I don't even think I was ready to be out on my own at fourteen. I don't know what I would have done.

TROY. I got up from the creek and walked on down to Mobile. I was through with farming. Figured I could do better in the city. So I walked the two hundred miles to Mobile.
LYONS. Wait a minute . . . you ain't walked no two hundred miles, Pop. Ain't nobody gonna walk no two hundred miles. You talking about some walking there.
BONO. That's the only way you got anywhere back in them days.
LYONS. Shhh. Damn if I wouldn't have hitched a ride with somebody!
TROY. Who you gonna hitch it with? They ain't had no cars and things like they got now. We talking about 1918.
ROSE (*entering*). What you all out here getting into?
TROY (*to Rose*). I'm telling Lyons how good he got it. He don't know nothing about this I'm talking.
ROSE. Lyons, that was Bonnie on the phone. She say you supposed to pick her up.
LYONS. Yeah, okay, Rose.
TROY. I walked on down to Mobile and hitched up with some of them fellows that was heading this way. Got up here and found out . . . not only couldn't you get a job . . . you couldn't find no place to live. I thought I was in freedom. Shhh. Colored folks living down there on the riverbanks in whatever kind of shelter they could find for themselves. Right down there under the Brady Street Bridge. Living in shacks made of sticks and tarpaper. Messed around there and went from bad to worse. Started stealing. First it was food. Then I figured, hell, if I steal money I can buy me some food. Buy me some shoes too! One thing led to another. Met your mama. I was young and anxious to be a man. Met your mama and had you. What I do that for? Now I got to worry about feeding you and her. Got to steal three times as much. Went out one day looking for somebody to rob . . . that's what I was, a robber. I'll tell you the truth. I'm ashamed of it today. But it's the truth. Went to rob this fellow . . . pulled out my knife . . . and he pulled out a gun. Shot me in the chest. I felt just like somebody had taken a hot branding iron and laid it on me. When he shot me I jumped at him with my knife. They told me I killed him and they put me in the penitentiary and locked me up for fifteen years. That's where I met Bono. That's where I learned how to play baseball. Got out that place and your mama had taken you and went on to make life without me. Fifteen years was a long time for her to wait. But that fifteen years cured me of that robbing stuff. Rose'll tell you. She asked

me when I met her if I had gotten all that foolishness out of my system. And I told her, "Baby, it's you and baseball all what count with me." You hear me, Bono? I meant it too. She say, "Which one comes first?" I told her, "Baby, ain't no doubt it's baseball . . . but you stick and get old with me and we'll both out-live this baseball." Am I right, Rose? And it's true.

ROSE. Man, hush your mouth. You ain't said no such thing. Talking about, "Baby you know you'll always be number one with me." That's what you was talk-ing.

TROY. You hear that, Bono. That's why I love her.

BONO. Rose'll keep you straight. You get off the track, she'll straighten you up.

ROSE. Lyons, you better get on up and get Bonnie. She waiting on you.

LYONS (gets up to go). Hey, Pop, why don't you come on down to the Grill and hear me play?

TROY. I ain't going down there. I'm too old to be sitting around in them clubs.

BONO. You got to be good to play down at the Grill.

LYONS. Come on, Pop . . .

TROY. I got to get up in the morning.

LYONS. You ain't got to stay long.

TROY. Naw, I'm gonna get my supper and go on to bed.

LYONS. Well, I got to go. I'll see you again.

TROY. Don't you come around my house on my payday.

ROSE. Pick up the phone and let somebody know you coming. And bring Bonnie with you. You know I'm always glad to see her.

LYONS. Yeah, I'll do that, Rose. You take care now. See you, Pop. See you, Mr. Bono. See you, Uncle Gabe.

GABRIEL. Lyons! King of the Jungle!

Lyons exits.

TROY. Is supper ready, woman? Me and you got some business to take care of. I'm gonna tear it up too.

ROSE. Troy, I done told you now!

TROY (puts his arm around Bono). Aw hell, woman . . . this is Bono. Bono like family. I done known this nig-ger since . . . how long I done know you?

BONO. It's been a long time.

TROY. I done know this nigger since Skippy was a pup. Me and him done been through some times.

BONO. You sure right about that.

TROY. Hell, I done know him longer than I known you. And we still standing shoulder to shoulder. Hey, look here, Bono . . . a man can't ask for no more than that. (Drinks to him.) I love you, nigger.

BONO. Hell, I love you too . . . I got to get home see my woman. You got yours in hand. I got to get mine.

Bono starts to exit as Cory enters the yard, dressed in his football uniform. He gives Troy a hard, un-compromising look.

CORY. What you do that for, Pop?

He throws his helmet down in the direction of Troy.

ROSE. What's the matter? Cory . . . what's the matter?

CORY. Papa done went up to the school and told Coach Zellman I can't play football no more. Wouldn't even let me play the game. Told him to tell the recruiter not to come.

ROSE. Troy . . .

TROY. What you Troying me for. Yeah, I did it. And the boy know why I did it.

CORY. Why you wanna do that to me? That was the one chance I had.

ROSE. Ain't nothing wrong with Cory playing football, Troy.

TROY. The boy lied to me. I told the nigger if he wanna play football . . . to keep up his chores and hold down that job at the A&P. That was the conditions. Stopped down there to see Mr. Stawicki . . .

CORY. I can't work after school during the football sea-son, Pop! I tried to tell you that Mr. Stawicki's hold-ing my job for me. You don't never want to listen to nobody. And then you wanna go and do this to me!

TROY. I ain't done nothing to you. You done it to yourself.

CORY. Just cause you didn't have a chance! You just scared I'm gonna be better than you, that's all.

TROY. Come here.

ROSE. Troy . . .

Cory reluctantly crosses over to Troy.

TROY. All right! See. You done made a mistake.

CORY. I didn't even do nothing!

TROY. I'm gonna tell you what your mistake was. See . . . you swung at the ball and didn't hit it. That's strike one. See, you in the batter's box now. You swung and you missed. That's strike one. Don't you strike out!

Lights fade to black.

ACT II

SCENE 1

The following morning. Cory is at the tree hitting the ball with the bat. He tries to mimic Troy, but his swing is awkward, less sure. Rose enters from the house.

ROSE. Cory, I want you to help me with this cupboard.

CORY. I ain't quitting the team. I don't care what Poppa say.

ROSE. I'll talk to him when he gets back. He had to see about your Uncle Gabe. The police done arrested him. Say he was disturbing the peace. He'll be back directly. Come on in here and help me clean out the top of this cupboard.

Cory exits into the house. Rose sees Troy and Bono coming down the alley.

Troy . . . what they say down there?

TROY. Ain't said nothing. I give them fifty dollars and they let him go. I'll talk to you about it. Where's Cory?

ROSE. He's in there helping me clean out these cupboards.

TROY. Tell him to get his butt out here.

Troy and Bono go over to the pile of wood. Bono picks up the saw and begins sawing.

TROY (*to Bono*). All they want is the money. That makes six or seven times I done went down there and got him. See me coming they stick out their hands.

BONO. Yeah. I know what you mean. That's all they care about . . . that money. They don't care about what's right. (*Pause.*) Nigger, why you got to go and get some hard wood? You ain't doing nothing but building a little old fence. Get you some soft pine wood. That's all you need.

TROY. I know what I'm doing. This is outside wood. You put pine wood inside the house. Pine wood is inside wood. This here is outside wood. Now you tell me where the fence is gonna be?

BONO. You don't need this wood. You can put it up with pine wood and it'll stand as long as you gonna be here looking at it.

TROY. How you know how long I'm gonna be here, nigger? Hell, I might just live forever. Live longer than old man Horsely.

BONO. That's what Magee used to say.

TROY. Magee's damn fool. Now you tell me who you ever heard of gonna pull their own teeth with a pair of rusty pliers.

BONO. The old folks . . . my granddaddy used to pull his teeth with pliers. They ain't had no dentists for the colored folks back then.

TROY. Get clean pliers! You understand? Clean pliers! Sterilize them! Besides we ain't living back then. All Magee had to do was walk over to Doc Goldblum's.

BONO. I see where you and that Tallahassee gal . . . that Alberta . . . I see where you all done got tight.

TROY. What you mean "got tight"?

BONO. I see where you be laughing and joking with her all the time.

TROY. I laughs and jokes with all of them, Bono. You know me.

BONO. That ain't the kind of laughing and joking I'm talking about.

Cory enters from the house.

CORY. How you doing. Mr. Bono?

TROY. Cory? Get that saw from Bono and cut some wood. He talking about the wood's too hard to cut. Stand back there, Jim, and let that young boy show you how it's done.

BONO. He's sure welcome to it.

Cory takes the saw and begins to cut the wood.

Whew-e-e! Look at that. Big old strong boy. Look like Joe Louis. Hell, must be getting old the way I'm watching that boy whip through that wood.

CORY. I don't see why Mama want a fence around the yard noways.

TROY. Damn if I know either. What the hell she keeping out with it? She ain't got nothing nobody want.

BONO. Some people build fences to keep people out . . . and other people build fences to keep people in. Rose wants to hold on to you all. She loves you.

TROY. Hell, nigger, I don't need nobody to tell me my wife loves me. Cory . . . go on in the house and see if you can find that other saw.

CORY. Where's it at?

TROY. I said find it! Look for it till you find it!

Cory exits into the house.

What's that supposed to mean? Wanna keep us in?

BONO. Troy . . . I done known you seem like damn near my whole life. You and Rose both. I done know both of you all for a long time. I remember when you met Rose. When you was hitting them baseball out the park. A lot of them old gals was after you then. You had the pick of the litter. When you picked Rose, I was happy for you. That was the first time I knew you had any sense. I said . . . My man Troy knows what he's doing . . . I'm gonna follow this nigger . . . he might take me somewhere. I been following you too. I done learned a whole heap of things about life watching you. I done learned how to tell where the shit lies. How to tell it from the alfalfa. You done learned me a lot of things. You showed me how to not make the same mistakes . . . to take life as it comes along and keep putting one foot in front of the other. (*Pause.*) Rose a good woman, Troy.

TROY. Hell, nigger, I know she a good woman. I been married to her for eighteen years. What you got on your mind, Bono?

BONO. I just say she a good woman. Just like I say anything. I ain't got to have nothing on my mind.

TROY. You just gonna say she a good woman and leave it hanging out there like that? Why you telling me she a good woman?

BONO. She loves you, Troy. Rose loves you.

TROY. You saying I don't measure up. That's what you trying to say. I don't measure up cause I'm seeing this other gal. I know what you trying to say.

BONO. I know what Rose means to you, Troy. I'm just trying to say I don't want to see you mess up.

TROY. Yeah, I appreciate that, Bono. If you was messing around on Lucille I'd be telling you the same thing.

BONO. Well, that's all I got to say. I just say that because I love you both.

TROY. Hell, you know me . . . I wasn't out there looking for nothing. You can't find a better woman than Rose. I know that. But seems like this woman just stuck onto me where I can't shake her loose. I done wrestled with it, tried to throw her off me . . . but she just stuck on tighter. Now she's stuck on for good.

BONO. You's in control . . . that's what you tell me all the time. You responsible for what you do.

TROY. I ain't ducking the responsibility of it. As long as it sets right in my heart . . . then I'm okay. Cause that's all I listen to. It'll tell me right from wrong every time. And I ain't talking about doing Rose no bad turn. I love Rose. She done carried me a long ways and I love and respect her for that.

BONO. I know you do. That's why I don't want to see you hurt her. But what you gonna do when she find out? What you got then? If you try and juggle both of them . . . sooner or later you gonna drop one of them. That's common sense.

TROY. Yeah, I hear what you saying, Bono. I been trying to figure a way to work it out.

BONO. Work it out right, Troy. I don't want to be getting all up between you and Rose's business . . . but work it so it come out right.

TROY. Ah hell, I get all up between you and Lucille's business. When you gonna get that woman that refrigerator she been wanting? Don't tell me you ain't got no money now. I know who your banker is. Mellon don't need that money bad as Lucille want that refrigerator. I'll tell you that.

BONO. Tell you what I'll do . . . when you finish building this fence for Rose . . . I'll buy Lucille that refrigerator.

TROY. You done stuck your foot in your mouth now!

Troy grabs up a board and begins to saw. Bono starts to walk out the yard.

Hey, nigger . . . where you going?

BONO. I'm going home. I know you don't expect me to help you now. I'm protecting my money. I wanna see you put that fence up by yourself. That's what I want to see. You'll be here another six months without me.

TROY. Nigger, you ain't right.

BONO. When it comes to my money . . . I'm right as fireworks on the Fourth of July.

TROY. All right, we gonna see now. You better get out your bankbook.

Bono exits, and Troy continues to work. Rose enters from the house.

ROSE. What they say down there? What's happening with Gabe?

TROY. I went down there and got him out. Cost me fifty dollars. Say he was disturbing the peace. Judge set up a hearing for him in three weeks. Say to show cause why he shouldn't be recommitted.

ROSE. What was he doing that cause them to arrest him?

TROY. Some kids was teasing him and he run them off home. Say he was howling and carrying on. Some folks seen him and called the police. That's all it was.

ROSE. Well, what's you say? What'd you tell the judge?

TROY. Told him I'd look after him. It didn't make no sense to recommit the man. He stuck out his big greasy palm and told me to give him fifty dollars and take him on home.

ROSE. Where's he at now? Where'd he go off to?

TROY. He's gone about his business. He don't need nobody to hold his hand.

ROSE. Well, I don't know. Seem like that would be the best place for him if they did put him into the hospital. I know what you're gonna say. But that's what I think would be best.

TROY. The man done had his life ruined fighting for what? And they wanna take and lock him up. Let him be free. He don't bother nobody.

ROSE. Well, everybody got their own way of looking at it I guess. Come on and get your lunch. I got a bowl of lima beans and some cornbread in the oven. Come and get something to eat. Ain't no sense you fretting over Gabe.

Rose turns to go into the house.

TROY. Rose . . . got something to tell you.

ROSE. Well, come on . . . wait till I get this food on the table.

TROY. Rose!

She stops and turns around.

I don't know how to say this. (*Pause.*) I can't explain it none. It just sort of grows on you till it gets out of hand. It starts out like a little bush . . . and the next thing you know it's a whole forest.

ROSE. Troy . . . what is you talking about?

TROY. I'm talking, woman, let me talk. I'm trying to find a way to tell you . . . I'm gonna be a daddy. I'm gonna be somebody's daddy.

ROSE. Troy . . . you're not telling me this? You're gonna be . . . what?

TROY. Rose . . . now . . . see . . .

ROSE. You telling me you gonna be somebody's daddy? You telling your *wife* this?

Gabriel enters from the street. He carries a rose in his hand.

GABRIEL. Hey, Troy! Hey, Rose!

ROSE. I have to wait eighteen years to hear something like this.

GABRIEL. Hey, Rose . . . I got a flower for you. (*He hands it to her.*) That's a rose. Same rose like you is.

ROSE. Thanks, Gabe.

GABRIEL. Troy, you ain't mad at me is you? Them bad mens come and put me away. You ain't mad at me is you?

TROY. Naw, Gabe, I ain't mad at you.

ROSE. Eighteen years and you wanna come with this.

GABRIEL (*takes a quarter out of his pocket*). See what I got? Got a brand new quarter.

TROY. Rose . . . it's just . . .

ROSE. Ain't nothing you can say, Troy. Ain't no way of explaining that.

GABRIEL. Fellow that give me this quarter had a whole mess of them. I'm gonna keep this quarter till it stop shining.

ROSE. Gabe, go on in the house there. I got some watermelon in the Frigidaire. Go on and get you a piece.

GABRIEL. Say, Rose . . . you know I was chasing hellhounds and them bad mens come and get me and take me away. Troy helped me. He come down there and told them they better let me go before he beat them up. Yeah, he did!

ROSE. You go on and get you a piece of watermelon, Gabe. Them bad mens is gone now.

GABRIEL. Okay, Rose . . . gonna get me some watermelon. The kind with the stripes on it.

Gabriel exits into the house.

ROSE. Why, Troy? Why? After all these years to come dragging this in to me now. It don't make no sense at your age. I could have expected this ten or fifteen years ago, but not now.

TROY. Age ain't got nothing to do with it, Rose.

ROSE. I done tried to be everything a wife should be. Everything a wife could be. Been married eighteen years and I got to live to see the day you tell me you been seeing another woman and done fathered a child by her. And you know I ain't never wanted no half nothing in my family. My whole family is half. Everybody got different fathers and mothers . . . my two sisters and my brother. Can't hardly tell who's who. Can't never sit down and talk about Papa and Mama. It's your papa and your mama and my papa and my mama . . .

TROY. Rose . . . stop it now.

ROSE. I ain't never wanted that for none of my children. And now you wanna drag your behind in here and tell me something like this.

TROY. You ought to know. It's time for you to know.

ROSE. Well, I don't want to know, goddamn it!

TROY. I can't just make it go away. It's done now. I can't wish the circumstance of the thing away.

ROSE. And you don't want to either. Maybe you want to wish me and my boy away. Maybe that's what you want? Well, you can't wish us away. I've got eighteen years of my life invested in you. You ought to have stayed upstairs in my bed where you belong.

TROY. Rose . . . now listen to me . . . we can get a handle on this thing. We can talk this out . . . come to an understanding.

ROSE. All of a sudden it's "we." Where was "we" at when you was down there rolling around with some godforsaken woman? "We" should have come to an understanding before you started making a damn fool of yourself. You're a day late and a dollar short when it comes to an understanding with me.

TROY. It's just . . . She gives me a different idea . . . a different understanding about myself. I can step out of this house and get away from the pressures and problems . . . be a different man. I ain't got to wonder how I'm gonna pay the bills or get the roof fixed. I can just be a part of myself that I ain't never been.

ROSE. What I want to know . . . is do you plan to continue seeing her. That's all you can say to me.

TROY. I can sit up in her house and laugh. Do you understand what I'm saying. I can laugh out loud . . . and it feels good. It reaches all the way down to the bottom of my shoes. (*Pause.*) Rose, I can't give that up.

ROSE. Maybe you ought to go on and stay down there with her . . . if she's a better woman than me.

TROY. It ain't about nobody being a better woman or nothing. Rose, you ain't the blame. A man couldn't ask for no woman to be a better wife than you've been. I'm responsible for it. I done locked myself into a pattern trying to take care of you all that I forgot about myself.

ROSE. What the hell was I there for? That was my job, not somebody else's.

TROY. Rose, I done tried all my life to live decent . . . to live a clean . . . hard . . . useful life. I tried to be a good husband to you. In every way I knew how. Maybe I come into the world backwards, I don't know. But . . . you born with two strikes on you before you come to the plate. You got to guard it closely . . . always looking for the curve ball on the inside corner. You can't afford to let none get past you. You can't afford a call strike. If you going down . . . you going down swinging. Everything lined up against you. What you gonna do. I fooled them, Rose. I bunted. When I found you and Cory and a halfway decent job . . . I was safe. Couldn't nothing touch me. I wasn't gonna strike out no more. I wasn't going back to the penitentiary. I wasn't gonna lay in the streets with a bottle of wine. I was safe. I had me a family. A job. I wasn't gonna get that last strike. I was on first looking for one of them boys to knock me in. To get me home.

ROSE. You should have stayed in my bed, Troy.

TROY. Then when I saw that gal . . . she firmed up my backbone. And I got to thinking that if I tried . . . I just might be able to steal second. Do you understand after eighteen years I wanted to steal second.

ROSE. You should have held me tight. You should have grabbed me and held on.

TROY. I stood on first base for eighteen years and I thought . . . well, goddamn it . . . go on for it!

ROSE. We're not talking about baseball! We're talking about you going off to lay in bed with another woman . . . and then bring it home to me. That's what we're talking about. We ain't talking about no baseball.

TROY. Rose, you're not listening to me. I'm trying the best I can to explain it to you. It's not easy for me to admit that I been standing in the same place for eighteen years.

ROSE. I been standing with you! I been right here with you, Troy. I got a life too. I gave eighteen years of my life to stand in the same spot with you. Don't you think I ever wanted other things? Don't you think I had dreams and hopes? What about my life? What about me. Don't you think it ever crossed my mind to want to know other men? That I wanted to lay up somewhere and forget about my responsibilities? That I wanted someone to make me laugh so I could feel good? You not the only one who's got wants and needs. But I held on to you, Troy. I took all my feelings, my wants and needs, my dreams . . . and I buried them inside you. I planted a seed and watched and prayed over it. I planted myself inside you and waited to bloom. And it didn't take me no eighteen years to find out the soil was hard and rocky and it wasn't never gonna bloom.

But I held on to you, Troy. I held you tighter. You was my husband. I owed you everything I had. Every part of me I could find to give you. And upstairs in that room . . . with the darkness falling in on me . . . I gave everything I had to try and erase the doubt that you wasn't the finest man in the world. And wherever you was going . . . I wanted to be there with you. Cause you was my husband. Cause that's the only way I was gonna survive as your wife. You always talking about what you give . . . and what you don't have to give. But you take too. You take . . . and don't even know nobody's giving!

Rose turns to exit into the house; Troy grabs her arm.

TROY. You say I take and don't give!

ROSE. Troy! You're hurting me!

TROY. You say I take and don't give!

ROSE. Troy . . . you're hurting my arm! Let go!

TROY. I done give you everything I got. Don't you tell that lie on me.

ROSE. Troy!

TROY. Don't you tell that lie on me!

Cory enters from the house.

CORY. Mama!

ROSE. Troy. You're hurting me.

TROY. Don't you tell me about no taking and giving.

Cory comes up behind Troy and grabs him. Troy, surprised, is thrown off balance just as Cory throws a glancing blow that catches him on the chest and knocks him down. Troy is stunned, as is Cory.

ROSE. Troy. Troy. No!

Troy gets to his feet and starts at Cory.

Troy . . . no. Please! Troy!

Rose pulls on Troy to hold him back. Troy stops himself.

TROY (*to Cory*). All right. That's strike two. You stay away from around me, boy. Don't you strike out. You living with a full count. Don't you strike out.

Troy exits out the yard as the lights go down.

SCENE 2

It is six months later, early afternoon. Troy enters from the house and starts to exit the yard. Rose enters from the house.

ROSE. Troy, I want to talk to you.

TROY. All of a sudden, after all this time, you want to talk to me, huh? You ain't wanted to talk to me for months. You ain't wanted to talk to me last night. You ain't wanted no part of me then. What you wanna talk to me about now?

ROSE. Tomorrow's Friday.

TROY. I know what day tomorrow is. You think I don't know tomorrow's Friday? My whole life I ain't done nothing but look to see Friday coming and you got to tell me it's Friday.

ROSE. I want to know if you're coming home.

TROY. I always come home, Rose. You know that. There ain't never been a night I ain't come home.

ROSE. That ain't what I mean . . . and you know it. I want to know if you're coming straight home after work.

TROY. I figure I'd cash my check . . . hang out at Taylors' with the boys . . . maybe play a game of checkers . . .

ROSE. Troy, I can't live like this. I won't live like this. You livin' on borrowed time with me. It's been going on six months now you ain't been coming home.

TROY. I be here every night. Every night of the year. That's 365 days.

ROSE. I want you to come home tomorrow after work.

TROY. Rose . . . I don't mess up my pay. You know that now. I take my pay and I give it to you. I don't have no money but what you give me back. I just want to have a little time to myself . . . a little time to enjoy life.

ROSE. What about me? When's my time to enjoy life?

TROY. I don't know what to tell you, Rose. I'm doing the best I can.

ROSE. You ain't been home from work but time enough to change your clothes and run out . . . and you wanna call that the best you can do?

TROY. I'm going over to the hospital to see Alberta. She went into the hospital this afternoon. Look like she might have the baby early. I won't be gone long.

ROSE. Well, you ought to know. They went over to Miss Pearl's and got Gabe today. She said you told them to go ahead and lock him up.

TROY. I ain't said no such thing. Whoever told you that is telling a lie. Pearl ain't doing nothing but telling a big fat lie.

ROSE. She ain't had to tell me. I read it on the papers.

TROY. I ain't told them nothing of the kind.

ROSE. I saw it right there on the papers.

TROY. What it say, huh?

ROSE. It said you told them to take him.

TROY. Then they screwed that up, just the way they screw up everything. I ain't worried about what they got on the paper.

ROSE. Say the government send part of his check to the hospital and the other part to you.

TROY. I ain't got nothing to do with that if that's the way it works. I ain't made up the rules about how it work.

ROSE. You did Gabe just like you did Cory. You wouldn't sign the paper for Cory . . . but you signed for Gabe. You signed that paper.

The telephone is heard ringing inside the house.

TROY. I told you I ain't signed nothing, woman! The only thing I signed was the release form. Hell, I can't read, I don't know what they had on that paper! I ain't signed nothing about sending Gabe away.

ROSE. I said send him to the hospital . . . you said let him be free . . . now you done went down there and signed him to the hospital for half his money. You went back on yourself, Troy. You gonna have to answer for that.

TROY. See now . . . you been over there talking to Miss Pearl. She done got mad cause she ain't getting Gabe's rent money. That's all it is. She's liable to say anything.

ROSE. Troy, I seen where you signed the paper.

TROY. You ain't seen nothing I signed. What she doing got papers on my brother anyway? Miss Pearl telling a big fat lie. And I'm gonna tell her about it too! You ain't seen nothing I signed. Say . . . you ain't seen nothing I signed.

Rose exits into the house to answer the telephone. Presently she returns.

ROSE. Troy . . . that was the hospital. Alberta had the baby.

TROY. What she have? What is it?

ROSE. It's a girl.

TROY. I better get on down to the hospital to see her.

ROSE. Troy . . .

TROY. Rose . . . I got to go see her now. That's only right . . . what's the matter . . . the baby's all right, ain't it?

ROSE. Alberta died having the baby.

TROY. Died . . . you say she's dead? Alberta's dead?

ROSE. They said they done all they could. They couldn't do nothing for her.

TROY. The baby? How's the baby?

ROSE. They say it's healthy. I wonder who's gonna bury her.

TROY. She had family, Rose. She wasn't living in the world by herself.

ROSE. I know she wasn't living in the world by herself.

TROY. Next thing you gonna want to know if she had any insurance.

ROSE. Troy, you ain't got to talk like that.

TROY. That's the first thing that jumped out your mouth. "Who's gonna bury her?" Like I'm fixing to take on that task for myself.

ROSE. I am your wife. Don't push me away.

TROY. I ain't pushing nobody away. Just give me some space. That's all. Just give me some room to breathe.

Rose exits into the house. Troy walks about the yard.

TROY (*with a quiet rage that threatens to consume him*). All right . . . Mr. Death. See now . . . I'm gonna tell you what I'm gonna do. I'm gonna take and build me a fence around this yard. See? I'm gonna build me a fence around what belongs to me. And then I want you to stay on the other side. See? You stay over there until you're ready for me. Then you come on. Bring your army. Bring your sickle. Bring your wrestling clothes. I ain't gonna fall down on my vigilance this time. You ain't gonna sneak up on me no more. When you ready for me . . . when the top of your list say Troy Maxson . . . that's when you come around here. You come up and knock on the front door. Ain't nobody else got nothing to do with this. This is between you and me. Man to man. You stay on the other side of that fence until you ready for me. Then you come up and knock on the front door. Anytime you want. I'll be ready for you.

The lights go down to black.

SCENE 3

The lights come up on the porch. It is late evening three days later. Rose sits listening to the ball game waiting for Troy. The final out of the game is made and Rose switches off the radio. Troy enters the yard carrying an infant wrapped in blankets. He stands back from the house and calls.

Rose enters and stands on the porch. There is a long, awkward silence, the weight of which grows heavier with each passing second.

TROY. Rose . . . I'm standing here with my daughter in my arms. She ain't but a wee bittie little old thing. She don't know nothing about grownups' business. She innocent . . . and she ain't got no mama.

ROSE. What you telling me for, Troy?

She turns and exits into the house.

TROY. Well . . . I guess we'll just sit out here on the porch.

He sits down on the porch. There is an awkward indelicateness about the way he handles the baby. His largeness engulfs and seems to swallow it. He speaks loud enough for Rose to hear.

A man's got to do what's right for him. I ain't sorry for nothing I done. It felt right in my heart. (*To the baby.*) What you smiling at? Your daddy's a big man. Got these great big old hands. But sometimes he's scared. And right now your daddy's scared cause we sitting out here and ain't got no home. Oh, I been homeless before. I ain't had no little baby with me. But I been homeless. You just be out on the road by your lonesome and you see one of them trains coming and you just kinda go like this . . .

He sings as a lullaby.

> Please, Mr. Engineer let a man ride the line
> Please, Mr. Engineer let a man ride the line
> I ain't got no ticket please let me ride the blinds.

Rose enters from the house. Troy, hearing her steps behind him, stands and faces her.

She's my daughter, Rose. My own flesh and blood. I can't deny her no more than I can deny them boys. (*Pause.*) You and them boys is my family. You and them and this child is all I got in the world. So I guess what I'm saying is . . . I'd appreciate it if you'd help me take care of her.

ROSE. Okay, Troy . . . you're right. I'll take care of your baby for you . . . cause . . . like you say . . . she's innocent . . . and you can't visit the sins of the father upon the child. A motherless child has got a hard time. (*She takes the baby from him.*) From right now . . . this child got a mother. But you a womanless man.

Rose turns and exits into the house with the baby. Lights go down to black.

SCENE 4

It is two months later. Lyons enters the street. He knocks on the door and calls.

LYONS. Hey, Rose! (*Pause.*) Rose!

ROSE (*from inside the house*). Stop that yelling. You gonna wake up Raynell. I just got her to sleep.

LYONS. I just stopped by to pay Papa this twenty dollars I owe him. Where's Papa at?

ROSE. He should be here in a minute. I'm getting ready to go down to the church. Sit down and wait on him.

LYONS. I got to go pick up Bonnie over her mother's house.

ROSE. Well, sit it down there on the table. He'll get it.

LYONS (*enters the house and sets the money on the table*). Tell Papa I said thanks. I'll see you again.

ROSE. All right, Lyons. We'll see you.

Lyons starts to exit as Cory enters.

CORY. Hey, Lyons.

LYONS. What's happening, Cory? Say man, I'm sorry I missed your graduation. You know I had a gig and couldn't get away. Otherwise, I would have been there, man. So what you doing?

CORY. I'm trying to find a job.

LYONS. Yeah I know how that go, man. It's rough out here. Jobs are scarce.

CORY. Yeah, I know.

LYONS. Look here, I got to run. Talk to Papa . . . he know some people. He'll be able to help get you a job. Talk to him . . . see what he say.

CORY. Yeah . . . all right, Lyons.

LYONS. You take care. I'll talk to you soon. We'll find some time to talk.

Lyons exits the yard. Cory wanders over to the tree, picks up the bat, and assumes a batting stance. He studies an imaginary pitcher and swings. Dissatisfied with the result, he tries again. Troy enters. They eye each other for a beat. Cory puts the bat down and exits the yard. Troy starts into the house as Rose exits with Raynell. She is carrying a cake.

TROY. I'm coming in and everybody's going out.

ROSE. I'm taking this cake down to the church for the bake sale. Lyons was by to see you. He stopped by to pay you your twenty dollars. It's laying in there on the table.

TROY (*going into his pocket*). Well . . . here go this money.

ROSE. Put it in there on the table, Troy. I'll get it.

TROY. What time you coming back?

ROSE. Ain't no use in you studying me. It don't matter what time I come back.

TROY. I just asked you a question, woman. What's the matter . . . can't I ask you a question?

ROSE. Troy, I don't want to go into it. Your dinner's in there on the stove. All you got to do is heat it up. And don't you be eating the rest of them cakes in there. I'm coming back for them. We having a bake sale at the church tomorrow.

Rose exits the yard. Troy sits down on the steps, takes a pint bottle from his pocket, opens it, and drinks. He begins to sing.

TROY.

> Hear it ring! Hear it ring!
> Had an old dog his name was Blue
> You know Blue was mighty true
> You know Blue was a good old dog
> Blue trees a possum in a hollow log
> You know from that he was a good old dog.

Bono enters the yard.

BONO. Hey, Troy.

TROY. Hey, what's happening, Bono?

BONO. I just thought I'd stop by to see you.

TROY. What you stop by and see me for? You ain't stopped by in a month of Sundays. Hell, I must owe you money or something.

BONO. Since you got your promotion I can't keep up with you. Used to see you every day. Now I don't even know what route you working.

TROY. They keep switching me around. Got me out in Greentree now . . . hauling white folks' garbage.

BONO. Greentree, huh? You lucky, at least you ain't got to be lifting them barrels. Damn if they ain't getting heavier. I'm gonna put in my two years and call it quits.

TROY. I'm thinking about retiring myself.

BONO. You got it easy. You can drive for another five years.

TROY. It ain't the same, Bono. It ain't like working the back of the truck. Ain't got nobody to talk to . . . feel like you working by yourself. Naw, I'm thinking about retiring. How's Lucille?

BONO. She all right. Her arthritis get to acting up on her sometime. Saw Rose on my way in. She going down to the church, huh?

TROY. Yeah, she took up going down there. All them preachers looking for somebody to fatten their pockets. (*Pause.*) Got some gin here.

BONO. Naw, thanks. I just stopped by to say hello.

TROY. Hell, nigger . . . you can take a drink. I ain't never known you to say no to a drink. You ain't got to work tomorrow.

BONO. I just stopped by. I'm fixing to go over to Skinner's. We got us a domino game going over his house every Friday.

TROY. Nigger, you can't play no dominoes. I used to whup you four games out of five.

BONO. Well, that learned me. I'm getting better.

TROY. Yeah? Well, that's all right.

BONO. Look here . . . I got to be getting on. Stop by sometime, huh?

TROY. Yeah, I'll do that, Bono. Lucille told Rose you bought her a new refrigerator.

BONO. Yeah, Rose told Lucille you had finally built your fence . . . so I figured we'd call it even.

TROY. I knew you would.

BONO. Yeah . . . okay. I'll be talking to you.

TROY. Yeah, take care, Bono. Good to see you. I'm gonna stop over.

BONO. Yeah. Okay, Troy.

Bono exits. Troy drinks from the bottle.

TROY.

>Old Blue died and I dig his grave
>Let him down with a golden chain
>Every night when I hear old Blue bark
>I know Blue treed a possum in Noah's Ark.
>Hear it ring! Hear it ring!

Cory enters the yard. They eye each other for a beat. Troy is sitting in the middle of the steps. Cory walks over.

CORY. I got to get by.

TROY. Say what? What's you say?

CORY. You in my way. I got to get by.

TROY. You got to get by where? This is my house. Bought and paid for. In full. Took me fifteen years. And if you wanna go in my house and I'm sitting on the steps . . . you say excuse me. Like your mama taught you.

CORY. Come on, Pop . . . I got to get by.

Cory starts to maneuver his way past Troy. Troy grabs his leg and shoves him back.

TROY. You just gonna walk over top of me?

CORY. I live here too!

TROY (*advancing toward him*). You just gonna walk over top of me in my own house?

CORY. I ain't scared of you.

TROY. I ain't asked if you was scared of me. I asked you if you was fixing to walk over top of me in my own house? That's the question. You ain't gonna say excuse me? You just gonna walk over top of me?

CORY. If you wanna put it like that.

TROY. How else am I gonna put it?

CORY. I was walking by you to go into the house cause you sitting on the steps drunk, singing to yourself. You can put it like that.

TROY. Without saying excuse me???

Cory doesn't respond.

I asked you a question. Without saying excuse me???

CORY. I ain't got to say excuse me to you. You don't count around here no more.

TROY. Oh, I see . . . I don't count around here no more. You ain't got to say excuse me to your daddy. All of a sudden you done got so grown that your daddy don't count around here no more . . . Around here in his own house and yard that he done paid for with the sweat of his brow. You done got so grown to where you gonna take over. You gonna take over my house. Is that right? You gonna wear my pants. You gonna go in there and stretch out on my bed. You ain't got to say excuse me cause I don't count around here no more. Is that right?

CORY. That's right. You always talking this dumb stuff. Now, why don't you just get out my way?

TROY. I guess you got someplace to sleep and something to put in your belly. You got that, huh? You got that? That's what you need. You got that, huh?

CORY. You don't know what I got. You ain't got to worry about what I got.

TROY. You right! You one hundred percent right! I done spent the last seventeen years worrying about what you got. Now it's your turn, see? I'll tell you what to do. You grown . . . we done established that. You a man. Now, let's see you act like one. Turn your behind around and walk out this yard. And when you get out there in the alley . . . you can forget about this house. See? Cause this is my house. You go on and be a man and get your own house. You can forget about this. Cause this is mine. You go on and get yours cause I'm through with doing for you.

CORY. You talking about what you did for me . . . what'd you ever give me?

TROY. Them feet and bones! That pumping heart, nigger! I give you more than anybody else is ever gonna give you.

CORY. You ain't never gave me nothing! You ain't never done nothing but hold me back. Afraid I was gonna be better than you. All you ever did was try and make me scared of you. I used to tremble every time you called my name. Every time I heard your footsteps in the house. Wondering all the time . . . what's Papa gonna say if I do this? . . . What's he gonna say if I do that? . . . What's Papa gonna say if I turn on the radio? And Mama, too . . . she tries . . . but she's scared of you.

TROY. You leave your mama out of this. She ain't got nothing to do with this.

CORY. I don't know how she stand you . . . after what you did to her.

TROY. I told you to leave your mama out of this!

He advances toward Cory.

CORY. What you gonna do . . . give me a whupping? You can't whup me no more. You're too old. You just an old man.

TROY (*shoves him on his shoulder*). Nigger! That's what you are. You just another nigger on the street to me!

CORY. You crazy! You know that?

TROY. Go on now! You got the devil in you. Get on away from me!

CORY. You just a crazy old man . . . talking about I got the devil in me.

TROY. Yeah, I'm crazy! If you don't get on the other side of that yard . . . I'm gonna show you how crazy I am! Go on . . . get the hell out of my yard.

CORY. It ain't your yard. You took Uncle Gabe's money he got from the army to buy this house and then you put him out.

TROY (*advances on Cory*). Get your black ass out of my yard!

Troy's advance backs Cory up against the tree. Cory grabs up the bat.

CORY. I ain't going nowhere! Come on . . . put me out! I ain't scared of you.

TROY. That's my bat!

CORY. Come on!

TROY. Put my bat down!

CORY. Come on, put me out.

Cory swings at Troy, who backs across the yard.

What's the matter? You so bad . . . put me out!

Troy advances toward Cory.

CORY (*backing up*). Come on! Come on!

TROY. You're gonna have to use it! You wanna draw that bat back on me . . . you're gonna have to use it.

CORY. Come on! . . . Come on!

Cory swings the bat at Troy a second time. He misses. Troy continues to advance toward him.

TROY. You're gonna have to kill me! You wanna draw that bat back on me. You're gonna have to kill me.

Cory, backed up against the tree, can go no farther. Troy taunts him. He sticks out his head and offers him a target.

Come on! Come on!

Cory is unable to swing the bat. Troy grabs it.

TROY. Then I'll show you.

Cory and Troy struggle over the bat. The struggle is fierce and fully engaged. Troy ultimately is the stronger and takes the bat from Cory and stands over him ready to swing. He stops himself.

Go on and get away from around my house.

Cory, stung by his defeat, picks himself up, walks slowly out of the yard and up the alley.

CORY. Tell Mama I'll be back for my things.

TROY. They'll be on the other side of that fence.

Cory exits.

TROY. I can't taste nothing. Helluljah! I can't taste nothing no more. (*Troy assumes a batting posture and begins to taunt Death, the fastball on the outside corner.*) Come on! It's between you and me now! Come on! Anytime you want! Come on! I be ready for you . . . but I ain't gonna be easy.

The lights go down on the scene.

SCENE 5

The time is 1965. The lights come up in the yard. It is the morning of Troy's funeral. A funeral plaque with a light hangs beside the door. There is a small garden plot off to the side. There is noise and activity in the house as Rose, Lyons, and Bono have gathered. The door opens and Raynell, seven years old, enters dressed in a flannel nightgown. She crosses to the garden and pokes around with a stick. Rose calls from the house.

ROSE. Raynell!

RAYNELL. Mam?

ROSE. What you doing out there?

RAYNELL. Nothing.

Rose comes to the door.

ROSE. Girl, get in here and get dressed. What you doing?

RAYNELL. Seeing if my garden growed.

ROSE. I told you it ain't gonna grow overnight. You got to wait.

RAYNELL. It don't look like it never gonna grow. Dag!

ROSE. I told you a watched pot never boils. Get in here and get dressed.

RAYNELL. This ain't even no pot, Mama.

ROSE. You just have to give it a chance. It'll grow. Now you come on and do what I told you. We got to be getting ready. This ain't no morning to be playing around. You hear me?

RAYNELL. Yes, mam.

Rose exits into the house. Raynell continues to poke at her garden with a stick. Cory enters. He is dressed in a Marine corporal's uniform, and carries a duffel-bag. His posture is that of a military man, and his speech has a clipped sternness.

CORY (*to Raynell*). Hi. (*Pause.*) I bet your name is Raynell.

RAYNELL. Uh huh.

CORY. Is your mama home?

Raynell runs up on the porch and calls through the screen door.

RAYNELL. Mama . . . there's some man out here. Mama?

Rose comes to the door.

ROSE. Cory? Lord have mercy! Look here, you all!

Rose and Cory embrace in a tearful reunion as Bono and Lyons enter from the house dressed in funeral clothes.

BONO. Aw, looka here . . .

ROSE. Done got all grown up!

CORY. Don't cry, Mama. What you crying about?

ROSE. I'm just so glad you made it.

CORY. Hey Lyons. How you doing, Mr. Bono.

Lyons goes to embrace Cory.

LYONS. Look at you, man. Look at you. Don't he look good, Rose. Got them Corporal stripes.

ROSE. What took you so long?

CORY. You know how the Marines are, Mama. They got to get all their paperwork straight before they let you do anything.

ROSE. Well, I'm sure glad you made it. They let Lyons come. Your Uncle Gabe's still in the hospital. They don't know if they gonna let him out or not. I just talked to them a little while ago.

LYONS. A Corporal in the United States Marines.

BONO. Your daddy knew you had it in you. He used to tell me all the time.

LYONS. Don't he look good, Mr. Bono?

BONO. Yeah, he remind me of Troy when I first met him. (*Pause.*) Say, Rose, Lucille's down at the church with the choir. I'm gonna go down and get the pallbearers lined up. I'll be back to get you all.

ROSE. Thanks, Jim.

CORY. See you, Mr. Bono.

LYONS (*with his arm around Raynell*). Cory . . . look at Raynell. Ain't she precious? She gonna break a whole lot of hearts.

ROSE. Raynell, come and say hello to your brother. This is your brother, Cory. You remember Cory.

RAYNELL. No, Mam.

CORY. She don't remember me, Mama.

ROSE. Well, we talk about you. She heard us talk about you. (*To Raynell.*) This is your brother, Cory. Come on and say hello.

RAYNELL. Hi.

CORY. Hi. So you're Raynell. Mama told me a lot about you.

ROSE. You all come on into the house and let me fix you some breakfast. Keep up your strength.

CORY. I ain't hungry, Mama.

LYONS. You can fix me something, Rose. I'll be in there in a minute.

ROSE. Cory, you sure you don't want nothing? I know they ain't feeding you right.

CORY. No, Mama . . . thanks. I don't feel like eating. I'll get something later.

ROSE. Raynell . . . get on upstairs and get that dress on like I told you.

Rose and Raynell exit into the house.

LYONS. So . . . I hear you thinking about getting married.

CORY. Yeah, I done found the right one, Lyons. It's about time.

LYONS. Me and Bonnie been split up about four years now. About the time Papa retired. I guess she just got tired of all them changes I was putting her through. (*Pause.*) I always knew you was gonna make something out yourself. Your head was always in the right direction. So . . . you gonna stay in . . . make it a career . . . put in your twenty years?

CORY. I don't know. I got six already, I think that's enough.

LYONS. Stick with Uncle Sam and retire early. Ain't nothing out here. I guess Rose told you what happened with me. They got me down the workhouse. I thought I was being slick cashing other people's checks.

CORY. How much time you doing?

LYONS. They give me three years. I got that beat now. I ain't got but nine more months. It ain't so bad. You learn to deal with it like anything else. You got to take the crookeds with the straights. That's what Papa used to say. He used to say that when he struck out. I seen him strike out three times in a row . . . and the next time up he hit the ball over the grandstand. Right out there in Homestead Field. He wasn't satisfied hitting in the seats . . . he want to hit it over everything! After the game he had two hundred people standing around waiting to shake his hand. You got to take the crookeds with the straights. Yeah, Papa was something else.

CORY. You still playing?

LYONS. Cory . . . you know I'm gonna do that. There's some fellows down there we got us a band . . . we gonna try and stay together when we get out . . . but yeah, I'm still playing. It still helps me to get out of bed in the morning. As long as it do that I'm gonna be right there playing and trying to make some sense out of it.

ROSE (calling). Lyons, I got these eggs in the pan.

LYONS. Let me go on and get these eggs, man. Get ready to go bury Papa. (Pause.) How you doing? You doing all right?

Cory nods. Lyons touches him on the shoulder and they share a moment of silent grief. Lyons exits into the house. Cory wanders about the yard. Raynell enters.

RAYNELL. Hi.

CORY. Hi.

RAYNELL. Did you used to sleep in my room?

CORY. Yeah . . . that used to be my room.

RAYNELL. That's what Papa call it. "Cory's room." It got your football in the closet.

Rose comes to the door.

ROSE. Raynell, get in there and get them good shoes on.

RAYNELL. Mama, can't I wear these? Them other one hurt my feet.

ROSE. Well, they just gonna have to hurt your feet for a while. You ain't said they hurt your feet when you went down to the store and got them.

RAYNELL. They didn't hurt then. My feet done got bigger.

ROSE. Don't you give me no backtalk now. You get in there and get them shoes on.

Raynell exits into the house.

Ain't too much changed. He still got that piece of rag tied to that tree. He was out here swinging that bat. I was just ready to go back in the house. He swung that bat and then he just fell over. Seem like he swung it and stood there with this grin on his face . . . and then he just fell over. They carried him on down to the hospital, but I knew there wasn't no need . . . why don't you come on in the house?

CORY. Mama . . . I got something to tell you. I don't know how to tell you this . . . but I've got to tell you . . . I'm not going to Papa's funeral.

ROSE. Boy, hush your mouth. That's your daddy you talking about. I don't want hear that kind of talk this morning. I done raised you to come to this? You standing there all healthy and grown talking about you ain't going to your daddy's funeral?

CORY. Mama . . . listen . . .

ROSE. I don't want to hear it, Cory. You just get that thought out of your head.

CORY. I can't drag Papa with me everywhere I go. I've got to say no to him. One time in my life I've got to say no.

ROSE. Don't nobody have to listen to nothing like that. I know you and your daddy ain't seen eye to eye, but I ain't got to listen to that kind of talk this morning. Whatever was between you and your daddy . . . the time has come to put it aside. Just take it and set it over there on the shelf and forget about it. Disrespecting your daddy ain't gonna make you a man, Cory. You got to find a way to come to that on your own. Not going to your daddy's funeral ain't gonna make you a man.

CORY. The whole time I was growing up . . . living in his house . . . Papa was like a shadow that followed you everywhere. It weighed on you and sunk into your flesh. It would wrap around you and lay there until you couldn't tell which one was you anymore. That shadow digging in your flesh. Trying to crawl in. Trying to live through you. Everywhere I looked, Troy Maxson was staring back at me . . . hiding under the bed . . . in the closet. I'm just saying I've got to find a way to get rid of that shadow, Mama.

ROSE. You just like him. You got him in you good.

CORY. Don't tell me that, Mama.

ROSE. You Troy Maxson all over again.

CORY. I don't want to be Troy Maxson. I want to be me.

ROSE. You can't be nobody but who you are, Cory. That shadow wasn't nothing but you growing into yourself. You either got to grow into it or cut it down to fit you. But that's all you got to make life with. That's all you got to measure yourself against that world out there. Your daddy wanted you to be everything he wasn't . . . and at the same time he tried to make you into everything he was. I don't know if he was right or wrong . . . but I do know he meant to do more good than he meant to do harm. He wasn't always right. Sometimes when he touched he bruised. And sometimes when he took me in his arms he cut.

When I first met your daddy I thought . . . Here is a man I can lay down with and make a baby. That's the first thing I thought when I seen him. I was thirty years old and had done seen my share of men. But when he walked up to me and said, "I can dance a waltz that'll make you dizzy," I thought, Rose Lee, here is a man that you can open yourself up to and be filled to bursting. Here is a man that can fill all them empty spaces you been tipping around the edges of. One of them empty spaces was being somebody's mother.

I married your daddy and settled down to cooking his supper and keeping clean sheets on the bed. When your daddy walked through the house he was so big he filled it up. That was my first mistake. Not to make him leave some room for me. For my part in the matter. But at that time I wanted that. I wanted a house that I could sing in. And that's what your daddy gave me. I didn't know to keep up his strength I had to give up little pieces of mine. I did that. I took on his life as mine and mixed up the pieces so that you couldn't hardly tell which was which anymore. It was my choice. It was my life and I didn't have to live it like that. But that's what life offered me in the way of being a woman and I took it. I grabbed hold of it with both hands.

By the time Raynell came into the house, me and your daddy had done lost touch with one another. I didn't want to make my blessing off of nobody's misfortune . . . but I took on to Raynell like she was all them babies I had wanted and never had.

The phone rings.

Like I'd been blessed to relive a part of my life. And if the Lord see fit to keep up my strength . . . I'm gonna do her just like your daddy did you . . . I'm gonna give her the best of what's in me.

RAYNELL (*entering, still with her old shoes*). Mama . . . Reverend Tollivier on the phone.

Rose exits into the house.

RAYNELL. Hi.
CORY. Hi.
RAYNELL. You in the Army or the Marines?
CORY. Marines.
RAYNELL. Papa said it was the Army. Did you know Blue?

CORY. Blue? Who's Blue?
RAYNELL. Papa's dog what he sing about all the time.
CORY (*singing*).
> Hear it ring! Hear it ring!
> I had a dog his name was Blue
> You know Blue was mighty true
> You know Blue was a good old dog
> Blue treed a possum in a hollow log
> You know from that he was a good old dog.
> Hear it ring! Hear it ring!

Raynell joins in singing.

CORY and RAYNELL.
> Blue treed a possum out on a limb
> Blue looked at me and I looked at him
> Grabbed that possum and put him in a sack
> Blue stayed there till I came back
> Old Blue's feets was big and round
> Never allowed a possum to touch the ground.

> Old Blue died and I dug his grave
> I dug his grave with a silver spade
> Let him down with a golden chain
> And every night I call his name
> Go on Blue, you good dog you
> Go on Blue, you good dog you.

RAYNELL.
> Blue laid down and died like a man
> Blue laid down and died . . .

BOTH.
> Blue laid down and died like a man
> Now he's treeing possums in the Promised Land
> I'm gonna tell you this to let you know
> Blue's gone where the good dogs go
> When I hear old Blue bark
> When I hear old Blue bark
> Blue treed a possum in Noah's Ark
> Blue treed a possum in Noah's Ark.

Rose comes to the screen door.

ROSE. Cory, we gonna be ready to go in a minute.
CORY (*to Raynell*). You go on in the house and change them shoes like Mama told you so we can go to Papa's funeral.
RAYNELL. Okay, I'll be back.

Raynell exits into the house. Cory gets up and crosses over to the tree. Rose stands in the screen door watching him. Gabriel enters from the alley.

GABRIEL (*calling*). Hey, Rose!
ROSE. Gabe?

GABRIEL. I'm here, Rose. Hey Rose, I'm here!

Rose enters from the house.

ROSE. Lord . . . Look here, Lyons!

LYONS. See, I told you, Rose . . . I told you they'd let him come.

CORY. How you doing, Uncle Gabe?

LYONS. How you doing, Uncle Gabe?

GABRIEL. Hey, Rose. It's time. It's time to tell St. Peter to open the gates. Troy, you ready? You ready, Troy. I'm gonna tell St. Peter to open the gates. You get ready now.

Gabriel, with great fanfare, braces himself to blow. The trumpet is without a mouthpiece. He puts the end of it into his mouth and blows with great force, like a man who has been waiting some twenty-odd years for this single moment. No sound comes out of the trumpet. He braces himself and blows again with the same result. A third time he blows. There is a weight of impossible description that falls away and leaves him bare and exposed to a frightful realization. It is a trauma that a sane and normal mind would be unable to withstand. He begins to dance. A slow, strange dance, eerie and life-giving. A dance of atavistic signature and ritual. Lyons attempts to embrace him. Gabriel pushes Lyons away. He begins to howl in what is an attempt at song, or perhaps a song turning back into itself in an attempt at speech. He finishes his dance and the gates of heaven stand open as wide as God's closet.

That's the way that go!

Blackout

COMMENTARY

Note: The following essay represents a single interpretation of the play. For other perspectives on Fences, *consult the essays listed below.*

Fences is in many ways similar to *Death of a Salesman*, particularly in its portrait of the clash between a domineering father and his athletically gifted son. Like Willy, Troy Maxson is a man who cannot adapt to a changing world, who is involved with another woman, and who ultimately drives his son away by his stubbornness. Furthermore, as in *Salesman*, we meet a ne'er-do-well son (cf. Happy and Lyons) and a long-suffering, dutiful wife (cf. Linda and Rose). And both plays are set in the so-called "boom" years after World War II, when many prospered while others were left behind.

But whereas Miller's near-tragic hero, Willy Loman, is the essence of "the little [low] man," Wilson invests Troy with a larger-than-life ("maximum") quality. Like Prometheus, Troy is a Titan who rails against the injustices heaped on the black man. Note that in virtually every confrontation in which Troy engages himself, his opponent is aligned with superhuman values: Mr. Death, the Devil, and "the Boss" for whom he works as a trash man (Troy's heroic stand at work is truly Promethean in its sheer audacity). Even the furniture salesman he battles is described in supernatural terms ("devil standing there bigger than life"). The great baseball players with whom Troy aligns himself—Josh Gibson, the ageless Satchel Paige, the trail-blazing Jackie Robinson, and the young Hank Aaron—emerge as godlike beings. Thus Wilson creates in Troy a modern mythic hero who tries to shake a universe filled with injustice and inequality. The playwright even assigns him a trumpet-playing brother, Gabriel, who tries to blow down the gates of heaven itself. Troy is one of Wilson's finest creations, and he stands among the most compelling characters to emerge in the contemporary American theater.

But Troy is as flawed as he is heroic. His "errors in judgment," to use an apt Aristotelian term, are many. Because of his own failed career as an athlete, he stifles Cory's ambitions to escape the destitution in which he lives. Though he proclaims his love for Rose, he condemns her to a life of servitude ("You supposed to come when I call you, woman"); ironically, he treats her much as his boss treats him. In short, he doesn't let her "drive the truck." He possesses a destructive temper and a pride that ultimately destroys him—and his family. Wilson's refusal to render his protagonist in only heroic terms makes Troy all the more universal and sympathetic. Through Troy's weaknesses, Wilson argues that the most divisive and dangerous threats to the African-American community stem from internal conflicts. To be sure, they are exacerbated by the rage fostered by a racist society, but Wilson represents a new strain of African-American playwriting. Unlike the works of LeRoi Jones, Ed Bullins, and other early Black Power dramatists, Wilson argues that the enemy is as often within as it is without the black community.

Rose Maxson also emerges as an extraordinary being, another in a long line of memorable American stage mothers (Amanda Winfield, Mama Younger, Linda Loman). Rose is uncommonly heroic in her acceptance of Raynell and, of course, in the manner in which she preserves a quiet dignity in the face of Troy's chauvinism. Her monologue at the end of Act II, Scene 1 is a masterpiece of self-realization, and her dismissal of Troy at the end of Act II, Scene 3 ("you a womanless man") is as powerful as Nora Helmer's famed "door slam" at the end of *A Doll's House*.

Cory, like Biff, is repulsed by his father's hypocrisy and heavy-handed justice; ironically, Troy is just as angered at the "unfairness" of his boss. And Cory, like Biff, is condemned to walk in his father's shoes: "I got to the place where I could feel [Troy] kicking in my blood and knew that the only thing that separated us was the matter of a few years." And, true to the form of dramas about generational warfare, Wilson provides us with an obligatory scene in which father and son square off in an archetypal battle in which a baseball bat is as potent a weapon as a broadsword.

It may be tempting to assume that Cory "wins" the battle because our final view of him is as a smartly dressed corporal in the United States Marine Corps. He has escaped the "fence" of Pittsburgh's "Hill," and he is clearly admired by Bono, Raynell, and Rose. But the reality is that Cory is a Marine in 1965, and his escape from the Hill most likely will lead him to the rice paddies of Vietnam. For Wilson, although military service seemed an attractive alternative to life in the inner city, the reality was that "a whole bunch of blacks went over and died in the Vietnam War. The survivors came back to the same street corners and found nothing had changed. They still couldn't get a job." Cory, then, is also condemned to an institution, as are the other principal characters: Rose at her church, Lyons in jail, and Gabriel in a mental hospital. Even Bono remains trapped on the Hill, his only respite the Friday evening paycheck that brings a few hours solace.

Despite the bleak ending, Wilson—as is typical of his work—intimates some hope throughout, largely in his well-chosen music. In addition to his use of baseball (along with boxing, the first mainstream sporting enterprise to employ African-Americans and thus change perceptions about minorities in America), Wilson also uses the songs of black Americans liberally throughout his scripts for both thematic and cultural purposes. Each song in *Fences* comments on the action just as the ancient Greek choral odes did. But the music is also a manifestation of the characters' abilities to persevere amidst hardship. In his earliest full-length play, *Ma Rainey's Black Bottom*, the title character (an actual historical figure who is recognized as "the Mother of the Blues") declares that "you don't sing to feel better—you sing because that's a way of understanding life." The line is an apt prologue to Wilson's ten-play cycle—especially *Fences*—in which he explores the black experience through the lens of various cultural phenomena that simultaneously enrich and exploit African-Americans. To paraphrase Ma Rainey, Wilson doesn't write to entertain, but he writes because it is a proven way for audiences of all colors to understand life. And in that understanding of the pain of rejection, injustice, and human error emerges a kind of hope that the world's imperfections, on the Hill and elsewhere, will diminish, just as surely as baseball's color line was broken in Brooklyn in 1947.

Other perspectives on *Fences*:

Awkward, Michael. "The Crookeds and the Straights: *Fences*, Race and the Politics of Adaptation." In Alan Nadel (ed.), *May All Your Fences Have Gates*. Iowa City: University of Iowa Press, 1994, 204–29.

Wolfe, Peter. "The House of Maxson." In *August Wilson*. New York: Twain, 1999, 55–75.

Another play by Wilson on video:

The Piano Lesson. Dir. Lloyd Richards. Perf. Charles Dutton, Alfre Woodard, and Courtney Vance. Hallmark Home Entertainment, 99 min., 1995.

Videos about August Wilson:

August Wilson: The American Dream, in Black and White. Films for the Humanities, 52 min., 1990.

August Wilson: Writing and the Blues. (Interview with Bill Moyers.) Films for the Humanities, 30 min., 1988.

by Heather Henderson

When August Wilson's Fences *opened at the Yale Rep last May under the direction of Lloyd Richards, it featured remarkable performances by two actors: James Earl Jones (as Troy Maxson) and Mary Alice (as Troy's wife, Rose).*

Mary Alice has appeared previously at the Yale Rep in Lorraine Hansberry's A Raisin in the Sun, *and in* Fences *she worked once again under her former acting teacher (later Yale Rep Artistic Director), Lloyd Richards. She has appeared on Broadway in Charles Gordone's* No Place to Be Somebody; *Off-Broadway in* Zooman and the Sign, Julius Caesar, Miss Julie, Spell #7; *in resident theater productions of* Open Admissions, King Lear, *and* The Blacks; *on television in* The Sty of the Blind Pig, The Killing Mission, Requiem for a Nun, The Resurrection of Lady Lester, *and* All My Children, *and on film in* Sparkle *and* Beat Street. *She has also toured Australia in* For Colored Girls . . .

James Earl Jones appeared at the Yale Rep. as Steve Daniels in the American premier of Fugard's A Lesson from Aloes, *as Julius Nkumbi in* The Day of the Picnic, *and as Judge Brack in* Hedda Gabler. *He won Broadway's Tony and was nominated for an Oscar for* The Great White Hope; *and he received an Obie Award for his performances in* Baal *and* Othello. *Among his extensive film credits are leading roles in* Dr. Strangelove *and* Claudine *(for which he won the Golden Globe Award); and he*

was the voice of Darth Vader in the Star Wars *series. Most recently, Mr. Jones has performed on Broadway and on international tour with* "MASTER HAROLD" . . . and the boys.

The following conversation took place in New Haven on May 10, 1985, following a performance of Fences.

What has it been like to work in an August Wilson play?

JONES: A dear friend of mine, a director, came back stage today and said that the play is unusual, and I agreed. You don't often find this kind of play. Steinbeck used to write about this stratum of life, but among American playwrights, it is rare. Few writers can capture dialect as dialogue in a manner as interesting and accurate as August's. My first experience with a play with the black sound was by a white writer, Howard Sackler—in *The Great White Hope*. That dialogue was not identifiable as Galveston, Texas; it was a poetic rendering of, an *idea* of, Southern dialect. August's dialogue is less "invented." Howard's dialogue was invented totally out of his imagination, which I admired. But August's language has a certain root—I've *heard* other people speak with the same kind of inarticulateness. You find it in other cultures— the uneducated Irish too sometimes speak with great floweriness, they use language very richly—and I think August is catching this sort of speech. My dad, who was a Mississippian before I was, said, "Don't ever lose touch with that sound; don't let your children lose touch with it. People do get educated out of it."

ALICE: I have found this with other writers, too—Charles Gordone, who wrote *No Place to Be Somebody*, Lorraine Hans-

berry, Charles Fuller—the wonderful thing is that because they are writing about material they're very familiar with, they can create the proper language, which is very important. Also—and August has admitted this—they love actors. So they write interesting characters. No matter how small the roles are, the characters are always complete.

Was Troy's character difficult for you to realize, James?

JONES: There are certain things that I find very difficult to achieve, and certain things in Troy that I haven't yet resolved. But overall, I love the person. I have known men similar to him, although their characters were not as rich. It's been hard to modulate Troy's levels of energy, to measure the extent to which he is deeply angry and the extent to which he is just loud-mouthing. I have not found yet where his depths and his highs are. He's like a manic-depressive; he's up and he's down. His relationship to his son is the most complicated one—I don't believe I have yet solved that. The love relationships he has with Rose, with Bono, and even with the older son are a lot easier to achieve than those he has with his younger son and his daughter. That is probably because an actor draws from his own experience, and unless you have things in your own life that can enlighten you, you have to search and search until you understand it.

[To Jones] Your two-year-old hasn't quite reached Cory's age yet?

ALICE: In fifteen years.

JONES: (laughing) Maybe it is all sitting there and I haven't found the connection yet. We share something with you. When I was thirteen, I was being raised by my maternal grandfather. We lived in the country, in both Mississippi and Michigan. In Michigan, my folks were church people—Southern Methodists, but they'd shout and holler and roll on the floor. They invented their own churches, or they would engage circuit preachers, black ministers who would ride by horse or car to a different church every Sunday. The preacher we had engaged that season was attending the chicken dinner one Sunday, and I overheard a conversation between him and my grandfather about men in one household. The preacher was saying, "Now, the boy's thirteen, and he's going to be fourteen." He didn't use the expression "smelling his piss," but he might well have used what August uses in this play. He said, "Sooner or later he's got to go, because two men in one house don't cut it." I was devastated to hear this; I loved my grandfather more than anybody, I couldn't imagine that there would be a conflict between him and me that would force me to leave or force him to make that decision. I read this play and I see there it is again. Is it inevitable?

Did it happen to you and your grandfather?

JONES: No, but I assumed that it would be inevitable. And of course in the animal kingdom it is inevitable that young males are driven away, unless they prove themselves strong enough. I'm haunted by that: by the past and by the prospects of it in the future. Will I have a conflict with my own son? I guess it is so prevalent in the animal kingdom that it is certainly worth holding up as a prototype of a conflict.

And not just the animal kingdom—it's in the Bible. You're supposed to leave your parents' house or—put away childish things. . . .

ALICE: "When I was a child I behaved as a child, but when I became a man I put away childish things." It's from *Corinthians*.

JONES: You know the Bible, don't you?

What about you, Mary? How did you approach your role in this play?

ALICE: In terms of how I approached work, it was not too different from most characters that I have played. I tried to *come* to it very openly, and I also came to this one willingly, because it's a play I love. Then, of course, I looked forward to being the wife of James, unlike sometimes when I am playing the wife of actors and they're difficult. Necessarily interpersonally difficult, but when you have to work at making the other actor your husband, I didn't have this difficulty with James at all. But basically I just started with what had been given by the writer, what Rose says, what is said about her. I suppose I somehow used women I knew, women I knew in 1957. Pittsburgh is not too far removed from Chicago, where I grew up. I didn't have any real difficulty creating her in the atmosphere of rehearsals and in Lloyd's direction. I just trusted Lloyd, which is very important; whatever he said I accepted.

A lot of who *I* am is also Rose. I know many women who are waiting, as she says, "to bloom," and many will never bloom. I have bloomed as a person, more than Rose, I feel, because I have at least to some degree been able to follow my dreams. So there are little petals sticking up somewhere. Rose is not unhappy being the wife and the mother. She is contented, but this is something that people do; they say, this is my place in life, and they accept it. She is able to be happy with this until she finds out that her husband has betrayed her. And it's only then that she begins to deal with what she really wants, with the sacrifices she made in giving all, putting everything into her marriage. There was so much there, already in the script, and given a good director, it was very, very clear.

Some audience members seeing *Fences* have said they see their own lives portrayed by it. You remember the audience member who told us that her parents were Portuguese immigrants and saw her own life on the stage. What of *your* lives did you find in the play, if you found any of your life there?

ALICE: Having to deal with the racism, like the way Troy is trying to break into baseball. When I grew up, I attended an all-girls school that was predominantly white, and I began to see that there are at least two cultures in America. I can also relate to the oral tradition: my grandfather, my father, even my mother, were always telling stories. That is a very African tradition. Dark people did not write it; it was passed on orally. That's very much a part of what I heard in the play.

[To Jones] You have said you've known men like Troy.

JONES: Yes. My summer nights in Michigan were very similar to this play's situation. I don't remember who *wouldn't* take it upon himself to entertain or tell a story. On summer nights the gatherings would happen on a porch. Somebody would end up telling a story, and someone else—visitors, guest—would counter with another story.

ALICE: I remember we used to sit out in front of the house a lot—every night, especially in summer. Everybody would sit out there. People don't do that anymore. I guess they're more afraid now.

Within the limits of blocking and specific direction in *Fences*, I've enjoyed the spontaneity that you bring to your roles—from rehearsal right into performance. How have you found that freshness in this play?

ALICE: In rehearsals Lloyd had a firm hand on the direction, but it was like you didn't feel it. It was always there, shaping the play, but within that, within whatever he wanted, there was so much freedom allowed *to* the actors. I still feel that.

JONES: Lloyd has a word he used to me and one or two other actors; he said it as an admonition. He would tell us, "Don't *manage* it. Let it happen to you." Then we relaxed enough so we developed a certain energy, and that got built into the production. Lloyd would make directorial choices by reminding us of things that we had done and saying he still wanted them. But a lot of his directorial choices were the things that he got us free and spontaneous enough to find. So he didn't have to say, "Do it this way, do it that way."

The greatest reward to come out of our spontaneity was after I had found the extent to which I thought I could take Troy's exposing himself when he says, "I'm going to be a daddy." I made it quite large, and Mary was engaging at quite a full level, too. And then one day in rehearsal, Russell [who played Gabriel] suddenly came in holding a real rose when he said his line about having a flower for Rose. Whatever was happening to Mary, in response to what I had just said to her, stopped. The flower filled the void. I don't know how a director could have managed that.

Has August's play affected you emotionally in any special way? Do you invest more or less emotional energy than is usual in your performances?

JONES: I feel a fatigue that does not occur in a play where the character resolves his situation before the end. Here Troy dies before the last scene, so he does not resolve things onstage. I bring a lot of stuff offstage with me after my last scene, and then I don't know what to do with it. In serious plays, especially tragedies, the actor undergoes a resolution, and he can go home. I can't quite feel that. It helps when I sit backstage and listen to the last scene when they sort things out about me before my funeral. Then I feel better about going home. For a long time in the rehearsal period I did not watch the last scene, and I was missing something: that resolve. For an audience there has to be a kind of catharsis, but an actor has to have it, too.

In a "conventional" tragedy, as the actor, you would go through that catharsis with the audience.

JONES: Yes. The first time I watched the rehearsal of the last scene, I was crying—not just for what I should have been crying about, I was crying for all the times that I should have been watching it and hadn't. There are three moments that trigger the ending catharsis: the moment when Rose acknowledges Troy has died, Cory's tribute, and Gabe's blowing the trumpet.

ALICE: Unlike Jimmy, I think I *have* a catharsis. I have mine at the top of the second act. I don't feel it in the evening, but more when I wake up the next morning—then I feel drained. I usually don't feel like being with people after the show, because all of that stuff that is set up from the first scene onward is still operating. The play requires such concentration and takes such energy. Not effort—but it *is* draining. After the play is over there is a residue; the character does not leave me right away. Regardless of what Mary Alice's behavior is after the show, inside, Rose is still there.

JONES: Is it possible that most plays or their stories demand only an aspect of the character, whereas this play demands the total character? There is not much more to Troy than what we are given, in spite of this private life he has with another woman. Troy speaks of her as something new—he thinks he has discovered something new. He says he laughs at home, but then he talks about another kind of laughter, another part of himself that he never knew before. I think that may just be a fantasy on his part. I think this play, this story, demands all of what this man is, and it asks its actors to make a commitment larger than you would make even in a Shakespeare play.

ALICE: There was a moment in the show today when I was looking at Troy sitting on the sawhorse—you know, when Lyons comes in and Bono tells him Troy has been promoted. Jimmy was just sitting there, and I thought, "Troy is really a great man." But he doesn't think of himself as a great man.

JONES: No.

ALICE: But he has been trying to be something. Not just for himself. He is trying to make it better for others working. And he is sitting there modestly, kind of laughing about it. And I just looked at him, thought, "This is really a great man."

JONES: That's curious, because that is one moment he is not shooting his mouth.

ALICE: Yes; he is just sitting there, having gotten the promotion, and they're teasing him and he takes the teasing.

JONES: There isn't much subtext or hidden parts to these people; they are all out there. They have private thoughts, but not as you would have them in most modern plays.

ALICE: They are very open. The subtext is there, but you don't have to play that, don't have to worry about it. You know who you are, what you want, what your relationship is, and before you know it the moment changes; you're laughing at one moment and the next moment it's serious. It's so real, that's how people are. That's what is beautiful about this play: the moments. And no matter how many times we have done it, it's still fresh.

PERSONAL EFFECTS

("Efectos Personales")

GRISELDA GAMBARO

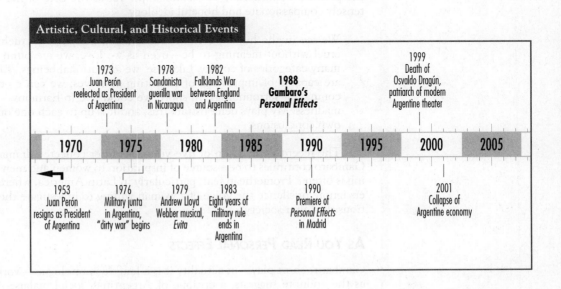

Artistic, Cultural, and Historical Events

1973
Juan Perón
reelected as President
of Argentina

1978
Sandanista
guerilla war
in Nicaragua

1982
Falklands War
between England
and Argentina

1988
Gambaro's
Personal Effects

1999
Death of
Osvaldo Dragún,
patriarch of modern
Argentine theater

| 1970 | 1975 | 1980 | 1985 | 1990 | 1995 | 2000 | 2005 |

1953
Juan Perón
resigns as President
of Argentina

1976
Military junta
in Argentina,
"dirty war" begins

1979
Andrew Lloyd
Webber musical,
Evita

1983
Eight years of
military rule
ends in
Argentina

1990
Premiere of
Personal Effects
in Madrid

2001
Collapse of
Argentine economy

GRISELDA GAMBARO (1928–)

Born in Argentina, Griselda Gambaro is the most prolific and accomplished Latin American woman dramatist. A professional novelist, short fiction writer, and author and lyricist of children's narratives, Gambaro has written over 30 full-length plays, one-acts, and brief dramatic sketches. Although she began her playwriting career in the early 1960s with the well-known *Las Parades* ("The Walls"), she did not attain international recognition until the mid-1970s. The winner of many literary honors, Gambaro has lectured extensively throughout Latin America, Canada, France, Italy, and Spain. She has taught at several universities in the United States, notably Yale, Cornell, and Rice. To escape Argentina's catastrophic political events in the 1970s, Gambaro lived in Barcelona from 1977 until 1980, when democracy was restored in her homeland.

It is difficult to assess Gambaro's dramatic and theatrical styles because she eludes stylistic and thematic comparisons. For example, she stated in a recent interview: "I remember that after the opening of *The Walls*, critics compared me to [Harold] Pinter, even though I had not read one Pinter play." Often labeled an absurdist, an expressionist, or an antirealist, Gambaro rejects such descriptions, as she said in an interview in the *Latin American Theater Review*:

I am more interested in the comic, the farcical and in the grotesque. But when I listen to critical comparisons to Absurdism, I feel a certain degree of convolutedness since the Theatre of the Absurd is not an influence on my work. But there are elements of the Grotesque in my work . . . that is the mixture of pathos, the tragic and the tragicomic that tend to appear in many of my plays.

Gambaro has also spoken frankly of her European and American literary influences: Shakespeare, Molière, Chekhov, Pirandello, Brecht, and O'Neill. She also acknowledges her indebtedness to the Argentinean masters, Armando Discépolo (1887–1971), Florencio Sánchez (1875–1910), and her contemporary, Osvaldo Dragún.

Gambaro's themes are similar to those of her Argentine countryman, Dragún: the devastating effects of urbanization; the inability to communicate; destructive psychological games that avoid honest relationships; the inner strength of humans who must survive the political conditioning of dictatorships. Yet at the core of her worldview lies an intensely compassionate and hopeful ideology.

We see in the human condition a series of inseparable cruelties; often we are cruel without meaning to be—even as we love, we are often cruel. One finds many categories of cruelty. Likewise, we are rational beings, thinking beings; we are capable of improving, of educating ourselves; we can co-exist, live, in our communal surroundings. In short, we could live in harmony—a special kind of madness. My plays demonstrate this, and it is up to each one of us to extract our own conclusions.

The recent publication of five volumes of her collected dramatic works attests that Gambaro continues to be a source of inspiration to women and men who realize that writing is often a Promethean feat, particularly in Latin America, where commercial publishers ignore or silence the voice of a woman willing to investigate the sociopolitical conditions that alter society.

As You Read *Personal Effects*

Gambaro's short play—in actuality it is a lengthy monologue—works on two levels. It is, as the endnote suggests, a critique of Argentina's social malaise, which has been well chronicled in the news. But you need not concern yourself with that aspect of the play as you read it because, on a higher level, the play is a tragicomedy in the absurdist tradition. Its central character might have been created by Samuel Beckett (see Part II), and the dilemmas portrayed are universal. We all carry "excess baggage" that weighs us down. The play depends on the interaction of the actor and the audience, and it is therefore imperative that you imagine a first-rate comedian, skilled in physical comedy, speaking to you. And, of course, you must see the deserted, dilapidated train station—and that enormous pile of "personal effects."

PERSONAL EFFECTS

GRISELDA GAMBARO

Translated by Roberto Darío Pomo

PERSONAL EFFECTS premiered on March 30, 1990, in the Teatro de Alfil in Madrid, Spain. The role of the Man was performed by Alejandro Creste. Scenography and costumes were designed by Roberto Villanueva.

A deserted train station in a small town. There are no benches, only a small drinking fountain next to a wall. Pasted on the walls, a few public announcements that are faded and semi-peeled. A man enters running—out of breath—as if he attempts to catch a departing train. Over his shoulder is a rather large duffel-bag. Under one of his arms and in his hand he carries a variety of suitcases of different sizes, while with his other hand he drags a large and heavy suitcase by a rope. He stops and looks around at the station's platform with a sense of relief. He dumps his entire baggage on the ground. A pause. He exits. He re-enters—this time with much more luggage and carrying a torn violin case. Again he drags yet another large suitcase by a thick rope. It's too much for him. He drops everything in a pile next to the other pieces of luggage. He turns to the large suitcase he has been dragging behind. With both hands he drags the suitcase towards the other suitcases. A pause. He looks all around desperately looking for something, pushing and kicking the suitcases until he locates his violin case. Relieved and content now, he picks it up, brushes the case off, embraces it and places the case on top of the heap with care. A pause. He stares at the railroad tracks. He exits. He enters again carrying an arm-load full of more suitcases which he dumps on top on the existing pile and on top of the violin case. A pause. He wipes the perspiration off his forehead as he stares into the distance. A pause.

What luck! I didn't miss the train. I'm a lucky man.

(He sits on top of one of the large suitcases and rests. He notices the schedule posted on one of the walls, walks to it, reads it. He looks at his watch, outraged.)

Why did they make me rush? Two hours.

(A tense smile)

Two hours. I didn't even get breakfast. What am I doing in this desert? Let me put some order here.

This one on the ground, and this one tied with rope so I won't lose it.

(He ties the suitcase with the rope.)

This one here, and this one . . .

(He holds a worn-out rectangular small suitcase in his hands.)

What did I put in here?

(He looks at it, turns it upside down, places his ear next to it then shakes it.)

No, I'm not going to open it . . . I'm curious, but not THAT curious. If I'm going to open every single suitcase to see what's inside . . .

(He laughs. Places the suitcase on the ground a bit apart from the other ones. He sits and stares at the suitcase through the corner of his eye.)

It's not that heavy. It's old. What did I put in it?

(He sniffs. Suddenly fear overcomes him.)

Did I catch a cold? And I don't have any aspirin.

(He stares at the suitcase.)

No, I didn't pack any aspirin in there. I'm certain.

(He stares at the suitcase with irritation.)

This suitcase is good for everything, except aspirin.

(Brusquely)

Socks, underwear. That's what I packed in it. No. Socks, underwear, the first change of clothing, always here.

(He looks through the pile and locates the duffel-bag. Opens it.)

Here we go.

(He takes out a sandwich, unwraps and stares at it.)

Salami and cheese? I told them no salami.

(Unhappily)

I don't like salami. I'll eat it anyway.

(He sits on one of the suitcases and proceeds to eat the sandwich.)

I know what's in every suitcase.

Only a fool doesn't know what's inside his own luggage.

(Pointing at one of the suitcases)

Inside that one, gifts. All junk. The town's coat of arms. What do I want with the town's coat of arms? They should have given me a ham sandwich with fresh lettuce. I didn't buy any gifts. What could anyone buy here? A cow. Just what I needed. To buy a cow! A mule, yes. To carry everything for me. But then they wouldn't let me on the train! As if there's a difference between me and a mule. What's the difference? To a mule, there's no difference. A mule sees a man and says, "That's a mule." Or it could say, "It's a horse." It has no sense of . . . of the world! What time is it? It's been ten minutes.

(Distracted, he straightens out other suitcases. He belches.)

This sandwich has settled in my stomach like lead.

(Screaming)

WATER!

(He crosses to the drinking fountain, but there's no water. He's dumbfounded.)

I could die of thirst here!

(He collapses on top of the large suitcase and then jumps up.)

We could all die of thirst! The old, the young, me! Universal dehydration! Bums. Why can't people make things work right? They dug, put in pipes, installed this shitty

little sink, connected it to a spring, to a well; they paid wages, made people get up at five in the morning, for what? All that effort, all that sweat, for what? So you can turn the faucet and get no water! I can't stand this! An earthquake one understands, things that happen under the earth, whims of nature, mischief, but this, so much human effort to provide a service, water for the thirsty, and nothing!

(He laughs hysterically. Attempts to move the drinking fountain. Kicks it.)

Not even a drop. The thirsty dies of thirst! And they didn't even see me to the station! I walked like Jesus at Calvary, with all these suitcases. It doesn't matter. I played for a small town, to deaf ears.

(Speaking to his suitcase)

What do you have in here? The gray suit, neatly folded.

(Looks at another suitcase. A sense of doubt registers on his face.)

Or did I put it . . . in there?

(Slowly he crosses to the suitcase. A pause. He stares at it intently.)

No, it's the small one that I remember. I'm positive. Absolutely certain. In this one, I packed three wool blazers and a jacket.

(He kneels by and opens the suitcase. Rummages through its contents and takes out a pair of pants and a gray jacket.)

I was wrong. It's in here, neatly folded . . . didn't want to get it wrinkled. I was tempted to put it inside the small one, but at the last minute I realized. How could I have packed a nice suit like that in this tiny suitcase? It'd come out looking like an accordion!

(As he speaks, he nervously places the contents back into the suitcase. He smoothes out the wrinkles of the jacket by hitting it rapidly. The nervous tension increases. He rolls and shoves the pair of pants into the suitcase—attempts to close it, but is unable to do so. He sits on top of it and finally manages to close it. Pieces of clothing are seen peering out from all around the suitcase.)

The gray suit for these people! I'm an idiot. I'll give myself a concert! Just for me. My gift to myself. Free of charge! To me, music brings joy to the soul. And I need some joy after the mule, the salami sandwich, the faucet with no water, the clothes that don't fit in the suitcase!

(He pulls at a protruding piece of clothing.)

And don't come out either.

(He madly struggles with the suitcase.)

What aggression!

(He kicks it. After a few seconds he attempts to control himself.)

Think about your soul, the serenity of music.

(He looks at the heap of luggage, then scatters the pieces around. His nervousness increases again.)

Where is it? But, I put it right here, on top of . . .

(He locates the violin case, dusts it with his sleeve. Places the case under his arm and applauds loudly. With modesty he takes a bow and salutes.)

That's enough now, thank you, please, thank you, thank you all.

(He opens the case, takes out the violin. A pause. He's speechless and dumbfounded.)

My God, the string's broken! It broke! My God. God, why did you do this to me? Am I not your child, a mortal, just a regular guy? Why pick on me? So it's all right if these train people don't know my mule or the mule doesn't know me either, but you'd think . . . there are other categories right? Don't answer! I don't want to hear excuses. Save it. Sorry doesn't make it better either. The string's broken. Why did this have to happen to me? Why didn't it happen to the mule? It wouldn't make any difference to the mule.

(A pause)

But I have to think! There are other possibilities here, right? No don't answer me! I don't want to hear any excuses! Save them! Repentance doesn't do any good! The string's broken! Why did it have to happen to me? Why didn't it happen to the damn mule? She wouldn't care!

(Looking at another suitcase)

And what did I pack in here? I don't know. I, who know everything about the others, do not know!

(He laughs with a false sense of cheerfulness. He kisses the violin case and speaks to it as he carefully puts it down.)

Don't suffer . . . a broken string is not the end of the world.

(Offended)

Why did this have to happen to me?

(Pause. In a lowered voice)

People who don't know me can think whatever they want. But the truth is: here I am, waiting for the train, with an as yet undigested cheese and salami sandwich in my stomach, thirsty for a drink of water, on the verge of catching a cold, and, nonetheless, I am . . . I am. I can't give myself a concert. I, who know how to play, I cannot. The string has snapped!

(He laughs hysterically and looks at another suitcase.)

I'm not going to open you. I know what's inside you. I'm just having a bit of amnesia. It's O.K. There's time. Ten minutes have passed. For the next ten minutes, I'm going to straighten up my luggage. Let me find a tip for the porter. I need a hand here. Since I don't have a mule. Ha ha.

(He takes out a few coins from his pockets. He realizes that they're only a few. He looks at them and places them back inside his pocket.)

No, I can do this by myself . . . the train won't leave without me. I have everything ready to go. From the platform I'll open up the window, and bam bam, throw the suitcases in one by one.

(He gestures as he talks.)

I'll get them organized. The shoes are in here. This one has the ceramic plate the club president gave me . . .

(Shaking a smaller suitcase)

It's rattling . . . It must be broken . . . fortunately. It looked more like brick. In here, the umbrella, the shaving kit . . . the pot to heat water for tea . . . books and magazines. Medicine here. But no aspirin!

(He jumps over the suitcases.)

I know, the Scottish blanket!

(Laughing)

I said to myself, "Not on this trip. I'll be safe and not sorry." That's what I put in there. All this hullabaloo when . . . *(He continues the momentum but meanwhile the smile freezes on his face.)* the solution is right . . . at hand . . . Or is it? *(He looks at another, larger suitcase.)* Doubt is not ignorance. Doubt is the cornerstone of intelligence. Did I pack it in there, the Scottish blanket with the blue wool bedspread that itches? I brought both, and an overcoat, in case it was cold. It was hot. Or did I pack them separately? All that bulk. Doubt is the cornerstone of . . . Don't repeat yourself!

(He crosses to the suitcase and opens it. He takes out the Scottish blanket and throws it up in the air. Immediately he takes out the blue bedspread.)

Didn't I know it? They're here. They picked this beautiful suitcase!

(He laughs as he kicks them around. After a few seconds he straightens out the Scottish blanket and picks up the blue bedspread. As if in a trance, he wrestles with it. He stops and places the blanket inside the suitcase. He does not close the suitcase but walks away from it.)

Done!

(He looks at the suitcase with disdain.)

You go on being mysterious. If I had a stethoscope or an x-ray machine or a laser gun. You'd see where your pride has got you. I played and they chitchatted, coughed, fidgeted in their seats, and some of them came in late, boom boom boom, like they had boots on, like they were goose stepping, that's what they were doing!

(Laughing)

Who would have thought it, eh? To come to this measly little town? But, there was this sweet little thing, seated in the front row . . . but I lost sight of her. And the dogs followed me here! So, what have you got in there? Tell me. Don't be so proud . . . I'm not going to open you up. I'm not going to please you in this way. Who the hell pleases me, eh? The string is broken . . . I have a cold . . . that sweet thing never took her eyes off me . . . so I missed a few notes in my performance . . . so what? The *Flight of the Bumble Bee* was perfect, but in the end, the fly goes splat on the wall.

(He hums a few bars of the Flight of the Bumble Bee *until he muddles the song.)*

The audience didn't even notice. She didn't either. She was a small-town girl, out of step with fashions, so beautiful . . .

(A long pause)

And she applauded . . . she waited around . . . the rest left right away, like bats out of hell.

(A jubilant laughter)

I starched two shirts and an undershirt.

(He sits on top of a large suitcase.)

I play by memory, so don't go thinking I'm going to forget anything.

(He grows somber. A long pause. He restrains himself.)

No, not this time. I'm not about to repeat this damn game! I'm sure . . . most sure of it. It's not just a matter of intuition . . . it's an absolute conviction . . . the solution to the mysteries of the universe. I'll specify the exact details: the white shirt has two buttons missing, the light blue striped shirt and the starched undershirt with holes in the elbows . . . I should have sewn them . . . I know. But that's not here or there. Maybe I didn't pack the undershirt in there. Could be. I don't like mixing things.

(Pointing at another suitcase)

I'll look! That way, I'll put all doubts to rest.

(To the smaller suitcase)

Your doubts. Not mine. Although doubt is the cornerstone of . . . *(He realizes he's repeating himself and stops. He opens the suitcase and takes out an alarm clock, a saucepan, a spatula and various garments.)*

See? It's not in here . . .

(He holds the undershirt in his hand. Pretending to be cheerful)

Here! I don't own two undershirts, so this must be the one with the elbows . . . Let's see the elbows. Worn out.

(He places the undershirt aside while continuing to extract pieces of clothing out of the suitcase.)

But an undershirt is not a shirt.

(Holding up two shirts)

Shirts are different, more elegant . . .

(Sees he has them in his hands)

They are . . .

(He puts everything inside without even closing the suitcase. He stands up straight.)

It's getting dark . . . I'm forty years old now.

(Genuinely surprised)

Me?

(Taking out his identification from his pocket. He stares at the papers for a few seconds)

It seems like I was born only yesterday. Now, I'm forty years old . . . I'm going bald, and I haven't accomplished much, have I? She looked at me, at me!

(A long pause)

Why didn't she wait for me after the performance? I walked around the block three times hoping to find her again, and not even a dog was around. Well, yes, dogs were around . . . dogs here . . . dogs there . . . but not even the dogs looked at me . . . they played by themselves . . . moronic animals . . . smelling each other . . . smelling each other's hind parts like they were delicacies.

(Looking at the suitcase out of the corner of his eyes)

I know, enough of this hypothesizing. Let the subconscious work on it. I'll go for a little walk.

(Humming as he walks)

Why did I study the violin?

(Answering himself)

Because you enjoyed music!

Why did you enjoy music?

(Answering himself)

Because I had a sensitive soul. . . . Yes, I'm sensitive . . . it's true. My fingers failed me, not my soul. At times it's probably better if the soul fails you, that goes unnoticed.

(Lifting his shoulders)

This town is truly radiant! The streets are bustling with life! What hustle and bustle!

(His enthusiasm collapses.)

I don't remember a thing. What if I open it? After all, that's what it's waiting for. It's playing hard to get. To make me give in. And then it'll say, "I win!" Well, you're dead wrong.

(He stands and crosses to the suitcase. He embraces it.)

You foolish thing, foolish, stubborn, obstinate. I know what you have inside. Trying to fool me, your daddy, your master, let's go for a walk, you and me. (*Pointing at the other suitcases on the ground*) Look. I'm leaving the others behind. I kick them, I hate them.

(Walking with it clutched to his chest)

You and I together.

(Pointing at the other suitcases on the ground)

See? These other ones I'll leave behind. I'll kick them . . . I detest them! If they're offended, that's their problem. Whisper in my ear . . . tell me . . . don't be ashamed . . . tell me . . .

(He positions his ear next to the suitcase. He listens. A long pause)

That's all? That and nothing more?

(Clutching it, he sits on top of the large suitcase.)

All this, for . . . well, all right. No need to be ashamed . . . You did what you could. No, no. It was a lot . . . A little nothing . . . It was a lot . . .

(He stands still embracing the suitcase. Slowly and with a deep feeling of sadness, he exits.)

After a few seconds

Blackout

COMMENTARY

Note: This essay represents a single interpretation of the play. For other perspectives on Personal Effects, *consult the essays listed below.*

Written in 1988, *Personal Effects* premiered in Madrid, Spain, in March 1990. A tragicomedy with Beckett-like themes and style, the play is a brief, albeit expansive, journey into the mind of a seemingly failed musician awaiting the arrival of a train so that he may be transported from his provincial surroundings back to his cosmopolitan dreamland. The violinist contemplates his existence while surrounded by a pile of luggage amidst a desolate landscape. A clownish figure reminiscent of Chaplin's Little Tramp or Beckett's grotesque clowns, the musician is also a volatile, self-indulgent, paranoid, and retentive personality.

Gambaro immediately establishes a relationship between the musician-performer and the audience. He directly communicates his psychological and spiritual displacement, and we are invited to share in his suffering, just as his fictional audience was invited, only hours before the curtain rises, to share in his musical communication. But as we learn of his apparent failure to reach an appreciative musical audience, we begin to understand that his disconnected narrative is truly an act of confession in which this postmodern clown proceeds to "unrobe" himself.

Just as Lucky in Beckett's *Waiting for Godot* carries with him the remnants of Western civilization in the form of a rope, a bag, and a picnic basket, so does our musician carry quantities of luggage symbolizing the residue of a nation unable to assemble the missing pieces of a once rich and democratic society. The "heavy baggage" of recent Argentine history carries with it numerous military coups, deposed presidencies, dictatorships, civil war, and the disappearance of thousands at the hands of the military. The disastrous defeat of the Argentine army by British forces during the brief Falklands-Malvinas War (1982) was the baggage that broke the nation's back, a problem compounded by the current economic crisis. As the musician busily rearranges the suitcases during the play's climactic moments, he mutters:

> You foolish thing, foolish, stubborn, obstinate. I know what you have inside. Trying to fool me . . . (*Walking with [a case] clutched to his chest*) You and I together. (*Pointing at the other suitcases on the ground*) See? These other ones I'll leave behind. I'll kick them . . . I detest them! If they're offended, that's their problem.

If the musician is unable to come to terms with his own loneliness and inertia, likewise, Gambaro suggests that certain pieces of historical baggage can never be discarded—that cultural signifiers have, for better or worse, been stored away, compartmentalized and appropriated into a landscape of the contemporary Argentine social fiber.

Additional difficulties arise for the musician because the railway station lacks water—an emblem of a society lacking a socioeconomic structure. Gambaro implies that for Argentina, in spite of a developed labor force and a highly educated population, nothing seems to function properly. The richest country in Latin America during the early twentieth century, contemporary Argentina is a dried-out shell seemingly incapable of reinventing itself. Or as the musician laments:

> Why can't people make things work right? They dug, put in pipes, installed this shitty little sink, connected it to a spring . . . they paid wages, made people get up at five in the morning, for what? All that effort, all that sweat, for what? So you can turn the faucet and get no water!

The impending arrival of the train—which never materializes—is yet another imposing image in Gambaro's play. Again, just as Gogo and Didi await Godot as the salvation of their distress, Gambaro's musician waits, and waits, and waits. Didi and Gogo find refuge in each other as they pass time, but the musician relies only on the companionship of his "personal effects" to make time bearable. The locomotive (like the bus in Gao Xingjian's *The Bus Stop*) becomes a symbol of psychological torture—somewhere in the distance perhaps it makes its way. But its motion is circular, just as the musician's attempted escape from his provincial environment is circular in nature. The first lines of the play are intriguing: "What luck! I didn't miss the train. I'm a lucky man." Yet, one might ask: Did he miss the train? Will the train ever arrive? After all, the station is deserted, its walls faded and covered with outdated announcements. There is not an attendant in sight. The present becomes the past, while the past becomes the future. Thus Gambaro's train metamorphoses into a torture chamber; ironically, it can never be a means of escape from the musician's plight.

For all its implications concerning Argentina's internal dilemmas, *Personal Effects* is ultimately a universal tragicomedy about the inability of a human being to understand fully the resonance of memory or the collective history of human experience. Shackled to the past—and its volumes of baggage—the human cannot move beyond self-destruction. Gambaro argues that:

if one looks at the condition of world politics, one sees a road heading towards death—it is not a road towards personal growth or maturity, or a road towards the possibilities that life offers; on the contrary, it is a road in search of an arms buildup, a war, a road heading towards world hunger, towards power plays and interests that are egotistical in nature. And all of us continue to protect our small pieces of turf thinking that it will never affect us.

Gambaro's musician is an artistically stilted, psychologically displaced, and personally marginalized individual who, through the accumulation of excess baggage, continues to attempt to find a way out of his own discord. Yet, through laughter and poignant theatrical moments, we see a mirror image of ourselves as we, too, attempt to find solace in a world quickly crumbling beneath our feet. Our baggage—our personal effects—is equally taxing.

Other perspectives on *Personal Effects* and Gambaro's dramaturgy:

Boyle, Catherine. "Griselda Gambaro: The Female Dramatist and the Audacious Trespasser." In Susan Bassnett (ed.), *Knives and Angels: Women Writers in Latin America.* Garden City, NJ: Zed, 1990, 145–47.

Postena, Rosalea. "Space and Spectator in the Theater of Griselda Gambaro." *Latin American Theater Review* 14:1 (Fall 1980): 35–46.

ANGELS IN AMERICA
PART ONE: MILLENNIUM APPROACHES

TONY KUSHNER

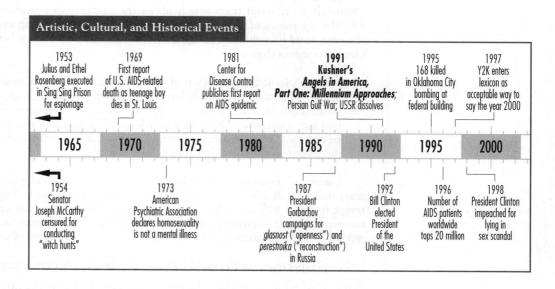

Artistic, Cultural, and Historical Events

1953	1969	1981	**1991**	1995	1997
Julius and Ethel Rosenberg executed in Sing Sing Prison for espionage	First report of U.S. AIDS-related death as teenage boy dies in St. Louis	Center for Disease Control publishes first report on AIDS epidemic	**Kushner's** ***Angels in America, Part One: Millennium Approaches***; Persian Gulf War; USSR dissolves	168 killed in Oklahoma City bombing at federal building	Y2K enters lexicon as acceptable way to say the year 2000

1965	1970	1975	1980	1985	1990	1995	2000

1954	1973	1987	1992	1996	1998
Senator Joseph McCarthy censured for conducting "witch hunts"	American Psychiatric Association declares homosexuality is not a mental illness	President Gorbachov campaigns for *glasnost* ("openness") and *perestroika* ("reconstruction") in Russia	Bill Clinton elected President of the United States	Number of AIDS patients worldwide tops 20 million	President Clinton impeached for lying in sex scandal

TONY KUSHNER (1956–)

Tony Kushner burst onto the American theatrical scene with a brilliance, exuberance, and political engagement unparalleled since the 1960s. *Millennium Approaches*, the first part of his two-part epic *Angels in America*, won virtually every theatrical award for the 1992 and 1993 seasons in the United States and England. Despite its potentially divisive emphasis on gay men and other marginalized communities—socialists, Jews, agnostics, political activists, drag queens, and artists—the play was embraced by audiences, academics, and mainstream critics alike. It proved just as popular and thought-provoking during a nationwide American tour when it was paired with its companion, *Perestroika*.

Born in Manhattan in 1956, Kushner grew up in Lake Charles, Louisiana, the son of musician parents of a decidedly liberal stripe. As an undergraduate at Columbia University in New York, Kushner saw director Richard Foreman's staging of Brecht's *The Threepenny Opera* for the Public Theatre at Lincoln Center. He was "devastated" by the production, saw it six times, and became interested in both the political philosophy and the dramaturgy of Brecht from that point on.

At Columbia too, he directed his first play, became involved in the antiapartheid movement, and joined a political theater collective, Three P Productions. The Ps stood for popcorn (entertainment), politics (engagement), and poetics (artistic beauty). For three summers after his graduation he directed youngsters back home in Louisiana in plays by Shakespeare and Brecht. His interests led him to New York University for graduate studies. He also worked at the Repertory Theater of St. Louis, at the New York Theater Workshop (which still supports his work), and at the Theater Communications Group before his playwriting generated enough income for him to write full-time.

Kushner gave *Angels in America* a subtitle: *A Gay Fantasia on National Themes*. The play opens with characters whose stage lives begin in 1985. The venal lawyer Roy M. Cohn, based on the real-life attorney who made his reputation in the anti-Communist hearings of the 1950s, is living high in Washington. He wants to plant young Joe Pitt, an appeals court law clerk from Salt Lake City, in the Justice Department. Pitt's wife Harper is depressed and given to Valium-fueled hallucinations that take her to Antarctica. She also wonders where Joe goes at night when he leaves her to walk alone. Cohn and Pitt are both closeted homosexuals, and much of *Millennium Approaches* anatomizes the psychic and political costs of living such a lie. But the play's main plot, which meshes with the others, involves Prior Walter and his lover, Louis Ironson, who deserts Walter when he discovers he has AIDS. Walter is haunted by visitations from thirteenth- and eighteenth-century ancestors who were also born into a time of plague; he also hears an unseen voice which urges him to— like John the Baptist—"prepare the way." When the play ends, an angel arrives from above in a blast of music and light, which Walter, in Brechtian ironic fashion, calls "*Very* Steven Spielberg." The angel greets him as a prophet and announces: "The Great Work begins." Kushner never defines the agenda of that Great Work, but his epic is wide in its thematic reach and highly entertaining as it careens from melodrama to low comedy to high comedy to camp, propelled by a singular combination of intelligence, ebullience, and rage directed at the conservative "revolution" wrought by President Ronald Reagan and his allies.

Kushner has said that anyone interested in exploring alternatives to individualism and the political economy it serves, capitalism, has to be willing to ask tough questions, not only about government but also about the self and community. The structure of *Millennium Approaches* reflects that kind of questioning as characters often are deployed in two- and three-character scenes for passionate debate.

The development and production process for *Millennium* was long. The play was commissioned in 1987 by the Eureka Theatre in San Francisco, then had a private, first-draft workshop production at the Mark Taper Forum in Los Angeles, followed a year later by a full production at the Eureka. London's National Theatre staged the first major production, a revised *Millennium*, in 1992. Later that year the Taper staged *Millennium* with the still unfinished *Perestroika*. In the spring of 1993, after its Broadway opening, *Millennium* won the Pulitzer Prize and the Tony Award for best play.

Kushner's other works include the early *A Bright Room Called Day* about the Hitler era; a comedy about post-glasnost Russia, *Slavs: or Thinking about the Longstanding Problems of Virtue and Happiness*; and adaptations of Corneille's *The Illusion* and Brecht's *The Good Woman of Setzuan*. He proved eerily prescient with his 2002 work *Homebody/Kabul*, a dazzling and devastating two-act play about a woman obsessed with Taliban-era Afghanistan; she then suffers violent consequences when she visits there. The play was completed long before the terrorist attacks of September 11, when national attention—and certainly that of most artists—was focused elsewhere.

AS YOU READ *ANGELS IN AMERICA, PART ONE: MILLENNIUM APPROACHES*

For all its postmodern sensibilities (see endnote for specific examples), *Millennium Approaches*, which can be appreciated as a work unto itself, emerges as a traditional play in its treatment of human isolation. It is the successor of the works of O'Neill and Williams, in its psychological (and perhaps autobiographical) portraiture of several couples in different parts of America who are tormented by personal problems in the last years of the millennium. The principal characters are Kushner's invention, save one: Roy Cohn (1927–86), a lawyer who worked for the infamous Senator McCarthy during the "Red Scare" witch-hunts of the 1950s. Cohn was the prosecutor in the famous trial of Julius and Ethel Rosenberg, who were accused of treason. Cohn won his (still controversial) case, and the Rosenbergs were sentenced to death. One of Kushner's masterstrokes is a scene in which Ethel Rosenberg's spirit visits Cohn as he is dying. Later Cohn worked in the Nixon Administration and became a symbol among liberals, and especially gays, for the cruel, dispassionate attitudes they associated with conservative Republicans. Kushner's Cohn—whom he describes as "a work of dramatic fiction"—is simultaneously the most reprehensible and pitiful character in the play.

ANGELS IN AMERICA, PART ONE: MILLENNIUM APPROACHES

T O N Y   K U S H N E R

T H E   C H A R A C T E R S

ROY M. COHN, *a successful New York lawyer and unofficial power broker.*

JOSEPH PORTER PITT, *chief clerk for Justice Theodore Wilson of the Federal Court of Appeals, Second Circuit.*

HARPER AMATY PITT, *Joe's wife, an agoraphobic with a mild Valium addiction.*

LOUIS IRONSON, *a word processor working for the Second Circuit Court of Appeals.*

PRIOR WALTER, *Louis's boyfriend. Occasionally works as a club designer or caterer, otherwise lives very modestly but with great style off a small trust fund.*

HANNAH PORTER PITT, *Joe's mother, currently residing in Salt Lake City, living off her deceased husband's army pension.*

BELIZE, *a former drag queen and former lover of Prior's. A registered nurse. Belize's name was originally Norman Arriaga; Belize is a drag name that stuck.*

THE ANGEL, *four divine emanations, Fluor, Phosphor, Lumen and Candle; manifest in One: the Continental Principality of America. She was magnificent in steel-gray wings.*

O T H E R   C H A R A C T E R S   I N   P A R T   O N E

RABBI ISIDOR CHEMELWITZ, *an orthodox Jewish rabbi, played by the actor playing Hannah.*

MR. LIES, *Harper's imaginary friend, a travel agent, who in style of dress and speech suggests a jazz musician; he always wears a large lapel badge emblazoned "IOTA" (The International Order of Travel Agents). He is played by the actor playing Belize.*

THE MAN IN THE PARK, *played by the actor playing Prior.*

THE VOICE, *the voice of The Angel.*

HENRY, *Roy's doctor, played by the actor playing Hannah.*

EMILY, *a nurse, played by the actor playing The Angel.*

MARTIN HELLER, *a Reagan Administration Justice Department flackman, played by the actor playing Harper.*

SISTER ELLA CHAPTER, *a Salt Lake City real-estate saleswoman, played by the actor playing The Angel.*

PRIOR 1, *the ghost of a dead Prior Walter from the 13th century, played by the actor playing Joe. He is a blunt, gloomy medieval farmer with a guttural Yorkshire accent.*

PRIOR 2, *the ghost of a dead Prior Walter from the 17th century, played by the actor playing Roy. He is a Londoner, sophisticated, with a High British accent.*

THE ESKIMO, *played by the actor playing Joe.*

THE WOMAN IN THE SOUTH BRONX, *played by the actor playing The Angel.*

ETHEL ROSENBERG, *played by the actor playing Hannah.*

PLAYWRIGHT'S NOTES
A DISCLAIMER

Roy M. Cohn, the character, is based on the late Roy M. Cohn (1927–1986), who was all too real; for the most part the acts attributed to the character Roy, such as his illegal conferences with Judge Kaufmann during the trial of Ethel Rosenberg, are to be found in the historical record. But this Roy is a work of dramatic fiction; his words are my invention, and liberties have been taken.

A NOTE ABOUT THE STAGING

The play benefits from a pared-down style of presentation, with minimal scenery and scene shifts done rapidly (no blackouts!), employing the cast as well as stagehands—which make for an actor-driven event, as this must be. The moments of magic—the appearance and disappearance of Mr. Lies and the ghosts, the Book hallucination, and the ending—are to be fully realized, as bits of wonderful theatrical illusion—which means it's OK if the wires show, and maybe it's good that they do, but the magic should at the same time be thoroughly amazing.

> In a murderous time
> the heart breaks and breaks
> and lives by breaking.
> —Stanley Kunitz, "The Testing-Tree"

ACT I: BAD NEWS

October–November 1985

SCENE 1

The last days of October. Rabbi Isidor Chemelwitz alone onstage with a small coffin. It is a rough pine box with two wooden pegs, one at the foot and one at the head, holding the lid in place. A prayer shawl embroidered with a Star of David is draped over the lid, and by the head a yarzheit candle is burning.

RABBI ISIDORE CHEMELWITZ (*He speaks sonorously, with a heavy Eastern European accent, unapologetically consulting a sheet of notes for the family names*). Hello and good morning. I am Rabbi Isidor Chemelwitz of the Bronx Home for Aged Hebrews. We are here this morning to pay respects at the passing of Sarah Ironson, devoted wife of Benjamin Ironson, also deceased, loving and caring mother of her sons Morris, Abraham, and Samuel, and her daughters Esther and Rachel; beloved grandmother of Max, Mark, Louis, Lisa, Maria . . . uh . . . Lesley, Angela, Doris, Luke and Eric. (*Looks more closely at paper*) Eric? This is a Jewish name? (*Shrugs*) Eric. A large and loving family. We assemble that we may mourn collectively this good and righteous woman.

(*He looks at the coffin*)

This woman. I did not know this woman. I cannot accurately described her attributes, nor do justice to her dimensions. She was. . . . Well, in the Bronx Home of Aged Hebrews are many like this, the old, and to many I speak but not to be frank with this one. She preferred silence. So I do not know her and yet I know her. She was . . .

(*He touches the coffin*)

. . . not a person but a whole kind of person, the ones who crossed the ocean, who brought with us to America the villages of Russia and Lithuania—and how we struggled, and how we fought, for the family, for the Jewish home, so that you would not grow up here, in this strange place, in the melting pot where nothing melted. Descendants of this immigrant woman, you do not grow up in America, you and your children and their children with the goyische names. You do not live in America. No such place exists. Your clay is the clay of some Litvak shtetl, your air the air of the steppes—because she carried the old world on her back across the ocean, in a boat, and she put it down on Grand Concourse Avenue, or in Flatbush, and she worked that earth into your bones, and you pass it to your children, this ancient, ancient culture and home.

(*Little pause*)

You can never make that crossing that she made, for such Great Voyages in this world do not any more exist. But every day of your lives the miles that voyage between that place and this one you cross. Every day. You understand me? In you that journey is.
So . . .
She was the last of the Mohicans, this one was. Pretty soon . . . all the old will be dead.

SCENE 2

Same day. Roy and Joe in Roy's office. Roy at an impressive desk, bare except for a very elaborate phone system, rows and rows of flashing buttons which bleep and beep and whistle incessantly, making chaotic music underneath Roy's conversations. Joe is sitting, waiting. Roy conducts business with great energy, impatience and sensual abandon: gesticulating, shouting, cajoling, crooning, playing the phone, receiver and hold button with virtuosity and love.

ROY (*Hitting a button*). Hold. (*To Joe*) I wish I was an octopus, a fucking octopus. Eight loving arms and all those suckers. Know what I mean?

JOE. No, I . . .

ROY (*Gesturing to a deli platter of little sandwiches on his desk*). You want lunch?

JOE. No, that's OK really I just . . .

ROY (*Hitting a button*). Ailene? Roy Cohn. Now what kind of a greeting is. . . . I thought we were friends, Ai.

. . . Look Mrs. Soffer, you don't have to get. . . . You're upset. You're yelling. You'll aggravate your condition, you shouldn't yell, you'll pop little blood vessels in your face if you yell. . . . No that was a joke, Mrs. Soffer, I was joking. . . . I already apologized sixteen times for that, Mrs. Soffer, you . . . (*While she's fulminating, Roy covers the mouthpiece with his hand and talks to Joe*) This'll take a minute, *eat* already, what is this tasty sandwich here it's— (*He takes a bite of a sandwich*) Mmmmm, liver or some. . . . Here.

(*He pitches the sandwich to Joe, who catches it and returns it to the platter.*)

ROY (*Back to Mrs. Soffer*). Uh huh, uh huh. . . . No, I already told you, it wasn't a vacation, it was business, Mrs. Soffer, I have clients in Haiti, Mrs. Soffer, I. . . . Listen, AILENE, YOU THINK I'M THE ONLY GODDAM LAWYER IN HISTORY EVER MISSED A COURT DATE? Don't make such a big fucking. . . . Hold. (*He hits the hold button*) You HAG!

JOE. If this is a bad time . . .

ROY. *Bad time?* This is a good time! (*Button*) Baby doll, get me. . . . Oh fuck, wait . . . (*Button, button*) Hello? Yah. Sorry to keep you holding, Judge Hollins, I. . . . Oh *Mrs.* Hollins, sorry dear deep voice you got. Enjoying your visit? (*Hands over mouthpiece again, to Joe*) She sounds like a truck-driver and he sounds like Kate Smith, very confusing. Nixon appointed him, all the geeks are Nixon appointees . . . (*To Mrs. Hollins*) Yeah yeah right good so how many tickets dear? Seven. For what, *Cats, 42nd Street,* what? No you wouldn't like *La Cage,* trust me, I know. Oh for godsake. . . . Hold. (*Button, button*) Baby doll, seven for *Cats* or something, anything hard to get, I don't give a fuck what and neither will they. (*Button; to Joe*) You see *La Cage?*

JOE. No I . . .

ROY. Fabulous. Best thing on Broadway. Maybe ever. (*button*) Who? Aw, Jesus H. Christ, Harry, *no,* Harry, Judge John Francis Grimes, Manhattan Family Court. Do I have to do every goddam thing myself? *Touch* the bastard, Harry, and don't call me on this line again, I told you not to . . .

JOE (*Starting to get up*). Roy, uh, should I wait outside or . . .

ROY (*To Joe*). Oh sit. (*To Harry*) You hold. I pay you to hold fuck you Harry you jerk. (*Button*) Half-wit dick-brain. (*Instantly philosophical*) I see the universe, Joe, as a kind of sandstorm in outer space with winds of

mega-hurricane velocity, but instead of grains of sand it's shards and splinters of glass. You ever feel that way? Ever have one of those days?

JOE. I'm not sure I . . .

ROY. So how's life in Appeals? How's the Judge?

JOE. He sends his best.

ROY. He's a good man. Loyal. Not the brightest man on the bench, but he has manners. And a nice head of silver hair.

JOE. He gives me a lot of responsibility.

ROY. Yeah, like writing his decisions and signing his name.

JOE. Well . . .

ROY. He's a nice guy. And you cover admirably.

JOE. Well, thanks, Roy, I . . .

ROY (*Button*). Yah? Who is *this?* Well who the fuck are *you?* Hold—(*Button*) Harry? Eighty-seven grand, something like that. Fuck him. Eat me. New Jersey, chain of porno film stores in, uh, Weehawken. That's—Harry, that's the beauty of the law. (*Button*) So, baby doll, what? *Cats?* Bleah. (*Button*) *Cats!* It's about cats. Singing cats, you'll love it. Eight o'clock, the theatre's always at eight. (*Button*) Fucking tourists. (*Button, then to Joe*) Oh live a little, Joe, *eat* something for Christ sake—

JOE. Um, Roy, could you . . .

ROY. What? (*To Harry*) Hold a minute. (*Button*) Mrs. Soffer? *Mrs.* . . . (*Button*) God-fucking-dammit to hell, where is . . .

JOE (*Overlapping*). Roy, I'd really appreciate it if . . .

ROY (*Overlapping*). Well she was here a minute ago, baby doll, see if . . .

(*The phone starts making three different beeping sounds, all at once.*)

ROY (*Smashing buttons*). Jesus fuck this goddam thing . . .

JOE (*Overlapping*). I really wish you wouldn't . . .

ROY (*Overlapping*). Baby doll? Ring the *Post* get me Suzy see if . . .

(*The phone starts whistling loudly.*)

ROY. CHRIST!

JOE. *Roy.*

ROY (*Into receiver*). Hold. (*Button; to Joe*) What?

JOE. Could you please not take the Lord's name in vain?

(*Pause*)

I'm sorry. But please. At least while I'm . . .

ROY (*Laughs, then*). Right. Sorry. Fuck.
Only in America. (*Punches a button*) Baby doll, tell 'em all to fuck off. Tell 'em I died. You handle Mrs.

Soffer. Tell her it's on the way. Tell her I'm schtup-
ping the judge. I'll call her back. I *will* call her. I know
how much I borrowed. She's got four hundred times
that stuffed up her. . . . Yeah, tell her I said that. (*Button. The phone is silent*)
So, Joe.

JOE. I'm sorry Roy, I just . . .

ROY. No no no no, principles count, I respect principles,
I'm not religious but I like God and God likes me.
Baptist, Catholic?

JOE. Mormon.

ROY. Mormon. Delectable. Absolutely. Only in America.
So, Joe. Whattya think?

JOE. It's . . . well . . .

ROY. Crazy life.

JOE. Chaotic.

ROY. Well but God bless chaos. Right?

JOE. Ummm . . .

ROY. Huh. Mormons. I knew Mormons, in um, Nevada.

JOE. Utah, mostly.

ROY. No, these Mormons were in Vegas.
So. So, how'd you like to go to Washington and work
for the Justice Department?

JOE. Sorry?

ROY. How'd you like to go to Washington and work for
the Justice Department? All I gotta do is pick up the
phone, talk to Ed, and you're in.

JOE. In . . . what, exactly?

ROY. Associate Assistant Something Big. Internal Affairs, heart of the woods, something nice with clout.

JOE. Ed . . . ?

ROY. Meese. The Attorney General.

JOE. Oh.

ROY. I just have to pick up the phone . . .

JOE. I have to think.

ROY. Of course.

(*Pause*)

It's a great time to be in Washington, Joe.

JOE. Roy, it's incredibly exciting . . .

ROY. And it would mean something to me. You understand?

(*Little pause.*)

JOE. I . . . can't say how much I appreciate this Roy, I'm
sort of . . . well, stunned, I mean. . . . Thanks, Roy.
But I have to give it some thought. I have to ask my
wife.

ROY. Your wife. Of course.

JOE. But I really appreciate . . .

ROY. Of course. Talk to your wife.

SCENE 3

*Later that day. Harper at home, alone. She is listen-
ing to the radio and talking to herself, as she often
does. She speaks to the audience.*

HARPER. People who are lonely, people left alone, sit
talking nonsense to the air, imagining . . . beautiful
systems dying, old fixed orders spiraling apart . . .
When you look at the ozone layer, from outside,
from a spaceship, it looks like a pale blue halo, a
gentle, shimmering aureole encircling the atmosphere encircling the earth. Thirty miles above our
heads, a thin layer of three-atom oxygen molecules,
product of photosynthesis, which explains the fussy
vegetable preference for visible light, its rejection of
darker rays and emanations. Danger from without.
It's a kind of gift, from God, the crowning touch to
the creation of the world: guardian angel, hands
linked, makes a spherical net, a blue-green nesting
orb, a shell of safety for itself. But everywhere, things
are collapsing, lies surfacing, systems of defense giving way. . . . This is why, Joe, this is why I shouldn't
be left alone.

(*Little pause*)

I'd like to go traveling. Leave you behind to worry. I'll
send postcards with strange stamps and tantalizing messages on the back. "Later maybe." "Nevermore . . ."

(*Mr. Lies, a travel agent, appears.*)

HARPER. Oh! You startled me!

MR. LIES. Cash, check or credit card?

HARPER. I remember you. You're from Salt Lake. You
sold us the plane tickets when we flew here. What
are you doing in Brooklyn?

MR. LIES. You said you wanted to travel . . .

HARPER. And here you are. How thoughtful.

MR. LIES. Mr. Lies. Of the International Order of Travel
Agents. We mobilize the globe, we set people adrift,
we stir the populace and send nomads eddying
across the planet. We are adepts of motion, acolytes
of the flux. Cash, check or credit card. Name your
destination.

HARPER. Antarctica, maybe. I want to see the hole in the
ozone. I heard on the radio . . .

MRI. LIES (*He has a computer terminal in his briefcase*). I
can arrange a guided tour. Now?

HARPER. Soon. Maybe soon. I'm not safe here you see.
Things aren't right with me. Weird stuff happens . . .

MR. LIES. Like?

HARPER. Well, like you, for instance. Just appearing. Or last week . . . well never mind. People are like planets, you need a thick skin. Things get to me, Joe stays away and now. . . . Well look. My dreams are talking back to me.

MR. LIES. It's the price of rootlessness. Motion sickness. The only cure: to keep moving.

HARPER. I'm undecided. I feel . . . that something's going to give. It's 1985. Fifteen years till the third millennium. Maybe Christ will come again. Maybe seeds will be planted, maybe there'll be harvest then, maybe early figs to eat, maybe new life, maybe fresh blood, maybe companionship and love and protection, safety from what's outside, maybe the door will hold, or maybe . . . maybe the troubles will come, and the end will come, and the sky will collapse and there will be terrible rains and showers of poison light, or maybe my life is really fine, maybe Joe loves me and I'm only crazy thinking otherwise, or maybe not, maybe it's even worse than I know, maybe . . . I want to know, maybe I don't. The suspense, Mr. Lies, it's killing me.

MR. LIES. I suggest a vacation.

HARPER (*Hearing something*). That was the elevator. Oh God, I should fix myself up, I, . . . You have to go, you shouldn't be here . . . you aren't even real.

MR. LIES. Call me when you decide . . .

HARPER. Go!

(*The Travel Agent vanishes as Joe enters.*)

JOE. Buddy?
   Buddy? Sorry I'm late. I was just . . . out. Walking. Are you mad?

HARPER. I got a little anxious.

JOE. Buddy kiss.

(*They kiss.*)

JOE. Nothing to get anxious about.
   So. So how'd you like to move to Washington?

SCENE 4

Same day. Louis and Prior outside the funeral home, sitting on a bench, both dressed in funereal finery, talking. The funeral service for Sarah Ironson has just concluded and Louis is about to leave for the cemetery.

LOUIS. My grandmother actually saw Emma Goldman speak. In Yiddish. But all Grandma could remember was that she spoke well and wore a hat.
   What a weird service. That rabbi . . .

PRIOR. A definite find. Get his number when you go to the graveyard. I want him to bury me.

LOUIS. Better head out there. Everyone gets to put dirt on the coffin once it's lowered in.

PRIOR. Oooh. Cemetery fund. Don't want to miss that.

LOUIS. It's an old Jewish custom to express love. Here, Grandma, have a shovelful. Latecomers run the risk of finding the grave completely filled.
   She was pretty crazy. She was up there in the home for ten years, talking to herself. I never visited. She looked too much like my mother.

PRIOR (*Hugs him*). Poor Louis. I'm sorry your grandma is dead.

LOUIS. Tiny little coffin, huh?
   Sorry I didn't introduce you to. . . . I always get so closety at these family things.

PRIOR. Butch. You get butch. (*Imitating*) "Hi Cousin Doris, you don't remember me I'm Lou, Rachel's boy." Lou, not Louis, because if you say Louis they'll hear the sibilant S.

LOUIS. I don't have a . . .

PRIOR. I don't blame you, hiding. Bloodlines, Jewish curses are the worst. I personally would dissolve if anyone ever looked me in the eye and said "Feh." Fortunately WASPs don't say "Feh." Oh and by the way, darling, cousin Doris is a dyke.

LOUIS. No.
   Really?

PRIOR. You don't notice anything. If I hadn't spent the last four years fellating you I'd swear you were straight.

LOUIS. You're in a pissy mood. Cat still missing?

(*Little pause.*)

PRIOR. Not a furball in sight. It's your fault.

LOUIS. It is?

PRIOR. I warned you, Louis. Names are important. Call an animal "Little Sheba" and you can't expect it to stick around. Besides, it's a dog's name.

LOUIS. I wanted a dog in the first place, not a cat. He sprayed my books.

PRIOR. He was a female cat.

LOUIS. Cats are stupid, high-strung predators, Babylonians sealed them up in bricks. Dogs have brains.

PRIOR. Cats have intuition.

LOUIS. A sharp dog is as smart as a really dull two-year-old child.

PRIOR. Cats know when something's wrong.

LOUIS. Only if you stop feeding them.

PRIOR. They know. That's why Sheba left, because she knew.

LOUIS. Knew what?

(Pause.)

PRIOR. I did my best Shirley Booth this morning, floppy slippers, housecoat, curlers, can of Little Friskies; "Come back, Little Sheba, come back. . . ." To no avail. Le chat, elle ne reviendra jamais, jamais . . .

(He removes his jacket, rolls up his sleeve, shows Louis a dark-purple spot on the underside of his arm near the shoulder)

See.

LOUIS. That's just a burst blood vessel.

PRIOR. Not according to the best medical authorities.

LOUIS. What?

(Pause)

Tell me.

PRIOR. K. S., baby. Lesion number one. Lookit. The wine-dark kiss of the angel of death.

LOUIS (Very softly, holding Prior's arm). Oh please . . .

PRIOR. I'm a lesionnaire. The Foreign Lesion. The American Lesion. Lesionnaire's disease.

LOUIS. Stop.

PRIOR. My troubles are lesion.

LOUIS. Will you stop.

PRIOR. Don't you think I'm handling this well?
      I'm going to die.

LOUIS. Bullshit.

PRIOR. Let go of my arm.

LOUIS. No.

PRIOR. Let go.

LOUIS (Grabbing Prior, embracing him ferociously). No.

PRIOR. I can't find a way to spare you baby. No wall like the wall of hard scientific fact. K. S. Wham. Bang your head on that.

LOUIS. Fuck you. (Letting go) Fuck you fuck you fuck you.

PRIOR. Now that's what I like to hear. A mature reaction.
      Let's go see if the cat's come home.
      Louis?

LOUIS. When did you find this?

PRIOR. I couldn't tell you.

LOUIS. Why?

PRIOR. I was scared, Lou.

LOUIS. Of what?

PRIOR. That you'll leave me.

LOUIS. Oh.

(Little pause.)

PRIOR. Bad timing, funeral and all, but I figured as long as we're on the subject of death . . .

LOUIS. I have to go bury my grandma.

PRIOR. Lou?

(Pause)

Then you'll come home?

LOUIS. Then I'll come home.

SCENE 5

Same day, later on. Split scene: Joe and Harper at home; Louis at the cemetery with Rabbi Isidor Chemelwitz and the little coffin.

HARPER. Washington?

JOE. It's an incredible honor, buddy, and . . .

HARPER. I have to think.

JOE. Of course.

HARPER. Say no.

JOE. You said you were going to think about it.

HARPER. I don't want to move to Washington.

JOE. Well I do.

HARPER. It's a giant cemetery, huge white graves and mausoleums everywhere.

JOE. We could live in Maryland. Or Georgetown.

HARPER. We're happy here.

JOE. That's not really true, buddy, we . . .

HARPER. Well happy enough! Pretend happy. That's better than nothing.

JOE. It's time to make some changes, Harper.

HARPER. No changes. Why?

JOE. I've been chief clerk for four years. I make twenty-nine thousand dollars a year. That's ridiculous. I graduated fourth in my class and I make less than anyone I know. And I'm . . . I'm tired of being a clerk, I want to go where something good is happening.

HARPER. Nothing good happens in Washington. We'll forget church teachings and buy furniture at . . . at Conran's and become yuppies. I have too much to do here.

JOE. Like what?

HARPER. I do have things . . .

JOE. What things?

HARPER. I have to finish painting the bedroom.

JOE. You've been painting in there for over a year.

HARPER. I know, I. . . . It just isn't done because I never get time to finish it.

JOE. Oh that's . . . that doesn't make sense. You have all the time in the world. You could finish it when I'm at work.

HARPER. I'm afraid to go in there alone.

JOE. Afraid of what?

HARPER. I heard someone in there. Metal scraping on the wall. A man with a knife, maybe.

JOE. There's no one in the bedroom, Harper.

HARPER. Not now.

JOE. Not this morning either.

HARPER. How do you know? You were at work this morning. There's something creepy about this place. Remember *Rosemary's Baby*?

JOE. *Rosemary's Baby*?

HARPER. Our apartment looks like that one. Wasn't that apartment in Brooklyn?

JOE. No, it was . . .

HARPER. Well, it looked like this. It did.

JOE. Then let's move.

HARPER. Georgetown's worse. *The Exorcist* was in Georgetown.

JOE. The devil, everywhere you turn, huh, buddy.

HARPER. Yeah. Everywhere.

JOE. How many pills today, buddy?

HARPER. None. One. Three. Only three.

LOUIS (*Pointing at the coffin*). Why are there just two little wooden pegs holding the lid down?

RABBI ISIDOR CHEMELWITZ. So she can get out easier if she wants to.

LOUIS. I hope she stays put.

I pretended for years that she was already dead. When they called to say she had died it was a surprise. I abandoned her.

RABBI ISIDOR CHEMELWITZ. "Sharfer vi di tson fun a shlang iz n umdankbar kind!"

LOUIS. I don't speak Yiddish.

RABBI ISIDOR CHEMELWITZ. Sharper than the serpent's tooth is the ingratitude of children. Shakespeare. *King Lear*.

LOUIS. Rabbi, what does the Holy Writ say about someone who abandons someone he loves at a time of great need?

RABBI ISIDOR CHEMELWITZ. Why would a person do such a thing?

LOUIS. Because he has to.

Maybe because this person's sense of the world, that it will change for the better with struggle, maybe a person who has this neo-Hegelian positivist sense of constant historical progress towards happiness or perfection or something, who feels very powerful because he feels connected to these forces, moving uphill all the time . . . maybe that person can't, um, incorporate sickness into his sense of how things are supposed to go. Maybe vomit . . . and sores and disease . . . really frighten him, maybe . . . he isn't so good with death.

RABBI ISIDOR CHEMELWITZ. The Holy Scriptures have nothing to say about such a person.

LOUIS. Rabbi, I'm afraid of the crimes I may commit.

RABBI ISIDOR CHEMELWITZ. Please, mister. I'm a sick old rabbi facing a long drive home to the Bronx. You want to confess, better you should find a priest.

LOUIS. But I'm not a Catholic, I'm a Jew.

RABBI ISIDOR CHEMELWITZ. Worse luck for you, bubbulah. Catholics believe in forgiveness. Jews believe in Guilt. (*He pats the coffin tenderly*)

LOUIS. You just make sure those pegs are in good and tight.

RABBI ISIDOR CHEMELWITZ. Don't worry, mister. The life she had, she'll stay put. She's better off.

JOE. Look, I know this is scary for you. But try to understand what it means to me. Will you try?

HARPER. Yes.

JOE. Good. Really try.

I think things are starting to change in the world.

HARPER. But I don't want . . .

JOE. Wait. For the good. Change for the good. America has rediscovered itself. Its sacred position among nations. And people aren't ashamed of that like they used to be. This is a great thing. The truth restored. Law restored. That's what President Reagan's done, Harper. He says, "Truth exists and can be spoken proudly." And the country responds to him. We become better. More good. I need to be part of that, I need something big to lift me up. I mean, six years ago the world seemed in decline, horrible, hopeless, full of unsolvable problems and crime and confusion and hunger and . . .

HARPER. But it still seems that way. More now than before. They say the ozone layer is . . .

JOE. Harper . . .

HARPER. And today out the window on Atlantic Avenue there was a schizophrenic traffic cop who was making these . . .

JOE. Stop it! I'm trying to make a point.

HARPER. So am I.

JOE. You aren't even making sense, you . . .

HARPER. My point is the world seems just as . . .

JOE. It only seems that way to you because you never go out in the world, Harper, and you have emotional problems.

HARPER. I do so get out in the world.

JOE. You don't. You stay in all day, fretting about imaginary . . .

HARPER. I get out. I do. You don't know what I do.

JOE. You don't stay in all day.

HARPER. No.

JOE. Well. . . . Yes you do.

HARPER. That's what you think.

JOE. Where do you go?

HARPER. Where do *you* go? When you walk.
(*Pause, then angrily*) And I DO NOT have emotional problems.

JOE. I'm sorry.

HARPER. And if I do have emotional problems it's from living with you. Or . . .

JOE. I'm sorry buddy, I didn't mean to . . .

HARPER. Or if you do think I do then you should never have married me. You have all these secrets and lies.

JOE. I want to be married to you, Harper.

HARPER. You shouldn't. You never should.

(*Pause*)

Hey buddy. Hey buddy.

JOE. Buddy kiss . . .

(*They kiss.*)

HARPER. I heard on the radio how to give a blowjob.

JOE. What?

HARPER. You want to try?

JOE. You really shouldn't listen to stuff like that.

HARPER. Mormons can give blowjobs.

JOE. *Harper.*

HARPER (*Imitating his tone*). *Joe.*
It was a little Jewish lady with a German accent. This is a good time. For me to make a baby.

(*Little pause. Joe turns away.*)

HARPER. Then they went on to a program about holes in the ozone layer. Over Antarctica. Skin burns, birds go blind, icebergs melt. The world's coming to an end.

SCENE 6

First week of November. In the men's room of the offices of the Brooklyn Federal Court of Appeals; Louis is crying over the sink; Joe enters.

JOE. Oh, um. . . . Morning.

LOUIS. Good morning, counselor.

JOE (*He watches Louis cry*). Sorry, I. . . . I don't know your name.

LOUIS. Don't bother. Word processor. The lowest of the low.

JOE (*Holding out hand*). Joe Pitt. I'm with Justice Wilson . . .

LOUIS. Oh, I know that. Counselor Pitt. Chief Clerk.

JOE. Were you . . . are you OK?

LOUIS. Oh, yeah. Thanks. What a nice man.

JOE. Not so nice.

LOUIS. What?

JOE. Not so nice. Nothing. You sure you're . . .

LOUIS. Life sucks shit. Life . . . just sucks shit.

JOE. What's wrong?

LOUIS. Run in my nylons.

JOE. Sorry . . . ?

LOUIS. Forget it. Look, thanks for asking.

JOE. Well . . .

LOUIS. I mean it really is nice of you.

(*He starts crying again*)

Sorry, sorry, sick friend . . .

JOE. Oh, I'm sorry.

LOUIS. Yeah, yeah, well, that's sweet.
Three of your colleagues have preceded you to this baleful sight and you're the first one to ask. The others just opened the door, saw me, and fled. I hope they had to pee real bad.

JOE (*Handing him a wad of toilet paper*). They just didn't want to intrude.

LOUIS. Hah. Reaganite heartless macho asshole lawyers.

JOE. Oh, that's unfair.

LOUIS. What is? Heartless? Macho? Reaganite? Lawyer?

JOE. I voted for Reagan.

LOUIS. You did?

JOE. Twice.

LOUIS. Twice? Well, oh boy. A Gay Republican.

JOE. Excuse me?

LOUIS. Nothing.

JOE. I'm not . . .
Forget it.

LOUIS. Republican? Not Republican? Or . . . What?

JOE. Not gay. I'm not gay.

LOUIS. Oh, sorry.
(*Blows his nose loudly*) It's just . . .

JOE. Yes?

LOUIS. Well, sometimes you can tell from the way a person sounds that . . . I mean you *sound* like a . . .

JOE. No I don't. Like what?

LOUIS. Like a Republican.

(*Little pause. Joe knows he's being teased; Louis knows he knows. Joe decides to be a little brave.*)

JOE (*Making sure no one else is around*). Do I? Sound like a . . . ?

LOUIS. What? Like a . . . ? Republican, or . . . ? Do *I*?

JOE. Do you what?

LOUIS. Sound like a . . . ?

JOE. Like a . . . ?
I'm . . . confused.

LOUIS. Yes.

My name is Louis. But all my friends call me Louise. I work in Word Processing. Thanks for the toilet paper.

(*Louis offers Joe his hand, Joe reaches. Louis feints and pecks Joe on the cheek, then exits.*)

SCENE 7

A week later. Mutual dream scene. Prior is at a fantastic makeup table, having a dream, applying the face. Harper is having a pill-induced hallucination. She has these from time to time. For some reason, Prior has appeared in this one. Or Harper has appeared in Prior's dream. It is bewildering.

PRIOR (*Alone, putting on makeup, then examining the results in the mirror; to the audience*): "I'm ready for my closeup, Mr. DeMille."

One wants to move through life with elegance and grace, blossoming infrequently but with exquisite taste, and perfect timing, like a rare bloom, a zebra orchid. . . . One wants. . . . But one so seldom gets what one wants, does one? No. One does not. One gets fucked. Over. One . . . dies at thirty, robbed of . . . decades of majesty.

Fuck this shit. Fuck this shit.

(*He almost crumbles; he pulls himself together; he studies his handiwork in the mirror*)

I look like a corpse. A corpsette. Oh my queen; you know you've hit rock-bottom when even drag is a drag.

(*Harper appears*)

HARPER. Are you. . . . Who are you?

PRIOR. Who are you?

HARPER. What are you doing in my hallucination?

PRIOR. I'm not in your hallucination. You're in my dream.

HARPER. You're wearing makeup.

PRIOR. So are you.

HARPER. But you're a man.

PRIOR (*Feigning dismay, shock, he mimes slashing his throat with his lipstick and dies, fabulously tragic. Then*). The hands and feet give it away.

HARPER. There must be some mistake here. I don't recognize you. You're not. . . . Are you my . . . some sort of imaginary friend?

PRIOR. No. Aren't you too old to have imaginary friends?

HARPER. I have emotional problems. I took too many pills. Why are you wearing makeup?

PRIOR. I was in the process of applying the face, trying to make myself feel better—I swiped the new fall colors at the Clinique counter at Macy's. (*Showing her*)

HARPER. You stole these?

PRIOR. I was out of cash; it was an emotional emergency!

HARPER. Joe will be so angry. I promised him. No more pills.

PRIOR. These pills you keep alluding to?

HARPER. Valium. I take Valium. Lots of Valium.

PRIOR. And you're dancing as fast as you can.

HARPER. I'm not *addicted*. I don't believe in addiction, and I never . . . well, I *never* drink. And I never take drugs.

PRIOR. Well, smell *you*, Nancy Drew.

HARPER. Except Valium.

PRIOR. Except Valium; in wee fistfuls.

HARPER. It's terrible. Mormons are not supposed to be addicted to anything. I'm a Mormon.

PRIOR. I'm a homosexual.

HARPER. Oh! In my church we don't believe in homosexuals.

PRIOR. In my church we don't believe in Mormons.

HARPER. What church do . . . oh! (*She laughs*) I get it.

I don't understand this. If I didn't ever see you before and I don't think I did then I don't think you should be here, in this hallucination, because in my experience the mind, which is where hallucinations come from, shouldn't be able to make up anything that wasn't there to start with, that didn't enter it from experience, from the real world. Imagination can't create anything new, can it? It only recycles bits and pieces from the world and reassembles them into visions. . . . Am I making sense right now?

PRIOR. Given the circumstances, yes.

HARPER. So when we think we've escaped the unbearable ordinariness and, well, untruthfulness of our lives, it's really only the same old ordinariness and falseness rearranged into the appearance of novelty and truth. Nothing unknown is knowable. Don't you think it's depressing?

PRIOR. The limitations of the imagination?

HARPER. Yes.

PRIOR. It's something you learn after your second theme party: It's All Been Done Before.

HARPER. The world. Finite. Terribly, terribly. . . . Well . . . This is the most depressing hallucination I've ever had.

PRIOR. Apologies. I do try to be amusing.

HARPER. Oh, well, don't apologize, you. . . . I can't expect someone who's really sick to entertain me.

PRIOR. How on earth did you know . . .

HARPER. Oh that happens. This is the very threshold of revelation sometimes. You can see things . . . how sick you are. Do you see anything about me?

PRIOR. Yes.

HARPER. What?

PRIOR. You are amazingly unhappy.

HARPER. Oh big deal. You meet a Valium addict and you figure out she's unhappy. That doesn't count. Of course I. . . . Something else. Something surprising.

PRIOR. Something surprising.

HARPER. Yes.

PRIOR. Your husband's a homo.

(Pause.)

HARPER. Oh, ridiculous.

(Pause, then very quietly)

Really?

PRIOR *(Shrugs)*. Threshold of revelation.

HARPER. Well I don't like your revelations. I don't think you intuit well at all. Joe's a very normal man, he . . . Oh God. Oh God. He. . . . Do homos take, like, lots of long walks?

PRIOR. Yes. We do. In stretch pants with lavender coifs. I just looked at you, and there was . . .

HARPER. A sort of blue streak of recognition.

PRIOR. Yes.

HARPER. Like you knew me incredibly well.

PRIOR. Yes.

HARPER. Yes.

I have to go now, get back, something just . . . fell apart.

Oh God, I feel so sad . . .

PRIOR. I . . . I'm sorry. I usually say, "Fuck the truth," but mostly, the truth fucks you.

HARPER. I see something else about you . . .

PRIOR. Oh?

HARPER. Deep inside you, there's a part of you, the most inner part, entirely free of disease. I can see that.

PRIOR. Is that. . . . That isn't true.

HARPER. Threshold of revelation.

Home . . .

(She vanishes.)

PRIOR. People come and go so quickly here . . .

(To himself in the mirror) I don't think there's any uninfected part of me. My heart is pumping polluted blood. I feel dirty.

(He begins to wipe makeup off with his hands, smearing it around. A large gray feather falls from up above. Prior stops smearing the makeup and looks at the feather. He goes to it and picks it up.)

A VOICE *(It is an incredibly beautiful voice)*. Look up!

PRIOR *(Looking up, not seeing anyone)*. Hello?

A VOICE. Look up!

PRIOR. Who is that?

A VOICE. Prepare the way!

PRIOR. I don't see any . . .

(There is a dramatic change in lighting, from above.)

A VOICE.

    Look up, look up,
    prepare the way
    the infinite descent
    A breath in air
    floating down
    Glory to . . .

(Silence.)

PRIOR. Hello? Is that it? Helloooo!

What the fuck . . . ? *(He holds himself)*

Poor me. Poor poor me. Why me? Why poor poor me? Oh I don't feel good right now. I don't.

SCENE 8

That night. Split scene: Harper and Joe at home; Prior and Louis in bed.

HARPER. Where were you?

JOE. Out.

HARPER. Where?

JOE. Just out. Thinking.

HARPER. It's late.

JOE. I had a lot to think about.

HARPER. I burned dinner.

JOE. Sorry.

HARPER. Not my dinner. My dinner was fine. Your dinner. I put it back in the oven and turned everything up as high as it could go and I watched till it burned black. It's still hot. Very hot. Want it?

JOE. You didn't have to do that.

HARPER. I know. It just seemed like the kind of thing a mentally deranged sex-starved pill-popping housewife would do

JOE. Uh huh.

HARPER. So I did it. Who knows anymore what I have to do?

JOE. How many pills?

HARPER. A bunch. Don't change the subject.

JOE. I won't talk to you when you . . .

HARPER. No. No. Don't do that! I'm . . . I'm fine, pills are not the problem, not our problem, I WANT TO KNOW WHERE YOU'VE BEEN! I WANT TO KNOW WHAT'S GOING ON!

JOE. Going on with what? The job?

HARPER. Not the job.

JOE. I said I need more time.

HARPER. Not the job!

JOE. Mr. Cohn, I talked to him on the phone, he said I had to hurry . . .

HARPER. Not the . . .

JOE. But I can't get you to talk sensibly about anything so . . .

HARPER. SHUT UP!

JOE. Then what?

HARPER. Stick to the subject.

JOE. I don't know what that is. You have something you want to ask me? Ask me. Go.

HARPER. I . . . can't. I'm scared of you.

JOE. I'm tired, I'm going to bed.

HARPER. Tell me without making me ask. Please.

JOE. This is crazy, I'm not . . .

HARPER. When you come through the door at night your face is never exactly the way I remembered it. I get surprised by something . . . mean and hard about the way you look. Even the weight of you in the bed at night, the way you breathe in your sleep seems unfamiliar. You terrify me.

JOE (*Cold*). I know who you are.

HARPER. Yes. I'm the enemy. That's easy. That doesn't change.

You think you're the only one who hates sex; I do; I hate it with you; I do. I dream that you batter away at me till all my joints come apart, like wax, and I fall into pieces. It's like a punishment. It was wrong of me to marry you. I knew you . . . (*She stops herself*) It's a sin, and it's killing us both.

JOE. I can always tell when you've taken pills, because it makes you red-faced and sweaty and frankly that's very often why I don't want to . . .

HARPER. Because . . .

JOE. Well, you aren't pretty. Not like this.

HARPER. I have something to ask you.

JOE. Then ASK! ASK! What in hell are you . . .

HARPER. Are you a homo?

(*Pause*)

Are you? If you try to walk out right now I'll put your dinner back in the oven and turn it up so high the whole building will fill with smoke and everyone in it will asphyxiate. So help me God I will.

Now answer the question.

JOE. What if I . . .

(*Small pause.*)

HARPER. Then tell me, please. And we'll see.

JOE. No, I'm not.

I don't see what difference it makes.

LOUIS. Jews don't have any clear textual guide to the afterlife; even that it exists. I don't think much about it. I see it as a perpetual rainy Thursday afternoon in March. Dead leaves.

PRIOR. Enough. Very Greco-Roman.

LOUIS. Well for us it's not the verdict that counts, it's the act of judgment. That's why I could never be a lawyer. In court all that matters is the verdict.

PRIOR. You could never be a lawyer because you are oversexed. You're too distracted.

LOUIS. Not distracted: *abstracted*. I'm trying to make a point:

PRIOR. Namely:

LOUIS. It's the judge in his or her chambers, weighing, books open, pondering the evidence, ranging freely over categories: good, evil, innocent, guilty; the judge in the chamber of circumspection, not the judge on the bench with the gavel. The shaping of the law, not its execution.

PRIOR. The point, dear, the point . . .

LOUIS. That it should be the questions and shape of a life, its total complexity gathered, arranged and considered, which matters in the end, not some stamp of salvation or damnation which disperses all the complexity in some unsatisfying decision—balancing of the scales . . .

PRIOR. I like this; very zen; it's . . . reassuringly incomprehensible and useless. We who are about to die thank you.

LOUIS. You are not about to die.

PRIOR. It's not going well, really . . . two new lesions. My leg hurts. There's protein in my urine, the doctor says, but who knows what the fuck that portends. Anyway it should be there, the protein. My butt is chapped from diarrhea and yesterday I shat blood.

LOUIS. I really hate this. You don't tell me . . .

PRIOR. You get too upset, I wind up comforting you. It's easier . . .

LOUIS. Oh thanks.

PRIOR. If it's bad I'll tell you.

LOUIS. Shitting blood sounds bad to me.

PRIOR. And I'm telling you.

LOUIS. And I'm handling it.

PRIOR. Tell me some more about justice.

LOUIS. I *am* handling it.

PRIOR. Well Louis you win Trooper of the Month.

(Louis starts to cry.)

PRIOR. I take it back. You aren't Trooper of the Month.
This isn't working . . .
Tell me some more about justice.

LOUIS. You are not about to die.

PRIOR. Justice . . .

LOUIS. . . . is an immensity, a confusing vastness. Justice
is God.
Prior?

PRIOR. Hmmm?

LOUIS. You love me.

PRIOR. Yes.

LOUIS. What if I walked out on this?
Would you hate me forever?

(Prior kisses Louis on the forehead.)

PRIOR. Yes.

JOE. I think we ought to pray. Ask God for help. Ask him
together . . .

HARPER. God won't talk to me. I have to make up people
to talk to me.

JOE. You have to keep asking.

HARPER. I forgot the question.
Oh yeah, God, is my husband a . . .

JOE *(Scary)*. Stop it. Stop it. I'm warning you.
Does it make any difference? That I might be one
thing deep within, no matter how wrong or ugly that
thing is, so long as I have fought, with everything I
have, to kill it. What do you want from me? What do
you want from me, Harper? More than that? For
God's sake, there's nothing left, I'm a shell. There's
nothing left to kill.
As long as my behavior is what I know it has to be.
Decent. Correct. That alone in the eyes of God.

HARPER. No, no, not that, that's Utah talk, Mormon
talk, I hate it, Joe tell me, say it . . .

JOE. All I will say is that I am a very good man who has
worked very hard to become good and you want to
destroy that. You want to destroy me, but I am not
going to let you do that.

(Pause.)

HARPER. I'm going to have a baby.

JOE. Liar.

HARPER You liar.

A baby born addicted to pills. A baby who does not
dream but who hallucinates, who stares up at us with
big mirror eyes and who does not know who we are.

(Pause.)

JOE. Are you really . . .

HARPER. No. Yes. No. Yes. Get away from me.
Now we both have a secret.

PRIOR. One of my ancestors was a ship's captain who made
money bringing whale oil to Europe and returning
with immigrants—Irish mostly, packed in tight, so
many dollars per head. The last ship he captained
foundered off the coast of Nova Scotia in a winter
tempest and sank to the bottom. He went down with
the ship—la Grande Geste—but his crew took seventy women and kids in the ship's only longboat, this
big, open rowboat, and when the weather got too
rough, and they thought the boat was overcrowded,
the crew started lifting people up and hurling them
into the sea. Until they got the ballast right. They
walked up and down the longboat, eyes to the water-
line, and when the boat rode low in the water they'd
grab the nearest passenger and throw them into the
sea. The boat was leaky, see; seventy people; they arrived in Halifax with nine people on board.

LOUIS. Jesus.

PRIOR. I think about that story a lot now. People in a
boat, waiting, terrified, while implacable, unsmiling
men, irresistibly strong, seize . . . maybe the person
next to you, maybe you, and with no warning at all,
with time only for a quick intake of air you are
pitched into freezing, turbulent water and salt and
darkness to drown.
I like your cosmology, baby. While time is running
out I find myself drawn to anything that's suspended,
that lacks an ending—but it seems to me that it lets
you off scot-free.

LOUIS. What do you mean?

PRIOR. No judgment, no guilt or responsibility.

LOUIS. For me.

PRIOR. For anyone. It was an editorial "you."

LOUIS. Please get better. Please.
Please don't get any sicker.

SCENE 9

*Third week in November, Roy and Henry, his doc-
tor, in Henry's office.*

HENRY. Nobody knows what causes it. And nobody
knows how to cure it. The best theory is that we

blame a retrovirus, the Human Immunodeficiency Virus. Its presence is made known to us by the useless antibodies which appear in reaction to its entrance into the bloodstream through a cut, or an orifice. The antibodies are powerless to protect the body against it. Why, we don't know. The body's immune system ceases to function. Sometimes the body even attacks itself. At any rate it's left open to a whole horror house of infections from microbes which it usually defends against.

Like Kaposi's sarcomas. These lesions. Or your throat problem. Or the glands.

We think it may also be able to slip past the blood-brain barrier into the brain. Which is of course very bad news.

And it's fatal in we don't know what percent of people with suppressed immune responses.

(Pause.)

ROY. This is very interesting, Mr. Wizard, but why the fuck are you telling me this?

(Pause.)

HENRY. Well, I have just removed one of three lesions which biopsy results will probably tell us is a Kaposi's sarcoma lesion. And you have a pronounced swelling of glands in your neck, groin, and armpits—lymphadenopathy is another sign. And you have oral candidiasis and maybe a little more fungus under the fingernails of two digits on your right hand. So that's why . . .

ROY. This disease . . .

HENRY. Syndrome.

ROY. Whatever. It afflicts mostly homosexuals and drug addicts.

HENRY. Mostly. Hemophiliacs are also at risk.

ROY. Homosexuals and drug addicts. So why are you implying that I . . .

(Pause)

What are you implying, Henry?

HENRY. I don't . . .

ROY. I'm not a drug addict.

HENRY. On come on Roy.

ROY. What, what, come on Roy what? Do you think I'm a junkie, Henry, do you see tracks?

HENRY. This is absurd.

ROY. Say it.

HENRY. Say what?

ROY. Say, "Roy Cohn, you are a . . ."

HENRY. Roy.

ROY. "You are a. . . ." Go on. Not "Roy Cohn you are a drug fiend." "Roy Marcus Cohn, you are a . . ."

Go on, Henry, it starts with an "H."

HENRY. Oh I'm not going to . . .

ROY. *With an "H,"* Henry, and it isn't "Hemophiliac." Come on . . .

HENRY. What are you doing, Roy?

ROY. No, say it. I mean it. Say: "Roy Cohn, you are a homosexual."

(Pause)

And I will proceed, systematically, to destroy your reputation and your practice and your career in New York State, Henry. Which you know I can do.

(Pause.)

HENRY. Roy, you have been seeing me since 1958. Apart from the facelifts I have treated you for everything from syphilis . . .

ROY. From a whore in Dallas.

HENRY. From syphilis to venereal warts. In your rectum. Which you may have gotten from a whore in Dallas, but it wasn't a female whore.

(Pause.)

ROY. So say it.

HENRY. Roy Cohn, you are . . .

You have had sex with men, many many times, Roy, and one of them, or any number of them, has made you very sick. You have AIDS.

ROY. AIDS.

Your problem, Henry, is that you are hung up on words, on labels, that you believe they mean what they seem to mean. AIDS. Homosexual. Gay. Lesbian. You think these are names that tell you who someone sleeps with, but they don't tell you that.

HENRY. No?

ROY. No. Like all labels, they tell you one thing and one thing only: where does an individual so identified fit in the food chain, in the pecking order? Not ideology, or sexual taste, but something much simpler: clout. Not who I fuck or who fucks me, but who will pick up the phone when I call, who owes me favors. This is what a label refers to. Now to someone who does not understand this, homosexual is what I am because I have sex with men. But really this is wrong. Homosexuals are not men who sleep with other men. Homosexuals are men who in fifteen years of trying cannot get a pissant antidiscrimination bill through City Council. Homosexuals are men who know nobody and who nobody knows. Who have zero clout. Does this sound like me, Henry?

HENRY. No.

ROY. No. I have clout. A lot. I can pick up this phone, punch fifteen numbers, and you know who will be on the other end in under five minutes, Henry?

HENRY. The President.

ROY. Even better, Henry. His wife.

HENRY. I'm impressed.

ROY. I don't want you to be impressed. I want you to understand. This is not sophistry. And this is not hypocrisy. This is reality. I have sex with men. But unlike nearly every other man of whom this is true, I bring the guy I'm screwing to the White House and President Reagan smiles at us and shakes his hand. Because *what* I am is defined entirely by *who* I am. Roy Cohn is not a homosexual. Roy Cohn is a heterosexual man, Henry, who fucks around with guys.

HENRY. OK, Roy.

ROY. And what is my diagnosis, Henry?

HENRY. You have AIDS, Roy.

ROY. No, Henry, no. AIDS is what homosexuals have. I have liver cancer.

(Pause.)

HENRY. Well, whatever the fuck you have, Roy, it's very serious, and I haven't got a damn thing for you. The NIH in Bethesda has a new drug called AZT with a two-year waiting list that not even I can get you onto. So get on the phone, Roy, and dial the fifteen numbers, and tell the First Lady you need in on an experimental treatment for liver cancer, because you can call it any damn thing you want, Roy, but what it boils down to is very bad news.

ACT II: IN VITRO

December 1985–January 1986

SCENE 1

Night, the third week in December. Prior alone on the floor of his bedroom; he is much worse.

PRIOR. Louis, Louis, please wake up, oh God.

(Louis runs in.)

PRIOR. I think something horrible is wrong with me I can't breathe . . .

LOUIS *(Starting to exit)*. I'm calling the ambulance.

PRIOR. No, wait, I . . .

LOUIS. *Wait?* Are you fucking crazy? Oh God you're on fire, your head is on fire.

PRIOR. It hurts, it hurts . . .

LOUIS. I'm calling the ambulance.

PRIOR. I don't want to go to the hospital, I don't want to go to the hospital please let me lie here, just . . .

LOUIS. No, no, God, Prior, stand up . . .

PRIOR. DON'T TOUCH MY LEG!

LOUIS. We have to . . . oh God this is so crazy.

PRIOR. I'll be OK if I just lie here Lou, really, if I can only sleep a little . . .

(Louis exits.)

PRIOR. Louis?

No! No! Don't call, you'll send me there and I won't come back, please, please Louis I'm begging, baby, please . . .

(Screams) LOUIS!!

LOUIS *(From off; hysterical)*. WILL YOU SHUT THE FUCK UP!

PRIOR *(Trying to stand)*. Aaaah, I have . . . to go to the bathroom. Wait. Wait, just . . . oh. Oh God. *(He shits himself.)*

LOUIS *(Entering)*. Prior? They'll be here in . . . Oh my God.

PRIOR. I'm sorry, I'm sorry.

LOUIS. What did . . . ? What?

PRIOR. I had an accident?

(Louis goes to him.)

LOUIS. This is blood.

PRIOR. Maybe you shouldn't touch it . . . me. . . . I . . . *(He faints)*

LOUIS *(Quietly)*. Oh help. Oh help. Oh God oh God oh God help me I can't I can't I can't.

SCENE 2

Same night. Harper is sitting at home, all alone, with no lights on. We can barely see her. Joe enters, but he doesn't turn on the lights.

JOE. Why are you sitting in the dark? Turn on the light.

HARPER. *No.* I heard the sounds in the bedroom again. I know someone was in there.

JOE. No one was.

HARPER. Maybe actually in the bed, under the covers with a knife.

Oh, boy. Joe. I, um, I'm thinking of going away. By which I mean: I think I'm going off again. You . . . you know what I mean?

JOE. Please don't. Stay. We can fix it. I pray for that. This is my fault, but I can correct it. You have to try too . . .

(He turns on the light. She turns it off again.)

HARPER. When you pray, what do you pray for?

JOE. I pray for God to crush me, break me up into little pieces and start all over again.

HARPER. Oh. Please. Don't pray for that.

JOE. I had a book of Bible stories when I was a kid. There was a picture I'd look at twenty times every day: Jacob wrestles with the angel. I don't really remember the story, or why the wrestling—just the picture. Jacob is young and very strong. The angel is . . . a beautiful man, with golden hair and wings, of course. I still dream about it. Many nights, I'm . . . It's me. In that struggle. Fierce, and unfair. The angel is not human, and it holds nothing back, so how could anyone human win, what kind of a fight is that? It's not just. Losing means your soul thrown down in the dust, your heart torn out from God's. But you can't not lose.

HARPER. In the whole entire world, you are the only person, the only person I love or have ever loved. And I love you terribly. Terribly. That's what's so awfully, irreducibly real. I can make up anything but I can't dream that away.

JOE. Are you . . . are you really going to have a baby?

HARPER. It's my time, and there's no blood. I don't really know. I suppose it wouldn't be a great thing. Maybe I'm just not bleeding because I take too many pills. Maybe I'll give birth to a pill. That would give a new meaning to pill-popping, huh?

I think you should go to Washington. Alone. Change, like you said.

JOE. I'm not going to leave you, Harper.

HARPER. Well maybe not. But I'm going to leave you.

SCENE 3

One AM, the next morning. Louis and a nurse, Emily, are sitting in Prior's room in the hospital.

EMILY. He'll be all right now.

LOUIS. No he won't.

EMILY. No. I guess not. I gave him something that makes him sleep.

LOUIS. Deep asleep?

EMILY. Orbiting the moons of Jupiter.

LOUIS. A good place to be.

EMILY. Anyplace better than here. You his . . . uh?

LOUIS. Yes, I'm his uh.

EMILY. This must be hell for you.

LOUIS. It is. Hell. The After Life. Which is not at all like a rainy afternoon in March, by the way, Prior. A lot more vivid than I'd expected. Dead leaves, but the crunchy kind. Sharp, dry air. The kind of long, luxurious dying feeling that breaks your heart.

EMILY. Yeah, well we all get to break our hearts on this one. He seems like a nice guy. Cute.

LOUIS. Not like this.
Yes, he is. Was. Whatever.

EMILY. Weird name. Prior Walter. Like, "The Walter before this one."

LOUIS. Lots of Walters before this one. Prior is an old old family name in an old old family. The Walters go back to the Mayflower and beyond. Back to the Norman Conquest. He says there's a Prior Walter stitched into the Bayeux tapestry.

EMILY. Is that impressive?

LOUIS. Well, it's old. Very old. Which in some circles equals impressive.

EMILY. Not in my circle. What's the name of the tapestry?

LOUIS. The Bayeux tapestry. Embroidered by La Reine Mathilde.

EMILY. I'll tell my mother. She embroiders. Drives me nuts.

LOUIS. Manual therapy for anxious hands.

EMILY. Maybe you should try it.

LOUIS. Mathilde stitched while William the Conqueror was off to war. She was capable of . . . more than loyalty. Devotion.

She waited for him, she stitched for years. And if he had come back broken and defeated from war, she would have loved him even more. And if he had returned mutilated, ugly, full of infection and horror, she would still have loved him; fed by pity, by a sharing of pain, she would love him even more, and even more, and she would never, never have prayed to God, please let him die if he can't return to me whole and healthy and able to live a normal life . . . If he had died, she would have buried her heart with him. So what the fuck is the matter with me?

(Little pause)

Will he sleep through the night?

EMILY. At least.

LOUIS. I'm going.

EMILY. It's one AM. Where do you have to go at . . .

LOUIS. I know what time it is. A walk. Night air, good for the. . . . The park.

EMILY. Be careful.

LOUIS. Yeah, Danger.

Tell him, if he wakes up and you're still on, tell him goodbye, tell him I had to go.

SCENE 4

An hour later. Split scene: Joe and Roy in a fancy (straight) bar; Louis and a Man in the Rambles in Central Park, Joe and Ray are sitting at the bar; the place is brightly lit. Joe has a plate for food in front of him but he isn't eating. Roy occasionally reaches over the table and forks small bites off Joe's plate. Roy is drinking heavily. Joe not at all. Louis and the Man are eyeing each other, each alternating interest and indifference.

JOE. The pills were something she started when she miscarried or . . . no, she took some before that. She had a really bad time at home, when she was a kid, her home was really bad. I think a lot of drinking and physical stuff. She doesn't talk about that, instead she talks about . . . the sky falling down, people with knives hiding under sofas. Monsters. Mormons. Everyone thinks Mormons don't come from homes like that, we aren't supposed to behave that way, but we do. It's not lying, or being two-faced. Everyone tries very hard to live up to God's strictures, which are very . . . um . . .

ROY. Strict.

JOE. I shouldn't be bothering you with this.

ROY. No, please. Heart to heart. Want another. . . . What is that, seltzer?

JOE. The failure to measure up hits people hard. From such a strong desire to be good they feel very far from goodness when they fail.

   What scares me is that maybe what I really love in her is the part of her that's farthest from the light, from God's love; maybe I was drawn to that in the first place. And I'm keeping it alive because I need it.

ROY. Why would you need it?

JOE. There are things. . . . I don't know how well we know ourselves. I mean, what if? I know I married her because she . . . because I love it that she was always wrong, always doing something wrong, like one step out of step. In Salt Lake City that stands out. I never stood out, on the outside, but inside, it was hard for me. To pass.

ROY. Pass?

JOE. Yeah.

ROY. Pass as what?

JOE. Oh. Well. . . . As someone cheerful and strong. Those who love God with an open heart unclouded by secrets and struggles are cheerful; God's easy simple love for them shows in how strong and happy they are. The saints.

ROY. But you had secrets? Secret struggles . . .

JOE. I wanted to be one of the elect, one of the Blessed. You feel you ought to be, that the blemishes are yours by choice, which of course they aren't. Harper's sorrow, that really deep sorrow, she didn't choose that. But it's there.

ROY. You didn't put it there.

JOE. No.

ROY. You sound like you think you did.

JOE. I am responsible for her.

ROY. Because she's your wife.

JOE. That. And I do love her.

ROY. Whatever. She's your wife. And so there are obligations. To her. But also to yourself.

JOE. She'd fall apart in Washington.

ROY. Then let her stay here.

JOE. She'll fall apart if I leave her.

ROY. Then bring her to Washington.

JOE. I just can't, Roy. She needs me.

ROY. Listen, Joe. I'm the best divorce lawyer in the business.

(Little pause.)

JOE. Can't Washington wait?

ROY. You do what you need to do, Joe. What *you* need. *You.* Let her life go where it wants to go. You'll be better for that. *Somebody* should get what they want.

MAN. What do you want?

LOUIS. I want you to fuck me, hurt me, make me bleed.

MAN. I want to.

LOUIS. Yeah?

MAN. I want to hurt you.

LOUIS. Fuck me.

MAN. Yeah?

LOUIS. Hard.

MAN. Yeah? You been a bad boy?

(Pause. Louis laughs, softly.)

LOUIS. Very bad. Very bad.

MAN. You need to be punished, boy?

LOUIS. Yes. I do.

MAN. Yes what?

(Little pause.)

LOUIS. Um, I . . .

MAN. Yes *what*, boy?

LOUIS. Oh. Yes sir.

MAN. I want you to take me to your place, boy.

LOUIS. No, I can't do that.

MAN. No *what?*

LOUIS. No sir, I can't, I . . .

   I don't live alone, sir.

MAN. Your lover know you're out with a man tonight, boy?

LOUIS. No sir, he . . .

   My lover doesn't know.

MAN. Your lover know you . . .

LOUIS. Let's change the subject, OK? Can we go to your place?

MAN. I live with my parents.

LOUIS. Oh.

ROY. Everyone who makes it in this world makes it because somebody older and more powerful takes an interest. The most precious asset in life, I think is the ability to be a good son. You have that, Joe. Somebody who can be a good son to a father who pushes them farther than they would otherwise go. I've had many fathers, I owe my life to them, powerful, powerful men. Walter Winchell, Edgar Hoover. Joe McCarthy most of all. He valued me because I am a good lawyer, but he loved me because I was and am a good son. He was a very difficult man, very guarded and cagey; I brought out something tender in him. He would have died for me. And me for him. Does this embarrass you?

JOE. I had a hard time with my father.

ROY. Well sometimes that's the way. Then you have to find other fathers, substitutes, I don't know. The father-son relationship is central to life. Women are for birth, beginning, but the father is continuance. The son offers the father his life as a vessel for carrying forth his father's dream. Your father's living?

JOE. Um, dead.

ROY. He was . . . what? A difficult man?

JOE. He was in the military. He could be very unfair. And cold.

ROY. But he loved you.

JOE. I don't know.

ROY. No, no, Joe, he did, I know this. Sometimes a father's love has to be very, very hard, unfair even, cold to make his son grow strong in a world like this. This isn't a good world.

MAN. Here, then.

LOUIS. I. . . . Do you have a rubber?

MAN. I don't use rubbers.

LOUIS. You should. (*He takes one from his coat pocket*) Here.

MAN. I don't use them.

LOUIS. Forget it, then. (*He starts to leave*)

MAN. No, wait.

   Put it on me. Boy.

LOUIS. Forget it, I have to get back. Home. I must be going crazy.

MAN. Oh come on please he won't find out.

LOUIS. It's cold. Too cold.

MAN. It's never too cold, let me warm you up. Please?

   (*They begin to fuck.*)

MAN. Relax.

LOUIS (*A small laugh*). Not a chance.

MAN. It . . .

LOUIS. What?

MAN. I think it broke. The rubber. You want me to keep going? (*Little pause*) Pull out? Should I . . .

LOUIS. Keep going.

   Infect me.

   I don't care. I don't care.

   (*Pause. The Man pulls out.*)

MAN. I . . . um, look, I'm sorry, but I think I want to go.

LOUIS. Yeah.

   Give my best to mom and dad.

   (*The Man slaps him.*)

LOUIS. Ow!

   (*They stare at each other.*)

LOUIS. It was a joke.

   (*The Man leaves.*)

ROY. How long have we known each other?

JOE. Since 1980.

ROY. Right. A long time. I feel close to you, Joe. Do I advise you well?

JOE. You've been an incredible friend, Roy, I . . .

ROY. I want to be family. Familia, as my Italian friends call it. La Familia. A lovely word. It's important for me to help you, like I was helped.

JOE. I owe practically everything to you, Roy.

ROY. I'm dying, Joe. Cancer.

JOE. Oh my God.

ROY. Please. Let me finish.

   Few people know this and I'm telling you this only because. . . . I'm not afraid of death. What can death bring that I haven't faced? I've lived; life is the worst. (*Gently mocking himself*) Listen to me, I'm a philosopher.

JOE. You must do this. You must must must. Love; that's a trap. Responsibility; that's a trap too. Like a father to a son I tell you this: Life is full of horror; nobody escapes, nobody; save yourself. Whatever pulls on you, whatever needs from you, threatens you.

Don't be afraid; people are so afraid; don't be afraid to live in the raw wind, naked, alone. . . . Learn at least this: What you are capable of. Let nothing stand in your way.

SCENE 5

Three days later. Prior and Belize in Prior's hospital room. Prior is very sick but improving. Belize has just arrived.

PRIOR. Miss Thing.

BELIZE. Ma cherie bichete.

PRIOR. Stella.

BELIZE. Stella for star. Let me see. (*Scrutinizing Prior*) You look like shit, why yes indeed you do, comme la merde!

PRIOR. Merci.

BELIZE (*Taking little plastic bottles from his bag, handing them to Prior*). Not to despair, Belle Reeve. Lookie! Magic goop!

PRIOR (*Opening a bottle, sniffing*). Pooh! What kinda crap is that?

BELIZE. Beats me. Let's rub it on your poor blistered body and see what it does.

PRIOR. This is not Western medicine, these bottles . . .

BELIZE. Voodoo cream. From the botanica 'round the block.

PRIOR. And you a registered nurse.

BELIZE (*Sniffing it*). Beeswax and cheap perfume. Cut with Jergen's Lotion. Full of good vibes and love from some little black Cubana witch in Miami.

PRIOR. Get that trash away from me, I am immune-suppressed.

BELIZE. I *am* a health professional. I *know* what I'm doing.

PRIOR. It stinks. Any word from Louis?

(*Pause. Belize starts giving Prior a gentle massage.*)

PRIOR. Gone.

BELIZE. He'll be back. I know the type. Likes to keep a girl on edge.

PRIOR. It's been . . .

(*Pause.*)

BELIZE (*Trying to jog his memory*). How long?

PRIOR. I don't remember.

BELIZE. How long have you been here?

PRIOR (*Getting suddenly upset*). I don't remember, I don't give a fuck. I want Louis. I want my fucking boyfriend, where the fuck is he? I'm dying, I'm dying, where's Louis?

BELIZE. Shhhh, shhh . . .

PRIOR. This is a very strange drug, this drug. Emotional liability, for starters.

BELIZE. Save a tab or two for me.

PRIOR. Oh no, not this drug, ce n'est pas pour la joyeux noël et la bonne année, this drug she is serious poisonous chemistry, ma pauvre bichette.
And not just disorienting. I hear things. Voices.

BELIZE. Voices.

PRIOR. A voice.

BELIZE. Saying what?

(*Pause.*)

PRIOR. I'm not supposed to tell.

BELIZE. You better tell the doctor. Or I will.

PRIOR. No no don't. Please. I want the voice; it's wonderful. It's all that's keeping me alive. I don't want to talk to some intern about it.
You know what happens? When I hear it, I get hard.

BELIZE. Oh my.

PRIOR. Comme ça. (*He uses his arm to demonstrate*) And you know I am slow to rise.

BELIZE. My jaw aches at the memory.

PRIOR. And would you deny me this little solace—betray my concupiscence to Florence Nightingale's storm troopers?

BELIZE. Perish the thought, ma bébé.

PRIOR. They'd change the drug just to spoil the fun.

BELIZE. You and your boner can depend on me.

PRIOR. Je t'adore, ma belle nègre.

BELIZE. All this girl-talk shit is politically incorrect, you know. We should have dropped it back when we gave up drag.

PRIOR. I'm sick, I get to be politically incorrect if it makes me feel better. You sound like Lou.

(*Little pause*)

Well, at least I have the satisfaction of knowing he's in anguish somewhere. I loved his anguish. Watching him stick his head up his asshole and eat his guts out over some relatively minor moral conundrum—it was the best show in town. But Mother warned me: if they get overwhelmed by the little things . . .

BELIZE. They'll be belly-up bustville when something big comes along.

PRIOR. Mother warned me.

BELIZE. And they do come along.

PRIOR. But I didn't listen.

BELIZE. No. (*Doing Hepburn*) Men are beasts.

PRIOR (*Also Hepburn*). The absolute lowest.

BELIZE. I have to go. If I want to spend my whole lonely life looking after white people I can get underpaid to do it.

PRIOR. You're just a Christian martyr.

BELIZE. Whatever happens, baby, I will be here for you.

PRIOR. Je t'aime.

BELIZE. Je t'aime. Don't go crazy on me, girlfriend, I already got enough crazy queens for one lifetime. For two. I can't be bothering with dementia.

PRIOR. I promise.

BELIZE (*Touching him; softly*). Ouch.

PRIOR. Ouch. Indeed.

BELIZE. Why'd they have to pick on you?

And eat more, girlfriend, you really do look like shit.

(*Belize leaves.*)

PRIOR (*After waiting a beat*). He's gone.

Are you still . . .

VOICE. I can't stay. I will return.

PRIOR. Are you one of those "Follow me to the other side" voices?

VOICE. No. I am no nightbird. I am a messenger . . .

PRIOR. You have a beautiful voice, it sounds . . . like a viola, like a perfectly tuned, tight string, balanced, the truth. . . . Stay with me.

VOICE. Not now. Soon I will return, I will reveal myself to you; I am glorious, glorious; my heart, my countenance and my message. You must prepare.

PRIOR. For what? I don't want to . . .

VOICE. No death, no:

A marvelous work and a wonder we undertake, an edifice awry we sink plumb and straighten, a great Lie we abolish, a great error correct, with the rule, sword and broom of Truth!

PRIOR. What are you talking about, I . . .

VOICE.

I am on my way; when I am manifest, our Work begins:

Prepare for the parting of the air,

The breath, the ascent,

Glory to . . .

SCENE 6

The second week of January. Martin, Roy and Joe in a fancy Manhattan restaurant.

MARTIN. It's a revolution in Washington, Joe. We have a new agenda and finally a real leader. They got back the Senate but we have the courts. By the nineties the Supreme Court will be block-solid Republican appointees, and the Federal bench—Republican judges like land mines, everywhere, everywhere they turn. Affirmative action? Take it to court. Boom! Land mine.

And we'll get our way on just about everything: abortion, defense, Central America, family values, a live investment climate. We have the White House locked till the year 2000. And beyond. A permanent fix on the Oval Office? It's possible. By '92 we'll get the Senate back, and in ten years the South is going to give us the House. It's really the end of Liberalism. The end of New Deal Socialism. The end of ipso facto secular humanism. The dawning of a genuinely American political personality. Modeled on Ronald Wilson Reagan.

JOE. It sounds great, Mr. Heller.

MARTIN. Martin. And Justice is the hub. Especially since Ed Meese took over. He doesn't specialize in Fine Points of the Law. He's a flatfoot, a cop. He reminds me of Teddy Roosevelt.

JOE. I can't wait to meet him.

MARTIN. Too bad, Joe, he's been dead for sixty years.

(*There is a little awkwardness. Joe doesn't respond.*)

MARTIN. Teddy Roosevelt. You said you wanted to. . . . Little joke. It reminds me of the story about the . . .

ROY (*Smiling, but nasty*). Aw shut the fuck up Martin.

(*To Joe*) You see that? Mr. Heller here is one of the mighty, Joseph, in D.C. he sitteth on the right hand of the man who sitteth on the right of The Man. And yet I can say "shut the fuck up" and he will take no offense. Loyalty. He . . .

Martin?

MARTIN. Yes, Roy?

ROY. Rub my back.

MARTIN. Roy . . .

ROY. No no really, a sore spot, I get them all the time now, these. . . . Rub it for me darling, would you do that for me?

(*Martin rubs Roy's back. They both look at Joe.*)

ROY (*To Joe*). How do you think a handful of Bolsheviks turned St. Petersburg into Leningrad in one afternoon? *Comrades.* Who do for each other. Marx and Engels. Lenin and Trotsky. Josef Stalin and Franklin Delano Roosevelt.

(*Martin laughs.*)

ROY. *Comrades*, right, Martin?

MARTIN. This man, Joe, is a Saint of the Right.

JOE. I know, Mr. Heller, I . . .

ROY. And you see what I mean, Martin? He's special, right?

MARTIN. Don't embarrass him, Roy.

ROY. Gravity, decency, smarts! His strength is as the strength of ten because his heart is pure! *And* he's a Royboy, one hundred percent.

MARTIN. We're on the move, Joe. On the move.

JOE. Mr. Heller, I . . .

MARTIN (*Ending backrub*). We can't wait any longer for an answer.

(*Little pause.*)

JOE. Oh. Um, I . . .

ROY. Joe's a married man, Martin.

MARTIN. Aha.

ROY. With a wife. She doesn't care to go to D.C., and so Joe cannot go. And keeps us dangling. We've seen that kind of thing before, haven't we? These men and their wives.

MARTIN. Oh yes. Beware.

JOE. I really can't discuss this under . . .

MARTIN. Then *don't* discuss. Say yes, Joe.

ROY. Now.

MARTIN. Say yes I will.

ROY. Now.

Now. I'll hold my breath till you do, I'm turning blue waiting. . . . Now, goddammit!

MARTIN. Roy, calm down, it's not . . .

ROY. Aw, fuck it. (*He takes a letter from his jacket pocket, hands it to Joe.*)

Read. Came today.

(*Joe reads the first paragraph, then looks up.*)

JOE. Roy. This is . . . Roy, this is terrible.

ROY. You're telling me.

A letter from the New York State Bar Association, Martin.

They're gonna try and disbar me.

MARTIN. Oh my.

JOE. Why?

ROY. Why, Martin?

MARTIN. Revenge.

ROY. The whole Establishment. Their little rules. Because I know no rules. Because I don't see the Law as a dead and arbitrary collection of antiquated dictums, thou shall, thou shalt not, because, because I know the Law's a pliable, breathing, sweating . . . *organ*, because, because . . .

MARTIN. Because he borrowed half a million from one of his clients.

ROY. Yeah, well, there's that.

MARTIN. *And* he forgot to *return* it.

JOE. Roy, that's. . . . You borrowed money from a client?

ROY. I'm deeply ashamed.

(*Little pause.*)

JOE (*Very sympathetic*). Roy, you know how much I admire you. Well I mean I know you have unorthodox

ways, but I'm sure you only did what you thought at the time you needed to do. And I have faith that . . .

ROY. Not so damp, please. I'll deny it was a loan. She's got no paperwork. Can't prove a fucking thing.

(*Little pause. Martin studies the menu.*)

JOE (*Handing back the letter, more official in tone*). Roy I really appreciate your telling me this, and I'll do whatever I can to help.

ROY (*Holding up a hand, then, carefully*). I'll tell you what you can do.

I'm about to be tried, Joe, by a jury that is not a jury of my peers. The disbarment committee: genteel gentleman Brahmin lawyers, country-club men. I offend them, to these men . . . I'm what, Martin, some sort of filthy little Jewish troll?

MARTIN. Oh well, I wouldn't go so far as . . .

ROY. Oh well I would.

Very fancy lawyers, these disbarment committee lawyers, fancy lawyers with fancy corporate clients and complicated cases. Antitrust suits. Deregulation. Environmental control. Complex cases like these need Justice Department cooperation like flowers need the sun. Wouldn't you say that's an accurate assessment, Martin?

MARTIN. I'm not here, Roy. I'm not hearing any of this.

ROY. No. Of course not.

Without the light of the sun, Joe, these cases, and the fancy lawyers who represent them, will wither and die.

A well-placed friend, someone in the Justice Department, say, can turn off the sun. Cast a deep shadow on my behalf. Make them shiver in the cold. If they overstep. They would fear that.

(*Pause.*)

JOE. Roy. I don't understand.

ROY. You do.

(*Pause.*)

JOE. You're not asking me to . . .

ROY. Ssshhhh. Careful.

JOE (*A beat, then*). Even if I said yes to the job, it would be illegal to interfere. With the hearings. It's unethical. No. I can't.

ROY. Un-ethical.

Would you excuse us, Martin?

MARTIN. Excuse you?

ROY. Take a walk, Martin. For real.

(*Martin leaves.*)

ROY. Un-ethical. Are you trying to embarrass me in front of my friend?

JOE. Well it is unethical, I can't . . .

ROY. Boy, you are really something. What the fuck do you think this is, Sunday School?

JOE. No, but Roy this is . . .

ROY. This is . . . this is gastric juices churning, this is enzymes and acids, this is intestinal is what this is, bowel movement and blood-red meat—this stinks, this is *politics*, Joe, the game of being alive. And you think you're. . . . What? Above that? Above alive is what? Dead! In the clouds! You're on earth, goddammit! Plant a foot, stay a while.

I'm sick. They smell I'm weak. They want blood this time. I must have eyes in Justice. In Justice you will protect me.

JOE. Why can't Mr. Heller . . .

ROY. Grow up, Joe. The administration can't get involved.

JOE. But I'd be part of the administration. The same as him.

ROY. Not the same. Martin's Ed's man. And Ed's Reagan's man. So Martin's Reagan's man.

And you're mine.

(Little pause. He holds up the letter)

This will never be. Understand me?

(He tears the letter up)

I'm gonna be a lawyer, Joe, I'm gonna be a lawyer, Joe, I'm gonna be a goddam motherfucking legally licensed member of the bar lawyer, just like daddy was, till my last bitter day on earth, Joseph, until the day I die.

(Martin returns.)

ROY. Ah, Martin's back.

MARTIN. So are we agreed?

ROY. Joe?

(Little pause.)

JOE. I will think about it.
      (To Roy) I will.

ROY. Huh.

MARTIN. It's the fear of what comes after the doing that makes the doing hard to do.

ROY. Amen.

MARTIN. But you can almost always live with the consequences.

SCENE 7

That afternoon. On the granite steps outside the Hall of Justice, Brooklyn. It is cold and sunny. A Sabrett wagon is selling hot dogs. Louis, in a shabby overcoat, is sitting on the steps contemplatively eating one. Joe enters with three hot dogs and a can of Coke.

JOE. Can I . . . ?

LOUIS. Oh, sure. Sure. Crazy cold sun.

JOE *(Sitting)*. Have to make the best of it.
      How's your friend?

LOUIS. My . . . ? Oh. He's worse. My friend is worse.

JOE. I'm sorry.

LOUIS. Yeah, well. Thanks for asking. It's nice, You're nice. I can't believe you voted for Reagan.

JOE. I hope he gets better.

LOUIS. Reagan?

JOE. Your friend.

LOUIS. He won't. Neither will Reagan.

JOE. Let's not talk politics, OK?

LOUIS *(Pointing to Joe's lunch)*. You're eating *three* of those?

JOE. Well . . . I'm . . . hungry.

LOUIS. They're really terrible for you. Full of rat-poo and beetle legs and wood shavings 'n' shit.

JOE. Huh.

LOUIS. And . . . um . . . irridium, I think. Something toxic.

JOE. You're eating one.

LOUIS. Yeah, well, the shape, I can't help myself, plus I'm *trying* to commit suicide, what's your excuse?

JOE. I don't have an excuse. I just have Pepto-Bismol.

(Joe takes a bottle of Pepto-Bismol and chugs it. Louis shudders audibly.)

JOE. Yeah I know but then I wash it down with Coke.

(He does this. Louis mimes barfing in Joe's lap. Joe pushes Louis's head away.)

JOE. Are you *always* like this?

LOUIS. I've been worrying a lot about his kids.

JOE. Whose?

LOUIS. Reagan's. Maureen and Mike and little orphan Patti and Miss Ron Reagan Jr., the you-should-pardon-the-expression heterosexual.

JOE. Ron Reagan Jr. is *not*. . . . You shouldn't just make these assumptions about people. How do you know? About him? What he is? You don't know.

LOUIS *(Doing Tallulah)*. Well darling he never sucked *my* cock but . . .

JOE. Look, if you're going to get vulgar . . .

LOUIS. No no really I mean. . . . What's it like to be the child of the Zeitgeist? To have the American Animus as your dad? It's not really a *family*, the Reagans. I read *People*, there aren't any connections there, no love, they don't even speak to each other except through their agents. So what's it like to be Reagan's kid? Enquiring minds want to know.

JOE. You can't believe everything you . . .

LOUIS (*Looking away*). But . . . I think we all know what that's like. Nowadays. No connections. No responsibilities. All of us . . . falling through the cracks that separate what we owe to our selves and . . . and what we owe to love.

JOE. You just. . . . Whatever you feel like saying or doing, you don't care, you just . . . do it.

LOUIS. Do what?

JOE. It. Whatever. Whatever it is you want to do.

LOUIS. Are you trying to tell me something?

(*Little pause, sexual. They stare at each other. Joe looks away.*)

JOE. No, I'm just observing that you . . .

LOUIS. Impulsive.

JOE. Yes, I mean it must be scary, you . . .

LOUIS (*Shrugs*). Land of the free. Home of the brave. Call me irresponsible.

JOE. It's kind of terrifying.

LOUIS. Yeah, well, freedom is. Heartless, too.

JOE. Oh you're not heartless.

LOUIS. You don't know.
Finish your weenie.

(*He pats Joe on the knee, starts to leave.*)

JOE. Um . . .

(*Louis turns, looks at him. Joe searches for something to say.*)

JOE. Yesterday was Sunday but I've been a little unfocused recently and I thought it was Monday. So I came here like I was going to work. And the whole place was empty. And at first I couldn't figure out why, and I had this moment of incredible . . . fear and also. . . . It just flashed through my mind: The whole Hall of Justice, it's empty, it's deserted, it's gone out of busines. Forever. The people that make it run have up and abandoned it.

LOUIS (*Looking at the building*). Creepy.

JOE. Well yes but. I felt that I was going to scream. Not because it was creepy, but because the emptiness felt so *fast*.
And . . . well, good. A . . . happy scream.
I just wondered what a thing it would be . . . if overnight everything you owe anything to, justice, or love, had really gone away. Free.

It would be . . . heartless terror. Yes. Terrible, and . . . Very great. To shed your skin, every old skin, one by one then walk away, unencumbered, into the morning.

(*Little pause. He looks at the building*)

I can't go in there today.

LOUIS. Then don't.

JOE (*Not really hearing Louis*). I can't go in, I need . . .

(*He looks for what he needs. He takes a swig of Pepto-Bismol*)

I can't *be* this anymore. I need . . . a change, I should just . . .

LOUIS (*Not a come-on, necessarily; he doesn't want to be alone*). Want some company? For whatever?

(*Pause. Joe looks at Louis and looks away, afraid. Louis shrugs.*)

LOUIS. Sometimes, even if it scares you to death, you have to be willing to break the law. Know what I mean?

(*Another little pause.*)

JOE. Yes.

(*Another little pause.*)

LOUIS. I moved out. I moved out on my . . .
I haven't been sleeping well.

JOE. Me neither.

(*Louis goes up to Joe, licks his napkin and dabs at Joe's mouth.*)

LOUIS. Antacid moustache.
(*Points to the building*) Maybe the court won't convene. Ever again. Maybe we are free. To do whatever. Children of the new morning, criminal minds. Selfish and greedy and loveless and blind. Reagan's children.
You're scared. So am I. Everybody is in the land of the free. God help us all.

SCENE 8

Late that night. Joe at a payphone phoning Hannah at home in Salt Lake City.

JOE. Mom?

HANNAH. Joe?

JOE. Hi.

HANNAH. You're calling from the street. It's . . . it must be four in the morning. What's happened?

JOE. Nothing, nothing, I . . .

HANNAH. It's Harper. Is Harper. . . . Joe? Joe?

JOE. Yeah, hi. No, Harper's fine. Well, no, she's . . . not fine. How are you, Mom?

HANNAH. What's happened?

JOE. I just wanted to talk to you. I, uh, wanted to try something out on you.

HANNAH. Joe, you haven't . . . have you been drinking, Joe?

JOE. Yes ma'am. I'm drunk.

HANNAH. That isn't like you.

JOE. No. I mean, who's to say?

HANNAH. Why are you out on the street at four AM? In that crazy city. It's dangerous.

JOE. Actually, Mom, I'm not on the street. I'm near the boathouse in the park.

HANNAH. What park?

JOE. *Central Park.*

HANNAH. CENTRAL PARK! Oh my Lord. What on earth are you doing in Central Park at this time of night? Are you . . .

Joe, I think you ought to go home right now. Call me from home.

(Little pause)

Joe?

JOE. I come here to watch, Mom. Sometimes. Just to watch.

HANNAH. Watch what? What's there to watch at four in the . . .

JOE. Mom, did Dad love me?

HANNAH. What?

JOE. Did he?

HANNAH. You ought to go home and call from there.

JOE. Answer.

HANNAH. Oh now really. This is maudlin. I don't like this conversation.

JOE. Yeah, well, it gets worse from here on.

(Pause)

HANNAH. Joe?

JOE. Mom. Momma. I'm a homosexual, Momma. Boy, did that come out awkward.

(Pause)

Hello? Hello?
I'm a homosexual.

(Pause)

Please, Momma. Say something.

HANNAH. You're old enough to understand that your father didn't love you without being ridiculous about it.

JOE. What?

HANNAH. You're ridiculous. You're being ridiculous.

JOE. I'm . . .
What?

HANNAH. You really ought to go home now to your wife. I need to go to bed. This phone call. . . . We will just forget this phone call.

JOE. Mom.

HANNAH. No more talk. Tonight. This . . .
(Suddenly very angry) Drinking is a sin! A sin! I raised you better than that.

(She hangs up)

SCENE 9

The following morning, early. Split scene: Harper and Joe at home; Louis and Prior in Prior's hospital room. Joe and Louis have just entered. This should be fast and obviously furious; overlapping is fine; the proceedings may be a little confusing but not the final results.

HARPER. Oh God. Home. The moment of truth has arrived.

JOE. Harper.

LOUIS. I'm going to move out.

PRIOR. The fuck you are.

JOE. Harper. Please listen. I still love you very much. You're still my best buddy; I'm not going to leave you.

HARPER. No, I don't like the sound of this. I'm leaving.

LOUIS. I'm leaving.
I already have.

JOE. Please listen. Stay. This is really hard. We have to talk.

HARPER. We are talking. Aren't we. Now please shut up. OK?

PRIOR. Bastard. Sneaking off while I'm flat out here, that's low.
If I could get up now I'd beat the holy shit out of you.

JOE. Did you take pills? How many?

HARPER. No pills. Bad for the . . . *(Pats stomach)*

JOE. You aren't pregnant. I called your gynecologist.

HARPER. I'm seeing a new gynecologist.

PRIOR. You have no right to do this.

LOUIS. Oh, that's ridiculous.

PRIOR. No right. It's criminal.

JOE. Forget about that. Just listen. You want the truth. This is the truth.

    I knew this when I married you. I've known this I guess for as long as I've known anything, but . . . I don't know, I thought maybe that with enough effort and will I could change myself . . . but I can't . . .

PRIOR. Criminal.

LOUIS. There oughta be a law.

PRIOR. There is a law. You'll see.

JOE. I'm losing ground here, I go walking, you want to know where I walk, I . . . go to the park, or up and down 53rd Street, or places where. . . . And I keep swearing I won't go walking again, but I just can't.

LOUIS. I need some privacy.

PRIOR. That's new.

LOUIS. Everything's new, Prior.

JOE. I try to tighten my heart into a knot, a snarl, I try to learn to live dead, just numb, but then I see someone I want, and it's like a nail, like a hot spike through my chest, and I know I'm losing.

PRIOR. Apartment too small for three? Louis and Prior comfy but not Louis and Prior and Prior's disease?

LOUIS. Something like that.

    I won't be judged by you. This isn't a crime, just—the inevitable consequence of people who run out of— whose limitations . . .

PRIOR. Bang bang bang. The court will come to order.

LOUIS. I mean let's talk practicalities, schedules; I'll come over if you want, spend nights with you when I can, I can . . .

PRIOR. Has the jury reached a verdict?

LOUIS. I'm doing the best I can.

PRIOR. Pathetic. Who cares?

JOE. My whole life has conspired to bring me to this place, and I can't despise my whole life. I think I believed when I met you I could save you, you at least if not myself, but . . .

    I don't have any sexual feelings for you, Harper. And I don't think I ever did.

(Little pause.)

HARPER. I think you should go.

JOE. Where?

HARPER. Washington. Doesn't matter.

JOE. What are you talking about?

HARPER. Without me.

    Without me, Joe. Isn't that what you want to hear?

(Little pause.)

JOE. Yes.

LOUIS. You can love someone and fail them. You can love someone and not be able to . . .

PRIOR. You *can*, theoretically, yes. A person can, maybe an editorial "you" can love, Louis, but not *you*, specifically you, I don't know, I think you are excluded from that general category.

HARPER. You were going to save me, but the whole time you were spinning a lie. I just don't understand that.

PRIOR. A person could theoretically love and maybe many do but we both know now you can't.

LOUIS. I do.

PRIOR. You can't even say it.

LOUIS. I love you, Prior.

PRIOR. I repeat. Who cares?

HARPER. This is so scary, I want this to stop, to go back . . .

PRIOR. We have reached a verdict, your honor. This man's heart is deficient. He loves, but his love is worth nothing.

JOE. Harper . . .

HARPER. Mr. Lies, I want to get away from here. Far away. Right now. Before he starts talking again. Please, please . . .

JOE. As long as I've known you Harper you've been afraid of . . . of men hiding under the bed, men hiding under the sofa, men with knives.

PRIOR (*Shattered; almost pleading; trying to reach him*). I'm dying! You stupid fuck! Do you know what that is! Love! Do you know what love means? We lived together four-and-a-half years, you animal, you idiot.

LOUIS. I have to find some way to save myself.

JOE. Who are these men? I never understood it. Now I know.

HARPER. What?

JOE. It's me.

HARPER. It is?

PRIOR. GET OUT OF MY ROOM!

JOE. I'm the man with the knives.

HARPER. You are?

PRIOR. If I could get up now I'd kill you. I would. Go away. Go away or I'll scream.

HARPER. Oh God . . .

JOE. I'm sorry . . .

HARPER. It is you.

LOUIS. Please don't scream.

PRIOR. Go.

HARPER. I recognize you now.

LOUIS. Please . . .

JOE. Oh. Wait, I. . . . Oh!

(*He covers his mouth with his hand, gags, and removes his hand, red with blood*)

I'm bleeding.

(*Prior screams.*)

HARPER. Mr. Lies.

MR. LIES (*Appearing, dressed in antarctic explorer's apparel*). Right here.

HARPER. I want to go away. I can't see him anymore.

MR. LIES. Where?

HARPER. Anywhere. Far away.

MR. LIES. Absolutamento.

(*Harper and Mr. Lies vanish. Joe looks up, sees that she's gone.*)

PRIOR (*Closing his eyes*). When I open my eyes you'll be gone.

(*Louis leaves.*)

JOE. Harper?

PRIOR (*Opening his eyes*). Huh. It worked.

JOE (*Calling*). Harper?

PRIOR. I hurt all over. I wish I was dead.

SCENE 10

The same day, sunset. Hannah and Sister Ella Chapter, a real-estate saleswoman, Hannah Pitt's closest friend, in front of Hannah's house in Salt Lake City.

SISTER ELLA CHAPTER. Look at that view! A view of heaven. Like the living city of heaven, isn't it, it just fairly glimmers in the sun.

HANNAH. Glimmers.

SISTER ELLA CHAPTER. Even the stone and brick it just glimmers and glitters like heaven in the sunshine. Such a nice view you get, perched up on a canyon rim. Some kind of beautiful place.

HANNAH. It's just Salt Lake, and you're selling the house *for* me, not *to* me.

SISTER ELLA CHAPTER. I like to work up an enthusiasm for my properties.

HANNAH. Just get me a good price.

SISTER ELLA CHAPTER. Well, the market's off.

HANNAH. At least fifty.

SISTER ELLA CHAPTER. Forty'd be more like it.

HANNAH. Fifty.

SISTER ELLA CHAPTER. Wish you'd wait a bit.

HANNAH. Well I can't.

SISTER ELLA CHAPTER. Wish you would. You're about the only friend I got.

HANNAH. Oh well now.

SISTER ELLA CHAPTER. Know why I decided to like you? I decided to like you 'cause you're the only unfriendly Mormon I ever met.

HANNAH. Your wig is crooked.

SISTER ELLA CHAPTER. Fix it.

(*Hannah straightens Sister Ella's wig.*)

SISTER ELLA CHAPTER. New York City. All they got there is tiny rooms.

I always thought: People ought to stay put. That's why I got my license to sell real estate. It's a way of saying: Have a house! Stay put! It's a way of saying traveling's no good. Plus I needed the cash. (*She takes a pack of cigarettes out of her purse, lights one, offers pack to Hannah*).

HANNAH. Not out here, anyone could come by.

There's been days I've stood at this ledge and thought about stepping over.

It's a hard place, Salt Lake: baked dry. Abundant energy; not much intelligence. That's a combination that can wear a body out. No harm looking someplace else. I don't need much room.

My sister-in-law Libby thinks there's radon gas in the basement.

SISTER ELLA CHAPTER. Is there gas in the . . .

HANNAH. Of course not. Libby's a fool.

SISTER ELLA CHAPTER. 'Cause I'd have to include that in the description.

HANNAH. There's no gas, Ella. (*Little pause*) Give a puff. (*She takes a furtive drag of Ella's cigarette*) Put it away now.

SISTER ELLA CHAPTER. So I guess it's goodbye.

HANNAH. You'll be all right, Ella, I wasn't ever much of a friend.

SISTER ELLA CHAPTER. I'll say something but don't laugh, OK?

This is the home of saints, the godliest place on earth, they say, and I think they're right. That means there's no evil here? No. Evil's everywhere. Sin's everywhere. But this . . . is the spring of sweet water in the desert, the desert flower. Every step a Believer takes away from here is a step fraught with peril. I fear for you, Hannah Pitt, because you are my friend. Stay put. This is the right home of saints.

HANNAH. Latter-day saints.

SISTER ELLA CHAPTER. Only kind left.

HANNAH. But still. Late in the day . . . for saints and everyone. That's all. That's all. Fifty thousand dollars for the house, Sister Ella Chapter; don't undersell. It's an impressive view.

ACT III: NOT-YET-CONSCIOUS,
FORWARD DAWNING

January 1986

SCENE 1

Late night, three days after the end of Act Two. The stage is completely dark. Prior is in bed in his apartment, having a nightmare. He wakes up, sits up and switches on a nightlight. He looks at his clock. Seated by the table near the bed is a man dressed in the clothing of a 13th-century British squire.

PRIOR (*Terrified*). Who are you?
PRIOR 1. My name is *Prior Walter*.

(*Pause.*)

PRIOR. My name is Prior Walter.
PRIOR 1. I know that.
PRIOR. Explain.
PRIOR 1. You're alive. I'm not. We have the same name. What do you want me to explain?
PRIOR. A ghost?
PRIOR 1. An ancestor.
PRIOR. Not *the* Prior Walter? The Bayeux tapestry Prior Walter?
PRIOR 1. His great-great grandson. The fifth of the name.
PRIOR. I'm the thirty-fourth, I think.
PRIOR 1. Actually the thirty-second.
PRIOR. Not according to Mother.
PRIOR 1. She's including the two bastards, then; I say leave them out. I say no room for bastards. The little things you swallow . . .
PRIOR. Pills.
PRIOR 1. Pills. For the pestilence. I too . . .
PRIOR. Pestilence. . . . You too what?
PRIOR 1. The pestilence in my time was much worse than now. Whole villages of empty houses. You could look outdoors and see Death walking in the morning, dew dampening the ragged hem of his black robe. Plain as I see you now.
PRIOR. You died of the plague.
PRIOR 1. The spotty monster. Like you, alone.
PRIOR. I'm not alone.
PRIOR 1. You have no wife, no children.
PRIOR. I'm gay.
PRIOR 1. So? Be gay, dance in your altogether for all I care, what's that to do with not having children?
PRIOR. Gay homosexual, not bonny, blithe and . . . never mind.

PRIOR 1. I had twelve. When I died.

(*The second ghost appears, this one dressed in the clothing of an elegant 17th-century Londoner.*)

PRIOR 1 (*Pointing to Prior 2*). And I was three years younger than him.

(*Prior sees the new ghost, screams.*)

PRIOR. Oh God another one.
PRIOR 2. Prior Walter. Prior to you by some seventeen others.
PRIOR 1. He's counting the bastards.
PRIOR. Are you having a convention?
PRIOR 2. We've been sent to declare her fabulous incipience. They love a well-paved entrance with lots of heralds, and . . .
PRIOR 1. The messenger come. Prepare the way. The infinite descent, a breath of in air . . .
PRIOR 2. They chose us, I suspect, because of the mortal affinities. In a family as long-descended as the Walters there are bound to be a few carried off by plague.
PRIOR 1. The spotty monster.
PRIOR 2. Black Jack. Came from a water pump, half the city of London, can you imagine? His came from fleas. Yours, I understand, is the lamentable consequence of venery . . .
PRIOR 1. Fleas on rats, but who knew that?
PRIOR. Am I going to die?
PRIOR 2. We aren't allowed to discuss . . .
PRIOR 1. When you do, you don't get ancestors to help you through it. You may be surrounded by children but you die alone.
PRIOR. I'm afraid.
PRIOR 1. You should be. There aren't even torches, and the path's rocky, dark and steep.
PRIOR 2. Don't alarm him. There's good news before there's bad.
We two come to stew rose petal and palm leaf before the triumphal procession. Prophet. Seer. Revelator. It's a great honor for the family.
PRIOR 1. He hasn't got a family.
PRIOR 2. I meant for the Walters, for the family in the larger sense.
PRIOR (*Singing*).
    All I want is a room somewhere,
    Far away from the cold night air . . .
PRIOR 2 (*Putting a hand on Prior's forehead*). Calm, calm, this is no brain fever . . .

(*Prior calms down, but keeps his eyes closed. The lights begin to change. Distant Glorious Music.*)

PRIOR 1 (*Low chant*).
    Adonai, Adonai,
    Olam ha-yichud,
    Zefirot, Zazahot,
    Ha-adam, ha-gadol
    Daughter of Light,
    Daughter of Splendors,
    Fluor! Phosphor!
    Lumen! Candle!

PRIOR 2 (*Simultaneously*).
    Even now,
    From the mirror-bright halls of heaven,
    Across the cold and lifeless infinity of space,
    The Messenger comes
    Trailing orbs of light,
    Fabulous, incipient,
    Oh Prophet,
    To you . . .

PRIOR 1 AND PRIOR 2.
    Prepare, prepare,
    The Infinite Descent,
    A breath, a feather,
    Glory to . . .

(*They vanish.*)

SCENE 2

The next day. Split scene: Louis and Belize in a coffee shop. Prior is at the outpatient clinic at the hospital with Emily, the nurse; she has him on a pentamidine IV drip.

LOUIS. Why has democracy succeeded in America? Of course by succeeded I mean comparatively, not literally, not in the present, but what makes for the prospect of some sort of radical democracy spreading outward and growing up? Why does the power that was once so carefully preserved at the top of the pyramid by the original framers of the Constitution seem drawn inexorably downward and outward in spite of the best effort of the Right to stop this? I mean it's the really hard thing about being Left in this country, the American Left can't help but trip over all these petrified little fetishes: freedom, that's the worst; you know, *Jeane Kirkpatrick* for God's sake will go on and on about freedom and so what does that mean, the word freedom, when she talks about it, or human rights; you have Bush talking about human rights, and so what are these people talking about, they might as well be talking about the mating habits of Venusians, these people don't begin to know what, ontologically, freedom is or human rights, like they see these bourgeois property-based Rights-of-Man-type rights but that's not enfranchisement, not democracy, not what's implicit, what's potential within the idea, not the idea with blood in it. That's just liberalism, the worst kind of liberalism, really, bourgeois tolerance, and what I think is that what AIDS shows us is the limits of tolerance, that it's not enough to be tolerated, because when the shit hits the fan you find out how much tolerance is worth. Nothing. And underneath all the tolerance is intense, passionate hatred.

BELIZE. Uh huh.

LOUIS. Well don't you think that's true?

BELIZE. Uh huh. It is.

LOUIS. *Power* is the object, not being tolerated. Fuck assimilation. But I mean in spite of all this the the thing about America, I think, is that ultimately we're different from every other nation on earth, in that, with people here of every race, we can't. . . . Ultimately what defines us isn't race, but politics. Not like any European country where there's an insurmountable fact of a kind of racial, or ethnic, monopoly, or monolith, like all Dutchmen, I mean Dutch people, are well, Dutch, and the Jews of Europe were never Europeans, just a small problem. Facing the monolith. But here there are so many small problems, it's really just a collection of small problems, the monolith is missing. Oh, I mean, of course I suppose there's the monolith of White America. White Straight Male America.

BELIZE. Which is not unimpressive, even among monoliths.

LOUIS. Well, no, but when the race thing gets taken care of, and I don't mean to minimize how major it is, I mean I know it is, this is a really, really incredibly racist country but it's like, well, the British. I mean, all these blue-eyed pink people. And it's just weird, you know, I mean I'm not all that Jewish-looking, or . . . well, maybe I am but, you know, in New York, everyone is . . . well, not everyone, but so many are but so but in England, in London I walk into bars and I feel like Sid the Yid, you know I mean like Woody Allen in *Annie Hall*, with the payess and the gabardine coat, like never, never anywhere so much—I mean, not actively despised, not like they're Germans, who I think are still terribly anti-Semitic, and racist too, I mean black-racist, they pretend otherwise but, anyway, in London, there's just . . . and at one point I met this black gay guy from Jamaica who talked with a lilt but he said his family'd been living in London since before the Civil War—the American one—and how the English never let him forget for a minute that he wasn't blue-eyed and pink and I said yeah, me too, these people are anti-Semites and he said yeah but the British Jews have the clothing business all sewed up and blacks here can't get a foothold. And it was an incredibly awkward moment of just. . . . I mean here we were, in this bar that was gay but it was a *pub*, you know, the beams and the plaster and those horrible little, like, two-day-old fish and egg sandwiches—and just so British, so *old*, and I felt, well, there's no way out of this because both of us are, right now, too much immersed in this history, hope is dissolved in the sheer age of this place, where race is what counts and there's no real hope of change—it's the racial destiny of the Brits that matters to them, not their political destiny, whereas in America . . .

BELIZE. Here in America race doesn't count.

LOUIS. No, no, that's not. . . . I mean you *can't* be hearing that . . .

BELIZE. I . . .

LOUIS. It's—look, race, yes, but ultimately race here is a political question, right? Racists just try to use race here as a tool in a political struggle. It's not really about race. Like the spiritualists try to use that stuff, are you enlightened, are you centered, channeled, whatever, this reaching out for a spiritual past in a country where no indigenous spirits exist—only the Indians, I mean Native American spirits and we killed them off so now, there are no gods here, no ghosts and spirits in America, there are no angels in America, no spiritual past, no racial past, there's only the political, and the decoys and the ploys to maneuver around the inescapable battle of politics, the shifting downwards and outwards of political power to the people . . .

BELIZE. POWER to the People! AMEN! (*Looking at his watch*) OH MY GOODNESS! Will you look at the time. I gotta . . .

LOUIS. Do you. . . . You think this is, what, racist or naive or something?

BELIZE. Well it's certainly *something*. Look, I just remembered I have an appointment . . .

LOUIS. What? I mean I really don't want to, like, speak from some position of privilege and . . .

BELIZE. I'm sitting here, thinking, eventually he's *got* to run out of steam, so I let you rattle on and on saying about maybe seven or eight things I find really offensive.

LOUIS. What?

BELIZE. But I know you, Louis, and I know the guilt fueling this peculiar tirade is obviously already swollen bigger than your hemorrhoids.

LOUIS. I don't have hemorrhoids.

BELIZE. I hear different. May I finish?

LOUIS. Yes, but I don't have hemorrhoids.

BELIZE. So finally, when I . . .

LOUIS. Prior told you, he's an asshole, he should have . . .

BELIZE. You promised, Louis. Prior is not a subject.

LOUIS. You brought him up.

BELIZE. I brought up hemorrhoids.

LOUIS. So it's indirect. Passive-aggressive.

BELIZE. Unlike, I suppose, banging me over the head with your theory that America doesn't have a race problem.

LOUIS. Oh be fair I never said that.

BELIZE. Not exactly, but . . .

LOUIS. I said . . .

BELIZE. . . . but it was close enough, because if it'd been that blunt I'd've just walked out and . . .

LOUIS. You deliberately misinterpreted! I . . .

BELIZE. Stop interrupting! I haven't been able to . . .

LOUISE. Just let me . . .

BELIZE. NO! What, *talk?* You've been running your mouth nonstop since I got here, yaddadda yaddadda blah blah blah, up the hill, down the hill, playing with your MONOLITH . . .

LOUIS (*Overlapping*). Well, you could have joined in at any time instead of . . .

BELIZE (*Continuing over Louis*). . . . and girlfriend it is truly an *awesome* spectacle but I got better things to do with my time than sit here listening to this racist bullshit just because I feel sorry for you that . . .

LOUIS. I am not a racist!

BELIZE. Oh come on . . .

LOUIS. So maybe I am a racist but . . .

BELIZE. Oh I really hate that! It's no fun picking on you Louis; you're so guilty, it's like throwing darts at a glob of jello, there's no satisfying hits, just quivering, the darts just blop in and vanish.

LOUIS. I just think when you are discussing lines of oppression it gets very complicated and . . .

BELIZE. Oh is that a fact? You know, we black drag queens have a rather intimate knowledge of the complexity of the lines of . . .

LOUIS. *Ex*-black drag queen.

BELIZE. Actually ex-ex.

LOUIS. You're doing drag again?

BELIZE. I don't. . . . Maybe. I don't have to tell you. Maybe.

LOUIS. I think it's sexist.

BELIZE. I didn't ask you.

LOUIS. Well it is. The gay community, I think, has to adopt the same attitude towards drag as black women have to take towards black women blues singers.

BELIZE. Oh my we *are* walking dangerous tonight.

LOUIS. Well, it's all internalized oppression, right, I mean the masochism, the stereotypes, the . . .

BELIZE. Louis, are you deliberately trying to make me hate you?

LOUIS. No, I . . .

BELIZE. I mean, are you deliberately transforming yourself into an arrogant, sexual-political Stalinist-slash-racist flagwaving thug for my benefit?

(*Pause.*)

LOUIS. You know what I think?

BELIZE. What?

LOUIS. You hate me because I'm a Jew.

BELIZE. I'm leaving.

LOUIS. It's true.

BELIZE. You have no basis except your . . .
Louis, it's good to know you haven't changed; you are still an honorary citizen of the Twilight Zone, and after your pale, pale white polemics on behalf of racial insensitivity you have a flaming *fuck* of a lot of nerve calling me an anti-Semite. Now I really gotta go.

LOUIS. You called me Lou the Jew.

BELIZE. That was a joke.

LOUIS. I didn't think it was funny. It was hostile.

BELIZE. It was three years ago.

LOUIS. So?

BELIZE. You just called yourself Sid and Yid.

LOUIS. That's not the same thing.

BELIZE. Sid the Yid is different from Lou the Jew.

LOUIS. Yes.

BELIZE. Someday you'll have to explain that to me, but right now . . .
You hate me because you hate black people.

LOUIS. I do not. But I do think most black people are anti-Semitic.

BELIZE. "Most black people." *That's* racist, Louis, and *I* think most Jews . . .

LOUIS. Louis Farrakhan.

BELIZE. Ed Koch.

LOUIS. Jesse Jackson.

BELIZE. Jackson. Oh really, Louis, this is . . .

LOUIS. Hymietown! Hymietown!

BELIZE. Louis, you voted for Jesse Jackson. You send checks to the Rainbow Coalition.

LOUIS. I'm ambivalent. The checks bounced.

BELIZE. All your checks bounce, Louis; you're ambivalent about everything.

LOUIS. What's that supposed to mean?

BELIZE. You may be dumber than shit but I refuse to believe you can't figure it out. Try.

LOUIS. I was never ambivalent about Prior. I love him. I do. I really do.

BELIZE. Nobody said different.

LOUIS. Love and ambivalence are. . . . Real love isn't ambivalent.

BELIZE. "Real love isn't ambivalent." I'd swear that's a line from my favorite bestselling paperback novel, *In Love with the Night Mysterious*, except I don't think you ever read it.

(*Pause.*)

LOUIS. I never read it, no.

BELIZE. You ought to. Instead of spending the rest of your life trying to get through *Democracy in America*. It's about this white woman whose Daddy owns a plantation in the Deep South in the years before the Civil War—the American one—and her name is Margaret, and she's in love with her Daddy's number-one slave, and his name is Thaddeus, and she's married but her white slave-owner husband has AIDS: Antebellum Insufficiently Developed Sexorgans. And there's a lot of hot stuff going down when Margaret and Thaddeus can catch a spare torrid ten under the cotton-picking moon, and then of course the Yankees come, and here they set the slaves free, and the slaves string up old Daddy, and so on. Historical fiction. Somewhere in there I recall Margaret and Thaddeus find the time to discuss the nature of love; her face is reflecting the flames of the burning plantation—you know, the way white people do—and his black face is dark in the night and she says to him, "Thaddeus, real love isn't ever ambivalent."

(*Little pause. Emily enters and turns off IV drip.*)

BELIZE. Thaddeus looks at her; he's contemplating her thesis; and he isn't sure he agrees.

EMILY (*Removing IV drip from Prior's arm*). Treatment number . . . (*Consulting chart*) four.

PRIOR. Pharmaceutical miracle. Lazarus breathes again.

LOUIS. Is he. . . . How bad is he?

BELIZE. You want the laundry list?

EMILY. Shirt off, let's check the . . .

(*Prior takes his shirt off. She examines his lesions.*)

BELIZE. There's the weight problem and the shit problem and the morale problem.

EMILY. Only six. That's good. Pants.

(*He drops his pants. He's naked. She examines.*)

BELIZE. And. He thinks he's going crazy.

EMILY. Looking good. What else?

PRIOR. Ankles sore and swollen, but the leg's better. The nausea's mostly gone with the little orange pills. BM's pure liquid but not bloody anymore, for now, my eye doctor says everything's OK, for now, my dentist says "Yuck!" when he sees my fuzzy tongue, and now he wears little condoms on his thumb and forefinger. And a mask. So what? My dermatologist is in Hawaii and my mother . . . well leave my mother out of it. Which is usually where my mother is, out of it. My glands are like walnuts, my weight's holding steady for week two, and a friend died two days ago of bird tuberculosis; bird tuberculosis; that scared me and I didn't go to the funeral today because he was an Irish Catholic and it's probably open casket and I'm afraid of . . . something, the bird TB or seeing him or. . . . So I guess I'm doing OK. Except for of course I'm going nuts.

EMILY. We ran the toxoplasmosis series and there's no indication . . .

PRIOR. I know, I know, but I feel like something terrifying is on its way, you know, like a missile from outer space, and its plummeting down towards the earth, and I'm ground zero, and . . . I am generally known where I am known as one cool, collected queen. And I am ruffled.

EMILY. There's really nothing to worry about. I think that shochen bamromim hamtzeh menucho nechono al kanfey haschino.

PRIOR. What?

EMILY. Everything's fine. Bemaalos k'doshim ut'horim kezohar horokeea mazhirim . . .

PRIOR. Oh I don't understand what you're . . .

EMILY. Es nishmas Prior sheholoch leolomoh, baavur shenodvoo z'dokoh b'ad hazkoras nishmosoh.

PRIOR. Why are you doing that? Stop it! Stop it!

EMILY. Stop what?

PRIOR. You were just . . . weren't you just speaking in Hebrew or something.

EMILY. *Hebrew?* (*Laughs*) I'm basically Italian-American. No. I didn't speak in Hebrew.

PRIOR. Oh no, oh God please I really think I . . .

EMILY. Look, I'm sorry, I have a waiting room full of. . . . I think you're one of the lucky ones, you'll live for years, probably—you're pretty healthy for someone with no immune system. Are you seeing someone? Loneliness is a danger. A therapist?

PRIOR. No, I don't need to see anyone, I just . . .

EMILY. Well think about it. You aren't going crazy. You're just under a lot of stress. No wonder . . . (*She starts to write in his chart*)

(*Suddenly there is an astonishing blaze of light, a huge chord sounded by a gigantic choir, and a great book with steel pages mounted atop a molten-red pillar pops up from the stage floor. The book opens; there is a large Aleph inscribed on its pages, which bursts into flames. Immediately the book slams shut and disappears instantly under the floor as the lights become normal again. Emily notices none of this, writing. Prior is agog.*)

EMILY (*Laughing, exiting*). Hebrew . . .

(*Prior flees.*)

LOUIS. Help me.

BELIZE. I beg your pardon?

LOUIS. You're a nurse, give me something, I . . . don't know what to do anymore, I. . . . Last week at work I screwed up the Xerox machine like permanently and so I . . . then I tripped on the subway steps and my glasses broke and I cut my forehead, here, see, and now I can't see much and my forehead . . . it's like the Mark of Cain, stupid, right, but it won't heal and every morning I see it and I think, Biblical things, Mark of Cain, Judas Iscariot and his silver and his noose, people who . . . in betraying what they love betray what's truest in themselves, I feel . . . nothing but cold for myself, just cold, and every night I miss him, I miss him so much but then . . . those sores, and the smell and . . . where I thought it was going. . . . I could be . . . I could be sick too, maybe I'm sick too. I don't know.

Belize. Tell him I love him. Can you do that?

BELIZE. I've thought about it for a long time, and I still don't understand what love is. Justice is simple. Democracy is simple. Those things are unambivalent. But love is very hard. And it goes bad for you if you violate the hard law of love.

LOUIS. I'm dying.

BELIZE. He's dying. You just wish you were.

Oh cheer up, Louis. Look at that heavy sky out there.

LOUIS. Purple.

BELIZE. *Purple?* Boy, what kind of a homosexual are you, any way? That's not purple, Mary, that color up there is (*very grand*) *mauve.*

All day today it's felt like Thanksgiving. Soon, this . . . ruination will be blanketed white. You can smell it—can you smell it?

LOUIS. Smell what?

BELIZE. Softness, compliance, forgiveness, grace.

LOUIS. No . . .

BELIZE. I can't help you learn that. I can't help you, Louis. You're not my business. (*He exits*)

(Louis puts his head in his hands, inadvertently touching his forehead.)

LOUIS. Ow FUCK! (*He stands slowly, looks towards where Belize is seated*) Smell what?

(He looks both ways to be sure no one is watching, then inhales deeply, and is surprised.) Huh. Snow.

SCENE 3

Same day. Harper in a very white, cold place, with a brilliant sky above; a delicate snowfall. She is dressed in a beautiful snowsuit. The sound of the sea, faint.

HARPER. Snow! Ice! Mountains of ice! Where am I? I . . . I feel better, I do. I . . . feel better. There are ice crystals in my lungs, wonderful and sharp. And the snow smells like cold, crushed peaches. And there's something . . . some current of blood in the wind, how strange, it has that iron taste.

MR. LIES. Ozone.

HARPER. Ozone! Wow! Where am I?

MR. LIES. The Kingdom of Ice, the bottommost part of the world.

HARPER (*Looking around, then realizing*). Antarctica. This is Antarctica!

MR. LIES. Cold shelter for the shattered. No sorrow here, tears freeze.

HARPER. Antarctica, Antarctica, oh boy oh boy, LOOK at this, I. . . . Wow, I must've really snapped the tether, huh?

MR. LIES. Apparently . . .

HARPER. That's great. I want to stay here forever. Set up camp. Build things. Build a city, an enormous city made up of frontier forts, dark wood and green roofs and high gates made of pointed logs and bonfires burning on every street corner. I should build by a river. Where are the forests?

MR. LIES. No timber here. Too cold. Ice, no trees.

HARPER. Oh details! I'm sick of details! I'll plant them and grow them. I'll live off caribou fat, I'll melt it over the bonfires and drink it from long, curved goat-horn cups.

It'll be great. I want to make a new world here. So that I never have to go home again.

MR. LIES. As long as it lasts. Ice has a way of melting . . .

HARPER. No. Forever. I can have anything I want here—maybe even companionship, someone who has . . . desire for me. You, maybe.

MR. LIES. It's against the by-laws of the International Order of Travel Agents to get involved with clients. Rules are rules. Anyway, I'm not the one you really want.

HARPER. There isn't anyone . . . maybe an Eskimo. Who could ice-fish for food. And help me build a nest for when the baby comes.

MR. LIES. There are no Eskimo in Antarctica. And you're not really pregnant. You made that up.

HARPER. Well all of this is made up. So if the snow feels cold I'm pregnant. Right? Here, I can be pregnant. And I can have any kind of a baby I want.

MR. LIES. This is a retreat, a vacuum, its virtue is that it lacks everything; deep-freeze for feelings. You can be numb and safe here, that's what you came for. Respect the delicate ecology of your delusions.

HARPER. You mean like no Eskimo in Antarctica.

MR. LIES. Correcto. Ice and snow, no Eskimo. Even hallucinations have laws.

HARPER. Well then who's that?

(The Eskimo appears.)

MR. LIES. An Eskimo.

HARPER. An antarctic Eskimo. A fisher of the polar deep.

MR. LIES. There's something wrong with this picture.

(The Eskimo beckons.)

HARPER. I'm going to like this place. It's my own National Geographic Special! Oh! Oh! (*She holds her stomach*) I think . . . I think I felt her kicking. Maybe I'll give birth to a baby covered with thick white fur, and that way she won't be cold. My breasts will be full of hot cocoa so she doesn't get chilly. And if it gets really cold, she'll have a pouch I can crawl into. Like a marsupial. We'll mend together. That's what we'll do; we'll mend.

SCENE 4

Same day. An abandoned lot in the South Bronx. A homeless Woman is standing near an oil drum in which a fire is burning. Snowfall. Trash around. Hannah enters dragging two heavy suitcases.

HANNAH. Excuse me? I said excuse me? Can you tell me where I am? Is this Brooklyn? Do you know a Pineapple Street? Is there some sort of bus or train or . . . ? I'm lost, I just arrived from Salt Lake. City. Utah? I took the bus that I was told to take and I got off—well it was the very last stop, so I had to get off, and I *asked* the driver was this Brooklyn, and he nodded yes but he was from one of those foreign countries where they think it's good manners to nod at everything even if you have no idea what it is you're nodding at, and in truth I think he spoke no English at all, which I think would make him ineligible for employment on public transportation. The public being English-speaking, mostly. Do you speak English?

(*The Woman nods.*)

HANNAH. I was supposed to be met at the airport by my son. He didn't show and I don't wait more than three and three-quarters hours for *anyone*. I should have been patient, I guess, I. . . . Is this . . .

WOMAN. Bronx.

HANNAH. Is that. . . . The *Bronx*? Well how in the name of Heaven did I get to the Bronx when the bus driver said . . .

WOMAN (*Talking to herself*). Slurp slurp slurp will you STOP that disgusting slurping! YOU DISGUSTING SLURPING FEEDING ANIMAL! Feeding yourself, just feeding yourself, what would it matter, to you or to ANYONE, if you just stopped. Feeding. And DIED?

(*Pause.*)

HANNAH. Can you just tell me where I . . .

WOMAN. Why was the Kosciusko Bridge named after a Polack?

HANNAH. I don't know what you're . . .

WOMAN. That was a joke.

HANNAH. Well what's the punchline?

WOMAN. I don't know.

HANNAH (*Looking around desperately*). Oh for pete's sake, is there anyone else who . . .

WOMAN (*Again, to herself*). Stand further off you fat loathsome whore, you can't have any more of this soup, slurp slurp slurp you animal, and the—I know you'll just go pee it all away and where will you do that? Behind what bush? It's FUCKING COLD out here and I . . .
Oh that's right, because it was supposed have been a tunnel!
That's not very funny.
Have you read the prophecies of Nostradamus?

HANNAH. Who?

WOMAN. Some guy I went out with once somewhere, Nostradamus. Prophet, outcast, eyes like. . . . Scary shit, he . . .

HANNAH. Shut up. Please. Now I want you to stop jabbering for a minute and pull your wits together and tell me how to get to Brooklyn. Because you know! And you are going to tell me! Because there is no one else around to tell me and I am wet and cold and I am

very hungry! So I am sorry you're psychotic but just make the effort—take a deep breath—DO IT!

(*Hannah and the Woman breathe together.*)

HANNAH. That's good. Now exhale.

(*They do.*)

HANNAH. Good. Now how do I get to Brooklyn?

WOMAN. Don't know. Never been. Sorry. Want some soup?

HANNAH. Manhattan? Maybe you know . . . I don't suppose you know the location of the Mormon Visitor's . . .

WOMAN. 65th and Broadway.

HANNAH. How do you . . .

WOMAN. Go there all the time. Free movies. Boring, but you can stay all day.

HANNAH. Well. . . . So how do I . . .

WOMAN. Take the D Train. Next block make a right.

HANNAH. Thank you.

WOMAN. Oh yeah. In the next century I think we will all be insane.

SCENE 5

Same day. Joe and Roy in the study of Roy's brownstone. Roy is wearing an elegant bathrobe. He has made a considerable effort to look well. He isn't well, and he hasn't succeeded much in looking it.

JOE. I can't. The answer's no. I'm sorry.

ROY. Oh, well, apologies . . .
I can't see that there's anyone asking for apologies.

(*Pause.*)

JOE. I'm sorry, Roy.

ROY. Oh, well, apologies.

JOE. My wife is missing, Roy. My mother's coming from Salt Lake to . . . to help look, I guess. I'm supposed to be at the airport now, picking her up but. . . . I just spent two days in a hospital, Roy, with a bleeding ulcer, I was spitting up blood.

ROY. Blood, huh? Look, I'm very busy here and . . .

JOE. It's just a job.

ROY. A job? A *job*? *Washington*! Dumb Utah Mormon hick shit!

JOE. Roy . . .

ROY. WASHINGTON! When Washington called me I was younger than you, you think I said, "Aw fuck no I can't go I got two fingers up my asshole and a little moral nosebleed to boot!" When Washington calls you my pretty young punk friend you go or you can go fuck yourself sideways 'cause the train has pulled out of the station, and you are *out*, nowhere, out in the cold. Fuck you, Mary Jane, get outta here.

JOE. Just let me . . .

ROY. Explain? Ephemera. You broke my heart. Explain that. Explain that.

JOE. I love you. Roy.

There's so much that I want, to be . . . what you see in me, I want to be a participant in the world, in your world, Roy, I want to be capable of that, I've tried, really I have but . . . I can't do this. Not because I don't believe in you, but because I believe in you so much, in what you stand for, at heart, the order, the decency. I would give anything to protect you, but. . . . There are laws I can't break. It's too ingrained. It's not me. There's enough damage I've already done. Maybe you were right, maybe I'm dead.

ROY. You're not dead, boy, you're a sissy.

You love me; that's moving, I'm moved. It's nice to be loved. I warned you about her, didn't I, Joe? But you don't listen to me, why, because you say Roy is smart and Roy's a friend but Roy . . . well, he isn't nice, and you wanna be nice. Right? A nice, nice man!

(Little pause)

You know what my greatest accomplishment was, Joe, in my life, what I am able to look back on and be proudest of? And I have helped make Presidents and unmake them and mayors and more goddam judges than anyone in NYC ever—AND several million dollars, tax-free—and what do you think means the most to me?

You ever hear of Ethel Rosenberg? Huh, Joe, huh?

JOE. Well, yeah, I guess I. . . . Yes.

ROY. Yes. Yes. You have heard of Ethel Rosenberg. Yes. Maybe you even read about her in the history books. If it wasn't for me, Joe, Ethel Rosenberg would be alive today, writing some personal-advice column for *Ms.* magazine. She isn't. Because during the trial, Joe, I was on the phone every day, talking with the judge . . .

JOE. Roy . . .

ROY. Every day, doing what I do best, talking on the telephone, making sure that timid Yid nebbish on the bench did his duty to America, to history. That sweet unprepossessing woman, two kids, boo-hoo-hoo, reminded us all of our little Jewish mamas—she came this close to getting life; I pleaded till I wept to put her in the chair. Me. I did that. I would have fucking pulled the switch if they'd have let me. Why? Be-

cause I fucking hate traitors. Because I fucking hate communists. Was it legal? Fuck legal. Am I a nice man? Fuck nice. They say terrible things about me in the *Nation*. Fuck the *Nation*. You want to be Nice, or you want to be Effective? Make the law, or subject to it. Choose. Your wife chose. A week from today, she'll be back. SHE knows how to get what SHE wants. Maybe I ought to send *her* to Washington.

JOE. I don't believe you.

ROY. Gospel.

JOE. You can't possibly mean what you're saying.

Roy, you were the Assistant United States Attorney on the Rosenberg case, ex parte communication with the judge during the trial would be . . . censurable, at least, probably conspiracy and . . . in a case that resulted in execution, it's . . .

ROY. What? Murder?

JOE. You're not well is all.

ROY. What do you mean, not well? Who's not well?

(Pause.)

JOE. You said . . .

ROY. No I didn't. I said what?

JOE. Roy, you have cancer.

ROY. No I don't.

(Pause.)

JOE. You told me you were dying.

ROY. What the fuck are you talking about Joe? I never said that. I'm in perfect health. There's not a goddam thing wrong with me.

(He smiles)

Shake?

(Joe hesitates. He holds out his hand to Roy. Roy pulls Joe into a close, strong clinch.)

ROY *(More to himself than to Joe)*. It's OK that you hurt me because I love you, baby Joe. That's why I'm so rough on you.

(Roy releases Joe. Joe backs away a step or two.)

ROY. Prodigal son. The world will wipe its dirty hands all over you.

JOE. It already has, Roy.

ROY. Now go.

(Roy shoves Joe, hard. Joe turns to leave. Roy stops him, turns him around.)

ROY *(Smoothing Joe's lapels, tenderly)*. I'll always be here, waiting for you . . .

(Then again, with sudden violence, he pulls Joe close, violently)

What did you want from me, what was all this, what do you want, you treacherous ungrateful little . . .

(Joe, very close to belting Roy grabs him by the front of his robe, and propels him across the length of the room. He holds Roy at arm's length, the other arm ready to hit.)

ROY *(Laughing softly, almost pleading to be hit)*. Transgress a little, Joseph.

(Joe releases Roy.)

ROY. There are so many laws; find one you can break.

(Joe hesitates, then leaves, backing out. When Joe has gone, Roy doubles over in great pain, which he's been hiding throughout the scene with Joe.)

ROY. Ah, Christ . . .
Andy! Andy! Get in here! Andy!

(The door opens but it isn't Andy. A small Jewish Woman dressed modestly in a fifties hat and coat stands in the doorway. The room darkens.)

ROY. Who the fuck are you? The new nurse?

(The figure in the doorway says nothing. She stares at Roy. A pause. Roy looks at her carefully, gets up, crosses to her. He crosses back to the chair, sits heavily.)

ROY. Aw, fuck. Ethel.

ETHEL ROSENBERG *(Her manner is friendly, her voice is ice-cold)*. You don't look good, Roy.

ROY. Well, Ethel. I don't feel good.

ETHEL ROSENBERG. But you lost a lot of weight. That suits you. You were heavy back then. Zaftig, mit hips.

ROY. I haven't been that heavy since 1960. We were all heavier back then, before the body thing started. Now I look like a skeleton. They stare.

ETHEL ROSENBERG. That shit's really hit the fan, huh, Roy?

(Little pause. Roy nods.)

ETHEL ROSENBERG. Well, the fun's just started.

ROY. What is this, Ethel, Halloween? You trying to scare me?

(Ethel says nothing.)

ROY. Well you're wasting your time! I'm scarier than you any day of the week! So beat it, Ethel! BOOO! BET-TER DEAD THAN RED! Somebody trying to shake

me up? HAH HAH! From the throne of God in heaven to the belly of hell, you can all fuck your-selves and then go jump in the lake because I'M NOT AFRAID OF YOU OR DEATH OR HELL OR ANYTHING!

ETHEL ROSENBERG. Be seeing you soon, Roy. Julius sends his regards.

ROY. Yeah, well send this to Julius!

(He flips the bird in her direction, stands and moves towards her. Halfway across the room he slumps to the floor, breathing laboriously, in pain.)

ETHEL ROSENBERG. You're a very sick man, Roy.

ROY. Oh God . . . ANDY!

ETHEL ROSENBERG. Hmmm. He doesn't hear you, I guess. We should call the ambulance.

(She goes to the phone)

Hah! Buttons! Such things they got now.
What do I dial, Roy?

(Pause. Roy looks at her, then)

ROY. 911.

ETHEL ROSENBERG. *(Dials the phone)*? It sings!
(Imitating dial tones) La la la . . .
Huh.
Yes, you should please send an ambulance to the home of Mister Roy Cohn, the famous lawyer.
What's the address, Roy?

ROY *(A beat, then)*. 244 East 87th.

ETHEL ROSENBERG. 244 East 87th Street. No apartment number, he's got the whole building.
My name? *(A beat)* Ethel Greenglass Rosenberg.
(Small smile) Me? No I'm not related to Mr. Cohn. An old friend.

(She hangs up)

They said a minute.

ROY. I have all the time in the world.

ETHEL ROSENBERG. You're immortal.

ROY. I'm immortal. Ethel. *(He forces himself to stand)* I have forced my way into history. I ain't never gonna die.

ETHEL ROSENBERG *(A little laugh, then)*. History is about to crack wide open. Millennium approaches.

SCENE 6

Late that night. Prior's bedroom. Prior 1 watching Prior in bed, who is staring back at him, terrified. Tonight Prior 1 is dressed in weird alchemical robes and hat over his historical clothing and he carries a long palm-leaf bundle.

PRIOR 1. Tonight's the night! Aren't you excited? Tonight she arrives! Right through the roof! Ha-adam, Ha-gadol . . .

PRIOR 2 (*Appearing similarly attired*). Lumen! Phosphor! Fluor! Candle! An unending billowing of scarlet and . . .

PRIOR. Look. Garlic. A mirror. Holy water. A crucifix. FUCK OFF! Get the fuck out of my room! GO!

PRIOR 1 (*To Prior 2*). Hard as a hickory knob, I'll bet.

PRIOR 2. We all tumesce when they approach. We wax full, like moons.

PRIOR 1. Dance.

PRIOR. Dance?

PRIOR 1. Stand up, dammit, give us your hands, dance!

PRIOR 2. Listen . . .

(*A lone oboe begins to play a little dance tune.*)

PRIOR 2. Delightful sound. Care to dance?

PRIOR. Please leave me alone, please just let me sleep . . .

PRIOR 2. Ah, he wants someone familiar. A partner who knows his steps. (*To Prior*) Close your eyes. Imagine . . .

PRIOR. I don't . . .

PRIOR 2. Hush. Close your eyes.

(*Prior does.*)

PRIOR 2. Now open them.

(*Prior does. Louis appears. He looks gorgeous. The music builds gradually into a full-blooded, romantic dance tune.*)

PRIOR. Lou.

LOUIS. Dance with me.

PRIOR. I can't, my leg, it hurts at night . . .
Are you . . . a ghost, Lou?

LOUIS. No. Just spectral. Lost to myself. Sitting all day on cold park benches. Wishing I could be with you. Dance with me, babe . . .

(*Prior stands up. The legs stop hurting. They begin to dance. The music is beautiful.*)

PRIOR 1 (*To Prior 2*). Hah. Now I see why he's got no children. He's a sodomite.

PRIOR 2. Oh be quiet, you medieval gnome, and let them dance.

PRIOR 1. I'm not interfering, I've done my bit. Hooray, hooray, the messenger's come, now I'm blowing off. I don't like it here.

(*Prior 1 vanishes.*)

PRIOR 2. The twentieth century. Oh dear, the world has gotten so terribly, terribly old.

(*Prior 2 vanishes. Louis and Prior waltz happily. Lights fade back to normal. Louis vanishes.*

Prior dances alone.

Then suddenly, the sound of wings fills the room.)

SCENE 7

Split scene: Prior alone in his apartment; Louis alone in the park.

Again, a sound of beating wings.

PRIOR. Oh don't come in here don't come in . . . LOUIS!!
No. My name is Prior Walter, I am . . . the scion of an ancient line, I am . . . abandoned I . . . no, my name is . . . is . . . Prior and I live . . . *here and now*, and . . . in the dark, in the dark, the Recording Angel opens its hundred eyes and snaps the spine of the Book of Life and . . . hush! Hush!
I'm talking nonsense, I . . .
No more mad scene, hush, hush . . .

(*Louis in the park on a bench. Joe approaches, stands at a distance. They stare at each other, then Louis turns away.*)

LOUIS. Do you know the story of Lazarus?

JOE. Lazarus?

LOUIS. Lazarus. I can't remember what happens, exactly.

JOE. I don't. . . . Well, he was dead, Lazarus, and Jesus breathed life into him. He brought him back from death.

LOUIS. Come here often?

JOE. No. Yes. Yes.

LOUIS. Back from the dead. You believe that really happened?

JOE. I don't know anymore what I believe.

LOUIS. This is quite a coincidence. Us meeting.

JOE. I followed you.
From work. I . . . followed you here.

(*Pause.*)

LOUIS. You followed me.
You probably saw me that day in the washroom and thought: there's a sweet guy, sensitive, cries for friends in trouble.

JOE. Yes.

LOUIS. Well I fooled you. Crocodile tears. Nothing . . .

(*He touches his heart, shrugs*)

(*Joe reaches tentatively to touch Louis's face.*)

LOUIS (*Pulling back*). What are you doing? Don't do that.

JOE (*Withdrawing his hand*). Sorry. I'm sorry.

LOUIS. I'm . . . just not . . . I think, if you touch me, your hand might fall off or something. Worse things have happened to people who have touched me.

JOE. Please.

Oh, boy . . .

Can I . . .

I . . . want . . . to touch you. Can't I please just touch you . . . um, here?

(*He puts his hand on one side of Louis's face. He holds it there*)

I'm going to hell for doing this.

LOUIS. Big deal. You think it could be any worse than New York City?

(*He puts his hand on Joe's hand. He takes Joe's hand away from his face, holds it for a moment, then*) Come on.

JOE. Where?

LOUIS. Home. With me.

JOE. This makes no sense. I mean I don't know you.

LOUIS. Likewise.

JOE. And what you do know about me you don't like.

LOUIS. The Republican stuff?

JOE. Yeah, well for starters.

LOUIS. I don't not like that. I *hate* that.

JOE. So why on earth should we . . .

(*Louis goes to Joe and kisses him.*)

LOUIS. Strange bedfellows. I don't know. I never made it with one of the damned before. I would really rather not have to spend tonight alone.

JOE. I'm a pretty terrible person, Louis.

LOUIS. Lou.

JOE. No, I really am. I don't think I deserve being loved.

LOUIS. There? See? We already have a lot in common.

(*Louis stands, begins to walk away. He turns, looks back at Joe, Joe follows. They exit.*)

(*Prior listens. At first no sound, then once again, the sound of beating wings, frighteningly near.*)

PRIOR. That sound, that sound, it. . . . What is that, like birds or something, like a *really* big bird, I'm fright-

ened, I . . . no, no fear, find the anger, find the . . . anger, my blood is clean, my brain is fine, I can handle pressure, I am a gay man and I am used to pressure, to trouble, I am tough and strong and. . . . Oh. Oh my goodness. I . . . (*He is washed over by an intense sexual feeling*) Ooohhhh. . . . I'm hot, I'm . . . so . . . aw Jeez what is going on here I . . . must have a fever I . . .

(*The bedside lamp flickers wildly as the bed begins to roll forward and back. There is a deep bass creaking and groaning from the bedroom ceiling, like the timbers of a ship under immense stress, and from above a fine rain of plaster dust.*)

PRIOR. OH!

PLEASE, OH PLEASE! Something's coming in here, I'm scared, I don't like this at all, something's approaching and I. . . . OH!

(*There is a great blaze of triumphal music, heralding. The light turns an extraordinary harsh, cold, pale blue, then a rich, brilliant warm golden color, then a hot bilious green, and then finally a spectacular royal purple. Then silence.*)

PRIOR (*An awestruck whisper*). God almighty . . .
Very Steven Spielberg.

(*A sound, like a plummeting meteor, tears down from very, very far above the earth, hurtling at an incredible velocity towards the bedroom; the light seems to be sucked out of the room as the projectile approaches; as the room reaches darkness, we hear a terrifying CRASH as something immense strikes earth; the whole building shudders and a part of the bedroom ceiling, lots of plaster and lathe and wiring, crashes to the floor. And then in a shower of unearthly white light, spreading great opalescent gray-silver wings, the Angel descends into the room and floats above the bed.*)

ANGEL.

Greetings, Prophet;
The Great Work begins:
The Messenger has arrived.

(*Blackout.*)

END OF PART ONE

COMMENTARY

Note: The following essay represents a single interpretation of the play. For other perspectives on Angels in America, Part One: Millennium Approaches, *consult the essays listed below.*

Although *Angels in America* has emerged as the most decorated and widely accepted play about gay issues, it is not the first to portray the subject sympathetically. As early as 1592 Christopher Marlowe wrote about the relationship between King Edward II and Piers Gaveston in *Edward II*. Shakespeare addresses the subject in *Troilus and Cressida* in the Achilles-Patroclus subplot, and there have been a number of recent studies exploring homoeroticism in his works. Subsequent playwrights, such as Oscar Wilde, Noel Coward, Robert Anderson, Tennessee Williams, and Edward Albee (all open about their homosexuality), have included gay issues in their works. But these works are not generally considered as "gay plays" in the manner we recognize *Angels in America* as such.

Mart Crowley's *The Boys in the Band* (1968) was the first Broadway play to place the gay community and its distinctive subculture at center stage. Crowley's success paved the way for such respected playwrights as Terence McNally, Harvey Fierstein, and Lanford Wilson. Gay musicals, such as *La Cage aux Folles* (*The Bird Cage*, 1983), were also accepted within Broadway's mainstream. The AIDS crisis, which surfaced in the early 1980s, prompted many dramatic responses, most notably Larry Kramer's *The Normal Heart* and William Hoffman's *As Is*. By 1993 the American mainstream eagerly embraced *Angels in America*, not as a "trailblazer" but as a necessary play about the state of the union as it entered the third millennium.

Kushner subtitled his two-part, seven-hour epic *A Gay Fantasia on National Themes*. The "themes" in question concern the AIDS crisis; religious, racial, and sexual bigotry; drug addiction; and contemporary American politics, specifically the "conservative revolution" fostered by the Reagan presidency. Kushner attacks the belief that it is "OK to be AIDS-phobic and homophobic," and he advocates federal intervention to achieve equal rights for gay men and lesbians. Although *Millennium Approaches* is a play about despair, its sequel, *Perestroika*, ends with what Kushner calls "great quiet and hope." "Perestroika" is a Russian term coined by former Premier Gorbachev to describe a major change in political attitudes. In it, Kushner has found "a more perfect metaphor for human change than it was in the heady days of 1990 when the world seemed to have miraculously transformed." Hence the "hope" that pervades *Perestroika*.

The success of *Angels in America*, however, transcends any political message ("I don't think art is a public service announcement," Kushner says). Rather, its appeal derives from its audacious scope, its extraordinary mixture of styles, and ultimately its sympathetic portrait of people—straights as well as gays—who suffer unbearable loneliness, uncertainty, and pain.

Angels in America is a virtual casebook of contemporary (specifically postmodern) theatrical technique.

- It is episodic, even cinematic, in structure. Events fade, blur, and merge into one another, and they often occur simultaneously. One set of characters discusses an issue that is echoed by another conversation in a different locale. See especially Act II, Scene 9 which, according to Kushner, should be played "fast and obviously furious; overlapping is fine; the proceedings may be a little confusing but not the final result."
- Locales—Salt Lake City; Washington, DC; the Arctic Circle; Central Europe; even Heaven itself—segue into one another almost seamlessly. One senses that the whole world, if not the universe, is in disarray.
- The public world of history overlaps the private world of the individual (a rather Shakespearean concept); ultimately, the history of America at the end of the millennium is the history of individuals in conflict with personal as well as larger social issues.
- Kushner freely mixes styles and genres. The issues are serious, nearly tragic, yet comedy in all its forms dominates the play. Even as Prior lies dying of AIDS, Belize, a campy

ex–drag queen, upstages the action. Realism, Expressionism, fantasy, agit-prop, vaude-ville sketch, and—most importantly—a grand theatricality meld with one another to create one of the most ambitious plays in the history of the American theater.

- Actors are asked to play multiple roles. The actor who plays the Angel is also seen, quite deliberately, as the homeless lady in the South Bronx, the grotesquely hilarious real estate saleswoman in Salt Lake City, and the nurse. One actor plays a man (Rabbi Chemelwitz) and a woman (Hannah), a Jew and a Christian. We see variants on the same character simultaneously: the dying Prior is visited by his ancestors, a medieval monk and a fop out of the Restoration Theatre.

- Pop culture (i.e., references to such film stars as Judy Garland and Steven Spielberg) complements Marxist political tracts, biblical allusions, and other notable literature; vulgarity coexists with some of the most poetic stage language since Tennessee Williams. The result is a multilayered text that defies categorization.

- Despite its much-praised language, the play's most memorable moments are visual, even ritualistic: the descent of a single feather from on high, the eruption of a sacred book from the bowels of the earth, and—most famously—the apparition of the angel with "great opalescent gray-silver wings" in the final moment. Kushner's is very much "a theater of images."

Kushner's multifaceted dramaturgy, heightened by an inventive showmanship unseen in most recent nonmusical theater, creates an ambience that transcends the particular "national themes" he explores. By mixing styles and theatrical effects, the play emerges as something more profound than a contemporary political tract. Its use of archetypes, most notably the Angel of Death and her intimations of "the Continental Principality of America," extends the parameters of the playwright's message that "everywhere things are collapsing."

Kushner's drama follows a cross-section of tormented Americans who epitomize that collapse. Joe and Harper Pitt, staid Mormons, must confront their sexuality and mental deterioration. Harper's Valium-induced hallucinations are among the most troubling—and comic—in the play. Joe's mother, Hannah, can confront her son's dilemma only by denying it. Similarly, Louis, Prior's lover, chooses to leave his dying companion rather than face the reality of their situation. The mutual scenes shared by this quartet of lovers are the most moving in the play.

Still, it is Roy Cohn, a character of Shakespearean dimensions, who dominates the play. He is dying of AIDS, yet he denies his reality ("It's just liver cancer"). He does not want to be branded as a homosexual because homosexuals are—in his mind—only weak men "who in fifteen years of trying cannot get a pissant antidiscrimination bill through City Council." In his twisted logic, he is "a heterosexual man . . . who fucks around with guys." And in Kushner's mind Cohn is the quintessential hypocrite who justifies his ruthless actions as serving the public good, even as he practices the very acts he condemns. Cohn is the dark angel hovering over the American landscape, and his hypocrisy is seen as more destructive than Harper's drug addiction, Joe's sexual ambiguity, Louis's callousness toward his dying lover, or the purportedly indecent acts committed by consenting adults. It is Cohn's viciousness and contradictions that make his the most memorable and disturbing role in a memorable, disturbing, and entertaining play.

Other perspectives on Angels in America, Part One: Millennium Approaches

Geis, Deborah R., and Steven F. Kruger (eds.). *Millennium Approaches: Essays on Angels in America.* Ann Arbor: University of Michigan Press, 1997.

Rogoff, Gordon. "Angels in America, Devils in the Wings." *Theater* 24 (1993): 21–29.

Vorlicky, Robert (ed.). *Tony Kushner in Conversation.* Ann Arbor: University of Michigan Press, 1998.

SHOWCASE ■ TONY KUSHNER ON BERTOLT BRECHT AND ALTERNATIVES TO CAPITALISM

The interviews in this Showcase were conducted by theater critics Anne Marie Welsh and Michael Phillips and first appeared in the San Diego Union-Tribune; they are reprinted with the newspaper's permission.

"Things are going very badly all over the world," Tony Kushner said in the summer of 1995, two years after his *Angels in America* won every major theater award in England and America. "I'm beginning to reach a point," he continued, "when I think of optimism as obscene. The world is in the worst shape now it's ever been in. One has the responsibility of not despairing. But there's a difference between not despairing and being silly." And why, the playwright was asked, are things going so badly all over the world? "Because we've stopped looking for alternatives to capitalism," he answered readily. "As long as we've lost that ability, then we're in unimaginable trouble."

Kushner came to this conclusion around the time of the West Coast premiere of his *Slavs!*, before he began work on his Afghanistan-set *Homebody/Kabul*, and long before the terrorist attacks of September 11. Yet by spring of 2002, when he gave the commencement address at Vassar College, Kushner had pushed through towards hope which he called "not a choice, [but a] moral obligation, an obligation to the cells in your body. Hope is a function of those cells, it's a bodily function the same as breathing and eating and sleeping. Hope is not naïve, hope grapples endlessly with despair. . . . lose your hope and you lose your soul." Even as his plays anatomize the world's political economies, with their terrible injustices and oppressions, Kushner sows the seeds of that hope, rooted in moral choice. *Slavs!* began, for instance, as a series of leftover scenes from the *Perestroika* half of the two-part *Angels*. In near burlesque style (the old Bolshevik Prelapsarianov, for instance, drops dead of talking too much), *Slavs!* explores

the fate of post-perestroika Russia. Its director Michael Greif, then of La Jolla Playhouse, said in a press interview that the play, which changes tone as it progresses, shares certain traits with those of the left-leaning British playwright Caryl Churchill [see *Top Girls*]—"the same pointedness, spareness, the same fierce intelligence, and a great huge heart apparent as well in his sympathy for those suffering injustice."

A news and political junkie, Kushner referred to the clippings scattered about his New York desk. One described three Greek men arrested there after they had bought eight tons of bomb-grade zirconium from a general in the Ukraine, stored it in a warehouse in Queens, and spread the word they would sell it to the highest bidder, namely Iraq. Another described the non-personhood of women and other horrors of Taliban rule in Afghanistan. Characteristically, Kushner sensed troublespots before conflict with Western capitalist democracies erupted.

Although Kushner was not cynical about the success of his radically liberal *Angels in America*, he viewed its acceptance as conditioned by the 1992 election results. "*Angels in America* plugged into the Clinton fifteen minutes," he explained, placing a different spin on the popularity of a work that had extended runs in London, New York and San Francisco before it toured the U.S. "I was naïve enough to think that the public believed 13 years of Reagan and Bush were enough. I didn't think much of Clinton as a man but thought he would be a fairly good liberal, an alternative to the crazy nihilism behind Newt Gingrich," leader of the conservative Republicans who took over the Congress during the mid-term elections of 1994. "Our society has mobilized itself to deny people an education. When you do that, you deny them the right to choose good leaders. It was the abolitionists who made Abe Lincoln become Abraham Lincoln. He was just a backwoods lawyer with a capacity for moral vision and a command of rhetoric until his vision was awakened."

A charming man with a squinty grin and a fierce interest in Marx, the self-described "nerd," a New Yorker, gay, Jewish and agnostic, said the sources of *Angels in America* go far back into his childhood. When he was 11, he said, his music teacher father gave him the book *The Nightmare Decade*, about Sen. Joseph McCarthy's Red Menace campaign. He recalled being mesmerized by the spectre of Roy Cohn, McCarthy's right-hand man. (In *Angels*, one of the characters describes Cohn as "the polestar of human evil.")

Kushner became aware of his own homosexuality when he was a teenager but didn't come out to his parents until his early 20s, having shelved the notion proposed to him by one therapist of "curing" his gay orientation. After graduating in medieval studies from Columbia University and enrolling at New York University's graduate theater program, he wrote and directed throughout the 1980s, before completing his first play. It was inspired by Brecht's *Fear and Misery in the Third Reich* and called *A Bright Room Called Day*, an over-the-top drama which pilloried the Reagan administration in cruder and less sophisticated ways than *Angels* does.

After *Slavs!* Kushner set out "to cleanse the palette" by creating a faithful adaptation of a major work by his favorite playwright—*The Good Woman of Setzuan* by Bertolt Brecht. Of Brecht, Kushner said, "He's saying some incredibly simple things in it—that there's something terribly wrong with the world when human pity, the pity one feels when one sees a child eating garbage, for instance, becomes a kind of monstrous weakness. A world where the good do so badly and the wicked do so well . . . He's simply saying: what is this? Why are we living in a world like this?" Kushner added that he hesitated at first to tackle the Brecht play because "I do think Brecht is the greatest playwright since Shakespeare, and I think he's without question the greatest writer for the theater of this century. And he's the most important writer of any writer to me . . . It would be like translating Shakespeare: You just have to know that what you're touching is something immeasurably greater than yourself."

Like many of his contemporaries, Kushner saw director Richard Foreman's Public Theatre revival of Brecht and Kurt Weill's *The Threepenny Opera* in the 1970s and was changed by it. The cynicism, the dark exuberance, the deceptively seductive tactics of the brilliant score all came through. Soon Kushner came to see Brecht as proof that leftist politics could inform dramatic work without falling back on tired bourgeois theatrical forms. Still, Kushner expressed wariness of such phrases as "Brechtian" or "the alienation effect" because they imply that "you're supposed to alienate the audience, or that people aren't supposed to feel anything. So you often see Brecht productions where people are just acting badly and stupidly. Or: On the other hand people say, 'Well, it's just like any other play, let's just do it that way'."

Kushner pointed to Brecht's journal descriptions of the frankly artifical quality of the alienation effect. To achieve it, he said, "The actor must give up his complete conversion into the stage character. He shows the character, he quotes his lines, he repeats a real-life incident." And the audience is purposely not carried away. Kushner pointed to Anna Deavere Smith [see Showcase on Docudrama] as a great contemporary exponent of the A-effect,

in her "gestic acting. She's completely in a role and a little bit outside of it at the same time. It's presentational as well as representational. And it's marvelously precise," the admiring playwright said.

After these projects, Kushner turned to a rewrite of his earlier *Hydriotaphia*, a comic pastiche about the roots of capitalism in the life of the 17th century English scientist, writer and eccentric, Sir Thomas Browne. And then, in 1999, Kushner began researching and writing a contemporary play, its divergent acts set in London and Kabul. The first act, which has echoes of Virginia Woolf's subtle novel of consciousness *Mrs. Dalloway*, is a long monologue for a curious Englishwoman who's preparing for a party, reading a guidebook about Kabul, and gathering fezzes from an Afghani shopkeeper. The second act takes the woman's husband and daughter to Afghanistan, to search for her. It's a country which the aid worker character Quongo calls "a populated disaster," and what the woman's family finds there, besides a report of her beating and dismembering, is a confrontation with The Other that subtly opens and changes them. Critics noted how "eerily prescient" Kushner was in his awareness of the violent destructiveness of the Taliban and the global significance of its takeover when Western forces abandoned the region; the remark was so often repeated that in the published script of *Homebody/Kabul*, Kushner

writes that a friend suggested he adopt the drag stage name Eara Lee Prescent. The play had a praised run at New York's Public Theatre where it was met by rave reviews for the first act and a more mixed response to the second and third. It was scheduled to open in Los Angeles soon after, but Kushner pulled the play and instead went to work on a revision.

Having burlesqued the collapse of the Soviet Union as it attempted to adopt Western style capitalism, and having sensed the ferocious hostility that the Taliban and other fundamentalist groups would spread globally, Kushner now saw the condition of the world as even worse than when he spoke up in 1994 and 1995. But the poetic vitality of language, the generosity of emotion, and the sheer, dazzling theatricality of *Homebody/Kabul* remains, as in *Angels in America*, its own antidote to dread. Towards the end of his "Afterword" to *Homebody/Kabul*, Kushner quotes what he calls Brecht's "immortal phrase" to describe our own times: "There is injustice everywhere/and no rebellion." But after reminding us that legend names Kabul as the burial place of the primal murderer Cain, Kushner also quotes from the Talmud: "I read the following sentence, which suggests another kind of prologue to creation, perhaps offers hope for some prelude other than destruction, some other way for the future to commence: 'Repentance preceded the world'."

THE WOMAN WHO WAS A RED DEER DRESSED FOR THE DEER DANCE

DIANE GLANCY

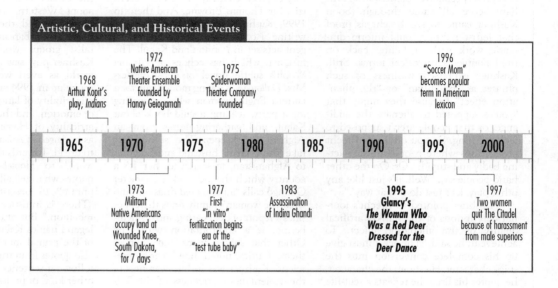

Artistic, Cultural, and Historical Events

1968 Arthur Kopit's play, *Indians*

1972 Native American Theater Ensemble founded by Hanay Geiogamah

1975 Spiderwoman Theater Company founded

1996 "Soccer Mom" becomes popular term in American lexicon

1965 — 1970 — 1975 — 1980 — 1985 — 1990 — 1995 — 2000

1973 Militant Native Americans occupy land at Wounded Knee, South Dakota, for 7 days

1977 First "in vitro" fertilization begins era of the "test tube baby"

1983 Assassination of Indira Ghandi

1995 Glancy's *The Woman Who Was a Red Deer Dressed for the Deer Dance*

1997 Two women quit The Citadel because of harassment from male superiors

DIANE GLANCY (1941–)

Part Cherokee, part German/English poet, Diane Glancy, a novelist, playwright, and screenwriter, is emerging as among the most respected voices of the new generation of Native American artists. Although her writing style appears to be experimental in nature, nevertheless Glancy's descriptive landscapes are symbols of an America that is redefining itself as it enters a new millennium. Glancy's vision, however, never becomes didactic; rather, she allows the humanity of her dramas and poetry to penetrate our emotional and psychological reality. Often, her plays juxtapose a skewed contemporary society with an American Indian culture, which is usually ignored or relegated to the kitsch of Hollywood.

An interview conducted by Roberto Pomo in September 2002 reveals Glancy's thematic and artistic concerns.

Given your deep commitment to dramatic discourse, in your opinion, is there a specific aesthetic generally found in the writing of Native American theater and drama?

I don't know what to say about a specific dramatic aesthetic. Words like "dream-like," "violent," "alcoholic" come to mind. There are similarities in native writing: the importance of family, the importance of land, and the importance of the spirit world—the extended world of the unseen, whether spirits, animal spirits, ancestors, or whatever. The presence of visions is another important aspect. Something unseen can appear anytime. Many native novels have several narrators and are not chronological—and that feel of a community narrative and something moving in and out of time is there. There is a magic realism in native drama for which I have tried to find another name than *magic realism*: maybe *realized improbabilities* or *implausible realities* is close. I have an essay on native dramatic theory called, "Further (Farther): Creating Dialogue to Talk about Native American Plays," where I talk about these issues. [See Commentary for citation.]

As a writer having to confront, for example, issues of gender and cultural assimilation, do you, therefore, view dramatic writing from a political point of view?

I believe that the politics of a creative piece should be indirect. I am thinking of two South African writers: Nadine Gordimer, who faces apartheid head-on and beats away at it, and J.M. Coetzee, who imbeds the issues in the art of his text. I prefer Coetzee's approach.

Do you approach the writing of poetry in the same manner as you do a dramatic text? A screenplay?

Poetry and drama are different. In drama the conflict/resolution, the character change and epiphany are utmost. Drama revolves around the characters in conflict with one another, or a conflict from something within. Poetry is an abstraction, such as a dream, that leaves its residue in the waking world. I also said earlier that native drama is dreamlike. So there is a contradiction, which is another trademark of native drama.

A screenplay is least artistic—it serves as blueprint for something else and follows a prescription. I'm working on a screenplay, *Flutie*, about a young, mixed-blood girl who is so shy she can't speak in front of others, though she speaks to her family. It is the story of how she finds her voice through circumstance and an act of the will. I was talking to someone about the script, and they asked, where is the murder? The sex? The violence? Well, the actions of a dysfunctional family are there, but that is not the main story—it's the character development of Flutie and her interface between past and present that is the main concern.

To what do you attribute the lack of a vital Native American voice in the landscape of the professional and commercial American theater?

I agree there is a lack of a vital Native American voice in the landscape of professional and commercial American theater. As popular as native mythology is, usually in connection with a pseudo native spirituality, no one seems too interested in the realities and struggles of native life. Perhaps it is the implication of guilt. There is still so much explanation and propaganda in current native scripts. It takes a long time for the essence to come through in that indirect way I mentioned earlier. All the students in my Native American Literature and Film course ask, "Where are more Indian movies made by Indians?" That same question applies to plays. It may take the multiple input of writer, choreographer, musician, to uncover the heart of native theater. I'm not talking about a musical, but a multi-layered drama where sound and image interact with the words. I recently had an experience with Native Voices at the Autry, a native theater group that works with the Autry Museum of Western Heritage in Los Angeles. In producing one of my plays, *Jump Kiss*, they pulled a string of words through the intersection of mythology and technology. Maybe acting companies like Native Voices will be the warriors of native theater.

Glancy's eclectic writings include a number of fictional works: *The Only Piece of Furniture* (1996), *Pushing the Bear: A Novel of the Trail of Tears* (1996), *Fuller Man: A Novel*

(1998), *Claiming Breath* (1999), and *The Closets of Heaven* (1999). Her poetry includes *Iron Woman* (1990), *(Ado)ration* (1999), and *The Relief of America* (2000). An anthology of Glancy's plays, *American Gypsy* (2002), reflects a strong commitment to a multicultural theater. A highly successful novel, *Flutie* (1998), has been adapted as a screenplay through a Sundance Screenwriting Fellowship. Glancy's numerous literary prizes include the American Book Award, the National Federation of State Poetry Societies Award, the Native American Prose Award, the Capricorn Award from the Writers Voice, and a National Endowment for the Humanities Award. A Master of Fine Arts graduate of the influential Writer's Workshop of the University of Iowa, Glancy is presently Professor of English at Macalester College in St. Paul, Minnesota.

AS YOU READ *THE WOMAN WHO WAS A RED DEER DRESSED FOR THE DEER DANCE*

Glancy herself provides us with the most useful guide to understanding both the structure and meaning of her play.

> *My deer dress is the way I felt,*
> *transformed by the power of ceremony.*

This dramatic/poetic piece is an intermixing of ethnographic material (the story of *Ahw'uste* was taken from Doi on Ahu'usti and Asudi on Ahw'usti in *Friends of Thunder, Tales of the Oklahoma Cherokees* (Frank and Anna Kilpatrick, eds., University of Oklahoma Press, Norman, 1995), pieces of the old language (Cherokee), and contemporary materials (the granddaughter's life in a soup kitchen and dance bars). It is a dialogue/monologue between a grandmother and her granddaughter, each arguing against the other for her own way of life. The grandmother talks about stories and the spirits and the red deer dress she has made to feel more in tune with *Ahw'uste*, a mythological spirit deer. The granddaughter talks about the problems of a contemporary life, including her experiences with several men. The grandmother continues talking about *Ahw'uste* and the spirits, who in the end, she realizes, let her down. "Damned spirits. Didn't always help out. Let us have it rough sometimes," she says as she talks of hunger and the uncertainty she faced in her life. The granddaughter says she has to look for work, which she can't find, and says she doesn't have time for the *Ahw'uste* and the spirits, and longs for more practical help from her grandmother. In the end, the granddaughter enters some of her grandmother's world and says, "You know, I've learned she told me more without speaking than she did with her words."

THE WOMAN WHO WAS A RED DEER DRESSED FOR THE DEER DANCE

DIANE GLANCY

*My deer dress is the way I felt,
transformed by the power of ceremony.*

In this I try. Well, I try. To combine the overlapping realities of myth, imagination and memory with spaces for the silences. To make a story. The voice speaking in different agencies. Well, I try to move on with the voice in its guises. A young woman and her grandmother in a series of scenelets. Divided by a line of flooring. Shifting between dialogue and monologue. Not with the linear construct of conflict/resolution, but with the story moving like rain on a windshield, between differing and unreliable experiences.

GIRL. Have you heard of *Ahw'uste?*
GRANDMOTHER. I have, but I've forgotten.
GIRL. They said they fed her.
GRANDMOTHER. Yes, they did.
GIRL. What was she?
GRANDMOTHER. I don't know.
GIRL. A deer?
GRANDMOTHER. Yes, a deer. A small deer.
GIRL. She lived in the house, didn't she?
GRANDMOTHER. Yes, she did. She was small.
GIRL. They used to talk about her a long time ago, didn't they?
GRANDMOTHER. Yes, they did.
GIRL. Did you ever see one of the deer?
GRANDMOTHER. I saw the head of one once. Through the window. Her head was small, and she had tiny horns.
GIRL. Like a goat?
GRANDMOTHER. Yes, like that.
GIRL. Where did you see her?
GRANDMOTHER. I don't know. Someone had her. I just saw her. That's all.

GIRL. You saw the head?
GRANDMOTHER. Yes, just the head.
GIRL. What did they call her?
GRANDMOTHER. A small deer.
GIRL. Where did you see her?
GRANDMOTHER. What do they call it down there?
GIRL. Deer Creek.
GRANDMOTHER. Yes, that's where I saw her.
GIRL. What did they use her for?
GRANDMOTHER. I don't know. There were bears there, too. And larger deer.
GIRL. Elk maybe?
GRANDMOTHER. Yes, they called them elk.
GIRL. Why did they have them?
GRANDMOTHER. They used them for medicine.
GIRL. How did they use them?
GRANDMOTHER. They used their songs.
GIRL. The deer sang?
GRANDMOTHER. No, they were just there. They made the songs happen.
GIRL. The elk, too?
GRANDMOTHER. Yes, the elk, too.
GIRL. And the moose?
GRANDMOTHER. Yes, the moose.

GIRL. It was like talking to myself when I stayed with her. If I asked her something, she answered flat as the table between us.

Open your deer mouth and talk. You never say anything on your own. I could wear a deer dress. I could change into a deer like you. We could deer dance in the woods under the red birds. The blue jay. The finch.

U-da-tlv:da de-s-gi-ne-hv'-si, E-li'-sin
Pass me the cream, Grandmother.

My cup and saucer on the oilcloth.

How can you be a deer? You only have two legs.

GRANDMOTHER. I keep the others under my dress.

GIRL. It was a wordless world she gave me. Not silent, but wordless. Oh, she spoke, but her words seemed hollow. I had to listen to her deer noise. I had to think what she meant. It was like having a conversation with myself. I asked. And I answered. Well—I could hear what I wanted.

When I was with her, I talked and never stopped because her silence ate me like buttered toast.

What was she saying? Her words were in my own hearing?

I had to know what she said before I could hear it?

GRANDMOTHER. I don't like this world anymore. We're reduced to what can be seen and felt. We're brought from the universe of the head into the kitchen full of heat and cold.

GIRL. She fought to live where we aren't tied to table and fork and knife and chair.

It was her struggle against what happens to us.

Why can't you let me in just once and speak to me as one of your own? You know I have to go into the *seeable*—live away from the world of imagination. You could give me more.

GIRL. You work the church soup kitchen before? You slop up the place, and I get to clean up. You night shifts think you're tough shit. But I tell you, you don't know nothing. I think you took my jean jacket. The one with Jesus on the cross in sequins on the back. Look—I see your girl wearing it, I'll have you on the floor.

Don't think I don't know who's taking the commodities—I'm watching those boxes of macaroni and cheese disappear.

I know it was you who lost the key to the storeroom, and I had to pay for the locksmith to change the lock. They kept nearly my whole check. I couldn't pay rent. I only got four payments left on my truck. I'm not losing it.

GIRL. She said once, there were wings the deer had when it flew. You couldn't see them, but they were there. They pulled out from the red deer dress. Like leaves opened from the kitchen table—

Like the stories that rode on her silence. You knew they were there. But you had to decide what they meant. Maybe that's what she gave me—the ability to fly when I knew I had no wings. When I was left out of the old world that moved in her head. When I had to go on without her stories.

They get crushed in this *seeable* world.

But they're still there. I hear them in the silence sometimes.

I want to wear a deer dress. I want to deer dance with *Ahw'uste.* . . .

GIRL. What does *Ahw'uste* mean in English?

GRANDMOTHER. I don't know what the English was. But *Ahw'uste* was a spirit animal.

GIRL. What does that mean?

GRANDMOTHER. She was only there for some people to see.

GIRL. She was only there when you thought she was?

GRANDMOTHER. She had wings, too. If you thought she did. She was there to remind us—you think you see something you're not sure of. But you think it's there anyway.

GIRL. Maybe Jesus used wings when he flew to heaven. Ascended right up the air. Into holy Heaven. Floating and unreachable. I heard them stories at church when I worked the soup kitchen.

Or maybe they're wings like the spirits use when they fly between the earth and sky. But when you pick up a spirit on the road, you can't see his wings—he's got them folded into his jacket.

GRANDMOTHER. They say rocket ships go there now.

GIRL. The ancestors?

GRANDMOTHER. Yes, all of them wear red deer dresses.

GIRL. With two legs under their dresses?

GRANDMOTHER. In the afterworld they let them down.

GIRL. A four-legged deer with wings—wearing a red deer dress with shoes and hat? Dancing in the leaves—red maple, I suppose. After they're raked up to the sky? Where they stay red forever only if they think they do?

Sometimes your hooves are impatient inside your shoes. I see them move. You stuff twigs in your shoes to make them fit your hooves. But I know hooves are there.

Why would I want to be a deer like you?

Why would I want to eat without my hands?

Why would I want four feet?

What would I do with a tail? It would make a lump behind my jeans.

Do you know what would happen if I walked down the street in a deer dress?

If I looked for a job?

I already know I don't fit anywhere—I don't need to be reminded—I'm at your house, Grandma, with my sleeping bag and old truck—I don't have any place else to go. . . .

_____

GIRL (*Angrily*). OK, dude. Dudo. I pick you up on the road. I take you to the next town to get gas for your van, take you back when it still won't start. I pull you to town 'cause you don't have money for a tow truck. I wait two hours while you wait. Buy you supper. I give you love, what do you want? Hey, dude, your cowboy boots are squeaking, your hat with the beaded band. Your CB's talking to the highway, the truckers, the girls driving by themselves, that's what you look for. You take what we got. While you got one eye on your supper, one eye on your next girl.

I could have thought you were a spirit. You could have been something more than a dude. . . .

_____

GRANDMOTHER. The leaves only get to be red for a moment. Just a moment, and then the tree grieves all winter until the leaves come back. But they're green through the summer. The maple waits for the leaves to turn red. All it takes is a few cold mornings. A few days left out of the warmth.

Then the maple tree has red leaves for a short while.

_____

GIRL (*Angrily*). I can't do it your way, Grandma. I have to find my own trail—is that why you won't tell me? Is that why you won't speak? I'm caught? I have no way through? But there'll be a way through—I just can't see it yet. And if I can't find it, it's still there. I speak it through. Therefore, it is. If not now, then later. It's coming—if not for me—then for others.

I have to pass through this world not having a place, but I'll go anyway.

GRANDMOTHER. That's *Ahw'uste.*

GIRL. I'll speak these stories I don't know. I'll speak because I don't know them.

GRANDMOTHER. We're like the tree waiting for the red leaves. We count on what's not there as though it is, because the maple has red leaves—only you can't always see them.

GIRL. You'd rather live with what you can't see—is that the point of your red-leaf story?

GRANDMOTHER. I was trying to help you over the hard places.

GIRL. I can get over them myself.

GRANDMOTHER. I wanted you to look for the red leaves instead of the dudes on the highway.

GIRL. A vision is *not* always enough—

GRANDMOTHER. It's all I had.

GIRL. You had me—is a vision worth more than me?

GRANDMOTHER. I wanted to keep the leaves red for you.

GIRL. I don't want you to do it for me.

GRANDMOTHER. What am I supposed to do?

GIRL. Find someone else to share your silence with.

_____

GIRL. I was thinking we could have gone for a drive in my old truck.

GRANDMOTHER. I thought we did.

_____

GRANDMOTHER. *Ahw'uste*'s still living. Up there on the hill, straight through (*Indicating*) near Asuwosg' Precinct. A long time ago, I was walking by there, hunting horses. There was a trail that went down the hill. Now there's a highway on that hill up there, but, then, the old road divided. Beyond that, in the valley near Ayohli Amayi, I was hunting horses when I saw them walking and I stopped.

They were this high (*Indicating*), and had horns. They were going that direction. (*Indicating*). It was in the forest, and I wondered where they were going. They were all walking. She was going first, just this high (*Indicating*), and she had little horns. Her horns were just as my hands are shaped—five points, they call them five points. That's the way it was. Just this high. (*Indicating*) And there was a second one, a third one, and a fourth one. The fifth one was huge, and it also had horns with five points. They stopped a while, and they watched me. I was afraid of the large one! They were turning back, looking at me. They were pawing with their feet, and I was afraid. They were showing their anger then. First they'd go (*Indicates pawing*) with the right hoof and then with the left, and they'd go: *Ti! Ti! Ti! Ti!* They kept looking at me and pawing, and I just stood still.

They started walking again and disappeared away off, and I wondered where they went. I heard my horses over there, and I went as fast as I could. I caught a horse to ride and took the others home.

There was a man named Tseg' Ahl'tadeg, and when I got there, at his house, he asked me: What did you see?

I saw something down there, I told him.

What was it?

A deer. She was just this high (*Indicating*), and she had horns like this (*Indicating*), and she was walking in front. The second one was this high (*Indicating*), and the third one was this high (*Indicat-*

ing), and the fourth one (*Indicating*)—then the rest were large.

It was *Ahw'uste*, he said.

GIRL. I thought you said *Ahw'uste* lived in a house in Deer Creek.

GRANDMOTHER. Well, she did, but these were her tribe. She was with them sometimes.

GIRL. She's the only one who lived in a house?

GRANDMOTHER. Yes.

GIRL. In Deer Creek?

GRANDMOTHER. Yes, in Deer Creek.

GIRL. Your deer dress is the way you felt when you saw the deer?

GRANDMOTHER. When I saw *Ahw'uste*, yes. My deer dress is the way I felt, transformed by the power of ceremony. The idea of it in the forest of my head.

GIRL. Speak without your stories. Just once. What are you without your deer dress? What are you without your story of *Ahw'uste*?

GRANDMOTHER. We're carriers of our stories and histories. We're nothing without them.

GIRL. We carry ourselves. Who are you besides your stories?

GRANDMOTHER. I don't know—no one ever asked.

GIRL. OK, bucko. I find out you're married. But not living with her. *You aren't married in your heart,* you say. *It's the same as not being married.* And you got kids, too? Yeah, several, I'm sure. Probably left more of them behind to take care of themselves than you admit. You think you can dance me backwards around the floor, bucko?

GRANDMOTHER. Why would I want to be like you?

GRANDMOTHER. Why can't my granddaughter wait on the spirit? Why is she impatient? It takes a while sometimes. She says, *Hey spirit, what's wrong? Your wings broke down? You need a jumper cable to get them started?*

My granddaughter wants to do what she wants. Anything that rubs against her, well, she bucks. Runs the other way. I'm not going to give her my deer dress to leave in a heap on some dude's floor. It comes from long years from my grandmother. . . .

I have to live so far away from you. Take me where you are—I feel the pull of the string. (*She touches her breastbone*) Reel me in. Just pull. I want out of here. I want to see you ancestors. Not hear the tacky world. No more.

GIRL. You always got your eye on the next world.

GRANDMOTHER. I sit by the television, watch those stupid programs.

GIRL. What do you want? Weed the garden. Do some beans for supper. Set a trap for the next spirit to pass along the road.

GRANDMOTHER. The spirits push us out so we'll know what it's like to be without them. So we'll struggle all our lives to get back in—

GIRL. Is that what life is for you? No—for me—I get busy with day-to-day stuff until it's over.

I told 'em at church I didn't take the commodities—well not all those boxes—I told 'em—shit—what did it matter?

Have you ever lost one job after another?

GRANDMOTHER. Have you eaten turnips for a week? Because that was all you had in your garden. In your cupboard. Knowing your commodities won't last because you gave them to the next family on the road? They got kids and you can hear them crying.

GIRL. Well, just step right off the earth. That's where you belong. With your four deer feet.

GRANDMOTHER. Better than your two human ones. All you do is walk into trouble.

GIRL. Because I pick up someone now and then? Didn't you know what it was like to want love?

GRANDMOTHER. Love—ha! I didn't think of that. We had children one after another. We were cooking supper or picking up some crying child or brushing the men away. Maybe we did what we didn't want to do. And we did it every day.

GIRL. Well, I want something more for my life.

GRANDMOTHER. A trucker dude or two to sleep with till they move on? Nights in a bar. The jukebox and cowboys rolling you over.

GIRL (*She slaps her*). What did I do? Slap my grandmother? That felt good!

You deserved it. Sitting there in your smug spirit mode. I don't curl up with stories. I live in the world I see.

I've got to work. Christ—where am I going to find another job?

GRANDMOTHER. You can't live on commods alone.

GIRL. You can't drive around all day in your spirit mobile either.

GIRL. I been paying ten years on my truck, bub. You think I need a new transmission? 'Cause I got 180,000 miles on the truck and it's in the garage? You think you can sell me a new one, bubby? My truck'll run another hundred thousand. I don't have it paid for yet. You think you can sell me a used truck? You couldn't sell me mud flaps. Just get it running—try something else or my grandma'll stomp you with her hooves. My truck takes me in a vision. You got a truck that has visions? I don't see it on the list of options, bubby.

_____

GRANDMOTHER. *Gu'-s-di i-da-da-dv-hni.* My relatives—I'm making medicine from your songs. Sometimes I feel it. But mostly I have to know it's there without seeing. I go there from the hurts he left me with—all those kids and no way to feed them but by the spirit. Sometimes I think the birds brought us food. Or somehow we weren't always hungry. That's not true. Mostly we were on our own. Damned spirits. Didn't always help out. Let us have it rough sometimes. All my kids are gone. Run off. One of my daughters calls from Little Falls sometimes. Drunk. Drugged. They all have accidents. One got shot.

    What was that? *E-li'-sin*—Grandmother?

    No, just the blue jay. The finch.

    Maybe the ancestors—I hear them sometimes—out there, raking leaves—or I hear them if I think I do. *Hey—quiet out there,* my granddaughter would say. *Just reel me in, Grandmother,* I say.

_____

GIRL. So I told 'em at my first job interview: No, I hadn't worked that kind of machine—but I could learn.

    I told 'em at my second interview the same thing . . . .

I told 'em at the third . . .

    At the fourth I told 'em—my grandmother was a deer. I could see her change before my eyes. She caused stories to happen. That's how I knew she could be a deer.

    At the fifth I continued—I'm sewing my own red deer dress. It's different than my grandma's. Mine is a dress of words. I see *Ahw'uste* also.

    At the rest of the interviews I started right in—let me talk for you, that's what I can do.

    My grandma covered her trail. Left me without knowing how to make a deer dress. Left me without covering.

    But I make a covering she could have left me if only she knew how.

    I think I hear her sometimes—that crevice you see through into the next world. You look again, it's gone.

    My heart has red trees. The afterworld must be filling up with leaves.

    You know, I've learned she told me more without speaking than she did with her words.

End of Play

COMMENTARY

Note: The following essay represents a single interpretation of the play. For other perspectives on Native American literature and drama, consult the essays listed below.

> I have trouble with the spoken word. I talk, but often
> do not have the word I want to carry the meaning.
> Often it is a macaronic breach of two languages—
> or the snagging of one into a shortened branding-iron insignia.
> Pocal is the local cowpoke.
>   Chowdhurry is a quick bowl of soup.
> I wonder if this happens in the transfer of two heritages
> into one vessel—
> a bifurcation of thought not only from within
> but also pressed inward from the out—
>   Diane Glancy
>   *Some Thoughts on Our Uncommon Language*

The existence of the silent "minority" in America is the history of our rich nation, and the calculated and violent displacement of Native Americans continues to be overshadowed by a Western desire to assimilate and become self-sufficient in our search for "progress." The extermination and uprooting of American Indian populations have become the silenced reality; we acknowledge it, but only in private and pensive moments. The language of silence, therefore, is bearable.

The language of the throat is the language of oral tradition, a way of finding meaning through the dissemination of the spoken word, through storytelling, through a chant, a prayer, so that a history of an entire people can be recited in orchestrated dialogue. Myths, legends, beliefs, and traditions are passed on to the next generation by storytellers who are able to recollect entire generations, if not centuries, of ideology. It is the religion of the tribe. *The Woman Who Was a Red Deer Dressed for the Deer Dance* explores issues of generational differences, gender, cultural assimilation, and socioeconomic disintegration through a poetic language that transcends ordinary dialogue into the realm of naturalistic, spiritual eloquence. Glancy calls her stylistic theatrical language "Native spoken-word art" and allows her characters to gravitate between spatial and psychic realities, in verbal clashes, inner monologues, and realistic and representational dialogue. She asks the viewer to listen to the voices (words) "moving like rain on a windshield, between differing and unreliable experiences."

Although they coexist under the same roof and consistently shift between the past and the present, the Girl and the Grandmother trace their individual journeys as they attempt to comprehend their present state of affairs. The Girl's emotional makeup continues to shift because of her confusion and inability to find meaning in human relationships. Blaming her Grandmother for their ties bathed in silence and coded exchanges, she utters: "It was like talking to myself when I stayed with her. If I asked her something, she answered flat as the table between us." It is the vivid metaphor of the "table" that firmly establishes the break with cultural traditions. The distance between them is firmly rooted in the Grandmother's maternal and tribal past, which contrasts pointedly with the Girl's desperate search for purpose. Yet it is the Grandmother's inability to accept her earthly condition that batters her psyche: "I don't like this world anymore. We're reduced to what can be seen and felt. We're brought from the universe of the head into the kitchen full of heat and cold." Like the Girl, she is displaced, but unlike her granddaughter, she finds solace in death: "I feel the pull of the string. (*She touches her breastbone*) Reel me in. Just pull. I want out of here. I want to see you ancestors. Not hear the tacky world. No more."

Glancy's astute symbolism juxtaposes religion with the tastelessness of our culture. The Girl compares her jean jacket ("with Jesus on the cross in sequins on the back") to the presence of *Ahw'uste* in the Grandmother's spiritual realm; westernized religion and ancient mythology, therefore, clash in the argument.

As the "scenelets" shift, the play's subtext becomes clear. In their ambiguity, both the Girl and the Grandmother do find a sense of common ground in the love they share for one another. In the end, the Girl's realization ("I've learned she told me more without speaking than she did with her words") is a clear reflection of Glancy's belief that the "transfer of two heritages into one vessel" can indeed transform humanity. *The Woman Who Was a Red Deer Dressed for the Deer Dance* suggests that the shadows of the Native American past may, after all, coexist with our cultural geography, but only if we remain united by a respectful understanding of our common origins.

Other perspectives on Native American literature and drama:

Curtis, Natalie. "The People of the Totem Poles: Their Art and Legends." *The Craftsman* 16 (1999): 612–21.

Glancy, Diane. "Further (Farther): Creating Dialogue to Talk about Native American Plays." *Journal of Dramatic Theory and Criticism*, XIV:1 (Fall 1999): 5–14.

D'Aponte, Mimi Gisolfi, and Charles Gattnig. "The Route of Evanescence: Sand and Sawdust in Rituals of Transformation." *Centerpoint* (Winter 1975–76): 17–28.

SHOWCASE   NATIVE AMERICAN THEATER

Because of film and television—which are not necessarily accurate in their portrayals of the lives and customs of indigenous peoples—you may be familiar with some types of performance by Native Americans, many of which are rooted in communal celebrations and ancient rituals of cosmic significance. Because the indigenous peoples of North America belonged to literally hundreds of nations (each with its own language and customs), performances by Native Americans are diverse and cannot be neatly categorized. They are as rich and varied as the culture itself.

Among the best-known performance rituals of Native Americans (though similar examples may be found in other cultures) is the so-called "rain dance" in which dancers imitate the action of falling rain in the hope that nature itself will imitate them and send rain. This is among the oldest forms of performance impulses known to humans, and it is called "sympathetic (or homeopathic) magic." Other dances, such as the Hopi Corn Dance or the Sioux Buffalo Dance, also have roots in sympathetic magic. Healing dances and songs were also common; a shaman or other healer attempted to drive impurities from a sick body through the performance of dances, chants, and prayer. After the massacre of Native Americans at Wounded Knee (Christmas Day, 1890), an Indian seer named Black Elk had a vision in which native peoples would reclaim their land. And, it must be stressed, Black Elk did not merely tell his people of his vision; he performed it through a dance that is still repeated by Native Americans. The Ghost Dance is, in essence, a communal healing dance. Again, we see that cleansing and catharsis are integral elements of ritual and the drama from which it evolved.

Storytelling, either as highly polished one-person dramas or improvisations by shamans, is also central to Native American performances. The Navajos of the Southwest United States developed *chantways*, 100-hour

performances involving whole communities that carefully planned every aspect of this storytelling ritual. The Pawnee of the Northern Plains danced the Hako, a three-day ceremony performed for Mother Corn under the direction of a single person (the *kurahus*) entrusted with the "memory" of the ceremony. The dance gave promise of children and longevity, and it established a social bond among the various elements within the nation. The Hako was performed by one group—collectively known as "the Father"—for the benefit of another, "the Son." The structure of the Hako was not unlike that of the medieval liturgical plays because it was comprised of many rituals and tales, each complete unto itself. Yet each unit was related to a controlling idea, and the combined rituals formed an unbroken sequence that created a cosmic whole in the mind of the Pawnee.

While we may think of Native American dances, rituals, and ceremonies as austere and solemn occasions, they often contained comedic elements. The Cherokee Booger Dance typifies clowning dances found among Native Americans. Though its roots can be traced to pre-Columbian times, the dance changed with the arrival of white settlers who were made the objects of satire. A company of masked men—the "boogers," representing non-Indians—invaded a dance party in a raucous display of striking spectators, grabbing women, acting insane, stumbling, and laughing. Asked to identify themselves, the dancers farted and gave nonsensical names such as "Black Buttocks" and "Big Testicles," or they imitated the guttural sounds of the white invaders. They also abducted women and carried them away from the performance site. The dancers often wore gourds about their loins, reminiscent of the phalli of the classical theater of Greece. Elders, who proclaimed they were peaceable and nonviolent, drove off the boogers and restored order to the Cherokee nation.

Today a Native American theater does exist, though its development was seriously curtailed by a long history of anti-Indian policies. As early as 1646 the Massachusetts Bay Colony prohibited curing ceremonies among the indigenous peoples, and in 1865 the Office of Indian Affairs issued a proclamation outlawing "any (religious) dance . . . and frequent or prolonged periods of celebration . . . any disorderly or plainly excessive performance that promotes superstitious cruelty, licentiousness, idleness, danger to health, and shiftless indifference to family welfare." While such ignorant legislation has been eradicated, there are still barriers that inhibit the development of a truly Native American theater, most notably the confinement of many Indians to reservations (see Diane Glancy's comments in the introduction to *The Woman Who Was a Red Deer Dressed for the Deer Dance*).

In the twentieth century, R. Lynn Riggs, an Oklahoman whose mother was Cherokee, was among the first descendants of Native Americans to write for the theater. In 1922 he wrote a popular melodrama with folk songs called *Green Grow the Lilacs*. In 1943 the play was transformed by Richard Rogers and Oscar Hammerstein into *Oklahoma!*, often cited as "the Granddaddy of the modern American musical."

Particularly in the past thirty years a number of playwrights have fostered both traditional and contemporary theater and drama as a voice for Native Americans. In 1972 Hanay Geiogamah founded the Native American Theater Ensemble to develop traditional myths and plays that would restore ethnic pride in Indian audiences; today Geiogamah heads the American Indian Dance Theatre, which regularly performs works from an intertribal repertory. In 1975 Lisa Mayo and sisters Gloria and Muriel Miguel of the Kuna-Rappahannock nation formed the Spiderwoman Theater, a combination of Native American and feminist theater. Spiderwoman is the Hopi goddess of creation noted for her weaving, and thus this innovative company weaves traditional stories into performance pieces that fuse indigenous rites with Western theater practice. One of Spiderwoman's most noted pieces was *Lysistrata Numbah*, an updating of the ancient Greek comedy in which women force their men to stop fighting a war by refusing to have sex with them. The company also creates works such as *Winnetou's Snake-Oil Show from Wigwam City*, a caustic satire that exposes the treatment of Native Americans in general and woman in particular.

Today many playwrights, such as Diane Glancy, address problems encountered by Native Americans. Among the most noteworthy of these are Canadians Tomson Highway (Cree) and David Daniel Moses (Delaware); William S. Yellow Robe, Jr. (Assiniboone-Nakota); Bunky Echo Hawke (Pawnee); LeAnne Howe (Choctaw); Drew Hayden Taylor (Ojibway); and Monique Mojica (Kuna-Rappahannock).

For an outstanding collection of plays by Native American playwrights:

Gisolfi D'Aponte, Mimi (ed). *Seventh Generation: An Anthology of Native American Plays*. New York: Theatre Communications Group, 1999.

See the *Ghost Dance* on video:

Tahtonka: The American Indian Buffalo and Ghost Dances. Dir. Charles Nauman. Nauman Films, 30 min., 1991.

The West: Ghost Dance (Volume 8). Dir. Stephen Ives. Narr. Peter Coyote. Insight Media, 60 min., 1996.

TOPDOG/UNDERDOG
SUZAN-LORI PARKS

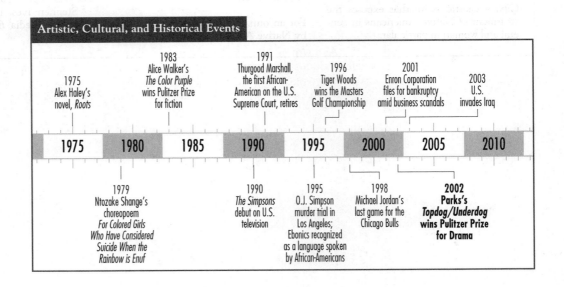

Artistic, Cultural, and Historical Events

1975
Alex Haley's
novel, *Roots*

1983
Alice Walker's
The Color Purple
wins Pulitzer Prize
for fiction

1991
Thurgood Marshall,
the first African-
American on the U.S.
Supreme Court, retires

1996
Tiger Woods
wins the Masters
Golf Championship

2001
Enron Corporation
files for bankruptcy
amid business scandals

2003
U.S.
invades Iraq

| 1975 | 1980 | 1985 | 1990 | 1995 | 2000 | 2005 | 2010 |

1979
Ntozake Shange's
choreopoem
*For Colored Girls
Who Have Considered
Suicide When the
Rainbow is Enuf*

1990
The Simpsons
debut on U.S.
television

1995
O.J. Simpson
murder trial in
Los Angeles;
Ebonics recognized
as a language spoken
by African-Americans

1998
Michael Jordan's
last game for the
Chicago Bulls

**2002
Parks's
Topdog/Underdog
wins Pulitzer Prize
for Drama**

SUZAN-LORI PARKS (1961–)

Novelist James Baldwin nudged Suzan-Lori Parks into playwriting. While she was a student at Mount Holyoke College in Massachusetts, she took a creative writing course from Baldwin, the famed author of *Native Son* and *The Fire Next Time*, at nearby Hampshire College. As the career he influenced unfolded and Parks published her first anthology of plays and essays in 1995, Baldwin called her (in an often-quoted preface to the anthology) "an utterly astounding and beautiful creature who may become one of the most valuable artists of our time."

Her theater works play with traditional notions of history and historical meaning; her language riffs off these and other themes as if she were a jazz musician improvising within the framework of a theatrical combo. Other musical metaphors are pertinent to experiencing her work—the call-and-response structure derived from African music and dance, and what Parks calls "Rep & Rev," the repetition of phrases, speeches, or scenes with only slight variations that build their cumulative impact and can gradually change their meaning and emotional effect. Instead of a linear plot with a beginning, middle, and end, Parks often creates a drama of accumulation, as a choreographer might construct a dance from movement phrases. In her early plays, beginning with *The Sinners Place* (1983) through *The America Play* (1993), she favors sound over logical sense. "Musicians," she wrote in her essay "Elements of Style," do that "all the time, they don't follow the standard melody line. James Joyce did in *Finnegan's Wake*." African-American director Marion McClinton described the style of *The America Play* to a Los Angeles critic as a combination of blues and bebop: "A lot of her language is old black English juxtaposed against modern language, so it has both an old blues feel and an avant-garde jazz feel to it." The "avant-garde" dropped away from descriptions of her 2002 Topdog/Underdog, however, for here Parks constructed a straight-ahead narrative, revisiting the Lincoln impersonator of The America Play by making him one of two battling brothers in her Pulitzer-winning Cain-and-Abel drama.

Parks was born into a military family in Fort Knox, Kentucky. She lived on various military bases in the United States and spent most of her teen years in what was then West Germany. She gathered from these years of exile an outsider's perspective and a keen, playful sense of language. Her family eventually settled in Syracuse, New York, and Parks attended Mount Holyoke, majoring in English and German, and graduated cum laude and Phi Beta Kappa in 1985. Parks studied acting for a year in London, though she says she never wanted to be an actor; she simply wanted to become a better writer for the theater. She also taught for a time at the Yale School of Drama.

"As a writer," she proclaimed in a 1994 essay, "my job is to write good plays. It's also to defend dramatic literature against becoming 'Theater of Schmaltz.' For while there are some playwrights whose work I love, love, love, it also seems that in no other form of writing these days is the writing so awful—so intended to produce some reaction of sorts, to discuss some issue: theater as the-wrapping-paper-version-of-some-hot-newspaper-headline."

Parks remains less interested in political issues affecting African-Americans than in the nature of history itself and in the musicality of language. Her characters are often "chased" by history, attempting to find the cracks or holes in official history through which their own stories can be glimpsed. "The mission of many plays," she has written, "is to tell a known history. But there are a lot of things that black people have done that haven't been written down, haven't been chronicled, are not remembered. . . . The unchronicled events are what I'm interested in writing about." In another discussion about making theater, Parks—who reveals influences from novelist Toni Morrison and experimental modernists Gertrude Stein and James Joyce—described her wish to "locate the ancestral burial ground, dig for bones, find bones, hear the bones sing, write it down." In two of her plays characters literally dig in real dirt onstage.

Parks's first play to be professionally produced, Imperceptible Mutabilities in the Third Kingdom (1989), received positive notices and gave her career a strong launch when it premiered in Brooklyn's experimental theater, BACA Downtown. However, its difficult leaps of language, its unconventional structure, and its dramatic personae who were "figures," not psychologically rounded characters, meant that the play initially appealed to a small group—artists, audiences, and critics with a taste for the new and a liking for poetry, music, and dance as well as theater. Mutabilities, with its dreams and ghosts and its pervading sense of loss, also presents black people brought low "as slugs." It is her "first and last play," Parks has said "to deal with black people as an oppressed group. I thought about it, I did it, it was interesting. But it is no longer." In an essay written soon after, "An Equation for Black People Onstage," she outlined a new kind of drama in which black people could be represented as something other than "Oppressed by/Obsessed with 'Whitey.'" Her writing is rich, dense, and poetic, she contended, because African-Americans are not an impoverished people: "We are a rich people fallen on hard times." And just as there is no single black experience, she argued, there is no single black aesthetic, no single way "to write or think or feel or dream or interpret or be interpreted." She called upon African-Americans to recognize the "insidious essentialism" of narrow stereotyping for what it is: "a trap to reduce us to only one way of being. We should endeavor to show the world and ourselves our beautiful and powerfully infinite variety."

Parks follows in the innovative poetic tradition of Adrienne Kennedy as opposed to the naturalism of Lorraine Hansberry, whose A Raisin in the Sun was the first play by an African-American woman to be produced on Broadway. The more adventurous group of writers to which Parks belongs spans two generations and includes Laurie Carlos, Robbie Macauley, and Ntozake Shange. The latter's for colored girls who have considered suicide/when the rainbow is enuf is usually defined as a "choreopoem" and has been much produced in the

United States, Europe, and Africa since a successful New York run in 1979. Parks and the Chicago-based Regina Taylor are from a younger generation than Shange; along with realists Pearle Cleage and Cheryl West and the famed monologist Anna Deavere Smith (see Showcase: "Docudrama") they comprise a small roster of African-American women whose work is occasionally produced in America's regional theaters.

Among Parks's plays after *Imperceptible Mutabilities* are *The Death of the Last Black Man in the Whole Entire World* (1990–92), which features characters named Black Man with Watermelon, Lots of Grease and Lots of Pork, and Old Man River Jordan; the more traditionally structured *Venus* (1996), about Saartjie Baartman, the nineteenth-century sideshow freak who reinvented herself as the celebrity, the Venus Hottentot; and *In the Blood* (1999), a freehand contemporary response to Nathaniel Hawthorne's classic novel *The Scarlet Letter*. The Hawthorne-based play was a finalist for the 2000 Pulitzer Prize, as Parks's evolving work sidled closer to the mainstream. *Topdog/Underdog* (2001–02) is a more linear second look at two characters with the historically charged names—central to *The America Play*—of Lincoln and Booth. This time, however, they are two black brothers who explore family secrets, three-card monte, and their lifelong rivalry. The play moved from New York's Off-Broadway Public Theatre, where artistic director George C. Wolfe has been a key supporter of Parks, to Broadway in spring 2002. One day later it won the Pulitzer Prize for Drama, making Parks the first African-American woman ever to win that award.

Parks heads the Writing for Performance program at California Institute for the Arts in Valencia, California. She has begun to demonstrate the "beautiful and powerfully infinite variety" of which she wrote by supplying the screenplay for the Spike Lee movie *Girl 6* and accepting a commission from Disney Theatricals to write a musical about the Harlem Globetrotters, *Hoopz*.

AS YOU READ *TOPDOG/UNDERDOG*

To understand *Topdog*, it helps to know something about *The America Play*, one of Parks's most produced early works. On the surface, it follows a somewhat traditional plot progression. A black gravedigger named the Foundling Father decides to capitalize on his resemblance to Abraham Lincoln. He leaves his wife Lucy and son Brazil to fulfill his dream, creating a kind of surreal sideshow in which he dresses like President Lincoln and reenacts, for a fee, the Great Man's assassination by John Wilkes Booth: the customers get to shoot him. But a mere look at the cast of characters and the setting of Parks's play in the Great Hole of History immediately indicates its unconventional nature. In the more traditionally structured *Topdog/Underdog*, set in a decrepit boarding house, the main characters are the brothers Lincoln and Booth, given those names as a joke by the father who abandoned them. The older Link works as an Abraham Lincoln impersonator in a penny arcade, dressing in a stovepipe hat and beard, wearing white face, and getting paid to let customers shoot him with a cap gun. The less assured brother Booth wants to be a master of three-card monte, the hand-is-quicker-than-the-eye card game Link long ago perfected hustling on the street. Much of the early part of Scene 1 is taken up with demonstrations of the classic con as Booth even changes his name to 3-Card in his increasingly desperate attempt to unseat his firstborn brother as the Topdog.

TOPDOG/UNDERDOG

S U Z A N - L O R I P A R K S

THE PLAYERS
LINCOLN, the topdog
BOOTH (AKA 3-CARD), the underdog

AUTHOR'S NOTES: From the "Elements of Style"

I'm continuing the use of my slightly unconventional theatrical elements. Here's a road map.

- (*Rest*)
  Take a little time, a pause, a breather; make a transition

- A Spell
  An elongated and heightened (*Rest*). Denoted by repetition of figures' names with no dialogue. Has sort of an architectural look:

  LINCOLN
  BOOTH
  LINCOLN
  BOOTH

  This is a place where the figures experience their pure true simple state. While no action or stage business is necessary, directors should fill this moment as they best see fit.

- [Brackets in the text indicate optional cuts for production]

- (Parentheses around dialogue indicate softly spoken passages (asides; sotto voce)).

> I am God in nature;
> I am a week by the wall.
>
> —Ralph Waldo Emerson
> From "Circles"
> *Essays: First Series* (1841)

SCENE 1

Thursday evening. A seedily furnished rooming house room. A bed, a reclining chair, a small wooden chair, some other stuff but not much else. Booth, a black man in his early 30's practices his 3-card monte scam on the classic setup: 3 playing cards and the cardboard playing board atop 2 mismatched milk crates. His moves and accompanying patter are, for the most part, studied and awkward.

BOOTH. Watch me close watch me close now: who-see-thuh-red-card-who-see-thuh-red-card? I-see-thuh-red-card. Thuh-red-card-is-thuh-winner. Pick-thuh-red-card-you-pick-uh-winner. Pick-uh-black-card-you-pick-uh-loser. Theres-thuh-loser, yeah, theres-thuh-black-card, theres-thuh-other-loser-and-theres-thuh-red-card, thuh-winner.

(Rest)

Watch me close watch me close now: 3-Card-throws-thuh-cards-lightning-fast. 3-Card-that's-me-and-Ima-last. Watch-me-throw-cause-here-I-go. One-good-pickll-get-you-in, 2-good-picks-and-you-gone-win. See-thuh-red-card-see-thuh-red-card-who-see-thuh-red-card?

(Rest)

Don't touch my cards, man, just point to thuh one you want. You-pick-that-card-you-pick-a-loser, yeah, that-cards-a-loser. You-pick-that-card-that's-thuh-other-loser. You-pick-that-card-you-pick-a-winner. Follow that card. You gotta chase that card. You-pick-thuh-dark-deuce-that's-a-loser-other-dark-deuces-thuh-other-loser, red-deuce, thuh-deuce-of-heartsll-win-it-all. Follow thuh red card.

(Rest)

Ima show you thuh cards: 2 black cards but only one heart. Now watch me now. Who-sees-thuh-red-card-who-knows-where-its-at? Go on, man, point to thuh card. Put yr money down cause you aint no clown. No? Ah you had thuh card, but you didn't have thuh heart.

(Rest)

You wanna bet? 500 dollars? Shoot. You musta been watching 3-Card real close. Ok. Lay the cash in my hand cause 3-Cards thuh man. Thank you, mister. This card you say?

(Rest)

Wrong! Sucker! Fool! Asshole! Bastard! I bet yr daddy heard how stupid you was and drank himself to death just cause he didn't wanna have nothing to do witchu! I bet yr mama seen you when you comed out and she walked away from you with thuh afterbirth still hanging from out twixt her legs, sucker! Ha Ha Ha! And 3-Card, once again, wins all thuh money!!

(Rest)

What? Cops looking my way? Fold up thuh game, and walk away. Sneak outa sight. Set up on another corner.

(Rest)

Yeah.

(Rest)

Having won the imaginary loot and dodged the imaginary cops, Booth sets up his equipment and starts practicing his scam all over again. Lincoln comes in quietly. He is a black man in his later 30's. He is dressed in an antique frock coat and wears a top hat and fake beard, that is, he is dressed to look like Abraham Lincoln. He surreptitiously walks into the room to stand right behind Booth, who, engrossed in his cards, does not notice Lincoln right away.

BOOTH. Watch me close watch me close now: who-see-thuh-red-card-who-see-thuh-red-card? I-see-thuh-red-card. Thuh-red-card-is-thuh-winner. Pick-thuh-red-card-you-pick-uh-winner. Pick-uh-black-card-you-pick-uh-loser. Theres-thuh-loser-yeah-theres-thuh-black-card, theres-thuh-other-loser-and-theres-thuh-red-card, thuh-winner. Don't touch my cards, man, don't—

(Rest)

Dont do that shit. Dont do that shit. Dont do that shit!

Booth, sensing someone behind him, whirls around, pulling a gun from his pants. While the presence of Lincoln doesn't surprise him, the Lincoln costume does.

BOOTH. And woah, man dont *ever* be doing that shit! Who thuh fuck you think you is coming in my shit all spooked out and shit. You pull that one more time I'll shoot you!
LINCOLN. I only had a minute to make the bus.
BOOTH. Bullshit.
LINCOLN. Not completely. I mean, its either bull or shit, but not a complete lie so it aint bullshit, right?

(Rest)

Put yr gun away.
BOOTH. Take off the damn hat at least.

Lincoln takes off the stovepipe hat. Booth puts his gun away.

LINCOLN. Its cold out there. This thing kept my head warm.
BOOTH. I don't like you wearing that bullshit, that shit that bull that disguise that getup that motherdisfuckinguise anywhere in the vicinity of my humble abode.
LINCOLN. Better?
BOOTH. Take off the damn coat too. Damn, man. Bad enough you got to wear that shit all day you come up in here wearing it. What my women gonna say?
LINCOLN. What women?
BOOTH. I got a date with Grace tomorrow. Shes in love with me again but she dont know it yet. Aint no man can love her the way I can. She sees you in that getup its gonna reflect bad on me. She coulda seen you coming down the street. Shit. Could be standing outside right now taking her ring off and throwing it on the sidewalk.

Booth takes a peek out the window.

BOOTH. I got her this ring today. Diamond. Well, diamond-esque, but it looks just as good as the real thing. Asked her what size she wore. She say 7 so I go boost a size 6 and a half, right? Show it to her and she loves it and I shove it on her finger and it's a tight fit right, so she cant just take it off on a whim, like she did the last one I gave her. Smooth, right?

Booth takes another peek out the window.

LINCOLN. She out there?
BOOTH. Nope. Coast is clear.

LINCOLN. You boosted a ring?

BOOTH. Yeah. I thought about spending my inheritance on it but—take off that damn coat, man, you make me nervous standing there looking like a spook, and that damn face paint, take it off. You should take all of it off at work and leave it there.

LINCOLN. I dont bring it home someone might steal it.

BOOTH. At least *take it off* there, then.

LINCOLN. Yeah.

(Rest)

Lincoln takes off the frock coat and applies cold cream, removing the whiteface.

LINCOLN. I was riding the bus. Really I only had a minute to make my bus and I was sitting in the arcade thinking, should I change into my street clothes or should I make the bus? Nobody was in there today anyway. Middle of week middle of winter. Not like on weekends. Weekends the place is packed. So Im riding the bus home. And this kid asked me for my autograph. I pretended I didnt hear him at first. I'd had a long day. But he kept asking. Theyd just done Lincoln in history class and he knew all about him, he'd been to the arcade but, I dunno, for some reason he was tripping cause there was Honest Abe right beside him on the bus. I wanted to tell him to go fuck hisself. But then I got a look at him. A little rich kid. Born on easy street, you know the type. So I waited until I could tell he really wanted it, the autograph, and I told him he could have it for 10 bucks. I was gonna say 5, cause of the Lincoln connection but something in me made me ask for 10.

BOOTH. But he didnt have a 10. All he had was a penny. So you took the penny.

LINCOLN. All he had was a 20. So I took the 20 and told him to meet me on the bus tomorrow and Honest Abe would give him the change.

BOOTH. Shit.

LINCOLN. Shit is right.

(Rest)

BOOTH. Whatd you do with thuh 20?

LINCOLN. Bought drinks at Luckys. A round for everybody. They got a kick out of the getup.

BOOTH. You shoulda called me down.

LINCOLN. Next time, bro.

(Rest)

You making bookshelves? With the milk crates, you making bookshelves?

BOOTH. Yeah, big bro, Im making bookshelves.

LINCOLN. What's the cardboard part for?

BOOTH. Versatility.

LINCOLN. Oh.

BOOTH. I was thinking we dont got no bookshelves we dont got no dining room table so Im making a sorta modular unit you put the books in the bottom and the table top on top. We can eat and store our books. We could put the photo album in there.

Booth gets the raggedy family photo album and puts it in the milk crate.

BOOTH. Youd sit there, I'd sit on the edge of the bed. Gathered around the dinner table. Like old times.

LINCOLN. We just gotta get some books but thats great, Booth, thats real great.

BOOTH. Don't be calling me Booth no more, K?

LINCOLN. You changing yr name?

BOOTH. Maybe.

LINCOLN.

BOOTH.

LINCOLN. What to?

BOOTH. Im not ready to reveal it yet.

LINCOLN. You already decided on something?

BOOTH. Maybe.

LINCOLN. You gonna call yrself something african? That be cool. Only pick something that's easy to spell and pronounce, man, cause you know, some of them african names, I mean, ok, Im down with the power to the people thing, but, no ones gonna hire you if they cant say yr name. And some of them fellas who got they african names, no one can say they names and they cant say they names neither. I mean, you dont want yr new handle to obstruct yr employment possibilities.

BOOTH.

LINCOLN.

BOOTH. You bring dinner?

LINCOLN. "Shango" would be a good name. The name of the thunder god. If you aint decided already Im just throwing it in the pot. I brought chinese.

BOOTH. Let's try out the table.

LINCOLN. Cool.

They both sit at the new table. The food is far away near the door.

LINCOLN.

BOOTH.

LINCOLN. I buy it you set it up. Thats the deal. Thats the deal, right?

BOOTH. You like this place?

LINCOLN. Ssallright.

BOOTH. But a little cramped sometimes, right?

LINCOLN. You dont hear me complain. Although that recliner sometimes Booth, man—no Booth, right—
man, Im too old to be sleeping in that chair.

BOOTH. Its my place. You dont got a place. Cookie, she
threw you out. And you cant seem to get another
woman. Yr lucky I let you stay.

LINCOLN. Every Friday you say *mi casa es su casa*.

BOOTH. Every Friday you come home with yr paycheck.
Today is Thursday and I tell you brother, it's a long
way from Friday to Friday. All kinds of things can happen. All kinds of bad feelings can surface and erupt
while yr little brother waits for you to bring in yr share.

(Rest)

I got my Thursday head on, Link. Go get the food.

Lincoln doesn't budge.

LINCOLN. You dont got no running water in here, man.

BOOTH. So?

LINCOLN. You dont got no toilet you dont got no sink.

BOOTH. Bathrooms down the hall.

LINCOLN. You living in thuh Third World, fool! Hey, I'll
get thuh food.

*Lincoln goes to get the food. He sees a stray card on
the floor and examines it without touching it. He
brings the food over, putting it nicely on the table.*

LINCOLN. You been playing cards?

BOOTH. Yeah.

LINCOLN. Solitaire?

BOOTH. Thats right. Im getting pretty good at it.

LINCOLN. Thats soup and thats sauce. I got you the meat
and I got me the skrimps.

BOOTH. I wanted the skrimps.

LINCOLN. You said you wanted the meat. This morning
when I left you said you wanted the meat.

(Rest)

Here man, take the skrimps. No sweat.

*They eat. Chinese food from styrofoam containers,
cans of soda, fortune cookies. Lincoln eats slowly
and carefully, Booth eats ravenously.*

LINCOLN. Yr getting good at solitaire?

BOOTH. Yeah. How about we play a hand after eating?

LINCOLN. Solitaire?

BOOTH. Poker or rummy or something.

LINCOLN. You know I dont touch thuh cards, man.

BOOTH. Just for fun.

LINCOLN. I dont touch thuh cards.

BOOTH. How about for money?

LINCOLN. You dont got no money. All the money you got
I bring in here.

BOOTH. I got my inheritance.

LINCOLN. Thats like saying you dont got no money cause
you aint never gonna do nothing with it so its like
you dont got it.

BOOTH. At least I still got mines. You blew yrs.

LINCOLN.

BOOTH.

LINCOLN. You like the skrimps?

BOOTH. Ssallright.

LINCOLN. Whats yr fortune?

BOOTH. "Waste not want not." Whats yrs?

LINCOLN. "Your luck will change!"

*Booth finishes eating. He turns his back to Lincoln
and fiddles around with the cards, keeping them on
the bed, just out of Lincolns sight. He mutters the
3-card patter under his breath. His moves are still
clumsy. Every once and a while he darts a look over
at Lincoln who does his best to ignore Booth.*

BOOTH. ((((Watch me close watch me close now: who-
see-thuh-red-card-who-see-thuh-red-card? I-see-thuh-
red-card. Thuh-red-card-is-thuh-winner. Pick-thuh-
red-card-you-pick-uh-winner. Pick-uh-black-card-you-
pick-uh-loser. Theres-thuh-loser, yeah, theres-thuh-
black-card, theres-thuh-other-loser-and-theres-thuh-
red-card, thuh-winner! Cop C, Stick, Cop C! Go
on—))))

LINCOLN. ((Shit.))

BOOTH. (((((((One-good-pickll-get-you-in, 2-good-picks-
and-you-gone-win. Dont touch my cards, man, just
point to thuh one you want. You-pick-that-card-you-
pick-uh-loser, yeah, that-cards-uh-loser. You-pick-
that-card-thats-thuh-other-loser. You-pick-that-card-
you-pick-uh-winner. Follow-that-card. You-gotta-chase-
that-card!)))))))

LINCOLN. You wanna hustle 3-card monte, you gotta do it
right, you gotta break it down. Practice it in smaller
bits. Yr trying to do the whole thing at once thats
why you keep fucking it up.

BOOTH. Show me.

LINCOLN. No. Im just saying you wanna do it you gotta do
it right and if you gonna do it right you gotta work on
it in smaller bits, thatsall.

BOOTH. You and me could team up and do it together.
We'd clean up, Link.

LINCOLN. I'll clean up—bro.

*Lincoln cleans up. As he clears the food, Booth goes
back to using the "table" for its original purpose.*

BOOTH. My new names 3-Card. 3-Card, got it? You wanted to know it so now you know it. 3-card monte by 3-Card. Call me 3-Card from here on out.

LINCOLN. 3-Card. Shit.

BOOTH. Im getting everybody to call me 3-Card. Grace likes 3-Card better than Booth. She says 3-Cards got something to it. Anybody not calling me 3-Card gets a bullet.

LINCOLN. Yr too much, man.

BOOTH. Im making a point.

LINCOLN. Point made, 3-Card. Point made.

Lincoln picks up his guitar. Plays at it.

BOOTH. Oh, come on, man, we could make money you and me. Throwing down the cards. 3-Card and Link: look out! We could clean up you and me. You would throw the cards and I'd be your Stickman. The one in the crowd who looks like just an innocent passerby, who looks like just another player, like just another customer, but who gots intimate connections with you, the Dealer, the one throwing the cards, the main man. I'd be the one who brings in the crowd, I'd be the one who makes them want to put they money down, you do yr moves and I do mines. You turn yr head and I turn the card—

LINCOLN. It aint as easy as all that. Theres—

BOOTH. We could be a team, man. Rake in the money! Sure thered be some cats out there with fast eyes, some brothers and sisters who would watch real close and pick the right card, and so thered be some days when we would lose money, but most of the days we would come out on top! Pockets bulging, plenty of cash! And the ladies would be thrilling! You could afford to get laid! Grace would be all over me again.

LINCOLN. I thought you said she was all over you.

BOOTH. She is she is. Im seeing her tomorrow but today we gotta solidify the shit twixt you and me. Big brother Link and little brother Booth—

LINCOLN. 3-Card.

BOOTH. Yeah. Scheming and dreaming. No one throws the cards like you, Link. And with yr moves and my magic, and we get Grace and a girl for you to round out the posse. We'd be golden, bro! Am I right?

LINCOLN.

LINCOLN.

BOOTH. Am I right?

LINCOLN. I dont touch thuh cards, 3-Card. I dont touch thuh cards no more.

LINCOLN.

BOOTH.

LINCOLN.

BOOTH.

BOOTH. You know what Mom told me when she was packing to leave? You was at school motherfucker you was at school. You got up that morning and sat down in yr regular place and read the cereal box while Dad read the sports section and Mom brought you yr dick toast and then you got on the damn school bus cause you didn't have the sense to do nothing else you was so into yr own shit that you didnt have the sense to feel nothing else going on. I had the sense to go back cause I was feeling something going on man, I was feeling something changing. So I—

LINCOLN. Cut school that day like you did almost every day—

BOOTH. She was putting her stuff in bags. She had all them nice suitcases but she was putting her stuff in bags.

(Rest)

Packing up her shit. She told me to look out for you. I told her I was the little brother and the big brother should look out after the little brother. She just said it again. That I should look out for you. Yeah. So who gonna look out for me. Not like you care. Here I am interested in an economic opportunity, willing to work hard, willing to take risks and all you can say you shiteating motherfucking pathetic limpdick uncle tom, all you can tell me is how you dont do no more what I be wanting to do. Here I am trying to earn a living and you standing in my way. YOU STANDING IN MY WAY, LINK!

LINCOLN. Im sorry.

BOOTH. Yeah, you sorry all right.

LINCOLN. I cant be hustling no more, bro.

BOOTH. What you do all day aint no hustle?

LINCOLN. Its honest work.

BOOTH. Dressing up like some crackerass white man, some dead president and letting people shoot at you sounds like a hustle to me.

LINCOLN. People know the real deal. When people know the real deal it aint a hustle.

BOOTH. We do the card game people will know the real deal. Sometimes we will win sometimes they will win. They fast they win, we faster we win.

LINCOLN. I aint going back to that, bro. I aint going back.

BOOTH. You play Honest Abe. You aint going back but you going all the way back. Back to way back then when folks was slaves and shit.

LINCOLN. Dont push me.

BOOTH.

LINCOLN.

BOOTH. You gonna have to leave.

LINCOLN. I'll be gone tomorrow.
BOOTH. Good. Cause this was only supposed to be a temporary arrangement.
LINCOLN. I will be gone tomorrow.
BOOTH. Good.

Booth sits on his bed. Lincoln, sitting in his easy chair with his guitar, plays and sings.

LINCOLN.
My dear mother left me, my father's gone away.
My dear mother left me and my fathers gone away.
I dont got no money, I dont got no place to stay.

My best girl, she threw me into the street.
My favorite horse, they ground him into meat.
Im feeling cold from my head down to my feet.

My luck was bad but now it turned to worse.
My luck was bad but now it turned to worse.
Dont call me up a doctor, just call me up a hearse.
BOOTH. You just made that up?
LINCOLN. I had it in my head for a few days.
BOOTH. Sounds good.
LINCOLN. Thanks.

(Rest)

Daddy told me once why we got the names we do.
BOOTH. Yeah?
LINCOLN. Yeah.

(Rest)

He was drunk when he told me, or maybe I was drunk when he told me. Anyway he told me, may not be true, but he told me. Why he named us both. Lincoln and Booth.
BOOTH. How come. How come, man?
LINCOLN. It was his idea of a joke.

(Both men relax back as the lights fade)

SCENE 2

Friday evening. The very next day. Booth comes in looking like he is bundled up against the cold. He makes sure his brother isn't home, then stands in the middle of the room. From his big coat sleeves he pulls out one new shoe then another, from another sleeve come two more shoes. He then slithers out a belt from each sleeve. He removes his coat. Underneath he wears a very nice new suit. He removes the jacket and pants revealing another new suit underneath. The suits still have the price tags

on them. He takes two neckties from his pockets and two folded shirts from the back of his pants. He pulls a magazine from the front of his pants. Hes clearly had a busy day of shoplifting. He lays one suit out on Lincolns easy chair. The other he lays out on his own bed. He goes out into the hall returning with a folding screen which he sets up between the bed and the recliner creating 2 separate spaces. He takes out a bottle of whiskey and two glasses, setting them on the two stacked milk crates. He hears footsteps and sits down in the small wooden chair reading the magazine. Lincoln, dressed in street clothes, comes in.

LINCOLN. Taaaaadaaaaaaaa!
BOOTH. Lordamighty, Pa, I smells money!
LINCOLN. Sho nuff, Ma. Poppas brung home thuh bacon.
BOOTH. Bringitherebringitherebringithere.

With a series of very elaborate moves Lincoln brings the money over to Booth.

LINCOLN. Put it in my hands, Pa!
BOOTH. I want ya tuh smells it first, Ma!
BOOTH. Put it neath my nose then, Pa!
LINCOLN. Take yrself a good long whiff of them greenbacks.
BOOTH. Oh lordamighty Ima faint, Pa! Get me muh med-sin!

Lincoln quickly pours two large glasses of whiskey.

LINCOLN. Dont die on me, Ma!
BOOTH. Im fading fast, Pa!
LINCOLN. Thinka thuh children, Ma! Thinka thuh farm!
BOOTH. 1-2-3.
LINCOLN AND BOOTH.

AAAAAAAAAAAAAAAAAAAAAH!
Lots of laughing and slapping on the backs.

LINCOLN. Budget it out man budget it out.
BOOTH. You in a hurry?
LINCOLN. Yeah. I wanna see how much we got for the week.
BOOTH. You rush in here and dont even look around. Could be a fucking A-bomb in the middle of the floor you wouldnt notice. Yr wife, Cookie—
LINCOLN. X-wife—
BOOTH. —could be in my bed you wouldnt notice—
LINCOLN. She was once—
BOOTH. Look the fuck around please.

Lincoln looks around and sees the new suit on his chair.

LINCOLN. Wow.
BOOTH. Its yrs.
LINCOLN. Shit.
BOOTH. Got myself one too.

LINCOLN. Boosted?

BOOTH. Yeah, I boosted em. Theys stole from a big-ass department store. That store takes in more money in one day than we will in our whole life. I stole and I stole generously. I got one for me and I got one for you. Shoes belts shirts ties socks in the shoes and everything. Got that screen too.

LINCOLN. You all right, man.

BOOTH. Just cause I aint good as you at cards dont mean I cant do nothing.

LINCOLN. Lets try em on.

They stand in their separate sleeping spaces, Booth near his bed, Lincoln near his recliner, and try on their new clothes.

BOOTH. Ima wear mine tonight. Gracell see me in this and *she* gonna ask me tuh marry *her.*

(Rest)

I got you the blue and I got me the brown. I walked in there and walked out and they didnt as much as bat an eye. Thats how smooth lil bro be, Link.

LINCOLN. You did good. You did real good, 3-Card.

BOOTH. All in a days work.

LINCOLN. They say the clothes make the man. All day long I wear that getup. But that dont make me who I am. Old black coat not even real old just fake old. Its got worn spots on the elbows, little raggedy places thatll break through into holes before the winters out. Shiny strips around the cuff and the collar. Dust from the cap guns on the left shoulder where they shoot him, where they shoot me I should say but I never feel like they shooting me. The fella who had the gig before I had it wore the same coat. When I got the job they had the getup hanging there waiting for me. Said thuh fella before me just took it off one day and never came back.

(Rest)

Remember how Dads clothes used to hang in the closet?

BOOTH. Until you took em outside and burned em.

(Rest)

He had some nice stuff. What he didnt spend on booze he spent on women. What he didnt spend on them two he spent on clothes. He had some nice stuff. I would look at his stuff and calculate thuh how long it would take till I was big enough to fit it. Then you went and burned it all up.

LINCOLN. I got tired of looking at em without him in em.

(Rest)

They said thuh fella before me—he took off the getup one day, hung it up real nice, and never came back. And as they offered me thuh job, saying of course I would have to wear a little makeup and accept less than what they would offer a—another guy—

BOOTH. Go on, say it. "White." Theyd pay you less than theyd pay a white guy.

LINCOLN. I said to myself thats exactly what I would do: wear it out and then leave it hanging there and not come back. But until then, I would make a living at it. But it dont make me. Worn suit coat, not even worn by the fool that Im supposed to be playing, but making fools out of all those folks who come crowding in for a chance to play at something great. Fake beard. Top hat. Dont make me into no Lincoln. I was Lincoln on my own before any of that.

The men finish dressing. They style and profile.

BOOTH. Sharp, huh?

LINCOLN. Very sharp.

BOOTH. You look sharp, too, man. You look like the real you. Most of the time you walking around all bedraggled and shit. You look good. Like you used to look back in thuh day when you had Cookie in love with you and all the women in the world was eating out of yr hand.

LINCOLN. This is real nice, man. I dont know where Im gonna wear it but its real nice.

BOOTH. Just wear it around. Itll make you feel good and when you feel good yll meet someone nice. Me I aint interested in meeting no one nice, I mean, I only got eyes for Grace. You think she'll go for me in this?

LINCOLN. I think thuh tie you gave me'll go better with what you got on.

BOOTH. Yeah?

LINCOLN. Grace likes bright colors dont she? My ties bright, yrs is too subdued.

BOOTH. Yeah. Gimmie yr tie.

LINCOLN. You gonna take back a gift?

BOOTH. I stole the damn thing didnt I? Gimmie yrs! I'll give you mines.

They switch neckties. Booth is pleased. Lincoln is more pleased.

LINCOLN. Do thuh budget.

BOOTH. Right. Ok lets see: we got 314 dollars. We put 100 aside for the rent. 100 a week times 4 weeks makes the rent and—

LINCOLN AND BOOTH. —we don't want thuh rent spent.

BOOTH. That leaves 214. We put aside 30 for the electric leaving 184. We put aside 50 for thuh phone leaving 134.

LINCOLN. We dont got a phone.

BOOTH. We pay our bill theyll turn it back on.

LINCOLN. We dont need no phone.

BOOTH. How you gonna get a woman if you dont got a phone? Women these days are more cautious, more whaddacallit, more circumspect. You go into a club looking like a fast daddy, you get a filly to give you her numerophono and gone is the days when she just gives you her number and dont ask for yrs.

LINCOLN. Like a woman is gonna call me.

BOOTH. She dont wanna call you she just doing a preliminary survey of the property. Shit, Link, you dont know nothin no more.

(Rest)

She gives you her number and she asks for yrs. You give her yr number. The phone number of yr home. Thereby telling her 3 things: 1) you got a home, that is, you aint no smooth talking smooth dressing *homeless* joe; 2) that you is in possession of a telephone and a working telephone number which is to say that you got thuh cash and thuh wherewithal to acquire for yr self the worlds most revolutionary communication apparatus and you together enough to pay yr bills!

LINCOLN. Whats 3?

BOOTH. You give her yr number you telling her that its cool to call if she should so please, that is, that you aint got no wife or wife approximation on the premises.

(Rest)

50 for the phone leaving 134. We put aside 40 for "med-sin."

LINCOLN. The price went up. 2 bucks more a bottle.

BOOTH. We'll put aside 50, then. That covers the bills. We got 84 left. 40 for meals together during the week leaving 44. 30 for me 14 for you. I got a woman I gotta impress tonight.

LINCOLN. You didnt take out for the phone last week.

BOOTH. Last week I was depressed. This week things is looking up. For both of us.

LINCOLN. Theyre talking about cutbacks at the arcade. I only been there 8 months, so—

BOOTH. Dont sweat it man, we'll find something else.

LINCOLN. Not nothing like this. I like the job. This is sit down, you know, easy work. I just gotta sit there all day. Folks come in kill phony Honest Abe with the phony pistol. I can sit there and let my mind travel.

BOOTH. Think of women.

LINCOLN. Sometimes.

(Rest)

All around the whole arcade is buzzing and popping. Thuh whirring of thuh duckshoot, baseballs smacking the back wall when someone misses the stack of cans, some woman getting happy cause her fella just won the ring toss. The Boss playing the barker talking up the fake freaks. The smell of the ocean and cotton candy and rat shit. And in thuh middle of all that, I can just sit and let my head go quiet. Make up songs, make plans. Forget.

(Rest)

You should come down again.

BOOTH. Once was plenty, but thanks.

(Rest)

Yr Best Customer, he come in today?

LINCOLN. Oh, yeah, he was there.

BOOTH. He shoot you?

LINCOLN. He shot Honest Abe, yeah.

BOOTH. He talk to you?

LINCOLN. In a whisper. Shoots on the left whispers on the right.

BOOTH. Whatd he say this time?

LINCOLN. "Does thuh show stop when no ones watching or does thuh show go on?"

BOOTH. Hes getting deep.

LINCOLN. Yeah.

BOOTH. Whatd he say, that one time? "Yr only yrself—"

LINCOLN. "—when no ones watching," yeah.

BOOTH. Thats deep shit.

(Rest)

Hes a brother, right?

LINCOLN. I think so.

BOOTH. He know yr a brother?

LINCOLN. I dunno. Yesterday he had a good one. He shoots me, Im playing dead, and he leans in close then goes: "God aint nothing but a parasite."

BOOTH. Hes one *deep* black brother.

LINCOLN. Yeah. He makes the day interesting.

BOOTH.

(Rest)

That's a fucked-up job you got.

LINCOLN. Its a living.

BOOTH. But you aint living.

LINCOLN. Im alive aint I?

(Rest)

One day I was throwing the cards. Next day Lonny died. Somebody shot him. I knew I was next, so I quit. I saved my life.

(Rest)

The arcade gig is the first lucky break Ive ever had. And Ive actually grown to like the work. And now theyre talking about cutting me.

BOOTH. You was lucky with thuh cards.

LINCOLN. Lucky? Aint nothing lucky about cards. Cards aint luck. Cards is work. Cards is skill. Aint never nothing lucky about cards.

(Rest)

I dont wanna lose my job.

BOOTH. Then you gotta jazz up yr act. Elaborate yr moves, you know. You was always too stiff with it. You cant just sit there! Maybe, when they shoot you, you know, leap up flail yr arms then fall down and wiggle around and shit so they gotta shoot you more than once. Blam Blam Blam! Blam!

LINCOLN. Help me practice. I'll sit here like I do at work and you be like one of the tourists.

BOOTH. No thanks.

LINCOLN. My paychecks on the line, man.

BOOTH. I got a date. Practice on yr own.

(Rest)

I got a rendezvous with Grace. Shit she so sweet she makes my teeth hurt.

(Rest)

Link, uh, howbout slipping me an extra 5 spot. Its the biggest night of my life.

LINCOLN.
BOOTH.

Lincoln gives Booth a 5er.

BOOTH. Thanks.

LINCOLN. No sweat.

BOOTH. Howabout I run through it with you when I get back. Put on yr getup and practice till then.

LINCOLN. Sure.

Booth leaves. Lincoln stands there alone. He takes off his shoes, giving them a shine. He takes off his socks and his fancy suit, hanging it neatly over the little wooden chair. He takes his getup out of his shopping bag. He puts it on, slowly, like an actor preparing for a great role: frock coat, pants, beard, top hat, necktie. He leaves his feet bare. The top hat has an elastic band which he positions securely underneath his chin. He picks up the white pancake makeup but decides against it. He sits. He pretends to get shot, flings himself on the floor and thrashes around. He gets up, considers giving

the new moves another try, but instead pours himself a big glass of whiskey and sits there drinking.

SCENE 3

Much later that same Friday evening. The recliner is reclined to its maximum horizontal position and Lincoln lies there asleep. He wakes with a start. He is horrific, bleary eyed and hungover, in his full Lincoln regalia. He takes a deep breath, realizes where he is and reclines again, going back to sleep. Booth comes in full of swagger. He slams the door trying to wake his brother who is dead to the world. He opens the door and slams it again. This time Lincoln wakes up, as hung over and horrid as before. Booth swaggers about, his moves are exaggerated, rooster-like. He walks round and round Lincoln making sure his brother sees him.

LINCOLN. You hurt yrself?

BOOTH. I had me an "evening to remember."

LINCOLN. You look like you hurt yrself.

BOOTH. Grace Grace Grace. *Grace.* She wants me back. She wants me back so bad she wiped her hand over the past where we wasnt together just so she could say we aint never been apart. She wiped her hand over our breakup. She wiped her hand over her childhood, her teenage years, her first boyfriend, just so she could say that she been mine since the dawn of time.

LINCOLN. Thats great, man.

BOOTH. And all the shit I put her through: she wiped it clean. And the women I saw while I was seeing her—

LINCOLN. Wiped clean too?

BOOTH. Mister Clean, Mister, Mister Clean!

LINCOLN. Whered you take her?

BOOTH. We was over at her place. I brought thuh food. Stopped at the best place I could find and stuffed my coat with only the best. We had candlelight, we had music we had—

LINCOLN. She let you do it?

BOOTH. Course she let me do it.

LINCOLN. She let you do it without a rubber?

BOOTH. —Yeah.

LINCOLN. Bullshit.

BOOTH. I put my foot down—and she *melted.* And she was—huh—she was something else. I dont wanna get you jealous, though.

LINCOLN. Go head, I dont mind.

BOOTH.

(Rest)

Well, you know what she looks like.

LINCOLN. She walks on by and the emergency room fills up cause all the guys get whiplash from lookin at her.

BOOTH. Thats right thats right. Well—she comes to the door wearing nothing but her little nightie, eats up the food I'd brought like there was no tomorrow and then goes and eats on me.

(Rest)

LINCOLN. Go on.

BOOTH. I dont wanna make you feel bad, man.

LINCOLN. Ssallright. Go on.

BOOTH.

(Rest)

Well, uh, you know what shes like. Wild. Good-looking. So sweet my teeth hurt.

LINCOLN. Sexmachine.

BOOTH. Yeah.

LINCOLN. Hotsy-Totsy.

BOOTH. Yeah.

LINCOLN. Amazing Grace.

BOOTH. Amazing Grace! Yeah. Thats right. She let me do her how I wanted. And no rubber.

(Rest)

LINCOLN. Go on.

BOOTH. You dont wanna hear the mushy shit.

LINCOLN. Sure I do.

BOOTH. You hate mushy shit. You always hated thuh mushy shit.

LINCOLN. Ive changed. Go head. You had "an evening to remember," remember? I was just here alone sitting here. Drinking. Go head. Tell Link thuh stink.

(Rest)

Howd ya do her?

BOOTH. Dogstyle.

LINCOLN. Amazing Grace.

BOOTH. In front of a mirror.

LINCOLN. So you could see her. Her face her breasts her back her ass. Graces got a great ass.

BOOTH. Its all right.

LINCOLN. Amazing Grace!

Booth goes into his bed area and takes off his suit, tossing the clothes on the floor.

BOOTH. She said next time Ima have to use a rubber. She let me have my way this time, but she said that next time I'd have to put my boots on.

LINCOLN. Im sure you can talk her out of it.

BOOTH. Yeah.

(Rest)

What kind of rubbers you use, I mean, when you was with Cookie.

LINCOLN. We didnt use rubbers. We was married, man.

BOOTH. Right. But you had other women on the side. What kind you use when you was with them?

LINCOLN. Magnums.

BOOTH. Thats thuh kind I picked up. For next time. Grace was real strict about it.

While Booth sits on his bed fiddling with his box of condoms, Lincoln sits in his chair and resumes drinking.

LINCOLN. Im sure you can talk her out of it. You put yr foot down and she'll melt.

BOOTH. She was real strict. Sides I wouldnt wanna be taking advantage of her or nothing. Putting my foot down and her melting all over thuh place.

LINCOLN. Magnums then.

(Rest)

They're for "the larger man."

BOOTH. Right. Right.

Lincoln keeps drinking as Booth, sitting in the privacy of his bedroom, fiddles with the condoms, perhaps trying to put one on.

LINCOLN. Thats right.

BOOTH. Graces real different from them fly-by-night gals I was making do with. Shes in school. Making something of herself. Studying cosmetology. You should see what she can do with a womans hair and nails.

LINCOLN. Too bad you aint a woman.

BOOTH. What?

LINCOLN. You could get yrs done for free, I mean.

BOOTH. Yeah. She got this way of sitting. Of talking. Everything she does is. Shes just so hot.

(Rest)

We was together 2 years. Then we broke up. I had my little employment difficulty and she needed time to think.

LINCOLN. And shes through thinking now.

BOOTH. Thats right.

LINCOLN.

BOOTH.

LINCOLN. Whatcha doing back there?

BOOTH. Resting. That girl wore me out.

LINCOLN. You want some med-sin?

BOOTH. No thanks.

LINCOLN. Come practice my moves with me, then.

BOOTH. Lets hit it tomorrow, K?

LINCOLN. I been waiting. I got all dressed up and you said if I waited up—come on, man, they gonna replace me with a wax dummy.

BOOTH. No shit.

LINCOLN. Thats what theyre talking about. Probably just talk, but—come on, man, I even lent you 5 bucks.

BOOTH. Im tired.

LINCOLN. You didnt get shit tonight.

BOOTH. You jealous, man. You just jail-us.

LINCOLN. You laying over there yr balls blue as my boosted suit. Laying over there waiting for me to go back to sleep or black out so I wont hear you rustling thuh pages of yr fuck book.

BOOTH. Fuck you, man.

LINCOLN. I was over there looking for something the other week and theres like 100 fuck books under yr bed and theyre matted together like a bad fro, bro, cause you spunked in the pages and didnt wipe them off.

BOOTH. Im hot. I need constant sexual release. If I wasnt taking care of myself by myself I would be out there running around on thuh town which costs cash that I dont have so I would be doing worse: I'd be out there doing who knows what, shooting people and shit. Out of a need for unresolved sexual release. I'm a hot man. I aint apologizing for it. When I dont got a woman, I gotta make do. Not like you, Link. When you dont got a woman you just sit there. Letting yr shit fester. Yr dick, if it aint falled off yet, is hanging there between yr legs, little whiteface shriveled-up blank-shooting grub worm. As goes thuh man so goes thuh mans dick. Thats what I say. Least my shits intact.

(Rest)

You a limp dick jealous whiteface motherfucker whose wife dumped him cause he couldnt get it up and she told me so. Came crawling to me cause she needed a man.

(Rest)

I gave it to Grace good tonight. So goodnight.

LINCOLN.

(Rest)

Goodnight.

LINCOLN.
BOOTH.
LINCOLN.
BOOTH.
LINCOLN.
BOOTH.

Lincoln sitting in his chair. Booth lying in bed. Time passes. Booth peeks out to see if Lincoln is asleep. Lincoln is watching for him.

LINCOLN. You can hustle 3-card monte without me you know.

BOOTH. Im planning to.

LINCOLN. I could contact my old crew. You could work with them. Lonny aint around no more but theres the rest of them. Theyre good.

BOOTH. I can get my own crew. I dont need yr crew. Buncha has-beens. I can get my own crew.

LINCOLN. My crews experienced. We usedta pull down a thousand a day. Thats 7 G a week. That was years ago. They probably do twice, 3 times that now.

BOOTH. I got my own connections, thank you.

LINCOLN. Theyd take you on in a heartbeat. With my say. My say still counts with them. They know you from before, when you tried to hang with us but—wernt ready yet. They know you from then, but I'd talk you up. I'd say yr my bro, which they know, and I'd say youd been working the west coast. Little towns. Mexican border. Taking tourists. I'd tell them you got moves like I dreamed of having. Meanwhile youd be working out yr shit right here, right in this room, getting good and getting better every day so when I did do the reintroductions youd have some marketable skills. Youd be passable.

BOOTH. I'd be more than passable, I'd be the be all end all.

LINCOLN. Youd be the be all end all. And youd have my say. If yr interested.

BOOTH. Could do.

LINCOLN. Youd have to get a piece. They all pack pistols, bro.

BOOTH. I *got* a piece.

LINCOLN. Youd have to be packing something more substantial than that pop gun, 3-Card. These hustlers is upper echelon hustlers they pack upper echelon heat, not no Saturday night shit, now.

BOOTH. Whata you know of heat? You aint hung with those guys for 6, 7 years. You swore off em. Threw yr heat in thuh river and you "Don't touch thuh cards." I know more about heat than you know about heat.

LINCOLN. Im around guns every day. At the arcade. Theyve all been reworked so they only fire caps but I see guns every day. Lots of guns.

BOOTH. What kinds?

LINCOLN. You been there, you seen them. Shiny deadly metal each with their own deadly personality.

BOOTH. Maybe I *could* visit you over there. I'd boost one of them guns and rework it to make it shoot for real again. What kind you think would best suit my personality?

LINCOLN. You aint stealing nothing from the arcade.

BOOTH. I go in there and steal if I want to go in there and steal I go in there and steal.

LINCOLN. It aint worth it. They dont shoot nothing but blanks.

BOOTH. Yeah, like you. Shooting blanks.

(Rest)

(Rest)

You ever wonder if someones gonna come in there with a real gun? A real gun with real slugs? Someone with uh axe tuh grind or something?

LINCOLN. No.

BOOTH. Someone who hates you come in there and guns you down and gets gone before anybody finds out.

LINCOLN. I dont got no enemies.

BOOTH. Yr X.

LINCOLN. Cookie dont hate me.

BOOTH. Yr Best Customer? Some miscellaneous stranger?

LINCOLN. I cant be worrying about the actions of miscellaneous strangers.

BOOTH. But there they come day in day out for a chance to shoot Honest Abe.

(Rest)

Who are they mostly?

LINCOLN. I dont really look.

BOOTH. You must see something.

LINCOLN. Im supposed to be staring straight ahead. Watching a play, like Abe was.

BOOTH. All day goes by and you never ever take a sneak peek at who be pulling the trigger.

Pulled in by his own curiosity, Booth has come out of his bed area to stand on the dividing line between the two spaces.

LINCOLN. Its pretty dark. To keep thuh illusion of the whole thing.

(Rest)

But on thuh wall opposite where I sit theres a little electrical box, like a fuse box. Silver metal. Its got uh dent in it like somebody hit it with they fist. Big old dent so everything reflected in it gets reflected upside down. Like yr looking in uh spoon. And that's where I can see em. The assassins.

(Rest)

Not behind me yet but I can hear him coming. Coming in with his gun in hand, thuh gun he already picked out up front when he paid his fare. Coming on in. But not behind me yet. His dress shoes making too much noise on the carpet, the carpets too thin, Boss should get a new one but hes cheap. Not behind me yet. Cheap lightbulb just above my head.

(Rest)

And there he is. Standing behind me. Standing in position. Standing upside down. Theres some feet shapes on the floor so he knows just where he oughtta stand. So he wont miss. Thuh gun is always cold. Winter or summer thuh gun is always cold. And when the gun touches me he can feel that I'm warm and he knows I'm alive. And if I'm alive then he can shoot me dead. And for a minute, with him hanging back there behind me, its real. Me looking at him upside down and him looking at me looking like Lincoln. Then he shoots.

(Rest)

I slump down and close my eyes. And he goes out thuh other way. More come in. Uh whole day full. Bunches of kids, little good for nothings, in they school uniforms. Businessmen smelling like two for one martinis. Tourists in they theme park t-shirts trying to catch it on film. Housewives with they mouths closed tight, shooting more than once.

(Rest)

They all get so into it. I do my best for them. And now they talking about replacing me with uh wax dummy. Itll cut costs.

BOOTH. You just gotta show yr boss that you can do things a wax dummy cant do. You too dry with it. You gotta add spicy shit.

LINCOLN. Like what.

BOOTH. Like when they shoot you, I dunno, scream or something.

LINCOLN. Scream?

Booth plays the killer without using his gun.

BOOTH. Try it. I'll be the killer. Bang!

LINCOLN. Aaaah!

BOOTH. That's good.

LINCOLN. A wax dummy can scream. They can put a voicebox in it and make it like its screaming.

BOOTH. You can curse. Try it. Bang!

LINCOLN. Motherfucking cocksucker!

BOOTH. Thats good, man.

LINCOLN. They aint going for that, though.

BOOTH. You practice rolling and wiggling on the floor?

LINCOLN. A little.

BOOTH. Lemmie see. Bang!

Lincoln slumps down, falls on the floor and silently wiggles around.

BOOTH. You look more like a worm on the sidewalk. Move yr arms. Good. Now scream or something.

LINCOLN. Aaaah! Aaaaah! Aaaah!

BOOTH. A little tougher than that, you sound like yr fucking.

LINCOLN. Aaaaaah!

BOOTH. Hold yr head or something, where I shotcha. Good. And look at me! I am the assassin! *I am Booth!!* Come on man this is life and death. Go all out!

Lincoln goes all out.

BOOTH. Cool, man thats cool. Thats enough.

LINCOLN. Whatdoyouthink?

BOOTH. I dunno, man. Something about it. I dunno. It was looking too real or something.

LINCOLN. They dont want it looking too real. I'd scare the customers. Then I'd be out for sure. Yr trying to get me fired.

BOOTH. I'm trying to help. Cross my heart.

LINCOLN. People are funny about they Lincoln shit. Its historical. People like they historical shit in a certain way. They like it to unfold the way they folded it up. Neatly like a book. Not raggedy and bloody and screaming. You trying to get me fired.

(Rest)

I am uh brother playing Lincoln. Its uh stretch for anyones imagination. And I aint easy for me neither. Every day I put on that shit, I leave my own shit at the door and I put on that shit and I go out there and I make it work. I make it look easy but its hard. That shit is hard. But it works. Cause I work it. And you trying to get me fired.

(Rest)

I swore off them cards. Took nowhere jobs. Drank. Then Cookie threw me out. What thuh fuck was I gonna do? I seen that "Help Wanted" sign and I went up in there and I looked good in the getup and agreed to the whiteface and they really dug it that me and Honest Abe got the same name.

(Rest)

It's a sit down job. With benefits. I dont wanna get fired. They wont give me a good reference if I get fired.

BOOTH. Iffen you was tuh get fired, then, well—then you and me could—hustle the cards together. We'd have to support ourselves somehow.

(Rest)

Just show me how to do the hook part of the card hustle, man. The part where the Dealer looks away but somehow he sees—

LINCOLN. I couldnt remember if I wanted to.

BOOTH. Sure you could.

LINCOLN. No

(Rest)

Night, man.

BOOTH. Yeah.

Lincoln stretches out in his recliner. Booth stands over him waiting for him to get up, to change his mind. But Lincoln is fast asleep. Booth covers him with a blanket then goes to his bed, turning off the lights as he goes. He quietly rummages underneath his bed for a girlie magazine which, as the lights fade, he reads with great interest.

SCENE 4

Saturday. Just before dawn. Lincoln gets up. Looks around. Booth is fast asleep, dead to the world.

LINCOLN. No fucking running water.

He stumbles around the room looking for something which he finally finds: a plastic cup, which he uses as a urinal. He finishes peeing and finds an out of the way place to stow the cup. He claws at his Lincoln getup, removing it and tearing it in the process. He strips down to his t-shirt and shorts.

LINCOLN. Hate falling asleep in this damn shit. Shit. Ripped the beard. I can just hear em tomorrow. Busiest day of the week. They looking me over to make sure Im presentable. They got a slew of guys working but Im the only one they look over every day. "Yr beards ripped, pal. Sure, we'll getcha new one but its gonna be coming outa yr pay." Shit. I should quit right then and there. I'd yank off the beard, throw it on the ground and stomp it, then go strangle the fucking boss. Thatd be good. My hands around his neck and his bug eyes bugging out. You been ripping me off since I took this job and now Im gonna have to take it outa yr pay, motherfucker. Shit.

(Rest)

Sit down job. With benefits.

(Rest)

Hustling. Shit, I was good. I was great. Hell I was the be all end all. I was throwing cards like throwing cards was made for me and me alone. I was the best anyone ever seen. Coast to coast. Everybody said so. And I never lost. Not once. Not one time. Not never. Thats how much them cards was mines. I was the be all end all. I was that good.

(Rest)

Then you woke up one day and you didnt have the taste for it no more. Like something in you knew—. Like something in you knew it was time to quit. Quit while you was still ahead. Something in you was telling you—. But hells no. Not Link thuh stink. So I went out there and threw one more time. What thuh fuck. And Lonny died.

(Rest)

Got yrself a good job. And when the arcade lets you go yll get another good job. I dont gotta spend my whole life hustling. Theres more to Link than that. More to me than some cheap hustle. More to life than cheating some idiot out of his paycheck or his life savings.

(Rest)

Like that joker and his wife from out of town. Always wanted to see the big city. I said you could see the bigger end of the big city with a little more cash. And if they was fast enough, faster than me, and here I slowed my moves I slowed em way down and my Lonny, my right hand, my Stickman, spanish guy who looked white and could draw a customer in like nothing else, Lonny could draw a fly from fresh shit, he could draw Adam outa Eve just with that look he had, Lonny always got folks playing.

(Rest)

Somebody shot him. They dont know who. Nobody knows nobody cares.

(Rest)

We took that man and his wife for hundreds. No, thousands. We took them for everything they had and everything they ever wanted to have. We took a father for the money he was gonna get his kids new bikes with and he cried in the street while we vanished. We took a mothers welfare check, she pulled a knife on us and we ran. She threw it but her aim werent shit. People shopping. Greedy. Thinking they could take me and they got took instead.

(Rest)

Swore off thuh cards. Something inside me telling me—. But I was good.

LINCOLN.
LINCOLN.

He sees a packet of cards. He studies them like an alcoholic would study a drink. Then he reaches for them, delicately picking them up and choosing 3 cards.

LINCOLN. Still got my moves. Still got my touch. Still got my chops. Thuh feel of it. And I aint hurting no one, God. Link is just here hustling hisself.

(Rest)

Lets see whatcha got.

He stands over the monte setup. Then he bends over it placing the cards down and moving them around. Slowly at first, aimlessly, as if hes just making little ripples in water. But then the game draws him in. Unlike Booth, Lincolns patter and moves are deft, dangerous, electric.

LINCOLN. (((Lean in close and watch me now: who see thuh black card who see thuh black card I see thuh black card black cards thuh winner pick thuh black card thats thuh winner pick thuh red card thats thuh loser pick thuh other red card that's thuh other loser pick thuh black card you pick thuh winner. Watch me as I throw thuh cards. Here we go.)))

(Rest)

(((Who see thuh black card who see thuh black card? You pick thuh red card you pick a loser you pick that red card you pick a loser you pick thuh black card thuh deuce of spades you pick a winner who sees thuh deuce of spades thuh one who sees it never fades watch me now as I throw thuh cards. Red losers black winner follow thuh deuce of spades chase thuh deuce. Dark deuce will get you thuh win.)))

Even though Lincoln speaks softly, Booth wakes and, unbeknownst to Lincoln, listens intently.

(Rest)

LINCOLN.
((10 will get you 20, 20 will get you 40.))

(Rest)

((Ima show you thuh cards: 2 red cards but only one spade. Dark winner in thuh center and thuh red losers on thuh sides. Pick uh red card you got a loser pick thuh other red card you got a loser pick thuh black card you got a winner. One good pickll get you in, 2 good picks and you gone win. Watch me come on watch me now.))

(Rest)

((Who sees thuh winner who knows where its at? You do? You sure? Go on then, put yr money where yr mouth is. Put yr money down you aint no clown. No? Ah, you had thuh card but you didnt have the heart.))

(Rest)

((Watch me now as I throw thuh cards watch me real close. Ok, man, you know which card is the deuce of spades? Was you watching Links lightning fast express? Was you watching Link cause he the best? So you sure, huh? Point it out first, then place yr bet and Linkll show you yr winner.))

(Rest)

((500 dollars? You thuh man of thuh hour you thuh man with thuh power. You musta been watching Link real close. You must be thuh man who know thuh most. Ok. Lay the cash in my hand cause Link the man. Thank you, mister. This card, you say?))

(Rest)

((Wrong! Ha!))

(Rest)

((Thats thuh show. We gotta go.))

Lincoln puts the cards down. He moves away from the monte setup. He sits on the edge of his easy chair, but he can't take his eyes off the cards.

INTERMISSION

SCENE 5

Several days have passed. Its now Wednesday night. Booth is sitting in his brand new suit. The monte setup is nowhere in sight. In its place is a table with two nice chairs. The table is covered with a lovely tablecloth and there are nice plates, silverware, champagne glasses and candles. All the makings of a very romantic dinner for two. The whole apartment takes its cue from the table. Its been cleaned up considerably. New curtains on the windows, a doily-like object on the recliner. Booth sits at the table darting his eyes around, making sure everything is looking good.

BOOTH. Shit.

He notices some of his girlie magazines visible from underneath his bed. He goes over and nudges them

out of sight. He sits back down. He notices that theyre still visible. He goes over and nudges them some more, kicking at them finally. Then he takes the spread from his bed and pulls it down, hiding them. He sits back down. He gets up. Checks the champagne on much melted ice. Checks the food.*

BOOTH. Foods getting cold, Grace!! Don't worry man, she'll get here, she'll get here.

He sits back down. He goes over to the bed. Checks it for springiness. Smoothes down the bedspread. Double-checks 2 matching silk dressing gowns, very expensive, marked "His" and "Hers." Lays the dressing gowns across the bed again. He sits back down. He cant help but notice the visibility of the girlie magazines again. He goes to the bed, kicks them fiercely, then on his hands and knees shoves them. Then he begins to get under the bed to push them, but he remembers his nice clothing and takes off his jacket. After a beat he removes his pants and, in this half-dressed way, he crawls under the bed to give those telltale magazines a good and final shove. Lincoln comes in. At first Booth, still stripped down to his underwear, thinks its his date. When he realizes its his brother, he does his best to keep Lincoln from entering the apartment. Lincoln wears his frock coat and carries the rest of his getup in a plastic bag.

LINCOLN. You in the middle of it?

BOOTH. What the hell you doing here?

LINCOLN. If yr in the middle of it I can go. Or I can just be real quiet and just—sing a song in my head or something.

BOOTH. The casas off limits to you tonight.

LINCOLN. You know when we lived in that 2-room place with the cement backyard and the frontyard with nothing but trash in it, Mom and Pops would do it in the middle of the night and I would always hear them but I would sing in my head, cause, I dunno, I couldnt bear to listen.

BOOTH. You gotta get out of here.

LINCOLN. I would make up all kinds of songs. Oh, sorry, yr all up in it. No sweat, bro. No sweat. Hey, Grace, howyadoing?!

BOOTH. She aint here yet, man. Shes running late. And its a good thing too cause I aint all dressed yet. Yr gonna spend thuh night with friends?

LINCOLN. Yeah.

Booth waits for Lincoln to leave. Lincoln stands his ground.

LINCOLN. I lost my job.

BOOTH. Hunh.

LINCOLN. I come in there right on time like I do every day and that motherfucker gives me some song and dance about cutbacks and too many folks complaining.

BOOTH. Hunh.

LINCOLN. Showd me thuh wax dummy—hes buying it right out of a catalog.

(Rest)

I walked out still wearing my getup.

(Rest)

I could go back in tomorrow. I could tell him I'll take another pay cut. Thatll get him to take me back.

BOOTH. Link. Yr free. Dont go crawling back. Yr free at last! Now you can do anything you want. Yr not tied down by that job. You can—you can do something else. Something that pays better maybe.

LINCOLN. You mean Hustle.

BOOTH. Maybe. Hey, Graces on her way. You gotta go.

Lincoln flops into his chair. Booth is waiting for him to move. Lincoln doesnt budge.

LINCOLN. I'll stay until she gets here. I'll act nice. I wont embarrass you.

BOOTH. You gotta go.

LINCOLN. What time she coming?

BOOTH. Shes late. She could be here any second.

LINCOLN. I'll meet her. I met her years ago. I'll meet her again.

(Rest)

How late is she?

BOOTH. She was supposed to be here at 8.

LINCOLN. Its after 2 a.m. Shes—shes late.

(Rest)

Maybe when she comes you could put the blanket over me and I'll just pretend like I'm not here.

(Rest)

I'll wait. And when she comes I'll go. I need to sit down. I been walking around all day.

BOOTH.

LINCOLN.

Booth goes to his bed and dresses hurriedly.

BOOTH. Pretty nice, right? The china thuh silver thuh crystal.

LINCOLN. It's great.

(Rest)

Boosted?

BOOTH. Yeah.

LINCOLN. Thought you went and spent yr inheritance for a minute, you had me going I was thinking shit, Booth—3-Card—that 3-Cards gone and spent his inheritance and the gal is—late.

BOOTH. It's boosted. Every bit of it.

(Rest)

Fuck this waiting bullshit.

LINCOLN. She'll be here in a minute. Dont sweat it.

BOOTH. Right.

Booth comes to the table. Sits. Relaxes as best he can.

BOOTH. How come I got a hand for boosting and I dont got a hand for throwing cards? Its sorta the same thing—you gotta be quick—and slick. Maybe yll show me yr moves sometime.

LINCOLN.

BOOTH.

LINCOLN.

BOOTH.

LINCOLN. Look out the window. When you see Grace coming, I'll go.

BOOTH. Cool. Cause youd jinx it, youd really jinx it. Maybe you being here has jinxed it already. Naw. Shes just a little late. You aint jinxed nothing.

Booth sits by the window, glancing out, watching for his date. Lincoln sits in his recliner. He finds the whiskey bottle, sips from it. He then rummages around, finding the raggedy photo album. He looks through it.

LINCOLN. There we are at that house. Remember when we moved in?

BOOTH. No.

LINCOLN. You were 2 or 3.

BOOTH. I was 5.

LINCOLN. I was 8. We all thought it was the best fucking house in the world.

BOOTH. Cement backyard and a frontyard full of trash, yeah, dont be going down memory lane man, yll jinx thuh vibe I got going in here. Gracell be walking in here and wrinkling up her nose cause you done jinxed up thuh joint with yr raggedy recollections.

LINCOLN. We had some great times in that house, bro. Selling lemonade on thuh corner, thuh treehouse out back, summers spent lying in thuh grass and looking at thuh stars.

BOOTH. We never did none of that shit.

LINCOLN. But we had us some good times. That row of nails I got you to line up behind Dads car so when he backed out the driveway to work—

BOOTH. He came back that night, only time I ever seen his face go red, 4 flat tires and yelling bout how thuh white man done sabotaged him again.

LINCOLN. And neither of us flinched. Neither of us let on that itd been us.

BOOTH. It was at dinner, right? What were we eating?

LINCOLN. Food.

BOOTH. We was eating pork chops, mashed potatoes and peas. I remember cause I had to look at them peas real hard to keep from letting on. And I would glance over at you, not really glancing not actually turning my head, but I was looking at you out thuh corner of my eye. I was sure he was gonna find us out and then he woulda whipped us good. But I kept glancing at you and you was cool, man. Like nothing was going on. You was cooooool.

(Rest)

What time is it?

LINCOLN. After 3.

(Rest)

You should call her. Something mighta happened.

BOOTH. No man, Im cool. She'll be here in a minute. Patience is a virtue. She'll be here.

LINCOLN. You look sad.

BOOTH. Nope. Im just, you know, Im just—

LINCOLN. Cool.

BOOTH. Yeah. Cool.

Booth comes over, takes the bottle of whiskey and pours himself a big glassful. He returns to the window looking out and drinking.

BOOTH. They give you a severance package, at thuh job?

LINCOLN. A weeks pay.

BOOTH. Great.

LINCOLN. I blew it. Spent it all.

BOOTH. On what?

LINCOLN. —. Just spent it.

(Rest)

It felt good, spending it. Felt really good. Like back in thuh day when I was really making money. Throwing thuh cards all day and strutting and rutting all night. Didnt have to take no shit from no fool, didnt have to worry about getting fired in favor of some damn wax dummy. I was thuh shit and they was my fools.

(Rest)

Back in thuh day.

(Rest)

(Rest)

Why do you think they left us, man?

BOOTH. Mom and Pops? I dont think about it too much.

LINCOLN. I dont think they liked us.

BOOTH. Naw. That aint it.

LINCOLN. I think there was something out there that they liked more than they liked us and for years they was struggling against moving towards that more liked something. Each of them had a special something that they was struggling against. Moms had hers. Pops had his. And they was struggling. We moved out of that nasty apartment into a house. A whole house. It werent perfect but it was a house and theyd bought it and they brought us there and everything we owned, figuring we could be a family in that house and them things, them two separate things each of them was struggling against, would just leave them be. Them things would see thuh house and be impressed and just leave them be. Would see thuh job Pops had and how he shined his shoes every night before he went to bed, shining them shoes whether they needed it or not, and thuh thing he was struggling against would see all that and just let him be, and thuh thing Moms was struggling against, it would see the food on the table every night and listen to her voice when she'd read to us sometimes, the clean clothes, the buttons sewed on all right and it would just let her be. Just let us all be, just regular people living in a house. That wernt too much to ask.

BOOTH. Least we was grown when they split.

LINCOLN. 16 and 13 aint grown.

BOOTH. 16s grown. Almost. And I was ok cause you were there.

(Rest)

Shit man, it aint like they both one day both, together packed all they shit up and left us so they could have fun in thuh sun on some tropical island and you and me would have to grub in thuh dirt forever. They didnt leave together. That makes it different. She left. 2 years go by. Then he left. Like neither of them could handle it no more. She split then he split. Like thuh whole family mortgage bills going to work thing was just too much. And I dont blame them. You dont see me holding down a steady job. Cause its bullshit and I know it. I seen how it cracked them up and I aint going there.

(Rest)

It aint right me trying to make myself into a one woman man just because she wants me like that. One woman

971

rubber-wearing motherfucker. Shit. Not me. She gonna walk in here looking all hot and shit trying to see how much she can get me to sweat, how much she can get me to give her before she gives me mines. Shit.

LINCOLN.

BOOTH.

LINCOLN. Moms told me I shouldnt never get married.

BOOTH. She told me thuh same thing.

LINCOLN. They gave us each 500 bucks then they cut out.

BOOTH. Thats what Im gonna do. Give my kid 500 bucks then cut out. Thats the way to do it.

LINCOLN. You dont got no kids.

BOOTH. Im gonna have kids then Im gonna cut out.

LINCOLN. Leaving each of yr offspring 500 bucks as yr splitting.

BOOTH. Yeah.

(Rest)

Just goes to show Mom and Pops had some agreement between them

LINCOLN. How so.

BOOTH. Theyd stopped talking to eachother. Theyd stopped *screwing* eachother. But they had an agreement. Somewhere in there when it looked like all they had was hate they sat down and did thuh "split" budget.

(Rest)

When Moms splits she gives me 5 hundred-dollar bills rolled up and tied up tight in one of her nylon stockings. She tells me to put it in a safe place, to spend it only in case of an emergency, and not to tell nobody I got it, not even you. 2 years later Pops splits and before he goes—

LINCOLN. He slips me 10 fifties in a clean handkerchief: "Hide this somewheres good, dont go blowing it, dont tell no one you got it, especially that Booth."

BOOTH. Theyd been scheming together all along. They left separately but they was in agreement. Maybe they arrived at the same place at the same time, maybe they renewed they wedding vows, maybe they got another family.

LINCOLN. Maybe they got 2 new kids. 2 boys. Different than us, though. Better.

BOOTH. Maybe.

Their glasses are empty. The whiskey bottle is empty too. Booth takes the champagne bottle from the ice tub. He pops the cork and pours drinks for his brother and himself.

BOOTH. I didnt mind them leaving cause you was there. Thats why Im hooked on us working together. If we could work together it would be like old times. They split and we got that room downtown. You was done with school and I stopped going. And we had to run around doing odd jobs just to keep the lights on and the heat going and thuh child protection bitch off our backs. It was you and me against the world, Link. It could be like that again.

LINCOLN.

BOOTH.

LINCOLN.

BOOTH.

LINCOLN. Throwing cards aint as easy as it looks.

BOOTH. I aint stupid.

LINCOLN. When you hung with us back then, you was just on thuh sidelines. Thuh perspective from thuh sidelines is thuh perspective of a customer. There was all kinds of things you didnt know nothing about.

BOOTH. Lonny would entice folks into thuh game as they walked by. Thuh 2 folks on either side of ya looked like they was playing but they was only pretending tuh play. Just tuh generate excitement. You was moving thuh cards as fast as you could hoping that yr hands would be faster than yr customers eyes. Sometimes you won sometimes you lost what else is there to know?

LINCOLN. Thuh customer is actually called the "Mark." You know why?

BOOTH. Cause hes thuh one you got yr eye on. You mark him with yr eye.

LINCOLN.

LINCOLN.

BOOTH. Im right, right?

LINCOLN. Lemmie show you a few moves. If you pick up these yll have a chance.

BOOTH. Yr playing.

LINCOLN. Get thuh cards and set it up.

BOOTH. No shit.

LINCOLN. Set it up set it up.

In a flash, Booth clears away the romantic table setting by gathering it all up in the tablecloth and tossing it aside. As he does so he reveals the "table" underneath: the 2 stacked monte milk crates and the cardboard playing surface. Lincoln lays out the cards. The brothers are ready. Lincoln begins to teach Booth in earnest.

LINCOLN. Thuh deuce of spades is the card tuh watch.

BOOTH. I work with thuh deuce of hearts. But spades is cool.

LINCOLN. Theres thuh Dealer, thuh Stickman, thuh Sides, thuh Lookout and thuh Mark. I'll be thuh Dealer.

BOOTH. I'll be thuh Lookout. Lemmie be thuh Lookout, right? I'll keep an eye for thuh cops. I got my piece on me.

LINCOLN. You got in on you right now?

BOOTH. I always carry it.

LINCOLN. Even on a date? In yr own home?

BOOTH. You never know, man.

(Rest)

So Im thuh Lookout.

LINCOLN. Gimmie yr piece.

Booth gives Lincoln his gun. Lincoln moves the little wooden chair to face right in front of the setup. He then puts the gun on the chair.

LINCOLN. We dont need nobody standing on the corner watching for cops cause there aint none.

BOOTH. I'll be the thuh Stickman, then.

LINCOLN. Stickman knows the game inside and out. You aint there yet. But you will be. You wanna learn good, be my Sideman. Playing along with the Dealer, moving the Mark to lay his money down. You wanna learn, right?

BOOTH. I'll be thuh Side.

LINCOLN. Good.

(Rest)

First thing you learn is what is. Next thing you learn is what aint. You dont know what is you dont know what aint, you dont know shit.

BOOTH. Right.

LINCOLN.

BOOTH.

BOOTH. Whatchu looking at?

LINCOLN. Im sizing you up.

BOOTH. Oh yeah?!

LINCOLN. Dealer always sizes up thuh crowd.

BOOTH. Im yr Side, Link, Im on yr team, you dont go sizing up yr own team. You save looks like that for yr Mark.

LINCOLN. Dealer always sizes up thuh crowd. Everybody out there is part of the crowd. His crew is part of the crowd, he himself is part of the crowd. Dealer always sizes up thuh crowd.

Lincoln looks Booth over some more then looks around at an imaginary crowd.

BOOTH. Then what then what?

LINCOLN. Dealer dont wanna play.

BOOTH. Bullshit man! Come on you promised!

LINCOLN. Thats thuh Dealers attitude. He *acts* like he dont wanna play. He holds back and thuh crowd,

with their eagerness to see his skill and their willingness to take a chance, and their greediness to win his cash, the larceny in their hearts, all goad him on and push him to throw his cards, although of course the Dealer has been wanting to throw his cards all along. Only he dont never show it.

BOOTH. Thats some sneaky shit, Link.

LINCOLN. It sets thuh mood. You wanna have them in yr hand before you deal a hand, K?

BOOTH. Cool. —K.

LINCOLN. Right.

LINCOLN.

BOOTH.

BOOTH. You sizing me up again?

LINCOLN. Theres 2 parts to throwing thuh cards. Both parts are fairly complicated. Thuh moves and thuh grooves, thuh talk and thuh walk, thuh patter and thuh pitter pat, thuh flap and thuh rap: what yr doing with yr mouth and what yr doing with yr hands.

BOOTH. I got thuh words down pretty good.

LINCOLN. You need to work on both.

BOOTH. K.

LINCOLN. A goodlooking walk and a dynamite talk captivates their entire attention. The Mark focuses with 2 organs primarily: his eyes and his ears. Leave one out you lose yr shirt. Captivate both, yr golden.

BOOTH. So them times I seen you lose, them times I seen thuh Mark best you, that was a time when yr hands werent fast enough or yr patter werent right.

LINCOLN. You could say that.

BOOTH. So, there were plenty of times—

Lincoln moves the cards around.

LINCOLN. You see what Im doing? Dont look at my hands, man, look at my eyes. Know what is and know what aint.

BOOTH. What is?

LINCOLN. My eyes.

BOOTH. What aint?

LINCOLN. My hands. Look at my eyes not my hands. And you standing there thinking how thuh fuck I gonna learn how tuh throw thuh cards if I be looking in his eyes? Look into my eyes and get yr focus. Dont think about learning how tuh throw thuh cards. Dont think about nothing. Just look into my eyes. Focus.

BOOTH. Theyre red.

LINCOLN. Look into my eyes.

BOOTH. You been crying?

LINCOLN. Just look into my eyes, fool. Now. Look down at thuh cards. I been moving and moving and moving them around. Ready?

BOOTH. Yeah.

LINCOLN. Ok, Sideman, thuh Marks got his eye on you. Yr gonna show him its easy.

BOOTH. K.

LINCOLN. Pick out thuh deuce of spades. Don't pick it up just point to it.

BOOTH. This one, right?

LINCOLN. Don't ask thuh Dealer if yr right, man, point to yr card with confidence.

Booth points.

BOOTH. That one.

(Rest)

Flip it over, man.

Lincoln flips over the card. It is in fact the deuce of spades. Booth struts around gloating like a rooster. Lincoln is midly crestfallen.

BOOTH. Am I right or am I right?! Make room for 3-Card! Here comes thuh champ!

LINCOLN. Cool. Stay focused. Now we gonna add the second element. Listen.

Lincoln moves the cards and speaks in a low hypnotic voice.

LINCOLN. Lean in close and watch me now: who see thuh black card who see thuh black card I see thuh black card black cards thuh winner pick thuh black card thats thuh winner pick thuh red card thats thuh loser pick thuh other red card thats thuh other loser pick thuh black card you pick thuh winner. Watch me as I throw thuh cards. Here we go.

(Rest)

Who see thuh black card who see thuh black card? You pick thuh red card you pick a loser you pick that red card you pick a loser you pick thuh black card thuh deuce of spades you pick a winner who sees the deuce of spades thuh one who sees it never fades watch me now as I throw thuh cards. Red losers black winner follow thuh deuce of spades chase thuh black deuce. Dark deuce will get you thuh win. One good pickll get you in 2 good picks you gone win. 10 will get you 20, 20 will get you 40.

(Rest)

Ima show you thuh cards: 2 red cards but only one spade. Dark winner in thuh center and thuh red losers on thuh sides. Pick uh red card you got a loser pick thuh other red card you got a loser pick thuh

black card you got a winner. Watch me watch me watch me now.

(Rest)

Ok, 3-Card, you know which cards thuh deuce of spades?

BOOTH. Yeah.

LINCOLN. You sure? Yeah? You sure you sure or you just think you sure? Oh you sure you sure huh? Was you watching Links lightning fast express? Was you watching Link cause he the best? So you sure, huh? Point it out. Now, place yr bet and Linkll turn over yr card.

BOOTH. What should I bet?

LINCOLN. Dont bet nothing man, we just playing. Slap me 5 and point out thuh deuce.

Booth slaps Lincoln 5, then points out a card which Lincoln flips over. It is in fact again the deuce of spades.

BOOTH. Yeah, baby! 3-Card got thuh moves! You didnt know lil bro had thuh stuff, huh? Think again, Link, think again.

LINCOLN. You wanna learn or you wanna run yr mouth?

BOOTH. Thought you had fast hands. Wassup? What happened tuh "Links Lightning Fast Express"? Turned into uh local train looks like tuh me.

LINCOLN. Thats yr whole motherfucking problem. Yr so busy running yr mouth you aint never gonna learn nothing! You think you something but you aint shit.

BOOTH. I aint shit, I am *The* Shit. Shit. Wheres thuh dark deuce? Right there! Yes, baby!

LINCOLN. Ok, 3-Card. Cool. Lets switch. Take thuh cards and show me whatcha got. Go on. Dont touch thuh cards too heavy just—its a light touch. Like yr touching Graces skin. Or, whatever, man, just a light touch. Like uh whisper.

BOOTH. Like uh whisper.

Booth moves the cards around, in an awkward imitation of his brother.

LINCOLN. Good.

BOOTH. Yeah. All right. Look into my eyes.

Booths speech is loud and his movements are jerky. He is doing worse than when he threw the cards at the top of the play.

BOOTH. Watch-me-close-watch-me-close-now: who-see-thuh-dark-card-who-see-thuh-dark-card? I-see-thuh-dark-card. Here-it-is. Thuh-dark-card-is-thuh-winner. Pick-thuh-dark-card-and-you-pick-uh-winner. Pick-uh-red-card-and-you-pick-uh-loser. Theres-thuh-loser-yeah-theres-thuh-red-card, theres-thuh-other-loser-

and-theres-thuh-black-card, thuh-winner. Watch-me-close-watch-me-close-now: 3-Card-throws-thuh-cards-lightning-fast. 3-Card-thats-me-and-Ima-last. Watch-me-throw-cause-here-I-go. See thuh black card? Yeah? Who see I see you see thuh black card?

LINCOLN. Hahahahhahahahahahahah!

Lincoln doubles over laughing. Booth puts on his coat and pockets his gun.

BOOTH. What?

LINCOLN. Nothing, man, nothing.

BOOTH. *What?!*

LINCOLN. Yr just, yr just a little wild with it. You talk like that on thuh street cards or no cards and theyll lock you up, man. Shit. Reminds me of that time when you hung with us and we let you try being the Stick cause you wanted to so bad. Thuh hustle was so simple. Remember? I told you that when I put my hand in my left pocket you was to get thuh Mark tuh pick thuh card on that side. You got to thinking something like Links left means my left some dyslexic shit and turned thuh wrong card. There was 800 bucks on the line and you fucked it up.

(Rest)

But it was cool, little bro, cause we made the money back. It worked out cool.

(Rest)

So, yeah, I said a light touch, little bro. Throw thuh cards light. Like uh whisper.

BOOTH. Like Graces skin.

LINCOLN. Like Graces skin.

BOOTH. What time is it?

Lincoln holds up his watch. Booth takes a look.

BOOTH. Bitch. *Bitch!* She said she was gonna show up around 8. 8-a-fucking-clock.

LINCOLN. Maybe she meant 8 *a.m.*

BOOTH. Yeah. She gonna come all up in my place talking bout how she *love* me. How she cant stop *thinking* bout me. Nother mans shit up in her nother mans thing in her nother mans dick on her breath.

LINCOLN. Maybe something happened to her.

BOOTH. Something happened to her all right. She trying to make a chump outa me. I aint her chump. I aint nobodys chump.

LINCOLN. Sit. I'll go to the payphone on the corner. I'll—

BOOTH. Thuh world puts its foot in yr face and you dont move. You tell thuh world tuh keep on stepping. But Im my own man, Link. I aint you.

Booth goes out, slamming the door behind him.

LINCOLN. You got that right.

After a moment Lincoln picks up the cards. He moves them around fast, faster, faster.

SCENE 6

Thursday night. The room looks empty, as if neither brother is home. Lincoln comes in. Hes fairly drunk. He strides in, leaving the door slightly ajar.

LINCOLN. Taaadaaaa!

(Rest)

(Rest)

Taadaa, motherfucker. Taadaa!

(Rest)

Booth—uh, 3-Card—you here? Nope. Good. Just as well. Ha Ha *Ha Ha Ha!*

He pulls an enormous wad of money from his pocket. He counts it, slowly and luxuriously, arranging and smoothing the bills and sounding the amounts under his breath. He neatly rolls up the money, secures it with a rubber band and puts it back in his pocket. He relaxes in his chair. Then he takes the money out again, counting it all over again, but this time quickly, with the touch of an expert hustler.

LINCOLN. You didnt go back, Link, you got back, you got it back you got yr shit back in thuh saddle, man, you got back in business. Walking in Luckys and you seen how they was looking at you? Lucky starts pouring for you when you walk in. And the women. You see how they was looking at you? Bought drinks for everybody. Bought drinks for Lucky. Bought drinks for Luckys damn dog. Shit. And thuh women be hanging on me and purring. And I be feeling that old call of thuh wild calling. I got more phone numbers in my pockets between thuh time I walked out that door and thuh time I walked back in than I got in my whole life. Cause my shit is *back.* And back better than it was when it left too. Shoot. Who thuh man? Link. Thats right. Purrrrring all up on me and letting me touch them and promise them shit. 3 of them sweethearts in thuh restroom on my dick all at once and I was *there* my shit was there. And Cookie just went out of my mind which is cool which is very cool. 3 of them. Fighting over it. Shit. Cause they knew I'd been throwing thuh cards. Theyd seen me on thuh corner with thuh old crew or if they aint seed me with they own eyes theyd heard word. Links thuh stink! Theyd heard word and they seed uh sad face on some poor sucker or a tear in thuh eye of some stupid fucking tourist and they figured it was me whod just took thuh suckers last dime, it was me who had all thuh suckers loot. They knew. They knew.

Booth appears in the room. He was standing behind the screen, unseen all this time. He goes to the door, soundlessly, just stands there.

LINCOLN. And they was all in Luckys. Shit. And they was waiting for me to come in from my last throw. Cant take too many fools in one day, its bad luck, Link, so they was all waiting in there for me to come in thuh door and let thuh liquor start flowing and thuh music start going and let thuh boys who dont have thuh balls to get nothing but a regular job and uh weekly paycheck, let them crowd around and get in some- how on thuh excitement, and make way for thuh ladies, so they can run they hands on my clothes and feel thuh magic and imagine thuh man, with plenty to go around, living and breathing underneath.

(Rest)

LINCOLN. They all thought I was down and out! They all thought I was some NoCount HasBeen LostCause motherfucker. But I got my shit back. Thats right. They stepped on me and kept right on stepping. Not no more. Who thuh man?! Goddammit, who thuh—

Booth closes the door.

LINCOLN.
BOOTH.

(Rest)

LINCOLN. Another evening to remember, huh?
BOOTH.

(Rest)

Uh—yeah, man, yeah. Thats right, thats right.
LINCOLN. Had me a memorable evening myself.
BOOTH. I got news.

(Rest)

What you been up to?
LINCOLN. Yr news first.
BOOTH. Its good.

LINCOLN. Yeah?
BOOTH. Yeah.
LINCOLN. Go head then.
BOOTH.

(Rest)

Grace got down on her knees. Down on her knees, man. Asked *me* tuh marry *her*.
LINCOLN. Shit.
BOOTH. Amazing Grace!
LINCOLN. Lucky you, man.
BOOTH. And guess where she was, I mean, while I was here waiting for her. She was over at her house watching tv. I'd told her come over Thursday and I got it all wrong and was thinking I said Wednesday and here I was sitting waiting my ass off and all she was doing was over at her house just watching tv.
LINCOLN. Howboutthat.
BOOTH. She wants to get married right away. Shes tired of waiting. Feels her clock ticking and shit. Wants to have my baby. But dont look so glum man, we gonna have a boy and we gonna name it after you.
LINCOLN. Thats great, man. Thats really great.
BOOTH.
LINCOLN.
BOOTH. Whats yr news?
LINCOLN.

(Rest)

Nothing.
BOOTH. Mines good news, huh?
LINCOLN. Yeah, real good news, bro.
BOOTH. Bad news is—well, shes real set on us living to- gether. And she always did like this place.

(Rest)

Yr gonna have to leave. Sorry.
LINCOLN. No sweat.
BOOTH. This was only a temporary situation anyhow.
LINCOLN. No sweat man. You got a new life opening up for you, no sweat. Graces moving in today? I can leave right now.
BOOTH. I dont mean to put you out.
LINCOLN. No sweat. I'll just pack up.

Lincoln rummages around finding a suitcase and be- gins to pack his things.

BOOTH. Just like that, huh? "No sweat"?! Yesterday you lost yr damn job. You dont got no cash. You dont got no friends, no nothing, but you clearing out just like that and its "no sweat"?!

LINCOLN. Youve been real generous and you and Grace need me gone and its time I found my own place.

BOOTH. No sweat.

LINCOLN. No sweat.

(Rest)

K. I'll spill it. I got another job, so getting my own place aint gonna be so bad.

BOOTH. You got a new job! Doing what?

LINCOLN. Security guard.

BOOTH.

(Rest)

Security guard. Howaboutthat.

Lincoln continues packing the few things he has. He picks up a whiskey bottle.

BOOTH. Go ahead, take thuh med-sin, bro. You gonna need it more than me. I got, you know, I got my love to keep me warm and shit.

LINCOLN. You gonna have to get some kind of work, or are you gonna let Grace support you?

BOOTH. I got plans.

LINCOLN. She might want you now but she wont want you for long if you dont get some kind of job. Shes a smart chick. And she cares about you. But she aint gonna let you treat her like some pack mule while shes out working her ass off and yr laying up in here scheming and dreaming to cover up thuh fact that you dont got no skills.

BOOTH. Grace is very cool with who I am and where Im at, thank you.

LINCOLN. It was just some advice. But, hey, yr doing great just like yr doing.

LINCOLN.

BOOTH.

LINCOLN.

BOOTH.

BOOTH. When Pops left he didn't take nothing with him. I always thought that was fucked-up.

LINCOLN. He was a drunk. Everything he did was always half regular and half fucked-up.

BOOTH. Whyd he leave his clothes though? Even drunks gotta wear clothes.

LINCOLN. Whyd he leave his clothes whyd he leave us? He was uh drunk, bro. He—whatever, right? I mean, you aint gonna figure it out by thinking about it. Just call it one of thuh great unsolved mysteries of existence.

BOOTH. Moms had a man on thuh side.

LINCOLN. Yeah? Pops had side shit going on too. More than one. He would take me with him when he went to visit them. Yeah.

(Rest)

Sometimes he'd let me meet the ladies. They was all very nice. Very polite. Most of them real pretty. Sometimes he'd let me watch. Most of thuh time I was just outside on thuh porch or in thuh lobby or in thuh car waiting for him but sometimes he'd let me watch.

BOOTH. What was it like?

LINCOLN. Nothing. It wasnt like nothing. He made it seem like it was this big deal this great thing he was letting me witness but it wasnt like nothing.

(Rest)

One of his ladies liked me, so I would do her after he'd done her. On thuh sly though. He'd be laying there, spent and sleeping and snoring and her and me would be sneaking it.

BOOTH. Shit.

LINCOLN. It was alright.

BOOTH.

LINCOLN.

Lincoln takes his crumpled Abe Lincoln getup from the closet. Isnt sure what to do with it.

BOOTH. Im gonna miss you coming home in that getup. I don't even got a picture of you in it for the album.

LINCOLN.

(Rest)

Hell, I'll put it on. Get thuh camera get thuh camera.

BOOTH. Yeah?

LINCOLN. What thuh fuck, right?

BOOTH. Yeah, what thuh fuck.

Booth scrambles around the apartment and finds the camera. Lincoln quickly puts on the getup, including 2 thin smears of white pancake makeup, more like war paint than whiteface.

LINCOLN. They didnt fire me cause I wasnt no good. They fired me cause they was cutting back. Me getting dismissed didnt have no reflection on my performance. And I was a damn good Honest Abe considering.

BOOTH. Yeah. You look great man, really great. Fix yr hat. Get in thuh light. Smile.

LINCOLN. Lincoln didnt never smile.

BOOTH. Sure he smiled.

LINCOLN. No he didnt, man, you seen thuh pictures of him. In all his pictures he was real serious.

BOOTH. You got a new job, yr having a good day, right?

LINCOLN. Yeah.

BOOTH. So smile.

LINCOLN. Snapshots gonna look pretty stupid with me—

Booth takes a picture.

BOOTH. Thisll look great in thuh album.

LINCOLN. Lets take one together, you and me.

BOOTH. No thanks. Save the film for the wedding.

LINCOLN. This wasnt a bad job. I just outgrew it. I could put in a word for you down there, maybe when business picks up again theyd hire you.

BOOTH. No thanks. That shit aint for me. I aint into pretending Im someone else all day.

LINCOLN. I was just sitting there in thuh getup. I wasnt pretending nothing.

BOOTH. What was going on in yr head?

LINCOLN. I would make up songs and shit.

BOOTH. And think about women.

LINCOLN. Sometimes.

BOOTH. Cookie.

LINCOLN. Sometimes.

BOOTH. And how she came over here one night looking for you.

LINCOLN. I was at Lucky's.

BOOTH. She didn't know that.

LINCOLN. I was drinking.

BOOTH. All she knew was you couldnt get it up. You couldnt get it up with her so in her head you was tired of her and had gone out to screw somebody new and this time maybe werent never coming back.

(Rest)

She had me pour her a drink or 2. I didnt want to. She wanted to get back at you by having some fun of her own and when I told her to go out and have it, she said she wanted to have her fun right here. With me.

(Rest)

[And then, just like that, she changed her mind.

(Rest)

But she'd hooked me. That bad part of me that I fight down everyday. You beat yrs down and it stays there dead but mine keeps coming up for another round. And she hooked the bad part of me. And the bad part of me opened my mouth and started promising her things. Promising her things I knew she wanted and you couldnt give her. And the bad part of me took her clothing off and carried her into thuh bed and had her, Link, yr Cookie. It wasnt just thuh bad part of me it was all of me, man,] I had her. Yr damn wife. Right in that bed.

LINCOLN. I used to think about her all thuh time but I dont think about her no more.

BOOTH. I told her if she dumped you I'd marry her but I changed my mind.

LINCOLN. I dont think about her no more.

BOOTH. You dont go back.

LINCOLN. Nope.

BOOTH. Cause you cant. No matter what you do you cant get back to being who you was. Best you can do is just pretend to be yr old self.

LINCOLN. Yr outa yr mind.

BOOTH. Least Im still me!

LINCOLN. Least I work. You never did like to work. You better come up with some kinda way to bring home the bacon or Gracell drop you like a hot rock.

BOOTH. I got plans!

LINCOLN. Yeah, you gonna throw thuh cards, right?

BOOTH. That's right!

LINCOLN. You a double left-handed motherfucker who dont stand a chance in all get out out there throwing no cards.

BOOTH. You scared.

LINCOLN. Im gone.

Lincoln goes to leave.

BOOTH. Fuck that!

LINCOLN. Yr standing in my way.

BOOTH. You scared I got yr shit.

LINCOLN. The only part of my shit you got is the part of my shit you think you got and that aint shit.

BOOTH. Did I pick right them last times? Yes. Oh, I got yr shit.

LINCOLN. Set up the cards.

BOOTH. Thought you was gone.

LINCOLN. Set it up.

BOOTH. I got yr shit and Ima go out there and be thuh man and you aint gonna be nothin.

LINCOLN. Set it up!

Booth hurriedly sets up the milk crates and cardboard top. Lincoln throws the cards.

LINCOLN. Lean in close and watch me now: who see thuh black card who see thuh black card I see thuh black card black cards thuh winner pick thuh black card thats thuh winner pick thuh red card thats thuh loser pick thuh other red card thats thuh other loser pick thuh black card you pick thuh winner. Who see thuh black card who see thuh black card? You pick thuh red card you pick a loser you pick that red card you pick a loser you pick thuh black card thuh deuce of spades you pick a winner who sees thuh deuce of spades thuh one who sees it never fades watch me now as I throw thuh cards. Red losers black winner follow thuh deuce of spades chase thuh black deuce. Dark deuce will get you thuh win. One good pickll get you in 2 good picks you gone win.

(Rest)

Ok, man, wheres thuh black deuce?

Booth points to a card. Lincoln flips it over. It is the deuce of spades.

BOOTH. Who thuh man?!

Lincoln turns over the other 2 cards, looking at them confusedly.

LINCOLN. Hhhhh.

BOOTH. Who thuh man, Link?! Huh? Who thuh man, Link?!?!

LINCOLN. You thuh man, man.

BOOTH. I got yr shit down.

LINCOLN. Right.

BOOTH. "Right"? All you saying is "right"?

(Rest)

You was out on the street throwing. Just today. Werent you? You wasnt gonna tell me.

LINCOLN. Tell you what?

BOOTH. That you was out throwing.

LINCOLN. I was gonna tell you, sure. Cant go and leave my little bro out thuh loop, can I? Didnt say nothing cause I thought you heard. Did all right today but Im still rusty, I guess. But hey—yr getting good.

BOOTH. But I'll get out there on thuh street and still fuck up, wont I?

LINCOLN. You seem pretty good, bro.

BOOTH. You gotta do it for real, man.

LINCOLN. I am doing it for real. And yr getting good.

BOOTH. I dunno. It didnt feel real. Kinda felt—well it didnt feel real.

LINCOLN. We're missing the essential elements. The crown, the street, thuh traffic sounds, all that.

BOOTH. We missing something else too, thuh thing thatll really make it real.

LINCOLN. Whassat, bro?

BOOTH. Thuh cash. Its just bullshit without thuh money. Put some money down on thuh table then itd be real, then youd do it for real, then I'd win it for real.

(Rest)

And dont be looking all glum like that. I know you got money. A whole pocketful. Put it down.

LINCOLN.

BOOTH.

BOOTH. You scared of losing it to thuh man, chump? Put it down, less you think thuh kid who got two left hands is gonna give you uh left hook. Put it down, bro, put it down.

Lincoln takes the roll of bills from his pocket and places it on the table.

BOOTH. How much you got there?

LINCOLN. 500 bucks.

BOOTH. Cool.

(Rest)

Ready?

LINCOLN. Does it feel real?

BOOTH. Yeah. Clean slate. Take it from the top. "One good pickll get you in 2 good picks and you gone win."

(Rest)

Go head.

LINCOLN. Watch me now:

BOOTH. Woah, man, woah.

(Rest)

You think Ima chump.

LINCOLN. No I dont.

BOOTH. You aint going full out.

LINCOLN. I was just getting started.

BOOTH. But when you got good and started you wasnt gonna go full out. You wasnt gonna go all out. You was gonna do thuh the pussy shit, not thuh real shit.

LINCOLN. I put my money down. Money makes it real.

BOOTH. But not if I don't put no money down tuh match it.

LINCOLN. You dont got no money.

BOOTH. I got money!

LINCOLN. You aint worked in years. You dont got shit.

BOOTH. I got money.

LINCOLN. Whatcha been doing, skimming off my weekly paycheck and squirreling it away?

BOOTH. I got money.

(Rest)

They stand there sizing eachother up. Booth breaks away, going over to his hiding place from which he gets an old nylon stocking with money in the toe, a knot holding the money secure.

LINCOLN.

BOOTH.

BOOTH. You know she was putting her stuff in plastic bags? She was just putting her stuff in plastic bags not putting but shoving. She was shoving her stuff in plastic bags and I was standing in thuh doorway watching her and she was so busy shoving thuh shit she didnt see me. "I aint made of money," thats what he always saying. The guy she had on the side. I would catch them together sometimes. Thuh first time I cut school I got tired of hanging out so I goes home—figured I could tell Mom I was sick and cover my ass. Come in thuh house real slow cause Im sick and moving slow and quiet. He had her bent over. They both had all they clothes on like they was about to do something like go out dancing cause they was dressed to thuh 9s but at thuh last minute his pants had fallen down and her dress had flown up and theyd ended up doing something else.

(Rest)

They didnt see me come in, they didnt see me watching them, they didnt see me going out. That was uh Thursday. Something told me tuh cut school thuh next Thursday and sure enough—. He was her Thursday man. Every Thursday. Yeah. And Thursday nights she was always all cleaned up and fresh and smelling nice. Serving up dinner. And Pops would grab her cause she was all bright and she would look at me, like she didnt know that I knew but she was asking me not to tell nohow. She was asking me to— oh who knows.

(Rest)

She was talking with him one day, her sideman, her Thursday dude, her backdoor man, she needed some money for something, thered been some kind of problem some kind of mistake had been made some kind of mistake that needed cleaning up and she was asking Mr. Thursday for some money to take care of it. "I aint made of money," he says. He was putting his foot down. And then there she was 2 months later not showing yet, maybe she'd got rid of it maybe she hadnt maybe she'd stuffed it along with all her other things in them plastic bags while he waited outside in thuh car with thuh motor running. She musta known I was gonna walk in on her this time cause she had my payoff—my *inheritance*— she had it all ready for me. 500 dollars in a nylon stocking. Huh.

He places the stuffed nylon stocking on the table across from Lincolns money roll.

BOOTH. Now its real.
LINCOLN. Dont put that down.

BOOTH. Throw thuh cards.
LINCOLN. I dont want to play.
BOOTH. Throw thuh fucking cards, man!!
LINCOLN.

(Rest)

2 red cards but only one black. Pick thuh black you pick thuh winner. All thuh cards are face down you point out thuh cards and then you move them around. Now watch me now, now watch me real close. Put thuh winning deuce down in the center put thuh loser reds on either side then you just move thuh cards around. Move them slow or move them fast, Links thuh king he gonna last.

(Rest)

Wheres thuh deuce of spades?

Booth chooses a card and chooses correctly.

BOOTH. HA!
LINCOLN. One good pickll get you in 2 good picks and you gone win.
BOOTH. I know man I know.
LINCOLN. Im just doing thuh talk.
BOOTH. Throw thuh fucking cards!

Lincoln throws the cards.

LINCOLN. Lean in close and watch me now: who see thuh black card who see thuh black card I see thuh black card black cards thuh winner pick thuh black card thats thuh winner pick thuh red card thats thuh loser pick thuh other red card thats thuh other loser pick thuh black card you pick thuh winner. Watch me as I throw thuh cards. Here we go.

(Rest)

Ima show you thuh cards: 2 red cards but only one spade. Dark winner in thuh center and thuh red losers on thuh sides. Pick uh red card you got a loser pick thuh other red card you got a loser pick thuh black card you got a winner. Watch me watch me watch me now.

(Rest)

Who see thuh black card who see thuh black card? You pick thuh red card you pick a loser you pick that red card you pick a loser you pick thuh black card thuh deuce of spades you pick a winner who sees the deuce of spades thuh one who sees it never fades watch me now as I throw thuh cards. Red losers black winner follow thuh deuce of spades chase thuh black deuce. Dark deuce will get you thuh win.

(Rest)

Ok, 3-Card, you know which cards thuh deuce of spades? This is for real now, man. You pick wrong Im in yr wad and I keep mines.

BOOTH. I pick right I got yr shit.

LINCOLN. Yeah.

BOOTH. Plus I beat you for real.

LINCOLN. Yeah.

(Rest)

You think we're really brothers?

BOOTH. Huh?

LINCOLN. I know we *brothers*, but is we really brothers, you know, blood brothers or not, you and me, what-duhyathink?

BOOTH. I think we're brothers.

BOOTH.

LINCOLN.

BOOTH.

LINCOLN.

BOOTH.

LINCOLN.

LINCOLN. Go head man, wheres thuh deuce?

In a flash Booth points out a card.

LINCOLN. You sure?

BOOTH. Im sure!

LINCOLN. Yeah? Dont touch thuh cards, now.

BOOTH. Im sure.

The 2 brothers lock eyes. Lincoln turns over the card that Booth selected and Booth, in a desperate break of concentration, glances down to see that he has chosen the wrong card.

LINCOLN. Deuce of hearts, bro. Im sorry. Thuh deuce of spades was this one.

(Rest)

I guess all this is mines.

He slides the money toward himself.

LINCOLN. You were almost right. Better luck next time.

(Rest)

Aint yr fault if yr eyes aint fast. And you cant help it if you got 2 left hands, right? Throwing cards aint thuh whole world. You got other shit going for you. You got Grace.

BOOTH. Right.

LINCOLN. Whassamatter?

BOOTH. Mm.

LINCOLN. Whatsup?

BOOTH. Nothing.

LINCOLN.

(Rest)

It takes a certain kind of understanding to be able to play this game.

(Rest)

I still got thuh moves, dont I?

BOOTH. Yeah you still got thuh moves.

Lincoln cant help himself. He chuckles.

LINCOLN. I aint laughing at you, bro, Im just laughing. Shit there is so much to this game. This game is—there is just so much to it.

Lincoln, still chuckling, flops down in the easy chair. He takes up the nylon stocking and fiddles with the knot.

LINCOLN. Woah, she sure did tie this up tight, didnt she?

BOOTH. Yeah. I aint opened it since she gived it to me.

LINCOLN. Yr kidding. 500 and you aint never opened it? Shit. Sure is tied tight. She said heres 500 bucks and you didnt undo thuh knot to get a look at the cash? You aint needed to take a peek in all these years? Shit. I woulda opened it right away. Just a little peek.

BOOTH. I been saving it.

(Rest)

Oh, dont open it, man.

LINCOLN. How come?

BOOTH. You won it man, you dont gotta go opening it.

LINCOLN. We gotta see whats in it.

BOOTH. We *know* whats in it. Dont open it.

LINCOLN. You are a chump, bro. There could be millions in here! There could be nothing! I'll open it.

BOOTH. Don't.

LINCOLN.

BOOTH.

(Rest)

LINCOLN. Shit this knot aint coming out. I could cut it, but that would spoil the whole effect, wouldn't it? Shit. Sorry. I aint laughing at you Im just laughing. Theres so much about those cards. You think you can learn them just by watching and just by playing but there is much more to them cards than that. And—. Tell me something, Mr. 3-Card, she handed you this stocking and she said there was money in it and then she split and you say you didnt open it. Howd you know she was for real?

BOOTH. She was for real.

LINCOLN. How you know? She coulda been jiving you, bro. Jiving you that there really *was* money in this thing. Jiving you big time. It's like thuh cards. And ooooh you certainly was persistent. But you was in such a hurry to learn thuh last move that you didn't bother learning thuh first one. That was yr mistake. Cause its thuh first move that separates thuh Player from thuh Played. And thuh first move is to know that there aint no winning. It may look like you got a chance but the only time you pick right is when thuh man lets you. And when its thuh real deal, when its thuh real fucking deal, bro, and thuh moneys on thuh line, thats when thuh man wont want you picking right. He will want you picking wrong so he will make you pick wrong. Wrong wrong wrong. Ooooh, you thought you was finally happening, didnt you? You thought yr ship had come in or some shit, huh? Thought you was uh Player. But I played you, bro.

BOOTH. Fuck you. Fuck you FUCK YOU *FUCK YOU*!!!

LINCOLN. Whatever, man. Damn this knot is tough. Ima cut it.

Lincoln reaches in his boot, pulling out a knife. He chuckles all the while.

LINCOLN. Im not laughing at you, bro, Im just laughing.

Booth chuckles with him. Lincoln holds the knife high, ready to cut the stocking.

LINCOLN. Turn yr head. You may not wanna look.

Booth turns away slightly. They both continue laughing. Lincoln brings the knife down to cut the stocking.

BOOTH. I popped her.

LINCOLN. Huh?

BOOTH. Grace. I popped her. Grace.

(Rest)

Who thuh fuck she think she is doing me like she done? Telling me I dont got nothing going on. I showed her what I got going on. Popped her good. Twice. 3 times. Whatever.

(Rest)

She aint dead.

(Rest)

She werent wearing my ring I gived her. Said it was too small. Fuck that. Said it hurt her. Fuck that. Said she was into bigger things. *Fuck* that. Shes alive not

to worry, she aint going out that easy, shes alive shes shes—.

LINCOLN. Dead. Shes—

BOOTH. Dead.

LINCOLN. Ima give you back yr stocking, man. Here, bro—

BOOTH. Only so long I can stand that little brother shit. Can only take it so long. Im telling you—

LINCOLN. Take it back, man—

BOOTH. That little bro shit had to go—

LINCOLN. Cool—

BOOTH. Like Booth went—

LINCOLN. Here, 3-Card—

BOOTH. That Booth shit is over. 3-Cards thuh man now—

LINCOLN. Ima give you yr stocking back, 3-Card—

BOOTH. Who thuh man now, huh? Who thuh man now?! Think you can fuck with me, motherfucker think again motherfucker think again! Think you can take me like Im just some chump some two lefthanded pussy dickbreath chump who you can take and then go laugh at. Aint laughing at me you was just laughing bunch uh bullshit and you know it.

LINCOLN. Here. Take it.

BOOTH. I aint gonna be needing it. Go on. You won it you open it.

LINCOLN. No thanks.

BOOTH. Open it open it open it open it. *OPEN IT!!!*

(Rest)

Open it up, bro.

LINCOLN.

BOOTH.

Lincoln brings the knife down to cut the stocking. In a flash, Booth grabs Lincoln from behind. He pulls his gun and thrusts it into the left side of Lincolns neck. They stop there poised.

LINCOLN. Dont.

Booth shoots Lincoln. Lincoln slumps forward, falling out of his chair and onto the floor. He lies there dead. Booth paces back and forth, like a panther in a cage, holding his gun.

BOOTH. Think you can take my shit? My shit. That shit was mines. I kept it. Saved it. All this while. Through thick and through thin. Through fucking thick and through fucking thin, motherfucker. And you just gonna come up in here and mock my shit and call me two lefthanded talking bout how she coulda been jiving me then go steal from me? My *inheritance*. You stole my *inheritance*, man. That aint right. That aint right and you know it. You had yr own. And you blew it. You *blew it*, motherfucker! I saved mines and you blew yrs. Thinking you all that and blew yr shit. And I *saved* mines.

(*Rest*)

You aint gonna be needing yr fucking money-roll no more, dead motherfucker, so I will pocket it thank you.

(*Rest*)

Watch me close watch me close now: Ima go out there and make a name for myself that dont have nothing to do with you. And 3-Cards gonna be in everybodys head and in everybodys mouth like Link was.

(*Rest*)

Ima take back my inheritance too. It was mines anyhow. Even when you stole it from me it was still mines cause she gave it to me. She didnt give it to you. And I been saving it all this while.

He bends to pick up the money-filled stocking. Then he just crumples. As he sits beside Lincolns body, the money-stocking falls away. Booth holds Lincolns body, hugging him close. He sobs.

BOOTH. AAAAAAAAAAAAAAAAAAAAAH!

End of play

COMMENTARY

Note: This essay represents a single interpretation of the play. For other perspectives on Parks, consult the essays listed below.

Parks has said that writing can be torture for her, and that each of the four plays in the cycle she began with *Mutabilities* and completed with *Venus* took three to four years to complete. *Topdog/Underdog* came more easily to her, but reading her lyrical, looping, and strangely comic writing in any of her plays need not be torture, especially if you read the play out loud. The speech rhythms feel natural and even the words in old black dialect are easy to pronounce when spoken. The text also contains the directions Parks uses to cue actors. These are not stage directions but vocal cues such as "*Rest,*" which means to pause, as in a musical rest. Occasionally there are wordless exchanges between characters indicated by the appearance of the character's name and a blank, then another character's name and a blank, as in this exchange in the third scene of Act I when the brothers are trying to get to sleep.

LINCOLN.
BOOTH.
LINCOLN.
BOOTH.
LINCOLN.
BOOTH.

As in Harold Pinter's plays, some important shift occurs during those back-and-forth silences. Parks calls these moments of elongated and heightened rest "a spell" when there is no action or stage business but the figures may be experiencing themselves in their "pure simple true state. I don't explode the form because I find traditional plays 'boring'— I don't really," Parks wrote in one of the introductory essays of her first volume of plays. "It's just that those structures never could accommodate the figures which take up residence in me."

The younger brother of *Topdog* mocks Lincoln for "dressing up like a white man" when he could still be the monte master he once was. Booth (played by rapper Mos Def in the Broadway production) proves inept, almost a klutz at the quick-shuffling, jive-talking game that Lincoln (film star Jeffrey Wright in the Broadway staging) so skillfully and kinetically demonstrates. Director George C. Wolfe's pacing of this premier production mirrored the quickly moving rhythms of the card game, creating the illusion that more than two characters are moving the cards in this scintillating theatrical con. Everyone else in the game is offstage. The mother and the father, who separately abandoned the brothers, emerge in the second act as we hear their history slowly, and painfully, get spliced into the game when the action devolves into violence. Also offstage is the Man, whoever that authority figure might be—whitey or big brother or an unfeeling god—a force that Booth ultimately believes he can't please. Lincoln has the richer part in *Topdog/Underdog*, and Wright gave a subtly layered performance, radiating vitality whether soberly showing his brother the nuances of the card game or drunkenly demonstrating all the ways that Honest Abe can get shot or fiercely raging against his "sit-down job with benefits." The petty thief Booth has his own repertory of slides, shuffles, spins, and shrugs that underscore the energetic high comedy of some scenes.

The fatal love-hate these abandoned brothers bear toward one another is encapsulated in the names Parks so boldly gives them. And these lonely battling blacks join a long line of such theatrical siblings—in Sam Shepard's *True West*, Pinter's *The Caretaker*, and Martin McDonagh's *Lonesome West*—as archetypal men whose power struggles come to represent conflicts tearing and dividing their nations. The members of this family struggle and suffer, but they are not depicted as a representative "black family" facing oppression together; they are not heroes or victims or political advocates as they might be in works by Lorraine Hansberry or August Wilson. They are viewed instead with affectionate, absurdist, and often comic irony. Set in a seedy room the brothers are forced to share, *Topdog/Underdog* is less dense and original than Parks's earlier works, but it carries a deep emotional charge that has brought her ferocious talent to the wider public her work has long deserved.

Other perspectives on Suzan-Lori Parks and her plays:

Fanger, Iris. "Pultizer Prize Winner Shakes Off Labels." *The Christian Science Monitor* (12 April 2002): 19.

Garrett, Shawn-Marie. "The Possession of Suzan-Lori Parks." *American Theatre* 17:8 (October 2000): 22–26.

APPENDIX

GLOSSARY OF TERMS

Words in boldface type within an entry are defined elsewhere in the glossary.

act: the primary division in the action of a play. A play can consist of a single act, or it may have two, three, four, or five acts. Also: to represent or perform an action on stage.

action: what happens in the story line of a play; a **plot** consists of events that create the play's action.

acto: Spanish term for an act of a play; in contemporary American theater, it is usually a short satiric play on social issues important to Chicanos.

agit-prop: short for "agitation-propaganda," a form of drama that incites the emotions of its audience ("agitation") and then teaches them social and political lessons to encourage them to engage in a particular political action. Clifford Odets's play *Waiting for Lefty* and the *actos* of Luis Valdez typify agit-prop.

agon: Greek term for "debate" or "contest"; both tragedies and comedies had formal agons in which the central idea of the drama was debated.

alienation effect: from the German term *verfrumdungseffekt* ("to make strange"); Brecht's technique for making the audience members stand back and objectively observe the action of a play so that they might judge its social issues. Such things as songs, political speeches, signboards, storytellers, direct address, etc. "alienate" the audience from the action of the play.

allegory: a play in which symbolic fictional characters portray truths or generalizations about human existence; the medieval **morality plays** were allegories, as is Dickens's famous story, *A Christmas Carol*. Shaw's *Heartbreak House* is a modern allegory.

alternative theater: generic term for theater practice and theory that is outside the traditional commercial theater; it is usually *avant-garde* and experimental, and it depends on collective creation by its practiners, most of whom are bound by a common ideology.

antagonist: the character who opposes the **protagonist** or central character of a play; e.g., Torvald and Krogstad in *A Doll's House*.

apron: the part of the stage closest to the audience and in front of the **proscenium**. In theaters without a proscenium (such as the Elizabethan theater), virtually the entire stage becomes an **apron stage** (sometimes called a **thrust stage**).

archetypal character: a recurring figure who transcends the particulars of time and place to take on a symbolic value with universal appeal; a primary example; e.g., Prometheus is the archetype of the human who takes on suffering for the greater good.

arena theater: theater configuration in which the audience sits on all sides of the stage; sometimes referred to as "theater in the round."

ariyetos: ritual dramas using song, dance, mime, and the spoken word that were performed in Cuba, Puerto Rico, and other parts of the Caribbean in pre-Columbian times; they represent some of the first performances recorded by Europeans in the New World.

aside: a performance convention in which a character speaks directly to the audience while the other characters do not hear him or her.

atmosphere: the mood of a play created by scenery, lighting, sound, movement, and other effects.

avant-garde: an intelligencia that develops new or experimental forms, especially in the arts.

bailetes: dance musicals in the Spanish language theater.

beat: the smallest motivational unit of a play script; it may be a only a phrase or sentence in which a character manifests a particular need that must be fulfilled.

bill: the list and order of acts in a vaudeville show; also, the order of acts in a theatrical presentation.

biomechanics: a style, developed by the Russian director Meyerhold, in which actors perform in machine-like movements on a space reflecting the machinery of the Industrial Age.

blocking: the movement and positioning of actors on the stage, usually denoted as crosses.

burlesque: 1. a comic parody of a serious work; 2. a theatrical entertainment comprised of broadly humorous skits and short turns (blackouts), songs, dances, and frequently striptease acts.

business: actions performed by actors, such as drinking, smoking, comic beatings, etc.

987

cabaret: variety show, associated with the German theater, in which political skits and songs are performed in a restaurant and/or barroom.

catharsis: the emotional cleansing initiated by the tragic experience; for the character it is the recognition and acceptance of his or her error; for the audience, it is the sum total of the pity and fear created by the play.

ceremony: an action performed formally meant to sanction a political, social, or religious concept; it usually lacks the deeper significance of a **ritual**. Examples of a ceremony include a graduation or swearing-in.

character: 1. a person in a play; 2. the personality of such a person. (See also **stock character** and **archetypal character**.)

choreography: the arrangement and movement of performers on stage; though the term customarily applies to dancers, it is also used to denote the orchestrated movement of actors, especially in stage combat.

choric speech: a speech spoken by a group; also, a speech that describes off-stage action.

chorus: a group of singer-dancers in Greek drama participating in or commenting on the action of the play; in other ages the Chorus is a single figure who speaks the prologue, epilogue, and comments on the action.

Classicism: a dramatic style that emphasizes order, harmony, balance, and the unities of time, place, and action. Characteristically, classical plays use few characters and follow a single line of action. *Oedipus the King* typifies the classical play.

climax: the resolution of the protagonist's principal conflict; it usually grows out of the **crisis**, and it brings about a play's **denouement** or falling action.

cocoliche: comic dramas from Argentina dealing with the problems of immigrants.

comedia: generic Spanish term for a "play," both comic and serious.

comedy: one of the primary dramatic genres, which usually ends happily and treats its subject matter lightly.

comedy of manners: comic genre that satirizes the behaviors, fashions, and mores of a given social class or set. Such plays demand a sophisticated and knowledgeable audience.

comic relief: humorous scenes inserted in tragic or serious dramas that provide emotional relief from the play's weighty issues; comic relief can, however, also provide an alternate perspective to the serious issues of the play. The Grave Digger in *Hamlet* provides both comic relief and a commentary on death.

conflict: the opposition of forces. In drama, there are two types of conflict: external conflict occurs when an individual is at odds with another person, society, or nature; internal conflict is when an individual is at odds with himself or herself.

Constructivism: a movement in nonobjective art and performance that flourished in Soviet Russia in the 1920s and reflected modern industry; both the acting (see **biomechanics**) and the scenography portrayed human experience in mechanistic terms.

context: the "given circumstances" of a text; this includes the historical, social, and interpersonal backgrounds of the characters.

convention: an established technique or device that the audience agrees to accept as "real" in a performance; the "ground rules" under which a particular play will be performed. Examples include asides, soliloquies, the use of mime, and shifting scenery in view of the audience. Conventions change from age to age, from performance to performance.

costumbristas: popular entertainments in Latin America that reflect the manners, dress, music, and dance of the common people.

coup de théâtre: French for "stroke of theater"; it is either a sudden sensational turn in a play (e.g., when Nora walks out on her husband at the end of *A Doll's House*) or a spectacular moment that stops the show (e.g., the appearance of the Angel at the end of *Angels in America, Part One: Millennium Approaches*).

crisis: that moment in a play at which the protagonist faces the greatest conflict; it is the turning point of the play and precipitates the **climax**.

curtain line: 1. the point where the curtain falls and meets the stage floor, usually marking the line between the auditorium and the playing space in realistic theater; 2. a contrived line spoken as the curtain falls to end an act, usually to heighten the dramatic impact of a scene (especially in melodrama).

cyclic plot: a form of plotting especially popular in the modern theater in which the end of a play repeats the opening action, usually to show that there are no resolutions to life's problems and that humans are trapped in their existence.

Dadaism: an early-twentieth-century "anti-art" movement of the *avant-garde* that attempted to show the irrationality of the world by avoiding all logic in their work. Randomness and chaos created a surrealistic view of the world.

deconstructionism: a postmodern critical approach that "constructs" new meanings of old texts by subverting (or "deconstructing") them; it is based on the premise that language is an imprecise instrument that has been manipulated by the traditional Eurocentric worldview. Theater productions, as well as written criticism, can be deconstructionist.

decorum: a Neoclassic belief that characters were required to behave according to expectations based on their social status, sex, age, etc.

denouement (falling action): the final outcome of the dramatic action in which the fates of the characters are determined, harmony is restored, and destinies are settled; it follows the climax.

deus ex machina: literally, "the god from the machine," a reference to the practice of lowering a god onto the stage in the ancient Greek and Roman theaters; as a literary term it refers to a character that is introduced late in the play to provide a contrived solution to an apparently insolvable problem. The three gods in Brecht's *The Good Woman of Setzuan* are a parody of the deus ex machina ending.

deuteragonist(s): secondary character(s) in a play.

dialogue: the exchange of speeches by two or more characters in a play. Also, a generic term referring to the words in a script.

diction: one of the six Aristotelian elements of the drama; it deals with the language of a play and the manner in which characters speak; as an acting term it refers to the clarity with which an actor speaks.

didactic theater: propagandistic theater whose primary aim is to "instruct" or "teach." Most medieval religious plays were didactic in that they "instructed" audiences about the Bible or morality. Most modern didactic theater, such as Brecht's, is political.

Dionysus (Roman: Bacchus): Greek god of wine and—by extension—creativity, passion, and irrational behavior.

diorama: a scenic representation in which sculptured figures and miniatures are displayed against a painted background; the effect suggests a realistic panorama.

director: the theatrical artist most responsible for coordinating the work of the actors, designers, and technicians as they interpret the work of the playwright.

directorial concept: the director's interpretation of the play and the means by which he or she achieves it.

distributed exposition: background material revealed throughout the course of a play, as opposed to conventional exposition, in which the material is presented largely in the first act; the plays of Ibsen are noted for their distributed exposition.

docudrama: a play, television, or film that deals with historical events; dialogue is taken from interviews, court transcripts, newspaper articles, etc., and visual effects rely on photographs or film of the actual event; e.g., *The Laramie Project*.

down stage line: a performance mode in which the actors stand in a semi-circle on the forestage and deliver their lines; the style was popular in France in the seventeenth and eighteenth centuries.

drama: a composition in verse or prose that portrays the actions of characters in conflict; the literary form of a play; a series of events involving intense conflict.

dramatis personae: a list of characters appearing in a play; the Latin term for "persons of the drama." Characters may be listed by order of importance to the play, order of appearance, or (as in the Renaissance) in a hierarchical order.

dramaturgy: the art of writing and crafting plays.

drao: a Greek word meaning "to act" or "to do"; **drama** derives from this term.

emotion memory: an acting technique in which the performer summons up the memory of a particular emotional experience and transfers it to the emotional life of the character he or she portrays.

Enlightenment: the eighteenth-century philosophic movement characterized by an emphasis on rationalism and a rejection of traditional religious, political, and social beliefs in favor of empiricism and the new science.

environmental theater: a performance mode in which the action is not confined to a traditional stage but uses the entire "environment" for the presentation of the play; the action frequently takes place in and around the spectators (who are often encouraged to participate in the play).

ensemble pathos: a term coined by Francis Ferguson to describe a playwriting style that does not focus on the plight of a single individual but on a group of people; the audience's emotional response is therefore dispersed among the group. The plays of Chekhov are especially typical of ensemble pathos.

entre'acts: short entertainments (such as a song or dance) inserted between the acts of a play; also, the musical overture preceding the second act of a musical theater piece.

Epic Theatre: non-Aristotelian theater espoused by Bertolt Brecht aimed at the audience's intellect rather than its emotions; it seeks to instruct audiences so that they may deal with contemporary moral problems and social realities but in nonrealistic modes of performance.

epilogue: a formal speech, usually in verse, addressed to the audience by an actor after a play; often called a "curtain speech."

episodic plot: a story with a series of events, often unrelated, which can take place over great periods of time and in many locales; the events of an episodic plot are not necessarily causally related. Epic dramas, the history plays of Shakespeare, and the works of Brecht are episodic in structure.

Existentialism: a predominantly twentieth-century philosophy that argues that humans define themselves (i.e., their "existence" rather than their "essence") by the choices and actions they freely and consciously make. Existentialism has influenced much mid-twentieth-century drama, especially that of the Absurdists.

exposition: essential information that an audience needs to know about a character or events (particularly those that happen prior to the first scene). Usually exposition is found in the first act or scene, but **distributed exposition** may be found throughout the play.

Expressionism: an early-twentieth-century literary and performance style that attempted to create the inner workings of the human mind by showing subjective states of reality through distortion, nightmarish images, etc.

external actor: an actor whose primary emphasis and training are on such things as voice, physicality, gesture, etc.

extravaganzas: lavish and spectacular stage shows, often recreating famous military battles or stories from the Wild West.

falling action: see **denouement**

famileinstucke: a form of German domestic drama that focused on the plight of families in crisis (e.g., losing the family homestead); it influenced the melodrama and subsequently the realistic theater. Lorraine Hansberry's *A Raisin in the Sun* is a modern *famileinstucke*.

farce: a comic genre that depends on an elaborately contrived, usually improbable plot, broadly drawn stock characters, and physical humor. Most farces are amoral and exist to entertain.

feminist theater: theater practice, theory, and criticism devoted to drama by women and/or about the problems of women in society.

floorplan: a set designer's drawing of the layout of the stage to show the spatial relationships between set pieces, the placement of platforms, entrances, exits, etc. The rehearsal room floor is usually taped to designate the various elements of the floorplan.

foil: a character who serves as a contrast to another (and usually central) character; e.g., Willy Loman's neighbor, Charlie, is a foil to Willy, and Charlie's son, Bernard, is a foil to Biff.

foreshadowing: hints of events or actions to come in a play; usually foreshadowing helps create suspense.

Formalism: a late-twentieth-century performance style that emphasizes external and visual elements. The works of Robert Wilson typify Formalism.

fourth wall: a convention of the realistic theater in which the audience assumes it is looking through an invisible wall into an actual room; this wall is determined by the opening in the proscenium arch.

Futurism: an early-twentieth-century art and performance movement, originating in Italy, that glorified science and machines, especially speed and efficiency. Futurist plays employed mechanistic performance techniques, simultaneity of action, and abstraction.

gauchescos: Argentine plays about gauchos (cowboys), comparable to westerns of the United States.

genero chico: a Spanish-American variety show similar to the vaudeville or music hall; also known as a *puchero* ("stew").

genre: a category of play characterized by a particular style, form, and content, e.g., tragedy, comedy, tragicomedy, melodrama, farce.

gestus: the most important term in Brecht's vocabulary for actors; it refers to the social reality the character is asked to play (as opposed to the psychological reality of Stanislavskian acting).

"given circumstances": Stanislavsky's term for the contextual background of a play and its characters; these include social situation, personal characteristic, conflict, etc. (See "Magic If.")

griot: African term for a storyteller.

hamartia: Greek term (which means "missing the mark") that is usually applied to the flaw or error in judgment that leads to the downfall of the tragic hero.

hero (fem. **heroine**): the central character of a play, usually the character who undergoes the most pronounced change; in romantic drama and melodrama the "hero" is usually the person who embodies "good." The twentieth century has seen the emergence of the anti-hero, a character who may not be "good" but who is still the central figure in the drama. Willy Loman is an anti-hero.

high comedy: sophisticated comedy that depends on witty dialogue, social satire, and sophisticated characters for their impact. The plays of George Bernard Shaw typify high comedy.

historification: setting the action of a play in the historic past to draw parallels with contemporary events; among Brecht's favorite devices for creating an **alienation effect** for his audience.

hubris: the most common form of tragic flaw, usually ascribed to excessive pride or arrogance.

hypokrites: the original Greek term for "actor"; originally it meant "answerer."

imitation: the act of representing (or recreating) another person through voice and gesture; see *mimesis*. Imitation is one of the founding principles of the theatrical arts.

independent theater(s): generic term for (mostly) small theaters at the end of the nineteenth century whose aim was not commercial success but artistic and social drama. The Théâtre Libre in Paris, the Abbey Theatre in Ireland, and the Provincetown Playhouse in America typify the independent theater movement.

integrated actor: an actor who combines both internal and external techniques as the basis of his or her work.

internal actor: an actor who relies on inner technique as the source of his or her performance; such things as emotion memory, subtext, and psychological motivations are central to the internal approach.

irony: 1. an unexpected reversal of fortune (or *peripeteia*) in a drama in which characters expect exactly the opposite of what occurs; 2. dramatic irony occurs when a character is deprived of knowledge that other characters and the audience share.

lazzi: Italian term for "comic stage business" (e.g., a beating, a pratfall). The Italian playwright and performance artist Dario Fo uses *lazzi* in his political comedies.

linear plot: the most traditional form of plotting, which begins with exposition and builds through a series of minor crises to a major crisis and climax. Linear plots are usually based on causality, that is, one event "causes" another to happen.

low comedy: comedy that usually relies on physical humor or crude word play, as opposed to the more sophisticated **high comedy**.

"Magic If": Stanislavsky's term for the trigger that allows the actor to enter into the emotional life of a character: "Under these **given circumstances**, what would I do if I were this character?"

mask: 1. a device that hides the face to conceal an identity; 2. a pose or false front, especially true of a "psychological mask."

masquerades: theatrical activities characterized by the use of elaborate masks, oversized costumes, and vigorous physical dancing and other mimetic actions; the Carnival in Trinidad, the New Orleans *Mardi Gras*, and the Yoruban Festival are examples of masquerades.

masques: spectacular entertainments held in the English courts in the sixteenth and seventeenth centuries; they were performed for and often by royalty.

melodrama: the dramatic genre characterized by an emphasis on plot over characterization; typically, characters are defined as heroes or villains, conflicts are defined along moral lines, and the resolution rewards the good and punishes the wicked. Spectacle and action are important to the melodramatic effect.

mestizo: Spanish term for "of mixed blood"; refers to plays that are a mixture of the drama of Spain and indigenous dramas of Latin America.

metanarrative(s): postmodern term for the "new myths" created by a synthesis of traditional stories and modern sensibilities. Stoppard's *Rosencrantz and Guildenstern Are Dead* is a metanarrative on *Hamlet*.

"Method" acting: strongly internalized acting that emphasizes emotion memory and personal experience in creating a character. The term is most associated with Lee Strasberg's teaching at New York's Actors Studio.

mimesis: Greek term referring to the art of imitation through physical and vocal means.

mise en scène: the spectacle in a theater event; it includes costumes, makeup, scenery, properties, and lighting effects.

monologue: a lengthy speech spoken by a single character, usually to other characters (see **soliloquy**).

morality plays: medieval dramas that portrayed moral dilemmas through allegorical figures such as Everyman and various virtues (strength, beauty) and vices (gluttony, rumor). Most moralities dealt with the way the Christian meets death. Shaw's *Heartbreak House* retains elements of the morality play. See **allegory**.

multiculturalism: the incorporation into an artwork of the values and modes of expression of those other than traditional Eurocentricism. Soyinka's *Death and the King's Horseman* and Valdez's *Zoot Suit* are multicultural works.

music: one of the six Aristotelian elements of the drama; it refers to song, melody, rhythm, etc.

musical theater: a genre that uses song, music, and dance as an integral part of the play's action; it is not usually as elevated as **opera** or even **operetta**. Musical theater can be further divided into musical drama (e.g., *West Side Story*) or musical comedy (e.g., *Guys and Dolls*).

Naturalism: a particular form of Realism that emphasizes environment; Naturalism was also a philosophical movement that saw humans as products of their heredity and environment. *Cat on a Hot Tin Roof* has many naturalistic elements.

Neoclassicism: a Renaissance movement that consciously imitated the classical style of the Greeks and Romans; it is noted for its strict adherence to the rules of dramatic writing and its emphasis on morality and decorum. The plays of Jean Racine epitomize Neoclassicism.

New Comedy: post-Aristophanic comedy dealing with the lives and actions of common people; usually New Comedy is apolitical and focuses on the follies of ordinary people. Menander is said to have originated New Comedy, and the Roman playwrights Plautus and Terence perfected it. Most television "sit coms" are derived from New Comedy.

New Stagecraft: an early-twentieth-century movement that moved away from pictorial realism to more abstract settings designed to evoke mood and place emphasis on the language of a play.

Noh (No) theater: the classical dance-drama of Japan, distinguished by a fusion of dance, poetry, music, mime, and meditation.

obligatory scene (also *scene à faire*): the climactic scene, which the audience comes to expect; usually, the ultimate confrontation between the protagonist and antagonist which leads to the resolution of the play's conflict; in the **well-made play**, the obligatory scene is often marked by the revelation of a secret.

opera: a drama, set to music, that almost exclusively uses vocal pieces and orchestral music; operas usually deal with tragic and heroic themes, e.g., *Madame Butterfly* or *The Ring Cycle*.

opera bouffe: satirical comic operas, e.g., *Orpheus in Hades*.

operetta: a "little opera," or romantic and comic play that uses considerable music, song, and dance, e.g., *The Merry Widow* or *The Mikado*.

overture: an orchestral piece played before the beginning of an opera, operetta, or musical play; overtures were also often played before nonmusical plays in the eighteenth and nineteenth centuries.

pantomimes: dumb shows that place an emphasis on spectacle.

pastiche: a postmodern playwriting technique that fuses a variety of styles, genres, and story lines to create a new form. Stoppard's *Rosencrantz and Guildenstern Are Dead* is a pastiche of Shakespeare's *Hamlet*, Beckett's *Waiting for Godot*, absurdist theater, vaudeville, and existentialist tract.

Peking opera: a generic term for populist Chinese theater, originating in the eighteenth century, which uses song, dance, and nonrealistic means to tell melodramatic stories; the national theater form of China.

performance art: a post-1960s movement that combines visual and verbal performance with popular culture (pop music, film, video, and other electronic media) and topical material with the artist's body as the primary medium; performance art is usually ideological and uses the body as a political agent. Laurie Anderson and Karen Finley are notable performance artists.

peripeteia: Aristotelian term for "reversal" in a play, that is, the moment when the fortunes of the protagonist are drastically changed.

perspective: the technique, used by scenic designers, of representing on a flat surface (such as a canvas drop) the spatial relation of objects as they might appear to the eye.

pictorial realism: the attempt to suggest "real life" on the stage through painterly devices.

play: a literary genre in which a story (plot) is presented by actors imitating characters before an audience. One might say that a "play" is a script "on its feet."

play-within-the-play: a usually brief play inserted into the action of a larger play, typically to comment on or illuminate the primary play. The performance of the "panto" in Walcott's *Pantomime* is a play-within-the-play.

plot: the structure of a play's story line; see **praxis**.

pluralism: the inclusion of many cultures, races, and lifestyles into an enterprise; for the theater, this includes multicultural/racial drama, feminist drama, gay and lesbian drama; in general, pluralism is an alternative to traditional male-dominated, Eurocentric art.

poetic justice: a moral doctrine that requires that the good be rewarded for their benevolent deeds and that the wicked be punished for their transgressions; the doctrine is particularly influential on the resolution of melodramas and sentimental comedies.

The Poetics: Aristotle's treatise on dramatic theory and stage practice; in particular, it defines and discusses tragedy. It was written in the middle of the fourth century, BC, and is the seminal work on dramatic theory in Western theater.

point of attack: that moment nearest the beginning of the play in which the major conflict to be resolved occurs; sometimes called the "inciting moment."

Poor Theatre: Jerzy Grotowski's term for a theater that seeks (by choice or necessity) to eliminate everything not entirely essential to the performance (e.g., scenery, elaborate costumes, makeup, high-tech lighting); "found" objects and costumes are used, and the actors themselves create effects to support the production. (See also *via negativa*.)

Postmodernism: a late-twentieth-century critical, literary, and performance movement that reacts to modern art and literature; postmodernists suggest that truth is no longer verifiable and that new art forms are best created by freely mixing previous styles and themes.

praxis: the "action" of a story, i.e., the arrangement of the events of the story calculated to bring about a desired response from the audience.

presentational style: a performance mode in which the actors openly acknowledge the presence of the audience and play to it. Much Brechtian drama is performed in a presentational style.

prologue: originally, the opening action of a Greek play; it usually is a dialogue between two or three characters and establishes the problem of the play. It now refers to an opening section of a play that is not part of the first scene or act.

proscenium: in modern theaters, the wall that separates the stage from the auditorium and provides the arch that frames it; often referred to as the "picture frame" stage.

protagonist: literally, "the first debater," but the term applies to the central character in a drama.

queer theater/theory: drama, theory, and criticism concerned with gay men and lesbians in society.

quid pro quo: Latin for "something for something"; a playwriting term applied to a situation in which one, two, or more characters unknowingly misunderstand a situation, which further enmeshes them in the play's action.

raisoneur: a common term applied to a character who speaks for society or the playwright; customarily, the raisoneur gives advice to the protagonist. Dr. Rank in *A Doll's House* is a raisoneur.

Realism: an attempt to recreate actual life on stage in a manner that employs the details of daily dress, speech, environment, and situations. All is calculated to give the illusion of real life on stage. Ibsen's social dramas typify Realism. (See also **Naturalism**.)

recognition (*anagnorisis*): a character discovers a truth previously unknown; in tragedy it is the awareness of the error in judgment that leads to the character's downfall. Originally, it referred to the recognition of one character by another (e.g., Electra recognizes her long-lost brother, Orestes), but the term now applies to the discovery of an error or a truth about oneself. The lengthy scene between Big Daddy and Brick in Act II of *Cat on a Hot Tin Roof* is a "recognition scene."

renderings: a scenery or costume designer's drawings of the set or costumes; these are usually colored or painted to suggest how the finished product will look.

regisseur: a continental term for the stage director.

repartee: witty verbal exchanges between characters, especially in high comedy. Many of the exchanges between the title characters in Tom Stoppard's *Rosencrantz and Guildenstern Are Dead* typify repartee.

representational style: a performance mode in which the actors seem to ignore the presence of the audience; *A Doll's House* is customarily performed in a representational style.

revenge tragedy: Elizabethan- and Jacobean-era dramas that depended on sensational events, murders, and revenge for their plotting; the Roman tragedies of Seneca were the models for revenge tragedies.

reversal (*peripeteia*): a drastic change in fortune, usually for the protagonist of a play. In tragedy the reversal is calamitous and leads to the downfall of the principal character; in comedy, the reversal usually brings about good fortune and a happy resolution to the play.

reviewer: a theater critic who attends a play in performance and assesses the quality of the script, the performances and designs, and the overall experience.

revistas: Brazilian popular entertainments, usually musicals.

rising action: the series of minor crises in a plot that build toward the major crisis and climax.

ritual: a formal and customarily repeated act, usually according to religious or social customs; a ritual generally has greater significance than a **ceremony**, e.g., a baptism or wedding. Early rituals often were intended to control the outcome of events.

ritualized enactment: symbolic actions performed in a pattern and progression that eventually become highly controlled and precise in their execution.

Romanticism: a late-eighteenth- and early-nineteenth-century philosophical and artistic movement marked by an emotional appeal to the heroic, adventurous, remote, mysterious, or idealized. Romanticism celebrated the common people and is aligned with the democratic revolution.

sainetes: short farces in Spanish-language theater.

satire: a species of comic drama that holds human follies and institutions up to ridicule and scorn; the use of wit, irony, or sarcasm to expose vice and folly.

scenario: an outline of a play that denotes the principal actions of the plot.

scene: 1. the secondary division of a play; acts may be divided into scenes; 2. the locale of a play's action.

scenery: the backdrops, furniture, and other visual accessories that help define the locale and mood of a play.

sets: the scenery constructed for a particular play; usually, it is three dimensional (as opposed to painted drops).

setting: the locale of a play's action and the scenic elements that help define it.

shaman: a holy person who uses magic and ritual for the purpose of curing the sick, divining hidden mysteries, or controlling events. Shamans are often storytellers who preserve a community's myths.

slapstick: a form of comedy that depends exclusively on physical humor such as beatings, chases, pratfalls, etc. The term is derived from a prop devised by actors in the *commedia dell'arte* that was used to administer beatings. The films of the Three Stooges epitomize slapstick comedy.

soliloquy: a theater convention in which a character speaks his or her thoughts aloud to the audience; it is particularly associated with Elizabethan drama, although the postmodern theater uses soliloquies generously.

spectacle: one of the six elements of theater defined by Aristotle; it refers to the visual elements of scenery and costume (and in the modern theater, lighting).

spine: see **superobjective**.

spirit cult performances: theatricalized rituals in which a medium, thought to be possessed by spirits of the dead, assumes a character while in a trance state.

stage direction: the playwright's instructions to the actors, designers, and directors concerning setting, motivations, characterization, etc.

stichomythia: stage dialogue in which characters alternate single lines; it is used to increase dramatic tension. Though the term is Greek in origin, it may be found in many eras of theater.

stock character: an instantly recognizable type of figure that reoccurs in many works, e.g., the young lover, the grouchy old man, the sassy servant, the braggart soldier.

storytelling performance: a preliterate form of drama, especially common in Africa, in which a narrator tells a story while enacting the central roles; others may play roles as well as providing song and dance to accompany the tale.

Sturm und Drang: German for "storm and stress," a philosophical and artistic movement in the late eighteenth century characterized by high emotion and rousing action that often dealt with an individual's revolt against society; the forerunner of **Romanticism**.

style: the manner in which a play is performed. The two principal styles are **presentational**, in which the actors openly acknowledge the presence of the audience and play to it, and **representational**, in which the actors seem to ignore the presence of the audience. Style implies the degree of "reality" or artificiality of a performance.

subplot: a secondary plot in a play that often parallels the major plot; e.g., in *Angels in America, Part One: Millennium Approaches*, the story of the Mormon couple is a subplot.

subtext: the underlying meaning of a speech in a play, i.e., what the text implies; sometimes referred to as the intentional meaning of a speech.

superobjective: Stanislavsky's term for the primary motivation of a character. Willy Loman's superobjective may be stated by an actor as "to preserve Willy's dignity."

Surrealism: an early-twentieth-century art and performance movement in which irrational juxtapositions of real and unreal objects produced fantasy images to create a highly subjective, dream-like effect.

suspension of disbelief: Coleridge's term for an audience's willingness to accept the events on stage as true or plausible during the course of a play.

Symbolism: a literary or theatrical device in which an object or action suggests another meaning beyond its literal meaning. Willy's worn suitcases in *Death of a Salesman* symbolize his life and failures. Also, a theatrical style popular in the early twentieth century that relied almost exclusively on symbols for its impact; such plays as García Lorca's *Blood Wedding* typify symbolist drama.

sympathetic (homeopathic) magic: when humans imitate an act of nature in the hope that nature, in turn, will imitate humans and thereby produce a desired result, e.g., a Native American rain dance.

the System: the term applied to Stanislavsky's approach to actor training at the Moscow Art Theatre; it blends external technique with strong psychological analysis of the character.

tableau vivants: French for "living pictures," spectacular scenes that often created historical events or violent situations (such as guillotining a character). Today a tableau refers to a "freeze" in which the actors do not move.

text: the printed version of a play; a script. (See also **context** and **subtext**.)

theater: the art form by which drama is realized; also, the formal space in which a drama is performed.

theater collectives: alternative theater companies, usually bound by a common ideology, that create works collectively; often they live in communes. The Living Theatre (United States), the Theatre du Soleil (France), Committed Artists (South Africa), and Grupo Teatro Escambray (Cuba) are examples of collectives.

Theatre of Cruelty: a movement associated with the theories of Antonin Artaud, who forced audiences to purge their inhumanity ("the Plague") by stripping away their defense mechanisms through an assault on the senses.

Theater of the Absurd: a dramatic movement of the mid-twentieth century concerned with the metaphysical anguish of the human condition in a world that defies rational sense; it relies on plotless dramas, discursive dialogue, motiveless behavior, and ambiguity. The plays of Samuel Beckett are especially representative of absurdist drama.

theatrical (theatricality): the formal and stylized use of costumes, makeup, scenery, properties, lighting, and sound as a means of performance; with theatricality there is no pretense of realism.

thesis play (also *pièce à thèse* and "discussion drama"): social dramas in which contemporary problems are illustrated and discussed; typified by the early works of Ibsen, Shaw, Odets, etc. Most thesis plays are presented in a realistic or naturalistic style.

thought: one of the six Aristotelian elements of the drama; it deals with the idea or thematic values of a play.

thrust stage: a stage or acting area that is projected into the audience and is usually surrounded by the audience on three sides. The classical Greek theater and the Elizabethan public theaters used thrust stages. Many theaters built since the 1960s have returned to the thrust stage.

tirade: a lengthy, highly emotional speech most often associated with the French Neoclassic theater; a strong outpouring of emotion. Many of the lengthy speeches in *Cat on a Hot Tin Roof* are modern versions of the tirade.

tlatquetzque: professional entertainers or actors in the Mayan culture, often dressed as ocelots, sacred snakes, or colorful birds.

Total Theater: a twentieth-century performance mode that employs multisensory, multimedia techniques to assault the audience's senses. Traditional performance techniques are often combined with film, video, slide shows, electronic sound tracks, light shows, etc.

township theater: performances derived from the townships of South Africa in which actors often improvise dialogue and stories and use "found" materials for costumes and props.

tragedy: one of the principal dramatic genres, in which a central character is in conflict with an external, as well as internal, force; the conflict ends disastrously for the character and provokes pity and fear in the audience.

tragicomedy: one of the principal dramatic genres, which blends serious and comic elements; frequently the serious is treated comically, while the comic is given a more somber treatment. The plays of Anton Chekhov and Samuel Beckett typify tragicomedy.

trilogy: a collection of three plays usually related by theme or characters. Aeschylus's *Orestia* is a trilogy dealing with the fall of the House of Atreus. Neil Simon's *Brighton Beach* trilogy portrays the playwright's early life.

unities: refer to the time, place, and action of a drama. The Neoclassicists believed that a play ought to be confined to a single action that takes place in a single location and occurs within a short time span.

vaudeville: stage entertainment comprised of a variety of unrelated acts such as songs, dances, magic, comedy, etc. Originally, a **vaudeville** was a French entertainment that combined pantomime, dance, and music to tell a simple story.

verfrumdungseffekt: Brecht's term for the **alienation affect**.

verisimilitude: "likeness to truth," i.e., the attempt to put a truthful picture of life on stage. Although it purported to "realism," verisimilitude, especially in the Renaissance, offered an idealized view of real life.

via negativa: Grotowski's motto for the **Poor Theatre**, which means "to refrain from doing." It encourages actors to rely solely on their resources, and not externals, for the creation of the theater act. Plays performed in South Africa's township theater and by the Mexican-American collective, El Teatro Campesino, embody this principle.

well-made play (also *pièce à bien fait*): a drama in which a carefully constructed plot is designed to create suspense and forward movement, often at the expense of characterization. Such plays frequently employ a withheld secret, confrontations between heros and villains, and a series of minor crises building to a climax and resolution in which all the conflicts are neatly worked out. Although *Oedipus the King* is the prototype of the well-made play, it is a genre that flourished in the nineteenth century, especially in the works of Eugene Scribe. *A Doll's House* retains many elements of the well-made play.

zarzuela: Spanish term applied to "musical comedy"; begun by Calderon in seventeenth-century Spain and brought to the New World by Spanish colonists. *Zarzuela bufas* are "comical musicals," while *bailetes* are "dance musicals." Such works are still popular throughout Latin America.

CREDITS

Credits

Federico García Lorca. *Blood Wedding* by Frederico García Lorca, translation by James Graham-Lujan and Richard L. O'Connell, from THREE TRAGEDIES, copyright © 1947 by New Directions Publishing Corp. Reprinted by permission of New Directions Publishing Corp.

Bonnie Marranca. Introduction to the *Theatre of Images*, edited with introductory essays by Bonnie Marranca © 1977, 1996 by Bonnie Marranca. Reprinted by permission of the author.

Jo Mielziner. *Designing for the Theatre* by Jo Mielziner. Reprinted with the permission of Scribner, a Division of Simon and Schuster Adult Publishing Group for DESIGNING FOR THE THEATRE by Jo Mielziner. Copyright © 1965 Jo Mielziner.

Heiner Müller. *Hamletmachine* in *Hamletmachine and Other Texts for the Stage*. © Copyright 1984 by Performing Arts Journal Publications. © Copyright 1984 Translation by Carl Weber. Reprinted by permission of PAJ Publications.

Eugene O'Neill. *A Moon for the Misbegotten* by Eugene O'Neill. Copyright © 1945, © 1952 by Eugene O'Neill, renewed 1973, 1980 by Oona O'Neill Chaplin and Shane O'Neill. Reprinted by permission of William Morris Agency, Inc. on behalf of the Author.

Suzan-Lori Parks. *Topdog/Underdog* by Suzan-Lori Parks, copyright © by the author. Published by Theatre Communications Group. Used by permission.

Harold Pinter. *The Birthday Party* by Harold Pinter. Copyright © 1959 by Harold Pinter. Used by permission of Grove/Atlantic, Inc.

Bernard Shaw. *Heartbreak House*. © Copyright 1919, 1930, 1948 George Bernard Shaw. © Copyright 1957 The Public Trustee as Executor of the Estate of George Bernard Shaw. Reprinted by permission of The Society of Authors on behalf of the Estate of Bernard Shaw.

Sam Shepard. *True West*, copyright © 1981 by Sam Shepard, from SEVEN PLAYS by Sam Shepard. Used by permission of Bantam Books, a division of Random House, Inc.

Wole Soyinka. DEATH AND THE KING'S HORSEMAN by Wole Soyinka. Copyright © 1975 by Wole Soyinka. Used by permission of W.W. Norton & Company, Inc.

Tom Stoppard. *Rosencrantz and Guildenstern Are Dead*. Copyright © 1967 by Tom Stoppard. Reprinted by permission of Grove/Atlantic, Inc.

August Strinberg. *The Ghost Sonata* by August Strindberg. Copyright © 1955 by August Strindberg. Translated by Elizabeth Sprigge. Reprinted by permission of Curtis Brown, Ltd.

Sophie Treadwell. *Machinal* by Sophie Treadwell. Reprinted with permission.

Luis Valdez. *Zoot Suit* by Luis Valdez is reprinted with permission from the publisher of *Zoot Suit and Other Plays* (Houston: Arte Público Press—University of Houston, 1992).

Derek Walcott. *Pantomime* from REMEMBRANCE AND PANTOMIME: TWO PLAYS by Derek Walcott. Reprinted by permission of Farrar, Straus, and Giroux, LLC.

Tennessee Williams. *Cat on a Hot Tin Roof* by Tennessee Williams from CAT ON A HOT TIN ROOF, copyright © 1954, 1955, 1971, 1975 by The University of the South. Reprinted by permission of New Directions Publishing Corp.

August Wilson. FENCES by August Wilson, copyright © 1986 by August Wilson. Used by permission of Dutton Signet, a division of Penguin Putnam, Inc.

Egon Wolff. *Paper Flowers: A Play in Six Scenes* by Egon Wolff, translated by Margaret Sayers Peden, by permission of the University of Missouri Press. Copyright © 1971 by the Curators of the University of Missouri.

PHOTO CREDITS

PROLOGUE
Page 2 © Jack Vartoogian.

PART I
Page 32 J. Petersen & Son/Royal Theatre Archives and Library Copenhagen, Denmark.
Page 122 © Donald Cooper, Photostage.
Page 191 Billy Rose Theatre Collection, New York Public Library for the Performing Arts, Astor, Lenox, and Tilden Foundations.

PART II
Page 194 Billy Rose Theatre Collection, New York Public Library for the Performing Arts, Astor, Lenox, and Tilden Foundations.

Page 197 © Gerry Goodstein.
Page 319 © 1978 Lois Greenfield.
Page 461 © Gerry Goodstein.

PART III
Page 484 © Richard Feldman.
Page 504 Jay Thompson.
Page 648 © George E. Joseph.
Page 653 Jay Thompson.

INDEX

Index